Hoover's Handbook of

Private Companies

2006

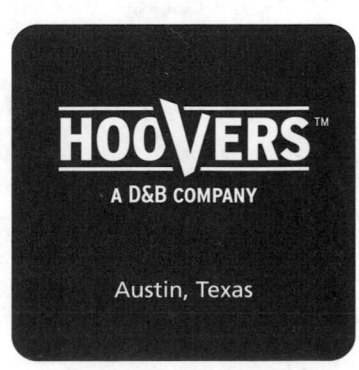

HOOVERS™

A D&B COMPANY

Austin, Texas

Hoover's Handbook of Private Companies 2006 is intended to provide readers with accurate and authoritative information about the enterprises covered in it. Hoover's asked all companies and organizations profiled to provide information. Many did so; a number did not. The information contained herein is as accurate as we could reasonably make it. In many cases we have relied on third-party material that we believe to be trustworthy, but were unable to independently verify. We do not warrant that the book is absolutely accurate or without error. Readers should not rely on any information contained herein in instances where such reliance might cause loss or damage. The publisher, the editors, and their data suppliers specifically disclaim all warranties, including the implied warranties of merchantability and fitness for a specific purpose. This book is sold with the understanding that neither the publisher, the editors, nor any content contributors are engaged in providing investment, financial, accounting, legal, or other professional advice.

The financial data (Historical Financials sections) in this book are from the companies profiled or from trade sources deemed to be reliable. Hoover's, Inc., is solely responsible for the presentation of all data.

Many of the names of products and services mentioned in this book are the trademarks or service marks of the companies manufacturing or selling them and are subject to protection under US law. Space has not permitted us to indicate which names are subject to such protection, and readers are advised to consult with the owners of such marks regarding their use. Hoover's is a trademark of Hoover's, Inc.

10 9 8 7 6 5 4 3 2 1

Publishers Cataloging-in-Publication Data

Hoover's Handbook of Private Companies 2006

   Includes indexes.

   ISBN 1-57311-109-0

   ISSN 1073-6433

   1. Business enterprises — Directories. 2. Corporations — Directories.

HF3010 338.7

Hoover's Company Information is also available on the Internet at Hoover's Online (www.hoovers.com). A catalog of Hoover's products is available on the Internet at www.hooversbooks.com.

The Hoover's Handbook series is edited by George Sutton and is produced for Hoover's Business Press by:

Sycamore Productions, Inc.
5808 Balcones Drive, Suite 205
Austin, Texas 78731
info@sycamoreproductions.com

Cover design is by John Baker. Electronic prepress and printing are by Von Hoffman Corporation, Owensville, Missouri.

U.S. AND WORLD BOOK SALES

Hoover's, Inc.
5800 Airport Blvd.
Austin, TX 78752
Phone: 512-374-4500
Fax: 512-374-4538
e-mail: orders@hoovers.com
Web: www.hooversbooks.com

EUROPEAN BOOK SALES

William Snyder Publishing Associates
5 Five Mile Drive
Oxford OX2 8HT
England
Phone & fax: +44-186-551-3186
e-mail: snyderpub@aol.com

Hoover's, Inc.

Founder: Gary Hoover
President: Dwayne H. Spradlin
EVP International: Russell Secker
EVP Marketing and Product: Paul Pellman
EVP Technology: Jeffrey (Jeff) Guillot
VP US Sales and Support: John Lysinger
VP Finance: Charles (Chuck) Harvey
VP Human Resources: Gillian Felix
VP Product Design and Creative Services: Michael Reiff
VP Acquisition Marketing: Chris Warwick
VP Strategic Accounts and Channel Sales: George Kanuck
VP Subscription Sales and Support: Mel Yarbrough

EDITORIAL

VP Content: Rachel Brush
Director, Content Acquisition and Management: Valerie Pearcy
Senior Editors: Margaret Claughton, Kathleen Kelly, Laurie Najjar, Barbara Redding, Dennis Sutton
Library Research Manager: Gina Leiss
Content Operations Analyst: Alison Stoeltje
Team Leads: Linnea Anderson Kirgan, Larry Bills, Troy Bryant, Carrie Geis, Zack Gonzales, Nancy Kay, Julie Krippel, Greg Perliski
Editors: Sally Alt, Adam Anderson, Alex Biesada, Joe Bramhall, James Bryant, Ryan Caione, Jason Cella, Catherine Colbert, Elizabeth Cornell, Danny Cummings, Jeff Dorsch, Michaela Drapes, Bobby Duncan, Lesley Epperson, Marcus Gould, David Hamerly, Stuart Hampton, Rosie Hatch, Donna Iroabuchi, Jessica Jimenez, Maggie Jimenez, Kenny Jones, Anne Law, Tara LoPresti, Josh Lower, John MacAyeal, Michael McLellan, Rachel Meyer, Barbara Murray, Nell Newton, Kristi Park, Peter Partheymuller, David Ramirez, Melanie Robertson, Belen Rodriguez, Matt Saucedo, Amy Schein, Seth Shafer, Lee Simmons, Joe Simonetta, Katherine Smith, Paula Smith, Betsy Staton, Diane Stimets, Barbara Strickland, Daysha Taylor, Vanita Trippe, Tim Walker, Kathi Whitley, Randy Williams, David Woodruff
Content Manager: Jannell Chester
QA Editors: Jason Cother, Emily Domaschk, Lisa Goodgame, Allan Gill, Diane Lee, John Willis
Financial Editors: Adi Anand, Jim Harris, Chris Huston, Anthony Staats
Editorial Projects Analyst: Karin Marie
Editorial Projects Specialist: Rob Mellett
Editorial Customer Advocates: Amy Davison, Anna Porlas

HOOVER'S BUSINESS PRESS

Distribution Manager: Rhonda Mitchell
Fulfillment and Shipping Manager: Michael Febonio
Shipping Clerk: Paul Olvera

ABOUT HOOVER'S, INC. — THE BUSINESS INFORMATION AUTHORITY™

Hoover's, a D&B company, gives its customers a competitive edge with insightful information about industries, companies, and key decision makers. Hoover's provides this updated information for sales, marketing, business development, and other professionals who need intelligence on U.S. and global companies, industries, and the people who lead them. This information, along with powerful tools to search, sort, download, and integrate the content, is available through Hoover's (www.hoovers.com), the company's premier online service. Hoover's business information is also available through corporate intranets and distribution agreements with licensees, as well as via Hoover's books. The company is headquartered in Austin, Texas.

Abbreviations

AFL-CIO – American Federation of Labor and Congress of Industrial Organizations
AMA – American Medical Association
AMEX – American Stock Exchange
ARM – adjustable-rate mortgage
ASP – application services provider
ATM – asynchronous transfer mode
ATM – automated teller machine
CAD/CAM – computer-aided design/ computer-aided manufacturing
CD-ROM – compact disc – read-only memory
CD-R – CD-recordable
CEO – chief executive officer
CFO – chief financial officer
CMOS – complimentary metal oxide silicon
COO – chief operating officer
DAT – digital audiotape
DOD – Department of Defense
DOE – Department of Energy
DOS – disk operating system
DOT – Department of Transportation
DRAM – dynamic random-access memory
DSL – digital subscriber line
DVD – digital versatile disc/digital video disc
DVD-R – DVD-recordable
EPA – Environmental Protection Agency
EPROM – erasable programmable read-only memory
EPS – earnings per share
ESOP – employee stock ownership plan
EU – European Union
EVP – executive vice president
FCC – Federal Communications Commission
FDA – Food and Drug Administration

FDIC – Federal Deposit Insurance Corporation
FTC – Federal Trade Commission
FTP – file transfer protocol
GATT – General Agreement on Tariffs and Trade
GDP – gross domestic product
HMO – health maintenance organization
HR – human resources
HTML – hypertext markup language
ICC – Interstate Commerce Commission
IPO – initial public offering
IRS – Internal Revenue Service
ISP – Internet service provider
kWh – kilowatt-hour
LAN – local-area network
LBO – leveraged buyout
LCD – liquid crystal display
LNG – liquefied natural gas
LP – limited partnership
Ltd. – limited
mips – millions of instructions per second
MW – megawatt
NAFTA – North American Free Trade Agreement
NASA – National Aeronautics and Space Administration
NASDAQ – National Association of Securities Dealers Automated Quotations
NATO – North Atlantic Treaty Organization
NYSE – New York Stock Exchange
OCR – optical character recognition
OECD – Organization for Economic Cooperation and Development
OEM – original equipment manufacturer
OPEC – Organization of Petroleum Exporting Countries

OS – operating system
OSHA – Occupational Safety and Health Administration
OTC – over-the-counter
PBX – private branch exchange
PCMCIA – Personal Computer Memory Card International Association
P/E – price to earnings ratio
RAID – redundant array of independent disks
RAM – random-access memory
R&D – research and development
RBOC – regional Bell operating company
RISC – reduced instruction set computer
REIT – real estate investment trust
ROA – return on assets
ROE – return on equity
ROI – return on investment
ROM – read-only memory
S&L – savings and loan
SCSI – Small Computer System Interface
SEC – Securities and Exchange Commission
SEVP – senior executive vice president
SIC – Standard Industrial Classification
SOC – system on a chip
SVP – senior vice president
USB – universal serial bus
VAR – value-added reseller
VAT – value-added tax
VC – venture capitalist
VoIP – Voice over Internet Protocol
VP – vice president
WAN – wide-area network
WWW – World Wide Web

Contents

Companies Profiled

Companies Profiled (continued)

Companies Profiled (continued)

Companies Profiled (continued)

Companies Profiled (continued)

About Hoover's Handbook of Private Companies 2006

Publishing current, relevant information about non-public companies can be a challenge, as many of these organizations see secrecy as a competitive strategy. Thus it is with pride that we offer this 11th edition of *Hoover's Handbook of Private Companies*. We do the tough work for you of compiling the hard-to-find facts which makes this volume one of the premier sources of business information on privately held enterprises in the US.

In this edition we bring you the facts on 900 of the largest and most influential enterprises in the US. As we did last year, we have dropped the past distinction between companies with in-depth profiles and those with shorter, capsule profiles. Some larger and more visible companies will continue to have an additional History section, but now all companies will have up to 10 years of financial information, product information where available, and a longer list of company executives.

By doing this, we achieve our goal of adding even more value to this already valuable resource.

HOOVER'S ONLINE FOR BUSINESS NEEDS

In addition to the 2,550 companies featured in our handbooks, coverage of some 40,000 business enterprises is available in electronic format on our Web site, Hoover's Online (www.hoovers.com). Our goal is to provide one site that offers authoritative, updated intelligence on US and global companies, industries, and the people who shape them. Hoover's has partnered with other prestigious business information and service providers to bring you all the right business information, services, and links in one place.

We welcome the recognition we have received as the premier provider of high-quality company information — online, electronically, and in print — and continue to look for ways to make our products more available and more useful to you.

Hoover's Handbook of Private Companies is one of our four-title series of handbooks that covers, literally, the world of business. The series is available as an indexed set, and also includes *Hoover's Handbook of American Business*, *Hoover's Handbook of World Business*, and *Hoover's Handbook of Emerging Companies*. This series brings you information on the biggest, fastest-growing, and most influential enterprises in the world.

We believe that anyone who buys from, sells to, invests in, lends to, competes with, interviews with, or works for a company should know all there is to know about that enterprise. Taken together, this book and the other Hoover's products and resources represent the most complete source of basic corporate information readily available to the general public.

HOW TO USE THIS BOOK

This book has four sections:

1. "Using Hoover's Handbooks" describes the contents of our profiles and explains the ways in which we gather and compile our data.

2. "A List-Lover's Compendium" contains lists of the largest and fastest-growing private companies. The lists are based on the information in our profiles, or compiled from well-known sources.

3. The company profiles section makes up the largest and most important part of the book — 900 profiles of major private enterprises, arranged alphabetically.

4. Three indexes complete the book. The first sorts companies by industry groups, the second by headquarters location. The third index is a list of all the executives found in the Executives section of each company profile.

As always, we hope you find our books useful. We invite your comments via phone (512-374-4500), fax (512-374-4538), mail (5800 Airport Boulevard, Austin, Texas 78752), or e-mail (custsupport@hoovers.com).

The Editors,
Austin, Texas,
December 2005

Using Hoover's Handbooks

SELECTION OF THE COMPANIES PROFILED

The 900 enterprises profiled in this book include the largest and most influential private enterprises in America. Among them are:

- private companies, from the giants (Cargill and Koch) to the colorful and prominent (Helmsley Enterprises and L.L. Bean)
- mutuals and cooperative organizations owned by their customers (State Farm Insurance, Ace Hardware, Ocean Spray Cranberries)
- not-for-profits (American Red Cross, Kaiser Foundation Health Plan, Smithsonian Institution)
- joint ventures (Motiva Enterprises, Dow Corning)
- partnerships (Baker & McKenzie, Kohlberg Kravis Roberts & Co.)
- universities (Columbia, Harvard, University of California)
- government-owned corporations (US Postal Service and New York City's Metropolitan Transportation Authority)
- and a selection of other enterprises (National Basketball Association, AFL-CIO, Texas Lottery Commission).

ORGANIZATION

The profiles are presented in alphabetical order. You will find the commonly used name of the enterprise at the beginning of the profile; the full, legal name is found in the Locations section. If a company name is also a person's name, such as Henry Ford Health System or Mary Kay, it will be alphabetized under the first name; if the company name starts with initials, for example, L.L. Bean or S.C. Johnson, look for it under the combined initials (in the above examples, LL and SC, respectively).

Basic financial data are listed under the heading Historical Financials. The annual financial information contained in the profiles is current through fiscal year-ends occurring as late as October 2005. We have included certain nonfinancial developments, such as officer changes, through November 2005.

OVERVIEW

In the first section of the profile, we have tried to give a thumbnail description of the company and what it does. The description will usually include information on the company's strategy, reputation, and ownership. We recommend that you read this section first.

HISTORY

This extended section, which is available for some of the larger and more well-known companies, reflects our belief that every enterprise is the sum of its history and that you have to know where you came from in order to know where you are going. While some companies have limited historical awareness and were unable to help us much and other companies are just plain boring, we think the vast majority of the enterprises in this book have colorful backgrounds. We have tried to focus on the people who made the enterprises what they are today. We have found these histories to be full of twists and ironies; they make fascinating reading.

EXECUTIVES

Here we list the names of the people who run the company, insofar as space allows. In the few cases where available, we have shown the ages and pay of key officers. In some instances the published data is for the previous year although the company has announced promotions or retirements since year-end. The pay represents cash compensation, including bonuses, but excludes stock option programs.

Although companies are free to structure their management titles any way they please, most modern corporations follow standard practices. The ultimate power in any corporation lies with the shareholders, who elect a board of directors, usually including officers or "insiders" as well as individuals from outside the company. The chief officer, the person on whose desk the buck stops, is usually called the chief executive officer (CEO). Often, he or she is also the chairman of the board.

As corporate management has become more complex, it is common for the CEO to have a "right-hand person" who oversees the day-to-day operations of the company, allowing the CEO plenty of time to focus on strategy and long-term issues. This right-hand person is usually designated the chief operating officer (COO) and is often the president of the company. In other cases one person is both chairman and president.

A multitude of other titles exists, including chief financial officer (CFO), chief administrative officer, and vice chairman. We have always tried to include the CFO, the chief legal officer, and the chief human resources or personnel officer.

The people named in the Executives section are indexed at the back of the book.

The Executives section also includes the name of the company's auditing (accounting) firm, where available.

LOCATIONS

Here we include the company's full legal name and its headquarters, street address, telephone and fax numbers, and Web site, as available. The back of the book includes an index of companies by headquarters locations.

In some cases we have also included information on the geographic distribution of the company's business, including sales and profit data. Note that these profit numbers, like those in the Products/Operations section below, are usually operating or pretax profits rather than net profits. Operating profits are generally those before financing costs (interest income and payments) and before taxes, which are considered costs attributable to the whole company rather than to one division or part of the world. For this reason the net income figures (in the Historical Financials section) are usually much lower, since they are after interest and taxes. Pretax profits are after interest but before taxes.

Headquarters for companies that are incorporated in Bermuda, but whose operational headquarters are in the US, are listed under their US address. The same applies for companies with joint US and non-US headquarters (such as KPMG International).

PRODUCTS/OPERATIONS

This section lists as many of the company's products, services, brand names, divisions, subsidiaries, and joint ventures as we could fit. We have tried to include all of its major lines and all familiar brand names.

The nature of this section varies by company and the amount of information available. If the company publishes sales and profit information by type of business, we have included it.

COMPETITORS

In this section we have listed companies that compete with the profiled company. This feature is included as a quick way to locate similar companies and compare them. The universe of competitors includes all public companies and all private companies with sales in excess of $500 million. In a few instances we have identified smaller private companies as key competitors.

HISTORICAL FINANCIALS

Here we have tried to present as much data about each enterprise's financial performance as we could compile in the allocated space. The information varies somewhat from industry to industry and is less complete in the case of private companies that do not release data (although we have always tried to provide annual sales and employment). There are a few industries, venture capital and investment banking, for example, for which revenue numbers are not reported as a rule. In the case of private companies that do not publicly disclose financial information, we have gathered estimates of sales and other statistics from numerous sources.

The following information is generally present.

A 10-year table, with relevant annualized compound growth rates, covers:

- Sales — fiscal year sales (year-end assets for most financial companies)
- Net income — fiscal year net income (before accounting changes)
- Income as a percent of sales — fiscal year net income as a percent of sales (as a percent of assets for most financial firms)
- Employees — fiscal year-end or average number of employees

The information on the number of employees is intended to aid the reader interested in knowing whether a company has a long-term trend of increasing or decreasing employment. As far as we know, we are the only company that publishes this information in print format.

The numbers on the left in each row of the Historical Financials section give the month and the year in which the company's fiscal year actually ends. Thus, a company with a March 31, 2005, year-end is shown as 3/05. The last item in the Financials section is a graph, which for private companies shows net income, or, if that is unavailable, sales.

Key year-end statistics are included in this section for insurance companies and companies required to file reports with the SEC. They generally show the financial strength of the enterprise, including:

- Debt ratio (long-term debt as a percent of shareholders' equity)
- Return on equity (net income divided by the average of beginning and ending common shareholders' equity)
- Cash and cash equivalents
- Current ratio (ratio of current assets to current liabilities)
- Total long-term debt (including capital lease obligations)
- Fiscal year sales for financial institutions.

Hoover's Handbook of

Private Companies

A List-Lover's Compendium

The 300 Largest Companies by Sales in
Hoover's Handbook of Private Companies 2006

Rank	Company	Sales ($ mil.)	Rank	Company	Sales ($ mil.)	Rank	Company	Sales ($ mil.)
1	Blue Cross	182,700	51	Science Applications Intl.	7,187	101	Hearst	4,100
2	Cargill	71,066	52	NewYork-Presbyterian Healthcare	7,060	102	Major League Baseball	4,100
3	U.S. Postal Service	68,996	53	Guardian Life Insurance	7,021	103	Graybar Electric	4,080
4	State Farm	56,100	54	Dairy Farmers of America	6,933	104	Levi Strauss	4,073
5	Koch Industries	40,000	55	Regence Group	6,700	105	QuikTrip	4,051
6	Cellco Partnership	27,662	56	American Family Insurance	6,607	106	Bill & Melinda Gates Foundation	4,010
7	Federal Reserve	26,847	57	Wakefern Food	6,578	107	Guardian Industries	4,000
8	Kaiser Foundation Health Plan	25,300	58	MidAmerican Energy	6,553	108	Schwan Food	4,000
9	Kaiser Permanente	25,300	59	S.C. Johnson	6,500	109	Transammonia	4,000
10	IGA	21,000	60	Marmon Group	6,400	110	Gulf States Toyota	3,800
11	Liberty Mutual	19,641	61	Blue Shield of California	6,203	111	University of Pennsylvania	3,786
12	Cingular Wireless	19,436	62	Alticor	6,200	112	Providence Health System	3,780
13	Motiva Enterprises	19,300	63	State University of New York	6,176	113	Stater Bros.	3,705
14	Massachusetts Mutual Life Insurance	18,705	64	Catholic Health Initiatives	6,121	114	Mutual of Omaha	3,656
15	Publix Super Markets	18,686	65	National Football League	6,000	115	Wegmans	3,600
16	Mars	18,000	66	Visa	6,000	116	Hyatt	3,600
17	New York Life	17,330	67	Menard	6,000	117	Gulf Oil	3,600
18	Ernst & Young	16,902	68	Advance Publications	5,909	118	SunGard Data Systems	3,556
19	Nationwide Mutual	16,803	69	Unisource	5,900	119	Mervyn's	3,553
20	Northwestern Mutual	16,545	70	New York State Lottery	5,848	120	Bloomberg	3,500
21	Deloitte	16,400	71	Boise Cascade	5,735	121	H.T. Hackney	3,500
22	Bechtel	16,337	72	Catholic Health East	5,700	122	84 Lumber	3,460
23	PricewaterhouseCoopers	16,283	73	MacAndrews & Forbes	5,700	123	Center Oil	3,400
24	University of California	15,122	74	Sutter Health	5,672	124	Milliken	3,400
25	Penske	14,000	75	Tenaska	5,600	125	University of Michigan	3,384
26	Blue Cross Blue Shield of Michigan	13,716	76	Southern Wine & Spirits	5,400	126	Health Insurance of New York	3,370
27	C&S Wholesale Grocers	13,600	77	Catholic Healthcare West	5,397	127	TAP Pharmaceutical	3,362
28	KPMG	13,440	78	Dole Food	5,316	128	Peter Kiewit Sons'	3,352
29	TIAA-CREF	12,815	79	Trinity Health	5,287	129	Ace Hardware	3,289
30	Meijer	11,900	80	University of Texas	5,235	130	University of Wisconsin	3,273
31	Cox Enterprises	11,552	81	VT	5,229	131	Intermountain Health Care	3,267
32	Carlson Wagonlit	11,500	82	Giant Eagle	5,100	132	ESPN	3,223
33	Toys "R" Us	11,100	83	Horizon Healthcare Services, Inc.	5,082	133	RaceTrac Petroleum	3,200
34	USAA	10,593	84	Sony BMG	5,000	134	Bonneville Power	3,198
35	H. E. Butt Grocery	10,500	85	Mayo Foundation	4,822	135	JohnsonDiversey	3,169
36	Adventist Health System	10,123	86	Roundy's	4,777	136	J.R. Simplot	3,100
37	Chevron Phillips Chemical	9,558	87	MBM	4,744	137	Eby-Brown	3,100
38	FMR	9,200	88	Auto-Owners Insurance	4,714	138	Ohio State University	3,060
39	Highmark	9,118	89	New United Motor Manufacturing	4,699	139	Unified Western Grocers	3,040
40	Ascension Health	9,054	90	Pacific Mutual	4,668	140	Salvation Army	3,040
41	CCA Global	8,700	91	Reyes Holdings	4,630	141	American Red Cross	3,034
42	Trump Organization	8,500	92	Topco Associates	4,600	142	Alliance Capital Management	3,027
43	Carlson	8,400	93	Associated Wholesale Grocers	4,570	143	Sisters of Mercy Health System	3,003
44	Health Care Service	8,190	94	Metropolitan Transportation Authority	4,523	144	NASCAR	3,000
45	Army and Air Force Exchange	7,905	95	Platinum Equity	4,500	145	E. & J. Gallo	3,000
46	JM Family Enterprises	7,700	96	Hy-Vee	4,500	146	National Basketball Association	3,000
47	Land O'Lakes	7,677	97	Thrivent Financial	4,469	147	Kohler	3,000
48	TVA	7,533	98	Hallmark	4,400	148	McKinsey & Company	3,000
49	Enterprise Rent-A-Car	7,400	99	Delta Dental of California	4,300	149	Security Benefit Group	2,969
50	Flying J	7,301	100	New York City Health and Hospitals	4,200	150	Texas Lottery	2,966

SOURCE: HOOVER'S, INC., DATABASE, OCTOBER 2005

The 300 Largest Companies by Sales in
Hoover's Handbook of Private Companies 2006 (continued)

Rank	Company	Sales ($ mil.)	Rank	Company	Sales ($ mil.)	Rank	Company	Sales ($ mil.)
151	Cook Inlet Energy Supply	2,950	201	Hunt Consolidated	2,250	251	US Oncology	1,966
152	Kinray	2,910	202	Western Refining	2,215	252	Structure Tone	1,950
153	Schneider National	2,900	203	Sentry Insurance	2,213	253	Demoulas Super Markets	1,950
154	University of Illinois	2,900	204	Goodwill	2,210	254	Allina Hospitals	1,940
155	Sinclair Oil	2,900	205	H Group Holding	2,200	255	DynCorp International	1,921
156	California State University	2,900	206	Schreiber Foods	2,200	256	California Dairies	1,916
157	Jones Financial	2,891	207	ContiGroup	2,200	257	Rich Products	1,910
158	Catholic Healthcare Partners	2,874	208	Ingram Industries	2,200	258	Love's Travel Stops	1,900
159	Dow Corning	2,873	209	JELD-WEN	2,200	259	Texas Health Resources	1,900
160	Wawa	2,819	210	HP Hood	2,200	260	Dr Pepper/Seven Up Bottling	1,900
161	Red Apple Group	2,800	211	Glazer's Wholesale Drug	2,200	261	SSM Health Care	1,900
162	Perdue Farms	2,800	212	Save Mart	2,194	262	Central National-Gottesman	1,900
163	A-Mark Financial	2,800	213	Quintiles Transnational	2,146	263	Westcon	1,885
164	Keystone Foods	2,800	214	F. Dohmen Co.	2,141	264	Whiting-Turner Contracting	1,876
165	Lefrak Organization	2,800	215	Ag Processing	2,127	265	Spectrum Health	1,868
166	Hendrick Automotive	2,783	216	Solo Cup	2,116	266	Minnesota Mutual	1,827
167	Port Authority of NY and NJ	2,764	217	Cumberland Farms	2,100	267	UniGroup	1,809
168	Swinerton	2,751	218	Golden State Foods	2,100	268	University of Rochester	1,809
169	Clark Enterprises	2,750	219	Gilbane	2,100	269	J.M. Huber	1,805
170	Allegis Group	2,750	220	Fry's Electronics	2,100	270	CARQUEST	1,800
171	Advocate Health Care	2,716	221	National Hockey League	2,100	271	EBSCO	1,800
172	CH2M HILL	2,715	222	AMTRAK	2,077	272	Bashas'	1,800
173	FM Global	2,700	223	Columbia University	2,074	273	Kingston Technology	1,800
174	Booz Allen Hamilton	2,700	224	Texas Genco	2,054	274	Asplundh Tree Expert	1,800
175	TravelCenters of America	2,678	225	Vanguard Group	2,044	275	Mary Kay	1,800
176	Henry Ford Health System	2,600	226	Holman Enterprises	2,042	276	General Parts	1,800
177	J.F. Shea	2,597	227	True Value	2,024	277	Hensel Phelps Construction	1,800
178	George E. Warren	2,586	228	Hexion Specialty Chemicals	2,019	278	Illinois Lottery	1,799
179	Yale University	2,565	229	DeBruce Grain	2,018	279	Memec	1,798
180	Cornell University	2,510	230	Forever Living	2,012	280	ABC Supply	1,793
181	Springs Industries	2,500	231	CalPERS	2,006	281	AMC Entertainment	1,783
182	Golub	2,500	232	New York University	2,005	282	Vanguard Health Systems	1,783
183	BJC HealthCare	2,500	233	Houchens	2,005	283	Walsh Group	1,725
184	International Data Group	2,500	234	Metaldyne	2,004	284	Metro-Goldwyn-Mayer	1,725
185	Vistar	2,500	235	Lanoga	2,000	285	Charmer-Sunbelt	1,700
186	Harvard University	2,473	236	Irvine Company	2,000	286	Purdue Pharma	1,700
187	Belk	2,447	237	NextiraOne	2,000	287	Ashley Furniture	1,700
188	CUNA Mutual	2,416	238	Scoular	2,000	288	Delaware North	1,700
189	Discovery Communications	2,365	239	Grant Thornton International	2,000	289	A. G. Spanos	1,700
190	Pennsylvania Lottery	2,352	240	Quad/Graphics	2,000	290	Purity Wholesale Grocers	1,700
191	Energy Transfer Equity	2,347	241	WinCo Foods	2,000	291	Bose	1,700
192	Alex Lee	2,320	242	Andersen	2,000	292	University of Chicago	1,699
193	Stanford University	2,300	243	Follett	2,000	293	Adventist Health	1,690
194	Sheetz	2,300	244	AECOM Technology	2,000	294	Dunavant Enterprises	1,664
195	Connell Company	2,300	245	Tishman Realty & Construction	2,000	295	Dresser	1,657
196	Consolidated Electrical	2,300	246	Ergon	2,000	296	Dunn Industries	1,655
197	Tufts Associated Health Plans	2,300	247	Vanderbilt University	1,971	297	Software House	1,652
198	New York Power Authority	2,292	248	Vision Service Plan	1,970	298	Parsons	1,651
199	Bill Heard Enterprises	2,279	249	Sammons Enterprises	1,969	299	Vertis	1,645
200	University of Washington	2,263	250	Group Health Cooperative of Puget Sound	1,966	300	Larry H. Miller Group	1,608

The 300 Largest Employers in
Hoover's Handbook of Private Companies 2006

Rank	Company	Employees	Rank	Company	Employees	Rank	Company	Employees
1	U.S. Postal Service	707,485	51	Burger King	32,600	101	Perdue Farms	18,000
2	Carlson	190,000	52	Providence Health System	32,526	102	AECOM Technology	18,000
3	Toys "R" Us	157,000	53	Wegmans	32,000	103	Hallmark	18,000
4	Blue Cross	150,000	54	Platinum Equity	32,000	104	Belk	17,900
5	Kaiser Permanente	147,000	55	Jones Financial	31,400	105	AMC Entertainment	17,200
6	Publix Super Markets	128,000	56	Catholic Healthcare Partners	30,524	106	Springs Industries	17,000
7	Cargill	124,000	57	Delaware North	30,000	107	Carrols Holdings	17,000
8	PricewaterhouseCoopers	122,471	58	Life Care Centers	30,000	108	Quintiles Transnational	16,986
9	University of California	120,786	59	Nationwide Mutual	30,000	109	Texas Health Resources	16,800
10	Deloitte	115,000	60	Koch Industries	30,000	110	Lefrak Organization	16,200
11	Ernst & Young	106,650	61	FMR	29,424	111	24 Hour Fitness	16,000
12	KPMG	93,983	62	Advance Publications	29,200	112	Hobby Lobby	16,000
13	IGA	92,000	63	Mervyn's	29,000	113	Stater Bros.	15,700
14	Ascension Health	87,469	64	Asplundh Tree Expert	28,948	114	ContiGroup	15,500
15	Goodwill	82,370	65	University of Wisconsin	28,030	115	New York University	15,010
16	State Farm	79,000	66	Giant Eagle	28,000	116	Wawa	15,000
17	Cox Enterprises	77,000	67	Kohler	28,000	117	Trump Organization	15,000
18	Meijer	75,000	68	Menard	27,000	118	KB Toys	15,000
19	Cingular Wireless	70,300	69	University of Washington	26,750	119	Indiana University	15,000
20	University of Texas	66,845	70	Sisters of Mercy Health System	26,000	120	Sentara Healthcare	15,000
21	Dole Food	64,000	71	BJC HealthCare	25,525	121	Booz Allen Hamilton	14,800
22	H. E. Butt Grocery	60,000	72	Metromedia	25,500	122	Detroit Medical Center	14,311
23	Enterprise Rent-A-Car	57,300	73	Advocate Health Care	25,000	123	Vanguard Health Systems	14,300
24	Kaiser Foundation Health Plan	54,300	74	Texas A&M	24,500	124	DynCorp International	14,100
25	NewYork-Presbyterian Healthcare	53,562	75	Schwan Food	24,000	125	Peter Kiewit Sons'	14,000
26	Catholic Health Initiatives	53,459	76	University of Missouri	23,513	126	CH2M HILL	14,000
27	Wakefern Food	50,000	77	University of Illinois	23,483	127	Milliken	14,000
28	Cellco Partnership	49,800	78	SSM Health Care	23,300	128	University of Southern California	14,000
29	Army and Air Force Exchange	47,323	79	Buffets Holdings	23,000	129	Spectrum Health	14,000
30	Chick-fil-A	46,500	80	Allina Hospitals	22,583	130	AMF Bowling	13,800
31	Hy-Vee	46,000	81	AMTRAK	22,000	131	Cornell University	13,677
32	Trinity Health	44,100	82	Golub	22,000	132	International Data Group	13,510
33	Adventist Health System	44,000	83	Marmon Group	22,000	133	Inova Health System	13,500
34	California State University	44,000	84	Roundy's	21,855	134	Harman Management	13,500
35	Bechtel	44,000	85	University of Nebraska	21,624	135	General Parts	13,500
36	Catholic Health East	43,000	86	Grant Thornton International	21,500	136	Bashas'	13,200
37	Mayo Foundation	42,620	87	USAA	21,000	137	Cinemark	13,200
38	Salvation Army	42,530	88	JELD-WEN	21,000	138	Flying J	13,000
39	Science Applications Intl.	42,400	89	Schneider National	20,733	139	Whataburger	13,000
40	H Group Holding	42,000	90	UNICCO Service	20,500	140	SunGard Data Systems	13,000
41	Sutter Health	41,000	91	Federal Reserve	20,448	141	Health Care Service	13,000
42	American Red Cross	40,000	92	ClientLogic	20,300	142	Alticor	13,000
43	Catholic Healthcare West	40,000	93	Federal Prison Industries	20,274	143	TVA	12,742
44	Hyatt	40,000	94	Hearst	20,000	144	Henry Ford Health System	12,700
45	Mars	39,000	95	Day & Zimmermann	20,000	145	New York Life	12,650
46	Liberty Mutual	38,000	96	MacAndrews & Forbes	19,800	146	University of Chicago	12,623
47	CARQUEST	36,500	97	Guardian Industries	19,000	147	LPA Holding	12,000
48	Penske	36,000	98	Adventist Health	18,823	148	Quad/Graphics	12,000
49	Ohio State University	34,000	99	Vanderbilt University	18,551	149	C&S Wholesale Grocers	12,000
50	City University of New York	33,460	100	ClubCorp	18,500	150	Philip Services	12,000

SOURCE: HOOVER'S, INC., DATABASE, OCTOBER 2005

The 300 Largest Employers in
Hoover's Handbook of Private Companies 2006 (continued)

Rank	Company	Employees
151	JohnsonDiversey	12,000
152	Turner Industries	12,000
153	S.C. Johnson	12,000
154	University of Pennsylvania	11,949
155	White Castle	11,815
156	Captain D's	11,590
157	MidAmerican Energy	11,540
158	TravelCenters of America	11,510
159	Solo Cup	11,500
160	J.R. Simplot	11,500
161	Mashantucket Pequot Gaming	11,500
162	McKinsey & Company	11,500
163	VICORP Restaurants	11,382
164	Foster Poultry Farms	11,000
165	Harvard University	11,000
166	Highmark	11,000
167	Boscov's Department Store	11,000
168	Bass Pro Shops	10,700
169	Ritz Camera	10,700
170	Brookdale Senior Living	10,500
171	Michigan State University	10,500
172	Boise Cascade	10,494
173	Concentra	10,370
174	Alex Lee	10,300
175	Mohegan Tribal Gaming	10,300
176	Stream	10,149
177	MediaNews	10,000
178	Sony BMG	10,000
179	Vanguard Group	10,000
180	Massachusetts Mutual Life Insurance	10,000
181	SSA Marine	10,000
182	Follett	10,000
183	Sheetz	9,950
184	Texas Pacific Group	9,900
185	Barnes & Noble College Bookstores	9,900
186	Group Health Cooperative of Puget Sound	9,708
187	SAS Institute	9,528
188	Discount Tire	9,500
189	Save Mart	9,417
190	Ashley Furniture	9,300
191	Houchens	9,229
192	Amsted Industries	9,100
193	Zachry Construction	9,096
194	Battelle Memorial	9,034
195	Haworth	9,000
196	NextiraOne	9,000
197	Parsons	9,000
198	Dr Pepper/Seven Up Bottling	8,900
199	Levi Strauss	8,850
200	Graham Packaging	8,600

Rank	Company	Employees
201	Big Y Foods	8,600
202	Musicland	8,500
203	Blue Cross Blue Shield of Michigan	8,500
204	The Restaurant Company	8,400
205	Baker & McKenzie	8,400
206	Towers Perrin	8,384
207	Dresser	8,300
208	Memorial Sloan-Kettering	8,255
209	American Family Insurance	8,238
210	J. Crew	8,200
211	Dow Corning	8,200
212	Uno Restaurant Holdings	8,200
213	US Oncology	8,096
214	Yale University	8,071
215	Renco	8,000
216	Lanoga	8,000
217	ValleyCrest	8,000
218	Metaldyne	8,000
219	Vertis	8,000
220	Andersen	8,000
221	Key Safety Systems	8,000
222	Bloomberg	8,000
223	84 Lumber	8,000
224	Southern Wine & Spirits	8,000
225	Land O'Lakes	8,000
226	Bose	8,000
227	BE&K	7,700
228	Graybar Electric	7,700
229	Timex	7,500
230	WinCo Foods	7,500
231	Mark IV	7,500
232	Spansion	7,500
233	Town Sports International Holdings	7,440
234	Pella	7,400
235	University of Iowa Hospitals and Clinics	7,229
236	Quality Dining	7,176
237	Northwestern University	7,100
238	Unisource	7,100
239	Carlson Wagonlit	7,047
240	United Supermarkets	7,000
241	QuikTrip	7,000
242	Cumberland Farms	7,000
243	Family Sports Concepts	7,000
244	McWane	7,000
245	Sinclair Oil	7,000
246	Port Authority of NY and NJ	7,000
247	Academy	6,995
248	Crown Equipment	6,900
249	Hexion Specialty Chemicals	6,900
250	W. L. Gore & Associates	6,900

Rank	Company	Employees
251	Remy	6,800
252	Ingram Industries	6,730
253	MTD Products	6,600
254	Sbarro	6,500
255	Jordan Industries	6,500
256	Rich Products	6,500
257	Keystone Foods	6,500
258	NCH	6,500
259	Sealy	6,399
260	Bertucci's	6,307
261	Duane Reade	6,300
262	Jostens	6,300
263	Black & Veatch	6,200
264	Outsourcing Solutions	6,100
265	Southeastern Freight Lines	6,000
266	GENCO Distribution System	6,000
267	Regence Group	6,000
268	Sydran Services	6,000
269	Visa	6,000
270	TIAA-CREF	6,000
271	McKee Foods	6,000
272	Fry's Electronics	6,000
273	CUNA Mutual	6,000
274	Jamba Juice	5,880
275	Team Health	5,800
276	Atrium Hotels	5,800
277	GeoLogistics	5,700
278	Rooms To Go	5,700
279	Larry H. Miller Group	5,700
280	University of Louisville	5,521
281	Culligan	5,500
282	Glazer's Wholesale Drug	5,500
283	Chevron Phillips Chemical	5,300
284	Princeton University	5,291
285	TriMas Corporation	5,200
286	ICON Health	5,142
287	EBSCO	5,000
288	Dart Container	5,000
289	Real Mex Restaurants	5,000
290	Ace Hardware	5,000
291	Brand Intermediate	5,000
292	King Kullen Grocery	5,000
293	Consolidated Electrical	5,000
294	HP Hood	5,000
295	Guardian Life Insurance	5,000
296	Davey Tree	5,000
297	Caribou Coffee	4,934
298	Scott Fetzer	4,889
299	J.M. Huber	4,850
300	NUMMI	4,800

The *Inc.* 500 Fastest-Growing Private Companies in America

Rank	Company	Headquarters	Sales Growth Increase (%)*	Rank	Company	Headquarters	Sales Growth Increase (%)*
1	Video Gaming Technologies	Roebuck, SC	9,720.5	51	Mirifex Systems	Strongsville, OH	1,373.7
2	Merlin Technical Solutions	Greenwood Vil., CO	7,978.9	52	Mont Blanc Gourmet	Denver, CO	1,335.1
3	eSilicon	Sunnyvale, CA	7,088.5	53	SurePayroll	Skokie, IL	1,302.3
4	ADS	Virginia Beach, VA	6,028.5	54	MarketerNet	Chicago, IL	1,299.9
5	Bankers Healthcare Group	Weston, FL	5,817.8	55	CustomInk.com	Falls Church, VA	1,293.6
6	Meridias Capital	Henderson, NV	5,575.0	56	Outsourcing Solutions	Jupiter, FL	1,272.4
7	180solutions	Bellevue, WA	5,418.7	57	WhitePages.com	Seattle, WA	1,265.6
8	Object Sciences	Kingstowne, VA	4,939.8	58	Tri-Auto Enterprises	Indianapolis, IN	1,257.9
9	Arbor Networks	Lexington, MA	4,650.9	59	Zantaz	Pleasanton, CA	1,207.9
10	OptionsXpress	Chicago, IL	4,370.2	60	FXCM	New York City, NY	1,189.7
11	Moe's	Atlanta, GA	3,583.4	61	Alere Medical	Reno, NV	1,189.1
12	Evolve Manufacturing Technologies	Mountain View, CA	3,311.6	62	Metronome	Irvine, CA	1,139.3
13	NexTag	San Mateo, CA	3,247.5	63	Duck Creek Technologies	Bolivar, MO	1,131.4
14	Garden of Life	West Palm Beach, FL	2,865.5	64	ONI Medical Systems	Wilmington, MA	1,125.8
15	Coventry First	Fort Washington, PA	2,857.9	65	Intelligent Software Solutions	Colorado Springs, CO	1,124.4
16	Spheris	Franklin, TN	2,710.8	66	CharterAuction	Quincy, MA	1,108.6
17	iDirect Technologies	Herndon, VA	2,573.1	67	DriveCam	San Diego, CA	1,105.6
18	Gratis Internet	Washington, DC	2,349.8	68	SeamlessWeb	New York City, NY	1,104.9
19	United Bank Card	Hampton, NJ	2,319.1	69	Peak 10	Charlotte, NC	1,085.4
20	C&S Marketing	Sacramento, CA	2,314.6	70	Die Cuts With a View	Provo, UT	1,074.9
21	Purcell Systems	Spokane Valley, WA	2,273.0	71	ZeroChaos	Orlando, FL	1,070.3
22	Commodity Sourcing Group	Detroit, MI	2,121.0	72	GamePlan Financial Marketing	Woodstock, GA	1,057.6
23	Zappos.com	Las Vegas, NV	2,118.7	73	Allconnect	Atlanta, GA	1,052.5
24	WageWorks	San Mateo, CA	2,116.9	74	Logic Trends	Atlanta, GA	1,049.1
25	Sirius Solutions	Houston, TX	2,111.7	75	Buycostumes.com	New Berlin, WI	1,046.1
26	PreCash	Houston, TX	2,098.2	76	GTCI	Richardson, TX	1,028.4
27	NetSuite	San Mateo, CA	1,924.1	77	Athenahealth	Watertown, MA	1,025.8
28	Telesis	Rockville, MD	1,894.0	78	Pinnacle Technical Resources	Dallas, TX	1,024.9
29	OpenPages	Waltham, MA	1,876.4	79	SecureWorks	Atlanta, GA	1,011.9
30	MDVIP	Boca Raton, FL	1,841.1	80	STG International	Alexandria, VA	1,009.1
31	Epam Systems	Lawrenceville, NJ	1,840.8	81	CodeCorrect	Yakima, WA	1,007.8
32	Albridge Solutions	Lawrenceville, NJ	1,787.7	82	BullsEye Telecom	Oak Park, MI	1,006.9
33	Kineticom	San Diego, CA	1,759.7	83	EmailLabs	Menlo Park, CA	1,006.2
34	Guy Brown Products	Brentwood, TN	1,755.3	84	eNeighborhoods	Boca Raton, FL	985.9
35	LanceSoft	Reston, VA	1,737.7	85	TriVirix	Durham, NC	983.4
36	Convergenz	McLean, VA	1,724.0	86	Gain Capital Group	Bedminster, NJ	981.9
37	CaseStack	Santa Monica, CA	1,718.2	87	Liquidity Services	Washington, DC	976.1
38	Intellimar	Sykesville, MD	1,703.4	88	MBI	Waltham, MA	960.5
39	Khimetrics	Scottsdale, AZ	1,675.1	89	Edge Products	Ogden, UT	955.2
40	SkinMedica	Carlsbad, CA	1,641.0	90	Aagard Group	Alexandria, MN	927.4
41	OnFiber Communications	Austin, TX	1,587.8	91	Actcom Security Solutions	Virginia Beach, VA	926.2
42	Health Market Science	King of Prussia, PA	1,547.3	92	MaxStream	Lindon, UT	923.7
43	NetQoS	Austin, TX	1,541.0	93	TSC Band-All	Rock Island, IL	919.4
44	FX Solutions	Ridgewood, NJ	1,516.9	94	EMA Design Automation	Rochester, NY	915.1
45	Petron Pacific	Chantilly, VA	1,468.8	95	Salary.com	Needham, MA	914.7
46	Summit Mortgage	Boston, MA	1,463.2	96	Protomold	Maple Plain, MN	912.6
47	Xpress Source	Dothan, AL	1,462.2	97	U.S. Tech Solutions	Jersey City, NJ	910.2
48	EFG Leasing	Fresno, CA	1,449.2	98	R&L Construction	Yonkers, NY	910.1
49	Attache	Columbus, OH	1,403.2	99	Ameresco	Framingham, MA	908.4
50	eTelecare Global Solutions	Monrovia, CA	1,391.5	100	Blue Canopy	Reston, VA	907.1

*Average annual sales growth measured over a three-year period.

SOURCE: *INC.*; FALL, 2005

The *Inc.* 500 Fastest-Growing Private Companies in America (continued)

Rank	Company	Headquarters	Sales Growth Increase (%)	Rank	Company	Headquarters	Sales Growth Increase (%)
101	2Wire	San Jose, CA	896.6	151	DSLExtreme.com	Winnetka, CA	697.3
102	The Go Daddy Group	Scottsdale, AZ	892.2	152	LatiNode	Miami, FL	689.5
103	EVault	Emeryville, CA	880.3	153	Sauna Warehouse	Lake Forest, CA	686.8
104	NextWeb	Fremont, CA	871.4	154	New Media Strategies	Arlington, VA	686.4
105	Picis	Wakefield, MA	868.6	155	NextGen Information Services	St. Louis, MO	679.7
106	SmartPak Equine	Plymouth, MA	868.2	156	Budget Blinds	Orange, CA	678.8
107	Smooth Corp.	Bellevue, WA	866.1	157	Intuitive Research and Technology	Huntsville, AL	676.3
108	Educational Outfitters	Chattanooga, TN	851.5	158	National Atlantic Holdings	Freehold, NJ	670.7
109	Medical Education Broadcast Network	Londonderry, NH	849.1	159	Ensynch	Tempe, AZ	667.9
110	Just Marketing	Indianapolis, IN	849.0	160	Ameridian Specialty Services	Cincinnati, OH	666.2
111	Outsource Partners International	Los Angeles, CA	841.8	161	Peoplelink	South Bend, IN	659.9
112	Repipe Specialists	Glendale, CA	841.1	162	LoanBright	Evergreen, CO	659.4
113	Orizon	Rockville, MD	840.8	163	Theprinters.com	State College, PA	657.5
114	The Great American Hanger Co.	Miami, FL	838.2	164	STOPS	Titusville, FL	653.9
115	PaySource	Dayton, OH	837.2	165	S.M. Stoller	Lafayette, CO	645.3
116	GlobeNet	Alexandria, VA	827.9	166	Advanced Patient Advocacy	Annapolis, MD	643.7
117	SecureUSA	Cumming, GA	827.6	167	Big Communications	Ferndale, MI	642.7
118	Hire Expectations	Northville, MI	818.1	168	KnowledgeStorm	Alpharetta, GA	633.1
119	FlexCorp Systems	New York City, NY	815.7	169	Günther Douglas	Denver, CO	629.9
120	Intellidyn	Hingham, MA	815.4	170	Shutterfly	Redwood City, CA	626.8
121	EveryTicket.com	Miami Beach, FL	811.6	171	VeriCenter	Houston, TX	625.9
122	MILA	Mountlake Terrace, WA	802.5	172	SDI Networks	Greenville, SC	625.2
123	Arena Communications	Salt Lake City, UT	799.8	173	Oregon Aero	Scappoose, OR	618.3
124	AbsoluteHire	Roseville, CA	795.0	174	Octagon Research Solutions	Wayne, PA	616.5
125	Deco Security Services	Baxter, MN	793.6	175	Marketing Informatics	Indianapolis, IN	614.5
126	Red Peacock International	Glendale, CA	784.2	176	The Westwood Group	Washington, DC	608.9
127	Dynetech	Orlando, FL	779.2	177	Red Hawk Industries	Greenwood Village, CO	602.3
128	Magnetech Integrated Services	South Bend, IN	773.4	178	Platinum Holdings	Indianapolis, IN	600.8
129	Fastclick	Santa Barbara, CA	770.2	179	PremierGarage	Phoenix, AZ	600.2
130	Union Equity	Indianapolis, IN	766.2	180	American Capital Financial Services	Sacramento, CA	597.3
131	iSqFt	Cincinnati, OH	763.2	181	Neumann Enterprises	Waukesha, WI	596.6
132	MindLance	Hoboken, NJ	760.0	182	Innovative Solutions Consulting	Hollywood, MD	592.4
133	Pacific Property Assets	Irvine, CA	753.1	183	Information Transport Solutions	Wetumpka, AL	591.9
134	Video Networks	Gaithersburg, MD	752.3	184	Premier Environmental Services	Marietta, GA	588.0
135	AdminServer	Chester, PA	751.4	185	Esys	Auburn Hills, MI	580.4
136	Ascentium	Bellevue, WA	743.0	186	Vintage IT Services	Austin, TX	580.1
137	StarMine	San Francisco, CA	729.9	187	IDEAS	Uniontown, OH	579.0
138	Liquidnet Holdings	New York City, NY	725.7	188	JLT Mobile Computers	Chandler, AZ	579.0
139	Call Inc.	Doylestown, PA	725.7	189	Primescape Solutions	Arlington, VA	577.8
140	Intercept Interactive	New York City, NY	722.8	190	HostMySite.com	Newark, DE	573.5
141	Academic Superstore	Austin, TX	720.2	191	Coastal Technologies Group	Boca Raton, FL	573.1
142	Allied Home Medical	Cookeville, TN	719.5	192	UpStream Software	Rochester, MI	570.9
143	Mighty Leaf Tea	San Rafael, CA	716.2	193	Financial Recovery Services	Edina, MN	569.4
144	InfoReliance	Fairfax, VA	712.3	194	Apartment Express Corporate Housing	Tampa, FL	567.4
145	TransDimension	Irvine, CA	710.7	195	MarketRx	Bridgewater, NJ	567.3
146	Equity Plus	San Diego, CA	709.2	196	TX Air Composites	Desoto, TX	565.8
147	Strategic Business Systems	Herndon, VA	704.1	197	Argotek	South Riding, VA	561.5
148	Radiance Technologies	Huntsville, AL	701.7	198	Ambient Weather	Phoenix, AZ	559.2
149	The Planet	Dallas, TX	698.3	199	Ad-Base Systems	Pittsburgh, PA	557.8
150	PCPC Direct	Houston, TX	697.5	200	HSU Development	Rockville, MD	557.7

Rank	Company	Headquarters	Sales Growth Increase (%)	Rank	Company	Headquarters	Sales Growth Increase (%)
201	HireQuest	Irvine, CA	549.7	251	K & Co.	Parkville, MO	483.8
202	Vineyard Vines	Stamford, CT	547.0	252	BoDeans Baking Co.	Le Mars, IA	483.5
203	DataCert	Houston, TX	545.7	253	iBahn	South Jordan, UT	482.4
204	ePrize	Pleasant Ridge, MI	543.2	254	Oasis Semiconductor	Waltham, MA	482.3
205	Quintum Technologies	Eatontown, NJ	542.1	255	FirstComp	Omaha, NE	478.9
206	PriceGrabber.com	Los Angeles, CA	539.2	256	CarterBaldwin	Roswell, GA	478.8
207	Underground Technologies	Maryville, TN	536.7	257	Epocrates	San Mateo, CA	473.6
208	Who's Calling	Kirkland, WA	536.1	258	FootBridge	Andover, MA	472.7
209	Mortgage Store, The	St. Louis, MO	533.7	259	Omniture	Orem, UT	472.0
210	Smart Carpet	Manasquan, NJ	530.2	260	Netconn Solutions	Hagerstown, MD	470.9
211	Correct Building Products	Biddeford, ME	530.0	261	U.S. Legal Forms	Flowood, MS	469.1
212	ReQuest	Ballston Spa, NY	528.7	262	Brownwood Acres Foods	Eastport, MI	468.2
213	Media Temple	Culver City, CA	526.7	263	Autobase	Indianapolis, IN	467.3
214	Silver State Mortgage	Las Vegas, NV	526.4	264	Jasa Transit	Blair, NE	466.4
215	BuyOnlineNow.com	Rochester, MN	526.3	265	Vocollect	Pittsburgh, PA	466.0
216	RagingWire Enterprise Solutions	Sacramento, CA	525.5	266	SiloSmashers	Fairfax, VA	466.0
217	Jarrett Logistics Systems	Orrville, OH	524.8	267	VisionIT	Detroit, MI	465.8
218	American Apparel	Los Angeles, CA	524.6	268	Capital Field Services	Columbus, OH	464.3
219	Arrowhead Global Solutions	Falls Church, VA	522.5	269	Jobing.com	Phoenix, AZ	463.8
220	HRsmart	Richardson, TX	522.1	270	TechDisposal	Columbus, OH	462.6
221	SM Consulting	Linthicum, MD	520.9	271	Integrated Management Services	Jackson, MS	459.5
222	GeoLearning	West Des Moines, IA	520.1	272	Omega Systems	Phoenix, AZ	456.5
223	Edge Development	Temecula, CA	518.7	273	CBay Systems	Annapolis, MD	456.4
224	METI	El Paso, TX	514.0	274	BCS Industries	Memphis, TN	454.6
225	SP Systems	Greenbelt, MD	513.5	275	The Newberry Group	St. Charles, MO	452.9
226	Starizon	Keystone, CO	512.3	276	Restaurant Technologies	Eagan, MN	452.2
227	ClearSource	Natick, MA	511.6	277	Mimeo.com	New York City, NY	452.0
228	ScriptLogic	Boca Raton, FL	511.2	278	MTC Performance	Schaumburg, IL	447.1
229	Dynarand	San Francisco, CA	510.7	279	EnvoyWorldWide	Bedford, MA	447.1
230	Bodybuilding.com	Boise, ID	509.5	280	Family First Mortgage	Palm Coast, FL	446.1
231	Contours Express	Nicholasville, KY	507.9	281	UniScripts	North Huntingdon, PA	446.1
232	Mary Frances Accessories	Lafayette, CA	507.4	282	Access Systems	Reston, VA	443.7
233	Wholesale Carrier Services	Boca Raton, FL	502.8	283	New Edge Networks	Vancouver, WA	442.2
234	Mythics	Virginia Beach, VA	501.9	284	Payerpath	Richmond, VA	441.4
235	Networks Plus Technology Group	San Diego, CA	500.9	285	C&B Services	Port Neches, TX	441.1
				286	ISR	Liberty Lake, WA	440.1
236	High Power Technical Services	Louisville, KY	499.3	287	Clear!Blue	Birmingham, MI	438.7
237	Insulair	Vernalis, CA	498.4	288	Genscape	Louisville, KY	437.8
238	Visionary Solutions	Oak Ridge, TN	498.1	289	Beacon Hill Staffing Group	Boston, MA	436.4
239	Kara Homes	East Brunswick, NJ	498.0	290	Avail Workforce Management Solutions	Atlanta, GA	434.0
240	Harbor Payments	Atlanta, GA	496.5				
241	ECS	Fairfax, VA	492.6	291	Summit Energy	Park City, UT	434.0
242	Campbellsville Apparel	Campbellsville, KY	491.2	292	ProSight	Portland, OR	432.4
243	Sedona Staffing Services	Frankfort, IL	489.5	293	VitalSmarts	Provo, UT	432.0
244	Thralow	Duluth, MN	488.0	294	Marlabs	Edison, NJ	431.1
245	Labor Staffing	Chamblee, GA	487.9	295	The Christmas Light Co.	Phoenix, AZ	431.0
246	The Active Network	San Diego, CA	487.2	296	Resolution Consulting	Broomfield, CO	430.4
247	Headsets.com	San Francisco, CA	487.1	297	DataStream Market Intelligence	Owasso, OK	430.0
248	Intellect Technical Solutions	Clearwater, FL	486.0	298	Resource Options	Needham, MA	429.5
249	S.A. Robotics	Loveland, CO	485.5	299	Nappanee Window	Nappanee, IN	428.1
250	CITI	Arlington, VA	485.4	300	Netspoke	Woburn, MA	427.7

Rank	Company	Headquarters	Sales Growth Increase (%)
301	Möbius Partners Enterprise Solutions	San Antonio, TX	426.9
302	Employer Solutions Group	Bakersfield, CA	426.8
303	Century Gaming	Missoula, MT	425.6
304	Super D	Irvine, CA	425.5
305	ChromaDex	Santa Ana, CA	425.1
306	McKnight Associates	Plano, TX	425.0
307	ViaCell	Cambridge, MA	424.5
308	ShowMe Tickets	Columbia, IL	424.3
309	Motor Car Auto Carriers	Commerce City, CO	424.0
310	Artel	Reston, VA	423.4
311	Ventech Solutions	Columbus, OH	422.3
312	Eoscene	Renton, WA	421.5
313	Global eProcure	Clark, NJ	421.4
314	HTP	Columbus, OH	419.9
315	Line Systems	Newtown Square, PA	419.3
316	Griffin International Cos.	Minneapolis, MN	418.6
317	NFM	Baltimore, MD	416.4
318	Active Motif	Carlsbad, CA	416.4
319	SCI Real Estate Investments	Los Angeles, CA	416.0
320	Alternate Solutions	Kettering, OH	411.3
321	Simonini Builders of South Carolina	Charleston, SC	411.0
322	Consultants & Builders	Duluth, GA	410.1
323	Authsec	Columbia, MD	409.8
324	Green Mountain Energy	Austin, TX	409.0
325	Thomas & Herbert Consulting	Silver Spring, MD	404.6
326	Asynchrony Solutions	St. Louis, MO	404.2
327	Home Tech Innovation	Albion, IL	402.3
328	QuantumDirect	Austin, TX	399.7
329	First Fidelity Centers	Tarzana, CA	399.7
330	Recruitmax Software	Jacksonville, FL	399.3
331	RideGear.com	Santa Cruz, CA	399.2
332	JT Packard	Verona, WI	398.7
333	Asset Protection	Corpus Christi, TX	397.5
334	FMF Capital Group	Southfield, MI	395.3
335	G&A Partners	Houston, TX	393.4
336	American Reading Co.	King of Prussia, PA	392.7
337	Atlanta Refrigeration Service	Doraville, GA	392.4
338	Intelli-Tech	San Dimas, CA	392.0
339	LiquidHub	King of Prussia, PA	392.0
340	Vosges Haut-Chocolat	Chicago, IL	391.7
341	Toyos Clinic	Jackson, TN	391.4
342	LTM	Havelock, NC	391.3
343	Dogfish Head Craft Brewery	Milton, DE	391.2
344	Human Resource Staffing	St. Peters, MO	390.9
345	Ameritrend Homes	Vero Beach, FL	390.8
346	BestNest	Cincinnati, OH	390.4
347	Röhe & Wright Builders	Houston, TX	389.0
348	Maxim Enterprises	North Canton, OH	387.6
349	Lydian Trust	Palm Beach, FL	387.0
350	AFMS	Portland, OR	386.7
351	Signature Wines	Hayward, CA	385.7
352	Curley Insurance Group	Dallas, TX	385.6
353	Integrity Applications	Chantilly, VA	382.0
354	Legg Inc.	Livermore, CA	381.1
355	Science & Engineering Services	Columbia, MD	379.4
356	Milestone Group	Arlington, VA	378.1
357	McDowell Research	Waco, TX	375.3
358	Cascades Technologies	Sterling, VA	373.6
359	Coast to Coast Tickets	Austin, TX	372.6
360	MobilityWorks	Akron, OH	371.4
361	Quality Assured Services	Orlando, FL	370.7
362	Bart Larsen Trucking	Roberts, ID	370.7
363	Icat Logistics	Linthicum, MD	369.2
364	Taleo	San Francisco, CA	367.4
365	Cross Telecom	Eden Prairie, MN	367.3
366	FastBucks	Dallas, TX	367.1
367	Homefield Financial	Irvine, CA	367.0
368	Buck Engineering	Cary, NC	366.6
369	TroyResearch	Gahanna, OH	365.2
370	Ability Services Network	Duluth, GA	365.1
371	Click Tactics	Waltham, MA	364.4
372	Atrilogy Solutions Group	Irvine, CA	364.3
373	MediNotes	West Des Moines, IA	364.0
374	Total Quality Logistics	Milford, OH	363.8
375	Cole & Co.	Dallas, TX	363.6
376	Event Network	San Diego, CA	363.3
377	Shred First	Spartanburg, SC	362.9
378	3D Research	Huntsville, AL	362.6
379	Conduant	Longmont, CO	362.5
380	Counsel on Call	Brentwood, TN	360.5
381	Prism Innovations	Deerfield, IL	358.9
382	FreeOffice	Phoenix, AZ	357.0
383	KellyMitchell	Clayton, MO	357.0
384	Round Table Group	Chicago, IL	356.9
385	Empyrean Management Group	Blue Bell, PA	354.0
386	Skoda, Minotti & Co.	Mayfield Village, OH	352.9
387	Métier	Washington, DC	352.6
388	Fagen	Granite Falls, MN	351.1
389	Back to Basics	Bluffdale, UT	350.0
390	Hostopia	Fort Lauderdale, FL	350.0
391	McDonald Bradley	Herndon, VA	348.7
392	Clover Technologies Group	Ottawa, IL	348.6
393	GECC	Woodstock, GA	348.2
394	DSR Management	Evanston, IL	347.8
395	Environmental Products & Services of Vermont	Syracuse, NY	346.2
396	Corporate Research International	Findlay, OH	346.1
397	TeamWorld	Binghamton, NY	345.0
398	Magnum Logistics	Indianapolis, IN	344.7
399	MagnaDrive	Bellevue, WA	344.3
400	Netuno USA	Miami, FL	343.9

The *Inc.* 500 Fastest-Growing Private Companies in America (continued)

Rank	Company	Headquarters	Sales Growth Increase (%)	Rank	Company	Headquarters	Sales Growth Increase (%)
401	Treetop Technologies	Boise, ID	341.7	451	Gray Hawk Systems	Alexandria, VA	317.6
402	LocalNet	Williamsville, NY	341.6	452	eTrials Worldwide	Morrisville, NC	316.8
403	Vitacost.com	Boynton Beach, FL	341.2	453	Long Wave	Oklahoma City, OK	315.6
404	National Link	San Dimas, CA	340.9	454	GTRI	Denver, CO	315.4
405	That's Good HR	Indianapolis, IN	340.5	455	Hiller Plumbing, Heating & Cooling	Nashville, TN	315.3
406	Innovative Lighting	Roland, IA	340.1	456	MoreVisibility	Boca Raton, FL	314.5
407	Welocalize	Frederick, MD	339.5	457	Executive Management Associates	Darnestown, MD	313.9
408	Quantech Services	Bedford, MA	339.1	458	East West Connection	Pittstown, NJ	313.4
409	Georgia Cabling & Electric	Norcross, GA	338.1	459	Healthx	Indianapolis, IN	313.0
410	Inlet Medical	Eden Prairie, MN	337.7	460	Applied Global Technologies	Rockledge, FL	312.5
411	Appletree Answering Services	Wilmington, DE	336.7	461	Edison Automation	Nashville, TN	312.3
412	Gartner Studios	Stillwater, MN	336.6	462	Silicon Mountain Memory	Boulder, CO	312.3
413	Regency Technologies	Bedford, TX	336.6	463	Northstar Aerospace	Duluth, MN	311.3
414	United Pacific Mortgage	Woodland Hills, CA	336.0	464	NSI Software	Hoboken, NJ	311.3
415	ath Power Consulting	Andover, MA	335.9	465	Affinity Internet	Fort Lauderdale, FL	309.8
416	China United Transport	City of Industry, CA	335.9	466	DazMedia	River Edge, NJ	309.2
417	Movex	Tampa, FL	334.6	467	WebSurveyor	Herndon, VA	307.3
418	Broadlane	San Francisco, CA	333.9	468	Karl R. Johnson Trucking	Lyndonville, VT	306.4
419	Builder Homesite	Austin, TX	333.5	469	Campbell Roofing & Construction	Warner Robins, GA	306.3
420	MTC Services	Chula Vista, CA	333.1	470	RTG Medical	Fremont, NE	306.0
421	Schaller Anderson	Phoenix, AZ	333.1	471	RealCapitalMarkets.com	Carlsbad, CA	305.6
422	iDirect Marketing	Irvine, CA	332.2	472	Eagle Systems & Services	Lawton, OK	305.3
423	LinkEdge Technologies	Chatsworth, CA	332.0	473	Ceiba Technologies	Chandler, AZ	305.1
424	Cold Stone Creamery	Scottsdale, AZ	331.4	474	RxUSA	Port Washington, NY	304.7
425	Cosentino USA	Stafford, TX	331.1	475	Intranets.com	Burlington, MA	304.2
426	McKeough Land Co.	Grand Haven, MI	330.3	476	Intelliseek	Cincinnati, OH	303.7
427	US Labs	Irvine, CA	329.4	477	All Fund Mortgage	Tacoma, WA	301.1
428	XOS Technologies	Sanford, FL	329.3	478	CEI Boston	East Walpole, MA	301.0
429	SouthStar Funding	Atlanta, GA	329.2	479	MNdustries	Suwanee, GA	300.9
430	LoopNet	San Francisco, CA	328.1	480	AmeriQuest Transportation and Logistics Resources	Cherry Hill, NJ	300.9
431	Alpine Access	Golden, CO	327.9	481	DMinSite	Cincinnati, OH	300.8
432	Cardtronics	Houston, TX	327.9	482	Solid Earth	Huntsville, AL	299.1
433	Health Dialog Services	Boston, MA	327.6	483	B2B Technologies	Atlanta, GA	298.5
434	Dynamic Restoration	West Chester, PA	326.3	484	Century Bankcard Services	Chatsworth, CA	297.4
435	Pacific Pavingstone	Sun Valley, CA	325.7	485	DiskFaktory.com	Irvine, CA	297.1
436	Allied Solutions Group	Richfield, OH	325.7	486	Diagnostic Hybrids	Athens, OH	297.0
437	LHC Group	Lafayette, LA	325.0	487	Ameritrust Mortgage	Charlotte, NC	295.6
438	Digineer	St. Louis Park, MN	324.2	488	Capella Education	Minneapolis, MN	294.9
439	Newcastle Construction	Birmingham, AL	322.9	489	Cynergy Data	New York City, NY	294.5
440	Calypso Technology	San Francisco, CA	322.7	490	Phoenix Personnel	Wyoming, MI	294.4
441	Quantec	Portland, OR	321.2	491	Alienware	Miami, FL	293.9
442	Packaging Resources	Lyons, IL	321.2	492	VitesseLearning	San Francisco, CA	293.6
443	PaymentOne	San Jose, CA	321.1	493	MicroPact Engineering	Herndon, VA	293.3
444	Plateau Systems	Arlington, VA	320.9	494	Fetch Logistics	Amherst, NY	293.1
445	Hi-Tec Systems	Egg Harbor Twp., NJ	320.1	495	Fieldstone Investment	Columbia, MD	292.9
446	California Numismatic Investments	Los Angeles, CA	319.6	496	Directed Energy Solutions	Colorado Springs, CO	291.0
447	Managed Care Network	Niagara Falls, NY	319.5	497	SpectorSoft	Vero Beach, FL	290.6
448	21st Century Systems	Herndon, VA	319.4	498	PostcardMania	Clearwater, FL	289.8
449	Automation Technologies	Vienna, VA	318.6	499	Guaranteed Home Mortgage	White Plains, NY	288.3
450	iPlacement	Orlando, FL	318.6	500	Partners Human Resources	Oklahoma City, OK	288.3

The *Forbes* Largest Private Companies in the US

Rank	Company	Sales ($ mil.)	Rank	Company	Sales ($ mil.)	Rank	Company	Sales ($ mil.)
1	Cargill	66,669	51	Allegis Group	3,600	101	Aecom	2,500
2	Koch Industries	60,000	52	Colonial Group	3,600	102	Alex Lee	2,500
3	Mars	19,100	53	Kohler	3,600	103	Andersen	2,500
4	PricewaterhouseCoopers	18,700	54	Wegmans Food Markets	3,600	104	Grant Thornton International	2,500
5	Publix Super Markets	18,686	55	SunGard Data Systems	3,556	105	Heico Cos.	2,500
6	Bechtel	17,378	56	Kinray	3,510	106	Kingston Technology	2,500
7	Ernst & Young	16,900	57	OSI Group	3,500	107	Save Mart Supermarkets	2,500
8	C&S Wholesale Grocers	15,200	58	84 Lumber	3,452	108	Services Group of America	2,500
9	SemGroup	12,574	59	Battelle Memorial Institute	3,400	109	Belk	2,447
10	Meijer	12,500	60	Mervyns	3,400	110	ContiGroup Cos.	2,400
11	H.E. Butt Grocery	11,500	61	Milliken & Co.	3,397	111	E&J Gallo Winery	2,400
12	Cox Enterprises	11,162	62	Schwan Food	3,385	112	JM Huber	2,400
13	Toys "R" Us	11,100	63	Peter Kiewit Sons'	3,352	113	Quality King Distributors	2,400
14	Fidelity Investments	10,470	64	HT Hackney	3,350	114	Red Apple Group	2,400
15	Swift & Co.	9,669	65	RaceTrac Petroleum	3,310	115	Texas Genco	2,334
16	Enterprise Rent-A-Car	8,230	66	Booz Allen Hamilton	3,300	116	Ingram Industries	2,305
17	JM Family Enterprises	8,200	67	Raley's	3,300	117	HP Hood	2,300
18	Platinum Equity	8,000	68	Stater Bros Markets	3,250	118	Jeld-Wen	2,300
19	Capital Group Cos.	7,770	69	Eby-Brown	3,200	119	Vanguard Health Systems	2,269
20	SAIC	7,187	70	Schneider National	3,198	120	US Oncology	2,260
21	Reyes Holdings	7,000	71	JohnsonDiversey	3,169	121	Fry's Electronics	2,250
22	Tenaska Energy	6,668	72	McKinsey & Co.	3,150	122	Tishman Construction	2,246
23	Menard	6,508	73	Perdue Farms	3,100	123	Graham Packaging Holdings	2,239
24	S.C. Johnson & Son	6,500	74	J.R. Simplot	3,100	124	DeBruce Grain	2,218
25	Alticor	6,400	75	Wawa	3,083	125	Love's Travel Stops	2,211
26	Marmon Group	6,336	76	JF Shea	3,079	126	Golden State Foods	2,200
27	Advance Publications	6,276	77	VWR International	3,005	127	Petters Group Worldwide	2,200
28	Murdock Holding Company	6,250	78	Cumberland Farms	3,000	128	Sammons Enterprises	2,200
29	Unisource Worldwide	6,000	79	InterTech Group	3,000	129	Schnuck Markets	2,200
30	Flying J	5,906	80	Keystone Foods	3,000	130	Southwire	2,200
31	Southern Wine & Spirits	5,900	81	Springs Industries	3,000	131	WinCo Foods	2,200
32	QuikTrip	5,863	82	Carlson Cos.	2,900	132	Houchens Industries	2,180
33	Boise Cascade	5,735	83	Edward Jones	2,891	133	Rich Products	2,180
34	Giant Eagle	5,401	84	Glazer's Wholesale Drug	2,800	134	NewPage	2,176
35	Transammonia	5,341	85	Clark Enterprises	2,796	135	Quintiles Transnational	2,146
36	Guardian Industries	5,000	86	Lanoga	2,750	136	Solo Cup	2,116
37	Gulf Oil	5,000	87	Sheetz	2,730	137	Affinia Group	2,106
38	Hy-Vee	4,850	88	CH2M Hill Cos.	2,715	138	DeMoulas Super Markets	2,100
39	MBM	4,800	89	Global Hyatt	2,700	139	Structure Tone	2,100
40	Roundy's	4,777	90	Golub	2,700	140	Rooney Holdings	2,095
41	Hallmark Cards	4,159	91	Schreiber Foods	2,700	141	Hensel Phelps Construction	2,088
42	Hexion Specialty Chemicals	4,100	92	Ergon	2,680	142	Asplundh Tree Expert	2,083
43	Graybar Electric	4,080	93	International Data Group	2,680	143	Amsted Industries	2,072
44	Levi Strauss & Co.	4,072	94	TravelCenters of America	2,678	144	Bass Pro	2,050
45	Hearst	4,038	95	Vistar	2,650	145	ABC Supply	2,042
46	Gulf States Toyota	4,000	96	Whiting-Turner Contracting	2,624	146	Follett	2,023
47	Sinclair Oil	3,950	97	Consolidated Elec. Distributors	2,600	147	Metaldyne	2,004
48	Neiman Marcus Group	3,822	98	Leprino Foods	2,600	148	Ashley Furniture Industries	2,000
49	Gordon Food Service	3,625	99	Gilbane	2,580	149	Bashas'	2,000
50	Bloomberg	3,610	100	Hunt Consolidated/Hunt Oil	2,530	150	Central National-Gottesman	2,000

SOURCE: *FORBES*; NOVEMBER 28, 2005

The *Forbes* Largest Private Companies in the US (continued)

Rank	Company	Sales ($ mil.)	Rank	Company	Sales ($ mil.)	Rank	Company	Sales ($ mil.)
151	Dr Pepper/7 Up Bottling Group	2,000	201	CC Industries	1,500	251	New Balance Athletic Shoe	1,289
152	General Parts	2,000	202	FHC Health Systems	1,500	252	Day & Zimmermann	1,283
153	Mary Kay	2,000	203	Flex-N-Gate	1,500	253	Houghton Mifflin	1,283
154	Rosen's Diversified	2,000	204	National Gypsum	1,500	254	American Tire Distributors	1,282
155	Scoular	2,000	205	Sierra Pacific Industries	1,500	255	Key Safety Systems	1,280
156	UniGroup	1,995	206	Tang Industries	1,500	256	O'Neal Steel	1,272
157	Parsons	1,994	207	Young's Market	1,500	257	D&H Distributing	1,270
158	Dresser	1,965	208	Berwind Group	1,489	258	Haworth	1,260
159	Brookshire Grocery	1,964	209	Wilbur-Ellis	1,474	259	Brasfield & Gorrie	1,258
160	Walsh Group	1,950	210	Shamrock Foods	1,471	260	Dart Container	1,250
161	Dot Foods	1,926	211	AG Spanos Cos.	1,460	261	Musicland Group	1,250
162	Ebsco Industries	1,900	212	SSA Marine	1,449	262	Purity Wholesale Grocers	1,250
163	Medline Industries	1,900	213	North Pacific Group	1,447	263	Esselte	1,242
164	Software House Intl.	1,897	214	Yates Cos.	1,441	264	Burger King	1,230
165	Grocers Supply	1,878	215	Maines Paper & Food Service	1,440	265	Maritz	1,230
166	Cooper-Standard Automotive	1,864	216	Skadden Arps	1,440	266	Austin Industries	1,227
167	Swinerton	1,844	217	WinWholesale	1,440	267	Watkins Associated Industries	1,222
168	W.L. Gore & Associates	1,840	218	L.L. Bean	1,407	268	Big Y Foods	1,220
169	Ben E. Keith	1,822	219	McCarthy Building Cos.	1,403	269	Academy Sports & Outdoors	1,216
170	Quad/Graphics	1,811	220	Black & Veatch	1,400	270	Vought Aircraft Industries	1,215
171	AMC Entertainment	1,807	221	Purdue Pharma	1,400	271	Gould Paper	1,210
172	Bose	1,800	222	Rooms to Go	1,400	272	Dawn Food Products	1,200
173	Life Care Centers of America	1,800	223	World Wide Technology	1,400	273	Pella	1,200
174	Renco Group	1,780	224	Parsons Brinckerhoff	1,390	274	Washington Cos.	1,200
175	G-I Holdings	1,773	225	Dunavant Enterprises	1,388	275	International Specialty Products	1,194
176	Sunbelt Beverage	1,765	226	Great Lakes Cheese	1,375	276	Ritz Camera Centers	1,185
177	Brightstar	1,743	227	Republic Beverage	1,375	277	Kum & Go	1,150
178	F. Dohmen	1,734	228	Warren Equities	1,356	278	Les Schwab Tire Centers	1,150
179	Frank Consolidated Enterprises	1,733	229	Baker & McKenzie	1,352	279	Wirtz	1,150
180	Metro-Goldwyn-Mayer	1,725	230	Hobby Lobby Stores	1,349	280	Red Chamber Group	1,143
181	Delaware North Cos.	1,700	231	SSP Partners	1,347	281	Honickman Affiliates	1,130
182	Truman Arnold Cos.	1,700	232	GNC	1,345	282	Topa Equities	1,121
183	McWane	1,686	233	Conair	1,343	283	Alsco	1,118
184	Nortek	1,679	234	Bradco Supply	1,340	284	GSC Enterprises	1,117
185	Discount Tire	1,666	235	Goodman Manufacturing	1,318	285	Bartlett & Co.	1,110
186	Foster Farms	1,664	236	Arctic Slope Regional	1,316	286	DreamWorks SKG	1,107
187	Select Medical	1,661	237	Michael Foods	1,314	287	ViewSonic	1,104
188	National Distributing	1,645	238	Sealy	1,314	288	Concentra Operating	1,102
189	Vertis	1,645	239	Hampton Affiliates	1,312	289	Beall's	1,101
190	Dunn Industries	1,633	240	K-VA-T Food Stores	1,310	290	McKee Foods	1,101
191	Towers Perrin	1,620	241	Oxbow	1,307	291	Bozzuto's	1,100
192	Soave Enterprises	1,609	242	Holiday Cos.	1,305	292	Genmar Holdings	1,100
193	Ardent Healthcare Services	1,607	243	Anderson News	1,301	293	Jones Day	1,100
194	Hunt Construction Group	1,600	244	Bellco Health	1,300	294	LPL Financial Services	1,100
195	Taylor	1,600	245	Boar's Head Provisions	1,300	295	Printpack	1,100
196	Barnes & Noble College Booksellers	1,541	246	Boston Consulting Group	1,300	296	Progress Rail Services	1,100
197	Iasis Healthcare	1,534	247	Carpenter	1,300	297	TIC Holdings	1,100
198	SAS Institute	1,530	248	Koch Foods	1,300	298	Associated Materials	1,094
199	National Waterworks	1,522	249	Di Giorgio	1,297	299	M. A. Mortenson	1,085
200	Baker & Taylor	1,500	250	Crown Equipment	1,293	300	McJunkin	1,081

The *Forbes* Largest Private Companies in the US (continued)

Rank	Company	Sales ($ mil.)	Rank	Company	Sales ($ mil.)	Rank	Company	Sales ($ mil.)
301	Boscov's Department Store	1,071	316	Goya Foods	1,040	331	Plastipak Packaging	1,004
302	ASI	1,060	317	David Weekley Homes	1,031	332	Walbridge Aldinger	1,003
303	Doane Pet Care	1,051	318	Williamson-Dickie Mfg.	1,030	333	Beaulieu of America Group	1,000
304	Remy International	1,051	319	Sidley Austin Brown & Wood	1,029	334	Crowley Maritime	1,000
305	Klein Wholesale Distributors	1,050	320	United Components	1,027	335	M. Fabrikant & Sons	1,000
306	MA Laboratories	1,050	321	Barton Malow	1,024	336	Meridian Automotive Systems	1,000
307	Micro Electronics	1,050	322	Cinemark USA	1,024	337	Plastech Engineered Products	1,000
308	MTD Products	1,050	323	Long & Foster Cos.	1,023	338	Sutherland Lumber	1,000
309	Peerless Importers	1,050	324	Connell Limited Partnership	1,020	339	Swagelok	1,000
310	Sigma Plastics Group	1,050	325	Suffolk Construction	1,020			
311	US Oil	1,047	326	Chemcentral	1,019			
312	Columbia Forest Products	1,046	327	24 Hour Fitness Worldwide	1,015			
313	TriMas	1,045	328	Drees Co.	1,013			
314	Petro Stopping Centers	1,044	329	Team Health	1,009			
315	Freeman Cos.	1,041	330	Estes Express Lines	1,004			

Top 20 US Law Firms

Rank	Law Firm	Gross Revenue ($ mil.)	Number of lawyers
1	Skadden, Arps, Slate, Meagher & Flom	1,440.0	1,554
2	Baker & McKenzie	1,228.0	2,992
3	Latham & Watkins	1,206.0	1,502
4	Jones Day	1,190.0	2,076
5	Sidley Austin Brown & Wood	1,029.5	1,405
6	White & Case	953.0	1,685
7	Mayer, Brown, Rowe & Maw	911.0	1,258
8	Weil, Gotshal & Manges	905.0	1,080
9	Kirkland & Ellis	835.0	897
10	Sullivan & Cromwell	833.0	589
11	Shearman & Sterling	775.0	963
12	Wilmer Cutler	750.5	960
13	McDermott, Will & Emery	745.0	975
14	Morgan, Lewis & Bockius	723.5	1,112
15	Greenberg Traurig	712.0	1,149
16	O'Melveny & Myers	697.0	910
17	Cleary, Gottlieb, Steen & Hamilton	695.0	844
18	Gibson, Dunn & Crutcher	693.0	745
19	Simpson Thacher & Bartlett	691.0	632
20	Hogan & Hartson	630.0	898

SOURCE: *AMERICAN LAWYER*, JULY 2005

Top 20 Tax & Accounting Firms by US Revenue

Rank	Firm	Headquarters	2004 US Revenue ($ mil.)
1	Deloitte & Touche	New York	6,876.0
2	Ernst & Young	New York	5,511.4
3	PricewaterhouseCoopers	New York	5,189.5
4	KPMG	New York	4,115.0
5	H&R Block	Kansas City, MO	4,108.0
6	Grant Thornton	Chicago	634.8
7	RSM McGladrey/ McGladrey & Pullen	Bloomington, MN	585.8
8	Jackson Hewitt Inc.	Parsippany, NJ	460.1
9	American Express Tax & Business Services	New York	385.0
10	CBiz/Mayer Hoffman McCann	Cleveland	373.5
11	BDO Seidman	Chicago	365.0
12	Crowe Group	South Bend, IN	286.2
13	BKD	Springfield, MO	230.6
14	Moss Adams	Seattle	199.0
15	Plante & Moran	Southfield, MI	198.6
16	UHY Advisors	Chicago	174.2
17	Clifton Gunderson	Peoria, IL	160.0
18	Virchow, Krause & Co.	Madison, WI	136.3
19	LarsonAllen	Minneapolis	105.0
20	J.H. Cohn	Roseland, NJ	103.1

SOURCE: *ACCOUNTING TODAY*, MARCH 2005

Top 20 Universities

Rank	School
1	Harvard University
1	Princeton University
3	Yale University
4	University of Pennsylvania
5	Duke University
5	Stanford University
7	California Institute of Technology
7	Massachusetts Inst. of Technology
9	Columbia University
9	Dartmouth College
11	Washington University in St. Louis
12	Northwestern University
13	Cornell University
13	Johns Hopkins University
15	Brown University
15	University of Chicago
17	Rice University
18	University of Notre Dame
18	Vanderbilt University
20	Emory University

Ranked by composite score, including such factors as graduation and retention rates, faculty resources, and student-to-faculty ratio.

SOURCE: *U.S. NEWS AND WORLD REPORT*, AUGUST 29, 2005

Top 20 US Foundations

Rank	Name	State	Assets ($ mil.)
1	Bill & Melinda Gates Foundation	WA	26,810.5
2	The Ford Foundation	NY	10,686.0
3	J. Paul Getty Trust	CA	9,100.2
4	The Robert Wood Johnson Foundation	NJ	8,982.8
5	Lilly Endowment Inc.	IN	8,585.0
6	W. K. Kellogg Foundation	MI	6,801.8
7	The William and Flora Hewlett Foundation	CA	6,489.2
8	The David and Lucile Packard Foundation	CA	5,328.3
9	The Andrew W. Mellon Foundation	NY	5,301.1
10	Gordon and Betty Moore Foundation	CA	4,846.1
11	John D. and Catherine T. MacArthur Foundation	IL	4,530.4
12	The Pew Charitable Trusts	PA	4,118.8
13	The Starr Foundation	NY	3,577.4
14	The California Endowment	CA	3,572.4
15	The Rockefeller Foundation	NY	3,210.1
16	The Annie E. Casey Foundation	MD	3,106.5
17	The Kresge Foundation	MI	2,752.3
18	The Annenberg Foundation	PA	2,695.8
19	The Duke Endowment	NC	2,542.6
20	Charles Stewart Mott Foundation	MI	2,527.9

SOURCE: THE FOUNDATION CENTER (WWW.FOUNDATIONCENTER.ORG), AUGUST 1, 2005

Hoover's Handbook of

Private Companies

The Companies

24 Hour Fitness

If you're holding too much weight, 24 Hour Fitness Worldwide has the solution. It owns and operates more than 350 fitness centers that offer aerobic, cardiovascular, and weight lifting activities to the company's more than 3 million members. Some facilities also feature squash, racquetball, and basketball courts; swimming pools; steam and sauna rooms; tanning rooms; and whirlpools. It is one of the only fitness chains open 24 hours a day. The centers are located in 16 states in the US, as well as in Asia. Investment partnership McCown De Leeuw & Co. is the leading investor in 24 Hour Fitness, which was founded in 1983 by CEO Mark Mastrov. Financier Theodore J. Forstmann acquired the company for $1.6 billion.

The company has a history of linking with celebrities such as basketball stars Magic Johnson and Shaquille O'Neal as well as tennis great Andre Agassi. In 2005 the chain joined with champion cyclist Lance Armstrong to create clubs called 24 Hour Fitness Lance Armstrong Sports Clubs, which will feature large cycling rooms.

The company expanded into Asia and Europe in the 1990s, but later decided to pull out of Europe. It kept its clubs in Asia.

EXECUTIVES

Chairman and CEO: Mark S. Mastrov
EVP and CFO: Colin Heggie
VP and Assistant General Counsel: Joseph Freschi
VP Human Resources: Dan Abfalter
VP Sports Marketing: Kevin D. Steele
CIO: Lee Kennedy
President, 24 Hour Fitness USA: Brian Bouma
Corporate Account Director, Central California Division: Jad Hassan
Corporate Director, Group Exercise: Donna Meyer
Senior Director of Corporate Group Sales, Northern California Division: Ben Midgley
Director of Corporate Group Sales, Central Midwest Division: Eric Frazier
Director of Corporate Group Sales, Pacific Northwest Division: Michelle Briede
Director of Corporate Group Sales, Southern California Division: Daryl Hawkins
Director of Team Sports: Chris Feder
Public Relations Manager: Shannon May
Auditors: Deloitte & Touche

LOCATIONS

HQ: 24 Hour Fitness Worldwide, Inc.
   12647 Alcosta Blvd., 5th Fl., San Ramon, CA 94583
Phone: 925-543-3100   **Fax:** 925-543-3200
Web: www.24hourfitness.com

24 Hour Fitness Worldwide operates clubs in China, Malaysia, Singapore, Taiwan, and the US.

COMPETITORS

Bally Total Fitness
Curves International
Gold's Gym
Jazzercise
Lady of America
Physical Spa & Fitness
The Sports Club
World Gym
YMCA
YWCA

HISTORICAL FINANCIALS

Company Type: Private

Income Statement

FYE: December 31

	REVENUE ($ mil.)	NET INCOME ($ mil.)	NET PROFIT MARGIN	EMPLOYEES
12/03	1,000	—	—	16,000
12/02	1,000	—	—	20,000
12/01	1,029	—	—	27,000
12/00	911	—	—	26,794
12/99	736	—	—	19,500
12/98	330	—	—	15,000
12/97	262	—	—	11,500
12/96	180	—	—	—
12/95	98	—	—	—
12/94	41	—	—	—
Annual Growth	**42.5%**	**—**	**—**	**5.7%**

Revenue History

---

84 Lumber

With its no-frills stores (most don't have air conditioning or heating), 84 Lumber has built itself to be a leading low-cost provider of lumber and building materials. Through some 500 stores, the company, which is the nation's largest privately held building-materials supplier, sells lumber, siding, drywalls, windows, and other supplies, as well as kits to make barns, play sets, decks, and even homes. Its stores are in about 35 states, mainly in the East, Southeast, and Midwest; 84 Lumber also sells products internationally. CEO Joseph Hardy Sr. founded 84 Lumber in 1956.

Founded to serve professionals, 84 Lumber expanded its product offering to attract more DIY consumers. It has since re-shifted its focus to professional builders and remodelers, with 95% of 2004 sales going to residential and commercial builders and remodelers. While the professional market is less profitable and more cyclic than the DIY segment, it has the advantage of being less crowded with heavy competitors such as The Home Depot and Lowe's.

To foster growth and better manage the company, the building materials retailer is splitting into two divisions (northeastern and southeastern) and adding a new Midwest region.

A sister company, 84 Components, operates 15 floor, truss, and wall-panel plants with plans to build another 15. The company has also expanded to provide professional services, including financing, risk insurance, and travel through 84 Travel.

84 Lumber plans to open more than 50 stores in 2005, extending its reach to 41 states.

HISTORY

In 1956 Joseph Hardy Sr. opened the first 84 Lumber store in Eighty Four, Pennsylvania, a town near Pittsburgh. Hardy epitomized the bare-bones approach, keeping a tight rein on his company and paying cash for new building sites.

The strategy was successful, and for the next two decades 84 Lumber prospered, growing steadily to more than 350 stores in the early 1980s. But the 1980s brought trouble, not only for 84 Lumber but also within the Hardy family. Paul Hardy, the second-eldest son, left the company after continued sparring with Hardy Sr. Another son, Joe Hardy Jr., seemed to be his father's handpicked successor: He had worked for 84 Lumber since 1967, rising to the level of COO. However, Joe Jr. and Joe Sr. clashed and under pressure from his father, Joe Jr. resigned in 1988.

Joe Sr. also underwent a transformation during this time, opening his once-tight purse strings to buy himself an honorary English title — lord of the manor of Henley-in-Arden — for about $170,000. In 1987 he paid $3.1 million to purchase a retreat in southwestern Pennsylvania, the Nemacolin Woodlands. He placed the renovation of the resort (at the cost of some $100 million) in the hands of his daughter Maggie, who was in her early twenties at the time.

While Hardy was transforming, so was 84 Lumber. The company started moving away from its traditional approach in an attempt to gain a piece of the budding yuppie market. This approach, along with an ill-timed expansion, led to a loss of customers and falling profits. Earnings fell from $52 million in 1987 to $22 million in 1989.

84 Lumber started to right itself in 1991. Hardy transferred stock to Maggie, his heir apparent. While running luxury resort Nemacolin Woodlands, Maggie strove to emulate her father's business style, including obscenity-laced staff meetings. 84 Lumber shut stores and returned to its basic operating scheme as a low-cost provider of lumber in small towns. The company also added do-it-yourself (DIY) building kits for kitchens and baths that year, and it expanded that DIY concept a year later in 1992, with home building kits.

Under new president Maggie, 84 Lumber's sales topped the $1 billion mark in 1993 and the company refocused on its professional contractor customers. The company first shipped its building materials internationally in 1996 (to New Zealand) and added customers in China, South Korea, Switzerland, and Australia in the late 1990s.

In 1997 84 Lumber opened Maggie's Building Solutions Showroom, a 7,500-sq.-ft. remodeling center featuring upscale home products. By 1997 84 Lumber was the US's largest dealer of building supplies to professional contractors.

In a further effort to attract contractors' business, 84 Lumber introduced a builder financing program in 1999 and began converting some of its stores to an 84-Plus store format, in which its traditional lumberyard setup is matched with a 10,000-sq.-ft. hardware store.

In an effort to reach more professionals, the company increased outside sales staff by 25% in 2000.

The next year the company bought 15 stores from Payless Cashways, which went out of business, a move that extended 84 Lumber's operations to Oklahoma, Nevada, and Nebraska.

The company added two red-letter dates to its company history in 2002. On April 3 of that year, 84 Lumber opened 20 new stores throughout the US, increasing its store count by 5%. Thanks in part to added revenue from those stores, on December 7, 2002, company cash registers went past the $2 billion mark in sales for the year.

In June 2004, 84 Lumber opened a distribution center in Auburn, New York. The facility supplies vinyl siding and roofing materials to stores in Rochester and Syracuse.

EXECUTIVES

CEO: Joseph A. Hardy Sr., age 81
President: Maggie Hardy Magerko, age 38
COO: Bill J. Myrick
CFO: Dan Wallach
VP, Communications: Jeff Nobers
VP, Human Resources: Brian Kelly
VP, Store Operations: Frank Cicero
Manager, Public Relations: Robyn Hall

LOCATIONS

HQ: 84 Lumber Company
1019 Rte. 519, Eighty Four, PA 15330
Phone: 724-228-8820   **Fax:** 724-228-8058
Web: www.84lumber.com

84 Lumber operates stores in about 35 states and sells its products in Australia, China, South Korea, and Switzerland.

PRODUCTS/OPERATIONS

Selected Products
Doors
Drywall
Flooring
Insulation
Lumber
Plywood
Project kits
  Barns (pole and storage)
  Decks
  Garages
  Houses
  Kitchens
  Play sets
Roofing
Room additions
Siding
Skylights
Trim
Trusses
Ventilation
Windows

COMPETITORS

Ace Hardware	Grossman's
Builders FirstSource	Home Depot
Building Materials	Lanoga
Holding	Lowe's
Carter Lumber	McCoy
Contractors' Warehouse	Menard
Cox Lumber	Stock Building Supply
Do it Best	Sutherland Lumber
Foxworth-Galbraith	True Value
Lumber	Wolohan Lumber
Futter Lumber	

HISTORICAL FINANCIALS

Company Type: Private

Income Statement   FYE: First Sunday following December 31

	REVENUE ($ mil.)	NET INCOME ($ mil.)	NET PROFIT MARGIN	EMPLOYEES
12/04	3,460	—	—	8,000
12/03	2,538	—	—	6,500
12/02	2,139	—	—	5,800
12/01	1,847	—	—	5,400
12/00	1,850	—	—	5,000
12/99	1,800	—	—	4,500
12/98	1,625	—	—	4,400
12/97	1,600	—	—	4,815
12/96	1,590	—	—	4,500
12/95	1,275	—	—	3,500
Annual Growth	**11.7%**	**—**	**—**	**9.6%**

Revenue History

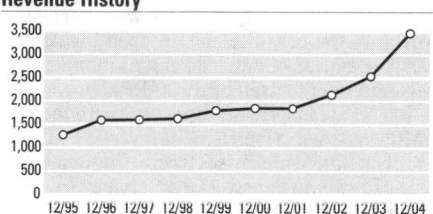

A. G. Spanos

Spanning the land from California to Florida, A.G. Spanos Companies bridges many operations: from building, managing, and selling multi-family housing units to constructing master-planned communities, to developing land. The firm has built more than 100,000 apartments in 18 states since its founding in 1960. Major projects include Spanos Park, a $1 billion master-planned community on 3,000 acres in founder and chairman Alex Spanos' hometown of Stockton, California, as well as the construction of luxury apartments across the nation. Alex Spanos, owner of the NFL's San Diego Chargers, operates the company with his sons Dean (president and CEO) and Michael Spanos (EVP).

EXECUTIVES

Chairman: Alexander Gus (Alex) Spanos, age 82
President and CEO: Dean A. Spanos, age 55
EVP: Michael A. Spanos, age 45
CFO: Jeremiah T. Murphy
Financial Officer and CTO: Steven L. Cohen
VP Marketing and Sales: Nick Faklis
Director, Public Relations: Natalia Orfanos
Manager, Human Resources: Charlene Flynn
Manager, Land Development Division:
 Jim Panagopoulos
Manager, Florida and Texas Division: Charlie Raffo
Manager, Georgia Division: Jim Kourafas
Manager, Nevada Division: George Filios
Manager, Southern California, Arizona, and New Mexico Division: Ray Hanes

LOCATIONS

HQ: A. G. Spanos Companies
10100 Trinity Pkwy., Stockton, CA 95219
Phone: 209-478-7954   **Fax:** 209-473-3703
Web: www.agspanos.com

The A.G. Spanos Companies operates offices in Arizona (Phoenix/Tempe), California (Fairfield, Riverside, and Stockton), Florida (Tampa), Georgia (Atlanta/Marietta), Indiana (Fishers), Kansas (Overland), Nevada (Las Vegas), North Carolina (Charlotte), and Texas (Austin, Dallas/Irving).

PRODUCTS/OPERATIONS

Selected Subsidiaries
A. G. Spanos Construction
A. G. Spanos Development, Inc.
A. G. Spanos Enterprises, Inc.
A. G. Spanos Management, Inc.
A. G. Spanos Realty, Inc.
A. G. Spanos Securities
A. G. Spanos Ventures
AGS Financial Corporation
AGS International Corporation
The Spanos Corporation

Other Ownership Interests
A. G. Spanos Aviation (Stockton, California)
San Diego Chargers National Football League Team

COMPETITORS

Barratt Developments
Calprop
Centex
Del Webb
D.R. Horton, Schuler
Edward Rose
Irvine Company
Lennar
Morrison Homes
Perini
Pinnacle West
Pulte Homes
William Lyon Homes

HISTORICAL FINANCIALS

Company Type: Private

Income Statement   FYE: September 30

	REVENUE ($ mil.)	NET INCOME ($ mil.)	NET PROFIT MARGIN	EMPLOYEES
9/04	1,700	—	—	600
9/03	1,700	—	—	600
9/02	1,400	—	—	600
9/01	1,560	—	—	600
9/00	1,590	—	—	600
9/99	1,440	—	—	600
9/98	1,175	—	—	600
9/97	964	—	—	600
9/96	950	—	—	600
9/95	947	—	—	—
Annual Growth	**6.7%**	**—**	**—**	**0.0%**

Revenue History

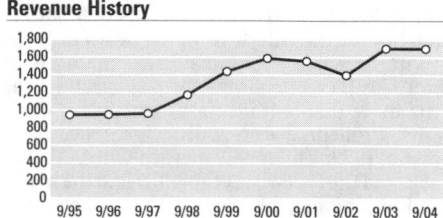

AARP

AARP is gearing up for the geezer boom. Open to anyone age 50 or older (dues are $12.50 per year), the not-for-profit organization is the largest organization of older adults in the US with about 36 million members and is also the largest lobby for the elderly (it spends about $60 million on lobbying and related activities). On a mission to enhance the quality of life for older Americans, AARP is active in four areas: information and education, community service, advocacy, and member services. It is organized into 3,500 local chapters and publishes the monthly *AARP Bulletin* and the bimonthly *AARP The Magazine*.

AARP may not be the most exclusive club around, but it is one of the most powerful. As the largest advocacy group in the US, the organization has a loud (and sometimes feared) voice on Capitol Hill. Its policy recommendations address such issues as the national budget, Medicare, elder abuse, and Social Security.

AARP attracted baby boomers with its 50+ campaign (a five-year plan begun in 2000) and turned quickly to develope a 10-year agenda designed to address the massive impact of the first wave of boomers reaching age 65 in 2011.

AARP disseminates information in a variety of formats (a Web site, public policy agendas, and radio and TV spots) and pursues educational and research efforts through the AARP Andrus Foundation, the Research Information Center, and the Public Policy Institute. Members are eligible for services including savings on prescription drugs, travel, investment opportunities, and health, life, and auto insurance. Retired educators who join the National Retired Teachers Association (a division of AARP) can receive both AARP services and other benefits designed specifically for them.

HISTORY

Ethel Andrus, a retired Los Angeles high school principal who founded the National Retired Teachers Association (NRTA) in 1947, founded the American Association of Retired Persons (AARP) in 1958 with the assistance of Leonard Davis, a New York insurance salesman who had helped her find an underwriter for the NRTA. The new organization's goal: to "enhance the quality of life" for older Americans and "improve the image of aging."

Andrus offered members the same low rates for health and accident insurance provided to NRTA members. She also started publishing AARP's bimonthly magazine, *Modern Maturity*, in 1958. The organization's first local chapter opened in Youngstown, Arizona, in 1960. Still an insurance man, Davis formed Colonial Penn Insurance in 1963 to take over the AARP account. Andrus led the AARP and its increasingly powerful lobby for the elderly until her death in 1967.

With criticism of Colonial Penn mounting in the 1970s (critics charged the organization was little more than a front for the insurance company), Prudential won AARP's insurance business in 1979. The NRTA merged with AARP in 1982, and the following year it lowered the membership eligibility age from 55 to 50. The organization continued to expand its offerings, adding an auto club and financial products such as mutual funds and expanded insurance policies. The organization also started a federal credit union

for members in 1988, but despite rosy projections, it ceased operations two years later.

AARP forked over $135 million to the IRS in 1993 as part of a settlement regarding the tax status of profits from some of its activities, but the dispute remained unresolved. AARP switched insurance providers again in 1996 (New York Life) and started offering discounted legal services. Also that year, AARP said it would let HMOs offer managed-care services to members. The plan drew objections over its potential violation of Medicare anti-kickback laws and AARP developed a revised payment plan in 1997.

AARP's image was bruised in 1998 when Dale Van Atta wrote a scathing account of the organization, *Trust Betrayed: Inside the AARP*. The book accused the organization of operating out of lavish accommodations, acting as a shill for businesses to hawk their wares, and concealing a drop in membership. Also in 1998, recognizing that nearly a third of its members were working, the organization dropped the American Association of Retired Persons moniker and began to refer to itself by the AARP abbreviation.

To end the long-running dispute with the IRS, AARP reached a settlement over its alleged profit-making enterprises by creating a new taxable subsidiary called AARP Services in 1999. The following year AARP initiated a five-year plan to attract aging baby boomers. AARP launched its new *My Generation* magazine in 2001; two years later the organization combined *My Generation* with its *Modern Maturity* magazine to form a single publication: *AARP The Magazine*.

In 2005 the group named Marie Smith president. Smith is a former Social Security Administration employee with additional experience in Medicare and Medicaid.

EXECUTIVES

VP, Board Governance/Board Chairman: Charles Leven
CEO: William D. (Bill) Novelli
President: Marie F. Smith
COO: Thomas C. Nelson
CFO: Robert R. Hagans Jr.
VP Membership and Director: W. Lee Hammond
President, AARP Services: Dawn M. Sweeney
Chief Communications Officer: Christine Donohoo
Associate Executive Director, Membership; Director, AARP Foundation: Jerry Florence
Associate Executive Director, Operations: Richard Henry
Associate Executive Director, State and National Initiatives: Christopher W. (Chris) Hansen
Director Policy and Strategy: John Rother
General Counsel: Joan S. Wise
Chief People Officer: Ellie Hollander
Director Communications: Lisa R. Davis

LOCATIONS

HQ: AARP
   601 E. St. NW, Washington, DC 20049
Phone: 202-434-2277   **Fax:** 202-434-6548
Web: www.aarp.org

AARP has offices in all 50 states, the District of Columbia, Puerto Rico, and the Virgin Islands.

PRODUCTS/OPERATIONS

2003 Sales

	$ mil.	% of total
Royalties	300.4	39
Membership dues	210.8	27
Advertising	77.6	10
Federal & other grants	76.2	10
Investment income	60.3	8
Program income	20.8	3
Other	23.5	3
Total	**769.6**	**100**

2003 Expenses

	$ mil.	% of total
Programs & field services	201	30
Member services	148	21
Publications	146	21
Membership & general	79	12
Legislation & research	58	8
Membership development	57	8
Total	**689**	**100**

Selected Operations and Programs

55 ALIVE/Mature Driving
AARP Andrus Foundation (gerontology research)
AARP Bulletin (monthly news update)
AARP Legal Services Network
AARP Services (taxable product management, marketing & e-commerce subsidiary)
AARP The Magazine (bimonthly magazine)
Financial Planning
Mature Focus Radio (daily news program)
National Retired Teachers Association
Public Policy Institute
Research Information Center
Senior Community Service Employment Program
Tax-Aide

HISTORICAL FINANCIALS

Company Type: Association

Income Statement

FYE: December 31

	REVENUE ($ mil.)	NET INCOME ($ mil.)	NET PROFIT MARGIN	EMPLOYEES
12/03	770	—	—	—
12/02	636	—	—	1,800
12/01	595	—	—	1,800
12/00	580	—	—	2,000
12/99	486	—	—	2,000
12/98	541	—	—	2,000
12/97	529	—	—	1,900
12/96	475	—	—	1,850
12/95	506	—	—	1,800
12/94	469	—	—	1,752
Annual Growth	5.7%	—	—	0.3%

Revenue History

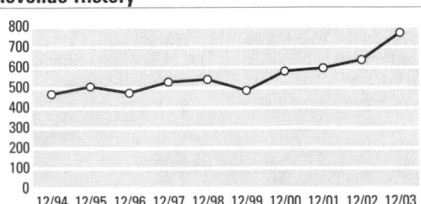

Aavid Thermal Technologies

Aavid Thermal Technologies is avid about keeping cool. The company's Aavid Thermalloy subsidiary makes heat sinks, fans, heat spreaders, liquid cooling products, cooling assemblies, and other devices used in computer, networking, and industrial electronic systems. Aavid Thermalloy's Enductive Solutions subsidiary provides thermal management systems consulting and design services. Aavid's Fluent subsidiary makes computational fluid dynamics (CFD) software for analyzing heat transfer. Customers include 3M, Agilent, Dow Chemical, General Motors, IBM, Lockheed Martin, and Solectron. Heat Holdings, which is 73% owned by private investment firm Willis Stein & Partners, owns Aavid.

Enductive Solutions, once known as the Applied Thermal Technologies unit, was spun off in 2001 to establish a separate corporate brand for its services. The subsidiary works with Fluent and such software vendors as ANSYS to provide design tools for its consulting clients. Enductive has offices in California and New Hampshire.

EXECUTIVES

Chairman, President, and CEO; CEO, Fluent: Bharatan R. (Bart) Patel, age 56, $750,676 pay
VP, Finance and CFO: Brian A. Byrne, age 57, $367,062 pay
VP, General Counsel, and Secretary: John W. Mitchell, age 56, $382,166 pay
Managing Director, Europe: Luca Rossi
President and COO, Fluent: H. Ferit Boysan, age 57, $387,259 pay
VP and CFO, Fluent: Peter L. Christie, age 59, $285,945 pay
Auditors: Ernst & Young LLP

LOCATIONS

HQ: Aavid Thermal Technologies, Inc.
1 Eagle Sq., Ste. 509, Concord, NH 03301
Phone: 603-224-1117　　**Fax:** 603-224-6673
Web: www.aatt.com

Aavid Thermal Technologies has operations in Belgium, Canada, China, France, Germany, India, Italy, Japan, Mexico, Singapore, Taiwan, the UK, and the US.

2004 Sales

	$ mil.	% of total
US	114.6	40
China	28.5	10
UK	24.3	8
Italy	22.6	8
Taiwan	19.8	7
Japan	17.6	6
Mexico	9.1	3
Other countries	51.4	18
Adjustments	(60.8)	—
Total	**227.1**	**100**

PRODUCTS/OPERATIONS

2004 Sales

	$ mil.	% of total
Thermal products	122.7	54
CFD software	104.4	46
Total	**227.1**	**100**

Selected Operations

Thermal Products
　Services
　　Consulting
　　Thermal management systems design
　Thermal management products
　　Fans
　　Heat sinks, fan heat sinks, and heat spreaders
　　Interface materials and attachment accessories
　　Liquid cooling and phase change devices
CFD (computational fluid dynamics) Software
　Electronics cooling design (Icepak)
　Flow simulation (FIDAP)
　General-purpose CFD software (Fluent)
　Interface tool (GAMBIT, G/Turbo, and TGrid)
　Mixing vessel design (Mixsim)
　Polymer processing analysis (Polyflow)
　Ventilation system design (Airpak)

COMPETITORS

ANSYS
APW
Blue Ridge Numerics
Hon Hai
Molex
SEMX
TAT Technologies
Wakefield Thermal Solutions

HISTORICAL FINANCIALS

Company Type: Private

Income Statement

FYE: December 31

	REVENUE ($ mil.)	NET INCOME ($ mil.)	NET PROFIT MARGIN	EMPLOYEES
12/04	227	8	3.4%	2,157
12/03	188	(4)	—	1,837
12/02	162	(13)	—	1,834
12/01	209	(184)	—	2,218
12/00	294	(49)	—	3,219
12/99	214	7	3.1%	3,012
12/98	209	8	3.9%	2,243
12/97	168	9	5.1%	1,934
12/96	107	(0)	—	1,279
12/95	91	(2)	—	1,034
Annual Growth	**10.7%**	**—**	**—**	**8.5%**

2004 Year-End Financials

Debt ratio: —　　　　Current ratio: 0.88
Return on equity: —　　Long-term debt ($ mil.): 130
Cash ($ mil.): 28

Net Income History

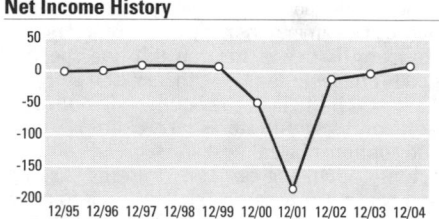

ABC Supply

American Builders & Contractors Supply Co. (better known as ABC Supply) has put roofs over millions of heads. A leading supplier of roofing, siding, windows and doors, and related builder's supplies, ABC Supply operates more than 250 outlets in 44 US states. It carries its own brand of products under the Amcraft name, as well as offering products from outside vendors. The company, which markets its products mostly to small and medium-sized professional contractors, was founded in 1982 by CEO Ken Hendricks. Hendricks and his wife, EVP Diane, own ABC Supply.

In 2004 the company acquired Paco Building Supply (distributor of exterior siding and windows in Missouri) and Mansion Supply (a New Jersey window company).

EXECUTIVES

Chairman and CEO: Kenneth A. (Ken) Hendricks, age 64, $1,861,538 pay
President, COO, and Director: David A. Luck, age 54, $1,230,506 pay
CFO, Treasurer, and Director: Kendra A. Story, age 44, $502,273 pay
EVP, Secretary, and Director: Diane M. Hendricks, age 56, $385,577 pay
SVP Manufacturing Operations: Robert Bartels, age 55, $481,504 pay
VP Branch Operations: Kevin Hendricks, age 39
VP Strategic Marketing and Planning: Keith Rozolis, age 44
MIS Director: Kathy Murray
Director Human Resources: Lisa Indgjer, age 40
Auditors: Ernst & Young LLP

LOCATIONS

HQ: American Builders & Contractors Supply Co., Inc.
1 ABC Pkwy., Beloit, WI 53511
Phone: 608-362-7777　　**Fax:** 608-362-2717
Web: www.abc-supply.com

PRODUCTS/OPERATIONS

Selected Products

Roofing materials
Siding materials
Tools and equipment
Windows and doors

COMPETITORS

Bradco Supply
Emco Corporation
Georgia-Pacific Corporation
Guardian Building Products Distribution
Huttig Building Products
North Pacific Group
Pacific Coast Building Products
PrimeSource Building

HISTORICAL FINANCIALS

Company Type: Private

Income Statement

FYE: December 31

	REVENUE ($ mil.)	NET INCOME ($ mil.)	NET PROFIT MARGIN	EMPLOYEES
12/03	1,793	67	3.8%	4,128
12/02	1,425	41	2.9%	3,711
12/01	1,382	42	3.1%	3,188
12/00	1,239	14	1.1%	3,121
12/99	1,198	7	0.6%	3,239
12/98	1,162	(3)	—	3,100
Annual Growth	9.1%	—	—	5.9%

2003 Year-End Financials

Debt ratio: 205.1%
Return on equity: 57.1%
Cash ($ mil.): 6

Current ratio: 2.39
Long-term debt ($ mil.): 275

Net Income History

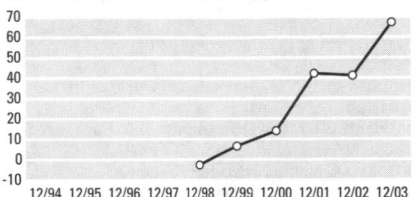

ABP

If you're looking for good bread, ABP Corporation is a good place to start. ABP operates and franchises more than 230 Au Bon Pain bakery cafes in the US and internationally. The bistros offer a wide range of sandwiches, soups, salads, and baked goods, as well as coffee and other cafe beverages. Most of the restaurants are located in downtown areas, but it also has on-site locations in airports, shopping malls, and on university campuses. Au Bon Pain was founded in 1978 by Louis Kane. UK-based Compass Group acquired the chain in 2000. In 2005 ABP management bought 75% of the company for an undisclosed amount, leaving former parent, Compass, with a 25% stake.

Au Bon Pain's company-owned sites are concentrated in the Boston, Chicago, New York, Philadelphia, and Washington, DC, areas. Franchisee sites are located in 19 US states. Its foreign locations include South Korea, Taiwan, and Thailand. Bowing to customer demand, the company's bagels, cookies, and muffins now contain zero grams of trans fat.

The company has shifted away from its long-time strategy of focusing on downtown and airport locations for its restaurants and is concentrating, instead, on opening suburban locations.

EXECUTIVES

Acting CEO and VP Special Projects: Sue Morelli
CFO: Tim Oliveri
VP Communications: Jim Fisher
VP Food and Beverage and Executive Chef: Thomas John
VP Human Resources: Susie Gorsline
VP Information Technology: Ed Mockler
VP Operations: R. J. Deurney
VP Real Estate and Development: John Billingsley
Auditors: Deloitte & Touche LLP

LOCATIONS

HQ: ABP Corporation
1 Au Bon Pain Way, Boston, MA 02210
Phone: 617-423-2100   **Fax:** 617-423-7879
Web: www.aubonpain.com

COMPETITORS

AFC Enterprises	New World Restaurants
Atlanta Bread	Panera Bread
Bruegger's	Peet's
Camille's Sidewalk Cafe	Port of Subs
Diedrich Coffee	Pret A Manger
Krispy Kreme	Starbucks
La Madeleine	Tully's Coffee

HISTORICAL FINANCIALS

Company Type: Private

Income Statement

FYE: September 30

	ESTIMATED REVENUE ($ mil.)	NET INCOME ($ mil.)	NET PROFIT MARGIN	EMPLOYEES
9/04*	41	—	—	1,500
9/02	120	—	—	3,500
Annual Growth	(65.8%)	—	—	(57.1%)

*Irregular reporting interval

Revenue History

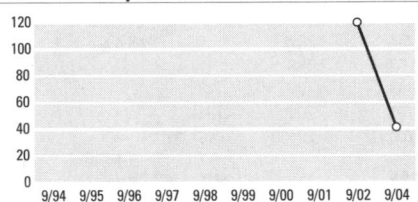

Academy

Academy Sports & Outdoors is near the head of the class among sporting goods retailers. The company is one of the top full-line sporting goods chains in the US with some 80 stores in 10 states throughout the South and Southwest. Academy's low-frills stores carry clothing, shoes, and equipment for almost any sport and outdoor activity, including camping, hunting, fishing, and boating. The company dates back to a San Antonio tire shop opened by Max Gochman in 1938. The business moved into military surplus items and during the 1980s began focusing on sports and outdoor merchandise. The Gochman family still owns Academy.

The regional sporting goods chain is expanding by building larger stores (up to 82,000 sq. ft.) and opening outlets in new markets, such as Georgia and Missouri.

EXECUTIVES

Chairman and CEO: David Gochman
President: Arthur Gochman
EVP, Apparel: Robert Frennea
EVP, Footwear: Beth Menuet
EVP, Hardgoods: A. J. Blanchard
VP and CFO: Michael Ondruch
VP and General Counsel: Elise Neal
VP, Administrative Resources: Sylvia Barrera-Moses
VP, Chief Audit Officer: David Pittman
VP, Information Technology: Mike Marrie
VP, Logistics and Distribution: Kal Patel
VP, Store Development: Greg Miller
VP, Store Operations: Allen McConnell

LOCATIONS

HQ: Academy Sports & Outdoors, Ltd.
1800 N. Mason Rd., Katy, TX 77449
Phone: 281-646-5200   **Fax:** 281-646-5000
Web: www.academy.com

Academy Sports & Outdoors operates stores in Alabama, Arkansas, Florida, Georgia, Louisiana, Mississippi, Missouri, Oklahoma, Tennessee, and Texas.

COMPETITORS

Bass Pro Shops
Finish Line
Foot Locker
Hibbett Sporting Goods
Kmart
REI
Sears
Sports Authority
Target
Wal-Mart

HISTORICAL FINANCIALS

Company Type: Private

Income Statement

FYE: January 31

	REVENUE ($ mil.)	NET INCOME ($ mil.)	NET PROFIT MARGIN	EMPLOYEES
1/04	1,059	—	—	6,995
1/03	1,000	—	—	6,000
1/02	775	—	—	5,000
1/01	720	—	—	4,748
1/00	612	—	—	4,745
1/99	499	—	—	4,500
1/98	435	—	—	3,200
1/97	367	—	—	2,800
1/96	315	—	—	2,500
1/95	268	—	—	1,700
Annual Growth	16.5%	—	—	17.0%

Revenue History

Academy of Motion Picture Arts and Sciences

And the Oscar goes to . . . the Academy of Motion Picture Arts and Sciences (AMPAS). The not-for-profit organization promotes the movie industry by recognizing excellence, fostering cultural progress, providing a forum for various crafts, and cooperating in technical research. It is best known for the annual Academy Awards in which a britannia metal trophy (known as the Oscar) is awarded for outstanding achievement in the motion picture industry. The more than 6,000 AMPAS members (who pick the Oscar winners) represent 14 branches of the industry, including actors, directors, and producers. The organization was founded in 1927 and is governed by seven officers and a board of governors.

EXECUTIVES

Chairman: Fay Kanin
Vice Chairman: Charles Bernstein
Vice Chairman: Arthur Hamilton
Executive Director and Executive Secretary of the Board of Trustees: Bruce Davis
Executive Administrator: Ric Robertson
Controller: Andrew Horn
Academy Film Archive Director: Michael Pogorzelski
Awards Administration Director: Richard Miller
Communications Director: John M. Pavlik
Educational Programs and Special Projects Director: Randy Haberkamp
Marketing Director: Beth Harris
Margaret Herrick Library Director: Linda Harris Mehr
Science and Technology Council Director: Andrew Maltz
Awards Coordinator: Torene Svitil
Credits Coordinator: Howard Loberfeld
Film Department Coordinator: D. J. Ziegler
Program Coordinator, Grants and Nicholl Fellowships: Greg Beal
Auditors: PricewaterhouseCoopers LLP

LOCATIONS

HQ: Academy of Motion Picture Arts and Sciences
8949 Wilshire Blvd., Beverly Hills, CA 90211
Phone: 310-247-3000   **Fax:** 310-859-9351
Web: www.oscars.org

Academy of Television Arts & Sciences

And the award for best organization that honors the television industry goes to: the Academy of Television Arts & Sciences (ATAS). Founded in 1946, ATAS, which has more than 12,000 members, presents the annual Emmy Awards and sponsors various television-related conferences and activities. The organization also oversees the Daytime Emmy Awards and the L.A. Area Emmy Awards, publishes *emmy* magazine, and oversees a number of television archives and educational programs through its ATAS Foundation. The Emmy statuette features a winged woman holding an atom aloft to symbolize the melding of art and science. The award's name is a deviation of "Immy," an early television camera.

The organization's members are divided into 27 peer groups including animation, cinematographers, daytime programming, makeup, performers, and writers. Benefits of membership include Emmy voting, travel and other discounts, seminars, and other educational activities. ATAS also hosts private film screenings, family events, and behind the scenes events for TV shows.

EXECUTIVES

Chairman and CEO: Richard H. (Dick) Askin Jr.
First Vice Chair: John Shaffner
Second Vice Chair: Karen Miller
President and COO: Todd Leavitt
CFO and Chief Administrative Officer: Frank Kohler
VP Marketing: Laurel Whitcomb
Director of Human Resources: Gregory Sims
Director of Membership: Barbara Chase
Secretary: Dan Birman

LOCATIONS

HQ: Academy of Television Arts & Sciences, Inc.
5220 Lankershim Blvd.,
North Hollywood, CA 91601
Phone: 818-754-2800   **Fax:** 818-761-2827
Web: www.emmys.org

Accentia

Accentia BioPharmaceuticals emphasizes runny noses. The company develops treatments for respiratory conditions, pain management, and cancer. Accentia has about 10 products on the market, including the Histex line of antihistamines and pain reliever XODOL. Its development-stage drugs include SinuNase, a potential treatment for sinus inflammation, and Biovaxid, a possible vaccine for non-Hodgkin's lymphoma. In addition to its drug offerings, the company offers biologic manufacturing services, including cell-line development, purification, and viral validation. It also develops cell production instruments, including the miniMAX, ResCu-Primer, and Xcellerator.

Once Accentia goes public, biotech investor The Hopkins Capital Group will own 14% of the company, and Pharmaceutical Product Development will have a 10% stake. Timothy Ryll, son of director Dennis Ryll, will control a 12.5% stake.

EXECUTIVES

Chairman and CEO: Francis E. O'Donnell Jr., age 55
CFO and Director: Alan Pearce, age 55
Director; President and COO, Commercial Operations and Business Development: Martin G. Baum, age 39
Director; President and COO, Product Development and Market Services: Steven R. (Steve) Arikian
General Counsel and Secretary: Samuel S. Duffey
Auditors: Aidman, Piser & Company, P.A.

LOCATIONS

HQ: Accentia BioPharmaceuticals, Inc.
5310 Cypress Center Dr., #101, Tampa, FL 33609
Phone: 813-864-2554   **Fax:** 813-287-6642
Web: www.accentia.net

Accentia BioPharmaceuticals has operations in Florida, Massachusetts, New York, and North Carolina.

PRODUCTS/OPERATIONS

2004 Sales

	$ mil.	% of total
Biopharmaceuticals products & services	14.0	54
Specialty pharmaceuticals	11.9	46
Total	**25.9**	**100**

Selected Products

Approved
Histex (antihistamine/decongestant)
Histex CT (antihistamine)
Histex HC (cough suppressant/antihistamine/decongestant)
Histex I/E (allergy antihistamine)
Histex Pd (antihistamine)
Histex Pd 12 (antihistamine)
Histex SR (antihistamine/decongestant)
Respi-TANN (antitussive/decongestant)
XODOL (pain reliever)
In Development
Biovaxid (non-Hodgkin's lymphoma)
SinuNase (chronic rhinosinusitis)

COMPETITORS

3M
Antigenics
Biogen Idec
Corixa
Dey
Favrille
Genitope
GlaxoSmithKline
Immunomedics
IVAX
Large Scale Biology

HISTORICAL FINANCIALS

Company Type: Private

Income Statement

FYE: September 30

	REVENUE ($ mil.)	NET INCOME ($ mil.)	NET PROFIT MARGIN	EMPLOYEES
9/04	26	(23)	—	259
9/03	10	(17)	—	—
9/02	6	(9)	—	—
Annual Growth	**115.1%**	**—**	**—**	**—**

2004 Year-End Financials

Debt ratio: —
Return on equity: —
Cash ($ mil.): 2

Current ratio: 0.20
Long-term debt ($ mil.): 7

Net Income History

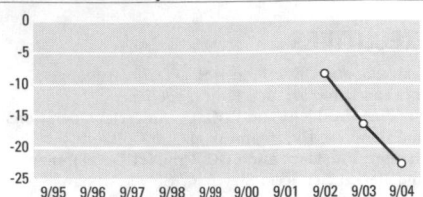

Ace Hardware

Luckily, Ace has John Madden up its sleeve. Despite the growth of warehouse-style competitors, Ace Hardware has remained a household name, thanks to ads featuring Madden, a former Oakland Raiders football coach and TV commentator. By sales the company is the #1 hardware co-operative in the US, ahead of Do It Best. Ace dealer-owners operate more than 4,700 Ace Hardware stores, home centers, and lumber and building materials locations in all 50 US states and about 70 other countries. From about 15 warehouses Ace distributes such products as electrical and plumbing supplies, garden equipment, hand tools, housewares, and power tools. Ace's paint division is the 12th largest paint manufacturer in the US.

It also makes its own brand of paint and offers thousands of other Ace-brand products. Ace additionally provides training programs and advertising campaigns for its dealers.

Challenged by big-box chains such as The Home Depot and Lowe's, Ace has unveiled its Next Generation store concept, which calls for signage with detailed product descriptions and different flooring to set off departments, among other features. Ace dealers own the company and receive dividends from Ace's profits.

In its most ambitious expansion plan to date, Ace Hardware will add 150 to 200 stores. The company is also increasing the size of its stores. The average store is 10,000 sq. ft., but newer stores are about 14,000 sq. ft.

HISTORY

A group of Chicago-area hardware dealers — William Stauber, Richard Hesse, Gern Lindquist, and Oscar Fisher — decided in 1924 to pool their hardware buying and promotional costs. In 1928 the group incorporated as Ace Stores, named in honor of the superior WWI fliers dubbed aces. Hesse became president the following year, retaining that position for the next 44 years. The company also opened its first warehouse in 1929, and by 1933 it had 38 dealers.

The organization had 133 dealers in seven states by 1949. In 1953 Ace began to allow dealers to buy stock in the company through the Ace Perpetuation Plan. During the 1960s Ace expanded into the South and West, and by 1969 it had opened distribution centers in Georgia and California — its first such facilities outside Chicago. In 1968 it opened its first international store in Guam.

By the early 1970s the do-it-yourself market began to surge as inflation pushed up plumber and electrician fees. As the market grew, large home center chains gobbled up market share from independent dealers such as those franchised through Ace. In response, Ace and its dealers became a part of a growing trend in the hardware industry — cooperatives.

Hesse sold the company to its dealers in 1973 for $6 million (less than half its book value), and the following year Ace began operating as a co-operative. Hesse stepped down in 1973. In 1976 the dealers took full control when the company's first Board of Dealer-Directors was elected.

After signing up a number of dealers in the eastern US, Ace had dealers in all 50 states by 1979. The co-op opened a plant to make paint in Matteson, Illinois, in 1984. By 1985 Ace had reached $1 billion in sales and had initiated its Store of the Future Program, allowing dealers to borrow up to $200,000 to upgrade their stores and conduct market analyses. Former head coach John Madden of the National Football League's Oakland Raiders signed on as Ace's mouthpiece in 1988.

A year later the co-op began to test ACENET, a computer network that allowed Ace dealers to check inventory, send and receive e-mail, make special purchase requests, and keep up with prices on commodity items such as lumber. In 1990 Ace established an International Division to handle its overseas stores. (It had been exporting products since 1975.) EVP and COO David Hodnik became president in 1995. That year the co-op added a net of 67 stores, including a three-store chain in Russia. Expanding further internationally, Ace signed a five-year joint-supply agreement in 1996 with Canadian lumber and hardware retailer Beaver Lumber. Hodnik added CEO to his title in 1996.

Ace fell further behind its old rival, True Value, in 1997 when ServiStar Coast to Coast and True Value merged to form TruServ (renamed True Value in 2005), a hardware giant that operated more than 10,000 outlets at the completion of the merger.

Late in 1997 Ace launched an expansion program in Canada. (The co-op already operated distribution centers in Ontario and Calgary.) In 1999 Ace merged its lumber and building materials division with Builder Marts of America to form a dealer-owned buying group to supply about 2,700 retailers. In 2000, Ace gained 208 member outlet stores, but saw 279 member outlets terminated. The next year it gained 220, but lost 255.

Sodisco-Howden bought all the shares of Ace Hardware Canada in February 2003. To better serve international members, Ace opened its first international buying office, in Hong Kong, in April 2004.

After 33 years with the company, David F. Hodnik retired as president and CEO of Ace Hardware on April 1, 2005. He was succeeded by COO Ray A. Griffith.

EXECUTIVES

Chairman: J. Thomas (Tom) Glenn, age 46
President and CEO: Ray A. Griffith, age 51
EVP (Principal Financial Officer): Rita D. Kahle
SVP, General Counsel, and Secretary:
  Arthur J. McGivern
SVP, International and Paint: David F. Myer

VP, Marketing, Advertising, and Company Stores:
  Michael C. Bodzewski, age 53
VP, Retail Operations: Kenneth L. (Ken) Nichlos
VP, Merchandising: Lori L. Bossmann
VP, Retail Development and New Business:
  Michael A. Zipser
VP and Controller: Ronald J. (Ron) Knutson, age 39
VP, Human Resources: Jimmy Alexander
VP, Information Technology: Michael J. Altendorf
VP, Retail Support — West: William J. (Bill) Bauman
VP, Retail Support — East: Daniel C. Prochaska
President, Ace International: Murray Armstrong
Treasurer: Sandy Brandt
Manager, Corporate Communications and Public Relations: Paula K. Erickson, age 34
Auditors: KPMG LLP

LOCATIONS

HQ: Ace Hardware Corporation
  2200 Kensington Ct., Oak Brook, IL 60523
Phone: 630-990-6600   **Fax:** 630-990-6838
Web: www.acehardware.com

2004 Sales

	$ mil.	% of total
US	3,163.6	96
Other countries	125.1	4
Total	**3,288.7**	**100**

PRODUCTS/OPERATIONS

2004 Sales

	$ mil.	% of total
Wholesale	3,219.6	98
Paint manufacturing	24.8	1
Other	44.3	1
Total	**3,288.7**	**100**

COMPETITORS

84 Lumber	Lowe's
Akzo Nobel	McCoy
Benjamin Moore	Menard
Building Materials	Northern Tool
Holding	Orgill
Costco Wholesale	Réno-Dépôt
Do it Best	Sears
Fastenal	Sherwin-Williams
Grossman's	Stock Building Supply
Handy Hardware	Sutherland Lumber
Wholesale	True Value
Home Depot	United Hardware
ICI American	Distributing
Kmart	Wal-Mart
Lanoga	Wolohan Lumber

HISTORICAL FINANCIALS

Company Type: Cooperative

Income Statement		FYE: Saturday nearest December 31		
	REVENUE ($ mil.)	**NET INCOME ($ mil.)**	**NET PROFIT MARGIN**	**EMPLOYEES**
12/04	3,289	102	3.1%	5,000
12/03	3,159	101	3.2%	5,100
12/02	3,029	82	2.7%	5,268
12/01	2,894	73	2.5%	5,229
12/00	2,945	80	2.7%	5,513
12/99	3,182	93	2.9%	5,180
12/98	3,120	88	2.8%	4,672
12/97	2,907	76	2.6%	4,685
12/96	2,743	72	2.6%	4,352
12/95	2,436	64	2.6%	3,917
Annual Growth	**3.4%**	**5.4%**	**—**	**2.7%**

2004 Year-End Financials

Debt ratio: 56.7%
Return on equity: 34.2%
Cash ($ mil.): 43

Current ratio: 1.44
Long-term debt ($ mil.): 172

Net Income History

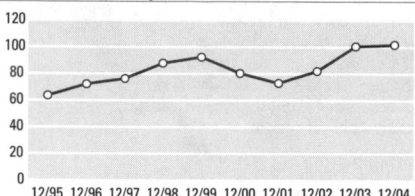

12/95 12/96 12/97 12/98 12/99 12/00 12/01 12/02 12/03 12/04

Activant Solutions

Activant Solutions Holdings wants all parts of a business holding hands, singing in perfect harmony. The company provides vertical enterprise resource planning (ERP) software for more than 20,000 small and medium-sized business locations in the automotive parts aftermarket, hardware and home center, wholesale trade, and lumber and building materials industries. Activant's software automates functions such as inventory management, parts selection, general accounting, and point-of-sale analysis. Customers include members of the Ace Hardware, True Value, and Do it Best cooperatives. Hicks, Muse, Tate & Furst owns nearly all of Activant's stock.

Activant has grown through its acquisitions of enterprise resource planning software maker Speedware and the assets of The Systems House, a developer of software for distributors in the automotive aftermarket and office products industries. Part of the company's strategy for growth is to continue pursuing acquisitions that will help it expand into new vertical markets. In 2005 Activant bought distribution software maker Prophet 21 in a deal worth $215 million.

EXECUTIVES

Chairman: Jack D. Furst, age 45
President, CEO, and Director:
A. Laurence (Larry) Jones, age 52, $375,000 pay
Managing Director, Activant Europe: Jon Goodchild
SVP and COO: Pervez Qureshi, age 48, $476,754 pay
SVP and CFO: Greg B. Petersen, age 42, $461,750 pay
SVP and General Manager, Automotive: Hoon Chung, age 45, $382,047 pay
SVP Automotive: Scott D. Thompson
SVP Business Development: Mary Beth Loesch, age 44
VP and General Manager, Triad Denver:
Steve McLaughlin
VP Customer Services, Hardlines and Lumber:
Kraig Hall
VP Finance, Treasurer, and Assistant Secretary:
Christopher Speltz, age 42, $256,669 pay
VP Information Technology: Gary Cowsert, age 47
General Counsel and Secretary: Richard Rew II, age 37, $192,112 pay
Auditors: Ernst & Young LLP

LOCATIONS

HQ: Activant Solutions Holdings Inc.
804 Las Cimas Pkwy., Ste. 200, Austin, TX 78746
Phone: 512-328-2300 **Fax:** 512-278-5223
Web: www.activant.com

Activant Solutions Holdings has offices in Canada, France, Ireland, the UK, and the US.

2004 Sales

	$ mil.	% of total
Americas	219.1	97
Europe	6.7	3
Total	**225.8**	**100**

PRODUCTS/OPERATIONS

2004 Sales

	$ mil.	% of total
Wholesale distribution, building materials & hardware	119.9	53
Automotive	105.9	47
Total	**225.8**	**100**

2004 Sales

	$ mil.	% of total
Systems	82.0	36
Product support	79.2	35
Content & data services	57.3	26
Other	7.3	3
Total	**225.8**	**100**

Selected Products

Automotive
Activant A-DIS (warehouse management)
Activant J-CON (inventory management and electronic purchasing)
Activant The Paperless Warehouse (warehouse operations management system)
Activant PRISM (distribution management system)
Activant Ultimate (centralized business solution)
Industry Solutions
Activant CSD (building materials management system)
Activant Eagle (comprehensive set of Windows applications business management software)
Activant Falcon (management system for large multi-location lumber and building material dealers)
Activant Gemini (ERP system for multi-store hardware and lumber retail stores)

COMPETITORS

CAM Commerce Solutions	JDA Software
CarParts Technologies	Manugistics Group
Catalyst International	Prophet 21
i2 Technologies	Reynolds and Reynolds
Intuit	Wrenchead, Inc.

HISTORICAL FINANCIALS

Company Type: Private

Income Statement

FYE: September 30

	REVENUE ($ mil.)	NET INCOME ($ mil.)	NET PROFIT MARGIN	EMPLOYEES
9/04	226	17	7.4%	1,200
9/03	222	8	3.5%	1,300
9/02	219	9	4.3%	1,300
9/01	211	(13)	—	1,400
9/00	224	(33)	—	1,700
9/99	241	(40)	—	1,900
9/98	227	0	—	1,800
9/97	214	(43)	—	1,900
9/96	176	1	0.7%	1,400
9/95	175	8	4.6%	410
Annual Growth	**2.9%**	**8.6%**	**—**	**12.7%**

2004 Year-End Financials

Debt ratio: —
Return on equity: —
Cash ($ mil.): 32

Current ratio: 1.59
Long-term debt ($ mil.): 155

Net Income History

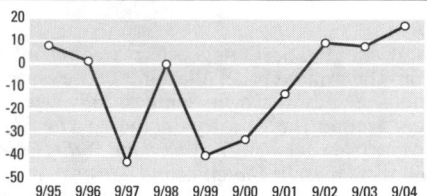

9/95 9/96 9/97 9/98 9/99 9/00 9/01 9/02 9/03 9/04

Adams Homes of Northwest Florida

Adams Homes of Northwest Florida's name is slightly deceiving. The company does build homes in northwestern Florida, but it also operates in other areas of Florida and in Alabama and Mississippi. Adams Homes constructs and sells pre-planned residential homes, specializing in first time homebuyers and those looking for larger or smaller houses. It also offers warranty and mortgage assistance. The company was founded in 1991 by president Wayne Adams.

EXECUTIVES

President: Wayne Adams
Production Manager, Port St. Lucie: Michael Alvarez
Financial Manager: Brian Stringfellow

LOCATIONS

HQ: Adams Homes of Northwest Florida, Inc.
1101 Gulf Breeze Pkwy., Ste. 229,
Gulf Breeze, FL 32561
Phone: 850-934-0470 **Fax:** 850-934-5533
Web: www.adamshomes.com

COMPETITORS

Caribe Homes
Centex
Century Homebuilders
Engle Homes
Lennar
Mercedes Homes
Pulte Homes
Standard Pacific

HISTORICAL FINANCIALS

Company Type: Private

Income Statement

FYE: December 31

	REVENUE ($ mil.)	NET INCOME ($ mil.)	NET PROFIT MARGIN	EMPLOYEES
12/04	138	—	—	200

Advance Publications

Advance Publications gets its marching orders from the printed page. A leading US newspaper publisher, Advance owns some 25 daily newspapers around the country, including *The Star-Ledger* (New Jersey), *The Cleveland Plain Dealer*, and its namesake *Staten Island Advance*. It also owns American City Business Journals (more than 40 weekly papers) and Parade Publications (*Parade Magazine* Sunday insert). Aside from print publishing, Advance is a major online publisher with 10 regional news Web sites. Samuel "Si" Newhouse Jr. and his brother, Donald, own the company.

It runs Internet properties Epicurious (food and dining) and Concierge (travel). The company also has stakes in cable TV systems (33%, with Time Warner) and cable broadcaster Discovery Communications (about 25%).

Advance had been a top magazine publisher in the US (along with Time, Inc.) through units Condé Nast Publications, with its popular titles such as *Allure, Glamour,* and *Vanity Fair,* and trade journal publisher Fairchild Publications (*Women's Wear Daily*). In 2005 the company announced that all magazines would be combined under the Condé Nast company.

HISTORY

Solomon Neuhaus (later Samuel I. Newhouse) got started in the newspaper business after dropping out of school at age 13. He went to work at the *Bayonne Times* in New Jersey and was put in charge of the failing newspaper in 1911; he managed to turn the paper around within a year. In 1922 he bought the *Staten Island Advance* (founded in 1886) and formed the Staten Island Advance Company in 1924. After buying up more papers, he changed the name of the company to Advance Publications in 1949. By the 1950s the company had local papers in New York, New Jersey, and Alabama.

In 1959 Newhouse bought magazine publisher Condé Nast as an anniversary gift for his wife. (He joked that she had asked for a fashion magazine, so he bought her *Vogue*.) His publishing empire continued to grow with the addition of the *Times-Picayune* (New Orleans) in 1962 and *The Cleveland Plain Dealer* in 1967. In 1976 the company paid more than $300 million for Booth Newspapers, publisher of eight Michigan papers and *Parade Magazine*.

Newhouse died in 1979, leaving his sons Si and Donald to run the company, which encompassed more than 30 newspapers, a half-dozen magazines, and 15 cable systems. The next year Advance bought book publishing giant Random House from RCA. Si resurrected the Roaring Twenties standard *Vanity Fair* in 1983 and added *The New Yorker* under the Condé Nast banner in 1985. The Newhouses scored a victory over the IRS in 1990 after a long-running court battle involving inheritance taxes. Condé Nast bought Knapp Publications (*Architectural Digest*) in 1993 and Advance later acquired American City Business Journals in 1995.

In 1998 the company sold the increasingly unprofitable Random House to Bertelsmann for about $1.2 billion. It later bought hallmark Internet magazine *Wired* (though it passed on

Wired Ventures' Internet operations). That year revered *New Yorker* editor Tina Brown, credited with jazzing up the publication's content and increasing its circulation, left the magazine; staff writer and Pulitzer Prize winner David Remnick was named as Brown's replacement.

In 1999 Advance joined Donrey Media Group (now called Stephens Media Group), E.W. Scripps, Hearst Corporation, and MediaNews Group to purchase the online classified advertising network AdOne (later named PowerOne Media). It also bought Walt Disney's trade publishing unit, Fairchild Publications, for $650 million. In 2000 the company shifted *Details* from Condé Nast to Fairchild and relaunched the magazine as a fashion publication. Later that year the company announced it would begin creating Web versions of its popular magazine titles.

In 2001 Condé Nast bought a majority stake in Miami-based Ideas Publishing Group (Spanish language versions of US magazines; its name was later changed to Condé Nast Americas). Also that year Advance bought four golf magazines, including *Golf Digest,* from the New York Times Company for $430 million. Condé Nast picked up *Modern Bride* magazine from PRIMEDIA in 2002 for $52 million.

Richard Diamond, a Newhouse relative who'd been publisher of the *Staten Island Advance* since 1979, died in 2004.

EXECUTIVES

Chairman and CEO; Chairman, Condé Nast Publications: Samuel I. (Si) Newhouse Jr., age 76
President: Donald E. Newhouse, age 72
COO; CEO, Condé Nast: Charles H. (Chuck) Townsend, age 61
CFO, Advance Media Group; EVP and COO, Condé Nast: John Bellando, age 47
Chairman and CEO, American City Business Journals: Ray Shaw
Chairman, CEO, and Publisher, Parade Publications: Walter Anderson
President, Advance Internet: Peter Weinberger
President, CondéNet: Sarah Chubb
SVP Consumer Marketing; SVP Circulation, Condé Nast Publications: Peter A. Armour
VP Marketing, Staten Island Advance: Jack Furnari
Comptroller, Staten Island Advance: Arthur Silverstein
Director of Retail, Classified, and National Sales, Staten Island Advance: Gary Cognetta

LOCATIONS

HQ: Advance Publications, Inc.
950 Fingerboard Rd., Staten Island, NY 10305
Phone: 212-286-2860 **Fax:** 718-981-1456
Web: www.advance.net

PRODUCTS/OPERATIONS

Broadcasting and Communications
Cartoonbank.com (database of cartoons from *The New Yorker*)
Discovery Communications (25%, cable TV channel)
Newhouse Broadcasting (33%, cable TV joint venture with Time Warner)
Newhouse News Service
Religion News Service

Newspaper Publishing
American City Business Journals
(41 weekly titles in 22 states)
Street & Smith's Sports Business Group
Newhouse Newspapers (25 papers across the US)
The Birmingham News (Alabama)
The Oregonian (Portland)
The Plain Dealer (Cleveland)
The Star-Ledger (Newark, NJ)
Staten Island Advance (New York)
The Times-Picayune (New Orleans)
Parade Publications

Online Publishing
Advance Internet
al.com (Alabama)
cleveland.com
MassLive.com (Massachusetts)
MLive (Michigan)
NJ.com (New Jersey)
NOLA.com (New Orleans)
OregonLive.com
PennLive.com (Pennsylvania)
SILive (New York)
Syracuse.com (New York)
CondéNet
Concierge (travel information)
Epicurious (recipes and fine dining)
STYLE.com (fashion and beauty)

COMPETITORS

American Express	Martha Stewart Living
American Media	McClatchy Company
Crain Communications	Meredith
Dow Jones	New York Times
E. W. Scripps	News Corp.
Essence Communications	Newsweek
F+W Publications	North Jersey Media
Forbes	PRIMEDIA
Freedom Communications	Reader's Digest
Gannett	Reed Elsevier Group
Gruner + Jahr	Rodale
Hachette Filipacchi Médias	Time
Hearst	Tribune
Johnson Publishing	Washington Post
Knight-Ridder	Wenner Media

HISTORICAL FINANCIALS

Company Type: Private

Income Statement

FYE: December 31

	REVENUE ($ mil.)	NET INCOME ($ mil.)	NET PROFIT MARGIN	EMPLOYEES
12/03	5,909	—	—	29,200
12/02	5,565	—	—	27,585
12/01	4,200	—	—	22,785
12/00	4,542	—	—	23,000
12/99	4,228	—	—	26,300
12/98	3,859	—	—	24,000
12/97	3,669	—	—	24,000
12/96	4,250	—	—	24,000
12/95	5,349	—	—	24,000
12/94	4,855	—	—	19,000
Annual Growth	2.2%	—	—	4.9%

Revenue History

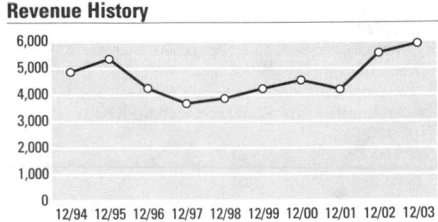

Advanced Lighting Technologies

And then there was metal halide light. Advanced Lighting Technologies' (ADLT) metal halide simulates sunlight more closely than other lighting technologies. Through subsidiary Venture Lighting, ADLT makes metal halide lamps ranging from 32 to 2,000 watts. Other lighting products include lamp components, power supplies, and lamp-making equipment. A vertically integrated company, ADLT makes the metal halide salts used in its own products; metal halide salts are also sold to other manufacturers. ADLT's Deposition Sciences subsidiary makes passive optical telecommunications devices and deposition coating equipment. After a rough patch, the company has reorganized and has paid off 100% of its debt.

With its plans for reorganization approved, ADLT has emerged from Chapter 11 and was taken private after an investment from Saratoga Lighting Holdings, an affiliate of the New York-based private equity investment firm Saratoga Partners. Saratoga Lighting has invested a reported $30 million for the company's preferred stock; Wells Fargo Foothill has also entered into a $30 million senior secured credit facility. Additionally, ADLT has sold off all of its lighting fixture interests in order to focus on metal halide lighting products.

EXECUTIVES

Chairman and CEO: Wayne R. Hellman, age 58, $2,627,914 pay
COO and Director: Sabu Krishnan, age 46, $416,154 pay
EVP and Treasurer: Wayne J. Vespoli
EVP: Wayne L. Platt, age 65, $285,731 pay
VP and Chief Accounting Officer: Christopher F. Zerull, age 45
VP; President, Deposition Sciences, Inc.: Lee A. Bartolomei, age 65, $253,261 pay
VP: James L. Schoolenberg, age 61
Director, Human Resources: Ken Hawley
Corporate Communications: Lisa Barry
Auditors: Grant Thornton LLP

LOCATIONS

HQ: Advanced Lighting Technologies, Inc.
32000 Aurora Rd., Solon, OH 44139
Phone: 440-519-0500 **Fax:** 440-519-0501
Web: www.adlt.com

Advanced Lighting Technologies maintains manufacturing facilities in California, Illinois, and Ohio, as well as in India.

2004 Sales

	% of total
US	58
Canada	18
UK	15
Australia	7
Other countries	2
Total	**100**

COMPETITORS

Corning	Magnetek
EI Products	Nortel Networks
GE	Philips Electronics
JDS Uniphase	Siemens
LSI Industries	SLI International Holdings

HISTORICAL FINANCIALS

Company Type: Private

Income Statement

FYE: June 30

	REVENUE ($ mil.)	NET INCOME ($ mil.)	NET PROFIT MARGIN	EMPLOYEES
6/04	145	(14)	—	1,480
6/03	145	(29)	—	1,425
6/02	167	(101)	—	1,329
6/01	219	0	0.1%	2,088
6/00	225	2	0.8%	2,020
6/99	189	(84)	—	1,731
6/98	164	(26)	—	1,776
6/97	87	7	8.2%	1,182
6/96	55	2	4.4%	564
6/95	41	3	7.6%	540
Annual Growth	**15.1%**	**—**	**—**	**11.9%**

2004 Year-End Financials

Debt ratio: 10,000.0%
Return on equity: —
Cash ($ mil.): 5
Current ratio: 1.74
Long-term debt ($ mil.): 127

Net Income History

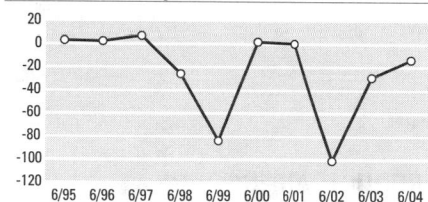

Advanstar Communications

Advanstar Communications offers a constellation of business-to-business publishing and marketing services. The company has a portfolio of 55 publications and directories and 75 electronic publications and Web sites. It also stages some 50 expositions and conferences annually. Titles include *Motor Age*, *Spectroscopy*, and *Dermatology Times;* trade shows include apparel show MAGIC; and marketing offerings include direct mail services and custom publishing. In 2005 the company slimmed down considerably when it sold assets not related to fashion, life sciences, and powersports. Investment firm Hellman & Friedman Capital Partners sold Advanstar to the merchant banking affiliate of Donaldson, Lufkin & Jenrette in 2000.

In 2003 Advanstar purchased health care publications from Thomson Healthcare, a subsidiary of The Thomson Corporation, for $135 million. Advanstar also purchased the Institute of Validation Technology, a source of FDA information, in 2004 to strengthen its pharmaceutical business.

The company shed some of its automotive and technology titles and trade shows, as well as

some art industry specific titles and shows in 2003 and 2004. In 2004 the company formed a unit devoted to off-road vehicles, as part of its Powersports division. It subsequently launched its first consumer-based magazine, *DIRTsports*, covering the off-road motor sports market.

In 2005 Advanstar disposed of assets yet again when it sold its technology, travel, portfolio, beauty, and home entertainment groups (which comprised 23 trade publications, 50 Web sites, 21 exhibitions, and 25 conferences) to another business-to-business media firm, Questex Media Group.

EXECUTIVES

Chairman and VP: James M. (Jim) Alic, age 62, $225,000 pay
CEO: Joseph (Joe) Loggia, age 45, $964,016 pay
EVP Corporate Development, General Counsel, and Assistant Secretary: Eric I. Lisman, age 47, $506,800 pay
EVP Healthcare, Portfolio, and Marketing Services Markets: Alexander S. DeBarr, age 44
EVP Information Technology, Call Center, Telecom, and Powersports Markets: Daniel M (Danny) Phillips, age 42
EVP: Scott E. Pierce, age 46
EVP Life Sciences Group: Annie Callanan
VP Finance, CFO, and Secretary: David W. (Dave) Montgomery, age 47, $418,462 pay
VP and CTO: Rick Treese, age 34, $323,731 pay
VP, Treasurer, and Controller: Adele D. Hartwick
VP Market Development: R. Steven (Steve) Morris, age 53
Corporate Communications Manager: Marc Merrill
Auditors: PricewaterhouseCoopers LLP

LOCATIONS

HQ: Advanstar Communications Inc.
1 Park Ave., New York, NY 10016
Phone: 212-951-6600 **Fax:** 212-951-6793
Web: www.advanstar.com

Advanstar Communications has 21 US offices and five international locations in Asia, Europe, and Latin America.

PRODUCTS/OPERATIONS

2004 Sales

	% of total
Publications	54
Trade shows & conferences	40
Direct marketing & other	6
Total	**100**

Selected Products and Services

Marketing services
  Classified advertising
  Database marketing
  Direct mail services
  Directories
  Guides and reference books
  Reprints
Trade, business, and professional publications
Trade shows and conferences

Selected Trade Shows and Conferences

International Powersports Dealer Expo (powersports accessories trade show)
MAGIC (men's apparel trade show)

Selected Publications

Dental Product Reports
Dermatology Times
DIRTsports
Drug Topics
Motor Age
Spectroscopy

COMPETITORS

Access Intelligence	Lebhar-Friedman
Cadmus Communications	McGraw-Hill
Crain Communications	MediaLive International
Fairchild Publications	Penton Media
Freeman Companies	PRIMEDIA
George P. Johnson	Reed Elsevier Group
Hanley Wood	Thomas Publishing
Harte-Hanks	United Business Media
IHS	Verticalnet
Informa	VNU
International Data Group	Wolters Kluwer

HISTORICAL FINANCIALS

Company Type: Private

Income Statement

FYE: December 31

	REVENUE ($ mil.)	NET INCOME ($ mil.)	NET PROFIT MARGIN	EMPLOYEES
12/04	381	(67)	—	1,400
12/03	326	(70)	—	1,400
12/02	307	(124)	—	1,200
12/01	347	(28)	—	1,300
12/00	378	(17)	—	1,500
12/99	328	(2)	—	1,470
12/98	260	(28)	—	1,300
12/97	188	(9)	—	—
12/96	151	(6)	—	—
12/95	145	(1)	—	—
Annual Growth	11.3%	—	—	1.2%

2004 Year-End Financials

Debt ratio: 2,867.8%
Return on equity: —
Cash ($ mil.): 41
Current ratio: 0.72
Long-term debt ($ mil.): 752

Net Income History

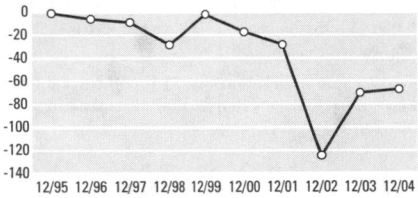

| 12/95 | 12/96 | 12/97 | 12/98 | 12/99 | 12/00 | 12/01 | 12/02 | 12/03 | 12/04 |

Advantis Real Estate Services

Advantis Real Estate Services (Advantis/GVA) finds its advantage in commercial real estate. The company offers brokerage, property management, construction management, and consulting services to commercial property owners and developers, primarily in the southeast US. Advantis/GVA also provides brokerage services for tenants. It leases and manages some 30 million sq. ft. of commercial space including office, industrial, and retail properties. The company has 13 offices in Florida (5); Georgia; Maryland; North Carolina; Virginia (4); and Washington, DC. Advantis/GVA is a member of global brokerage partnership GVA Worldwide.

Previously a subsidiary of St. Joe, Advantis/GVA was sold to company management in 2005. The firm continued to provide leasing and property management duties for much of St. Joe's portfolio.

EXECUTIVES

President and CEO: Petch Gibbons
SVP, COO, and CFO: John Hutcheson
VP, Construction Services: Paul Thomann
VP, Human Resources: Karen McWeeny
VP, Management Services: Bruce Ford
Senior Director, Management Services: Susan (Sue) Higgins
Senior Director, Office Services: Gerard F. Crum
Managing Director, Atlanta, Georgia: Thad Ellis
Executive Director and Regional Director, Corporate Services, Atlanta, Georgia: Scott W. Nelson
Executive Director, Office Properties, Atlanta, Georgia: Dan Granot
Executive Director, Real Estate Investment Banking, Atlanta, Georgia: C. Matthew (Matt) Tritschler
Auditors: KPMG LLP

LOCATIONS

HQ: Advantis Real Estate Services Company
3455 Peachtree Rd., Ste. 400, Atlanta, GA 30326
Phone: 404-262-2828 **Fax:** 404-262-1083
Web: www.advantisgva.com

2004 Properties Managed

	% of total
Virginia	37
Florida	36
North Carolina	13
Georgia	7
Maryland	6
Washington, DC	1
Total	100

PRODUCTS/OPERATIONS

2004 Property Types Managed

	% of total
Office	57
Industrial	21
Retail	16
Facilities management	5
Residential	1
Total	100

COMPETITORS

Carter
Divaris Real Estate
Donohoe Companies
Flagler Development
Great Atlantic Management
Levitt Commercial
Lincoln Property
Opus
Stiles
Weichert

HISTORICAL FINANCIALS

Company Type: Private

Income Statement

FYE: December 31

	REVENUE ($ mil.)	NET INCOME ($ mil.)	NET PROFIT MARGIN	EMPLOYEES
12/04	98	—	—	500

Adventist Health

Adventist Health is the West Coast wing of an international organization with strong ties to the Seventh-Day Adventist Church that operates Adventist health care providers around the globe. Adventist Health runs 20 hospitals (with some 3,100 beds), almost 20 home health services agencies, and various other outpatient facilities and hospices in California, Hawaii, Oregon, and Washington. The organization also works with its own churches and those of other denominations to offer such preventative health services as medical screenings, immunizations, and health education.

Adventist Health has joint ventures to operate independent and assisted-living centers in California, Oregon, and Washington. With Loma Linda University Medical Center, the health system has a behavioral care provider and a managed care organization.

EXECUTIVES

Chairman: Thomas J. Mostert Jr.
President, CEO, and Director: Donald R. Ammon
EVP, COO, and Director: Robert G. Carmen
SVP and CFO: Douglas E. Rebok
SVP; Chairman, Hanford Community Medical Center, Central Valley General Hospital, and Selma Hospital: Alan J. Rice
SVP: Larry D. Dodds
VP and CIO: Brett Spenst
VP and Treasurer: Rodney Wehtje
VP Delivery of Care: Wynelle J. Huff
VP Finance: James Brewster
VP Government Relations: Everett Gooch
VP Hospital Finance: Teresa M. Day
VP Hospital Finance Region II: Harry Weis
VP Hospital Finance: Stan Adams
VP Marketing and Communications, Adventist Health and Adventist Medical Center: Monty Knittel
VP Rural Health Clinics: Darwin Remboldt
Assistant VP Human Resources: Roger Ashley
Assistant VP Corporate Communications: Rita Waterman
Auditors: Ernst & Young LLP

LOCATIONS

HQ: Adventist Health
2100 Douglas Blvd., Roseville, CA 95661
Phone: 916-781-2000 **Fax:** 916-783-9909
Web: www.adventisthealth.org

Selected Facilities

California
San Joaquin Community Hospital (Bakersfield)
Redbud Community Hospital (Clearlake)
St. Helena Hospital (Deer Park)
Glendale Adventist Medical Center (Glendale)
Central Valley General Hospital (Hanford)
Hanford Community Medical Center (Hanford)
South Coast Medical Center (Laguna Beach)
White Memorial Medical Center (Los Angeles)
Paradise Valley Hospital (National City)
Feather River Hospital (Paradise)
Selma Community Hospital (Selma)
Simi Valley Hospital (Simi Valley)
Sonora Regional Medical Center (Sonora)
Ukiah Valley Medical Center (Ukiah)
Frank R. Howard Memorial Hospital (Willits)

Hawaii
Castle Medical Center (Kailua)
North Hawaii Community Hospital (Kamuela)

Oregon
Adventist Medical Center (Portland)
Tillamook County General Hospital (Tillamook)

Washington
Walla Walla General Hospital (Walla Walla)

COMPETITORS

Catholic Healthcare West	PacifiCare
HCA	Providence Health System
Kaiser Foundation	Province Healthcare
Health Plan	Sisters of Charity
Legacy Health System	of Leavenworth
LifePoint	Sutter Health
Los Angeles County	Tenet Healthcare
Health Department	Triad Hospitals
Memorial Health Services	Trinity Health (Novi)
	VITAS Healthcare

HISTORICAL FINANCIALS

Company Type: Not-for-profit

Income Statement

FYE: December 31

	REVENUE ($ mil.)	NET INCOME ($ mil.)	NET PROFIT MARGIN	EMPLOYEES
12/04	1,690	—	—	18,823
12/03	5,237	—	—	18,352
12/02	3,822	—	—	17,200
12/01	2,869	—	—	16,500
12/00	2,510	—	—	16,500
12/99	2,045	—	—	16,477
12/98	1,740	—	—	17,129
12/97	1,090	—	—	16,567
12/96	980	—	—	15,351
12/95	981	—	—	14,610
Annual Growth	6.2%	—	—	2.9%

Revenue History

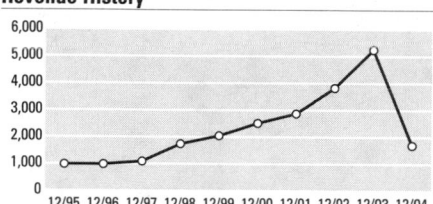

Adventist Health System

Adventist Health System (AHS) operates nearly 40 hospitals and about two dozen long-term care facilities located in about 10 states, mostly in the midwestern and southeastern US. Its acute care hospitals have nearly 6,300 beds combined, and its nursing homes offer more than 2,500 beds total. Florida is a key market: Its Florida Hospital system serves residents of the central part of the state and has nearly 1,800 beds. The AHS system includes about two dozen home health care agencies. The health system is sponsored by the Seventh-Day Adventist Church.

EXECUTIVES

President and CEO: Thomas L. (Tom) Werner
EVP, Florida Division: Des D. Cummings Jr.
EVP; COO, Florida Hospital: Lars D. Houmann
EVP; President and CEO, Florida Division and Florida Hospital: Donald L. Jernigan
SVP, Administration: Robert R. Henderschedt
SVP and CFO: Terry D. Shaw
SVP, Information Services and Senior Financial Officer; CFO, Multistate Hospital Division: Brent G. Snyder

VP, Home Care Services: La Donna R. Blom-Antonio
VP, Medical Affairs and Chief Medical Officer: Loran D. Hauck
VP, Human Resources: Donald G. (Don) Jones
VP, Mission and Ministries: Benjamin F. Reaves
VP and Treasurer: Gary C. Skilton
VP, Legal Services: T. L. Trimble

LOCATIONS

HQ: Adventist Health System
111 N. Orlando Ave., Winter Park, FL 32789
Phone: 407-647-4400   **Fax:** 407-975-1469
Web: www.ahss.org

Hospitals

Colorado
Porter Adventist Hospital (Denver)
Littleton Adventist Hospital (Littleton)
Avista Adventist Hospital (Louisville)
Florida
Florida Hospital Altamonte (Altamonte Springs)
Florida Hospital Apopka (Apopka)
Florida Hospital Celebration Health (Celebration)
Florida Hospital DeLand (DeLand)
Florida Hospital Kissimmee (Kissimmee)
Florida Hospital Lake Placid (Lake Placid)
Florida Hospital Fish Memorial (Orange City)
Florida Hospital East Orlando (Orlando)
Florida Hospital Orlando (Orlando)
Florida Hospital — Oceanside (Ormond Beach)
Florida Hospital — Ormond Memorial (Ormond Beach)
Florida Hospital — Flagler (Palm Coast)
Florida Hospital Heartland Medical Center (Sebring)
Florida Hospital Waterman (Tavares)
Florida Hospital Wauchula (Wauchula)
Winter Park Memorial Hospital (Winter Park)
East Pasco Medical Center (Zephyrhills)
Georgia
Gordon Hospital (Calhoun)
Emory-Adventist Hospital (Smyrna)
Illinois
Bolingbrook Medical Center (Bolingbrook)
GlenOaks Hospital (Glendale Heights)
Hinsdale Hospital (Hinsdale)
La Grange Memorial Hospital (La Grange)
Kansas
Shawnee Mission Medical Center (Shawnee Mission)
Kentucky
Manchester Memorial Hospital (Manchester)
North Carolina
Park Ridge Hospital (Fletcher)
Tennessee
Takoma Adventist Hospital (Greeneville)
Jellico Community Hospital (Jellico)
Tennessee Christian Medical Center — Madison (Madison)
Tennessee Christian Medical Center — Portland (Portland)
Texas
Huguley Memorial Medical Center (Fort Worth)
Metroplex Hospital (Killeen)
Rollins-Brook Community Hospital (Lampasas)
Central Texas Medical Center (San Marcos)
Wisconsin
Chippewa Valley Hospital (Durand)

HISTORICAL FINANCIALS

Company Type: Not-for-profit

Income Statement

FYE: December 31

	REVENUE ($ mil.)	NET INCOME ($ mil.)	NET PROFIT MARGIN	EMPLOYEES
12/03	10,123	—	—	44,000
12/02	8,433	—	—	42,000
12/01	6,655	—	—	—
12/00	5,285	—	—	—
Annual Growth	24.2%	—	—	4.8%

Revenue History

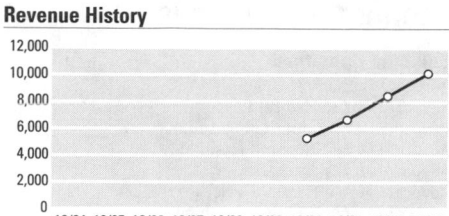

Advocate Health Care

Advocating wellness in Chicagoland from Palos Heights to Palatine, Advocate Health Care is an integrated health care network with more than 200 sites serving the Chicago area. Advocate's operations include eight acute care hospitals (including Christ Medical Center and Lutheran General Hospital) with 3,500 beds, and two children's hospitals, as well as home health care and ambulatory care services. Advocate also has teaching affiliations with area medical schools such as the University of Illinois at Chicago. The health system's Advocate Medical Group has nearly 200 physician members serving northwest Chicago.

Advocate Health Care has ties to both the United Church of Christ and the Evangelical Lutheran Church in America.

EXECUTIVES

President and CEO: James H. (Jim) Skogsbergh
EVP and COO: William P. (Bill) Santulli
EVP and CFO: Lawrence J. Majka
EVP and Chief Medical Officer; President, Advocate Health Partners: Lee B. Sacks
SVP and CIO: Bruce Smith
SVP Human Resources: Ben Grigaliunas
SVP Mission and Spiritual Care: Rev Jerry A. Wagenknecht
VP Business Development: Sara Moser
VP Communications and Government Relations: Tony Mitchell
VP Finance and Corporate Controller: Dominic J. Nakis
Chairperson, Advocate Charitable Foundation: William Graft
Chief Legal Officer and General Counsel: Gail D. Hasbrouck
Director Public Relations: Mike Maggio
Auditors: Ernst & Young

LOCATIONS

HQ: Advocate Health Care
2025 Windsor Dr., Oak Brook, IL 60523
Phone: 630-572-9393   **Fax:** 630-572-9139
Web: www.advocatehealth.com

PRODUCTS/OPERATIONS

Selected Operations
Advocate Bethany Hospital
Advocate Christ Medical Center
Advocate Good Samaritan Hospital
Advocate Good Shepherd Hospital
Advocate Health Centers
Advocate Home Health Services
Advocate Hope Children's Hospital
Advocate Illinois Masonic Medical Center
Advocate Lutheran General Hospital
Advocate Lutheran General Children's Hospital
Advocate Medical Group
Advocate South Suburban Hospital
Advocate Trinity Hospital
Dreyer Clinic, Inc.

COMPETITORS

Alexian Brothers
  Health System
Covenant Ministries
HCA
Provena Health
Rush System for Health
SSM Health Care

HISTORICAL FINANCIALS

Company Type: Not-for-profit

Income Statement

	REVENUE ($ mil.)	NET INCOME ($ mil.)	NET PROFIT MARGIN	EMPLOYEES
12/03	2,716	124	4.6%	25,000
12/02	2,604	(7)	—	25,293
12/01	2,467	108	4.4%	24,500
12/00	1,675	(7)	—	24,500
12/99	1,600	—	—	23,000
12/98	1,390	—	—	21,000
12/97	1,636	—	—	21,000
12/96	1,522	—	—	21,054
12/95	1,421	—	—	21,145
12/94	1,340	—	—	20,400
Annual Growth	8.2%	—	—	2.3%

FYE: December 31

2003 Year-End Financials

Debt ratio: 36.7%
Return on equity: 8.5%
Cash ($ mil.): —
Current ratio: 0.98
Long-term debt ($ mil.): 590

Net Income History

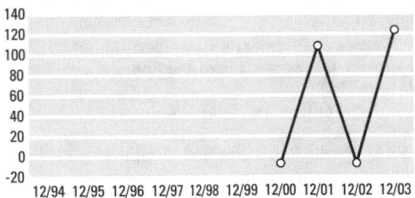

Aearo

When the sparks fly, it helps to be under the aegis of Aearo. The company makes and sells personal protection equipment in more than 70 countries under brand names such as AOSafety, E-A-R, Peltor, and SafeWaze. Products include earplugs, goggles, face shields, respirators, hard hats, safety clothing, first-aid kits, and communication headsets. Aearo also sells safety prescription eyewear and makes energy-absorbing foams that control noise, vibration, and shock for use in its own and other manufacturers' products. Bear Stearns Merchant Banking owns an 80% stake in Aearo.

Bear Stearns Merchant Banking acquired its stake in Aearo in 2004. Other investors include Vestar Capital Partners, which owns about 10% of the company, and members of Aearo's management team.

EXECUTIVES

Chairman, President, and CEO: Michael A. McLain, age 54, $1,020,604 pay
SVP, CFO, Secretary, and Treasurer: Jeffrey S. Kulka, age 47, $363,257 pay
SVP and Chief Marketing Officer: James H. Bernhardt, age 60, $336,257 pay
SVP Corporate Development and Chief Strategy Officer: Rahul Kapur, age 53, $327,610 pay
SVP Operations and Research and Development: Joseph C. Marlette, age 60
SVP Specialty Composites: M. Rand Mallitz, age 62, $344,458 pay
SVP Operations and Research and Development: Thomas R. D'Amico
SVP Human Resources: James M. Phillips, age 52
President, North American Safety Products Group: D. Garrad (Gary) Warren III, age 52, $479,312 pay
President, Aearo Europe; Managing Director, International: James H. Floyd, age 48, $413,066 pay
VP, Canadian Industrial: Dave Savage
VP, Category Management: Tim Millar
VP, National Accounts: Jay Kastan
VP, U.S. Industrial: Daryl Charton
Auditors: Deloitte & Touche LLP

LOCATIONS

HQ: Aearo Company I
  5457 W. 79th St., Indianapolis, IN 46268
Phone: 317-692-6666   **Fax:** 317-692-3088
Web: www.aearo.com

Aearo operates manufacturing facilities in Canada, Sweden, the UK, and the US.

2004 Sales

	$ mil.	% of total
US	218.9	60
Canada	27.1	8
UK	18.3	5
Sweden	15.9	4
France	14.9	4
Germany	13.9	4
Italy	5.3	2
Other countries	48.5	13
Total	**362.8**	**100**

PRODUCTS/OPERATIONS

2004 Sales

	$ mil.	% of total
Safety products	274.4	76
Specialty composites	48.6	13
Safety prescription eyewear	39.8	11
Total	**362.8**	**100**

COMPETITORS

3M
Bontex
Jackson Products
Lakeland Industries
Mine Safety Appliances

HISTORICAL FINANCIALS

Company Type: Private

Income Statement

	REVENUE ($ mil.)	NET INCOME ($ mil.)	NET PROFIT MARGIN	EMPLOYEES
9/04	363	4	1.0%	1,582
9/03	316	21	6.5%	1,603
9/02	287	9	3.2%	1,510
9/01	284	(2)	—	1,519
9/00	305	9	3.0%	1,657
9/99	290	7	2.4%	1,728
9/98	293	(11)	—	1,947
9/97	286	(7)	—	2,151
9/96	244	2	0.9%	2,000
9/95	257	4	1.6%	—
Annual Growth	3.9%	(2.0%)	—	(2.9%)

FYE: September 30

2004 Year-End Financials

Debt ratio: 368.9%
Return on equity: 1.9%
Cash ($ mil.): 28
Current ratio: 2.23
Long-term debt ($ mil.): 303

Net Income History

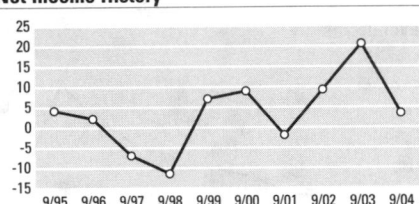

AECOM Technology

AECOM Technology means never having to say Architecture, Engineering, Consulting, Operations, and Maintenance. One of the world's leading engineering and design groups, AECOM offers a range of professional technical services, mostly to government agencies and large corporations. It is a top design firm in Asia and the Middle East and a global leader in the water, transportation, and wastewater sectors. It has expanded in Europe by acquiring UK-based companies such as transportation infrastructure groups Maunsell and Oscar Faber and water and wastewater construction firm Metcalf & Eddy UK. When AECOM withdrew its IPO in 2002, chairman Richard Newman and former vice chairman Joseph Incaudo owned major stakes.

AECOM has vied for some of the management and construction work to be had in Iraq; its activities there include contracts to support management activities for several public works. The company has also helped the Pentagon to buy goods and services and assisted in auditing projects of other contractors working on Iraq's reconstruction.

The group expanded in 2004 with the addition of Australian mechanical and electrical engineering firm Bassett, which joined the Maunsell group to become part of AECOM. The same year AECOM also acquired PADCO, a company that provides management and consulting services in developing countries; and UMA Group, a Canadian infrastructure engineering company.

EXECUTIVES

Chairman and CEO: Richard G. Newman, age 69
President, Corporate Development:
Raymond W. Holdsworth
EVP and COO: John M. Dionisio
SVP and CFO: Glenn R. Robson
SVP, Chief Administrative Officer, and Corporate Secretary: Stephanie A. Hunter
SVP Corporate Finance and General Counsel: Eric Chen
Chairman, Asia and Australia; Director:
Francis S. Y. Bong
Chairman, AECOM Global: David N. Odgers
CEO, Americas Transportation and Environmental Group: Robert H. Fischer
President, DMJM Harris: Frederick W. (Fred) Werner
CEO, Americas Facilities, Regional and Government Services Groups: James R. Royer
CEO, Australia, New Zealand, Asia, and Middle East Group: Nigel C. Robinson
CEO, Hong Kong and China Group: Tony C. K. Shum
CEO, United Kingdom Group: Kennedy F. (Ken) Dalton
Director of Corporate Communications: Jill Groswirth
Auditors: Ernst & Young LLP

LOCATIONS

HQ: AECOM Technology Corporation
555 S. Flower St., Ste. 3700, Los Angeles, CA 90071
Phone: 213-593-8000 **Fax:** 213-593-8730
Web: www.aecom.com

AECOM Technology has more than 150 major operating offices worldwide.

PRODUCTS/OPERATIONS

Selected Operations

AGS (government services)
Austin AECOM (architecture, engineering, construction, and consulting)
CTE (formerly Consoer Townsend Envirodyne; transportation and environmental engineering)
DMJM Aviation (consulting and engineering for aviation industry)
DMJM H&N (architecture, engineering, construction services)
DMJM Harris (construction and engineering)
Faber Maunsell (construction, transportation, environmental, and facilities consulting)
Maunsell (environmental, facilities, transportation, and consulting)
Maunsell AECOM (infrastructure, transportation, environmental, and facilities)
Metcalf & Eddy (wastewater engineering and environmental consulting)
PADCO (international development consulting)
TCB (formerly Turner Collie & Braden Inc.; engineering and project management)
UMA (environmental, transportation, and development)

COMPETITORS

ABB	MWH Global
AMEC	Parsons
Bechtel	Parsons Brinckerhoff
Black & Veatch	The PBSJ Corporation
Earth Tech	Perini
Fluor	Skidmore Owings
Foster Wheeler	STV
Henkels & McCoy	Terracon
Jacobs Engineering	Thorton-Tomasetti
Lockwood Greene	URS
Louis Berger	

HISTORICAL FINANCIALS

Company Type: Private

Income Statement
FYE: September 30

	REVENUE ($ mil.)	NET INCOME ($ mil.)	NET PROFIT MARGIN	EMPLOYEES
9/04	2,000	—	—	18,000
9/03	1,850	—	—	17,100
9/02	1,700	—	—	15,500
9/01	1,530	—	—	12,700
9/00	1,402	—	—	12,100
Annual Growth	**9.3%**	**—**	**—**	**10.4%**

Revenue History

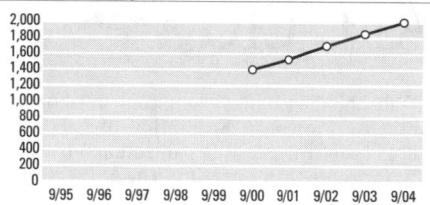

AESP

AESP wants to put networking equipment in your hands ASAP. The company makes computer connectivity and networking devices, including cable assemblies, adapters, interface cards, hubs, transceivers, and repeaters. AESP also offers audio/video connectivity products and accessories such as surge protectors and cable testers. It provides support and training services to its customers, which include retailers and computer manufacturers. The company sells products under its Signamax brand, and manufactures products for customers that attach their own brands. AESP has sold or shuttered all of its European subsidiaries due to losses by those units. CEO Slav Stein and EVP Roman Briskin each own about 24% of the company.

EXECUTIVES

President, CEO, and Director: Slav Stein, age 60, $205,256 pay
EVP, Secretary, Treasurer, and Director:
Roman Briskin, age 55, $205,256 pay
CFO: John F. Wilkens, age 46, $140,037 pay
VP, Network Group: Stephen Daily, age 47, $125,550 pay
Controller and Human Resources: David Jupiter
Auditors: Rachlin Cohen & Holtz LLP

LOCATIONS

HQ: AESP, Inc.
1810 NE 144th St., North Miami, FL 33181
Phone: 305-944-7710 **Fax:** 305-949-4483
Web: www.aesp.com

AESP has offices and plants in Florida and Pennsylvania, with distributors in Russia and Ukraine.

2004 Sales

	$ mil.	% of total
US	10.4	66
Russia & Ukraine	5.4	34
Total	**15.8**	**100**

PRODUCTS/OPERATIONS

Selected Products

Cables
Hubs
Interface cards
Patch cables
Patch panels
Plugs
Repeaters
Routers
Transceivers
Wallplates

COMPETITORS

3Com
Adaptec
Allied Telesyn
Cisco Systems
Communications Systems
Digi International
D-Link
Enterasys
Finisar
Leviton
Metrobility
NETGEAR
Ortronics
Riverstone Networks
Tyco

HISTORICAL FINANCIALS

Company Type: Private

Income Statement
FYE: December 31

	REVENUE ($ mil.)	NET INCOME ($ mil.)	NET PROFIT MARGIN	EMPLOYEES
12/04	16	(4)	—	72
12/03	32	(3)	—	117
12/02	30	(2)	—	139
12/01	30	(4)	—	134
12/00	30	1	2.3%	156
12/99	27	0	1.5%	149
12/98	22	(5)	—	112
12/97	21	1	2.8%	96
12/96	14	1	8.0%	62
12/95	14	—	—	62
Annual Growth	**1.6%**	**—**	**—**	**1.7%**

2004 Year-End Financials

Debt ratio: — Current ratio: 0.76
Return on equity: — Long-term debt ($ mil.): 0
Cash ($ mil.): 0

Net Income History

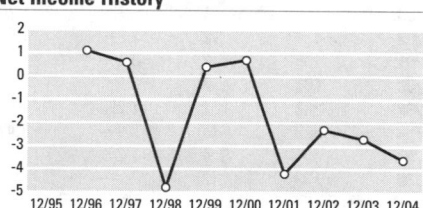

Affinity Group

Recreation is serious business for Affinity Group (AGI). The direct marketing company sells goods and services through its clubs, such as Good Sam, Coast to Coast, President's Club (which provides discounts for the RV crowd), and Golf Card (discounts for green fees). It also runs 30 Camping World retail stores, which sell RV products (air conditioners, sanitation systems, repair items, and furnishings) not usually found in general merchandise stores. In addition, AGI publishes magazines and travel guides, from which it derives subscription fees and ad sales revenue. Former parent, Affinity Group Holding (AGHI), was merged into AGI (surviving corporate entity) in 2004. Chairman Steve Adams is the majority owner.

EXECUTIVES

Chairman; Chairman, Affinity Group, Inc.:
  Stephen Adams
President and CEO, Affinity Group, Inc.:
  Michael Schneider
SVP and CFO: Thomas F. Wolfe
SVP, Affinity Group, Inc.: Michael Blumer
SVP, Marketing, Affinity Group, Inc.: Murray S. Coker
President and CEO, Camping World: Mark J. Boggess
Auditors: Ernst & Young LLP

LOCATIONS

HQ: Affinity Group, Inc.
  2575 Vista Del Mar, Ventura, CA 93001
Phone: 805-667-4100   **Fax:** 805-667-4419
Web: www.affinitygroup.com

COMPETITORS

International Leisure
KOA
Outdoor Resorts
REI
Thousand Trails

HISTORICAL FINANCIALS

Company Type: Private

Income Statement

FYE: December 31

	REVENUE ($ mil.)	NET INCOME ($ mil.)	NET PROFIT MARGIN	EMPLOYEES
12/04	465	10	2.2%	1,800
12/03	425	24	5.7%	1,701
12/02	431	12	2.8%	1,627
12/01	405	1	0.1%	1,514
12/00	405	3	0.8%	1,608
12/99	382	7	1.7%	1,565
12/98	359	(5)	—	1,471
12/97	301	4	1.2%	—
12/96	139	(2)	—	—
Annual Growth	**16.3%**	**—**	**—**	**3.4%**

2004 Year-End Financials

Debt ratio: —   Current ratio: 0.91
Return on equity: —   Long-term debt ($ mil.): 313
Cash ($ mil.): 25

Net Income History

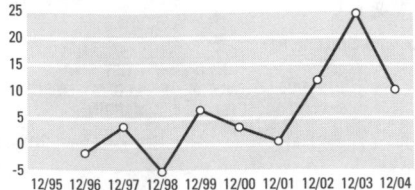

25
20
15
10
5
0
-5

12/95 12/96 12/97 12/98 12/99 12/00 12/01 12/02 12/03 12/04

AFL-CIO

Talk about spending a long time in labor: The AFL-CIO (American Federation of Labor and Congress of Industrial Organizations) has been at it for more than a century. The AFL-CIO is an umbrella organization for more than 60 autonomous national and international unions representing more than 10 million workers — ranging from actors and airline pilots to marine engineers and machinists — and fights to improve wages and working conditions. The organization charters 51 state federations and nearly 580 central labor councils. Union members generally receive about 33% higher pay and more benefits than nonmembers.

The organization's membership has been decreasing because of the decline in manufacturing jobs and the increased use of temporary workers and automation. Despite president John Sweeney's aggressive plans to increase recruiting, the Teamsters and the Service Employees International Union (SEIU) left the AFL-CIO in 2005 over the issues of plummeting membership and the future course of the labor movement. They took 3.3 million members with them.

HISTORY

The American Federation of Labor (AFL) was formed in 1886 in Columbus, Ohio, by the merger of six craft unions and a renegade craft section of the Marxist-oriented Knights of Labor. Samuel Gompers, a New York cigar factory worker who headed the AFL until his death in 1924, initiated the AFL's pragmatic focus: to work within the economic system to increase wages, improve working conditions, and abolish child labor.

Gompers' successes incensed employers, whose arsenal, supported by the US courts and public opinion, included injunctions, government-backed police forces to crush strikes, and the Sherman Anti-Trust Act (used to assail union monopoly powers).

WWI's production needs boosted AFL membership to 4 million by 1919. Labor clashes with management were widespread in the 1920s amid the fear of Bolsheviks. As part of open-shop drives, employers replaced strikers with southern African-Americans and Mexican workers.

The Great Depression brought more supportive public and pro-labor laws, including the National Industrial Recovery Act (NIRA, 1933), which allowed union organizing and collective bargaining. After NIRA was declared unconstitutional, the Wagner Act (1936) restated many of NIRA's provisions and established the legal basis for unions.

Union power split in 1935 when AFL coal miner John L. Lewis began organizing unskilled workers. Lewis and his allies, expelled from the AFL, formed the Congress of Industrial Organizations (CIO, 1938) and enjoyed success in unionizing the auto, steel, textile, and other industries. By 1946 the AFL and CIO had 9 million and 5 million members, respectively.

Amid postwar concern over rising prices, communist infiltration, and union corruption, Congress passed the Taft-Hartley Act in 1947 (which outlawed closed shops). The new climate of hostility led the AFL (headed by plumber George Meany) and the CIO (headed by autoworker Walter Reuther) to merge in 1955. The AFL-CIO soon expelled the Teamsters and other unions on charges of corruption. (The Teamsters reaffiliated in 1987.)

AFL-CIO membership jumped after President Kennedy gave federal employees the right to unionize (1962); state, county, and municipal workers soon followed.

Union membership, which peaked in the mid-1940s with more than a third of the US labor force, was particularly hurt by a jump in imported goods in the 1970s and automation's triumph over manual labor in the 1980s. Legislation supported by the AFL-CIO included a law requiring 60 days' notice for plant closings (1988) and the Family Medical Leave Act (1993). But labor lost its battle against NAFTA (North American Free Trade Agreement), which it feared would export jobs to Mexico.

In 1995 John Sweeney, former head of the Service Employees International Union, became president of the AFL-CIO in its first contested election. Under Sweeney the union spent $35 million in advertising in 1996 to draw attention to issues. After years with little focus on organizing, in 1997 the AFL-CIO launched a massive campaign to organize construction, hospital, and hotel workers in Las Vegas, and committed a third of its budget to recruiting and reorganizing. It supported the Teamsters' successful strike against UPS in 1997 and in 1998 threw its weight behind the Air Line Pilots Association's walkout on Northwest Airlines. It approved a restructuring plan in 1999 and the next year spent significant time and money rallying members all across the US in support of losing presidential candidate Al Gore. In 2002 AFL-CIO announced its pledge of $750 million to create affordable housing in New York City.

At the group's 2005 convention, the Teamsters and the SEIU broke ranks over Sweeney's inability to stem the tide of falling membership. They joined a rival group, Change to Win Coalition, led by SEIU's Andrew Stern.

EXECUTIVES

President: John J. Sweeney, age 71
EVP: Linda Chavez-Thompson, age 61
Secretary and Treasurer: Richard L. Trumka, age 56
VP; President, International Association of Machinists and Aerospace Workers: R. Thomas Buffenbarger
VP; President, International Brotherhood of Electrical Workers: Edwin D. Hill
VP; President Sheet Metal Workers Union:
  Mike Sullivan
President, Transportation Trades Department:
  Ed Wytkind
Director Corporate Affairs: Ron Blackwell
Director International Affairs: Barbara Shailor
Director Human Resources: Karla Garland
General Counsel: Jonathan Hiatt
Investment Officer: Brandon Rees
Director, Legislative: Bill Samuel

LOCATIONS

HQ: AFL-CIO
815 16th St. NW, Washington, DC 20006
Phone: 202-637-5000 **Fax:** 202-637-5058
Web: www.aflcio.org

PRODUCTS/OPERATIONS

Selected Trades and Workers Represented

Acting
Airline pilots
Broadcasting
Building trades
Education
Electrical trades
Engineering
Farmworkers
Firefighters
Flight attendants
Food trades
Government workers
Hotel employees
Industrial trades
Maritime trades
Metal trades
Mining
Music
Office employees
Police
Postal employees
Restaurant employees
Teachers
Transportation trades
Utility workers
Writers

HISTORICAL FINANCIALS

Company Type: Labor union

Income Statement				FYE: June 30
	REVENUE ($ mil.)	NET INCOME ($ mil.)	NET PROFIT MARGIN	EMPLOYEES
6/03	145	—	—	480

Ag Processing

Soy far, soy good for Ag Processing (AGP), one of the largest soybean processors in the US. AGP's chief soybean products include vegetable oil and commercial animal feeds. It also provides grain marketing and transportation services. The cooperative is promoting its corn-based ethanol and soybean oil-based bio-fuels, fuel additives, and solvents. AGP processes some 15,000 acres of soybeans a day from its members' farms. The co-op's owners include 200,000 members from 16 US states and Canada. The members, mostly in the Midwest, are represented through 238 local co-ops and eight regional co-ops.

AGP also turns its products into food ingredients, such as lethicin and meat extenders for ground beef. To capitalize on new EPA emission limits and mandates, the co-op is lobbying to increase retail demand for ethanol. Additionally, AGP is promoting methyl ester, a by-product of soy oil refining, for use as a clean fuel and fuel additive, agricultural spray, and non-toxic solvent to replace petroleum-based products.

HISTORY

Seeking strength in numbers, Ag Processing (AGP) was formed in 1983 when agricultural cooperatives Land O' Lakes and Farmland Industries merged their money-losing soybean operations into similarly struggling Boone Valley Cooperative.

Separately, AGP's six soybean mills had been unable to compete successfully against each other and larger corporations. The entire industry had been hampered by the Soviet grain embargoes imposed by the US in 1973 and 1979, and US government policies had contributed to increased competition from heavily subsidized soy producers in Argentina and Brazil. Soy exports from the US had fallen dramatically, leading to a production capacity surplus.

Collectively, AGP was able to attract a stronger management staff than its predecessors had; it hired 21-year Archer Daniels Midland (ADM) veteran James Lindsay as CEO and general manager. With operations scattered over four states, AGP placed its headquarters in Omaha, Nebraska — chosen for its central location and close proximity to the co-op's main bank.

In its first two years, AGP cut employee rolls by 20% and scaled back production, thus trimming costs and squeezing higher prices for finished products. A turnaround came quickly, and in 1985 members received a dividend from the co-op's $8 million pretax profit. That year AGP purchased two Iowa plants from AGRI Industries.

AGP dismantled two plants in 1987. By the next year the co-op witnessed an increase in domestic demand and had resumed selling to the Soviet Union. It generated additional sales by further processing soybean oil into food-grade products like hydrogenated oil and lecithin.

With an eye on diversification and value-added products, by 1991 AGP had expanded to eight soybean plants and two vegetable oil refineries; it also acquired the feed and grain business of International Multifoods that year through an 80%-owned joint venture with ADM. The acquisition included 29 feed plants in the US and Canada, 26 retail centers, 18 grain elevators, and the brands Supersweet and Masterfeeds. In 1994 AGP formed feed manufacturer Consolidated Nutrition, a 50-50 joint-venture with ADM.

Consolidated Nutrition introduced a Swine Operations program in 1996. The program quickly grew through the development of PORK PACT, a partnership to serve pork producers. (The co-op has since exited the swine business.) The next year AGP's grain division sold nine grain elevators in Ohio and Indiana to Cargill. That year the co-op gained control of Venezuelan feed manufacturer Proagro.

By 1998 passage of the Freedom to Farm Act and growing demand had spurred soybean planting. The co-op in 1998 opened an additional processing plant in Emmetsburg, Iowa, followed by another in Eagle Grove, Iowa. AGP sold off its pet food operations in 1998 to Windy Hill, which was later acquired by Doane Pet Care Enterprises. Also that year Consolidated Nutrition combined its Master Mix and Supersweet feed brands into the Consolidated Nutrition label.

In 1999 the company added the Garner-Klemme-Meservey cooperative to its grain operations. It opened a new plant late that year in St. Joseph, Missouri, to make value-added products such as hardfat (used in emulsifiers).

In June 2001 AGP sold its 50% share of Consolidated Nutrition to ADM. In 2002 the co-op's Masterfeeds business acquired four feed mills and a merchandising operation from Saskatchewan Wheat Pool. In 2003 AGP opened the Port of Grays Harbor vessel-loading terminal in Aberdeen, Washington, that year.

EXECUTIVES

Chairman: Bradley T. Davis
Vice Chairman: Lowell D. Wilson
CEO and General Manager: Martin P. (Marty) Reagan
SVP and Corporate Controller: Tim E. Witty
SVP, Corporate and Member Relations:
 Michael L. Maranell
SVP, Engineering and Environment:
 Charles A. Janiszewski
SVP, Human Resources: Judith V. Ford
SVP, Transportation: Terry J. Voss
Group VP, Animal Nutrition; President, Masterfeeds:
 Robert J. Flack
Group VP, Finance, CFO, Assistant Secretary, and Assistant Treasurer: J. Keith Spackler
Group VP, Food and Industrial: George L. Hoover
Group VP, Grain: Michael J. (Mike) Knobbe
Group VP, Processing Soybean and Corn:
 Calvin J. Meyer
VP, Corporate General Counsel, and Assistant Secretary: Larry J. Steier
Auditors: Deloitte & Touche LLP

LOCATIONS

HQ: Ag Processing Inc
 12700 W. Dodge Rd., Omaha, NE 68154
Phone: 402-496-7809 **Fax:** 402-498-2215
Web: www.agp.com

PRODUCTS/OPERATIONS

Selected Brands
AMINOPLUS (dairy feed additive)
Masterfeeds (feeds, Canada)
Progtinal/Proagro (poultry and feed, Venezuela)
SOYGOLD (bio-diesel, solvents, fuel additives)

Selected Operations
Commercial feeds
Food (lecithin, soybean oil, vegetable oil)
Grain
Industrial products (ethanol, methyl ester)
Soybean processing
Transportation (barge, rail, truck)

Selected Subsidiaries
Ag Environmental Products
 (soybean methyl ester products)
AGP Grain, Ltd.
AGP Grain Marketing, Inc.
Intellectual Property Holdings LLC

COMPETITORS

Abengoa Bioenergy
ADM
Andersons
Bunge Limited
Cargill
CHS
ConAgra
Corn Products International
DeBruce Grain
Griffin Industries
MFA
Riceland Foods
Southern States
SunOpta

HISTORICAL FINANCIALS

Company Type: Cooperative

Income Statement

FYE: August 31

	REVENUE ($ mil.)	NET INCOME ($ mil.)	NET PROFIT MARGIN	EMPLOYEES
8/03	2,127	11	0.5%	1,500
8/02	1,802	32	1.8%	2,500
8/01	1,789	27	1.5%	2,500
8/00	1,962	—	—	2,500
8/99	2,095	—	—	2,500
8/98	2,615	—	—	2,550
8/97	2,948	—	—	3,000
8/96	2,765	—	—	3,050
8/95	2,132	—	—	—
8/94	1,377	—	—	—
Annual Growth	4.9%	(36.1%)	—	(9.6%)

2003 Year-End Financials

Debt ratio: 19.5%
Return on equity: 2.7%
Cash ($ mil.): 7

Current ratio: 1.62
Long-term debt ($ mil.): 79

Net Income History

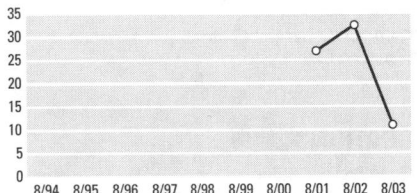

Airxcel

Airxcel Holdings, operating through Airxcel, Inc., manufactures air conditioners, furnaces, water heaters, cooking appliances, and compressor refrigeration units mainly for recreational vehicle OEMs (almost 70% of sales), including Fleetwood Enterprises, Thor Industries, and Winnebago. The RV products unit makes Coleman-brand air-conditioning equipment; the Marvair unit makes specialty wall-mount ACs, environmental control units, and heat pumps for utilities and schools and for modular construction and telecom companies. Subsidiary Suburban Manufacturing Company makes RV gas furnaces, water heaters, ranges, and cooktops; the InstaFreeze unit makes compressor refrigerators for RV, marine, and ambulance OEMs.

EXECUTIVES

President, CEO, and Director: Melvin L. (Mel) Adams, age 59, $521,280 pay
CFO, Secretary, and Treasurer: Richard L. Schreck, age 52, $287,916 pay
VP; President, RV Products: Gregory G. Guinn, age 56, $289,860 pay
VP, RV Manufacturing and Engineering: Lonnie L. Snook, age 69, $233,660 pay
Auditors: Ernst & Young LLP

LOCATIONS

HQ: Airxcel Holdings Corporation
3050 N. St. Francis, Wichita, KS 67219
Phone: 316-832-3400   **Fax:** 316-832-3493
Web: www.airxcel.com

Airxcel has facilities in Cordele, Georgia; Dayton, Tennessee; Elkhart, Indiana; and Wichita, Kansas.

COMPETITORS

American Standard
Carrier
Hughes Supply
Johns Manville
Lennox
Nortek
York International

HISTORICAL FINANCIALS

Company Type: Private

Income Statement

FYE: December 31

	REVENUE ($ mil.)	NET INCOME ($ mil.)	NET PROFIT MARGIN	EMPLOYEES
12/04	184	5	2.8%	864
12/03	161	3	2.0%	889
12/02	159	(19)	—	923
12/01	145	2	1.2%	812
Annual Growth	8.3%	44.2%	—	2.1%

2004 Year-End Financials

Debt ratio: —
Return on equity: —
Cash ($ mil.): —

Current ratio: —
Long-term debt ($ mil.): 89

Net Income History

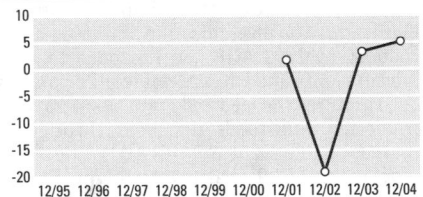

Alex Lee

The George family mixed wholesale and retail food well before it was a consolidation trend. Founded by Alex and Lee George in 1931, Alex Lee is a holding company for four food and warehousing companies located in the southeast US: Consolidation Services (warehousing); Institution Food House, Inc., or IFH (foodservice distributor); Lowe's Food Stores, Inc. (supermarkets); and Merchants Distributors, Inc., or MDI, (wholesale food and related merchandise supplier). The company serves more than 600 retailers in the mid-Atlantic and Southeast, including IGA stores and Galaxy Food Centers. The George family controls Alex Lee.

The company became a foodservice supplier in the 1960s with the purchase of Institution Food House. In 1984 Alex Lee bought the Lowe's food chain, which has more than 100 stores in North and South Carolina and Virginia. In 1998 the company started Consolidation Services to provide logistics services to vendors, distributors, and manufacturers.

EXECUTIVES

Chairman and CEO: Boyd L. George
President: Dennis G. Hatchell
EVP and CFO: Ronald W. Knedlik
VP, Human Resources: Glenn DeBiasi
VP, Information Systems: Jay Schwarz
President, Institution Food House:
David A. (Dave) Stansfield
President, Lowe's Foods: Curtis Oldenkamp

LOCATIONS

HQ: Alex Lee, Inc.
120 4th St. SW, Hickory, NC 28603
Phone: 828-323-4424   **Fax:** 828-323-4435
Web: www.alexlee.com

COMPETITORS

Ahold USA
ARAMARK
C&S Wholesale
Ingles Markets
Kroger
K-VA-T Food Stores
McLane Foodservice
Nash Finch
Ruddick
SUPERVALU
SYSCO
U.S. Foodservice
Winn-Dixie

HISTORICAL FINANCIALS

Company Type: Private

Income Statement

FYE: September 30

	REVENUE ($ mil.)	NET INCOME ($ mil.)	NET PROFIT MARGIN	EMPLOYEES
9/04	2,320	—	—	10,300
9/03	2,140	—	—	9,500
9/02	1,980	—	—	9,000
9/01	1,890	—	—	8,500
9/00	1,690	—	—	8,500
9/99	1,588	—	—	7,154
9/98	1,516	—	—	7,482
9/97	1,315	—	—	6,143
9/96	1,300	—	—	5,400
9/95	1,270	—	—	5,400
Annual Growth	6.9%	—	—	7.4%

Revenue History

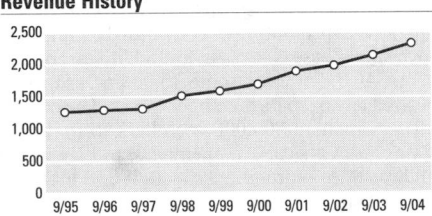

AlgoRx Pharmaceuticals

AlgoRx Pharmaceuticals wants to pinpoint your pain and make it "all gone." The pain management company has three drugs in development, including ALGRX 4975, which could treat postsurgical pain as well as pain associated with osteoarthritis. Another drug, ALGRX 3268 or PowderJect Dermal Lidocaine, is a needle-free anesthetic that could reduce pain that occurs when blood is drawn or when intravenous lines are inserted. AlgoRx's third drug candidate, ALGRX 1207, is a topical local anesthetic that could treat chronic pain related to skin diseases. The company focuses on acquiring or licensing products to treat acute and chronic pain. AlgoRx plans to acquire drug maker Corgentech.

AlgoRx's shareholders will control more than 60% of the new company. Corgentech shareholders will control about 38%. The deal will significantly increase AlgoRx's late-stage drug pipeline.

Venture capital firms InterWest and J.P. Morgan Partners each own about 20% of the company.

EXECUTIVES

Chairman: Charles M. Cohen, age 54
CEO and Director: Ronald M. Burch, age 50, $349,000 pay
President and COO: Paul R. Hamelin, age 50, $141,250 pay (partial-year salary)
SVP, Clinical Research and Regulatory Affairs: Jeffrey D. Lazar, age 58, $295,700 pay
VP, Finance and CFO: Jeffrey A. Rona, age 36, $222,000 pay
VP, Manufacturing and Process Development: Badri N. Dasu, age 41
VP, Marketing: Diana Davidson, age 49
VP, Regulatory Affairs: Steven I. Engel, age 50
Auditors: Ernst & Young LLP

LOCATIONS

HQ: AlgoRx Pharmaceuticals, Inc.
500 Plaza Dr., 2nd Fl., Secaucus, NJ 07094
Phone: 201-325-6900   **Fax:** 201-325-6909
Web: www.algorx.com

PRODUCTS/OPERATIONS

Drug candidates

ALGRX 1207 (skin pain)
ALGRX 3268 or PowderJect Dermal Lidociane (pain from drawing blood and intravenous line insertions)
ALGRX 4975 (postsurgery pain and osteoarthritis)

COMPETITORS

Abbott Labs
Johnson & Johnson
Pfizer
Purdue Pharma

HISTORICAL FINANCIALS

Company Type: Private

Income Statement
FYE: December 31

	REVENUE ($ mil.)	NET INCOME ($ mil.)	NET PROFIT MARGIN	EMPLOYEES
12/04	0	(23)	—	23
12/03	0	(16)	—	23
12/02	0	(20)	—	—
12/01	0	(1)	—	—
Annual Growth	—	—		0.0%

2004 Year-End Financials

Debt ratio: 0.0%   Current ratio: 11.69
Return on equity: —   Long-term debt ($ mil.): 0
Cash ($ mil.): 14

Net Income History

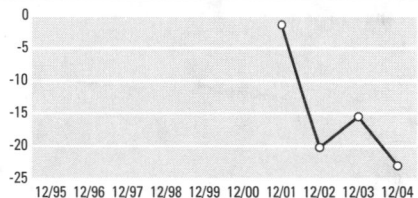

12/95 12/96 12/97 12/98 12/99 12/00 12/01 12/02 12/03 12/04

Alion Science and Technology

This company creates an alliance between science, technology, and big government. Alion Science and Technology is a development and research firm that provides consulting and technology services primarily to federal agencies (the majority of its revenues comes from contracts with the US Department of Defense). Its practice areas include industrial engineering, modeling and simulation software, transportation systems, and wireless communication systems. Other skill areas include advanced materials research, explosive decontamination and demolition, and defense-related strategic planning and decision support services. Employee-owned Alion was spun off from the IIT Research Institute in 2003.

Alion counts on the US government for nearly all of its business. The company plans on expanding its client base to include more civilian agencies and to build its organization through strategic acquisitions.

Alion acquired information technology and management service provider Identix Public Sector (IPS) for $8.9 million in early 2004.

EXECUTIVES

Chairman and CEO: Bahman Atefi
Group SVP and Group Manager, National Security: John Otjen
Group SVP and Group Manager, Operational Solutions: Phillip (Phil) Abold
Group SVP and Group Manager, Spectrum Engineering: Richard Meidenbauer
Group SVP and Group Manager, Spectrum International: Lynn Cumberpatch
Group SVP and Group Manager, Strategic Operations: Joe Owen
Group SVP and Group Manager, Strategic Systems: Scott Fry
Group SVP and Group Manager, Technology Solutions: Christopher Amos
SVP, CFO, and Treasurer: John (Jack) Hughes
SVP, Administration: Gary N. Armstutz
SVP and Chief Administrative Officer: Stacy Mendler
SVP, General Counsel, and Secretary: James C. (Jim) Fontana
Corporate VP, Administration and Director, Human Resources: Katherine C. Madeleno
Assistant VP, Administration and Director, Marketing and Communications: Peter J. Jacobs
Auditors: KPMG LLP

LOCATIONS

HQ: Alion Science and Technology Corporation
1750 Tysons Blvd., Ste. 1300, McLean, VA 22102
Phone: 703-918-4480   **Fax:** 703-714-6508
Web: www.alionscience.com

COMPETITORS

Anteon	Lockheed Martin
Booz Allen	ManTech
CACI International	MTC Technologies
Capgemini	Northrop Grumman
Computer Sciences Corp.	Perot Systems
EDS	SAIC
General Dynamics	SI International
IBM	Unisys
L-3 Titan	

HISTORICAL FINANCIALS

Company Type: Private

Income Statement
FYE: September 30

	REVENUE ($ mil.)	NET INCOME ($ mil.)	NET PROFIT MARGIN	EMPLOYEES
9/04	270	(15)	—	1,880
9/03	166	(13)	—	1,604
9/02	202	5	2.3%	1,622
9/01	193	9	4.9%	1,458
9/00	156	4	2.7%	1,334
9/99	118	4	3.1%	1,074
9/98	94	4	4.2%	1,013
9/97	108	3	2.4%	1,099
Annual Growth	14.1%	—	—	8.0%

2004 Year-End Financials

Debt ratio: 1,006.5%   Current ratio: 1.57
Return on equity: —   Long-term debt ($ mil.): 98
Cash ($ mil.): 5

Net Income History

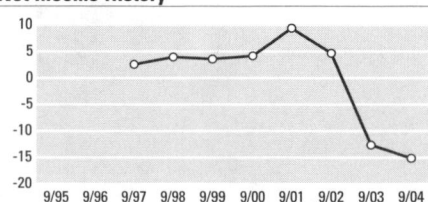

9/95 9/96 9/97 9/98 9/99 9/00 9/01 9/02 9/03 9/04

Allbritton Communications

Allbritton Communications helps bring a little of the Magic Kingdom to its television markets. The company owns (either wholly or partially) and operates about nine TV stations in markets in Alabama, Arkansas, Oklahoma, Pennsylvania, South Carolina, Virginia, and Washington, DC. All of its stations are affiliates of ABC (which is owned by Walt Disney). The company also owns a 24-hour cable news channel (NewsChannel 8) that serves the Washington, DC, area. NewsChannel 8 shares facilities with the company's Washington, DC station WJLA. More than a quarter of the company's revenue comes from automotive-related advertising.

EXECUTIVES

Chairman and CEO: Robert L. Allbritton, age 37, $325,000 pay
Vice Chairman, President, COO, and Director: Frederick J. Ryan Jr., age 49, $317,500 pay
EVP and Director: Barbara B. Allbritton, age 67
SVP and CFO: Stephen P. Gibson, age 39, $266,000 pay
SVP Legal and Strategic Affairs and General Counsel: Jerald N. Fritz, age 53, $276,500 pay
VP Human Resources and Employee Benefits: Phyllis Schwartz
VP Sales: James C. Killen Jr., age 42
Auditors: PricewaterhouseCoopers LLP

LOCATIONS

HQ: Allbritton Communications Company
808 17th St. NW, Ste. 300, Washington, DC 20006
Phone: 202-789-2130   **Fax:** 202-822-6749
Web: www.allbritton.com

PRODUCTS/OPERATIONS

Selected Station Operations
KATV (Little Rock, Arkansas)
KTUL (Tulsa, Oklahoma)
NewsChannel 8 (cable news based in Washington, DC)
WBMA (80%-owned; Birmingham, Alabama)
WCFT (Tuscaloosa, Alabama)
WCIV (Charleston, South Carolina)
WHTM (80%-owned; Harrisburg, Pennsylvania)
WJLA (Washington, DC, operations integrated with NewsChannel 8)
WJSU (80%-owned; Anniston, Alabama)
WSET (Roanoke/Lynchburg, Virginia)

COMPETITORS

Belo
Cox Enterprises
Equity Broadcasting
Fox Entertainment
Gannett
Hearst-Argyle Television
LIN TV
NBC
Tribune
Viacom
Young Broadcasting

HISTORICAL FINANCIALS

Company Type: Private

Income Statement

FYE: September 30

	REVENUE ($ mil.)	NET INCOME ($ mil.)	NET PROFIT MARGIN	EMPLOYEES
9/04	203	14	6.7%	936
9/03	203	—	—	936
9/02	196	—	—	—
9/01	191	—	—	856
9/00	205	—	—	889
9/99	187	—	—	890
9/98	183	—	—	806
9/97	173	—	—	814
9/96	156	—	—	—
9/95	138	—	—	—
Annual Growth	**4.4%**	**—**	**—**	**2.0%**

Revenue History

(Line graph showing revenue in $ mil. from 9/95 to 9/04, ranging approximately 138 to 205)

Allegis Group

Clients in need of highly skilled technical and other personnel might want to take the pledge of Allegis. Allegis Group is one of the world's largest staffing and recruitment firms, with more than 220 offices in North America and Europe. Among its operating companies are Aerotek (engineering, automotive, and scientific professionals for short- and long-term assignments), Mentor 4 (recruitment for accounting, human resources, and customer support positions), and TEKsystems (IT staffing and consulting). In 1983 CEO Steve Bisciotti and Jim Davis established the company to provide contract engineering personnel to two clients in the aerospace industry; Bisciotti and Davis still control Allegis.

EXECUTIVES

CEO: Steve Bisciotti
CFO: Dave Seandeven
EVP Human Resources: Neil Mann
CIO: Kevin Apperson
CEO, TEKsystems: Mike Salandra
President, Aerotek: Tom Thornton
President, Mentor 4: Mike McSally
Product Manager: Ethan Griffin
General Counsel: Randy Sones

LOCATIONS

HQ: Allegis Group, Inc.
7301 Parkway Dr., Hanover, MD 21076
Phone: 410-579-4800   **Fax:** 410-540-7556
Web: www.allegisgroup.com

PRODUCTS/OPERATIONS

Operating Companies
Aerotek (engineering, automotive, and scientific personnel for short- and long-term assignments)
MarketSource (outsourced sales support, training, recruiting, and program management)
Mentor 4 (recruitment for accounting, human resources, and customer support positions)
Contacteam
Option One
TEKsystems (IT staffing and consulting)

COMPETITORS

Adecco	Randstad
ASG Renaissance	RDL Group
CDI	Robert Half
Innovative Management Solutions	Snelling and Snelling
Kelly Services	Spherion
Manpower	Vedior
MPS	Volt Information

HISTORICAL FINANCIALS

Company Type: Private

Income Statement

FYE: December 31

	ESTIMATED REVENUE ($ mil.)	NET INCOME ($ mil.)	NET PROFIT MARGIN	EMPLOYEES
12/03	2,750	—	—	4,600
12/02	2,035	—	—	4,600
12/01	2,700	—	—	8,000
12/00	3,700	—	—	8,800
Annual Growth	**(9.4%)**	**—**	**—**	**(19.4%)**

Revenue History

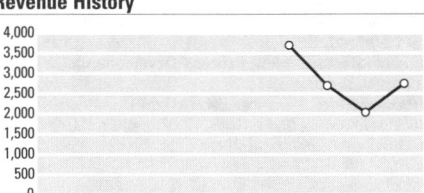

(Line graph showing estimated revenue in $ mil. from 12/94 to 12/03)

Alliance Capital Management

Alliance Capital Management has tons of funds. As one of the world's largest investment managers, Alliance Capital Management administers more than 100 domestic and international mutual funds. The company primarily serves such institutional investors as pension funds, foundations, endowments, government entities, and insurance firms. For individual investors, it provides private client services, managed accounts, annuities, retirement plans, and college savings plans. Alliance Capital also owns money manager and research firm Sanford C. Bernstein. French insurer AXA holds approximately 60% of Alliance Capital Management; publicly traded Alliance Capital Management Holding owns more than 30%.

Alliance Capital Management is active in North America, Europe, Australia, and Asia.

Long known as a growth investor, Alliance Capital is trying to cast itself in a more conservative light. Institutional customers — which include public retirement funds in approximately 40 states and for about 40 of the *FORTUNE* 100 companies — account for more than 55% of Alliance Capital's more than $500 billion in assets under management, most of which are invested in fixed income and value equity products.

In 2003 Alliance Capital came under investigation as instances of improper market-timing trades came to light. The firm's president, the head of its mutual fund distribution unit, and some additional employees were ousted amidst the scandal. In late 2003, the company reached a $600 million settlement with regulators, also agreeing to cut its fund fees and freeze the rates at that level for a five-year period.

Alliance Capital in 2005 sold its cash management business to Federated Investors; the sale includes the assets under management of 22 third-party-distributed money market funds.

HISTORY

Alliance Capital Management began in 1962 as the management department of Donaldson, Lufkin & Jenrette, now Credit Suisse First Boston (USA). The company opened its first international office in the UK in 1978. Also that year the company introduced its first money market fund. In 1983 the company debuted its first mutual fund. The Equitable acquired Alliance as part of its DLJ acquisition in 1985.

In an attempt to raise money, cash-strapped Equitable sold 40% of the company in a 1988 public offering of Alliance stock. The company acquired Shields Asset Management in 1994 and bought Cursitor-Eaton two years later. Poor performance of the Cursitor unit forced the company to take a $121 million charge in 1997.

In 1998 the Taxpayer Relief Act of 1997 removed Alliance's Master Limited Partnership tax status and increased the company's tax rate to that of a regular partnership, a 3.5% increase. The next year the company organized a holding company and transferred its operations and old name to a new limited partnership, Alliance Capital Management Holding, to help provide tax relief for parent company The Equitable (renamed AXA Financial in 1999).

The firm continued to bolster its reputation as a global investor, expanding its operations in Asia, Europe, the UK, and South America, where it targeted privatized pension funds. As deregulation opened the Japanese mutual fund market in 1998, the company worked to rapidly establish a major presence there. Alliance's global vision played into the strategy of its ultimate parent, AXA. As one of the world's largest insurers, AXA began building its brand, using Alliance to help establish itself in global financial services.

In 2000 the company bought money manager Sanford C. Bernstein, a firm noted for its research.

EXECUTIVES

Chairman and CEO: Lewis A. (Lew) Sanders, age 59, $275,002 pay
Vice Chairman, Institutional and Private Asset Management Sales and Marketing: Roger Hertog, age 63
President, COO, and Director: Gerald M. Lieberman, age 58, $2,500,000 pay
EVP and CTO: Lawrence H. (Larry) Cohen, age 43
EVP and General Counsel: Laurence E. Cranch, age 58
EVP and Chief Investment Officer — Global, UK, and European Value Equities: Sharon E. Fay, age 44, $2,511,538 pay

EVP, Head of Bernstein Value Equities Business, and Chief Investment Officer — US Value Equities: Marilyn G. Fedak, age 58, $2,511,538 pay
EVP, Director of Global Quantitative Research, and Chief Investment Officer — Absolute Return Strategy: Mark R. Gordon, age 51
EVP; President, Bernstein Investment Research and Management: Thomas S. Hexner, age 48
EVP and Chief Investment Officer — Style Blend and Core Equity: Seth J. Masters, age 45
EVP; Chairman, AllianceBernstein Investment and Research Management: Marc O. Mayer, age 47
EVP and Co-Head and Chief Investment Officer, Alliance Capital Fixed Income: Douglas J. (Doug) Peebles, age 39
EVP and Co-Head and Chief Investment Officer, Alliance Capital Fixed Income: Jeffrey S. (Jeff) Phlegar, age 38
EVP and Head of US Large-Cap Growth: James G. Reilly, age 44
EVP and Director of Research — Global Growth Equities: Paul C. Rissman, age 48, $2,500,000 pay
SVP and CFO: Robert H. Joseph Jr., age 57
SVP and Chief Accounting Officer: Edward J. Farrell
SVP, Counsel, and Secretary: Adam Spilka
Auditors: KPMG LLP

LOCATIONS

HQ: Alliance Capital Management L.P.
1345 Avenue of the Americas, New York, NY 10105
Phone: 212-969-1000   **Fax:** 212-969-2229
Web: www.alliancecapital.com

2004 Sales

	% of total
US	78
Other countries	22
Total	**100**

PRODUCTS/OPERATIONS

2004 Sales

	$ mil.	% of total
Investment advisory & service fees		
Institutional investment management	758.9	26
Retail	727.0	24
Private client	627.5	21
Distribution revenues	447.3	15
Institutional research services	303.6	10
Shareholder servicing fees	87.5	3
Other	75.1	2
Total	**3,026.9**	**100**

2004 Sales

	% of total
Retail	42
Institutional investment management	25
Private client	21
Institutional research services	10
Other	2
Total	**100**

COMPETITORS

Affiliated Managers Group	Janus Capital
AIG	Legg Mason
AIG Retirement Services	Merrill Lynch
American Century	MFS
AMVESCAP	Neuberger Berman
BlackRock	Nuveen
Eaton Vance	Principal Financial
Federated Investors	Raymond James Financial
FMR	T. Rowe Price
Franklin Resources	UBS Financial Services
GAMCO Investors	Vanguard Group
ING	Waddell & Reed

HISTORICAL FINANCIALS

Company Type: Private

Income Statement

FYE: December 31

	ASSETS ($ mil.)	NET INCOME ($ mil.)	INCOME AS % OF ASSETS	EMPLOYEES
12/04	8,779	705	8.0%	4,100
12/03	8,172	330	4.0%	4,096
12/02	7,218	611	8.5%	4,172
12/01	8,175	615	7.5%	4,542
12/00	8,271	669	8.1%	4,438
12/99	1,661	462	27.8%	2,396
Annual Growth	39.5%	8.8%	—	11.3%

2004 Year-End Financials

Equity as % of assets: 47.7%   Long-term debt ($ mil.): 408
Return on assets: 8.3%   Sales ($ mil.): 3,027
Return on equity: 17.7%

Net Income History

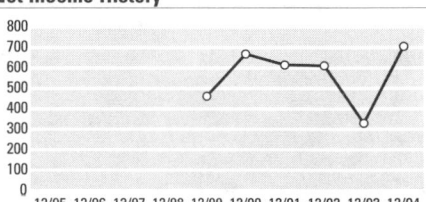

800									
700									
600									
500									
400									
300									
200									
100									
0									

12/95 12/96 12/97 12/98 12/99 12/00 12/01 12/02 12/03 12/04

Alliance Laundry

Alliance Laundry Holdings makes commercial laundry equipment used in North American laundromats, multi-housing laundry facilities (apartments, dormitories, military bases), and on-premise laundries (hotels, hospitals, prisons). Its washers and dryers are made under the brands Huebsch, Speed Queen, and UniMac. In addition, Alliance offers laundry and dry-cleaning presses and shirt finishing equipment under the Ajax brand. Founded in 1908, Alliance Laundry was sold to private investment firm Teachers' Private Capital (private equity arm of Ontario Teachers' Pension Plan) for about $450 million in early 2005.

Alliance got its start with the introduction of the hand-operated washer. The company was sold to McGraw Electric in 1956 and later Raytheon (1979); in 1998 Raytheon exited the commercial laundry business and spun off the company.

EXECUTIVES

Chairman and CEO: Thomas F. (Tom) L'Esperance, age 55, $800,066 pay
SVP, Sales and Marketing: Jeffrey J. (Jeff) Brothers, age 57
VP and CFO: Bruce P. Rounds, age 47
VP and Corporate Controller: Robert T. Wallace, age 48
VP and General Manager, Marianna Operations: William J. Przybysz, age 59
VP and General Manager, Ripon Operations: R. Scott Gaster, age 51
VP, Law and Human Resources: Scott L. Spiller, age 53
Auditors: PricewaterhouseCoopers LLP

LOCATIONS

HQ: Alliance Laundry Holdings LLC
Shepard Street, Ripon, WI 54971
Phone: 920-748-3121   **Fax:** 920-748-4334
Web: www.comlaundry.com

Alliance Laundry operates a network of more than 200 North American distributors and over 150 international distributors, serving more than 100 countries globally.

COMPETITORS

American Dryer
Maytag
Whirlpool

HISTORICAL FINANCIALS

Company Type: Private

Income Statement

FYE: December 31

	REVENUE ($ mil.)	NET INCOME ($ mil.)	NET PROFIT MARGIN	EMPLOYEES
12/04	281	12	4.2%	1,312
12/03	268	16	5.9%	1,309
12/02	255	1	0.5%	1,300
Annual Growth	4.9%	201.3%	—	0.5%

2004 Year-End Financials

Debt ratio: —
Return on equity: —
Cash ($ mil.): 11
Current ratio: 1.33
Long-term debt ($ mil.): 258

Net Income History

12/95 12/96 12/97 12/98 12/99 12/00 12/01 12/02 12/03 12/04

Allina Hospitals

Allina Hospitals and Clinics is a not-for-profit health care system that focuses on protecting people's number one asset — "Their Good Health." Allina Hospitals and Clinics owns and operates 11 hospitals and medical centers, and about 80 clinics, hospice services, and pharmacies. The Allina network serves Minnesota and western Wisconsin. Allina Hospitals and Clinics also provides disease prevention programs, specialized inpatient and outpatient services, medical equipment, and emergency medical transportation service. About 5,000 physicians provide services through the health care system.

EXECUTIVES

Chairman Emeritus: Michael E. Dougherty, age 64
Chairman: Rollin H. (Rollie) Crawford
Vice Chairman: John M. Morrison
President, CEO, and Director:
Richard R. (Dick) Pettingill, age 56
COO: Ken Paulus

EVP and CFO: Mark G. Harrison
EVP Hospital and Specialty Operations: Rickie Ressler
EVP Human Resources and Culture and Chief Talent Officer: Michael W. Howe
EVP Nursing and Chief Nursing Officer: Christine Seitz
EVP Public Policy and Compliance and Corporate Compliance Officer: David B. Orbuch
EVP Safety and Quality Systems: Barbara Balik
CIO: Robert Plaszcz
Chief Medical Officer: Brian Anderson
Corporate Secretary and General Counsel:
Mary P. Foarde
Media Relations: Jennifer Syltie Johnson
Auditors: Deloitte & Touche LLP

LOCATIONS

HQ: Allina Hospitals and Clinics
710 E. 24th St., Minneapolis, MN 55404
Phone: 612-775-5000   **Fax:** 612-863-5667
Web: www.allina.com

PRODUCTS/OPERATIONS

Selected Hospitals

Abbott Northwestern Hospital (Minneapolis, MN)
Buffalo Hospital (Buffalo, MN)
Cambridge Medical Center (Cambridge, MN)
Mercy Hospital (Coon Rapids, MN)
New Ulm Medical Center (New Ulm, MN)
Owatonna Hospital (Owatonna, MN)
Phillips Eye Institute (Minneapolis, MN)
River Falls Area Hospital (River Falls, WI)
St. Francis Regional Medical Center (Shakopee, MN)
United Hospital (St. Paul, MN)
Unity Hospital (Fridley, MN)

COMPETITORS

Alexian Brothers
Health System
Catholic Health Initiatives
HCA
Mayo Foundation
SSM Health Care

HISTORICAL FINANCIALS

Company Type: Not-for-profit

Income Statement

FYE: December 31

	REVENUE ($ mil.)	NET INCOME ($ mil.)	NET PROFIT MARGIN	EMPLOYEES
12/03	1,940	—	—	22,583
12/02	1,800	—	—	22,347
12/01	1,700	—	—	22,102
12/00	2,600	—	—	21,500
12/99	2,600	—	—	22,546
12/98	2,550	—	—	22,000
12/97	2,500	—	—	21,200
12/96	2,400	—	—	20,800
12/95	2,100	—	—	20,000
Annual Growth	(1.0%)	—	—	1.5%

Revenue History

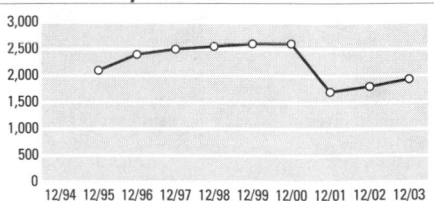

12/94 12/95 12/96 12/97 12/98 12/99 12/00 12/01 12/02 12/03

Allstates WorldCargo

No relation to insurance giant Allstate, Allstates WorldCargo uses its "good hands" to provide freight forwarding and logistics services. The company arranges the transportation of its customers' cargo by plane, ship, and truck. Rather than maintaining its own transportation assets, Allstates WorldCargo uses a network of air, ocean, and over-the-road carriers. The company operates from a network of some 20 offices in the US, and it maintains partnerships and agency relationships with freight forwarders in Europe, South America, and the Asia/Pacific region. Chairman Joseph Guido owns 57% of the company.

A subsidiary, Audiogenesis Systems, distributes protective clothing and other safety equipment to employees of a pharmaceutical company.

Audiogenesis Systems bought Allstates Air Cargo in a reverse acquisition in 1999, and the combined company took the name Allstates WorldCargo. Guido, a former freight supervisor for AMR's American Airlines, founded Allstates Air Cargo in 1961.

Company CEO Sam DiGiralomo, a veteran employee of Audiogenesis Systems and its predecessor, Genesis Safety Systems, owns 15% of Allstates WorldCargo.

EXECUTIVES

Chairman: Joseph M. Guido, age 70, $329,811 pay
President, CEO, and Director: Sam DiGiralomo, age 61, $216,000 pay
EVP, COO, and Director: Barton C. Theile, age 58, $213,948 pay
CFO, Secretary, Treasurer, and Director:
Craig D. Stratton, age 53, $148,077 pay
Auditors: Cowan, Gunteski & Co., P.A.

LOCATIONS

HQ: Allstates WorldCargo, Inc.
4 Lakeside Dr. South, Forked River, NJ 08731
Phone: 609-693-5950   **Fax:** 609-693-5550
Web: www.allstatesair.com

COMPETITORS

BAX Global
C.H. Robinson Worldwide
EGL
Expeditors
FedEx Trade Networks Transport & Brokerage
GeoLogistics
Menlo Worldwide
UPS Supply Chain Solutions

HISTORICAL FINANCIALS

Company Type: Private

Income Statement

FYE: September 30

	REVENUE ($ mil.)	NET INCOME ($ mil.)	NET PROFIT MARGIN	EMPLOYEES
9/04	55	0	0.4%	93
9/03	46	(1)	—	98
9/02	36	0	0.3%	—
Annual Growth	22.6%	41.4%	—	(5.1%)

Debt ratio: —   Current ratio: —
Return on equity: —   Long-term debt ($ mil.): 2
Cash ($ mil.): —

Net Income History

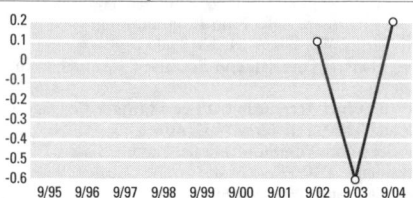

Alticor

At the core of Alticor, there is Amway. Alticor was formed in 2000 as a holding company for four businesses: direct-selling giant Amway, Web-based sales firm Quixtar, Pyxis Innovations (corporate development for Alticor and affiliates), and Access Business Group (manufacturing, logistics services). Access Business' biggest customers are Amway and Quixtar, but Access also serves outsiders. Amway, which accounts for the bulk of Alticor's revenues, sells more than 450 different products through 3 million independent distributors. Quixtar sells Amway and other products online. Amway China Co. is fueling Alticor's sales growth. Alticor is owned by Amway founders, the DeVos and Van Andel families.

The company also owns the Amway Grand Plaza Hotel, located in Grand Rapids, Michigan. The hotel houses the state's first AAA Five-Diamond-designated restaurant, the 1913 Room.

EXECUTIVES

Chairman: Steve Van Andel
President and Director; President, Amway; and President, Quixtar: Doug DeVos
EVP and CFO: Lynn Lyall
SVP and Managing Director, Quixtar: Ken McDonald
VP, Corporate Communications: Mark Bain
VP, Human Resources: Robin Horder-Koop
VP, Public Policy: Richard Holwill
COO, Access Business Group LLC: Al Koop
Chief Information Officer: Kelly Savage
Chief Marketing Officer: John Parker
Chief of Staff: William R. (Bill) Payne
Manager, Brand Communications: Amy Scott
Corporate General Counsel: Michael Mohr
Supervisor, Voice-Telecommunications Services: Gerard Wood

LOCATIONS

HQ: Alticor Inc.
7575 Fulton St. East, Ada, MI 49355
Phone: 616-787-1000   **Fax:** 616-682-4000
Web: www.alticor.com

Alticor operates in more than 80 countries worldwide. It has manufacturing facilities in the US, China, and South Korea and farming operations in the US, Mexico, and Brazil.

PRODUCTS/OPERATIONS

Selected Amway Products

Catalog Products
    Appliances
    Electronics
    Fashions
    Home furnishings
    Office supplies
    Toys
Home Care Products
    Dishwashing liquid
    Laundry detergent
    Multi-purpose cleaner
Home Living/Home Tech Products
    Cookware
    Water-treatment systems
Nutrition and Wellness Products
    Beverages
    Dietary supplements
    Meals
    Snacks
    Weight-control products
Personal Care Products
    Body washes
    Deodorants
    Hair care products
    Lotions
    Toothpaste
Skin Care and Cosmetics Products
    Cleansers
    Color cosmetics
    Moisturizers
    Toners

COMPETITORS

Avon	Kao
Bath & Body Works	L'Oréal
Body Shop	MacAndrews & Forbes
Brown-Forman	Mary Kay
CCL Industries	Newell Rubbermaid
Clorox	Nikken
Colgate-Palmolive	Nu Skin
Daiei	PFSweb
Estée Lauder	Procter & Gamble
Fingerhut	S.C. Johnson
Forever Living	Shaklee
GNC	Tom's of Maine
Henkel	Tupperware
Herbalife	Unilever
Johnson & Johnson	

HISTORICAL FINANCIALS

Company Type: Private

Income Statement   FYE: August 31

	REVENUE ($ mil.)	NET INCOME ($ mil.)	NET PROFIT MARGIN	EMPLOYEES
8/04	6,200	—	—	13,000
8/03	4,900	—	—	11,500
8/02	4,500	—	—	10,500
8/01	3,500	—	—	10,500
8/00	3,500	—	—	10,000
8/99	3,000	—	—	10,000
8/98	2,900	—	—	14,000
8/97	5,780	—	—	13,000
8/96	5,352	—	—	13,000
8/95	4,958	—	—	13,000
Annual Growth	2.5%	—	—	0.0%

Revenue History

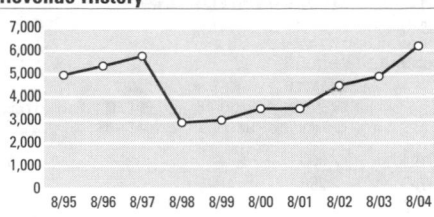

A-Mark Financial

Calling all gold bugs: A-Mark Financial trades, markets, and finances rare coins, precious metals, and collectibles. A-Mark Precious Metals trades in gold, silver, platinum, and palladium coins, bars, ingots, and medallions for central banks, corporations, and individuals around the world. A-Mark Financial distributes coins for government mints, including those of Australia, Canada, South Africa, and the US. Subsidiary Goldline International sells rare and collectible coins and bullion, while A-M Handling provides melting and assay services. Chairman and owner Steven Markoff founded A-Mark Financial in 1965; it is now among the 10 largest privately held companies in Los Angeles county.

EXECUTIVES

President and CEO: Steven C. Markoff
Controller: Dennis Lautzenheiser
Chief Administrative Officer: Joseph P. Ozaki
President and CEO, Goldline International: Mark Albarian
EVP, Marketing, Goldline International: Joseph C. Battaglia
Auditors: Deloitte & Touche LLP

LOCATIONS

HQ: A-Mark Financial Corporation
100 Wilshire Blvd., 3rd Fl., Santa Monica, CA 90401
Phone: 310-260-0315   **Fax:** 310-319-0310
Web: www.amark.com

PRODUCTS/OPERATIONS

Selected Services

Deferred pricing transactions
Inventory financing
Leasing and consignment
Market making
Marketing support
New product announcements
Order execution
Platinum market updates
Refining
Storage

COMPETITORS

Anglo American
Degussa
DGSE Companies
Tumba Bruk

HISTORICAL FINANCIALS

Company Type: Private

Income Statement

FYE: July 31

	ESTIMATED REVENUE ($ mil.)	NET INCOME ($ mil.)	NET PROFIT MARGIN	EMPLOYEES
7/04	2,800	—	—	112
7/03	2,200	—	—	118
7/02	2,600	—	—	102
7/01	1,812	—	—	106
7/00	2,446	—	—	120
7/99	1,500	—	—	100
7/98	1,000	—	—	100
7/97	1,000	—	—	120
7/96	1,000	—	—	110
7/95	1,000	—	—	121
Annual Growth	**12.1%**	**—**	**(0.9%)**	

Revenue History

AMC Entertainment

AMC Entertainment shines when the lights go down. The #2 movie theater chain in the US (behind Regal), the firm owns about 230 theaters that house almost 3,550 screens, about 75% of which are in multiplexes and megaplexes (units with more than 14 screens and stadium seating). Its theaters can be found in 27 states and the District of Columbia, as well as in Canada, France, Hong Kong, Japan, Portugal, Spain, and the UK. The firm also teamed with other media and theater firms such as Famous Players (bought by Cineplex Entertainment in 2005), Hollywood Media, and National Amusements to launch MovieTickets.com, of which AMC Entertainment owns about a quarter. AMC in 2005 agreed to buy rival Loews Cineplex.

AMC Entertainment generates more than two-thirds of its revenue from ticket sales, while more than 25% comes from the concession stand. The company also sells digitally projected on-screen advertising and pre-show entertainment videos through its National CineMedia joint venture with Regal Entertainment and Cinemark. National CineMedia was formed in early 2005 when AMC merged its National Cinema Network with Regal's Regal CineMedia subsidiary. The new company can now deliver ads and programming to more than 13,000 screens in North America. (Cinemark later bought a 21% stake in National Cinemedia. The deal reduced AMC's initial interest in the venture to 29%.)

The unbridled expansion of megaplexes (and the failure to close smaller, older locations) had left the theater industry with a glut of screens. However, as one of the few theater chains to avoid Chapter 11 in the last few years, AMC En-

tertainment has expanded with the purchases of rival exhibitors Gulf States Theatres and GC Companies. Merger talks with Loews Cineplex were once abandoned in 2004, but AMC finally agreed to purchase Loews the following year. The combined company will retain the AMC Entertainment name, and AMC CEO Peter Brown would also continue in his position.

Marquee Holdings, an investment vehicle controlled by affiliates of J.P. Morgan Partners and Apollo Advisors, purchased AMC Entertainment for about $2 billion at the close of 2004.

HISTORY

After performing in tent shows around the Midwest, Edward Dubinsky settled in Kansas City, Missouri, and opened his first movie theater in 1920. Dubinsky, who later changed his name to Durwood, had opened about a dozen theaters and drive-ins by the 1950s. After he died in 1960, his son Stanley took control of the business. Three years later Stanley Durwood ushered in a new age of movie viewing by opening the first mall-based theater with multiple screens. The company, which became American Multi-Cinema in 1968, expanded the multiplex concept throughout the 1970s. In 1983 American Multi-Cinema shortened its name to AMC and went public.

The company opened theaters at a furious rate, growing at about 100 screens a year for five years. This left it with a massive debt, however, and AMC posted little or no profit between 1988 and 1992. The company later restructured, laying off employees and reducing its total number of screens to 1,600 in 1994. AMC opened a 24-screen theater in Dallas in 1995. A year later a new AMC theater in Ontario, California, became the first to have 30 screens. In 1997 AMC teamed with Planet Hollywood to develop Planet Movies, a restaurant, theater, and retail concept.

To reduce debt, the next year AMC transferred 13 theaters to a real estate investment trust it had created; it then leased the theaters back to AMC. In 1999 the US Justice Department filed a lawsuit against AMC claiming the company's theaters denied handicapped individuals access to better, stadium-style seats. The first Planet Movie opened that summer in Columbus, Ohio, but financial problems at Planet Hollywood put further projects on hold. Stanley Durwood died later that year after a long battle with cancer. He was replaced by co-chairman Peter Brown.

In early 2000 AMC partnered with entertainment companies to form MovieTickets.com, a joint venture created to sell movie tickets over the Web. The company also began experimenting with the digital distribution of movies via satellite. In 2002 AMC acquired Gulf States Theatres (which included five theatres in the New Orleans area) and the bankrupt rival exhibitor GC Companies (which included 66 theatres throughout the US).

The following year a federal court ruled AMC violated regulations regarding accommodations for people in wheelchairs. As a result, the company announced plans to spend $21 million over five years to modify 113 stadium-style theaters.

At the end of 2004 AMC ceased to be publicly traded after it was purchased by affiliates of J.P. Morgan Partners and Apollo Advisors. Early the next year, AMC combined its National Cinema Network movie theater advertising sales business with Regal Entertainment's Regal CineMedia to form the jointly owned National CineMedia.

EXECUTIVES

Chairman, President, and CEO: Peter C. Brown, age 46, $1,134,000 pay
EVP and CFO: Craig R. Ramsey, age 53, $507,800 pay
EVP; President and COO, AMC Theatres: Philip M. Singleton, age 58, $733,600 pay
EVP; Chairman, AMC Film Programming: Richard T. Walsh, age 51, $518,800 pay
SVP, General Counsel, and Secretary: Kevin M. Connor, age 42
VP and Chief Accounting Officer: Chris A. Cox, age 39
VP and Treasurer: Terry W. Crawford
VP Corporate Communications: Pamela Blase
President, AMC Film Group: Sonny Gourley
President and CEO, National CineMedia: Kurt C. Hall, age 45
EVP International Operations, AMC Entertainment International: Mark A. McDonald, age 46, $455,800 pay
EVP North American Operations, AMC Theatres: John D. McDonald, age 48
Auditors: PricewaterhouseCoopers LLP

LOCATIONS

HQ: AMC Entertainment Inc.
920 Main St., Kansas City, MO 64105
Phone: 816-221-4000   **Fax:** 816-480-4617
Web: www.amctheatres.com

AMC Entertainment has movie theaters in Canada, France, Hong Kong, Japan, Portugal, Spain, the UK, and the US.

PRODUCTS/OPERATIONS

Selected Subsidiaries

MovieTickets.com (online tickets and movie information, 27%)
National CineMedia (on-screen advertising, joint venture with Regal Entertainment)

COMPETITORS

Carmike Cinemas
Century Theatres
Cinemark
CinemaStar
Cineplex Galaxy
Clearview Cinemas
Hoyts Cinemas
Landmark Theatres
Loews Cineplex
National Amusements
Pacific Theatres
Regal Entertainment

HISTORICAL FINANCIALS

Company Type: Private

Income Statement

FYE: Thursday nearest March 31

	REVENUE ($ mil.)	NET INCOME ($ mil.)	NET PROFIT MARGIN	EMPLOYEES
3/04	1,783	(11)	—	17,200
3/03	1,792	(20)	—	18,300
3/02	1,342	(12)	—	17,700
3/01	1,215	(106)	—	13,900
3/00	1,123	(55)	—	12,800
3/99	1,027	(16)	—	12,300
3/98	847	(25)	—	12,700
3/97	750	19	2.5%	10,300
3/96	658	8	1.2%	9,500
3/95	565	34	6.0%	8,000
Annual Growth	**13.6%**	**—**	**—**	**8.9%**

2004 Year-End Financials

Debt ratio: 265.7%
Return on equity: —
Cash ($ mil.): 333

Current ratio: 1.46
Long-term debt ($ mil.): 745

Net Income History

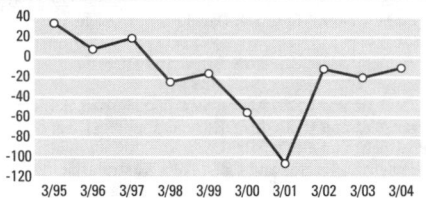

AmCOMP

AmCOMP helps make on-the-job injuries less painful for employers. The holding company's subsidiaries specialize in all aspects of workers' compensation insurance operations, including underwriting, claims management, premium collection, loss control and prevention, employer education, and provision of network providers. Client industries include construction, manufacturing, retail, and farming. The company markets its products through independent agents associated with about 250 agencies in the Southeast, Midwest, Mid-Atlantic, and Texas. Directors Sean Traynor and Paul Queally are partners in equity firm Welsh, Carson, Anderson & Stowe, which owns 35% of AmCOMP. Director Sam Stephens owns 26% of the company.

The construction industry accounts for the largest portion of AmCOMP's premiums; member companies include AmCOMP Assurance, AmCOMP Preferred, Pinnacle Administrative, and AmSERV.

AmCOMP was founded in 1982 as the Florida Air Conditioning Contractors Association Self-Insurers Fund.

EXECUTIVES

Chairman, President, and CEO: Fred R. Lowe, age 70, $325,000 pay
EVP, COO, and Director; President and COO, AmCOMP Assurance; Vice Chairman and President, AmCOMP Preferred: Debra Cerre-Ruedisili, age 50, $285,450 pay
SVP, CFO, and Treasurer: Kumar Gursahaney, age 49, $155,450 pay
SVP, Claims: Alan N. Duggan
VP and Actuary: Hayden Burrus
VP, Finance and Controller: Jennifer Wiedrick
VP, Human Resources: Laura Newstead
VP, Information Technology: Debbie Brenner
VP, Regulatory Reporting and Compliance and Corporate Secretary: Melody Misiaszek
President, Mid-Atlantic Region: Antonio (Tony) Faillaci, age 59, $180,416 pay
President, Midwest Region: Lisa Perrizo, age 40
President, Texas Region: Colin Williams, age 53, $201,025 pay
Auditors: Deloitte & Touche LLP

LOCATIONS

HQ: AmCOMP Incorporated
701 US Hwy. 1, North Palm Beach, FL 33408
Phone: 561-840-7171   **Fax:** 800-226-1805
Web: www.amcomp.com

AmCOMP has operations in Alabama, Florida, Georgia, Illinois, Indiana, Kentucky, North Carolina, South Carolina, Tennessee, Texas, Virginia, and Wisconsin.

PRODUCTS/OPERATIONS

2004 Premiums Written by Industry

	% of total
Contracting	35
Goods & services	28
Manufacturing	20
Office & clerical	6
Miscellaneous	6
Other	5
Total	**100**

COMPETITORS

Acordia
AMERISAFE
Argonaut Group
Fremont General
Highlands Insurance
NCCI Holdings
PAULA Financial
PMA Capital
Royal & SunAlliance USA
St. Paul Travelers
State Auto Financial
WellPoint
Zenith National

HISTORICAL FINANCIALS

Company Type: Private

Income Statement

	ASSETS ($ mil.)	NET INCOME ($ mil.)	INCOME AS % OF ASSETS	EMPLOYEES
12/04	544	5	0.90%	432
12/03	457	1	0.20%	—
12/02	413	3	0.80%	—
12/01	357	(10)	—	—
12/00	310	6	2.00%	—
12/99	260	7	2.60%	—
12/98	236	8	3.50%	—
12/97	223	5	2.40%	175
12/96	136	5	4.00%	—
12/95	3	1	18.20%	—
Annual Growth	**78.2%**	**19.6%**	**—**	**13.8%**

FYE: December 31

2004 Year-End Financials

Equity as % of assets: 10.7%
Return on assets: 1.0%
Return on equity: 8.8%

Long-term debt ($ mil.): 42
Sales ($ mil.): 189

Net Income History

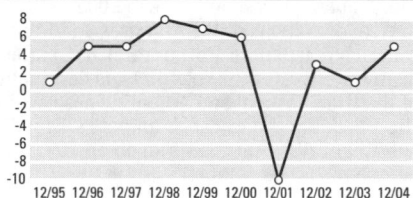

American Achievement

American Achievement wants you to wear its class ring and sign its yearbook. Scholastic products account for nearly 90% of the company's sales. These include class rings (American Achievement, with its ArtCarved and Balfour brands, is the #2 US maker of class rings, after Jostens), Taylor Publishing (yearbooks), and graduation products (caps and gowns, diplomas, and announcements). The company also produces achievement publications such as *Who's Who in American High Schools* (through Educational Communications) and commemorative jewelry for families, sports fans, employee awards, and professional sports events such as the World Series and the Super Bowl. American Achievement is majority-owned by Fenway Partners.

EXECUTIVES

CEO: Donald A. Percenti, age 48
CFO, Secretary, and Treasurer: Sherice P. Bench, age 45
SVP, Manufacturing Operations: Charlyn A. Daugherty, age 56
SVP, Retail Products: Parke H. Davis, age 62
VP, Human Resources: Sharon Brown
Auditors: Deloitte & Touche LLP

LOCATIONS

HQ: American Achievement Corporation
7211 Circle S Rd., Austin, TX 78745
Phone: 512-444-0571   **Fax:** 512-443-5213

PRODUCTS/OPERATIONS

2004 Sales

	% of total
Scholastic products	88
Recognition & affinity products	12
Total	**100**

Selected Products

Scholastic Products
Class rings
Graduation products
  Appreciation gifts
  Caps and gowns
  Certificates
  Diploma covers
  Diplomas
  Graduation announcements
  Graduation name cards
  Thank-you stationery
Yearbooks

Recognition and Affinity Products
Achievement publications
  Who's Who Among American High School Students
  Who's Who Among American Teachers
  The National Dean's List
Fan affinity jewelry
Jewelry commemorating family events
Professional sports championship rings
  Stanley Cup
  Super Bowl
  World Series

COMPETITORS

CA Short
Jostens
Michael Anthony Jewelers

Taylor Corporation
Walsworth

HISTORICAL FINANCIALS

Company Type: Private

Income Statement

FYE: Last Saturday in August

	REVENUE ($ mil.)	NET INCOME ($ mil.)	NET PROFIT MARGIN	EMPLOYEES
8/04	314	1	0.4%	2,170
8/03	308	11	3.5%	2,344
8/02	304	(6)	—	2,400
8/01	282	(3)	—	2,525
8/00	182	7	3.7%	—
8/99	160	(4)	—	1,575
8/98	151	(5)	—	1,809
8/97	88	(9)	—	1,602
Annual Growth	20.0%	—	—	4.4%

2004 Year-End Financials

Debt ratio: 284.9%
Return on equity: 1.3%
Cash ($ mil.): 3
Current ratio: 1.35
Long-term debt ($ mil.): 309

Net Income History

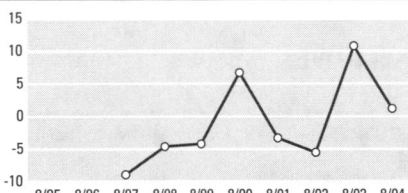

15 · 10 · 5 · 0 · -5 · -10 | 8/95 8/96 8/97 8/98 8/99 8/00 8/01 8/02 8/03 8/04

American Automobile Association

This isn't your father's American Automobile Association (commonly known as AAA). The not-for-profit organization still offers its trademark emergency roadside assistance to members, but it has expanded its offerings to include various financial services as well. AAA Financial Services offers credit cards, personal loans, online banking, and vehicle financing and leasing. AAA also sells insurance, operates more than 1,100 travel agencies, and publishes TourBook and TravelBook guides and maps. The organization's 48 million members can take advantage of AAA's travel benefits in 110 countries.

Founded in Chicago in 1902 by nine auto clubs, AAA has about 80 clubs and about 100 US and Canadian offices. The company coordinates its emergency roadside assistance through a network of about 13,000 independent and AAA-owned service providers. With an estimated 24% of all US households holding a AAA membership, the company responds to roughly 28 million service calls a year. AAA's roadside services include towing, tire repair, minor mechanical repairs, and jump starts. In addition to its roadside services, the company has a network of about 7,400 "AAA Approved" repair shops in the US and Canada that offer special benefits to AAA members.

EXECUTIVES

President and CEO: Robert L. Darbelnet
CFO: John Schaffer
EVP Administration and Publishing: Richard D. Rinner
EVP Association and Club Services: Mark H. Brown
VP and CIO: Satish D. Mahajan
VP Automotive Services: Marshall L. Doney
VP Public Affairs: Susan G. Pikrallidas
VP Travel Services: Sandra S. Hughes
National Director, Traffic Safety Policy: Bella Dinh-Zarr
Managing Director, AAA Financial Services: Scott Denman
Managing Director, Emergency Road Service: Margaret Pittelkow
Managing Director, Human Resources: Carol Droessler
Managing Director, Partnership Programs: Tom Wilt
Managing Director, Public Relations: Tom Calcagni

LOCATIONS

HQ: American Automobile Association
1000 AAA Dr., Heathrow, FL 32746
Phone: 407-444-7000   **Fax:** 407-444-7380
Web: www.aaa.com

COMPETITORS

Allstate
American Express
APCO
Carlson Wagonlit
Cendant
General Motors
Mercury General
Miller Industries
Shell
State Farm
USAA
WorldTravel

American Banknote

Take note! American Banknote Corporation foils counterfeiters. American Banknote, through its subsidiaries, prints secure financial- and identification-related documents, including stock certificates, car titles, smart cards, ID cards, bank checks, and college transcripts. These products typically require treatments that deter counterfeiting, such as detailed hand engraving, serial numbering, microprinting, prismatic backgrounds, bar coding, and specialized inks. The company also offers graphic design, prepress, database management, and fulfillment services. American Banknote reorganized under Chapter 11 bankruptcy protection in 2005 and emerged as a private company.

In 2002 the company emerged from Chapter 11 bankruptcy, which it entered in 1998, only to file Chapter 11 a second time in 2005.

With operations in the Americas and Europe, American Banknote Corporation has suffered from the effects of the volatility and devaluation of the Brazilian real and Argentine peso against the US dollar. American Banknote's Brazilian subsidiary, ABNB, accounts for about 70% of the company's total revenue.

EXECUTIVES

Chairman Emeritus and Director: C. Gerald Goldsmith, age 77
Chairman and CEO: Steven G. Singer, age 44, $716,687 pay
EVP and CFO: Patrick J. Gentile, age 46, $398,620 pay
VP and General Counsel: David M. Kober, age 41, $76,588 pay
President and CEO, ABN Brazil and Director: Sidney Levy, age 48, $421,328 pay
President and CEO, ABN Argentina: Hernan Daniele
President and CEO, ABN Europe: Philippe Delanoue
President and CEO, ABN USA: Joseph Caffarella
Managing Director and CEO, ABN Australasia: David Head
Chief Administrative Officer and Corporate Secretary: Elaine Lazaridis, age 42
Acting Treasurer: Craig D. Weiner, age 39
Auditors: Friedman LLP

LOCATIONS

HQ: American Banknote Corporation
560 Sylvan Ave., Englewood Cliffs, NJ 07632
Phone: 201-568-4400   **Fax:** 201-568-4577
Web: www.americanbanknote.com

The company has operations in Argentina, Brazil, France, and the US.

2004 Sales

	$ mil.	% of total
Brazil	112.3	70
US	24.9	15
France	16.8	10
Argentina	8.3	5
Total	162.3	100

PRODUCTS/OPERATIONS

2004 Sales

	$ mil.	% of total
Security printing solutions	71.2	44
Transaction cards & systems	62.2	38
Printing services & document management	28.9	18
Total	162.3	100

Selected Products and Services

Car titles
Checks
College transcripts
Coupons
Gift certificates
ID cards
Money orders
Smart cards
Stock and bond certificates

Subsidiaries

American Bank Note Company (US)
American Bank Note Ltda. (Brazil, 77.5%)
CPS Technologies, S.A. (France)
Transtex S.A. (Argentina)

COMPETITORS

De La Rue
Deluxe
John Harland
Liberty Enterprises
MDC

HISTORICAL FINANCIALS
Company Type: Private

Income Statement
FYE: December 31

	REVENUE ($ mil.)	NET INCOME ($ mil.)	NET PROFIT MARGIN	EMPLOYEES
12/04	162	46	28.5%	2,520
12/03	223	(47)	—	2,950
12/02	202	222	109.5%	2,990
12/01	221	(6)	—	3,110
12/00	260	(17)	—	3,060
12/99	275	—	—	3,100
12/98	300	—	—	3,100
12/97	336	—	—	3,390
12/96	310	—	—	3,260
12/95	206	—	—	2,380
Annual Growth	(2.6%)	—	—	0.6%

2004 Year-End Financials
Debt ratio: 14.9%
Return on equity: —
Cash ($ mil.): 14
Current ratio: 0.48
Long-term debt ($ mil.): 1

Net Income History

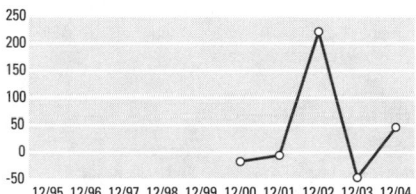

250 200 150 100 50 0 -50
12/95 12/96 12/97 12/98 12/99 12/00 12/01 12/02 12/03 12/04

American Bar Association

The American Bar Association (ABA) is the nation's largest organization of lawyers. Its roster of more than 400,000 members includes judges, court administrators, law professors, and nonpracticing attorneys. The ABA seeks to promote improvements in the American justice system and develop guidelines for the advancement of the legal profession and legal education. It provides law school accreditation, continuing legal education, legal information, and other services to assist legal professionals. All lawyers in good standing with any US state or territory bar are eligible for membership in the ABA. The ABA cannot discipline lawyers, nor can it enforce its rules; it can only develop rules as guidelines.

The ABA releases about 100 books and numerous magazines, journals, and newsletters through its ABA Publishing division. Popular materials run the gamut of topics, from administrative practices for lobbyists to immigration law guides for criminal lawyers to leadership and empowerment for women lawyers.

EXECUTIVES

Chair, House of Delegates: Stephen N. Zack
President: Michael S. Greco
President-Elect: Karen J. Mathis
Executive Director: Robert A. Stein, age 66
Secretary: Armando Lasa-Ferrer
Treasurer: William T. Robinson III
Auditors: Ernst & Young LLP

LOCATIONS

HQ: American Bar Association
321 N. Clark St., Chicago, IL 60610
Phone: 312-988-5000 **Fax:** 312-988-5177
Web: www.abanet.org

The American Bar Association has offices in Chicago and Washington, DC.

PRODUCTS/OPERATIONS

Selected Commissions, Forums, and Other Groups
American Bar Endowment
Board of Governors
Business Law Section
Center for Professional Responsibility
Children and the Law
Commission on Domestic Violence
Commission on Legal Problems of the Elderly
Commission on Mental and Physical Disability Law
Commission on Opportunities For Minorities in the Profession
Commission on Women in the Profession
Coordinating Committee on Gun Violence
Council on Legal Education Opportunity
Council on Racial & Ethnic Justice
Death Penalty Representation Project
Forum on Affordable Housing and Community Development Law
Forum on Entertainment and Sports Industries
House Of Delegates
Judicial Division
Law Student Division
Legislative and Governmental Advocacy
Office of the President
Section of Administrative Law
Section of Antitrust Law
Section of Labor and Employment Law
Senior Lawyers Division
Standing Committee on Judicial Independence
Standing Committee on Lawyers' Professional Liability
Standing Committee on Legal Assistants
Standing Committee on Pro Bono and Public Service
Young Lawyers Division

HISTORICAL FINANCIALS
Company Type: Association

Income Statement
FYE: August 31

	REVENUE ($ mil.)	NET INCOME ($ mil.)	NET PROFIT MARGIN	EMPLOYEES
8/02	160	—	—	900
8/01	100	—	—	900
8/00	100	—	—	750
8/99	125	—	—	800
8/98	140	—	—	750
8/97	139	—	—	750
8/96	135	—	—	750
8/95	113	—	—	750
8/94	114	—	—	700
8/93	110	—	—	—
Annual Growth	4.2%	—	—	3.2%

Revenue History

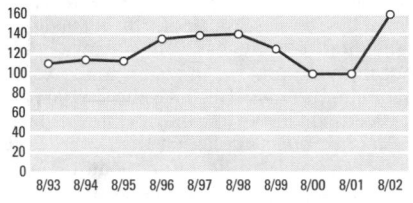

160 140 120 100 80 60 40 20 0
8/93 8/94 8/95 8/96 8/97 8/98 8/99 8/00 8/01 8/02

American Cancer Society

The American Cancer Society (ACS) works as a firefighter for your lungs. Dedicated to the elimination of cancer, the not-for-profit organization is staffed by professionals and more than 2 million volunteers at some 3,400 local units across the country. ACS is the largest source of private cancer research funds in the US. Recipients of the society's funding include 32 Nobel Prize laureates. In addition to research, the ACS supports detection, treatment, and education programs. The organization encourages prevention efforts with programs such as the Great American Smokeout. Patient services include moral support, transportation to and from treatment, and camps for children who have cancer.

The ACS has generated considerable income by marketing its name for antismoking nicotine patches and orange juice, and is contemplating even more lucrative deals. Programs account for 72% of expenses; 28% goes to administration and fund raising.

HISTORY

Concerned over the lack of progress in detecting and treating cancer, a group of 10 physicians and five laymen met in New York City in 1913 to form the American Society for the Control of Cancer (ASCC). Because public discussion of cancer was taboo, the group struggled with how to educate people without raising unnecessary fears. Some physicians even preferred keeping knowledge of the disease from the public. In the 1920s the ASCC began sponsoring cancer clinics and collecting statistics on the disease. By 1923 some states reported improvements in early diagnosis and treatment. In 1937 the ASCC started its first nationwide public education program, with the help of volunteers known as the Women's Field Army. President Franklin Roosevelt named April National Cancer Control Month, a practice since followed by every president.

By 1944 some cancer rates were rising but the word "cancer" still couldn't be mentioned on radio. Mary Lasker, wife of prominent ad executive Albert Lasker, was instrumental in getting information about cancer broadcast. At her insistence, in 1945 the newly renamed American Cancer Society began donating at least 25% of its budget to research. The society raised $4 million in its first major national fund-raising campaign.

The link between smoking and lung cancer became known after a study in the early 1950s by ACS medical director Charles Cameron. That information became part of the Surgeon General's Report of 1964. In 1973 an ACS branch in Minnesota held the first Great American Smokeout to encourage people to quit smoking.

The ACS backed the 1971 congressional bill that inaugurated the War on Cancer. The society was attacked in the 1970s for emphasizing cures rather than prevention because, critics claimed, research would reveal environmental causes from industrial products made by companies with connections to ACS directors. In the 1970s and 1980s, the ACS backed tougher restrictions on tobacco and, in response to earlier criticism, directed research toward prevention as well as treatment. The society played a major role in the 1989 airline smoking ban.

John Seffrin, a former Indiana University professor, was named CEO of ACS in 1992. The first of several genetic breakthroughs came in the 1990s when ACS grantees isolated genes believed to be responsible for triggering various types of cancer. In 1995 the ACS accused the tobacco industry of infiltrating its offices in the 1970s and using its papers to aid in the early marketing of low-tar cigarettes.

In 1996 the ACS announced that new data showed a drop in the US cancer death rate for the first time ever. The ACS entered agreements with SmithKline Beecham (NicoDerm antismoking patches) and the Florida Department of Citrus in 1996 to allow the use of the American Cancer Society name in marketing.

The proposed $369 billion settlement between the attorneys general of 40 states and the tobacco industry was big news in 1997. The ACS had wanted more concessions, such as a $2-per-pack tax increase, more power for industry regulation by the FDA, and underage use rate-reduction targets for smokeless tobacco products as stringent as those for cigarettes.

In 1998 the ACS launched a $5 million national advertising campaign to combat what it sees as "misleading" information spread by the tobacco industry. It argued in Supreme Court in 1999 to help the FDA gain control over cigarette production and distribution. In 2000 ACS restructured its $50-million-a-year research program to increase the size of individual grants; it also awarded its largest-ever award, $1.7 million, to study the side effects of cancer treatment. In 2001 ACS filed petitions to the FDA urging them to regulate new tobacco products marketed as being safer than traditional cigarettes. In 2002 ACS and The Robert Wood Johnson Foundation launched the Center for Tobacco Cessation to help people quit smoking. In 2003 ACS published strategic guides to help countries in early stages of tobacco control.

EXECUTIVES

Chairman: Thomas G. Burish
First VP: Stephen F. Sener
CEO: John R. Seffrin
National Director, Media Relations: Anne Isenhower
Treasurer: G. Van Velsor Wolf Jr.
Second VP: Carolyn D. Runowicz
Secretary: Marion E Morra

LOCATIONS

HQ: American Cancer Society, Inc.
1599 Clifton Rd. NE, Atlanta, GA 30345
Phone: 404-320-3333 **Fax:** 404-982-3677
Web: www.cancer.org

PRODUCTS/OPERATIONS

Selected Patient Services Programs

Children's Camps (for children and teens with cancer; some for siblings)
Hope Lodge (housing assistance)
I Can Cope (education and support classes on living with cancer)
Look Good . . . Feel Better (cosmetics and beauty techniques for women experiencing side effects of cancer treatment)
Man To Man Prostate Cancer Support
Pamphlets and brochures for cancer patients and their families
Reach to Recovery (support for women with breast cancer and their families)
Road to Recovery (transportation services)

Selected Public Education Programs and Publications

Great American Smokeout (national stop-smoking-for-a-day event)
Making Strides Against Breast Cancer (fund-raiser)
Relay for Life (fund-raiser)

Selected Research Grants and Awards

Clinical Research Professorships
Clinical Research Training Grants
Institutional research grants
Postdoctoral fellowships
Research Opportunity Grants
Research Professorships

HISTORICAL FINANCIALS

Company Type: Not-for-profit

Income Statement

FYE: August 31

	REVENUE ($ mil.)	NET INCOME ($ mil.)	NET PROFIT MARGIN	EMPLOYEES
8/03	836	—	—	
8/02	813	—	—	6,500
8/01	822	—	—	6,500
8/00	812	—	—	6,000
8/99	672	—	—	4,500
8/98	677	—	—	4,500
8/97	602	—	—	4,418
8/96	458	—	—	4,500
8/95	420	—	—	4,656
8/94	392	—	—	4,100
Annual Growth	8.8%	—	—	5.9%

Revenue History

900	
800	
700	
600	
500	
400	
300	
200	
100	
0	

8/94 8/95 8/96 8/97 8/98 8/99 8/00 8/01 8/02 8/03

American Crystal Sugar

Call it saccharine, but for American Crystal Sugar, business is all about sharing. The sugar beet cooperative is owned by more than 3,000 growers in the Red River Valley of North Dakota and Minnesota. American Crystal, formed in 1899 and converted into a co-op in 1973, divides the 35-mile-wide valley into five districts, each served by a processing plant. During an annual eight-month "campaign," the plants operate continuously, producing sugar, molasses, and beet pulp. Its products (under the Crystal name, the licensed Pillsbury brand, and private labels) are sold through marketing the co-ops United Sugars and Midwest Agri-Commodities. American Crystal also owns 51% of corn sweeteners joint venture ProGold.

EXECUTIVES

President and CEO: James J. Horvath, age 59, $776,527 pay
VP, Administration: Brian F. Ingulsrud, age 41, $142,627 pay (partial-year salary)
VP, Agriculture: Tom Astrup, age 34, $279,523 pay (partial-year salary)
VP, Factory Operations Crookston: David A. Walden, age 50, $275,628 pay (partial-year salary)
VP, Finance and CFO: Joseph J. Talley, age 44, $357,373 pay
VP, Operations: David A. Berg, age 50, $337,731 pay (partial-year salary)
Director, Business Development, Assistant Treasurer, and Assistant Secretary: David L. Malmskog, age 47
Director, Government Affairs: Kevin Price
Corporate Controller, Assistant Secretary, and Assistant Treasurer: Mark P. Kalvoda, age 32
Secretary and General Counsel: Daniel C. Mott, age 45
Treasurer and Assistant Secretary: Samuel S. M. Wai, age 50
Specialist, Public Relations: Jeff Schweitzer
Auditors: Eide Bailly LLP

LOCATIONS

HQ: American Crystal Sugar Company
101 N. Third St., Moorhead, MN 56560
Phone: 218-236-4400 **Fax:** 218-236-4422
Web: www.crystalsugar.com

COMPETITORS

ADM	NutraSweet
Alberto-Culver	Südzucker
Alexander & Baldwin	SMBSC
Amalgamated Sugar	Sterling Sugars
C&H Sugar	Sugar Cane Growers
Cargill	Cooperative of Florida
Cumberland Packing	Sugar Foods
Florida Crystals	Tate & Lyle
Imperial Sugar	U.S. Sugar
M A Patout	Western Sugar
Michigan Sugar Company	Cooperative
Nippon Beet Sugar	

HISTORICAL FINANCIALS

Company Type: Cooperative

Income Statement

FYE: August 31

	REVENUE ($ mil.)	NET INCOME ($ mil.)	NET PROFIT MARGIN	EMPLOYEES
8/04	1,033	473	45.8%	1,359
8/03	829	362	43.6%	1,231
8/02	775	399	51.4%	1,243
8/01	866	389	44.9%	1,250
8/00	731	358	49.0%	1,294
8/99	844	370	43.8%	1,292
8/98	677	306	45.2%	1,263
8/97	677	367	54.2%	1,202
8/96	688	310	45.1%	2,437
8/95	606	321	52.9%	2,000
Annual Growth	6.1%	4.4%	—	(4.2%)

2004 Year-End Financials

Debt ratio: 94.3%   Current ratio: 1.33
Return on equity: 190.3%   Long-term debt ($ mil.): 250
Cash ($ mil.): 0

Net Income History

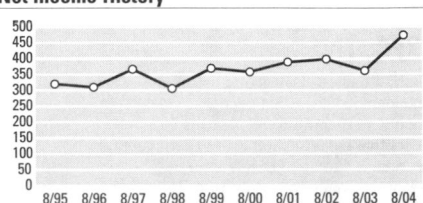

500	
450	
400	
350	
300	
250	
200	
150	
100	
50	
0	

8/95 8/96 8/97 8/98 8/99 8/00 8/01 8/02 8/03 8/04

American Family Insurance

Even confirmed bachelors can get insured through American Family Insurance. The company specializes in property & casualty insurance, but also offers life, health, and homeowners coverage, as well as investment and retirement-planning products. It is among the largest US mutual companies that concentrate on auto insurance (State Farm is the biggest). American Family Insurance also provides coverage for apartment owners, restaurants, contractors, and other businesses. Through the company's consumer finance division, agents can also offer their customers home equity and personal lines of credit.

American Family Insurance has around 4,000 independent agents operating primarily in the Midwest. Unlike many of its competitors, The company has said it has no plans to demutualize.

Benefitting from a rebounding stock market and a favorable insurance market (especially for auto and health lines), American Family Insurance grew its net revenues by some $100 million in 2003. It followed that with record operating gains ($703 million) in 2004, more than double the previous year's gain.

HISTORY

In 1927 Herman Wittwer founded Farmers Mutual Automobile Insurance to sell coverage to Wisconsin farmers. As farms became mechanized in the 1920s, the insurance market grew. Low-density rural traffic reduced the potential for accidents, a fact that attracted Wittwer and others, such as State Farm (founded in 1922) to serve the similar markets. Wittwer also noted that rural Wisconsin's severe winters made cars unusable for a good part of the year, further reducing risk.

Farmers Mutual grew despite the Depression and WWII, spreading to Minnesota (1933); Missouri (1939); Nebraska and the Dakotas (1940); and Indiana, Iowa, and Kansas (1943). The war years were generous to insurers: Rising incomes allowed people to insure their cars, but rationing programs limited use of the cars. The postwar suburban boom — when cars became a necessity rather than a luxury — also helped auto insurers.

Growing prosperity for single-earner households in the 1950s helped boost the demand for life insurance. In 1958 Farmers Mutual formed American Family Life Insurance. The company wrote $1.6 million in insurance on its first day in the life insurance business. During that decade, Farmers Mutual moved into Illinois.

The 1960s brought growth and change. To capture more auto business, it founded American Standard Insurance to write nonstandard auto insurance. The firm also launched consumer finance operations for insurance customers and noncustomers alike, departing from standard industry practice by selling through agents rather than offices. In 1963, in recognition of its growing diversification, Farmers Mutual changed its name to American Family Mutual Insurance.

During the 1970s and 1980s, the firm strengthened its infrastructure and added regional offices.

It moved into Arizona and later formed American Family Brokerage to fill in gaps in its own coverage by obtaining insurance for clients through other insurers.

During this period American Family suffered cultural pains. It moved beyond its traditional rural clientele and into the urban unknown as it sought to increase its market share. In 1981 community groups questioned whether the company was adequately serving racially mixed neighborhoods. In 1988 the US Justice Department began investigating allegations that the firm engaged in redlining (offering inferior or no service for minority neighborhoods); a class-action suit based on similar claims was filed in 1990. The suit went all the way to the Supreme Court, which ruled that insurance sales must comply with the Fair Housing Act.

The company had begun rectifying its practices before the case was decided. Nevertheless, when American Family settled the case in 1995, it agreed to pay a $14.5 million settlement plus about $2 million in court costs. Part of the settlement was to compensate people who had suffered from the company's discrimination. But most of the money went to fund community programs begun in 1996 to promote home ownership among minorities. In 1997 trouble came from within and without: One lawsuit claimed the company falsely promised to shrink premiums as policies earned dividends, and two dissident agents filed a civil complaint for wrongful termination (the latter case was settled the next year).

The company's profits tumbled in 1998 due to severe storms in Minnesota and Wisconsin. The next year American Family expanded its operations in Colorado and moved into Cleveland.

In 2000 Wisconsin was again pounded by hail, high winds, and floods. American Family Insurance announced $100 million in expected losses from the event. Streamlining claims processing, the company closed nine of its offices in 2001.

American Family Insurance grew its policy count by almost 10% in 2002 but the volatile stock market hurt the company's net result. By 2004 the company had regained financial strength to the tune of $4.2 billion in policyholder equity, primarily due to record gains in operations.

EXECUTIVES

Chairman and CEO: Harvey R. Pierce
President, COO, and Director: David R. Anderson
EVP: Daniel R. DeSalvo
EVP: Darnell Moore
EVP: Jack C. Salzwedel
EVP and Secretary: James F. Eldridge
EVP and Treasurer: J. Brent Johnson
VP and Controller: Daniel R. Schultz
VP, Actuarial: Bradley J. Gleason
VP, American Family Financial Services:
  R. D. Boschulte
VP, Claims: Terese A. Taarud
VP, Commercial, Farm and Ranch: Jerry G. Rekowski
VP, Education: Ann M. Hamilton
VP, Government Affairs and Compliance: Mark V. Afable
VP, Human Resources: Vicki L. Chvala
VP, Information Services: Byrne W. Chapman
VP, Investments: Thomas S. King
VP, Legal: Christopher S. Spencer
VP, Marketing: Jeffrey E. Burke
VP, Public Relations: Richard A. Fetherston
Auditors: PricewaterhouseCoopers LLP

LOCATIONS

HQ: American Family Insurance Group
  6000 American Pkwy., Madison, WI 53783
Phone: 608-249-2111   **Fax:** 608-243-4921
Web: www.amfam.com

American Family Insurance Group operates in Arizona, Colorado, Idaho, Illinois, Indiana, Iowa, Kansas, Minnesota, Missouri, Nebraska, Nevada, North Dakota, Ohio, Oregon, South Dakota, Utah, and Wisconsin.

PRODUCTS/OPERATIONS

2004 Assets

	$ mil.	% of total
Bonds	8,685.6	64
Stocks	1,564.8	12
Premiums receivable	950.9	7
Deferred policy-acquisition costs	836.0	6
Real estate	257.2	2
Mortgages	193.9	1
Policy loans	183.4	1
Other	969.4	7
Total	**13,641.2**	**100**

2004 Sales

	$ mil.	% of total
Property & casualty premiums	5,788.7	88
Investment income	462.6	7
AFLIC premiums	298.9	4
Finance charges	9.3	—
Other	47.3	1
Total	**6,606.8**	**100**

COMPETITORS

21st Century	Liberty Mutual
AIG	Lincoln Financial Group
AIG American General	Loews
Allstate	Mutual of Omaha
American Financial	Nationwide
Berkshire Hathaway	Ohio Casualty
Chubb	Old Republic
CIGNA	Progressive Corporation
Cincinnati Financial	Prudential
Citigroup	Safeco
CNA Financial	St. Paul Travelers
General Re	State Farm
The Hartford	USAA
Kemper Insurance	

HISTORICAL FINANCIALS

Company Type: Mutual company

Income Statement

FYE: December 31

	ASSETS ($ mil.)	NET INCOME ($ mil.)	INCOME AS % OF ASSETS	EMPLOYEES
12/04	13,641	564	4.1%	8,238
12/03	12,239	155	1.3%	8,100
12/02	10,840	58	0.5%	7,500
12/01	10,275	100	1.0%	7,431
12/00	9,970	237	2.4%	7,300
12/99	9,569	282	2.9%	7,247
12/98	8,949	40	0.4%	6,940
12/97	8,348	252	3.0%	6,800
12/96	6,836	55	0.8%	6,506
12/95	6,256	219	3.5%	6,411
Annual Growth	**9.0%**	**11.1%**	**—**	**2.8%**

2004 Year-End Financials

Equity as % of assets: 30.9% Long-term debt ($ mil.): 2,148
Return on assets: 4.4%   Sales ($ mil.): 6,607
Return on equity: 14.4%

Net Income History

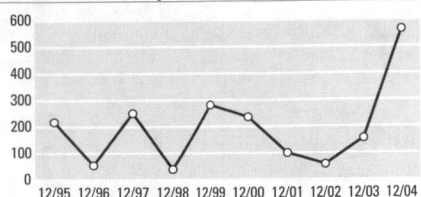

American Foods

American Foods Group is a bona fide Green Bay packer. It slaughters cattle and produces branded and private label bacon, beef cuts, deli meats, ham, and sausage for sale to the grocery and foodservice industries. Its beef plant cranks out 4 million pounds of ground beef each week. The company operates refrigerated trucking unit America's Service Lines. CEO and owner Carl Kuehne purchased American Foods in 1985 and grew it through acquisitions and product development. After nixing plans to be acquired by Smithfield Foods, the company set up a joint venture with an Iowa beef producers cooperative. In 2005 American Foods Group merged with Rosen's Diversified.

EXECUTIVES

Co-Chairman and Co-CEO: Carl W. Kuehne
Co-Chairman and Co-CEO: Tom Rosen
CFO: Doug Hagen
CFO: Robert Hovde
COO: Greg Benedict
Chief Sales and Marketing Officer: Joseph P. Baker
VP, Human Resources: Trudy Kamps
Controller: Dave Schuldt
Director, Case Ready Meats: Mike Zimmerman
Director, Information Technology: LouAnn Bannow
Director, International Sales: Mike Stone
Director, Purchasing: Ron Bouche

LOCATIONS

HQ: American Foods Group, LLC
544 Acme St., Green Bay, WI 54308
Phone: 920-437-6330   **Fax:** 920-436-6510
Web: www.americanfoodsgroup.com

Since the merger with Rosen's, American Foods Group operates facilities in Minnesota, Nebraska, Ohio, South Dakota, Virginia, and Wisconsin.

PRODUCTS/OPERATIONS

Selected Brands

American Foods Group
American Foods Specialties
Black Angus Reserve Beef
Dakota Supreme
Dakota Valley
Golden Prairie
Golden Superb
Green Bay Dressed Beef
Server's Choice
Sheboygan Deli Superb

Company Divisions

America's Service Line (refrigerated transportation)
American Foods, Kosher Processing
American Foods Specialties

COMPETITORS

Alexander & Hornung   Swift
Smithfield Beef   Tyson Fresh Meats
  Enterprises   U.S. Premium Beef

HISTORICAL FINANCIALS

Company Type: Private

Income Statement

FYE: June 30

	REVENUE ($ mil.)	NET INCOME ($ mil.)	NET PROFIT MARGIN	EMPLOYEES
6/04	1,000	—	—	2,000
6/03	850	—	—	2,625
6/02	655	—	—	1,800
6/01	650	—	—	1,500
6/00	580	—	—	1,450
6/99	510	—	—	1,250
6/98	520	—	—	1,450
6/97	600	—	—	2,000
6/96	575	—	—	1,800
6/95	555	—	—	1,800
Annual Growth	**6.8%**	**—**	**—**	**1.2%**

Revenue History

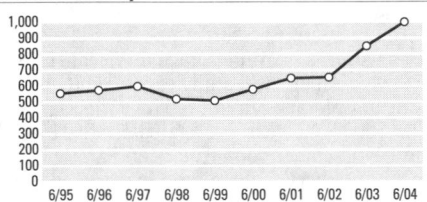

American Homestar

Stormy weather in the manufactured housing market hasn't snowed American Homestar. Out of bankruptcy and reorganized, it produces factory-built, multi-section and single-section single-family homes that sell for about half the price of comparable site-built homes. Its homes average about $55,500; multi-section homes make up about 63% of its new home retail sales. The company sells its homes through a network of 30 retail centers; 126 independent retailers and developers in Colorado, Kansas, Louisiana, New Mexico, Oklahoma, and Texas; and through displays in more than 35 manufactured housing communities. Other operations include financing, insurance, rental communities, and residential subdivision development.

Acquisitions during the 1990s expanded American Homestar's operations to 28 states, mainly in the US South and West. When the manufactured housing market went bust around 2000, American Homestar suffered and filed for bankruptcy in early 2001, but has since exited bankruptcy and is now owned mostly by its creditors.

As part of its reorganization, the company began downsizing. It dramatically cut back from 150 company-owned or franchised (Oak Creek Village) retail centers in 2000 to about 30 in 2004 (located in New Mexico, Oklahoma, and Texas). The company reduced its manufacturing facilities from 10 to two, one of which is used for refurbishing repossessions. American Homestar continues to provide insurance through its affiliation with Western Insurance Agency and provides financing services through its American Homestar Mortgage joint venture.

The Northwestern Mutual Life Insurance Company owns approximately 20% of the company; Kemper Investors Life Insurance Co. owns 16%; and Allstate Life Insurance Company owns about 15%. Company president and CEO Finis "Buck" Teeter owns roughly 7%, with options that could increase his share of the company to about 23%.

EXECUTIVES

President, CEO, and Director: Finis F. (Buck) Teeter, age 61
EVP, CFO, and Secretary: Craig A. Reynolds, age 54
VP, COO — Manufacturing Operations: Jackie H. Holland, age 58
VP, COO — Retail Operations: Charles N. Carney Jr., age 50
Auditors: UHY Mann Frankfort Stein & Lipp CPAs, LLP

LOCATIONS

HQ: American Homestar Corporation
2450 South Shore Blvd., Ste. 300,
League City, TX 77573
Phone: 281-334-9700   **Fax:** 281-334-9737
Web: www.americanhomestar.com

American Homestar owns two plants in Fort Worth and Lancaster, Texas, and leases a facility to refurbish lender repossessions in Burleson, Texas.

PRODUCTS/OPERATIONS

2005 New Home Sales

	% of total
Multi-section	63
Single-section	37
Total	**100**

Selected Subsidiaries and Affiliates

114 Starwood Development, LTD (manufactured housing rental community development in Houston)
American Homestar Mortgage, LLP (50%)
Oak Creek Home Centers
Oak Creek Manufactured Homes
Oak Creek Modular Homes
Western Insurance Agency, Inc. (property/casualty and credit life insurance)

COMPETITORS

Cavalier Homes
Cavco
Champion Enterprises
Clayton Homes
Coachmen
Elixir Industries
Fairmont Homes
Fleetwood Enterprises
Liberty Homes
Nobility Homes
Palm Harbor
Patriot Homes
Skyline

HISTORICAL FINANCIALS

Company Type: Private

Income Statement

FYE: Friday nearest June 30

	REVENUE ($ mil.)	NET INCOME ($ mil.)	NET PROFIT MARGIN	EMPLOYEES
6/05	79	(2)	—	637
6/04	72	(1)	—	568
6/03	92	(2)	—	672
6/02	109	158	144.5%	770
6/01	242	(179)	—	727
6/00*	574	(48)	—	3,934
5/99	612	18	2.9%	5,049
5/98	482	18	3.7%	3,803
5/97	314	15	4.7%	2,661
5/96	209	10	4.7%	1,500
Annual Growth	**(10.2%)**	**—**	**—**	**(9.1%)**

*Fiscal year change

2005 Year-End Financials

Debt ratio: 0.0% Current ratio: 3.27
Return on equity: — Long-term debt ($ mil.): 0
Cash ($ mil.): 12

Net Income History

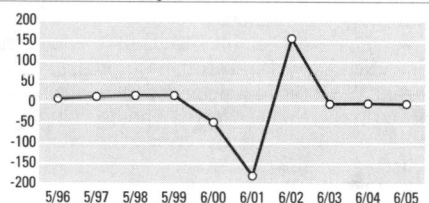

LOCATIONS

HQ: American Library Association
  50 E. Huron St., Chicago, IL 60611
Phone: 312-944-6780 **Fax:** 312-440-9374
Web: www.ala.org

The American Library Association has offices in Chicago and Washington, DC.

PRODUCTS/OPERATIONS

Selected Divisions

American Association of School Librarians
Association of College and Research Libraries
Library and Information Technology Association
Public Library Association

HISTORICAL FINANCIALS

Company Type: Association

Income Statement

FYE: August 31

	REVENUE ($ mil.)	NET INCOME ($ mil.)	NET PROFIT MARGIN	EMPLOYEES
8/00	40	—	—	260
8/99	38	—	—	270
8/98	36	—	—	270
8/97	35	—	—	267
8/96	34	—	—	265
8/95	23	—	—	286
Annual Growth	**11.8%**	**—**	**—**	**(1.9%)**

Revenue History

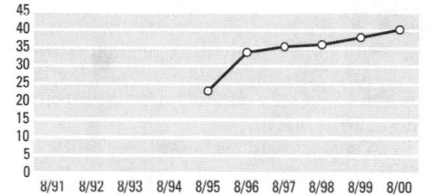

EXECUTIVES

Chairman: William G. Plested III
Chairman Elect: J. James Rohack
President: John C. Nelson
EVP: Michael D. Maves
CFO and VP Finance: Denise Hagerty
Deputy EVP: Robert W. Gilmore
VP; EVP and CEO Operations: Maria Maher
SVP Advocacy: Lee J. Stillwell
SVP Communications and Core Identity: Linn A. Weiss
SVP Governance and Operations: Todd Vande Hey
SVP Human Resources: Rhonda Rhodes
SVP Membership, Publishing, and Business Services: Robert A. Musacchio
SVP Professional Standards: Michael J. Scotti Jr.
SVP Scientific Publications and Multimedia Applications; Editor JAMA: Catherine D. De Angelis
General Counsel: Jon Ekdahl
Auditors: Deloitte & Touche LLP

LOCATIONS

HQ: American Medical Association
  515 N. State St., Chicago, IL 60610
Phone: 312-464-5000 **Fax:** 312-464-4184
Web: www.ama-assn.org

HISTORICAL FINANCIALS

Company Type: Association

Income Statement

FYE: December 31

	REVENUE ($ mil.)	NET INCOME ($ mil.)	NET PROFIT MARGIN	EMPLOYEES
12/02	251	(17)	—	—
12/01	249	7	2.9%	—
12/00	257	3	1.1%	—
12/99	250	—	—	—
12/98	240	—	—	—
12/97	236	—	—	1,205
12/96	209	—	—	1,200
12/95	199	—	—	1,175
12/94	187	—	—	1,100
Annual Growth	**3.7%**	**—**	**—**	**3.1%**

Net Income History

American Library Association

Shhhh! The American Library Association (ALA) is an organization dedicated to the development, improvement, and promotion of library and information services. Founded in 1876 and governed by an elected council, the ALA works with libraries of all types, from public to academic to prison. The more than 64,000-member organization consists of 11 divisions, about 25 affiliated organizations, and chapters in all 50 states, all working to advance ALA causes, such as Banned Books Week, an annual event promoting awareness about efforts to ban certain books from libraries. The ALA's Washington, DC office tries to influence federal legislative policy to ensure the public's right to free access to information.

EXECUTIVES

Executive Director: Keith Michael Fiels
President: Michael Gorman
President-Elect: Leslie Burger
Treasurer: Teri Switzer
Associate Executive Director for Finance: Gregory (Greg) Calloway
Director Human Resources: Dorothy Ragsdale

American Medical Association

The AMA knows whether there's a doctor in the house. The American Medical Association (AMA) prescribes the standards for the medical profession. The membership organization's activities include advocacy for physicians, promoting ethics standards in the medical community, and improving health care education. It also publishes books and products for physicians, is a partner in the Medem online physician network, sells medical malpractice insurance, and helps doctors fight legal claims. The organization was founded in 1847 to establish a medical code of ethics.

American Railcar

American Railcar Industries doesn't make the little engine that could or the little red caboose — just the cars that go in between. The company is a leading manufacturer of covered hopper cars, used for dry bulk commodities, and tank cars, used for liquid and compressed bulk commodities. American Railcar Industries also makes railcar components and offers railcar maintenance and fleet management services. It operates two manufacturing facilities in Arkansas, and manufacturing operations account for about 90% of the company's sales. The company's main customers are railcar leasing companies, rail shippers, and railroads. Financier Carl Icahn controls American Railcar Industries.

Icahn also controls railcar lessors ACF Industries and American Railcar Leasing, which together accounted for about 25% of American Railcar Industries' sales in 2004. Lessor CIT Group, which accounted for about 15% of sales in 2004, has agreed to buy at least 9,000 railcars from the company by the end of 2008.

EXECUTIVES

Chairman: Carl C. Icahn, age 69
President, CEO, and Director: James J. Unger, age 57, $350,000 pay
SVP and CFO: William P. Benac, age 58
SVP Sales, Marketing and Services: Alan C. Lullman, age 50, $160,000 pay
Director Railcar Manufacturing: Jackie R. Pipkin, age 55
VP Engineering and Manufacturing:
  Michael R. Williams, age 44
Auditors: Grant Thornton LLP

LOCATIONS

HQ: American Railcar Industries, Inc.
  100 Clark St., St. Charles, MO 63301
Phone: 636-940-6000   **Fax:** 636-940-6030
Web: www.americanrailcar.com

PRODUCTS/OPERATIONS

2004 Sales

	$ mil.	% of total
Manufacturing operations	316.5	89
Railcar services	38.6	11
Total	**355.1**	**100**

COMPETITORS

Greenbrier
Meridian Rail
Millennium Rail
Miner Enterprises
Trinity Industries
Union Tank Car

HISTORICAL FINANCIALS

Company Type: Private

Income Statement

FYE: December 31

	REVENUE ($ mil.)	NET INCOME ($ mil.)	NET PROFIT MARGIN	EMPLOYEES
12/04	355	2	0.6%	2,372
12/03	218	1	0.6%	—
12/02	169	(4)	—	—
Annual Growth	45.0%	—	—	—

2004 Year-End Financials

Debt ratio: 582.2%
Return on equity: 15.5%
Cash ($ mil.): 7
Current ratio: 1.77
Long-term debt ($ mil.): 139

Net Income History

| | 12/95 | 12/96 | 12/97 | 12/98 | 12/99 | 12/00 | 12/01 | 12/02 | 12/03 | 12/04 |

American Red Cross

When it comes to disaster, the Red Cross is the master. The American Red Cross is a member of the International Red Cross and Red Crescent Movement, a not-for-profit organization that offers disaster relief and other humanitarian services through more than 1,000 chapters nationwide. Chartered by Congress in 1905, the American Red Cross isn't a government agency. Its staff is largely volunteer — more than 1.2 million strong. Aside from helping victims of about 70,000 disasters each year, the Red Cross teaches CPR, first aid, and AIDS awareness courses; provides counseling for US military personnel; and maintains some of the largest blood and plasma banks in the nation. It spends 91% of its funds on programs.

To fund its activities, the Red Cross relies primarily on its biomedical operation, which supplies blood and tissue to some 3,000 hospitals and accounts for about two-thirds of the Red Cross' revenue. Contributions from organizations such as the United Way, grants, and other sources make up the rest of its operating fund.

The organization was stretched to its limits, however, due to five hurricanes that ravaged coastal areas in Florida and other parts of the Southeast during a two-month period in 2004. Nearly 26,000 Red Cross disaster workers were called out to help more than 400,000 victims of the storms. To help cover the costs, the group was forced to seek additional money from the federal government.

Red Cross aid workers know there's little or no rest for the weary, as evidenced by the need for emergency assistance following the Indian Ocean earthquake and tsunami in December 2004. The Red Cross responded to the disaster (that claimed the lives of more than 220,000 victims in South Asia) by rolling out a plan for short- and long-term aid; the plan called for an estimated $400 million of public and private contributions.

In the years since the 2001 terrorist attacks, the organization has been engaged in a campaign to raise the nation's emergency preparedness, both for government agencies and individuals. It also handles the $1 billion Liberty Fund, donations made to the Red Cross specifically for the September 11 victims and their families.

HISTORY

The Red Cross traces its start to a trip made in 1859 by Jean-Henri Dunant, a Swiss businessman. Dunant was traveling in northern Italy when he saw the aftermath of the Battle of Solferino — 40,000 dead or wounded troops, left without help. He published a pamphlet three years later calling for the formation of international volunteer societies to aid wounded soldiers.

In 1863 a five-member committee (including Dunant) formed the International Committee of the Red Cross in Geneva. Delegates of 16 countries attended the first conference, which resulted in the formation of national Red Cross societies across Europe. A red cross on a white background (the reverse of the Swiss flag) was chosen as the organization's symbol; the Red Crescent symbol was added in 1876 by Muslim relief workers during the Russo-Turkish War. In 1864 the group's principles were codified into international law —

initially signed by 12 nations — through the Geneva Convention.

Clara Barton, famous for her aid to soldiers during the US Civil War, learned about the Red Cross when she assisted with relief efforts during the Franco-Prussian War (1870-71). After the war, Barton returned home and persuaded Congress to support the Geneva Convention. In 1881 she and some friends founded the American Association of the Red Cross, with the first chapter in Dansville, New York. The US signed the Geneva Convention in 1882.

Barton soon expanded the Red Cross' mission to include aiding victims of natural disasters. The group received a congressional charter in 1905, making it responsible for providing assistance to the US military and disaster relief in the US and overseas.

Membership soared during WWI as the number of chapters jumped from 107 to 3,864, and volunteers from the US and other nations served with the armed forces in Europe. After the war, the American Red Cross helped refugees in Europe, recruited thousands of nurses to improve the health and hygiene of rural Americans, and provided food and shelter to millions during the Depression.

The Red Cross established its first blood center, in New York's Presbyterian Hospital, in 1941. During WWII the American Red Cross again mobilized massive relief efforts. At home, volunteers taught nutrition courses, served in hospitals, and collected blood.

In 1956 the Red Cross began research to increase the safety of its blood supply. It also continued to provide assistance during natural disasters, as well as during the Korean and Vietnam Wars and other US military conflicts.

During the 1980s the Red Cross was criticized for moving too slowly to improve testing of its blood supply for the HIV virus. Elizabeth Dole, named the organization's president in 1991, reorganized the blood collection program.

In 1996 *Money* magazine reported that the Red Cross spent more than 91 cents of every dollar on programs, the best ratio of any major charity. The next year HemaCare settled a blood-product-pricing lawsuit against the Red Cross without disclosing terms.

In 1999 Dole resigned from the Red Cross and followed in her husband's footsteps by making her own bid for the US presidency in 2000 (she later dropped out of the race). Dole was succeeded by Dr. Bernadine Healy, a former dean of the Ohio State University College of Medicine and the first physician to head the association.

The mission of the American Red Cross was highlighted after the 2001 terrorist attacks on New York City and Washington, DC, gaining praise for its quick response immediately afterwards. Soon after, however, it drew fire from critics over a proposal to use some donations for a blood bank reserve instead of it all going to families of those killed and injured in the attacks. In the wake of those critical reports, Healy was given her walking papers.

General Counsel Harold Decker was tapped to replace Healy at the end of 2001. The American Red Cross appointed Marsha Johnson Evans as president and CEO in 2002. In 2005 the organization announced a termination of its tissue programs to concentrate on disaster relief. That year it launched major relief efforts in the wake of Hurricanes Katrina, Rita, and Wilma.

EXECUTIVES

Chair: Bonnie McElveen-Hunter
President and CEO: Marsha J. (Marty) Evans, age 57
COO: R. Alan McCurry
CFO: Robert P. (Bob) McDonald
EVP Biomedical Services: John F. (Jack) McGuire III
EVP Chapter Services: James Krueger
EVP Disaster Services: Terry Sicilia
Acting EVP Human Resources: Carol Miller
SVP Communications and Marketing:
  Charles D. Connor
SVP Quality Assurance and Regulatory Affairs:
  C. William Cherry
VP Communications and Marketing: Deborah Daley
Chief Diversity Officer: Anthony J. Polk
Director of Creative Resources: Carol Robinson
Director of Media Relations: Pat McCrummen
Director of Community Development, Badger Chapter:
  Jane Richardson
General Counsel and Corporate Secretary:
  Mary S. Elcano
Information Technology: Christine Brown
National Chair of Volunteers: Kathryn A. Forbes
Auditors: KPMG LLP

LOCATIONS

HQ: The American Red Cross
  2025 E St., NW, Washington, DC 20006
Phone: 202-303-4498   **Fax:** 202-942-2024
Web: www.redcross.org

The American Red Cross has chapters nationwide. In addition it has international chapters in Germany, Italy, and Japan.

PRODUCTS/OPERATIONS

2004 Revenue

	$ mil.	% of total
Products & services		
Biomedical	2,119.3	68
Program materials	145.1	5
Public support		
Corporate, foundation,		
& individual donations	275.0	9
United Way & other federated	163.8	5
Legacies & bequests	93.6	3
Grants	73.9	2
Services & materials	62.5	2
Investment income	62.3	2
Contracts	46.8	2
Other	49.2	2
Total	**3,091.5**	**100**

2004 Program Expenditures

	% of total
Biomedical services	73
Domestic disaster services	9
Health & safety services	7
Community services	5
Armed Forces emergency services	2
International services	2
Liberty disaster relief (Sept. 11 response)	2
Total	**100**

Selected Programs and Services

Biomedical services
  Blood
  Clinical services
  Plasma
  Testing
Disaster relief
Health and safety services
  Care giving and babysitting
  CPR training
  First aid
  Lifeguard training
  Swimming lessons
  Youth programs
Community services
  Food and nutrition
  Homeless shelters
  Hospitals and nursing homes
  Senior services
  Transportation services
Military services
  Counseling
  Emergency communications
  Financial assistance
  Veterans services
International services

HISTORICAL FINANCIALS

Company Type: Not-for-profit

Income Statement

FYE: June 30

	REVENUE ($ mil.)	NET INCOME ($ mil.)	NET PROFIT MARGIN	EMPLOYEES
6/04	3,092	—	—	—
6/03	3,034	—	—	40,000
6/02	4,117	—	—	40,000
6/01	2,743	—	—	35,000
6/00	2,529	—	—	35,000
6/99	2,422	—	—	35,000
6/98	2,080	—	—	30,000
6/97	1,940	—	—	29,850
6/96	1,814	—	—	30,021
6/95	1,724	—	—	31,000
Annual Growth	**6.7%**	**—**	**—**	**3.2%**

Revenue History

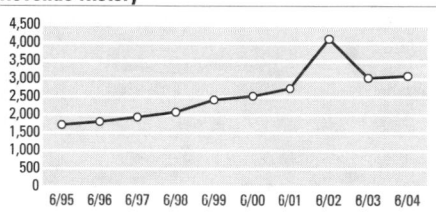

American Seafoods

With operations in both the northern Pacific and Atlantic oceans, and catfish farms in the southern US, American Seafoods Holdings has cast its nets wide. The company focuses on frozen and processed white fish such as pollock, cod, and sole, and operates a fleet that includes several ships that process and freeze the catch while at sea. Its Frionor and Bayside Bistro branded products include surimi (fish paste), breaded and battered filets, and nuggets, which are sold to the food service and grocery industries. The company has grown rapidly through acquisitions. Chairman and CEO Bernt O. Bodal owns 23% of the company.

Much of the fish caught and processed at sea is sold to restaurants and other food service outlets for use in breaded and battered fish entrees. Fish eggs also are harvested and primarily sold to markets in Japan. American Seafoods has land-based operations for processing catfish and scallops.

EXECUTIVES

Chairman and CEO: Bernt O. Bodal, age 51,
  $1,482,031 pay
CFO and Treasurer, American Seafoods Group:
  Brad D. Bodenman, age 41, $709,679 pay
VP and Group Controller, American Seafoods Group:
  Glenn Sumida
VP, Finance and Corporate Development, American Seafoods Group: Amy Humphreys, age 38,
  $384,707 pay
VP, Human Resources, American Seafoods Group:
  Tammy French
VP, IT: Dar Khalighi
President, American Pride Seafoods: John Cummings
President, American Seafoods Company:
  Inge Andreassen, age 41
VP and General Manager, Southern Pride Catfish:
  Benny Bishop
General Manager, American Seafoods Company:
  Bill Stokes
VP, Development, American Pride Seafoods:
  David Bleth
VP, Finance and Administration, American Pride Seafoods: Bob Myatt
Chief Legal Officer and General Counsel:
  Matthew D. Latimer, age 37
Auditors: KPMG LLP

LOCATIONS

HQ: American Seafoods Holdings LLC
  Marketplace Tower, 2025 1st Ave., Ste. 1200,
  Seattle, WA 98121
Phone: 206-374-1515   **Fax:** 206-374-1516
Web: www.americanseafoods.com

American Seafoods Holdings has processing facilities aboard its fishing vessels in Alaska and on land in Greensboro, Alabama, and New Bedford, Massachusetts.

2004 Sales

	% of total
North America	46
Asia	
Japan	27
Other countries	11
Europe	16
Total	**100**

PRODUCTS/OPERATIONS

2004 Sales

	$ mil.	% of total
At-sea processing	265.5	58
Land-based processing	196.1	42
Total	**461.6**	**100**

Selected Subsidiaries

American Seafoods Company LLC
American Seafoods International LLC
Southern Pride Catfish Company
Southern Pride Trucking, Inc.

COMPETITORS

Alyeska Seafoods
Icelandic Group
Icicle Seafoods
Maruha Group
Pacific Seafood
Red Chamber Co.
Trident Seafoods

HISTORICAL FINANCIALS

Company Type: Private

Income Statement
FYE: December 31

	REVENUE ($ mil.)	NET INCOME ($ mil.)	NET PROFIT MARGIN	EMPLOYEES
12/04	462	(29)	—	2,000
12/03	411	13	3.0%	2,400
12/02	333	9	2.6%	1,100
12/01	337	20	6.0%	—
Annual Growth	11.1%	—	—	34.8%

2004 Year-End Financials

Debt ratio: —
Return on equity: —
Cash ($ mil.): 1

Current ratio: 1.43
Long-term debt ($ mil.): 455

Net Income History

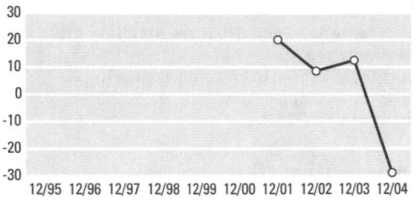

30 20 10 0 -10 -20 -30
12/95 12/96 12/97 12/98 12/99 12/00 12/01 12/02 12/03 12/04

American Tire

American Tire Distributors' business starts where the rubber meets the road. The company, formerly Heafner Tire, is one of the largest independent distributors of tires and related products in the US. Tire brands include industry leaders Michelin and Bridgestone/Firestone as well as Goodyear, which also makes American Tire's Monarch house brand through its Kelly-Springfield subsidiary. American Tire's distribution business is conducted through about 70 distribution centers that serve about 40 states. Investment firm Investcorp S.A purchased the company from Charlesbank Capital Partners in 2005 for an undisclosed sum.

Investcorp now controls 100% of American Tire Distributors' shares.

The company is growing steadily through the acquisition of smaller, regional players. It extended its reach in 2004 with the acquisition of Texas Market Tire. The deal gave American Tire Distributors an additional nine distribution centers in Texas, Oklahoma, and New Mexico. The company grew again just a few months later with the purchase of Target Tire and its 11 distribution centers in Georgia, North Carolina, South Carolina, Tennessee, and Virginia. American Tire Distributors consolidated Target Tire's operations with its existing network and closed 10 of the 11 distribution centers.

EXECUTIVES

Chairman and CEO: Richard P. (Dick) Johnson, age 57, $1,054,400 pay
President and COO: William E. Berry, age 50, $547,500 pay
EVP, General Counsel, and Secretary: J. Michael (Mike) Gaither, age 52, $418,500 pay
SVP, Procurement: Daniel K. Brown, age 51, $398,500 pay
SVP, Sales and Marketing: Phillip E. Marrett, age 54, $373,500 pay
VP, Credit and Financial Services: Jack Phillips
VP, Equipment and Supply: Gary Reed
VP, Heafner Worldwide: Lee Fishkin
Auditors: PricewaterhouseCoopers LLP

LOCATIONS

HQ: American Tire Distributors, Inc.
12200 Herbert Wayne Ct., Ste. 150,
Huntersville, NC 28070
Phone: 704-992-2000   **Fax:** 704-992-1384
Web: www.americantiredistributors.com

PRODUCTS/OPERATIONS

2004 Sales

	% of total
Tires	88
Wheels, service equipment & other parts	12
Total	**100**

Selected Products and Brands

Equipment	Firestone
Ammco	General
Hunter	Gillette
Lincoln	Goodyear
Magnum	Michelin
Supplies	Monarch
Tires	Pirelli
BF Goodrich	UniRoyal
Bridgestone	Yokohama
Continental	Wheels
Dunlop	

COMPETITORS

BFS Retail & Commercial Operations
Cooper Tire & Rubber
Discount Tire
Sears
TBC

HISTORICAL FINANCIALS

Company Type: Private

Income Statement
FYE: December 31

	REVENUE ($ mil.)	NET INCOME ($ mil.)	NET PROFIT MARGIN	EMPLOYEES
12/04	1,282	25	1.9%	2,071
12/03	1,113	16	1.4%	1,894
12/02	1,060	37	3.5%	1,915
12/01	1,108	(31)	—	2,025
12/00	1,087	(43)	—	2,600
12/99	908	(7)	—	—
Annual Growth	7.1%	—	—	(5.5%)

2004 Year-End Financials

Debt ratio: 10,000.0%
Return on equity: —
Cash ($ mil.): 3

Current ratio: 1.54
Long-term debt ($ mil.): 231

Net Income History

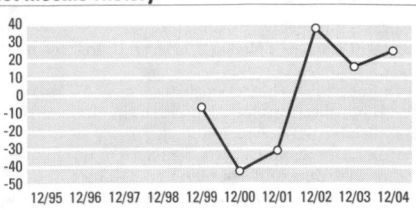

40 30 20 10 0 -10 -20 -30 -40 -50
12/95 12/96 12/97 12/98 12/99 12/00 12/01 12/02 12/03 12/04

American Wholesale Insurance

The American Wholesale Insurance Group is an independent lot. The company is the largest independent wholesale insurance broker in the US and the second-largest overall (after Swett & Crawford). Also known as AmWINS, the group provides insurance services to independent agents and brokers across the country. It offers expertise in property/casualty and group benefits brokerage and specialty underwriting. The company also provides actuarial services. Chairman Ernie Telford and CEO Steve DeCarlo founded American Wholesale Insurance Group in 2002 by combining several specialty wholesale insurance firms.

The American Wholesale Insurance Group in 2005 acquired Stewart Smith Group, the US wholesale insurance unit of Willis Group Holdings as part of an industry-wide trend by retail insurance brokers to divest wholesale holdings to remove any appearance of a conflict of interest.

EXECUTIVES

Chairman: Ernie Telford
President and CEO: M. Steven (Steve) DeCarlo
Division President, Group Benefits Brokerage: Samuel H. Fleet
Division President, Specialty Underwriting: Stephen J. Vaccaro Jr.
Division President, AmWINS Brokerage: Mark M. Smith
CFO: Scott Purviance
Chief Actuary and Chief Administrative Officer: J. Scott Reynolds
Chief Marketing and Sales Officer: Gregg Calestini

LOCATIONS

HQ: American Wholesale Insurance Group Inc.
4064 Colony Rd., Ste. 450, Charlotte, NC 28211
Phone: 704-943-2000   **Fax:** 704-943-9000
Web: www.amwins.com

PRODUCTS/OPERATIONS

Selected Subsidiaries and Affiliates

Custom Products & Services
AmWINS Actuarial Services

Group Benefits Brokerage
BrokerNetUSA
National Employee Benefit Companies, Inc. (NEBCO)

Property/Casualty Brokerage
  AmWINS Brokerage of Arizona
  AmWINS Brokerage of the Carolinas
  AmWINS Brokerage of Georgia
  AmWINS Brokerage of Illinois
  AmWINS Brokerage of New Jersey
  AmWINS Brokerage of New York
  AmWINS Brokerage of Texas
  AmWINS Healthcare
  AmWINS Insurance Brokerage of California
  Property Risk Services
Specialty Underwriting
  Americana Program Underwriters
  Lambert Green Limited
  Seaboard Underwriters
  Specialty Programs & Facilities Managers
  Woodus K. Humphrey & Co.

COMPETITORS

BISYS	Crump Insurance Services
CRC Insurance	Swett & Crawford

HISTORICAL FINANCIALS

Company Type: Private

Income Statement

FYE: December 31

	ESTIMATED REVENUE ($ mil.)	NET INCOME ($ mil.)	NET PROFIT MARGIN	EMPLOYEES
12/04	163	—	—	695

AmeriPath

Pickled organs and preserved tissues are AmeriPath's favorite things. The firm contracts with more than 200 hospitals to manage their anatomic pathology practices in more than 20 states. The more than 400 pathologists in AmeriPath's network diagnose diseases by examining tissue samples; work is performed in hospital and outpatient laboratories. Ameripath operates more than 40 outpatients labs and the Center for Advanced Diagnostics, which provides advanced pathology testing and disease management services. The company also manages the non-medical aspects of the practices, including payroll, staffing, supply, and financial reporting. The company has agreed to acquire Specialty Laboratories.

AmeriPath's Dermpath Diagnostics unit is focused exclusively on dermatology pathology services. The company also operates institute for gastrointestinal and digestive diseases, as well as one for urologic and renal diseases.

The firm is developing its regional network of practices through acquisitions. AmeriPath itself was acquired in 2003 by Welsh, Carson, Anderson & Stowe. The decision to go private was primarily due to years of stagnant stock prices. Welsh, Carson, Anderson & Stowe owns more than 95% of the company.

EXECUTIVES

Chairman and CEO: Donald E. (Don) Steen, age 58
President: Joseph A. Sonnier, $500,000 pay
EVP and CFO: David L. Redmond, age 54, $145,000 pay
SVP, Human Resources: Stephen V. (Steve) Fuller, age 48
VP, Business Development: Steven E. Casper
Regional President, Northeast Region: Bruce C. Walton
VP and CIO: Bob J. Copeland
Chief Medical Officer: Jeffrey A. Mossler, age 51, $461,058 pay (partial-year salary)
Medical Director, DermPath Diagnostics: Clay J. Cockerell
Auditors: Ernst & Young LLP

LOCATIONS

HQ: AmeriPath, Inc.
  7289 Garden Rd., Ste. 200, Riviera Beach, FL 33404
Phone: 561-712-6200   **Fax:** 561-845-0129
Web: www.ameripath.com

AmeriPath has offices in Alabama, California, Colorado, Florida, Georgia, Indiana, Kentucky, Massachusetts, Michigan, Mississippi, New York, North Carolina, Ohio, Oklahoma, Pennsylvania, South Carolina, Tennessee, Texas, Utah, West Virginia, and Wisconsin.

PRODUCTS/OPERATIONS

2004 Sales

	$ mil.	% of total
Net patient services	483.0	95
Net management services	24.3	5
Total	**507.3**	**100**

COMPETITORS

Bio-Reference Labs	Per-Se Technologies
Esoterix	Quest Diagnostics
LabCorp	Specialty Laboratories

HISTORICAL FINANCIALS

Company Type: Private

Income Statement

FYE: December 31

	REVENUE ($ mil.)	NET INCOME ($ mil.)	NET PROFIT MARGIN	EMPLOYEES
12/04	507	2	0.3%	2,729
12/03	485	23	4.8%	2,685
12/02	479	45	9.3%	2,945
12/01	419	23	5.6%	2,515
12/00	330	13	4.0%	2,325
12/99	233	23	9.9%	1,595
12/98	177	19	10.5%	1,346
12/97	108	7	6.7%	994
12/96	43	2	4.7%	688
12/95	16	1	5.6%	565
Annual Growth	**46.8%**	**5.8%**	**—**	**19.1%**

2004 Year-End Financials

Debt ratio: 138.3%
Return on equity: —
Cash ($ mil.): —
Current ratio: —
Long-term debt ($ mil.): 495

Net Income History

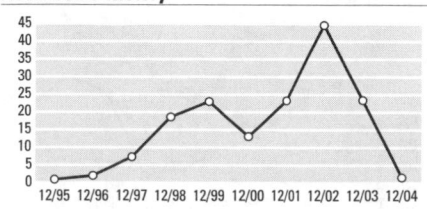

AMERISAFE

Keeping Americans safe since 1986, AMERISAFE specializes in providing workers' compensation insurance for businesses in hazardous industries. Some of the industries served include agriculture, manufacturing, construction, logging, oil and gas, and trucking. The company writes coverage (through subsidiary American Interstate Insurance) for approximately 15,000 employers (mainly small and mid-sized firms with 10-50 employees) through some 1,300 agents. In addition, AMERISAFE offers loss prevention and claims management services. AMERISAFE operates in some 45 states and Washington, DC. Private investment concern Welsh, Carson, Anderson & Stowe is putting up its 68% stake in the company for sale.

Louisiana accounts for 11% of AMERISAFE's business, the largest of any state. Georgia follows close behind with 10% of all business.

Director Jared Morris controls 16% of AMERISAFE's shares.

EXECUTIVES

Chairman: Mark R. Anderson, age 53, $392,000 pay
President, CEO, and Director: C. Allen Bradley Jr., age 54, $400,000 pay
EVP and CFO: Geoffrey R. (Geoff) Banta, age 56, $280,000 pay
EVP, Sales and Marketing: Craig P. Leach, age 55, $285,000 pay
EVP, General Counsel, and Secretary: Arthur L. Hunt, age 60, $295,000 pay
SVP, Claims Operations: Henry O. Lestage IV, age 44
SVP, Enterprise Risk Management: Allan E. Farr, age 46
SVP, Human Resources and Client Services: Cynthia P. Harris, age 51
SVP, Information Technology: Edwin R. Longanacre, age 47
SVP, Premium Audit: Lasa L. Simmons, age 48
SVP, Underwriting Operations: Kelly R. Goins, age 39
SVP, Safety Operations: Leon J. Lagneaux, age 54
VP and Treasurer: Angela S. Lannen, age 59
Auditors: Ernst & Young LLP

LOCATIONS

HQ: AMERISAFE, Inc.
  2301 Hwy. 190 West, DeRidder, LA 70634
Phone: 337-463-9052   **Fax:** 337-463-7298
Web: www.amerisafe.com

PRODUCTS/OPERATIONS

2004 Sales

	$ mil.	% of total
Premiums earned	234.8	94
Net investment income	12.2	5
Net realized gains on investments	1.4	1
Fees & other	0.6	—
Total	**249.0**	**100**

COMPETITORS

Aetna
AmCOMP
Farm Family Holdings
The Hartford
Highlands Insurance
Liberty Mutual
Mutual Risk Management
Nationwide
Zenith National

HISTORICAL FINANCIALS

Company Type: Private

Income Statement

FYE: December 31

	REVENUE ($ mil.)	NET INCOME ($ mil.)	NET PROFIT MARGIN	EMPLOYEES
12/04	249	11	4.3%	465
12/03	191	9	4.5%	—
12/02	175	5	3.0%	—
12/01	182	—	—	650
12/00	196	—	—	650
12/99	157	—	—	654
12/98	200	—	—	625
12/97	150	—	—	600
12/96	96	—	—	—
12/95	70	—	—	315
Annual Growth	**15.2%**	**42.8%**	**—**	**4.4%**

2004 Year-End Financials

Debt ratio: —
Return on equity: —
Cash ($ mil.): —

Current ratio: —
Long-term debt ($ mil.): 0

Net Income History

12/95 12/96 12/97 12/98 12/99 12/00 12/01 12/02 12/03 12/04

AMF Bowling

AMF Bowling Worldwide is looking to hit some strikes after a string of gutterballs. After years of rapid expansion, the company is the largest operator of bowling centers in the world with more than 370 facilities in the US. In addition to operating bowling alleys, AMF sells goods such as shoes and ball bags and provides equipment such as pinsetters and ball returns to other bowling centers. The company makes billiard tables under the brands Highland, Renaissance, and Play Master, though the Billiards & Games unit may be up for sale. Private investment firm Code Hennessy & Simmons bought AMF in 2004.

After growing too far too fast, AMF is trimming down. The company has shed nearly all its foreign bowling center operations and is contemplating a sale of its billiard supplies business.

EXECUTIVES

President and CEO: Frederick R. (Fred) Hipp, age 53, $242,308 pay
SVP, CFO, and Treasurer: Christopher F. Caesar, age 39, $307,043 pay
VP Human Resources: Anthony (Tony) Ponsiglione
VP North America Sales: Jay Buhl
President and COO, AMF Bowling Products: John B. Walker, age 48, $270,003 pay
VP Sales, AMF Bowling Products: Jon Farinholt
Director Marketing: Joan Phares
VP Food & Beverage, AMF U.S. Bowling Centers: Joseph (Joe) Scarnaty
Auditors: KPMG LLP

LOCATIONS

HQ: AMF Bowling Worldwide, Inc.
8100 AMF Dr., Richmond, VA 23111
Phone: 804-730-4000 **Fax:** 804-559-6276
Web: www.amf.com

PRODUCTS/OPERATIONS

Selected Operations

AMF Bowling Centers
Billiard tables
 Highland
 PlayMaster
 Renaissance
Bowling equipment

COMPETITORS

Bowl America
Brunswick
Dave & Buster's
Haw Par
Jillian's Billiards
Vulcan International

HISTORICAL FINANCIALS

Company Type: Private

Income Statement

FYE: June 30

	REVENUE ($ mil.)	NET INCOME ($ mil.)	NET PROFIT MARGIN	EMPLOYEES
6/04	679	(67)	—	13,800
6/03	668	3	0.5%	15,361
6/02*	342	(35)	—	14,500
12/01	695	(217)	—	16,500
12/00	715	(201)	—	16,386
12/99	733	(162)	—	15,568
12/98	738	(126)	—	14,489
12/97	714	(56)	—	18,415
12/96	385	(20)	—	13,929
12/95	565	97	17.1%	—
Annual Growth	**2.1%**	**—**	**—**	**(0.1%)**

*Fiscal year change

2004 Year-End Financials

Debt ratio: 257.1%
Return on equity: —
Cash ($ mil.): 13

Current ratio: 0.85
Long-term debt ($ mil.): 287

Net Income History

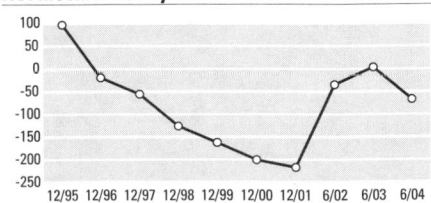

12/95 12/96 12/97 12/98 12/99 12/00 12/01 6/02 6/03 6/04

Amscan

Amscan caters to the party animal in all of us. The firm produces more than 400 specially designed ensembles of party accessories and novelties, including balloons, invitations, piñatas, stationery, and tableware. Amscan's products are sold to more than 20,000 retail outlets worldwide, mainly party goods superstores, mass merchandisers, and other distributors. Its largest customer, Party City, accounts for about 14% of sales. Amscan itself makes party items (which bring in about 60% of sales) and buys the rest from other manufacturers, primarily in Asia. It has production and distribution facilities in Asia, Australia, Europe, and North America. Berkshire Partners and Weston Presidio are Amscan's principal owners.

Amscan expanded into metallic balloons by acquiring M&D Balloons (since renamed M&D Industries) in February 2002. M&D also possesses a portfolio of character licenses, including Disney and Nickelodeon.

The company filed to go public in June 2002 but later decided not to pursue a public offering.

EXECUTIVES

Chairman: Robert J. Small, age 38
CEO and Director: Gerald C. Rittenberg, age 53, $830,000 pay
President, COO, and Director: James M. Harrison, age 53, $747,000 pay
CFO: Michael A. Correale, age 47, $265,000 pay
SVP: Garry Kieves, age 54
SVP Operations, Amscan Inc.: Willard D. Finch
SVP Party Division, Amscan Inc.: Diane D. Spaar
SVP Sales, Amscan Inc.: Sheldon Babyatsky
VP Marketing: Craig Leaf
VP and General Manager, Anagram International: James Plutt
CIO: Michael Mostrom
Controller: John Conlon
Human Resources Manager: Laura Bucci
Auditors: Ernst & Young LLP

LOCATIONS

HQ: Amscan Holdings, Inc.
80 Grasslands Rd., Ste. 4, Elmsford, NY 10523
Phone: 914-345-2020 **Fax:** 914-345-3884
Web: www.amscan.com

Amscan Holdings has manufacturing, distribution, and sales operations in the US, as well as in Australia, Canada, France, Japan, Mexico, and the UK. Its products are sold around the world.

PRODUCTS/OPERATIONS

2004 Sales

	% of total
Party goods	68
Metallic balloons	24
Stationery	5
Gift	3
Total	**100**

Selected Products

Gift
  Ceramic giftware
  Decorative candles
  Decorative frames
  Mugs
  Plush toys
  Wedding accessories and cake tops
Party Goods
  Candles
  Cascades and centerpieces
  Crepe
  Cutouts
  Decorative and solid color tableware
  Flags and banners
  Guest towels
  Latex balloons
  Party favors
  Party hats
  Piñatas
Stationery
  Baby and wedding memory books
  Decorative tissues
  Gift wrap, bows, and bags
  Invitations, notes, and stationery
  Photograph albums
  Ribbons
  Stickers and confetti

COMPETITORS

American Greetings
CSS Industries
CTI Industries
Hallmark
Solo Cup

HISTORICAL FINANCIALS

Company Type: Private

Income Statement

FYE: December 31

	REVENUE ($ mil.)	NET INCOME ($ mil.)	NET PROFIT MARGIN	EMPLOYEES
12/04	399	8	1.9%	1,750
12/03	403	17	4.3%	1,900
12/02	386	17	4.3%	2,000
12/01	345	11	3.3%	1,830
12/00	324	8	2.5%	1,830
12/99	305	10	3.3%	1,800
12/98	235	7	2.8%	1,500
12/97	210	(0)	—	1,100
12/96	193	2	1.1%	1,100
12/95	167	14	8.5%	1,100
Annual Growth	10.1%	(6.6%)	—	5.3%

2004 Year-End Financials

Debt ratio: 262.4%
Return on equity: 11.2%
Cash ($ mil.): 4
Current ratio: 2.94
Long-term debt ($ mil.): 385

Net Income History

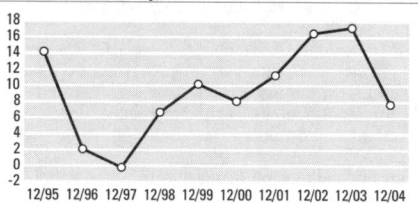

Amsted Industries

Wilbur and Orville Wright's first flight might never have succeeded without an assist from Amsted Industries' Diamond Chain subsidiary. A maker of roller chains for a variety of equipment and machinery, Diamond Chain also produced the propeller chain for the Wright brothers' aircraft. Other subsidiaries include ASF-Keystone (side frames, bolsters, and cast steel freight car components), Griffin Pipe Products (ductile iron pressure and sewer pipe), and Means Industries (automotive steering and transmission components).

The company sells its products to industrial distributors, locomotive and railcar manufacturers, and automotive OEMs. Employee-owned, Amsted Industries has some 50 plants worldwide.

EXECUTIVES

Chairman, President, and CEO: W. Robert Reum, age 62
VP and CFO: Paul F. Fischer
VP, Chief Accounting Officer: Richard A. (Rick) Nunemaker
VP, General Counsel, and Secretary: Thomas C. Berg
President, ASF-Keystone, North America: John Wories Jr.
President, Baltimore Aircoil: Steven S. Duerwachter
President, Brenco Incorporated: Dave Liming
President, Burgess-Norton Mfg. Co.: John F. Carroll
President, Consolidated Metco: Ed Oeltjen
President, Diamond Chain Company: Brett Vasseur
President, Griffin Pipe Products: Paul T. Ciolino
President, Griffin Wheel Company: William J. Demmert
President, Means Industries, Inc.: D. W. (Bill) Shaw
Treasurer: Matthew J. Hower
Director, Human Resources: Shirley J. Whitesell
Auditors: PricewaterhouseCoopers

LOCATIONS

HQ: Amsted Industries Incorporated
  205 N. Michigan Ave., 44th Fl., Chicago, IL 60601
Phone: 312-645-1700   **Fax:** 312-819-8494
Web: www.amsted.com

Amsted Industries has 47 manufacturing facilities in 11 countries.

PRODUCTS/OPERATIONS

Selected Products

Construction and industrial products
  Closed circuit cooling towers
  Cooling towers
  Ductile iron pressure pipe and fittings
  Evaporative condensers
  Ice thermal storage units
  Roller chains
Railroad products
  Center plates
  Constant contact side bearings
  Couplers and connectors
  Draft gears and cushion units
  Draft sills
  Locomotive draft gears
  Rail anchors
  Springs
  Tapered roller bearings
  Truck systems
  Wheels

Vehicular products
  Aluminum and iron wheel hubs
  Aluminum castings
  Automatic transmission reaction plates
  Brake drums
  Fifth wheels
  Molded plastic components
  One-way clutches
  Piston pins
  Powder metal parts
  Steering column components

COMPETITORS

BorgWarner
Columbus Stainless
Evapco
Gunite
McWane
Timken
U.S. Pipe
U.S. Tsubaki

HISTORICAL FINANCIALS

Company Type: Private

Income Statement

FYE: September 30

	REVENUE ($ mil.)	NET INCOME ($ mil.)	NET PROFIT MARGIN	EMPLOYEES
9/04	1,600	—	—	9,100
9/03	2,000	—	—	9,200
9/02	1,360	—	—	9,000
9/01	1,650	—	—	10,300
9/00	1,774	—	—	11,200
9/99	1,370	—	—	12,600
9/98	1,252	—	—	9,100
9/97	1,105	—	—	8,500
9/96	1,140	—	—	8,700
9/95	1,165	—	—	9,300
Annual Growth	3.6%	—	—	(0.2%)

Revenue History

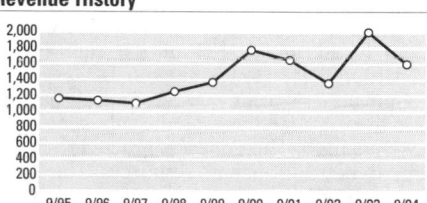

AMTRAK

Fueled by government dollars, Amtrak keeps on chugging, hoping to operate under its own steam. The National Railroad Passenger Corporation, better known as Amtrak, carries more than 24 million passengers a year in 46 states — Alaska, Hawaii, South Dakota, and Wyoming are excluded. The company's system includes more than 22,000 route miles, nearly all of which are owned by freight railroads. A for-profit company that has never been profitable, Amtrak is almost wholly owned by the US Department of Transportation and receives large subsidies from the federal government. Some government officials have called for Amtrak to be self-sufficient.

Under CEO David Gunn, Amtrak has moved to cut costs by reducing its workforce. Nevertheless, the railroad needs subsidies to maintain its operations. For fiscal 2004, Amtrak asked for $1.8 billion from the federal government and was granted $1.2 billion. With more cash, Amtrak officials say, the railroad could put more cars on the tracks in high-traffic areas such as the northeastern US.

The Bush administration wanted to reform Amtrak and cut its budget, and the US House seemed to be on board with that plan. That is until the House voted to approve a $1.2 billion budget. Amtrak's board has voted, in accordance with the wishes of the Bush administration, to spin off Amtrak's Northeast corridor service as a separate entity that would be funded and maintained by the states. Many who are dependent on Amtrak for their daily commute are vehemently opposed to such a plan. Amtrak's future rests in the hands of Congress.

HISTORY

US passenger train travel peaked in 1929, with 20,000 trains in operation. But the spread of automobiles, bus service, and air travel cut into business, and by the late 1960s only about 500 passenger trains remained running in the country. In 1970 the combined losses of all private train operations exceeded $1.8 billion in today's dollars. That year Congress passed the Rail Passenger Service Act, which created Amtrak to preserve America's passenger rail system. Although railroads were offered stock in the corporation for their passenger equipment, most just wrote off the loss.

Amtrak began operating in 1971 with 1,200 cars, most built in the 1950s. Although the company lost money from the outset ($153 million in 1972), it continued to be bankrolled by Uncle Sam, despite much criticism. Amtrak ordered its first new equipment in 1973, the year it also began taking over stations, yards, and service staff. The company didn't own any track until 1976, when it purchased hundreds of miles of right-of-way track from Boston to Washington, DC.

After a 1979 study showed Amtrak passengers to be by far the most heavily subsidized travelers in the US, Congress ordered the company to better utilize its resources. The 1980s saw Amtrak leasing its rights-of-way along its tracks in the Northeast corridor to telecommunications companies, which installed fiber-optic cables, and beginning mail and freight services for extra revenue.

In the early 1990s Amtrak faced a number of challenges: Midwest flooding, falling airfares, and safety concerns over a number of rail accidents, particularly the 1993 wreck of the Sunset Limited near Mobile, Alabama, in which 47 people were killed (the worst accident in Amtrak's history). In 1994 Amtrak's board of directors (at Congress' behest) adopted a plan to be free of federal support by 2002. In 1995 the company began planning high-speed trains for its heavily traveled East Coast routes.

In 1997 Amtrak finalized agreements to buy the high-speed cars and locomotives central to its self-sufficiency plan. It also began increasing its freight hauling and had its first profitable offering: the Metroliner route between New York and Washington, DC.

Amtrak's board of directors was replaced by Congress in 1997 with a seven-member Reform Board appointed by President Clinton. Chairman and president Thomas Downs resigned that year, and Tommy Thompson, then governor of Wisconsin, took over as chairman. Former Massachusetts governor Michael Dukakis was named vice chairman, and George Warrington stepped in as Amtrak's president and CEO.

Technical problems in 1999 delayed Amtrak's introduction of the Acela high-speed train in the Northeast until late 2000, when service began in the Boston-Washington corridor. In 2001 Amtrak pitched a 20-year plan, involving an annual outlay of $1.5 billion in federal funds, for expanding and modernizing its passenger service to help alleviate highway and airport congestion nationwide.

Thompson left the Amtrak board in 2001 after he was named US secretary of health and human services.

Realizing Amtrak would not meet its end-of-the-year deadline to be self-sufficient, in 2002 the Amtrak Reform Council sent a proposal to Congress that Amtrak be divided into three groups: one to oversee operations and funding, a second to maintain certain Amtrak-owned tracks and properties, and a third to operate trains. It also called for competition to be allowed on some passenger routes within two to three years.

Also in 2002 Warrington resigned and was replaced by David Gunn, who formerly headed the metropolitan transit systems in New York and Toronto. Gunn began moving to cut costs, and he worked to secure new federal money to avert a threatened shutdown of rail service in July 2002.

EXECUTIVES

Chairman: David M. Laney
President and CEO: David L. Gunn
CFO: David N. Smith
SVP Operations: William L. (Bill) Crosbie
VP Business Diversity: Gerri Mason Hall
VP Government Affairs and Policy:
 Joseph H. (Joe) McHugh
VP Human Resources: Lorraine A. Green
VP Labor Relations: Joseph M. Bress
VP Marketing and Sales: Barbara J. Richardson
VP Procurement and Materials Management:
 Michael J. Rienzi
VP Strategic Planning and Contract Administration:
 Gilbert O. (Gil) Mallery
CIO: Steve Emanuel
General Counsel and Corporate Secretary:
 Alicia M. Serfaty
Inspector General: Fred E. Weiderhold
Auditors: KPMG LLP

LOCATIONS

HQ: National Railroad Passenger Corporation
 60 Massachusetts Ave. NE, Washington, DC 20002
Phone: 202-906-3000   **Fax:** 202-906-3306
Web: www.amtrak.com

PRODUCTS/OPERATIONS

2004 Sales

	% of total
Passenger related	78
Commuter	6
Other	15
State capital payments	1
Total	**100**

COMPETITORS

AMR Corp.	Norfolk Southern
Burlington Northern	Northwest Airlines
Santa Fe	Southwest Airlines
Continental Airlines	UAL
CSX	Union Pacific
Delta Air	US Airways
Greyhound	

HISTORICAL FINANCIALS

Company Type: Government-owned

Income Statement

FYE: September 30

	REVENUE ($ mil.)	NET INCOME ($ mil.)	NET PROFIT MARGIN	EMPLOYEES
9/04	1,865	(1,309)	—	19,700
9/03	2,077	(1,274)	—	22,000
9/02	2,228	(1,132)	—	22,000
9/01	2,109	(1,248)	—	24,600
9/00	2,111	(768)	—	25,000
9/99	2,042	(702)	—	25,000
9/98	2,285	(353)	—	24,000
9/97	1,674	(762)	—	23,000
9/96	1,555	(764)	—	23,000
9/95	1,497	(808)	—	24,100
Annual Growth	2.5%	—	—	(2.2%)

2004 Year-End Financials

Debt ratio: (51.5%)   Current ratio: 0.50
Return on equity: —   Long-term debt ($ mil.): 3,673
Cash ($ mil.): 247

Net Income History

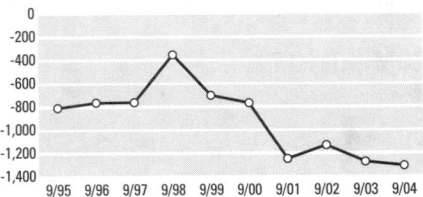

AMTROL

AMTROL will help you to not sweat the small stuff. The company manufactures HVAC (heating/ventilation/air conditioning) expansion and pressure control products used in water systems as well as well water accumulators, hot water expansion controls, and indirect-fired water heaters. Its brands include CHAMPION, EXTROL, Therm-X-Trol, Water Worker, and Well-X-Trol. AMTROL's distribution network of independent dealers reaches 1,600 customers in North America alone. Investment firm The Cypress Group controls the company through AMTROL Holdings Inc.

EXECUTIVES

Chairman, President, and CEO: Albert D. Indelicato, age 54, $400,000 pay
EVP, CFO, and Treasurer: Larry T. Guillemette, age 49, $194,375 pay
SVP Operations: Christopher A. Laus, $168,004 pay
VP Finance and Controller: Joseph L. (Joe) DePaula, age 50, $182,654 pay
VP Human Resources: Michael Montigny
President Alfa European Operations: William Chohfi, $296,700 pay
Secretary and General Counsel: Patricia A. Pickrel, age 54
Auditors: Ernst & Young LLP

LOCATIONS

HQ: AMTROL Inc.
1400 Division Rd., West Warwick, RI 02893
Phone: 401-884-6300   **Fax:** 401-884-4773
Web: www.amtrol.com

AMTROL has manufacturing and distribution operations in the US in Kentucky, Maryland, Ohio, and Rhode Island, as well as in Canada, Poland, and Portugal. The company has sales offices in Singapore and the UK.

2004 Sales

	$ mil.	% of total
North America		
US	120.5	61
Other countries	7.3	3
Europe		
Portugal	69.3	35
Other countries	1.3	1
Total	**198.4**	**100**

PRODUCTS/OPERATIONS

2004 Sales

	$ mil.	% of total
Water technologies	105.2	53
Cylinders	93.2	47
Total	**198.4**	**100**

Selected Products and Brands

Hot water expansion control tanks (EXTROL)
Indirect-fired residential and commercial water heaters
Pressure-rated cylinders
Thermal expansion accumulators (Therm-X-Trol)
Well water accumulators (CHAMPION, Well-X-Trol)

COMPETITORS

A. O. Smith	Mobile Mini
Emerson Electric	Pentair
GE	Worthington Industries
Indeck	

HISTORICAL FINANCIALS

Company Type: Private

Income Statement

FYE: December 31

	REVENUE ($ mil.)	NET INCOME ($ mil.)	NET PROFIT MARGIN	EMPLOYEES
12/04	198	(22)	—	1,318
12/03	196	(2)	—	1,722
12/02	187	(45)	—	1,718
12/01	182	(9)	—	1,574
12/00	198	(4)	—	1,714
12/99	212	2	0.9%	1,856
12/98	202	(13)	—	1,875
12/97	176	(8)	—	1,650
12/96	171	10	5.7%	915
12/95	173	9	5.3%	950
Annual Growth	**1.6%**	**—**	**—**	**3.7%**

2004 Year-End Financials

Debt ratio: —   Current ratio: 1.43
Return on equity: —   Long-term debt ($ mil.): 171
Cash ($ mil.): 12

Net Income History

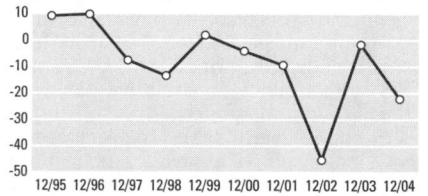

12/95 12/96 12/97 12/98 12/99 12/00 12/01 12/02 12/03 12/04

Andersen

Windows of opportunity open and shut daily for Andersen, a leading and well-known maker of wood-clad windows and patio doors in the US. Andersen offers window designs from hinged, bay, and double-hung to skylight, gliding, and picture windows. It operates nearly 90 Renewal by Andersen window replacement stores in 30 states. Andersen's EMCO subsidiary makes storm and screen doors. Through independent and company-owned distributorships, the company sells to architects, general contractors, and building owners throughout the Americas, Europe, Asia, and the Middle East. Andersen Logistics operates in 16 states. The company is equally owned by the Andersen family, the Andersen Foundation, and company employees.

Andersen competes in the marketplace by building strong brand recognition for its products. Acquisitions play an important role in the company's growth strategy, and Andersen has been buying many of the independent distributorships that carry its products, including Morgan Products (now operating as Andersen Logistics), the largest US distributor of its products. The company has also expanded its manufacturing operations through acquisitions.

Through its Aspen Research subsidiary, the company analyzes composite materials development, product life-cycle management, and waste elimination and reclamation.

HISTORY

Danish immigrant Hans Andersen and his two sons, Fred and Herbert, founded Andersen in 1903. Andersen's first words in English, "All together, boys," became the company motto. Andersen arrived in Portland, Maine, in 1870 and worked as a lumber dealer and manufacturer. In the 1880s he bought a sawmill in St. Cloud, Minnesota, and later managed one in Hudson, Wisconsin. When the Hudson mill owners asked him to let workers go during the off season, Andersen refused and then resigned. He subsequently launched his own lumber business — Andersen Lumber Company — in 1903 and hired some of the men who had been laid off. He opened a second lumberyard, in Afton, Minnesota, in 1904. Andersen and his sons revolutionized the window industry in the early 1900s by introducing a standardized window frame with interchangeable parts. Buoyed by success, the Andersens sold their lumberyards in 1908 to focus on the window-frame business. (Andersen purchased lumberyards again in 1916 before exiting the lumberyard business for good in the 1930s.) Around 1913 the company moved from Hudson to South Stillwater (now Bayport), Minnesota.

Thrifty Hans launched the company's first (and the US's third) profit-sharing plan shortly before his death in 1914. Herbert became VP, secretary, treasurer, and factory manager, and Fred became president. Herbert died in 1921 (at age 36), but Fred proved to be a versatile and capable successor. Among his accomplishments, Fred came up with the tag line "Only the rich can afford poor windows."

In 1929 the company changed its name to Andersen Frame Corporation. In the following decade Andersen introduced a number of innovations, including Master Frame (a frame with a locked sill joint, 1930); a casement window, the industry's first complete factory-made window

unit (1932); and a basement window (1934). The company adopted its current name in 1937.

Andersen introduced the gliding window concept in the early 1940s. It also launched the Home Planners Scrap Book consumer ad campaign in 1943. During the 1950s Andersen's new products included the Flexivent awning window, which featured welded insulating glass that served as an alternative to traditional storm windows. In the 1960s the company produced a gliding door and introduced the Perma-Shield system. The system featured easy-to-maintain vinyl cladding to protect wood frames from weathering. By 1978 Perma-Shield products accounted for three-quarters of sales. Fred, who had run the company as president until 1960 and had subsequently held the positions of chairman and chairman emeritus, died in 1979 at age 92.

Between 1984 and 1994 the company increased its sales threefold by introducing additional customized and state-of-the-art products, including patio doors. In 1995 it launched Renewal by Andersen, a retail window-replacement business.

Andersen acquired former long-term strategic partner Aspen Research (materials testing, research, and product development) in 1997. Among its jointly developed products is Fibrex, a composite material used in replacement windows. Also in 1997 the company moved its international division office from Bayport, Minnesota, to the Minnesota World Trade Center in St. Paul to help boost its export drive.

In 1998 company veteran Donald Garofalo succeeded Andersen's president and CEO Jerold Wulf, who retired after 39 years with the company. Andersen reinforced its company-owned distributorships in 1999 when it bought millwork distributors Morgan Products and Independent Millwork.

Expanding its product offerings, Andersen purchased privately held EMCO Enterprises (storm doors and accessories, Iowa) in 2001. Other acquisitions from about 1993 to 2003 have included Dashwood Industries (windows, skylights, roof windows, doors; Canada) and KML Windows (architectural windows and doors, Canada). The company also opened a new production facility in Menomonie, Wisconsin.

At the close of 2002, Andersen's COO James Humphrey was promoted to president, becoming the company's ninth president; he gained the added role of chief executive the next year. Garofalo retained the position of vice chair of the board; he later became chair of the board. Andersen celebrated its 100th year in 2003, publishing a book on its history, and the company kicked off a community project to build 100 Habitat for Humanity homes throughout North America over the next five years.

Andersen completed construction of a 150,000-sq.-ft. facility for wood composite profile extrusion in North Branch, Minnesota in 2004. The company shut down its plant in White Bear Lake and relocated approximately 40 employees to North Branch. Andersen also reorganized its distribution centers.

In 2005 Andersen purchased Iowa-based Eagle Window & Door, Inc., which manufactures aluminum-clad wood windows and patio doors, to operate as a subsidiary.

EXECUTIVES

Board Chair: Donald L. Garofalo
President and CEO: James E. (Jim) Humphrey, age 57
SVP and CFO: Philip (Phil) Donaldson
SVP Human Resources and Corporate Administration: Mary D. Carter
SVP Manufacturing: Gary Berndt
SVP Research, Technology and Engineering: Mary J. Schumacher, age 46
SVP Sales and Marketing: Jay Lund
VP and General Counsel: Alan Bernick
VP Marketing: J. Glasnapp
VP Sales: Steve Mog
President, Renewal by Andersen: Craig Evanich
Director, Corporate Communications: Maureen McDonough
Director, Marketing Communications and Services: Frank Quadflieg

LOCATIONS

HQ: Andersen Corporation
100 4th Ave. North, Bayport, MN 55003
Phone: 651-264-5150   **Fax:** 651-264-5107
Web: www.andersencorp.com

Andersen markets its products in Brazil, the Caribbean, China, Guatemala, Honduras, Ireland, Israel, Japan, Kuwait, Mexico, Poland, Portugal, South Korea, Spain, Taiwan, Turkey, the UK, and the US.

PRODUCTS/OPERATIONS

Selected Products and Brands

Doors
  Patio doors
    Art glass (Frank Lloyd Wright designs)
    Frenchwood Collection (gliding, hinged, and outswing)
    Narroline gliding patio doors
    Perma-Shield gliding patio doors
  Screen doors
  Storm doors
Windows
  Aluminum-clad
  Art glass
  Awning
  Basement
  Bay and bow
  Casement
  Double-hung
  Fixed
  Gliding
  Horizontal sliding
  Picture
  Skylights and roof windows
  Transom
  Utility
  Wood

COMPETITORS

Bocenor
CertainTeed
JELD-WEN
JELD-WEN UK.
JS Group
Marshfield DoorSystems
MI Windows and Doors
Owens Corning
Pella
Royal Group Technologies
Sierra Pacific Industries
Silver Line Building
  Products
Simonton Windows
Thermal Industries
UIS

HISTORICAL FINANCIALS

Company Type: Private

Income Statement

FYE: December 31

	ESTIMATED REVENUE ($ mil.)	NET INCOME ($ mil.)	NET PROFIT MARGIN	EMPLOYEES
12/03	2,000	—	—	8,000
12/02	2,000	—	—	8,000
12/01	1,800	—	—	7,000
12/00	1,700	—	—	6,000
12/99	1,500	—	—	6,000
12/98	1,400	—	—	3,700
12/97	1,300	—	—	3,700
12/96	1,250	—	—	3,700
12/95	1,200	—	—	3,700
12/94	1,100	—	—	3,700
Annual Growth	**6.9%**	**—**	**—**	**8.9%**

Revenue History

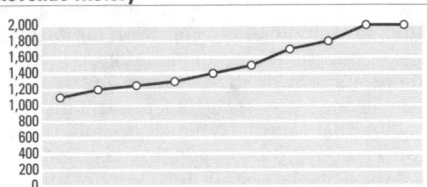

Anna's Linen

Motherly devotion paid off for entrepreneur and company founder, Alan Gladstone. Anna's Linen is a specialty retailer of discounted home furnishings, including bed linens, window coverings, and bath accessories, featuring brand names such as Wamsutta and Grand Patrician. Its more than 180 retail locations in 12 US states have expanded their offerings to include additional home décor items such as area rugs, decorative pillows, housewares, and kitchen textiles. Chairman, president, and CEO Gladstone (who named the company after his mother, Anna, whose picture graces its direct mail advertising, Web site, and store marketing materials) envisions Anna's Linen eventually growing to 1,000 storefronts nationwide.

Its stores currently average about 9,700 sq. ft. Their larger size (some are as big as 15,000 sq. ft.) allows the company to experiment with its lineup of home décor offerings. Its target markets are African-American and Hispanic populations with household incomes between $35,000 and $75,000. In addition to growing in number, these demographics' home ownership rates are rising more quickly than those of the rest of the US population.

EXECUTIVES

Chairman, President, and CEO: Alan Gladstone, age 57, $850,000 pay
SVP Finance and CFO: Michael C. Harnetiaux, age 53, $196,000 pay
SVP Marketing and Merchandising: Carie Doll, age 33, $160,000 pay

VP Real Estate: Patrick Barber, age 53, $230,000 pay
VP Store Operations: Russell Brown, age 58, $172,500 pay
VP and Chief Administrative Officer: Scott Gladstone, age 35
VP General Merchandise: Kevin McLain, age 39, $160,000 pay
Auditors: Deloitte & Touche LLP

LOCATIONS

HQ: Anna's Linen Company
3550 Hyland Ave., Costa Mesa, CA 92626
Phone: 714-850-0504   **Fax:** 714-850-9170
Web: www.annaslinens.com

COMPETITORS

Bed Bath & Beyond
Federated
J. C. Penney Company
Kohl's
Linens 'n Things
Sears Holdings
Target
Wal-Mart

HISTORICAL FINANCIALS

Company Type: Private

Income Statement

FYE: Sunday nearest January 31

	REVENUE ($ mil.)	NET INCOME ($ mil.)	NET PROFIT MARGIN	EMPLOYEES
1/05	225	5	2.4%	1,620
1/04	155	4	2.8%	—
1/03	108	3	2.4%	—
Annual Growth	**44.2%**	**44.1%**	**—**	**—**

2005 Year-End Financials

Debt ratio: 164.5%
Return on equity: —
Cash ($ mil.): 2
Current ratio: 1.41
Long-term debt ($ mil.): 2

Net Income History

Apex Systems

Your career has to start somewhere, so why not start at the Apex? Founded in 1995, Apex Systems specializes in the placement of information technology, telecommunications, and engineering professionals. The company finds people for temporary or contract assignments, as well as temp-to-hire and permanent placements. It uses Internet job boards, print ads, its own existing database of candidates, extensive networking through user groups, referrals, and other methods to find its recruits. The company operates from about 20 offices located across the US filling midsized to large companies' staffing needs.

EXECUTIVES

CEO: Brian Callaghan
President: Jeff Veatch
COO: Win Sheridan
CFO: Theodore Hanson
Controller: L. Paige Kerr
Auditors: KPMG LLP

LOCATIONS

HQ: Apex Systems, Inc.
4400 Cox Rd., Ste. 200, Glen Allen, VA 23060
Phone: 804-342-9090   **Fax:** 804-254-7920
Web: www.apexsystemsinc.com

Apex Systems has offices in Washington, DC, as well as in California, Colorado, Florida, Georgia, Illinois, Maryland, Massachusetts, Missouri, New York, North Carolina, Pennsylvania, Texas, Virginia, and Washington.

COMPETITORS

Adecco
Butler International
CDI
COMFORCE
Kelly Services
Kforce
Manpower
MPS
Randstad
Spherion
StarTek
TAC Worldwide
Technisource
VistaRMS
Volt Information

HISTORICAL FINANCIALS

Company Type: Private

Income Statement

FYE: December 31

	REVENUE ($ mil.)	NET INCOME ($ mil.)	NET PROFIT MARGIN	EMPLOYEES
12/04	120	—	—	325
12/03	82	—	—	225
12/02	61	—	—	205
12/01	46	—	—	205
12/00	38	—	—	145
Annual Growth	32.8%	—	—	22.4%

Revenue History

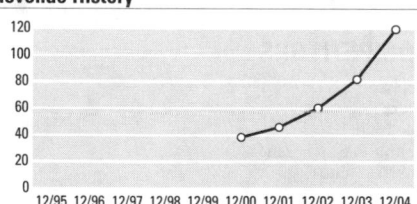

Appleton Papers

Appleton Papers hasn't fallen far from the tree. The company manufactures and distributes a variety of specialty paper products. Its primary revenue generator is carbonless paper (sold under the NCR Paper brand), which is used for business forms. Appleton also makes thermal paper and related products that are used in point-of-sale receipts and coupons, tickets (including event, lottery, and transportation tickets), and labels. Other units make security products (checks and documents designed to be resistant to counterfeiting) and plastic packaging films for use in the food processing, household, and industrial products industries. Appleton is owned by its employees.

Employees own Appleton through a holding company, Paperweight Development. Money from employee retirement savings plans was used to fund Paperweight Development's purchase of Appleton from ArjoWiggins (then known as Arjo Wiggins Appleton) in 2001. On average, Appleton employees invested about 75% of their 401(k) retirement plan balances in the deal.

Though the company's legal name remains Appleton Papers Inc., in 2003 it began referring to itself as simply "Appleton" for branding purposes.

EXECUTIVES

President and CEO: Mark R. Richards, age 45
VP, Finance, CFO and Director: Dale E. Parker, age 53, $361,398 pay
VP, Human Resources and Law, Secretary, and Director: Paul J. Karch, age 48, $317,371 pay
VP and General Manager, Thermal and Advanced Technical Products: John R. Depies, age 48, $318,525 pay
VP and General Manager, Coated Solutions Sales and Marketing: James H. (Jim) McDermott, age 48, $319,097 pay
VP, Market Transformation: Ann M. Whalen, age 45
VP, Performance Packaging: Stephen P. Sakai, age 51
VP, Technology: Ted E. Goodwin, age 48
CEO, BemroseBooth Limited: Graham Bennington, age 54
Director, Manufacturing and Mill Manager, West Carrollton Mill: Todd Downey, age 46
Manager, Corporate Communications: Bill Van Den Brandt
Auditors: PricewaterhouseCoopers LLP

LOCATIONS

HQ: Appleton Papers Inc.
825 E. Wisconsin Ave., Appleton, WI 54911
Phone: 920-734-9841   **Fax:** 920-991-8080
Web: www.appletonideas.com

Appleton operates from facilities in Canada, the UK, and the US.

PRODUCTS/OPERATIONS

2004 Sales

	$ mil.	% of total
Coated solutions	602.1	61
Thermal & advanced technical products	209.1	21
Security products	131.3	13
Other	47.0	5
Total	**989.5**	**100**

Selected Products

Coated solutions
  Carbonless paper
  Inkjet printing
  Point-of-sale displays
Thermal and advanced technical products
  Non-thermal products
  Thermal business products
    Point-of-sale receipts and coupons
    Label products
    Lotteries and gaming tickets
    Tags for airline baggage
    Tickets
Security products
  Brand protection products
  Business documents
  Checks
  Government documents
  High-integrity mailing and niche publishing
  Mass transit and car parking tickets
  Security printed vouchers and payment cards
Performance packaging
  Flexible packaging materials
  Multilayered films

COMPETITORS

ArjoWiggins
Boise Cascade
communisis
Curwood
De La Rue
Imation
Kanzaki Specialty Papers
MeadWestvaco
Mitsubishi Paper Mills
Pliant
Ricoh
Winpak

HISTORICAL FINANCIALS

Company Type: Private

Income Statement

FYE: Saturday nearest December 31

	REVENUE ($ mil.)	NET INCOME ($ mil.)	NET PROFIT MARGIN	EMPLOYEES
12/04	990	(25)	—	3,406
12/03	862	11	1.3%	3,348
12/02	898	10	1.1%	2,500
12/01	956	40	4.2%	—
Annual Growth	1.2%	—	—	16.7%

2004 Year-End Financials

Debt ratio: 545.0%
Return on equity: —
Cash ($ mil.): 70
Current ratio: 2.26
Long-term debt ($ mil.): 591

Net Income History

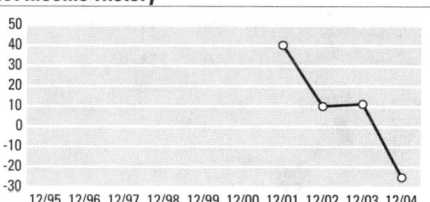

ArcSoft

ArcSoft develops multimedia software and firmware for personal computers, mobile devices, and consumer electronics manufacturers. The company's software line enables users to edit, enhance, and manage their digital photos and videos. Its products are available in multiple languages and are bundled with digital video and still cameras, mobile phones, PDAs, printers, scanners, computers, and other consumer electronic devices. The company receives most of its revenue from license fees from OEM customers. It collaborates with large device manufacturers such as Canon, Epson, Hewlett-Packard, Matsushita Kotobuki Electronics (Panasonic brands), Motorola, Nikon, and Palm.

Based on the company's preliminary IPO filing in August 2004, CEO and President Michael Deng owned 18% of the company, Pacific One international controlled 13%, and private investor Sam Zheng held 12%.

The company withdrew its planned IPO filing in July 2005.

EXECUTIVES

Chairman: David C. (Dave) Nagel, age 60
President, CEO, and Director: Hui (Michael) Deng, age 42, $350,000 pay
SVP and COO: Todd J. Rumaner, age 35, $355,000 pay
SVP and CFO: Alfred V. Larrenaga, age 57
VP; General Manager, ArcSoft (Hangzhou) Company, Limited: Hua (James) Zhong, age 38
VP, Engineering: Liangkui (Frank) Feng, age 38
VP, Retail Sales and Operations: Larry Swensen
Media Relations: Karen Cheung
Auditors: Deloitte & Touche LLC

LOCATIONS

HQ: ArcSoft, Inc.
46601 Fremont Blvd., Fremont, CA 94538
Phone: 510-440-9901 **Fax:** 510-440-1270
Web: www.arcsoft.com

ArcSoft has offices in China, Japan, Taiwan, the UK, and the US.

2004 Sales

	$ mil.	% of total
US	12.0	54
Japan	7.2	33
UK	0.4	2
Other countries	2.5	11
Total	**22.1**	**100**

PRODUCTS/OPERATIONS

2004 Sales

	$ mil.	% of total
Product	19.0	86
Internet services	3.1	14
Total	**22.1**	**100**

Selected Products

Photo Software
  Collage Creator
  Funhouse
  Greeting Card Creator
  Media Card Companion
  Multimedia E-mail
  Panorama Maker
  PhotoBase
  PhotoImpression
  PhotoMontage
  PhotoPrinter
  PhotoStudio
  Total Media
Video/DVD Software
  DVD SlideShow
  QuickDVD
  Showbiz DVD
  VideoImpression
  Video Stabilizer
Phone/PDA Software
  PhotoBase for Palm OS
  PhotoBase for Pocket PC
  PhotoBAse for Nokia 3650, 7650

COMPETITORS

Adobe
Apple Computer
InterVideo
Microsoft
Pinnacle Entertainment
Sonic Solutions
Ulead

HISTORICAL FINANCIALS

Company Type: Private

Income Statement

FYE: June 30

	REVENUE ($ mil.)	NET INCOME ($ mil.)	NET PROFIT MARGIN	EMPLOYEES
6/04	22	(1)	—	394
6/03	19	(2)	—	—
6/02	19	(4)	—	—
Annual Growth	**8.1%**	**—**	**—**	**—**

2004 Year-End Financials

Debt ratio: (25.4%)
Return on equity: —
Cash ($ mil.): 3
Current ratio: 0.91
Long-term debt ($ mil.): 2

Net Income History

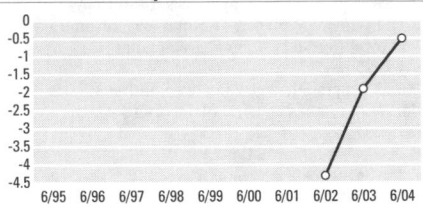

Argo-Tech

Argo-Tech helps keep aircraft aloft with its fuel-flow devices. The company makes main engine fuel pumps and accessories and commercial and military airframe fuel pumps and fuel distribution products. Argo-Tech also makes ground fueling equipment and cryogenic pumps. On the service side, Argo-Tech provides aerospace maintenance, overhauling, testing, plating, and surface treatment. Customers include military and commercial engine and airframe makers such as Airbus, Boeing, GE Aircraft Engines, Lockheed Martin, and Rolls-Royce. Argo-Tech employees own about 54% of the company. Masashi Yamada, who controls distributor Upsilon International (a major customer), owns about 35% of Argo-Tech.

Argo-Tech's sales to commercial aerospace customers dropped with the decline in air travel that followed the September 11, 2001, terrorist attacks, but have since recovered. Rising sales to military and industrial customers partially offset the decrease in the commercial aerospace market.

When commercial sales *do* get made, Argo-Tech is the sole supplier of main engine fuel pumps for the CFM56 series engine, which powers several Airbus models (A-318, A-319, A-320, A-321, A-340) and the Boeing 737. Argo-Tech is also the sole supplier of main engine fuel pumps for the Boeing 777. On the regional and business jet side, its pumps are used on the BR700 (Bombardier Global Express, Gulfstream V, Boeing 717) and GE CF34-8 engines (Bombardier CRJ700 and CRJ900, Embraer ERJ-170).

Upsilon International accounts for about 11% of Argo-Tech's sales.

EXECUTIVES

Chairman, President, and CEO: Michael S. Lipscomb, age 58, $830,351 pay
EVP, CFO, and Director: Frances S. St. Clair, age 49, $366,188 pay
EVP, Secretary, General Counsel, and Director: Paul R. Keen, age 55, $401,146 pay
VP, Human Resources: James Cummingham
Auditors: Deloitte & Touche LLP

LOCATIONS

HQ: Argo-Tech Corporation
23555 Euclid Ave., Cleveland, OH 44117
Phone: 216-692-6000 **Fax:** 216-692-5293
Web: www.argo-tech.com

Argo-Tech operates from facilities in the US (Arizona, California, and Ohio) and in the UK.

2004 Sales

	$ mil.	% of total
US	107.1	57
Europe	32.8	18
Other regions	47.4	25
Total	**187.3**	**100**

PRODUCTS/OPERATIONS

2004 Sales

	$ mil.	% of total
Aerospace	138.2	74
Industrial	49.1	26
Total	**187.3**	**100**

Selected Products

Airframe boost and transfer pumps
Lube oil and scavenge pumps
Main engine fuel pumps
Small main engine pumps

Selected Services

Aerospace material testing and analysis
Field service
Maintenance
Overhaul services
Plating and surface treatment
Technical support

COMPETITORS

Cobham
Ebara
Goodrich
Hamilton Sundstrand
Intertechnique
Meggitt
Parker Hannifin

HISTORICAL FINANCIALS

Company Type: Private

Income Statement

FYE: Last Saturday in October

	REVENUE ($ mil.)	NET INCOME ($ mil.)	NET PROFIT MARGIN	EMPLOYEES
10/04	187	(1)	—	690
10/03	161	5	2.8%	654
10/02	155	6	3.8%	664
10/01	173	11	6.2%	696
10/00	159	1	0.5%	707
10/99	177	5	3.0%	790
10/98	174	4	2.2%	773
10/97	117	8	6.7%	772
10/96	96	6	5.8%	—
10/95	87	2	2.5%	—
Annual Growth	**8.9%**	**—**	**—**	**(1.6%)**

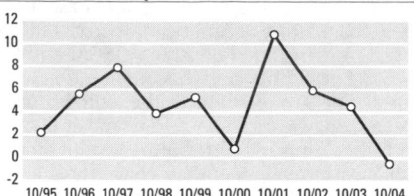
Army and Air Force Exchange

Be all that you can be and buy all that you can buy at the PX (Post Exchange). The Army and Air Force Exchange Service (AAFES) runs more than 3,100 facilities — including PXs and BXs (Base Exchanges) — at US Army and Air Force bases in about 30 countries (including locations in Iraq) and 49 US states. Its outlets range from tents to shopping centers that have retail stores, fast-food outlets (brand names like Burger King and proprietary brands like Anthony's Pizza), movie theaters, beauty shops, and gas stations. AAFES serves active-duty military personnel, reservists, retirees, and their family members. A government agency under the Department of Defense (DOD), it receives no funding from the department.

While the AAFES receives no federal money, it pays neither taxes nor rent to occupy US government property. Its retail prices average 22% less than the competition, and nearly 70% of AAFES's profits go into Morale, Welfare, and Recreation (MWR) programs for amenities such as libraries and youth centers. Other profits are used to renovate or build new stores. Active military personnel head AAFES, but its staff consists mostly of military family members and other civilians.

A proposal made in May 2003 by then-Deputy Secretary of Defense Paul Wolfowitz to explore a merger of AAFES with the Navy Exchange Service Command and the Marine Corps Personnel Support has been tabled for now. Nevertheless, the military shops are facing increased competition from Wal-Mart Stores, which is luring soldiers off base with its everyday low prices. Texas officials had lobbied members of Congress charged with exploring ways to integrate the three exchange services to keep the AAFES in Dallas and consolidate shared functions in Texas.

To better compete with discounters, AAFES has begun adding dollar sections to about 150 of its stores worldwide.

HISTORY

During the American Revolution, peddlers known as sutlers followed the Army, selling items such as soap, razors, and tobacco. The practice lasted until after the Civil War, when post traders replaced sutlers. This system was replaced in 1889 when the War Department authorized canteens at military bases.

The first US military exchanges were established in 1895, creating a system to supply military personnel with personal items on US Army bases around the world. The exchanges were run independently, with each division creating a Post Exchange (PX) to serve its unit. The post commander would assign an officer to run the PX (usually along with other duties) and would decide how profits were spent.

In 1941 the Army Exchange Service was created, and the system was reorganized. A five-member advisory committee made up of civilian merchandisers was created to provide recommendations for the reorganization. The restructuring made the system more like a chain store business. The independent PXs were bought by the War Department from the individual military organizations that ran them. Civilian personnel were brought in to staff the PXs, and a brigadier general was named to head an executive staff made up of Army officers and civilians that provided centralized control of the system. The Army also created a special school to train officers to run the PXs.

Sales at the PXs skyrocketed during WWII; a catalog business was added so soldiers could order gifts to send home to their families. The Department of the Air Force was established in 1947, and the exchange system organization was renamed the Army and Air Force Exchange Service (AAFES) the next year.

In 1960 the government allowed the overseas exchanges to provide more luxury items in an effort to keep soldiers from buying foreign-made goods. By the time the military had been cranked up again for the Vietnam War, big-ticket items such as TVs, cameras, and tape recorders were among the exchanges' best-sellers. In 1967 AAFES moved its headquarters from New York City to Dallas.

By 1991 the exchanges were open to the National Guard and the Reserve; AAFES's customer base had grown to 14 million. When the military began downsizing during the 1990s following the end of the Cold War, AAFES's customer base shrank by 35%.

AAFES stores sold more than $12 million of pornographic materials in 1995. The House of Representatives passed the Military Honor and Decency Act the next year prohibiting the sale of pornography on US military property, including AAFES stores; this ban was struck down as unconstitutional in 1997. That year AAFES was approved as a provider of medical equipment covered by federal CHAMPUS/TRICARE insurance. It also created a Web site to offer online shopping in 1997.

The Supreme Court upheld the 1996 porn ban in 1998; the Pentagon banned the sale of more than 150 sexually explicit magazines (such as Penthouse), while a military board permitted the continued sale of certain publications (including Playboy). Maj. Gen. Barry Bates took over as AAFES's commander and CEO in 1998. To better battle other retailers, that year AAFES announced its stores would offer best-price guarantees, matching prices of local stores and refunding price differences if customers found lower prices within 30 days of buying products.

In 1999 AAFES expanded to Macedonia and Kosovo, providing its services to military personnel in Operation Joint Guardian. In 2000 Bates was replaced as AAFES commander and CEO by Maj. Gen. Charles J. Wax.

Wax stepped down as commander and CEO in August 2002 and was replaced by Maj. Gen. Kathryn Frost of the US Army.

EXECUTIVES

Chairman: Claude V. Christianson
Commander: Paul W. (Bill) Essex
Vice Commander and Director, Equal Opportunity: Toreraser A. Steele
COO: Marilyn Iverson
CFO: Jerry Justus
SVP, Human Resources: Ronnie D. Compton
SVP, Management Information Systems: Terry B. Corley
SVP, Marketing: Mark Westphal
SVP, Sales: Karen Stack
VP, Corporate Compliance: Matt Dromey
VP, Food and Theater Division: Richard Sheff
VP, Main Stores and Hardlines: Jacquie Waelde
VP, Main Store/Soft-lines Division: James Moon
VP, Sales: Dale Linebarger
VP, Services: Craig Sewell
Chief of Business Planning: Nick Williams
Chief of Communications: Debra L. Pressley
Chief Technology Officer: Tony Levister
General Counsel: Col. Athena Jones, USAF
Public Affairs Specialist: Judd Anstey
Auditors: Ernst & Young LLP

LOCATIONS

HQ: Army and Air Force Exchange Service
3911 S. Walton Walker Blvd., Dallas, TX 75236
Phone: 214-312-2011   **Fax:** 214-312-3000
Web: www.aafes.com

The Army and Air Force Exchange Service has operations in 49 states and in more than 30 countries and overseas areas.

PRODUCTS/OPERATIONS

Selected Merchandise and Services

Barber and beauty shops
Books, newspapers, and magazines
Catalog services
Class Six stores
Concessions
Food facilities (mobile units, snack bars, name-brand fast-food franchises, and concession operations)
Gas stations and auto repair
Military clothing stores
Movie theaters
Retail stores
Vending centers

COMPETITORS

7-Eleven	METRO AG
Best Buy	Sears
Costco Wholesale	Supercuts
J. C. Penney	Target
Kmart	Wal-Mart
Kroger	

HISTORICAL FINANCIALS

Company Type: Government agency

Income Statement   FYE: January 31

	REVENUE ($ mil.)	NET INCOME ($ mil.)	NET PROFIT MARGIN	EMPLOYEES
1/04	7,905	485	6.1%	47,323
1/03	7,323	416	5.7%	49,861
1/02	7,133	373	5.2%	52,400
1/01	7,369	381	5.2%	52,400
1/00	6,992	362	5.2%	54,000
1/99	6,783	343	5.1%	54,000
1/98	6,620	337	5.1%	53,946
1/97	6,874	348	5.1%	57,583
1/96	6,710	228	3.4%	56,495
1/95	6,746	269	4.0%	58,556
Annual Growth	1.8%	6.8%	—	(2.3%)

2004 Year-End Financials

Debt ratio: 0.0%   Current ratio: 1.97
Return on equity: 12.6%   Long-term debt ($ mil.): 0
Cash ($ mil.): 110

Net Income History

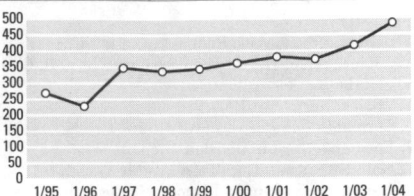

ASC

When it comes to developing new car models, ASC and ye shall receive. Formerly a sunroof maker, ASC — the name now stands for American Specialty Cars — works with carmakers to deliver entire specialty vehicles. Models ASC has helped bring to life include the BMW Z3, Chevrolet SSR, Dodge Viper, and Pontiac Firebird. In addition to offering design, modeling, and prototyping services, ASC delivers sunroofs, entertainment systems, convertible tops, and exterior styling components to carmakers' assembly lines. The company maintains facilities in the US, Canada, Germany, and South Korea. Investment firm Questor Management owns the company.

Convertible tops, which have grown in popularity since nearly disappearing from production cars in the 1970s — have helped make ASC's reputation. Leading buyers of the company's convertible systems have included BMW, Toyota, and Mitsubishi.

EXECUTIVES

President and CEO: Paul B. Wilbur
Vice Chairman, Product Development:
 J. E. (Ted) Robertson
CFO: Patrick (Pat) Aubry
EVP and Chief Marketing Officer: Jeffrey (Jeff) Steiner
VP Human Resources: Ronda Coogan
VP Program Management: Vimal Khanna
VP Purchasing: Mike Lingo
VP and General Manager, Ford and New Domestics
 Account: Vanessa Gordon
VP and General Manager, DaimlerChrysler Account:
 Steve Laurain
General Manager, ASC West Coast Design and
 Technical Center: Thomas (Tom) Pavlak
CIO: Michael Ziethlow
Chief Administration Officer: Kathy Steiger
Director Business Development; VP and General
 Manager, General Motors Account: James Puscas
Director Business and Product Planning:
 Marques B. McCammon
Director Marketing and Communications:
 Timothy L. (Tim) Yost

LOCATIONS

HQ: ASC Incorporated
 1 ASC Center, Southgate, MI 48195
Phone: 734-285-4911   **Fax:** 734-246-2735
Web: www.ascglobal.com

PRODUCTS/OPERATIONS

Selected Products and Capabilities

Composites and Finishing
 Assembly
 Bonding
 Low-pressure sheet molded composite
 Preforming
 Resin transfer molding
 Rigid foam core molding
Creative Services
 Design-to-production
 Mid-cycle enhancement programs
 Program management
Open-Air Systems
 Convertible systems
 Formed boot systems
 Mobile entertainment systems
 Performance systems
 Removable hardtop systems
 Retractable hardtop systems
 Sunroof systems
 Uniquely styled body panel systems
Specialty Customization
 Assembly of niche open-air systems
 Complete assembly of small-series specialty vehicles
 Dual-stage vehicle conversion and assembly
 Second stage vehicle conversion
Total Vehicle Integration
 Advanced concepts
 Design
 Engineering
 Manufacturing engineering
 Plant set-up
 Production management
 Prototyping

COMPETITORS

ArvinMeritor, Inc.   Regal-Beloit
Delphi   Robert Bosch
Magna International   Webasto Sunroofs

HISTORICAL FINANCIALS

Company Type: Private

Income Statement

FYE: December 31

	ESTIMATED REVENUE ($ mil.)	NET INCOME ($ mil.)	NET PROFIT MARGIN	EMPLOYEES
12/04	493	—	—	1,221
12/03	428	—	—	815
12/02	413	—	—	904
12/01	406	—	—	—
12/00	400	—	—	—
12/99	300	—	—	2,200
12/98	300	—	—	2,200
12/97	323	—	—	2,200
12/96	370	—	—	2,200
12/95	330	—	—	2,000
Annual Growth	4.6%	—	—	(5.3%)

Revenue History

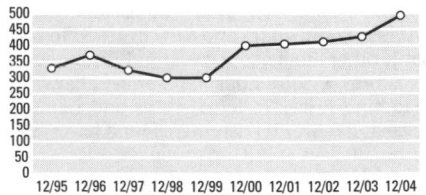

ASCAP

While Frank Sinatra got the glory, Johnny Mercer got some of the money, and his estate still does, thanks to the American Society of Composers, Authors and Publishers (ASCAP). ASCAP is the #1 performance rights organization in the world. The group protects the rights of composers, songwriters, lyricists, and music publishers by licensing and distributing royalties for the public performances of their copyrighted works. Be they played in a stadium, on the radio or Internet, on an airplane, or in a bar, songs of more than 200,000 members are covered. The group also lobbies Congress on behalf of its constituency.

ASCAP no longer charges annual membership dues. Founded in 1914, the not-for-profit organization is run entirely by members who serve on the board of directors. About 85% of collected funds are paid out to members; the remainder covers operating expenses.

The group also serves musicians with showcases, workshops, publications, health insurance, and a credit union.

EXECUTIVES

Chairman and President: Marilyn Bergman
Vice Chairman: Jay Morgenstern
CEO: John LoFrumento
EVP Membership Group, Los Angeles: Todd Brabec
EVP Performing Rights Group: Al Wallace
SVP Licensing, Performing Rights Group:
 Vincent Candilora
SVP and Chief Economist, Performing Rights Group:
 Peter Boyle
SVP Information Services and CIO, Performing Rights
 Group: Tina Barber
SVP International, Headquarters Group:
 Roger Greenaway
SVP Marketing, Headquarters Group: Philip Crosland
SVP Creative Affairs, Membership Group, Los Angeles:
 John Alexander
SVP Industry Affairs and VP and Executive Director,
 ASCAP Foundation: Karen Sherry
SVP Membership Group, Nashville: Connie Bradley
SVP Director Membership Film and Television
 Repertory, Membership Group: Nancy Knutsen
SVP Enterprises Group: Chris Amenita
VP and CFO: Bob Candela
VP General Licensing, Performing Rights Group:
 Bonnie King
VP Human Resources: Carolyn Jensen
VP Legal Services, Headquarters Group:
 Richard Reimer
Director Media Relations, Headquarters Group:
 Jim Steinblatt

LOCATIONS

HQ: American Society of Composers, Authors and
 Publishers
 1 Lincoln Plaza, New York, NY 10023
Phone: 212-621-6000   **Fax:** 212-724-9064
Web: www.ascap.com

PRODUCTS/OPERATIONS

Selected Past and Present Members

Beck
Leonard Bernstein
Garth Brooks
Duke Ellington
George Gershwin
James Horner
Lyle Lovett
Madonna
Henry Mancini
Tito Puente
Stevie Wonder

HISTORICAL FINANCIALS

Company Type: Not-for-profit

Income Statement

FYE: December 31

	ESTIMATED REVENUE ($ mil.)	NET INCOME ($ mil.)	NET PROFIT MARGIN	EMPLOYEES
12/03	700	—	—	630
12/02	635	—	—	600
12/01	600	—	—	600
12/00	500	—	—	500
12/99	500	—	—	500
12/98	500	—	—	600
12/97	500	—	—	583
12/96	483	—	—	588
12/95	437	—	—	566
12/94	423	—	—	688
Annual Growth	5.8%	—	—	(1.0%)

Revenue History

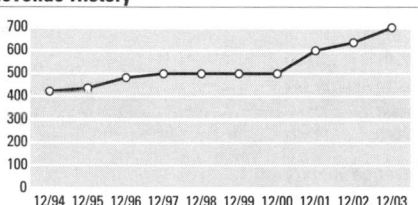

Ascension Health

Ascension Health has ascended to the pinnacle of not-for-profit health care. One of the largest Catholic hospital systems in the US, and thus one of the top providers of charity care in the nation, the organization's health care network consists of some 65 general acute care hospitals along with a dozen long-term care, rehabilitation, and psychiatric hospitals. Ascension Health also operates nursing homes, community clinics, and other health care facilities in about 20 states and the District of Columbia. The organization's facilities have more than 16,700 licensed beds.

Ascension's facilities are primarily located in the Southern, Midwestern, and Northeastern areas of the US.

The system takes to heart the words of St. Vincent de Paul, co-founder of the Daughters of Charity, who advised the order to serve "the poor sick bodily, ministering to them in all their needs, and spiritually also so that they will live and die well."

As such, nuns from Ascension's sponsoring religious orders sit on its governing board, which is led by non-clergy Chairman Jack Mudd.

In this age of high-cost health care, Ascension realizes the need for fiscal health. In addition to selling money-losing hospitals, Ascension has reorganized its facilities by geographic regions, with each region headed by a VP who controls costs and speeds decision making.

In response to rising health care costs, Ascension merged with national Catholic health care provider Carondelet Health System in 2003.

HISTORY

The Daughters of Charity order was formed in France in 1633 when St. Vincent de Paul recruited a rich widow (St. Louise de Marillac) to care for the sick on battlefields and in their homes.

Elizabeth Ann Seton, America's first saint (canonized 1974), brought the order to the US. In 1809 Seton earned the title of mother and started the Sisters of Charity. The Sisters adopted the vows of the Daughters of Charity, adding "service" to them in 1812.

The Sisters officially became part of the Daughters of Charity in 1850. The Daughters cared for soldiers during the Civil War and were responsible for training Florence Nightingale. In the late 1800s the Daughters pioneered exclusive provider arrangements (similar to today's managed care contracts) with railroads, lumber camps, and the like. During the next 100 years, the order furthered its mission of caring for the sick and the poor. To support their efforts, the nuns founded hospitals (44 by 1911), schools, and other charity centers.

In 1969 the charity association formed a health care services cooperative, which became the Daughters of Charity National Health System (DCNHS). DCNHS operated as two regional institutions (one based in Maryland, the other in Missouri) until 1986, when the systems merged. The first task was to balance their holy mission with the need to make money. With competition from managed care companies increasing, DCNHS responded by cutting staff and diversifying into nursing homes and retirement centers.

The Daughters of Charity's western unit combined its six hospitals in California with Mullikin Centers (a physician-owned medical group) in 1993 to form one of the largest health care associations in the state.

DCNHS expanded its network in 1995 by merging its hospitals with and becoming a co-sponsor of San Francisco-based Catholic Healthcare West. That year it joined with Catholic Relief Services to operate a hospital in war-torn Angola.

In 1996 DCNHS dropped a proposed merger of its struggling 221-bed Carney Hospital in Boston with Quincy Hospital because the municipally owned Quincy facility was required by law to provide abortions. Instead, DCNHS sold Carney Hospital to Caritas Christi Health Care System (owned by the Boston Roman Catholic archdiocese), one of about a dozen hospital sales by DCNHS in the mid-1990s.

DCNHS reorganized its leadership in 1997, creating SVP positions for system direction and policy and for program development to strengthen and update its programs. In 1998 Sister Irene Kraus, who had founded DCNHS and led it through its expansion, died.

In 1999 DCNHS merged with fellow Catholic caregiver Sisters of St. Joseph Health System, then Michigan's largest health care system.

In 2000 Ascension saw the collapse of a five-hospital merger in Florida between subsidiary St. Vincent's Health System and Baptist Health System. The organization also launched the Voice for the Voiceless initiative, which combines private monies and federal grants to fund programs for the uninsured in Detroit, New Orleans, and Austin, Texas.

EXECUTIVES

Chairman: John O. (Jack) Mudd
President and CEO: Anthony R. (Tony) Tersigni, age 55
COO: Robert J. (Bob) Henkel, age 51
SVP and CFO: Anthony J. (Tony) Speranzo
SVP and CIO: Sherry L. Browne
SVP and Chief Risk Officer: James K. Beckmann Jr.
SVP, Legal Services and General Counsel: Joseph R. Impicciche
SVP, Strategic Business Development and Innovation; President, Ascension Health Ventures: John D. Doyle
SVP, Advocacy and External Relations: Susan Nestor Levy
SVP and Chief Supply Chain Officer: Michael T. (Mike) Langlois
SVP, Clinical Excellence: David B. Pryor
SVP, Mission Integration: Sister Maureen McGuire
SVP, Governance and Sponsor Relations: Rex P. Killian
VP, Advocacy, Ascension Health-Michigan: Sean Gehle
VP, Communications: Steve LeResche
Manager, Human Resources: Kate Brandt
Auditors: Ernst & Young LLP

LOCATIONS

HQ: Ascension Health
4600 Edmundson Rd., St. Louis, MO 63134
Phone: 314-733-8000　　**Fax:** 314-733-8013
Web: www.ascensionhealth.org

COMPETITORS

Beverly Enterprises	HealthSouth
Catholic Health East	Kindred Healthcare
Catholic Health Initiatives	Life Care Centers
Catholic Healthcare Partners	Tenet Healthcare
HCA	Triad Hospitals
Health Management Associates	Trinity Health (Novi)
	Universal Health Services

HISTORICAL FINANCIALS

Company Type: Not-for profit

Income Statement

FYE: June 30

	REVENUE ($ mil.)	NET INCOME ($ mil.)	NET PROFIT MARGIN	EMPLOYEES
6/03	9,054	—	—	87,469
6/02	7,666	—	—	83,412
6/01	6,853	—	—	83,412
6/00	6,400	—	—	67,000
6/99	6,400	—	—	67,000
6/98	6,170	—	—	65,000
6/97	5,700	—	—	60,000
6/96	5,700	—	—	61,100
6/95	6,200	—	—	62,300
6/94	7,000	—	—	67,400
Annual Growth	2.9%	—	—	2.9%

Revenue History

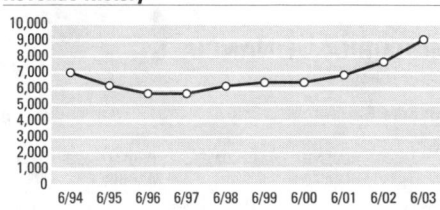

Ashley Furniture

Furniture buyers took a shine to Ashley Furniture Industries when it added a tough, high-gloss polyester finish to its furniture in 1986. The firm is one of the nation's largest furniture manufacturers. Ashley Furniture makes and imports upholstered, leather, and hardwood furniture, as well as bedding. It has manufacturing plants and distribution centers throughout the country and overseas. It runs nearly 100 Ashley Furniture HomeStores — independently owned shops that sell only Ashley Furniture products — in the US, Canada, and Japan. Founded by Carlyle Weinberger in 1945, Ashley Furniture is owned by father-and-son duos Ron and Todd Wanek and Chuck and Ben Vogel.

The company has three operating divisions: Ashley Casegoods, Ashley Upholstery, and Millennium. About 40% of the company's furniture is manufactured in Asia (half of that in China). It also maintains 3 million sq. ft. of facilities spanning six locations.

In November 2002 the Vogels (who own 25% of Ashley Furniture) filed a lawsuit against the Waneks (who own 75%), alleging that the Waneks were trying to squeeze the Vogel father and son out of the business. The Vogels and Waneks settled out of court in May 2005.

EXECUTIVES

Chairman: Ronald G. (Ron) Wanek
CEO: Todd Wanek
CFO: Dale Barneson
CIO: Dwain Jansson
President, Casegoods Division: Rob Hoffman
Director of Corporate Marketing: Bill Napier
Credit Manager: Jim Evanson
Human Resources Manager: Jim Dotta

LOCATIONS

HQ: Ashley Furniture Industries, Inc.
1 Ashley Way, Arcadia, WI 54612
Phone: 608-323-3377   **Fax:** 608-323-6008
Web: www.ashleyfurniture.com

COMPETITORS

Bassett Furniture	Hooker Furniture
Berkline/BenchCraft	IKEA
Bombay Company	Kimball International
Brown Jordan	Klaussner Furniture
International	La-Z-Boy
Ethan Allen	Natuzzi
Euromarket Designs	Pulaski Furniture
Furniture Brands	Rowe Companies
International	Williams-Sonoma

HISTORICAL FINANCIALS

Company Type: Private

Income Statement

FYE: December 31

	REVENUE ($ mil.)	NET INCOME ($ mil.)	NET PROFIT MARGIN	EMPLOYEES
12/03	1,700	—	—	9,300
12/02	1,400	—	—	8,000
12/01	1,090	—	—	6,000
12/00	952	—	—	5,000
12/99	816	—	—	5,691
12/98	650	—	—	4,567
12/97	540	—	—	2,100
12/96	450	—	—	—
Annual Growth	**20.9%**	—	—	**28.1%**

Revenue History

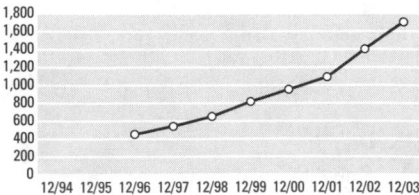

| 12/94 | 12/95 | 12/96 | 12/97 | 12/98 | 12/99 | 12/00 | 12/01 | 12/02 | 12/03 |

ASI Corp.

ASI, a wholesale distributor of computer software, hardware, and accessories, sells more than 3,000 products, including CD-ROM drives, modems, monitors, PCs, networking equipment, and storage devices. The company also boasts a dedicated motherboard catalog site, motherboardmaster.com, and offers standard and custom configurations. ASI sells to systems integrators and resellers throughout North America. Vendor partners include 3Com, Microsoft, Samsung, and Toshiba. Top officers Marcel and Christine Liang founded ASI in 1987; they own the company.

A family connection exists between ASI and one of its many vendors: Christine Liang, president and co-founder of ASI, is a sister of James Chu, CEO of ViewSonic.

EXECUTIVES

Chairman and CEO: Marcel Liang
President: Christine Liang
VP Product Management and Marketing: Brian Paterson
Human Resources: Veronica Contreras

LOCATIONS

HQ: ASI Corp.
48289 Fremont Blvd., Fremont, CA 94538
Phone: 510-226-8000   **Fax:** 510-226-8858
Web: www.asipartner.com

ASI has sales offices and warehouses in California, Florida, Georgia, Illinois, Kansas, New Jersey, Oregon, and Texas, as well as in Canada.

PRODUCTS/OPERATIONS

Selected Products

Cables	Notebooks
Cameras	Optical drives
CD-ROM drives	PCs
Central processing units	Printers
Controller cards	Projectors
DVD	Removable drives
Hard drives	and media
Keyboards	Scanners
Memory	Software
Mice	Sound cards
Modems	Speakers
Monitors	Storage devices
Motherboards	Tape back-up products
MP3 players	Video cards
Multimedia products	Zip drives
Network connectivity products	

COMPETITORS

Agilysys	Ingram Micro
Arrow Electronics	Merisel
Avnet	MicroAge
CompuCom	MTM Technologies
D&H Distributing	Pacific Magtron
Dell	SED International
En Pointe	Softmart
Gateway	Software House
Hewlett-Packard	Supercom
IBM	Tech Data

HISTORICAL FINANCIALS

Company Type: Private

Income Statement

FYE: December 31

	REVENUE ($ mil.)	NET INCOME ($ mil.)	NET PROFIT MARGIN	EMPLOYEES
12/04	1,060	—	—	500
12/03	1,200	—	—	550
12/02	866	—	—	530
12/01	1,000	—	—	500
12/00	818	—	—	500
12/99	730	—	—	610
12/98	730	—	—	560
12/97	540	—	—	400
12/96	426	—	—	350
12/95	326	—	—	300
Annual Growth	**14.0%**	—	—	**5.8%**

Revenue History

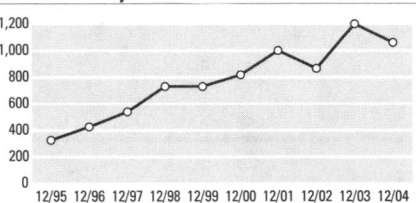

| 12/95 | 12/96 | 12/97 | 12/98 | 12/99 | 12/00 | 12/01 | 12/02 | 12/03 | 12/04 |

Asplundh Tree Expert

How much wood would a woodchuck chuck, if a woodchuck could chuck wood? A lot, if the woodchuck were named Asplundh. The company is the world's largest tree-trimming business, clearing tree limbs from power lines for utilities and municipalities in Australia, Canada, New Zealand, and the US. Asplundh also offers utility-related services such as meter reading, pipeline maintenance, storm emergency services, street light maintenance and construction, underground pipeline location, and utility pole maintenance. The company also holds an interest in fountains plc, a utility services and vegetation management company in the UK. The Asplundh family owns and manages the company, which was founded in 1928.

EXECUTIVES

Chairman and CEO: Christopher B. Asplundh
President: Scott M. Asplundh
Treasurer and Secretary: Joseph P. Dwyer
Manager Field Personnel: Ryan Swier

LOCATIONS

HQ: Asplundh Tree Expert Co.
708 Blair Mill Rd., Willow Grove, PA 19090
Phone: 215-784-4200 **Fax:** 215-784-4493
Web: www.asplundh.com

Asplundh has operations in Australia, Canada, New Zealand, and the US.

PRODUCTS/OPERATIONS

Selected Subsidiaries

American Lighting & Signalization (traffic signal services)
Asplundh Construction (utility and heavy construction)
Blume Tree Services (line clearance and vegetation management)
Central Locating Service (locating underground utility pipes and lines)
Utility Line Construction Service (line construction)
Utility Meter Services (meter reading and installation)
Utility Pole Technologies (pole inspection and restoration)

COMPETITORS

Davey Tree
Dow AgroSciences
Wright Tree Service

HISTORICAL FINANCIALS

Company Type: Private

Income Statement FYE: December 31

	REVENUE ($ mil.)	NET INCOME ($ mil.)	NET PROFIT MARGIN	EMPLOYEES
12/03	1,800	—	—	28,948
12/02	1,678	—	—	27,978
12/01	1,557	—	—	26,385
12/00	1,473	—	—	25,500
12/99	1,251	—	—	24,000
12/98	1,026	—	—	25,000
12/97	1,000	—	—	22,000
12/96	936	—	—	18,000
12/95	868	—	—	18,500
12/94	856	—	—	19,200
Annual Growth	8.6%	—	—	4.7%

Revenue History

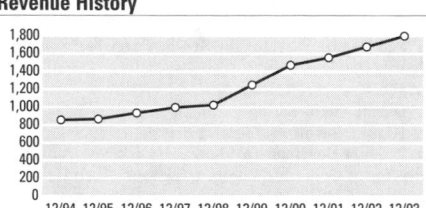

Associated Materials

Associated Materials Incorporated (AMI) is quick to side with its customers. Through its Alside and Gentek divisions, AMI makes and distributes vinyl siding and windows; vinyl fencing, decking, and railing (UltraGuard brand); and aluminum and steel siding, aluminum trim coil, and accessories (Revere and Gentek brands), mainly for the home remodeling and new construction markets (about two-thirds of sales). AMI owns about 125 supply centers that generate roughly 70% of sales. It also distributes building products made by other OEMs. AMI is an indirectly owned subsidiary of AMH Holdings, Inc., which is owned by AMH Holdings II, Inc. (which is controlled by Investcorp S.A. and Harvest Partners, Inc.).

Associated Materials sold its AmerCable division to AmerCable Incorporated and members of AmerCable's management in June 2002.

In 2003 AMI acquired Gentek Holdings, Inc. (vinyl, aluminum, and steel siding and vinyl windows), including its Gentek Building Products, Inc., and Gentek Building Products Limited subsidiaries, for about $118 million.

AMI's plans to reduce its fixed costs included closing its vinyl siding manufacturing plant in Freeport, Texas, in 2005.

EXECUTIVES

President, CEO, and Director, Associated Materials Incorporated, AMH Holdings, Inc., and Associated Materials Holdings; CEO and Director, Alside: Michael J. (Mike) Caporale Jr., age 53, $1,500,004 pay
VP, CFO, Secretary, and Treasurer: D. Keith LaVanway, age 40, $550,004 pay
VP, Human Resources: John F. Haumesser, age 40, $288,252 pay
President, Manufacturing and Supply Chain Management; President, Alside Siding & Window Company: Kenneth L. Bloom, age 42, $460,005 pay
President, Alside Supply Centers: Robert M. Franco, age 51, $422,505 pay
Auditors: Ernst & Young LLP

LOCATIONS

HQ: Associated Materials Incorporated
3773 State Rd., Cuyahoga Falls, OH 44223
Phone: 330-929-1811 **Fax:** 330-922-2354
Web: www.associatedmaterials.com

Associated Materials has plants in Iowa, New Jersey, North Carolina, Ohio, Texas, Virginia, and Washington in the US, and in Ontario and Quebec, Canada.

2004 Sales

	% of total
US	85
Canada	15
Total	**100**

PRODUCTS/OPERATIONS

2004 Sales

	% of total
Vinyl windows & vinyl siding	60
Other products	40
Total	**100**

Selected Products

Aluminum siding
Aluminum trim coil
Steel siding
Vinyl fencing, decking, and railing
Vinyl siding
Vinyl windows

COMPETITORS

Andersen Corporation	Owens Corning
CertainTeed	Royal Group Technologies
JELD-WEN	Silver Line
Louisiana-Pacific	Building Products
MMI Products	ThermoView Industries
Nortek	

HISTORICAL FINANCIALS

Company Type: Private

Income Statement FYE: Saturday nearest December 31

	REVENUE ($ mil.)	NET INCOME ($ mil.)	NET PROFIT MARGIN	EMPLOYEES
12/04	1,094	(11)	—	3,137
12/03	780	25	3.1%	3,173
12/02	630	6	1.0%	2,550
12/01	596	25	4.3%	2,140
12/00	499	24	4.7%	2,000
12/99	453	21	4.5%	1,800
12/98	408	9	2.2%	2,440
12/97	398	13	3.3%	1,500
12/96	357	9	2.5%	2,215
12/95	350	1	0.4%	2,310
Annual Growth	13.5%	—	—	3.5%

2004 Year-End Financials

Debt ratio: 130.3% Current ratio: 2.41
Return on equity: — Long-term debt ($ mil.): 339
Cash ($ mil.): 58

Net Income History

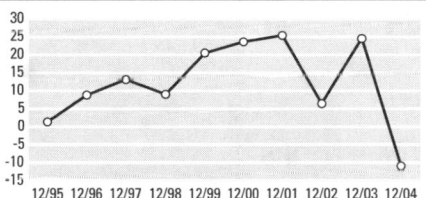

Associated Milk Producers

Associated Milk Producers Inc. (AMPI) might wear a cheesy grin, but it churns up solid sales. Shying away from the liquid stuff, it transforms more than 5 billion pounds of milk into butter, cheese, and other solid milk products each year. A regional cooperative of 4,600 dairy farms from Iowa, Minnesota, Missouri, Nebraska, North and South Dakota, and Wisconsin, AMPI operates 14 manufacturing plants. The co-op produces 60% of all the instant milk sold in the US and is a major cheddar producer. Aside from its own State brand of cheese and butter, AMPI primarily makes private-label products for retailers and foodservice customers.

AMPI has upgraded its 14 plants to produce additional value-added dairy products such as shredded cheese, aseptic-packaged cheese sauces (in coated cardboard containers for stable shelf life), and individually wrapped butter pats. Only one plant produces fluid milk.

AMPI's 93,000-sq.-ft. plant in New Ulm, Minnesota, is the biggest butter barn in the US and was originally able to whip up nearly 20,000 pounds of butter per hour. However, a fire at that plant in December 2004 melted nearly 3 million pounds of butter and left the facility badly damaged. AMPI has said it will rebuild the plant.

EXECUTIVES

President: Paul Toft
CFO: Brian J. Tomm
VP: Roger Lyon
General Manager: Mark Furth
Secretary: Phil Johnson
Treasurer: Greg Zwald
Director, Procurement: Donn DeVelder
Director, Fluid Marketing: Neil Gulden
Director, Quality Assurance: Tom Honce
Director, Information Technology: Jon Nelson
Director, Marketing: Jim Walsh
Plant Manager, AMPI Butter: William (Bill) Swan

LOCATIONS

HQ: Associated Milk Producers Inc.
315 N. Broadway, New Ulm, MN 56073
Phone: 507-354-8295   **Fax:** 507-359-8651
Web: www.ampi.com

Associated Milk Producers Incorporated has 14 milk processing plants in Iowa, Minnesota, South Dakota, and Wisconsin.

PRODUCTS/OPERATIONS

Selected Products

Butter
Cheese
Cheese Sauce
Dry milk
Fluid milk
Pudding

COMPETITORS

California Dairies Inc.	Leprino Foods
Dairy Farmers of America	Marathon Cheese
Dairylea	MMPA
Dean Foods	Prairie Farms Dairy
Foremost Farms	Saputo
Great Lakes Cheese	Saputo Cheese USA Inc.
Land O'Lakes	Schreiber Foods

HISTORICAL FINANCIALS

Company Type: Cooperative

Income Statement

FYE: December 31

	REVENUE ($ mil.)	NET INCOME ($ mil.)	NET PROFIT MARGIN	EMPLOYEES
12/03	1,057	—	—	1,700
12/02	981	—	—	1,700
12/01	1,200	—	—	1,600
12/00	1,000	—	—	1,600
12/99	1,100	—	—	1,600
12/98	1,100	—	—	1,600
12/97	928	—	—	1,600
12/96	2,189	—	—	4,500
12/95	2,555	—	—	4,500
12/94	2,629	—	—	4,500
Annual Growth	(9.6%)	—	—	(10.3%)

Revenue History

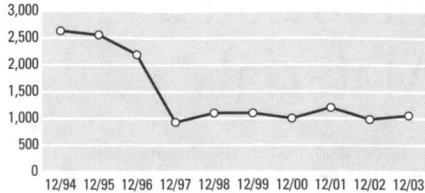

Associated Press

This just in: The Associated Press (AP) is reporting tonight and every night wherever news is breaking. AP is one of the world's largest news-gathering organizations, with about 240 news bureaus serving more than 120 countries. It provides news, photos, graphics, and audiovisual services that reach people daily through print, radio, television, and the Web. In addition to traditional news services, it operates an international television division (AP Television News), photo archives, and a continuous online news service (The WIRE). It also offers advertising management and distribution services. The not-for-profit cooperative was founded in 1848 and is owned by 1,700 member newspapers.

AP has been focused on maintaining its edge in the newsgathering business in a new, digital environment. In 2004 it relocated from Rockefeller Plaza (its home for the last 65 years) to a new headquarters on the west side of Manhattan that features a 105,000-sq-ft newsroom and serves as a central hub of digital news streams. At the same time, it is clamping down on costs and financial controls to strengthen its bottom line. The company moved to strengthen its sports information coverage in 2005, merging its AP MegaSports operation with News Corporation's STATS, Inc. to form STATS, LLC, a 50-50 joint venture.

CEO Tom Curley, who took the helm of the association in 2003 after a tenure at Gannet as publisher of *USA TODAY*, has presided over these developments as part of a strategy to keep pace with changes in how and where consumers get their news. AP faces the challenge of delivering information to customers accustomed to having greater choice and control when it comes to digesting news and other content. More importantly, it must also anticipate how those delivery channels will change in the coming years.

HISTORY

The Associated Press was formed in 1848 when six New York City newspapers joined to share news that arrived by telegraph wire. Two years later AP began selling wire reports to other papers and before long started creating regional associations. Adapting to changing technologies and public interests, AP began covering sports, financial, and public interest stories in the 1920s and was selling news reports to radio stations in the 1940s. Advancements during WWII included using transatlantic cable and radio-teletype circuits to deliver news and photos.

In the late 1960s AP and Dow Jones introduced services to improve business and financial reporting. AP improved photo delivery, reception, and storage in the 1970s with the advent of

Laserphoto and the Electronic Darkroom. It began transmitting news by satellite and offering color photographs to newspapers in the 1980s. In 1985 Louis Boccardi took over the job as president and CEO of AP.

AP adjusted to the media-heavy culture of the 1990s by launching the APTV international news video service and the All News Radio network in 1994. It then moved onto the Internet with The WIRE in 1996 and began offering online access to its Photo Archive in 1997. It bought Worldwide Television News in 1998, combining it with APTV to form Associated Press Television News (APTN). The following year it purchased the radio news contracts of UPI after the rival organization announced it was getting out of broadcast news.

In 2000 AP created an Internet division, AP Digital, to focus on marketing news to online providers. The cooperative continued its Internet focus the following year, launching AP Online en Español (news for Spanish-language Web sites) and AP Entertainment Online (multimedia entertainment news for Web sites). Also that year AP bought the Newspaper Industry Communication Center from the Newspaper Association of America.

In 2002 the company launched an expanded editorial partnership with Dow Jones Newswires, increasing the amount of financial news distributed on AP wires. Later that year it acquired Capitolwire, a provider of state government news. Boccardi stepped down as CEO in 2003, handing the reigns to former *USA TODAY* publisher Tom Curley. The following year AP relocated to Manhattan's West Side from Rockefeller Plaza, where it had resided for more than 65 years.

EXECUTIVES

Chairman: Burl Osborne
Vice Chairman: Lissa Walls Vahldiek
President, CEO, and Director: Thomas (Tom) Curley, age 56
SVP and CFO: Kenneth (Ken) Dale
SVP and Director of Newspapers and New Media Markets: Thomas R. (Tom) Brettingen
SVP and Executive Editor: Kathleen Carroll
SVP, General Counsel, and Corporate Secretary: John R. Keitt Jr.
SVP International Business: James M. (Jim) Donna, age 58
SVP Services and Technology: John Reid
VP; Managing Director, International Television: J. Eric Braun, age 55
VP and Director of Broadcast Division: James R. Williams III
VP and Director of Strategic Planning: James M. Kennedy
VP and Deputy Director for Services and Technology: Jeffrey Hastie
VP and Managing Editor: Mike Silverman
VP Global Business: Joy Jackson
VP Human Resources: Jessica Bruce, age 39
VP Product Development: Lorraine Cichowski, age 51
Director of Corporate Communications: Ellen Hale
Director of Media Relations: Jack Stokes
Auditors: Ernst & Young LLP

LOCATIONS

HQ: The Associated Press
450 W. 33rd St., New York, NY 10001
Phone: 212-621-1500   **Fax:** 212-621-5447
Web: www.ap.org

The Associated Press has about 240 news bureaus serving more than 120 countries.

PRODUCTS/OPERATIONS

Selected Products and Services
AP AdVantage (advertising placement)
AP AdSEND (ad delivery service)
AP Digital (Internet and wireless news delivery)
AP Information Services (corporate, government, and online distribution)
AP Photo Archive
AP Telecommunications (land-based and satellite information networks)
AP Wide World Photos (image licensing services)
APTN (AP Television News, international television news service)
ENPS (electronic news production system)
The WIRE (24-hour news service)

COMPETITORS

Agence France-Presse
Bloomberg
Business Wire
Comtex
Corbis
Dow Jones
E. W. Scripps
Gannett
Getty Images
Knight-Ridder
New York Times
PR Newswire
Reuters
Tribune
UPI

HISTORICAL FINANCIALS
Company Type: Cooperative

Income Statement
FYE: December 31

	REVENUE ($ mil.)	NET INCOME ($ mil.)	NET PROFIT MARGIN	EMPLOYEES
12/04	630	—	—	3,700
12/03	593	—	—	3,700
12/02	554	—	—	3,500
12/01	575	—	—	3,500
12/00	574	—	—	3,700
12/99	572	—	—	3,500
12/98	495	—	—	3,500
12/97	441	—	—	3,500
12/96	418	—	—	3,000
12/95	390	—	—	3,150
Annual Growth	5.5%	—	—	1.8%

Revenue History

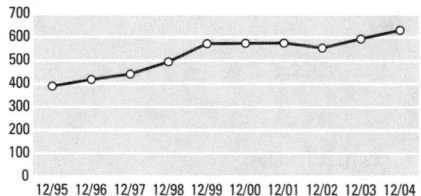

700	
600	
500	
400	
300	
200	
100	
0	

12/95 12/96 12/97 12/98 12/99 12/00 12/01 12/02 12/03 12/04

Associated Wholesale Grocers

Associated Wholesale Grocers (AWG) knows its customers can't live by bread and milk alone. One of the largest US retailer-owned cooperatives, AWG supplies more than 1,300 member-stores in 21 states with grocery merchandise, and such services as advertising, electronic data interchange, education and training, insurance, member services, printing, real estate, reclamation, retail systems support, store design and décor, and engineering. It offers the use of the banners ALPS (Always Low Priced Store), Apple Market, CashSaver, Country Mart, Price Chopper/Price Mart, Sunfresh, and Thriftway.

AWG supplies members with brand-name and private-label food (Always Save and Best Choice) and nonfood items; other services the co-op provides include property and casualty insurance, employee benefits packages, loan programs, and real estate lease assistance. It also helps its members appeal to specfic customer groups, offering more than 7,000 specialty food items.

AWG also operates about 30 of its own Falley's and Food 4 Less stores in Kansas and Missouri, as well as some 45 Homeland stores throughout Oklahoma.

HISTORY

About 20 Kansas City, Kansas-area grocers met in a local grocery in 1924 and organized the Associated Grocers Company to get better deals on purchases and advertising. They elected J. C. Harline president, and each chipped in a few hundred dollars to make their first purchases. It took a while to find a manufacturer who would sell directly to them; a local soap maker was finally convinced, and others gradually followed.

In 1926 the group was incorporated as Associated Wholesale Grocers (AWG). It outgrew two warehouses in four years, finally moving to a 16,000-sq.-ft. facility big enough to add new lines and more products. Membership doubled between 1930 and 1932 as grocers moved from ordering products a year ahead to the new wholesale concept, and members took seriously the slogan: "Buy, Sell, Buy Some More." They met every week to plan how to sell their products, and buyer and advertising manager Harry Small gave sales presentations and advertising ideas (his trade-in plan for old brooms sold more than two train-carloads of brooms in two weeks). Heavy newspaper advertising also paid off; AWG topped $1 million in sales in 1933.

The cooperative made its first acquisition in 1936, buying Progressive Grocers, a warehouse in Joplin, Missouri; the next year a second such warehouse named Associated Grocers was acquired in Springfield, Missouri. AWG continued building and expanding warehouses, and annual sales were at $11 million by 1951.

Louis Fox became CEO in 1956. Fox maximized year-end rebates for members, led several acquisitions, and formed a new subsidiary for financing stores and small shopping centers where AWG members had a presence (Supermarket Developers). Sales increased nearly fifteen fold to over $200 million in his first 15 years.

James Basha, who succeeded Fox when he retired in 1984, saw sales reach $2.4 billion by his own retirement in 1992.

Basha was followed by former COO Mike DeFabis, once a deputy mayor of Indianapolis. DeFabis orchestrated several acquisitions, including 41 Kansas City-area stores — most of which were quickly bought by members — from bankrupt Food Barn Stores in 1994 and 29 Oklahoma stores and a warehouse from Safeway spinoff Homeland Stores in 1995 (members bought all the stores).

AWG's nonfood subsidiary, Valu Merchandisers Co., was established in 1995; its new Kansas warehouse began shipping health and beauty aids and housewares the following year to help members battle big discounters. Members narrowly defeated a proposal in late 1996 to convert the cooperative into a public company. Proponents promptly petitioned for a second vote, which was defeated early the next year.

AWG veteran Doug Carolan succeeded DeFabis in 1998, becoming only the fifth CEO in the cooperative's history. The company bought five Falley's and 33 Food 4 Less stores in Kansas and Missouri from Fred Meyer in 1998 for $300 million. In a break with tradition, AWG began operating the stores rather than selling them to members.

In 2000, after a months-long labor dispute with the Teamsters was resolved, Carolan left AWG. The company's CFO, Gary Phillips, was named president and CEO later that year. In 2001 the company debuted a new format, ALPS (Always Low Price Stores) — small stores that carry a limited selection of grocery top-sellers. Also that year AWG's Kansas City division began distributing to more than 10 new stores that had formerly been served by Fleming, the #1 US wholesale food distributor.

In 2002 supermarket operator Homeland Stores, which operates stores in Oklahoma, emerged from bankruptcy as a fully owned subsidiary of AWG. AWG formed a new subsidiary, Associated Retail Grocers, to oversee Homeland and its Falley's chain.

As a result of the 2003 sale of Fleming Companies' wholesale distribution business, AWG picked up food distribution centers in Nebraska (two), Oklahoma (one), and Tennessee (two) and general-merchandise distribution centers in Tennessee and Kansas.

Introducing a "dollar" section in its stores in 2004 proved successful and AWG now offers more than 1,000 food and non-food items priced at $1.

EXECUTIVES

Chairman: J. Fred Ball
President and CEO: Gary A. Phillips
EVP and CFO: Robert C. Walker
EVP, Marketing: Jerry Garland
EVP, Operations Wholesale: Mike Rand
SVP, Grocery Products: Dennis Kinser
SVP, General Counsel, and Corporate Secretary: Frances Pellegrino Puhl
SVP, Perishables: Lucky Hicks
SVP, Real Estate and Store Engineering: Scott Wilmoski
Corporate VP, Human Resources: Frank Tricamo
VP, Corporate Sales: Bill Lancaster
VP, Corporate Sales Development: Steve Dillard
VP, Distribution: John Lane
VP, Finance: David Carl
VP, Sales Value Merchandisers Inc.: Joe Bush
VP, Store Engineering: John Crumley
VP and Corporate Controller: Gary Koch
Auditors: KPMG LLP

LOCATIONS

HQ: Associated Wholesale Grocers, Inc.
 5000 Kansas Ave., Kansas City, KS 66106
Phone: 913-288-1000   **Fax:** 913-288-1508
Web: www.awginc.com

Associated Wholesale Grocers serves grocers in Alabama, Arkansas, Georgia, Illinois, Indiana, Iowa, Kansas, Kentucky, Louisiana, Mississippi, Missouri, Nebraska, New Mexico, North Carolina, Oklahoma, Ohio, South Carolina, Tennessee, Texas, Virginia, and West Virginia. The cooperative has seven distribution centers in Kansas, Mississippi, Missouri, Oklahoma, and Tennessee.

PRODUCTS/OPERATIONS

Selected Operations/Subsidiaries
Associated Retail Grocers
Benchmark Insurance Company
Valu Merchandisers Inc. (health and beauty supplies, general merchandise, and pharmacy products)

Selected Private-Label Brands
Always Save
Best Choice

Selected Retail Store Concepts
ALPS
Apple Market
CashSaver
Country Mart
Price Chopper
Price Mart
Sun Fresh
Thriftway

Selected Services
Advertising
Category management
Employee training
Financial planning
In-store marketing
Insurance
Market research & analysis
Merchandising advice
Printing
Private-label products
Product positioning
Real estate lease assistance
Reclamation
Site acquisition
Store engineering & construction
Store financing
Store franchise formats
Store remodeling

COMPETITORS

Affiliated Foods
Albertson's
Alex Lee
C&S Wholesale
Delhaize America
Grocers Supply
GSC Enterprises
H.T. Hackney
Hy-Vee
IGA
Kroger
Nash Finch
Purity Wholesale Grocers
Roundy's
S. Abraham & Sons
Schnuck Markets
Shurfine International
Spartan Stores
SUPERVALU
Wakefern Food
Wal-Mart

HISTORICAL FINANCIALS
Company Type: Cooperative

Income Statement

	REVENUE ($ mil.)	NET INCOME ($ mil.)	NET PROFIT MARGIN	EMPLOYEES
12/04	4,570	—	—	—
12/03	3,721	—	—	6,171
12/02	3,139	—	—	5,727
12/01	3,097	—	—	3,300
12/00	3,267	—	—	3,300
12/99	3,370	—	—	3,300
12/98	3,180	—	—	3,100
12/97	3,129	—	—	3,000
12/96	3,096	—	—	2,797
12/95	2,970	—	—	—
Annual Growth	**4.9%**	**—**	**—**	**12.0%**

FYE: Last Saturday in December

Revenue History

(chart: Revenue from 12/95 to 12/04, $ mil., range 0–5,000)

Astaris

Astaris is phosphorific! A 50-50 joint venture between FMC and Solutia, Astaris produces phosphorus chemicals, phosphoric acid, and phosphate salts. The chemicals are used in foods, cleaners, water treatment, and pharmaceuticals. Astaris was formed in 2000. Industrywide overcapacity led the company to undergo a restructuring in late 2003, which included the closing of four facilities and ramping down of various others. The company operates four manufacturing facilities and maintains another four sourcing facilities in the US and one of each in Brazil. In 2005 the parent companies reached an agreement to sell Astaris to Israel Chemicals Limited for $255 million.

Solutia has been in bankruptcy since December 2003 and has been looking to lighten its load a bit. ICL, on the other hand, is wanting to expand its international business. It will add Astaris to its ICL Performance Products segment.

EXECUTIVES

President and CEO: Paul L. Howes, age 46
VP and CFO: Paul M. Schlessman, age 45
VP, Operations and Technology: James J. Kaiman
VP, Legal, Human Resources Services, and Secretary: Robert Ashton
VP, Sales and Marketing: Jim Moffatt
South America Business Director: Flavio Pinho Filho
Director, Europe: Luigi Logato
Food Business Director: Paul Gillstrom
Technical and Phosphoric Acid Business Director: Angela Schewe
Director, Marketing Technical Services: Nancy Stachiw
Fire Safety Business Director: Edward Goldberg
Human Resources: Michael (Mike) Bork

LOCATIONS

HQ: Astaris LLC
 622 Emerson Rd., St. Louis, MO 63141
Phone: 314-983-7500   **Fax:** 314-983-7638
Web: www.astaris.com

Astaris maintains operations in California, Florida, Idaho, Illinois, Kansas, Michigan, Missouri, New Jersey, West Virginia, and Wyoming in the US, as well as in Brazil.

PRODUCTS/OPERATIONS

Selected Products
Food grade products
 Adipic acid
 Diammonium phosphate
 Dipotassium phosphate
 Monoammonium phosphate anhydrous
 Monocalcium phosphate
 Phosphoric acid
Pharmaceutical grade products
 Dicalcium phosphate anhydrous powder
 Dicalcium phosphate dihydrate
 Tricalcium phosphate
Technical grade products
 Dipotassium phosphate
 Disodium phosphate anhydrous
 Phosphoric acid
 Phosphorus pentasulfide

COMPETITORS

Ferro
Innophos
Mosaic Company
PotashCorp
Rasa

HISTORICAL FINANCIALS
Company Type: Joint venture

Income Statement

	REVENUE ($ mil.)	NET INCOME ($ mil.)	NET PROFIT MARGIN	EMPLOYEES
12/04*	350	—	—	570
12/02	446	—	—	600
12/01	486	—	—	—
Annual Growth	**(15.2%)**	**—**	**—**	**(5.0%)**

FYE: December 31

*Irregular reporting interval

Revenue History

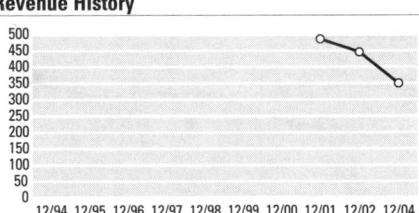

(chart: Revenue from 12/94 to 12/04, $ mil., range 0–500)

Atlanta Spirit

Atlanta Spirit is the wind beneath the wings of the Atlanta Hawks. The Hawks first shot baskets in 1946 as the Tri-Cities Blackhawks of the National Basketball League. The team joined the NBA in 1949, shortened its name, and roosted in Milwaukee and St. Louis (where it won its only title in 1958) before settling in Atlanta in 1968. The Hawks were playoff contenders in the 1980s and 1990s, thanks to players such as Dominique Wilkins (now a team executive), but never made the Finals. Turner Sports, a unit of television firm Turner Broadcasting, sold the Hawks, as well as hockey's Atlanta Thrashers, to private investment group Atlanta Spirit, led by entrepreneur Bruce Levenson, for $250 million.

The franchise is hanging its hopes for a high-flying future on a pair of Joshes — Josh Smith and Josh Childress, both selected to 2005's All-Rookie second team.

After much public feuding that included a lawsuit, an injunction, and power plays of all sorts over the signing of guard Joe Johnson, Steve Belkin agreed to sell his 30% stake in Atlanta Spirit to the other owners.

EXECUTIVES

President and CEO: Bernard J. (Bernie) Mullin
EVP and General Manager: Billy Knight, age 53
President, Philips Arena: Bob Williams
EVP and CFO: Bill Duffy, age 49
EVP Business Development: Lee Douglas, age 53
SVP Broadcast and Corporate Partnerships:
 Tracy White
SVP Philips Arena: Mike Oshust
SVP Communications: Tom Hughes
VP and General Counsel: T. Scott Wilkinson
VP Basketball: Dominique Wilkins, age 45
VP Hawks Public Relations: Arthur Triche
VP Operations, Philips Arena: Patrick Lane
VP Community Development: Tiffany Stone
VP Marketing, Advertising, and Branding: Jim Pfeifer
VP and Assistant General Manager, Basketball Operations: Chris Grant, age 33
Head Coach, Basketball Operations: Mike Woodson, age 47
Corporate Communications Publicist: Katie McLennan
Director Human Resources: Ginni Siler

LOCATIONS

HQ: Atlanta Spirit, L.L.C.
 Centennial Tower, 101 Marietta St. NW, Ste. 1900,
 Atlanta, GA 30303
Phone: 404-827-3800   **Fax:** 404-827-4229
Web: www.hawks.com

The Atlanta Hawks play at the 20,000-seat Philips Arena in Atlanta.

COMPETITORS

Charlotte Bobcats
Miami Heat
Orlando Magic
Washington Wizards

HISTORICAL FINANCIALS

Company Type: Private

Income Statement

FYE: December 31

	REVENUE ($ mil.)	NET INCOME ($ mil.)	NET PROFIT MARGIN	EMPLOYEES
12/04	83	—	—	—
12/03	78	—	—	—
12/02	79	—	—	—
12/01	76	—	—	—
12/00	50	—	—	—
12/99	50	—	—	—
12/98	29	—	—	—
12/97	47	—	—	75
12/96	41	—	—	75
12/95	41	—	—	—
Annual Growth	**8.2%**	**—**	**—**	**0.0%**

Revenue History

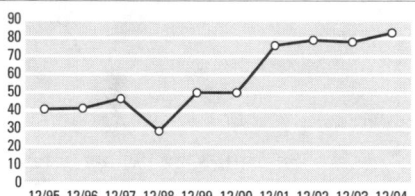

Atrium Hotels

Atrium Hotels has several rooms with a view. The company owns and operates more than 40 upscale hotels in about 20 states and manages about a dozen additional locations. Most of its properties operate under the Embassy Suites, Holiday Inn, and Marriott banners, and many are located near convention centers, universities, and corporate headquarters. Atrium also owns resorts in Branson, Missouri (Chateau on the Lake), and St. Augustine, Florida (World Golf Renaissance Resort). In 2005, the company's founder John Hammons sold the company to JQH Acquisitions, a group that includes investor Jonathan Eilian and GIC Real Estate, a subsidiary of Singapore-based Prime Properties.

Hotel management firm Barceló Crestline tried to acquire the company in October 2004 but withdrew the offer three months later. JQH Acquisition LLC offered $3 more a share than Barceló. JQH previously owned about 20% of the company. Hammons is expected to remain in a leadership role and retain a stake in the firm.

EXECUTIVES

Chairman and CEO: John Q. Hammons, age 86,
 $596,124 pay
President: Louis (Lou) Weckstein, age 68, $518,006 pay
EVP and CFO: Paul E. Muellner, age 48, $314,014 pay
SVP and Corporate Controller: Pat A. Shivers, age 53
SVP and General Counsel: Debra M. Shantz, age 41,
 $250,527 pay
SVP Architecture: Steven E. Minton, age 53
SVP Sales and Marketing: L. Scott Tarwater, age 56
VP Capital Planning and Asset Management:
 William T. George Jr., age 53
VP Human Resources: Kent S. Foster, age 45
Regional VP, Eastern Region: William A. Mead, age 51,
 $240,957 pay
Secretary and Director: Jacqueline A. Dowdy, age 61
Auditors: Deloitte & Touche LLP

LOCATIONS

HQ: Atrium Hotels, Inc.
 300 John Q. Hammons Pkwy., Ste. 900,
 Springfield, MO 65806
Phone: 417-864-4300   **Fax:** 417-873-3540
Web: www.jqhhotels.com

PRODUCTS/OPERATIONS

2004 Sales

	$ mil.	% of total
Rooms	266.8	62
Food & beverage	112.4	26
Meeting room rental & other	51.6	12
Total	**430.8**	**100**

Select Hotel Brands

Capitol Plaza
Chateau on the Lake
Embassy Suites
Homewood Suites
Holiday Inn
Marriott
Radisson
Sheraton
World Golf Renaissance Resort

COMPETITORS

Carlson Hotels
Choice Hotels
Doubletree Corporation
Hilton
Marriott
Ramada
Sheraton

HISTORICAL FINANCIALS

Company Type: Private

Income Statement

FYE: Friday nearest December 31

	REVENUE ($ mil.)	NET INCOME ($ mil.)	NET PROFIT MARGIN	EMPLOYEES
12/04	431	(1)	—	5,800
12/03	431	(7)	—	6,000
12/02	440	(3)	—	5,900
12/01	437	(3)	—	7,000
12/00	437	(1)	—	7,000
12/99	356	(1)	—	8,000
12/98	326	(1)	—	8,000
12/97	302	2	0.8%	8,000
12/96	269	5	1.9%	5,200
12/95	235	5	2.2%	8,000
Annual Growth	**7.0%**	**—**	**—**	**(3.5%)**

2004 Year-End Financials

Debt ratio: —   Current ratio: 1.22
Return on equity: —   Long-term debt ($ mil.): 740
Cash ($ mil.): 41

Net Income History

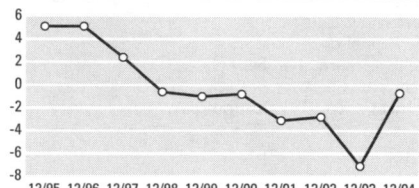

Attorneys' Title Insurance Fund

Sunshine State attorneys know where to go for title insurance services. Attorneys' Title Insurance Fund (The Fund) provides title insurance-related products to its 6,000 member attorneys throughout Florida and in several other states. The Fund is owned by a business trust created in 1947. Membership in the trust is limited to Florida attorneys, although The Fund serves non-member customers as well. Products include property information, property ownership verification, real estate closing software, and a variety of industry-related marketing tools.

EXECUTIVES

Chair: Thomas D. Wright
President: Charles J. Kovaleski
SVP Financial Services and Treasurer: Jimmy R. Jones
SVP Legal Services, General Counsel, and Corporate Secretary: R. Norwood Gay III
SVP Branch Operations: Sharon Priest
SVP Employee Services: B. Gwen Geier
SVP Information Services: Jeannie L. Calabrese
SVP Marketing Services: Michael R. Hammond
VP Examination Standards: Daniel L. Adams
VP Legal Services and Associate General Counsel: Louis B. Guttmann III
VP Special Legal Services: G. Robert Arnold
VP Special Projects Manager: Sue Ellen Foreman
VP Underwriting: Patricia P. Jones
Auditors: PricewaterhouseCoopers LLP

LOCATIONS

HQ: Attorneys' Title Insurance Fund, Inc.
6545 Corporate Centre Blvd., Orlando, FL 32822
Phone: 407-240-3863   **Fax:** 407-240-0750
Web: www.thefund.com

PRODUCTS/OPERATIONS

2004 Sales

	$ mil.	% of total
Insurance premiums	134.5	72
Title information revenue	38.4	20
Realized investment gains	5.8	3
Investment income	2.5	1
Other	6.9	4
Total	**188.1**	**100**

COMPETITORS

American Pioneer Title Insurance
Capital Title
First American
Investors Title
LandAmerica Financial Group
North American Title
Old Republic
Stewart Information Services
Ticor Title Co.
United General Title Insurance

HISTORICAL FINANCIALS

Company Type: Private

Income Statement

FYE: December 31

	ASSETS ($ mil.)	NET INCOME ($ mil.)	INCOME AS % OF ASSETS	EMPLOYEES
12/04	282	33	11.7%	844
12/03	243	26	10.8%	875
12/02	184	10	5.4%	900
12/01	158	(4)	—	—
Annual Growth	**21.3%**	**—**	**—**	**(3.2%)**

2004 Year-End Financials

Equity as % of assets: 47.7%   Long-term debt ($ mil.): 0
Return on assets: 12.5%   Sales ($ mil.): 188
Return on equity: 27.5%

Net Income History

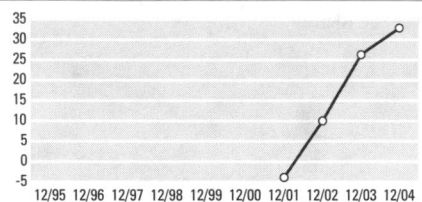

Auntie Anne's

You don't have to be twisted to enjoy one of Auntie Anne's Hand-Rolled Soft Pretzels. The company franchises more than 850 pretzel stores in malls, airports, train stations, and stadiums throughout 42 states and a dozen countries. Auntie Anne's offers a variety of pretzel flavors, including original, almond, whole wheat, and parmesan herb. Former CEO Anne Beiler and husband Jonas started the Gap Family Center to assist families in need after the death of their daughter. Anne Beiler started the company in 1988 to fund the center. She sold the company outright to its president, Sam Beiler (a cousin), for an undisclosed sum in early 2005 so she and her husband could concentrate on their charity work.

The company started as a pretzel stand which Anne Beiler set up at a farmer's market to fund the faith-based Gap Family Center. The center opened in 1992.

EXECUTIVES

President and CEO: Samuel R. (Sam) Beiler
COO, CFO, Secretary, and Treasurer: Grant S. Markley
EVP Training: Becky Stoltzfus
VP and Director of Human Resources and Administration: Gerard G. (Jere) Wiegand
VP Business Development: J. Richard Sauder
VP System Relations and Communications: Scot Crain
Director Advertising and Marketing Services: Judy Shaffer
Director Food Science and Technology: John Haggerty
Director International Development and General Counsel: John Roda
Director Information Systems: Chuck Blair
Director Purchasing: Dale Smucker
Director Accounting: Denise Fulmer
Public Relations Manager: Valerie Kinney
Supply Chain Manager: Christopher J. Martin
Auditors: Beard Miller Company LLP

LOCATIONS

HQ: Auntie Anne's, Inc.
160-A Rte. 41, Gap, PA 17527
Phone: 717-442-4766   **Fax:** 717-442-4139
Web: www.auntieannes.com

COMPETITORS

Cinnabon
Cinnaroll Bakeries
Dairy Queen
Dippin Dots
Dunkin
Freshëns

J & J Snack Foods
Krispy Kreme
Mrs. Fields
Starbucks
Triarc
Wetzel's Pretzels

HISTORICAL FINANCIALS

Company Type: Private

Income Statement

FYE: December 31

	REVENUE ($ mil.)	NET INCOME ($ mil.)	NET PROFIT MARGIN	EMPLOYEES
12/04	36	—	—	568
12/03	34	—	—	596
12/02	35	—	—	629
12/01	33	—	—	569
12/00	29	—	—	603
12/99	29	—	—	404
12/98	20	—	—	300
12/97	20	—	—	275
Annual Growth	**8.5%**	**—**	**—**	**10.9%**

Revenue History

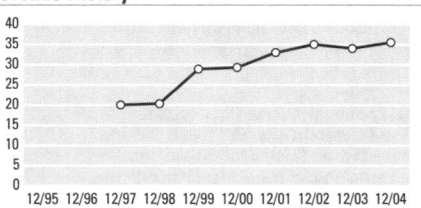

Autocam

Members of both the UAW and the AMA use Autocam's products. The company makes precision components for the automotive and medical device industries. Autocam makes parts used in automotive air bags, brake systems, electric motors, fuel systems, and power steering systems. The company's medical components include stents (used to keep human blood vessels open after balloon angioplasty), as well as ophthalmic and surgical devices. Autocam also offers machined components for power tools. Investment firm Aurora Capital Group sold Autocam in 2004 to investors including GS Capital, Roger Penske, and Autocam CEO John Kennedy.

Aurora Capital Group's investment in Autocam paid off handsomely. The investment firm paid $20 million for the company in 2000 and sold it for about $390 million.

Penske, a former race car driver and the CEO of Penske Corporation, is investing in Autocam through private equity fund Transportation Resource Partners, which focuses on companies engaged in transportation and related services.

Major Autocam customers include Tier 1 auto industry suppliers ZF Friedrichshafen, Delphi, TRW Automotive, and Robert Bosch, which together account for about 60% of Autocam's sales.

EXECUTIVES

Chairman, President, and CEO: John C. Kennedy, age 44
COO: John Buchan
CFO and Treasurer: Warren A. Veltman
Director, Human Resources: Jim Wojczynski

LOCATIONS

HQ: Autocam Corporation
    4436 Broadmoor SE, Kentwood, MI 49512
Phone: 616-698-0707   **Fax:** 616-698-6876
Web: www.autocam.com

Autocam has facilities in Brazil, China, France, and the US (California and Michigan).

2004 Sales

	$ mil.	% of total
Europe	184.2	53
North America	143.9	41
South America	22.2	6
Total	**350.3**	**100**

PRODUCTS/OPERATIONS

2004 Sales

	% of total
Power steering	34
Fuel injection	31
Electric motors	11
Braking	9
Air bags	5
Medical devices	3
Other	7
Total	**100**

Selected Automotive Products

Air bag systems
Braking system components
Electric motors
Fuel system components
Steering system components

Selected Medical Products

Ophthalmic devices
    Cataract
    Retinal
Stents
    Aortic
    Cardiovascular
    Peripheral
Surgical devices
    Orthopedic
    Urinary

COMPETITORS

Autoliv
Boston Scientific
Dana
DENSO
Hilite Industries
Key Safety Systems
Mark IV
Medtronic
Remy
Smiths Group
Visteon

HISTORICAL FINANCIALS

Company Type: Private

Income Statement

FYE: December 31

	REVENUE ($ mil.)	NET INCOME ($ mil.)	NET PROFIT MARGIN	EMPLOYEES
12/04	350	3	0.8%	2,578
12/03*	323	7	2.2%	2,300
6/02	250	—	—	1,800
6/01	250	—	—	1,800
6/00	200	—	—	1,800
6/99	180	—	—	1,773
6/98	90	—	—	953
6/97	62	—	—	373
6/96	58	—	—	255
6/95	54	—	—	240
Annual Growth	**23.0%**	**(61.4%)**	**—**	**30.2%**

*Fiscal year change

2004 Year-End Financials

Debt ratio: 166.8%
Return on equity: 1.6%
Cash ($ mil.): —
Current ratio: —
Long-term debt ($ mil.): 276

Net Income History

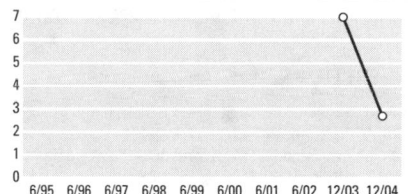

6/95 6/96 6/97 6/98 6/99 6/00 6/01 6/02 12/03 12/04

Auto-Owners Insurance

There's more to Auto-Owners Insurance Group than the name implies. In addition to auto coverage, the company provides personal products such as universal and whole life, homeowners, and long-term care insurance through its predictably named subsidiaries (including Home-Owners Insurance Company and Property-Owners Insurance Company). Auto-Owners Insurance Group also sells commercial auto, liability, and workers' compensation policies.

With almost 34,000 independent agents in more than 5,000 different locations, the company operates in some 25 states nationwide.

EXECUTIVES

CEO: Roger L. Looyenga
President: John W. Fisher
SVP Personnel: Dan Thelen
First VP and Treasurer: Ron Simon

LOCATIONS

HQ: Auto-Owners Insurance Group
    6101 Anacapri Blvd., Lansing, MI 48917
Phone: 517-323-1200   **Fax:** 517-323-8796
Web: www.auto-owners.com

Auto-Owners Insurance has full-service offices in Montgomery, Alabama; Mesa, Arizona; Westminster, Colorado; Lakeland, Florida; Duluth, Georgia; Peoria, Illinois; Marion, Indiana; West Des Moines, Iowa; Lexington, Kentucky; Lansing and Traverse City, Michigan; White Bear Lake, Minnesota; Charlotte, North Carolina; Fargo, North Dakota; Lima, Ohio; Columbia, South Carolina; Brentwood, Tennessee; and Appleton, Wisconsin; it also has claim offices in 68 cities.

PRODUCTS/OPERATIONS

Selected Subsidiaries

Auto-Owners Insurance Company
Auto-Owners Life Insurance Company
Home-Owners Insurance Company
Owners Insurance Company
Property-Owners Insurance Company
Southern-Owners Insurance Company

COMPETITORS

ACE Limited	Progressive Corporation
AIG	Prudential
Allstate	Safeco
Farmers Group	St. Paul Travelers
GEICO	State Farm
MetLife	

HISTORICAL FINANCIALS

Company Type: Private

Income Statement

FYE: December 31

	ASSETS ($ mil.)	NET INCOME ($ mil.)	INCOME AS % OF ASSETS	EMPLOYEES
12/04	10,835	191	1.8%	3,270

Avalon Pharmaceuticals

Avalon Pharmaceuticals doesn't mind if genes express themselves — but they should know that anything they express can and could be used against them if they lead to cancer. The development-stage biotech studies changes in gene expression using its proprietary AvalonRx analysis system to discover disease pathways and targets; it then bombards these targets with various compounds to try to change them in an effort to stop cancer's growth. Avalon Pharmaceuticals is initially focusing on blood cancers. The company's lead drug candidate AVN944 could help patients suffering from various forms of leukemia by preventing lymphoid and myeloid cells from overproducing.

The firm's AvalonRx technology may not only be useful for discovering new therapies but also for discovering new disease markers and diagnostic tools to help doctors better classify cancer patients and determine how they will respond to certain therapies.

Avalon Pharmaceuticals licensed its lead drug candidate from Vertex Pharmaceuticals. The company aims to have the candidate in phase I trials later in 2005.

In addition to developing cancer therapies and prognostic and diagnostic tools, Avalon Pharmaceuticals is teaming with other drugmakers to develop therapeutic antibodies. In collaboration with Medarex, the firm has discovered a protein associated with cancer. Another partner is Sanofi-Aventis; their collaboration contributed most of Avalon Pharmaceuticals' revenues in 2004.

Investors in the company include Belgian investment firm GIMV (which has a 12% stake in the company), Forward Ventures (8%), AIG Global Investment Group (8%), and MDS Capital (6%).

EXECUTIVES

Chairman: Alan G. Walton, age 69
President, CEO, and Director: Kenneth C. Carter, age 45, $304,500 pay
CFO: Gary Lessing, age 39, $215,250 pay
SVP, Operations, and General Counsel: Thomas G. David, age 58, $236,250 pay
VP, Business Development: James H. Meade, age 56
VP, Pharmaceutical Development: David K. Bol, age 39
VP, Research: Paul E. Young, age 41, $195,000 pay
Auditors: Ernst & Young LLP

LOCATIONS

HQ: Avalon Pharmaceuticals, Inc.
20358 Seneca Meadows Pkwy.,
Germantown, MD 20876
Phone: 301-556-9900   **Fax:** 301-556-9910
Web: www.avalonrx.com

COMPETITORS

Amgen
ARIAD Pharmaceuticals
ArQule
Array BioPharma
Cell Therapeutics
Merck

Millennium
Pharmaceuticals
Onyx Pharmaceuticals
OSI Pharmaceuticals
OXiGENE
Telik

HISTORICAL FINANCIALS

Company Type: Public

Income Statement

FYE: December 31

	REVENUE ($ mil.)	NET INCOME ($ mil.)	NET PROFIT MARGIN	EMPLOYEES
12/04	2	(14)	—	45
12/03	0	(17)	—	—
12/02	0	(16)	—	—
Annual Growth	—	—	—	—

2004 Year-End Financials

Debt ratio: (16.6%)
Return on equity: —
Cash ($ mil.): 2
Current ratio: 2.69
Long-term debt ($ mil.): 11

Net Income History

NASDAQ: AVRX

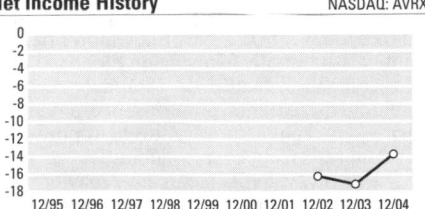

Avondale

Family-owned Avondale has fabric in its genes . . . er, jeans. The vertically integrated company makes apparel fabrics (cotton and cotton-blend piece-dyed fabrics, indigo-dyed denim), greige fabrics (undyed, unfinished cotton and cotton blends), specialty fabrics (such as coated materials for awnings, boat covers, and tents), and yarns. Leading apparel makers such as VF Corporation (maker of Lee, Chic, and Wrangler jeans, among others) buy from Avondale. VF accounts for about 10% of sales. The company operates about 17 manufacturing facilities in Alabama, Georgia, and North and South Carolina. Avondale was founded in Georgia in 1895 and is headed by G. Stephen Felker, great-grandson of the founder.

Avondale believes 2005 will be a financially difficult year because of a worldwide over-supply of textile and apparel products and the strength of the US dollar compared to the Chinese yuan. The elimination of all textile import quotas under the World Trade Organization beginning in 2005 will add further uncertainties.

EXECUTIVES

Chairman and CEO: G. Stephen Felker, age 53, $800,016 pay (prior to title change)
Vice Chairman and CFO, Avondale and Avondale Mills: Jack R. Altherr Jr., age 55, $775,008 pay
President and COO: Keith M. Hull, age 52, $388,032 pay (prior to promotion)
VP, Avondale Mills; President, Manufacturing Operations: T. Wayne Spraggins, age 67, $371,016 pay
VP, Secretary, and Controller, Avondale Mills and Avondale: M. Delen Boyd, age 48
VP, Human Resources, Avondale Mills: Sharon L. Rodgers, age 48, $167,088 pay
Auditors: Dixon Hughes PLLC

LOCATIONS

HQ: Avondale Incorporated
506 S. Broad St., Monroe, GA 30655
Phone: 770-267-2226   **Fax:** 770-267-5196
Web: www.avondalemills.com

Avondale operates about 17 manufacturing facilities in Alabama, Georgia, North Carolina, and South Carolina.

2004 Sales

	$ mil.	% of total
US	475.4	84
Other countries	89.4	16
Total	**564.8**	**100**

PRODUCTS/OPERATIONS

2004 Sales

	$ mil.	% of total
Apparel fabric	420.3	64
Yarns	178.6	27
Other fabric	59.8	9
Adjustments	(93.9)	—
Total	**564.8**	**100**

COMPETITORS

Burlington Industries
Concord Fabrics
Cone Denim
Galey & Lord Swift Denim
Greenwood Mills
Guilford Mills

Johnston Textiles
Milliken
Parkdale Mills
R. B. Pamplin
Springs Industries

HISTORICAL FINANCIALS

Company Type: Private

Income Statement

FYE: Last Friday in August

	REVENUE ($ mil.)	NET INCOME ($ mil.)	NET PROFIT MARGIN	EMPLOYEES
8/04	565	(6)	—	4,300
8/03	591	(8)	—	5,000
8/02	660	(0)	—	5,700
8/01	773	1	0.2%	5,800
8/00	837	33	3.9%	6,600
8/99	881	10	1.1%	6,800
8/98	1,056	34	3.2%	7,000
8/97	1,050	23	2.2%	7,500
8/96	706	14	1.9%	—
8/95	539	21	3.9%	—
Annual Growth	0.5%	—	—	(7.6%)

2004 Year-End Financials

Debt ratio: 131.4%
Return on equity: —
Cash ($ mil.): 5
Current ratio: 2.69
Long-term debt ($ mil.): 141

Net Income History

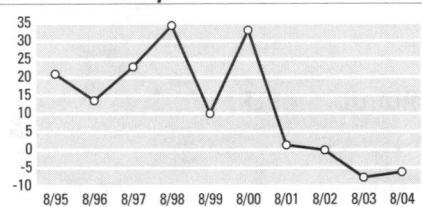

Bad Boy Worldwide Entertainment

From music to fashion to food, Bad Boy Worldwide Entertainment Group is always selling attitude and image. The company oversees a variety of business interests engaged in by its founder, owner, and CEO Sean "Diddy" Combs, a music impresario, fashion designer, and now business mogul. Combs' core business is Bad Boy Records, founded in 1994 with Craig Mack and the late Notorious B.I.G., which produces such artists as Eightball & MJG, Mario Winans, and Mase. Combs also markets branded clothing through Sean John Clothing and operates two upscale restaurants called Justin's in New York City and Atlanta. Bad Boy also offers advertising and marketing services through its Blue Flame Marketing unit.

Bad Boy Records was originally a joint venture between Combs and Arista Records, an imprint of Sony Music (now Sony BMG). Arista, however, dropped the label in 2002 due to lagging sales. Combs considered selling the business but instead inked a three-year distribution deal with Universal Records (a unit of Universal Music Group) in 2003. Bad Boy Records switched alliances again two years later, joining into a partnership with Warner Music Group (WMG) to distribute albums through its Atlantic Records unit. The $30 million distribution deal also gives WMG a 50% stake in the record company.

In addition to producing records, Bad Boy has a co-publishing agreement with EMI Music Publishing through Janice Combs Music Publishing, and it manages young producers through Janice Combs Management. (Both units are named after Combs' mother.) In 2005 the company joined with MTV Networks and MTV Films to produce a series of television and movie projects.

Diddy (who has also gone by the monikers Puffy, Puff Daddy, and most recently P. Diddy) opened his first Justin's restaurant in Manhattan in 1997 and expanded with a second location in Atlanta in 1999. (Bad Boy is looking to franchise the concept.) Sean John was started in 1998, garnering distribution through such retailers as Bloomingdale's, Macy's, and Fred Segal.

EXECUTIVES

Chairman and CEO, Bad Boy Worldwide Entertainment Group and Sean John Clothing; CEO, Blue Flame Marketing + Advertising: Sean (Diddy) Combs, age 35
CFO: Derek Ferguson
Chief Marketing Officer; President, Blue Flame Marketing + Advertising: Jameel Spencer, age 36
EVP and COO, Sean John Clothing: Todd Kahn
VP A&R, Bad Boy Records: Harve Pierre
VP Marketing, Bad Boy Records: Tracey Waples
VP Promotions, Bad Boy Records: Mel Smith
General Manager, Bad Boy Records: Lewis Tucker

LOCATIONS

HQ: Bad Boy Worldwide Entertainment Group
1440 Broadway, 16th Fl., New York, NY 10018
Phone: 212-381-1540   **Fax:** 212-381-1599
Web: www.badboyonline.com

PRODUCTS/OPERATIONS

Selected Operations

Blue Flame Marketing + Advertising
Justin's (restaurant)
Music
  Bad Boy Records
  Daddy's House Studios
  Janice Combs Management
  Janice Combs Music Publishing
Sean John Clothing

COMPETITORS

Armani
Capitol Records
Columbia Records
Comet Intercontinental
Epic Records
FUBU
Hugo Boss
Interscope Geffen A&M
Island Def Jam
Karl Kani Infinity
Motown Records
Phat
Rush Communications
Tha Row
Tommy Boy
TVT Records
Zomba

HISTORICAL FINANCIALS

Company Type: Private

Income Statement

	ESTIMATED REVENUE ($ mil.)	NET INCOME ($ mil.)	NET PROFIT MARGIN	EMPLOYEES
12/04	300	—	—	600
12/03	300	—	—	400
12/02	500	—	—	600
12/01	300	—	—	600
12/00	300	—	—	—
12/99	200	—	—	—
12/98	150	—	—	—
12/97	122	—	—	—
Annual Growth	**13.7%**	—	—	**0.0%**

FYE: December 31

Revenue History

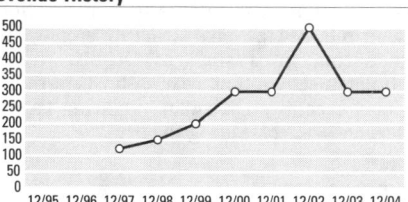

Badger State Ethanol

Badger State Ethanol hopes to badger gasoline consumers into using its ethanol. The company manufactures fuel-grade ethanol (a performance-enhancing gasoline additive derived from processing corn into ethyl alcohol) at the rate of approximately 49 million gallons per year at its ethanol plant in Monroe, Wisconsin. Badger State Ethanol also sells distillers grains (an animal feed supplement) and carbon dioxide, two by-products of the ethanol production process. Another source of income is state and federal incentive payments designed to foster alternative fuel research. The company was formed in 2000 and opened its ethanol plant in 2002.

EXECUTIVES

Chairman and CEO: John L. Malchine, age 66, $9,000 pay
President and General Manager: Gary L. Kramer, age 55, $62,154 pay
Secretary: David Kolsrud
Treasurer: Donald (Don) Endres
Controller: James (Jim) Leitzinger, $28,750 pay
Commodity Manager: Erik Huschitt
Sales and Marketing: George Drewry
Auditors: Grant Thornton LLP

LOCATIONS

HQ: Badger State Ethanol, LLC
820 W. 17th St., Monroe, WI 53566
Phone: 608-329-3900   **Fax:** 608-329-3866
Web: www.badgerstateethanol.com

PRODUCTS/OPERATIONS

2004 Sales

	% of total
Ethanol	78
Distillers grains	17
Corn	2
Ethanol supports	2
Carbon dioxide	1
Total	**100**

COMPETITORS

Abengoa Bioenergy	Lake Area Corn Processors
ADM	Little Sioux
Cargill	Corn Processors
Iogen	Northern Growers
Iroquois Bio-Energy	United Wisconsin

HISTORICAL FINANCIALS

Company Type: Private

Income Statement

	REVENUE ($ mil.)	NET INCOME ($ mil.)	NET PROFIT MARGIN	EMPLOYEES
12/04	92	12	13.5%	36
12/03	74	12	16.1%	34
12/02	10	(2)	—	34
Annual Growth	**202.0%**	—	—	**2.9%**

FYE: December 31

2004 Year-End Financials

Debt ratio: 51.8%
Return on equity: 40.9%
Cash ($ mil.): 4
Current ratio: 1.73
Long-term debt ($ mil.): 18

Net Income History

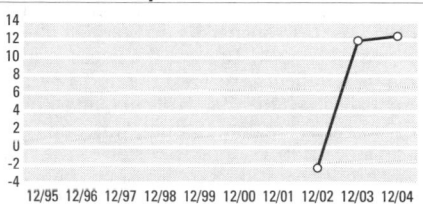

Baker & McKenzie

Baker & McKenzie knows that size has its advantages (and disadvantages). The firm is one of the world's largest law practices with more than 3,000 lawyers and nearly 70 offices in almost 40 countries. It offers expertise in such areas as intellectual property law, antitrust law, international trade, mergers and acquisitions, and tax law. Although Baker & McKenzie's size helps attract attorneys as well as clients, the firm also has had to fight the image that it is focused more on franchising than quality legal work. Russell Baker and John McKenzie founded the firm in 1949 with a focus on building an international practice.

The firm is known for the global scale of its practice, with some 80% of Baker & McKenzie attorneys practicing outside the US. However, it is beginning to face new competition on the global scene from firms such as Clifford Chance (which merged with two other practices in 2000 to create a network larger than Baker's). Its global operations have also increased the firm's risk to liability, leading Baker & McKenzie to reorganize itself as a Swiss Verein in 2004. Under the new structure, which is used by accounting firms such as Deloitte Touche Tohmatsu, its member firms operate as separate entities, protecting the parent firm from liability issues. Baker is the first international law firm to organize itself under the Verein structure.

In 2004 John Conroy was selected to replace Christine Lagarde as executive chairman. Elected in 1999, Lagarde was not only one of the first women to lead a major law firm but also one of the youngest partners to reach that high office.

The half-century-old firm has handled the legal affairs of such heavy-duty clients as Chase Manhattan (now J.P. Morgan Chase), Honeywell, and Ingersoll-Rand.

HISTORY

Russell Baker traveled from his native New Mexico to Chicago on a railroad freight car to attend law school. Upon graduation in 1925 he started practicing law with his classmate Dana Simpson under the name Simpson & Baker. Inspired by Chicago's role as a manufacturing and agricultural center for the world and influenced by the international focus of his alma mater, the University of Chicago, Baker dreamed of creating an international law practice. He began developing an expertise in international law, and in 1934 Abbott Laboratories retained him to handle its worldwide legal affairs. Baker was on his way to fulfilling his dream.

Baker joined forces with Chicago litigator John McKenzie in 1949, forming Baker & McKenzie. In 1955 the firm opened its first foreign office in Caracas, Venezuela, to meet the needs of its expanding US client base. Over the next 10 years it branched out into Asia, Australia, and Europe, with offices in London, Manila, Paris, and Tokyo. Baker's death in 1979 neither slowed the firm's growth nor changed its international character. The next year it expanded into the Middle East and opened its 30th office in 1982 (Melbourne). To manage the sprawling law firm, Baker & McKenzie created the position of chairman of the executive committee in 1984.

In late 1991 the firm dropped the Church of Scientology as a client, losing an estimated $2 million in business. It was speculated that pressure from client Eli Lilly (maker of the drug Prozac, which Scientologists actively oppose) influenced the decision. In 1992 Baker & McKenzie was ordered to pay $1 million for wrongfully firing an employee who later died of AIDS. (The case became the basis for the 1993 film *Philadelphia*.) The firm fought the verdict but eventually settled for an undisclosed amount in 1995.

In 1994 Baker & McKenzie closed its Los Angeles office (the former MacDonald, Halsted & Laybourne; acquired 1988) amid considerable rancor. Also that year a former secretary at the firm received a $7.1 million judgment for sexual harassment by a partner. (A San Francisco Superior Court judge later reduced the award to $3.5 million.)

John Klotsche, a senior partner from the firm's Palo Alto, California, office was appointed chairman in 1995. The following year the firm began a major expansion into California's Silicon Valley as part of an initiative to serve technology companies around the world. It also expanded its Warsaw, Poland, office through a merger with the Warsaw office of Dickinson, Wright, Moon, Van Dusen & Freman.

In 1998 Baker & McKenzie formed a special unit in Singapore to deal with business generated by the financial troubles in Asia. The opening of offices in Taiwan and Azerbaijan in 1998 brought the firm's total number of offices to 59. Klotsche stepped down in 1999 as the firm celebrated its 50th anniversary; Christine Lagarde replaced him. In early 2001 Baker & McKenzie created a joint venture practice with Singapore-based associate firm Wong & Leow. Also that year it merged with Madrid-based Briones Alonso y Martin to create the largest independent law firm in Spain.

In 2004 the firm reorganized as a Swiss Verein to protect itself from potential liability issues faced by its growing international operations. Baker & McKenzie was the first international law firm to use the legal structure employed by accounting firms such as Deloitte Touche Tohmatsu. Later that year, John Conroy was elected executive chairman, replacing Lagarde after five years of leading the firm.

EXECUTIVES

Chairman of the Executive Committee: John Conroy
COO: Craig Courter
CFO: Robert S. Spencer, age 57
Chair, North American Intellectual Property Practice: John Flaim
CTO: Sue Hall
Director of Business Development: Rob Gijsen
Director of Professional Responsibility: William J. Linklater
Director of Knowledge Management: Jason Marty
Director of Marketing: David Tabolt
Regional IT Director, the Americas: Michael J. Flanders
Regional IT Director, Europe, Middle East and Central Asia: Brian McShea
Regional IT Director, Asia Pacific: Martin Telfer
Marketing Manager, North America: Heidi Bouldin
Marketing Manager, Latin America: Graciela Maronna
Marketing Director, Asia Pacific: Kevin Nudd
General Counsel: Edward J. Zulkey
Human Resources, Chicago: Eleonora Nikol
Chief Global Press Officer: Judith Green
Senior Public Relations Coordinator: Sam Gregg

LOCATIONS

HQ: Baker & McKenzie
130 E. Randolph Dr., Ste. 2500, Chicago, IL 60601
Phone: 312-861-8800   **Fax:** 312-861-8823
Web: www.bakernet.com

Baker & McKenzie has nearly 70 offices throughout Asia, Australia, Europe, Latin America, the Middle East, and North America.

PRODUCTS/OPERATIONS

Selected Practice Areas

Banking and finance
Corporate and securities
E-commerce
International commercial arbitration
International trade
Intellectual property, information technology, and communications
Labor and employment
Tax
US litigation

COMPETITORS

Clifford Chance
Jones Day
Kirkland & Ellis
Latham & Watkins
Mayer, Brown, Rowe & Maw
McDermott, Will

Shearman & Sterling
Sidley Austin Brown & Wood
Skadden, Arps
Sullivan & Cromwell
Weil, Gotshal
White & Case

HISTORICAL FINANCIALS

Company Type: Partnership

Income Statement				FYE: June 30
	REVENUE ($ mil.)	NET INCOME ($ mil.)	NET PROFIT MARGIN	EMPLOYEES
6/04	1,228	—	—	8,400
6/03	1,134	—	—	8,401
6/02	1,060	—	—	8,000
6/01	1,000	—	—	8,000
6/00	940	—	—	8,000
6/99	818	—	—	6,900
6/98	785	—	—	6,700
6/97	697	—	—	6,100
6/96	646	—	—	5,680
6/95	594	—	—	5,248
Annual Growth	8.4%	—	—	5.4%

Revenue History

Baker & Taylor

If you've strolled through a library recently, you likely saw a lot of Baker & Taylor (B&T) without knowing it. The #1 book supplier to libraries, B&T primarily serves two types of markets. Its primary business distributes books, calendars, music, and DVDs to about 8,000 school, public, and specialty libraries around the world. The firm's retail unit supplies storefront and Internet retailers, as well as independent booksellers, with some 4 million book titles and more than 135,000 video, DVD, and CD titles. On the Internet (which formerly operated as Informata.com), B&T offers B2B e-commerce fulfillment services. The Carlyle Group sold the company to investment firm Willis Stein & Partners in 2003.

B&T's library unit also offers acquisition and collection management support services to libraries through its YBP Library Services subsidiary. B&T's fulfillment customers include such companies as barnesandnoble.com and Amazon.com. The retail unit also handles the company's international operations.

B&T offers automatic shipping of books and books-on-tape by popular authors (mailed as soon as they are published), and its J.A. Majors Company subsidiary is a major supplier of medical books to the educational and professional health markets.

EXECUTIVES

Chairman, President, and CEO: Richard Willis
EVP and CFO: Robert E. Agres
EVP and COO: Marshall A. (Arnie) Wight
SVP and General Counsel: Bradley D. Murchison
SVP Entertainment Group: Frank Wolbert
SVP Human Resources: Claudette Hampton
SVP Merchandising: Jean Srnecz
SVP Operations: James Benjamin
SVP Retail and International Sales:
William (Bill) Preston
President, Baker & Taylor Institutional: George Coe
President and COO, YBP Library Services:
Gary M. Shirk

LOCATIONS

HQ: Baker & Taylor Corporation
2550 W. Tyvola Rd., Ste. 300, Charlotte, NC 28217
Phone: 704-998-3100   **Fax:** 704-998-3316
Web: www.btol.com

Baker & Taylor has operations in Georgia, Illinois, Nevada, New Hampshire, New Jersey, North Carolina, Pennsylvania, and Texas, and has sales offices in Australia and Japan.

PRODUCTS/OPERATIONS

Selected Products and Services

Accessories
Audiocassettes
Calendars
Cataloging database (B&T MARC)
CD-ROM and Internet database and ordering software
(Title Source II)
CDs
DVDs
Hardcover and paperback books
Library acquisition and collection management
services (YBP Library Services)
Medical books (J.A. Majors Company)
Spoken-word audiocassettes
Standing-order service (Compass)
Videos

COMPETITORS

Advanced Marketing
Alliance Entertainment
Chas. Levy
Dawson Holdings
East Texas Distributing
Educational Development
Follett
Handleman
Ingram Industries
Navarre
Rentrak

HISTORICAL FINANCIALS

Company Type: Subsidiary

Income Statement

FYE: Last Friday in June

	REVENUE ($ mil.)	NET INCOME ($ mil.)	NET PROFIT MARGIN	EMPLOYEES
6/04	1,300	—	—	2,700
6/03	1,203	—	—	2,850
6/02	1,122	—	—	2,750
6/01	1,000	—	—	2,500
6/00	1,130	—	—	2,700
6/99	1,021	—	—	2,500
6/98	883	—	—	—
6/97	829	—	—	—
6/96	751	—	—	—
6/95	784	—	—	—
Annual Growth	**5.8%**	**—**	**—**	**1.6%**

Revenue History

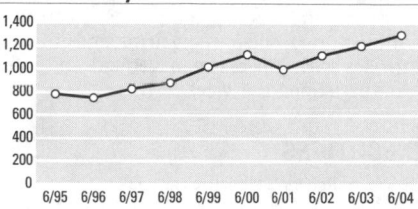

1,400	
1,200	
1,000	
800	
600	
400	
200	
0	6/95 6/96 6/97 6/98 6/99 6/00 6/01 6/02 6/03 6/04

Baker Botts

Baker Botts is a Lone Star legal legend. The law firm's history stretches back to 1840, when founding partner Peter Gray was admitted to the bar of the Republic of Texas. The firm became Baker & Botts after Walter Browne Botts and James Addison Baker, great-grandfather of former US secretary of state and current partner James A. Baker III, joined the partnership. Its nearly 700 lawyers specialize in practice areas ranging from banking to litigation to tax. It's no surprise that Texas-based Baker Botts has carved a niche in the energy industry, representing such clients as Halliburton, Centerpoint Energy, and ExxonMobil.

As its energy practice has evolved, the firm has also grown its global footprint, setting up offices in London, Moscow, Hong Kong, and Dubai.

EXECUTIVES

Managing Partner: Walter J. (Walt) Smith
CFO: Lydia Companion
Partner-In-Charge, Austin: Jim Cannon
Partner-In-Charge, Baku: Kevin B. Dent
Partner-In-Charge, Dallas: Jack L. Kinzie
Partner-In-Charge, Houston: Gregory V. (Greg) Nelson
Partner-In-Charge, London: Antony (Tony) Higginson
Partner-In-Charge, Moscow: Steven (Steve) Wardlaw
Partner-In-Charge, New York: Lee D. Charles
Partner-In-Charge, Riyadh: Stephen P. Matthews
Partner-In-Charge, Washington: James A. Baker IV
Chief Administrative Officer: Mark White
Director of Client Relations: Catherine Austin
Director of Human Resources: Sue Robinson Moss
Director of IT: Mark Hendrick
Public Relations: Mike Cinelli

LOCATIONS

HQ: Baker Botts L.L.P.
1 Shell Plaza, 910 Louisiana St., Houston, TX 77002
Phone: 713-229-1234   **Fax:** 713-229-1522
Web: www.bakerbotts.com

Baker Botts has US offices in Austin, Dallas, and Houston, Texas; New York City; and Washington, DC. The firm has international offices in Baku, Azerbaijan; Dubai, UAE; London; Moscow; and Riyadh, Saudi Arabia.

PRODUCTS/OPERATIONS

Selected Practice Areas

Antitrust
Appellate
Banking
Bankruptcy
Business and estate planning
Corporate
Energy and natural resources
Environmental
Government contracts
Intellectual property
Labor and employment
Litigation
Media and entertainment
Oil and gas
Project development and project finance
Real estate
Tax

COMPETITORS

Akin Gump
Andrews Kurth
Bracewell & Patterson
Fulbright & Jaworski

Jenkens & Gilchrist
Locke Liddell
Thompson and Knight
Vinson & Elkins

HISTORICAL FINANCIALS

Company Type: Partnership

Income Statement

FYE: December 31

	REVENUE ($ mil.)	NET INCOME ($ mil.)	NET PROFIT MARGIN	EMPLOYEES
12/04	420	—	—	1,601
12/03	394	—	—	1,582
12/02	365	—	—	—
12/01	334	—	—	—
12/00	312	—	—	1,500
12/99	260	—	—	1,500
12/98	230	—	—	1,500
12/97	206	—	—	1,460
12/96	178	—	—	—
12/95	171	—	—	—
Annual Growth	**10.5%**	**—**	**—**	**1.3%**

Revenue History

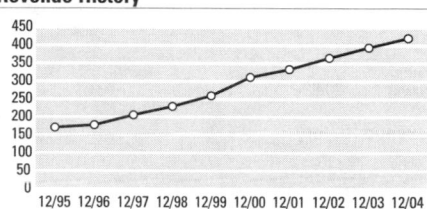

450	
400	
350	
300	
250	
200	
150	
100	
50	
0	12/95 12/96 12/97 12/98 12/99 12/00 12/01 12/02 12/03 12/04

Baker, Donelson

Baker, Donelson, Bearman, Caldwell & Berkowitz is a part of the Ol' South. Founded in 1888, the law firm boasts more than 400 attorneys in its 12 US offices, many of which are in the Southeast; it also operates out of Washington, DC and has a representative office in Beijing. Baker, Donelson's practice areas include public policy, health care, securities, and intellectual property.

EXECUTIVES

Chairman and CEO: Ben C. Adams Jr.
CFO: Jim Hughes
Chief Marketing Officer: Laura Hine
Director Human Resources: Caroline Boswell
Director, Attorney Recruitment & Development:
Sue S. Hunter

LOCATIONS

HQ: Baker, Donelson, Bearman,
Caldwell & Berkowitz, PC
165 Madison Ave., Ste. 2000, Memphis, TN 38103
Phone: 901-526-2000   **Fax:** 901-577-2303
Web: www.bakerdonelson.com

PRODUCTS/OPERATIONS

Selected Practice Areas

Antitrust
Bankruptcy and creditors' rights
Business and technology
Business and transactions
Construction
Eminent domain
Employee benefits and executive compensation
Environmental, health and safety
Equipment leasing
Estate planning
Health law
Immigration
Intellectual property
Labor & employment
Litigation
Public policy
Transportation

COMPETITORS

Alston & Bird	Powell Goldstein
Carlton Fields	Troutman Sanders
Husch & Eppenberger	Womble Carlyle
Nelson Mullins Riley	
& Scarborough	

HISTORICAL FINANCIALS

Company Type: Partnership

Income Statement

FYE: January 31

	REVENUE ($ mil.)	NET INCOME ($ mil.)	NET PROFIT MARGIN	EMPLOYEES
1/05	139	—	—	—
1/04	116	—	—	—
1/03	87	—	—	—
Annual Growth	26.8%	—	—	—

Revenue History

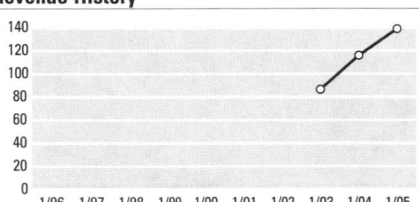

140
120
100
80
60
40
20
0

1/96 1/97 1/98 1/99 1/00 1/01 1/02 1/03 1/04 1/05

BancTec

BancTec keeps tabs on all sorts of financial transactions. The company offers electronic processing systems, software, and services for government agencies, banks, utility and telecommunications companies, and other organizations that do high-volume financial transactions. BancTec's systems and software capture and process checks, bills, and other documents; products include digital archiving systems, workflow software, and scanners. BancTec's services include cost estimates and contingency planning, resource use, systems integration, and maintenance. Founded in 1972, BancTec is owned by investment firm Welsh, Carson, Anderson & Stowe, which took BancTec private in 1999.

In addition to its information capture and management business lines, BancTec offers more general IT services through its Computer & Network Services (CNS) division. CNS provides aerospace and defense companies, electronics manufacturers, outsourcing firms, and other enterprises with process management and infrastructure support services.

EXECUTIVES

Chairman: Robert A. Minicucci, age 52
President and CEO: J. Coley Clark, age 59, $128,077 pay
SVP and CFO: Jeffrey D. Cushman, age 43
SVP; General Manager, Computer and Network Services Division: Mark Spire
SVP, Global Products and Operations: Mark D. Fairchild
VP; General Manager, Sales: Chuck Corbin
SVP, European Operations Group: Michael D. Peplow
SVP, Human Resources and Chief Administrative Officer: Lin M. Held
VP, Software Development: Neil Snowdon
General Manager, Plexus Software Division: Jim Forkin
Corporate Controller: Cathy Hauslein
Auditors: KPMG LLP

LOCATIONS

HQ: BancTec, Inc.
2701 E. Grauwyler Rd., Irving, TX 75061
Phone: 972-579-6000   **Fax:** 972-579-6448
Web: www.banctec.com

2004 Sales

	$ mil.	% of total
US	234.9	65
UK	60.6	17
Other countries	65.2	18
Total	**360.7**	**100**

PRODUCTS/OPERATIONS

2004 Sales

	$ mil.	% of total
Computer & network services	127.1	35
International	123.7	34
US Solutions	109.9	31
Total	**360.7**	**100**

Selected Products

Check processing
    Check repair and preprocessing system (CheckMender)
    High-speed archiving system (OpenARCHIVE)
    Item processing transport (X-Series Transport, E-Series Transport)
Document management
    Document organization system (ImageFIRST Office)
    Electronic data management applications (eFIRST)
    Image processing and workflow tools (Plexus)
    Image quality assurance application (Image Sentry)
    Scanning (DocuScan and S-Series Scanner)
    Workflow automation (FloWare)
Payment processing
    Remittance processing suite (PayCourier)

COMPETITORS

BISYS
CheckFree
Documentum
EDS
Equifax
FileNet
First Data
Fiserv
IBM
Jack Henry
NCR
Top Image Systems
TSYS
Unisys

HISTORICAL FINANCIALS

Company Type: Private

Income Statement

FYE: December 31

	REVENUE ($ mil.)	NET INCOME ($ mil.)	NET PROFIT MARGIN	EMPLOYEES
12/04	361	(17)	—	3,000
12/03	379	18	4.7%	3,100
12/02	379	—	—	3,200
12/01	506	—	—	3,200
12/00	488	—	—	3,700
12/99	535	—	—	3,900
12/98	598	—	—	4,100
12/97	604	—	—	4,000
12/96	554	—	—	3,650
12/95	384	—	—	2,274
Annual Growth	(0.7%)	—	—	3.1%

2004 Year-End Financials

Debt ratio: —
Return on equity: —
Cash ($ mil.): 51
Current ratio: 1.10
Long-term debt ($ mil.): 198

Net Income History

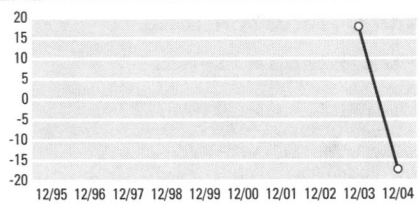

20
15
10
5
0
-5
-10
-15
-20

12/95 12/96 12/97 12/98 12/99 12/00 12/01 12/02 12/03 12/04

Barnes & Noble College Bookstores

Barnes & Noble College Bookstores is the scholastic sister company of Barnes & Noble (B&N), the US's largest bookseller. Started in 1873, the company operates more than 500 campus bookstores nationwide, selling textbooks, trade books, school supplies, collegiate clothing, and emblematic merchandise. Universities, medical and law schools, and community colleges hire Barnes & Noble College Bookstores to replace traditional campus cooperatives. (The schools get a cut of the sales.) Its College Marketing Network division offers on-campus marketing opportunities to businesses. B&N's chairman, Leonard Riggio, owns a controlling interest in the company.

Barnes & Noble College Bookstores often goes above and beyond when it takes over an old co-op location, adding Starbucks cafes, media centers where students can try out high tech gadgets like laptops and handheld devices from Dell and Apple, and school related decor like the eight-person rowing scull suspended from the ceiling at Georgia Tech's bookstore.

EXECUTIVES

Chairman; Chairman, Barnes & Noble, Inc.:
Leonard S. Riggio, age 64
President and COO: Max J. Roberts
EVP and General Merchandise Manager: Jade Roth
SVP and CFO: Jack A. Dill
SVP Marketing: Bill Maloney
VP, Book Merchandising: Joel Friedman
VP, General Merchasing and Manager:
Janine von Juergensonn
Auditors: BDO Seidman, LLP

LOCATIONS

HQ: Barnes & Noble College Bookstores, Inc.
120 Mountain View Blvd., Basking Ridge, NJ 07920
Phone: 908-991-2665   **Fax:** 212-780-1866
Web: www.bkstore.com

COMPETITORS

Amazon.com   Nebraska Book
Borders   Varsity Group
Ecampus.com   Wal-Mart
Follett

HISTORICAL FINANCIALS

Company Type: Private

Income Statement

FYE: April 30

	ESTIMATED REVENUE ($ mil.)	NET INCOME ($ mil.)	NET PROFIT MARGIN	EMPLOYEES
4/04	1,300	—	—	9,900
4/03	1,300	—	—	9,700
4/02	1,250	—	—	9,500
4/01	1,200	—	—	9,000
4/00	920	—	—	6,500
4/99	830	—	—	6,000
4/98	800	—	—	5,500
4/97	725	—	—	5,000
4/96	700	—	—	4,000
4/95	700	—	—	—
Annual Growth	7.1%	—	—	12.0%

Revenue History

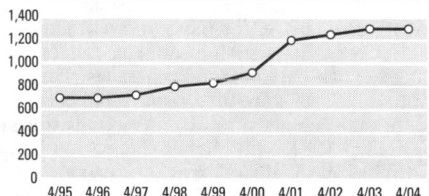

Barton Malow

Barton Malow scores by building end zones and home plates. The general contracting and construction management firm also makes points for its schools, hospitals, offices, and plants. It is a top automotive contractor. Its services range from planning to completion on projects in 37 states and Washington, DC. These include Atlanta's Phillips Arena, Boston's Shriners Hospital, and General Motors' Truck Product Center. Barton Malow Design provides architecture and engineering services, and the Barton Malow Rigging unit installs process

equipment and machinery. Chairman Ben Maibach III and his family own a majority stake in the company, which Carl Osborn Barton began as C.O. Barton Company in Detroit in 1924.

EXECUTIVES

Chairman, President, and CEO: Ben C. Maibach III
Vice Chairman: Mark A. Bahr
EVP, Chief Legal Officer, and Secretary:
Thomas (Tom) Porter
SVP and CFO: Lori R. Howlett
SVP Central Region: Lester (Les) Snyder III
SVP Health Facilities Group: Richard (Dick) Miller
SVP K12 Education, Historic Renovations:
Richard (Dick) Snider
SVP Sports Facilities: Bob Wyatt
VP and Treasurer: Edward R. (Ed) Jarchow
VP and General Counsel: Ronald J. Torbert
VP Energy: Bill Mallory
VP Health Facilities: Dave Imesch
VP Higher Education: Todd Ketola
VP Human Resources: Judith Willard
VP Sales and Marketing: Sheryl B. Maibach
President, Barton Malow Design: George L. Houhanisin
CIO: Phil Go
Public Relations Manager: Anne-Marie Poltorak
Auditors: Grant Thornton LLP

LOCATIONS

HQ: Barton Malow Company
26500 American Dr., Southfield, MI 48034
Phone: 248-436-5000   **Fax:** 248-436-5001
Web: www.bmco.com

Barton Malow has offices in Atlanta; Chantilly and Charlottesville, Virginia; Columbus, Ohio; Linthicum, Maryland (near Baltimore); Detroit, Oak Park, and Southfield, Michigan; and Phoenix.

PRODUCTS/OPERATIONS

Primary Services

Architecture/design
Concrete subcontracting
Construction management
Design/build
Facility audits
Facility services
General contracting
Interior design
Program management
Project planning
Rigging/millwright
Technology consulting

COMPETITORS

Alberici
BE&K
Clark Enterprises
Fluor
Gilbane
Hensel Phelps Construction
H.J. Russell
Hunt Construction
M. A. Mortenson
McCarthy Building
Skanska USA Building
Turner Corporation
Walbridge Aldinger
Walsh Group
Whiting-Turner
Zachry

HISTORICAL FINANCIALS

Company Type: Private

Income Statement

FYE: March 31

	REVENUE ($ mil.)	NET INCOME ($ mil.)	NET PROFIT MARGIN	EMPLOYEES
3/04	1,100	—	—	1,250
3/03	1,350	—	—	1,550
3/02	1,251	—	—	1,264
3/01	1,160	—	—	1,640
3/00	1,026	—	—	1,500
3/99	821	—	—	1,350
3/98	727	—	—	1,300
3/97	565	—	—	896
3/96	669	—	—	754
3/95	634	—	—	762
Annual Growth	6.3%	—	—	5.7%

Revenue History

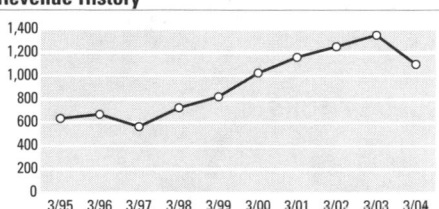

Bashas'

Bashas' has blossomed in the Arizona desert. Founded in 1932 and still owned by the Basha family, the food retailer has grown to nearly 150 stores located primarily in Arizona, as well as a few stores in California and New Mexico. Its holdings include Bashas' traditional supermarkets, AJ's Fine Foods (gourmet-style supermarkets), Bashas' Dine Markets, and Food City supermarkets (which cater to Hispanics in southern Arizona). Bashas' has opened more than 30 Natural Choice in-store departments that feature natural and organic items. It also operates a handful of supermarkets (including its New Mexico store) in the Navajo Nation. Bashas' offers online grocery shopping through its Groceries On The Go service.

The third-largest grocery retailer in Arizona, Bashas' trails rivals Fry's Food Stores (owned by The Kroger Co.) and Safeway, and is feeling the heat from Wal-Mart Stores, which is rapidly expanding in the state. Bashas' outspoken CEO Eddie Basha has likened the Wal-Mart juggernaut to an economic blitzkrieg. Wal-Mart has more than 50 locations in Arizona.

EXECUTIVES

Chairman and CEO: Edward N. (Eddie) Basha Jr., age 66
Vice Chairman and SVP Real Estate: Johnny Basha
President and COO: Mike Proulx, age 55
SVP Finance and CFO: James (Jim) Buhr, age 55
SVP Human Resources: Michael Gantt
SVP Legal and Financial Affairs: Edward N. Basha III
SVP Logistics: Mike Basha
SVP Marketing: Christie Frazier-Coleman
SVP Retail Operations: Ralph Woodward
SVP Sales and Merchandising: Mark Barnett
SVP Support Services: Ike Basha
SVP Warehouse and Distribution: Sonny Felix
VP Finance: Barbara Jefferson
VP Information Services: Jim Clendenen
VP Marketing: Dallas Bennewitz
Director Public Relations: Diana Medina

LOCATIONS

HQ: Bashas' Inc.
22402 S. Basha Rd., Chandler, AZ 85248
Phone: 480-895-9350   **Fax:** 480-895-5371
Web: www.bashas.com

COMPETITORS

Albertson's
Fry's Food
Safeway
Smart & Final
SUPERVALU
Trader Joe's
Wal-Mart
Whole Foods
Wild Oats Markets

HISTORICAL FINANCIALS

Company Type: Private

Income Statement

FYE: December 31

	ESTIMATED REVENUE ($ mil.)	NET INCOME ($ mil.)	NET PROFIT MARGIN	EMPLOYEES
12/03	1,800	—	—	13,200
12/02	1,600	—	—	12,500
12/01	1,359	—	—	10,500
12/00	1,200	—	—	8,800
12/99	1,210	—	—	8,000
12/98	1,000	—	—	7,600
12/97	870	—	—	7,600
12/96	800	—	—	6,600
12/95	675	—	—	5,600
12/94	650	—	—	5,000
Annual Growth	12.0%	—	—	11.4%

Revenue History

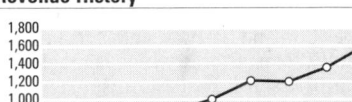

1,800
1,600
1,400
1,200
1,000
800
600
400
200
0
12/94 12/95 12/96 12/97 12/98 12/99 12/00 12/01 12/02 12/03

Basic Energy Services

Oil and gas producers turn to Basic Energy Services for the fundamentals. The company provides well site services with its fleet of well-servicing rigs (at more than 300, the third-largest in the US behind Key Energy Services and Nabors Industries), fluid service trucks, and related equipment. These services include acidizing, cementing, fluid handling, fracing, well construction, well maintenance, and workover. Basic Energy Services serves producers operating in Louisiana, New Mexico, Oklahoma, and Texas. It is a consolidator in the fragmented well services industry and has acquired more than 30 rivals since 1996. Investment firm DLJ Merchant Banking Partners III, L.P., controls the company.

Basic Energy Services has pursued a strategy of growth through acquisitions. In 2004 the company acquired underbalanced drilling services company Energy Air Drilling Service, and wireline firm AWS Wireline Services.

EXECUTIVES

Chairman: Steven A. Webster, age 53
President, CEO, and Director:
Kenneth V. (Ken) Huseman, age 53, $827,884 pay
EVP and Secretary: James J. (Jim) Carter, age 60, $368,846 pay (prior to title change)
VP, CFO, and Treasurer: Alan Krenek, age 50
VP, Business Development: Mark D. Rankin, age 51
VP, Equipment and Safety: Dub W. Harrison, age 47, $201,789 pay
VP, Human Resources: James E. Tyner, age 55, $112,735 pay
VP, Permian Basin: Charles W. (Charlie) Swift, age 56, $221,818 pay
Controller: David M. Dunn, age 60
Business Development Director: Charley D. Gregg
Safety Director: Lyn Sockwell
Human Resources Manager: Vicki Burdette
Credit/Collections: Judy McPeters
Auditors: KPMG LLP

LOCATIONS

HQ: Basic Energy Services, Inc.
400 W. Illinios, Ste. 800, Midland, TX 79701
Phone: 432-620-5500   **Fax:** 432-570-0437
Web: www.basicenergyservices.com

Basic Energy Services operates in Louisiana, New Mexico, Oklahoma, and Texas.

PRODUCTS/OPERATIONS

2004 Sales

	$ mil.	% of total
Well servicing	142.6	46
Fluid services	98.7	32
Well site construction services	40.9	13
Drilling & completion services	29.3	9
Total	311.5	100

COMPETITORS

BJ Services
Halliburton
Key Energy
Nabors Industries
Pride International
Schlumberger
Weatherford International

HISTORICAL FINANCIALS

Company Type: Private

Income Statement

FYE: December 31

	REVENUE ($ mil.)	NET INCOME ($ mil.)	NET PROFIT MARGIN	EMPLOYEES
12/04	312	13	4.1%	2,800
12/03	181	3	1.8%	—
12/02	109	(1)	—	—
12/01	100	6	6.0%	1,200
12/00	56	—	—	646
12/99	37	—	—	646
12/98	45	—	—	—
12/97	26	—	—	—
12/96	8	—	—	—
12/95	4	—	—	—
Annual Growth	60.5%	29.1%	—	34.1%

2004 Year-End Financials

Debt ratio: 140.3%   Current ratio: 1.98
Return on equity: 11.3%   Long-term debt ($ mil.): 171
Cash ($ mil.): 20

Net Income History

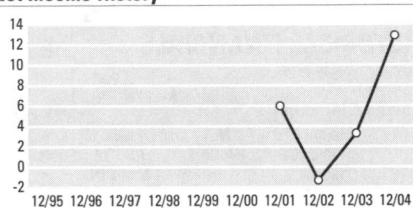

14
12
10
8
6
4
2
0
-2
12/95 12/96 12/97 12/98 12/99 12/00 12/01 12/02 12/03 12/04

Bass Pro Shops

Bass Pro Shops (BPS) knows how to reel in the shoppers. Each of its 25-plus Outdoor World stores (in 17 states) covers about 280,000 sq. ft. The cavernous outlets sell boats, campers, equipment, and apparel for most outdoor activities and offer features such as archery ranges, fish tanks, snack bars, and video arcades. The first Outdoor World store (in Missouri) has been one of the state's biggest tourist attractions since it opened in 1981. BPS catches shoppers at home with its seasonal and specialty catalogs and through its TV and radio programs. It owns Tracker Marine (boat manufacturing) and American Rod & Gun (sporting goods wholesale) and runs a resort in the Ozark Mountains. Founder John Morris owns BPS.

The company introduced its private label credit card in partnership with GE Consumer Finance in three markets in May 2005.

Bass Pro Shops is also an Internet retailer.

EXECUTIVES

Founder: John L. (Johnny) Morris
President and COO: James (Jim) Hagale
VP and CFO: Toni Miller
VP, Construction: Sean Easter
VP of Human Resources: Mike Roland
VP, Marketing: Stan Lippleman
Director of Corporate Public Relations:
Martin Mac Donald
Manager of Corporate Public Relations: Larry Whitely

LOCATIONS

HQ: Bass Pro Shops, Inc.
2500 E. Kearney, Springfield, MO 65898
Phone: 417-873-5000   **Fax:** 417-873-4672
Web: www.basspro.com

2004 Stores

	No.
US	
Florida	4
Georgia	2
Missouri	2
Tennessee	2
Texas	2
Illinois	1
Louisiana	1
Maryland	1
Michigan	1
Nevada	1
New York	1
North Carolina	1
Ohio	1
Oklahoma	1
Pennsylvania	1
South Carolina	1
Virginia	1
Canada	
Toronto	1
Total	**25**

PRODUCTS/OPERATIONS

Selected Merchandise Categories

Apparel
Boats
Camping and auto
Fishing
Fly fishing
Footwear
Gifts and home decor
Hunting
Marine and electronics
Saltwater fishing

Other Operations

American Rod & Gun (sporting goods wholesale)
Bass Pro Shops (sporting goods catalog)
Bass Pro Shops Outdoor World (magazine and radio and TV programs)
Big Cedar Lodge (resort)
Outdoor World (retail stores)
Tracker Marine (sport boat manufacturing)

COMPETITORS

Academy Sports & Outdoors	MarineMax
Cabela's	REI
Camping World	Sears
Cruise America	Sports Authority
Dick's Sporting Goods	Sportsman's Guide
Gander Mountain	Travis Boats & Motors
Hibbett Sporting Goods	Wal-Mart
Kmart	West Marine
	Winmark

HISTORICAL FINANCIALS

Company Type: Private

Income Statement

FYE: December 31

	ESTIMATED REVENUE ($ mil.)	NET INCOME ($ mil.)	NET PROFIT MARGIN	EMPLOYEES
12/03	1,600	—	—	10,700
12/02	1,400	—	—	11,400
12/01	1,100	—	—	8,800
12/00	990	—	—	8,200
12/99	950	—	—	7,900
12/98	311	—	—	
12/97	270	—	—	
Annual Growth	**34.5%**	**—**	**—**	**7.9%**

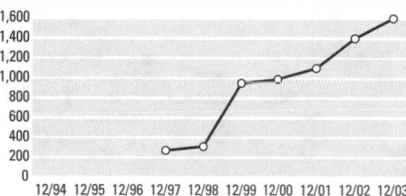

Revenue History

Battelle Memorial

When you use a copier, hit a golf ball, or listen to a CD, you're using technologies developed by Battelle Memorial Institute. The not-for-profit trust operates one of the world's largest research enterprises, with more than 16,000 scientists and engineers serving some 2,000 corporate and government customers in the US and Europe. Battelle operates three of its own research facilities and manages four other government-sponsored labs, including Brookhaven National Laboratory, Oak Ridge National Laboratory, and Pacific Northwest National Laboratory. The company was established in 1929 by the family of Gordon Battelle, an early leader in the steel industry.

While contract research and development remains the core activity of the company, Battelle is becoming more and more involved in managing laboratory operations for the government. In 2004 it was awarded a 10-year contract from the Department of Energy to establish a new national lab, Idaho National Laboratory, for nuclear energy research and development. Battelle will operate the lab through Battelle Energy Alliance, a partnership formed with BWX Technologies, Washington Group International, Electric Power Research Institute, and a consortium of universities including MIT, Ohio State, and the University of Idaho. Battelle is also in the running to take over management of Los Alamos National Laboratory (currently operated by the University of California).

Through its Battelle Ventures unit, the company also serves as a nesting ground for new businesses formed to commercialize discoveries and technologies Battelle owns or has rights to. In addition, the company invests in math and science education, both financially and through the volunteer efforts of its staff members.

Originally formed to promote metallurgy and related industries, the institute has diversified into research and development in other areas such as agriculture, energy, software, and medicine. Among other notable milestones, Battelle's research was instrumental in developing the photocopy machine, optical digital recording (used with compact discs), and bar codes.

HISTORY

Battelle Memorial Institute was founded with a $1.5 million trust willed by Gordon Battelle, who died in 1923. Battelle was a champion of research for the advancement of humankind, and before taking his father's place as president of several Ohio steel mills, he had funded a former university professor's successful work to extract useful chemicals from mine waste. Battelle's mother, upon her death in 1925, left the institute an additional $2.1 million. The institute opened in 1929.

The institute took on perhaps the most important project in its history in 1944 when it helped an electronics company's patent lawyer, Chester Carlson, find practical uses for his invention, called xerography. Eventually Battelle developed the first photocopy machine, and in 1955 it sold the patent rights for the machine to Haloid (now Xerox) in exchange for royalties.

During WWII Battelle worked on uranium refining for the Manhattan Project, and in the early 1950s it established the world's first private nuclear research facility. The company also set up operations in Germany and Switzerland.

The tax man came knocking in 1961, questioning the tax-free status of some of Battelle's activities. The organization eventually had to pay $47 million. In 1965 Battelle developed a coin with a copper core and a copper-and-nickel-alloy cladding for the US Treasury.

As the result of a ruling that reinterpreted a clause in Gordon Battelle's will, in 1975 the institute gave $80 million to philanthropic enterprises. This ruling, coupled with the taxes that the organization was still unaccustomed to paying, forced Battelle to reexamine its strategy.

Battelle co-developed the Universal Product Code (the bar code symbol found today on nearly all consumer goods packaging) in the 1970s. The institute also landed a lucrative contract from the US Department of Energy (DOE) to manage its commercial nuclear waste isolation program.

In 1987 Battelle chose Douglas Olesen — a 20-year veteran of the institute — to replace retiring CEO Ronald Paul. An Ohio court in 1997 approved a seven-page agreement with the institute outlining the key principles that must be followed according to Gordon Battelle's will. This agreement replaced the 1975 decree and ended more than 20 years of scrutiny by the state attorney general's office.

In 1998 the DOE contracted Brookhaven Science Associates — a partnership between the State University of New York and Battelle — to operate Brookhaven National Laboratory. That year a Battelle contract to dispose of Vietnam War-era napalm drew national attention when subcontractor Pollution Control Industries backed out of the project, citing safety concerns. Under Battelle's direction, Houston-based GNI Group took the 3.4 million gallons of napalm off the US Navy's hands.

Battelle and the University of Tennessee in 1999 won a five-year contract to operate the US government's Oak Ridge National Laboratory. That year the institute made several breakthroughs in cancer research, including FDA approval to test an inhalation delivery system for treating lung cancer.

In 2000 the company spun off OmniViz (data mining software) and Battelle Pulmonary Therapeutics (pulmonary and drug delivery technology) as wholly owned subsidiaries. In 2001 Battelle chose former Kodak EVP and chief technology officer Carl Kohrt to replace Olesen.

Battelle and several partners, including BWX Technologies, Washington Group International, and Electric Power Research Institute, won a 10-year contract to operate Idaho National Laboratory, a research facility established to focus on nuclear energy research and related technologies.

EXECUTIVES

Chairman: John B. McCoy Jr.
First Vice Chairman: John J. Hopfield
Second Vice Chairman: W. George Meredith
President and CEO: Carl F. Kohrt, age 61
EVP and CFO: Martin Inglis
EVP Laboratory Operations: William J. Madia
SVP and CTO, Core Technology Development:
  Richard C. Adams
SVP Administration, General Counsel, and Secretary:
  Jerome R. Bahlmann
SVP Organizational Development: Robert W. Smith Jr.
**SVP; General Manager, Army/Marines/Office of
  Secretary of Defense Market Sector:** Stephen E. Kelly
**SVP; General Manager, Chemical Products Market
  Sector:** Benjamin G. Maiden
VP: Bernhard Metzger
VP External Business Relations:
  Richard D. (Rich) Rosen
VP Strategic Planning and Business Development:
  Dennis McGinn, age 57
VP Strategy Development: Pete Hennessey
VP Technology and Product Development Support:
  James Sonnett
Director of Information Management: Lynn Davison
Media Relations Manager: Mark Berry, age 36

LOCATIONS

HQ: Battelle Memorial Institute
  505 King Ave., Columbus, OH 43201
Phone: 614-424-6424   **Fax:** 614-424-5263
Web: www.battelle.org

Battelle Memorial Institute has about 40 offices and
research facilities in the US and Europe.

PRODUCTS/OPERATIONS

Selected Laboratories and Research Facilities
Battelle Eastern Science and Technology Center
  (Aberdeen, MD)
Brookhaven National Laboratory (Upton, NY)
Human Factors Transportation Center (Seattle)
Marine Science Laboratory (Sequim, WA)
National Energy Renewable Laboratory (Golden, CO)
Oak Ridge National Laboratory (Oak Ridge, TN)
Ocean Sciences Laboratory (Duxbury, MA)
Pacific Northwest National Laboratory (Richland, WA)

Selected Inventions
Automobile cruise control (1960s)
Exploded-tip paintbrush (nylon brush for
  Wooster Brush Co., 1950)
Golf ball coatings (1965)
Heat Seat (microwaveable heated
  stadium cushion, 1990s)
Holograms (work began in the 1970s)
Insulin injection pen (for Eli Lilly, 1990s)
Oil spill outline monitor (1992)
PCB-cleaning chemical process (1992)
Photocopy machine (with Haloid, 1940s)
Plastic breakdown process (1990s)
"Sandwich" coins (copper/copper and nickel alloy
  cladding design for US Treasury, 1965)
SenSonic toothbrush (with Teledyne/WaterPik, 1990s)
Smart cards (cards embedded with tiny computer chips
  that store information, 1980s)
SnoPake (correction fluid, 1955)
Universal Product Code (co-creator; bar code, 1970s)

COMPETITORS

Aerospace Corporation	Raytheon
Charles Stark Draper	Research Triangle Institute
Laboratory	SAIC
General Dynamics	Southwest Research
Lockheed Martin	Institute
MITRE	SRI International
Northrop Grumman	Universities Research
QinetiQ	Association
RAND	

HISTORICAL FINANCIALS

Company Type: Not-for-profit

Income Statement

FYE: September 30

	REVENUE ($ mil.)	NET INCOME ($ mil.)	NET PROFIT MARGIN	EMPLOYEES
9/04	1,440	—	—	9,034
9/03	1,350	—	—	8,900
9/02	1,176	—	—	8,700
9/01	1,029	—	—	7,607
9/00	950	—	—	7,100
9/99	901	—	—	7,060
9/98	710	—	—	7,250
9/97	946	—	—	7,060
9/96	945	—	—	7,163
9/95	974	—	—	7,500
Annual Growth	**4.4%**	**—**		**2.1%**

Revenue History

1,600	
1,400	
1,200	
1,000	
800	
600	
400	
200	
0	
9/95 9/96 9/97 9/98 9/99 9/00 9/01 9/02 9/03 9/04	

BE&K

A busy bee in the power plant industry, BE&K
is a top US engineering and construction contractor. Through a network of subsidiaries,
BE&K provides engineering, procurement, and
construction and maintenance services worldwide for power plants and other industrial
process facilities, including the cement, chemical, petrochemical, pharmaceutical, and pulp
and paper industries. It also serves the telecommunications, manufacturing, environmental,
and commercial sectors. Founded in 1972 by
partners Peter Bolvig, William Edmonds, and
Ted Kennedy, the company initially worked primarily for the pulp and paper industry. Overseas
operations began in Poland in 1984 through a
strategic relationship with International Paper.

EXECUTIVES

Chairman and CEO: T. Michael (Mike) Goodrich, age 59
**EVP and COO; President, BE&K Construction
  Company:** John W. Redmon
EVP and CFO: Clyde M. Smith
SVP Human Resources: Kimberly S. Patterson
VP Sales and Marketing: Tom Freeland
VP; General Manager, BE&K Houston: Gerry L. Turner
VP; General Manager, BE&K Raleigh: Paul Turner
VP; Manager, Delaware Operations: Robert Pinson
VP Industrial Services: Susan M. (Sue) Steele
VP Construction Services: Bryson Edmonds
VP, AllStates Technical Services: John Sanborn
VP, BE&K Construction Co.: Randy Evans
VP, BE&K Hydrocarbons Business Units:
  Stephen H. (Steve) Grote
VP Power: Don Beebe
Controller: Joe McCarty
Director Corporate Communications: Susan Wasley
General Counsel: Ed Cassady
Manager Human Resources: Bruce May
Auditors: Ernst & Young LLP

LOCATIONS

HQ: BE&K, Inc.
  2000 International Park Dr., Birmingham, AL 35243
Phone: 205-972-6000   **Fax:** 205-972-6651
Web: www.bek.com

BE&K and its subsidiaries operate from offices in the
US in Alabama, California, Colorado, Delaware, Florida,
Georgia, Maine, Nevada, New York, North Carolina,
Pennsylvania, South Carolina, Tennessee, Texas,
Virginia, Washington, and Washington, DC. The
company has international offices in Finland and Poland.

PRODUCTS/OPERATIONS

Selected Services
Bio-pharmaceutical facility design and construction
Boiler and auxiliary equipment installation,
  repair, and replacement
Computer-aided design (CAD) engineering
Construction design, engineering, and building
Environmental consulting and engineering
Industrial contract maintenance and plant support
International industrial design,
  engineering, and construction
Process industries design, construction,
  and maintenance

COMPETITORS

AMEC	Halliburton
ARCADIS	HOCHTIEF
Bechtel	Jacobs Engineering
Black & Veatch	McClier
CH2M HILL	Parsons
Day & Zimmermann	Parsons Brinckerhoff
Dick Corporation	Perini
E M C Engineers	Peter Kiewit Sons'
Eichleay Corporation	Skanska
Fluor	Tetra Tech
Foster Wheeler	URS
Gilbane	Washington Group

HISTORICAL FINANCIALS

Company Type: Private

Income Statement

FYE: March 31

	REVENUE ($ mil.)	NET INCOME ($ mil.)	NET PROFIT MARGIN	EMPLOYEES
3/04	1,000	—	—	7,700
3/03	1,098	—	—	8,212
3/02	1,478	—	—	8,822
3/01	1,776	—	—	10,799
3/00	1,370	—	—	10,525
3/99	960	—	—	8,617
3/98	1,061	—	—	8,159
3/97	960	—	—	7,872
3/96	807	—	—	7,600
3/95	828	—	—	7,303
Annual Growth	**2.1%**	**—**		**0.6%**

Revenue History

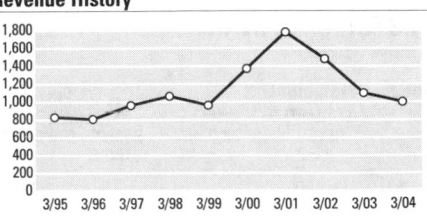

1,800	
1,600	
1,400	
1,200	
1,000	
800	
600	
400	
200	
0	
3/95 3/96 3/97 3/98 3/99 3/00 3/01 3/02 3/03 3/04	

Beacon Technologies

Beacon Technologies provides IT services to Tennessee businesses and organizations. Through its five divisions (Audio-Video, Cabling, IT, Security, and Telephony/VOIP), the company designs, installs, and supports video teleconferencing systems, cabling networks, and video surveillance systems. Other services include computer telephony integration, Internet and intranet services, and consulting. Beacon Technologies' customers include the Tennessee Valley Authority and Vanderbilt Law School.

EXECUTIVES

CEO: William J. (Bill) Hapner
President and Chief Organizational Officer:
Tony Wakefield
VP Client Strategy and Enablement: David D. White
VP Procurement and Facilities: Joe Culver
Chief Administration Officer and CIO:
Sam Shallenberger

LOCATIONS

HQ: Beacon Technologies, Inc.
911 Twin Elms Ct., Nashville, TN 37210
Phone: 615-301-5020   **Fax:** 615-301-5023
Web: www.beacontech.net

HISTORICAL FINANCIALS

Company Type: Private

Income Statement

	REVENUE ($ mil.)	NET INCOME ($ mil.)	NET PROFIT MARGIN	EMPLOYEES
12/04	13	—	—	85
12/03	8	—	—	80
12/02	5	—	—	55
Annual Growth	55.0%	—	—	24.3%

FYE: December 31

Revenue History

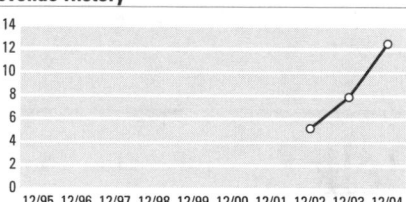

12/95 12/96 12/97 12/98 12/99 12/00 12/01 12/02 12/03 12/04

Bechtel

Whether the job is raising an entire city or razing a nuclear power plant, you can bet the Bechtel Group will be there to bid on the business. The firm is the US's #1 contractor (ahead of Fluor). The engineering, construction, and project management firm operates worldwide and has participated in such notable projects as the construction of Hoover Dam and the cleanup of the Chernobyl nuclear plant. Subsidiary Bechtel Enterprises invests in infrastructure projects and arranges financing for its clients. The group is in its fourth generation of leadership by the Bechtel family, with chairman and CEO Riley Bechtel at the helm. The billionaire Bechtel family owns a controlling stake in the firm.

Bechtel has made a name for itself by participating in mega-projects. It completes more than 1,000 projects a year. In addition to providing its core project management and design services, it offers such services as environmental restoration and remediation, telecommunications infrastructure (installing cable-optic networks and constructing data centers), and e-business infrastructure (including design, systems integration, and commissioning).

Among Bechtel's more traditional infrastructure projects has been its involvement in the "Big Dig," Boston's Central Artery/Tunnel project. Bechtel, in a joint venture with Parsons Brinckerhoff, has served as lead contractor on the $14.6 billion project, which has been the subject of much dispute over cost overruns. In 2003 the Massachusetts inspector general issued a report that blamed the venture for more than $1 billion in cost overruns for the project, which has been under construction for almost 20 years.

Other major projects of the group are its buildouts of the Cingular Wireless networks (including those of former AT&T Wireless before its 2004 acquisition). In Europe it is expanding its rail business by participating in the construction of the Channel Tunnel Rail Link, the UK's first major new railroad project in a century. It has also joined a consortium to renovate part of London's 140-year-old subway.

The mother of all mega-projects for Bechtel might turn out to be its involvement in the rehabilitation and repair of Iraq's infrastructure system. Its government services company, Bechtel National, Inc. (BNI), has been managing engineering and construction projects for public works in the war-ravaged country, including power systems, water and sanitation systems, roads and bridges, public buildings, airports, and ports. The group's work in Iraq helped contribute to a 40% spike in Bechtel's annual revenues in 2003.

BNI has also been the prime contractor for design and construction of the Hanford Waste Treatment Plant in Washington State, one of the DOE's most complex cleanup projects. The project's aim is to treat 53 million gallons of high-level radioactive waste stored at the Hanford site. BNI also helps the US Army in destroying mustard agent weapons stored in a Pueblo, Colorado, chemical depot.

Bechtel and joint venture partner Shell Oil agreed to sell InterGen, its power production joint venture, for about $1.75 billion in 2005. Shell owns 68% of the company; Bechtel, 32%.

HISTORY

In 1898 25-year-old Warren Bechtel left his Kansas farm to grade railroads in the Oklahoma Indian territories, then followed the rails west. Settling in Oakland, California, he founded his own contracting firm. Foreseeing the importance of roads, oil, and power, he won big projects such as the Northern California Highway and the Bowman Dam. By 1925, when he incorporated his company as W.A. Bechtel & Co., it ranked as the West's largest construction company. In 1931 Bechtel helped found the consortium that built Hoover Dam.

Under the leadership of Steve Bechtel (president after his father's death in 1933), the company obtained contracts for large infrastructure projects such as the San Francisco-Oakland Bay Bridge. Noted for his friendships with influential people, including Dwight Eisenhower, Adlai Stevenson, and Saudi Arabia's King Faisal, Steve developed projects that spanned nations and industries, such as pipelines in Saudi Arabia and numerous power projects. By 1960, when Steve Bechtel Jr. took over, the company was operating on six continents.

In the next two decades, Bechtel worked on transportation projects — such as San Francisco's Bay Area Rapid Transit (BART) system and the Washington, DC, subway system — and power projects, including nuclear plants. After the 1979 Three Mile Island accident, Bechtel tried its hand at nuclear cleanup. With nuclear power no longer in vogue, it focused on other markets, such as mining in New Guinea (gold and copper, 1981-84) and China (coal, 1984). Bechtel's Jubail project in Saudi Arabia, begun in 1976, raised an entire industrial port city on the Persian Gulf.

The US recession and rising developing-world debt of the early 1980s sent Bechtel reeling. It cut its workforce by 22,000 and stemmed losses by piling up small projects.

Riley Bechtel, great-grandson of Warren, became CEO in 1990. After the 1991 Gulf War, Bechtel extinguished Kuwait's flaming oil wells and worked on the oil-spill cleanup. During the decade it also worked on such projects as the Channel tunnel (Chunnel) between England and France, the new Hong Kong airport, and pipelines in the former Soviet Union.

Bechtel was part of the consortium contracted in 1996 to build a high-speed passenger rail line between London and the Chunnel. International Generating (InterGen), Bechtel's joint venture with Pacific Gas and Electric (PG&E), was chosen to help build Mexico's first private power plant. In 1998 it joined Battelle and Electricité de France in project management of a long-term plan to stabilize the damaged reactor of the Chernobyl nuclear plant in Ukraine.

In 1999 Bechtel was hired to decommission the Connecticut Yankee nuclear plant. The next year Bechtel teamed up with Shell Oil to build a $400 million power plant in Baja California.

In 2002 Bechtel took over management of the upgrade of the UK's West Coast main line from financially troubled Railtrack. As part of a consortium with UK facilities management giants Jarvis and Amey, Bechtel began work that year on a 30-year project to modernize part of London's aging subway system.

In 2003 and 2004, a group led by Bechtel received contracts (worth $1 billion and $1.8 billion, respectively) by the U.S. Agency for International Development to manage construction projects for the rebuilding of Iraq's infrastructure.

EXECUTIVES

Chairman Emeritus: Stephen D. (Steve) Bechtel Jr., age 80
Chairman and CEO: Riley P. Bechtel, age 52
President and COO: Adrian Zaccaria
EVP and Deputy COO: Jude Laspa
EVP; President, Bechtel National, Inc.; President, Bechtel Systems and Infrastructure: Thomas F. (Tom) Hash
EVP; President, Petroleum and Chemical and Pipeline: Bill Dudley
EVP; President, Telecommunications: Tim Statton
EVP; Manager of Special Operations: Mike Thiele
SVP and CFO: Peter Dawson
SVP and General Counsel: Rick Burt
SVP Human Resources: Chuck Redman
SVP; President, Power Global Business Unit: Scott Ogilvie
CIO and Manager Information Systems & Technology: Geir Ramleth
Secretary: Foster Wollen
Manager, Human Resources, Six Sigma: Mary Moreton
Public Affairs and Information Manager: Jeff H. Berger
Auditors: PricewaterhouseCoopers LLP

LOCATIONS

HQ: Bechtel Group, Inc.
50 Beale St., San Francisco, CA 94105
Phone: 415-768-1234   **Fax:** 415-768-9038
Web: www.bechtel.com

Bechtel Group operates worldwide from offices in 11 states in the US, along with international offices in Argentina, Australia, Brazil, Canada, Chile, China, Egypt, France, India, Indonesia, Japan, Korea, Malaysia, Mexico, Oman, Peru, the Philippines, Russia, Saudi Arabia, Singapore, Spain, Taiwan, Thailand, Turkey, United Arab Emirates, the UK, and Venezuela.

PRODUCTS/OPERATIONS

Selected Services

Construction
Engineering
Financing and development
Procurement
Project management
Safety
Technology

Selected Markets

Civil infrastructure
Development, financing, and ownership (Bechtel Enterprises)
Federal government
Industrial
Mining and metals
Petroleum and chemicals
Pipelines
Power (fossil and nuclear)
Telecommunications

COMPETITORS

ABB Lummus Global	Kajima
Aker Kværner	Marelich Mechanical
AMEC	Parsons
Black & Veatch	Perini
Bouygues	Peter Kiewit Sons'
Centerline Piping	RWE
Centex Construction	Schneider
CH2M HILL	Shaw Group
Chiyoda Corp.	Siemens
EIFFAGE	Skanska
Fluor	Technip
Foster Wheeler	URS
Halliburton	VINCI
HOCHTIEF	Vinnell Corporation
Hyundai Engineering and Construction	Washington Group
	Weston
ITOCHU	WFI Government Services
Jacobs Engineering	

HISTORICAL FINANCIALS

Company Type: Private

Income Statement

FYE: December 31

	REVENUE ($ mil.)	NET INCOME ($ mil.)	NET PROFIT MARGIN	EMPLOYEES
12/03	16,337	—	—	44,000
12/02	11,622	—	—	47,000
12/01	13,400	—	—	50,000
12/00	14,287	—	—	40,000
12/99	15,108	—	—	40,000
12/98	12,645	—	—	30,000
12/97	11,329	—	—	30,000
12/96	8,157	—	—	30,000
12/95	8,504	—	—	29,400
12/94	7,885	—	—	29,200
Annual Growth	8.4%	—		4.7%

Revenue History

18,000
16,000
14,000
12,000
10,000
8,000
6,000
4,000
2,000
0

12/94 12/95 12/96 12/97 12/98 12/99 12/00 12/01 12/02 12/03

Belden & Blake

It may sound like a law firm, but Belden & Blake is in fact an energy company that obeys the laws of supply and demand in the oil and gas market. It acquires properties, explores for and develops oil and gas reserves, and gathers and markets natural gas in the Appalachian and Michigan basins. Belden & Blake has interests in more than 4,120 wells, holds leases on 565,060 net acres, and owns and operates more than 1,260 miles of gas gathering lines. The company has estimated proved reserves of 284.8 billion cu. ft. of gas equivalent. Belden & Blake is controlled by Capital C, an affiliate of Carlyle/Riverstone Global Energy and Power Fund II, L.P.

EXECUTIVES

Chairman and CEO: James A. Winne III, age 53, $103,836 pay (partial-year salary)
President, COO, and Director: Michael Becci, age 48
SVP and CFO: Robert W. Peshek, age 50, $735,491 pay
VP and Corporate Controller: Frederick J. Stair, age 45
VP and General Manager, Michigan Exploration and Production: David M. Becker, age 43, $532,814 pay
VP Administration: Patricia A. Harcourt, age 41
VP Legal Affairs and Gas Marketing: Duane D. Clark, age 49, $142,594 pay
Auditors: Ernst & Young LLP

LOCATIONS

HQ: Belden & Blake Corporation
5200 Stoneham Rd., North Canton, OH 44720
Phone: 330-499-1660   **Fax:** 330-497-5463

Belden & Blake has operations in Kentucky, Michigan, New York, Ohio, Pennsylvania, and West Virginia.

PRODUCTS/OPERATIONS

2004 Sales

	$ mil.	% of total
Oil & gas	90.7	89
Gas gathering & marketing	10.0	10
Other	1.1	1
Total	**101.8**	**100**

COMPETITORS

Cabot Oil & Gas	Quicksilver Resources
Equitable Resources	Range Resources
Petroleum Development	

HISTORICAL FINANCIALS

Company Type: Private

Income Statement

FYE: December 31

	REVENUE ($ mil.)	NET INCOME ($ mil.)	NET PROFIT MARGIN	EMPLOYEES
12/04	102	13	12.5%	180
12/03	109	(2)	—	305
12/02	114	3	2.2%	301
12/01	132	7	4.9%	391
12/00	118	3	2.5%	393
12/99	136	(18)	—	429
12/98	155	(131)	—	574
12/97	164	(21)	—	625
12/96	153	15	9.7%	602
12/95	110	5	4.7%	576
Annual Growth	(0.9%)	10.4%	—	(12.1%)

2004 Year-End Financials

Debt ratio: 483.6%   Current ratio: 0.94
Return on equity: 3,227.5% Long-term debt ($ mil.): 281
Cash ($ mil.): 18

Net Income History

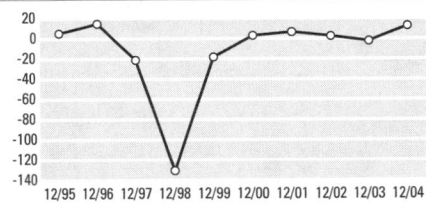

20
0
-20
-40
-60
-80
-100
-120
-140

12/95 12/96 12/97 12/98 12/99 12/00 12/01 12/02 12/03 12/04

Belk

Belk has shed a lot of bulk. Now a relatively svelte 275-store retailer operating in 14 states, the chain was a confederation of 112 separate companies, formed over the past century, before its 1998 reorganization. Belk stores, located in the Southeast and Mid-Atlantic (primarily in the Carolinas and Georgia), offer mid-priced brand-name and private-label apparel, shoes, cosmetics, gifts, and home furnishings. Its stores usually anchor malls or shopping centers in small to medium-sized markets and target 35-to-54-year-old middle- and upper-income women. The Belk family runs the show and owns most of the company, which is the largest privately owned department store chain in the US.

In July 2005 Belk began bulking up again with the acquisition of the McRae's and Proffitt's divisions of Saks for about $622 million. The 47

Proffitt's and McRae's stores are located in 11 southeastern states.

Larger Belk stores may also contain hair salons, restaurants, and optical centers. Belk plans to open 14 new stores in 2005. Its first store in Missouri is set to debut in the spring of 2006. Belk is focusing its expansion efforts in medium-sized markets.

While some might say a public offering is the logical next step, former chairman and octogenarian John Belk vowed that would never happen while he is alive. The Belk brood has not always brimmed with brotherly love, but there is no need to call in Richard Dawson to settle the Belk family feud.

HISTORY

William Henry Belk didn't mind being known as a cheapskate. At 26 he opened his first store, New York Racket, in 1888 in Monroe, North Carolina. He nicknamed the tiny shop "The Cheapest Store on Earth" and created the slogan "Cheap Goods Sell Themselves." In 1891 Belk convinced his brother John to give up a career as a doctor and join him in the retail business.

The new company, Belk Brothers, opened stores in North and South Carolina, often with partners who were family members or former employees, resulting in many two-family store names such as Belk-Harry and Hudson-Belk.

The Belks formed a partnership with the Leggett family (John's in-laws) in 1920. But feuding between the two families led to a split in 1927. The Leggetts agreed that the Belk family could keep a 20% share of the Leggett stores. John died the next year.

A strict no-credit policy worked in William's favor during the Depression, when he was able to buy out his more lenient competitors for rock-bottom prices. The shrewd businessman grew the chain from 29 stores in 1929 to about 220 stores by 1945, employing concepts such as a no-haggling policy and easy returns. William died in 1952.

That year one of his six children, William Henry Jr., opened a Belk-Lindsey store in Florida using a new format that featured, among other things, an Oriental design. Most of his siblings balked at the store's new look, but William Jr. opened another store in 1953 following the same format.

Two years later four of William Jr.'s siblings — John, Irwin, Tom, and Sarah — cut ties with the Florida stores and formed Belk Stores Services to organize their other stores. Angry at the rebuke, William Jr. and another brother, Henderson, sued the rest of the family, but they later dropped the lawsuit. In 1956 Belk Stores, with John at the helm, bought out 50-store rival chain Effird.

John had political ambitions and was elected mayor of Charlotte, North Carolina, in 1969, despite attempts by his brother William Jr. to foil the campaign. He remained mayor until 1977. Tom became the company's president in 1980.

Belk Stores continued to hold its own in the 1980s against larger department store chains on the prowl for acquisitions, but the company was stung by family discord and a loose ownership structure. Some relatives sold Belk stores to competitors such as Proffitt's (now Saks Inc.) and Dillard's. Irwin and his family, discouraged about the company's direction, sold their stock to John. In 1996 the Leggetts came back into the fold when Belk Stores bought out their 30-store chain.

Tom died in 1997 after complications from gall bladder surgery. His three sons, Tim,

Johnny, and McKay, stepped up as co-presidents but continued to answer to their uncle John, the CEO. Also in 1997 Belk Stores closed its struggling 13 Tags off-price outlets.

A year later the firm reorganized and brought all 112 separate corporations under one company, streamlining the company's accounting (previously it had to fill out tax forms for all 112 businesses) and other operations. Soon after, Belk consolidated its 13 divisional offices into four regional units. Also in 1998 it traded several store locations with Dillard's.

In 1999 Belk formed Belk National Bank in Georgia to manage its credit card operations. In 2001 the company closed four of its distribution centers, consolidating their operations into its new Blythewood, South Carolina center.

The company opened nine new department stores in 2002 and shut down two others. In 2003 it opened eight stores and completed major renovation on four existing stores.

After serving over 50 years as the company's CEO and close to 25 years as chairman, John Belk retired in May 2004. Nephew Tim Belk was named the new chairman and CEO, and his brothers McKay and Johnny were promoted to co-presidents of the company.

On July 2, 2005 Belk acquired the Proffitt's and McRae's department store business from Saks Inc. for about $622 million. Proffitt's/McRae's operates 47 stores in 11 southeastern states.

EXECUTIVES

Chairman and CEO: Thomas M. (Tim) Belk Jr., age 49, $1,047,835 pay
Vice Chairman: B. Frank Matthews II, age 76
Co-President, COO, and Director:
  John R. (Johnny) Belk, age 46, $1,047,835 pay
Co-President, Chief Merchandising Officer, and Director: H. W. McKay Belk, age 47, $1,047,835 pay
EVP, Finance: Brian T. Marley, age 46
EVP, General Counsel, and Secretary: Ralph A. Pitts, age 49, $774,549 pay
EVP, General Merchandise Manager, Men's, Young Men's and Home: Bill Roberts
EVP, Human Resources: Stephen J. (Steve) Pernotto
EVP, Private Brands: Paul Thum Suden
EVP, Real Estate and Store Planning:
  William L. (Bill) Wilson, age 54
EVP, Systems: Robert K. (Roddy) Kerr Jr., age 53
SVP, Brands Management: Michael N. (Mike) Restaino
SVP, Director of Stores, Northern Division:
  John F. Hering
SVP, Sales Promotion and Marketing: Paul Michelle
VP, Financial Planning: Trey Noonan
VP, Marketing, Administration and Budgeting:
  Steve Kelly
Auditors: KPMG LLP

LOCATIONS

HQ: Belk, Inc.
  2801 W. Tyvola Rd., Charlotte, NC 28217
Phone: 704-357-1000   **Fax:** 704-357-1876
Web: www.belk.com

2005 Stores

	No.
North Carolina	74
Georgia	40
South Carolina	37
Florida	19
Virginia	19
Tennessee	8
Texas	8
Alabama	5
Arkansas	5
Kentucky	4
Maryland	2
Mississippi	2
West Virginia	2
Louisiana	1
Total	**226**

PRODUCTS/OPERATIONS

Private Labels

Home Accents
J.Khaki
Kim Rogers
Madison Studio
Meeting Street
Saddlebred

COMPETITORS

Dillard's
Elder-Beerman Stores
Federated
J. C. Penney
Kohl's
May
Saks Inc.
Sears
Stein Mart
Target
TJX Companies
Wal-Mart

HISTORICAL FINANCIALS

Company Type: Private

Income Statement

FYE: Saturday closest to January 31

	REVENUE ($ mil.)	NET INCOME ($ mil.)	NET PROFIT MARGIN	EMPLOYEES
1/05	2,447	124	5.1%	17,900
1/04	2,265	112	4.9%	17,200
1/03	2,242	84	3.7%	17,800
1/02	2,243	63	2.8%	18,500
1/01	2,270	57	2.5%	21,000
1/00	2,145	71	3.3%	21,000
1/99	2,091	57	2.7%	22,000
1/98	1,974	54	2.8%	29,000
1/97	1,773	101	5.7%	25,000
1/96	1,686	44	2.6%	—
Annual Growth	**4.2%**	**12.3%**	**—**	**(4.1%)**

2005 Year-End Financials

Debt ratio: 27.5%
Return on equity: 12.2%
Cash ($ mil.): 232
Current ratio: 3.56
Long-term debt ($ mil.): 293

Net Income History

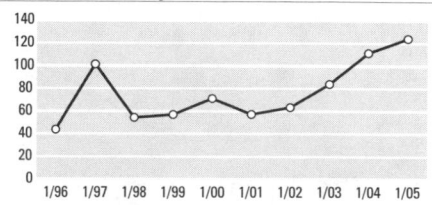

Bellco Health

Bellco Health is no baby. The company operates through three divisions. Its Bellco Drug division is an independent drug distributor selling primarily to pharmacies and retailers on Long Island and in New York City. The company distributes various name-brand and generic pharmaceutical products, as well as over-the-counter drugs and sundries. Its American Medical Distributors division sells professional products to specialty clinics and physicians. The company's third division, Dialysis Purchasing Alliance, is a group purchasing organization focusing on dialysis equipment and supplies. The Schuss family, which founded Bellco in 1955, owns the company.

EXECUTIVES

Chairman: Eric Schuss
CEO: Neal Goldstein
President and CFO: Vincent Russo
COO: David J. Schuss
Managing Director, Dialysis Purchasing Alliance: William Venus
Director, Group Purchasing, Dialysis Purchasing Alliance: Karen Girillo
Director, Marketing: Jennifer Corbett
Manager, Human Resources: Christine Brown
Clinical Services: Jennifer Vavrinchik
Senior Contract Coordinator, Dialysis Purchasing Alliance: Lorraine Scozzari

LOCATIONS

HQ: Bellco Health Corp.
5500 New Horizons Blvd.,
North Amityville, NY 11701
Phone: 631-789-6300   **Fax:** 631-841-6185
Web: www.bellcohealth.com

COMPETITORS

AmerisourceBergen
Cardinal Health
Caremark

McKesson
Quality King

HISTORICAL FINANCIALS

Company Type: Private

Income Statement

FYE: June 30

	REVENUE ($ mil.)	NET INCOME ($ mil.)	NET PROFIT MARGIN	EMPLOYEES
6/04	1,215	—	—	205
6/03	1,050	—	—	185
6/02	1,000	—	—	160
6/01	775	—	—	156
6/00	659	—	—	215
6/99	560	—	—	145
6/98	462	—	—	145
6/97	345	—	—	100
6/96	210	—	—	—
Annual Growth	**24.5%**	**—**	**—**	**10.8%**

Revenue History

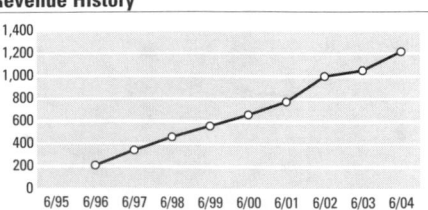

Ben E. Keith

Ben E. Keith is your bud if you like eating out and drinking brew. The firm delivers a full line of foods (produce, dry groceries, frozen food, meat), paper goods, equipment, and supplies to more than 12,000 customers in about 10 states. It is one of the world's largest Anheuser-Busch distributors, delivering beer in some 50 Texas counties. Ben E. Keith's customers include restaurants, hospitals, schools, and other institutional businesses. Founded in 1906 as Harkrider-Morrison, the company assumed its current name in 1931 in honor of Benjamin Ellington Keith, who served as the firm's president until 1959. Its owners include executives Robert and Howard Hallam.

EXECUTIVES

Chairman and CEO: Robert Hallam
President and COO: Howard Hallam
CFO: Mel Cockrell
President, Ben E. Keith Beers: Kevin Bartholomew
President, Ben E. Keith Foods: Mike Roach
VP, Produce and Training, Ben E. Keith Foods: Floyd Warner
Corporate Secretary and General Counsel: David Greenlee
Director, Human Resources: Sam Reeves
General Manager, Ben E. Keith Foods, Amarillo: Jeff Yarber
General Manager, Ben E. Keith Foods, Oklahoma Division: Kirk Purnell
District Sales Representative, Ben E. Keith Foods, San Antonio and Victoria Area: Bob Daniels

LOCATIONS

HQ: Ben E. Keith Company
601 E. 7th St., Fort Worth, TX 76102
Phone: 817-877-5700   **Fax:** 817-338-1701
Web: www.benekeith.com/main.html

Ben E. Keith serves 10 US states from six distribution centers in Arkansas, New Mexico, Oklahoma, and Texas.

COMPETITORS

Gambrinus
MBM
McLane Foodservice
Morrison
 Management Specialists

Southern Wine & Spirits
SYSCO
U.S. Foodservice

HISTORICAL FINANCIALS

Company Type: Private

Income Statement

FYE: June 30

	REVENUE ($ mil.)	NET INCOME ($ mil.)	NET PROFIT MARGIN	EMPLOYEES
6/04	1,500	—	—	2,800
6/03	1,335	—	—	2,618
6/02	1,185	—	—	2,526
6/01	1,068	—	—	2,347
6/00	959	—	—	2,160
6/99	787	—	—	2,000
6/98	682	—	—	1,800
6/97	630	—	—	1,626
6/96	580	—	—	1,600
6/95	542	—	—	1,513
Annual Growth	**12.0%**	**—**	**—**	**7.1%**

Revenue History

```
1,600
1,400
1,200
1,000
 800
 600
 400
 200
   0
    6/95 6/96 6/97 6/98 6/99 6/00 6/01 6/02 6/03 6/04
```

Berkline/ BenchCraft

Berkline/Benchcraft would be tickled for you to kick back, slip off your tired loafers, and recline in one of its upholstered chairs. The company, made up of sister companies Berkline and BenchCraft, makes mid-priced upholstered furniture for the home. Berkline makes specialty motion upholstery and reclining chairs, while BenchCraft primarily makes stationary fabric and leather pieces. In addition to its upholstered offerings, the company also makes occasional tables and complementary pieces including its Natural Elements line. With manufacturing facilities in Tennessee, Mississippi, and Montreal, it sells through independent, regional, and national furniture retailers.

In 2002 executives Wittenberg (CEO), Eckhard (EVP), and Musick (EVP), in partnership with Code Hennessy & Simmons, bought Berkline and BenchCraft from now-defunct LifeStyle Furnishings International. The two companies merged to form Berkline/BenchCraft Holdings.

EXECUTIVES

President, CEO, and Director: C. William (Bill) Wittenberg Jr., age 48, $562,500 pay
EVP Operations: Larry R. Musick, age 59, $450,000 pay
EVP Sales and Marketing: Dalthard (Dal) Eckard, age 62, $450,000 pay
SVP Corporate Business Development: Grey Hunsucker
SVP Corporate Marketing and Merchandising: Larry Smith, age 49
SVP Corporate National Accounts: William Harding, age 48
SVP Corporate Procurement: Lamont Hope, age 54
SVP Corporate Sales: Dennis Valkanoff, age 53
SVP Finance, CFO, and Treasurer: Phillip J. (Phil) Pacey, age 40
SVP Human Resources: Dennis Carper, age 52
SVP International Division and Corporate Counsel: David Popkin, age 52
SVP Manufacturing and Industrial Engineering: Wayne Burnett, age 47
SVP Operations Services: David Hood, age 54
VP Finance and Controller: Gary Cox
Auditors: Ernst & Young LLP

LOCATIONS

HQ: Berkline/BenchCraft Holdings, Inc.
1 Berkline Dr., Morristown, TN 37813
Phone: 423-585-1500   **Fax:** 423-585-4420
Web: www.berkline.com

COMPETITORS

Ashley Furniture	Furniture
Bassett Furniture	Brands International
Brown Jordan	Hooker Furniture
International	Klaussner Furniture
Chromcraft Revington	La-Z-Boy
Ethan Allen	Rowe Companies

HISTORICAL FINANCIALS

Company Type: Private

Income Statement

FYE: December 31

	REVENUE ($ mil.)	NET INCOME ($ mil.)	NET PROFIT MARGIN	EMPLOYEES
12/04	500	(19)	—	3,763
12/03	456	7	1.5%	—
12/02	339	(2)	—	—
Annual Growth	21.4%	—	—	—

2004 Year-End Financials

Debt ratio: —   Current ratio: 2.13
Return on equity: —   Long-term debt ($ mil.): 162
Cash ($ mil.): 6

Net Income History

Bertucci's

New Englanders in need of a taste of Italy can turn to Bertucci's. The company owns and operates more than 90 Italian casual-dining establishments operating under the Bertucci's Brick Oven Pizzeria banner. The restaurants, located primarily in the northeast, feature a wide array of Tuscan-style dishes, including pasta, chicken, and seafood dishes, as well as appetizers and desserts. It also offers premium, brick oven pizza. Chairman Benjamin Jacobson owns 32% of the company via his investment partnership, J.P. Acquisition Fund.

The company has invested in a new interior and exterior design and overhauled the menu, transforming Bertucci's from a gourmet pizza chain into a full-service casual-dining establishment. Bertucci's is looking to franchise its concept.

EXECUTIVES

Chairman: Benjamin R. (Ben) Jacobson, age 60
President and CEO: Stephen Clark
CFO: David G. Lloyd
VP and Controller: Dan E. Shea
VP Construction: Lewis P. Holt, age 50
VP Executive Chef: Stefano Cordova
VP Information Technology: James D. Lux, age 38
VP Operations, Region 2: Francis Christman
VP Purchasing and Distribution: Kevin Connelly
Director Employee Benefits, Relations, and Licensing: Bryan Schwanke

Office Manager and Executive Assistant: Lori-Ann Braley
Director, Marketing: Nancy Barrett
Area Director, Training: Christine San Juan
Recruiting Manager: Joanne Barnes
Director, Culinary Operations: Martha Leahy
Auditors: Deloitte & Touche LLP

LOCATIONS

HQ: Bertucci's Corporation
   155 Otis St., Northborough, MA 01532
Phone: 508-351-2500   **Fax:** 508-393-8046
Web: www.bertuccis.com

2004 Locations	No.
Massachusetts	39
Connecticut	11
Virginia	8
Pennsylvania	7
Maryland	6
New Jersey	6
New Hampshire	3
New York	3
Delaware	2
District of Columbia	2
North Carolina	2
Rhode Island	2
Total	**91**

COMPETITORS

Applebee's	Cheesecake Factory
Back Bay Restaurant	Darden
Boston Restaurant	Donatos Pizzeria
Associates	Legal Sea Foods
Brinker	Outback Steakhouse
BUCA	Ruby Tuesday
California Pizza Kitchen	Uno Restaurants
Carlson Restaurants	

HISTORICAL FINANCIALS

Company Type: Private

Income Statement

FYE: Wednesday nearest December 31

	REVENUE ($ mil.)	NET INCOME ($ mil.)	NET PROFIT MARGIN	EMPLOYEES
12/04	200	(15)	—	6,307
12/03	186	(9)	—	6,275
12/02	162	(5)	—	6,060
12/01	187	15	8.0%	6,440
12/00	285	(3)	—	10,112
12/99	268	(7)	—	8,550
12/98	161	(2)	—	2,450
12/97	81	2	2.6%	—
12/96	70	2	2.9%	—
12/95	60	1	2.3%	—
Annual Growth	14.3%	—	—	17.1%

2004 Year-End Financials

Debt ratio: —   Current ratio: 0.74
Return on equity: —   Long-term debt ($ mil.): 92
Cash ($ mil.): 12

Net Income History

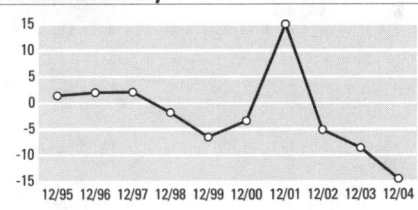

Best Western

Western hospitality has really spread. Begun in 1946 by hotelier M. K. Guertin and named for its California origins, Best Western now has more than 4,100 independently owned and operated hotels (2,400-plus in the US alone), making it the world's largest hotel brand (by number of rooms). Hotels sport its flag in about 80 countries; Australia and France have the most outside the US. Best Western is organized as a not-for-profit membership association, with most of its sales coming from monthly fees and annual dues.

In December 2004 the company announced that due to a steep decline in phone reservations, it would cut 480 jobs at its headquarters location and outsource the work (call center and information technology) to India and the Philippines. The drop in phone reservations was balanced with a significant increase in electronic reservations.

The company also gave $1 million to the children's organization UNICEF and Habitat for Humanity International after the South Asia tsunami the same year. Two Best Western hotels were damaged in the disaster.

EXECUTIVES

Chairman: Larry McRae
Vice Chairman: Raymond Johnston
President and CEO: David Kong
SVP Brand Quality and Member Services: Ric Leutwyler
SVP Marketing: Dorothy Dowling
VP and General Counsel: Kris Schloemer
VP International Operations: Suzi Yoder
VP Member Operations Support: Loyd Nygaard
VP North American Development: Mark E. Williams
VP Procurement: Rich Bennett
VP Worldwide Reservation Services: William (Will) Jansen
Secretary and Treasurer: Charles Helm
Director E-Customer Contact: Karmela Gaffney
Director Education and Cultural Diversity: John Hogan
Director External Communications: David Trumble
Director Marketing Strategy and Planning: Matthew Clyde
Auditors: Mukai, Greenlee & Company, P.C.

LOCATIONS

HQ: Best Western International, Inc.
   6201 N. 24th Pkwy., Phoenix, AZ 85016
Phone: 602-957-4200   **Fax:** 602-957-5641
Web: www.bestwestern.com

COMPETITORS

Accor
Arlington Hospitality
Cendant
Choice Hotels
Hilton
HVM
InterContinental Hotels
La Quinta
Marriott
Prime Hospitality
Scandic Hotels
ShoLodge
Starwood Hotels & Resorts
Sunburst Hospitality

HISTORICAL FINANCIALS

Company Type: Association

Income Statement

FYE: November 30

	REVENUE ($ mil.)	NET INCOME ($ mil.)	NET PROFIT MARGIN	EMPLOYEES
11/04	190	(4)	—	1,200
11/03	179	4	2.2%	1,200
11/02	165	0	0.2%	1,200
11/01	157	0	0.3%	1,300
11/00	157	1	0.8%	1,200
11/99	155	2	1.3%	1,130
11/98	161	1	0.4%	1,000
Annual Growth	2.8%	—	—	3.1%

2004 Year-End Financials

Debt ratio: 0.0%
Return on equity: —
Cash ($ mil.): 16
Current ratio: 0.92
Long-term debt ($ mil.): 0

Net Income History

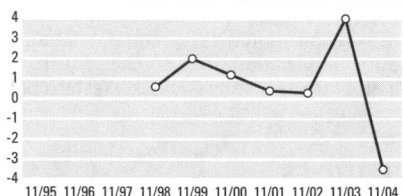

11/95 11/96 11/97 11/98 11/99 11/00 11/01 11/02 11/03 11/04

Big Y Foods

Why call it Big Y? Big Y Foods began as a 900 sq. ft. grocery at a Y intersection in Chicopee, Massachusetts. It now operates about 50 super-markets in Massachusetts and Connecticut. More than half of its stores are Big Y World Class Markets, offering specialty areas such as bakeries and floral shops, as well as banking. The rest consist of Big Y Supermarkets and two gourmet food and wine stores (Table & Vine, Town & Country). Some Big Y stores provide child care, dry cleaning, photo processing, and even propane sales, and their delis and Food Courts offer to-go foods. Big Y is owned and run by the D'Amour family.

EXECUTIVES

Chairman and CEO: Donald H. D'Amour
EVP and COO: Charles L. D'Amour
SVP, CFO: Herbert T. (Herb) Dotterer
SVP, Merchandising: Daniel (Dan) Lescoe
VP, Center Store: Phill Schneider
VP, Corporate Communications:
  Claire H. D'Amour-Daley
VP, Employee Services: Jack Henry
VP, Information Systems: John N. Sarno
VP, Store Operations: David Brunelle
VP, Real Estate and Development: Peter J. Thomas
Auditors: Deloitte & Touche LLP

LOCATIONS

HQ: Big Y Foods, Inc.
  2145 Roosevelt Ave., Springfield, MA 01102
Phone: 413-784-0600   **Fax:** 413-732-7350
Web: www.bigy.com

PRODUCTS/OPERATIONS

Selected Products and Services

Babysitting
Bakery
Banking
Bottle redemption
Coin sorting and counting
Deli
Dry cleaning
Florist
General merchandise
Gourmet food
Knife sharpening
Liquor
Lottery tickets
Meat
Money orders
Phone cards
Photo processing
Postage stamps
Poultry
Produce
Propane
Seafood
Sushi
Western Union
Wine

COMPETITORS

Cumberland Farms
DeMoulas Super Markets
Golub
Hannaford Bros.
Shaw's
Stop & Shop
SUPERVALU
Wal-Mart

HISTORICAL FINANCIALS

Company Type: Private

Income Statement

FYE: June 30

	REVENUE ($ mil.)	NET INCOME ($ mil.)	NET PROFIT MARGIN	EMPLOYEES
6/04	1,210	—	—	8,600
6/03	1,190	—	—	8,500
6/02	1,200	—	—	7,850
6/01	1,200	—	—	7,800
6/00	1,083	—	—	7,600
6/99	1,010	—	—	7,000
6/98	1,009	—	—	7,200
6/97	914	—	—	7,173
6/96	789	—	—	6,253
6/95	735	—	—	3,940
Annual Growth	5.7%	—	—	9.1%

Revenue History

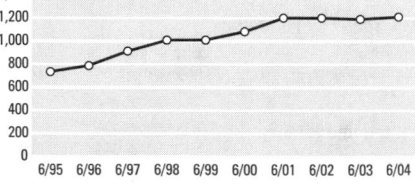

6/95 6/96 6/97 6/98 6/99 6/00 6/01 6/02 6/03 6/04

Bill & Melinda Gates Foundation

You don't have to be one of the richest men in the world to attract attention to your charitable foundation, but it doesn't hurt. Established in 1994, The William H. Gates Foundation was thrust into the spotlight in 1999 after receiving more than $2 billion from Microsoft chairman and foundation namesake Bill Gates. Later that year it merged with affiliate Gates Learning Foundation to form the Bill & Melinda Gates Foundation. Its contributions fund work in the areas of world health (vaccine research and distribution) and education; it also supports community service initiatives in the Pacific Northwest. William Gates, Sr., runs the foundation, the largest in the US, with an endowment of about $27 billion.

In 2005 the Bill & Melinda Gates Foundation granted nearly $43 million to the Institute for OneWorld Health, a not-for-profit pharmaceutical company. The grant will be applied to research and develop an affordable cure for malaria.

The foundation also has established the Gates Millennium Scholars Program, which plans to provide scholarships to minority students over the next 20 years.

Bill Gates has said he would like to give away most of his fortune while he is still living.

HISTORY

Bill Gates created the William H. Gates Foundation in 1994 with $106 million. During the next four years, he added about $2 billion to the charity. He appointed his father the head of the foundation, and the foundation at first was housed in Bill Gates Sr.'s basement. In 1997 Gates established the Gates Learning Foundation (originally called the Gates Library Foundation), a philanthropic effort to improve library systems. It was Gates' goal to improve technology and Internet access at libraries, which some critics saw as a way for him to plant Microsoft software at libraries nationwide. Patty Stonesifer, a former executive at Microsoft, ran the organization from an office above a pizza parlor.

Bill and his wife Melinda contributed some $16 billion to the foundation in 1999. That year Gates decided to merge his two charity programs into one entity: the Bill & Melinda Gates Foundation, to be run by the elder Gates and Stonesifer.

In early 2000 Gates made another $5 billion gift of stock to the foundation. That year a federal judge ordered that Microsoft be split up — the effect, if any, on the foundation is unclear. (Most of its donations come in the form of stock that is then converted to cash.) In 2000 the foundation pledged $10 million toward construction of an underground visitors center at Capitol Hill in Washington, DC. The Bill & Melinda Gates Foundation donated another $10 million in 2001 to be awarded over three years to the Hope for African Children Initiative, which will help African children affected by AIDS. In 2002 the Bill & Melinda Gates Foundation pledged more than $100 million over 10 years to reduce the spread of AIDS in India. The foundation awarded a $70 million grant to the departments of genome sciences and bioengineering at the University of Washington in 2003.

The Bill & Melinda Gates Foundation donated $750 million to be given over 10 years to the Global Alliance for Vaccines & Immunization in 2005. This follows its $750 million gift to the organization when it was established in 2000.

EXECUTIVES

Co-Founder: William H. (Bill) Gates III, age 49
Co-Founder: Melinda French Gates, age 39
Co-Chairman: William H. (Bill Sr.) Gates Sr., age 78
Co-Chairman and President:
 Patricia Q. (Patty) Stonesifer, age 48
COO and Executive Director: Sylvia M. Mathews, age 39
CFO and Chief Administrative Officer: Allan C. Golston
Executive Director, Education: Tom Vander Ark
Executive Director, Global Health: Richard D. Klausner
Program Director, Pacific Northwest Program:
 Greg Shaw
Director, Global Libraries: Martha Choe
Director, Research and Evaluation: David J. Ferrero
Deputy Director, Pacific Northwest Program:
 Katie Hong
Auditors: KPMG LLP

LOCATIONS

HQ: Bill & Melinda Gates Foundation
 1551 Eastlake Ave. East, Seattle, WA 98102
Phone: 206-709-3100   **Fax:** 206-709-3180
Web: www.gatesfoundation.org

PRODUCTS/OPERATIONS

2004 Grants by Program

	$ mil.	% of total
Education	720.9	57
Global Health	447.0	36
Pacific Northwest	38.2	3
Global Libraries	25.2	2
Special Projects & Other	29.8	2
Total	**1,261.1**	**100**

2004 Sales

	$ mil.	% of total
Net investment income	2,632.0	79
Contributions	711.5	21
Total	**3,343.5**	**100**

Selected Beneficiaries

Alliance for Cervical Cancer Prevention ($3.9 million over two years)
Gay City Health Project ($30,000 over three years)
Global Alliance for Vaccines & Immunization ($1.5 billion over 15 years)
Global Health Council ($4.8 million over three years)
Helen Keller International ($5 million over five years)
International Planned Parenthood Federation ($8.8 million over five years)
International Tuberculosis Foundation ($1.9 million over five years)
International Vaccine Institute ($40 million over five years)
Library and Information Commission ($4.2 million over one year)
National Institute of Child Health and Human Development ($15 million over five years)
Oxfam ($2.9 million over four years)
Pacific Institute for Women's Health ($1 million over three years)
Population Council ($4 million over two years)
Portland Children's Museum ($600,000 over three years)
United Negro College Fund ($1 billion over 20 years)
US Fund for UNICEF ($15 million over five years)

HISTORICAL FINANCIALS

Company Type: Foundation

Income Statement

FYE: December 31

	REVENUE ($ mil.)	NET INCOME ($ mil.)	NET PROFIT MARGIN	EMPLOYEES
12/04	3,344	—	—	234
12/03	4,010	—	—	184
12/02	2,048	—	—	—
12/01	1,182	—	—	—
12/00	304	—	—	6
12/99*	276	—	—	4
3/98	128	—	—	2
Annual Growth	**72.3%**	**—**	**—**	**121.2%**

*Fiscal year change

Revenue History

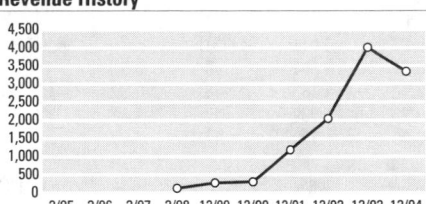

Bill Heard Enterprises

The Southern hills (and Western deserts) are alive with the sound of Chevys — music to the ears of Bill Heard Enterprises. The nation's leading chain of Chevrolet franchises, Bill Heard has more than 15 dealerships in Alabama, Arizona, Florida, Georgia, Nevada, Tennessee, and Texas. The dealer sells both new and used vehicles and auto supplies and offers repair services; it also owns Saab and Cadillac franchises in Georgia. William Heard Sr. opened his first dealership in 1919. He switched to selling Chevrolets exclusively in 1932, and his son and grandsons, who now run the family-owned business, continue to focus on Chevy sales.

EXECUTIVES

CEO: William T. (Bill) Heard
CFO: Ronald A. (Ron) Feldner
Corporate Services Administrator: Jim Matthews

LOCATIONS

HQ: Bill Heard Enterprises, Inc.
 200 Brookstone Center Pkwy., Ste. 205,
 Columbus, GA 31904
Phone: 706-323-1111   **Fax:** 706-321-9488
Web: www.billheard.com

COMPETITORS

AutoNation	McCombs Enterprises
CarMax	Morse Operations
Charlie Thomas Dealer Group	Red McCombs Automotive Group
Gulf States Toyota	Sonic Automotive
Hendrick Automotive	United Auto Group
JM Family Enterprises	

HISTORICAL FINANCIALS

Company Type: Private

Income Statement

FYE: December 31

	ESTIMATED REVENUE ($ mil.)	NET INCOME ($ mil.)	NET PROFIT MARGIN	EMPLOYEES
12/03	2,279	—	—	3,500
12/02	2,411	—	—	4,000
12/01	2,600	—	—	4,000
12/00	1,796	—	—	3,100
12/99	1,433	—	—	3,100
12/98	1,200	—	—	2,000
12/97	1,100	—	—	2,000
12/96	950	—	—	1,800
12/95	875	—	—	1,600
12/94	800	—	—	1,600
Annual Growth	**12.3%**	**—**	**—**	**9.1%**

Revenue History

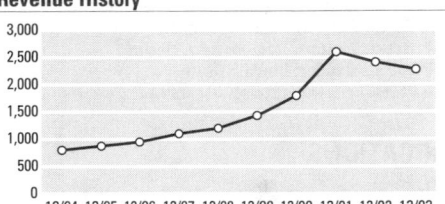

Birds Eye Foods

Whether from a bird's eye or with eyes on the bottom line, the view is excellent at Birds Eye Foods (formerly Agrilink Foods). As the #1 US maker of store-brand frozen vegetables, company brands include McKenzie's and its flagship brand Birds Eye. The company also makes pie fillings, chili and chili ingredients, salad dressings, and salty snacks. In addition, it produces private-label, food service, and industrial market foods. In 2002 Vestar Holdings acquired control of Birds Eye from Pro-Fac Cooperative. Vestar holds approximately 99% of Birds Eye.

The company, which changed its name to reflect the company's success with its Birds Eye brands, has production facilities across the US. Its brands include Comstock and Wilderness canned pie fillings; Brooks and Nalley chili and chili ingredients; Bernstein's salad dressings; and Husman's, Tim's, and Snyder of Berlin snacks. Its Birds Eye brands include Birds Eye Voila! and Birds Eye Simply Grillin'. The Birds Eye brands were named after company founder Clarence Birdseye.

Birds Eye's private label and industrial products include frozen vegetables, salad dressings, salsa, fruit fillings and toppings, and frozen vegetable specialty products.

In a move to concentrate on its frozen vegetables, in 2003 the company sold its applesauce business to Knouse Foods and its popcorn business to Gilster-Mary Lee. Also that year, the company sold its Veg-All canned vegetable unit to Arkansas-based Allen Canning Company for an undisclosed amount. In 2004 Birds Eye exited the canned vegetable business entirely with the sale of its Freshlike operations to Allen Canning. Moving into the West Coast market, in 2004 the company acquired California & Washington Company (C&W), a frozen vegetable and fruit company based in San Francisco.

EXECUTIVES

Chairman, President, and CEO: Neil Harrison, age 52
EVP, Finance, CFO, and Secretary: Earl L. Powers, age 61, $426,473 pay
EVP, Operations: Carl W. Caughran, age 52, $394,000 pay
EVP, Marketing and Business Development: David E. (Dave) Hogberg, age 52, $421,244 pay
SVP, Retail Sales: Robert Montgomery, age 52
VP, Commodity Management: Paul DeGenova
VP, Corporate Communications: Bea Slizewski
VP, Human Resources: Lois Warlick-Jarvie
VP, Marketing: Randy Zeno
VP, Sales, Central Region: Bill Kalaf
VP, Sales, Eastern Region: Larry Hahn
VP, Sales, Western Region: John Heslin
VP and Controller: Linda Nelson
Auditors: PricewaterhouseCoopers LLP

LOCATIONS

HQ: Birds Eye Foods, Inc.
90 Linden Oaks, Rochester, NY 14625
Phone: 585-383-1850   **Fax:** 585-385-2857
Web: www.birdseyefoods.com

PRODUCTS/OPERATIONS

2005 Sales

	$ mil.	% of total
Branded Frozen	356.1	41
Non-Branded	299.2	35
Branded Dry	203.4	24
Total	**858.7**	**100**

Selected Brands

Bernstein's
Birds Eye
Brooks
Comstock
C&W
Erin's
Flavor Destinations
Freshlike
Globe
Gold King
Greenwood
Husman's
La Restaurante
Mariner's Cove
McKenzie's
Nalley
Naturally Good
Riviera
Snyder of Berlin
Southern Farms
Southland
Thank You
Tim's Cascade Snacks
Tropic Isle
Wilderness

COMPETITORS

Chiquita Brands	JR Simplot
ConAgra	Kraft Foods
Del Monte Foods	Michael Foods, Inc.
Dole Food	Nestlé USA
Fyffes	Ocean Spray
General Mills	Seneca Foods
Hanover Foods	Unilever

HISTORICAL FINANCIALS

Company Type: Private

Income Statement

FYE: Last Saturday in June

	REVENUE ($ mil.)	NET INCOME ($ mil.)	NET PROFIT MARGIN	EMPLOYEES
6/05	859	19	2.2%	2,730
6/04	843	32	3.8%	2,750
6/03	878	21	2.4%	3,200
6/02	1,011	(131)	—	4,000
6/01	1,303	0	0.0%	4,685
6/00	1,183	6	0.5%	5,289
6/99	1,239	17	1.4%	—
6/98	720	17	2.4%	—
Annual Growth	**2.6%**	**1.2%**	**—**	**(12.4%)**

2005 Year-End Financials

Debt ratio: 116.0%
Return on equity: 7.4%
Cash ($ mil.): 36
Current ratio: 2.12
Long-term debt ($ mil.): 301

Net Income History

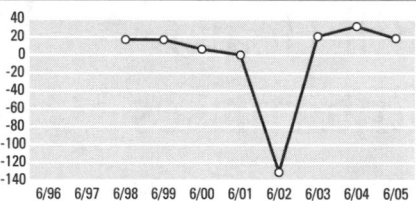

BISSELL Homecare

A pioneer in the carpet-cleaning industry, BISSELL Homecare produces a full line of vacuum cleaners, sweepers, steam cleaners, deep cleaners, and cleaning chemicals for the home. Its models include the Powersteamer, Little Green, and Spotlifter machines. The company sells its products worldwide under the BISSELL brand name, through mass merchandisers (Best Buy, Target, Wal-Mart), home centers (Lowe's, Home Depot), and hardware stores (Ace Hardware); its product are also sold online at BISSELL.com. Founded in 1876 by Melville and Anna Bissell, the company is still owned and operated by the Bissell family.

The company has shed its health care unit (rehabilitation and patient-assistance products), as well as its graphics businesses (imaging, check-reading). In November 2004 Bissell acquired the Woolite rug and upholstery cleaning business from Playtex Products.

EXECUTIVES

Chairman: John M. Bissell
President and CEO: Mark J. Bissell
EVP Product Development, Sales, and Marketing: James A. (Jim) Krzeminski
SVP Administration and CFO: Daniel T. Caldon
SVP Operations: Lawrence W. McDonough
VP and Corporate Controller: Timothy E. Bosscher
VP and General Counsel: William J. Brennan
Director Human Resources: Thomas P. McInerney

LOCATIONS

HQ: BISSELL Homecare, Inc.
2345 Walker St. NW, Grand Rapids, MI 49544
Phone: 616-453-4451   **Fax:** 616-453-1383
Web: www.bissell.com

PRODUCTS/OPERATIONS

Selected Products

Accessories and replacement parts
Bags, belts, and filters
Bare floor products
Cleaning formulas (machine, manual application, bare floor)
Deep cleaners (uprights, canisters, compacts)
Steam cleaners
Sweepers
Vacuums (canisters, stick vacs, uprights)

COMPETITORS

Aerus
Black & Decker
Candy
Electrolux
Kirby Company
Maytag
Panasonic Corporation of North America
Royal Appliance

HISTORICAL FINANCIALS

Company Type: Private

Income Statement

FYE: December 31

	ESTIMATED REVENUE ($ mil.)	NET INCOME ($ mil.)	NET PROFIT MARGIN	EMPLOYEES
12/04	700	—	—	1,800
12/03	535	—	—	—
12/02	500	—	—	—
12/01	500	—	—	1,700
12/00	500	—	—	1,700
12/99	500	—	—	2,500
12/98	450	—	—	2,250
12/97	450	—	—	2,250
12/96	443	—	—	2,250
12/95	425	—	—	2,450
Annual Growth	**5.7%**	**—**	**—**	**(3.4%)**

Revenue History

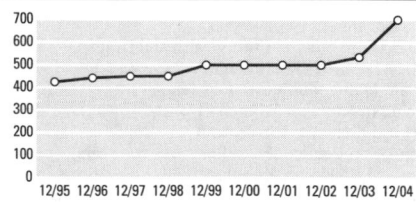

BJC HealthCare

BJC HealthCare brings Jews and Christians together for the good of its patients. The system operates more than a dozen hospitals — including Barnes-Jewish Hospital, Boone Hospital Center, and Christian Hospital — and about 100 primary care and home health facilities in and around St. Louis. BJC HealthCare's facilities have more than 4,300 beds. Specialized services include hospice care, along with long-term care and about half a dozen nursing facilities. The company's BarnesCare and OccuMed subsidiaries offer occupational health and workers' compensation services. BJC HealthCare is affiliated with Washington University Medical Center.

After a long, contentious battle with rival SSM Health Care System, the hospital operator in March 2004 won approval to build a new hospital in O'Fallon, one of Missouri's fastest growing cities.

BJC HealthCare is the product of the June 1993 merger of Barnes-Jewish, Inc., and Christian Health Services.

BJC HealthCare brought on Missouri Baptist Medical Center and St. Louis Children's Hospital and now calls the two entities BJC HealthCare.

EXECUTIVES

Chairman: Paul McKee Jr.
President and CEO: Steven H. Lipstein
Senior Executive Officer; President, Barnes-Jewish Hospital: Andrew Ziskind
Senior Executive Officer; President, Boone Hospital Center: Michael B. Shirk
Senior Executive Officer; President, St. Louis Children's Hospital: Lee F. Fetter
SVP and General Counsel: Michael A. (Mike) DeHaven
VP and CFO: Patrick Dupuis, age 42
VP and CIO: David A. Weiss
VP and Chief Human Resources Officer: JoAnn Shaw
VP, Business Development, Planning, and Physician Services: Joan R. Magruder
VP, Capital Asset Management: Robert W. Cannon
VP, Corporate and Public Communications: June McAllister Fowler
Medical Director, BJC Medical Group: John T. Ellena

LOCATIONS

HQ: BJC HealthCare
4444 Forest Park Ave., St. Louis, MO 63108
Phone: 314-286-2000 **Fax:** 314-286-2060
Web: www.bjc.org

Selected Facilities

Illinois
  Alton Memorial Hospital (Alton)
  Eunice C. Smith Home (Alton)
  Clay County Hospital (Flora)
  Fayette County Hospital (Vandalia)
Missouri
  Boone Hospital Center (Columbia)
  Parkland Health Center (Farmington)
  Village North Manor (Florissant)
  Barnes-Jewish Extended Care (St. Louis)
  Barnes-Jewish Hospital (St. Louis)
  Barnes-Jewish West County Hospital (St. Louis)
  Christian Hospital (St. Louis)
  Missouri Baptist Medical Center (St. Louis)
  St. Louis Children's Hospital
  Barnes-Jewish St. Peters Hospital (St. Peters)
  Missouri Baptist Hospital-Sullivan

COMPETITORS

Alexian Brothers Health System
Ascension Health
Catholic Health Initiatives
HCA
Sisters of Mercy Health System
SSM Health Care
Tenet Healthcare
Universal Health Services

HISTORICAL FINANCIALS

Company Type: Not-for-profit

Income Statement

FYE: December 31

	REVENUE ($ mil.)	NET INCOME ($ mil.)	NET PROFIT MARGIN	EMPLOYEES
12/03	2,500	—	—	25,525
12/02	2,400	—	—	25,993
12/01	2,200	—	—	25,801
12/00	2,100	—	—	26,038
12/99	1,608	—	—	27,071
12/98	1,561	—	—	25,853
12/97	1,587	—	—	25,500
12/96	1,553	—	—	23,696
12/95	1,530	—	—	24,975
12/94	1,413	—	—	—
Annual Growth	**6.5%**	—	—	**0.3%**

Revenue History

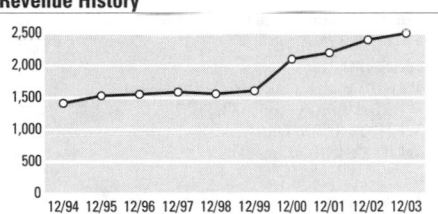

Black & Veatch

From Argentina to Zimbabwe, Black & Veatch provides the ABCs of construction, engineering, and consulting. The international group is one of the largest private companies in the US. Targeting infrastructure development for the energy, water, services, and information markets, the group engages in all phases of building projects, including design and engineering, financing and procurement, and construction. Among its services are environmental consulting, operations and maintenance, security design and consulting, and management consulting. It also offers IT services. Founded in 1915 in Kansas City by engineers E. B. Black and Tom Veatch, the firm is now employee-owned and has more than 90 offices worldwide.

Black & Veatch is involved worldwide in three major market sectors: energy, water, and information. For its part in the energy market, the company claims to have built more gas turbine projects than anyone else in the world. It also says it has been involved in more megawatts of power generation. In addition, it says it is a leader in sulfur recovery and NGL (natural gas liquids) fractionation markets. Supporting those claims is its rankings as one of the top design firms in the power, operations and maintenance, fossil fuel facilities, and transmission and distribution sectors.

The group's operations in the global water markets affect water quality and quantity throughout the water cycle: from source to treatment, to delivery, to wastewater collection and treatment. A key player in water treatment and wastewater treatment design, Black & Veatch's water sector division works with utilities, governments, and industries worldwide. Its expertise has gained it one of the largest design/build/operate contracts in North America for an advanced water treatment plant in Phoenix.

To support its clients' needs for more advanced information technologies and networks, Black & Veatch has an IT division. The company has been involved with the design and construction of wireless, fiber, and integrated networks, as well as mission-critical facilities.

EXECUTIVES

Chairman, President, and CEO:
Leonard C. (Len) Rodman
EVP and CFO: Karen L. Daniel
Chief Administrative Officer: Howard G. Withey
Chief Human Resources officer: Shirley Gaufin
VP Brand Management and Communications:
Corrine Smith
SVP, CTO, and Chief Knowledge Officer:
John G. Voeller
Strategic Sales & Marketing: Kim I. Mastalio
Auditors: KPMG LLP

LOCATIONS

HQ: Black & Veatch Holding Company
11401 Lamar Ave., Overland Park, KS 66211
Phone: 913-458-2000 **Fax:** 913-458-2934
Web: www.bv.com

Black & Veatch Holding has more than 90 offices worldwide.

PRODUCTS/OPERATIONS

Major Divisions

Energy Sector
  Engineering & Construction
  Energy Services
  Gas, Oil & Chemicals
  Power Delivery
Information Sector
  BV Solutions Group
  Telecommunications
Services Sector
  Construction
  Enterprise Consulting
  Environmental
  US Government
  Startup & Commissioning
  Transportation
Water Sector
  Potable Water
  Research
  Wastewater
  Water Resources

COMPETITORS

AECOM	Malcolm Pirnie
AMEC	McDermott
Bechtel	Michael Baker
Burns and Roe	MWH Global
CH2M HILL	Parsons
EA Engineering	Parsons Brinckerhoff
Fluor	Shaw Group
Foster Wheeler	SNC-Lavalin
Halcrow Group	Tetra Tech
Halliburton	TIC Holdings
HNTB	Washington Group
Louis Berger	Zachry

HISTORICAL FINANCIALS

Company Type: Private

Income Statement

FYE: December 31

	REVENUE ($ mil.)	NET INCOME ($ mil.)	NET PROFIT MARGIN	EMPLOYEES
12/03	1,400	—	—	6,200
12/02	2,000	—	—	7,124
12/01	2,224	—	—	8,500
12/00	2,358	—	—	8,500
12/99	2,375	—	—	9,000
12/98	2,100	—	—	9,000
12/97	1,860	—	—	8,000
12/96	1,400	—	—	6,500
12/95	1,102	—	—	4,400
12/94	985	—	—	4,900
Annual Growth	4.0%	—	—	2.6%

Revenue History

Block Communications

Block Communications Incorporated (BCI) is hardly the new kid on the block. The company has owned and operated Toledo, Ohio's newspaper, *The Blade,* since 1926 and the *Pittsburgh Post-Gazette* since 1927. BCI also owns a handful of broadcast TV stations, Ohio cable service provider Buckeye CableSystem, a security company (Corporate Protection Services), and other operations. Block family patriarch Paul Block launched the family fortune when he bought *The Blade* for $4.5 million in 1926. A year later he bought the *Post-Gazette.* After his death in 1941, Block's sons took over the family-owned business. BCI bought *Post-Gazette* rival *The Press* from Scripps Howard in 1992 and discontinued the paper.

EXECUTIVES

Chairman: Allan J. Block, age 50, $499,446 pay (prior to promotion)
Vice Chairman and Editorial Director; Publisher and Editor-in-Chief, *Pittsburgh Post-Gazette* and *The Blade:* John R. Block, age 50, $499,446 pay
President: David G. Huey, age 57, $414,125 pay
VP and CFO: Gary J. Blair, age 59
Secretary and General Counsel: Fritz Byers, age 49
Treasurer and Principal Accounting Officer: Jodi L. Miehls, age 33
Director Corporate Citizenship: Karen Block Johnese

President and General Manager, Buckeye CableSystem; President, Metro Fiber and Cable Construction: Walter H. (Chip) Carstensen
President and General Manager, Community Communication Services: Gloria Shank
President and General Manager, WAND-TV: T. J. Vaughan
President and General Manager, WLIO-TV: Bruce Opperman
President, Buckeye TeleSystem: Joe Jensen
President, Corporate Protection Services: Kim Klewer
President, *Pittsburgh Post-Gazette:* David (Dave) Beihoff
VP and General Manager, *Pittsburgh Post-Gazette:* Diana E. Block, age 32, $499,446 pay
Director Human Resources, *The Toledo Blade:* Barbara F. Gessel

LOCATIONS

HQ: Block Communications, Inc.
541 N. Superior St., Toledo, OH 43660
Phone: 419-724-6000 **Fax:** 419-724-6080
Web: www.blockcommunications.com

PRODUCTS/OPERATIONS

Selected Operations

Cable
Buckeye CableSystem

Newspapers
The Blade (Toledo, OH)
Pittsburgh Post-Gazette

Television stations
WAND-TV (ABC; Springfield/Decatur, IL)
WDRB-TV (FOX; Lousiville, KY)
WFTE-TV (UPN; Louisville, KY)
WLIO-TV (NBC; Lima, OH)

Other
Buckeye Access (dial-up Internet service)
Buckeye Express (high-speed Internet service)
Buckeye TeleSystem (telephone services)
Corporate Protection Services (Toledo, OH)

COMPETITORS

Advance Publications
Belo
Cablevision Systems
Comcast
Dispatch Printing
Gannett
Hearst-Argyle Television
Knight-Ridder
Liberty Corporation
New York Times
Raycom
Time Warner Cable
Washington Post

HISTORICAL FINANCIALS

Company Type: Private

Income Statement

FYE: December 31

	REVENUE ($ mil.)	NET INCOME ($ mil.)	NET PROFIT MARGIN	EMPLOYEES
12/04	438	(7)	—	3,000
12/03	420	(41)	—	2,900
12/02	419	3	0.6%	—
12/01	407	(18)	—	—
12/00	411	—	—	3,200
12/99	400	—	—	—
12/98	393	—	—	2,700
12/97	375	—	—	1,600
12/96	349	—	—	1,600
12/95	318	—	—	1,600
Annual Growth	3.6%	—	—	7.2%

2004 Year-End Financials

Debt ratio: —
Return on equity: —
Cash ($ mil.): 4
Current ratio: 1.06
Long-term debt ($ mil.): 264

Net Income History

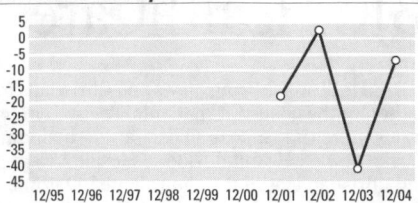

Bloomberg

What do you do when you've conquered Wall Street? You become mayor of the city the famous financial district calls home. After leading his financial news and information company to success, founder Michael Bloomberg left Bloomberg to lead the Big Apple. The Bloomberg Professional service's terminals provide real-time, around-the-clock financial news, market data, and analysis. Bloomberg is among the world's largest providers of such devices. The company also has a syndicated news service, publishes books and magazines, and disseminates business information via TV, radio, and the Web. Michael Bloomberg, inaugurated New York City mayor in 2002, owns about 70% of the company.

Bloomberg serves more than 260,000 customers in more than 125 countries. Although terminals generate most of the company's sales (Bloomberg charges a monthly fee per terminal for multiple system clients), the company distributes financial news and information through many other media channels in an effort to build its brand and keep up with the intense competition. In addition to the company's media products, Bloomberg also offers an order-matching system, the Bloomberg Tradebook. The company's Bloomberg Index License creates and licenses indices to fund managers, stock exchanges, and other clients.

In 2005 the company left Park Avenue and moved into the new Bloomberg Tower on Lexington Avenue. The 53-story building is also home to retail and residential space. There is speculation that Mayor Bloomberg, who is running for re-election in 2005, will sell the business when he leaves public office because he wants to fund a foundation.

Merrill Lynch has an ownership stake in the company.

HISTORY

By the mid-1970s ambitious Michael Bloomberg had worked his way up to head of equity trading and sales at New York investment powerhouse Salomon Brothers. He left Salomon in 1981, just after the firm went private, cashing out with $10 million for his partnership interest.

Bloomberg founded Innovative Marketing Systems and spent the next year developing the Bloomberg terminal, which allowed users to manipulate bond data. In 1982 he pitched it to Merrill Lynch, which bought 20 machines. Regular production of the terminals began in 1984, and in 1985 Merrill Lynch invested $39 million in the company to gain a 30% stake. The company prospered during the 1980s boom, and over time the data, not the machines, became the heart of the business, which was renamed Bloomberg L.P. in 1986.

The company weathered the stock market crash of 1987, opening offices in London and Tokyo. Bloomberg made its entry into newsgathering and delivery in 1990 when Bloomberg News began broadcasting on its terminals. The company built its news organization from scratch, hiring away reporters from such publications as *The Wall Street Journal* and *Forbes*. Bloomberg bought a New York radio station in 1992 and converted it to an all-news format. The next year it built an in-house TV studio and created a business news show for PBS. A satellite TV station followed in 1994, along with the *Bloomberg Personal Finance* magazine.

In 1995 Bloomberg began offering business information via its Web site. The company also introduced the Bloomberg Tradebook, an electronic securities-trading venue designed to compete with Reuters' Instinet. (In 1997 Tradebook was approved by the SEC for use in connection with some Nasdaq-listed stocks.) Bloomberg also started offering its services to subscribers in a PC-compatible format and selling its data to other news purveyors, such as LexisNexis (an online information service).

In 1996 the company went further into financial publishing, issuing *Swap Literacy: A Comprehensive Guide* and *A Common Sense Guide to Mutual Funds.* That year Michael Bloomberg bought back 10% of the company from Merrill Lynch for $200 million, giving Bloomberg L.P. an estimated market value of $2 billion. The company agreed in 1997 to supply the daytime programming for Paxson Communications' New York TV station WPXN.

When Bridge Information Systems bought Dow Jones Markets from Dow Jones in 1998, Bridge surpassed Bloomberg in number of financial information terminals installed, bumping Bloomberg from the #2 spot into third place. But Bloomberg continued expanding its offerings through strategic agreements with Internet companies such as America Online and CNET Networks, and through the introduction of new magazines such as *Bloomberg Money* in 1998 as well as *On Investing* and *Bloomberg Wealth Manager* in 1999.

Also in 1999 Bloomberg secured a deal with the Australian stock exchange that would allow its terminals to facilitate international order routing into the Australian market. The company also expanded its presence in the Spanish-language market through its agreement with CBS Telenoticias to produce a TV news program (*Noticiero Financiero*). In 2000 Bloomberg joined with Merrill Lynch to make Merrill Lynch's institutional e-commerce portal available to Bloomberg customers. The company shuttered its *Bloomberg Personal Finance* magazine in early 2003. The next year Bloomberg announced that it would provide financial programming to E! Entertainment Television during the early morning on weekdays in a three-year deal.

EXECUTIVES

Founder: Michael R. (Mike) Bloomberg, age 63
Chairman: Peter T. Grauer, age 59
CEO: Lex Fenwick, age 45
Editor-in-Chief: Matthew Winkler
Director of Worldwide Sales: Tom Secunda

LOCATIONS

HQ: Bloomberg L.P.
731 Lexington Ave., New York, NY 10022
Phone: 212-318-2000 **Fax:** 917-369-5000
Web: www.bloomberg.com

Bloomberg has offices worldwide.

PRODUCTS/OPERATIONS

Selected Products and Services

Bloomberg Custom Publishing Services
Bloomberg Data License (financial database service)
Bloomberg Investimenti (financial publication focusing on Italian finance)
Bloomberg Markets (financial magazine)
Bloomberg Money (financial magazine for European investors)
Bloomberg News (syndicated news service)
Bloomberg Portfolio Trading System (asset management tool)
Bloomberg Press (book publishing)
Bloomberg Professional (24-hour, real-time financial information system)
Bloomberg Radio (syndicated radio news service)
Bloomberg Roadshows (presentation service)
BLOOMBERG TELEVISION (24-hour news channel and syndicated reports)
Bloomberg Tradebook (equities trading technology)
Bloomberg Trading System (Bloomberg information combined with trading technology)
Bloomberg Wealth Manager (magazine for financial planners and investment advisers)
Bloomberg.com (Web site)

COMPETITORS

Agence France-Presse	Intuit
Associated Press	MarketWatch
Dow Jones	Media General
FactSet	Reuters
Forbes	TheStreet.com
Interactive Data	Thomson Corporation

HISTORICAL FINANCIALS

Company Type: Private

Income Statement

FYE: December 31

	ESTIMATED REVENUE ($ mil.)	NET INCOME ($ mil.)	NET PROFIT MARGIN	EMPLOYEES
12/04	3,500	—	—	8,000
12/03	3,250	—	—	8,200
12/02	3,000	—	—	8,200
12/01	2,600	—	—	7,200
12/00	2,800	—	—	7,200
12/99	2,300	—	—	5,150
12/98	1,500	—	—	4,900
12/97	1,300	—	—	4,000
12/96	760	—	—	3,000
12/95	650	—	—	2,500
Annual Growth	**20.6%**	**—**	**—**	**13.8%**

Revenue History

Blue Cross

The rise of managed health care has had some of its members singing the blues, but the Blue Cross and Blue Shield Association still has major market power. The Blue Cross and Blue Shield Association coordinates about 40 chapters that provide health care coverage to over 90 million Americans through indemnity insurance, Health Maintenance Organizations (HMOs), preferred provider organizations (PPOs), point-of-service (POS) plans, and fee-for-service plans. Blue Cross and Blue Shield Association chapters also administer Medicare plans for the federal government.

While some Blues always faced competition head-on, most received tax benefits for taking all comers. But as lower-cost plans attracted the hale and hearty, the Blues' customers became older, sicker, and more expensive. With their quasi-charitable status and outdated rate structures, many Blues lost market share.

The Blues have fought back by updating their technology and rate structures, merging among themselves, creating for-profit subsidiaries, forming alliances with for-profit enterprises, or (in some cases) dropping their not-for-profit status and going public — while still using the Blue Cross Blue Shield name. A history of tax breaks complicates these efforts and usually requires the creation of charitable foundations. As a result, the umbrella association is becoming a licensing and brand-marketing entity. The conversion of the Blues to for-profit status is sparking a backlash by consumer organizations and lawmakers due to the rising cost of health care.

The Blues' efforts seem to be paying off as evidenced by increased enrollment and lower administration costs.

HISTORY

Blue Cross was born in 1929, when Baylor University official Justin Kimball offered schoolteachers 21 days of hospital care for $6 a year. A major plan feature was a community rating system that based premiums on the community claims experience rather than members' conditions.

The Blue Cross symbol was devised in 1933 by Minnesota plan executive E. A. van Steenwyck. By 1935 many of the 15 plans in 11 states used the symbol. Many states gave the plans nonprofit status, and in 1936 the American Hospital Association formed the Committee on Hospital Service (renamed the Blue Cross Association in 1948) to coordinate them.

As Blue Cross grew, state medical societies sponsored prepaid plans to cover doctors' fees. In 1946 they united under the aegis of the American Medical Association (AMA) as the Associated Medical Care Plans (later the Association of Blue Shield Plans).

In 1948 the AMA thwarted a Blue Cross attempt to merge with Blue Shield. But the Blues increasingly cooperated on public policy matters while competing for members, and each Blue formed a not-for-profit corporation to coordinate its plan's activities.

By 1960 Blue Cross insured about a third of the US. Over the next decade the Blues started administering Medicare and other government health plans, and by 1970 half of Blue Cross' premiums came from government entities.

In the 1970s the Blues adopted such cost-control measures as review of hospital admissions; many plans even abandoned the community rating system. Most began emphasizing preventive care in HMOs or PPOs. The two Blues finally merged in 1982, but this had little effect on the associations' bottom lines as losses grew.

By the 1990s the Blues were big business. Some of the state associations offered officers high salaries and perks but still insisted on special regulatory treatment.

Blue Cross of California became the first chapter to give up its tax-free status when it was bought by WellPoint Health Networks, a managed care subsidiary it had founded in 1992. In a 1996 deal, WellPoint became the chapter's parent and converted it to for-profit status, assigning all of the stock to a public charitable foundation which received the proceeds of its subsequent IPO. WellPoint also bought the group life and health division of Massachusetts Mutual Life Insurance.

The for-profit switches picked up in 1997. Blue Cross of Connecticut merged with insurance provider Anthem (now WellPoint), and other mergers followed. Half the nation's Blues formed an alliance called BluesCONNECT, competing with national health plans by offering employers one nationwide benefits organization. The association also pursued overseas licensing agreements in Europe, South America, and Asia, assembling a network of Blue Cross-friendly caregivers aiming for worldwide coverage.

In 1998 Blues in more than 35 states sued the nation's big cigarette companies to recoup costs of treating smoking-related illnesses. In a separate lawsuit, Blue Cross and Blue Shield of Minnesota received nearly $300 million from the tobacco industry. In 1999, Anthem moved to acquire or affiliate with Blues in Colorado, Maine, and New Hampshire.

In 2000, after years of discussions, the New York attorney general permitted Empire Blue Cross and Blue Shield to convert to for-profit status.

In 2003, the Blues had to deal with controversy as former Blues members Anthem and WellPoint announced plans to merge, and become the largest for-profit health insurer in the nation.

EXECUTIVES

President and CEO: Scott P. Serota, $1,307,804 pay
SVP and CFO: Kathryn M. Sullivan, age 48
SVP and Chief Information Officer:
  Robert D. Rosencrans
SVP and Chief Medical Officer: Allan M. Korn
SVP, Corporate Secretary, and General Counsel:
  Roger G. Wilson
SVP, Human Resources and Administration:
  William (Bill) Colbourne
SVP, National Programs: Steve W. Gammarino
SVP, Policy and Representation: Mary Nell Lehnhard
SVP, Strategic Services: Maureen Sullivan
VP, Finance and Administration: Ralph Rambach
VP, Deputy General Counsel, and Assistant Corporate Secretary: Paul F. Brown
VP, Inter-Plan Programs: Frank Coyne
Executive Director, Branding and Market Intelligence: Kathy Wall
Executive Director, Corporate Communications and Public Affairs: Bill Hensley
Executive Director, External Affairs: Bryan Quigley
Executive Director, Marketing and Communications: Joe Bogardas
Auditors: PricewaterhouseCoopers LLP

LOCATIONS

HQ: Blue Cross and Blue Shield Association
  225 N. Michigan Ave., Chicago, IL 60601
Phone: 312-297-6000   **Fax:** 312-297-6609
Web: www.bcbs.com

The Blue Cross and Blue Shield Association has offices in Chicago and Washington, DC, with licensees operating throughout the US as well as in Africa, Asia, Australia, Canada, Latin America, the Middle East, and Western Europe.

PRODUCTS/OPERATIONS

2004 Health Care Members

	Members (mil.)	% of total
PPO	57.5	62
HMO	16.5	18
Traditional Indemnity	13.5	14
POS (Point of Sale)	5.5	6
Total	**93.0**	**100**

Selected Operations

BlueCard Worldwide (care of US members in foreign countries)
BluesConnect (nationwide alliance)
Federal Employee Health Benefits Program (federal employees and retirees)
Health maintenance organizations
Medicare management
Point-of-service programs
Preferred provider organizations

COMPETITORS

Aetna
CIGNA
Health Net
Highmark
Humana
Kaiser Foundation Health Plan
Oxford Health
PacifiCare
Prudential
UniHealth
UnitedHealth Group

HISTORICAL FINANCIALS

Company Type: Association

Income Statement

FYE: December 31

	REVENUE ($ mil.)	NET INCOME ($ mil.)	NET PROFIT MARGIN	EMPLOYEES
12/03	182,700	—	—	150,000
12/02	162,800	—	—	150,000
12/01	143,200	—	—	150,000
12/00	126,000	—	—	150,000
12/99	93,700	—	—	150,000
12/98	94,700	—	—	150,000
12/97	76,500	—	—	150,000
12/96	75,200	—	—	150,000
12/95	74,400	—	—	146,000
12/94	71,414	—	—	146,352
Annual Growth	11.0%	—	—	0.3%

Revenue History

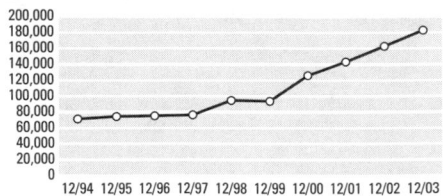

Blue Cross Blue Shield of Michigan

Blue Cross Blue Shield of Michigan is one of the nation's top Blue Cross Blue Shield health insurance associations, serving more than 4.7 million members, including autoworkers for GM and Ford. The company's insurance plans include traditional indemnity, Blue Preferred (PPO), and Blue Care Network (HMO). Blue Cross Blue Shield of Michigan also offers dental, vision, and Medicare supplement coverage, as well as workers' compensation insurance, health assessment, and health care management services. For-profit subsidiary Preferred Provider Organization of Michigan offers private health care management services.

For Blue Cross Blue Shield of Michigan, operating a "profitable" not-for-profit is a constant struggle.

While other Blues have converted to for-profit status or have teamed up with for-profit companies to become more competitive, BCBSM is committed to remaining not-for-profit. Rate hikes have helped get the company's insurance operations back into the black, and it plans to continue raising rates to keep up with the sky-rocketing costs of health care.

EXECUTIVES

Chairman: Greg Sudderth
Vice Chairman: John MacKeigan
President and CEO: Richard E. Whitmer
EVP and CFO: Mark R. Bartlett
SVP and CIO: William P. Smith
SVP and Chief Administration Officer:
  George F. Francis III
SVP and Chief Medical Officer: Thomas L. Simmer
SVP and Chief of Staff: Daniel J. Loepp
SVP, General Counsel, and Corporate Secretary:
  Lisa S. DeMoss
SVP, Auto/National Business Unit: Leslie A. Viegas
SVP, Health Care Products and Provider Services:
  Marianne Udow
SVP, Michigan Sales and Services: J. Paul Austin
VP and Deputy Counsel: Jeffrey P. Rumley
VP and Treasurer: Carolyn Walton
VP, Corporate Communications: R. Andrew Hetzel
Auditors: Deloitte & Touche LLP

LOCATIONS

HQ: Blue Cross Blue Shield of Michigan
  600 E. Lafayette Blvd., Detroit, MI 48226
Phone: 313-225-9000   **Fax:** 313-225-5629
Web: www.bcbsm.com

PRODUCTS/OPERATIONS

Selected Health Care Plans

Blue Care Network (health maintenance)
Blue Choice (point of service)
Blue MedSave (prescription plan)
Blue Preferred PPO (preferred provider for auto industry workers)
Blue Traditional (prepayment)
Blue Vision PPO
Community Blue PPO

Community Dental
Medicare Blue HMO
Personal Plus HMO
Preferred Rx (prescription plan)
Traditional Dental
Traditional Rx (prescription plan)
Traditional Vision Coverage

COMPETITORS

Aetna	United American
CIGNA	Healthcare
Henry Ford Health System	UnitedHealth Group
Humana	WellPoint

HISTORICAL FINANCIALS

Company Type: Not-for-profit

Income Statement

FYE: December 31

	REVENUE ($ mil.)	NET INCOME ($ mil.)	NET PROFIT MARGIN	EMPLOYEES
12/03	13,716	368	2.7%	8,500
12/02	12,511	161	1.3%	8,500
12/01	11,883	56	0.5%	8,500
12/00	10,507	65	0.6%	8,500
12/99	9,487	89	0.9%	8,500
12/98	8,432	83	1.0%	8,500
12/97	7,731	43	0.6%	8,827
12/96	7,001	101	1.4%	7,980
12/95	6,926	154	2.2%	6,500
12/94	6,411	71	1.1%	8,415
Annual Growth	8.8%	20.0%	—	0.1%

2003 Year-End Financials

Debt ratio: —
Return on equity: —
Cash ($ mil.): 511
Current ratio: —
Long-term debt ($ mil.): —

Net Income History

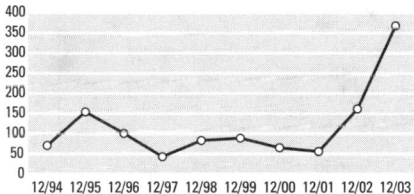

12/94 12/95 12/96 12/97 12/98 12/99 12/00 12/01 12/02 12/03

Blue Martini Software

Blue Martini Software wants to stir up all sorts of customer interactions — ensuring satisfied, not shaken, customers. The company's customer relationship management (CRM) software enables companies to manage a variety of functions, including phone and Web-based customer service interactions, call center operations, loyalty program management, marketing, and online sales efforts. Blue Martini offers industry-specific versions of its software for manufacturers and retailers. Blue Martini has been acquired by Multi-Channel Holdings, a private company backed by equity firm Golden Gate Capital, in a deal valued at about $54 million.

Blue Martini's software encompasses a variety of customer interactions, including communication via Web sites, call centers, wireless devices, e-mail, and retail storefronts. The company's customers come from industries such as telecommunications, health care, and financial services; clients include Masco, Starbucks, and America Online.

In May 2005 Blue Martini was acquired by Multi-Channel Holdings (which is a portfolio company of Golden Gate Capital). Multi-Channel plans to merge the company's operations with those of Ecometry.

EXECUTIVES

Chairman: Monte Zweben, age 41, $300,000 pay
President and CEO: John A. Marrah
CFO: Eran Pilovsky, age 44, $276,500 pay
VP and General Manager, Europe: Pascal Podvin
VP, Global Marketing and Business Development: Russell (Rocky) Gunderson, age 51, $140,192 pay
VP, North American Sales: Rob Neibauer
VP, Product Development: Eugene (Gene) Davis, age 42, $59,295 pay
VP, Professional Services: Ron Franks
Auditors: KPMG LLP

LOCATIONS

HQ: Blue Martini Software, Inc.
2600 Campus Dr., San Mateo, CA 94403
Phone: 650-356-4000   **Fax:** 650-356-4001
Web: www.bluemartini.com

Blue Martini Software has offices in France, Japan, the UK, and the US.

2004 Sales

	% of total
US	71
Other countries	29
Total	**100**

PRODUCTS/OPERATIONS

2004 Sales

	$ mil.	% of total
Professional services	11.8	42
Maintenance	9.2	32
Licenses	7.3	26
Total	**28.3**	**100**

Selected Software

Blue Martini Channels (management of trading partners and online marketplaces)
Blue Martini Commerce (personalization of customer transactions)
Blue Martini Marketing (creation of targeted marketing campaigns)
Blue Martini Service (management of customer service functions)

Selected Services

Analytic
Consulting
Training
Support

COMPETITORS

Art Technology Group	Oracle
BroadVision	Pinpoint Selling
Chordiant Software	Retek
Epiphany	salesforce.com
Firepond	SAP
JDA Software	Selectica
KANA	Siebel Systems
Microsoft	Trilogy
Oncontact	Unica
Onyx Software	Vignette

HISTORICAL FINANCIALS

Company Type: Private

Income Statement

FYE: December 31

	REVENUE ($ mil.)	NET INCOME ($ mil.)	NET PROFIT MARGIN	EMPLOYEES
12/04	28	(12)	—	95
12/03	33	(18)	—	210
12/02	34	(59)	—	255
12/01	58	(70)	—	355
12/00	74	(62)	—	473
12/99	11	(10)	—	235
12/98	0	(1)	—	—
Annual Growth	—	—	—	(16.6%)

2004 Year-End Financials

Debt ratio: 0.0%
Return on equity: —
Cash ($ mil.): 3
Current ratio: 3.71
Long-term debt ($ mil.): 0

Net Income History

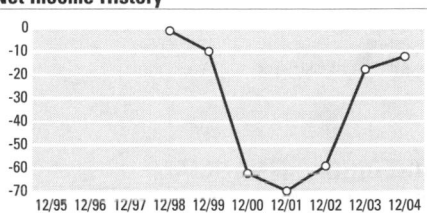

12/95 12/96 12/97 12/98 12/99 12/00 12/01 12/02 12/03 12/04

Blue Shield of California

Blue Shield Of California (a.k.a. California Physicians' Service) provides health insurance products and related services to more than 3 million members in the state of California. The not-for-profit organization's health insurance products include HMO, preferred provider organization (PPO), dental, and a Medicare supplemental plan. Accidental death and dismemberment, executive medical reimbursement, life insurance, vision, and short-term health plans are provided by the company's Blue Shield of California Life & Health Insurance subsidiary. Blue Shield of California is a Blue Cross and Blue Shield Association member.

A key component of Blue Shield of California's strategy for growth consists of expanding its large group accounts. The company's strategy is paying off as evidenced by its becoming a vendor of Calpers in 2003.

EXECUTIVES

Chairman, President, and CEO; Chairman, Blue Shield of California Life & Health Insurance: Bruce G. Bodaken
EVP and COO: Kenneth F. Wood
EVP and CFO, Blue Shield of California and Blue Shield of California Life & Health Insurance: Heidi Kunz, age 50
EVP, Corporate Development: Paul Swenson
EVP, Customer Services and Corporate Marketing: Bob Novelli
SVP and Chief Analytics Officer: Cliff Lange
SVP and Chief Information Officer: David Bowen
SVP and Chief Medical Officer: Eric Book

SVP; President and CEO, Blue Shield of California Life & Health Insurance: Debra Bowles
SVP, General Counsel, and Corporate Secretary, Blue Shield of California and Blue Shield of California Life & Health Insurance Company: Seth Jacobs
SVP, Large Group Business Unit and Ancillary Business Unit: Paul Markovich
SVP and CEO, Individual and Government Business Unit: Lisa Rubino
SVP, Human Resources: Marianne Jackson
SVP, Network Services: David S. Joyner
VP, Corporate Controller: Emmalee Noble
VP, Public Affairs: Tom Epstein

LOCATIONS

HQ: Blue Shield Of California
    50 Beale St., San Francisco, CA 94105
Phone: 415-229-5000   **Fax:** 415-229-5744
Web: www.mylifepath.com

COMPETITORS

Aetna
CIGNA
Health Net
Health Net of California
Kaiser Foundation
  Health Plan
PacifiCare
WellPoint

HISTORICAL FINANCIALS

Company Type: Not-for-profit

Income Statement

	REVENUE ($ mil.)	NET INCOME ($ mil.)	NET PROFIT MARGIN	EMPLOYEES
12/03	6,203	314	5.1%	4,200
12/02	4,624	—	—	4,200
Annual Growth	**34.1%**	—	—	**0.0%**

FYE: December 31

Revenue History

7,000 6,000 5,000 4,000 3,000 2,000 1,000 0
12/94 12/95 12/96 12/97 12/98 12/99 12/00 12/01 12/02 12/03

Blue Tee

Blue Tee has stayed out of the rough through diversification. The company, operating its subsidiaries, distributes steel and scrap metal and manufactures a variety of industrial equipment. Blue Tee's Brown-Strauss Steel subsidiary is a leading distributor of steel products (beams, pipe, tubing) in the western US. Other operations include AZCON (scrap metal sales and rail cars and parts), GEFCO (portable drilling rigs), Standard Alloys (pump parts), and Steco (dump-truck trailers). Union Tractor provides replacement parts for construction and transportation equipment in western Canada. Blue Tee is owned by its employees.

EXECUTIVES

Chairman and CEO: Richard A. Secrist
President and COO: William M. Kelly
VP and Treasurer: Glenn A. Smith
SVP: David P. Alldian

LOCATIONS

HQ: Blue Tee Corp.
    250 Park Ave. South, New York, NY 10003
Phone: 212-598-0880   **Fax:** 212-598-0896
Web: www.bluetee.com

Blue Tee has operations in the US (Arizona, California, Illinois, Massachusetts, Minnesota, New York, North Carolina, Oklahoma, Oregon, Pennsylvania, Texas, and Utah) and in Canada (Alberta and British Columbia).

PRODUCTS/OPERATIONS

Selected Subsidiaries

AZCON Corporation (ferrous and nonferrous scrap; rail cars, locomotives, and parts; relay and reroll rail)
Brown-Strauss Steel (steel distribution, including angles, beams, channels, pipe, and tubing)
GEFCO (The George E. Failing Company, portable drilling rigs)
PUMPSTAR (truck-mounted concrete boom pumps)
Southco, Inc. (distribution of pipe and reinforcing bar)
Standard Alloys (pump parts and repairs)
Steco (dump trailers, transfer trailers, and trailer parts)
Union Tractor Ltd. (Canada)
  Delta Warehouses (replacement parts for construction and transportation equipment)
  United Diesel Injection (parts and service for fuel-injection systems and turbochargers)

COMPETITORS

A. M. Castle
APi Group
Dover
Furukawa
ITT Industries
Kreher Steel
OmniSource
Philip Services
Reliance Steel
RTI International Metals
Russel Metals
Supreme Industries
Trinity Industries
TTX
United Technologies
Utility Trailer
Wescast Industries

HISTORICAL FINANCIALS

Company Type: Private

Income Statement

	REVENUE ($ mil.)	NET INCOME ($ mil.)	NET PROFIT MARGIN	EMPLOYEES
12/04	741	36	4.9%	—
12/03	379	5	1.2%	—
12/02	300	—	—	870
12/01	315	—	—	870
12/00	371	—	—	850
12/99	310	—	—	850
12/98	305	—	—	800
12/97	330	—	—	800
Annual Growth	**12.2%**	**670.2%**	—	**1.7%**

FYE: December 31

Net Income History

40 35 30 25 20 15 10 5 0
12/93 12/94 12/97 12/98 12/99 12/00 12/01 12/02 12/03 12/04

BMI

The hills may be alive with the sound of music, but all Broadcast Music, Inc. (BMI) hears is "ka-ching!" The not-for-profit organization collects licensing fees from a host of outlets and venues (such as radio stations, TV programs, Web sites, restaurants, and nightclubs) that play the music of the more than 300,000 songwriters, composers, and music publishers it represents. Its catalog of compositions includes more than 6.5 million works by a diverse range of artists including Danny Elfman, Marilyn Manson, Willie Nelson, Sting, and Shania Twain.

BMI is working to eliminate online piracy and ensure that its clients get a cut of the proceeds when their music is downloaded on the Internet. The organization monitors music played over the Web and has created a digital licensing center to license music played online.

BMI has acquired digital audio recognition technology from the UK-based Shazam Entertainment. The company subsequently formed a wholly owned subsidiary, Landmark Digital Services, to own, deploy, and exploit the technology.

EXECUTIVES

Chairman: Cecil L. Walker
President, CEO, and Director: Del R. Bryant
COO: John Cody
CFO: Bruce Esworthy
SVP and General Counsel: Marvin Berenson
SVP Government Relations: Fred Cannon
SVP International: Ron Solleveld
SVP Media Licensing: John Shaker
SVP Operations and Information Technology: Bob Barone
SVP Performing Rights: Alison Smith
SVP Writer/Publisher Relations: Phillip R. Graham
VP Corporate Relations: Robbin Ahrold
VP New Media: Richard Conlon
VP Business Affairs, Media Licensing: Michael Steinberg, age 38
Executive Director Media Relations: Hanna Pantle
Senior Attorney: John Coletta

LOCATIONS

HQ: Broadcast Music, Inc.
    320 W. 57th St., New York, NY 10019
Phone: 212-586-2000   **Fax:** 212-245-8986
Web: www.bmi.com

Broadcast Music has offices in Atlanta, London, Los Angeles, Miami, Nashville, New York City, and Puerto Rico.

PRODUCTS/OPERATIONS

Selected BMI Artists

The Beach Boys
The Beatles
Chuck Berry
David Bowie
Brooks & Dunn
James Brown
Dave Brubeck
Mariah Carey
Eric Clapton
Sheryl Crow
Dixie Chicks
Eagles
Eminem
Elton John
Kid Rock
Little Richard
Jennifer Lopez
Marilyn Manson
matchbox twenty
Tim McGraw
Sarah McLachlan
Moby
Willie Nelson
Santana
Smash Mouth
Sting
Shania Twain

HISTORICAL FINANCIALS

Company Type: Not-for-profit

Income Statement				FYE: June 30
	ESTIMATED REVENUE ($ mil.)	NET INCOME ($ mil.)	NET PROFIT MARGIN	EMPLOYEES
6/04	673	—	—	700
6/03	630	—	—	700
6/02	574	—	—	700
6/01	541	—	—	700
6/00	500	—	—	700
6/99	450	—	—	700
6/98	425	—	—	500
6/97	400	—	—	650
6/96	375	—	—	500
6/95	355	—	—	568
Annual Growth	7.4%	—	—	2.3%

Revenue History

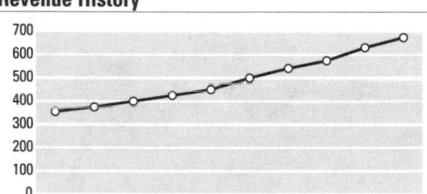

Boise Cascade

Boise Cascade Holdings maintains a perpetual tidal wave of wood and paper products. It manufactures and distributes lumber, plywood, particleboard, and engineered products such as wood I-joists and laminated lumber. It operates about 30 wholesale building material distribution centers throughout the US. Boise Cascade also makes and sells office papers, uncoated free sheet papers, envelopes, forms bond, and printing papers, as well as newsprint, market pulp, containerboard, and corrugated containers. It has sold its timberland assets. Formerly part of Boise Cascade Corporation (now OfficeMax), the company is controlled by private investment firm Madison Dearborn Partners through Forest Products Holdings, L.L.C.

Boise Cascade had a long history under the name Boise Cascade Corporation; however, the corporation's paper, forest products, and timber assets were purchased by Madison Dearborn Partners in late 2004, forming Boise Cascade Holdings. During this transaction, the old Boise Cascade Corporation's office products distribution business changed its name to OfficeMax Incorporated.

To reduce outstanding debt, the company sold its US timberland assets (2.2 million acres in Alabama, Idaho, Louisiana, Minnesota, Oregon, and Washington) to investment company Forest Capital Partners for $1.65 billion in 2005. The transaction includes an agreement in which Forest Capital will supply fiber and wood products to Boise Cascade's mills and manufacturing plants.

Boise Cascade has also changed its business unit structure. It formerly operated through two divisions (Boise Paper Solutions and Boise Building Solutions); it now functions through four divisions (paper, packaging and newsprint, building materials distribution, and wood products).

The firm filed an IPO registration statement, but canceled the IPO in May 2005; it had planned to change its name to Boise Cascade Company upon becoming a public company.

HISTORY

Boise Cascade got its start as the old Boise Cascade Corporation in 1957 with the merger of two small lumber companies — Boise Payette Lumber Company (based in Boise, Idaho) and Cascade Lumber Company (Yakima, Washington). The business diversified in the 1960s under the leadership of Robert Hansberger, moving into office-products distribution in 1964. A number of acquisitions followed, including Ebasco Industries (1969), a consulting, engineering, and construction firm. By 1970 Boise Cascade had made more than 30 buys to diversify into building materials, paper products, real estate, recreational vehicles (RVs), and publishing.

In the early 1970s the company suffered a timber shortage as its access to public timberlands dwindled. Its plans to develop recreational communities in California, Hawaii, and Washington met opposition from residents, causing Boise Cascade to scrap all but six of the 29 projects.

In 1972 high costs related to the remaining projects left the company in debt. John Fery replaced Hansberger as president that year and sold companies not directly related to the company's core forest-product operations.

In the late 1980s and early 1990s Boise sold more nonstrategic operations, including its Specialty Paperboard Division in 1989. It sold more than half of its corrugated-container plants in 1992 to focus on manufacturing forest products and distributing building materials and office supplies.

Boise Cascade also sold its wholesale office-product business in 1992 to focus on direct sales to big buyers such as IBM and Boeing. The company sold off its Canadian subsidiary, Rainy River Forest Products, during 1994 and 1995. Resurgent paper prices resulted in a profit in 1995, Boise Cascade's first since 1990.

Also in 1995, in a move into the international paper market, Boise Cascade signed a joint venture agreement with Shenzhen Leasing to form Zhuhai Hiwin Boise Cascade, a Chinese manufacturer of carbonless paper. That year it sold a minority stake in Boise Cascade Office Products (BCOP) to the public.

The company sold its coated-papers business to paper and packaging heavyweight Mead in 1996 for $639 million. The following year Boise began harvesting its first quick-growth cottonwood trees (specially grown to cut the cost of harvesting from traditional slow-growth hardwood plantations). Also in 1997 BCOP bought Jean-Paul Guisset, an office-products direct marker in France. Although this acquisition boosted sales and increased the company's European presence, company profits suffered that year because of weak paper prices.

The low price of paper in 1998 prompted the company to close four sawmills and a research and development center. Restructuring costs associated with the closures and a fire at the company's Medford, Oregon, plywood plant led to a net income loss for the year.

In 1999 Boise bought Wallace Computer Services, a contract stationer business, and broadened its building-supply distribution network nationwide by acquiring Furman Lumber, a building-supplies distributor. In 2000 Boise Cascade completed the purchase of the 19% of Boise Office Solutions that it didn't already own. The company also sold its European office products operations for $335 million and then turned around and purchased the Blue Star Business Supplies Group of US Office Products in Australia and New Zealand for about $115 million.

Because of the decline in federal timber sales, in 2001 the company closed its plywood mill and lumber operations in Emmett, Idaho, and a sawmill in Cascade, Idaho. In 2002 lagging profits prompted Boise to implement cost-cutting procedures. In 2003 the company pinned its hopes for growth on the office product segment with the acquisition of OfficeMax for nearly $1.2 billion in cash and stock. The deal put Boise Cascade's office products business on par with industry leaders Staples and Office Depot. The deal would also seriously alter the way the company began to run its business (office products versus timber and wood products) in the future.

Investment firm Madison Dearborn Partners purchased Boise Cascade's paper, forest products, and timberland assets for $3.7 billion in October 2004 and changed the name of the company to Boise Cascade Holdings, L.L.C. Thomas Stephens became the new CEO.

EXECUTIVES

Chairman and CEO: William Thomas (Tom) Stephens, age 62, $358,795 pay
EVP, Administration, and Chief Legal Officer: John W. Holleran, age 50, $201,632 pay
SVP and CFO: Thomas E. Carlile, age 53, $191,297 pay
SVP, Building Materials Distribution: Stanley R. (Stan) Bell, age 58, $141,947 pay
SVP, Boise Paper Solutions, White Paper: Miles A. Hewitt, age 46
SVP, Wood Products: Thomas A. (Tom) Lovlien, age 49, $126,723 pay
VP and Controller: Samuel K. Cotterell, age 53
VP and Treasurer: Wayne M. Rancourt, age 42
VP, General Counsel, and Secretary: Karen E. Gowland, age 46
VP, Packaging and Newsprint: Judith M. (Judy) Lassa, age 46
VP, Packaging and Newsprint: Robert E. (Bob) Strenge, age 51
VP, Boise Building Solutions, Engineered Wood Products: Tom Corrick
VP, Boise Paper Solutions, Officer Papers: Rob Sommer
VP, Boise Paper Solutions, Printing and Converting Papers: George Jendrzejewski
Manager, Boise Paper Solutions, Pulp: Ric Sandstrom
Auditors: KPMG LLP

LOCATIONS

HQ: Boise Cascade Holdings, L.L.C.
1111 W. Jefferson St., Boise, ID 83702
Phone: 208-384-6161   **Fax:** 208-384-7189
Web: www.bc.com

Boise Cascade Holdings owns manufacturing and distribution facilities in Brazil, Canada, and the US.

PRODUCTS/OPERATIONS

2004 Sales

	$ mil.	% of total
Building material distribution	2,844	45
Paper	1,370	22
Wood products	1,360	21
Packaging & newsprint	695	11
Corporate & other	90	1
Adjustments	(624)	—
Total	**5,735**	**100**

Selected Products and Operations

Building materials distribution
  Composite decking
  Engineered wood products (EWP)
  Framing accessories
  Insulation
  Lumber
  Oriented strand board (OSB)
  Plywood
  Roofing
  Siding

Paper
  Business forms and envelopes
  Commercial printing paper
  Cut-size office paper
  Uncoated free sheet
  Value-added papers
    Colored papers
    Specialty papers

Wood
  Dimension lumber
  Engineered wood products (EWP)
  Laminated veneer lumber
  Plywood
  Ponderosa pine lumber

Packaging and newsprint
  Containerboard
  Corrugated containers
  Linerboard
  Newsprint

COMPETITORS

Abitibi-Consolidated	Louisiana-Pacific
Bowater	MeadWestvaco
Domtar	Potlatch
Georgia-Pacific	Smurfit-Stone Container
Corporation	Temple-Inland
International Paper	Weyerhaeuser

HISTORICAL FINANCIALS

Company Type: Private

Income Statement

FYE: December 31

	REVENUE ($ mil.)	NET INCOME ($ mil.)	NET PROFIT MARGIN	EMPLOYEES
12/04	5,735	94	1.6%	10,494
12/03	4,654	(47)	—	—
12/02	4,276	(61)	—	—
12/01	4,252	(78)	—	—
Annual Growth	**10.5%**	**—**	**—**	**—**

2004 Year-End Financials

Debt ratio: 531.8%
Return on equity: 17.2%
Cash ($ mil.): 163
Current ratio: 2.54
Long-term debt ($ mil.): 1,967

Net Income History

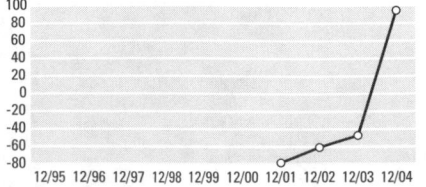

Bonneville Power

Bonneville Power Administration (BPA) keeps the lights on in the Pacific Northwest. The US Department of Energy power marketing agency operates a 15,000-mile high-voltage transmission grid that delivers about 40% of the electrical power consumed in the region. The electricity that BPA wholesales is generated primarily by 31 federal hydroelectric plants and one private nuclear facility. BPA also purchases power from other hydroelectric, gas-fired, and wind and solar generation facilities in North America. Founded in 1937, the utility sells power primarily to public and investor-owned utilities, as well as some industrial customers.

EXECUTIVES

Administrator and CEO: Stephen J. (Steve) Wright, age 44
Deputy Administrator: Steven G. (Steve) Hickok
COO: Ruth B. Bennett
EVP, Industry Restructuring: Allen L. Burns
SVP and General Counsel: Randy A. Roach
SVP, Employee and Business Resources: Terence G. (Terry) Esvelt
VP, Finance and CFO: James H. (Jim) Curtis
VP, Strategic Planning: Pamela J. (Pam) Marshall
VP, National Relations: Jeffrey K. (Jeff) Stier
CIO: Brian Furumasu
Chief Press Officer: Ed Mosey
Chief Risk Officer: Eric Larson
SVP, Power Business Line: Paul E. Norman
SVP, Transmission Business Line: Mark W. Maher
VP, Bulk Marketing and Transmission Services, Power Business Line: Stephen R. (Steve) Oliver
VP, Energy Efficiency, Power Business Line: Michael J. Weedall
VP, Generation Supply, Power Business Line: Gregory K. Delwiche
VP, Engineering and Technical Services, Transmission Business Line: Alan L. Courts
VP, Marketing and Sales, Transmission Business Line: Charles E. (Chuck) Meyer
Human Resources Diversity and EEO: Godfrey Beckett
Auditors: PricewaterhouseCoopers LLP

LOCATIONS

HQ: Bonneville Power Administration
  905 NE 11th Ave., Portland, OR 97208
Phone: 503-230-3000   **Fax:** 503-230-5884
Web: www.bpa.gov

Bonneville Power Administration carries electricity to California, Idaho, Montana, Nevada, Oregon, Utah, Washington, and Wyoming.

PRODUCTS/OPERATIONS

2004 Sales

	$ mil.	% of total
Power	2,662.0	83
Transmission	535.9	17
Total	**3,197.9**	**100**

COMPETITORS

AEP	IDACORP
AES	NW Natural
Avista	PacifiCorp
Black Hills	PG&E
CenterPoint Energy	Portland General Electric
Duke Energy	Puget Energy
Dynegy	Sempra Energy

HISTORICAL FINANCIALS

Company Type: Government-owned

Income Statement

FYE: September 30

	REVENUE ($ mil.)	NET INCOME ($ mil.)	NET PROFIT MARGIN	EMPLOYEES
9/04	3,198	504	15.8%	3,153
9/03	3,612	555	15.4%	3,121
9/02	3,534	10	0.3%	2,878
9/01	4,279	(169)	—	2,878
9/00	3,041	241	7.9%	2,732
9/99	2,619	123	4.7%	—
9/98	2,313	(49)	—	2,797
9/97	2,273	118	5.2%	2,929
9/96	2,428	96	4.0%	3,152
9/95	2,386	99	4.1%	3,271
Annual Growth	**3.3%**	**19.9%**	**—**	**(0.4%)**

2004 Year-End Financials

Debt ratio: 34.0%
Return on equity: 7.0%
Cash ($ mil.): 654
Current ratio: 1.13
Long-term debt ($ mil.): 2,462

Net Income History

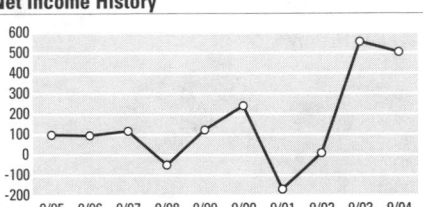

Booth Creek Ski Holdings

Booth Creek Ski Holdings caters to those fond of testing their skills against a frozen mountainside. With six ski resorts and more than 6,500 acres of ski terrain, Booth Creek is one of the largest ski companies in the US. The company focuses on regional resorts near major skiing populations, such as Boston, San Francisco, and Seattle. The resorts offer a range of services, including equipment rentals, restaurants, retail sales, and skiing lessons; some are open in the summer for golf, mountain biking, and conferences. Booth Creek also is engaged in residential real estate development at its resorts. Chairman George Gillett (who also owns the Montreal Canadiens NHL team) owns all of Booth Creek's voting shares.

EXECUTIVES

Chairman, CEO, and Assistant Secretary: George N. Gillett Jr., age 65
President, COO, and Assistant Secretary: Christopher P. Ryman, age 52, $400,000 pay
EVP, CFO, Treasurer, and Assistant Secretary: Elizabeth J. Cole, age 43, $350,000 pay
EVP Planning: Timothy H. Beck, age 53, $230,000 pay
VP, General Counsel, and Secretary: Ross D. Agre, age 35
VP Accounting and Finance, Assistant Treasurer, and Assistant Secretary: Brian J. Pope, age 41, $235,000 pay
VP Guest Experience and Product Development: Susie Tjossem, age 50

VP Human Resources: Laura B. Moriarty, age 48
VP Marketing and Sales: Julianne Maurer, age 47
VP Resort Development: David G. Corbin, age 51
VP Risk Management: Mark Petrozzi, age 44
Director of Purchasing: Kim Wall
Information Technology Manager: Frank Richey
Auditors: Ernst & Young LLP

LOCATIONS

HQ: Booth Creek Ski Holdings, Inc.
   1000 S. Frontage Rd. West, Ste. 100, Vail, CO 81657
Phone: 530-550-7112   Fax: 530-550-9455
Web: www.boothcreek.com

Resorts

Loon Mountain (New Hampshire)
Mt. Cranmore Resort (New Hampshire)
Northstar-at-Tahoe (California)
Sierra-at-Tahoe (California)
The Summit at Snoqualmie (Washington)
Waterville Valley (New Hampshire)

PRODUCTS/OPERATIONS

2004 Sales

	$ mil.	% of total
Resort operations		
Lift tickets	35.2	31
Season passes	22.1	19
Food & beverage	15.3	11
Equipment rental	7.8	8
Snow school	7.7	7
Retail	4.9	4
Other	12.4	11
Real estate & other	10.0	9
Total	**115.4**	**100**

COMPETITORS

American Skiing Company	Sinclair Oil
Aspen Skiing	Snowdance
Crested Butte	Vail Resorts
Intrawest	Winter Sports
Resorts of the	
Canadian Rockies	

HISTORICAL FINANCIALS

Company Type: Private

Income Statement

FYE: October 31

	REVENUE ($ mil.)	NET INCOME ($ mil.)	NET PROFIT MARGIN	EMPLOYEES
10/04	115	(2)	—	4,109
10/03	115	(5)	—	4,398
10/02	121	(2)	—	4,940
10/01	122	(14)	—	6,036
10/00	139	(0)	—	5,549
10/99	126	(19)	—	5,975
10/98	105	(18)	—	6,254
10/97	72	(17)	—	5,118
Annual Growth	**7.0%**	**—**	**—**	**(3.1%)**

2004 Year-End Financials

Debt ratio: —
Return on equity: —
Cash ($ mil.): 1
Current ratio: 0.09
Long-term debt ($ mil.): 81

Net Income History

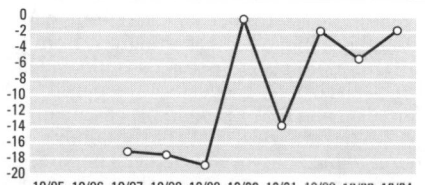

Booz Allen Hamilton

Consultants at Booz Allen Hamilton serve the needs of big business and big government. One of the world's leading management consulting firms, Booz Allen provides strategic and technology consulting services though nearly 60 offices located around the world. Its commercial sector business provides management consulting and technology integration services to help *FORTUNE* 500 companies improve their business processes. Booz Allen's government sector business provides similar services for government agencies and organizations, including the Department of Defense and the General Services Administration, as well as foreign governments and institutions. The firm was founded by Edwin Booz in 1914.

One of the largest government prime contractors, Booz Allen has seen an increase in work related to defense and national security in the time since the terrorist attacks of September 11, 2001. The firm has won work related to the reconstruction of Iraq (as a subcontractor on telecommunications projects managed by Lucent), and in 2003 it was awarded a contract from the Health Resources and Services Administration to help establish and operate a bioterrorism technical support center. Outside of the defense and security area, Booz Allen is helping the Department of Energy manage its technology infrastructure and it won a $15 million contract from the National Science Foundation to restructure its human resources operation. Work for US government agencies accounts for about 30% of the firm's business.

In the private sector, Booz Allen has performed work for such companies as Boeing, Ford, and BP. In 2003 it was hired by R.J. Reynolds Tobacco to help the cigarette maker revitalize its struggling business, and was retained by the government of Greece to help that country upgrade its transportation systems in preparation for the 2004 Olympics.

HISTORY

Edwin Booz graduated from Northwestern University in 1914 with degrees in economics and psychology and started a statistical analysis firm in Chicago. After serving in the army during WWI, he returned to his firm, renamed Edwin Booz Surveys. In 1925 Booz hired his first full-time assistant, George Fry, and in 1929 he hired a second, James Allen. By then the company had a long list of clients, including U.S. Gypsum, the *Chicago Tribune*, and Montgomery Ward, which was losing a retail battle with Sears, Roebuck and Co.

In 1935 Carl Hamilton joined the partnership, and a year later it was renamed Booz, Fry, Allen & Hamilton. The firm prospered well into the next decade by providing advice based on "independence that enables us to say plainly from the outside what cannot always be said safely from within," according to a company brochure.

During WWII the firm worked increasingly on government and military contracts. Fry opposed the pursuit of such work for consultants and left in 1942. The firm was renamed Booz, Allen & Hamilton. Hamilton died in 1946, and the following year Booz retired (he died in 1951), leav-

ing Allen as chairman. He successfully steered the firm into lucrative postwar work for clients such as Johnson Wax, RCA, and the US Air Force.

A separate company, Booz, Allen Applied Research, Inc. (BAARINC), was formed in 1955 for technical and government consulting, including missile and weaponry work, as well as consulting with NASA. By the end of the decade, *Time* had dubbed Booz Allen "the world's largest, most prestigious management consultant firm." The partnership was incorporated as a private company in 1962, and in 1967 commissioner Pete Rozelle requested its services for the merger of the National Football League and American Football League.

When Allen retired in 1970, Charlie Bowen became the new chairman, and the company went public. However, as the economy stalled during the energy crisis, spending for consultants plunged. Jim Farley replaced Bowen in 1975, and the company was taken private again in 1976. A turnaround was engineered, and the firm was soon helping Chrysler through its historic bailout and developing strategies for the breakup of AT&T.

Booz Allen again experienced trouble in the 1980s after Farley instituted a competition to select his successor. Michael McCullough was eventually chosen in 1984, but the ten-month election process turned into a dogfight that pitted partner against partner, taking an enormous toll on morale. McCullough began restructuring the firm along industry lines, creating a department store of services in an industry characterized by boutique houses. The turmoil was too much, and by 1988 nearly a third of the partners had quit.

William Stasior became chairman in 1991 and reorganized Booz Allen yet again, splitting it down public and private sector lines. James Allen died in 1992, the same year the firm moved to McLean, Virginia. The company began privatization work in the former Soviet Union and in Eastern Europe in 1992 and continued to emphasize government business, including contracts with the IRS (1995) for technology modernization and with the General Services Administration (1996) to provide technical and management support for all federal telecommunications users.

In 1998 the company won a 10-year, $200 million contract with the US Defense Department to establish a scientific and technical data warehouse. Ralph Shrader was appointed CEO in early 1999; Stasior retired as chairman later that year. Booz Allen acquired Scandinavian consulting firm Carta in 1999 and formed a venture capital firm for startups with Lehman Brothers in 2000. The company announced in late 2000 that it would spin off Aestix, its e-commerce business, but reconsidered amid a general economic slowdown and hostile IPO market. (The unit was integrated back into Booz Allen in 2002.)

EXECUTIVES

Chairman and CEO: Ralph W. Shrader, age 60
President, Worldwide Commercial Business:
  Daniel C. Lewis
President, Worldwide Technology Business:
  Dennis O. Doughty
CFO: Doug Swenson
SVP and Chief Administrative Officer:
  Samuel R. Strickland
SVP and General Counsel: C.G. Appleby
SVP: Heather L. Burns
SVP: Joyce C. Doria
SVP: Mark J. Gerencser
SVP: Paul Kocourek, age 54

SVP: Mike McConnell
SVP: Keith Oliver
SVP: Bruce Pasternack
SVP San Francisco: DeAnne Aguirre
VP and CIO: George Tillmann
Senior Director, Administrative Services: Gary Lance
Chief Personnel Officer: Horacio Rozanski
Auditors: Deloitte & Touche LLP

LOCATIONS

HQ: Booz Allen Hamilton Inc.
8283 Greensboro Dr., McLean, VA 22102
Phone: 703-902-5000　　**Fax:** 703-902-3333
Web: www.boozallen.com

PRODUCTS/OPERATIONS

Selected Services
Consulting
　Commercial services
　Corporate strategy
　E-business strategy
　Innovation
　Knowledge management
　Productivity improvement
　Strategic security
Technology services
　Engineering
　Information technology
　Systems development and integration

COMPETITORS

Accenture	L-3 Titan
Anteon	Lockheed Martin
A.T. Kearney	MAXIMUS
BAE SYSTEMS	McKinsey & Company
Bain & Company	Mercer
BearingPoint	Northrop Grumman
Boston Consulting	PA Consulting
CACI International	PRTM
Capgemini	QinetiQ
Computer Sciences Corp.	RAND
Deloitte Consulting	Raytheon
EDS	SAIC
General Dynamics	Towers Perrin
IAP Worldwide Services	Unisys
IBM	

HISTORICAL FINANCIALS

Company Type: Private

Income Statement　　　　　　　　　FYE: March 31

	REVENUE ($ mil.)	NET INCOME ($ mil.)	NET PROFIT MARGIN	EMPLOYEES
3/04	2,700	—	—	14,800
3/03	2,200	—	—	12,600
3/02	2,038	—	—	11,510
3/01	2,052	—	—	11,045
3/00	1,800	—	—	9,800
3/99	1,600	—	—	9,000
3/98	1,400	—	—	8,000
3/97	1,300	—	—	7,500
3/96	1,100	—	—	6,700
3/95	989	—	—	6,000
Annual Growth	11.8%	—	—	10.6%

Revenue History

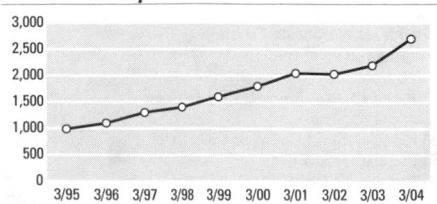

Boscov's Department Store

Outlet mall capital Reading, Pennsylvania, has conceived more than bargain shopping. It's given us Boscov's Department Store, which operates about 40 department stores that anchor malls mainly in Pennsylvania, but also in Delaware, Maryland, New Jersey, and New York. The stores sell men's, women's, and children's apparel, shoes, and accessories; also jewelry, cosmetics, housewares, appliances, toys, and sporting goods. Some stores also feature travel agencies, vision centers, hair salons, and restaurants. The firm's charge card services are handled by its Boscov's Receivable Finance subsidiary. Boscov's was founded by Solomon Boscov in 1911 and is owned by the families of Albert Boscov and Edwin Lakin.

EXECUTIVES

Chairman, Boscov's, Inc.: Albert R. (Al) Boscov
President, Boscov's, Inc.: Edwin A. Lakin
Chairman and CEO, Boscov's Department Store, LLC: Kenneth S. Lakin
President and Chief Merchandising Officer, Boscov's Department Store, LLC: Burton C. Krieger
SVP and CIO: Harry Roberts
SVP and Controller: Raymond J. Douglass
SVP and Director of Retail Merchandise Planning: Sam Flamholz
SVP and Director of Stores: Joseph M. Fabrizio
SVP and Treasurer: Russell C. Diehm
SVP, Credit and Customer Relations Management: Dean Sheaffer
SVP, Finance and Administration: Peter Lakin
SVP, Human Resources: Ed Elko
SVP, Marketing and Internet Services: Maralyn Lakin
Auditors: PricewaterhouseCoopers LLP

LOCATIONS

HQ: Boscov's Department Store
4500 Perkiomen Ave., Reading, PA 19606
Phone: 610-779-2000　　**Fax:** 610-370-3495
Web: www.boscovs.com

COMPETITORS

Bon-Ton Stores
Federated
J. C. Penney
Kmart
Kohl's
May
Sears
Target
Toys "R" Us
Wal-Mart

HISTORICAL FINANCIALS

Company Type: Private

Income Statement　　　　　　　　　FYE: January 31

	REVENUE ($ mil.)	NET INCOME ($ mil.)	NET PROFIT MARGIN	EMPLOYEES
1/04	1,051	—	—	11,000
1/03	1,016	—	—	10,500
1/02	1,000	—	—	12,000
1/01	1,000	—	—	10,000
1/00	958	—	—	10,000
1/99	1,000	—	—	10,000
1/98	846	—	—	9,000
1/97	811	—	—	8,500
1/96	783	—	—	8,500
1/95	750	—	—	6,500
Annual Growth	3.8%	—	—	6.0%

Revenue History

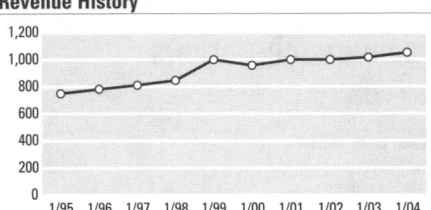

Bose

Bose has been making noise in the audio products business for some time. The company is one of the world's leading manufacturers of speakers for the home entertainment, automotive, and pro audio markets. It makes a variety of consumer models for stereo systems and home theaters, including its compact Wave radio system. For sound professionals, Bose offers loudspeakers and amplifiers, as well as products designed for musicians. Bose sells its products at more than 100 factory and showcase stores and through affiliated retailers. In addition, subsidiary EnduraTEC Systems makes biomedical testing equipment and other electronics. Founder Amar Bose, a former MIT professor, owns the company.

Bose has built a reputation for making high-quality products through its commitment to research in electronics and acoustical engineering. The expertise of its engineers proved invaluable to the new Boston Convention & Exhibition Center, which brought in Bose to revamp its public address system.

Its research focus has taken the company into new fields in recent years: Bose has been developing an electromagnetic suspension system for automobiles since the 1980s and in 2004 it acquired testing equipment maker EnduraTEC.

HISTORY

Music and electronics struck a chord in Amar Bose, the son of an Indian emigrant from Calcutta. As a youngster he studied violin and liked fixing electronic gadgets. A teenaged Bose started a radio repair shop in his basement during WWII that turned out to be the family's main source of income when his father's import business faltered during the war. Bose's interest in electronics led him to college at Massachusetts Institute of Technology (MIT) in 1947.

His quest to develop a better sound system began nearly a decade later when the hi-fi stereo he bought as a reward for doing well in his graduate studies made his violin record sound shrill. MIT allowed Bose to research the topic while he taught there. He formed his namesake company in 1964 and hired as its first employee Sherwin Greenblatt, a former student who later became company president.

Bose discovered that most speaker systems funneled sound directly at the listener, while live concerts sent sound directly and indirectly by bouncing it off walls, floors, and ceilings. He designed a system in which only some speakers are aimed at the listener while others reflect the sounds around the room. Calling the concept "reflected sound," Bose began selling his 901 stereo speakers in 1968.

A feud with *Consumer Reports* showed the arrogant side of the self-made entrepreneur. After the magazine concluded in a 1970 review that Bose speakers created a sound that tended to "wander around the room," Bose sued, claiming product disparagement. (The lawsuit was settled 13 years later when the Supreme Court ruled in favor of *Consumer Reports*.) Bose began making professional loudspeakers in 1972.

After trying and failing to gain market share in Japan throughout the 1970s, in 1978 Bose hired sales executive Sumi Sakura, who convinced 400 Japanese dealers to find space in their jam-packed stores for Bose products. Sales jumped within months. Bose also turned his attention to car stereos in the 1970s. After promising talks with General Motors in 1979, he risked $13 million and four years developing a stereo that could be custom-designed for cars. The first one was offered in 1983 in a Cadillac Seville. Contracts with other major carmakers followed, usually for their top-of-the-line models.

In the 1980s the company took its technology to TVs. With an agreeable guinea pig in Zenith, Bose developed a speaker tube that could coil inside the set without adding much bulk. The set was a hit, even with a price tag of more than $1,400 (in 1987). The firm's speakers were also used in several space shuttle flights, beginning in 1992 with *Endeavour.*

The critically acclaimed Wave radio was introduced in 1993 and has been a huge success ever since. A year later Bose acquired professional loudspeaker maker US Sound from Carver. In 1996 it teamed up with satellite TV firm PRIMESTAR to offer the home theater Companion systems. (The systems were discontinued in 1999, dissolving the partnership.) The next year Bose and IBM paired up to upgrade the quality of PC sound systems.

Bose upped the ante on its retail operations in 1997 when it began opening more upscale showcase stores where audiophiles could test sound systems at in-store music theaters. The company began making its sound systems for more mainstream cars, such as the Chevrolet Blazer, the following year. In 1999 Bose began selling its products online and introduced a new version of its popular Wave radio (with a CD player). In 2001 Bose introduced the Bose Wave/PC interactive system that provides one-touch access to Internet radio, digital audio files, AM/FM radio, and CDs through a personal computer.

EXECUTIVES

Chairman and CEO: Amar G. Bose
President and Director: John T. Coleman
VP, Engineering: Joseph (Joe) Veranth
VP, Finance and CFO: Daniel A. Grady, age 67
VP, Finance and Assistant Treasurer:
  Herbert W. Batchelder
VP, Human Resources: John C. Ferrie
VP, Manufacturing: Thomas Beeson
VP, Manufacturing: Bryan Fontaine
VP, Research and Director: Thomas A. Froeschle
VP: Sumiyoshi Sakura
VP, Bose Europe: Nic A. Merks
General Manager, Bose Corporation India:
  Ratish Pandey
General Manager, EnduraTEC Systems Group:
  Ed Moriarty
**Chief Engineer and Director, Bose Live Music
  Technology Group:** Ken Jacob
Secretary: Mark E. Sullivan
Treasurer: Mario J. Cornacchio Jr.
Director of Americas Professional Systems:
  Mitch Nollman
Director of Public Relations: Carolyn Cinotti
Auditors: PricewaterhouseCoopers LLP

LOCATIONS

HQ: Bose Corporation
  The Mountain, Framingham, MA 01701
Phone: 508-879-7330   **Fax:** 508-766-7543
Web: www.bose.com

Bose has manufacturing facilities in Columbia, South Carolina; Framingham, Massachusetts; Hillsdale, Michigan; and Yuma, Arizona; and in Ireland and Mexico. It also has international sales operations in Australia, Austria, Belgium, China, Denmark, France, Germany, India, Italy, Japan, the Netherlands, Norway, Sweden, Switzerland, and the UK.

PRODUCTS/OPERATIONS

Selected Products

Automotive sound systems
Aviation and military headsets
Home entertainment
  Headphones and headsets
  Home stereo speakers
  Home theater speakers
  Multimedia speakers
  Outdoor and marine speakers
  Wave systems
Professional audio
  Amplifiers
  Loudspeakers

COMPETITORS

Aiwa Business
Boston Acoustics
Cambridge SoundWorks
Eminence
Harman International
Kenwood
Klipsch
Koss
Mitek
Phoenix Gold
Pioneer
Polk Audio
QSC Audio
Rockford
SpeakerCraft
Stanton Group
Telex Communications

HISTORICAL FINANCIALS

Company Type: Private

Income Statement

FYE: March 31

	REVENUE ($ mil.)	NET INCOME ($ mil.)	NET PROFIT MARGIN	EMPLOYEES
3/04	1,700	—	—	8,000
3/03	1,600	—	—	8,000
3/02	1,300	—	—	7,000
3/01	1,250	—	—	7,000
3/00	1,100	—	—	6,000
3/99	950	—	—	4,000
3/98	850	—	—	4,000
3/97	750	—	—	4,000
3/96	700	—	—	3,500
3/95	600	—	—	3,100
Annual Growth	12.3%	—	—	11.1%

Revenue History

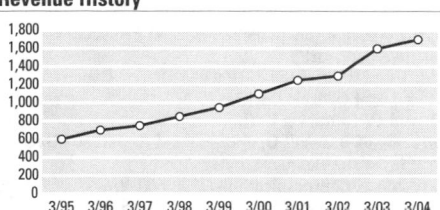

Boston Red Sox

The Curse has been lifted from Boston baseball fans. The Boston Red Sox in 2004 won their first World Series title since 1918, an 86-year drought popularly attributed to "The Curse of the Bambino." The championship capped off a season in which the franchise recorded sellouts of all its home games at venerable Fenway Park, the oldest stadium in Major League Baseball. The record-setting attendance was spurred by improvements made by owner John Henry to both team and stadium. Henry, who once owned the Florida Marlins, bought the Red Sox in 2002. The franchise was founded as a charter member of the American League in 1901 and won five championships before falling under its star-crossed hex.

Through the holding company New England Sports Ventures, Henry and his partners (which include The New York Times) paid about $660 million for the storied franchise, a record sum for a baseball team. The new ownership group upgraded the team's 90-year-old stadium with new concessions areas and seats atop the Green Monster — the left field wall which measures 37 feet high. The team's curse-breaking title run two years later saw the BoSox recover from a three-game deficit to defeat the Evil Empire (the New York Yankees) for the AL pennant, and then go on to win a four-game sweep of the St. Louis Cardinals in the World Series.

New England Sports Ventures also owns an 80% stake in New England Sports Network along with Boston Bruins owner Jeremy Jacobs. The Red Sox's former ownership group, led by John Harrington, sold the team after plans to build a 44,000-seat stadium to replace Fenway fell through. Neighborhood opposition scuttled plans to tear down Fenway and build a larger park so Sox management is buying real estate around the stadium and moving support and storage functions to make room for more seats at the park. The urban renewal extends to participation in a program aimed at cleaning up the area and bringing in restaurants, cafes, and up-scale bars.

EXECUTIVES

Principal Owner: John W. Henry
Chairman: Thomas C. Werner
Vice Chairman: David I. Ginsberg
Vice Chairman: Phillip H. Morse
Vice Chairman: Leslie B. Otten
President and CEO: Larry Lucchino, age 60
COO: Mike Dee
EVP Public Affairs: Charles S. Steinberg
SVP and General Manager: Theo Epstein, age 29
Assistant General Manager: Josh Byrnes
Manager: Terry John Francona
SVP Corporate Relations and Special Projects:
 Meg Vaillancourt
SVP Fenway Affairs: Lawrence C. (Larry) Cancro
Chief Legal Officer: Lucinda K. Treat
VP and CFO: Robert C. (Bob) Furbush
Director of Baseball Operations and Assistant Director of Player Development: Peter Woodfork
Director of Communications: Glenn Geffner
Director of Fan and Neighborhood Services:
 Sarah M. McKenna
Director of Human Resources and Office Management:
 Michele Julian
Traveling Secretary: John F. (Jack) McCormick

LOCATIONS

HQ: The Boston Red Sox
 4 Yawkey Way, Boston, MA 02215
Phone: 617-267-9440   **Fax:** 617-375-0944
Web: boston.redsox.mlb.com

The Boston Red Sox play at 33,871-seat capacity Fenway Park.

PRODUCTS/OPERATIONS

Championship Titles

World Series (1903, 1912, 1915-16, 1918, 2004)
American League Pennant (1903-04, 1912, 1915-16,
 1918, 1946, 1967, 1975, 1986, 2004)
American League East Division
 (1975, 1986, 1988, 1990, 1995)

COMPETITORS

Baltimore Orioles	Tampa Bay Devil Rays
New York Yankees	Toronto Blue Jays

HISTORICAL FINANCIALS

Company Type: Private

Income Statement

FYE: December 31

	REVENUE ($ mil.)	NET INCOME ($ mil.)	NET PROFIT MARGIN	EMPLOYEES
12/04	220	—	—	—
12/03	190	—	—	—
12/02	171	—	—	—
12/01	152	—	—	—
12/00	126	—	—	—
12/99	123	—	—	—
12/98	107	—	—	—
12/97	92	—	—	150
12/96	88	—	—	—
12/95	68	—	—	—
Annual Growth	14.0%	—	—	—

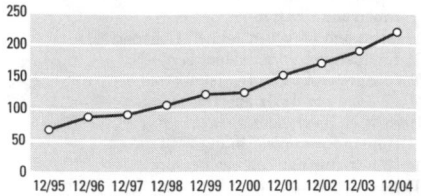

Revenue History

12/95 12/96 12/97 12/98 12/99 12/00 12/01 12/02 12/03 12/04

Boy Scouts of America

They enter on tender feet but leave flying like eagles. Boy Scouts of America (BSA) is one of the nation's largest youth organizations, with nearly 5 million members in about 128,000 units. Incorporated by Chicago publisher William Boyce in 1910, BSA offers educational and character-building programs emphasizing leadership, citizenship, personal development, and physical fitness. In addition to traditional scouting programs, it offers the Venturing program for boys and girls ages 14-20. BSA generates revenue through membership and council fees, supply and magazine sales, and contributions. In 2000 the Supreme Court ruled that the organization could legally bar homosexuals from becoming troop leaders.

BSA continues to finds itself embroiled in legal battles, charging that local and state governments have restricted the organization's access to charitable funds and public meeting locations.

Membership in most youth programs (with the exception of Tiger Cubs) is trending downward.

EXECUTIVES

Chief Scout Executive: Roy L. Williams
President: John C. Cushman III, age 64
EVP: Wiliiam F. Cronk III, age 62
National Commissioner: Donald D. Belcher
Assistant Treasurer: R. Thomas Buffenbarger
International Commissioner: Richard L. Burdick
VP, Program: Terrence P. Dunn
VP, Administration: John Gottschalk
Treasurer: Aubrey B. Harwell Jr., age 61
VP, Relationships and Publishing: Drayton McLane Jr., age 69
VP, Development and Strategic Initiatives:
 John F. Smith
VP, Human Resources: James S. Turley
National Director, Supply Group: Mark Ashline

LOCATIONS

HQ: Boy Scouts of America
 1325 W. Walnut Hill Ln., Irving, TX 75015
Phone: 972-580-2000   **Fax:** 972-580-2502
Web: www.scouting.org

PRODUCTS/OPERATIONS

2004 Youth Membership

	No.
Cub Scout-age youth	
Cub Scouts	885,341
Webolos Scouts	725,383
Tiger Cubs	265,028
Boy Scout-age youth	
Boy Scouts	922,323
Varsity Scouts	66,672
Venturers	280,584
Total	**3,145,331**

2004 Adult Membership

	No.
Boy Scout leaders	520,124
Cub Scout leaders	517,449
Venturing leaders	65,504
Council leaders	46,624
Varsity Scout leaders	23,363
Total	**1,173,064**

HISTORICAL FINANCIALS

Company Type: Not-for-profit

Income Statement

FYE: December 31

	REVENUE ($ mil.)	NET INCOME ($ mil.)	NET PROFIT MARGIN	EMPLOYEES
12/04	270	—	—	—
12/03	298	—	—	500
12/02	226	—	—	500
12/01	244	—	—	500
12/00	242	—	—	487
12/99	232	—	—	500
12/98	252	—	—	500
12/97	252	—	—	500
12/96	93	—	—	—
Annual Growth	14.2%	—	—	0.0%

Revenue History

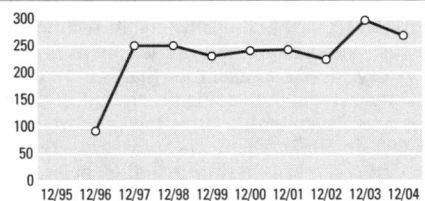

12/95 12/96 12/97 12/98 12/99 12/00 12/01 12/02 12/03 12/04

BPC Holding

The BPC in BPC Holding stands for the company's main subsidiary, Berry Plastics Corporation, a leading maker of injection-molded plastic products. Berry Plastics makes three types of products: containers (more than half of sales), closures, and consumer products such as plastic drink cups and housewares. Its containers hold items ranging from dairy products to chemicals. Products of Berry Plastics' closures unit include overcaps for aerosol cans and caps for mouthwash and detergent containers. Fast-food restaurants, convenience stores, and stadiums use the company's plastic drink cups. Funds associated with Goldman Sachs control 60% of BPC Holding; funds associated with J.P. Morgan Partners control 27%.

BPC Holding was formed in 1990 to acquire Berry Plastics, which has grown primarily through acquisitions. Berry Plastics acquired Landis Plastics, a leading manufacturer of containers for the yogurt business, for about $230 million in November 2003.

Internationally, Berry Plastics operates facilities in the UK and Italy. In addition, it has launched a manufacturing joint venture in China.

EXECUTIVES

Chairman, BPC Holding and Berry Plastics: Joseph H. Gleberman, age 48
President, CEO, and Director, BPC Holding and Berry Plastics: Ira G. Boots, age 51, $656,426 pay
EVP, CFO, Secretary, and Treasurer, BPC Holding and Berry Plastics: James M. Kratochvil, age 48, $422,609 pay
EVP; EVP and General Manager, Closures: William J. (Bill) Herdrich, age 54, $416,646 pay
EVP; President, Containers and Consumer Products, Berry Plastics: Ralph Brent Beeler, age 52, $502,498 pay
Director; President, Container Division, Berry Plastics: Gregory (Greg) Landis, age 54, $349,866 pay
VP and Controller: Mark Miles
VP and Plant Manager, Henderson: Donald R. Abney
VP and Plant Manager, Evansville: Fredrick A. Heseman
VP, Corporate Development: Brett C. Bauer
VP, Finance and Business Planning: Rodgers K. Greenwalt
VP, Global Purchasing: Scott Farmer
VP, Human Resources: Marcia C. Jochem
Auditors: Ernst & Young LLP

LOCATIONS

HQ: BPC Holding Corp.
101 Oakley St., Evansville, IN 47710
Phone: 812-424-2904   **Fax:** 812-424-0128
Web: www.berryplastics.com

PRODUCTS/OPERATIONS

2004 Sales

	$ mil.	% of total
Containers	518.3	64
Consumer products	130.4	16
Closures	127.5	15
International	38.0	5
Total	**814.2**	**100**

Selected Products

Containers
  Dairy
  Industrial Specialty
  Polypropylene
  Pry-off
  Thinwall
Consumer products
  Drink cups
  Housewares
    Bowls
    Outdoor flowerpots
    Pitchers
    Plates
    Tumblers
Closures
  Aerosol overcaps
  Continuous thread
  Child resistant
  Cups and spouts (for liquid laundry detergent)
  Dispensing
  Dropper bulb assemblies
  Fitments and plugs (for medical applications)
  Tamper evident

COMPETITORS

Berlin Packaging	Owens-Illinois
Dart Container	Polytainers
Dopaco	Portola Packaging
Huhtamäki	Radnor Holdings
International Paper	Rexam Beverage
Kerr Group	Can Americas
Letica	Silgan closures

HISTORICAL FINANCIALS

Company Type: Private

Income Statement

FYE: Last Saturday in December

	REVENUE ($ mil.)	NET INCOME ($ mil.)	NET PROFIT MARGIN	EMPLOYEES
12/04	814	23	2.8%	4,550
12/03	552	13	2.4%	4,700
12/02	494	(33)	—	3,250
12/01	462	(2)	—	3,100
12/00	409	(23)	—	3,100
12/99	329	(9)	—	2,800
12/98	272	(8)	—	2,300
12/97	227	(14)	—	2,100
12/96	151	(3)	—	1,040
12/95	141	6	4.5%	1,100
Annual Growth	**21.5%**	**15.4%**	**—**	**17.1%**

2004 Year-End Financials

Debt ratio: 373.7%   Current ratio: 1.69
Return on equity: 13.6%   Long-term debt ($ mil.): 687
Cash ($ mil.): 0

Net Income History

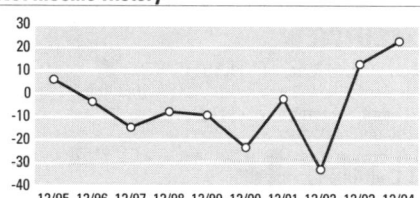

Brand Intermediate

Unlike Superman, Brand Intermediate Holdings cannot leap tall buildings in a single bound, but it can provide a way to get you to the top of a tall building. The company, doing business as Brand Services, provides industrial construction services through more than 80 international locations. It mainly sells, rents, and services scaffolding equipment to companies in the chemical, oil, paper, and petrochemical industries for nonresidential building renovation and maintenance projects. Brand Services also provides insulation services. Directors John Breckenridge, Christopher Behrens, and Sean Epps share, by affiliation, in the 73% ownership of the company held by investment firm J. P. Morgan Partners (BHCA), L.P.

Brand Services pumped up its operations in 2005, when it acquired Aluma Enterprises, Inc. The company expanded its business internationally and added concrete construction to its capabilities through the acquisition.

EXECUTIVES

Chairman: John W. Breckenridge
President, CEO, and Director: Paul T. Wood, age 44
VP, Finance and CFO: Anthony A. Rabb
VP, Operations Support Services and Secretary: Raymond L. (Ray) Edwards, age 50, $174,428 pay
VP, Business Development: Scott M. Robinson, age 56, $172,432 pay
VP, Operations - Southwest Region: Guy S. Huelat, age 42, $166,857 pay
VP, Operations - Northern Region: David R. Cichy, age 53, $165,963 pay
VP, Operations - Southeast Region: James (Marty) McGee, age 48, $166,940 pay
Auditors: Ernst & Young LLP

LOCATIONS

HQ: Brand Intermediate Holdings, Inc.
15450 S. Outer Hwy. 40, Ste. 270, Chesterfield, MO 63017
Phone: 636-519-1000   **Fax:** 636-519-1505
Web: www.brandscaffold.com

Brand Intermediate Holdings operates from more than 80 locations in the US, Canada, Latin America, the Middle East, and Asia.

COMPETITORS

Basic Industries
PDM Steel Service Centers
Safway Services
United Scaffolding
Varley and Gulliver

HISTORICAL FINANCIALS

Company Type: Private

Income Statement

FYE: December 31

	REVENUE ($ mil.)	NET INCOME ($ mil.)	NET PROFIT MARGIN	EMPLOYEES
12/04	334	(7)	—	5,000
12/03	348	(6)	—	4,900
12/02	305	—	—	219
Annual Growth	**4.6%**	**—**	**—**	**377.8%**

Net Income History

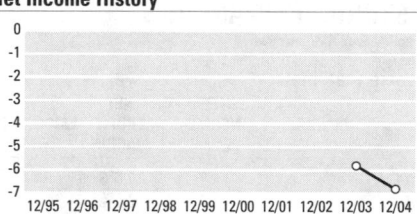

Breda Telephone

At its founding in 1905, Breda Telephone was named for its Iowa hometown. But in 2001 the telephone cooperative adopted a winning acronym when it began using the Western Iowa Networks (W.I.N.) brand. The company provides rural local-exchange carrier services to Breda and the surrounding rural towns of southern and central Iowa including local exchange and long-distance access. It also offers cable TV and Internet access services in some locations and offers the retail sale of telecommunications equipment, including wireless services and equipment. The telephone co-op is owned by its customers.

EXECUTIVES

VP (Vice Chairman): Dean Schettler, age 52
Co-CEO and COO: Robert J. Boeckman, age 42, $99,390 pay
Co-CEO and CFO: Jane A. Morlok, age 50, $91,025 pay
Treasurer and Director: Dave Grabner, age 56
Marketing and Sales Manager: Deb Lucht

LOCATIONS

HQ: Breda Telephone Corporation
112 E. Main, Breda, IA 51436
Phone: 712-673-2311 **Fax:** 712-673-2800
Web: www.win-4-u.com

PRODUCTS/OPERATIONS

2004 Sales

	% of total
Local-exchange carrier revenues	78
Broadcast revenues	13
Internet service revenues	9
Total	**100**

Selected Subsidiaries

Prairie Telephone Co., Inc. (local-exchange carrier)
Tele-Services, Ltd. (cable TV)
Westside Independent Telephone Company (local-exchange carrier)

COMPETITORS

ALLTEL	MCI
AT&T	Sprint Nextel

HISTORICAL FINANCIALS

Company Type: Cooperative

Income Statement

FYE: December 31

	REVENUE ($ mil.)	NET INCOME ($ mil.)	NET PROFIT MARGIN	EMPLOYEES
12/04	7	1	20.6%	35
12/03	6	1	19.0%	—
Annual Growth	7.9%	16.7%	—	—

2004 Year-End Financials

Debt ratio: — Current ratio: —
Return on equity: 9.1% Long-term debt ($ mil.): —
Cash ($ mil.): —

Net Income History

Broder Bros.

Selling clothes is in the genes of sportswear distributor Broder Bros. Begun as a haberdashery in 1919, the company evolved from hats and gloves to distributing imprintable sportswear such as golf shirts, T-shirts, sweatshirts, and jerseys. Broder Bros. also offers its private-label Luna Pier outerwear. Customers, mostly small retailers in the US, can view and order merchandise through seasonal catalogs or online. Broder Bros. bought rival Full Line Distributors in August 2001, and in September 2003 acquired Philadelphia-based Alpha Shirt. The company bought NES Clothing Company in 2004. Private investment firm Bain Capital has held a majority interest of the company since May 2000.

EXECUTIVES

CEO: Vincent Tyra, age 39, $911,000 pay
President: Mark Barrocas, age 33, $490,000 pay
CFO and Secretary: David Hollister, age 39, $490,000 pay
EVP, Purchasing: Glenn Putnam, age 51, $457,000 pay
VP, Controller: Diane Miller
VP, Distribution: Tim VandeMerkt
VP, Finance: Dan Shear
VP, Human Resources: Richard Emrich
VP, IT: Mike Fabrico
VP, Operations: Norman Hullinger, age 45, $392,000 pay
VP Sales, Alpha Division: David Grobison
VP Sales, Broder Division: Dori Bennett
Director, Human Resources: Linda MacEllven
Director, Purchasing: Kurt Schloss
Auditors: PricewaterhouseCoopers LLP

LOCATIONS

HQ: Broder Bros. Co.
6 Neshaminy Interplex, 6th Fl., Trevose, PA 19053
Phone: 215-291-6140 **Fax:** 800-521-1251
Web: www.broderbros.com

Broder Bros. Co. has distribution centers in Albany, New York; Atlanta, Georgia; Charlotte, North Carolina; Cleveland; Dallas; Detroit; Fresno, California; Fullerton, California; Houston; Louisville, Kentucky; Miami; Orlando, Florida; St. Louis, Missouri; Wadesboro, North Carolina; and Plymouth, Michigan.

COMPETITORS

Delta Apparel
Dickie Walker Marine
Drew Pearson Marketing
Fruit of the Loom
Gildan Activewear
PremiumWear
Russell
VF

HISTORICAL FINANCIALS

Company Type: Private

Income Statement

FYE: December 31

	REVENUE ($ mil.)	NET INCOME ($ mil.)	NET PROFIT MARGIN	EMPLOYEES
12/04	877	(2)	—	1,498
12/03	488	(13)	—	—
12/02	430	(1)	—	—
12/01	486	—	—	815
12/00	439	—	—	797
12/99	344	—	—	675
12/98	328	—	—	552
12/97	270	—	—	500
Annual Growth	18.3%	—	—	17.0%

2004 Year-End Financials

Debt ratio: 181.6% Current ratio: —
Return on equity: — Long-term debt ($ mil.): 138
Cash ($ mil.): —

Net Income History

Brookdale Senior Living

Brookdale Senior Living makes the old folks feel at home. The company operates assisted and independent living centers, retirement communities, and a nursing home for middle- and upper-income elderly clients. Brookdale Senior Living has more than 380 facilities in 32 states, offering studio, one-bedroom, and two-bedroom units, as well as meal service, 24-hour emergency response, housekeeping, concierge services, transportation, and recreational activities. The company also provides facilities designed for the treatment of Alzheimer's patients. Chairman Wesley Edens and director Randal Nardone own about 74% of the company through Fortress Investment Holdings.

Brookdale Senior Living generates more than 98% of its revenue through private-pay customers.

EXECUTIVES

Chairman: Wesley R. Edens, age 43
Vice Chairman: William B. Doniger, age 39
CEO: Mark J. Schulte, age 51, $1,164,738 pay
  (prior to title change)
Co-President: Mark W. Ohlendorf, age 45, $713,986 pay
  (prior to title change)
Co-President: John P. Rijos, age 52, $1,138,728 pay
  (prior to title change)
EVP and CFO: R. Stanley Young, age 53, $909,876 pay
  (prior to title change)
EVP, Secretary, and General Counsel:
  Deborah C. Paskin, age 53, $571,319 pay
EVP and Treasurer: Kristin A. Ferge, age 32,
  $331,822 pay
VP and Controller: Thomas W. Girard
VP, Dining Services: Joska J.W. Hajdu
VP, Human Resources: Pamela Dietmeyer
VP, Information Technology: Paul N. Nigro
VP, Treasury Operations: Jeffrey S. Carroll
Auditors: Ernst & Young LLP

LOCATIONS

HQ: Brookdale Senior Living Inc.
  330 N. Wabash, Ste. 1400, Chicago, IL 60611
Phone: 312-977-3700   **Fax:** 312-977-3701
Web: www.brookdaleliving.com

Selected Properties
The Brendenwood Retirement Community (New Jersey)
The Classic at West Palm Beach (Florida)
The Devonshire (Illinois)
Edina Park Plaza (Minnesota)
The Gables at Brighton (New York)
The Gables at Farmington (Connecticut)
The Hallmark (Illinois)
Hawthorn Lakes (Illinois)
The Heritage (Illinois)
The Kenwood (Minnesota)
The Park Place (Washington)
The Springs of East Mesa (Arizona)

COMPETITORS

American Retirement	Holiday Retirement
Atria Senior Living Group	Sunrise Senior Living
Colson & Colson	

HISTORICAL FINANCIALS

Company Type: Private

Income Statement   FYE: December 31

	REVENUE ($ mil.)	NET INCOME ($ mil.)	NET PROFIT MARGIN	EMPLOYEES
12/04	661	(22)	—	10,500
12/03	223	(13)	—	—
12/02	162	12	7.2%	—
Annual Growth	102.3%	—	—	—

2004 Year-End Financials

Debt ratio: 513.8%   Current ratio: 1.15
Return on equity: —   Long-term debt ($ mil.): 367
Cash ($ mil.): 87

Net Income History

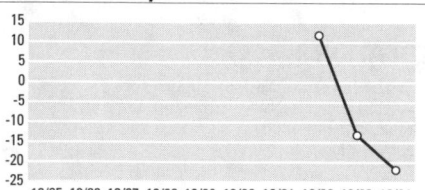

12/95 12/96 12/97 12/98 12/99 12/00 12/01 12/02 12/03 12/04

Brown Brothers Harriman

Brown Brothers Harriman is one of the largest, most prestigious private banks in the US. As a private partnership, the bank is not insured by the FDIC, and each of its some 40 partners has unlimited liability. The company provides investment management, brokerage, banking, mutual funds, and trust services to financial institutions, corporations, and well-off families and individuals around the world. It also performs merger and acquisition advisory, securities lending, foreign exchange, alternative investment, and corporate financing services. Founded in 1818 and known for its conservative investment approach, Brown Brothers Harriman has nearly $3 billion in assets.

EXECUTIVES

Managing Partner: Michael W. (Mike) McConnell, age 62
Partner; Chairman, Alternative Investments Group:
  Robert R. Gould
Partner and Chief Equity Strategist: Ronald J. Hill
Partner and Head of Systems: J. William Anderson
Partner, Global Custody: Douglas A. Donahue Jr.
Partner, Mergers and Acquisitions: John P. Molner,
  age 40
Partner, Relationship Management and Marketing, Asia/Pacific and Head of Network Management:
  Susan C. Livingston
Partner, Relationship Management and Marketing, Europe and the Americas (excluding the US) and Head of New Product Development: Andrew J.F. Tucker
Partner, Banking: William J. (Bill) Whelan Jr., age 50
Managing Director and Controller: Maroa C. Velez
Managing Director and General Counsel:
  James I. Kaplan, age 50
Managing Director and Equity Strategist:
  Charles H. Blood
Managing Director, Alternative Investments Group:
  John R. Hass
Managing Director, Banking: J. Edward (Jed) Hall
Managing Director, Private Equity: Walter W. Grist,
  age 63
Managing Director, Private Equity: Mark W. Johnson
Auditors: PricewaterhouseCoopers

LOCATIONS

HQ: Brown Brothers Harriman & Co.
  140 Broadway, New York, NY 10005
Phone: 212-483-1818   **Fax:** 212-493-8545
Web: www.bbh.com

PRODUCTS/OPERATIONS

Selected Mutual Funds
BBH Broad Market Fund
BBH Inflation-Indexed Securities Fund
BBH International Equity Fund
BBH Money Market Fund
BBH Tax-Efficient Equity Fund
BBH Tax Exempt Money Market Fund
BBH Tax Free Short/Intermediate Fixed Income Fund
BBH US Treasury Money Market Fund

COMPETITORS

Bank of New York	Goldman Sachs
Bear Stearns	J.P. Morgan Private Bank
Citigroup Global Markets	Lehman Brothers
Citigroup Private Bank	Mellon Financial
CSFB (USA)	Northern Trust
Deutsche Bank	Pequot Capital

HISTORICAL FINANCIALS

Company Type: Private

Income Statement   FYE: December 31

	REVENUE ($ mil.)	NET INCOME ($ mil.)	NET PROFIT MARGIN	EMPLOYEES
12/03	1,300	—	—	3,000
12/02	1,300	—	—	3,100
Annual Growth	0.0%	—	—	(3.2%)

Revenue History

1,400	
1,200	○——○
1,000	
800	
600	
400	
200	

12/94 12/95 12/96 12/97 12/98 12/99 12/00 12/01 12/02 12/03

Bruster's Real Ice Cream

It may have an ice cream flavor called Chocolate Lover's Trash, but Bruster's doesn't feed its customers any scraps. Bruster's Real Ice Cream operates and franchises more than 200 ice cream parlors in about 15 states. Its shops offer cones, shakes, and sundaes, as well as frozen yogurt, sherbet, and cakes. Bruster's makes its ice cream fresh each day. Bruce Reed opened the first Bruster's in Bridgewater, Pennsylvania in 1989, and the company began franchising in 1993. Bruster's intends to open 200 new stores by 2006.

EXECUTIVES

Founder: Bruce Reed
CEO: Jim Sahene
VP Operations: Geoff Goodman
VP Finance: Jeff Peterson
VP Franchise Development: Wayne Vincent
VP Marketing: Kim Piper
VP Training: Lynn Marie Nixon
Finance/Accounting: Judy Galand
Finance and Accounting: Jim Westover
Human Resources and Legal: Kathy Ragozzino
Franchise Development: Lori Molnar
Project Management: Mark Oldaker
Real Estate: Jim Graham
Training: Barbara (Barb) Dunlap

LOCATIONS

HQ: Bruster's Real Ice Cream, Inc.
  730 Mulberry St., Bridgewater, PA 15009
Phone: 724-774-4250   **Fax:** 724-774-0666
Web: www.brustersicecream.com

Bruster's Real Ice Cream owns and franchises more than 200 ice cream shops in Alabama, Florida, Georgia, Indiana, Maryland, Mississippi, New Hampshire, New York, North Carolina, Ohio, Pennsylvania, South Carolina, Tennessee, Virginia, and West Virginia.

COMPETITORS

Ben & Jerry's
Carvel
Cold Stone Creamery
CoolBrands
Dairy Queen
Dippin Dots
Dunkin
Friendly Ice Cream

KaleidoScoops
Marble Slab
Mrs. Fields
Nestlé
Planet Smoothie
Ritter's Frozen Custard
YoCream

HISTORICAL FINANCIALS

Company Type: Private

Income Statement
FYE: August 31

	REVENUE ($ mil.)	NET INCOME ($ mil.)	NET PROFIT MARGIN	EMPLOYEES
8/04	39	—	—	1,700

Buffets Holdings

Corn bread dressing, fish patties, baked beans, hot wings . . . kneel and pray to the almighty buffet. Buffets Holdings operates one of the country's largest portfolios of buffet restaurants, with about 360 locations in 38 states. Operating mostly under the Old Country Buffet and HomeTown Buffet brands, the company's locations are self-service buffets featuring entrees, sides, and desserts for an all-inclusive price. Its other brands include Granny's Buffet, Country Roadhouse Buffet & Grill, and Tahoe Joe's Famous Steakhouse. In addition to its company-owned restaurant operations, Buffets franchises about 20 locations.

Buffet Holdings offers a lot of food at a low cost. With more than 100 dishes filling its buffet, the average customer check is $7.42. Private equity firm Caxton-Iseman Capital owns 79% of the company. Sentinel Capital owns an additional 7% of Buffets Holdings, while vice chairman and CEO Roe Hatlen has a 6% stake.

EXECUTIVES

Chairman: Frederick J. (Fred) Iseman, age 51
Vice Chairman and CEO: Roe H. Hatlen, age 61, $638,000 pay (partial-year salary)
EVP, CFO, and COO: R. Michael Andrews Jr., age 40, $224,640 pay
EVP, General Counsel, and Secretary: H. Thomas Mitchell, age 46, $194,324 pay
EVP, Marketing: Karlin A. Linhardt
EVP, Human Resources: K. Michael Shrader
VP, Development: Janet Astor
VP, Workforce Excellence: Nancy Rich
Senior Director of Field Training: Linda Allison
COO, Tahoe Joe's Famous Steakhouse: Loret Carbone
Director of Food Services, Tahoe Joe's Famous Steakhouse: Porfirio Aldape
Director of Operations, Tahoe Joe's Famous Steakhouse: Curt Cappello
Human Resources, Tahoe Joe's Famous Steakhouse: Lorie Ruth
Auditors: Deloitte & Touche

LOCATIONS

HQ: Buffets Holdings, Inc.
1460 Buffet Way, Eagan, MN 55121
Phone: 651-994-8608 **Fax:** 651-365-2356
Web: www.buffet.com

2005 Locations

	No.
California	96
Illinois	32
Michigan	20
Pennsylvania	20
Ohio	16
New York	16
Washington	16
Minnesota	15
Arizona	13
Colorado	12
Wisconsin	12
Indiana	11
Missouri	10
Virginia	9
Massachusetts	9
Maryland	9
New Jersey	8
Oregon	7
Connecticut	6
Iowa	5
Texas	5
Kentucky	3
Nebraska	3
Other states	19
Total	**372**

PRODUCTS/OPERATIONS

2005 Locations

	No.
Company-owned	354
Franchised	18
Total	**372**

COMPETITORS

Applebee's
Barnhill's Buffet
Bob Evans
Boston Market
Buffet Partners
Carlson Restaurants
CBRL Group
CiCi Enterprises
Denny's
Frisch's
Garden Fresh Restaurants
Golden Corral

Luby's
Metromedia Restaurant Group
Pancho's Mexican Buffet
Piccadilly Cafeterias
Ryan's
Shoney's
Star Buffet
VICORP Restaurants
Western Sizzlin
Worldwide Restaurant Concepts

HISTORICAL FINANCIALS

Company Type: Private

Income Statement
FYE: Wednesday nearest June 30

	REVENUE ($ mil.)	NET INCOME ($ mil.)	NET PROFIT MARGIN	EMPLOYEES
6/04	943	8	0.8%	23,000
6/03	985	13	1.3%	23,000
6/02*	527	(7)	—	24,000
12/01	1,045	13	1.2%	25,000
12/00	1,021	32	3.1%	25,200
12/99	937	42	4.5%	25,000
12/98	869	39	4.5%	24,350
12/97	809	29	3.5%	24,830
12/96	751	(7)	—	24,100
12/95	510	27	5.3%	15,540
Annual Growth	**7.1%**	**(12.6%)**	**—**	**4.5%**

*Fiscal year change

2004 Year-End Financials

Debt ratio: —
Return on equity: —
Cash ($ mil.): 42

Current ratio: 0.75
Long-term debt ($ mil.): 496

Net Income History

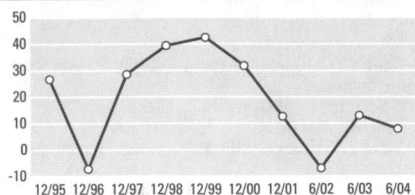

Bureau of National Affairs

The Bureau of National Affairs (BNA) might sound like one of Orwell's worst nightmares, but it produces more than 200 news and information services and dailies for professionals in business and government, including *Daily Labor Report* and *Daily Report for Executives*. Covering public policy and regulatory issues in areas such as law, labor, tax, and environment and safety, it maintains some 600 reporters and editors in Washington, DC. Its information is available in print (books, newsletters), on CD-ROM, and online. BNA also offers commercial printing services and markets tax and financial planning software. Founded in 1929, BNA is one of the oldest employee-owned companies in the US.

EXECUTIVES

Chairman, Bureau of National Affairs and Tax Management: Sandra C. Deglar, age 65
Vice Chairman, President, and CEO: Paul N. Wojcik, age 56, $507,258 pay
VP, COO, and Director; President, Tax Management: Gregory C. McCaffery, age 44, $302,367 pay
VP, CFO, and Director: George J. Korphage, age 58, $265,666 pay
VP, Corporate Secretary, and Director: Cynthia J. Bolbach, age 57
VP, General Counsel, and Director: Eunice L. Bumgardner, age 44
VP Human Resources: Jacqueline Blanchard
VP Resource Management: Carol A. Clark, age 48, $235,907 pay
VP Strategic Development and Director: Robert L. Velte, age 57, $255,894 pay
VP Subscriber Relations: Mary Patricia Swords, age 57
Treasurer: Gilbert S. Lavine, age 53
Controller: James R. Schneble
Auditors: KPMG LLP

LOCATIONS

HQ: The Bureau of National Affairs, Inc.
1231 25th St. NW, Washington, DC 20037
Phone: 202-452-4200 **Fax:** 202-452-4226
Web: www.bna.com

PRODUCTS/OPERATIONS

Selected Publications

Antitrust & Trade Regulation Daily (Web)
Bulletin to Management (Web)
Corporate Practice Series (print and Web)
Daily Labor Report (print and Web)
Daily Report for Executives (print and Web)
Daily Tax Report (print and Web)
Environmental Compliance Bulletin (print and Web)
Health Care Fraud Report (print and Web)
Money & Politics Report (Web)
Payroll Administration Library
   (CD-ROM, print, and Web)
WTO Reporter (Web)

COMPETITORS

American Lawyer Media
Daily Journal
IHS
Informa
Inside Washington Publishers
National Journal
Phillips International
Reed Elsevier Group
Thomson Corporation
Wolters Kluwer

HISTORICAL FINANCIALS

Company Type: Private

Income Statement

FYE: December 31

	REVENUE ($ mil.)	NET INCOME ($ mil.)	NET PROFIT MARGIN	EMPLOYEES
12/04	321	23	7.0%	1,802
12/03	312	16	5.2%	1,878
12/02	310	14	4.6%	1,999
12/01	306	13	4.3%	2,121
12/00	297	16	5.3%	2,085
12/99	281	21	7.5%	2,007
12/98	269	20	7.3%	2,055
12/97	244	20	8.0%	1,893
12/96	233	15	6.3%	1,915
12/95	227	12	5.3%	1,863
Annual Growth	4.0%	7.2%		(0.4%)

2004 Year-End Financials

Debt ratio: 413.9%
Return on equity: 114.1%
Cash ($ mil.): 8

Current ratio: 0.43
Long-term debt ($ mil.): 63

Net Income History

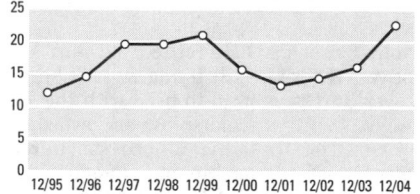

25
20
15
10
5
0

12/95 12/96 12/97 12/98 12/99 12/00 12/01 12/02 12/03 12/04

Burger King

This king commands a whopper of a fast food empire. Burger King operates the world's #2 hamburger chain (behind McDonald's) with more than 11,200 restaurants across the US and in about 60 other countries. In addition to its popular Whopper sandwich, the chain offers a variety of burgers, chicken sandwiches, salads, and breakfast items. Most of Burger King's freestanding units offer drive-through service as well as dine-in seating; about 90% of its restaurants are operated by franchisees. Founded by James McLamore and David Edgerton in 1954, Burger King was owned by UK-based Diageo until 2002 when an investment group led by Texas Pacific Group bought the company for about $1.5 billion and took it private. The company is owned by Bain Capital, Texas Pacific Group, and Goldman Sachs Capital Partners.

The fast food giants have been embroiled in a down-and-dirty price war trying to steal market share while consumers have started to abandon greasy menus in search of healthier alternatives. And while all the big chains have experienced declining same-store sales, Burger King has also suffered from several failed attempts to redesign its brand and, worst of all, a revolving door in the board room.

The company has welcomed nine CEOs since 1989, with the latest CEO to come and go being Brad Blum, former Darden Restaurants vice chairman. Appointed late in 2002, Blum attempted to turn the chain around through a focus on quality and the introduction of new products, such as the Angus Steak Burger and Fire-Grilled Salads. Despite some improvement in sales, he resigned the post after just 18 months, citing strategic differences with the company's board. Later, Bob Nilsen, a veteran of the Taco Bell chain brought in to be president of the company, also unexpectedly resigned.

Shortly after, in 2004 the company announced Greg Brenneman as its latest CEO; he is best known for his turnaround work at Continental Airlines. Brenneman immediately set to work on hiring his new executive team, in particular VP Audit and Risk Management Betty Ann Blandon — whose hiring sparked rumors that Burger King would ready itself for a public offering by 2006. In 2005 Brenneman was appointed chairman of the company.

Also in 2005, the company has introduced a new prototype restuarant in Miami, which is described as industrial chic and which is cheaper to build than the old-style buildings.

HISTORY

In 1954 restaurant veterans James McLamore and David Edgerton opened the first Burger King in Miami. Three years later the company added the Whopper sandwich (which then sold for 37 cents) to its menu of hamburgers, shakes, and sodas. Burger King used television to help advertise the Whopper (its first TV commercial appeared in 1958). During its infancy Burger King was the first chain to offer dining rooms.

Looking to expand nationwide, Burger King turned to franchising in 1959. McLamore and Edgerton took a hands-off approach, allowing franchises to buy large territories and operate with autonomy. Although their technique spurred growth, it also created large service inconsistencies among Burger Kings across the US; this gaffe

would haunt the company for years. Having grown to 274 stores in the US and abroad, Burger King was sold to Pillsbury in 1967.

During the early 1970s Burger King continued to add locations. The company did well during this time, launching its successful "Have It Your Way" campaign in 1974 and introducing drive-through service a year later. Yet parent Pillsbury had to fight to rein in large franchisees who argued they could run their Burger Kings better than a packaged-goods company. In 1977 Pillsbury handed control of Burger King to Donald Smith, a McDonald's veteran, who soon silenced the insurrection. Smith tightened franchising regulations, created 10 regional management offices, and instituted annual visits.

Smith left for Pizza Hut in 1980, and by 1982 Burger King had reached the #2 hamburger chain plateau, trailing only McDonald's. The company struggled through the rest of the 1980s, hurt by high management turnover and a string of unsuccessful ad campaigns (such as the ill-fated 1986 NFL Super Bowl "Herb the Nerd" concept). Pillsbury became the target of a hostile takeover by UK-based Grand Metropolitan, and in 1988 Grand Met acquired Pillsbury along with its 5,500 Burger King restaurants.

Grand Met bolstered Burger King's foreign operations in 1990 by converting about 200 recently acquired UK-based Wimpey hamburger stores into Burger Kings. International expansion increased with new restaurants in Mexico (1991), Saudi Arabia (1993), and Paraguay (1995).

In 1997 Grand Met and Guinness combined their operations to form Diageo, making Burger King a subsidiary. That year Dennis Malamatinas left Grand Met's Asian beverage division to become Burger King's CEO.

Late in 2000 Diageo announced plans to spin off Burger King, but the burger chain's slow sales delayed action. Malamatinas resigned as CEO and was replaced in 2001 by John Dasburg, former CEO of Northwest Airlines. Late that year Burger King took its cue from McDonald's popular New Tastes Menu and introduced 14 new items to its menu, including a vegetarian burger.

An investment group led by Texas Pacific Group acquired Burger King for $1.5 billion in 2002. Earlier that year Texas Pacific had agreed to pay $2.26 billion but renegotiated amid falling sales and a downturn in the burger market. Shortly after the purchase, Dasburg was ousted and Brad Blum, vice chairman of Darden Restaurants, was named as his replacement.

Miami-based Crispin Porter Bogusky took over creative work for the hamburger chain in 2004 and created a series of successful advertisements for Burger King, which targeted the male mid-to-late-20s demographic.

In 2004 Burger King began serving its Angus Steak Burger, which includes one-third of a pound of Angus beef. The next month Steak n Shake sued Burger King for allegedly infringing on its trademark by using the words "steak burger" in its advertising. After just 18 months on the job, Blum resigned his post as CEO in 2004, citing differences with the company's board. He was replaced by Greg Brenneman.

Burger King had consistent sales growth in 2004, and Brenneman's presence was a boost for the company. That year the company signed a deal (with rancher Luiz Eduardo Batalha) to develop about 50 restaurants in Brazil over a five-year period.

EXECUTIVES

Chairman and CEO: Gregory D. (Greg) Brenneman
President and CFO: John W. Chidsey
EVP, Chief Global Marketing Officer, and President, Burger King Brands, Inc.: Russ Klein
EVP, General Counsel, and Chief Ethics and Compliance Officer: Anne Chwat
EVP and Chief Human Resources Officer: Peter (Pete) Smith
EVP and Chief Global Operations Officer: Jim Hyatt
EVP and President, EMEA and Asia Pacific: Steve C. DeSutter
SVP, European Franchised Markets and Burger King UK: Martin Brok
SVP, Global Communications and External Affairs: Clyde Rucker
SVP, Global Communications: Edna Boone Johnson
SVP, Franchise Operations, Eastern Division: Enrique (Rick) Silva
SVP, Franchise Operations, Western Division: Joe Soraci
SVP, Operations and Training North America: Dave Gagnon
SVP, North America Development: Robert Gumm
SVP and CIO: Rajesh (Raj) Rawal
SVP and Chief Concept Officer: Denny Marie Post
SVP and Treasurer: Ben K. Wells
SVP and President, Latin America/Caribbean Region: Julio Ramirez

LOCATIONS

HQ: Burger King Corporation
5505 Blue Lagoon Dr., Miami, FL 33126
Phone: 305-378-3000 **Fax:** 305-378-7262
Web: www.burgerking.com

Selected International Locations

Asia
Australia
China
Guam
Japan
Malaysia
New Zealand
Philippines
Singapore
Republic Korea
Taiwan
Thailand

Canada

Europe/Middle East/Africa
Austria
Bahrain
Cyprus
Denmark
Germany
Gibraltar
Hungary
Iceland
Republic of Ireland
Israel
Italy
Kuwait
Jordan
Lebanon
Malta
Netherlands
Norway
Portugal
Qatar
Saudi Arabia
Spain
Sweden
Switzerland
Turkey
United Kingdom
United Arab Emirates

Latin America/Caribbean
Argentina
Aruba
Bahamas
Bolivia
Brazil
Chile
Costa Rica
Curacao
Dominican Republic
Ecuador
El Salvador
Freeport
Grand Cayman
Guatemala
Honduras
Jamaica
Mexico
Nicaragua
Panama
Paraguay
Peru
Puerto Rico
St. Lucia
St. Maarten
Trinidad/Tobago
Uruguay
Venezuela

COMPETITORS

AFC Enterprises
Chick-fil-A
CKE Restaurants
Dairy Queen
Domino's
Jack in the Box
Little Caesar's
McDonald's
Papa John's
Sonic
Subway
Triarc
Wendy's
Whataburger
YUM!

HISTORICAL FINANCIALS

Company Type: Private

Income Statement

	REVENUE ($ mil.)	NET INCOME ($ mil.)	NET PROFIT MARGIN	EMPLOYEES
6/04	1,300	—	—	32,600
6/03	1,100	—	—	32,000
6/02	1,721	—	—	31,000
6/01	1,474	—	—	30,166
6/00	1,427	—	—	28,432
6/99	1,379	—	—	26,000
6/98	1,449	—	—	27,149
6/97	1,396	—	—	29,590
6/96	1,342	—	—	—
Annual Growth	(0.4%)	—	—	1.4%

FYE: June 30

Revenue History

```
1,800
1,600
1,400
1,200
1,000
  800
  600
  400
  200
    0
     6/95 6/96 6/97 6/98 6/99 6/00 6/01 6/02 6/03 6/04
```

Burrell Communications

Corporate America comes to Burrell to get some street cred. Burrell Communications Group specializes in developing advertising and marketing campaigns targeted to African-American consumers and the urban market. It also offers its expertise in reaching consumers in the general and youth marketplaces. The advertising agency offers such services as brand consulting, account planning, public relations, event marketing, and research in addition to its creative ad work. Founded by Thomas Burrell in 1971, the shop is 49%-owned by French ad giant Publicis Groupe.

EXECUTIVES

Chairman Emeritus: Thomas J. (Tom) Burrell
Managing Partner: Fay H. Ferguson
Managing Partner: McGhee Williams
Managing Partner and Chief Creative Officer: Steve Conner
SVP and CFO: Lou DiSilvestro
SVP Media Services: Linda Jefferson
VP and Director of Engagement Marketing: Kelly Williams
VP and Director of Human Resources: Charlene Guss
Director of Administrative Operations: Janice Kelly

LOCATIONS

HQ: Burrell Communications Group, LLC
233 N. Michigan Ave., Chicago, IL 60602
Phone: 312-297-9600 **Fax:** 312-297-9601
Web: www.burrell.com

Burrell Communications Group has offices in Atlanta and Chicago.

COMPETITORS

Blue Flame Marketing
DDB
E. Morris Communications
GlobalHue
SWG&M
UniWorld Group

HISTORICAL FINANCIALS

Company Type: Private

Income Statement

	REVENUE ($ mil.)	NET INCOME ($ mil.)	NET PROFIT MARGIN	EMPLOYEES
12/04	28	—	—	150
12/03	21	—	—	129
12/02	25	—	—	127
12/01	24	—	—	127
12/00	24	—	—	—
12/99	23	—	—	160
12/98	22	—	—	158
12/97	21	—	—	150
Annual Growth	4.2%	—	—	0.0%

FYE: December 31

Revenue History

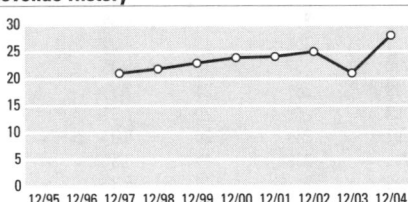

```
30
25
20
15
10
 5
 0
  12/95 12/96 12/97 12/98 12/99 12/00 12/01 12/02 12/03 12/04
```

Burt Automotive

John Elway may have retired, but Burt Automotive Network is still trying to sack him. In Denver Burt goes head-to-head with the John Elway AutoNation dealerships once owned (and still named for) the former Broncos star. Burt operates about 10 dealerships in Colorado that sell new cars from Ford, GM, Mazda, Toyota, and Subaru. It also sells commercial trucks and used cars and offers parts and repair services. With Kuni Automotive, Burt operates Burt Kuni Honda in Centennial, Colorado. Burt, owned by CEO Lloyd G. Chavez, is one of the largest Hispanic-owned businesses in the US. A salesman with Burt since 1950, Chavez became the majority owner in 1982 and bought the rest of the company in 1987.

EXECUTIVES

Chairman: Lloyd G. Chavez Sr.
President and CEO: Lloyd G. Chavez Jr., age 55
CFO: Robin Helms
SVP, General Manager, and Corporate Legal Counsel: John Held
Marketing Director: Deborah Brown Garrity
Human Resources Manager: Todd van Maldeghem
Executive Administrative Assistant: Patty Hara

LOCATIONS

HQ: Burt Automotive Network
10301 E. Arapahoe Rd., Centennial, CO 80112
Phone: 303-789-6700   **Fax:** 303-789-6706
Web: www.burt.com

COMPETITORS

AutoNation	MNL, Inc.
Larry H. Miller Group	Phil Long Dealerships

HISTORICAL FINANCIALS

Company Type: Private

Income Statement

FYE: December 31

	REVENUE ($ mil.)	NET INCOME ($ mil.)	NET PROFIT MARGIN	EMPLOYEES
12/03	1,575	—	—	1,000
12/02	1,478	—	—	1,032
12/01	1,317	—	—	1,350
12/00	1,130	—	—	1,200
12/99	1,004	—	—	1,184
12/98	838	—	—	1,019
12/97	867	—	—	875
12/96	813	—	—	849
12/95	576	—	—	790
12/94	423	—	—	719
Annual Growth	**15.7%**	**—**	**—**	**3.7%**

Revenue History

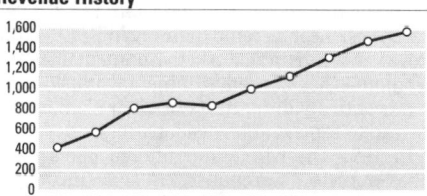

Buy.com

Buy what.com you ask? E-tailer Buy.com sells books, cell phones and services, computer hardware and software, electronics, DVDs, music, toys (in a partnership with eToys Direct), and more. Founded in 1997, Buy.com initially made a splash by selling products below cost. It has since raised its prices but maintains an edge by offering to match any qualified competitor's price. The company distributes *BuyMagazine* (a monthly digital publication featuring product reviews) to its 3.5 million customers. Founder Scott Blum left in 1999, just before the company first filed to go public. After debuting high, stock values plummeted and in 2001 Blum reacquired Buy.com and took it private.

Also in 2001 the company sold its UK operations to UK department store operator John Lewis Partnership. A year later, citing fraud, Buy.com closed its export operations in the UK, Canada, and Australia. The e-tailer then built a more secure export system and expanded its shipping throughout Europe, North America, and the UK, as well as Australia and New Zealand.

The company ventured into the travel industry briefly, with BuyTravel.com, an online discount travel store. Buy.com's partnership with United Airlines was begun and ended within the year; a volatile online travel industry was cited as the reason for the closure.

Buy.com is working hard to give Amazon.com a run for its money. In 2002 Buy.com watched its book sales soar when the company offered all of its book titles at 10% below Amazon.com's prices. A month later, Blum debuted a unique marketing approach, addressing Amazon.com customers in an open letter in *The Wall Street Journal*, expressing his intention to earn their business and save them money.

Blum keeps the hits coming: In 2002 the team that powered Buy.com's Web site was spun off as BuyServices, and has since taken over the e-commerce operations for companies including MTV.com and VH1.com. The following year Blum launched BuyMusic.com, a site that offers music downloads to Windows users.

In October 2004 the company acquired Metals.com which operates a Web site providing rewards (gift certificates and checks) to customers who recommend products to other customers.

EXECUTIVES

Chairman and CEO: Scott A. Blum, age 41
President, COO, Secretary and Director: Neel Grover, age 34, $166,731 pay
CFO: Robert R. (Rob) Price, age 52, $159,051 pay (prior to title change)
CIO: Roger Andelin, age 41, $144,420 pay
CTO: Robb Brock, age 41
SVP Sales: Keith Allen
VP Legal Affairs and General Counsel: Greg Giraudi, age 37, $154,168 pay
VP Marketing: Larisa Hall
VP Sales and Merchandising: Scott Reedy
Director Human Resources: Monika Malone
Auditors: Mayer Hoffman McCann P.C.

LOCATIONS

HQ: Buy.com Inc.
85 Enterprise, Ste. 100, Aliso Viejo, CA 92656
Phone: 949-389-2000   **Fax:** 949-389-2800
Web: www.buy.com

COMPETITORS

Amazon.com
barnesandnoble.com
Best Buy
Blockbuster
Borders
CDNOW
CDW
Circuit City
CompUSA
Cyberian Outpost
Dell
Fry's Electronics
Gateway
Musicland
Overstock.com
PC Connection
Tower Records
Wal-Mart

HISTORICAL FINANCIALS

Company Type: Private

Income Statement

FYE: December 31

	REVENUE ($ mil.)	NET INCOME ($ mil.)	NET PROFIT MARGIN	EMPLOYEES
12/04	291	(15)	—	121
12/03	238	(26)	—	—
12/02	302	(23)	—	—
12/01	400	—	—	200
12/00	788	—	—	258
12/99	597	—	—	230
12/98	125	—	—	196
12/97	1	—	—	—
Annual Growth	**128.3%**	**—**	**—**	**(7.7%)**

2004 Year-End Financials

Debt ratio: —
Return on equity: —
Cash ($ mil.): 0
Current ratio: 0.17
Long-term debt ($ mil.): 0

Net Income History

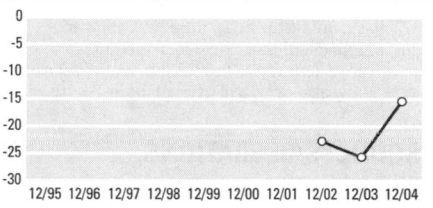

BWAY

BWAY helps keep coffee fresh and ammo dry. The company manufactures steel containers such as aerosol cans, pails, specialty cans, oblong cans, and ammunition boxes. Its products package items from paints, lubricants, and roof and driveway sealants to food, coffee, vegetable oil, and aerosol products. The company also provides material center services such as coating, lithography, and metal shearing. NAMPAC is the company's main subsidiary (metal and rigid plastic container manufacturing). Private investment firm Kelso & Company bought the company in 2002 in partnership with BWAY's chairman and CEO Jean-Pierre Ergas, vice chairman Warren Hayford, and other members of management.

BWAY has moved into the plastic container manufacturing industry through the acquisition of SST Industries, a maker of rigid plastic containers. It also acquired North America Packaging Corporation (NAMPAC), a provider of molded plastic pails, tighthead containers, plastic bottles, and drums in mid-2004. BWAY eventually formed a NAMPAC Packaging division by merging NAMPAC with its newly acquired SST Industries subsidiary later that same year.

Now functioning as two divisions, BWAY Packaging focuses on metal containers while selling and marketing its products under the BWAY name, and the newly created NAMPAC Division focuses on plastic containers, selling its products under the NAMPAC brand name. Still, BWAY's most lucrative segment remains its metal containers, bringing in almost 85% of total sales; the US market accounts for more than 95% of sales.

EXECUTIVES

Chairman and CEO: Jean-Pierre M. Ergas, age 65, $881,250 pay
Vice Chairman: Warren J. Hayford, age 75
SVP; President and COO, BWAY Packaging Division: Kenneth M. (Ken) Roessler, age 42, $418,750 pay
SVP; President and COO, NAMPAC Packaging Division: Thomas K. (Tom) Linton, age 51, $220,161 pay
VP and Treasurer: Jeffrey M. (Jeff) O'Connell, age 51, $268,125 pay
VP, Sales, Aerosols: Sean Fitzgerald
VP, Administration and CFO: Kevin C. Kern, age 45, $421,250 pay
VP, Sales, General Line: Robert C. (Bob) Coleman
Director, Engineering: Dennis Dettmer
Director, Human Resources: Joe Frabotta
Auditors: Deloitte & Touche LLP

LOCATIONS

HQ: BWAY Corporation
8607 Roberts Dr., Ste. 250, Atlanta, GA 30350
Phone: 770-645-4800   **Fax:** 770-645-4810
Web: www.bwaycorp.com

BWAY has manufacturing facilities in California, Georgia, Indiana, Illinois, New Jersey, Ohio, Pennsylvania, Tennessee, Texas, Utah, and Wisconsin; the company also owns a plastics plant in Puerto Rico.

PRODUCTS/OPERATIONS

2004 Sales

	$ mil.	% of total
Metal packaging		
General line containers	472.7	77
Material center services	31.8	5
Coffee containers	14.1	2
Plastic packaging		
Open-head containers	66.9	11
Tight-head containers	11.4	2
Other containers	14.6	3
Total	**611.5**	**100**

Selected Products and Services

Aerosol cans
Ammunition boxes
Coffee cans
Material centers (cut, coil, coat, and lithograph sheets of steel)
Oblong cans
Pails
Paint cans
Specialty cans (utility cans with screw-cap tops and applicator brushes; cone top cans)

COMPETITORS

Amcor
Ball Corporation
CLARCOR
Consolidated Container
Crown
Jarden
Silgan
U.S. Can

HISTORICAL FINANCIALS

Company Type: Private

Income Statement

FYE: Sunday nearest September 30

	REVENUE ($ mil.)	NET INCOME ($ mil.)	NET PROFIT MARGIN	EMPLOYEES
9/04	612	6	0.9%	2,966
9/03	551	(3)	—	1,993
9/02	528	12	2.3%	1,868
9/01	475	(17)	—	1,726
9/00	461	(3)	—	1,954
9/99	467	6	1.2%	2,176
9/98	401	2	0.4%	1,898
9/97	402	13	3.3%	2,097
9/96	283	1	0.4%	1,695
9/95	248	9	3.6%	1,155
Annual Growth	**10.6%**	**(4.7%)**	**—**	**11.0%**

2004 Year-End Financials

Debt ratio: 343.7%
Return on equity: 5.9%
Cash ($ mil.): 27

Current ratio: 1.40
Long-term debt ($ mil.): 395

Net Income History

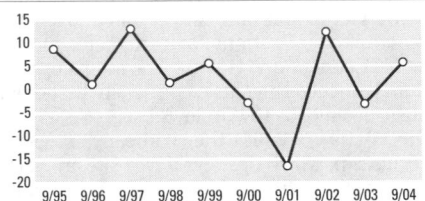

C&S Wholesale Grocers

C&S Wholesale Grocers is at the bottom of the food chain — and likes it that way. The company is New England's largest food wholesaler and second in the US (behind SUPERVALU), delivering groceries to approximately 4,000 independent supermarkets, major supermarket chains (including Safeway), mass marketers, and wholesale clubs. The company distributes more than 53,000 items, including groceries, produce, and non-food items from its more than 50 warehouses. C&S also sells groceries through Grand Union supermarkets. Chairman and CEO Richard Cohen owns the company, which his grandfather started in 1918.

Under pressure from the rapid growth of self-distributing grocery chains (most notably Wal-Mart Supercenters), C&S Wholesale has grown by providing outsourced distribution and logistics services to its retailer customers through its logistics service provider ES3. The wholesaler has taken over the facilities and runs distribution and logistics for customers including the A&P Food Mart, BJ's Warehouse, Giant Food Stores, Stop & Shop, Pathmark, and Safeway.

To avoid losing one of its top customers, the company, through affiliate GU Markets, bought bankrupt supermarket chain The Grand Union Company's assets in 2001, expanding C&S Wholesale into retailing. However, C&S Wholesale has since closed or sold off most of Grand Union's 170 stores. The 2002 acquisition of Tops'

distribution operations, with facilities in Buffalo, New York, and the Cleveland area, opened up new markets for C&S Wholesale. In keeping with its buying surge, C&S in 2003 purchased parts of the wholesale grocery division of Fleming Companies.

HISTORY

Israel Cohen and Abraham Siegel began C&S Wholesale Grocers in 1918 in Worcester, Massachusetts. Cohen ran the company for more than 50 years after buying out Siegel in 1921. It became a family concern in 1972 when Cohen turned the company over to his son Lester, who soon brought in his sons, Jim and Rick.

C&S Wholesale expanded over the years, growing along with its customers. It had $98 million in sales in 1981, the year its skyrocketing growth began. Also in 1981 Rick, now the company's chairman, president, and CEO, engineered a move to Brattleboro, in southern Vermont, where it had better access to interstate highways and a larger workforce.

After attending a seminar hosted by management whiz Tom Peters, in 1987 Cohen set up self-managed teams of three to eight employees who would act as small business units responsible for a customer's order from the time it was received to when it was delivered. Team members were paid for the amount of time they worked and were given bonuses for error-free operations and penalties for errors or damaged goods. His plan saw an immediate response in terms of increased sales, and by 1992 C&S Wholesale had more than $1 billion in sales. Rick bought out his father in 1989 and the next year became the company's single shareholder when he bought out his brother.

C&S Wholesale started its produce business in 1990 (by 1994 it was the major purchaser of locally grown fruits and vegetables) and began making plans to build an 800,000-sq.-ft. refrigerated warehouse near a scenic highway in Brattleboro. However, it ran up against environmentalists and Vermont's Act 250 environmental impact law, and eventually dropped its original plan, opting instead to expand at its headquarters.

In 1992 the wholesaler offered plans for a smaller, revised warehouse, but again met opposition. After a two-year battle, C&S Wholesale gave up and said it would build elsewhere. (Most of its employees and warehouses are now in Massachusetts and New Jersey.)

The following year C&S Wholesale welcomed 127 Grand Union stores and several East Coast Wal-Mart stores as customers. The next year the company picked up another 103 Grand Union stores; Grand Union said it was closing two distribution centers and shifting distribution to C&S Wholesale in a deal worth $500 million a year. A $650 million-per-year contract with Edwards stores was inked in 1996, the year C&S Wholesale's sales topped $3 billion.

The company acquired ice-cream distributor New England Frozen Foods in 1997. Continuing its move toward the mid-Atlantic, C&S Wholesale took over the distribution and supply operations of New Jersey-based grocery chain Pathmark Stores in 1998 for $60 million. In 1999 C&S Wholesale purchased Shaw's Supermarkets' Star Markets' wholesale division and moved into Pennsylvania with a facility in York.

In 2001 the company, through affiliate GU Markets, bought most of the assets of one of its biggest customers, bankrupt The Grand Union Company. C&S acquired about 170 of Grand

Union's 197 stores in the purchase. It transferred most of the stores to third-party purchasers, but continued operating about 20 of them.

In 2002 C&S Wholesale formed a new holding company, called C&S Holdings, and reorganized its management to better oversee its various businesses. Also that summer the company acquired the grocery distribution operations of Tops Markets, a division of Dutch supermarket giant Royal Ahold.

In 2003 C&S acquired the New England operations of SUPERVALU. President and COO Edward Albertian resigned in 2004 after just three years with the company. He was replaced by Ron Wright, a 20-year veteran with the company. In 2005 C&S acquired the warehouse facilities and distribution functions of supermarket chains Bi-Lo and Bruno's. Later that year C&S subsidiary Southern Family Markets bought about 140 Bi-Lo and Bruno's stores.

EXECUTIVES

Chairman and CEO: Richard B. (Rick) Cohen
Vice Chairman: Reuben T. Harris
Co-President; President, GU Family Markets and Southern Family Markets: Mark Gross
Co-President and COO; President, C&S Holdings: Ronald (Ron) Wright
EVP, Distribution and Supply Chain Management: Nat Silverman
EVP, ES3 One Source: Geoff Davis
SVP, Chain Sales and Customer Service: Marilyn Tillinghast
SVP, Retail: Frank Curci
SVP, Finance and Supply Chain: Jim Weidenheimer
SVP, Legal and Human Resources: Carl G. Wistreich
SVP, Merchandising: Michael Papaleo
SVP, Merchandising Logistics: George Semanie
SVP, Procurement: Robert (Bob) Palmer
SVP, Strategic Planning: William Hamlin
VP, Produce: Albert Grimaldi
Chief Administrative Officer: William C. (Bill) Copacino
Director, Corporate Giving: Gina Goff
CIO: Joe Carracappa

LOCATIONS

HQ: C&S Wholesale Grocers, Inc.
7 Corporate Dr., Keene, NH 03431
Phone: 603-354-7000   **Fax:** 603-354-6488
Web: www.cswg.com

C&S Wholesale Grocers has more than 50 warehouses operations located throughout the US.

PRODUCTS/OPERATIONS

Selected Customers
A&P Food Mart
Big Y Foods
BJ's Warehouse
Demoulas
Giant Food Stores
Great American
Pathmark
Safeway
SavMart/Foodmax
Shaw's
Stop and Shop

COMPETITORS

Alex Lee	McLane
Associated Wholesalers	Nash Finch
AWG	Roundy's
Bozzuto's	SUPERVALU
Di Giorgio	Unified Western Grocers
IGA	Wakefern Food
Krasdale Foods	White Rose Food

HISTORICAL FINANCIALS
Company Type: Private

Income Statement
FYE: September 30

	REVENUE ($ mil.)	NET INCOME ($ mil.)	NET PROFIT MARGIN	EMPLOYEES
9/04	13,600	—	—	12,000
9/03	13,500	—	—	9,000
9/02	9,700	—	—	7,500
9/01	8,500	—	—	7,000
9/00	7,000	—	—	5,000
9/99	6,050	—	—	4,000
9/98	5,120	—	—	3,800
9/97	3,665	—	—	3,000
9/96	3,348	—	—	2,850
9/95	2,650	—	—	2,000
Annual Growth	**19.9%**	**—**	**—**	**22.0%**

Revenue History

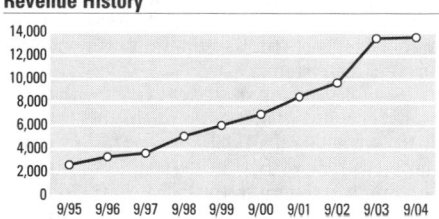

California Dairies

Herding dairies to give them greater "ag"-gregate strength has made California Dairies one of the largest dairy cooperatives in the US. Formed from the 1999 merger of three California dairy cooperatives (California Milk Producers, Danish Creamery Association, and San Joaquin Valley Dairymen), California Dairies' nearly 700 members account for more than 40% of its home state's milk production. The co-op's five plants process milk, cheese, butter, and powdered milk. California Dairies' subsidiaries includes Challenge Dairy Products (retail and foodservice butter products) and Los Banos Foods (cheddar cheese for food manufacturing).

California Dairies is also a majority owner of DairyAmerica, Inc., which markets dairy products, including over 60% of all milk powder produced in the US, to over 40 countries worldwide.

EXECUTIVES

Chairman: George Borba
First Vice Chairman: Tony Mendes
Second Vice Chairman: Dan Macedo
President and CEO: Gary L. Korsmeier
SVP and COO; President, DairyAmerica: Keith Gomes
SVP, CFO: Joe Heffington
SVP, Producer and Government Relations: Richard Cotta
SVP, Marketing and Sales: Jim Gomes
VP, Human Resources: Holly Misenhimer
Treasurer: Gerben Leyendekker
Secretary: Steve Maddox
Director, Information Technology: Scott McDonald
President, Challenge Dairy Products: John Whetten

LOCATIONS

HQ: California Dairies Inc.
11709 E. Artesia Blvd., Artesia, CA 90701
Phone: 562-865-1291   **Fax:** 562-860-8633
Web: www.californiadairies.com

COMPETITORS

AMPI	Foster Dairy Farms
Dairy Farmers of America	Land O'Lakes
Dean Foods	Northwest Dairy
Foremost Farms	

HISTORICAL FINANCIALS
Company Type: Cooperative

Income Statement
FYE: April 30

	REVENUE ($ mil.)	NET INCOME ($ mil.)	NET PROFIT MARGIN	EMPLOYEES
4/04	1,916	—	—	600
4/03	1,870	—	—	565
4/02	2,240	—	—	560
4/01	2,000	—	—	530
4/00	1,832	—	—	550
4/99	1,900	—	—	550
4/98	1,680	—	—	500
4/97	962	—	—	150
4/96	800	—	—	150
4/95	800	—	—	138
Annual Growth	**10.2%**	**—**	**—**	**17.7%**

Revenue History

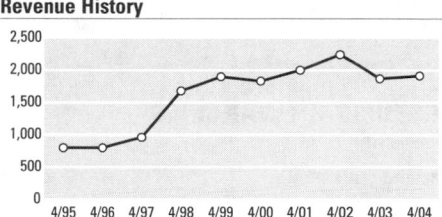

California Software

Founded in 1975, the company now known as California Software (CalSoft) developed a language compiler for the original IBM PC in 1980. When that business waned, CalSoft shifted its focus to software tools supporting the enormous installed base of IBM midrange computers, such as the AS/400 (now called the iSeries). The company also provides software for processing mortgage loan applications. CalSoft went public in 1998, acquired the assets of its bankrupt predecessor company in 1999, then went private again in 2002. CalSoft has offices in Argentina, France, Germany, Italy, Mexico, Singapore, the UK, and the US. CEO Bruce Acacio and president Carol Conway together own about half of the company.

HISTORICAL FINANCIALS

Company Type: Private

Income Statement

FYE: December 31

	REVENUE ($ mil.)	NET INCOME ($ mil.)	NET PROFIT MARGIN	EMPLOYEES
12/04*	23	—	—	150
12/01	6	—	—	38
12/00	2	—	—	67
Annual Growth	**257.5%**	—	—	**49.6%**

*Irregular reporting interval

Revenue History

12/93 12/94 12/95 12/96 12/97 12/98 12/99 12/00 12/01 12/04

California State University

California State University (CSU) turns students into teachers. The university traces its roots to the state's teaching colleges and trains some 87% of California's teachers and staff. CSU is neck and neck with the State University of New York (SUNY) as the nation's largest university system. With some baby boomers' children reaching college age and college participation increasing among adults, CSU's student body has grown to about 400,000. The system has campuses in 23 cities, including Bakersfield, Los Angeles, San Francisco, and San Jose. The university primarily awards bachelor's and master's degrees in about 240 subject areas, leaving higher levels of study to the University of California (UC) system.

CSU is developing strategies to cope with an expected enrollment increase of about 40% through 2010 — what it calls Tidal Wave II. The first waves started with more than 20,000 additional students flooding the system in the fall of 2001. To battle the crippling influx of new students, CSU has begun offering distance-education programs in which students are taught via teleconferencing and the Internet. Other strategies involve adding a summer semester to create year-long schooling, and expanding the use of off-campus centers.

HISTORY

In 1862 San Francisco's Normal School, a training center for elementary teachers, became California's first state-founded school for higher education. Six students attended its first classes, but there were 384 by 1866. It later moved to San Jose to escape the bustle of San Francisco.

In the late 1880s State Normal Schools opened in Chico, San Diego, and San Francisco, followed in 1901 by California State Polytechnic Institute, which offered studies in agriculture, business, and engineering. Other new colleges included Fresno State (1911) and Humboldt State (1913). Most of the schools offered four-year programs and admitted any student with eight years of grammar school education.

The Normal Schools were renamed Teachers Colleges in 1921 to reflect their role in teacher education. Two years later the colleges began awarding bachelor of arts degrees in education.

In 1935 the schools were renamed State Colleges and expanded into liberal arts. In 1947 they were authorized to confer master's degrees in education.

After WWII, students on the GI Bill helped increase enrollment, and campuses opened in Los Angeles, Sacramento, and Long Beach. The prospect of the first baby boomers reaching college age prompted the founding of more campuses in the late 1950s. Russia's 1957 launch of Sputnik spurred additional focus on science and math at all education levels. The next year the colleges began awarding master's degrees in subjects unrelated to teacher education.

During the Red Scare, the system's first chancellor, Buell Gallagher, was accused by the press of being soft on communism. Other faculty were subpoenaed to appear before the House Committee on Un-American Activities.

In 1961 the system became the California State Colleges (CSC) and the board of trustees was created, giving the schools more independence from state government. In 1969 student and faculty groups seeking ethnic studies departments went on strike in San Francisco; the unrest closed the campus.

In 1972 CSC became known as the California State University and Colleges. Ten years later it adopted the California State University as its name.

Barry Munitz became chancellor in 1991, taking over a system that had become oppressive due to a heavy-handed administration. Munitz, who came from corporate America, brought his business sense to the university and increased private fund raising, among other activities. He used words like "consumer" and "product" to describe his job. Munitz also increased tuition, which caused enrollments to drop from 1991-1995.

CSU added two new campuses in 1995, including CSU Monterey Bay, the first military base to be converted into a university since the end of the Cold War.

In 1997 Charles Reed was named to replace Munitz as chancellor, effective the following year. That year CSU proposed the California Educational Technology Initiative (CETI), a plan to build high-speed computer and telephone networks linking its campuses. CETI failed in 1998 after Microsoft and other investors pulled out. In 1999, after lengthy contract negotiations between Reed and faculty members failed to produce accord over teacher salaries and employment conditions, Reed imposed his own merit-based plan. The faculty responded with official rebukes and a vote of no confidence in Reed. The two sides eventually settled on a new three-year contract with provisions that salary and benefits may be negotiated annually.

The rancor over pay continued in 2000 when the California Faculty Association issued a report claiming women were discriminated against and the merit system was inherently unfair. CSU issued its own report denying the charges. In 2001 Reed, stirring up more controversy, began a new quest that would allow CSU to offer doctorate degrees. The move is bitterly opposed by the competing University of California system. In 2002 CSU started a program funded by a federal grant to reduce the harmful effects of alcohol on its students. CSU received a nearly $24 million budget cut in 2003, which led to a reduction in its enrollment growth.

EXECUTIVES

Chair: Murray L. Galinson
Vice Chair: Roberta Achtenberg
Chancellor and Ex-Officio Board Member:
Charles B. Reed, age 64
Executive Vice Chancellor and CFO: Richard P. West
Vice Chancellor, Human Resources: Jackie McClain

President, **California Polytechnic State University, San Luis Obispo:** Warren J. Baker
President, **California Maritime Academy:** William B. Eisenhardt
President, **Cal State Bakersfield:** Horace Mitchell
President, **Cal State Chico:** Paul J. Zingg
President, **Cal State Channel Islands:** Richard Rush
President, **CSU Dominguez Hills:** James E. Lyons Sr.
President, **Cal State Fresno:** John D. Welty, age 61
President, **Cal State Fullerton:** Milton A. Gordon, age 70
President, **Cal State Hayward:** Norma S. Rees
President, **Cal State Long Beach:** Robert C. Maxson
President, **Cal State Los Angeles:** James M. Rosser
Interim President, **Cal State Monterey Bay:** Diane Cordero de Noriega
President, **Cal State Northridge:** Jolene Koester
President, **Cal State Polytechic University, Pomona:** J. Michael Ortiz
President, **Cal State Sacramento:** Alexander Gonzalez
President, **Cal State San Bernardino:** Albert K. Karnig
President, **Cal State San Marcos:** Karen S. Haynes
President, **Humboldt State University:** Rollin C. Richmond
President, **San Diego State University:** Stephen L. (Steve) Weber
President, **San Francisco State University:** Robert A. (Bob) Corrigan, age 70
President, **San Jose State University:** Don W. Kassing
President, **Cal State Stanislaus:** Hamid (Ham) Shirvani
President, **Sonoma State University:** Ruben Armiñana, age 58
General Counsel: Christine Helwick, age 58
University Auditor: Larry Mandel
Director, Public Affairs: Colleen Bentley-Adler
Auditors: KPMG LLP

LOCATIONS

HQ: Trustees of the California State University
401 Golden Shore, Long Beach, CA 90802
Phone: 562-951-4000   **Fax:** 562-951-4949
Web: www.calstate.edu

California State University has campuses in 23 cities.

California State University Campuses

California Maritime Academy
California Polytechnic State University, San Luis Obispo
California State Polytechnic University, Pomona
California State University
  Bakersfield
  Channel Islands
  Chico
  Dominguez Hills
  Fresno
  Fullerton
  Hayward
  Long Beach
  Los Angeles
  Monterey Bay
  Northridge
  Sacramento
  San Bernardino
  San Marcos
  Stanislaus
Humboldt State University
San Diego State University
San Francisco State University
San Jose State University
Sonoma State University

PRODUCTS/OPERATIONS

Selected Majors

Agriculture	History
Anthropology	Latin American studies
Asian studies	Mathematics
Business administration	Nursing
Chemistry	Philosophy
Communications	Physics
Computer science	Psychology
Economics	Public administration
Education	Theater arts

HISTORICAL FINANCIALS

Company Type: School

Income Statement

FYE: June 30

	REVENUE ($ mil.)	NET INCOME ($ mil.)	NET PROFIT MARGIN	EMPLOYEES
6/04	2,900	—	—	44,000
6/03	4,499	—	—	42,000
6/02	4,286	—	—	40,000
6/01	4,050	—	—	40,000
6/00	3,804	—	—	40,000
6/99	3,272	—	—	40,323
6/98	2,612	—	—	39,000
6/97	2,522	—	—	38,512
6/96	3,889	—	—	37,360
6/95	3,121	—	—	33,000
Annual Growth	**(0.8%)**	**—**	**—**	**3.2%**

Revenue History

[Bar/line chart: Revenue ($ mil.) from 6/95 to 6/04, scale 0 to 4,500]

California Steel

California Steel Industries (CSI) is into slab and steel slab. The company uses steel slab produced by third parties to manufacture steel products such as hot-rolled and cold-rolled steel, galvanized coils and sheets, and electric resistance weld (ERW) pipe. Its customers include aftermarket automotive manufacturers, oil and gas producers, roofing makers, tubing manufacturers, and construction and building suppliers. CSI serves the western region of the US. The company operates slitting, shearing, coating, and single-billing services for third parties. JFE Steel, a subsidiary of Japan's JFE Holdings and Brazilian iron ore miner Companhia Vale do Rio Doce (CVRD) each own 50% of CSI.

The majority of sales come from within the US; CSI does sell to foreign customers, primarily in Canada (about 1% of tons). It buys about half of its steel slab from Ispat Mexicana (Imexsa). The purchased slab is transported to the Port of Los Angeles and then sent by train to CSI's facilities.

EXECUTIVES

Chairman: Vicente Wright, age 52, $388,676 pay
President and CEO: Masakazu Kurushima, age 56, $185,771 pay (partial-year salary)
EVP and CFO: Ricardo Bernandes, age 41, $250,688 pay
EVP, Operations: Tashiyuki (Ted) Tamai, age 53, $267,560 pay
VP, Administration and Corporate Secretary: Brett Guge, age 50, $247,626 pay
VP, Sales: James Wilson, age 56, $233,996 pay

Communications Manager: Kyle Schulty
Manager Customer Service, ERW Pipe Products: Martha Martinez
Manager, ERW Pipe Products: Ray Dubreuil
Manager, Manufacturing and OEM Industries: Bob Swist
Manager, Northern Locale Service Centers: Jim Marovich
Manager, Southern Locale Service Center: Al Plummer
Auditors: PricewaterhouseCoopers LLP

LOCATIONS

HQ: California Steel Industries, Inc.
14000 San Bernardino Ave., Fontana, CA 92335
Phone: 909-350-6200   **Fax:** 909-350-6223
Web: www.californiasteel.com

California Steel Industries sells steel products in 11 US states located west of the Rocky Mountains.

PRODUCTS/OPERATIONS

2004 Sales

	$ mil.	% of total
Hot-rolled coil & sheet	565.7	45
Galvanized coil & sheet	440.0	35
Cold-rolled coil & sheet	138.3	11
Electric resistance weld (ERW) pipe	113.0	9
Total	**1,257.0**	**100**

COMPETITORS

AK Steel Holding Corporation
Earle M. Jorgensen
Imsa
Nucor
O'Neal Steel
Oregon Steel Mills
Reliance Steel
Slater Steel
Steel Dynamics
Steelscape
USS-POSCO Industries

HISTORICAL FINANCIALS

Company Type: Joint venture

Income Statement

FYE: December 31

	REVENUE ($ mil.)	NET INCOME ($ mil.)	NET PROFIT MARGIN	EMPLOYEES
12/04	1,257	109	8.7%	944
12/03	764	5	0.6%	921
12/02	754	35	4.6%	929
12/01	640	(4)	—	952
12/00	721	35	4.8%	973
12/99	687	47	6.8%	952
12/98	673	20	2.9%	—
12/97	723	29	4.0%	—
Annual Growth	**8.2%**	**21.0%**	**—**	**(0.2%)**

2004 Year-End Financials

Debt ratio: 50.8%   Current ratio: 3.96
Return on equity: 42.5%   Long-term debt ($ mil.): 154
Cash ($ mil.): 1

Net Income History

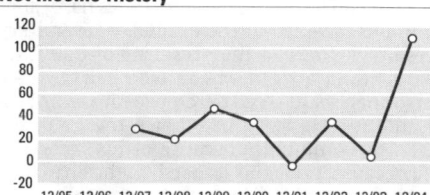

[Chart: Net income ($ mil.) from 12/95 to 12/04, scale -20 to 120]

CalPERS

California's public-sector retirees already have a place in the sun; CalPERS gives them the money to enjoy it. CalPERS is the California Public Employees' Retirement System, one of the largest public pension systems in the US. It manages retirement and health plans for more than 1.4 million beneficiaries (employees, retirees, and their dependents) from more than 2,500 government agencies and school districts. Even though the system's beneficiaries are current or former employees of the Golden State, CalPERS brings its influence to bear in all 50 states and beyond.

With nearly $190 billion in assets, CalPERS uses its clout to sway such corporate governance issues as company performance, executive compensation, and even social policy. In the absence of a strong federal effort to purge corporations of corruption, CalPERS has often acted as a force for reform; urging companies to remove conflicts of interest and make themselves more accountable to shareholders, employees, and the public.

As an example, CalPERS in 2003 sued the New York Stock Exchange and several specialist firms, including Bear Wagner Specialists; Fleet Specialist; LaBranche & Co; Spear, Leeds & Kellogg; and Van der Moolen Holding's Van Der Moolen Specialists USA. The pension fund's suit accuses the exchange and the specialists of using the trading system for their own gain at the expense of investors. (CalPERS found itself on the receiving end of a corporate governance issue in 2004 when a media group sued, demanding CalPERS make public the fees it pays to venture capital firms and hedge funds. CalPERS settled the suit by disclosing the fees.)

CalPERS is also a powerful negotiator for such services as insurance; rates established by the system serve as benchmarks for employers throughout the nation. In 2005 CalPERS, General Motors, and Ford decided to use their purchasing clout to tackle rising health care costs.

Most of CalPERS' revenue comes from its enormous investment program: It has interests in US and foreign securities, real estate development and investment, and even hedge funds and venture capital activities. CalPERS has steadily increased its investments in private equity, looking to take ownership stakes in more firms.

During the coming years CalPERS may be forced to sell assets, as it is expected to be hit with a wave of early retirements by middle-aged workers. In the meantime it is eyeing more short-term investments with higher returns.

CalPERS' board consists of six elected, three appointed, and four designated members (the director of the state's Department of Personnel Administration, the state controller, the state treasurer, and a member of the State Personnel Board). The board has seen its share of disputes, on issues ranging from staff salaries to how to invest assets. The public and sometimes nasty donnybrooks have led to the exodus of several key personnel. In 2004 the president of CalPERS' board, Sean Harrigan, was ousted when the State Personnel Board voted to remove him as its representative. Harrigan had drawn the ire of the business community because of his labor ties and because, under his leadership, the board had withheld votes for directors of most of the companies in which CalPERS invests.

HISTORY

The state of California founded CalPERS in 1931 to administer a pension fund for state employees. By the 1940s the system was serving other public agencies and educational institutions on a contract basis.

When the Public Employees' Medical and Hospital Care Act was passed in 1962, CalPERS added health coverage. The fund was conservatively managed in-house, with little exposure to stocks. Despite slow growth, the state used the system's funds to meet its own cash shortfalls.

CalPERS became involved in corporate governance issues in the mid-1980s, when California treasurer Jesse Unruh became outraged by corporate greenmail schemes. In 1987 he hired as CEO Wisconsin pension board veteran Dale Hanson, who led the movement for corporate accountability to institutional investors.

In the late 1980s CalPERS moved into real estate and Japanese stocks. When both crashed around 1990, Hanson came under pressure. CalPERS was twice forced to take major writedowns for its real estate holdings and turned to expensive outside fund managers, but its investment performance deteriorated and member services suffered.

Legislation in 1990 enabled CalPERS to offer long-term health insurance. Governor Pete Wilson's 1991 attempt to use $1.6 billion from CalPERS to help meet a state budget shortfall resulted in legislation banning future raids. CalPERS made its first direct investment in 1993, an energy-related infrastructure partnership with Enron.

CalPERS suffered in the 1994 bond crash. That year Hanson resigned amid criticism that his focus on corporate governance had depressed fund performance. The system moved to an indexing strategy.

CalPERS eased its corporate relations stance, creating a separate office to handle investor issues and launching an International Corporate Governance Program. However, the next year CalPERS was uninvited from a KKR investment pool because of criticism of its fund management and fee structure.

In 1996 the system teamed with the Asian Development Bank to invest in the Asia/Pacific region; it took a major hit in the Asian financial crisis the next year, but used the downturn as an opportunity to expand its position there in undervalued stocks.

In 2000 the system raised health care premiums almost 10% to keep up with rising care costs. It widened the scope of its direct investments with stakes in investment bank Thomas Weisel Partners (10%) and asset manager Arrowstreet Capital (15%); it also moved into real estate development, buying Genstar Land Co. with Newland Communities. CalPERS said that year it would sell off more than $500 million in tobacco holdings.

In 2001 California state controller and CalPERS board member Kathleen Connell successfully sued the system for not following state-sanctioned rules regarding pay increases. CalPERS was forced to cut salaries for investment managers, a move that prompted chief investment officer Daniel Szente to resign.

In 2003 CalPERS agreed to a record $250 million settlement relating to an age-discrimination suit brought by the Equal Employment Opportunity Commission. Also in 2003, CalPERS clamored for (and got) the resignation of New York Stock Exchange chairman Richard Grasso.

CalPERS and others claimed Grasso's pay of $140 million a year made it impossible for him to effectively monitor the exchange's member companies for corruption.

EXECUTIVES

President, Board: Rob Feckner, age 47
VP, Board: Robert F. Carlson
CEO: Fred R. Buenrostro Jr., age 53
Deputy Executive Officer, Operations: Gloria Moore Andrews
Deputy Executive Officer, Benefits Administration: Jarvio A. Grevious
Assistant Executive Officer, Financial and Administration Services: Vincent P. Brown
Assistant Executive Officer, Public Affairs: Patricia K. Macht
Assistant Executive Officer, Planning and Organizational Development: Allen P. Goldstein
Assistant Executive Officer, Information Technology Services: Ronald E. (Gene) Reich
Assistant Executive Officer, Investment Operations: Anne Stausboll
Assistant Executive Officer, Member and Benefit Services: Kathie Vaughn
Assistant Executive Officer, Governmental, Administrative & Planning Services: Robert D. Walton
Assistant Executive Officer, Health Benefits: Terri Westbrook
Chief Investment Officer: Mark J.P. Anson
Chief, Human Resources: Patricia Chappie
General Counsel: Peter H. Mixon
Auditors: PricewaterhouseCoopers LLP

LOCATIONS

HQ: California Public Employees' Retirement System
Lincoln Plaza, 400 P St., Sacramento, CA 95814
Phone: 916-795-3829   **Fax:** 916-795-4001
Web: www.calpers.ca.gov

PRODUCTS/OPERATIONS

2003 Assets

	$ mil.	% of total
Cash & equivalents	27,155	16
Bonds	38,080	22
Stocks	86,571	50
Other investments	7,385	4
Real estate	11,596	7
Receivables	2,376	1
Other assets	170	—
Total	**173,333**	**100**

Selected Retirement Plans

Defined Benefit Plans
  Judges' Retirement Fund
  Judges' Retirement Fund II
  Legislators' Retirement System
  Public Employees' Retirement Fund
  Volunteer Firefighters' Length of Service Award System
Defined Contribution Plans
  State Peace Officers' and Firefighters' Defined Contribution Plan Fund
Health Care Plans
  Public Employees' Health Care Fund
  Public Employees' Contingency Reserve Fund
Others
  Replacement Benefit Fund
  Public Employees' Long-Term Care Fund
  Public Employees' Deferred Compensation Fund
  Old Age & Survivors' Insurance Revolving Fund

COMPETITORS

A.G. Edwards	Morgan Stanley
Alliance Capital	Nationwide Financial
Management	Principal Financial
AXA Financial	Putnam
Charles Schwab	Raymond James Financial
Citigroup Global Markets	State Street
FMR	T. Rowe Price
Franklin Resources	TIAA-CREF
Janus Capital	UBS Financial Services
Legg Mason	USAA
Mellon Financial	VALIC
Merrill Lynch	Vanguard Group
MFS	

HISTORICAL FINANCIALS

Company Type: Government-owned

Income Statement

FYE: June 30

	ASSETS ($ mil.)	NET INCOME ($ mil.)	INCOME AS % OF ASSETS	EMPLOYEES
6/03	173,333	—	—	1,687
6/02	162,167	—	—	1,614
6/01	173,717	—	—	1,614
6/00	191,157	—	—	1,594
6/99	172,446	—	—	1,500
6/98	156,643	—	—	1,247
6/97	128,880	—	—	1,089
6/96	102,797	—	—	1,037
6/95	90,417	—	—	1,000
6/94	76,935	—	—	900
Annual Growth	**9.4%**	**—**	**—**	**7.2%**

Asset History

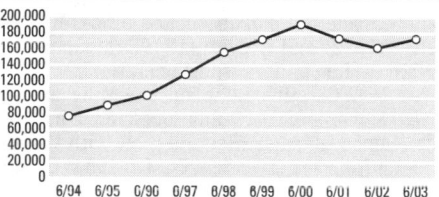

Capella Education

Capella Education gets students ready to wear a graduation cap. The fast-growing company operates Capella University, an online university that offers undergraduate and graduate degree programs in business, organization and management, education, psychology, human services, and information technology. More than 12,000 students are enrolled in the school, which employs about 740 faculty members. Students seeking doctoral degrees account for 47% of enrollment. Nearly 70% of revenues are from federal student financial aid programs. Chairman and CEO Steve Shank (who founded the company in 1993) owns 21% of Capella.

EXECUTIVES

Chairman and CEO; Chancellor, Capella University: Stephen G. (Steve) Shank, age 61, $549,175 pay
SVP Business Management: Paul A. Schroeder, age 45, $327,486 pay
SVP and CFO: Lois M. Martin, age 42
SVP; President and CEO, Capella University: Michael J. (Mike) Offerman, age 57, $327,613 pay
SVP Marketing: Heidi K. Thom, age 41, $307,948 pay
VP and CIO: Scott M. Henkel, age 50, $227,600 pay
VP Government Affairs, General Counsel, and Secretary: Gregory W. (Greg) Thom, age 48
VP Human Resources: Elizabeth M. (Betsy) Rausch, age 52
VP Service Operations: Elizabeth A. Nordin, age 49
Provost, Capella University: Karen Viechnicki
Vice Provost Academic Affairs, Capella University: Ron Anderson
Vice Provost Assessment and Institutional Research, Capella University: Dana Offerman
Media Relations: Maureen Chura
Auditors: Ernst & Young LLP

LOCATIONS

HQ: Capella Education Company
225 S. 6th St., 9th Fl., Minneapolis, MN 55402
Phone: 612-339-8650   **Fax:** 612-977-5060
Web: www.capellauniversity.edu

PRODUCTS/OPERATIONS

Selected Schools and Colleges

Harold Abel School of Psychology
School of Business
School of Education
School of Human Services
School of Technology

Degree Plans

Bachelor's
Certificates
Master's
MBA
PhD
PsyD

Areas of Study

Business
Counseling
Criminal Justice
Health Care Administration
Higher Education
Human Resources & Training
Human Services
Information Technology
Instructional Design for Online Learning
K-12 Education
Non-Profit Management
Project Management
Psychology
Social & Community Services

COMPETITORS

Apollo Group
Cardean Learning Group
The College Network
Corinthian Colleges
DeVry
eCollege.com
Laureate Education
Strayer Education
VCampus

HISTORICAL FINANCIALS

Company Type: Private

Income Statement

FYE: December 31

	REVENUE ($ mil.)	NET INCOME ($ mil.)	NET PROFIT MARGIN	EMPLOYEES
12/04	118	19	16.0%	1,372
12/03	82	4	5.4%	540
12/02	35	(6)	—	380
12/01	30	—	—	350
12/00	16	—	—	181
Annual Growth	**64.9%**	**—**	**—**	**65.9%**

2004 Year-End Financials

Debt ratio: (0.1%)   Current ratio: 2.70
Return on equity: —   Long-term debt ($ mil.): 0
Cash ($ mil.): 5

Net Income History

Captain D's

This captain is hardly a proponent of catch and release. Captain D's is a leading quick-service seafood chain with more than 580 locations in about two dozen states (primarily in the South) as well as overseas. Its menu features fried and broiled fish, shrimp, and chicken, as well as French fries, hush puppies, and corn on the cob. The company operates more than 300 of its restaurants, while the rest are owned by franchisees. Founded in 1969, Captain D's was a sister chain to Shoney's Restaurants before their parent company was acquired by investment firm Lone Star Funds in 2002. Equity firms Charlesbank Capital Partners and Grotech Capital Group acquired the company (for about $150 million) in 2004.

Started by Ray Danner in 1969, Captain D's was originally called Mr. D's. The chain was renamed in 1974. The company has plans to refresh its branding as it adds new menu items and retools advertising.

EXECUTIVES

Chairman: Ron Powell
President and COO: Ronald E. Walker, age 54
CFO: Michael (Mike) Payne, age 53
SVP Operations: Alan Caldwell
SVP Purchasing: Paula Vissing
VP Tax: Donna Adams
VP Real Estate: David Bunch
VP Information Systems: J. Chris Crabtree
VP and General Counsel: Michael T. (Mike) Folks
VP Training: E. Wayne Harris
VP Accounting: Deborah S. (Debbie) Locke
VP Franchise Operations: William E. (Bill) Nelson
VP Franchise Development: Mike Pearce
VP Purchasing: Jeff B. Suber
Chief Marketing Officer: Bob Kendzior

LOCATIONS

HQ: Captain D's, Inc.
1717 Elm Hill Pike, Ste. A-1, Nashville, TN 37210
Phone: 615-391-5461   **Fax:** 615-231-2309
Web: www.captainds.com

Captain D's operates and franchises more than 580 quick-service seafood restaurants in Alabama, Arizona, Arkansas, California, Colorado, Florida, Georgia, Illinois, Indiana, Kansas, Kentucky, Louisiana, Mississippi, Missouri, Nevada, New Mexico, North Carolina, Ohio, Oklahoma, South Carolina, Tennessee, Texas, Virginia, and West Virginia, and also in Japan.

COMPETITORS

AFC Enterprises
Back Yard Burgers
Burger King
Checkers Drive-In
Chick-fil-A
CKE Restaurants
Dairy Queen
Jack in the Box
Krystal
Long John Silver's
McDonald's
Subway
Triarc
TruFoods
Wendy's
White Castle
YUM!

HISTORICAL FINANCIALS

Company Type: Private

Income Statement   FYE: October 31

	ESTIMATED REVENUE ($ mil.)	NET INCOME ($ mil.)	NET PROFIT MARGIN	EMPLOYEES
10/04	506	—	—	11,590
10/03	450	—	—	9,500
10/02	400	—	—	9,000
Annual Growth	12.5%	—	—	13.5%

Revenue History

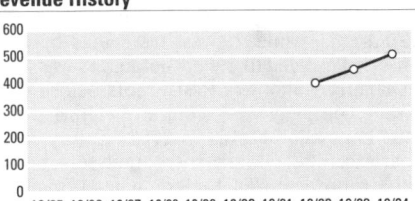

600										
500										
400										
300										
200										
100										
0										
	10/95	10/96	10/97	10/98	10/99	10/00	10/01	10/02	10/03	10/04

Car Toys

When you grow out of toy cars, you will find Car Toys. Car Toys sells car audio components and systems, security systems, navigation systems, radar detectors, wireless phones, and phone plans. The company sells its products at nearly 60 retail locations in Colorado, Oregon, Texas, and Washington, as well as through its Web site. Car Toys stores carry such brands as Alpine, Audiovox, JBL, Motorola, Panasonic, Pioneer, T-Mobile, and Verizon Wireless. As well as selling electronics, Car Toys stores offer advice and installation. CEO and president Dan Brettler founded the company in Bellevue, Washington, in 1987.

EXECUTIVES

Chairman, President, and CEO: Daniel Brettler
SVP and CFO: Robert (Rob) Jensen
SVP, Marketing: Theron Andrews
SVP, Merchandising: James (Jim) Warren
SVP, Stores: Andrew Steele
VP, Best Practices and Controls: Patricia DuBois Harris
VP, Human Resources: Jan Fitzgerald
Director of E-Commerce: Glen Hamilton

LOCATIONS

HQ: Car Toys, Inc.
20 W. Galer St., Seattle, WA 98119
Phone: 206-443-0980   **Fax:** 206-443-2525
Web: www.cartoys.com

COMPETITORS

Best Buy
Circuit City
Good Guys
RadioShack

HISTORICAL FINANCIALS

Company Type: Private

Income Statement   FYE: December 31

	REVENUE ($ mil.)	NET INCOME ($ mil.)	NET PROFIT MARGIN	EMPLOYEES
12/04	169	—	—	1,100

Cargill

Cargill may be private, but it's highly visible. The US's largest private corporation, Cargill's diversified operations include grain, cotton, sugar, and petroleum trading; financial trading; food processing; futures brokering; and feed and fertilizer production. The company is the leading grain producer in the US, and its Excel unit is one of the top US meatpackers. Cargill's brands include Diamond Crystal (salt), Gerkens (cocoa), Honeysuckle White (poultry), and Sterling Silver (fresh meats). Descendants of the founding Cargill and MacMillan families own about 85% of Cargill.

Being private doesn't mean Cargill is cut off from the world. The agribusiness giant has operations in 67 countries throughout the world. Along with its grain and meatpacking businesses, Cargill is a commodity trader and a producer of animal feed and crop fertilizers. It is also a global supplier of oils, syrups, flour, and other products used in food processing.

Cargill also is involved in petroleum trading, financial trading, futures brokering, and shipping. To focus on processing, Cargill sold its seed operations and coffee trading business and is selling part of its steel business. It formed a joint venture with Hormel Foods to market fresh beef, along with pork, under the Always Tender brand.

In 2004 Cargill announced the discovery of genetic markers in cattle that predict whether or not a specific steer will produce good-tasting meat. It plans to introduce a prototype blood test for the marker and will use it to screen cattle in its feedlots to see if it proves economical.

In conjunction with Monsanto, in 2004 Cargill announced the introduction of a low-linolenic

soybean, which can be used to produce soybean oil that helps reduce trans-fats in food products. Also that year Cargill combined its crop-nutrition segment with phosphate fertilizer maker IMC Global to form a new, publicly traded company called Mosaic. Cargill owns about 66% of the company. This is the first time privately held Cargill has ventured into the public sector.

Cargill announced in 2005 that it plans to acquire the global pectin business of Citrico and the food-ingredients operations of Degussa.

In 2005 Cargill announced it was acquiring Ontario's largest beef processor, Ontario Beef Limited.

HISTORY

William W. Cargill founded Cargill in 1865 when he bought his first grain elevator in Conover, Iowa. He and his brother Sam bought grain elevators all along the Southern Minnesota Railroad in 1870, just as Minnesota was becoming an important shipping route. Sam and a third brother, James, expanded the elevator operations while William worked with the railroads to monopolize transport of grain to markets and coal to farmers.

Around the turn of the century, William's son William S. invested in a number of ill-fated projects. William W. found that his name had been used to finance the projects; shortly afterward, he died of pneumonia. Cargill's creditors pressed for repayment, which threatened to bankrupt the company. John MacMillan, William W.'s son-in-law, took control and rebuilt Cargill. It had recovered by 1916 but lost its holdings in Mexico and Canada. MacMillan opened offices in New York (1922) and Argentina (1929), expanding grain trading and transport operations.

In 1945 Cargill bought Nutrena Mills (animal feed) and entered soybean processing; corn processing began soon after and grew with the demand for corn sweeteners. In 1954 Cargill benefited when the US began making loans to help developing countries buy American grain. Subsidiary Tradax, established in 1955, became one of the largest grain traders in Europe. A decade later Cargill began trading sugar by purchasing sugar and molasses in the Philippines and selling them abroad.

Cargill made its finances public in 1973 (as a requirement for its unsuccessful takeover bid of Missouri Portland Cement), revealing it to be one of the US's largest companies, with $5.2 billion in sales. In the 1970s it expanded into coal, steel, and waste disposal and became a major force in metals processing, beef, and salt.

In the early 1990s Cargill began selling branded meats and packaged foods directly to supermarkets. To placate family heirs who wanted to take Cargill public, CEO Whitney MacMillan, grandson of John, created an employee stock plan in 1991 that allowed shareholders to cash in their shares. He also boosted dividends and reorganized the board, reducing the family's control. MacMillan retired in 1995 and non-family member Ernest Micek became CEO and chairman.

The firm bought Akzo Nobel's North American salt operations in 1997, becoming the #2 US salt company. Micek resigned as CEO in 1999 and was replaced by Warren Staley. Also in 1999 Cargill fessed up to misappropriating some genetic seed material from rival Pioneer Hi-Bred, killing the $650 million sale of its North American seed assets to Germany's AgrEvo. Cargill sold its North American hybrid seed business to

Dow Chemical in 2000 (Cargill had sold its foreign seed operations to Monsanto in 1998).

In 2002 Cargill purchased a 56% stake in Cerestar (starches, syrups, feeds) from Montedison SpA, the Italian agriculture and energy conglomerate. It subsequently purchased the bulk of the company's publicly held stock, increasing its ownership of Cerestar to approximately 97%.

As part of a joint venture with Mitsubishi Chemical, in 2004 Cargill opened a manufacturing plant for erythritol, a sweetener that is claimed to taste like sugar but contain no calories. Entering into the European ingredients market, that year Cargill also acquired The Duckworth Group, a UK flavor company with facilities in Africa, China, India, and the UK. Later in 2004, Cargill took over Canadian frozen beef-patty maker Caravelle Foods.

In 2005 Cargill acquired The Dow Chemical Company's interest in the two companies' 50-50 plastics business joint venture, Cargill Dow LLC, and renamed it NatureWorks. It also broke ground for its first oil refinery in Russia. The company also added to its European cocoa presence with the 2005 purchase of East German industrial chocolate maker Schierstedter Schokoladefabrik. It also added to its beef-processing holdings with the purchase of Canadian company Better Beef, and to its bakery systems with the purchase of Integrated Bakery Resources.

That year it also sold its subsidiary Cargill Investor Services (CIS) to financial-services company REFCO for $208 million cash and future cash payments of between $67 million and $192 million, contingent on CIS's performance.

EXECUTIVES

Chairman and CEO: Warren R. Staley
Vice Chairman: Robert L. Lumpkins
Vice Chairman: F. Guillaume (Bassy) Bastiaens
Vice Chairman and Executive Supervisor, Cargill Asia: David W. Raisbeck
President and COO: Gregory R. Page
EVP: David M. Larson
SVP: David W. Rogers
SVP, Director of Corporate Affairs: Robbin S. Johnson Sr.
SVP and CFO: William W. Veazey
Corporate VP and Controller: Galen G. Johnson
Corporate VP and CTO: Ronald L. Christenson
Corporate VP, General Counsel, and Company Secretary: Steven C. Butler
Corporate VP, Human Resources: Nancy P. Siska
Corporate VP, Information Technology, and CIO: Rita J. Heise
Corporate VP, Public Affairs: Bonnie E. Raquet
Executive Director, Cargill Foundation: Mark Murphy
Auditors: KPMG LLP

LOCATIONS

HQ: Cargill, Incorporated
15407 McGinty Rd. West, Wayzata, MN 55391
Phone: 952-742-7575   **Fax:** 952-742-7393
Web: www.cargill.com

Cargill has operations in about 60 countries worldwide.

PRODUCTS/OPERATIONS

Selected Divisions and Products

Agriculture
　Caprock Industries
　Cargill AgHorizons
　Cargill Animal Nutrition
　Cargill Fertilizer
　Cargill Ventures
　Champions Choice

Financial and Risk Management
　Black River Asset Management
　Cargill Financial Markets Group
　Cargill Value Investment
　Cargill Ventures
Food/Food Processing
　Caravelle Foods
　Cargill Dry Corn Ingredients
　Duckworth Group
　Fermentation Solutions
　Cargill Foods
　Popwise Popping Oil
　Cargill Foodservice
　Cargill Juice
　Cargill Malt
　Cargill Salt
　Cargill Sweeteners
　Chocolate
　　Wilbur Chocolate
　　Peter's Chocolate
　　Schierstedter Schokoladefabrik
　Cocoa Processing
　　Fennema
　　Gerkens
　Excel
　Health & Food Technologies
　Honeysuckle White
　Horizon Milling
　Industrial Oils & Lubricants
　Progressive Baker
　Specialty Food Ingredients
　Sterling Silver Premium Meats
　Starches & Sweeteners
　Sun Valley Foods
　Sunny Fresh Foods
Industrial
　Cargill Industrial Oils
　NatureWax
Trading
　Cargill Cotton
　Cargill Energy
　Cargill Ferrous International
　Cargill Petroleum
　Cargill Power & Gas Markets
　Cargill Sugar
　Cargill World Trading Unit — Malaysia

COMPETITORS

ADM	King Arthur Flour
Ag Processing	Koch
BASF AG	Land O'Lakes Purina Feed
Bunge Limited	Morton Salt
CHS	Nippon Steel
COFCO	Nucor
ConAgra	Perdue
ContiGroup	Rohm and Haas
Corn Products	Saskatchewan Wheat Pool
International	Smithfield Foods
Dow Chemical	Tate & Lyle
DuPont	Tyson Foods
General Mills	Tyson Fresh Meats
Hormel	United States Steel

HISTORICAL FINANCIALS

Company Type: Private

Income Statement

FYE: May 31

	REVENUE ($ mil.)	NET INCOME ($ mil.)	NET PROFIT MARGIN	EMPLOYEES
5/05	71,066	2,103	3.0%	124,000
5/04	62,907	1,331	2.1%	101,000
5/03	59,894	1,290	2.2%	98,000
5/02	50,826	827	1.6%	97,000
5/01	49,204	358	0.7%	90,000
5/00	47,602	480	1.0%	84,000
5/99	45,697	597	1.3%	84,000
5/98	51,418	468	0.9%	80,600
5/97	56,000	814	1.5%	79,000
5/96	56,000	902	1.6%	76,000
Annual Growth	2.7%	9.9%	—	5.6%

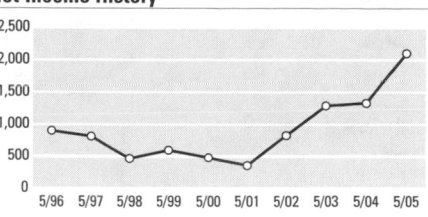

Net Income History

Caribou Coffee

Caribou Coffee Company serves hot Joe to the Java herd. The company operates the second largest non-franchised coffee chain in the US (behind Starbucks), based on the number of locations, with 322 stores in 12 states and the District of Columbia. The outlets, which resemble ski lodges and Alaskan cabins, offer various coffee blends, as well as specialty coffee drinks, teas, and baked goods. The company also sells whole bean coffee and brewing supplies. Its products are available in offices, and to the food-service and retail food industries. Caribou Coffee was founded in 1992 by John and Kim Puckett. Bahrain-based investment group Arcapita owns 84% of Caribou Coffee, which filed an IPO in July 2005.

Of Caribou's 322 locations, three are licensed and four are joint ventures. Under the leadership of chairman and CEO Michael Coles (founder of the Great American Cookie Company, now owned by Mrs. Fields' Original Cookies), the company has added 107 locations during the past two years. It plans to add about 80 in 2005 and about 110 in 2006. Caribou also plans to license its brand internationally, with an emphasis on the Middle East.

In its first foray into the western US, in 2005 Caribou became the in-flight coffee of Frontier Airlines. The company's other commercial-channel customers include Independence Air and foodservice provider ARAMARK.

EXECUTIVES

Chairman, President, and CEO: Michael J. Coles, age 61
CFO: George E. Mileusnic, age 50
SVP, Store Operations: Amy O'Neil, age 35
VP, Business Development and Commercial Sales: Henry A. Stein, age 48
VP, Human Resources: Karen E. McBride-Raffel, age 39
VP, Global Franchising: Bachir A. Mihoubi, age 47
VP, Marketing: Kathy F. Hollenhorst, age 43
VP, Real Estate and Store Development: Janet D. Astor, age 39
VP, Research and Development: Edward T. (Eddie) Boyle, age 43
VP, Support Operations: R. Paul Turek, age 50
VP, Training: Deborah K. (Deb) Jones, age 51
VP and Controller: Michael E. (Mike) Peterson, age 42
Senior Director, Coffee and Tea: Chad Trewick
Senior Director, IS: Scott Ficek
Director, Marketing: Jeremy Kugel
Auditors: Ernst & Young LLP

LOCATIONS

HQ: Caribou Coffee Company, Inc.
3900 Lakebreeze Ave. North,
Brooklyn Center, MN 55429
Phone: 763-592-2200   **Fax:** 763-592-2300
Web: www.cariboucoffee.com

2004 Locations

	No.
Minnesota	151
Illinois	54
Ohio	28
Michigan	23
North Carolina	19
Georgia	13
Maryland	9
Wisconsin	7
Virginia	6
Washington, DC	5
Pennsylvania	3
Iowa	2
North Dakota	2
Total	**322**

PRODUCTS/OPERATIONS

2004 Sales

	$ mil.	% of total
Coffeehouses	157.5	98
Other	3.3	2
Total	**160.8**	**100**

COMPETITORS

Big Apple Bagels	Kraft Foods
Bruegger's	Krispy Kreme
The Coffee Bean	Mars
Coffee Beanery	Nestlé
Community Coffee	New World Restaurants
Diedrich Coffee	Peet's
Dunkin	Procter & Gamble
Dunn Bros Coffee	Restaurant Developers
Farmer Bros.	Starbucks
Green Mountain Coffee	Tim Hortons
It's A Grind	Tully's Coffee
Coffee Franchise	

HISTORICAL FINANCIALS

Company Type: Public

Income Statement

FYE: Sunday nearest Dec. 31

	REVENUE ($ mil.)	NET INCOME ($ mil.)	NET PROFIT MARGIN	EMPLOYEES
12/04	161	(2)	—	4,934
12/03	124	(1)	—	3,900
12/02	108	3	2.9%	3,000
12/01	80	—	—	2,200
12/00	80	—	—	2,200
12/99	65	—	—	1,800
Annual Growth	**19.9%**	**—**	**—**	**22.3%**

2004 Year-End Financials

Debt ratio: 59.0%
Return on equity: —
Cash ($ mil.): 8

Current ratio: 0.78
Long-term debt ($ mil.): 20

Net Income History

NASDAQ: CRGU

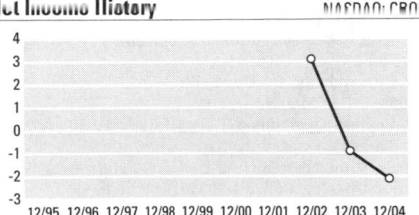

4		
3		
2		
1		
0		
-1		
-2		
-3		

12/95 12/96 12/97 12/98 12/99 12/00 12/01 12/02 12/03 12/04

Caritor

Caritor definitely cares about the state of your technology. The company provides a variety of information technology (IT) services and products including software product development, software application development, and application management and technology integration services. The company has locations in the US, the UK, India, Singapore, and South Africa.

EXECUTIVES

Chairman and CEO: Mani Subramanian
CFO: Chris Setterington
SVP Global Client Management: Jim Puthuff
SVP Client Management: Krishna Prabhu
SVP Human Capital and Quality: Srikanth Rao
SVP Infrastructure: Pradeep Srinivas
SVP Sales and Marketing: S. G. Raja (Raj) Sekharan

LOCATIONS

HQ: Caritor, Inc.
210 Porter Dr., Ste. 315, San Ramon, CA 94583
Phone: 925-838-8600   **Fax:** 925-838-7138
Web: www.caritor.com

COMPETITORS

Computer Sciences Corp.
EDS
IBM Global Services
SAIC
Siemens Business Services

HISTORICAL FINANCIALS

Company Type: Private

Income Statement

FYE: December 31

	REVENUE ($ mil.)	NET INCOME ($ mil.)	NET PROFIT MARGIN	EMPLOYEES
12/04	87	—	—	2,250
12/03	58	—	—	—
12/02	40	—	—	1,500
Annual Growth	**47.5%**	**—**	**—**	**22.5%**

Revenue History

90	
80	
70	
60	
50	
40	
30	
20	
10	
0	

12/95 12/96 12/97 12/98 12/99 12/00 12/01 12/02 12/03 12/04

Carlson

Carlson Companies began in 1938 as the Gold Bond Stamp Company, but has evolved into a leisure services juggernaut. The company owns 50% of travel giant Carlson Wagonlit (French hotelier Accor owns the rest). It also owns more than 900 hotels in about 70 countries under brands such as Radisson, Country Inns & Suites By Carlson, Park Inn, and Park Plaza. Carlson's restaurant empire includes the 750-unit T.G.I. Friday's chain. A specialist in relationship marketing, Carlson Marketing Group offers services such as sales promotion and customer loyalty programs. CEO Marilyn Carlson Nelson and director Barbara Carlson Gage, the daughters of founder Curtis Carlson, each own half of the company.

Carson Wagonlit is one of the largest business travel firms in the world, counting AT&T, General Electric, and IBM among its clients. For leisure vacationers, the Carlson Leisure Group operates a network of 1,700 travel agency locations under a variety of names.

In 2002 the company announced it was building about 20 new hotels, largely Radisson and Country Inns & Suites, in India. The move is part of a larger strategy to enhance Carlson's brand presence in the Asia/Pacific region. Carlson also spent the last few years becoming active in cruise operations through its Radisson Seven Seas Cruises, which offers one all-suite and five deluxe ships sailing to over 300 destinations.

HISTORY

Curtis Carlson, the son of Swedish immigrants, graduated from the University of Minnesota in 1937 and went to work selling soap for Procter & Gamble in the Minneapolis area. In 1938 he borrowed $55 and formed Gold Bond Stamp Company to sell trading stamps. His wife, Arleen, dressed as a drum majorette and twirled a baton to promote the concept. By 1941 the company had 200 accounts. Business was slowed by WWII but took off in the 1950s. During the 1960s the company began diversifying into other enterprises such as travel, marketing, hotels, and real estate.

In 1962 Gold Bond Stamp bought the Radisson Hotel in Minneapolis and began expanding the chain. The company adopted the Carlson Companies name in 1973. Carlson Companies continued expanding its holdings during the 1970s, buying the 11-unit T.G.I. Friday's chain, as well as Country Kitchen International, a string of family restaurants.

In 1979 Carlson bought First Travel Corp., which owned travel agency Ask Mr. Foster and Colony Hotels. Carlson Companies slowed the pace of its acquisitions in the 1980s. Hired in 1984, Juergen Bartels changed the hospitality division's strategy from building and owning hotels to franchising and managing them. This enabled Carlson to weather the crash that followed the 1980s hotel building boom.

The company took T.G.I. Friday's public to fund expansion in 1983, but it reacquired all outstanding shares in 1989. Carlson launched its cruise ship business in 1992, when the luxury liner SSC *Radisson Diamond* set sail.

The company made a major international advance in 1994 when it formed joint venture Carlson Wagonlit Travel, with France's Accor. In 1997 Carlson expanded into the luxury hotel business when it bought Regent International from Four

Seasons. In a nod to its roots, the company also unveiled the Gold Points Reward guest loyalty system to reward customers who frequent its hotels and restaurants.

In 1998 Curtis Carlson appointed his daughter, Marilyn Carlson Nelson, as the company's chief executive (he remained chairman). The following year Carlson Companies merged its UK leisure travel business with UK-based travel and financial services firm Thomas Cook. Founder Curtis Carlson died that year and Nelson added chairman to her title. The company later filed to spin off its T.G.I. Friday's unit as Carlson Restaurants Worldwide.

In 2001 Carlson Companies sold its 22% stake in Thomas Cook Holdings to German tour company C&N (which then changed its name to Thomas Cook AG). In mid-2001 the company bought 52-unit Asian restaurant chain Pick Up Stix. The following year Carlson Companies announced a major expansion initiative into the Asia/Pacific region. The company bought customer-based business strategy firm Peppers & Rogers in 2003, and the next year completed the purchase of the business travel subsidiary of Maritz Travel.

EXECUTIVES

Chairman and CEO: Marilyn Carlson Nelson, age 65
President and COO: Curtis C. Nelson
EVP and CFO: Trudy Rautio
EVP, CIO, and Customer Technology Officer: Jeffrey A. (Jeff) Balagna, age 44
SVP and General Counsel: William A. Van Brunt
SVP Human Resources: Jim Porter
VP and Chief Communications Officer: Kim Olson
VP and Treasurer: John M. Diracles Jr.
VP Assurance and Business Risk Management: Vicki Rasmusen
VP Business Process Improvement: Joseph Dehler
VP Corporate Human Resources: Charles Montreuil
VP Enterprise Supply Chain Management: Larry Taylor
VP Enterprise Transformation and Integration: Steve Geiger
VP Executive Communications: Douglas R. Cody
VP External Affairs: Deborah Cundy
VP Finance and Chief Accounting Officer: Robert Kleinschmidt
VP Financial Shared Services, Carlson Shared Services: Jim Hotze
VP Human Resources Shared Services, Carlson Shared Services: Greg Peters
VP Leadership and Organizational Development: Rick Clevette
VP Legal and Corporate Secretary: Ralph Beha

LOCATIONS

HQ: Carlson Companies, Inc.
701 Carlson Pkwy., Minnetonka, MN 55305
Phone: 763-212-1000 **Fax:** 763-212-2219
Web: www.carlson.com

Carlson Companies has operations in more than 140 countries.

PRODUCTS/OPERATIONS

Selected Operations

Cruises
Cruise Holidays
Radisson Seven Seas Cruises
SeaMaster Cruises
Hotels
Country Inns & Suites By Carlson
Park Inn Hotels
Park Plaza Hotels & Resorts
Radisson Hotels & Resorts
Regent International Hotels

Management Consulting
Peppers & Rogers Group
Marketing
Carlson Marketing Group
Gold Points Rewards Network
Restaurants
Pick Up Stix
T.G.I. Friday's
Travel
Carlson Leisure Travel Services
Carlson Wagonlit Travel (50%)
CW Government Travel
Results! Travel

COMPETITORS

American Express
Applebee's
Brinker
Carnival
Darden
Denny's
Fairmont Hotels
Four Seasons Hotels
Gage Marketing
Hilton
Hyatt
Interpublic Group
Marriott
Metromedia
Mitchells & Butlers
O'Charley's
Omni Hotels
Omnicom
Outback Steakhouse
Ritz-Carlton
Royal Caribbean Cruises
Starwood Hotels & Resorts
Sunterra
WorldTravel
WPP Group

HISTORICAL FINANCIALS

Company Type: Private

Income Statement				FYE: December 31
	REVENUE ($ mil.)	NET INCOME ($ mil.)	NET PROFIT MARGIN	EMPLOYEES
12/04	8,400	—	—	190,000
12/03	6,800	—	—	190,000
12/02	6,700	—	—	180,000
12/01	6,800	—	—	188,000
12/00	9,800	—	—	192,000
12/99	9,800	—	—	188,000
12/98	7,800	—	—	147,000
12/97	6,600	—	—	68,530
12/96	4,900	—	—	65,462
12/95	4,500	—	—	69,000
Annual Growth	**7.2%**	**—**	**—**	**11.9%**

Revenue History

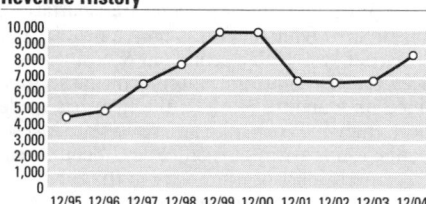

Carlson Wagonlit

History was bunk for Henry Ford, but for Carlson Wagonlit Travel it was a bunk bed. Carlson Wagonlit (pronounced Vah-gon-LEE) Travel descends from Europe's Wagons-Lits (literally, sleeping cars) company, which was founded by the creator of the Orient Express, and from the US's oldest travel agency chain (Ask Mr. Foster). It manages business travel from more than 3,000 travel offices in more than 140 countries. The company is the #2 travel firm in the world behind American Express. It is co-owned by the US firm Carlson Companies (whose US leisure and franchise operations also fall under the Carlson Wagonlit brand) and France's Accor.

Carlson Companies is a service conglomerate with nonbusiness travel operations such as hospitality (it franchises Radisson Hotels, T.G.I. Friday's and Italianni's restaurants, and luxury cruise lines) and marketing services (motivational and incentive programs for businesses). Accor is reaping the benefits of training the company's travel agents in booking Accor hotel rooms. The company's two parents have invested $100 million to get Carlson Wagonlit online with business-to-consumer and business-to-business sites.

The company's joint venture project with China Air Service (51% owned by CAS; 49% Carlson Wagonlit) opened offices in Shanghai and Guangzhou in 2004, further strengthening its position as China's leading corporate travel management company. In the spring of 2004 Carlson Wagonlit purchased Maritz Travel's US corporate travel subsidiary (MCT).

HISTORY

Belgian inventor Georges Nagelmackers' first enterprise was adding sleeping compartments to European trains in 1872. Nagelmackers later created the Orient Express. Over the years his Wagons-Lits company expanded its mission to become Wagonlit Travel.

While Nagelmackers was establishing his business in Europe, Ward G. Foster was giving out steamship and train schedules from his gift shop facing the stately Ponce de Leon Hotel in St. Augustine, Florida. As legend has it, hotel patrons with travel questions were directed to Foster's shop with: "Ask Mr. Foster. He'll know." In 1888 he founded Ask Mr. Foster Travel (it became the oldest travel agency in the US). By 1913 the company had offices located in pricey department stores and in the lobbies of upscale hotels and resorts throughout the country. After 50 years at the helm, Foster sold his business in 1937, three years before his death.

After suffering hard times during WWII and into the 1950s, the company changed hands again in 1957 when Donald Fisher and Thomas Orr, two Ask Mr. Foster shareholders, bought controlling interests for $157,000. In 1972 Peter Ueberroth (future Major League Baseball commissioner and Los Angeles Olympic Organizing Committee president) bought the company, then sold it in 1979 to Carlson Companies. In 1990 Ask Mr. Foster became Carlson Travel Network. Also that year Carlson Companies acquired the UK's A.T. Mays, the Travel Agents — a leading UK seller of vacation and tour packages. By 1992 Carlson Companies, besides adding a travel agency a day to the 2,000-plus it already owned, was adding a new hotel every 10 days.

In 1994 Carlson Companies joined with French hotelier Accor to form the joint venture Carlson Wagonlit Travel. (Accor had acquired a majority stake in Wagonlit Travel in 1990.) Under a dual-president ownership, the parent companies owned operations in specific world regions. The two companies began developing new business technology and expanded into new global business markets. Carlson Wagonlit acquired Germany's Brune Reiseburo travel agency and opened a branch office in Moscow. Through 1995 and 1996 acquisitions targeted the Asia/Pacific region, including Hong Kong's and Japan's Dodwell Travel and the corporate travel business of Singapore's Jetset Travel. The joint venture also formed a partnership with Traveland, an Australian travel agency.

In 1997 Carlson and Accor finalized the integration of their travel businesses and named Carlson Travel veteran Travis Tanner global CEO. The following year the new company acquired Florida's Travel Agents International, with more than 300 franchised operations and $600 million in annual sales. Also in 1998 Jon Madonna, formerly KPMG International chairman, was named CEO of Carlson Wagonlit. In 1999 three travel agencies in eastern Canada consolidated under the Carlson Wagonlit Travel brand, creating the largest travel network in that region. That same year Carlson Companies founder and Carlson Wagonlit Travel chairman Curtis Carlson died.

In 2000 Madonna was replaced as CEO by former European operations chief Herve Gourio. The following year Carlson Wagonlit joined with Japan Travel Bureau (now JTB Corp.) to form JTB Business Travel Solutions, a Japan-based travel management joint venture. The arrangement increased Carlson Wagonlit's presence in Asia while increasing the number of JTB locations in North America. In 2001 Carlson Wagonlit cut jobs because of a slowdown in business travel.

In 2003 the company formed a joint venture with China Air Service, creating China's leading corporate travel management company. In 2004 the joint venture project opened offices in Shanghai and Guangzhou. That same year, Gourio stepped down as CEO and was replaced by former Vivendi Universal executive Hubert Joly.

EXECUTIVES

President and CEO: Hubert Joly, age 46
CFO: Tim Hennessy
COO Asia Pacific: Berthold Trenkel
COO Europe, Middle East, and Africa: Richard Lovell
COO North America: Jack O'Neill
President Latin America and Partners Network:
Geoffrey Marshall
EVP Account Management, Europe, Middle East, and Africa: Jim Tweedie
EVP Business Travel Services: Dan Miles
EVP Europe, Middle East, and Africa:
August Gossewisch
EVP Global Accounts and Solutions: Martin Warner
EVP Global Account Management and Solutions Group:
Liliana Frigerio
EVP Human Resources: Philippe Vinay
EVP Supplier Relations, Industry Relations and Solutions Group, North America:
Robert (Rob) Deliberto
EVP Technology and Product Management; and CIO:
Loren Brown
CIO North America: Shawn Smith
VP Corporate Communication: Nicolas Brun
VP Finance, North America: Nicholas C. (Nick) Bluhm
VP Marketing and Support Services, North America:
Mark Carter

LOCATIONS

HQ: Carlson Wagonlit
31 rue du Colonel Pierre Avia, 75904 Paris, France
Phone: +33-01-41-33-65-00   **Fax:** +33-01-41-33-60-66
US HQ: 701 Carlson Pkwy., Minneapolis, MN 55459-8208
US Phone: 763-212-2100   **US Fax:** 763-212-2409
Web: www.carlsonwagonlit.com

COMPETITORS

American Express	Thomas Cook AG
JTB	TUI
Kuoni Travel	WorldTravel
Ovation Travel Group	

HISTORICAL FINANCIALS

Company Type: Joint venture

Income Statement

FYE: December 31

	REVENUE ($ mil.)	NET INCOME ($ mil.)	NET PROFIT MARGIN	EMPLOYEES
12/03	11,500	—	—	7,047
12/02	10,700	—	—	7,504
12/01	11,000	—	—	8,083
12/00	12,000	—	—	7,702
12/99	11,000	—	—	7,015
12/98	11,000	—	—	20,100
12/97	10,600	—	—	20,000
12/96	9,500	—	—	20,000
Annual Growth	**2.8%**	**—**	**—**	**(13.8%)**

Revenue History

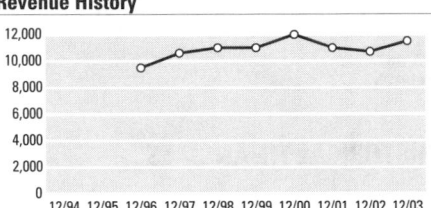

Carlyle Group

The Carlyle Group, with more than $30 billion under management, is one of the world's largest private investment firms. Moreover, it seems that Carlyle likes to keep all options open: Undertakings include management-led buyouts, minority equity investments, real estate, venture capital, and leveraged finance opportunities in the aerospace & defense, automotive & transportation, consumer & retail, energy & power, health care, industrial, real estate, technology & business services, and telecommunications & media sectors. Since its founding in 1987, the firm has made more than 400 corporate and real estate investments; it now maintains offices in 14 countries.

Formerly a list of who's-who in the aerospace & defense sector, Carlyle has unloaded a lot of assets in the sector (including United Defense Industries) and remade its management board, which has seen the departure of former British Prime Minister John Major, former President of the Philippines Fidel Ramos, former Secretary of State James Baker, former US Secretary of Defense Frank Carlucci, and Anand Panyarachun, former Prime Minister of Thailand. Meanwhile,

the founders are trying to set up a succession plan for the firm's next generation of managers.

Notable investments have included such names as United Defense Industries (now BAE Systems Land and Armaments), Dr Pepper/Seven Up Bottling Group, and MedPointe.

Although the majority of the firm's money is in North America, it is also pushing more intensely overseas, launching funds aimed at Asia, Europe, Latin America, and Russia. One of the company's larger moves overseas is the purchase of the transportation business of The Daiei, Japan's #2 retailer in which the company has a 90% stake. The firm's first European energy deal was the buyout of Petroplus International, a Dutch oil refiner.

Its moves overseas haven't all been as easy as picking up the phone or as lucrative, however. Carlyle, along with investment firm Welsh, Carson, Anderson & Stowe, bought Dex Media, the yellow pages business of the financially strapped Qwest Communications, but quickly flipped that investment through an IPO less than a year after the acquisition.

Carlyle is keeping an eye on the transportation and health care industries as possible candidates for deal making, but the maturing buy-out market creates fewer prize deals and more competitors. And the firm is still active in the telecommunications industry: It has bought Verizon Hawaii and 60% of DDI Pocket, the mobile phone division of Japanese telecom concern KDDI. In mid-2005 Carlyle also agreed to buy hospital operator LifeCare Holdings for about $555 million.

The partnership began raising money for Carlyle Partners IV in late 2004; by March of 2005 the fund had commitments of $7.85 billion. Carlyle's latest European fund, Europe Partners II, has commitments of $2.2 billion.

In 2005 The Carlyle Group agreed to team up with Clayton, Dubilier & Rice and Merrill Lynch Global Private Equity to buy Hertz from Ford Motor Company in a deal worth about $15 billion.

California Public Employees' Retirement System (CalPERS) owns more than 5% of Carlyle.

HISTORY

In 1987 T. Rowe Price director Edward Mathias brought together David Rubenstein, a former aide to President Carter; Stephen Norris and Daniel D'Aniello, both executives with Marriott; William Conway Jr., the CFO of MCI; and Greg Rosenbaum, a VP with a New York investment firm. They pooled their experience along with a load of money from T. Rowe Price Associates, Alex. Brown & Sons (now Deutsche Banc Alex. Brown), First Interstate (now part of Wells Fargo) and Pittsburgh's Mellon family to form a buyout firm.

Named after the Carlyle Hotel in New York, the firm opted to make Washington, DC, its headquarters so it wouldn't get lost in the crowd of New York investment firms. The company spent its first years investing in a mish-mash of companies, using Norris' and D'Aniello's Marriott experience to focus primarily on restaurant and food service companies (including Mexican restaurant chain Chi-Chi's).

In 1989 it wooed the well-connected Frank Carlucci, who had served as President Reagan's secretary of defense, to join the group. Soon thereafter, Carlyle began making more high-profile deals. That year it acquired Coldwell Banker's commercial real estate operations (sold

1996) and Caterair International, Marriott's airline food services (sold 1995).

Carlucci helped redirect the firm's focus to the downsizing defense industry. Among its targets were Harsco (1990), BDM International (1991), and LTV's missile and aircraft units (1992). Carlyle helped overhaul their operations and make them attractive (for the right price) to the industry's elite, including Boeing and Lockheed Martin.

As the company's reputation grew, so did its cast of players. Among its new backers were James Baker and Richard Darman (both Reagan and Bush administration alums) and investor George Soros, who chipped some $100 million into the Carlyle Partners L.P. buyout fund. With the help of its "access capitalists" such as Baker and Saudi Prince al-Waleed bin Talal (the firm helped add to his fortune in a 1991 Citicorp stock transaction), Carlyle made deals in the Middle East and Western Europe (including a bailout of Euro Disney) in the mid-1990s.

While the firm continued to be a side in the iron triangle, acquiring such defense companies as aircraft castings maker Howmet in 1995, it picked up a grab bag of holdings, such as natural food grocer Fresh Fields Markets (1994; sold 1996); the quick turnaround helped build Carlyle's war chest. In 1999, the firm acquired automobile engine parts manufacturer Honsel International Technologies in Germany's first public-to-private transaction. (It later sold this investment to Ripplewood Holdings in 2004.)

As Carlyle's esteem rose, so did the number of its investors. In the late 1990s the firm launched buyout funds targeting Asia (closed 1999), Europe (closed 1998), Russia, and Latin America. At home, it faced a dwindling number of opportunities as the long-running bull market drove up prices and more investors chased fewer deals. Among those was its partnership with Cadbury Schweppes to buy the Dr Pepper Bottling Co. of Texas and merge it with its own American Bottling Co.

Carlyle began the new century by launching Carlyle Asset Management Group, selling its stake in Le Figaro to Socpresse, and acquiring Rexnord and a majority stake in CSX Lines.

EXECUTIVES

Chairman: Louis V. Gerstner Jr., age 63
Managing Director and CFO: John F. Harris
Managing Director and General Counsel:
  Jeffrey W. Ferguson
Managing Director: Curt Buser
Managing Director: Daniel A. D'Aniello
Managing Director: David M. Rubenstein
Senior Advisor, Aerospace & Defense, Europe Buyout:
  Julian Browne
Senior Advisor, Aerospace & Defense, US Buyout:
  Thomas A. (Tom) Corcoran, age 60
Senior Advisor, Energy & Power, US Venture, Asia Venture, and Global Energy and Power:
  Richard G. Darman, age 61
Senior Advisor, US High Yield: Wilfred A. Finnegan
Senior Advisor, Aerospace & Defense, US Buyout:
  Kent Kresa, age 67
Senior Advisor, Telecom & Media: Duncan Lewis
Senior Advisor: Arthur Levitt Jr., age 71
Senior Advisor, Buyout Opportunities, Mexico:
  Thomas F. (Mack) McLarty III, age 59
Senior Advisor, Technology & Business Services, US Buyout and US Venture: Charles O. Rossotti, age 64
Senior Advisor, Aerospace & Defense, Automotive & Transportation, and Industrial, US Buyout:
  David L. Squier
Senior Advisor, Industrial, Europe Buyout:
  Robert Coxon
VP, Corporate Communications: Chris Ullman

LOCATIONS

HQ: The Carlyle Group
  1001 Pennsylvania Ave. NW, Washington, DC 20004
Phone: 202-729-5626   **Fax:** 202-347-1818
Web: www.thecarlylegroup.com

US Offices

Bellevue, WA	Newport Beach, CA
Charlotte, NC	San Francisco
Dallas	Tysons Corner, VA
New York	Washington, DC

International Offices

Bangalore, India	Moscow
Barcelona, Spain	Munich
Frankfurt	Paris
Hong Kong	Seoul
London	Singapore
Luxembourg	Tokyo
Milan, Italy	

PRODUCTS/OPERATIONS

Selected Portfolio Companies

Aerospace & Defense
  Aviall Services, Inc.
  Avio SpA (Italy)
  Firth Rixson (UK)
  QinetiQ (UK)
  Stellex Aerostructures
  United Defense Industries, Inc.
  Vought Aircraft Industries, Inc.

Automotive
  Edscha AG (Germany)
  Key Plastics, LLC
  Key Saftey Systems, Inc.
  United Components, Inc.

Consumer & Industrial
  Boto International (artificial Christmas trees, China)
  Custom Alloy (France)
  Dr. Pepper/Seven Up Bottling Group
  Duratek, Inc. (23%, disposal of radioactive materials)
  Groupe Genoyer (France)
  Kito Corp. (cranes and hoists, Japan)
  Kuhlman Electric Corporation
  Messner Eutectic Castolin Group (Germany)
  Otor (Corrugated board and recycled containerboard, France)
  Pacific China Holdings (department stores, China)
  Panolam Industries International, Inc. (decorative laminate paneling)
  Rexnord Corporation
  Tecnoforge Group (Italy)
  Terreal (clay roof tile and bricks, France)

Energy & Power
  CDM Resource Management Ltd.
  Frontier Drilling ASA (Norway)
  InTank, Inc.
  Legend Natural Gas (natural gas and crude oil exploration)
  Magellan Midstream Partners, L.P.
  Seabulk International, Inc. (marine support and transportation services)

Healthcare
  Acufocus, Inc.
  Align Technology, Inc.
  Apteka Holding ZAO (Russia)
  Colin Medical Technology Corporation (Japan)
  ConnectiCare Holdings, Inc.
  Endius, Inc.
  Heritage Health Systems, Inc.
  The Innovation Factory
  InteliStaf Group, Inc.
  MedPointe, Inc.
  NeoVista, Inc.
  Primary Health, Inc.
  Sight Resource Corporation

Telecom & Media
  Actelis Networks, Inc.
  Aprovia (business publishing, France)
  Bredbandsbolaget AB (Sweden)
  Casema BV (cable television, The Netherlands)
  Hawaiian Telecom, Inc.
  LinkAir Communications, Inc. (China)
  Mercury Corporation (South Korea)
  Orthogon Systems (UK)
  Taiwan Broadband Communications
  Vidéotron Telecom (Canada)
  WCI Cable, Inc.

Transportation
  Air Cargo, Inc. (ground transportation services)
  Garrett Aviation Services
  Gemini Air Cargo, Inc.
  Grand Vehicle Works, LLC
  Piedmont Hawthorne Holdings, Inc.
  TrenStar, Inc.

COMPETITORS

Bain Capital
Blackstone Group
CSFB (USA)
Forstmann Little
Goldman Sachs
Hicks Muse
Investcorp
J.P. Morgan Partners
KKR
Lehman Brothers
Texas Pacific Group
Thomas H. Lee Partners

CARQUEST

Searching for a sensor, solenoid, or switches? CARQUEST can steer you in the right direction. The replacement auto parts distribution group is owned by its five member warehouse distributors (the largest is North Carolina-based General Parts). The CARQUEST group includes a network of about 60 distribution centers serving about 4,000 distributor-owned and independent jobbers in the US and Canada. The company sells its own line of auto parts (made by Moog Automotive, Dana, Gabriel, and others) to the jobbers, as well as wholesalers, for eventual resale to professional repair centers, service stations, dealerships, and, to a lesser degree, do-it-yourself (DIY) customers.

General Parts owns more than 1,400 stores across the US and Canada and has bought two fellow CARQUEST distributors in the last two years. The average CARQUEST store carries about 18,000 parts, while a distribution center carries some 150,000 items.

To strengthen ties with service shops, CARQUEST offers the Tech-Net Professional Auto Service program. The program provides a national computer base of more than 600,000 repair records as well as a full guarantee on parts; signage and other marketing tools are also included.

Consolidation in the aftermarket industry has blurred the lines of distribution between wholesalers and retailers, causing all segments of the industry to scramble for ways to gain or maintain market share. CARQUEST focuses on professional mechanics, but it is being squeezed as retailers such as AutoZone look beyond their regular DIY customers for a piece of the commercial pie. At the same time, chains such as The Pep Boys — Manny, Moe & Jack are chipping away at service stations' business by offering parts and service.

HISTORY

Even though he didn't know the auto parts business, Temple Sloan recognized America's infatuation with the automobile and started distributor General Parts in 1961 at age 21. By 1972 he had acquired enough warehouse space to supply the entire state of North Carolina. Determined to get bigger faster, Sloan studied auto parts kingpin Genuine Parts, digging through its annual reports and uncovering tricks of the trade, while working on a few of his own. To compete in what was then a fast-growing industry, Genuine Parts had created a marketing alliance, NAPA, that used mass buying power to garner better pricing and service from manufacturers that often wouldn't recognize individual companies.

Sloan recruited friends and fellow distributors Dan Bock, president of Bobro Products, and Joe Hughes, president of Indiana Parts Warehouse, and together they formed CARQUEST in 1974. The company was designed to help jobbers (middlemen between distributors and mechanics) being threatened by retailers attempting to get a piece of the commercial business market traditionally served by jobbers. CARQUEST began recruiting other distributors and achieved first-year sales of $29 million. In the first five years, almost 1,500 jobbers committed to CARQUEST. Leadership rotated among distributor members until Bock became president in 1984.

As CARQUEST grew, the need for a unifying private-label line became apparent. In the 1970s it developed the Proven Value line of do-it-yourself-oriented products such as oils and filters. The establishment of the CARQUEST brand in the mid-1980s gave the company complete control over quality, coverage, price, and promotions, giving CARQUEST jobbers an advantage in the marketplace. Private-label sales grew from 20%-25% of business to 70% by 1996.

That year CARQUEST relocated its national headquarters from Tarrytown, New York, to Lakewood, Colorado, and Peter Kornafel became president and CEO, replacing Bock. Kornafel had been president of Hatch Grinding, a Denver distributor that merged with General Parts in 1996. The next year the firm moved into Canada, as General Parts bought half of the McKerlie-Millen subsidiary of Acklands (more than 400 parts stores). In 1998 CARQUEST launched its Tech-Net Professional Service program.

Also in 1998 CARQUEST added about 150 new stores to its network when General Parts bought bankrupt APS Holding; it also added 75 stores and eight DCs from Republic Auto. In 1999 General Parts bought The Parts Source, which included 41 Ace Auto Parts stores in Florida.

In January 2000 General Parts bought Acktion Corp's 50% interest in CARQUEST Canada, giving them complete ownership. Later in the year, General Parts also bought St. Louis-based distributor A.E. Lottes Co. In 2001 the company moved its headquarters to Raleigh, North Carolina, and Art Lottes III succeeded Kornafel as president.

In 2005 General Parts purchased long-time San Antonio, Texas, parts distributor Straus-Frank Co., leaving just five distributors in the CARQUEST chain.

EXECUTIVES
Chairman: Neil Stockel
Vice Chairman, Secretary, and Treasurer: Pete Kornafel
President: A.E. Lottes III
EVP: Todd Hack
CFO, CARQUEST and General Parts: John Gardner
Advertising Director: Scott Ginsburg
Human Resources Director: Ed Whirty

LOCATIONS
HQ: CARQUEST Corporation
2635 E. Millbrook Rd., Raleigh, NC 27604
Phone: 919-573-3000   **Fax:** 919-573-2501
Web: www.carquest.com

CARQUEST operates some 60 warehouse distribution centers serving about 4,000 stores in the US and Canada.

PRODUCTS/OPERATIONS

Member Warehouse Distributors
Automotive Warehouse, Inc.
BWP Distributors, Inc.
CAP Warehouse
CARQUEST Canada, Ltd. (owned by General Parts)
General Parts, Inc.
Muffler Warehouse

Selected Manufacturers of CARQUEST Products
Airtex
Cardone Industries
Dana
Federal Mogul Corporation
Gates
Maremont/Gabriel
Melling
Moog Automotive
NEAPCO
Standard Motor Products
WIX

COMPETITORS

Advance Auto Parts	Pep Boys
AutoZone	Sears
CSK Auto	Target
Genuine Parts	Wal-Mart
Hahn Automotive	

HISTORICAL FINANCIALS
Company Type: Private

Income Statement				FYE: December 31
	ESTIMATED REVENUE ($ mil.)	NET INCOME ($ mil.)	NET PROFIT MARGIN	EMPLOYEES
12/03	1,800	—	—	36,500
12/02	2,500	—	—	36,500
12/01	2,200	—	—	36,000
12/00	2,000	—	—	36,000
12/99	2,000	—	—	36,000
12/98	1,400	—	—	35,000
12/97	1,300	—	—	35,000
12/96	1,200	—	—	26,000
12/95	940	—	—	26,000
12/94	860	—	—	—
Annual Growth	**8.6%**	—	—	**4.3%**

Revenue History

Carrols Holdings

Carrols has some quick-service royalty in its blood. Through subsidiary Carrols Corporation, the company is the #1 Burger King franchisee in the US, with more than 360 units in 13 states. Carrols Holdings also owns and franchises quick-service chains Taco Cabana and Pollo Tropical. Its more than 130 Taco Cabana units (10 are franchised) offer Tex-Mex and Mexican dishes, such as tacos and quesadillas. The 80-plus-unit Pollo Tropical chain (20 are franchised) serves fresh grilled chicken and Caribbean side dishes. Carrols Holdings, started in 1968 by Herbert Slotnick, is controlled by investment firms BIB Holdings, which owns about 42% of Carrols, and Madison Dearborn Partners, which also owns about 42%.

While its Burger King operations are very profitable, Carrols is focused on growing its other two quick-service chains, Taco Cabana and Pollo Tropical.

EXECUTIVES
Chairman and CEO: Alan Vituli, age 63
President and COO: Daniel T. Accordino
EVP, Pollo Tropical: James E. (Jim) Tunnessen
EVP, Taco Cabana: Michael A. Biviano
VP, CFO, and Treasurer: Paul R. Flanders
VP and Controller: Timothy J. LaLonde
VP, General Counsel, and Secretary: Joseph A. Zirkman
VP, Human Resources: Jerry Digenova, age 47
VP, Information Services: John Lukas, age 43
Chief Concept Officer, Hispanic Brands: Lewis Shaye
Auditors: Deloitte & Touche LLP

LOCATIONS
HQ: Carrols Holdings Corporation
968 James St., Syracuse, NY 13203
Phone: 315-424-0513   **Fax:** 315-425-8874
Web: www.carrols.com

COMPETITORS
AFC Enterprises
Boston Market
B.T. Woodlipp
California Pizza Kitchen
Checkers Drive-In
Chick-fil-A
CKE Restaurants
Consolidated Restaurant Operations
Dairy Queen
Jack in the Box
McDonald's
Pancho's Mexican Buffet
Subway
Triarc
Wendy's
YUM!

HISTORICAL FINANCIALS

Company Type: Private

Income Statement
FYE: Sunday nearest December 31

	REVENUE ($ mil.)	NET INCOME ($ mil.)	NET PROFIT MARGIN	EMPLOYEES
12/04	700	—	—	17,000
12/03	645	—	—	15,900
12/02	657	—	—	16,100
12/01	656	—	—	16,100
12/00	467	—	—	17,200
12/99	457	—	—	13,200
12/98	417	—	—	12,725
12/97	295	—	—	11,700
12/96	241	—	—	8,400
12/95	226	—	—	7,500
Annual Growth	**13.4%**	—	—	**9.5%**

Revenue History

Catholic Health East

Catholic Health East doesn't believe prayers to St. Jude are necessary to continue providing health care to any person in need. Catholic Health East is one of the top religious health systems in the US. The company carries out its mission of serving the poor and the old by offering health care through more than 30 hospitals, about 45 nursing homes, and some 20 independent- and assisted-living facilities, primarily on the East Coast. The network also operates behavioral health facilities and offers adult day care, home health services, and hospice care. Catholic Health East is sponsored by 15 religious communities.

Catholic Health East is governed by a board composed of 10 nuns, eight secular health care professionals, and one reverend.

Like many religious health care systems, Catholic Health East continues to struggle with the problem of keeping both the faith and the bottom line intact. Providing indigent care is becoming increasingly difficult thanks to the ever-rising costs of health care coupled with cuts in reimbursements that have hurt not only the system's hospital services but its nursing home and outpatient services as well.

Catholic Health East expanded in mid-2004 when Pennsylvania's Maxis Health joined the organization.

HISTORY

It was three easy pieces that made up Catholic Health East in 1997. Allegany Health System, Eastern Mercy Health System, and Sisters of Providence Health System operated almost en-

tirely in separate, but adjacent, geographic areas on the East Coast, overlapping only in Florida.

Catholic Health East's history goes as far back as 1831, when the Sisters of Mercy was founded in Dublin, Ireland, by Catherine McAuley, who established a poorhouse using her inheritance. Some of the sisters hopped the Pond in 1843, establishing the first Catholic hospital in the US, the Mercy Hospital of Pittsburgh, four years later. Over the years the Sisters of Mercy expanded throughout the US. By 1991 there were 25 Sisters of Mercy congregations; they united that year under the newly formed Institute of the Sisters of Mercy of the Americas.

The Sisters of Providence came from Kingston, Ontario, to found the first hospital in Holyoke, Massachusetts. Having established their own ministry, the sisters in Holyoke became a separate congregation in 1892. The congregation expanded slowly, moving into North Carolina in 1956, eventually forming the Sisters of Providence Health System.

A Polish nun, Mother Colette Hilbert, formed a new congregation in Pittsburgh in 1897 after the other members of her former parish were recalled to Poland. The new congregation entered health care in 1926, establishing a home for the elderly in New York. In honor of Hilbert's favorite saint, the order became the Franciscan Sisters of St. Joseph in 1934.

The Franciscan Sisters of St. Joseph and the Sisters of Mercy united to form the ministry that became Pittsburgh Mercy Health System in 1983. In 1986 the congregations formed Eastern Mercy Health System as a holding company for the health concern. The consolidation served to cut costs, as well as to preserve the organization's religious mission.

The Franciscan Sisters of Allegany congregation got its start in 1859 teaching children in Buffalo, New York. In 1883 the order took over St. Elizabeth Hospital in Boston, expanding its health care services ministry throughout New York, New Jersey, and Florida by the 1930s. In 1986 the sisters organized the operations as Allegany Health System.

In the early 1990s Catholic health care systems underwent a round of consolidation. Allegany Health Systems and Eastern Mercy Health Systems combined services, aiming to lower costs through economies of scale.

The mid-1990s also brought consolidation, but this time operational costs weren't the major problem; Catholic health systems across the nation were facing a shortage of sisters. To have a sufficient number of sisters to keep the "Catholic" in Catholic health care, the three health systems merged in 1997, becoming Catholic Health East.

After the merger, the company continued to build its network through acquisitions, including Mercy Health in Miami (1998) and a suffering, secular Cooper Health System in Camden, New Jersey (1999). In 2000 it gained control of two troubled hospitals in Palm Beach, Florida, only to sell them the following year. Catholic Health East remains focused on reducing costs as it expands.

EXECUTIVES

Chairman: Earle L. Bradford Jr.
President and CEO: Robert V. Stanek
EVP and COO: Mark O'Neil
EVP and CFO: Peter L. (Pete) DeAngelis Jr.
EVP and Chief Administration Officer: Stanley T. Urban
EVP, Mission Integration: Sister Juliana M. Casey
EVP, Continuing Care Division: Robert H. Morrow
EVP, Mid-Atlantic Division: Judith M. (Judy) Persichilli

EVP, Northeast Division: Sister Kathleen Popko
EVP, Southeast Division: Howard Watts
VP, Advocacy and Government Relations: Kenneth A. Becker
VP, Strategy Development: Elaine Bauer
VP, Ethics: Philip Boyle
VP, Mission Services: Mary Ann Carter
VP, Quality and Patient Safety: Diane S. Denny
VP, System Communications: Salvatore C. (Sal) Foti
VP, System Compliance and Legal Services and General Counsel: Michael C. Hemsley
VP, Information Technology and CIO: Jack Hueter
Director, Human Resources and Administration: Lisa Bond

LOCATIONS

HQ: Catholic Health East
14 Campus Blvd., Ste. 300,
Newtown Square, PA 19073
Phone: 610-355-2000 **Fax:** 610-355-2050
Web: www.che.org

Divisions

Northeast
  Mercy Health System of Maine (Portland)
  Sisters of Providence Health System (Springfield, MA)
  St. Peter's Health Care Services (Albany, NY)
  Catholic Health System (Buffalo, NY)
  St. James Mercy Health System (Hornell, NY)
Mid-Atlantic
  St. Francis Healthcare Services (Wilmington, DE)
  Our Lady of Lourdes Health System (Camden, NJ)
  St. Francis Medical Center (Trenton, NJ)
  Mercy Health System of Southeastern Pennsylvania (Conshohocken, PA)
  Maxis Health System (Carbondale, PA)
  St. Mary Medical Center (Langhorne, PA)
  Pittsburgh Mercy Health System
Southeast
  BayCare Health Systems (Clearwater, FL)
  Holy Cross Health Ministries (Fort Lauderdale, FL)
  Mercy Hospital (Miami)
  St. Mary's Health Care System, Inc. (Athens, GA)
  Saint Joseph's Health System (Atlanta)
Continuing Care
  Mercy Medical (Daphne, AL)
  Mercy Community Health, Inc. (West Hartford, CT)
  Mercy Uihlein Health Corporation (Lake Placid, NY)
  St. Joseph of the Pines (Southern Pines, NC)

PRODUCTS/OPERATIONS

Supporting Congregations

Franciscan Sisters of Allegany (St. Bonaventure, NY)
Franciscan Sisters of St. Joseph (Hamburg, NY)
Sisters of Charity of Seton Hill (Greensburg, PA)
Sisters of Mercy of the Americas (Albany, NY)
Sisters of Mercy of the Americas (Baltimore)
Sisters of Mercy of the Americas (Orchard Park, NY)
Sisters of Mercy of the Americas (Hartsdale, NY)
Sisters of Mercy of the Americas (Merion, PA)
Sisters of Mercy of the Americas (Pittsburgh)
Sisters of Mercy of the Americas (Portland, ME)
Sisters of Mercy of the Americas (Rochester, NY)
Sisters of Mercy of the Americas (West Hartford, CT)
Sisters of Providence (Holyoke, MA)
Sisters of St. Joseph (St. Augustine, FL)

COMPETITORS

Ascension Health
Bon Secours Health
Catholic Health Initiatives
HCA
Triad Hospitals

HISTORICAL FINANCIALS

Company Type: Not-for-profit

Income Statement

FYE: December 31

	REVENUE ($ mil.)	NET INCOME ($ mil.)	NET PROFIT MARGIN	EMPLOYEES
12/03	5,700	—	—	43,000
12/02	5,000	—	—	43,000
12/01	4,300	—	—	43,000
12/00	4,300	—	—	44,000
12/99	4,300	—	—	45,000
12/98	3,800	—	—	45,000
12/97	3,000	—	—	31,838
12/96	2,700	—	—	—
Annual Growth	**11.3%**	**—**	**—**	**5.1%**

Revenue History

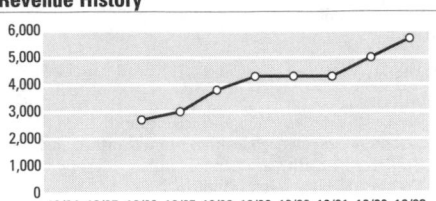

| | 12/94 | 12/95 | 12/96 | 12/97 | 12/98 | 12/99 | 12/00 | 12/01 | 12/02 | 12/03 |

(chart values: 6,000 / 5,000 / 4,000 / 3,000 / 2,000 / 1,000 / 0)

Catholic Health Initiatives

"And he sent them out to preach the Kingdom of God and to heal the sick" (Luke 9:2). Catholic Health Initiatives (CHI) hopes to make those words the driving force behind its initiative. The giant not-for-profit Roman Catholic health system is one of the largest in the US. CHI operates nearly 70 hospitals and more than 40 long-term care, assisted-living, and residential facilities. Combined, the health system has more than 8,300 beds. The organization is sponsored by 12 different congregations and serves communities in some 20 states, primarily in the Midwest.

CHI is an amalgamation of four Roman Catholic health care systems: Catholic Health Corporation of Omaha, Nebraska; Franciscan Health System of Aston, Pennsylvania; Sisters of Charity Health Care Systems of Cincinnati; and Sisters of Charity of Nazareth Health Care System of Bardstown, Kentucky. As a reflection of its divine purpose in a mundane health care market, the company's governing board is made up of both religious and lay officers.

Catholic Health Initiatives has to deal with the conundrum facing many Catholic health systems: Their religious mission — to care for the "unserved and underserved" (and underinsured) members of its communities — is financially uncompetitive. CHI offsets the expense of its mission by also providing health care to the general public and by making business decisions more often associated with secular business (cutting staff, centralizing functions, and joining with other Catholic health care institutions to drive harder bargains with medical suppliers).

HISTORY

In 1860 the Sisters of St. Francis established a hospital in Philadelphia, laying the foundation for a larger health care organization. In 1981 Franciscan Health System was formally established to be a national holding company for Catholic hospitals and related organizations. By the mid-1990s the system consisted of 12 member and two affiliate hospitals and 11 long-term-care facilities located in the mid-Atlantic states and the Pacific Northwest.

Sisters of Charity of Cincinnati and the Sisters of St. Francis Perpetual Adoration of Colorado Springs co-sponsored The Sisters of Charity Health Care Systems, incorporated in 1979 as a multi-institutional health care network. By the mid-1990s the system included 20 hospitals in Colorado, Kentucky, Nebraska, New Mexico, and Ohio.

Three congregations collaborated to form Catholic Health Corporation in 1980, one of the first such health care partnerships between religious communities within the Roman Catholic Church in the US. By 1996 this coalition operated 100 health care facilities in 12 states.

The development of modern managed care health care systems put pressure on the smaller Catholic hospital operations, so the three systems established Catholic Health Initiatives (CHI) in 1996 as a national entity serving five geographic regions. Patricia Cahill, a lay health care veteran who previously served the Archdiocese of New York, was appointed president and CEO of CHI. The following year CHI absorbed the 10-hospital Sisters of Charity of Nazareth Health Care System, based in Bardstown, Kentucky (founded in a log cabin in 1812).

That year CHI continued to seek new partnerships to improve efficiency. With Alegent Health it formed provider network Midwest Select with nearly 200 hospitals, marketing discounted rates to businesses. CHI allied with the Daughters of Charity to form for-profit joint venture Catholic Healthcare Audit Network to provide operational, financial, compliance, and information systems audits, as well as due diligence reviews. CHI also joined insurance joint venture NewCap Insurance with the Daughters of Charity and Catholic Health East; the firm allowed CHI to operate independently of commercial insurers.

CHI made a secular tie-in with the University of Pennsylvania Health System in 1998, whereby the university's system would offer care through five Catholic hospitals (CHI made plans to transfer these hospitals to Catholic Health East in 2001). The next year CHI announced its first loss, due to lackluster performance in the Midwest. During 2000 the company responded by streamlining operations and changing management, resulting in a positive bottom line. In 2001 it sold three hospitals in Pennsylvania, one in Delaware, and one in New Jersey to Catholic Health East.

EXECUTIVES

President and CEO: Kevin E. Lofton
EVP and COO: Michael T. Rowan
SVP and Chief Medical Officer: John F. Anderson
SVP and Chief Nursing Officer: Victoria M. George
SVP and Chief Human Resource Officer, Kentucky: Herbert J. Vallier
SVP, Advocacy: M. Colleen Scanlon
SVP, Communications: Joyce M. Ross
SVP, Finance and Treasury and CFO: Colleen M. Blye
SVP, Legal Services and General Counsel: Paul G. Neumann
SVP, Mission: Rev Thomas R. Kopfensteiner

SVP, Performance Management: Susan E. Peach
SVP, Sponsorship and Governance: Sister Peggy Ann Martin
SVP, Supply Chain: Phillip W. Mears
SVP, Information Technology and Chief Information Officer: Christopher J. Macmanus
SVP and Chief Risk Officer, Kentucky: Mitch H. Melfi
Chief Administrative Officer: Michael L. Fordyce
Auditors: Ernst & Young LLP

LOCATIONS

HQ: Catholic Health Initiatives
  1999 Broadway, Ste. 2600, Denver, CO 80202
Phone: 303-298-9100   **Fax:** 303-298-9690
Web: www.catholichealthinit.org

PRODUCTS/OPERATIONS

Sponsoring Congregations

Benedictine Sisters of Mother of God Monastery (Watertown, SD)
Congregation of the Dominican Sisters of St. Catherine of Siena (Kenosha, WI)
Franciscan Sisters of Little Falls (Little Falls, MN)
Nuns of the Third Order of St. Dominic (Great Bend, KS)
Sisters of Charity of Cincinnati
Sisters of Charity of Nazareth (Bardstown, KY)
Sisters of the Holy Family of Nazareth (Philadelphia, PA)
Sisters of Mercy of the Americas, Regional Community of Omaha (Omaha, NE)
Sisters of the Presentation of the Blessed Virgin Mary (Fargo, ND)
Sisters of St. Francis of Colorado Springs
Sisters of St. Francis of the Immaculate Heart of Mary (Hankinson, ND)
Sisters of St. Francis of Philadelphia

COMPETITORS

Allina Hospitals
Ascension Health
Baxter Regional Medical Center
Beverly Enterprises
BJC HealthCare
Catholic Healthcare Partners
HCA
Health Management Associates
Life Care Centers
Mayo Foundation
OhioHealth
Presbyterian Healthcare Services
Tenet Healthcare

HISTORICAL FINANCIALS

Company Type: Not-for-profit

Income Statement

FYE: June 30

	REVENUE ($ mil.)	NET INCOME ($ mil.)	NET PROFIT MARGIN	EMPLOYEES
6/04	6,121	770	12.6%	53,459
6/03	6,072	203	3.3%	54,979
6/02	5,900	117	2.0%	67,000
6/01	5,742	167	2.9%	66,000
6/00	5,551	97	1.7%	56,100
6/99	5,000	—	—	50,000
6/98	4,500	—	—	44,000
6/97	4,002	—	—	—
6/96	3,755	—	—	—
6/95	3,800	—	—	—
Annual Growth	**5.4%**	**68.1%**	**—**	**3.3%**

2004 Year-End Financials

Debt ratio: 43.8%
Return on equity: 18.6%
Cash ($ mil.): 282

Current ratio: 1.64
Long-term debt ($ mil.): 1,987

Net Income History

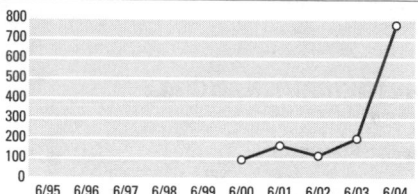

| | 6/95 | 6/96 | 6/97 | 6/98 | 6/99 | 6/00 | 6/01 | 6/02 | 6/03 | 6/04 |

Catholic Healthcare Partners

Catholic Healthcare Partners offers health care services, primarily in Ohio but also in Indiana, Kentucky, Pennsylvania, and Tennessee through the more than 100 corporations that comprise its system. Facilities include about 30 hospitals, more than a dozen stand-alone long-term care facilities, housing sites for the elderly, and wellness centers. The system also offers physician practices, hospice and home health care, and outreach services. Catholic Healthcare Partners is co-sponsored by the Sisters of Mercy communities of Cincinnati and Dallas, Pennsylvania; the Sisters of the Humility of Mary of Villa Maria, Pennsylvania; the Franciscan Sisters of the Poor; and Covenant Health Systems.

Catholic Healthcare Partners organizes its operations into nearly 10 regions to better serve the communities where its facilities are located. In addition to these regions, the system operates Laurel Lake Retirement Community, a senior citizen home in northeast Ohio that offers various levels of care, as well as Providence Retirement Home and Sacred Heart Village.

The health system lost one of its members at the end of 2004. St. Elizabeth Health Partners, which serves Northern Kentucky, bowed out when it announced plans to regain its independence. The loss hasn't hurt Catholic Healthcare Partners, as the member's financial assets were never combined with those of its parent.

EXECUTIVES

Vice Chairman: Anthony L. Barbato
Chairman: Sister Mildred Ely
President and CEO: Michael D. Connelly
EVP: Jane Durney Crowley
EVP: A. David Jimenez
EVP: Susan Smith Makos

SVP and CFO: William Shuttleworth
SVP and CIO: Rebecca (Becky) Sykes
SVP and Chief Medical Officer: Donald E. Casey Jr.
SVP and General Counsel: Michael A. Bezney
SVP, Human Resources and Organization Effectiveness: Jon C. Abeles
SVP, Insurance and Physician Services: R. Jeffrey Copeland
SVP, Mission and Values Integration: Sister Doris Gottemoeller
SVP; President and CEO, Community Health Partners: Brian C. Lockwood
Corporate Director, Communications: Greg Smith
Auditors: Ernst & Young LLP

LOCATIONS

HQ: Catholic Healthcare Partners
615 Elsinore Place, Cincinnati, OH 45202
Phone: 513-639-2800   **Fax:** 513-639-2700
Web: www.health-partners.org

PRODUCTS/OPERATIONS

Regions

Community Health Partners (North Central Ohio)
Humility of Mary Health Partners (Northeast Ohio)
Mercy Health Partners Kentucky/Indiana Region
Mercy Health Partners Northeast Region (Northeast Pennsylvania)
Mercy Health Partners Northern Region (Northwest Ohio and Southern Michigan)
Mercy Health Partners Southwest Ohio Region
Mercy Health Partners Western Ohio Region
St. Mary's Health Partners (Eastern Tennessee)
West Central Ohio Health Partners

COMPETITORS

Ascension Health
Catholic Health Initiatives
HCA
Kindred Healthcare
NeighborCare
OhioHealth
Tenet Healthcare
Universal Health Services

HISTORICAL FINANCIALS

Company Type: Not-for-profit

Income Statement

FYE: December 31

	REVENUE ($ mil.)	NET INCOME ($ mil.)	NET PROFIT MARGIN	EMPLOYEES
12/03	2,874	—	—	30,524
12/02	2,715	—	—	30,524
12/01	2,602	—	—	30,000
12/00	2,373	—	—	27,941
12/99	1,984	—	—	30,800
12/98	1,821	—	—	29,000
12/97	1,778	—	—	23,920
12/96	1,909	—	—	24,000
12/95	2,246	—	—	18,100
12/94	1,045	—	—	15,739
Annual Growth	11.9%	—	—	7.6%

Revenue History

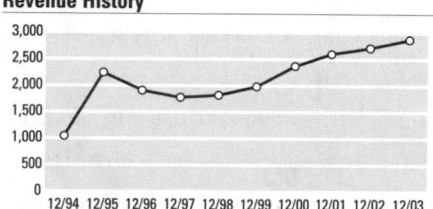

| | 12/94 | 12/95 | 12/96 | 12/97 | 12/98 | 12/99 | 12/00 | 12/01 | 12/02 | 12/03 |

Catholic Healthcare West

Catholic Healthcare West (CHW) has found it takes a lot of nunsense to become one of the largest private, not-for-profit health care providers in the state of California. CHW has a network of some 40 facilities in California, Arizona, and Nevada. CHW's health care system consists of acute care hospitals, skilled nursing facilities, and medical centers. CHW also has an alliance with Scripps, a major San Diego-based health care provider. The organization has nearly 7,100 acute care beds and almost 1,200 skilled nursing beds. CHW is sponsored by seven religious congregations.

With both clergy and laity on its governing board, CHW has grown by consolidating hospitals owned by Roman Catholic women's religious orders. Additional affiliations with non-Catholic institutions have raised some hackles because Catholic doctrine opposes abortion, most forms of birth control, and in-vitro fertilization.

In 2004 CHW joined other Catholic hospitals in announcing plans to charge uninsured patients the same rates charged to patients on Medicare, Medicaid, and other government-funded health care programs. The announcement came, in part, as a response to criticism that hospitals across the country charge uninsured patients much higher rates for services and aggressively seek payment.

The hospital operator has expanded its California presence. CHW bought two hospitals from Universal Health Services: French Medical Center in San Luis Obispo and Arroyo Grande Community Hospital in Arroyo Grande. The two facilities combined have almost 180 beds.

HISTORY

Catholic Healthcare West traces its roots to 1857, when the Sisters of Mercy founded St. Mary's Hospital in San Francisco. The order expanded in that area, and in 1986 two different communities of the Sisters of Mercy merged their hospitals into an organization with one retirement home and 10 hospitals from the Bay Area to San Diego. Declining membership in Roman Catholic religious orders, combined with consolidation in the field, led the orders to see merger as their only route to survival.

Rising medical costs, slow payers, and merger expenses dropped the organization's combined net income to $20 million in 1988 (from nearly $58 million in 1986). One of the hardest-hit CHW affiliates was Mercy Healthcare Sacramento, which lost $4.2 million between 1986 and 1987. In 1988 Mercy Healthcare restructured along regional lines.

The next year the Sisters of St. Dominic brought two hospitals into the alliance. CHW launched the Community Economic Assistance program, which provided $220,000 in grants to 16 human service and health care agencies in its first year.

CHW continued to add facilities, including AMI Community Hospital in Santa Cruz, California, in 1990. Since CHW already owned the area's only other acute care hospital, Dominican Santa Cruz Hospital, CHW in 1993 was ordered not to acquire any more acute care hospitals in Santa Cruz County without FTC approval.

As the trend to managed care became a stampede in the 1990s, CHW moved more into preventive care and began reining in costs through productivity improvement plans. It continued to add hospitals, including tax-supported institutions trying to compete with national for-profit systems.

The network increased its medical clout in 1994 by allying with San Diego-based Scripps, one of the state's largest HMO systems. In 1995 the Daughters of Charity Province of the West realigned its six-hospital operation with CHW. The next year the Dominican Sisters (California), the Dominican Sisters of St. Catherine of Siena (Wisconsin), and the Sisters of Charity of the Incarnate Word allied their California hospitals with CHW. New community hospitals included Bakersfield Memorial, Sierra Nevada Memorial (Grass Valley), Sequoia Hospital (Redwood City), and Woodland Healthcare.

Charity and cost-consciousness clashed in 1996 when union members staged a walkout to protest nonunion outsourcing of vocational nursing, housekeeping, and kitchen jobs. This dispute was settled, but CHW continued to be a target for union organizers, with a bitter battle against the Service Employees International Union (SEIU) starting in 1998.

CHW agreed in 1996 to merge with Samaritan Health Systems (now Banner Health System) in a move that would have made CHW one of the US's top five providers, but the deal fell apart in 1997. In 1998 CHW merged with UniHealth, a group with eight facilities in Los Angeles and Orange counties. Mounting costs forced CHW to post a loss, and in 1999 it cut some managerial positions and reorganized to recover.

The year 2000 brought CHW more problems with labor relations: SEIU argued that the organization was resistant to unionization. Continued losses led the organization to implement major restructuring the following year, as its 10 regional divisions were consolidated into four.

In 2001, CHW stepped up donations, grants, and other sponsorship efforts designed to benefit areas served by its hospitals and clinics. However, the rapid expansion that made the system a name in the California health care industry also left it bloated. Rising health care costs and trouble with its physician management groups cut deeply into earnings. Management casualties occurred as CHW reorganized that year.

Two years later, the company parted ways with one of its sponsoring organizations, the Franciscan Sisters of the Sacred Heart of Frankfort, Illinois. The sponsorship ended when CHW closed St. Francis Medical Center of Santa Barbara. However, the hospital operator that fiscal year posted its first operating profit since 1996.

EXECUTIVES

Chairperson: Adrienne Y. Crowe
President and CEO: Lloyd H. Dean
EVP and COO: Michael Erne
EVP and CFO: Michael D. Blaszyk
SVP and Chief Administrative Officer: Elizabeth Shih
SVP, Chief Human Resources Officer:
Ernest (Ernie) Urquhart
SVP and Chief Medical Officer: George Bo-Linn
SVP and Chief Strategy Officer: Charles P. Francis
SVP and General Counsel: Derek F. Covert
SVP, Corporate Relations: Alan Iftiniuk
SVP, Managed Care: John Wray
SVP, Sponsorship and Mission Integration:
Sister Bernita McTernan
President, Marian Medical Center:
Charles (Chuck) Cova, age 49

CEO, Saint Francis Memorial Hospital: Cheryl Fama
CEO, St. Mary's Medical Center: Ken Steele
President, Mercy Healthcare Sacramento and Mercy San Juan Medical Center: Mike Uboldi
Secretary: Charles H. Chapman
Manager, Workers' Compensation: Barbara Pelletreau
Media Relations: Tricia Griffin
Auditors: Deloitte & Touche LLP

LOCATIONS

HQ: Catholic Healthcare West
185 Berry St., Ste. 300, San Francisco, CA 94107
Phone: 415-438-5500   **Fax:** 415-438-5724
Web: www.chw.edu

Facilities

Arizona
  Barrow Neurological Institute (Phoenix)
  Chandler Regional Hospital (Phoenix)
  Chandler Regional Medical Center (Phoenix)
  CHW Business Services Center (Phoenix)
  St. Joseph's Hospital and Medical Center (Phoenix)

California
  Arroyo Grande Community Hospital (Arroyo Grande)
  Bakersfield Memorial Hospital (Bakersfield)
  Mercy Southwest Hospital (Bakersfield)
  Mercy Hospital (Bakersfield)
  St. John's Pleasant Valley Hospital (Camarillo)
  Mercy San Juan Medical Center (Carmichael)
  Mercy Hospital of Folsom (Folsom)
  Glendale Memorial Hospital and
    Health Center (Glendale)
  Sierra Nevada Memorial Miners Hospital (Grass Valle)
  St. Mary Medical Center (Long Beach)
  California Hospital Medical Center (Los Angeles)
  St. Dominic's Hospital (Manteca)
  Mercy Medical Center Merced (Merced)
  Mercy Medical Center Mt. Shasta (Mt. Shasta)
  Northridge Hospital Medical Center-Roscoe Blvd.
    Campus (Northridge)
  Oak Valley Hospital District (Oakdale)
  St. John's Regional Medical Center (Oxnard)
  St. Elizabeth Community Hospital (Red Bluff)
  Mercy Medical Center Redding (Redding)
  Sequoia Hospital (Redwood City)
  Mercy General Hospital (Sacramento)
  Methodist Hospital of Sacramento (Sacramento)
  Mark Twain St. Joseph's Hospital (San Andreas)
  Community Hospital of San
    Bernardino (San Bernardino)
  St. Bernardine Medical Center (San Bernardino)
  Saint Francis Memorial Hospital (San Francisco)
  St. Mary's Medical Center (San Francisco)
  San Gabriel Valley Medical Center (San Gabriel)
  French Hospital Medical Center (San Luis Obispo)
  Dominican Hospital (Santa Cruz)
  Marian Medical Center (Santa Maria)
  St. Joseph's Behavioral Health Center (Stockton)
  St. Joseph's Medical Center (Stockton)
  Mercy Westside Hospital (Taft)
  Woodland Healthcare (Woodland)

Nevada
  St. Rose Dominican Hospital Rose de
    Lima Campus (Henderson)
  St. Rose Dominican Hospital Siena Campus
    (Henderson)

PRODUCTS/OPERATIONS

Sponsoring Organizations

Auburn Regional Community of the Sisters of Mercy
  (Auburn, CA)
Burlingame Regional Community of the Sisters of Mercy
  (Burlingame, CA)
Congregation of the Dominican Sisters of St. Catherine
  of Siena of Kenosha (Kenosha, WI)
Congregation of the Sisters of Charity of the Incarnate
  Word (Houston)
Sisters of St. Dominic, Congregation of the Most Holy
  Rosary (Adrian, MI)
Sisters of St. Francis of Penance and Christian Charity,
  St. Francis Province (Redwood City, CA)
Sisters of the Third Order of St. Dominic, Congregation
  of the Most Holy Name (San Rafael, CA)

COMPETITORS

Adventist Health
Catholic Health Initiatives
HCA
Los Angeles County
  Health Department

Memorial Health Services
Sutter Health
Tenet Healthcare
Triad Hospitals

HISTORICAL FINANCIALS

Company Type: Not-for-profit

Income Statement

FYE: June 30

	REVENUE ($ mil.)	NET INCOME ($ mil.)	NET PROFIT MARGIN	EMPLOYEES
6/04	5,397	246	4.6%	40,000
6/03	4,989	51	1.0%	36,000
6/02	4,502	(51)	—	36,000
6/01	4,807	(87)	—	36,000
6/00	4,513	(47)	—	40,000
6/99	4,200	82	2.0%	38,000
6/98	3,301	73	2.2%	20,000
6/97	2,749	36	1.3%	17,451
6/96	2,688	161	6.0%	21,495
6/95	2,674	99	3.7%	20,000
Annual Growth	8.1%	10.6%	—	8.0%

2004 Year-End Financials

Debt ratio: 111.3%   Current ratio: 1.84
Return on equity: 11.6%   Long-term debt ($ mil.): 2,610
Cash ($ mil.): 293

Net Income History

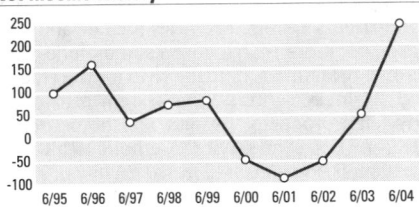

Cavaliers/Gund Arena

The Cavaliers/Gund Arena Company has far from a cavalier attitude toward roundball. Its Cleveland Cavaliers joined the NBA in 1970 as part of an expansion that included the Portland Trail Blazers and Buffalo Braves (now the Los Angeles Clippers). The team spent much of the 1990s providing highlight footage for Michael Jordan and tied for the worst record in the NBA in the 2002-03 season, resulting in coach John Lucas being replaced with Paul Silas, former New Orleans Hornets head coach. Things began looking up on the court with the drafting of high school sensation LeBron James in 2003. The family of chairman Gordon Gund owns part of the team but Quicken Loans founder Dan Gilbert holds the majority.

Attendance figures for the Cavaliers have consistently been among the worst in the league. In the 2002-03 season, the team averaged only 11,497 fans a game and had only 4,500 season ticket holders. But the dreadful days have actually worked in the team's favor as it scored the first pick in the 2003 NBA draft and quickly snatched

James. The deal helped to drastically increase the Cavaliers' season ticket sales for the 2003-04 season. The team missed the playoffs that season but James was named Rookie of the Year.

Attendance and revenues continued to climb the following season, prompting the Gunds to explore selling the team. Gilbert bought the team (and Gund Arena) for about $375 million in 2005. The Gunds and hip hop star Usher, who also came on board in 2005, have minority stakes.

EXECUTIVES

Chairman: Gordon Gund, age 65
Vice Chairman: George Gund III
Vice Chairman: James C. Boland, age 65
CEO: Mark Stornes
President: Len Komoroski
General Manager: Danny Ferry
Head Coach: Mike Brown
Assistant Coach: Hank Egan
VP Communications: Tad Carper
VP Finance and Administration: John Wolf
VP Marketing: Tracy Marek
VP Operations: Pat Fitzgerald
Senior Director of Broadcasting Services: Dave Dombrowski
Director of Basketball Operations: Mike Bratz
Director of Communications and Public Relations: Bill Evans
Director of Human Resources: Farrell Finnin
Director of Player Personnel: Mark Warkentien
Director of Sales and Service: Mike Ostrowski

LOCATIONS

HQ: Cavaliers/Gund Arena Company
1 Center Ct., Cleveland, OH 44115
Phone: 216-420-2000 **Fax:** 216-420-2101
Web: www.gundarena.com

COMPETITORS

Chicago Bulls
Detroit Pistons
Indiana Pacers
Milwaukee Bucks

HISTORICAL FINANCIALS
Company Type: Private

Income Statement
FYE: October 31

	REVENUE ($ mil.)	NET INCOME ($ mil.)	NET PROFIT MARGIN	EMPLOYEES
10/04	93	—	—	—
10/03	72	—	—	—
10/02	79	—	—	—
10/01	75	—	—	—
10/00	69	—	—	—
10/99	38	—	—	150
10/98	62	—	—	100
10/97	60	—	—	—
10/96	65	—	—	—
10/95	66	—	—	—
Annual Growth	**3.9%**	**—**	**—**	**50.0%**

Revenue History

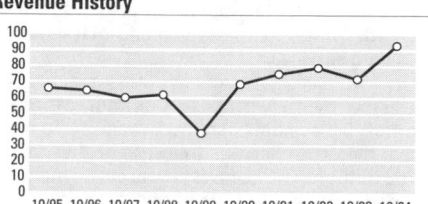

10/95 10/96 10/97 10/98 10/99 10/00 10/01 10/02 10/03 10/04

Cbeyond Communications

Cbeyond Communications isn't looking past the 25 million small businesses in the US to find customers for its broadband services. The facilities-based Voice over Internet Protocol (VoIP) carrier provides local and long-distance services and broadband Internet access over its own private IP network. The company hopes to side-step stiff competition from incumbent carriers by focusing on the traditionally underserved small-business market. Cbeyond offers services in the Atlanta, Dallas, Denver, Chicago, and Houston metro areas and plans to expand services to six additional markets. Investors in the company include Madison Dearborn Partners, Battery Ventures, and VantagePoint Ventures Partners.

EXECUTIVES

Chairman, President, and CEO: James F. (Jim) Geiger, age 46, $303,955 pay
COO: Richard Batelaan, age 39, $197,866 pay
EVP and CFO: J. Robert (Bob) Fugate, age 44, $236,537 pay
EVP Sales and Service: Robert R. (Bob) Morrice, age 57, $236,537 pay
VP and CTO: Christopher C. (Chris) Gatch, age 33
VP and Chief Marketing Officer: Brooks A. Robinson, age 33
VP and CIO: Joe Oesterling, age 38
VP Finance and Chief Accounting Officer: Henry C. Lyon, age 40
VP Regulatory and Legislative Affairs: Julia Strow
VP Sales: Brian E. Craver, age 36
VP Human Resources: Joan L. Tolliver
VP Marketing Communications: Terry Trout
Auditors: Ernst & Young LLP

LOCATIONS

HQ: Cbeyond Communications, Inc.
320 Interstate N. Pkwy. SE, Ste. 300, Atlanta, GA 30339
Phone: 678-424-2400 **Fax:** 678-424-2500
Web: www.cbeyond.net

2004 Sales

	$ mil.	% of total
Atlanta	42.2	37
Denver	35.1	31
Dallas	33.1	29
Houston	2.9	3
Total	**113.3**	**100**

PRODUCTS/OPERATIONS

Selected Services
Broadband Internet access
Calling cards
Conference calling
E-mail
Local voice access
Long-distance voice
Toll-free
Virtual private network (VPN)
Voicemail
Web hosting

COMPETITORS

8x8	ICG Communications
AT&T	ITC^DeltaCom
BellSouth	MCI
Birch	McLeodUSA
Cablevision Systems	NuVox
Comcast	Qwest
Covad Communications Group	SBC Communications
Cox Communications	Time Warner Cable
Deltathree	Time Warner Telecom
DSL.net	US LEC
Eschelon	Vonage
	XO Communications

HISTORICAL FINANCIALS
Company Type: Private

Income Statement
FYE: December 31

	REVENUE ($ mil.)	NET INCOME ($ mil.)	NET PROFIT MARGIN	EMPLOYEES
12/04	113	(12)	—	634
12/03	66	(30)	—	—
12/02	21	(47)	—	380
Annual Growth	**132.3%**	**—**	**—**	**29.2%**

2004 Year-End Financials

Debt ratio: (77.5%)
Return on equity: —
Cash ($ mil.): 23

Current ratio: 1.24
Long-term debt ($ mil.): 57

Net Income History

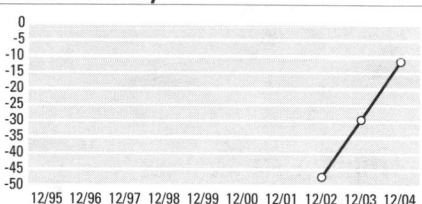

12/95 12/96 12/97 12/98 12/99 12/00 12/01 12/02 12/03 12/04

CBOT Holdings

CBOT Holdings (formerly The Board of Trade of the City of Chicago, and familiarly the Chicago Board of Trade) facilitates more than the agriculture-based trading for which it's famous. Founded in 1848, it operates one of the world's largest futures exchanges (subsidiary The Board of Trade of the City of Chicago), helping businesses manage risk by locking in commodity prices. In 2005 it restructured, converting its organization from a nonstock, not-for-profit company with members into a stock, for-profit holding company with stockholders, and a nonstock, for-profit derivatives exchange subsidiary with members. The board of trade's members became stockholders of CBOT Holdings and remain members of its exchange.

Some 3,600 members trade futures and options ranging from precious metals to live hogs to US Treasury bonds. Although most members trade verbally and use an elaborate hand-signal system, CBOT also offers electronic trading.

The board of trade has teamed with Chicago Board Options Exchange and Chicago Mercantile Exchange to introduce single-stock futures contracts through joint venture OneChicago.

EXECUTIVES

Chairman: Charles P. Carey, age 51
Vice Chairman: Robert F. Corvino, age 47
President, CEO, and Director: Bernard W. Dan, age 44, $1,500,000 pay
EVP and COO: Bryan T. Durkin, age 44, $675,000 pay
EVP and Chief of Staff: Carol A. Burke, age 54, $825,000 pay
EVP: William M. (Bill) Farrow III, age 50, $825,000 pay
EVP, Marketing and Business Development: Christopher (Chris) Malo, age 48
SVP and CFO: Glen M. Johnson, age 57
SVP, Business Development: Robert Ray
SVP, Government Relations: Celesta S. Jurkovich, age 54
SVP, Technical Solutions: James G. (Chip) Bennett, age 51, $444,000 pay
VP, Human Resources: Debra Dana
Shareholder Relations: Victoria Pizzirulli
Auditors: Deloitte & Touche LLP

LOCATIONS

HQ: CBOT Holdings, Inc.
141 W. Jackson Blvd., Chicago, IL 60604
Phone: 312-435-3500 **Fax:** 312-341-3392
Web: www.cbot.com

CBOT Holdings has offices in Chicago, London, New York, and Washington, DC.

COMPETITORS

AMEX
CBOE
Chicago Mercantile Exchange
Deutsche Börse
LIFFE
NASD
NYSE

HISTORICAL FINANCIALS

Company Type: Public

Income Statement

FYE: December 31

	REVENUE ($ mil.)	NET INCOME ($ mil.)	NET PROFIT MARGIN	EMPLOYEES
12/04	380	42	11.0%	828
12/03	381	31	8.1%	—
12/02	308	34	11.1%	—
12/01	244	4	1.8%	—
12/00	213	(10)	—	711
12/99	185	(10)	—	846
12/98	184	7	3.6%	853
12/97	165	10	5.9%	805
12/96	155	20	12.7%	811
Annual Growth	11.9%	10.0%	—	0.3%

2004 Year-End Financials

Debt ratio: 10.6%
Return on equity: 15.1%
Cash ($ mil.): 105
Current ratio: 1.85
Long-term debt ($ mil.): 21

Net Income History

NYSE: BOT

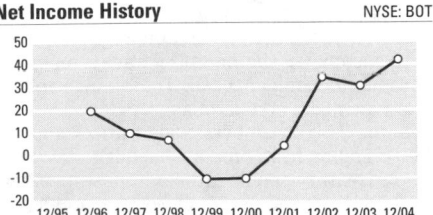

CCA Global

Business is "floor"ishing at CCA Global Partners. Formerly Carpet Co-op, the firm operates more than 3,600 retail stores in the US and abroad in the floor covering and various other specialties. Many stores operate under the Carpet One name; other names include Flooring America, Flooring One, ProSource, and International Design Guild (high-end showrooms). The world's largest floor covering retailer (with stores in the US, Canada, Australia, and New Zealand), Carpet One is the exclusive US marketer of Bigelow and the LEES For Living carpet brands. CCA Global has also made forays into bicycle retailing, mortgage banking, and men's formalwear. Executives Howard Brodsky and Alan Greenberg founded the co-op in 1984.

CCA Global's Lenders One division operates as an aggregator of mortgage loans. Its Lighting One division (bought by CCA in 2001) has about 100 locations selling lamps, ceiling fans, and accessories.

In 2003 CCA Global expanded into formalwear with its acquisition of Tuxedo America Group, a cooperative of more than 300 independently owned retailers of men's formalwear. Today the independent retailers are known collectively as Savvi Formalwear and operate more than 400 stores.

EXECUTIVES

Co-Chairman and Co-CEO: Howard Brodsky
Co-Chairman and Co-CEO: Alan Greenberg
President: Sandy Mishkin
COO: Bob Wilson
CFO: Ed Muchnick
COO, Carpet One; President, Carpet One Canada: Charlie Dilks
SVP, Training: Brian Metcalf
VP, CCA Global Partners University: Tony Perry
VP Hard Surfaces: Randy Gum
VP, Soft Surface Products: Mike Englert
Director of Human Resources: Lisa Miles

LOCATIONS

HQ: CCA Global Partners
4301 Earth City Expwy., Earth City, MO 63045
Phone: 314-506-0000 **Fax:** 314-291-6674
Web: www.ccaglobal.com

PRODUCTS/OPERATIONS

Selected Companies

US Flooring
  Carpet One
  FloorExpo
  Flooring America
  International Design Guild
  ProSource Wholesale Floorcoverings
  Rug Décor
  Stone Mountain's Carpet Mill Outlet/GCO Carpet Outlet
International Flooring
  Carpet One (Canada, Australia, New Zealand)
  Flooring One (UK)
  Flooring Canada (Canada)
Bicycle Retail
  The Biking Solution
Mortgage Banking
  Lenders One
Specialty Lighting
  Lighting One
Men's Formalwear
  Savvi Formalwear

COMPETITORS

Abbey Carpet	Home Depot
After Hours	Lowe's
Federated	May
Formal Specialist	Menard

HISTORICAL FINANCIALS

Company Type: Cooperative

Income Statement

FYE: September 30

	REVENUE ($ mil.)	NET INCOME ($ mil.)	NET PROFIT MARGIN	EMPLOYEES
9/04	8,700	—	—	—
9/03	8,000	—	—	350
9/02	6,000	—	—	550
9/01	5,000	—	—	450
9/00	4,000	—	—	350
9/99	3,100	—	—	300
9/98	2,450	—	—	265
9/97	2,000	—	—	150
9/96	1,600	—	—	—
Annual Growth	23.6%	—	—	15.2%

Revenue History

Cellco Partnership

Cellco Partnership, which does business as Verizon Wireless, is the #2 US mobile phone operator (after rival Cingular Wireless acquired AT&T Wireless) serving 45.5 million customers nationwide. Verizon Wireless began operations in 2000 when Bell Atlantic and Vodafone combined their US wireless assets, including their PrimeCo partnership. Verizon Wireless gained GTE's US wireless operations when Bell Atlantic bought GTE to form Verizon Communications, which owns 55% of the company; Vodafone owns 45%. Plans for an IPO, postponed in 2001, were revived but finally withdrawn in 2003 citing lack of funding needs.

The company is developing third-generation wireless services based on CDMA (code division multiple access) technology. It also has teamed up with Microsoft to develop and market wireless data services.

In late 2002 Verizon Wireless reached an agreement with Northcoast Communications, a unit of Cablevision Systems, to acquire 50 radio wave spectrum licenses in a cash deal valued at $762 million. The licenses cover several lucrative markets, including Boston and New York City, which reach a population of some 47 million. Following the deal's completion in 2003 Verizon Wireless announced plans to introduce a national service in direct competition with rival

Nextel's "push to talk" feature. (Nextel has since become Sprint Nextel.)

The company has announced plans to spend $1 billion over two years on the development of a nationwide broadband wireless Internet data network. It also has acquired the wireless assets of Qwest Communications in a cash deal valued at about $418 million.

Verizon Wireless hoped to bolster its coverage in the New York metropolitan area by agreeing to acquire licenses held by NextWave Telecom in that company's bankruptcy auction. It later acquired the bankrupt company in a deal valued at $3 billion. At that time NextWave's assets consisted only of spectrum licenses in 23 US markets, including Boston, Los Angeles, New York, and Washington, DC. Verizon Wireless also has agreed to buy 23 spectrum licenses for markets in upstate New York, Michigan, Wisconsin, Arkansas, Mississippi, and Alabama, from Leap Wireless. The deal, valued at $102.5 million, includes a swap of spectrum in Buffalo, New York.

EXECUTIVES

Chairman: Ivan G. Seidenberg, age 58
President, CEO, and Director: Dennis F. (Denny) Strigl, age 58, $2,415,000 pay
EVP, COO, and Director: Lowell C. McAdam, age 50, $1,312,950 pay
EVP and CTO: Richard J. (Dick) Lynch, age 56, $837,550 pay
VP and CFO: John Townsend, age 42
VP and Chief Marketing Officer: John G. Stratton, age 44
VP Business Development: Margaret P. (Molly) Feldman, age 47
VP Corporate Communications: James J. (Jim) Gerace, age 41
VP Enterprise Data Sales: Cindy Patterson
VP Legal and External Affairs, General Counsel, and Secretary: Steven E. Zipperstein, age 45
VP Messaging: Todd Buchanan
VP Human Resources: Martha Delehanty, age 39
VP and Controller: Michael T. Stefanski, age 39
Auditors: Deloitte & Touche LLP

LOCATIONS

HQ: Cellco Partnership
180 Washington Valley Rd., Bedminster, NJ 07921
Phone: 908-306-7000   **Fax:** 908-306-6927
Web: www.verizonwireless.com

PRODUCTS/OPERATIONS

2004 Sales

	$ mil.	% of total
Service revenues	24,400	88
Equipment & other revenues	3,262	12
Total	**27,662**	**100**

Selected Services

Cellular
Equipment sales
Paging
PCS (personal communications services)
Wireless data and Internet

COMPETITORS

ALLTEL
Cingular Wireless
SkyTel Communications
Sprint Nextel
T-Mobile USA
U.S. Cellular
Western Wireless

HISTORICAL FINANCIALS

Company Type: Joint venture

Income Statement

FYE: December 31

	REVENUE ($ mil.)	NET INCOME ($ mil.)	NET PROFIT MARGIN	EMPLOYEES
12/04	27,662	4,698	17.0%	49,800
12/03	22,489	3,083	13.7%	43,900
12/02	19,260	2,584	13.4%	39,300
12/01	17,393	1,300	7.5%	40,000
12/00	14,222	1,528	10.7%	38,000
12/99	7,659	932	12.2%	32,500
12/98	6,641	906	13.6%	—
12/97	6,196	737	11.9%	—
Annual Growth	**23.8%**	**30.3%**	**—**	**8.9%**

2004 Year-End Financials

Debt ratio: 5.9%
Return on equity: 14.8%
Cash ($ mil.): 171
Current ratio: 0.29
Long-term debt ($ mil.): 2,495

Net Income History

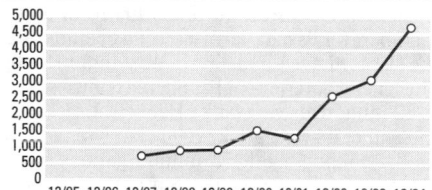

Center Oil

Center Oil's core business is peddling petroleum. The company is one of the largest private wholesale distributors of gasoline and other petroleum products to customers primarily in the eastern region of the US. Center Oil owns nine storage terminals capable of storing more than 1.5 million barrels of petroleum product. It also has access to 36 terminals in 10 states, as well as access to the Williams, Texas Eastern, Kinder Morgan Chicago, and Kaneb pipeline systems. Its products are also distributed through a fleet of ships, barges, and trucks. The company was founded in 1986 by president and CEO Gary Parker.

EXECUTIVES

President and CEO: Gary R. Parker
VP and CFO: John R. Niemi
Secretary: Christine K. Moyer
Treasurer: Richard I. (Rick) Powers
Controller: Joseph (Joe) Beck
Finance Manager: Brian Skoff
Sales Manager: Rob Kraeger
Manager Business Development: Chris Pelligreen
Manager Operations and Scheduling: Jerry Jost
Manager Terminal Operations: Ray Idzior
General Counsel: Michael Aufdenspring

LOCATIONS

HQ: Center Oil Company
600 Mason Ridge Center Dr., St. Louis, MO 63141
Phone: 314-682-3500   **Fax:** 314-682-3599
Web: www.centeroil.com

Center Oil operates storage terminals in Baltimore; Chillicothe, Illinois; Cleveland; Hartford; Indianapolis; Madison, Wisconsin; Newark; St. Louis; and Wichita, Kansas.

COMPETITORS

Apex Oil
Colonial Group
George Warren
Gulf Oil
U.S. Oil

HISTORICAL FINANCIALS

Company Type: Private

Income Statement

FYE: December 31

	REVENUE ($ mil.)	NET INCOME ($ mil.)	NET PROFIT MARGIN	EMPLOYEES
12/03	3,400	—	—	50
12/02	2,600	—	—	44
Annual Growth	**30.8%**	**—**	**—**	**13.6%**

Revenue History

Central National-Gottesman

All the news that fit to print (or at least some of it) shows up on Central National-Gottesman's products. The paper-maker distributes pulp, paper, paperboard, and newsprint in more than 75 countries worldwide. In addition to its North American operations, the company operates about 23 offices in 22 countries located in Asia, Europe, and Latin America. The Central National-Gottesman network includes the Lindenmeyr family of companies, which specialize in the distribution of fine paper as well as papers for books and magazines. The company's extensive list of suppliers includes paper industry leaders International Paper (#1) and Weyerhaeuser. The family-owned company was founded in 1886.

EXECUTIVES

President and CEO: Kenneth L. Wallach
VP, Human Resources: Louise Caputo
Treasurer: Steven Eigen

LOCATIONS

HQ: Central National-Gottesman Inc.
3 Manhattanville Rd., Purchase, NY 10577
Phone: 914-696-9000   **Fax:** 914-696-1066
Web: www.cng-inc.com

Central National-Gottesman has operations in the Americas, Asia, Australia, and Europe including 24 overseas sales offices.

COMPETITORS

Clifford Paper	Ris Paper
International Paper	Smurfit-Stone Container
Midland Paper	Unisource
Pope & Talbot	

HISTORICAL FINANCIALS

Company Type: Private

Income Statement

FYE: December 31

	REVENUE ($ mil.)	NET INCOME ($ mil.)	NET PROFIT MARGIN	EMPLOYEES
12/03	1,900	—	—	850
12/02	1,600	—	—	850
12/01	1,700	—	—	900
12/00	1,825	—	—	900
12/99	1,660	—	—	900
12/98	1,600	—	—	900
12/97	2,000	—	—	900
12/96	2,000	—	—	900
12/95	2,000	—	—	900
12/94	2,000	—	—	900
Annual Growth	**(0.6%)**	**—**	**—**	**(0.6%)**

Revenue History

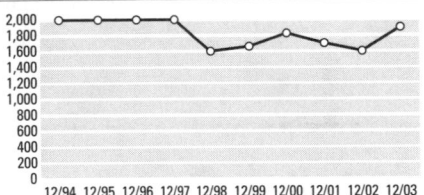

CH2M HILL

Catchy, no; descriptive, yes. CH2M HILL's name is a amalgam of initials from its founders — Cornell, Howland, Hayes, and Merryfield — plus HILL, from its first merger. The group offers engineering consulting related to industrial facility design, transportation, water treatment, and environmental remediation. Specialties include sewer and waste-treatment design, hazardous-waste cleanup, and transportation projects such as highways and bridges. CH2M HILL is also involved in federal nuclear waste cleanup projects, facilities operations and management, and security and emergency management services. Founded in 1946 in Corvallis, Oregon, the firm is employee-owned and operates from about 200 offices worldwide.

CH2M HILL's full range of integrated services enables it to offer clients support for projects throughout several cycles — from concept, planning, and financing through design, implementation, and providing operations and maintenance. The company resides at the top levels of industry rankings of environmental consulting and engineering firms for several sectors: hazardous waste, water, sewer/waste, telecommunications, and transportation. The group is also one of the largest environmental firms to serve state and local governments, as well as federal clients.

It also holds lofty rankings among the US construction management-for-fee firms. CH2M HILL is one of the largest contractors in the nuclear waste, site assessment and compliance, clean air compliance, water treatment plants, and hazardous waste sectors. It is the largest privately held firm in Colorado, as well as one of the largest private construction companies in the US. With its 2003 acquisition of engineering and construction firm Lockwood Greene, the company has enhanced its offerings to the industrial and power markets worldwide. Lockwood Greene has annual revenues of some $600 million and about 2,500 employees.

Although the group was selected as one of *FORTUNE*'s "100 Best Companies to Work For" in 2003, it has also come under fire from union members for its tank-farm cleaning operations at the Hanford nuclear facility in Washington State. The federal government has offered bonuses of up to $2 million for each tank CH2M HILL cleans by the end of its contract in 2006. The site has 177 tanks, holding about 53 million gallons of radioactive and toxic waste from plutonium produced for nuclear weapons. At issue are allegations of worker injuries from tank vapors. Federal and state investigations have been conducted, but the Energy Department's investigation cleared CH2M HILL of any criminal conduct regarding ammonia vapor readings. Despite steps taken by the company to strengthen its safety practices, CH2M workers at Hanford were exposed to higher-than-normal levels of radiation in July 2004 and were not wearing protective leaded gloves. By October 2004, CH2M HILL had identified 52 chemicals of "potential concern" that might pose a threat to workers at the site.

In 2004 the group restructured its operations according to three main client groups: civil infrastructure (state and local governments), federal (US and international governments), and industrial (private-sector clients). Its federal business segment includes environmental and nuclear services and outsourcing services. Late in the year CEO Ralph Peterson was treated for stomach cancer; CFO Samuel Iapalucci was named interim president and CEO while Peterson recovers.

EXECUTIVES

Chairman, President, and CEO: Ralph R. Peterson, age 60, $1,348,670 pay
Vice Chairman and SVP: Joseph A. (Bud) Ahearn, age 68, $494,807 pay
EVP, CFO, and Secretary: Samuel H. (Sam) Iapalucci, age 52, $704,430 pay
EVP: Alan M. Parker
CIO: Robert (Bob) Bullock
SVP Finance and Director: M. Catherine Santee, age 43
SVP and Director; President and CEO, Civil Infrastructure Client Group: Donald S. (Don) Evans, age 54, $663,814 pay
SVP and Director; President and CEO, Federal Client Group and Industrial Client Group: James J. (Jim) Ferris, age 61, $704,525 pay
SVP; President, Industrial Business Group and Industrial Design and Construction: Kenneth F. Durant
SVP; President, Transportation Business Group: Michael D. (Mike) Kennedy, age 55
SVP and Director; President, Water Business Group: Thomas G. (Tom) Searle, age 51

SVP, CH2M HILL Hanford Group: Dale Allen
VP and Controller: Vern L. Nelson
VP and Treasurer: Stanley W. (Stan) Vinson
VP Human Resources: Robert C. (Bob) Allen
Director Marketing Communications: Cary Baird
Auditors: KPMG LLP

LOCATIONS

HQ: CH2M HILL Companies, Ltd.
9191 S. Jamaica St., Englewood, CO 80112
Phone: 303-771-0900   **Fax:** 720-286-9250
Web: www.ch2m.com

CH2M HILL Companies operates in more than 30 countries.

PRODUCTS/OPERATIONS

2004 Sales

	$ mil.	% of total
Federal	993.0	37
Industrial	870.3	31
Civil Infrastructure	852.1	32
Total	**2,715.4**	**100**

COMPETITORS

AECOM
Bechtel
Black & Veatch
Earth Tech
ERM
Fluor
Foster Wheeler
Jacobs Engineering
MWH Global
Parsons
Parsons Brinckerhoff
Shaw Group
Tetra Tech
URS

HISTORICAL FINANCIALS

Company Type: Private

Income Statement

FYE: December 31

	REVENUE ($ mil.)	NET INCOME ($ mil.)	NET PROFIT MARGIN	EMPLOYEES
12/04	2,715	32	1.2%	14,000
12/03	2,154	24	1.1%	14,000
12/02	1,999	30	1.5%	10,600
12/01	1,941	28	1.4%	10,500
12/00	1,707	25	1.4%	10,600
12/99	1,185	14	1.1%	9,200
12/98	932	6	0.6%	7,000
12/97	918	5	0.5%	7,200
12/96	937	5	0.5%	7,026
12/95	805	5	0.7%	6,876
Annual Growth	**14.5%**	**22.0%**	**—**	**8.2%**

2004 Year-End Financials

Debt ratio: 1.8%
Return on equity: 15.0%
Cash ($ mil.): 56

Current ratio: 1.18
Long-term debt ($ mil.): 4

Net Income History

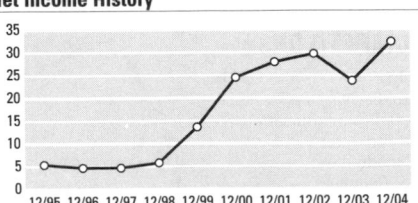

Charmer-Sunbelt

The Charmer-Sunbelt Group has become one of the biggest swigs in its business. A leading wine and spirits wholesaler, the company operates through a number of joint ventures and subsidiaries including Charmer Industries (New York), Premier Beverage (Florida), Reliable Churchill (Maryland), Ben Arnold-Sunbelt Beverage (South Carolina), and others in Alabama, Arizona, Colorado, Connecticut, Mississippi, Pennsylvania, and Washington, DC. Division management bought the group from McKesson (drugs and sundries wholesaler) and took it private in 1988. Herman Merinoff has a majority stake in the company.

The Charmer-Sunbelt Group handles 15% of Southcorp Limited's US wine business and has exclusive rights to Allied Domecq brands in Maryland, Florida, upstate New York, and Washington, DC.

EXECUTIVES

CEO: Charles Merinoff
EVP and CFO: Gene Luciano
VP, Human Resources: Ann Giambusso
Vice Chairman, Charmer Industries: Steve Drucker
President, Ben Arnold Beverage Company:
  William Tovell
President, Capital Wine and Spirits Company:
  Robert Storey
President, Bacchus Importers: Bruce Gearhart
President, Premier Beverage Company: Bob Drinon
President, Charmer Industries: E. Lloyd Sobel
Chairman and CEO, Reliable Churchill: Jim Smith

LOCATIONS

HQ: The Charmer Sunbelt Group
  60 E. 42nd St., New York, NY 10165
Phone: 212-699-7000   **Fax:** 212-699-7099
Web: www.charmer-sunbelt.com

PRODUCTS/OPERATIONS

Selected Subsidiaries

Bacchus Importers
Ben Arnold-Sunbelt Beverage
Capital Wine & Spirits
Charmer Industries
Premier Beverage Company
Reliable Churchill, LLP

COMPETITORS

Bacardi USA
Constellation Brands
Glazer's Wholesale Drug
Johnson Brothers
National Distributing
Southern Wine & Spirits
Young's Market

HISTORICAL FINANCIALS

Company Type: Private

Income Statement

FYE: March 31

	ESTIMATED REVENUE ($ mil.)	NET INCOME ($ mil.)	NET PROFIT MARGIN	EMPLOYEES
3/04	1,700	—	—	3,000
3/03	2,200	—	—	3,800
3/02	950	—	—	1,700
3/01	910	—	—	1,700
3/00*	850	—	—	1,500
12/99	820	—	—	1,500
12/98	770	—	—	1,700
12/97	700	—	—	1,485
12/96	675	—	—	1,485
12/95	665	—	—	1,485
Annual Growth	**11.0%**	—	—	**8.1%**

*Fiscal year change

Revenue History

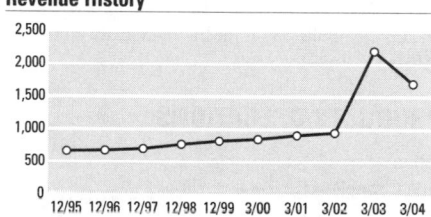

Chevron Phillips Chemical

A coin toss determined which company's name would go first when Chevron and Phillips Petroleum (now ConocoPhillips) formed a new 50-50 joint venture, Chevron Phillips Chemical Company (CP Chem), in 2000. Among the largest US petrochemical firms, CP Chem produces ethylene, propylene, polyethylene, and polypropylene — sometimes used as building blocks for the company's other products such as pipe. CP Chem also produces aromatics such as benzene and styrene, specialty chemicals such as acetylene black (a form of carbon black), and drilling and mining chemicals. The company has formed several petrochemicals joint ventures in the Middle East. Most of CP Chem's operations are located in the US.

After an improved but still unprofitable 2002, CP Chem turned a small profit in 2003 and a much larger profit the following year. The good news comes as a result of across-the-board price increases, higher volumes, and good years from its affiliates in the Middle East (Saudi Chevron Phillips Company, in which it has a 50% stake, and Qatar Chemical Company, in which it has a 60% stake).

The company is North America's largest producer of high-density polyethylene (HDPE) — used in blow/injection molding, plastic bags and pipes, and films. CP Chem also is near the top in styrene, ethylene, and aromatics production.

Chevron Phillips Chemical Company LP is the US operating subsidiary of CP Chem, which also includes foreign ventures, mainly those in Asia and the Middle East. Chevron Phillips Chemical Company LP accounts for about 85% of its parent's revenues.

EXECUTIVES

President and CEO: James L. (Jim) Gallogly, age 53, $1,009,679 pay
SVP, CFO, and Controller: Greg G. Maxwell, age 48
SVP, Aromatics and Styrenics: J. M. (Mike) Parker, age 58, $372,979 pay
SVP, Manufacturing: R. L. (Rick) Roberts, age 51, $464,253 pay
SVP, Olefins and Polyolefins: Timothy G. (Tim) Taylor, age 51, $533,186 pay
SVP, Planning and Specialty Projects: Greg C. Garland, age 47, $539,013 pay
SVP, General Counsel, and Secretary: Craig B. Glidden, age 47, $523,558 pay
VP, Human Resources: Don F. Kremer, age 53
VP and Treasurer: Joseph M. (Joe) McKee, age 54
VP, Technology: Mary Jane Hagenson
VP, Environment, Health, and Safety: Greg Hanggi
CIO: Larry R. Frazier
General Tax Counsel: Bruce E. Waits
Market Development Manager: Greg Collins
Auditors: Ernst & Young LLP

LOCATIONS

HQ: Chevron Phillips Chemical Company LLC
  10001 6 Pines Dr., The Woodlands, TX 77380
Phone: 832-813-4100   **Fax:** 800-231-3890
Web: www.cpchem.com

Chevron Phillips Chemical Company operates about 30 manufacturing facilities and five research and technical centers, including facilities in Belgium, China, Mexico, Qatar, Saudi Arabia, Singapore, South Korea, and the US.

2004 Sales

	% of total
US	84
Other	16
Total	**100**

PRODUCTS/OPERATIONS

2004 Sales

	$ mil.	% of total
Olefins & polyolefins	6,018	61
Aromatics & styrenics	3,357	34
Specialty products	481	5
Adjustments	(298)	—
Total	**9,558**	**100**

Selected Products

Olefins and polyolefins
  Ethylene
  Polyethylene
  Polyethylene pipe
  Polypropylene
  Propylene
Aromatics and styrenics
  Benzene
  Cumene
  Cyclohexane
  Paraxylene
  Styrene
Specialty products
  Acetylene black
  Alpha olefins
  Dimethyl sulfide
  Drilling specialty chemicals
  High-purity hydrocarbons and solvents
  Mining chemicals
  Neohexene
  Performance and reference fuels
  Polyalpha olefins
  Polystyrene

COMPETITORS

Basell	Lyondell Chemical
Dow Chemical	NOVA Chemicals
DuPont	SABIC
Equistar Chemicals	Sasol
ExxonMobil Chemical	Sterling Chemicals
Innovene	Sunoco Chemicals
Jilin Chemical	Westlake Chemical
KRATON	

HISTORICAL FINANCIALS

Company Type: Joint venture

Income Statement

FYE: December 31

	REVENUE ($ mil.)	NET INCOME ($ mil.)	NET PROFIT MARGIN	EMPLOYEES
12/04	9,558	605	6.3%	5,300
12/03	7,018	7	0.1%	5,451
12/02	5,473	(30)	—	5,517
12/01	6,010	(480)	—	6,056
Annual Growth	16.7%	—	—	(4.3%)

2004 Year-End Financials

Debt ratio: 35.0%
Return on equity: 16.2%
Cash ($ mil.): 63

Current ratio: 1.61
Long-term debt ($ mil.): 1,390

Net Income History

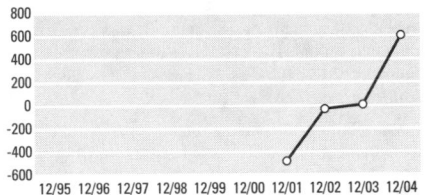

12/95 12/96 12/97 12/98 12/99 12/00 12/01 12/02 12/03 12/04

Chicago Bulls

The Chicago Bulls no longer charge to The Finals. The Bulls won six titles between 1991 and 1998, led by five-time MVP Michael Jordan. "Da Bulls" struggled for most of its first 20 years (the team joined the NBA in 1966) until drafting Jordan from North Carolina in 1984. After Jordan retired (he returned to the NBA briefly with the Washington Wizards in 2001), the Bulls gutted their championship squad, replacing coach Phil Jackson with former Iowa State coach Tim Floyd, who lasted only four losing seasons. His successor, Bill Cartwright, also got the ax in 2003. Former Phoenix Suns head coach Scott Skiles now leads the team. Chairman Jerry Reinsdorf (who also owns the Chicago White Sox) owns the Bulls.

While the Bulls hadn't won more than 30 games since 1998 (Jordan's last year) until 2004-05, the team has managed to still pull in about 19,600 fans a year, third in the league. The club attributes the attendance figures to the fact that it has frozen ticket prices since the Bulls entered its Jordan-less slump.

EXECUTIVES

Chairman: Jerry Reinsdorf, age 69
EVP Basketball Operations: John Paxson
EVP Business Operations: Steve Schanwald
SVP Financial and Legal: Irwin Mandel
Head Coach: Scott Skiles, age 41
VP, Ticket Sales: Keith Brown
Controller: Stu Bookman
Senior Director of Public and Media Relations: Tim Hallam
Senior Director of Ticket Operations: Joe O'Neil
Director of Community Relations: David Kurland
Senior Manager of Basketball Operations: Matt Lloyd
Senior Manager, Corporate Communications: Marianne Caponi

LOCATIONS

HQ: Chicago Bulls
United Center, 1901 W. Madison St.,
Chicago, IL 60612
Phone: 312-455-4000   **Fax:** 312-455-4198
Web: www.nba.com/bulls

The Chicago Bulls play at the 21,700-capacity United Center in Chicago.

PRODUCTS/OPERATIONS

Titles

NBA Champions (1991-93, 96-98)

COMPETITORS

Cavaliers/Gund
Detroit Pistons
Indiana Pacers
Milwaukee Bucks

HISTORICAL FINANCIALS

Company Type: Private

Income Statement

FYE: July 31

	REVENUE ($ mil.)	NET INCOME ($ mil.)	NET PROFIT MARGIN	EMPLOYEES
7/04	123	—	—	—
7/03	119	—	—	—
7/02	115	—	—	—
7/01	117	—	—	—
7/00	112	—	—	—
7/99	110	—	—	—
7/98	112	—	—	60
7/97	83	—	—	60
7/96	87	—	—	65
7/95	70	—	—	—
Annual Growth	6.5%	—	—	(3.9%)

Revenue History

140
120
100
80
60
40
20
0
7/95 7/96 7/97 7/98 7/99 7/00 7/01 7/02 7/03 7/04

Chick-fil-A

Beloved by bovines, Chick-fil-A operates the nation's second-largest fast-food chain that specialize in chicken dishes. (It is #2 in sales behind leader KFC.) With about 1,200 restaurants, Chick-fil-A serves chicken entrees, sandwiches, and salads, along with its popular waffle fries and fresh-squeezed lemonade. The chain is made up primarily of mall-based stores, but it also includes free-standing units that offer drive-through service as well as dine-in seating. Chick-fil-A also licenses its concept to foodservice operators for high-traffic areas, such as schools and airports. All of its restaurants are closed on Sundays, a policy insisted upon by founder (and devout Baptist) S. Truett Cathy.

Unlike most fast-food franchises, Chick-fil-A owns most of its restaurants and licenses franchisees to run the units for a fixed annual income plus a share in the profits. This unique arrangement lowers the initial cost to its franchisees and has resulted in less operator turnover than in other chains.

The company has 40% of its restaurants located in three southern states (Florida, Georgia, and Texas). Chick-fil-A has been focusing its expansion efforts on opening more free-standing restaurants — most recently in Southern California — as well as licensed units in non-traditional locations. It has also developed a "lunch counter" design concept for use in office buildings. Overall, Chick-fil-A plans to open about 80 restaurants in 2005 — seeking to increase its total number of stores to about 2,300 by 2010.

As part of its marketing strategy, Chick-fil-A is a big sponsor of athletic events, including the annual Peach Bowl college football game. It also supports leadership training and scholarship programs through the WinShape Centre Foundation.

The company also operates two full-service restaurant concepts, Chick-fil-A Dwarf Houses and Truett's Grill.

EXECUTIVES

Chairman: S. Truett Cathy, age 83
President and COO: Dan T. Cathy
SVP, Design and Construction: Perry A. Ragsdale
SVP, Finance, and CFO: James B. (Buck) McCabe
SVP, Marketing, and Chief Marketing Officer: Steve A. Robinson
SVP, Operations: Timothy P. (Tim) Tassopoulos
SVP, Real Estate, and General Counsel: Bureon E. Ledbetter Jr.
SVP; President, Dwarf House: Donald M. (Bubba) Cathy
VP, Brand Development: Woody Faulk
VP, Public Relations: Don Perry
VP, Training and Development: Mark Miller
VP and CIO: Jon Bridges
Director, Field Operations: Cheryl Dick
Manager, Human Resources: Andy Lorenzen

LOCATIONS

HQ: Chick-fil-A, Inc.
5200 Buffington Rd., Atlanta, GA 30349
Phone: 404-765-8038   **Fax:** 404-765-8971
Web: www.chick-fil-a.com

Chick-fil-A operates more than 1,100 restaurants in 38 states.

COMPETITORS

AFC Enterprises
Blimpie
Boston Market
Burger King
Captain D's
CKE Restaurants
Dairy Queen
Freshëns
Jack in the Box
KFC
Krystal
McDonald's
Panasonic Mobile Communications
Quiznos
Sonic
Subway
Triarc
Wendy's
YUM!
Zaxby's

HISTORICAL FINANCIALS

Company Type: Private

Income Statement

FYE: December 31

	REVENUE ($ mil.)	NET INCOME ($ mil.)	NET PROFIT MARGIN	EMPLOYEES
12/03	1,534	—	—	46,500
12/02	1,373	—	—	45,000
12/01	1,242	—	—	43,000
12/00	1,082	—	—	40,000
12/99	750	—	—	35,000
12/98	650	—	—	35,000
12/97	672	—	—	28,500
12/96	570	—	—	25,000
12/95	502	—	—	—
12/94	451	—	—	—
Annual Growth	**14.6%**	—	—	**9.3%**

Revenue History

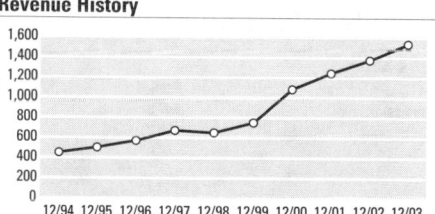

The Chimes

The sound of bells can induce a message of hope. The Chimes is a private agency serving the needs of people with mental and physical disabilities. The organization offers a wide range of health, education, job training and placement, housing, and social services in the mid-Atlantic states of the US and in Tel Aviv, Israel. The Chimes offers similar services through two subsidiaries, Developmental Services of New Jersey and Holcomb Behavioral Health Systems. The agency was established in 1947 when a group of Baltimore parents used space in a church to found a school for their mentally disabled children.

EXECUTIVES

Chairperson: Stephen S. Kramer
Vice Chairperson: Patrick Bagley
Vice Chairperson: Bobby Edmondson
Vice Chairperson: Arthur C. George
Vice Chairperson: Julius B. Margolis
President and CEO: Terry Allan Perl
COO and Secretary: Albert Bussone
CFO and CIO: Martin (Marty) Lampner
VP Human Resources: Martha Loveman Perl
Treasurer: Martin S. Lampner
Director Development and Corporate Communications: Marge Wisnom

LOCATIONS

HQ: The Chimes, Inc.
4815 Seton Dr., Baltimore, MD 21215
Phone: 410-358-6400 **Fax:** 410-358-8546
Web: www.chimes.org

PRODUCTS/OPERATIONS

The Chimes has facilities in Delaware, Maryland, New Jersey, North Carolina, Pennsylvania, Virginia, and Washington, DC. It also has a location in Tel Aviv, Israel.

HISTORICAL FINANCIALS

Company Type: Not-for-profit

Income Statement

FYE: June 30

	REVENUE ($ mil.)	NET INCOME ($ mil.)	NET PROFIT MARGIN	EMPLOYEES
6/04*	129	(4)	—	—
7/02	93	—	—	2,000
Annual Growth	**38.1%**	—	—	—

*Fiscal year change

Revenue History

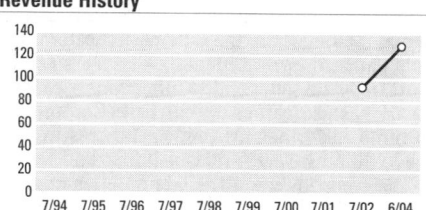

Choice Homes

Choice Homes is the builder of choice for many first-time buyers and first-time move-up homeowners in Texas and Georgia. The privately held builder of affordable homes and single-family townhomes is one of the largest home-builders in the Dallas/Fort Worth area. It maintains more than 140 communities in and around Amarillo, Austin, Dallas/Fort Worth, Galveston, Houston, Lubbock, and San Antonio, Texas, and 16 Georgia communities in Atlanta, Athens, and Macon. Customers may choose from more than 200 floor plans with a variety of options. The company, which began in 1987, builds about 4,400 homes annually. For five consecutive years *Builder* magazine has ranked it as one of the top 25 builders in the US.

Consistent with its philosophy to share its success with the people who helped make it happen, Choice Homes incorporates a companywide dividend program that divides equally among its

employees a percentage of the company's profits each year. The company presented over $1.5 million in performance bonuses to its employees in 2002 and more than $1.2 million in 2003.

The company's plan for growth targets Houston, West Texas, and San Antonio markets, as well as the greater Atlanta area. Choice Homes is expanding into the New Braunfels market in Texas and entered Lubbock in 2004.

EXECUTIVES

President and CEO: Bob Ladd
VP and CFO: Steve Garza
Regional VP, Tarrant, Parker, Hood, and Denton Counties, Texas: Daniel D. Couture
Regional VP, Georgia: Kelly Dempsey
Regional VP, Dallas and East Texas: Zack Jones
Regional VP, Houston: Marc Jungers
Regional VP, San Antonio: Frank Prince
Treasurer: Betty Floyd
Director, IT: Andrew Brimberry
Director, Marketing and Advertising: Kristina (Kris) Densing
Land Acquisition Manager, Houston: Mary Daily

LOCATIONS

HQ: Choice Homes, Inc.
1600 East Lamar Blvd., Arlington, TX 76011
Phone: 817-652-5100 **Fax:** 817-633-2925
Web: www.choicehomes.com

Choice Homes builds in and around Amarillo, Austin, Dallas/Fort Worth, Galveston, Houston, Lubbock, and San Antonio, Texas, and in Atlanta, Athens, and Macon, Georgia. It has offices in Arlington (near Dallas/Fort Worth), Houston, San Antonio, and Atlanta.

COMPETITORS

Beazer Homes
Centex
David Weekley Homes
D.R. Horton
KB Home
Kimball Hill Inc
Lennar
Pulte Homes

HISTORICAL FINANCIALS

Company Type: Private

Income Statement

FYE: December 31

	REVENUE ($ mil.)	NET INCOME ($ mil.)	NET PROFIT MARGIN	EMPLOYEES
12/04	497	—	—	452
12/03	541	—	—	485
12/02	466	—	—	440
Annual Growth	**3.2%**	—	—	**1.4%**

Revenue History

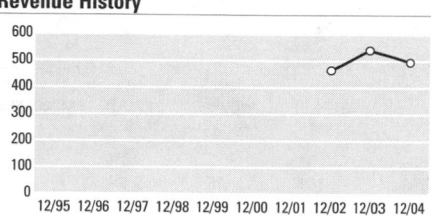

Chugach Electric

Deriving its name from an old Eskimo tribal word, Chugach Electric Association generates, transmits, distributes, and sells electricity in Alaska's railbelt region. This area extends from the coastal Chugach Mountains into central Alaska and includes the state's two largest cities (Anchorage and Fairbanks). The member-owned cooperative utility has 530 MW of generating capacity from its natural gas-fired and hydroelectric power plants. Serving 75,500 retail customers, Chugach Electric, the largest electric utility in Alaska, also sells wholesale power to other municipal and cooperative utilities in the region.

Chugach Electric was formed in 1948 as a Rural Electrification Administration cooperative to create an electrical distribution system to meet the growing power needs of the Greater Anchorage region.

EXECUTIVES

Chairman: Jeffrey W. (Jeff) Lipscomb, age 54
Vice Chairman: Alan Christopherson
CFO: Michael R. Cunningham, age 55, $132,316 pay
SVP Services Division: William R. Stewart, age 58
General Manager G&T Division: Bradley W. Evans, age 49
General Manager Distribution Division: Lee D. Thibert, age 49
Secretary and Director: David Cottrell, age 57
Treasurer and Director: Liz Vazquez
Public Relations Contact: Patti Bogan
Auditors: KPMG LLP

LOCATIONS

HQ: Chugach Electric Association, Inc.
5601 Electron Dr., Anchorage, AK 99518
Phone: 907-563-7494   **Fax:** 907-762-4678
Web: www.chugachelectric.com

PRODUCTS/OPERATIONS

2004 Sales

	$ mil.	% of total
Retail		
Residential	65.7	33
Commercial	59.1	29
Wholesale	64.8	32
Other	11.7	6
Total	**201.3**	**100**

COMPETITORS

SEMCO Energy

HISTORICAL FINANCIALS

Company Type: Cooperative

Income Statement				FYE: December 31
	REVENUE ($ mil.)	NET INCOME ($ mil.)	NET PROFIT MARGIN	EMPLOYEES
12/04	201	8	3.8%	355
12/03	184	6	3.4%	353
12/02	172	(2)	—	—
Annual Growth	8.2%	—	—	0.6%

Net Income History

Cinemark

Cinemark has left its mark on the cinema landscape. The third-largest movie exhibitor in the US (following Regal Entertainment and AMC) has more than 3,200 screens in more than 300 theaters in the US and several other countries, mostly in Latin America. Cinemark operates multiplex theaters (the ratio of screens to theaters is about 12 to 1) in smaller cities and suburban areas of major metropolitan markets. Some larger theaters operate under the Tinseltown name; others are "discount" theaters showing no first-run films. Chairman and CEO Lee Roy Mitchell shares ownership of the company with private investment firm Madison Dearborn Partners which paid about $1.5 billion for a stake in Cinemark.

All of Cinemark's theaters are multiplexes, many of which sport neon color schemes not found in nature. About 15% of its theaters are "discount" cinemas. The company prefers to build new theaters in midsized markets or in suburbs of major cities where the Cinemark theater is the only game in town. Cinemark's theaters can be found in 33 US states and 14 other countries. Cinemark has also teamed up with Imax Corporation to build five Cinemark IMAX Theatres in Colorado, Illinois, New York, Oklahoma, and Texas.

The company spent the late nineties upgrading into one of the most modern and technologically advanced movie chains. (About two-thirds of the current screens have been built since 1996; about 65% of its North American first run screens and 75% of its international screens feature stadium seating — a trend that began in the 1990s.) In 2005 it joined Regal Entertainment and AMC Entertainment in National CineMedia, a joint venture that delivers ads and pre-movie entertainment to more than 13,000 screens in the US and Canada via a private digital network. Regal owns 50%, AMC 29%, and Cinemark 21%.

Cinemark, along with the rest of the movie theater industry, struggled through the late 1990s as numerous bankruptcies abounded thanks to overbuilding. Things seemed to be on the upswing in early 2002, and Cinemark responded by filing an IPO. However, the overall decline of the stock market forced the firm to postpone its offering later that year. Cinemark has since abandoned plans to take the company public in favor of bringing in major investors. Investment firms Madison Dearborn and Quadrangle Group both bought seats in the Cinemark show.

EXECUTIVES

Chairman and CEO: Lee Roy Mitchell, age 68, $1,134,151 pay
President and COO: Alan W. Stock, age 44, $671,170 pay
EVP and Assistant Secretary: Tandy Mitchell, age 54
SVP, Treasurer, CFO, and Assistant Secretary: Robert D. Copple, age 46, $490,084 pay
SVP Operations: Robert F. Carmony, age 47, $472,460 pay
SVP; President Cinemark International: Tim Warner, age 60, $544,267 pay
VP, General Counsel, and Assistant Secretary: Michael Cavalier, age 38
VP Construction: Don Harton, age 47
VP Development: Tom Owens, age 48
VP Film Licensing: John Lundin, age 55
VP Purchasing: Walter Hebert III, age 59
VP Marketing and Communications: Terrell Falk, age 54
VP Real Estate and Assistant Secretary: Margaret E. Richards, age 46
Controller: Joe Manzi
Director Human Resources: Brad Smith
Auditors: Deloitte & Touche LLP

LOCATIONS

HQ: Cinemark, Inc.
3900 Dallas Pkwy., Ste. 500, Plano, TX 75093
Phone: 972-665-1000   **Fax:** 972-665-1004
Web: www.cinemark.com

Cinemark has theaters in Argentina, Brazil, Canada, Chile, Colombia, Costa Rica, Ecuador, El Salvador, Honduras, Nicaragua, Mexico, Panama, Peru, and 32 states in the US.

2004 Sales

	$ mil.	% of total
US and Canada	783.4	77
Brazil	90.9	9
Mexico	76.1	7
Other regions	75.2	7
Eliminations	(1.4)	—
Total	**1,024.2**	**100**

PRODUCTS/OPERATIONS

2004 Sales

	$ mil.	% of total
Admissions	647.0	63
Concession	321.6	31
Other	55.6	6
Total	**1,024.2**	**100**

COMPETITORS

AMC Entertainment	Loews Cineplex
Carmike Cinemas	National Amusements
Clearview Cinemas	Pacific Theatres
Hoyts Cinemas	Regal Entertainment

HISTORICAL FINANCIALS

Company Type: Private

Income Statement				FYE: December 31
	REVENUE ($ mil.)	NET INCOME ($ mil.)	NET PROFIT MARGIN	EMPLOYEES
12/04	1,024	45	4.4%	13,200
12/03	958	45	4.7%	12,700
12/02	939	39	4.2%	12,500
12/01	854	(4)	—	8,000
12/00	786	(10)	—	8,000
12/99	713	1	0.1%	8,000
12/98	571	11	1.9%	8,000
12/97	435	15	3.5%	7,000
12/96	342	15	4.3%	6,500
12/95	299	13	4.4%	7,000
Annual Growth	14.7%	14.5%	—	7.3%

2004 Year-End Financials

Debt ratio: 377.4%   Current ratio: 0.98
Return on equity: 36.3%   Long-term debt ($ mil.): 637
Cash ($ mil.): 100

Net Income History

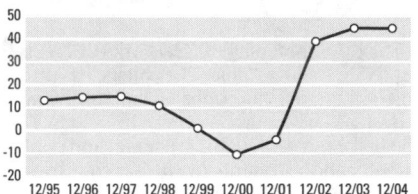

Cingular Wireless

BellSouth *plus* SBC *times* wireless assets *equals* Cingular Wireless. With a name chosen to emphasize unity and the individual customer, the two regional Bell companies have combined assets and joined forces to acquire rival AT&T Wireless, thus creating the #1 wireless carrier in the US, overtaking Verizon Wireless. With more than 50 million customers, including subscribers to its Mobitex wireless data services network, the joint venture is 60%-owned by SBC and 40% by BellSouth, according to the contributions made by the two companies, which share control. Eleven brand names used by the SBC and BellSouth units have been replaced by the Cingular Wireless brand and AT&T Wireless customers are now being integrated.

Cingular won a bidding war with UK-based wireless operator Vodafone Group to acquire AT&T Wireless as part of a long-anticipated consolidation within the mobile phone industry. The cash deal was valued at $41 billion. Prior to the deal, Cingular had formed a joint venture with AT&T Wireless to work on the development of advanced networks. The two wireless carriers use the same network technology.

To accommodate the deal to acquire AT&T Wireless, Cingular agreed to sell some assets, including a wireless network in California and Nevada to T-Mobile USA. That deal, valued at $2.5 billion, includes a $200 million payment to T-Mobile USA to end a venture in which the two companies shared each other's networks. The company also announced it would cut about 10% of the 68,000 workers over the next 18 months as it combines operations. Cingular had earlier held merger talks with VoiceStream Wireless, now T-Mobile USA.

The company also has agreed to sell its Cingular Interactive subsidiary, which provides wireless corporate e-mail and messaging services, to a unit of Cerberus Partners. It also is selling its one-third stake in India's Idea Cellular to its current partners in the wireless operator, the industrial families Tata Group and A. V. Birla Group, in a deal valued at about $300 million.

Cingular Wireless also has acquired additional licenses from bankrupt NextWave Telecom. The deal, valued at $1.4 billion, sent 34 licenses to Cingular for markets that include 83 million potential customers. These markets are primarily areas where Cingular already operates. In another

deal, Cingular has completed a swap of some cellular properties in northwest Michigan to Dobson Communications in exchange for properties along the eastern Maryland shore. It also has acquired 16,000 customers in Louisiana, as well as spectrum and operations in Louisiana, Texas, and Arkansas, from US Unwired in a cash deal valued at $27.6 million.

EXECUTIVES

Chairman: Ronald M. Dykes, age 58
President and CEO: Stanley T. (Stan) Sigman, age 58, $2,291,442 pay
COO: Ralph de la Vega, age 53, $1,245,192 pay
CFO: Peter A. (Pete) Ritcher, age 44, $710,612 pay (partial-year salary)
EVP and General Counsel: Joaquin R. Carbonell III, age 52, $685,477 pay
EVP Human Resources: Rickford D. (Rick) Bradley, age 53
EVP International: William W. Hague, age 49
EVP External Affairs and Public Relations: Paul R. Roth, age 46
EVP Treasury and Corporate Development: Sean P. Foley, age 46
SVP Sales Operations: Larry Carter
SVP Customer Service: Kathleen L. (Kathy) Dowling
VP Advertising and Marketing Communications: Daryl Evans
VP and Controller: Gregory T. Hall, age 49
VP, Assistant General Counsel, Corporate Secretary, and Chief Compliance Officer: Carol L. Tacker, age 56
Chief Marketing Officer: Marc Lefar
CIO: F. Thaddeus Arroyo, age 41, $818,592 pay
CTO: Kristin S. Rinne
Senior Director, Media Relations: Clay Owen
Executive Director, Investor Relations: Kent Evans
Auditors: Ernst & Young LLP

LOCATIONS

HQ: Cingular Wireless LLC
Glenridge Highlands Two, 5565 Glenridge Connector, Atlanta, GA 30342
Phone: 404-236-6000   **Fax:** 404-236-6005
Web: www.cingular.com

PRODUCTS/OPERATIONS

2004 Sales

	$ mil.	% of total
Services		
Local		
Voice	14,839	76
Data	892	5
Incollect roamer	764	4
Outcollect	585	3
Long-distance	229	1
Other services	164	1
Equipment sales	1,963	10
Total	**19,436**	**100**

Selected Services

Analog wireless access
Digital wireless access
Interactive messaging
Short text messaging
Wireless data
Wireless Internet access

Selected Subsidiaries

Cingular Wireless Corporation (managing entity)

COMPETITORS

ALLTEL
Centennial
  Communications
CenturyTel
Sprint Nextel

Telephone & Data Systems
T-Mobile USA
U.S. Cellular
Verizon Wireless
Western Wireless

HISTORICAL FINANCIALS

Company Type: Joint venture

Income Statement

FYE: December 31

	REVENUE ($ mil.)	NET INCOME ($ mil.)	NET PROFIT MARGIN	EMPLOYEES
12/04	19,436	201	1.0%	70,300
12/03	15,483	1,022	6.6%	39,400
12/02	14,727	1,207	8.2%	33,800
12/01	14,108	1,692	12.0%	—
12/00	3,055	127	4.2%	—
12/99	9,042	—	—	—
12/98	7,988	—	—	—
12/97	7,433	—	—	—
Annual Growth	**14.7%**	**12.2%**	**—**	**44.2%**

2004 Year-End Financials

Debt ratio: 53.6%   Current ratio: 0.70
Return on equity: 0.8%   Long-term debt ($ mil.): 23,857
Cash ($ mil.): 352

Net Income History

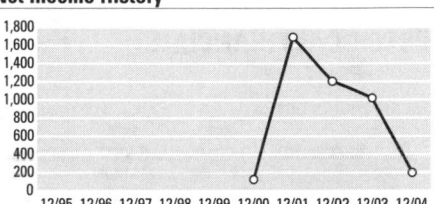

Circus and Eldorado

Circus and Eldorado Joint Venture owns and operates the Silver Legacy Resort Casino in Reno, Nevada. The Silver Legacy, which features a nineteenth century silver mining theme, offers a more than 87,000-sq.-ft. casino with about 1,800 slot machines and nearly 75 table games. The casino's hotel boasts some 1,700 guest rooms and 15 penthouse and hospitality suites. Silver Legacy also houses six restaurants. MGM MIRAGE (through Galleon, Inc.) and Eldorado Resorts each own 50% of Circus and Eldorado Joint Venture. (MGM MIRAGE's stake was owned by Mandalay Resort Group until MGM bought Mandalay in 2005.)

The company markets the Silver Legacy to a select group of patrons including preferred casino customers, convention groups, and specialty Internet travel groups.

EXECUTIVES

CEO; General Manager, Silver Legacy: Gary L. Carano, age 52, $400,000 pay
CFO, Treasurer, and Controller; Director of Finance and Administration, Silver Legacy: Bruce C. Sexton, age 51, $175,000 pay
Secretary; Executive Director of Marketing, Silver Legacy: Glen T. Carano, age 49, $400,000 pay
Auditors: Deloitte & Touche LLP

LOCATIONS

HQ: Circus and Eldorado Joint Venture
    407 N. Virginia St., Reno, NV 89501
Phone: 775-325-7401   **Fax:** 775-325-7330
Web: www.silverlegacyreno.com

PRODUCTS/OPERATIONS

2004 Sales

	$ mil.	% of total
Casino	85.5	51
Hotel	38.5	23
Food & beverage	35.3	21
Other	8.6	5
Promotional allowances	(14.2)	—
Total	**153.7**	**100**

COMPETITORS

Boomtown
Harrah's Entertainment
Sands Regent

HISTORICAL FINANCIALS

Company Type: Joint venture

Income Statement   FYE: December 31

	REVENUE ($ mil.)	NET INCOME ($ mil.)	NET PROFIT MARGIN	EMPLOYEES
12/04	154	11	7.0%	2,105
12/03	152	10	6.3%	2,061
12/02	159	17	10.5%	—
Annual Growth	(1.8%)	(20.2%)	—	2.1%

Net Income History

12/95 12/96 12/97 12/98 12/99 12/00 12/01 12/02 12/03 12/04

City National Bancshares

City National Bancshares is the holding company for City National Bank of New Jersey, which serves minority and low- to middle-income urban neighborhoods in New Jersey and New York through about 10 locations. It offers traditional deposit accounts including checking, savings, IRAs, CDs, and money markets. Real estate loans make up nearly 85% of the bank's portfolio, including commercial real estate (40%) and single-family mortgages (25%). Charles Whigham founded City National Bank in 1973.

EXECUTIVES

President, CEO, and Director, City National Bancshares and City National Bank: Louis E. Prezeau, age 62, $271,500 pay
SVP and CFO, City National Bancshares and City National Bank of New Jersey: Edward R. Wright, age 59, $123,305 pay
SVP and Chief Credit Officer, City National Bank of New Jersey: Stanley Weeks, age 48, $145,672 pay
SVP, City National Bank of New Jersey: Veronica T. Gilbert, age 45, $116,228 pay
VP, City National Bank of New Jersey: Raul Oseguera, $103,670 pay
Auditors: KPMG LLP

LOCATIONS

HQ: City National Bancshares Corporation
    900 Broad St., Newark, NJ 07102
Phone: 973-624-0865   **Fax:** 973-624-5754
Web: www.citynatbank.com

City National Bank has New Jersey offices in Hackensack, Newark (3), and Paterson; it also operates New York branches in Brooklyn, Hempstead, Manhattan (Harlem), and Roosevelt.

PRODUCTS/OPERATIONS

2004 Sales

	$ mil.	% of total
Interest		
Loans	8.8	52
Investment securities	5.0	29
Other	0.6	4
Noninterest		
Deposit service charges	1.2	7
Other	1.4	8
Total	**17.0**	**100**

COMPETITORS

Banco Popular North America
Bank of America
Hudson City Bancorp
Hudson United
Independence Community Bank
New York Community Bancorp
PennFed Financial
PNC Financial
Valley National Bancorp
Wachovia

HISTORICAL FINANCIALS

Company Type: Private

Income Statement   FYE: December 31

	ASSETS ($ mil.)	NET INCOME ($ mil.)	INCOME AS % OF ASSETS	EMPLOYEES
12/04	325	2	0.6%	93
12/03	236	2	0.7%	97
12/02	215	2	0.8%	90
12/01	222	1	0.6%	—
Annual Growth	13.5%	17.3%	—	1.7%

2004 Year-End Financials

Equity as % of assets: 4.7%   Long-term debt ($ mil.): 23
Return on assets: 0.7%   Sales ($ mil.): 17
Return on equity: 14.2%

Net Income History

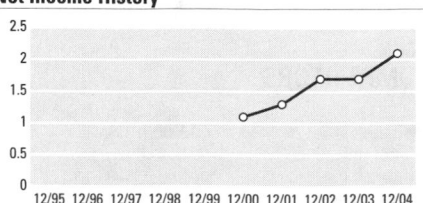

12/95 12/96 12/97 12/98 12/99 12/00 12/01 12/02 12/03 12/04

City University of New York

The City University of New York (CUNY) is the big "U" in the Big Apple. The college has 20 campuses in the five boroughs of New York City and is the US's largest urban university system. About 450,000 undergraduate, graduate, and continuing education students (from 145 countries) are enrolled at CUNY, which has 11 senior colleges, six community colleges, a doctoral-granting graduate school, a law school, and The Sophie Davis School of Biomedical Education. Its 1,400 academic programs range from specialized, career-oriented courses to traditional liberal arts curricula. CUNY employs over 14,000 faculty members, more than half of which are part-time.

CUNY has made some big changes, including tougher admission standards that critics feared would hurt the university's ethnic diversity, a hallmark of the school (enrollment numbers have proven otherwise). Notable CUNY alumni include novelist Oscar Hijuelos, General Colin Powell, comedian Jerry Seinfeld, and 11 Nobel laureates.

As with many public universities throughout the US, CUNY is enduring tough times economically. In order to free up the money to hire more full-time professors, the university has had to end a 10-year tradition of not charging four-year students for the last semester of their senior year.

HISTORY

The New York State Legislature first created a municipal college system in New York City in 1926, when it formed the New York City Board of Higher Education to manage the operations of the City College of New York and Hunter College. City College's roots were established in 1847 when New York passed a referendum creating the Free Academy, a tuition-free school. Hunter College was founded in 1870 as a women's college, and it was the first free teachers college in the US.

The Board of Higher Education authorized City College to create the Brooklyn Collegiate Center (a two-year men's college) in 1926; Hunter established a similar two-year women's branch in Brooklyn. Four years later the schools merged to create the Brooklyn College of the City of New York, the city's first public, coed liberal arts college. Other schools added to the municipal system included Queens College (1937), New York City Community College (1947), Staten Island Community College (1955), Bronx Community College (1957), and Queensborough Community College (1958).

The state legislature renamed New York City's municipal college system The City University of New York (CUNY) in 1961 and ordered its board of trustees to expand the system's facilities and scope. One of the first actions was to create a graduate school. CUNY chartered a number of new schools during the 1960s, including Richmond College (1965), York College (1966), Medgar Evers College (1968), and several community colleges. CUNY took over management of the New York State Institute of Applied Arts and Sciences (renamed New York City Technical College) in 1964 and established the John Jay College of Criminal Justice. CUNY became affiliated with Mount Sinai School of Medicine in 1967.

Despite its expansion, the university system had difficulty keeping up with demand, particularly after 1970, when it established an open admissions policy for all New York City high school graduates. Richmond College and Staten Island Community College became the College of Staten Island in 1976. Both CUNY and the City of New York ran into serious financial problems in the mid-1970s, spelling the end of CUNY's tradition of free undergrad tuition for New York City residents. To increase state financial support for CUNY, the legislature signed the City University Governance and Financing Act in 1979.

The City University School of Law held its first classes in 1983. The following year the state board of regents authorized CUNY to offer a doctor of medicine degree. CUNY's law school received accreditation from the American Bar Association in 1992. Since abandoning the free enrollment policy in the 1970s, the university's tuition continued to increase. In 1992, after presenting a nearly $600 increase in tuition, CUNY initiated its "last semester free" program, whereby four-year students did not have to pay tuition for the last semester of their senior year.

After several years of budget cuts and steadily increasing enrollment, CUNY declared a state of financial emergency in 1995. The following year New York's Governor George Pataki proposed new budget cuts, and in 1997 he called for tuition hikes. CUNY's board of trustees introduced a resolution calling for the elimination of remedial education programs at the senior college level in 1998. The state Board of Regents approved the plan in 1999 (most remedial classes were phased out by 2001). Matthew Goldstein was appointed chancellor in 1999 and has worked to increase CUNY's budget to hire more full-time faculty.

Belt-tightening continued in 2002. The university was forced to begin charging four-year students for the last semester of their senior year in order to earn more money.

EXECUTIVES

Chairperson: Benno C. Schmidt Jr., age 61
Chancellor: Matthew Goldstein
Executive Vice Chancellor, Academic Affairs:
  Selma Botman
Senior Vice Chancellor and COO: Allan H. Dobrin
Vice Chancellor, Academic Administration and Planning: Michael J. Zavelle
Vice Chancellor, Budget and Finance: Ernesto Malave
Vice Chancellor, Facilities Planning, Construction, and Management: Emma Espino Macari
Vice Chancellor, Faculty and Staff Relations:
  Brenda Richardson Malone
Vice Chancellor, Legal Affairs and General Counsel:
  Frederick P. Schaffer
Vice Chancellor, Student Development and Enrollment Management: Otis Hill
Vice Chancellor, University Relations and Secretary:
  Jay Hershenson
CIO: Brian Cohen
Senior University Dean, Academic Affairs; Dean, School of Professional Studies: John Mogulescu
Dean, Academic Affairs: Ann Cohen
Dean and Deputy to the Vice Chancellor for Faculty and Staff Relations: Gloriana Waters
Dean, Institutional Research and Assessment:
  David Crook
Dean, The Executive Office: Robert Ptachik
Dean, The Graduate School of Journalism:
  Stephen B. Shepard
Dean, Undergraduate Education: Judith Summerfield
Director Media Relations: Michael Arena
Auditors: KPMG LLP

LOCATIONS

HQ: The City University of New York
  535 E. 80th St., New York, NY 10021
Phone: 212-794-5555   **Fax:** 212-209-5600
Web: www.cuny.edu

The City University of New York has schools serving the Bronx, Brooklyn, Manhattan, Queens, and Staten Island boroughs of New York City.

PRODUCTS/OPERATIONS

Senior Colleges
Bernard M. Baruch College
Brooklyn College
City College
City University School of Law at Queens College
The College of Staten Island
The Graduate School and University Center
Herbert H. Lehman College
Hunter College
John Jay College of Criminal Justice
Medgar Evers College
New York City College of Technology
Queens College
York College

Community Colleges
Borough of Manhattan Community College
Bronx Community College
Hostos Community College
Kingsborough Community College
LaGuardia Community College
Queensborough Community College

HISTORICAL FINANCIALS

Company Type: School

Income Statement				FYE: June 30
	REVENUE ($ mil.)	NET INCOME ($ mil.)	NET PROFIT MARGIN	EMPLOYEES
6/04	1,371	(1,003)	—	33,460
6/03	1,192	—	—	32,638
6/02	1,041	—	—	30,000
6/01	1,927	—	—	30,000
6/00	1,900	—	—	30,000
6/99	1,873	—	—	28,000
6/98	1,784	—	—	28,000
6/97	1,729	—	—	27,900
6/96	1,756	—	—	25,800
6/95	1,722	—	—	25,800
Annual Growth	(2.5%)	—	—	2.9%

Revenue History

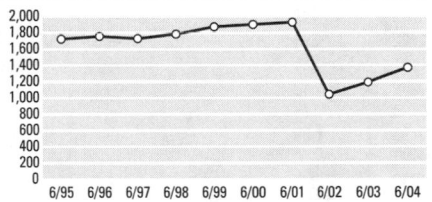

Clark Enterprises

Like Clark Kent, this firm holds some super powers. Clark Enterprises, one of the largest privately held companies in the metro Washington, DC area, provides ownership, investment, and asset management services to its subsidiaries. It holds interests in real estate, private equities, technology development, and construction companies. The Clark Construction Group, its main subsidiary, is a top US contractor and works on commercial, institutional, and heavy construction projects. Other units include residential developer Clark Realty Capital, heavy contractor Atkinson Construction, and highway construction company Shirley Contracting. Chairman and CEO James Clark owns the company, which was founded in 1972.

EXECUTIVES

Chairman and CEO: A. James Clark
President and COO: Lawrence C. Nussdorf, age 58
EVP: Robert J. (Bob) Flanagan, age 48
SVP and General Counsel: Rebecca L. Owen, age 43
VP and Treasurer: Sandy R. Garchik
VP: Terri D. Klatzkin
Deputy General Counsel: David H. Brody
Chairman, Clark Construction Group: Peter C. Forster
President and COO, Clark Construction Group:
  Dan T. Montgomery
President, Clark Realty Builders: Glenn Ferguson
President, Clark Realty Management: Douglas Sandor
President and CEO, Atkinson Construction: Scott Lynn
President, Seawright Corp.: D. Stephen Seawright
Executive Assistant to President and Office Manager:
  Connie Pumphrey

LOCATIONS

HQ: Clark Enterprises, Inc.
  7500 Old Georgetown Rd., 15th Fl.,
  Bethesda, MD 20814
Phone: 301-657-7100   **Fax:** 301-657-7263
Web: www.clarkenterprisesinc.com

PRODUCTS/OPERATIONS

Selected Subsidiaries
Atkinson Construction (heavy contractor)
The Clark Construction Group, Inc. (commercial, institutional, and heavy construction)
Clark Realty Capital, LLC (residential development)
Clark Realty Management, LLC (property management)
CNF Investments LLC (private equity investment)
Shirley Contracting (highway and heavy construction)

COMPETITORS

Barton Malow	Hunt Construction
Bechtel	Perini
Bovis Lend Lease	Peter Kiewit Sons'
Centex	Skanska
Donohoe Companies	Turner Corporation
FaulknerUSA	Tutor-Saliba
Fluor	Webcor Builders
Gilbane	Whiting-Turner
Hensel Phelps Construction	

HISTORICAL FINANCIALS

Company Type: Private

Income Statement

FYE: December 31

	ESTIMATED REVENUE ($ mil.)	NET INCOME ($ mil.)	NET PROFIT MARGIN	EMPLOYEES
12/03	2,750	—	—	4,200
12/02	2,800	—	—	4,500
12/01	2,500	—	—	4,000
12/00	2,400	—	—	4,500
12/99	1,800	—	—	5,000
12/98	1,500	—	—	5,000
12/97	1,330	—	—	3,500
12/96	1,400	—	—	4,500
12/95	1,500	—	—	5,000
12/94	1,500	—	—	5,000
Annual Growth	7.0%	—	—	(1.9%)

Revenue History

```
3,000
2,500
2,000
1,500
1,000
 500
   0
    12/94 12/95 12/96 12/97 12/98 12/99 12/00 12/01 12/02 12/03
```

ClientLogic

This company tries to prove to its clients the logic behind outsourcing. ClientLogic is a leading provider of outsourced teleservices, including customer care and support, customer acquisition and retention, and other telemarketing services. It also offers a range of fulfillment services, from outsourced catalog and e-commerce operations to logistics and shipping. Customers include DIRECTV, Hewlett-Packard, Sony, and TiVo. ClientLogic has more than 50 customer care and fulfillment centers in about a dozen countries. Founded in 1990, it is 68%-owned by Canadian holding company Onex.

With interest in outsourcing continuing to grow, ClientLogic has been expanding its international call-center operations in such likely places as India and the Philippines, but it has also been adding new centers in Canada and expanding its operations in some US cities. It can offer teleservices in more than 16 languages.

ClientLogic traces its roots to Buffalo, New York-based Upgrade Corp. of America, founded by Ronald Schreiber and Jordan Levy. Upgrade (later known as SOFTBANK Services Group) marketed software upgrades for such clients as Microsoft. It was acquired in 1998 by Onex and merged with North Direct Response to create ClientLogic. A plan to spin-off the call-center operation was shelved in 2000, but ClientLogic did raise more than $250 million from such private equity investors as Toronto-Dominion Bank.

EXECUTIVES

Chairman: Harvey Golub, age 65
Vice Chairman: Thomas O. Harbison
President and CEO: David E. Garner
CFO: Paul R. Stone
Chief Human Resources Officer: Ginni Goldsberry
Chief Legal Officer and Corporate Secretary: Terrence Leve
Chief Sales and Marketing Officer: Julie M. Casteel
CEO, Continental Europe: Enno Osinga
CEO, Northern Europe: Glenn Timms
COO, Americas: Chad Carlson
COO, Europe: Thomas O. Hillmer
CIO, Americas: Dave Eckert
CIO, International Operations: Sytze Koopmans
Senior Marketing Services Director: Robin Neal
Public Relations: Amit Shankardass

LOCATIONS

HQ: ClientLogic Corporation
3102 West End Ave., Ste. 900, Nashville, TN 37203
Phone: 615-301-7100   **Fax:** 615-301-7150
Web: www.clientlogic.com

ClientLogic has operations in Austria, Canada, France, Germany, India, Ireland, Mexico, Morocco, the Netherlands, the Philippines, Poland, the UK, and the US.

COMPETITORS

Accenture
Acxiom
APAC Customer Services
Convergys
EDS
IBM Global Services
ICT Group
NCO Group
SITEL
SR.Teleperformance
StarTek
Stream
Sykes Enterprises
TeleTech
West Corporation
Wipro Technologies

HISTORICAL FINANCIALS

Company Type: Private

Income Statement

FYE: December 31

	REVENUE ($ mil.)	NET INCOME ($ mil.)	NET PROFIT MARGIN	EMPLOYEES
12/04	562	—	—	20,300
12/03	433	—	—	14,400
12/02	399	—	—	11,400
12/01	385	—	—	10,500
12/00	282	—	—	8,200
12/99	178	—	—	7,129
12/98	29	—	—	—
12/97	0			
12/96	0			
Annual Growth	—	—	—	23.3%

Revenue History

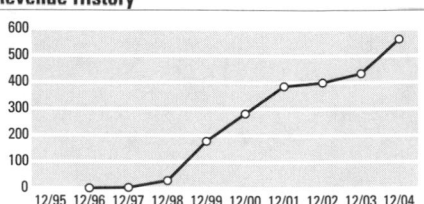
```
600
500
400
300
200
100
  0
   12/95 12/96 12/97 12/98 12/99 12/00 12/01 12/02 12/03 12/04
```

ClubCorp

ClubCorp makes its green from the green — the golf green, that is. The world's largest operator of golf courses, its holdings include country clubs, private clubs, and resorts. The company owns and operates about 200 properties in the US and three other countries. Its holdings include Mission Hills Country Club near Palm Springs, California, and North Carolina's Pinehurst Resort and Country Club (site of the 1999 and 2005 US Opens). The company's nearly 70 clubs include the Boston College Club, the Metropolitan Club in Chicago, and the City Club of Washington, DC. The family of late founder Robert Dedman owns 46% of ClubCorp.

Striving to stay on top of the game, the company has been acquiring new properties and is building new ones through Bear's Best, a joint venture with golf legend Jack Nicklaus. Robert Dedman, who was named by *Forbes* magazine as one of the 400 wealthiest Americans, died in 2002. His son, Robert Jr., took over as CEO, but passed those duties to president John Beckert in 2004. (Dedman Jr. remains chairman.) ClubCorp's other shareholders include The Cypress Group, which owns about 16%.

HISTORY

Though his childhood in Depression-era Arkansas was dominated by intense poverty, ClubCorp founder Robert Dedman knew how to dream big. At a young age he vowed to become "very, very rich," and the scrappy Dedman embarked on achieving that goal by earning a college scholarship, obtaining a law degree, and eventually launching a flourishing Dallas law practice.

Dedman's law firm was successful, but he realized that it wouldn't bring him the $50 million he wanted to earn by age 50. In 1957 he formed Country Clubs, Inc., to venture into the country club business. At that time, doctors and lawyers working on a volunteer basis were managing most clubs, and Dedman believed his new company could bring professional management expertise to these facilities. The company opened its first country club, Dallas' Brookhaven Country Club, in 1957. Through the subsequent purchase of 20 more clubs, Country Clubs refined its management style, implementing unique practices such as reducing playing time on the golf course and developing specialized training for club staff.

In 1965 the company expanded into city and athletic clubs and assumed the Club Corporation of America name. The expansion drive that followed fueled a 30% growth rate that the company maintained from the 1960s through the 1980s. In 1985 the company was restructured and divided into a handful of separate companies owned by the newly formed Club Corporation International holding company.

In 1988 the company bought an 80% interest in Franklin Federal Bancorp. The bank's club properties had initially caught his eye, but Dedman also believed that the 400,000 members of his clubs might prove fertile ground for the marketing of financial services. In 1996, however, Club Corporation International sold the financial institution to Norwest. Although Franklin Federal was turning a profit, losses from investment in derivatives, coupled with the bank's inability to compete with larger competitors, prompted the company to sell the bank and refocus on its core club and resort business.

In 1996 Japanese cookie-maker Tohato sued the company, claiming that it intentionally mismanaged the Pinewild Country Club. Pinewild was owned by Tohato, managed by Club Corporation International, and located next door to Club Corporation International's Pinehurst Resort and Country Club. Tohato alleged that the company's mismanagement was part of a scheme to eventually buy Pinewild at a reduced price. The case was eventually settled, but the nasty legal wrangling that ensued cast a pall over the impending 1999 US Open at Pinehurst.

In 1998 the company was reincorporated as ClubCorp International, Inc. It expanded its international base that year by purchasing nearly 30% of PGA European Tour Courses. The company also entered into a joint venture with Jack Nicklaus to develop three dozen new golf courses.

The company shortened its moniker to ClubCorp in 1999. Among the additions ClubCorp made to its holdings that year were 22 properties acquired from The Meditrust Companies. The company also increased its ownership of Canadian club developer ClubLink to 25%. An influx of funds for further expansion came in 1999 after investment firm The Cypress Group took a stake. In 2001 the company sold its interests in ClubLink and PGA European Tour Courses.

Robert Dedman died in 2002. His son, Robert Dedman Jr., took over as CEO for a time, but relinquished those duties to president John Beckert in 2004. Dedman Jr. remains chairman of ClubCorp.

EXECUTIVES

Chairman: Robert H. Dedman Jr., age 47, $789,900 pay
President, CEO, and COO: John A. Beckert, age 51, $853,731 pay
CFO: Jeffrey P. Mayer, age 48, $580,049 pay
EVP, Secretary, and General Counsel: Thomas T. Henslee, age 45
EVP ClubCorp USA: Douglas T. Howe, age 47, $427,446 pay
EVP ClubCorp USA: Frank C. Gore, age 55, $453,592 pay
EVP Operations: Richard N. Beckert, age 48, $517,079 pay
EVP Strategic Operations: Murray S. Siegel, age 59
EVP: Mark W. Dietz, age 51
SVP, Controller, and Chief Accounting Officer: Angela A. Stephens
SVP Business and Sports Division: David B. Woodyard
SVP Human Resources: John Longstreet
SVP Marketing: Lisa H. Kislak
SVP Purchasing: William T. Walden
CIO: Colby H. Springer, age 54
President, The Pinehurst Company: Patrick A. (Pat) Corso, age 52, $365,940 pay
Auditors: Deloitte & Touche LLP

LOCATIONS

HQ: ClubCorp, Inc.
3030 LBJ Fwy., Ste. 600, Dallas, TX 75234
Phone: 972-243-6191   **Fax:** 972-888-7700
Web: www.clubcorp.com

ClubCorp has operations in Australia, China, Mexico, and the US.

PRODUCTS/OPERATIONS

Selected Clubs

Aspen Glen Country Club (Colorado)
The Athletic and Swim Club at Equitable Center (New York)
Columbia Tower Club (Washington)
The Hills Country Club (Texas)
Mission Hills Country Club (California)
Pinehurst Resort and Country Club (North Carolina)
Teal Bend Golf Club (California)

COMPETITORS

American Golf
Club Med
Four Seasons Hotels
Hillman
Hilton
Hyatt
Marriott
ResortQuest International
Sandals Resorts
Silverleaf Resorts
Starwood Hotels & Resorts

HISTORICAL FINANCIALS

Company Type: Private

Income Statement

	REVENUE ($ mil.)	NET INCOME ($ mil.)	NET PROFIT MARGIN	EMPLOYEES
				FYE: December 31
12/04	944	(6)	—	18,500
12/03	912	(105)	—	19,000
12/02	947	(62)	—	20,000
12/01	1,015	(106)	—	23,000
12/00	1,069	(17)	—	24,000
12/99	1,028	12	1.1%	23,000
12/98	851	38	4.5%	21,000
12/97	840	122	14.5%	20,000
12/96	784	29	3.7%	19,000
12/95	761	(11)	—	19,800
Annual Growth	2.4%	—	—	(0.8%)

2004 Year-End Financials

Debt ratio: 263.4%
Return on equity: —
Cash ($ mil.): 125

Current ratio: 0.98
Long-term debt ($ mil.): 685

Net Income History

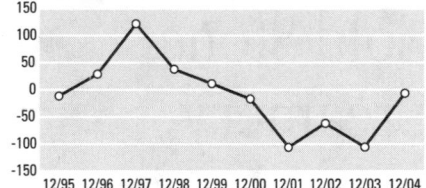

12/95 12/96 12/97 12/98 12/99 12/00 12/01 12/02 12/03 12/04

Cogdell Spencer

Cogdell Spencer puts it money where your health is. Cogdell Spencer owns, develops, renovates, and manages health care properties, including hospitals, medical office buildings, and diagnostic centers. It owns or manages nearly 75 properties in five southeastern states (Georgia, Kentucky, Louisiana, North Carolina, and South Carolina), totaling approximately 3.4 million sq. ft. of space. Working closely with its tenants, the company has developed more than 70 properties since its predecessor was founded in 1972. Cogdell Spencer intends to operate as a self-advised real estate investment trust (REIT) for tax purposes. Chairman James Cogdell owns 25% of the company.

Cogdell Spencer has a diverse tenant base of nearly 500 occupants. The largest tenant, NorthEast Medical Center, accounts for 6% of rental revenues.

The REIT has provided repeat development services for several health care systems, including NorthEast Medical Center and Roper St. Francis Healthcare (nine and four projects completed, respectively). It also acquires existing properties.

CEO Frank Spencer owns 6% of Cogdell Spencer; directors and officers collectively own 32% of the company.

EXECUTIVES

Chairman: James W. Cogdell, age 64, $430,000 pay
President, CEO, and Director: Frank C. Spencer, age 44, $430,000 pay
SVP, CFO, and Secretary: Charles M. Handy, age 43, $225,000 pay
VP, Capital Markets and Acquisitions: Matthew Nurkin, age 34
VP, Development: Devereaux Gregg, age 47
VP, Management: Rex A. Noble, age 41
VP, Management: Mary J. Surles, age 48
Chief Accounting Advisor: Andrew Prentice
Auditors: Deloitte & Touche LLP

LOCATIONS

HQ: Cogdell Spencer Inc.
4401 Barclay Downs Dr., Ste. 300, Charlotte, NC 28209
Phone: 704-940-2900   **Fax:** 704-940-2959

2004 Properties

	% of total
South Carolina	41
North Carolina	36
Georgia	15
Louisiana	6
Kentucky	2
Total	**100**

PRODUCTS/OPERATIONS

2004 Sales

	$ mil.	% of total
Rent	40.5	91
Expense reimbursements	0.8	2
Fees	0.5	1
Interest & other	2.9	6
Total	**44.7**	**100**

COMPETITORS

Cousins Properties
DASCO
Duke Realty
Health Care Property Investors
Healthcare Realty
Lauth
Medical Properties Trust
National Health Investors
Omega Healthcare Investors
Universal Health Realty
Windrose Medical Properties

HISTORICAL FINANCIALS

Company Type: Private

Income Statement				FYE: December 31
	REVENUE ($ mil.)	NET INCOME ($ mil.)	NET PROFIT MARGIN	EMPLOYEES
12/04	45	8	17.9%	75
12/03	42	4	8.8%	—
12/02	41	0	1.0%	—
Annual Growth	4.0%	347.2%	—	—

2004 Year-End Financials

Debt ratio: —
Return on equity: —
Cash ($ mil.): —
Current ratio: —
Long-term debt ($ mil.): 215

Net Income History

Cold Heading Company

The cold, hard truth about Cold Heading Company is that it makes a range of fasteners and other hardware through its Freemont Heading, Fremont Rolling, Hudson, STG Nut, and Warren Pack & Ship divisions. It specializes in hex flange bolts, hex flange engine fasteners, wheel and staking bolts, nuts, and special heading parts. The company produces more than a billion fasteners annually. Major customers include Daimler Chrysler, Ford, General Motors, Nissan, and Subaru. Cold Heading affiliate Ajax Metal Processing offers annealing, electroplating, heat treating, and pickling services. Another affiliate, Direct Tool, offers grinding, sinking, and finishing services.

Cold Heading was founded in 1914 and was originally called Ajax Bolt & Screw; it wasn't until 1951 that it adopted the Cold Heading Company name. The company established Ajax Metal Processing in 1973, and Direct Tool in 1994.

EXECUTIVES

Chairman: Elizabeth Stevens
President: Derek J. Stevens
COO: Elmer Cecil
CFO: Edward E. Miller
VP, Sales: Anthony Cebrian
Office Manager: Brigid Loffreda
Auditors: Ernst & Young LLP

LOCATIONS

HQ: Cold Heading Company
    21777 Hoover Rd., Warren, MI 48089
Phone: 586-497-7000   **Fax:** 586-497-7007
Web: www.coldheading.com

COMPETITORS

Illinois Tool Works
MacLean-Fogg
MNP
Textron

HISTORICAL FINANCIALS

Company Type: Private

Income Statement				FYE: December 31
	REVENUE ($ mil.)	NET INCOME ($ mil.)	NET PROFIT MARGIN	EMPLOYEES
12/04	129	—	—	315
12/03	117	—	—	300
12/02	120	—	—	307
Annual Growth	3.7%	—	—	1.3%

Revenue History

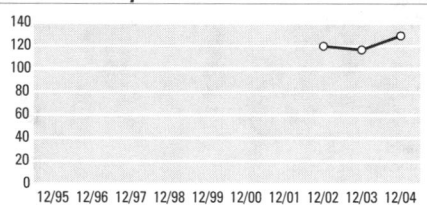

Cold Stone Creamery

This chain of ice cream shops is known for its use of mineral assets. Cold Stone Creamery franchises 1,000 premium ice cream outlets in more than 47 US states as well as in the Caribbean and Guam. True to its name, the company's ingredients are blended into the ice cream on a cold stone. Patrons can create their own flavors by choosing from a variety of mix-ins, such as candy, fruit, and cookie dough. The shops also offer yogurt, sorbet, and other frozen treats. A small number of locations are operated by the company. Founders Donald and Susan Sutherland opened their first Cold Stone Creamery in Tempe, Arizona, in 1988.

A rolling Cold Stone gathers no moss, cold or otherwise; thus, the company added 362 stores in 2004 and plans to add about 400 more in 2005. In May 2005 Cold Stone added its 1,000th store, located in Columbus, Ohio. The company has announced an expansion to Asia, with plans to open stores in China, Japan, and South Korea, as well as Puerto Rico and the Virgin Islands.

EXECUTIVES

Chairman and CEO: Doug Ducey
President: Sheldon Harris
COO: David Andow
CFO: Steve S. Krell
VP, Creamery Operations: Kim Cramton
VP, Franchise Development: John Wuycheck
VP, Franchise Relations: James (Jim) Valentino
VP, Operations and Area Developer Support:
  Lee E. Knowlton
VP, Special Projects: Sally Bell
VP, Supply Chain Management and Purchasing:
  Bruce Burnham
VP, Training: Susan Landgraf
Director, Public Relations: Kevin Donnellan
General Counsel: Melanie Hansen

LOCATIONS

HQ: Cold Stone Creamery
    9311 E. Via De Ventura, Scottsdale, AZ 85258
Phone: 480-362-4800   **Fax:** 480-362-4812
Web: www.coldstonecreamery.com

COMPETITORS

Ben & Jerry's
Braum's
Bruster's
Carvel
CoolBrands
Dairy Queen
Dippin Dots
Dunkin
Friendly Ice Cream
Happy Joe's
KaleidoScoops
MaggieMoo's
Marble Slab
Mrs. Fields
Nestlé
YoCream

HISTORICAL FINANCIALS

Company Type: Private

Income Statement				FYE: December 31
	REVENUE ($ mil.)	NET INCOME ($ mil.)	NET PROFIT MARGIN	EMPLOYEES
12/04	285	—	—	225
12/03	156	—	—	115
12/02	88	—	—	73
12/01	45	—	—	41
Annual Growth	85.0%	—	—	76.4%

Revenue History

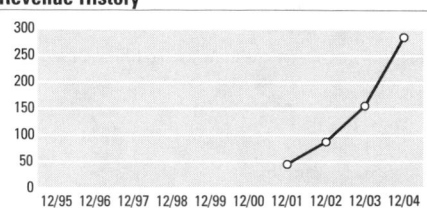

Colorado Avalanche

You'd be wrong to think this avalanche is headed downhill. The Colorado Avalanche, which represents the Denver area in the National Hockey League, makes regular appearances in the NHL playoffs and won Stanley Cup championships in 1996 and 2001. Backed by a $60 million payroll (among the highest in the league) the Avalanche is succeeding at the turnstiles as well, boasting regular sellouts at its home arena. The team, which took the ice in 1979 as the Quebec Nordiques, is owned by Wal-Mart heir and St. Louis Rams part-owner Stan Kroenke's Kroenke Sports Enterprises. KSE also owns the NBA's Denver Nuggets and the Pepsi Center, the home arena for both teams.

EXECUTIVES

Owner: E. Stanley (Stan) Kroenke
President and General Manager: Pierre Lacroix, age 46
Head Coach: Joel Quenneville, age 47
Assistant Coach: Tony Granato, age 41
Assistant Coach: Jacques Cloutier, age 44
SVP Communications and Team Services:
Jean Martineau
SVP Sports Finance: Mark Waggoner
VP Business Affairs and Treasurer: Mike Benson
VP Community Relations: Deb Dowling-Canino
VP Corporate Sales and Partnership Marketing:
Mike Kurowski
VP Player Personnel: Michel Goulet
Executive Director of Sports Finance: Jerry Girkin
Senior Director of Human Resources: Cheryl Miller
Director of Hockey Operations: Eric Lacroix
Director of Special Projects and Communications:
Hayne Ellis

LOCATIONS

HQ: Colorado Avalanche, LLC
Pepsi Center, 1000 Chopper Circle,
Denver, CO 80204
Phone: 303-405-1100   **Fax:** 303-575-1920
Web: www.coloradoavalanche.com

The Colorado Avalanche play at the 18,001-seat capacity Pepsi Center in Denver.

PRODUCTS/OPERATIONS

Championship Trophies

Stanley Cup (1996, 2001)
Clarence S. Campbell Bowl (1996, 2001)
Presidents' Trophy (1997, 2001)

COMPETITORS

Calgary Flames
Edmonton Oilers
Minnesota Wild
Vancouver Canucks

HISTORICAL FINANCIALS

Company Type: Private

Income Statement

FYE: June 30

	REVENUE ($ mil.)	NET INCOME ($ mil.)	NET PROFIT MARGIN	EMPLOYEES
6/04	99	—	—	—
6/03	88	—	—	—
6/02	93	—	—	—
6/01	93	—	—	—
6/00	82	—	—	—
6/99	70	—	—	—
6/98	57	—	—	—
6/97	37	—	—	—
6/96	19	—	—	—
Annual Growth	22.8%	—	—	—

Revenue History

100										
90										
80										
70										
60										
50										
40										
30										
20										
10										
0										
6/95	6/96	6/97	6/98	6/99	6/00	6/01	6/02	6/03	6/04	

Colt Defense

Today's soldier needs more than a horse and a Colt .45-caliber handgun, and fortunately Colt Defense has changed with the times. The company produces small arms and weapons systems for the US, Canadian, and other NATO-member military forces and for law enforcement agencies. Colt Defense holds multiyear contracts as a prime contractor to the US Department of Defense (its largest customer with 54% of sales) and the Canadian Department of National Defence. The company's products include military rifles (M4 carbine rifles and M16 rifles), auxiliary weapon systems (M203 grenade launchers), law enforcement rifles, and spare parts and replacement kits.

In 2005 Colt Defense acquired small-caliber firearms and weapon systems maker Diemaco, a division of Héroux-Devtek Inc., and renamed the company Colt Canada Corporation. Colt Canada serves Canadian military and law enforcement agencies and other militaries outside the US.

Outside North America, the United Arab Emirates and Denmark each account for about 10% of Colt Defense's sales.

Colt Defense traces its lineage to frontier days — a corporate predecessor began supplying weapons to the US military in 1847. Colt Defense was spun off from Colt's Manufacturing in 2002.

EXECUTIVES

President, CEO, and Director: William M. Keyes,
age 68, $421,860 pay
EVP and COO: James R. Battaglini, age 55, $77,858 pay
VP and CFO: Richard J. Nadeau, age 50
VP, General Counsel, and Secretary: Carlton S. Chen,
age 54, $182,863 pay
Executive Director — Sales and Marketing:
Michael P. Reissig, age 51
Executive Director — Military Programs:
Kevin J. Brown, age 53
Auditors: Ernst & Young LLP

LOCATIONS

HQ: Colt Defense Inc.
547 New Park Ave., West Hartford, CT 06110
Phone: 860-232-4489   **Fax:** 860-244-1442
Web: www.colt.com

Colt Defense operates manufacturing facilities in West Hartford, Connecticut, in the US and in Kitchener, Ontario, in Canada.

PRODUCTS/OPERATIONS

2004 Sales

	$ mil.	% of total
US government rifles	31.0	41
Direct foreign rifles	14.7	20
US law enforcement rifles	9.4	13
Spares & contract management	16.0	21
Other	4.0	5
Total	**75.1**	**100**

2004 Sales

	% of total
US government	54
International military	30
US law enforcement	16
Total	**100**

Selected Subsidiaries

Colt Canada Corporation
Colt Rapid Mat LLC

COMPETITORS

Beretta USA
Browning
Bushmaster Firearms
Glock
Herstal
Marlin Firearms
Remington Arms
Ruger
Savage Arms
Smith & Wesson Holding
Springfield Armory

HISTORICAL FINANCIALS

Company Type: Private

Income Statement

FYE: December 31

	REVENUE ($ mil.)	NET INCOME ($ mil.)	NET PROFIT MARGIN	EMPLOYEES
12/04	75	10	13.3%	380
12/03	67	3	4.8%	—
12/02	53	5	10.1%	—
Annual Growth	18.7%	36.1%	—	—

2004 Year-End Financials

Debt ratio: —
Return on equity: —
Cash ($ mil.): 0
Current ratio: 0.97
Long-term debt ($ mil.): 38

Net Income History

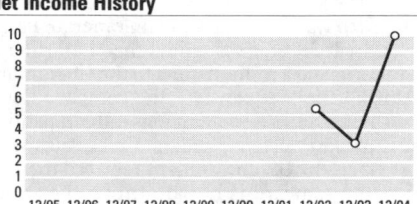

10										
9										
8										
7										
6										
5										
4										
3										
2										
1										
0										
12/95	12/96	12/97	12/98	12/99	12/00	12/01	12/02	12/03	12/04	

Colt's Manufacturing

The Colt .45 may have won the West, but it took a New York investment firm to save Colt's Manufacturing from a post-Cold War decline in weapons sales and tough foreign competition. Through its subsidiaries, Colt's Manufacturing makes handguns (Cowboy, Defender) and semi-automatic rifles for civilian use and military weapons (M-16, M-4 Carbine) for the US and other governments. The company has distributors throughout Europe, Asia, and Australia. Founded in 1836 by Samuel Colt, the company is about 85%-owned by investment firm Zilkha & Co., who has been reviving the company since 1994 when it bought the firm out of bankruptcy.

With the firearms industry taking cover from safety and health care expense-related lawsuits filed by cities and counties across the US, Colt's is discontinuing a number of handguns it makes for the consumer market. The company spun off its "smart gun" division as iColt, but the division closed soon after.

In 2003 the company began reproduction of its classic WWI military sidearm, the 1911. The original 1911 and its descendants have been used by servicemen during WWI and WWII, as well as in Korea and Vietnam.

HISTORY

After waiting four years for a patent, Samuel Colt started the Patent Arms Manufacturing Company in 1836 to make his revolutionary handgun, a revolver. The newfangled gun was slow to catch on (the company went bankrupt in 1842), but it gained fame after being adopted by the Texas Rangers. The US Army delegated Capt. Samuel Walker to work with Colt to improve the design, and sales of the resulting "Walker Colt" enabled Colt to set up a factory in Hartford, Connecticut.

In 1851 the company was the first American manufacturer to open a plant in England. Patent Arms Manufacturing was renamed Colt's Patent Fire Arms Manufacturing Co. four years later. Colt was a millionaire when he died in 1862 at age 47.

Colt's introduced the six-shot Colt .45 Army Model, "the gun that won the West," in 1873. More products followed, including machine guns and automatic pistols designed by inventor John Browning. Colt's widow sold the firm to an investor group in 1901.

Business boomed during both world wars, but by the 1940s labor strife and outmoded equipment began to take a toll, and Colt's lost money during the last years of WWII. In 1955 the struggling firm was acquired by conglomerate Penn-Texas. In 1959 Colt's patented the M-16 rifle; in 10 years it sold a million units to the US military.

During the Vietnam War the company flourished, but the 1980s brought low-end competition and shrinking defense orders. Colt's sales were hurt when the US government replaced the Colt .45 as the standard-issue sidearm for the armed forces. A three-year strike prompted the Army to shift its M-16 contract to Belgium's FN Herstal in 1988.

Two years later Colt's was acquired by private investors and a Connecticut state pension fund and was renamed Colt's Manufacturing. Sales remained flat, however, forcing the company to seek bankruptcy protection in 1992. There Colt's remained until New York investment firm Zilkha & Co. bailed it out in 1994, reorganizing the company. The new management made an offer for rival FN Herstal in 1997, but the deal was blocked by the Belgian government and fell through. Late that year the company won a contract to supply M-4 rifles to the Army.

Colt's bought military weapons specialist Saco Defense, maker of MK 19 and Striker grenade launchers, in 1998. Also that year Steven Sliwa succeeded retiring CEO Ronald Stewart.

As US cities began suing Colt's and other makers of firearms in attempts to recover safety and health expenses attributed to gun violence, the company stepped up lobbying in 1999 and said it would increase gun safety efforts, including development of its "smart gun" technology.

A restructuring in 1999 ended most of Colt's consumer handgun business. It also spun off its smart gun technology as a separate company, iColt. Sliwa left to head iColt, and retired US Marine Lieutenant General William Keys was named president and CEO of Colt's. Also in 1999 Colt's bought Ultra-Light Arms, a maker of upscale hunting rifles, and said it would buy Heckler & Koch, a small arms manufacturer based in Germany. By 2000 the company had withdrawn iColt (investors didn't seem interested in a lawsuit laden industry) and stepped away from the Heckler & Koch deal. The company continues to focus on weapons for the military and police, but in 2001 it lost out to CAPCO Inc. in a bid for a contract to upgrade M16 rifles used by the Air Force.

EXECUTIVES

Chairman: Donald Zilkha
President and CEO: William M. (Bill) Keys
CFO: Rick Nadeau
Director, Human Resources: Mike Magouirk
Director, Marketing: Mike Reissig
Director, Materials: John Ibbotson

LOCATIONS

HQ: Colt's Manufacturing Company, LLC
545 New Park Ave., West Hartford, CT 06110
Phone: 860-236-6311   **Fax:** 860-244-1442
Web: www.coltsmfg.com

PRODUCTS/OPERATIONS

Selected Products and Brands

Classics
  Anaconda
  Colt 1911 WWI replica
  Python
Commercial rifles
  Colt accurized rifles
  Match target rifles
Law enforcement
  AR15
  Carbine
  Commando
  M-16A2
  M203 Grenade Launchers
  M-4 Carbine
  Submachine guns
Performance products
  Colt Gunsite Pistol
  Colt XSE Series
  Gold Cup Trophy
  Special Combat Government Competition
Personal protection
  Colt Defender
  M1991A1
Western
  Colt Cowboy
  Model Ps

COMPETITORS

Beretta	Remington Arms
Browning	Ruger
FN Manufacturing	SIG
Glock	Smith & Wesson Holding
Marlin Firearms	Springfield Inc.
Mauser-Werke	U.S. Repeating Arms

HISTORICAL FINANCIALS

Company Type: Private

Income Statement

FYE: December 31

	ESTIMATED REVENUE ($ mil.)	NET INCOME ($ mil.)	NET PROFIT MARGIN	EMPLOYEES
12/03	95	—	—	700
12/02	95	—	—	700
12/01	95	—	—	700
12/00	95	—	—	700
12/99	95	—	—	700
12/98	96	—	—	700
12/97	92	—	—	700
Annual Growth	0.5%	—	—	0.0%

Revenue History

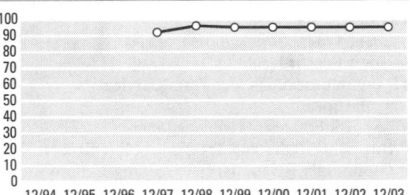

Columbia University

Predating the American Revolution, Columbia University (founded as King's College in 1754) is the fifth-oldest institution of higher learning in the US. With a student population of more than 23,000 students and a campus spread across 36 acres in Manhattan, Columbia's 16 schools and colleges grant undergraduate and graduate degrees in about 100 disciplines, including its well-known programs in journalism, law, and medicine. The Ivy League university's more than 3,000-member faculty has included 70 Nobel laureates and former Vice President Al Gore. Columbia also has a strong reputation for research.

Columbia has forged affiliations with nearby institutions such as Barnard College, Teachers College, Union Theological Seminary, and The Jewish Theological Seminary. Columbia-Presbyterian Medical Center, the result of more than 75 years of partnership between Columbia and New York Presbyterian Hospital, helped pioneer the concept of academic medical centers.

Columbia's list of alumni includes such luminaries as Yankee great Lou Gehrig, Supreme Court Justice Ruth Bader Ginsberg, and President Franklin Roosevelt. Columbia has gone to the alumni well (and others sources) often over the past 10 years, with an endowment valued at $4.3 billion.

HISTORY

Created by royal charter of King George II of England, the university was founded in 1754 as King's College. Its first class of eight students met in a schoolhouse adjacent to Trinity Church (in what is now Manhattan). Some of the university's earliest students included Alexander Hamilton and John Jay. King's College was renamed Columbia College in 1784, a name that symbolized the patriotic mind-set of the age.

The college moved to 49th Street and Madison Avenue in 1849. The School of Law was founded in 1858, followed by the predecessor to the School of Engineering and Applied Science in 1864. The Graduate School of Arts and Sciences was established in 1880, and Columbia became affiliated with Barnard College in 1889.

Columbia College became Columbia University in 1896, and the following year it moved to its present location, the former site of the Bloomingdale Insane Asylum. Columbia continued to expand during the early 20th century. It added the School of Journalism in 1912 with funding from publishing magnate Joseph Pulitzer. Other additions included the School of Business (1916), the School of Public Health (1921), and the School of International and Public Affairs (1946).

Dwight Eisenhower became president of Columbia in 1948, retaining the position until becoming President of the United States in 1953. During the late 1960s Columbia gained a reputation for student political action, and in 1968 students closed down the university for several days in protest of the Vietnam War.

Facing financial woes, an escalating New York City crime rate, and contention among its faculty, Columbia struggled to maintain its reputation during the 1970s and 1980s. With this challenge as a backdrop, the university continued to evolve, welcoming its first coed freshman class in 1983.

Still facing economic pressures and reductions in government research spending, Columbia was forced to cut costs, eliminating its linguistics and geography departments in 1991. George Rupp became Columbia's president in 1993. Columbia took over operation of the controversial Biosphere 2 laboratory in Arizona in 1996 (the university had been associated with the lab since 1994, when it formed a consortium with other universities to overhaul the ailing science experiment).

By the late 1990s Columbia had begun to recover from its financial and academic decline. Under the leadership of president Rupp, the university improved its fund-raising efforts and became more selective in student admissions. Microsoft founder Bill Gates donated $50 million to Columbia's School of Public Health in 1999 for research into the prevention of death and disability from childbirth in developing countries. That year Columbia created Morningside Ventures, a for-profit company focused on producing educational materials.

Columbia partnered in 2000 with the British Library, Cambridge University Press, the London School of Economics, the New York Public Library, and the Smithsonian to form another for-profit venture, Fathom.com, a site offering online access to various scholarly resources from each institution. Although the Web site served more than 65,000 people, Fathom.com discontinued operations in 2003. Columbia refocused its online efforts through its Columbia Digital Knowledge Ventures (DKV), a Web site created in 2000, but updated to include e-learning tools in 2003.

In 2001, the National Science Foundation awarded Columbia a $90,000 grant to gather personal accounts and create an oral history piece on the World Trade Center attacks of September 11. In 2002 Columbia University received a pledge of $8 million from Bernard Spitzer for stem cell research to develop new treatments for Parkinson's disease and other neurological disorders. Also that year Lee Bollinger replaced Rupp as president.

EXECUTIVES

Chair Emeritus: David J. Stern, age 63
Chair: William V. (Bill) Campbell, age 65
Vice Chair: Evan A. Davis
Vice Chair: Michael E. Patterson, age 57
President and Trustee: Lee C. Bollinger
Provost: Alan Brinkley
SEVP: Robert A. Kasdin
EVP and Secretary: R. Keith Walton
EVP Government and Community Affairs: Emily Lloyd
EVP Finance: Albert G. (Al) Horvath
EVP Health and Biomedical Sciences:
  Gerald D. Fischbach
EVP Research: David Hirsh
VP Government and Community Affairs:
  Maxine Griffith
VP Human Resources: Colleen M. Crooker
VP Information Services and University Librarian:
  James G. (Jim) Neal
VP University Development and Alumni Relations:
  Susan K. Feagin
Treasurer: Gail Hoffman
Controller: Cheryl Ross
Director Financial Reporting: Ed Hamilton
Director Human Resources and Budget: Kate Sheeran
Director Treasury Operations: Alik O. Hinckson
General Counsel: Elizabeth J. Keefer
Auditors: Deloitte & Touche LLP

LOCATIONS

HQ: Columbia University
  2690 Broadway, New York, NY 10027
Phone: 212-854-1754   **Fax:** 212-749-0397
Web: www.columbia.edu

Columbia University in the City of New York is located in the Morningside Heights section of Manhattan.

PRODUCTS/OPERATIONS

Selected Schools, Colleges, and Programs
Continuing Education
Graduate and Professional Schools
  College of Physicians and Surgeons
    Human Nutrition
    Occupational Therapy
    Physical Therapy
  The Fu Foundation School of Engineering
    & Applied Science
  Mailman School of Public Health
  School of Architecture, Planning & Preservation
  School of the Arts
  School of Arts and Sciences
  School of Business
    Executive Education Program
    Executive MBA Program
  School of Dental & Oral Surgery
  School of International and Public Affairs
  School of Journalism
  School of Law
  School of Nursing
  School of Social Work
Undergraduate Schools
  Columbia College
  The Fu Foundation School of Engineering
    and Applied Science
  School of General Studies

COMPETITORS

Brown University
Cornell University
Dartmouth
Harvard University

Princeton University
University of Pennsylvania
Yale University

HISTORICAL FINANCIALS

Company Type: School

Income Statement

FYE: June 30

	REVENUE ($ mil.)	NET INCOME ($ mil.)	NET PROFIT MARGIN	EMPLOYEES
6/03	2,074	—	—	—
6/02	2,009	—	—	15,300
6/01	1,934	—	—	7,072
6/00	1,790	—	—	15,000
6/99	1,574	—	—	15,000
6/98	1,448	—	—	15,300
6/97	1,339	—	—	17,930
6/96	1,234	—	—	16,300
6/95	1,160	—	—	16,565
6/94	1,103	—	—	14,639
Annual Growth	7.3%	—	—	0.6%

Revenue History

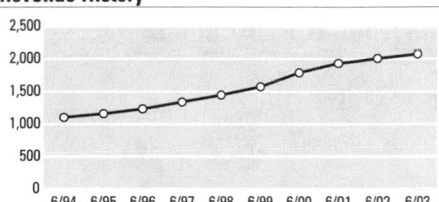

Columbus Blue Jackets

This hockey team puts a new spin on the term sport coat. The Columbus Blue Jackets are the latest addition to the National Hockey League (along with the Minnesota Wild), joining the NHL as an expansion team in 2000. Playing in Columbus' Nationwide Arena, the team has already attracted a strong following despite its limited success on the ice. Worthington Industries founder John McConnell helped bring the franchise to Columbus and worked with local insurance giant Nationwide and newspaper publisher Dispatch Printing to get the team's arena built. He also has a stake in the Columbus Destroyers, the Arena Football League franchise that also plays at Nationwide Arena.

McConnell established the Columbus Blue Jackets Foundation to serve as the team's charity. Its Sticks With Kids program helps combat pediatric cancer and provide educational opportunities for kids. It also uses about a quarter of its yearly budget to promote youth hockey.

EXECUTIVES

Chairman and Governor: John H. McConnell, age 82
Alternate Governor: John P. McConnell, age 51
President, General Manager, and Alternate Governor:
 Doug MacLean, age 51
CFO: T. J. LaMendola
EVP and Assistant General Manager: Jim Clark, age 51
Head Coach: Gerard Gallant, age 42
VP Corporate Development: Paul D'Aiuto
VP Marketing: David Paitson
VP Ticketing: Dan Froehlich
General Counsel: Greg Kirstein
Director of Communications: Todd Sharrock
Director of Human Resources: Kelley Walton
Director of Player Development: Paul Castron
Marketing Manager: Nathaniel Ferrall

LOCATIONS

HQ: The Columbus Blue Jackets
 200 W. Nationwide Blvd., Columbus, OH 43125
Phone: 614-246-4625   **Fax:** 614-246-4007
Web: www.bluejackets.com

COMPETITORS

Chicago Blackhawks   Nashville Predators
Detroit Red Wings   St. Louis Blues

HISTORICAL FINANCIALS

Company Type: Private

Income Statement

FYE: June 30

	REVENUE ($ mil.)	NET INCOME ($ mil.)	NET PROFIT MARGIN	EMPLOYEES
6/04	66	—	—	—
6/03	66	—	—	—
6/02	64	—	—	—
Annual Growth	1.6%	—	—	—

Revenue History

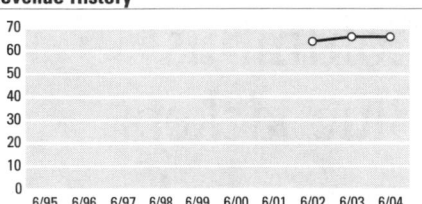

CombinatoRx

CombinatoRx is looking for the right one-two punch combo. The company develops combinations of already approved drugs to target multiple disease pathways rather than the traditional way of singling out genes or proteins for modification. Because the compounds in development have already received regulatory approval in the US, Europe, or Japan, CombinatoRx can move quicker and cheaper through the drug development process: It already has half a dozen candidates in early clinical trials. Its drug candidates could treat cancer, type 2 diabetes, rheumatoid arthritis, and other immuno-inflammatory diseases.

Investors in CombinatoRx include TL Ventures, Canaan Partners, and Boston Millennia Partners.

The company has signed an agreement with HenKan Pharmaceutical giving that company the rights to develop and distribute CRx-026, CombinatoRx's anti-cancer drug in Taiwan, China, and South Korea.

Another deal inked in 2005 with Angiotech could prove to be CombinatoRx's most lucrative. In exchange for a $27 million up-front licensing fee and a $15 million equity stake in CombinatoRx, Angiotech gets to license up to 10 compounds, but it doesn't stop there. Angiotech will also fork out $30 million in milestone payments for each new product it selects for further development. Add a pinch of royalties to the mix, and CombinatoRx could potentially earn as much as $500 million during the five-year period of the agreement.

EXECUTIVES

President, CEO, and Director: Alexis Borisy, age 33, $302,777 pay
EVP and CFO: Robert Forrester, age 41, $225,568 pay
EVP and Chief Medical Officer: Jan N. Lessem, age 56, $336,441 pay
EVP, Product Development: Peter Elliott, age 46, $250,250 pay
SVP, Clinical Development: R. Eric McAllister, age 62
SVP, Discovery: Curtis T. Keith, age 34, $207,607 pay
VP, Corporate Development and Strategy: Daniel Grau
Auditors: Ernst & Young LLP

LOCATIONS

HQ: CombinatoRx, Incorporated
 650 Albany St., Boston, MA 02118
Phone: 617-425-7000   **Fax:** 617-425-7010
Web: www.combinatorx.com

PRODUCTS/OPERATIONS

Drug Candidates

CRx-026 (metastic solid tumors)
CRx-102 (rheumatoid arthritis, osteoarthritis)
CRx-119 (rheumatoid arthritis)
CRx-139 (rheumatoid arthritis)
CRx-140 (psoriasis)
CRx-150 (rheumatoid arthritis)
CRx-170 (asthma)

COMPETITORS

Abbott Labs   Genentech
Amgen   Scios
Biogen Idec   Wyeth Pharmaceuticals
Centocor

HISTORICAL FINANCIALS

Company Type: Private

Income Statement

FYE: December 31

	REVENUE ($ mil.)	NET INCOME ($ mil.)	NET PROFIT MARGIN	EMPLOYEES
12/04	0	(22)	—	72
12/03	0	(16)	—	68
12/02	0	(14)	—	70
12/01	0	(6)	—	—
Annual Growth	—	—	—	1.4%

2004 Year-End Financials

Debt ratio: (2.5%)
Return on equity: —
Cash ($ mil.): 2
Current ratio: 8.74
Long-term debt ($ mil.): 2

Net Income History

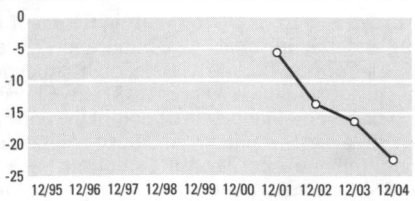

Computer Generated Solutions

Computer Generated Solutions (CGS) can generate beaucoup computer services. CGS offers a myriad of technical services such as network services, call center management, training, and Internet consulting. Through a partnership with IBM, CGS provides software and services for Big Blue's midrange AS/400 computer. The company also offers its own software for enterprise resource planning, online sales, and supply chain management. CGS has expanded through acquisitions, including its purchases of Allstate's computer services subsidiary and Garpac Corporation's supply chain management software for the sewn products industry. CEO Philip Friedman founded CGS in 1984.

In 2002, Computer Generated Solutions established a portal for IBM's WebSphere software suite, a site that provides "e-tutorials" for WebSphere capabilities.

The company in 2005 acquired the assets of Connectrix Systems, adding capabilities to CGS's BlueCherry Enterprise Suite for the fashion industry. The Connectrix acquisition adds merchandise line management, merchandise planning and forecasting, and inventory and brand management.

CGS moved its corporate headquarters in New York City from Midtown to Lower Manhattan. The company applied to New York State's Empire State Development Corp. for a $2 million grant meant to retain and create jobs in the business district devastated by the terrorist attacks of 2001.

EXECUTIVES

President and CEO: Philip (Phil) Friedman, age 56
SVP and CFO: Jeffrey (Jeff) White, age 60
SVP, Application Solutions Division: Paul Magel
SVP: Michael Wilding
VP and Legal Counsel: Carl Heringer
VP, Human Resources: Dan Beards
CTO: Joel Bastow
Controller: Peter Kalotschke
Country Manager, India: Pradeep Tandon
Auditors: Ernst & Young LLP

LOCATIONS

HQ: Computer Generated Solutions, Inc.
3 World Financial Center, 27th Fl.,
New York, NY 10281
Phone: 212-408-3800   **Fax:** 212-977-7474
Web: www.cgsinc.com

Computer Generated Solutions has about 30 offices in Canada, India, and the US.

PRODUCTS/OPERATIONS

Software and Services

Applications outsourcing
Business intelligence applications
Call center management
Document management
Enterprise resource planning applications and support
Hardware support
Help desk support
Legacy systems outsourcing
Network support
Sales force automation and e-business applications
Supply chain management applications and support
Systems development and integration
Technical and end user training

COMPETITORS

Accenture	EDS
Analysts International	IBM Global Services
BearingPoint	Infocrossing
BrightStar Information	Keane
Technology	Perot Systems
California Software	Stream
Canterbury Consulting	Sykes Enterprises
Capgemini	TACT
CHC	Technology Solutions
Computer Sciences Corp.	Tier Technologies
Deloitte Consulting	WidePoint

HISTORICAL FINANCIALS

Company Type: Private

Income Statement

FYE: December 31

	REVENUE ($ mil.)	NET INCOME ($ mil.)	NET PROFIT MARGIN	EMPLOYEES
12/04	113	—	—	1,600
12/03	83	—	—	1,200
12/02	100	—	—	1,200
12/01	110	—	—	1,200
12/00	110	—	—	1,500
12/99	120	—	—	—
12/98	123	—	—	1,300
12/97	64	—	—	1,000
12/96	58	—	—	890
12/95	36	—	—	900
Annual Growth	**13.6%**	**—**	**—**	**6.6%**

Revenue History

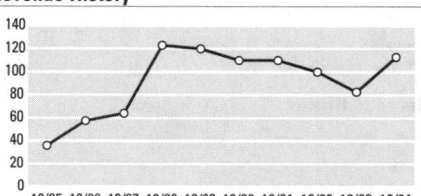

Conair

Counterintelligence has shown that Conair has a place in many bathrooms and kitchens. Personal products by Conair include curling irons, hair dryers, mirrors, shavers, and salon products (Jheri Redding, Rusk) designed for both home and professional salon use. Its Cuisinart and Waring divisions produce blenders, food processors, and other small kitchen appliances. Conair also sells telephones, answering machines, Interplak electric toothbrushes, and Scunci hair accessories. Products are sold at discount chains, department stores, and mass merchants (Bed Bath & Beyond, Target, Wal-Mart) throughout the US. Lee Rizzuto, who founded Conair in 1959 with his parents, pleaded guilty to tax evasion in 2002.

Scunci is Conair's largest acquisition to date; the company is the top-selling brand of hair accessories at food, drug, and discount retailers. Conair plans to expand the Scunci brand into hair appliances and bring it to overseas markets.

Conair also manufactures and distributes hairstyling appliances (hairdryers, curling irons, and straightening irons) for teenage girls marketed under teenage superstars Mary-Kate and Ashley Olsen's eponymous brand.

EXECUTIVES

Co-President: Ronald T. Diamond
Co-President: Barry Haber
CFO: Pat Yannotta
SVP Administration: John Mayorek
VP Chemical Product Development: Lou Salce
VP Research and Development: Jules Nachtigal
VP Sales and Marketing: Frank Lindsey
Marketing Manager: Joni Bologna

LOCATIONS

HQ: Conair Corporation
150 Milford Rd., East Windsor, NJ 08520
Phone: 609-426-1300   **Fax:** 609-426-9475
Web: www.conair.com

PRODUCTS/OPERATIONS

Selected Brands

BaByliss
Conair
ConairPro
Cuisinart
Grand Finale
Interplak
Jheri Redding
Pollenex
Rusk
Scunci
Waring

Selected Divisions and Products

Conair Appliance Manufacturing (worldwide production)
Conair Packaging (health and beauty aid products)
Consumer Electronics (telephones)
Cuisinart (kitchen appliances)
Interplak (electric toothbrushes)
Liquids (hair care)
Personal Care (hair dryers, curling irons, health and wellness appliances)
Professional Products (toiletries and appliances)
Rusk (hair care products)
Scunci International (hair accessories)
Waring (kitchen appliances)

COMPETITORS

Alberto-Culver	Newell Rubbermaid
Applica	Philips Electronics
Braun GmbH	Philips Oral
Claire's Stores	Professional
Gillette	Dental Technologies
Global-Tech Appliances	Revlon
Goody	Salton
Helen of Troy	Spectrum Brands
John Paul Mitchell	Stephan
L'Oréal	Sunbeam
National Presto Industries	Water Pik Technologies

HISTORICAL FINANCIALS

Company Type: Private

Income Statement

FYE: December 31

	REVENUE ($ mil.)	NET INCOME ($ mil.)	NET PROFIT MARGIN	EMPLOYEES
12/03	1,277	—	—	4,000
12/02	1,176	—	—	4,373
12/01	1,151	—	—	4,592
12/00	1,082	—	—	4,461
12/99	928	—	—	3,676
12/98	787	—	—	3,898
12/97	716	—	—	3,652
12/96	655	—	—	3,175
12/95	614	—	—	3,431
Annual Growth	**9.6%**	**—**	**1.9%**	

Revenue History

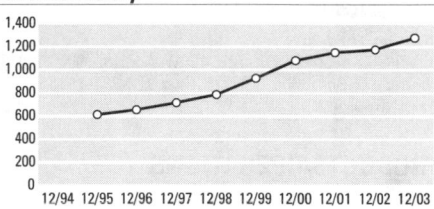

Concentra

Concentra concentrates on controlling costs. Through subsidiary Concentra Operating Corp. and other units, the firm provides cost containment and case management services to employers and to occupational, auto, and group health payors throughout the US. Concentra offers specialized cost-containment services for occupational and auto injury cases, preferred provider network management, telephone case management, and medical bill review. Its Concentra Health Services operates more than 250 medical centers in about 35 states, providing occupational health care, including pre-employment screening, injury care, and loss prevention. Welsh, Carson, Anderson & Stowe owns nearly 65% of Concentra.

The company counts among its clients some 3,500 insurance companies, health care plans, and benefits administrators.

Concentra's health service centers provide such services as drug testing, treatment for work related injuries, and physical therapy. These services account for nearly 50% of the firm's sales. The company aims to grow by expanding its health services offerings.

Concentra Operating Corporation has agreed to acquire Occupational Health + Rehabilitation, expanding its network of occupational health centers into new markets in six states (Maine, Massachusetts, New Hampshire, New York, Rhode Island, and Vermont).

Another member of the family, First Notice Systems, provides outsourced claims reporting services to insurance companies, third-party administrators, and other clients.

EXECUTIVES

Chairman: Paul B. Queally, age 41
President, CEO, and Director: Daniel J. (Dan) Thomas, age 46, $1,418,654 pay
EVP, Corporate Development: James M. (Jim) Greenwood, age 44, $508,789 pay
EVP, CFO, and Treasurer: Thomas E. (Tom) Kiraly, age 45, $787,077 pay
EVP, General Counsel, and Secretary: Richard A. Parr II, age 45, $485,636 pay
SVP and CIO: Laura Ciavola
SVP and Chief Medical Officer: W. Tom Fogarty
SVP and Corporate Controller: Douglas C. Rice
SVP, Business Development and Chief Marketing Officer: Andrew R. (Andy) Daniels, age 46
SVP, Human Resources and Compliance Officer: Tammy Steele
SVP, National Sales: Kenneth Loffredo
SVP, Regional Sales: Mark Farrell
SVP, Risk Management: John T. Berry
Auditors: PricewaterhouseCoopers

LOCATIONS

HQ: Concentra Inc.
5080 Spectrum Dr., Ste. 400W, Addison, TX 75001
Phone: 972-364-8000   **Fax:** 972-387-1938
Web: www.concentra.com

PRODUCTS/OPERATIONS

2004 Sales

	$ mil.	% of total
Health services	576.9	52
Case management services	281.4	26
Network services	244.0	22
Total	**1,102.3**	**100**

Selected Operations

Concentra Case Management Services
Concentra Health Services
Concentra Medical Examinations
Concentra Preferred Systems
First Notice Systems, Inc.
   (claims reporting services and software products)
FOCUS HealthCare Management

COMPETITORS

CorVel
Crawford & Company
First Health Group
GENEX Services
NDCHealth
Occupational Health & Rehab
Per-Se Technologies
RTW

HISTORICAL FINANCIALS

Company Type: Private

Income Statement

FYE: December 31

	REVENUE ($ mil.)	NET INCOME ($ mil.)	NET PROFIT MARGIN	EMPLOYEES
12/04	1,102	(10)	—	10,370
12/03	1,051	43	4.1%	10,000
12/02	999	(4)	—	10,254
12/01	843	(10)	—	10,500
12/00	752	(7)	—	8,800
12/99	681	(27)	—	8,800
12/98	617	23	3.6%	7,800
12/97	459	3	0.6%	7,270
12/96	170	11	6.5%	2,725
12/95	109	6	5.6%	2,125
Annual Growth	**29.3%**	**—**	**—**	**19.3%**

2004 Year-End Financials

Debt ratio: —
Return on equity: —
Cash ($ mil.): 61
Current ratio: 1.71
Long-term debt ($ mil.): 700

Net Income History

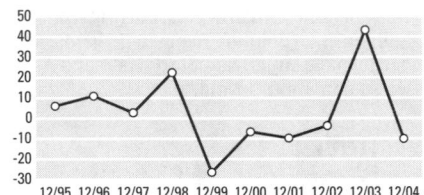

Connecticut Lottery

The Connecticut Lottery gives residents of the Constitution State a chance to amend their incomes. The organization operates a variety of scratch-off instant games and daily numbers games (Cash 5, Nightly Numbers, Play 4). It also offers Classic Lotto twice-a-week jackpot games and the multistate Powerball Lottery. Players who buy Instant Powerball TV Game scratch-off tickets also are eligible to win a chance to get their 15 minutes of fame by competing on *Powerball Instant Millionaire*, a weekly lottery game show operated by the Multi-State Lottery Association. The Connecticut Lottery pays out about 60% of lottery revenue in prizes and about 30% to Connecticut's general fund.

In June 2005 a Connecticut man was the lone winner of a Powerball drawing, which brought him a $60 million jackpot.

The Connecticut Lottery employs Cashman +Katz of Glastonbury, Connecticut to manage its $5 million advertising and public relations budget.

EXECUTIVES

President and CEO: James (Jim) Vance
VP Sales and Marketing: Dennis Chapman
VP Operations: Barabara Porto
Director, Sales: Gloria Donnelly
Drawing Coordinator: Richard Wiszniak
Lottery Ambassador: Bill Hennessey
Auditors: State of Connecticut Auditor of Public Accounts

LOCATIONS

HQ: Connecticut Lottery Corporation
270 John Downey Dr., New Britain, CT 06051
Phone: 860-348-4001   **Fax:** 860-348-4015
Web: www.ctlottery.org

PRODUCTS/OPERATIONS

2004 Sales

	% of total
Prizes	59
General fund	31
Retailers	6
Operating costs	4
Total	**100**

Selected Games

Cash 5
Classic Lotto
Mid-day 3
Mid-day 4
Play 4
Powerball
Powerball Instant Millionaire
Scratch-off games

COMPETITORS

Loto-Québec
Mashantucket Pequot Gaming
Massachusetts State Lottery
New Jersey Lottery
New York State Lottery
Pennsylvania Lottery

HISTORICAL FINANCIALS

Company Type: Government-owned

Income Statement

FYE: June 30

	REVENUE ($ mil.)	NET INCOME ($ mil.)	NET PROFIT MARGIN	EMPLOYEES
6/04	912	—	—	120
6/03	858	—	—	120
6/02	850	—	—	120
6/01	840	—	—	120
6/00	838	—	—	120
6/99	871	—	—	120
6/98	806	—	—	115
6/97	772	—	—	105
6/96	707	—	—	100
6/95	671	—	—	—
Annual Growth	**3.5%**	**—**	**—**	**2.3%**

Revenue History

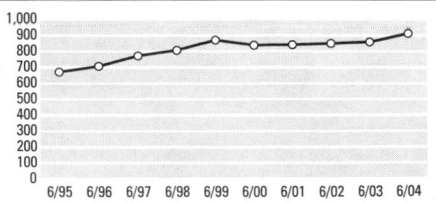

Connell Company

The Connell Company can sell you a boatload of rice or lend you money for that power plant you've been meaning to install. Connell's core business is rice distribution, conducted through subsidiary Connell Rice & Sugar. The company's support operations have grown into full subsidiaries including brokerage of flour and sweeteners, export sales of food manufacturing equipment, commercial real estate development, heavy equipment leasing, exporting, and financial services (such as underwriting airlines' purchases of aircraft). The company has offices in Taiwan, Thailand, and the US. Connell has remained a family-owned business since it was founded in 1926.

EXECUTIVES

President: Grover Connell
CFO: Terry Connell
SEVP and President, Connell Rice & Sugar:
 Ted Connell
EVP: George Alayeto
EVP: Duane Connell
EVP and President, Connell Technologies:
 Shane Connell
SVP and General Counsel: Mark Decker
VP and Controller: Vincent (Vince) Krzywosz
VP, Human Resources: Maureen Waldron
General Manager, Connell Purchasing Services:
 Randy Briesath

LOCATIONS

HQ: The Connell Company
 1 Connell Dr., Berkeley Heights, NJ 07922
Phone: 908-673-3700   **Fax:** 908-673-3800
Web: www.connellco.com/TCC.htm

PRODUCTS/OPERATIONS

Selected Divisions and Subsidiaries
Connell & Co. (flour, sugar brokerage services)
Connell Finance Company, Inc.
 (financial advisory services)
 Connell Equipment Leasing Company
 Connell Technologies Company
 (asset management services)
Connell GATCO Company (heavy equipment
 distribution)
Connell International Co. (exporting)
Connell Realty & Development Co.
 (commercial and corporate buildings)
Connell Rice & Sugar Co.

COMPETITORS

American Rice
Atlas Copco
Cargill
Deere
Man Group
Merrill Lynch
Riceland Foods
Riviana Foods

HISTORICAL FINANCIALS
Company Type: Private

Income Statement

FYE: December 31

	REVENUE ($ mil.)	NET INCOME ($ mil.)	NET PROFIT MARGIN	EMPLOYEES
12/03*	2,300	—	—	220
12/01	2,525	—	—	245
12/00	2,425	—	—	240
12/99	2,300	—	—	220
12/98	2,100	—	—	225
12/97	1,275	—	—	225
12/96	1,300	—	—	220
12/95	1,200	—	—	200
12/94	1,100	—	—	200
12/93	1,050	—	—	200
Annual Growth	9.1%	—	—	1.1%

*Irregular reporting interval

Revenue History

Consolidated Container

Being flexible allowed Consolidated Container to can its former name (Continental Can). Consolidated Container is one of the largest manufacturers of rigid plastic containers in the US. The company markets its products to the dairy, water, agricultural, food, and industrial chemical industries and manufactures containers for a variety of products, including water, milk, ketchup, salsa, soap, motor oil, antifreeze, insect repellent, fertilizers, and medical supplies. Procter & Gamble is a major customer. Consolidated Container was formed when Suiza Foods merged its plastics business with Reid Plastics. Dean Foods owns 40% of Consolidated Container.

Besides Dean Foods and Procter & Gamble, major customers of Consolidated Container include Coca-Cola North America, Colgate-Palmolive, Kroger, Nestle Waters North America, National Dairy Holdings, PepsiCo, and Scotts.

Consolidated Container expanded its West Coast operations in 2005 by acquiring two California-based companies, Mayfair Plastics and STC Plastics.

EXECUTIVES

Chairman: James P. Kelley, age 50
Vice Chairman: B. Joseph Rokus, age 50
President and CEO: Stephen E. (Steve) Macadam,
 age 44, $1,054,800 pay
SVP, Finance and Accounting, Chief Accounting
 Officer, and CFO: Richard P. Sehring, age 42
SVP, Consumer Packaging Group: Jeff Greene
SVP, General Counsel, and Secretary: Louis Lettes,
 age 40, $239,615 pay

SVP, Operations Services, and Procurement:
 Robert Keith Brower, age 56, $378,848 pay
SVP, Human Resources: Laura H. Fee, age 45,
 $245,404 pay
Assistant Secretary and Director: John R. Woodard,
 age 40
VP, Information Services: Andrew Ziegele
Auditors: Deloitte & Touche LLP

LOCATIONS

HQ: Consolidated Container Company LLC
 3101 Towercreek Pkwy., Ste. 300, Atlanta, GA 30339
Phone: 678-742-4600   **Fax:** 678-742-4750
Web: www.cccllc.com

Consolidated Container has more than 60 manufacturing plants in North America.

PRODUCTS/OPERATIONS

2004 Sales

	% of total
Dairy	27
Water	17
Other beverage	15
Household Chemicals & Personal Care	15
Agricultural, Industrial & Other	10
Food	9
Automotive	7
Total	**100**

Selected Products
Antifreeze containers
Bleach bottles
Dishwashing liquid bottles
Edible oil containers
Fertilizer containers
Fruit juice bottles
Insect repellent containers
Ketchup bottles
Laundry detergent bottles
Maple syrup containers
Milk bottles
Motor oil containers
Salsa bottles
Water bottles
Windshield wash solvent bottles

COMPETITORS

Ball Corporation	Plastipak Holdings, Inc.
Crown	RPC Group
Graham Packaging	Silgan
Krones	Silgan Plastics
Owens-Illinois	Corporation

HISTORICAL FINANCIALS
Company Type: Private

Income Statement

FYE: December 31

	REVENUE ($ mil.)	NET INCOME ($ mil.)	NET PROFIT MARGIN	EMPLOYEES
12/04	761	(16)	—	3,500
12/03	740	(17)	—	4,000
12/02	747	(300)	—	4,130
12/01	787	(31)	—	4,650
12/00	755	23	3.1%	4,400
12/99	474	2	0.4%	4,500
12/98	175	0	0.2%	—
12/97	546	8	1.5%	3,442
12/96	585	(6)	—	3,463
12/95	614	1	0.1%	3,796
Annual Growth	2.4%	—	—	(0.9%)

2004 Year-End Financials

Debt ratio: —   Current ratio: 1.34
Return on equity: —   Long-term debt ($ mil.): 562
Cash ($ mil.): 8

Net Income History

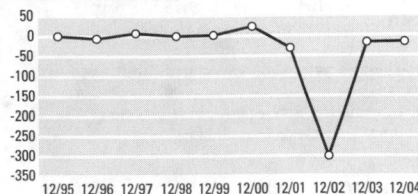

Consolidated Electrical

Electrical equipment wholesaler Consolidated Electrical Distributors (CED) has US distribution wired. With more than 500 locations nationwide, the family-owned business is one of the largest distributors of electrical products in the country. CED supplies load centers, panelboards, transformers, switches, motor controls, drives, and similar products to residential and commercial contractors and industrial customers. Founded in 1957 as The Electric Corporation of San Francisco, the company has grown by acquiring electrical distributors; since it usually keeps the acquired firm's name and management team, CED now does business under about 80 names. The Colburn family owns CED.

EXECUTIVES

President: H. Dean Bursch
CFO: Jeff Wofford
Secretary: David C. Verbeck
Treasurer: John D. Parish
Recruiting Coordinator: Marie Lipp

LOCATIONS

HQ: Consolidated Electrical Distributors, Inc.
31356 Via Colinas, Ste. 107,
Westlake Village, CA 91362
Phone: 818-991-9000 **Fax:** 818-991-6842
Web: www.cedcareers.com

Consolidated Electrical Distributors has more than 500 US locations in 44 states.

PRODUCTS/OPERATIONS

Selected Products

Adjustable frequency drives
Circuit breakers
Control transformers
Load centers
Metering equipment
Motor control centers
Open starters/contractors
Panelboards
Power outlet panels
Pushbuttons
Relays
Safety switches
Starters
Switchboards
Switchgear
Timers
Transformers

COMPETITORS

Anixter International	North Coast Electric
CLS	One Source Distributors
Electrocomponents	Rexel Canada
Fastenal	Rexel, Inc.
GE Supply	Sonepar USA
General Cable	Stuart C. Irby
Graybar Electric	SUMMIT Electric Supply
Home Depot Supply	Thomas & Betts
Hubbell	United Electric Supply
Hughes Supply	Walters Wholesale Electric
McJunkin	WESCO International
McNaughton-McKay	W.W. Grainger

HISTORICAL FINANCIALS

Company Type: Private

Income Statement

FYE: December 31

	ESTIMATED REVENUE ($ mil.)	NET INCOME ($ mil.)	NET PROFIT MARGIN	EMPLOYEES
12/03	2,300	—	—	5,000
12/02	2,300	—	—	5,000
12/01	2,400	—	—	5,350
12/00	2,500	—	—	5,500
12/99	2,700	—	—	5,000
12/98	2,600	—	—	4,500
12/97	1,925	—	—	4,500
12/96	1,900	—	—	4,000
12/95	1,600	—	—	4,000
12/94	1,600	—	—	3,700
Annual Growth	**4.1%**	—	—	**3.4%**

Revenue History

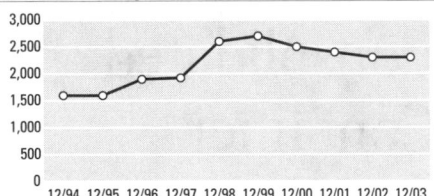

Consumers Union

Consumers Union of United States (CU) inspires both trust and fear. Best known for publishing *Consumer Reports* magazine (4 million subscribers), the not-for-profit organization also serves as a consumer watchdog through newsletters, books, TV and radio programming, and the *Consumer Reports for Kids Online* site. Its subscriber Web site (more than 1 million paid subscribers) rates products ranging from candy bars to cars. The company tests and rates thousands of products annually. Its Consumer Policy Institute conducts research and education projects on issues such as air pollution, biotechnology, food safety, and right-to-know laws.

It maintains 50 laboratories within its National Testing and Research Center in Yonkers, New York. In addition to conducting its own product testing, CU gathers product information by surveying the readers of its publications.

CU derives revenue from sales of its publications, from car and insurance pricing services, and from contributions, grants, and fees. The company has revamped its *Consumer Reports* publication with additional content and a new look aimed at improving the magazine's layout and organization.

Retailer Sharper Image sued CU over an article unflattering to the company's popular air purifier device, but a judge threw out the suit in late 2004.

The organization testifies before legislative and regulatory entities and files lawsuits on behalf of consumers. CU is governed by an 18-member board. To preserve its independence, CU accepts no advertising and does not permit its ratings or comments to be used commercially.

HISTORY

In 1926 engineer Frederick Schlink organized a "consumer club" (in White Plains, New York), which distributed lists of recommended and non-recommended products. The lists led to the founding of Consumers' Research and a magazine devoted to testing products.

Schlink moved the group to Washington, New Jersey, in 1933. In 1935 three employees formed a union. Schlink fired them. Faced with another strike that year, Schlink accused the strikers of being "Red" and responded with strikebreakers and armed detectives. The next year the strikers set up their own organization, the Consumers Union of United States (CU).

CU's first magazine, *Consumers Union Reports*, came out three months later and rated products that the fledgling organization could afford to test, such as soap and breakfast cereals. Subsequent issues focused on food and drug regulation and working conditions for women in textile mills.

The organization drew the wrath of both *Reader's Digest* and *Good Housekeeping* (which accused it in 1939 of prolonging the Depression). The next year the House Un-American Activities Committee put CU on its list of suspect organizations. CU cut staff and dropped "Union" from its magazine title, but circulation remained low until after WWII.

By 1950, however, Americans began consuming again, helping to boost circulation to almost 400,000. During the 1950s CU published a series of reports on the health hazards of smoking.

In 1960 CU helped found the International Organization of Consumers Unions (now Consumers International) to foster the consumer movement worldwide. Rhoda Karpatkin was hired as publisher in 1974. During the 1970s CU established consumer advocacy offices in California, Texas, and Washington, DC.

Recession and an increase in not-for-profit mailing rates caused the company to lose money in the early 1980s. CU looked to its readers, who donated more than $3 million. The organization was hit by a 13-week strike in 1984 by union members calling for more say in management.

In 1996 CU slapped "not acceptable" ratings on the Isuzu Trooper and the Acura SLX. The next year the National Highway Traffic Safety Administration declared that CU's testing procedure of the Trooper was flawed, but CU stood by its tests of the vehicle.

CU hit another bump in 1998 when it was compelled to retract a story on the nutritional value of Iams and Eukanuba pet food. Admitting its test results were incorrect, CU's retraction of the story was something of a rarity — its last retraction had occurred almost 20 years earlier when the organization retracted a story on condoms.

In 1999 the company defended itself in court against allegations by Isuzu and Suzuki that their companies were defamed through negative reviews by Consumer Reports. The following year a jury found CU guilty of falsely reporting on the Isuzu but declined to impose fines on the publisher. Also in 2000 a district court upheld the dismissal of Suzuki's suit against CU (based on CU's 1988 rating of the Suzuki Samurai as "not acceptable" due to rollover risks); Suzuki appealed the decision. Karpatkin announced she would step down as president in 2001. Later that year CU agreed to license its content to Internet portal Yahoo! James Guest, CU's chairman since 1980, took over as president in 2001.

Suzuki and CU settled their legal dispute in 2004.

EXECUTIVES

Chairman, President, and CEO: James A. (Jim) Guest
EVP: Joel Gurin
VP and CFO: Richard (Rich) Gannon
VP and Technical Director: Jeffrey A. (Jeff) Asher
VP Administration and Human Resources: Richard (Rick) Lustig
VP Publishing: John J. Sateja
VP Web Information Systems: Michael (Mike) D'Alessandro
Senior Director and General Manager, Consumer Reports Information Products, Web Publishing: Jerry Steinbrink
Senior Director and General Manager, Product and Market Development, Publishing: Paige Amidon
Senior Director and Editor, Consumer Reports, Editorial: Margot Slade
Director and Editor, ConsumerReports.org and New Media, Web Editorial: Laura R. Bona
Director, Strategic Technology Development: Frank Iacopelli
Senior Director and Controller: Connie Tucker
Senior Director, Treasury and Chief Investment Officer: Eric Wayne
Director, Business Planning and Analysis: JoAnne Boyd
Director, Human Resources: Milca Esdaille
Director, Facilities Management: Al Rizzotti
Auditors: KPMG LLP

LOCATIONS

HQ: Consumers Union of United States, Inc.
101 Truman Ave., Yonkers, NY 10703
Phone: 914-378-2000   **Fax:** 914-378-2900
Web: www.consumersunion.org

Consumers Union of United States performs most product tests at a renovated warehouse in Yonkers, New York. It has consumer advocacy offices in Austin, Texas; San Francisco; and Washington, DC.

PRODUCTS/OPERATIONS

Selected Operations

Auto Services
   CR New Car Price Service
   CR Used Car Price Service
Books and Buying Guides
   Auto Books
      New Car Buying Guide
      New Car Preview
      Used Car Buying Guide
      Used Car Yearbook
   House and Home
      Best Buys for Your Home Buying Guide
      Home Computer Buying Guide
   Money
      Consumer Reports Money Book
      How to Plan for a Secure Retirement
   Personal and Leisure
      Consumer Drug Reference
      Guide to Baby Products
      Guide to Health Care for Seniors
      Travel Well for Less

Magazines and Newsletters
   Consumer Reports Magazine
TV and Radio
   Consumer Reports on TV (video segments)
   CR Radio (daily radio feature)
Web Sites
   ConsumerReports.org
   Consumer Reports for Kids Online (zillions.org)

COMPETITORS

Consumers' Research	PRIMEDIA
Hearst	Reader's Digest
International Data Group	Reed Elsevier Group
J.D. Power	Shopping.com
National Technical Systems	Underwriters Labs

HISTORICAL FINANCIALS
Company Type: Not-for-profit

Income Statement — FYE: May 31

	REVENUE ($ mil.)	NET INCOME ($ mil.)	NET PROFIT MARGIN	EMPLOYEES
5/03	157	43	27.1%	450
5/02	151	30	19.6%	450
5/01	161	38	23.5%	450
5/00	140	—	—	450
5/99	140	—	—	482
5/98	140	—	—	475
5/97	135	—	—	461
5/96	136	—	—	451
5/95	129	—	—	453
5/94	124	—	—	451
Annual Growth	2.6%	5.8%	—	(0.0%)

Net Income History

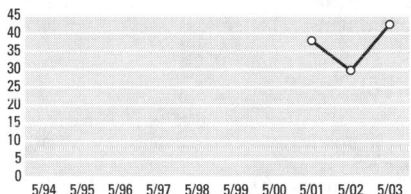

Container Store

With its packets, pockets, and boxes, The Container Store has the storage products niche well-contained. Its merchandise ranges from backpacks to recipe holders. The home organization pioneer operates about 35 stores, mostly in major cities in California, Colorado, Georgia, Illinois, Maryland, New York, and Texas. The stores carry more than 10,000 items; the company's Elfa brand wire shelving accounts for about one-fifth of sales. The company touts a low employee turnover rate, thanks in part to high wages. Chairman Garrett Boone and president and CEO Kip Tindell own most of the company's stock. They met in 1969 working in a Montgomery Ward paint department and opened their first store in Dallas in 1978.

The Container Store has been expanding in New England, most recently in Boston. The company plans to open a second store in Manhattan — where space-starved New Yorkers have embraced its first The Container Store — in 2006.

Texas billionaire Robert Bass and two other Texas investors have purchased a 10% stake in the storage and organizing products company.

EXECUTIVES

Chairman: Garrett Boone
President and CEO: Kip Tindell
CFO: Sharon Ellis
EVP, Merchandising: Sharon Tindell
EVP, Stores and Marketing: Melissa Reiff
VP and CTO: Thomas (Tom) Birmingham
VP, Marketing: Casey Priest
VP, Stores: John Thrailkill

LOCATIONS

HQ: The Container Store
500 Freeport Pkwy., Coppell, TX 75019
Phone: 972-538-6000   **Fax:** 972-538-7623
Web: www.containerstore.com

COMPETITORS

Bed Bath & Beyond
Euromarket Designs
Garden Ridge
Home Depot
IKEA
Linens 'n Things
Newell Rubbermaid
Pier 1 Imports
Restoration Hardware
Sterilite
Target
Tupperware
Wal-Mart
Williams-Sonoma

HISTORICAL FINANCIALS
Company Type: Private

Income Statement — FYE: March 31

	REVENUE ($ mil.)	NET INCOME ($ mil.)	NET PROFIT MARGIN	EMPLOYEES
3/05	425	—	—	—
3/04*	375	—	—	3,926
3/02	250	—	—	—
3/01	260	—	—	1,500
3/00	240	—	—	1,473
3/99	214	—	—	1,400
3/98	168	—	—	1,200
3/97	150	—	—	1,100
3/96	120	—	—	950
3/95	86	—	—	875
Annual Growth	19.4%	—	—	20.6%

*Irregular reporting interval

Revenue History

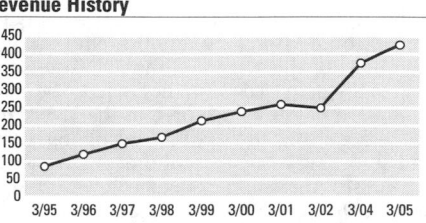

ContiGroup

Making its way up the food chain, ContiGroup Companies (CGC) is focusing on meat production. CGC operates through subsidiary Wayne Farms, a major poultry processor; majority-owned Premium Standard Farms, the #2 US fresh pork producer (after Smithfield Foods); and Five Rivers Ranch Cattle Feeding, a joint venture with Smithfield Foods that is the #1 global cattle feedlot operator. The company has exited its grain trading, chemicals, and animal nutrition operations. Overseas it has interests in flour milling, animal feed, aquaculture, and pork and poultry processing. CGC's investment arm, ContiInvestments, manages diverse holdings. CEO Paul Fribourg (a descendant of founder Simon Fribourg) and his family own CGC.

CGC entered the Five Rivers joint venture with Smithfield Foods in 2005. The two companies combined their respective feedlot operations to form the new entity, which operates 10 cattle feedlots with a capacity of more than 800,000 head in Colorado, Idaho, Kansas, Oklahoma, and Texas. CGC contributed six of the 10 feedlots, which were previously operated by its former ContiBeef subsidiary.

HISTORY

Simon Fribourg founded a commodity trading business in Belgium in 1813. It operated domestically until 1848, when a drought in Belgium caused it to buy large stocks in Russian wheat.

As the Industrial Revolution swept across Europe and populations shifted to cities, people consumed more traded grain. In the midst of such rapid changes, the company prospered. After WWI, Russia, which had been Europe's primary grain supplier, ceased to be a major player in the trading game, and Western countries picked up the slack. Sensing the shift, Jules and Rene Fribourg reorganized the business as Continental Grain and opened its first US office in Chicago in 1921.

Throughout the Depression the company bought US grain elevators, often at low prices. Through its purchases, Continental Grain built a North American grain network that included major locations like Kansas City, Missouri; Nashville, Tennessee; and Toledo, Ohio.

In Europe, meanwhile, the Fribourgs were forced to endure constant political and economic upheaval, often profiting from it (they supplied food to Republican forces during the Spanish Civil War). When Nazis invaded Belgium in 1940, the Fribourgs were forced to flee, but they reorganized the business in New York City after the war.

Following the war, Continental Grain pioneered US grain trade with the Soviets. The company went on a buying spree in the 1960s and 1970s, acquiring Allied Mills (feed milling, 1965) and absorbing many agricultural and transport businesses, including Texas feedlots, a bakery, and the Quaker Oats agricultural products unit.

During the 1980s Continental Grain sold its baking units (Oroweat and Arnold) and its commodities brokerage house. Amid an agricultural bust, it formed ContiFinancial and other financial units.

Michel Fribourg stepped down as CEO in 1988 and was succeeded by Donald Staheli, the first outside CEO. The company entered a grain-handling and selling joint venture with Scoular in 1991. Three years later Staheli added the title of

chairman, and Michel's son Paul became president. Continental Grain sold a stake in ContiFinancial (home equity loans and investment banking) to the public in 1996. Also in 1996 the firm formed ContiInvestments, an investment arm geared toward the parent company's areas of expertise.

That year Continental Grain and an overseas affiliate (Arab Finagrain) agreed to pay the US government $35 million, which included a $10 million fine against Arab Finagrain, to settle a fraud case involving commodity sales to Iraq.

Paul succeeded Staheli as CEO in 1997. The company bought Campbell Soup's poultry processing units that year, and in 1998 it bought a 51% stake in pork producer/processor Premium Standard Farms. Meanwhile, ContiFinancial diversified into retail home mortgage and home equity lending.

Continental Grain sold its commodities marketing business in July 1999 to #1 grain exporter Cargill. With its grain operations gone, in 1999 the company renamed itself ContiGroup Companies.

During 2000 ContiFinancial declared bankruptcy, and ContiGroup sold its Animal Nutrition Division (Wayne Foods) to feed manufacturer Ridley Inc. for $37 million. In mid-2000, Premium Standard Farms doubled its processing capacity with the purchase of Lundy Packing Company. Chairman emeritus Michel Fribourg, the founder's great-great-grandson, died in 2001. That same year ContiSea, the salmon and seafood processing joint venture between ContiGroup and Seaboard, was sold to Norway's Fjord Seafood, giving ContiGroup a significant share of Fjord.

To better focus on its food and agribusiness holdings, in early 2003 ContiGroup sold off its ContiChem LPG business.

EXECUTIVES

Chairman, President, and CEO: Paul J. Fribourg, age 51
EVP, Human Resources and Information Systems:
  Teresa E. McCaslin
EVP, Investments and Strategy and CFO; President, ContiInvestments: Michael J. Zimmerman, age 54
CEO, ContiBeef: Mike Thoren
CEO, Premium Standard Farms: John M. Meyer, age 42
CEO, Wayne Farms: Elton Maddox
SVP and Managing Director, ContiAsia: Michael A. Hoer
VP and General Manager, ContiLatin: Brian Anderson

LOCATIONS

HQ: ContiGroup Companies, Inc.
  277 Park Ave., New York, NY 10172
Phone: 212-207-5100   **Fax:** 212-207-5499
Web: www.contigroup.com

In addition to the US, ContiGroup has operations in China, Ecuador, the French West Indies, Haiti, Peru, and Venezuela.

PRODUCTS/OPERATIONS

Major Business Units

ContiAsia (feed milling, pork production, and poultry production; China)
ContiInvestments, LLC (investment management)
ContiLatin (feed and flour milling, poultry operations, and shrimp farming; Caribbean and Latin America)
Five Rivers Ranch Cattle Feeding LLC (joint venture with Smithfield Foods, cattle feedlot operations)
Premium Standard Farms, Inc.
  (53%, hog and pork production)
Wayne Farms, LLC (poultry production)

COMPETITORS

AzTx Cattle	Hormel
Brawley Beef	King Ranch
Cactus Feeders	Pilgrim's Pride
Cargill	Seaboard
CHS	Smithfield Foods
ConAgra	Tyson Foods
Gold Kist	

HISTORICAL FINANCIALS

Company Type: Private

Income Statement

FYE: March 31

	ESTIMATED REVENUE ($ mil.)	NET INCOME ($ mil.)	NET PROFIT MARGIN	EMPLOYEES
3/04	2,200	—	—	15,500
3/03	2,000	—	—	13,500
3/02	3,300	—	—	14,500
3/01	4,000	—	—	14,500
3/00	10,000	—	—	13,500
3/99	10,500	—	—	14,000
3/98	15,000	—	—	17,500
3/97	16,000	—	—	16,800
3/96	15,000	—	—	16,000
3/95	14,000	—	—	16,000
Annual Growth	**(18.6%)**	**—**	**—**	**(0.4%)**

Revenue History

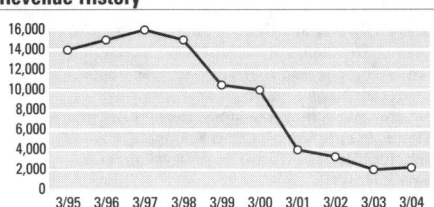

Cook Inlet Energy Supply

Captain Cook would have been proud. Named for the area of Alaska explored by the global navigator in 1778, Cook Inlet Energy Supply is one of the largest privately owned energy trading companies in the US. The company primarily buys and sells natural gas on the wholesale market, and it provides storage, transportation, hedging, and asset management services. Customers include municipal and regional utilities, power producers, industrial end-users, government and financial institutions, and other energy marketers. Cook Inlet Energy operates in Canada, Mexico, and the US. Inupiat Energy Corporation, which is controlled by Cook Inlet CEO Gregory Craig, owns a majority stake in the company.

Cook Inlet Energy was originally a partnership of more than 6,700 Alaskan Eskimos, and remains the largest minority-owned energy business in the US. Its employees are fluent in more than 20 languages.

EXECUTIVES

CEO: Gregory L. Craig, age 40
President: Hans O. Saeby
EVP: Suyen E. Pell
VP Trading: Cindy Khek
Chief Risk Officer: Neelesh (Neel) Pinge
Controller: Meehee Voelzke
Director, Contract Administration: Angela Jones
Director, East Coast and Gulf Coast Trading and Marketing: Mark Gazzilli
Director, MidContinent Trading and Marketing: Scott Biscoe
Director, Quality Control: Aamer Khan
Director, Pacific Northwest and Southwest Trading and Marketing: Sabrina Bienstock

LOCATIONS

HQ: Cook Inlet Energy Supply L.L.C.
10100 Santa Monica Blvd., 18th Fl.,
Los Angeles, CA 90067
Phone: 310-789-3900   **Fax:** 310-789-3901
Web: www.cook-inlet.com

COMPETITORS

Constellation
Energy Commodities
Mirant
Sempra Commodities

HISTORICAL FINANCIALS

Company Type: Private

Income Statement

FYE: December 31

	REVENUE ($ mil.)	NET INCOME ($ mil.)	NET PROFIT MARGIN	EMPLOYEES
12/03	2,950	—	—	62
12/02	2,870	—	—	58
Annual Growth	2.8%	—	—	6.9%

Revenue History

Cooperative Regions of Organic Producers

Cooperative Regions of Organic Producers Pool (CROPP) is the largest organic farmer's cooperative in the US. Its nearly 700 farmer-members produce the Organic Valley Family of Farms brand of fluid milk, cheeses, butter, and soy milk. Beyond the dairy barn, the cooperative also produces organic citrus juices, eggs, and meats. Organic Valley retail products are sold at grocers, while its industrial ingredients are marketed to other organic food processors. Founded in 1988, CROPP's leap into national supermarket chains has propelled the company's rapid growth. A processing partnership with Guida's Milk & Ice Cream is helping the company expand its regional reach into the Northeastern US.

EXECUTIVES

CEO: George Siemon
CFO: Mike Bedessem
COO: Louise Hemstead
VP, Sales: Eric Newman
Chief Marketing Executive: Theresa Marquez
Manager, Human Resources: Bob Brague
Manager, Food Service Sales: Derek Lee
President, The Organic Meat Company of Organic Valley: Michael Levine
Manager, Public Relations: Sue McGovern
Manager, Information Technology: George Neill
Manager, Industrial Sales: Kreigh Rasikas

LOCATIONS

HQ: Cooperative Regions of Organic Producers Pool
1 Organic Way, LaFarge, WI 54639
Phone: 608-625-2602   **Fax:** 608-625-2600
Web: www.organicvalley.coop

COMPETITORS

Aurora Organic Dairy
Berkeley Farms
Coleman Natural Products
Crowley Foods
Dakota
Dean Foods
Egg Innovations
Foster Dairy Farms
Keller's Creamery
Laura's Lean Beef
Maverick Ranch
Niman Ranch
Odwalla
Stonyfield Farm
Straus Family Creamery

HISTORICAL FINANCIALS

Company Type: Cooperative

Income Statement

FYE: December 31

	REVENUE ($ mil.)	NET INCOME ($ mil.)	NET PROFIT MARGIN	EMPLOYEES
12/04	208	—	—	—
12/03	156	—	—	—
12/02	125	—	—	—
Annual Growth	29.0%	—	—	—

Revenue History

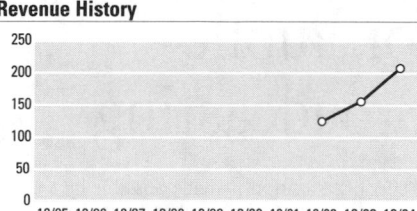

Cornell University

To excel at Cornell, you'll need every one of your brain cells. The Ivy League university has been educating young minds since its founding in 1865. Its more than 20,000 students can select from 14 undergraduate, graduate, and professional colleges and schools. In addition to its Ithaca, New York, campus the university has medical programs in New York City and Doha, Qatar. Cornell's faculty includes a handful of Nobel laureates, and the university has a robust research component studying everything from animal health to space to waste management; the university's 19 libraries hold more than 7 million volumes. Notable alumni include author E. B. White and US Supreme Court Justice Ruth Bader Ginsburg.

Cornell awarded the nation's first university degree in veterinary medicine and first doctorates in electrical engineering and industrial engineering. It awarded the world's first degree in journalism (and taught the first university course in that subject), and established the first four-year schools of hotel administration and industrial and labor relations.

EXECUTIVES

Chairman Emeritus: Austin H. Kiplinger
Chairman Emeritus: Harold Tanner
Chairman Emeritus: Stephen H. Weiss, age 70
Chairman: Peter C. Meinig
Vice Chairman: Diana M. Daniels, age 55
Vice Chairman: Samuel C. Fleming, age 64
Interim President: Hunter R. Rawlings III, age 60
Provost: Carolyn A. (Biddy) Martin
EVP Finance and Administration: Stephen T. (Steve) Golding, age 56
VP Financial Affairs and University Controller: Joanna M. DeStefano
VP Human Resources: Mary G. Opperman
VP Student and Academic Services: Susan H. Murphy, age 53
VP University Communications: Thomas W. Bruce
University Counsel and Secretary: James J. Mingle
Auditors: KPMG LLP

LOCATIONS

HQ: Cornell University
Cornell University Campus, 305 Day Hall,
Ithaca, NY 14853
Phone: 607-255-2000   **Fax:** 607-255-5396
Web: www.cornell.edu

PRODUCTS/OPERATIONS

Selected Undergraduate Colleges and Schools

College of Agriculture and Life Sciences
College of Architecture, Art, and Planning
College of Arts and Sciences
College of Engineering
School of Hotel Administration
College of Human Ecology
School of Industrial and Labor Relations

Selected Graduate and Professional Colleges and Schools

College of Veterinary Medicine
Graduate School
Johnson Graduate School of Management
Law School
Weill Graduate School of Medical Sciences (New York City)
Weill Medical College (New York City and Doha, Qatar)

COMPETITORS

Brown University
Columbia University
Dartmouth
Harvard University
Ithaca College
Princeton University
University of Pennsylvania
Yale University

HISTORICAL FINANCIALS

Company Type: School

Income Statement

FYE: June 30

	REVENUE ($ mil.)	NET INCOME ($ mil.)	NET PROFIT MARGIN	EMPLOYEES
6/04	2,510	478	19.0%	13,677
6/03	1,903	3	0.1%	13,517
6/02	1,666	—	—	13,319
6/01	1,459	—	—	12,866
6/00	2,352	—	—	12,468
6/99	1,856	—	—	12,207
6/98	1,899	—	—	11,873
6/97	1,709	—	—	11,757
6/96	1,747	—	—	11,481
6/95	1,378	—	—	9,600
Annual Growth	6.9%	17,585.2%	—	4.0%

2004 Year-End Financials

Debt ratio: —
Return on equity: 9.1%
Cash ($ mil.): —

Current ratio: —
Long-term debt ($ mil.): —

Net Income History

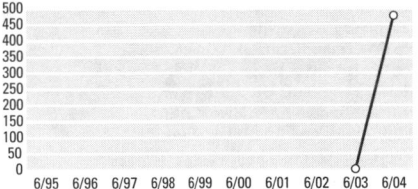

500
450
400
350
300
250
200
150
100
50
0

6/95 6/96 6/97 6/98 6/99 6/00 6/01 6/02 6/03 6/04

Cornerstone Bancorp

Cornerstone Bancorp is the holding company for Cornerstone National Bank, which has three branches in northwestern South Carolina. The bank offers traditional products and services, including checking and savings accounts, money markets, CDs, and credit cards. Commercial real estate loans comprise the largest portion of its lending portfolio (about 33%); other offerings include residential mortgages (22%), business and industrial loans (19%), and consumer loans (4%). Cornerstone National Bank has offices in Easley, Greenville, and Powdersville, South Carolina.

EXECUTIVES

President and CEO: J. Rodger Anthony, age 58, $135,592 pay
CFO: Jennifer M. Champagne, age 36
President, Cornerstone National Bank: Ben L. Garvin, age 59, $113,897 pay
Auditors: Elliott Davis LLC

LOCATIONS

HQ: Cornerstone Bancorp
1670 E. Main St., Easley, SC 29640
Phone: 864-306-1444   **Fax:** 864-306-1473
Web: www.cornerstonenatlbank.com

PRODUCTS/OPERATIONS

2004 Sales

	$ mil.	% of total
Interest		
Loans, including fees	4.0	75
Securities & other	0.6	11
Noninterest		
Mortgage loan origination fees	0.4	8
Dposit service fees & other	0.3	6
Total	**5.3**	**100**

COMPETITORS

First Citizens
Bancorporation

Peoples Bancorporation
South Financial

HISTORICAL FINANCIALS

Company Type: Private

Income Statement

FYE: December 31

	ASSETS ($ mil.)	NET INCOME ($ mil.)	INCOME AS % OF ASSETS	EMPLOYEES
12/04	101	1	0.7%	31
12/03	85	0	0.5%	30
12/02	67	0	0.3%	27
Annual Growth	22.8%	87.1%	—	7.2%

2004 Year-End Financials

Equity as % of assets: 8.7%
Return on assets: 0.8%
Return on equity: 8.3%

Long-term debt ($ mil.): —
Sales ($ mil.): 5

Net Income History

0.7
0.6
0.5
0.4
0.3
0.2
0.1
0

12/95 12/96 12/97 12/98 12/99 12/00 12/01 12/02 12/03 12/04

Corporation for Public Broadcasting

This organization is made possible by a grant from the federal government and by support from viewers like you. The Corporation for Public Broadcasting (CPB) is a private, not-for-profit corporation (not a government agency) created by the federal government that receives appropriations from Congress to help fund programming for more than 1,000 member-owned stations of the Public Broadcasting Service, National Public Radio, Public Radio International, and other organizations. The organization's funding is

often a political hot potato (frequently a target of Republicans who are opposed to government funding of educational, informational, and cultural programming). CPB was created by Congress in 1967.

Contributions from CPB represent about 15% of public broadcasting's revenues. In 2005 a House subcommittee proposed eliminating within two years all federal money for the CPB starting with a 25% reduction in CPB's budget for 2006, from $400 million to $300 million, representing a rollback of money that Congress had promised in 2004. A national outcry followed, and the House subsequently voted to restore the $100 million cut. CPB has received additional funding that will keep it rolling through fiscal 2005.

Also in 2005 former Republican National Committee co-chairwoman Patricia Harrison became CEO of CPB. Harrison's appointment was criticized on the grounds that she will inject partisanship into the CPB. The decision comes on the heels of inquiries into chairman Kenneth Tomlinson's possible partisan interference within the agency. Tomlinson, a Republican, has pressed public television to correct what he considers a liberal bias.

HISTORY

As commercial radio began to fill the radio dial, the FCC in 1945 reserved 20 channels from 88 FM to 92 FM for noncommercial, educational broadcasts. The first public television station started broadcasting in 1953, and by 1965 there were 124 public TV stations across the country. To help allocate government funds to these public TV and radio stations, Congress created the Corporation for Public Broadcasting (CPB) in 1967. CPB created the Public Broadcasting Service (PBS) in 1969 and National Public Radio (NPR) in 1970.

CPB has always been politically controversial; critics have often charged it with elitism, cultural bias, and liberalism. When Republicans gained control of Congress in 1994, their laundry list of grievances included government cultural spending. They were foiled in their effort to eliminate funding for CPB, however, in part because of public support for public television. Congress still cut funding by $100 million, forcing CPB to reduce its staff by almost 25% and introduce performance criteria for stations seeking grant money, including listenership and community financial support minimums.

Robert Coonrod was promoted to CEO in 1997. The following year Congress approved additional funding to help public television's transition from analog to digital broadcasting. Frank Cruz was appointed chairman of CPB in 1999. At about the same time, increased funding for 2003 (funding is approved two years in advance) was threatened when it was discovered that some PBS stations were giving their mailing lists to the Democratic party for fundraising purposes. Nevertheless, funding for CPB was increased in the 2001 budget.

In late 2001 businesswoman Katherine Milner Anderson was voted in as chairman, taking over for Cruz (who remained on the board). After serving two consecutive terms as chairman, Anderson was replaced by veteran journalist Kenneth Y. Tomlinson in 2003.

CPB's funding was approved at $350 million for 2002 and $365 million for 2003. Funding was approved through 2003 despite a 1999 investigation that revealed some PBS stations had given their mailing lists to the Democratic party for fundraising purposes.

In 2004 Coonrod left the company. Former COO Kathleen Cox and CPB agreed to a one-year contract for her to serve as president and chief executive officer. After nine months she left the post. Former Republican National Committee co-chairwoman Patricia Harrison became CEO in 2005.

EXECUTIVES

Chair: Cheryl Halpern
Vice Chair: Gay Hart Gaines
President and CEO: Patricia S. (Pat) Harrison
EVP and Senior Adviser to the President:
  Frederick L. DeMarco
SVP and General Counsel:
  H. Westwood (West) Smithers Jr.
SVP Business Affairs: Steven J. Altman
SVP Corporate and Public Affairs:
  Nancy Risque Rohrbach
SVP Educational Programming and Services:
  Peggy O'Brien
SVP Media: Andrew L. Russell
SVP Radio: Vincent Curren
SVP Television Programming: Michael Pack
VP Finance and Administration and Treasurer:
  David Creekmore
VP Legal and Regulatory Affairs and General Counsel:
  Donna Coleman Gregg
VP Media Strategies: Terry Bryant
VP Television Program Development: John Prizer
Corporate Secretary: Teresa Safon
Ombudsmen: Ken A. Bode
Ombudsmen: William Schulz
Corporate and Public Affairs: Michael Levy
Auditors: Deloitte & Touche LLP

LOCATIONS

HQ: Corporation for Public Broadcasting
  401 9th St., Northwest, Washington, DC 20004
Phone: 202-879-9600   **Fax:** 202-879-9700
Web: www.cpb.org

PRODUCTS/OPERATIONS

Selected Affiliations

American Public Television
  (programs for public television)
The Annenberg/CPB Projects (telecourses
  and education programs)
Association of America's Public Television Stations
  (organization of public TV stations)
Independent Television Service (independent creative
  programming for public TV)
National Public Radio (radio programming distribution)
Public Broadcasting Service (TV distribution)
Public Radio International
  (international radio distribution)

HISTORICAL FINANCIALS

Company Type: Not-for-profit

Income Statement

FYE: September 30

	REVENUE ($ mil.)	NET INCOME ($ mil.)	NET PROFIT MARGIN	EMPLOYEES
9/03	426	—	—	100
9/02	400	—	—	100
9/01	398	—	—	110
9/00	384	—	—	100
9/99	283	—	—	90
9/98	285	—	—	90
9/97	282	—	—	90
9/96	296	—	—	85
9/95	286	—	—	95
9/94	275	—	—	100
Annual Growth	**5.0%**	**—**	**—**	**0.0%**

Revenue History

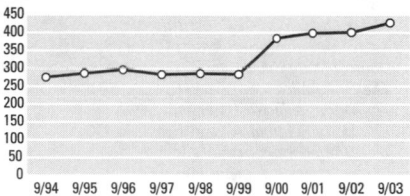

450
400
350
300
250
200
150
100
50
0

9/94 9/95 9/96 9/97 9/98 9/99 9/00 9/01 9/02 9/03

Cox Enterprises

The Cox family has been working at this enterprise for more than 100 years. One of the largest media conglomerates in the US, family-owned Cox Enterprises publishes 17 daily newspapers (including *The Atlanta Journal-Constitution*) and about 25 weeklies and shoppers and owns 15 TV stations through Cox Television. It also owns Cox Communications (which was a public company until a Cox Enterprises buyout in late 2004), one of the US's largest cable systems with more than 6.6 million subscribers in about 22 states. Other operations include 62% of Cox Radio, owner of about 80 radio stations; Manheim, which sells 10 million vehicles through auctions worldwide; and a majority stake in AutoTrader.com.

While Cox Communications is the company's biggest revenue generator (55% of sales), Cox Enterprises has been spending a lot of money and time driving on the information superhighway. AutoTrader.com, which the company operates in conjunction with Manheim, is one of the few profitable Internet companies. Manheim is the world's largest used-car auctioneer and the combination of the businesses has proved lucrative for Cox Enterprises.

Fed up with the demands of running a publicly traded cable company, Cox Enterprises in 2004 bought the 38% of Cox Communications that it didn't already own for $8.5 billion. The move gives Cox Enterprises complete control over its cable systems as it offers more and more broadband Internet services, VoIP (Voice over Internet Protocol) digital telephone services, and digital video recorders and related entertainment-on-demand services.

Barbara Cox Anthony (mother of chairman and CEO James Kennedy) and Anne Cox Chambers, daughters of founder James Cox, control 98% of the company. The sisters were recently ranked high on *Forbes'* list of the richest Americans.

HISTORY

James Middleton Cox, who dropped out of school in 1886 at 16, had worked as a teacher, reporter, and congressional secretary before buying the *Dayton Daily News* in 1898. After acquiring the nearby *Springfield Press-Republican* in 1905, he took up politics, serving two terms in the US Congress (1909-1913) and three terms as Ohio governor (1913-1915; 1917-1921). He even ran for president in 1920 (his running mate was future President Franklin Roosevelt) but lost to rival Ohio publisher Warren G. Harding.

Once out of politics, Cox began building his media empire. He bought the *Miami Daily News* in 1923 and founded WHIO (Dayton, Ohio's first

---

radio station). He bought Atlanta's WSB ("Welcome South, Brother"), the South's first radio station, in 1939 and added WSB-FM and WSB-TV, the South's first FM and TV stations, in 1948. Cox founded Dayton's first FM and TV stations (WHIO-FM and WHIO-TV) the next year, and *The Atlanta Constitution* joined his collection in 1950. Cox died in 1957.

The company continued to expand its broadcasting interests in the late 1950s and early 1960s. It was one of the first major broadcasting companies to expand into cable TV when it purchased a system in Lewistown, Pennsylvania, in 1962. The Cox family's broadcast properties were placed in publicly held Cox Broadcasting in 1964. Two years later its newspapers were placed into privately held Cox Enterprises, and the cable holdings became publicly held Cox Cable Communications. The broadcasting arm diversified, buying Manheim Services (auto auctions, 1968), Kansas City Automobile Auction (1969), and TeleRep (TV ad sales, 1972).

Cox Cable had 500,000 subscribers in nine states when it rejoined Cox Broadcasting in 1977. Cox Broadcasting was renamed Cox Communications in 1982, and the Cox family took the company private again in 1985, combining it with Cox Enterprises. James Kennedy, grandson of founder James Cox, became chairman and CEO in 1987.

Expansion became the keyword for Cox in the 1990s. The company merged its Manheim unit with the auto auction business of Ford Motor Credit and GE Capital in 1991. It also formed Sprint Spectrum in 1994, a partnership with Sprint, TCI (now part of AT&T), and Comcast to bundle telephone, cable TV, and other communications services (Sprint bought out Cox in 1999). Then, in one of its biggest transactions, Cox bought Times Mirror's cable TV operations for $2.3 billion in 1995 and combined them with its own cable system into a new, publicly traded company called Cox Communications. The following year it spun off its radio holdings into a public company called Cox Radio.

To expand its online presence, the company formed Cox Interactive Media in 1996, establishing a series of city Web sites and making a host of investments in various Internet companies, including Career Path, ExciteHome, iVillage, MP3.com, and Tickets.com. Cox also applied the online strategy to its automobile auction businesses, establishing AutoTrader.com in 1998 and placing the Internet operations of Manheim Auctions (now just Manheim) into a new company, Manheim Interactive, in 2000.

In 2002 Cox dropped plans to expand its local Internet city guide business nationwide and moved its Interactive Media operations to other parts of the company. Two years later, Cox bought the 38% of Cox Communications that it didn't already own for $8.5 billion, thus ending the cable subsidiary's status as a public company.

EXECUTIVES

**Chairman and CEO; Chairman, Cox Communications
  and Cox Radio:** James C. Kennedy, age 57
Vice Chairman: David E. Easterly, age 61
President, COO, and Director: G. Dennis Berry, age 60
EVP: Jimmy W. Hayes, age 52
EVP, CFO, and Director: Robert C. (Bob) O'Leary,
  age 66
SVP Administration: Timothy W. Hughes, age 61
SVP Public Policy: Alexander V. Netchvolodoff, age 68
VP and CIO: Gregory B. Morrison, age 45
VP and General Tax Counsel: Preston B. Barnett, age 58
VP and Treasurer: Richard J. Jacobson, age 48

VP Business Development: Sanford (Sandy) Schwartz, age 52
VP Development: Richard D. (Dick) Huguley, age 57
VP Development: Lacey Lewis
VP Direct Marketing and Database Management: Tom Whitfield, age 48
VP Human Resources: Marybeth H. Leamer, age 48
VP Legal Affairs, General Counsel, and Secretary: Andrew A. Merdek, age 54
VP Marketing: John C. Williams, age 56

LOCATIONS

HQ: Cox Enterprises, Inc.
6205 Peachtree Dunwoody Rd., Atlanta, GA 30328
Phone: 678-645-0000   **Fax:** 678-645-1079
Web: www.coxenterprises.com

PRODUCTS/OPERATIONS

2004 Sales

	$ mil.	% of total
Cable TV	6,400	55
Auctions	2,400	21
Newspapers	1,400	12
TV stations	694	6
Radio stations	438	4
Internet auto classifieds	190	2
Adjustments	30	—
Total	**11,552**	**100**

Selected Operations

Cox Broadcasting
Cox Television
Harrington, Righter & Parsons (TV ad sales)
MMT Sales (TV ad sales)
TeleRep (TV ad sales)
Television Stations
KAME (Reno, NV; UPN)
KFOX (El Paso, TX; FOX)
KICU (San Francisco/San Jose, CA; Independent)
KIRO (Seattle, CA; CBS)
KRXI (Reno, NV; FOX)
KTVU (Oakland/San Francisco, CA; FOX)
PCNC (cable channel, Pittsburgh, Independent)
UPN 17 (cable channel; Dayton, OH; UPN)
WAXN (Charlotte, NC; Independent)
WFTV (Orlando, FL; ABC)
WHIO (Dayton, OH; CBS)
WJAC (Johnstown, PA; NBC)
WPXI (Pittsburgh, NBC)
WRDQ (Orlando, FL; Independent)
WSB-TV (Atlanta, ABC)
WSOC (Charlotte, NC; ABC)
WTOV (Steubenville, OH; NBC)
Cox Communications (cable television systems)
Cox Radio (62%)
Atlanta (WBTS-FM, WSB-AM, WSB-FM)
Birmingham, AL (WBHJ-FM, WBHK-FM, WZZK-FM)
Bridgeport/New Haven, CT (WEZN-FM)
Dayton, OH (WHIO-AM, WHKO-FM)
Greenville/Spartanburg, SC (WJMZ-FM)
Honolulu (KRTR-FM, KXME-FM)
Houston (KLDE-FM)
Jacksonville (WAPE-FM, WFYV-FM, WKQL-FM)
Long Island, NY (WBAB-FM, WBLI-FM)
Louisville, KY (WRKA-FM, WVEZ-FM)
Miami (WEDR-FM, WHQT-FM)
New Haven, CT (WPLR-FM)
Orlando, FL (WHTQ-FM, WWKA-FM)
Richmond, VA (WKLR-FM)
San Antonio (KCYY-FM, KISS-FM, KONO-FM)
Stamford/Norwalk, CT (WEFX-FM, WNLK-AM)
Tampa (WDUV-FM, WWRM-FM)
Tulsa, OK (KRAV-FM, KRMG-AM, KRTQ-FM, KWEN-FM)

Cox Newspapers
Daily Newspapers
The Atlanta Journal-Constitution
Austin American-Statesman (Texas)
Dayton Daily News (Ohio)
The Daily Advance (Elizabeth City, NC)
The Daily Reflector (Greenville, NC)
The Daily Sentinel (Grand Junction, CO)
The Daily Sentinel (Nacogdoches, TX)
Longview News-Journal (Texas)
The Lufkin Daily News (Texas)
The Middleton Journal (Ohio)
News Messenger (Marshall, TX)
Palm Beach Daily News (Florida)
The Palm Beach Post (Florida)
Rocky Mount Telegram (North Carolina)
Springfield News Sun (Ohio)
Waco Tribune-Herald (Texas)
Cox Custom Media (commercial newsletters)
PAGAS Mailing Services
SP Newsprint (33%)
Trader Publishing (50%, classified advertising)
Valpack (direct mail advertisements)
Manheim
Manheim Interactive (online auto auctions)
AutoTrader.com (majority owned, online auto sales)
Sports Teams
Atlanta Beat (women's professional soccer)
San Diego Spirit (women's professional soccer)

COMPETITORS

Advance Publications	Hearst
Austin Chronicle	Knight-Ridder
Belo	Media General
Clear Channel	Morris Communications
Columbus Fair Auto	New York Times
Auction	News Corp.
Comcast	Ticketmaster
Disney	Time Warner Cable
Dow Jones	Tribune
E. W. Scripps	Viacom
Gannett	Washington Post

HISTORICAL FINANCIALS

Company Type: Private

Income Statement
FYE: December 31

	REVENUE ($ mil.)	NET INCOME ($ mil.)	NET PROFIT MARGIN	EMPLOYEES
12/04	11,552	—	—	77,000
12/03	10,700	—	—	77,000
12/02	9,900	—	—	77,000
12/01	8,693	—	—	76,000
12/00	7,824	—	—	74,000
12/99	6,097	—	—	61,000
12/98	5,355	—	—	55,500
12/97	4,936	—	—	50,000
12/96	4,591	—	—	43,000
12/95	3,806	—	—	38,000
Annual Growth	**13.1%**	—	—	**8.2%**

Revenue History

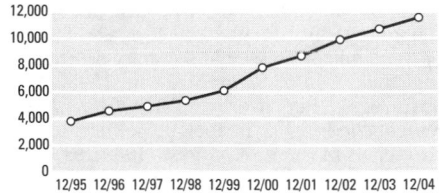

Coyotes Hockey

The desert heat hasn't stopped Arizona hockey fans from howling for more. Coyotes Hockey owns and operates the Phoenix Coyotes professional hockey franchise, which draws respectable crowds at home despite a downward trend in wins over the past few seasons. A group led by developer Steve Ellman and hockey great Wayne Gretzky owns the club, which moved into the $220 million Glendale Arena (built by Ellman's development company) in 2003. The team began playing in 1972 as the Winnipeg Jets in the fledgling World Hockey League. Since joining the National Hockey League in 1979, it has made 14 playoff appearances but has yet to capture the Stanley Cup.

Richard Burke and Steven Gluckstern bought the Jets in 1996 and moved the failing franchise to Phoenix. (Gluckstern sold his share to Burke in 1998 and bought the New York Islanders.) Ellman and Gretzky (the Great One), along with trucking magnate Jerry Moyes, later bought the franchise for $125 million in 2001.

EXECUTIVES

Chairman and Governor: Steve Ellman
President and COO: Douglas (Doug) Moss
SEVP Hockey Operations: Cliff Fletcher
General Manager and Alternate Governor: Michael Barnett
Head Coach: Wayne Gretzky
SVP and Chief Marketing Officer: Mike Bucek
SVP and General Manager, Glendale Arena: Ron Woodbridge
SVP Corporate Sales: Dave Groff
SVP Finance and Administration: Vaibhav Gupta
VP and Controller: Joe Leibfried
VP Communications: Richard Nairn
Director of Community Relations, Publicity and Managing, and Coyotes Charities: Barb Kozuh
Director of Human Resources: Julie Atherton
General Counsel: Bob Kaufman

LOCATIONS

HQ: Coyotes Hockey, LLC
9375 E. Bell Rd., Scottsdale, AZ 85260
Phone: 480-473-5600   **Fax:** 480-473-5699
Web: www.phoenixcoyotes.com

The Phoenix Coyotes play at the 17,500-seat capacity Glendale Arena in Glendale, Arizona.

COMPETITORS

Dallas Stars	Mighty Ducks
Los Angeles Kings	San Jose Sharks

HISTORICAL FINANCIALS

Company Type: Private

Income Statement
FYE: June 30

	REVENUE ($ mil.)	NET INCOME ($ mil.)	NET PROFIT MARGIN	EMPLOYEES
6/04	57	—	—	—
6/03	43	—	—	—
6/02	42	—	—	—
6/01	39	—	—	—
6/00	42	—	—	—
6/99	43	—	—	—
6/98	41	—	—	120
6/97	30	—	—	—
6/96	21	—	—	—
Annual Growth	**13.6%**	—	—	—

Revenue History

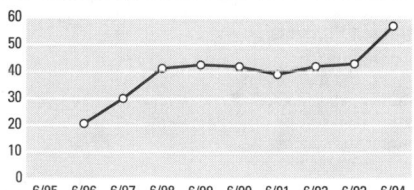

2004 Year-End Financials

Debt ratio: (39.2%) Current ratio: 0.80
Return on equity: — Long-term debt ($ mil.): 1
Cash ($ mil.): 1

Net Income History

PRODUCTS/OPERATIONS

2004 Sales

	$ mil.	% of total
Liner services	632.3	63
Oil & chemical distribution & transportation services	213.4	21
Energy & marine services	79.0	8
Ship assist & escort services	75.0	8
Total	**999.7**	**100**

Major Subsidiaries

Crowley Liner Services, Inc.
Crowley Logistics Inc.
Crowley Marine Services, Inc.
Crowley Petroleum Transport, Inc.
Marine Transport Corporation
Vessel Management Services, Inc.

Crocs

Though they don't promise protection if you encounter the real thing, Crocs and its trademark slip-on shoes are quickly gaining popularity in the watersports arena. The shoes, sold under the crocs brand name, are made of its proprietary closed-cell resin and are renowned for their comfort. The company operates manufacturing facilities in China and Mexico, as well as Italy and Canada and distributes through retailers including Dillard's, Nordstrom, REI, and The Sports Authority. Crocs' shoes, designed for men, women, and children, feature a rear handle and are sold in 17 different colors. The company is aggressively expanding on both domestic and international fronts.

EXECUTIVES

Chairman: Richard L. Sharp, age 58
President, CEO and Director: Ronald R. (Ron) Snyder, age 48
CFO and Treasurer: Caryn D. Ellison, age 53
VP, Asian and Australian Operations: John C. McCarvel, age 49
VP, Manufacturing: Lyndon V. (Duke) Hanson III, age 43
VP, Sales and Marketing: Michael C. Margolis, age 54
Auditors: Deloitte & Touche LLP

LOCATIONS

HQ: Crocs, Inc.
  6273 Monarch Park Place, Niwot, CO 80503
Phone: 303-468-4260 **Fax:** 303-468-4266
Web: www.crocs.com

COMPETITORS

adidas-Salomon
Birkenstock
Columbia Sportswear
Deckers Outdoor
L.L. Bean
NIKE
R. Griggs
Timberland
Wolverine World Wide

HISTORICAL FINANCIALS

Company Type: Private

Income Statement

FYE: December 31

	REVENUE ($ mil.)	NET INCOME ($ mil.)	NET PROFIT MARGIN	EMPLOYEES
12/04	14	(2)	—	260
12/03	1	(1)	—	—
12/02	0	(0)	—	8
Annual Growth	—	—	—	470.1%

Crowley Maritime

Crowley Maritime has pushed and pulled its way into prominence as one of the largest tug and barge operators in the world. The company's Liner Services unit provides scheduled transportation of containers, trailers, and other cargo, mainly between ports in the US, the Caribbean, and Latin America, plus logistics services. Other Crowley Maritime units transport oil and chemical products and oil field equipment and provide ship escort services. Besides tugs and barges, the company's fleet of some 265 vessels includes roll-on/roll-off vessels, tank ships, and oil spill cleanup vessels. Chairman and CEO Thomas Crowley (grandson of the founder), his family, and employees own the company, which was founded in 1892.

EXECUTIVES

Chairman and CEO: Thomas B. (Tom) Crowley Jr., age 38
Vice Chairman and EVP: William A. Pennella, age 59
SVP and Controller: John Calvin, age 45
SVP and General Counsel: William P. Verdon, age 63
SVP and General Manager, Latin America Services: John Hourihan
SVP and General Manager, Petroleum Transportation and Distribution: Rockwell (Rocky) Smith
SVP and General Manager, Ship Assist and Escort Services and Energy and Marine Services: John Douglass
SVP Administration: Susan Rodgers, age 55
SVP and General Manager, Logistics: Rinus Schepen
Corporate Secretary: Bruce Love
Director Human Resources: Bryan R. Lee
Director Corporate Communications: Mark Miller
Auditors: Deloitte & Touche LLP

LOCATIONS

HQ: Crowley Maritime Corporation
  155 Grand Ave., Oakland, CA 94612
Phone: 510-251-7500 **Fax:** 510-251-7788
Web: www.crowley.com

COMPETITORS

A.P. Møller — Mærsk
APL
APL Logistics
Exel plc
Foss Maritime
Horizon Lines
Hornbeck Offshore
K-Sea Transportation
Maritrans
Sea Star Line
Seabulk
SEACOR
Tidewater
Trailer Bridge
UPS Supply Chain Solutions
U.S. Shipping

HISTORICAL FINANCIALS

Company Type: Private

Income Statement

FYE: December 31

	REVENUE ($ mil.)	NET INCOME ($ mil.)	NET PROFIT MARGIN	EMPLOYEES
12/04	1,000	25	2.5%	4,268
12/03	978	13	1.3%	4,000
12/02	978	17	1.8%	3,913
12/01	1,001	20	2.0%	3,800
12/00	799	20	2.5%	5,000
12/99	775	—	—	3,300
12/98	1,100	—	—	5,000
12/97	1,100	—	—	5,000
12/96	1,100	—	—	5,000
12/95	1,100	—	—	5,000
Annual Growth	(1.1%)	5.2%	—	(1.7%)

2004 Year-End Financials

Debt ratio: 116.8% Current ratio: 1.80
Return on equity: 8.9% Long-term debt ($ mil.): 341
Cash ($ mil.): 143

Net Income History

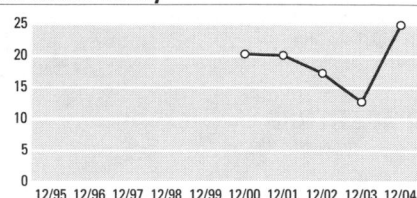

Crown Equipment

The jewels in the crown of Crown Equipment Corporation are electric heavy-duty lift trucks used for maneuvering goods in warehouses and distribution centers. A market leader, the company's products include narrow-aisle stacking equipment, powered pallet trucks, order-picking equipment, and forklift trucks. Its equipment can move four-ton loads and stack pallets nearly 45 feet high. Crown Equipment sells its products globally through retailers. The company, founded in 1945 by brothers Carl and Allen Dicke, originally made temperature controls for coal furnaces. It began making material-handling equipment in the 1950s. The Dicke family still controls Crown Equipment.

Crown offers customers a wide range of electric fork lift trucks (from hand pallet trucks to very narrow-aisle (VNA) turret trucks) and extensive maintenance and repair services through its global dealer network.

EXECUTIVES

Chairman Emeritus: James F. Dicke
Chairman and CEO: James F. Dicke II, age 59
President: James F. Dicke III, age 34
SVP: Donald E. Luebrecht
SVP: James D. Moran
VP and General Counsel: John G. Maxa
VP, Engineering: Timothy S. Quellhorst
VP, Finance: Kent W. Spille
VP, Human Resources: Randy W. Niekamp
VP, Information Services: Mark A. Manuel
Corporate Controller: Craig Seitz
Publicity Administrator: David Helmstetter
Auditors: Deloitte & Touche

LOCATIONS

HQ: Crown Equipment Corporation
44 S. Washington St., New Bremen, OH 45869
Phone: 419-629-2311   **Fax:** 419-629-2900
Web: www.crown.com

Crown Equipment has 77 factory-owned sales and service facilities and more than 160 independent dealers worldwide.

PRODUCTS/OPERATIONS

Selected Products
Counterbalanced trucks
Hand pallet trucks
Narrow-aisle reach trucks
Rider pallet trucks
Stockpickers
Tow tractors
Very narrow-aisle turret trucks
Walkie pallet trucks
Walkie stackers

COMPETITORS

Caterpillar
Jungheinrich
Komatsu
Linde Material Handling
NACCO Industries
Toyota Material Handling

HISTORICAL FINANCIALS

Company Type: Private

Income Statement

FYE: March 31

	REVENUE ($ mil.)	NET INCOME ($ mil.)	NET PROFIT MARGIN	EMPLOYEES
3/04	1,090	—	—	6,900
3/03	1,000	—	—	6,800
3/02	966	—	—	6,500
3/01	1,127	—	—	7,290
3/00	1,010	—	—	6,510
3/99	968	—	—	6,440
3/98	855	—	—	6,050
3/97	781	—	—	5,975
3/96	707	—	—	5,800
3/95	607	—	—	5,000
Annual Growth	**6.7%**	**—**	**—**	**3.6%**

Revenue History

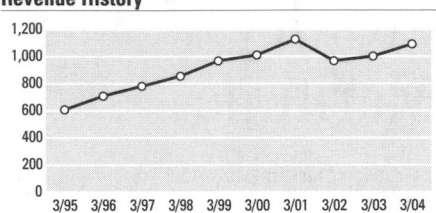

Culligan

"Hey Culligan Man!" To be sure, the phrase made famous by an ad campaign still rings in the ears of Culligan International workers. Formerly a subsidiary of Veolia Environnement, Culligan produces filters for tap water, household water softeners, microfiltration products, desalination systems, and portable deionization services for commercial and industrial users. The franchised "Culligan Man" noted in the advertising phrase delivers bottled water and water systems to consumers and businesses throughout the US and in more than 90 other countries. Besides Culligan, the company's brand names include Everpure, Elga, and Bruner. Buyout firm Clayton, Dubilier & Rice acquired the company for $610 million in 2004.

EXECUTIVES

Chairman: George W. Tamke, age 57
CEO: Mark Seals
COO: Mike Kachmer
CFO: Joe Morrison
VP Sales: Larry Holzman
VP Human Resources: Wayne Bosch

LOCATIONS

HQ: Culligan International Company
1 Culligan Pkwy., Northbrook, IL 60062
Phone: 847-205-6000   **Fax:** 847-205-6030
Web: www.culligan.com

Culligan has offices in more than 100 countries in Africa, the Americas, Asia, and Europe.

PRODUCTS/OPERATIONS

Selected Products
Bottled water
Commercial dealkalizers
Commercial deionizers
Commercial reverse osmosis systems
Counter top systems
Drinking water systems
Faucet mount systems
Household filters
Replacement filter cartridges
Softeners

COMPETITORS

AquaCell	Millipore
BRITA	Pall
Calgon Carbon	Procter & Gamble
CUNO	USFilter
GE Infrastructure	

HISTORICAL FINANCIALS

Company Type: Private

Income Statement

FYE: June 30

	REVENUE ($ mil.)	NET INCOME ($ mil.)	NET PROFIT MARGIN	EMPLOYEES
6/04	718	—	—	5,500

Cumberland Farms

Once a one-cow dairy, Cumberland Farms now owns more than 1,100 outlets, operating about 650 convenience stores (three-fourths of which sell gasoline) in 11 eastern seaboard states from Maine to Florida. The company has its own grocery distribution and bakery operations to supply its stores. Cumberland owns a two-thirds limited partnership in petroleum wholesaler Gulf Oil, giving it the right to use and license Gulf trademarks in Delaware, New Jersey, New York, most of Ohio, Pennsylvania, and the New England states. The first convenience-store operator in New England, Cumberland was founded in 1938 by Vasilios and Aphrodite Haseotes. The Haseotes' children, including CEO Lily Haseotes Bentas, own the company.

EXECUTIVES

Chairman, President, and CEO: Lily Haseotes Bentas
EVP and COO: Harry J. Brenner
SVP and CFO: Stephen Winslow
SVP, Retail Operations: Daniel D. Phaneuf
VP, Information Technology: John Carroll
VP, Human Resources: Foster G. Macrides
VP, Marketing: Alvin (Al) McKay
VP, Wholesale Petroleum: George P. Haseotes
Controller: Kevin Johnson
Senior Corporate Recruiter: Stephen Dolinich
Manager, Training Systems and Development:
Sheree Beissner
Manager, Fleet Administration: Edward Potkay
Administrative Secretary: Debra Sprout

LOCATIONS

HQ: Cumberland Farms, Inc.
777 Dedham St., Canton, MA 02021
Phone: 781-828-4900 **Fax:** 781-828-9624
Web: www.cumberlandfarms.com

Cumberland Farms operates about 650 convenience stores in Connecticut, Delaware, Florida, Maine, Massachusetts, New Hampshire, New Jersey, New York, Pennsylvania, Rhode Island, and Vermont.

COMPETITORS

7-Eleven	Golub
BP	Motiva Enterprises
Chevron	Racetrac Petroleum
DeMoulas Super Markets	Sheetz
Exxon Mobil	Stewart's Shops
Gate Petroleum	Wawa, Inc.
Getty Realty	

HISTORICAL FINANCIALS

Company Type: Private

Income Statement

FYE: September 30

	REVENUE ($ mil.)	NET INCOME ($ mil.)	NET PROFIT MARGIN	EMPLOYEES
9/04	2,100	—	—	7,000
9/03	2,000	—	—	6,976
9/02	1,700	—	—	6,976
9/01	1,500	—	—	6,545
9/00	950	—	—	6,200
9/99	1,140	—	—	6,900
9/98	1,387	—	—	6,800
9/97	1,469	—	—	7,100
9/96	1,396	—	—	7,100
9/95	1,321	—	—	7,200
Annual Growth	**5.3%**	**—**	**—**	**(0.3%)**

Revenue History

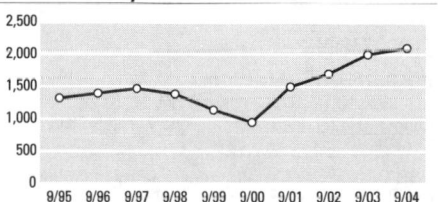

CUNA Mutual

CUNA would soonah eat tuna than make its products available to banks. CUNA Mutual offers the more than 9,500 credit unions in the US (as well as those in 30 other countries) a range of products and services, including life insurance, investment advisory, and information technology. Entities that make up the group include CUNA Mutual Insurance Society (accident, health, and life insurance) and CUNA Mutual Mortgage Corporation (mortgage loan origination, purchasing, and servicing). The group also offers customers such technology services as Web site enhancement and automated lending software. CUNA Mutual was founded in 1935 by pioneers of the credit union movement and is owned by its credit union policyholders.

CUNA Mutual is selling CUNA Mutual Mortgage to PHH Mortgage in what promises to be the first in a series of restructuring moves for the company.

CFO Jeff Holley temporarily moved into CUNA Mutual's CEO office in 2004 after Mike Kitchen resigned under pressure in relation to allegations of anti-labor union activity. In early 2005 the company brought on Jeff Post to serve as its new CEO.

EXECUTIVES

Chairman: Loretta M. Burd
Vice Chairman: Eldon R. Arnold
President, CEO, and Director: Jeff Post
EVP and CFO: Jeffrey D. (Jeff) Holley
EVP and Chief Administrative Officer: David Lundgren
EVP, Sales: Robert Trunzo
SVP, Corporate Strategy and Transition: David Sargent
SVP, Human Resources: Keith Williams
VP, Corporate Credit Union Relations: Dan Kavanaugh
Regional VP, Member-Solutions Group: Mark Wilson
CTO: Rick R. Roy
Chief Sales and Marketing Officer: Jim Gowan
Assistant VP, Public Relations: Sydney Lindner
Auditors: Deloitte & Touche LLP

LOCATIONS

HQ: CUNA Mutual Group
5910 Mineral Point Rd., Madison, WI 53701
Phone: 608-238-5851
Web: www.cunamutual.com

CUNA Mutual has offices in Rancho Cucamonga, California; Madison, Wisconsin (headquarters); and Waverly, Iowa.

PRODUCTS/OPERATIONS

2004 Sales

	$ mil.	% of total
Life & health premiums	1,213	49
Property/casualty premiums	525	21
Net investment income	374	15
Other	369	15
Total	**2,481**	**100**

Selected Subsidiaries and Affiliates

CMG Mortgage Insurance Co.
CUMIS Insurance Society, Inc. (property/casualty)
CUNA Mutual Insurance Society
CUNA Mutual Life Insurance Company
CUNA Mutual Mortgage Corp.
Members Life Insurance Co.

COMPETITORS

BISYS	PrimeVest
Certegy	SEI
Online Resources	U.S. Central

HISTORICAL FINANCIALS

Company Type: Mutual company

Income Statement

FYE: December 31

	ASSETS ($ mil.)	NET INCOME ($ mil.)	INCOME AS % OF ASSETS	EMPLOYEES
12/04	14,004	136	1.0%	6,000
12/03	12,885	134	1.0%	6,000
12/02	11,009	(9)	—	5,000
Annual Growth	**12.8%**	**—**	**—**	**9.5%**

2004 Year-End Financials

Equity as % of assets: —
Return on assets: 1.0%
Return on equity: —
Long-term debt ($ mil.): —
Sales ($ mil.): 2,481

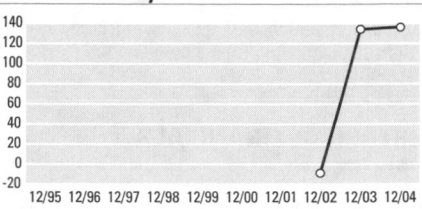

Cynosure

If famed bearded Lady Olga had been around today, she might have had a few more career options with the help of Cynosure. The company makes laser and pulsed-light devices used to perform non-invasive procedures to remove hair, treat varicose veins, and reduce the appearance of cellulite. Cynosure's 15 different systems are marketed under such names as Apogee, Cynergy, and PhotoGenica. The company, along with its six subsidiaries, sells its systems to doctors, health spas, and veterinarians in nearly 50 countries from sales offices located in more than 30 countries. North American sales, however, accounted for more than half of 2004 sales. Italian laser maker El. En. controls nearly 80% of the company.

EXECUTIVES

Chairman, President, and CEO: Michael R. Davin, age 47, $342,768 pay
COO: John T. Theroux, age 52, $129,423 pay (partial-year salary)
EVP, CFO, and Treasurer: Timothy W. Baker, age 44, $149,038 pay (partial-year salary)
EVP, Sales: Douglas J. Delaney, age 38, $425,114 pay (prior to title change)
SVP, International Sales: Kenji Shimizu, age 52
SVP, Medical Technology and Regulatory Affairs and Director: George Cho, age 61
VP, Marketing: Marina Kamenakis, age 46
VP, Operations: David Mackie, age 43
CTO: Rafael Sierra, age 55
Auditors: Ernst & Young LLP

LOCATIONS

HQ: Cynosure, Inc.
5 Carlisle Rd., Westford, MA 01886
Phone: 978-256-4200 **Fax:** 978-256-6556
Web: www.cynosurelaser.com

2004 Sales

	% of total
North America	55
Europe	24
Asia/Pacific	16
Other	5
Total	**100**

PRODUCTS/OPERATIONS

Selected Subsidiaries

Cynosure France
Cynosure GmbH (German)
Cynosure K.K. (Japan)
Cynosure UK Ltd.
Cynosure U.K. Ltd. Sucursal Espana (Spain)
Suzhou Cynosure Medical Devices Company Ltd. (China)

COMPETITORS

Candela Corporation
Cutera
Laserscope

Palomar Medical
PhotoMedex

HISTORICAL FINANCIALS

Company Type: Private

Income Statement

FYE: December 31

	REVENUE ($ mil.)	NET INCOME ($ mil.)	NET PROFIT MARGIN	EMPLOYEES
12/04	40	5	13.1%	178
12/03	27	(1)	—	155
12/02	23	(2)	—	138
Annual Growth	32.5%	—	—	13.6%

2004 Year-End Financials

Debt ratio: 3.3%
Return on equity: 48.3%
Cash ($ mil.): 4

Current ratio: 1.85
Long-term debt ($ mil.): 0

Net Income History

12/95 12/96 12/97 12/98 12/99 12/00 12/01 12/02 12/03 12/04

Cypress Communications

Cypress Communications Holding has undergone a transformation from an owner to a doer. The company, formerly U.S. RealTel, used to own and sublease telecommunications rights for properties in Argentina and Brazil. But with the acquisition of Cypress Communications in 2002, the company shuttered its Latin American operations and took on its subsidiary's business full-time — that of providing telecom services via in-building networks to small and midsized businesses. The company designs, installs, and operates broadband networks in more than 1,000 office buildings to more than 8,000 business customers nationwide. Cypress Holding has been acquired by an affiliate of investment firm Arcapita and taken private.

EXECUTIVES

Chairman: Ross J. Mangano, age 59
President, CEO, and Director:
  Gregory P. (Greg) McGraw
EVP and COO: Salvatore W. (Sam) Collura, age 50
EVP and CFO: Neal L. Miller
SVP and Chief Marketing Officer:
  Michael A. (Tony) Floyd
SVP Network Operations: Thomas J. (Tom) Francis
VP and Corporate Controller: Peter W. Pamplin
Director, Legal and Business Affairs: Deena Snipes
Auditors: Deloitte & Touche LLP

LOCATIONS

HQ: Cypress Communications Holding Co., Inc.
  15 Piedmont Center, Ste. 100, Atlanta, GA 30305
Phone: 404-869-2500   **Fax:** 404-869-2525
Web: www.cypresscom.net

Cypress Communications Holding Co., Inc. has operations in Atlanta; Birmingham, Alabama; Boston; Chicago; Dallas; Denver; Hartford, Connecticut; Houston; Indianapolis; Los Angeles and Orange County; Miami; Minneapolis; Nashville; New Orleans; New Jersey; New York; Orlando, Florida; Philadelphia; Phoenix; Pittsburgh; Portland, Oregon; San Francisco; Seattle; Tampa; and Washington, DC.

PRODUCTS/OPERATIONS

Selected Services

Data
  Colocation
  Dedicated connectivity
  Internet access
  Web conferencing
  Web site hosting
Voice
  Audio conferencing and Web conferencing
  Digital telephone system
  Integrated voicemail
  Local exchange access
  Long-distance
Other
  Bundled voice and data services (EZ Office Suite)
  Voice over Internet Protocol (VoIP)

COMPETITORS

ALLTEL
AT&T
BellSouth
Broadwing
Cbeyond
Cogent Communications Group
EarthLink
Eureka Networks

ICG Communications
Level 3 Communications
MCI
Qwest
SBC Communications
Sprint Nextel
Verizon
Vonage
Winstar
XO Communications

HISTORICAL FINANCIALS

Company Type: Private

Income Statement

FYE: December 31

	REVENUE ($ mil.)	NET INCOME ($ mil.)	NET PROFIT MARGIN	EMPLOYEES
12/04	79	0	0.5%	331
12/03	85	(4)	—	311
12/02	52	(2)	—	343
12/01	0	(8)	—	103
12/00	2	3	158.8%	—
Annual Growth	161.1%	(38.0%)	—	47.6%

2004 Year-End Financials

Debt ratio: —
Return on equity: —
Cash ($ mil.): 0

Current ratio: 0.37
Long-term debt ($ mil.): 10

Net Income History

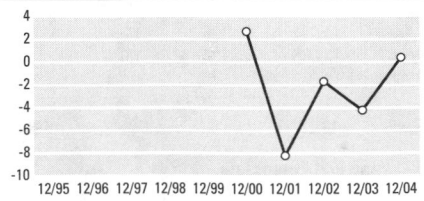

12/95 12/96 12/97 12/98 12/99 12/00 12/01 12/02 12/03 12/04

D&H Distributing

D&H Distributing sells more than 10,000 computer and electronics products to resellers nationwide. Clients include small and large resellers and retailers, system builders, and college bookstores. D&H also targets schools and government agencies. The company operates through divisions dedicated to academic resellers, campus bookstores, computer products, consumer electronics, elementary and secondary schools, government resellers, security products, and video games. Suppliers include Hewlett-Packard, Intel, and Microsoft. D&H has been employee-owned since 1999.

D&H was founded in 1918 as a tire retreader; the company entered the electronics business in 1926. Dave Schwab and Harry Spector were the original D&H.

EXECUTIVES

Chairman and CEO: Israel (Izzy) Schwab
President: Gary Brothers
EVP and Treasurer: James F. (Jimmy) Schwab
VP, Sales: Jeff Davis
VP and Controller: Robert J. Miller Jr.
VP, Marketing: Daniel (Dan) Schwab
VP, Purchasing: Michael (Mike) Schwab
Director, Credit and Financial Services: Joe Chaudoin
Director, Inside Sales: Pat Donavan
Director, Purchasing: Rob Eby
Director, Government Services Division: John Alifano
Manager, Home Entertainment and Security Products Division: Jeff Stevenson
Manager, National VAR Sales and Systems:
  Art Steinberg

LOCATIONS

HQ: D&H Distributing Co., Inc.
  2525 N. 7th St., Harrisburg, PA 17110
Phone: 717-236-8001   **Fax:** 717-255-7838
Web: www.dandh.com

D&H Distributing operates from facilities in California, Florida, Illinois, Pennsylvania, and Texas.

COMPETITORS

Agilysys
Arrow Electronics
ASI Corp.
Avnet
Elcom International
Electrograph Technologies
Ingram Micro
Merisel
New Age Electronics
Sayers Group
SED International
Sirius Computer Solutions
Solarcom
Supercom
Tech Data
ZT Group

HISTORICAL FINANCIALS

Company Type: Private

Income Statement

FYE: April 30

	ESTIMATED REVENUE ($ mil.)	NET INCOME ($ mil.)	NET PROFIT MARGIN	EMPLOYEES
4/04	1,070	—	—	618
4/03	857	—	—	550
4/02	760	—	—	—
4/01	637	—	—	—
4/00	643	—	—	400
4/99	620	—	—	400
4/98	600	—	—	360
4/97	550	—	—	400
4/96	490	—	—	400
4/95	430	—	—	375
Annual Growth	10.7%	—	—	5.7%

Revenue History

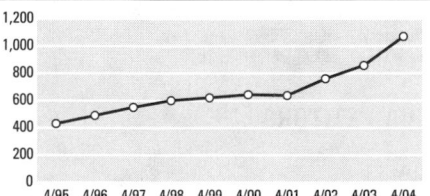

Dairy Farmers of America

The members of the Dairy Farmers of America (DFA) are partners in cream. DFA is one of the world's largest dairy cooperatives, with almost 22,000 members in 49 states. The co-op produces 33% of the US milk supply with an annual pool of about 57 billion pounds of milk. Along with fresh and shelf-stable fluid milk, the co-op also produces cheese, butter, and other products for industrial, wholesale, and retail customers worldwide. DFA is seeking strength by adding value-added products and seeking joint ventures to distribute its milk and milk-based food ingredients to wider regions.

While DFA is a major supplier to the #1 US milk processor, Dean Foods, it also owns half of what will likely become another US milk powerhouse, National Dairy Holdings. DFA's American Dairy Brands makes and markets Borden cheeses, and its Formulated Dairy Food Products group bottles up Starbucks' Frappuccino coffee drink. In addition, the co-op provides marketing, research and development, and legislative lobbying on behalf of its members.

American dairy farmers have had to come to terms with consolidation in the retail industry, dissolving government milk price supports, and increased foreign competition. To better compete with other dairy processors and soften the swings of the commodity markets, DFA has invested heavily in facilities and joint ventures to process its fluid milk into value-added products and high-end dairy-based ingredients.

DFA's sheer size makes it a frequent target of anti-trust investigations. Recent investigations sought to determine if the cooperative bullied farmers and smaller cooperatives to join it, and paid out below-market prices to its members.

HISTORY

Mid-America Dairymen (Mid-Am), the largest of the cooperatives that merged to form Dairy Farmers of America (DFA), was born in 1968. At that time, several Midwestern dairy co-ops banded together to attack common economic problems, such as reduced government subsidies, price drops resulting from a rising milk surplus, dealer consolidation, and improvements in production, processing, and packaging. The merging organizations — representing 15,000 dairy farmers — were Producers Creamery Company (Springfield, Missouri), Sanitary Milk Producers (St. Louis), Square Deal Milk Producers (Highland, Illinois), Mid-Am (Kansas City, Missouri), and Producers Creamery Company of Chillicothe (north central Missouri).

During the early 1970s Mid-Am struggled with internal restructuring. Most dairy farmers and co-ops were hit hard by the energy crisis and the government's decision to allow increased dairy imports in 1973, the same year the US Justice Department filed an antitrust suit against Mid-Am. (A judge cleared the co-op 12 years later.)

In 1974 Mid-Am lost almost $8 million on revenues of $625 million, chalked up to record-high feed prices, a weakened economy, a milk surplus, and a massive inventory loss. Co-op veteran Gary Hanman was named CEO that year. Over the next two years, Mid-Am cut costs, sold corporate frills, downsized management, and began marketing more of its own products under the Mid-America Farms label, thus reducing dependency on commodity sales.

Mid-Am expanded its research and development efforts throughout the 1980s. The co-op opened its services to farmers in California and New Mexico in 1993, and a series of mergers in 1994 and 1995 nearly doubled its size. In 1997 it purchased some of Borden's dairy operations, including rights to the valuable Elsie the Cow and Borden's trademarks.

Wary of falling milk prices, Mid-Am merged with Western Dairymen Cooperative, Milk Marketing, and the Southern Region of Associated Milk Producers at the end of 1997 to form DFA. Hanman moved into the seat of CEO at the new co-op. DFA began a series of joint ventures with the #1 US dairy processor, Suiza Foods.

DFA added California Gold (more than 330 farmers, 1998) and Independent Cooperative Milk Producers Association (730 dairy farmer members in Michigan and parts of Ohio and Indiana, 1999). In another joint venture with Suiza, in early 2000 DFA sold its 50% stake in the US's #3 fluid milk processor, Southern Foods, in exchange for 34% of a new company named Suiza Dairy Group.

After mollifying the government's antitrust fears, DFA acquired the butter operations of Sodial North America in mid-2000. It then molded all its butter businesses into a new entity, Keller's Creamery. However, another acquisition did not fare as well. In February 2000 DFA acquired controlling interest in Southern Belle Dairy only to have the merger challenged three years later by the Department of Justice. Arguing that the merger formed a monopoly in school milk sales in several states, the Department of Justice filed suit which a federal judge later dismissed.

During 2001 the cooperative went in with Land O'Lakes 50/50 to purchase a cheese plant from Kraft. Later in the year as Suiza Foods acquired Dean Foods (and took on its name), DFA sold back its stake in Suiza Dairy Group to the new Dean Foods. DFA then teamed up with a group of dairy investors to form a new 50/50 joint venture, National Dairy Holdings, which received 11 processing plants from Dean Foods as part of the exchange for Suiza Dairy.

Weak milk prices and a drop in demand during 2002 caused DFA's revenues to slide. DFA has typically grown by inviting smaller dairy co-ops to merge with it, including the Black Hills Milk Producers Cooperative in 2002. However, to better secure milk sources for its customers in the northeastern US, that same year DFA welcomed two regional co-ops, Dairylea and St. Albans, to join as members. The two co-ops remain as separate but affiliated organizations.

At the start of 2005 DFA acquired full ownership of what had been a joint venture in Keller's Creamery.

EXECUTIVES

Chairman: Tom Camerlo
President and CEO: Gary E. Hanman
COO and CEO, Dairylea: Richard P. (Rick) Smith
CFO: Gerald L. (Jerry) Bos
EVP: Donald H. (Don) Schriver
SVP: John I. Collins
SVP and COO, Southwest Area: David C. Jones
Corporate VP, Human Resources & Administration: Harold Papen
Corporate VP, Marketing and Economic Analysis: John J. Wilson
Corporate VP and Legal Counsel: David A. Geisler
VP, Communications and Public Relations: Agnes Schafer
VP, Quality Assurance and Regulatory Affairs: James F. (Jim) Carroll
VP and COO, Central Area: Randall S. (Randy) McGinnis
VP and COO, Western Area: David L. Parrish
President, American Dairy Brands and EVP, Dairy Food Products Group: Mark Korsmeyer
President, Dairy Food Products: Sam E. McCroskey
Market Information: Elvin Hollon
Member Relations: Melissa Lascon
Auditors: Deloitte & Touche LLP

LOCATIONS

HQ: Dairy Farmers of America, Inc.
10220 N. Ambassador Dr., Kansas City, MO 64153
Phone: 816-801-6455   **Fax:** 816-801-6456
Web: www.dfamilk.com

PRODUCTS/OPERATIONS

Selected Brands

Borden	Jacobo
Breakstone's	Keller's
CalPro	Mid-America Farms
Elsie	Sport Shake
Enricco	VitaCal
Golden Cheese	

Selected Products

Butter
Cheese dips
Cheeses
Coffee creamer
Condensed milk
Cream
Dehydrated dairy products
Infant formula
Nonfat dry milk powder
Shelf-stable nutritional beverages
Whey products

COMPETITORS

AMPI	Lactalis
Arla Foods	Land O'Lakes
California Dairies Inc.	Northwest Dairy
Darigold, Inc.	Parmalat
Dean Foods	Prairie Farms Dairy
Fonterra	Quality Chekd
Foremost Farms	Saputo
Glanbia	Schreiber Foods
Kraft Foods North America	Unilever

HISTORICAL FINANCIALS

Company Type: Cooperative

Income Statement
FYE: December 31

	REVENUE ($ mil.)	NET INCOME ($ mil.)	NET PROFIT MARGIN	EMPLOYEES
12/03	6,933	56	0.8%	4,000
12/02	6,448	50	0.8%	4,000
12/01	7,902	62	0.8%	4,000
12/00	6,586	39	0.6%	4,000
12/99	7,483	43	0.6%	5,000
12/98	7,284	70	1.0%	5,300
12/97	3,818	26	0.7%	5,300
12/96	4,085	17	0.4%	3,200
12/95	3,681	14	0.4%	3,100
12/94	2,491	12	0.5%	3,000
Annual Growth	12.0%	18.6%	—	3.2%

Net Income History

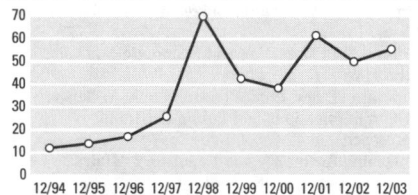

Dairylea Cooperative

Yes, the farmer takes a wife, then hi-ho, the dairy-o, the farmer takes membership in milk marketing organizations such as Dairylea Cooperative. Owned by more than 2,500 dairy farmers in the northeastern US, Dairylea markets 5.5 billion pounds of milk for its farmers annually to food manufacturers. Its Agri-Services holding company provides members with financial and farm management services as well as insurance. Its Empire Livestock unit operates a livestock auction market. Dairylea, a leading milk marketer in the Northeast, has a joint marketing venture with Dairy Farmers of America.

EXECUTIVES

Chairman and President: Clyde E. Rutherford
CEO: Richard P. (Rick) Smith
COO: Greg Wickham
VP, Finance and Administration: Edward Bangel
VP and Secretary: William Beeman
VP, Finance: Ellen Gall
Treasurer and Director: David R. Chamberlain
Director, Communications: Monica Coleman

LOCATIONS

HQ: Dairylea Cooperative Inc.
5001 Brittonfield Pkwy., East Syracuse, NY 13057
Phone: 315-433-0100   **Fax:** 315-433-2345
Web: www.dairylea.com

COMPETITORS

Agri-Mark
AMPI
Dairy Farmers of America
Foremost Farms
Land O'Lakes
Quality Chekd

HISTORICAL FINANCIALS

Company Type: Cooperative

Income Statement
FYE: March 31

	REVENUE ($ mil.)	NET INCOME ($ mil.)	NET PROFIT MARGIN	EMPLOYEES
3/04	963	1	0.1%	115
3/03	852	1	0.1%	115
3/02	941	1	0.1%	115
3/01	803	1	0.1%	107
3/00	812	—	—	205
3/99	881	—	—	250
3/98	750	—	—	200
3/97	699	—	—	150
3/96	594	—	—	80
Annual Growth	6.2%	3.6%	—	4.6%

Net Income History

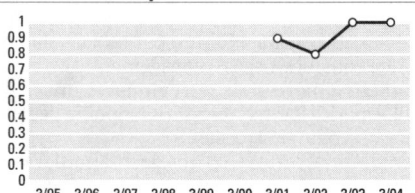

Dakota Growers Pasta Company

Dakota Growers Pasta Company puts an *al dente* in the noodle market. The company is a leading supplier of branded and private-label pasta products and flours, all of which are certified organic, to retail, foodservice, and ingredient markets in North America. Its brand names include Dreamfields, Pasta Growers, Pasta Sanita, Primo Piatto, and Zia Briosa. Dakota Growers began operations in 1991 as a wheatgrowers co-operative; in 2002 it converted to a private corporation. In 2004 the company took over New World Pasta's food service operations and now distributes Ronzoni, Price, and San Georgio brands.

EXECUTIVES

Chairman: John S. (Jack) Dalrymple III, age 56
President and CEO: Timothy J. Dodd, age 49, $202,566 pay
CFO: Thomas P. Friezen, age 45, $173,268 pay
VP, Finance, and Chief Accounting Officer: Edward O. Irion, age 33
VP, Human Resources and Administration: Susan M. Clemens, age 43
VP, Manufacturing and Special Projects: David E. Tressler, age 50, $115,840 pay
VP, Operations, Minnesota: Eldon Buschbom, age 56
VP, Quality Assurance: Radwan Ibrahim, age 60
VP, Sales and Marketing: Jack B. Hasper, age 63, $144,288 pay
VP, Supply Chain: James D. Cochran, age 36, $115,840 pay
Auditors: Eide Bailly LLP

LOCATIONS

HQ: Dakota Growers Pasta Company, Inc.
One Pasta Ave., Carrington, ND 58421
Phone: 701-652-2855   **Fax:** 701-652-3552
Web: www.dakotagrowers.com

COMPETITORS

A. Zerega's Sons	ConAgra
ADM	Kraft Foods
American Italian Pasta	Luigino's
Barilla	Nestlé
Campbell Soup	New World Pasta
CHS	Provena Foods

HISTORICAL FINANCIALS

Company Type: Private

Income Statement
FYE: July 31

	REVENUE ($ mil.)	NET INCOME ($ mil.)	NET PROFIT MARGIN	EMPLOYEES
7/04	145	0	0.2%	367
7/03	137	(0)	—	388
7/02	153	2	1.2%	430
7/01	136	(2)	—	423
7/00	139	—	—	460
7/99	125	—	—	456
7/98	120	—	—	500
7/97	71	—	—	—
7/96	51	—	—	—
7/95	41	—	—	—
Annual Growth	15.0%	—	—	(5.0%)

2004 Year-End Financials

Debt ratio: 36.0%   Current ratio: 1.57
Return on equity: 0.5%   Long-term debt ($ mil.): 21
Cash ($ mil.): 1

Net Income History

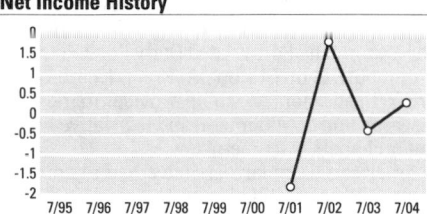

Dallas Mavericks

The Dallas Mavericks have bucked the image of a losing team. Formed in 1980 by millionaire Donald Carter, the franchise contended seriously only twice for a conference title in its history. After struggling with losing seasons through the 1990s, the Mavs returned to playoff contention in the 2000s. Millionaire Mark Cuban (co-founder of HDNet) bought the team in 2000 for $280 million and has since gone on to develop a reputation as an outspoken critic of league officiating and rack up over $1 million in fines from commissioner David Stern. The team plays in the $420 million AmericanAirlines Center, built partially with public funds.

EXECUTIVES

Owner: Mark Cuban, age 45
President and CEO: Terdema L. Ussery II
Head Coach: Avery Johnson
President Basketball Operations: Donnie Nelson
SVP Human Resources: Buddy Pittman
SVP Marketing and Communications: Matt Fitzgerald
VP and CFO: Floyd Jahner
VP Corporate Sponsorships: George Killebrew
VP Merchandising: Steve Shilts
VP Ticket Sales and Services: George Prokos
Controller: Ronnie Fauss
Director of Corporate Communications and Community Relations: Dawn Holgate Turner
Director of Marketing: Paul Monroe

LOCATIONS

HQ: Dallas Mavericks
The Pavilion, 2909 Taylor St., Dallas, TX 75226
Phone: 214-747-6287   **Fax:** 214-752-3860
Web: www.dallasmavericks.com

PRODUCTS/OPERATIONS

Post Season Appearances

1984 (Western Conference Semifinals, lost to Los Angeles Lakers)
1985 (Western Conference First Round, lost to Portland Trail Blazers)
1986 (Western Conference Semifinals, lost to Los Angeles Lakers)
1987 (Western Conference First Round, lost to Seattle SuperSonics)
1988 (Western Conference Finals, lost to Los Angeles Lakers)
2001 (Western Conference Semifinals, lost to San Antonio Spurs)
2002 (Western Conference Semifinals, lost to Sacramento Kings)
2003 (Western Conference Finals, lost to San Antonio Spurs)

COMPETITORS

Houston Rockets
Memphis Grizzlies
New Orleans Hornets
San Antonio Spurs

HISTORICAL FINANCIALS

Company Type: Private

Income Statement

FYE: June 30

	REVENUE ($ mil.)	NET INCOME ($ mil.)	NET PROFIT MARGIN	EMPLOYEES
6/04	117	—	—	—
6/03	117	—	—	—
6/02	105	—	—	—
6/01	68	—	—	—
6/00	60	—	—	85
6/99	50	—	—	85
6/98	41	—	—	85
6/97	40	—	—	85
6/96	42	—	—	83
6/95	39	—	—	55
Annual Growth	**13.1%**	**—**	**—**	**9.1%**

Revenue History

	6/95	6/96	6/97	6/98	6/99	6/00	6/01	6/02	6/03	6/04
120										

Damon's

At Damon's, all the world's a grill, and the men and women merely ribs. Damon's International operates and franchises more than 120 Damon's Grill casual-dining restaurants in 24 states, mostly in and around the Great Lakes area. Its eateries feature grilled steaks, ribs, chicken, and seafood, as well as appetizers, such as the onion loaf. Each location also offers a dining room along with a sports-themed bar and entertainment area called Damon's Clubhouse. The restaurant chain was started in 1979.

Damon's added 13 new stores in 2003 and about 15 new locations in 2004. However, it is pulling out of some markets, such as Toledo, Ohio, due to declining sales.

EXECUTIVES

President and CEO: Shannon R. Foust
CFO: Stuart G. Laws
COO: Carl T. Howard
EVP Development: Ed Williams
VP Purchasing: Tanny Feerer
VP Quality Assurance: Will Liphart
VP Franchise Sales and General Counsel: Jim Meaney
VP Marketing: Jon Quinn, age 37
VP Franchise Operations: John Votino
Research and Development Chef: Brett Freifeld

LOCATIONS

HQ: Damon's International, Inc.
4645 Executive Dr., Columbus, OH 43220
Phone: 614-442-7900   **Fax:** 614-442-7787
Web: www.damons.com

Restaurant Locations

Arizona	New York
Colorado	North Carolina
Delaware	Ohio
Florida	Oregon
Illinois	Pennsylvania
Indiana	South Carolina
Kentucky	Tennessee
Maryland	Texas
Michigan	Virginia
Minnesota	West Virginia
New Jersey	Wisconsin

COMPETITORS

Applebee's	Houlihan's
Avado Brands	Jillian's Billiards
Brinker	Landry's
Buffalo Wild Wings	Metromedia Restaurant Group
Carlson Restaurants	
Champps Entertainment	O'Charley's
Darden	Outback Steakhouse
Dave & Buster's	RARE Hospitality
Famous Dave's	Rock Bottom Restaurants
Fox & Hound Restaurant	Ruby Tuesday
Hooters	Stuart Anderson's

HISTORICAL FINANCIALS

Company Type: Private

Income Statement

FYE: June 30

	ESTIMATED REVENUE ($ mil.)	NET INCOME ($ mil.)	NET PROFIT MARGIN	EMPLOYEES
6/04	77	—	—	3,350
6/03	75	—	—	3,200
6/02	75	—	—	3,200
6/01	50	—	—	2,300
6/00	50	—	—	2,000
Annual Growth	**11.4%**	**—**	**—**	**13.8%**

Revenue History

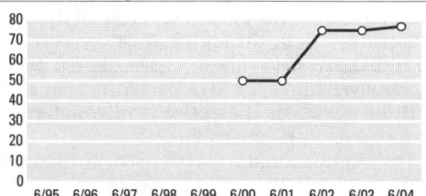

	6/95	6/96	6/97	6/98	6/99	6/00	6/01	6/02	6/03	6/04
80										

Dart Container

Dart Container is a world cup winner — maybe not in soccer, but it is the world's top maker of foam cups and containers, with about half of the global market in cups. The company uses a secret method of molding expandable polystyrene to make its products, which include cups, lids, dinnerware, and cutlery for customers such as hospitals, schools, and restaurants. To cut costs, Dart Container builds its own molding machinery and operates its own distribution trucks. The firm sells its recycled polystyrene to companies that make such items as insulation material and egg cartons. Although often embroiled in litigation, the Dart family continues to own the company.

In terms of Dart's products, the company is moving into foam lid and plastic containers for industrial or retail use.

The company runs four polystyrene-recycling plants and operates in the US and through subsidiaries in Argentina, Australia, Canada, Mexico, and the UK.

The king of cups has a simple strategy — secrecy. The cup-making machine developed by the Darts was never patented to avoid revealing how it works. Most of its factory workers have never seen the machines, and the firm's salespeople are not allowed inside the plants. After years of legal battles, the Darts have reached an agreement regarding alleged discrepancies in the family inheritance. The terms of the settlement are, naturally, secret.

In 2003 Ken Dart added to the family fortune, winning a $700 million lawsuit against Argentina in a dispute over the country's decision to default on its bonds in 1991.

HISTORY

William F. Dart founded a Michigan firm to make steel tape measures in 1937. Dart's son William A. started experimenting with plastics in 1953, and in the late 1950s the two devised a cheap way to mold expandable polystyrene and built a cup-making machine. Dart Container was incorporated in Mason, Michigan, in 1960 and shipped its first cups that year. By the late 1960s the rising demand for plastic-foam products sparked an increase in R&D. In 1970 the company built a plant in Corona, California.

It was a family feud in the making in 1974, as William F. divided the business among his grandsons — Tom, Ken, and Robert — in separate trusts that named William A. trustee for all. Tom branched out in 1975 and founded oil and gas company Dart Energy, which was later absorbed into Dart Container. William F. died the next year. Following the oil market crash of the early 1980s, Tom went through a sticky divorce and admitted to cocaine abuse. His father temporarily removed him as head of Dart Energy in 1982, and the next year the entire family underwent group psychiatric counseling.

The family reorganized its assets in 1986, giving Ken and Robert the cup business and Tom the energy business plus $58 million in cash. In 1987 Ken began to swell the family fortune with a series of successful investments. Better tax rates motivated Dart family members to move to Sarasota, Florida, in 1989. They set up shop in an unmarked building behind a sporting-goods store. By the late 1980s Dart Container commanded more than 50% of the worldwide market for foam cups.

In 1990 the company paid $250,000 to settle a factory worker's minority discrimination lawsuit. The next year Ken bought 11% of the Federal Home Loan Mortgage Corp. (Freddie Mac), as well as portions of Salomon and Brazil's foreign debt. According to Tom, that year Ken also financed brain research in hopes of finding a way to keep his brain alive after the death of his body in an attempt to avoid future estate taxes.

Tom sued his brothers and father in 1992 for allegedly cheating him out of millions in trust money in the 1986 reorganization. Ken turned a $300 million investment into $1 billion by selling the Freddie Mac shares. The next year he and Robert renounced their US citizenship to avoid paying taxes. Ken also made a failed attempt to block the restructuring of Brazil's debt (of which Dart owned 4%). That year Ken's new $1 million

Sarasota home was firebombed (the case remains unsolved), and Robert moved to Britain, where he soon filed for divorce.

Ken began hiring bodyguards, and he moved his family to the Cayman Islands in 1994. Dart then shelled out $230,000 to settle yet another discrimination case. In 1995 Tom was fired from Dart Energy, and Ken tried — and failed — to return to the US as a diplomat of Belize. In 1996 Tom accused Judge Donald Owens of being biased in favor of William A. The judge succumbed to the pressure in 1997 and removed himself from the proceedings, only to be ordered back on the case by Michigan's Court of Appeals. The lawsuit was settled in 1998 before going to trial, but the terms were kept secret. The following year saw yet another series of lawsuits for the container company. In 1999 Dart Container filed an appeal to an IRS demand to pay $31 million in back taxes from 1994 and late penalties. The legal wrangling continued through 2001, but in 2002 the company agreed to pay $26 million to settle the issue. Meanwhile, the company has expanded their foam lid and container products for wholesale industrial or retail use.

EXECUTIVES

Chairman: William Dart
CEO: Kenneth B. Dart
President: Robert C. Dart
CFO and Treasurer: William (Bill) Myers
VP and COO: George Jenkins
VP, Administration and General Counsel: Jim Lammers
VP, Manufacturing: Dan Calkins
VP, Manufacturing: John M. Murray
VP, Technology: Ralph MacKenzie
Director, Human Resources: Mark Franks
Director, Sales: Robert Williams

LOCATIONS

HQ: Dart Container Corporation
500 Hogsback Rd., Mason, MI 48854
Phone: 517-676-3800   **Fax:** 517-676-3883
Web: www.dartcontainer.com

Dart Container has four recycling centers in Canada and the US, and manufacturing operations in Argentina, Australia, Canada, Mexico, the UK, and the US.

PRODUCTS/OPERATIONS

Selected Products

Clear containers
Container lids
Deli containers and lids
Dinnerware
Foam cups
Hinged containers
Paper cups and lids
Plastic cups and lids
Plastic cutlery

Selected Services

CARE (Cups Are REcyclable) Program (provides densifier to larger customers to compact their polystyrene, which Dart then picks up)
Foam-Recycling (four plants in Canada, Florida, Michigan, and Pennsylvania and a drop-off site in Georgia)
Recycla-Pak (provides small-volume businesses with cup-shipping containers that double as recycling bins)

COMPETITORS

Berry Plastics
Huhtamäki
NOVA Chemicals
Radnor Holdings
Smurfit-Stone Container
Sonoco Products
Temple-Inland

HISTORICAL FINANCIALS

Company Type: Private

Income Statement

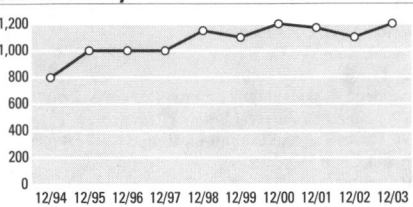

	ESTIMATED REVENUE ($ mil.)	NET INCOME ($ mil.)	NET PROFIT MARGIN	EMPLOYEES
12/03	1,200	—	—	5,000
12/02	1,100	—	—	4,950
12/01	1,170	—	—	5,000
12/00	1,200	—	—	5,000
12/99	1,100	—	—	5,000
12/98	1,150	—	—	5,000
12/97	1,000	—	—	5,000
12/96	1,000	—	—	4,300
12/95	1,000	—	—	4,300
12/94	800	—	—	3,600
Annual Growth	4.6%	—	—	3.7%

FYE: December 31

Revenue History

Datatel

Datatel provides information management software for higher education institutions. The company's Datatel Colleague platform integrates applications for managing information about students, finances, financial aid, human resources, and advancement. Subsidiary LiquidMatrix provides e-communications, content management, and Web services software designed to help universities meet their enrollment and fundraising goals. In 2005 Datatel's executive team, led by CEO Russ Griffith and backed by Thoma Cressey Equity Partners and Trident Capital, bought the company from Ken Kendrick and Tom Davidson, who founded the company in 1968.

EXECUTIVES

Chairman, President, and CEO: H. Russ Griffith
SVP Finance and Administration: Vernon R. Hollidge Jr.
VP, Accounting: Ginger L. Piercy
VP, Professional Services: Elizabeth A. Murphy
VP, Sales: John P. Opgen III
VP, Software Development: Thomas A. (Tom) Reynolds
VP, Strategic Planning and Marketing: Jayne W. Edge
Director, Sales: Steve Boller
Director, Client Business Relations: Bill Knight
Director, Technology Product Management: Sue Kumpf
Director, Partner Programs: Kyran Kennedy
Public Affairs Specialist: Tricia Jo Score

LOCATIONS

HQ: Datatel, Inc.
4375 Fair Lakes Ct., Fairfax, VA 22033
Phone: 703-968-9000
Web: www.datatel.com

COMPETITORS

Blackbaud   Jenzabar
Blackboard   SunGard SCT
Collegis

HISTORICAL FINANCIALS

Company Type: Private

Income Statement

FYE: December 31

	REVENUE ($ mil.)	NET INCOME ($ mil.)	NET PROFIT MARGIN	EMPLOYEES
12/04*	95	—	—	—
12/02	75	—	—	470
Annual Growth	26.7%	—	—	—

*Irregular reporting interval

Revenue History

100
90
80
70
60
50
40
30
20
10
0

12/94 12/95 12/96 12/97 12/98 12/99 12/00 12/01 12/02 12/04

Daubert Industries

If you're Daubert Industries, metal health is the top concern. Its three subsidiaries protect metals by different methods. Daubert VCI (volatile corrosion inhibitors) makes protective coatings for almost every metal — ferrous, nonferrous, and multi-metal. Its transparent coatings protect metal that is stored or shipped until it is unwrapped and the coatings break down. ECP (Entire Car Protection) offers paints, carpet dyes, detailing products, and under-the-hood cleaners. Daubert Chemical focuses on developing corrosion prevention, industrial anti-skid, and sound-deadening coatings. Daubert Industries was formed in 1935 by George A. Daubert; the company is controlled by Daubert's descendants.

EXECUTIVES

Chairman: Harry A. Fischer Jr.
Vice Chairman: Andrew M. Fischer
Vice Chairman: Harry A. (Fritz) Fischer III
Vice Chairman: Peter D. Fischer
President, CEO, and Director; President and CEO, Daubert VCI: M. Lawrence Garman
SVP, Finance and Administration and CFO: Peter Miehl
VP, Treasurer, and Secretary: John R. Cosbey
President and CEO, Daubert Chemical: Michael Dwyer
President and CEO, ECP: Lawrence Bettendorf
EVP, Operations, Daubert Chemical: Mark Pawelski
EVP, Sales, ECP: Michael Feely
Director, Human Resources: Ginny Winkelmann
Auditors: McGladrey & Pullen, LLP

LOCATIONS

HQ: Daubert Industries, Inc.
1333 Burr Ridge Pkwy., Ste. 200,
Burr Ridge, IL 60521
Phone: 630-203-6800   **Fax:** 630-203-6907
Web: www.daubert.com

Daubert has manufacturing operations in Illinois and Indiana. It has distributors throughout Canada and the US.

PRODUCTS/OPERATIONS

Selected Operations and Products

Daubert Chemical Company
    Corrosion prevention coatings
    Industrial anti-skid coatings
    Penetrating oil
    Sound deadening coatings
Daubert VCI
    Coating papers — ferrous metals
    Coating papers — nonferrous and multi-metals
    Liquid coating — ferrous and nonferrous metals
Entire Car Protection
    Buffers
    Car soaps, shampoos, detergents
    Chamois and wash mits
    Cleaners, solvents, degreasers
    Lubricants and protectants
    Paint
    Paint correction compounds
    Underhood cleaners
    Vinyl, plastic, carpet dyes
    Wax specialty applicators

COMPETITORS

Atlantis Plastics   Huntsman
Bodycote   ICG/Holliston
Enerchem International   Norman Hay
General Magnaplate   Quaker Chemical

HISTORICAL FINANCIALS

Company Type: Private

Income Statement

FYE: December 31

	REVENUE ($ mil.)	NET INCOME ($ mil.)	NET PROFIT MARGIN	EMPLOYEES
12/04*	68	—	—	171
12/02	61	—	—	209
12/01	59	—	—	209
12/00	58	—	—	215
12/99	54	—	—	203
12/98	47	—	—	165
12/97	136	—	—	490
12/96	130	—	—	480
12/95	117	—	—	459
12/94	110	—	—	472
Annual Growth	(5.2%)	—	—	(10.7%)

*Irregular reporting interval

Revenue History

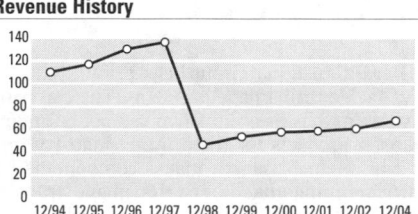

140
120
100
80
60
40
20
0

12/94 12/95 12/96 12/97 12/98 12/99 12/00 12/01 12/02 12/04

Davey Tree Expert

Business at The Davey Tree Expert Company is as green as grass. The company's roots extend back to 1880 when John Davey founded the horticultural services company, which branched into residential, commercial, utility, and other natural resource management services. Among the services Davey offers are the treatment, planting, and removal of trees, shrubs, and other plant life; landscaping; tree surgery; and the application of fertilizers, herbicides, and insecticides. Other services include line clearing for public utilities, urban and utility forestry research and development, and environmental planning. Pacific Gas and Electric accounts for about 15% of sales. Davey has been employee-owned since 1979.

EXECUTIVES

Chairman and CEO: R. Douglas Cowan, age 64, $493,858 pay
President, COO, and Director: Karl J. Warnke, age 53, $391,592 pay
EVP, CFO, and Secretary: David E. Adante, age 52, $275,923 pay
SVP and General Manager, Davey Tree Surgery Company: Howard D. Bowles, age 61, $275,392 pay
SVP and General Manager, Residential and Commercial Services: C. Kenneth Celmer, age 58, $258,638 pay
VP, Personnel Recruiting and Development: Gordon L. Ober, age 55
Treasurer: Bradley L. Comport, age 53
Controller: Nicholas R. Sucic, age 58
General Auditor: Kenneth P. Bechtol
Auditors: Ernst & Young LLP

LOCATIONS

HQ: The Davey Tree Expert Company
1500 N. Mantua St., Kent, OH 44240
Phone: 330-673-9511   **Fax:** 330-673-9843
Web: www.davey.com

The Davey Tree Expert Company has operations in the US and Canada.

2004 Sales

	$ mil.	% of total
US	370.6	93
Canada	28.0	7
Total	**398.6**	**100**

PRODUCTS/OPERATIONS

2004 Sales

	$ mil.	% of total
Residential & commercial services	182.1	46
Utility services	173.2	43
Other	43.3	11
Total	**398.6**	**100**

COMPETITORS

Arbor Tree Surgery
Asplundh
TruGreen Landcare
UNICCO Service
ValleyCrest Companies

HISTORICAL FINANCIALS

Company Type: Private

Income Statement

	REVENUE ($ mil.)	NET INCOME ($ mil.)	NET PROFIT MARGIN	EMPLOYEES
12/04	399	12	3.1%	5,000
12/03	346	9	2.5%	5,100
12/02	319	7	2.3%	6,000
12/01	321	7	2.1%	6,000
12/00	322	(2)	—	6,000
12/99	308	4	1.2%	6,000
12/98	314	11	3.4%	6,000
12/97	295	11	3.8%	5,900
12/96	267	9	3.3%	5,800
12/95	230	6	2.8%	5,200
Annual Growth	**6.3%**	**7.5%**	**—**	**(0.4%)**

FYE: December 31

2004 Year-End Financials

Debt ratio: 28.2%
Return on equity: 18.6%
Cash ($ mil.): 1
Current ratio: 1.38
Long-term debt ($ mil.): 20

Net Income History

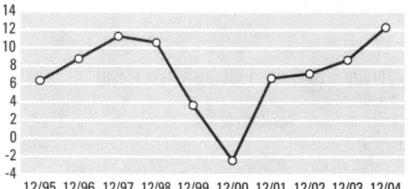

14 12 10 8 6 4 2 0 -2 -4
12/95 12/96 12/97 12/98 12/99 12/00 12/01 12/02 12/03 12/04

Day & Zimmermann

The Day & Zimmermann Group offers services as distinct as day and night. The company provides engineering and construction, design, plant maintenance, security, staffing, munitions, validation, and asset management services worldwide. A top global contractor, Day & Zimmermann provides operations, contract support, and maintenance services to US and foreign governments, as well as commercial customers. The group has been selling noncore divisions to integrate its operations and focus on its strategic businesses, particularly technical staffing unit Yoh Company. Founded in 1901, Day & Zimmermann is owned and managed by the Yoh family, which has headed the firm for three generations.

EXECUTIVES

Chairman and CEO: Harold L. (Hal) Yoh III, age 44
EVP Commercial Operations: Joseph J. Ucciferro
SVP Administration: William R. (Bill) Hamm
VP Finance and CFO: Joseph W. (Joe) Ritzel
VP and Executive Committee Member: John Dabek
VP and CIO: Anthony J. Bosco Jr.
VP and Group Controller: Joseph E. McKinney
VP Corporate Marketing and Communications: Sharon Gosdeck
VP Human Resources: Belen J. Acosta
VP Government Affairs: James (Jim) Hickey
VP Strategy and Marketing, Yoh Group: Jim Lanzalotto
Auditors: Deloitte & Touche

LOCATIONS

HQ: The Day & Zimmermann Group, Inc.
1818 Market St., Fl. 22, Philadelphia, PA 19103
Phone: 215-299-8000   **Fax:** 215-299-8030
Web: www.dayzim.com

The Day & Zimmermann Group operates from more than 150 locations worldwide.

COMPETITORS

Adecco	Louis Berger
Alliant Techsystems	Manpower
AMEC	McCarthy Building
Bechtel	McDermott
CDI	Parsons
Fluor	Peter Kiewit Sons'
Foster Wheeler	URS
Halliburton	Washington Group
Jacobs Engineering	WS Atkins
Johnson Controls	

HISTORICAL FINANCIALS

Company Type: Private

Income Statement

	REVENUE ($ mil.)	NET INCOME ($ mil.)	NET PROFIT MARGIN	EMPLOYEES
12/03	1,300	—	—	20,000
12/02	1,351	—	—	21,000
12/01	1,300	—	—	20,000
12/00	1,554	—	—	26,000
12/99	1,650	—	—	24,000
12/98	1,080	—	—	16,500
12/97	995	—	—	15,000
12/96	812	—	—	14,000
12/95	766	—	—	13,800
12/94	706	—	—	12,000
Annual Growth	**7.0%**	**—**	**—**	**5.8%**

FYE: December 31

Revenue History

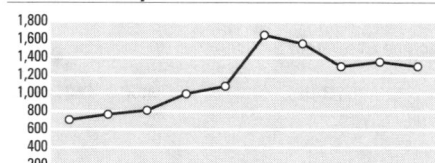

1,800 1,600 1,400 1,200 1,000 800 600 400 200 0
12/94 12/95 12/96 12/97 12/98 12/99 12/00 12/01 12/02 12/03

Day International

Day International Group helps printing companies tackle their image problems. The company divides its business into two segments: image transfer products for the printing industry, and textile products, which makes components for yarn spinning machinery. Its image transfer products segment manufactures and sells offset-printing blankets and sleeves (which transfer ink from printing plates to paper) and pressroom chemicals. Customers include advertising, magazine, newspaper, and packaging printers. Its textile products unit makes rubber cots (rollers),

aprons (belts), and other components used in textile machinery. Investment firms GSC Partners and SG Capital Partners LLC own almost all of the company.

Day International's current business operations began in 1938 with the production of synthetic roll covers. The company was originally founded in 1905 as the Dayton Rubber Company, a maker of garden hoses and fruit jar sealing rings.

EXECUTIVES

Chairman: William C. Ferguson, age 74
President, CEO, and Director: Dennis R. Wolters, age 58, $410,000 pay
SVP: Scott D. Morrison, age 47
SVP and Managing Director, Flexographic Products: Mario Busshoff, age 32
SVP and General Manager, Textile Products Group: Norbert P. Kroner, age 54
SVP, General Manager, Transfer Media and Chemical Products, North America: John W. Frazier, age 41
SVP, Sales and Marketing, Image Transfer Group North America: Mark Barrington
VP and CFO: Thomas J. Koenig, age 43, $249,640 pay
VP, Human Resources and Assistant Secretary: Dwaine R. Brooks, age 61
VP Marketing and National Accounts: Mike Neroni
Group VP and General Manager, Textiles and Flexographic Products: David B. Freimuth, age 51, $269,364 pay
Group VP and General Manager, Image Transfer Group: Stephen P. Noe, age 47, $336,162 pay
Managing Director, Europe: Dermot J. Healy, age 49, $326,439 pay
Managing Director, Pacific Rim: Brent A. Stephen, age 53, $217,006 pay
Auditors: Ernst & Young LLP

LOCATIONS

HQ: Day International Group, Inc.
130 W. Second St., Dayton, OH 45402
Phone: 937-224-4000   **Fax:** 937-226-1855
Web: www.dayintl.com

2004 Sales

	$ mil.	% of total
US	187.9	49
Germany	82.1	21
UK	44.6	11
Other countries	72.3	19
Adjustments	(24.2)	—
Total	**362.7**	**100**

PRODUCTS/OPERATIONS

2004 Sales

	$ mil.	% of total
Image transfer	313.7	86
Textile products	49.0	14
Total	**362.7**	**100**

Selected Operations

Image transfer
Pressroom chemicals (roller and blanket washes, fountain solutions)
Transfer media (blankets, sleeves)

Textile products
Aprons (flexible belts)
Cots (rubber rollers)

COMPETITORS

HUBER + SUHNER
MacDermid
Reeves
Rycoline

HISTORICAL FINANCIALS

Company Type: Private

Income Statement

FYE: December 31

	REVENUE ($ mil.)	NET INCOME ($ mil.)	NET PROFIT MARGIN	EMPLOYEES
12/04	363	(10)	—	1,470
12/03	289	(6)	—	1,470
12/02	260	10	3.8%	1,350
12/01	254	(5)	—	1,350
Annual Growth	12.6%	—	—	2.9%

2004 Year-End Financials

Debt ratio: (182.2%)
Return on equity: —
Cash ($ mil.): 1

Current ratio: 2.47
Long-term debt ($ mil.): 248

Net Income History

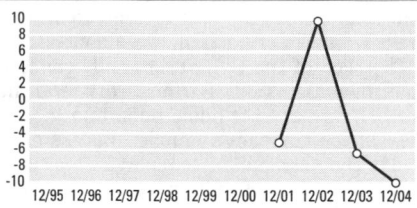

12/95 12/96 12/97 12/98 12/99 12/00 12/01 12/02 12/03 12/04

Dayton Superior

Superior products are all in a day's work for Dayton Superior. The company makes metal accessories and forms for keeping concrete and masonry structures in place while under construction. Dayton Superior's products include concrete accessories (anchoring and bracing for walls, positioning steel reinforcing bars, and supporting bridge framework), masonry products (wire support for masonry walls), welded dowel assemblies (metal dowels), paving products, and corrosive-preventing epoxy coatings and other chemicals. The company's rental equipment includes concrete forming systems and shoring systems. Odyssey Investment Partners controls 92% of the company.

The company's structures are primarily used in building highways, bridges, and commercial buildings.

Dayton Superior sells and rents through 22 service centers in North America. Customers include rebar fabricators, precast and prestressed concrete manufacturers, and general contractors.

In 2003 Dayton Superior acquired the fixed assets and rental fleet assets of Safway Formwork Systems, L.L.C. (concrete forming and shoring systems, Wisconsin), a subsidiary of Safway Services, Inc. (whose ultimate parent is ThyssenKrupp AG).

EXECUTIVES

Chairman, Interim President and CEO: John A. (Chic) Ciccarelli, age 65
VP and CFO: Edward J. Puisis, age 44, $450,000 pay
VP General Counsel, and Secretary: Steven C. Huston, age 50
VP Corporate Accounting: Thomas W. Roehrig, age 39
VP Engineering: Peter J. Astrauskas, age 54

VP Sales and Marketing: Raymond E. Bartholomae, age 58, $425,000 pay
VP and General Manager, American Highway Technology: Mark K. Kaler, age 47, $327,000 pay
VP Supply Chain Management: Dennis P. Haggerty, age 53, $335,000 pay
Manager Human Resources: Douglas (Doug) Good
Auditors: Deloitte & Touche LLP

LOCATIONS

HQ: Dayton Superior Corporation
7777 Washington Village Dr., Ste. 130, Dayton, OH 45459
Phone: 937-428-6360   **Fax:** 937-428-9115
Web: www.daytonsuperior.com

Dayton Superior Corporation has 14 manufacturing/distribution plants and eight service/distribution centers in North America. Principal facilities are located in Alabama, Arizona, California, Georgia, Illinois, Kansas, Ohio, Pennsylvania, Texas, and Washington, as well as in Canada and Mexico.

PRODUCTS/OPERATIONS

2004 Sales

	$ mil.	% of total
Product sales	348.0	83
Rental revenues	42.2	10
Used rental equipment	28.4	7
Total	**418.6**	**100**

Selected Products and Services

Product Sales
Concrete accessories
Chemicals
Masonry products
Paving products

Rental Revenues and Sales of Used Rental Equipment
Concrete forming systems
Shoring systems
Tilt-up construction products

COMPETITORS

Ameron
Commercial Metals
Gerdau AmeriSteel
MMI Products
Simpson Manufacturing
Smith-Midland

HISTORICAL FINANCIALS

Company Type: Private

Income Statement

FYE: December 31

	REVENUE ($ mil.)	NET INCOME ($ mil.)	NET PROFIT MARGIN	EMPLOYEES
12/04	419	(48)	—	1,700
12/03	378	(17)	—	1,900
12/02	378	(20)	—	1,900
12/01	394	(4)	—	2,200
12/00	368	(4)	—	2,400
12/99	322	15	4.6%	2,250
12/98	283	10	3.6%	2,080
12/97	167	7	4.2%	1,834
12/96	125	2	1.8%	862
12/95	93	4	4.0%	838
Annual Growth	18.2%	—	—	8.2%

2004 Year-End Financials

Debt ratio: —
Return on equity: —
Cash ($ mil.): 5

Current ratio: 2.87
Long-term debt ($ mil.): 375

Net Income History

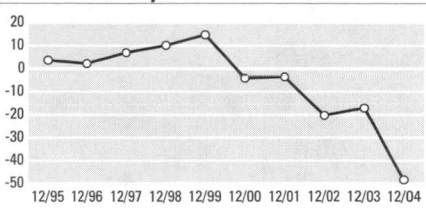

12/95 12/96 12/97 12/98 12/99 12/00 12/01 12/02 12/03 12/04

DCP Midstream Partners

The D in DCP Midstream Partners is for Duke Energy, and the CP, ConocoPhillips. These two energy majors own parent Duke Energy Field Services, a joint venture which formed DCP Midstream Partners in 2005 to control, manage, and expand a portfolio of related midstream energy assets. DCP Midstream Partners is engaged in natural gas gathering, compressing, treating, processing, transporting, and selling. It also transports and sells natural gas liquids (NGLs). The company operates a 1,430-mile integrated natural gas pipeline system in Louisiana and Arkansas. Its NGLs logistics business unit includes the Seabreeze NGLs pipeline (Texas) and the 50%-owned Black Lake NGLs pipeline (Louisiana and Texas).

Parent Duke Energy Field Services is one of the largest natural gas gatherers in North America. It is also the largest producer and one of the largest marketers of NGLs.

EXECUTIVES

Chairman, DCP Midstream GP: Jim W. Mogg, age 56
President and CEO, DCP Midstream GP: Michael J. (Mike) Bradley, age 51
VP and CFO, DCP Midstream GP: Thomas E. Long, age 48
VP, General Counsel, and Secretary, DCP Midstream GP: Michael S. Richards, age 45
VP, Business Development, DCP Midstream GP: Greg K. Smith, age 38
VP and Controller, DCP Midstream GP: Patrick J. Welch
Auditors: Deloitte & Touche LLP

LOCATIONS

HQ: DCP Midstream Partners, LP
370 17th St., Ste. 2775, Denver, CO 80202
Phone: 303-633-2900   **Fax:** 303-605-2225

COMPETITORS

Dynegy
El Paso
Enterprise Products
Williams Companies
XTO Energy

HISTORICAL FINANCIALS

Company Type: Partnership

Income Statement

FYE: December 31

	REVENUE ($ mil.)	NET INCOME ($ mil.)	NET PROFIT MARGIN	EMPLOYEES
12/04	510	20	4.0%	65
12/03	475	10	2.1%	—
12/02	297	9	2.9%	—
Annual Growth	30.9%	54.9%	—	—

2004 Year-End Financials

Debt ratio: 0.0%
Return on equity: 10.2%
Cash ($ mil.): 0

Current ratio: 1.43
Long-term debt ($ mil.): 0

Net Income History

12/95 12/96 12/97 12/98 12/99 12/00 12/01 12/02 12/03 12/04

DealerTrack

DealerTrack Holdings helps car dealers play their cards right in the financing game. The company provides Web-based software that links automotive dealerships with banks, finance companies, credit unions, credit reporting agencies, and other players in the car sales and financing process. Through its software, DealerTrack connects clients to its network of more than 20,000 auto dealers, 140 financing sources, and other service and information providers. The company, which generates revenues through subscriptions and transaction-based fees, also offers tools that automate credit application processing, ensure document legal compliance, and execute electronic financing contracts. JPMorgan owns 26% of DealerTrack.

DealerTrack is looking for growth by expanding its customer base through its direct sales force and by selling additional products to its more than 20,000 existing customers. The company's current customers are primarily franchised car dealerships — a market which DealerTrack has successfully penetrated — but it is working to build its clientele among independent dealers.

DealerTrack has also been using acquisitions to build its business. In 2005 the company bought the assets of Automotive Lease Guide (a provider of lease residual value data for automobiles), North American Advanced Technology (tools for automating after-market product administration), and Chrome Systems (data collection and enhancement tools for vertical industries).

First American owns 20% of DealerTrack; AmeriCredit owns 12%; Wells Fargo owns 9%; GRP owns 8%; and CapitalOne Auto Finance and WFS Financial each own 7%.

EXECUTIVES

Chairman, President and CEO: Mark F. O'Neil, age 47, $1,007,201 pay
SVP, CFO and Treasurer: Robert J. Cox III, age 39, $345,696 pay
SVP, General Counsel and Secretary: Eric D. Jacobs, age 38, $361,048 pay
President, Deal Track, Inc.: Vincent Passione, age 43, $587,195 pay
SVP and CIO, Dealer Track, Inc.: Charles J. Giglia, age 54, $372,757 pay
VP Marketing: Alexi Venneri
Auditors: PricewaterhouseCoopers LLP

LOCATIONS

HQ: DealerTrack Holdings, Inc.
1111 Marcus Ave., Ste. M04,
Lake Success, NY 11042
Phone: 516-734-3600
Web: www.dealertrack.com

DealerTrack Holdings has offices in California, Florida, Illinois, New York, and Oregon, and in Canada.

PRODUCTS/OPERATIONS

2004 Sales

	$ mil.	% of total
Transaction services	51.7	74
Subscription services	17.0	24
Other	1.3	2
Total	70.0	100

COMPETITORS

ADP
Auto Data Network
Microsoft
  Business Solutions

NSB Retail Systems
Reynolds and Reynolds
TSA

HISTORICAL FINANCIALS

Company Type: Private

Income Statement

FYE: December 31

	REVENUE ($ mil.)	NET INCOME ($ mil.)	NET PROFIT MARGIN	EMPLOYEES
12/04	70	11	16.1%	499
12/03	39	(3)	—	—
12/02	12	(17)	—	—
Annual Growth	144.6%	—	—	—

2004 Year-End Financials

Debt ratio: (1.7%)
Return on equity: —
Cash ($ mil.): 22

Current ratio: 2.30
Long-term debt ($ mil.): 0

Net Income History

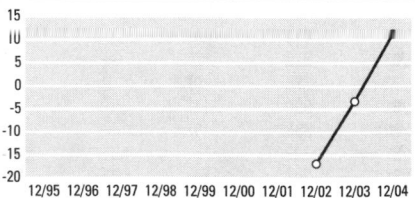

12/95 12/96 12/97 12/98 12/99 12/00 12/01 12/02 12/03 12/04

DeBartolo Corporation

Real estate holdings, gambling, horse racing, a felony conviction, and warring siblings surrounded by a storied NFL franchise — sounds like an old episode of *Dallas*. But the story of The DeBartolo Corporation takes place in Youngstown, Ohio (where the company is based), via San Francisco (where the company owns the 49ers football team). The company also provides management services to the Louisiana Downs racetrack in Bossier City. The firm's other interests include a software firm in Tennessee and a few health care companies in Oklahoma and Pennsylvania. DeBartolo Corp. is also trying to bring an Arena Football League team to San Francisco.

The saga of the DeBartolo family concerns chairman Denise DeBartolo York and her brother, former CEO Eddie DeBartolo Jr., children of the company's founder. Eddie's guilty plea to charges of failing to report a felony led to his ouster and a lawsuit from his sister to recover a $94 million debt he owed the company. Eddie countersued, and after much wrangling, the siblings reached an agreement whereby Denise took the company name, the 49ers, and the racetrack (which it later sold but still operates), and Eddie received real estate and the firm's minority stake in Simon Property Group, one of North America's largest public real estate companies.

HISTORY

Edward J. DeBartolo left his stepfather's paving business in 1944 and established the eponymous Edward J. DeBartolo Corporation. DeBartolo's foresight about the growth of the suburbs led him to build one of the first strip-style malls outside California, the Belmont Plaza, near Youngstown, Ohio, in 1949. Over the next 15 years, the company built 45 more strip centers throughout the US. In the 1960s DeBartolo became one of the first to develop large, covered regional malls in many parts of the nation. DeBartolo opened the Louisiana Downs racetrack in 1974 and moved the company into the sports business in 1977 when he helped his son, Edward Jr. (Eddie), buy the San Francisco 49ers.

When the management of Allied Stores asked DeBartolo to help fend off a bid by real estate developer Robert Campeau, DeBartolo thought that control of Allied's department store chains would provide anchor stores for his mall developments and loaned Campeau $150 million for the takeover instead. Two years later DeBartolo borrowed $480 million and lent it to Campeau for his acquisition of Federated Department Stores.

The company reached its zenith in the late 1980s (opening the Rivercenter in San Antonio and Lakeland Square in Florida), but Campeau was in trouble — the highly leveraged Allied and Federated went bankrupt and threatened to take DeBartolo with them. As part of the bankruptcy settlement, DeBartolo took a 60% interest in California-based Ralphs supermarket (since sold) and started selling off assets in 1991 to cover the loan he made to Campeau and the company's own $4 billion debt. The fire sale included his private jet, three malls, two office buildings, a 50% stake in Higbee's department stores, and the Rivercenter.

Edward died in 1994. His daughter, Denise DeBartolo York, became chairman, and his son, Eddie (who was also chairman and CEO of the 49ers) became president and CEO. Eddie reshuffled the company's assets with most of its real estate holdings turned into DeBartolo Realty, a real estate investment trust that went public that year, raising $575 million. Mounting tensions between the siblings intensified in 1995 when Eddie formed DeBartolo Entertainment, his own separate company in the gaming business (Denise tried to distance the family business from Eddie's new company in a press release). DeBartolo Realty merged with Simon Property Group the following year.

Eddie ran into trouble in 1997 when an investigation revealed that he had paid former Louisiana governor Edwin Edwards $400,000 in an effort to obtain a riverboat gambling license for DeBartolo Entertainment. (Before the gambling fraud probe became public, San Francisco voters approved a $100 million bond issue to help finance a $525 million stadium/shopping mall for the 49ers. Those plans were put on ice.) Eddie pleaded guilty to felony charges of concealing wrongdoing the next year, was fined $2 million, and stepped down from DeBartolo Corp. (His later testimony against Gov. Edwards helped lead to the government official's conviction on extortion charges.) The NFL then fined Eddie another $1 million and banned him from the 49ers in 1999. Later that year Denise sued Eddie for debt owed to the company and he countersued. DeBartolo Corp. also sold two of its racetracks (Thistledown and Remington Park).

In 2001 the DeBartolos completed the division of the company's assets between them. DeBartolo York also shortened the company's name to The DeBartolo Corporation.

EXECUTIVES

Chairman: Marie Denise DeBartolo York, age 54
President: John C. York II
Head Coach: Mike Nolan

LOCATIONS

HQ: The DeBartolo Corporation
7620 Market St., Youngstown, OH 44512
Phone: 330-965-2000   **Fax:** 330-965-2077
Web: http://www.49ers.com/team

The DeBartolo Corporation has operations in California, Louisiana, Ohio, Oklahoma, Pennsylvania, and Tennessee.

COMPETITORS

Arizona Cardinals
Harrah's Entertainment
Oakland Raiders
Seattle Seahawks
St. Louis Cardinals

HISTORICAL FINANCIALS

Company Type: Private

Income Statement

FYE: June 30

	ESTIMATED REVENUE ($ mil.)	NET INCOME ($ mil.)	NET PROFIT MARGIN	EMPLOYEES
6/01	250	—	—	4,000
6/00	250	—	—	4,000
6/99	254	—	—	4,000
6/98	250	—	—	4,000
6/97	250	—	—	3,000
6/96	220	—	—	3,000
6/95	230	—	—	3,000
6/94	550	—	—	3,800
6/93	525	—	—	—
6/92	500	—	—	—
Annual Growth	**(7.4%)**	**—**	**—**	**0.7%**

Revenue History

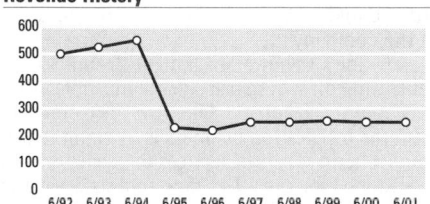

DeBruce Grain

Got a few tons of wheat and no place to keep it? DeBruce Grain stores, handles, and sells grain and fertilizer for the agribusiness industry. The company runs 10 grain-handling facilities, 13 grain elevators (with a storage capacity of 60 million bushels), a fertilizer distribution terminal, and seven retail fertilizer operations in five US states, as well as an office in Mexico, which serves its international customers. The company also markets both wholesale and retail fertilizer. DeBruce paid a $685,000 fine in relation to the 1998 explosion, which killed seven workers, of its Haysville, Kansas, facility — the largest grain elevator in the world. Owner and CEO Paul DeBruce founded the company in 1978.

EXECUTIVES

CEO: Paul DeBruce
President: Larry Kittoe
CFO: Curt Heinz
Manager, DeBruce Grain De México, S.A. de C.V.: Cristopher Brown
Manager, Creston Bean Processing: Weldon Sander
Manager, Abilene: Brent Martin
Manager, Amarillo: Lee Kleman
Manager, Creston: Dean Michealson
Manager, Dimmitt: Rodney Hunter
Manager, Etter: Rango Springer
Manager, Fremont: Chris Faust
Manager, Lexington: Carey Williams
Manager, Maceo: Larry Lenning
Manager, Nebraska City: Darin Hanson
Manager, Percival: Darin Hanson
Manager, Shenandoah: Ray Pinney
Manager, Thumel: Beau Hepler
Manager, Wichita: Neil Schwemmer

LOCATIONS

HQ: DeBruce Grain, Inc.
4100 N. Mulberry Dr., Kansas City, MO 64116
Phone: 816-421-8182   **Fax:** 816-584-2350
Web: www.debruce.com

PRODUCTS/OPERATIONS

Selected Divisions

DeBruce Fertilizer Inc.
DeBruce Grain Inc.
DeBruce Transportation Inc.

COMPETITORS

ADM	Cargill
Ag Processing	CHS
Bartlett and Company	ConAgra
Bunge Limited	Scoular

HISTORICAL FINANCIALS

Company Type: Private

Income Statement

FYE: March 31

	REVENUE ($ mil.)	NET INCOME ($ mil.)	NET PROFIT MARGIN	EMPLOYEES
3/04	2,018	—	—	420
3/03	1,729	—	—	420
3/02	1,378	—	—	400
3/01	1,201	—	—	330
3/00	879	—	—	300
3/99	772	—	—	250
3/98	723	—	—	200
3/97	865	—	—	200
3/96	688	—	—	150
3/95	507	—	—	130
Annual Growth	**16.6%**	**—**	**—**	**13.9%**

Revenue History

DecisionOne

Haven't decided which computer technology support services to use? Try DecisionOne. The company offers computer maintenance and technology support services for large businesses, manufacturers, Internet service providers, and software developers such as Motorola, Sony, Nortel Networks, and Sprint. DecisionOne's services include planning and consulting, call center support, deployment, network support, and logistics. In 2000 a group of investors, including Bear Stearns and Goldman Sachs, took DecisionOne private as it emerged from Chapter 11 bankruptcy.

The company has over 5,000 technicians working out of more than 150 North American offices. DecisionOne was founded in 1969 as Decision Data, a provider of keypunch machines.

EXECUTIVES

Chairman: Michael S. Williams
CEO and Director: Neal Bibeau
EVP and COO: Stephen W. (Steve) Martin
EVP and CFO: Paul H. Snyder, age 56
EVP, Business Development: John Rooney
VP and General Manager: Tom Praschak
VP, Major Account Sales and Marketing: Frank Tait
VP, Operations, Western Region: Nancy Alm
Manager, Marketing Communications: Dana Melia
Auditors: Deloitte & Touche LLP

LOCATIONS

HQ: DecisionOne Corporation
   426 W. Lancaster Ave., Devon, PA 19333
Phone: 610-296-6000 **Fax:** 610-296-2910
Web: www.decisionone.com

DecisionOne has offices in Canada and the US.

PRODUCTS/OPERATIONS

Services

Call center support
Deployment
Logistics
Network support
Planning and consulting
Technical support

COMPETITORS

Affiliated Computer Services	Data Systems & Software
Aquent	EDS
CHC	Getronics
CIBER	IBM
Computer Enterprises	Perot Systems
Computer Sciences Corp.	Sapient
CTG	u1.net
	Unisys

HISTORICAL FINANCIALS

Company Type: Private

Income Statement

FYE: June 30

	REVENUE ($ mil.)	NET INCOME ($ mil.)	NET PROFIT MARGIN	EMPLOYEES
6/04	363	—	—	4,500
6/03	500	—	—	4,400
6/02	450	—	—	4,000
6/01	490	—	—	4,000
6/00	528	—	—	4,000
6/99	726	—	—	5,110
6/98	806	—	—	6,500
6/97	786	—	—	6,560
6/96	540	—	—	5,600
6/95	163	—	—	5,900
Annual Growth	**9.3%**	**—**	**—**	**(3.0%)**

Revenue History

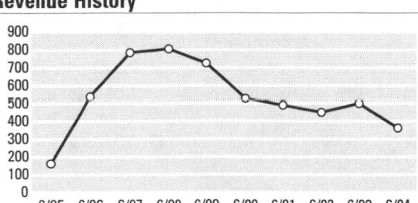

DeCrane Aircraft Holdings

DeCrane Aircraft Holdings makes big-wigs comfy jetting from coast-to-coast. Its largest operating group, Cabin Management, accounts for three-fourths of sales and offers products for corporate aircraft interiors, including furnishings, in-flight entertainment systems, composite components, and seating products. DeCrane's other operating group, Systems Integration, provides auxiliary fuel and power systems and offers engineering and installation services. Aircraft manufacturers Boeing, Bombardier, and Textron, which owns Cessna, account for about half of DeCrane's sales. Investment firm DLJ Merchant Banking Partners owns a controlling stake in the company.

DeCrane's Cabin Management group is concentrating on selling packages of multiple products to more customers. Likewise, the company's Systems Integration business is working to sell comprehensive sets of services to its customers.

Strapped for cash, DeCrane sold its Specialty Avionics division in 2003.

EXECUTIVES

Chairman: Thompson Dean, age 47
CEO and Director: R. Jack DeCrane, age 58, $546,406 pay
SVP, CFO, Secretary, Treasurer, and Director: Richard J. Kaplan, $307,389 pay
SVP and Group President, Systems Integration: Robert G. (Bob) Martin, age 67, $316,933 pay
SVP and Group President, Cabin Management Group: Donald G. Zerbe, age 58, $288,846 pay
VP Information Technology and Shared Services: Eric D. Steidl
VP Sales and Marketing, Audio International: Mike Hammers
VP Sales & Marketing, DeCrane Aircraft Seating Company, Inc.: Mark Anderson
Auditors: PricewaterhouseCoopers LLP

LOCATIONS

HQ: DeCrane Aircraft Holdings, Inc.
   8425 Pulsar Pl., Ste. 340, Columbus, OH 43240
Phone: 614-848-7700
Web: www.decraneaircraft.com

2004 Sales

	$ mil.	% of total
US	206.2	96
Mexico	7.5	4
Total	**213.7**	**100**

PRODUCTS/OPERATIONS

2004 Sales

	$ mil.	% of total
Cabin management	158.6	73
Systems integration	58.0	27
Adjustments	(2.9)	—
Total	**213.7**	**100**

Selected Products and Services

Cabin Management Group
   Composite components
   Entertainment and cabin-control systems
   Interior furnishings
   Seating
Systems Integration Group
   Auxiliary fuel systems
   Integration of cabin and flight-deck systems
   Power units

COMPETITORS

AAR
BE Aerospace
C&D Aerospace
Honeywell Aerospace
Jet Aviation
NORDAM
Weber Aircraft

HISTORICAL FINANCIALS

Company Type: Private

Income Statement

FYE: December 31

	REVENUE ($ mil.)	NET INCOME ($ mil.)	NET PROFIT MARGIN	EMPLOYEES
12/04	214	(43)	—	1,529
12/03	170	(73)	—	1,296
12/02	326	(66)	—	2,176
12/01	395	(19)	—	2,647
12/00	347	1	0.4%	2,865
12/99	244	(4)	—	2,536
12/98	150	(3)	—	1,451
12/97	109	3	2.9%	1,243
12/96	65	(6)	—	927
12/95	56	(3)	—	982
Annual Growth	**16.1%**	**—**	**—**	**5.0%**

2004 Year-End Financials

Debt ratio: —
Return on equity: —
Cash ($ mil.): 1
Current ratio: 1.89
Long-term debt ($ mil.): 339

Net Income History

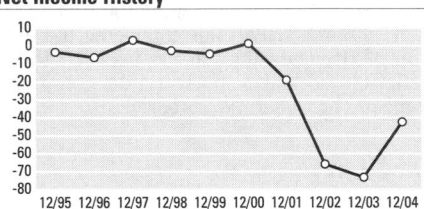

Delaware North

When it comes to corn dogs and nachos, Delaware North makes a lot of concessions. The firm has a string of subsidiaries ready to make hungry folks happy. Among the company's holdings are Sportservice (food service at sports stadiums), CA One Services (airport food service), and Delaware North Parks & Resorts (visitor services for national parks and tourist attractions). It also operates Boston's TD Banknorth Garden (formerly the FleetCenter). In addition, the company owns and operates a number of pari-mutuel racetracks nationwide through its Gaming & Entertainment division, a steamboat firm (Delta Queen), and American Park 'n Swap.

Delaware North has operations in Canada, Europe, the Pacific Rim, and the US. The company was founded in 1915 by brothers Charles, Louis, and Marvin Jacobs. The Jacobs family (including CEO Jeremy Jacobs, owner of the NHL's Boston Bruins) still controls it.

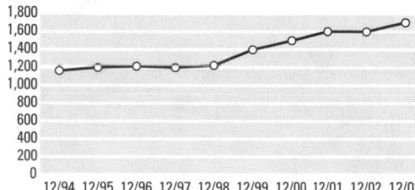

Revenue History

Deloitte

This company is "deloitted" to make your acquaintance, particularly if you're a big business in need of accounting services. Deloitte Touche Tohmatsu (now doing business simply as Deloitte) is one of accounting's Big Four, along with Ernst & Young, KPMG, and PricewaterhouseCoopers. Deloitte offers traditional audit and fiscal-oversight services to a multinational clientele. It also provides human resources and tax consulting services, as well as services to governments and international lending agencies working in emerging markets. (China and India are important markets.) Units include Deloitte & Touche (the US accounting arm) and Deloitte Consulting. Consulting services account for 25% of Deloitte's sales.

Deloitte spent the 1980s and 1990s pursuing a strategy of using accountants and consultants in concert to provide seamless service in auditing, accounting, strategic planning, information technology, financial management, and productivity. Deloitte Consulting became Deloitte's fastest-growing line, offering strategic and management consulting as well as information technology and human resources consulting.

Increasingly, though, Deloitte and its peers came under fire for their combined accounting/consulting operations; regulators and observers wondered whether accountants could maintain objectivity when they were auditing clients for whom they also provided consulting services. Criticism mounted after Enron's collapse capsized Arthur Andersen and put the entire accounting industry under scrutiny. (Deloitte picked up new business and members in Andersen's wake.)

Deloitte in 2002 announced it would spin off its consulting business, becoming the last of the big accountants to do so; a year later it called off the split, citing a weakened market for consulting, among other woes.

Deloitte was in the headlines again in late 2003, when auditing client Parmalat filed for bankruptcy in the midst of a $12 billion financial scandal, then dropped Deloitte as its auditor. Parmalat sued Deloitte in 2004, claiming its auditing procedures were inadequate and should have uncovered the fraud at Parmalat earlier.

HISTORY

In 1845 William Deloitte opened an accounting office in London, at first soliciting business from bankrupts. The growth of joint stock companies and the development of stock markets in the mid-19th century created a need for standardized financial reporting and fueled the rise of auditing, and Deloitte moved into the new field. The Great Western Railway appointed him as its independent auditor (the first anywhere) in 1849.

In 1890 John Griffiths, who had become a partner in 1869, opened the company's first US office in New York City. Four decades later branches had opened throughout the US. In 1952 the firm partnered with Haskins & Sells, which operated 34 US offices.

Deloitte aimed to be "the Cadillac, not the Ford" of accounting. The firm, which became Deloitte Haskins & Sells in 1978, began shedding its conservatism as competition heated up; it was the first of the major accountancy firms to use aggressive ads.

In 1984 Deloitte Haskins & Sells tried to merge with Price Waterhouse, but the deal was dropped after Price Waterhouse's UK partners objected.

In 1989 Deloitte Haskins & Sells joined the flamboyant Touche Ross (founded 1899) to become Deloitte & Touche. Touche Ross's Japanese affiliate, Ross Tohmatsu (founded 1968) rounded out the current name. The merger was engineered by Deloitte's Michael Cook and Touche's Edward Kangas, in part to unite the former firm's US and European strengths with the latter's Asian presence. Cook continued to oversee US operations, with Kangas presiding over international operations. Many affiliates, particularly in the UK, rejected the merger and defected to competing firms.

As auditors were increasingly held accountable for the financial results of their clients, legal action soared. In the 1990s Deloitte was sued because of its actions relating to Drexel Burnham Lambert junk bond king Michael Milken, the failure of several savings and loans, and clients' bankruptcies.

Nevertheless, in 1995 the SEC chose Michael Sutton, the firm's national director of auditing and accounting practice, as its chief accountant. That year Deloitte formed Deloitte & Touche Consulting to consolidate its US and UK consulting operations; its Asian consulting operations were later added to facilitate regional expansion.

In 1996 the firm formed a corporate fraud unit (with special emphasis on the Internet) and bought PHH Fantus, the leading corporate relocation consulting company. The next year Deloitte and Thurston Group (a Chicago-based merchant bank) teamed up to form NetDox, a system for delivering legal, financial, and insurance documents via the Internet. In 1997, amid a new round of industry mergers, rumors swirled that a Deloitte and Ernst & Young union had been scrapped because the firms could not agree on ownership issues. Deloitte disavowed plans to merge and launched an ad campaign directly targeted against its rivals.

The Asian economic crisis hurt overseas expansion in 1998, but provided a boost in restructuring consulting. In 1999 the firm sold its accounting staffing service unit (Resources Connection) to its managers and Evercore Partners, citing possible conflicts of interest with its core audit business. Also that year Deloitte Consulting decided to sell its computer programming subsidiary to CGI Group, and Kangas stepped down as CEO to be succeeded by James Copeland; the following year Kangas ceded the chairman's seat to Piet Hoogendoorn.

In 2001 the SEC forced Deloitte & Touche to restate the financial results of Pre-Paid Legal Services. In an unusual move, Deloitte & Touche publicly disagreed with the SEC's findings.

The accountancy put some old trouble to bed in 2003 when it agreed to pay $23 million to settle claims it had been negligent in its auditing of failed Kentucky Life Insurance, a client in the 1980s. Later that year the UK's High Court found Deloitte negligent in audits related to the failed Barings Bank; however, the ruling was considered something of a victory for the accountancy because it essentially cleared Deloitte of the majority of charges against it and effectively limited its financial liability in the matter. Copeland retired from the global CEO's office that year and handed the reins over to Bill Parrett, who had formerly served as managing director for the US and the Americas.

EXECUTIVES

Chairman: Piet Hoogendoorn
CEO; Senior Partner, US: William G. (Bill) Parrett, age 59
CFO and Managing Partner, Global Office: William A. Fowler
CIO: Wolfgang Richter
Global Managing Partner, Reputation, Excellence, and Practice Protection; Managing Partner, Netherlands: Willy A. Biewinga
Global Managing Partner, Innovation and Investment; Managing Partner, Germany and Regional Managing Partner, Europe/Middle East/Africa: Wolfgang Grewe
Global Managing Partner, Client Service Excellence; Tohmatsu Representative to DTT, and Regional Managing Partner, Japan: Shuichiro Sekine
Global Managing Partner, Brand and Eminence; Chief Executive and Managing Partner, Canada and Regional Managing Partner, North America: Colin Taylor
Global Managing Partner, Intellectual Capital, Inclusion, and Development; Chief Executive, France: Philippe Vassor
Global Managing Partner, Financial Advisory Services: Ralph G. Adams
Global Managing Partner, Audit: Stephen Almond
Global Managing Partner, Tax & Legal Services: Alan Schneier
Global Managing Partner, Human Resources: Conrad Venter
Managing Director, Finance and Administration: S. Ashish Bali
General Counsel: Joseph J. Lambert

LOCATIONS

HQ: Deloitte Touche Tohmatsu
1633 Broadway, New York, NY 10019
Phone: 212-436-2000   **Fax:** 212-436-5000
Web: www.deloitte.com

Deloitte Touche Tohmatsu operates through about 670 offices in nearly 150 countries.

2004 Sales

	$ mil.	% of total
Americas	8,200	50
Europe/Middle East/Africa	6,600	40
Asia-Pacific/Japan	1,600	10
Total	**16,400**	**100**

PRODUCTS/OPERATIONS

2004 Sales

	$ mil.	% of total
Audit	7,400	45
Consulting	4,000	25
Tax	3,800	23
Financial advisory services	1,200	7
Total	**16,400**	**100**

Selected Products and Services

Audit
Auditing services
Global offerings services
International financial reporting conversion services
Consulting
Enterprise applications
Human capital
Outsourcing
Strategy and operations
Technology integration
Enterprise Risk Services
Capital markets
Control assurance
Environment and sustainability
Internal audit
Regulatory consulting
Security services
Financial Advisory
Corporate finance
Forensic services
Reorganization services
Transaction services
Tax
Comprehensive tax solutions
Corporate tax
European Union services
Indirect tax
International assignment services
International tax
Mergers and acquisitions
Research and development credits
Tax technology solutions
Transfer pricing

COMPETITORS

Accenture	H&R Block
BDO International	KPMG
Booz Allen	Marsh & McLennan
Boston Consulting	McKinsey & Company
Capgemini	PricewaterhouseCoopers
EDS	Towers Perrin
Ernst & Young	Watson Wyatt
Grant Thornton	
International	

HISTORICAL FINANCIALS

Company Type: Partnership

Income Statement

FYE: May 31

	REVENUE ($ mil.)	NET INCOME ($ mil.)	NET PROFIT MARGIN	EMPLOYEES
5/04	16,400	—	—	115,000
5/03	15,100	—	—	119,237
5/02	12,500	—	—	98,000
5/01	12,400	—	—	95,000
5/00*	11,200	—	—	90,000
8/99	10,600	—	—	90,000
8/98	9,000	—	—	82,000
8/97	7,400	—	—	65,000
8/96	6,500	—	—	60,110
8/95	5,950	—	—	59,000
Annual Growth	11.9%	—	—	7.7%

*Fiscal year change

Revenue History

Delta Dental of California

Delta Dental of California (formerly Delta Dental Plan of California) doesn't just help keep the mouths of movie stars clean. A not-for-profit organization, the company is a member of the Delta Dental Plans Association and has affiliates nationwide. Delta Dental of California provides dental coverage through HMOs, preferred provider plans (PPOs), and such government programs as California's Denti-Cal. The company serves about 18 million enrollees in California; its programs cover more than one-third of California residents. Together with Delta Dental of Pennsylvania, Delta Dental of California formed Dentegra Group, a holding company that serves nearly 20 million members throughout the US.

Delta Dental of California also provides information technology services to other Delta Plan affiliates across the nation through its for-profit subsidiary, DeltaNet.

EXECUTIVES

President and CEO: Gary D. Radine
EVP and COO: Anthony S. (Tony) Barth
EVP and CFO: Michael J. Castro, age 42
EVP and CIO: Patrick S. Steele, age 54
EVP and Chief Dental Officer: Marilynn Belek
EVP and Chief Legal Officer: Robert G. Becker
SVP and Associate General Counsel: Charles Lamont
SVP Administration: Jerry Holcombe
SVP Enterprise Dental Affairs: Michael McGinley
SVP Sales and Marketing: Robert B. Elliot
SVP Sales and Marketing: Belinda Martinez
SVP State Government Programs: Michael Kaufmann
Manager Media and Affiliate Communications: Elizabeth Risberg
Director Public Affairs: Jeff Album

LOCATIONS

HQ: Delta Dental of California
100 1st St., San Francisco, CA 94105
Phone: 415-972-8300   **Fax:** 415-972-8466
Web: www.deltadentalca.org

PRODUCTS/OPERATIONS

Selected Products

DeltaCare (dental plans for groups in more than one state)
DeltaCare USA (group and individual dental HMOs)
DeltaVision (group vision HMO)

COMPETITORS

Aetna
CIGNA
Health Net
MetLife
PacifiCare
SafeGuard Health Enterprises
WellPoint

HISTORICAL FINANCIALS

Company Type: Not-for-profit

Income Statement				FYE: December 31
	REVENUE ($ mil.)	NET INCOME ($ mil.)	NET PROFIT MARGIN	EMPLOYEES
12/03	4,300	—	—	2,500
12/02	4,000	—	—	2,500
12/01	3,300	—	—	2,400
12/00	2,800	—	—	2,400
12/99	2,700	—	—	2,400
12/98	2,440	—	—	2,400
12/97	2,315	—	—	2,115
12/96	2,114	—	—	1,960
12/95	2,145	—	—	1,800
12/94	2,025	—	—	1,649
Annual Growth	8.7%	—	—	4.7%

Revenue History

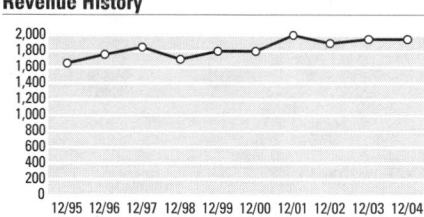

Demoulas Super Markets

Supermarket or soap opera? Demoulas Super Markets runs about 60 grocery stores under the Market Basket and Demoulas Super Market names in Massachusetts and New Hampshire. The firm also has real estate interests. The company was founded in 1954 when brothers George and Mike Demoulas bought their parents' mom-and-pop grocery. The men agreed that, upon one brother's death, the other would care for the deceased's family and maintain the firm's 50-50 ownership. In 1990 George's family alleged that Mike had defrauded them of all but 8% of the company's stock; the 10-year court battle was decided in favor of George's family, giving it 51% of the company. By then Mike had resigned as CEO; the post remains vacant.

EXECUTIVES

EVP: Julien Lacourse
EVP: James Miamis
VP, Finance and Treasurer: Donald Mulligan
VP, Grocery Sales and Merchandising: Joseph Rockwell
VP and Treasurer, Retail Management and Development Inc.: Michael Kettenbach
Corporate Counsel: Sumner Darman
Payroll Administrator: Lucille Lopez
Coffee and Beverage Buyer: Jim Lacourse

LOCATIONS

HQ: Demoulas Super Markets Inc.
875 East St., Tewksbury, MA 01876
Phone: 978-851-8000 **Fax:** 978-640-8390

COMPETITORS

Big Y Foods	IGA
BJ's Wholesale Club	Shaw's
Costco Wholesale	Stop & Shop
Cumberland Farms	SUPERVALU
Golub	Wal-Mart
Hannaford Bros.	

HISTORICAL FINANCIALS

Company Type: Private

Income Statement				FYE: December 31
	ESTIMATED REVENUE ($ mil.)	NET INCOME ($ mil.)	NET PROFIT MARGIN	EMPLOYEES
12/04	1,950	—	—	—
12/03	1,950	—	—	12,900
12/02	1,900	—	—	12,700
12/01	2,000	—	—	12,700
12/00	1,800	—	—	12,500
12/99	1,800	—	—	12,500
12/98	1,700	—	—	12,350
12/97	1,850	—	—	12,300
12/96	1,760	—	—	11,900
12/95	1,650	—	—	11,700
Annual Growth	1.9%	—	—	1.2%

Revenue History

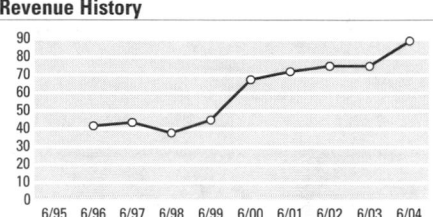

Denver Nuggets

The mother lode of the NBA has eluded the Denver Nuggets for more than 30 years. The franchise was founded in 1967 as the Denver Rockets and backed by trucking magnate J. W. "Bill" Ringsby. A charter member of the American Basketball Association, the team (renamed the Nuggets in 1974) joined the NBA in 1976. While the Nuggets prospered early in the NBA, the franchise has toiled in defeat for much of its history. Behind the talents of forward Carmelo Anthony, the team made the playoffs in 2004 for the first time in nine years. In 2005 the team named confrontational NBA veteran George Karl head coach. He led them to the playoffs that year. Wal-Mart heir Stan Kroenke owns the team and its home, the Pepsi Center.

EXECUTIVES

Owner: E. Stanley (Stan) Kroenke
General Manager: Ernest M. (Kiki) Vandeweghe III
Assistant General Manager: David Fredman, age 48
Assistant General Manager: Jeff Weltman
Head Coach: George Karl, age 54
Assistant Coach: Scott Brooks
Assistant Coach: Adrian Dantley
Assistant Coach: Doug Moe
SVP Sports Finance: Mark Waggoner
SVP Ticket Sales and Service: Paul Andrews
Senior Director, Communications: Teri Washington
Director, Human Resources: Cheryl Miller

LOCATIONS

HQ: Denver Nuggets
1000 Chopper Circle, Denver, CO 80204
Phone: 303-405-1100 **Fax:** 303-575-1920
Web: www.nba.com/nuggets

The Denver Nuggets play at the 19,099-capacity Pepsi Center in Denver.

COMPETITORS

Minnesota Timberwolves	Seattle SuperSonics
Portland Trail Blazers	Utah Jazz

HISTORICAL FINANCIALS

Company Type: Private

Income Statement				FYE: June 30
	REVENUE ($ mil.)	NET INCOME ($ mil.)	NET PROFIT MARGIN	EMPLOYEES
6/04	89	—	—	—
6/03	75	—	—	—
6/02	75	—	—	—
6/01	72	—	—	—
6/00	68	—	—	—
6/99	45	—	—	120
6/98	38	—	—	100
6/97	44	—	—	—
6/96	42	—	—	—
Annual Growth	9.9%	—	—	20.0%

Revenue History

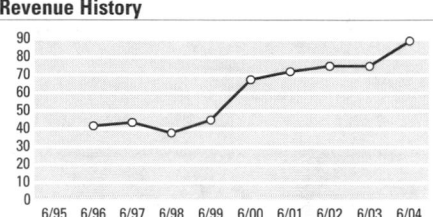

Derive Technologies

Derive Technologies provides network integration services, such as infrastructure development, maintenance, and security. The company installs and maintains IT products from a variety of vendors, including Cisco Systems, Citrix Systems, Computer Associates, Hewlett-Packard, IBM, Microsoft, and VERITAS Software. CEO Kirit Desai owns about 40% of the company; Lawrence Marcus (COO), Mitchell Martinez (EVP Sales), Darius Stafford (CTO), John Wood (VP Business Development and Sales), and Madhu Royal (VP Sales) together own about 60%. Derive Technologies was founded in 1987.

EXECUTIVES

CEO: Kirit Desai
COO: Lawrence Marcus
EVP Sales: Mitch Martinez
VP Business Development and Sales: John Wood
VP Sales: Madhu Royal
CTO: Darius Stafford

LOCATIONS

HQ: Derive Technologies LLC
116 John St., New York, NY 10038
Phone: 212-363-1111 **Fax:** 212-363-6188
Web: www.derivetech.com

COMPETITORS

ePlus
Software House
Westcon

HISTORICAL FINANCIALS

Company Type: Private

Income Statement

FYE: December 31

	REVENUE ($ mil.)	NET INCOME ($ mil.)	NET PROFIT MARGIN	EMPLOYEES
12/04	63	—	—	95
12/03	39	—	—	70
12/02	64	—	—	75
Annual Growth	(0.8%)	—	—	12.5%

Revenue History

70									
60									
50									
40									
30									
20									
10									
0									

12/95 12/96 12/97 12/98 12/99 12/00 12/01 12/02 12/03 12/04

Desert Island Restaurants

Being marooned at one of this company's restaurants might not be such a bad experience. Desert Island Restaurants operates a small chain of upscale Asian-themed restaurants under the name Thaifoon — Taste of Asia. Borrowing from the cuisines of several Asian countries, the restaurants serve lunch and dinner and offer take-out service. The company has four Thaifoon locations in Arizona, California, and Utah. Desert Island also operates three Ruth's Chris Steak House franchises in Hawaii and its own Franco's Italian Café in Phoenix. CEO Randy Schoch founded the company in 1998 and opened the first Thaifoon restaurant in 2001.

EXECUTIVES

CEO: W. Randall (Randy) Schoch
VP and CFO: Robert (Bob) Snyder
Controller: Angela Larson
Director of Human Resources: Linda Eckert
Director of Marketing and Public Relations: Adeline Lui
General Manager, Irvine: Mike Kinsella
General Manager, Newport Beach: Tim Rodney
General Manager, Scottsdale: Jim Duginski
General Manager, Salt Lake City: Patti Rasmussen
Chef, Newport Beach: Luis Zaragoza
Chef, Scottsdale: Andy Adams
Chef, Irvine: Erik Kronquist
Chef, Salt Lake City: Greg Smith
Group Sales Manager, Irvine: Ashley Van Asten

LOCATIONS

HQ: Desert Island Restaurants, L.L.C.
6263 N. Scottsdale Rd., Ste. 374,
Scottsdale, AZ 85250
Phone: 480-945-0088 **Fax:** 480-945-4747
Web: www.thaifoon.com

Selected Thaifoon Locations

Irvine, CA
Newport Beach, CA
Salt Lake City
Scottsdale, AZ

COMPETITORS

Benihana
BUCA
California Pizza Kitchen
Carlson Restaurants
Cheesecake Factory
Darden
Leeann Chin
Lettuce Entertain You
Noodles & Company
Outback Steakhouse
P.F. Chang's
Romacorp
Ruby Tuesday

HISTORICAL FINANCIALS

Company Type: Private

Income Statement

FYE: December 31

	REVENUE ($ mil.)	NET INCOME ($ mil.)	NET PROFIT MARGIN	EMPLOYEES
12/04	24	—	—	500
12/03	25	—	—	500
12/02	30	—	—	500
Annual Growth	(10.6%)	—	—	0.0%

Revenue History

30									
25									
20									
15									
10									
5									
0									

12/95 12/96 12/97 12/98 12/99 12/00 12/01 12/02 12/03 12/04

Desert Schools Federal Credit Union

One of the largest credit unions in Arizona, Desert Schools operates some 45 locations in the Phoenix area, serving more than 285,000 members. Founded in 1939 by a group of 15 teachers, the credit union offers banking products and services including checking and savings accounts, IRAs, and CDs. Subsidiary Desert Schools Financial Services sells insurance products and investment services. On top of the organization's core clientele of school employees and retirees, membership is available to any individual living, working, or attending church or school in Gila, Maricopa, or Pinal counties.

EXECUTIVES

Chairman: G. Frank Davidson
Vice Chairman: Richard Johnson
President and CEO: Susan C. Frank
Secretary: Claudette M. Gronksi
Treasurer: Michael J. Konen
Auditors: McGladrey & Pullen, LLP

LOCATIONS

HQ: Desert Schools Federal Credit Union
148 N. 48th St., Phoenix, AZ 85034
Phone: 602-433-7000 **Fax:** 602-246-8339
Web: www.desertschools.org

PRODUCTS/OPERATIONS

2004 Sales

	$ mil.	% of total
Interest		
Loans to members	92.5	65
Investments & cash equivalents	14.6	10
Noninterest		
Service charges & other fees	29.7	21
Net gains on sales of loans	2.6	2
Other	3.5	2
Total	**142.9**	**100**

COMPETITORS

Bank of America
Compass Bancshares
JPMorgan Chase
Marshall & Ilsley
Ohio Savings Bank
Washington Mutual
Wells Fargo
Western Alliance
Zions Bancorporation

HISTORICAL FINANCIALS

Company Type: Not-for-profit

Income Statement

FYE: December 31

	ASSETS ($ mil.)	NET INCOME ($ mil.)	INCOME AS % OF ASSETS	EMPLOYEES
12/04	2,212	28	1.3%	1,000
12/03	1,979	27	1.4%	700
12/02	1,755	27	1.5%	—
Annual Growth	12.3%	1.8%	—	42.9%

2004 Year-End Financials

Equity as % of assets: 10.8%   Long-term debt ($ mil.): 50
Return on assets: 1.3%   Sales ($ mil.): 143
Return on equity: 12.4%

Net Income History

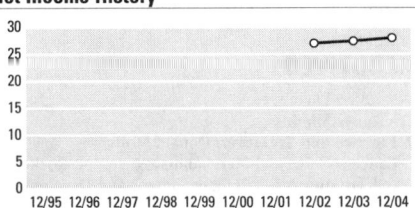

30									
25									
20									
15									
10									
5									
0									

12/95 12/96 12/97 12/98 12/99 12/00 12/01 12/02 12/03 12/04

Detroit Medical Center

The seeds for the Detroit Medical Center were planted in 1955, when four Detroit hospitals joined efforts to provide coordination between the hospitals and Wayne State University's medical school. Today the medical center (which became a not-for-profit corporation in 1985) serves patients in southeastern Michigan with more than 2,000 beds and some 3,000 physicians. The center is made up of seven hospitals, more than 100 outpatient facilities, and two nursing centers. The Detroit Medical Center is the teaching and clinical research site for Wayne State, now one of the US's largest medical schools; it is also allied with the Barbara Ann Karmanos Cancer Institute and the Kresge Eye Institute.

EXECUTIVES

President and CEO: Michael E. Duggan
EVP and COO: Benjamin Carter, age 46
EVP and CFO: Christopher J. (Chris) Palazzoo
EVP and Chief Administrative Officer: Richard T. Cole
EVP and Chief Medical Officer: Thomas A. Malone
VP Human Resources: Ruthann Liagre
VP Laboratory Services, DMCUL: Verdell Tolbert
CIO: Michael LeRoy
Director Communication: Emery King
Director Marketing and Communication: Sharyl Smith
Director Sales and Marketing, DMCUL: Donna Hekker
General Counsel: Floyd Allen

LOCATIONS

HQ: Detroit Medical Center
3990 John R. St., Detroit, MI 48201
Phone: 313-578-2000   **Fax:** 313-578-3225
Web: www.dmc.org

PRODUCTS/OPERATIONS

Hospitals

Children's Hospital of Michigan (Detroit)
Detroit Receiving Hospital and University Health Center
Harper Hospital (Detroit)
Huron Valley-Sinai Hospital (Commerce, MI)
Hutzel Women's Hospital (Detroit)
Rehabilitation Institute of Michigan (Detroit)
Sinai-Grace Hospital (Detroit)

Selected Affiliates

Barbara Ann Karmanos Cancer Institute
DMC Health Care Centers
DMC Nursing Centers
International Center
Kresge Eye Institute
Renaissance Home Health Care

COMPETITORS

Ascension Health
Catholic Health Initiatives
HCA
Henry Ford Health System
Trinity Health (Novi)
William Beaumont Hospital

HISTORICAL FINANCIALS

Company Type: Not-for-profit

Income Statement				FYE: December 31
	REVENUE ($ mil.)	NET INCOME ($ mil.)	NET PROFIT MARGIN	EMPLOYEES
12/03	1,600	—	—	14,311
12/02	1,600	—	—	13,000
12/01	1,600	—	—	14,000
12/00	1,600	—	—	16,500
12/99	1,453	—	—	16,500
12/98	1,573	—	—	16,500
12/97	1,448	—	—	16,288
12/96	1,300	—	—	13,879
12/95	1,200	—	—	10,000
12/94	1,161	—	—	12,000
Annual Growth	3.6%	—	—	2.0%

Revenue History

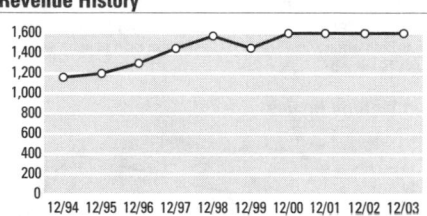

Dewey Ballantine

International law firm Dewey Ballantine, which has changed its name about a dozen times in its 90-plus years of existence, has 550 lawyers in more than a dozen offices worldwide. Its areas of expertise include antitrust, corporate, tax, and trade law, as well as mergers and acquisitions (Dewey Ballantine has overseen some of the larger M&A deals in recent history, including Chrysler's merger with Daimler Benz). Dewey Ballantine was founded in 1909 by three Harvard Law School grads; the Dewey in the name refers to former partner Thomas Dewey, famous for the "Dewey Defeats Truman" headline from the 1948 presidential election.

EXECUTIVES

Chairman: Morton A. Pierce
Executive Director: Dennis D'Alessandro
Director of Finance: Peter Casey
Director of Global Operations: Thomas Van Buskirk
Director of Human Resources: Mary Ellen Ciafardini
Director of Information Technology: Eva Steiner
Director of Library Services: Gitelle Seer
Partner: Seth Farber
Recruiting, Administrative Staff, New York Office: Patrizia DeGennaro
Recruiting, Legal, New York Office: Nicole Gunn
Recruiting, Paralegal Staff, New York Office: Eva Lantos
Professional Development and Training, New York Office: Susan Briggs
Director of Marketing and Communications: Jason S. Dinwoodie

LOCATIONS

HQ: Dewey Ballantine LLP
1301 Avenue of the Americas, New York, NY 10019
Phone: 212-259-8000   **Fax:** 212-259-6333
Web: www.deweyballantine.com

Dewey Ballantine has offices in Austin and Houston, Texas; Beijing; East Palo Alto and Los Angeles, California; Frankfurt; London; Milan and Rome, Italy; New York City; Warsaw; and Washington, DC.

PRODUCTS/OPERATIONS

Selected Practice Areas

Antitrust
Banking and financial institutions
Corporate
Employment law
Energy
Intellectual property
International trade
Litigation
Mergers and acquisitions
Public policy
Real estate
Tax
Technology
White collar crime

COMPETITORS

Baker & McKenzie
Cleary Gottlieb
Cravath, Swaine
Davis Polk
Fried, Frank, Harris
Jones Day
Kirkland & Ellis
Shearman & Sterling
Skadden, Arps
White & Case
Willkie Farr

HISTORICAL FINANCIALS

Company Type: Partnership

Income Statement				FYE: September 30
	REVENUE ($ mil.)	NET INCOME ($ mil.)	NET PROFIT MARGIN	EMPLOYEES
9/04	381	—	—	—
9/03	374	—	—	—
9/02	350	—	—	—
9/01	328	—	—	—
9/00	307	—	—	—
9/99	202	—	—	1,000
9/98	250	—	—	976
9/97	228	—	—	951
9/96	202	—	—	—
9/95	174	—	—	—
Annual Growth	9.1%	—	—	2.5%

Revenue History

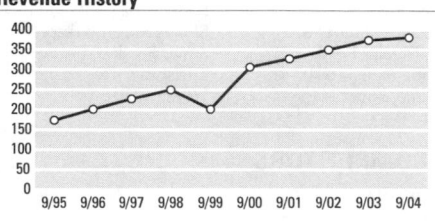

Di Giorgio

Di Giorgio delivers little apples (and other foods) to the Big Apple. Founded in 1920, the firm is a food wholesaler and distributor primarily in New York City, Long Island, New Jersey, and the greater Philadelphia area. It offers more than 24,000 products to food retailers ranging from independents and members of co-ops to regional chains. (Associated Food Stores accounts for 19% of sales.) Although Di Giorgio distributes national brands, it also supplies frozen and refrigerated products under its White Rose brand, a name known in New York for well over a century. Di Giorgio co-chairman and CEO Richard Neff owns approximately 99% of the company, primarily through his sole general partnership in Rose Partners.

Capitalizing on the popularity of ethnic and organic foods, Di Giorgio has launched a new division called DGI Specialty Foods, which offers a complete line of specialty food products including ethnic, gourmet, and organic products. Di Giorgio lost its largest customer A&P in October 2003.

EXECUTIVES

Co-chairman: Richard B. Neff, age 56, $660,000 pay
Co-chairman, President and COO: Stephen R. Bokser, age 62, $840,000 pay
SVP and CFO: Lawrence S. (Larry) Grossman, age 43, $286,000 pay
EVP, Finance and Treasurer: Robert A. Zorn, age 50, $332,100 pay
SVP, Distribution: Joseph R. DeSimone, age 65
SVP and General Manager, White Rose Dairy Division and DGI Specialty Foods: Joseph Fantozzi, age 43, $294,000 pay
SVP and General Manager, White Rose Frozen Division: John Annetta, age 53, $285,500 pay
SVP: John J. Zumba, age 67
VP, General Counsel, and Secretary: Harlan Levine, age 43
VP, Logistics: George Conklin, age 44
Assistant VP, Human Resources: Jackie Simmons
Auditors: Deloitte & Touche LLP

LOCATIONS

HQ: Di Giorgio Corporation
380 Middlesex Ave., Carteret, NJ 07008
Phone: 732-541-5555   **Fax:** 732-541-3590
Web: www.whiterose.com

PRODUCTS/OPERATIONS

Selected Customers

Associated Foods Stores	Met
Bravo	Pioneer
C-Town	Scaturros
Foodtown	Shop 'N Bag
Grande (Puerto Rico)	Sloans Supermarkets
Gristede's Foods	Super Food
King Kullen	Thristway
Kings Super Markets	Western Beef

COMPETITORS

Associated Wholesalers
Bozzuto's
C&S Wholesale
General Trading
Key Food
Krasdale Foods
SGA Sales & Mktg
SUPERVALU
Wakefern Food

HISTORICAL FINANCIALS

Company Type: Private

Income Statement
FYE: Saturday nearest December 31

	REVENUE ($ mil.)	NET INCOME ($ mil.)	NET PROFIT MARGIN	EMPLOYEES
12/04	1,297	8	0.6%	1,201
12/03	1,544	14	0.9%	1,238
12/02	1,560	13	0.8%	1,288
12/01	1,539	12	0.8%	1,353
12/00	1,488	11	0.7%	1,373
12/99	1,414	10	0.7%	1,275
12/98	1,197	4	0.4%	1,229
12/97	1,072	(3)	—	1,156
12/96	1,050	5	0.5%	1,123
12/95	1,020	0	—	1,135
Annual Growth	2.7%	—	—	0.6%

2004 Year-End Financials

Debt ratio: 484.2%
Return on equity: 25.7%
Cash ($ mil.): 8
Current ratio: 1.58
Long-term debt ($ mil.): 148

Net Income History

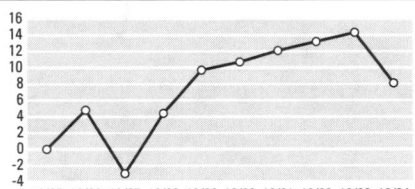

Directed Electronics

Please step away from the vehicle. Directed Electronics, one of the world's top manufacturers of auto security systems, delivers products with a bite — or sting — intended to keep would-be car thieves at arm's length. Brand names include Viper, Python, and Hornet. Directed Electronics also makes keyless entry and remote start systems for automobiles and offers GPS tracking systems. In addition, the company manufactures car audio equipment, including speakers and amplifiers. Directed Electronics, which was founded in 1982, is controlled by Miami-based investment firm Trivest.

Other Directed Electronics offerings include mobile video systems, speakers for home audio systems, and Sirius satellite radio products.

The company sells its products through a variety of channels, including automotive parts retailers, car dealers, electronics chains, and mass merchandisers. Best Buy and Circuit City are major customers.

EXECUTIVES

Chairman: Troy D. Templeton, age 44
President, CEO, and Director: James E. (Jim) Minarik, age 52, $901,122 pay
EVP, Home Audio: Sanford M. Gross
SVP, Sales and Marketing: Glenn R. Busse, age 43, $370,327 pay
VP, Finance and CFO: Richard J. (Rich) Hirshberg, age 51, $313,159 pay
VP and General Counsel: K. C. Bean, age 41
VP, Engineering and Product Development: Mark E. Rutledge, age 35, $319,890 pay
VP, Strategy and Corporate Development: Kevin P. Duffy, age 30, $281,819 pay
VP, Operations and Management Information Systems: Michael N. Smith, age 39
Director Communications: Kennedy Gammage
Director Human Resources: Pat Merson
Director Marketing: Jim Jardin
Auditors: PricewaterhouseCoopers LLP

LOCATIONS

HQ: Directed Electronics, Inc.
1 Viper Way, Vista, CA 92081
Phone: 760-598-6200   **Fax:** 760-598-6400
Web: www.directed.com

COMPETITORS

Audiovox
Bose
Clarion
Harman International
Kenwood
Phoenix Gold
Pioneer
Rockford
SANYO
Winner International

HISTORICAL FINANCIALS

Company Type: Private

Income Statement
FYE: December 31

	REVENUE ($ mil.)	NET INCOME ($ mil.)	NET PROFIT MARGIN	EMPLOYEES
12/04	190	14	7.4%	235
12/03	132	13	9.5%	225
12/02	124	13	10.3%	210
12/01	120	—	—	190
12/00	101	—	—	170
12/99	87	—	—	170
12/98	79	—	—	170
12/97	75	—	—	150
12/96	68	—	—	137
12/95	64	—	—	90
Annual Growth	12.8%	4.6%	—	11.3%

2004 Year-End Financials

Debt ratio:
Return on equity: 37.6%
Cash ($ mil.): 4
Current ratio: 1.66
Long-term debt ($ mil.): 226

Net Income History

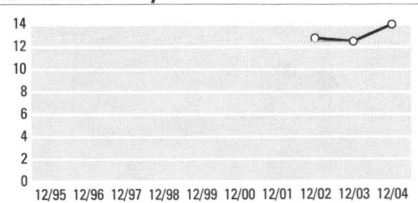

Discount Tire

Concerned about that upcoming "re-tirement"? Discount Tire Co., one of the largest independent tire dealers in the US, can provide several options. With more than 600 stores in 18 states, the company sells such leading brands as Michelin, Goodyear, and Uniroyal, as well as wheels. Discount Tire operates mostly in the Midwest and Southwest. Some of the company's West Coast stores operate as America's Tire Co. because of a name conflict. Customers can search for tires by make and model on the company's Web site. Chairman and owner Bruce Halle founded the company in 1960 with six tires — four of them recaps.

EXECUTIVES

CEO: Tom Englert
Chairman: Bruce Halle
Vice Chairman: Gary T. Van Brunt
CFO: Christian Roe
EVP and Chief Administrative Officer: Bob Holman
Assistant Vice President, Human Resources and Payroll: Staci Adams

LOCATIONS

HQ: Discount Tire Co. Inc.
20225 N. Scottsdale Rd., Scottsdale, AZ 85255
Phone: 480-606-6000 **Fax:** 480-606-4401
Web: www.discounttire.com

Discount Tire Co. and America's Tire Co. have stores in Arizona, California, Colorado, Florida, Georgia, Illinois, Indiana, Michigan, Minnesota, Nevada, New Mexico, North Carolina, Ohio, Oregon, South Carolina, Texas, Utah, and Washington.

COMPETITORS

BFS Retail & Commercial Operations
Les Schwab Tire Centers
Penske
Pep Boys
Sears
TBC
TCI Tire Centers
Wal-Mart

HISTORICAL FINANCIALS

Company Type: Private

Income Statement

FYE: December 31

	REVENUE ($ mil.)	NET INCOME ($ mil.)	NET PROFIT MARGIN	EMPLOYEES
12/03	1,541	—	—	9,500
12/02	1,417	—	—	8,944
12/01	1,320	—	—	8,415
12/00	1,192	—	—	8,987
12/99	1,031	—	—	8,100
12/98	900	—	—	6,500
12/97	864	—	—	6,200
12/96	739	—	—	5,154
12/95	658	—	—	4,714
12/94	590	—	—	4,200
Annual Growth	**11.3%**	**—**	**—**	**9.5%**

Revenue History

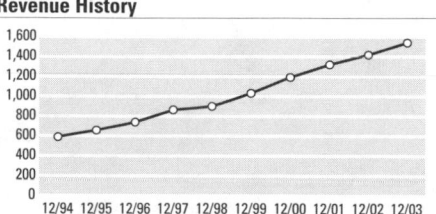

Discovery Communications

Discover science and nature in the comfort of your living room with Discovery Communications (DCI). Reaching more than 86 million households, its Discovery Channel is one of the top-rated cable networks in the US. DCI owns other cable networks as well, including The Learning Channel (which faces tough times due to the declining popularity of its *Trading Spaces* program), Travel Channel, and Animal Planet. Internationally, DCI's channels reach 160 countries. DCI also operates Discovery Channel retail stores, and its Internet unit, Discovery.com, houses various nature and science Web sites. Discovery Holding (50%), Cox Communications (25%), and Advance/Newhouse Communications (25%) own DCI.

The company also operates five digital Discovery cable channels focused on specific topics such as science and home and health. In a joint venture, Discovery and The New York Times Company have launched the news-oriented Discovery Times Channel, which took the place of the Discovery Civilization Channel. The company also launched a new digital cable network called Discovery HD Theater, which features high-definition quality television. In addition, it rebranded the aviation-themed Discovery Wings channel as the Military Channel, focusing on the armed forces.

Once Discovery's most popular network, The Learning Channel (TLC) has seen its popularity decline rapidly as the network broadcast a glut of home makeover programming to cash in on the success of *Trading Spaces*. The overexposure led to lower ratings at TLC virtually across the board, leading Discovery to dump *Trading Spaces*' perky host Paige Davis in favor of a hostless format. Several top executives have also left the channel.

Building on its name brand, DCI creates original programming, games, and activities for a series of science and nature Web sites under the Discovery.com name and publishes videos, books, and CD-ROMs. It also operates about 165 Discovery Channel retail stores.

Speculation about whether DCI would be acquired has run rampant in recent years, but founder John Hendricks always denied reports of a sale. Hendricks did, however, step down as the firm's CEO in mid-2004 (he remains chairman). President Judy McHale replaced him. Early the next year, former majority owner Liberty Media placed its interest in Discovery, as well as its Ascent Media film and video post-production subsidiary, into a new company called Discovery Holding, which it is spun off to Liberty Media shareholders.

HISTORY

John Hendricks, a history graduate who wanted to expand the presence of educational programming on TV, founded Cable Educational Network in 1982. Three years later he introduced the Discovery Channel. Devoted entirely to documentaries and nature shows, the channel premiered in 156,000 US homes. After dodging bankruptcy (it had $5,000 cash and $1 million in debt to the BBC), within a year the Discovery Channel had 7 million subscribers and a host of new investors,

including Cox Cable Communications and TCI (now AT&T Broadband). It expanded its programming from 12 hours to 18 hours a day in 1987.

Discovery continued to attract subscribers, reaching more than 32 million by 1988. The next year it launched Discovery Channel Europe to more than 200,000 homes in the UK and Scandinavia. The company began selling home videos in 1990 and entered the Israeli market. The following year Discovery Communications, Inc. (DCI) was formed to house the company's operations, and it bought The Learning Channel (TLC, founded in 1980). The company revamped TLC's programming, and in 1992 introduced a daily, six-hour, commercial-free block of children's programs. The next year it introduced its first CD-ROM title, *In the Company of Whales*, based on the Discovery Channel documentary.

DCI increased its focus on international expansion in 1994, moving into Asia, Latin America, the Middle East, North Africa, Portugal, and Spain. The next year the company introduced its Web site and began selling company merchandise such as CD-ROMs and videos. DCI solidified its move into the retail sector in 1996 with the acquisition of The Nature Company and Scientific Revolution chains (renamed Discovery Channel Store). Also that year it launched its third major cable channel, Animal Planet.

The company continued expanding internationally throughout the mid-1990s, establishing operations in Australia, Canada, India, New Zealand, and South Korea (1995); Africa, Brazil, Germany, and Italy (1996); and Japan and Turkey (1997). DCI also added to its stable of cable channels with the purchase of 70% of Paxson Communications' Travel Channel in 1997 (it acquired the rest in 1999). The company's 1997 original production, "Titanic: Anatomy of a Disaster," attracted 3.2 million US households, setting a network ratings record.

DCI spent $330 million launching its new health and fitness channel, Discovery Health, in 1999 and formed partnerships with high-speed online service Road Runner (to provide interactive information and services to Road Runner customers) and Rosenbluth Travel (to provide vacation packages based on DCI programming).

DCI reorganized its Internet activities into one unit called Discovery.com in 2000 with plans to eventually take it public. Later that year the Discovery Channel set back-to-back records with the two highest-rated documentaries ever on cable, "Raising the Mammoth" (10.1 million people) and "Walking With Dinosaurs" (10.7 million people). In 2001 the company cut about 50 jobs as part of a restructuring. Later that year Discovery Communications struck a three-year deal to lease time from NBC on Saturday mornings (paying $6 million per season) to show its Discovery Kids programs.

In 2002 the company launched a 24-hour high-definition television network called Discovery HD Theater. Two years later founder John Hendricks relinquished his CEO duties (he remains chairman). President Judy McHale replaced him.

DCI started off 2005 by re-branding its aviation-themed Discovery Wings channel as the Military Channel. Later that year, former majority owner Liberty Media placed its stake in DCI into a new company called Discovery Holding, which it then spun off to Liberty shareholders.

EXECUTIVES

Chairman: John S. Hendricks, age 52
President and CEO: Judith A. McHale, age 58
President, Affiliate Sales and Marketing: Bill Goodwyn
President, Discovery Commerce: Frank Rosales
President, Discovery Networks International:
Dawn L. McCall
President, Discovery Networks, US:
William M. (Billy) Campbell III
President, Discovery Networks US Production:
Clark Bunting
SEVP Corporate Operations and General Counsel:
Mark Hollinger
SEVP Human Resources and Administration:
Pandit F. Wright
SEVP Strategy and Development: Donald A. Baer
EVP and CFO: Barbara (Barb) Bennett
EVP New Media and Network Services: Mona Abutaleb
EVP and General Manager, Animal Planet, US:
Maureen Smith
EVP Production: Carole Tomko
EVP Advertising Sales: Scott McGraw
EVP Marketing, Discovery Networks US: Ken Dice
SVP Corporate Affairs and Communications:
David Leavy

LOCATIONS

HQ: Discovery Communications, Inc.
1 Discovery Place, Silver Spring, MD 20910
Phone: 240-662-2000   **Fax:** 240-662-1868
Web: www.discovery.com

PRODUCTS/OPERATIONS

Selected Operations

Discovery Commerce
  Discovery Consumer Products
    Discovery Channel Catalog (product catalog)
    Discovery Channel Stores (approximately 165
      Discovery Channel retail outlets)
    Discovery Education (educational video productions)
    Discovery.com (online store)
Discovery HD Theater (digital channel featuring high-
  definition TV programming)
Discovery Networks International (35 languages, 160
  countries)
Discovery Networks US
  Animal Planet
  BBC America (markets and distributes for the BBC)
  Discovery Channel
  Discovery en Español
  Discovery Health Channel
  Discovery Kids
  Discovery Times Channel
  FitTV
  The Learning Channel
  Military Channel
  The Science Channel
  Travel Channel

COMPETITORS

A&E Networks
American Institute Of Physics
CPB
Crown Media
Disney
Imaginova
Lifetime
National Geographic
NBC Universal
News Corp.
Oxygen Media
PBS
Scripps Networks
Time Warner
Univision
Viacom

HISTORICAL FINANCIALS

Company Type: Joint venture

Income Statement

FYE: December 31

	REVENUE ($ mil.)	NET INCOME ($ mil.)	NET PROFIT MARGIN	EMPLOYEES
12/04	2,365	—	—	—
12/03	1,995	—	—	5,000
12/02	1,717	—	—	5,000
12/01	1,800	—	—	4,000
12/00	1,730	—	—	4,000
12/99	1,400	—	—	3,500
12/98	1,100	—	—	3,000
12/97	860	—	—	3,000
12/96	662	—	—	1,900
12/95	452	—	—	500
Annual Growth	**20.2%**	**—**	**—**	**33.4%**

Revenue History

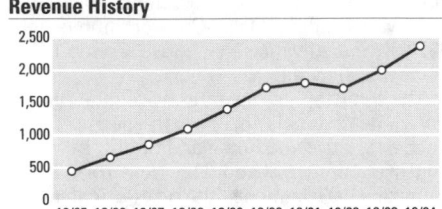

DMX MUSIC

DMX MUSIC is giving elevator music a high-tech twist. Formed in 2001 through the merger of AEI Music Network and Liberty Media Group, it's a leading distributor of commercial-free music to homes, businesses, and airlines in the US, Europe, Asia, Australia, and South America. It offers more than 500 styles of music organized into a variety of channels delivered by digital cable, satellite, DVD, and the Internet. DMX serves some 180,000 businesses, including retail chains (The Limited, Macy's, Nine West), as well as 11 million homes and 30 airlines. Liberty Media is its majority shareholder. DMX filed for Chapter 11 bankruptcy protection and was sold to THP Capstar for $75 million during a bankruptcy auction.

CEO Steve Hicks, who took control of DMX MUSIC in June 2005, has a reputation for buying radio stations and selling them for a profit. He's the brother of Tom Hicks, a Dallas-based billionaire investor. The new owners of the company plan to move its headquarters from Los Angeles to Austin, Texas.

EXECUTIVES

CEO: Steve Hicks
President: John D. Cullen, age 45
COO: Paul D. Stone, age 38
SVP and CFO: Robert Baxter
SVP Content: Alan Furst
VP Business Affairs: Margaret McAusland
SVP Brand Marketing and Music Programming:
Christy Noel

VP Business Development: Michael Quigley
VP Music & Entertainment: Rick Gillette
VP Finance and Corporate Controller:
Michele Nadelmman
Regional President, Northeast: Simon Bexon
CTO: Nick Wilson
President, Worldwide: Barry Knittel
Senior Director of Payroll: Rebecca Molina

LOCATIONS

HQ: DMX MUSIC, Inc.
11400 W. Olympic Blvd., Ste. 1100,
Los Angeles, CA 90064
Phone: 310-444-1744   **Fax:** 310-444-1717
Web: www.dmxmusic.com

DMX MUSIC has about 40 offices across the US and overseas offices in Australia, Belgium, Brazil, Canada, The Czech Republic, France, Germany, Holland, Hungary, New Zealand, Japan, Poland, South Africa, and the UK.

PRODUCTS/OPERATIONS

Selected Customers

Abercrombie & Fitch	Pier 1 Imports
Bloomingdale's	Pottery Barn
Brinker International	Saks Fifth Avenue
Macy's	The Limited
Nine West Group	Tommy Hilfiger
Nordstrom	Victoria's Secret
Olive Garden	

COMPETITORS

Cox Radio
MP3.com
Muzak
PlayNetwork
TM Century

HISTORICAL FINANCIALS

Company Type: Private

Income Statement

FYE: December 31

	REVENUE ($ mil.)	NET INCOME ($ mil.)	NET PROFIT MARGIN	EMPLOYEES
12/04*	186	—	—	—
12/00	101	—	—	544
12/99	103	—	—	650
12/98	110	—	—	500
12/97	100	—	—	500
12/96	97	—	—	500
12/95	98	—	—	—
Annual Growth	**11.3%**	**—**	**—**	**2.1%**

*Fiscal year change

Revenue History

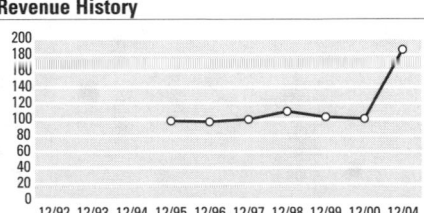

Doane Pet Care

Doane Pet Care has no quibble with kibble. The largest maker of private-label dog and cat food in Europe and North America, the company makes dry (more than 70% of sales) and semi-moist foods, soft treats, and dog biscuits. Doane also makes products for other pet food companies. Its customers include mass merchandisers such as Wal-Mart (about 40% of sales), grocery and pet store chains, and farm and feed stores. The company has expanded into Asia, Europe, and Latin America through acquisitions. Doane is owned by private equity investors, as well as investment companies including J.P. Morgan Partners and Bruckmann, Rosser, Sherrill. In 2005 Doane agreed to be acquired by Teachers' Private Capital.

The purchase price for the company is approximately $840 million. Teachers' Private Capital, the private investment arm of the Ontario Teachers' Pension Plan, plans to execute a recapitalization plan upon completion of the deal.

EXECUTIVES

Chairman: George B. Kelly, age 55
President and CEO: Douglas J. (Doug) Cahill, age 45, $1,180,000 pay
VP, Finance and CFO: Philip K. Woodlief, age 51, $495,625 pay
VP and General Manager, North American Operations: David L. Horton, age 44, $495,625 pay
VP, Co-Manufacturing and Specialty: Richard A. Hannasch, age 51
VP, Doane Europe: Kenneth H. Koch, age 47, $387,500 pay
VP, Supply Chain, Quality and CIO: Joseph J. Meyers, age 43, $380,000 pay
Corporate Controller and Principal Accounting Officer: Stephen P. Havala
Auditors: KPMG LLP

LOCATIONS

HQ: Doane Pet Care Company
210 Westwood Place South, Ste. 400, Brentwood, TN 37027
Phone: 615-373-7774   **Fax:** 615-309-1187
Web: www.doanepetcare.com

Doane Pet Care has about 25 manufacturing and distribution facilities in Alabama, California, Colorado, Florida, Georgia, Indiana, Iowa, Minnesota, Missouri, New York, Ohio, Oklahoma, Pennsylvania, South Carolina, Tennessee, Texas, Virginia, and Wisconsin. It also has facilities in Austria, Denmark, Italy, Spain, and the UK.

2004 Sales

	$ mil.	% of total
US	763.2	73
Denmark	207.9	20
Spain	61.6	6
UK	18.5	1
Total	**1,051.2**	**100**

PRODUCTS/OPERATIONS

2004 Sales

	% of total
Dry pet food	71
Wet, semi-moist & other	21
Biscuits & treats	8
Total	**100**

Selected Brands

Bonkers
Country Prime
Dura Life
Kozy Kitten
Maxximum Nutrition
NutriCare
Ol' Roy
Pet Lovers
Pet Pride
PMI-Nutrition
Retriever
Special Kitty
Sportsmans Choice
TrailBlazer

COMPETITORS

Colgate-Palmolive
Del Monte Foods
Hartz Mountain
Hill's Pet Nutrition
Iams
Nestlé Purina PetCare
Nutro Products
Royal Canin

HISTORICAL FINANCIALS

Company Type: Private

Income Statement

	REVENUE ($ mil.)	NET INCOME ($ mil.)	NET PROFIT MARGIN	EMPLOYEES
12/04	1,051	(46)	—	2,392
12/03	1,014	(68)	—	2,671
12/02	887	15	1.7%	2,707
12/01	896	(22)	—	2,730
12/00	892	(5)	—	3,585
12/99	771	21	2.8%	2,286
12/98	687	(22)	—	2,453
12/97	565	6	1.1%	2,330
12/96	513	(2)	—	—
Annual Growth	**9.4%**	**—**	**—**	**0.4%**

FYE: December 31

2004 Year-End Financials

Debt ratio: 9,633.9%
Return on equity: —
Cash ($ mil.): 29
Current ratio: 1.33
Long-term debt ($ mil.): 687

Net Income History

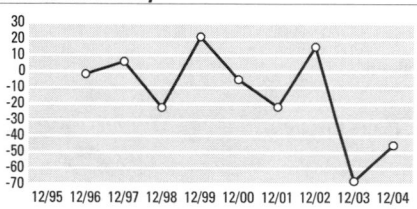

Doctor's Associates

You don't have to go underground to catch this subway. Doctor's Associates operates the Subway chain of sandwich shops, the second-largest chain behind McDonald's. It boasts more than 22,000 locations in 79 countries, with more US locations than the Golden Arches. Virtually all Subway restaurants are franchised and offer such fare as hot and cold sandwiches, turkey wraps, and salads. Subways are located in freestanding buildings, as well as in airports, convenience stores, sports facilities, and other locations. The company is owned by co-founders Fred Deuce and Peter Buck, who opened the first Subway in 1965.

With a low initial franchise cost and simple operations (minimum space requirements and little on-site cooking), Subway has been one of the fastest-growing franchises in the world. Doctor's Associates saw more than 2,000 Subway franchises open in 2003. Its popularity as a healthy alternative to burgers and fries has also increased with the help of an advertising campaign featuring Jared Fogle, a customer who claims to have lost 245 pounds on a diet of Subway sandwiches. Subway now controls about a third of the sandwich market.

The company is focused on increasing its international presence, having opened more than 100 locations in the UK and 400 in Australia. In the US it is seeking to outpace its competition in key markets, including deli-rich New York City. The chain is also introducing new menu items, such as wrap sandwiches endorsed by Atkins Nutritionals, to satisfy the health concerns of fast-food consumers.

The chain, staying competitive with the likes of Quiznos and Jimmy John's, developed a sandwich-toasting oven for use in every Subway location.

HISTORY

In 1965 17-year-old Fred DeLuca dreamed of becoming a doctor and worked as a stock boy in a Bridgeport, Connecticut, hardware store to earn college tuition. It wasn't enough, so he cornered family friend Peter Buck at a backyard barbecue and asked for advice. Buck, a nuclear physicist, suggested DeLuca open a submarine sandwich shop and put up $1,000 to get him started.

As the summer of 1965 was coming to an end, DeLuca rented a small location in a remote area of Bridgeport, opened Pete's Super Submarines, and there he sold foot-long sandwiches. On the first day the sandwiches were so popular that DeLuca hired his own customers to work behind the counter; by the end of the day, he had sold out of all his supplies. The sandwiches continued to be popular for a while, but within a few months the shop started losing money, and DeLuca and Buck found that selling submarine sandwiches was a seasonal business. They decided they could create an illusion of success by opening a second location and then a third. The third store was finally successful, partly because of its more visible location and increased marketing and partly because of a new name — Subway.

DeLuca and Buck had set a goal of 32 shops opened by 1975, but they had only 16 by 1974. They realized that the only way they could reach their goal in one year was to license the Subway name. The first franchise opened that year in Wallingford, Connecticut, and they opened 32 by the end of 1975. The partners hit 100 by 1978, then 200 by 1983, and DeLuca set a new goal: 5,000 Subway shops by 1994. The first international Subway opened in Bahrain in 1984, and DeLuca achieved his goal of 5,000 shops by 1990.

During the 1990s, DeLuca experimented with several other franchise concepts, including We Care Hair (budget styling salons), Cajun Joe's (spicy fried chicken), and Q Burgers. But none of these ventures fared as well as his sandwich empire. As Subway grew, however, controversy surrounding its treatment of franchisees began to surface. A Federal Trade Commission investigation of the company was dropped in 1993, but Subway continued to battle franchisees complaining about broken contracts, market over-saturation (and, therefore, too much competition and self-cannibalization), and what the franchisees viewed as unreasonably high royalty fees.

In spite of its franchising troubles, Subway kept growing. It expanded into Russia and China in the mid-1990s, and opened its 11,000th restaurant in 1995. In 1997 Subway inked deals with the Army, Navy, and Air Force exchange services to bring Subway units to military bases. Two years later the company opened its 14,000th restaurant in Mount Gambier, Australia, an event that coincided with Subway's renewed push to expand internationally.

The company got some unexpected publicity in 1999 when 22 year-old Jared Fogle claimed that he dropped 245 pounds from his 425-pound frame by subsisting on a diet of Subway turkey sandwiches. Subway helped Fogle extend his 15 minutes of fame by featuring him and his oversized pants in a TV commercial. (The company has since built an entire campaign around Fogle which features other weight watchers attributing their success to Jared and Subway.) Subway introduced its largest menu initiative ever in 2000 when it unveiled its Subway Selects Gourmet Sandwiches, adding 13 items to the menu. In April 2001 the company opened its 15,000th store.

Also that year, Buck retired as chairman, but stayed on as a member of the board of directors. Becoming one of the fastest-growing franchises in the world, Subway expanded from 16,000 locations in 2002 to more than 22,000 stores by the end of 2004.

EXECUTIVES

President: Frederick A. (Fred) DeLuca, age 56
Controller: David Worroll
Chief Marketing Officer: Bill Schettini
CEO and Executive Director, Subway Franchisee Advertising Fund Trust: Tom Seddon
SVP and Chief Administrative Officer, Subway Franchisee Advertising Fund Trust: Steven Safier
President, Subway Development Corporation: Deep Dhindsa
Director, Corporate Communications: Michele DiNello
Director, Development: Don Fertman
Director, International: Patricia Demarais
Director, Research and Development: Suzanne Greco
Manager, Marketing and Profitability, Subway Australia: Lincoln Patterson
Manager, Public Relations: Kevin Kane

LOCATIONS

HQ: Doctor's Associates Inc.
325 Bic Dr., Milford, CT 06460
Phone: 203-877-4281   **Fax:** 203-876-6674
Web: www.subway.com

2004 Locations

	No.
US	17,919
Canada	1,993
Australia	745
UK	366
Mexico	188
Puerto Rico	180
Germany	166
New Zealand	123
Japan	95
Venezuela	71
South Korea	39
Taiwan	39
India	37
China	32
Spain	27
United Arab Emirates	24
Ireland	23
El Salvador	22
Singapore	22
Costa Rica	21
Brazil	20
Philippines	20
The Netherlands	18
Bahamas	17
Finland	16
Kuwait	15
Iceland	14
Saudi Arabia	14
Guam	13
France	12
Guatemala	11
Netherlands Antilles	10
Other countries	165
Total	**22,477**

COMPETITORS

AFC Enterprises	Jersey Mike's	Quiznos
Blimpie	Jimmy John's	Triarc
Burger King	Maid-Rite	Wall Street Deli
Chick-fil-A	McDonald's	Wendy's
CKE Restaurants	Mr. Goodcents	YUM!
Dairy Queen	Port of Subs	
Jack in the Box	Potbelly	

HISTORICAL FINANCIALS

Company Type: Private

Income Statement

FYE: December 31

	ESTIMATED REVENUE ($ mil.)	NET INCOME ($ mil.)	NET PROFIT MARGIN	EMPLOYEES
12/03	468	—	—	638
12/02	500	—	—	730
12/01	400	—	—	730
12/00	350	—	—	730
12/99	300	—	—	
12/98	300	—	—	
12/97	300	—	—	
12/96	250	—	—	
12/95	250	—	—	
12/94	200	—	—	
Annual Growth	**9.9%**	—	—	**(4.4%)**

Revenue History

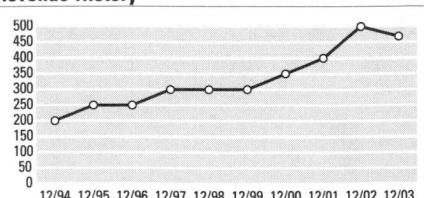

Dole Food

Bananas might be Dole Food's favorite fruit because they have "a-peel," but as the world's largest producer of fresh fruits and vegetables, it grows and markets much more than the slipper-peeled fruit. The company is one of the world's leading producers of bananas and pineapples, and also markets citrus, table grapes, dried fruits, nuts, and fresh-cut flowers. Dole has added value-added products (packaged salads, novelty canned pineapple shapes) to insulate itself from fluctuating commodity markets. Cost-cutting measures, including job cuts, have helped boost Dole's earnings. CEO David Murdock took the company private in 2003 and is its sole owner.

Along with being the world's largest producer of fresh fruits and vegetables, Dole is also a world-leading producer of fresh-cut flowers. The company has been introducing convenience-oriented products such as bagged vegetables, ready-to-eat salads, and individual fruit servings packaged in plastic cups, as well as niche products such as organic bananas. It is adding to its distribution channels, with a significant share of its products now available in drug and convenience stores, club stores, and mass merchandisers.

HISTORY

James Dole embarked on an unlikely career in a faraway land when he graduated from Harvard College in 1899 and sailed to Hawaii. He bought 61 acres of farmland for $4,000 in 1900 and the next year organized the Hawaiian Pineapple Company, announcing that the island's pineapples would eventually be in every US grocery store.

Others had tried and failed to sell fresh fruit to the mainland. Dole decided he would succeed by canning pineapples. He built his first cannery in 1903 and introduced a national magazine advertising campaign in 1908 designed to make consumers associate Hawaii with pineapples (then considered exotic fruits).

In 1922 Dole expanded his production by buying the island of Lanai, where he set up a pineapple plantation. He financed the purchase by selling a third interest in Hawaiian Pineapple to Waialua Agricultural Company, which was part of Castle & Cooke (C&C). Samuel Castle and Amos Cooke, missionaries to Hawaii, formed C&C in 1851 to manage their church's failing depository, which supplied outlying mission posts with staple goods. In 1858 they entered the sugar business and within 10 years served as agents for several Hawaiian sugar plantations and the ships that carried their cargoes.

C&C gained control of Hawaiian Pineapple in 1932 when it acquired an additional 21% interest in the business. The company began using the Dole name on packaging the next year. Dole became chairman of the board of the reorganized company in 1935 but pursued other business interests until he retired in 1948.

Hawaiian Pineapple was run separately until C&C bought the remainder in 1961. The company started pineapple and banana farms in the Philippines in 1963 to supply markets in East Asia. C&C began importing bananas when it purchased 55% of Standard Fruit of New Orleans in 1964. (It purchased the remainder four years later.)

Heavily in debt and limping from two hostile takeover attempts, C&C agreed in 1985 to merge with Flexi-Van, a container leasing company. The merger brought with it needed capital, Flexi-Van owner David Murdock (who became C&C's CEO), and a fleet of ships to transport produce. Murdock began trimming back, leaving C&C with its fruit and real estate operations. He then decided to end all pineapple operations on Lanai to concentrate on tourist properties. (The company took a $168 million write-off on them in 1995, when it spun off its real estate and resort operations as Castle & Cooke.)

C&C became Dole Food in 1991. The company expanded at home and internationally, adding SAMICA (dried fruits and nuts, Europe, 1992), Dromedary (dates, US, 1994), Chiquita's New Zealand produce operations (1995), and SABA Trading (60%, produce importing and distribution, Sweden, 1998; Dole acquired 100% of SABA in 2005).

In 1995 Dole sold its juice business to Seagram's Tropicana Products division, keeping its pineapple juices and licensing the Dole name to Seagram. (PepsiCo bought Tropicana in 1998.) Dole entered the fresh-flower trade in 1998 by acquiring four major growers and marketers. It is now the world's largest producer of freshly cut flowers.

A worldwide banana glut, Hurricane Mitch, and severe freezes in California hit the company hard in late 1998. The next year Dole launched cost-cutting measures, which by early 2000 had ripened into better earnings. Nonetheless, cutbacks and disposals continued throughout 2001.

In 2002 Murdock made a cash and debt takeover bid for the company worth about $2.5 billion. However, at least one minority shareholder was dissatisfied with the offer and filed a proposal calling for Murdock's resignation. The company rejected Murdock's $29.50 per share offer and negotiated with him regarding a larger price-per-share offer. In December Dole and Murdock finally signed a merger agreement. The deal, which gave stockholders $33.50 per share in cash, was approved by company stockholders in March 2003 and left Murdock in sole control of the company.

When Maui Land & Pineapple decided to sell off its Costa Rican subsidiary, Dole scooped it up in late 2003, paying $15.3 million for the pineapple-growing and marketing business. In 2004 Lawrence Kern, Dole's president and COO, left the company and chairman, CEO, and sole owner Murdock took over as president. In July 2004 CFO Richard Dahl became president. Also in 2004 the company acquired frozen fruit manufacturer J.R. Wood, Inc. and fresh berry producer Coastal Berry Company, which made Dole a top North American strawberry producer.

EXECUTIVES

Chairman and CEO: David H. Murdock, age 81, $2,037,750 pay
President, COO, and Director: Richard J. Dahl, age 53, $1,464,519 pay
EVP, Chief of Staff, and Director: Roberta Wieman, age 59
EVP, Corporate Development, and Director: Scott A. Griswold, age 51
EVP, General Counsel, Corporate Secretary, and Director: C. Michael Carter, age 61, $912,981 pay
SVP, Human Resources: Sue Hagen
SVP, Manufacturing: Danko Stambuk
SVP, Marketing and Sales: Brad Bartlett

VP, Corporate Controller, and Chief Accounting Officer: Yoon J. Hugh
VP, Sales and Marketing, Foodservice: Chris Lock
VP, Worldwide Applied Research: Thomas Farewell
VP and CFO: Joseph S. Tesoriero, age 51, $545,265 pay
VP and CFO, Dole Worldwide Packaged Foods: Allan M. Dicks
VP and Treasurer: Beth Potillo
Director, Corporate Communications: Freya Maneki
Auditors: Deloitte & Touche LLP

LOCATIONS

HQ: Dole Food Company, Inc.
1 Dole Dr., Westlake Village, CA 91362
Phone: 818-879-6600   **Fax:** 818-879-6615
Web: www.dole.com

Dole Food distributes its more than 200 products in more than 90 countries worldwide.

2004 Sales

	$ mil.	% of total
US	2,302.6	43
EU countries	1,036.4	19
Japan	673.8	13
Sweden	462.8	9
Canada	99.5	2
South Korea	93.0	2
Other regions	648.1	12
Total	**5,316.2**	**100**

PRODUCTS/OPERATIONS

2004 Sales

	$ mil.	% of total
Fresh fruit	3,535.7	66
Fresh vegetables	887.4	17
Packaged foods	691.8	13
Fresh-cut flowers	169.8	3
Other	31.5	1
Total	**5,316.2**	**100**

Divisions and Selected Products

Dried fruit and nuts
Almonds	Prunes
Dates	Raisins
Pistachios	

Fresh flowers
Carnations
Chrysanthemums
Roses

Fresh fruit
Apples	Melons
Bananas	Oranges
Cherries	Papayas
Cranberries	Pears
Grapefruit	Pineapples
Grapes	Raspberries
Kiwi	Strawberries
Lemons	Tangelos
Mangoes	

Fresh vegetables
Artichokes	Lettuce
Asparagus	Onions
Broccoli	Snow peas
Carrots	Spinach
Celery	

Ready-to-eat foods
Coleslaw
Peeled mini-carrots
Salad mixes
Shredded lettuce

Packaged foods
Canned mandarin-orange segments
Canned mixed fruits
Canned pineapple
Pineapple juice

COMPETITORS

Blue Diamond Growers	The Nunes Company
Chiquita Brands	Ocean Mist Farms
Del Monte Foods	Ocean Spray
Earthbound Farm	Performance Food
Fresh Del Monte Produce	Seneca Foods
Fyffes	Sun Growers
Geest	Sunkist
Global Berry Farms	Tanimura & Antle
John Sanfilippo & Son	UniMark Group
Maui Land & Pineapple	United Foods

HISTORICAL FINANCIALS

Company Type: Private

Income Statement

FYE: Saturday closest to December 31

	REVENUE ($ mil.)	NET INCOME ($ mil.)	NET PROFIT MARGIN	EMPLOYEES
12/04	5,316	134	2.5%	64,000
12/03	4,773	84	1.8%	59,000
12/02	4,392	36	0.8%	57,000
12/01	4,449	150	3.4%	59,000
12/00	4,763	68	1.4%	61,000
12/99	5,061	49	1.0%	59,500
12/98	4,424	12	0.3%	53,500
12/97	4,336	160	3.7%	44,000
12/96	3,840	89	2.3%	46,000
12/95	3,804	23	0.6%	43,000
Annual Growth	**3.8%**	**21.5%**	**—**	**4.5%**

2004 Year-End Financials

Debt ratio: 271.0%   Current ratio: 1.49
Return on equity: 23.7%   Long-term debt ($ mil.): 1,837
Cash ($ mil.): 79

Net Income History

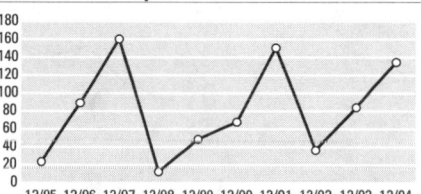

Dot Foods

Dot Foods, the largest food service redistributor in the US, began as a station wagon that hauled dairy goods around as Associated Dairy Products. The company now runs hundreds of trucks (under the name Dot Transportation) that distribute foods, flatware, serve ware, and janitorial supplies to food processors and food service distributors. Dot owns distribution facilities in California, Georgia, Illinois, Maryland, and Missouri that serve customers throughout the US. Its edotfoods subsidiary handles Dot's e-commerce. Dot also owns Principle Resource, a provider of marketing services to food manufacturers. Robert and Dorothy Tracy founded the family-owned company in 1960.

EXECUTIVES

Chairman and CEO: Patrick F. (Pat) Tracy
President: John Tracy
CFO: William (Bill) Metzinger
VP, Business Development: Mike Buckley
VP, Distribution Centers: John Long

VP, Human Resources: Mike Hulsen
VP, Information Technology Systems: Mark Read
VP, Marketing: Scott Stamerjohn
VP, Quality: Dan Koch
VP, Sales: Michael (Mike) Duggan
President, Tracy Family Foundation: Jean Buckley
National Sales Manager: Dick Tracy
Aviation: Ted Irons
Human Resources: Erin Tracy

LOCATIONS

HQ: Dot Foods, Inc.
  Route 99 South, Mt. Sterling, IL 62353
Phone: 217-773-4411   **Fax:** 217-773-3321
Web: www.dotfoods.com

COMPETITORS

Associated Wholesalers   McLane Foodservice
C.D. Hartnett   Purity Wholesale Grocers

HISTORICAL FINANCIALS

Company Type: Private

Income Statement
FYE: December 31

	REVENUE ($ mil.)	NET INCOME ($ mil.)	NET PROFIT MARGIN	EMPLOYEES
12/03	1,573	—	—	2,200
12/02	1,410	—	—	2,000
12/01	1,500	—	—	1,750
12/00	1,107	—	—	1,607
12/99	986	—	—	1,468
12/98	814	—	—	1,307
Annual Growth	**14.1%**	**—**	**—**	**11.0%**

Revenue History

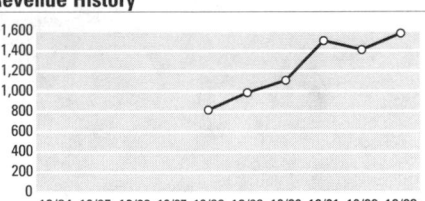

DoubleClick

Help with online advertising is only a DoubleClick away. The company provides targeted online advertising placement and scheduling services for both advertisers and Web site publishers through its TechSolutions business unit. It also offers e-mail marketing, search engine results placement, and other electronic marketing services. In addition, DoubleClick offers traditional database marketing services to direct marketers through its Abacus and Data Management divisions. In addition to North America, the company has operations in Asia and Europe. DoubleClick was taken private in 2005 by investment firms Hellman & Friedman and JMI Equity.

Having survived the boom-to-bust Internet bubble, DoubleClick faces increasing challenges as the focus in online advertising shifts from traditional banner ads to text-based ads targeted by keywords and search results. The new ad format, pioneered and popularized by search engine Google, has displaced much of the interest in traditional banner ads, the format DoubleClick helped champion in the early heyday of Internet publishing. To meet this challenge, the company acquired Performics, a search engine marketing firm, in 2004 for about $60 million. While the deal has helped DoubleClick's bottom line, the company continues to trail the burgeoning industry.

It agreed to the $1.1 billion buyout by Hellman and JMI after putting itself up for sale in 2004. Company veteran Kevin Ryan left his post as CEO following the completion of the deal, leaving division heads David Rosenblatt and Brian Rainey to oversee the company.

EXECUTIVES

CEO, Abacus: Brian M. Rainey, age 43
CEO, DoubleClick Digital Advertising:
  David S. Rosenblatt, age 37, $407,667 pay
CIO: Mok Choe, age 46, $408,000 pay
CTO: Dwight A. Merriman, age 36
Chief Marketing Officer: Peter (Pete) Krainik, age 46
Chief Privacy Officer: Bennie Smith
SVP and General Counsel: Hillary Smith
SVP and General Manager, Ad Management:
  Doug Knopper
SVP and General Manager, E-mail Solutions: Eric Kirby
SVP; General Manager, Performics: Stuart B. Frankel, age 33
SVP Global Human Resources: Melanie Hughes
SVP Global Technical Services: John Rehl
SVP Marketing Automation:
  Courtland B. (Court) Cunningham, age 34
Director of Marketing: Lynn Tornabene
Corporate Communications: Jennifer Blum
Auditors: PricewaterhouseCoopers LLP

LOCATIONS

HQ: DoubleClick Inc.
  111 8th Ave., 10th Fl., New York, NY 10011
Phone: 212-683-0001   **Fax:** 212-287-1203
Web: www.doubleclick.com

DoubleClick has operations in Australia, China, France, Germany, Ireland, Japan, Spain, the UK, and the US.

2004 Sales

	$ mil.	% of total
US	246.0	82
International	55.6	18
Total	**301.6**	**100**

PRODUCTS/OPERATIONS

2004 Sales

	$ mil.	% of total
TechSolutions	196.3	65
Data	105.3	35
Total	**301.6**	**100**

Selected Services and Operations

TechSolutions
  Advertising management
    DART for Publishers
    DART for Advertisers
    DART Enterprise Software
    DART Motif
    MediaVisor
  Marketing automation
    DARTmail (e-mail marketing)
  Performics
    Affiliate marketing
    Search engine marketing
Data
  Abacus
    Business-to-business marketing
    Consumer database marketing information
  Data Management (database marketing tools)

COMPETITORS

24/7 Real Media   Harte-Hanks
Acxiom   infoUSA
Advertising.com   Mediaplex
aQuantive   Microsoft
Digital Impact   ValueClick
Fastclick   Yahoo! Search Marketing
Google

HISTORICAL FINANCIALS

Company Type: Private

Income Statement
FYE: December 31

	REVENUE ($ mil.)	NET INCOME ($ mil.)	NET PROFIT MARGIN	EMPLOYEES
12/04	302	38	12.4%	1,541
12/03	271	17	6.2%	1,223
12/02	300	(118)	—	1,111
12/01	406	(266)	—	1,450
12/00	506	(156)	—	1,929
12/99	258	(56)	—	1,386
12/98	80	(18)	—	482
12/97	31	(8)	—	185
12/96	7	(3)	—	13
Annual Growth	**61.6%**	**—**	**—**	**81.6%**

2004 Year-End Financials

Debt ratio: 23.3%   Current ratio: 4.65
Return on equity: 6.1%   Long-term debt ($ mil.): 135
Cash ($ mil.): 126

Net Income History

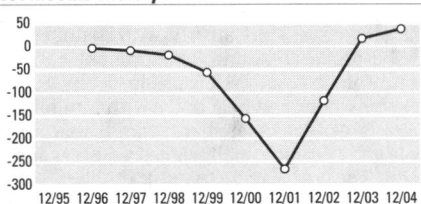

Dover Saddlery

Dover Saddlery is an upscale specialty retailer and direct marketer of equestrian products. The company's specialty is English-style riding gear, and its selection features riding apparel, tack, and stable supplies, as well as horse health care products. Its brand-name products, which include names such as Ariat, Grand Prix, Hermes, Mountain Horse, Passier, Prestige, and Smith Brothers, account for about 75% of company sales. Dover sells through catalogs, a Web site, and four retail stores operating under the Dover Saddlery and Smith Brothers banners. The company was founded in 1975 by US Equestrian Team members, including Jim and Dave Powers who (along with CEO Stephen Day) own nearly 50% of Dover Saddlery.

EXECUTIVES

President, CEO, Treasurer, and Director:
  Stephen L. Day, age 59, $258,200 pay
VP, COO, Secretary, and Director: Jonathan A. R. Grylls, age 40, $217,200 pay
CFO: Michael W. Bruns, age 48, $115,982 pay
VP, Operations: William Schmidt, age 56, $208,400 pay
Auditors: Ernst & Young LLP

Dow Corning

Break out the streamers and party hats for Dow Corning. In June 2004 the 50-50 joint venture of chemical titan Dow and glass giant Corning emerged from nine years of bankruptcy protection that had come about as a result of thousands of claims alleging the company's silicone-gel breast implants were harmful. Dow Corning produces about 7,000 silicone-based products such as adhesives, insulating materials, and lubricants for aerospace, automotive, and electrical uses. Because silicone does not conduct electricity, it is also used in its hard polycrystalline form (silicon) as the material on which semiconductors are built. With plants worldwide, the company sells more than half of its products outside the US.

Having filed for bankruptcy protection in 1995, Dow Corning appeared close to a settlement that would help it emerge from Chapter 11 in 1998. The settlement would provide $2.35 billion for breast implant claims over a 16-year period. A bankruptcy court approved the settlement in 1999 (paving the road for the company's exit from bankruptcy), but the deal fell through when the judge ruled that women who did not agree to the settlement could still sue Dow Corning's corporate parents. Dow Corning and about 94% of the women who had sued it appealed the judge's ruling.

In October 2003 an advisory panel recommended the FDA approve the use of silicone implants made by another company, Inamed, a move that might have protected Dow Corning from further lawsuits. The FDA, though, ruled against that recommendation, keeping the implants illegal except in trials.

Finally, in April 2004, a bankruptcy court judge ruled that the re-approved settlement would go through effective June 1. The move allows the money Dow Corning set aside for the settlement to be dispersed to claimants and for the company to exit Chapter 11, which finally occurred June 2004.

Corning, Inc., has been suffering from weak sales in telecommunications markets, and Dow Corning's exit from bankruptcy could help Corning back to profitability.

HISTORY

Dow Corning was founded in 1943 as a joint venture between Dow Chemical and Corning Glass Works. Corning, founded by Amory Houghton in 1875, provided Thomas Edison with glass for the first light bulbs. It developed Pyrex heat-resistant glass in 1915.

Corning made its first silicone resin samples in 1938. It teamed with a group of Dow Chemical scientists who were also working on silicone products in 1940. Dow Chemical president Willard Dow and Corning Glass Works president Glen Cole shook hands on the idea of a joint venture in 1942, and 10 months later Dow Corning was formed. Its first product, the engine grease DOW CORNING 4, enabled B-17s to fly at 35,000 feet (a major contribution to the Allied war effort). In 1945 DOW CORNING 35 (an emulsifier used in tire molds) and Pan Glaze (which made baking pans stick-proof and easier to clean) were instant successes on the home front.

Dow Corning expanded rapidly in international markets and in 1960 set up Dow Corning International to handle sales and technical service in markets outside North America. By 1969 the company had operations worldwide.

Dow Corning's first breast implants went on the market in 1964. Since then Dow Corning and other silicone makers have sold silicone breast implants to more than a million women in the US. In the early 1980s breast-implant recipients began suing Dow Corning and other implant makers, claiming that the silicone gel in the implants leaked and caused health problems. Dow Corning, the leading implant maker, defended the devices as safe. Dow Corning stopped making implants in 1992, after the Food and Drug Administration called for a moratorium on silicone-gel implants.

In 1993 Baxter International, Bristol-Myers Squibb, and Dow Corning offered $4.2 billion to settle thousands of claims. The corporation declared bankruptcy in 1995 to buy time for financial reorganization. A federal judge stripped Dow Chemical of its protection from direct liability, and the company was later ordered to pay a Nevada couple $4.1 million in damages (other jurisdictions did not follow suit). Dow Corning sold its Polytrap polymer technology to Advanced Polymer, maker of polymer-based pharmaceutical delivery systems, in 1996. The following year the company sold Bisco Products, its silicone-foam business, to Rogers Corporation for $12 million.

Dow Corning's $3.7 billion bankruptcy reorganization plan, offered in 1997, allowed for $2.4 billion to be set aside to settle most implant lawsuits against the corporation. However, a federal bankruptcy judge found legal flaws in the proposal and refused to allow claimants to vote on it. In 1998 Dow Corning upped the ante to $4.4 billion — $3 billion to the silicone claimants and the rest to creditors.

Both sides later agreed to a $3.2 billion compensation package, and in 1999 the plan received approval from a bankruptcy judge and creditors. However, the settlement stalled when the judge ruled that women who disagreed with the settlement could sue Dow Chemical and Corning (Dow Corning appealed). Despite its court battles, in 2000 the company acquired the 51% of Universal Silicones & Lubricants (high-tech lubricants and silicone sealants) it did not own and renamed the company Dow Corning India. Dow Corning finally emerged from Chapter 11 in mid-2004.

PRODUCTS/OPERATIONS

Selected Products and Applications

Aerospace
  Adhesives
  Encapsulants
  Exotic composite materials
  Greases
  High-purity fluids
  Primers
  Protective coatings
  Sealants

Automotive
  Body components
  Brake systems
  Chassis
  Electrical component
  Electronic components
  Engine/drivetrain
  Exterior lighting
  Fuel systems

Chemical and Material Manufacturing
  Agrochemicals
  Auto appearance chemicals
  Industrial release agents
  Materials treatment
  Oil and gas
  Process aid antifoams
  Pulp manufacturing

Cleaning Products
  Dry cleaning
  Laundry detergents
  Polishes and hard surface cleaners

Coatings and Plastics
  Caulks
  Coatings
  Sealants

Electrical/Electronics
  Adhesives and sealants
  Conformal coatings
  Dielectric gels
  High-voltage insulators
  Hyperpure polycrystalline silicon
  Interlayer dielectric and passivation materials
  Liquid transformer fluid
  Silicone encapsulants
  Silicone grease for insulators
  Silicone RTV coating for insulators
  Silicone rubber insulators
  Thermally conductive adhesives

Food and Beverage
  Defoamers
  Packaging

Health Care
  Hydrocephalus shunts
  Pacemaker leads
  Tubing for dialysis

Paper Manufacturing & Finishing
  Release coatings for label-backing paper, pressure-sensitive adhesives, and paper coatings

Personal Care
  Materials for deodorants, cosmetics, and lotions

Plastics

Textiles
  Waterproofing agents

COMPETITORS

3M	Goldschmidt
Asahi Glass	H.B. Fuller
BASF AG	Hexcel
Bayer MaterialScience	Honeywell Specialty
Bostik	Materials
Cytec	Imperial Chemical
Cytec Engineered	Industries
Materials	National Starch and
Degussa	Chemical
Dynea	PRC-DeSoto
Eastman Chemical	Rhodia
Formosa Plastics	Shin-Etsu Chemical
GE Industrial	Wacker-Chemie

HISTORICAL FINANCIALS

Company Type: Joint venture

Income Statement

FYE: December 31

	REVENUE ($ mil.)	NET INCOME ($ mil.)	NET PROFIT MARGIN	EMPLOYEES
12/03	2,873	177	6.1%	8,200
12/02	2,610	59	2.2%	8,200
12/01	2,438	(23)	—	7,500
12/00	2,751	105	3.8%	9,000
12/99	2,603	110	4.2%	9,000
12/98	2,568	207	8.0%	9,000
12/97	2,644	238	9.0%	9,100
12/96	2,532	222	8.8%	8,900
12/95	2,493	(31)	—	8,500
12/94	2,205	(7)	—	8,300
Annual Growth	3.0%	—	—	(0.1%)

2003 Year-End Financials

Debt ratio: 6.2%
Return on equity: 25.5%
Cash ($ mil.): 462

Current ratio: 2.14
Long-term debt ($ mil.): 52

Net Income History

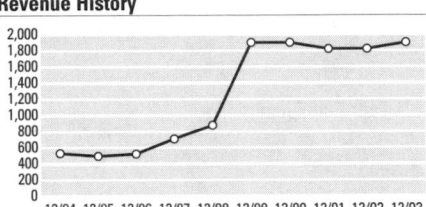

COMPETITORS

Buffalo Rock	Pepsi Bottling
Coca-Cola Bottling	Pepsi Bottling of Knoxville
Consolidated	Pepsi Bottling Ventures
Coca-Cola Bottling of	Pepsi MidAmerica
Northern New England	Pepsi-Cola Bottling
Coca-Cola Enterprises	Company of NY
Coke United	Pepsi-Cola of Ft.
Cott	Lauderdale
National Beverage	Philadelphia Coca-Cola

HISTORICAL FINANCIALS

Company Type: Private

Income Statement

FYE: December 31

	REVENUE ($ mil.)	NET INCOME ($ mil.)	NET PROFIT MARGIN	EMPLOYEES
12/03	1,900	—	—	8,900
12/02	1,820	—	—	8,800
12/01	1,820	—	—	8,800
12/00	1,900	—	—	8,000
12/99	1,900	—	—	3,000
12/98	878	—	—	2,700
12/97	709	—	—	2,500
12/96	523	—	—	1,567
12/95	496	—	—	1,535
12/94	532	—	—	1,400
Annual Growth	15.2%	—	—	22.8%

Revenue History

Dr Pepper/Seven Up Bottling

Dr Pepper/Seven Up Bottling Group (DPSUBG) rings up sweet results for Cadbury Schweppes, the world's #3 soft-drink firm. It is a leading bottler of soft drinks in the US, distributing in 21 states. Besides the Dr Pepper and 7 UP brands (owned by Cadbury Schweppes), it also bottles the lesser-known Big Red and Crush brands, as well as Clearly Canadian bottled water. Cadbury Schweppes and The Carlyle Group own 40% and 51% of the company, respectively. The company, formed from the 1999 merger of Turner Beverage Group and American Bottling Co., continues to grow by acquiring other bottlers. Longtime president and CEO Jim Turner retired in 2005.

EXECUTIVES

Chairman: John Franklin Brock, age 57
President and CEO: Larry D. Young, age 49
CFO: Holly Lovvorn
EVP, Administration: Tom Taszarek
VP, Information Systems: Gerry Mecca
VP, Human Resources: Kellie Defratus
VP, Sales and Marketing: Guy Mueller

LOCATIONS

HQ: Dr Pepper/Seven Up Bottling Group, Inc.
  5950 Sherry Ln., Ste. 500, Dallas, TX 75225
Phone: 214-530-5000 **Fax:** 214-530-5036

DreamWorks

DreamWorks L.L.C has moguls times three. Created in 1994 by Steven Spielberg (famed film director/producer), Jeffrey Katzenberg (former Disney film executive and animation guru), and David Geffen (recording industry maven), DreamWorks produces live action movies (*The Terminal, The Ring*) and TV shows (*Las Vegas*). It produced computer-animated features through DreamWorks Animation, until spinning off the unit to shareholders in 2004. DreamWorks also pulled out of the GameWorks video arcade business it started with SEGA and Universal Pictures, and has sold its music business to Universal Music. The three founders collectively own the majority of DreamWorks; Microsoft co-founder Paul Allen also owns a stake.

The company had once dared to dream of operating a media empire with movie, animation, and television production units, as well as music and Internet holdings. And though its live-action movie unit has generated successes such as *Old School* and *Road to Perdition,* and its animation unit has produced hits including *Chicken Run* and *Shrek,* DreamWorks has been less successful in other areas.

DreamWorks Records, which produced the soundtracks to all DreamWorks films and albums for popular artists, never caught fire and the company sold the unit to Universal Music Group for an estimated $100 million.

The company's TV unit has produced only one notable hit (*Spin City*, whose six-year series-run ended in 2002). DreamWorks' TV has signed a development pact with NBC, in which NBC pays DreamWorks a fee to cover production costs and gets first look at any new series created by DreamWorks. NBC then finances and owns a majority stake in the projects it chooses to develop. DreamWorks hoped the NBC pact would help kick start its television division, but the first project, the animated *Father of the Pride,* tanked and has since been cancelled.

The DreamWorks Animation division turned out to be the firm's most successful business. Released in 2004, *Shrek 2* surpassed previous records as one of the most successful animated films of all time. The company spun off DreamWorks Animation later that year in an effort to better compete with rival Pixar. DreamWorks no longer holds any ownership interest in the animation company, but continues to market and distribute its features.

Japanese media firm Kadokawa Holdings invested $100 million in DreamWorks, giving Kadokawa a 3% stake in the studio. Its investment gives Kadokawa exclusive rights to distribute DreamWorks films, videos, DVDs, and other products in Japan.

HISTORY

Before pooling their collective talents in 1994, Steven Spielberg, Jeffrey Katzenberg, and David Geffen had each established an impressive track record. Spielberg had spawned such blockbusters as *Jaws, The Indiana Jones Trilogy,* and *Jurassic Park.* Katzenberg had guided Walt Disney's return to animation (*The Lion King, Aladdin*) before a falling out with former Disney CEO Michael Eisner. Music guru Geffen had helped make superstars of the Eagles and Nirvana.

A high-tech who's who embraced the SKG dream. Microsoft invested around $30 million to develop video games, while Microsoft co-founder Paul Allen shelled out nearly $500 million for a stake in the new company. Soon DreamWorks had arranged a $100 million programming deal with ABC, a 10-year HBO licensing agreement worth an estimated $1 billion, and co-founded a $50 million animation studio with Silicon Graphics. DreamWorks then announced plans in 1995 to build the first new studio since the 1930s, just outside of Los Angeles in Playa Vista. In 1996 the company purchased a stake in the Sunnyvale, California-based computer animation firm PDI to form PDI/DreamWorks.

DreamWorks produced a string of TV flops before finding success with the Michael J. Fox comedy *Spin City* in 1996. Later that year it released the first record under its new label, a dud from pop star George Michael, and it announced its partnership with SEGA and MCA (now Universal Studios) to develop SEGA GameWorks (video arcade super-centers featuring SEGA titles and games designed by Spielberg). It finally released its first three movies in 1997 (*The Peacemaker, Amistad,* and *Mouse Hunt*) to mixed critical reviews and mediocre box office performances. Combined with DreamWorks' less-than-stellar offerings in TV and music, buzz circulated that the meeting of the minds at DreamWorks wasn't all it cracked up to be.

But DreamWorks started showing signs of life in 1998 with the comet disaster film *Deep Impact* and Spielberg's Oscar-winning *Saving Private Ryan,* the highest grossing film of the year. It also introduced the first of its animated films that year, which included the successful *Antz.* DreamWorks finished the year with the highest average gross per film of all the major studios.

After facing a multitude of environmental protests, cost overruns, and construction delays, DreamWorks scrapped its Playa Vista studio plans in 1999. Around the same time, Katzenberg settled his high-profile lawsuit against Disney over a bonus owed him when he resigned. Later that year DreamWorks announced a five-picture deal with Academy Award-winning animation firm Aardman Animations, with which it co-produced *Chicken Run* (released in 2000).

DreamWorks and Microsoft sold DreamWorks Interactive, their video game joint venture, to Electronic Arts in 2000. Later that year *American Beauty* took home the Oscar for Best Picture of 1999, and the studio continued its successful box-office run with three films that grossed more than $100 million (*Gladiator,* which scored the studio its second Best Picture Oscar, *Chicken Run,* and *What Lies Beneath*).

The studio won big in 2001 with *Shrek,* which became one of that year's highest grossing films with more than $265 million at the box office. *A Beautiful Mind,* its co-production with Universal Pictures, won one of the company's films yet another Best Picture Oscar. Also that year the company exited the GameWorks venture when the arcades failed to catch on quickly.

In 2003 the company exited the music business with the sale of DreamWorks records to Universal Music's Interscope Records. DreamWorks scored another hit with the 2004 release of *Shrek 2,* one of the highest grossing animated films of all time. The company spun off DreamWorks Animation in an IPO that raised $812 million. DreamWorks no longer owns any percentage of DreamWorks Animation, but it continues to market and distribute the new company's features.

EXECUTIVES

Principal: David Geffen, age 62
Principal: Jeffrey Katzenberg, age 54
Principal: Steven Spielberg, age 59
President and COO: Rick Sands
Head of Marketing: Terry Press
Head of Theatrical Distribution: Jim Tharp
Head of International Marketing and Distribution: Stephen Basil-Jones
Co-Head of DreamWorks Television: Justin Falvey
Co-Head of DreamWorks Television: Darryl Frank
Co-Head of Motion Picture Division: Laurie MacDonald
Co-Head of Motion Picture Division: Walter Parkes, age 52
Head of PDI/DreamWorks: Patti Burke
Head of Domestic Home Entertainment: Kelly Sooter
Head of Worldwide Home Entertainment: Kelley Avery
President of Production: Adam Goodman

LOCATIONS

HQ: DreamWorks L.L.C.
1000 Flower St., Glendale, CA 91201
Phone: 818-733-7000   **Fax:** 818-695-7574
Web: www.dreamworks.com

DreamWorks has operations in Beverly Hills, Glendale, and Universal City, California; Nashville; New York City; London; and Toronto.

PRODUCTS/OPERATIONS

Selected Films and Television Shows

DreamWorks Pictures
Almost Famous (2000)
American Beauty (1999)
Amistad (1997)
Antz (1998)
A Beautiful Mind (2001, co-produced with Universal Studios)
Catch Me if You Can (2002)
Chicken Run (2000, co-produced with Aardman Animation)
Collateral (2004, co-produced with Paramount Pictures)
Deep Impact (1998, co-produced with Paramount Pictures)
Galaxy Quest (1999)
Gladiator (2000, co-produced with Universal Studios)
House of Sand and Fog (2003)
The Legend of Bagger Vance (2000)
Minority Report (2002)
Mouse Hunt (1997)
Old School (2003)
The Peacemaker (1997)
The Prince of Egypt (1998)
The Ring (2002)
The Ring Two (2005)
Road to Perdition (2002)
Road Trip (2000)
Saving Private Ryan (1998, co-produced with Paramount Pictures)
Shark Tale (2004)
Shrek (2001)
Shrek 2 (2004)
Sinbad: Legend of the Seven Seas (2003)
Small Time Crooks (2000)
The Terminal (2004)
War of the Worlds (2005, co-produced with Paramount Pictures)
DreamWorks Television
Boomtown (2002-2003)
Freaks and Geeks (1999-2000)
The Job (2001)
Las Vegas (2003)
Oliver Beene (2003)
Spin City (1996-2002)
Undeclared (2001)

COMPETITORS

Carsey-Werner	NBC Universal
Fox Filmed Entertainment	Paramount Pictures
Lions Gate Entertainment	Sony Pictures
Lucasfilm	Entertainment
MGM	Universal Pictures
Miramax	Warner Bros.

HISTORICAL FINANCIALS

Company Type: Private

Income Statement

FYE: December 31

	REVENUE ($ mil.)	NET INCOME ($ mil.)	NET PROFIT MARGIN	EMPLOYEES
12/03	1,250	—	—	1,100
12/02	1,813	—	—	1,600
12/01	2,219	—	—	1,500
12/00	1,873	—	—	1,500
Annual Growth	(12.6%)	—	—	(9.8%)

Revenue History

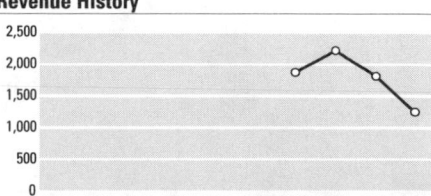

Drees Co.

A family-operated enterprise since its founding by Theodore Drees in 1928, The Drees Co. builds about 3,100 homes annually. Customers may choose from more than 100 floor plans for homes that range in price from about $100,000 to more than $800,000. Drees is a leading homebuilder in Cincinnati. It also builds condominiums, apartments, and commercial buildings through its nine divisions. The company is expanding through acquisitions such as the additions of the homebuilding assets of Zaring National in Cincinnati (Zaring Premier Homes), Indianapolis, and Nashville, and Ausherman Homes in Frederick, Maryland (near Washington, DC). Drees offers financing through its First Equity Mortgage subsidiary.

The Drees Co. also purchases land to develop as homesites in southeastern Indiana, northern Kentucky, Maryland, North Carolina, Ohio, Tennessee, Texas, eastern West Virginia, and Washington, DC.

EXECUTIVES

Chairman: Ralph Drees
President and CEO: David Drees
EVP and CFO: Mark Williams
SVP Marketing: Jack Miller
VP Human Resources: Effie McKeehan
Director, Marketing: Barbara Drees
Director, IS: Mike Rulli
Secretary and Treasurer: Lawrence G. Herbst

LOCATIONS

HQ: The Drees Co.
211 Grandview Dr., Ste. 300,
Fort Mitchell, KY 41017
Phone: 859-578-4200   **Fax:** 859-341-5854
Web: www.dreeshomes.com

The Drees Co. has operations in Indiana, Kentucky, Maryland, North Carolina, Ohio, Tennessee, Texas; Virginia, and Washington, DC.

Division Office Locations

Austin Division (Austin, Texas)
Cincinnati Division (Fort Mitchell, Kentucky)
Cleveland Division (North Canton, Ohio)
Dallas Division (Irving, Texas)
Dayton Division (Centerville, Ohio)
Indianapolis Division (Indianapolis, Indiana)
Nashville Division (Brentwood, Tennessee)
Raleigh Division (Raleigh, North Carolina)
Washington, DC, Division (Alexandria, Virginia)

COMPETITORS

Centex
D.R. Horton
Engle Homes
Fischer Homes
KB Home
Lennar
M/I Homes
Pulte Homes
Ryland

HISTORICAL FINANCIALS

Income Statement

FYE: March 31

	REVENUE ($ mil.)	NET INCOME ($ mil.)	NET PROFIT MARGIN	EMPLOYEES
3/04	978	—	—	1,200
3/03	822	—	—	1,232
3/02	848	—	—	1,100
3/01	527	—	—	850
3/00	515	—	—	—
3/99	366	—	—	700
3/98	343	—	—	685
3/97	301	—	—	675
3/96	253	—	—	675
3/95	236	—	—	625
Annual Growth	**17.1%**	**—**	**—**	**7.5%**

Revenue History

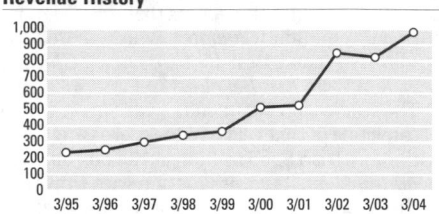

Dresser

Is your energy business all dressed up with no place to flow? Not if Dresser can help it. The company, formerly Dresser Industries (and once a part of Halliburton), makes flow control products (valves, actuators, and the like for oil and gas exploration), measurement systems (gas pumps and point of sale terminals for gas stations and convenience stores made by Dresser Wayne), and power systems (Waukesha engines and ROOTS blowers and compressors). Dresser's flow control segment also makes diagnostic equipment, injection pumps, and valves. The company maintains a presence in more than 100 countries, with manufacturing or support facilities in 22.

First Reserve Corporation, a US-based investment firm, owns more than 90% of Dresser. Morgan Stanley and Credit Suisse First Boston are representing the underwriters for the proposed IPO of the company.

The public offering has been put on hold pending restatements of financial results following disclosure of accounting problems. Dresser also announced in late 2004 that the company may come in for criminal charges involving improper sales to US government-sanctioned countries like Iran, Sudan, and Iraq.

In 2005 the company agreed to sell its On/Off valve business, which caters primarily to the oil and gas exploration industry, to Cooper Cameron. The deal is for $224 million. While the business accounts for about a fifth of Dresser's total sales, its margins are awfully low. And so Dresser is concentrating on its more profitable operations. It then announced an agreement to sell Dresser Instruments in order to concentrate on its core, energy industry business. Dresser Instruments makes pressure gauges, transmitters, and temperature switches. Dresser Inc. plans to use much of what it receives from the sale of the two divisions to pay down up to $250 million in debt.

EXECUTIVES

Chairman and CEO: Patrick M. Murray, age 62, $747,500 pay (prior to title change)
President and COO: John P. Ryan, age 52, $376,113 pay (prior to promotion)
EVP, Ethics and Compliance and CFO: James A. Nattier, age 43
SVP, Finance and Accounting: Robert D. (Bob) Woltil, age 50
SVP, Corporate Development: J. Scott Matthews, age 58
SVP, Human Resources: Mark J. Scott, age 50
VP and CIO: Troy D. Matherne, age 41
VP, General Counsel, and Secretary: Frank P. Pittman, age 57
VP, Finance: Michael R. Skelton
VP; President, Dresser Flow Solutions: Andrew E. Graves, age 45, $289,872 pay (partial-year salary)
VP; President, Dresser Instruments: John T. McKenna
VP; President, Waukesha Engine: Thomas J. Laird, age 54
VP; President, Dresser Wayne: Neil H. Thomas, age 36
VP, Investor Relations and Corporate Communications: Jenny Haynes
Chief Accounting Officer and Corporate Controller: Thomas J. Kanuk, age 52
Corporate Secretary and Associate General Counsel: David M. Dolan
Auditors: PricewaterhouseCoopers LLP

LOCATIONS

HQ: Dresser, Inc.
15455 Dallas Pkwy., Ste. 1100, Addison, TX 75001
Phone: 972-361-9800   **Fax:** 972-361-9903
Web: www.dresser.com

Dresser has manufacturing facilities around the globe.

2003 Sales

	$ mil.	% of total
US	716	43
Europe & Africa	450	27
Canada & Latin America	224	14
Other regions	267	16
Total	**1,657**	**100**

PRODUCTS/OPERATIONS

2003 Sales

	$ mil.	% of total
Flow control	996	60
Measurement systems	391	23
Compression & power systems	277	17
Adjustments	(7)	—
Total	**1,657**	**100**

COMPETITORS

Caterpillar
Cooper Cameron
Danaher
Datamarine
Dover Resources
Emerson Electric
Flowserve
IDEX
ITT Industries
Pentair
Rotork
SPX
Tyco

HISTORICAL FINANCIALS

Company Type: Private

Income Statement

	REVENUE ($ mil.)	NET INCOME ($ mil.)	NET PROFIT MARGIN	EMPLOYEES
12/03	1,657	(45)	—	8,300
12/02	1,589	(23)	—	7,900
12/01	1,546	57	3.7%	8,500
Annual Growth	3.5%	—	—	(1.2%)

FYE: December 31

2003 Year-End Financials

Debt ratio: —
Return on equity: —
Cash ($ mil.): 149
Current ratio: 1.87
Long-term debt ($ mil.): 941

Net Income History

12/94 12/95 12/96 12/97 12/98 12/99 12/00 12/01 12/02 12/03

Duane Reade

Duane Reade is the Big Apple of drugstores. Named after the two streets where its first store was located, the company is the market leader in the densely populated Manhattan area. The company operates about 250 stores in New York and New Jersey. More than half of the company's stores are in high-traffic Manhattan (giving the firm more sales per square foot than any other US drugstore chain). Duane Reade's stores vary greatly in size (1,600-14,700 sq. ft.). The company sells prescription drugs, but nearly 60% of sales come from items such as over-the-counter medications, food and beverages, and health and beauty aids. Duane Reade was taken private in mid-2004 by equity group Oak Hill Capital Partners.

Oak Hill Capital is led by Texas investor Robert M. Bass. In return for each share, stockholders received $16.50 in cash for a transaction valued at about $700 million — including debt — for the company.

Much of Duane Reade's growth has been through new store openings, including what it terms "planned cannibalization," where new stores are opened near crowded older stores to relieve traffic. However, the company has slowed the pace of its store openings. Duane Reade plans to open only about 10 new stores in 2005 (down from 16 last year), and to introduce new in-store services, including professional tooth whitening and diet planning. Duane Reade is also experimenting with ATM-like movie vending machines, coffee kiosks, and "Skin Fitness Centers" to boost sales. The focus on services as a revenue source is a result of the industrywide decline in pharmacy margins.

New York's ban on smoking in some public places has cut into the chain's front-end sales.

The firm buys most of its non-pharmacy products directly from manufacturers and distributes those items through its warehouses in New

Jersey and Queens. Duane Reade fills about 1,700 called-in prescriptions a day from its midtown central fill station. The company also offers more than 800 private-label products (including its "apt.5" line of cosmetics), which account for about 7% of non-pharmacy sales.

A ruling by the National Labor Relations Board could force the regional drugstore chain to pay out more than $25 million in unpaid benefit contributions to its unionized employees. The ruling is part of an ongoing labor dispute between Duane Reade and 2,600 members of Local 338, which the company no longer recognizes.

EXECUTIVES

Chairman, President, and CEO: Anthony J. (Tony) Cuti, age 57, $850,000 pay
EVP, Sales and Marketing: Gary Charboneau, age 58, $450,000 pay
SVP, CFO, and Assistant Secretary: John K. Henry, age 53, $350,000 pay
SVP, Merchandising: Timothy R. (Tim) LaBeau, age 49, $385,000 pay
SVP, Store and Pharmacy Operations: Jerry M. Ray, age 55, $350,000 pay
VP, General Counsel, and Secretary: Michelle D. Bergman, age 37
VP and Controller: Chris Darrow
VP, Finance: Anthony M. Goldrick
VP, Management Information Systems: Joseph S. Lacko, age 61, $258,536 pay
VP, Human Resources and Administration: James M. Rizzo
Auditors: PricewaterhouseCoopers LLP

LOCATIONS

HQ: Duane Reade Inc.
440 9th Ave., New York, NY 10001
Phone: 212-273-5700   **Fax:** 212-244-6527
Web: www.duanereade.com

Duane Reade operates about 250 drugstores in New York and New Jersey; it also has a central fill station in Manhattan and distribution facilities in North Bergen, New Jersey, and Queens, New York.

2004 Stores

	No.
New York	236
New Jersey	13
Total	**249**

PRODUCTS/OPERATIONS

Selected Merchandise and Services

Automated teller machines
Cosmetics
Food and beverage items
Greeting cards
Health and beauty aids
Hosiery
Housewares
Lottery ticket sales
Nutritional products
Over-the-counter medications
Photo supplies
Photofinishing
Prescription drugs
Seasonal merchandise
Tobacco products
Vitamins

COMPETITORS

A&P	Pathmark
Brooks Pharmacy	Rite Aid
CVS	Walgreen
drugstore.com	

HISTORICAL FINANCIALS

Company Type: Private

Income Statement

	REVENUE ($ mil.)	NET INCOME ($ mil.)	NET PROFIT MARGIN	EMPLOYEES
12/04	1,600	—	—	6,300
12/03	1,384	—	—	6,100
12/02	1,275	—	—	6,000
12/01	1,144	—	—	5,100
12/00	1,000	—	—	5,500
12/99	840	—	—	5,000
12/98	587	—	—	3,500
12/97	430	—	—	2,000
12/96	382	—	—	2,000
12/95	337	—	—	—
Annual Growth	18.9%	—	—	15.4%

FYE: Saturday nearest December 31

Revenue History

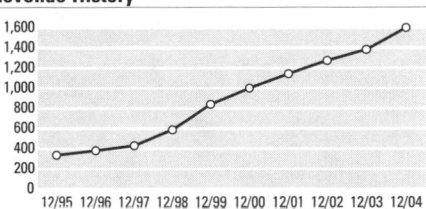

12/95 12/96 12/97 12/98 12/99 12/00 12/01 12/02 12/03 12/04

Duke University Health System

At the core of the Duke University Health System is the Duke University Medical Center. The system also includes two community hospitals in Durham and Raleigh, North Carolina. Its network of medical facilities provides such services as primary and specialty care, home and hospice care, clinical research, and public education programs. The emergency department treats more than 58,800 patients each year.

EXECUTIVES

President and CEO: Victor J. Dzau
SVP, CFO, and Treasurer: Kenneth C. Morris
VP, Acute Care Division; CEO, Duke University Hospital: William J. Fulkerson Jr.
VP, Administration; Vice Chancellor, Operations, Duke University Medical Center; Vice Dean, Administration and Finance, Duke University School of Medicine: Gordon D. Williams
VP, Ambulatory Care; Executive Director, Duke Private Diagnostic Clinic and Duke Patient Revenue Management Organization: Paul R. Newman
VP, Business Development and Chief Strategic Planning Officer; Vice Chancellor, Duke University Medical Center: Molly K. O'Neill
VP and CIO; VP and CIO, Duke University Medical Center: Asif Ahmad
VP, Medical Affairs: Michael Cuffe
Associate VP and Chief Compliance Officer: Lori Feezor
President and CEO, Durham Regional Hospital: David P. McQuaid
CEO, Duke Health Raleigh Hospital: James P. Knight
Chief Patient-Safety Officer: Karen Frush

LOCATIONS

HQ: Duke University Health System
3701 Duke Medical Center, Durham, NC 27706
Phone: 919-684-8111
Web: dukehealth.org

HISTORICAL FINANCIALS

Company Type: Private

Income Statement

FYE: June 30

	ESTIMATED REVENUE ($ mil.)	NET INCOME ($ mil.)	NET PROFIT MARGIN	EMPLOYEES
6/04	1,400	—	—	—
6/03	1,300	—	—	—
Annual Growth	**7.7%**	—	—	—

Revenue History

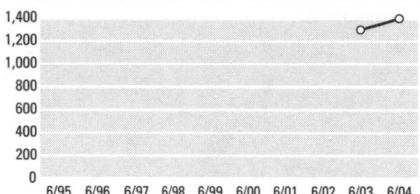

Dunavant Enterprises

King Cotton is alive and well in Memphis. Homegrown Dunavant Enterprises is one of the largest cotton traders in the world. Dunavant was founded in 1960 by William Dunavant, his son Billy (who is allergic to cotton), and Samuel T. Reeves. (The elder Dunavant died shortly after the founding, and Reeves left in 1995 to form Pinnacle Trading.) The company, which grew by selling aggressively to China and the Soviet Union, maintains offices in Africa, Asia, Australia, Europe, Mexico, South America, the former Soviet Union, and the southern US. The company's other business interests include cotton ginning, trucking, and warehousing. Dunavant Enterprises is owned by the Dunavant family and company employees.

EXECUTIVES

Chairman and CEO: William B. (Billy) Dunavant Jr.
President: William B. Dunavant III
President, Dunavant of California: Roger Glaspey
Manager, Human Resources: Mike Andereck
Secretary and General Counsel:
William (Bill) Stubblefield

LOCATIONS

HQ: Dunavant Enterprises, Inc.
3797 New Getwell Rd., Memphis, TN 38118
Phone: 901-369-1500   **Fax:** 901-369-1608
Web: www.dunavant.com

Dunavant has offices in all of the major cotton producing areas of the US, including Alabama, Arkansas, California, Georgia, Louisiana, Mississippi, North Carolina, Tennessee, and Texas. International offices are found in Argentina, Australia, Brazil, China, Guatemala, Mexico, Paraguay, Switzerland, Tajikistan, Turkmenistan, Uzbekistan, and Zambia.

COMPETITORS

Calcot	Southwestern
Cargill	Irrigated Cotton
J.G. Boswell Co.	Staplcotn
King Ranch	Weil Brothers Cotton
Plains Cotton	

HISTORICAL FINANCIALS

Company Type: Private

Income Statement

FYE: June 30

	ESTIMATED REVENUE ($ mil.)	NET INCOME ($ mil.)	NET PROFIT MARGIN	EMPLOYEES
6/04	1,664	—	—	2,115
6/03	1,099	—	—	2,000
6/02	1,000	—	—	2,000
6/01	1,030	—	—	2,400
6/00	1,022	—	—	950
6/99	1,065	—	—	700
6/98	1,200	—	—	700
6/97	1,250	—	—	950
6/96	1,300	—	—	920
6/95	1,300	—	—	—
Annual Growth	**2.8%**	—	—	**11.0%**

Revenue History

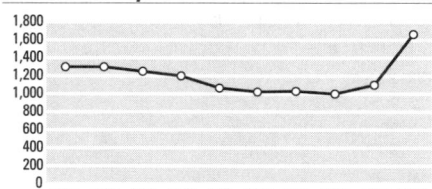

Dunn Industries

Although its beginnings date back to 1924, this company is far from done. Dunn Industries, owned by descendants of founder John E. Dunn, holds the J. E. Dunn Group of construction companies, including flagship J. E. Dunn Construction and Atlanta-based R.J. Griffin & Company. The group builds institutional, commercial, and industrial structures; it also provides construction and program management and design/build services. J. E. Dunn Construction, which ranks among the top 10 US general builders, was one of the first contractors to offer the construction management delivery method. Projects include Sprint's world headquarters, one of the Midwest's largest construction projects, in Overland Park, Kansas.

EXECUTIVES

Chairman Emeritus: William H. Dunn Sr.
Chairman: Stephen D. (Steve) Dunn
Vice Chairman: Robert A. (Bob) Long
President: Jack Nix
CEO: Terrence P. (Terry) Dunn
EVP: William H. Dunn Jr.
SVP, Finance: Gordon E. Lansford III
SVP and General Counsel: Casey S. Halsey
SVP, Corporate Development:
Charles J. (Chuck) Cianciaruso
SVP, Human Resources: Rick Beyer
VP, Community Affairs: Robert P. Dunn
VP, Marketing: John Brake
Corporate Secretary: Barbara G. Hachey

LOCATIONS

HQ: Dunn Industries, Inc.
929 Holmes, Kansas City, MO 64106
Phone: 816-474-8600   **Fax:** 816-391-2510
Web: www.jedunn.com

Dunn Industries has 14 offices throughout the US: Atlanta; Charlotte, North Carolina; Colorado Springs, Colorado; Dallas; Denver; Des Moines, Iowa; Houston; Kansas City, Missouri; Minneapolis; Nashville, Tennessee; Orlando, Florida; Portland, Oregon; Seattle; and Topeka, Kansas.

COMPETITORS

Alberici
Bovis Lend Lease
Clark Enterprises
Hensel Phelps Construction
Rudolph & Sletten
Skanska USA Building
Turner Corporation
Washington Group

HISTORICAL FINANCIALS

Company Type: Private

Income Statement

FYE: December 31

	REVENUE ($ mil.)	NET INCOME ($ mil.)	NET PROFIT MARGIN	EMPLOYEES
12/03	1,655	—	—	3,000
12/02	1,655	—	—	3,000
12/01	1,533	—	—	3,000
12/00	1,311	—	—	3,000
12/99	1,063	—	—	2,000
12/98	871	—	—	2,000
12/97	386	—	—	2,000
12/96	632	—	—	1,700
Annual Growth	**14.7%**	—	—	**8.5%**

Revenue History

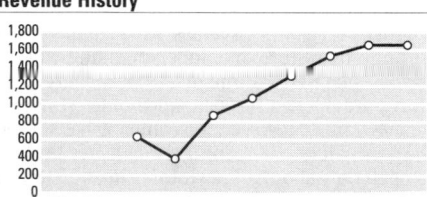

DynCorp International

DynCorp International works behind the scenes to support US military and diplomatic efforts on the front lines. The company's International Technical Services division, which accounts for more than 60% of DynCorp International's sales, provides base operations, drug eradication, law enforcement training, logistics, and security services. Contracts with the US Department of State to train police officers overseas constitute the unit's largest business. DynCorp International's Field Technical Services division offers engineering and maintenance services for aircraft, support equipment, and weapons systems. Investment firm Veritas Capital owns DynCorp International.

Veritas Capital bought the businesses that make up DynCorp International from information technology giant Computer Sciences Corporation (CSC) in February 2005. The DynCorp International operations had been part of another company, DynCorp, which was acquired by CSC in March 2003. CSC kept DynCorp's information technology operations but sold the company's security- and maintenance-related units.

The Department of State and the US Department of Defense each account for about half of DynCorp International's sales; commercial contracts make up the balance.

EXECUTIVES

Chairman: Robert B. McKeon, age 51
President, CEO, and Director: Stephen J. Cannon, age 51, $695,568 pay
EVP and COO: Jay K. Gorman, age 47, $397,196 pay
SVP and CFO: Michael J. Thorne, age 48, $241,375 pay
SVP Special Programs: Charles C. Cannon, $300,017 pay
SVP Strategic Business Development: Edward Phelan
SVP and Chief Accounting Officer: W. Bryan Hill, age 38
SVP Operations: Jeffrey E. Scheferman
President, Field Technical Services: Natale S. DiGesualdo, age 65, $289,615 pay
President, International Technical Services: Robert B. Rosenkranz, age 66
VP Communications: Gregory Lagana
Auditors: Deloitte & Touche LLP

LOCATIONS

HQ: DynCorp International Inc.
8445 Freeport Pkwy., Ste. 400, Irving, TX 75063
Phone: 817-302-1460
Web: www.dyn-intl.com

PRODUCTS/OPERATIONS

2005 Sales

	$ mil.	% of total
International Technical Services	1,232.7	64
Field Technical Services	688.2	36
Total	**1,920.9**	**100**

Selected Operations

International Technical Services
　Contingency services (peacekeeping support, humanitarian relief, de-mining, worldwide contingency planning, and other rapid response services)
　Infrastructure development (infrastructure engineering and construction management)
　International narcotics (drug eradication and host nation pilot and crew training)
　Law enforcement training (international police training, judicial support, immigration support, and base operations)
　Logistics support services (procurement, parts tracking, property control, inventory, and equipment maintenance)
　Marine services (ship logistics and maintenance, communications services, and oil spill response fleet operations)
　Military facility operations (facility and equipment maintenance, facility management, engineering, and custodial and administrative services)
　Security services (security for diplomats, personal protection and security system design, installation and operations)
　Security technology (installation, maintenance and upgrades of physical and software access control points and development of security software, smart cards, and biometrics)

Field Technical Services
　Aviation engineering (design and kit manufacturing, avionics upgrades, field installations, cockpit/fuselage design, and configuration management)
　Aviation ground equipment support (ground equipment support, maintenance and overhaul, and modifications and upgrades)
　Aviation services (aircraft fleet maintenance and modifications, depot augmentation, aftermarket logistics support, and aircrew services and training)
　Ground vehicle maintenance (maintenance of wheeled and tracked vehicles, scheduling, and work flow management)
　Range services (information processing, range technical support, test-and-train range operations, and maintenance, engineering and analysis)

COMPETITORS

General Dynamics	Securitas
Group 4 Securicor	UPS Supply Chain
Lockheed Martin	Solutions
Northrop Grumman	

HISTORICAL FINANCIALS

Company Type: Private

Income Statement

FYE: Friday nearest March 31

	REVENUE ($ mil.)	NET INCOME ($ mil.)	NET PROFIT MARGIN	EMPLOYEES
3/05	1,921	57	2.9%	14,100
3/04	1,214	31	2.6%	—
3/03	918	20	2.2%	—
Annual Growth	**44.6%**	**67.8%**	**—**	**—**

2005 Year-End Financials

Debt ratio: 814.5%　　　　Current ratio: 1.77
Return on equity: 22.9%　　Long-term debt ($ mil.): 789
Cash ($ mil.): 13

Net Income History

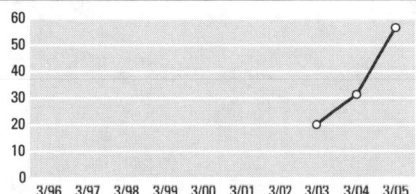

E. & J. Gallo

E. & J. Gallo Winery brings merlot to the masses. The company is one of the world's largest wine makers and the largest in the US by cases sold, thanks in part to its inexpensive jug and box brands Carlo Rossi and Peter Vella. It also makes the fortified Thunderbird brand. The vintner cultivates more than 3,000 acres in the Napa and Sonoma valleys in California. It is the leading US wine exporter. Among its premium wines and imports are those of Gallo of Sonoma and Italian wine Ecco Domani. For those who prefer a little kick to their wine, Gallo distills several lines of brandy. The company makes its own labels and bottles at subsidiary Gallo Glass. The Gallo family owns E. & J. Gallo.

Gallo once only sold wine in the low-to-moderate price range, but now sells about 45 brands over a wide price range, from alcohol-added wines and wine coolers to upscale varietals that fetch more than $50 a bottle. It has successfully expanded premium wines such as Turning Leaf and Gossamer Bay, which don't have the Gallo name on the label. The vintner's strong affiliation with Wal-Mart has boosted wine sales in new Wal-Mart markets such as Germany and the UK.

In addition to using its own grapes, Gallo buys the fruit from other Sonoma County growers. Its 2002 purchase of fellow Sonoma County vintner Louis M. Martini Winery marked the first time Gallo bought another winery rather than land or wine labels. Gallo invested about $1 million in capital improvements at the winery with plans to ramp up production of cabernet under the Martini label.

HISTORY

Giuseppe Gallo, the father of Ernest and Julio Gallo, was born in 1882 in the wine country of northwest Italy. Around 1900 he and his brother, Michelo (they called themselves Joe and Mike), traveled to America seeking fame and fortune in San Francisco. Both brothers became wealthy growing grapes and anticipating the growth of the market during Prohibition (homemade wine was legal and popular).

Giuseppe's eldest sons, Ernest and Julio, worked with their father from the beginning, but their relationship was strained. The father was reluctant to help his sons, particularly Ernest, in business. However, the mysterious murder-suicide that ended the lives of Giuseppe and his wife in 1933 eliminated that problem: the sons inherited the business their father had been unwilling to share.

From then on Ernest ran the business end, assembling a large distribution network and building a national brand, while Julio made the wine and Joe Jr., the third, much younger, brother, worked for them. In the early 1940s Gallo opened bottling plants in Los Angeles and New Orleans, using screw-cap bottles, which then seemed more hygienic and modern than corks. Gallo lagged during WWII, when alcohol was diverted for the military. Under Julio's supervision, it upgraded its planting stock and refined its technology.

In an attempt to capitalize on the sweet wines popular in the 1950s, Gallo introduced Thunderbird, a fortified wine (its alcohol content boosted to 20%), in 1957. In the 1960s Gallo spurred its growth by heavily advertising and keeping prices low. It introduced Hearty Burgundy, a jug wine, in 1964, along with Ripple. Gallo introduced the carbonated, fruit-flavored Boone's Farm Apple Wine in 1969, creating short-term interest in "pop" wines.

The company introduced its first varietal wines in 1974. In the 1970s Gallo field workers switched unions, from the United Farm Workers to the Teamsters. Repercussions included protests and boycotts, but sales were largely unaffected. From 1976 to 1982 Gallo operated under an FTC order limiting its control over wholesalers. The order was lifted after the industry's competitive balance changed.

Through the 1970s and 1980s, Gallo expanded its production of varietals; in 1988 it began adding vintage dates to labels. But it also kept a hand in the lower levels of the market, introducing Bartles & Jaymes wine coolers.

Gallo began a legal battle in 1986 with Joe, who had been eased out of the business, over the use of the Gallo name. In 1992 Joe lost the use of his name for commercial purposes. Julio died the next year when his Jeep overturned on a family ranch.

In 1996 rival Kendall-Jackson sued Gallo for trademark infringement over Gallo's new wine brand, Turning Leaf, claiming Gallo copied its Vintner's Reserve bottle and label. A jury ruled in Gallo's favor in 1997; a federal appeals court supported that decision in 1998.

In May 2000 Gallo announced plans to promote wine-cooler market leader Bartles & Jaymes with a new advertising campaign, although the category continued to wane. The next year Gallo expanded the technological end of the wine business. Gallo's research team patented a number of tools licensed to winemakers around the world; one tool, for example, can diagnose a sick vine in a matter of hours, rather than years.

Gallo bought the Louis M. Martini Winery in Napa Valley in 2002, furthering its expansion into premium wines. In 2004 it bought the brand name and stocks of San Jose-based wine producer Mirassou Vineyards, one of the oldest wineries in California, and Santa Barbara company Bindlewood Weste Winery. In 2005 Gallo added Grape Links, Inc., maker of Barefoot Cellars, to its stable of holdings.

EXECUTIVES

Chairman: Ernest Gallo
Co-President and CEO: Joseph E. Gallo
Co-President: James E. Coleman
Co-President: Robert J. (Bob) Gallo
CFO: Anthony (Tony) Youga
EVP, Marketing: Albion Fenderson
EVP and General Counsel: Jack B. Owens
VP, Creative Services: Joseph Visola
VP, Cella Class: John Cells
VP, Global Chain Accounts: Steve Sprinkle
VP, Human Resources: Mike Chase
VP, Marketing: Iain Douglas
VP, Marketing: Gerry Glasgow
VP, Marketing International Americas: Tim Roach
VP, Media: Sue McClelland
VP, National Sales: Gary Ippolito
VP, Viticulture: Nick Dokoŏzlian
VP, Wine Growing: Tom Smith
VP and CIO: Kent Kushar
CTO: Mary Wagner

LOCATIONS

HQ: E. & J. Gallo Winery
600 Yosemite Blvd., Modesto, CA 95354
Phone: 209-341-3111   **Fax:** 209-341-3569
Web: www.gallo.com

E. & J. Gallo Winery has wineries in the California counties of Fresno, Livingston, Modesto, and Sonoma, and vineyards throughout the region. Its wine is sold throughout the US and in more than 85 countries.

PRODUCTS/OPERATIONS

Selected Products and Labels

Bargain generic & varietals (Carlo Rossi, Livingston Cellars, Peter Vella, Twin Valley, Wild Vines)
Brandy (E & J, E&J Cask & Cream, E&J VSOP)
Flagship (Gallo of Sonoma — County, Estate, and Single Vineyard series)
Fortified & jug (Night Train, Ripple, Thunderbird)
French wines (Red Bicyclette, Pont d'Avignon)
Hospitality industry (Burlwood, Copperidge by E&J Gallo, Liberty Creek, William Wycliff Vineyards)
Imported varietals (Bella Sera, Ecco Domani, McWilliams Hanwood Estate)
Mid-priced varietals (Redwood Creek, Turning Leaf)
Sparkling (André, Ballatore, Indigo Hills, Tott's)
Premium (Anapamu, Frei Brothers Reserve, Indigo Hills, Marcelina, Rancho Zabaco, Turning Leaf Coastal Reserve)

COMPETITORS

Allied Domecq	Kendall-Jackson
Asahi Breweries	Kirin
Bacardi	LVMH
Bacardi USA	Pernod Ricard
Brown-Forman	Premier Pacific
Chalone Wine	Ravenswood Winery
Concha y Toro	R.H. Phillips
Constellation Brands	Sebastiani Vineyards
Diageo	Taittinger
Foster's	Terlato Wine
Foster's Wine Estates Americas	Trinchero Family Estates
GIV	UST
Heaven Hill Distilleries	Vincor
Jim Beam Brands	Wine Group

HISTORICAL FINANCIALS

Company Type: Private

Income Statement				FYE: December 31
	ESTIMATED REVENUE ($ mil.)	NET INCOME ($ mil.)	NET PROFIT MARGIN	EMPLOYEES
12/04	3,000	—	—	—
12/03	2,000	—	—	4,600
12/02	1,800	—	—	4,600
12/01	1,700	—	—	3,500
12/00	1,610	—	—	3,600
12/99	1,520	—	—	5,250
12/98	1,500	—	—	5,000
12/97	1,300	—	—	5,000
12/96	1,200	—	—	5,000
12/95	1,100	—	—	4,000
Annual Growth	**11.8%**	—	—	**1.8%**

Revenue History

(chart: Revenue History, $ values from 3,000 down to 0, years 12/95 through 12/04)

eAcceleration

eAcceleration understands your need for speed. The company's products — such as Webcelerator, Superfassst, and Net Butler — help Web surfers put the e-pedal to the metal and speed up online browsing and downloading. The company also provides professional services such as online technical support and virus protection to subscribers through its eAnthology service. Husband and wife Clinton Ballard (CEO) and Diana Ballard (chairman) own 99% of the company.

EXECUTIVES

Chairman, President, and CEO: Clinton (Clint) Ballard, age 42, $360,644 pay
CFO: E. Edward Ahrens, age 57, $104,478 pay
Auditors: Peterson Sullivan P.L.L.C.

LOCATIONS

HQ: eAcceleration Corp.
1050 NE Hostmark St., Ste. 100B, Poulsbo, WA 98370
Phone: 360-779-6301   **Fax:** 360-598-2450
Web: www.eacceleration.com

COMPETITORS

McAfee
Symantec
Trend Micro
Zix

HISTORICAL FINANCIALS

Company Type: Private

Income Statement				FYE: December 31
	REVENUE ($ mil.)	NET INCOME ($ mil.)	NET PROFIT MARGIN	EMPLOYEES
12/04	13	(2)	—	169
12/03	8	0	—	83
12/02	3	(3)	—	79
12/01	3	(1)	—	48
12/00	8	(1)	—	58
12/99	5	1	14.6%	39
12/98	2	0	21.1%	35
12/97	2	1	61.1%	—
Annual Growth	**32.2%**	—	—	**30.0%**

Net Income History

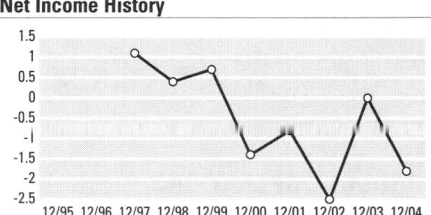

(chart: Net Income History, values from 1.5 to −2.5, years 12/95 through 12/04)

Eagle Family Foods

The holidays wouldn't be the same without Eagle Family Foods. The company manufactures a number of familiar Borden branded products, including sweetened condensed milk (Eagle Brand, Magnolia, Meadow Gold), and mincemeat pie filling (None Such). The company also markets Borden Eggnog and Kava instant coffee. With fewer people stirring up desserts from scratch, the company has launched a line of dessert kits based upon Eagle Brand sweetened condensed milk. Nearly half of the company's sales occur in November and December. Dairy Farmers of America has swapped Eagle Family Foods a manufacturing plant and $14 million to fix it up, in exchange for 44% of Eagle's voting equity and supply agreements.

The company bought Milnot Holding Corporation's canned milk division (condensed and evaporated milk in which the fat is replaced by soybean oil) in 2005.

EXECUTIVES

President, CEO, CFO, Treasurer, and Director:
 Craig A. Steinke, age 48, $527,408 pay
VP, Finance: Michael P. Conti, age 36, $228,762 pay
VP, Marketing: Kelly J. Crouse, age 42, $236,411 pay
VP, Supply Chain: Ronald E. Hord Jr., age 43, $236,680 pay
VP, Sales: Harold G. M. Strunk, age 48, $255,411 pay
Secretary and Controller: Lori S. Snowden, age 45
Auditors: Grant Thornton LLP

LOCATIONS

HQ: Eagle Family Foods Holdings, Inc.
 735 Taylor Rd., Ste. 200, Gahanna, OH 43230
Phone: 614-501-4200 **Fax:** 614-501-4299
Web: www.eaglebrand.com

Eagle Family Foods has offices in Ohio and manufacturing plants in Mississippi, Pennsylvania, and Texas.

PRODUCTS/OPERATIONS

2005 Sales

	$ mil.	% of total
Canned milk	139.5	93
Niche brand products	10.2	7
Total	**149.7**	**100**

Selected Products

Borden egg nog
Eagle Brand sweetened condensed milk
Kava instant coffee
Magnolia sweetened condensed milk
None Such pie filling

COMPETITORS

Dean Foods
E.D. Smith
Kraft Foods
Nestlé USA

HISTORICAL FINANCIALS

Company Type: Private

Income Statement

FYE: Saturday nearest June 30

	REVENUE ($ mil.)	NET INCOME ($ mil.)	NET PROFIT MARGIN	EMPLOYEES
6/05	150	(9)	—	158
6/04	116	(2)	—	163
6/03	129	(55)	—	165
6/02	144	(32)	—	247
6/01	221	(5)	—	362
Annual Growth	**(9.2%)**	**—**	**—**	**(18.7%)**

2005 Year-End Financials

Debt ratio: — Current ratio: 0.58
Return on equity: — Long-term debt ($ mil.): 127
Cash ($ mil.): 2

Net Income History

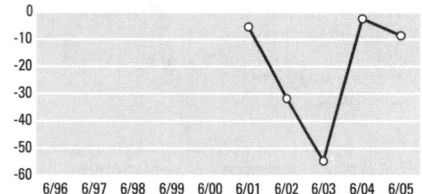

Eastern Bank

Mutually owned Eastern Bank has about 75 banking offices and in-store locations in Massachusetts. The bank offers retail and commercial banking products, as well as trust and investment management services through Eastern Investment Advisors. Its lending activities focus on consumer loans, including indirect auto and education loans. The bank's loan portfolio also includes residential mortgage and commercial real estate loans, as well as business and equipment lease financing loans. Treasury services include cash management and escrow accounts. Its insurance agency subsidiary Eastern Insurance offers personal, commercial, and specialty lines.

Eastern Bank bought mutually owned Plymouth Savings Bank in early 2005, stretching its branch network from Newburyport to Cape Cod. Plymouth will operate separately until integration is completed later in the year. The company also opened eight new branch locations during 2003 and 2004.

Eastern Bank's operations date back to 1818.

EXECUTIVES

Chairman and CEO, Eastern Bank Corporation, Eastern Bank, and Plymouth Savings Bank:
 Stanley J. Lukowski
Vice Chairman: Thomas S. Olsen
President and COO, Eastern Bank Corporation and Eastern Bank: Richard E. Holbrook
CFO and Treasurer; EVP and CFO, Eastern Bank and Plymouth Savings Bank: Charles M. Johnston
VP; Managing Director, Eastern Investment Advisors: W. David Brennan
VP; EVP, Commercial Banking, Eastern Bank and Plymouth Savings Bank: Robert E. Griffin
VP; EVP, Corporate Services, Eastern Bank and Plymouth Savings Bank: Lloyd L. Hamm Jr.
VP; President, Plymouth Savings Bank: Charles H. Ritch

Chairman, Fantini & Gorga: George J. Fantini Jr.
SVP, Human Resources, Eastern Bank and Plymouth Savings Bank: Nancy Huntington Stager
SVP, Marketing, Eastern Bank and Plymouth Savings Bank: Krista L. Lane
Auditors: Ernst & Young LLP

LOCATIONS

HQ: Eastern Bank Corporation
 265 Franklin St., Boston, MA 02110
Phone: 617-897-1008 **Fax:** 617-897-1105
Web: www.easternbank.com

PRODUCTS/OPERATIONS

2004 Sales

	$ mil.	% of total
Interest		
Loans	183.6	60
Securities	41.9	14
Other	0.1	—
Noninterest		
Insurance commissions	29.8	10
Service charges	15.3	5
Trust & investment advisory	9.9	3
Processing fees & other	23.3	8
Total	**303.9**	**100**

COMPETITORS

Bank of America	Independent Bank (MA)
Brookline Bancorp	Service Bancorp
Capital Crossing Bank	Sovereign Bancorp
Century Bancorp (MA)	Wainwright Bank
Citizens Financial Group	Washington Mutual

HISTORICAL FINANCIALS

Company Type: Mutual company

Income Statement

FYE: December 31

	ASSETS ($ mil.)	NET INCOME ($ mil.)	INCOME AS % OF ASSETS	EMPLOYEES
12/04	5,126	43	0.8%	1,462
12/03	4,475	48	1.1%	1,295
12/02	4,113	45	1.1%	1,102
12/01	4,055	36	0.9%	1,200
12/00	3,510	34	1.0%	—
12/99	2,861	31	1.1%	876
12/98	2,689	28	1.0%	908
12/97	2,103	28	1.3%	—
12/96	2,044	23	1.1%	—
12/95	2,110	22	1.1%	—
Annual Growth	**10.4%**	**7.6%**	**—**	**8.3%**

2004 Year-End Financials

Equity as % of assets: 9.8% Long-term debt ($ mil.): 421
Return on assets: 0.9% Sales ($ mil.): 304
Return on equity: —

Net Income History

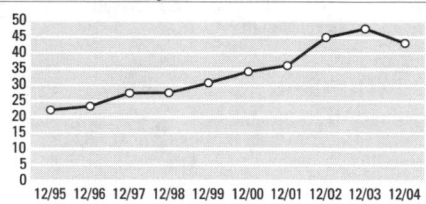

EBSCO

Few portfolios are more diverse than that of EBSCO Industries (short for Elton B. Stephens Company). Among the conglomerate's more than 20 information services, manufacturing, and sales subsidiaries are magazine subscription and fulfillment firms, a fishing lure manufacturer, a rifle manufacturer, a specialty office and computer furniture retailer, and a real estate company. Its main businesses revolve around the publishing industry: EBSCO operates a subscription management agency and is one of the largest publishers of information online and on CD-ROM. The family of founder Elton B. Stephens Sr. owns the company.

EBSCO provides bulk subscription services for print and electronic journals, technical reports, books, and other publications to schools, libraries, and professional offices. It offers sales, promotion, telemarketing, and fulfillment services to publishers, and it owns commercial printers and supplies bindery and packaging products.

Among EBSCO's eclectic subsidiaries are promotional products manufacturers Four Seasons and Vitronic; PRADCO, which makes fishing tackle; Valley Joist, which produces steel construction materials; Vulcan Industries, which makes point-of-purchase displays; Knight & Hale, which makes hunting accessories; specialty furniture makers H. Wilson and Luxor; and real estate unit EBSCO Development.

In 2003 EBSCO acquired the European operations of RoweCom, a company that provided libraries with an online service giving subscribers access to more than 240,000 periodicals. In 2005 EBSCO expanded its medicine and consumer health data when it agreed to purchase the assets of HealthGate Data's patient content repository business for $8.1 million in cash.

EXECUTIVES

Chairman: James T. (J.T.) Stephens
President and CEO: F. Dixon Brooke Jr.
VP and CFO: Richard L. (Rick) Bozzelli
VP and Director Marketing: Jack H. Breard Jr.
VP Corporate Communications: Joe K. Weed
VP Human Resources and Training: John Thompson
VP; General Manager, Administrative Services:
  Becky Caldarello
VP; General Manager, EBSCO Information Services:
  Allen Powell
VP; General Manager, EBSCO Publishing:
  Timothy R. (Tim) Collins
VP; General Manager, EBSCO Realty:
  Elton B. Stephens Jr.
VP; General Manager, EBSCO TeleServices:
  Robert (Bob) Prosise
**VP; General Manager, Information Systems and
  Services:** John R. Pitts
VP; General Manager, MetaPress: Mark Williams
President and General Manager, S.S. Nesbitt:
  Steven S. (Steve) Nesbitt

LOCATIONS

HQ: EBSCO Industries Inc.
  5724 Hwy. 280 East, Birmingham, AL 35242
Phone: 205-991-6600   **Fax:** 205-995-1636
Web: www.ebscoind.com

PRODUCTS/OPERATIONS

Selected Operations

Information Services
  EBSCO Information Services (reference databases, online journals, and subscription services)
  EBSCO Publishing (database publishing and information retrieval services)
  EBSCO Subscription Services (subscription services for libraries and institutions)
Manufacturing
  EBSCO Media (commercial printer)
  Four Seasons (promotional products)
  H. Wilson Co. (audiovisual and computer products and furniture)
  Knight & Hale Game Calls
  Knight Rifles
  Luxor (specialty furniture for offices, schools, libraries, and health care facilities)
  PRADCO Outdoor Brands (fishing lures, fishing line, and related products)
  Valley Joist (steel joists, girders, and metal decks for the construction industry)
  Vitronic (promotional products)
  Vulcan Industries (point-of-purchase displays)
  Wayne Industries (point-of-purchase advertising and signs)
Sales
  EBSCO Development Co. (real estate development)
  EBSCO Magazine Express (direct-marketing subscription agency)
  EBSCO Realty (real estate broker)
  EBSCO TeleServices (telemarketing services)
  Military Service Company (producer and manufacturers' representative serving military base exchanges)
  Publisher Promotion and Fulfillment (promotion and fulfillment services)
  S.S. Nesbitt & Co. (insurance)
  Vulcan Service (magazine subscription sales)

COMPETITORS

ACI Telecentrics
AMREP
APAC Customer Services
Bowne
Brunswick
Dai Nippon Printing
General Binding
HALO
Johnson Outdoors
McGraw-Hill
Quebecor
Reed Elsevier Group
Roanoke Electric Steel
R.R. Donnelley
Scholastic
Simon Worldwide
SITEL
TELESPECTRUM
Thomson Corporation

HISTORICAL FINANCIALS
Company Type: Private

Income Statement
FYE: June 30

	REVENUE ($ mil.)	NET INCOME ($ mil.)	NET PROFIT MARGIN	EMPLOYEES
6/04	1,800	—	—	5,000
6/03	1,400	—	—	4,500
6/02	1,400	—	—	5,000
6/01	1,375	—	—	4,500
6/00	1,375	—	—	4,200
6/99	1,210	—	—	4,200
6/98	1,000	—	—	4,000
6/97	1,000	—	—	4,000
6/96	900	—	—	4,000
Annual Growth	9.1%	—	—	2.8%

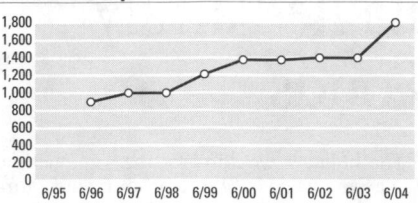

Revenue History

| | 6/95 | 6/96 | 6/97 | 6/98 | 6/99 | 6/00 | 6/01 | 6/02 | 6/03 | 6/04 |

Eby-Brown

Eby-Brown makes its money on vices such as munchies and nicotine. The company is a leading convenience-store supplier of more than 11,000 name-brand products, including tobacco, candy, snacks, health and beauty aids, and general merchandise. The company's eight distribution centers serve 28 states and more than 25,000 stores, including the Speedway and SuperAmerica chains owned by Marathon Ashland Petroleum. Eby-Brown also has a marketing division that offers its customers advertising and promotion services. The century-old company is family-owned and run. Co-CEOs Tom and Dick Wake succeeded their father, William Wake Jr., in 1983. William died in 2004 at the age of 78.

EXECUTIVES

Co-President and Co-CEO: Richard (Dick) Wake
Co-President and Co-CEO: Thomas G. (Tom) Wake
CFO: Mark Smetana
EVP, Sales: Al Palma
VP, Advertising and Sales Promotions: Ralph Kallmann
VP, Business Development: Ron Coppel
Employment Contact: Joan Nauman
Auditors: Deloitte & Touche

LOCATIONS

HQ: Eby-Brown Company
  280 W. Shuman Blvd., Ste. 280,
  Naperville, IL 60566
Phone: 630-778-2800   **Fax:** 630-778-2830
Web: www.eby-brown.com

Eby-Brown's distribution centers are located in Florida, Georgia, Illinois, Indiana, Maryland, Michigan, Ohio, and Wisconsin.

COMPETITORS

AMCON Distributing
C&S Wholesale
C.D. Hartnett
GSC Enterprises
H.T. Hackney
McLane
Nash Finch
Purity Wholesale Grocers
S. Abraham & Sons
Spartan Stores
SUPERVALU

HISTORICAL FINANCIALS

Company Type: Private

Income Statement

FYE: September 30

	REVENUE ($ mil.)	NET INCOME ($ mil.)	NET PROFIT MARGIN	EMPLOYEES
9/04	3,100	—	—	2,100
9/03	3,670	—	—	2,100
9/02*	3,600	—	—	2,100
12/01	3,670	—	—	2,100
12/00	3,400	—	—	2,011
12/99	2,773	—	—	2,011
12/98	1,700	—	—	1,550
12/97	1,650	—	—	1,450
12/96	1,670	—	—	1,395
12/95	1,550	—	—	1,411
Annual Growth	8.0%	—	—	4.5%

*Fiscal year change

Revenue History

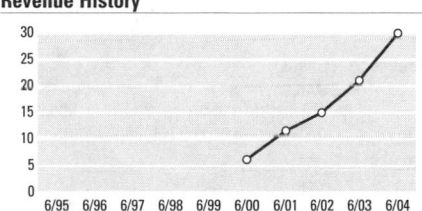

| | 12/95 | 12/96 | 12/97 | 12/98 | 12/99 | 12/00 | 12/01 | 9/02 | 9/03 | 9/04 |

---

eCopy

eCopy turns the stacks of paper on your desk into digital documents. The company offers document distribution and integration software that customers use to convert paper-based documents into digital files, which can then be distributed over the Internet or integrated into enterprise applications. eCopy's offerings, which work with digital copiers and scanners, include eCopy Desktop, which enables users to view, edit, annotate, forward, print, and archive digital files. The company targets the financial services, health care, insurance, legal, and manufacturing industries. Customers include General Electric, Intuit, and Time Warner. CEO Edward Schmid founded eCopy in 1992.

eCopy has received venture capital investments from Ascent Venture Partners, Landmark Partners, and Canon U.S.A., as well as a local group of private investors. The company has offices in Australia, Japan, the UK, and the US.

EXECUTIVES

President and CEO: Edward (Ed) Schmid, age 58
SVP, Worldwide Sales: Tim Corkery
VP and CFO: Denis E. Liptak
VP, Engineering: Michael (Mike) Conley
VP, North American Sales: Tim James
VP, Product Marketing: David Toub
Controller: Karen Dumont
Director, Human Resources: Susan L. Herman
General Manager, Europe: Joachim Twelmeyer
General Manager, Japan: Tatsuo Yazaki
Public Relations Manager: Bill Brikiatis
Manager, Japanese Marketing: Naohiko Yamanouchi
Senior Marketing Specialist: Angela Heenan

LOCATIONS

HQ: eCopy, Inc.
1 Oracle Dr., Nashua, NH 03062
Phone: 603-881-4450 **Fax:** 603-881-4399
Web: www.ecopy.com

PRODUCTS/OPERATIONS

Software

eCopy Suite
Desktop (editing, annotation, distribution, and archiving of digital files)
ScanStation (touch-screen panel attached to digital copiers)
ShareScan (document distribution and scanning)

COMPETITORS

Adobe	FormScape
Arbortext	Mitek Systems
Captiva Software	Ricoh
Documentum	ScanSoft
FileNet	Xerox

HISTORICAL FINANCIALS

Company Type: Private

Income Statement

FYE: June 30

	ESTIMATED REVENUE ($ mil.)	NET INCOME ($ mil.)	NET PROFIT MARGIN	EMPLOYEES
6/04	30	—	—	135
6/03	21	—	—	100
6/02	15	—	—	90
6/01	12	—	—	80
6/00	6	—	—	47
Annual Growth	48.3%	—	—	30.2%

Revenue History

| | 6/95 | 6/96 | 6/97 | 6/98 | 6/99 | 6/00 | 6/01 | 6/02 | 6/03 | 6/04 |

Edelbrock

Speed demon Edelbrock makes performance-enhancing parts for cars, light trucks, recreational vehicles, race cars, and motorcycles. Its products include carburetors, intake manifolds, cylinder heads, air cleaners, camshafts, exhaust systems, and a wide array of other aftermarket parts. The company markets its products mainly through automotive chain stores, mail-order houses, and warehouse distributors. Edelbrock also makes a line of aftermarket engine parts specifically for Harley-Davidson motorcycles. The Edelbrock family — led by company chairman, president, and CEO Victor Edelbrock — controls the company.

To maintain control over the cast-aluminum components of its products, Edelbrock operates its own foundry. The company manufactures more than half of the products it sells and relies on third-party suppliers for the rest.

Edelbrock used to be a publicly traded company, but because the Edelbrock family and other insiders controlled so much of its stock, the company attracted little attention from Wall Street. Believing its shares were undervalued, Victor Edelbrock took the company private in December 2004.

EXECUTIVES

Chairman, President, and CEO: O. Victor Edelbrock, age 67, $698,443 pay
EVP, COO, General Manager, and Director: Jeffrey L. Thompson, age 51, $424,200 pay
VP of Advertising, Secretary, and Director: Cathleen Edelbrock, age 44
VP of Finance, CFO, and Director: Aristedes T. Feles, age 36, $171,637 pay
VP of Manufacturing: Wayne P. Murray, age 52, $226,850 pay
VP of Purchasing: Christina Edelbrock, age 43
VP, Research and Development: Jack B. Mayberry, age 57
VP of Sales: Steve Whipple, age 46
Treasurer: Nancy M. Edelbrock, age 67
Controller: Rodney T. Teraishi, age 38
Director of Human Resources: Jackie Langlais
Auditors: Grant Thornton LLP

LOCATIONS

HQ: Edelbrock Corporation
2700 California St., Torrance, CA 90503
Phone: 310-781-2222 **Fax:** 310-320-1187
Web: www.edelbrock.com

Edelbrock maintains manufacturing facilities in Torrance, California, and foundry operations in San Jacinto, California.

PRODUCTS/OPERATIONS

Selected Products

Air cleaners
Aluminum cylinder heads (for Harley-Davidson motorcycles)
Brake parts (sold under the Russell brand)
Breathers
Camshafts
Carburetors
Cylinder heads
Exhaust systems
Intake manifolds
Shock absorbers
Valve covers

COMPETITORS

Competition Cams
Crane Cams
Federal-Mogul
Harley-Davidson
Holley Performance Products
Moroso Performance Products

HISTORICAL FINANCIALS

Company Type: Private

Income Statement

FYE: June 30

	REVENUE ($ mil.)	NET INCOME ($ mil.)	NET PROFIT MARGIN	EMPLOYEES
6/04	126	4	2.8%	722
6/03	115	3	2.6%	691
6/02	124	5	4.4%	679
6/01	116	5	4.2%	645
6/00	121	8	6.6%	691
6/99	109	7	6.8%	592
6/98	96	6	6.1%	563
6/97	87	7	8.2%	531
6/96	79	7	8.2%	485
6/95	69	6	9.3%	463
Annual Growth	7.0%	(6.5%)	—	5.1%

2004 Year-End Financials

Debt ratio: 0.2%
Return on equity: 3.9%
Cash ($ mil.): 13
Current ratio: 4.39
Long-term debt ($ mil.): 0

Net Income History

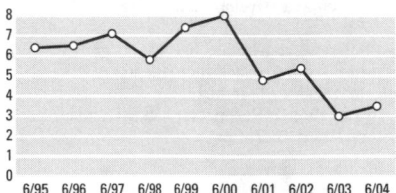

El Pollo Loco

This chicken restaurant chain is crazy from the Mexican heat. El Pollo Loco (which means "The Crazy Chicken" in Spanish) operates and franchises more than 320 fast-casual restaurants that specialize in Mexican-style chicken dishes. The chain's menu includes chicken burritos and tacos, as well as salads and a complete chicken dinner. Most of El Pollo Loco's outlets are in California, while a small number can be found in Arizona, Nevada, and Texas. More than half of its locations are operated by franchisees. Juan Francisco Ochoa started the chain in Mexico in 1975; it is owned by Trimaran Capital Partners.

Growing to more than 80 locations by 1980, El Pollo Loco was acquired by family-dining chain operator Denny's in 1983. (The Ochoa family retained the rights to the name in Mexico.) The chain slowly expanded through the 1990s before it was sold to company management and New York-based American Securities Capital in 1999.

The company plans to grow in and outside its current market. Among the new territories it hopes to enter are Colorado and areas east of the Mississippi River, including Chicago. The goal is to add more than 130 locations (mostly franchised) by 2009.

Trimaran Capital Partners purchased El Pollo Loco for $415 million from American Securities Capital in the fall of 2005.

EXECUTIVES

President and CEO: Stephen E. (Steve) Carley
VP, Finance and CFO: Joseph N. Stein
VP, Human Resources and Training: Jeanne Scott
VP, Marketing and Chief Marketing Officer: Karen B. Eadon
VP, Development: Brian Berkhausen
VP, Operations: Kenneth W. (Ken) Clark
VP and General Counsel: Pamela R. Milner
Director, Communications: Julie L. Weeks
Director, Franchise Operations: Michael Wildman
Director, Information Technology: Tom Giannetti
Director, Operations: David Wetzel
Director, Retail Marketing: Mark Hardison
Co-Director, Franchise Sales and Development: Marcelino Contreras
Co-Director, Franchise Sales and Development: Scott Gillie
Controller: Robert Gossman

LOCATIONS

HQ: El Pollo Loco, Inc.
3333 Michelson Dr., Ste. 550, Irvine, CA 92612
Phone: 949-399-2000   **Fax:** 949-399-2025
Web: www.elpolloloco.com

COMPETITORS

Boston Market
Brinker
Chevys
Chipotle
Del Taco
Fresh Enterprises
Juan Pollo
KFC
Qdoba
Rubio's Restaurants
Taco Bell

HISTORICAL FINANCIALS

Company Type: Private

Income Statement

FYE: December 31

	ESTIMATED REVENUE ($ mil.)	NET INCOME ($ mil.)	NET PROFIT MARGIN	EMPLOYEES
12/04	219	—	—	3,600
12/03	206	—	—	3,600
12/02	150	—	—	4,000
12/01	150	—	—	4,000
12/00	150	—	—	3,800
12/99	125	—	—	3,500
Annual Growth	11.9%	—	—	0.6%

Revenue History

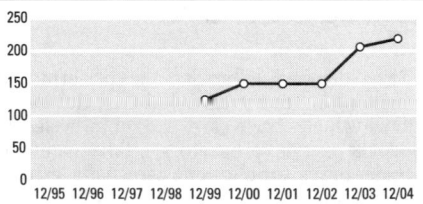

Electrograph Technologies

If you're reading this on a big screen, you or someone you know might have done business with Electrograph Technologies (formerly Manchester Technologies). The company resells LCD flat panels, plasma displays, projectors, and other computer-related products. Electrograph serves customers throughout North America via a network of 10 US sales offices. Private equity firm Caxton-Iseman Capital acquired the former Manchester Technologies for about $56 million in cash in August 2005. In conjunction with the acquisition, Caxton-Iseman brought in new management and changed the name of the company. Electrograph had been the main business unit of Manchester Technologies.

In 2003, the former Manchester Technologies closed its Donovan Consulting Group unit, acquired two years earlier. In 2004, it sold its IT fulfillment, professional services, and enterprise software development and operations consulting businesses to ePlus, a provider of enterprise cost management software.

EXECUTIVES

CEO: Alan M. Smith, age 40
President: Sam Taylor
VP, Finance, CFO, and Assistant Secretary: Elan Yaish, age 34, $375,000 pay
Director, Business Development and Marketing: Richard G. Vestuto
Director, Human Resources: Rose Ann Gordon
Auditors: KPMG LLP

LOCATIONS

HQ: Electrograph Technologies Corp.
160 Oser Ave., Hauppauge, NY 11788
Phone: 631-435-1199   **Fax:** 631-435-2113
Web: www.electrograph.com

COMPETITORS

ASI Corp.
CompuCom
D&H Distributing
Dell
En Pointe
Hartford Computer
Ingram Micro
Merisel
PC Warehouse
Pomeroy IT
Resilien
SARCOM
Sayers Group
SED International
Software House
Software Spectrum
Tech Data
Westcon
ZT Group

HISTORICAL FINANCIALS

Company Type: Private

Income Statement

FYE: July 31

	REVENUE ($ mil.)	NET INCOME ($ mil.)	NET PROFIT MARGIN	EMPLOYEES
7/04	173	(3)	—	96
7/03	286	(3)	—	278
7/02	262	1	0.3%	348
7/01	280	2	0.6%	325
7/00	300	4	1.4%	385
7/99	229	2	1.0%	339
7/98	203	2	1.1%	322
7/97	188	4	1.9%	263
7/96	190	2	1.1%	222
7/95	171	2	1.0%	240
Annual Growth	**0.1%**	**—**	**—**	**(9.7%)**

2004 Year-End Financials

Debt ratio: 18.3%   Current ratio: 2.59
Return on equity: —   Long-term debt ($ mil.): 8
Cash ($ mil.): 17

Net Income History

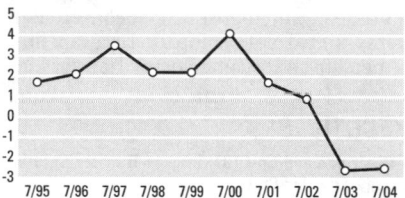

7/95 7/96 7/97 7/98 7/99 7/00 7/01 7/02 7/03 7/04

Elgin National Industries

Managing more than a dozen businesses is all in a day's work for Elgin National Industries, which operates a diverse group of manufacturing and engineering services companies. Through its Manufactured Products division, the company makes highly engineered products such as centrifuges, fasteners, and electrical switch gear equipment. Its Engineering Services division provides bulk materials handling systems, as well as design, engineering, procurement, and construction management services for mineral processors. The electric utility, industrial equipment, mining, and mineral processing industries use the company's products and services. Chairman and CEO Fred Schulte owns 58% of the company.

The company's engineering services segment has been seeking to diversify its markets and expand internationally. During 2004, about 25% of the net sales of this segment came from international projects.

EXECUTIVES

Chairman and CEO: Fred C. Schulte
President, COO, and Director: Charles D. Hall
VP, CFO, Treasurer, and Director: Wayne J. Conner
VP, Controller, and Secretary (HR): Lynn C. Batory
VP, Manufacturing: David Hall
Auditors: McGladrey & Pullen, LLP

LOCATIONS

HQ: Elgin National Industries, Inc.
2001 Butterfield Rd., Ste. 1020,
Downers Grove, IL 60515
Phone: 630-434-7200   **Fax:** 630-434-7272
Web: www.eni.com

Elgin National Industries operates manufacturing facilities in Indiana, Illinois, Missouri, Ohio, Tennessee, Utah, Virginia, and West Virginia, and in Australia.

2004 Sales

	$ mil.	% of total
US	171.1	82
Other countries	37.0	18
Total	**208.1**	**100**

PRODUCTS/OPERATIONS

2004 Sales

	$ mil.	% of total
Manufactured products	108.4	52
Engineering services	99.7	48
Total	**208.1**	**100**

Selected Subsidiaries

Manufactured Products
  Best Metal Finishing Inc.
  Centrifugal and Mechanical Industries
  Centrifugal Services, Inc.
  Chandler Products
  Clinch River Corporation
  Leland Powell Fasteners, Inc.
  Mining Controls, Inc.
  Norris Screen and Manufacturing Inc.
  Ohio Rod Products Company
  Tabor Machine Company
  Vanco International, Inc.

Engineering Services
  Roberts & Schaefer Company
  Soros Associates, Inc.

COMPETITORS

Illinois Tool Works   Sumitomo
Indel   Heavy Industries
Morton Industrial Group   Synalloy
NACCO Industries

HISTORICAL FINANCIALS

Company Type: Private

Income Statement

FYE: December 31

	REVENUE ($ mil.)	NET INCOME ($ mil.)	NET PROFIT MARGIN	EMPLOYEES
12/04	208	(3)	—	790
12/03	145	(2)	—	690
12/02	149	(2)	—	690
12/01	192	4	1.8%	780
12/00	163	4	2.4%	670
12/99	150	4	2.3%	650
12/98	156	3	2.0%	650
12/97	140	5	3.2%	673
12/96	136	5	3.6%	—
12/95	127	(0)	—	—
Annual Growth	**5.7%**	**—**		**2.3%**

2004 Year-End Financials

Debt ratio: —   Current ratio: 1.51
Return on equity: —   Long-term debt ($ mil.): 103
Cash ($ mil.): 0

Net Income History

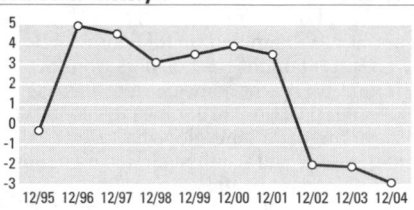

12/95 12/96 12/97 12/98 12/99 12/00 12/01 12/02 12/03 12/04

Encyclopaedia Britannica

Encyclopaedia Britannica thinks it knows everything, and it probably does. The company publishes reference works including its flagship 32-volume *Encyclopaedia Britannica* (first published in 1768), *The Annals of America,* and *Great Books of the Western World.* It also publishes a variety of dictionaries (*Merriam Webster's Collegiate Dictionary, Merriam Webster's Biographical Dictionary*) through its Merriam-Webster subsidiary. Most of the company's products are available online, as well as on CD-ROM and DVD. Swiss financier Jacob Safra (a nephew of the late banking king Edmond Safra) owns the company.

Its Britannica.com Web site offers access for a fee to its entire collection of encyclopedia articles, an editorially reviewed Web site directory, and third-party content from *The New York Times* and other providers. Britannica's site also features an online store where users can buy its print and interactive products.

After initially being late to the CD-ROM and dot-com party, Encyclopaedia Britannica decided to commit to Britannica.com, a sister firm devoted to electronic content which was to be spun off in an IPO. But the idea turned out to be disastrous (in part because of bad publicity over traffic jams at the site and a downturn in online advertising), and the company has since focused back on its core business with a renewed interest in print products. The company is considering selling its Merriam-Webster subsidiary to raise capital.

Trying a new approach to reach consumers, the company began selling its products on TV home shopping network QVC in 2003.

HISTORY

Engraver Andrew Bell and printer and bookseller Colin Macfarquhar created the first edition of the *Encyclopaedia Britannica* in Scotland, releasing the three-volume set in weekly installments between 1768 and 1771. Benjamin Franklin and John Locke were among early contributors. The second edition, completed in 1784, expanded to 10 volumes; the fourth (1809) contained 20. The ninth edition (1889) captured the scientific spirit of the age with articles by Thomas Henry Huxley and James Clerk Maxwell.

American businessmen Horace Hooper and Walter Jackson purchased the *Encyclopaedia* in 1901 and established the Encyclopaedia Britannica Company in the US. It published the first *Britannica Book of the Year* in 1913. Sears chairman Julius Rosenwald bought the company in

1920 and tried to market *Britannica* through Sears' retail operations, as well as with door-to-door sales. William Benton (of Benton & Bowles Advertising) bought the business from Sears in 1941 and built a nationwide sales force with a hard-sell reputation. Britannica released its first foreign-language encyclopedia, *Enciclopedia Barsa,* in 1957 and acquired dictionary publisher G. & C. Merriam in 1964.

When Benton died in 1974, he bequeathed the operation to the non-profit William Benton Foundation, the sole beneficiary of which was the University of Chicago. Britannica later bought out rival Compton's Encyclopedia in the mid-1970s. The 1989 CD-ROM release of *Compton's MultiMedia Encyclopedia* was a first for the industry, but Britannica sold Compton's NewMedia division to Chicago's Tribune Company in 1993 just before the CD-ROM market exploded. The company also promised not to release a competing multimedia version of Encyclopaedia Britannica for two years. Not realizing that the electronic revolution was upon them and reluctant to change its established and profitable door-to-door sales techniques, the conservative company fell behind challengers who offered CD-ROMs including Microsoft and its *Funk & Wagnalls* product (later relaunched as *Encarta*).

Jacob Safra, a *Britannica* lover since childhood, led a group that paid $135 million for the struggling company in 1996. With book sales dwindling and heavy competition, Britannica cut its prices and ceased its door-to-door marketing that year. It agreed to sell both its CD-ROM and print encyclopedias in retail stores in 1997, and lured publisher Paul Hoffman away from Walt Disney's successful *Discover* magazine. Britannica Internet Guide (BIG), a free Internet search engine, launched that year. Britannica added guest columns and other features to BIG in 1998 and renamed it eBlast (it changed the site's name again to Britannica the following year).

Encyclopaedia Britannica Holdings (Safra's umbrella firm for the publisher) launched a sister firm, Britannica.com, in 1999 to oversee the company's electronic and Internet products and services. CEO Don Yannias resigned his post with the print company and took the reins of the new digital firm, allowing Hoffman to take over as the publisher's president. Britannica.com struggled with the rest of the Internet industry in 2000, laying off almost 25% of its staff.

In 2001 Yannias left the company entirely and was replaced by Ilan Yeshua, an executive from an Israeli educational technology firm. Later that year, the company integrated Britannica.com back into the encyclopedia unit of Encyclopaedia Britannica, a move that involved severely downsizing the Web staff. Yeshua departed the company in 2003 and was replaced by Britannica executive Jorge Cauz.

EXECUTIVES

Chairman: Jacob E. Safra
President: Jorge Cauz
EVP, Secretary, and General Counsel: William J. Bowe
SVP and Editor: Dale Hoiberg
SVP Corporate Development: Michael Ross
SVP International: Leah Mansoor
SVP Sales and Marketing: Patti Ginnis
VP Operations and Finance: Richard Anderson
President and Publisher, Merriam-Webster: John Morse
Director, Corporate Communications: Tom Panelas
Executive Director, Technology: Tom Lang
Marketing Manager, Consumer Sales: Elizabeth Arnold
Direct Marketing Manager: Christine Hodgson
Auditors: PricewaterhouseCoopers

LOCATIONS

HQ: Encyclopaedia Britannica, Inc.
310 S. Michigan Ave., Chicago, IL 60604
Phone: 312-347-7000   **Fax:** 312-347-7399
Web: corporate.britannica.com

Encyclopaedia Britannica makes its headquarters in Chicago and maintains offices in London, New Delhi, Paris, Seoul, Sydney, Taipei, Taiwan; Tel Aviv, and Tokyo.

PRODUCTS/OPERATIONS

Selected Products
Dictionaries
  Merriam Webster's Biographical Dictionary
  Merriam Webster's Collegiate Dictionary
  Merriam Webster's Collegiate Thesaurus
  Merriam Webster's Dictionary of Law
Encyclopedias
  Britannica First Edition Replica Set
  Encyclopaedia Britannica
  The Encyclopedia of Popular Music
Other reference works
  The Annals of America
  Gray's Anatomy
  Great Books of the Western World

COMPETITORS

Dow Jones
Editis
Franklin Electronic Publishers
Harcourt Education
LexisNexis
McGraw-Hill
Microsoft
National Geographic
Pearson
Random House
Scholastic Library Publishing
Thomson Corporation
Time
Wikimedia Foundation
World Book

HISTORICAL FINANCIALS

Company Type: Private

Income Statement

FYE: December 31

	REVENUE ($ mil.)	NET INCOME ($ mil.)	NET PROFIT MARGIN	EMPLOYEES
12/01	225	—	—	260
12/00	275	—	—	300
12/99*	279	—	—	350
9/98	300	—	—	400
9/97	325	—	—	400
9/96	375	—	—	700
9/95	400	—	—	800
9/94	453	—	—	900
9/93	540	—	—	1,000
9/92	586	—	—	1,100
Annual Growth	(10.1%)	—	—	(14.8%)

*Fiscal year change

Revenue History

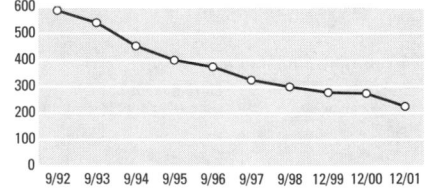

Energy Transfer Equity

Energy Transfer Equity is transferring some equity to get more out of its midstream energy assets. The company acts as the general partner of Energy Transfer Partners, which sells nearly 400 million gallons of propane a year to more than 700,000 customers in 34 states. It also operates about 11,700 miles of natural gas pipelines. Through its Energy Transfer Partners GP unit, Energy Transfer Equity owns a 2% general partnership stake in Energy Transfer Partners, and 50% of its outstanding incentive distribution rights. Following the closing of its IPO, Energy Transfer Equity will directly own 33% of Energy Transfer Partners. Energy Transfer Equity is managed by general partner LE GP.

The company was formed in 2002 as La Grange Energy, a Texas limited partnership. In early 2005 it changed its name to Energy Transfer Company. In August 2005 it converted from a Texas limited partnership to a Delaware limited partnership and became Energy Transfer Equity.

EXECUTIVES

Co-Chairman and Co-CEO, Energy Transfer Equity and Energy Transfer Partners: Ray C. Davis, age 63, $943,462 pay
Co-Chairman and Co-CEO, Energy Transfer Equity and Energy Transfer Partners: Kelcy L. Warren, age 49, $925,000 pay
President, CFO, and Director, Energy Transfer Partners GP: H. Michael Krimbill, age 52, $650,000 pay
President and CFO, Energy Transfer Equity and LE GP, LLC; Director, Energy Transfer Partners: John W. McReynolds, age 54
EVP and COO, Energy Transfer Partners: R.C. Mills, age 67, $435,000 pay
VP, Corporate Development, Energy Transfer Partners: Bradley K. Atkinson, age 50
VP and Treasurer, Energy Transfer Partners: John W. Daigh, age 49
VP, Administration, and Controller, Energy Transfer Partners: Karen Z. Hicks, age 42
SVP, Commercial Development, Energy Transfer Partners: Marshall S. (Mackie) McCrea, age 46, $484,923 pay
VP, General Counsel, and Secretary, Energy Transfer Partners: Robert A. Burk, age 48, $296,538 pay
Auditors: Deloitte & Touche LLP

LOCATIONS

HQ: Energy Transfer Equity, L.P.
2828 Woodside St., Dallas, TX 75204
Phone: 214-981-0700   **Fax:** 214-981-0703
Web: www.energytransfer.com

COMPETITORS

All Star Gas
AmeriGas Partners
Atmos Energy
Duke Energy Field Services
Enbridge
Ferrellgas Partners
Star Gas Partners
Suburban Propane

HISTORICAL FINANCIALS

Company Type: Private

Income Statement

FYE: August 31

	REVENUE ($ mil.)	NET INCOME ($ mil.)	NET PROFIT MARGIN	EMPLOYEES
8/04	2,347	450	19.2%	3,114
8/03	931	46	5.0%	—
Annual Growth	152.1%	874.5%	—	—

2004 Year-End Financials

Debt ratio: 290.8%
Return on equity: 163.4%
Cash ($ mil.): 83

Current ratio: 1.19
Long-term debt ($ mil.): 1,071

Net Income History

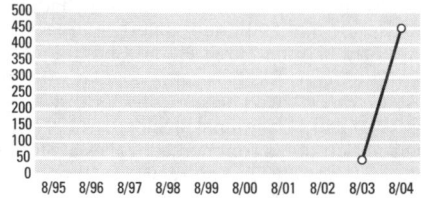

500
450
400
350
300
250
200
150
100
50
0

8/95 8/96 8/97 8/98 8/99 8/00 8/01 8/02 8/03 8/04

Engineous Software

Engineous Software provides design and optimization software for engineering design firms. The company's iSIGHT and FIPER tools help integrate various commercial CAD/CAM/CAE tools, internally developed software, and applications such as Microsoft's Excel spreadsheet program. Customers include 3M, Boeing, Computer Sciences Corp. (CSC), DaimlerChrysler, and Ishikawajima-Harima Heavy Industries (IHI). Founded in 1996, Engineous Software has offices in Asia, Europe, and North America. In 2004 the company acquired Synaps, Inc., an Atlanta-based design optimization software and services firm specializing in the aerospace industry.

EXECUTIVES

Chairman: Siu S. Tong
President and CEO: Janet C. Wylie
COO and CFO: Wade Ficken
EVP, Sales, Europe and North America: Alan (Al) Wojcik
VP, Automotive Industry: Mike Sheh
VP, Business Development: Glenn Reis
VP, Engineering: Alex Van der Velden
VP, Human Resources and Operations Support: Mike Lemmons
VP, Marketing Communications and Product Management: J. P. Evans
Controller: Denis A. Brichford

LOCATIONS

HQ: Engineous Software, Inc.
2000 CentreGreen Way, Ste. 100, Cary, NC 27513
Phone: 919-677-6700 **Fax:** 919-677-8911
Web: www.engineous.com

COMPETITORS

Altair Engineering
Kubotek USA
UGS Corp.

HISTORICAL FINANCIALS

Company Type: Private

Income Statement

FYE: June 30

	REVENUE ($ mil.)	NET INCOME ($ mil.)	NET PROFIT MARGIN	EMPLOYEES
6/04*	12	—	—	88
12/03	9	—	—	80
Annual Growth	33.3%	—	—	10.0%

*Fiscal year change

Revenue History

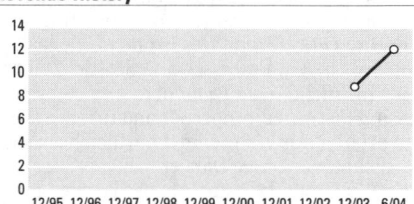

14
12
10
8
6
4
2
0

12/95 12/96 12/97 12/98 12/99 12/00 12/01 12/02 12/03 6/04

Enterprise Rent-A-Car

This Enterprise is boldly going where it hasn't gone before — the airport. The company, which offers to ferry customers to the rental office, says it is the largest car rental firm in the US. With more than 600,000 cars in its fleet, Enterprise operates in the US, Canada, Germany, Ireland, and the UK. The company targets customers whose own cars are in the shop or who need a rental for short trips; it also has begun serving the airport market. Controlled by founder Jack Taylor and his family, Enterprise has spun off its non-automotive operations (balloons, footwear, a golf course, hotel amenities, and prison supplies) as Centric Group.

The company also leases vehicles and manages fleets for other companies (Enterprise Fleet Services), and when it's ready to refresh its fleet, Enterprise sells its cars (Enterprise Car Sales) through a nationwide program. Potential customers can shop by make and model through the Enterprise Web site.

In March 2004 Enterprise announced plans to hire some 6,500 additional employees over the course of the year, citing new branch openings of about one per business day as the reason. Enterprise opened 300 new locations during 2003.

Founder John Taylor's son Andrew is the company's chairman and CEO.

HISTORY

In 1957 Jack Taylor, the sales manager for a Cadillac dealership in St. Louis, hit on the idea that leasing cars might be an easier way to make money than selling them. Taylor's idea sounded good to his boss, Arthur Lindburg, who agreed to set Taylor up in the leasing business. In return for a 50% pay cut, Taylor received 25% of the new enterprise, called Executive Leasing, which began in the walled-off body shop of a car dealership.

In the early 1960s Taylor started renting cars for short periods as well as leasing them. When his leasing agents expressed annoyance with the rental operation, Taylor turned that business over to Don Holtzman. Holtzman realized that his 17-car rental operation was too little to take on industry giants like Hertz and Avis; instead, he concentrated on the "home city" or replacement market. He offered competitive rates to insurance adjusters who needed to find cars for policyholders whose vehicles were damaged or stolen.

Propelled by court decisions that required casualty companies to pay for loss of transportation, Taylor expanded from his St. Louis base in 1969 with a branch office in Atlanta. Since another car leasing outfit in Georgia was already named Executive, Taylor changed the name of his company to Enterprise Rent-A-Car.

The company expanded into Florida and Texas in the early 1970s, targeting garages and body shops that performed repairs for insured drivers. Oil price shocks of that period compelled Taylor to diversify his operations. In 1974 Enterprise acquired Keefe Coffee and Supply, a supplier of coffee, packaged foods, and beverages to prison commissaries. To service *FORTUNE* 1000 companies wanting to lease or buy more than 50 vehicles, the company started Enterprise Fleet Services in 1976.

Enterprise acquired Courtesy Products (coffee and tea for hotel guests) in 1980, and the following year sales reached the $100 million mark. It acquired ELCO Chevrolet in 1986, the same year it formed Crawford Supply (hygiene products for prisons). Taylor bought out the Lindburg family's interest in Enterprise the next year. In 1989 Enterprise raised its brand recognition with a national TV campaign that focused on an older and higher-income audience by showing its commercials exclusively on CBS. Also in the late 1980s, the company began targeting "discretionary rentals" to families with visiting relatives or with children home for the holidays.

Taylor's son, Andrew, became CEO of Enterprise in 1991, and sales topped $1 billion for the first time. By 1994 sales had passed $2 billion, and the company had expanded into Canada and the UK. By 1996 Enterprise had a fleet of more than 300,000 vehicles. That year it opened several locations in the UK. In 1997 the company opened locations in Ireland, Germany, Scotland, and Wales.

In 1998 Enterprise battled other rental firms over use of the advertising tagline, "We'll pick you up," which it had trademarked. Rent-A-Wreck lost a court case over the matter; Hertz settled with Enterprise over use of the phrase.

In 1999 the company more than doubled the number of its airport locations in an attempt to woo occasional travelers (rather than hard-core corporate fliers). That year the Taylor family split off their non-automotive operations (including companies involved in prison supplies, hotel amenities, a golf course, mylar balloons, and athletic shoes) as Centric Group.

In 2001 the company's COO, Donald Ross, became the first non-Taylor to be promoted to president after Jack Taylor was named chairman emeritus and Andrew gave up the president title to assume the company's chairmanship while remaining as CEO.

EXECUTIVES

Chairman and CEO: Andrew C. (Andy) Taylor
Vice Chairman and President: Donald L. Ross
EVP and COO: Pamela M. (Pam) Nicholson
EVP and CFO: William W. (Bill) Snyder
SVP and CIO: Craig Kennedy
SVP and Chief Administrative Officer: Lee R. Kaplan
SVP, Car Sales: Tim Walsh
SVP, Corporate Strategy: M.W. (Sandy) Rogers
SVP, European Operations: James (Jim) Burrell
SVP, Fleet Services: Steven E. (Steve) Bloom
SVP, Human Resources: Edward (Ed) Adams
VP, Corporate Communications: Pat Farrell
Senior Marketing Manager: Barry Dvoracek
Auditors: Ernst & Young LLP

LOCATIONS

HQ: Enterprise Rent-A-Car Company
600 Corporate Park Dr., St. Louis, MO 63105
Phone: 314-512-5000   **Fax:** 314-512-4706
Web: www.enterprise.com

Enterprise Rent-A-Car has about 5,500 locations in the US (in all 50 states), Canada, Germany, Ireland, and the UK.

PRODUCTS/OPERATIONS

Operations

ELCO Chevrolet Inc. (car dealership, St. Louis)
Enterprise Car Sales (used car sales)
Enterprise Fleet Services (vehicle leasing)
Enterprise Rent-A-Car

COMPETITORS

Alamo Rent A Car
Avis Europe
Avis Group
Budget
Dollar Thrifty Automotive
Hertz
Rent-A-Wreck
Sixt
Vanguard Car Rental

HISTORICAL FINANCIALS

Company Type: Private

Income Statement

FYE: July 31

	REVENUE ($ mil.)	NET INCOME ($ mil.)	NET PROFIT MARGIN	EMPLOYEES
7/04	7,400	—	—	57,300
7/03	6,900	—	—	53,500
7/02	6,500	—	—	50,000
7/01	6,300	—	—	50,000
7/00	5,600	—	—	45,000
7/99	4,730	—	—	40,000
7/98	4,180	—	—	37,000
7/97	3,680	—	—	35,182
7/96	3,127	—	—	28,806
7/95	2,464	—	—	21,703
Annual Growth	**13.0%**	—	—	**11.4%**

Revenue History

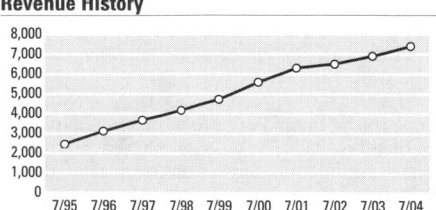

Equity Group Investments

Equity Group Investments is the apex of financier Sam Zell's pyramid of business holdings. The Chicago-based private investment group controls a multi-billion dollar mix of businesses, including real estate investment trusts (REITs), restaurants, and cruise ships. Zell's REIT portfolio makes him the US's largest owner of property leased by manufactured homeowners (Equity Lifestyle Properties, formerly Manufactured Home Communities), office buildings (Equity Office Properties Trust), and apartments (Equity Residential Properties Trust). Sam Zell has a controlling interest in Equity Group Investments.

Equity Office Properties is one of the largest landlords in San Francisco and Seattle. Zell has made his niche — and a lot of money — by purchasing distressed properties and turning them into profitable investments (for which he earned the nickname "Grave Dancer").

Equity Group Investments has rescued many companies floundering in bankruptcy and often buys during downturns. Many acquisitions are made through the Zell/Chilmark Fund. Zell's Equity Residential Properties continues to build its portfolio through acquisitions.

Subsidiary Equity International Properties invests in Latin American commercial and residential real estate. It has established Mexico Retail Partners, a joint venture with the Black Creek Group, to develop big-box retail south of the border.

Zell has made forays into other investments with mixed success. He bought into sugar mills in Mexico that were nationalized by the government. Another holding, American Classic Voyages, suffered a combo of misfortune with the soft Hawaiian cruise market on one side and the impact of September 11 on travel on the other. The cruise operator has filed for Chapter 11 bankruptcy protection.

HISTORY

Sam Zell's first business endeavor was photographing his eighth-grade prom. In 1953 he graduated to reselling 50-cent *Playboy* magazines to schoolmates at a 200% markup.

While at the University of Michigan in the 1960s, Zell teamed with fraternity brother Robert Lurie to manage off-campus student housing. In graduate school, they invested in residential properties and formed Equity Financial and Management Co. after graduation. Their collection of distressed properties grew in the 1970s as Zell made the deals and Lurie made them work. Zell's hands-off management style had its drawbacks, however. In 1976 Zell and three others (including his brother-in-law) were indicted on federal tax-related charges after selling a Reno, Nevada, hotel and apartment complex. The charges were later dropped against Zell and another defendant (only the brother-in-law was convicted).

In the 1980s tax-law changes led the team to begin buying troubled companies. They started in 1983 with Great American Management and Investment, a foundering real estate manager they turned into an investment vehicle. Other targets included Itel (1984, now Anixter International) and oil and gas company Nucorp (1988,

now part of insurer CNA Surety). The true attraction in many of these acquisitions, however, lay in tax-loss carryforwards that could be applied against future earnings.

Lurie died in 1990, after which Zell began to consolidate his power and ease out old friends. (Lurie's estate still owns shares of many Zell enterprises.) That year Zell and David Schulte formed the Zell/Chilmark Fund, which soon owned or controlled such companies as Schwinn (sold 1997), Sealy (sold 1997), and Revco (sold 1997). Among the fund's failures was West Coast retailer Broadway Stores, which Zell bought out of bankruptcy in 1992; when California's slumping economy prevented a rapid turnaround, Zell sold it (once again near bankruptcy) in 1995.

Starting in 1987, Zell formed four real estate funds with Merrill Lynch; six years later, both Equity Residential and Equity Lifestyle Properties (formerly Manufactured Home Communities) went public. As REITs became popular with investors, more trusts began vying for distressed assets — Zell's traditional lifeblood. In 1997 Zell melded four of his commercial real estate funds into another REIT, Equity Office Properties Trust, and took it public.

In 1998, as investors and financiers looked for fresh opportunities, Zell launched Equity International Properties, a fund targeting acquisitions in Latin America and elsewhere. That year a civil racketeering suit brought against Zell by former executive Richard Perlman shed light on "handshake" loans to top executives and other informal business deals. In 1999 Zell sold Jacor Communications to radio industry consolidator Clear Channel Communications. Equity Group Investments remained diversified, however. That year Equity Office Properties teamed with venture capital firm Kleiner Perkins Caufield & Byers to form Broadband Office to offer Internet and phone services to Zell's tenants and those of other property owners. Not surprisingly, Broadband Office bit the dust in the dot-com blowout.

Equity Office Properties Trust continued its buying into the 21st century, claiming New York-based Cornerstone Properties (2000) and California's Spieker Properties (2001).

Equity International Properties continues to expand its holdings in Mexico and the rest of Latin America, targeting both the commercial and residential sectors.

EXECUTIVES

Chairman: Samuel (Sam) Zell, age 63
President: Donald J. (Don) Liebentritt, age 54
CFO: Philip Tinkler
Managing Director: William C. Pate

LOCATIONS

HQ: Equity Group Investments, L.L.C.
2 N. Riverside Plaza, Ste. 600, Chicago, IL 60606
Phone: 312-454-0100   **Fax:** 312-454-0335

PRODUCTS/OPERATIONS

Selected Affiliates

Angelo & Maxie's, Inc. (38%, restaurants)
Anixter International, Inc.
(14%, communications network equipment)
Capital Trust, Inc. (commercial real estate finance)
Davel Communications, Inc.
(14%, pay-telephone operator)
Equity International Properties (overseas buyout fund)

Equity Office Properties Trust (4%, office property REIT)
Equity Residential Properties Trust
(3%, apartments REIT)
Equity International Properties, Ltd.
(Latin American property investment)
Manufactured Home Communities, Inc.
(15%, mobile home communities REIT)
Transmedia Network (40%, consumer savings programs)
Zell/Chilmark Fund L.P. (investment vulture fund)

COMPETITORS

Apollo Advisors	JMB Realty
Blackstone Group	KKR
Carlyle Group	Thomas H. Lee Partners
CD&R	Trump
Goldman Sachs	

Ergon

When it comes to work, Ergon (named after the Greek word for work) has it covered. Ergo, Ergon operates in six major business segments: asphalt and emulsions; information technology; oil and gas; real estate; refining and marketing; and transportation and terminaling. In addition to providing a range of petroleum products and services, the company manufactures and markets computer technology services and sells road maintenance systems, including emulsions and special coatings. Ergon also provides truck, rail, and marine transport services and sells residential and commercial real estate properties.

EXECUTIVES

CEO: Leslie B. Lampton Sr.
CFO: A. Patrick Busby
President, Asphalt Division: Bill Lampton
VP, Environment, Health, and Safety, Ergon Refining:
Paul Young
VP, Marine Operations, Magnolia Marine Transport:
Roger Harris
Media Relations Manager: Jim Temple

LOCATIONS

HQ: Ergon, Inc.
2829 Lakeland Dr., Ste. 2000, Jackson, MS 39232
Phone: 601-933-3000   **Fax:** 601-933-3350
Web: www.ergon.com

PRODUCTS/OPERATIONS

Major Operations
Asphalt and Emulsions
Crafco, Inc.
Ertech
Information Technology
Diversified Technology, Inc.
Oil and Gas
Lampton-Love, Inc.
Real Estate
Ergon Properties, Inc.
Refining and Marketing
Ergon Refining, Inc.
Ergon-West Virginia, Inc.
Lion Oil Company
Petroleum Specialties Marketing Division
Transportation and Terminaling
Ergon Rail
Ergon Terminals
Ergon Trucking, Inc.
Magnolia Marine Transport Company

COMPETITORS

AmeriGas Partners	Koch
Ferrellgas Partners	Marathon Oil
Kirby	

HISTORICAL FINANCIALS

Company Type: Private

Income Statement

FYE: December 31

	ESTIMATED REVENUE ($ mil.)	NET INCOME ($ mil.)	NET PROFIT MARGIN	EMPLOYEES
12/03	2,000	—	—	2,300
12/02	1,380	—	—	2,000
12/01	1,460	—	—	2,000
12/00	1,900	—	—	2,000
12/99	1,400	—	—	2,000
Annual Growth	9.3%	—	—	3.6%

Revenue History

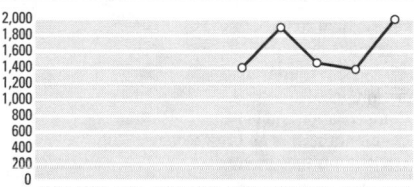

Ernst & Young

Accounting may actually be the *second*-oldest profession, and Ernst & Young is one of the oldest practitioners. Ernst & Young is also one of the world's largest accounting firms with some 700 offices in 140 countries, offering auditing and accounting services. The firm also provides legal services and services relating to emerging growth companies, human resources issues, and corporate transactions (mergers and acquisitions, IPOs, and the like). Ernst & Young has one of the world's largest tax practices, serving multinational clients that have to comply with multiple local tax laws.

After spending decades building their consultancies, the big accountancies have all moved toward shedding them, because of internal and regulatory pressures, as well as the perceived conflict of interest in providing auditing and consulting services to the same clients. Ernst & Young was the first to split off its consultancy, selling it in 2000 to what is now Cap Gemini Ernst & Young.

Ernst & Young, which gained an impressive amount of weight in former rival Andersen's diaspora, has also boosted its legal services, assembling some 2,000 lawyers in dozens of countries.

But Ernst & Young has faced Andersen-style trouble of its own. Federal regulators in 2002 sued the firm for its alleged role in the failure of Superior Bank FSB, and threatened civil charges for purported fraud relating to Cendant. In the UK, insurer Equitable Life in 2003 sued the accountancy for professional negligence related to work performed when Ernst & Young was its auditor. More problems followed with clients HealthSouth and America Online; Ernst & Young faces a lawsuit in relation to its work for the former company. Rick Bobrow retired as the firm's global CEO after just a year on the job; the departure was presumed to have been related to the airing of previously unpublicized Ernst & Young financial information during Bobrow's divorce proceedings. In 2004 the firm agreed to sell its Ernst & Young Corporate Finance unit to Giuliani Partners (along with its stake in that firm) as part of former New York City mayor Rudolph Giuliani's bid to launch an investment banking firm.

HISTORY

In 1494 Luca Pacioli's *Summa di Arithmetica* became the first published text on double-entry bookkeeping, but it was almost 400 years before accounting became a profession.

In 1849 Frederick Whinney joined the UK firm of Harding & Pullein. His ledgers were so clear that he was advised to take up accounting, which was a growth field as stock companies proliferated. Whinney became a name partner in 1859 and his sons followed him into the business. The firm became Whinney, Smith & Whinney (WS&W) in 1894.

After WWII, WS&W formed an alliance with Ernst & Ernst (founded in Cleveland in 1903 by brothers Alwin and Theodore Ernst), with each firm operating on the other's behalf across the Atlantic.

Whinney merged with Brown, Fleming & Murray in 1965 to become Whinney Murray. In 1979 Whinney Murray, Turquands Barton Mayhew (also a UK firm), and Ernst & Ernst merged to form Ernst & Whinney.

But Ernst & Whinney wasn't done merging. Ten years later, when it was the fourth-largest accounting firm, it merged with #5 Arthur Young, which had been founded by Scotsman Arthur Young in 1895 in Kansas City. Long known as "old reliable," Arthur Young fell on hard times in the 1980s because its audit relationships with failed S&Ls led to expensive litigation (settled in 1992 for $400 million).

Thus the new firm of Ernst & Young faced a rocky start. In 1990 it fended off rumors of collapse. The next year it slashed payroll, even thinning its partner roster. Exhausted by the S&L wars, in 1994 the firm replaced its pugnacious general counsel, Carl Riggio, with the more cost-conscious Kathryn Oberly.

In the mid-1990s Ernst & Young concentrated on consulting, particularly in software applications, and grew through acquisitions. In 1996 the firm bought Houston-based Wright Killen & Co., a petroleum and petrochemicals consulting firm, to form Ernst & Young Wright Killen. It also entered new alliances that year, including ones with Washington-based ISD/Shaw, which provided banking industry consulting, and India's Tata Consulting.

In 1997 Ernst & Young was sued for a record $4 billion for its alleged failure to effectively handle the 1993 restructuring of the defunct Merry-Go-Round Enterprises retail chain (it settled for $185 million in 1999). On the heels of a merger deal between Coopers & Lybrand and Price Waterhouse, Ernst & Young agreed in 1997 to merge with KPMG International. But Ernst & Young called off the negotiations in 1998, citing the uncertain regulatory process they faced.

In 1999 the firm reached a settlement in lawsuits regarding accounting errors at Informix and Cendant and sold its UK and southern African trust and fiduciary businesses to Royal Bank of Canada (now RBC Financial Group).

In 2000 Ernst & Young became the first of the (then) Big Five firms to sell its consultancy, dealing it to France's Cap Gemini Group for about $11 billion. The following year the UK accountancy watchdog group announced it would investigate Ernst & Young for its handling of the accounts of UK-based The Equitable Life Assurance Society. The insurer was forced to close to new business in 2000 because of massive financial difficulties.

Ernst & Young made headlines and gave competitors plenty to talk about in 2002 when closely held financial records were made public during a divorce case involving executive Rick Bobrow (who in 2003 abruptly retired as global CEO after just a year on the job). The firm in 2002 also formed an alliance with former New York City mayor Rudy Giuliani to help launch a business consultancy and an investment firm bearing the Giuliani name.

EXECUTIVES

Global Chairman and CEO; Chairman for the Americas: James S. (Jim) Turley, age 50
COO: Paul J. Ostling
Global Managing Partner, Quality & Risk Management: Sue Frieden
Global Managing Partner, Client Service and Accounts: Thomas P. (Tom) McGrath
Global CFO and Global Managing Partner, Finance and Infrastructure: Jeffrey H. (Jeff) Dworken
Global Managing Partner, People: Pierre Hurstel
Global Managing Partner — Markets: Mike Cullen
Global Managing Partner — Practice Integration: Jean-Charles Raufast
Deputy Global Managing Partner — Infrastructure; VC of Knowledge & Technology, Ernst & Young LLP: John G. Peetz Jr.
Global Director — Business Risk Services: Thomas Bussa
Vice Chairman — Strategy: Beth A. Brooke
Vice Chairman — Assurance and Advisory Business Services: James A. Hassett
Vice Chairman — Global Financial Services: Robert W. (Bob) Stein
Vice Chairman — Tax: Karl Johansson
Vice Chairman — Technology, Communications, and Entertainment: Stephen E. Almassy
Vice Chairman — Law: Patrick Bignon
Vice Chairman — Sales: Patrick J.P. Flochel
Vice Chairman — Corporate Finance: Francis Small
Global Director, Insurance Industry Services: Peter Porrino
Director, Entrepreneur of the Year Program: Nancy Clark

LOCATIONS

HQ: Ernst & Young International
   5 Times Square, New York, NY 10036
Phone: 212-773-3000   **Fax:** 212-773-6350
Web: www.eyi.com

Ernst & Young International has approximately 700 offices in 140 countries.

2005 Sales

	$ mil.	% of total
Europe, Middle East & Africa	7,636	45
Americas	7,400	44
Asia/Pacific	1,866	11
Total	**16,902**	**100**

PRODUCTS/OPERATIONS

2005 Sales

	$ mil.	% of total
Assurance & advisory business services	11,131	64
Tax & law services	4,489	26
Transaction advisory services	1,667	9
Other	180	1
Adjustment	(565)	—
Total	**16,902**	**100**

Selected Services

Assurance and Advisory
   Actuarial services
   Audits
   Accounting advisory
   Business risk services
   Internal audit
   Real estate advisory services
   Technology and security risk services

Emerging Growth Companies
   Corporate finance services
   Mergers and acquisitions advisory
   Operational consulting
   Strategic advisory
   Transactions advisory

Human Capital
   Compensation and benefits consulting
   Cost optimization and risk management
   Transaction support services

Law
   Corporate and M&A
   Employment
   Finance
   Information technology services
   Intellectual property
   International trade and anti-trust
   Litigation and arbitration
   Real estate

Tax
   Global tax operations
   Indirect tax
   International tax

Transactions
   Capital management
   Corporate development advisory
   Financial and business modeling
   M&A advisory
   Post-deal advisory
   Strategic finance
   Transaction management
   Valuation

COMPETITORS

Bain & Company
BDO International
Deloitte
Grant Thornton International
IBM
KPMG
PricewaterhouseCoopers

HISTORICAL FINANCIALS

Company Type: Partnership

Income Statement

FYE: June 30

	REVENUE ($ mil.)	NET INCOME ($ mil.)	NET PROFIT MARGIN	EMPLOYEES
6/05	16,902	—	—	106,650
6/04	14,547	—	—	100,601
6/03	13,136	—	—	103,000
6/02	10,124	—	—	87,206
6/01	9,900	—	—	82,000
6/00*	9,500	—	—	88,625
9/99	12,500	—	—	97,800
9/98	10,900	—	—	85,000
9/97	9,100	—	—	79,750
9/96	7,800	—	—	72,000
Annual Growth	**9.0%**	**—**	**—**	**4.5%**

*Fiscal year change

Revenue History

ESPN

ESPN is a superstar of the sports broadcasting world. The company is the leading cable sports broadcaster with seven domestic networks — including its flagship ESPN, ESPN2 (sporting events, news, and original programming), ESPN Classic (historical sports footage), ESPN HD, and ESPNEWS (24-hour news and information) — that reach more than 89 million US homes. It also reaches another 190 countries through ESPN International. In addition, ESPN creates content for TV and radio and operates one of the most popular sports sites on the Internet. ESPN also has lent its name to a magazine and a chain of sports-themed restaurants. ESPN is 80% owned by Walt Disney (through Disney ABC Cable); Hearst has a 20% stake.

After buying domestic rights from the National Basketball Association in 2002, ESPN became the first network ever to have contracts to televise all four professional sports leagues — baseball, football, basketball, and hockey. (However, in 2005 the channel let its option to continue broadcasting NHL games expire after the 2004-05 season was lost to a labor dispute.) The company launched a high definition service, called ESPN HD, in spring 2003. In addition to its heavily watched sports wrap-up shows, the company has tried its hand at original programming including movies *Season on the Brink* and *The Junction Boys*. It plans to use ESPN2 as its primary outlet for original programming. In 2005 ESPN launched a 24-hour channel devoted to college sports called ESPNU.

ESPN will gain *Monday Night Football* from sister company ABC beginning in 2006. ABC loses about $150 million a year on the venerable program, and the network decided it would fare better on cable. ESPN will pay the NFL $1.1 billion a year (for eight years) for the broadcasting rights.

For those curious about the roots of the company's name: the network's original name was the Entertainment and Sports Programming Network when it was formed in 1979. The network adopted the new name — ESPN, Inc. — in 1985.

EXECUTIVES

Chairman and President; President, ABC Sports:
George W. Bodenheimer, age 45
EVP and CFO: Christine Driessen
EVP Administration: Ed Durso
EVP Content: John Skipper, age 49
EVP Sales and Marketing: Sean H. R. Bratches
EVP and Managing Director, ESPN International:
Russell Wolff
EVP ESPN Enterprises: Salil Mehta
EVP National Sales and Customer Marketing:
Lou Koskovolis
EVP National Sales and Event Marketing: David Rotem
EVP Marketing: Lee Ann Daly
EVP Studio and Remote Production: Norby Williamson
EVP Technology: Chuck Pagano
SVP and Controller: Tony Waggoner
SVP Corporate Communications and Outreach:
Rosa Gatti
VP Human Resources: Milton C. Anderson

LOCATIONS

HQ: ESPN, Inc.
ESPN Plaza, 935 Middle St., Bristol, CT 06010
Phone: 860-766-2000   **Fax:** 860-766-2213
Web: espn.go.com

PRODUCTS/OPERATIONS

Selected TV Operations

ESPN (sporting events and news channel)
ESPN Classic (archival sports footage channel)
ESPN Deportes (Spanish-language sports network)
ESPN Extra (pay-per-view events)
ESPN HD (high definition channel)
ESPN Now (scheduling information channel)
ESPN Original Programming
(original content for cable channels)
ESPN Today (interactive television sports channel)
ESPN2 (sporting events and news channel)
ESPNEWS (24-hour sports news channel)
ESPNU (college sports)

Other Operations

BASS (bass fishing organization)
ESPN.com (sports information site)
ESPN Outdoors
ESPN Radio
ESPN The Magazine (magazine)
ESPN Wireless
ESPN Zone (sports-themed restaurants)
SportsTicker (provider of sports news and scores)

COMPETITORS

CBS
Comcast Spectacor
CSTV Networks
Fox Entertainment
NBC
SportsLine.com
Turner Broadcasting
Vulcan Sports Media
Yahoo!

HISTORICAL FINANCIALS

Company Type: Joint venture

Income Statement				FYE: September 30
	REVENUE ($ mil.)	NET INCOME ($ mil.)	NET PROFIT MARGIN	EMPLOYEES
9/04	3,223	—	—	—
9/03	2,869	—	—	3,400
9/02	2,120	—	—	—
9/01	2,500	—	—	—
9/00	2,600	—	—	2,500
Annual Growth	5.5%	—	—	10.8%

Revenue History

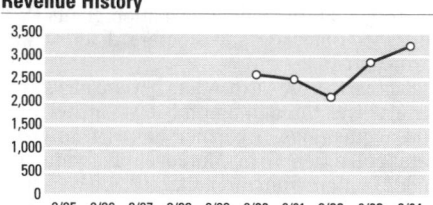

EXCO Resources

EXCO Resources puts extra effort into oil and gas exploration and production operations in Colorado, Ohio, Pennsylvania, Texas, and West Virginia. The company, which has an ongoing acquisition program, has proved reserves of 686 billion cu. ft. of natural gas equivalent. EXCO Resources holds interests in more than 5,800 wells. Chairman and CEO Douglas Miller bought EXCO Resources in 2003 and took it private. In 2004 the company acquired Appalachian explorer North Coast Energy for $164 million. EXCO Resources had expanded into Canada by buying Addison Energy, but subsequently sold the company in 2005.

In 2005 EXCO Resources sold Addison Energy to NAL Oil and Gas Trust for $442.7 million. The company is also considering a spin-off of its Appalachian properties into a master limited partnership.

EXECUTIVES

Chairman and CEO: Douglas H. Miller, age 56,
$722,495 pay
President, Treasurer, and Director: T. W. Eubank,
age 61, $355,000 pay
VP and COO: Charles R. Evans, age 50, $290,000 pay
VP, CFO, and Director: J. Douglas Ramsey, age 43,
$212,500 pay
VP, Secretary, and General Counsel: Richard E. Miller,
age 50, $212,500 pay
VP and Chief Accounting Officer: J. David Choisser,
age 52
Auditors: PricewaterhouseCoopers LLP

LOCATIONS

HQ: EXCO Resources, Inc.
12377 Merit Dr., Ste. 1700, Dallas, TX 75251
Phone: 214-368-2084   **Fax:** 214-368-2087
Web: www.excoresources.com

EXCO Resources operates in Colorado, Ohio, Pennsylvania, Texas, and West Virginia.

2004 Sales

	% of total
US	60
Canada	40
Total	**100**

PRODUCTS/OPERATIONS

COMPETITORS

Belden & Blake
Burlington Resources
Cabot Oil & Gas
Petroleum Development

HISTORICAL FINANCIALS

Company Type: Private

Income Statement				FYE: December 31
	REVENUE ($ mil.)	NET INCOME ($ mil.)	NET PROFIT MARGIN	EMPLOYEES
12/04	178	6	3.5%	284
12/03	96	5	5.4%	132
12/02	66	(1)	—	119
12/01	61	(39)	—	93
12/00	29	9	29.4%	68
12/99	5	5	88.7%	25
12/98	1	(1)	—	19
12/97	1	(0)	—	7
12/96	1	(0)	—	—
Annual Growth	93.7%	—	—	69.7%

2004 Year-End Financials

Debt ratio: 245.6%   Current ratio: 0.72
Return on equity: 3.2%   Long-term debt ($ mil.): 500
Cash ($ mil.): 26

Net Income History

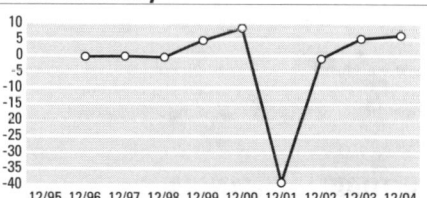

F. Dohmen Co.

The F. Dohmen Co. helps pharmacists with just about everything except interpreting handwriting. The company is one of the largest private pharmaceutical wholesalers in the US. Its Dohmen Medical division distributes brand name and generic products, including medical and surgical supplies. F. Dohmen also makes pharmaceutical management systems that perform an array of services, including prescription processing, physician and insurer information management, and chronic disease management. The company's additional services include advertising assistance; it sells National Brand Equivalent products that permit pharmacies to use their own store labels. German immigrant Frederick Dohmen founded the firm in 1858.

EXECUTIVES

Chairman, President, and CEO: John F. Dohmen
EVP: Robert C. Dohmen
VP, Purchasing and Marketing: Jim Grigg
CIO: Thomas (Tom) Farrington
President, Sales: Tracy Pearson
Director, Operations: Jeff Grogan
Manager, Human Resources: Shannon Brown

LOCATIONS

HQ: The F. Dohmen Co.
W194 N11381 McCormick Dr.,
Germantown, WI 53022
Phone: 262-255-0022   **Fax:** 262-255-0041
Web: www.dohmen.com

PRODUCTS/OPERATIONS

Selected Company Divisions

DDN Pharmaceutical Logistics
(pharmaceutical distribution)
Dohmen Distribution Partners, LLC
(pharmacy management services)
jASCorp (pharmaceutical management systems)
RESTAT (prescription benefits management)

Selected Products

DotConnect (central prescription editing, messaging,
and data analysis system)
Encounter Pro (disease management system)
Encounter Rx (prescription processing system)
Enhance Pro (pharmacy counseling system)
HealthCare America Ad Program (advertising assistance)
HealthCare America private labels
(National Brand Equivalent products)
Impact (insurer/physician/patient information
management system)
Infonet EC (electronic ordering system)
P3 Performance Plan (program that assists pharmacists
with marketing and provides product information)

COMPETITORS

AmerisourceBergen	Kinray
Cardinal Health	McKesson
D & K	Owens & Minor
Healthcare Resources	QK Healthcare

HISTORICAL FINANCIALS

Company Type: Private

Income Statement

FYE: April 30

	REVENUE ($ mil.)	NET INCOME ($ mil.)	NET PROFIT MARGIN	EMPLOYEES
4/04	2,141	—	—	950
4/03	1,400	—	—	500
4/02	838	—	—	450
4/01	748	—	—	450
4/00	655	—	—	480
4/99	524	—	—	430
Annual Growth	32.5%	—	—	17.2%

Revenue History

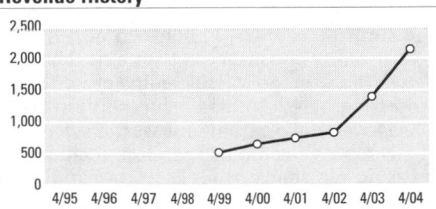

Factiva

This company is helping people get their facts straight. Dow Jones Reuters Business Interactive, which does business as Factiva, is a leading provider of news articles and business information. The company's Web-based service aggregates information from more than 9,000 sources, including the *Financial Times, New York Times, Wall Street Journal,* and *Yomiuri Shimbun*, as well as 500 newswire services. It also offers business intelligence tools and provides corporate and industry information. A joint venture between global news and information giants Dow Jones & Company and Reuters, Factiva was formed in 1999.

Factiva has been expanding beyond news article archives through a number of partnerships and acquisitions. A partnership with Internet data collection firm Moreover Technologies added content from more than 10,000 Web sites to Factiva's business intelligence offering, while its acquisition of Synapse in 2005 expanded the company's corporate taxonomy consultancy. Later that year, Factiva joined with Web search powerhouse Yahoo! to make its content available through a new subscription search service.

EXECUTIVES

Chairman: L. Gordon Crovitz, age 46
President and CEO: Clare Hart
Deputy CEO: Claude Green
CFO: Richard Hanks
Chief Product Officer: Karin Borchert
Chief Marketing Officer: Alan C. Scott
VP and Director of Global Sales:
William H. (Bill) Voltmer
VP and Director of Human Resources: Kerrie Coleman
VP Content: Simon Alterman
General Counsel: Matthew (Matt) Hamel
Director of Global Public Relations: Diane Thieke
Auditors: PricewaterhouseCoopers LLP

LOCATIONS

HQ: Dow Jones Reuters Business Interactive LLC
4300 N. Rte. 1, South Brunswick, NJ 08852
Phone: 609-627-2000   **Fax:** 609-627-2310
Web: www.factiva.com

Dow Jones Reuters Business Interactive has offices in Australia, Austria, Belgium, Canada, China, France, Germany, Japan, the Netherlands, Singapore, South Africa, Spain, Sweden, Switzerland, the UK, and the US.

PRODUCTS/OPERATIONS

Selected Products

Factiva Companies & Industries
(corporate and industry information)
Factiva Insight (business intelligence)
Factiva iWorks (data integration software)
Factiva SalesWorks (sales prospecting)
Factiva.com (Web-based news and information portal)

COMPETITORS

Alacra	Hoover's, Inc.
Bloomberg	LexisNexis
Capital IQ	OneSource
D&B	ProQuest
EDGAR Online	Thomson Corporation
FactSet	YellowBrix

HISTORICAL FINANCIALS

Company Type: Joint venture

Income Statement

FYE: December 31

	REVENUE ($ mil.)	NET INCOME ($ mil.)	NET PROFIT MARGIN	EMPLOYEES
12/04	250	—	—	750
12/03	245	—	—	800
12/02	249	—	—	800
12/01	250	—	—	800
12/00	240	—	—	800
12/99	225	—	—	700
12/98	225	—	—	950
Annual Growth	1.8%	—	—	(3.9%)

Revenue History

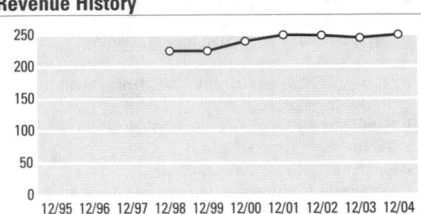

Family Sports Concepts

Irish luck and American comfort await the customers of this company. Family Sports Concepts operates a chain of nearly 200 wholly franchised Beef O'Brady's family-style pubs in about 15 states nationwide, primarily in Florida. The restaurants feature buffalo-style chicken wings along with sandwiches, burgers, and a selection of appetizers. The late Jim Mellody started Beef O'Brady's in 1985 and sold it to former Chili's Grill & Bar franchisees Chuck Winship and Gene Knippers in 1998.

EXECUTIVES

President: Nicholas Vojnovic, age 45
CFO: Jim Humboldt
SVP Business Development: Scott Taylor
VP Marketing: Ken Hall
Director, Human Resources: Karen Skop

LOCATIONS

HQ: Family Sports Concepts, Inc.
5510 W. LaSalle St., Ste. 200, Tampa, FL 33607
Phone: 813-226-2333   **Fax:** 813-226-0030
Web: www.beefobradys.com

Family Sports Concepts franchises Beef O'Brady's locations in Alabama, Arkansas, Florida, Georgia, Indiana, Kentucky, Louisiana, Michigan, Mississippi, North Carolina, Ohio, South Carolina, Tennessee, Texas, Virginia, West Virginia, and Wisconsin.

COMPETITORS

Applebee's
Brinker
Buffalo Wild Wings
Carlson Restaurants
Champps Entertainment
Damon's
Darden
Fox & Hound Restaurant
Hooters
Hops Grillhouse
Jillian's Billiards
Miller's Ale House
Wing Zone
Wingstop

HISTORICAL FINANCIALS

Company Type: Private

Income Statement

FYE: N/A

	REVENUE ($ mil.)	NET INCOME ($ mil.)	NET PROFIT MARGIN	EMPLOYEES
2004	78	—	—	7,000

Fatburger

It's a little more expensive than 99 cents, but you don't need to be a real fat cat to enjoy a Fatburger. The company operates and franchises more than 70 hamburger stands known for their 5-ounce signature sandwich. Located primarily in Southern California, the 50s-style stands also offer a 6-ounce Kingburger and 2-ounce Baby Fat burger, as well as a variety of side orders and other sandwiches. Franchisees own and operate about half of the company's locations. Lovie Yancey opened the first Fatburger in 1952 when "fat" was often used as slang for "good." The company is owned by a management group led by CEO Keith Warlick and backed by Fog Cutter Capital Group.

Fatburger is gearing up for nationwide growth. With a new funding deal from GE Franchise Finance, the company intends to develop its executive infrastructure and open 200 new units over the next four years. Helping out with that growth is East Coast Foods, which plans 20 restaurants in the Northeast.

EXECUTIVES

President and CEO: Keith A. Warlick
VP Operations: John Anderson
VP Construction and Purchasing: Bentley Hetrick
VP Marketing and Public Relations: Elaine Patel
Director of Franchising: Michelle Wilkins
Human Resources: Victor Santillan

LOCATIONS

HQ: Fatburger Corporation
   301 Arizona Ave., Ste. 200, Santa Monica, CA 90401
Phone: 310-319-1850   **Fax:** 310-319-1863
Web: www.fatburger.com

2005 Locations

	No.
California	46
Nevada	11
Arizona	5
Washington	4
Colorado	3
Florida	2
Louisiana	2
New Jersey	2
Georgia	1
Pennsylvania	1
Virginia	1
Total	**78**

COMPETITORS

5 & Diner
Battleground Restaurants
Burger King
Checkers Drive-In
CKE Restaurants
Dairy Queen
Del Taco
Farmer Boys
Fuddruckers
Harman Management
In-N-Out Burgers
Jack in the Box
Johnny Rockets
McDonald's
Quiznos
Red Robin
Subway
Triarc
Wendy's
Whataburger
YUM!

HISTORICAL FINANCIALS

Company Type: Private

Income Statement

FYE: June 30

	ESTIMATED REVENUE ($ mil.)	NET INCOME ($ mil.)	NET PROFIT MARGIN	EMPLOYEES
6/04	21	—	—	540
6/03	20	—	—	500
6/02	20	—	—	400
6/01	10	—	—	300
6/00	10	—	—	210
6/99	10	—	—	225
6/98	9	—	—	275
Annual Growth	**14.7%**	**—**	**—**	**11.9%**

Revenue History

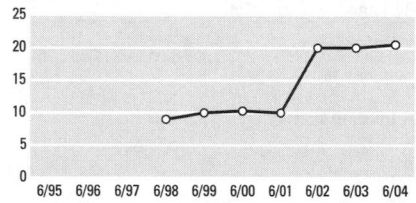

Federal Prison Industries

Some businesses benefit from captive audiences; this company benefits from captive employees. Federal Prison Industries (FPI), known by its trade name UNICOR, uses prisoners to make products and provide services, mainly for the US government. More than 19,300 inmates (about 13% of the total eligible inmate population) are employed in more than 100 FPI factories at 71 prisons. UNICOR, which is part of the Justice Department's Bureau of Prisons, manufactures products such as office furniture, clothing, beds and linens, electronics equipment, and eyewear. It also offers services including data entry, bulk mailing, laundry services, printing, recycling, and refurbishing vehicle components.

Federal law mandates that government buyers consider UNICOR products first; the company is allowed to sell services (but not products) to the private sector. FPI already produces most of the products the federal government buys, and it is benefiting from a growing prison population and the cheap cost of its labor (pay ranges from 23 cents to $1.15 per hour). The company is also tapping into the commercial market by offering services. Self-supporting, UNICOR is overseen by a governing board that is appointed by the US president.

Rep. Peter Hoekstra of Michigan has been pushing for legislation that would make UNICOR compete with private companies for government contracts.

HISTORY

FPI was established by President Franklin Roosevelt in 1934 to teach job skills at men's and women's federal prisons. During WWII, 95% of FPI's output was dedicated to the war effort — the company's products included parachutes and munitions. In the late 1950s and early 1960s, FPI built or renovated structures at 18 of the 31 federal prisons. In 1974 it established regional sales offices, and in 1977 it took the name UNICOR.

Although self-supporting, UNICOR remained necessarily inefficient because of its goal to put as many inmates as possible to work. However, as the prison population increased, the company underwent rapid expansion and added skilled services in the 1980s.

UNICOR put its product catalog online in 1996. The next year the Senate authorized a study of ways to make UNICOR more competitive, after private businesses had complained that the booming prison population, low wages (23 cents to $1.15 per hour), and government preferential treatment gave UNICOR an unfair advantage. Legislation to force FPI to bid against the private sector for government contracts was brought before Congress in 1999; at the same time, a bill was introduced to allow the company to offer its products to the private sector. Meanwhile, FPI began selling services such as data entry to private-sector customers.

In 2003 Dell Computer dropped UNICOR as the vendor for its computer recycling program.

EXECUTIVES

CEO: Harley G. Lappin
COO: Steve Schwalb
Controller: Bruce Long
Regional Manager, Office Furniture Sales Offices, Texas: Katherine Allen
Regional Manager, Office Furniture Sales Offices, Washington: Richard Balch
Design Manager, Office Furniture Sales Offices, Alabama: Amy McGowan
Group Manager, Order Processing: Mark Barnes
Install Manager, Office Furniture Sales Offices, Texas: Brian Schneider
Sales Manager, Office Furniture Sales Offices, Alabama: Diane Stabinski
Sales Manager, Office Furniture Sales Offices, New York: Michael Walsh
Administrator, Customer Service: Randy Toy
Assistant Director, Human Resources: Keith Hall
Chief, Policy and Field Support: Lisabeth Day
Auditors: PricewaterhouseCoopers LLP

LOCATIONS

HQ: Federal Prison Industries, Inc.
320 1st St. NW, Washington, DC 20534
Phone: 202-305-3500   **Fax:** 202-305-7340
Web: www.unicor.gov

Federal Prison Industries operates 102 factories at 71 prisons in the US.

PRODUCTS/OPERATIONS

2004 Sales

	$ mil.	% of total
Electronics	255.2	29
Clothing & textiles	184.5	21
Office furniture	140.9	16
Fleet management	129.1	15
Industrial products	45.8	5
Graphics	23.7	3
Services	13.6	1
Recycling	10.0	1
Other revenue	76.6	9
Total	**879.4**	**100**

Selected Products

Clothing and textiles
  Apparel
  Draperies and curtains
  Embroidery and screen printing on textiles
  Mattresses, bedding, linens, and towels

Electronics
  Electrical cables (both braided and cord assemblies)
  Electrical components and connectors
  Lighting systems
  Wire harness assemblies and circuit boards

Office furniture
  Casegoods and training table products
  Filing and storage products
  Office furniture and accessories
  Office system products
  Packaged office solutions
  Seating products

Fleet management
  Fleet management customized services
  New-vehicle retrofit services
  Rebuilt and refurbished vehicle components

Industrial products
  Custom fabricated industrial products, lockers, and storage cabinets
  Dorm and quarters furnishings and packaged room solutions
  Industrial racking catwalks, mezzanines, and shelving
  Optical eyewear (safety and prescription)
  Replacement filters
  Security fencing

Graphics
  Custom engraving and printing on awards, promotional gifts, and license plates
  Interior and exterior architectural, safety, and recreational signs
  Printing and creative design services
  Remanufacturing of toner cartridges

Services
  Assembly and packing services
  Call center and order fulfillment services
  Distribution and mailing services
  Document conversion
  Laundry services

Recycling
  Recycling of electronic components
  Reuse and recovery of usable components for resale

COMPETITORS

Anderson Hickey
Avnet
CPAC
Deere
Federal Signal
Global Furniture
Haworth
Herman Miller
HighPoint Furniture
HNI
Kimball International
Matthews International
Mine Safety Appliances
Molex
Steelcase
Tyco
WestPoint Stevens

HISTORICAL FINANCIALS

Company Type: Government agency

Income Statement

FYE: September 30

	REVENUE ($ mil.)	NET INCOME ($ mil.)	NET PROFIT MARGIN	EMPLOYEES
9/04	879	64	7.2%	19,337
9/03	722	2	0.3%	20,274
9/02	717	9	1.3%	21,778
9/01	602	5	0.8%	22,560
9/00	546	(12)	—	21,688
9/99	566	17	2.9%	20,966
9/98	534	(2)	—	21,800
9/97	513	3	0.6%	18,414
9/96	496	12	2.4%	17,379
9/95	459	—	—	16,780
Annual Growth	**7.5%**	**23.2%**	**—**	**1.6%**

2004 Year-End Financials

Debt ratio: 5.7%
Return on equity: 19.8%
Cash ($ mil.): 184
Current ratio: 2.74
Long-term debt ($ mil.): 20

Net Income History

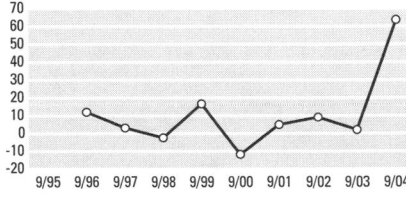

Federal Reserve

Where do banks go when they need a loan? To the Federal Reserve System, which sets the discount interest rate, the base rate at which its member banks may borrow. Known as the Fed, the system oversees a network of 12 Federal Reserve Banks located in major US cities; these in turn regulate banks in their districts and ensure they maintain adequate reserves. The Fed also clears money transfers, issues currency, and buys or sells government securities to regulate the money supply. Through its powerful New York bank, the Fed conducts foreign currency transactions, trades on the world market to support the US dollar's value, and stores gold for foreign governments and international agencies.

The seven-member Board of Governors, chaired by former Ayn Rand compadre Alan Greenspan since the Reagan administration, oversees the Fed's activities. As chairman under four different presidents, Greenspan has wielded more power than perhaps any Fed chief in history and securities markets virtually dangle on his every word. Greenspan will end his reign as chairman in January 2006; President Bush has appointed former Fed board member and chairman of his Council of Economic Advisers Ben Bernanke to replace Greenspan. The appointment is subject to Senate confirmation.

Fed members are appointed by the US president and confirmed by the Senate for one-time 14-year terms, staggered at two-year intervals to prevent political stacking. The seven governors comprise the majority of the 12-person Federal Open Market Committee, which determines monetary policy. The five remaining members are reserve bank presidents who rotate in one-year terms, with New York always holding a place. Although the Fed enjoys significant political and financial freedom (it even operates at a profit), the chairman is required to testify before Congress twice a year. National member banks must own stock in their Federal Reserve Bank, though it is optional for state-chartered banks.

By setting the discount rate and the federal funds rate (the rate at which banks borrow from each other), the Fed influences the pace of lending and, many believe, the pace of the economy itself. After slashing the federal funds rate in 2001 to its lowest point in some 40 years via an unprecedented skein of cuts, the Fed cut the rate another half-point in November 2002 to an infinitesimal 1.25% in hopes of fueling growth. The economy showed few signs of rebound by June 2003, so the Fed cut the federal funds rate again, to 1%.

A year later, with the economy in a tentative upturn in June 2004, the Fed began a series of bumps to the rate, and by late 2005 it had reached 3.75%, the highest level in almost four years.

HISTORY

When New York's Knickerbocker Trust Company failed in 1907, it brought on a panic that was stemmed by J. P. Morgan, who strong-armed his fellow bankers into supporting shaky New York banks. The incident showed the need for a central bank.

Morgan's actions sparked fears of his economic power and spurred congressional efforts to establish a central bank. After a six-year struggle between eastern money interests and populist monetary reformers, the 1913 Federal

Reserve Act was passed. Twelve Federal Reserve districts were created, but New York's economic might ensured it would be the most powerful.

New York bank head Benjamin Strong dominated the Fed in the 1920s, countering the glut of European gold flooding the US in 1923 by selling securities from the Fed's portfolio. After he died in 1928, the Fed couldn't stabilize prices. Such difficulty, along with low rates encouraging members to use Fed loans for stock speculation, helped set the stage for 1929's crash.

During the Depression and WWII, the Fed yielded to the demands of the Treasury to buy bonds. But after WWII it sought independence, cultivating Congress to help free it from Treasury demands. This effort was led by chairman William McChesney Martin, with the assistance of New York bank president Alan Sproul (also a rival for the chairmanship). Martin diluted Sproul's influence by governing by consensus with the other bank leaders.

The Fed managed the economy successfully in the postwar boom, but it was stymied by inflation in the late 1960s. In the early 1970s the New York bank also faced the collapse of the fixed currency exchange-rate system and the growth of currency trading. Its role as foreign currency trader became even more crucial as the dollar's value eroded amid rising oil prices and a slowing economy.

The US suffered from double-digit inflation in 1979 as President Jimmy Carter appointed New York Fed president Paul Volcker as chairman. Volcker, believing that raising interest rates a few points would not suffice, allowed the banks to raise their discount rates and increased bank reserve requirements to reduce the money supply. By the time inflation eased, Ronald Reagan was president.

During the 1980s and 1990s, US budget fights limited options for controlling the economy through spending decision, so the Fed's actions became more important. Its higher profile brought calls for more access to its decision-making processes. Alan Greenspan took over as chairman in 1987 after being designated by Reagan (and has since been reappointed by presidents George H. W. Bush and Bill Clinton).

While the US economy seemed immune to the Asian currency crisis of 1997 and 1998, the Federal Reserve remained relatively quiescent. But when Russia defaulted on some of its bonds in 1998, leading to the near-collapse of hedge fund Long-Term Capital Management, the New York Federal Reserve Bank brokered a bailout by the fund's lenders and investors.

This led in 1999 to new guidelines for banks' risk management. The next year, the Fed faced up to the Internet age, taking a look at e-banking supervision. After raising interest rates to stave off inflation during the go-go late 1990s, the Fed cut rates an unprecedented 11 times in 2001 (to a 40-year low of 1.75%) to help spur the flagging post-boom economy.

EXECUTIVES

Chairman of the Board of Governors: Alan Greenspan, age 79, $171,900 pay
Chairman Elect: Ben S. Bernanke, age 51
Vice Chairman of the Board of Governors: Roger W. Ferguson Jr., age 53
Director, Division of Consumer and Community Affairs: Sandra F. Braunstein
General Counsel, Legal Division: Scott G. Alvarez
President, Federal Reserve Bank of Dallas: Richard W. Fisher, age 55
President, Federal Reserve Bank of New York: Timothy F. Geithner, age 44

President, Federal Reserve Bank of Atlanta: Jack Guynn, age 62
President, Federal Reserve Bank of Kansas City: Thomas M. Hoenig, age 59
President, Federal Reserve Bank of Richmond: Jeffrey M. (Jeff) Lacker, age 50
President, Federal Reserve Bank of Boston: Cathy E. Minehan, age 58
President, Federal Reserve Bank of Chicago: Michael H. Moskow
President, Federal Reserve Bank of Cleveland: Sandra Pianalto, age 51
President, Federal Reserve Bank of St. Louis: William Poole, age 68
President, Federal Reserve Bank of Philadelphia: Anthony M. Santomero, age 59
President, Federal Reserve Bank of Minneapolis: Gary H. Stern
President, Federal Reserve Bank of San Francisco: Janet L. Yellen, age 59
Comptroller of the Currency: John C. Dugan
CIO: Jackie Fletcher
Chief of Staff and Public Affairs: Mark A. Nishan
Secretary: Jennifer J. Johnson
Auditors: PricewaterhouseCoopers LLP

LOCATIONS

HQ: Federal Reserve System
20th Street and Constitution Avenue NW, Washington, DC 20551
Phone: 202-452-3000
Web: www.federalreserve.gov

Federal Reserve Banks
Atlanta
Boston
Chicago
Cleveland
Dallas
Kansas City, Missouri
Minneapolis
New York
Philadelphia
Richmond, Virginia
St. Louis
San Francisco

PRODUCTS/OPERATIONS

2003 Sales

	$ mil.	% of total
Interest		
US government & federal agency securities	22,597	84
Investments denominated in foreign currencies	260	1
Loans to depository institutions	1	—
Noninterest		
Net foreign currency gains	2,695	10
Income from services	887	3
Other	407	2
Total	**26,847**	**100**

HISTORICAL FINANCIALS
Company Type: Government agency

Income Statement
FYE: December 31

	ASSETS ($ mil.)	NET INCOME ($ mil.)	INCOME AS % OF ASSETS	EMPLOYEES
12/03	771,487	23,006	3.0%	20,448
12/02	730,977	26,048	3.6%	21,208
12/01	654,949	28,035	4.3%	22,000
12/00	609,877	29,868	4.9%	23,056
12/99	674,460	26,262	3.9%	—
Annual Growth	**3.4%**	**(3.3%)**	**—**	**(3.9%)**

2003 Year-End Financials

Equity as % of assets: 2.3%
Return on assets: 3.1%
Return on equity: 133.5%
Long-term debt ($ mil.): 689,757
Sales ($ mil.): 26,847

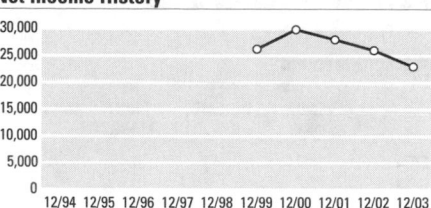
Feed The Children

Tuppence a bag may feed birds, but it takes more to help children. Feed The Children (FTC) is a not-for-profit Christian charity that provides physical, spiritual, and educational support worldwide. The organization collects donated items like food, medicine, and clothes and distributes them through approved organizations to children and families dealing with famine, war, poverty, and natural disasters. In Kenya, FTC runs a home for babies and toddlers abandoned as a result of the AIDS pandemic; it also organizes medical expeditions and community development projects around the globe. As part of its continuous fundraising efforts, FTC offers supporters a chance to sponsor a child with an $8 per month donation.

EXECUTIVES

Chairman: Dwight Powers
Founder, President, and CEO: Larry Jones, $125,721 pay
CFO: Christy Tharp, $77,423 pay
EVP: Frances Jones, $100,577 pay
VP and General Counsel: Larri Sue Jones, $109,022 pay
VP International Public Relations: Steven Whetstone
VP Management Information Systems: Larry Correa, $107,840 pay
Director, Human Resources: Diane Hardin
Director, Development: Charles Schillings, $100,538 pay

LOCATIONS

HQ: Feed The Children, Inc.
333 N. Meridian Ave., Oklahoma City, OK 73107
Phone: 405-942-0228   **Fax:** 405-945-4177
Web: www.feedthechildren.org

PRODUCTS/OPERATIONS

2004 Support and Revenue

	$ mil.	% of total
Gifts-in-kind	865.4	89
Contributions	87.8	9
Investment income	5.3	1
Government grants	1.6	—
Donated services	0.2	—
Other revenues	6.8	1
Total	**967.1**	**100**

2004 Expenses for Program Services

	$ mil.	% of total
Childcare, food & medical	680.4	80
Disaster relief	8.4	1
Education & community development	156.9	19
Total	**845.7**	**100**

HISTORICAL FINANCIALS

Company Type: Not-for-profit

Income Statement

FYE: June 30

	REVENUE ($ mil.)	NET INCOME ($ mil.)	NET PROFIT MARGIN	EMPLOYEES
6/04	967	43	4.4%	160
6/03	576	5	0.8%	160
6/02	553	—	—	160
Annual Growth	32.2%	826.1%	—	0.0%

2004 Year-End Financials

Debt ratio: —
Return on equity: 35.7%
Cash ($ mil.): —

Current ratio: —
Long-term debt ($ mil.): —

Net Income History

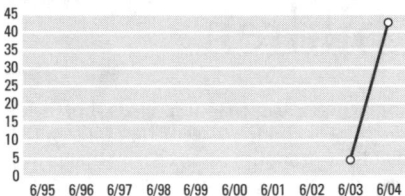

45									
40									
35									
30									
25									
20									
15									
10									
5									
0									
6/95	6/96	6/97	6/98	6/99	6/00	6/01	6/02	6/03	6/04

Feld Entertainment

A lot of clowning around has helped Feld Entertainment become one of the largest live entertainment producers in the world. The company entertains some 10 million people each year through its centerpiece, Ringling Bros. and Barnum & Bailey Circus, which visits about 90 locations. Feld also produces several touring ice shows, including Disney On Ice shows such as *Beauty and the Beast* and *Toy Story*. Feld's Siegfried & Roy show at The Mirage in Las Vegas closed after Roy Horn was mauled by a tiger in 2003. (The Mirage is replacing it with a Cirque du Soleil show.) Chairman and CEO Kenneth Feld, whose father, Irvin, began managing the circus in 1956, owns the company and personally oversees most of its productions.

Feld has engaged in some high-profile battles lately with animal rights activists. In 2001 a district court judge dismissed a complaint filed against the company by several animal activist groups, who claimed that Feld Entertainment didn't comply with federal regulations regarding the care of Asian elephants. The lawsuit was reinstated in early 2003 due to a procedural technicality.

HISTORY

When five-year-old Irvin Feld found a $1 bill in 1923, he told his mother, "I'm going to buy a circus." He started by working the sideshows of traveling circuses before settling in Washington, DC, in 1940. Feld, who was white, opened the Super Cut-Rate Drugstore in a black section of the segregated city with the backing of the NAACP. In 1944 he opened the Super Music City record store and started his own record company, Super Disc. Feld and his brother Israel also began promoting outdoor concerts. When rock

and roll became popular in the 1950s, Feld promoted Chubby Checker and Fats Domino, among others.

Feld came a step closer to his dream in 1956 when he began managing the Ringling Bros. and Barnum & Bailey Circus for majority owner John Ringling North. North's circus traced its roots back to 1871 and P. T. Barnum's Grand Traveling Museum, Menagerie, Caravan, and Circus. Barnum's circus merged with James Bailey's circus in 1881, creating Barnum & Bailey. In 1907 Bailey's widow sold Barnum & Bailey to North's uncles, the Ringling brothers, who had started their circus in 1884.

Among Feld's suggestions to North was moving the circus into air-conditioned arenas, saving $50,000 a week because 1,800 roustabouts were no longer needed to set up tents. Feld continued to promote music acts, but he suffered a serious blow in 1959 when three of his stars — Buddy Holly, Ritchie Valens, and J. P. Richardson (the Big Bopper) — died in a plane crash.

Feld's dream of owning a circus finally was realized in 1967 when he and investors paid $8 million for Ringling Brothers. He fired most of the circus' performers and opened a Clown College to train new ones. Feld bought a German circus the following year to obtain animal trainer Gunther Gebel-Williams (who then spent the next 30 years with Ringling Brothers). Feld split Ringling into two units in 1969, so he could book it in two parts of the country at the same time and double his profits. Feld took the company public that year.

Feld and the other stockholders sold the circus to Mattel in 1971 for $47 million in stock; Feld stayed on as manager and held on to the lucrative concession business, Sells-Floto. He persuaded Mattel to buy the Ice Follies, Holiday on Ice, and the Siegfried & Roy magic show in 1979. Mattel sold the circus back to Feld in 1982 for $22.5 million, along with the ice shows and the magic show. Feld died two years later, and his son Kenneth became head of the company. A chip off the old block, Kenneth fired almost all the circus performers when he took over.

In an attempt to leverage the Barnum & Bailey brand, the company opened four retail store locations in 1990, but the venture failed and the stores were closed two years later. A constant target of animal rights activists, Feld began backing conservation efforts on behalf of the endangered Asian elephant and established the Center for Elephant Conservation in Florida in 1995. The next year the company changed its name to Feld Entertainment.

Under increasing pressure as the company's creative guru and managerial boss, Feld hired Turner Home Entertainment executive Stuart Snyder as president and COO in 1997, so he could focus on the creative side of the business. That focus produced Barnum's Kaleidoscape in 1999, an upscale version of the original circus, featuring specialty acts, gourmet food, plush seats, and audience interaction. Plus, for the first time since 1956, a Feld circus was performed under a tent. (The company later shut down the tour of the Kaleidoscape, but claims it will return.) Snyder resigned later in 1999.

In an effort to inject new life into the 130-year-old Ringling Bros. and Barnum & Bailey Circus, Feld Entertainment launched two new marketing campaigns (one aimed at adults, the other aimed at children) in 2001.

Feld Entertainment's popular Siegfried & Roy show suffered a tragedy in 2003 when Roy Horn was mauled by a white tiger during a perfor-

mance. He later suffered a stroke that left him partially paralyzed, and the Siegfried & Roy show is closed indefinitely.

In 2004 the company battled a potential ban on exotic animal acts in Denver. A 15-year-old student led the charge, getting the initiative on the ballot. Feld hired political consultants and handily defeated the measure by a 72% vote.

EXECUTIVES

Chairman and CEO: Kenneth Feld, age 56
CFO: Mike Ruch
SVP Field Marketing and Sales, North America: Jeff Meyer
SVP Marketing: Julie Robertson
VP Creative Development: Jerry Bilik
VP International Sales and Business Development: Robert McHugh
VP and Corporate Counsel: Julie Alexa Strauss
Director of Corporate Communications: Catherine Ort-Mabry
Director of Human Resources: Kirk McCoy
Executive Director of Animal Stewardship: John Kirtland
Public Relations, Siegfried & Roy: Frank H. Lieberman
National Director of Public Relations: Mark Riddell

LOCATIONS

HQ: Feld Entertainment, Inc.
8607 Westwood Center Dr., Vienna, VA 22182
Phone: 703-448-4000   **Fax:** 703-448-4100
Web: www.feldentertainment.com

Feld Entertainment produces shows in 48 countries on six continents.

PRODUCTS/OPERATIONS

Selected Attractions

Disney On Ice
 Beauty and the Beast
 The Jungle Book
 The Lion King
 Tarzan
 Toy Story 2
 Walt Disney's 100 Years of Magic
Ringling Bros. and Barnum & Bailey Circus

Other Operations

Feld Consumer Products (concessions operations)
Hagenbeck-Wallace (prop design studio)

COMPETITORS

CIE
Cirque du Soleil
Clear Channel Entertainment
Harlem Globetrotters
HIT Entertainment
On Stage Entertainment
Renaissance Entertainment
Six Flags
TBA Global
Tom Collins

HISTORICAL FINANCIALS

Company Type: Private

Income Statement

FYE: January 31

	ESTIMATED REVENUE ($ mil.)	NET INCOME ($ mil.)	NET PROFIT MARGIN	EMPLOYEES
1/02	780	—	—	1,550
1/01	776	—	—	2,500
1/00	675	—	—	2,500
1/99	645	—	—	2,500
1/98	630	—	—	2,500
1/97	550	—	—	2,500
1/96	625	—	—	2,500
1/95	600	—	—	2,500
1/94	570	—	—	2,500
1/93	500	—	—	2,500
Annual Growth	5.1%	—	—	(5.2%)

Revenue History

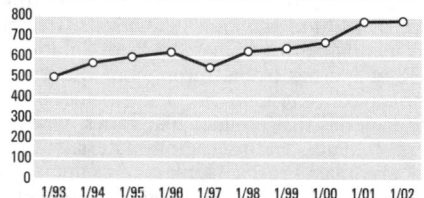

First Banks

Family comes first at First Banks. The holding company for First Bank is owned by chairman James Dierberg and his family, and a number of its branches and ATMs are located in Dierbergs Markets, a Missouri-based grocery chain owned by Dierberg's brother Robert. First Bank has nearly 170 branches in California, Illinois, Missouri, and Texas offering deposit products and loans, as well as securities brokerage, insurance, trust, private banking, and institutional money management services. Commercial real estate loans account for about 30% of the bank's loan book, as do business operating loans. Its portfolio is rounded out by residential mortgages, and consumer and construction loans.

First Banks expanded its branch network in the Chicago metropolitan area by an additional 16 branches when it acquired CIB Marine Bancshares, the largest acquisition in the company's history.

Next First Banks announced plans to buy FBA Bancorp, holding company for First Bank of the Americas, an Illinois savings bank that operates three branches in southwestern Chicago and caters to the metropolitan area's growing Hispanic population. FBA opens accounts for immigrants using matricula identification cards issued by Mexico, and lends money to them with taxpayer ID numbers issued by the Internal Revenue Service. Consequently, FBA is considered a pioneer of alternate IDs and remittance products. First Banks will likely institute similar policies in its Texas and California branches where a high concentration of Hispanics bank.

Now First Banks plans to acquire Northway State Bank, its fourth acquisition in the metropolitan Chicago area in a year.

EXECUTIVES

Chairman: James F. (Jim) Dierberg, age 67, $610,000 pay
President, CEO, Secretary, and Director: Allen H. Blake, age 62, $426,000 pay
SEVP, COO, and Director; Chairman, President, and CEO, First Bank: Terrance M. (Terry) McCarthy, age 50, $367,500 pay
EVP and CIO: Russell L. Goldammer, age 48
EVP and Director of Operations: Mary P. Sherrill, age 50
EVP and Chief Credit Officer; EVP, First Bank: Daniel W. Jasper, age 59, $209,500 pay
EVP and Director of Sales, Marketing, and Products: F. Christopher McLaughlin, age 51, $212,800 pay
EVP, Mortgage Banking; EVP, First Bank: Mark T. Turkcan, age 48, $250,700 pay
SVP, CFO, and Director; SVP, Private Banking, Wealth Management, and Trust Services, First Bank; Manager, First Brokerage America: Steven F. Schepman, age 33
SVP, Customer Support Services: James F. Klein
SVP, General Counsel, and Corporate Secretary: Peter D. Wimmer
SVP and Director of Human Resources: John D. Kitson
SVP and Controller: Lisa K. Vansickle
General Counsel: Michael J. Dierberg, age 32
Auditors: KPMG LLP

LOCATIONS

HQ: First Banks, Inc.
135 N. Meramec Ave., Clayton, MO 63105
Phone: 314-854-4600   **Fax:** 314-592-6840
Web: www.firstbanks.com

2004 Branch Locations

	No.
Central & southern Illinois	34
Southern California	32
Northern Illinois	31
St. Louis metropolitan area	29
Northern California	16
Eastern Missouri	15
Texas	10
Total	**167**

PRODUCTS/OPERATIONS

2004 Sales

	$ mil.	% of total
Interest		
Loans, including fees	341.5	71
Investment securities	51.7	11
Other	1.6	—
Noninterest		
Deposit service charges & customer service fees	38.2	8
Gain on loans sold & held for sale	18.5	4
Investment management income	6.9	2
Bank-owned life insurance	5.2	1
Other	14.7	3
Total	**478.3**	**100**

COMPETITORS

Bank of America
Citigroup
Commerce Bancshares
JPMorgan Chase
UMB Financial
U.S. Bancorp
Washington Mutual
Wells Fargo

HISTORICAL FINANCIALS

Company Type: Private

Income Statement

FYE: December 31

	ASSETS ($ mil.)	NET INCOME ($ mil.)	INCOME AS % OF ASSETS	EMPLOYEES
12/04	8,733	83	0.9%	2,350
12/03	7,107	63	0.9%	2,160
12/02	7,351	45	0.6%	2,200
12/01	6,779	65	1.0%	2,350
12/00	5,877	56	1.0%	1,985
12/99	4,868	44	0.9%	1,670
12/98	4,555	34	0.7%	1,739
Annual Growth	11.5%	16.3%	—	5.1%

2004 Year-End Financials

Equity as % of assets: 6.9%
Return on assets: 1.0%
Return on equity: 14.4%
Long-term debt ($ mil.): 1,485
Sales ($ mil.): 478

Net Income History

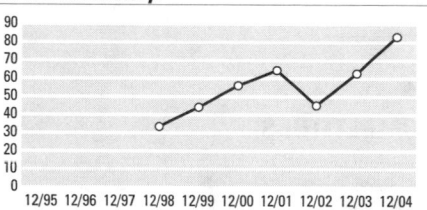

First Interstate BancSystem

First Interstate BancSystem is the holding company for First Interstate Bank, which has almost 60 branches in Montana and Wyoming. It offers individuals and businesses traditional banking services, including deposit accounts and agricultural, consumer, commercial, and real estate loan products. Real estate loans make up about 60% of the bank's loan portfolio. The company also owns i_Tech, a provider of information processing services for financial institutions and ATMs. The Scott family, including brothers Thomas (chairman), James (vice chairman), and Homer, owns about 80% of First Interstate BancSystem.

EXECUTIVES

Chairman: Thomas W. Scott, age 60, $590,000 pay
Vice Chairman: James R. Scott, age 54
President, CEO, and Director: Lyle R. Knight, age 58, $465,000 pay
SVP and CFO: Terrill R. Moore, age 51, $268,500 pay
SVP and Chief Credit Officer: Edward Garding, age 54, $269,400 pay
SVP, Human Asset Management Group: Robert A. Jones, age 57, $227,000 pay
SVP and Director of Marketing: Neil W. Klusmann, age 52
SVP and Chief Information Officer: Kevin Guenthner, age 40
Auditors: McGladrey & Pullen, LLP

LOCATIONS

HQ: First Interstate BancSystem, Inc.
401 N. 31st St., Billings, MT 59116
Phone: 406-255-5390   **Fax:** 406-255-5160
Web: www.firstinterstatebank.com

PRODUCTS/OPERATIONS

2004 Sales

	$ mil.	% of total
Interest		
Loans	161.8	61
Investment securities	29.7	11
Other	1.4	1
Noninterest		
Service charges on deposit accounts	18.9	7
Other service charges, commissions & fees	19.2	7
Technology services	13.2	5
Income from origination and sale of loans	8.4	3
Fiduciary activities	5.7	2
Investment securities gains (losses)	(0.8)	—
Other income	6.6	3
Total	**264.1**	**100**

COMPETITORS

Glacier Bancorp
U.S. Bancorp
Wells Fargo

HISTORICAL FINANCIALS

Company Type: Private

Income Statement				FYE: December 31
	REVENUE ($ mil.)	NET INCOME ($ mil.)	NET PROFIT MARGIN	EMPLOYEES
12/04	264	45	17.2%	1,574
12/03	259	41	15.7%	—
12/02	262	35	13.2%	—
Annual Growth	**0.4%**	**14.7%**	**—**	**—**

2004 Year-End Financials

Debt ratio: —   Current ratio: —
Return on equity: 15.6%   Long-term debt ($ mil.): —
Cash ($ mil.): —

Net Income History

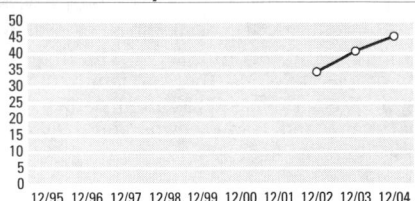

FLAVORx

It takes a spoonful from FLAVORx to help the medicine go down. The company offers a medical flavoring system which makes medicine more palatable for children (and some adults). The company doesn't neglect our furry friends either, as the product is also available to veterinarians. Using 42 flavors to sweeten some 600 human and nearly 400 animal medications, FLAVORx sells its products to some 25,000 pharmacies located in the US, Canada, Bahamas, the UK, New Zealand, and Australia. CEO Kenny Kramm started the company out of the need to hide the bitter taste of his daughter's cerebral palsy medicine.

EXECUTIVES

CEO: Kenneth Kramm
EVP Sales: Richard Levin
CFO: Woodie Neiss
Chief Information Officer: Ashton Maaraba
Marketing: Orsi Winhoffer
Public Relations: Stephany Boettner
Human Resources: Shelli Colemen

LOCATIONS

HQ: FLAVORx, Inc.
8120 Woodmont Ave., Ste. 600, Bethesda, MD 20814
Phone: 800-884-5771   **Fax:** 301-654-1117
Web: www.flavorx.com

COMPETITORS

ICC Industries
Lyne
Senomyx
zuChem

HISTORICAL FINANCIALS

Company Type: Private

Income Statement				FYE: June 30
	REVENUE ($ mil.)	NET INCOME ($ mil.)	NET PROFIT MARGIN	EMPLOYEES
6/04	6	—	—	43
6/03	5	—	—	—
6/02	3	—	—	—
Annual Growth	**46.1%**	**—**	**—**	**—**

Revenue History

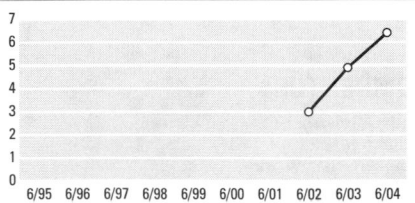

Flint Ink

The world's #2 ink maker (behind Sun Chemical), Flint Ink produces inks and coatings for a variety of applications, including packaging, publication, commercial uses, and digital printing. It operates nine divisions: North America, Latin America, Asia, India/Pacific, Flint-Schmidt (Europe), Jetrion (digital ink), Precisia (printed electronics), Progressive Color Media (color management), and CDR Pigments and Dispersions (colorants for ink and other uses). The company's products include sheetfed and web offset, gravure, ultraviolet and electronic beam (UV/EB) curable, and flexographic inks. Flint Ink was acquired by CVC Capital Partners in 2005.

The company announced in May 2005 that it was considering acquisition or merger options. In October of that year CVC acquired Flint Ink. CVC plans to merge Flint Ink with its German ink manufacturing unit, XSYS Print Solutions.

Flint Ink has plants throughout the world. The company's primary customers include printing facilities that produce magazines, newspapers, catalogs, and packaging materials. Flint Ink also makes specialty inks (for example, for printing lottery tickets) and environment-friendly vegetable oil-based inks.

Although the world's #1 privately held maker of inks, Flint Ink has drawn a bull's-eye on becoming the #1 ink maker, regardless of ownership. The company has been growing through acquisitions, joint ventures, and partnerships. Flint Ink acquired one of Europe's largest ink makers, German-based Gebr. Schmidt GmbH, in 2002.

In 2003 Flint launched two new subsidiaries: Jetrion is a digital ink manufacturer and Precisia makes conductive and advanced inks for electronics uses. The company also opened a new production facility in China, and in 2004 it formed subsidiary Progressive Color Media to provide workflow management solutions.

H. Howard Flint founded Flint Ink in 1920; the founder's grandson, H. Howard Flint II, who served as the company's CEO from 1992 until January 2005, died of pancreatic cancer in June 2005 while serving as chairman.

EXECUTIVES

Chairman and CEO: Leonard D. (Dave) Frescoln
President and COO: Linda J. Welty, age 47
EVP: David B. Flint
SVP, Finance and CFO: Michael J. Gannon
SVP, Research and New Product Development: Joseph W Raksis
VP and General Manager, North American Publication and Commercial Ink Divisions: Susan Kuchta
VP and Chief Technology Officer; President, Precisia: Graham Battersby
VP, Corporate Communications: Rita Conrad
VP, Human Resources: Glenn T. Autry

LOCATIONS

HQ: Flint Ink Corporation
4600 Arrowhead Dr., Ann Arbor, MI 48105
Phone: 734-622-6000   **Fax:** 734-622-6131
Web: www.flintink.com

Flint Ink has operations in Africa, the Americas, Asia, Australia, and Europe.

PRODUCTS/OPERATIONS

Selected Products and Brands
Commercial inks
Digital inks
Flexographic news inks
Flexo/Gravure packaging inks
High-performance inks and coatings
Inkjet inks
Offset news inks
Packaging inks
Publication gravure inks
Sheetfed inks
UV/EB curable inks
Web offset heatset inks

COMPETITORS

Akzo Nobel
Americhem
Cabot
Engelhard
Field Container
Magruder Color
Mitsubishi Chemical America
Sakata Inx
Sun Chemical

HISTORICAL FINANCIALS

Company Type: Private

Income Statement

FYE: December 31

	REVENUE ($ mil.)	NET INCOME ($ mil.)	NET PROFIT MARGIN	EMPLOYEES
12/03	1,454	—	—	4,600
12/02	1,400	—	—	4,600
12/01	1,400	—	—	4,000
12/00	1,080	—	—	3,700
12/99	1,200	—	—	3,500
12/98	1,216	—	—	3,500
12/97	924	—	—	3,500
12/96	836	—	—	2,730
12/95	875	—	—	2,700
12/94	634	—	—	2,613
Annual Growth	**9.7%**	**—**		**6.5%**

Revenue History

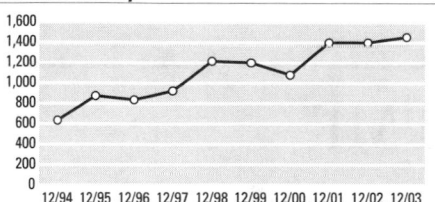

Florida Panthers

South Florida sports fans have given these Panthers a cool reception. The Florida Panthers Hockey Club entered the National Hockey League as an expansion franchise in 1993, but has produced little action on or off the ice. The team has made a handful of playoff appearances and reached the Stanley Cup finals once in 1996 (losing to the Colorado Avalanche). With a lack of winning seasons, the franchise has annually posted losses as ticket sales have fallen short of expectations. A group of investors led by Alan Cohen bought the Panthers from Wayne Huizenga's Boca Resorts in 2001. Huizenga, who owns the Miami Dolphins football team, retains a minority interest in the club.

EXECUTIVES

Chairman, CEO, and Governor: Alan P. Cohen, age 47
Alternate Governor: William A. Torrey
Alternate Governor: Jordan Zimmerman
COO: Michael Yormark
General Manager: Mike Keenan, age 55
Assistant General Manager: Grant Sonier
Head Coach: Jacques Martin, age 53
EVP Business Operations and Chief Marketing Officer: Christopher (Chris) Overholt
EVP and General Manager, Office Depot Center: Steve Dangerfield
SVP Corporate Partnerships & Building Operations: Chris Hibbs
SVP Sales and Service: Chad Johnson
VP Communications: Randy Sieminski
VP Finance and CFO: Evelyn Lopez
VP Human Resources: Carol Duncanson
VP Marketing and Communications: Alon Marcovici
Controller and Senior Director of Accounting: Phillip Reitz

LOCATIONS

HQ: Florida Panthers Hockey Club
1 Panther Pkwy., Sunrise, FL 33323
Phone: 954-835-7000   **Fax:** 954-835-7600
Web: www.flpanthers.com

The Florida Panthers play at the 19,250-seat capacity Office Depot Center in Sunrise, Florida.

PRODUCTS/OPERATIONS

Championship Trophies
Prince of Wales Trophy (1996)

COMPETITORS

Atlanta Thrashers   Tampa Bay Lightning
Carolina Hurricanes   Washington Capitals

HISTORICAL FINANCIALS

Company Type: Private

Income Statement

FYE: June 30

	REVENUE ($ mil.)	NET INCOME ($ mil.)	NET PROFIT MARGIN	EMPLOYEES
6/04	60	—	—	—
6/03	57	—	—	—
6/02	67	—	—	—
6/01	64	—	—	—
Annual Growth	**(2.1%)**	**—**	**—**	**—**

Revenue History

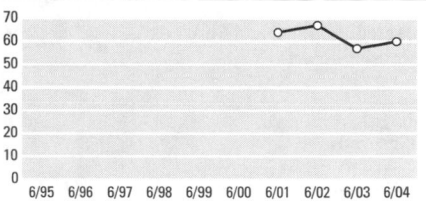

Flying J

Flying J puts out a welcome mat for truckers in North America. From its beginnings in 1968 with four locations, the company is now the #1 distributor of diesel fuel and a leading truck-stop operator in the US — with nearly 170 amenity-loaded Flying J Travel Plazas in 44 states and Canada. Flying J goes beyond the usual truck-stop fare (food, fuel, showers) by offering extra services, including banking, bulk-fuel programs, communications (wireless Internet connections), fuel cost analysis, insurance, and truck fleet sales. The company also owns oil and gas reserves and two refineries, which together produce 100,000 barrels of oil a day. Founder and chairman Jay Call died in a plane crash in 2003.

Flying J, together with oil-and-gas company Shell Canada, opened its first co-branded travel plaza in Edmonton in June 2005, bringing the number of travel plazas the company operates in Canada to four. A second co-branded site, under development in Calgary, is scheduled to open in 2006. (Shell Canada has been the official fuel supplier to Flying J in Canada since 1998.)

Flying J subsidiary Big West Oil is involved in crude oil purchasing and transportation in Utah, Wyoming, and Colorado.

EXECUTIVES

President and CEO: J Phillip (Phil) Adams
CFO and Treasurer: Scott Clayson
SVP, General Counsel, and Secretary: Barre G. Burgon
SVP, Supply & Distribution, and Petroleum Marketing: Richard D. Peterson
VP, Financial Services: J. J. Singh
VP, Retail Operations: James (Jim) Baker
VP, Transportation, Communication, and Logistics Services: Jeff Foote
VP, Real Estate: Ronald R. (Ron) Parker
VP, Food Service Operations: Ron DeJuncker
CIO: Bron McCall
Director, Human Resources: Jerry Beckman
Director, Marketing: Virginia Parker

LOCATIONS

HQ: Flying J Inc.
1104 Country Hills Dr., Ogden, UT 84403
Phone: 801-624-1000   **Fax:** 801-624-1587
Web: www.flyingj.com

Flying J operates travel plazas in the US and Canada, oil refineries in California and Utah, and oil and gas reserves in Utah.

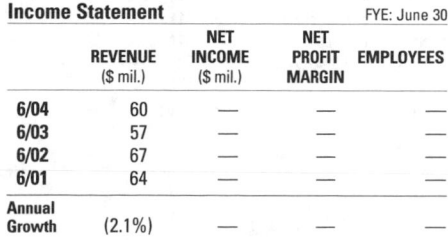

PRODUCTS/OPERATIONS

Selected Products and Services

Advertising services
ATMs
Banking
Bulk-fuel programs
Calling cards
Credit cards
Fleet financing
Food
Freight matching
Fuel
Insurance
Laundry facilities
Load and equipment postings
Lube centers
Motels
Restaurants
Showers
Truck washes

COMPETITORS

Exxon Mobil
FFP Operating
Love's Country Stores
Marathon Oil
Petro Stopping Centers
Pilot
Rip Griffin Truck Service Center
Stuckey's
TravelCenters of America

HISTORICAL FINANCIALS

Company Type: Private

Income Statement

FYE: January 31

	REVENUE ($ mil.)	NET INCOME ($ mil.)	NET PROFIT MARGIN	EMPLOYEES
1/05	7,301	—	—	13,000
1/04	5,586	—	—	12,000
1/03	4,637	—	—	11,750
1/02	4,225	—	—	11,500
1/01	4,349	—	—	11,000
1/00	2,953	—	—	10,000
1/99	2,345	—	—	9,000
1/98	2,298	—	—	8,000
1/97	2,120	—	—	8,000
1/96	1,806	—	—	7,600
Annual Growth	16.8%	—	—	6.1%

Revenue History

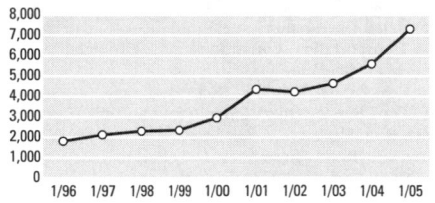

FM Global

If you're looking to protect your corporation, turn your insurance dial to FM Global. Factory Mutual Insurance (operating as FM Global) provides commercial and industrial property insurance and a variety of risk management services, ranging from all-risk programs to specialized products for ocean cargo and machinery equipment, as well as property loss prevention engineering and research. FM Global operates through such subsidiaries as Factory Mutual Insurance, Mutual Boiler Re, Affiliated FM Insurance, and Bermuda-based New Providence Mutual (which offers alternative risk financing for hard-to-find coverage). In addition to the US, the company has offices in Asia, Australia, Canada, Europe, and South America.

FM Global operates a business model that promotes proactive loss prevention rather than actuarial loss predictions. The company helps its clients improve and strengthen facilities, minimizing the damage that can result from such events as fires, explosions, and hurricanes. Its engineering expertise is provided by FM Global Research Campus, a research and testing complex.

EXECUTIVES

Chairman and CEO: Shivan S. Subramaniam
EVP: Ruud H. Bosman
EVP: Brian J. Hurley
SVP, Claims: Dennis J. Hedden
SVP, Commercial Lines: Carol G. Barton
SVP, Corporate Training: Daniel W. Schaffer
SVP, Engineering and Research: Thomas A. Lawson
SVP, Finance: Jeffrey A. Burchill
SVP, Human Resources: Enzo Rebula
SVP, Information Services: Jeanne R. Lieb
SVP, Investments: Paul E. LaFleche
SVP, Law and Governmental Affairs: John J. Pomeroy
SVP, Marketing: Roland J. Bonitati
SVP, Underwriting and Reinsurance: Robert E. Bean
Auditors: Ernst & Young LLP

LOCATIONS

HQ: Factory Mutual Insurance Company
  1301 Atwood Ave., Johnston, RI 02919
Phone: 401-275-3000 **Fax:** 401-275-3029
Web: www.fmglobal.com

FM Global offers its products and services in about 90 countries around the world.

PRODUCTS/OPERATIONS

2004 Assets

	$ mil.	% of total
Investments		
Debt securities	3,396.2	36
Equity securities		
Common	2,928.0	31
Other	116.6	1
Real estate	320.3	3
Recoverable from reinsurers	1,414.2	15
Premiums receivable	547.9	6
Cash & equivalents	224.3	2
Other	536.9	6
Total	**9,484.4**	**100**

2004 Sales

	$ mil.	% of total
Net premiums	2,440.8	90
Investment income	234.7	9
Fees	24.9	1
Total	**2,700.4**	**100**

Selected Subsidiaries

Affiliated FM Insurance
FM Global Research
FM Insurance Company, Limited (UK)
Mutual Boiler Re
New Providence Mutual (Bermuda)
TSB Loss Control Consultants, Inc.

COMPETITORS

ACE Limited
AIG
Allianz
CNA Financial
GE Insurance Solutions
Gerling
The Hartford
Nationwide
Royal & SunAlliance USA
St. Paul Travelers
Zurich Financial Services

HISTORICAL FINANCIALS

Company Type: Mutual company

Income Statement

FYE: December 31

	ASSETS ($ mil.)	NET INCOME ($ mil.)	INCOME AS % OF ASSETS	EMPLOYEES
12/04	9,484	558	5.9%	4,700
12/03	8,250	666	8.1%	4,400
12/02	7,189	244	3.4%	4,400
12/01	6,516	(132)	—	4,000
12/00	5,673	345	6.1%	—
Annual Growth	13.7%	12.7%	—	5.5%

2004 Year-End Financials

Equity as % of assets: 39.0%
Return on assets: 6.3%
Return on equity: 16.5%
Long-term debt ($ mil.): 121
Sales ($ mil.): 2,700

Net Income History

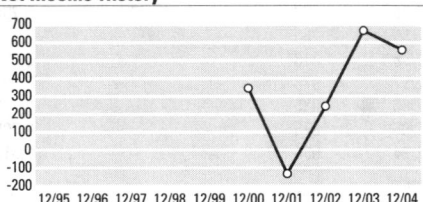

FMR

FMR is *semper fidelis* (ever faithful) to its core business. The financial services conglomerate, better known as Fidelity Investments, is the world's #1 mutual fund company. Serving more than 19 million individual and institutional clients, Fidelity manages approximately 360 funds and has more than $1 trillion of assets under management. Among its notable offerings is the Magellan Fund, which was for many years the largest in the US. The founding Johnson family controls most of FMR; Abigail Johnson, CEO Ned's daughter and heir apparent, is the largest single shareholder with about 25%.

Fidelity's nonfund offerings include life insurance, trust services, securities clearing, retirement services, and a leading online discount brokerage. It is one of the largest administrators of 401(k) plans, and the firm continues to grow this segment, which includes other services related to benefits outsourcing. It has investor centers in about 100 cities throughout the US and Canada, as well in Europe and Asia.

FMR has major holdings in telecommunications (COLT Telecom Group) and transportation (BostonCoach). Like many institutional investors, Fidelity uses its clout to sway the boards of companies in which it has significant holdings.

FMR acquired about a 15% stake in venerable British investment bank Lazard in 2005.

HISTORY

Boston money management firm Anderson & Cromwell formed Fidelity Fund in 1930. Edward Johnson became president of the fund in 1943, when it had $3 million invested in Treasury bills. Johnson diversified into stocks, and by 1945 the fund had grown to $10 million. In 1946 he established Fidelity Management and Research to act as its investment adviser.

In the early 1950s Johnson hired Gerry Tsai, a young immigrant from Shanghai, to analyze stocks. He put Tsai in charge of Fidelity Capital Fund in 1957. Tsai's brash, go-go investment strategy in such speculative stocks as Xerox and Polaroid paid off; by the time he left to form his own fund in 1965, he was managing more than $1 billion.

The Magellan Fund started in 1962. The company entered the corporate pension plans market (FMR Investment Management) in 1964, and retirement plans for self-employed individuals (Fidelity Keogh Plan) in 1967. It began serving investors outside the US (Fidelity International) in 1968.

Holding company FMR was formed in 1972, the same year Johnson gave control of Fidelity to his son Ned, who vertically integrated FMR by selling directly to customers rather than through brokers. In 1973 he formed Fidelity Daily Income Trust, the first money market fund to offer check writing.

Peter Lynch was hired as manager of the Magellan Fund in 1977. During his 13-year tenure, Magellan grew from $20 million to $12 billion in assets and outperformed all other mutual funds. Fidelity started Fidelity Brokerage Services in 1978, becoming the first mutual fund company to offer discount brokerage.

In 1980 the company launched a nationwide branch network and in 1986 entered the credit card business. The Wall Street crash of 1987 forced its Magellan Fund to liquidate almost $1 billion in stock in a single day. That year FMR moved into insurance by offering variable life, single premium, and deferred annuity policies. In 1989 the company introduced the low-expense Spartan Fund, targeted toward large, less-active investors.

Magellan's performance faded in the early 1990s, dropping from #1 performer to #3. Most of Fidelity's best performers were from its 36 select funds, which focus on narrow industry segments. FMR founded London-based COLT Telecom in 1993. In 1994 Johnson gave his daughter and heir apparent, Abigail, a 25% stake in FMR.

Jeffrey Vinik resigned as manager of Magellan in 1996, one of more than a dozen fund managers to leave the firm that year and the next. Robert Stansky took the helm of the $56 billion fund, which FMR decided to close to new investors in 1997. Fidelity had a first that year when it went with an outside fund manager, hiring Bankers Trust (now part of Deutsche Bank) to manage its index funds.

FMR did some housecleaning in the late 1990s. It sold its Wentworth art galleries (1997) and *Worth* magazine (1998). Despite continued management turnover, it entered Japan and expanded its presence in Canada.

In 1999 the firm formed a joint venture with Charles Schwab; Donaldson, Lufkin & Jenrette, known now as Credit Suisse First Boston (USA); and Spear, Leeds & Kellogg to form electronic communications network REDIBook ECN (now part of Archipelago) to trade Nasdaq stocks online. That year Fidelity teamed with Internet portal Lycos (now part of Terra Networks) to develop its online brokerage.

FMR opened savings and loan Fidelity Personal Trust Co. in 2000. That year the Magellan Fund for a time lost its longtime title as the US's largest mutual fund to the Vanguard Index 500 Fund. In 2001 the company teamed up with Frank Russell to offer a new fund for wealthy clients.

EXECUTIVES

Chairman and CEO: Edward C. (Ned) Johnson III
Vice Chairman and COO: Robert L. (Bob) Reynolds
CFO: Clare S. Richer
Executive Director, Fidelity Management and Research: Stephen P. Jonas
Vice Chairman, Fidelity Management and Research: Peter S. Lynch
President, Fidelity Employer Services: Abigail P. (Abby) Johnson, age 43
President, Fidelity Real Estate: Sarah K. Abrams
President, Registered Investment Advisor Group: William C. (Bill) Carey, age 44
President, Fidelity Personal Investments: Jeffrey R. (Jeff) Carney
President, National Financial Markets Group: Robert DiFazio
President, Fidelity Investment Operations: Timothy F. Hayes
President, Fidelity Strategic Investments: Robert A. Lawrence
President, Fidelity Investments Institutional Services: Joseph P. LoRusso
President, Fidelity Brokerage Company: Ellyn A. McColgan
President, Fidelity Investments Life Insurance: Jon J. Skillman
President, Fidelity Institutional Asset Management Group: Peter J. Smail
Managing Partner, Fidelity Ventures: Robert C. (Rob) Ketterson
EVP, Corporate Services: Steven P. (Steve) Akin
EVP and Director, Corporate Affairs: Thomas E. Eidson
EVP and General Counsel: Lena G. Goldberg
EVP and Head of Human Resources: D. Ellen Wilson
Auditors: PricewaterhouseCoopers LLP

LOCATIONS

HQ: FMR Corp.
  82 Devonshire St., Boston, MA 02109
Phone: 617-563-7000   **Fax:** 617-476-6150
Web: www.fidelity.com

PRODUCTS/OPERATIONS

Selected Subsidiaries and Divisions

Fidelity Employer Services Company
Fidelity Institutional Retirement Services Company
Fidelity Investments Canada, Limited
Fidelity Investments Institutional
  Services Company, Inc.
Fidelity Management and Research Company
Fidelity Management Trust Company
Fidelity Personal Investments
Fidelity Registered Investment Advisor Group
Fidelity Ventures
National Financial
National Financial Markets Group

COMPETITORS

Alliance Capital	MassMutual
American Century	Merrill Lynch
Ameritrade	MetLife
AXA Financial	Morgan Stanley
Barclays	Northwestern Mutual
Charles Schwab	Prudential
Citigroup	Putnam
Dow Jones	Raymond James Financial
E*TRADE Financial	T. Rowe Price
Goldman Sachs	TD Waterhouse
John Hancock Financial	TIAA-CREF
Services	UBS Financial Services
Lehman Brothers	Vanguard Group
Marsh & McLennan	

HISTORICAL FINANCIALS

Company Type: Private

Income Statement

FYE: December 31

	REVENUE ($ mil.)	NET INCOME ($ mil.)	NET PROFIT MARGIN	EMPLOYEES
12/03	9,200	908	9.9%	29,424
12/02	8,900	808	9.1%	29,000
12/01	9,800	1,320	13.5%	31,033
12/00	11,096	2,170	19.6%	33,186
12/99	8,845	1,008	11.4%	30,000
12/98	6,776	446	6.6%	28,000
12/97	5,878	536	9.1%	25,000
12/96	5,080	423	8.3%	23,300
12/95	4,277	431	10.1%	18,000
12/94	3,530	315	8.9%	14,600
Annual Growth	**11.2%**	**12.5%**	**—**	**8.1%**

Net Income History

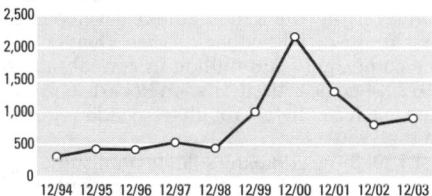

Follett

Not all kids like to read, but (fortunately for Follett) by the time they reach college, they don't have a choice. Follett is the #1 operator of US college bookstores with over more than 700 campus bookstores in 48 states, as well as Canada. The company's business groups, which reach about 60 countries, also provide books and audiovisual materials to grade school and public libraries, library automation and management software, textbook reconditioning, and other services. Its efollett.com Web site sells new and used college textbooks (its database has about 16 million titles). The Follett family has owned and managed the company for four generations.

In addition to books, campus stores sell items such as clothing, school supplies, and software. The company has capitalized on the growing trend of universities farming out operations to independent operators.

HISTORY

Follett began in 1873 as a small bookstore opened by the Rev. Charles Barnes in his Wheaton, Illinois, home. By 1893 a recession had rocked the business, and Barnes sought investment from his wife's family, for which he gave up controlling interest. Sales topped $237,000 in 1899.

Initially hired by Barnes in 1901 to help move the store to a new location in Chicago, 18-year-old C. W. Follett stayed on as both salesman and stock clerk. Barnes retired the following year and left the business to his son William and his father-in-law, John Wilcox, who was a major shareholder. In 1917 C. W. bought into the company when William moved to New York (he started what became one of Follett's biggest competitors, Barnes & Noble), and he renamed it J. W. Wilcox & Follett Company. Wilcox died in 1923, and C. W. bought the Wilcox family shares and shortened the name to Wilcox & Follett.

C. W.'s sons were brought into the business, and each was instrumental in shaping the company's future. Garth created Follett Library Resources, a wholesale service for libraries. Dwight started the elementary textbook publishing division. But Robert would have the most influence: He began wholesaling college textbooks, which led to the establishment of Follett College Stores and Follett Campus Resources.

Wilcox & Follett expanded throughout the Depression. During WWII it began publishing kids' books, which were in demand because of a metal toy shortage. C. W. died in 1952 and Dwight took over. Five years later the firm organized into divisions; Follett was created as the parent company. During the 1960s Follett developed the first multi-racial textbook series. Dwight built the company to $50 million in annual sales by 1977, when he retired. His son Robert succeeded him and led Follett through tremendous growth in the 1980s.

In 1983 the company sold its publishing division to Esquire Education Group; using funds from this sale, it began acquiring college bookstore chains such as Campus Services. In 1989 Follett developed Tom-Tracks, a computerized textbook system for college bookstores. A year later the company acquired Brennan College Service, adding 57 stores to its chain. Robert's son-in-law Richard Traut, named chairman in 1994, was the first person without the Follett name to hold that position. By 1994 Tom-Tracks had been installed in over 500 bookstores across the country. That year Follett introduced Sneak Preview Plus, a CD-ROM product designed to enhance the acquisition process in libraries.

The company acquired used-textbook reseller Western Textbook Exchange (1996), juvenile-book distributor Book Wholesalers (1997), and coursepack printer CAPCO (1998). In early 1998 Follett reorganized its corporate structure by market segments, establishing three divisions: the Elementary/High School Group, the Higher Education Group, and the Library Group. Later that year the Follett Campus Resources unit agreed to pay the University of Tennessee $380,000 after the school discovered that the firm had been underpaying students in a book-buyback program for several years. Adding to its bevy of campus bookstores, it signed a contract the same year to build a $5 million bookstore at the University of Texas at Arlington.

Also in 1998 CFO Kenneth Hull replaced Richard Litzsinger as CEO. Follett launched efollett.com in early 1999 to sell college textbooks online. That year Hull became chairman upon Richard Traut's departure. In November 2000 Christopher Traut became CEO; Hull remained chairman.

In April 2001 Hull retired, and Mark Litzsinger succeeded him as chairman.

EXECUTIVES

Chairman: R. Mark Litzsinger
President and CEO: Christopher D. Traut
EVP Finance and CFO: Kathryn A. Stanton
EVP Human Resources: Richard Ellspermann
President and CEO, School and Library Group:
  Ross Follett
President, BWI: John Nelson
President, Follett Educational Distribution Group:
  Bob Mallo, age 47
President, Higher Education Group:
  Thomas A. (Tom) Christopher
EVP Library and School Group: Chuck Follett, age 52

LOCATIONS

HQ: Follett Corporation
  2233 West St., River Grove, IL 60171
Phone: 708-583-2000   **Fax:** 708-452-9347
Web: www.follett.com

PRODUCTS/OPERATIONS

Company Divisions
Elementary/High School Group
  Follett Educational Services
    (K-12 textbooks and workbooks)
  Follett Software Company (library automation)
Higher Education Group
Library Group
  Book Wholesalers, Inc. (BWI) (public libraries)
  Follett Library Resources (school libraries)

COMPETITORS

Baker & Taylor	Educational Development
Barnes & Noble College	Ingram Industries
Bookstores	Nebraska Book
Brodart	Varsity Group
Ecampus.com	Wal-Mart

HISTORICAL FINANCIALS

Company Type: Private

Income Statement

FYE: March 31

	REVENUE ($ mil.)	NET INCOME ($ mil.)	NET PROFIT MARGIN	EMPLOYEES
3/05	2,000	—	—	10,000
3/04	1,899	—	—	10,000
3/03	1,851	—	—	10,000
3/02	1,733	—	—	10,000
3/01	1,554	—	—	8,000
3/00	1,401	—	—	8,000
3/99	1,200	—	—	8,000
3/98	1,073	—	—	7,500
3/97	916	—	—	8,000
3/96	811	—	—	7,500
Annual Growth	10.5%	—	—	3.2%

Revenue History

Ford Foundation

As one of the US's largest philanthropic organizations with a more than $9.5 billion diversified investment portfolio, The Ford Foundation can afford to be generous. The not-for-profit foundation offers grants to individuals and institutions in the US and abroad that meet its stated goals of strengthening democratic values, reducing poverty and injustice, promoting international cooperation, and advancing human achievement. The Ford Foundation's charitable giving covers a wide spectrum, from A (Association for Asian Studies) to Z (Zanzibar International Film Festival).

The Ford Foundation gives to a variety of causes in one of three areas: Asset Building and Community Development (designed to help expand opportunities for the poor and reduce hardship); Peace and Social Justice (promotes peace and the rule of law, human rights, and freedom); and Knowledge, Creativity, and Freedom (aimed at strengthening education and the arts and at building identity and community). Following the September 11 terrorist attacks in 2001, The Ford Foundation joined other philanthropic organizations in providing disaster relief.

The foundation is governed by an international board of trustees and no longer has stock in Ford Motor Company or ties to the Ford family. Funds are derived from a diversified investment portfolio that includes publicly traded equity and fixed-income securities.

HISTORY

Henry Ford and his son Edsel gave $25,000 to establish The Ford Foundation in Michigan in 1936, followed the next year by 250,000 shares of nonvoting stock in the Ford Motor Company. The foundation's activities were limited mainly to Michigan until the deaths of Edsel (1943) and Henry (1947) made the foundation the owner of 90% of the automaker's nonvoting stock (catapulting the endowment to $474 million, the US's largest).

In 1951, under a new mandate and president (Paul Hoffman, former head of the Marshall Plan), Ford made broad commitments to the promotion of world peace, the strengthening of democracy, and the improvement of education. Early education program grants overseen by University of Chicago chancellor Robert Maynard Hutchins ($100 million between 1951 and 1953) helped establish major international programs (e.g., Harvard's Center for International Legal Studies) and the National Merit Scholarships.

Under McCarthyite criticism for its experimental education grants, the foundation in 1956 granted $550 million (after selling 22% of its Ford shares) to noncontroversial recipients such as liberal arts colleges and not-for-profit hospitals. The organization's money set up the Radio and Television Workshop (1951); public TV support became a foundation trademark.

International work, begun in Asia and the Middle East (1950) and extended to Africa (1958) and Latin America (1959), focused on education and rural development. The foundation also supported the Population Council and research in high-yield agriculture with The Rockefeller Foundation.

In the early 1960s Ford targeted innovative approaches to employment and race relations. McGeorge Bundy (former national security adviser to President John Kennedy), named president of the foundation in 1966, increased the activist trend with grants for direct voter registration; the NAACP; public-interest law centers serving consumer, environmental, and minority causes; and housing for the poor.

The early 1970s saw support for black colleges and scholarships, child care, and job training for women, but by 1974 inflation, weak stock prices, and overspending had eroded assets. Programs were cut, but continued support for social justice issues led Henry Ford II to quit the board in 1976.

Under lawyer Franklin Thomas (named president in 1979), Ford established the nation's largest community development support organization, Local Initiatives Support. Thomas, the first African-American to lead the foundation, was a catalyst in a series of meetings between white and black South Africans in the mid-1980s.

Thomas stepped down in 1996, and new president Susan Berresford, formerly EVP, consolidated the foundation's grant programs into three areas: Asset Building and Community Development; Peace and Social Justice; and Education, Media, Arts, and Culture. In the late 1990s Ford was surpassed by various other foundations and had to relinquish its 30-year title as the biggest charitable organization in the US.

In 2000 the foundation announced its largest grant ever, the 10-year, $330 million International Fellowship Program to support graduate students studying in 20 countries. The Ford Foundation provided aid to people affected by the September 11 attacks in 2001, committing grants of $10 million in New York City and more than $1 million in Washington, DC.

EXECUTIVES

Chair: Kathryn S. Fuller, age 58
President: Susan V. Berresford
EVP, Secretary, and General Counsel: Barron M. Tenny
SVP: Barry D. Gaberman
VP and Chief Investment Officer: Linda B. Strumpf
VP Asset Building and Community Development: Pablo Farias
VP Communications: Marta L. Tellado
VP Knowledge, Creativity, and Freedom: Alison R. Bernstein
VP Peace and Social Justice: Bradford K. Smith
Treasurer and Director Financial Services: Nicholas M. Gabriel
Director Human Resources: Bruce D. Stuckey
Assistant Secretary and Associate General Counsel: Nancy P. Feller
Auditors: PricewaterhouseCoopers LLP

LOCATIONS

HQ: The Ford Foundation
320 E. 43rd St., New York, NY 10017
Phone: 212-573-5000   **Fax:** 212-351-3677
Web: www.fordfound.org

The Ford Foundation has offices in New York City, as well as Beijing; Cairo; Hanoi, Vietnam; Jakarta, Indonesia; Johannesburg; Lagos, Nigeria; Mexico City; Moscow; Nairobi, Kenya; New Delhi; Rio de Janeiro; and Santiago, Chile. It closed its Manila, Philippines, office in 2003.

PRODUCTS/OPERATIONS

Program Area Grants

Asset Building and Community Development
  Community and Resource Development
  Economic Development

Knowledge, Creativity, and Freedom
  Education, Sexuality, and Religion
  Media, Arts, and Culture

Peace and Social Justice
  Governance and Civil Society
  Human Rights

HISTORICAL FINANCIALS

Company Type: Foundation

Income Statement

FYE: September 30

	REVENUE ($ mil.)	NET INCOME ($ mil.)	NET PROFIT MARGIN	EMPLOYEES
9/03	261	—	—	—
9/02	289	—	—	400
9/01	992	—	—	500
9/00	2,432	—	—	600
9/99	1,785	—	—	576
9/98	1,087	—	—	580
9/97	1,005	—	—	574
9/96	899	—	—	570
9/95	586	—	—	587
9/94	489	—	—	597
Annual Growth	(6.8%)	—	—	(4.9%)

Revenue History

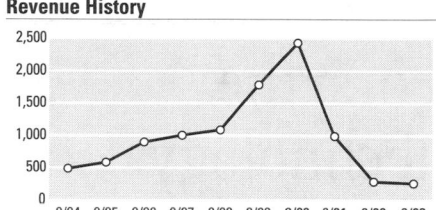

Forever 21

You don't have to be over 21 to buy something at Forever 21's stores — you just need your wallet. The company operates more than 200 mainly mall-based US stores, many in California, (plus one in Canada) under the Forever 21 name, offering cheap and chic fashions for women and junior girls. Its trendy clothes are priced 2% lower than its competitors. Most of the retailer's apparel is private label and made in Southern California. Forever 21 has also opened a series of new concept stores (nine in total) called Fashion XXI that offers men's and women's fashions, as well as lingerie, footwear, cosmetic items, and other accessories. Owner and CEO Don Chang and his wife founded the company as Fashion 21 in 1984.

In mid-2003 the company extended its reach in the junior market by acquiring Reference Clothing Co. Reference had a similar product offering of inexpensive trendy clothes; all of its stores were converted into Forever 21 stores. Continuing its expansion spree, in March 2005 the chain acquired the assets of bankrupt teen retailer Gadzooks for about $33 million. The purchase of 150 Gadzooks stores in 36 states greatly expands Forever 21's retail presence. The retailer

has been opening about 35 stores a year. It recently opened its first accessories-only format called ForLove21. The fast-growing company plans to eventually go public. It may also expand its line of cheap fast fashions to men.

Forever 21 also has two stores in the United Arab Emirates and one in Singapore.

Under fire from the animal rights activist group People for the Ethical Treatment of Animals (PETA), Forever 21 has banned clothing with fur from its shelves.

EXECUTIVES

CEO: Do Won (Don) Chang, age 48
SVP and CFO: Lawrence (Larry) Meyer
Head Buyer: Jin Sook Chang
Human Resources Manager: Kate Chun

LOCATIONS

HQ: Forever 21, Inc.
2001 S. Alameda St., Los Angeles, CA 90058
Phone: 213-741-5100   **Fax:** 213-741-5161
Web: www.forever21.com

COMPETITORS

Charlotte Russe Holding
Charming Shoppes
Claire's Stores
dELiA*s
Gap
H&M
Limited Brands
Old Navy
Urban Outfitters
Wet Seal

HISTORICAL FINANCIALS

Company Type: Private

Income Statement

FYE: December 31

	REVENUE ($ mil.)	NET INCOME ($ mil.)	NET PROFIT MARGIN	EMPLOYEES
12/04	640	—	—	—
12/03*	506	—	—	—
2/02	307	—	—	—
2/01	190	—	—	—
Annual Growth	49.9%	—	—	—

*Fiscal year change

Revenue History

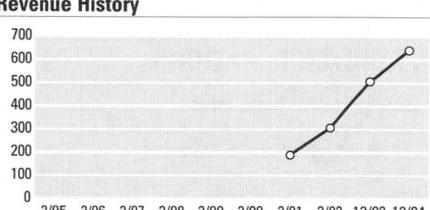

Forever Living

Forever Living Products International might not lead you to immortality, but its aloe vera-based health care products are intended to improve your well-being. The firm sells aloe vera drinks, as well as aloe vera-based aromatherapy products, cosmetics, dietary and nutritional supplements, lotion, soap, and tooth gel products. Owner Rex Maughan also owns aloe vera plantations in the Dominican Republic, Mexico, and Texas; Aloe Vera of America, a processing plant; and Forever Resorts' US resorts and marinas, including Dallas-area Southfork Ranch (of *Dallas* TV show fame). Forever Living Products, founded in 1978, sells its goods through a global network of independent distributors.

Subsidiary Forever Resorts has more than 50 locations (lodges and marinas) in the US and Africa. Forever Living's resort subsidiary expanded into Africa in July 2003 when Rex Maughan bought 10 resorts there.

EXECUTIVES

Chairman, President, and CEO: Rex Gene Maughan
Vice Chairman, CFO, General Counsel, and Secretary: Rjay Lloyd
EVP: Navaz Ghaswala
EVP Sales: Gregg Maughan
SVP Sales, North America: Harold Greene
SVP Human Resources and Risk Management: Glen B. Banks
VP Finance: Dave Hall
VP Information Technology: Steve Itami
VP Marketing: Aidan O'Hare
Director, Distributor Support and Customer Service: Marcy Rivera
Managing Director and Engineer, Forever Living Products Nigeria Limited: Wale Oyemade

LOCATIONS

HQ: Forever Living Products International, Inc.
7501 E. McCormick Pkwy., Ste. 135S,
Scottsdale, AZ 85258
Phone: 480-998-8888 **Fax:** 480-998-8887
Web: www.foreverliving.com

Forever Living Products has distributors worldwide. The company operates two facilities in the Rio Grande Valley area of Texas. One produces raw aloe gel primarily for cosmetics and the second makes aloe juice. From its Dominican Republic plant, Forever Living Products runs one of the largest aloe vera farms in the world.

PRODUCTS/OPERATIONS

Selected Product Categories
Aloe vera drinks
Bee products
Cosmetics
Nutrition
Resorts
Skin care
Weight loss

COMPETITORS

Alticor	Mannatech
Amway	Nature's Sunshine
Avon	NBTY
Body Shop	Shaklee
Burt's Bees	Sunrider
GNC	Whole Foods
Herbalife	Wild Oats Markets
Jafra	

HISTORICAL FINANCIALS

Company Type: Private

Income Statement
FYE: December 31

	REVENUE ($ mil.)	NET INCOME ($ mil.)	NET PROFIT MARGIN	EMPLOYEES
12/03	2,012	—	—	4,100
12/02	1,773	—	—	4,000
12/01	1,489	—	—	2,000
12/00	1,200	—	—	1,901
12/99	1,100	—	—	932
12/98	1,000	—	—	1,700
12/97	950	—	—	1,200
12/96	900	—	—	1,360
12/95	800	—	—	750
12/94	750	—	—	—
Annual Growth	11.6%	—	—	23.7%

Revenue History

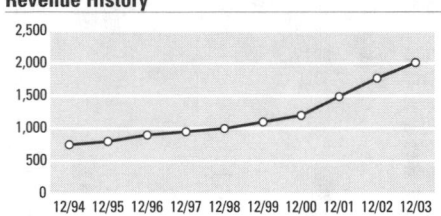

2,500	
2,000	
1,500	
1,000	
500	
0	

12/94 12/95 12/96 12/97 12/98 12/99 12/00 12/01 12/02 12/03

Forsythe Technology

Forsythe Technology believes it has the foresight to provide valuable information technology (IT) consulting services. Its Forsythe Solutions Group works on companies' IT infrastructure elements, including servers, storage, and networks, and clients can lease computer equipment through the Forsythe McArthur subsidiary. Forsythe Technology customers include Aflac, Outback Steakhouse, and TriZetto. In 2004 the company acquired security services firm National Business Group, which expanded Forsythe's offerings in the area of IT risk management. CEO Richard Forsythe holds a majority interest in the employee-owned company.

Richard Forsythe founded the company in 1971, starting off with $200 and a telephone on a dining room table. The company now works with vendors such as Cisco Systems, Hewlett-Packard, and Sun Microsystems, and it serves more than 3,000 clients from offices throughout the US.

EXECUTIVES

Chairman; Chairman, Forsythe Solutions; Chairman and CEO, Forsythe McArthur: Richard A. (Rick) Forsythe
President and Director; President and Director, Forsythe Solutions: William P. (Bill) Brennan, age 49
EVP, Finance and Administration, CFO, and Director; President, Forsythe McArthur: Albert L. (Al) Weiss
SVP and General Counsel: R. Thomas (Tom) Hoffman
SVP and Sales Manager, Western Region: Robert D. (Bob) Dvorak
SVP, Financial Services: John D. Carcone
SVP, Systems Solutions and Technology Products: Michael J. (Mike) Qualley

VP and Chief Accounting Officer: Thomas R. (Tom) Ehmann
VP and Treasurer, Forsythe Technology and Forsythe McArthur: Raymond L. (Ray) Ellingsen
VP, Corporate Development: Richard A. (Rick) Finocchi
VP, Human Resources: Julie A. Fusco
VP, Marketing; SVP, Marketing, Forsythe Solutions: Sally Knapp Buchanan
VP, Sales Administration: Michelle M. Coffield
VP, Tax Administration and Assistant Secretary: Steven M. (Steve) Avrick
Senior Communications Specialist: Kyra Auslander

LOCATIONS

HQ: Forsythe Technology, Inc.
7770 Frontage Rd., Skokie, IL 60077
Phone: 847-213-7000 **Fax:** 847-213-7922
Web: www.forsythe.com

Forsythe Technology has offices throughout the US.

PRODUCTS/OPERATIONS

Selected Services
Forsythe Solutions
Back-up and recovery
Database and application development
Internet application integration
Network design and security
Software and systems benchmarking
Storage systems integration
Systems analysis and management
Systems consolidation
Training
Forsythe McArthur
Computer equipment leasing

COMPETITORS

Affiliated Computer Services	GCI Systems
ATEL Capital	HP Technology Solutions Group
Black Box	IBM Global Services
Blackwell Consulting	ICON Capital
Computer Sciences Corp.	Keane
Dell	Meridian Group
EDS	ORIX
Electro Rent	Perot Systems
ePlus	Sayers Group
FAEF	Unisys
GATX	

HISTORICAL FINANCIALS

Company Type: Private

Income Statement
FYE: December 31

	REVENUE ($ mil.)	NET INCOME ($ mil.)	NET PROFIT MARGIN	EMPLOYEES
12/04	449	6	1.3%	639
12/03	444	24	5.4%	549
12/02	568	20	3.5%	535
12/01	691	34	5.0%	521
12/00	631	24	3.8%	562
12/99	536	25	4.6%	393
12/98	448	22	4.9%	363
12/97	280	14	5.1%	302
12/96	189	12	6.3%	230
12/95	151	8	5.0%	150
Annual Growth	12.9%	(3.1%)	—	17.5%

2004 Year-End Financials

Debt ratio: —
Return on equity: 4.0%
Cash ($ mil.): —

Current ratio: —
Long-term debt ($ mil.): —

Net Income History

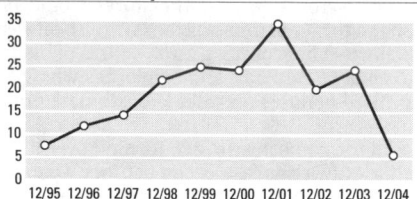

Foster Poultry Farms

As the West Coast's top poultry company, Foster Poultry Farms has a secure place in the pecking order. The company's vertically integrated operations see chickens and turkeys from the incubator to grocers' meat cases (under the Foster Farms brand). In addition to hatching, raising, slaughtering, and processing chickens and turkeys for the grocery and food service industries, the company grinds its own feeds. Already #1 in its home state, Foster Poultry Farms grew larger when it bought the chicken operations of local rival Zacky Farms. Max and Verda Foster founded the company in 1939; it is still owned by the Foster family, which also operates sister company Foster Dairy Farms.

EXECUTIVES

Director: Ron Foster
President: Don Jackson
CFO: Larry Keillor
VP Foodservice: Bob Wangerien
VP Human Resources: Tim Walsh
VP Marketing: David Schanzer
VP Sales: Bob Kellert
Director of Corporate Accounting: Troy Mangrum
Business Manager, Expansion Markets:
Matthew McIntire
Business Manager, Foodservice: Mark Staub
Consumer Affairs Manager: Teresa Lenz
Auditors: Deloitte & Touche LLP

LOCATIONS

HQ: Foster Poultry Farms
1000 Davis St., Livingston, CA 95334
Phone: 209-394-7901 **Fax:** 209-394-6342
Web: www.fosterfarms.com

Foster Poultry Farms has operations in California, Oregon, and Washington.

COMPETITORS

Cagle's
ConAgra
Farmers Pride, Inc.
Gold Kist
Hormel
Murphy-Brown

Pilgrim's Pride
Randall Foods
Shelton's
Tyson Foods
Zacky Farms

HISTORICAL FINANCIALS

Company Type: Private

Income Statement

FYE: December 31

	REVENUE ($ mil.)	NET INCOME ($ mil.)	NET PROFIT MARGIN	EMPLOYEES
12/03	1,520	—	—	11,000
12/02	1,434	—	—	11,000
12/01	1,269	—	—	11,000
12/00	1,127	—	—	9,500
12/99	1,100	—	—	7,500
12/98	990	—	—	7,000
12/97	1,000	—	—	7,200
12/96	925	—	—	6,800
12/95	825	—	—	6,700
12/94	800	—	—	6,600
Annual Growth	**7.4%**	**—**	**—**	**5.8%**

Revenue History

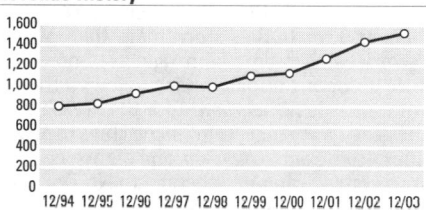

Frank Consolidated Enterprises

Frank Consolidated Enterprises has an old lease on life. Its Wheels subsidiary, which claims to have pioneered the auto leasing concept, provides fleet management services — administrative, management, and financing services to help corporations manage their vehicle fleets. The company manages more than 240,000 vehicles. It operates in the US as Wheels and in other countries through Fleet Synergy International, an alliance of international fleet management and leasing companies. Wheels was founded in 1939 by Zollie Frank. Frank's family still owns the parent company; his widow serves as its chair, and son Jim is the president and CEO.

EXECUTIVES

Chairman: Elaine S. Frank
President and CEO: James S. (Jim) Frank
EVP and COO, Wheels: Ford Pearson
SVP, Finance and Operations and CFO, Wheels:
Mary Ann O'Dwyer, age 49
SVP, Sales, Marketing, and Account Management, Wheels: Scott Pattullo
VP, Client Relations: Norman Din
VP, IT and CIO, Wheels: Larry Buettner
VP, Human Resources, Wheels: Joan Richards
VP, International Sales, Wheels: Peter Egan
VP, Maintenance Assistance Program Operations, Wheels: John Frank
VP, Sales, Wheels: Michael Christian
VP, Sales, Wheels: Prentiss Harvey

LOCATIONS

HQ: Frank Consolidated Enterprises
666 Garland Place, Des Plaines, IL 60016
Phone: 847-699-7000 **Fax:** 847-699-6494
Web: www.wheels.com

COMPETITORS

Donlen
Emkay
Enterprise Rent-A-Car
GE Equipment Services

Holman Enterprises
Jordan Automotive
PHH corp
Sixt

HISTORICAL FINANCIALS

Company Type: Private

Income Statement

FYE: August 31

	REVENUE ($ mil.)	NET INCOME ($ mil.)	NET PROFIT MARGIN	EMPLOYEES
8/04	1,600	—	—	550
8/03	1,500	—	—	550
8/02	1,575	—	—	550
8/01	1,500	—	—	600
8/00	1,431	—	—	591
8/99	1,364	—	—	562
8/98	1,181	—	—	574
8/97	1,025	—	—	600
8/96	1,200	—	—	675
8/95	1,165	—	—	675
Annual Growth	**3.6%**	**—**	**—**	**(2.2%)**

Revenue History

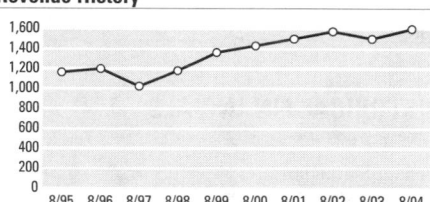

Fresh Concepts

Let there be no confusion about this company's food fusion. Founded in 1997 by brothers Larry and Bruce Reinstein, Fresh Concepts operates about 15 Fresh City restaurants in five northeastern states. The food is presented in a cafeteria-cum-marketplace atmosphere, with food and drink "stations" dotting the stores. Offerings include wrap sandwiches, juices and smoothies, salads, and homemade soups. Menu items are also thematically diverse — burritos, Asian noodles, Italian pasta. The freshness and healthfulness of the ingredients are heavily emphasized to customers. Fresh Concepts also operates 10 Souper Salad restaurants in Massachusetts.

In 1976 the Reinstein brothers' father founded the Souper Salad chain; two years later the San Antonio, Texas-based Souper Salad chain secured the national trademark for the name, preventing the Reinstein's from ever growing the concept outside of Massachusetts.

Some restaurant locations also offer catering services.

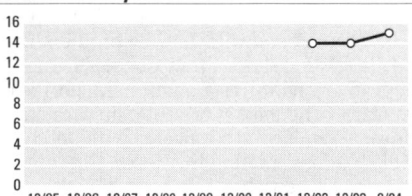
Fry's Electronics

Trying to catalog all the things this superstore carries could fry your brain. Fry's Electronics is a leading big-box retailer of computers, consumer electronics, and appliances with more than 30 stores in about 10 states. The chain's extensive inventory includes computer software and components, magazines, movies and music, refrigerators, small appliances, stereo equipment, and televisions. In addition, each store typically stocks a variety of snacks and other impulse items. The technogeek's dream store began in 1985 as the brainchild of CEO John Fry (with brothers Randy and Dave) and EVP Kathryn Kolder. The Fry brothers, who got their start at Fry's Food Stores, still own the company.

Its mammoth stores, some swallowing almost 200,000 sq. ft., cater to the intensely technical shopper. Fry's outlets stock more than 50,000 low-priced electronic items and are known for their decor and displays. Each follows a theme, from *Alice in Wonderland* to a UFO crash site. The geek-gaws range from silicon chips to potato chips, from *Byte* to *Playboy,* and high-speed PCs (plus software and peripherals) to No-Doz (and other over-the-counter drugs).

In addition to its retail outlets, Fry's sells electronics online through Fry's Outpost.com (acquired in 2001) and it offers dial-up Internet access services in more than 40 states.

Fry's stores' extensive inventories are said to be the company's strongest draw, unlike its reputation for poor customer service. This reputation, combined with Fry's bemoaned system for returning items, has left the company a target of many gripe-filled Web sites.

HISTORY

The Fry brothers — David, John, and Randy — wear genes stitched of retailing. Their father, Charles, started Fry's Food Stores supermarket chain in the 1950s in South Bay, California. The 40-store chain was sold for $14 million in 1972 to Dillion (now part of grocery store giant The Kroger Co.) before Charles' progeny heard the retail calling.

Charles gave each of his sons $1 million from the sale of the supermarkets. His oldest, John, who had gained technical expertise while running the supermarket's computer system, convinced his siblings of the viability of a hard-core computer retail store. The brothers pooled their funds and in 1985 started the first in Sunnyvale, California, along with Kathryn Kolder (now EVP). They added a store in Fremont in 1988; the Palo Alto store was completed two years later.

John mixed his supermarket sales experience with a sharp marketing acumen, selling prime shelf space at smart prices to suppliers. He stocked the stores with everything for a computer user's survival and slashed prices. The first Los Angeles-area store opened in 1992; a second one opened the following year. Hiring an ex-Lucasfilm designer, John spent $1 million on each location, decorating stores like medieval castles, Mayan temples, Wild West saloons, and other individual fantasy themes.

In 1994 the Los Angeles computer retail market began to see increased competition from nationwide discount computer superstores. The next year Fry's responded by opening a new store in Woodland Hills with an *Alice in Wonderland* motif. It was the first Southern California Fry's

Electronics store to offer appliances and an expanded music department.

The chain continued to gain notoriety for the contempt it seemed to show its customers. Local Better Business Bureaus started ranking Fry's "unsatisfactory" because the stores would not respond to complaints. Patrons with a beef were usually met by security guards, scores of hidden surveillance cameras, and employees who were promised bonuses for talking customers out of cash returns.

Still the company thrived, turning over its inventories twice as fast as competitors. One customer who sued Fry's for injuries allegedly received at the hands of store security guards went back for deals soon thereafter. Fry's went on an expansion frenzy in 1996, opening new California stores in Burbank, San Jose, and Anaheim. Moving beyond its Pacific roots, the company in 1997 spent $118 million to buy six of Tandy's failed Incredible Universe retail mega-outlets in Arizona, Oregon, and Texas. The company also won a legal battle with Frenchy Frys, a Seattle vending machine maker, for the right to own and use the frys.com URL. The company in 1998 continued to restructure its new stores into Fry's outlets.

Fry's opened a new store (complete with gushing oil derricks) in Houston in 2001. That year it pulled out of a deal to acquire all of the assets of technology products marketer Egghead.com and bought competitor Cyberian Outpost instead. In 2003 Fry's set up shop in Las Vegas; the entrance features a two-story neon slot machine.

PRODUCTS/OPERATIONS

Selected Products

Appliances (coffeemakers, blenders, vacuums)
Cameras
CD players
Computer components (hard drives, routers)
Computers (PCs, notebooks)
DVD players
DVDs
MP3 players
Office products (printers, copiers, fax machines)
PDAs
Software
Toys
Video games

COMPETITORS

Amazon.com
Apple Computer
Best Buy
Buy.com
CDW
Circuit City
CompUSA
Dell
Electronics Boutique
GameStop
Gateway
Hastings Entertainment
Musicland
Office Depot
PC Mall
PC Warehouse
RadioShack
Staples
Tower Records
Trans World Entertainment
Tweeter Home Entertainment
Wal-Mart
Zones

HISTORICAL FINANCIALS

Company Type: Private

Income Statement				FYE: December 31
	ESTIMATED REVENUE ($ mil.)	NET INCOME ($ mil.)	NET PROFIT MARGIN	EMPLOYEES
12/03	2,100	—	—	6,000
12/02	2,000	—	—	5,650
12/01	1,900	—	—	4,900
12/00	1,500	—	—	4,450
12/99	1,420	—	—	4,100
12/98	1,250	—	—	4,000
12/97	950	—	—	4,000
12/96	535	—	—	2,000
12/95	414	—	—	1,500
12/94	327	—	—	1,500
Annual Growth	23.0%	—	—	16.7%

Revenue History

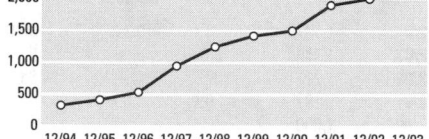

GENCO Distribution System

GENCO Distribution System provides third-party logistics services, including direct logistics (warehousing and distribution services), reverse logistics (processing of goods returned by consumers), supply chain analysis, transportation management (including parcel management), and unsaleables (analyzing causes of damage to customers' product). The company maintains some 23 million sq. ft. of warehouse space at more than 85 locations in the US and Canada; it also has operations in Australia and the UK. Customers include manufacturers, retailers, and government agencies. CEO Herb Shear owns the company, which was founded in 1898 by his grandfather Hyman Shear.

EXECUTIVES

Chairman and CEO: Herbert (Herb) Shear
Vice Chairman: Larry Sur
Vice Chairman: William G. (Gus) Pagonis, age 63
Vice Chairman: James Adams
CFO: Rick Roadarmel
SVP Business Development and Marketing: Glenn Mauney
President, Business Development: Curtis Greve
President, Customer Solutions: Dwight (Buzzy) Wyland
President, Direct Solutions: Jim Polacheck
President, GENCO Infrastructure Solutions: Enzo Zoratto
President, Reverse Solutions: Steven South
President, SCM Solutions: Larry Chaplin
President, Value Added Solutions: Dan Eisenhuth
Director, Corporate Communications: Donald Rendulic

LOCATIONS

HQ: GENCO Distribution System, Inc.
100 Papercraft Park, Pittsburgh, PA 15238
Phone: 412-820-3923   **Fax:** 412-820-3689
Web: www.genco.com

COMPETITORS

APL Logistics
Caterpillar Logistics Services
DSC Logistics
Exel plc
Kenco Group
Kuehne & Nagel, Inc.
Ozburn-Hessey Logistics
Roadway Express
TNT Logistics North America
UPS Supply Chain Solutions
UTi Integrated Logistics

HISTORICAL FINANCIALS

Company Type: Private

Income Statement				FYE: December 31
	REVENUE ($ mil.)	NET INCOME ($ mil.)	NET PROFIT MARGIN	EMPLOYEES
12/04	458	—	—	6,000
12/03	409	—	—	5,000
12/02	373	—	—	—
Annual Growth	10.8%	—	—	20.0%

Revenue History

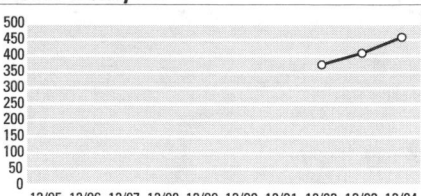

General Parts

Feel free to salute General Parts, distributor of replacement automotive parts, supplies, and tools for every make and model of foreign and domestic car, truck, bus, and farm or industrial vehicle. The largest member of the CARQUEST network, employee-owned General Parts, with more than 1,400 company-owned stores, distributes its products to about 4,000 CARQUEST and other auto parts stores across North America through 41 distribution centers. The company, which has been growing through acquisitions, sells its parts to do-it-yourself mechanics, professional installers, body shops, farmers, and fleet owners (commercial customers account for about 70% of sales). The company owns CARQUEST Canada.

EXECUTIVES

Chairman and CEO: O. Temple Sloan Jr., age 66
Vice Chairman: Joe Owen
President: O. Temple Sloan III
CFO: John Gardner
VP Administration and Accounting: William Kuykendall
VP Human Resources: Ed Whirty
President, Stores Group: Wayne Lavrack

LOCATIONS

HQ: General Parts, Inc.
2635 Millbrook Rd., Raleigh, NC 27604
Phone: 919-573-3000   **Fax:** 919-573-3553

COMPETITORS

Advance Auto Parts
AutoZone
CSK Auto
Genuine Parts
Hahn Automotive
Pep Boys

HISTORICAL FINANCIALS

Company Type: Private

Income Statement

FYE: December 31

	REVENUE ($ mil.)	NET INCOME ($ mil.)	NET PROFIT MARGIN	EMPLOYEES
12/03	1,800	—	—	13,500
12/02	1,650	—	—	14,000
12/01	1,562	—	—	13,000
12/00	1,459	—	—	12,000
12/99	1,462	—	—	12,700
12/98	1,248	—	—	10,150
12/97	1,060	—	—	6,700
12/96	818	—	—	6,700
12/95	680	—	—	4,700
12/94	612	—	—	4,670
Annual Growth	**12.7%**	**—**	**—**	**12.5%**

Revenue History

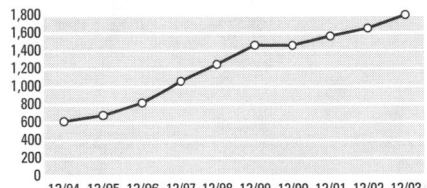

Genomic Health

Genomic Health believes the genome is key to good health. The company conducts genomic research to develop molecular diagnostics and assays that can predict the likelihood of disease recurrence and response to therapy and treatments. Genomic Health's Onco*type* DX assay is used to predict the likelihood of breast cancer recurrence in women with newly diagnosed, early stage invasive breast cancer. Genomic Health was founded in 2000 and has received funding from firms including Kleiner Perkins Caufield & Byers, Versant Ventures, Texas Pacific Group, J.P. Morgan Partners, and Credit Suisse First Boston.

Kleiner Perkins Caufield & Byers and Versant Partners each own 13% of the company, with TPG Ventures holding a 10% stake. Individuals that hold significant stakes include directors Brook Byers (13%), Samuel Colella (13%), and Fred Cohen (10%).

EXECUTIVES

Chairman and CEO: Randal W. (Randy) Scott, age 47, $200,000 pay
President, COO, and Director: Kimberly J. (Kim) Popovits, age 46, $275,000 pay
EVP, CFO, and Secretary: G. Bradley (Brad) Cole, age 49, $120,311 pay (partial-year salary)
Chief Medical Officer: Steven (Steve) Shak, age 54, $275,000 pay
Chief Scientific Officer: Joffre B. Baker, age 57, $275,000 pay
Media Relations: Kathleen Rinehart
Media Relations: Jim Weiss
Auditors: Ernst & Young LLP

LOCATIONS

HQ: Genomic Health, Inc.
301 Penobscot Dr., Redwood City, CA 94063
Phone: 650-556-9300   **Fax:** 650-556-1132
Web: www.genomichealth.com

PRODUCTS/OPERATIONS

2004 Sales

	$ mil.	% of total
Product revenues	0.2	67
Contract revenues	0.1	33
Total	**0.3**	**100**

COMPETITORS

Applera	LabOne
Genzyme	Quest Diagnostics
Johnson & Johnson	Roche Diagnostics
LabCorp	

HISTORICAL FINANCIALS

Company Type: Public

Income Statement

FYE: December 31

	REVENUE ($ mil.)	NET INCOME ($ mil.)	NET PROFIT MARGIN	EMPLOYEES
12/04	0	(25)	—	101
12/03	0	(15)	—	—
12/02	0	(11)	—	—
Annual Growth	**—**	**—**	**—**	**—**

2004 Year-End Financials

Debt ratio: 0.0%
Return on equity: —
Cash ($ mil.): 38
Current ratio: 15.83
Long-term debt ($ mil.): 0

Net Income History

NASDAQ: GHDX

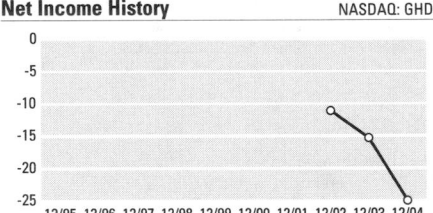

GeoLogistics

GeoLogistics gets goods going, globally. The company's offerings include freight forwarding, customs brokerage, warehousing and distribution, supply chain management, and trade-show logistics. As a freight forwarder, GeoLogistics buys transportation capacity from air, ocean, and over-the-road carriers and resells that capacity to customers. The company does business from a network of some 250 offices in more than 25 countries and about 150 agent-owned branches in more than 65 countries. Operations outside the US account for most of the company's sales. Kuwait-based PWC Logistics acquired GeoLogistics in September 2005.

PWC Logistics, which specializes in supply chain management and warehousing, bought GeoLogistics for $454 million from a group led by investment firm Questor Management. The price represented a significant return on

Questor's original investment in GeoLogistics, a $67.5 million purchase of the company's preferred stock that was made in 2001.

PWC said GeoLogistics would operate under its own name and that the unit's senior management team would stay in place.

EXECUTIVES

President, CEO, and Director: William J. (Bill) Flynn
EVP and CFO: Stephen P. (Steve) Bishop, age 48
SVP Marketing: Christopher Logan
VP and General Counsel: Ronald (Ron) Jackson
Chief Information Officer: Charles Kirk, age 56
CEO, Americas Region: Alex Leivici, age 44
CEO, Asia Pacific Region: Wolfgang Hollermann, age 56
CEO, Europe/Middle East/Africa Region: Karl Nutzinger, age 47
Auditors: Ernst & Young LLP

LOCATIONS

HQ: GeoLogistics Corporation
1251 E. Dyer Rd., Ste. 200, Santa Ana, CA 92705
Phone: 714-513-3000   **Fax:** 714-513-3120
Web: www.geo-logistics.com

2004 Sales

	$ mil.	% of total
Europe, Middle East & Africa	802.5	51
Asia/Pacific	484.3	31
Americas	290.1	18
Total	**1,576.9**	**100**

PRODUCTS/OPERATIONS

Selected Services

Air and ocean freight forwarding
Customs brokerage
Distribution and warehousing
Inventory management
Packaging, transportation, unpacking
Packing and crating
Real-time shipment tracking
Trade show and exhibition services

COMPETITORS

APL Logistics	Kuehne & Nagel
BAX Global	Nippon Express
C.H. Robinson Worldwide	Panalpina
DHL	Schenker
EGL	Sinotrans
Exel plc	TNT
Expeditors	UPS Supply
FedEx Trade Networks	Chain Solutions
Kintetsu World Express	UTi Worldwide

HISTORICAL FINANCIALS

Company Type: Private

Income Statement

FYE: December 31

	REVENUE ($ mil.)	NET INCOME ($ mil.)	NET PROFIT MARGIN	EMPLOYEES
12/04	1,577	4	0.3%	5,700
12/03	1,375	(30)	—	5,600
12/02	1,227	(37)	—	6,000
12/01	1,192	9	0.8%	6,000
12/00	1,500	—	—	6,000
12/99	1,558	—	—	6,200
12/98	1,600	—	—	6,300
12/97	1,525	—	—	6,000
12/96	1,639	—	—	6,352
Annual Growth	**(0.5%)**	**(23.7%)**	**—**	**(1.3%)**

2004 Year-End Financials

Debt ratio: 724.6%
Return on equity: —
Cash ($ mil.): 22

Current ratio: 1.05
Long-term debt ($ mil.): 60

Net Income History

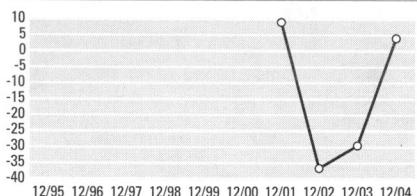

George E. Warren

By barge, by pipeline, by tank truck, by George; George E. Warren is a major private wholesale distributor of petroleum in the eastern US. Founded in Boston by George E. Warren in 1907 as a coal and oil distributor, it moved to Florida in the early 1990s.

The company distributes its products mostly by barge and pipeline, though it uses some tank trucks as well. Warren has distribution facilities in the southeastern and southwestern US. It distributes products including ethylene and heating oil to various industries.

George E. Warren is one of the largest private companies in Florida. In addition to its Vero Beach office, the wholesale fuel distributor also has an office in the UK. President and CEO Thomas Corr owns the company.

EXECUTIVES

President and CEO: Thomas L. Corr
CFO and Controller: Michael E. George
Director Human Resources: Martin Paris

LOCATIONS

HQ: George E. Warren Corporation
3001 Ocean Dr., Vero Beach, FL 32963
Phone: 772-778-7100 **Fax:** 772-778-7171
Web: www.gewarren.com

COMPETITORS

Center Oil
ConocoPhillips
Crown Central Petroleum
Exxon Mobil
Martin Resource Management
Penn Octane
Sun Coast Resources
Western Gas
Williams Companies

HISTORICAL FINANCIALS

Company Type: Private

Income Statement

FYE: December 31

	REVENUE ($ mil.)	NET INCOME ($ mil.)	NET PROFIT MARGIN	EMPLOYEES
12/03	2,586	—	—	32
12/02	3,000	—	—	25
12/01	3,200	—	—	25
12/00	2,000	—	—	25
12/99	1,281	—	—	25
12/98	1,406	—	—	25
12/97	2,602	—	—	24
12/96	2,313	—	—	23
Annual Growth	1.6%	—	—	4.8%

Revenue History

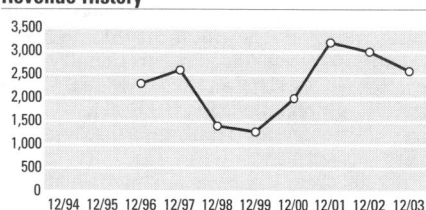

G-I Holdings

G-I Holdings (formerly GAF Corporation) is one of the US's oldest sources for commercial and residential roofing materials. Subsidiary Building Materials Corporation of America makes flashing, vents, and complete roofing systems. Other products include residential shingles (Timberline and Sovereign brands) and GAF CompositeRoof for commercial asphalt roofing. The company operates more than 25 plants in the US. Its customers include contractors, distributors, and retail outlets such as The Home Depot. G-I Holdings has filed for bankruptcy protection due to asbestos liability claims. Chairman Samuel Heyman owns 99% of the company and all of affiliate International Specialty Products Inc.

EXECUTIVES

Chairman, G-I Holdings Inc., and International Specialty Products Inc.; President and CEO, GAF:
Samuel J. Heyman, age 66
Director; EVP, General Counsel, and Secretary, International Specialty Products Inc.:
Richard A. Weinberg, age 43
SVP, CFO, and Treasurer: Susan B. Yoss, age 46
VP Human Resources: Gary Schneid

LOCATIONS

HQ: G-I Holdings Inc.
1361 Alps Rd., Wayne, NJ 07470
Phone: 973-628-3000 **Fax:** 973-628-3326

G-I Holdings operates 26 plants throughout the US.

PRODUCTS/OPERATIONS

Selected Residential Products

Laminated shingles (Timberline)
Roofing systems (Weather Stopper)
Specialty shingles (Slateline)
Strip shingles (Sovereign)

COMPETITORS

Bridgestone Americas
Carlisle Companies
ElkCorp
Formica

Johns Manville
NCI Building Systems
Owens Corning

HISTORICAL FINANCIALS

Company Type: Private

Income Statement

FYE: December 31

	REVENUE ($ mil.)	NET INCOME ($ mil.)	NET PROFIT MARGIN	EMPLOYEES
12/03	1,608	—	—	3,500
12/02	1,361	—	—	3,400
12/01	1,293	—	—	3,400
12/00	1,200	—	—	3,500
12/99	1,140	—	—	3,500
12/98	1,088	—	—	3,300
12/97	945	—	—	3,000
12/96	1,568	—	—	5,209
12/95	1,339	—	—	5,400
12/94	1,156	—	—	4,500
Annual Growth	3.7%	—	—	(2.8%)

Revenue History

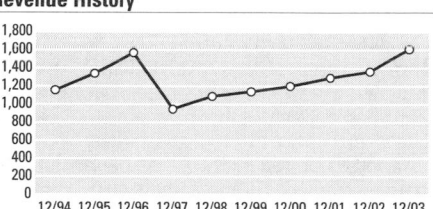

Giant Eagle

With its talons firmly wrapped around western Pennsylvania, Giant Eagle is eyeing new territory. The grocery chain is the #1 food retailer in Pittsburgh. It operates nearly 140 corporate and about 80 franchised supermarkets (about 60,000 sq. ft. in size) and convenience stores throughout Maryland, western Pennsylvania, Ohio, and north central West Virginia. In addition to food, many Giant Eagle stores feature video rental, banking, photo processing, and ready-to-eat meals. Giant Eagle is also a wholesaler to the licensed stores and sells groceries to other retail chains. Chairman and CEO David Shapira is the grandson of one of the five men who founded the company in 1931. The founders' families own Giant Eagle.

As with other birds of the retailing feather, Giant Eagle's supermarkets carry private-label merchandise (Eagle Valley and Giant Eagle brands) and nonfood items; many have pharmacies.

Giant Eagle became the #1 food seller in eastern Ohio through a 1997 acquisition, and the supermarket chain has expanded to Cleveland, Columbus, and Toledo. The company's goal is to grow Giant Eagle food and drug sales through a combination of acquisitions and organic growth to $9 billion by 2007. To that end, in 2002 Giant Eagle launched a successful bid for the remaining assets of bankrupt discount drugstore chain Phar-Mor. It also acquired and converted eight Big Bear grocery stores in the Columbus area from bankrupt supermarket operator Penn Traffic, which has sold off its Big Bear chain.

The company operates a convenience store chain called GetGo from Giant Eagle. Of the 70-plus stores, some 40 are located in western Pennsylvania. (The rest are in Ohio.) GetGo stores feature fresh foods and sell gas a steeply discounted prices through the popular fuel-perks! program. Some of the stores offer "healthy" kids meals.

The supermarket chain has shifted the start of its weekly sales specials from Sunday to Thursday to match its customers' changing shopping patterns and better compete with nontraditional grocery chains, such as Costco Wholesale and Wal-Mart Supercenters. Giant Eagle has also cut prices an average of 7% on some 3,000 items to better compete with discount grocery chains.

HISTORY

When Joe Porter, Ben Chait, and Joe Goldstein sold their chain of 125 Eagle grocery stores in Pittsburgh to Kroger in 1928, the agreement stated that the men would have to leave the grocery business for three years. In retrospect, Kroger should have made the term last for the length of their lives, because in 1931 the three men joined the owners of OK Grocery — Hyman Moravitz and Morris Weizenbaum — and launched a new chain of grocery stores called Giant Eagle. Eventually, the chain would knock Kroger out of the Pittsburgh market.

Although slowed by the Great Depression, the chain expanded, fighting such large rivals as Acme, A&P, and Kroger for Pittsburgh's food shoppers. The stores were mom-and-pop operations with over-the-counter service until they began converting to self-service during the 1940s. Store sizes expanded to nearly 15,000 sq. ft. in the 1950s. During that time Giant Eagle, with about 30 stores, launched Blue Stamps in answer to Green Stamps and other loyalty programs.

It phased out trading stamps in the 1960s in lieu of everyday low prices. To accommodate its growth, in 1968 Giant Eagle acquired a warehouse in Lawrenceville, Pennsylvania, that more than doubled its storage area. Also that year the firm opened its first 20,000-sq.-ft. Giant Eagle store.

During the inflationary 1970s Giant Eagle introduced generic items and began offering the Food Club line, a private-label brand, in conjunction with wholesaler Topco. It continued its expansion, and by 1979 it had become Pittsburgh's #1 supermarket chain, as chains such as Kroger, Acme, and A&P were leaving the city. In 1981 Giant Eagle, with 52 stores, acquired Tamarkin, a wholesale and retail chain in Youngstown, Ohio, part-owned by the Monus family. The purchase moved it into the franchise business, and later that year the first independent Giant Eagle store opened in Monaca (outside Pittsburgh).

The Tamarkin purchase brought together Mickey Monus and Giant Eagle CEO David Shapira, grandson of founder Goldstein. In 1982 they created Phar-Mor, a deep-discount drugstore chain (Wal-Mart's Sam Walton once said it was the only competitor he truly feared). From a single store in Niles, Ohio, Phar-Mor grew rapidly to 310 outlets in 32 states in the early 1990s.

Phar-Mor president Monus helped found the World Basketball League (WBL) in 1987 and became the owner of three teams. In 1992 an auditor discovered two unexplainable Phar-Mor checks to the WBL totaling about $100,000. Investigators soon uncovered three years of over-

stated inventories and a false set of books; Shapira (who was also CEO of Phar-Mor), Giant Eagle owners (which held a 50% stake in Phar-Mor until 1992), and other investors had been duped of more than $1 billion. Shapira fired Monus and his cronies on July 31, 1992. The next day the WBL folded; about two weeks after that Phar-Mor filed for Chapter 11 bankruptcy. A mistrial in 1994 couldn't save Monus from prison; he was reindicted in 1995 and sentenced to 20 years (later reduced to 12).

Giant Eagle made its largest acquisition in 1997, paying $403 million for Riser Foods, a wholesaler (American Seaway Foods) with 35 company-owned stores under the Rini-Rego Stop-n-Shop banner. The stores were converted to the Giant Eagle banner in 1998 (another 18 independent Stop-n-Shop stores were also converted).

In 2000 Giant Eagle opened several stores in Columbus, Ohio. The grocer moved into Maryland in 2001 when it acquired six Country Market stores in Maryland and Pennsylvania. Also in 2001, the grocer founded ECHO Real Estate Services Co. to develop retail, housing, and golf course projects.

In 2002 Giant Eagle was among the winning bidders for the remaining assets of bankrupt Phar-Mor. Giant Eagle acquired leases to 10 Phar-Mor stores and the inventory and prescription lists for 27 stores.

The retailer scrapped its plan to sell its transportation business and signed a new five-year contract with its union delivery drivers in September 2003.

In mid-2005 the grocery chain acquired four CoGo convenience stores, which it will convert to its fast-growing GetGo banner.

EXECUTIVES

Chairman and CEO: David S. (Dave) Shapira, age 63
Vice Chairman: Anthony C. Rego
President and COO: Raymond Burgo
EVP, Business Systems: Jack Flanagan
EVP, Sales: Laura Karet
SVP and CFO: Mark Minnaugh
SVP, Distribution and Logistics: Larry Baldauf
SVP and CIO: Russ Ross
VP, Marketing: Kevin Srigley
VP, Meat and Seafood Merchandising: Ed Steinmetz
VP, Application Engineering: Mike Krugle
VP, Columbus Operations: David (Dave) Daniel
VP, Foods and Convenience: Daniel Pastor
VP, Logistics: Bill Parry
VP, Nonfoods: Tina Flowers
VP, Pharmacy Merchandising: Randy Heiser
Director, Communications: Rob Borella
Director, Customer Relationships and Target Marketing: Rebecca Kane
Director, Human Resources Services: Vicki Clites

LOCATIONS

HQ: Giant Eagle, Inc.
   101 Kappa Dr., Pittsburgh, PA 15238
Phone: 412-963-6200   **Fax:** 412-968-1617
Web: www.gianteagle.com

2005 Stores

	No.
Ohio	112
Pennsylvania	100
West Virginia	4
Maryland	3
Total	**219**

PRODUCTS/OPERATIONS

Private Labels
Eagle Valley
Giant Eagle

Selected Services
Bakery
Banking services
Childcare
Deli department
Dry cleaning
Fresh seafood
Greeting cards
Pharmacy
Photo developing
Ready-to-eat meals
Ticketmaster outlet
Video rental

COMPETITORS

7-Eleven
A&P
Giant Food
Heinen's
IGA
Kroger
Shop 'N Save
Tops Markets
Wal-Mart
Wegmans
Weis Markets
Whole Foods

HISTORICAL FINANCIALS

Company Type: Private

Income Statement

FYE: June 30

	REVENUE ($ mil.)	NET INCOME ($ mil.)	NET PROFIT MARGIN	EMPLOYEES
6/05	5,500	—	—	36,000
6/04	5,100	—	—	28,000
6/03	4,739	—	—	26,000
6/02	4,415	—	—	26,000
6/01	4,435	—	—	25,600
6/00	4,221	—	—	25,600
6/99	4,360	—	—	25,600
6/98	4,050	—	—	25,000
6/97	3,800	—	—	19,200
6/96	2,200	—	—	12,000
Annual Growth	**10.7%**	**—**	**—**	**13.0%**

Revenue History

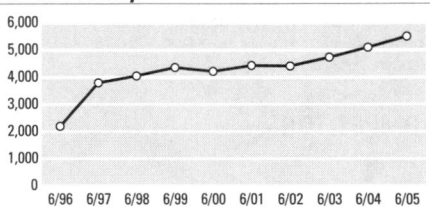

GiftCertificates.com

The folks at GiftCertificates.com pride themselves on keeping other companies' employees smiling. The firm serves its corporate clients through employee incentive and customer loyalty programs, as well as through marketing promotions. In addition, GiftCertificates.com's Web site allows customers to order gift certificates from a wide variety of airlines, boutiques, hotels, movie theaters, national and local stores, and restaurants including Blockbuster, Gap, and Williams-Sonoma. Its SuperCertificates are redeemable from all vendors represented on its site. The company, established in 1997, acquired rivals GiftSpot.com and Giftpoint.com in 2000.

EXECUTIVES

Chairman: Robert D. Stone
CEO and Director: Timothy (Tim) Barefield
EVP, Operations: Dennis Wildsmith
VP, Marketing: Jill Ambrose
VP Sales: Michael Andrews
VP, Legal and Human Resources and Chief Legal Officer: Julie A. Brooks
Auditors: KPMG

LOCATIONS

HQ: GiftCertificates.com, Inc.
315 Fifth Ave. South, Ste. 700, Seattle, WA 98104
Phone: 206-568-2500 **Fax:** 206-568-2525
Web: www.giftcertificates.com

COMPETITORS

1-800-FLOWERS.COM
Carlson
Hallmark
IncentOne
Maritz
NBO Systems
RedEnvelope

HISTORICAL FINANCIALS

Company Type: Private

Income Statement				FYE: December 31
	REVENUE ($ mil.)	NET INCOME ($ mil.)	NET PROFIT MARGIN	EMPLOYEES
12/04	100	—	—	125
12/03	95	—	—	125
12/02	70	—	—	130
12/01	53	—	—	120
12/00	45	—	—	260
12/99	10	—	—	260
12/98	3	—	—	—
12/97	0	—	—	—
Annual Growth	143.0%	—	—	(13.6%)

Revenue History

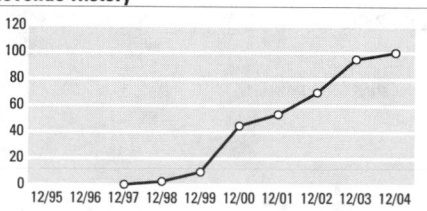

Gilbane

Family-owned Gilbane has been the bane of its rivals for four generations. Subsidiary Gilbane Building provides construction management, contracting, and design and build services to construct office buildings, manufacturing plants, schools, prisons, and more for the firm's governmental, commercial, and industrial clients. Landmark projects include work on the National Air and Space Museum, Lake Placid's 1980 Winter Olympics facilities, and the new WWII memorial in Washington, DC. Another subsidiary, Gilbane Development Company, develops and finances public and private projects and acts as a property manager. William Gilbane founded the firm in 1873.

EXECUTIVES

Chairman and CEO, Gilbane and Gilbane Building Company: Paul J. Choquette Jr., age 66
VP; President and CEO, Gilbane Properties: Robert V. Gilbane
VP; President and COO, Gilbane Building Company: William J. Gilbane Jr., age 58
VP; Chairman and CEO, Gilbane Building Company: Thomas F. Gilbane Jr., age 56
CFO and Treasurer: Ken Alderman
VP, General Counsel, and Secretary: Brad A. Gordon
Senior Business Development Manager: Karl Schon

LOCATIONS

HQ: Gilbane, Inc.
7 Jackson Walkway, Providence, RI 02903
Phone: 401-456-5800 **Fax:** 401-456-5936
Web: www.gilbaneinc.com

PRODUCTS/OPERATIONS

Selected Markets

Aviation
Corporate
Criminal justice
Cultural
Education
Government
Health care
Life sciences
Pharmaceutical
Public assembly
Recreation
Sports
Technology
Transportation

Subsidiaries

Gilbane Building Company
Gilbane Development Company

COMPETITORS

Barton Malow	KBR
BE&K	M. A. Mortenson
Bechtel	McCarthy Building
Bernards Brothers	Parsons
Bovis Lend Lease	Perini
Centex	Skanska USA Building
Clark Enterprises	Structure Tone
Fluor	Swinerton
Hunt Construction	Turner Corporation
Jacobs Engineering	Whiting-Turner

HISTORICAL FINANCIALS

Company Type: Private

Income Statement				FYE: December 31
	REVENUE ($ mil.)	NET INCOME ($ mil.)	NET PROFIT MARGIN	EMPLOYEES
12/03	2,100	—	—	1,700
12/02	2,771	—	—	1,700
12/01	2,658	—	—	1,700
12/00	2,388	—	—	1,510
12/99	2,179	—	—	900
12/98	2,200	—	—	1,200
12/97	1,923	—	—	1,148
12/96	1,848	—	—	993
12/95	1,371	—	—	1,000
12/94	1,249	—	—	958
Annual Growth	5.9%	—	—	6.6%

Revenue History

Girl Scouts USA

Choose your president wisely, because his wife is likely to become honorary president of the Girl Scouts of the United States of America. The group known for selling 200 million boxes of cookies annually is the world's largest organization for girls. All told the Girl Scouts have about 2.8 million members, not to mention 986,000 adult volunteers. It is open to girls between ages 5 and 17 and strives to build character and leadership skills through projects involving technology, sports, the environment, literacy, the arts, and the sciences. The group is part of the World Association of Girl Guides and Girl Scouts. The nation's First Lady customarily has adopted its honorary leadership.

EXECUTIVES

National Honorary President: Laura W. Bush
Chair, National Board of Directors: Patricia Diaz-Dennis
CEO: Kathy Cloninger
CFO and SVP Business Services: Florence Corsello
SVP Communications and Marketing: Courtney Shore
SVP Information and Technology: Marcia Balestrino
SVP Corporate Relations and Administration: Deborah Long
SVP Program, Membership and Research: Sharon Hussey
SVP Council Services: Carol McMillan
SVP Fund Development: Mary Lee Hoffman
SVP Human Resources: Michael Watson
Auditors: Ernst & Young LLP

LOCATIONS

HQ: Girl Scouts of the United States of America
420 5th Ave., New York, NY 10018
Phone: 212-852-8000 **Fax:** 212-852-6514
Web: www.girlscouts.org

Girl Scouts of the United States of America operates more than 236,000 troops throughout the US and in more than 80 other countries.

PRODUCTS/OPERATIONS

Girl Scout Programs
Daisy Girl Scouts (ages 5-6)
Brownie Girl Scouts (ages 6-8)
Junior Girl Scouts (ages 8-11)
Cadette Girl Scouts (ages 11-14)
Senior Girl Scouts (ages 14-17)

Best-Selling Girl Scout Cookie Flavors
Caramel deLites (Samoas)
Peanut Butter Patties (Tagalongs)
Peanut Butter Sandwich (Do-si-dos)
Shortbread (Trefoils)
Thin Mints

HISTORICAL FINANCIALS
Company Type: Not-for-profit

Income Statement
FYE: September 30

	REVENUE ($ mil.)	NET INCOME ($ mil.)	NET PROFIT MARGIN	EMPLOYEES
9/01	42	—	—	480
9/00	64	—	—	—
9/99	48	—	—	—
9/98	50	—	—	—
9/97	99	—	—	400
9/96*	82	—	—	—
9/94	43	—	—	—
9/93	43	—	—	—
Annual Growth	(0.5%)	—	—	4.7%

*Fiscal year change

Revenue History

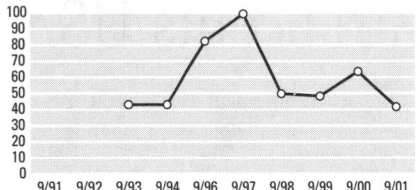

Glazer's Wholesale Drug

Glazer's Wholesale Drug, named during Prohibition when only drugstores and drug wholesalers could deal in liquor, is a wholesale distributor of alcoholic beverages. In Texas it is the largest company of its kind and one of the largest wine and spirits distributors in the US. The company distributes Robert Mondavi wines, Brown-Forman and Bacardi spirits, and Diageo products. CEO Bennett Glazer and family own Glazer's.

In 2003 Glazer's bought a 50% stake in Union Beverage Co. (a subsidiary of National Wine & Spirits, Inc.) to move distribution into Illinois. In June 2003 the company became the sole provider of Diageo brands in Dallas and Houston as part of Diageo's consolidation of its Texas distributors. Glazer's has been acquiring wholesalers and distributors in the Midwest, including Mid-Continent Distributor (Missouri). Glazer's is expanding in Oklahoma, having bought Reliance Wine & Spirits Co. It also has purchased Hirst Imports Co. In Arkansas, Glazer's is consolidating three distributors: Little Rock-Silbernagel, Barrett Hamilton, and Strauss Distributors.

EXECUTIVES
Chairman: R.L. Glazer
Chairman and CEO: Bennett Glazer
President: Jerry Cargill
EVP and COO: Barkley J. Stuart
EVP and Secretary: Mike Glazer
VP and CFO: Cary Rossel
VP and CIO: Mike Adams
VP, Operations: Jack Westenborg
VP, Business and Marketing: George Trilikis
VP, Corporate Accounts: Jim Grace
VP, Corporate Accounts: Mike Williams
VP, Corporate Strategy: Louis Zweig
VP, Human Resources and Development: Terri Lowell
VP, Logistics: Gregg Mitchell
VP, Supplier Relations: Mike Lorence

LOCATIONS
HQ: Glazer's Wholesale Drug Company, Inc.
14911 Quorum Dr., Dallas, TX 75254
Phone: 972-392-8200   **Fax:** 972-702-8508
Web: www.glazers.com

Glazer's Distributors operates in 11 US states, including Arizona, Arkansas, Illinois, Indiana, Iowa, Kansas, Louisiana, Missouri, Ohio, Oklahoma, and Texas.

COMPETITORS
Ben E. Keith
Gallo
Gambrinus
Hensley & Company
Johnson Brothers
National Distributing
National Wine & Spirits
Republic
Beverage Company
Southern Wine & Spirits
Tarrant Distributors
Wirtz

HISTORICAL FINANCIALS
Company Type: Private

Income Statement
FYE: December 31

	REVENUE ($ mil.)	NET INCOME ($ mil.)	NET PROFIT MARGIN	EMPLOYEES
12/03	2,200	—	—	5,500
12/02	1,750	—	—	3,900
12/01	1,600	—	—	3,600
12/00	1,480	—	—	3,200
12/99	1,110	—	—	2,700
12/98	855	—	—	2,700
12/97	758	—	—	2,500
12/96	670	—	—	1,850
12/95	590	—	—	1,100
12/94	520	—	—	1,000
Annual Growth	17.4%	—	—	20.9%

Revenue History

Global Secure

Fighting fires that fuel fears, Global Secure Corp. provides data management, analysis, and dissemination services for the BioWatch program for detecting airborne biological agents. It also sells software for real-time collaboration and communication between public health agencies and other federal, state, and local emergency management and homeland security professionals. Additionally, the company provides hazardous materials management services and offers training programs and customized exercises for responding to critical incidents. It also makes filtered-air respirators for protection in harmful environments. Cofounder and former director Ross Mandell and Sky Capital Enterprises own 27% of the company.

Global Secure Corp.'s largest contract is with the US Department of Defense, whereby it provides hazardous materials management services for the US Navy. The company also provides responder training for handling potential incidents involving weapons of mass destruction to the US Department of Justice, its largest training client. The US Department of Homeland Security is budgeted to be the company's largest account in 2006.

In addition to preventing and limiting the potential effects of terrorist acts, the company offers products and services that aid in natural disasters and other threats to public safety and health. It also provides equipment and training to firefighting, medical, and law enforcement communities.

Former CEO and director C. Thomas McMillen owns 12% of the company.

EXECUTIVES
Chairman: Gene W. Ray, age 67
President, CEO, and Director; President, Global Secure Safety: Craig R. Bandes, age 36, $272,500 pay
CFO and Director: Charles A. Hasper, age 50
President, Global Secure Systems: Eric D. Shaffer, age 35
President, Global Secure Training: Timothy J. Czysz, age 37, $209,539 pay
SVP, General Counsel, and Secretary: Eric S. Galler, age 41
VP, Marketing: Kay Bransford
VP, Finance and Controller: Michael Homon
VP, Business Development: Jack Sawicki
Auditors: Eisner LLP

LOCATIONS
HQ: Global Secure Corp.
2600 Virginia Ave. NW, Ste. 600,
Washington, DC 20037
Phone: 202-333-8400   **Fax:** 202-333-0082
Web: www.globalsecurecorp.com

PRODUCTS/OPERATIONS

2004 Sales

	$ mil.	% of total
Product/safety	2.6	50
Software & services/training	2.5	50
Total	**5.1**	**100**

COMPETITORS

3M	GP Strategies
3M Health Care	L-3 Titan
3M Health Care UK	Lockheed Martin
Aearo	Mine Safety Appliances
Avon Rubber	Northrop Grumman TASC
Bacou-Dalloz	SAIC
Battelle Memorial	SRA International

HISTORICAL FINANCIALS

Company Type: Private

Income Statement
FYE: June 30

	REVENUE ($ mil.)	NET INCOME ($ mil.)	NET PROFIT MARGIN	EMPLOYEES
6/04	5	(3)	—	147
6/03	1	(0)	—	—
Annual Growth	920.0%	—	—	—

2004 Year-End Financials

Debt ratio: 16.2%
Return on equity: —
Cash ($ mil.): 3
Current ratio: 1.40
Long-term debt ($ mil.): 1

Net Income History

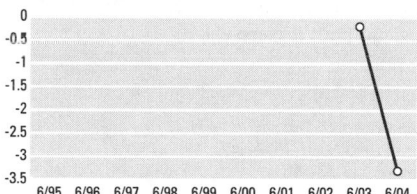

	6/95	6/96	6/97	6/98	6/99	6/00	6/01	6/02	6/03	6/04

Golden State Foods

Food processor and distributor Golden State Foods puts the gold in McDonald's golden arches. The firm provides McDonald's with more than 130 products, including beef patties, Big Mac sauce (which it helped formulate), buns, ketchup, and mayonnaise. Golden State Foods has 11 distribution centers in the US and overseas (Australia, Egypt, and Mexico) and operates two US processing plants. The company was founded in 1947 by the late William Moore. Investment firm Yucaipa owned 51% of the firm until 2004 when CEO Mark Wetterau led a management buyout of Yucaipa's shares. Wetterau Associates now owns 100% of Golden State Foods.

Golden State Foods supplies more than 2,900 McDonald's restaurants throughout the US and worldwide. McDonald's and its suppliers have established a symbiotic relationship. Golden State Foods adheres to McDonald's standards and gears its operations toward furthering the restaurant chain's interests. The company serves McDonald's without the benefit of a long-term, written contract, but McDonald's is known for its loyalty to its suppliers.

HISTORY

In 1947 William Moore founded Golden State Meat, a small meat-supply business that served restaurants and hotels in the Los Angeles area. In 1954 he added several new clients to his business — franchisees of a new chain of hamburger stands called McDonald's that was founded in San Bernardino, California in 1948. In 1961 Ray Kroc, a franchisee from Illinois, bought out the founding McDonald brothers, and the next year he moved to California to oversee a massive expansion in that state.

Moore and Kroc met, were mutually impressed, and became friends. Moore, at first, tried to get Kroc to buy him out, but Kroc's view of McDonald's did not include micromanaging its supply operations. He wanted to find suppliers the company could trust, and preferred smaller ones that weren't intent on breaking into the retail market. Golden State's relationship with McDonald's was sealed by a handshake between Kroc and Moore.

Moore and a partner bought a McDonald's franchise in 1965; two years later they had five. When Moore's partner died, McDonald's bought the units back for stock, which Moore later sold, using the proceeds to finance a new meat processing plant and warehouse. In 1969 Golden State Meat incorporated as Golden State Foods.

In 1972, after the new facilities were completed, Moore introduced the idea of total distribution. In addition to processing and distributing meat (by now delivered as frozen patties rather than fresh meat, which had limited delivery ranges in the 1950s and 1960s), Moore began supplying most of the needs of the McDonald's stores, making and delivering ketchup, mayonnaise, packaging, and syrup base for soft drinks. This allowed clients to reduce the number of weekly deliveries they received from as many as 30 to about three. The company went public in 1972, and two years later it dropped all of its other clients to cater exclusively to McDonald's.

Golden State grew in the 1970s, supplying a large share of the millions of McDonald's hamburgers sold every day. Moore died in 1978. Soon thereafter, a group of executives led by newly appointed CEO James Williams began exploring the possibility of taking the company private. In 1980, with backing from Butler Capital, they paid $29 million for the company, which then had sales of $330 million.

During the next decade Golden State expanded its relationship with McDonald's (and with the buying co-ops that supply stores operated by franchisees), opening facilities in other parts of the country. In 1990 the owners of Golden State tried to cash out by putting the company up for sale, but they withdrew it from the market within two years.

Golden State moved its headquarters from Pasadena to Irvine in 1992. In 1996 the company opened a distribution center in Portland, Oregon, and international expansion followed.

Yucaipa and Wetterau Associates, whose management hails from a major midwestern food wholesaler sold to SUPERVALU in 1992, bought Golden State in 1998 for about $400 million. The purchase represented Yucaipa's first significant acquisition outside the supermarket arena. James

Williams, who had been with Golden State Foods for 38 years and served as its CEO for more than two decades, resigned in 1999. He was replaced by Mark Wetterau, who is a partner in Wetterau Associates with his brother Conrad Wetterau.

In early 2004 investor Ron Burkle and his Yucaipa investment firm sold its 50.3% stake of Golden State for $110 million (and bought a $100 million piece of Sean John Clothing, owned by Sean "P. Diddy" Combs) to Wetterau Associates, giving Wetterau Associates 70% of the firm and its management and employees 30%.

EXECUTIVES

Chairman and CEO: Mark S. Wetterau
SEVP, Liquid Products Group: Frank Listi
EVP and CFO: Mike Waitukaitis
VP, Accounting and Information Services: Richard D. Moretti
VP, Human Resources: Steve Becker
VP, International: Phillip Crane
VP, Legal Affairs, General Counsel, and Assistant Secretary: Michael J. Hoppe Jr.
President, Distribution: Robert (Bob) Jorge
President, Meat Group: David H. Gilbert
Assistant VP, Technical Services: T. Webber Neal
Director of Development: John Walter
West Coast Director, Liquid Products: Kevin Deary
West Coast Director, Meat Operations: Lenny Goler
Manager, Human Resources, City of Industry Manufacturing Facility: Nancy Shepherd

LOCATIONS

HQ: Golden State Foods
18301 Von Karman Ave., Ste. 1100,
Irvine, CA 92612
Phone: 949-252-2000   **Fax:** 949-252-2080
Web: www.goldenstatefoods.com

Golden State Foods has distribution and processing facilities in Arizona, California, Georgia, Hawaii, New York, North Carolina, Oregon, South Carolina, Virginia, and Washington as well as Australia, Egypt, and Mexico.

PRODUCTS/OPERATIONS

Selected Products

Beef patties
Buns
Ketchup
Jelly
Lettuce
Mayonnaise
Onions
Salad dressing
Sundae toppings

COMPETITORS

Anderson-DuBose
JR Simplot
Keystone Foods
Martin-Brower
MBM
McLane Foodservice
OSI Group LLC
Reyes Holdings
Services Group
Shamrock Foods
SYSCO
U.S. Foodservice

HISTORICAL FINANCIALS

Company Type: Private

Income Statement

FYE: December 31

	ESTIMATED REVENUE ($ mil.)	NET INCOME ($ mil.)	NET PROFIT MARGIN	EMPLOYEES
12/03	2,100	—	—	2,500
12/02	1,700	—	—	2,000
12/01	1,800	—	—	2,000
12/00	1,764	—	—	2,000
12/99	1,750	—	—	2,000
12/98	1,600	—	—	1,800
12/97	1,500	—	—	2,000
12/96	1,450	—	—	2,000
12/95	1,340	—	—	1,700
12/94	1,260	—	—	1,700
Annual Growth	**5.8%**	**—**	**—**	**4.4%**

Revenue History

2,500
2,000
1,500
1,000
500
0
12/94 12/95 12/96 12/97 12/98 12/99 12/00 12/01 12/02 12/03

Golden State Warriors

The Golden State Warriors look more yellow than golden of late. The team has suffered through 10 straight losing seasons, and no end to the drought is in sight. Golden State was organized in 1946 as the Philadelphia Warriors in the Basketball Association of America. After a stint in San Francisco, the team in 1971 jumped the bay to Oakland and became the Golden State Warriors. It won the NBA Championship in 1975. The team's only real notable event in the last decade was the 1997 choking of former head coach P. J. Carlesimo by player Latrell Sprewell (who was suspended and later traded). The team is 80%-owned by former cable mogul Chris Cohan and plays in The Arena in Oakland.

EXECUTIVES

Majority Owner and Chairman: Christopher Cohan
President: Robert Rowell
EVP Basketball Operations: Chris Mullin, age 40
EVP Team Marketing: Travis Stanley
General Manager: Rod Higgins
VP and Assistant General Manager: Alvin Attles
Head Coach: Mike Montgomery, age 58
Executive Director of Business Development: Neda Kia
Executive Director of Corporate Sales and Services: Victor Pelt
Executive Director of Finance: Dwayne Redmon
Executive Director of Public Relations: Raymond Ridder
Director of Human Resources: Erika Brown

LOCATIONS

HQ: Golden State Warriors
1011 Broadway, Oakland, CA 94607
Phone: 510-986-2200   **Fax:** 510-452-0132
Web: www.nba.com/warriors

The Golden State Warriors play at the 18,500-seat The Arena in Oakland.

PRODUCTS/OPERATIONS

Championship Titles

NBA Champions (1975)
Western Conference Champions (1975)

COMPETITORS

Los Angeles Clippers   Phoenix Suns
Los Angeles Lakers   Sacramento Kings

HISTORICAL FINANCIALS

Company Type: Private

Income Statement

FYE: June 30

	REVENUE ($ mil.)	NET INCOME ($ mil.)	NET PROFIT MARGIN	EMPLOYEES
6/04	76	—	—	—
6/03	70	—	—	—
6/02	71	—	—	—
6/01	69	—	—	—
6/00	67	—	—	100
6/99	32	—	—	—
6/98	48	—	—	100
6/97	48	—	—	—
6/96	46	—	—	—
Annual Growth	**6.4%**	**—**	**—**	**0.0%**

Revenue History

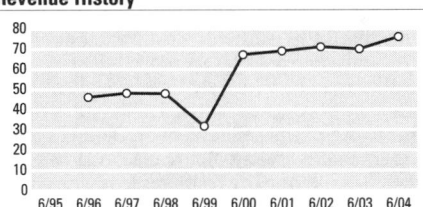

80
70
60
50
40
30
20
10
0
6/95 6/96 6/97 6/98 6/99 6/00 6/01 6/02 6/03 6/04

Golfsmith

You might not be so quick to wrap that 5-iron around a tree if you'd made it yourself. Golfsmith International began in 1967 as a mail-order seller of custom-made golf clubs, and it still teaches golfers how to craft their own irons, woods, and putters. The company sells its products through its catalogs, Web site, and nearly 50 golf superstores in the US. The company's stores — averaging about 25,000 sq. ft. — sell private-label and brand-name golf equipment, accessories, and related paraphernalia and offer such services as swing analysis. Golfsmith also operates the Harvey Penick Golf Academy, an instructional school for golfers. Atlantic Equity Partners owns the majority of the company.

Golfsmith's instructional school is named after the late Harvey Penick and incorporates the techniques of the well known golf instructor into its curriculum.

In 2003 Golfsmith purchased Don Sherwood Golf, a chain of six California golf stores. The company plans on opening between eight to 12 new superstores in 2005. Golfsmith also plans to add tennis centers in up to 60% of its stores that are located in major tennis markets during 2005. The company already operates tennis centers in Atlanta; Austin, Texas; Dallas; Denver; Houston; Orlando, Florida; and the San Francisco Bay area.

EXECUTIVES

President, CEO, and Director:
James D. (Jim) Thompson, age 42, $325,654 pay
VP and CFO: Virginia (Ginger) Bunte, age 39, $187,512 pay
VP and Chief Information Officer: Kiprian (Kip) Miles, age 43, $181,731 pay
VP, Secretary, and Director: James Grover, age 33
VP and Director: Noel E. Wilens
VP, Marketing: Matthew (Matt) Corey, age 38
VP, Merchandising: Fred Quandt, age 35, $167,981 pay
VP, Research and Development: Jeff Sheets, age 45
VP, Store Development: Romi Bodin, age 40
VP, Store Operations and Guest: Daniel Stevens, age 54
VP, Store Operations and Real Estate:
Kenneth (Ken) Brugh, age 54, $207,692 pay
VP, Supply Chain: Jerry Dent Jr., age 39
Director, Human Resources: Jan Petty
Media Relations: Andy Craig
Auditors: Ernst & Young LLP

LOCATIONS

HQ: Golfsmith International Holdings, Inc.
11000 N. IH-35, Austin, TX 78753
Phone: 512-837-4810   **Fax:** 512-837-1245
Web: www.golfsmith.com

In addition to Golfsmith's operations in Austin, Texas, the company also operates facilities in Canada and the UK.

2004 Stores

	No.
California	13
Texas	9
Illinois	4
Arizona	3
Colorado	3
Georgia	3
Michigan	3
New Jersey	2
New York	2
Connecticut	1
Florida	1
Minnesota	1
Ohio	1
Total	**46**

PRODUCTS/OPERATIONS

2004 Sales

	% of total
Superstores	69
Direct-to-consumer	29
International	2
Harvey Penick Academy	—
Total	**100**

Selected Brands

Proprietary	Non-proprietary
GearForGolf	Callaway
GiftsForGolf	Cobra
Golfsmith	FootJoy
Killer Bee	Nike
Lynx	Ping
Snake Eyes	TaylorMade
Zevo	Titleist

COMPETITORS

Academy Sports & Outdoors
Dick's Sporting Goods
Eaton
Edwin Watts Golf
Golf Galaxy
Hanover Direct
Las Vegas Golf & Tennis
MacGregor
McHenry Metals Golf
Nevada Bob's
Sports Authority

HISTORICAL FINANCIALS

Company Type: Private

Income Statement

	REVENUE ($ mil.)	NET INCOME ($ mil.)	NET PROFIT MARGIN	EMPLOYEES
12/04	296	(5)	—	1,297
12/03	258	1	0.4%	1,178
12/02	218	(2)	—	1,000
12/01	221	7	3.3%	1,021
12/00	275	—	—	1,800
12/99	285	—	—	1,600
12/98	257	—	—	1,800
12/97	180	—	—	1,500
12/96	117	—	—	653
12/95	90	—	—	398
Annual Growth	14.2%	—	—	14.0%

FYE: Last Saturday in December

2004 Year-End Financials

Debt ratio: 146.9%
Return on equity: —
Cash ($ mil.): 15
Current ratio: 1.36
Long-term debt ($ mil.): 80

Net Income History

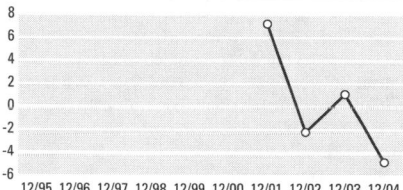

Golub

Supermarket operator The Golub Corporation offers tasty come-ons such as table-ready meals, gift certificates, automatic discount cards, and a hotline where cooks answer food-related queries. Golub operates 100-plus Price Chopper supermarkets in Connecticut, Massachusetts, New Hampshire, upstate New York, northeastern Pennsylvania, and Vermont. It also runs Mini Chopper service stations and convenience stores. Golub has discontinued its HouseCalls home delivery service. Brothers Bill and Ben Golub founded the company in 1932. The Golub family owns 45% of the firm and has turned down offers to sell it. Employees own the remaining 55% of The Golub Corp.

EXECUTIVES

Chairman: Lewis Golub
President and CEO: Neil M. Golub
CFO: John Endres
EVP and COO: Lawrence Zettle
EVP, Secretary, and General Counsel: William Kenneally
SVP, Information Systems and CIO, Price Chopper: Tom Nowak
VP and Treasurer, Price Chopper: Jennifer Kenneally
VP, Distribution: Ron Cellupica
VP, Human Resources: Margaret Davenport
VP, Merchandising Strategy: Nancy Stanton
VP, Operations: Mark E. Boucher
VP, Real Estate: Don Orlando
VP, Store Operations: David (Dave) Hepfinger
VP, Transportation: Robert Doyle
Director, Public Relations and Consumer Services: Mona J. Golub
Auditors: PricewaterhouseCoopers LLP

LOCATIONS

HQ: The Golub Corporation
501 Duanesburg Rd., Schenectady, NY 12306
Phone: 518-355-5000 **Fax:** 518-379-3515
Web: www.pricechopper.com

2005 Stores

	No.
New York	68
Massachusetts	14
Vermont	12
Pennsylvania	8
Connecticut	6
New Hampshire	1
Total	**109**

COMPETITORS

7-Eleven	Penn Traffic
A&P	Shaw's
Big Y Foods	Stop & Shop
Cumberland Farms	Tops Markets
DeMoulas Super Markets	Wal-Mart
Hannaford Bros.	Wegmans

HISTORICAL FINANCIALS

Company Type: Private

Income Statement

	ESTIMATED REVENUE ($ mil.)	NET INCOME ($ mil.)	NET PROFIT MARGIN	EMPLOYEES
4/04	2,500	—	—	22,000
4/03	2,100	—	—	20,000
4/02	2,100	—	—	19,700
4/01	2,000	—	—	19,500
4/00	1,800	—	—	18,500
4/99	1,710	—	—	18,000
4/98	1,610	—	—	18,000
4/97	1,600	—	—	17,500
4/96	1,375	—	—	15,500
4/95	1,200	—	—	9,000
Annual Growth	8.5%	—	—	10.4%

FYE: April 30

Revenue History

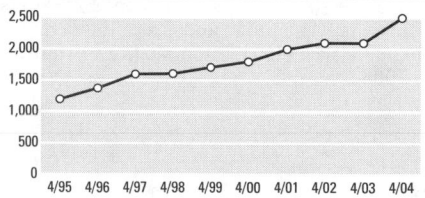

Goodwill

Founded to give those in need "a hand up, not a handout," Goodwill Industries International supports the operations of about 210 independent Goodwill chapters worldwide. Though known mainly for its some 2,000 thrift stores, Goodwill focuses on providing rehabilitation, training, placement, and employment services for those with disabilities and other barriers to employment. Goodwill is one of the world's largest providers of such services, as well as one of the world's largest employers of the physically, mentally, and emotionally disabled. Funding comes primarily from the retail stores, contract services provided to local employers, and grants.

Goodwill has chapters in Canada, South Korea, Mexico, the US, and nearly 25 other countries. It uses 84% of its funds on programs. Roughly half its revenue comes from the retails stores that carry everything from kitchenware to sporting goods and clothing to computers.

EXECUTIVES

Chairman: Edward A. Osborne
President and CEO: George W. Kessinger
VP Operations: Linda Chandler
VP Membership Support Services: John Huber
Auditors: Deloitte & Touche

LOCATIONS

HQ: Goodwill Industries International, Inc.
15810 Indianola Ave., Rockville, MD 20855
Phone: 301-530-6500 **Fax:** 301-530-1516
Web: www.goodwill.org

PRODUCTS/OPERATIONS

2004 Revenue

	$ mil.	% of total
Retail sales	1,370.0	57
Industrial & service contract work	422.1	18
Employment & training fees/government grants	356.9	15
Public support (monetary contributions)	53.0	2
Other	188.0	8
Total	**2,390.0**	**100**

HISTORICAL FINANCIALS

Company Type: Not-for-profit

Income Statement

	REVENUE ($ mil.)	NET INCOME ($ mil.)	NET PROFIT MARGIN	EMPLOYEES
12/04	2,390	—	—	—
12/03	2,210	—	—	82,370
12/02	2,055	—	—	140,023
12/01	1,940	—	—	61,766
12/00	1,850	—	—	77,895
12/99	1,650	—	—	60,000
12/98	1,507	—	—	60,000
12/97	1,361	—	—	60,000
12/96	1,200	—	—	60,679
12/95	1,038	—	—	64,403
Annual Growth	9.7%	—	—	3.1%

FYE: December 31

Revenue History

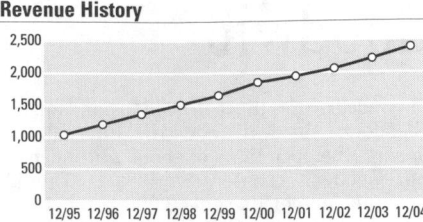

Revenue History chart (12/95–12/04), values 0 to 2,500.

Goya Foods

Whether you call 'em *frijoles* or *habichuelas*, beans are beans, and Goya's got 'em. Goya Foods produces approximately 1,200 Hispanic and Caribbean grocery items, including canned and dried beans, canned meats, fruit nectars, olives, rice, seasonings and sauces, plantain and yucca chips, and frozen entrees. It sells more than 20 rice products and 30 types of beans and peas. Brands include Goya and Canilla. It also sells beverages such as tropical fruit nectars and juices, tropical sodas, and coffee. Goya is owned by one of the richest Hispanic *familias* in the US, the Unanues, which founded the company in 1936.

Goya has historically served the Hispanic communities in the Northeast and Florida with mostly Cuban, Dominican, and Puerto Rican customers. The company now has products geared toward the tastes of Hispanics in California and the Southwest with roots in Mexico and Central and South America. A growing taste for ethnic foods across the US has fueled Goya's growth beyond its Hispanic roots. In addition, its "all-in-one-aisle" product placement in food stores has proven very successful.

Continued growth at Goya is evidenced by the fact that the company announced a plan in 2005 to expand its distribution space by 1 million sq. ft. Part of this plan includes operations in Virginia and Texas.

However, the company still faces competition from food giants such as Kraft Foods, which have lines of Hispanic specialty products. It's also challenged by food manufacturers from Mexico who are turning north to tap the pocketbooks of US consumers. Goya is one of the largest Hispanic-owned companies in the US.

HISTORY

Immigrants from Spain by way of Puerto Rico, husband and wife Prudencio Unanue and Carolina Casal founded Unanue & Sons in New York City in 1936. The couple imported sardines, olives, and olive oil from Spain, but when the Spanish Civil War (1936-1939) interrupted supply lines, they began importing from Morocco.

In 1949 the company established a cannery in Puerto Rico; the Puerto Rican imports were distributed to local immigrants from the West Indies. Each of the couple's four sons eventually joined the family business, and in 1958 the firm relocated to Brooklyn. The company took its current name, Goya Foods, in 1962 when the family bought the Goya name — originally a brand of sardines — for $1.

The oldest Unanue son, CEO Charles, was fired from Goya in 1969 — and subsequently cut out of Prudencio's will — when he spoke out about

an alleged tax evasion scheme. (Legal wrangling between Charles and the rest of the family continued into the late 1990s.) Goya moved to its present New Jersey headquarters in 1974.

Another son, Anthony, died in 1976, as did Prudencio. That year Joseph, another sibling, was named president and CEO. Along with his brother Francisco (Frank), president of Goya Foods de Puerto Rico, he began a cautious expansion campaign by adding traditional products to the company's existing line of Latin Caribbean and Spanish favorites.

Buoyed by the growing popularity of Mexican food, in 1982 Goya began distributing its products in Texas, targeting the region's sizable Mexican and Central American population. At first, the move proved a disaster. Goya's products were not suited to the Mexican palate, which generally preferred spicier food. Likewise, a similar strategy to capture a portion of Florida's huge Cuban market share initially met with only moderate success, but Goya persevered, eventually turning the tables in its favor.

During the 1980s the company also attempted to woo the non-Hispanic market. While Goya's cream of coconut — a key ingredient in piña coladas — found a broader market, its ad campaign featuring obscure actress Zohra Lampert did little to attract a large following of non-Hispanic customers.

Success in that market came in the 1990s. America's interest in the reportedly healthier "Mediterranean diet" boosted sales of Goya's extra-virgin olive oil. Recommendations for low-fat, high-fiber diets prompted the company's launch of the "For Better Meals, Turn to Goya" advertising campaign — its first in English — in 1992.

Three years later the company released a line of juice-based beverages. In 1996 Goya sponsored an exhibition of the works of the Spanish master Goya at the New York Metropolitan Museum of Art. Continuing its efforts to reach out to non-Hispanics and English-dominant Hispanics, in 1997 the company began including both English and Spanish on the front of its packaging.

To lure more snackers, the next year Goya added yucca (a.k.a. cassava) chips to its line. In 1999 Goya began packaging its frozen entrees in microwaveable trays. In 2001 it bought a new factory in Spain.

In 2002 Goya added 12 flavors (including guava, mandarin orange, and tamarind) to its line of Refresco Goya Fruit Sodas, thus joining the beverage industry trend toward offering more diverse flavors. In 2002, the president of the company's Puerto Rican division, Francisco J. Unanue, died.

In 2004 long-time chairman, CEO, and president Joseph Unanue and his son, COO Andy Unanue, were forced out of family-owned Goya by Joseph's two nephews, Robert I. and Francisco R. Unanue. Robert is now president and Francisco took over the Florida division of the company. Lawsuits to regain control of the company filed by Joseph followed but were eventually dropped.

In order to handle its expansion in Arkansas, Louisiana, Oklahoma, and Texas, the company opened a new distribution facility in Houston in 2005.

EXECUTIVES

President: Robert I. (Bob) Unanue
VP, Logistics: Peter Unanue
VP, MIS: David Kinkela
VP, Purchasing: Joseph Perez
VP, Sales & Marketing: Conrad O. Colon
VP and General Manager, Goya Foods Puerto Rico: Carlos Unanue
VP, Operatons Goya Foods Puerto Rico: Jorge Unanue
Director, Finance: Miguel Lugo
Director, Human Resources: Tony Rico
Director, Public Relations: Rafael Toro
Director, Purchasing Goya Foods Florida: Tom Unanue
Director, Sales: John Hernandez
Controller: Tony Diaz
General Manager, Goya Foods Great Lakes: Robert Drago
General Manager, Goya Foods Texas: Evelio Fernandez
General Manager, Production: Benjamin Spinnickie
General Counsel: Carlos Ortiz
Assistant, Public Relations: Jeanette Ojeda

LOCATIONS

HQ: Goya Foods, Inc.
100 Seaview Dr., Secaucus, NJ 07096
Phone: 201-348-4900   **Fax:** 201-348-6609
Web: www.goya.com

Goya has 13 plants located in the Dominican Republic, Puerto Rico, Spain, and the US.

PRODUCTS/OPERATIONS

Selected Products

Beverages
  Café Goya
  Coconut Water
  Malta (malt beverage)
  Nectars and juices (apple, apricot, banana, guanabana, guava, mango, passion fruit, papaya, peach, pear, pear/passion, pineapple, pineapple/guava, pineapple/passion, strawberry, strawberry/banana, tamarind, tropical fruit punch)
  Tropical sodas (apple, coconut, cola champagne, fruit punch, ginger beer, grape, guaraná, guava, lemon lime, mandarin orange, pineapple, strawberry, tamarind)
Foods & Other Products
  Beans (black-eyed peas, chick peas, lentils, refried)
  Bouillon
  Cooking sauces
  Cooking wine
  Cornmeal
  Devotional candles
  Flour
  Frozen foods
  Marinades
  Meat (chorizo, corned beef, potted, Vienna sausage)
  Olive oil
  Olives
  Pasta
  Plantain chips
  Rice
  Seafood
  Seasonings
  Spices
  Yucca chips

COMPETITORS

American Rice	Hormel
Authentic Specialty Foods	Kraft Foods
Bimbo	La Tortilla Factory
Casa de Oro Foods	McCormick
Chiquita Brands	Nestlé
ConAgra	Ole' Mexican Foods
Del Monte Foods	Pro-Fac
Dole Food	Reser's
Don Miguel Mexican Foods	Riceland Foods
El Dorado Mexican Food	Riviana Foods
Products	Ruiz Mexican Foods
Frito-Lay	Seneca Foods
Herdez	Unilever

HISTORICAL FINANCIALS

Company Type: Private

Income Statement

FYE: May 31

	REVENUE ($ mil.)	NET INCOME ($ mil.)	NET PROFIT MARGIN	EMPLOYEES
5/04	850	—	—	2,500
5/03	750	—	—	2,500
5/02	750	—	—	2,500
5/01	715	—	—	2,500
5/00	695	—	—	2,500
5/99	653	—	—	2,200
5/98	620	—	—	3,000
5/97	600	—	—	3,000
5/96	560	—	—	2,200
5/95	528	—	—	2,000
Annual Growth	**5.4%**	**—**	**—**	**2.5%**

Revenue History

(Graph: Revenue rising from ~520 in 5/95 to ~850 in 5/04, y-axis 0–900, x-axis 5/95 through 5/04)

Graham Packaging

Grocery stockers and mechanics handle Graham Packaging's products every day. The company makes blow-molded plastic containers for food and beverages, automotive lubricants, household products, and personal care and specialty products. Major customers include PepsiCo, which accounts for about 15% of sales, and Danone, which accounts for about 10%. Graham Packaging operates some 90 manufacturing plants, about 30% of which are located on the grounds of its customers' production facilities. Investment firm Blackstone Group owns a controlling stake in Graham Packaging.

In 2004 Graham Packaging doubled its size by buying blow-molded plastic container operations in North America, South America, and Europe from glass manufacturing giant Owens-Illinois for about $1.2 billion. Graham Packaging hopes this transaction will solidify its presence as one of the global leaders in plastic packaging.

The next year Graham Packaging agreed to buy four blow-molded plastic container plants from Sweden's Tetra Pak.

EXECUTIVES

Chairman and CEO: Philip R. Yates, age 57, $1,670,143 pay
President and COO: Roger M. Prevot, age 46, $1,149,535 pay
CFO: John E. Hamilton, age 46, $750,586 pay
SVP and General Manager, North America Automotive and South America: G. Robinson Beeson, age 56, $436,707 pay
SVP and General Manager, Global Food and Beverage: Ashok Sudan, age 51, $591,511 pay
SVP, Global People Resources: George Lane

VP and General Manager, Personal Care/Specialty: David L. Andrulonis, age 47
VP and General Manager, Household: Peter T. Lennox, age 42
VP, Finance and Administration: Jay W. Hereford, age 54
Investor Relations: Mark Leiden
Auditors: Deloitte & Touche LLP

LOCATIONS

HQ: Graham Packaging Holdings Company
2401 Pleasant Valley Rd., York, PA 17402
Phone: 717-849-8500   **Fax:** 717-848-4836
Web: www.grahampackaging.com

Graham Packaging has manufacturing facilities in Argentina, Belgium, Brazil, Canada, Ecuador, Finland, France, Hungary, Mexico, the Netherlands, Poland, Spain, Turkey, the UK, the US, and Venezuela.

2004 Sales

	$ mil.	% of total
North America	1,136.5	84
Europe	173.4	13
South America	43.6	3
Adjustments	(0.5)	—
Total	**1,353.0**	**100**

PRODUCTS/OPERATIONS

2004 Sales

	$ mil.	% of total
Food & beverage	769.9	57
Automotive lubricants	274.0	20
Household	240.6	18
Personal care & specialty	68.5	5
Total	**1,353.0**	**100**

COMPETITORS

Amcor	Constar International
Ball Corporation	Plastipak Holdings, Inc.
Consolidated Container	Silgan

HISTORICAL FINANCIALS

Company Type: Private

Income Statement

FYE: December 31

	REVENUE ($ mil.)	NET INCOME ($ mil.)	NET PROFIT MARGIN	EMPLOYEES
12/04	1,353	(41)	—	8,600
12/03	979	10	1.0%	3,900
12/02	907	8	0.8%	3,900
12/01	923	(44)	—	4,100
12/00	825	(46)	—	4,000
12/99	716	1	0.2%	4,000
12/98	588	(28)	—	—
12/97	522	11	2.0%	—
12/96	460	21	4.6%	—
12/95	467	19	4.0%	—
Annual Growth	**12.6%**	**—**	**—**	**16.5%**

2004 Year-End Financials

Debt ratio: —
Return on equity: —
Cash ($ mil.): 22
Current ratio: 1.62
Long-term debt ($ mil.): 2,440

Net Income History

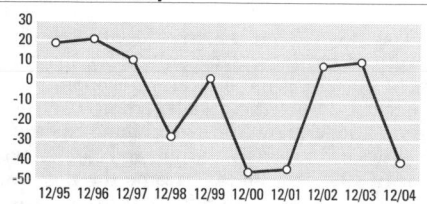

(Graph: Net income history, y-axis -50 to 30, x-axis 12/95 through 12/04)

Grande Communications

Grande Communications' grand vision is to become a big player in the Texas telecommunications arena. By building its own fiber-optic network and bundling telephone services, Internet access, and cable TV into one package, the company hopes it can grab market share from incumbent cable and telecom providers. Grande Communications also provides wholesale communications services to other telecoms and ISPs.

The company has operations in Austin-San Marcos, Corpus Christi, Dallas, Midland-Odessa, San Antonio, and Waco. Grande's investors include Whitney & Co. (23%), The Centennial Funds (22%), and Austin Ventures (7%).

Grande Communications expanded with the acquisition of broadband services provider ClearSource and it expanded its fiber-optic network by purchasing assets from utility firms that are exiting the telecommunications market. These acquisitions include 3,000 fiber-miles of network from C3 Communications, a unit of America Electric Power (AEP). This purchase expands the company's network from the Rio Grande Valley of south Texas to parts of Oklahoma, Arkansas, and Louisiana, and connects Texas' major markets, including Houston, Dallas, Austin, San Antonio, and Corpus Christi. The company also has acquired telecom properties from TXU and has agreed to acquire Advantex Communications, which operates in the Dallas area.

Grande Communications got a jump-start on its operations in 2000 with the purchase of San Marcos, Texas-based integrated network services provider Thrifty Call.

EXECUTIVES

Chairman: James M. Mansour, age 46
Interim President and CEO: W.K.L. (Scott) Ferguson Jr., age 45
Special Counsel to The President: Joe C. Ross, age 35
CFO: Michael L. (Mike) Wilfley, age 48, $258,704 pay
EVP Corporate Policy and Services: Martha E. Smiley, age 56, $258,455 pay
EVP Network Services: Stephen M. Wagner
General Counsel: Andy Sarwal
VP Network Services: Jared P. Benson
VP People and Culture: Kay Stroman
VP Retail Sales and Marketing: Eileen Bustamante-Kret
Treasurer: Douglas T. (Doug) Brannagan
Auditors: Ernst & Young LLP

LOCATIONS

HQ: Grande Communications Holdings, Inc.
401 Carlson Circle, San Marcos, TX 78666
Phone: 512-878-4000   **Fax:** 512-878-4010
Web: www.grandecom.com

Selected Services

Broadband Internet access
Cable TV
Local telephone access
Long-distance
Network services
  Data services
  Managed services
  Switched carrier services
Wholesale services

HISTORICAL FINANCIALS

Company Type: Private

Income Statement
FYE: December 31

	REVENUE ($ mil.)	NET INCOME ($ mil.)	NET PROFIT MARGIN	EMPLOYEES
12/04	179	(55)	—	873
12/03	182	(38)	—	811
12/02	147	(29)	—	700
12/01	96	(27)	—	490
Annual Growth	23.0%	—	—	21.2%

2004 Year-End Financials

Debt ratio: 36.7%
Return on equity: —
Cash ($ mil.): 41

Current ratio: 2.08
Long-term debt ($ mil.): 128

Net Income History

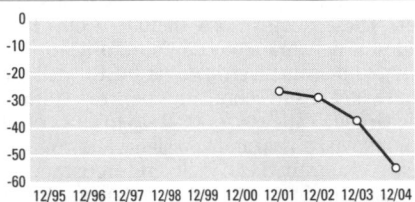

| | 12/95 | 12/96 | 12/97 | 12/98 | 12/99 | 12/00 | 12/01 | 12/02 | 12/03 | 12/04 |

Grant Thornton International

Grant Thornton International is a kid brother to the Big Four. The umbrella organization of accounting and management consulting firms operates from nearly 600 offices in 109 countries worldwide, making it one of the top second-tier companies that trail around behind the biggest of the big guys (Deloitte Touche Tohmatsu, Ernst & Young International, KPMG International, and PricewaterhouseCoopers). Grant Thornton International's member firms elect representatives to an international policy board that runs the day-to-day operations of the accounting company.

Industry consolidation prompted Grant Thornton International and other second-tier firms to enter such niche areas as information technology and corporate finance. And while the Big Four focus on large corporations, Grant Thornton locks in on owner-managed companies, helping them with accounting, audit, and tax issues, as well as growth strategies. It is facing new competitors for its target market; such firms as H&R Block and American Express have been adding accounting, tax planning, and consulting services.

With the lowering of trade barriers in Latin America and Europe, Grant Thornton has been focusing on developing business in emerging markets. Member firms have been working to increase cross-border cooperation by pooling resources and cutting costs. The organization also

helped pick up the pieces as Andersen crumbled, acquiring employees, offices, and clients from the felled giant.

Like Andersen before it, Grant Thornton felt the red-hot glare of unwanted media attention as Italian food giant Parmalat (a former auditing client) fell into bankruptcy amidst an Enron-style scandal in late 2003. Grant Thornton's Italian unit had remained the auditor for Parmalat subsidiary Bonlat, which played a central role in the unfolding scandal. The Italian affiliate, which has been expelled from Grant Thornton's global network, maintains it was a victim of fraud in the case. Parmalat in 2004 filed suit against the Italian accountancy, claiming two of its partners were involved in the fraud; the two also face criminal charges.

HISTORY

Cameron, Missouri accountant Alexander Grant founded Alexander Grant & Co. in 1924 with William O'Brien. They built their firm in Chicago and concentrated on providing services to midwestern clients.

In the 1950s and 1960s, the firm began expanding both domestically and internationally. Alexander Grant & Co. continued to focus on manufacturing and distribution companies.

In 1973 O'Brien died. In 1979 the company began publishing its well-known (and sometimes controversial) index of state business climates. An attempt to merge with fellow second-tier accounting firm Laventhol & Horwath failed that year. The next year Grant Thornton International was formed when Alexander Grant & Co. and its British affiliate, Thornton Baker, combined their offices around the world to form a network. The UK and US branches, however, kept their respective names.

The 1980s brought turmoil and change for the firm. Financial scandals led investors and the government to hold accounting firms liable for their audits. Along with the (then) Big Six, Alexander Grant & Co. was hit with several lawsuits alleging fraud and cover-ups. One case marred the firm's squeaky-clean image and caused dozens of clients to jump ship: Just days after Alexander Grant issued it a clean audit, a Florida trading firm was shut down by the SEC. Jilted investors sued to reclaim lost money; Alexander Grant settled for $160 million. Chairman Herbert Dooskin and other leaders also left the company; although they denied it was because of the scandal, their departures left Alexander Grant rudderless during a critical time.

Meanwhile, the company merged with Fox & Co. to create the US's #9 accounting firm. With scandal-scared partners leaving (and taking clients), Fox looked to the merger to shore up its reputation. But Alexander Grant's auditing troubles led some Fox partners and clients to flee from the merged company.

After the fallout from the lawsuits and the merger, the company began rebuilding, taking on new clients, reclaiming lost ones, and refocusing on midsized companies. In 1986 both Alexander Grant & Co. and Thornton Baker took the Grant Thornton name.

The early 1990s recession reduced accounting revenues but increased demand for management consulting. As political and economic barriers fell during the decade, Grant Thornton International grew. The firm entered emerging markets in Africa, Asia, Europe, and Latin America. In 1998 the Big Six became the Big Five; Grant Thornton added refugee firms and part-

ners to its global network. In 1999 the firm's US branch entertained merger offers from H&R Block and PricewaterhouseCoopers, but instead announced plans to reposition itself as a corporate services firm to better compete.

In 2000 the company pulled out of its advisory position to companies involved in controversial diamond mining in war-torn portions of Africa. It also agreed to merge its UK operations with those of HLB Kidsons; the merged firm retained the Grant Thornton name.

The following year, after disagreements about strategy, US CEO Dom Esposito resigned. UK partner David McDonnell was named the global CEO. In 2002, Grant Thornton grew by picking up pieces of Andersen that fell away as a result of the Enron scandal. Andersen's fall also winnowed out Grant Thornton's competitors (at least in the numeric sense), as the Big Five became the Big Four.

EXECUTIVES

Global CEO: David C. McDonnell
Divisional Director, Asia Pacific: Gabriel Azedo
Divisional Director, Europe, Middle East and Africa: Sören Carlsson
Divisional Director, The Americas: Bob Leavy
Worldwide Director, Audit and Risk Management: Barry Barber
International Director, Corporate Finance: David Spence
International Director, Development: Paul Andrews
International Director, Marketing Communication: Sue Palmer
Director, Client Service, Grant Thornton Corporate Finance: Tim Blois
Director, International Financial Reporting: April Mackenzie
Director, Human Resources, Grant Thornton LLP: Jill Osborn
Head of International and European Services: Andrew Godfrey
Head of Client Service, Recovery and Reorganization: Mark Byers

LOCATIONS

HQ: Grant Thornton International
175 W. Jackson Blvd., Chicago, IL 60604
Phone: 312-856-0001   **Fax:** 312-565-4719
Web: www.gti.org

Grant Thornton International has offices in about 110 countries worldwide

2004 Locations

	No.
Europe, Middle East & Africa	279
Americas	224
Asia Pacific	94
Total	**597**

PRODUCTS/OPERATIONS

Selected Services

Assurance
Corporate finance
Corporate recovery and business reorganization
International tax
PRIMA (people and relationship issues in management)

COMPETITORS

American Express Tax and Business Services
Baker Tilly International
BDO International
Deloitte
Ernst & Young
H&R Block
KPMG

McGladrey & Pullen
McKinsey & Company
Moore Stephens International
Moores Rowland
PricewaterhouseCoopers
RSM McGladrey

HISTORICAL FINANCIALS

Company Type: Not-for-profit

Income Statement

FYE: July 31

	REVENUE ($ mil.)	NET INCOME ($ mil.)	NET PROFIT MARGIN	EMPLOYEES
7/03	2,000	—	—	21,500
7/02	1,840	—	—	21,500
7/01	1,700	—	—	21,879
7/00	1,690	—	—	20,300
7/99	1,800	—	—	20,000
7/98	1,600	—	—	20,160
7/97	1,405	—	—	18,562
7/96	1,285	—	—	18,300
Annual Growth	6.5%	—	—	2.3%

Revenue History

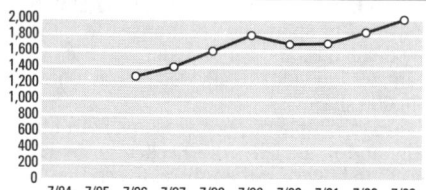

Graybar Electric

There's no gray area when it comes to describing Graybar Electric's main business: it's one of the largest distributors of electrical products in the US. Purchasing from thousands of manufacturers, the employee-owned company distributes nearly 1 million types of electrical and communications components, including wire, cable, and lighting products. Its customers include electrical contractors, industrial plants, power utilities, and telecommunications providers. Subsidiary Graybar Financial Services offers equipment leasing and financing, as well as complete project funding.

Graybar maintains distribution networks — each comprising a main facility and supporting branch locations — in 13 regional districts throughout the US. Its distribution facilities are supported by 14 warehouses. Graybar's largest group of customers, electrical contractors, account for 45% of the company's sales.

To help bring supply, distribution, and inventory costs down, the company uses electronic data interchange and supplier-assisted inventory management. Graybar has looked to new technologies to streamline its supply chain. In 2004 the company completed a multi-year project to implement an enterprise resource planning (ERP) system that links its entire network of warehouses and distribution facilities.

HISTORY

After serving as a telegrapher during the Civil War, Enos Barton borrowed $400 from his widowed mother in 1869 and started an electrical equipment shop in Cleveland with George Shawk. Later that year Elisha Gray, a professor of physics at Oberlin College who had several inventions (including a printing telegraph) to his credit, bought Shawk's interest in the shop, and

the firm moved to Chicago, where a third partner joined.

The company incorporated as the Western Electric Manufacturing Co. in 1872, with two-thirds of the company's stock held by two Western Union executives. As the telegraph industry took off, the enterprise grew rapidly, providing equipment to towns and railroads in the western US.

Gray and his company missed receiving credit for inventing the telephone in 1875 when Gray's patent application for a "harmonic telegraph" reached the US Patent Office a few hours after Bell's application for his telephone. However, the telephone and the invention of the light bulb in 1879 opened new doors for Western Electric. The company began to grow into a major corporation, selling and distributing a variety of electrical equipment, including batteries, telegraph keys, and fire-alarm boxes. By 1900 the firm was the world's #1 maker of telephone equipment.

Western Electric formed a new distribution business in 1926, Graybar Electric Co. (from "Gray" and "Barton"), the world's largest electrical supply merchandiser. In 1929 employees bought the company from Western Electric for $3 million in cash and $6 million in preferred stock. During the 1930s it marketed a line of appliances and sewing machines under the Graybar name.

In 1941 the company bought the outstanding shares of stock from Western Electric for $1 million. Graybar Electric was a vital link between manufacturers and US defense needs during WWII. Its men and equipment wired the Panama Canal with telephone cable; it also helped the US military during the Korean conflict and the Vietnam War.

By 1980 Graybar Electric had reached nearly $1.5 billion in sales. Business was hurt when construction slowed in the late 1980s and the early 1990s, and the company reorganized in 1991, closing regional offices and cutting jobs. Rebounding in 1992 as the US economy improved, Graybar acquired New Jersey-based Square Electric Co.

In 1994 the company acquired a minority interest in R.E.D. Electronics, a Canadian data communications and computer networking company, and realigned its operations into two business segments: electrical products and communications and data products.

In 1995 Graybar Electric formed the Solutions Providers Alliance with wholesale distributors Kaman Industrial Technologies, VWR Scientific Products, and Vallen Corporation. In 1996 AT&T's Global Procurement Group named the company as one of only three suppliers for its electrical products. The next year Graybar Electric upped its stake in one of its Canadian operations, Harris & Roome Supply Limited.

Graybar Electric in 1998 opened a subsidiary in Chile and formed a joint venture, Graybar Financial Services, with Newcourt Financial (formerly AT&T Capital). The next year Graybar Electric bought the Connecticut-based electrical wholesaler Frank A. Blesso, Inc., and it expanded its distribution partnership with wire and cable manufacturer Belden Electronics in 2000.

In 2001 Graybar opened a new distribution location in northeastern Pennsylvania. The following year Graybar increased its presence in the telecommunications industry when it inked a deal to distribute products made by Copper Mountain Networks, a US-based broadband equipment manufacturer.

EXECUTIVES

Chairman, President, and CEO: Robert A. Reynolds Jr., age 56, $897,019 pay
SVP, CFO, and Director: D. Beatty D'Alessandro, age 44
SVP, Sales and Distribution and Director: Dennis E. DeSousa, age 46, $380,624 pay
SVP, Electrical Business and Director: Charles R. Udell, age 60, $322,113 pay
SVP, Operations and Director: Lawrence R. (Larry) Giglio, age 50, $341,250 pay
SVP, Sales and Marketing and Director: Richard D. Offenbacher, age 54
VP, Secretary, General Counsel, and Director: Thomas F. Dowd, age 61, $354,051 pay
VP, Human Resources and Strategic Planning and Director: Kathleen M. Mazzarella, age 45
VP, Human Resources and Director: Jack F. Van Pelt, age 66, $333,132 pay
President and CEO, Graybar Electric Canada and Director: F. H. Hughes
Commercial Market Manager: Bob Weiland
VP and Controller: Martin J. Beagen, age 48
Auditors: Ernst & Young LLP

LOCATIONS

HQ: Graybar Electric Company, Inc.
34 N. Meramec Ave., St. Louis, MO 63105
Phone: 314-512-9200 **Fax:** 314-573-9455
Web: www.graybar.com

Graybar Electric Company has distribution facilities in Canada, Mexico, Puerto Rico, and the US.

PRODUCTS/OPERATIONS

2004 Sales by Customer

	% of total
Electrical contractors	45
Commercial & industrial	22
Voice & data communications	21
Other	12
Total	**100**

Selected Products

Ballasts	Industrial fans
Batteries	Lighting
Cable	Lubricants
Conduit	Paints
Connectors	Patch cords
Emergency lighting	Smoke detectors
Enclosures	Testing and measuring
Fiber optic cable	instruments
Fittings	Timers
Fluorescent lighting	Transfer switches
Fuses	Transformers
Hand tools	Utility products
Hangers/fasteners	Wire
Heating and ventilating equipment	

COMPETITORS

Agilysys	Premier Farnell
Anixter International	Rexel, Inc.
Communications Supply	Siemens
Consolidated Electrical	Sonepar USA
Cooper Industries	SPX
Eaton	SUMMIT Electric Supply
Emerson Electric	Tech Data
GE Supply	Tyco
Hagemeyer	WESCO International
Matsushita	W.W. Grainger
Molex	

HISTORICAL FINANCIALS

Company Type: Private

Income Statement

FYE: December 31

	REVENUE ($ mil.)	NET INCOME ($ mil.)	NET PROFIT MARGIN	EMPLOYEES
12/04	4,080	14	0.3%	7,700
12/03	3,803	9	0.2%	7,900
12/02	3,975	11	0.3%	8,300
12/01	4,815	32	0.7%	9,800
12/00	5,214	66	1.3%	10,500
12/99	4,300	65	1.5%	8,900
12/98	3,744	60	1.6%	7,900
12/97	3,338	53	1.6%	7,200
12/96	2,991	45	1.5%	6,600
12/95	2,765	37	1.3%	6,200
Annual Growth	4.4%	(10.2%)	—	2.4%

2004 Year-End Financials

Debt ratio: 52.4%
Return on equity: 3.6%
Cash ($ mil.): 10
Current ratio: 1.54
Long-term debt ($ mil.): 206

Net Income History

70 60 50 40 30 20 10 0

12/95 12/96 12/97 12/98 12/99 12/00 12/01 12/02 12/03 12/04

Great Western Bancorporation

Great Western Bancorporation (formerly Spectrum Bancorporation) is the holding company for Great Western Bank, which has more than 70 offices in Nebraska, South Dakota, southern Iowa, northern Missouri, and Kansas.

In addition to checking, savings, and individual retirement acccounts the bank offers loans for consumers and businesses. Commercial and agricultural loans make up more than 80% of the bank's loan portfolio. Great Western also offers insurance, trust, and investment services through affiliate Spectrum Capital.

Chairman and founder Deryl Hamann and his family own a majority of Great Western Bancorporation. Founded in 1907, Great Western Bank is one of the largest privately-owned banks in Nebraska.

EXECUTIVES

Chairman and CEO: Deryl F. Hamann, age 71, $711,947 pay
President and COO: Daniel A. Hamann, age 46, $368,500 pay
CFO, Secretary, and Treasurer: James R. Clark, age 53, $176,833 pay
EVP; President and CEO, Great Western Bank, Omaha: Daniel J. Brabec, age 45, $410,078 pay
SVP and Assistant Sercretary; President, Spectrum Financial Services: Thomas B. Fischer, age 57
Auditors: BKD, LLP

LOCATIONS

HQ: Great Western Bancorporation, Inc.
10834 Old Mill Rd., Ste. 1, Omaha, NE 68154
Phone: 402-333-8330   **Fax:** 402-333-8339
Web: www.greatwesternbank.com

PRODUCTS/OPERATIONS

2005 Sales

	$ mil.	% of total
Interest		
Loans	130.2	74
Securities	14.2	8
Other	0.9	1
Noninterest		
Service charges & other fees	18.0	10
Net gains from sales of loans	3.8	2
Trust department income	2.2	1
Insurance commissions	1.7	1
Other	5.6	3
Total	**176.6**	**100**

COMPETITORS

Commercial Federal
First National of Nebraska
Pinnacle Bancorp
TierOne
U.S. Bancorp
Wells Fargo

HISTORICAL FINANCIALS

Company Type: Private

Income Statement

FYE: June 30

	ASSETS ($ mil.)	NET INCOME ($ mil.)	INCOME AS % OF ASSETS	EMPLOYEES
6/05	2,740	30	1.1%	883
6/04	2,430	25	1.0%	793
6/03	2,148	16	0.7%	—
Annual Growth	12.9%	37.4%	—	11.3%

2005 Year-End Financials

Equity as % of assets: 5.8%
Return on assets: 1.2%
Return on equity: 20.1%
Long-term debt ($ mil.): 316
Sales ($ mil.): 177

Net Income History

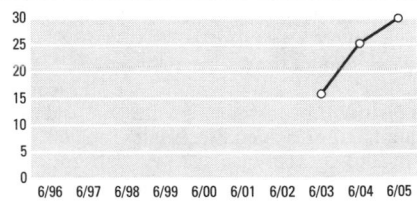

30 25 20 15 10 5 0

6/96 6/97 6/98 6/99 6/00 6/01 6/02 6/03 6/04 6/05

Green Bay Packers

On the frozen tundra of Lambeau Field, the Green Bay Packers battle for pride in the National Football League. The team, founded in 1919 by Earl "Curly" Lambeau, has been home to such football icons as Bart Starr, Ray Nitschke, and legendary coach Vince Lombardi. Current head cheeses include coach Mike Sherman and quarterback Brett Favre. The Packers boast a record 12 championship titles, including three Super Bowl victories. The team is also the NFL's only community-owned franchise, being a not-for-profit corporation with about 111,500 shareholders. The shares do not increase in value nor pay dividends, and can only be sold back to the team. No individual is allowed to own more than 200,000 shares.

After a couple of poor seasons, both athletically and financially, the Packers organization has high hopes for the future. Green Bay voters approved public financing for a $295 million renovation of historic Lambeau Field (which the city owns) in 2000, and the completed project added 10,000 seats to the stadium as well as additional luxury suites. The team's waiting list for season tickets boasts more than 56,000 names. Further proof of the team's popularity is its perch on top of the merchandise sales charts for the NFL at $17 million per year.

HISTORY

In 1919 Earl "Curly" Lambeau helped organize a professional football team in Green Bay, Wisconsin, with the help of George Calhoun, the sports editor of the *Green Bay Press-Gazette*. At 20 years old, Lambeau was elected team captain and convinced the Indian Packing Company to back the team, giving the squad its original name, the Indians. The local paper, however, nicknamed the team the Packers and the name stuck. Playing on an open field at Hagemeister Park, the team collected fees by passing the hat among the fans. In 1921 the team was admitted into the American Professional Football Association (later called the National Football League), which had been organized the year before.

The Packers went bankrupt after a poor showing its first season in the league and Lambeau and Calhoun bought the team for $250. With debts continuing to mount, *Press-Gazette* general manager Andrew Turnbull helped reorganize the team as the not-for-profit Green Bay Football Corporation and sold stock at $5 a share. Despite winning three straight championships from 1929-31, the team again teetered on the brink of bankruptcy, forcing another stock sale in 1935. With fortunes on and off the field dwindling, Lambeau retired in 1950 after leading the team to six NFL championships (prior to the creation of the Super Bowl which pitted the NFL against rival American Football League). A third stock sale was called for that year, raising $118,000. City Stadium (renamed Lambeau Field in 1965) was opened in 1957. In 1959 the team hired New York Giants assistant Vince Lombardi as head coach.

Under Lombardi, the Packers dominated football in the 1960s, winning five NFL titles. With players such as Bart Starr and Ray Nitschke, the team defeated the Kansas City Chiefs in the first

Super Bowl after the 1966 season. Lombardi resigned after winning Super Bowl II and five NFL championships. He died in 1970 and football commissioner Pete Rozelle named the Super Bowl championship trophy the Vince Lombardi trophy. But the team again fell into mediocrity. Former MVP Starr was called upon to coach in 1974 but couldn't turn the tide before he was released in 1983.

Bob Harlan, who had joined the Packers as assistant general manager in 1971, became president and CEO in 1989. He hired Ron Wolf as general manager in 1991, who in turn hired Mike Holmgren as head coach early the next year. With a roster including Brett Favre, Reggie White, and Robert Brooks, the Packers posted six straight playoff appearances and won its third Super Bowl in 1997. A fourth stock sale (preceded by a 1,000:1 stock split) netted the team more than $24 million.

After Holmgren resigned in 1999 (he left to coach the Seattle Seahawks), former Philadelphia Eagles coach Ray Rhodes tried to lead the team but lasted only one dismal season. In 2000 Mike Sherman, a former Holmgren assistant, was named the team's 13th head coach. Prompted by falling revenue, the team announced plans to renovate Lambeau Field, and voters in Brown County later approved a sales tax increase to help finance the $295 million project. (The project was completed in 2003.) The next year Wolf retired and coach Sherman added general manager to his title. The team also signed quarterback Favre to a 10-year, $100 million contract extension.

While Sherman managed to lead the team to the playoffs in four of his first five seasons, the Packers were a disappointing 2-4 in postseason play. In 2005 team president Harlan decided to restructure the general manager and head coaching duties, with Sherman remaining as head coach and Ted Thompson, hired from Seattle, taking over as the team's new general manager.

EXECUTIVES

President and CEO: Robert E. Harlan, age 69
EVP and COO: John M. Jones, age 53
EVP, General Manager, and Director of Football Operations: Ted Thompson, age 52
EVP and Head Coach: Michael F. (Mike) Sherman, age 50
VP Player Finance and General Counsel: Andrew Brandt, age 45
Director of Accounting: Duke Copp
Director of Administrative Affairs: Mark Schiefelbein
Director of College Scouting: John Dorsey, age 45
Director of Corporate Security: Jerry Parins
Director of Finance: Vicki Vannieuwenhoven
Director of Marketing and Corporate Sales: Craig Benzel
Director of Player Development: Edgar Bennett, age 36
Director of Public Relations: Jeff Blumb
Team Historian: Lee Remmel, age 81
Human Resources Generalist: Nicole Chaloupka
Auditors: Wipfli Ullrich Bertelson LLP

LOCATIONS

HQ: The Green Bay Packers, Inc.
 1265 Lombardi Ave., Green Bay, WI 54304
Phone: 920-569-7500   **Fax:** 920-569-7301
Web: www.packers.com

The Green Bay Packers play at 72,601-seat Lambeau Field in Green Bay, Wisconsin. The team holds its training camp at St. Norbert College in De Pere, Wisconsin.

PRODUCTS/OPERATIONS

Championship Titles
Super Bowl I (1967)
Super Bowl II (1968)
Super Bowl XXXI (1997)
NFC Championships (1996-97)
NFC Central Division (1972, 1995-97)
NFC North Division (2002-04)
NFL Championships
 (1929-31, 1936, 1939, 1944, 1961-62, 1965)
NFL Western Conference
 (1936, 1938-39, 1944, 1960-62, 1965-67)

COMPETITORS

Chicago Bears
Detroit Lions
Minnesota Vikings

HISTORICAL FINANCIALS

Company Type: Not-for-profit

Income Statement

FYE: March 31

	REVENUE ($ mil.)	NET INCOME ($ mil.)	NET PROFIT MARGIN	EMPLOYEES
3/04	179	29	16.2%	150
3/03	153	15	9.9%	150
3/02	132	4	2.9%	150
3/01	124	9	7.0%	140
3/00	109	3	2.5%	95
3/99	103	7	6.3%	95
3/98	82	6	7.7%	92
3/97	75	—	—	90
3/96	70	—	—	82
3/95	62	—	—	80
Annual Growth	12.5%	29.1%	—	7.2%

Net Income History

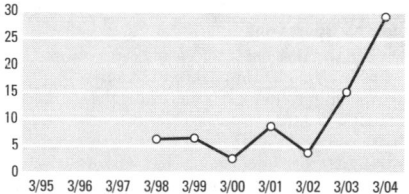

Customers include Boeing, Hewlett-Packard, and Motorola.

Rival Wind River Systems filed a patent infringement lawsuit against Green Hills Software in 2001, but dropped the suit in 2002. The competitors were back in court in early 2005, as Wind River sued Green Hills to force the termination of a 99-year cooperative agreement between the two companies. Green Hills and Wind River had agreed a decade earlier on cooperatively supporting joint customers, who used the software development tools of both companies for military contracts involving the F-15 and F/A-18 aircraft, among other projects. Green Hills fired back with an antitrust complaint against Wind River, saying its competitor was trying to monopolize the very specialized market. The two companies reached a legal settlement in mid-2005, with no money changing hands and Wind River providing object code for its VxWorks real-time operating system to Green Hills. The agreement means Wind River will extend to Green Hills the same kind of technical support it gives to its VxWorks customers.

Green Hills and Wind River are at cross purposes when it comes to open-source software, as well. As vendors of proprietary software development tools, the two companies had little commercial incentive to join in the industry trend toward incorporating the Linux operating system and various open-source utilities, developed by volunteer programmers around the world. Under a new CEO in early 2004, Wind River publicly embraced Linux and open source, striking a cooperative agreement with Red Hat, the leading distributor of Linux. Green Hills CEO Dan O'-Dowd took the opposite tack, going on a public-relations campaign against open-source software, asserting in white papers distributed by his company that open-source software shouldn't be used in software developed for national-security programs. The reason? Enemies of the US and other Western powers could exploit the transparent nature of open-source software projects to insert malicious code. The solution? Using Green Hills Software tools, such as INTEGRITY PC, of course. While Green Hills primarily promotes its INTEGRITY real-time operating system for embedded software projects, the company does support Linux with certain tools.

EXECUTIVES

Vice Chairman: John B. (Jack) Douglas III, age 51
President and CEO: Daniel D. (Dan) O'Dowd, age 49
CFO: Jeffrey R. Hazarian, age 49
VP, Advanced Products: Craig Franklin, age 59
VP, Engineering: David Kleidermacher, age 36
VP, European Operations: Martin V. Nappi, age 47
VP, Marketing: Christopher Smith, age 44
VP, Sales: David Chandler, age 42
Manager, Marketing Communications: Lynn J. Robinson
Auditors: Ernst & Young

LOCATIONS

HQ: Green Hills Software, Inc.
 30 W. Sola St., Santa Barbara, CA 93101
Phone: 805-965-6044   **Fax:** 805-965-6343
Web: www.ghs.com

Green Hills Software has offices in France, Germany, Israel, the Netherlands, Sweden, the UK, and the US.

Green Hills Software

Green Hills Software can't help with planning an African hunting safari, but it can come to the rescue of embedded systems developers. The company provides a variety of software tools for developers of embedded systems (combinations of microprocessors and components used in diverse products including disk drives, cellular phones, video games, braking, and avionics systems). Green Hills' products include real-time operating systems (INTEGRITY), development environments (MULTI2000), debugging devices, and optimizing compilers, as well as custom software development services. Green Hills Software was founded in 1982 by president and CEO Dan O'-Dowd, who owns 97% of the company.

PRODUCTS/OPERATIONS

Selected Products

Development environments
  AdaMULTI2000
  MULTI2000

Optimizing Compilers
  Optimizing Ada 95 Compiler
  Optimizing C Compiler
  Optimizing C++, Embedded C++ Compilers
  Optimizing FORTRAN Compiler

Real-time operating systems
  INTEGRITY
  ThreadX

Target Debug Devices
  Green Hills Probe
  Slingshot

Selected Services

Advanced debugging
Consulting
Custom compiler development
Digital signal processor (DSP) software development
Technical support

COMPETITORS

BSQUARE
CodeWeavers
Core Mobility
Insyde Technology
LynuxWorks
Mentor Graphics
Microsoft
Mistral Software
MontaVista Software
OSA Technologies
QNX Software
RadiSys
Red Hat
Sun Microsystems
VaST Systems
Wind River

HISTORICAL FINANCIALS

Company Type: Private

Income Statement

FYE: December 31

	REVENUE ($ mil.)	NET INCOME ($ mil.)	NET PROFIT MARGIN	EMPLOYEES
12/04	72	—	—	200
12/03	51	—	—	200
12/02	41	—	—	185
12/01	45	—	—	—
12/00	40	—	—	150
Annual Growth	15.7%	—	—	7.5%

Revenue History

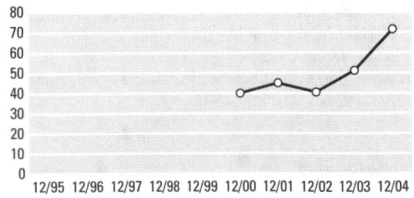

Greenville Hospital System

Greenville Hospital System is a not-for-profit community hospital system serving South Carolina's "Golden Strip" (the I-85 corridor connecting Charlotte, North Carolina, and Atlanta). Founded in 1912 as a community hospital, the system today includes four acute-care hospitals (about 900 beds), as well as a children's hospital, a cancer center, and a nursing home. Greenville Hospital System offers a full range of services, including a primary-care physician network, a health plan, and outpatient care. The company, which also operates a charitable foundation, has teaching affiliations with two medical schools and a research affiliation with Clemson University.

EXECUTIVES

President: Frank D. Pinckney
VP, Financial Services, CFO, and Treasurer: Susan Bichel
VP, Human Resources: Douglas Dorman
CIO: Doran Dunaway
Auditors: Ernst & Young LLP

LOCATIONS

HQ: Greenville Hospital System
  701 Grove Rd., Greenville, SC 29605
Phone: 864-455-7000   **Fax:** 864-455-6218
Web: www.ghs.org

Greenville Hospital System operates in South Carolina.

PRODUCTS/OPERATIONS

Selected Operations

Allen Bennett Hospital (Greer, acute care)
Greenville Memorial Hospital (acute care)
Hillcrest Hospital (Simpsonville, acute care)
Marshall I. Pickens Hospital
  (Greenville, psychiatric care)
North Greenville Hospital (Travelers Rest, acute care)
Roger C. Peace Rehabilitation Hospital
  (Greenville, rehab)
Roger Huntington Nursing Center
  (Greer, assisted living)

COMPETITORS

Bon Secours Health
Health Management Associates
Novant Health

HISTORICAL FINANCIALS

Company Type: Not-for-profit

Income Statement

FYE: September 30

	REVENUE ($ mil.)	NET INCOME ($ mil.)	NET PROFIT MARGIN	EMPLOYEES
9/04	789	21	2.7%	7,500
9/03	754	53	7.0%	6,500
9/02	710	33	4.7%	6,500
9/01	691	34	4.9%	6,500
9/00	592	35	5.9%	6,200
9/99	541	10	1.8%	6,000
9/98	494	—	—	5,700
9/97	453	—	—	5,500
9/96	430	—	—	5,500
9/95	399	—	—	5,000
Annual Growth	7.9%	16.8%	—	4.6%

2004 Year-End Financials

Debt ratio: 116.2%
Return on equity: 5.8%
Cash ($ mil.): 64
Current ratio: 2.02
Long-term debt ($ mil.): 429

Net Income History

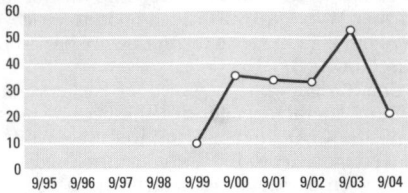

Gristede's Foods

New York City never sleeps, but eating is another matter. Gristede's Foods feeds hungry New Yorkers with nearly 50 area supermarkets (most are located in Manhattan), including new Gristede's Mega Stores. The stores offer fresh meats, produce, dairy products, baked goods, frozen foods, gourmet foods, and nonfood items. Gristede's also operates three stand-alone pharmacies and XpressGrocer.com, for online grocery shopping. The company owns City Produce Operating, which supplies the supermarkets with groceries and produce and sells wholesale fresh produce to third parties. Chairman and CEO John Catsimatidis and Gristede's other major shareholders took the grocery chain private in November 2004.

Gristede's recently launched XpressGrocer.com, its Internet grocery delivery service, partly in response to the entry of upstart Web grocer FreshDirect into the New York grocery market. The New York grocery chain has also begun filling Internet orders via the Amazon.com Web site. In addition to new online competition, Gristede's Foods's business is coming under assault from non-traditional players, including drugstores, big box retailers Costco Wholesale and Wal-Mart Stores (which wants to open a store in Queens, NY), and high-end specialty supermarkets such as Balducci's and Whole Foods.

Gristede's is adding in-store pharmacies to select supermarkets. It's also modernizing and expanding some locations and reopening them as Gristede's Mega Stores, which average sales increases of more than 50% following the makeover. Gristede's acquired three Food Emporium stores from troubled rival The Great Atlantic & Pacific Tea Company, aka A&P, in 2002 for $5.5 million and has reopened them as Gristede's stores.

Gristede's and its New York rival D'Agostino Supermarkets both made competing offers for Kings Super Markets, which is owned by the UK clothing retailer Marks and Spencer. Ultimately, both companies failed to acquire the New Jersey chain.

EXECUTIVES

Chairman, President, and CEO: John A. Catsimatidis, age 56, $100,000 pay
EVP, CFO, and Director: Kishore Lall, age 57
CIO: Don Winant
EVP: Robert (Bob) Schwartz
VP, Operations: Gallo Balseca
Director, Human Resources: John Gildea
Director, Marketing: Michael Criscuolo
Auditors: BDO Seidman, LLP

LOCATIONS

HQ: Gristede's Foods, Inc.
    823 11th Ave., New York, NY 10019
Phone: 212-956-5803   **Fax:** 212-247-4509
Web: www.gristedes.com

COMPETITORS

A&P	Key Food
D'Agostino Supermarkets	King Kullen Grocery
Duane Reade	Pathmark
Food Emporium	Rite Aid
FreshDirect	Western Beef
Jetro Cash & Carry	Whole Foods

HISTORICAL FINANCIALS

Company Type: Private

Income Statement

FYE: November 30

	REVENUE ($ mil.)	NET INCOME ($ mil.)	NET PROFIT MARGIN	EMPLOYEES
11/04	300	—	—	4,000
11/03	280	—	—	2,180
11/02	251	—	—	2,288
11/01	230	—	—	1,748
11/00	216	—	—	1,533
11/99	182	—	—	1,528
11/98	158	—	—	1,323
11/97*	9	—	—	385
2/97	52	—	—	—
2/96	50	—	—	—
Annual Growth	21.9%	—	—	39.7%

*Fiscal year change

Revenue History

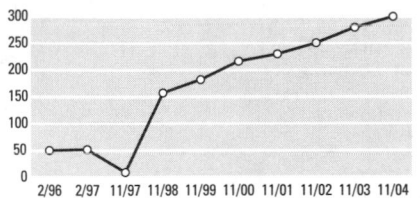

Grocers Supply

Need crackers in Caracas or vanilla in Manila? Grocers Supply Co. distributes groceries near and far. The company (not to be confused with fellow Texas distributor GSC Enterprises) transports food, health and beauty items, household products, and school and office supplies to more than 1,200 convenience stores, 650 grocery stores, and 200 schools within a 350-mile radius of Houston. Its Grocers Supply International (GSI) division ships supplies to oil company operations, other commercial customers, and US embassies around the world. GSI boasts that it will buy anything to ship anywhere for anyone, including macaroons in Rangoon, or even oleo in Tokyo. Grocers Supply is owned by the Levit family.

The company's subsidiary Bexar County Markets runs 10 Handy Andy Supermarkets in the San Antonio area. The company owns the Garland, Texas, operations of the now defunct Fleming Companies. It also owns Fiesta Mart, which operates ethnic food stores throughout Texas.

EXECUTIVES

President: Max Levit, age 70
SVP, Accounting: Michael Castleberry, age 47
SVP, Buying: Tom Becker, age 63
SVP, Financial Services: Jim Nelson, age 59
SVP, Operations: Robert Hunt, age 57
SVP, Sales: Dave Hoffman, age 59
VP, Human Resources: Terry Collins, age 49
VP, Management Information Systems: David Bash, age 49
VP, Real Estate: James Arnold, age 59
VP, Sales: Jim Davenport, age 56
President, Bexar County Markets: Terry Warrren
Secretary: Tracy Levit-Larner, age 41
Controller: Bill Stewart, age 53
Auditors: PricewaterhouseCoopers

LOCATIONS

HQ: The Grocers Supply Co., Inc.
    3131 E. Holcombe Blvd., Houston, TX 77221
Phone: 713-747-5000   **Fax:** 713-746-5611
Web: www.grocerssupply.com

COMPETITORS

Affiliated Foods	Kroger
AWG	McLane
Brenham Wholesale	Nash Finch
C.D. Hartnett	Randall's
GSC Enterprises	SUPERVALU
H-E-B	Wal-Mart

HISTORICAL FINANCIALS

Company Type: Private

Income Statement

FYE: December 31

	REVENUE ($ mil.)	NET INCOME ($ mil.)	NET PROFIT MARGIN	EMPLOYEES
12/03	1,500	—	—	2,000
12/02	1,500	—	—	2,538
12/01*	1,500	—	—	2,400
5/00	1,400	—	—	2,000
5/99	1,400	—	—	1,800
5/98	1,400	—	—	1,938
5/97	1,300	—	—	1,200
5/96	1,200	—	—	1,200
5/95	1,500	—	—	1,200
5/94	1,450	—	—	1,200
Annual Growth	0.4%	—	—	5.8%

*Fiscal year change

Revenue History

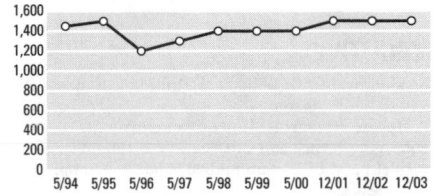

Group Health Cooperative of Puget Sound

Group Health Cooperative of Puget Sound is a not-for-profit managed health care group serving counties in Washington and northern Idaho. Members may participate in HMO, PPO, or point-of-service health plans. The co-op is governed by an 11-person board elected by the organization's members. Specialized services include mental health and substance abuse treatment, hospice services, women's health, and emergency medicine.

Group Health Cooperative of Puget Sound has an alliance with Virginia Mason Medical Center (to share medical centers and hospitals), as well as with Kaiser Permanente, one of the nation's largest nonprofit health care systems. The organization is owned by its nearly 540,000 members.

Group Health Cooperative of Puget Sound is one of the largest consumer-owned health care companies in the nation. The managed health care group was founded in 1947.

EXECUTIVES

Chairman: Ruth Ballweg
President and CEO: Scott Armstrong
EVP and CFO: Jim Truess
EVP and Chief Marketing Officer; President and CEO, Group Health Options: Maureen McLaughlin
EVP, Integrated Group Practice: Peter G. Adler
VP and General Counsel: Rick Woods
VP and Chief Information Officer: Janice Newell
VP Public Affairs and Governance: Pam MacEwan
VP Human Resources: Brenda Tolbert
Auditors: Deloitte & Touche

LOCATIONS

HQ: Group Health Cooperative of Puget Sound
    521 Wall St., Seattle, WA 98121
Phone: 206-448-5600   **Fax:** 206-448-4010
Web: www.ghc.org

PRODUCTS/OPERATIONS

Selected Services

The Adolescent Center
Alternative Care
Behavioral health
Consulting nurse service
Cosmetic dermatology
Emergency care
Eye care services
Home and long-term care
Maternity services
Smoking cessation
Specialty care
Transplant program
Women's health

COMPETITORS

Aetna
CIGNA
PacifiCare
UnitedHealth Group

HISTORICAL FINANCIALS

Company Type: Cooperative

Income Statement

FYE: December 31

	REVENUE ($ mil.)	NET INCOME ($ mil.)	NET PROFIT MARGIN	EMPLOYEES
12/03	1,966	156	7.9%	9,708
12/02	1,760	—	—	10,519
12/01	1,436	—	—	10,500
12/00	1,400	—	—	9,873
12/99	1,400	—	—	9,746
12/98	1,323	—	—	9,602
12/97	1,016	—	—	8,300
12/96	927	—	—	7,179
12/95	1,039	—	—	7,100
12/94	1,013	—	—	7,100
Annual Growth	7.6%	—	—	3.5%

Revenue History

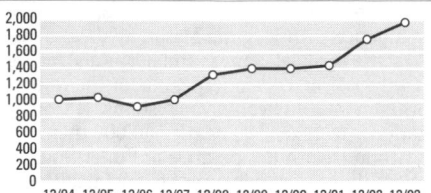

Guardian Industries

Giving its customers a break would never occur to Guardian Industries, one of the world's largest glassmakers. With more than 60 facilities on five continents, Guardian primarily produces float glass and fabricated glass products for the automobile and construction markets. It also makes architectural glass, fiberglass, and automotive trim parts. Through its Guardian Building Products Group, the company operates Guardian Fiberglass, Builder Marts of America, Guardian Building Products Distribution, and Ashley Aluminum. President and CEO William Davidson took Guardian Industries public in 1968 and bought it back for himself in 1985. Davidson is also the managing partner of the Detroit Pistons NBA team.

Guardian has been expanding primarily through international acquisitions and by increasing its already significant position in the building materials business. The company added business in Egypt (a stake in Egyptian Glass Company) and has been opening float glass plants and treatment facilities on a regular basis. It added float plants in Poland (2002), the UK (2003), and Mexico (2004).

HISTORY

Guardian Glass began as a small maker of car windshields in Detroit in 1932 during the Great Depression. The company spent the 1930s and 1940s building its business to gain a foothold in glassmaking, historically one of the world's most monopolized industries. In 1949 PPG Industries and Libbey-Owens-Ford (now owned by the UK's Pilkington) agreed to stop their alleged monopolistic activity. William Davidson took over Guardian Glass from his uncle in 1957. As president, he tried to boost the enterprise's standing in the windshield niche, but PPG and Libbey-Owens-Ford refused to sell him raw glass. That year Guardian Glass filed for bankruptcy to reorganize.

The company emerged from bankruptcy in 1960 (the same year Pilkington developed the float process for glassmaking), and in 1965 it was hit with its first patent-infringement lawsuit. Three years later the company went public, changed its name to Guardian Industries, and was refused a license to use Pilkington's float technology. Guardian began an aggressive acquisition strategy in 1969, and in 1970 it hired Ford's top glass man (who knew the float process) and proceeded to build its first float-glass plant in Michigan. PPG sued Guardian in 1972. Davidson bought the Detroit Pistons in 1974. He applied a do-or-die style that might best be illustrated by the 1979 firing of Piston's coach Dick Vitale, who claims Davidson axed him on his own front doorstep while a curbside limo waited with the motor running.

In 1980 Guardian started making fiberglass and began hiring former workers from insulation maker Manville to duplicate that company's patented technology for fiberglass insulation. Manville successfully sued Guardian in 1981. Guardian opened a Luxembourg plant that year. Pilkington sued Guardian in 1983, but the case was settled out of court three years later. Davidson took Guardian private in 1985, and in 1988 he bought an Indiana auto trim plant. He also built The Palace of Auburn Hills sports arena in 1988.

The 1990s brought more international expansion for Guardian, with plants added in India, Spain, and Venezuela. It also set up a distribution center in Japan, a country known for its tight control of the glass industry. In 1992 Guardian bought OIS Optical Imaging Systems, a maker of computer display screens. Guardian moved its headquarters to Auburn Hills, Michigan, in 1995. Its 1996 purchase of Automotive Moulding boosted its position in the auto plastics and trim market.

Guardian booted its OIS Optical Imaging Systems unit in 1998, citing ongoing losses. That year the company's fiberglass subsidiary bought 50% of building materials buying group Builder Marts of America, giving Guardian a foothold in the markets for lumber and roofing products. Also in 1998 Davidson made a failed attempt to buy the Tampa Bay Lightning hockey team.

In 1999 Guardian bought Siam Guardian Glass Ltd. from Siam Cement Plc, the company's partner in Thailand. The next year Guardian acquired Cameron Ashley Building Products (renamed Ashley Aluminum), a distributor with more than 160 branches in the US and Canada. In 2002 the company expanded to Poland where it built a float glass plant; Guardian also opened float glass plants in the UK in 2003 and in Mexico in 2004.

EXECUTIVES

President and CEO: William M. (Bill) Davidson, age 81
EVP: Ralph J. Gerson
VP, Human Resources: Bruce Cummings
Group VP, Finance and CFO: Jeffrey A. Knight
President and CEO, Automotive Products Group: D. James Davis
President, Building Products Group: Duane H. Faulkner
President, Glass Group: Russell J. Ebeid

LOCATIONS

HQ: Guardian Industries Corp.
2300 Harmon Rd., Auburn Hills, MI 48326
Phone: 248-340-1800   **Fax:** 248-340-9988
Web: www.guardian.com

Guardian Industries has operations in 21 countries.

PRODUCTS/OPERATIONS

Selected Products and Services

Architectural Glass
Custom fabrication
Float glass
Insulating glass
Laminated glass
Mirrors
Patterned glass
Reflective coated glass
Tempered glass

Automotive Systems
Bodyside (mud flaps, wheel covers)
Front and rear end (grilles, rub strips)
Side window (door-frame moldings)
Windshield (window-surround moldings)

Guardian Building Products
Aluminum screen doors
Carports
Ceiling tile
Door frames
Doors
Fiberglass insulation
Formica
Metal roofing
Patio covers
Plywood
Rebar
Sheetrock
Storm doors
Windows

Guardian Fiberglass
Fiberglass insulation

Retail Auto Glass
Auto glass
Auto glass repair and replacement
Insurance claim processing

COMPETITORS

Apogee Enterprises
Asahi Glass
Corning
CRH
Johns Manville
Magna Donnelly
Nippon Sheet Glass
Owens Corning
Pilkington
PPG
Safelite Group
Saint-Gobain
Vitro

HISTORICAL FINANCIALS

Company Type: Private

Income Statement

FYE: December 31

	ESTIMATED REVENUE ($ mil.)	NET INCOME ($ mil.)	NET PROFIT MARGIN	EMPLOYEES
12/03	4,000	—	—	19,000
12/02	3,950	—	—	19,000
12/01	4,000	—	—	19,000
12/00	4,000	—	—	20,000
12/99	3,650	—	—	15,000
12/98	2,200	—	—	15,000
12/97	2,000	—	—	14,000
12/96	1,900	—	—	13,000
12/95	1,700	—	—	12,000
12/94	1,500	—	—	10,000
Annual Growth	11.5%	—	—	7.4%

Revenue History

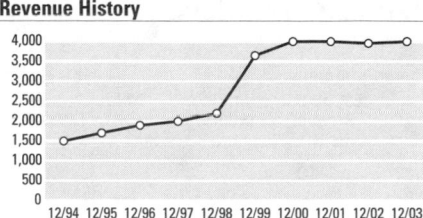

Revenue History chart ($ mil.), 12/94–12/03

Guardian Life Insurance

When your guardian angel fails you, there's Guardian Life Insurance Company of America. The mutual company, owned by its policy holders, offers life insurance, disability income insurance, and — more recently — retirement programs. Guardian Life Insurance Company of America's employee health indemnity plans provide HMO, PPO, and dental and vision plans, as well as disability plans. In the retirement area, Guardian has long offered the Park Avenue group of mutual funds and annuity products, managed by its Guardian Investor Services.

To meet competition in the quickly deregulating financial services area, the company is building its wealth management capabilities to target baby boomers getting ready for retirement. It created broker-dealer Park Avenue Securities and launched Guardian Trust Company to offer trust and investment management services. The company has also added long-term care insurance to its product line.

Guardian has also grown through acquisition, buying complementary firms, such as disability insurance specialist Berkshire Life Insurance.

HISTORY

Hugo Wesendonck came to the US from Germany in 1850 to escape a death sentence for his part in an abortive 1848 revolution. After working in the silk business in Philadelphia, he moved to New York, which was home to more ethnic Germans than any city save Berlin and Vienna.

In 1860 Wesendonck and other expatriates formed an insurance company to serve the German-American community. Germania Life Insurance was chartered as a stock mutual, which paid dividends to shareholders and policy owners. Wesendonck was its first president.

The Civil War blocked the company's growth in the South, but it expanded in the rest of the US and by 1867 even operated in South America.

After the Civil War, many insurers foundered from high costs. Wesendonck battled this by implementing strict cost controls and limiting commissions, allowing the company to continue issuing dividends and rebates on its policyholders' premiums.

In the 1870s Germania opened offices in Europe, and for the next few decades much of the company's growth was there. By 1910, 46% of sales originated in Europe. The company's target clientele in the US decreased between the 1890s and WWI as German immigration slowed,

and its market share dropped from ninth in 1880 to 21st in 1910.

During WWI the company lost contact with its German business. Prodded by anti-German sentiment in the US, the company changed its name to The Guardian Life Insurance Company of America in 1917. After WWI the company began winding down its German business (a process that lasted until 1952).

In 1924 Guardian began mutualizing but could not complete the process until 1944 because of probate problems with a shareholder's estate.

After WWII, Guardian offered noncancelable medical insurance (1955) and group insurance (1957). The company formed Guardian Investor Services in 1969 to offer mutual funds; two years later it established Guardian Insurance & Annuity to sell variable contracts. In 1989 it organized Guardian Asset Management to handle pension funds.

In 1993, as indemnity health costs rose, the company moved into managed care via its membership in Private Health Care Systems, a consortium of commercial insurance carriers offering managed health care products and services. This allowed Guardian to offer HMO and PPO products.

Guardian entered a joint marketing agreement in 1995 with HMO Physicians Health Services, which contracts with physicians and hospitals in the New York tri-state area. In 1996 the company acquired Managed Dental Care of California and an interest in Physicians Health Services.

Facing deregulation and consolidation in the financial services area, as well as the demutualization of some of its largest competitors, Guardian in the late 1990s decided to add depth to its employee benefits lines and breadth to its wealth management lines.

In 1999 Guardian formed its broker-dealer subsidiary and received a thrift license to facilitate creation of a trust business. Acquisitions included Innovative Underwriters Services, Fiduciary Insurance Co. of America, and managed dental care companies First Commonwealth and First Choice Dental Network. In 2001 the company moved to boost its disability business with the purchase of Berkshire Life Insurance.

EXECUTIVES

President, CEO, and Director: Dennis J. Manning
EVP and CFO: Robert E. Broatch, age 49
EVP and CIO: Dennis S. Callahan
EVP and Chief Actuary: Armand M. de Palo
EVP, Risk Management Products: Gary B. Lenderink
EVP, Equity Products: Bruce C. Long
EVP and Chief Investment Officer; President, The Park Avenue Portfolio: Thomas G. Sorell
SVP, Individual Markets: David W. Allen
SVP, Corporate Secretary, and Director: Joseph A. Caruso
SVP, Group Pensions: Dennis P. Mosticchio
SVP, Human Resources: James D. (Jim) Ranton
SVP, Corporate Marketing: Nancy F. Rogers
SVP, Group Insurance: Richard A. White
VP and General Counsel: John Peluso
VP, Agency Growth and Development: Thomas W. Slack
VP, Reinsurance: Jeremy Starr
President, Berkshire Life Insurance Company of America: Joan Bancroft
Auditors: PricewaterhouseCoopers LLP

LOCATIONS

HQ: The Guardian Life Insurance Company of America
7 Hanover Sq., New York, NY 10004
Phone: 212-598-8000   **Fax:** 212-919-2170
Web: www.guardianlife.com

Guardian Life Insurance Company of America has operations throughout the US.

PRODUCTS/OPERATIONS

2004 Sales

	$ mil.	% of total
Premiums, annuity considerations & fund deposits	5,607	80
Net investment income	1,188	17
Other income	226	3
Total	**7,021**	**100**

Selected Subsidiaries and Affiliates

Berkshire Life Insurance Company of America
First Commonwealth, Inc.
Guardian Baillie Gifford Limited
The Guardian Insurance & Annuity Company, Inc.
Guardian Investor Services LLC
Guardian Trust Company, FSB
Innovative Underwriters, Inc.
Managed Dental Care (California)
Managed DentalGuard (New Jersey)
Managed DentalGuard (Texas)
Park Avenue Life Insurance Company
Park Avenue Securities LLC

COMPETITORS

Aetna	MassMutual
AIG American General	Merrill Lynch
Allstate	MetLife
AXA Financial	Nationwide
Charles Schwab	New York Life
CIGNA	Northwestern Mutual
Citigroup	Oxford Health
CNA Financial	Pacific Mutual
FMR	Principal Financial
General Re	Prudential
The Hartford	UBS Financial Services
John Hancock Financial Services	UnitedHealth Group
	UnumProvident
Liberty Mutual	USAA
Lincoln Financial Group	WellPoint

HISTORICAL FINANCIALS

Company Type: Mutual company

Income Statement
FYE: December 31

	REVENUE ($ mil.)	NET INCOME ($ mil.)	NET PROFIT MARGIN	EMPLOYEES
12/04	7,021	286	4.1%	5,000
12/03	6,732	218	3.2%	5,500
12/02	7,192	(283)	—	5,500
12/01	6,947	170	2.5%	6,000
12/00	6,569	563	8.6%	6,000
12/99	6,283	325	5.2%	5,465
12/98	8,499	160	1.9%	—
12/97	7,180	299	4.2%	4,800
12/96	6,904	173	2.5%	5,155
12/95	6,195	125	2.0%	5,322
Annual Growth	**1.4%**	**9.6%**	**—**	**(0.7%)**

Net Income History

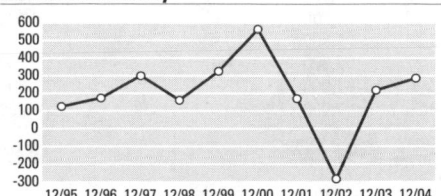

Net Income History chart, 12/95–12/04

Gulf Oil

Gulf Oil bridges the gap between petroleum producers and retail sales outlets. The petroleum wholesaler distributes gasoline and diesel fuel to about 1,800 Gulf-brand stations in 11 northeastern states. Gulf Oil, which owns and operates 12 storage terminals, also distributes motor oils, lubricants, and heating oil to commercial, industrial, and utility customers. The company has alliances with terminal operators in areas in the Northeast where it does not have a proprietary terminal. Gulf Oil boasts one of the oldest and most recognizable brands in the oil business.

Gulf Oil traces its roots to the famous 1901 oil strike in Spindletop, Texas. At one time one of the largest integrated oil concerns in the world, Gulf Oil Corporation restructured into seven operating companies in the 1970s, the bulk of which were acquired by Chevron in 1984.

EXECUTIVES

CEO: John Kaneb
President: Gary Kaneb
Controller: Alice Kuhne
Director Human Resources: Karen Channel

LOCATIONS

HQ: Gulf Oil Limited Partnership
90 Everett Ave., Chelsea, MA 02150
Phone: 617-889-9000   **Fax:** 617-884-0637
Web: www.gulfoil.com

Gulf Oil operates in 11 northeastern US states.

PRODUCTS/OPERATIONS

Selected Products

Antifreeze	Kerosene
Gasoline	Synthetic lubricants
Grease	Transmission fluid
Heating oil	Zinc-free oils

COMPETITORS

Amerada Hess	Getty Petroleum
BP	Marketing
CITGO	Global Partners
Consolidated Beacon	Motiva Enterprises
Exxon Mobil	Sunoco

HISTORICAL FINANCIALS

Company Type: Partnership

Income Statement

FYE: September 30

	ESTIMATED REVENUE ($ mil.)	NET INCOME ($ mil.)	NET PROFIT MARGIN	EMPLOYEES
9/04	3,600	—	—	350
9/03	2,100	—	—	150
9/02	1,680	—	—	150
9/01	1,970	—	—	200
9/00	1,800	—	—	185
9/99	1,808	—	—	185
9/98	1,800	—	—	185
9/97	2,300	—	—	200
9/96	1,900	—	—	200
9/95	2,000	—	—	200
Annual Growth	**6.7%**	**—**	**—**	**6.4%**

Revenue History

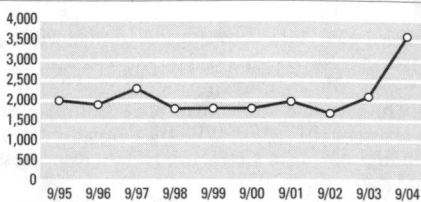

Gulf States Toyota

Even good ol' boys buy foreign cars from Gulf States Toyota (GST). One of only two US Toyota distributors not owned by Toyota Motor Sales (the other is JM Family Enterprises' Southeast Toyota Distributors), the company distributes Toyota cars, trucks, and sport utility vehicles in Arkansas, Louisiana, Mississippi, Oklahoma, and Texas. Founded in 1969 by Thomas Friedkin and still owned by The Friedkin Companies, GST distributes new Toyotas, parts, and accessories to around 150 dealers in its region.

EXECUTIVES

President and General Manager: Toby Hynes
CFO: Frank Gruen
VP, Human Resources: Dominic Gallo
VP, Marketing: J.C. Fassino
VP, Sales Operations: Tom Bittenbender
Director, Administration: David Copeland
Marketing Support Senior Manager: Eric Williamson
Scion Marketing Manager: Tom Lauterbach
Technical Capacity Manager: Don Cole
Truck and Sport Utility Vehicle Marketing Manager: Rick Humphreys

LOCATIONS

HQ: Gulf States Toyota, Inc.
7701 Wilshire Place Dr., Houston, TX 77040
Phone: 713-580-3300   **Fax:** 713-580-3332

COMPETITORS

BMW
DaimlerChrysler
David McDavid Auto Group
Ford
General Motors
Honda
Kia Motors
Mazda
Nissan North America
Volkswagen
Volvo

HISTORICAL FINANCIALS

Company Type: Private

Income Statement

FYE: December 31

	ESTIMATED REVENUE ($ mil.)	NET INCOME ($ mil.)	NET PROFIT MARGIN	EMPLOYEES
12/03	3,800	—	—	3,100
12/02	3,700	—	—	3,000
12/01	3,800	—	—	3,000
12/00	3,250	—	—	1,650
12/99	3,158	—	—	1,600
12/98	2,500	—	—	1,600
12/97	2,300	—	—	1,600
12/96	1,700	—	—	1,500
12/95	1,600	—	—	1,500
12/94	1,800	—	—	1,500
Annual Growth	**8.7%**	**—**	**—**	**8.4%**

Revenue History

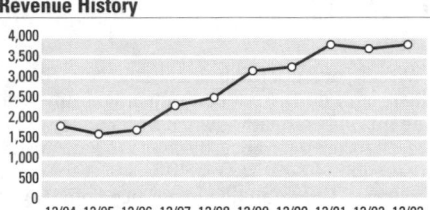

Gundle/SLT Environmental

Oil and water don't mix, and Gundle/SLT Environmental (GSE) plans to keep it that way. The company makes and installs synthetic liners used to prevent groundwater contamination. Waste-management firms, mining companies, and government agencies use these liners at garbage dumps and water-containment facilities. GSE's high-density polyethylene smooth-sheet liners account for more than half of sales. The company also makes textured sheets and geosynthetic clay liners. The US accounts for more than half of sales. Private equity firm Code Hennessy & Simmons bought GSE and took it private in 2004.

GSE went ahead with the Code Hennessy transaction even though some shareholders had filed suit to block the deal. The company was able to settle out of court, and the acquisition closed in the spring of 2004. Code Hennessy kept prior management in place with one exception; Daniel Hennessy was named chairman of GSE after closing of the deal.

EXECUTIVES

Chairman: Daniel J. Hennessy, age 48
President and CEO: Samir Badawi, age 65, $743,660 pay (prior to title change)
VP and CFO: Kelvin R. Collard, age 47
VP, Corporate Counsel, and Secretary: C. Wayne Case
VP, General Manager, Asia/Pacific Region: James T. (Jim) Steinke, age 58, $221,008 pay
VP, General Manager, Europe/Middle East/Africa Region: Paul A. Firrell, age 38, $269,599 pay
VP, General Manager, North America Operations: Ernest C. (Ernie) English Jr., age 52, $255,977 pay
VP, General Manager, U.S. Installation Services Division: Gerald (Gerry) Hersh, age 61, $244,563 pay

VP, Bentofix Technologies, Inc.: Scott Lucas
VP, Engineering and Quality Control: Ed Zimmel
VP, Manufacturing: Rick Schaefer
VP, North American Dealer Sales: David Leggett
VP, Sales and Marketing: Gary R. Joachim
VP, Technical Sales: Boyd J. Ramsey
Chief Information Officer: Dan Mastin
Auditors: Ernst & Young LLP

LOCATIONS

HQ: Gundle/SLT Environmental, Inc.
19103 Gundle Rd., Houston, TX 77073
Phone: 281-443-8564 **Fax:** 281-230-2504
Web: www.gseworld.com

Gundle/SLT Environmental has manufacturing operations in Canada, Egypt, Germany, Thailand, the UK, and the US.

2004 Sales

	$ mil.	% of total
US	163.1	56
Europe	62.1	22
Latin & South America	20.2	7
Asia/Pacific	19.5	7
Africa & Middle East	15.3	5
Other regions	7.7	3
Total	**287.9**	**100**

PRODUCTS/OPERATIONS

2004 Sales

	$ mil.	% of total
Solid waste containment	195.0	68
Liquid containment	40.1	14
Mining	30.0	10
Other applications	22.8	8
Total	**287.9**	**100**

Selected Products

Concrete protection liners
Drainage nets
Geocomposites
Geosynthetic clay liners
Vertical barrier walls

Selected Subsidiaries

Bentofix Technologies (USA) Inc.
Bentofix Technologies, Inc. (Canada)
Deposita Folientechnik GmbH (Germany)
Geoplastics Gesellschaft Fur Abdichtungssysteme GmbH (Germany)
GSE (UK) Limited
GSE Australia Pty Ltd
GSE Clay Lining Technology Co.
GSE Lining Technology (Canada) LTD
GSE Lining Technology Company Ltd.
Hyma/GSE Lining Technology Co. (Egypt)
Hyma/GSE Manufacturing Co. (Egypt)

COMPETITORS

Baker Hughes
Bechtel
BJ Services
Black & Veatch
Butyl
Fluor
FMC
Halliburton
McDermott
Nabors Industries
Peter Kiewit Sons'
Raytheon
Schlumberger
Smith International
Weatherford International

HISTORICAL FINANCIALS

Company Type: Private

Income Statement				FYE: December 31
	REVENUE ($ mil.)	**NET INCOME** ($ mil.)	**NET PROFIT MARGIN**	**EMPLOYEES**
12/04	288	2	0.7%	1,045
12/03	275	21	7.6%	1,127
12/02	267	39	14.6%	1,081
12/01	173	1	0.8%	764
12/00	191	4	1.9%	901
12/99	179	5	2.7%	788
12/98	180	4	2.2%	824
12/97	199	5	2.3%	851
12/96	209	12	5.5%	843
12/95	248	(2)	—	833
Annual Growth	1.7%	—	—	2.6%

2004 Year-End Financials

Debt ratio: 227.4%
Return on equity: 1.7%
Cash ($ mil.): 24
Current ratio: 2.74
Long-term debt ($ mil.): 168

Net Income History

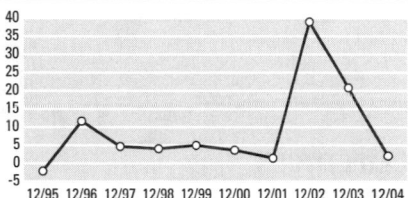

H. E. Butt Grocery

The Muzak bounces between Tejano and country, and the warm tortillas and marinated fajita meat are big sellers at H. E. Butt Grocery (H-E-B). Texas' largest private company and the #1 food retailer in South and Central Texas, H-E-B owns more than 300 supermarkets, including a growing number of large (70,000 sq. ft.) gourmet Central Market stores in major metropolitan areas and more than 80 smaller (24,000-30,000 sq. ft.) Pantry Foods stores, often in more rural areas. H-E-B also has about 20 upscale and discount stores in Mexico. H-E-B processes some of its own bread, dairy products, meat, and tortillas. The 100-year-old company is owned by the Butt family, which founded H-E-B in Kerrville, Texas, in 1905.

To cement its #1 spot in Central Texas and fend off Wal-Mart, which is expanding its supercenter presence in the region, H-E-B plans to open several 160,000-sq.-ft. stores in 2006; a considerably larger footprint than those of its H-E-B Plus stores, which measure about 109,000 sq. ft. and are about 20% larger than average H-E-B outlets and devote considerable space to nonfood items, including furniture. Two of the Wal-Mart-sized stores will be in the San Antonio market, where H-E-B has acquired stores from ailing rival Albertson's to bolster its position there and elsewhere in the Texas market. H-E-B has lowered prices on some 12,000 items in the Austin market.

Since entering the Houston market in 2001, the Texas grocery chain has invested heavily to add 11 large combination food and drug stores, while closing some of its smaller Pantry supermarkets in the area. H-E-B has set a goal of 25% market share in Houston by 2010. (Currently, H-E-B's Houston market share is nearly 14%, behind Kroger's 27% and Wal-Mart's 22%.) To gain an edge on its competition, H-E-B plans to incorporate aspects of its upscale Central Market format, including cafes, into the new Houston stores.

H-E-B currently operates seven Central Market stores in five Texas markets, with plans to open an eighth store in the Dallas-Fort Worth area in 2006.

H-E-B is familiar with the tastes of Latinos as about half of its market is Hispanic. South of the border H-E-B has moved into Monterrey's more affluent neighborhoods, with stores operating under the H-E-B banner and the Economax name (a discount supermarket format).

More than 40% of the H-E-B stores have gasoline outlets, and about 190 have pharmacies, which are being remodeled to include drive-through windows and enlarged health and beauty aid selections. The retailer recently opened its first Payless Express shoe department in a Laredo store, and has plans to open more.

HISTORY

Charles C. Butt and his wife, Florence, moved to Kerrville, in the Texas Hill Country, in 1905, hoping the climate would help Charles' tuberculosis. Since Charles was unable to work, Florence began peddling groceries door-to-door for A&P. Later that year she opened a grocery store, C. C. Butt Grocery. However, Florence, a dyed-in-the-wool Baptist, refused to carry such articles of vice as tobacco. The family lived over the store, and all three of the Butt children worked there. The youngest son, Howard, began working in the business full-time in his teens and took over the business after WWI.

By adopting modern marketing methods such as price tagging (and deciding to sell tobacco), the Butts earned enough to begin expanding. In 1927 Howard opened a second store in Del Rio in West Texas, and over the next few years he opened other stores in the Rio Grande Valley. The company gained patron loyalty by making minimal markups on staples. It moved from Kerrville to Harlingen, Texas, in 1928 (it moved to Corpus Christi, Texas, in 1940 and to San Antonio in 1985).

The company began manufacturing foods in the 1930s, and it invested in farms and orchards. In 1935 Howard (who had adopted the middle name Edward) rechristened the chain the H. E. Butt Grocery Company (H-E-B). He put his three children to work for the company, grooming son Charles for the top spot after Howard Jr. took over the H. E. Butt Foundation from his mother.

While other chains updated their stores during the 1960s, H-E-B plodded. Howard Sr. resigned in 1971 and Charles took over, bringing in fresh management. But this was not enough. Studies showed that the reasons for its lagging market share were its refusal to stock alcohol and its policy of Sunday closing; it abandoned these policies in 1976. It also drastically undercut competitors, driving many independents out of business. Winning the price wars, H-E-B emerged the dominant player in its major markets.

H-E-B's first superstore, a 56,000-sq.-ft. facility offering general merchandise, photofinishing, and a pharmacy, opened in Austin, Texas, in 1979, and it concentrated on building more superstores over the next decade. It also installed in-store video rentals and added 35 freestanding Video Central locations (sold to Hollywood Entertainment in 1993).

In 1988 H-E-B launched its H-E-B Pantry division, which remodeled and built smaller supermarkets, mostly in rural Texas towns. Three years later it launched another format, the 93,000-sq.-ft. H-E-B Marketplace in San Antonio, which included restaurants. It also opened the upscale Central Market in Austin with extensive cheese, produce, and wine departments in 1994 (it later opened similar stores in San Antonio and Houston).

Chairman and CEO Charles retired as president in 1996, and James Clingman became the first non-family member to assume the office. That year H-E-B opened its first non-Texas store, in Lake Charles, Louisiana. In 1997 it opened its first Mexican store in an affluent area of Monterrey, followed the next year by a discount supermarket there under the Economax banner. The company said it would expand further in Mexico with six to eight new stores per year. In 2001 H-E-B opened its first store — a Central Market — in the Dallas/Fort Worth area.

In mid-2002 H-E-B opened a new Central Market in Dallas, its seventh Central Market in Texas and the company's 300th store. The company also acquired five San Antonio stores from Albertson's and reopened them as H-E-B stores.

In early 2004, H-E-B opened its first H-E-B Plus store in San Juan, Texas. In 2005 the company celebrated its centennial.

EXECUTIVES

Chairman and CEO: Charles C. Butt
COO: Robert D. (Bob) Loeffler, age 52
Chief Administration Officer and CFO:
  John C. (Jack) Brouillard, age 57
EVP, Food Manufacturing, Procurement, and Merchandising: Steve Harper
SVP, General Manager, Central Texas: Jeff Thomas
SVP, General Manager, San Antonio/West Region: Paul Madura
SVP, General Merchandise, San Antonio Region: Greg Souquette
SVP, Human Resources: Todd Piland
SVP, Operations, Central Market, and Dallas-Fort Worth Region: Stephen Butt
SVP, Supply Chain and Logistics: Kenneth Allen
Group VP, Manufacturing: Bob McCullough
Group VP, Marketing, Advertising, and Branding: Cory J. Basso
Group VP, Public Affairs and Diversity: Winell Herron
VP, Information Solutions: Shawn Sedate
VP, Meat Merchandising, Procurement, and Product Development: Randy Vaclavik
VP, Shopping Experience: Jaren Shaw
VP, Innovation; VP, Procurement/Merchandising, Central Market: John Campbell
VP, Quality Assurance and Environmental Affairs: Bill Fry, age 62
President, H-E-B Houston and Central Market Stores: Scott McClelland, age 47
Director General, Mexican Division: Howard Butt III

LOCATIONS

HQ: H. E. Butt Grocery Company
  646 S. Main Ave., San Antonio, TX 78204
Phone: 210-938-8000   **Fax:** 210-938-8169
Web: www.heb.com

H. E. Butt Grocery Company operates 300-plus grocery stores and gas stations throughout Texas; and in Mexico. The company also operates bakeries; a photo processing lab; and meat, milk, and ice cream plants.

PRODUCTS/OPERATIONS

Private Labels

Central Market All Natural
Central Market Organics
H-E-B Own Brand
Hill Country Fare

Store Formats

Central Market (about 70,000 sq. ft., upscale
  supermarkets with expanded organic and
  gourmet foods; located in
major metropolitan markets)
Economax (discount supermarkets, Mexico)
Gas 'N Go (gas stations)
H-E-B (large supermarkets)
H-E-B Marketplace (large supermarkets
  with specialty departments)
H-E-B Pantry (24,000-30,000 sq. ft., no-frills
  supermarkets with basic groceries; often located in
  rural or suburban areas)

COMPETITORS

7-Eleven	Kmart
Albertson's	Kroger
Brookshire Brothers	Minyard Group
Chedraui	Randall's
Comerci	Rice Food Markets
Costco Wholesale	Soriana
Fiesta Mart	Target
Foodarama Supermarkets	Walgreen
Gerland's Food Fair	Wal-Mart
Gigante	Wal-Mart de México
Grupo Corvi	Whole Foods
IGA	Wild Oats Markets

HISTORICAL FINANCIALS

Company Type: Private

Income Statement

FYE: October 31

	REVENUE ($ mil.)	NET INCOME ($ mil.)	NET PROFIT MARGIN	EMPLOYEES
10/04	10,500	—	—	60,000
10/03	10,700	—	—	56,000
10/02	9,900	—	—	60,000
10/01	8,965	—	—	60,000
10/00	8,200	—	—	50,000
10/99	7,500	—	—	45,000
10/98	7,000	—	—	45,000
10/97	6,500	—	—	45,000
10/96	5,800	—	—	42,000
10/95	5,137	—	—	25,000
Annual Growth	8.3%	—	—	10.2%

Revenue History

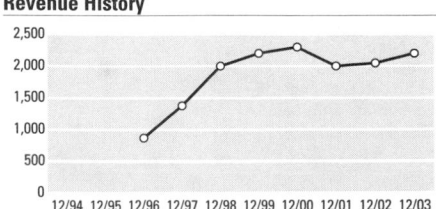

H Group Holding

Owned and operated by the Pritzkers, Chicago's financial super-family, H Group Holding is the holding company for Global Hyatt Corporation (hospitality operations), Conwood tobacco company, and Classic Residence senior communities. Since the death of Jay Pritzker in 1999, family squabbles over their vast $15 billion fortune have led to talks of breaking up the empire and taking Hyatt public. The Pritzker portfolio also includes the Marmon Group (including credit check subsidiary Trans Union), Pritzker Realty, and a stake in the Royal Caribbean cruise ship line. The family is active in philanthropic circles through the Pritzker Foundation.

EXECUTIVES

President: Daniel Azark
VP and Treasurer: John Stellato
Secretary: Harold S. (Hank) Handelsman
Director: Nicholas J. (Nick) Pritzker

LOCATIONS

HQ: H Group Holding, Inc.
  200 W. Madison St., Ste. 3800, Chicago, IL 60606
Phone: 312-873-4900   **Fax:** 312-873-4983

COMPETITORS

Cendant
Four Seasons Hotels
GE
Henry Crown
Hilton
Host Marriott
ITT Industries
Marriott
Starwood Hotels & Resorts
Swisher International
UST

HISTORICAL FINANCIALS

Company Type: Private

Income Statement

FYE: December 31

	REVENUE ($ mil.)	NET INCOME ($ mil.)	NET PROFIT MARGIN	EMPLOYEES
12/03	2,200	—	—	42,000
12/02	2,047	—	—	41,000
12/01	2,000	—	—	41,000
12/00	2,300	—	—	70,000
12/99	2,200	—	—	70,000
12/98	2,000	—	—	70,000
12/97	1,378	—	—	43,000
12/96	869	—	—	—
Annual Growth	14.2%	—	—	(0.4%)

Revenue History

Hallmark

As the #1 producer of warm fuzzies, Hallmark Cards is the Goliath of greeting cards. The company's cards are sold under brand names such as Hallmark, Shoebox, and Ambassador and can be found in more than 42,000 US retail stores (about 4,100 of these stores bear the Hallmark Gold Crown name; the majority of these stores are franchised). Hallmark also owns Binney & Smith (maker of Crayola brand crayons) and portrait studio chain The Picture People. It offers electronic greeting cards and flowers through its Web site and produces television movies through Hallmark Entertainment and its 84%-owned Crown Media unit, which it is considering selling. Members of the founding Hall family own two-thirds of Hallmark.

Not resting on well-engraved laurels, Hallmark has announced its intention to triple its revenue by 2010. While it plans to continue expanding its greeting card empire, the company is also intent on stretching its reach in markets such as personal development and family entertainment. Hallmark brought a literary slant to its products with a line of cards and products developed by Pulitzer Prize nominee and poet Maya Angelou. The company is working on the image of its Gold Crown stores, changing store designs and layouts to reflect a homier image and differentiate the stores from other retail shops.

Hallmark decided to move some of its IT operations to Affiliated Computer Services in a seven-year deal worth $230 million; the Dallas-based company will open a center near the Hallmark headquarters to handle the work.

In 2005 the company's Crown Media unit sold its overseas operations as well as foreign rights to its program library.

HISTORY

Eighteen-year-old Joyce Hall started selling picture postcards from two shoe boxes in his room at the Kansas City, Missouri, YMCA in 1910. His brother Rollie joined him the next year, and the two added greeting cards to their line in 1912. The brothers opened Hall Brothers, a store that sold postcards, gifts, books, and stationery, but it was destroyed in a 1915 fire. The Halls got a loan, bought an engraving company, and produced their first original cards in time for Christmas.

In 1921 a third brother, William, joined the firm, which started stamping the backs of its cards with the phrase "A Hallmark Card." By 1922 Hall Brothers had salespeople in all 48 states. The firm began selling internationally in 1931.

Hall Brothers patented the "Eye-Vision" display case for greeting cards in 1936 and sold it to retailers across the country. The company aired its first radio ad in 1938. The next year it introduced a friendship card, displaying a cart filled with purple pansies. The card became the company's best-seller. During WWII Joyce Hall persuaded the government not to curtail paper supplies, arguing that his greeting cards were essential to the nation's morale.

The company opened its first retail store in 1950. The following year marked the first production of *Hallmark Hall of Fame,* TV's longest-running dramatic series and winner of more Emmy awards than any other program. Hall Brothers changed its name to Hallmark Cards in

1954 and introduced its Ambassador line of cards five years later.

Hallmark introduced paper party products and started putting *Peanuts* characters on cards in 1960. Donald Hall, Joyce Hall's son, was appointed CEO in 1966. Two years later Hallmark opened Crown Center, which surrounded company headquarters in Kansas City. Disaster struck in 1981 when two walkways collapsed at Crown Center's Hyatt Regency hotel, killing 114 and injuring 225.

Joyce Hall died in 1982, and Donald Hall became both chairman and CEO. Hallmark acquired Crayola Crayon maker Binney & Smith in 1984. It introduced Shoebox Greetings, a line of nontraditional cards, in 1986. Irvine Hockaday replaced Donald Hall as CEO the same year (Hall continued as chairman).

The company joined with Information Storage Devices in 1993 to market recordable greeting cards. It unveiled its Web site, Hallmark.com, in 1996 and began offering electronic greeting cards. Hallmark's 1998 acquisition of UK-based Creative Publications boosted the company into the top spot in the British greeting card market. The following year the company acquired portrait studio chain The Picture People and Christian greeting card maker DaySpring Cards. Hallmark also introduced Warm Wishes, a line of 99-cent cards. The company also unveiled the Hallmark Home Collection, a line of home furnishings.

The company began testing overnight flower delivery in the US just in time for Valentine's Day 2000. Hallmark Entertainment subsidiary Crown Media went public in that same year. Hockaday retired as president and CEO at the end of 2001; vice chairman Donald Hall Jr. took the additional title of CEO in early 2002.

EXECUTIVES

Chairman: Donald J. Hall
Vice Chairman, President, and CEO:
  Donald J. (Don) Hall Jr., age 49
EVP and CFO: Robert J. Druten, age 58
EVP and General Counsel: Brian E. Gardner, age 52
EVP Corporate Strategy: Anil Jagtiani, age 43
SVP Creative Product Development: Paul Barker
SVP Human Resources: Tom Wright
SVP Information Technology: Steve Hawn
SVP Public Affairs and Communication: Steve Doyal
SVP Sales: Steve Paoletti
**VP Business Research and One-to-One Consumer
  Marketing:** Jay Dittmann
VP Operations: Margaret Keating
VP Supermarket Sales: Marc Woodward
VP Trade Development: Vince G. Burke
Director of Marketing: Jim Welch
**Public Relations Director, Public Affairs and
  Communications:** Julie O'Dell

LOCATIONS

HQ: Hallmark Cards, Inc.
  2501 McGee St., Kansas City, MO 64108
Phone: 816-274-5111   **Fax:** 816-274-5061
Web: www.hallmark.com

Hallmark Cards has operations in Australia, Belgium, Canada, Denmark, Japan, Mexico, the Netherlands, New Zealand, Puerto Rico, Spain, the UK, and the US.

PRODUCTS/OPERATIONS

Selected Product Lines

Ambassador (greeting cards)
Fresh Ink (greeting cards)
Life Mosaic (cards and gifts by poet Maya Angelou)
Hallmark.com (electronic greeting cards, gifts, flowers)
Hallmark Flowers (flower delivery)
Keepsake (holiday ornaments and other collectibles)
Mahogany (products celebrating
  African-American heritage)
Nature's Sketchbook (cards and gifts)
Shoebox (greeting cards)
Sinceramente (Spanish-language greeting cards)
Tree of Life (products celebrating Jewish heritage)

Selected Subsidiaries

Binney & Smith (Crayola brand crayons and markers)
Crown Center Redevelopment (retail complex)
DaySpring Cards (Christian greeting cards)
Gift Certificate Center (business and
  consumer certificates)
Hallmark Entertainment (television, movies, and home
  video production)
  Crown Media Holdings (79%, pay television channels)
Halls Merchandising (department store)
Image Arts (discount greeting card distribution)
InterArt (specialized cards)
Irresistible Ink (handwriting and marketing service)
Litho-Krome (lithography)
The Picture People (portrait studio chain)
William Arthur (invitations, stationery)

COMPETITORS

1-800-FLOWERS.COM	Lifetouch
American Greetings	Nobleworks
Amscan	Olan Mills
Andrews McMeel Universal	Paramount Cards
Blyth	Party City
CPI Corp.	PCA International
CSS Industries	SPS Studios
Disney	Syratech
Dixon Ticonderoga	Thomas Nelson
Enesco Group	Time Warner
Faber-Castell	Viacom

HISTORICAL FINANCIALS

Company Type: Private

Income Statement

FYE: December 31

	REVENUE ($ mil.)	NET INCOME ($ mil.)	NET PROFIT MARGIN	EMPLOYEES
12/04	4,400	—	—	18,000
12/03	4,300	—	—	18,000
12/02	4,000	—	—	18,645
12/01	4,000	—	—	20,000
12/00	4,200	—	—	24,500
12/99	4,200	—	—	21,000
12/98	3,900	—	—	20,945
12/97	3,700	—	—	12,554
12/96	3,600	—	—	12,600
12/95	3,400	—	—	12,100
Annual Growth	2.9%	—	—	4.5%

Revenue History

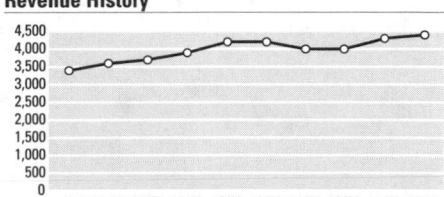

Hampton Affiliates

As a vertically integrated lumber company, Hampton Affiliates knows trees from the seedling to the stud. One of Oregon's top timber firms, Hampton produces about 900 million board ft. of lumber annually. The company has more than 180,000 acres of timberland and owns tree farms and mills in Oregon and Washington. Through its Hampton Distribution Companies division, it distributes doors, windows, and other building materials. Hampton supplies homebuilding centers through its stud lumber and distribution operations. L. M. "Bud" Hampton founded the company in 1942, and the Hampton family continues to own the enterprise.

Hampton Affiliates has grown primarily by adding timberland and increasing its manufacturing capacity and distribution operations. Its plan for future growth includes expanding its resource base, adding manufacturing plants, and investing in new technologies and equipment upgrades. The company also plans to diversify into new market segments and opportunities throughout the Pacific Rim region.

During 2002 the company acquired Darrington Lumber Mills and completed a timberland exchange of 92,000 acres. In 2004 the company added 12,000 acres in Northwest Oregon through its purchase of Wilson River Tree Farm. It also closed its Fort Hill sawmill that year due to uncertain supply and maket conditions. Hampton Affiliates sold its Lane Stanton Vance hardwoods distribution business to BlueLinx in 2005.

EXECUTIVES

Vice Chairman: Ronald C. (Ron) Parker
CEO: Steven J. (Steve) Zika
CTO: Andy McNiece
VP Finance and CFO: Robert Bluhm
VP Manufacturing: Bruce Mallory
Controller: Arvid Lacy
President, HLS: Michael (Mike) Phillips
General Sales Manager: Carter Stinton
Director, Human Resources: Dave Salmon
General Manager, HDC Sacramento: Jeff Wedge
Director, Distribution and Financial Analysis, HDC Sacramento: Chris Walton

LOCATIONS

HQ: Hampton Affiliates
9600 SW Barnes Rd., Ste. 200, Portland, OR 97225
Phone: 503-297-7691   **Fax:** 503-203-6607
Web: www.hamptonlumber.com

Hampton Affiliates owns sawmills in Oregon and Washington, and distribution facilities in California.

PRODUCTS/OPERATIONS

Selected Products
Clear and industrial lumber
Dimensional lumber
Engineered wood
Panel products
Residential doors
Siding and trim
Stud lumber
Timbers
Wood windows

Selected Services
Custom milling
Design floor and roof systems
Engineered wood take-offs
Overseas delivery
Rail car delivery
Reloading
Softwood remanufacturing
Truck delivery
Warehousing

COMPETITORS

Georgia-Pacific Corporation
International Paper
Louisiana-Pacific
OfficeMax
Roseburg Forest Products
Sierra Pacific Industries
Simpson Investment
TreeSource
West Fraser Timber
Western Forest Products
Weyerhaeuser

HISTORICAL FINANCIALS

Company Type: Private

Income Statement

FYE: January 31

	REVENUE ($ mil.)	NET INCOME ($ mil.)	NET PROFIT MARGIN	EMPLOYEES
1/04	700	—	—	1,300
1/03	700	—	—	1,300
1/02	700	—	—	1,300
1/01	721	—	—	1,300
1/00	715	—	—	1,100
1/99	525	—	—	900
1/98	500	—	—	800
Annual Growth	5.8%	—	—	8.4%

Revenue History

```
800
700                   o---o---o---o---o
600
500           o---o
400
300
200
100
  0
   1/95 1/96 1/97 1/98 1/99 1/00 1/01 1/02 1/03 1/04
```

Hard Rock Hotel

This might be one of the only times in your life that you can find a Rolling Stone pinned to *The Wall* as you contemplate the glamour of Ziggy Stardust. Hard Rock Hotel, Inc. owns and operates the Hard Rock Hotel and Casino in Las Vegas. Using the successful cafe with the same name as its inspiration, the hotel boasts a collection of rock memorabilia as well as the giant outside guitar synonymous with the Hark Rock name.

The hotel and casino is also home to a nightclub, concert hall, several restaurants, and a spa, as well as several other retail establishments.

The company plans to open its second location, a Roman-themed casino and hotel, outside San Diego in late 2006. A third location, planned to open in September 2005 in Biloxi, Mississippi, will now open in 2006. The complex was nearly destroyed when Hurricane Katrina made landfall in August 2005.

EXECUTIVES

Chairman, CEO, and Secretary: Peter A. Morton
President and COO: Kevin Kelley
CFO, VP of Finance, and Treasurer:
James D. (Jim) Bowen
SVP: Brian D. Ogaz
Director, Marketing and Public Relations:
Dallas Orchard
Auditors: Deloitte & Touche LLP

LOCATIONS

HQ: Hard Rock Hotel, Inc.
4455 Paradise Rd., Las Vegas, NV 89109
Phone: 702-693-5000   **Fax:** 702-693-5021
Web: www.hardrockhotel.com

COMPETITORS

Harrah's Entertainment
Isle of Capri Casinos
Las Vegas Sands
MGM MIRAGE
Riviera Holdings
Trump

HISTORICAL FINANCIALS

Company Type: Private

Income Statement

FYE: December 31

	REVENUE ($ mil.)	NET INCOME ($ mil.)	NET PROFIT MARGIN	EMPLOYEES
12/04	151	3	1.7%	1,735
12/03	139	2	1.5%	1,646
12/02	128	3	2.0%	—
Annual Growth	8.5%	0.0%	—	5.4%

Net Income History

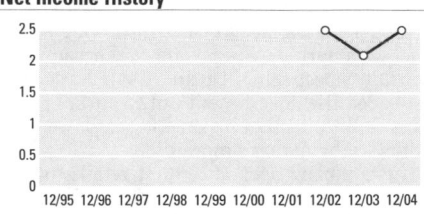

```
2.5                            o
  2                              o---o
1.5
  1
0.5
  0
   12/95 12/96 12/97 12/98 12/99 12/00 12/01 12/02 12/03 12/04
```

Harman Management

This company helped a colonel get started in the chicken business. Harman Management, one of the largest franchisees of KFC (a division of YUM! Brands), was founded by Leon Harman — the first person to buy a franchise from Colonel Sanders, the chain's founder. The company now has more than 340 fried chicken units in California, Colorado, Utah, and Washington, along with several locations co-branded with Taco Bell, Pizza Hut, and A&W units. Harman, who ran a cafe in Salt Lake City, was awarded his franchise in 1952. He coined the name Kentucky Fried Chicken and popularized the concept of selling the chicken in a bucket.

EXECUTIVES

Chairman and President: James Olson
COO: Vern Wardle
VP Finance: James Jackson
VP Operations: Jim Beglin
Director of Real Estate: Karen Bellini
Director of Human Resources: Shawn Grady

LOCATIONS

HQ: Harman Management Corporation
199 1st St., Ste. 212, Los Altos, CA 94022
Phone: 650-941-5681   **Fax:** 650-948-7532

COMPETITORS

AFC Enterprises	In-N-Out Burgers
Burger King	Jack in the Box
Chick-fil-A	K-MAC
CKE Restaurants	McDonald's
Dairy Queen	Subway
Del Taco	Wendy's
El Pollo Loco	

HISTORICAL FINANCIALS

Company Type: Private

Income Statement

FYE: June 30

	REVENUE ($ mil.)	NET INCOME ($ mil.)	NET PROFIT MARGIN	EMPLOYEES
6/04	391	—	—	13,500
6/03	377	—	—	13,000
6/02	378	—	—	13,000
6/01	335	—	—	
Annual Growth	5.3%	—	—	1.9%

Revenue History

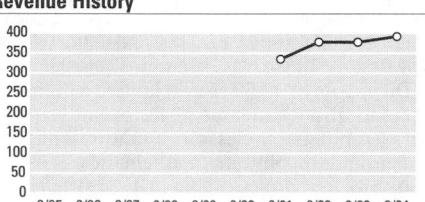

Harpo

Everyone knows Oprah Winfrey is an exceptional businesswoman; there's no need to Harpo on it. Unrelated to the silent Marx brother, Harpo controls the entertainment interests of talk show host/actress/producer Oprah Winfrey. *The Oprah Winfrey Show* is the highest-rated TV talk show in history, seen in almost every US market and in 110 countries. Winfrey's show has ranked number one among all talk shows for virtually every season of its long run (it is currently in its 19th season). Harpo also produces feature films (*Beloved,* which also starred Winfrey) and made-for-TV movies (*Oprah Winfrey Presents: Tuesdays with Morrie*) and publishes *O, The Oprah Magazine* with Hearst at a circulation of about 2.7 million.

Winfrey is worth about $1 billion according to *Forbes* magazine's list of billionaires. (She is the first black woman to join the ranks.) Her innovative ideas (such as Oprah's Book Club, which sent many previously little known titles to the top of bestseller lists) have earned *The Oprah Winfrey Show* about 40 Emmys. Each week her show has some 30 million viewers in the US, about three-fourths of whom are women. The talk show icon had previously announced that her show would end in 2006, the 20th anniversary of the program; however, she has since signed a new contract to keep it on the air into 2011. (Windrey claims she will retire that year as well.)

Winfrey also owns a significant stake in women's cable channel operator Oxygen Media. The Oxygen network airs her *Oprah After the Show* program, where viewers can see candid conversations Oprah has with her studio audience.

Winfrey founded Harpo (Oprah spelled backwards) in 1986.

HISTORY

Oprah Winfrey began her broadcasting career in 1973 at age 19 as a news anchor at Nashville's WTVF-TV. She became an evening news co-anchor in Baltimore in 1976, where she was recruited to co-host WJZ-TV's local talk show *People Are Talking*. She moved to Chicago in the early 1980s to host ABC affiliate WLS-TV's *AM Chicago,* which quickly became the city's top morning talk show. It was renamed *The Oprah Winfrey Show* in 1985.

Winfrey's performance in Steven Spielberg's *The Color Purple* in 1985 (her first ever acting role) won her an Oscar nomination and boosted her ratings when *The Oprah Winfrey Show* debuted nationally in 138 cities the following year thanks to a syndication deal with King World Productions secured by her agent (later Harpo's president and COO) Jeffrey Jacobs. Harpo was founded that year.

Winfrey obtained full ownership of her program in 1988. Two years later Harpo Films was created, and Winfrey bought a Chicago studio to produce *Oprah,* becoming only the third woman to own her own production studio (Mary Pickford and Lucille Ball were the others). She introduced the popular Oprah's Book Club in 1996. Also that year Texas cattlemen filed a lawsuit claiming she had caused a drop in beef futures prices after a show on the UK outbreak of mad cow disease (Winfrey didn't emphasize that the disease had not appeared in the US). But jurors ruled in her favor in early 1998. Winfrey also re-

newed her contract that year until the 2001-2002 TV season.

In 1998 Winfrey agreed to produce original programming for Oxygen, a new cable network for women, in exchange for an equity stake. CBS bought King World in 1999, and the deal gave King World stockholder Winfrey a $100 million stake in CBS (which is now a stake in Viacom following its buy of CBS). The following year Winfrey launched with Hearst her own magazine (*O, The Oprah Magazine*) that focuses on relationships, health, and fashion.

In 2002 the talk show diva decided that Oprah's Book Club would be an occasional, instead of a regular, segment on her TV program (much to the dismay of many book publishers). In addition, a spinoff talk show hosted by Dr. Phil McGraw (a regular on the Oprah show) premiered that year. In 2003 Winfrey announced that she was reviving her book club (with an emphasis on classic literature rather than books authored by contemporary writers). She also signed a contract to keep her TV program on the air into 2008. The next year Winfrey extended the contract even further, striking a deal to keep gabbing until 2011.

EXECUTIVES

Chairman: Oprah Winfrey, age 50
CFO: Doug Pattison
President, Harpo Productions: Tim Bennett
President, Harpo Films: Kate Forte
Director of Ad Sales, Oprah.com, Harpo Interactive: Doug Weiner
Director of Media and Corporate Relations: Lisa Halliday
Director of Harpo Interactive: Jessica DeVlieger
Director of Human Resources: Bernice Smith
Creative Services and Program Development: Harriet Seitler

LOCATIONS

HQ: Harpo, Inc.
110 N. Carpenter St., Chicago, IL 60607
Phone: 312-633-1000   **Fax:** 312-633-1976
Web: www.oprah.com

PRODUCTS/OPERATIONS

Selected Operations

Harpo Entertainment Group
Harpo Films
    Beloved (1998)
    Oprah Winfrey Presents: Before Women Had Wings (1997)
    Oprah Winfrey Presents: The Wedding (1998)
    Overexposed (1992)
    There Are No Children Here (1993)
Harpo Productions
    Oprah After the Show
    Oprah Winfrey Presents: Amy & Isabelle (2001)
    Oprah Winfrey Presents: David and Lisa (1998)
    Oprah Winfrey Presents: Tuesdays with Morrie (1999)
    The Oprah Winfrey Show
    The Women of Brewster Place (1989)
Harpo Video
O, The Oprah Magazine (joint venture with Hearst Corporation)
Oprah's Angel Network (charitable organization)
Oprah's Book Club (reading club featured on *The Oprah Winfrey Show*)
Oprah Boutique (consumer products)
Oprah.com

COMPETITORS

Hallmark	Rainbow Media
iVillage	Sony Pictures
Lifetime	Entertainment
Martha Stewart Living	Time Warner
NBC Universal TV Studio	Viacom
News Corp.	

HISTORICAL FINANCIALS

Company Type: Private

Income Statement

FYE: December 31

	REVENUE ($ mil.)	NET INCOME ($ mil.)	NET PROFIT MARGIN	EMPLOYEES
12/03	275	—	—	250
12/02	225	—	—	240
12/01	200	—	—	221
12/00	180	—	—	200
12/99	170	—	—	200
12/98	162	—	—	190
12/97	150	—	—	175
12/96	140	—	—	176
12/95	130	—	—	166
12/94	120	—	—	141
Annual Growth	9.7%	—	—	6.6%

Revenue History

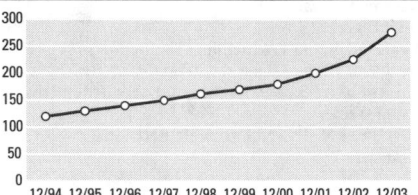

Harry & David Holdings

Harry & David Holdings (formerly Bear Creek Holdings) wants customers to enjoy the fruits — and flowers — of its labors. Its Harry and David Direct Marketing catalog and Intenet unit offers gift baskets filled with gourmet foods, most notably its Royal Riviera pears and chocolates. Harry and David Stores sell fruit and flowers at about 140 locations across the US. It also owns Jackson & Perkins, a mail-order nursery specializing in roses, and rose wholesaler Jackson & Perkins Wholesale. Bear Creek had been owned by Yamanouchi (now Astellas), but was sold in 2004 to New York investment firm Wasserstein & Co. for about $260 million. The company's new owners filed in August 2005 to take the company public.

Following the sale to Wasserstein & Co., Nancy Tait and John Dailey (CEO and CFO, respectively) retired from the company in July 2004 and were replaced by a former Yamanouchi executive Bill Williams (as the new CEO) and Wasserstein executive Steve O'Connell as the company's new chief financial and administrative officer. A month later, the company laid off 60 employees in the finance, information technology, and human resources departments.

Beginning in 2003 Lowe's became the exclusive home center retailer of Jackson & Perkins roses.

About 95% of the company's crop is sold from September through December. Harry and David Stores have locations in 35 states.

EXECUTIVES

President, CEO, and Director: William H. (Bill) Williams, age 57, $837,104 pay (partial-year salary)

CFO, Chief Administrative Officer, and Director: Stephen V. (Steve) O'Connell, age 46, $575,000 pay (partial-year salary)

EVP, Human Resources: Rudd C. Johnson, age 55, $337,050 pay (partial-year salary)

SVP and General Manager, Direct Marketing: William C. (Bill) Michel, age 53, $416,080 pay

SVP and General Manager, Stores: Cathy J. Fultineer, age 47, $434,000 pay

SVP and General Manager, Product Supply: Peter Kratz, age 51

SVP and General Manager, Customer Operations: Donald Cato, age 55

SVP and General Manager, Wholesale: Alfred M. Multari, age 45

SVP, General Counsel, and Secretary: Robert E. (Bob) Bluth

SVP, Corporate Relations: William J. (Bill) Ihle

SVP, Agricultural Operations: Ron Henri

Auditors: Ernst & Young LLP

LOCATIONS

HQ: Harry & David Holdings, Inc.
2500 S. Pacific Hwy., Medford, OR 97501
Phone: 541-864-2362   **Fax:** 541-864-2742
Web: www.bco.com

PRODUCTS/OPERATIONS

2005 Sales

	% of total
Harry and David Direct Marketing	62
Harry and David Stores	23
Jackson & Perkins	13
Other	2
Total	**100**

COMPETITORS

1-800-FLOWERS.COM	Lindt & Sprüngli
Burpee & Co.	Lowe's
Calloway's Nursery	Martha Stewart Living
Dean & DeLuca	Omaha Steaks
FTD	See's Candies
Godiva Chocolatier	Skinner Nurseries
Hickory Farms	Smith & Hawken
Home Depot	Tastefully Simple

HISTORICAL FINANCIALS

Company Type: Private

Income Statement

FYE: Last Saturday in June

	REVENUE ($ mil.)	NET INCOME ($ mil.)	NET PROFIT MARGIN	EMPLOYEES
3/05	562	(4)	—	1,507
3/04	522	11	2.1%	—
3/03	515	10	2.0%	—
3/02	489	—	—	—
3/01	455	—	—	—
3/00	464	—	—	—
3/99	369	—	—	—
3/98	332	—	—	—
Annual Growth	7.8%	—	—	—

2005 Year-End Financials

Debt ratio: 1,951.6%   Current ratio: 1.44
Return on equity: —   Long-term debt ($ mil.): 245
Cash ($ mil.): 60

Net Income History

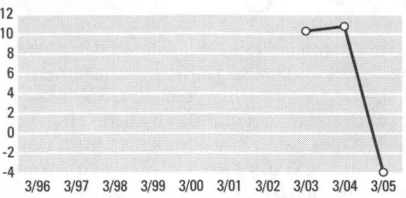

Harvard University

Many parents dream of sending their children to Harvard; some even dream of being able to afford it at about $27,500 a year (undergraduate). Harvard, the oldest institution of higher learning in the US, is home to Harvard College (undergraduate studies) and 10 graduate schools including the John F. Kennedy School of Government and the Harvard Business, Law, and Medical Schools. The Radcliffe Institute for Advanced Study at Harvard was created when Radcliffe College and Harvard University merged in 1999. Harvard has more than 19,700 students, about two-thirds of whom are enrolled in graduate programs. Harvard's endowment of almost $26 billion is the largest of any university in the world. (Yale ranks #2).

It's usually a toss-up whether Harvard or one of its Ivy League rivals Princeton or Yale will rank at the top of the list of America's premiere schools or programs, but the university's reputation for academic excellence is well-founded. More than 40 Harvard faculty members have won Nobel Prizes over the years. Additionally, among Harvard's alumni are six US presidents — John Adams, John Quincy Adams, Rutherford B. Hayes, John F. Kennedy, Franklin Delano Roosevelt, and Theodore Roosevelt.

HISTORY

In 1636 the General Court of Massachusetts appropriated 400 pounds sterling for the establishment of a college. The first building was completed at Cambridge in 1639 and was named for John Harvard, who had willed his collection of about 400 books and half of his land to the school. The first freshman class had four students.

During its first 150 years, Harvard adhered to the education standards of European schools, with emphasis on classical literature and languages, philosophy, and mathematics. It established its first professorship in 1721 (the Hollis Divinity Professorship) and soon after added professorships in mathematics and natural philosophy. In 1783 the school appointed its first professor of medicine.

Harvard updated its curriculum in the early 1800s, after professor Edward Everett returned from studying abroad with reports of the modern teaching methods in Germany. The university established the Divinity School in 1816, the

Law School in 1817, and two schools of science in the 1840s.

In 1869 president Charles Eliot began engineering the development of graduate programs in arts and sciences, engineering, and architecture. He raised standards at the medical and law schools and laid the groundwork for the Graduate School of Business Administration and the School of Public Health. Radcliffe College was founded as "Harvard Annex" in 1879, 15 years after a group of women had begun studying privately with Harvard professors in rented rooms.

Harvard's enrollment, faculty, and endowment grew tremendously throughout the 20th century. The Graduate School of Education opened in 1920, and the first undergraduate residential house opened in 1930. In the 1930s and 1940s, the school established a scholarship program and a general education curriculum for undergraduates. During WWII Harvard and Radcliffe undergraduates began attending the same classes.

A quota limiting the number of female students was abolished in 1975, and in 1979 Harvard introduced a new core curriculum. Princeton-educated Neil Rudenstine became president in 1991 and vowed to cut costs and to seek additional funding so that no one should be denied a Harvard education for financial reasons.

Harvard made dubious headlines during its 1994-95 academic year, enduring a bank robbery in Harvard Square, three student suicides, and one murder-suicide. The following year Harvard paid a fine of $775,000 after the US Attorney's Office claimed the school's pharmacy had not properly controlled drugs, including antidepressants and codeine cough syrup. The fine was the largest ever paid in the US under the Controlled Substance Act.

In 1998 Harvard's endowment fund acquired insurance services firm White River in one of the largest direct investments ever made by a not-for-profit institution. Also that year the school altered some of its graduation processes and introduced stress-reducing programs in the wake of another student suicide.

In 1999 Radcliffe College merged with Harvard and the Radcliffe Institute for Advanced Study at Harvard was established. In 2000 president Neil Rudenstine announced he would step down in 2001. Former US Treasury Secretary Lawrence Summers replaced him.

EXECUTIVES

President: Lawrence H. (Larry) Summers, age 51
Provost: Steven E. (Steve) Hyman
VP Administration: Sally H. Zeckhauser
VP Alumni Affairs and Development: Donella Rapier
VP Finance: Ann E. Berman
VP Government, Community, and Public Affairs: Alan Stone
VP Human Resources: Marilyn M. Hausammann
VP and General Counsel: Robert I. Iuliano
Assistant Provost and CIO: Dan Moriarty
Interim Chief Investment Officer: Peter A. Nadosy
Treasurer: James Rothenberg
Controller: Jay Bounty
Auditors: PricewaterhouseCoopers LLP

LOCATIONS

HQ: Harvard University
Massachusetts Hall, Cambridge, MA 02138
Phone: 617-495-1000   **Fax:** 617-495-0754
Web: www.harvard.edu

PRODUCTS/OPERATIONS

Selected Programs and Schools

Undergraduate
Harvard College

Graduate
Graduate School of Arts and Sciences
Graduate School of Design
Graduate School of Education
Harvard Business School
Harvard Divinity School
Harvard Law School
Harvard Medical School
Harvard School of Public Health
John F. Kennedy School of Government
School of Dental Medicine

HISTORICAL FINANCIALS

Company Type: School

Income Statement

FYE: June 30

	REVENUE ($ mil.)	NET INCOME ($ mil.)	NET PROFIT MARGIN	EMPLOYEES
6/03	2,473	—	—	11,000
6/02	2,357	—	—	15,000
6/01	2,228	—	—	15,000
6/00	2,023	—	—	11,360
6/99	1,788	—	—	10,500
6/98	1,679	—	—	9,701
6/97	1,565	—	—	12,782
6/96	1,519	—	—	12,150
6/95	1,467	—	—	11,100
6/94	1,377	—	—	11,000
Annual Growth	**6.7%**	**—**	**—**	**0.0%**

Revenue History

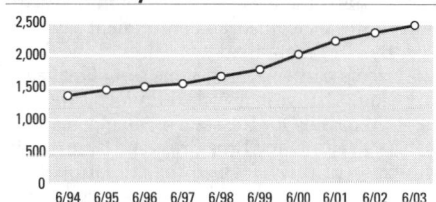

Haworth

Designers at Haworth sit at their cubicles and think about . . . more cubicles. The company is one of the top office furniture manufacturers in the US, behind #1 Steelcase and competing with HNI Corporation for the #2 position. Haworth offers a full range of furniture known for its innovative design, including partitions, desks, chairs, tables, and storage products. Brands include Berlin, if, PLACES, and X99. Dilbert and other long-suffering office drones have Haworth to thank for inventing the pre-wired partitions that make today's cubicled workplace possible. Haworth is owned by the family of Gerrard Haworth, who founded the company in 1948.

The company sells its products worldwide through more than 600 dealers. It has about 40 manufacturing locations and 60 showrooms worldwide.

Haworth, known as an aggressive competitor, has been expanding its presence in Europe, mostly through acquisitions. Operations include Germany's Roeder, Spain's Kemen, and Canada's SMED and Groupe Lacasse. In late 2003 Ha-

worth agreed to purchase the assets of flooring maker Interface Architectural Resources.

An extended decline in the office furniture industry is forcing the company to consolidate operations, including relocating its US manufacturing from four states (Arkansas, North Carolina, Pennsylvania, and Texas) to three plants in Michigan.

EXECUTIVES

Founding Chairman: G. W. Haworth
Chairman: Richard G. (Dick) Haworth
President and CEO: Franco Bianchi
VP, Global Human Resources: Nancy Teutsch
VP, Global Sales and Marketing: Gary Scitthelm
CFO and VP, International Sectors: Calvin W. (Cal) Kreuze
VP and General Manager, Asia Pacific: Frank Rexach
VP, Architecture and Design: Georgianna D. (Georgy) Olivieri
VP, European Operations: José Amaral
VP, Global Customer Service and Customer Processes: Al Lanning
VP, Global Information Systems: Micheal D. Moon
VP, Global Manufacturing: Robert J. (Bob) Stander
President, Groupe Lacasse: François Giroux
Manager, Corporate Communications: Susan Wray

LOCATIONS

HQ: Haworth, Inc.
1 Haworth Center, Holland, MI 49423
Phone: 616-393-3000   **Fax:** 616-393-1570
Web: www.haworth.com

Haworth operates in more than 120 countries throughout the Americas, Asia, the Caribbean, Europe, and the Middle East.

PRODUCTS/OPERATIONS

Products

Desks and casegoods
Files and storage
Seating
Systems
Tables
Work tools

Selected Brands

Accolade	Neon
Berlin	PLACES
DataThing	PREMISE
Forenze	RACE
Hello	Richmond
Huit	Tas
if	Tempo
Jump Stuff	Tripoli
LOOK	Tuscany
Maria	Varia
Monaco	X99

COMPETITORS

Falcon Products
Global Group
Herman Miller
HNI
Inscape
Jami
KI
Kimball International
Knoll
Neutral Posture
Norstar Office Products
Skandinavisk Group
Steelcase
Teknion
Trendway
Virco Mfg.

HISTORICAL FINANCIALS

Company Type: Private

Income Statement
FYE: December 31

	REVENUE ($ mil.)	NET INCOME ($ mil.)	NET PROFIT MARGIN	EMPLOYEES
12/03	1,230	—	—	9,000
12/02	1,320	—	—	9,500
12/01	1,710	—	—	10,000
12/00	2,065	—	—	14,500
12/99	1,580	—	—	10,000
12/98	1,540	—	—	10,000
12/97	1,510	—	—	10,000
12/96	1,370	—	—	9,000
12/95	1,150	—	—	8,900
12/94	1,005	—	—	7,400
Annual Growth	2.3%	—	—	2.2%

Revenue History

Health Care Service

Health Care Service Corporation (HCSC) has the Blues. HCSC is made up of Blue Cross Blue Shield of Illinois (that state's oldest and largest health insurer), Blue Cross and Blue Shield of Texas, and Blue Cross and Blue Shield of New Mexico. A licensee of the Blue Cross and Blue Shield Association, the mutual company provides a range of group and individual insurance and medical plans to nearly 10 million members, including indemnity insurance and managed care programs. HCSC also offers prescription drug plans, Medicare supplement insurance, dental and vision coverage, life and disability insurance, workers' compensation, retirement services, and medical financial services through subsidiaries.

HCSC also covers federal employees in its three states through the Federal Employee Program, a contract with the US government.

HCSC's strategy for growth consists of making strategic acquisitions of other independent Blue Cross companies, as well as other health and insurance companies that complement the company's core product offerings.

This strategy has allowed HCSC to better compete in the health care industry by benefiting from economies of scale.

HISTORY

The seeds of the Blue Cross organization were sown in 1929, when an official at Baylor University Hospital in Dallas began offering schoolteachers 21 days of hospital care for $6 a year. Fundamental to its coverage was a community rating system, which based premiums on the community's claims experience rather than subscribers' conditions.

In 1935 Elgin Watch Co. owner Taylor Strawn, Charles Schweppe, and other Chicago civic leaders pooled resources to form Hospital Services Corporation to provide the same type of coverage. (The firm adopted the Blue Cross symbol in 1939.) Employees of the Rand McNally cartography company were the first to be covered by the plan.

Soon, four similar plans were launched in other Illinois towns. Between 1947 and 1952, Hospital Services Corp. and these other four joined forces, offering coverage nearly statewide.

Meanwhile, Blue Shield physician's fee plans in several cities were incorporated as Illinois Medical Service. Hospital Services Corp. and Illinois Medical Service operated independently but shared office space and personnel.

A 1975 change in state legislation let the entities merge to become Health Care Service Corp. (HCSC), which offered both Blue Cross and Blue Shield coverage. Following the merger, the company's board of directors (which had been primarily composed of care providers) became dominated by consumers, which helped HCSC become more responsive to its members.

For the next six years, the state denied HCSC any rate increases, leaving it with a frighteningly low $12 million in reserves in 1982.

HCSC achieved statewide market presence in 1982 when it merged with Illinois' last independent Blue Cross plan, Rockford Blue Cross. In 1986, as managed care swept through the health care industry, only 14% of HCSC's members were enrolled in managed care plans. HCSC created its Managed Care Network Preferred point-of-service plan in 1991; the idea caught on with both employers and individuals and enrollment skyrocketed. By 1994 more than two-thirds of the firm's subscribers participated in some sort of managed care plan. That year it picked up Medicare payment processing for the state of Michigan.

In 1995 HCSC and Blue Cross and Blue Shield of Texas (BCBST) formed an affiliation they hoped would culminate in a merger giving the combined company $6 billion in sales and reserves of more than $1 billion. Texas consumer groups objected to the merger, claiming that Texas residents own BCBST and that Texans should be compensated for the transfer of ownership — especially since BCBST had received state tax breaks for decades in exchange for accepting all applicants. (A Texas judge ruled in favor of the merger in 1998.)

Citing high risks and low margins, HCSC in 1997 dropped its Medicare payment processing contract, which it had held for some 30 years. The next year HCSC agreed to pay $144 million after it pleaded guilty to covering up its poor performance in processing Medicare claims.

In 1998 HCSC acquired Blue Cross and Blue Shield of Texas.

In 1999 HCSC agreed to buy Aetna's NylCare of Texas, giving it large, profitable HMOs in Houston and Dallas (completed in 2000). The next year it bested Anthem (now WellPoint) and Wellmark in wooing the troubled Blue Cross Blue Shield of New Mexico (completed in 2001).

EXECUTIVES

President and CEO: Raymond F. McCaskey
EVP and COO: Sherman M. Wolff
SVP and CFO: Denise A. Bujack
SVP and Chief Information Officer: Patrick E. Moroney, age 48
SVP, Human Resources: Patrick O'Conner

President, Blue Cross and Blue Shield of Illinois: Gail K. Boudreaux, age 44
President, Blue Cross and Blue Shield of New Mexico: Liz Watrin, age 40
President, Blue Cross and Blue Shield of Texas: Patricia A. Hemingway Hall
VP and Treasurer: Brian A. Kennedy
VP and Actuary: Kenneth Avner
VP, Sales and Marketing Division, Blue Cross and Blue Shield of New Mexico: Dorane Wintermeyer
VP, Member Services Division, Blue Cross and Blue Shield of New Mexico: Linda Amburn
VP, National and Major Accounts: Paul Boulis
VP, Public Affairs and Advertising: John Ori
Director, Human Resources: Robert Ernst
Auditors: Ernst & Young LLP

LOCATIONS

HQ: Health Care Service Corporation
300 E. Randolph St., Chicago, IL 60601
Phone: 312-653-6000   **Fax:** 312-819-1220
Web: www.hcsc.net

PRODUCTS/OPERATIONS

Selected Products and Services

Dental insurance
Disability insurance
Indemnity insurance
Life insurance
Managed health care plans
Supplemental Medicare coverage
Prescription drug coverage
Retirement plans
Vision insurance
Workers' compensation

Selected Subsidiaries

Group Medical and Surgical Service
Preferred Financial Group
  Colorado Bankers Life Insurance Company
  Fort Dearborn Life Insurance Co.
  Medical Life Insurance Company
Rio Grande HMO, Inc.
Texas Gulf Coast HMO, Inc.
Texas Health Plan, Inc.
West Texas Health Plans, L.C.

COMPETITORS

Aetna	Mutual of Omaha
Aflac	New York Life
CIGNA	Prudential
Guardian Life	UnitedHealth Group
Humana	WellPoint
Kaiser Foundation Health Plan	

HISTORICAL FINANCIALS

Company Type: Mutual company

Income Statement
FYE: December 31

	REVENUE ($ mil.)	NET INCOME ($ mil.)	NET PROFIT MARGIN	EMPLOYEES
12/03	8,190	625	7.6%	13,000
12/02	7,312	246	3.4%	—
12/01	6,198	387	6.2%	—
12/00	10,430	174	1.7%	—
12/99	8,980	111	1.2%	—
12/98	7,819	50	0.6%	—
12/97	5,107	71	1.4%	5,700
12/96	4,478	89	2.0%	5,650
12/95	4,201	139	3.3%	5,600
12/94	3,930	166	4.2%	—
Annual Growth	8.5%	15.9%	—	11.1%

Debt ratio: 18.7%   Current ratio: —
Return on equity: 34.7%   Long-term debt ($ mil.): 400
Cash ($ mil.): 502

Net Income History

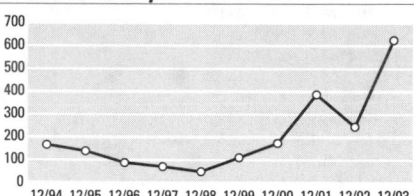

| | 12/94 | 12/95 | 12/96 | 12/97 | 12/98 | 12/99 | 12/00 | 12/01 | 12/02 | 12/03 |

Health Insurance of New York

This firm says it's HIP to be healthy. Health Insurance Plan of Greater New York (HIP) is a not-for-profit HMO founded in 1947 to provide low-cost health care to New York City employees. HIP now boasts more than 1 million members and is the largest HMO in the New York metro area, as well as New York state's biggest Medicare provider. The organization also provides medical, lab, and pharmacy services through some 41,000 physicians and about 61,000 locations in New York. HIP serves employer groups ranging from small firms to *FORTUNE* 500 companies.

HIP's efforts in the 1990s to expand out-of-state proved disastrous; its New Jersey effort was closed by regulators, and HIP sold its Florida affiliate after accumulating huge losses. Back home, HIP has faced allegations from regulators of lavish executive lifestyles and too-cozy relationships with contractors.

The company still dominates the New York metro HMO market, and is nationally recognized for its efficient use of information technology to reduce its operating costs and improve patient care.

To expand its presence in the Northeast, HIP acquired ConnectiCare. HIP has agreed to merge with Group Health (GHI).

EXECUTIVES

Chairman and CEO: Anthony L. Watson, age 64
President and COO: Daniel T. McGowan
EVP, CFO, General Counsel, and Corporate Secretary: Michael D. Fullwood
EVP, Brand Leadership: Thomas J. Mcateer Jr.
EVP, Medical Affairs and Chief Medical Officer: Ronald Platt
EVP, Operations and Chief Information Officer: John H. Steber
SVP, Information Technology and Chief Technology Officer: Pedro Villalba
SVP, Corporate Compliance and Internal Audit: Valerie A. Reardon
SVP, Finance and Corporate Controller: Dominic F. D'Adamo

SVP, External Affairs and Corporate Contributions: Arthur H. Barnes
SVP, Human Resources: Fred Blickman
SVP, Marketing and Sales, and Chief Marketing Officer: Larry G. Posner
SVP, Operations, Public Policy and Regulatory Affairs: David S. Abernethy
SVP, Public Affairs and Operations Advisor to the Chairman: Ronald Maiorana
VP and Treasurer: Michael S. Vincent
Auditors: Deloitte & Touche LLP

LOCATIONS

HQ: Health Insurance Plan of Greater New York
55 Water St., New York, NY 10041
Phone: 212-630-5000
Web: www.hipusa.com

PRODUCTS/OPERATIONS

2004 Sales

	$ mil.	% of total
Premiums	3,599.0	99
Investment income	34.0	1
Administrative services & other fees	16.7	—
Other	4.5	—
Total	**3,654.2**	**100**

Selected Health Plans

HIPaccess I & II (Traditional)
HIP Prime Dental
HIP Prime EPO/PPO
HIP Prime (HMO)
HIP Prime POS (point-of-service)
HIP VIP (Medicare)

COMPETITORS

Aetna   Oxford Health
CIGNA   Prudential
Health Net   UnitedHealth Group
Humana   WellChoice

HISTORICAL FINANCIALS

Company Type: Not-for-profit

Income Statement   FYE: December 31

	REVENUE ($ mil.)	NET INCOME ($ mil.)	NET PROFIT MARGIN	EMPLOYEES
12/04	3,654	215	5.9%	3,000
12/03	3,370	275	8.2%	2,000
12/02	2,902	178	6.1%	2,000
12/01	2,600	—	—	2,000
12/00	2,410	—	—	2,000
12/99	2,223	—	—	1,500
12/98	2,000	—	—	1,500
12/97	1,568	—	—	1,483
12/96	1,734	—	—	1,500
12/95	1,777	—	—	1,500
Annual Growth	8.3%	9.9%		8.0%

2004 Year-End Financials

Debt ratio: 0.7%   Current ratio: 2.27
Return on equity: 25.3%   Long-term debt ($ mil.): 6
Cash ($ mil.): 467

Net Income History

| | 12/95 | 12/96 | 12/97 | 12/98 | 12/99 | 12/00 | 12/01 | 12/02 | 12/03 | 12/04 |

Hearst

Like legendary founder William Randolph Hearst's castle, The Hearst Corporation is sprawling. The company owns 12 daily newspapers (the *San Francisco Chronicle;* the *Houston Chronicle*) and 14 weekly newspapers, 18 US consumer magazines (such as *Cosmopolitan* and *Esquire*) with more than 100 international editions, TV and radio stations (through 68%-owned Hearst Argyle Television), and a cartoon and features syndication service (King Features). Hearst is also active in cable networks through stakes in A&E, Lifetime, and ESPN; online services including a 25% stake in women's Web network iVillage; and business information publishing. The company is owned by the Hearst family, but managed by a board of trustees.

Using the selling power of its popular *Cosmopolitan* magazine, the company has capitalized with a TV channel in Spain based on the magazine. The company then added another one in Latin America and is considering a US launch. Hearst hasn't been so lucky when trying to take the trend in the other direction. The firm launched *Lifetime* magazine in 2003 with women's cable channel Lifetime. However, the magazine fared poorly and ceased publication in late 2004. This came on the heels of the high-profile failure of *Talk* magazine, a joint venture with movie studio Miramax. Led by Tina Brown, the famous former editor of *The New Yorker*, the magazine only lasted two years before the partners shut it down, citing the downturn in the economy and poor circulation.

Hearst further expanded its potent stable of magazines in 2003 by purchasing *Seventeen* magazine from PRIMEDIA. In addition to the magazine, the deal (valued at $182 million) includes the purchase of *Teen* magazine and school marketing business Cover Concepts. Hearst also became a major player in yellow page publishing with its 2004 purchase of White Directory Publishers, one of the largest telephone directory companies in the US.

Although it no longer owns Hearst Castle (deeded to the State of California in 1951), the company has extensive real estate holdings.

Upon his death, William Randolph Hearst left 99% of the company's common stock to two charitable trusts controlled by a 13-member board that includes five family and eight non-family members. The will includes a clause that allows the trustees to disinherit any heir who contests the will.

HISTORY

William Randolph Hearst, son of a California mining magnate, started as a reporter — having been expelled from Harvard in 1884 for playing jokes on professors. In 1887 he became editor of the *San Francisco Examiner,* which his father had obtained as payment for a gambling debt. In 1895 he bought the *New York Morning Journal* and competed against Joseph Pulitzer's *New York World.* The "yellow journalism" resulting from that rivalry characterized American-style reporting at the turn of the century.

Hearst branched into magazines (1903), film (1913), and radio (1928). Also during this time it created the Hearst International News Service (it was sold to E.W. Scripps' United Press in 1958 to form United Press International). By 1935 Hearst was at its peak, with newspapers in

19 cities, the largest syndicate (King Features), international news and photo services, 13 magazines, eight radio stations, and two motion picture companies. Two years later Hearst relinquished control of the company to avoid bankruptcy, selling movie companies, radio stations, magazines, and, later, most of his San Simeon estate. (Hearst's rise and fall inspired the 1941 film *Citizen Kane.*)

In 1948 Hearst became the owner of one of the US's first TV stations, WBAL-TV in Baltimore. When Hearst died in 1951, company veteran Richard Berlin became CEO. Berlin sold off failing newspapers, moved into television, and acquired more magazines.

Frank Bennack, CEO since 1979, expanded the company, acquiring newspapers, publishing firms (notably William Morrow, 1981), TV stations, magazines (*Redbook,* 1982; *Esquire,* 1986), and 20% of cable sports network ESPN (1991). Hearst branched into video via a joint venture with Capital Cities/ABC (1981) and helped launch the Lifetime and Arts & Entertainment cable channels (1984).

In 1991 Hearst launched a New England news network with Continental Cablevision. The following year Hearst brought on board former Federal Communications Commission chairman Alfred Sikes, who quickly moved the company onto the Internet. In 1996 Randolph A. Hearst passed the title of chairman to nephew George Hearst (the last surviving son of the founder, Randolph died in 2000). Broadcaster Argyle Television merged with Hearst's TV holdings in 1997 to form publicly traded Hearst-Argyle Television.

In 1999 Hearst combined its HomeArts Web site with Women.com to create one of the largest online networks for women. It also joined with Walt Disney's Miramax Films to publish entertainment magazine *Talk* (shut down in 2001) and Oprah Winfrey's Harpo Entertainment to publish *O, The Oprah Magazine* (launched in 2000). In 1999 the company sold its book publishing operations to News Corp.'s HarperCollins unit. It also agreed to buy the *San Francisco Chronicle* from rival Chronicle Publishing. That deal was called into question over concerns that the *San Francisco Examiner* would not survive and the city would be left with one major paper. To resolve the issue, the next year Hearst sold the *Examiner* to ExIn (a group of investors affiliated with the Ted Fang family and other owners of the *San Francisco Independent*). Also in 2000 Hearst bought the UK magazines of Gruner + Jahr, the newspaper and magazine unit of German media juggernaut Bertelsmann.

The following year Hearst gained a 30% stake in iVillage following that company's purchase of rival Women.com Networks. In mid-2002 Victor Ganzi took over as CEO and president following Bennack's retirement from these positions. Hearst expanded further into entertaining the younger generation in 2003 with the purchase of *Seventeen* magazine from PRIMEDIA.

EXECUTIVES

Chairman: George R. Hearst Jr., age 77
Vice Chairman: Frank A. Bennack Jr., age 72
President and CEO; Chairman, Hearst-Argyle Television: Victor F. Ganzi, age 58
SVP and CFO: Ronald J. Doerfler
SVP and Chief Legal and Development Officer: James M. Asher
SVP; President, Hearst Newspapers: George B. Irish
SVP; President and Group Head, Hearst Entertainment and Syndication: Raymond E. Joslin

VP; President and CEO, Hearst Magazines International; EVP, Hearst Magazines: George Green
VP; VP and Deputy Group Head, Hearst Entertainment and Syndication; President, Hearst Entertainment: Bruce Paisner
VP and Chief Communications Officer: Debra Shriver
Manager of Corporate Communications: Alex Steinberg
Chairman and Editor In Chief, SmartMoney: Edwin A. Finn Jr.
President and CEO, Hearst-Argyle Television: David J. Barrett, age 57
President, Hearst Business Media: Richard P. Malloch
President, Hearst Interactive Media: Kenneth A. Bronfin, age 45
President, Hearst Magazines: Cathleen P. (Cathie) Black, age 60
EVP, Hearst Newspapers: Steven R. Swartz

LOCATIONS

HQ: The Hearst Corporation
959 8th Ave., New York, NY 10019
Phone: 212-649-2000   **Fax:** 212-649-2108
Web: www.hearstcorp.com

Hearst newspapers are located throughout the US. Hearst Magazines are distributed in more than 100 countries.

PRODUCTS/OPERATIONS

Selected Operations
Broadcasting
  Hearst-Argyle Television (68%)
Business Publications
  Black Book
  Diversion
  Electronic Products
  First DataBank
  Motor Magazine
Entertainment and Syndication
  A&E Television Networks (37.5%, with ABC & NBC)
    A&E
    The Biography Channel
    The History Channel
    History Channel International
    The Military History Channel
  Cosmopolitan Television Iberia
    (Spain and Latin America)
  ESPN (20%)
  King Features Syndicate
  Lifetime Entertainment Services (50%, with ABC)
  Locomotion (50%; all animation TV)
  New England Cable News (with Comcast)
Interactive Media
  Circles (online loyalty marketing programs)
  drugstore.com (online pharmacy site)
  Hire.com (job site)
  iVillage (25%, Internet site geared towards women)
Magazines
  Best (UK magazine)
  Company (UK magazine)
  CosmoGIRL!
  Cosmopolitan
  Country Living
  Country Living GARDENER
  Esquire
  Good Housekeeping
  Harper's Bazaar
  House Beautiful
  Marie Claire (with Marie Claire Album)
  O, The Oprah Magazine (with Harpo)
  Popular Mechanics
  Prima (UK magazine)
  Redbook
  Seventeen
  She (UK magazine)
  SmartMoney (with Dow Jones)
  Teen
  Town & Country TRAVEL
  Veranda
  Your Home (UK magazine)
  Zest (UK magazine)

Major Newspapers
  Albany Times Union (New York)
  Houston Chronicle
  Huron Daily Tribune (Michigan)
  Laredo Morning Times (Texas)
  Midland Daily News (Michigan)
  San Antonio Express-News
  San Francisco Chronicle
  Seattle Post-Intelligencer
Real Estate
  Hearst Realties
  San Francisco Realties
  Sunical Land & Livestock Division
Other Operations
  Cover Concepts (in-school marketing)
  Reed Brennan Media Associates (custom electronic and pagination services for newspapers)
  White Directory Publishers (telephone directories)

COMPETITORS

Advance Publications	McGraw-Hill
Andrews McMeel Universal	MediaNews
Belo	Meredith
Bertelsmann	New York Times
Bloomberg	News Corp.
Cox Enterprises	PRIMEDIA
Dennis Publishing	Reader's Digest
Disney	Reed Elsevier Group
E. W. Scripps	Rodale
Emap	Seattle Times
Freedom Communications	Time Warner
Gannett	TransWestern Publishing
Hachette Filipacchi Médias	Tribune
infoUSA	Viacom
IPC Group	Washington Post
Knight-Ridder	Yellow Book USA
Liberty Media	

HISTORICAL FINANCIALS

Company Type: Private

Income Statement

FYE: December 31

	REVENUE ($ mil.)	NET INCOME ($ mil.)	NET PROFIT MARGIN	EMPLOYEES
12/03	4,100	—	—	20,000
12/02	3,565	—	—	17,320
12/01	3,300	—	—	17,170
12/00	3,400	—	—	18,300
12/99	2,740	—	—	14,000
12/98	2,200	—	—	13,555
12/97	2,833	—	—	15,000
12/96	2,568	—	—	14,000
12/95	2,513	—	—	14,000
12/94	2,299	—	—	14,000
Annual Growth	6.6%	—	—	4.0%

Revenue History

The Heat Group

The Miami Heat hope to blaze a trail to the NBA title. The team acquired All-Star Shaquille O'Neal from the Los Angeles Lakers in 2004 and played hot in the 2004-05 season before losing to the Detroit Pistons in the Eastern Conference finals. The team is owned by The Heat Group, organized by former 76ers head coach Billy Cunningham as part of the NBA's 1988 expansion. The Heat generated little until 1995 when Pat Riley, former coach of the NBA Champion Lakers, was named head coach and made the team a post season contender. In 2003 Riley resigned as coach but remains president. Stan Van Gundy replaced him on the court. The Heat warm up and play in AmericanAirlines Arena. Carnival CEO Micky Arison owns the firm.

EXECUTIVES

Owner and Managing General Partner: Micky Arison, age 55
President, Basketball Operations: Pat Riley, age 60
President, Business Operations: Eric Woolworth
EVP and Chief Marketing Officer: Michael McCullough
Head Coach: Stan Van Gundy, age 43
EVP Heat Group Enterprises: Mike Walker
SVP and CFO: Sammy Schulman
SVP and General Counsel: Raquel Libman
SVP Basketball Operations: Andy Elisburg
SVP Sales: Stephen Weber
VP and Chief Technology Officer: Tony Coba
VP Arena Marketing and Bookings: Eric Bresler
VP Business Development and Chief of Staff: Kim Stone
VP Facilities and General Manager, AmericanAirlines Arena: Alexander M Diaz
VP Marketing: Jeff Craney

LOCATIONS

HQ: The Heat Group
AmericanAirlines Arena, 601 Biscayne Blvd., Miami, FL 33132
Phone: 786-777-1000   **Fax:** 786-777-1615
Web: www.nba.com/heat

The Miami Heat play at 19,600-seat AmericanAirlines Arena in Miami.

COMPETITORS

Atlanta Hawks
Charlotte Bobcats
Orlando Magic
Washington Wizards

HISTORICAL FINANCIALS

Company Type: Private

Income Statement

FYE: July 1

	REVENUE ($ mil.)	NET INCOME ($ mil.)	NET PROFIT MARGIN	EMPLOYEES
6/04	93	—	—	—
6/03	91	—	—	—
6/02	96	—	—	—
6/01	99	—	—	—
6/00	90	—	—	80
6/99	33	—	—	60
6/98	50	—	—	95
6/97	44	—	—	87
6/96	39	—	—	80
Annual Growth	11.4%	—	—	0.0%

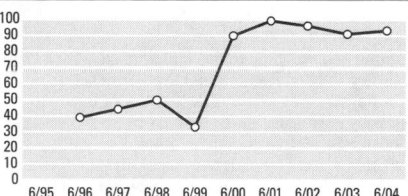

Revenue History

Heifer Project International

It's not just a handout; it's a new way of life. Heifer Project International (known as Heifer International) has helped some 4 million impoverished families from 115 countries and 35 states become self-sufficient. The charity provides more than 25 different kinds of breeding livestock that can be used for food, income, or plowing power in addition to training in sustainable agriculture techniques. In exchange, the family agrees to pass on not only the animals' first female offspring to another needy family, but their knowledge, too. Heifer International was established in 1944.

EXECUTIVES

President and CEO: Jo Luck, age 64
SVP, External Relations: Mark Schnarr
SVP, Internal Operations: Tanya Wright
SVP, Programs: James (Jim) De Vries
VP, Communications and Marketing: Tom Peterson
Director of Finance: Kit Smith
Director of Marketing: Mike Matchett
Auditors: BKD, LLP

LOCATIONS

HQ: Heifer Project International
1015 Louisiana St., Little Rock, AR 72202
Phone: 501-907-2600   **Fax:** 501-907-2805
Web: www.heifer.org

HISTORICAL FINANCIALS

Company Type: Not-for-profit

Income Statement

FYE: June 30

	REVENUE ($ mil.)	NET INCOME ($ mil.)	NET PROFIT MARGIN	EMPLOYEES
6/04	69	—	—	304
6/03	58	—	—	—
6/02	46	—	—	—
Annual Growth	22.7%	—	—	—

Revenue History

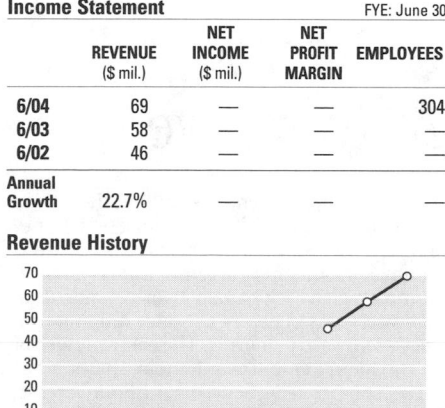

Helmsley

What word rhyming with "itch" describes Leona Helmsley? Rich! Helmsley Enterprises is the repository of the real estate empire amassed by the late Harry Helmsley over a period of 50 years. Helmsley's widow and heir, Leona, has interests in such high-profile properties as Carlton House, the Helmsley Park Lane, and the Helmsley Windsor. Other holdings include apartment buildings and millions of square feet of primarily New York real estate, not to mention a lease held on the Empire State Building until 2075. The portfolio was valued at $5 billion before Harry Helmsley's death in 1997. Leona Helmsley has sold more than $2 billion worth of property since.

Helmsley has ended a relatively quiet half-decade of staying out of the limelight. After quietly selling off a number of properties, many at a premium in New York's stratospheric real estate market, the "Queen of Mean" is grabbing headlines again: She won a public fight with Donald Trump over the terms of the Empire State Building lease (he sold his ownership interest in 2002), but was sued in separate actions for wrongful termination by the company's former chief operating officer and a former employee.

Leona's holdings may be eroding even further; the Helmsley Middletowne is up for sale, Helmsley hotels no longer hold coveted slots on the *Zagat Survey of Top U.S. Hotels*, and occupancy levels are below those of Manhattan's new trendy boutique hotels.

At its apex, Helmsley's real estate empire included interests in more than 25 million sq. ft. of office space, more than 20,000 apartments, some 7,500 hotel rooms, 50 retail projects, warehouse space, land, garages, restaurants, and real estate companies. To keep the money in the family, the properties were managed by Helmsley-Spear (then 99%-owned by Helmsley, sold in 1997) and Helmsley-Noyes.

HISTORY

In 1925 Harry Helmsley began his career as a Manhattan rent collector; the work, then done in person, taught him to evaluate buildings and acquainted him with their owners. During the Depression, Helmsley obtained property at bargain prices. He paid $1,000 down for a building with a $100,000 mortgage and later quipped that he did so to provide a job for his father, whom he hired as superintendent. In 1946 he sold the building for $165,000.

In the late 1940s Helmsley teamed up with lawyer Lawrence Wien. Helmsley located properties; Wien financed them through a device of his own invention, the loan syndicate. Prominent properties Helmsley bought into in the 1950s included the Flatiron (1951), Berkeley (1953), and Equitable (1957) buildings. He moved into management in 1955 with the purchase of Leon Spear's property management firm. In 1961 Helmsley bought the Empire State Building for $65 million and sold it to Prudential for $29 million with a 114-year leaseback (which expires in 2075); a public offering for the newly created Empire State Building Co. made up the balance.

In the mid-1960s Helmsley moved into property development, erecting office buildings and shopping centers. He bought the 30-building Furman and Wolfson trust, borrowing $78 million of the $165 million price on the strength of his reputation — the largest signature loan ever.

In 1969 Spear introduced Helmsley to Leona Roberts, a real estate broker who had sold Spear an apartment. Helmsley hired Leona and promoted her to SVP at his Brown, Harris, Stevens real estate brokerage. He divorced his wife and married Leona in 1971. In 1974 he leased an historic building and delegated the renovation to Leona (who built the company's hotel business). The Helmsley Palace opened in 1980 (now the New York Palace, sold 1993).

As Harry's health began to fail in the 1980s, Leona gained control of the empire. Maintenance deteriorated, bookkeeping went lax, and the couple's lavish spending became notorious. In 1988 they were charged with tax evasion. Harry was ruled incompetent to stand trial, but in 1989 Leona was convicted, fined $7.1 million, and sentenced to jail. She spent 21 months incarcerated, the last part of it in a halfway house.

After her 1994 release, Leona was banned from management of the hotels by laws forbidding felon involvement in businesses that serve liquor. She became more involved in the management of Harry's interests and began reshuffling assets, moving management contracts from Helmsley-Spear to Helmsley-Noyes, and selling buildings.

A 1995 suit brought by Harry's partners in Helmsley-Spear accused Leona of looting the company by depriving it of management contracts and loading it with debt to render worthless their right to buy the company under a 1970 option agreement.

In 1997 Harry died, and Leona announced she would sell the 125-property Helmsley portfolio. Wien's son-in-law Peter Malkin, partner in 13 top-notch Manhattan buildings, contested the control granted to her by Harry's will. They resolved their differences late that year. Leona also settled her differences with the Helmsley-Spear partners in 1997, agreeing to sell them the firm for less than $1 million.

Leona sold her favorite, the Helmsley Building on 230 Park Place, in 1998 to the Bass family on condition the building retain the name. That year, partly to avoid estate taxes, she formed the Harry and Leona Helmsley Foundation, a charity to which she contributed more than $30 million in 1999.

Leona moved closer to a deal in 2000 to buy back the Empire State Building from then-owner Donald Trump and partners. The following year Malkin moved to challenge her, forming a plan to buy the skyscraper himself; Leona vowed to block his proposal. In 2002, Trump agreed to sell the building to Malkin for $57.5 million.

EXECUTIVES

Chairman, President, and CEO: Leona Helmsley, age 82
VP and CFO: Abe Wolf
Human Resources Director: Yogesh Mathur
Auditors: Eisner & Lubin LLP

LOCATIONS

HQ: Helmsley Enterprises, Inc.
230 Park Ave., New York, NY 10169
Phone: 212-679-3600 **Fax:** 212-953-2810

Helmsley Enterprises operates primarily in New York City.

PRODUCTS/OPERATIONS

Selected Properties

Empire State Building (office building, New York City)
Helmsley Carlton House (hotel, New York City)
Helmsley Middletowne (hotel, New York City)
Helmsley Park Lane (hotel, New York City)
Helmsley Sandcastle (hotel, Sarasota, Florida)
Helmsley Windsor (hotel, New York City)
Lincoln Building (office building, New York City)
New York Helmsley (hotel, New York City)

COMPETITORS

Accor	Ritz-Carlton
Four Seasons Hotels	Shorenstein
Hyatt	SL Green Realty
JMB Realty	Tishman
Lefrak Organization	Trammell Crow Company
Lincoln Property	Trizec Properties
Macklowe Properties	Trump
Marriott	Vornado Realty Trust

HISTORICAL FINANCIALS

Company Type: Private

Income Statement   FYE: December 31

	ESTIMATED REVENUE ($ mil.)	NET INCOME ($ mil.)	NET PROFIT MARGIN	EMPLOYEES
12/02	1,000	—	—	3,500
12/01	1,000	—	—	3,000
12/00	1,000	—	—	3,000
12/99	1,000	—	—	3,000
12/98	1,000	—	—	7,800
12/97	1,000	—	—	7,800
12/96	1,900	—	—	13,000
12/95	1,770	—	—	13,000
12/94	1,700	—	—	13,000
12/93	1,200	—	—	13,000
Annual Growth	(2.0%)	—	—	(13.6%)

Revenue History

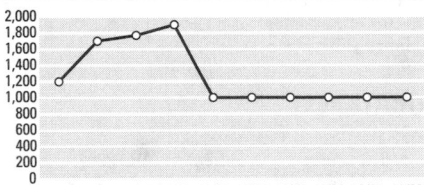

Hendrick Automotive

For megadealer Hendrick Automotive Group, variety is the spice of life. The company sells new and used cars and light trucks from more than 20 automakers, running the gamut from Hyundai to Hummer. Hendrick has a network of more than 60 dealerships in nearly 10 states ranging from the Carolinas to California. The company also offers financing, as well as automobile parts, accessories, service, and body repair. Founder Rick Hendrick pleaded guilty in 1997 to mail fraud relating to alleged bribes of American Honda executives; he was later pardoned by President Bill Clinton. Hendrick owns the company, which

began in 1976 as a single dealership in Bennettsville, South Carolina.

Rick Hendrick leads the group as chairman, but he is known for granting a large measure of autonomy and ultimate responsibility for results to the general manager of each dealership. His hands-off policy does seem to have achieved results. Hendrick Acura, for instance, has increased its sales count from more than 380 new cars a month in 1997 to more than 1,100 a month in 2003.

In 2004 Hendrick lost his son, brother, and other members of his family in the crash of a private plane carrying members of his NASCAR racing team Hendrick Motorsports.

EXECUTIVES

Chairman: J.R. (Rick) Hendrick III
CEO: Jim C. Perkins
EVP and CFO: James F. Huzl
VP of Accounting, Audits, and Taxes: Veronica Zayatz
Director, Human Resources: Tim Taylor
General Manager, Hendrick Motorsports:
Marshall Carlson

LOCATIONS

HQ: Hendrick Automotive Group
6000 Monroe Rd., Charlotte, NC 28212
Phone: 704-568-5550 **Fax:** 704-566-3295
Web: www.hendrickauto.com

Hendrick Automotive Group operates in California, Georgia, Kansas, Missouri, North Carolina, South Carolina, Tennessee, Texas, and Virginia.

COMPETITORS

Asbury Automotive	Morse Operations
AutoNation	Sonic Automotive
Bill Heard	United Auto Group
CarMax	VT Inc.
Holman Enterprises	

HISTORICAL FINANCIALS

Company Type: Private

Income Statement   FYE: December 31

	REVENUE ($ mil.)	NET INCOME ($ mil.)	NET PROFIT MARGIN	EMPLOYEES
12/03	2,783	—	—	4,700
12/02	2,491	—	—	4,700
12/01	2,639	—	—	4,700
12/00	2,483	—	—	4,500
12/99	2,522	—	—	4,500
12/98	2,434	—	—	4,300
12/97	2,455	—	—	4,500
12/96	2,250	—	—	4,500
12/95	2,315	—	—	4,500
12/94	1,800	—	—	4,500
Annual Growth	5.0%	—	—	0.5%

Revenue History

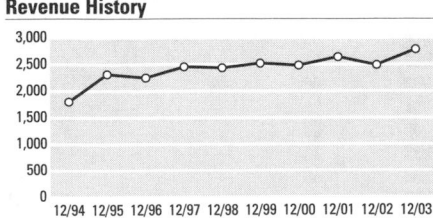

Henry County Bancshares

Henry County Bancshares is the holding company for First State Bank, which serves the area south of Atlanta through six branch locations. It offers standard deposit products, including checking and savings accounts, money market accounts, IRAs, and CDs. Lending activities are heavily focused on real estate: construction loans account for nearly half of total loans, while mortgages account for another 40%. The company also provides mortgage banking products and services through subsidiary First Metro Mortgage; it originates loans for sale on the secondary market.

Chairman Robert Linch owns 6% of Henry County Bancshares; executive officers and directors collectively own 10% of the company.

EXECUTIVES

Chairman: Robert O. Linch, age 75
President, CEO, and Director; President and CEO, First State Bank: David H. Gill, age 50, $283,576 pay
VP and CFO: Thomas L. Redding, age 46, $111,125 pay
Secretary and Director; EVP and Chief Credit Officer, First State Bank: William C. Strom Jr., age 55, $208,340 pay
Auditors: Mauldin & Jenkins, LLC

LOCATIONS

HQ: Henry County Bancshares, Inc.
4806 N. Henry Blvd., Stockbridge, GA 30281
Phone: 770-474-7293   **Fax:** 770-474-8053
Web: www.firststateonline.com

PRODUCTS/OPERATIONS

2004 Sales

	$ mil.	% of total
Interest		
Loans, including fees	26.9	82
Securities	1.4	4
Other	0.4	1
Noninterest		
Service charges on		
deposit accounts	2.3	7
Mortgage banking income	1.2	4
Other service charges & fees	0.8	2
Total	**33.0**	**100**

COMPETITORS

BB&T
RBC Centura Banks
Regions Financial
SunTrust
Wachovia

HISTORICAL FINANCIALS

Company Type: Private

Income Statement

	ASSETS ($ mil.)	NET INCOME ($ mil.)	INCOME AS % OF ASSETS	EMPLOYEES
				FYE: December 31
12/04	571	8	1.5%	156
12/03	515	8	1.5%	152
12/02	489	7	1.5%	146
Annual Growth	**8.0%**	**7.3%**	**—**	**3.4%**

2004 Year-End Financials

Equity as % of assets: 9.9%   Long-term debt ($ mil.): —
Return on assets: 1.5%   Sales ($ mil.): 33
Return on equity: 15.6%

Net Income History

Henry Ford Health System

In 1915 automaker Henry Ford founded the hospital that would be the starting point for southeastern Michigan's not-for-profit Henry Ford Health System (HFHS), a hospital network that is also involved in medical research and education. The system's hospital network includes Henry Ford Hospital, Henry Ford Wyandotte Hospital, and Kingswood Hospital, which specializes in treating mental health patients. HFHS also operates nursing homes, hospice and home health care providers, and a medical supply retailer. The system's Health Alliance Plan of Michigan provides managed care and health insurance to more than 500,000 members.

HFHS has a joint venture with Bon Secours Health System, Bon Secours Cottage Health Services, to operate Cottage Hospital and Bon Secours Hospital, both located northeast of Detroit. In 2004 an audit of the joint venture's books revealed its former CFO had misstated revenues and assets for the previous seven years.

The Henry Ford Health Sciences Center Research Institute, the Josephine Ford Cancer Center, and other research centers and affiliated hospitals are also part of the health care system.

After posting a $75 million loss in 2002, the health system began a turnaround initiative that reaped rewards with a profit posted in 2003. To achieve the return to fiscal fitness, HFHS cut more than 1,000 jobs, trimmed some services, and closed one of its facilities. About half of the company's revenue in 2003 came from Health Alliance Plan of Michigan.

EXECUTIVES

President Emeritus: Gail L. Warden, age 67
President and CEO: Nancy M. Schlichting
COO: Robert (Bob) Riney
EVP; CEO, Henry Ford Medical Group: Mark A. Kelley
SVP and CFO: James M. Connelly
SVP and Chief Administrative Officer: Robert (Bob) Rieny
SVP and Chief Human Resources Officer: Ronald Waetzman
SVP Special Projects: Vinod K. Sahney

President and CEO, Henry Ford Hospital and Health Network: Anthony (Tony) Armada
VP Behavioral Health, Henry Ford Hospital: Edward Coffey
VP Human Resources and Chief Learning Officer: John Hayden
VP Retail Pharmacies, Henry Ford Hospital: John Polanski
CIO: Arthur Gross

LOCATIONS

HQ: Henry Ford Health System
1 Ford Place, Detroit, MI 48202
Phone: 313-876-8700   **Fax:** 313-876-9243
Web: www.henryfordhealth.org

PRODUCTS/OPERATIONS

Selected Operations

Bon Secours Cottage Health Services (joint venture with Bon Secours Health System)
Health Alliance Plan of Michigan
Henry Ford Bi-County Community Hospital (osteopathic hospital)
Henry Ford Hospital
Henry Ford Medical Group
Henry Ford Mercy Health Network (joint venture with Trinity Health)
Henry Ford Wyandotte Hospital
Kingswood Hospital (mental health care)
Virginia Park/Henry Ford Hospital Non-Profit Housing Corp.

COMPETITORS

Ascension Health
Blue Cross (MI)
Detroit Medical Center
Healthplus of Michigan
Trinity Health (Novi)
William Beaumont Hospital

HISTORICAL FINANCIALS

Company Type: Not-for-profit

Income Statement

	REVENUE ($ mil.)	NET INCOME ($ mil.)	NET PROFIT MARGIN	EMPLOYEES
				FYE: December 31
12/03	2,600	—	—	12,700
12/02	2,400	—	—	12,600
12/01	2,000	—	—	15,000
12/00	1,900	—	—	16,000
12/99	1,229	—	—	16,000
12/98	1,303	—	—	17,000
12/97	2,200	—	—	17,000
12/96	1,980	—	—	17,000
12/95	1,750	—	—	17,000
12/94	1,525	—	—	15,000
Annual Growth	**6.1%**	**—**	**—**	**(1.8%)**

Revenue History

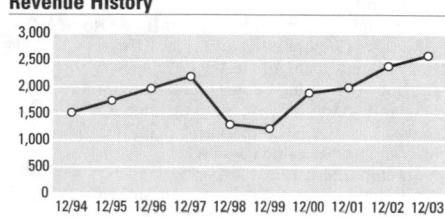

Hensel Phelps Construction

Hensel Phelps Construction builds it all, from the courthouse to the Big House. Launched as a homebuilding firm by Hensel Phelps in 1937, the employee-owned general contractor now focuses on institutional and commercial projects: prisons, airport facilities, hotels, government and corporate complexes, convention centers, sport arenas, and department stores. It also works on mass transportation, educational, residential, and health care projects. Hensel Phelps offers design/build and construction management services. Recent projects include the Hyatt Denver Convention Center Hotel and the new headquarters for Whole Foods Market in Austin, Texas.

EXECUTIVES

President and CEO: Jerry L. Morgensen
EVP and Manager, Eastern Division and Mid-Atlantic District: Robert E. Daniels
EVP and Manager, Western Division; President, Phelps Program Management: Robert J. (Bob) Pesavento
VP Finance and CFO: Stephen J. (Steve) Carrico
VP and General Counsel: Eric L. Wilson
Auditors: KPMG LLP

LOCATIONS

HQ: Hensel Phelps Construction Co.
420 6th Ave., Greeley, CO 80632
Phone: 970-352-6565   **Fax:** 970-352-9311
Web: www.henselphelps.com

Hensel Phelps Construction has offices in Arkansas, California, Colorado, Florida, Texas, and Virginia.

PRODUCTS/OPERATIONS

Selected Services
Building operation
Commissioning
Estimating
Feasibility studies
Financing
Land acquisition
Leasing
Moving services
Scheduling
Subcontractor management
Warranty programs
Zoning and code compliance

Selected Projects
Capital Square Office Tower (Sacramento)
Colorado Convention Center Expansion and Renovation Project (Denver)
Denver Center of the Performing Arts
Excelsior Hotel & Convention Center (Little Rock, AR)
J.D. Edwards Corporate Headquarters (Denver)
Neiman Marcus (Palo Alto, CA)
Paseo Nuevo Shopping Center (Santa Barbara, CA)
Pentagon Renovation Wedges 2-5 (Arlington, VA)
Riverport Casino Center (Maryland Heights, MO)
Sahara Hotel and Casino (Las Vegas)
San Antonio International Airport
Sea World New Friends Stadium (San Antonio)
University of Texas at Dallas School of Management
New Midfield Concourse, Washington Dulles Airport
Youth Services Center (Washington, DC)

COMPETITORS

C.F. Jordan	Perini
Clark Enterprises	Rooney Holdings
Dick Corporation	Skanska USA Building
Hunt Construction	Turner Corporation
M. A. Mortenson	Walbridge Aldinger
McCarthy Building	Walsh Group
PCL	Whiting-Turner

HISTORICAL FINANCIALS

Company Type: Private

Income Statement

FYE: May 31

	REVENUE ($ mil.)	NET INCOME ($ mil.)	NET PROFIT MARGIN	EMPLOYEES
5/04	1,800	—	—	2,500
5/03	1,872	—	—	2,500
5/02	1,771	—	—	2,200
5/01	1,368	—	—	2,200
5/00	1,357	—	—	2,200
5/99	1,165	—	—	2,151
5/98	934	—	—	1,926
5/97	876	—	—	1,535
5/96	726	—	—	1,540
5/95	734	—	—	1,400
Annual Growth	10.5%	—	—	6.7%

Revenue History

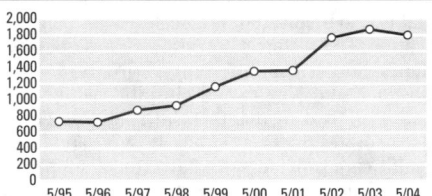

Herbalife

Rooted in the medicinal value provided by Mother Nature, Herbalife International sells more than 100 products containing herbal and other natural ingredients. The company's products include weight-control mixes and tablets, nutritional supplements specifically designed for men and women, food, shampoos, lotions, sunscreens, and body oils. The multi-level marketer sells its products through a network of independent distributors in nearly 60 countries; salespeople earn money from their own efforts, as well as from the sales of those whom they have recruited into the organization.

Distributors in emerging markets in Africa, Asia, and Eastern Europe have been attracted to Herbalife by the low startup costs. After buying promotional materials (average cost: $60), distributors buy products from Herbalife at a discount of up to 50% and resell them at retail prices.

After founder Mark Hughes passed away in 2000, the company slumped, and was subsequently acquired by a group of venture capital firms including Whitney & Co. and Golden Gate Capital. Striving to reclaim the success it had in the 1980's, the company brought in fresh management in 2003, including several former Dis-

ney executives. The company is currently dealing with litigation brought on by users of its ephedra-based weight loss products; the herbal supplement has been banned in the US.

HISTORY

Mark Hughes' mother's death from an overdose of prescription diet pills was the catalyst for Herbalife. Hughes, a high-school dropout, founded the company with diet supplement maker Richard Marconi in 1980. Herbalife went public in 1986 after rapid growth, but it got into trouble for some of its product claims. Following federal and state investigations and US Senate hearings, Herbalife paid a hefty fine and removed some of its products from the market. Hughes was able to resurrect the firm by taking it overseas. Sales also got a boost from the success of the Thermojetics weight-control systems.

In 1995 Herbalife introduced a line of herbal and botanical skin care products (Dermajetics). In 1997 insider selling of stock prompted a major slide in the price of Herbalife shares. Earnings tanked in 1998 when economic crises hit such big revenue contributors as Russia and Asia.

In 1999 Hughes planned to buy the company's outstanding shares and take the company private; investors sued. In 2000 he dropped the attempt. That year 44-year-old Hughes died in what was ruled an accidental death caused by a combination of alcohol and antidepressant medication. Hughes' longtime associate and former Herbalife COO Christopher Pair moved into the positions of president and CEO. He stepped down a year later after the company's board criticized his management.

Later that year, the Mark Hughes Family Trust turned down a $173 million bid for control of the company from Internet retailer Rbid.com. A group of investment firms bought the company in 2002 and Hughes' hopes to take the company private came to fruition without him. In 2004 Herbalife was hit with multiple lawsuits related to its ephedra-based weight-loss products. The FDA banned ephedra after it was linked to more than 150 deaths between 1994 and 2004.

EXECUTIVES

Chairman: Peter M. Castleman, age 49
Vice Chairman: Henry S. Burdick, age 63
CEO: Michael O. Johnson, age 51
COO: Gregory (Greg) Probert, age 48
CFO: Richard (Rich) Goudis, age 43
SVP, Regional Operations, The Americas: Robert (Rob) Levy
SVP, Scientific Affairs and Medical Affairs Advisor: Janice E. Thompson
SVP and Managing Director, Herbalife Japan: William M. Rahn
VP, Event Management and Communications: Randall (Randy) Brogna
General Manager, Herbalife Canada: Melanie Hayden
General Counsel: Brett R. Chapman, age 49
Executive Director, Herbalife Family Foundation: Joan Kardashian
Director, Public Relations, US: George Fischer
Director, Public Relations, Europe: Karen White
Auditors: Deloitte & Touche LLP

LOCATIONS

HQ: Herbalife International, Inc.
9800 S. La Cienega Blvd., Inglewood, CA 90301
Phone: 310-216-9661   **Fax:** 310-216-7019
Web: www.herbalife.com

Herbalife International's products are available through independent distributors in 59 countries worldwide.

PRODUCTS/OPERATIONS

Selected Products
Nutritional Supplements
21-Day Herbal Cleansing Program
Activated Fiber
Active Fiber Powder
AM Replenishing Formula
Aminogen
Bulk & Muscle Formula Protein Drink Mix
Cardio ToconOx
Dinomins
Florafiber
Garden 7
Herbal Aloe Drink
Herbal Concentrate
Herbalifeline
Joint Support-Glucosamine with Herbs
Kindermins
Male Factor 1000
Mega Garlic Plus
Mega Ginseng Blend
Niteworks
N-R-G Tablets
N-R-G Tea
Ocular Defense Formula
PM Cleansing Formula
Prelox Blue
Relax Now
RoseOx
Schizandra Plus
Sleep Now
Specialized Internal Program
Tang Kuei Plus
Triple Berry Complex
Ultimate Prostate Formula
Woman's Choice
Xtra-Cal

Weight Management
Activated Fiber
Active Fiber Powder
Aminogen
Beige Herbal Tablets
Beverage Mix Packets
Cell Activator
Cell-U-Loss
Formula 1 Nutritional Shake Mix
Formula 2 Multivitamin Complex
Formula 3 Personalized Protein Powder
Herbal Aloe Drink
Herbal Concentrate
N-R-G Tablets
N-R-G Tea
Protein Bar
Protein Drink Mix (formerly HPLC Shake Mix)
Roasted Soy Nuts with Cardia Salt
Sampler Pack
ShapeWorks Advanced
ShapeWorks QuickStart
ShapeWorks Ultimate
Snack Defense
Snack Pack
Soup Mix
Thermo-Bond Fiber Tablets
Total Control

Personal Care
Body Buffing Scrub
Body Contouring Creme
Herbal Aloe Bath and Body Bar
Herbal Aloe Everyday
Herbal Aloe Hand Cream
Herbal Aloe Moisturizing Conditioner
Herbal Aloe Moisturizing Shampoo
Herbal Aloe Soft Hold Hair Spray
Mystic Mask
Nature's Mirror
Night Companion
Radiant C Body Lotion SPF 15
Skin Activator Daily Replenishing Cream
Skin-Survival Kit

COMPETITORS

Alticor	The Right Solution
GNC	Schiff Nutrition
Jenny Craig	International
Mannatech	Shaklee
Nature's Sunshine	Slim-Fast
NBTY	Sunrider
Nu Skin	Vitamin Shoppe
Reliv'	Whole Living
Rexall Sundown	Wyeth

HISTORICAL FINANCIALS

Company Type: Private

Income Statement
FYE: December 31

	REVENUE ($ mil.)	NET INCOME ($ mil.)	NET PROFIT MARGIN	EMPLOYEES
12/03	1,159	—	—	2,254
12/02	1,094	—	—	2,625
12/01	1,020	—	—	2,445
12/00	944	—	—	2,391
12/99	956	—	—	2,170
12/98	867	—	—	1,742
12/97	783	—	—	1,459
12/96	632	—	—	1,180
12/95	489	—	—	1,060
12/94	467	—	—	862
Annual Growth	10.6%	—	—	11.3%

Revenue History

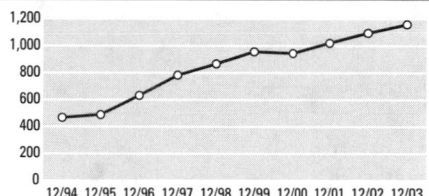

1,200	
1,000	
800	
600	
400	
200	
0	

12/94 12/95 12/96 12/97 12/98 12/99 12/00 12/01 12/02 12/03

Hercules Offshore

"With the strength of 10, ordinary men . . . " Hercules Offshore, through its subsidiaries, provides shallow-water drilling and liftboat services to major integrated energy companies and independent oil and natural gas exploration and production companies in the US Gulf of Mexico. It owns and operates the fourth-largest fleet of jackup rigs that can operate in water depths up to 250 ft. and the largest fleet of self-propelled, self-elevating liftboats in the region. The holding company generally contracts its jackup rigs and liftboats under short-term, daily rental agreements at fixed rental rates. Hercules Offshore was established by Thomas Seward II as Hercules Offshore Drilling Company in 2004.

Through acquisitions of complementary assets or businesses, Hercules Offshore plans to add to its fleet of eight jackup rigs that can drill in water depths that range from 85 ft. to 250 ft.,

and its fleet of about 40 self-propelled, self-elevating liftboats with leg lengths that range from 105 ft. to 260 ft. The company has agreed to acquire eight liftboats from Danos & Curole by the end of 2005.

The company makes about 75% of its revenues from drilling services and the remainder from marine services. Some of the company's largest customers are Chevron, Bois d'Arc Offshore, Noble Energy, and PetroQuest Energy.

EXECUTIVES

Chairman: John T. Reynolds, age 35
President, CEO, and Director:
Randall D. (Randy) Stilley, age 51, $121,692 pay (partial-year salary)
CFO: Steven A. Manz, age 39
President, Hercules Liftboat Company: Randal R. Reed, age 48, $51,250 pay (partial-year salary)
President, Hercules Drilling Company:
Thomas J. Seward II, age 74, $142,050 pay (partial-year salary)
VP Operations and COO, Hercules Drilling Company:
Thomas E. Hord, age 53, $131,779 pay (partial-year salary)
VP Finance, Hercules Liftboat Company:
Renee M. Pitre, age 43
VP Finance, Hercules Drilling Company:
Don P. Rodney, age 57, $74,037 pay (partial-year salary)
General Manager, Hercules Liftboats: Raywood Menard
Operations Manager, Hercules Liftboats: Teryl Ryder
Auditors: Grant Thornton LLP

LOCATIONS

HQ: Hercules Offshore, Inc.
2929 Briarpark Dr., Ste. 435, Houston, TX 77042
Phone: 713-952-4176   **Fax:** 713-952-4342
Web: www.herculesoffshore.com

PRODUCTS/OPERATIONS

2004 Sales

	$ mil.	% of total
Contract drilling services	24.0	76
Marine services	7.7	24
Total	**31.7**	**100**

Selected Subsidiaries
Hercules Drilling Company LLC
Hercules Liftboat Company LLC

COMPETITORS

Abdon Callais
GlobalSantaFe
Horizon Offshore
Kiewit Offshore
Noble Energy
Parker Drilling

HISTORICAL FINANCIALS

Company Type: Private

Income Statement
FYE: December 31

	REVENUE ($ mil.)	NET INCOME ($ mil.)	NET PROFIT MARGIN	EMPLOYEES
12/04	32	8	25.6%	700

Hexion Specialty Chemicals

Hexion Specialty Chemicals is trying to put a curse on the competition. The company joins together the forces of the former Borden Chemical, Resolution Performance Products, Resolution Specialty Materials, and Bakelite. All these companies were owned by private investment goliath Apollo when it announced the formation of Hexion in 2005. The new company is the world's largest thermosetting resins (or thermosets) maker, ahead of the likes of Georgia-Pacific. Thermosets add a desired quality (heat resistance, gloss, adhesion) to a number of different paints and adhesives. Hexion also is among the largest makers of formaldehyde and other forest product resins, epoxy resins, and raw materials for coatings and inks.

Its business is divided into two segments.

The Adhesive and Structural unit (accounting for about three-quarters of sales) includes the manufacture of formaldehyde, epoxy resins and intermediates, molding compounds, and composite resins. These products go into plywood and particle board, carbon and glass fiber composites, oil and gas field proppants, electronic laminates, and automotive friction materials.

The other, smaller segment is Coating, which also includes epoxy resins in addition to acrylic and polyester resins, versatic acids, and resins and additives for inks. These products are used in paints and coatings for the automotive, marine, construction, and maintenance industries as well as in printing inks.

Half of its business comes from North America. Customers include global giants like 3M, BASF, Sumitomo, and General Electric.

EXECUTIVES

Chairman, President, and CEO: Craig O. Morrison, age 49, $1,433,260 pay
Vice Chairman: Marvin O. Schlanger, age 57
EVP, CFO, and Director: William H. (Bill) Carter, age 51, $974,438 pay
EVP; President, Coatings and Inks: Jeffrey M. (Jeff) Nodland, age 49
EVP; President, Epoxy and Phenolic Resins: Layle K. (Kip) Smith, age 50
EVP; President, Formaldehyde and Forest Products Resins: Joseph P. (Jody) Bevilaqua, age 50, $578,195 pay
EVP; President, Performance Products: Sarah R. Coffin, age 52
EVP, Environmental Health and Safety: Richard L. Monty, age 57
EVP and General Counsel: Mark S. Antonvich, age 44
EVP, Procurement: Nathan E. Fisher, age 39
SVP, Finance and Treasurer: George F. Knight
VP, Human Resources: Judith A. (Judy) Sonnett, age 47, $410,970 pay
VP, Manufacturing: C. Hugh Morton, age 52, $430,080 pay (prior to title change)
Director, Public Affairs and Investor Relations: Peter F. (Pete) Loscocco
Auditors: PricewaterhouseCoopers LLP

LOCATIONS

HQ: Hexion Specialty Chemicals, Inc.
   180 E. Broad St., Columbus, OH 43215
Phone: 614-225-4000
Web: www.bordenchem.com

Hexion Specialty Chemicals operates 86 manufacturing facilities in 18 countries worldwide.

PRODUCTS/OPERATIONS

2004 Sales by End Market

	% of total
Industrial & marine	20
Construction	15
Consumer & durable goods	14
Automotive	10
Electronics	7
Architectural	6
Civil engineering	5
Repair & remodel	5
Other	18
Total	**100**

Business Segments and Selected Products

Adhesives and Structural
   Composite resins
   Epoxy resins
   Formaldehyde-based resins and intermediates
   Molding compounds
   Phenolic encapsualted substrates

Coating
   Acrylic resins
   Alkyd resins
   Epoxy resins
   Ink resins and additives
   Polyester resins
   Versatic acids and derivatives

COMPETITORS

A. Schulman
Akzo Nobel
Arkema US
Ashland
Bayer MaterialScience
Celanese
Dainippon Ink
DuPont
Dynea
ExxonMobil Chemical
GE Industrial
Georgia-Pacific Corporation
Huntsman Corp
Mitsui Chemicals
Rohm and Haas

HISTORICAL FINANCIALS

Company Type: Private

Income Statement

FYE: December 31

	REVENUE ($ mil.)	NET INCOME ($ mil.)	NET PROFIT MARGIN	EMPLOYEES
12/04	2,019	(114)	—	6,900
12/03	782	(83)	—	—
12/02	740	(14)	—	—
Annual Growth	65.2%	—	—	—

2004 Year-End Financials

Debt ratio: —
Return on equity: —
Cash ($ mil.): 152

Current ratio: 1.66
Long-term debt ($ mil.): 1,834

Net Income History

Hicks, Muse, Tate & Furst

These Texas Hicks know an investment pool ain't no cement pond and like to buy, buy & buy. (They sell sometimes, too.) Hicks, Muse, Tate & Furst creates investment pools in the form of limited partnerships. Investors are mostly pension funds but also include financial institutions and wealthy private investors. The leveraged buyout firm assembles limited partnership investment pools, targets underperforming companies in specific niches, builds them up, and uses them to form a nucleus for other investments. Hicks Muse also has holdings in manufacturing and real estate. Thomas Hicks retired at the end of 2004; co-founder John Muse replaced him at the helm of the firm.

It's "back to basics" for Hicks, Muse, Tate & Furst — media, branded food, and basic component manufacturing; it reevaluated its investments after some dramatic dot-com and telecommunications losses and a spoiled cinematic adventure with Kohlberg Kravis Roberts (the firms bought Regal Cinemas, but it went bankrupt, leaving a $500 million crater in Hicks Muse's pocket). The firm responded by moving away from telecoms and into Europe and Latin America.

Cable television has been in favor with Hicks Muse over the past 10 years. The firm bought its first cable company, Marcus Cable, in 1995 and has since bought nearly a dozen. Recent deals include Centennial Puerto Rico Cable TV and Canadian company Persona.

The company, along with Colorado-based Booth Creek Management, bought a 54% share of ConAgra's meatpacking operations. Hicks Muse also owns the North American assets of bankrupt Vlasic Foods International, including Vlasic pickles, Open Pit barbecue sauces, and Swanson Frozen Food. After bolstering the holdings of Premier International Foods, which bought up troubled, but well-known English food brands from firms like Nestlé, Cadbury Schweppes, and Unilever, it shepherded the company through an IPO, selling off its entire stake.

The London-based European arm of Hicks Muse, which has been lauded for its deal-making, formally split from the company in early 2005. In September of the same year a group led by Hicks Muse agreed to buy wholesale insurance broker Swett & Crawford from Aon Corporation.

HISTORY

The son of a Texas radio station owner, Thomas Hicks became interested in leveraged buyouts as a member of First National Bank's venture capital group. Hicks and Robert Haas formed Hicks & Haas in 1984; the next year that firm bought Hicks Communications, a radio outfit run by Hicks' brother Steven. (This would be the first of many media companies bought or created by the buyout firm, often with Steven Hicks' involvement.)

Hicks & Haas' biggest coup was its mid-1980s buy of several soft drink makers, including Dr Pepper and Seven-Up. The firm took Dr Pepper/Seven-Up public just 18 months after merging the two companies. In all, Hicks & Haas turned $88 million of investor funding into $1.3 billion. The pair split up in 1989; Hicks wanted to raise a large pool to invest, but Haas preferred to work deal by deal.

Hicks raised $250 million in 1989 and teamed with former Prudential Securities banker John Muse. Early investments included Life Partners Group (life insurance, 1990; sold 1996). In 1991 Morgan Stanley's Charles Tate and First Boston's Jack Furst became partners.

As part of its buy-and-build strategy, Hicks Muse bought DuPont's connector systems unit in 1993, renamed it Berg Electronics, added six more companies to it, and doubled its earnings before selling it in 1998. Not every move was a star in the Hicks Muse crown. Less-than-successful purchases included bankrupt brewer G. Heileman, bought in 1994 and sold two years later for an almost $100 million loss.

The buyout firm's Chancellor Media radio company went public in 1996. That year Hicks Muse gained entry into Latin America with its purchases of cash-starved Mexican companies, including Seguros Commercial America, one of the country's largest insurers. That year also brought International Home Foods (Jiffy Pop, Chef Boyardee) into the Hicks Muse fold.

In 1997 Chancellor and Evergreen Media merged to form Chancellor Media (renamed AMFM in 1999). The next year Hicks Muse continued buying US and Latin American media companies, as well as a few oddities (a UK software maker, a Danish seed company, and US direct-seller Home Interiors & Gifts). Hicks Muse and Kohlberg Kravis Roberts merged their cinema operations to form the US's largest theater chain. The company that year also moved into the depressed energy field (Triton Energy) and formed a $1.5 billion European fund.

Buys in 1999 included UK food group Hillsdown Holdings, one-third of Mexican flour maker Grupo Minsa, and (just in time for millennial celebrations) popular champagne brands Mumm and Perrier-Jouët (it quadrupled its investment when it sold the champagne houses in late 2000).

Hicks Muse, along with UK-based Apax Partners, bought BT's yellow pages firm Yell for roughly $3.5 billion, making it the largest noncorporate LBO in European history. Yell bought US directories publisher McLeodUSA for about $600 million, and floated in 2003.

Hicks Muse spotted a tasty deal and bought Nestlé's Ambient Food Business in 2002, which added well-known UK brands Crosse & Blackwell, Branston Pickle, Chivers (marmalade), Sun-Pat (peanut butter), Gale's (honey), Sarson's (vinegar) and Rowntree's (jelly) to the Premier Foods stable. Cereal maker Weetabix and Unilever's cast-offs Ambrosia (creamed rice and puddings) and Brown & Polson, rounded out Premier Foods' portfolio in 2003.

Acquisitions in 2004 included Kerns Oil & Gas (renamed Blackbrush Energy — natural gas production), Persona (Canadian cable television company), Regency Gas Services (gas processing and distribution), and Centennial Puerto Rico Cable TV (Puerto Rican cable television company). It also agreed to buy a majority stake in trendy luxury shoemaker Jimmy Choo. Disposals during the year included the company's remaining stake in Yell and its stake in Premier Foods. Thomas Hicks retired at the end of 2004; co-founder John Muse replaced him at the helm of the firm.

The company's European arm, which has been on a roll, split from the company in January 2005.

EXECUTIVES

Chairman: John R. Muse, age 54
COO and Partner: Jack D. Furst, age 45
CFO and CIO: Darron Ash, age 40
Partner: Peter S. Brodsky, age 34
Partner: Joe Colonnetta, age 43
Partner: Eric C. Neuman, age 60
Partner: Andrew S. Rosen, age 36
Principal: Marcos A. Clutterbuck, age 34
Principal: Jason Downie, age 34
Principal: Edward Herring, age 34
Principal: Eric Lindberg, age 33
Principal: Stephan Lobmeyr
Principal: Christina Weaver, age 34
IS/IT: Clark Sandlin
Treasurer: Dave Knickel
Counsel: Eric Allen
Human Resources: Lynnita Jessen
Investor Relations: Michelle Westfall
Auditors: KPMG

LOCATIONS

HQ: Hicks, Muse, Tate & Furst Incorporated
200 Crescent Ct., Ste. 1600, Dallas, TX 75201
Phone: 214-740-7300 **Fax:** 214-720-7888
Web: www.hmtf.com

PRODUCTS/OPERATIONS

Selected Holdings

Aster City Cable (21%, cable broadcasting, Poland)
Cablevision (50%, Argentina)
Claxson Interactive Group (Latin American media and cable)
Glass's Group (automotive information services software)
Grupo Minsa, S.A. de C.V. (32%, corn flour producer, Mexico)
Grupo MVS SA (23%, pay-TV provider and radio station owner, Mexico)
Grupo Vidrio Formas (69%, glass container supplier, Mexico)
Hedstrom Corp. (playground equipment)
Hillsdown Holdings PLC (food production)
Home Interiors & Gifts, Inc. (80%, direct-selling of decorative accessories and gift items)
International Outdoor Advertising (97%; billboards in Argentina, Chile, and Uruguay)
International Wire Holdings Corp. (60%; wire, wire harnesses, and cable)
Jimmy (51%, women's shoes)
LIN TV Corp. (46%, television stations)
Pan-American Sports Network (80%, regional cable sports network)
Swift Foods (beef and pork processing)
United Biscuits (Holdings) plc (87%, with Finalrealm; food products; UK)
Viasystems Group (printed circuit boards)
Walden (residential real estate)

COMPETITORS

Bain Capital
Berkshire Hathaway
Boston Ventures
CD&R
Equity Group Investments
Haas Wheat
Hellman & Friedman
Investcorp
Jordan Company
KKR
Texas Pacific Group
Thomas H. Lee Partners
Vestar Capital Partners
Vsm Investors
Wingate Partners

Highmark

Rated as one of the nation's top health plans, Highmark gets an A+ for customer satisfaction. The company provides health-related coverage to some 25 million customers, primarily in Pennsylvania. Highmark offers medical, dental, vision, life, casualty, and other health insurance, as well as such community service programs as the Western Pennsylvania Caring Foundation, which offers free health care coverage to children whose parents earn too much to qualify for public aid but too little to afford private programs. Highmark also processes Medicare claims (Veritus Medicare and HGSAdministrators Medicare Services).

Highmark continues to operate in western Pennsylvania under the Highmark Blue Cross Blue Shield name, and as Highmark Blue Shield in Central, Eastern and Northeastern Pennsylvania. National subsidiaries include United Concordia Companies (dental coverage), Highmark Life and Casualty Group (disability and life insurance), and Medmark (specialty pharmacy).

As a result of some belt-tightening in 2004, the company shut down its Alliance Ventures (administrative and information services) and Lifestyle Advantage subsidiaries.

HISTORY

Highmark was created from the merger of Blue Cross of Western Pennsylvania (founded in 1937) and Pennsylvania Blue Shield, created in 1964 when the Medical Service Association of Pennsylvania (MSAP) adopted the Blue Shield name.

The Pennsylvania Medical Society, in conjunction with the state of Pennsylvania, had formed MSAP to provide medical insurance to the poor and indigent. MSAP borrowed $25,000 from the Pennsylvania Medical Society to help set up its operations, and Chauncey Palmer (who had originally proposed the organization) was named president. Individuals paid 35 cents per month, and families paid $1.75 each month to join MSAP, which initially covered mainly obstetrical and surgical procedures.

In 1945 Arthur Daugherty replaced Palmer as president (he served until his death in 1968) and helped MSAP recruit major new accounts, including the United Mine Workers and the Congress of Industrial Organizations. MSAP in 1946 became a chapter of the national Blue Shield association, which was started that year by the medical societies of several states to provide prepaid health insurance plans.

In 1951 MSAP signed up the 150,000 employees of United States Steel, bringing its total enrollment to more than 1.6 million. Growth did not lead to prosperity, though, as the organization had trouble keeping up with payments to its doctors. This shortfall in funds led MSAP to raise its premiums in 1961, at which point the state reminded the association of its social mission and suggested it concentrate on controlling costs instead of raising rates.

MSAP changed its name to Pennsylvania Blue Shield in 1964. Two years later the association began managing the state's Medicare plan and started the 65-Special plan to supplement Medicare coverage. In the 1970s Pennsylvania Blue Shield again could not keep up with the cost of paying its doctors, which led to more rate increases and closer scrutiny of its expenses. Competition increased in the 1980s as HMOs cropped up around the state. Pennsylvania Blue Shield fought back by creating its own HMO plans — some of which it owned jointly with Blue Cross of Western Pennsylvania — in the 1980s.

After years of slowly collecting noninsurance businesses, Blue Cross of Western Pennsylvania changed its name to Veritus in 1991 to reflect the growing importance of its for-profit operations.

In 1996 Pennsylvania Blue Shield overcame physicians' protests and state regulators' concerns to merge with Veritus. The company adopted the name Highmark to represent its standards for high quality; it took a loss as it failed to meet cost-cutting goals and suffered early-retirement costs related to the merger consolidation. To gain support for the merger, Highmark sold for-profit subsidiary Keystone Health Plan East to Independence Blue Cross in 1997.

In 1999 Highmark teamed with Mountain State Blue Cross Blue Shield to become West Virginia's primary licensee. Rate hikes and investment returns helped propel the company into the black as the decade closed.

In 2001 Highmark announced that it had uncovered almost $5 million in health care insurance fraud against the company over the course of the previous year.

EXECUTIVES

Chairman: J. Robert Baum
President, CEO, and Director: Kenneth R. Melani, age 48
EVP, Human Resources and Administrative Services: S. Tyrone Alexander
EVP, Finance and Subsidiary Services, CFO, and Treasurer: Robert C. Gray
EVP, Health Services: James Klingensmith
EVP, Government Services: David M. O'Brien
SVP and Chief Audit Executive: Elizabeth A. Farbacher
SVP and Corporate Compliance Officer: Michael A. Romano
SVP, Corporate Secretary, and General Counsel: Gary R. Truitt
SVP, Corporate Affairs: Aaron A. Walton
Assistant Secretary: Carrie J. Pecht
SVP and Chief Medical Officer: Donald R. Fischer
Assistant Treasurer: Joseph F. Reichard
Auditors: PricewaterhouseCoopers LLP

LOCATIONS

HQ: Highmark Inc.
120 5th Ave., Pittsburgh, PA 15222
Phone: 412-544-7000   **Fax:** 412-544-8368
Web: www.highmark.com/hmk2/index.shtml

PRODUCTS/OPERATIONS

Selected Subsidiaries

Clarity Vision, Inc.
Davis Vision, Inc.
Gateway Health Plan
HealthGuard of Lancaster, Inc.
HGSAdministrators
Highmark Blue Cross Blue Shield
Highmark Blue Shield
The Highmark Life and Casualty Group, Inc.
Keystone Health Plan West, Inc.
Medmark, Inc.
Mountain State Blue Cross Blue Shield
United Concordia Companies, Inc.
Veritus Medicare Services
Viva Optique, Inc.

COMPETITORS

Aetna
CIGNA
Guardian Life
HealthAmerica
Humana
Independence Blue Cross
New York Life
Prudential
UnitedHealth Group
UPMC
U.S. Healthcare, Inc.

HISTORICAL FINANCIALS

Company Type: Not-for-profit

Income Statement

FYE: December 31

	REVENUE ($ mil.)	NET INCOME ($ mil.)	NET PROFIT MARGIN	EMPLOYEES
12/04	9,118	311	3.4%	11,000
12/03	8,140	76	0.9%	11,000
12/02	7,482	(83)	—	11,000
12/01	6,799	132	1.9%	11,000
12/00	9,000	242	2.7%	11,000
12/99	8,190	69	0.8%	11,000
12/98	7,544	62	0.8%	12,000
12/97	7,405	101	1.4%	12,000
12/96	6,619	(50)	—	10,500
12/95	3,367	43	1.3%	8,000
Annual Growth	11.7%	24.6%	—	3.6%

2004 Year-End Financials

Debt ratio: 20.6%
Return on equity: 11.9%
Cash ($ mil.): —
Current ratio: —
Long-term debt ($ mil.): 583

Net Income History

350		
300		
250		
200		
150		
100		
50		
0		
-50		
-100	12/95 12/96 12/97 12/98 12/99 12/00 12/01 12/02 12/03 12/04	

Hillman Companies

If you were to *label* it, the *key* to success — according to distributor The Hillman Companies — is doing things by the *numbers*. Operating through subsidiary The Hillman Group, it distributes small hardware merchandise such as fasteners, keys, key duplication systems, signs, letters, numbers, and identification tags to home centers, hardware stores, pet stores, and grocery stores; customers include Wal-Mart, Home Depot, Lowe's, Sears, and PETsMART. The company also makes picture hanging wire and hooks sold under the Anchor Wire name. The Hillman Companies was acquired by investment firm Allied Capital in 2001; in 2004 Hillman was sold to private equity company Code Hennessy & Simmons for about $510 million.

Code Hennessy & Simmons (CHS) now owns 54% of the Hillman's voting stock. CHS tends to avoid volatile businesses, focusing instead on the more predictable manufacturing, service, and distribution industries.

EXECUTIVES

Chairman: Peter M. Gotsch, age 41
President and CEO: Max W. Hillman Jr., $742,530 pay
CFO and Secretary: James P. Waters, age 43, $259,946 pay
President, The Hillman Group: Richard P. Hillman, age 56, $376,750 pay
SVP, Engraving, The Hillman Group: George L. Heredia, age 46, $277,972 pay
SVP, National Account Sales, The Hillman Group: Terry R. Rowe, age 50, $259,972 pay
Auditors: PricewaterhouseCoopers LLP

LOCATIONS

HQ: The Hillman Companies, Inc.
10590 Hamilton Ave., Cincinnati, OH 45231
Phone: 513-851-4900   **Fax:** 513-851-4997
Web: www.hillmangroup.com

The Hillman Companies operates facilities in Canada and the US.

2004 Sales

	% of total
US	98
Other countries	2
Total	**100**

PRODUCTS/OPERATIONS

Selected Products and Services

Anchors
Brads
Fasteners
In-store service
Keys
Key duplication systems
Letters
Merchandising systems
Numbers
Picture hanging wire
Signs
Tacks
Tags

COMPETITORS

Applied Industrial Technologies
C&H Distributors
Endries
Fastenal
Genuine Parts
Handy & Harman
H.C. Slingsby
IBT
Lawson Products
MNP
MSC Industrial Direct
NCH
Park-Ohio Holdings

HISTORICAL FINANCIALS

Company Type: Private

Income Statement

FYE: December 31

	REVENUE ($ mil.)	NET INCOME ($ mil.)	NET PROFIT MARGIN	EMPLOYEES
12/04	352	(19)	—	1,794
12/03	318	(5)	—	1,760
12/02	287	6	2.1%	1,800
12/01	401	(4)	—	1,460
12/00	460	25	5.4%	2,100
12/99	556	(37)	—	4,010
12/98	713	14	1.9%	4,070
12/97	698	29	4.2%	3,900
12/96	649	19	3.0%	3,984
12/95	600	45	7.5%	3,843
Annual Growth	(5.8%)	—	—	(8.1%)

2004 Year-End Financials

Debt ratio: 327.1%
Return on equity: —
Cash ($ mil.): 33

Current ratio: 2.52
Long-term debt ($ mil.): 262

Net Income History

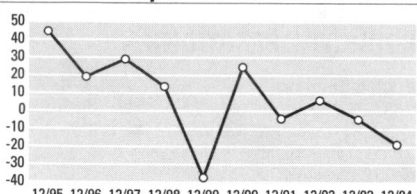

PRODUCTS/OPERATIONS

2004 Sales

	$ mil.	% of total
Interest		
Loans	57.6	74
Securities & other	7.7	10
Noninterest		
Service charges & fees	5.2	7
Trust fees	2.7	3
Gain on loan sales	1.5	2
Other	3.1	4
Total	**77.8**	**100**

COMPETITORS

Commercial Federal	U.S. Bancorp
Iowa First	Wells Fargo
North Central Bancshares	West Bancorporation

Hills Bancorporation

This company urges you to run for the hills! Hills Bancorporation is the holding company for Hills Bank and Trust, which has about a dozen branches located in the eastern Iowa counties of Johnson, Linn, and Washington. The bank specifically targets individuals, businesses, government entities, and institutional customers, offering them demand, savings, and time deposits, as well as agricultural, commercial, consumer, and real estate loans. It also administers estates, personal trusts, and pension plans, and provides farm management and investment advisory and custodial services to corporations, individuals, and not-for-profits.

Real estate mortgages account for nearly 80% of Hills Bancorporation's loan portfolio, which is rounded out by agricultural, commercial, construction, and consumer loans.

EXECUTIVES

Director and President, Hills Bancorporation and Hills Bank and Trust: Dwight O. Seegmiller, age 52, $319,369 pay
VP and Director; Chairman, Hills Bank and Trust: Willis M. Bywater, age 66
Secretary and Treasurer; SVP and CFO, Hills Bank and Trust: James G. Pratt, $235,219 pay
VP and Senior Lending Officer, Hills Bank and Trust: John A. Benson
VP and Human Resource Director, Hills Bank and Trust: Joan M. Wagner
VP and Senior Trust Officer, Hills Bank and Trust: Bradford C. Zuber
Senior Information Systems Officer, Hills Bank and Trust: Rodney L. Jensen
Auditors: KPMG LLP

LOCATIONS

HQ: Hills Bancorporation
131 Main St., Hills, IA 52235
Phone: 319-679-2291   **Fax:** 319-679-2251
Web: www.hillsbank.com

HISTORICAL FINANCIALS

Company Type: Private

Income Statement

FYE: December 31

	ASSETS ($ mil.)	NET INCOME ($ mil.)	INCOME AS % OF ASSETS	EMPLOYEES
12/04	1,290	14	1.1%	407
12/03	1,183	14	1.2%	411
12/02	1,099	12	1.0%	394
Annual Growth	8.4%	11.1%	—	1.6%

2004 Year-End Financials

Equity as % of assets: 8.0%
Return on assets: 1.1%
Return on equity: 14.2%

Long-term debt ($ mil.): 168
Sales ($ mil.): 78

Net Income History

Hobby Lobby

If something wicker this way comes, Hobby Lobby Stores may be the source. The firm operates more than 360 stores in 28 Southern and Midwestern states and sells arts and crafts supplies, baskets, candles, frames, home-decorating accessories, and silk flowers. The #3 craft retailer (behind Michaels Stores and Jo-Ann Stores), it prefers to set up shop in second-generation retail sites (such as vacated supermarkets and superstores). Sister companies supply Hobby Lobby stores with merchandise, received from its Oklahoma distribution facility. CEO David Green, who owns the company with his wife Barbara, founded the company in 1972 and operates it according to biblical principles, including closing stores on Sunday.

Hobby Lobby began as a picture frame manufacturing company. Today David Green's son Steven is president of the fast-growing retail chain.

The company also has operations in Hong Kong, mainland China and the Philippines. It also is expanding its 3 million sq. ft. of warehouse, corporate office, and distribution space in Oklahoma City.

EXECUTIVES

CEO: David Green
President: Steven Green, age 41
CFO: John Cargill
SVP Operations: Ken Haywood
VP and Director of Real Estate: Bill Darrow
VP Advertising: John Schumacher
VP Construction: Steve Seay
VP Legal: Peter Dobelbower
Assistant VP, Real Estate: Scott Nelson
Director of Recruiting: Bill Owens

LOCATIONS

HQ: Hobby Lobby Stores, Inc.
7707 SW 44th St., Oklahoma City, OK 73179
Phone: 405-745-1100   **Fax:** 405-745-1636
Web: www.hobbylobby.com

Hobby Lobby Stores has locations in Alabama, Arkansas, Colorado, Florida, Georgia, Illinois, Indiana, Iowa, Kansas, Kentucky, Louisiana, Michigan, Minnesota, Mississippi, Missouri, Nebraska, New Mexico, North Carolina, North Dakota, Ohio, Oklahoma, South Carolina, South Dakota, Tennessee, Texas, Wisconsin, and Wyoming.

PRODUCTS/OPERATIONS

Selected Products

Arts and crafts supplies
Baskets
Candles
Cards
Furniture
Home accent pieces
Jewelry-making supplies
Memory books
Model kits
Needlework
Party supplies
Picture frames and framing
Rubber stamping supplies
Seasonal items
Sewing materials (fabric, patterns, notions)
Silk flowers
Wearable art

Selected Affiliates

Basket Market (retail basket sales)
Bearing Fruit Communications (Christian advertising agency)
Crafts, Etc! (online sales and wholesale distribution of domestic and imported arts, crafts, and jewelry-making and hobby materials to Hobby Lobby and other retailers)
Greco Frame & Supply (custom-made and ready-made frames)
Hemispheres (home furnishings and accessories)
HL Construction (remodels and redesigns sites to become Hobby Lobby stores)
HL Realty (handles the real estate and property management for Hobby Lobby)
Mardel Christian Office & Educational Supply (Christian materials, office supplies, and educational products)
Worldwood Industries (manufacturer of wood products, T-shirts and sweatshirts, and home accessories)

COMPETITORS

A.C. Moore	Jo-Ann Stores
Burnes	Kirkland's
Family Christian Stores	Longaberger
Garden Ridge	Michaels Stores
Hancock Fabrics	Old Time Pottery
HobbyTown USA	Rag Shops
Home Interiors & Gifts	Wal-Mart

HISTORICAL FINANCIALS

Company Type: Private

Income Statement

FYE: December 31

	REVENUE ($ mil.)	NET INCOME ($ mil.)	NET PROFIT MARGIN	EMPLOYEES
12/04	1,400	—	—	16,000
12/03	1,300	—	—	15,000
12/02	1,164	—	—	13,500
12/01	1,015	—	—	15,000
12/00	905	—	—	13,500
12/99	798	—	—	12,000
12/98	664	—	—	11,000
12/97	590	—	—	7,500
12/96	540	—	—	7,500
Annual Growth	12.6%	—	—	9.9%

Revenue History

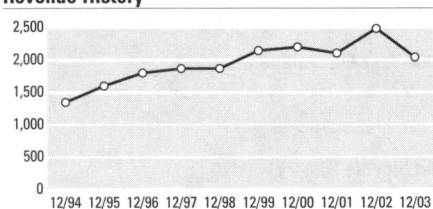

Holman Enterprises

Holman sells a whole lot of cars. Family-owned Holman Enterprises owns more than 10 car and truck dealerships in southern New Jersey and another 10 or so in southern Florida. Founded in 1924, Holman sells BMW, Ford, Infiniti, Jaguar, Lincoln, Mercury, Rolls-Royce, and Saturn cars, as well as Ford and Sterling trucks. The company also offers collision repair services. Holman's RMP engine and parts distributor sells small parts and engines authorized by Ford. Its Automotive Resources International unit, one of the largest independently owned fleet leasing groups in the world, also operates a truck parts and accessories company and offers vehicle financing with Fourth Fleet Financial.

EXECUTIVES

Chairman: Joseph S. Holman
Vice Chairwoman, CEO, and President: Mindy Holman
VP, Finance and Assistant Secretary: Robert Campbell
Corporate Secretary: Albert V. Andreola
Assistant Secretary: Kathy A. Mullin
Treasurer: Scott A. Naugel
Corporate Controller: Laird T. Poinsett
VP, Dealership Operations: Bill Cariss
VP: Glenn A. Gardner
VP: Henry H. Herrington

LOCATIONS

HQ: Holman Enterprises
7411 Maple Ave., Pennsauken, NJ 08109
Phone: 856-663-5200   **Fax:** 856-665-3444
Web: www.holmanauto.com

COMPETITORS

AMERCO
AutoNation
CarMax
Cendant
Enterprise Rent-A-Car
Hendrick Automotive
JM Family Enterprises
Morse Operations
Penske
Planet Automotive Group
Ryder
Sansone Auto Network
Toresco Enterprises
United Auto Group
Wheels

HISTORICAL FINANCIALS

Company Type: Private

Income Statement

FYE: December 31

	REVENUE ($ mil.)	NET INCOME ($ mil.)	NET PROFIT MARGIN	EMPLOYEES
12/03	2,042	—	—	2,700
12/02	2,483	—	—	2,700
12/01	2,105	—	—	2,600
12/00	2,200	—	—	2,800
12/99	2,146	—	—	2,718
12/98	1,870	—	—	2,700
12/97	1,870	—	—	2,800
12/96	1,800	—	—	2,700
12/95	1,600	—	—	2,500
12/94	1,350	—	—	2,870
Annual Growth	4.7%	—	—	(0.7%)

Revenue History

Holthouse Carlin & Van Trigt

Tune in to HCVT for a little professional advice. Holthouse Carlin & Van Trigt (also known as HCVT) provides accounting, tax planning, business consulting, litigation support, technology consulting, and related services. The firm, which has three offices in Southern California, serves such clients as privately owned businesses and high-net-worth individuals. Target industries include real estate, hospitality, entertainment, manufacturing, distribution, and technology, as well as retirement plans. Holthouse Carlin & Van Trigt was founded in 1991.

EXECUTIVES

President: Philip J. (Phil) Holthouse
Partner: James S. Carlin
Partner: John E. Van Trigt
Partner: David L. (Dave) Bierhorst
Partner: Blake E. Christian

LOCATIONS

HQ: Holthouse Carlin & Van Trigt LLP
100 Oceangate Rd., Ste. 800, Long Beach, CA 90802
Phone: 562-590-9535   **Fax:** 562-590-0395
Web: www.hcvt.com

PRODUCTS/OPERATIONS

Selected Services

401(k)/benefit plan audits
Affordable housing/IRC Section 42 tax credit projects
Business management
Financial reporting
Litigation support
Mergers, acquisitions, and business restructuring
Sales, use, and local tax planning
Tax planning and compliance
Technology information consulting
Valuations

COMPETITORS

Diehl, Evans & Company
Hutchinson and Bloodgood
Macias, Gini & Company
Moss Adams LLP
RBZ
Windes & McClaughry
Zdonek & Wolowicz

HISTORICAL FINANCIALS

Company Type: Private

Income Statement

FYE: December 31

	REVENUE ($ mil.)	NET INCOME ($ mil.)	NET PROFIT MARGIN	EMPLOYEES
12/04	19	—	—	95
12/03	17	—	—	83
Annual Growth	10.1%	—	—	14.5%

Revenue History

Home Interiors & Gifts

Home Interiors & Gifts is knocking. The company makes decorating accessories, which are sold by nearly 100,000 representatives through home parties in the US, Canada, Mexico, and Puerto Rico. Its product lines include artificial flowers, candles, framed artwork, lighting sconces, mirrors, plaques, small furniture, and shelves. The firm buys almost all of its products from subsidiaries such as Dallas Woodcraft Company and Laredo Candle Company. Mary Crowley, sister-in-law of makeup maven Mary Kay Ash, founded Home Interiors in 1957. Executives led by Joey Carter (Crowley's grandson) and buyout firm Hicks, Muse, Tate & Furst recapitalized Home Interiors in 1998. Hicks, Muse owns more than 75% of the company.

EXECUTIVES

Chairman: Joseph (Joe) Colonnetta, age 43
Vice Chairman: Barbara J. Hammond, age 74
Vice Chairman: Christina L. (Christi) Carter Urschel, age 40
President, CEO, and Director:
Michael D. (Mike) Lohner, age 42, $1,489,916 pay
COO: Mary-Knight Tyler, age 43, $181,194 pay
SVP Finance and CFO: Keith Krzeminski
SVP Sales and Marketing: Eugenia B. (Jeannie) Price, age 39, $267,358 pay (prior to promotion)
VP IT: Alan Boyer
Director, Human Resources: Carla Fulton
Media Contact: Carol Eichinger
Auditors: PricewaterhouseCoopers LLP

LOCATIONS

HQ: Home Interiors & Gifts, Inc.
1649 Frankford Rd. West, Carrollton, TX 75007
Phone: 972-695-1000 **Fax:** 972-695-1112
Web: www.homeinteriors.com

PRODUCTS/OPERATIONS

Selected Products

Artificial floral displays
Candle holders
Candles
Figurines
Framed artwork and mirrors
Planters
Plaques
Sconces
Small furniture
Tableware
Wall shelves

COMPETITORS

Alticor
Avon
Blyth
Garden Ridge
Hanover Direct
Hobby Lobby
Lancaster Colony
Lillian Vernon
Mary Kay
Michaels Stores
Pier 1 Imports
Pinnacle Frames
Wal Mart
Yankee Candle

HISTORICAL FINANCIALS

Company Type: Private

Income Statement

FYE: December 31

	REVENUE ($ mil.)	NET INCOME ($ mil.)	NET PROFIT MARGIN	EMPLOYEES
12/04	550	(4)	—	1,400
12/03	617	32	5.2%	3,700
12/02	575	36	6.2%	2,400
12/01	462	4	0.8%	1,300
12/00	460	10	2.1%	1,200
12/99	503	52	10.3%	1,400
12/98	490	48	9.9%	1,400
12/97	469	62	13.3%	—
12/96	434	54	12.5%	—
12/95	483	50	10.2%	—
Annual Growth	1.4%	—	—	0.0%

2004 Year-End Financials

Debt ratio: — Current ratio: 1.37
Return on equity: — Long-term debt ($ mil.): 450
Cash ($ mil.): 28

Net Income History

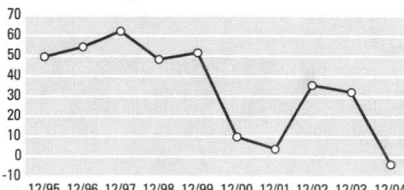

12/95 12/96 12/97 12/98 12/99 12/00 12/01 12/02 12/03 12/04

Home Products International

Home Products International (HPI) helps folks get it together — and has done the same to its industry. A consolidator in the housewares field, HPI is one of the leading manufacturers of ironing boards and covers in the US. It also makes other laundry products, plastic containers and carts, clothes hangers, shower organizers, food storage items, and organizers for children's belongings. All HPI products are sold under the Homz brand name. HPI sells to hotels, discounters, and other retailers (Wal-Mart, Kmart, and Target bring in more than 70% of its sales). In 2004 HPI was acquired by Storage Acquisition Company, which comprises a group of investors including chairman Joseph Gantz.

EXECUTIVES

Chairman: Joseph (Joe) Gantz
CEO and Director: Doug Ramsdale, $8,931 pay (partial-year salary)
COO: Rich Hassert
EVP, CFO, and Secretary: James E. (Jim) Winslow, age 49, $561,102 pay
SVP, Marketing: Park Owens
VP, Operations, Chicago: Joseph Lacambra, age 63
Manager, Human Resources: Jovita Folis

LOCATIONS

HQ: Home Products International, Inc.
4501 W. 47th St., Chicago, IL 60632
Phone: 773-890-1010 **Fax:** 773-890-0523
Web: www.hpii.com

2004 Sales

	% of total
US	97
Other countries	3
Total	**100**

PRODUCTS/OPERATIONS

2004 Sales

	$ mil.	% of total
General storage	122.7	47
Laundry management	77.8	30
Closet storage	35.8	14
Bathware	13.5	5
Kitchen storage	10.5	4
Total	**260.3**	**100**

COMPETITORS

Dynatec
Knape & Vogt
Myers Industries
Newell Rubbermaid
Owens-Illinois
Sterilite
SunLink Health Systems
Tupperware
ZAG Industries

HISTORICAL FINANCIALS

Company Type: Private

Income Statement

FYE: Last Saturday in December

	REVENUE ($ mil.)	NET INCOME ($ mil.)	NET PROFIT MARGIN	EMPLOYEES
12/04	260	(5)	—	1,042
12/03	234	(11)	—	1,202
12/02	249	14	5.7%	1,255
12/01	250	17	6.8%	1,215
12/00	297	(72)	—	1,345
12/99	294	2	0.7%	1,576
12/98	252	4	1.5%	1,465
12/97	129	7	5.6%	1,240
12/96	38	1	2.1%	493
12/95	41	(4)	—	368
Annual Growth	22.8%	—	—	12.3%

2004 Year-End Financials

Debt ratio: 5,090.9% Current ratio: 1.31
Return on equity: — Long-term debt ($ mil.): 121
Cash ($ mil.): 1

Net Income History

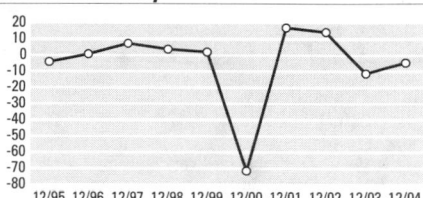

12/95 12/96 12/97 12/98 12/99 12/00 12/01 12/02 12/03 12/04

Horizon Healthcare Services, Inc.

Horizon Healthcare Services is New Jersey's top not-for-profit health insurance provider, serving more than 3 million members. The company's insurance plans include traditional indemnity, Horizon HMO, Horizon PPO, and Horizon Direct Access (Open Access). Horizon Healthcare Services also offers dental, Medicare, and behavioral health coverage, as well as workers' compensation insurance. The company's Horizon Healthcare Insurance Agency subsidiary provides life, long-term disability, and long-term care coverage. Its Horizon/Mercy subsidiary participates in the state of New Jersey's Medicaid program.

Although it was once considered a prime candidate for conversion to a for-profit public company (like Anthem (now WellPoint), WellChoice, and WellPoint), Horizon Healthcare Services has decided to remain not-for-profit.

EXECUTIVES

President and CEO: William J. Marino, age 61
SVP, Administration, CFO, and Treasurer:
  Robert J. Pures
SVP, General Counsel, and Secretary: John W. Campbell
SVP, Healthcare Management: Christy W. Bell
SVP, Information Systems and Chief Information
  Officer: Charles C. Emery Jr.
SVP, Market Business Units: Robert A. Marino
SVP, Service: Patrick J. Gerghty
VP, Corporate Marketing and Communications:
  Lawrence B. Altman
VP, Actuarial and Chief Actuary: John J. Lynch
VP, Customer Service: Jackie R. Jennifer
VP, Health Affairs and Chief Medical Officer:
  Richard G. Popiel
VP, Human Resources: Carole Czar Soldo
Auditors: PricewaterhouseCoopers LLP

LOCATIONS

HQ: Horizon Healthcare Services, Inc.
  3 Penn Plaza East, Newark, NJ 07101
Phone: 973-466-4000   Fax: 973-466-4317
Web: www.horizon-bcbsnj.com

Horizon Healthcare Services operations area includes
the state of New Jersey and surrounding counties.

PRODUCTS/OPERATIONS

2004 Sales

	$ mil.	% of total
Premiums	5,077.3	92
Administrative service fees	319.4	6
Investments	86.9	2
Other	20.6	—
Total	**5,504.2**	**100**

Selected Subsidiaries

Horizon Casualty Services (workers'
  comp and TPA services)
Horizon Healthcare (managed care plans and services)
Horizon/Mercy (Medicaid HMO)
Horizon Healthcare Dental (managed dental
  care plans and services)
Horizon Healthcare Insurance Agency (Life,
  LTD, and LTC)

COMPETITORS

Aetna
CIGNA
UnitedHealth Group

HISTORICAL FINANCIALS

Company Type: Not-for-profit

Income Statement				FYE: December 31
	REVENUE ($ mil.)	NET INCOME ($ mil.)	NET PROFIT MARGIN	EMPLOYEES
12/04	5,504	173	3.1%	4,400
12/03	5,082	171	3.4%	4,600
12/02	4,098	114	2.8%	4,600
12/01	3,534	106	3.0%	—
12/00	3,079	117	3.8%	—
Annual Growth	**15.6%**	**10.2%**	**—**	**(2.2%)**

2004 Year-End Financials

Debt ratio: 2.6%
Return on equity: 17.2%
Cash ($ mil.): 172

Current ratio: 1.02
Long-term debt ($ mil.): 29

Net Income History

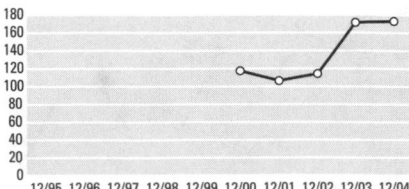

12/95 12/96 12/97 12/98 12/99 12/00 12/01 12/02 12/03 12/04

Houchens

Houchens Industries operates stores for shoppers more interested in supper than super. Eschewing the industry trend toward massive superstores, its 40 Houchens Markets in Kentucky average less than 20,000 sq. ft. The grocery chain also runs about 100 other supermarkets under the Food Giant and IGA banners. Its 200-plus Save-A-Lot discount grocery stores in 13 states offer limited selections and cover 15,000 sq. ft. or less. Houchens also owns about 40 Jr. Foods convenience stores and 23 Tobacco Shoppe discount cigarette outlets, mostly in Kentucky and Tennessee. It bought cigarette maker Commonwealth Brands in 2001. Founded as BG Wholesale in 1918 by Ervin Houchens, the company is owned by its employees.

Houchens Industries acquired Food Giant Supermarkets, the operator of 90 Food Giant and Piggly Wiggly supermarkets in eight states, in mid-2004. The Food Giant acquisition increased Houchens store count to nearly 400 locations. In December 2004 the company also acquired Scotty's Contracting & Stone — a Central Kentucky highway-construction company — in a stock swap between the two employee-owned companies. Connected with the Scotty's transaction, Houchens also acquired TS Trucking.

The regional grocery chain continues to grow its Save-A-Lot grocery store business. Most recently Houchens acquired 14 Save-A-Lot stores mostly in eastern Kentucky, but also in South Carolina and Virginia.

Houchens Industries is a diversified company operating subsidiaries in the construction, insurance, recycling, tobacco, and warehousing businesses, among others.

EXECUTIVES

Chairman, President, and CEO: James (Jimmie) Gipson
CFO: Mark Iverson
Director of Advertising: Venus Popplewell
Director of Benefits: Sharon Grooms
Director of Marketing and Merchandising: Alan Larsen
Information Systems Manager: David Puckett

LOCATIONS

HQ: Houchens Industries Inc.
  900 Church St., Bowling Green, KY 42101
Phone: 270-843-3252   Fax: 270-780-2877

Houchens Industries has stores in Alabama, Georgia, Illinois, Indiana, Kentucky, New York, North Carolina, Ohio, South Carolina, Tennessee, Texas, Virginia, and West Virginia.

COMPETITORS

7-Eleven	Meijer
ALDI	Sheetz
Alliance Tobacco	Smokin Joes
Cigarettes Cheaper	Vector
Cumberland Farms	Wal-Mart
Delhaize America	Weis Markets
Kroger	Winn-Dixie
K-VA-T Food Stores	

HISTORICAL FINANCIALS

Company Type: Private

Income Statement				FYE: September 30
	ESTIMATED REVENUE ($ mil.)	NET INCOME ($ mil.)	NET PROFIT MARGIN	EMPLOYEES
9/04	2,005	—	—	9,229
9/03	1,913	—	—	7,760
9/02	1,727	—	—	5,850
9/01	820	—	—	5,200
9/00	735	—	—	4,800
9/99	585	—	—	4,200
9/98	515	—	—	3,860
9/97	450	—	—	3,600
9/96	400	—	—	3,100
Annual Growth	**22.3%**	**—**	**—**	**14.6%**

Revenue History

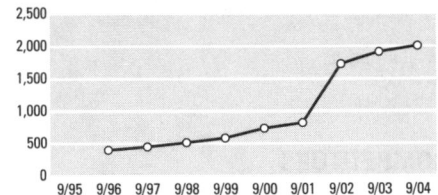

9/95 9/96 9/97 9/98 9/99 9/00 9/01 9/02 9/03 9/04

Houghton Mifflin

Alice Cooper's 1972 album *School's Out* probably doesn't get much play around the offices of Houghton Mifflin. A top publisher of textbooks for the K-12 and college markets, the company also offers fiction and nonfiction books for adults and children and reference works such as the *American Heritage Dictionary*. Major divisions include McDougal Littell (secondary school textbooks), Riverside Publishing (educational testing), and Great Source Education Group (supplemental school materials for grades K-12). It also operates a digital publishing business. Vivendi Universal Publishing (now Editis), formerly the publishing arm of French media giant Vivendi Universal, sold Houghton to several investment firms in 2002.

The company's trade fiction and nonfiction lines, although small, still produce the occasional best seller. In 2004 sales of *The Gourmet Cookbook*, Philip Roth's *The Plot Against America*, and children's book *The Polar Express* were brisk.

Houghton Mifflin is working on building up the company's college, trade and reference, and workplace assessments units. The publisher currently relies heavily on its K-12 publishing business, which makes up 65% of sales.

After 150 years in business as an independent company, the company has had several changes of ownership in recent years. Houghton Mifflin was acquired by French media giant Vivendi Universal in 2001 for $2.2 billion (which included the assumption of $500 million in debt). Houghton Mifflin was placed under Vivendi Universal's publishing unit, which in 2002 decided to sell off most of its assets as part of Vivendi Universal's $9.8 billion sale of assets. Two investment firms (Thomas H. Lee and Bain Capital) bought Houghton Mifflin. Vivendi Universal Publishing sold off its non-US-based publishing assets to an investment bank firm, which then sold the assets to Lagardère.

Parent company HM Publishing Corp. owns Houghton Mifflin.

EXECUTIVES

CEO: Anthony (Tony) Lucki
EVP, CFO, and COO: Stephen Richards
EVP; President, Assessment Group: Sylvia Metayer
SVP and CIO: Patrick J. (Pat) Meehan
SVP Administration: Gary L. Smith, age 56
SVP, Clerk, Secretary, and General Counsel:
 Paul D. Weaver, age 58
SVP Educational and Governmental Affairs:
 Maureen DiMarco
SVP Human Resources: Gerald T. Hughes, age 44
VP Corporate Communications: Collin Earnst
President, Trade and Reference: Theresa (Terri) Kelly
President, Edusoft: Iwan Streichenberger
President, College Division: June Smith, age 57
President, Great Source Education Group:
 Stephen Zukowski
President, McDougal Littell Inc.: Rita H. Schaefer,
 age 47
President, School Division: Donna Lucki
President, Riverside Publishing Company: Lee Jones
Auditors: Ernst & Young LLP

LOCATIONS

HQ: Houghton Mifflin Company
 222 Berkeley St., Boston, MA 02116
Phone: 617-351-5000   **Fax:** 617-351-1105
Web: www.hmco.com

PRODUCTS/OPERATIONS

Selected Operations

Education
 Classwell (online pre K-12 educational resources)
 Edusoft (assessment tools)
 Great Source Education Group (supplemental
  education materials)
 McDougal Littell (secondary textbooks)
 Promissor (test administration
  technology and services)
 The Riverside Publishing Company (testing materials)
Professional Development
 Calabash (professional development resources)
Trade and Reference Division

COMPETITORS

Educational Testing
 Service
Everyday Learning
Goodheart-Willcox
Harcourt Education
HarperCollins
John Wiley
McGraw-Hill
Pearson
Random House

Scholastic
Scholastic Library
 Publishing
Time Warner Book Group
Touchstone Applied
 Science
Verlagsgruppe Georg von
 Holtzbrinck
W.W. Norton

HISTORICAL FINANCIALS

Company Type: Private

Income Statement

FYE: December 31

	REVENUE ($ mil.)	NET INCOME ($ mil.)	NET PROFIT MARGIN	EMPLOYEES
12/04	1,283	(58)	—	3,554
12/03	1,264	(72)	—	3,459
12/02	1,195	(790)	—	3,550
12/01	1,129	(26)	—	3,500
12/00	1,028	56	5.4%	3,500
12/99	920	76	8.3%	3,300
12/98	862	64	7.4%	2,830
12/97	797	50	6.2%	2,550
12/96	718	44	6.1%	2,420
12/95	529	(7)	—	2,350
Annual Growth	10.3%	—	—	4.7%

2004 Year-End Financials

Debt ratio: 233.6%
Return on equity: —
Cash ($ mil.): 206

Current ratio: 1.89
Long-term debt ($ mil.): 1,137

Net Income History

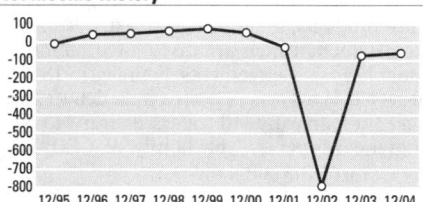

Houlihan's Restaurants

Casual dining has been on Houlihan's menu for more than 30 years. Houlihan's Restaurants operates and franchises about 75 casual eateries in some 20 states and in Mexico, most of them operating under the Houlihan's Restaurant & Bar name. The restaurants offer a variety of main dishes, including burgers, pasta, and steaks, as well as several appetizers and salads. The company also operates a small number of other dining concepts, including Bristol Bar & Grill, Darryl's, Devon, Chequers, and J. Gilbert's Wood-Fired Steaks. Houlihan's emerged from bankruptcy in 2002 with management owning 51% of the company. Restaurant firm Gilbert-Robinson opened the first Houlihan's restaurant in 1972.

Houlihan's is focusing on a new franchising strategy, intending to open a series of new restaurants inside hotels. It inked a partnership with a Wyndham Hotel in Ohio and Hilton Hotels in Washington, DC, and it intends to open at many as 55 new locations nationwide by 2006.

EXECUTIVES

President and CEO: Robert (Bob) Hartnett
CFO: Robert (Rob) Ellis
SVP, Operations: Dan Clay
VP, Operations, Fine Dining: Lou Ambrose
VP, Purchasing: Murray Meikenhous
VP and General Counsel: Paul Strasen
Director, Corporate Systems: Chris Corp
Director, Human Resources: Francis King
Director, Recruiting: Thuan Nguyen
Culinary Director: Dan Admire
Creative Director and Brand Manager: Jen Gulvik

LOCATIONS

HQ: Houlihan's Restaurants, Inc.
 8700 State Line Rd., Ste. 100, Leawood, KS 66206
Phone: 913-901-2500   **Fax:** 913-901-2666
Web: www.houlihans.com

COMPETITORS

Applebee's
Brinker
Carlson Restaurants
CBRL Group
Cheesecake Factory
Darden
Hillstone Restaurant Group
Hooters
Landry's
Lone Star Steakhouse
Metromedia Restaurant Group
O'Charley's
Outback Steakhouse
RARE Hospitality
Roadhouse Grill
Romacorp
Ruby Tuesday
Stuart Anderson's
Texas Roadhouse

HISTORICAL FINANCIALS

Company Type: Private

Income Statement

FYE: Last Monday in December

	REVENUE ($ mil.)	NET INCOME ($ mil.)	NET PROFIT MARGIN	EMPLOYEES
12/04	225	—	—	—
12/03	225	—	—	—
12/02	145	—	—	3,500
12/01	209	—	—	2,800
12/00	300	—	—	3,600
12/99	241	—	—	2,900
12/98	272	—	—	3,700
12/97	280	—	—	8,400
12/96	275	—	—	—
12/95	268	—	—	—
Annual Growth	(1.9%)	—	—	(16.1%)

Revenue History

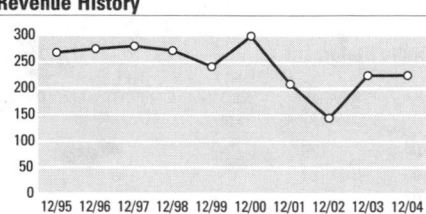

Houston Rockets

The Houston Rockets first took to the court in 1967 but never really left the launching pad as the San Diego Rockets, despite the best efforts of center Elvin Hayes. The team moved to Houston after four years, but it wasn't until 1976, when the Rockets picked up center Moses Malone (who bypassed college to play pro ball), that the team became a force in the NBA. Under the leadership of former head coach and Rocket Rudy Tomjanovich, the team won repeat titles in 1994 and 1995. The Rockets squad has lost some star power in recent years but made up for it in 2004 when it acquired guard Tracy McGrady to join popular center Yao Ming. Former Wall Street securities trader Leslie Alexander owns the team.

EXECUTIVES

Owner: Leslie L. Alexander, age 61
President and CEO: George Postolos
General Manager: Carroll Dawson
Head Coach: Jeff Van Gundy, age 43
CFO: Marcus Jolibois
SVP Sales and Marketing: Thaddeus B. (Tad) Brown
VP and General Counsel: Mark Biskamp
VP Basketball Operations: Keith Jones
VP Basketball Operations and Player Personnel: Dennis Lindsey
VP Marketing: Tim McDougal
VP Sales and Service: Mark Norelli
Director of Community Relations: Sarah Joseph
Director of Finance: David Jackson
Director of Human Resources: Vivian LeFlour
Director of Media Relations: Nelson Luis

LOCATIONS

HQ: Houston Rockets
    1510 Polk St., Houston, TX 77002
Phone: 713-758-7200   **Fax:** 713-758-7315
Web: www.nba.com/rockets

The Houston Rockets play in the 18,300-capacity Toyota Center in Houston.

PRODUCTS/OPERATIONS

Titles
NBA Champions (1994-95)
Western Conference Champions (1981, 1986, 1994-95)

COMPETITORS

Dallas Mavericks
Memphis Grizzlies
New Orleans Hornets
San Antonio Spurs

HISTORICAL FINANCIALS

Company Type: Private

Income Statement

FYE: June 30

	REVENUE ($ mil.)	NET INCOME ($ mil.)	NET PROFIT MARGIN	EMPLOYEES
6/04	125	—	—	—
6/03	82	—	—	—
6/02	82	—	—	—
6/01	81	—	—	—
6/00	79	—	—	—
6/99	44	—	—	75
6/98	72	—	—	90
6/97	67	—	—	—
6/96	63	—	—	—
6/95	57	—	—	60
Annual Growth	9.1%	—	—	5.7%

Revenue History

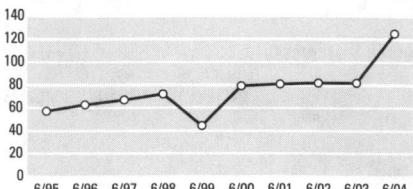

HP Hood

HP Hood is busily trying to cream its competition — with ice cream, sour cream, and whipping cream. The company, one of New England's leading dairies, also produces milk, cottage cheese, and juices. Besides its own brands, HP Hood makes private-label, licensed, and franchise products. It specializes in extended-shelf-life products, which are distributed nationally under licensing agreements. Founded in 1846 by Harvey P. Hood as a one-man milk delivery service, the company still offers delivery to New England residents. The family of CEO John Kaneb owns the company.

HP Hood bought dairy producers Crowley Foods and Marigold Foods (now Kemps LLC) from National Dairy Holdings in 2004. The purchase brought the Kemps, Heluva, Axelrod, Maggio, Brown's Velvet, and Dairymens brands into the HP Hood fold, among others. That same year, HP Hood forged a partnership with Stonyfield Farm to market organic fluid milk.

EXECUTIVES

Chairman, President, and CEO: John A. Kaneb
CFO: Gary R. Kaneb
EVP, Sales: James F. Walsh
VP, Operations Services: Francis V. Torgerson
VP, Order Fulfillment and Logistics: Jeffrey J. Kaneb
VP, Milk Procurement and Processing — West: Mike J. Suever
VP, Processing — New England: H. Scott Blake
VP, Research, Development, and Quality Control: Margaret A. Poole
VP, Human Resources: Bruce W. Bacon
VP, Marketing: Barry C. Boehme
Treasurer: Theresa M. Bresten
Controller: James A. Marcinelli
Director, Information Systems: Jack Billiel
Director, Public Relations and Government Affairs: Lynne M. Bohan
General Counsel: Paul C. Nightingale

LOCATIONS

HQ: HP Hood LLC
    90 Everett Ave., Chelsea, MA 02150
Phone: 617-887-3000   **Fax:** 617-887-8484
Web: www.hphood.com

HP Hood has plants in Connecticut, Maine, Massachusetts, New Hampshire, New York, Vermont, and Virginia.

PRODUCTS/OPERATIONS

Selected Brands

Axelrod
Booth Brothers
Brown's Velvet
Dairymens
Gillette Milk
Hawaiian Punch (license)
Heluva
Hood
Kemp
Lactaid
LifeSavers (license)
Maggio
Oak Grove

COMPETITORS

Brigham's
Dean Foods
Dreyer's
Guida's
National Dairy Holdings
Organic Valley
Parmalat Canada
Stew Leonard's
Unilever

HISTORICAL FINANCIALS

Company Type: Private

Income Statement

FYE: December 31

	REVENUE ($ mil.)	NET INCOME ($ mil.)	NET PROFIT MARGIN	EMPLOYEES
12/03	2,200	—	—	5,000
12/02	1,000	—	—	1,700
12/01	800	—	—	1,600
12/00	700	—	—	1,439
12/99	600	—	—	1,450
12/98	500	—	—	1,300
12/97	500	—	—	1,200
Annual Growth	28.0%	—	—	26.9%

Revenue History

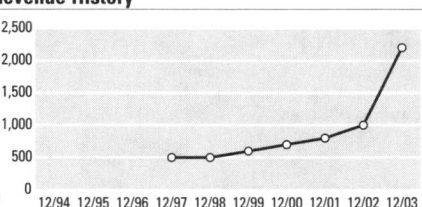

H.T. Hackney

The H.T. Hackney Company began delivering goods to small grocers by horse and buggy in 1891; it now supplies more than 20,000 independent grocers and convenience stores in about 20 states east of the Mississippi. H.T. Hackney distributes more than 30,000 items, including frozen food, tobacco products, health and beauty items, and deli products. In addition it owns Tennessee-based Natural Springs Water Group and has furniture-making operations (Holland House and Volunteer Fabricators). Looking to expand its convenience store business, in 2000 the company acquired six gas stations from Aztex Enterprises and two supply centers from Spartan Stores in 2003. Chairman and CEO Bill Sansom owns H.T. Hackney.

EXECUTIVES

Chairman and CEO: William B. (Bill) Sansom
VP and CFO: Mike Morton
VP and COO: Dean Ballinger
VP, Administration: Leonard Robinette
VP, Sales: Tommy Thomas

LOCATIONS

HQ: H.T. Hackney Company
502 S. Gay St., Knoxville, TN 37902
Phone: 865-546-1291 **Fax:** 865-546-1501
Web: www.hthackney.com

H.T. Hackney serves retailers in Alabama, Arkansas, Florida, Georgia, Illinois, Indiana, Iowa, Kentucky, Louisiana, Maryland, Michigan, Mississippi, Missouri, North Carolina, Ohio, Pennsylvania, South Carolina, Tennessee, Virginia, West Virginia, and Wisconsin.

PRODUCTS/OPERATIONS

Selected Subsidiaries

Holland House Furniture
(wholesale furniture distributor)
Natural Springs Water Group, LLC (bottles water)
Volunteer Fabricators (manufactures furniture
component parts)

COMPETITORS

Alex Lee
AMCON Distributing
AWG
C&S Wholesale
Eby-Brown
GSC Enterprises
McLane
Nash Finch
Roundy's
S. Abraham & Sons
Spartan Stores
SUPERVALU

HISTORICAL FINANCIALS

Company Type: Private

Income Statement

FYE: March 31

	REVENUE ($ mil.)	NET INCOME ($ mil.)	NET PROFIT MARGIN	EMPLOYEES
3/04	3,500	—	—	3,600
3/03*	3,300	—	—	3,500
12/01	2,500	—	—	3,100
12/00	2,300	—	—	3,100
12/99	2,000	—	—	3,000
12/98	1,818	—	—	2,900
12/97	1,623	—	—	2,643
12/96	1,800	—	—	1,900
Annual Growth	**10.0%**	—	—	**9.6%**

*Fiscal year change

Revenue History

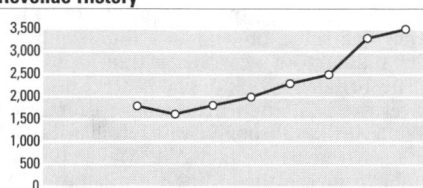

Hungry Howie's Pizza & Subs

Hungry Howie's Pizza & Subs operates a chain of more than 475 franchised pizza parlors in about a dozen states. The carry-out and delivery pizzerias offer several varieties of pizza, as well as calzone-style sub sandwiches, salads, and chicken wings. It also offers flavored crusts for its pies. James Hearn opened the first Hungry Howie's in 1973; company president Steve Jackson got his start at Hungry Howie's delivering pizzas.

EXECUTIVES

President: Steven E. (Steve) Jackson
VP Franchise Development: Bob Cuffaro
VP Operations: Paul Pfeiffer

LOCATIONS

HQ: Hungry Howie's Pizza & Subs, Inc.
30300 Stephenson Hwy.,
Madison Heights, MI 48071
Phone: 248-414-3300 **Fax:** 248-414-3301
Web: www.hungryhowies.com

Hungry Howie's Pizza & Subs franchises more than 450 restaurants in Alabama, Arizona, California, Florida, Georgia, Illinois, Indiana, Maryland, Michigan, Nevada, North Carolina, Ohio, and South Carolina.

COMPETITORS

Bellacino's	Noble Roman's
B.R. Associates	Papa John's
CEC Entertainment	Peter Piper Pizza
CiCi Enterprises	Pizza Factory
Domino's	Pizza Hut
Fox's Pizza Den, Inc.	Pizza Inn
Godfather's Pizza	Pizza Magia
Happy Joe's	Pizza Patrón
Jet's Pizza	Pizza Pro
LaRosa's	RedBrick Pizza
Little Caesar's	Sbarro
Mr. Gatti's	Shakey's
Mr. Goodcents	Simple Simon's
Nick-N-Willy's	Straw Hat

HISTORICAL FINANCIALS

Company Type: Private

Income Statement

FYE: September 30

	ESTIMATED REVENUE ($ mil.)	NET INCOME ($ mil.)	NET PROFIT MARGIN	EMPLOYEES
9/04	20	—	—	20
9/03	20	—	—	20
9/02	10	—	—	20
9/01	10	—	—	—
9/00	10	—	—	—
Annual Growth	**18.9%**	—	—	**0.0%**

Revenue History

Hunt Consolidated

Hunt Consolidated is a holding company for the oil and real estate businesses of Ray Hunt, son of legendary Texas wildcatter and company founder H.L. Hunt. Founded in 1934 (reportedly with H.L.'s poker winnings), Hunt Oil is an oil and gas production and exploration company with primary interests in North and South America. Hoping to repeat huge discoveries in Yemen, Hunt is exploring in Canada, Ghana, Madagascar, and Oman. It has also teamed up with Repsol YPF and SK Corporation on an exploration project in Peru, and has expanded its Canadian operations through the acquisition of Chieftain International. Hunt Realty handles commercial and residential real estate investment management activities.

EXECUTIVES

Chairman, President, and CEO: Ray L. Hunt, age 61
SVP Financial Operations: Harry Dombroski
SVP Special Projects and New Business Development:
Thomas A. (Tom) Meurer, age 63
SVP and Tax Counsel: W. Kirk Baker
SVP and General Counsel: Richard A. Massman
VP and CIO: Kevin P. Campbell
VP Global Security: Mike Pritchard
VP Human Resources: Laura S. Weaver

LOCATIONS

HQ: Hunt Consolidated Inc.
Fountain Place, 1445 Ross at Field, Ste. 1400,
Dallas, TX 75202
Phone: 214-978-8000 **Fax:** 214-978-8888
Web: www.huntoil.com

PRODUCTS/OPERATIONS

Selected Subsidiaries and Affiliates

Hunt Oil Company (integrated oil company)
Hunt Oil Company of Canada
Hunt Power L.P. (utility projects and services)
Hunt Private Equity Group
Hunt Realty Corporation (acquires real estate and
manages investments)
Hunt Refining Co. Inc.
Hunt Ventures, L.P. (diversified investments)
Yemen Hunt Oil Co.

COMPETITORS

Anadarko Petroleum
BP
Exxon Mobil
Houston Exploration
Kerr-McGee
Lincoln Property
Murphy Oil
Nexen
Royal Dutch/Shell Group
TOTAL

HISTORICAL FINANCIALS

Company Type: Private

Income Statement

	REVENUE ($ mil.)	NET INCOME ($ mil.)	NET PROFIT MARGIN	EMPLOYEES
FYE: December 31				
12/03	2,250	—	—	2,900
12/02	1,930	—	—	2,500
12/01	1,500	—	—	2,600
12/00	2,000	—	—	2,500
12/99	1,200	—	—	2,600
12/98	700	—	—	2,600
12/97	1,000	—	—	2,600
12/96	1,000	—	—	2,600
12/95	1,000	—	—	2,600
12/94	1,000	—	—	2,600
Annual Growth	9.4%	—	—	1.2%

Revenue History

2,500	
2,000	
1,500	
1,000	
500	
0	
12/94 12/95 12/96 12/97 12/98 12/99 12/00 12/01 12/02 12/03	

Hurricanes Hockey

Hurricanes Hockey hopes to blow away the competition. The company owns and operates the Carolina Hurricanes professional hockey franchise, which plays host at the RBC Center in Raleigh, North Carolina. Formerly the Hartford Whalers, the team was bought by a group led by Compuware founder and chairman Peter Karmanos for $47.5 million in 1994. Karmanos moved the team to Greensboro, North Carolina, in 1997, but a cool reception from fans brought losses of $30 million that year. The Hurricanes took up residence in Raleigh two seasons later. The team made its first Stanley Cup appearance in 2002, but lost to the Detroit Red Wings.

The Whalers franchise was founded in 1971 as the New England Whalers by Howard Baldwin and originally represented Boston in the World Hockey Association (WHA). The team moved to Hartford, Connecticut, in 1975, and joined the National Hockey League in 1979 when the WHA folded.

EXECUTIVES

CEO and Governor: Peter (Pete) Karmanos Jr., age 62
President and General Manager: Jim Rutherford
Head Coach: Peter Laviolette, age 40
CFO: Michael (Mike) Amendola
VP and Assistant General Manager: Jason Karmanos
VP and General Manager, RBC Center: Davin Olsen
VP Business Operations: Matt West
Director of Information Technology: Glenn Johnson
Director of Media Relations: Mike Sundheim
Community Relations Manager: Emma Bennett
Marketing Manager: Sheila Carter
Human Resources Coordinator: Irene Cantelli
Human Resources Coordinator: Carrie Hubinek

LOCATIONS

HQ: Hurricanes Hockey Limited Partnership
1400 Edwards Mill Rd., Raleigh, NC 27607
Phone: 919-467-7825   **Fax:** 919-462-7030
Web: www.caneshockey.com

PRODUCTS/OPERATIONS

Championship Trophies
Prince of Wales Trophy (2002)

COMPETITORS

Atlanta Thrashers	Tampa Bay Lightning
Florida Panthers	Washington Capitals

HISTORICAL FINANCIALS

Company Type: Private

Income Statement

	REVENUE ($ mil.)	NET INCOME ($ mil.)	NET PROFIT MARGIN	EMPLOYEES
FYE: June 30				
6/04	52	—	—	—
6/03	57	—	—	—
6/02	67	—	—	—
6/01	52	—	—	—
6/00	45	—	—	100
6/99	47	—	—	100
6/98	25	—	—	105
6/97	24	—	—	90
Annual Growth	11.8%	—	—	3.6%

Revenue History

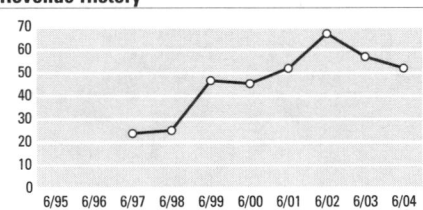

70	
60	
50	
40	
30	
20	
10	
0	
6/95 6/96 6/97 6/98 6/99 6/00 6/01 6/02 6/03 6/04	

Hyatt

Travelers interested in luxury lodgings can check in for the Hyatt touch. Global Hyatt is one of the world's top operators of full-service luxury hotels and resorts with more than 200 locations in about 40 countries. Its core hotel brand, Hyatt Regency, offers well-appointed rooms, fine dining, and exceptional service targeted primarily to business travelers and upscale vacationers. The company also operates properties under the names Grand Hyatt and Park Hyatt. Its resort destinations offer golfing, spas, and other upmarket rest and relaxation activities. Although Global Hyatt was formed in 2004, the Hyatt chain traces its roots back to 1957. The company is owned by the wealthy Pritzker family of Chicago.

As part of an ongoing effort to restructure H Group Holding, the holding company that oversees the family's various business enterprises, Global Hyatt was formed to consolidate the Pritzker's hospitality interests. The reorganization brought together the operations of Hyatt Hotels Corporation (domestic hotels), Hyatt In-

ternational, Hyatt Equities (hotel ownership), and Hyatt Vacation Club.

Global Hyatt's operations also include U.S. Franchise Systems, which franchises three smaller chains: America's Best Inns & Suites, Hawthorn Suites, and Microtel Inns & Suites. The subsidiary, founded in 1995, was acquired by the Pritzker family in 2000.

In 2005 Hyatt expanded its reach into the limited-service hotel business when it acquired the AmeriSuites chain previously owned by Prime Hospitality. The upscale hotelier announced a $175 million initiative to rebrand the more than 140 locations under the Hyatt Place banner, a new brand designed to attract Generation X travelers with wireless Internet access, flat screen televisions, and contemporary interiors.

HISTORY

Nicholas Pritzker left Kiev for Chicago in 1881, where his family's ascent to the ranks of America's wealthiest families began. His son A. N. left the family law practice in the 1930s and began investing in a variety of businesses. He turned a 1942 investment (Cory Corporation) worth $25,000 into $23 million by 1967. A. N.'s son Jay followed in his father's wheeling-and-dealing footsteps. In 1953, with the help of his father's banking connections, Jay purchased Colson Company and recruited his brother Bob, an industrial engineer, to restructure a company that made tricycles and US Navy rockets. By 1990 Jay and Bob had added 60 industrial companies, with annual sales exceeding $3 billion, to the entity they called The Marmon Group.

The family's connection to Hyatt hotels was established in 1957 when Jay Pritzker bought a hotel called Hyatt House, located near the Los Angeles airport, from Hyatt von Dehn. Jay added five locations by 1961 and hired his gregarious youngest brother, Donald, to manage the hotel company. Hyatt went public in 1967, but the move that opened new vistas for the hotel chain was the purchase that year of an 800-room hotel in Atlanta that both Hilton and Marriott had turned down. John Portman's design, incorporating a 21-story atrium, a large fountain, and a revolving rooftop restaurant, became a Hyatt trademark.

The Pritzkers formed Hyatt International in 1969 to operate hotels overseas, and the company grew rapidly in the US and abroad during the 1970s. Donald Pritzker died in 1972, and Jay assumed control of Hyatt. The family decided to take the company private in 1979. Much of Hyatt's growth in the 1970s came from contracts to manage Hyatt hotels built by other investors. When Hyatt's earnings on those contracts shrank in the 1980s, the company launched its own hotel and resort developments under Nick Pritzker, a cousin to Jay and Bob. In 1988, with US and Japanese partners, it built the Hyatt Regency Waikoloa on Hawaii's Big Island for $360 million — a record at the time for a hotel.

The Pritzkers took a side-venture into air travel in 1983 when they bought bedraggled Braniff Airlines through Hyatt subsidiaries as it emerged from bankruptcy. After a failed 1987 attempt to merge the airline with Pan Am, the Pritzkers sold Braniff in 1988.

Hyatt opened Classic Residence by Hyatt, a group of upscale retirement communities, in 1989. The company joined Circus Circus (now part of MGM MIRAGE) in 1994 to launch the Grand Victoria, the nation's largest cruising gaming vessel. The next year, as part of a new strategy to manage both freestanding golf courses and those near Hyatt hotels, the company opened its first freestanding course: an 18-hole, par 71 championship course in Aruba.

President Thomas Pritzker, Jay's son, took over as Hyatt chairman and CEO following his father's death in early 1999. In 2000 Hyatt announced plans to join rival Marriott International in launching an independent company to provide an online procurement network serving the hospitality industry. The following year the company announced plans to build a 47-story skyscraper in downtown Chicago. Construction for the new building, named the Hyatt Center, began at the end of 2002.

In 2004 the Pritzker family consolidated its hospitality holdings to form Global Hyatt Corporation. The following year the company bought the AmeriSuites limited-service hotel chain from Prime Hospitality.

EXECUTIVES

Chairman and CEO; Chairman, Hyatt International Corporation: Thomas J. Pritzker, age 54
Vice Chairman; Chairman and CEO, Hyatt Development and Hyatt Equities: Nicholas J. (Nick) Pritzker
President: Douglas G. (Doug) Geoga, age 49
EVP Acquisitions and Development: Steve Goldman
SVP and General Counsel: Susan T. Smith, age 53
SVP Acquisitions and Development:
  James R. (Jim) Abrahamson, age 49
President and CEO, U.S. Franchise Systems:
  Michael A. (Mike) Leven, age 67
President, Hyatt Hotels: Edward W. Rabin Jr., age 57
President, Hyatt International Corporation:
  Bernd Chorengel
SVP Marketing, Hyatt Hotels: Thomas F. (Tom) O'Toole, age 46
SVP Operations, Hyatt Hotels: Chuck Floyd
VP Corporate Communications: Katie Meyer
VP Electronic Distribution, Hyatt Hotels: Joan Lowell
VP Finance: Kirk A. Rose
VP Human Resources, Hyatt Hotels: Doug Patrick
VP Marketing, Hyatt Hotels: Amy Weyman
Executive Director of Sales, Individual Travel:
  Kevin Kelly
Director of Corporate Public Relations: Lori Armon

LOCATIONS

HQ: Global Hyatt Corporation
  71 S. Wacker Dr., Chicago, IL 60606
Phone: 312-750-1234   **Fax:** 312-750-8550
Web: www.hyatt.com

Global Hyatt Corporation operates more than 200 hotels and resorts in nearly 40 countries.

PRODUCTS/OPERATIONS

Selected Operations

AmeriSuites (limited-service hotels)
Camp Hyatt (activities for children)
Classic Residence by Hyatt (upscale
  retirement communities)
Grand Hyatt (large business and convention hotels)
Hyatt Casinos (gaming resorts)
Hyatt Regency (core hotel format)
Park Hyatt (small luxury hotels)

COMPETITORS

Accor	LXR Luxury Resorts
Carlson Hotels	Marriott
Club Med	Millennium &
Four Seasons Hotels	Copthorne Hotels
Hilton	Starwood Hotels &
Hilton Group	Resorts
InterContinental Hotels	Wyndham

HISTORICAL FINANCIALS

Company Type: Private

Income Statement				FYE: January 31
	ESTIMATED REVENUE ($ mil.)	NET INCOME ($ mil.)	NET PROFIT MARGIN	EMPLOYEES
1/03	3,600	—	—	40,000
1/02	3,400	—	—	37,000
1/01	3,500	—	—	36,632
1/00	3,950	—	—	80,000
1/99	3,400	—	—	80,000
1/98	3,000	—	—	80,000
1/97	2,900	—	—	80,000
1/96	2,500	—	—	65,000
1/95	1,240	—	—	54,000
1/94	950	—	—	47,000
Annual Growth	**16.0%**	**—**	**—**	**(1.8%)**

Revenue History

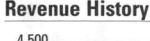

Hy-Vee

Give Hy-Vee a high five for being one of the largest privately owned US supermarket chains, despite serving some modestly sized towns in the Midwest. The company runs about 220 Hy-Vee supermarkets in Illinois, Iowa, Kansas, Minnesota, Missouri, Nebraska, and South Dakota. About half of its supermarkets are in Iowa, as are most of its 25-plus Drug Town drugstores. It distributes products to its stores through several subsidiaries, including Lomar Distributing (specialty foods), Perishable Distributors of Iowa (fresh foods), and Florist Distributing (flowers). Charles Hyde and David Vredenburg founded the employee-owned firm in 1930. The company's moniker is a combination of the founders' names.

In 2004, Hy-Vee spent more than $200 million to open eight new supermarkets and to relocate or expand about 15 existing stores. It also acquired an Osco drugstore in Council Bluffs, Iowa from food-and-drug retail giant Albertson's.

In mid-2005 the company began renaming its 26 Drug Town stores Hy-Vee Drugstores, to capitalize on Hy-Vee's strong brand recognition in the region.

Going beyond traditional grocery fare, the company has been focusing on adding Hy-Vee Gas units, wine and spirits stores, pharmacies, and Hy-Vee HealthMarket departments. Many Hy-Vee stores also have seasonal garden centers.

EXECUTIVES

Chairman: Ronald D. (Ron) Pearson
President, CEO, and COO: Richard N. (Ric) Jurgens
EVP: Charlie Bell
EVP: Raymond (Ray) Stewart
EVP: Ken Waller
SVP, CFO, and Treasurer: John Briggs
VP, General Merchandise: Jon Wendel
VP, Human Resources: Jane Knaack-Esbeck
VP, Management Information Systems: Eric Smith
VP, Purchasing and Marketing: Ron Taylor
President, Perishable Distributors of Iowa:
  Andy McCann
Assistant VP, Communications: Ruth Comer
Auditors: McGladrey & Pullen, LLP

LOCATIONS

HQ: Hy-Vee, Inc.
  5820 Westown Pkwy., West Des Moines, IA 50266
Phone: 515-267-2800   **Fax:** 515-267-2817
Web: www.hy-vee.com

PRODUCTS/OPERATIONS

Selected Subsidiaries

D & D Foods, Inc.
Florist Distributing, Inc.
Hy-Vee Weitz Construction, L.C.
Lomar Distributing, Inc.
Meyocks Group, Inc.
Midwest Heritage Bank, FSB
Perishable Distributors of Iowa, Ltd.

COMPETITORS

Albertson's	Nash Finch
AWG	Niemann Foods
Ball's Food	Rite Aid
Casey's General Stores	Roundy's
CVS	SUPERVALU
Dahl's Foods	Target
Fareway Stores	Walgreen
Kmart	Wal-Mart
Kroger	

HISTORICAL FINANCIALS

Company Type: Private

Income Statement				FYE: September 30
	ESTIMATED REVENUE ($ mil.)	NET INCOME ($ mil.)	NET PROFIT MARGIN	EMPLOYEES
9/04	4,500	—	—	46,000
9/03	4,230	—	—	46,000
9/02	4,100	—	—	46,000
9/01	3,900	—	—	46,000
9/00	3,600	—	—	44,000
9/99	3,500	—	—	42,900
9/98	3,200	—	—	41,200
9/97	2,900	—	—	38,400
9/96	2,800	—	—	36,000
9/95	2,700	—	—	30,000
Annual Growth	**5.8%**	**—**	**—**	**4.9%**

Revenue History

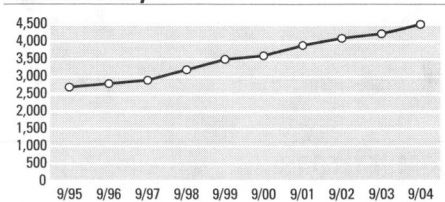

ICON Health

ICON Health & Fitness has brawn as one of the leading US makers of home fitness equipment. Its products include treadmills, elliptical trainers, and weight benches. Brands include HealthRider, NordicTrack, and ProForm. ICON also offers fitness accessories, spas (unit being sold to Keys Fitness), and commercial fitness gear. It makes most of its products in Utah and sells them through retailers, infomercials, the Web, and its catalog Workout Warehouse. Sears (which accounts for about 40% of sales) has an exclusive license to sell NordicTrack brand apparel.

Bain Capital, Credit Suisse, and founders Scott Watterson and Gary Stevenson collectively own over 90% of ICON.

The company plans to license its brands.

EXECUTIVES

Chairman and CEO: David J. Watterson, age 46, $550,000 pay
President and Chief Merchandising Officer: Matthew N. Allen, age 41
COO: M. Joseph Brough, age 41
VP, CFO, Chief Accounting Officer, and Treasurer: S. Fred Beck, age 47, $358,076 pay
SVP; President, JumpKing: Jace Jergensen, age 42
SVP, Manufacturing: Jon M. White, age 57
VP, Business Development: Lynn C. Brenchley
VP, Imports, Transportation, and New Business Development: Jeff Carmignani
VP, Purchasing: Douglas L. Clausen
VP, Design: William T. Dalebout, age 57
President, ICON Canada: Richard Hebert, age 60, $697,627 pay
President, ICON Europe: Giovanni Lato, $303,540 pay
COO, ICON Europe: Daniele Di Carmine, $248,255 pay
Secretary and General Counsel: Brad H. Bearnson, age 51
Auditors: PricewaterhouseCoopers LLP

LOCATIONS

HQ: ICON Health & Fitness, Inc.
1500 S. 1000 West, Logan, UT 84321
Phone: 435-750-5000 **Fax:** 435-750-3917
Web: www.iconfitness.com

ICON has facilities in Canada, China, Europe, and the US.

2004 Sales

	$ mil.	% of total
US	988.9	90
Other countries	106.8	10
Total	**1,095.7**	**100**

PRODUCTS/OPERATIONS

Selected Brands

Epic
Free Motion Fitness
Gold's Gym (licensed)
HealthRider
Image
JumpKing
NordicTrack
ProForm
Reebok (licensed)
Weider

COMPETITORS

Bell Sports	Life Fitness
Cybex International	Nautilus
Escalade	Precor
Fitness Quest	Soloflex
Keys Fitness	

HISTORICAL FINANCIALS

Company Type: Private

Income Statement

FYE: May 31

	REVENUE ($ mil.)	NET INCOME ($ mil.)	NET PROFIT MARGIN	EMPLOYEES
5/04	1,096	23	2.1%	5,142
5/03	1,012	28	2.8%	4,569
5/02	871	20	2.2%	4,800
5/01	797	13	1.6%	4,200
5/00	733	—	—	3,952
5/99	710	—	—	4,328
5/98	749	—	—	4,200
5/97	836	—	—	5,400
5/96	748	—	—	4,300
5/95	531	—	—	3,437
Annual Growth	**8.4%**	**22.3%**	**—**	**4.6%**

2004 Year-End Financials

Debt ratio: 227.4%
Return on equity: 41.9%
Cash ($ mil.): 5
Current ratio: 1.34
Long-term debt ($ mil.): 153

Net Income History

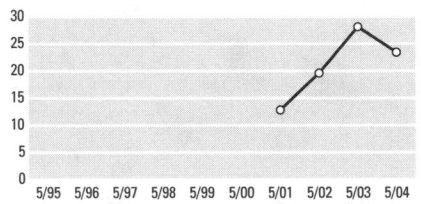

IGA

IGA grocers are independent, but not that independent. The world's largest voluntary supermarket network, IGA has more than 4,000 stores, including members in nearly all 50 states and about 45 other countries. Collectively, its members are among North America's leaders in terms of supermarket sales. IGA (for either International or Independent Grocers Alliance, the company says) is owned by 36 worldwide distribution companies, including SUPERVALU. Members can sell IGA Brand private-label products (2,300 items) and take advantage of joint operations and services, such as advertising and volume buying. Some stores in the IGA alliance, which primarily caters to smaller towns, also sell gas.

The first US grocer in China and Singapore, IGA has moved into Europe with its operations in Poland and Spain. Its international operations account for more than 60% of its total sales. IGA realigned its corporate structure in 2001, setting up IGA North America, IGA Southern Hemisphere/Europe/Caribbean, and IGA Asia, each with its own president.

HISTORY

IGA was founded in Chicago in 1926 by a group led by accountant Frank Grimes. During the 1920s chains began to dominate the grocery store industry. Grimes, an accountant for many grocery wholesalers, saw an opportunity to develop a network of independent grocers that could compete with the burgeoning chains. Grimes and five associates — Gene Flack, Louis

Groebe, W. K. Hunter, H. V. Swenson, and William Thompson — created IGA.

Their idea was to "level the playing field" for independent grocers and chain stores by taking advantage of volume buying and mass marketing. IGA originally acted as a purchasing agent for its wholesalers but eventually passed that duty to the wholesalers. The group's first members were Poughkeepsie, New York-based grocery distributor W. T. Reynolds Company and the 69 grocery stores it serviced.

IGA focused on adding distributors and retailers, and it soon added wholesaler Fleming-Wilson (now Fleming Companies) and Winston & Newell (now SUPERVALU). In 1930 it hired Babe Ruth as a spokesman; other celebrity endorsers during the period included Jackie Cooper, Jack Dempsey, and Popeye. IGA also sponsored a radio program called the IGA Home Town Hour.

In 1945 the company introduced the Foodliner format, a design for stores larger than 4,000 sq. ft. The next year IGA introduced the 30-foot-by-100-foot Precision Store — designed so customers had to pass all the other merchandise in the store to get to the dairy and bread sections.

Grimes retired as president in 1951. He was succeeded by his son, Don, who continued to expand the company. Don was succeeded in 1968 by Richard Jones, head of IGA member J. M. Jones Co.

Thomas Haggai was named chairman of the company in 1976. A Baptist minister, radio commentator, and former CIA employee, Haggai had come to the attention of Grimes in 1960 when he praised Christian Scientists in one of his radio broadcasts. Grimes, a Christian Scientist, asked Haggai to speak at an IGA convention and eventually asked him to join the IGA board. Haggai, who became CEO in 1986, tightened the restrictions for IGA members, weeding out many of the smaller, low-volume mom-and-pop stores making up much of the group's network.

Haggai also began a push for international expansion. In 1988 the organization signed a deal with Japanese food company C. Itoh (now ITOCHU) to open a distribution outlet in Tokyo.

The 1990s saw expansion into Australia, Papua New Guinea, the Caribbean, China, Singapore, South Africa, and Brazil. IGA also expanded outside the continental US when it entered Hawaii. In 1993 IGA began an international television advertising campaign, a first for the supermarket industry. The next year the company launched its first line of private-label products for an ethnic food market, introducing several Mexican food products. In 1998 the group developed a new format for its stores that included on-site gas pumps.

SUPERVALU signed 54 independent grocery stores (primarily in Mississippi and Arkansas, and Trinidad in the Caribbean) to the IGA banner in August 1999.

With more than 60% of sales coming from international operations, IGA realigned its corporate structure in 2001, setting up IGA North America, IGA Southern Hemisphere/Europe/Caribbean, and IGA Asia, each with its own president.

IGA suffered the loss of Fleming (one of the grocery chain's principal wholesale distributors) and 300 stores in 2003. On the plus side, four Julian's Supermarkets on the Caribbean island of St. Lucia converted to IGA, giving IGA a presence in 45 countries worldwide.

EXECUTIVES

Chairman and CEO: Thomas S. Haggai
EVP and Chief Growth Officer: William (Bill) Benzing
CFO: Robert (Bob) Grottke
National Accounts Manager: Jim Collins
EVP, IGA International, and President, IGA Institute:
Paulo Goelzer
VP, Administration, Events, and Communication:
Barbara G. Wiest
VP, Buying Group Operations, IGA Canada:
Randy Huckvale
VP, Information Technology: Nick Liakopulos
VP, Red Oval Family Relations: Thomas (Tom) Zatina
VP, U.S. Chief Growth Officer: Doug Fritsch
CEO, IGA Distribution, Australia: Lou Jardin, age 47
Senior Director, Branding and Business Development:
James J. (Jim) Walz
Director, International: Jose Brinson
Director, Marketing Events and Editor-at-large IGA
Grocerygram: Patrick Sylvester
Director, Packaging: Tim Considine
Manager, Events Marketing: Zorona Chapman
International Coordinator: Jerry Pinney

LOCATIONS

HQ: IGA, Inc.
8725 W. Higgins Rd., Chicago, IL 60631
Phone: 773-693-4520 **Fax:** 773-693-4532
Web: www.igainc.com

IGA has operations in 48 states and about 45 countries, including Anguilla, Antigua, Aruba, Australia, Barbados, Barbuda, Botswana, Brazil, Cambodia, Canada, Cayman Islands, China, the Czech Republic, Dominica, the Dominican Republic, Grenada, Indonesia, Jamaica, Japan, Kenya, Lesotho, Malawi, Malaysia, Mauritius, Mozambique, Namibia, Papua New Guinea, Philippines, Poland, St. Kitts, Singapore, South Africa, South Korea, Spain, St. Lucia, Swaziland, Thailand, Trinidad and Tobago, the Turks and Caicos, Vietnam, Zambia, and Zimbabwe, and is served by 37 independent distribution companies.

PRODUCTS/OPERATIONS

Distributors/Owners

Bozzuto's Inc.
C.I. Foods Systems Co., Ltd. (Japan)
The Copps Corporation
Davids Limited (Australia)
Foodland Associated Limited (Australia)
Great North Foods
IGA Brasil (includes 16 individual companies)
Ira Higdon Grocery Company
Laurel Grocery Company
Martahari Putra Prima Tbk (Indonesia)
McLane Polska (Poland)
Merchants Distributors, Inc.
Metro Cash & Carry (Africa)
Nash Finch Company
NTUC Fairprice (Singapore)
Pearl River Distribution Ltd. (China)
SUPERVALU INC.
Tasmania Independent Wholesalers (Australia)
Tripifoods, Inc.
Villa Market JP Co., Ltd. (Thailand)
W. Lee Flowers & Co., Inc.
WALTERMART SUPERMARKETS (Philippines)

Affiliates

H.Y. Louie (fraternal relationship, Canada)
Sobey's (fraternal relationship, Canada)

Selected Joint Operations and Services

Advertising
Community service programs
Equipment purchase
IGA Brand (private-label products)
IGA Grocergram (in-house magazine)
Internet services
Marketing & merchandising
Red Oval Family (manufacturer/IGA collaboration on
sales, marketing, and other activities)
Volume buying

COMPETITORS

A&P	Ito-Yokado
Albertson's	Kroger
AWG	Meijer
BJ's Wholesale Club	Metro Cash and Carry
C&S Wholesale	Penn Traffic
Carrefour	Publix
Casino Guichard	Roundy's
Coles Myer	Royal Ahold
Daiei	Safeway
Dairy Farm International	Spartan Stores
Delhaize	Wakefern Food
George Weston	Wal-Mart
Hannaford Bros.	Winn-Dixie
H-E-B	

HISTORICAL FINANCIALS

Company Type: Holding company

Income Statement

FYE: December 31

	REVENUE ($ mil.)	NET INCOME ($ mil.)	NET PROFIT MARGIN	EMPLOYEES
12/03	21,000	—	—	92,000
12/02	21,000	—	—	92,000
12/01	21,000	—	—	92,000
12/00	21,000	—	—	92,000
12/99	19,000	—	—	92,000
12/98	18,000	—	—	92,000
12/97	18,000	—	—	135,000
12/96	16,800	—	—	128,000
12/95	17,100	—	—	130,000
12/94	17,000	—	—	—
Annual Growth	**2.4%**	**—**	**—**	**(4.2%)**

Revenue History

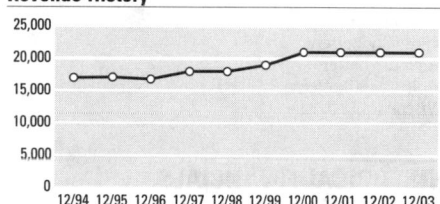

IHS

IHS Inc. (Information Handling Services Inc.) handles the hottest commodity around: information. A publisher of technical documents focusing on engineering, energy, and regulatory issues, the company distributes its data in several electronic formats (Internet, intranet, extranet, CD-ROM). Products such as collections of technical standards, safety publications, design guidelines, vendor and logistics information, and software are sold through its IHS Engineering unit. IHS also provides operational, research, and strategic advisory services and has an IHS Energy division devoted to the oil and gas market. IHS, a unit of German-based Thyssen-Bornemisza Group, has more than 55,000 customers in some 100 countries.

International activities account for about half of IHS's sales. The company specializes in delivering information to engineers, designers, technical professionals, senior managers, compliance officers, marketing executives, and strategic planners at both small and large businesses. Customers come from a number of industries, including energy, defense, aerospace, construction, electronics, and automotive. More than 75% of revenues come from subscriptions to IHS products.

The company's IHS Energy division provides information products and services — such as consulting and well and production data — to professionals in the oil and gas industry, focusing on issues relating to geology, technology, and reserves potential. It also assesses the economic impact of political, fiscal, and environmental risks.

IHS has made several recent purchases, including the 2004 acquisitions of USA Information Systems and Intermat, and the 2005 acquisition of American Technical Publishers.

The company is undergoing a reorganization, which includes job cuts and office closings in its Engineering segment, and putting certain IHS Energy assets up for sale.

EXECUTIVES

Chairman: Jerre L. Stead, age 62, $800,000 pay
President, CEO, and Director: Charles A. Picasso, age 63, $614,903 pay (prior to promotion)
SVP and CFO: Michael J. (Mike) Sullivan, age 40, $427,679 pay
SVP and CIO: H. John Oechsle, age 42, $360,075 pay
SVP Global Human Resources: Jeffrey (Jeff) Sisson, age 48
SVP and General Counsel: Stephen (Steve) Green, age 52, $475,264 pay
SVP Investor Relations and Corporate Communications: Jane Okun, age 42
SVP Corporate Development and Strategic Planning: Matthew (Matt) Levin, age 31
SVP Human Resources: Susan J. Auxer
President and COO, IHS Engineering: Jeffrey R. (Jeff) Tarr, age 42
President and COO, IHS Energy: Ron Mobed, age 45
Press Contact: Tim Stack
Auditors: Ernst & Young LLP

LOCATIONS

HQ: IHS Inc.
15 Inverness Way East, Englewood, CO 80112
Phone: 303-790-0600 **Fax:** 303-754-3940
Web: www.ihsgroup.com

IHS distributes its publications in more than 100 countries.

2004 Sales

	$ mil.	% of total
US	196.7	50
UK	84.4	21
Canada	41.8	11
Switzerland	33.6	8
Other countries	38.1	10
Total	**394.6**	**100**

PRODUCTS/OPERATIONS

2004 Sales

	$ mil.	% of total
Engineering	208.2	53
Energy	186.4	47
Total	**394.6**	**100**

COMPETITORS

Advanstar	John Wiley
Bonnierforetagen	McGraw-Hill
Bureau of National Affairs	Pearson
Crain Communications	Penton Media
Divestco	PRIMEDIA
GlobalSpec	Reed Elsevier Group
Hearst	Thomson Corporation
i2 Technologies	United Business Media
IBC	VNU
Informa	Wolters Kluwer
International Data Group	W.W. Norton

HISTORICAL FINANCIALS

Company Type: Private

Income Statement
FYE: November 30

	REVENUE ($ mil.)	NET INCOME ($ mil.)	NET PROFIT MARGIN	EMPLOYEES
11/04	395	61	15.5%	2,300
11/03	346	43	12.3%	2,200
11/02	339	30	8.8%	2,500
11/01	400	—	—	2,700
11/00	400	—	—	3,000
11/99	450	—	—	3,200
11/98	475	—	—	3,200
11/97	324	—	—	3,000
11/96	289	—	—	2,000
11/95	257	—	—	1,800
Annual Growth	4.9%	43.2%	—	2.8%

2004 Year-End Financials

Debt ratio: 0.1%
Return on equity: 15.5%
Cash ($ mil.): 124

Current ratio: 1.07
Long-term debt ($ mil.): 1

Net Income History

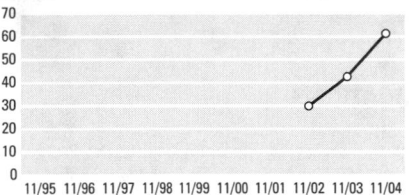

```
70
60
50
40
30
20
10
 0
   11/95 11/96 11/97 11/98 11/99 11/00 11/01 11/02 11/03 11/04
```

Illinois Lottery

Just because the Cubs can't win in Illinois doesn't mean you can't. Created in 1974, the Illinois Department of the Lottery runs numbers games, including Pick 3 and Pick 4, and participates in the seven-state Big Game in which players can win jackpots starting at $5 million (odds of winning: 1 in 76 million). It also offers instant-win scratch-off games. Of the money collected from ticket sales, 56% is paid in prizes and 34% goes to the state's Common School Fund, which helps finance K-12 public education. The rest covers retailer commissions and expenses. The Illinois Lottery operates through more than 8,400 retail businesses.

EXECUTIVES

Superintendent: Carolyn Adams
Public Information Officer: Anne Plohr Rayhill
Director, Marketing: Sarah Cummins
Director, Sales: Kris Hanlon
Budget Liaison: Dennis Wright
Acting Springfield Chief of Staff and Legal Assistant: Lisa Crites
Product Manager, Instant Games: Michele Eichhom
Director, Promotions: Paul Arnell
Auditors: McGladrey & Pullen, LLP

LOCATIONS

HQ: Illinois Department of the Lottery
   101 W. Jefferson St., Springfield, IL 62702
Phone: 217-524-5250
Web: www.illinoislottery.com

PRODUCTS/OPERATIONS

Selected Games

Numbers games
   Big Game (multistate drawing with Georgia, Maryland, Massachusetts, Michigan, New Jersey, and Virginia)
   Little Lotto
   Lotto
   Pick 3
   Pick 4
Scratch-off games
   Add 'Em Up
   Beat Score
   Match 3
   Tic Tac Toe

COMPETITORS

Hoosier Lottery
Kentucky Lottery
Missouri Lottery
Multi-State Lottery
Wisconsin Lottery

HISTORICAL FINANCIALS

Company Type: Government-owned

Income Statement
FYE: June 30

	REVENUE ($ mil.)	NET INCOME ($ mil.)	NET PROFIT MARGIN	EMPLOYEES
6/04	1,799	—	—	151
6/03	1,590	—	—	151
6/02	1,590	—	—	290
6/01	1,550	—	—	—
6/00	1,503	—	—	—
6/99	1,520	—	—	290
6/98	1,577	—	—	284
6/97	1,624	—	—	290
6/96	1,637	—	—	284
6/95	1,630	—	—	281
Annual Growth	1.1%	—	—	(6.7%)

Revenue History

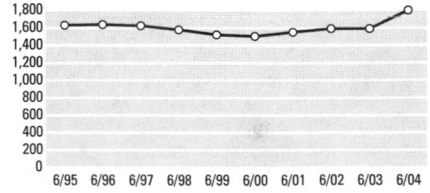

```
1,800
1,600
1,400
1,200
1,000
  800
  600
  400
  200
    0
    6/95  6/96  6/97  6/98  6/99  6/00  6/01  6/02  6/03  6/04
```

IMPAC Medical Systems

IMPAC Medical Systems packs a technological punch. Founded in 1990, the company provides clinical and administrative management systems for cancer care facilities. Its products combine business functions such as scheduling, billing, and records management with specialized features for chemotherapy and radiation therapy treatment. IMPAC's clients include hospitals, cancer care centers, private practices, and government entities in some 55 countries; the company markets both directly and through a distribution relationship with Siemens Medical Solutions. IMPAC, which offers maintenance and support services, was acquired in 2005 by Sweden-based Elekta Group, a provider of clinical systems for radiation treatment.

While IMPAC has continued its trend of overall sales growth, the company's core oncology software business has slowed down due in part to increased competition, and more of the company's revenues (43%) are coming from maintenance and other services. Looking to grow its product offerings, IMPAC has purchased the pathology information systems and cancer registry information assets of bankrupt cancer information company IMPATH. The company has also been searching for growth in international markets, establishing direct sales and marketing programs in Europe and the Asia/Pacific. More than 90% of IMPAC's sales come from customers in the US.

EXECUTIVES

Chairman, President, and CEO:
 Joseph K. (Joe) Jachinowski, age 48, $471,958 pay
EVP, COO, and Director: James P. (Jay) Hoey, age 45, $471,958 pay
EVP, Treasurer, Secretary, and Director; President, IMPAC Global Systems: David A. Auerbach, age 44, $471,958 pay
CFO: Kendra A. Borrego, age 35, $214,100 pay
SVP, Worldwide Sales: Robert L. Shaw
VP, Business Development: George L. Rugg
VP, Client Services: Cornelius L. (Leonard) Lyons
VP, Engineering: Todd M. Powell
VP, Marketing: Suzanne M. Hoey
VP, Medical Affairs: Joel W. Goldwein
VP, North America Sales: Scott T. Soehl
Public Relations Manager: Julie DeSantis
Auditors: Burr, Pilger & Mayer LLP

LOCATIONS

HQ: IMPAC Medical Systems, Inc.
   100 W. Evelyn Ave., Mountain View, CA 94041
Phone: 650-623-8800   **Fax:** 650-428-0721
Web: www.impac.com

IMPAC Medical Systems sells its products in the Asia/Pacific, Europe, and North America. It has facilities in California, Massachusetts, Nevada, New Jersey, Virginia, and the UK.

2004 Sales

	% of total
US	93
Other countries	7
Total	**100**

PRODUCTS/OPERATIONS

2004 Sales

	$ mil.	% of total
Software licences	39.7	57
Maintenance & services	29.5	43
Total	**69.2**	**100**

Selected Software

Cancer registry
Electronic data interchange
Electronic medical records
Lab information systems
Medical oncology charting
Oncology informatics
Practice management
Radiation therapy
Urology charting

COMPETITORS

Cerner
Eclipsys
IDX Systems
NDCHealth
Nucletron Electronic
QuadraMed
Siemens Medical
Varian Medical Systems

HISTORICAL FINANCIALS

Company Type: Private

Income Statement

FYE: September 30

	REVENUE ($ mil.)	NET INCOME ($ mil.)	NET PROFIT MARGIN	EMPLOYEES
9/04	69	4	5.8%	430
9/03	61	9	14.2%	308
9/02	46	5	11.4%	262
9/01	34	3	8.8%	211
9/00	28	3	11.2%	—
9/99	21	3	15.0%	—
Annual Growth	**27.3%**	**5.2%**	**—**	**26.8%**

2004 Year-End Financials

Debt ratio: 0.0% Current ratio: 1.43
Return on equity: 6.8% Long-term debt ($ mil.): 0
Cash ($ mil.): 55

Net Income History

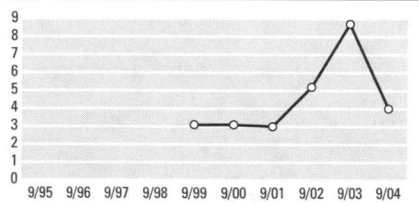

Indiana Pacers

Despite the storied achievements of Hoosier basketball teams, Pacers Sports & Entertainment has yet to produce an NBA championship. After a dismal beginning (entering the NBA in 1976), the Pacers made the playoffs every year except one since 1990, earning their first trip to the finals in 2000 (they lost to the LA Lakers). Former Detroit Pistons head coach Rick Carlisle runs the team. Pacers Sports & Entertainment is owned by shopping-center magnates Melvin and Herbert Simon (who bought the team in 1983) and includes the WNBA's Indiana Fever and the Conseco Fieldhouse arena.

At the beginning of the 2004-05 season, an ugly brawl erupted between several Pacers and rowdy fans at the end of a Detroit Pistons home game. A fight amongst the players on the court soon spilled into the stands after a fan hit Pacers forward Ron Artest with a cup of ice. Artest charged into the stands and started swinging, and teammates including Stephen Jackson and Jermaine O'Neal followed suit, leading to three minutes of mayhem throughout the arena.

Afterwards, the NBA cracked down hard and suspended Artest for the rest of the season. Jackson and O'Neal received 30- and 15-game suspensions, respectively. Detroit area authorities filed assault and battery charges against five Pacers (Artest, Jackson, O'Neal, David Harrison, and Anthony Johnston) and seven Pistons fans.

In early 2005, just weeks after vehemently denying rumors of his retirement, popular guard Reggie Miller, the Pacer's all-time leading scorer, announced (via his sister, Cheryl Miller, a reporter for Turner Broadcasting's TNT network) that it would be his final season.

EXECUTIVES

Co-Owner: Herbert Simon, age 70
Co-Owner: Melvin Simon, age 78
President and CEO: Donnie Walsh
President of Basketball Operations: Larry Bird, age 48
Head Coach: Rick Carlisle, age 46
Assistant Coach: Chuck Person
ESVP; Executive Director, Conseco Fieldhouse: Rick Fuson
SVP Finance and CFO: Kevin Bower
SVP Basketball Administration: David Morway
SVP Marketing: Larry Mago
VP and Controller: Doug McKee
VP Budget: Jane Wardle
VP Entertainment: Jamie Berns
VP Event Services and Merchandising: Rich Kapp
VP Facilities Administration: Harry James
VP Human Resources: Donna Wilkinson
Director of Community Relations: Vonda Brooks
Director of Public Information: David Benner

LOCATIONS

HQ: Pacers Sports & Entertainment
125 S. Pennsylvania St., Indianapolis, IN 46204
Phone: 317-917-2500   **Fax:** 317-917-2599
Web: www.consecofieldhouse.com

The Indiana Pacers play at the 18,500-capacity Conseco Fieldhouse in Indianapolis.

COMPETITORS

Boston Celtics
Cavaliers/Gund
Chicago Bulls
Detroit Pistons
Miami Heat
Milwaukee Bucks

HISTORICAL FINANCIALS

Company Type: Private

Income Statement

FYE: June 30

	REVENUE ($ mil.)	NET INCOME ($ mil.)	NET PROFIT MARGIN	EMPLOYEES
6/04	104	—	—	—
6/03	94	—	—	—
6/02	91	—	—	—
6/01	89	—	—	—
6/00	86	—	—	—
6/99	34	—	—	—
6/98	56	—	—	128
6/97	52	—	—	—
6/96	48	—	—	—
6/95	45	—	—	—
Annual Growth	**9.7%**	**—**	**—**	**—**

Revenue History

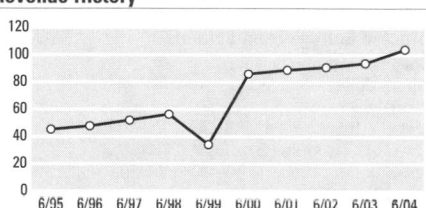

Indiana University

Indiana University has been educating residents of the Hoosier State since its founding in 1820. With a total student population of more than 98,000, the university has eight campuses including flagship institution IU-Bloomington and seven commuter campuses in Fort Wayne, Gary, Indianapolis, Kokomo, New Albany, Richmond, and South Bend. IU-Bloomington offers students more than 100 undergraduate majors. Its graduate schools offer advanced degrees in a variety of areas ranging from business to music to law. IU-Bloomington also is home to a string of centers and institutes including the Advanced Research & Technology Institute and the Center for International Business Education and Research.

An 1820 statute created the Indiana Seminary, the predecessor to Indiana University. In 1828 the legislature changed the name of the institution to Indiana College, and in 1838 it established Indiana University.

EXECUTIVES

President, Board of Trustees: Frederick F. Eichhorn Jr.
VP, Board of Trustees: Stephen L. Ferguson
President: Adam W. Herbert Jr.
VP, CFO, and Interim Treasurer: Judith G. Palmer
VP and Chief Administrative Officer: J. Terry Clapacs
VP Research and Information Technology and CIO: Michael A. McRobbie
VP Government Relations: Tom Healy
VP Institutional Development and Student Affairs: Charlie Nelms
VP University Relations: Michael M. Sample, age 52

Chancellor, IU-Perdue University Indianapolis:
 Charles R. Bantz
Chancellor, IU-Purdue University Fort Wayne:
 Michael A. Wartell
Chancellor, IU Kokomo: Ruth J. Person, age 59
Chancellor, IU Northwest: Bruce W. Bergland
Chancellor, IU South Bend: Una Mae Reck
Chancellor, IU Southeast: Sandra R. Patterson-Randles
Auditors: Indiana State Board of Accounts

LOCATIONS

HQ: Indiana University
     107 S. Indiana Ave., Bloomington, IN 47405
Phone: 812-855-4848   **Fax:** 812-855-7002
Web: www.indiana.edu

Indiana University has campuses in Bloomington, Fort Wayne, Gary, Indianapolis, Kokomo, New Albany, Richmond, and South Bend, Indiana.

PRODUCTS/OPERATIONS

Selected Colleges and Schools

College of Arts and Sciences
Honors College
Graduate School
School of Business
School of Continuing Studies
School of Education
School of Fine Arts
School of Informatics
School of Journalism
School of Library and Information Science
School of Medicine
School of Music
School of Nursing
School of Optometry
School of Public and Environmental Affairs
School of Social Work

COMPETITORS

Ball State	University of Illinois
Michigan State	University of Iowa
Northwestern University	University of Michigan
Ohio State University	University of Minnesota
Penn State University	University of
Purdue University	Wisconsin-Madison
University of Evansville	

HISTORICAL FINANCIALS

Company Type: School

Income Statement

FYE: June 30

	REVENUE ($ mil.)	NET INCOME ($ mil.)	NET PROFIT MARGIN	EMPLOYEES
6/04	1,494	115	7.7%	15,000
6/03	1,374	—	—	15,000
6/02	1,261	—	—	16,500
6/01	1,783	—	—	16,070
6/00	1,658	—	—	16,000
6/99	1,541	—	—	15,000
6/98	1,470	—	—	14,458
6/97	1,379	—	—	15,000
6/96	1,280	—	—	17,000
6/95	1,216	—	—	17,000
Annual Growth	2.3%	—	—	(1.4%)

Revenue History

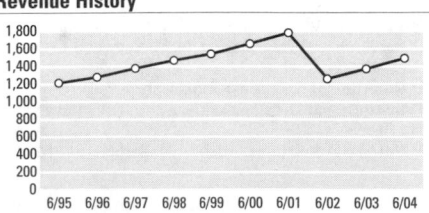

InfoCision

InfoCision provides telemarketing services for other companies as well as not-for-profits and political organizations. It provides outbound and inbound call center service as well as support in e-commerce and for the Web. The company can also create, produce, and mail marketing items, such as flyers and brochures, through their fulfillment services.

EXECUTIVES

Chairman: Gary L. Taylor
President: Carl Albright
CFO: Forrest Thompson
SVP Marketing: Ken Dawson
SVP Call Center Operations: Mike Langenfeld
SVP Corporate Affairs: Steve Brubaker
Director Client Services: Jim Moran

LOCATIONS

HQ: InfoCision Management Corporation
     325 Springside Dr., Akron, OH 44333
Phone: 330-668-1400   **Fax:** 330-668-1401
Web: www.infocision.com

COMPETITORS

Advanced Data-Comm
iSYNERGISTICS
LiveBridge

HISTORICAL FINANCIALS

Company Type: Private

Income Statement

FYE: December 31

	REVENUE ($ mil.)	NET INCOME ($ mil.)	NET PROFIT MARGIN	EMPLOYEES
12/04	128	—	—	2,783
12/03	117	—	—	2,500
12/02	100	—	—	2,500
Annual Growth	13.1%	—	—	5.5%

Revenue History

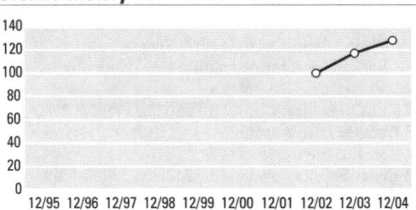

InfoReliance

If you need to rely on information technology services, InfoReliance could be the contractor you want. Founded in 2000, the firm provides commercial and government customers with custom software development, creating Web portals, and other IT services including systems integration, network design, project management, consulting, and training. Clients have included the US departments of Agriculture, Commerce, Defense, Interior, Justice, State, and Transportation; the US Army, Marine Corps, and Navy; the Centers for Disease Control and Prevention; the FBI; and the Drug Enforcement Administration. The majority owners of InfoReliance are Bill Williams (CEO) and Andrew Butler (president).

The company's commercial customers come from a wide range of industries including financial services, health care, and manufacturing, as well as government agencies and other public sector organizations.

EXECUTIVES

CEO: William T. (Bill) Williams
President: Andrew J. Butler
CFO: Matthew Toloczko

LOCATIONS

HQ: InfoReliance Corporation
     9990 Lee Hwy., Ste. 450, Fairfax, VA 22030
Phone: 703-246-9360   **Fax:** 703-246-9331
Web: www.inforeliance.com

COMPETITORS

Global TechPro
International Software Systems
Zolon Tech

HISTORICAL FINANCIALS

Company Type: Private

Income Statement

FYE: December 31

	ESTIMATED REVENUE ($ mil.)	NET INCOME ($ mil.)	NET PROFIT MARGIN	EMPLOYEES
12/04	22	—	—	115
12/03	12	—	—	50
Annual Growth	80.0%	—	—	130.0%

Revenue History

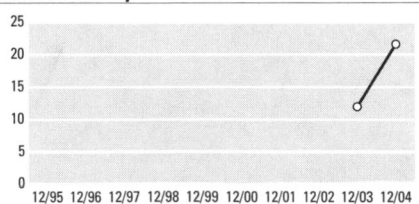

Ingram Industries

Ingram Industries is heavy into books and boats. Ingram Book Group is one of the largest wholesale book distributors in the US; it ships more than 175 million books and audiotapes annually (representing about 17,000 publishers) to more than 30,000 retail outlets. Ingram Marine Group operates Ingram Barge and ships grain, ore, and other products through about 3,700 barges and 100 boats. The Ingram family, led by chairman Martha Ingram (one of America's wealthiest active businesswomen), owns and runs Ingram Industries and controls about 20% of the shares of Ingram Micro (a top computer products wholesaler).

Ingram Book Group (operating out of four fulfillment centers) is also a leading distributor to libraries, and the entire book division accounts for over half of Ingram Industries' total sales. Its Lightning Source subsidiary is a leader in print on demand services with over 100,000 titles (including e-books) from more than 2,300 publishing partners.

The company sold its Permanent General Insurance business (which covers high-risk drivers in about seven states) to Capital Z Financial Services Partners and PGC Holdings in late 2004.

HISTORY

Orrin Ingram and two partners founded the Dole, Ingram & Kennedy sawmill in 1857 in Eau Claire, Wisconsin, on the Chippewa River, about 50 miles upstream from the Mississippi River. By the 1870s the company, renamed Ingram & Kennedy, was selling lumber as far downstream as Hannibal, Missouri.

Ingram's success was noticed by Frederick Weyerhaeuser, a German immigrant in Rock Island, Illinois, who, like Ingram, had worked in a sawmill before buying one of his own. In 1881 Ingram and Weyerhaeuser negotiated the formation of Chippewa Logging (35%-owned by up-river partners, 65% by down-river interests), which controlled the white pine harvest of the Chippewa Valley. In 1900 Ingram paid $216,000 for 2,160 shares in the newly formed Weyerhaeuser Timber Company. Ingram let his sons and grandsons handle the investment and formed O.H. Ingram Co. to manage the family's interests. He died in 1918.

In 1946 Ingram's descendants founded Ingram Barge, which hauled crude oil to the company's refinery near St. Louis. After buying and then selling other holdings, in 1962 the family formed Ingram Corp., consisting solely of Ingram Barge. Brothers Bronson and Fritz Ingram (the great-grandsons of Orrin) bought the company from their father, Hank, before he died in 1963, and in 1964 they bought half of Tennessee Book, a textbook distributing company founded in 1935. In 1970 they formed Ingram Book Group to sell trade books to bookstores and libraries.

Ingram Barge won a $48 million Chicago sludge-hauling contract in 1971, but later the company was accused of bribing city politicians with $1.2 million in order to land the contract. The brothers stood trial in 1977 for authorizing the bribes; Bronson was acquitted, but the court convicted Fritz on 29 counts. Before Fritz entered prison (he served 16 months of a four-

year sentence), he and his brother split their company. Fritz took the energy operations and went bust in the 1980s. Bronson took the barge and book businesses and formed Ingram Industries.

The new company formed computer products distributor Ingram Computer in 1982 and between 1985 and 1989 bought all the stock of Micro D, a computer wholesaler. Ingram Computer and Micro D merged to form Ingram Micro. In 1992 it acquired Commtron, the world's #1 wholesaler of prerecorded videocassettes, and merged it into Ingram Entertainment.

When Bronson died in mid-1995, his wife Martha (the PR director) became chairman and began a restructuring. Ingram Industries closed its non-bookstore rack distributor (Ingram Merchandising) in 1995 and sold its oil-and-gas machinery subsidiary (Cactus Co.) in 1996. It spun off Ingram Micro in 1996, followed in 1997 by Ingram Entertainment. Ingram Industries purchased Christian books distributor Spring Arbor that year and also introduced an on-demand book publishing service (Lightning Print).

The company in late 1998 agreed to sell its book group to Barnes & Noble for $600 million, but FTC pressure killed the deal in mid-1999. With customers and competitors increasing distribution capacity in the western US, a resulting drop in business led Ingram Industries to cut more than 100 jobs at an Oregon warehouse in 1999.

In early 2000 Ingram renamed Lightning Print as Lightning Source. Also that year Ingram announced plans to distribute products other than books for e-tailers (starting with gifts). In March 2001 Ingram took over the specialty-book distribution for Borders.

In July 2002 Ingram completed its acquisition of Midland Enterprises LLC, a leading US inland marine transportation company that includes The Ohio River Company LLC and Orgulf Transport LLC. In an effort to streamline its distribution network, in mid-2002 Ingram Book Group consolidated its eight distribution centers into four super centers, including a new facility in Pennsylvania.

In late 2003 the company's Lightning Source subsidiary celebrated the printing of its 10 millionth book.

EXECUTIVES

Chairman: Martha R. Ingram
Vice Chairman; Chairman, Ingram Book Group: John R. Ingram, age 43
President and CEO; Chairman, Ingram Barge Company: Orrin H. Ingram II, age 44
EVP and CFO: Mary K. Cavarra
VP, Human Resources: Dennis Delaney
President and CEO, Ingram Barge: Craig E. Philip
President and CEO, Ingram Book Group: James E. (Jim) Chandler
President and CEO, Ingram Library Services; CEO, Ingram Periodicals; and President, Ingram International: Peter Clifton
President and CEO, Lightning Source: J. Kirby Best
President, Ingram Periodicals: Robert Kerekes
President, Tennessee Book Company: John D. Reed III
Managing Director, Lightning Source UK: David Taylor
SVP, Operations and Administration, Tennessee Book Company: Randy S. Collignon
VP and General Manager, Spring Arbor Distributors: Janet McDonald

LOCATIONS

HQ: Ingram Industries Inc.
1 Belle Meade Place, 4400 Harding Rd.,
Nashville, TN 37205
Phone: 615-298-8200   **Fax:** 615-298-8242

PRODUCTS/OPERATIONS

Selected Operations

Ingram Book Group
  Ingram Book Company (wholesaler of trade books and audiobooks)
  Ingram Customer Systems (computerized systems and services)
  Ingram Fulfillment Services (book shipping)
  Ingram International (international distribution of books and audiobooks)
  Ingram Library Services (distributes books, audiobooks, and videos to libraries)
  Ingram Periodicals (direct distributor of specialty magazines)
  Lightning Source (on-demand printing and electronic publishing)
  Spring Arbor Distributors (products and services for Christian retailers)
  Tennessee Book Company (Tennessee school system textbook depository)
Ingram Marine Group
  Custom Fuel Services (provides midstream fueling services to inland marine operations)
  Ingram Barge (ships grain, ore, and other products)
  Ingram Materials (produces construction materials such as sand and gravel)

COMPETITORS

Advanced Marketing	Jim Pattison Group
American Commercial	Kirby
Lines	Media Source
Baker & Taylor	Safeco
Chas. Levy	Thomas Nelson
Follett	Times Publishing
Hudson News	

HISTORICAL FINANCIALS

Company Type: Private

Income Statement

FYE: December 31

	REVENUE ($ mil.)	NET INCOME ($ mil.)	NET PROFIT MARGIN	EMPLOYEES
12/03	2,200	—	—	6,730
12/02	2,200	—	—	6,900
12/01	1,929	—	—	6,148
12/00	2,075	—	—	6,494
12/99	2,135	—	—	6,080
12/98	2,000	—	—	6,500
12/97	1,796	—	—	6,362
12/96	1,463	—	—	5,300
12/95	11,000	—	—	13,000
12/94	8,010	—	—	10,000
Annual Growth	(13.4%)	—	—	(4.3%)

Revenue History

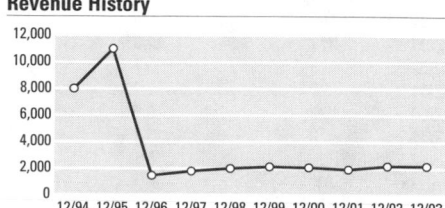

Inland Retail Real Estate Trust

Inland Retail is a closely held real estate investment trust (REIT) that invests in, develops, renovates, and manages retail properties in the US. Its portfolio includes about 275 shopping centers and free-standing retail properties encompassing about 35 million sq. ft. of leasable space. Inland Retail's major tenants include Publix Super Markets, Wal-Mart, Kohl's, and Lowe's. Although its holdings are concentrated in the Southeast, the highly acquisitive REIT has begun expanding into northeastern states, especially New Jersey and Pennsylvania. The company is part of The Inland Group of real estate companies.

In 2004 Inland Retail Real Estate Trust acquired a slew of property management and advisory firms as a part of its plan to become a self-administered and self-managed REIT. These included such Inland entities as Inland Retail Real Estate Advisory Services, Inland Southern Management, and Inland Mid-Atlantic Management.

EXECUTIVES

Chairman: Robert D. Parks, age 61
President, CEO, and Director: Barry L. Lazarus, age 57
COO: Thomas P. McGuinness, age 49
SVP, General Counsel, and Corporate Secretary:
 Robert J. Walner, age 58
VP and CFO: James W. Kleifges
VP Administration: Roberta S. Matlin, age 59
VP Acquisitions: Steven D. Sanders, age 54
Secretary: Scott Wilton, age 44
Auditors: KPMG LLP

LOCATIONS

HQ: Inland Retail Real Estate Trust, Inc.
 2901 Butterfield Rd., Oak Brook, IL 60523
Phone: 630-218-8000 **Fax:** 630-954-5693
Web: www.inland-retail.com

COMPETITORS

AmREIT	Lincoln Property
Commercial Net Lease	Regency Centers
Cousins Properties	Simon Property Group
Equity One	Sizeler Property Investors
Kimco Realty	Weingarten Realty

HISTORICAL FINANCIALS

Company Type: Private

Income Statement

FYE: December 31

	REVENUE ($ mil.)	NET INCOME ($ mil.)	NET PROFIT MARGIN	EMPLOYEES
12/04	464	(81)	—	135
12/03	318	70	22.0%	1
12/02	116	28	23.7%	1
12/01	38	8	21.2%	1
12/00	22	2	9.5%	1
12/99	6	0	3.3%	1
Annual Growth	138.6%	—	—	166.7%

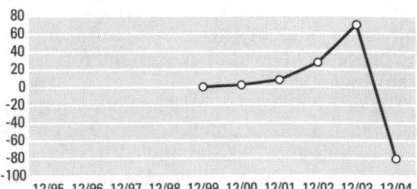

Net Income History

Inova Health System

Inova keeps NoVa (northern Virginia) healthy. Founded in 1956 as a country hospital in Fairfax, Virginia, Inova Health System is a not-for-profit health care provider, offering acute care, long-term care, home health care, mental health, and satellite emergency care services in the northern Virginia suburbs of Washington, DC. Inova's network consists of five hospitals (including a children's hospital) with about 1,600 beds, as well as assisted living centers for seniors and family practice locations. Through the Inova Health System Foundation, the company coordinates philanthropy programs for the community.

Inova Health System also offers wellness classes for the public as well as continuing education classes for health care professionals. In addition, the health system provides cancer, pregnancy, women's health, orthopedics, and heart resource centers.

EXECUTIVES

President and CEO: J. Knox Singleton
SVP and CFO: Richard Magenheimer
SVP Legal Affairs and General Counsel: James Hughes
SVP Human Resources: Ellen Menard
Media Relations Manager: Kathleen Thomas
Media Relations Specialist: Beth Visioli

LOCATIONS

HQ: Inova Health System
 2990 Telestar Ct., Falls Church, VA 22042
Phone: 703-289-2000 **Fax:** 703-205-2161
Web: www.inova.org

PRODUCTS/OPERATIONS

Selected Facilities

Inova Alexandria Hospital (Alexandria, VA)
Inova Fair Oaks Hospital (Fairfax, VA)
Inova Fairfax Hospital (Falls Church, VA)
Inova Fairfax Hospital for Children (Fairfax, VA)
Inova Mount Vernon Hospital (Alexandria, VA)

COMPETITORS

Bon Secours Health	Johns Hopkins Medicine
Carilion Health System	MedStar Health
HCA	

HISTORICAL FINANCIALS

Company Type: Not-for-profit

Income Statement

FYE: December 31

	REVENUE ($ mil.)	NET INCOME ($ mil.)	NET PROFIT MARGIN	EMPLOYEES
12/03	1,289	86	6.7%	13,500
12/02	1,248	(15)	—	13,000
12/01	1,154	26	2.2%	13,000
12/00	1,046	139	13.3%	13,000
12/99	963	—	—	13,000
12/98	908	—	—	13,000
12/97	900	—	—	13,000
12/96	700	—	—	9,500
12/95	644	—	—	9,500
Annual Growth	9.1%	(14.8%)	—	4.5%

Net Income History

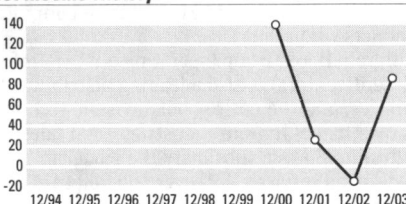

InSight Health Corp.

With its MRI, computed tomography (CT), and PET imaging equipment, InSight Health knows what evil lurks within the hearts, brains, and pancreases of men. The company offers diagnostic services to hospitals and HMOs through some 130 fixed-site centers, and more than 110 mobile MRI units. InSight also provides conventional X-ray, mammogram, nuclear medicine, and ultrasound services. InSight's Gamma Knife uses high dosages of focused radiation to treat brain lesions. InSight operates one of the largest diagnostic imaging networks in the US, with facilities in more than 30 states. Company management took InSight private in 2001 with financing from investment firms J.W. Childs Associates and Halifax Group.

InSight Health Services primarily serves patients in Arizona, California, and Texas, as well as the Mid-Atlantic, New England, and the Southeast.

The company plans to grow by acquiring and developing new diagnostic imaging facilities in order to expand its regional diagnostic imaging networks.

EXECUTIVES

Chairman: Michael N. Cannizzaro, age 55
President, CEO, and Director: Bret W. Jorgensen
EVP and CFO: Mitch C. Hill
EVP and Chief Strategy Officer: Kip Hallman
EVP, General Counsel, and Corporate Secretary:
 Marilyn U. MacNiven-Young, age 52
EVP, Enterprise Development: Michael A. Boylan, age 48
EVP, Enterprise Operations: Patricia R. Blank, age 54

SVP and Chief Accounting Officer: Brian G. Drazba,
  age 42
SVP, Mobile Operations: Robert J. Mentzer
VP, Design and Construction: Robert J. Armstrong
VP, Human Resources: William E. Brewer
Treasurer: Kent E. Tuholsky
Auditors: PricewaterhouseCoopers LLP

LOCATIONS

HQ: InSight Health Corp.
  26250 Enterprise Ct., Ste. 100,
  Lake Forest, CA 92630
Phone: 949-282-6000   Fax: 949-462-3292
Web: www.insighthealthcorp.com

PRODUCTS/OPERATIONS

Selected Services

Bone Densitometry
Computed tomography (CT)
Fluoroscopy
Lithotripsy
Magnetic resonance imaging (MRI)
Mammography
Nuclear medicine
Open MRI
Positron emission tomography (PET)
Radiation therapy
Radiography (x-rays)
Ultrasound

COMPETITORS

Alliance Imaging
HealthSouth
Medical Resources
Primedex Health
Radiologix
Raytel

HISTORICAL FINANCIALS

Company Type: Private

Income Statement   FYE: June 30

	REVENUE ($ mil.)	NET INCOME ($ mil.)	NET PROFIT MARGIN	EMPLOYEES
6/04	291	3	1.0%	2,290
6/03	238	5	2.1%	1,780
6/02	155	0	—	1,630
6/01	212	14	6.5%	1,620
6/00	189	7	3.8%	1,510
6/99	162	6	3.8%	1,100
6/98	114	1	0.4%	850
6/97	91	1	1.4%	624
6/96*	26	(1)	—	776
12/95	51	(4)	—	—
Annual Growth	21.5%	—	—	14.5%

*Fiscal year change

2004 Year-End Financials

Debt ratio: 560.4%   Current ratio: 2.11
Return on equity: 3.1%   Long-term debt ($ mil.): 532
Cash ($ mil.): 30

Net Income History

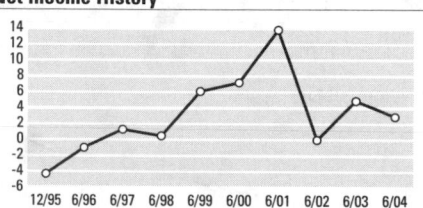
12/95 6/96 6/97 6/98 6/99 6/00 6/01 6/02 6/03 6/04

Interactive Brokers

Interactive Brokers Group (IBG) serves investors who interact with world markets. Through affiliates Interactive Brokers LLC (IB) and Timber Hill LLC, the company executes more than 340,000 trades daily in stocks, options, futures, and foreign exchange and corporate bonds. Customers may trade on more than 50 exchanges and market centers in about 15 countries. IB caters to experienced individual and institutional investors who trade via the Internet or who use its TraderWorkstation software. IB, the Bourse de Montréal, and the Boston Stock Exchange formed a partnership to launch the Boston Options Exchange (BOX). IBG is majority-owned by founder and chairman Thomas Peterffy.

EXECUTIVES

Chairman: Thomas Peterffy
CFO: Paul J. Brody
CTO: Thomas Frank
Managing Director, Business Development and
  Marketing: Steve Sanders
Communications Director: Isabelle Clary
Auditors: Deloitte & Touche LLP

LOCATIONS

HQ: Interactive Brokers Group LLC
  1 Pickwick Plaza, Greenwich, CT 06830
Phone: 203-618-5700   Fax: 203-618-5770
Web: www.interactivebrokers.com

Interactive Brokers Group LLC operates through offices in the US in Chicago and Greenwich, Connecticut, and internationally in Hong Kong, London, Montréal, Sydney, and Zug, Switzerland.

COMPETITORS

Banc of America Investment Services
Charles Schwab
CIBC World Markets
Citigroup Global Markets
CSFB
CyberTrader
Goldman Sachs
ICAP
Instinet
Jefferies Group
Knight Capital
Lehman Brothers
Man Group
Merrill Lynch
Morgan Stanley
optionsXpress
UBS Financial Services
Vining-Sparks
William Blair

HISTORICAL FINANCIALS

Company Type: Private

Income Statement   FYE: December 31

	REVENUE ($ mil.)	NET INCOME ($ mil.)	NET PROFIT MARGIN	EMPLOYEES
12/04	700	—	—	455
12/03	720	—	—	450
12/02	643	—	—	419
12/01	746	—	—	479
12/00	707	—	—	400
Annual Growth	(0.2%)	—	—	3.3%

Revenue History

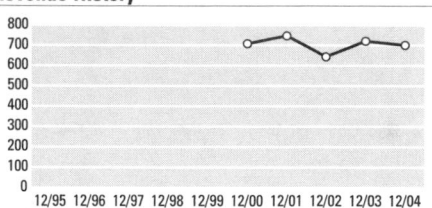
12/95 12/96 12/97 12/98 12/99 12/00 12/01 12/02 12/03 12/04

Interconnect Devices

Interconnect Devices, Inc. (IDI) makes spring contact probes used in automated test equipment (ATE), as well as semiconductor test probes and sockets. A sister company, Synergetix, makes connectors, sockets, and interfaces used by manufacturers in aerospace, ATE, automobiles, medical equipment, and telecommunications. Synergetix was established in 1994. IDI was founded in 1979 and is owned by its officers.

EXECUTIVES

President and CEO: Edward (Ed) Schifman, age 56
SVP of Operations: Howard Weiner
VP and CFO: Jerry Meisenheimer, age 57
VP of Human Resources: Marianne Russell
VP of Marketing: Karen Bock
Senior Director of Sales: Bill Oxley
Director of Business Development: Jon Diller
Director of Operations: Mary Zeljeznjak
Director of Product Design Engineering: Bill Thurston
Director of Quality: Ron Meek
National Sales Manager: Jeff Tamasi

LOCATIONS

HQ: Interconnect Devices, Inc.
  5101 Richland Ave., Kansas City, KS 66106
Phone: 913-342-5544   Fax: 913-342-7043
Web: www.idinet.com

COMPETITORS

Agilent Technologies
Cascade Microtech
Everett Charles Technologies
FormFactor
inTEST
Keithley Instruments
Tektronix
Teradyne

HISTORICAL FINANCIALS

Company Type: Private

Income Statement
FYE: December 31

	REVENUE ($ mil.)	NET INCOME ($ mil.)	NET PROFIT MARGIN	EMPLOYEES
12/04	13	—	—	230
12/03	13	—	—	250
Annual Growth	6.4%	—	—	(8.0%)

Revenue History

12/95 12/96 12/97 12/98 12/99 12/00 12/01 12/02 12/03 12/04

Intercontinental Exchange

If there was money to be made in ice futures, IntercontinentalExchange (ICE) would probably trade that as well. The company is a leading on-line marketplace for global commodity trading, primarily of electricity, natural gas, crude oil, refined petroleum products, precious metals, and weather and emission credits. It also owns the International Petroleum Exchange, a leading European energy futures and options platform. ICE's 10x Group subsidiary provides real-time market data reports, and the company's eConfirm platform provides electronic trade confirmations. ICE offers real-time OTC clearing and credit and risk management services. The company was formed by a group of top financial and energy firms in 2000.

EXECUTIVES

Chairman and CEO: Jeffrey C. Sprecher, age 50, $1,035,431 pay
SVP and COO: Charles A. (Chuck) Vice, age 41, $651,000 pay
SVP and CFO: Richard V. Spencer, age 51, $651,000 pay
SVP and CTO: Edwin Marcial, age 37, $542,500 pay
SVP, Business Development and Sales: David S. Goone, age 44, $523,900 pay
SVP, General Counsel, and Secretary: Jonathan H. Short, age 39
CEO, IPE: Richard Ward, age 48, $638,759 pay
Auditors: Ernst & Young LLP

LOCATIONS

HQ: IntercontinentalExchange, Inc.
2100 RiverEdge Pkwy., Ste. 500, Atlanta, GA 30328
Phone: 770-857-4700   **Fax:** 770-951-1307
Web: www.theice.com

PRODUCTS/OPERATIONS

2004 Sales

	$ mil.	% of total
Futures	55.5	51
OTC	52.9	49
Total	**108.4**	**100**

Founding Partners

BP p.l.c.
Deutsche Bank AG
The Goldman Sachs Group, Inc.
Morgan Stanley Dean Witter & Co.
Royal Dutch/Shell Group
Société Générale
TOTAL S.A.

Other Partners

American Electric Power Company, Inc.
Duke Energy Corporation
El Paso Energy Partners
Mirant

COMPETITORS

APX	NYMEX Holdings
Bloomberg	Prebon Yamane
CHOICE! Energy	Reuters
Enporion	TradeSpark
ICAP	Unitil

HISTORICAL FINANCIALS

Company Type: Private

Income Statement
FYE: December 31

	REVENUE ($ mil.)	NET INCOME ($ mil.)	NET PROFIT MARGIN	EMPLOYEES
12/04	108	22	20.2%	200
12/03	94	13	14.3%	—
12/02	126	35	27.6%	204
Annual Growth	(7.1%)	(20.6%)	—	(1.0%)

2004 Year-End Financials

Debt ratio: 8.7%
Return on equity: 13.0%
Cash ($ mil.): 61
Current ratio: 2.90
Long-term debt ($ mil.): 13

Net Income History

12/95 12/96 12/97 12/98 12/99 12/00 12/01 12/02 12/03 12/04

Intermountain Health Care

Intermountain Health Care (IHC) operates some 20 hospitals, more than a dozen home health care agencies, an air ambulance service, and more than 100 physician and urgent care clinics, counseling offices, rehabilitation centers, and other health care facilities in Utah and southern Idaho. IHC has affiliations with more than 2,000 physicians, including about 400 in its IHC Physician Division. IHC Health Plans offers health insurance programs to large and small employers and to individuals. Affiliate IHC/AmeriNet is a group purchasing organization.

The company was formed in 1975 when the Church of Jesus Christ of Latter Day Saints (the Mormons) decided to donate 15 of its hospitals to the communities they served.

EXECUTIVES

Chairman: Merrill Gappmayer
Vice Chairman: Kent H. Murdock
President and CEO: William H. (Bill) Nelson
CFO: Burt Zimmerly
CEO, IHC Health Plans: Sidney C. Paulson
CEO, IHC Physician Division: Linda C. Leckman
CEO, Urban Central Region: H. Gary Pehrson
CEO, Primary Children's Medical Center: Joseph R. (Joe) Horton
CEO, Urban North Region: Thomas F. Hanrahan
CEO, Urban South Region: Chris Coons
Director, Planning: Steven Vance
General Counsel: Jane Reister
Media Relations: Daron Cowley

LOCATIONS

HQ: Intermountain Health Care, Inc.
36 S. State St., Fl. 22, Salt Lake City, UT 84111
Phone: 801-442-2000   **Fax:** 801-442-3327
Web: www.ihc.com

Hospitals

Cassia Regional Medical Center (Burley, ID)
American Fork Hospital (American Fork, UT)
Valley View Medical Center (Cedar City, UT)
Delta Community Medical Center (Delta, UT)
Heber Valley Medical Center (Heber City, UT)
Logan Regional Hospital (Logan, UT)
Sanpete Valley Hospital (Mt. Pleasant, UT)
Cottonwood Hospital (Murray, UT)
The Orthopedic Specialty Hospital (Murray, UT)
McKay-Dee Hospital Center (Ogden, UT)
Orem Community Hospital (Orem, UT)
Garfield Memorial Hospital (Panguitch, UT)
Utah Valley Regional Medical Center (Provo, UT)
Sevier Valley Hospital (Richfield, UT)
Dixie Regional Medical Center (St. George, UT)
LDS Hospital (Salt Lake City)
Primary Children's Medical Center (Salt Lake City)
Alta View Hospital (Sandy, UT)
Bear River Valley Hospital (Tremonton, UT)

COMPETITORS

Aetna	LifePoint
Blue Cross	Sierra Health
CHRISTUS Health	Trinity Health (Novi)
HCA	UnitedHealth Group
Iasis Healthcare	

HISTORICAL FINANCIALS

Company Type: Not-for-profit

Income Statement
FYE: December 31

	REVENUE ($ mil.)	NET INCOME ($ mil.)	NET PROFIT MARGIN	EMPLOYEES
12/03	3,267	893	27.3%	—
12/02	2,847	—	—	25,000
12/01	2,652	—	—	23,000
12/00	2,552	—	—	23,000
12/99	2,390	—	—	23,000
12/98	2,156	—	—	23,000
12/97	2,009	—	—	22,000
12/96	1,758	—	—	20,000
12/95	1,589	—	—	20,000
12/94	1,380	—	—	19,000
Annual Growth	10.0%	—	—	3.5%

Revenue History

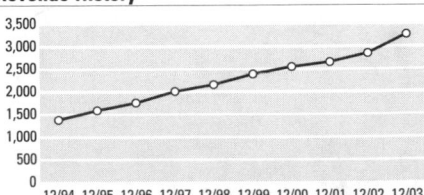

12/94 12/95 12/96 12/97 12/98 12/99 12/00 12/01 12/02 12/03

International Coal Group

International Coal Group focuses its energy on one nation, the US. The company produces coal from 11 mining complexes in Northern and Central Appalachia (Kentucky, Maryland, and West Virginia) and from one complex in the Illinois Basin. International Coal Group produces low-sulfur steam coal, which is sold mainly to electric utilities, and metallurgical coal, which is sold to steelmakers. The company controls reserves of more than 700 million tons of coal. International Coal Group was formed in May 2004 when investor Wilbur Ross led a group that bought many of the assets of Horizon Natural Resources in a bankruptcy auction. International Coal Group is buying more coal properties from Anker and CoalQuest.

EXECUTIVES

Non-Executive Chairman: Wilbur L. Ross Jr., age 67
President and CEO: Bennett K. (Ben) Hatfield, age 48
SVP and General Counsel: Roger L. Nicholson, age 44
SVP Kentucky and Illinois Operations:
  William Scott Perkins, age 49
SVP Mining Services: Oren Eugene Kitts, age 50
SVP Sales and Marketing: Michael Hardesty, age 42
SVP West Virginia and Maryland Operations:
  Samuel R. Kitts, age 43
VP, Treasurer, and Secretary: William D. Campbell, age 57
Auditors: Deloitte & Touche LLP

LOCATIONS

HQ: International Coal Group, Inc.
  2000 Ashland Dr., Ashland, KY 41101
Phone: 606-920-7400

PRODUCTS/OPERATIONS

2004 Sales

	$ mil.	% of total
Coal sales	130.4	96
Freight & handling	0.9	1
Other	4.8	3
Total	**136.1**	**100**

COMPETITORS

Alliance Resource	Drummond
Alpha Natural	Foundation Coal
Arch Coal	Massey Energy
CONSOL Energy	Peabody Energy

HISTORICAL FINANCIALS

Company Type: Private

Income Statement

FYE: December 31

	REVENUE ($ mil.)	NET INCOME ($ mil.)	NET PROFIT MARGIN	EMPLOYEES
12/04	136	4	3.1%	1,425

International Data Group

International Data Group (IDG) is a publishing giant with digital appeal. The world's top technology publisher, IDG produces more than 300 magazines and newspapers (including *PC World* and *CIO*) in 85 countries and in dozens of languages. In addition to publishing, IDG provides technology market research through its IDC unit and produces a number of industry events. The company also offers career services through JobUniverse.com and ITcareers.com and operates 400 Web sites featuring technology content. Chairman Patrick McGovern, who founded IDG in 1964, holds a majority stake in the company; an employee stock plan owns the rest.

While a downturn in the economy hurt publishers in 2000 and 2001, IDG weathered the storm in part by concentrating on growing its market research and event marketing businesses. The company's IDC research unit has more than 600 analysts in more than 40 countries, and its industry events include Macworld Expo and the Bio-IT World Conference & Expo.

With traditional business-to-business technology titles still in a slump industry wide, the company is turning to expanding its video games titles and developing additional international titles (for its *PC World* and *ComputerWorld* magazines). In addition, IDG has launched *Digital World*, a "wired home"-type title devoted to consumers with home technology, and *Playlist*, a digital music magazine.

The company announced in 2005 that it would establish a joint venture with VNU Business Media Europe for their French publishing operations.

HISTORY

Patrick McGovern began his career in publishing as a paperboy for the *Philadelphia Bulletin*. As a teenager in the 1950s, McGovern was inspired by Edmund Berkeley's book *Giant Brains; or Machines That Think*. He later built a computer and won a scholarship to MIT. There he edited the first computer magazine, *Computers and Automation*. McGovern started market research firm International Data Corporation in 1964 after interviewing the president of computer pioneer UNIVAC. Three years later he launched *Computerworld*, and within a few weeks the eight-page tabloid had 20,000 subscribers. Combined under the name International Data Group, McGovern's company reached $1 million in sales by 1968.

Taking the "International" in its name to heart, IDG began publishing in Japan in 1971 and expanded to Germany in 1975. Following the collapse of communism, the company had 10 publications in Russia and Eastern Europe by 1990. That year two teenage hackers broke into the company's voice mail system and erased orders from customers and messages from writers. The prank cost IDG about $2.4 million. Also in 1990, IDG launched IDG Books Worldwide (renamed Hungry Minds in 2000), which hit it big the next year with *DOS for Dummies*.

With the technology boom of the 1990s, competition in tech publishing heated up. By 1993 several of IDG's magazines, including *InfoWorld*, *Macworld*, and *PC World*, began losing ad pages to rivals Ziff-Davis and CMP Media. To help stem advertiser attrition, IDG started an incentive program tied to its new online service. In 1995 IDG bought a stake in software companies Architect Software (now ExciteHome) and Netscape (now owned by America Online) as part of its move toward Internet-based services.

In 1996 IDG launched *Netscape World: The Web*, a magazine covering the Internet, and introduced more than 30 industry newsletters delivered by e-mail. The company also bought *PC Advisor*, the UK's fastest-growing computer magazine. IDG kicked off its online ad placement service, Global Web Ad Network, in 1997. That year IDG merged *Macworld* with rival Ziff-Davis' *MacUser* in a joint venture called Mac Publishing.

In 1998 IDG pledged $1 billion in venture capital for high-tech startups in China. It also introduced new publications in China, including a Chinese edition of *Cosmopolitan* (with Hearst Magazines) and *China Computer Reseller World*. Later that year the company launched *The Industry Standard* and spun off 25% of IDG Books to the public.

In 1999 it sold a 20% stake in Industry Standard Communications (renamed Standard Media International) to private investors and began laying plans for a possible spinoff in 2000. However, a weakening economy and slowing ad sales in 2000 quieted those plans.

The next year both Standard Media and Hungry Minds announced staff cuts and restructuring. IDG eventually sold its majority interest in Hungry Minds to John Wiley & Sons for about $90 million. Standard Media filed for bankruptcy and liquidated its assets, some of which were bought by IDG. The company also purchased Ziff Davis' 50% stake in their joint venture Mac Publishing. In 2002 IDG CEO Kelly Conlin left the business and was replaced by company executive Pat Kenealy, who had previously founded the now-defunct *Digital News* magazine.

EXECUTIVES

Chairman: Patrick J. (Pat) McGovern
CEO: Pat Kenealy
CFO: Ted Bloom
VP Business Development and Operations:
  Colin Crawford
VP Human Resources: Richard Willoughby
President and CEO, CXO Media: Walter Manninen
President and CEO, IDC: Kirk Campbell
President and CEO, IDG International Publishing Services: David F. Hill
President and CEO, IDG World Expo: David Korse
President and Publisher, Bio-IT World: Alan Bergstein
President, IDG Communications: Bob Carrigan
President, IDG Communications List Services:
  Deb Goldstein
President, IDG Global Solutions: John P. O'Malley
President, IDG Research Services: Kathy Dinneen
Corporate Communications Director: Howard Sholkin
Corporate Communications Manager: Susanna Hinds
Auditors: Deloitte & Touche LLP

LOCATIONS

HQ: International Data Group, Inc.
  1 Exeter Plaza, 15th Fl., Boston, MA 02116
Phone: 617-534-1200   **Fax:** 617-423-0240
Web: www.idg.com

International Data Group publishes more than 300 magazines and newspapers in 85 countries.

PRODUCTS/OPERATIONS

Selected Operations
IDC (market research)
IDG Communications List Services
IDG Events & Conferences
IDG Global Solutions
IDG Publications (periodical publishing)
IDG Recruitment Solutions (employment services)
IDG Research Services Group
IDG.net (online publications hub)

Selected Events
Bio-IT World Conference & Expo
COMNET Conference & Expo
Demo
The European Telecoms Forum
LinuxWorld Conference & Expo
Macworld Conference & Expo
Storage Forum

Selected Periodicals
Bio-IT World
CIO
CSO
Computerworld
GamePro
InfoWorld
Macworld
Network World
PC World

COMPETITORS

101communications	MediaLive International
CNET Networks	Microsoft
Editis	Pearson
Forrester Research	Penton Media
Freeman Companies	Reed Elsevier Group
Future	SYS-CON Media
Gartner	United Business Media
Jupitermedia	VNU
McGraw-Hill	Ziff Davis Media

HISTORICAL FINANCIALS
Company Type: Private

Income Statement
FYE: September 30

	REVENUE ($ mil.)	NET INCOME ($ mil.)	NET PROFIT MARGIN	EMPLOYEES
9/04	2,500	—	—	13,510
9/03	2,410	—	—	13,450
9/02	2,580	—	—	13,050
9/01	3,010	—	—	13,200
9/00	3,100	—	—	13,400
9/99	2,560	—	—	12,000
9/98	2,050	—	—	11,500
9/97	1,876	—	—	9,500
9/96	1,700	—	—	8,500
9/95	1,400	—	—	8,200
Annual Growth	6.7%	—	—	5.7%

Revenue History

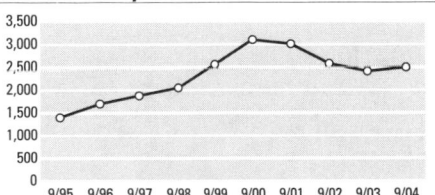

Interstate Battery

Interstate Battery System of America offers a battery of batteries. The company can provide the electrical juice for everything from calculators and radios to automobiles and lawn equipment. Interstate Battery has distributors throughout the US; consumers can purchase Interstate Battery's products at more than 200,000 retail locations, including a growing number of Interstate All Battery Centers. The company makes the official replacement battery for the vehicles of companies such as Land Rover, Subaru, and Toyota. Interstate Battery sponsors the Joe Gibbs Racing team on the NASCAR circuit. Chairman Norm Miller owns the company, which was founded in 1952.

Interstate sells batteries that carry its own brand as well as products with manufacturers' labels. Johnson Controls supplies Interstate's automotive line.

EXECUTIVES

Chairman: Norm Miller
President and CEO: Carlos Sepulveda
VP, Corporate Accounting and Services: Lisa Huntsberry
VP, Advertising and Public Relations: Charles Suscavage
VP, All Battery: Mickey Elam
VP, Independent Distributor Development: Jeff Haddock
VP, Information Technology and CIO: Merv Tarde
VP, Interstate Owned Territories: Alex Louis
VP, Interstate Owned Territories: Neal Holford
VP, Human Resources and Powercare and General Counsel: Walter Holmes
VP, Marketing and E-Commerce: Dennis Brown
VP, National Accounts: William (Billy) Norris
VP, Procurement and Distribution: Ray Krusing

LOCATIONS

HQ: Interstate Battery System of America, Inc.
12770 Merit Dr., Ste. 400, Dallas, TX 75251
Phone: 972-991-1444 **Fax:** 972-458-8288
Web: www.ibsa.com

Interstate Battery System of America has distributors in Canada, the Dominican Republic, Guam, Jamaica, Puerto Rico, and the US.

PRODUCTS/OPERATIONS

Selected Applications
Automotive/truck
Calculators
Camcorders
Cellular phones
Chargers
Commercial equipment
Computers/laptops
Cordless phones
Cordless tools
Flashlights
Household batteries
Lawn and garden
Marine/RV
Medical equipment
Motorcycles
Pagers
Photo batteries
Radio batteries
Sealed lead/SLA
Watches

COMPETITORS

Advance Auto Parts	O'Reilly Automotive
AutoZone	Pep Boys
Costco Wholesale	Sears
Genuine Parts	Target
Kmart	Wal-Mart

HISTORICAL FINANCIALS
Company Type: Private

Income Statement
FYE: April 30

	REVENUE ($ mil.)	NET INCOME ($ mil.)	NET PROFIT MARGIN	EMPLOYEES
4/04	700	—	—	900
4/03	680	—	—	900
4/02	650	—	—	800
4/01	526	—	—	685
4/00	531	—	—	655
4/99	473	—	—	502
4/98	467	—	—	430
Annual Growth	7.0%	—	—	13.1%

Revenue History
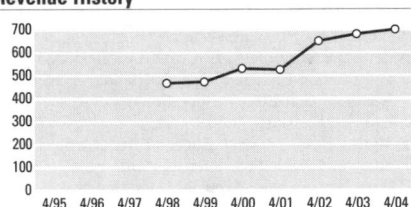

IntraLinks

IntraLinks wants high volumes of confidential information to travel comfortably online. The company provides its clients with secure, collaborative online digital workspaces for conducting financial transactions, exchanging documents, and collaborating with advisers, customers, and suppliers. Intralinks sells its business-to-business collaboration system as a subscription service to 150,000 users from more than 13,000 companies in the financial services, life sciences, and mergers and acquisitions markets. Leading customers include JPMorgan Chase (11% of sales) and Bank of America. Rho Ventures owns about one-third of IntraLinks, while TowerBrook Investors holds around 21%.

IntraLinks has a strong position within the banking industry, where its technologies are used primarily for conducting loan syndication deals. IntraLinks is branching out into other fields, such as accounting, corporate governance, insurance, life sciences, pharmaceuticals, private equity investing, and real estate.

Former banking executives Mark Adams, John Muldoon, Arthur Sculley, and CEO Patrick Wack co-founded the company in 1996.

Reuters holds an equity stake of about 12% in IntraLinks. Apax Partners owns around 9% of the company.

EXECUTIVES

Chairman: Peter J. Boni, age 59
President and CEO: Patrick J. Wack Jr., age 38,
$347,500 pay
CFO and Chief Administrative Officer:
Anthony C. Plesner, age 46
EVP, Business Development: Christopher Thomas,
age 37
EVP, Finance and Administration: Andrew Goldman,
age 43
EVP, Product Marketing: Julian Henkin, age 45
EVP, Sales and Marketing: J. Andrew Damico, age 42
EVP, Service Delivery: William (Bill) Conklin, age 47
SVP, New Markets: Adam Sloan
VP and General Counsel: Gary Hirsch, age 42
VP, Marketing and Communications: Diane Carlson,
age 41
Director Human Resources: Melissa Bruno-Torres
Auditors: PricewaterhouseCoopers LLP

LOCATIONS

HQ: IntraLinks, Inc.
1372 Broadway, 11th Fl., New York, NY 10018
Phone: 212-543-7700   **Fax:** 212-543-7978
Web: www.intralinks.com

IntraLinks has offices in Boston and New York, and
in London.

2004 Sales

	% of total
North America	89
Other regions	11
Total	**100**

PRODUCTS/OPERATIONS

2004 Sales

	$ mil.	% of total
Debt capital markets	22.1	59
Mergers & acquisitions	10.8	29
Other	4.3	12
Total	**37.2**	**100**

COMPETITORS

Documentum	Open Text
Fidelity National	Plumtree Software
GXS	SAP
IBM Global Services	Sterling Commerce
Internet Commerce Corp.	Tumbleweed
Lotus	Communications
Merrill	Viador
Microsoft	

HISTORICAL FINANCIALS

Company Type: Private

Income Statement

	REVENUE ($ mil.)	NET INCOME ($ mil.)	NET PROFIT MARGIN	EMPLOYEES
12/04	37	(10)	—	214
12/03	26	(4)	—	148
12/02	20	(7)	—	100
12/01	18	—	—	150
12/00	13	—	—	180
12/99	4	—	—	131
12/98	1	—	—	73
12/97	0	—	—	—
Annual Growth	**132.9%**	**—**	**—**	**19.6%**

FYE: December 31

2004 Year-End Financials

Debt ratio: (1.1%)   Current ratio: 1.09
Return on equity: —   Long-term debt ($ mil.): 1
Cash ($ mil.): 8

Net Income History

0	
-2	
-4	
-6	
-8	
-10	
-12	

12/95 12/96 12/97 12/98 12/99 12/00 12/01 12/02 12/03 12/04

IPC Acquisition

IPC wants movers and shakers to trade up to its
products. IPC Acquisition Corp., which operates
through its IPC Information Systems subsidiary,
makes and services "turret" communications systems, also called dealerboards, that combine PBX,
data switching, computer telephony, voice recording, and multimedia capabilities. Its products are
used by financial institutions for voice and data
transmission and routing in their trading environments. These products are designed to integrate with products from major technology
vendors such as IBM and Cisco. IPC's customers
include such banks, foreign exchange and commodity brokers, and insurance companies as
Goldman Sachs, JP Morgan, and the New York
Stock Exchange.

EXECUTIVES

CEO and Director: Lance B. Boxer, age 50, $350,000 pay
President, COO, and Director: Gregg Kenepp, age 43
CFO: Timothy (Tim) Whelan, age 38
SVP, Marketing and Corporate Development:
Don Carlos Bell III, age 35
SVP, Global Network Operations: Phil Lines
SVP, Global Trading Systems Operations: Pete Simms
President, Europe, Middle East, and Africa:
Colin Knight, age 63, $237,200 pay
Managing Director, Asia/Pacific: Stephen Phillips
Managing Director, Global Sales: Michael Sheehan,
age 52
General Counsel and Secretary: John McSherry
Auditors: Ernst & Young LLP

LOCATIONS

HQ: IPC Acquisition Corp.
88 Pine St., Wall Street Plaza, New York, NY 10005
Phone: 212-825-9060   **Fax:** 212-344-5106
Web: www.ipc.com

IPC operates from 20 offices worldwide.

2004 Sales

	$ mil.	% of total
Americas	159.2	60
Europe	72.7	28
Asia/Pacific	31.3	12
Total	**263.2**	**100**

PRODUCTS/OPERATIONS

2004 Sales

	$ mil.	% of total
Services	148.7	57
Products & installations	114.5	43
Total	**263.2**	**100**

Selected Products

Trading Systems
Computer telephony software (TradeSmart,
WorldTurret)
Digital recording systems (Enhanced Alliance)
Hoot and holler systems
Multimedia communications equipment
(TradeCentral)
Network switches and routers
Servers
Telephone instruments (IQmx, MX Slimline, ICMX
Intercom, TradePhone)
Trading communications platfom (Alliance MX)

COMPETITORS

Alcatel	France Telecom
BT	Hitachi Telecom
BT Consulting and	Siemens Communications
Systems Integration	

HISTORICAL FINANCIALS

Company Type: Private

Income Statement

	REVENUE ($ mil.)	NET INCOME ($ mil.)	NET PROFIT MARGIN	EMPLOYEES
9/04	263	7	2.7%	765
9/03	265	4	1.5%	650
9/02	233	(9)	—	—
Annual Growth	**6.3%**	**—**	**—**	**17.7%**

FYE: September 30

2004 Year-End Financials

Debt ratio: —   Current ratio: —
Return on equity: —   Long-term debt ($ mil.): 47
Cash ($ mil.): —

Net Income History

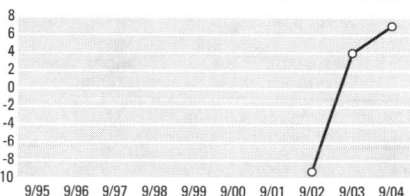

8	
6	
4	
2	
0	
-2	
-4	
-6	
-8	
-10	

9/95 9/96 9/97 9/98 9/99 9/00 9/01 9/02 9/03 9/04

---

iRobot

If you're a Jetsons fan, you'll likely appreciate
iRobot Corporation. The company makes robots
for all sorts of applications, from government
and military to toys and appliances. Its Roomba
FloorVac, launched in 2002, is the first vacuum
that automatically cleans floors. In addition iRobot has introduced its Scooba floor washing
robot and PackBot tactical military robots, which
perform battlefield reconnaissance and bomb
disposal. The firm has offices in California, Massachusetts, Virginia, and Hong Kong and sells
through more than 7,000 retail outlets globally.
iRobot was founded in 1990 by robot engineers
who performed research at the Massachusetts
Institute of Technology.

The company is in the process of developing
the "Small Unmanned Ground Vehicle" reconnaissance robot for the US Army and another
unmanned ground vehicle model with Deere
& Company.

Irvine Company

At The Irvine Company, everything goes according to plan. Master plan, that is. The company creates master-planned communities in well-heeled Orange County, where it owns nearly 50,000 acres (making it a top California landowner). Its Irvine Ranch includes the US's largest planned community, Irvine, with more than 240,000 residents; about 50,000 acres under the company's stewardship have been set aside as permanent open space or for recreational uses. The Irvine Ranch covers 93,000 acres — a drop from its original 120,000 acres back in the mid-1800s, when James Irvine bought out the debts of Mexican land-grant holders. Chairman Donald Bren, one of America's wealthiest men, owns the company.

The Irvine Company's portfolio includes Irvine Spectrum, one of the nation's largest high-tech research and business centers, as well as two hotels, four marinas, and three golf courses. Irvine Spectrum encompasses some 40 million sq. ft. and counts some 2,500 companies as tenants. The company's 35 retail centers include Fashion Island and Market Place.

The Irvine Company also owns Irvine Apartment Communities, a residential management firm that owns more than 80 apartment complexes — located on Irvine Ranch as well as in Northern California, San Diego, and Santa Monica, California.

The University of California, Irvine is built on company-donated land.

Chairman Donald Bren has continued the 35-year-old master plan created by the Irvine Foundation (the former parent of The Irvine Company), which calls for gradual development of rigorously planned communities. The plan — which has so far helped form the communities of Laguna Beach, Newport Beach, Orange, and Tustin, as well as centerpiece Irvine — has entered its final phase (set for completion around 2040), but the company faces increasing political opposition to its plans from area residents, who tend to become development-weary after they get their piece of the Irvine Ranch. In a move to prevent unchecked growth, the company has stopped selling desirable Irvine Spectrum land to small commercial building developers.

With most of its developments complete, The Irvine Company has increasingly focused on property investment and management. In 2003 the company took over the management of its industrial and office buildings, and in 2004 started managing its retail properties.

HISTORY

A wholesale merchant in San Francisco during the gold rush, James Irvine and two others assembled vast holdings in Southern California in the mid-1800s by buying out the debts of Mexican and Spanish land-grant holders. Irvine bought his partners' shares in 1876 and passed the ranch of 120,000 acres to his son, James II, upon his death in 1886. Eight years later James II incorporated the ranch as The Irvine Company and began turning it into an agribusiness empire, shifting from sheep ranching to cash crop farming.

James II owned the ranch and company until the 1930s, when the death of his son, James III, prompted him to transfer a controlling interest in the company to the not-for-profit Irvine Foundation. James III's wife, Athalie, and daughter, Joan, inherited 22% of Irvine.

In 1959 company president Myford Irvine, a grandson of James I and uncle to Joan, was found dead from two shotgun wounds. Officials ruled it a suicide, but others weren't so sure.

With Athalie and Joan's encouragement, the company donated land in the early 1960s for the construction of the University of California, Irvine. The company would continue contributing to educational and philanthropic causes as well as donating property for green space to improve Orange County's suburban areas.

The 1960s also saw the Irvine Foundation forming its definitive master plan for pre-arranged communities and marked the company's entry into the real estate development sector. The plan was designed to anticipate and control growth, with provisions for green space and a mix of pricing levels.

Superrich firebrand Joan, who had long accused Irvine Foundation officers of serving their own interests at the expense of other stockholders, lobbied Congress in the late 1960s to change tax laws pertaining to the foundation. Along with a group of investors led by Donald Bren, Alfred Taubman, and Herbert Allen, Joan trumped a bid by Mobil Oil and in 1977 wrested control of the company from the foundation.

When California's real estate market went sour in 1983, Bren bought out his fellow shareholders, and increased his ownership stake from 34% to 95%. Joan returned to court to protest the price, gaining extra money when the court valued the land at $1.4 billion.

In 1993 Bren sought cash from his holdings by offering apartment developments as a real estate investment trust (REIT), Irvine Apartment Communities.

Orange County's record-setting bankruptcy in 1994 (the county lost $1.7 billion in risky investments) threatened the value of The Irvine Company's property portfolio, most of which is located in Orange County. Thanks in part to a frothy economy and settlements from brokerage firms, Orange County and The Irvine Company were spared another 1983-esque bust.

In 1996 Bren bought the company's remaining stock. As part of its expansion into R&D, retail, and office properties in the Silicon Valley area, The Irvine Company opened an office in San Jose the next year, followed by its Eastgate Technology Park in San Diego in 1998. An industrywide slide in REIT stock prices prompted Bren to take Irvine Apartment Communities private in 1999.

The company continued to expand its retail and office holdings into the aughts — including the purchase of Century City's Fox Plaza. In 2002, the Irvine City Council approved The Irvine Company's plans to develop the last phase of the company's master plan (to be completed in 2040) — bringing over 12,000 homes, 730,000 sq. ft. of retail space, and 6.57 million sq. ft. of industrial space to the city's Northern Sphere area.

EXECUTIVES

Chairman: Donald L. Bren, age 73
Vice Chairman and COO: Michael D. McKee, age 58
EVP, Entitlement and Public Affairs:
 Daniel (Dan) Young
Group SVP and CFO: Marc Ley, age 40
Group SVP, Corporate Communications: Larry Thomas
Group SVP, Urban Planning and Design:
 Robert N. Elliott
President, Apartment Communities: Max L. Gardner,
 age 51
SVP, Capital Markets and Treasurer: Don McNutt
President, Investment Properties Group:
 Clarence W. Barker
President, Irvine Community Development:
 Joseph D. Davis
President, Office Properties: William (Bill) Halford
President, Resort Properties: L. K. Eric Prevette
President, Retail Properties: Keith Eyrich
SVP, Operations, Retail Properties: Russell Lowe
VP, Commercial Land Sales: Larry Williams

LOCATIONS

HQ: The Irvine Company
 550 Newport Center Dr., Newport Beach, CA 92660
Phone: 949-720-2000   **Fax:** 949-720-2218
Web: www.irvinecompany.com

The Irvine Company owns about 50,000 acres
in Orange County, California, including the City of
Irvine and parts of Anaheim, Laguna Beach, Newport
Beach, Orange, and Tustin. It also owns properties
in Los Angeles, San Diego, and San Jose.

PRODUCTS/OPERATIONS

Selected Divisions

Investment Properties Group
 Apartment Communities
 Commercial Land Sales
 Resort Properties (hotels, marinas, and golf courses)
 Office Properties
 Retail Properties
Irvine Community Development

COMPETITORS

Arden Realty	The Koll Company
California Coastal	Majestic Realty
Communities	MBK Real Estate
C.J. Segerstrom & Sons	Mission West Properties
Corky McMillin	Newhall Land
Intergroup	Pan Pacific
KB Home	Rancho Mission Viejo
Kilroy Realty	Tejon Ranch

HISTORICAL FINANCIALS

Company Type: Private

Income Statement
FYE: June 30

	REVENUE ($ mil.)	NET INCOME ($ mil.)	NET PROFIT MARGIN	EMPLOYEES
6/03	2,000	—	—	—
6/02	1,700	—	—	762
6/01	1,500	—	—	470
6/00	1,305	—	—	435
6/99	1,100	—	—	250
6/98	1,000	—	—	236
6/97	816	—	—	200
6/96	710	—	—	190
6/95	700	—	—	200
6/94	800	—	—	200
Annual Growth	10.7%	—	—	18.2%

Revenue History

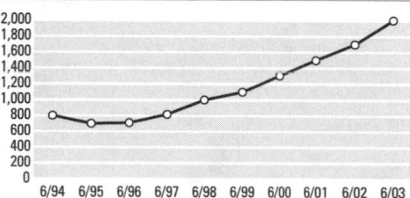

It's A Grind Coffee Franchise

Do you swim sips of coffee across your palate
as if it were a classic vintage of wine? Then It's A
Grind has a cup for you. The company operates
and franchises about 140 coffee houses in 11
states nationwide. It serves a variety of coffee
drinks, teas, and baked goods — it even has a
decaf kid's menu. An online company store is in
the works. In 1994, company president Marty
Cox opened the first location in California with
his wife Louise Montgomery.

EXECUTIVES

CEO: Steve Shoeman
President: Marty Cox
COO: Dave Wetzel
CFO: Ernest T. Klinger
SVP Franchise Development: Steve Olson
Director of Identity and Marketing: Bob Phibbs
Director of Training: Meghan Hunt Rider
Office Manager: Karen Fernandez
Franchise Development Administrator: Shawnna Volpe
Administrative Assistant: Michelle Glynn

LOCATIONS

HQ: It's A Grind Coffee Franchise LLC
 6272 E. Pacific Coast Hwy., Ste. E,
 Long Beach, CA 90803
Phone: 562-594-5600   **Fax:** 562-594-4100
Web: www.itsagrind.com

It's A Grind Coffee Franchise LLC is a franchisor of
coffee houses in Arizona, California, Colorado, Georgia,
Michigan, Missouri, Nevada, Pennsylvania, Tennessee,
and Texas.

COMPETITORS

Caribou Coffee
The Coffee Bean
Diedrich Coffee
Le Boulanger
New World Restaurants
Peet's
Restaurant Developers
Starbucks
Tully's Coffee

HISTORICAL FINANCIALS

Company Type: Private

Income Statement
FYE: August 31

	REVENUE ($ mil.)	NET INCOME ($ mil.)	NET PROFIT MARGIN	EMPLOYEES
8/04	13	—	—	3,000

It's Just Lunch

It's Just Lunch (IJL) doesn't offer high-tech
hook-ups. The matchmaking service sets up
busy, professional singles for lunch dates based
on personal interviews instead of the much ma-
ligned introduction videos or online dating
pools. The company, which franchises more than
75 offices across the US and in Singapore and
Canada, charges singles around $1,500 for a se-
ries of dates (prices vary by location). It boasts
more than 2 million dates and 9,500 marriages
and engagements since its inception. Former
chairman Andrea McGinty founded IJL in 1992
after her fiancé jilted her six weeks before their
wedding. McGinty is now married to CEO Daniel
Dolan, who met her in 1994 after reading a news
story on the company.

EXECUTIVES

Chairman and CEO: Daniel G. Dolan, age 42
President and COO: Irene LaCota
SVP: Nancy Kirsch
Senior Manager, Communications: Alana Beyer

LOCATIONS

HQ: It's Just Lunch International LLC
 600 B St., Ste. 1850, San Diego, CA 92101
Phone: 619-234-7200   **Fax:** 619-234-8500
Web: www.itsjustlunch.com

COMPETITORS

eHarmony.com
Lavalife
Match.com
Spark Networks
Spring Street
Tickle
Together
Yahoo!

HISTORICAL FINANCIALS

Company Type: Private

Income Statement
FYE: December 31

	REVENUE ($ mil.)	NET INCOME ($ mil.)	NET PROFIT MARGIN	EMPLOYEES
12/04	30	—	—	20
12/03	20	—	—	15
12/02	15	—	—	15
Annual Growth	41.4%	—	—	15.5%

Revenue History

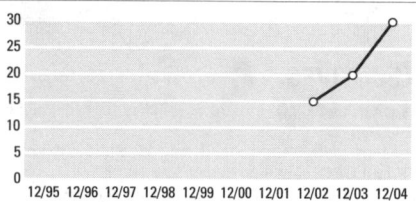

J. Crew

The crews depicted in the flashy catalogs of the J. Crew Group are far from motley. The retailer is known for its preppy fashions, including jeans, khakis, and other basic (but pricey) items sold to young professionals through its catalogs, Web site, and some 200 retail and factory stores in the US. It also has about 45 outlets in Japan through a joint venture with ITOCHU. Asian contractors produce about 80% of the company's merchandise. In 2003 Millard "Mickey" Drexler was brought in from The Gap as CEO to try to revive J. Crew's ailing retail fortunes. Private equity firm Texas Pacific Group owns more than 50% of J. Crew, which has filed an initial public offering of as much as $200 million in common stock.

Other J. Crew shareholders include director Emily Scott, with 16% of the company's shares, and Drexler, who owns 15% of the stock.

J. Crew has gone through some tough times since the Texas Pacific Group bought a majority stake in the family-run company in 1997. A previous plan to take the company public was shelved amid declining sales and profitability as the company fell farther behind rivals such as Abercrombie & Fitch and American Eagle Outfitters. However, Drexler and company president Jeff Pfeifle, also formerly of The Gap, have met with some success in their effort to turn the company around.

Almost three-quarters of J. Crew's sales come from retail; about 25% of sales come from the 16 catalog editions that reach about 50 million people each year. Hemmed by the stagnant growth of its catalog operations, the New York City-based company has sold or closed two of its noncore catalog businesses, Popular Club Plan and Clifford & Wills, leaving it with only its namesake operations.

Just in time for Fashion Week in 2004, Drexler led J. Crew down the wedding aisle by introducing an abbreviated collection of wedding ensembles for men and women. The success of the wedding line prompted the company to launch a bridal-only catalog "J. Crew Wedding" in April 2005. The company has increased its focus on accessories, shoes, and expensive limited-edition items. It also began offering jewelry in May 2005 and has plans to expand into the children's apparel market.

J. Crew expects to add seven new stores this year, and between 15 and 25 new outlets in 2006. Thereafter, the company plans to add as many as 35 stores annually.

Also in 2005 the company brought its J. Crew factory business to the Internet when it launched jcrewfactory.com.

EXECUTIVES

Chairman and CEO: Millard S. (Mickey) Drexler, age 61, $200,000 pay
President: Jeffrey (Jeff) Pfeifle, age 46, $1,260,000 pay
EVP and CFO: James S. Scully, age 40
EVP Merchandising, Planning, and Production: Tracy Gardner, age 41, $848,100 pay (partial-year salary)
SVP, Manufacturing: Scott D. Hyatt, age 47, $535,000 pay
VP, Corporate Controller, and Acting CFO: Nicholas Lamberti, age 62
SVP, Women's Design: Jenna Lyons
VP, Men's Design: Todd Snyder
VP Real Estate, Planning, and Construction: Holly Cohen
Auditors: KPMG LLP

LOCATIONS

HQ: J. Crew Group, Inc.
770 Broadway, New York, NY 10003
Phone: 212-209-2500   **Fax:** 212-209-2666
Web: www.jcrew.com

2005 Stores

	No.
California	23
New York	20
Pennsylvania	11
New Jersey	10
Illinois	9
Massachusetts	8
Texas	8
Connecticut	7
Florida	7
Michigan	7
Virginia	7
Colorado	6
Georgia	6
Ohio	6
Arizona	4
Maryland	4
Minnesota	4
North Carolina	4
South Carolina	4
Tennessee	4
Washington	4
Alabama	3
Missouri	3
New Hampshire	3
Other states	25
Total	**197**

PRODUCTS/OPERATIONS

2005 Sales

	$ mil.	% of total
J. Crew Retail	579.8	72
J. Crew Direct		
Internet	122.0	15
Catalog	76.5	10
Other	25.9	3
Total	**804.2**	**100**

COMPETITORS

Abercrombie & Fitch	J. C. Penney
Aéropostale	Lands' End
American Eagle Outfitters	Limited Brands
AnnTaylor	Liz Claiborne
Benetton	L.L. Bean
Burberry	Loehmann's
Calvin Klein	Marks & Spencer
Chadwick's of Boston	May
Coldwater Creek	Men's Wearhouse
Dillard's	Nautica Enterprises
Eddie Bauer	Neiman Marcus
Eddie Bauer Holdings	New York & Company
Esprit Holdings	Nordstrom
Federated	Polo Ralph Lauren
French Connection	Saks Inc.
Gap	Sears
Guess	Talbots
Hartmarx	Target
Inditex	Tommy Hilfiger
Intimate Brands	

HISTORICAL FINANCIALS

Company Type: Private

Income Statement

FYE: Saturday nearest January 31

	REVENUE ($ mil.)	NET INCOME ($ mil.)	NET PROFIT MARGIN	EMPLOYEES
1/05	804	(100)	—	8,200
1/04	690	(50)	—	5,500
1/03	768	(41)	—	8,200
1/02	778	(11)	—	7,800
1/01	826	22	2.6%	7,600
1/00	717	(7)	—	8,400
1/99	824	(15)	—	8,900
1/98	834	(27)	—	6,200
1/97	809	13	1.5%	6,100
1/96	746	6	0.9%	5,600
Annual Growth	**0.8%**	**—**	**—**	**4.3%**

2005 Year-End Financials

Debt ratio: —
Return on equity: —
Cash ($ mil.): 24
Current ratio: 1.09
Long-term debt ($ mil.): 577

Net Income History

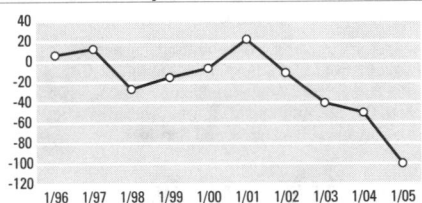

Jack's Family Restaurants

This Alabama company had a 1970's regional TV character named for it — Sergeant Jack. Jack's Family Restaurants operates a chain of about 70 hamburger joints in Alabama, Mississippi, and Tennessee. The restaurants serve standard fast-food fare, including hamburgers, cheeseburgers, and chicken sandwiches, along with such breakfast items as biscuits, scrambled eggs, and hash browns. Seven of the Alabama locations are franchised. Jack Caddell, an entrepreneur who was impressed by the early success of McDonald's, opened the first Jack's in Homewood, Alabama, in 1960. Former franchisee Benny LaRussa later bought the chain in 1989.

EXECUTIVES

CEO: Benny LaRussa
President: Charles Mizerany
VP, Operations: Billy Wentz
Director, Accounting: Cheryl Ledbetter
Director, Marketing: Pam Measel
Public Relations: Debbie Horst

LOCATIONS

HQ: Jack's Family Restaurants, Inc.
133 W. Oxmoor Rd., Ste. 215,
Birmingham, AL 35209
Phone: 205-945-8167   **Fax:** 205-945-9820
Web: www.eatatjacks.com

COMPETITORS

Back Yard Burgers	McDonald's
Burger King	Popeyes
Captain D's	Red Robin
Checkers Drive-In	Sonic
Chick-fil-A	Steak n Shake
CKE Restaurants	Subway
Dairy Queen	Triarc
Del Taco	Wendy's
Hardee's	Whataburger
Jack in the Box	YUM!
Krystal	Zaxby's

HISTORICAL FINANCIALS

Company Type: Private

Income Statement

FYE: September 30

	ESTIMATED REVENUE ($ mil.)	NET INCOME ($ mil.)	NET PROFIT MARGIN	EMPLOYEES
9/04	50	—	—	2,000
9/03	50	—	—	2,000
9/02	50	—	—	2,000
9/01	50	—	—	1,900
Annual Growth	0.0%	—	—	1.7%

Revenue History

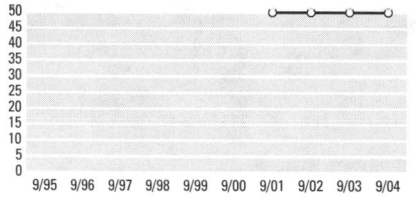

Jacobs Entertainment

Jacobs Entertainment wants you to come out and play. The company operates The Lodge Casino and Gilpin Hotel Casino in Black Hawk, Colorado and the Gold Dust West Casino in Reno, Nevada. The company also has nearly 15 truck stop video gaming facilities throughout Louisiana; the Colonial Downs horseracing track in New Kent, Virginia; and six satellite pari-mutuel wagering locations throughout Virginia. Chairman, president, and CEO Jeffrey Jacobs owns 50% of the company. His father, Richard Jacobs, who co-founded Jacobs Entertainment, owns the other half.

Jacobs Entertainment looks to add to its holdings with the addition of New York's Vernon Downs. The purchase would be subject to approval of a bankruptcy judge overseeing the affairs of Vernon Downs owner, Mid-State Raceway. Also, its Colonial Downs subsidiary plans to buy Maryland-Virginia Racing Circuit from Magna Entertainment.

EXECUTIVES

Chairman, President, CEO, Secretary, and Treasurer: Jeffrey P. Jacobs, age 52, $750,000 pay
CFO and President of Casino Operations: Stephen R. Roark, age 57, $422,700 pay
President of Pari-Mutuel Wagering and Video Poker Operations: Ian M. Stewart, age 50, $280,000 pay
VP, Casino Operations: Michael T. Shubic, age 50, $299,440 pay
General Manager, The Lodge Casino: Michael Frawley
VP, Louisiana Operations: Stan Guidroz
Auditors: Deloitte & Touche LLP

LOCATIONS

HQ: Jacobs Entertainment, Inc.
   240 Main St., Black Hawk, CO 80422
Phone: 303-582-1117   **Fax:** 303-582-0239
Web: www.thelodgecasino.com

PRODUCTS/OPERATIONS

2004 Sales

	$ mil.	% of total
Gaming		
Casinos	108.4	57
Pari-mutuel	32.9	17
Truck stops	24.3	13
Convenience store — fuel	18.4	10
Food and beverage	17.8	9
Other	8.0	4
Adjustments	(20.1)	(10)
Total	**189.7**	**100**

COMPETITORS

Ameristar Casinos
Boyd Gaming
Harrah's Entertainment
Isle of Capri Casinos
MGM MIRAGE
Penn National Gaming
Pinnacle Entertainment
Station Casinos

HISTORICAL FINANCIALS

Company Type: Private

Income Statement

FYE: December 31

	REVENUE ($ mil.)	NET INCOME ($ mil.)	NET PROFIT MARGIN	EMPLOYEES
12/04	190	5	2.6%	1,365
12/03	172	3	1.6%	1,365
12/02	154	3	1.9%	1,350
Annual Growth	11.1%	31.3%	—	0.6%

2004 Year-End Financials

Debt ratio: 203.0%
Return on equity: 7.2%
Cash ($ mil.): 21
Current ratio: 1.20
Long-term debt ($ mil.): 147

Net Income History

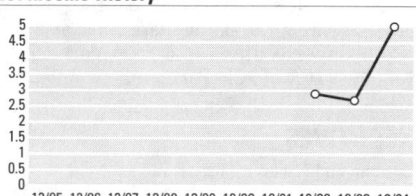

Jamba Juice

The blenders at Jamba Juice are running at high speed. The company is the leading outlet for blended fruit drinks, with more than 500 smoothie stands in two dozen states and the District of Columbia. Its menu includes more than 20 varieties of custom smoothies (including Kiwi Berry Buster, Mango-A-Go-Go, and Orange Dream Machine) and Jamba Boosts (smoothies made with vitamin and protein supplements), along with other fruit juices and baked goods. Jamba Juice locations include freestanding units as well as on-site kiosks in high traffic areas, such as college campuses, gyms, and airports. About half of its units are franchised. Chairman and fitness fanatic Kirk Perron founded the chain in 1990.

Jamba Juice is expanding rapidly through franchising and licensing agreements, primarily with existing companies interested in building multiple locations within a new market. It already has licensing agreements with grocery store operator Whole Foods. The company also offers delivery and catering services through its Jamba Go-Go subsidiary.

Perron opened his first smoothie stand in San Luis Obispo, California. Originally called Juice Club, the chain expanded to three stores by 1993 and changed its name to Jamba Juice two years later. (Jamba means "to celebrate" in Swahili.) CEO Paul Clayton joined the company in 2000 from #2 US hamburger chain Burger King.

In 2005 the company opened its 500th store; it plans to open between 80 and 100 more in 2006 and hopes to be a $1 billion company by 2010.

EXECUTIVES

Founder: Kirk J. Perron
CEO: Paul E. Clayton Jr.
CFO: Don Breen
VP, Development: Beth Lombard
VP, Emerging Markets: Charles (Chuck) Dooly
VP, Human Resources: Russ Testa
VP, Marketing and Brand Development: T.J. Williams
VP, Operations: Karen Kelley
VP, Stores, Human Resources, and Training: Becky Iliff
Director, Product Marketing: Rosa Compean
Director, Real Estate: Susan Young
Director, Regional Marketing: Renee Kempler
Auditors: Deloitte & Touche LLP

LOCATIONS

HQ: Jamba Juice Company
   1700 17th St., San Francisco, CA 94103
Phone: 415-865-1100   **Fax:** 415-487-1143
Web: www.jambajuice.com

COMPETITORS

American Dairy Queen	Maui Wowi
Bahama Buck's	Mrs. Fields
Blimpie	New World Restaurants
CoolBrands	Panera Bread
Dairy Queen	Planet Smoothie
Dunkin	Shake's Frozen Custard
Garden Fresh Restaurants	Smoothie King
Juice It Up!	Starbucks
Kahala	Taco Maker

HISTORICAL FINANCIALS

Company Type: Private

Income Statement

FYE: June 30

	ESTIMATED REVENUE ($ mil.)	NET INCOME ($ mil.)	NET PROFIT MARGIN	EMPLOYEES
6/04	135	—	—	5,880
6/03	100	—	—	5,000
6/02	100	—	—	4,700
6/01*	100	—	—	4,600
12/00	97	—	—	4,400
Annual Growth	8.6%	—	—	7.5%

*Fiscal year change

Revenue History

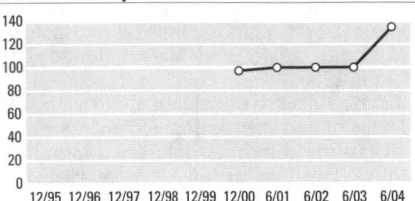

Jazzercise

Jazzercise has shown people how to shake their booties toward fitness for more than 30 years. The company's franchised fitness classes, taught by over 5,000 instructors, blend jazz dancing with an aerobic workout for nearly a half million students worldwide. Franchise fees to Jazzercise outlets account for about 60% of sales; the sale of clothing, books, and other merchandise online and through catalogs brings 25%. Its JM DigitalWorks unit produces Jazzercise workout tapes and provides video production services to other clients. Its Jazzertogs division offers fitness apparel and accessories. President and CEO Judi Sheppard Missett, a professional dancer, founded Jazzercise in 1969 and began franchising in 1980.

EXECUTIVES

CEO: Judi Sheppard Missett
EVP: Shanna Missett Nelson
VP, Finance: Sally Baldrige
VP, International and Corporate Events: Kenny Harvey
VP, Marketing: Kathy Missett
VP, Technology: Brad Jones
Director, Management Information Systems: David West
Director, Human Resources: Rick Colson
Director, Public Relations: Denice Menard

LOCATIONS

HQ: Jazzercise, Inc.
2460 Impala Dr., Carlsbad, CA 92008
Phone: 760-476-1750   **Fax:** 760-602-7180
Web: www.jazzercise.com

PRODUCTS/OPERATIONS

2004 Sales

	% of total
Franchise fees	59
Merchandise	25
JM DigitalWorks & other income	16
Total	**100**

COMPETITORS

24 Hour Fitness	Town Sports
Bally Total Fitness	International Holdings
Curves International	YMCA
Gold's Gym	YWCA
The Sports Club	

HISTORICAL FINANCIALS

Company Type: Private

Income Statement

FYE: June 30

	REVENUE ($ mil.)	NET INCOME ($ mil.)	NET PROFIT MARGIN	EMPLOYEES
6/04	20	—	—	—
6/03	19	—	—	—
Annual Growth	4.8%	—	—	—

Revenue History

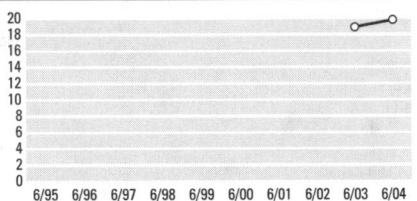

JCM Partners

JCM Partners invests in, renovates, manages, markets, and sells multifamily residential and commercial real estate in Northern California. It owns about 50 properties, including nearly 45 apartment communities, a multi-tenant office/retail property, and six industrial properties. About half of the residential properties are located in Sacramento County. The company plans to continue focus its portfolio on apartments, punctuated with commercial properties within the same geographical markets. JCM Partners is the result of a reorganization of IRM Corporation, which emerged from bankruptcy in 2000.

JCM Partners owns apartment properties in Concord/Antioch (4), Fairfield/Vacaville (5), Modesto/Turlock (6), Sacramento (21), Stockton (3), and Tracy/Manteca (4), California; altogether, the properties have some 5,200 individual units.

In 2004, the company sold a San Francisco office property and three apartment complexes. While it holds properties for long-term investments, the firm's management has the power to sell assets without attaining shareholder approval.

Company executives and managers collectively own 16% of JCM Partners.

EXECUTIVES

Chairman and Manager: Michael W. Vanni, age 65
Vice Chairman and Manager: Marvin J. Helder, age 55
President, CEO, Secretary, Manager, and Tax Matters Partner: Gayle M. Ing, age 55, $350,000 pay
COO and Director, Property Management: Brian S. Rein, age 47, $205,000 pay
CFO and Director, Property Management: Cornelius Stam, age 57, $165,000 pay
Auditors: Moss Adams, LLP

LOCATIONS

HQ: JCM Partners, LLC
2151 Salvio St., Ste. 325, Concord, CA 94520
Phone: 925-676-1966   **Fax:** 925-676-1744

PRODUCTS/OPERATIONS

2004 Sales

	$ mil.	% of total
Rent		
Apartments	47.2	94
Other	3.0	6
Interest	0.1	—
Total	**50.3**	**100**

COMPETITORS

AvalonBay	Pacific Property Company
BRE Properties	United Dominion Realty
Intergroup	

HISTORICAL FINANCIALS

Company Type: Private

Income Statement

FYE: December 31

	REVENUE ($ mil.)	NET INCOME ($ mil.)	NET PROFIT MARGIN	EMPLOYEES
12/04	50	6	11.7%	205
12/03	52	2	3.1%	222
12/02	51	1	1.2%	—
Annual Growth	(1.0%)	213.6%	—	(7.7%)

Net Income History

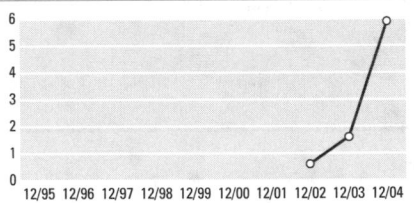

JELD-WEN

JELD-WEN can improve your outlook by providing new windows and doors for your home or by offering accommodations at a scenic resort. A leading manufacturer of windows and doors, JELD-WEN offers aluminum, vinyl, and wood windows; interior and exterior doors; garage doors; swinging and sliding patio doors; and door frames and moldings. If you get tired of looking out your own doors and windows, JELD-WEN owns several resorts in Arizona, Idaho, Oregon, and Washington, including Oregon's Eagle Crest Resort and Running Y Ranch. Jeld-Wen also owns Contractors' Warehouse, a retail chain of seven building materials stores in California. Chairman Richard Wendt and his siblings founded JELD-WEN in 1960.

In 2003 JELD-WEN had some 27 door and window brand names in North America. The company decided that year to bring all of its brands under the JELD-WEN name to decrease confusion and increase JELD-WEN brand awareness and recognition. The change maintains some of the oldest and best-known brands in the industry, but brings them all under the JELD-WEN "master brand" umbrella.

In the ensuing months JELD-WEN launched a marketing campaign and rebranded all products as JELD-WEN or linked them to JELD-WEN through labeling, transportation, and packaging.

JELD-WEN added to its specialty line of doors and windows by acquiring Seasonshield, Inc. in 2004. The Florida-based company makes windows and patio doors that are engineered and tested to withstand hurricane conditions.

EXECUTIVES

Chairman: Richard L. Wendt, age 74
President: Roderick C. (Rod) Wendt
EVP and CFO: Douglas P. (Doug) Kintzinger
EVP and COO: Robert Turner
VP and Treasurer: Karen Hoggarth
VP Door Marketing: James (Jim) Hackett
VP Marketing: Peter Dempsey
European Technical Director: Ian Purkis
Marketing Director, Europe: Joanne Mitchell
Coordinating General Manager, Wood Fiber Divisions: Ken Kiest
Corporate Communications Manager: Teri Cline

LOCATIONS

HQ: JELD-WEN, inc.
    401 Harbor Isles Blvd., Klamath Falls, OR 97601
Phone: 541-882-3451   **Fax:** 541-885-7454
Web: www.jeld-wen.com

JELD-WEN has divisions and companies in Argentina, Australia, Canada, Chile, France, Indonesia, Japan, Latvia, Lebanon, Malaysia, Morocco, Poland, Singapore, South Korea, Spain, Thailand, Turkey, the UK, and the US.

PRODUCTS/OPERATIONS

Selected Products

Doors
    Exterior (wood, custom fiberglass, fiberglass, and steel)
    Garage (wood composite)
    Interior (wood, custom-carved, molded, and flush)
    Patio (wood, vinyl, aluminum, and steel)
Millwork
    Columns
    Posts
    Spindles
    Stair parts
Windows
    Aluminum clad wood
    Energy-efficient
    Replacement
    Wood

Real Estate

AmeriTitle (real estate)
JELD-WEN Real Estate (buying, selling, leasing, financing, and developing industrial real estate properties)

Resorts

Brasada Ranch (Oregon)
Eagle Crest Resort (Oregon)
The Running Y Ranch Resort (Oregon)
Silver Mountain Ski Resort (Idaho)
Suncadia (Washington)
Windmill Inns of America (Arizona, Oregon)

Retail

Contractors' Warehouse (seven building supply locations in California)
CW Bargain Outlet (single location; discount building supplies in North Highlands, California)

COMPETITORS

Andersen Corporation	Marshfield DoorSystems
Designer Doors	Nortek
Fairfield Resorts	Owens Corning
Guardian Building	Pella
Products Distribution	Sierra Pacific Industries
Home Depot	Simonton Windows
Lane Industries	Thermal Industries
Lowe's	

HISTORICAL FINANCIALS

Company Type: Private

Income Statement

FYE: December 31

	ESTIMATED REVENUE ($ mil.)	NET INCOME ($ mil.)	NET PROFIT MARGIN	EMPLOYEES
12/03	2,200	—	—	21,000
12/02	2,000	—	—	20,000
12/01	2,040	—	—	20,000
12/00	2,000	—	—	20,000
12/99	2,000	—	—	15,000
12/98	1,500	—	—	11,000
12/97	1,400	—	—	10,400
12/96	850	—	—	7,100
12/95	750	—	—	7,050
12/94	800	—	—	7,650
Annual Growth	11.9%	—	—	11.9%

Revenue History

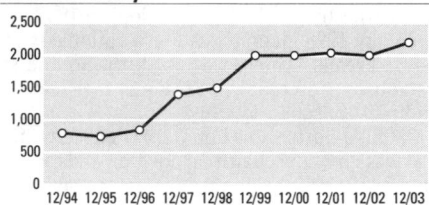

J.F. Shea

J.F. Shea helped construct the Washington, DC, subway system, the Golden Gate Bridge, and the Hoover Dam, and now it wants to build your house. Its Shea Homes division builds single-family houses and planned communities. Flagship unit J.F. Shea Construction is involved in commercial and civil engineering projects and offers design/build services. The group's Heavy Civil Engineering division works on underground projects, including dams and tunnels, and its Redding division produces gravel, asphalt, and concrete products. Other interests include real estate property management, electrical contracting, and concrete guns and pumps. Founded as a plumbing company in 1876, J.F. Shea is still owned by the Shea family.

EXECUTIVES

President and CEO: John F. Shea
COO: Peter O. Shea Jr.
CFO and Secretary: James G. Shontere
EVP; President, J.F. Shea Construction: Peter O. Shea
EVP: Edmund H. Shea Jr.
VP Taxes: Ron Lakey
President and CEO, Shea Homes: Bert Selva
Treasurer: Robert R. O'Dell
Senior Technical Manager: Mike Little
Director, Finance: Andy Roundtree

LOCATIONS

HQ: J.F. Shea Co., Inc.
    655 Brea Canyon Rd., Walnut, CA 91789
Phone: 909-594-9500   **Fax:** 909-594-0914
Web: www.jfshea.com

PRODUCTS/OPERATIONS

Major Units

J.F. Shea Construction, Inc. (commercial buildings, subways, and civil engineering projects)
    J.F. Shea Heavy Civil Engineering (bridges, tunnels, and transit systems)
Redding Construction (sand, gravel, asphalt, and concrete products; highway construction)
Reed Manufacturing (concrete guns and pumps and concrete-placing equipment)
Shasta Electric LLP (full-service electrical contractor for commercial and industrial projects)
Shea Homes (residential units, developed and master-planned communities)
Shea Mortgage (mortgage lender)
Shea Properties (apartment and industrial and commercial building management)
Venture Capital (investment firm)

COMPETITORS

Austin Industries
Bechtel
Black & Veatch
Centex
Del Webb
Dick Corporation
D.R. Horton
Granite Construction
Hyundai Engineering and Construction
KB Home
Lennar
M.D.C. Holdings
Parsons
Peter Kiewit Sons'
Pulte Homes
Ryland
Shapell Industries
Standard Pacific
Tutor-Saliba
Washington Group

HISTORICAL FINANCIALS

Company Type: Private

Income Statement

FYE: December 31

	REVENUE ($ mil.)	NET INCOME ($ mil.)	NET PROFIT MARGIN	EMPLOYEES
12/03	2,597	—	—	2,685
12/02	1,994	—	—	2,315
12/01	1,968	—	—	2,288
12/00	1,863	—	—	2,200
12/99	1,794	—	—	2,100
12/98	1,621	—	—	2,000
12/97	1,001	—	—	1,420
12/96	957	—	—	1,200
12/95	687	—	—	1,100
Annual Growth	18.1%	—	—	11.8%

Revenue History

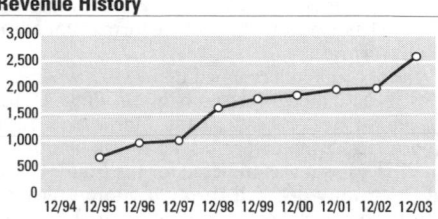

JM Family Enterprises

Founder and honorary chairman Jim Moran and chairman Pat Moran (Jim's daughter) make JM Family Enterprises a family affair. JM, owned by the Moran family, is a holding company (Florida's second-largest private company, in fact, after Publix Super Markets) with about a dozen automotive-related businesses, including the world's largest-volume Lexus retailer, JM Lexus, in Margate, Florida. JM's major subsidiary, Southeast Toyota Distributors, is the nation's largest Toyota distribution franchise, delivering Toyota cars, trucks, and SUVs to more than 160 dealers in Alabama, Florida, Georgia, and North and South Carolina.

Among JM Family's other subsidiaries, JM&A Group provides insurance and warranty services to retailers nationwide. World Omni Financial handles leasing, dealer financing, and other financial services for US auto dealers.

JM Family Enterprises is one of the largest woman-owned companies in the US and consistently ranks in the top half on *FORTUNE* magazine's 100 Best Companies to Work For list on the strength of on-site medical, fitness, and day-care centers.

HISTORY

Jim Moran first became visible as "Jim Moran, the Courtesy Man" in Chicago TV advertisements in the 1950s. At that time he ran Courtesy Motors, where he was so successful as the world's #1 Ford dealer that *Time* magazine put his picture on its cover in 1961.

Moran had entered the auto sales business after fixing up and selling a car for more than three times the price he had paid for it. That profit was much better than what he made at the Sinclair gas station he had bought, so he opened a used-car lot. Later, he moved to new-car sales when he bought a Hudson franchise (Ford had rejected him).

Seeing the promise of TV advertising, in 1948 Moran pioneered the forum for Chicago car dealers, not only as an advertiser and program sponsor but also as host of a variety show and a country/western music barn dance. The increased visibility positioned Moran as Hudson's #1 dealer, but the sales tactics at Courtesy Motors earned an antitrust suit that was settled out of court.

In 1955 Moran started with Ford and, with his TV influence as host of *The Jim Moran Courtesy Hour,* he became the world's #1 Ford dealer in his first month.

He moved to Florida in 1966 after being diagnosed with cancer and given one year to live. Successfully fighting the disease, he bought a Pontiac franchise and later started Southeast Toyota Distributors. In 1969 he formed JM Family Enterprises.

Legal problems cropped up in 1973 when the IRS investigated a Nassau bank serving as a tax haven for wealthy Americans. Moran and three Toyota executives were linked to the bank, and in 1978 Moran was indicted for tax fraud. When an immunity deal fell through, Moran pleaded guilty to seven tax fraud charges in 1984 and was sentenced to two years (suspended), fined more than $12 million, and ordered to perform community service. Moran's legal problems threatened his association with Toyota and were blamed for causing his stroke in 1983.

JM's legal problems continued in the 1980s, partly because of the imposition of auto import restrictions. To get more cars to sell, some Southeast Toyota managers encouraged auto dealers to file false sales reports. Some North Carolina dealers resisted and one sued, settling out of court for $22 million. Other dealers alleged racketeering and fraud on the part of Southeast Toyota, and by the beginning of 1994, JM had paid more than $100 million in fines and settlements for cases stretching back to 1988. In spite of that, Toyota renewed its contract with the company in 1993, a year ahead of schedule.

Pat Moran succeeded her father as JM president in 1992. Between 1991 and 1994 three suits were filed against Jim and Southeast Toyota alleging racism against blacks in establishing Toyota dealerships. All three suits were settled.

Jim teamed with Wayne Huizenga in 1996 to launch a national chain of used-car megastores under the name AutoNation USA, which Jim expected would draw buyers to his own auto dealerships. (AutoNation USA's first store was built just two blocks from JM's Coconut Creek Lexus Dealership.) Jim's interest in AutoNation USA was converted into a small percentage (less than 5%) of Republic Industries stock after Huizenga merged AutoNation into waste hauler Republic Industries (now called AutoNation) in 1997.

In late 1998 JM embarked on a national strategy to expand its presence outside the Southeast, establishing an office in St. Louis that handles indirect consumer leasing.

In 2000 Jim became honorary chairman while Pat was given the chairman position and continued as CEO; COO Colin Brown was named president. Also that year the company was named the 51st Best Company to Work For in the United States by *FORTUNE* magazine. The company's rank in the Best Company to Work For list rose to 20th place in 2001.

In March 2003 Brown assumed the CEO title, with Pat Moran continuing in the chairman position. In 2004 the company ranked first in the nation in dealer service contract satisfaction according to J.D. Power and Associates and sat at 25 on *FORTUNE*'s Best Company to Work For list.

EXECUTIVES

Honorary Chairman: James M. (Jim) Moran
Chairman: Patricia (Pat) Moran, age 58
President and CEO: Colin Brown, age 53
EVP: Louis Feagles
EVP, Human Resources: Gary L. Thomas
EVP; President, JM Service Center: Scott Barrett
SVP: Jan Moran
SVP and CFO: Mark S. Walter
Group VP, Corporate Communications: Tony Stromberg
VP: Larry McGinnes
VP, Aviation: George Kokinakis
VP, Community Relations: Rick Noland
VP, Community Relations and Marine Departments: Kiernan P. Moylanhas
VP, Corporate Communications: Lisa Kitei
VP, Corporate Tax Services: Jorge Gonzalez
VP, Government Relations: Kienan Moylan
VP, Human Resources: John Heins
Director, Corporate Safety: Claude Revels
Director, Corporate Security: Roger Robbins
Director, Dealer Services: Wendy Smith

LOCATIONS

HQ: JM Family Enterprises, Inc.
100 Jim Moran Blvd., Deerfield Beach, FL 33442
Phone: 954-429-2000 **Fax:** 954-429-2300
Web: www.jmfamily.com

JM Family Enterprises operates auto retail, distribution, leasing, and financing businesses across the US, mainly in Alabama, Florida, Georgia, and North and South Carolina.

PRODUCTS/OPERATIONS

Selected Subsidiaries

Finance and Leasing
  Centerone Financial Services
  World Omni Financial Corp.
Insurance, Marketing, Consulting, and Related Companies
  Courtesy Administrative Services, Inc.
  Courtesy Insurance Company
  Fidelity Insurance Agency, Inc.
  Fidelity Warranty Services, Inc.
  Jim Moran & Associates, Inc.
  JM&A Group (auto service contracts, insurance)
  J.M.I.C. Life Insurance Co.
Retail Car Sales
  JM Lexus
Vehicle Processing and Distribution
  SET Inland Processing
  SET Parts Supply and Distribution
  SET Port Processing
  Southeast Toyota Distributors, LLC

COMPETITORS

AutoNation
CarMax
Gulf States Toyota
Hendrick Automotive
Holman Enterprises
Island Lincoln-Mercury
Morse Operations
United Auto Group

HISTORICAL FINANCIALS

Company Type: Private

Income Statement

FYE: December 31

	REVENUE ($ mil.)	NET INCOME ($ mil.)	NET PROFIT MARGIN	EMPLOYEES
12/03	7,700	—	—	3,700
12/02	7,600	—	—	3,500
12/01	7,800	—	—	3,227
12/00	7,100	—	—	3,400
12/99	6,600	—	—	3,304
12/98	6,200	—	—	3,000
12/97	5,400	—	—	2,900
12/96	5,100	—	—	3,000
12/95	4,500	—	—	2,000
12/94	4,200	—	—	2,000
Annual Growth	7.0%	—	—	7.1%

Revenue History

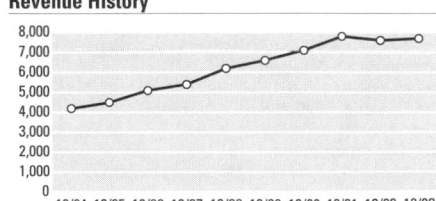

J.M. Huber

As great as toothpaste, paint, and tires are, J.M. Huber claims to make them even better. Hard to believe, we know. Founded in 1890 by Joseph M. Huber (and still owned by his heirs), the company makes specialty additives and minerals used to thicken and improve the cleaning properties of toothpaste, the brightness and gloss of paper, the strength and durability of rubber, and the flame retardant properties of wire and cable. The diverse company also makes oriented strand board (a plywood substitute), explores for and produces oil and gas, and provides technical and financial services. Huber has acquired hydrocolloids (thickeners for gums) maker CP Kelco from Lehman Brothers and Hercules.

Following the purchase of Hercules's 29% stake in CP Kelco in early 2004, Huber decided to buy out Lehman's 71% stake; the sale was made official in September 2004. The company has since combined its Noviant (hydrocolloids) business with CP Kelco; the companies will operate under the CP Kelco brand.

Huber also manages approximately 500,000 acres of timberland in Maine and the southeastern US, and has oil and gas operations in Texas, Colorado, Kansas, Utah, and Wyoming.

EXECUTIVES

Chairman, President, and CEO: Peter T. Francis
Director, Corporate Communications:
Robert (Bob) Currie
Manager, Human Resources: Gary Crowell
VP and General Manager, Paper, Engineered Materials:
John Takerer
President and CEO, CP Kelco: Thomas B. Lamb

LOCATIONS

HQ: J.M. Huber Corporation
333 Thornall St., Edison, NJ 08837
Phone: 732-549-8600   **Fax:** 732-549-7256
Web: www.huber.com

J. M. Huber Corporation has operations in Asia, Europe, Latin America, and North America.

PRODUCTS/OPERATIONS

Selected Operations

CP Kelco (food, pharmaceutical, household, and industrial gums)
Noviant (carboxymethl cellulose, hydrocolloids for paper, food, hygene, and industrial uses)
Demica (trade receivables securitization)
Huber Energy (oil and gas acquisition, exploration, and production)
Huber Engineered Materials (engineered minerals and specialty chemicals)
Huber Engineered Woods (high-performance specialty woods, including oriented strand board)
Huber Resources Corporation (yield maximization from timberland)
Huber Timber (timberland management)
Shelterwood Financial Services LLC (investment management and business consulting)

COMPETITORS

ADM	Ineos Silicas
Baker Hughes	Kerry Group
Cabot	Marathon Oil
Danisco	Minerals Technologies
Degussa	Occidental Petroleum
FMC	OfficeMax
Georgia-Pacific	Robert Weed
Corporation	Plywood Corp.
Imerys	

HISTORICAL FINANCIALS

Company Type: Private

Income Statement

FYE: December 31

	ESTIMATED REVENUE ($ mil.)	NET INCOME ($ mil.)	NET PROFIT MARGIN	EMPLOYEES
12/03	1,805	—	—	4,850
12/02	1,231	—	—	3,278
12/01	1,122	—	—	3,003
12/00	1,022	—	—	2,880
12/99	855	—	—	2,699
12/98	1,500	—	—	5,000
12/97	1,500	—	—	5,150
12/96	1,400	—	—	5,000
12/95	1,300	—	—	5,100
12/94	1,300	—	—	5,163
Annual Growth	3.7%	—	—	(0.7%)

Revenue History

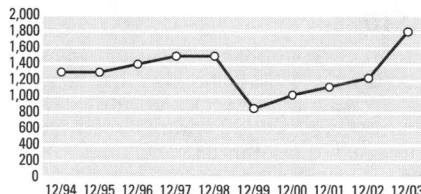

John Paul Mitchell

From pomades to pompadours, John Paul Mitchell Systems offers its best to those who do 'dos. The #1 privately owned hair care firm in the US makes more than 90 different hair care products that sell in about 90,000 hair salons worldwide. John Paul Mitchell was founded in Hawaii in 1980 by John Paul "J. P." DeJoria and the late Paul Mitchell. The company's signature white bottles with distinctive black lettering (because the founders couldn't afford color ink) have attracted the attention of counterfeiters on more than one occasion. Chairman and CEO DeJoria, a former gang member who sports a black ponytail and beard (and is seen in company TV commercials), is a vocal supporter for consumer-product safety.

EXECUTIVES

Chairman and CEO: John Paul (J. P.) DeJoria, age 60
Vice Chairman: Kenin M. Spivak
COO and Human Resources: Luke Jacobellis
VP, Advertising and Public Relations: Nanette Bercu
VP, Finance: Rick Battaglini
VP, Sales: Brent Golden
VP, Sports Marketing: Julie Solwold
CIO: Eric Peterson
Marketing Director, UK: Leslie George Spears
Public Relations Director: Isabelle Smith
Product Security Manager: Vikki Bresnahan
Company Secretary, UK: Peter Derald Barham
Corporate Counsel: Michaeline Re
Senior National Educator: Guadalupe Ovalles-Moore
National Educator: Jodi Bansley

LOCATIONS

HQ: John Paul Mitchell Systems
9701 Wilshire Blvd., Ste. 1205,
Beverly Hills, CA 90212
Phone: 310-248-3888   **Fax:** 310-248-2780
Web: www.paulmitchell.com

PRODUCTS/OPERATIONS

Selected Brands

Modern Elixirs
Paul Mitchell
Awapuhi
Baby Don't Cry
Shampoo One
Shampoo Three
Shampoo Two
Tea Tree
The Conditioner
The Cream
The Detangler
The Heat
The Masque
The Rinse
The Shine
The Wash
Paul Mitchell Professional Salon
XTG (Extreme Thickening Glue)

Selected Products

Conditioners
Finish sprays
Shampoos
Styling aids (gel, glaze, foam, lotion, spray, pomade, and wax)

COMPETITORS

Alberto-Culver	SoftSheen/Carson
L'Oréal	Stephan
Modern Organic Products	Unilever
Nexxus Products	Wella

HISTORICAL FINANCIALS

Company Type: Private

Income Statement

FYE: December 31

	ESTIMATED REVENUE ($ mil.)	NET INCOME ($ mil.)	NET PROFIT MARGIN	EMPLOYEES
12/03	800	—	—	—
12/02	700	—	—	—
12/01	600	—	—	100
12/00	600	—	—	100
12/99	600	—	—	97
12/98	200	—	—	110
12/97	185	—	—	100
12/96	165	—	—	89
Annual Growth	25.3%	—	—	2.4%

Revenue History

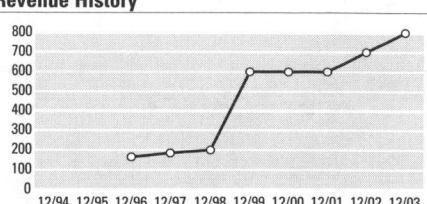

John Wieland Homes

John Wieland Homes and Neighborhoods (JW) develops land and builds cluster homes, townhomes, and more than 100 different types of upscale single-family homes in the Southeast US (in the metropolitan areas of Atlanta, Charleston, Charlotte, Raleigh, and Nashville). The company annually sells about 1,800 homes at an average sales price of $403,000. JW also provides remodeling and landscaping services. In cities where it builds, the company operates New Home Center design centers that provide interior and exterior design services. Wieland Financial Services offers mortgage lending to JW customers and others. Chairman John Wieland owns the firm, which he founded in 1970.

EXECUTIVES

Chairman and Chief Creative Officer: John Wieland
CEO and Director: Terry Russell
President, COO, and Director: Eric Price
EVP, General Counsel, and Director: Richard Bacon
SVP Land Development: Charlie Biele
VP and CFO: Doug Ray
VP Commercial Division: Jack Wieland
VP Organizational Development: Laura McMurrain
VP Human Resources: John Wood
Auditors: Birnbrey, Minsk & Minsk

LOCATIONS

HQ: John Wieland Homes and Neighborhoods, Inc.
1950 Sullivan Rd., Atlanta, GA 30337
Phone: 770-996-2400   **Fax:** 770-907-3419
Web: www.jwhomes.com

COMPETITORS

Beazer Homes
Centex
Del Webb
D.R. Horton
Engle Homes
M/I Homes
NVR
Oriole Homes
Pulte Homes

HISTORICAL FINANCIALS

Company Type: Private

Income Statement

FYE: September 30

	ESTIMATED REVENUE ($ mil.)	NET INCOME ($ mil.)	NET PROFIT MARGIN	EMPLOYEES
9/04	730	—	—	1,000
9/03	606	—	—	1,000
9/02	500	—	—	900
9/01	502	—	—	900
Annual Growth	13.3%	—	—	3.6%

Revenue History

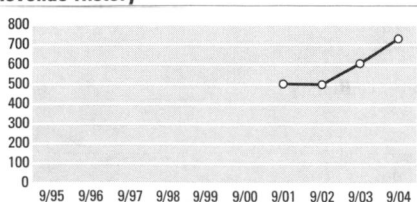

Johnson Publishing

Snubbed by advertisers when he founded his company 60 years ago, the late John Johnson pushed his magazine company to the front of the pack. Led by its flagship publication, *Ebony,* family-owned Johnson Publishing Company is the largest black-owned publishing firm in the country. It also publishes *Jet* and operates a book division. In addition, Johnson Publishing produces a line of hair care products (Supreme Beauty) and cosmetics (Fashion Fair) marketed for African-American women, and each year it hosts the Ebony Fashion Fair, a traveling fashion show that raises money for scholarships and charities in cities across the US and Canada.

The company's book division features titles such as *The New Ebony Cookbook* and the more controversial *Forced Into Glory: Abraham Lincoln's White Dream.*

Johnson Publishing is owned and controlled by family members of founder Johnson, who died in 2005. His daughter, Linda Johnson Rice, handles the day-to-day operations as president and CEO. His wife, Eunice, produces the Ebony Fashion Fair.

HISTORY

John H. Johnson launched his publishing business in 1942 while he was still in college in Chicago. The idea for a black-oriented magazine came to him while he was working part-time for Supreme Life Insurance Co. of America, where one of his jobs was to clip magazine and newspaper articles about the black community. Johnson used his mother's furniture as collateral to secure a $500 loan and then mailed $2 charter subscription offers to potential subscribers. He received 3,000 replies and used the $6,000 to print the first issue of *Negro Digest,* patterned after *Reader's Digest.* Circulation was 50,000 within a year.

Johnson started *Ebony* magazine in 1945 (which gained immediate popularity and is still the company's premier publication) and launched *Jet* in 1951, a pocket-sized publication containing news items and features. In the early days Johnson was unable to obtain advertising, so he formed his own Beauty Star mail-order business and advertised its products (dresses, wigs, hair care products, and vitamins) in his magazines. He won his first major account, Zenith Radio, in 1947; Johnson landed Chrysler in 1954, only after sending a salesman to Detroit every week for 10 years. For 20 years, *Ebony* and *Jet* were the only national publications targeting blacks in the US.

By the 1960s Johnson had become one of the most prominent black men in the US. He posed with John F. Kennedy in 1963 to publicize a special issue of *Ebony* celebrating the Emancipation Proclamation. US magazine publishers named him Publisher of the Year in 1972. Johnson launched *Ebony Jr!* (since discontinued) in 1973, a magazine designed to provide "positive black images" for black preteens. His first magazine, *Negro Digest* (renamed *Black World*), became known for its provocative articles, but its circulation dwindled from 100,000 to 15,000. Johnson retired the magazine in 1975.

Unable to find the proper makeup for his *Ebony* models, Johnson founded his own cosmetics business, Fashion Fair Cosmetics, that year, which carved out a niche beside Revlon (which introduced cosmetic lines for blacks) and another black cosmetics company, Johnson Products (unrelated) of Chicago. By 1982 Fashion Fair sales were more than $30 million.

The company got into broadcasting in 1972 when it bought Chicago radio station WGRT (renamed WJPC; that city's first black-owned station). It added WLOU (Louisville, Kentucky) in 1982 and WLNR (Lansing, Illinois; re-launched in 1991 as WJPC-FM) in 1985. By 1995, however, it had sold all of its stations.

Johnson and the company sold their controlling interest in the last minority-owned insurance company in Illinois (and Johnson's first employer), Supreme Life Insurance, to Unitrin (a Chicago-based life, health, and property insurer) in 1991. That year the company and catalog retailer Spiegel announced a joint venture to develop fashions for black women. The two companies launched a mail-order catalog called *E Style* in 1993 and an accompanying credit card the next year.

Johnson Publishing launched its South African edition of *Ebony* in 1995. Johnson was awarded the Presidential Medal of Freedom in 1996. The next year, however, circulation of *Ebony* fell 7% as mainstream magazines began covering black issues more thoroughly and a host of new titles appeared. In response, the company restructured its ventures and closed its *E Style* catalog. Johnson Publishing retired *Ebony Man* (launched in 1985) in 1998 and *Ebony South Africa* in 2000.

In 2002 John Johnson named his daughter Linda Johnson Rice as CEO of the company; Johnson kept the title of chairman and publisher. John Johnson died at the age of 87 in 2005.

EXECUTIVES

President and CEO: Linda Johnson Rice, age 47
Secretary and Treasurer; Producer and Director, EBONY Fashion Fair: Eunice W. Johnson
Executive Editor, EBONY: Lerone Bennett Jr.
SVP and General Counsel: June Acie Rhinehart
SVP and Midwest Advertising Director: Dennis H. Boston
SVP and Associate Publisher, Advertising: Jeff Burns Jr.
SVP, Fashion Fair Cosmetics: J. Lance Clark
VP and Director of Advertising Production: Tammy E. Rollé
VP and Director of Finance: Treka Owens
VP and Director of Promotions: Lydia J. Davis Eady
VP and Research Director: Barbara E. Rudd
VP and Western Advertising Director: John Cater
Director of Circulation: Kenneth C. Brooks
Telecommunications Manager: Sheila Jenkins
Purchasing Manager: Ruth Wagner
Senior Corporate Counsel: Lisa M. Butler

LOCATIONS

HQ: Johnson Publishing Company, Inc.
820 S. Michigan Ave., Chicago, IL 60605
Phone: 312-322-9200   **Fax:** 312-322-0918
Web: www.johnsonpublishing.com

PRODUCTS/OPERATIONS

Selected Operations

Fashion and Beauty Aids
Ebony Fashion Fair (traveling fashion show)
Fashion Fair Cosmetics (color cosmetics, fragrances, skincare)
Supreme Beauty Products (hair care)

Books
Magazines
  Ebony
  Jet

COMPETITORS

Advance Publications	Forbes
Alberto-Culver	Hearst Magazines
Avon	LFP
BET	L'Oréal
Earl G. Graves	Mary Kay
Essence Communications	Revlon
Estée Lauder	Time

HISTORICAL FINANCIALS
Company Type: Private

Income Statement
FYE: December 31

	REVENUE ($ mil.)	NET INCOME ($ mil.)	NET PROFIT MARGIN	EMPLOYEES
12/03	489	—	—	2,000
12/02	425	—	—	2,076
12/01	412	—	—	2,594
12/00	400	—	—	2,614
12/99	387	—	—	2,657
12/98	372	—	—	2,647
12/97	361	—	—	2,677
12/96	326	—	—	2,702
12/95	316	—	—	2,680
12/94	307	—	—	2,662
Annual Growth	5.3%	—	—	(3.1%)

Revenue History

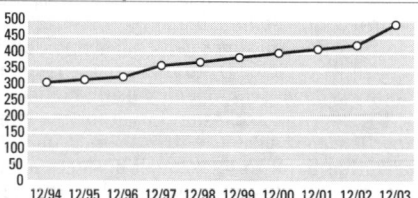

JohnsonDiversey

JohnsonDiversey is the industrial-strength version of S.C. Johnson & Son. Split off from the well-known private company in 1999, JohnsonDiversey consists of two units: Professional and Polymer. Professional provides commercial cleaning, hygiene, pest control, and food sanitation products to retailers, building service contractors, food service operators, and hospitality firms. Polymer produces acrylic resins used in printing, packaging, coatings, and adhesives. The Johnson family controls two-thirds of the company; Unilever controls the rest. The firm changed its name from S.C. Johnson Commercial Markets to JohnsonDiversey in 2002 after acquiring DiverseyLever, Unilever's industrial cleaning business.

The acquisition of DiverseyLever more than doubled the company's sales and made it the #2 industrial and institutional cleaning products firm behind Ecolab. JohnsonDiversey has an option to buy out Unilever's stake by 2007.

JohnsonDiversey dates back to the 1930s when S.C. Johnson became involved in commercial sales of cleaning products.

EXECUTIVES

Chairman: Samuel Curtis (Curt) Johnson III, age 49, $1,662,332 pay
President and CEO: Gregory E. (Greg) Lawton, age 54, $2,345,850 pay
EVP and CFO: Joseph F. (Joe) Smorada, age 58
EVP, Chief Administrative Officer, Secretary, and General Counsel: JoAnne Brandes, age 51, $867,313 pay
EVP, Corporate Development: Michael J. (Mike) Bailey, age 52, $862,042 pay
SVP, Chief Scientific Officer: Stephen A. Di Biase, age 52
SVP, Global Marketing and Coustomer Management, Group President, Latin America and Asia: Mark S. Cross, age 48
SVP, Global Human Resources: Diarmuid P. Ryan, age 53
VP, Global Communications, Public Affairs, and Administrative Services: John Matthews
Regional President, Asia Pacific: Paul A. Mathias, age 60
Regional President, Europe: Graeme D. Armstrong, age 42, $908,538 pay
Regional President, Japan: Morio Nishikawa, age 60
Regional President, Latin America: Jean-Max Teissier, age 60
Regional President, North America: Thomas M. Gartland, age 47
Auditors: Ernst & Young LLP

LOCATIONS

HQ: JohnsonDiversey, Inc.
  8310 16th St., Sturtevant, WI 53177
Phone: 262-631-4001   **Fax:** 262-631-4282
Web: www.johnsondiversey.com

JohnsonDiversey operates about 45 manufacturing facilities in 26 countries including Argentina, Brazil, Canada, China, France, Germany, Italy, Japan, the Netherlands, Spain, Switzerland, Turkey, the UK, and the US.

2004 Sales

	$ mil.	% of total
Europe	1,534.9	48
Americas		
North America	1,008.2	31
Central & South America	139.3	4
Asia		
Japan	348.8	11
Asia/Pacific	194.5	6
Adjustments	(56.4)	—
Total	**3,169.3**	**100**

PRODUCTS/OPERATIONS

2004 Sales

	$ mil.	% of total
Professional	2,861.4	90
Polymer	328.4	10
Adjustments	(20.5)	—
Total	**3,169.3**	**100**

COMPETITORS

Acuity Brands	Dainippon Ink
Acuity Specialty Products	Dow Chemical
Air Products	Eastman Chemical
Arrow-Magnolia	Ecolab
Avecia	Kimberly-Clark
BASF AG	NCH
Clorox	Procter & Gamble
Colgate-Palmolive	Rohm and Haas
Cytec Surface Specialties	

HISTORICAL FINANCIALS
Company Type: Private

Income Statement
FYE: December 31

	REVENUE ($ mil.)	NET INCOME ($ mil.)	NET PROFIT MARGIN	EMPLOYEES
12/04	3,169	14	0.4%	12,000
12/03	2,948	24	0.8%	13,000
12/02	2,196	30	1.3%	13,530
12/01*	549	11	2.0%	14,500
6/01	1,133	33	2.9%	3,600
6/00	1,028	50	4.8%	3,500
6/99	980	15	1.5%	3,000
Annual Growth	21.6%	(1.3%)	—	26.0%

*Fiscal year change

2004 Year-End Financials

Debt ratio: 121.7%
Return on equity: 1.3%
Cash ($ mil.): 28
Current ratio: 1.07
Long-term debt ($ mil.): 1,273

Net Income History

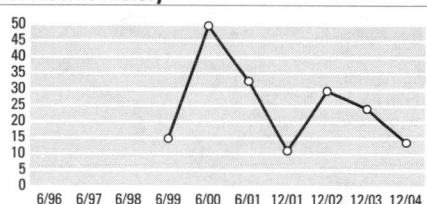

Jones Day

Legal leviathan Jones Day ranks as one of the world's largest law firms, providing counsel to about half of the *FORTUNE* 500 companies. It has more than 2,000 attorneys in some 30 offices across the US, as well as in Asia, Australia, Europe, and Latin America. The firm's practice groups include litigation, tax, government regulation, and business. Jones Day has counted Bridgestone/Firestone, General Motors, IBM, RJR Nabisco, and Texas Instruments among its top clients. The firm traces its roots to the Cleveland law partnership founded by Edwin Blandin and William Rice in 1893.

EXECUTIVES

Managing Partner: Stephen J. Brogan
CFO: David Post
Partner-in-Charge, International Region: David F. Clossey
Partner-in-Charge, New York: Dennis W. LaBarre, age 62
Partner-in-Charge, Paris: Wesley R. Johnson Jr.
Partner-In-Charge, Washington: Mary Ellen Powers
Director of Administration: William Gaskill

LOCATIONS

HQ: Jones Day
  Northpoint, 901 Lakeside Ave., Cleveland, OH 44114
Phone: 216-586-3939   **Fax:** 216-579-0212
Web: www.jonesday.com

Jones Day has US offices in Atlanta; Chicago; Cleveland; Columbus, Ohio; Dallas; Houston; Irvine, Los Angeles, Menlo Park, San Diego, and San Francisco, California; New York City; Pittsburgh; and Washington, DC. The firm has international offices in Beijing; Brussels; Frankfurt; Hong Kong; London; Madrid; Milan; Munich; Paris; Shanghai; Singapore; Sydney; Taipei, Taiwan; and Tokyo.

PRODUCTS/OPERATIONS

Selected Practice Areas

Antitrust & competition law
Business restructuring & reorganization
Capital markets
Complex commercial & multijurisdictional litigation
Corporate criminal investigations
Employee benefits & executive compensation
Energy delivery & power
Government regulation
Health care
Intellectual property
Labor & employment
Mergers & acquisitions
Oil & gas
Real estate
Securities & shareholder litigation
Tax

COMPETITORS

Akin Gump
Baker & McKenzie
Cleary Gottlieb
Clifford Chance
Holland & Knight
Latham & Watkins
Mayer, Brown, Rowe & Maw
Morgan, Lewis
Shearman & Sterling
Sidley Austin Brown & Wood
Skadden, Arps
White & Case

HISTORICAL FINANCIALS

Company Type: Partnership

Income Statement

FYE: December 31

	REVENUE ($ mil.)	NET INCOME ($ mil.)	NET PROFIT MARGIN	EMPLOYEES
12/03	1,035	—	—	4,700
12/02	908	—	—	4,500
12/01	790	—	—	4,000
12/00	675	—	—	3,200
12/99	595	—	—	3,200
12/98	530	—	—	3,200
12/97	490	—	—	3,092
12/96	450	—	—	2,880
12/95	400	—	—	2,800
12/94	384	—	—	468
Annual Growth	**11.6%**	—	—	**29.2%**

Revenue History

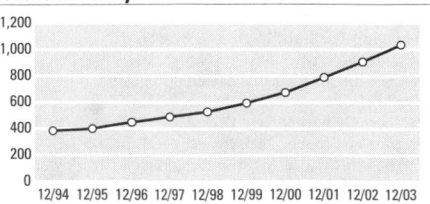

Jones Financial

This is not your father's broker. Well, maybe it is. The Jones Financial Companies is the parent of Edward Jones, an investment brokerage network catering to individual investors. Most of its clients are retirees and small-business owners in rural communities and suburbs. The "Wal-Mart of Wall Street" has thousands of satellite-linked offices in all 50 states plus Canada and the UK. Brokers preach a conservative buy-and-hold approach, offering relatively low-risk investment vehicles such as government bonds, blue-chip stocks, and high-quality mutual funds.

Edward Jones' network of some 9,000 offices — many of them with a single broker — makes it one of the largest brokerage networks in the world. The company also sells insurance and engages in investment banking for such clients as Wal-Mart and public agencies. The firm embraces technology, maintaining one of the industry's largest satellite networks (including a dish for each office).

Preferring to groom brokers internally, the firm accepts applicants with no previous experience, trains them extensively, and monitors investment patterns to prevent account churning and trading in risky low-cap stocks. Before they are given such luxuries as office space or assistants, new brokers must make 1,000 cold calls in their chosen community. Edward Jones' investment in training, backed by what's perceived to be old-school values and strong ethics, seems to be paying off: The firm is consistently ranked on *Fortune* magazine's "100 Best Companies to Work For."

The company's attempt to embrace old-fashioned traditions has not spared it from some modern-day issues. In 2004 Edward Jones was one of several brokerage firms investigated for allegedly failing to disclose the incentives its brokers received for certain mutual fund sales. To settle the matter, the firm paid a $75 million penalty distributed to Edward Jones customers.

The Jones Companies is the only major financial services firm still organized as a partnership, and it has said it has no plans to go public.

HISTORY

Jones Financial got its start in 1871 as bond house Whitaker & Co. In 1922 Edward D. Jones (no relation to the Edward D. Jones of Dow Jones fame) opened a brokerage in St. Louis. In 1943 the two firms merged.

Jones' son Edward "Ted" Jones Jr. joined the firm in 1948. Under Ted's leadership (and against his father's wishes), the company focused on rural customers, opening its first branch in the Missouri town of Mexico in 1955 and beginning its march across small-town America. Ted took over as managing partner in 1968, masterminding the company's small-town expansion. (The Wal-Mart comparison is apt; Ted Jones and Sam Walton were good friends.)

Almost from the start, the firm hammered home a conservative investment message focusing on blue-chip stocks and bonds. It expanded steadily throughout the years, adding offices with such addresses as Cedarburg, Wisconsin, and Paris, Illinois.

In the 1970s Edward D. Jones moved into underwriting with clients including Southern Co., Citicorp, and Humana. (It got burned in the

mid-1980s on one such deal, when the SEC accused the company of fraud in a bond offering for life insurer D.H. Baldwin Co., which later filed for bankruptcy.)

The company's technological bent was spurred in 1978 after its Teletype network couldn't handle the demand generated by the firm's 220 offices. As a stopgap, the company nixed use of the Teletype for stock quotes, telling its brokers to call Merrill Lynch's toll-free number instead.

Managing partner John Bachmann took over from Ted Jones in 1980. (Bachmann started at the company as a janitor.) A follower of management guru Peter Drucker, Bachmann inculcated the company's brokers with Drucker's customer- and value-oriented principles.

Edward D. Jones began moving into the suburbs and into less-than-posh sections of big cities in the mid-1980s. In 1986 the company started a mortgage program, but the plan was never successful and was ended in 1988. The company weathered the 1987 stock market crash (many brokerages did not), albeit with thinner profit margins.

In 1990 Ted Jones died. The first half of the decade was a time of great expansion for the company as it doubled its number of offices. In 1993 the company opened an office in Canada.

In 1994 Jones Financial's acquisition of Columbia, Missouri-based thrift Boone National gave it the ability to offer trust and mortgage services to its clients, which helped sales as Jones started facing competition from Merrill Lynch in its small-town niche. The company's rapid expansion and relatively expensive infrastructure (all those one-person offices add up) began to eat at the bottom line, and in 1995 Bachmann stopped expansion so the firm could catch its breath.

In 1997 Edward Jones (which had unofficially dropped its middle "D" to boost name recognition) moved overseas, opening its first offices in the UK, a prime expansion target for the company. The next year the firm teamed up with Mercantile Bank to offer small-business loans. Jones resumed its expansionist push in 1999 and 2000, adding offices in all its markets, but continued to resist online trading.

EXECUTIVES

Managing Partner: Douglas E. (Doug) Hill, age 60, $233,508 pay
Principal, Canadian Operations: Gary D. Reamey, $158,508 pay
Principal, Compliance: Pamela (Pam) Cavness
Principal, Finance and Accounting:
  Steven (Steve) Novik, age 55, $183,508 pay
Principal, Human Resources: Ken Dude
Principal, Information Systems:
  Richie L. (Rich) Malone, age 56, $183,508 pay
Principal, Internal Audit: Ann Ficken
Principal, Marketing: Dallas Kersey
Principal, Operations: Norman Eaker, age 48
Principal, Product and Sales: Brett Campbell
Principal, Product and Sales: James D. (Jim) Weddle, $183,508 pay
Principal, Products and Services: Ray Robbins
Principal, Sales Hiring and Training: Dann Timm
Principal, Service: Randy Haynes
Principal, United Kingdom Operations: Tim Kirley
General Counsel: Lawrence R. Sobol, age 54
Management Development: Robert (Bob) Virgil Jr.
Chief Market Strategist: Alan F. Skrainka
Auditors: PricewaterhouseCoopers LLP

LOCATIONS

HQ: The Jones Financial Companies, L.L.L.P.
12555 Manchester Rd., Des Peres, MO 63131
Phone: 314-515-2000 **Fax:** 314-515-2622
Web: www.edwardjones.com

PRODUCTS/OPERATIONS

2004 Sales

	$ mil.	% of total
Commissions		
Mutual funds	986.6	34
Listed brokerage transactions	249.4	9
Insurance	202.1	7
Over-the-counter transactions	66.0	2
Asset fees	581.8	20
Account & activity fees	304.6	11
Principal transactions	304.1	11
Interest & dividends	153.1	5
Investment banking	27.9	1
Other	15.8	—
Total	**2,891.4**	**100**

COMPETITORS

A.G. Edwards
Ameritrade
Charles Schwab
Citigroup
Merrill Lynch
Morgan Stanley
National Financial Partners
Oppenheimer Holdings
Piper Jaffray
Raymond James Financial
T. Rowe Price
TD Waterhouse
UBS Financial Services
Wells Fargo

HISTORICAL FINANCIALS

Company Type: Partnership

Income Statement

FYE: December 31

	REVENUE ($ mil.)	NET INCOME ($ mil.)	NET PROFIT MARGIN	EMPLOYEES
12/04	2,891	0	—	31,400
12/03	2,539	203	8.0%	29,200
12/02	2,270	149	6.6%	28,469
12/01	2,142	149	7.0%	26,460
12/00	2,212	230	10.4%	23,432
12/99	1,787	187	10.5%	20,541
12/98	1,450	199	13.7%	15,795
12/97	1,135	114	10.1%	13,691
12/96	952	93	9.8%	12,148
12/95	722	58	8.1%	11,717
Annual Growth	**16.7%**	—	—	**11.6%**

2004 Year-End Financials

Debt ratio: —   Current ratio: —
Return on equity: —   Long-term debt ($ mil.): 32
Cash ($ mil.): —

Net Income History

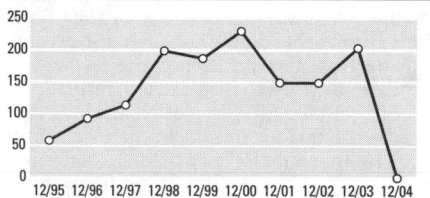

Jordan Industries

What has 18 operating companies that serve five industry segments, and has manufacturing plants in eight countries? Jordan Industries, which is engaged in markets as diverse as automotive products, bicycle reflector kits, software application development, electric motors, and specialty advertising products. Its five business units are: Consumer and Industrial Products (orthopedic supports and gift items); Kinetek (electric motors and gears), Jordan Auto Aftermarket (torque converters), Jordan Specialty Plastics (plastic products), and Specialty Printing and Labeling (promotional products). Director David Zalaznick owns 20% of the company; chairman and CEO John W. Jordan II owns 18%.

EXECUTIVES

Chairman and CEO: John W. (Jay) Jordan II, age 57
President, COO, and Director: Thomas H. Quinn, age 57, $1,000,000 pay
SVP, Business Development: Joseph C. (Joe) Linnen
SVP and Treasurer: Gordon L. Nelson Jr., age 47
VP, Assistant Secretary, and Director:
Jonathan F. Boucher, age 48
VP and CFO: Norman R. Bates
VP and Controller: Lisa M. Ondrula, age 34
CEO, GramTel USA: Tracy Graham
President, Beemak Plastics, Inc.: Chris Braun
President, Pamco Label Co.: Michael Blechman
President, Sate-Lite Manufacturing:
Richard (Dick) Van Deventer
General Counsel, Secretary, and Director:
G. Robert Fisher, age 64
Auditors: Ernst & Young LLP

LOCATIONS

HQ: Jordan Industries, Inc.
Arborlake Center, Ste. 550, 1751 Lake Cook Rd., Deerfield, IL 60015
Phone: 847-945-5591   **Fax:** 847-945-0198
Web: www.jordanindustries.com

Jordan Industries has facilities in Canada, China, France, Germany, Italy, Mexico, the UK, and the US.

2004 Sales

	$ mil.	% of total
US	611.4	84
Other countries	111.9	16
Total	**723.3**	**100**

PRODUCTS/OPERATIONS

2004 Sales

	$ mil.	% of total
Kinetek	313.9	40
Jordan Specialty Plastics	147.7	20
Jordan Auto Aftermarket	141.8	16
Consumer & industrial products	68.8	14
Specialty printing & labeling	51.1	10
Total	**723.3**	**100**

Selected Products and Operations

Kinetek
Advanced D.C. Motors
FIR (electric motors)
Imperial (electric motors, gears, motion control systems)
Merkle-Korff (electric motors)
Motion Control Engineering

Jordan Specialty Plastics
Beemak (point-of-purchase displays, brochure holders, sign holders)
Deflecto (injection-molded products)
Sate-Lite (bicycle products)
Jordan Auto Aftermarket
Alma (remanufactured drive trains)
Atco (mobile air conditioning components)
Dacco (remanufactured torque converters and hydraulic pumps and sealing rings, bearings, washers, filter kits)
Consumer and Industrial Products
Cho-Pat (orthopedic sports medicine devices)
GramTel (information technology outsourcing)
Welcome Home (imports gifts, wooden furniture, framed art)
Specialty Printing and Labeling
Pamco (printed tapes and labels)
Seaboard (printed folding cartons and boxes, insert packaging, blister pack cards)
Valmark (graphic panel overlays, membrane switch control panels, adhesive-backed labels)

COMPETITORS

Aftermarket Technology
Baldor Electric
Bed Bath & Beyond
BorgWarner
Dana
HMI Industries
Multi-Color
Red Man Pipe & Supply
Regal-Beloit
Tex Holdings
Thomas Nelson
Twin Disc
Tyco

HISTORICAL FINANCIALS

Company Type: Private

Income Statement

FYE: December 31

	REVENUE ($ mil.)	NET INCOME ($ mil.)	NET PROFIT MARGIN	EMPLOYEES
12/04	723	(20)	—	6,500
12/03	720	(33)	—	6,605
12/02	720	(64)	—	7,200
12/01	723	(58)	—	6,500
12/00	807	—	—	6,967
12/99	777	—	—	7,000
12/98	944	—	—	7,092
12/97	707	—	—	6,200
12/96	602	—	—	6,218
12/95	507	—	—	5,150
Annual Growth	**4.0%**	—	—	**2.6%**

2004 Year-End Financials

Debt ratio: —   Current ratio: 1.59
Return on equity: —   Long-term debt ($ mil.): 689
Cash ($ mil.): 15

Net Income History

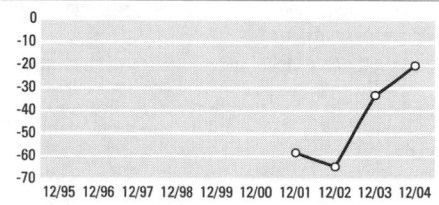

Jostens

Are you *sure* you want to remember high school? If so, look to Jostens, the leading US producer of yearbooks and class rings. Class rings are sold on school campuses and through bookstores, retail jewelers, and the Internet, while Jostens' sports rings commemorate professional sports champions (it has made 24 of 36 Super Bowl rings). Other graduation products include diplomas, announcements, caps, and gowns, and it takes and sells class and individual pictures for schools in the US and Canada. In 2003 Jostens was sold to a unit of CSFB. The next year Jostens was recapitalized and became part of a newly created printing and marketing services company co-owned by an affiliate of CSFB and Kohlberg Kravis Roberts.

Yearbooks (for all levels of schools from elementary through college) account for more than 40% of Jostens' sales. Representatives work closely with students and faculty advisors in all phases of yearbook creation — from planning, editing, and layout to production, printing, and distribution. The company also prints books, brochures, and promotional materials. Jostens exited the recognition business in 2001.

In conjunction with Jostens' sale to CSFB in 2003, a newly formed company (controlled by the private equity unit of CSFB), Ring Acquisition Corp., was merged with Jostens; Jostens continued as the surviving corporation. Visant, the specialty printing and marketing services company created in 2004, consists of Jostens, as well as Von Hoffmann Corporation (a leading printer of educational textbooks and supplemental materials) and Arcade Marketing (a printer and manufacturer of sampling products for the fragrance, cosmetics, consumer products, and food and beverage industries). DLJ Merchant Banking Partners III is the CSFB affiliate that co-owns Jostens.

EXECUTIVES

CEO: Michael L. Bailey, age 49
SVP and CFO: David A. Tayeh, age 38
SVP and General Manager, Printing and Emerging Markets: Timothy M. Larson, age 30
VP, Treasurer, and Corporate Controller: Marjorie J. Brown, age 50
VP and General Manager, Photography and Jostens Canada: Dick Lewis
Director, Communications: Richard (Rich) Stoebe
Communications Manager: Julie Goetz
Auditors: Ernst & Young LLP

LOCATIONS

HQ: Jostens, Inc.
   5501 American Blvd. West, Minneapolis, MN 55437
Phone: 952-830-3300   **Fax:** 952-830-3293
Web: www.jostens.com

Jostens sells its products and services throughout North America through independent and employee sales representatives. It has manufacturing facilities in California, Kansas, Massachusetts, Minnesota, North and South Carolina, Pennsylvania, Tennessee, and Texas, as well as in Canada.

PRODUCTS/OPERATIONS

Selected Products
Printing and publishing
   Books
   Commercial brochures
   Promotional books and materials
   Yearbooks (elementary, middle, and
      high schools; college)
Jewelry
   Athletic rings
   Class rings (high school and college)
Graduation products
   Announcements
   Caps and gowns
   Diplomas
Photography
   Class and individual school pictures
   Prom and special events pictures
   Senior portraits
   Student ID cards

COMPETITORS

American Achievement
Herff Jones
Lifetouch
Walsworth

HISTORICAL FINANCIALS

Company Type: Private

Income Statement			FYE: Saturday nearest December 31	
	REVENUE ($ mil.)	**NET INCOME** ($ mil.)	**NET PROFIT MARGIN**	**EMPLOYEES**
12/03	788	(26)	—	6,300
12/02	756	30	4.0%	6,700
12/01	737	4	0.6%	6,100
12/00	805	(19)	—	6,500
12/99	782	43	5.5%	6,700
12/98	771	42	5.4%	6,800
12/97	743	57	7.7%	6,500
12/96*	277	(1)	—	6,100
6/96	695	52	7.4%	5,600
6/95	665	50	7.6%	8,000
Annual Growth	**1.9%**	**—**	**—**	**(2.6%)**

*Fiscal year change

2003 Year-End Financials

Debt ratio: 213.4%   Current ratio: 0.73
Return on equity: —   Long-term debt ($ mil.): 821
Cash ($ mil.): 19

Net Income History

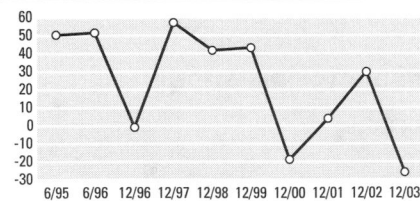

J.R. Simplot

J.R. Simplot hopes you'll have fries with that. Potato potentate J. R. "Jack" Simplot simply shook hands with McDonald's pioneer Ray Kroc in the mid-1960s, and his company's french fry sales have sizzled ever since. The company still remains the major french fry supplier for McDonald's and supplies Burger King and KFC as well. J.R. Simplot produces more than 3 billion pounds of french fries and hash browns annually, making it one of the world's largest processors of frozen potatoes. It offers its potato products mainly to food service and retail customers under its Simplot brand and private labels.

In addition to potatoes, J.R. Simplot also produces fruits and vegetables under the RoastWorks and Simplot Classic labels. The company's spuds sprouted other businesses as well, including cattle ranches and 150,000-head capacity feedlots (which use feed made from potato peels). Its AgriBusiness Group mines phosphates (for fertilizer and feed) and silica. The company's Turf and Horticulture Group produces grass and turf seed and fertilizer.

After being out of the dehydrated potato business for more than 30 years, Simplot acquired the dehydrated potato granule business of Nestlé USA in 2004; in addition, it reached an agreement with Idaho Fresh-Pak to distribute that company's dehydrated potatoes.

Officially retired since 1994, J.R. Simplot remains one of the wealthiest Americans. After amassing a mountain of potato money, the spudillionaire moved on to semiconductors and invested heavily in Boise-based Micron Technology.

HISTORY

J.R. Simplot was born in Dubuque, Iowa, in 1909. His family moved to the frontier town of Declo, Idaho, about a year later. Frustrated with school and an overbearing father, Simplot dropped out at age 14 and moved to a local hotel, where he made money by paying cash for teachers' wage scrip, at 50 cents on the dollar. Simplot then got a bank loan using the scrip as collateral and moved into farming, first by raising hogs and then by growing potatoes. He met Lindsay Maggart, a leading farmer in the area, who taught him the value of planting certified potato seed, rather than potatoes.

Simplot purchased an electric potato sorter in 1928 and eventually dominated the local market by sorting for neighboring farms. By 1940 his company, J.R. Simplot, operated 33 potato warehouses in Oregon and Idaho. The company moved into food processing in the 1940s, first by producing dried onions and other vegetables for Chicago-based Sokol & Co. and later by producing dehydrated potatoes. Between 1942 and 1945 J.R. Simplot produced more than 50 million pounds of dehydrated potatoes for the US military. During the war the company also expanded into fertilizer production, cattle feeding, and lumber. It moved to Boise, Idaho, in 1947.

In the 1950s J.R. Simplot researchers developed a method for freezing french fries. In the mid-1960s Simplot persuaded McDonald's founder, Ray Kroc, to go with his frozen fries, a handshake deal that practically guaranteed Simplot's success in the potato processing industry.

By the end of the 1960s, Simplot was the largest landowner, cattleman, potato grower, and employer in the state of Idaho. He also had established fertilizer plants, mining operations, and other businesses in 36 states, as well as in Canada and a handful of other countries.

During the oil crisis of the 1970s, J.R. Simplot began producing ethanol from potatoes. However, Simplot's empire-building was not without its rough edges. In 1977 he pleaded no contest to federal charges that he failed to report his income, and the next year he was forced to settle charges that he manipulated Maine potato futures.

The company entered the frozen fruit and vegetable business in 1983. Other ventures included using wastewater from potato processing for irrigation and using cattle manure to fuel methane gas plants. Simplot set up a Chinese joint venture in the 1990s to provide processed potatoes to McDonald's and other customers in East Asia.

The company bought the giant ZX cattle ranch near Paisley, Oregon, in 1994. Simplot retired from the board of directors that year to become chairman emeritus; Stephen Beebe was named president and CEO. The 1995 acquisition of the food operations of Pacific Dunlop (now Ansell) led to the creation of Simplot Australia, one of the largest food processors in Australia. Its 1997 stock swap with I. & J. Foods Australia enlarged the subsidiary's frozen food menu.

In 1999 the company sold its Simplot Dairy Products cheese business to France's Besnier Group, and it teamed with Dutch potato processor Farm Frites to enter new markets. In 2000 it launched agricultural Web site planetAg, bought the turf grass seed assets of AgriBioTech, and added the US potato operations of Nestlé to its pantry.

In 2001 the firm said it would build an $80 million potato-processing plant in Manitoba. Also that year the company said it would not increase the value of its contracts with growers struggling amid low prices in a glutted market.

In 2002 Simplot sold its Australian pudding maker Big Sister to the Fowlers Vacola Group and its Agrisource grain company to a private buyer. That same year Beebe retired and Lawrence Hlobik, president of the company's agribusiness unit, was named CEO. The company closed its only meat-processing plant in September 2003.

In 2004 the company began offering zero-gram trans-fat french fries, called Infinity Fries, for the foodservice market.

EXECUTIVES

Chairman: Scott R. Simplot
President and CEO: Lawrence S. (Larry) Hlobik
SVP, Finance and CFO: Annette Elg
SVP, Retail Operations, AgriBusiness Group: Pat Avery
SVP, Corporate Secretary, and General Counsel: Terry Uhling
VP, Special Projects: Rick Fisch
VP, Mining and Manufacturing: Martin Hunt
VP, Marketing, Food Group: Alan Kahn
VP, Sales, Food Group: Steve Patterson
VP, Human Resources: Mike Vasilenko
VP, Public Relations: Fred Zerza
VP and CIO: Roger Parks
Director, Energy and Natural Resources: David Hawk
President, Food Group: Kevin Storms
President, AgriBusiness Group: Bill Whitacre

LOCATIONS

HQ: J.R. Simplot Company
999 Main St., Ste. 1300, Boise, ID 83702
Phone: 208-336-2110   **Fax:** 208-389-7515
Web: www.simplot.com

In addition to the US, Simplot has operations in Australia, Canada, China, and Mexico.

PRODUCTS/OPERATIONS

Major Operating Groups

AgriBusiness Group
Nitrogen and phosphate fertilizers
Phosphate and silica ore mining

Corporate Group
Corporate Development Department
Corporate Information Systems
Simplot Aviation (in-company flight services)

Food Group (Simplot Foods)
Asparagus, avocadoes, broccoli, carrots, cauliflower, corn, peas, strawberries
Fresh potatoes (Blue Ribbon, Golden Classic)

Frozen Fruits and Vegetables
Frozen potato products (fries, nuggets, patties, sticks)

Roasted Foods
Roasted vegetables and potatoes

Land and Livestock Group
Cattle feeding
Hay, corn, grain production for feedlots

COMPETITORS

ADM
Cargill
ConAgra
ContiGroup
Del Monte Foods
Golden State Foods
Heinz
Martin-Brower
McCain Foods
Michael Foods, Inc.
PotashCorp
Pro-Fac
Seneca Foods

HISTORICAL FINANCIALS

Company Type: Private

Income Statement

FYE: August 31

	REVENUE ($ mil.)	NET INCOME ($ mil.)	NET PROFIT MARGIN	EMPLOYEES
8/04	3,100	—	—	11,500
8/03	3,100	—	—	12,000
8/02	3,000	—	—	13,000
8/01	3,000	—	—	13,000
8/00	2,700	—	—	12,000
8/99	2,730	—	—	12,000
8/98	2,800	—	—	12,000
8/97	2,800	—	—	12,000
8/96	2,700	—	—	13,000
8/95	2,200	—	—	10,000
Annual Growth	**3.9%**	—	—	**1.6%**

Revenue History

3,500	
3,000	
2,500	
2,000	
1,500	
1,000	
500	
0	
	8/95 8/96 8/97 8/98 8/99 8/00 8/01 8/02 8/03 8/04

K&W Cafeterias

K&W Cafeterias takes you back to the salad days of Salisbury steak and strawberry shortcake. The company, with operations in the southeastern US, serves trend-free cafeteria fare to groups of all ages and sizes. Founder Grady Allred Sr. purchased the original location from Messrs. Knight and Wilson (hence the company's name) in 1940. His family continues to own the company.

K&W Cafeterias operates more than 30 cafeteria-style restaurants in North Carolina, South Carolina, Virginia, and West Virginia. Locations offer take-out service in addition to its dining room meals.

EXECUTIVES

President: Jimmy Sizemore
VP Administration and Finance: Leo Sasaki

LOCATIONS

HQ: K&W Cafeterias Inc.
1391 Plaza West Dr., Winston-Salem, NC 27114
Phone: 336-760-0526   **Fax:** 336-659-0032
Web: www.kwcafeterias.com

K&W Cafeterias operates restaurants in North Carolina, South Carolina, Virginia, and West Virginia.

COMPETITORS

Buffet Partners
Buffets Holdings
Luby's
Piccadilly Cafeterias
Shoney's
Smith & Sons

HISTORICAL FINANCIALS

Company Type: Private

Income Statement

FYE: June 30

	REVENUE ($ mil.)	NET INCOME ($ mil.)	NET PROFIT MARGIN	EMPLOYEES
6/04	107	—	—	2,500
6/03	100	—	—	2,500
6/02	106	—	—	—
6/01	103	—	—	—
6/00	95	—	—	—
Annual Growth	**3.0%**	—	—	**0.0%**

Revenue History

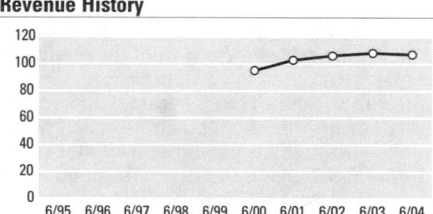

120	
100	
80	
60	
40	
20	
0	
	6/95 6/96 6/97 6/98 6/99 6/00 6/01 6/02 6/03 6/04

Kaiser Foundation Health Plan

Kaiser Foundation Health Plan aims to be the emperor of the HMO universe. With more than 8 million members in nine states and the District of Columbia, it is one of the largest not-for-profit managed health care companies in the US. Kaiser has an integrated care model, offering both hospital and physician care through a network of hospitals and physician practices operating under the Kaiser Permanente name. Members of Kaiser health plans have access to hospitals and some 400 other health care facilities operated by Kaiser Foundation Hospitals and Permanente Medical Groups, associations consisting of about 11,000 doctors.

California is the company's largest market, with more than 75% of its members.

A string of losses due to skyrocketing costs and stiff competition from commercial providers of managed care have prompted Kaiser to raise rates and divest under performing units.

Kaiser's strategy for growth and profitability consists of strengthening its integrated care model via increased use of technology, and construction of new health care facilities.

HISTORY

Henry Kaiser — shipbuilder, war profiteer, builder of the Hoover and Grand Coulee dams, and founder of Kaiser Aluminum — was a bootstrap capitalist who did well by doing good. A high school dropout from upstate New York, Kaiser moved to Spokane, Washington, in 1906 and went into road construction. During the Depression, he headed the consortium that built the great WPA dams.

It was in building the Grand Coulee Dam that, in 1938, Kaiser teamed with Dr. Sidney Garfield, who earlier had devised a prepayment health plan for workers on California public works projects. As Kaiser moved into steelmaking and shipbuilding during WWII (turning out some 1,400 bare-bones Liberty ships — one per day at peak production), Kaiser decided healthy workers produce more than sick ones, and he called on Garfield to set up on-site clinics funded by the US government as part of operating expenses. Garfield was released from military service by President Roosevelt for the purpose.

After the war, the clinics became war surplus. Kaiser and his wife bought them — at a 99% discount — through the new Kaiser Hospital Foundation. His vision was to provide the public with low-cost, prepaid medical care. He created the health plan — the self-supporting entity that would administer the system — and the group medical organization, Permanente (named after Kaiser's first cement plant site). He then endowed the health plan with $200,000. This health plan, the classic HMO model, was criticized by the medical establishment as socialized medicine performed by "employee" doctors.

But the plan flourished, becoming California's #1 medical system. In 1958 Kaiser retired to Hawaii and started his health plan there. But physician resistance limited national growth;

HMOs were illegal in some states well into the 1970s.

As health care costs rose, Congress legalized HMOs in all states. Kaiser expanded in the 1980s; as it moved outside its traditional geographic areas, the company contracted for space in hospitals rather than build them. Growth slowed as competition increased.

Some health care costs in California fell in the early 1990s as more medical procedures were performed on an outpatient basis. Specialists flooded the state, and as price competition among doctors and hospitals heated up, many HMOs landed advantageous contracts. Kaiser, with its own highly paid doctors, was unable to realize the same savings and was no longer the best deal in town. Its membership stalled.

To boost membership and control expenses, Kaiser instituted a controversial program in 1996 in which nurses earned bonuses for cost-cutting. Critics said the program could lead to a decrease in care quality; Kaiser later became the focus of investigations into wrongful death suits linked to cost-cutting in California (where it has since beefed up staffing and programs) and Texas (where it has agreed to pay $1 million in fines).

In 1997 Kaiser and Washington-based Group Health Cooperative of Puget Sound formed Kaiser/Group Health to handle administrative services in the Northwest. Kaiser also tried to boost membership by lowering premiums, but the strategy proved *too* effective: Costs linked to an unwieldy 20% enrollment surge brought a loss in 1997 — Kaiser's first annual loss ever.

A second year in the red in 1998 prompted Kaiser to sell its Texas operations to Sierra Health Services. It also entered the Florida market via an alliance with Miami-based AvMed Health Plan. In 1999 Kaiser announced plans to sell its unprofitable North Carolina operations (it closed the deal the following year).

In 2000 Kaiser announced plans to charge premiums for its Medicare HMO, Medicare Advantage, to offset the shortfall in federal reimbursements. Kaiser also responded to rising costs by selling its unprofitable operations in North Carolina (2000) and Kansas (2001). In 2001 the company's hospital division bought the technology and assets of defunct Internet grocer Webvan in an effort to increase its distribution activity. Also that year the son of a deceased anthrax victim sued a Kaiser facility for failing to recognize and treat his father's symptoms.

EXECUTIVES

Chairman and CEO: George C. Halvorson
SVP, Community Benefit: Raymond J. (Ray) Baxter
SVP, Research and Policy Development:
  Robert M. Crane
SVP, CIO, and Chief Administrative Officer:
  J. Clifford (Cliff) Dodd
SVP and Chief Compliance Officer:
  Daniel P. (Dan) Garcia
SVP, National Contracting Purchasing and Distribution:
  Joseph W. Hummel
SVP, Strategic Planning and Interim CFO:
  Kathy Lancaster
SVP, Sales and Account Management:
  Lawrence (Larry) Leisure
SVP, Quality and Clinical Systems Support:
  Louise L. Liang
SVP, Hospital Strategy and Operations Support:
  Christine Malcolm, age 55
SVP, Health Plan and Hospital Operations:
  Leslie A. Margolin
SVP, General Counsel, and Secretary: Kirk E. Miller
SVP, Human Resources: Laurence G. O'Neil
SVP and Director for Care and Services Quality:
  Patricia B. Siegel
SVP, Product and Market Management:
  Arthur M. Southam
SVP, Communications and External Relations:
  Bernard J. Tyson
SVP, Government Relations and Permanente Partnership Support: Steven (Steve) Zatkin
VP, National HIPAA Compliance and Kaiser Permanente Information Technology (KP-IT) Compliance: Mary Henderson
VP and Treasurer: Tom Meier
VP, Clinical Information System (CIS) Project:
  Bruce Turkstra
Auditors: KPMG LLP

LOCATIONS

HQ: Kaiser Foundation Health Plan, Inc.
  1 Kaiser Plaza, Oakland, CA 94612
Phone: 510-271-5800   **Fax:** 510-271-6493
Web: www.kaiserpermanente.org

Kaiser Foundation Health Plan operates in California, Colorado, Georgia, Hawaii, Maryland, Ohio, Oregon, Virginia, Washington, and the District of Columbia.

COMPETITORS

Aetna
Blue Cross
Blue Cross of California
Blue Shield Of California
CIGNA
Health Net
Humana
Molina Healthcare
Oxford Health
PacifiCare
PacifiCare of Colorado
Premera Blue Cross
Regence BlueShield
Regence Group
Sharp Health Plan
Sierra Health
UnitedHealth Group
WellPoint

HISTORICAL FINANCIALS

Company Type: Subsidiary

Income Statement

FYE: December 31

	REVENUE ($ mil.)	NET INCOME ($ mil.)	NET PROFIT MARGIN	EMPLOYEES
12/03	25,300	996	3.9%	54,300
12/02	22,500	70	0.3%	47,300
12/01	19,700	681	3.5%	111,000
12/00	17,700	590	3.3%	90,000
12/99	16,841	(6)	—	90,000
12/98	15,500	(288)	—	100,000
12/97	14,500	(270)	—	100,000
12/96	13,241	265	2.0%	90,000
12/95	12,290	550	4.5%	85,000
12/94	12,268	816	6.7%	84,845
Annual Growth	8.4%	2.2%	—	(4.8%)

Net Income History

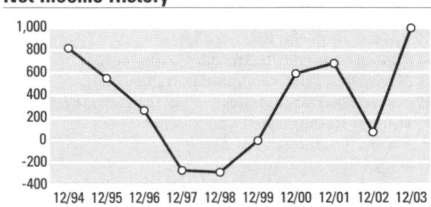

Kaiser Permanente

Kaiser Permanente hopes to be a permanent fixture in health care in the US. The not-for-profit entity is among the largest integrated health care systems in the US. The company offers health care services through a network of about 11,000 physicians belonging to Permanente Medical Groups; 30 medical centers and more than 430 medical offices that form the Kaiser Foundation Hospitals; and the Kaiser Foundation Health Plan, which covers more than 8 million lives (the bulk of which is in California). Kaiser Permanente is primarily bi-coastal, active in California, Colorado, Georgia, Hawaii, Maryland, Ohio, Oregon, Virginia, Washington, and Washington, DC.

The company's empire is divided into geographic regions: California Division (divided into Northern and Southern regions); Colorado Region; Georgia Region; Hawaii Region; Mid-Atlantic Region (Maryland, Virginia, and Washington, D.C.); Ohio Region; and the Northwest Region (Oregon and Washington). Although Kaiser Permanente owns hospitals only in California, Hawaii, and Oregon, it provides services to its members in the other areas it operates through contracts with health care facilities. The company has an alliance with Group Health Cooperative that extends its network in the Pacific Northwest.

To better serve its roughly 3.2 million participants in Northern California (about 40% of its total enrollment), Kaiser Permanente in 2004 reorganized its operations in the region, forming about a dozen service areas, each with a major Kaiser-affiliated medical center at its core. The company is doling out a fair amount of money in the state, spending more than $1.2 billion to build four new hospitals and bring its facilities up to earthquake safety codes.

In addition to providing health care plans and services, Kaiser Permanente conducts medical research and offers health education to the communities it serves. The organization is also something of a pioneer in health care administration: The automated electronic medical records system installed in 2003 is accessible to members and physicians and should help the company reap significant cost savings. (Kaiser plans to spend some $3 billion through 2013 on administrative technology.)

EXECUTIVES

Chairman, President, and CEO: George C. Halvorson
SVP and CFO: Kathy Lancaster
SVP, Community Benefit; Interim President, Kaiser Foundation Health Plan and Kaiser Foundation Hospitals, Southern California Region:
Raymond J. (Ray) Baxter
SVP, Research and Policy Development:
Robert M. Crane
SVP, Finance: Larry Wilson
SVP, CIO, and Chief Administrative Officer:
J. Clifford (Cliff) Dodd
SVP, Sales and Account Management:
Lawrence (Larry) Leisure

SVP, Quality and Clinical Systems Support:
Louise L. Liang
SVP, Health Plan and Hospital Operations:
Leslie A. Margolin
SVP, Human Resources: Laurence G. O'Neil
SVP, Product and Market Management:
Arthur M. Southam
SVP, Communications and External Relations:
Bernard J. Tyson
VP and CTO: David Watson
Auditors: KPMG LLP

LOCATIONS

HQ: Kaiser Permanente
1 Kaiser Plaza, Ste. 2600, Oakland, CA 94612
Phone: 510-271-5800   **Fax:** 510-267-7524
Web: www.kaiserpermanente.org

COMPETITORS

Aetna	The Cleveland Clinic
Blue Cross	HCA
Catholic Health Initiatives	Humana
Catholic Healthcare	PacifiCare
Partners	Sutter Health
Catholic Healthcare West	Tenet Healthcare
CIGNA	UnitedHealth Group

HISTORICAL FINANCIALS

Company Type: Not-for-profit

Income Statement

FYE: December 31

	REVENUE ($ mil.)	NET INCOME ($ mil.)	NET PROFIT MARGIN	EMPLOYEES
12/03	25,300	996	3.9%	147,000
12/02	22,500	70	0.3%	136,511
Annual Growth	12.4%	1,322.9%	—	7.7%

Net Income History

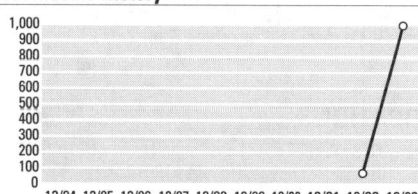

Kaiser Ventures

Recycled from the former Kaiser Steel, Kaiser Ventures oversees recycling and solid waste investments. The company's holdings include an 82% stake in Mine Reclamation Corporation (MRC) and a 50% stake in West Valley Materials Recovery Facility and Transfer Station, which separates waste materials for recycling or storage. Through MRC, the company has turned Kaiser Steel's iron-ore mining pits into a rail-accessible solid waste landfill at Eagle Mountain in the California desert; it has agreed to sell the landfill to County District No. 2 of Los Angeles County. Kaiser Ventures is owned mainly by former creditors of Kaiser Steel.

In addition to its waste management assets, Kaiser Ventures owns or controls about 5,400 acres of land at the Eagle Mountain site that is not included in the pending sale of the landfill.

Kaiser Steel filed for bankruptcy protection back in 1987. The mission of Kaiser Ventures is to manage the remaining Kaiser assets in order to maximize the amount of cash distributed to shareholders. Entities with stakes in what's left of Kaiser include an employee pension fund (10%) and the federal Pension Benefit Guaranty Corporation (6%).

EXECUTIVES

Chairman, President, and CEO: Richard E. Stoddard, age 54
Vice Chairman: Gerald A. Fawcett, age 72
EVP Finance and CFO: James F. Verhey, age 57
EVP Administration, General Counsel, and Corporate Secretary: Terry L. Cook, age 49
VP Finance: Paul E. Shampay, age 43
Manager and Director: Ronald E. Bitonti, age 72
Manager and Director: Todd G. Cole, age 84
Manager and Director: Marshall F. Wallach, age 62
Auditors: Moss Adams, LLP

LOCATIONS

HQ: Kaiser Ventures LLC
3633 East Inland Empire Blvd., Ste. 480, Ontario, CA 91764
Phone: 909-483-8500   **Fax:** 909-944-6605
Web: www.kaiserventures.com

COMPETITORS

Allied Waste
Norcal Waste
Republic Services
Waste Connections
Waste Management

HISTORICAL FINANCIALS

Company Type: Private

Income Statement

FYE: December 31

	REVENUE ($ mil.)	NET INCOME ($ mil.)	NET PROFIT MARGIN	EMPLOYEES
12/04	2	(0)	—	9
12/03	2	(4)	—	11
12/02	1	(0)	—	13
12/01	68	49	72.0%	16
12/00	8	13	175.0%	22
12/99	52	24	46.5%	28
12/98	10	1	12.1%	21
12/97	10	1	8.0%	27
12/96	15	3	16.9%	27
12/95	11	1	12.6%	30
Annual Growth	(17.8%)	—	—	(12.5%)

2004 Year-End Financials

Debt ratio: 0.0%
Return on equity: —
Cash ($ mil.): 4
Current ratio: 6.11
Long-term debt ($ mil.): 0

Net Income History

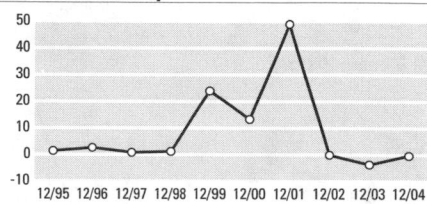

Kaleida Health

Operating five acute-care facilities with some 2,500 beds, Kaleida Health serves the residents of western New York. The health system's hospitals are Buffalo General Hospital, The Women & Children's Hospital of Buffalo, DeGraff Memorial Hospital, Millard Fillmore Gates Circle Hospital, and Millard Fillmore Suburban Hospital. Primary care needs are met through a network of community and school-based clinics. Kaleida Health also operates four skilled nursing care facilities and provides home health care. To help train future medical professionals, Buffalo General Hospital is a teaching affiliate of the State University of New York.

EXECUTIVES

Chair: Edward F. Walsh Jr.
Vice Chair: Brian J. Lipke, age 53
CEO: William D. (Bill) McGuire, age 61
President and COO: James R. (Jim) Kaskie, age 52
EVP and Chief Medical Officer: Margaret Paroski
EVP and CFO: Robert L. (Bob) Glenning
SVP and Chief Learning Officer: Connie Krasinksi
SVP, Public Affairs and Development:
 Stephen McClellan
SVP, Legal Services and General Counsel; Acting SVP, Human Resources: Robert Nolan
VP, Ambulatory Services and Business Development:
 Donald Boyd
Secretary: James A.W. McLeod
Treasurer: Robert M. Zak, age 47
Director, Public Relations: Michael Hughes
Auditors: KPMG LLP

LOCATIONS

HQ: Kaleida Health
 100 High St., Buffalo, NY 14203
Phone: 716-859-2834   **Fax:** 716-859-3323
Web: www.kaleidahealth.org

COMPETITORS

Catholic Health System

HISTORICAL FINANCIALS

Company Type: Not-for-profit

Income Statement

FYE: December 31

	REVENUE ($ mil.)	NET INCOME ($ mil.)	NET PROFIT MARGIN	EMPLOYEES
12/04	872	8	0.9%	10,000
12/03	824	2	0.2%	9,724
Annual Growth	5.8%	275.0%	—	2.8%

2004 Year-End Financials

Debt ratio: —   Current ratio: —
Return on equity: 4.1%   Long-term debt ($ mil.): —
Cash ($ mil.): —

Net Income History

12/95 12/96 12/97 12/98 12/99 12/00 12/01 12/02 12/03 12/04

KB Toys

KB Toys desperately hopes toy buyers will take their haul from the mall. One of the largest toy retailers in the US, mall-based KB Toys operates about 650 stores and KB Toy Express (in operation during the holiday season). The company filed for Chapter 11 bankruptcy in January 2004, resulting in nearly 600 store closures and 4,000 layoffs. In March 2004 KB Toys sold its KBToys.com Internet business to an affiliate of D. E. Shaw, which renamed the company eToys Direct. The Web site KBToys.com is now run by eToys Direct via a licensing agreement. KB emerged from Chapter 11 in August 2005 with a new owner, Prentice Capital Management, and a new CEO, Gregory Staley, former president of Toys "R" Us.

The company emerged from bankruptcy without more store closings or layoffs but had to settled lawsuits against executives and directors regarding use of company money prior to the Chapter 11 filing. The new owners brought in the toy-experienced CEO and another Toys "R" Us ex-exec as director and consultant.

EXECUTIVES

President and CEO: Greg Staley
EVP and COO: William L. (Bill) McMahon
EVP and CFO: Robert J. Feldman
EVP, Operations and Stores: James C. Solon
EVP, Corporate Buying Group: Sal Vasta
SVP, Human Resources: Gerald P. (Gerry) Murray, age 46
SVP, Merchandising: Charles (C.B.) Alberts
SVP, Product Development: Thomas J. (Tom) Alfonsi
VP and Controller: Joel Wiest
VP, Finance: David T. Pyne, age 36
VP, Marketing and Advertising: Bonnie Burton
VP, Sales: Pete Lungo
General Counsel and Secretary: Scott Z. Hochfelder, age 41

LOCATIONS

HQ: KB Toys, Inc.
 100 West St., Pittsfield, MA 01201
Phone: 413-496-3000   **Fax:** 413-496-3616
Web: www.kbtoys.com

KB Toys has distribution and fulfillment centers in Alabama, Arizona, Kentucky, Massachusetts, and New Jersey; it has store locations in Guam, Puerto Rico, and the US.

COMPETITORS

Amazon.com
GameStop
Gymboree
Kmart
Sears
Target
Toys "R" Us
Wal-Mart

HISTORICAL FINANCIALS

Company Type: Private

Income Statement

FYE: January 31

	ESTIMATED REVENUE ($ mil.)	NET INCOME ($ mil.)	NET PROFIT MARGIN	EMPLOYEES
1/04	1,200	—	—	15,000
1/03	2,000	—	—	24,000
1/02	2,000	—	—	25,000
1/01	2,000	—	—	16,000
1/00	1,767	—	—	13,000
Annual Growth	(9.2%)	—	—	3.6%

Revenue History

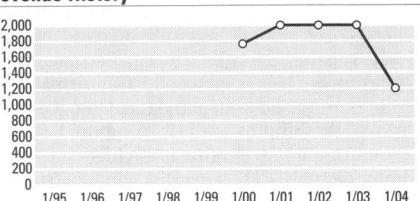

1/95 1/96 1/97 1/98 1/99 1/00 1/01 1/02 1/03 1/04

Kellogg Foundation

Charitable grants from W.K. Kellogg Foundation are gr-r-reat! Founded in 1930 by cereal industry pioneer Will Keith Kellogg, the foundation provides more than $200 million in grants each year to programs focused on youth and education, health, food systems and rural development, and philanthropy and volunteerism. Most of its grants go to initiatives in the US, though it also makes grants throughout Latin America and Africa. The foundation's work is funded primarily from its nearly $6 billion trust.

W.K. Kellogg Foundation is guided by its founder's desire "to help people help themselves" and prefers funding programs that offer long-term solutions rather than quick handouts. In 1934 Kellogg donated $66 million in stock to the foundation, which now ranks as one of the largest charitable organizations in the world.

W.K. Kellogg Foundation, which owns nearly a third of the Kellogg Company, is governed by an independent board of trustees.

HISTORY

Born in 1860, Will Keith Kellogg's early jobs included those of stock boy and traveling broom salesman. He also worked as a clerk (and, later, bookkeeper and manager) at the Battle Creek Sanitarium, a renowned homeopathic hospital where his older brother, John Harvey Kellogg, was physician-in-chief. The brothers' experiments to improve vegetarian diets led to a happy accident in 1894 that resulted in the first wheat flakes. In 1906 W.K. Kellogg started the Battle Creek Toasted Corn Flake Company. Through marketing genius and innovative products, Kellogg's company became a leader in the industry.

A philanthropist by inclination, Kellogg established the Fellowship Corporation in 1925 to build an agricultural school and a bird sanctuary, as well as to set up an experimental farm and a reforestation project. He also gave $3 million to hometown causes, such as the Ann J. Kellogg School for disabled children, and for the construction of an auditorium, a junior high school, and a youth recreation center.

After attending a White House Conference on Child Health and Protection, Kellogg established the W.K. Kellogg Child Welfare Foundation in 1930. A few months later he broadened the focus of the charter and renamed the institution the W.K. Kellogg Foundation. That year the foundation began its landmark Michigan Community Health Project (MCHP), which opened public health departments in counties once thought too small and poor to sustain them. In 1934 Kellogg placed more than $66 million in Kellogg Company stock and other investments in a trust to fund his foundation.

During WWII the foundation expanded its programming to Latin America, funding advanced schooling for dentists, physicians, and other health professionals. After the war, it broadened its programming to include agriculture to help war-torn Europe. It funded projects in Germany, Iceland, Ireland, Norway, and the UK. Following Kellogg's death in 1951, the organization began providing support for graduate programs in health and hospital administration, as well as for rural leadership and community colleges.

During the 1970s the foundation lent its support to the growing volunteerism movement and to aiding the disadvantaged, with a special emphasis on programs for minorities. A review of operations in the late 1970s led the Kellogg Foundation to reassert its emphasis on health, education, agriculture, and leadership. The foundation also expanded its programs to southern Africa.

In 1986 The Kellogg Foundation began funding the Rural America Initiative — a series of 28 projects meant to develop leadership, train local government officials, and revitalize rural areas. William Richardson became president and CEO of the foundation in 1995, leaving his post as president of The Johns Hopkins University. Also during the 1990s the foundation supported the Community-Based Public Health Initiative, which assisted universities in educating public health professionals by presenting community-based approaches to students and faculty.

In 1998 the organization announced a five-year, $55 million plan to bring health care to the nation's poor and homeless. Also that year it gave Portland State University a $600,000 grant to develop its Institute for Nonprofit Management. In 1999 the Kellogg Foundation started its first geographically based program, pledging $15 million in grants for development of Mississippi River Delta communities in Arkansas, Louisiana, and Mississippi. In 2001 the foundation pledged an additional $20 million to support economic growth in the region through the Emerging Markets Partnership. In 2002 the Kellogg Foundation awarded about $2 million in grants to SPARK (Supporting Partnerships to Assure Ready Kids) to help prepare low-income children for starting school. The organization funded a national campaign to improve men's health in 2003.

EXECUTIVES

President and CEO: William C. (Bill) Richardson, age 64
President and CEO: Sterling Speirn
SVP Programs: Anne C. Petersen
SVP and Corporate Secretary: Gregory A. Lyman
Interim SVP Programming: James E. McHale

VP and Chief Investment Officer: Paul J. Lawler
VP Finance and Treasurer: La June Montgomery-Talley
VP Philanthropy and Volunteerism: Robert Long
VP Programs: Richard M. Foster
VP Programs: Marguerite M. Johnson
VP Programs: Robert F. (Bob) Long
VP Programs: Gail D. McClure
Director Human Resources: Norm Howard
Director Marketing and Communications:
  Karen E. Lake
Director Technology: Tim Dechant
Portfolio and Investment Manager: Malcolm Goepfert
General Counsel and Assistant Corporate Secretary:
  Mary C. Cotter
Auditors: Deloitte & Touche LLP

LOCATIONS

HQ: W.K. Kellogg Foundation
  1 Michigan Ave. East, Battle Creek, MI 49017
Phone: 269-968-1611   **Fax:** 269-968-0413
Web: www.wkkf.org

2004 Grants

	$ mil.	% of total
US	177.3	81
Latin America & the Caribbean	21.8	10
Southern Africa	20.6	9
Total	**219.7**	**100**

PRODUCTS/OPERATIONS

2004 Grants

	$ mil.	% of total
Youth & education	40.4	19
Philanthropy and volunteerism	26.2	12
Program activities	24.7	11
Health	23.8	11
Latin America & the Caribbean	21.8	10
Southern Africa	20.6	9
Special opportunities	19.5	9
Food systems & rural development	19.3	9
Recurring grants	9.9	4
Greater Battle Creek	9.4	4
Cross Program/Detroit RiverWalk Project	4.1	2
Total	**219.7**	**100**

HISTORICAL FINANCIALS

Company Type: Foundation

Income Statement   FYE: August 31

	REVENUE ($ mil.)	NET INCOME ($ mil.)	NET PROFIT MARGIN	EMPLOYEES
8/04	328	—	—	—
8/03	277	—	—	203
8/02	250	—	—	200
8/01	223	—	—	209
8/00	277	—	—	250
8/99	327	—	—	290
8/98	330	—	—	286
8/97	374	—	—	280
8/96	298	—	—	276
8/95	271	—	—	264
Annual Growth	**2.1%**	**—**	**—**	**(3.2%)**

Revenue History

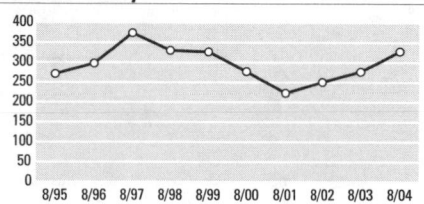

Kentucky Lottery

Kentucky's grass may be blue, but many Kentuckians prefer green — the kind they can stuff into their wallets. For optimists looking to bag some bucks, the Kentucky Lottery offers numbers games (Pick 3, Pick 4, Lotto South) and an array of scratch-off and pull-tab games (Hot Cherries, NutQuacker, Bluegrass Highway). Kentucky also participates in the multistate Powerball game. About a quarter of the lottery's proceeds go to education grants and scholarships, literacy programs for adults and children, and Kentucky's General Fund. Launched in 1989, the lottery has introduced new games as it struggles with intense competition from nearby casinos and nearby Tennessee's new lottery.

EXECUTIVES

President and CEO: Arthur L. (Arch) Gleason Jr.
EVP and COO: Margaret (Marty) Gibbs
SVP Finance and Administration: Howard Kline
SVP Information Systems: Harvey Roberts
SVP Marketing and Sales: Steve Casebeer
SVP Security: Bill Hickerson
VP Human Resources: Church Saufley
VP Internal Audit: Gale Vessels
VP Marketing: Betsy Paulley
VP Sales: Robert (Bob) Little
VP Systems Development: Linda Stark
Director Operations: Larry Smith
Director Planning and Research: Larry Newby
General Counsel: Mary Harville

LOCATIONS

HQ: Kentucky Lottery Corporation
  1011 W. Main St., Louisville, KY 40202
Phone: 502-560-1500   **Fax:** 502-560-1670
Web: www.kylottery.com

The Kentucky Lottery Corporation has regional offices in Bowling Green, Jefferson, Lexington, Louisville, Madisonville, and Prestonsburg, Kentucky.

PRODUCTS/OPERATIONS

Selected Games

Numbers Games	Scratch-offs
Kentucky Cash Ball	Beat the Heat
Kentucky Powerball	Blackjack 21
Lotto South	Hot Dice
Pick 3	In the Bank
Pick 4	Lucky Queen
Pull-Tabs	Rake in the Money
Ace in the Hole	Slots of Fun
Cherry Hearts	Vacation Cash
Lucky $599	Your Lucky Day
Sweet & Spicy 7's	

COMPETITORS

Argosy Gaming
Aztar
Churchill Downs
Hoosier Lottery
Illinois Lottery
Trump
Virginia Lottery

HISTORICAL FINANCIALS

Company Type: Government-owned

Income Statement

FYE: July 31

	REVENUE ($ mil.)	NET INCOME ($ mil.)	NET PROFIT MARGIN	EMPLOYEES
7/04	725	—	—	204
7/03	674	—	—	204
7/02*	600	—	—	200
6/01	591	—	—	200
6/00	584	—	—	200
6/99	583	—	—	200
6/98	585	—	—	205
6/97	569	—	—	210
6/96	543	—	—	205
6/95	513	—	—	205
Annual Growth	**3.9%**	**—**	**—**	**(0.1%)**

*Fiscal year change

Revenue History

```
800
700
600
500
400
300
200
100
  0
     6/95 6/96 6/97 6/98 6/99 6/00 6/01 7/02 7/03 7/04
```

Key Safety Systems

This Key won't start your car, but it will protect the occupants. Key Safety Systems is a leading maker of air bags and air bag components. The company also makes steering wheels and seat belts. Key Safety Systems' line of air bag products includes sensors, inflators, driver-side and steering-wheel air bag combinations, and side-impact air bag systems. The company supplies air bag systems to most of the world's carmakers. Key Safety Systems also makes a line of interior trim products, including automatic and manual shift knobs, parking brake handles, shift and brake boots, armrest covers, and pull handles. The company is part of Key Automotive Group, which is controlled by investment firm Ewing Management.

Carlyle Management Group, the turnaround arm of investment firm The Carlyle Group, bought Key Safety Systems (then known as BREED Technologies) in April 2003. Carlyle Management principal Edward Ewing became CEO and soon announced sweeping cost-cutting plans. The company cut 3,500 jobs across its global operations (27% of the workforce) and negotiated for price breaks from its suppliers.

The company changed its name to Key Safety Systems in September 2003 and was folded into Key Automotive Group, which also includes Key Plastics.

In 2004 Carlyle Management, led by Ewing, split off from Carlyle Group to form a new company, Ewing Management.

EXECUTIVES

Chairman and CEO: B. Edward Ewing
President and COO; President and COO, Asia: Jason Luo
SVP and CFO: Dave Smith
SVP, Human Resources: Rick Blough
SVP, Legal: Stuart D. Boyd
SVP, Global Sales and Marketing: Ron Feldeisen
VP, Public Relations: Peter McElroy
President and COO, North America; President, Airbags and Inflators North America: Greg Heald
President, Seat Belts and Steering Wheels, North America: Wendell C. Lane Jr.
President and COO, Europe; President, Airbags and Inflators Europe: Mark Wehner

LOCATIONS

HQ: Key Safety Systems, Inc.
7000 Nineteen Mile Rd., Sterling Heights, MI 48314
Phone: 586-726-3800
Web: www.keysafetyinc.com

PRODUCTS/OPERATIONS

Selected Products

Airbag systems, inflators, and modules
Armrest covers
Electronics (crash sensors)
Parking brake handles
Seat-belt systems
Shift and brake boots
Shift knobs
Steering wheels

COMPETITORS

Analog Devices	OZ Italy Wheel
Autocam	PerkinElmer
Autoliv	Robert Bosch
DENSO	SensoNor
Fondmetal	Siemens
Hi-Shear Technology	Temic
Honeywell International	Texas Instruments
Motorola	Tokai Rika
Oki Electric	

HISTORICAL FINANCIALS

Company Type: Private

Income Statement

FYE: June 30

	REVENUE ($ mil.)	NET INCOME ($ mil.)	NET PROFIT MARGIN	EMPLOYEES
6/04	1,100	—	—	8,000
6/03	1,100	—	—	10,000
6/02	1,100	—	—	16,000
6/01	1,422	—	—	16,000
6/00	1,400	—	—	16,100
6/99	1,400	—	—	16,200
6/98	1,385	—	—	16,300
6/97	795	—	—	11,100
6/96	432	—	—	7,000
6/95	401	—	—	4,800
Annual Growth	**11.9%**	**—**	**—**	**5.8%**

Revenue History

```
1,600
1,400
1,200
1,000
  800
  600
  400
  200
    0
     6/95 6/96 6/97 6/98 6/99 6/00 6/01 6/02 6/03 6/04
```

Keystone Foods

Keystone Foods hopes you won't just have the salad. The company is one of the largest makers of hamburger patties and processed poultry. It's a major supplier to McDonald's restaurants; in the 1970s Keystone persuaded McDonald's to switch to frozen beef to reduce the health risks associated with fresh beef. Overseas, operations include McKey Food Services and MacFood Services (some are joint ventures). In addition to its worldwide meat processing plants, which produce millions of burgers daily, Keystone also operates M&M Restaurant Supply and has begun to supply fresh beef to a US grocery retailer. Through subsidiary STI France, the company offers logistics services in Europe. Chairman and CEO Herb Lotman owns the company, which began as a beef-boning business in the 1960s.

EXECUTIVES

Chairman and CEO: Herbert (Herb) Lotman, age 70
President and COO: Jerry Dean
EVP and CFO: John Coggins
SVP and Controller: Paul McGarvie
VP, Human Resources: Jerry Gotro
VP, Information Systems: Ken Wierman
VP, Quality Assurance and Food Safety: Dane Bernard
CEO, STI France: Philippe Lejeune
Administrative and Financial Supervisor, STI France: Françoise Gauvreau
Road Chartering Officer, STI France: Pierre Borrego
Chartering Executive, STI France: Aziz Zahdane
Dedicated Fleet Executive, STI France: Christine Luquet
Sales Executive, STI France: Laurent Roussille
Auditors: Ernst & Young LLP

LOCATIONS

HQ: Keystone Foods LLC
300 Barr Harbor Dr., Ste. 600, West Conshohocken, PA 19428
Phone: 610-667-6700   **Fax:** 610-667-1460
Web: www.keystonefoods.com

Keystone Foods serves customers in Asia, Australia, Europe, the Middle East, and the US.

PRODUCTS/OPERATIONS

Selected Products

Beef
  Fajita strips
  Hamburger patties
Chicken
  Breaded patties
  Breast filets
  Diced
  Fajita strips
  Nuggets
  Wings
Fish
Pork

COMPETITORS

Anderson-DuBose	OSI Group LLC
ConAgra	Perdue
Gold Kist	Pilgrim's Pride
Golden State Foods	SYSCO
Lopez Foods	Tyson Foods
Martin-Brower	Tyson Fresh Meats
McLane Foodservice	U.S. Foodservice

HISTORICAL FINANCIALS

Company Type: Private

Income Statement
FYE: December 31

	ESTIMATED REVENUE ($ mil.)	NET INCOME ($ mil.)	NET PROFIT MARGIN	EMPLOYEES
12/03	2,800	—	—	6,500
12/02	2,600	—	—	6,700
12/01	2,700	—	—	6,700
12/00	2,650	—	—	6,700
12/99	2,594	—	—	6,700
12/98	2,342	—	—	4,300
12/97	2,184	—	—	4,300
12/96	1,900	—	—	4,000
12/95	1,700	—	—	2,000
12/94	1,600	—	—	—
Annual Growth	6.4%	—	—	15.9%

Revenue History

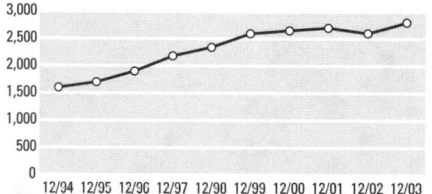

Kimball Hill

Chicagoland's GI generation and their off-spring, who have long thrived in the 'burbs, can thank lawyer-turned-builder D. Kimball Hill, a pioneer of the city's suburbs and founder of Kimball Hill, Inc. The company, still owned and operated by the Hill family, builds single-family detached homes, townhomes, and condominiums under the name Kimball Hill Homes in the Chicago area and in California, Florida, Nevada, Ohio, Oregon, Texas, Washington, and Wisconsin. It mainly targets first-time and move-up buyers, but also builds homes up to 4,100 sq. ft. in size and $800,000 in price.

Subsidiary KH Financial offers mortgage financing and refinancing of investment properties in five states.

EXECUTIVES

Chairman and CEO: David K. Hill Jr., age 63
President and COO: Isaac Heimbinder
CFO: Gene Rowehl
CIO: Frank Scaramuzza
VP Human Resources: JoAnn Peterson
Director, Sales and Marketing: Ray Wolford
Director, Customer Satisfaction Initiative: Brent Gustafson
Auditors: Deloitte & Touche LLP

LOCATIONS

HQ: Kimball Hill, Inc.
5999 New Wilke Rd., Ste. 504,
Rolling Meadows, IL 60008
Phone: 847-364-7300 **Fax:** 847-439-0875
Web: www.kimballhill.com

Kimball Hill has principal operations in Austin, Dallas/Fort Worth, Houston, and San Antonio, Texas; Chicago; Elk Grove, Sacramento, and Stockton, California; Bradenton, Marco Island/Naples, Sarasota, and Tampa, Florida; Las Vegas, Nevada; Cleveland; Portland, Oregon; Vancouver, Washington; and Saint Francis (a Milwaukee suburb), Wisconsin.

PRODUCTS/OPERATIONS

2004 Sales

	$ mil.	% of total
Homebuilding	920.9	99
Mortgage banking	6.4	1
Total	927.3	100

COMPETITORS

Beazer Homes
Centex
David Weekley Homes
D.R. Horton
D.R. Horton, Schuler
KB Home
Lennar
M.D.C. Holdings
Morrison Homes
Neumann Homes
Pulte Homes
Ryland
Town and Country Homes

HISTORICAL FINANCIALS

Company Type: Private

Income Statement
FYE: September 30

	REVENUE ($ mil.)	NET INCOME ($ mil.)	NET PROFIT MARGIN	EMPLOYEES
9/04	927	56	6.0%	700
9/03*	793	38	4.7%	700
6/02	700	—	—	654
6/01	673	—	—	546
6/00	580	—	—	510
6/99	490	—	—	427
6/98	410	—	—	320
6/97	296	—	—	280
6/96	224	—	—	240
Annual Growth	19.4%	47.9%	—	14.3%

*Fiscal year change

Net Income History

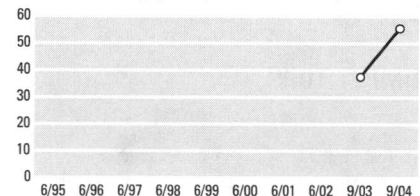

King Kullen Grocery

How's this for a crowning achievement? King Kullen Grocery Company claims to have been the originator of the supermarket format. Heralding itself as "America's first supermarket," the firm operates nearly 50 supermarkets, mainly on Long Island, New York. King Kullen also owns two Wild By Nature natural foods stores and offers a line of vitamins and supplements under the same name in some King Kullen stores. Most outlets average about 35,000 sq. ft., but it has a 62,000-sq.-ft. upscale market with features such as ethnic fare, catering, and a Wild By Nature section. Started in a Queens, New York warehouse in 1930 by Michael J. Cullen, the firm is owned and operated by Cullen's descendants.

EXECUTIVES

Chairman and CEO: Bernard D. Kennedy
Co-President and Co-COO: Brian C. Cullen
Co-President and Co-COO: J. D. Kennedy
SVP, Finance and Administration: James Flynn
SVP, Operations: Thomas (Tom) Massaro
VP, Real Estate: Ed Glackin
Director, Human Resources: Thomas Nagle
Auditors: Grant Thornton LLP

LOCATIONS

HQ: King Kullen Grocery Company, Inc.
185 Central Ave., Bethpage, NY 11714
Phone: 516-733-7100 **Fax:** 516-827-6325
Web: www.kingkullen.com

COMPETITORS

A&P	Kmart
Ahold USA	Man-dell Food Stores
C&S Wholesale	Pathmark
Gristede's Foods	Wakefern Food
IGA	Wal-Mart

HISTORICAL FINANCIALS

Company Type: Private

Income Statement
FYE: September 30

	ESTIMATED REVENUE ($ mil.)	NET INCOME ($ mil.)	NET PROFIT MARGIN	EMPLOYEES
9/04	800	—	—	5,000
9/03	800	—	—	—
9/02	790	—	—	4,800
9/01	782	—	—	4,579
9/00	720	—	—	4,400
9/99	714	—	—	4,100
9/98	725	—	—	4,500
9/97	750	—	—	4,400
9/96	724	—	—	4,500
9/95	706	—	—	4,500
Annual Growth	1.4%	—	—	1.2%

Revenue History

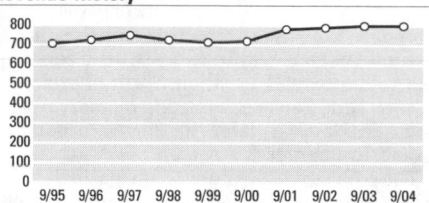

Kingston Technology

Kingston Technology cuts a regal figure in the realm of memory. The company is a top maker of memory modules — circuit boards loaded with DRAM (dynamic random-access memory) or other memory chips that increase the capacity and speed of printers and computers. Kingston also makes flash memory cards used in portable electronic devices such as digital cameras, wireless phones, and personal digital assistants. Kingston has taken on some manufacturing chores for customers through its sister company Payton Technology, which runs a specialized factory that tests and packages memory chips before assembling them into customized memory modules. Founders John Tu (president and CEO) and David Sun (COO) own the company.

Tu and Sun promote a casual atmosphere and treat employees as members of an extended family. (Their work cubicles are identical to their employees'.) Since 1996 they have given over $100 million in bonuses to workers; in some cases the bonuses have amounted to three times the employees' annual salaries.

Kingston is also known for its friendliness to business partners. It is sometimes the first to receive scarce components during shortages, thanks to the good relations it enjoys with its suppliers.

The company has inked a long-term deal with German chip heavyweight Infineon, under which Infineon is to supply much of Kingston's DRAM needs and Kingston is to provide Infineon with contract manufacturing and engineering services. Kingston has also made a $50 million investment in DRAM maker Elpida Memory.

HISTORY

Kingston Technology was founded in 1987 by Shanghai-born John Tu and Taiwan-born David Sun, both of whom had moved to California in the 1970s. The pair met in 1982 and started a memory upgrade company called Camminton Technology in Tu's garage. Sales had reached $9 million by 1986, when they sold the business to high-tech firm AST Research for $6 million. The two invested their money in stock market futures but suffered heavy losses when the market crashed in 1987.

That year PC makers were producing computers that lacked the memory needed to run the latest, hottest software, so Tu and Sun sprang into action. With just $4,000 in cash, they started another company that converted inexpensive, outdated chips into memory upgrades. Tu, who was educated in Europe, wanted to call the company Kensington after the gardens in London. A mouse pad company had that name, so Kingston was chosen.

Tu had doubts about the new company and bet Sun a Jaguar that it wouldn't survive the first year of operations. Sun won the car (which he later gave to a veteran employee who dreamed of owning one) and within two years the company had sold nearly $40 million worth of products. In 1989 Kingston began making memory system upgrades; a year later it started producing processor upgrades.

The company was #1 on *Inc.* magazine's list of fastest-growing private US companies in 1992.

The next year Kingston began marketing networking and storage products. Its vendor-friendly policy paid off that year, when demand for semiconductors far outstripped supply. Suppliers kept shipping to the company even when orders for other buyers were delayed.

In 1996 SOFTBANK paid $1.5 billion for 80% of the company but promised to preserve its culture and retain all management — including Tu and Sun — and employees. Sun and Tu set aside $100 million for employee bonuses.

In 1998 Kingston opened its first foreign manufacturing facilities, in Ireland and Taiwan. Also in 1998, in a unique arrangement suggesting that SOFTBANK overpaid when it bought Kingston, Tu and Sun agreed to forgo SOFTBANK's final $333 million payment. The following year Tu and Sun bought back SOFTBANK's stake for about $450 million. Also in 1999 the company opened a manufacturing plant in Malaysia.

After years of making computer storage devices, Kingston in 2000 formed a separate company, StorCase Technology, which specializes in storage equipment. The following year Kingston discontinued its Peripheral Products Division's offerings.

Also in 2001 Kingston launched a joint venture (and opened a new plant) in China with computer maker China Great Wall Computer Shenzhen Company.

Annual revenues topped $2 billion for the first time in 2004.

EXECUTIVES

President and CEO: John Tu, age 63
COO: David Sun
CFO: Koichi Hosokawa
SVP, Sales and Marketing: Mike Sager
VP, Administration (HR): Daniel Hsu
Digital Storage Product Manager: Mike Kuppinger

LOCATIONS

HQ: Kingston Technology Company, Inc.
17600 Newhope St., Fountain Valley, CA 92708
Phone: 714-435-2600 **Fax:** 714-435-2699
Web: www.kingston.com

Kingston Technology has operations in Australia, China, France, Germany, Ireland, Malaysia, Taiwan, the UK, and the US.

PRODUCTS/OPERATIONS

Selected Products

Flash memory cards (CompactFlash, DataFlash, MultiMediaCard)
Memory modules and add-on boards
Standard memory modules (ValueRAM)

COMPETITORS

AMD	Micron Technology
Amkor	M-Systems
ASE Test Limited	PNY Technologies
Centon	Samsung Electronics
Dataram	SanDisk
Elpida	Silicon Storage
Hynix	SimpleTech
Intel	Unigen
Lexar	Viking InterWorks
MA Laboratories	Wintec

HISTORICAL FINANCIALS

Company Type: Private

Income Statement

FYE: December 31

	REVENUE ($ mil.)	NET INCOME ($ mil.)	NET PROFIT MARGIN	EMPLOYEES
12/03	1,800	—	—	2,200
12/02	1,450	—	—	1,884
12/01	1,020	—	—	1,900
12/00	1,625	—	—	2,000
12/99	1,400	—	—	2,000
12/98	1,000	—	—	670
12/97	1,000	—	—	663
12/96	2,100	—	—	547
12/95	1,300	—	—	450
12/94	800	—	—	310
Annual Growth	**9.4%**	—	—	**24.3%**

Revenue History

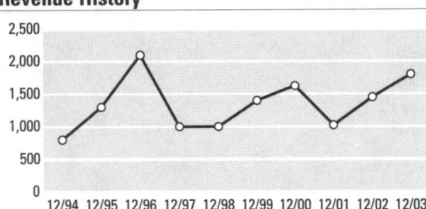

Kinray

Kinray, the US's top private wholesale drug distributor, is nothing if not independent. It provides generic, branded, and repackaged drugs, health and beauty products, medical equipment, vitamins and herbals, and diabetes-care products. The distributor also offers some 600 private label products under the Preferred Plus Pharmacy brand. It serves more than 3,000 pharmacies in seven northeastern US states. With the end of speculative buying that helped build the drug distribution industry, Kinray is looking to keep its spot at the top by increasing sales volume rather than by increasing prices. The firm was founded in 1944 by Joseph Rahr. His son, CEO and president Stewart Rahr, has owned Kinray since 1975.

Kinray spearheaded the creation of Wholesale Alliance, a group of 14 independent regional drug distributors that aims to help preserve the viability of independent pharmacies (who are customers to the wholesalers).

Stewart Rahr is one of the richest people in New York and made a splash when he paid $45 million (reportedly in cash) in early 2005 for an estate in East Hampton. The price tag made the purchase the most expensive home ever bought in the state of New York.

EXECUTIVES

President and CEO: Stewart Rahr
CFO: Howard Hirsch
EVP, Purchasing and Marketing: Sandy Greco
VP and General Manager: Bill Bodinger
VP, Sales and Marketing: Michael Rothstein
Director, Human Resources: Howard Hershberg
Design Manager: Marie McKinley
Senior Corporate Officer: Casey Bruno
Technology Officer: Michael Rapaport

LOCATIONS

HQ: Kinray Inc.
152-35 10th Ave., Whitestone, NY 11357
Phone: 718-767-1234 **Fax:** 718-767-4388
Web: www.kinray.com

Kinray operates in Connecticut, Delaware, Massachusetts, New Jersey, New York, Pennsylvania, and Rhode Island.

COMPETITORS

AmerisourceBergen
Cardinal Pharmaceutical
  Distribution
D & K
  Healthcare Resources

The F. Dohmen Co.
McKesson
QK Healthcare
Quality King

HISTORICAL FINANCIALS

Company Type: Private

Income Statement

FYE: December 31

	REVENUE ($ mil.)	NET INCOME ($ mil.)	NET PROFIT MARGIN	EMPLOYEES
12/03	2,910	—	—	700
12/02	2,500	—	—	800
12/01	2,000	—	—	600
12/00	1,710	—	—	400
12/99	1,510	—	—	350
12/98	900	—	—	275
12/97	735	—	—	250
12/96	750	—	—	225
12/95	610	—	—	210
12/94	460	—	—	170
Annual Growth	**22.7%**	**—**	**—**	**17.0%**

Revenue History

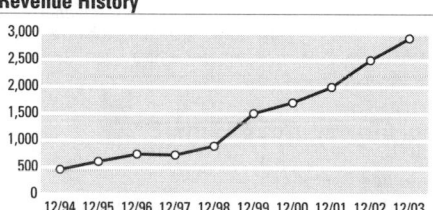

Kirkland & Ellis

Kirkland & Ellis is ready to go to court. The litigious law firm — home to former independent counsel Kenneth Starr — has been in the thick of several big courtroom battles, including defending Brown & Williamson Tobacco (it settled with the state of Minnesota for $6.5 billion in 1998). It serves other clients (Dow Corning, General Motors, Motorola) in areas such as intellectual property, antitrust, mergers and acquisitions, tort litigation, and employee benefits. Kirkland & Ellis has more than 950 lawyers in five US offices and two European offices. Founded in 1908, the firm rose to prominence with the free speech and libel law strides made by firm namesakes Weymouth Kirkland and Howard Ellis.

EXECUTIVES

Chairman: Thomas D. Yannucci
Firm Administrator: Douglas (Doug) McLemore
CFO: Nicholas J. (Nick) Willmott, age 44
CIO: Steve Novak
Director Human Resources: Wendy Cartland
Senior Marketing Manager: Maria Black
Manager Public Relations: Brian D. Pitts
Marketing Technology Coordinator: Joel Hjelmfelt

LOCATIONS

HQ: Kirkland & Ellis LLP
Aon Center, 200 E. Randolph Dr., Chicago, IL 60601
Phone: 312-861-2000 **Fax:** 312-861-2200
Web: www.kirkland.com

Kirkland & Ellis has offices in Chicago, Los Angeles, New York City, San Francisco, and Washington, DC, as well as in London and Munich, Germany.

PRODUCTS/OPERATIONS

Selected Practice Areas

Antitrust
Employee benefits
Energy
Intellectual property
Litigation
Mergers and acquisitions
Real estate
Tax
Trusts and estates
Venture capital
White-collar crime

COMPETITORS

Baker & McKenzie
Cravath, Swaine
Holland & Knight
Jenner & Block
Jones Day
Latham & Watkins
Mayer, Brown,
  Rowe & Maw

McDermott, Will
Morgan, Lewis
Shook, Hardy & Bacon
Sidley Austin
  Brown & Wood
Skadden, Arps

HISTORICAL FINANCIALS

Company Type: Partnership

Income Statement

FYE: January 31

	REVENUE ($ mil.)	NET INCOME ($ mil.)	NET PROFIT MARGIN	EMPLOYEES
1/04	725	—	—	—
1/03	611	—	—	—
1/02	530	—	—	—
1/01	470	—	—	—
1/00	410	—	—	700
1/99	310	—	—	600
1/98	255	—	—	552
1/97	229	—	—	504
1/96	220	—	—	—
1/95	215	—	—	—
Annual Growth	**14.5%**	**—**	**—**	**11.6%**

Revenue History

Kitchell

Not everything blooms in the Arizona desert, but Kitchell's buildings do. The employee-owned company, which operates in the western US, has two construction management and contracting services segments: Kitchell Contractors works with private customers in the health care, planned community, Native American, and custom home markets; Kitchell CEM works with public-sector clients, building schools, jails, municipal buildings, and performing arts centers. Kitchell also has a real estate development arm, Kitchell Development Company, that develops community, retail, office, and industrial projects. Lastly, American Refrigeration Supplies is a refrigeration and air conditioning equipment wholesaler.

The company has won a US Department of Defense contract to assist in program management for the Defense Commissary Agency. The company will help manage construction and remodeling of commissary and navy exchange projects, primarily in the US West. Kitchell currently manages more than $2 billion in new construction, expansion, or renovation projects for public-sector clients in Arizona, California, the Pacific Northwest, and the Midwest.

EXECUTIVES

Chairman Emeritus: Samuel F. Kitchell
Chairman, President, and CEO: William C. Schubert
EVP; President, Kitchell CEM: Gregory P. (Greg) Denk
VP, Marketing: Sandy Werthman
President, Kitchell Contractors: Mark J. Pendleton
President, Kitchell Custom Homes: Larry Butler
VP, Kitchell Development: Jeff Allen
VP, Kitchell Development: Don Glatthorn
Corporate Secretary: Karen S. Wolf
Controller: William (Bill) Judge
Director of Communications: Barbara Bean
Director of Human Resources: Marie Theel
Auditors: Mayer Hoffman McCann P.C.

LOCATIONS

HQ: Kitchell Corporation
1707 E. Highland Ave., Ste. 100, Phoenix, AZ 85016
Phone: 602-264-4411 **Fax:** 602-631-9112
Web: www.kitchell.com

Kitchell Corporation has offices in Carlsbad and Sacramento, California; Kansas City, Kansas; Las Vegas; and Phoenix.

PRODUCTS/OPERATIONS

Selected Subsidiaries

American Refrigeration Supplies (formerly Arizona Refrigeration Supplies; wholesale refrigeration and air-conditioning)
Kitchell CEM (design and construction of public facilities)
Kitchell Contractors (general contracting and construction management)
Kitchell Development Company (real estate development services)

COMPETITORS

Balfour Beatty
CORE Construction
Gilbane
Jacobs Engineering
McCarthy Building

Perini
Sundt
Swinerton
Turner Corporation

HISTORICAL FINANCIALS

Company Type: Private

Income Statement

FYE: December 31

	REVENUE ($ mil.)	NET INCOME ($ mil.)	NET PROFIT MARGIN	EMPLOYEES
12/04	436	—	—	758
12/03	519	—	—	944
12/02	463	—	—	850
12/01	475	—	—	900
12/00	500	—	—	1,000
Annual Growth	(3.4%)	—	—	(6.7%)

Revenue History

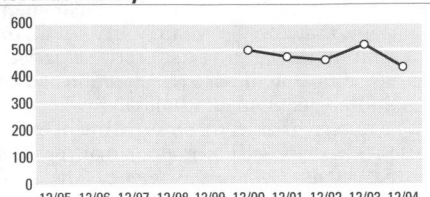

600									
500									
400									
300									
200									
100									
0									
	12/95	12/96	12/97	12/98	12/99	12/00	12/01	12/02	12/03 12/04

Koch Industries

Koch Industries is the real thing when there's money to be made. Koch (pronounced "coke") is the second-largest private US company, after Cargill. Koch Industries' operations (through its numerous subsidiaries) include asphalt, chemicals, energy, fertilizers, fibers and intermediates, finance, minerals, petroleum, pulp and paper, ranching, securities, and trading. A subsidiary owns three refineries that can process about 787,000 barrels of crude oil daily. Koch subsidiaries also process natural gas liquids, and operate gas gathering systems and pipelines across North America. Brothers Charles and David Koch control the company, which in 2004 acquired INVISTA for $4.2 billion and merged it with its KoSa unit.

Koch's business activities focus on three core competencies: Trading (many Koch companies are well-established traders of a wide range of commodities); Operations (Koch companies strive to be industry-leading, cost-efficient operators of their many plants and facilities); and Investments (Koch has equity investments in a variety of industries).

Koch combined its pipeline system and trading units with the power marketing businesses of electric utility Entergy in 2001 to form Entergy-Koch, a joint venture that ranked among the biggest energy commodity traders in the US. (It was sold to Merrill Lynch in 2004).

In 2002 Koch acquired Valero Energy's 40% stake in a Mont Belvieu, Texas, natural gas liquids fractionator, boosting its ownership to 80%.

HISTORY

Fred Koch grew up poor in Texas and worked his way through MIT. In 1928 Koch developed a process to refine more gasoline from crude oil, but when he tried to market his invention, the major oil companies sued him for patent infringement. Koch eventually won the lawsuits (after 15 years in court), but the controversy made it tough to attract many US customers. In 1929 Koch took his process to the Soviet Union, but he grew disenchanted with Stalinism and returned home to become a founding member of the anticommunist John Birch Society.

Koch launched Wood River Oil & Refining in Illinois (1940) and bought the Rock Island refinery in Oklahoma (1947). He folded the remaining purchasing and gathering network into Rock Island Oil & Refining (though he later sold the refineries).

After Koch's death in 1967, his 32-year-old son Charles took the helm and renamed the company Koch Industries. He began a series of acquisitions, adding petrochemical and oil trading service operations.

During the 1980s Koch was thrust into various arenas, legal and political. Charles' brother David, also a Koch Industries executive, ran for US vice president on the Libertarian ticket in 1980. That year the other two Koch brothers, Frederick and William (David's fraternal twin), launched a takeover attempt, but Charles retained control, and William was fired from his job as VP.

The brothers traded lawsuits, and in a 1983 settlement Charles and David bought out the dissident family members for just over $1 billion. William and Frederick continued to challenge their brothers in court, claiming they had been shortchanged in the deal (the two estranged brothers eventually lost their case in 1998, and their appeals were rejected in 2000). In 1987 they even sued their mother over her distribution of trust fund money.

Despite this legal wrangling, Koch Industries continued to expand, purchasing a Corpus Christi, Texas, refinery in 1981. It expanded its pipeline system, buying Bigheart Pipe Line in Oklahoma (1986) and two systems from Santa Fe Southern Pacific (1988).

In 1991 Koch purchased the Corpus Christi marine terminal, pipelines, and gathering systems of Scurlock Permian (a unit of Ashland Oil). In 1992 the company bought United Gas Pipe Line (renamed Koch Gateway Pipeline) and its pipeline system extending from Texas to Florida.

To strengthen its engineering services presence worldwide, Koch acquired Glitsch International (a maker of separation equipment) from engineering giant Foster Wheeler in 1997. It also acquired USX-Delhi Group, a natural gas processor and transporter.

In 1998 Koch bought Purina Mills, the largest US producer of animal feed, and formed the KoSa joint venture with Mexico's Saba family to buy Hoechst's Trevira polyester unit. (Koch acquired the Saba family's stake in KoSa in 2001.) Lethargic energy and livestock prices in 1998 and 1999, however, led Koch to lay off several hundred employees, sell its feedlots, and divest portions of its natural gas gathering and pipeline systems. Purina Mills filed for bankruptcy protection in 1999 (later, it emerged from bankruptcy and held an IPO in 2000, and was acquired by #2 US dairy co-op Land O'Lakes in 2001).

William Koch sued Koch Industries in 1999, claiming the company had defrauded the US government and Native Americans in oil payments on Indian lands. A jury found for William, but he, Charles, and David agreed to settle the case in 2001 — and sat down to dinner together for the first time in 20 years.

In other legal matters, in 2000 Koch agreed to pay a $30 million civil fine and contribute $5 million toward environmental projects to settle complaints over oil spills from its pipelines in the 1990s. The company agreed to pay $20 million in 2001 to settle a separate environmental case concerning a Texas refinery.

In 2005 SemGroup acquired all of Koch Materials Company's US and Mexico asphalt operations.

EXECUTIVES

Chairman and CEO: Charles G. Koch, age 69
President, COO, and Director: Joseph W. (Joe) Moeller
CFO: Steve Feilmeier
EVP and Director: David H. Koch, age 65
EVP Operations and Director: Bill R. Caffey
EVP and Director; President, Koch Mineral Services, LLC: Jeff Gentry
EVP and Director; Chairman, Flint Hills Resources, LP: David L. (Dave) Robertson
EVP: Rich Fink
SVP Corporate Strategy: John C. Pittenger
VP Business Development: Ron Vaupel
VP and General Counsel: Tye Darland
VP Human Resources: Dale Gibbens
Director of Corporate Compliance: Chris Wilkins
Controller: Richard Dinkel
Communication Coordinator and Public Affairs: Patti Parker
Auditors: Ernst & Young; KPMG LLP

LOCATIONS

HQ: Koch Industries, Inc.
4111 E. 37th St. North, Wichita, KS 67220
Phone: 316-828-5500 **Fax:** 316-828-5739
Web: www.kochind.com

Koch Industries has operations in Argentina, Australia, Belgium, Brazil, Canada, China, the Czech Republic, France, Germany, India, Italy, Japan, Luxembourg, the Netherlands, Poland, South Africa, Spain, Switzerland, the UK, the US, and Venezuela.

PRODUCTS/OPERATIONS

Selected Operations

Flint Hills Resources (formerly Koch Petroleum, crude oil and refined products)
Koch Exploration Company, LLC
Koch Agriculture Group
  Matador Cattle Co.
Koch Chemicals Group
  INVISTA Inc.
  Koch Chemicals (paraxylene)
  Koch Microelectronic Service Co. (semiconductor chemicals)
  Koch Specialty Chemicals (high-octane missile fuel)
Koch Chemical Technology Group (specialty equipment and services for refining and chemical industry)
  Brown Fintube Company
  Iris Power Engineering, Inc.
  The John Zink Company
  Koch-Glitsch, Inc.
  Koch Membrane Systems Inc.
  Koch Modular Process Systems, LLC
  Tru-Tec Services, Inc.
Koch Energy Group
Koch Financial Services, Inc.
  Koch Financial Corp.
Koch Gas Liquids Group
Koch Mineral Services (bulk ocean transportation and fuel supply)
  Koch Fertilizer Storage & Terminal Co.
  Koch Nitrogen Co.
Koch Pipeline Co. LP
Koch Supply & Trading, LLC
Koch Ventures LLC (investment in noncore businesses)

COMPETITORS

ADM	Kerr-McGee
AEP	King Ranch
Aquila	Lyondell Chemical
Ashland	Marathon Oil
Avista	Motiva Enterprises
BP	Occidental Petroleum
Cargill	Peabody Energy
CenterPoint Energy	PEMEX
Chevron	PG&E
ConocoPhillips	Royal Dutch/Shell Group
ContiGroup	Shell Oil Products
Duke Energy	Southern Company
Dynegy	SUEZ-TRACTEBEL
Enron	Sunoco
Exxon Mobil	Williams Companies
Imperial Oil	

HISTORICAL FINANCIALS

Company Type: Private

Income Statement

FYE: December 31

	REVENUE ($ mil.)	NET INCOME ($ mil.)	NET PROFIT MARGIN	EMPLOYEES
12/03	40,000	—	—	30,000
12/02	40,000	—	—	17,000
12/01	40,000	—	—	11,000
12/00	40,000	—	—	11,500
12/99	33,050	—	—	12,500
12/98	35,000	—	—	16,000
12/97	36,200	—	—	15,600
12/96	30,000	—	—	13,000
12/95	25,200	—	—	12,500
12/94	23,725	—	—	12,000
Annual Growth	6.0%	—	—	10.7%

Revenue History

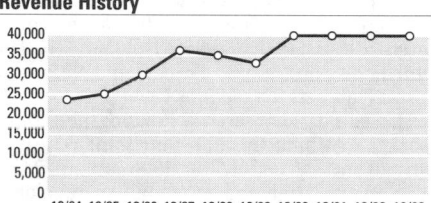

Kohlberg Kravis Roberts

The barbarians at the gate are now knocking politely. The master of the 1980s buyout universe, Kohlberg Kravis Roberts (popularly known as KKR) has shed its hostile takeover image for a kinder, gentler, buy-and-build strategy. In short, KKR assembles funds from institutional and wealthy investors to buy low and sell high. An active investor, the firm supervises or installs new management and revamps strategy and corporate structure, selling underperforming units or adding new ones. KKR profits from fund and company management fees as well as its direct interests. Cousins Henry Kravis and George Roberts are the senior partners in KKR, which is part of a group buying Toys "R" Us.

Recent investments include Masonite International (doors and door components), Duales System Deutschland (recycling in Germany), a stake in PanAmSat (satellite broadcasting; which it acquired with Carlyle and Providence Equity Partners) from DirecTV, and 92% of bedding manufacturer Sealy.

In a move that has the private equity world talking, KKR has abandoned plans to open a small part of its investment empire to the public markets. It has cancelled the planned IPO of KKR BDC, a business development company. Instead, KKR now has plans to start a private real estate investment trust (REIT) that will invest in mortgage-backed securities and other real estate-related debt. Kohlberg Kravis Roberts also has a joint venture with venture capital firm Accel Partners, Accel KKR, to provide support for companies integrating online and brick-and-mortar businesses.

Since 1976 KKR has invested about $140 billion in more than 115 deals, with investors historically receiving returns of around 23%. As the economy cooled down, though, the firm has weathered its fair share of tumult. KKR is no longer the top fund raiser in the investment industry and has written off investments in such firms as Birch Telecom, which subsequently slid into bankruptcy.

Early in 2005 KKR, Bain Capital, and Vornado Realty Trust agreed to buy Toys "R" Us, the #2 US toy retailer, for a reported $6.6 billion. KKR is also part of a group of seven private investment companies (led by Silver Lake Partners) that agreed in 2005 to acquire SunGard Data Systems for $11.3 billion. KKR filed a registration statement in 2005 to take its REIT, KKR Financial Corp., public.

The deals continued apace in the summer of 2005 as a group led by KKR agreed to pay about $1.3 billion for a 60% stake in General Motors Acceptance Corporation's (GMAC) commercial mortgage business. KKR also teamed up with Silver Lake Partners again to buy Agilent Technologies' chip business for $2.66 billion.

Late in 2005 a consortium made up of Blackstone Group, Hellman & Friedman, Kohlberg Kravis Roberts, and Texas Pacific Group agreed to sell Texas Genco (which it acquired for $3.65 billion in 2004) to NRG Energy for $5.8 billion ($4 billion in cash and $1.8 billion in stock). Around the same time, KKR also agreed to a pay about $1.27 billion for medical device maker Accellent.

HISTORY

In 1976 Jerome Kohlberg left investment bank Bear Stearns to form his own leveraged buyout firm; with him he brought protégé Henry Kravis and Kravis' cousin George Roberts. They formed Kohlberg Kravis Roberts & Co. (KKR).

Kohlberg believed LBOs, by giving management ownership stakes in their companies, would yield better results. KKR orchestrated friendly buyouts funded by investor groups and debt. The firm's first buyout was machine-toolmaker Houdaille Industries in 1979.

KKR lost money on its 1981 investment in the American Forest Products division of Bendix. But by 1984 the firm had raised its fourth fund and made its first $1 billion buyout: Wometco Enterprises.

The next year KKR turned mean with a hostile takeover of Beatrice. The deal depended on junk bond financing devised by Drexel Burnham Lambert's Michael Milken and on the sale of pieces of the company. KKR funded the buyouts of Safeway Stores and Owens-Illinois (1986), Jim Walter Homes (1987), and Stop & Shop (1988, sold in 1996).

Unhappy with the firm's hostile image, Kohlberg left in 1987 to form Kohlberg & Co. His suit against KKR over the alleged undervaluing of companies in relation to his departure settlement was resolved for an undisclosed amount.

The Beatrice LBO triggered a rash of similar transactions as the financial industry sought fat fees. The frenzy culminated in 1988 with the $31 billion RJR Nabisco buyout, which brought KKR $75 million in fees.

KKR made its first international foray in 1993 with Russian truck maker Kamaz; it later stalled when Kamaz refused to pay management fees. The next year it freed itself from the RJR morass by swapping its investment in RJR for troubled food company Borden.

In the latter half of the decade, KKR reaped mixed results on its investments, including what is now Spalding Holdings (sporting goods and Evenflo baby products), supermarket chain Bruno's, and KinderCare Learning Centers. The $600 million KKR had sunk into magazine group K-III (now PRIMEDIA) between 1990 and 1994 didn't revive interest in the stock, and Bruno's filed for bankruptcy in 1998.

Focused on Europe, in 2000 the firm claimed the telecommunications business of Robert Bosch (now Tenovis, and sold to Avaya in 2004), UK private equity fund Wassall PLC, and Siemens' banking systems unit. The next year it bought the specialty chemicals and pigments operations of Laporte plc to create Rockwood Specialties. Kohlberg acquired major divisions from Laporte for about $1.2 billion in 2001.

After a failed attempt to take Borden Chemical public in 2004, KKR sold the firm to private equity group Apollo Management. KKR acquired Masonite International, a profitable Canadian building products company in 2005 for about $2.66 billion. Meanwhile, in Europe, it acquired German recycler Duales System Deutschland GmbH. The same year KKR sold two-thirds of its stake in Dayton Power & Light Co. KKR also teamed with Permira Advisers Limited to acquire SBS Broadcasting.

EXECUTIVES

Founding Partner: Henry R. Kravis, age 61
Founding Partner, California: George R. Roberts
General Partner: Perry Golkin, age 51
General Partner, California:
James H. (Jamie) Greene Jr., age 54
General Partner, California: Robert I. MacDonnell, age 68
General Partner: Michael W. Michelson, age 54
General Partner: Paul E. Raether, age 58
General Partner: Scott M. Stuart, age 45
Managing Director, London: Jacques R. Garaïalde
Managing Director, California: Ned Gilhuly
Managing Director, London: Lord Clive R. Hollick, age 60
Managing Director, London: Johannes Huth, age 44
Managing Director, New York:
Kenneth W. (Ken) Freeman, age 54
Chairman, Accel-KKR: Paul M. Hazen, age 63
Office Manager: Sandy Petronella
Auditors: Deloitte & Touche LLP

LOCATIONS

HQ: Kohlberg Kravis Roberts & Co.
9 W. 57th St., Ste. 4200, New York, NY 10019
Phone: 212-750-8300 **Fax:** 212-750-0003
Web: www.kkr.com

Kohlberg Kravis Roberts & Co. has offices in London; Menlo Park, California; and New York City.

Kohler

Kohler's profits are in the toilet, literally. The company makes bathroom products under the names Hytec, Kohler, and Sterling (plumbing); Ann Sacks (ceramic tile, marble, stone); and Kallista (fixtures). European brands include Jacob Delafon and Neomediam (plumbing) and Sanijura (cabinetry). Kohler also makes furniture under such names as Baker and McGuire. Lesser-known Kohler operations include small engines, generators, and uninterruptible power supplies. Kohler's real estate operations include Destination Kohler, a giant resort in Wisconsin, and Old Course Hotel Golf Resort and Spa in Scotland. Chairman Herbert Kohler Jr. and his sister Ruth Kohler, grandchildren of the founder, control Kohler.

Kohler started out with bathroom fixtures, but it's become a huge private company with interests in both seemingly natural (furnishings) and unexpected (engines, resorts) businesses. Best known, of course, is the Kitchen & Bath Group, which includes fixtures, plumbing, and cabinetry products for residential, commercial, and industrial markets.

The Interiors Group got its start with the 1986 acquisition of Baker Furniture. Today, the division includes Milling Road Furniture, Dapha, Ltd. (custom upholstery), McGuire Furniture (rattan, teak, bamboo and Oriental hardwoods), and Ann Sacks (tile and stone).

The company's Global Power Group began making engines way back in the 1920s. Modern products include small 4-29 hp engines and generator sets up to 2,800 kW. Kohler also offers uninterruptible power systems through Kohler Rental Power.

Lastly, the Hospitality and Real Estate Group includes Destination Kohler, a luxury resort in Wisconsin that boasts a resort hotel, four golf courses, 26 specialty boutiques, a 500-acre wildlife preserve, and a fitness complex. The division also includes Village Realty & Development, a planned community adjacent to Destination Kohler.

Chairman Herbert Kohler Jr. breeds Morgan horses at Kohler Stables in Kentucky. In August 2004 the company hosted the PGA Championship.

HISTORY

In 1873, 29-year-old Austrian immigrant John Kohler and partner Charles Silberzahn founded Kohler & Silberzahn in Sheboygan, Wisconsin. That year they purchased a small iron foundry that made agricultural products for $5,000 from Kohler's father-in-law. In 1880, two years after Silberzahn left the firm, its machine shop was destroyed by fire.

The company introduced enameled plumbing fixtures in the rebuilt factory in 1883. The design caught on, and the business sold thousands of sinks, kettles, pans, and bathtubs. By 1887, when Kohler was incorporated, enameled items accounted for 70% of sales. By 1900 the 250-person company received 98% of its sales from enameled iron products. That year, shortly after John Kohler began building new facilities near Sheboygan (which later became the company village of Kohler), he died at age 56. More trouble followed: Kohler's new plant burned down in 1901, and two of the founder's sons died — Carl at age 24 in 1904 and Robert at age 35 in 1905.

Eldest surviving son Walter built a boarding hotel to house workers and introduced other employee-benefit programs. He also set up company-paid workmen's compensation before the state made it law in 1917.

By the mid-1920s, when Kohler premiered colors in porcelain fixtures and added brass fittings and vitreous china toilets and washbasins to its line, it was the #3 plumbing-product company in the US. As a testament to the design quality of its products, Kohler items were displayed at the New York Museum of Modern Art in 1929. The company also began developing products that would grow in importance in later decades: electric generators and small gasoline engines. During the 1950s Kohler's engines virtually conquered Southeast Asia, where they were used to power boats, drive air compressors, and pump water for rice paddies in Vietnam and Thailand. While strikes against Kohler in 1897 and 1934 had been resolved quickly, a 1954 strike against the firm lasted six years. The strike gave Kohler the dubious honor of enduring the longest strike in US history.

Small-engine use grew in the US in the 1960s, and Kohler's motors were used in lawn mowers, construction equipment, and garden tractors. The founder's last surviving son, Herbert (a child from John Kohler's second marriage), died in 1968. Under the leadership of Herbert's son, Herbert Jr. (appointed chairman 1972), Kohler expanded its operations and began to develop its resort business in the US with the restoration of The American Club hotel (1981); it bought Sterling Faucet (1984), Baker Furniture (1986), Knapp & Tubbs (1986), and Jacob Delafon (1986). Subsequent acquisitions have included Sanijura (bathroom furniture, France) in 1993; Osio (enamel baths, Italy) in 1994; Robern (mirrored cabinets) in 1995; Holdiam (baths, whirlpools, and sinks, France) in 1995; and Canac (cabinets, Canada) in 1996.

The company entered a growing plumbing market in China through four joint ventures formed in that country in 1996 and 1997. In 1998 several family and non-family shareholders claimed a reorganization plan unfairly forced them out and undervalued their stock. Legal battles over the stock's fair price continued in 1999, and a settlement was reached in 2000 that granted shareholders a fair price and Herbert Jr. and his sister Ruth gained firm control of the company. Herbert reorganized the company and vowed it would never go public.

In 2001 the company sued Canada-based Kohler International Ltd. for trademark infringement. Also that year Kohler acquired UK-based Mira Showers. Following the September 11 terrorist attacks, Kohler quickly created a mobile showering unit with nine shower stalls and four sinks within an enormous semi-trailer to provide hot showers for workers and volunteers at the World Trade Center.

In the fall of 2002 Kohler and about 3,450 United Auto Workers (UAW) union members who worked at the company's Village of Kohler and Town of Mosel plants agreed on a five-year labor contract that called for increases in wages and benefits.

Kohler expanded its resort business internationally in 2004 by purchasing the world-renowned Old Course Hotel Golf Resort and Spa in St. Andrews, Scotland, along with Golf Resorts International (GRI), Limited.

EXECUTIVES

Chairman and President: Herbert V. Kohler Jr., age 65
SVP Finance and CFO: Jeffrey P. Cheney
SVP Human Resources: Laura Kohler
VP Hospitality and Real Estate: Alice Edland
VP Marketing, Fixtures: Mike Chandler
President, Engine Business: James Doyle
President, Global Power Group:
  Richard J. (Dick) Fotsch, age 49
Director; President, Kitchen and Bath Group:
  David Kohler
**Manager, Environmental Health and Safety Technology
  Resources:** Paul Kubicek
Marketing Director, Sterling Brand: Gordon Wuthich
Communications, Kohler Global Power Group:
  Stephanie Dlugopolski
Public Relations, Kitchen and Bath Group: Todd Weber
Media Relations, Destination Kohler: Scott Silvestri
**Director of Communications, Kitchen & Bath Group
  and Interiors:** Elisabeth Sutton

LOCATIONS

HQ: Kohler Co.
  444 Highland Dr., Kohler, WI 53044
Phone: 920-457-4441   **Fax:** 920-457-1271
Web: kohlerco.com

Kohler Co. operates 44 manufacturing plants, 26
subsidiaries and affiliates, and sales offices worldwide.

PRODUCTS/OPERATIONS

Selected Operations

Engines
  Commercial turf equipment engines
  Consumer lawn and garden equipment engines
  Industrial, construction, and
    commercial equipment engines
  Recreational equipment engines
Furniture
  Baker Furniture
  McGuire Furniture Company
  Milling Road Furniture
Generators
  Kohler rental power
  Marine generators
  Mobile generators
  On-site power systems
    Automatic transfer switches
    Switchgear
  Residential generators
  Small business generators
Kitchen and Bath Products
  Cabinets and vanities
    Canac (bathroom cabinetry)
    Robern (lighting and mirrored bath cabinetry)
    Sanijura (vanities and other bath furniture)
  Plumbing products
    Jacob Delafon (bathtubs, faucets,
      lavatories, and toilets)
    Kohler (bath and shower faucets, baths, bidet
      faucets, bidets, body spa systems, glass showers
      and shower doors, kitchen and bathroom sinks
      and faucets, master baths, toilets, toilet seats,
      vanities, whirlpool baths)
    Kallista (bathroom and kitchen sinks and faucets)
    Sterling (bathing fixtures, faucets, sinks, tub/shower
      enclosures, vitreous china bath fixtures)
  Tile and stone products
    Ann Sacks (art tile, glazed tile, knobs and pulls,
      mosaics, terra cotta)
Real Estate and Hospitality (Destination Kohler)
  The American Club (resort hotel)
  Blackwolf Run golf course
  Golf Resorts International, Limited (Scotland)
  Inn on Woodlake
  Kohler Stables
  Kohler Waters Spa
  Old Course Hotel Golf Resort and Spa (Scotland)
  Riverbend (private club)
  River Wildlife
  The Shops at Woodlake Kohler
  Whistling Straits golf course

COMPETITORS

American Standard	Grohe
Armstrong Holdings	Honda
Armstrong World	Iberia Tiles
Industries	Jacuzzi Brands
Bassett Furniture	Klaussner Furniture
Black & Decker	Leggett & Platt
Briggs & Stratton	Masco
Carlson	Moen
Chicago Faucet	Mueller Industries
Cooper Industries	Newell Rubbermaid
Crane	NIBCO
Crane Plumbing	Price Pfister
Crossville	Samuel Heath
Dal-Tile	Starwood Hotels & Resorts
Dyson-Kissner-Moran	Tecumseh Products
Elkay Manufacturing	TOTO
Geberit	Villeroy & Boch
Geberit Manufacturing	Waxman
Gerber Plumbing Fixtures	Yamaha

HISTORICAL FINANCIALS

Company Type: Private

Income Statement

FYE: December 31

	ESTIMATED REVENUE ($ mil.)	NET INCOME ($ mil.)	NET PROFIT MARGIN	EMPLOYEES
12/04	3,000	—	—	28,000
12/03	3,005	—	—	25,000
12/02	3,000	—	—	25,000
12/01	3,000	—	—	22,000
12/00	2,700	—	—	20,000
12/99	2,500	—	—	20,000
12/98	2,400	—	—	18,000
12/97	2,210	—	—	18,000
12/96	2,020	—	—	18,000
12/95	1,850	—	—	15,000
Annual Growth	5.5%	—	—	7.2%

Revenue History

EXECUTIVES

Chairman, KI Holdings and Koppers Inc.: Robert Cizik,
  age 74
**President, CEO, and Director, KI Holdings and
  Koppers Inc.:** Walter W. Turner, age 58, $880,000 pay
VP and CFO, KI Holdings and Koppers Inc.:
  Brian H. McCurrie, age 44, $556,000 pay
**VP, Australasian Operations, Koppers Inc.; Managing
  Director, Koppers Australia Pty Ltd.:** Ernest S. Bryon,
  age 59
VP, European Operations, Koppers Inc.: David Whittle,
  age 63, $444,699 pay
**VP; General Manager, Carbon Materials and Chemicals
  Division, Koppers Inc.:** Kevin J. Fitzgerald, age 52,
  $334,960 pay
**VP; General Manager, Global Marketing, Sales, and
  Development Group, Koppers Inc.:**
  Mark R. McCormack, age 46
**VP; General Manager, Railroad Products and Services
  Division, Koppers Inc.:** Thomas D. Loadman, age 50
**VP; General Manager, Utility Poles and Piling Products,
  Koppers Inc.:** David T. Bryce, age 58
**SVP, Administration, General Counsel, and Secretary,
  KI Holdings and Koppers Inc.:** Steven R. Lacy, age 49,
  $590,640 pay
Auditors: Ernst & Young LLP

LOCATIONS

HQ: KI Holdings Inc.
  436 7th Ave., Pittsburgh, PA 15219
Phone: 412-227-2001   **Fax:** 412-227-2333
Web: www.koppers.com

KI Holdings operates 37 facilities in Australia, China,
Denmark, Fiji, Malaysia, New Zealand, South Africa,
Tasmania, the UK, and the US.

2004 Sales

	$ mil.	% of total
US	627.2	66
Australia & Asia/Pacific	197.4	21
Europe	127.9	13
Total	**952.5**	**100**

PRODUCTS/OPERATIONS

2004 Sales

	$ mil.	% of total
Carbon Materials & Chemicals	553.4	58
Railroad & Utility Products	399.1	42
Total	**952.5**	**100**

Selected Products

Carbon Materials and Chemicals
  Carbon black
  Carbon pitch
  Coal tar distillates
  Creosote
  Furnace coke
  Phthalic anhydride (PAA)
  Refined tars
  Roofing pitch
Railroad and Utility Products
  Crossties (wood and concrete)
  Pilings
  Track and switch preassemblies
  Utility poles

COMPETITORS

Arch Chemicals	North American
Cabot	Technologies
Cytec	Osmose
De Dietrich	RailWorks
Degussa	Steel Authority of India
Kerr-McGee	Stepan
KMG Chemicals	U.S. Plastic Lumber
McFarland Cascade	Usiminas
Mitsubishi Chemical	Velsicol Chemical

Koppers

Koppers treats wood right. KI Holdings (dba
Koppers) makes carbon compounds and treated-
wood products for the chemical, railroad, aluminum, utility, construction, and steel industries
around the world. Its carbon materials and chemicals unit makes materials for producing aluminum, polyester resins, plasticizers, and wood
preservatives. The railroad and utility products
unit supplies treated crossties and utility poles
and treats wood for vineyard, construction, and
other uses. KI Holdings owns 50% of KSA Limited Partnership, which produces about 100,000
concrete crossties annually. Investment firm
Saratoga Partners controls KI Holdings.

HISTORICAL FINANCIALS

Company Type: Private

Income Statement

FYE: December 31

	REVENUE ($ mil.)	NET INCOME ($ mil.)	NET PROFIT MARGIN	EMPLOYEES
12/04	953	11	1.2%	2,029
12/03	843	(37)	—	1,975
12/02	730	17	2.3%	2,057
12/01	708	13	1.9%	2,085
12/00	724	15	2.0%	2,155
12/99	664	24	3.6%	1,904
12/98	671	20	3.0%	1,927
12/97	593	(6)	—	1,990
12/96	589	14	2.4%	1,919
12/95	526	24	4.6%	2,104
Annual Growth	6.8%	(8.2%)	—	(0.4%)

2004 Year-End Financials

Debt ratio: —
Return on equity: —
Cash ($ mil.): 15

Current ratio: 1.70
Long-term debt ($ mil.): 363

Net Income History

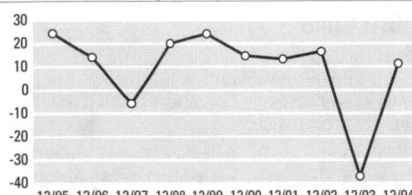

30									
20									
10									
0									
-10									
-20									
-30									
-40									

12/95 12/96 12/97 12/98 12/99 12/00 12/01 12/02 12/03 12/04

KPMG

Businesses all over the world count on KPMG for accounting. KPMG is the smallest, yet most geographically dispersed of accounting's Big Four, which also includes Deloitte Touche Tohmatsu, Ernst & Young, and PricewaterhouseCoopers. KPMG, a cooperative that operates as an umbrella organization for its member firms, has organized its structure into three operating regions: the Americas; Asia/Pacific; and Europe, Middle East, Africa. Member firms' offerings include audit, tax, and advisory services; KPMG focuses on clients in such industries as financial services, consumer products, government, health care, information, communications, and entertainment. KPMG has discontinued its KLegal International network.

After much regulatory pressure, KPMG separated its accounting and consulting operations; it sold a chunk of the consulting business to networking equipment maker Cisco Systems, then took it public and sold off its shares in 2002. The consulting unit, which in 2002 changed its name to BearingPoint, acquired KPMG's Austrian, German, and Swiss consulting businesses.

A run-in with the US government over questionable tax shelters characterized as abusive (costing the US more than $1 billion in tax revenues) led to a shakeup in the US firm's tax services unit in 2004 and the payment of a $456 million penalty in mid-2005. While KPMG appears to have headed off an indictment of the firm, eight former KPMG executives have been indicted and charged with conspiracy in connection with the tax shelters.

Lawsuits over KPMG's work for other former clients hit the accountancy's pocketbook. In 2003 KPMG agreed to pay $125 million to settle a dispute regarding work for Rite Aid. The next year, KPMG's Belgian and US units agreed to a $115 million settlement regarding now-defunct Lernout & Hauspie Speech Products.

HISTORY

Peat Marwick was founded in 1911, when William Peat, a London accountant, met James Marwick during an Atlantic crossing. University of Glasgow alumni Marwick and Roger Mitchell had formed Marwick, Mitchell & Company in New York in 1897. Peat and Marwick agreed to ally their firms temporarily, and in 1925 they merged as Peat, Marwick, Mitchell, & Copartners.

In 1947 William Black became senior partner, a position he held until 1965. He guided the firm's 1950 merger with Barrow, Wade, Guthrie, one of the US's oldest firms, and built its consulting practice. Peat Marwick restructured its international practice as PMM&Co. (International) in 1972 (renamed Peat Marwick International in 1978).

The next year several European accounting firms led by Klynveld Kraayenhoff (the Netherlands) and Deutsche Treuhand (Germany) began forming an international accounting federation. Needing an American member, the European firms encouraged the merger of two American firms founded around the turn of the century, Main Lafrentz and Hurdman Cranstoun. Main Hurdman & Cranstoun joined the Europeans to form Klynveld Main Goerdeler (KMG), named after two of the member firms and the chairman of Deutsche Treuhand, Reinhard Goerdeler. Other members were C. Jespersen (Denmark), Thorne Riddel (Canada), Thomson McLintok (UK), and Fides Revision (Switzerland).

Peat Marwick merged with KMG in 1987 to form Klynveld Peat Marwick Goerdeler (KPMG). KPMG lost 10% of its business as competing client companies departed. Professional staff departures followed in 1990 when, as part of a consolidation, the firm trimmed its partnership rolls.

In the 1990s the then-Big Six accounting firms all faced lawsuits arising from an evolving standard holding auditors responsible for the substance, rather than merely the form, of clients' accounts. KPMG was hit by suits stemming from its audits of defunct S&Ls and litigation relating to the bankruptcy of Orange County, California (settled for $75 million in 1998). Nevertheless KPMG kept growing; it expanded its consulting division with the acquisition of banking consultancy Barefoot, Marrinan & Associates in 1996.

In 1997, after Price Waterhouse and Coopers & Lybrand announced their merger, KPMG and Ernst & Young announced one of their own. But they called it quits the next year, fearing that regulatory approval of the deal would be too onerous.

The creation of PricewaterhouseCoopers (PwC) and increasing competition in the consulting sides of all of the Big Five brought a realignment of loyalties in their national practices. KPMG Consulting's Belgian group moved to PwC and its French group to Computer Sciences Corporation. Andersen nearly wooed away KPMG's Canadian consulting group, but the plan was foiled by the ever-sullen Andersen Consulting group (now Accenture) and by KPMG's promises of more money. Against this back-

ground, KPMG sold 20% of its consulting operations to Cisco Systems for $1 billion. In addition to the cash infusion, the deal allowed KPMG to provide installation and system management to Cisco's customers.

Even while KPMG worked on the IPO of its consulting group (which took place in 2001), it continued to rail against the SEC as it called for relationships between consulting and auditing organizations to be severed. In 2002 KPMG sold its British and Dutch consultancy units to France's Atos Origin.

In 2003 the SEC charged US member firm KPMG L.L.P. and four partners with fraud in relation to alleged profit inflation at former client Xerox in the late 1990s. (In April 2005 the accounting firm paid almost $22.5 million, including a $10 million civil penalty, to settle the charges.)

KPMG exited various businesses around the globe during fiscal 2004, including full-scope legal services and certain advisory services, to focus on higher-demand services.

EXECUTIVES

Chairman; Senior Partner, KPMG UK:
Michael (Mike) Rake, age 57
CEO: Robert W. (Bob) Alspaugh, age 58
COO: Colin Holland
Chairman and CEO, KPMG LLP: Timothy P. Flynn, age 48
Chairman, Europe, Middle East, and Africa:
Harald Wiedmann
Chairman, Asia Pacific: John Harrison
Vice Chairman: Ruth Anderson
Vice Chairman and Managing Partner, Global Markets:
Alistair Johnston
Vice Chairman: Philip Wallace
Vice Chairman: Derek Zissman
CEO, Switzerland: Hubert Achermann
Senior Partner, Brazil: David Bunce
Managing Partner, Singapore: Bobby Chin
President, France: Jean-Luc Decornoy
Senior Partner, Mexico: Guillermo Garcia-Naranjo
Chairman and Senior Partner, South Africa:
Tom Grieve
Senior Partner, Italy: Renato Guerini
National Chairman, Australia: Doug Jukes
Managing Partner, Ireland: Denis O'Connor
Chairman and CEO, Canada: Bill MacKinnon
Senior Partner, Denmark: Finn L. Meyer
Senior Partner, Sweden: Thomas Thiel
Chairman, Board of Management, Netherlands:
Ben van der Veer
Senior Partner and CEO, Japan: Masanori Sato
General Counsel: Tom Wethered
Secretary: Needra Patel

LOCATIONS

HQ: KPMG
Burgemeester Rijnderslaan 10, 1185 MC
Amstelveen, The Netherlands
Phone: +31-20-656-7890   **Fax:** +31-20-656-7700
US HQ: 345 Park Ave., New York, NY 10154-0102
US Phone: 212-758-9700   **US Fax:** 212-758-9819
Web: www.kpmg.com

KPMG International has offices in nearly 150 countries.

2004 Sales

	$ mil.	% of total
Europe, Middle East, South Asia & Africa	6,840	51
Americas	4,930	37
Asia/Pacific	1,670	12
Total	**13,440**	**100**

PRODUCTS/OPERATIONS

2004 Sales

	$ mil.	% of total
Audit services	6,420	48
Advisory services	3,910	29
Tax services	3,110	23
Total	**13,440**	**100**

2004 Sales by Customer Type

	$ mil.	% of total
Financial services	3,810	28
Infrastructure, government & health care	2,960	22
Industrial markets	2,900	22
Information, communications & entertainment	2,080	15
Consumer markets	1,690	13
Total	**13,440**	**100**

Selected Services

Audit services
  Financial statement audit
  Internal audit services

Tax services
  Corporate & business tax
  Global tax
  Indirect tax
  Personal tax

Advisory services
  Audit support services
  Financial risk management
  Information risk management
  Process improvement
  Regulatory & compliance

COMPETITORS

Aon	H&R Block
Bain & Company	Hewitt Associates
Baker Tilly International	Marsh & McLennan
BDO International	McKinsey & Company
Booz Allen	PricewaterhouseCoopers
Deloitte	Towers Perrin
Ernst & Young	Watson Wyatt
Grant Thornton International	

HISTORICAL FINANCIALS

Company Type: Partnership

Income Statement

FYE: September 30

	REVENUE ($ mil.)	NET INCOME ($ mil.)	NET PROFIT MARGIN	EMPLOYEES
9/04	13,440	—	—	93,983
9/03	12,160	—	—	93,470
9/02	10,720	—	—	98,000
9/01	11,700	—	—	103,000
9/00	10,700	—	—	108,000
9/99	12,200	—	—	102,000
9/98	10,600	—	—	85,300
9/97	9,200	—	—	83,500
9/96	8,100	—	—	77,000
9/95	7,500	—	—	72,000
Annual Growth	**6.7%**	**—**	**—**	**3.0%**

Revenue History

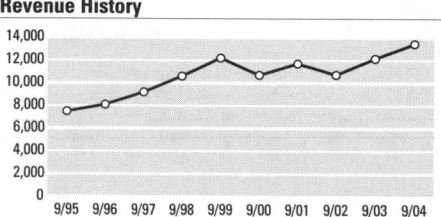

La Madeleine

La Madeleine hopes its crème brulee, croissants, and quiche prove as memorable as Proust's famous teacake. The privately held chain operates more than 60 namesake casual dining locations in six states, offering French country cuisine for breakfast, lunch, and dinner. The restaurants, which welcome patrons with such interior appointments as a stone hearth and handcrafted wood tables, use a cafeteria-style serving line and limited table service. Each location also sells a variety of fresh baked goods. Owned by Paris-based restaurant operator Groupe Le Duff, la Madeleine de Corps was founded in 1983 by French native Patrick Leon Esquerré.

With food service veteran Greg Buchanan at the helm, (formerly with Darden and Carlson Restaurants) the company has laid plans to expand to more than 100 restaurants during the next five years. It is also exploring the possibility of franchising new locations to accelerate the chain's growth.

Groupe Le Duff, which operates and franchises La Brioche Dorée bistros and Pizza Del Arte quick service restaurants in France, bought la Madeleine in 2001 for about $60 million.

EXECUTIVES

Chairman and CEO: Jean-Roch Vachon
President: Greg Buchanan
COO: Rosalyn (Roz) Mallet
Chief Marketing Officer: Debra Tippett
VP, Finance: Bill Schaffler
VP and General Counsel: Harry Martin
Senior Director, Information Systems Support: George Popson
Recruiting Manager: Jeff Erts
Senior Director, Culinary: Susan Dederan

LOCATIONS

HQ: la Madeleine de Corps, Inc.
6688 North Central Expwy., Ste. 700, Dallas, TX 75206
Phone: 214-696-6962　　**Fax:** 214-692-8496
Web: www.lamadeleine.com

La Madeleine operates more than 60 restaurants in Arizona, Georgia, Louisiana, Maryland, Texas, Virginia, and Washington, DC.

COMPETITORS

Applebee's	Lone Star Steakhouse
Atlanta Bread	Marie Callender
Avado Brands	Metromedia Restaurant Group
Benihana	Noodles & Company
Brinker	O'Charley's
BUCA	Outback Steakhouse
California Pizza Kitchen	Panera Bread
Carlson Restaurants	P.F. Chang's
Cheesecake Factory	RARE Hospitality
Consolidated Restaurant Operations	Rock Bottom Restaurants
Darden	Romacorp
Houlihan's	Ruby Tuesday
Landry's	

HISTORICAL FINANCIALS

Company Type: Private

Income Statement

FYE: June 30

	REVENUE ($ mil.)	NET INCOME ($ mil.)	NET PROFIT MARGIN	EMPLOYEES
6/05	120	—	—	2,350
6/04	119	—	—	2,350
6/03	125	—	—	2,300
6/02	122	—	—	2,300
6/01	121	—	—	2,781
6/00	117	—	—	2,701
6/99	110	—	—	2,800
6/98	100	—	—	2,000
6/97	100	—	—	2,000
Annual Growth	**2.3%**	**—**	**—**	**2.0%**

Revenue History

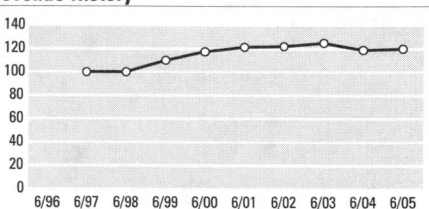

Lake Area Corn Processors

With soaring crude oil prices, ethanol is looking like a great investment for Lake Area Corn Processors, which produces ethanol and livestock feed. Through its Dakota Ethanol unit, the company produces nearly 50 million gallons of ethanol. Dakota Ethanol is a partnership between Lake Area Corn Processors and Broin Companies, a manufacturer of ethanol processing plants. Ethanol production at Dakota Ethanol uses 16 million bushels of corn a year. Ethanol is not only an environmentally friendly fuel, but is also used as a high quality livestock feed for local, regional, and national markets.

Dakota Ethanol operates the 11th ethanol plant built by the Broin Companies, which began building ethanol plants in 1983. Dakota Ethanol began operations in 2001.

EXECUTIVES

CEO: Doulgas L. (Doug) Van Duyn, age 50
CFO: Brian Woldt, age 38
VP: Dale L. Thompson, age 55
Secretary: Dale I. Schut, age 46
General Manager, Dakota Ethanol: Dean Frederickson, age 47
Controller, Dakota Ethanol: Rob Buchholtz, age 33
Membership Coordinator, Dakota Ethanol: Alan May, age 50
Auditors: Eide Bailly LLP

LOCATIONS

HQ: Lake Area Corn Processors, LLC
46269 S. Dakota Hwy. 34, Wentworth, SD 57075
Phone: 605-483-2676　　**Fax:** 605-483-2681
Web: www.dakotaethanol.com

HISTORICAL FINANCIALS

Company Type: Private

Income Statement				FYE: December 31
	REVENUE ($ mil.)	NET INCOME ($ mil.)	NET PROFIT MARGIN	EMPLOYEES
12/04	84	8	8.9%	38
12/03	69	5	6.6%	38
12/02	66	8	11.7%	—
Annual Growth	13.4%	(1.3%)	—	0.0%

Net Income History

12/95 12/96 12/97 12/98 12/99 12/00 12/01 12/02 12/03 12/04

LaMar's Donuts

LaMar's Donuts operates and franchises more than 30 doughnut shops in nine southern states. The company sells a variety of doughnuts, including bizmarks, fritters, knots, and the LaMar's Bar (a giant eclair). The late Ray Lamar, founder and former stockbroker, opened his first shop in Kansas City in 1960, and the chain quickly became an institution there. LaMar's has partnered with Denver's Dazbog Coffee Company in an agreement to exclusively sell its joe. LaMar's was acquired by a group led by Joseph Field in 1997. Ed Hughes and Jack Irwin acquired the company in April 2004.

EXECUTIVES

CEO: Anthony Bonelli
CFO: Thad Bagnado
Accounting Services: Sharon McCormick
Franchise Sales: Sheri Emerson
Store Operations: Matt Joslyn
Marketing, Communication, and Customer Service: Rachel Daughters

LOCATIONS

HQ: LaMar's Donuts
6551 Revere Pkwy., Ste. 250, Centennial, CO 80111
Phone: 303-792-9200 **Fax:** 303-790-0708
Web: www.lamars.com

COMPETITORS

Cinnabon	Starbucks
Dunkin	Tim Hortons
Krispy Kreme	Triarc
New World Restaurants	

HISTORICAL FINANCIALS

Company Type: Private

Income Statement				FYE: December 31
	ESTIMATED REVENUE ($ mil.)	NET INCOME ($ mil.)	NET PROFIT MARGIN	EMPLOYEES
12/04	13	—	—	250

Land O'Lakes

Land O'Lakes butters up its customers, and shows you what life is like if everyone cooperates. Owned by and serving more than 7,000 dairy farmer members and 1,300 community cooperatives, Land O'Lakes is the #3 dairy co-op in the US (behind Dairy Farmers of America and California Dairies). It provides its members with wholesale fertilizer and crop protection products, seed, and animal feed. Its oldest product, LAND O' LAKES butter, is the #1 butter brand in the US. Land O'Lakes also produces packaged milk, margarine, sour cream, and cheese. The co-op's animal feed division, Land O'Lakes Purina Feed, is a leading animal and pet food maker.

Land O'Lakes also holds about 57% of a joint venture in egg producer MoArk. The co-op's subsidiary Land O'Lakes Finance provides financing services for beef, dairy, pork, and poultry producers.

Outside of the US, Land O'Lakes has taken aim at the largest emerging market: China. The company's sales agent in China is working to establish the Land O'Lakes brand of cheese and cultured dairy products in supermarkets.

HISTORY

In the old days, grocers sold butter from communal tubs and it often went bad. Widespread distribution of dairy products had to await the invention of fast, reliable transportation. By 1921 the necessary transportation was available. That year about 320 dairy farmers in Minnesota formed the Minnesota Cooperative Creameries Association and launched a membership drive with $1,375, mostly borrowed from the US Farm Bureau.

The co-op arranged joint shipments for members; imposed strict hygiene and quality standards; and aggressively marketed its sweet cream butter nationwide, packaged for the first time in the familiar box of four quarter-pound sticks. A month after the co-op's New York sales office opened, it was ordering 80 shipments a week.

Minnesota Cooperative Creameries, as part of its promotional campaigns, ran a contest in 1924 to name that butter. Two contestants offered the winning name — Land O'Lakes. The distinctive Indian Maiden logo first appeared about the same time, and in 1926 the co-op changed its name to Land O'Lakes Creameries. By 1929, when it began supplying feed, its market share approached 50%.

During WWII civilian consumption dropped, but the co-op increased production of dried milk to provide food for soldiers and newly liberated concentration camp victims.

In the 1950s and 1960s, Land O'Lakes added ice cream and yogurt producers to its membership and fought margarine makers, yet butter's market share continued to melt. The co-op diversified in 1970 through acquisitions, adding feeds and agricultural chemicals. Two years later Land O'Lakes threw in the towel and came out with its own margarine. Despite the decreasing use of butter nationally, the co-op's market share grew.

Land O'Lakes formed a marketing joint venture, Cenex/Land O'Lakes Agronomy, with fellow co-op Cenex in 1987. As health consciousness bloomed in the 1980s, Land O'Lakes launched reduced-fat dairy products. It also purchased a California cheese plant, doubling its capacity. Land O'Lakes began ramping up its international projects at the same time: It built a feed mill in Taiwan, introduced feed products in Mexico, and established feed and cheese operations in Poland.

In 1997 the co-op bought low-fat cheese maker Alpine Lace Brands. Land O'Lakes took on the eastern US when it merged with the 3,600-member Atlantic Dairy Cooperative (1997), and it bulked up on the West Coast when California-based Dairyman's Cooperative Creamery Association joined its fold (1998).

During 2000 the co-op sold five plants to Dean Foods with an agreement to continue supplying the plants with raw milk. Also in 2000 Land O'Lakes combined its feed business with those of Farmland Industries to create Land O'Lakes Farmland Feed, LLC, with 69% ownership. That same year Cenex/Land O'Lakes Agronomy and Farmland Industries joined together their agronomy operations to create Agriliance LLC (now 50% owned).

In late 2001 the company spent $359 million to acquire Purina Mills (pet and livestock feeds). Purina Mills was folded into Land O'Lakes Farmland Feed and, as part of the purchase, Land O'Lakes increased its ownership of the feed business to 92%. In 2004 it purchased the remaining 8%.

To take advantage of its nationally recognized brand, Land O'Lakes formed an alliance with Dean Foods in 2002 to develop and market value-added dairy products.

Exiting the meat business, Land O'Lakes sold its swine operations in 2005 to private pork producer, Maschhoff West LLC, for an undisclosed sum. Later that year, it sold its interest in fertilizer manufacturer, CF Industries. Long-time president and CEO Jack Gherty retired that year; he was replaced by Chris Policinski.

EXECUTIVES

Chairman: Peter (Pete) Kappelman, age 42
President and CEO: Chris Policinski, age 46, $727,113 pay (prior to title change)
EVP and COO, Dairy Foods Industrial: Alan Pierson
EVP and COO, Dairy Foods Value-Added: Steve Dunphy
EVP, Feed: Fernando Palacios, age 45, $517,436 pay
SVP and CFO: Daniel E. Knutson, age 48, $660,497 pay
VP, Foodservice Sales: Mark Blabac
VP, Human Resources: Karen Grabow, age 55, $421,023 pay
VP, Public Affairs: James D. (Jim) Fife, age 55
VP, Seed: Dave Seehusen
VP, Strategy and Business Development: Barry Wolfish
VP and General Counsel: Peter Janzen, age 45
Director, Corporate Communications: Lydia Botham
Manager, Training Foodservice: Sally Leivermann
Auditors: KPMG LLP

LOCATIONS

HQ: Land O'Lakes, Inc.
   4001 Lexington Ave. North, Arden Hills, MN 55126
Phone: 651-481-2222   **Fax:** 651-481-2000
Web: www.landolakesinc.com

Land O'Lakes operates processing, manufacturing, warehousing, and distribution facilities across the US and internationally.

PRODUCTS/OPERATIONS

2004 Sales

	$ mil.	% of total
Dairy foods	3,956.9	52
Feed	2,626.6	34
Layers	541.3	7
Seed	538.4	7
Other	13.3	—
Total	**7,676.5**	**100**

Selected Brands

Alpine Lace (low-fat cheese)
CROPLAN GENETICS (crop seed)
Fresh Buttery Taste (butter-flavored spread)
LAND O' LAKES (consumer dairy products)
Land O'Lakes (animal feed)
New Yorker (cheese)
PMI Nutrition (animal feeds and pet foods)

Dairy Products

Butter
Cheese
Flavored butter
Light butter
Margarine
Milk
Sour cream

COMPETITORS

ADM	National Dairy Holdings
AMPI	Nestlé
California Dairies Inc.	Nestlé USA
Dairy Farmers of America	Northwest Dairy
Darigold, Inc.	Parmalat
Dean Foods	Pioneer Hi-Bred
Fonterra	Prairie Farms Dairy
Foremost Farms	Saputo
HP Hood	Schreiber Foods
Kraft Foods	Unilever
Milk Specialties	

HISTORICAL FINANCIALS

Company Type: Cooperative

Income Statement   FYE: December 31

	REVENUE ($ mil.)	NET INCOME ($ mil.)	NET PROFIT MARGIN	EMPLOYEES
12/04	7,677	21	0.3%	8,000
12/03	6,321	84	1.3%	8,000
12/02	5,847	99	1.7%	8,000
12/01	5,973	72	1.2%	8,600
12/00	5,756	103	1.8%	6,500
12/99	5,613	21	0.4%	6,500
12/98	5,174	69	1.3%	6,500
12/97	4,195	95	2.3%	5,500
12/96	3,486	119	3.4%	5,500
12/95	3,014	121	4.0%	5,500
Annual Growth	**10.9%**	**(17.5%)**	**—**	**4.3%**

2004 Year-End Financials

Debt ratio: 119.8%
Return on equity: 2.4%
Cash ($ mil.): 73
Current ratio: 1.29
Long-term debt ($ mil.): 1,024

Net Income History

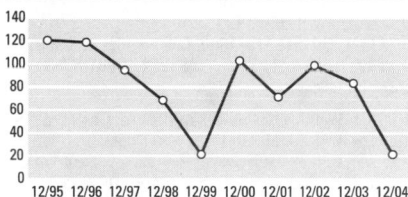

Lanoga

Lanoga is a lumbering giant. The company is one of the top US retailers of lumber and building materials, catering to professional contractors and consumers. Operating more than 300 stores in 20 US states, Lanoga has grown through dozens of small acquisitions. Its divisions include Dixieline (California), the Home Lumber Company (Colorado), Lumbermens Building Centers (Northwest, Arizona, and California), Spenard Builders Supply (Alaska), and United Building Centers (Midwest and Rocky Mountain states). Lanoga was founded in the mid-1850s by the Laird and Norton families, who were cousins. Descendants of the company's founders own Lanoga.

In 2004 Lanoga acquired nearly 30 Wickes locations in the Midwest. Lanoga subsidiary Hope Lumber & Supply additionally acquired more than 10 Wickes outlets in the South and Colorado. In 2005 Lanoga purchased almost all of the assets of door and window maker Bernco Inc.

EXECUTIVES

Chairman: Paul Brewer
President and CEO: Paul W. Hylbert
EVP, CFO, Secretary, and Treasurer:
  William (Bill) Brakken
EVP and COO: Mike Morehouse
VP, Market Development: George C. Finkenstaedt
President and CEO, Dixieline:
  William S. (Bill) Cowling II
President, Lumbermen's Building Centers:
  Dave Dittmer
President, Spenard Builders Supply: Ed Waite
President, United Building Centers: Dale Kukowski
IT Manager: Reba Mart

LOCATIONS

HQ: Lanoga Corporation
   17946 NE 65th St., Redmond, WA 98052
Phone: 425-883-4125   **Fax:** 425-882-2959
Web: lanoga.com

COMPETITORS

84 Lumber
Ace Hardware
Building Materials Holding
Home Depot
Lowe's
Menard
Stock Building Supply
True Value
Wolohan Lumber

HISTORICAL FINANCIALS

Company Type: Private

Income Statement   FYE: December 31

	REVENUE ($ mil.)	NET INCOME ($ mil.)	NET PROFIT MARGIN	EMPLOYEES
12/03	2,000	—	—	8,000
12/02	1,453	—	—	7,009
12/01	1,400	—	—	5,500
12/00	1,300	—	—	5,360
12/99	1,251	—	—	5,125
12/98	1,030	—	—	4,085
12/97	990	—	—	4,147
12/96	842	—	—	3,730
12/95	760	—	—	3,600
12/94	746	—	—	3,400
Annual Growth	**11.6%**	**—**	**—**	**10.0%**

Revenue History

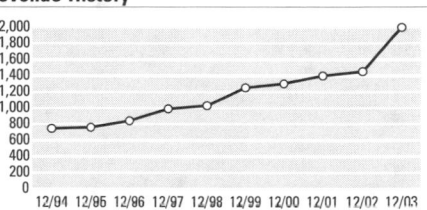

Larry H. Miller Group

You wouldn't hire the Larry H. Miller Group for your late night bebop, but the firm does know a little something about all that jazz. The company operates about 35 auto dealerships in Arizona, Colorado, Idaho, New Mexico, Oregon, and Utah. The company also owns the Utah Jazz, its home (the Delta Center arena), the WNBA's Utah Starzz, Fanzz retail stores, and Salt Lake City TV station KJZZ. In addition the Larry H. Miller Group operates three movie theatres with about 40 screens in Salt Lake City, Lehi, and Sandy, Utah. Also in Sandy the company owns Jordan Commons, an office and entertainment center. Owned by Larry H. Miller, the company was founded in 1979.

EXECUTIVES

CEO: Clark Whitworth
President: Karen G. Miller
COO: Richard Nelson
SVP and Operations Manager: Bryant Henrie
Director of Human Resources: Linda Jeppesen

LOCATIONS

HQ: Larry H. Miller Group
   9350 S. 150 East, Rte. 1000, Sandy, UT 84070
Phone: 801-563-4100   **Fax:** 801-563-4198
Web: www.lhm.com

COMPETITORS

AMC Entertainment	Minnesota Timberwolves
AutoNation	Phil Long Dealerships
Burt Automotive	Portland Trail Blazers
CarMax	Regal Entertainment
Denver Nuggets	Ron Tonkin
DriveTime	Seattle SuperSonics
Earnhardt's Auto Centers	United Auto Group
Loews Cineplex	VT Inc.

HISTORICAL FINANCIALS

Company Type: Private

Income Statement
FYE: December 31

	REVENUE ($ mil.)	NET INCOME ($ mil.)	NET PROFIT MARGIN	EMPLOYEES
12/03	1,608	—	—	5,700
12/02	1,631	—	—	—
12/01	1,550	—	—	—
12/00	1,367	—	—	—
12/99	1,361	—	—	—
12/98	1,200	—	—	—
12/97	1,019	—	—	3,200
12/96	842	—	—	2,200
12/95	926	—	—	1,700
12/94	700	—	—	1,720
Annual Growth	9.7%	—	—	14.2%

Revenue History

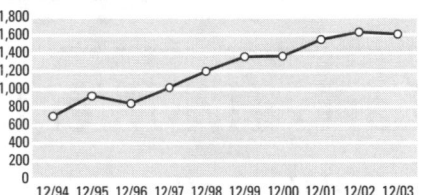

Latham & Watkins

Latham & Watkins' founders Dana Latham and Paul Watkins flipped a coin in 1934 to determine which of their names would go first on the company's shingle. From that coin toss, the law firm has grown into one of the largest in the US. With more than 1,500 lawyers, the firm ranks high in corporate finance, mergers and acquisitions, technology law, and litigation. Latham & Watkins was a key player in the financing for the Venetian Resort Hotel and Casino in Las Vegas and Gemstar's acquisition of TV Guide. Headquartered in Los Angeles, the firm has more than 20 locations worldwide. Latham & Watkins counts Amgen, Time Warner Inc., Lucent, and Morgan Stanley among its clients.

EXECUTIVES

Chairman and Managing Partner: Robert M. Dell
Executive Director: LeeAnn Black
Director Finance: Grant Johnson
Director Global Human Resources: Mimi Krumholz

LOCATIONS

HQ: Latham & Watkins LLP
633 W. 5th St., Ste. 4000, Los Angeles, CA 90071
Phone: 213-485-1234   **Fax:** 213-891-8763
Web: www.lw.com

Latham & Watkins has offices in Boston; Chicago; Costa Mesa, Los Angeles, Menlo Park, San Diego, and San Francisco, California; Newark, New Jersey; New York City; Reston, Virginia; and Washington, DC; as well as in Brussels; Frankfurt and Hamburg, Germany; Hong Kong; London; Milan; Moscow; Paris; Shanghai; Singapore; and Tokyo.

PRODUCTS/OPERATIONS

Selected Practice Areas

Corporate
Environmental
Finance and real estate
International
Litigation
Tax

COMPETITORS

Baker & McKenzie
Clifford Chance
Davis Polk
Gibson, Dunn & Crutcher
Holland & Knight
Kirkland & Ellis
O'Melveny & Myers
Paul, Hastings
Simpson Thacher
Skadden, Arps
Sullivan & Cromwell
Weil, Gotshal

HISTORICAL FINANCIALS

Company Type: Partnership

Income Statement
FYE: December 31

	REVENUE ($ mil.)	NET INCOME ($ mil.)	NET PROFIT MARGIN	EMPLOYEES
12/03	1,032	—	—	—
12/02	906	—	—	—
12/01	770	—	—	—
12/00	643	—	—	2,647
12/99	582	—	—	2,297
12/98	502	—	—	2,287
12/97	421	—	—	—
12/96	363	—	—	—
12/95	300	—	—	—
12/94	263	—	—	—
Annual Growth	16.4%	—	—	7.6%

Revenue History

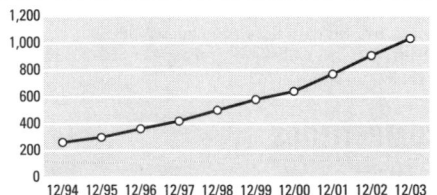

Lefrak Organization

Horace Greeley said "Go west, young man!" and The Lefrak Organization listened — if you take the famous *New Yorker* comic strip's view that you're in the Midwest once you cross the Hudson. The Lefrak Organization is one of the US's largest private landlords, owning and managing some 71,000 apartments (affordable and upscale) in New York City and New Jersey as well as millions of square feet of commercial space. Owned by the LeFrak family, the company's office and retail holdings include its flagship office tower at 40 West 57th Street in midtown Manhattan. Lefrak tenants include Nautica, Bank of America, and Infinity Broadcasting. The company was founded in 1901.

The Lefrak Organization has developed property solely in New Jersey since 1998, focusing on the $10 billion mixed-use Newport in Jersey City. The 600-acre community of apartments, shopping centers, hotels, and office buildings sits on the Hudson River waterfront overlooking Lower Manhattan. The company has built half a dozen office towers (occupied by CIGNA, U.S. Trust, and UBS Financial Services, among others) on the site, and plans for further developments are underway. When completed, the development will include 9,000 apartment units and 9 million sq. ft. of commercial space. Lefrak's flagship residential development, the 5,000-unit Lefrak City in Queens, has been home to successive waves of ethnic groups seeking a better life.

The company also has holdings in oil exploration (Lefrak Oil & Gas Organization, or LOGO) and entertainment (Lefrak Entertainment operates LMR, the record label that launched Barbra Streisand). It also owns stage and movie theaters and produces television programs, movies, and Broadway shows.

Chairman Samuel LeFrak, famed for his interpretation of the Golden Rule ("he who has the gold makes the rules"), died in April 2003. He was an active philanthropist, supporting the Guggenheim Museum and the American Museum of Natural History. He also contributed to the oceanographic studies of the late sea explorer Jacques Cousteau.

HISTORY

Harry Lefrak and his father Aaron came to the US from Palestine (or France — there are many conflicting versions of the Lefrak family history — Aaron's father Maurice is said to have been a developer there in the 1840s) around 1900. They began building tenements in Brooklyn's Williamsburg neighborhood to house the flood of immigrants then pouring into New York City.

In 1901, Harry and Aaron started what is now known as The Lefrak Organization. It diversified into glass and for some time provided raw material for the workshops of Louis Comfort Tiffany. After WWI the glass factory was sold, and the company expanded into Brooklyn, where it developed housing and commercial space in Bedford-Stuyvesant, among other areas.

Samuel, Harry's son, began working in the business early, assisting tradesmen at building sites. He then attended the University of Maryland, and shunning a future career in dentistry (family lore claims his left-handedness would have required special tools), returned to the business. Samuel's first project was a 120-unit apartment building in Brooklyn's Midwood — it was 1938, and he was 20 years old and still a university student.

During WWII, the firm built camps and housing for the Army. After the war, business took off, as the company began building low-cost housing. Samuel took over the company in 1948. To keep costs down, Samuel bought clay and gypsum quarries, forests, and lumber mills and cement plants, eventually achieving 70% vertical integration of his operations. This included the creation of in-house architectural, engineering, and construction departments that handled all aspects of building the LeFrak empire's properties — from initial designs to general contracting — from the ground up.

The 1950s building boom was in part spurred by new laws in New York authorizing the issue of state bonds for financing low-interest construction loans, which Lefrak used to build more than 2,000 apartments in previously undeveloped coastal sections of Brooklyn. At its peak, Lefrak turned out an apartment every 16 minutes for rents as low as $21 per room.

In 1960 Lefrak broke ground for Lefrak City, a 5,000-apartment development built on 40 acres in Queens (after four years of negotiations with the trustees of the William Waldorf Astor estate over the sale price — $6 million), which featured air-conditioned units and rented for $40 per room.

The next decade brought a real estate slump that endangered the organization's next project, Battery Park. Lefrak issued public bonds to save it. Samuel also picked up a few more properties during this period, and he capitalized the "F" in his family name but not the company name. (He later said that he did this to distinguish himself from other Lefraks at his club who had been posted for nonpayment of dues, though a conflicting story states that his mother's French-born physician originally capitalized the "F" on Samuel's birth certificate.)

Samuel's son Richard became president of the company in 1975. Richard oversaw an even bigger project: the 600-acre Newport City development, begun in 1989 with plans for some 10,000 apartments and retail and commercial space.

Meanwhile, Lefrak City had "turned," as its original Jewish occupants sought greener fields. As occupancy dropped, the company relaxed its tenant screening, and the development deteriorated (it was subsequently tagged "Crack City"). In the 1990s, however, it began attracting a mix of African, Jewish, and Central Asian immigrants, whose tightly-knit communities improved the development's safety and equilibrium.

Construction of the company's Newport project continued throughout the 1990s with construction of office buildings, apartments, and a hotel (completed in 2000) on the site. As a tight Manhattan office market drove up lease prices, Lefrak's new offices across the Hudson attracted companies in the finance and insurance sectors. Lefrak filled about 3 million sq. ft. in its Newport development during 1999 and 2000.

In 2001 the company's Gateway complex in Battery Park City was damaged in the World Trade Center terrorist attack. The tenants threatened a rent strike, prompting Lefrak to lower rents to compensate for the difficulties attributed to living near the site.

Samuel LeFrak died in April 2003 at the age of 85.

EXECUTIVES

President, CEO, and COO: Richard S. LeFrak, age 59
EVP and CFO: Richard N. Papert
Managing Director: Harrison LeFrak
Managing Director: James (Jamie) LeFrak
SVP Marketing and Public Relations: Edward Cortese
VP Commercial: Marsilia (Marcy) Boyle
VP Commercial: Irwin Granville
VP Construction and Engineering: Anthony Scavo
VP Finance and Administration and Treasurer: Mitchell Ingerman
General Counsel: Arnold S. Lehman
Director, Human Resources: John Farrelly
Director, Residential Leasing: Tom Pichi
Auditors: Lewis Goldberg

LOCATIONS

HQ: Lefrak Organization Inc.
9777 Queens Blvd., Rego Park, NY 11374
Phone: 718-459-9021   **Fax:** 718-897-0688
Web: www.lefrak.com

The Lefrak Organization operates primarily in New Jersey and New York.

Selected Properties

Commercial Space
  Jersey City, NJ
    Newport development
  New York City (Manhattan)
    40 W. 57th St.
    Gateway Plaza at Battery Park City
    James Tower
Residential Apartments
  Jersey City, NJ
    Atlantic
    East Hampton
    James Monroe
    Presidential Plaza
    Riverside
    Southampton
    Towers of America
  New York City (Manhattan)
    Gateway Plaza at Battery Park City
  New York City (Queens)
    Lefrak City
Residential Co-op Properties
  New York City (Brooklyn)
    Bay Ridge
    Bensonhurst
    Flatbush
    Park Slope
    Sheepshead Bay
  New York City (Queens)
    Elmhurst
    Flushing
    Forest Hills
    Key Gardens
    Rego Park
    Woodside
Retail
  Jersey City, NJ
    Newport Centre Mall

PRODUCTS/OPERATIONS

Selected Operations

Energy
  Lefrak Oil & Gas Organization
Entertainment
  Lefrak Entertainment Company
Real Estate
  Commercial properties
  Residential apartments
  Residential co-op properties
  Retail properties
Telecommunications
  Newport Telephone Company, Inc.

COMPETITORS

Alexander's	Related Capital
AvalonBay	Silverstein Properties
Boston Properties	SL Green Realty
Equity Office Properties	Starrett Corporation
Grenadier	Tishman
Hartz Mountain	Trizec Properties
Helmsley Enterprises	Trump
Mack-Cali	Vornado Realty Trust
Macklowe Properties	Witkoff Group
Reckson Associates Realty	

HISTORICAL FINANCIALS

Company Type: Private

Income Statement

FYE: Last Sunday in November

	REVENUE ($ mil.)	NET INCOME ($ mil.)	NET PROFIT MARGIN	EMPLOYEES
11/02	2,800	—	—	16,200
11/01	3,800	—	—	16,200
11/00	3,800	—	—	16,110
11/99	2,500	—	—	16,500
11/98	2,750	—	—	16,000
11/97	3,400	—	—	18,000
11/96	3,500	—	—	17,500
11/95	3,300	—	—	17,400
11/94	3,100	—	—	17,500
11/93	3,200	—	—	18,000
Annual Growth	(1.5%)	—	—	(1.2%)

Revenue History

Leslie's Poolmart

Leslie's Poolmart is the big fish of pool product retailers. The company sells pool chemicals, cleaning and testing equipment, covers, and recreational items through about 470 stores in more than 35 states, mostly in California, Texas, Arizona, and Florida. It also sells through catalogs and its Web site. Leslie's makes chlorine tablets and repackages other chemicals to be sold under the Leslie name. Pool chemicals, major equipment, and parts account for about 82% of sales. Founded in 1963, Leslie's went private in a 1997 management LBO backed by Leonard Green & Partners, which owns nearly 61% of the company.

EXECUTIVES

Chairman, President, and CEO: Lawrence H. Hayward, age 50, $922,445 pay
EVP and CFO: Steven L. Ortega
SVP, Merchandising and Marketing: Michael L. Hatch, age 51, $300,535 pay
SVP, Store Operations: Marvin D. Schutz, age 55, $284,380 pay
SVP and CIO: Janet I. McDonald, age 46, $245,585 pay
VP, Service and Commercial: Mark A. Lum, age 44
Director, Human Resources: Marie Sousa
Auditors: Ernst & Young LLP

HQ: Leslie's Poolmart, Inc.
   3925 E. Broadway Rd., Ste. 100, Phoenix, AZ 85040
Phone: 602-366-3999   **Fax:** 602-366-3934
Web: www.lesliespool.com

2004 Stores

	No.
California	109
Texas	83
Arizona	40
Florida	32
New Jersey	22
New York	21
Georgia	18
Pennsylvania	18
Nevada	14
Ohio	10
Connecticut	9
Massachusetts	9
Missouri	8
Michigan	7
Oklahoma	7
Tennessee	7
Virginia	7
Illinois	6
Indiana	6
Louisiana	6
Other states	35
Total	**474**

COMPETITORS

Home Depot
Kmart
SCP Pool
Wal-Mart

HISTORICAL FINANCIALS

Company Type: Private

Income Statement

FYE: Saturday nearest September 30

	REVENUE ($ mil.)	NET INCOME ($ mil.)	NET PROFIT MARGIN	EMPLOYEES
9/04	356	16	4.6%	1,892
9/03	327	10	3.1%	2,006
9/02	313	5	1.5%	1,843
9/01	302	1	0.4%	1,805
9/00	303	(5)	—	1,813
9/99	282	(1)	—	2,437
9/98	253	3	1.1%	1,906
9/97	196	9	4.5%	1,767
9/96	192	4	2.0%	1,055
9/95	163	3	2.1%	780
Annual Growth	**9.1%**	**18.9%**	**—**	**10.3%**

2004 Year-End Financials

Debt ratio: (152.2%)
Return on equity: —
Cash ($ mil.): 21
Current ratio: 1.55
Long-term debt ($ mil.): 59

Net Income History

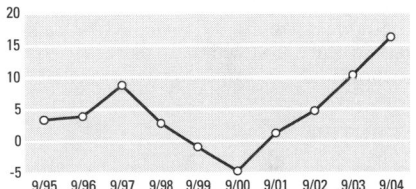

Levi Strauss

Levi Strauss & Co. (LS&CO.) strives to provide the world's casual workday wardrobe, inside and out. LS&CO., the world's #1 maker of brand-name clothing, sells jeans and sportswear under the Levi's, Dockers, and Levi Strauss Signature names in more than 110 countries. It also markets men's and women's underwear and loungewear. Levi's jeans — department store staples — were once the uniform of American youth, but LS&CO. lost touch with the trends in recent years. In response, the company has transformed its product offerings to include wrinkle-free and stain-resistant fabrics used in the making of some of its Levi's and Dockers slacks. The Haas family (relatives of founder Levi Strauss) owns LS&CO.

Hoping to regain some of the market share lost to VF Corporation (makers of Lee and Wrangler) and others over the past decade, the company has rolled out an array of new products the last few years. Levi's Superlow jeans and Levi Strauss Signature jeans were created for the mass market, though their distribution in the US was short-lived. Dockers Flat Front Mobile pants (with secret pockets for cell phones, PDAs, and other gadgets) and Dockers Go Khaki pants (with Stain Defender, a Teflon treatment preventing stains) target the 25 to 39 age group. Undaunted by a slate of disappointing and stale brands (including Levi's Engineered Jeans, the Type 1, and the Superlow), Levi Strauss revamped a number of its basic products, including Levi's 501, 550, and 515.

In 2004 the company announced a licensing agreement with Dehli, India-based M&B Footwear to manufacture men's and women's casual shoes and sneakers beginning in 2005. The line appears in 50 Levi's outlets and M&B's retail stores. Further expanding its product array, LS&CO. under license by Signature Apparel Group added Levi-brand underwear and loungewear to its portfolio in 2005 that will be carried by such mid-tier retailers as Kohl's, JCPenney, and Sears. To feed the country's need for American fashion, Levi Strauss in early 2005 opened its first jeans outlet in Vietnam — in a shopping center in Hanoi.

Due to substantial drops in net sales over the past seven years, Levi Strauss has also taken measures to recoup some of its losses, including closing 37 of its factories worldwide and, instead, using independent contract manufacturers. It closed its remaining North American manufacturing facilities; San Antonio and three Canadian operations shut down in early 2004. The closures affected some 2,000 employees. In Haiti, Levi Strauss is closing its production facility not because of budget cuts, but labor disputes, an action that will result in the loss of about 700 jobs.

Meanwhile, the company continues to suss out other cost-cutting measures during its internal restructuring process. The company reduced its workforce by 10% over a six-month period in 2004. In mid-2004 Levi Strauss announced plans to close its Spanish manufacturing facilities, resulting in the loss of more than 450 jobs. In Europe, in general, LS&CO. eliminated about 350 jobs that year.

Also in 2004 LS&CO. signed a licensing deal with Li & Fung for the production of men's tops under the Levi's, Red Tab, SILVER TAB, and Premium names.

HISTORY

Levi Strauss arrived in New York City from Bavaria in 1847. In 1853 he moved to San Francisco to sell dry goods to the gold rushers. Shortly after, a prospector told Strauss of miners' problems in finding sturdy pants. Strauss made a pair out of canvas for the prospector; word of the rugged pants spread quickly.

Strauss continued his dry-goods business in the 1860s. During this time he switched the pants' fabric to a durable French cloth called serge de Nimes, soon known as denim. He colored the fabric with indigo dye and adopted the idea from Nevada tailor Jacob Davis of reinforcing the pants with copper rivets. In 1873 Strauss and Davis produced their first pair of waist-high overalls (later known as jeans). The pants soon became *de rigueur* for lumberjacks, cowboys, railroad workers, oil drillers, and farmers.

Strauss continued to build his pants and wholesaling business until he died in 1902. Levi Strauss & Co. (LS&CO.) passed to four nephews who carried on their uncle's jeans business while maintaining the company's philanthropic reputation.

After WWII Walter Haas and Peter Haas (a fourth-generation Strauss family member) assumed leadership of LS&CO. In 1948 they ended the company's wholesaling business to concentrate on Levi's clothing. In the 1950s Levi's jeans ceased to be merely functional garments for workers: They became the uniform of American youth. In the 1960s LS&CO. added women's attire and expanded overseas.

The company went public in 1971. That year it added a women's career line and bought Koret sportswear (sold in 1984). By the mid-1980s profits declined. Peace Corps veteran-turned-McKinsey consultant Robert Haas (Walter's son) grabbed the reins of LS&CO. in 1984 and took the company private the next year. He also instilled a touchy-feely corporate culture often at odds with the bottom line.

In 1986 LS&CO. introduced Dockers casual pants. The company's sales began rising in 1991 as consumers forsook designer duds of the 1980s for more practical clothes. LS&CO. says seven out of every 10 American men own a pair of Dockers. However, LS&CO. missed out on the birth of another trend: the split between the fashion sense of US adolescents and their Levi's-loving, baby boomer parents.

In 1996 the company introduced Slates dress slacks. That year LS&CO. bought back nearly one-third of its stock from family and employees for $4.3 billion. Grappling with slipping sales and debt from the buyout, in 1997 LS&CO. closed 11 of its 37 North American plants, laying off 6,400 workers and 1,000 salaried employees; it granted generous severance packages even to those earning minimum wage.

In 1998, citing improved labor conditions in China, LS&CO. announced it would step up its use of Chinese subcontractors. Further restructuring added a third of its European plants to the closures list that year. LS&CO.'s sales fell 13% in fiscal 1998. The next year LS&CO. closed 11 of 22 remaining North American plants. It also unleashed several new jeans brands that eschewed the company's one-style-fits-all approach of old.

In 1999 Haas handed his CEO title to Pepsi executive Philip Marineau. In 2002 LS&CO. announced it would close six of its last eight US plants and cut 20% of its worldwide staff (3,300 workers). In 2003 it cut another 5% of its worldwide staff (650 workers).

EXECUTIVES

Chairman: Robert D. (Bob) Haas, age 62
President and CEO: Philip A. (Phil) Marineau, age 58, $4,047,992 pay
CFO: Hans Ploos van Amstel, age 40
SVP and CIO: David G. Bergen, age 49
SVP, General Counsel, and Assistant Secretary: Albert F. Moreno, age 61
SVP; Interim President, Levi Strauss Europe, Middle East and Africa (LSEMA); President, Levi Strauss Asia Pacific: R. John Anderson, age 53, $1,470,177 pay
SVP and President, Levi Strauss Europe: Paul Mason, age 44, $2,184,642 pay
SVP, Strategy and Planning: Lawrence W. Ruff, age 48
SVP, Worldwide Human Resources: Fred D. Paulenich, age 40
SVP, World Supply Chain: Paul Harrington, age 42
VP and Controller: Gary W. Grellman
VP, Global Tax Department: Paul Smith
VP, Worldwide and US Communications: Dan Chew
VP, Marketing, Dockers: Bill Stewart
VP, Marketing, Levi Strauss Signature: Sherri Phillips
President and General Manager, Dockers Commercial Business Unit, US: John D. Goodman, age 49
President, Dockers Brand, US: Roberta H. (Bobbi) Silten, age 44
President, Levi Strauss Signature Brand, US: Scott A. LaPorta, age 42, $1,010,822 pay
President, Levi's Brand, US: Robert L. Hanson, age 40, $1,308,542 pay
Auditors: KPMG LLP

LOCATIONS

HQ: Levi Strauss & Co.
   1155 Battery St., San Francisco, CA 94111
Phone: 415-501-6000   **Fax:** 415-501-7112
Web: www.levistrauss.com

Levi Strauss & Co. manufactures and sells its branded jeans, sportswear, and dress pants through retail locations and company-owned outlets in more than 100 countries.

2004 Sales

	$ mil.	% of total
North America	2,426.5	60
Europe	1,042.1	25
Asia/Pacific	603.9	15
Total	**4,072.5**	**100**

PRODUCTS/OPERATIONS

Selected Brand Names

501
505
Dockers
Dockers K-1
Dockers Premium
Dockers Recode
Dress Mobile
Flat Front Mobile
Go Khaki
Levi's
Levi's Engineered
Levi's Red
Levi's Silvertab
Levi's Type 1
ProStyle
Pure Blue
Red Tab
Superlow

COMPETITORS

Abercrombie & Fitch
adidas-Salomon
American Eagle Outfitters
Benetton
Calvin Klein
Diesel
Eddie Bauer
Fruit of the Loom
FUBU
Gap
Guess
Haggar
Hugo Boss
Innovo
J. C. Penney
J. Crew
Jockey International
Jones Apparel
Kmart
Lands' End
Limited Brands
Liz Claiborne
Nautica Enterprises
NIKE
OshKosh B'Gosh
Oxford Industries
Perry Ellis International
Playtex
Polo Ralph Lauren
Sears
Target
Tommy Hilfiger
Under Armour
VF
Victoria's Secret Stores
Wacoal
Wal-Mart
Warnaco Group

HISTORICAL FINANCIALS

Company Type: Private

Income Statement

FYE: Last Sunday in November

	REVENUE ($ mil.)	NET INCOME ($ mil.)	NET PROFIT MARGIN	EMPLOYEES
11/04	4,073	30	0.7%	8,850
11/03	4,091	(349)	—	12,300
11/02	4,137	25	0.6%	12,400
11/01	4,259	151	3.5%	16,700
11/00	4,645	223	4.8%	17,300
11/99	5,140	5	0.1%	30,000
11/98	5,959	103	1.7%	30,000
11/97	6,862	138	2.0%	37,000
11/96	7,136	465	6.5%	37,000
11/95	6,707	735	11.0%	37,700
Annual Growth	**(5.4%)**	**(29.8%)**	**—**	**(14.9%)**

2004 Year-End Financials

Debt ratio: —
Return on equity: —
Cash ($ mil.): 300
Current ratio: 1.57
Long-term debt ($ mil.): 2,255

Net Income History

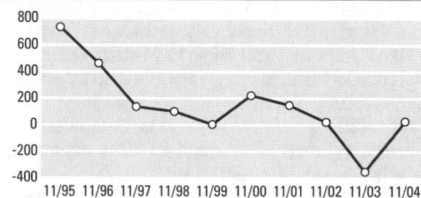

Levitz Home Furnishings

The lamps will stay lit at Levitz Home Furnishings (the holding company for Levitz Furniture Incorporated, LFI), but have gone out at sister chain Seaman Furniture. LFI (parent company of the Levitz Furniture Corp. chain) has about 120 stores mostly in the Northeast and on the West Coast, including 25 former Seaman stores that have been converted to the Levitz Home Furnishings name. The creation of Levitz Home Furnishings in 2001 allowed LFI to emerge from Chapter 11 bankruptcy (originally filed in 1997), in part by distributing management of its 15 East Coast stores to Seaman Furniture. Heavily leveraged and struggling, Levitz Home Furnishings itself filed for Chapter 11 bankruptcy protection in October 2005.

The closing of the 45-store Seaman Furniture chain in May 2005 was intended to strengthen Levitz Home Furnishings financially, but the recent bankruptcy filing suggests otherwise. Levitz Home Furnishings says it has arranged for a $90 million in debtor-in-possession financing package led by GE Commercial Finance. The furniture chain says it will continue to operate its stores during the reorganization. However, some stores are expected to be closed.

The company operates 43 stores in California.

Chairman and CEO Jay Carothers resigned abruptly in March 2005 after three years of slumping sales. (Company president C. Mark Scott is filling in as CEO on an interim basis.) Former CEO Alan Rosenberg, credited for taking the Seaman's chain out of bankruptcy and merging it with Levitz (also in bankruptcy), died in November 2003.

EXECUTIVES

President and Acting CEO: C. Mark Scott
COO: Sandeep Chugani
SVP, Strategic Sourcing: Hemant Kalbag
SVP, Supply Chain Operations: Shisir Agarwal
SVP, Finance: Coleen A. Colreavy
Divisional VP, Advertising: Greg Ackerman
General Counsel: Robert Webber
Executive Administration: Sybil Handwerker

LOCATIONS

HQ: Levitz Home Furnishings, Inc.
   300 Crossways Park Dr., Woodbury, NY 11797
Phone: 516-496-9560   **Fax:** 631-927-1780
Web: www.levitz.com

Levitz Home Furnishings operates 121 furniture showrooms in Arizona, California, Connecticut, Delaware, Minnesota, Nevada, New Jersey, New York, Oregon, Pennsylvania, and Washington.

COMPETITORS

Bombay Company
Cost Plus
Dillard's
Ethan Allen
Euromarket Designs
Federated
IKEA
J. C. Penney
Jennifer Convertibles
La-Z-Boy
Mattress Giant
May
Pier 1 Imports
Restoration Hardware
Sleepy's
Williams-Sonoma
Z Gallerie

HISTORICAL FINANCIALS

Company Type: Private

Income Statement

FYE: April 30

	ESTIMATED REVENUE ($ mil.)	NET INCOME ($ mil.)	NET PROFIT MARGIN	EMPLOYEES
4/04	1,000	—	—	4,000
4/03	1,000	—	—	4,000
4/02	915	—	—	4,900
4/01	920	—	—	4,400
Annual Growth	2.8%	—	—	(3.1%)

Revenue History

Liberty Mutual

Boston boasts of baked beans, the Red Sox, and the Liberty Mutual Group. Liberty Mutual Holding is the parent company for the Liberty Mutual Group and its three principal mutual insurance companies, Liberty Mutual Insurance, Liberty Mutual Fire Insurance, and Employers Insurance Company of Wausau. Liberty Mutual is one of the top property/casualty insurers in the US and a top 10 provider of automobile insurance. The company also offers homeowners' insurance and commercial lines for small to large companies. Liberty Mutual Group is a diversified global insurer with operations in 900 offices throughout the world.

The Commercial Markets division provides commercial property/casualty products and includes the National Market group, which serves large businesses, and the Business Market unit, serving businesses midsized enterprises. The Commercial Markets division also includes the Wausau Commercial Market unit, which provides workers' compensation, general liability, and other commercial insurance and relates products to midsized to large employers. This division also offers specialty risk products such as surety bonds and captive services as well as group disability and life insurance.

The Agency Markets (formerly called Regional Agency Markets) offers small commercial and personal lines coverage through independent agents and brokers throughout the US. The International division includes local companies that offer personal and commercial insurance to local markets around the globe and Liberty International Underwriters, which provides specialty commercial lines worldwide.

HISTORY

The need for financial aid to workers injured on the job was recognized in Europe in the late 19th century but did not make its way to the US until a workers' compensation law for federal employees was passed in 1908. Massachusetts was one of the first states to enact similar legislation. Liberty Mutual was founded in Boston in 1912 to fill this newly recognized niche.

Liberty Mutual followed the fire insurance practice of taking an active part in loss prevention. It evaluated clients' premises and procedures and recommended ways to prevent accidents. The company rejected the budding industry practice of limiting medical fees, instead studying the most effective ways to reduce the long-term cost of a claim by getting the injured party back to work.

In 1942 the company acquired the United Mutual Fire Insurance Company (founded 1908, renamed Liberty Mutual Fire Insurance Company in 1949). The next year it founded a rehabilitation center in Boston to treat injured workers and to test treatments.

In the 1960s and 1970s, Liberty Mutual expanded its line to include life insurance (1963), group pensions (1970), and IRAs (1975).

Seeking to increase its national presence, the company formed Liberty Northwest Insurance Corporation in 1983. It continued expanding its offerings, with new subsidiaries in commercial, personal, and excess lines and, in 1986, by moving into financial services by buying Stein Roe & Farnham (founded 1958).

The expansion/diversification strategy seemed to work. Earnings between 1984 and 1986 more than tripled. Then the downturn: Recession was followed by a string of natural disasters, and Liberty Mutual's income fell sharply between 1986 and 1988. In 1992 and 1993 the firm lost suits to Coors and Outboard Marine for failing to back those companies in environmental litigation cases.

Liberty Mutual restructured in 1994, withdrawing from the group health business and reorganizing claims operations into two units: Personal Markets and Business Markets. The next year it gained a foothold in the UK when it received permission to invest in a Lloyd's of London syndicate management company.

The company expanded its financial services operations in 1995 and 1996, merging its Liberty Financial subsidiary with the already-public Colonial Group; it also acquired American Asset Management and Newport Pacific Management.

In a soft workers' compensation market, the company tried to build its position through key market acquisitions. In 1997 Liberty Mutual acquired Société Générale's US mutual funds unit, led by international money dean Jean-Marie Eveillard. In 1998 the company was slammed by increased claims — many related to a Condé Nast Building construction accident that shut down New York City's Times Square that summer. Liberty Mutual acquired erstwhile competitor Employers Insurance of Wausau that year.

In 1999 the company bought Guardian Royal Exchange's US operations. In a new international initiative that year, Liberty Mutual bought 70% of Singapore-based insurer Citystate Holdings (to be renamed Liberty Citystate) as its foothold in Asia. Also in 1999 Liberty Mutual strengthened its US business insurance lineup by adding the Wausau Companies.

After failing to find a buyer, asset management subsidiary Liberty Financial in 2001 began liquidating assets. Canadian insurer Sun Life acquired Keyport Life Insurance and mutual fund distributor Independent Financial Marketing Group. Liberty Financial's investment management segment (including subsidiaries Crabbe Huston, Stein Roe & Farnham, and Liberty Wanger Asset Management) was snapped up by FleetBoston (now part of the Bank of America empire). Liberty Mutual then bought the nearly 30% of Liberty Financial it did not already own.

The company's diversification efforts included Liberty International, which expanded operations in such countries as Canada, Japan, Mexico, Singapore, and the UK. The company also grew its international presence in areas such as China and southern Europe.

Slumping property/casualty lines and the events of September 11 hit Liberty Mutual in 2001 (the company paid out some $500 million in claims). In 2001 and 2002 the company reorganized into a mutual holding company structure with its three principal operating companies (Liberty Mutual Insurance, Liberty Mutual Fire Insurance, and Employers Insurance Company of Wausau) each becoming separate stock insurance companies with Liberty Mutual Holding Company as the parent.

The company rebounded nicely in 2002-03, thanks to the rebounding stock market and strategic acquisitions worldwide. Strengthening its personal lines business, Liberty Mutual in 2003 bought Prudential's domestic property/casualty operations and MetLife's auto business in Spain.

EXECUTIVES

Chairman, President, and CEO: Edmund F. (Ted) Kelly, age 59
Special Consultant to the CEO: Roger L. Jean
EVP, Personal Markets: J. Paul Condrin III
EVP, Liberty International: Thomas C. Ramey
EVP; President and COO, Wausau Insurance: Mark Fiebrink
EVP and Chief Investment Officer: A. Alexander Fontanes
EVP, Agency Markets: Gary R. Gregg
EVP, Commercial Markets: David H. Long
SVP and CFO: Dennis J. Langwell
SVP and CIO: Stuart M. McGuigan
SVP and General Counsel: Christopher C. Mansfield
SVP and Corporate Actuary: Robert T. Muleski
SVP, Human Resources and Administration: Helen E. R. Sayles
SVP, Communications Services: Stephen G. Sullivan
VP and Director, Investor Relations: Matthew T. Coyle
Auditors: Ernst & Young LLP

LOCATIONS

HQ: Liberty Mutual Holding Company Inc.
175 Berkeley St., Boston, MA 02116
Phone: 617-357-9500   **Fax:** 617-350-7648
Web: www.libertymutual.com

Liberty Mutual Insurance has about 800 offices in the US, as well as in Argentina, Australia, Bermuda, Brazil, Canada, China, Colombia, Hong Kong, Ireland, Japan, Malaysia, Mexico, Portugal, Singapore, Spain, Thailand, the UK, and Venezuela.

PRODUCTS/OPERATIONS

2004 Assets

	$ mil.	% of total
Investments		
Fixed maturities	35,601	49
Equity securities	1,802	2
Trading securities	457	1
Short-term investments	687	1
Other investments	990	1
Cash & equivalents	2,590	4
Premium & other receivables	5,642	8
Reinsurance recoverables	14,209	20
Deferred income taxes	938	1
Deferred policy acquisition costs	1,354	2
Goodwill & intangible assets	824	1
Prepaid reinsurance premiums	1,330	2
Separate account assets	3,572	5
Other assets	2,363	3
Total	**72,359**	**100**

2004 Sales

	$ mil.	% of total
Premiums earned	16,563	84
Net investment income	2,102	11
Net realized investment gains	312	2
Fees & other revenues	664	3
Total	**19,641**	**100**

2004 Sales

	$ mil.	% of total
Personal market	5,931	30
Commercial markets	5,618	29
Agency markets	3,975	20
Liberty International	3,620	18
Other revenues	497	3
Total	**19,641**	**100**

Selected Product and Services

Personal market
  Homeowners' insurance
  Private passenger automobile insurance
Commercial markets (midsized to large businesses)
  Commercial Automobile
  Commercial property/casualty
  General liability
  Risk management
  Specialty risk
    Captive services
    Commercial and contract surety bonds
    Property insurance
  Workers' compensation
Agency markets (formerly regional agency markets;
  small businesses and individuals)
  Commercial automobile
  Commercial multi-peril
  General liability
  Personal lines coverage
    Personal automobile
    Homeowners
  Property insurance
  Workers' compensation
Liberty International
  Multi-line insurance
    Aviation
    Personal accident
    Property insurance
    Treaty casualty
  Reinsurance
  Specialty risk
    Aviation
    Casualty
    Directors and officers
    Energy
    Engineering
    Errors and omissions
    Excess casualty
    Marine
    Professional liability
    Property liability

COMPETITORS

21st Century	Lincoln Financial Group
ACE Limited	MassMutual
AEGON USA	MetLife
AIG	New York Life
Allianz	Northwestern Mutual
Allstate	Progressive Corporation
Charles Schwab	Prudential
CIGNA	Safeco
Citigroup	St. Paul Travelers
CNA Financial	State Farm
COUNTRY Insurance	T. Rowe Price
Fremont General	USAA
GenAmerica	Washington
The Hartford	National Corporation
ING	

HISTORICAL FINANCIALS
Company Type: Mutual company

Income Statement
FYE: December 31

	ASSETS ($ mil.)	NET INCOME ($ mil.)	INCOME AS % OF ASSETS	EMPLOYEES
12/04	72,359	1,245	1.7%	38,000
12/03	64,422	851	1.3%	38,000
12/02	55,877	508	0.9%	35,000
12/01	53,065	(289)	—	35,000
12/00	30,264	403	1.3%	37,000
12/99	55,259	501	0.9%	37,440
12/98	26,254	245	0.9%	24,000
12/97	25,230	412	1.6%	23,000
12/96	22,690	474	2.1%	23,000
12/95	21,791	457	2.1%	23,000
Annual Growth	**14.3%**	**11.8%**	**—**	**5.7%**

2004 Year-End Financials

Equity as % of assets: 12.0%   Long-term debt ($ mil.): 2,074
Return on assets: 1.8%   Sales ($ mil.): 19,641
Return on equity: 15.5%

Net Income History

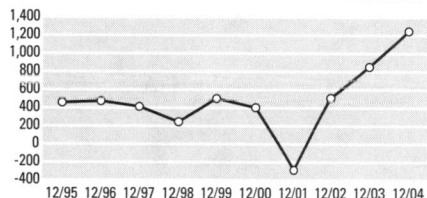

1,400
1,200
1,000
800
600
400
200
0
-200
-400

12/95 12/96 12/97 12/98 12/99 12/00 12/01 12/02 12/03 12/04

Life Care Centers

Life Care Centers of America is a privately owned operator of retirement and health care centers. The company manages more than 260 facilities in 28 states — including retirement communities, assisted-living facilities, and nursing homes — and provides specialized services such as home health care. Life Care also operates centers specifically for people with Alzheimer's disease or related dementia. Founder Forrest Preston opened his first center in 1970, and the company continues to tout a "corporate culture grounded in the Judeo-Christian ethic." However, Life Care has faced complaints of poor-quality care, part of a problem that plagues the industry overall.

EXECUTIVES

Chairman: Forrest L. Preston
President: Don J. Giardina
COO: Cathy Murray
CFO: Steve Ziegler
EVP: Beecher Hunter
EVP and Director of Operations, Garden Terrace Associates: Trent Tolbert
SVP, Operations West: James W. Scadlock
VP, Life Care at Home: Mary R. Maurer
Director, Public Relations: Sebrena Sawtell
Corporate Integrity Services Officer: Kim New
Webmaster: Paul Garner

LOCATIONS

HQ: Life Care Centers of America
  3570 Keith St. NW, Cleveland, TN 37320
Phone: 423-472-9585   **Fax:** 423-339-8337
Web: www.lcca.com

COMPETITORS

Advocat
Beverly Enterprises
Kindred Healthcare
Manor Care
Mariner
National HealthCare
Sun Healthcare

HISTORICAL FINANCIALS
Company Type: Private

Income Statement
FYE: December 31

	ESTIMATED REVENUE ($ mil.)	NET INCOME ($ mil.)	NET PROFIT MARGIN	EMPLOYEES
12/03	1,600	—	—	30,000
12/02	1,460	—	—	30,000
12/01	1,328	—	—	30,000
12/00	1,265	—	—	29,350
12/99	1,210	—	—	26,000
12/98	1,210	—	—	22,000
12/97	1,100	—	—	22,000
12/96	1,000	—	—	22,000
Annual Growth	**6.9%**	**—**	**—**	**4.5%**

Revenue History

1,600
1,400
1,200
1,000
800
600
400
200
0

12/94 12/95 12/96 12/97 12/98 12/99 12/00 12/01 12/02 12/03

Lifetime Entertainment

Lifetime Entertainment Services hopes viewers make a long-term commitment to its television programs. The company operates three woman-oriented cable-TV networks (Lifetime, Lifetime Movie Network, Lifetime Real Women) offering original movies, talk shows, and syndicated shows. Its Lifetime channel reaches 89 million US households and is one of the highest-rated cable networks in primetime. The Lifetime Online unit offers information and entertainment on the Web. The firm launched *Lifetime* magazine in 2003, but decided to halt publication in fall 2004.

Lifetime was formed by the merger of channels Daytime and Cable Health Network in 1984. It is jointly owned by Walt Disney (via Disney ABC Cable) and Hearst.

Longtime CEO Carole Black left the company in early 2005, replaced by former Turner Broadcasting executive Betty Cohen. Before she left the company, Black set Lifetime Entertainment on a new course in its programming for the 2005-06 television season. The company is boosting its original programming by about 33%, which will consist of Lifetime Entertainment's first forays into scripted comedies, miniseries, and limited series.

EXECUTIVES

President and CEO: Betty Cohen
President, Entertainment: Susanne Daniels
EVP and CFO: James Wesley
EVP Distribution and Business Development:
Louise Henry Bryson
EVP Legal, Business Affairs, and Human Resources:
Patricia Langer
EVP Public Affairs and Corporate Communications:
Meredith Wagner
EVP Research: Tim Brooks
EVP Sales; EVP and General Manager, Lifetime Television Network: Lynn Picard
SVP Finance: Paul Jennings
SVP Original Movies: Trevor Walton
SVP Publicity: Carla Princi
VP Corporate Communications: Katherine Urbon
VP Marketing: Catherine Moran

LOCATIONS

HQ: Lifetime Entertainment Services
309 W. 49th St., New York, NY 10019
Phone: 212-424-7000 **Fax:** 212-957-4449
Web: www.lifetimetv.com

PRODUCTS/OPERATIONS

Operations
Lifetime Books (publishing)
Lifetime Movie Network (cable network, 45 million households)
Lifetime Radio for Women (syndicated radio programming)
Lifetime Real Women (cable network, 10 million households)
Lifetime Television Network (cable network, 89 million households)
Lifetime TV Store

Selected Lifetime Programming
Any Day Now
Designing Women
The Division
Fit Forever with Denise Austin
Golden Girls
Intimate Portrait
Lifetime Now
Mad About You
Merge
MISSING
The Nanny
Providence
Speaking of Women's Health
Strong Medicine
What Should You Do?
Wild Card

COMPETITORS

A&E Networks	iVillage
CPB	Martha Stewart Living
Crown Media	NBC Universal
Discovery Communications	Oxygen Media
Disney	Paxson Communications
Fox Entertainment	Viacom
Harpo	WE: Women's Entertainment

HISTORICAL FINANCIALS
Company Type: Joint venture

Income Statement
FYE: December 31

	REVENUE ($ mil.)	NET INCOME ($ mil.)	NET PROFIT MARGIN	EMPLOYEES
12/04	850	—	—	—
12/03	820	—	—	—
12/02	790	—	—	—
12/01	727	—	—	—
12/00	661	—	—	—
12/99	528	—	—	—
12/98	468	—	—	—
12/97	398	—	—	300
12/96	257	—	—	270
12/95	271	—	—	—
Annual Growth	**13.6%**	—	—	**11.1%**

Revenue History

12/95	12/96	12/97	12/98	12/99	12/00	12/01	12/02	12/03	12/04

Linn Energy

It's a Linn-Linn situation. CEO Michael Linn's namesake company Linn Energy has successfully drilled for natural gas in the Appalachian Basin. The natural gas exploration and production company made seven property acquisitions (including more than 1,230 producing wells) between 2003 and 2005 in New York, Pennsylvania, Virginia, and West Virginia. The company, which has drilled 126 wells with a 100% success rate, reports proved reserves of 100.9 billion cu. ft. of natural gas equivalent. Linn Energy has focused on shallow drilling (2,500 to 5,500 ft.), and many of its wells are connected to multiple producing zones. Following its IPO, Quantum Energy Partners will control 45% of the company; CEO Linn, 14%.

Linn Energy has pursued a strategy of buying mature properties and extending the life of these natural gas fields by workovers and improved field operations, including the use of additional production equipment and drilling activities.

EXECUTIVES

Chairman: Toby R. Neugebauer, age 34
President, CEO, and Director: Michael C. Linn, age 53
EVP and Secretary: Roland P. (Chip) Keddie, age 52
EVP Engineering Operations: Gerald W. Merriam, age 47
VP Operations: Curtis L. Tipton, age 47
EVP and CFO: Kolja Rockov, age 34
Chief Accounting Officer: Donald T. Robinson, age 30
Auditors: KPMG LLP

LOCATIONS

HQ: Linn Energy, LLC
1700 N. Highland Rd., Ste. 100,
Pittsburgh, PA 15241
Phone: 412-854-0470 **Fax:** 412-854-0474

COMPETITORS

Belden & Blake	Petroleum Development
Cabot Oil & Gas	Range Resources
Equitable Resources	

HISTORICAL FINANCIALS
Company Type: Private

Income Statement
FYE: December 31

	REVENUE ($ mil.)	NET INCOME ($ mil.)	NET PROFIT MARGIN	EMPLOYEES
12/04	21	(4)	—	52
12/03	3	(1)	—	—
Annual Growth	**542.4%**	—	—	—

2004 Year-End Financials

Debt ratio: 763.7%
Return on equity: —
Cash ($ mil.): 2
Current ratio: 0.73
Long-term debt ($ mil.): 82

Net Income History

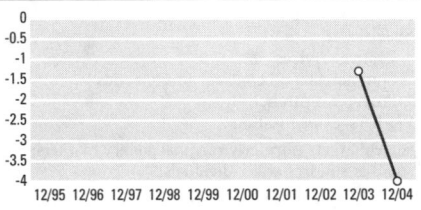

12/95	12/96	12/97	12/98	12/99	12/00	12/01	12/02	12/03	12/04

L.L. Bean

With L.L. Bean, you can tame the great outdoors — or just look as if you could. The outdoor apparel and gear maker mails more than 200 million catalogs per year. L.L. Bean's library includes about 10 specialty catalogs offering products in categories such as children's, fly-fishing, outerwear, sportswear, housewares, footwear, camping and hiking gear, and the Maine hunting shoe upon which the company was built. L.L. Bean also operates four retail and 15 factory outlets in the US, with nine additional stores in Japan. It also sells online through English- and Japanese-language Web sites. L.L. Bean was founded in 1912 by Leon Leonwood Bean and is controlled by his descendants.

From a pair of waterproof hunting boots in 1911, L.L. Bean's empire is based on catalogs mailed out under 95 different titles and advertising 16,000 products. Catalog sales account for 80% of L.L. Bean's revenue. L.L. Bean's flagship store in Freeport, Maine (known by locals as "the Bean") attracts 3 million visitors annually and is open 24 hours a day, 365 days a year. The company plans to open more retail outlets. Retail sales currently account for 20% of L.L. Bean's revenue; the company would like to see that number eventually rise to 50%. L.L. Bean also plans to scale back the number of catalog titles it offers. However, the retailer is adding a new title: L.L. Bean: Everyday Adventures, catering to women interested in yoga and fitness products.

L.L. Bean's famous customer service is exemplified by its liberal return policies and perpetual replacement of the rubber soles of its Maine Hunting Shoe. The company also offers seminars and events on such topics as fly fishing, sea kayaking, and outdoor photography.

In 2004 L.L. Bean pursued legal action against four retailers, including Nordstrom and J. C. Penney. The suit claims trademark infringement on the company's Web site connected with pop-up advertisements redirecting customer traffic to Web sites engineered by the alleged offenders. L.L. Bean claims that the actions of the pop-up advertisements appear to imply endorsement by L.L. Bean. The company hosting the pop-up advertisements filed a counter-suit a few weeks later, claiming that L.L. Bean's suit is frivolous in nature.

HISTORY

Leon Leonwood Bean started out as a storekeeper in Freeport, Maine. Tired of wet, leaky boots, he experimented with various remedies and in 1911 came up with the Maine Hunting Shoe, a boot with rubber soles and feet and leather uppers. It became his most famous product.

From its outset in 1912, Bean's company was a mail-order house. The first batch of boots was a disaster: Almost all of them leaked. But Bean's willingness to correct his product's defects quickly, at his own expense, saved the company.

Maine's hunting licensing system, implemented in 1917, provided the company with a mailing list of affluent recreational hunters in the Northeast, and that year Bean opened a showroom to accommodate the customers stopping by his Freeport workshop.

Bean cultivated the image of the folksy Maine guide, offering durable, comfortable, weather-resistant clothes and reliable camping supplies. In 1920 Bean built a store on Main Street in Freeport. L.L. Bean continued to grow and add products, even during the Depression, and sales reached $1 million in 1937.

During WWII Bean helped design the boots used by the US military, and his company manufactured them, thus remaining afloat as the war years and rationing brought cutbacks in materials and outdoor activities. He began keeping the retail store open 24 hours a day in 1951, noting that he had "thrown away the keys." Bean added a women's department three years later.

Sales rose to $2 million in the early 1960s and were at $4.8 million when Bean died in 1967 at age 94. (He had resisted growing the business bigger, saying, "I'm eating three meals a day; I can't eat four.") The new president was Bean's grandson Leon Gorman, who had started with L.L. Bean in 1960. His early attempts at updating the mailing operations (mailing labels typed by hand and correspondence kept in cardboard boxes) had been vetoed by his grandfather. Gorman brought in new people and made improvements, including automating the mailing systems, improving the manufacturing systems, and targeting new, nonsporting markets (like women's casual clothes).

L.L. Bean continued its transition by targeting more of its classic customer profile — upper-middle-class college graduates — and sales grew about 20% annually for most of the 1980s. By 1989, however, sales had slowed and growth flattened as the national economy slumped and imitators carried away market share.

Unsolicited catalog orders had been coming in from Japan since the late 1980s, so in 1992 L.L. Bean began a joint venture with Seiyu and Matsushita Electric Industrial. Their first store opened that year (the company opened a catalog

and service center in Japan in 1995). L.L. Kids began in 1993.

In 1996 the company began an online shopping service. Sparked by the success of its L.L. Kids division, which grew 300% in four years, the company opened a separate children's store in Freeport the next year. The company opened its second full-line store in 2000 near Washington, DC. L.L. Bean plans to continue opening retail stores in the eastern US.

L.L. Bean veteran Chris McCormick was named president and CEO in May 2001; Gorman remained chairman. McCormick is the first person outside of the Bean family to head the company.

In January 2002 L.L. Bean laid off 175 employees (about 4% of its workforce); in early 2003 it cut about 500 more jobs and offered an early retirement program which was accepted by an additional 200 employees.

In July 2004 L.L. Bean partly settled lawsuits filed against Atkins Nutritionals Inc. and Gevalia Kaffe, accusing those companies of using pop-up ads of Bean's Web site without its permission. The amount of the settlement was not disclosed.

EXECUTIVES

Chairman: Leon A. Gorman, age 67
President and CEO: Chris McCormick, age 46
SVP and COO: Bob Peixotto
SVP and CFO: Mark Fasold
SVP and General Manager, Retail: Ken Kacere
VP E-Commerce: Mary Lou Kelley
VP Finance: Daniel Love
VP Human Resources: Martha Cyr
Chief Merchandising Officer: Fran Philip
Chief Retail Officer: Edward R. (Ed) Howell
Director of IT Operations: Stafford Soule
Director of Logistics: James (Jim) Helming
Advertising Manager: Jennifer El-Hillow
CIT, Manager of Engineering, Distribution Operations: David Lockman
PR Spokesman: Rich Donaldson
Senior Product Developer: Sandra Rossi
Senior Systems Analyst: Patrick Carroll
Senior Analyst and Project Manager: Louise Grant

LOCATIONS

HQ: L.L. Bean, Inc.
   15 Casco St., Freeport, ME 04033
Phone: 207-865-4761   **Fax:** 207-552-6821
Web: www.llbean.com

L.L. Bean sells through direct-mail catalogs and has retail stores and outlet stores in the US and Japan. It manufactures some of its merchandise in Maine.

PRODUCTS/OPERATIONS

Selected Catalogs
Corporate Sales (custom embroidered clothing and luggage)
Fly Fishing (equipment, outer wear, and accessories)
Home (linens, pillows, and decorating)
L.L. Bean
L.L. Bean Hunting
L.L. Bean: Everyday Adventures (women's yoga and fitness products)
Outdoor Discovery Schools (classes and symposiums)
Outdoors (seasonal outdoor wear and accessories)
Traveler (clothing, luggage, and accessories)

Selected Products
Home and garden accessories
Men's, women's, and children's casual apparel
Outdoor classes
Outer wear
Shoes and boots
Sports gear and apparel
Travel apparel and luggage

COMPETITORS

Abercrombie & Fitch
American Eagle Outfitters
American Retail
Bass Pro Shops
Cabela's
Coldwater Creek
Coleman
Columbia Sportswear
Dillard's
Eddie Bauer
Eddie Bauer Holdings
Fast Retailing
Federated
Foot Locker
Gap
J. C. Penney
J. Crew
J. Jill Group
Johnson Outdoors
Lands' End
Levi Strauss
Limited Brands
May
Nautica Enterprises
Norm Thompson
North Face
Orvis Company
OshKosh B'Gosh
Patagonia
Polo Ralph Lauren
Redcats
REI
Sara Lee
Sears
Sports Authority
Sportsman's Guide
Talbots
Target
Timberland
Tommy Hilfiger

HISTORICAL FINANCIALS

Company Type: Private

Income Statement				FYE: February 28
	REVENUE ($ mil.)	NET INCOME ($ mil.)	NET PROFIT MARGIN	EMPLOYEES
2/04	1,150	—	—	3,800
2/03	1,070	—	—	3,800
2/02	1,140	—	—	4,500
2/01	1,100	—	—	4,700
2/00	1,100	—	—	4,000
2/99	1,070	—	—	4,000
2/98	1,068	—	—	3,600
2/97	1,040	—	—	3,500
2/96	1,078	—	—	3,800
2/95	976	—	—	3,800
Annual Growth	1.8%	—	—	0.0%

Revenue History

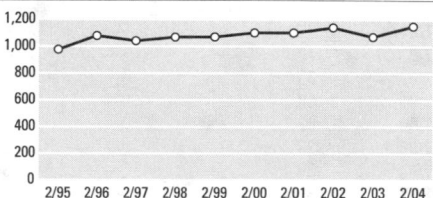

Los Angeles Clippers

With one winning season since moving to Los Angeles in 1984, many consider the Clippers the worst team in all of sports. Players come and go, and the most recent young star to find his way to another team was Lamar Odom (the Clippers managed to hang onto forward Elton Brand). The Clippers moved into the Staples Center in 1999 (along with the Los Angeles Lakers and Los Angeles Kings). In 2003 the team fired head coach Alvin Gentry after posting an 89-133 record on his watch. Former Trail Blazers coach Mike Dunleavy replaced him. The team started as the Buffalo Braves in 1970 and became the San Diego Clippers in 1978 before moving to LA. Real estate magnate Donald Sterling owns the team.

EXECUTIVES

Owner and Chairman: Donald T. Sterling
EVP: Andy Roeser
SVP Marketing and Sales: Carl Lahr
VP Basketball Operations: Elgin Baylor, age 71
Head Coach: Mike Dunleavy, age 51
VP Communications: Joe Safety
VP Finance: Donna Johnson
VP Marketing and Broadcasting: Christian Howard
General Counsel: Bob Platt
Director of Communications: Rob Raichlen
Director of Community Relations and Player Programs: Denise Booth
Director of Corporate Sales: Greg Flaherty

LOCATIONS

HQ: Los Angeles Clippers
Staples Center, 1111 S. Figueroa St., Ste. 1100, Los Angeles, CA 90015
Phone: 213-742-7500   **Fax:** 213-742-7570
Web: www.nba.com/clippers

The Los Angeles Clippers play at the 18,118-seat capacity Staples Center in Los Angeles.

COMPETITORS

Golden State Warriors	Phoenix Suns
Los Angeles Lakers	Sacramento Kings

HISTORICAL FINANCIALS

Company Type: Private

Income Statement

FYE: July 31

	REVENUE ($ mil.)	NET INCOME ($ mil.)	NET PROFIT MARGIN	EMPLOYEES
7/04	77	—	—	—
7/03	72	—	—	—
7/02	73	—	—	—
7/01	68	—	—	—
7/00	62	—	—	—
7/99	23	—	—	35
7/98	39	—	—	90
7/97	36	—	—	—
7/96	35	—	—	—
7/95	32	—	—	95
Annual Growth	10.3%	—	—	(22.1%)

Revenue History

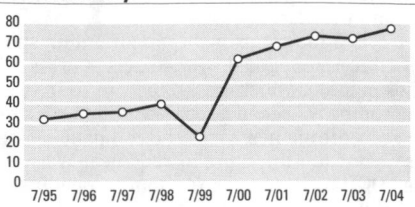

Los Angeles Kings

These kings have yet to be crowned Stanley Cup Champions. The Los Angeles Kings entered the National Hockey League in 1967 and has made just one appearance in the Stanley Cup finals. Led by the great Wayne Gretzky, the team reached the championship in 1993 but lost to the Montreal Canadiens in seven games. Despite the lack of championships, the franchise has not been too overshadowed by its Staples Center brethren, the title-laden Los Angeles Lakers, and continues to draw decent crowds. The team is owned by Denver billionaire Philip Anschutz and Los Angeles developer Edward Roski, who bought the team in 1995. The partners also own the Staples Center and a minority stake of the Lakers.

The Los Angeles hockey franchise was first awarded to Jack Kent Cooke (one-time owner of both the Los Angeles Lakers and the Washington Redskins) and played in the LA Forum for most of its history. Anschutz, who also controls Regal Entertainment and holds stakes in a host of other businesses through his Anschutz Company, and Roski acquired the team from Jeffrey Sudikoff and Joseph Cohen for about $110 million. After buying the team, they built the $300 million Staples Center in 1999 with the help of media giant News Corp. (Anschutz and Roski bought the media titan's 40% stake in the arena in 2004.)

EXECUTIVES

Owner: Philip F. Anschutz, age 65
Owner: Edward P. (Ed) Roski Jr.
President and Governor: Timothy J. (Tim) Leiweke
EVP and CFO: Dan Beckerman
EVP and Chief Administrative Officer: Kevin McDowell
EVP and General Counsel: Ted Fikre
SVP and General Manager: Dave Taylor
VP Hockey Operations and Assistant General Manager: Kevin Gilmore
Head Coach: Andy Murray, age 54
VP Communications and Broadcasting: Michael Altieri, age 39
VP Sales and Marketing: Chris McGowan
Director of Communications: Jeff Moeller

LOCATIONS

HQ: The Los Angeles Kings Hockey Club LP
1111 S. Figueroa St., Los Angeles, CA 90015
Phone: 213-742-7100   **Fax:** 213-742-7296
Web: www.lakings.com

The Los Angeles Kings play at the 18,118-seat capacity Staples Center in Los Angeles.

PRODUCTS/OPERATIONS

Championship Trophies
Clarence S. Campbell Bowl (1993)

COMPETITORS

Dallas Stars
Mighty Ducks
Phoenix Coyotes
San Jose Sharks

HISTORICAL FINANCIALS

Company Type: Private

Income Statement

FYE: July 31

	REVENUE ($ mil.)	NET INCOME ($ mil.)	NET PROFIT MARGIN	EMPLOYEES
7/04	80	—	—	—
7/03	78	—	—	—
7/02	81	—	—	120
7/01	73	—	—	—
7/00	64	—	—	—
7/99	34	—	—	70
7/98	39	—	—	75
7/97	42	—	—	—
7/96	50	—	—	—
7/95	27	—	—	100
Annual Growth	12.7%	—	—	2.6%

Revenue History

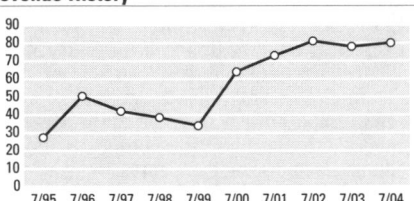

Los Angeles Lakers

If you find yourself under Shaq-attack, you're no longer playing the Los Angeles Lakers. After the Lakers lost the 2004 Finals to the Detroit Pistons, gargantuan center Shaquille O'Neal demanded a trade and was shipped to the Miami Heat, ending an era of dominance out West and leaving the team in the hands of guard Kobe Bryant. The team is the NBA's most valuable, estimated at more than $425 million. Los Angeles has won 14 titles since joining the league as the Minnesota Lakers in 1949. Chairman Jerry Buss, a real estate mogul who bought the Lakers in 1979, owns 70% of the team. Billionaire Philip Anschutz, developer Edward Roski, and hall of famer Earvin "Magic" Johnson also own minority stakes in the Lakers.

After getting slammed out of the playoffs in the second round in 2003, Jackson resigned, O'Neal and Payton left for other teams, and Malone opted out of his contract to become a free agent. The team hired former Houston Rockets head coach Rudy Tomjanovich to replace Jackson. Bryant re-signed with LA to the tune of $136 million over seven years.

Tomjanovich, who battled cancer in the 1990s, resigned as head coach midway through the season in early 2005 citing health reasons. While the team was watching the NBA finals on TV, management rehired Phil Jackson as head coach with a reported three-year deal worth $30 million — the league's highest salary for a coach.

The team also owns the WNBA's two-time champion Los Angeles Sparks.

EXECUTIVES

Chairman, President, and Majority Owner; Chairman, Los Angeles Sparks: Jerry Buss
EVP Basketball Operations and General Manager: Mitch Kupchak
Assistant General Manager: Jim Buss
Assistant General Manager: Ronnie Lester
EVP Business Operations: Jeanie Buss
EVP Marketing and Broadcasting: Frank Mariani
Head Coach: Phil Jackson, age 60
VP Finance: Joe McCormack
Assistant Coach: Frank Hamblen
Assistant Coach: Kurt Rambis
Assistant Coach: Brian Shaw
Executive Director of Corporate Sponsorships: Ron Rockoff
Executive Director of Multimedia Marketing: Keith Harris
Director of Human Resources: Joan McLaughlin
Director of Public Relations: John Black
President, Los Angeles Sparks: Johnny Buss

LOCATIONS

HQ: The Los Angeles Lakers, Inc.
555 N. Nash St., El Segundo, CA 90245
Phone: 310-426-6000   **Fax:** 310-426-6115
Web: www.nba.com/lakers

The Los Angeles Lakers and the Los Angeles Sparks play in the Staples Center in downtown Los Angeles.

PRODUCTS/OPERATIONS

Championship Titles

National Basketball League (NBL, 1947)
NBA Central Division (1950)
NBA Finals (1949-50, 1952-54, 1972, 1980, 1982, 1985, 1987-88, 2000-02)
NBA Pacific Division (1971-74, 1977, 1980, 1982-90, 1998, 2000-01, 2004)
NBA Western Conference (1972-73, 1980, 1982-85, 1987-89, 1991, 2000-02, 2004)
NBA Western Division (1951, 1953-54, 1962-63, 1965-66, 1969)

COMPETITORS

Golden State Warriors
Los Angeles Clippers
Phoenix Suns
Portland Trail Blazers
Sacramento Kings
Seattle SuperSonics

HISTORICAL FINANCIALS

Company Type: Private

Income Statement

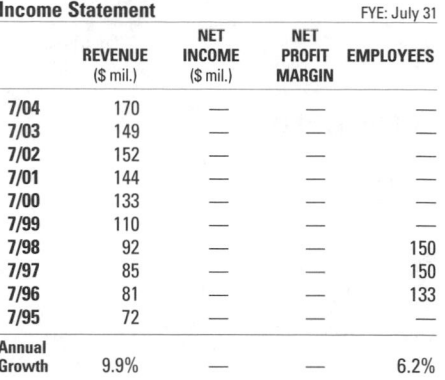

FYE: July 31

	REVENUE ($ mil.)	NET INCOME ($ mil.)	NET PROFIT MARGIN	EMPLOYEES
7/04	170	—	—	—
7/03	149	—	—	—
7/02	152	—	—	—
7/01	144	—	—	—
7/00	133	—	—	—
7/99	110	—	—	—
7/98	92	—	—	150
7/97	85	—	—	150
7/96	81	—	—	133
7/95	72	—	—	—
Annual Growth	9.9%	—	—	6.2%

Revenue History

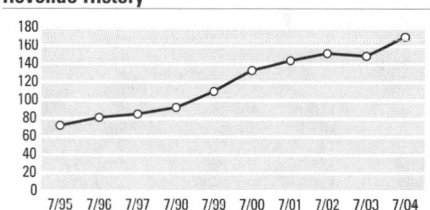

Louis Berger Group

What happens when you combine 100,000 miles of highway, 2,000 miles of railroad, 3,000 bridges, 100 airfields, seaports, dams, and water supply systems, as well as a passel of environmental projects with a bunch of engineers, scientists, economists, and archaeologists? You get The Louis Berger Group, a global engineering firm founded in 1953 by the late Dr. Louis Berger. The company — which provides civil, structural, mechanical, electrical, and environmental engineering services — has worked on high-profile projects such as the Pennsylvania Turnpike, the first toll expressway in the US. It has also won contracts to help rebuild Iraq's communications system, transportation infrastructure, and courthouses.

Among its recent projects in the US is work for the World Trade Center area. The Louis Berger Group, along with Hill International, was selected by the Port Authority of New York and New Jersey to provide program management services for the engineering, final design, and construction of its Downtown Restoration Program for redevelopment of the World Trade Center and the WTC transportation hub.

Iraq reconstruction contracts awarded to the group include two in 2004 by the U.S. Agency for International Development (USAID) to help restructure and privatize state-owned businesses, promote small businesses, and provide vocational training.

EXECUTIVES

Chairman and CEO: Derish M. Wolff
President and CEO: Nicolas J. (Nick) Masucci
CFO: Leon Marantz
EVP and COO; Group VP, International Operations: Michel Jichlinski
IT Director: Randy Morgan
Chief Engineer: Kent Lande
SVP Cultural Resources: John A. Hotopp
SVP Energy Services: Kevin Young
SVP Engineering Division (MidAtlantic): James (Jim) Stamatis
SVP Integrated Development; SVP Development Economics: Charles Bell
SVP Integrated Development: Julie Haines
SVP Integrated Development; SVP Southeast Asia: Richard Hirsch
SVP Justice Programs: Robert J. Nardi
SVP Ports, Waterways, and Airports: Isaac Shafran
SVP Transportation Planning, Economics and Environmental Science: Larry Pesesky
Manager Human Resources: Terry Williams
Auditors: PricewaterhouseCoopers

LOCATIONS

HQ: The Louis Berger Group, Inc.
100 Halsted St., East Orange, NJ 07018
Phone: 973-678-1960   **Fax:** 973-672-4284
Web: www.louisberger.com

The Louis Berger Group operates worldwide with offices in more than 60 countries.

PRODUCTS/OPERATIONS

Selected Services

Architecture
Construction management
Cultural resources
Development planning
Economic evaluations
Engineering design
Environmental compliance and analysis
Environmental permitting
Facilities and space planning
Geographic information systems
Maintenance management
Natural resource management
Operations planning and management
Pollution prevention
Privatization studies
Program management
Resident engineering and inspection
Urban planning
Water resources planning

Selected Subsidiaries and Affiliates

Amman & Whitney Consulting Engineers, P.C.
Berger/ABAM Engineers, Inc.
Berger Devine Yaeger, Inc.
Berger Klohn Crippen Holdings, Ltd. (Canada)
Berger, Lehman Associates, P.C.
CHELBI Engineering Consultants, Inc. (China)
Louis Berger SAS (France)
Urban Engineering Systems, Inc. (Thailand)

COMPETITORS

AECOM
Black & Veatch
CH2M HILL
Day & Zimmermann
Edwards and Kelcey
HNTB
Hyundai Engineering and Construction
Jacobs Engineering
Kajima
Nishimatsu Construction
Parsons
Parsons Brinckerhoff
URS
VINCI

HISTORICAL FINANCIALS

Company Type: Private

Income Statement

FYE: June 30

	REVENUE ($ mil.)	NET INCOME ($ mil.)	NET PROFIT MARGIN	EMPLOYEES
6/04	541	—	—	4,000
6/03	328	—	—	3,800
6/02	259	—	—	3,782
6/01	398	—	—	3,722
6/00	378	—	—	3,000
6/99	307	—	—	3,000
6/98	312	—	—	2,800
6/97	307	—	—	2,800
6/96	278	—	—	2,800
6/95	170	—	—	—
Annual Growth	13.7%	—	—	4.6%

Revenue History

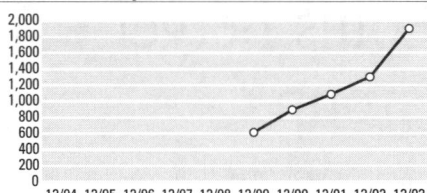

600
500
400
300
200
100
0
6/95 6/96 6/97 6/98 6/99 6/00 6/01 6/02 6/03 6/04

Love's Travel Stops

If you're a trucker or RVer on the road, all you need is Love's. Love's Travel Stops & Country Stores operates more than 150 travel stop locations throughout a swath of about 24 states from California to Virginia, including convenience stores in Colorado, Kansas, New Mexico, Oklahoma, and Texas. Each travel stop includes a convenience store, a fast-food restaurant, such as Taco Bell or Subway, and gas outlets for cars, trucks, and RVs. The travel stops also provide shower rooms, laundry facilities, game rooms, and mail drops. Love's Travel Stops & Country Stores is owned by the family of CEO Tom Love, who founded the company in 1964.

EXECUTIVES

Chairman and CEO: Tom Love
President and COO; President and COO, Love's Development Companies: Greg Love
President, Love's Operating Companies: Frank Love
EVP and CFO: Doug Stussi
EVP, Store Operations: Tom Edwards
VP, Accounting: Shane Wharton
VP and CIO: Jim Xenos
VP, Construction: Terry Ross
Director, Human Resources: Carl Martincich
Director, Legal Services: Amy Guzzy
Director, Marketing: Mark Romig
Director, Public Relations: Jenny Love Meyer
Director, Restaurant Services: Buster Walker
Director, Sales: Don Van Curen

LOCATIONS

HQ: Love's Travel Stops & Country Stores, Inc.
10601 N. Pennsylvania Ave.,
Oklahoma City, OK 73120
Phone: 405-751-9000   **Fax:** 405-749-9110
Web: www.loves.com

COMPETITORS

7-Eleven	Pilot
Allsup's	Racetrac Petroleum
Chevron	Rip Griffin Truck Service
Exxon Mobil	Center
E-Z Mart Stores	Royal Dutch/Shell Group
FFP Operating	Stuckey's
Flying J	TravelCenters of America
Marathon Oil	Valero Energy
Petro Stopping Centers	Walgreen

HISTORICAL FINANCIALS

Company Type: Private

Income Statement

FYE: December 31

	REVENUE ($ mil.)	NET INCOME ($ mil.)	NET PROFIT MARGIN	EMPLOYEES
12/03	1,900	—	—	3,500
12/02	1,300	—	—	3,800
12/01	1,086	—	—	3,200
12/00	894	—	—	3,150
12/99	614	—	—	2,500
Annual Growth	32.6%	—	—	8.8%

Revenue History

2,000
1,800
1,600
1,400
1,200
1,000
800
600
400
200
0
12/94 12/95 12/96 12/97 12/98 12/99 12/00 12/01 12/02 12/03

Lower Colorado River Authority

"The stars at night are big and bright" . . . but Texans in 58 counties still need electricity from the Lower Colorado River Authority (LCRA). The utility supplies wholesale electricity to 42 utility customers (primarily municipalities and cooperatives). The LCRA has interests in fossil-fueled, hydroelectric, and wind-powered generation facilities that give it a capacity of about 2,900 MW; it also has power transmission assets. The company's water unit operates 35 water and wastewater systems, three irrigation systems, and six dams in its service territory; it also monitors the water quality of the lakes formed by its dams. LCRA's revenues provide funding for its more than 40 recreation areas.

Founded by the Texas Legislature in 1934, the LCRA has pursued two complementary goals — providing reliable, low-cost utility and public services, and ensuring the protection of the area's natural resources. In the latter role, the LCRA owns or operates more than 16,600 acres of parks and recreational areas.

EXECUTIVES

Chair: Ray A. Wilkerson
Vice Chair: G. Hughes Abell
General Manager; CEO, LCRA Transmission Services, GenTex Power, and LCRA Wholesale Energy Services: Joseph J. (Joe) Beal
Deputy General Manager, CFO, and Diversity Leader; CFO, LCRA Transmission Services, GenTex Power, and LCRA Wholesale Energy Services: John M. Meismer
Deputy General Manager, Community Services and Employee Focus Leader: Donna K. Brasher
Deputy General Manager, Energy Services and Safety Leader: Marcus W. Pridgeon
Deputy General Manager, External Affairs and Customer Service Leader: Rick Bluntzer
Deputy General Manager, Water Services and Environment Leader: Paul D. Thornhill
Executive Manager, Communications: Robert Cullick
Executive Manager, Human Resources: Karen Farabee
Secretary: Connie Granberg
Treasurer: Brady Edwards
Controller: James D. Travis
General Counsel; Secretary, LCRA Transmission Services, GenTex Power, and LCRA Wholesale Energy Services: Thomas G. Mason
General Auditor: Philip J. Kolman
Auditors: Deloitte & Touche LLP

LOCATIONS

HQ: Lower Colorado River Authority
3700 Lake Austin Blvd., Austin, TX 78703
Phone: 512-473-3200   **Fax:** 512-473-3298
Web: www.lcra.org

Lower Colorado River Authority serves central and southern Texas.

PRODUCTS/OPERATIONS

2004 Sales

	% of total
Electric	90
Water, wastewater & irrigation	7
Other	3
Total	100

Selected Subsidiaries and Divisions

GenTex Power Corporation (power generation)
LCRA Transmission Services Corporation (power transmission services)
LCRA Water Services (water, wastewater, irrigation, and resource management services)
LCRA Wholesale Energy Services Corporation (generates and sells power to wholesale customers)

COMPETITORS

AEP
Brazos Electric Power
El Paso Electric
Entergy
Southwest Water
TNP Enterprises
TXU

HISTORICAL FINANCIALS

Company Type: Government-owned

Income Statement

FYE: June 30

	REVENUE ($ mil.)	NET INCOME ($ mil.)	NET PROFIT MARGIN	EMPLOYEES
6/04	694	34	5.0%	2,224
6/03	643	23	3.5%	2,211
6/02	556	50	9.0%	2,112
6/01	689	(17)	—	1,910
6/00	538	8	1.5%	1,724
6/99	455	26	5.6%	1,723
6/98	470	19	4.1%	1,655
6/97	478	57	11.9%	1,659
6/96	452	—	—	1,699
6/95	397	—	—	1,704
Annual Growth	6.4%	(6.9%)	—	3.0%

2004 Year-End Financials

Debt ratio: 258.2%
Return on equity: 5.3%
Cash ($ mil.): 57

Current ratio: 0.80
Long-term debt ($ mil.): 1,695

Net Income History

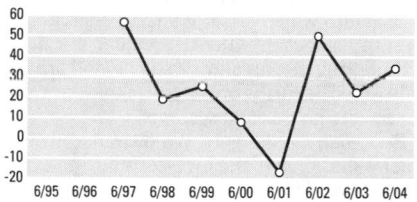

6/95 6/96 6/97 6/98 6/99 6/00 6/01 6/02 6/03 6/04

LPA Holding

When it comes to child care, La Petite Academy is Le Grand. LPA Holding Corp.'s main operating subsidiary, La Petite Academy, is a leading operator of preschool and child care facilities. Founded in 1968, the company provides both full- and part-time child care, educational and developmental programs, and workplace child care. Its nearly 650 centers (including 590 residential academies, 30 workplace academies, and 29 Montessori schools) enroll some 65,000 children ranging in age from six weeks to 12 years old. LPA's La Petite academies are located across the country in 36 states and Washington, DC.

During 2005, the company opened 10 new schools. Six of those school openings were through acquisitions.

Director Robert King owns a controlling interest in LPA Holding.

EXECUTIVES

Chairman: Stephen P. (Steve) Murray, age 42
President, CEO, and Director: Gary A. Graves, age 45, $590,000 pay
SVP and CFO: Neil P. Dyment, age 50, $295,721 pay
VP and CIO: Hugh W. (Walt) Tracy, age 43, $195,992 pay
VP and Chief Revenue Officer:
William H. (Bill) Van Huis, age 48
VP, General Counsel, and Secretary: Gregory S. Davis, age 43, $236,375 pay

VP, Field Support Services: Paul G. Kreuser
VP, People: William C. (Bill) Buckland, age 58
VP, Central Division: Lisa J. Miskimins, age 44
VP, Eastern Division: Stephan (Steve) Laudicino, age 55
VP, Florida Division: Leah L. Oliva, age 43
VP, Texas Division: Stephanie L. Pasche, age 42
VP, Western Division: Lawrence (Larry) Appell, age 55, $185,888 pay
Treasurer: Dan Knight
Auditors: Deloitte & Touche LLP

LOCATIONS

HQ: LPA Holding Corp.
130 S. Jefferson St., Ste. 300, Chicago, IL 60661
Phone: 312-798-1200　**Fax:** 312-382-1776
Web: www.lapetite.com

LPA Holding Corp. leases administrative office space in Burbank, California; Charlotte, North Carolina; Chicago; and Overland Park, Kansas.

PRODUCTS/OPERATIONS

Selected Services and Programs

Employer-based academies
Kids Station (curriculum for school-age children)
Journey (curriculum for pre-school children)
La Petite Academy
Montessori schools
Neighborhood-based academies
Private kindergarten

COMPETITORS

Bright Horizons Family Solutions
Child Development Schools
Childtime Learning Centers
KinderCare
Knowledge Learning
Nobel Learning Communities

HISTORICAL FINANCIALS

Company Type: Private

Income Statement

FYE: Saturday closest to June 30

	REVENUE ($ mil.)	NET INCOME ($ mil.)	NET PROFIT MARGIN	EMPLOYEES
6/04	384	(9)	—	12,000
6/03	390	(16)	—	12,800
6/02	391	(77)	—	13,500
6/01	385	(6)	—	12,000
6/00	371	(11)	—	13,000
6/99*	281	(1)	—	12,000
8/98	315	(13)	—	12,700
8/97	303	(1)	—	14,200
8/96	300	(4)	—	—
8/95	280	(12)	—	—
Annual Growth	3.6%	—	—	(2.4%)

*Fiscal year change

2004 Year-End Financials

Debt ratio: —
Return on equity: —
Cash ($ mil.): 7

Current ratio: 0.45
Long-term debt ($ mil.): 273

Net Income History

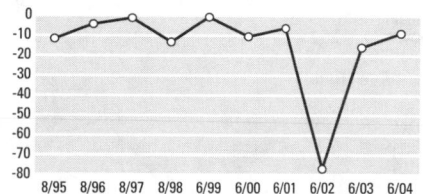

8/95 8/96 8/97 8/98 6/99 6/00 6/01 6/02 6/03 6/04

Lucasfilm

The Force is definitely with Emperor George Lucas. With five of the 30 highest-grossing movies of all time, Lucasfilm is one of the most successful independent production companies in the history of film. Owned by filmmaker George Lucas (the brains behind the *Star Wars* and *Indiana Jones* films), Lucasfilm's productions have won 19 Academy Awards. Its most recent movie is 2005's box office hit *Star Wars: Episode III — Revenge of the Sith*; Lucasfilm's 1999 release *Episode I — The Phantom Menace* has grossed more than $920 million worldwide and claims the #4 spot on the all-time list. Other subsidiaries in the Lucas empire are responsible for licensing, special effects, and software. Lucasfilm was created in 1971.

Lucasfilm consists of LucasArts (video games), Lucas Digital (special effects house Industrial Light + Magic and Skywalker Sound), Lucas Licensing (consumer products), and Lucas Online (e-commerce, news, and information). George Lucas also owns educational software firm Lucas Learning.

In 2002 Lucas spun off digital sound systems firm THX as an independent company. The following year the company formed its Lucasfilm Animation unit to create digitally animated feature films and television productions. The 2003 release of Lucasfilm's *The Adventures of Indiana Jones: The Complete DVD Movie Collection* made record-breaking sales, and the company hit gold again with the DVD release of *The Star Wars Trilogy* in 2004.

The company has also expanded into Asia with the creation of Lucasfilm Animation Singapore. The unit, which will produce digital animation for movies, television, and games, is 75% owned by Lucasfilm. The remainder is held by a Singapore state-led consortium.

Lucasfilm has built the Letterman Digital Arts Center, a new headquarters and production center at the Presidio, a former Army base in San Francisco, to bring Lucasfilm, ILM, LucasArts, and Lucas Online under one roof for the first time.

2005's final sequel to the *Star Wars* series, *Episode III — Revenge of the Sith*, earned a whopping $50 million in its first day of release. The post-*Star Wars* future of the company remains unclear, and the tight-lipped founder has shown little interest in collaborating with Hollywood producers.

HISTORY

After attending film school at the University of Southern California, George Lucas started his career as a documentary filmmaker, chronicling the production of Francis Ford Coppola's *Finian's Rainbow* in 1968. The two men became fast friends and founded American Zoetrope in 1969, which two years later released Lucas' feature film debut, the science-fiction film *THX 1138* (a full-length version of a student film he made at USC). The film flopped, and Coppola went into production on *The Godfather*. Lucas left American Zoetrope and created his own company, Lucasfilm, in 1971.

Two years later Lucas released *American Graffiti* through Universal Pictures (with some financial help from Coppola). The film was a smash hit; it raked in $115 million in the US and made him a millionaire before the age of 30. It also gave him the clout to try and get his most ambitious project off the ground, a space opera called *Star Wars.* Universal, frustrated with cost overruns on *Graffiti,* wanted no part of Lucas' seemingly ridiculous idea, so he went to 20th Century Fox, which agreed to finance the $10 million film. Lucas gave up his directing fee for a percentage of the box-office take and all merchandising rights. He created Industrial Light + Magic (ILM) and Sprocket Systems (later Skywalker Sound) in 1975 to produce the visual and sound effects needed for the film.

Star Wars cost about $12 million, and almost everyone involved was sure it would bomb. Released in 1977, the movie shattered every box-office record, and the merchandising rights Lucas obtained made him a multimillionaire. With his take from *Star Wars,* Lucas was able to finance the film's sequel, *The Empire Strikes Back* (1980), out of his own pocket, meaning he would receive most of the profits (it grossed more than $220 million domestically). Lucasfilm's next production was *Raiders of the Lost Ark* (1981), directed by Lucas' friend Steven Spielberg. It went on to gross more than $380 million worldwide.

The next year Lucas began developing the THX sound system in preparation for the 1983 release of the third *Star Wars* film, *Return of the Jedi* (which hauled in more than $260 million domestically). He also founded LucasArts in 1982 to develop video games. Lucasfilm completed Skywalker Ranch (a facility housing many of its various companies in Marin County, California) in the mid-1980s and filled out the decade with two *Raiders* sequels — *Indiana Jones and the Temple of Doom* (1984, $333 million worldwide) and *Indiana Jones and the Last Crusade* (1989, $495 million worldwide).

Lucasfilm reorganized in 1993 by spinning off LucasArts into a separate company and regrouping ILM and Skywalker Sound into a new company called Lucas Digital. Lucasfilm won local government approval to build an $87 million film studio near Skywalker Ranch in 1996, and the following year it re-released the *Star Wars Trilogy* to theaters with new special effects in celebration of the 20th anniversary, adding another $250 million to its take. Anticipating the release of the first of three prequels to the *Star Wars Trilogy,* Lucasfilm started signing marketing agreements in 1998 (including deals with Hasbro and Pepsi) that resulted in advance licensing of nearly $3 billion.

Star Wars: Episode I — The Phantom Menace opened in May 1999 and has grossed about $920 million worldwide (it finished its initial run second only to *Titanic*). Later in 1999 Lucas announced plans to develop a $250 million digital arts center at the old Presidio army base in San Francisco to house ILM, LucasArts, Lucas Learning, Lucas Online, THX, and the George Lucas Educational Foundation.

The next film in the *Star Wars* series, *Episode II — Attack of the Clones,* opened in May 2002. In early 2003 the company reorganized, bringing in Lucas Digital, LucasArts Entertainment, and Lucas Licensing (which had previously been operating as independent companies) as subsidiaries under the Lucasfilm umbrella.

In 2005 Lucasfilm released the third *Star Wars* movie, *Episode III — Revenge of the Sith.* Also that year the company opened its Letterman Digital Arts Center.

EXECUTIVES

Chairman and CEO: George W. Lucas Jr.
President and COO: Micheline (Mich) Chau
SVP; President, LucasArts: Jim Ward
VP Marketing: Joshua Katz
President, Industrial Light and Magic: Chrissie England
President, Lucas Licensing: Howard Rothman
VP and General Manager, Skywalker Sound:
  Glenn Kiser
Director Communications: Lynne Hale
**Director Content Management Marketing and Head of
  Fan Relations:** Steve Sansweet, age 59

LOCATIONS

HQ: Lucasfilm Ltd.
  5858 Lucas Valley Rd., Nicasio, CA 94946
Phone: 415-662-1800   **Fax:** 415-448-2495
Web: www.lucasfilm.com

PRODUCTS/OPERATIONS

Selected Productions

American Graffiti (1973)
Howard the Duck (1986)
Indiana Jones and the Last Crusade (1989)
Indiana Jones and the Temple of Doom (1984)
Labyrinth (1986)
More American Graffiti (1979)
Radioland Murders (1994)
Raiders of the Lost Ark (1981)
Star Wars: Episode I — The Phantom Menace (1999)
Star Wars: Episode II — Attack of the Clones (2002)
Star Wars: Episode III — Revenge of the Sith (2005)
Star Wars: Episode IV — A New Hope (1977)
Star Wars: Episode V — The Empire Strikes Back (1980)
Star Wars: Episode VI — Return of the Jedi (1983)
Tucker: The Man and His Dream (1988)
Willow (1988)
The Young Indiana Jones Chronicles
  (1992-96, TV movies)

COMPETITORS

Disney Studios	Paramount Pictures
DreamWorks	Pixar
Fox Filmed Entertainment	Sony Pictures
Lions Gate Entertainment	Entertainment
MGM	Universal Studios
New Line Cinema	

HISTORICAL FINANCIALS

Company Type: Private

Income Statement

FYE: March 31

	ESTIMATED REVENUE ($ mil.)	NET INCOME ($ mil.)	NET PROFIT MARGIN	EMPLOYEES
3/03	1,200	—	—	1,800
3/02	1,350	—	—	1,900
3/01	1,500	—	—	2,000
3/00	1,100	—	—	1,800
3/99	600	—	—	1,300
3/98	400	—	—	500
3/97	250	—	—	200
3/96	200	—	—	100
3/95	160	—	—	36
3/94	160	—	—	—
Annual Growth	**25.1%**	**—**	**—**	**63.1%**

Revenue History

MacAndrews & Forbes

Through MacAndrews & Forbes Holdings, financier Ron Perelman is focused on cosmetics and cash. The holding company has investments in an array of public and private companies, most notably 83%-owned Revlon (the #3 cosmetics company in the US), M&F Worldwide (licorice flavors), and WeddingChannel.com. Perelman is intent on reversing the fortunes of Revlon, which he has controlled since 1985. He made a hefty profit when Consolidated Cigar Holdings (the #1 US cigar maker) was sold to French tobacco maker Seita in 1999. Perelman got behind the wheel of AM General, manufacturer of Humvee and HUMMER vehicles, by acquiring a majority stake in the company in mid-2004 through MacAndrews AMG Holdings.

MacAndrews & Forbes' other holdings include the drug-development company TransTech Pharma (in which it is the largest shareholder); 83% of Panavision, the #1 provider of cameras for shooting movies and TV shows; and privately held Allied Security, one of the biggest providers of security guards and systems.

Perelman's holdings have dwindled in value since 1999. Most of the investor's business strategy involves improving his cash position and paying down debt — hence his IPO of Revlon (1996), the sale of The Coleman Company to American Household (formerly Sunbeam Corp., 1998), and the sale of two of Revlon's noncore units. Perelman has committed a $215 million debt-and-equity funding package to rescue Revlon, which is struggling with debt and dwindling market share.

Perelman's sale of The Coleman Company in the late 1990s is helping the investor improve his cash flow in 2005. In his suit against Morgan Stanley, Perelman alleged that the investment bank withheld its knowledge of Sunbeam's accounting fraud when Perelman sold The Coleman Company to Sunbeam in 1998 for about $1.5 billion. Perelman's investment (he held 14.1 million shares of Sunbeam stock as part of the sale) later tanked as news of the accounting irregularities broke. Despite an attempt to settle the dispute with Morgan Stanley in 2003 for $20 million, Perelman took the bank to court and was awarded more than $1.5 billion in damages by a Florida jury in mid-2005.

Perelman is still a media curiosity, largely because of his public courtship and wedding to wife #4, actress Ellen Barkin.

HISTORY

Ron Perelman grew up working in his father's Philadelphia-based conglomerate, Belmont Industries, but he left at the age of 35 to seek his fortune in New York. In 1978 he bought 40% of jewelry store operator Cohen-Hatfield Industries. The next year Cohen-Hatfield bought a minority stake in MacAndrews & Forbes (licorice flavoring). Cohen-Hatfield acquired MacAndrews & Forbes in 1980.

In 1984 Perelman reshuffled his assets to create MacAndrews & Forbes Holdings, which acquired control of Pantry Pride, a Florida-based supermarket chain, in 1985. Pantry Pride then bought Revlon for $1.8 billion with the help of (convicted felon) Michael Milken. After Perelman acquired Revlon, he added several other cosmetics vendors, including Max Factor and Yves Saint Laurent's fragrance and cosmetic lines.

In 1988 MacAndrews & Forbes agreed to invest $315 million in five failing Texas savings and loans (S&Ls), which Perelman combined and named First Gibraltar (sold to BankAmerica, now Bank of America, in 1993). The next year MacAndrews & Forbes bought The Coleman Company, a maker of outdoor equipment.

With a growing reputation for buying struggling companies, revamping them, and then selling them at a higher price, Perelman bought Marvel Entertainment Group (Marvel Comics) in 1989 and took it public in 1991. That year he sold Revlon's Max Factor and Betrix units to Procter & Gamble for more than $1 billion.

MacAndrews & Forbes acquired 37.5% of TV infomercial producer Guthy-Renker and SCI Television's seven stations and merged them to create New World Television. That company was combined with TV syndicator Genesis Entertainment and TV production house New World Entertainment to create New World Communications Group, which Perelman took public in 1994. That year MacAndrews & Forbes and partner Gerald J. Ford bought Ford Motor's First Nationwide, the US's fifth-largest S&L at that time.

Subsidiaries Mafco Worldwide and Consolidated Cigar Holdings merged with Abex (aircraft parts) to create Mafco Consolidated Group in 1995. Following diminishing comic sales, Perelman placed Marvel in bankruptcy in 1996 and subsequently lost control of the company.

In 1997 First Nationwide bought California thrift Cal Fed Bancorp for $1.2 billion. In addition, Perelman sold New World to Rupert Murdoch's News Corp.

In 1998 Perelman orchestrated a $1.8 billion deal in which First Nationwide merged with Golden State Bancorp to form the US's third-largest thrift. Sunbeam Corp. (now American Household) bought Perelman's stake in Coleman that year, making Perelman a major American Household shareholder. Also in 1998 MacAndrews & Forbes bought a 72% stake in Panavision (movie camera maker, later increased to 91%), invested in WeddingChannel.com, and sold its 64% stake in Consolidated Cigar to French tobacco giant Seita (netting Perelman a smoking $350 million profit).

Still burdened by debt, Revlon sold its professional products business in 2000.

Perelman's stock in American Household was rendered worthless when the company initiated bankruptcy proceedings in February 2001. (It would emerge from bankruptcy, however, in December 2002.) He also was sued by angry shareholders after the board of M&F Worldwide, the licorice company he controls, bought Perelman's stock in Panavision at more than five times its market value. In order to settle the litigation surrounding the purchase, in 2002 M&F agreed to return Perelman's 83% stake in Panavision to Mafco. Golden State Bancorp also left the MacAndrews fold in 2002 when it was acquired by Citigroup.

MacAndrews & Forbes Holdings acquired Allied Security, the largest independent provider of contract security services and products in the US, from Gryphon Investors in February 2003 for an undisclosed sum.

EXECUTIVES

Chairman and CEO: Ronald O. (Ron) Perelman, age 62
Co-Vice Chairman: Donald G. Drapkin, age 57
Co-Vice Chairman and Chief Administrative Officer: Howard Gittis, age 71
SVP, Corporate Affairs: James T. Conroy
SVP, Corporate Communications: Christine Taylor
VP: Matthew Adam Drapkin, age 31
VP and Controller: Norman J. Ginstling
Auditors: PricewaterhouseCoopers LLP

LOCATIONS

HQ: MacAndrews & Forbes Holdings Inc.
35 E. 62nd St., New York, NY 10021
Phone: 212-688-9000   **Fax:** 212-572-8400

MacAndrews & Forbes Holdings' consumer products operations are principally in the US.

PRODUCTS/OPERATIONS

Selected Holdings

Allied Security (leading provider of security guards and systems)
American Household (about 37%, small appliances and Coleman camping gear)
M&F Worldwide Corp. (32%, licorice extract)
Revlon Inc. (83%, cosmetics and personal care products)
TransTech Pharma (drug development company)
WeddingChannel.com

COMPETITORS

Alberto-Culver	Johnson & Johnson
Alticor	Kellwood
Avon	L'Oréal USA
Body Shop	LVMH
Chattem	Mary Kay
Colgate-Palmolive	Procter & Gamble
Dial	Ulta
Estée Lauder	Unilever
Guardsmark	Wackenhut

HISTORICAL FINANCIALS

Company Type: Private

Income Statement

FYE: December 31

	REVENUE ($ mil.)	NET INCOME ($ mil.)	NET PROFIT MARGIN	EMPLOYEES
12/02	5,700	—	—	19,800
12/01	5,700	—	—	19,800
12/00	5,500	—	—	19,500
12/99	5,400	—	—	19,500
12/98	4,900	—	—	19,500
12/97	6,071	—	—	29,854
12/96	6,196	—	—	30,000
12/95	4,413	—	—	22,800
12/94	3,030	—	—	22,328
12/93	2,748	—	—	23,500
Annual Growth	**8.4%**	**—**	**—**	**(1.9%)**

Revenue History

Major League Baseball

It may be the national pastime, but Major League Baseball (MLB) is a big business. MLB runs the game of professional baseball and oversees 30 franchises in 28 cities. Each team operates as a separate business, but each is regulated and governed by MLB. The league sets official rules, regulates team ownership, and collects licensing fees for merchandise. It also sells national broadcasting rights and distributes fees to the teams. (Regional broadcast rights are held by each franchise.) MLB was formed when the rival National and American Leagues joined together in 1903.

Baseball has been riding high on a resurgent wave of popularity since the disastrous players' strike of 1994. The work stoppage, which curtailed the season and led to the cancellation of the World Series, marked a low point in MLB history, but fans returned to the game in record numbers to watch sluggers Mark McGwire and Sammy Sosa chase Roger Maris' single-season home run record in 1998. The sport's popularity has also given its prosperity a shot in the arm: the league signed a $2.5 billion broadcasting contract with Fox Entertainment in 2000, sold the Japanese television rights to its games to advertising firm Dentsu for $275 million in 2003, and agreed to a $650 million deal with XM Satellite Radio in 2004.

Despite these healthy deals, the league and commissioner Bud Selig have had to make some tough decisions in recent years. The team owners and the league struggled throughout the 2002 season to negotiate a new labor agreement with players, avoiding another strike with a deal signed in late August at the 11th hour. The agreement forces MLB to delay its plans to eliminate two teams until 2006 (the league had planned on contraction as early as 2003) and also places a luxury tax on teams with high payrolls. The money acquired from the tax is distributed to smaller-market teams in an effort to allow those poorer clubs to compete with the high-priced talent of such teams as the New York Yankees.

However, MLB still has image problems that have to be addressed. Allegations that large numbers of players habitually abuse steroids and other performance enhancement drugs has hung over the league for years. After the *San Francisco Chronicle* reported in 2004 that New York Yankees star Jason Giambi admitted to using steroids during grand jury testimony investigating a California pharmaceuticals company, the league implemented stricter testing rules and penalties for steroid abuse. The new guidelines include mandatory annual tests for each player, and automatic suspensions for first time offenders.

The steroid problem was further exasperated by a tell-all book by ex-player Jose Canseco, who alleges that he personally injected McGwire with steroids, and that he also introduced several other stars (including Rafael Palmeiro, who later was suspended despite continuing denials, and Ivan Rodriguez) to performance enhancement drugs. Numerous MLB officials and players have vehemently denied Canseco's charges, saying he's desperate for attention and out to make a quick buck.

HISTORY

The first baseball team to field professional players was the Cincinnati Red Stockings (now the Cincinnati Reds) in 1869. Teams in Boston, New York City, and Philadelphia followed suit. In 1876 eight professional teams formed the National League. Competing leagues sprang up and folded, but Ban Johnson's Western League (formed in 1892) seized on territory abandoned by the National league in 1900 and began luring National League players with higher salaries. Renamed the American League, it also began drawing away fans. The two leagues agreed to join forces in 1903 by having their champions meet in the World Series.

The sport flourished until the "Black Sox" scandal of 1919, in which eight Chicago White Sox players were accused of taking bribes to throw the World Series. The owners hired Judge Kenesaw Mountain Landis as baseball's first commissioner in 1921 to clean up the game's image. He served until his death in 1944. A joint committee of owners and players introduced more reforms in 1947, including a player pension fund.

The players formed the Major League Baseball Players' Association (MLBPA) in 1954 and signed the first collective-bargaining agreement with the owners in 1968. The players called their first strike in 1972, a 13-day walkout that won an improved pension plan. They won the right to free agency in 1976; another seven-week strike interrupted the 1981 season.

Salary increases slowed, and the free agent market dried up in the mid-1980s, prompting the MLBPA to sue the owners for collusion. The owners agreed to a settlement of $280 million in 1990. Baseball's eighth commissioner, Fay Vincent, resigned in 1992 after the owners effectively removed all power from the commissioner's office. An executive council of owners led by Milwaukee Brewers owner Bud Selig took control.

Prompted by the owners' decision to unilaterally restrict free agency and withdraw salary arbitration, the players started a 232-day strike in August 1994 that forced the cancellation of the World Series and stretched into the 1995 season. Play resumed in 1995 when the owners and the MLBPA approved a new collective-bargaining agreement. Selig stepped down from the Brewers in 1998 to become the game's ninth commissioner. The next year MLB signed a new six-year, $800 million TV contract with ESPN.

Sweeping changes took place in 2000 when owners, who had voted the previous year to eliminate the American and National league offices (centralizing power with the commissioner's office), also voted to restore the "best interests of baseball" powers to the commissioner, giving Selig full authority to redistribute wealth, block trades, and fine teams and players. The MLB also scored a financial home run when Fox Entertainment agreed to pay $2.5 billion for exclusive rights to televise all postseason contests through the 2006 season.

Due to the consistent financial disparity between large- and small-market teams, the league in 2001 voted to eliminate two teams before the start of the 2003 season. A new labor agreement was eventually reached in 2002, however, avoiding another players' strike. The new agreement pushed back the league's contraction plans until 2006 and also placed a luxury tax (which is distributed to small-market franchises) on teams with high payrolls.

EXECUTIVES

Commissioner: Allan H. (Bud) Selig, age 70
President and COO: Robert A. (Bob) DuPuy
EVP Administration: John McHale Jr.
EVP Baseball Operations: Jimmie Lee Solomon
EVP Business: Timothy J. (Tim) Brosnan
EVP Finance and CFO: Jonathan D. Mariner, age 50
EVP Labor Relations and Human Resources:
 Robert D. (Rob) Manfred Jr.
Chief Legal Counsel: Thomas J. (Tom) Ostertag
SVP and General Counsel, Major League Baseball Properties: Ethan Orlinsky
SVP Advertising and Marketing: Jacqueline Parkes
SVP Baseball Operations: Joe Garagiola Jr.
SVP Corporate Sales and Marketing, Major League Baseball Properties: John S. Brody
SVP International Business Operations: Paul Archey
SVP Licensing: Howard Smith
SVP Media Relations: Richard (Rich) Levin
SVP Security and Facilities Management:
 Kevin M. Hallinan
VP Broadcasting: Bernadette McDonald
VP Community Affairs: Thomas C. Brasuell
VP Corporate Sales and Marketing: Justin Johnson
VP International Baseball Operations: Lou Melendez
Auditors: Deloitte & Touche LLP

LOCATIONS

HQ: Major League Baseball
 245 Park Ave., New York, NY 10167
Phone: 212-931-7800   **Fax:** 212-949-8636
Web: www.mlb.com

Major League Baseball has 30 franchises in 28 cities in the US and Canada.

PRODUCTS/OPERATIONS

Major League Franchises

American League
 Anaheim Angels (1965, California)
  Los Angeles Angels (1961)
 Baltimore Orioles (1954)
  St. Louis Browns (1902)
  Milwaukee Brewers (1901)
 Boston Red Sox (1901)
 Chicago White Sox (1901)
 Cleveland Indians (1915)
  Cleveland Spiders (1889)
 Detroit Tigers (1900)
 Kansas City Royals (1969, Missouri)
 Minnesota Twins (1961, Minneapolis)
  Washington Senators (1901; Washington, DC)
 New York Yankees (1913, New York City)
  New York Highlanders (1903, New York City)
  Baltimore Orioles (1901)
 Oakland Athletics (1968, California)
  Kansas City Athletics (1955, Missouri)
  Philadelphia Athletics (1901)
 Seattle Mariners (1977)
 Tampa Bay Devil Rays (1998)
 Texas Rangers (1972, Arlington)
  Washington Senators (1961; Washington, DC)
 Toronto Blue Jays (1977)

National League
 Arizona Diamondbacks (Phoenix, 1998)
 Atlanta Braves (1966)
  Milwaukee Braves (1953)
  Boston Braves (1912)
  Boston Beaneaters (1883)
  Boston Red Stockings (1871)
 Chicago Cubs (1903)
  Chicago Orphans (1898)
  Chicago Colts (1894)
  Chicago White Stockings (1871)
 Cincinnati Reds (1866)
 Colorado Rockies (1993, Denver)
 Florida Marlins (1993, Miami)
 Houston Astros (1964)
  Houston Colt .45s (1962)
 Los Angeles Dodgers (1958)
  Brooklyn Dodgers (1890, New York)
 Milwaukee Brewers (1970; switched from American
  League, 1998)
  Seattle Pilots (1969)
 New York Mets (1962, New York City)
 Philadelphia Phillies (1883)
 Pittsburgh Pirates (1887)
 St. Louis Cardinals (1900)
  St. Louis Brown Stockings (1882)
 San Diego Padres (1969)
 San Francisco Giants (1958)
  New York Giants (1883, New York City)
 Washington Nationals (2004, Washington DC)
  Montreal Expos (1969)

COMPETITORS

AFL
Indy Racing League
Major League Soccer
NASCAR
NBA
NFL
NHL
Open Wheel Racing
USSF
World Wrestling Entertainment

HISTORICAL FINANCIALS

Company Type: Association

Income Statement

FYE: October 31

	REVENUE ($ mil.)	NET INCOME ($ mil.)	NET PROFIT MARGIN	EMPLOYEES
10/04	4,100	—	—	—
10/03	3,800	—	—	—
10/02	3,547	—	—	—
10/01	3,500	—	—	—
10/00	3,178	—	—	—
10/99	2,838	—	—	—
10/98	3,174	—	—	—
10/97	2,216	—	—	200
10/96	1,847	—	—	200
10/95	1,411	—	—	170
Annual Growth	12.6%	—	—	8.5%

Revenue History

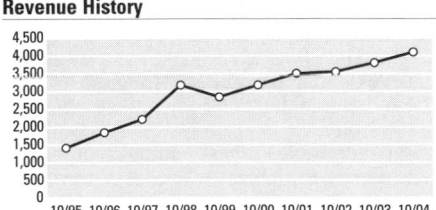

Marbo

Marbo manufactures juice drinks and juice concentrates that are available in a variety of serving sizes and flavors, including Kiwi Strawberry Guava. Marbo beverages, sold under the Tampico brand, are distributed throughout the US and 49 other countries in Central and South America and Africa. Marbo began making Tampico juice products in the early 1980s. Marbo also has licensed the Tampico name to a line of ice cream made through a joint venture with Dean Foods Midwest Division.

EXECUTIVES

CEO: Scott Miller
CFO: Bill White
SVP International Sales: Dan Weingart
Director, Marketing: Richard Ross

LOCATIONS

HQ: Marbo, Inc.
3106 N. Campbell Ave., Chicago, IL 60618
Phone: 773-296-0190   **Fax:** 773-296-0191
Web: www.tampico.com

COMPETITORS

Coca-Cola
Dole Food
Ocean Spray
Snapple
Tropicana

HISTORICAL FINANCIALS

Company Type: Private

Income Statement

	ESTIMATED REVENUE ($ mil.)	NET INCOME ($ mil.)	NET PROFIT MARGIN	EMPLOYEES	FYE: December 31
12/04	75	—	—	130	

Mariner Energy

Despite its name, oil and gas exploration and production company Mariner Energy is not all at sea. True, the independent explores in both the deep and shallow waters of the Gulf of Mexico, where it has more than half of its proved reserves. But the landlocked Permian Basin of West Texas accounts for 48% of reserves. The company has proved reserves of 237.5 billion cu. ft. of natural gas equivalent. Mariner Energy was owned by an Enron affiliate before the bankrupt Enron sold the company to Carlyle/Riverstone in 2004. Carlyle/Riverstone sold its controlling interest in Mariner Energy to institutional buyers in 2005 to help pay down the oil company's debt.

An early entrant in the Gulf of Mexico's growing deepwater exploration business, Mariner Energy has discovered seven new fields there since 1992. The company first filed to go public as Marine Energy, LLC, in 2000 but withdrew the offer in 2002.

EXECUTIVES

Chairman, President, and CEO: Scott D. Josey, age 47, $900,000 pay
VP, CFO, and Treasurer: Rick G. Lester, age 53
COO: Dalton F. Polasek Jr., age 53, $515,000 pay
VP, General Counsel, and Secretary:
Teresa G. Bushman, $405,000 pay
VP Chief Exploration Officer:
Michiel C. (Mike) van den Bold, age 43, $407,500 pay
VP Corporate Development: Jesus G. Melendrez, age 46
VP Deepwater Development: Cory Loegering, age 49
VP Shelf Operations: Judd A. Hansen, age 49, $406,023 pay
Executive Assistant: Maureen Calloway
Human Resources: Emily McClung
Auditors: Deloitte & Touche LLP

LOCATIONS

HQ: Mariner Energy, Inc.
2101 City West Blvd., Ste. 1900, Houston, TX 77042
Phone: 713-954-5500   **Fax:** 713-945-5517
Web: www.mariner-energy.com

Mariner Energy explores for and produces oil and gas in the Gulf of Mexico and West Texas.

2004 Proved Reserves

	% of total
Permian Basin	48
Deepwater Gulf of Mexico	37
Gulf of Mexico Shelf	15
Total	**100**

PRODUCTS/OPERATIONS

2004 Proved Reserves

	% of total
Natural gas	64
Crude oil & condensate	36
Total	**100**

COMPETITORS

Abraxas Petroleum
BP
Brigham Exploration
Chesapeake Energy
Chevron
Devon Energy
Exxon Mobil
Pioneer Natural Resources
Pogo Producing
Range Resources
Royal Dutch/Shell Group
Unocal

HISTORICAL FINANCIALS

Company Type: Private

Income Statement

	REVENUE ($ mil.)	NET INCOME ($ mil.)	NET PROFIT MARGIN	EMPLOYEES	FYE: December 31
12/04	214	68	31.9%	53	
12/03	143	38	26.8%	—	
12/02	158	30	19.0%	43	
12/01	155	12	8.0%	55	
12/00	121	22	18.1%	81	
12/99	53	(10)	—	74	
12/98	57	(58)	—	80	
12/97	63	(20)	—	—	
12/96	60	(16)	—	—	
Annual Growth	**17.1%**	**—**		**(6.6%)**	

2004 Year-End Financials

Debt ratio: 85.9%
Return on equity: 38.9%
Cash ($ mil.): 3
Current ratio: 0.65
Long-term debt ($ mil.): 115

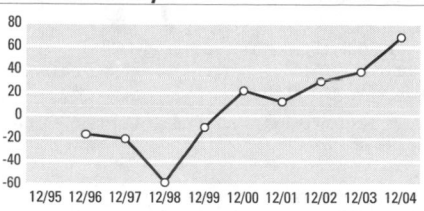

Net Income History

Maritz

Maritz may not be *sending* your employees on business trips, but it will still *motivate* them to go. The company designs employee incentive and reward programs (including incentive travel rewards), customer loyalty programs, plans corporate trade shows and events, and also offers traditional market research services such as the creation of product launch campaigns. Maritz's programs are designed to help its clients improve workforce quality and customer satisfaction. Maritz has phased out its corporate travel business; in 2004 it sold its TQ3 Travel Solutions division to Carlson Wagonlit Travel. The Maritz family owns the company.

Maritz's customers include a majority of the *Forbes* 500 (automakers, financial corporations, pharmaceutical and technology companies). In early 2004 Maritz sold Delve, its data collection unit, to Bush O'Donnell Capital Partners.

Chairman and CEO Steve Maritz controls 60% of the company's shares. His brothers, Peter and Philip Maritz, hold the remaining 40%, and have repeatedly sued the company over the past few years in an effort to unload their shares at a price they deem fair. The dispute stems partly from Maritz's 2002 purchase of incentive travel planner McGettigan (McGettigan works primarily for the pharmaceutical industry), a transaction Peter and Philip called wasteful. The brothers claim the acquisition's $48 million cost was $10 million higher than what was originally described to the company's board, and that the firm's shares declined in value as a result.

EXECUTIVES

Chairman and CEO: W. Stephen (Steve) Maritz, age 46
SEVP and CFO: James W. Kienker, age 56
SVP Marketing: William P. (Scott) Bush, age 41
VP Community Affairs and Organizational Development: Tom Tener
VP Human Resources: Con McGrath
VP Public Relations and Communications: Beth Rusert
VP Sales: Dennis Hummel
CIO: Gil Hoffman
President and CEO, Maritz Automotive Group:
Tim Rogers
President and CEO, Maritz Travel Company:
Christine Duffy
President, Maritz Incentives: Jane Herod
President, Maritz Research: Michael Brereton
Public Relations Director: Jennifer Larsen

LOCATIONS

HQ: Maritz Inc.
1375 N. Highway Dr., Fenton, MO 63099
Phone: 636-827-4000 **Fax:** 636-827-3312
Web: www.maritz.com

Maritz has offices in Canada, France, Germany, Spain, the UK, and the US.

PRODUCTS/OPERATIONS

Services

Marketing Research
Custom marketing research
Customer satisfaction and customer value analysis
Data collection (focus groups, telephone interviews)
Maritz Polls and Maritz Research Reports
Syndicated buyer research
Telecommunications research

Performance Improvement
Communications
e-Learning
Fulfillment
Internet consulting
Loyalty marketing
Measurement and feedback
Rewards and recognition

Travel
Consulting services
Corporate travel management
Group travel services
Travel award programs

COMPETITORS

ACNielsen
Franklin Covey
Gallup
GiftCertificates.com
Harris Interactive
IMS Health
Information Resources
J.D. Power
JTB
Landround
NFO WorldGroup
Opinion Research

HISTORICAL FINANCIALS

Company Type: Private

Income Statement

FYE: March 31

	REVENUE ($ mil.)	NET INCOME ($ mil.)	NET PROFIT MARGIN	EMPLOYEES
3/05	1,200	—	—	4,090
3/04	1,200	—	—	4,200
3/03	1,440	—	—	5,700
3/02	1,500	—	—	6,000
3/01	1,318	—	—	6,200
3/00	1,325	—	—	6,500
3/99	2,200	—	—	6,500
3/98	2,170	—	—	6,500
3/97	2,010	—	—	7,500
3/96	1,795	—	—	7,000
Annual Growth	(4.4%)	—	—	(5.8%)

Revenue History

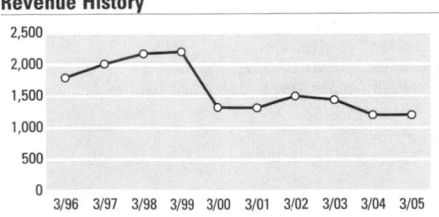

Mark IV

Mark IV Industries aims to hit the mark with engineered components and systems for the automotive, industrial machinery, and transportation management markets. The company's automotive products include aftermarket belts, hoses, and camshaft components, along with OEM power transmission systems, timing belts, engine cooling systems, and power steering systems. Mark IV's power train division makes diesel and gasoline engines for industrial, agricultural, and marine uses. Other products include information display systems (for buses, aircraft, and railcars) and traffic management equipment, including electronic toll-collection systems. European private equity firm BC Partners controls Mark IV Industries.

The North American and European markets each account for about half of Mark IV's sales, and European sales have been increasing relative to those in other parts of the world. Outside the US, Mark IV has regional headquarters in Sölvesborg, Sweden, and Airasca, Italy. The company operates in more than 15 countries overall.

EXECUTIVES

Chairman and Director: Kurt J. Johansson
CEO and Director: William P. Montague, age 58
President, COO, and Director: Giuliano Zucco
VP, CFO, and Treasurer: Mark G. Barberio
VP and Chief Accounting Officer: Richard L. Grenolds
VP, Human Resources: Steve Kerns
President — Power Train: Gianni Borghi
President — Transportation Technologies: Martin Capper
President — Heavy Duty and President — Power Transmission: Adriano Rolando
President — Aftermarket and Interim President — Platform: Dennis Welvaert
CFO — Europe and SA: Guiseppe Tranchini
General Manager — Air Admission and Cooling: Jean-Luc Dejean
Director, Communications: Colleen Pibollo

LOCATIONS

HQ: Mark IV Industries, Inc.
501 John James Audubon Pkwy.,
Amherst, NY 14226
Phone: 716-689-4972 **Fax:** 716-689-6098
Web: www.mark-iv.com

2004 Sales

	% of total
North America	50
Europe	46
Other regions	4
Total	**100**

PRODUCTS/OPERATIONS

2004 Sales

	% of total
Industrial & distribution	
Aftermarket	17
Power train	16
Transportation technologies	15
Heavy duty	6
Automotive	
Power transmission	19
Platform	17
Air admission & cooling	10
Total	**100**

Selected Products

Industrial and distribution
Aftermarket
Automotive belts and hoses
Camshaft and accessory drive components
Power Train
Diesel and small gasoline engines
Power Pacs (diesel engines with continuously variable transmissions)
Transportation technologies
Bus, rail, aircraft, and stationary signs and lighting systems
Intelligent Vehicle Highway Systems (IVHS)
Heavy duty
Power transmission systems for accessory and camshaft drives
Automotive
Power transmission
Automatic tensioning devices
Power transmission systems for accessory and camshaft drives
Pulleys, idlers, brackets, and dampers
Timing and poly-rib belts
Platform
Fuel filler systems and vapor recovery canisters
Power steering, air conditioning, and oil cooling systems
Air admission and cooling
Air intake manifolds
Brake fluid, surge, and power steering tanks and water pumps
Engine cooling systems

COMPETITORS

BorgWarner
Dana
Delphi
Eaton
Gates Corporation
Goodyear
Tesma
Tomkins
Visteon

HISTORICAL FINANCIALS

Company Type: Private

Income Statement

FYE: February 28

	REVENUE ($ mil.)	NET INCOME ($ mil.)	NET PROFIT MARGIN	EMPLOYEES
2/04	1,425	—	—	7,500
2/03	1,300	—	—	7,500
2/02	1,200	—	—	8,000
2/01	2,000	—	—	15,500
2/00	1,994	—	—	15,600
2/99	1,949	—	—	17,000
2/98	2,210	—	—	17,000
2/97	2,076	—	—	15,800
2/96	2,089	—	—	16,000
2/95	1,603	—	—	16,200
Annual Growth	(1.3%)	—	—	(8.2%)

Revenue History

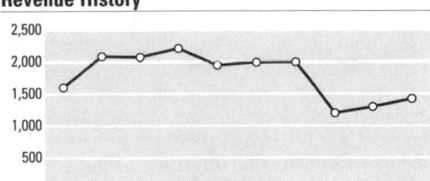

Market Strategies

Market Strategies Inc. (MSI) offers full service custom and syndicated research, as well as strategic consulting services to clients in such industries as energy, health care, and financial services, information technology and telecommunications. Its research specialties include customer satisfaction measurement, market segmentation, product and service evaluation, and e-commerce assessment. Founded in 1989, the firm has offices in Michigan; Oregon; Washington, DC; and New Jersey.

EXECUTIVES

Chairman and CEO: Andrew J. Morrison
COO; CEO, MSInteractive: Reginald Baker
CFO: Jack Vanden Berg
President: Janice A. Brown
Principal and Head of Services Group: Leona J. Foster
SVP and Head of Global Life Sciences Division: Peter E. Carlin
SVP Global Life Sciences Division: Larry Levin
SVP Government, Foundation, and Academic Research Division: Joseph K. Garrett
VP Human Resources: Robin J. Hembree
Auditors: Plante & Moran, PLLC

LOCATIONS

HQ: Market Strategies, Inc.
20255 Victor Parkway, Ste. 400, Livonia, MI 48152
Phone: 734-542-7600   **Fax:** 734-542-7620
Web: www.marketstrategies.com

COMPETITORS

Abt Associates	Maritz Research
Burke	MORPACE
C&R Research	NPD
Gallup	NRC
GfK	Opinion Research
GfK NOP	Press Ganey
Greenfield Consulting	Synovate
Harris Interactive	Taylor Nelson
IMS Health	VNU
Ipsos	Walker Information
Kantar Group	

HISTORICAL FINANCIALS

Company Type: Private

Income Statement

FYE: December 31

	REVENUE ($ mil.)	NET INCOME ($ mil.)	NET PROFIT MARGIN	EMPLOYEES
12/05	45	—	—	525
12/04	40	—	—	495
12/03	34	—	—	470
12/02	33	—	—	715
12/01	30	—	—	—
12/00	34	—	—	—
Annual Growth	**5.7%**	**—**	**—**	**(9.8%)**

Revenue History

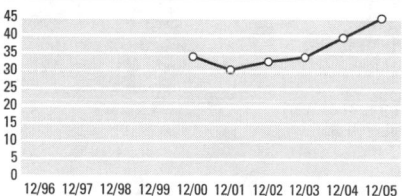

12/96 12/97 12/98 12/99 12/00 12/01 12/02 12/03 12/04 12/05

Marmon Group

With more monikers than most, The Marmon Group monitors a melange of more than 100 autonomous manufacturing and service companies. Marmon's manufacturing units make medical products, mining equipment, industrial materials and components, consumer products (including Wells Lamont gloves), transportation equipment, building products, and water-treatment products. Services include marketing and distribution. Overall, Marmon companies operate 300 facilities in more than 40 countries. Chicago's Pritzker family (owners of the Hyatt hotel chain) owns The Marmon Group. The company's services used to include providing consumer credit information through Trans Union, but the Pritzker family has spun off that business.

Each Marmon company works under its own management, and a small corporate office (fewer than 100 employees) oversees and pulls together the conglomerate, acting as combination CFO, tax lawyer, accountant, and broker to member companies.

Marmon continues to grow through acquisitions, largely to complement existing businesses in fields such as retail display equipment, fasteners and metal products, and consumer credit information.

The Pritzker family is preparing a plan to break up The Marmon Group and divide it among heirs. The Trans Union separation can be seen as a precursor to this, though the group assures that it is not planning to sell the credit-checking company. Penny Pritzker, the independent Trans Union's new chairman, said that the separation will better allow the company to grow, as Trans Union is a technology and information company as opposed to Marmon's stable of manufacturing businesses.

The eventual break up of Marmon Group, should it happen, will take place slowly over the course of a decade with an eye toward family inheritance issues as well as a possible public offering of parts of the business. The actual plans, though, are not known. The famously secretive company went so far as to drop a lawsuit asking for legal approval of the breakup plan when a judge ruled that the records would have to be unsealed if brought before the court.

HISTORY

Although the history of The Marmon Group officially begins in 1953, the company's roots are in the Chicago law firm Pritzker and Pritzker, started by Nicholas Pritzker in 1902. Through the firm the family made connections with First National Bank of Chicago, which A. N. Pritzker, Nicholas' son, used to get a line of credit to buy

real estate. By 1940 the firm had stopped accepting outside clients to concentrate on the family's growing investment portfolio.

In 1953 A. N.'s son Jay used his father's connections to get a loan to buy Colson Company, a small, money-losing manufacturer of bicycles, hospital equipment, and other products. Jay's brother, Robert, a graduate of the Illinois Institute of Technology, took charge of Colson and turned it around. Soon Jay began acquiring more companies for his brother to manage.

In 1963 the brothers paid $2.7 million for about 45% of the Marmon-Herrington Company (whose predecessor, Marmon Motor Car, built the car that in 1911 won the first Indianapolis 500). The family now had a name for its industrial holdings — The Marmon Group.

It became a public company in 1966 when it merged with door- and spring-maker Fenestra. However, Jay began to take greater control of the group through a series of stock purchases, and by 1971 The Marmon Group was private once again.

A year earlier, in 1970, the group acquired a promising industrial pipe supplier, Keystone Tubular Service (it later became Marmon/Keystone). In 1973 Marmon began to acquire stock in Cerro Corp., which had operations in mining, manufacturing, trucking, and real estate; by 1976 the group had bought all of Cerro, thereby tripling its revenues. The brothers sold Cerro's trucking subsidiary, ICX, in 1977 and bought organ maker Hammond Corp., along with Wells Lamont, Hammond's glove-making subsidiary.

Marmon acquired conglomerate Trans Union in 1981. Trans Union brought many operations, including railcar and equipment leasing, credit information services, international trading, and water- and wastewater-treatment systems. Jay acquired Ticketmaster in 1982.

The Pritzkers made a foray into the airline business in 1984 by buying Braniff Airlines. After unsuccessfully bidding for Pan Am in 1987, they sold Braniff in 1988. Disappointments in other Pritzker businesses didn't slow Marmon, which added to its transportation equipment business in 1984 with Altamil, a maker of products for the trucking and aerospace industries.

To mark its 40th anniversary, the company sponsored a car, the Marmon Wasp II, at the 1993 Indianapolis 500. That year the Pritzkers sold 80% of Ticketmaster to Microsoft co-founder Paul Allen but retained a minority interest. Marmon sold Arzco Medical Systems in 1995 and Marmon/Keystone acquired Anbuma Group, a Belgian steel tubing distributor.

The Anbuma purchase and Marmon/Keystone's 1997 acquisition of UK tube distributor Wheeler Group exemplify Marmon's practice of building strength through acquisitions in its established markets. In 1998 Marmon purchased more than 30 companies and opened a business development office in Beijing.

Marmon splashed out more than $500 million in 1999 to make 35 acquisitions, including Kerite (power cables), OsteoMed (specialty medical devices), and Bridport (medical and aviation products). Jay died that year, and the company announced that his title of chairman will not be filled.

In 2000 Marmon spent another $500 million on more than 20 acquisitions, buying operations engaged in the production of retail display equipment, tank containers, and metal products, among others. Former Illinois Tool Works chief John Nichols took over the Marmon CEO responsibilities from Robert Pritzker in 2001.

EXECUTIVES

President and CEO: John D. Nichols
EVP: Robert C. Gluth
SVP and CFO: Robert K. Lorch
SVP and General Counsel: Robert W. (Bob) Webb
SVP: Henry J. (Hank) West
President, Retail Services: Richard Winter
VP Human Resources: Larry Rist
Auditors: Ernst & Young LLP

LOCATIONS

HQ: The Marmon Group, Inc.
225 W. Washington St., Chicago, IL 60606
Phone: 312-372-9500   **Fax:** 312-845-5305
Web: www.marmon.com

PRODUCTS/OPERATIONS

Selected Member Companies

Automotive Equipment
Fontaine Modification Co.
Fontaine Trailer Co.
Marmon-Herrington Co.
Perfection HY-Test Co.

Building Products and Fasteners
Anderson Copper and Brass Co.
Atlas Bolt & Screw Company
Shepherd Caster Corporation
Shepherd Products Inc.

Consumer Products, Marketing, and Financial Services
Beijing Huilian Food Co., Ltd.
Getz Bros. & Co., Inc.
Great Lakes Consulting Group, Inc.
MarCap Corp.
Wells Lamont Corporation

Industrial Products
Amarillo Gear Co.
Bridport Aviation

Medical Products
American Medical Instruments, Inc.
B.G. Sulzle, Inc.
Medical Device Technologies, Inc. (MD Tech)
Pearsalls Limited
Surgical Specialties Corporation

Metal Products and Materials
Cerro Copper Products Co.
Cerro Metal Products Co.
Penn Aluminum International, Inc.

Pipe and Tube Distribution
Marmon/Keystone Corporation
Future Metals, Inc.
M/K Huron Steel

Railway and Transportation Services
Exsif Worldwide, Inc.
Penn Machine Co.
Railserve, Inc.
Trackmobile, Inc.
Union Tank Car Co.

Retail and Food-Service Equipment
Alexander-Otto Company
L.A. Darling Company
Store Opening Solutions, Inc.
Thorco Industries, Inc.

Seat Belts and Cargo Restraints
Am-Safe Inc.
Bridport Aviation

Water Treatment Systems
Ecodyne Limited
EcoWater Systems, Inc.
Spectrum Labs, Inc.

Wire and Cable Products
Cable USA, Inc.
Comtran Corporation
Hendrix Wire & Cable, Inc.
The Kerite Co.
Owl Wire and Cable, Inc.
Rockbestos-Surprenant Cable Corp.

COMPETITORS

Alcatel	Masco
Balfour Beatty	Nexans
Eaton	Pirelli & C.
GE	Superior Essex
Illinois Tool Works	Terex
Ingersoll-Rand	USG
ITT Industries	Wolverine Tube
LEONI	

HISTORICAL FINANCIALS

Company Type: Private

Income Statement

FYE: December 31

	REVENUE ($ mil.)	NET INCOME ($ mil.)	NET PROFIT MARGIN	EMPLOYEES
12/04	6,400	—	—	22,000
12/03	5,560	—	—	28,000
12/02	5,756	—	—	30,000
12/01	6,414	—	—	35,000
12/00	6,786	—	—	40,000
12/99	6,530	—	—	40,000
12/98	6,032	—	—	35,000
12/97	6,003	—	—	33,000
12/96	5,776	—	—	35,000
12/95	6,083	—	—	30,000
Annual Growth	0.6%	—	—	(3.4%)

Revenue History

Mars

Mars knows chocolate sales are nothing to snicker at. The company makes such worldwide favorites as M&M's, Snickers, and the Mars bar. Its other products include 3 Musketeers, Dove, Milky Way, Skittles, Twix, and Starburst sweets; Combos and Kudos snacks; Uncle Ben's rice; and pet food under the names Pedigree, Sheba, and Whiskas. Mars also makes drink vending equipment and electronic automated payment systems. The Mars family (including siblings and retired company CEO Forrest Mars Jr., chairman John Franklyn Mars, and VP Jacqueline Badger Mars) owns the highly secretive firm, making the Mars family one of the richest in the US.

Mars makes non-chocolate confections including breath mints such as AquaDrops, and snack foods like Combos and Kudos. It also makes ice-cream versions of several of its candy bars. Mars' Masterfoods USA swallows a large bite of the pet-food market with its Royal Canin, Pedigree, and Whiskas brands. Uncle Ben's and Seeds of Change also come under the Masterfoods umbrella.

Mars also owns Flavia Beverage Systems and its MEI subsidiary makes automated payment systems, including electronic coin-changers and bill-acceptors. Mars stays virtually debt free and uses its profits for international expansion. It sells its products in more than 100 countries on five continents.

HISTORY

Frank Mars invented the Milky Way candy bar in 1923 after his previous three efforts at the candy business left him bankrupt. After his estranged son, Forrest, graduated from Yale, Mars hired him to work at his candy operation. When Forrest demanded one-third control of the company and Frank refused, Forrest moved to England with the foreign rights to Milky Way and started his own company (Food Manufacturers) in the 1930s. He made a sweeter version of Milky Way for the UK, calling it a Mars bar. Forrest also ventured into pet food with the 1934 purchase of Chappel Brothers (renamed Pedigree). At one point he controlled 55% of the British pet food market.

During WWII Forrest returned to the US and introduced Uncle Ben's rice (the world's first brand-name raw commodity) and M&M's (a joint venture between Forrest and Bruce Murrie, son of Hershey's then-president). The idea for M&M's was borrowed from British Smarties, for which Forrest obtained rights (from Rowntree Mackintosh) by relinquishing similar rights to the Snickers bar in some foreign markets. The ad slogan "Melts in your mouth, not in your hand" (and the candy's success in non-air-conditioned stores and war zones) made the company an industry leader. Mars introduced M&M's Peanut in 1954. It was one of the first candy companies to sponsor a television show — *Howdy Doody* in the 1950s.

Forrest merged his firm with his deceased father's company in 1964, after buying his dying half-sister's controlling interest. (He renamed the business Mars at her request.) The merger was the end of an alliance with Hershey, who had supplied Frank with chocolate since his Milky Way inception.

In 1968 Mars bought Kal Kan. (The division now oversees all pet food operations.) In 1973 Forrest, then 69 years old, delegated his company responsibility to sons Forrest Jr. and John. Five years later the brothers, looking for snacks to offset dwindling candy sales from a more diet-conscious America, bought the Twix chocolate-covered cookie brand. During the late 1980s they bought ice-cream bar maker Dove Bar International and Ethel M Chocolates, producer of liqueur-flavored chocolates, a business their father had begun in his retirement.

Hershey passed Mars as the US's largest candy maker in 1988 when it acquired Cadbury Schweppes' US division (Mounds and Almond Joy). In response to the success of Hershey's Symphony Bar, Mars introduced its dark-chocolate Dove bar in 1991.

While Hershey chose to stick close to home, Mars ventured abroad. The company entered the huge confectionery market of India in 1989 by building a $10 million factory there. In 1996 the company opened a confectionery processing plant in Brazil. Back home, the company expanded its Starburst candy line in 1996 and in 1997 launched new ad campaigns, including M&M's spots featuring a trio of animated M&M candies. Mars introduced Uncle Ben's Rice Bowl frozen meals in the late 1990s.

Forrest Sr. died in 1999, spurring rumors that Mars would go public or be sold. Instead, the company dismantled most of its sales force, opting to use less costly food brokers. Also in 1999 Forrest Jr. retired, leaving brother John Franklyn as president and CEO. Still far behind its rival, Mars received a modest boost in US market share when Hershey experienced computer troubles.

In 2000 the company established a subsidiary, Effem India, to market Mars' products in India. In 2003 Mars acquired French pet food producer Royal Canin. That same year its Mexican subsidiary, Effem Mexico SA de CV, merged with Mexican confectioner Grupo Matre to form a partnership to produce candy for Hispanic markets. Also that year the company began making an energy bar, Snickers Marathon.

The company also acquired Japanese vending machine parts manufacturer Nippon Conlux in 2003. The deal was Mars' first takeover venture in Japan.

Moving into the drink sector, in 2004 Mars licensed its Milky Way, Starburst, and 3 Musketeers brands to Bravo!, which will market vitamin-enhanced milk drinks using the names. That year the company appointed two co-presidents, Peter Cheney and Paul Michaels, leaving John Franklyn Mars as chairman.

Responding to public concerns about healthy eating, Mars started phasing out its "king size" candy bars in 2005.

EXECUTIVES

Chairman: John Franklyn Mars, age 66
President: Paul S. Michaels
VP: Jacqueline Badger Mars, age 65
VP, Chocolate: Mark Mattia
VP, Marketing: Jim Cass
VP, Treasurer, and CFO: R. E. Barnes
Director, Science: Harold Schmitz
President, Gourmet Chocolate and Retail: John Haugh
President, Masterfoods Australia-New Zealand:
Andy Weston-Webb
President, Masterfoods Europe: Pierre Laubies
President, Masterfoods North America: Bob Gamgort
SVP, Marketing, Masterfoods USA:
Michael (Mike) Tolkowsky
VP and General Manager, Snackfoods, Masterfoods USA: Martyn Wilks
VP, Sales Strategy, Masterfoods USA: Timothy LeBel
Director, Masterfoods USA: Doug Milne
Director, Licensing, Masterfoods USA: Lynn Scott
Director, Marketing, Masterfoods Pet Food: Chris Jones
Director, Relationship Marketing, Masterfoods USA:
Robert DeSena

LOCATIONS

HQ: Mars, Incorporated
6885 Elm St., McLean, VA 22101
Phone: 703-821-4900   **Fax:** 703-448-9678
Web: www.mars.com

PRODUCTS/OPERATIONS

Selected Products
Candy
3 Musketeers	Milky Way
Bounty	Opal Fruit
Dove	Revels
Ethel M Chocolates	Skittles
Maltesers	Snickers
M&M's	Starburst
Mars	Twix

Ice-Cream Bars
3 Musketeers
DoveBars
M&M Cookie Ice Cream Sandwiches
Milky Way
Snickers
Starburst Ice Bars

Pet Food
Bounce	Loyal
Brekkies	My Dog
Cesar	Pedigree
Chappie	Sheba
Dine	Trill
Effem	Waltham
Frolic	Whiskas
KiteKat	

Snacks
Combos
Kudos

Rice and Other Food and Drinks
Dolmio sauces
Flavia drinks
Masterfoods condiments and sauces
Suzi Wan Chinese food
Uncle Ben's Rice

Other Products
Coin changers
Flavia office beverage systems
Klix beverage vending equipment
Smart card payment systems

Selected Divisions
Information Services International (information and systems technology for Mars units)
Masterfoods USA (US business units of M&M/Mars, Kal Kan, and Uncle Ben's)
MEI (electronic bill acceptors, coin changers, and card-based cashless payment systems)

COMPETITORS

Alpine Confections	Hershey
American Licorice	House of Brussels
Barry Callebaut	Kraft Foods
Brach's	Laura Secord
Butterfields Candy	Lindt & Sprüngli
Cadbury Schweppes	Meiji Seika
Campbell Soup	NECCO
Chupa Chups	Nestlé
Colgate-Palmolive	PEZ Candy
ConAgra	Riviana Foods
Concord Confections	Rocky Mountain Chocolate
CSM	Russell Stover
Doane Pet Care	See's Candies
Ezaki Glico	Sherwood Brands
Ferrara Pan Candy	Spangler Candy
Ferrero	SweetWorks
General Mills	Thorntons
Grupo Corvi	Tootsie Roll
Guittard	Unilever
Heinz	Wrigley

HISTORICAL FINANCIALS
Company Type: Private

Income Statement
FYE: December 31

	ESTIMATED REVENUE ($ mil.)	NET INCOME ($ mil.)	NET PROFIT MARGIN	EMPLOYEES
12/04	18,000	—	—	39,000
12/03	17,000	—	—	31,000
12/02	16,200	—	—	30,000
12/01	15,500	—	—	30,000
12/00	15,400	—	—	30,000
12/99	15,200	—	—	28,500
12/98	15,500	—	—	30,000
12/97	14,400	—	—	28,500
12/96	14,000	—	—	28,000
12/95	13,000	—	—	28,000
Annual Growth	3.7%	—	—	3.8%

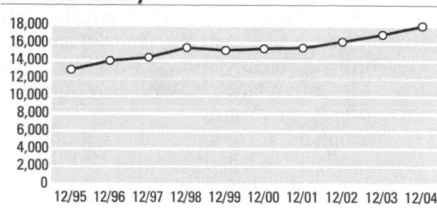

Revenue History

Mary Kay

Celebrating its 40th anniversary in 2003, Mary Kay is in the pink and in Avon's shadow (considering Avon's more than $6.8 billion in revenue in 2003) as the US's #2 direct seller of beauty products. It offers more than 200 products in six categories: body care, color cosmetics, facial skin care, fragrances, nail care, and sun protection. Some 1.3 million independent sales consultants demonstrate Mary Kay products in the US and about 30 other countries. Consultants vie for awards each year, ranging from jewelry to the company's trademark pink Cadillac (first awarded in 1969). The family of founder Mary Kay Ash owns most of the company.

Founded by a woman for women, Mary Kay has an overwhelmingly female independent sales force. Although the company stands by Mary Kay's original goal of providing financial and career opportunities for women, much of the company's executive population is male. Ash's son Richard Rogers (chairman and CEO) runs the company.

Mary Kay works hard to retain the feel of a small company, despite its more than 1-million-strong independent sales force and the firm's growing international reach. As part of this initiative, each beauty consultant receives the option to buy his or her own Web site to use for selling to clients.

During her lifetime, Mary Kay Ash was known for her religious nature as well as her generosity. She founded the Mary Kay Ash Charitable Foundation in 1996. She suffered a debilitating stroke later that year and died on Thanksgiving Day 2001.

HISTORY

Before founding her own company in 1963, Mary Kay Ash worked as a Stanley Home Products sales representative. Impressed with the alligator handbag awarded to the top saleswoman at a Stanley convention, Ash was determined to win the next year's prize — and she did. Despite that accomplishment and having worked at Stanley for 11 years, a male assistant she had trained was made her boss after less than a year on the job. Tired of not receiving recognition, Ash and her second husband used their life savings ($5,000) to go into business for themselves. Although her husband died of a heart attack shortly before the business opened, Ash forged ahead with the help of her two grown sons.

She bought a cosmetics formula invented years earlier by a hide tanner. (The mixture was originally used to soften leather, but the tanner noticed how the formula made his hands look younger, and he began applying the mixture to his face, with great results.) Ash kept her first line simple — 10 products — and packaged her wares in pink to complement the typically white bathrooms of the day. Ash also enlisted consultants, who held "beauty shows" with five or six women in attendance. Mary Kay grossed $198,000 in its first year.

The company introduced men's skin care products in 1964. Ash bought a pink Cadillac the following year and began awarding the cars as prizes in 1969. (By 1981 orders were so large — almost 500 — that GM dubbed the color "Mary Kay Pink.")

Ash became a millionaire when her firm went public in 1968. Mary Kay grew steadily through the 1970s. Foreign operations began in 1971 in Australia, and over the next 25 years the company entered 24 more countries, including nations in Asia, Europe, Central and South America, and the Pacific Rim.

Sales plunged in the early 1980s, along with the company's stock prices (from $40 to $9 between 1983 and 1985). Ash and her family reacquired Mary Kay in 1985 through a $375 million LBO. Burdened with debt, the firm lost money in the late 1980s. Mary Kay took a number of steps to boost sales and income, doing a makeover on the cosmetics line and advertising in women's magazines again (after a five-year hiatus) to counter its old-fashioned image. The company also introduced recyclable packaging and lipstick in a tube (replacing brush-on palettes). In 1989 Avon rebuffed a buyout offer by Mary Kay, and both companies halted animal testing.

In 1993 Mary Kay opened a subsidiary in Russia, which later became the company's fourth-largest international market (behind Mexico, China, and Canada). Ash suffered a debilitating stroke in 1996.

In 1998 Mary Kay began selling through retail boutiques in China because of a government ban on direct selling. Changing with the times, Mary Kay added a white sport utility vehicle and new shades of pink to its fleet of 10,000 GM cars that year.

Chairman John Rochon was named CEO in 1999. Also in 1999 Mary Kay launched *Women & Success* (a magazine for consultants) and Atlas (its electronic ordering system).

In June 2001 Richard Rogers, the company chairman and son of Ash, replaced Rochon as CEO. A month later Mary Kay introduced the Velocity Products line, targeting girls ages 14 to 24. Ash died on Thanksgiving Day 2001.

Mary Kay Poland, headquartered in Warsaw, became the company's 34th international market in mid-2003.

EXECUTIVES

Chairman and CEO: Richard R. Rogers
President and COO: David B. Holl
President, Global Sales: Tom Whatley
EVP and CIO: Kregg Jodie
EVP, Global Human Resources and Operations: Darrell Overcash
EVP, Global Manufacturing: Dennis Greaney
EVP, Global Marketing/R&D: Myra O. Barker
SVP, Finance: Terry Smith
SVP, General Counsel, and Secretary: Nathan P. Moore
SVP, Marketing: Rhonda Shasteen
VP, Global Corporate Communications: Randall G. Oxford
VP, Government Relations: Anne Crews
VP, Information Technology: Karen Calvert
VP, Sales Development and Administration: Sean Key
President, Mary Kay Europe: Tara Eustance
President, Mary Kay Greater China: Paul Mak
Director, Product Marketing: Lisa Cohorn
Corporate Communications: Shannon Summers

LOCATIONS

HQ: Mary Kay Inc.
16251 Dallas Pkwy., Addison, TX 75001
Phone: 972-687-6300   **Fax:** 972-687-1611
Web: www.marykay.com

Mary Kay has an independent sales force of more than 1 million that sells the company's products in more than 33 markets in Asia, Australia, Europe, North America, and South America.

PRODUCTS/OPERATIONS

Selected Product Lines

Body care
Cosmetics
Facial skin care
Fragrances (men's and women's)
Men's skin care
Nail care
Nutritional supplements for men
Nutritional supplements for women
Sun protection

COMPETITORS

Alberto-Culver	John Paul Mitchell
Alticor	Johnson & Johnson
Avon	L'Oréal
Bath & Body Works	Merle Norman
BeautiControl Cosmetics	Murad, Inc.
Body Shop	Nu Skin
Clarins	Perrigo
Colgate-Palmolive	Procter & Gamble
Coty Inc.	Reliv'
Dana Classic Fragrances	Revlon
Del Labs	Schwarzkopf & Henkel
Dial	Scott's Liquid Gold
Estée Lauder	Shaklee
Helen of Troy	Shiseido
Herbalife	Sunrider
Intimate Brands	Unilever

HISTORICAL FINANCIALS

Company Type: Private

Income Statement				FYE: December 31
	REVENUE ($ mil.)	NET INCOME ($ mil.)	NET PROFIT MARGIN	EMPLOYEES
12/03	1,800	—	—	3,600
12/02	1,560	—	—	3,600
12/01	1,300	—	—	3,600
12/00	1,200	—	—	3,600
12/99	1,000	—	—	3,250
12/98	1,000	—	—	3,500
12/97	1,050	—	—	3,500
12/96	1,000	—	—	3,000
12/95	950	—	—	2,800
12/94	850	—	—	2,400
Annual Growth	8.7%	—	—	4.6%

Revenue History

Maryland State Lottery

The Maryland State Lottery Agency offers players a variety of ways to amass a fortune. Among its games of chance are scratch-offs bearing titles such as Betty Boop, High Stakes, Hot Cherries, and Slingo. The agency's numbers games include Lotto, Pick 3, and Pick 4. Maryland State Lottery also participates in the seven-state The Big Game lottery. The agency, which was created in 1973, distributes about 57% of its revenue as prizes; the rest goes to state-funded programs, retailers, and operational expenses. Proceeds from lottery sales helped build Camden Yards, home of Major League Baseball's Baltimore Orioles.

EXECUTIVES

Chairman: Frank Bonaventure
Director: Buddy W. Roogow
Deputy Director and CFO: Gina M. Smith
Deputy Director and CIO: Sandra A. Johnson
Chief Security and Investigations: Nathaniel (Nate) Smoot
Director Creative Services: Jill Q. Baer
Director Policy and Development: Paul Dorsey
Director Human Resources: Lawrence J. Simpson
Director Communications: Hollis J. (Jimmy) White
Executive Associate: Marie Torosino
Principal Counsel: Andrea J. Johnson

LOCATIONS

HQ: Maryland State Lottery Agency
1800 Washington Blvd., Ste. 330,
Baltimore, MD 21230
Phone: 410-230-8800   **Fax:** 410-230-8728
Web: www.msla.state.md.us

PRODUCTS/OPERATIONS

Selected Games

Numbers games
  The Big Game
  Keno
  Lotto
  Pick 3
  Pick 4
Scratch-off games
  Betty Boop
  Fire n' Ice
  Hot Cherries
  Pharaoh's Gold
  Riverboat Riches
  Slingo
  Tropical Jackpot
  Vegas

COMPETITORS

Multi-State Lottery
New Jersey Lottery
Pennsylvania Lottery
Virginia Lottery

HISTORICAL FINANCIALS

Company Type: Government-owned

Income Statement
FYE: June 30

	REVENUE ($ mil.)	NET INCOME ($ mil.)	NET PROFIT MARGIN	EMPLOYEES
6/04	1,395	—	—	150
6/03	1,320	—	—	150
6/02	1,300	—	—	150
6/01	1,211	—	—	157
6/00	1,175	—	—	150
6/99	1,080	—	—	150
6/98	1,070	—	—	170
6/97	1,041	—	—	170
6/96	1,112	—	—	160
6/95	1,039	—	—	148
Annual Growth	3.3%	—	—	0.1%

Revenue History

(Line chart showing revenue from 6/95 to 6/04, rising from about 1,000 to 1,400)

| 6/95 | 6/96 | 6/97 | 6/98 | 6/99 | 6/00 | 6/01 | 6/02 | 6/03 | 6/04 |

Mashantucket Pequot Gaming

Mashantucket Pequot Gaming Enterprise has propelled the Mashantucket Pequot Tribal Nation (with roughly 700 members) from the depths of intense poverty to its lofty position as the wealthiest Native American tribe in the US. It owns and operates Foxwoods Resort Casino, one of the largest casinos in the world and, many believe, the most profitable. The complex offers more than 6,400 slot machines and 350 gaming tables in six casinos, three hotels (Grand Pequot Tower, Great Cedar Hotel, Two Trees Inn), 24 restaurants, live entertainment, and a string of retail shops.

The Mashantucket Pequot reservation is a sovereign nation, and the Pequot tribe is not obligated to pay local property or business taxes, or reveal all of its finances. However, estimates of Foxwoods' annual revenues exceed $1 billion. The state of Connecticut receives 25% of the casino's slot machine revenues.

In addition to its gaming operations, the Mashantucket Pequot Tribal Nation owns Fox Navigation (high-speed ferry service) and the Pequot Pharmaceutical Network (mail-order and discount pharmaceuticals). It also owns three Connecticut hotels (Hilton Mystic, Norwich Inn & Spa, Randall's Ordinary Inn) and two golf courses (Foxwoods Golf & Country Club at Boulder Hills and Pequot Golf Club). The Mashantucket Pequot Tribal Nation has even established the Mashantucket Pequot Museum and Research Center dedicated to the tribe's life and history.

Two books released in 2000 and 2001, which questioned the authenticity of the Mashantucket Pequot tribe and claimed that the government was duped into giving them more land for their reservation than they were entitled to, sparked a series of lawsuits from neighboring communities. In early 2002 the Mashantucket Pequot tribe announced it had withdrawn its application to annex 165 acres of land close to its Foxwood Resort Casino, ending nearly 10 years of legal battles.

HISTORY

Once a powerful tribe, the Pequots were virtually wiped out in the 17th century by disease and attacks from colonists. More than 350 years later, Richard "Skip" Hayward, a pipefitter making $15,000 a year, led the fight for federal recognition of his nearly extinct Mashantucket Pequot tribe. He was elected tribal chairman in 1975, and the US government officially recognized the tribe in 1983.

The Indian Gaming Regulatory Act of 1988 opened the door for legal gambling on reservations, but tribes still had to negotiate with state governments for authorization. Hayward hired G. Michael "Mickey" Brown as a consultant and lawyer. Brown took the tribe's legal battle to the US Supreme Court, which eventually ruled that the Pequots could build a casino. When some 30 banks turned down the Pequots for a construction loan, Brown introduced Hayward and his tribe to Lim Goh Tong, billionaire developer of the successful Gentings Highlands Casino resort in Malaysia. Tong invested approximately $60 million, and the Foxwoods casino opened in 1992.

Brown brought in Alfred J. Luciani to serve as president and CEO of Foxwoods. Luciani stayed less than a year, however, resigning because of what he called philosophical differences with tribe leadership. Brown took over as CEO in 1993. Although Foxwoods grew rapidly, Brown often wrestled with members of the tribal council over how the business should be run. The next year Brown rehired Luciani to oversee the development of the Grand Pequot Tower hotel.

Brown resigned and Luciani was fired in 1997 after it was revealed that Brown had not fully disclosed his ties with Lim Goh Tong and that, in 1992, Luciani had accepted a $377,000 loan from Gamma International, a vendor that provided keno services to Foxwoods. The Pequots considered these actions to be conflicts of interest. A new management team was brought in, and Floyd "Bud" Celey, a veteran of Hilton Hotels, was appointed CEO.

The Pequots opened the Mashantucket Pequot Museum and Research Center in 1998. When tribal elections were held later that year, Kenneth Reels was elected chairman of the Pequot's tribal governing body, ousting Hayward from the position he had held for more than 20 years. Hayward was elected vice chairman. Mashantucket Pequot Gaming Enterprise concentrated on improving financial accountability in 1999, and the tribe began cutting costs by shuttering unprofitable holdings, including Pequot River Shipworks, its shipbuilding business.

Former COO William Sherlock replaced Celey as CEO in 2000. That year the first of two books (the second was published in 2001), which questioned the tribe's legitimacy, created some controversy for the group. A federal audit in 2000 revealed that the tribe's pharmaceutical firm was giving discount drugs intended for Native Americans to its non-Native American employees. In 2002 the tribe withdrew its application to annex 165 acres of land close to its Foxwood Resort Casino after nearly 10 years of legal battles.

EXECUTIVES

Chairman: Michael J. Thomas
President and CEO: William (Bill) Sherlock
COO: Robert Sheldon
EVP Marketing: Robert De Salvio
SVP Administration: Bryce Kirchner
SVP Finance: John O'Brien
SVP Human Resources: Joanne Franks
Director, Media Relations and Advertising: Sandra Rios
Director, Poker Operations: Kathy Raymond
Chief Development Officer: Gary D. Armentrout

LOCATIONS

HQ: Mashantucket Pequot Gaming Enterprise Inc.
Rte. 2, Mashantucket, CT 06339
Phone: 860-312-3000   **Fax:** 860-312-1599
Web: www.foxwoods.com

The Mashantucket Pequot Gaming Enterprise has holdings in Connecticut and Rhode Island.

PRODUCTS/OPERATIONS

**Selected Mashantucket Pequot
Tribal Nation Holdings**

Fox Navigation (ferry service)
Hilton Mystic (Mystic, CT)
Mashantucket Pequot Gaming Enterprise (Foxwoods Resort Casino; Ledyard, CT)
Mashantucket Pequot Museum and Research Center (Mashantucket, CT)
Norwich Inn & Spa (Norwich, CT)
Pequot Golf Club (Stonington, CT)
Pequot Pharmaceutical Network (mail-order and discount pharmaceuticals)
Randall's Ordinary Inn (North Stonington, CT)

COMPETITORS

Aztar
Connecticut Lottery
Harrah's Entertainment
Kerzner International
Mohegan Tribal Gaming
New York State Lottery
Trump Resorts

HISTORICAL FINANCIALS

Company Type: Private

Income Statement
FYE: September 30

	ESTIMATED REVENUE ($ mil.)	NET INCOME ($ mil.)	NET PROFIT MARGIN	EMPLOYEES
9/02	1,000	—	—	11,500
9/01	1,500	—	—	11,500
9/00	1,300	—	—	11,500
9/99	1,200	—	—	11,500
9/98	1,000	—	—	11,500
9/97	1,000	—	—	11,180
9/96	1,100	—	—	12,000
9/95	1,030	—	—	11,000
9/94	1,000	—	—	10,000
9/93	1,000	—	—	9,100
Annual Growth	0.0%	—	—	2.6%

Revenue History

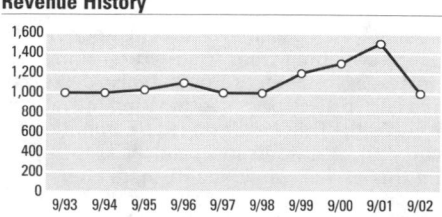

| 9/93 | 9/94 | 9/95 | 9/96 | 9/97 | 9/98 | 9/99 | 9/00 | 9/01 | 9/02 |

Massachusetts Mutual Life Insurance

Massachusetts Mutual Life Insurance (Mass-Mutual) is the flagship firm of the MassMutual Financial Group, a global organization of companies that provide financial services including life insurance, annuities, money management, and retirement planning. Founded in 1851, MassMutual's clients include individuals and businesses. The company also offers disability income insurance, long-term care insurance, structured settlement annuities, and trust services (through The MassMutualTrust Company). Other subsidiaries include OppenheimerFunds (mutual funds), David L. Babson & Co. (investor services), and Cornerstone Real Estate (real estate equities).

Like so many other insurance firms, Mass-Mutual is determined to transform into a financial services firm. However, you won't catch the firm issuing stock to get the job done; its management and policyholders have reaffirmed their intention to keep MassMutual a mutual company despite the efforts of some policyholders.

The company's board of directors terminated former CEO Robert O'Connell in 2005 citing a list of reasons that includes using company assets improperly and the use of retaliatory behavior against employees.

MassMutual has acquired the operations of Baring Asset Management from ING Groep.

MassMutual International is exporting the company's operations worldwide, having established subsidiaries in Asia, Europe, and South America. It focuses on new product development (the majority of sales come from products or channels developed within the last couple of years) and broadened distribution.

HISTORY

Insurance agent George Rice formed Massachusetts Mutual in 1851 as a stock company based in Springfield. The firm converted to a mutual in 1867. For its first 50 years MassMutual sold only individual life insurance, but after 1900 it branched out, offering first annuities (1917) and then disability coverage (1918).

The early 20th century was rough on MassMutual, which was forced to raise premiums on new policies during WWI, then faced the high costs of the 1918 flu epidemic. The firm endured the Great Depression despite policy terminations, expanding its product line to include income insurance. In 1946 MassMutual wrote its first group policy, for Jack Daniel's maker Brown-Forman Distillers. By 1950 the company had diversified into medical insurance.

MassMutual began investing in stocks in the 1950s, switching from fixed-return bonds and mortgages for higher returns. It also decentralized and in 1961 began automating operations. By 1970 the firm had installed a computer network linking it to its independent agents. During this period, whole life insurance remained the core product.

With interest rates increasing during the late 1970s, many insurers diversified by offering high-yield products like guaranteed investment contracts funded by high-risk investments. MassMutual resisted as long as it could, but as interest rates soared to 20%, the company experienced a rash of policy loans, which led to a cash crunch. In 1981, with its policy growth rate trailing the industry norm, MassMutual developed new products, including some that offered higher dividends in return for adjustable interest on policy loans.

In the 1980s MassMutual reduced its stock investment (to about 5% of total investments by 1987), allowing it to emerge virtually unscathed from the 1987 stock market crash.

The firm changed course in 1990 and entered financial services. It bought a controlling interest in mutual fund manager Oppenheimer Management. MassMutual announced in 1993 that, with legislation limiting rates, it would stop writing new individual and small-group policies in New York.

The next year the company targeted the neglected family-owned business niche; in 1995 it sponsored the American Alliance of Family-Owned Businesses and rolled out new whole life products aimed at this segment. That year it bought David L. Babson & Company, a Massachusetts-based investment management firm, and opened life insurance companies in Chile and Argentina.

In 1996 MassMutual merged with Connecticut Mutual. It also acquired Antares Leveraged Capital Corp. (commercial finance) and Charter Oak Capital Management (investment advisory services). The next year MassMutual sold its Life & Health Benefits Management subsidiary.

Still in the mood to merge, the company entered discussions with Northwestern Mutual in 1998, but culture clashes terminated the talks. Also that year the company helped push through legislation that would allow insurers to issue stock through mutual holding companies, a move which MassMutual itself contemplated in 1999.

MassMutual expanded outside the US at the turn of the century. In 1999 it issued securities in Europe, opened offices in such locales as Bermuda and Luxembourg, and bought the Argentina operations of Jefferson-Pilot. A year later it expanded into Asia when it bought Hong Kong-based CRC Protective Life Insurance (now MassMutual Asia). In 2001 the company entered the Taiwanese market, buying a stake in Mercuries Life Insurance (now MassMutual Mercuries Life Insurance) and acquired Japanese insurer Aetna Heiwa Life (a subsidiary of US health insurer Aetna).

Also in 2001 MassMutual policyholders defeated a proposal by some to convert the company to stockholder ownership.

EXECUTIVES

Chairman: James R. Birle
President and CEO: Stuart H. Reese
Chief Administrative Officer: Elaine Sarsynski
EVP and CFO; Office of the CEO: Howard E. Gunton
EVP and Chief Investment Officer; Office of the CEO: Roger Crandall
EVP, Retirement Services: Frederick C. Castellani
EVP and CIO: James E. Miller
EVP; Chairman, President, and CEO, OppenheimerFunds, Inc.; Office of the CEO: John V. Murphy
EVP, International, Large Corporate Markets, M&A, Income Management; President and CEO, MassMutual International, Inc.: Andrew Oleksiw
EVP, Retirement, Financial, Disability and Long-Term Care Products: Toby J. Slodden
EVP, Individual Insurance Group; Office of the CEO: Matthew E. Winter

SVP and Deputy CFO: Michael T. Rollings
SVP, Corporate Tax: Richard D. Bourgeois
SVP; Managing Director and CEO, MassMutual Asia Ltd.: Elroy Chan
SVP, Corporate Communications: Frances B. Emerson
SVP and General Auditor: Douglas J. Janik
SVP and General Counsel: Robert Liguori
SVP, Corporate Human Resources: Nancy M. Roberts
VP and Treasurer: Edward M. Kline
Auditors: PricewaterhouseCoopers LLP

LOCATIONS

HQ: Massachusetts Mutual Life Insurance Company
1295 State St., Springfield, MA 01111
Phone: 413-788-8411   **Fax:** 413-744-6005
Web: www.massmutual.com

PRODUCTS/OPERATIONS

2004 Sales

	$ mil.	% of total
Premium income	14,172	76
Net investment income	4,082	22
Fees & other income	451	2
Total	**18,705**	**100**

Selected Subsidiaries and Affiliates

Antares Capital Corporation (commercial finance)
Babson Capital Management LLC
Baring Asset Management
Baring Asset Management (Germany)
Baring Asset Management (UK)
Baring Asset Management France
Baring Asset Management (Japan)
Baring International Fund Managers (Hong Kong)
Baring SICE (Taiwan)
C.M. Life Insurance Company
Cornerstone Real Estate Advisers LLC
   (real estate equities)
David L. Babson and Company, Inc. (institutional
   investment services)
Fuh Hwa Securities Investment Trust Co., Ltd. (Taiwan)
MassMutual Asia Ltd. (Hong Kong)
MassMutual (Bermuda)
MassMutual Europe S.A. (Luxembourg)
MassMutual International, Inc.
MassMutual Life Insurance Company K.K. (Japan)
MassMutual Mercuries Life Insurance Co., Ltd. (Taiwan)
MassMutual Settlement Solutions
MassMutual Trust Company, F.S.B.
MML Bay State Life Insurance Company
MML Investors Services, Inc.
OFI Institutional Asset Management
OFI Institutional Asset Management (Europe)
OppenheimerFunds (Asia) (Hong Kong)
OppenheimerFunds, Inc. (mutual funds)
   Tremont Capital Management, Inc.
   OppenheimerFunds International (UK)
The MassMutual Trust Company, FSB
Vida Corp. (Chile)

COMPETITORS

AIG	John Hancock Financial
AIG American General	Services
Allianz	Liberty Mutual
Allstate	Mellon Financial
American Financial	Merrill Lynch
AXA Financial	MetLife
Charles Schwab	Nationwide
CIGNA	New York Life
Citigroup	Northwestern Mutual
CNA Financial	Principal Financial
Conseco	Prudential
FMR	St. Paul Travelers
Genworth Financial	State Farm
Guardian Life	TIAA-CREF
The Hartford	Torchmark
Jefferson-Pilot	UBS Financial Services

HISTORICAL FINANCIALS

Company Type: Mutual company

Income Statement

FYE: December 31

	ASSETS ($ mil.)	NET INCOME ($ mil.)	INCOME AS % OF ASSETS	EMPLOYEES
12/04	108,216	335	0.3%	10,000
12/03	96,779	461	0.5%	10,000
12/02	84,102	1,408	1.7%	9,000
12/01	78,934	791	1.0%	9,000
12/00	73,739	740	1.0%	8,000
12/99	70,586	441	0.6%	7,900
12/98	66,979	359	0.5%	7,885
12/97	61,069	262	0.4%	—
12/96	55,752	239	0.4%	—
12/95	38,632	159	0.4%	—
Annual Growth	12.1%	8.6%	—	4.0%

2004 Year-End Financials

Equity as % of assets: 5.8%
Return on assets: 0.3%
Return on equity: 5.3%
Long-term debt ($ mil.): 55,524
Sales ($ mil.): 18,705

Net Income History

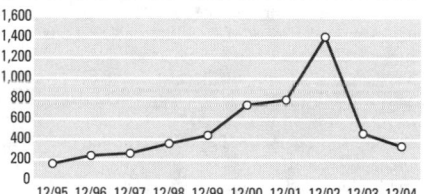

12/95 12/96 12/97 12/98 12/99 12/00 12/01 12/02 12/03 12/04

MathStar

No doubt MathStar has plenty of math stars on its engineering staff. The fabless semiconductor company designs reconfigurable logic chips, which it calls field-programmable object arrays, or FPOAs. These devices are designed to allow electronics makers to program them at low cost for various digital signal processing functions. MathStar is targeting applications in high-definition video, imaging, machine vision, military/aerospace, test and measurement, and wireless base stations. The development-stage company touts its approach as a lower-cost alternative to existing technologies in programmable logic, such as field-programmable gate arrays. MathStar was founded in 1997.

Since it was established, MathStar has tried its hand at a couple of semiconductor markets before finally focusing on the FPOA technology. In 2001, the company acquired Digital MediaCom, a developer of high-speed serial interface chips for the Gigabit Ethernet networking equipment market. Due to the dot-com/telecom bust that ensued, reducing the market opportunities for high-speed networking gear, MathStar sold the assets of the Digital MediaCom business in 2002. In early 2002, MathStar decided to discontinue development of the fixed-function chips it had been working on since its inception and to switch to the programmable semiconductor model. Its FPOA chips were first fabricated in late 2003, with the first working silicon delivered in early 2004. The company plans to sell a commercial version of the FPOA beginning in the first quarter of 2006.

The company is working on strategic development programs with Honeywell International and Valley Technologies. Honeywell is interested in radiation-hardened semiconductors that can be used in digital signal processing systems for satellite communications. Valley Technologies is developing reconfigurable computers meant for navigation, weather forecasting, and military applications.

Design tools are key to programmable logic devices, as seen by the emphasis put on design software at rivals Altera and Xilinx, which combine third-party tools and internally developed software for their customers. MathStar is working with Summit Design, a developer and vendor of electronic system-level design software, to provide design tools for its clients.

Fabrication of MathStar semiconductors is principally outsourced to Taiwan Semiconductor Manufacturing Co. (TSMC), the world's largest supplier of silicon foundry services.

MathStar CEO Douglas Pihl owns nearly 13% of the company.

EXECUTIVES

Chairman, President, and CEO:
Douglas M. (Doug) Pihl, age 65, $246,000 pay
COO: Daniel J. Sweeney, age 46
VP, Administration and CFO:
James W. (Jim) Cruckshank, age 50
VP, Engineering: Timothy A. Teckman, age 47
VP, Marketing: Sean P. Riley, age 36
VP, Sales: Dean J. Westman, age 49
CTO: Ronald K. (Ron) Bell, age 62, $240,000 pay
General Counsel and Secretary: Byron K. Bequette, age 46
Engineering Manager: Christopher (Chris) Sonnek
Auditors: PricewaterhouseCoopers LLP

LOCATIONS

HQ: MathStar, Inc.
5900 Green Oak Dr., Minnetonka, MN 55343
Phone: 952-746-2200 **Fax:** 952-746-2201
Web: www.mathstar.com

MathStar has offices in California, Minnesota, Oregon, and Texas.

COMPETITORS

3DSP	Lattice Semiconductor
Actel	Leopard Logic
Altera	LOGIC Devices
AMI Semiconductor	LSI Logic
Analog Devices	QuickLogic
Atmel	Texas Instruments
DSP Group	Xilinx
IBM Microelectronics	

HISTORICAL FINANCIALS

Company Type: Private

Income Statement

FYE: December 31

	REVENUE ($ mil.)	NET INCOME ($ mil.)	NET PROFIT MARGIN	EMPLOYEES
12/04	0	(9)	—	40
12/03	0	(11)	—	—
12/02	0	(30)	—	—
Annual Growth	—	—	—	—

2004 Year-End Financials

Debt ratio: 0.0%
Return on equity: —
Cash ($ mil.): 4
Current ratio: 9.02
Long-term debt ($ mil.): 0

Net Income History

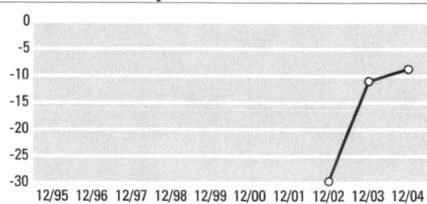

12/95 12/96 12/97 12/98 12/99 12/00 12/01 12/02 12/03 12/04

Mayer, Brown, Rowe & Maw

Practicing law is a supreme calling for many attorneys at Mayer, Brown, Rowe & Maw (formerly Mayer, Brown & Platt). One of the largest law firms in the US, Mayer, Brown was one of the first to specialize in arguing cases before the Supreme Court. The firm has over 1,300 lawyers at its 13 offices in the US and Europe, offering their expertise in corporate and securities law and litigation, global trade, and real estate. Founded in 1881 in Chicago, the firm has represented clients such as Dow Chemical, America Online (now Time Warner Inc.), and BMW.

Mayer, Brown is also noted for being one of the first of the top 20 law firms to elect a woman as managing partner (1991) and for having a large percentage of female lawyers. The firm was formed in 2002 with the merger of Mayer, Brown, Rowe & Maw (US based) with Mayer, Brown, Rowe & Maw (based in the UK).

EXECUTIVES

Chairman: Tyrone C. Fahner
Executive Director: Steven R. Wells
CFO: Alan S. Cohen
Director Human Resources: Coleen Callahan
Partner, Houston: Robert Gray Jr.

LOCATIONS

HQ: Mayer, Brown, Rowe & Maw LLP
190 S. LaSalle St., Chicago, IL 60603
Phone: 312-782-0600 **Fax:** 312-701-7711
Web: www.mayerbrownrowe.com

The firm has US offices in Charlotte, North Carolina; Chicago; Houston; Los Angeles; New York City; Palo Alto, California; and Washington, DC. International offices include Brussels; Cologne and Frankfurt, Germany; London and Manchester, UK; and Paris.

PRODUCTS/OPERATIONS

Selected Practice Areas

Bankruptcy
Corporate and securities
Environmental
Government relations
International trade
Labor
Litigation
Real estate
Taxation
Venture capital

HISTORICAL FINANCIALS

Company Type: Partnership

Income Statement

FYE: December 31

	REVENUE ($ mil.)	NET INCOME ($ mil.)	NET PROFIT MARGIN	EMPLOYEES
12/03	813	—	—	—
12/02	705	—	—	—
12/01	573	—	—	—
12/00	534	—	—	1,000
12/99	464	—	—	820
12/98	400	—	—	816
12/97	340	—	—	695
12/96	325	—	—	643
12/95	274	—	—	550
12/94	263	—	—	550
Annual Growth	13.4%	—	—	10.5%

Revenue History

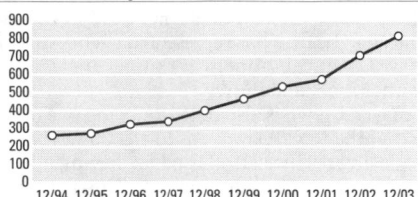

| 900 |
| 800 |
| 700 |
| 600 |
| 500 |
| 400 |
| 300 |
| 200 |
| 100 |
| 0 |

12/94 12/95 12/96 12/97 12/98 12/99 12/00 12/01 12/02 12/03

Mayo Foundation

Mayo can whip up a medical miracle. The not-for-profit Mayo Foundation for Medical Education and Research provides health care, most notably for complex medical conditions, through its renowned Mayo Clinic in Rochester, Minnesota. Other clinics are located in Arizona and Florida. The clinics' multidisciplinary approach to care attracts thousands of patients a year, including such notables as the late Ronald Reagan and the late King Hussein of Jordan. The Mayo Health System operates a network of affiliated community hospitals and clinics in Minnesota, Iowa, and Wisconsin. The Mayo Foundation also conducts research and trains physicians, nurses, and other health professionals.

In addition to the Mayo Clinics, the foundation operates other hospitals: Saint Marys and Rochester Methodist in Rochester; Mayo Clinic Hospital in Phoenix; and St. Luke's Hospital in Jacksonville. Mayo Health System includes five clinics in Iowa, five hospitals and some 20 clinics in Wisconsin, and nearly 50 facilities in Minnesota. At the University of Minnesota, the foundation's education programs include the Mayo Graduate School of Medicine and the Mayo School of Health-Related Sciences.

With managed care limiting patients' ability to use its facilities, Mayo forms referral alliances with hospital groups, HMOs, and other groups. Its charter prevents it from raising prices to compensate for rising health care costs, so the foundation commercializes medical technology, publishes medical literature, and invests in other medical startups to increase income. Also, affluent patients who can pay — well — for treatment (and who may contribute to the endowment) help subsidize care for those who can't pay.

The Mayo Foundation dates back to a frontier practice launched by William Mayo in 1863.

HISTORY

In 1845 William Mayo came to the US from England. He was a doctor, veterinarian, river boatman, surveyor, and newspaper editor before settling in Rochester, Minnesota, in 1863.

When a tornado struck Rochester in 1883, Mayo took charge of a makeshift hospital. The Sisters of St. Francis offered to replace the hospital that was lost in the disaster if Mayo would head the staff. He agreed reluctantly. Not only were hospitals then associated with the poor and insane, but his affiliation with the sisters raised eyebrows among Protestants and Catholics.

Saint Marys Hospital opened in 1889. Mayo's sons William and Charles, who were starting their medical careers, helped him. After the elder Mayo retired, the sons ran the hospital. Although the brothers accepted all medical cases, they made the hospital self-sufficient, attracting paying patients by pioneering in specialization at a time when physicians were jacks-of-all-medical-trades.

This specialization attracted other physicians, and by 1907 the practice was known as "the Mayo's clinic." The brothers, in association with the University of Minnesota, established the Mayo Foundation for Medical Research (now the Mayo Graduate School of Medicine), the world's first program to train medical specialists, in 1915.

In 1919 the brothers transferred the clinic properties and miscellaneous financial assets, primarily from patient care profits, into the Mayo Properties Association (renamed the Mayo Foundation in 1964). Under the terms of the endowment, all Mayo Clinic medical staff members became salaried employees. In 1933 the clinic established one of the first blood banks in the US. Both brothers died in 1939.

Part of the association's mission was to fund research. In 1950 two Mayo researchers won a Nobel Prize for developing cortisone to treat rheumatoid arthritis. The foundation opened its second medical school, the Mayo Medical School, in 1972.

As insurers in the 1980s pressured to cut hospital admissions and stays, the foundation diversified with for-profit ventures. In 1983 Mayo began publishing the *Mayo Clinic Health Letter*, its first subscription publication for a general audience, and the *Mayo Clinic Family Health Book*. It also began providing specialized lab services to other doctors and hospitals. The addition of Rochester Methodist Hospital (creating the largest not-for-profit medical group in the country) was also a response to financial pressures. Following the money south as affluent folks retired, the foundation opened clinics in Jacksonville (1986); Scottsdale, Arizona (1987); and in nearby Phoenix (1998).

Seeking to expand in its home market, Mayo in 1992 formed the Mayo Health System, a regional network of health care facilities and medical practices. In 1996 former patient Barbara Woodward Lips left $127.9 million to the foundation, the largest bequest in its history.

In the late 1990s the foundation increasingly looked to corporate partnerships to help defray costs and to expand research activities. In 1998 and 1999 Mayo boosted its presence overseas with nonmedical regional offices. Mayo scientists in 2000 announced they had regrown or repaired nerve coverings in mice; this type of damage in humans (caused by such conditions as multiple sclerosis) had been considered irreparable. The Mayo Foundation continues to push for breakthroughs in medical science.

EXECUTIVES

Chairman: Bert A. Getz, age 65
President and CEO: Denis A. Cortese
CFO: Jeffrey W. Bolton
VP; Chairman, Mayo Clinic Rochester: Hugh C. Smith
VP and Chief Administrative Officer: Robert K. Smoldt
Administrator, Mayo Clinic Scottsdale:
James G. Anderson
Chairman, Mayo Clinic Jacksonville: George B. Bartley
Director, Education: Thomas H. Berquist
Director, Mayo Clinic Cancer Center:
Franklyn G. Prendergast, age 59
**Chairman, Department of Facilities and Systems
Support Services:** Craig A. Smoldt
Chairman, Mayo Clinic Scottsdale: Victor F. Trastek
Chairman, Information Technology: Abdul Bengali
Chairman, Human Resources: Marita Heller
Secretary and Chairman, Legal Department:
Jonathan J. Oviatt
Director for Development: James C. Schroeder
Medical Director for Development: David A. Ahlquist
Chair, Department of Development:
Michael J. McNamara
Auditors: Ernst & Young LLP

LOCATIONS

HQ: Mayo Foundation for Medical Education
and Research
200 1st St. SW, Rochester, MN 55905
Phone: 507-284-2511   **Fax:** 507-284-0161
Web: www.mayo.edu

Selected Locations

Arizona
Mayo Clinic Hospital (Phoenix)
Mayo Clinic Scottsdale

Florida
Mayo Clinic Jacksonville
St. Luke's Hospital (Jacksonville)

Iowa
Amstrong Clinic (Armstrong)
Decorah Clinic (Decorah)
Lake Mills Clinic (Lake Mills)
New Hampton Clinic (New Hampton)
Franciscan Skemp Healthcare Waukon Clinic (Waukon)

Minnesota
Albert Lea Medical Center (Albert Lea)
Austin Medical Center (Austin)
Cannon Valley Clinic (Faribault)
Fairmont Medical Center (Fairmont)
Franciscan Skemp Healthcare Houston Clinic
(Houston)
Lake City Medical Center (Lake City)
Immanuel St. Joseph's (Mankato)
Fountain Centers Rochester (Rochester)
Mayo Clinic Rochester
Rochester Methodist Hospital
Saint Marys Hospital (Rochester)
Springfield Medical Center (Springfield)
Parkview Care Center (Wells)

Wisconsin
Barron Medical Center (Barron)
Bloomer Medical Center (Bloomer)
Midelfort Clinic (Cameron)
Luther Midelfort (Eau Claire)
Red Cedar Medical Center (Menomonie)
Franciscan Skemp Healthcare Onalaska Clinic
(Onalaska)

PRODUCTS/OPERATIONS

2003 Sales

	$ mil.	% of total
Medical services	4,081.3	85
Grants & contracts	222.2	5
Premiums	91.6	2
Contributions	78.1	1
Return on investments	65.2	1
Other	283.8	6
Total	**4,822.2**	**100**

2003 Sales

	% of total
Mayo Clinic Rochester	44
Mayo Health System	21
Mayo Clinic Jacksonville	10
Mayo Clinic Scottsdale	9
Research	5
Mayo Collaborative Services	4
Contributions	2
Investments	1
Other	4
Total	**100**

COMPETITORS

Allina Hospitals	Johns Hopkins Medicine
Ascension Health	Memorial Sloan-Kettering
Catholic Health Initiatives	Methodist Hospital System
Catholic	New York City Health
Healthcare Partners	and Hospitals
Detroit Medical Center	Rush System for Health
HCA	Scripps
Health Management	SSM Health Care
Associates	Tenet Healthcare
HealthSouth	Trinity Health (Novi)
Henry Ford Health System	Universal Health Services

HISTORICAL FINANCIALS

Company Type: Not-for-profit

Income Statement — FYE: December 31

	REVENUE ($ mil.)	NET INCOME ($ mil.)	NET PROFIT MARGIN	EMPLOYEES
12/03	4,822	349	7.2%	42,620
12/02	4,425	(212)	—	41,527
12/01	4,135	—	—	45,536
12/00	3,710	—	—	44,000
12/99	2,750	—	—	41,265
12/98	2,370	—	—	32,531
12/97	2,566	—	—	30,497
12/96	2,348	—	—	28,671
12/95	2,189	—	—	25,433
12/94	1,873	—	—	21,856
Annual Growth	**11.1%**	**—**	**—**	**7.7%**

2003 Year-End Financials

Debt ratio: 53.7%
Return on equity: 14.0%
Cash ($ mil.): 22
Current ratio: —
Long-term debt ($ mil.): 1,432

Net Income History

MBM

What's on the menu at your favorite restaurant? Just ask MBM Corporation, one of the largest privately owned custom food service distributors in the nation. The company specializes in providing food to national restaurant chains such as Arby's, Burger King, Captain D's, Chick-fil-A, and Darden Restaurants (Red Lobster, Olive Garden, Bahama Breeze). MBM fills its customers' orders through its network of about 30 distribution centers across the US. J. R. Wordsworth founded the company about 50 years ago as a retail food distributor. MBM made the transition to its present role in restaurant food distribution after Wordsworth's children bought the business in the 1970s.

Federal safety rules that took effect in January 2004 to reduce driver fatigue are expected to substantially increase trucking rates for MBM Corporation, as well as other large distributors, for the first time in two decades. MBM estimated that it would incur about $10 million in additional expenses to comply with the rules. The firm would need to add to its current fleet of some 800 trucks and 1,800 truck drivers.

EXECUTIVES

Chairman, President, and CEO: Jerry L. Wordsworth
CFO: Jeffrey M. (Jeff) Kowalk
EVP: Jim Sabiston
Executive Director, Human Resources: Tim Ozment
Executive Director, Operations: Andy Blanton
Director, Purchasing: Mitch Brantley
Secretary and Treasurer:
 Debbie Wordsworth-Daughtridge
Controller: Ernest Avent
President Assistant: Doug Martin

LOCATIONS

HQ: MBM Corporation
 2641 Meadowbrook Rd., Rocky Mount, NC 27802
Phone: 252-985-7200 **Fax:** 252-985-7241

COMPETITORS

Ben E. Keith	McLane Foodservice
Clark Products	Performance Food
Golden State Foods	Reyes Holdings
Gordon Food Service	Sodexho
Martin-Brower	SYSCO
McLane	U.S. Foodservice

HISTORICAL FINANCIALS

Company Type: Private

Income Statement — FYE: December 31

	REVENUE ($ mil.)	NET INCOME ($ mil.)	NET PROFIT MARGIN	EMPLOYEES
12/03	4,744	—	—	3,500
12/02	4,236	—	—	3,500
12/01	4,236	—	—	3,500
12/00	3,823	—	—	2,500
12/99	2,700	—	—	2,364
12/98	2,500	—	—	1,600
12/97	2,000	—	—	1,500
12/96	1,800	—	—	—
Annual Growth	**14.8%**	**—**	**—**	**15.2%**

Revenue History

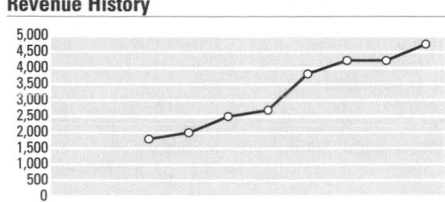

McCarthy Building

A company that was in construction before Reconstruction, McCarthy Building Companies is one of the oldest privately held builders in the US. The general contractor and construction manager has projects worldwide and ranks among the top builders of health care and education facilities in the US. Contracts include heavy construction projects (bridges and water and waste-treatment plants), industrial projects (biopharmaceutical, food processing, and microelectronics facilities), commercial projects (retail and office buildings), and institutional projects (airports, schools, and prisons). Timothy McCarthy founded the firm in 1864. His great-grandson, Michael McCarthy, sold the firm to its employees in 2002.

McCarthy Building Companies' clients include Kaiser Permanente, California State University, and the California Department of Corrections. Its projects include The Platinum condominium/hotel tower in Las Vegas and renovation and expansion of the National Baseball Hall of Fame and Museum in Cooperstown, New York.

EXECUTIVES

Chairman and CEO: Michael D. (Mike) Bolen
President, COO, and Director: Michael D. Hurst
EVP, CFO, Treasurer, and Director: George F. Scherer
EVP, Midwest Division: Derek W. Glanvill
EVP, Atlanta Office: Kevin Kuntz
SVP, Business Development, Laboratory/R&D, Midwest Division: Walter R. (Bud) Guest
SVP, Business Development, Southern California Division: Dennis F. Katovsich
SVP, Healthcare Services: Steven C. Mynsberge
SVP, General Counsel, Secretary, and Director:
 James A. Staskiel
VP, Corporate Safety: Gary Amsigner
VP, Human Resources: Jan Kraemer
Director Corporate Communications:
 Michael (Mike) Lenzen
Controller: J. Douglas Audiffred
Public Relations Manager: Susan Garritano
Auditors: Ernst & Young LLP

LOCATIONS

HQ: McCarthy Building Companies, Inc.
 1341 N. Rock Hill Rd., St. Louis, MO 63124
Phone: 314-968-3300 **Fax:** 314-968-3037
Web: www.mccarthy.com

McCarthy Building Companies has offices in Atlanta; Dallas; Detroit; Newport Beach, Sacramento, and San Francisco, California; Las Vegas; Phoenix; and St. Louis.

COMPETITORS

Barton Malow	Hensel Phelps
Bechtel	Construction
Bovis Lend Lease	Perini
Centex	Peter Kiewit Sons'
Clayco	Skanska
DPR Construction	Swinerton
Gilbane	Turner Corporation

HISTORICAL FINANCIALS

Company Type: Private

Income Statement

FYE: March 31

	REVENUE ($ mil.)	NET INCOME ($ mil.)	NET PROFIT MARGIN	EMPLOYEES
3/04	1,459	—	—	2,200
3/03	1,024	—	—	2,000
3/02	1,050	—	—	2,500
3/01	1,205	—	—	2,500
3/00	940	—	—	2,500
3/99	1,200	—	—	2,000
3/98	1,134	—	—	2,000
3/97	1,059	—	—	1,300
3/96	795	—	—	1,000
3/95	950	—	—	525
Annual Growth	**4.9%**	—	—	**17.3%**

Revenue History

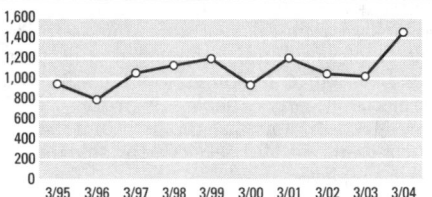

McFarland Cascade

McFarland Cascade produces wood products, including pressure-treated utility poles, cross-arms, lumber, and plywood. It also packages and distributes consumer-oriented outdoor living products and develops computer software packages for assisting consumers in designing, estimating, and constructing such outdoor projects as decks. The company operates in Tacoma, Curtis, and Spokane, Washington; Eugene, Oregon; Sandpoint, Idaho; Raynham, Massachusetts; Electric Mills, Mississippi; and Galloway, British Columbia. The company sells globally to customers in the US, Canada, the Middle East, and Asia. CEO Corry McFarland and EVP Greg McFarland own the company, which was founded in 1916.

EXECUTIVES

President and CEO: B. Corry McFarland
EVP: Gregory D. (Greg) McFarland
Controller: Al Boling
Human Resources Manager: Pat Marion
Auditors: BDO Seidman, LLP

LOCATIONS

HQ: McFarland Cascade
1640 East Marc St., Tacoma, WA 98421
Phone: 253-572-3033   **Fax:** 253-627-0764
Web: www.ldm.com

PRODUCTS/OPERATIONS

Selected Operations
McFarland Cascade Holdings Inc.
McFarland Cascade Pole & Lumber Company

Selected Trade Names
Cost Cutter
Drydek
McFarland Cascade
Rail-A-Deck
Universal Wood

COMPETITORS

Alamco Wood Products	Robbins Manufacturing
International Paper	Company
KI Holdings	Saint-Gobain plc
North Pacific Group	Stella-Jones
	Weyerhaeuser

HISTORICAL FINANCIALS

Company Type: Private

Income Statement

FYE: December 31

	REVENUE ($ mil.)	NET INCOME ($ mil.)	NET PROFIT MARGIN	EMPLOYEES
12/04	163	—	—	—
12/03	152	—	—	500
Annual Growth	**7.2%**	—	—	—

Revenue History

McIntosh Bancshares

McIntosh Bancshares is the holding company for McIntosh State Bank, which operates about five branch offices in central Georgia's Butts, Jasper, and Henry counties. The bank offers a variety of deposit products, including checking and savings accounts, IRAs, money market accounts, and NOW accounts. It uses funds from deposits to write business and consumer loans, including one- to four-family residential mortgages (some 30% of its loan portfolio), construction and land development loans (25%), and commercial mortgages (20%). Subsidiary McIntosh Financial Services provides financial planning and investment vehicles such as annuities, mutual funds, and life insurance.

EXECUTIVES

Chairman and CEO; Chairman, President, and CEO, McIntosh State Bank; Chairman, McIntosh Financial Services: William K. Malone, age 57, $216,652 pay
President, COO, and Director; President, McIntosh State Bank, Monticello and McIntosh Financial Services: Thurman L. Willis Jr., age 56, $184,142 pay
President, McIntosh State Bank, Jackson Office; Director, McIntosh Financial Services: Bruce E. Bartholomew, age 47, $146,479 pay
President, McIntosh State Bank, South Henry County; Director, McIntosh Financial Services: Robert C. Beall
SVP and Chief Credit Officer, McIntosh State Bank: Jason L. Patrick
VP and Senior Operations Officer, McIntosh State Bank: Jesse M. Roberts
Secretary; SVP, CFO, and Secretary, McIntosh State Bank: James P. Doyle, age 39, $133,997 pay
Auditors: Porter Keadle Moore, LLP

LOCATIONS

HQ: McIntosh Bancshares, Inc.
210 S. Oak St., Jackson, GA 30233
Phone: 770-775-8300   **Fax:** 770-775-8325
Web: www.mcintoshbancshares.com

McIntosh Bancshares has branches in Jackson, Locust Grove, McDonough, and Monticello, Georgia.

PRODUCTS/OPERATIONS

2004 Sales

	$ mil.	% of total
Interest		
Loans, including fees	15.3	74
Investment securities	1.8	9
Other	0.2	1
Noninterest		
Service charges on deposit accounts	2.0	10
Other	1.3	6
Total	**20.6**	**100**

COMPETITORS

Bank of America	SunTrust
BB&T	Wachovia
PAB Bankshares	

HISTORICAL FINANCIALS

Company Type: Private

Income Statement

FYE: December 31

	ASSETS ($ mil.)	NET INCOME ($ mil.)	INCOME AS % OF ASSETS	EMPLOYEES
12/04	311	4	1.2%	103
12/03	277	3	1.2%	90
12/02	243	3	1.3%	87
12/01	233	3	1.1%	—
Annual Growth	**10.2%**	**11.5%**	—	**8.8%**

2004 Year-End Financials

Equity as % of assets: 9.4%   Long-term debt ($ mil.): —
Return on assets: 1.2%   Sales ($ mil.): 21
Return on equity: 12.9%

Net Income History

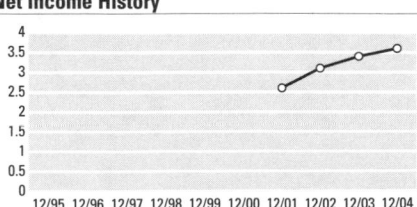

McKee Foods

When Little Debbie smiles up out of your lunch bag, you know you are loved. McKee Foods' Little Debbie is one of the US's leading brands of snack cakes, named for and featuring the smiling face of the company's founders' granddaughter. McKee makes snack cakes, creme-filled cookies, crackers, and candy. It also sells granola bars, fruit snacks, and cereals under its Sunbelt brand. Low prices and family packs of individually wrapped treats have driven sales. McKee Foods is the largest independent bakery in the US. The company started in 1934 with founder O. D. McKee and his wife, Ruth, selling nickel cakes from the back seat of their car. The company is still owned and operated by the McKee family.

The company has a fleet of trucks and brings home extra money through "backhauling" for other customers after delivering Little Debbie products. Employees who have worked for more than two years are eligible for profit-sharing bonuses. New product development is key in the highly competitive snack market, and McKee Foods steadily puts out variations such as its Cosmic Crispy bars with chocolate chips.

Ellsworth and Jack McKee, sons of the founders, are chairman and CEO, respectively. And, while Debbie herself doesn't hold an executive position with the company, third-generation Mike McKee is president.

EXECUTIVES

CEO: Jack C. McKee
President: Mike McKee
CFO: Barry Patterson
EVP and President, Blue Planet Foods: Rusty McKee
VP and General Manager: E. Ray Murphy
Manager, Corporate Communications and Public Relations: Ruth Garren
Manager, Corporate HR: Mark Newsome

LOCATIONS

HQ: McKee Foods Corporation
10260 McKee Rd., Collegedale, TN 37315
Phone: 423-238-7111   **Fax:** 423-238-7101
Web: www.mckeefoods.com

McKee Foods has baking facilities in Arkansas, Tennessee, and Virginia.

PRODUCTS/OPERATIONS

Selected Products

Heartland Brand
 Cereals (granola, oat bran, low fat)
 Granola pie crust
 Granola bars (apple crisp, maple crunch, oats and honey)
Little Debbie Brand
 Breakfast pastries (coffee cakes, honey buns, muffin loaves)
 Candy (Peanut Cluster, Star Crunch)
 Cookies and pies (Marshmallow Supremes, Nutty Bars, Oatmeal Creme Pies)
 Crackers (Toasty Crackers with Peanut Butter)
 Seasonal snacks (holiday-themed cakes and cookies)
 Snack cakes (Devil Squares, Swiss Cake Rolls)
Sunbelt Brand
 Cereal bars (with fruit filling)
 Fruit snacks
 Granola bars (chewy, fudge-dipped)

COMPETITORS

Chattanooga Bakery	Kellogg Snacks
Flowers Foods	Lance
General Mills	Otis Spunkmeyer
Grist Mill Company	Saputo
Interstate Bakeries	Tasty Baking
Kellogg	Weston Foods

HISTORICAL FINANCIALS

Company Type: Private

Income Statement

FYE: Friday nearest June 30

	REVENUE ($ mil.)	NET INCOME ($ mil.)	NET PROFIT MARGIN	EMPLOYEES
6/04	1,000	—	—	6,000
6/03	978	—	—	6,500
6/02	970	—	—	6,500
6/01	900	—	—	6,000
6/00	865	—	—	5,450
6/99	855	—	—	5,393
6/98	831	—	—	5,350
6/97	825	—	—	5,346
6/96	735	—	—	5,000
6/95	680	—	—	4,550
Annual Growth	**4.4%**	**—**	**—**	**3.1%**

Revenue History

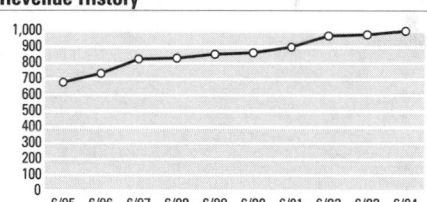

McKinsey & Company

How many McKinsey consultants does it take to screw in a light bulb? None. They would most likely advise rewiring the house. McKinsey & Company is one of the world's top management consulting firms with more than 80 offices in 44 countries. The company provides a full spectrum of consulting services to corporations, government agencies, and foundations, including leadership training, operations analysis, and strategic planning. Its practice areas include such industries as banking, energy, manufacturing, and media, among many others. McKinsey's consultants also dispense their knowledge in an avalanche of articles and books. Founded by James McKinsey in 1926, the company is owned by its partners.

In addition to being one of the largest consulting firms, McKinsey is also one of most well-respected and admired firms. It has earned a reputation for being the best through its accomplishments and history, but it also cultivates a certain mystique through its intense secrecy. Aspiring consultants often list it as the most desirable firm to work for, although McKinsey's rigorous up-or-out weeding process allows only the top 20% of new associates to become partners after five years. Notable McKinsey alumni include former American Express chairman Harvey Golub and former CBS chief Michael Jordan, as well as former Enron CEO Jeff Skilling.

Like its rivals in the consulting industry, McKinsey's business has taken a hit from the downturn in the economy. Many companies are shying away from costly consulting engagements, while bread-and-butter assignments, such as merger and acquisition business, have all but disappeared. Meanwhile, companies such as IBM and Accenture threaten to steal more traditional consulting business from the likes of McKinsey and its brethren. The consulting industry as a whole has also suffered a black eye in the wake of recent corporate scandals, and McKinsey has not been immune: its client list in the 1990s included the likes of Global Crossing, Swissair, and Enron. (The company has never been accused of any improprieties, however.)

Against this backdrop, Ian Davis was elected managing director in 2003 and given the task of leading the firm through uncertain times. A big part of McKinsey's survival could involve a reinforcement of the values of its spiritual leader, the late Marvin Bower, who dictated that the client's interests must come first and that the firm's consultants must be discreet and honest. As more companies seek to assuage regulators and gun-shy investors, an untarnished reputation will become a more valuable asset.

HISTORY

McKinsey & Company was founded in Chicago in 1926 by University of Chicago accounting professor James McKinsey. The company evolved from an auditing practice of McKinsey and his partners, Marvin Bower and A.T. Kearney, who began analyzing business and industry and offering advice. McKinsey died in 1937; two years later, Bower, who headed the New York office, and Kearney, in Chicago, split the firm. Kearney renamed the Chicago office A.T. Kearney & Co. (later acquired by Electronic Data Systems), and Bower kept the McKinsey name and built up a practice structured like a law firm.

Bower focused on the big picture instead of on specific operating problems, helping boost billings to $2 million by 1950. He hired staff straight out of prestigious business schools, reinforcing the firm's theoretical bent. Bower implemented a competitive up-or-out policy requiring employees who are not continually promoted to leave the firm.

The firm's prestige continued to grow during the booming 1950s along with demand for consulting services. Before becoming president in 1953, Dwight Eisenhower asked McKinsey to find out exactly what the government did. By 1959 Bower had opened an office in London, followed by others in Amsterdam; Dusseldorf, Germany; Melbourne; Paris; and Zurich.

In 1964 the company founded management journal *The McKinsey Quarterly*. When Bower retired in 1967, sales were $20 million, and McKinsey was the #1 management consulting firm. During the 1970s it faced competition from firms with newer approaches and lost market share. In response, then-managing director Ronald Daniel started specialty practices and expanded foreign operations.

The consulting boom of the 1980s was spurred by mergers and buyouts. By 1988 the firm had 1,800 consultants, sales were $620 million, and 50% of billings came from overseas.

The recession of the early 1990s hit white-collar workers, including consultants. McKinsey, scrambling to upgrade its technical side, bought Information Consulting Group (ICG), its first acquisition. But the corporate cultures did not meld, and most ICG people left by 1993.

In 1994 the company elected its first managing director of non-European descent, Indian-born Rajat Gupta. Two years later the traditionally hush-hush firm found itself at the center of that most public 1990s arena, the sexual discrimination lawsuit. A female ex-consultant in Texas sued, claiming McKinsey had sabotaged her career (the case was dismissed).

In 1998 McKinsey partnered with Northwestern University and the University of Pennsylvania to establish a world-class business school in India. The following year graduating seniors surveyed in Europe, the UK, and the US named the company as their ideal employer.

Also in 1999 the company created McKinsey to help "accelerate" Internet startups. The next year it increased salaries and offered incentives to better compete with Internet firms for employees. In 2001 the company expanded its branding business with the acquisition of Envision, a Chicago-based brand consultant.

In 2003 Ian Davis was elected as managing director of the firm, succeeding Rajat Gupta who had served as managing director for nine years. (The firm imposes a term limit on the position.) Davis had previously served as the head of the firm's UK office.

EXECUTIVES

Managing Director: Ian Davis, age 54
Senior Partner Worldwide: Rajat Gupta
Senior Partner: David Hunt
Director of External Relations: Anne Board
Director of External Relations: Michael Stewart
Director of McKinsey Global Institute: Diana Farrell
Director: Liz Lempres
Director: Kevin Sneader
Director: Jerome Vascellaro
Chairman of the Americas: Michael Patsalos-Fox
Chairman of Asia: Dominic Barton
Managing Partner, Australia and New Zealand: Adam Lewis
Managing Partner, UK and Middle East: Dominic Casserley
Director and Managing Partner, Media and Entertainment Practice: Michael J. Wolf
Partner, Johannesburg: David Fine
Director, European Chemical Practice: Florian Budde
Director, Germany: Thilo Mannhardt
German Office Manager: Jürgen Kluge
Senior Recruiter: Diane Black

LOCATIONS

HQ: McKinsey & Company
55 E. 52nd St., 21st Fl., New York, NY 10022
Phone: 212-446-7000   **Fax:** 212-446-8575
Web: www.mckinsey.com

PRODUCTS/OPERATIONS

Selected Practice Areas

Automotive and assembly	Metals and mining
Banking and securities	Nonprofit organizations
Chemicals	Petroleum
Consumer packaged goods	Pharmaceuticals
Electric power	and medical products
and natural gas	Private equity
Healthcare	Pulp and paper
Information technology	Retail
Insurance	Telecommunications
Media and entertainment	Travel and logistics

COMPETITORS

Accenture	ESource
A.T. Kearney	IBM
Bain & Company	Mercer
BearingPoint	PA Consulting
Booz Allen	Perot Systems
Boston Consulting	PRTM
Computer Sciences Corp.	Roland Berger
Deloitte Consulting	

HISTORICAL FINANCIALS

Company Type: Private

Income Statement

FYE: December 31

	REVENUE ($ mil.)	NET INCOME ($ mil.)	NET PROFIT MARGIN	EMPLOYEES
12/03	3,000	—	—	11,500
12/02	3,000	—	—	12,000
12/01	3,400	—	—	13,000
12/00	3,400	—	—	13,000
12/99	2,900	—	—	10,500
12/98	2,500	—	—	10,000
12/97	2,200	—	—	8,500
12/96	2,100	—	—	7,100
12/95	1,800	—	—	6,050
12/94	1,500	—	—	6,000
Annual Growth	**8.0%**	—	—	**7.5%**

Revenue History

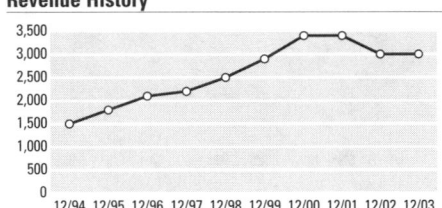

McWane

As a leading manufacturer of fire hydrants, McWane may just be a dog's best friend. Through its many divisions, McWane makes a variety of fluid control devices that include fire hydrants, industrial valves, pipes, and flanges. With the acquisition of Amerex in Trussville, Alabama, McWane has become one of the world's leading makers of fire extinguishers and fire suppression systems. Through its Manchester Tank division, the company also produces gas grills as well as propane tanks for recreational vehicles. Its M&H Valve Company, which makes industrial valves with waste-water applications and fire hydrants, has been in operation since 1854. McWane was founded in 1921 and continues to be family-owned.

Over the years McWane has grown by acquiring troubled companies, and turning them around with infusions of better equipment and streamlined management.

EXECUTIVES

Chairman: C. Phillip McWane, age 47
President: G. Ruffner Page Jr.
EVP: David Green
SVP and CFO: Charles F. (Charley) Nowlin
SVP and General Counsel: James M. Proctor II
SVP, Compliance and Corporate Affairs: Michael C. Keel
VP and General Manager, Pacific States Cast Iron Pipe: John Balian
Assistant VP and Director of Public Affairs: Michelle Clemon
Assistant VP, Employee and Community Relations: Donna S. Sanborn
Corporate Director, Human Resources: Darrell R. Witt

LOCATIONS

HQ: McWane, Inc.
2900 Hwy. 280, Ste. 300, Birmingham, AL 35223
Phone: 205-414-3100   **Fax:** 205-414-3170
Web: www.mcwane.com

McWane has operations in Alabama, Iowa, New Jersey, New York, Ohio, Texas, and Utah.

PRODUCTS/OPERATIONS

Selected Operations

Amerex Corporation (industrial and commercial fire extinguishers)
Clow Valve Company (fire hydrants and valves)
Clow Water Systems Company (ductile iron pipe and fittings)
Kennedy Valve (fire hydrants and valves)
M&H Valve Company (fire hydrants, gears and casings, stem guides, valves)
McWane Cast Iron Pipe Company
Pacific States Cast Iron Pipe Company (ductile iron pipe)
Tyler Pipe Company (cleanouts, drains, fittings, valves)

COMPETITORS

American Cast Iron Pipe	Margate Industries
Citation	McJunkin
Henry Technologies	Metallurg
Indeck	Northwest Pipe
INTERMET	Walter Industries
Kidde	

HISTORICAL FINANCIALS

Company Type: Private

Income Statement

FYE: December 31

	ESTIMATED REVENUE ($ mil.)	NET INCOME ($ mil.)	NET PROFIT MARGIN	EMPLOYEES
12/03	1,500	—	—	7,000
12/02	1,500	—	—	5,570
12/01	800	—	—	5,200
12/00	630	—	—	5,170
12/99	625	—	—	4,400
12/98	585	—	—	4,350
12/97	575	—	—	5,700
12/96	525	—	—	5,650
12/95	500	—	—	5,500
12/94	475	—	—	5,400
Annual Growth	**13.6%**	—	—	**2.9%**

Revenue History

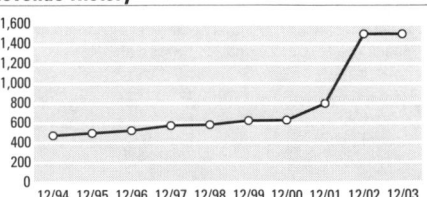

MediaNews

Paper cuts can really hurt, especially when they're made by newspaper group MediaNews Group. Known for ruthlessly cutting staff at unprofitable newspapers, the company publishes some 40 dailies (including *The Denver Post* and *The Salt Lake Tribune*) and about 65 non-daily newspapers in nine states. MediaNews Group operates Web sites for its daily papers that are hosted by its new media division, MediaNews Group Interactive. The company also operates a small number of radio stations in Texas and one television station, a CBS affiliate in Anchorage, Alaska. MediaNews Group is a joint venture of vice chairman and CEO Dean Singleton and chairman Richard Scudder, who began buying newspapers together in 1983.

Considered one of the nation's top 10 newspaper firms, MediaNews owns newspapers with a combined daily circulation of about 2 million. The company focuses on building newspaper clusters in specific geographic regions. Its clusters include Los Angeles Newspaper Group, New England Newspapers, Massachusetts Papers, Pennsylvania Newspaper Group, and Colorado Newspaper Group.

In addition, the company has a 33% interest in a partnership controlled by Gannett that operates six daily newspapers in Texas and New Mexico. MediaNews' papers in Denver, Salt Lake City, and Detroit operate under joint operating agency (JOA) agreements.

The Denver Post is part of the Denver Newspaper Agency, a JOA with E. W. Scripps (owner of the *Rocky Mountain News*) that combines the business operations of both papers.

In 2005 MediaNews announced the acquisition of *The Detroit News* from Gannett. The transaction is part of a deal in which Knight Ridder is selling partnership interest in the Detroit Newspaper Agency, the joint operating agency that handles business, advertising, production and delivery operations under a 1989 JOA. Under the new arrangement, Gannett is the general partner, and MediaNews Group is the limited partner.

The Salt Lake Tribune is also run under a JOA with The Deseret News Publishing Company (owner of the *Deseret News*). A legal dispute with the previous owners of *The Salt Lake Tribune* has resulted in a court order forcing the company to offer Utah newspaper back to the McCarthey family.

The families of Singleton and Scudder own MediaNews.

EXECUTIVES

Chairman: Richard B. Scudder, age 92
Vice Chairman and CEO: William D. (Dean) Singleton, age 54, $1,412,475 pay
President: Joseph J. (Jody) Lodovic IV, age 44, $1,039,600 pay
EVP and COO; President and CEO, Los Angeles Newspaper Group: Gerald E. (Jerry) Grilly, age 58, $746,875 pay
SVP Operations: Anthony F. Tierno, age 60, $401,250 pay
VP and CFO: Ronald A. (Ron) Mayo, age 44, $223,100 pay
VP and Controller: Michael J. Koren, age 38
VP Human Resources: Charles M. Kamen, age 57
President, MediaNews Group Interactive: Eric J. Grilly, age 34, $351,750 pay
Publisher, Eureka Times-Standard: David Lippman
Secretary: Patricia (Pat) Robinson, age 63
Treasurer: James L. McDougald, age 52
Auditors: Ernst & Young LLP

LOCATIONS

HQ: MediaNews Group, Inc.
1560 Broadway, Ste. 2100, Denver, CO 80202
Phone: 303-563-6360   **Fax:** 303-894-9327
Web: www.medianewsgroup.com

MediaNews Group publishes newspapers in California, Colorado, Connecticut, Massachusetts, Michigan, Pennsylvania, Texas, Utah, and Vermont. It also owns four radio stations in Texas and a television station in Alaska.

PRODUCTS/OPERATIONS

2005 Sales

	% of total
Advertising	78
Circulation	17
Other	5
Total	**100**

Selected Newspaper Holdings

California
  ANG Newspapers (San Francisco Bay Area)
    Oakland Tribune
    San Mateo County Times
  Daily News (Los Angeles)
  Press-Telegram (Long Beach)
  The Sun (San Bernardino)
Colorado
  The Denver Post (JOA)
Connecticut
  Connecticut Post
Massachusetts
  The Sun (Lowell)
Michigan
  The Detroit News (JOA)
Pennsylvania
  Lebanon Daily News
Texas-New Mexico Newspaper Partnership (34%-owned)
  Carlsbad Current-Argus
  El Paso Times
  Las Cruces Sun-Times
Utah
  The Salt Lake Tribune (JOA)
Vermont
  Bennington Banner

COMPETITORS

Copley Press	Lee Enterprises
E. W. Scripps	Liberty Group Publishing
Eagle Tribune Publishing	New Times
Freedom Communications	New York Times
Gannett	Pulitzer
Hearst	SF Newspaper Co.
Hearst Newspapers	Tribune
Journal Register	Village Voice Media
Knight-Ridder	

HISTORICAL FINANCIALS

Company Type: Private

Income Statement

FYE: June 30

	REVENUE ($ mil.)	NET INCOME ($ mil.)	NET PROFIT MARGIN	EMPLOYEES
6/05	779	40	5.1%	10,000
6/04	754	28	3.7%	10,000
6/03	739	41	5.5%	10,700
6/02	712	12	1.7%	11,200
6/01	853	25	3.0%	11,200
6/00	947	130	13.8%	8,939
6/99	1,010	—	—	8,997
6/98	850	—	—	8,800
6/97	620	—	—	8,000
6/96	545	—	—	7,000
Annual Growth	**4.1%**	**(21.1%)**	**—**	**4.0%**

2005 Year-End Financials

Debt ratio: 2,269.2%
Return on equity: 63.6%
Cash ($ mil.): 4
Current ratio: 1.26
Long-term debt ($ mil.): 873

Net Income History

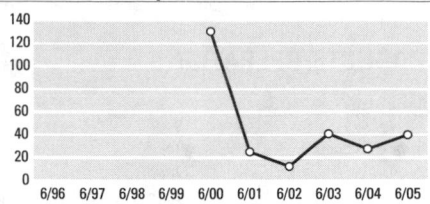

Medical Information Technology

Medical Information Technology (MEDITECH) prescribes a good dose of software to cure health care disorder. Founded in 1969, MEDITECH provides software and services for managing more than 1,900 hospitals, ambulatory care centers, doctors' offices, long-term care facilities, nursing homes, and home health care agencies in North America and the UK. The company's software includes applications for patient identification and scheduling, patient care management, clinical information management, long-term and ambulatory care, behavioral health, and financial and reimbursement management. CEO Neil Pappalardo, who co-founded MEDITECH along with Morton Ruderman and Edward Roberts, controls 37% of the company.

Ruderman owns 16% of MEDITECH.

EXECUTIVES

Chairman and CEO: A. Neil Pappalardo, age 62, $1,033,811 pay
Vice Chairman: Lawrence A. Polimeno, age 63, $653,811 pay
President and COO: Howard Messing, age 52, $713,811 pay
CFO, Treasurer, and Clerk: Barbara A. Manzolillo, age 52, $502,811 pay
SVP, Sales and Marketing: Edward G. (Ed) Pisinski, age 61, $502,811 pay
VP, Client Services: Joanne Wood, age 51
VP, Implementation: Steven B. (Steve) Koretz, age 52
VP, Marketing: Hoda Sayed-Friel, age 46
VP, Product Development: Robert S. Gale, age 58
VP, Sales: Stuart N. (Stu) Lefthes, age 51
VP, System Technology: Christopher (Chris) Anschuetz, age 52
Marketing and Public Relations Contact:
Paul Berthiaume
Auditors: Ernst & Young LLP

LOCATIONS

HQ: Medical Information Technology, Inc.
MEDITECH Circle, Westwood, MA 02090
Phone: 781-821-3000   **Fax:** 781-821-2199
Web: www.meditech.com

Medical Information Technology sells its software primarily in Canada, the UK, and the US.

2004 Sales

	% of total
US	86
Canada	12
Other countries	2
Total	**100**

PRODUCTS/OPERATIONS

2004 Sales

	$ mil.	% of total
Software products	148.3	53
Services	132.5	47
Total	**280.8**	**100**

Software Products

Ambulatory care applications
Behavioral health applications
Clinical applications
Decision support applications
Financial management applications
Long-term care information system
Patient care management applications
Patient identification and scheduling applications
Reimbursement applications

COMPETITORS

AMICAS	McKesson
CareCentric	Mediware
Cerner	MedPlus
CPSI	Misys Healthcare
Eclipsys	QuadraMed
Health Management	Quality Systems
Systems	Quovadx
IDX Systems	Siemens Medical
iSOFT	TriZetto

HISTORICAL FINANCIALS

Company Type: Private

Income Statement

FYE: December 31

	REVENUE ($ mil.)	NET INCOME ($ mil.)	NET PROFIT MARGIN	EMPLOYEES
12/04	281	71	25.4%	2,100
12/03	271	67	24.9%	2,000
12/02	256	64	24.9%	2,092
12/01	218	57	26.1%	1,800
12/00	211	55	26.2%	1,700
12/99	226	60	26.6%	—
12/98	204	53	26.2%	—
12/97	194	50	26.0%	—
Annual Growth	**5.4%**	**5.1%**	**—**	**5.4%**

2004 Year-End Financials

Debt ratio: 0.0%
Return on equity: 19.8%
Cash ($ mil.): 15
Current ratio: 5.53
Long-term debt ($ mil.): 0

Net Income History

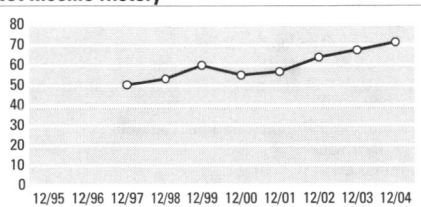

80	
70	
60	
50	
40	
30	
20	
10	
0	
12/95 12/96 12/97 12/98 12/99 12/00 12/01 12/02 12/03 12/04	

Medical Mutual of Ohio

Medical Mutual of Ohio (formerly Blue Cross and Blue Shield of Ohio) is a not-for-profit managed care company that provides health insurance products and related services to nearly 2 million members in Ohio and Pennsylvania. The company's health plans include HMO, PPO, POS, traditional indemnity, and supplemental Medicare. Medical Mutual of Ohio also provides dental, vision, and workers compensation plans, life insurance, and third-party administration (TPA) services. Founded in 1934, Medical Mutual of Ohio is not affiliated with the Blue Cross Blue Shield Association.

EXECUTIVES

Chairman, President, and CEO: Kent W. Clapp
EVP and CFO: Susan Tyler
EVP and Chief Information Officer; President, Antares Management Solutions: Kenneth Sidon
EVP, Sales and Customer Relations and Chief Marketing Officer: Errol D. Brick
EVP, Statewide Operations: Linda L. Johnson
EVP: Joseph Krysh
VP, Broker Sales: Charles Braschwitz
VP, Care Management: Paula Sauer
VP, Claims Operations: James Quiring
VP, Corporate Communications and Advertising, and Chief Communications Officer: Jared Chaney
VP, Finance: Rick Chiricosta
VP and General Auditor: William Allen
General Counsel and VP, Legal Affairs: John Dorrell

LOCATIONS

HQ: Medical Mutual of Ohio
2060 E. 9th St., Cleveland, OH 44115
Phone: 216-687-7000   **Fax:** 216-687-6044
Web: www.mmoh.com

PRODUCTS/OPERATIONS

Selected Insurance Products

SuperMed Classic (HMO)
SuperMed Dental
SuperMed HMO
SuperMed Plus (PPO)
SuperMed Select (Point-of Service)
SuperMed Vision
Medical Mutual's Greater Miami Valley Health Plan (Dayton Ohio Area Health Plan)

COMPETITORS

Aetna	Humana Health
CIGNA	Plan of Ohio
Highmark	UnitedHealth Group
Humana	WellPoint

HISTORICAL FINANCIALS

Company Type: Not-for-profit

Income Statement

FYE: December 31

	REVENUE ($ mil.)	NET INCOME ($ mil.)	NET PROFIT MARGIN	EMPLOYEES
12/03	1,600	—	—	2,500
12/02	1,500	—	—	2,500
Annual Growth	**6.7%**	**—**	**—**	**0.0%**

Revenue History

1,600	
1,400	
1,200	
1,000	
800	
600	
400	
200	
0	
12/94 12/95 12/96 12/97 12/98 12/99 12/00 12/01 12/02 12/03	

Medline Industries

Medline Industries, a private medical equipment distributor and manufacturer, goes toe-to-toe with the bigger guns, selling more than 100,000 products. The company's catalog includes such items as furnishings for hospital rooms, exam equipment, housekeeping supplies, and surgical gloves and garments. The firm manufactures about 70% of its products through its Dynacor unit and then distributes them to such customers as hospitals, extended care facilities, and home health care providers. Marketing efforts are handled by Medline's more than 750 sales representatives and roughly 30 distribution centers. The company is owned by the Mills family, which founded Medline in 1910 as a manufacturer of nurses' gowns.

Medline in late 2003 bought Maxxim Medical's surgical products business consisting of custom procedural trays, drapes, and gowns. Medline also bought Maxxim's medical products business and its vascular products business.

In a deal with medical supply distributor Novation, Medline's products are sold in group-purchasing contracts to organizations like the University Health System (which represents 2,400 hospitals nationwide).

About 97% of revenues come from sales in the US; the company also has operations in Canada and Europe.

EXECUTIVES

CEO: Charles S. (Charlie) Mills, age 43
President: Andy Mills
COO: Jim Abrams
CFO: Bill Abington
SVP, Corporate Sales: Tim Jacobson
VP, Human Resources: Joseph Becker
VP, National Accounts: Jack Hannemann
VP, National Accounts: Steve Heintze
President, Preferred Healthcare Division: Hunter Banks
President, Dermal Management Systems: Jonathan Primer
President, National Accounts: Kurt Krieghbaum
President, Operating Room Division: James Spann
President, Sales: Ray Swaback
VP, Marketing, Dynacor: Marc Lessem
Director, Corporate Communicatons: John J. Marks
Director, Marketing Communications: Lori Bolas

LOCATIONS

HQ: Medline Industries, Inc.
1 Medline Place, Mundelein, IL 60060
Phone: 847-949-5500   **Fax:** 800-351-1512
Web: www.medline.com

HISTORICAL FINANCIALS

Company Type: Private

Income Statement

FYE: December 31

	REVENUE ($ mil.)	NET INCOME ($ mil.)	NET PROFIT MARGIN	EMPLOYEES
12/03	1,600	—	—	4,200
12/02	1,450	—	—	3,800
12/01	1,231	—	—	3,500
12/00	1,016	—	—	3,277
12/99	905	—	—	2,600
12/98	756	—	—	2,300
12/97	655	—	—	2,700
12/96	600	—	—	2,383
12/95	560	—	—	2,200
12/94	476	—	—	2,000
Annual Growth	**14.4%**	**—**	**—**	**8.6%**

Revenue History

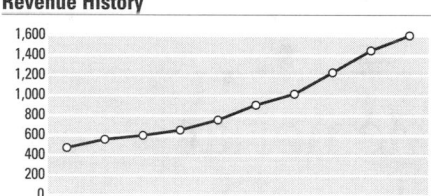

Meijer

Meijer (pronounced "Meyer") is the green giant of retailing in the Midwest. The company operates about 170 combination grocery and general merchandise stores; about half are in Michigan, while the rest are in Illinois, Indiana, Kentucky, and Ohio. Its huge stores (which average 200,000 to 250,000 sq. ft. each, or about the size of four regular grocery stores) stock about 120,000 items, including Meijer private-label products. Customers can choose from about 40 departments, including apparel, electronics, hardware, and toys. Most stores also sell gasoline, offer banking services, and have multiple in-store restaurants. Founder Hendrik Meijer opened his first store in 1934; the company is still family owned.

Although the discount superstore format is most often referred to in conjunction with its rival Wal-Mart, Meijer is its pioneer. But that hasn't stopped the world's #1 retailer from muscling in on Meijer's markets. Meijer competes with more than 50 supercenters and expects that number to reach 350 by 2007. The company is responding by cutting prices, putting some expansion plans on hold, and renovating its stores. It is also cutting jobs — eliminating about 1,900 management positions at its stores in January 2004 following a reduction of about 350 positions in 2003 — to become more efficient and competitive. On the plus side, Meijer plans to open nine new stores in 2005, which the company says will create about 6,500 new jobs. Meijer is also facing increased pressure from warehouse club stores, drugstores, and supermarket chains, like Kroger, that are expanding in its markets.

On the other hand, Kmart's woes have given Meijer a boost. With 35 of Kmart's store closings within 10 miles of a Meijer store, the company has begun filling prescriptions for former Kmart customers. Meijer also recently opened its first store in metropolitan Detroit in a former Kmart location.

HISTORY

Dutch immigrant and barber Hendrik Meijer owned a vacant space next to his barbershop in Greenville, Michigan. Because of the Depression, he couldn't rent it out. So in 1934 he bought $338.76 in merchandise on credit and started his own grocery store, Thrift Market, with the help of his wife, Gezina; son, Fred; and daughter, Johanna; he made $7 the first day. Meijer had 22 competitors in Greenville alone, but his dedication to low prices (he and Fred often traveled long distances to find bargains) attracted customers. In 1935, to encourage self-service, Meijer placed 12 wicker baskets at the front of the store and posted signs that read, "Take a basket. Help yourself."

A second store was opened in 1942. The company added four more in the 1950s. In 1962 Meijer — then with 14 stores — opened the first one-stop shopping Meijer Thrifty Acres store, similar to a hypermarket another operator had opened in Belgium a year earlier. By 1964, the year that Hendrik died and Fred took over, three of these general merchandise stores were operating. The company entered Ohio in the late 1960s.

In the early 1980s Meijer bought 14 Twin Fair stores in Ohio and 10 in Cincinnati. But it sold the stores by 1987 after disappointing results. Meijer had greater success in Columbus, Ohio, where it opened one store that year and immediately captured 20% of the market. In 1988 the company began keeping most stores open 24 hours a day.

Meijer annihilated competitors in Dayton, Ohio, in 1991, when it opened four stores that year. The company entered the Toledo market in 1993 with four stores; after one year it had taken 11.5% of the market. A foray into the membership warehouse market was abandoned in 1993, just a few months after they had opened, when Meijer said it would close all seven SourceClubs in Michigan and Ohio.

The company entered Indiana in 1994, opening 16 stores in less than two years; it also reached an agreement with McDonald's to open restaurants in several stores. The first labor strike in Meijer's history hit four stores in Toledo that year, leading to pickets at 14 others. Union officials accused the company of using intimidation tactics by its hiring of large, uniformed men in flak jackets and combat boots as security guards. After nine weeks Meijer agreed to recognize the workers' newly attained union affiliation.

In 1995 the company opened 13 stores, including its first in Illinois. It reentered the Cincinnati market in 1996, announcing the opening of two new stores there by mailing 80,000 videos to residents. By the end of the year, Meijer had a total of five stores in Cincinnati and had entered the Kentucky market.

Meijer opened a central kitchen in Indiana to prepare deli salads and some vegetables and process orange juice for its stores in 1997. It opened its first two stores in Louisville, Kentucky, the following year. Meijer broke into the tough Chicago-area market with its first store in 1999.

The next year Meijer opened several "village-style" stores — scaled-down versions (about 155,000 sq. ft.) of its larger stores. Later in 2000 Meijer unveiled what it claims is the largest superstore in North America. The 255,000-sq.-ft. behemoth (compared to a Wal-Mart Supercenter, which averages about 183,106 sq. ft.) features a gourmet coffee shop, a card shop, a bank open seven days a week, and restaurants serving pizza and sushi.

In February 2002 co-chairman Hank Meijer was named CEO, succeeding Jim McClean, who had run the company since 1999. The retailer launched a "reinvented superstore format" at six Dayton, Ohio-area stores in late 2002. The makeover emphasizes discount fashion (featuring brands such as Levi's, Dockers, and Gotcha) in a department store atmosphere.

In 2003 Meijer eliminated about 350 jobs to cut costs and opened two new stores.

Larry Zigerelli was promoted from EVP of Merchandising to president of the company in January 2005.

EXECUTIVES

Chairman Emeritus: Fred Meijer, age 84
Co-Chairman: Doug Meijer, age 50
Co-Chairman and Co-CEO: Hendrik G. (Hank) Meijer, age 53
Vice Chairman and Co-CEO: Paul Boyer, age 56
President: Larry Zigerelli
SVP, Finance and Administration, and CFO: Jim Walsh
SVP, Human Resources: Wendell (Windy) Ray
Division VP, Merchandising: Terry Griffith
Group VP, Grocery Merchandising: Ralph Fischer
Group VP, Hardlines and Drug Store: Tim Lesneski
Group VP, Softlines and Home: Rob Gruen
Group VP, Perishables Merchandising: Dave Prostko
VP, Drug Store: Nat Love
VP, Hardlines: Rob Atteberry
VP, Home: Ruth McCarthy
VP, Pharmacy Operations: Mike Major
VP, Real Estate: Mike Kinstle
VP, Service Operations: Carole Morgan
Director, Community and Customer Relations: John Zimmerman
Director, Marketing Strategy and Customer Relationship Management: Michael Ross

LOCATIONS

HQ: Meijer, Inc.
2929 Walker Ave. NW, Grand Rapids, MI 49544
Phone: 616-453-6711   **Fax:** 616-791-2572
Web: www.meijer.com

2005 Stores

	No.
Michigan	80
Ohio	39
Indiana	26
Illinois	10
Kentucky	8
Total	**163**

PRODUCTS/OPERATIONS

Selected Meijer Store Departments

Apparel	Jewelry
Auto supplies	Lawn and garden
Bakery	Music
Banking	Nutrition products
Books	Paint
Bulk foods	Pets and pet supplies
Coffee shop	Pharmacy
Computer software	Photo lab
Dairy	Portrait studio
Delicatessen	Produce
Electronics	Service meat and seafood
Floral	Small appliances
Food court	Soup and salad bar
Gas station	Sporting goods
Hardware	Tobacco
Health and beauty	Toys
products	Wall coverings
Home fashions	Wine

COMPETITORS

A&P	Kohl's
Albertson's	Kroger
ALDI	Marsh Supermarkets
Busch's	Retail Ventures
Costco Wholesale	Roundy's
CVS	SAM'S CLUB
D&W Food Centers	Schnuck Markets
Dollar General	Schottenstein Stores
Dominick's	Spartan Stores
Family Dollar Stores	SUPERVALU
Farmer Jack	Target
Giant Eagle	Walgreen
Home Depot	Wal-Mart
IGA	Whole Foods
Kmart	Winn-Dixie

HISTORICAL FINANCIALS

Company Type: Private

Income Statement

FYE: January 31

	ESTIMATED REVENUE ($ mil.)	NET INCOME ($ mil.)	NET PROFIT MARGIN	EMPLOYEES
1/05	11,900	—	—	75,000
1/04	11,900	—	—	75,000
1/03	10,900	—	—	83,402
1/02	10,600	—	—	83,402
1/01	10,000	—	—	80,000
1/00	9,500	—	—	80,000
1/99	8,300	—	—	80,000
1/98	6,900	—	—	77,000
1/97	6,000	—	—	73,000
1/96	5,640	—	—	65,000
Annual Growth	8.7%	—	—	1.6%

Revenue History

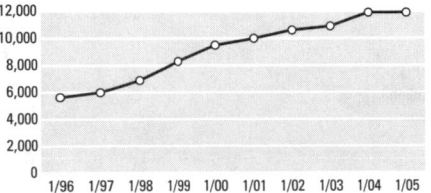

Memec

Active around the world, Memec and its subsidiaries provide logistics and distribution services to international manufacturers and suppliers in the semiconductor industry, including Xilinx, Actel, and Texas Instruments. Memec also provides IT, warehousing, and product packaging services to customers to help streamline their supply chains and lower cost. Each of the Memec group companies focuses on a limited number of suppliers within a specific industry. Investors in the company included London-based buyout firm Permira (which held 68% of the company) and Deutsche Bank. Memec has been acquired by Avnet for approximately $663 million in cash and stock, including the assumption of about $194 million in debt.

Memec is being integrated into the Avnet Electronics Marketing unit, with the integration expected to be completed by June 2006.

In addition to simply selling products to original equipment manufacturers, Memec works with its OEM customers during their design phases to drive demand for customized products.

EXECUTIVES

Chairman: Peter Smitham, age 63
President, CEO, and Director: David Ashworth, age 43, $707,093 pay
SVP, CFO, and Secretary: Doug Lindroth, age 38, $428,809 pay
SVP, Memec Global Supplier Group: Greg Provenzano, age 43, $473,841 pay (prior to promotion)
SVP; President, Memec Americas: Gerard (Gerry) Fay, age 46
SVP, Human Resources: William (Bill) O'Neill, age 48
SVP; President, Memec Asia-Pacific: Yang-Chiah Yee, age 38, $365,889 pay
SVP; President, Memec EMEA: Chris Page, age 47, $563,338 pay
VP; President, Memec Japan: Chris Norman
President and CEO, Memec Unique: Phil Sansone
VP Finance, Americas: Jeff Pace
SVP and CIO: Steve Phillips, age 40
Auditors: PricewaterhouseCoopers LLP

LOCATIONS

HQ: Memec Group Holdings Limited
3721 Valley Centre Dr., San Diego, CA 92121
Phone: 858-314-8800   **Fax:** 858-314-8850
Web: www.memec.com

Memec has operations in more than 30 countries, including presences in the Americas, Asia, Australia, Europe, and the Middle East.

2003 Sales

	$ mil.	% of total
Americas	774.1	43
Europe, Middle East & Africa	446.4	25
Asia/Pacific		
Japan	138.3	8
Other countries	439.0	24
Total	**1,797.8**	**100**

COMPETITORS

All American Semiconductor	Future Electronics
Arrow Electronics	Jaco Electronics
Avnet	Nu Horizons Electronics
Bell Microproducts	Premier Farnell
Digi-Key Electrocomponents	Richardson Electronics
	TTI Inc.

HISTORICAL FINANCIALS

Company Type: Private

Income Statement

FYE: December 31

	REVENUE ($ mil.)	NET INCOME ($ mil.)	NET PROFIT MARGIN	EMPLOYEES
12/03	1,798	(86)	—	2,425
12/02	1,609	(85)	—	2,700
12/01	2,065	(25)	—	2,800
12/00	3,700	—	—	—
Annual Growth	(21.4%)	—	—	(6.9%)

2003 Year-End Financials

Debt ratio: —
Return on equity: —
Cash ($ mil.): 42
Current ratio: 1.78
Long-term debt ($ mil.): 590

Net Income History

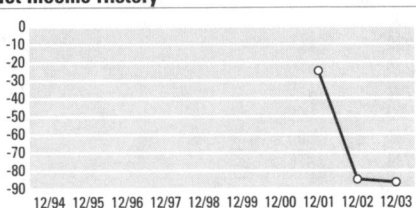

Memorial Sloan-Kettering

Ranked as one of the nation's top cancer centers, Memorial Sloan-Kettering Cancer Center includes Memorial Hospital for Cancer and Allied Diseases for pediatric and adult cancer care and the Sloan-Kettering Institute for cancer research activities. The cancer center specializes in bone-marrow transplants and chemotherapy and offers programs in cancer prevention, treatment, research, and education. Memorial Sloan-Kettering offers inpatient and outpatient services to about 20,100 patients every year. Other services include pain management, rehabilitation, and psychological programs.

Memorial Sloan-Kettering both gives and receives funding to further the fight against cancer and other diseases. Philanthropic contributions each year typically reach more than $100 million.

EXECUTIVES

Chairman: Douglas A. (Sandy) Warner III
Honorary Co-Chairman: James D. Robinson III
Vice Chairman; Chairman, Memorial Hospital: Richard I. (Dick) Beattie, age 66
Vice Chairman; Chairman, Sloan-Kettering Institute: Louis V. Gerstner Jr., age 63
President and CEO: Harold Varmus
President Emeritus and Head of Devlopmental Cell Biology Laboratory: Paul A. Marks
EVP and COO: John R. Gunn, age 62

SVP, Clinical Program Development:
Thomas J. Fahey Jr.
SVP, Finance and Assistant Treasurer:
Michael P. Gutnick
SVP and Hospital Administrator: Kathryn Martin
SVP and General Counsel: Roger N. Parker
SVP, Research Resources Management: James S. Quirk
VP, Information Systems and CIO: Patricia C. Skarulis
VP, Human Resources: Michael Browne
VP, Marketing: Ellen Miller Sonet
VP, Public Affairs: Anne Thomas
Secretary: Peter O. Crisp, age 72
Treasurer: Clifton S. Robbins

LOCATIONS

HQ: Memorial Sloan-Kettering Cancer Center
1275 York Ave., New York, NY 10021
Phone: 212-639-2000 **Fax:** 212-639-3576
Web: www.mskcc.org

COMPETITORS

Carilion Health System
Columbia University
Detroit Medical Center
Johns Hopkins Medicine
Mayo Foundation
New York City Health and Hospitals
Partners HealthCare
Rush System for Health
University of Texas

HISTORICAL FINANCIALS

Company Type: Not-for-profit

Income Statement

FYE: December 31

	REVENUE ($ mil.)	NET INCOME ($ mil.)	NET PROFIT MARGIN	EMPLOYEES
12/03	1,318	423	32.1%	8,255
12/02	1,088	(81)	—	7,953
12/01	959	(120)	—	7,609
12/00	876	64	7.3%	7,296
12/99	790	222	28.1%	7,133
12/98	747	204	27.3%	6,618
12/97	694	207	29.8%	6,142
12/96	640	178	27.5%	5,799
12/95	650	191	29.4%	6,050
12/94	637	21	3.4%	6,034
Annual Growth	8.4%	39.3%	—	3.5%

2003 Year-End Financials

Debt ratio: — Current ratio: —
Return on equity: 16.6% Long-term debt ($ mil.): —
Cash ($ mil.): —

Net Income History

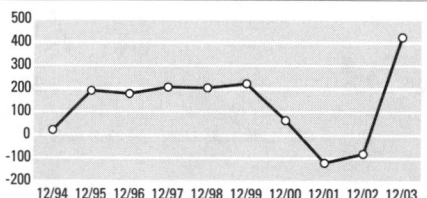

500
400
300
200
100
0
-100
-200
12/94 12/95 12/96 12/97 12/98 12/99 12/00 12/01 12/02 12/03

Memphis Grizzlies

Life's been pretty grisly for this team, but the Grizzlies' exodus from Canada improved their fortune. The Memphis Grizzlies (formerly of Vancouver) moved to Tennessee in 2001 after Chicago billionaire Michael Heisley bought the team for $160 million. The team was the first NBA franchise to relocate since 1985. The organization pinned its future on the hiring of Jerry West as president of basketball operations, and the team made the playoffs for the first time in 2004. Formed in 1995, it holds the dubious record for the longest losing streak in NBA history (23 games). The Grizzlies play host at the FedExForum, a $300 million publicly funded arena opened in 2004.

EXECUTIVES

Majority Owner: Michael Heisley Sr.
President of Basketball Operations: Jerry West, age 67
President of Business Operations: Andy Dolich
General Manager: Dick Versace
Assistant General Manager and Legal Counsel:
Tom Penn
Head Coach: Mike Fratello, age 57
SVP Business Operations: Mike Golub
SVP Broadcast: Randy Stephens
SVP Corporate Partnerships: Mike Redlick
SVP Ticket Sales and Services: Mike Levy
VP Arena Operations: Don Hardman, age 31
VP Finance: Todd Kobus
Senior Director of Marketing Communications:
Marla Taner
Director of Human Resources: Christy M. Haynes
Director of Media Relations: Kirk Clayborn

LOCATIONS

HQ: Memphis Grizzlies
175 Toyota Plaza, Ste. 150, Memphis, TN 38103
Phone: 901-888-4667 **Fax:** 901-205-1235
Web: www.nba.com/grizzlies

The Memphis Grizzlies play at the 20,000-seat FedExForum in Memphis.

COMPETITORS

Dallas Mavericks New Orleans Hornets
Houston Rockets San Antonio Spurs

HISTORICAL FINANCIALS

Company Type: Private

Income Statement

FYE: June 30

	REVENUE ($ mil.)	NET INCOME ($ mil.)	NET PROFIT MARGIN	EMPLOYEES
6/04	75	—	—	—
6/03	63	—	—	—
6/02	66	—	—	—
6/01	53	—	—	—
6/00	51	—	—	—
6/99	28	—	—	200
6/98	51	—	—	40
6/97	42	—	—	—
Annual Growth	8.5%	—	—	400.0%

Revenue History

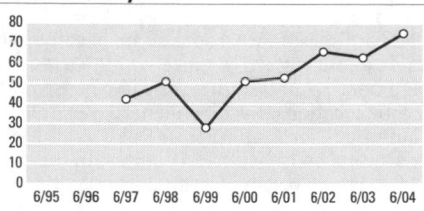

80
70
60
50
40
30
20
10
0
6/95 6/96 6/97 6/98 6/99 6/00 6/01 6/02 6/03 6/04

Menard

If sticks and stones break bones, what can two-by-fours and 2-in. nails do? That is what Menard is wondering now that its biggest rivals (#1 home improvement giant The Home Depot and #2 Lowe's) are hammering away at its home turf. The third-largest home improvement chain in the US, Menard has about 200 stores in Illinois, Indiana, Iowa, Michigan, Minnesota, Nebraska, North and South Dakota, Ohio, and Wisconsin. The stores sell home improvement products, such as floor coverings, hardware, millwork, paint, and tools. Unlike competitors, all the company's stores have full-service lumberyards. Menard is owned by president and CEO John Menard Jr., who founded the company in 1972.

Although Menard outlets are typically smaller than those of Home Depot, they offer a similar selection of products by building large warehouses adjacent to stores and then quickly restocking merchandise when it's sold. The company's products are laid out on easy-to-reach, supermarket-styled shelves. To help keep expenses low and prices cheap, Menard makes some of its merchandise, including doors and trusses.

The company is increasing its average store size to more than 220,000 sq. ft. It has opened its largest store ever — 250,000 sq. ft. — in Minnesota and is expanding 30 to 40 stores. Most of the the company's new stores will be more than 200,000 sq. ft. Besides stocking hardware and building supplies these new megastores will include garden centers and sell a large range of home appliances.

In addition to founder John Menard, other family members are engaged in its everyday operations. John Menard also owns Team Menard, an Indy car-racing team.

HISTORY

John Menard was the oldest of eight children on a Wisconsin dairy farm. To pay for attending the University of Wisconsin at Eau Claire, he and some fellow college students built pole barns in the late 1950s. Learning that other builders had trouble finding lumber outlets open on the weekends, Menard began buying wood in bulk and selling it to them. He added other supplies in 1960 and sold his construction business in 1970 as building supply revenues became his chief source of income.

He founded Menard in 1972 as the do-it-yourself craze was beginning, but he wanted an operation run more like mass merchandiser Target, with easy-to-reach shelves, wide aisles, and tile floors rather than the cold, cumbersome layout used by lumberyards. To realize that concept, Menard built warehouses and stockrooms behind the stores so he could re-stock merchandise quickly.

Menard's vision worked, and he began building his Midwestern empire, often acquiring abandoned retail sites that were inexpensive and in good locations. By 1986 Menard was in Iowa, Minnesota, North and South Dakota, and Wisconsin, and by 1990 it had 46 stores. In the early 1990s Menard began enlarging its operations to serve the ever-growing number of stores, opening a huge warehouse and distribution center and a manufacturing facility that made doors, Formica countertops, and other products. Menard entered Nebraska in 1990 and opened its first store in Chicago the next year. By 1992 there were more than 60 stores.

That year Menard made the National Enquirer with a story about the firing of a store manager who had built a wheelchair-accessible home for his 11-year-old daughter with spina bifida, violating a company theft-prevention policy forbidding store managers to build their own homes. The company insisted that the man was fired in part because of poor work performance.

Menard continued to expand to new areas, operating stores in Indiana and Michigan by 1992. As it continued expanding in the Chicago area, it offered varying store formats, ranging from a full line of building materials to smaller Menards Hardware Plus stores. By 1994 Menard had 85 stores, many bigger than 100,000 sq. ft.

In 1995 and 1996 the company was plagued with lawsuits filed by customers charging false arrest and imprisonment for shoplifting. An on-duty police officer apprehending a shoplifting suspect at a store was even stopped and searched.

Competition also heated up during that time. The Home Depot's push into the Midwest — including opening several stores directly across the street from Menard — spurred Menard to fight back by lowering prices and opening nearly 40 stores. The fight forced smaller chains like Handy Andy out of business.

In 1997 Menard and his company were fined $1.7 million after dumping bags of toxic ash from its manufacturing facility at residential trash pick-up sites rather than at properly regulated outlets (it had been fined for similar violations in 1989 and 1994). In response to a price war initiated by Home Depot, in 1998 Menard dropped sales prices by 10%.

In 1999 competitor Lowe's began moving into Menard's biggest market, Chicago. Menard began opening larger stores in 2000 (about 162,000 sq. ft., or some 74,000 sq. ft. bigger than the older stores). In 2001 it began beefing up its lines of home appliances, adding more washers, dryers, dishwashers, refrigerators, and ranges.

Menard opened a 225,000 sq. ft. store — larger by 50 sq. ft. than the original — in Indiana in 2003. It then opened a bigger store, at 250,000 sq. ft., in Minnesota in February 2004.

In January 2005, the Internal Revenue Service ruled the company owes $5.9 million in back taxes and fines because it paid John Menard too high a salary in 1998.

EXECUTIVES

President and CEO: John R. Menard Jr., age 65
CFO and Treasurer: Earl R. Rasmussen
VP of Merchandising: Ed Archibald
VP of Operations: Larry Menard
VP of Real Estate: Marv Prochaska
CTO: Dave Wagner
Payroll Manager: Terri Jain
General Counsel: Dawn M. Sands

LOCATIONS

HQ: Menard, Inc.
4777 Menard Dr., Eau Claire, WI 54703
Phone: 715-876-5911 **Fax:** 715-876-2868
Web: www.menards.com

Menard owns home improvement stores in Illinois, Indiana, Iowa, Michigan, Minnesota, Nebraska, North Dakota, Ohio, South Dakota, and Wisconsin.

PRODUCTS/OPERATIONS

Selected Operations
Menards (home improvement stores)
Midwest Manufacturing (product manufacturing)

Selected Departments
Appliances
Building materials
Electrical (wiring, lighting)
Floor coverings
Hardware
Lumberyard
Millwork (doors, cabinetry, molding)
Plumbing
Seasonal (Christmas, lawn and garden)
Tools
Wall coverings (wallpaper, paint)

COMPETITORS

84 Lumber
Ace Hardware
Carter Lumber
Do it Best
Fastenal
Home Depot
Lanoga
Lowe's
Sears
Seigle's
Sherwin-Williams
Stock Building Supply
Sutherland Lumber
True Value
Wal-Mart
WinWholesale
Wolohan Lumber

HISTORICAL FINANCIALS

Company Type: Private

Income Statement				FYE: January 31
	ESTIMATED REVENUE ($ mil.)	NET INCOME ($ mil.)	NET PROFIT MARGIN	EMPLOYEES
1/04	6,000	—	—	27,000
1/03	5,600	—	—	10,500
1/02	5,300	—	—	9,200
1/01	5,000	—	—	7,600
1/00	4,500	—	—	7,000
1/99	4,000	—	—	7,000
1/98	3,700	—	—	7,000
1/97	3,200	—	—	7,000
1/96	2,700	—	—	6,534
1/95	2,300	—	—	5,800
Annual Growth	11.2%	—	—	18.6%

Revenue History

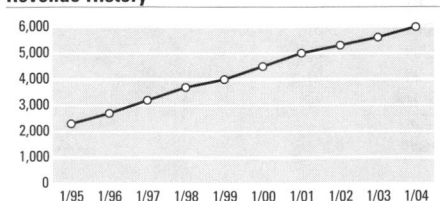

Merkel McDonald

Merkel McDonald (formerly Van Merkel) has figured out that the cookie might crumble, but it won't matter if the crumbs taste really good. Through its primary business, The Chippery, the company produces cookies and frozen cookie dough, which it sells to fundraising groups, food service operators, in-store bakeries, and direct to consumers nationwide through its Web site. Merkel McDonald was founded in 1984 and is owned by CEO Dave Merkel and president Jeffrey McDonald.

EXECUTIVES

CEO: Dave Merkel
President: Jeffrey (Jeff) McDonald
Controller: Mark Miller

LOCATIONS

HQ: Merkel McDonald, Inc.
6315 E. Stassney Ln., Ste. 100, Austin, TX 78744
Phone: 512-385-8822 **Fax:** 512-385-6025
Web: www.thechippery.com

COMPETITORS

Bama Pies
Jana's Classics
Mrs. Fields
Otis Spunkmeyer
Weston Foods

HISTORICAL FINANCIALS

Company Type: Private

Income Statement				FYE: December 31
	REVENUE ($ mil.)	NET INCOME ($ mil.)	NET PROFIT MARGIN	EMPLOYEES
12/04*	38	—	—	—
12/01	20	—	—	—
Annual Growth	90.0%	—	—	—

*Irregular reporting interval

Revenue History

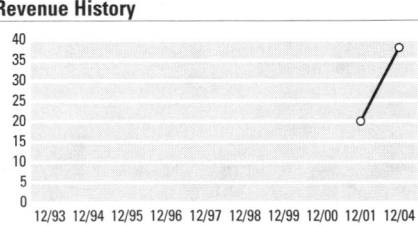

Merrill

Merrill manages documents, lock, stock, and barrel. Merrill Corporation is among the largest document management firms in the US and a leading provider of financial document services, such as preparing and delivering electronic filings to the SEC, producing annual reports, and creating other time-sensitive documents. It also provides business communications-related printing, graphic design, and fulfillment services. Other offerings include facilities management and legal support services. Its DataSite division offers online data rooms for due diligence and discovery. Customers include law firms, real estate companies, and financial services corporations.

With its stock price flagging, the company went private in 1999 through a recapitalization plan involving affiliates of Donaldson, Lufkin & Jenrette (later acquired by Credit Suisse First Boston). However, a weak market for financial document services limited the company's ability to pay down its growing debt load in 2000, and Merrill's lenders declared the company in default the next year. A second financial restructuring completed in 2002 helped the company to get back on track.

Employees own 47% of the company.

EXECUTIVES

CEO: John W. Castro, age 56
President and COO: Rick R. Atterbury
EVP and CFO: Robert H. Nazarian
EVP Human Resources: Brenda Vale
VP and Controller: Dean A. Niehus
VP DataSite Services: Paul Hartzell
VP Document Services: Peter J. Cawley
VP Document Services Operations: Nancee Ronning
VP Litigation Support Services: Joe Mann
VP Marketing: Leon S. DeMaille
CTO: John Stolle

LOCATIONS

HQ: Merrill Corporation
1 Merrill Cir., St. Paul, MN 55108
Phone: 651 646 4501   **Fax:** 651-646-5332
Web: www.merrillcorp.com

Merrill has offices in Canada, France, Germany, the UK, and the US.

PRODUCTS/OPERATIONS

Selected Products and Services
Legal
  Compliance and due diligence database
  Electronic discovery
  Securities Law database
Facilities management
  Copy centers
  Mailroom services
  Office services
  Records management
Financial
  Investor Relations services
  SEC documents, filing, and distribution
Printing
  Catalogs
  Corporate communications materials
  Direct mail
  Fulfillment
  Graphic design
  Marketing collateral
  Signage
Supply chain consulting
Translation services

Web-based tools
  MerrillConnect (sales and marketing analysis)
  MerrillReports (report automation
    for investment funds)
  net:MAIL (newsletters and mailers)
  net: PROSPECT (sales lead management)
Web site hosting
Workgroup Collaboration Web site

COMPETITORS

ADEXS	Quebecor World
Banta	North America
Bowne	R.R. Donnelley
Bowne Global Solutions	Service Point
Cenveo	St Ives
Dai Nippon Printing	Standard Register
Lionbridge	Toppan Printing
On-Site Sourcing	Workflow Management
Quad/Graphics	

HISTORICAL FINANCIALS
Company Type: Private

Income Statement   FYE: January 31

	REVENUE ($ mil.)	NET INCOME ($ mil.)	NET PROFIT MARGIN	EMPLOYEES
1/04	596	8	1.4%	4,200
1/03	582	—	—	4,070
1/02	603	—	—	4,086
1/01	650	—	—	4,100
1/00	588	—	—	4,157
1/99	510	—	—	3,933
1/98	460	—	—	3,838
1/97	354	—	—	2,804
1/96	245	—	—	2,253
1/95	237	—	—	1,739
Annual Growth	10.8%	—	—	10.3%

Revenue History

Mervyn's

Mervyn's is sure hoping that its change in ownership will get it back on target. The company operates some 260 midrange department stores in California and about a dozen other states, primarily in the West and South. In addition to name-brand apparel and housewares, Mervyn's offers goods under private labels, including Hillard & Hanson. About half of its stores are in regional malls and cater to working moms ages 25 to 49. Mervyn's has been squeezed by upscale department stores as well as discount chains. As a result, the retailer plans to close about a quarter of its stores. In 2004 former parent Target sold Mervyn's to an investment consortium of Sun Capital Partners, Cerberus Capital, and Lubert-Adler/Klaff.

Vanessa Castagna, former second-in-command at J. C. Penney, has joined Mervyn's as executive chairwoman. Castagna joined Cerberus Capital in early April 2005.

Mervyn's has agreed to sell the land underneath 36 of its stores to a team of developers for about $396 million. The sale, to Diversified Realty and Macquarie DDR Trust, is expected to close in mid-September. Also in September, Mervyn's announced plans to close 62 stores in eight states, including all of its Michigan and Oklahoma stores, and some outlets in Colorado, Louisiana, and Texas by February 2006. Some 4,800 employees face lay offs as a result of the closings. Following the closings, Mervyn's will operate 193 stores in 10 states.

The company plans to launch an exclusive collection of home products from HGTV host Susie Coelho, called Susie Coelho Style, in August.

Mervyn's credit card operation was sold to GE Consumer Finance in 2004.

EXECUTIVES

Executive Chairwoman and Acting CEO:
  Vanessa J. Castagna, age 54
President and Chief Merchandising Officer:
  Richard B. (Rick) Leto
CFO: Clay Creasey
EVP, Retail Operations: Beryl J. Buley, age 44
SVP and Chief Information Officer: Kurt Streitz
SVP and General Merchandise Manager, Home, Jewelry, Accessories, Shoes, and Intimates: Tom Tennyson
SVP, General Merchandise Manager, Women's Ready-to-Wear, Men's and Kids': Michael Wallen
SVP, Marketing: Terry McDonald
VP, Creative Marketing: Robert Raible
VP, Human Resources: Janna Adair
VP, Merchandise Planning: Lynn Schirmer
VP, Product Design and Development: Chris Daniel
Marketing and Media Relations: Michele Murphy
Senior Manager, Public Relations and Publicity:
  Katie Winter
Auditors: Ernst & Young LLP

LOCATIONS

HQ: Mervyn's, LLC
  22301 Foothill Blvd., Hayward, CA 94541
Phone: 510-727-3000   **Fax:** 510-727-2300
Web: www.mervyns.com

Mervyn's operates about 260 stores in Arizona, California, Colorado, Idaho, Louisiana, Michigan, Minnesota, Nevada, New Mexico, Oklahoma, Oregon, Texas, Utah, and Washington.

COMPETITORS

Burlington Coat Factory
Dillard's
Dress Barn
Federated
Gap
Gottschalks
J. C. Penney
Kmart
Kohl's
Limited Brands
May
Ross Stores
Sears
Target
TJX Companies
Wal-Mart

HISTORICAL FINANCIALS

Company Type: Private

Income Statement

FYE: Saturday nearest January 31

	REVENUE ($ mil.)	NET INCOME ($ mil.)	NET PROFIT MARGIN	EMPLOYEES
1/04	3,553	—	—	29,000
1/03	3,816	—	—	33,000
1/02	4,038	—	—	32,000
1/01	4,152	—	—	29,000
1/00	4,099	—	—	32,000
1/99	4,176	—	—	30,000
1/98	4,227	—	—	29,000
1/97	4,369	—	—	—
Annual Growth	**(2.9%)**	**—**	**—**	**0.0%**

Revenue History

```
4,500
4,000
3,500
3,000
2,500
2,000
1,500
1,000
  500
    0
     1/95 1/96 1/97 1/98 1/99 1/00 1/01 1/02 1/03 1/04
```

Metaldyne

Whether you're cruising down the highway or being towed, Metaldyne products may be involved. The metal-forming and -machining company's power train and chassis units make components for passenger cars and commercial vehicles. Products include components and assemblies for engines, noise and vibration control, transmissions, wheels, suspensions, axles, and drivelines. Major customers include the leading US automakers; DaimlerChrysler accounts for more than 20% of Metaldyne's sales. Private equity firm Heartland Industrial Partners, which controls Metaldyne, formed the company through the consolidation of MascoTech, Simpson Industries, and Global Metal Technologies.

Effective in January 2005, Metaldyne reorganized its operations from three segments into two. Its former driveline operations were split between the company's chassis segment and a new power train segment, which also includes the operations of the company's former engine segment.

EXECUTIVES

Chairman, President, and CEO: Timothy D. Leuliette, age 54
EVP and CFO: Jeffrey M. (Jeff) Stafeil, age 35
EVP, Commercial Operations: Thomas Amato, age 41
VP, Human Resources: Kim Kovac
VP, Corporate Affairs: Myra Moreland
VP and Treasurer: Karen A. Radtke, age 51
VP, Sales and Marketing: Roseann Stevens, age 49
VP, Supply Chain Management: Linda Theisen
President, Engine Group: Thomas V. Chambers, age 61
President, Chassis Group: Joseph Nowak, age 54
General Counsel: Jeffrey Pollock
Auditors: KPMG LLP

LOCATIONS

HQ: Metaldyne Corporation
47659 Halyard Dr., Plymouth, MI 48170
Phone: 734-207-6200   **Fax:** 734-207-6500
Web: www.metaldyne.com

2004 Sales

	$ mil.	% of total
North America		
US	1,580.1	78
Other countries	72.0	4
Europe	334.8	17
Other regions	17.4	1
Total	**2,004.3**	**100**

PRODUCTS/OPERATIONS

2004 Sales

	$ mil.	% of total
Driveline	784.5	39
Engine	636.2	32
Chassis	583.6	29
Total	**2,004.3**	**100**

COMPETITORS

American Axle & Manufacturing
Delphi
EaglePicher Hillsdale
GKN
Hayes Lemmerz
Tesma
Visteon

HISTORICAL FINANCIALS

Company Type: Private

Income Statement

FYE: Sunday nearest to December 31

	REVENUE ($ mil.)	NET INCOME ($ mil.)	NET PROFIT MARGIN	EMPLOYEES
12/04	2,004	(28)	—	8,000
12/03	1,508	(75)	—	7,900
12/02	1,793	(62)	—	7,100
12/01	2,128	(43)	—	12,500
12/00	1,650	56	3.4%	11,600
12/99	1,680	92	5.5%	9,500
12/98	1,636	98	6.0%	9,200
12/97	922	115	12.5%	9,000
12/96	1,281	52	4.0%	5,100
12/95	1,678	59	3.5%	10,800
Annual Growth	**2.0%**	**—**	**—**	**(3.3%)**

2004 Year-End Financials

Debt ratio: 157.8%
Return on equity: —
Cash ($ mil.): 0

Current ratio: 0.87
Long-term debt ($ mil.): 855

Net Income History

```
120
100
 80
 60
 40
 20
  0
-20
-40
-60
-80
    12/95 12/96 12/97 12/98 12/99 12/00 12/01 12/02 12/03 12/04
```

Metro-Goldwyn-Mayer

The name is Mayer. Metro-Goldwyn-Mayer (MGM). The studio that runs MGM Pictures and United Artists is the home of the valuable James Bond franchise. MGM makes and distributes movies (*Be Cool*, *The Amityville Horror*), TV shows (*Stargate SG-1*, *Stargate: Atlantis*) through MGM Television Entertainment, and DVDs through MGM Home Entertainment. Its MGM Consumer Products division markets products based on MGM films. MGM houses one of the largest post-1948 film library in the world with some 4,000 titles — including the Bond and Pink Panther series as well as hit titles such as *Rain Man* and *Rocky*. In 2005 billionaire Kirk Kerkorian sold the company to a consortium of investors led by Sony Corporation of America.

Kerkorian bought MGM three times since the late 1960s, most recently in 1996. In the past few years, Kerkorian frequently tried to sell MGM to a variety of buyers including NBC, Pixar, and Time Warner. Eventually an investment group made up of Sony and its equity partners Texas Pacific Group, Providence Equity Partners, Comcast Corporation, and DLJ Merchant Banking Partners (part of CSFB Private Equity), bought the company for $4.8 billion (including $2 billion of MGM debt). The deal coincides with Sony's agreement with Comcast to launch new channels and video on demand services featuring Sony and MGM's movie libraries. The two studios will also co-finance and co-produce new film projects. Harry Sloan joined MGM as CEO in late 2005, and also joined the ownership consortium.

MGM has adopted the strategy of attempting to generate higher profits through producing less expensive films. The lion roared with Reese Witherspoon's *Legally Blonde*, the most profitable non-Bond film in MGM's history. Its sequel, 2003's *Legally Blonde 2: Red, White and Blonde*, also preformed well at the box office. Other highlights include *Barbershop* and United Artists' hit documentary *Bowling for Columbine*. These welcome hits followed a string of duds (*Hart's War*, *Rollerball*, and *Windtalkers*). The company relied on 007 to save MGM's world with *Die Another Day* (2002), the franchise's 20th feature, which had the biggest opening of a James Bond film to date. The 2005 remake of *The Amityville Horror* also posted good numbers. Promising upcoming MGM releases include the next Bond film (*Casino Royale*) and a Steve Martin remake of *The Pink Panther*.

During their tenure, former studio bosses Alex Yemenidjian and Chris McGurk instituted major cost cuts, turned United Artists film production unit into a specialty film division with smaller budgets, and secured cable distribution of the company's films through 15 foreign channels.

MGM has also divested itself of numerous cable operations. In 2002 NBC purchased MGM's 20% stake in Bravo for $250 million, and the following year MGM sold its 20% stake in three other cable networks (now run by Rainbow Media) — American Movie Classics, The Independent Film Channel, and We: Women's Entertainment — back to Cablevision for $500 million. Proceeds from the sales helped eliminate some of MGM's debt.

EXECUTIVES

Chairman and CEO: Harry Sloan, age 55
President: Daniel J. Taylor, age 48, $1,381,561 pay
(prior to promotion)
SEVP and General Counsel: Jay Rakow, age 52,
$1,087,500 pay
EVP: Charles Cohen
SEVP and Secretary: William A. (Bill) Jones, age 63,
$1,030,600 pay
**EVP Consumer Products and Location-Based
Entertainment:** Travis Rutherford
EVP Corporate and Governmental Affairs:
Michael Smarinsky
EVP Home Entertainment Distribution: Blake Thomas
EVP Feature Post Production: Bruce Markoe
EVP Human Resources: Steve Shaw
EVP International Television: Simon Sutton
**EVP Investor Relations and Corporate
Communications:** Joseph M. (Joe) Fitzgerald
EVP Labor Relations: Mark B. Crowley
**EVP Marketing and Distribution and Head of United
Artists:** Daniel Rosett
EVP MGM Music: Anita Camarata
EVP MGM Networks: Bruce Tuchman
EVP Worldwide Publicity: Eric Kops
SVP Advertising Sales: Michael Daraio
SVP Domestic Distribution: Derek McLay
SVP Exhibitor Relations: Brett Fellman
SVP International Television Distribution:
Carolyn Stalins
VP Copyright and Trademark: Michael Moore
VP Intellectual Property: Laura Tunberg
Auditors: Ernst & Young LLP

LOCATIONS

HQ: Metro-Goldwyn-Mayer Inc.
10250 Constellation Blvd., Los Angeles, CA 90067
Phone: 310-449-3000   **Fax:** 310-449-8857
Web: www.mgm.com

Metro-Goldwyn-Mayer has operations in Los Angeles
and New York City. It also has international offices in
Amsterdam, Brussels, Frankfurt, London, Melbourne,
Paris, Sydney, and Toronto.

PRODUCTS/OPERATIONS

2004 Sales

	$ mil.	% of total
Feature films	1,438.6	83
Television programs	240.6	14
Other	45.6	3
Total	**1,724.8**	**100**

Selected Operations

MGM Consumer Products
MGM Distribution
MGM Home Entertainment
MGM Interactive (video games)
MGM Music (soundtracks)
MGM Pictures
MGM Television Entertainment
MGM Worldwide Television Distribution
Movielink (20%)
United Artists

COMPETITORS

Disney Studios
DreamWorks
Fox Filmed Entertainment
Lions Gate Entertainment
Lucasfilm
NBC Universal
Paramount Pictures
Universal Studios
Warner Bros.

HISTORICAL FINANCIALS

Company Type: Private

Income Statement

FYE: December 31

	REVENUE ($ mil.)	NET INCOME ($ mil.)	NET PROFIT MARGIN	EMPLOYEES
12/04	1,725	(29)	—	1,440
12/03	1,883	(162)	—	1,280
12/02	1,654	(142)	—	1,150
12/01	1,388	(438)	—	1,050
12/00	1,237	51	4.1%	973
12/99	1,142	(531)	—	890
12/98	1,241	(158)	—	870
12/97	831	(128)	—	1,020
12/96	1,141	(745)	—	900
12/95	861	(169)	—	700
Annual Growth	**8.0%**	**—**	**—**	**8.3%**

2004 Year-End Financials

Debt ratio: 615.6%   Current ratio: 3.11
Return on equity: —   Long-term debt ($ mil.): 1,984
Cash ($ mil.): 117

Net Income History

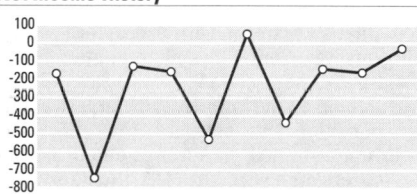

Metromedia

Metromedia Company has a lot of irons in a
lot of fires. The global giant is one of the US's
largest private companies. Subsidiary Metromedia International Group, a holding company in
which Metromedia owns a 20% stake, has interests in telecommunications ventures in Eastern Europe and the former Soviet Union,
including wireless and fixed-line phone and
cable TV systems. Other Metromedia units include Metromedia Restaurant Group, which
owns or franchises Ponderosa, Bennigan's, Bonanza, and Steak and Ale restaurants, and
Metromedia Energy, an independent energy
marketer. Chairman John Kluge and EVP and
partner Stuart Subotnick control about 20% of
Metromedia Company through a partnership.

Eatontown, New Jersey-based Metromedia
Energy delivers more than 20 billion cu. ft. per
year of commercial and industrial natural gas
to customers in the Northeast, Midwest, and
Mid-Atlantic.

In 2003 Metromedia sold a minority stake in
its restaurant subsidiary to Irving, Texas-based
Apex Restaurant Group, which assumed management of the chain operator.

HISTORY

German immigrant John Kluge, born in 1914,
came to Detroit at age eight with his mother and
stepfather. He later worked at the Ford assembly
line. At Columbia University he studied economics and (to the chagrin of college administrators)
poker, building a tidy sum with his winnings by

graduation. Kluge worked in Army intelligence
during WWII. After the war he bought WGAY
radio in Silver Spring, Maryland, and went on to
buy and sell other small radio stations.

Kluge began to diversify, entering the wholesale food business in the mid-1950s. In 1959 he
purchased control of Metropolitan Broadcasting, including TV stations in New York and
Washington, DC, and took it public. He renamed
the company Metromedia in 1960.

Metromedia added independent stations — to
the then-legal limit of seven — in other major
markets, paying relatively little compared to
network affiliate prices. The stations struggled
through years of infomercials but thrived in the
late 1970s and early 1980s. Metromedia's stock
price rose from $4.50 in 1974 to more than
$500 in 1983. The company also acquired
radio stations, the Harlem Globetrotters, and
the Ice Capades.

In 1983 Kluge bought paging and cellular telephone licenses across the US. He later acquired
long-distance carriers in Texas and Florida. In
1984 Metromedia went private in a $1.6 billion
buyout and began to sell off its assets in 1985. It
sold its Boston TV station to Hearst and its six
other TV stations to Rupert Murdoch for a total
of $2 billion. In 1986 it sold its outdoor advertis-
ing firm, nine of its 11 radio stations, and the
Globetrotters and Ice Capades. Kluge then sold
most of the company's cellular properties to SBC
Communications. In 1990 it sold its New York
cellular operations to LIN Broadcasting and its
Philadelphia cellular operations to Comcast.

Building what Kluge envisioned as his steak
house empire, the firm bought the Ponderosa
steak house chain (founded in the late 1960s) in
1988 from Asher Edelman and later added
Dallas-based USA Cafes (Bonanza steak houses,
founded 1964) and S&A Restaurant Corp. (Steak
and Ale, founded 1966; Bennigan's, founded
1976). Also in 1988 Kluge rescued friend Arthur
Krim, whose Orion Pictures was threatened by
Viacom, by buying control of the filmmaker.

Kluge's grand steak house vision did not come
to fruition. Increased competition squeezed profits at Ponderosa and Bonanza. The restaurant
group also was plagued by management shake-
ups, aging facilities, food-quality issues, and even
bad press. (Bennigan's was ranked the worst casual dining chain in the US in a 1992 Consumer
Reports poll.)

In 1989 Kluge merged Metromedia Long Distance with the long-distance operations of ITT.
Renamed Metromedia Communications in 1991,
the company merged with other long-distance
providers to become MCI WorldCom. (Kluge sold
his 16% of MCI WorldCom to the public in 1995.)

Kluge created Metromedia International
Group in 1995 by merging Orion Pictures,
Metromedia International Telecommunications,
MCEG Sterling (film and television production),
and Actava Group (maker of Snapper lawn mowers and sporting goods — sold 2002). Metromedia Restaurant Group announced a $190 million
refinancing agreement for S&A Restaurant Corp.
in 1998 to expand and refurbish its restaurants;
it closed 28 unprofitable restaurants that year
and launched a franchise program to grow its
Bennigan's and Steak and Ale chains.

Metromedia expanded its Bennigan's units in
South Korea in 1999 and the next year announced it would build 65 new restaurants in the
US and expand to more than 200 units internationally. In 2001 Verizon Communications invested nearly $2 billion in Metromedia unit
Metromedia Fiber Network (MFN), but MFN was

forced into Chapter 11 bankruptcy the following year. It blamed lower than expected demand for its metropolitan Internet services due to stiff competition, which drove down prices.

MFN (now AboveNet) emerged from bankruptcy in 2002 with a new owner. Kluge resigned from the Metromedia Fiber Network board that year and also stepped down from the Metromedia International Group board.

EXECUTIVES

Chairman and President: John W. Kluge, age 90
EVP; President and CEO, Metromedia International Group: Stuart Subotnick, age 63
SVP Finance and Treasurer: Robert A. Maresca
SVP, Secretary, and General Counsel: David A. Persing
SVP: Silvia Kessel
VP and Controller: David Gassler
VP Financial Reporting: Vincent D. Sasso Jr., age 42
VP: Mario P. Catuogno
Manager Human Resources: Jamie Smith-Wagner
Manager Pension and Profit Sharing: Patti Ann Kletz
CEO, Metromedia Restaurant Group: John J. Todd, age 44
Auditors: KPMG LLP

LOCATIONS

HQ: Metromedia Company
  1 Meadowlands Plaza, East Rutherford, NJ 07073
Phone: 201-531-8000   **Fax:** 201-531-2804

PRODUCTS/OPERATIONS

Selected Subsidiaries and Affiliates

Metromedia Energy, Inc. (independent energy marketer)
Metromedia International Group, Inc. (20%, telecommunications holdings)
Metromedia Restaurant Group (51%, Bennigan's, Bonanza, Ponderosa, and Steak and Ale owner and franchisee)

COMPETITORS

Applebee's	Lone Star Steakhouse
AT&T	MCI
Brinker	O'Charley's
BT	Outback Steakhouse
Buffets Holdings	Perkins
Carlson Restaurants	Rostelecom
Darden	Ryan's
Deutsche Telekom	Verizon
Hellenic	Worldwide
Telecommunications	Restaurant Concepts
Level 3 Communications	

HISTORICAL FINANCIALS

Company Type: Private

Income Statement

FYE: December 31

	ESTIMATED REVENUE ($ mil.)	NET INCOME ($ mil.)	NET PROFIT MARGIN	EMPLOYEES
12/03	1,500	—	—	25,500
12/02	1,450	—	—	29,500
12/01	1,400	—	—	28,500
12/00	1,500	—	—	29,500
12/99	1,610	—	—	32,000
12/98	1,500	—	—	62,700
12/97	1,950	—	—	63,000
12/96	1,900	—	—	
12/95	1,900	—	—	
12/94	2,000	—	—	
Annual Growth	(3.1%)	—	—	(14.0%)

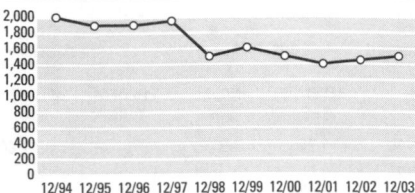

Revenue History

Metropolitan Transportation Authority

No Sigma Chi or Chi Omega chapter has anything on New York City's Metropolitan Transportation Authority (MTA) — it rushes millions of people on an average day. The largest public transportation system in the US, the government-owned MTA moves about 2.4 billion passengers a year. The MTA's New York City Transit Authority runs a fleet of about 4,900 buses in New York City's five boroughs, provides subway service to all but Staten Island, and operates the Staten Island Railway. Other MTA units offer bus and rail service to Connecticut and Long Island and maintains the Triborough system of toll bridges and tunnels.

The MTA, a public-benefit corporation chartered by the New York Legislature, is working to become more self-sufficient. It has attempted to cut expenses through more efficient administration and maintenance. But operating losses have persisted, and the MTA has increased fares and taken advantage of low interest rates to restructure its debt. The latest fare increase took effect in March 2005. The MTA also is considering bringing in cash by selling naming rights to subway stations, bus lines, bridges, and tunnels.

HISTORY

Mass transit began in New York City in the 1820s with the introduction of horse-drawn stagecoaches run by small private firms. By 1832 a horse-drawn railcar operating on Fourth Avenue offered a smoother and faster ride than its streetbound rivals.

By 1864 residents were complaining that horsecars and buses were overcrowded and that drivers were rude. (Horsecars were transporting 45 million passengers annually.) In 1870 a short subway under Broadway was opened, but it remained a mere amusement. Elevated steam railways were built, but people avoided them because of the smoke, noise, and danger from explosions. Cable cars arrived in the 1880s, and by the 1890s electric streetcars had emerged.

Construction of the first commercial subway line was completed in 1904. The line was operated by Interborough Rapid Transit (IRT), which leased the primary elevated rail line in 1903 and had effective control of rail transit in Manhattan and the Bronx. In 1905 IRT merged with the Metropolitan Street Railway, which ran most of the surface railways in Manhattan, giving the

firm almost complete control of the city's rapid transit. Public protests led the city to grant licenses to Brooklyn Rapid Transit (later BMT), creating the Dual System. The two rail firms covered most of the city.

By the 1920s the transit system was again in crisis, largely because the two lines were not allowed to raise their five-cent fares. With the IRT and BMT in receivership in 1932, the city decided to own and operate part of the rail system and organized the Independent (IND) rail line. Pressure for public ownership and operation of the transit system resulted in the city's purchase of all of IRT's and BMT's assets in 1940 for $326 million.

In 1953 the legislature created the New York City Transit Authority, the first unified system. In 1968, two years after striking transit workers left the city in a virtual gridlock, the Metropolitan Transit Authority began to coordinate the city's transit activities with other commuter services.

The 1970s and 1980s saw the city's transit infrastructure and service deteriorate as crime, accidents, and fares rose. But by the early 1990s a modernization program had begun to make improvements: Subway stations were repaired, graffiti was removed from trains, and service was extended. By 1994 the agency said subway crime was down 50% from 1990, and ridership had increased.

The MTA set up a five-year plan in 1995 to cut expenses by $3 billion. Only 18 months later and already two-thirds of the way to reaching the goal, the authority said it would cut another $230 million and return the savings to customers as fare discounts. The agency agreed in 1996 to sell Long Island Rail Road's freight operations. The next year it began selling its one-fare/free-transfer MetroCard Gold.

In 1998 the MTA capital program completed the $200 million restoration of the Grand Central Terminal. The next year the MTA ordered 500 new clean-fuel buses. But the agency suffered a setback when New York State's $3.8 billion Transportation Infrastructure Bond Act, which included $1.6 billion for MTA improvements, was rejected by voters in 2000.

MTA subway lines in lower Manhattan suffered extensive damage from the September 11, 2001, terrorist attacks that destroyed the World Trade Center's twin towers. The attacks left the MTA, which was already seeking billions of dollars for improvements, faced with $530 million worth of damage.

Confronted with a budget gap for the 2003 fiscal year, the MTA authorized the sale of nearly $2.9 billion worth of transportation bonds, the largest bond issue in the agency's history. The MTA had hoped the eventual proceeds from the bonds would help stave off a fare increase, but in 2003 the agency raised subway and bus fares from $1.50 to $2, among other fare and toll increases.

EXECUTIVES

Chairman: Peter S. Kalikow
Vice Chairman: Edward B. (Ted) Dunn
Vice Chairman: David S. Mack, age 62
Executive Director: Katherine N. Lapp, age 47
President, MTA Bus Company: Thomas J. Savage
CFO: Stephen L. Kessler
Corporate Secretary and Chief of Staff:
  Timothy A. O'Brien
Director of Budgets and Financial Management:
  Gary M. Lanigan

LOCATIONS

HQ: Metropolitan Transportation Authority
347 Madison Ave., New York, NY 10017
Phone: 212-878-7000   **Fax:** 212-878-0186
Web: www.mta.nyc.ny.us

PRODUCTS/OPERATIONS

Selected Operating Units

The Long Island Rail Road Company (MTA Long Island
Rail Road)
Metro-North Commuter Railroad Company (MTA Metro-
North Railroad)
Metropolitan Suburban Bus Authority (MTA Long Island
Bus)
New York City Transit Authority (MTA New York City
Transit)
Staten Island Rapid Transit Operating Authority (MTA
Staten Island Railway)
Triborough Bridge and Tunnel Authority (MTA Bridges
and Tunnels)

COMPETITORS

Amtrak
BostonCoach
Coach USA
Laidlaw International
Port Authority of NY & NJ
SuperShuttle International

HISTORICAL FINANCIALS

Company Type: Government-owned

Income Statement

	REVENUE ($ mil.)	NET INCOME ($ mil.)	NET PROFIT MARGIN	EMPLOYEES
12/04	4,837	83	1.7%	63,604
12/03	4,523	651	14.4%	63,884
12/02	4,053	360	8.9%	64,138
12/01	4,052	390	9.6%	64,169
12/00	4,033	(386)	—	62,800
12/99	5,590	(489)	—	58,000
12/98	5,707	(7)	—	57,551
12/97	5,511	(93)	—	57,563
12/96	5,381	440	8.2%	56,551
12/95	5,005	(154)	—	58,201
Annual Growth	(0.4%)	—	—	1.0%

2004 Year-End Financials

Debt ratio: 126.4%
Return on equity: 0.5%
Cash ($ mil.): 124
Current ratio: 1.02
Long-term debt ($ mil.): 22,243

Net Income History

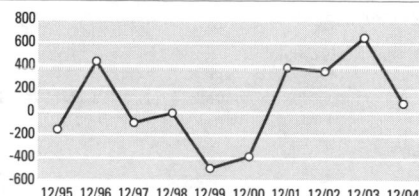

| 800 |
| 600 |
| 400 |
| 200 |
| 0 |
| -200 |
| -400 |
| -600 |

12/95 12/96 12/97 12/98 12/99 12/00 12/01 12/02 12/03 12/04

Michael Foods

With the help of willing hens, Michael Foods
is the leading US producer of egg products
(frozen, pre-cooked, dried). The food processor
and distributor has several divisions, but eggs account for 72% of its sales. Its Northern Star division pre-shreds and mashes potatoes. The
company also packages cheese and distributes
refrigerated foods. Customers include food
processors, foodservice distributors, and grocery
stores. The company sold its dairy products division (ice cream mixes, coffee creamers) to dairy
giant Dean Foods in 2003 for $155 million.
Thomas H. Lee Partners bought the company in
2003 from the Michael family and investors for
$1.05 billion.

EXECUTIVES

Chairman, President, and CEO: Gregg A. Ostrander,
age 52, $1,466,000 pay
COO: James D. Clarkson, age 52, $836,000 pay
EVP and CFO: John D. Reedy, age 59, $836,000 pay
SVP, Supply Chain: James G. Mohr, $349,630 pay
Treasurer and Secretary: Mark D. Witmer, age 47
Auditors: PricewaterhouseCoopers LLP

LOCATIONS

HQ: Michael Foods, Inc.
301 Carlson Pkwy., Ste. 400,
Minnetonka, MN 55305
Phone: 952-258-4000   **Fax:** 952-258-4911
Web: www.michaelfoods.com

Michael Foods has production facilities in Canada and
the US; it distributes its products in the US, with some
sales in Asia, Europe, and South America.

PRODUCTS/OPERATIONS

2004 Sales

	$ mil.	% of total
Egg products	941.4	72
Refrigerated distribution	288.3	22
Potato products	83.8	6
Total	**1,313.5**	**100**

Selected Brands

Egg products
  All Whites
  Better n Eggs
  Broke N' Ready
  Canadian Inovatech
  Centromay
  Chef's Omelet Brand
  Deep Chill
  Easy Eggs
  Emulsa

  Express Eggs
  Inovatech
  Logan Valley
  Michael Foods
  Quaker State Farms
  Simply Eggs Brand
  Sunny Side Up
  Table Ready

Potato products
  Diner's Choice
  Farm Fresh
  Northern Star
  Simply Potatoes
Refrigerated distribution
  Crystal Farms

Selected Products

Egg products
  Dried eggs
  Egg substitutes (Better 'n Eggs, All Whites)
  Extended shelf-life liquid eggs (Easy Eggs, Table
   Ready)
  Fresh eggs
  Frozen eggs
  Precooked eggs (hard boiled, patties, omelets)
Refrigerated potato products
  Hash browns
  Mashed potatoes
  Specialty potato products

COMPETITORS

Bob Evans
Cal-Maine Foods
Cargill
ConAgra
Heinz
JR Simplot
Kraft Foods
Land O'Lakes
McCain Foods
Primera Foods
Reser's
Rose Acre Farms
Sargento

HISTORICAL FINANCIALS

Company Type: Private

Income Statement

FYE: Saturday nearest December 31

	REVENUE ($ mil.)	NET INCOME ($ mil.)	NET PROFIT MARGIN	EMPLOYEES
12/04	1,314	34	2.6%	3,897
12/03	1,325	(23)	—	3,806
12/02	1,168	30	2.5%	4,371
12/01	1,161	4	0.4%	4,050
12/00	1,081	45	4.1%	4,100
12/99	1,053	44	4.2%	4,530
12/98	1,021	40	3.9%	4,160
12/97	956	32	3.4%	3,870
12/96	616	(3)	—	2,700
12/95	537	18	3.3%	2,600
Annual Growth	10.5%	7.4%	—	4.6%

2004 Year-End Financials

Debt ratio: 291.4%
Return on equity: 12.3%
Cash ($ mil.): 32
Current ratio: 1.35
Long-term debt ($ mil.): 750

Net Income History

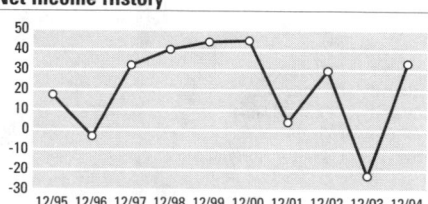

| 50 |
| 40 |
| 30 |
| 20 |
| 10 |
| 0 |
| -10 |
| -20 |
| -30 |

12/95 12/96 12/97 12/98 12/99 12/00 12/01 12/02 12/03 12/04

Michigan State University

The Spartan population is still growing today — in Michigan. With a population close to 45,000 students, Michigan State University dominates the small town of East Lansing. It offers more than 150 undergraduate programs among its 15 colleges and schools, with graduate and professional studies that include the arts, business, and law. The university also boasts three on-campus medical schools. MSU was founded in 1855 as a land-grant college under the name Agricultural College of the State of Michigan. It became a full university a century later.

EXECUTIVES

Chairperson: David L. Porteous, age 52
Vice Chairperson: Joel I. Ferguson, age 66
President: Lou Anna K. Simon
VP Academic Affairs and Provost: Kim Wilcox, age 51
Vice Provost for Libraries, Computing and Technology: David A. Gift
Assistant Provost and Dean of Graduate School: Karen L. Klomparens
Assistant Provost and Dean of Undergraduate Studies: June Youatt
Assistant Provost for Academic Services and University Registrar: Linda O. Stanford
Assistant Provost for University Outreach and Engagement: Hiram E. Fitzgerald
VP Finance and Operations and Treasurer: Fred L. Poston
VP Governmental Affairs: Steven M. Webster
VP Legal Affairs and General Counsel: Robert A. Noto
VP University Relations: Terry Denbow
Assistant VP, CFO, and Controller: David B. Brower
Assistant VP Finance and Operations: Kathryn E. Lindahl
Assistant VP Human Resources: Pamela S. Beemer
Auditors: KPMG LLP

LOCATIONS

HQ: Michigan State University
438 Administration Bldg., East Lansing, MI 48824
Phone: 517-355-6550   **Fax:** 517-355-9601
Web: www.msu.edu

COMPETITORS

Albion
Central Michigan University
Eastern Michigan University
Indiana University
Northwestern University
Ohio State University
Penn State University
Purdue University
UNC at Chapel Hill
University of Illinois
University of Iowa
University of Michigan
University of Minnesota
University of Pennsylvania
University of Virginia
University of Wisconsin-Madison

HISTORICAL FINANCIALS

Company Type: School

Income Statement

FYE: June 30

	REVENUE ($ mil.)	NET INCOME ($ mil.)	NET PROFIT MARGIN	EMPLOYEES
6/03	1,370	—	—	10,500
6/02	1,295	—	—	—
6/01	1,261	—	—	—
6/00	1,150	—	—	—
6/99	1,088	—	—	—
6/98*	1,034	—	—	—
8/97	973	—	—	—
8/96	946	—	—	—
8/95	902	—	—	—
Annual Growth	**5.4%**	—	—	—

*Fiscal year change

Revenue History

(chart: values 800–1,400 for 8/94 through 6/03)

Micro Electronics

There's nothing small about the way Micro Electronics sets up shop. The company has about 20 Micro Center computer retail stores which operate in about a dozen states. The stores range up to 62,000 sq. ft. and contain nearly 36,000 products organized in about a dozen specialized departments — an approach it calls "dedicated departments." Micro Electronics sells its own brands of notebook and desktop computers under the WinBook and PowerSpec names. Micro Center Online is the company's e-commerce operation. Micro Center was founded in 1979 by John Baker.

Store departments include PCs (desktops, laptops), Macintosh computers, digital imaging (cameras, camcorders), hardware (monitors, printers, keyboards), accessories (memory, CD and DVD drives), The Game Room (game systems and games), and supplies (blank media, printer cartridges). It even has a BYOPC (Build Your Own PC) department where customers can build a computer from scratch.

EXECUTIVES

Chairman, President, and CEO; President, Micro Center: Richard M. (Rick) Mershad
COO: Peggy Wolfe
CFO: James Koehler
VP Business Development: Kevin Hollingshead
VP Marketing: Mike Papai
VP Merchandising: Kevin Jones
CIO: Jim Gripshover
Chief CE Buyer: Sean Beaupre
Director, Human Resources: Angie Miller
Marketing Communications Manager: Ed Lukens

LOCATIONS

HQ: Micro Electronics, Inc.
4119 Leap Rd., Hilliard, OH 43026
Phone: 614-850-3000   **Fax:** 614-850-3001
Web: www.microelectronics.com

PRODUCTS/OPERATIONS

Selected Products

Accessories
  Cables
  Furniture
Books
Communications
  Handhelds
  PDAs
  Phones
Computers
  Desktops
  Notebooks
Digital imaging
  Camcorders
  Cameras
  Printers

Macintosh products
  Computers
  Notebooks
Peripherals
  Keyboards
  Monitors
  Printers
Software
Supplies
  Blank media
  Media storage
  Paper
  Printer cartridges
Upgrades
  Drives (CD, DVD)
  Memory

COMPETITORS

Best Buy
Buy.com
CDW
CompUSA
Dell
Fry's Electronics
Gateway
Insight Enterprises
PC Connection
RadioShack
Systemax

HISTORICAL FINANCIALS

Company Type: Private

Income Statement

FYE: September 30

	ESTIMATED REVENUE ($ mil.)	NET INCOME ($ mil.)	NET PROFIT MARGIN	EMPLOYEES
9/04	1,000	—	—	1,800
9/03	1,000	—	—	1,900
9/02	900	—	—	2,000
9/01	900	—	—	2,300
9/00	750	—	—	2,000
9/99	1,000	—	—	2,000
9/98	1,000	—	—	1,950
9/97	1,110	—	—	1,800
9/96	1,000	—	—	2,600
9/95	930	—	—	1,800
Annual Growth	**0.8%**	—	—	**0.0%**

Revenue History

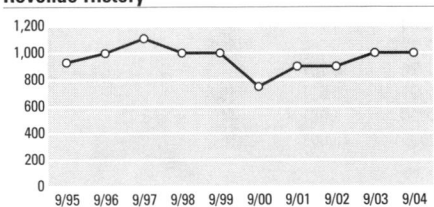

(chart: values 750–1,110 for 9/95 through 9/04)

MidAmerican Energy

There's a new kind of twister tearin' up Tornado Alley. MidAmerican Energy Holdings generates, transmits, and distributes electricity to 4.4 million customers and distributes natural gas to 680,000 customers in four Midwest states through subsidiary MidAmerican Energy Company. Its UK regional distribution subsidiaries, Northern Electric and Yorkshire Electricity, serve about 3.7 million electricity customers. MidAmerican Energy Holdings also has independent power production, real estate (HomeServices of America), and gas exploration, production, and pipeline operations. Warren Buffett's Berkshire Hathaway and other investors own the company.

MidAmerican Energy Company distributes electricity in Iowa, South Dakota, and Illinois, and it distributes natural gas in those three states plus Nebraska. It also generates 4,500 MW of electricity (primarily from coal-fired plants) and sells wholesale energy to other utilities and marketers. MidAmerican Energy Holdings' residential real estate brokerage, HomeServices of America (formerly HomeServices.Com), operates in 16 states in the US. Subsidiary CalEnergy has more than 2,000 MW of capacity from independent power projects in the US and the Philippines.

The company has signed a definitive agreement to acquire Oregon-based utility PacifiCorp, a subsidiary of Scottish Power, for a reported $9.4 billion (completion is expected by early 2006). Once complete, MidAmerican Energy Holdings will form a holding company that will serve approximately 3 million electric and natural gas customers.

MidAmerican Energy Holdings, which once focused on building and operating geothermal, hydroelectric, and natural gas power plants worldwide, now gets most of its revenues from its energy distribution operations. While deregulation led many regulated utilities into the independent power production business, MidAmerican Energy Holdings diversified by purchasing regulated utilities in the US and abroad. The company has also expanded its gas transportation operations through acquisitions; it operates nearly 18,000 miles of pipeline.

MidAmerican Energy Holdings was purchased by Berkshire Hathaway and other investors in 2000. Buffett owns about 10% of MidAmerican Energy Holdings. Buffett business partner and Berkshire director Walter Scott controls a majority of MidAmerican Energy Holdings' voting rights.

HISTORY

Amid oil shortages, polluted air, and concerns about the safety of nuclear power plants, Charles Condy formed California Energy in 1971 to sell oil and gas partnerships and to consult on the development of geothermal power plants.

In 1978 Congress passed the Public Utility Regulatory Policies Act (PURPA) to wean the US from foreign oil by encouraging efficient use of fossil fuels and development of renewable and alternative energy sources. Grasping the potential of the changing energy environment, CalEnergy signed a 30-year deal with the US government in 1979 to develop the geothermal Coso Project, northeast of Los Angeles. In the 1980s CalEnergy focused entirely on geothermal development and started producing power at the Coso Project in 1987, the year the company went public.

Omaha, Nebraska-based construction firm Peter Kiewit Sons' injected some much-needed capital when it began buying a stake in the company in 1990. CalEnergy restructured in 1991, moving its headquarters from San Francisco to Omaha. It also acquired Desert Peak and Roosevelt Hot Springs geothermal areas in the US and made plans to enter markets in Asia. In 1993 the Philippine government contracted CalEnergy to develop geothermal projects. CalEnergy also obtained the rights to exploit geothermal fields in Indonesia. In 1994 the company opened a geothermal plant in Yuma, Arizona.

In 1996 CalEnergy doubled its size by acquiring rival Magma Power, and it began geothermal projects in the Salton Sea and the Imperial Valley in California. It also took advantage of the growing deregulation trend in the UK by acquiring a controlling stake in Northern Electric, a major British regional electricity company with about 1.5 million customers in northeast England and Wales.

Completing its transformation into a global power player, CalEnergy acquired gas plants in Poland and Australia in 1997. It also attracted 300,000 new gas customers in the UK. The company bought back Kiewit's stake that year. In 1998 CalEnergy subsidiary CalEnergy International Ltd. was part of a consortium (the PowerBridge Group) that won a contract to develop, synchronize, and transmit up to 1,000 MW of electricity from Lithuania to Poland, at an estimated cost of $400 million.

The next year CalEnergy bought MidAmerican Energy Holdings, an electric utility, for about $2.4 billion. CalEnergy took the MidAmerican name and moved its headquarters to Des Moines, Iowa. Subsidiary MidAmerican Realty Services went public as HomeServices.Com; MidAmerican Energy Holdings retained a majority stake. In 2000 Warren Buffett's Berkshire Hathaway led an investor group, which included MidAmerican Energy Holdings CEO David Sokol, in purchasing MidAmerican Energy Holdings for about $2 billion and $7 billion in assumed debt.

In 2001 MidAmerican Energy Holdings bought out minority shareholders in HomeServices.Com, making it a wholly owned subsidiary. It also traded Northern Electric's electricity and gas retail supply operations for the distribution business of Yorkshire Electricity with Innogy (now RWE npower) in 2001.

The following year the company purchased The Williams Companies' Kern River Gas Transmission subsidiary, which operates a 926-mile interstate pipeline in the western US, in a $960 million deal. Also in 2002 MidAmerican Energy Holdings purchased the Northern Natural Gas pipeline from Dynegy for $928 million plus $950 million in assumed debt.

EXECUTIVES

Chairman and CEO: David L. Sokol, age 48, $3,300,000 pay
President, COO, and Director: Gregory E. Abel, age 42, $2,920,000 pay
SVP and CFO: Patrick J. Goodman, age 38, $585,000 pay
SVP, Communications, General Services, and Safety Audit and Compliance; SVP, MidAmerican Energy Company: Keith D. Hartje, age 54, $245,000 pay
SVP and Chief Procurement Officer: P. Eric Connor, age 52
SVP and General Counsel: Douglas L. Anderson, age 46, $510,000 pay

President and CEO, HomeServices of America: Ronald J. (Ron) Peltier
President and COO, CE Electric UK: Mark Horsley, age 45
President, CalEnergy US: Stefan Bird
President, CEGeneration Philippines: David A. Baldwin, age 40
President, Kern River Gas: Robert L. Sluder
President, MidAmerican Energy Company: Todd M. Raba, age 47
President, Northern Natural Gas: Mark A. Hewett
VP and Treasurer, MidAmerican Energy Company: Brian K. Hankel, age 42
VP and Controller, MidAmerican Energy Company: Thomas B. Specketer, age 47
VP Operations, Information Technology, and Engineering, Kern River Gas: Michael D. Falk
Director, Media Relations: Allan Urlis
Communications Manager: Mark Reinders
Wind Project Manager: Tom Budler
Auditors: Deloitte & Touche LLP

LOCATIONS

HQ: MidAmerican Energy Holdings Company
666 Grand Ave., Des Moines, IA 50309
Phone: 515-242-4300 **Fax:** 515-281-2389
Web: www.midamerican.com

MidAmerican Energy Holdings has energy operations in the US (Alabama, Arizona, California, Florida, Georgia, Illinois, Iowa, Kansas, Maryland, Minnesota, Missouri, Nebraska, North Carolina, South Dakota, Texas, and Utah), as well as in Australia, Bermuda, the Netherlands, the Philippines, Poland, and the UK.

PRODUCTS/OPERATIONS

2004 Sales

	$ mil.	% of total
MidAmerican Energy Co.	2,701.7	41
HomeServices	1,756.4	27
CE Electric UK	936.4	14
Northern Natural Gas	544.8	8
CalEnergy Generation		
Foreign	307.4	5
Domestic	39.0	1
Kern River	316.1	4
Adjustments	(48.4)	—
Total	**6,553.4**	**100**

Selected Subsidiaries

CalEnergy Generation — Domestic
  (independent power production)
CalEnergy Generation — Foreign (independent power production, the Philippines)
CE Electric UK Funding
  CalEnergy Gas (Holdings) Limited (exploration and production, Australia, Poland, and the North Sea)
  Northern Electric plc
    Northern Electric Distribution Ltd (NED, electricity distribution, UK)
  Yorkshire Electricity Group plc
    Yorkshire Electricity Distribution plc (YED, electricity distribution, UK)
HomeServices of America, Inc. (formerly HomeServices.Com, real estate brokerage)
Kern River Gas Transmission Company (natural gas pipeline)
MidAmerican Energy Company (electricity and natural gas distribution)
Northern Natural Gas Company (natural gas pipeline)

COMPETITORS

AES	Mirant
Alliant Energy	National Power
Ameren	Nebraska Public Power
Aquila	Nicor
Calpine	NRG Energy
Dynegy	Peoples Energy
Edison International	Scottish and
El Paso	Southern Energy
Entergy	Scottish Power
International Power	

HISTORICAL FINANCIALS

Company Type: Private

Income Statement
FYE: December 31

	REVENUE ($ mil.)	NET INCOME ($ mil.)	NET PROFIT MARGIN	EMPLOYEES
12/04	6,553	170	2.6%	11,540
12/03	6,145	416	6.8%	11,440
12/02	4,968	380	7.6%	10,985
12/01	5,337	143	2.7%	9,780
12/00	5,103	133	2.6%	9,550
12/99	4,399	167	3.8%	9,700
12/98	2,555	127	5.0%	3,703
12/97	2,166	(84)	—	4,300
12/96	519	93	17.8%	4,400
12/95	355	63	17.9%	593
Annual Growth	38.3%	11.6%	—	39.1%

2004 Year-End Financials

Debt ratio: 358.9%　　Current ratio: 0.83
Return on equity: 5.9%　　Long-term debt ($ mil.): 10,663
Cash ($ mil.): 961

Net Income History

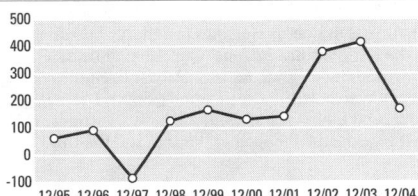

Midland Cogeneration Venture

Midland Cogeneration Venture has the power to go all the way. The company, formerly Midland Nuclear Power Plant, operates one of the largest cogeneration power plants in the US (at one time the largest gas-fired steam recovery power plant in the world). Midland Cogeneration Venture, with a generating capacity up to 1,500 MW, is responsible for about 11% of the electricity used in Michigan's lower peninsula. The company was the first nuclear power plant to be converted to one generating energy through more conventional means.

Midland Cogeneration Venture is jointly owned by CMS Energy (49%), El Paso Marketing (formerly El Paso Merchant Energy, 44%), and Dow Chemical (7%).

EXECUTIVES

President and CEO: James M. Kevra, age 56, $325,525 pay
VP, CFO, and Controller: James M. Rajewski, age 57, $250,331 pay
VP, General Counsel, and Secretary: Gary Pasek, age 49, $296,575 pay
VP, Human Resources, Communications, and Public Affairs: Bruce C. Grant, age 58, $154,433 pay
Treasurer: Laurie M. Valasek, age 37
Auditors: PricewaterhouseCoopers LLP

LOCATIONS

HQ: Midland Cogeneration Venture Limited Partnership
100 Progress Place, Midland, MI 48640
Phone: 989-839-6000　　**Fax:** 989-633-7935

COMPETITORS

ITC Holdings Corp.
Lansing Board of Water and Light
Wolverine Power Supply

HISTORICAL FINANCIALS

Company Type: Joint venture

Income Statement
FYE: December 31

	REVENUE ($ mil.)	NET INCOME ($ mil.)	NET PROFIT MARGIN	EMPLOYEES
12/04	650	(24)	—	113
12/03	584	60	10.2%	128
12/02	597	132	22.1%	131
12/01	611	48	7.9%	—
Annual Growth	2.1%	—	—	(7.1%)

Net Income History

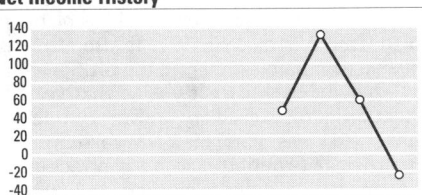

Midland Financial

Midland Financial is the holding company for MidFirst Bank and other financial services subsidiaries. One of the largest privately held banks in the US, MidFirst Bank has more than 40 branches throughout Oklahoma. It offers checking and savings accounts, CDs and IRAs, trust services, and mutual funds. In conjunction with its affiliate, Midland Mortgage, the bank has some 300,000 customers in 49 states. MidFirst Bank focuses on real estate lending — residential mortgages alone account for more than 70% of the bank's portfolio. Construction, commercial real estate, and multifamily residential real estate loans make up another 25%.

Midland has ventured outside its home state to open loan production offices in Phoenix and Denver. The company also is planning additional branches for Phoenix, Oklahoma City, and Tulsa, Oklahoma.

EXECUTIVES

Director; Chairman and CEO, MidFirst Bank:
George J. (Jeffrey) Records Jr., age 70
Director; President, MidFirst Bank: Robert F. (Bob) Dilg
EVP and CFO, MidFirst Bank: Todd A. Dobson
EVP, Mortgage Banking, MidFirst Bank; President, Midland Mortgage: Ken R. Clark
EVP, Retail Banking, MidFirst Bank: Dow R. Hughes
EVP, Commercial Banking, MidFirst Bank:
Alan H. Kraft
SVP, Administration, MidFirst Bank: Betty L. Rodgers
SVP and Chief Credit Officer, MidFirst Bank:
R. Wayne Booth
SVP, Commercial Banking, MidFirst Bank:
L. Randall Peck
SVP, Retail Banking, MidFirst Bank:
Garland W. Wilkinson
SVP and Treasurer, MidFirst Bank: Tim Tackett
SVP and Controller, MidFirst Bank: Stephen G. Martin
SVP, Human Resources, MidFirst Bank:
Dana M. Lorenson
VP and Marketing Director, MidFirst Bank:
Daniel Adams
Chairman and CEO, Midland Financial:
George J. Records Sr.

LOCATIONS

HQ: Midland Financial Co.
501 NW Grand Blvd., Oklahoma City, OK 73118
Phone: 405-840-7600　　**Fax:** 405-767-5426
Web: www.midfirst.com

PRODUCTS/OPERATIONS

2004 Sales

	$ mil.	% of total
Interest		
Loans	368.7	50
Investments & securities	187.8	26
Noninterest		
Loan administration	85.3	12
Other	90.5	12
Total	732.3	100

COMPETITORS

Arvest Holdings	Commercial Federal
BancFirst	International Bancshares
Bank of America	JPMorgan Chase
BOK Financial	UMB Financial

HISTORICAL FINANCIALS

Company Type: Private

Income Statement
FYE: December 31

	ASSETS ($ mil.)	NET INCOME ($ mil.)	INCOME AS % OF ASSETS	EMPLOYEES
12/04	9,509	372	3.9%	925
12/03	9,079	353	3.9%	1,036
12/02	8,575	222	2.6%	1,050
12/01	6,562	147	2.2%	885
Annual Growth	13.2%	36.3%	—	1.5%

2004 Year-End Financials

Equity as % of assets: 7.4%　　Long-term debt ($ mil.): 5,671
Return on assets: 4.0%　　Sales ($ mil.): 732
Return on equity: 56.2%

Net Income History

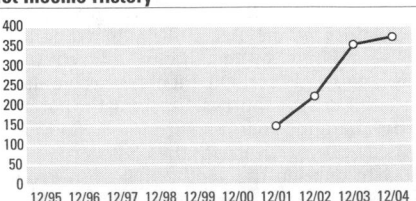

Midwest Research Institute

Midwest Research Institute (MRI) provides contract research services for private and government clients in the following areas: national defense, health sciences, agricultural and food safety, engineering, energy, environment, information technology, and analytical chemistry. The institute operates laboratories and agricultural research centers in Florida, Maryland, and Missouri. MRI also manages the US Department of Energy's National Renewable Energy Laboratory (NREL) located in Golden, Colorado. The not-for-profit organization was founded in 1944.

EXECUTIVES

Chairman: Louis W. Smith, age 62
Vice Chairman: William B. Neaves, age 62
President and CEO: James L. Spigarelli
CFO; Interim President, MRI Ventures:
Sandra A. J. Lawrence, age 47
SVP and Director Research Operations:
Michael F. Helmstetter
SVP; Director, National Renewable Energy Laboratory:
Dan E. Arvizu
Director Communications: Linda Cook
Director Corporate Human Resources and General Counsel: Gail M. Shrager

LOCATIONS

HQ: Midwest Research Institute
425 Volker Blvd., Kansas City, MO 64110
Phone: 816-753-7600 **Fax:** 816-753-8420
Web: www.mriresearch.org

HISTORICAL FINANCIALS

Company Type: Not-for-profit

Income Statement

FYE: June 30

	REVENUE ($ mil.)	NET INCOME ($ mil.)	NET PROFIT MARGIN	EMPLOYEES
6/04	288	—	—	1,500
6/03	270	—	—	1,200
Annual Growth	6.5%	—	—	25.0%

Revenue History

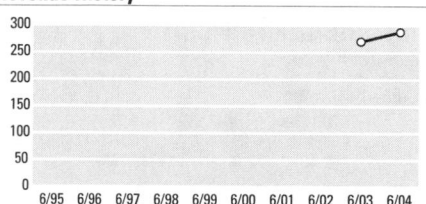

The Mighty Ducks of Anaheim

The Mighty Ducks have done all right despite not having Emilio Estevez as their coach. Entertainment goliath Walt Disney gave the world an example of life imitating art when it launched the National Hockey League expansion Mighty Ducks of Anaheim in 1993, taking the team's moniker from its 1992 hockey film. The Ducks made their first playoff appearance in 1997 and reached the Stanley Cup finals in 2003. (The team lost to the Dallas Stars.) Ticket sales, however, have not been buoyed much by the improvements on the ice, leading Disney to sell the team to billionaire Henry Samueli and his wife Susan in 2005.

After it launched the Ducks hockey franchise, Disney bought the Anaheim Angels baseball team as part of its expansion strategy. Its ABC and ESPN networks later paid $600 million for the television rights to hockey games, but ratings were so poor that ABC dropped out of the NHL broadcast scheme following the 2004 season. (Disney also sold the Angels.)

The Mighty Ducks lowered ticket prices for the 2005-06 season by 5%, and sales have picked up in spite of the last NHL labor dispute, which wiped out the entire 2004-05 season.

EXECUTIVES

Owner: Henry Samueli, age 50
Owner: Susan Samueli
CEO; and Chairman, Anaheim Arena Management:
Michael Schulman
EVP and COO; and President and CEO, Anaheim Arena Management: Tim Ryan
EVP and General Manager: Brian P. Burke, age 50
Assistant General Manager: David McNab
Head Coach: Randy Carlyle, age 49
SVP and Chief Marketing Officer: Bob Wagner
SVP and General Manager, Anaheim Arena Management: Mike O'Donnell
VP Sales and Marketing: Steve Obert
Director of Communications and Team Services:
Alex Gilchrist
Director of Finance: Mike McGee
Director of Human Resources: Jenny Price

LOCATIONS

HQ: The Mighty Ducks of Anaheim
2695 E. Katella Ave., Anaheim, CA 92806
Phone: 714-704-2700 **Fax:** 714-704-2754
Web: www.mightyducks.com

The Mighty Ducks of Anaheim play at the 17,174-seat capacity Arrowhead Pond of Anaheim in California.

COMPETITORS

Dallas Stars
Los Angeles Kings
Phoenix Coyotes
San Jose Sharks

HISTORICAL FINANCIALS

Company Type: Private

Income Statement

FYE: September 30

	REVENUE ($ mil.)	NET INCOME ($ mil.)	NET PROFIT MARGIN	EMPLOYEES
9/04	54	—	—	—
9/03	59	—	—	—
9/02	48	—	—	—
9/01	49	—	—	—
9/00	48	—	—	—
9/99	47	—	—	—
9/98	50	—	—	50
9/97	45	—	—	—
9/96	40	—	—	—
9/95	34	—	—	60
Annual Growth	5.3%	—	—	(5.9%)

Revenue History

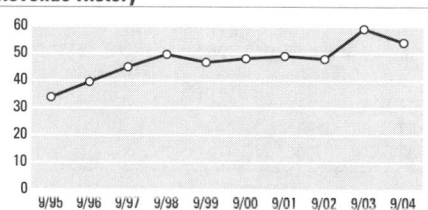

Milan Express Co.

This Milan Express is a trucking company from Tennessee, not a train from Rome. Milan Express provides less-than-truckload (LTL) and truckload freight transportation, along with logistics and warehousing and distribution services. The company operates primarily in the southeastern and midwestern US. Its service territory ranges from Florida to Wisconsin. Tommy Ross, now the chairman of Milan Express, founded the company in 1969 to serve an 87-mile route between Memphis and Milan, Tennessee. The Ross family owns the company, which has grown through acquisitions.

EXECUTIVES

Chairman: Tommy W. Ross
President: John W. Ross
CFO: Bruce F. Kalem
VP Corporate Services: Jim Szopinski
VP Distribution Services: Jeff Stinson
VP LTL Services: Robert Sullivan
VP LTL Sales and Marketing: Mitch Anderson
VP Operations, LTL Services: Mark Palmer
VP Properties: Barry Jones
VP TLS Services: Mike Stone
General Manager, Logistics: Roy Mabry
Manager, Payroll/Personnel: Debra Armstrong

LOCATIONS

HQ: Milan Express Co., Inc.
1091 Kefauver Dr., Milan, TN 38358
Phone: 731-686-7428 **Fax:** 731-686-8829
Web: www.milanexpress.com

HISTORICAL FINANCIALS

Company Type: Private

Income Statement

FYE: December 31

	REVENUE ($ mil.)	NET INCOME ($ mil.)	NET PROFIT MARGIN	EMPLOYEES
12/04	141	—	—	—
12/03	125	—	—	—
12/02	109	—	—	—
Annual Growth	**13.9%**	—	—	—

Revenue History

160
140
120
100
80
60
40
20
0

12/95 12/96 12/97 12/98 12/99 12/00 12/01 12/02 12/03 12/04

Milliken

Making tennis balls feel soft and Jell-O puddings taste smooth and creamy are just two of the things that Milliken & Company does. One of the world's largest textile companies, Milliken produces finished fabrics for rugs and carpets, as well as other synthetic fabrics used in such goods as apparel, automobiles, tennis balls, and specialty textiles. It also makes chemicals and petroleum products. Milliken's colorants infuse products such as Crayola markers, its clarifying agents make plastics clear, and its various other chemical products are used in the automotive, consumer products, and turf markets. Milliken operates more than 60 plants worldwide. The Milliken family controls the company.

Roger Milliken, a billionaire who is actively campaigning against the US trade policy and a fierce advocate for preserving American jobs, has led Milliken since 1947.

HISTORY

Seth Milliken and William Deering formed a company in 1865 to become selling agents for textile mills in New England and the southern US. Deering left the partnership, and in 1869 he founded Deering Harvester (now Navistar).

Milliken set up operations in New York before the turn of the century, began buying the ac-

counts receivable of cash-short textile mill operators, and invested in some of the companies.

In his position as agent and financier, Milliken was able to spot failing mills. He bought out the distressed owners at a discount and soon became a major mill owner himself. In 1905 Milliken and his allies waged a bitter proxy fight and court case to win control of two mills, earning Milliken a fearsome reputation.

H. B. Claflin, a New York dry-goods wholesaler that also operated department stores, owed money to Milliken. When Claflin went bankrupt in 1914, Milliken got some of the stores, which became Mercantile Stores. The Milliken family retained about 40% of the chain (sold to Dillard's in 1998).

Roger Milliken, grandson of the founder, became the president of the company in 1947 and has ruled with a firm hand. He fired brother-in-law W. B. Dixon Stroud in 1955, and none of Roger's children, nephews, or nieces has ever been allowed to work for the company. The workers at Milliken's Darlington, South Carolina, mill voted to unionize in 1956. The next day Milliken closed the plant, beginning 24 years of litigation that ended at the US Supreme Court. Milliken settled with its workers for $5 million.

In the 1960s the company introduced Visa, a finish for easy-care fabrics. Milliken launched its Pursuit of Excellence program in 1981; the program stressed self-managed teams of employees and eliminated 700 management positions. Tom Peters dedicated his 1987 bestseller, *Thriving on Chaos,* to Roger.

Away from that limelight, Milliken is (and has always been) a secretive, closely held business. In 1989 that secrecy and family control were threatened when members of the Stroud branch of the family sued the company in the Delaware courts and then sold a small number of shares to Erwin Maddrey and Bettis Rainsford, executives of Milliken competitor Delta Woodside. The courts ruled in favor of Milliken in 1992; Maddrey and Rainsford were required to sign confidentiality agreements before receiving Milliken information. Roger financially backed opponents of NAFTA in 1993.

Milliken is known by competitors for its unofficial motto: "Steal ideas shamelessly." Wovenfilament maker NRB sued Milliken in 1997 for corporate spying and the following year industrial textile maker Johnston Industries filed a similar lawsuit. Milliken settled both cases out of court.

In 1999 Milliken began using its Millitron dye technology to produce residential carpets and rugs. It also introduced new brands of patterned rugs (including Royal Dynasty, Prestige, American Heritage). In 2000 the company built a manufacturing facility in South Carolina to expand its production of Millard-brand clarifying agents. Milliken closed its Union and Saluda plants in 2004.

EXECUTIVES

Chairman and CEO: Roger Milliken
Vice Chairman: Thomas J. (Tom) Malone
President, COO, and CFO: Ashley Allen
VP, Human Resources: Tommy Hodge
VP, Quality & Milliken University: Craig Long
President, Milliken Chemical: John Rekers
Director, Public Affairs: Richard Dillard
Director, Safety and Health: Wayne Punch

LOCATIONS

HQ: Milliken & Company
 920 Milliken Rd., Spartanburg, SC 29304
Phone: 864-503-2020 **Fax:** 864-503-2100
Web: www.milliken.com

Milliken & Company has more than 60 manufacturing facilities worldwide, including operations in Australia, Belgium, Brazil, Denmark, France, Germany, Japan, Spain, the UK, and the US.

PRODUCTS/OPERATIONS

Selected Products

Chemicals
 Carpet cleaner (Capture)
 Clarifying agents for plastics (Millard)
 Colorants and tints (ClearTint, Liquitint,
  Palmer, Reactint)
 Electroconductive powders (Zelec)
 Resin intermediates
 Specialty chemicals
 Textile chemicals (Lubestat, SynFac, SynStat,
  Versatint)
 Turf maintenance chemicals
Fabrics, Carpet, and Rugs
 Area rugs
 Automotive fabrics
 Carpet and carpet tiles
 Drapery fabrics
 Knit and woven apparel fabrics
 Mats (Milliken KEX)
 Mops (Milliken KEX)
 Pool table cloth
 Table linen fabrics
 Tennis ball felt
 Towels
 Upholstery fabric

COMPETITORS

Asahi Kasei
Avondale Incorporated
Beaulieu
Burlington Industries
Collins & Aikman
Conso Products Company
Dixie Group
Dow Chemical
DuPont
Galey & Lord Swift Denim
Guilford Mills
Interface
Johnston Textiles
Mohawk Industries
Mount Vernon Mills
Reliance Industries
Shaw Industries
Springs Industries
W.L. Gore

HISTORICAL FINANCIALS

Company Type: Private

Income Statement

FYE: November 30

	ESTIMATED REVENUE ($ mil.)	NET INCOME ($ mil.)	NET PROFIT MARGIN	EMPLOYEES
11/03	3,400	—	—	14,000
11/02	3,600	—	—	14,000
11/01	3,900	—	—	20,000
11/00	4,000	—	—	21,000
11/99	3,500	—	—	18,000
11/98	3,100	—	—	16,000
11/97	3,200	—	—	16,000
11/96	3,000	—	—	15,000
11/95	2,800	—	—	13,500
11/94	2,706	—	—	13,500
Annual Growth	**2.6%**	—	—	**0.4%**

Revenue History

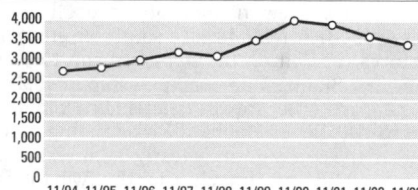

4,000
3,500
3,000
2,500
2,000
1,500
1,000
500
0

11/94 11/95 11/96 11/97 11/98 11/99 11/00 11/01 11/02 11/03

Milwaukee Bucks

The Milwaukee Bucks entered the NBA in 1968 and soon cashed in. After finishing its first season in last place, the team drafted Lew Alcindor (later Kareem Abdul-Jabbar), who wasted no time in leading the team to an NBA Championship in 1971. Abdul-Jabbar left for Los Angeles in a 1975 trade, and although the Bucks were somewhat successful in the late 1970s and 1980s under coach Don Nelson, they haven't won a championship since. After two consecutive playoff appearances, the Bucks are in a rebuilding phase and the team let go head coach George Karl (2003) then his replacement, former Portland Trail Blazer, Terry Porter (2005). Terry Stotts now holds the job. Sen. Herb Kohl of Wisconsin owns the Bucks.

EXECUTIVES

President and Owner: Herb Kohl
General Manager: Larry Harris
Assistant General Manager: Dan Kohl
Head Coach: Terry Stotts, age 47
Assistant Coach: Brian James, age 49
Assistant Coach: Lester Conner, age 46
Assistant Coach: Robert (Bob) Ociepka
Assistant Coach: Mike Sanders
CFO: Mike Burr
VP and Alternate Governor: Ron Walter
VP Business Operations: John Steinmiller
Director of Community Relations: Skip Robinson
Director of Finance: Jim Woloszyk
Director of Player Personnel: Dave Babcock
Director of Public Relations: Cheri Hanson
Director of Sales: Jim Grayson

LOCATIONS

HQ: Milwaukee Bucks
Bradley Center, 1001 N. 4th St.,
Milwaukee, WI 53203
Phone: 414-227-0500   **Fax:** 414-227-0543
Web: www.nba.com/bucks

The Milwaukee Bucks play at the 18,717-seat Bradley Center in Milwaukee.

PRODUCTS/OPERATIONS

Titles
NBA Champions (1971)
Western Conference Champions (1971, 1974)

COMPETITORS

Atlanta Hawks
Cavaliers/Gund
Chicago Bulls
Detroit Pistons
Indiana Pacers
New Orleans Hornets
Toronto Raptors

HISTORICAL FINANCIALS

Company Type: Private

Income Statement

FYE: June 30

	REVENUE ($ mil.)	NET INCOME ($ mil.)	NET PROFIT MARGIN	EMPLOYEES
6/04	77	—	—	—
6/03	70	—	—	—
6/02	67	—	—	—
6/01	65	—	—	—
6/00	55	—	—	50
6/99	26	—	—	50
6/98	43	—	—	38
6/97	36	—	—	
6/96	40	—	—	
Annual Growth	**8.5%**	**—**	**—**	**14.7%**

Revenue History

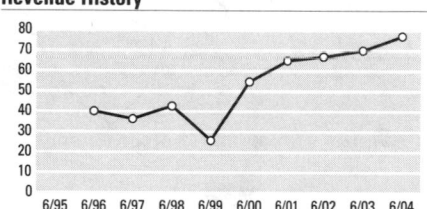

80
70
60
50
40
30
20
10
0

6/95 6/96 6/97 6/98 6/99 6/00 6/01 6/02 6/03 6/04

Minn-Dak Farmers Cooperative

Minn-Dak Farmers Cooperative is made up of farmers located in a nine-county area located in Minnesota, North Dakota, and South Dakota. The 488-member co-op processes beet crops into products such as molasses, pulp pellets, and sugar. Its subsidiary Minn-Dak Yeast produces fresh bakers' yeast.

EXECUTIVES

President and CEO: David H. Roche, age 57, $399,616 pay
EVP and CFO: Steven M. Caspers, age 54, $199,502 pay
VP, Agriculture: Thomas D. Knudsen, age 50, $137,084 pay
VP, Engineering: John R. Haugen, age 52, $131,900 pay
VP, Operations: Jeffrey L. (Jeff) Carlson, age 47, $140,901 pay
Director, HR: Greg J. Schmalz, age 53
Manager, Communications: Susan M. Johnson, age 57
Manager, Purchasing: John S. Nyquist, age 49
Controller and Chief Accounting Officer: Allen E. Larson, age 49, $131,193 pay
Assistant, Communications: Chris DeVries
Director, Safety: Kevin R. Shannon, age 50
Auditors: Eide Bailly LLP

LOCATIONS

HQ: Minn-Dak Farmers Cooperative
7525 Red River Rd., Wahpeton, ND 58075
Phone: 701-642-8411   **Fax:** 701-642-6814
Web: www.mdfarmerscoop.com

COMPETITORS

Amalgamated Sugar
American Crystal Sugar
Blanchard Valley Farmers Co-op
C&H Sugar
DeKalb Farmers Market
Farmers Cooperative Company
Florida Crystals
Imperial Sugar
SMBSC
United Farmers Cooperative

HISTORICAL FINANCIALS

Company Type: Cooperative

Income Statement

FYE: August 31

	REVENUE ($ mil.)	NET INCOME ($ mil.)	NET PROFIT MARGIN	EMPLOYEES
8/04	199	108	54.2%	284
8/03	194	110	56.6%	251
8/02	158	84	53.3%	—
Annual Growth	**12.2%**	**13.2%**	**—**	**13.1%**

Net Income History

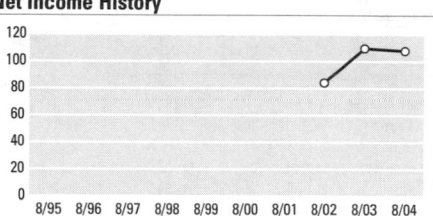

120
100
80
60
40
20
0

8/95 8/96 8/97 8/98 8/99 8/00 8/01 8/02 8/03 8/04

Minnesota Mutual

With 10,000 lakes in their state, Minnesotans have learned to be careful. Minnesota Mutual Companies helps them (and customers throughout the US) take care. Doing business as Minnesota Life, the company offers individual and group life and disability insurance and annuities, as well as retirement services and mortgage life insurance. The Advantus Capital Management unit provides mutual funds and institutional asset management services, while affiliated units of Securian Financial Group offer the company's insurance products, along with financial advisory, trust, and related services. Mutual holding company Minnesota Mutual Companies owns Minnesota Life through private stock company Securian Financial Group.

EXECUTIVES

Chairman, President, and CEO: Robert L. Senkler
EVP and Director: Robert E. Hunstad
EVP, Secretary, and General Counsel:
 Dennis E. Prohofsky
**EVP, Individual Financial Security and Retirement
 Services:** Randy F. Wallake
SVP, Financial Services: John F. Bruder
SVP, Securian Advisor Services: Thomas P. Burns
SVP, Human Resources and Corporate Services:
 Keith M. Campbell
SVP, Group Insurance: James E. Johnson
SVP, Asset Management: Dianne M. Orbison
SVP, Retirement Services: Bruce P. Shay
SVP and CFO: Gregory S. Strong
**VP and Actuary, Financial Services Financial
 Management:** Paul W. Anderson
**VP and Actuary, Retirement Services Financial
 Management:** Jenean C. Cordon
Second VP, Communications and Research:
 Mark B. Hier
Auditors: KPMG LLP

LOCATIONS

HQ: Minnesota Mutual Companies, Inc.
 400 Robert St. North, St. Paul, MN 55101
Phone: 651-665-3500   **Fax:** 651-665-4488
Web: www.minnesotamutual.com

Minnesota Mutual Companies operates nationwide and
in Puerto Rico.

PRODUCTS/OPERATIONS

2004 Sales

	$ mil.	% of total
Premiums	1,079.3	49
Net investment income	477.3	22
Policy & contract fees	381.9	18
Net realized investment gains	74.2	3
Commission income	65.4	3
Finance charge income	37.7	2
Other	64.5	3
Total	**2,180.3**	**100**

2004 Assets

	$ mil.	% of total
Separate account assets	9,563.4	44
Investments		
Fixed maturity securities		
available for sale	5,544.1	25
Fixed maturity securities on loan	1,152.1	5
Mortgage loans, net	810.5	4
Equity securities	749.9	3
Other	782.3	4
Securities held as collateral	1,276.8	6
Reinsurance recoverables	727.2	3
Deferred policy acquisition costs	721.4	3
Other	601.7	3
Total	**21,929.4**	**100**

COMPETITORS

American United Mutual
AmerUs
Conseco
COUNTRY Insurance
Guardian Life
Jefferson-Pilot
MetLife
National Western
Nationwide Life Insurance
New York Life
Northwestern Mutual
Pacific Mutual
Protective Life
Prudential
Torchmark

HISTORICAL FINANCIALS

Company Type: Private

Income Statement

FYE: December 31

	ASSETS ($ mil.)	NET INCOME ($ mil.)	INCOME AS % OF ASSETS	EMPLOYEES
12/04	21,929	137	0.6%	5,000
12/03	20,799	44	0.2%	4,400
12/02	17,695	4	0.0%	4,400
12/01	17,711	70	0.4%	4,400
12/00	17,900	235	1.3%	4,400
12/99	18,354	175	1.0%	4,400
12/98	16,434	163	1.0%	4,400
12/97	14,402	190	1.3%	2,187
12/96	12,443	131	1.0%	1,950
Annual Growth	**7.3%**	**0.6%**	**—**	**12.5%**

2004 Year-End Financials

Equity as % of assets: 10.7%   Long-term debt ($ mil.): 125
Return on assets: 0.6%   Sales ($ mil.): 2,180
Return on equity: 6.3%

Net Income History

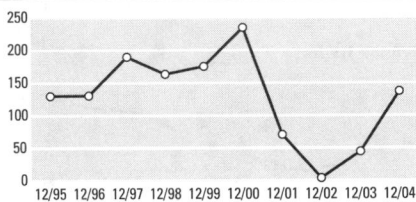

Minnesota Sports & Entertainment

The Stars might have gone to Dallas, but Minnesotans are still wild about hockey. Owned and operated by Minnesota Sports & Entertainment, the Minnesota Wild entered the National Hockey League in 2000 (along with the Columbus Blue Jackets), filling the void left after the Minnesota North Stars' franchise moved to Texas in 1993. Enthusiastic fans helped the Wild quickly set records for ticket sales by an expansion team, and the hockey faithful still come out in numbers despite the team's meager (but improving) results on the ice. Robert Naegele Jr., who once owned Rollerblade (now owned by the Benetton Group), controls the company, which also operates the team's Xcel Energy Center home arena.

The Wild has been one of the most financially successful expansion franchises in NHL history, boasting a string of sellouts and a list of more than 6,000 people waiting for season tickets.

Former North Stars owner Norm Green, and NHL officials, drew the ire of Minnesota hockey fans when their team headed south for greener pastures (in Dallas, the Stars went on to win their first Stanley Cup championship in 1999). Naegele and other investors, including Stanley Hubbard (CEO of Hubbard Broadcasting) and heirs of the Ordway family (early 3M investors), were awarded a new franchise for the Twin Cities market in 1997 as part of the league's expansion effort of the late 1990s.

EXECUTIVES

Chairman and Governor: Robert O. Naegele Jr.
Vice Chairman: Jac Sperling, age 56
President and General Manager: Doug Risebrough,
 age 51
Assistant General Manager of Hockey Operations:
 Tom Lynn, age 37
Assistant General Manager of Player Personnel:
 Tom Thompson, age 52
Head Coach: Rob Daum, age 47
Assistant Coach: Mike Ramsey, age 44
Assistant Coach: Mario Tremblay, age 49
EVP and CFO: Pamela Wheelock
EVP: Matt Majka, age 44
VP Administration: Mike Reeves, age 56
VP Communications and Broadcast: Bill Robertson,
 age 44
VP Sales and Service: Steve Griggs, age 37
VP Finance and Controller: Mike Nealy, age 40

LOCATIONS

HQ: Minnesota Sports & Entertainment
 317 Washington St., St. Paul, MN 55102
Phone: 651-602-6000   **Fax:** 651-222-1055
Web: www.wild.com

The Minnesota Wild play at the 18,064-seat
Xcel Energy Center in St. Paul, Minnesota.

COMPETITORS

Calgary Flames
Colorado Avalanche
Edmonton Oilers
Vancouver Canucks

HISTORICAL FINANCIALS

Company Type: Private

Income Statement

FYE: June 30

	REVENUE ($ mil.)	NET INCOME ($ mil.)	NET PROFIT MARGIN	EMPLOYEES
6/04	71	—	—	—
6/03	79	—	—	—
6/02	61	—	—	—
Annual Growth	**7.9%**	**—**	**—**	**—**

Revenue History

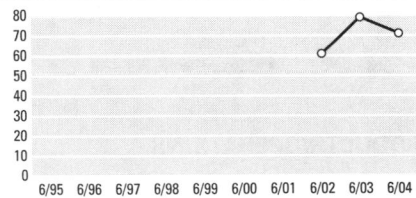

Minnesota Timberwolves

These wolves have basketball fans in the Twin Cities howling. The Minnesota Timberwolves franchise was awarded to local businessmen Harvey Ratner and Marv Wolfenson in 1988, returning NBA action to the Land of 10,000 Lakes for the first time since 1960, when the Minnesota Lakers (formed 1947) moved to Los Angeles. Former Minnesota Sen. Glen Taylor, chairman of printing giant Taylor Corporation, led a group of 14 investors who bought the team in 1995. After a heartbreaking string of first round playoff exits, the team advanced to the Western Conference Finals in 2004 behind the talents of MVP Kevin Garnett.

EXECUTIVES

Owner: Glen A. Taylor, age 63
President: Rob Moor
General Manager: James (Jim) Stack
VP Basketball Operations: Kevin McHale, age 47
Head Coach: Dwane Casey, age 48
VP Communications: Ted Johnson
VP Fan Relations: Jeff Munneke
VP Marketing: Jason LaFrenz
Director of Finance: Peter Stene
Timberwolves Strength and Conditioning Coach:
 Thomas McKinney
Assistant Coach: Johnny Davis, age 49
Assistant Coach: Jerry Sichting

LOCATIONS

HQ: Minnesota Timberwolves
 600 1st Ave. North, Minneapolis, MN 55403
Phone: 612-673-1600   **Fax:** 612-673-1699
Web: www.nba.com/timberwolves

The Minnesota Timberwolves play at the 18,500-seat Target Center in Minneapolis.

PRODUCTS/OPERATIONS

Titles
Midwest Division Champions (2004)

COMPETITORS

Denver Nuggets
Phoenix Suns
Portland Trail Blazers

San Antonio Spurs
Seattle SuperSonics
Utah Jazz

HISTORICAL FINANCIALS

Company Type: Private

Income Statement				FYE: June 30
	REVENUE ($ mil.)	NET INCOME ($ mil.)	NET PROFIT MARGIN	EMPLOYEES
6/04	97	—	—	—
6/03	85	—	—	—
6/02	85	—	—	—
6/01	77	—	—	—
6/00	70	—	—	—
6/99	42	—	—	70
6/98	52	—	—	65
6/97	44	—	—	60
6/96	47	—	—	—
Annual Growth	9.4%	—	—	8.0%

Revenue History

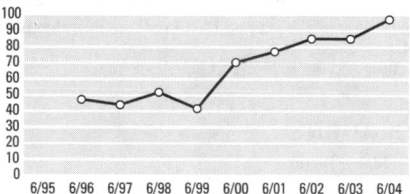

Minuteman International

Janitors with wood-handle mops and tin buckets dream about Minuteman International. The company makes commercial vacuums, floor and carpet care products, cleaning chemicals, biohazard vacuums, and litter vacuums, as well as lawn and carpet sweepers, scrubbers, and accessories. Brand names include Minuteman, Parker Sweeper, PowerBoss, and Multi-Clean. The company was founded in 1951 as American Cleaning Equipment Corporation. German cleaning equipment maker Hako-Werke International acquired Minuteman International in November 2004 and took it private.

The company has operations (manufacturing, warehouses) in the US (Illinois, Michigan, Minnesota, and North Carolina) and Toronto, Canada. It also has a subsidiary called Minuteman European B.V. in the Netherlands.

EXECUTIVES

President, CEO, and Director: Gregory J. Rau, age 45, $346,000 pay
VP, CFO, Secretary, Treasurer, and Director:
 Thomas J. Nolan, age 50, $216,000 pay
VP, Sales: Brian Slack, age 49
VP, Manufacturing: Dean W. Theobold, age 47, $173,000 pay
VP, Minuteman PowerBoss: James W. Van Dusen, age 45
VP, Multi-Clean Division: Michael A. Rau, age 44, $196,000 pay
Chief Accounting Officer: James A. Berg, age 40
Human Resources Manager: Kathy Duffy
Auditors: Ernst & Young LLP

LOCATIONS

HQ: Minuteman International, Inc.
 111 S. Rohlwing Rd., Addison, IL 60101
Phone: 630-627-6900   **Fax:** 630-627-1130
Web: www.minutemanintl.com

COMPETITORS

Aerus
Agri-Fab
BISSELL
HMI Industries
Royal Appliance
Tennant

HISTORICAL FINANCIALS

Company Type: Private

Income Statement				FYE: December 31
	REVENUE ($ mil.)	NET INCOME ($ mil.)	NET PROFIT MARGIN	EMPLOYEES
12/04	85	—	—	400
12/03	74	—	—	390
12/02	72	—	—	400
12/01	77	—	—	401
12/00	85	—	—	414
12/99	76	—	—	406
12/98	57	—	—	384
12/97	53	—	—	268
12/96	49	—	—	258
12/95	46	—	—	264
Annual Growth	7.0%	—	—	4.7%

Revenue History

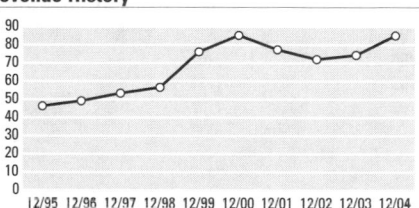

Mission Broadcasting

Mission Broadcasting finds that it's not impossible to broadcast TV in a handful of small and medium-sized markets. Mission owns and operates 14 television stations throughout the US. It has local service agreements with TV stations owned by Nexstar Broadcasting through which Nexstar provides programming, sales, and other services to Mission's stations. In 2005 Mission purchased WTVO, the ABC affiliate in Rockford, Illinois, from Young Broadcasting and Winnebago Television Corporation for about $21 million. President David Smith owns the company.

EXECUTIVES

President, Treasurer, and Director: David S. Smith, age 49, $330,000 pay
EVP and COO: Dennis Thatcher, age 57, $21,250 pay (partial-year salary)
VP and Secretary: Nancie J. Smith, age 51, $6,240 pay
Auditors: PricewaterhouseCoopers LLP

LOCATIONS

HQ: Mission Broadcasting, Inc.
 7650 Chippewa Rd., Ste. 305, Brecksville, OH 44141
Phone: 440-526-2227

Mission Broadcasting has TV stations in Illinois, Indiana, Kansas, Missouri, Montana, New York, Oklahoma, Pennsylvania, and Texas.

PRODUCTS/OPERATIONS

Selected Television Stations
KAMC (Lubbock, TX)
KHMT (Billings, MT)
KJTL (Wichita Falls, TX-Lawton, OK)
KODE (Joplin, MO-Pittsburg, KS)
KOLR (Springfield, MO)
KRBC (Abilene-Sweetwater, TX)
KSAN (San Angelo, TX)
WBAK (Terre Haute, IN)
WFXP (Erie, PA)
WTVO (Rockford, IL)
WUTR (Utica, NY)
WYOU (Wilkes Barre-Scranton, PA)

HISTORICAL FINANCIALS
Company Type: Private

Income Statement
FYE: December 31

	REVENUE ($ mil.)	NET INCOME ($ mil.)	NET PROFIT MARGIN	EMPLOYEES
12/04	37	(6)	—	31
12/03	28	(13)	—	99
12/02	28	(10)	—	—
Annual Growth	14.6%	—	—	(68.7%)

Net Income History

0
-2
-4
-6
-8
-10
-12
-14
12/95 12/96 12/97 12/98 12/99 12/00 12/01 12/02 12/03 12/04

MMI Products

No offense, but MMI Products likes concrete results. MMI operates in two segments: concrete construction products and fencing products. Concrete construction products include wire mesh and other products used to install reinforcing bars and grids. These products have applications in the construction of concrete pipe, bridges, and roads. The company's Merchants Metals fencing products include residential and commercial chain-link security fencing, aluminum and die-cast galvanized steel fencing fittings, and ornamental iron fence products. MMI sells its fencing products primarily to fence wholesalers and residential and commercial contractors. Court Square Capital controls about 66% of MMI's voting stock.

EXECUTIVES
Chairman: Julius S. Burns, age 72, $126,342 pay
President, CEO, and Director: John M. Piecuch, age 56, $1,762,600 pay
VP and CFO: Robert N. Tenczar, age 55, $302,025 pay
VP and Controller: Douglas L. White, age 36
VP, Manufacturing: Lyle D. Bumgarner, age 62
VP; President, Ivy Steel and Wire Division: James M. McCall, age 62, $369,300 pay
President Merchants Metals Division: Paul W. Harrison, age 56, $328,700 pay
President Meadow Burke Products Division: Walter E. Berner, age 52, $293,001 pay

---

Treasurer and Secretary: Tammy R. Hinkle, age 39
Director, Human Resources: Gary Hoffpauir
Sales Manager, Wood and PVC Products, Merchants Metals: Steve Colley
Auditors: Ernst & Young LLP

LOCATIONS
HQ: MMI Products, Inc.
400 N. Sam Houston Pkwy E., Ste. 1200, Houston, TX 77060
Phone: 281-876-0080 **Fax:** 281-876-1648
Web: www.merchantsmetals.com

MMI Products has 18 manufacturing plants and 63 distribution centers in the US and Mexico.

PRODUCTS/OPERATIONS

2004 Sales
	$ mil.	% of total
Concrete construction products	341.1	51
Fence products	332.8	49
Total	**673.9**	**100**

Selected Products
Aluminum die-cast fittings
Commodity building mesh
Galvanized chain-link fence fabric
Galvanized pressed-steel fittings
Heavy paving products
Masonry products
Ornamental iron fence products
Pipe mesh
Structural mesh
Vinyl-coated chain-link fence fabric
Vinyl-coated colored pipe
Vinyl fencing

COMPETITORS
Associated Materials	Keystone Consolidated
CertainTeed	Master-Halco
Dayton Superior	Oklahoma Steel and Wire
Insteel	Universal Forest Products

HISTORICAL FINANCIALS
Company Type: Private

Income Statement
FYE: Saturday closest to December 31

	REVENUE ($ mil.)	NET INCOME ($ mil.)	NET PROFIT MARGIN	EMPLOYEES
12/04	674	21	3.1%	2,300
12/03	503	(7)	—	2,300
12/02	505	(2)	—	2,400
12/01	502	10	2.0%	2,500
12/00	530	19	3.6%	2,590
12/99	481	19	3.9%	2,700
12/98	418	11	2.6%	2,200
12/97	347	8	2.2%	1,800
12/96	283	6	2.2%	1,400
12/95	201	—	—	1,282
Annual Growth	14.4%	16.2%	—	6.7%

2004 Year-End Financials
Debt ratio: 10,000.0%
Return on equity: —
Cash ($ mil.): 4
Current ratio: 3.36
Long-term debt ($ mil.): 304

Net Income History
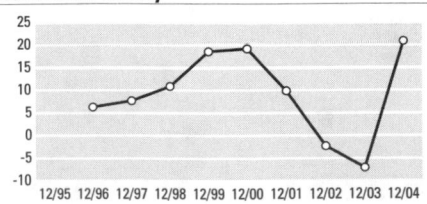

25
20
15
10
5
0
-5
-10
12/95 12/96 12/97 12/98 12/99 12/00 12/01 12/02 12/03 12/04

Model N

Model N wants to be your model of revenue management efficiency. The firm provides software that enables customers to align pricing, contract development and administration, payment of trade incentives, and government reimbursements. The company also offers professional services such as consulting, maintenance, installation, education, and support. Model N targets the life sciences industries; customers include Actelion, CoTherix, C.R. Bard, Boston Scientific, Medtronic, and Ortho-Clinical Devices. Model N has received funding from Accel Partners and Meritech Capital Partners.

EXECUTIVES
Chairman and CEO: Zack Rinat
COO: Kirk Bowman
VP Business Development: Nimrod Goor
VP Customer Services: Steven Yecies
VP Product Development: Yarden Malka
VP Sales and Marketing: Steve Zocchi
Corporate Controller: Annie Wayne
Director Human Resources: Rebecca Soler
Director National Sales: Robert Geist

LOCATIONS
HQ: Model N, Inc.
5000 Shoreline Ct., Ste. 301, South San Francisco, CA 94080
Phone: 650-808-8200 **Fax:** 650-808-8399
Web: www.modeln.com

PRODUCTS/OPERATIONS

Selected Software
Model N Compliance (compliance management)
Model N Contract (contract creation and management)
Model N Order (order management)
Model N Pricing (price plan creation, maintenance, and optimization)
Model N Reporting (reporting and analysis)

COMPETITORS
I-many
Metreo
SAP
Zilliant

HISTORICAL FINANCIALS
Company Type: Private

Income Statement
FYE: September 30

	ESTIMATED REVENUE ($ mil.)	NET INCOME ($ mil.)	NET PROFIT MARGIN	EMPLOYEES
9/04*	12	—	—	95
9/02	25	—	—	90
Annual Growth	(52.0%)	—	—	5.6%

*Irregular reporting interval

Revenue History
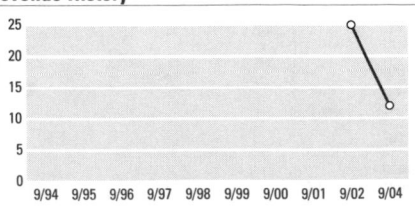

25
20
15
10
5
0
9/94 9/95 9/96 9/97 9/98 9/99 9/00 9/01 9/02 9/04

Mohegan Tribal Gaming

The sun also rises at Mohegan Sun Casino, a complex run by the Mohegan Tribal Gaming Authority for the Mohegan Indian tribe of Connecticut. The Native American-themed facility has about 6,100 slot machines, 280 tables, and simulcast horse race wagering. The facility also includes a 1,200-room luxury hotel, a 10,000-seat arena, a 300-seat cabaret, and dozens of stores and restaurants. Gambling revenues go to after-school and cultural programs for the tribe, financial assistance to other tribes, and college education for tribal members; a quarter of the slots revenue goes to the state.

In addition to operating casinos and hotels, the Mohegan Tribal Gaming Authority also owns the Connecticut Sun WNBA basketball team. Other operations include a subsidiary that plans to assist the Cowlitz Indian Tribe to open a casino in Clark County, Washington.

The company purchased horse racetrack Pocono Downs in Pennsylvania from Penn National Gaming for $175 million in early 2005. Plans call for building a gaming and entertainment facility on the site and renaming it Mohegan Sun at Pocono Downs.

EXECUTIVES

Chairman: Bruce (Two Dogs) Bozsum, age 45
Vice Chairman: Peter J. Schultz, age 50
CEO: William J. (Bill) Velardo, age 49, $1,440,000 pay
CFO: Leo M. Chupaska, age 56
President and CEO, Mohegan Sun: Mitchell G. Etess, age 46, $880,000 pay
EVP Finance and COO, Mohegan Sun:
 Jeffrey E. Hartmann, age 42, $855,000 pay
President and CEO, Pocono Downs: Robert J. Soper, age 32
SVP and CFO, Mohegan Sun: Alan J. Greenstein, age 45
SVP Food and Beverage, Mohegan Sun:
 Gary S. Crowder, age 54
SVP Hotel Operations, Mohegan Sun: Jon A. Arnesen, age 57, $275,000 pay
SVP Information Systems and CIO, Mohegan Sun:
 Daniel W. Garrow, age 54
SVP Marketing, Mohegan Sun: Michael W. Bloom, age 46, $319,000 pay
SVP Sports and Entertainment, Mohegan Sun:
 Paul S. Munick, age 51
Corresponding Secretary: Damon Damon-Murtha, age 56
Recording Secretary: Shirley M. Walsh, age 60
Treasurer: Maynard L. Strickland, age 64
Public Relations Ambassador, Mohegan Tribe:
 Jayne G. Fawcett, age 68
Auditors: PricewaterhouseCoopers LLP

LOCATIONS

HQ: Mohegan Tribal Gaming Authority
 1 Mohegan Sun Blvd., Uncasville, CT 06382
Phone: 860-862-8000   **Fax:** 860-862-7824
Web: www.mohegansun.com

PRODUCTS/OPERATIONS

2004 Sales

	$ mil.	% of total
Gaming	1,125.1	82
Retail & other	100.9	7
Food and beverage	89.9	7
Hotel	52.0	4
Adjustments	(111.0)	—
Total	**1,256.9**	**100**

Table Games

Baccarat
Blackjack
Caribbean stud poker
Craps
Pai Gow poker
Roulette

COMPETITORS

Aztar
Harrah's Entertainment
Mashantucket Pequot Gaming
Trump Resorts

HISTORICAL FINANCIALS

Company Type: Private

Income Statement

FYE: September 30

	REVENUE ($ mil.)	NET INCOME ($ mil.)	NET PROFIT MARGIN	EMPLOYEES
9/04	1,257	103	8.2%	10,300
9/03	1,189	96	8.1%	11,100
9/02	1,042	100	9.6%	10,203
9/01	787	205	26.0%	7,583
9/00	740	146	19.7%	6,202
9/99	682	(39)	—	5,703
9/98	575	(332)	—	5,065
9/97	466	37	7.9%	4,500
Annual Growth	**15.2%**	**15.9%**	**—**	**12.6%**

2004 Year-End Financials

Debt ratio: —
Return on equity: —
Cash ($ mil.): 61
Current ratio: 0.39
Long-term debt ($ mil.): 1,003

Net Income History

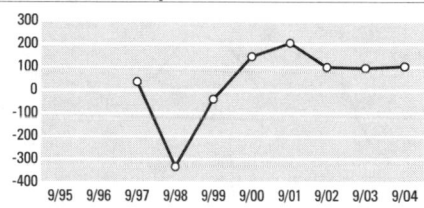

Monitronics

Monitronics International keeps its employees on guard while its customers are away. The company provides alarm system monitoring services to more than 470,000 customers throughout the US through its central monitoring station in Dallas. Monitronics operates through a network of authorized dealers, who sell, install, and service security systems and related equipment (manufactured by Ademco and GE Interlogix) to residential and commercial customers. Investors in Monitronics include ABRY Partners, Austin Ventures, and Capital Resource Partners. Monitronics was founded in 1994.

Nearly all of Monitronics' revenue is generated through its subscriber accounts, which are purchased from dealers in the company's network. The contracts generally run for three years.

Monitronics is working to acquire additional subscriber accounts from existing dealers and to expand its dealer network.

EXECUTIVES

President and CEO: James R. (Jim) Hull
VP and COO: Michael Haislip
VP and CFO: Michael R. Meyers
VP, Sales and Marketing: Michael Gregory
Director, Lead Development: Joe Russell
Regional Sales Director, West: Gordon Johnson
Regional Sales Manager, Northeast: Jason Keith
**Regional Sales Manager, Texas, New Mexico, and
 Oklahoma:** Chancy Pray
Human Resources: T. Harmon

LOCATIONS

HQ: Monitronics International, Inc.
 12801 N. Stemmons Fwy., Ste. 821,
 Dallas, TX 75234
Phone: 972-243-7443   **Fax:** 972-484-1393
Web: www.monitronics.com

COMPETITORS

ADT Security
Allied-Barton Security
Brink's Home Security
C.O.P.S. Monitoring
Honeywell ACS
Integrated Alarm
Protection One
Security Associates International

HISTORICAL FINANCIALS

Company Type: Private

Income Statement

FYE: June 30

	REVENUE ($ mil.)	NET INCOME ($ mil.)	NET PROFIT MARGIN	EMPLOYEES
6/04	150	(5)	—	500
6/03	126	4	3.0%	450
6/02	111	5	4.4%	467
Annual Growth	**16.2%**	**—**	**—**	**3.5%**

2004 Year-End Financials

Debt ratio: (463.7%)
Return on equity: —
Cash ($ mil.): 2
Current ratio: 0.74
Long-term debt ($ mil.): 379

Net Income History

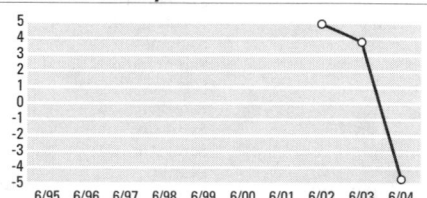

Morton's Restaurant Group

Morton's Restaurant Group offers eateries with an aura the Rat Pack would have loved. The company operates about 70 Morton's of Chicago locations in such cities as Atlantic City, Dallas, Los Angeles, New York, and, of course, Chicago. The well-known restaurants serve steak, lobster, and veal in an upscale setting featuring dark wooden interiors and background music by Sinatra. Morton's Restaurant Group also operates three more moderately priced Bertolini's Authentic Trattorias, which imitate the feel of an Italian street festival. The company is owned by private equity firm Castle Harlan.

Morton's intends to open five new restaurants nationwide by 2006. Each of the new units will include Morton's high-end bar concept, Bar 1221.

EXECUTIVES

Chairman, President, and CEO: Allen J. Bernstein, age 59, $1,146,000 pay
President, Morton's Steakhouse: Edie Garritano-Ames
Vice Chairman and President, Morton's of Chicago: Klaus W. Fritsch, age 62, $294,000 pay
EVP and CFO: Thomas J. Baldwin, age 49, $462,000 pay
SVP Development: Allan C. Schreiber, age 64, $281,000 pay
VP Communications: Roger J. Drake
VP Human Resources: Janet Hoffman
VP Marketing and Sales: Rick Weber
Director of Training: Steve Baker
Auditors: KPMG LLP

LOCATIONS

HQ: Morton's Restaurant Group, Inc.
3333 New Hyde Park Rd., Ste. 210,
New Hyde Park, NY 11042
Phone: 516-627-1515   **Fax:** 516-627-2050
Web: www.mortons.com

Select Markets

Atlanta	Minneapolis
Baltimore	Nashville
Beverly Hills, CA	New Orleans
Boca Raton, FL	New York
Boston	Orlando, FL
Charlotte, NC	Philadelphia
Chicago	Phoenix
Cincinnati	Pittsburgh
Cleveland	Portland, OR
Dallas	Sacramento, CA
Denver	San Antonio
Detroit	San Diego
Hackensack, NJ	San Francisco
Hartford, CT	San Juan, Puerto Rico
Honolulu	Santa Ana, CA
Houston	Seattle
Kansas City, MO	St. Louis
Las Vegas	Toronto
Los Angeles	Vancouver
Louisville, KY	Washington, DC
Miami	

COMPETITORS

Ark Restaurants	Palm Restaurants
B.R. Guest	Restaurant Associates
Cameron Mitchell	Restaurant
Restaurants	Development Group
CHT Corporation	Restaurants Unlimited
Clyde's Restaurant Group	Ruth's Chris Steak House
Il Fornaio	Smith & Wollensky
Keg Restaurants	Tavistock Restaurants
Levy Restaurants	Wolfgang Puck
Myriad Restaurant Group	

HISTORICAL FINANCIALS

Company Type: Private

Income Statement

	REVENUE ($ mil.)	NET INCOME ($ mil.)	NET PROFIT MARGIN	EMPLOYEES
12/04	276	2	0.6%	3,999
12/03	259	4	1.6%	3,859
12/02	238	(4)	—	4,000
12/01	237	1	0.4%	3,786
12/00	248	10	4.1%	3,696
12/99	207	8	4.1%	3,518
12/98	190	(2)	—	3,612
12/97	173	7	4.0%	3,312
12/96	193	2	0.9%	4,057
12/95	173	(14)	—	2,425
Annual Growth	5.3%	—	—	5.7%

FYE: Sunday nearest December 31

2004 Year-End Financials

Debt ratio: 101.0%
Return on equity: 1.7%
Cash ($ mil.): 10
Current ratio: 1.06
Long-term debt ($ mil.): 98

Net Income History

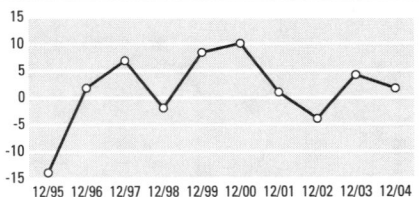

15									
10									
5									
0									
-5									
-10									
-15									

12/95 12/96 12/97 12/98 12/99 12/00 12/01 12/02 12/03 12/04

Motiva Enterprises

Making money is a major motive behind Motiva Enterprises, which operates the eastern and southeastern US refining and marketing businesses of Royal Dutch/Shell's Shell Oil unit and Saudi Aramco. The company operates three refineries with a total capacity of 865,000 barrels a day, and it sells fuel at 17,500 Shell and Texaco branded gas stations. In 2004 the company sold its Delaware refining complex to Premcor (now a part of Valero Energy) for $800 million. Motiva and sister company Shell Oil Products US (formerly Equilon), which operates in the West and Midwest, together make up the #1 US gasoline retailer. Motiva is a 50-50 joint venture of Shell and Saudi Aramco.

Motiva was formed in 1998 to combine the eastern and southeastern US refining and marketing businesses of Texaco, Shell Oil, and Saudi Aramco. Texaco and Saudi Aramco each owned

35% of Motiva, and Shell owned 30%. Texaco sold its stakes in Motiva (to Shell and Saudi Aramco) and Equilon (to Shell) to gain regulatory clearance to be acquired by Chevron. In 2002 Shell took full ownership of Equilon, which was renamed Shell Oil Products US.

HISTORY

Although Motiva was not created until the late 1990s, two of its key players, Texaco and Saudi Aramco, had been doing business together in various ventures since 1936. But they had never tried anything on the scale of the Star Enterprise joint venture approved by Texaco CEO James Kinnear and Saudi Oil Minister Hisham Nazer in late 1988. The deal, valued at nearly $2 billion, was the largest joint venture of its kind in the US.

The agreement to create Star Enterprise sprang, in part, from Texaco's tumultuous ride following its purchase of Getty Oil in 1983. Texaco was sued by Pennzoil for pre-empting Pennzoil's bid for Getty, and Pennzoil won a $10.5 billion judgment in 1985. Texaco filed for bankruptcy in 1987 and eventually settled with Pennzoil for $3 billion.

In 1988 Texaco emerged from bankruptcy after announcing a deal with Saudi Aramco at a stockholder meeting. Texaco got a much-needed injection of cash, and Saudi Aramco gained a steady US outlet for its supply of crude. The Saudis had been at odds with their OPEC partners for several years, and in late 1985 then-Saudi Oil Minister Sheikh Yamani and Saudi Aramco began increasing production, leading to an oil price crash in 1986. Nazer replaced Yamani and changed Saudi Aramco's strategy. To secure market share, the Saudis started signing long-term supply contracts.

The deal with Texaco gave Saudi Aramco a 50% interest in Texaco's refining and marketing operations in the East and on the Gulf Coast — about two-thirds of Texaco's US downstream operations — including three refineries and its Texaco-brand stations. In return, the Saudis paid $812 million cash and provided three-fourths of Star's initial inventory, about 30 million barrels of oil. They also agreed to a 20-year, 600,000-barrel-a-day commitment of crude. Each company named three representatives to Star's management.

The new company soon initiated a modernization and expansion program: It acquired 65 stations, built 30 new outlets, and remodeled another 172 during 1989. In 1994 the company began franchising its Texaco-brand Star Mart convenience stores. By mid-1995 it had sold 30 franchises.

Facing a more competitive oil marketing environment in the US, Shell Oil approached Texaco in 1996 with the possibility of merging some of their operations. In 1998 Shell and Texaco formed Equilon Enterprises, a joint venture that combined their western and midwestern refining and marketing activities.

Later that year Shell and Texaco/Saudi Aramco (Star Enterprises) formed Motiva to merge the companies' refining and marketing businesses on the East Coast and Gulf Coast. Shell and Texaco also formed two more Houston companies as satellite firms for Motiva and Equilon: Equiva Trading Company, a general partnership that provides supplies and trading services, and Equiva Services, which provides support services. Wilson Berry, the former president of Texaco Refining and Marketing, took over as CEO of Motiva.

In 1999 Motiva and Equilon together bought 15 product terminals from Premcor. To boost profits, the Motiva board appointed Texaco downstream veteran Roger Ebert as its new CEO in 2000, replacing Berry, who announced his resignation after a Motiva board meeting.

US government regulators in 2001 required that Texaco sell its Motiva and Equilon stakes in order to be acquired by Chevron. That year Texaco veteran John Boles replaced Ebert (who retired) as CEO. Shell and Saudi Aramco agreed to buy Texaco's stake in Motiva, and Shell agreed to buy Texaco's stake in Equilon. The deals were completed in 2002.

Boles retired in 2004.

EXECUTIVES

President and CEO: William B. (Bill) Welte
CFO: Ronald Langan
VP, Refining: Rudy Goetzee
VP, Commercial Marketing and Distribution: Ralph Grimmer
VP, Human Resources and Corporate Services: Elaine Guarrero
VP, Services: John Kiappes
VP, Supply: Brian Smith
VP, Retail: Ian Sutcliffe
Chief Diversity Officer: John Jefferson
General Manager Wholesale: Hugh Cooley
Treasurer and Director, Finance: James B. Castles
General Counsel: Lynda Irvine
General Manager, Business Development: Dan Grinstead
Business Ventures Manager, Florida: Joe Ahern
Business Ventures Manager, Texas: John Gray
Business Development Manager, Northeast: Steve Johnson
Business Development Manager, Mid Atlantic/Gulf Coast: Frank Rodriguez
Media Relations Advisor: Karyn Leonardi-Cattolica

LOCATIONS

HQ: Motiva Enterprises LLC
700 Milam St., Houston, TX 77002
Phone: 713-277-8000
Web: www.motivaenterprises.com

Motiva operates gas stations in the northeastern and southeastern US. It has refineries in Convent and Norco, Louisiana; and Port Arthur, Texas.

Major Operations

Alabama	New Hampshire
Arkansas	New Jersey
Connecticut	New York
Delaware	North Carolina
Florida	Pennsylvania
Georgia	Rhode Island
Louisiana	Tennessee
Maryland	Texas
Massachusetts	Vermont
Mississippi	Virginia

COMPETITORS

7-Eleven
BP
CITGO
Cumberland Farms
Exxon Mobil
Gulf Oil
Marathon Petroleum
Racetrac Petroleum
Sunoco
Valero Energy
Wawa, Inc.

HISTORICAL FINANCIALS

Company Type: Joint venture

Income Statement

FYE: December 31

	REVENUE ($ mil.)	NET INCOME ($ mil.)	NET PROFIT MARGIN	EMPLOYEES
12/03	19,300	—	—	3,600
12/02	16,700	—	—	3,800
12/01	18,000	—	—	5,000
12/00	19,446	—	—	8,000
12/99	12,196	—	—	6,000
12/98	5,371	—	—	3,750
Annual Growth	29.2%	—	—	(0.8%)

Revenue History

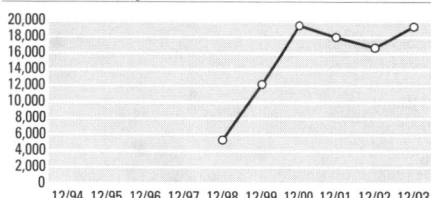

Mount Sinai Hospital

Mount Sinai Hospital opened its doors in 1919 with 60 beds to serve the burgeoning population of Eastern European immigrants in the Windy City. It is now a more than 430-bed teaching, research, and tertiary-care facility. Mount Sinai trains medical students from the Rosalind Franklin University of Medicine & Science (formerly the Finch University of Health Sciences/The Chicago Medical School). The hospital is a part of the Sinai Health System, which also includes the Schwab Rehabilitation Hospital, the Sinai Medical Group's primary-care clinics, and the Sinai Community Institute's health, wellness, and educational programs.

EXECUTIVES

Chairman: Bettylou K. Saltzman
President: Larry E. Volkmar
CFO: Charles (Chuck) Weis
VP, Corporate Services: David Hoekstra
Director, Human Resources: Andrew Wissle
Director, Risk Management: Robert Tarver
Auditors: Ernst & Young LLP

LOCATIONS

HQ: Mount Sinai Hospital
California Avenue at 15th Street, Chicago, IL 60608
Phone: 773-542-2000 **Fax:** 773-257-5145
Web: http://www.sinai.org/who/who_msh.asp

HISTORICAL FINANCIALS

Company Type: Not-for-profit

Income Statement

FYE: June 30

	REVENUE ($ mil.)	NET INCOME ($ mil.)	NET PROFIT MARGIN	EMPLOYEES
6/04	314	(6)	—	2,300
6/03	290	(16)	—	1,700
6/02	307	(12)	—	1,700
6/01	211	—	—	—
6/00	195	—	—	—
6/99	185	—	—	—
Annual Growth	11.1%	—	—	16.3%

Net Income History

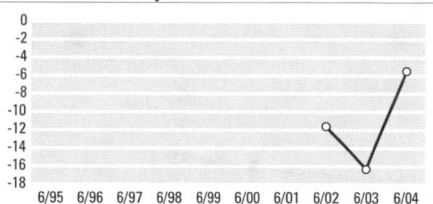

MTD Products

MTD Products wants to mow down its foes. The outdoor power equipment manufacturer makes walk-behind and tractor mowers, snow throwers, edgers, and tillers under the Cub Cadet, White Outdoor, Yard-Man, and Yard Machines brands. Its Cub Cadet line is aimed at landscapers. In 2001 MTD bought the Troy-Bilt tiller and mower business from Garden Way, which filed for bankruptcy. MTD was formed in 1932 by German immigrants Theo Moll, Emil Jochum, and Erwin Gerhard as the Modern Tool and Die Company. The Moll family, including CEO Curtis Moll, owns MTD.

EXECUTIVES

Chairman and CEO: Curtis E. Moll, age 66
CFO: Jeff Deuch
EVP Administration: Regis A. Dauk
EVP Marketing and Sales: Jean Hlay
EVP Operations and Global Supply: Theodore S. Moll, age 61
EVP Product Development: Hartmut Kaesgen
President Service: Gordon Manning
President Cub Cadet Corp.: Siva Sundarefan

LOCATIONS

HQ: MTD Products Inc.
5965 Grafton Rd., Valley City, OH 44280
Phone: 330-225-2600 **Fax:** 330-273-4617
Web: www.mtdproducts.com

MTD Products has manufacturing facilities in Canada, Europe, and the US.

COMPETITORS

Alamo Group	Exmark Manufacturing
Black & Decker	Honda
Blount	Metromedia International
Deere	Toro
Emak	

HISTORICAL FINANCIALS

Company Type: Private

Income Statement

FYE: July 31

	ESTIMATED REVENUE ($ mil.)	NET INCOME ($ mil.)	NET PROFIT MARGIN	EMPLOYEES
7/04	1,000	—	—	6,600
7/03	900	—	—	6,600
7/02	850	—	—	6,500
7/01	800	—	—	6,500
7/00	750	—	—	6,200
7/99	725	—	—	6,600
7/98	680	—	—	7,500
7/97	650	—	—	7,500
7/96	650	—	—	5,500
7/95	575	—	—	5,000
Annual Growth	6.3%	—	—	3.1%

Revenue History

1,000										
7/95	7/96	7/97	7/98	7/99	7/00	7/01	7/02	7/03	7/04	

Musicland

The Musicland Group prefers selling the blues, rather than singing them. As the top specialty retailer of prerecorded music and videos in the nation, the company operates more than 900 stores in nearly all 50 states, Puerto Rico, and the Virgin Islands. Its more than 450 Sam Goody mall-based stores sell new and vintage music, DVDs, videos, and other music-related items. The firm's stable of stores also includes about 400 Suncoast Motion Picture Company stores (videos, DVDs, magazines, movie memorabilia, and movie-themed apparel), also located in malls. Outside the mall, its 65-plus Media Play superstores offer music, videos, books, and software in more rural areas. Investment firm Sun Capital owns Musicland.

Media Play superstores average about 45,000 sq. ft., and in addition to their standard fare, sell musical instruments and toys.

In 2005 the company began experimenting with a new format for Sun Coast stores involving a brighter interior, better organization of products, and a home theater viewing area.

EXECUTIVES

Chairman and CEO: Jack Chadsey, age 57
President: Michael J. (Mike) Madden
CFO: Craig G. Wassenaar
CIO and SVP, Information Technology: Vladimir Bogdanov
SVP, Real Estate: Debra Brummer
SVP, Stores: Bruce Martin
SVP, Corporate Development: Rob Willey

VP, Human Resources: Curt Gray
VP and Controller: Doug Hamlin
VP and In-House Counsel: Kristin Peterson LeBre
VP, Marketing: Brian Miller
VP, Corporate Development: Aurora Toth
Public Relations: Laurie Bauer

LOCATIONS

HQ: The Musicland Group, Inc.
10400 Yellow Circle Dr., Minnetonka, MN 55343
Phone: 952-931-8000   **Fax:** 952-931-8300
Web: www.musicland.com

COMPETITORS

Amazon.com
Barnes & Noble
Blockbuster
Books-A-Million
Borders
Buy.com
CDNOW
Columbia House
CompUSA
Hastings Entertainment
Hollywood Entertainment
Kmart
Movie Gallery
Target
Tower Records
Trans World Entertainment
Virgin Group
Wal-Mart
Wherehouse Entertainment

HISTORICAL FINANCIALS

Company Type: Private

Income Statement

FYE: February 28

	REVENUE ($ mil.)	NET INCOME ($ mil.)	NET PROFIT MARGIN	EMPLOYEES
2/04	1,400	48	3.4%	8,500
2/03	1,727	(441)	—	10,000
2/02*	1,886	—	—	12,500
12/00	1,900	—	—	15,000
12/99	1,892	—	—	15,900
12/98	1,847	—	—	15,600
12/97	1,768	—	—	16,400
12/96	1,822	—	—	15,900
12/95	1,723	—	—	17,000
12/94	1,479	—	—	16,000
Annual Growth	(0.6%)	—	—	(6.8%)

*Fiscal year change

Net Income History

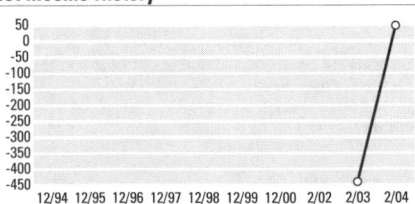

50									
12/94	12/95	12/96	12/97	12/98	12/99	12/00	2/02	2/03	2/04

Mutual of Omaha

In the wild kingdom that is today's insurance industry, The Mutual of Omaha Companies wants to distinguish itself from the pack. The company provides individual health and accident coverage (via subsidiary Mutual of Omaha Insurance); its United of Omaha Life Insurance unit offers life insurance and annuities. The firm also offers personal disability coverage, brokerage services, pension plans, mutual funds, and a range of employee benefits products and services. Mutual of Omaha, which is owned by its policyholders, offers its products mainly through agent networks.

In the health insurance arena, traditional indemnity insurers have less power to bargain for low-cost services and consequently have found themselves at a disadvantage against clout-wielding and increasingly cost-minded managed care organizations; state laws mandating coverage for persons regardless of underwriting policy have exacerbated the situation. Mutual of Omaha is exiting the health business in some areas and is adding managed care services. It is focused on growing its health care networks internally, rather than by acquisition, to ensure its standards are met. These networks are largely in underserved rural areas, where the firm has kept a strong presence. The insurer is also working to increase sales of its life insurance and annuities products.

Focusing on its core individual and employer-based lines, the company sold property & casualty and flood insurance operations to Fidelity National Financial. The UK's Beazley Group is buying subsidiary Omaha Property and Casualty Company.

Mutual of Omaha is involved in wildlife conservation and protection. Starting with sponsorship of the long-running *Mutual of Omaha's Wild Kingdom*, this interest has evolved into a grant and scholarship program run by the company's Wildlife Heritage Center.

HISTORY

Charter Mutual Benefit Health & Accident Association got its start in Omaha, Nebraska, in 1909. A year later half of its founders quit, leaving a group headed by pharmaceuticals businessman H. S. Weller in charge. He tapped C. C. Criss as principal operating officer, general manager, and treasurer. Criss brought in his wife, Mabel, and brother Neil to help run the business.

Formed to offer accident and disability protection at a time when there were many fraudulent benefit societies, Charter Mutual Benefit Health faced consumer resistance that slowed growth in its first 10 years. By 1920 it was licensed in only nine states. Experience helped it refine its products and improve its policies' comprehensibility. By 1924 the firm had more than doubled its penetration, gaining licensing in 24 states.

The US was nearing the depths of the Depression when Weller died in 1932. Criss succeeded him as president. The stock crash had brought a steep decline in the value of the firm's asset base, and premium income dropped (accompanied by an increase in claims). Even so, Mutual Benefit Health expanded its agency force, the scope of its benefits, and its operations. It went into Canada in 1935 and began a campaign to obtain licensing throughout the US.

By 1939 the company was licensed in all 48 states. During WWII it wrote coverage for civilians killed or injured in acts of war in the US (including Hawaii) and Canada. With paranoia running high and consumer goods in short supply, the insurance industry boomed during the war (and payouts on stateside act-of-war claims were low to nonexistent). Criss retired in 1949.

Gearing up its postwar sales efforts, in 1950 the company changed its name to Mutual of Omaha and adopted its distinctive chieftain logo. During the 1950s it added specialty accident and group medical coverage. In 1963 it made an advertising coup when it launched *Mutual of Omaha's Wild Kingdom.* Hosted by zoo director Marlin Perkins and, later, naturalist sidekick Jim Fowler, the show was one of the most popular nature programs of all time. Later that decade the company added investment management to its services.

Changes in the health care industry during the 1990s led Mutual of Omaha to de-emphasize its traditional indemnity products in favor of building managed care alternatives. In 1993 it joined with Alegent Health System to form managed care company Preferred HealthAlliance. Mutual of Omaha also stopped writing new major medical coverage in such states as California, Florida, New Jersey, and New York, where state laws made providing health care onerous. This led the company to cut its workforce by about 10% in 1996.

In 1999 it bought out Alegent's interest in their joint venture and entered the credit card business (offering First USA Visa cards). The firm also lifted its $25,000 limit for coverage of AIDS-related illnesses (its standard limit is $1 million); the company had been sued over the policy.

EXECUTIVES

Chairman and CEO: Daniel P. (Dan) Neary, age 53
EVP and CFO: David A. Diamond, age 49
EVP and Chief Actuary: Cecil D. Bykerk
EVP, Information Services: James L. Hanson
EVP, Corporate Services and Corporate Secretary: M. Jane Huerter
EVP, Group Benefit Services: Daniel Martin
EVP, Government Affairs: William C. Mattox
EVP and General Counsel: Thomas J. McCusker
EVP, Treasurer, and Comptroller: Tommie D. Thompson
EVP, Individual Financial Services: Mike Weekly
EVP and Chief Investment Officer; President, Mutual of Omaha Investor Services: Richard A. (Rick) Witt
SVP, Information Services: Steve Clauson
SVP, Group Health Plans: Joe Connolly
SVP, Special Markets: Gil Peers
SVP, Human Resources: Stacy Sholtz
SVP, Group Specialty Products: Robert Taylor
Auditors: Deloitte & Touche LLP

LOCATIONS

HQ: The Mutual of Omaha Companies
Mutual of Omaha Plaza, Omaha, NE 68175
Phone: 402-342-7600   **Fax:** 402-351-2775
Web: www.mutualofomaha.com

The Mutual of Omaha Companies operate throughout the US.

PRODUCTS/OPERATIONS

2004 Assets

	$ mil.	% of total
Investments		
Fixed maturities available for sale	12,972.6	70
Mortgage loans	866.8	5
Limited partnerships	306.6	2
Short-term investments	213.2	1
Policy loans	165.4	1
Other	66.0	—
Separate account assets	1,353.8	7
Deferred policy acquisition costs	1,300.3	7
Other	1,295.5	7
Total	**18,540.2**	**100**

2004 Sales

	$ mil.	% of total
Health & accident	1,742.4	47
Life & annuity	1,020.9	28
Net investment income	820.8	22
Other	98.2	3
Adjustments	(26.7)	—
Total	**3,655.5**	**100**

Selected Services and Products

401(k) plans
Annuities
Critical illness insurance
Defined benefit plans
Dental insurance
Disability insurance
Health & wellness programs
Health insurance products
Investments
Life insurance
Long-term-care insurance
Medicare supplement insurance
Prescription plans
Property & casualty insurance
Travel insurance

Selected Subsidiaries and Affiliates

Companion Life Insurance Company
innowave incorporated (water purification products)
Mutual of Omaha Insurance Company
Mutual of Omaha Investor Services, Inc. (mutual funds)
Omaha Property and Casualty Insurance Company
United of Omaha Life Insurance Company
United World Life Insurance Company

COMPETITORS

Aetna
Allstate
American National Insurance
Assurant
AXA Financial
Blue Cross
CIGNA
CNA Financial
Guardian Life
John Hancock Financial Services
Liberty Mutual
MassMutual
MetLife
Morgan Stanley
New York Life
Northwestern Mutual
Prudential
State Farm
USAA

HISTORICAL FINANCIALS

Company Type: Mutual company

Income Statement

FYE: December 31

	ASSETS ($ mil.)	NET INCOME ($ mil.)	INCOME AS % OF ASSETS	EMPLOYEES
12/04	18,540	125	0.7%	—
12/03	18,444	170	0.9%	5,847
12/02	15,203	(14)	—	6,600
12/01	11,533	49	0.4%	6,600
12/00	14,465	156	1.1%	7,000
12/99	13,959	90	0.6%	7,000
12/98	13,231	117	0.9%	7,111
12/97	12,639	181	1.4%	7,309
12/96	11,726	105	0.9%	7,047
12/95	10,659	122	1.1%	8,163
Annual Growth	6.3%	0.3%	—	(4.1%)

2004 Year-End Financials

Equity as % of assets: 17.7%
Return on assets: 0.7%
Return on equity: 3.8%
Long-term debt ($ mil.): 0
Sales ($ mil.): 3,656

Net Income History

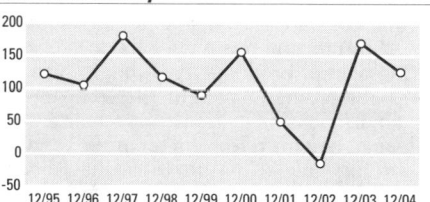

Muzak

The hills are alive with the sound of Muzak. Once the king of canned music, the company is working to transform its image. Muzak, famous for its instrumental versions of pop tunes, has turned its focus away from the elevator rider and toward the consumer as it pumps original songs (with lyrics) into retail stores, restaurants, and bars, as well as hotels, offices, and factories. It delivers about 70 programs via satellite, DVDs, Internet, and broadband connectivity. Some 100 million people hear Muzak tunes each day. The company also sells sound systems, intercoms, on-hold and in-store messaging systems, satellite TV programming, and plasma TVs. Media investment firm ABRY Partners owns a majority of Muzak.

Muzak made numerous acquisitions in the late 1990s and hopes to restore profitability by renewing its focus on its core services. Having suffered a decades-long stigma, the company's efforts to banish its reputation as a cheesy elevator-music label include hiring a design firm to overhaul its brand; moving its corporate headquarters to a futuristic-style building; and unveiling a re-designed corporate Web site.

Muzak brings music into homes via EchoStar Communications' DISH Network. However, the company continues to focus on commercial clients, and is played in retail outlets such as Gap, Barnes & Noble, and McDonald's.

Executive Lon Otremba joined the company from America Online in 2003. He became Muzak's CEO the following year. Also in 2004 he announced the addition of 150 jobs at the company's headquarters.

HISTORY

George Squier patented a system for transmitting phonograph music over electrical lines in 1922. He sold the rights to utility North American Company, and together they formed a subsidiary to begin testing the system in Cleveland. In 1934 Squier coined the term Muzak ("muz" from music and "ak" from Kodak, his favorite company) before he died that year. The company moved to New York in 1936.

During the 1930s Muzak was used in then-newfangled elevators to calm riders (hence the term "elevator music"). In 1938 Warner Bros. bought the company but sold it the next year to US Senator William Benton. Experiments showed that music could increase productivity, and during WWII Muzak systems were installed in factories.

After the war the company continued to work on "stimulus progression" — the idea of regulating worker productivity through music. In 1972 Teleprompter bought the company and began distributing its music via satellite. Westinghouse bought Teleprompter in 1981 and sold it to Marshall Field V in 1986. Field bought Seattle-based Yesco, a producer of "foreground" music for retailers, and merged the two the next year. Led by Yesco's management, Muzak began updating its sound to appeal to baby boomers. Field sold Muzak to its management and New York investment firm Centre Capital in 1992.

In 1996 the company called off plans to go public. Saddled with debt from the buyout and mounting losses, it ousted CEO John Jester in 1997 and replaced him with Bill Boyd, who refocused Muzak on its core music business. During 1998 the company began buying competitors and its own independent affiliates. In 1999 it merged with Audio Communications Network, a Muzak franchiser owned by media investment firm ABRY Partners, and the Muzak affiliates owned by Capstar (Capstar later became part of AMFM, which was subsequently acquired by radio station owner Clear Channel). Later that year Muzak made a string of acquisitions, including Data Broadcasting's (now Interactive Data Corporation) InStore Satellite Network, a music and ad business.

In 2000 Muzak moved its headquarters to Fort Mill, South Carolina. Extending its acquisitive streak, the company acquired Telephone Audio Productions (audio marketing and messaging) and Muzak franchisee Vortex Sound Communications.

EXECUTIVES

Chairman Emeritus: William A. (Bill) Boyd, age 62, $412,665 pay
CEO: Greg Rayburn
COO and CFO: Stephen P. (Steve) Villa, age 40, $319,746 pay
SVP Client Relations: Mary Ann Lusk
SVP Product and Marketing: Kenneth F. (Kenny) Kahn, age 41, $199,329 pay
SVP Sales: Scott Wolf
SVP Strategy and Brand: Alvin Collis

VP and Secretary: Peni A. Garber, age 42
VP, General Counsel, and Assistant Secretary: Michael F. Zendan II, age 40, $125,000 pay
CTO: David M. Moore, $119,995 pay
Treasurer: Catherin Walsh
Director Corporate Communications: Sumter Cox
Auditors: PricewaterhouseCoopers LLP

LOCATIONS

HQ: Muzak LLC
3318 Lakemont Blvd., Fort Mill, SC 29708
Phone: 803-396-3000   **Fax:** 803-396-3095
Web: www.muzak.com

PRODUCTS/OPERATIONS

2004 Sales

	$ mil.	% of total
Music & related services	184.4	75
Equipment sales & related services	61.5	25
Total	**245.9**	**100**

Selected Products

Audio Architecture (music programming)
Voice (music and messages for phone systems)

Selected Music Genres

Classical
Country
Jazz
Latin
Mature adult
Oldies
Popular contemporary
Popular contemporary instrumental
Specialty
Urban

COMPETITORS

DMX MUSIC	PlayNetwork
Music Choice	TM Century

HISTORICAL FINANCIALS

Company Type: Private

Income Statement

FYE: December 31

	REVENUE ($ mil.)	NET INCOME ($ mil.)	NET PROFIT MARGIN	EMPLOYEES
12/04	246	(46)	—	1,436
12/03	235	(35)	—	1,505
12/02	218	(30)	—	1,491
12/01	203	(44)	—	1,347
12/00	192	(44)	—	1,395
12/99	130	(22)	—	1,324
12/98	100	(12)	—	1,041
12/97	91	(13)	—	667
12/96	87	(11)	—	751
12/95	87	(6)	—	715
Annual Growth	**12.3%**	—	—	**8.1%**

2004 Year-End Financials

Debt ratio: —
Return on equity: —
Cash ($ mil.): —
Current ratio: —
Long-term debt ($ mil.): 429

Net Income History

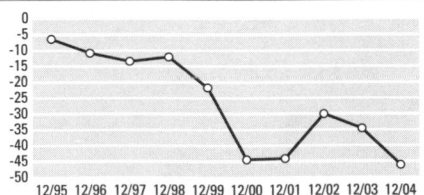

NAACP

The NAACP makes doubly sure that everyone is treated equally. The organization strives to ensure that all people are represented and have equal rights in American society and culture, regardless of race. The group works via political lobbies, legislation, speakers, and education and publishes *Crisis Magazine*. It registers African Americans to vote, encourages academic achievement among high-school students, and works with inmates to promote education and reduce recidivism. More than 500,000 people are members of the NAACP which was founded as the National Association for the Advancement of Colored People in 1909 by a group including W.E.B. DuBois, Thurgood Marshall, and Ida Wells-Barnett.

EXECUTIVES

Chairman: Julian Bond
Vice Chairwoman: Roslyn McCallister Brock
President: Bruce S. Gordon, age 59
COO: Rev Nelson B. Rivers III
Secretary: Angela Ciccolo
Treasurer and Director: Francisco L. Borges, age 53
General Counsel: Dennis C. Hayes
Assistant Treasurer: Jesse Turner Jr.
Special Assistant for Community Affairs and Director: Carolyn Q. Coleman

LOCATIONS

HQ: NAACP
4805 Mt. Hope Dr., Baltimore, MD 21215
Phone: 410-521-4939   **Fax:** 410-585-1310
Web: www.naacp.org

HISTORICAL FINANCIALS

Company Type: Association

Income Statement

FYE: December 31

	REVENUE ($ mil.)	NET INCOME ($ mil.)	NET PROFIT MARGIN	EMPLOYEES
12/04	28	—	—	138
12/03	42	—	—	138
Annual Growth	**(18.8%)**	—	—	**0.0%**

Revenue History

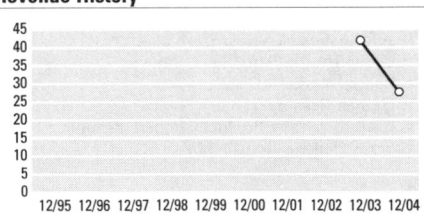

NASCAR

In the race for respectability in the sports world, NASCAR is on the right track. The National Association for Stock Car Auto Racing is one of the fastest-growing spectator sports in the US. NASCAR runs more than 100 races each year across the US through three racing circuits: the Busch, Craftsman Truck, and its signature Nextel Cup Series (formerly the Winston Cup). The Nextel Cup, featuring popular drivers like Jeff Gordon and Dale Jarrett, alone draws more than 7 million race fans each year. NBC, FOX, and Turner Broadcasting have taken note, paying $2.4 billion for broadcast rights. NASCAR was founded in 1948 by Bill France Sr. and is still owned by the France family.

Even though the networks have lost money on the NASCAR contract, they still have plenty of reason to be optimistic about the future of the partnership. Heading into the 2005 season, NASCAR ratings were second only to the NFL. In addition, as a younger generation of drivers pull in new fans (of which NASCAR says it has about 75 million), the sport's made inroads into parts of the country beyond its traditional fan base of the southern US.

NASCAR moved races out of some of the smaller markets for the 2004 season, a change that drew loud protests from racetrack owner and rival Speedway Motorsports. The France family also controls publicly traded International Speedway Corporation (ISC), the largest racetrack owner in the US. The reschedulings benefited International Speedway tracks, and a Speedway Motorsports shareholder filed a lawsuit against NASCAR on antitrust grounds. The parties settled the lawsuit by ISC selling North Carolina Speedway to Speedway Motorsports.

And in a surprise move, R.J. Reynolds dropped out as the sponsor for the title Winston Cup series. The tobacco company's wallet has seen better days thanks to tobacco lawsuits and restricted advertising. Reynolds had been the sponsor of the title race since 1971. Cell phone company Nextel signed a massive 10-year, $750 million deal with NASCAR to become the new sponsor. The agreement has silenced critics who question the racing circuit's longevity, as the Nextel deal is the biggest sports sponsorship deal in history.

NASCAR also changed its point system for the Nextel Cup. Under the new system, after 26 races the 10 leading drivers, and any other driver within 400 points of the leader, are eligible for the "Chase for the Championship." Those drivers then have their points adjusted so they can all be on more equal footing heading into the season's final races. The changes were spurred by a desire to make the late season races more exciting when NASCAR is forced to compete with the NFL and the World Series for television viewers.

HISTORY

Bill France Sr. founded the National Championship Stock Car Circuit (NCSCC) in 1947 as a place for ex-Prohibition-era moonshine runners to show off their driving skills. France, the son of a Washington, DC, banker, was a skilled mechanic and racecar builder. In 1934 he moved his family to Daytona Beach, Florida, which was nirvana for racecar drivers who used the hard beach as a speedway.

The City of Daytona Beach in 1938 approached France, who by then owned a successful gas sta-

tion and mechanic shop frequented by racers, and asked him to organize a race. France rounded up drivers and solicited local businesses to donate prizes such as beer and cigars. The event drew 4,500 fans. He organized another race the following year and turned a profit of a few thousand dollars.

WWII interfered with France's racing career when he was drafted and sent to work in a shipyard. Upon his return, lacking the money to put another race together in Florida, he sponsored a national championship race for stock cars (cars with standard auto bodies not specially designed for racing) in North Carolina. Since there was no national body governing the races and setting rules, France's championship idea drew little enthusiasm. So in 1947 he formed the NCSCC and set up a point system for drivers and a fund for prize money. Seeking to expand NCSCC's powers, France in 1948 gathered 35 prominent racing figures from all over the US, and they organized to form the National Association for Stock Car Auto Racing (NASCAR), of which France was elected president.

France tirelessly promoted the sport with the help of racetrack owners wanting NASCAR to make their races official, and as a result the sport grew rapidly in the 1950s and 1960s. Racetrack owners began upgrading their facilities or building new ones with paved tracks to replace the older dirt tracks. France in 1957 convinced Daytona Beach to allow him to replace the city's original beach track with a 2.5-mile paved raceway. It opened two years later to a crowd of 42,000.

In 1972, as France got more involved in operating specific tracks and having less time to focus on NASCAR, he passed the business on to his son, Bill France Jr. Bill Jr. signed R.J. Reynolds as a major sponsor in 1971, and NASCAR held the Winston 500 (the first incarnation of today's Winston Cup series) in Talladega, Alabama.

The company's first televised race, the Daytona 500, aired on the CBS Television Network in 1979 and drew about 16 million viewers. Cable sports network ESPN also began airing races in 1981. NASCAR came into its own as a major sports player in 2000 when NBC, FOX, and Turner Broadcasting agreed to pay the company $2.4 billion for the circuit's broadcasting rights until 2006. (FOX later extended its agreement until 2008.) And the inherent danger of stock car racing began to hit home with the racing related deaths of popular drivers such Adam Petty in 2000 and Dale Earnhardt in 2001.

In 2003 Bill France Jr. handed reins of the company to son Brian France by promoting him to chairman and CEO. Bill Jr. remains vice chairman. Also that year R.J. Reynolds dropped out as the sponsor for the Winston Cup series after more than 30 years with the race. Cell phone company Nextel took over as the new sponsor with the signing of a 10-year, $750 million deal.

The following year NASCAR announced that its Busch racing series would hold a race in Mexico City during the 2005 season, marking the first points-paying international event in about 50 years.

EXECUTIVES

Chairman and CEO: Brian Z. France, age 42
Vice Chairman: William C. (Bill) France Jr., age 70
Vice Chairman, EVP, and Secretary: Jim France
President: Mike Helton
SVP and COO: George Pyne
CFO, NASCAR, NASCAR Broadcasting, and NASCAR Digital Entertainment: R. Todd Wilson, age 41

VP Broadcasting: Paul Brooks
VP Competition: Robin Pemberton, age 48
VP Corporate Administration: Ed Bennett
VP Corporate Communications: Jim Hunter
VP Finance: Doris Rumery
VP Licensing and Consumer Products: Mark Dyer
VP Research and Development: Gary Nelson
President and CEO, NASCAR Images: Jay Abraham
Corporate Counsel: Gary Crotty
Treasurer: Tom Bledsoe
Managing Director of Brand and Consumer Marketing: Roger VanDerSnick
Director of Corporate Sales: Dan Lynch
Director of Human Resources: Starr George
Senior Public Relations Manager, Nextel Cup Series: John Dunlap

LOCATIONS

HQ: National Association for
Stock Car Auto Racing, Inc.
1801 W. International Speedway Blvd.,
Daytona Beach, FL 32115
Phone: 386-253-0611   **Fax:** 386-681-4041
Web: www.nascar.com

PRODUCTS/OPERATIONS

Selected Races
Busch Series
  Carquest Auto Parts 300
  Food City 250
  Ford 300
  Pepsi 300
  Sam's Town 300

Craftsman Truck Series
  Chevy Silverado 150
  Dodge Ram Tough 200
  Ford 200
  MBNA 200
  Toyota Tundra 200

Nextel Cup Series
  Coca-Cola 600
  Daytona 500
  Gatorade Duel at Daytona
  Pepsi 400
  Subway 500

COMPETITORS

AFL	NFL
Indy Racing League	NHL
Major League Baseball	World Wrestling
NBA	Entertainment

HISTORICAL FINANCIALS

Company Type: Private

Income Statement

FYE: December 31

	ESTIMATED REVENUE ($ mil.)	NET INCOME ($ mil.)	NET PROFIT MARGIN	EMPLOYEES
12/02	3,000	—	—	450
12/01	2,500	—	—	400
12/00	2,000	—	—	350
12/99	1,500	—	—	300
12/98	2,000	—	—	
Annual Growth	10.7%	—	—	14.5%

Revenue History

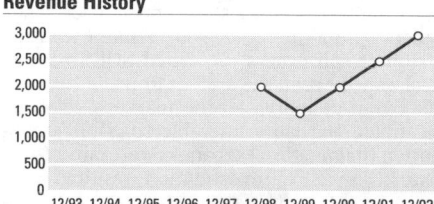

NASD

Bull market or bear, NASD will be there. NASD (previously The National Association of Securities Dealers) is the former parent of the #3 US stock market, the American Stock Exchange (AMEX), and former parent of the #2 market, Nasdaq. (Nasdaq was spun off through a series of private sales and now trades OTC; NASD still holds 55% of its stock.) Since Nasdaq's spinoff was completed in 2002, NASD has coped with its emptier nest by concentrating on its regulatory functions. Per SEC orders, NASD Regulation oversees OTC securities trading and disciplines traders; virtually all US securities dealers are members.

Even without stock market subsidiaries, NASD has plenty to keep it busy. More than 5,000 brokerages and some 660,000 registered securities representatives are under its jurisdiction. NASD writes rules, conducts investigations, and disciplines firms or individuals that don't comply. NASD also operates arbitration and mediation programs and offers educational services to industry professionals and to investors.

NASD in 2003 had planned to sell AMEX to GTCR Golder Rauner, but decided to sell AMEX to its members when the deal died.

HISTORY

NASD was founded in 1939 as a self-regulating entity for over-the-counter (OTC) securities traders who dealt directly with companies or with market makers authorized to trade their stock. Traders shopped by phone to get the best price from the market makers, and up-to-date OTC quotes were unobtainable. NASD set trading qualifications, administered licensing tests, set standards for underwriting compensation, and disciplined wayward traders.

In 1963 the SEC asked NASD to develop an automated OTC quotations system. Work began in 1968 on facilities in Trumbull, Connecticut, and Rockville, Maryland. The system went online in 1971 and soon turned into an electronic trading medium because it made dealer quotes more competitive and instantly visible. By 1972 volume exceeded 2 billion shares, and two years later the Nasdaq claimed a share volume nearly one-third of the New York Stock Exchange's. By 1980 it reported having almost 60% of the NYSE's volume, although Nasdaq counted both sides of many trades.

In 1975 Congress gave NASD responsibility for regulating the municipal securities market and asked the SEC to develop a national market system for share trading. The SEC handed the task to NASD. The market started trading in 1982 with 40 stocks, establishing a two-tier system: one for the crème de la crème, such as Microsoft, and one for smaller or newer issues. The system is continually updated; new technology made it a model for other markets.

To improve responsiveness to small investors, NASD instituted the SOES (small order entry system) after the 1987 stock crash, when many traders bailed themselves out before executing customer sell orders. So-called SOES bandits (dealers who used the system to make frequent small trades) increased the market's volatility and made Nasdaq vulnerable to NYSE's contention that auction exchanges were fairer to investors. An SEC investigation resulted in a requirement that dealers execute small customer orders along with their own and at the

best prices. In 1997 the new rules were phased in and spreads dropped by an average of 35% without affecting volume.

But NASD teetered between appeasing the public and looking out for its own. A 1997 proposal to cap investor arbitration awards at $750,000, regardless of actual damages, met with criticism, since arbitration had been instituted in 1987 because the parties could receive remedies comparable to those available in court.

Reform-minded Wall Streeter Frank Zarb took over in 1997. Nasdaq and the American Stock Exchange (AMEX) merged the next year. NASD reluctantly complied when the SEC asked it to join the NYSE in real-time trade price reporting.

With for-profit, around-the-clock competitors like The Island ECN and Archipelago in mind, NASD prepared in 1999 to spin off Nasdaq as a for-profit market (overwhelmingly approved in 2000). Nasdaq also extended official pricing to 6:30 p.m. (Eastern time) and agreed to share listings with the Hong Kong Stock Exchange.

In 2000 Nasdaq converted stock prices from fractions to decimals, mandated by regulators. That year it joined with SOFTBANK to build Nasdaq Japan, an Internet-based market of primarily Japanese tech companies. In 2001 the flaccid economy led Nasdaq to trim about 10% of its staff — its first job cuts since just after the 1987 crash. Zarb also retired that year.

In the wake of the terrorism attacks that shook Wall Street and the nation in 2001, Nasdaq and the NYSE began discussing a disaster plan under which the two would cooperate should a future incident cripple either market. It also continued to refine its focus toward regulation, with plans to dispose of AMEX, and a series of private stock sales that would ultimately separate Nasdaq from NASD in 2002.

EXECUTIVES

Chairman, President, and CEO: Robert R. Glauber, age 66
Vice Chairman; President, Regulatory Policy and Oversight: Mary L. Schapiro, age 49
SEVP and Chief Administrative Officer: Michael D. Jones
EVP and CFO: Todd T. DiGanci
EVP and CTO: Martin P. Colburn
EVP and Director Dispute Resolution: George H. Friedman
EVP and General Counsel: T. Grant Callery
EVP Compliance Information and Services: M. Ann Short
EVP Corporate Communications and Government Relations: Howard M. Schloss
EVP Enforcement: Barry R. Goldsmith
EVP Market Regulation and US Exchange Solutions: Stephen I. Luparello
EVP Member Regulation: Robert C. Errico
EVP Registration and Disclosure: Derek W. Linden
EVP Regulatory Policy and Programs: Elisse B. Walter
EVP Transparency Services: Steven A. (Steve) Joachim
SVP and Corporate Secretary: Barbara Z. Sweeney
SVP and Corporate Controller: Eileen M. Famiglietti
SVP and Investment Officer: James R. Allen
SVP Education and Training: Robert W. Gulick
SVP Human Resources: Andrew C. Goresh
Auditors: Ernst & Young LLP

LOCATIONS

HQ: NASD
1735 K St. Northwest, Washington, DC 20006
Phone: 202-728-8000　　**Fax:** 202-293-6260
Web: www.nasd.com

NASD has regulation and dispute resolution offices throughout the US.

PRODUCTS/OPERATIONS

Selected Subsidiaries and Affiliates
NASD Dispute Resolution, Inc.
NASD Regulation, Inc.

COMPETITORS

Bloomberg	Investment Technology
CBOT	Knight Capital
E*TRADE Financial	LaBranche & Co
Goldman Sachs	NYSE
Instinet	

HISTORICAL FINANCIALS

Company Type: Not-for-profit

Income Statement

FYE: December 31

	REVENUE ($ mil.)	NET INCOME ($ mil.)	NET PROFIT MARGIN	EMPLOYEES
12/03	1,028	(58)	—	2,000
12/02	1,238	(4)	—	2,087
12/01	1,539	112	7.3%	3,200
12/00	1,555	114	7.3%	3,200
12/99	1,177	154	13.1%	3,000
12/98	740	47	6.4%	2,900
12/97	634	36	5.7%	2,200
12/96	556	55	9.9%	2,218
12/95	438	17	3.9%	2,000
12/94	372	21	5.6%	2,328
Annual Growth	12.0%	—	—	(1.7%)

2003 Year-End Financials

Debt ratio: 22.9%　　　　Current ratio: 2.38
Return on equity: —　　　Long-term debt ($ mil.): 265
Cash ($ mil.): 333

Net Income History

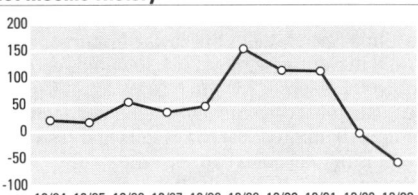

200										
150										
100										
50										
0										
-50										
-100										
	12/94	12/95	12/96	12/97	12/98	12/99	12/00	12/01	12/02	12/03

Nashville Hockey Club

Yeehaw, let's hit the ice! Nashville Hockey Club owns and operates the Nashville Predators professional hockey franchise, which entertains fans at the Music City's Gaylord Entertainment Center. The team has one of the smallest payrolls in the National Hockey League, lacking the deep pockets to spend heavily on free agent talent. Since entering the league as an expansion franchise in 1998, the Predators struggled for several seasons before posting its first playoff finish in 2004. Chairman Craig Leipold and his family own the team.

The team has recently settled a nasty lawsuit battle with former part-owner Gaylord Entertainment. In 2004, the entertainment company exercised an option to force the Predators to buy out Gaylord's stake in the team. Since the Predators could not get league approval for the deal, it refused to buy the stake, so Gaylord withheld its stadium naming rights payments. As a result, both parties dragged each other into court. The settlement agreement reached in early 2005 allowed the team to buy back Gaylord's 10% stake in exchange for Gaylord fulfilling and terminating its licensing agreement by making a one-time cash payment of $4 million and issuing a $5 million promissory note with interest. The Predators will begin securing a new naming rights partner for the stadium, which will continue under the Gaylord name until new arrangements are made.

The inspiration for the team's saber-toothed tiger logo came from a 9-in. fang of a 10,000-year-old saber-toothed tiger uncovered in the Nashville area in the 1970s.

EXECUTIVES

Chairman and Governor: Craig L. Leipold, age 50
President and COO: John C. (Jack) Diller
Assistant General Manager: Ray Shero
Head Coach: Barry Trotz, age 43
EVP Business Affairs: Steve Violetta
EVP Finance and Administration and CFO: Ed Lang
EVP Hockey Operations and General Manager: David Poile
SVP Communications and Development: Gerry Helper
VP Marketing: Randy Campbell
Senior Director of Finance: Beth Snider
Senior Director of Human Resources: Stephanie Ditenhafer
Director of Communications: Ken Anderson
Marketing and Special Events Manager: Christel Foley
Communications Coordinator: Tim Darling

LOCATIONS

HQ: Nashville Hockey Club Limited Partnership
501 Broadway, Nashville, TN 37203
Phone: 615-770-2300 **Fax:** 615-770-2309
Web: www.nashvillepredators.com

The Nashville Predators play at the 17,500-seat Gaylord Entertainment Center in Nashville.

COMPETITORS

Chicago Blackhawks	Detroit Red Wings
Columbus Blue Jackets	St. Louis Blues

HISTORICAL FINANCIALS

Company Type: Private

Income Statement

FYE: June 30

	REVENUE ($ mil.)	NET INCOME ($ mil.)	NET PROFIT MARGIN	EMPLOYEES
6/04	42	—	—	—
6/03	46	—	—	—
6/02	53	—	—	—
6/01*	53	—	—	—
7/00	52	—	—	—
7/99	48	—	—	80
Annual Growth	(2.8%)	—	—	—

*Fiscal year change

Revenue History

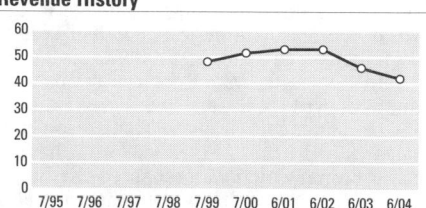

National Basketball Association

The National Basketball Association has shot a lot fewer airballs lately. The 30-team NBA is divided into the Eastern and Western conferences and includes one Canadian team. The league also operates the 13-team WNBA (women's basketball), as well as an eight-team development league. The league also launched NBA TV, its own cable channel devoted to all things basketball.

In 2002 the NBA cut a new six-year TV contract with Walt Disney's ABC and ESPN, and Time Warner's Turner Sports worth a reported $4.6 billion. Some fans are unhappy with the new TV contract as it puts a majority of the league's games almost exclusively on cable. The NBA further milked the new TV contract by expanding the first round of the playoffs from a best-of-five to a best-of-seven format.

Expansion is also still very much alive for the NBA. After the Charlotte Hornets moved to New Orleans for the 2002-03 season, the league voted to give the city another franchise that began play in 2004-05. Robert Johnson, founder of BET, is the majority owner of the new Charlotte Bobcats. He is the first African-American owner of a major league sports team. The addition of the Bobcats forced the league to realign into six divisions with five teams each.

In 2004 the NBA found itself mired in damage control after one of the worst brawls in the history of the league. During an Indiana Pacers/Detroit Pistons game in Motor City, a near riot erupted between Pistons fans and numerous Pacers players. After being hit by a cup of ice tossed from the crowd, Pacers forward Ron Artest charged into the stands and began throwing punches. Several of his teammates followed and also engaged in fisticuffs. The NBA handed down massive suspensions to all the players involved (Artest was booted for the rest of the season), while local authorities filed assault and battery charges against five Pacers (Artest, Jermaine O'Neal, David Harrison, Anthony Johnston, and Stephen Jackson) and seven Pistons fans.

The NBA has also rethought its strategy regarding the WNBA. The league restructured the previous ownership rules for a WNBA franchise that dictated only the current owners of NBA clubs could own a sister team. Now anyone can own a club, and the move allows the league to expand into cities where there isn't already an NBA franchise. But the new rules also force WNBA teams to find their own corporate sponsors and pay player salaries themselves, which prompted some teams to fold or find new homes.

HISTORY

Dr. James Naismith, a physical education teacher at the International YMCA Training School in Springfield, Massachusetts, invented basketball in 1891. Naismith nailed peach baskets at both ends of the school's gym, gave his students a soccer ball, and one of the world's most popular sports was born.

In the beginning many YMCAs deemed the game too rough and banned it, so basketball was limited to armories, gymnasiums, barns, and dance halls. To pay the rent for the use of the hall, teams began charging spectators fees for admission, and leftover cash was divided among the players. The first pro basketball game was played in 1896 in Trenton, New Jersey.

A group of arena owners looking to fill their halls when their hockey teams were on the road formed the Basketball Association of America in 1946. It merged with the midwestern National Basketball League in 1949 to form the 17-team National Basketball Association (NBA).

Six teams dropped out in 1950. The league got an unexpected boost the next year when a point-shaving scandal rocked college basketball. The bad publicity for the college game made the pros look relatively clean, and it helped attract more fans. Another boost came through innovation when the league introduced the 24-second shot clock in 1954, which sped up the game and increased scoring.

Basketball came into its own in the late 1950s and 1960s, thanks to the popularity of such stars as Wilt Chamberlain, Bill Russell, and Bob Cousy. A rival league, the American Basketball Association (ABA), appeared on the scene in 1967 with its red, white, and blue basketball. Salaries escalated as the two leagues competed for players. The leagues merged in 1976.

By the early 1980s the NBA was suffering major image problems (drugs, fighting, racial issues) and began to wane in popularity. The league was resuscitated by exciting new players such as Magic Johnson, Larry Bird, and Michael Jordan, and, in 1984, a new commissioner, David Stern. Although increased commercialism drove some purists crazy, big-name players and big-time rivalries helped sell the NBA's most important commodity — sport as entertainment.

Stern went to work cleaning up the league's image and financial problems, pushing through a strict anti-drug policy and a salary cap (the first such cap in major US sports). He also signed big marketing deals with such sponsors as Coca Cola and McDonald's. The NBA added its first two non-US teams in 1995, the Toronto Raptors and the Vancouver Grizzlies. (The Grizzlies moved to Memphis in 2001.) The league also created the Women's NBA (WNBA) in 1996.

On July 1, 1998, the NBA owners voted to lock out players, leading to the first work stoppage in the NBA's 52-year history. The dispute lasted six months, and the NBA's 1998-99 season was pared down to 50 games from the standard 82.

Concerned with the rash of players either leaving college early or skipping it entirely for the NBA, the league announced the formation of a developmental league (akin to baseball's minor leagues) in 2000, which started play in 2001. Also in 2001 the NBA got a much-needed shot in the arm when Michael Jordan came out of retirement for a second time to play for the Washington Wizards.

The following year the league signed a new TV contract. Former game telecaster NBC decided not to pursue the league after its $1.3 billion bid failed to measure up to a six-year, $4.6 billion deal offered by Walt Disney's ABC and ESPN, and Time Warner's Turner Sports.

In 2004 the league launched its 30th franchise, the Charlotte Bobcats. The move forced the league to realign into six divisions with five teams each.

EXECUTIVES

Commissioner: David J. Stern, age 63
Deputy Commissioner and COO: Russell T. Granik
EVP Global Media Properties and Marketing Partnerships: Heidi Ueberroth
EVP Strategic Planning and Business Development: Ed Desser
SVP Basketball Operations: Stu Jackson
SVP Business Affairs: Harvey E. Benjamin
SVP Communications: Timothy P. Andree
SVP Community Relations: Kathleen Behrens
SVP Finance: Robert Criqui
SVP Global Merchandising: Sal LaRocca
SVP International: Andrew Messick
SVP International Television and Marketing Partnerships: Scott Levy
SVP Marketing and Teams Business Operations: Scott O'Neil
SVP Operations and Technology: Steve Hellmuth
SVP Security: Bernie Tolbert
SVP and Chief Information Officer: Michael Gliedman
VP Business Development: Peter Farnsworth
VP Entertainment and Player Marketing: Charlie Rosenzweig
VP Global Media and NBA TV: Steve Justman
VP International Basketball Operations: Kim Bohuny
VP Marketing and Media: Ron Erskine
VP Operations: Carolyn Blitz
VP Production: Jared Franzreb

LOCATIONS

HQ: National Basketball Association
Olympic Tower, 645 5th Ave., New York, NY 10022
Phone: 212-826-7000   **Fax:** 212-754-6414
Web: www.nba.com

PRODUCTS/OPERATIONS

Eastern Conference

Atlantic Division
  Boston Celtics
  New Jersey Nets
  New York Knicks
  Philadelphia 76ers
  Toronto Raptors

Central Division
  Chicago Bulls
  Cleveland Cavaliers
  Detroit Pistons
  Indiana Pacers
  Milwaukee Bucks

Southeast Division
  Atlanta Hawks
  Charlotte Bobcats
  Miami Heat
  Orlando Magic
  Washington Wizards

Western Conference

Northwest Division
  Denver Nuggets
  Minnesota Timberwolves
  Portland Trail Blazers
  Seattle SuperSonics
  Utah Jazz

Pacific Division
  Golden State Warriors
  Los Angeles Clippers
  Los Angeles Lakers
  Phoenix Suns
  Sacramento Kings

Southwest Division
  Dallas Mavericks
  Houston Rockets
  Memphis Grizzlies
  New Orleans Hornets
  San Antonio Spurs

COMPETITORS

AFL	NHL
Major League Baseball	PGA
Major League Soccer	World Wrestling
NASCAR	Entertainment
NFL	

HISTORICAL FINANCIALS

Company Type: Association

Income Statement

FYE: August 31

	REVENUE ($ mil.)	NET INCOME ($ mil.)	NET PROFIT MARGIN	EMPLOYEES
8/04*	3,000	—	—	—
8/00	2,164	—	—	—
8/99	956	—	—	800
8/98	1,874	—	—	1,000
8/97	1,664	—	—	850
8/96	1,403	—	—	650
8/95	1,259	—	—	550
8/94	1,030	—	—	450
8/93	999	—	—	—
8/92	843	—	—	—
Annual Growth	15.1%	—	—	12.2%

*Irregular reporting interval

Revenue History

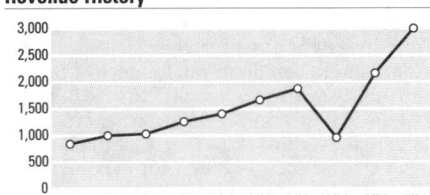

National Football League

In the world of professional sports, the National Football League (NFL) blitzes the competition. The organization oversees America's most popular spectator sport, acting as a trade association for 32 franchise owners. The teams operate as separate businesses but share much of the revenue generated through broadcasting and merchandising. The NFL was founded as the American Professional Football Association in 1920. The league reorganized its two conferences, the AFC and NFC, for the 2002-03 season when the Houston Texans joined the league as the latest expansion team. In 2004 and 2005, the NFL also negotiated new broadcasting contracts with Disney (owner of ESPN), CBS, FOX, NBC, and DIRECTV.

The NFL's primary operations consist of subsidiaries NFL Properties, which generates billions through merchandising and licensing, and NFL Enterprises, the entity that negotiates national broadcasting rights for the teams. During the past two years, the league got a jump on extending its broadcasting contracts. CBS and FOX agreed to a new deal for a combined $8 billion that will keep NFL games on their networks until 2011. The NFL also extended its exclusive deal with DIRECTV to broadcast NFL Sunday Ticket

until 2010 for $3.5 billion. The package allows DIRECTV subscribers to view any of the weekly Sunday telecasts, regardless of their local market. ABC decided to get out of the football business altogether by transferring the venerable *Monday Night Football* to sister network ESPN starting in 2006. (ABC has aired *Monday Night Football* since 1970.) NBC is returning to football with a six year deal (also beginning in 2006), picking up the Sunday night slack left by ESPN's move to Monday.

The NFL has also launched the NFL Network, a 24-hour football network. So far it's distributed primarily through DIRECTV, but Charter Communications, Comcast, and a couple of other smaller players have struck deals to air the network on their systems.

Other subsidiaries include NFL Charities and NFL Films. The league is also capitalizing on the Internet as a revenue source by signing deals with SportsLine.com, AOL, and CBS to promote and maintain the league's NLF.com site.

The NFL landed in the middle of a scandal during the 2004 Super Bowl when singer Janet Jackson exposed her breast during the halftime show. (Jackson claims the flashing was an accident.) The incident outraged much of the country and the league rethought its strategy of producing live entertainment aimed at younger viewers. It also set off a slew of congressional hearings into broadcasting indecency, and the FCC has significantly boosted fines for such violations.

HISTORY

Descended from the English game of rugby, American football was developed in the late 1800s by Walter Camp, a player from Yale University who is generally credited with introducing new rules for downs and scoring. Professional teams sprang up in the 1890s, but football remained relatively unorganized until 1920, when George Halas and college star Jim Thorpe helped organize the American Professional Football Association. The new league featured 14 teams from the Midwest and East, including Halas' Staleys (now the Chicago Bears) and the Racine Cardinals (now the Arizona Cardinals). In 1922 the association changed its name to the National Football League.

The new league suffered many growing pains over the next decade, but by the 1930s the NFL had settled on 10 teams, including the Green Bay Packers (joined in 1921), the New York Giants (1925), and the Philadelphia Eagles (1933). Interest in the game remained somewhat regional, however, until the late 1940s and 1950s. In 1946 the Cleveland Rams moved to Los Angeles, and in 1950 the NFL expanded with three teams joining from the defunct All-American Football Conference. Television showed its potential in 1958 when that year's championship game, the first to be televised nationally, kept audiences riveted with an overtime victory by the Baltimore Colts over the Giants. In 1962 the NFL signed its first league-wide television contract with CBS for $4.65 million.

The 1960s brought a new challenge in the form of the upstart American Football League (AFL). Concerned that the AFL would steal players with higher salaries and draw away fans, NFL commissioner Pete Rozelle negotiated a deal in 1966 to combine the leagues. That season concluded with the first AFL-NFL World Championship Game, which was renamed the Super Bowl in 1969. When the merger was completed in 1970, the new NFL sported 26 teams.

Football's popularity exploded during the 1970s, helped by the rise of franchise dynasties such as the Pittsburgh Steelers (four Super Bowl wins) and the Dallas Cowboys (five NFC titles). In 1982 the Oakland Raiders moved to Los Angeles after a jury ruled against the NFL's attempts to keep the team in Oakland. The decision prompted other teams to relocate in search of better facilities and more revenue. (The Raiders returned to Oakland in 1995.) Rozelle stepped down in 1989 and was replaced by Paul Tagliabue.

During the 1990s the league expanded to 30 teams, adding the Carolina Panthers and Jacksonville Jaguars in 1995. The next year Art Modell moved his Cleveland Browns franchise to Baltimore to become the Ravens (the city of Cleveland held onto the rights to the Browns name and history and the franchise was revived in 1999), and in 1997 the Houston Oilers defected to Tennessee and were later renamed the Titans. The next year brought new television deals worth $17.6 billion over eight years.

The NFL made plans for new expansion in 1999, awarding a franchise to Robert McNair of Houston, who paid a record $700 million franchise fee and $310 million for a new stadium. Named the Houston Texans, the team began play in 2002. (The NFL realigned the NFC and AFC in 2002, shifting to eight divisions with four teams each.) In 2003 the league launched its own television channel, the NFL Network.

EXECUTIVES

Commissioner: Paul J. Tagliabue, age 64
EVP and COO: Roger Goodell
EVP and General Counsel: Jeff Pash
EVP Communications and Government Affairs: Joe Browne
EVP Finance and Strategic Transactions: Eric P. Grubman
EVP Labor Relations; Chairman, NFL Management Council: Harold R. Henderson
SVP Broadcast Planning: Dennis Lewin
SVP Business Affairs: Frank Hawkins
SVP Consumer Products: Mark Holtzman
SVP Finance and NFL Business Ventures: Kimberly Williams
SVP Football Operations and Development: Art Shell
SVP Human Resources and Administration: Nancy Gill
SVP Marketing and Sales: Phil Guarascio
SVP Media Operations; and COO, NFL Films: Howard Katz
SVP New Media: Christopher J. Russo
VP Marketing Programs: Shawn Dennis
VP Partnership Marketing and Corporate Sales: Peter Murray
VP Public Relations: Greg Aiello
Auditors: Deloitte & Touche LLP

LOCATIONS

HQ: National Football League Inc.
280 Park Ave., New York, NY 10017
Phone: 212-450-2000   **Fax:** 212-681-7599
Web: www.nfl.com

The National Football League oversees 32 franchises in 31 cities. It also has six franchises in Europe.

PRODUCTS/OPERATIONS

American Football Conference
Baltimore Ravens (1996)
  Cleveland Browns (1944, joined the NFL from the AAFC in 1950)
Buffalo Bills (1959, joined the NFL from the AFL in 1970, New York)
Cincinnati Bengals (1968, joined the NFL from the AFL in 1970)
Cleveland Browns (1999)
Denver Broncos (1959, joined the NFL from the AFL in 1970)
Houston Texans (2002)
Indianapolis Colts (1984)
  Baltimore Colts (1953)
Jacksonville Jaguars (1995, Florida)
Kansas City Chiefs (1963, joined the NFL from the AFL in 1970, Missouri) Dallas Texans (1959)
Miami Dolphins (1966, joined the NFL from the AFL in 1970)
New England Patriots (1971; Foxboro, MA)
  Boston Patriots (1959, joined the NFL from the AFL in 1970)
New York Jets (1959, joined the NFL from the AFL in 1970)
Oakland Raiders (1995, California)
  Los Angeles Raiders (1982)
  Oakland Raiders (1959, joined the NFL from the AFL in 1970)
Pittsburgh Steelers (1940)
  Pittsburgh Pirates (1933)
San Diego Chargers (1961, joined the NFL from the AFL in 1970)
  Los Angeles Chargers (1959)
Tennessee Titans (1998, Nashville)
  Tennessee Oilers (1997, Memphis)
  Houston Oilers (1959, joined the NFL from the AFL in 1970)

National Football Conference
Arizona Cardinals (1994, Phoenix)
  Phoenix Cardinals (1988)
  St. Louis Cardinals (1960)
  Chicago Cardinals (1922)
  Racine Cardinals (1901, Chicago)
  Morgan Athletic Club (1898, Chicago)
Atlanta Falcons (1966)
Carolina Panthers (1995; Charlotte, NC)
Chicago Bears (1922)
  Chicago Staleys (1921)
  Decatur Staleys (1920, Illinois)
Dallas Cowboys (1960)
Detroit Lions (1934)
  Portsmouth Spartans (1930, Ohio)
Green Bay Packers (1919, Wisconsin)
Minnesota Vikings (1961, Minneapolis)
New Orleans Saints (1967)
New York Giants (1925)
Philadelphia Eagles (1933)
St. Louis Rams (1995)
  Los Angeles Rams (1946)
  Cleveland Rams (1937)
San Francisco 49ers (1946, joined the NFL from the AAFC in 1950)
Seattle Seahawks (1976)
Tampa Bay Buccaneers (1976)
Washington Redskins (1937; Washington, DC)
  Boston Redskins (1933)
  Boston Braves (1932)

Selected Business Units
NFL Charities
NFL Enterprises (media development)
NFL Films (highlight packages)
NFL Properties (licensing, marketing, promotions, and publishing)

COMPETITORS

AFL	NBA
FIFA	NHL
Major League Baseball	PGA
Major League Soccer	World Wrestling
NASCAR	Entertainment

HISTORICAL FINANCIALS

Company Type: Association

Income Statement

FYE: March 31

	REVENUE ($ mil.)	NET INCOME ($ mil.)	NET PROFIT MARGIN	EMPLOYEES
3/04	6,000	—	—	450
3/03	5,500	—	—	450
3/02	5,000	—	—	450
3/01	4,200	—	—	450
3/00	3,602	—	—	450
3/99	3,271	—	—	400
3/98	2,448	—	—	400
3/97	2,331	—	—	—
3/96	2,059	—	—	—
3/95	1,730	—	—	—
Annual Growth	**14.8%**	—	—	**2.0%**

Revenue History

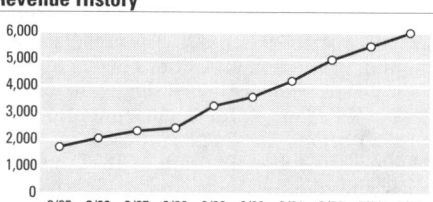

National Geographic

It's not your father's National Geographic Society anymore. Still publishing its flagship *National Geographic* magazine, the not-for-profit organization with more than 7 million members has expanded into an array of venues to enhance our knowledge of the big blue marble. Its National Geographic Ventures subsidiary is fortifying the organization's presence on television and the Web, as well as in map-making. The organization owns part of the National Geographic Channel US (a cable channel it operates jointly with FOX), which reaches 48 million households. It also supports geographic expeditions (it has funded more than 7,000 scientific research projects) and sponsors exhibits, lectures, and education programs.

National Geographic has focused on an international expansion strategy, launching its first local-language edition of *National Geographic* magazine for Japan in 1995. The organization now offers 25 local-language editions, with a circulation of more than 2 million. Readers from every country in the world subscribe to the magazine; 40% of readers live outside the US.

The organization also owns part of National Geographic Channels International (NGCI), which is operated jointly with NBC, FOX, and BskyB. NGCI, one of the fastest growing cable networks around the globe, airs in 145 countries in 26 languages, reaching more than 160 million households. In addition, National Geographic Global

Exploration Fun awards grants for international scientific research. Every month the National Geographic Society reaches more than 250 million people worldwide through its National Geographic Channel, magazines, maps, books, videos, and interactive media.

As competition from relative newcomers, such as Discovery Communications, intensifies, the diversification of the National Geographic Society has been accelerating.

HISTORY

In 1888 a group of scientists and explorers gathered in Washington, DC, to form the National Geographic Society. Gardiner Greene Hubbard was its first president. The organization mailed the first edition of its magazine, dated October 1888, to 165 members. The magazine was clothed in a brown cover and contained a few esoteric articles, such as "The Classification of Geographic Forms by Genesis." The organization's tradition of funding expeditions began in 1890 when it sent geologist Israel Russell to explore Alaska. It began issuing regular monthly editions of *National Geographic* in 1896.

Following Hubbard's death in 1897, his son-in-law, inventor Alexander Graham Bell, became president. Aiming to boost the magazine's popularity, he hired Gilbert Grosvenor (who later married Bell's daughter) as editor. Grosvenor turned the magazine from a dry, technical publication to one of more general interest.

Under Grosvenor the magazine pioneered the use of photography, including rare photographs of remote Tibet (1904), the first hand-tinted colored photos (1910), the first underwater color photos (1920s), and the first color aerial photographs (1930).

The organization sponsored Robert Peary's trek to the North Pole in 1909 and Hiram Bingham's 1912 exploration of Machu Picchu in Peru. National Geographic expanded into cartography with the creation of a maps division in 1915. Grosvenor became president in 1920.

By 1930 circulation was 1.2 million (up from 2,200 in 1900). Grosvenor's policy of printing only "what is of a kindly nature . . . about any country or people" resulted in two articles that were criticized for their kindly portrayal of pre-war Nazi Germany (however, National Geographic maps and photographs were used by the US government for WWII intelligence). That policy eased over the years, and in 1961 a *National Geographic* article described the growing US involvement in Vietnam.

Grosvenor retired in 1954. His son Melville Bell Grosvenor, who became president and editor in 1957, accelerated book publishing with the first edition of *National Geographic Atlas of the World*. In addition, he created a film unit that aired its first TV documentary in 1965. Melville retired in 1967.

Melville's son Gilbert Melville Grosvenor took over as president in 1970. The organization debuted its *National Geographic Explorer* television series in 1985. National Geographic branched into commercial ventures in 1995 when it created subsidiary National Geographic Ventures to expand its presence on television, the Internet, maps, and retail. That same year the *National Geographic* magazine began international circulation.

Grosvenor became chairman in 1996, and Reg Murphy took over as president. Murphy shook up the organization by laying off nearly a quarter of its staff and stepping up its profit-making activities. In 1997 National Geographic branched into cable television when it partnered with Fox, NBC, and BskyB to launch outside the US the National Geographic Channels International (NGCI).

John Fahey replaced Murphy as president in 1998. That same year National Geographic released *Mysteries of Egypt*, its first IMAX-style film. The following year National Geographic unveiled its *Adventure* magazine. The organization began offering *National Geographic* on newsstands for the first time in 1999. In 2000 National Geographic Ventures acquired recreational topographic map company Wildflower Productions. As part of an agreement to buy 30% of travel portal iExplore, National Geographic also agreed to license the use of its name. In 2001 National Geographic Channel US, a cable channel, was launched as a joint venture with FOX.

In 2002 National Geographic began using IBM software and hardware to digitize thousands of its culture and nature images to sell online. That same year *National Geographic World*, a magazine for young people, became *National Geographic Kids*. The organization also began a literacy campaign that included *National Geographic Explorer!* magazine and curriculum materials for classrooms. In 2003 it launched Hungarian, Romanian, Czech, Croatian, and Russian-language editions of *National Geographic* magazine.

EXECUTIVES

Chairman: Gilbert M. Grosvenor, age 73
Vice Chairman: Reg Murphy
President and CEO: John M. Fahey Jr., age 52
EVP and CFO: Christopher A. Liedel
EVP Law, Business, and Governmental Affairs: Terrence B. Adamson
EVP Mission Programs: Terry D. Garcia
EVP; President, Books and School Publishing: Nina D. Hoffman
EVP; President, Magazine Group: John Q. Griffin
EVP; President, National Geographic Enterprises: Linda Berkeley
SVP and Treasurer: H. Gregory Platts
SVP Communications: Betty Hudson
SVP Human Resources: Thomas A. (Tony) Sabló
SVP International Licensing: Robert W. (Rob) Hernandez
SVP Licensing: John Dumbacher
VP and Controller: Michael J. Cole
VP; Editor in Chief, *National Geographic Traveler*: Keith Bellows
VP Management Information Systems: Bernard B. Callahan
Chairman and CEO, National Geographic Ventures: Dennis Patrick
VP Education and Children's Programs: Barbara Chow
Chairman, Committee for Research and Exploration: Peter Raven

LOCATIONS

HQ: National Geographic Society
1145 17th St. NW, Washington, DC 20036
Phone: 202-857-7000   **Fax:** 202-775-6141
Web: www.nationalgeographic.com

PRODUCTS/OPERATIONS

Selected Operations

Books
  Cuba
  Eyewitness to the 20th Century
  Last Climb: The Legendary Everest Expeditions of George Mallory
  Return to Midway
  The World of Islam
Education products
Magazines
  Adventure
  National Geographic
  Traveler
  World
Maps and atlases
Sponsorship of expeditions, lectures, and education programs
Television
  National Geographic Channel
  National Geographic Explorer
  PBS specials
    Really Wild Animals
    Tales from the Wild

COMPETITORS

American Institute Of Physics
DeLorme
Discovery Communications
Educational Insights
Encyclopaedia Britannica
ESRI
Lonely Planet
MapQuest.com
Mariah Media
Rand McNally
Time
Time Warner

HISTORICAL FINANCIALS

Company Type: Not-for-profit

Income Statement

FYE: December 31

	REVENUE ($ mil.)	NET INCOME ($ mil.)	NET PROFIT MARGIN	EMPLOYEES
12/03	531	—	—	1,387
12/02	537	—	—	1,337
12/01	550	—	—	1,380
12/00	559	—	—	1,406
12/99	518	—	—	1,294
12/98	510	—	—	1,265
12/97	489	—	—	1,214
12/96	401	—	—	1,300
12/95	423	—	—	1,551
12/94	419	—	—	1,493
Annual Growth	2.7%	—	—	(0.8%)

Revenue History

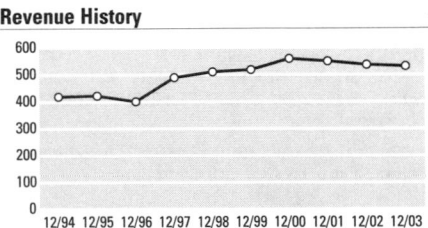

National Grape Cooperative

Well, of course grape growers want to hang out in a bunch! The 1,300 or so grower-owners in the National Grape Cooperative Association grow and harvest purple, red, and white grapes from almost 50,000 acres of vineyards in order to supply its well-known, wholly owned subsidiary Welch Foods. Welch's sells juices, jams, and jellies under the Welch's and BAMA brands. Other products include co-branded candy (with Russell Stover) and fresh grapes (distributed by C.H. Robinson Worldwide). The co-op's marketing arm Welch Foods sells products to retailers in about 40 countries worldwide.

Though jelly is a slowing market, new juice innovations, new packaging, and single-serving products are driving sales at Welch's. Following the trend of branded fresh produce, the Welch's brand now appears on fresh grapes sold in grocery stores nationwide. Recently publicized antioxidant health benefits of purple grape juice have helped spur sales of what was previously a dusty retail niche.

EXECUTIVES

President and Director: Randolph H. Graham
First VP and Director: Joseph C. Falcone
Second VP and Director: Harold H. Smith
Third VP and Director: James A. Schafer
General Manager, COO, and Treasurer: Brent J. Roggie
Financial and Accounting Officer: Albert B. Wright III
President and CEO, Welch Foods, Inc.: Daniel P. Dillon
Chief Legal Officer and Assistant Secretary: Vivian S. Y. Tseng
Secretary and Assistant Treasurer: Timothy A. Buss
Assistant Secretary: Richard H. Alpert
Assistant Treasurer: Richard C. Brouillette
Assistant Secretary: Thomas A. Bockhorst
Auditors: KPMG LLP

LOCATIONS

HQ: National Grape Cooperative Association, Inc.
2 S. Portage St., Westfield, NY 14787
Phone: 716-326-5200   **Fax:** 716-326-5494
Web: www.nationalgrape.com

National Grape Cooperative Association's members own almost 50,000 acres in Michigan, New York, Ohio, Pennsylvania, Washington, and Ontario, Canada.

PRODUCTS/OPERATIONS

Selected Products

Bulk Concord grape products (juice, puree, color extract)
Fresh grapes
Fruit juices (bottled, frozen, refrigerated, single-serve, shelf-stable concentrate)
Fruit spreads, jams, jellies, preserves
Juice cocktails (bottled, frozen, refrigerated, single-serve, shelf-stable concentrate)

COMPETITORS

B&G Foods
Cadbury Schweppes
Chiquita Brands
Coca-Cola
Constellation Brands
Del Monte Foods
Dole Food
Fresh Del Monte Produce
Goya
Hansen Natural
Nestlé USA
Northland Cranberries
Ocean Spray
Procter & Gamble
Ralcorp
Smucker
Tropicana

HISTORICAL FINANCIALS

Company Type: Cooperative

Income Statement

FYE: August 31

	REVENUE ($ mil.)	NET INCOME ($ mil.)	NET PROFIT MARGIN	EMPLOYEES
8/04	583	75	12.9%	1,390
8/03	579	76	13.1%	1,350
8/02	554	65	11.8%	1,264
8/01	650	67	10.4%	1,333
8/00	679	78	11.5%	1,308
8/99	631	71	11.2%	1,241
8/98	600	70	11.6%	1,258
8/97	573	56	9.8%	1,228
8/96	551	58	10.5%	1,224
8/95	509	56	11.1%	1,431
Annual Growth	1.5%	3.2%	—	(0.3%)

2004 Year-End Financials

Debt ratio: 41.2%
Return on equity: 74.8%
Cash ($ mil.): 3
Current ratio: 1.05
Long-term debt ($ mil.): 42

Net Income History

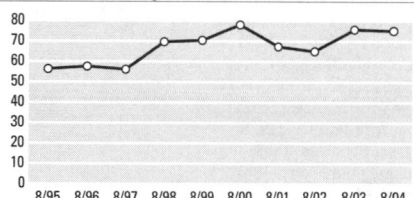

National Hockey League

Hockey is more than a cool sport for serious fans. The National Hockey League is one of the four major professional sports associations in North America, boasting 30 franchises in the US and Canada organized into two conferences with three divisions each. The NHL governs the game, sets and enforces rules, regulates team ownership, and collects licensing fees for merchandise. It also negotiates fees for national broadcasting rights. (Each team controls the rights to regional broadcasts.) In addition, five minor and semi-pro hockey leagues also fly under the NHL banner. The league was organized in Canada in 1917 and cancelled the 2004-05 season after disagreements between management and players over a salary cap.

Hockey boasts millions of fans throughout North America and the NHL has gone through a tremendous expansion under commissioner Gary Bettman. However, hockey still trails the other top sports in terms of attendance and revenue. Some critics have even suggested that Bettman's plan to add new franchises in the Southern US has hurt the league by spreading talent too thin and too far from hockey's traditional base in Canada. Meanwhile, the remaining Canadian teams (all six of them) are struggling to compete with the deeper pockets of their US competitors.

But Bettman's efforts at least netted the NHL greater exposure on the national sports stage and greater interest from broadcasters until the strike. A lucrative deal with ABC and ESPN never delivered the anticipated ratings and ABC decided to focus on the NBA. The NHL turned to NBC to take over broadcasting games under a two-year agreement unique in big league sports: the Peacock Network shares revenue from the broadcasts with the league instead of paying a large sum of money up front. After the strike, ESPN wanted a similar deal. When the NHL refused, the sports network walked away without agreeing to show any hockey for 2006. The Outdoor Living Network (OLN; owned by Comcast) picked up the slack in 2005, signing a deal to cover the league through 2007 with an option for the next year. OLN is paying an average of $70 million a year for the rights to show weeknight games and the first two playoff games. NBC has Saturday games and the deciding games of the finals.

When the 2004-2005 season was cancelled due to a dispute between the NHL and the NHL Players Association, the league picked up the dubious honor of being the first North American pro sports league to lose an entire season to a labor dispute. The main point of contention was a salary cap — management wanted it, the players didn't. In late July 2005, at nearly the last minute to start training camps in September, 87% of the players voted to get back on the ice, accepting a cap that ties salaries to league revenue.

HISTORY

The National Hockey League traces its heritage to 1893, when the Stanley Cup (donated by Lord Stanley, Governor General of Canada) was first awarded to the Montreal Amateur Athletic Association hockey club of the Amateur Hockey Association of Canada. The National Hockey Association (NHA) became the first professional league to award the Cup (a large silver chalice with a new layer added each year, passed to the winning team and engraved with the names of that team's players) in 1910. Five years later the NHA agreed to send its champion to play against the top team of the Pacific Coast Hockey Association (founded in 1911) for bragging rights to the Cup.

In the years leading up to WWI, however, disputes began to erupt between owners in the NHA, and, coupled with the call-up of many of its players for military service, the association decided to disband in 1917. Later that year Frank Calder, a British scholar and former sports journalist who came to Canada to be a soccer player, helped form the National Hockey League (NHL) and appointed himself president. The league originally consisted of five teams from the NHA that played a 22-game schedule.

The 1920s saw continued expansion — the Boston Bruins became the first US team in the league in 1925 — but the NHL remained amorphous as many teams joined up and dropped out during the decade.

The sport lost most of its talent to the military during WWII, forcing teams to field players who were often too young, too old, or who were barely able to skate. The league almost shut down, but the Canadian government encouraged play to continue, claiming it boosted national morale.

In the post-war years, the NHL consisted of just six teams: the Boston Bruins, the Chicago Blackhawks, the Detroit Red Wings, the Montreal Canadiens, the New York Rangers, and the Toronto Maple Leafs, known as the Original Six. The Canadiens began their three-decade domination of the NHL during this time, winning 17 championships from 1946 to 1979.

The league began expanding in 1967 when six US-based franchises were added to form the West Division, while the Original Six were placed in the East Division. More teams were slowly added through the 1970s and in 1979 the league absorbed four franchises from its rival professional league, the World Hockey Association (founded in 1972).

At the beginning of the 1980s the NHL consisted of 21 teams, including 15 franchises in the US. The NHL's shift towards the US market became more concrete when the league's headquarters moved from Montreal to New York City later in the decade.

In 1992, Gary Bettman, formerly assistant commissioner of the National Basketball Association, was hired as the NHL's first real commissioner. Under his leadership, the NHL began expanding to more southern locations in the US. The league's growth was temporarily slowed in 1994, however, by the first major labor dispute in NHL history. Team owners began a player lockout that delayed the start of the season until early 1995, but they ultimately failed in their goal of implementing a salary cap. In 1998 NHL team owners agreed to a $600 million, five-year television contract with Walt Disney's ABC and ESPN starting with the 2000-01 season.

In 2004 the NHL agreed to a two-year revenue-sharing deal to broadcast games on NBC, replacing former broadcasting partner ABC. A dispute that came down to management's demand for a salary cap and the players' rejection of a it lead to a lockout and eventual cancellation of the entire 2004-05 hockey season. In late 2005 (for hockey), the players accepted a cap, ending the lockout in time for a regular 2005-2006 season.

EXECUTIVES

Commissioner: Gary B. Bettman, age 53
EVP and CFO: Craig Harnett
EVP and Chief Legal Officer: William L. (Bill) Daly
EVP and Director of Hockey Operations:
 Colin Campbell
SVP and Director, Officiating: Stephen Walkom
SVP and General Counsel: David Zimmerman
SVP Finance: Joseph DeSousa
SVP Hockey Operations: James Gregory
**SVP New Business Development and President, NHL
 Interactive CyberEnterprises:** Keith Ritter
SVP Security: Dennis Cunningham
SVP Television and Media Ventures: Doug Perlman
VP Broadcasting and Programming: Adam Acone
VP Communications: Bernadette Mansur
VP Consumer Products Marketing: Jim Haskins
VP Strategic Development: Susan Cohig
Group VP; Managing Director, NHL International:
 Kenneth (Ken) Yaffe
Group VP Consumer Products Marketing:
 Brian Jennings
Group VP Corporate Marketing: Andrew Judelson
Group VP Events and Entertainment: Frank Supovitz
Group VP Information Technology: Peter DelGiacco
President, NHL Enterprises: Ed Horne
**EVP Legal and Business Affairs and General Counsel,
 NHL Enterprises:** Richard Zahnd
Auditors: Ernst & Young LLP

LOCATIONS

HQ: National Hockey League
 1251 Avenue of the Americas, 47th Fl.,
 New York, NY 10020
Phone: 212-789-2000 **Fax:** 212-789-2020
Web: www.nhl.com

The National Hockey League has 24 franchises in the US and six in Canada.

PRODUCTS/OPERATIONS

Teams

Atlanta Thrashers (1999)
Boston Bruins (1924)
Buffalo Sabres (1970)
Calgary Flames (1980)
 Atlanta Flames (1972)
Carolina Hurricanes (1997)
 Hartford Whalers (1975, joined the NHL from the
 World Hockey League in 1979)
 New England Whalers (1971)
Chicago Blackhawks (1926)
Colorado Avalanche (1995)
 Quebec Nordiques (1972, joined the NHL from the
 World Hockey League in 1979)
Columbus Blue Jackets (2000)
Dallas Stars (1993)
 Minnesota North Stars (1967)
Detroit Red Wings (1926)
Edmonton Oilers (1973, joined the NHL from the World
 Hockey League in 1979)
 Alberta Oilers (1972)
Florida Panthers (1993)
Los Angeles Kings (1967)
Mighty Ducks of Anaheim (1993)
Minnesota Wild (2000)
Montreal Canadiens (1909)
Nashville Predators (1998)
New Jersey Devils (1982)
 Colorado Rockies (1976)
 Kansas City Scouts (1974)
New York Islanders (1972)
New York Rangers (1926)
Ottawa Senators (1883)
Philadelphia Flyers (1967)
Phoenix Coyotes (1996)
 Winnipeg Jets (1972, joined the NHL from the World
 Hockey League in 1979)
Pittsburgh Penguins (1967)
St. Louis Blues (1967)
San Jose Sharks (1991)
Tampa Bay Lightning (1992)
Toronto Maple Leafs (1927)
Vancouver Canucks (1947, joined the NHL from the
 Western Hockey League in 1970)
Washington Capitals (1974)

COMPETITORS

AFL	NASCAR
FIFA	NBA
Indy Racing League	NFL
Major League Baseball	PGA
Major League Soccer	

HISTORICAL FINANCIALS

Company Type: Association

Income Statement

FYE: June 30

	REVENUE ($ mil.)	NET INCOME ($ mil.)	NET PROFIT MARGIN	EMPLOYEES
6/04	2,100	—	—	—
6/03	1,996	—	—	—
6/02	1,875	—	—	—
6/01	1,769	—	—	—
6/00	1,566	—	—	—
6/99	1,285	—	—	—
6/98	1,141	—	—	—
6/97	1,105	—	—	—
6/96	936	—	—	—
6/95	568	—	—	—
Annual Growth	**15.6%**	**—**	**—**	**—**

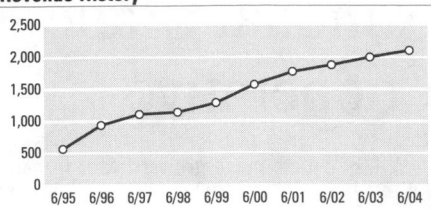

Revenue History

National Life Insurance

One nation, under insurance, with financial security for all. National Life Group, the marketing name for National Life Insurance Company and its affiliated companies, is a mutually owned insurer dating back to 1848. Today, National Life Group offers a range of insurance, investment, and savings products throughout the US through such subsidiaries and affiliates as The Sentinel Companies (mutual funds), Life Insurance Company of the Southwest (insurance and annuities), National Retirement Plan Advisors, and American Guaranty and Trust (trust and custody services).

National Life's Private Client Group (part of subsidiary NL Capital Management) was spun off to management in 2004 and renamed Maple Capital Management.

EXECUTIVES

Chairman, President, and CEO: Thomas H. MacLeay,
 age 53
**EVP; CEO, NL Capital Management and Sentinel
 Management:** Christian W. Thwaites
EVP and CFO: Edward J. Bonach
EVP, Corporate Services and General Counsel:
 Michele S. Gatto
SVP and CIO: Joel Conrad
SVP and Chief Investment Officer:
 Thomas H. (Tom) Brownell
SVP, Finance: Don W. Cummings
VP, Human Resources: Bill Decker
**President and CEO, Equity Services; SVP, NL Financial
 Alliance:** Kenneth R. Ehinger
President, Life & Annuity: Mehran Assadi, age 46
Auditors: PricewaterhouseCoopers LLP

LOCATIONS

HQ: National Life Insurance Company
 1 National Life Dr., Montpelier, VT 05604
Phone: 802-229-3333 **Fax:** 802-229-9281
Web: www.natlifeinsco.com

PRODUCTS/OPERATIONS

2004 Assets

	$ mil.	% of total
Cash & investments		
Available-for-sale debt securities	8,060.5	63
Mortgage loans	1,440.6	11
Policy loans	697.0	6
Other	638.9	5
Separate account assets	779.6	6
Deferred policy acquisition costs	680.8	5
Other	499.0	4
Total	**12,796.4**	**100**

2004 Sales

	$ mil.	% of total
Investment income	682.8	53
Insurance premiums	378.1	29
Policy & contract charges	123.1	9
Mutual fund commissions & fees	82.9	6
Realized investment gains	8.4	1
Other	19.9	2
Total	**1,295.2**	**100**

Selected Subsidiaries

American Guaranty & Trust
Equity Services, Inc.
Life Insurance Company of the Southwest
National Life Insurance Company
National Retirement Plan Advisors Inc.
NL Capital Management, Inc.
The Sentinel Companies

COMPETITORS

AIG American General
AmerUs
AXA Financial
CIGNA
Citigroup
CNA Financial
FMR
John Hancock Financial Services
MassMutual
MetLife
Minnesota Mutual
Mutual of Omaha
New York Life
Ohio National
Pacific Mutual
Principal Financial
Prudential
Sentry Insurance
Utica Mutual Insurance

HISTORICAL FINANCIALS

Company Type: Mutual company

Income Statement

FYE: December 31

	ASSETS ($ mil.)	NET INCOME ($ mil.)	INCOME AS % OF ASSETS	EMPLOYEES
12/04	12,796	86	0.7%	—
12/03	12,034	77	0.6%	1,000
12/02	10,739	26	0.2%	1,000
12/01	10,161	48	0.5%	1,000
12/00	9,618	61	0.6%	950
12/99	9,356	57	0.6%	900
12/98	9,206	20	0.2%	750
12/97	8,814	36	0.4%	750
12/96	8,304	17	0.2%	960
Annual Growth	**5.6%**	**22.4%**	**—**	**0.6%**

2004 Year-End Financials

Equity as % of assets: 9.6%
Return on assets: 0.7%
Return on equity: 7.3%
Long-term debt ($ mil.): 220
Sales ($ mil.): 1,295

Net Income History

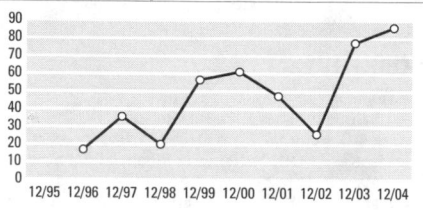

90
80
70
60
50
40
30
20
10
0

12/95 12/96 12/97 12/98 12/99 12/00 12/01 12/02 12/03 12/04

National Rural Utilities Cooperative

Cooperation may work wonders on *Sesame Street*, but in the real world it takes money to pay the power bill. The National Rural Utilities Cooperative Finance Corporation, or CFC, provides financing for electrical and telephone projects throughout the US. Owned by its more than 1,500 members, most of which are electric utility and telecommunications systems, the CFC supplements the government loans that traditionally have fueled rural electric utilities by selling commercial paper, medium-term notes, and collateral trust bonds for its loans. The CFC was formed in 1969 by the National Rural Electric Cooperative Association, a lobby representing the nation's electric co-ops.

EXECUTIVES

Governor and CEO: Sheldon C. Petersen, age 52, $628,105 pay
President and Director: James P. Duncan, age 58
VP and Director: Cletus Carter, age 64
Secretary-Treasurer and Director: Terryl Jacobs, age 46
SVP and CFO: Steven L. Lilly, age 55, $368,539 pay
SVP, Corporate Relations: Richard E. Larochelle, age 52
SVP, Credit Risk Management: John M. Borak, age 61
SVP, Member Services, and General Counsel: John J. List, age 58, $319,324 pay
SVP, Operations: John T. Evans, age 55, $319,324 pay
SVP, Rural Telephone Finance Cooperative: Lawrence Zawalick, age 47, $266,676 pay
VP and Controller: Steven L. Slepian
Auditors: Deloitte & Touche LLP

LOCATIONS

HQ: National Rural Utilities Cooperative Finance Corporation
2201 Cooperative Way, Herndon, VA 20171
Phone: 703-709-6700 **Fax:** 703-709-6778
Web: www.nrucfc.org

National Rural Utilities Cooperative Finance Corporation provides financing throughout the US.

PRODUCTS/OPERATIONS

Selected Subsidiaries and Affiliates

National Cooperative Services Corporation (debt refinancing and lending to electric co-ops)
Rural Telephone Finance Cooperative (rural telecommunications lending)

COMPETITORS

AgFirst
AgriBank
GE

HISTORICAL FINANCIALS

Company Type: Cooperative

Income Statement

FYE: May 31

	ASSETS ($ mil.)	NET INCOME ($ mil.)	INCOME AS % OF ASSETS	EMPLOYEES
5/04	21,350	(178)	—	218
5/03	20,974	652	3.1%	222
5/02	20,343	107	0.5%	215
5/01	19,999	133	0.7%	200
5/00	17,083	115	0.7%	186
5/99	13,925	76	0.5%	182
5/98	10,683	62	0.6%	164
5/97	9,058	55	0.6%	200
5/96	8,054	49	0.6%	—
5/95	7,081	45	0.6%	—
Annual Growth	**13.0%**	**—**	**—**	**1.2%**

2004 Year-End Financials

Equity as % of assets: 3.3%
Return on assets: —
Return on equity: —
Long-term debt ($ mil.): 16,659
Sales ($ mil.): 1,006

Net Income History

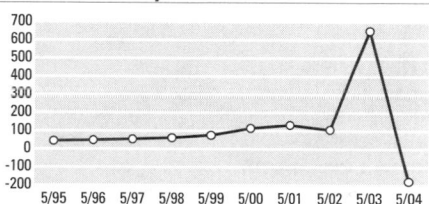

700
600
500
400
300
200
100
0
-100
-200

5/95 5/96 5/97 5/98 5/99 5/00 5/01 5/02 5/03 5/04

National Wine & Spirits

Bartender to the nation's breadbasket, National Wine & Spirits is one of the Midwest's largest wine and liquor distributors. Serving 36,000 locations, the company distributes to restaurants, liquor stores, and retailers in Illinois, Indiana, and Michigan and owns an interest in a Kentucky distributor. Its suppliers include Fortune Brands (Jim Beam), Diageo (Bailey's), and Beringer Blass Wine Estates. The company operates through several wholly owned subsidiaries. CEO James LaCrosse and director Norma Johnston own National Wine & Spirits, which was founded in 1934.

Major changes among suppliers of distilled spirits have National Wine & Spirits and other alcohol distributors across the country re-evaluating how they do business.

For example, Diageo is conducting a state-by-state review to determine the companies that have exclusive rights to distribute its products. In Illinois it has not granted such rights to National Wine & Spirits; two other suppliers, Future Brands and Canandaigua Wine Company, also have ended the company's Illinois distribution rights. As a result, National Wine & Spirits is scaling back operations and about 300 jobs in that state and forming a strategic alliance with Glazer's Wholesale Drug Company.

Both Glazer's and National Wine & Spirits have acquired parts of Johnson Brothers wine business in Illinois. As a result, National Wine &

Spirits will sell E & J Gallo brands in that state through its Union Beverage subsidiary.

However, in Michigan and Indiana, National Wine & Spirits does have exclusive rights to distribute Diageo products, which is likely to boost business in those areas.

To broaden its offerings, the company also sells imported and specialty beers through a subsidiary and in some markets sells cigars.

EXECUTIVES

Chairman, President, CEO, and CFO:
James E. LaCrosse, age 72, $440,300 pay
COO, Secretary, and Director: John J. Baker, age 35, $488,269 pay
EVP, Sales and Marketing: Gregory J. Mauloff, age 53, $488,817 pay
VP, Sales, Indiana Fine Wine and Director:
Catherine M. LaCrosse, age 38
President, National Wine and Spirits Illinois LLC:
John Wittig, age 45, $363,322 pay
President and CEO, US Beverage: Joseph J. Fisch Jr., age 56, $410,000 pay
Treasurer and Corporate Controller: Patrick A. Trefun, age 45
Auditors: Deloitte & Touche LLP

LOCATIONS

HQ: National Wine & Spirits, Inc
700 W. Morris St., Indianapolis, IN 46206
Phone: 317-636-6092   **Fax:** 317-685-8810
Web: www.nwscorp.com

PRODUCTS/OPERATIONS

Selected Brands

Indiana
  Absolut vodka
  Almaden wine
  Beringer wine
  Captain Morgan rum
  Crown Royal whiskey
  Jim Beam whiskey
  Jose Cuervo tequila
  Ravenswood wine
  Seagram's gin
  Smirnoff vodka
  Yellow Tail wine

Kentucky
  Absolut vodka
  Beringer wine
  Jim Beam whiskey
  Kendall-Jackson wine

Michigan
  Absolut vodka
  Captain Morgan rum
  Jim Beam whiskey
  Jose Cuervo tequila
  Smirnoff vodka

COMPETITORS

Glazer's Wholesale Drug
Johnson Brothers
Southern Wine & Spirits

HISTORICAL FINANCIALS

Company Type: Private

Income Statement

FYE: March 31

	REVENUE ($ mil.)	NET INCOME ($ mil.)	NET PROFIT MARGIN	EMPLOYEES
3/05	554	5	1.0%	1,435
3/04	541	(9)	—	1,388
3/03	713	16	2.2%	1,430
3/02	682	8	1.1%	1,618
3/01	661	15	2.3%	1,521
3/00	626	6	0.9%	1,550
3/99	553	—	—	1,550
3/98	521	—	—	1,517
3/97	491	—	—	—
3/96	443	—	—	—
Annual Growth	**2.5%**	**(1.8%)**	**—**	**(0.8%)**

2005 Year-End Financials
Debt ratio: 468.8%
Return on equity: 35.6%
Cash ($ mil.): 3
Current ratio: 1.77
Long-term debt ($ mil.): 83

Net Income History

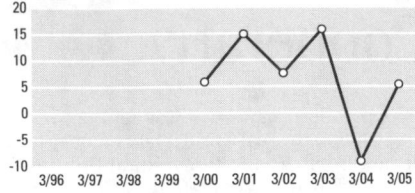

3/96	3/97	3/98	3/99	3/00	3/01	3/02	3/03	3/04	3/05	

Nationwide Mutual

Call it truth in advertising — Nationwide Mutual Insurance Company has offices throughout the US. The company is a leading US property/casualty insurer that, though still a mutual firm, operates in part through publicly held insurance subsidiary Nationwide Financial Services. In addition to personal and commercial property/casualty coverage, life insurance, and financial services, Nationwide offers surplus lines, professional liability, workers' compensation, managed health care, and other coverage. The company sells its products through such affiliates as ALLIED Group, Farmland Insurance, GatesMcDonald, Scottsdale Insurance, and asset manager Gartmore.

To enhance its focus on personal and small-business lines in the US, Nationwide bought specialty auto insurer THI from Prudential. Nationwide Financial also bought Provident Mutual Life Insurance (now Nationwide Financial Network); the acquisition made the company the fourth-largest US provider of variable life insurance.

HISTORY

In 1919 members of the Ohio Farm Bureau Federation, a farmers' consumer group, established their own automobile insurance company. (As rural drivers, they didn't want to pay city rates.) To get a license from the state, the company, called Farm Bureau Mutual, needed 100 policyholders. It gathered more than 1,000. Founder Murray Lincoln headed the company until 1964.

The insurer expanded into Delaware, Maryland, North Carolina, and Vermont in 1928 and began selling auto insurance in 1931 to city folks. It expanded into fire insurance in 1934 and life insurance the next year.

During WWII growth slowed, although the company had operations in 12 states and Washington, DC, by 1943. It diversified in 1946 when it bought a Columbus, Ohio, radio station. By 1952 the firm had resumed expansion and changed its name to Nationwide.

The company was one of the first auto insurance companies to use its agents to sell other financial products, adding life insurance and mutual funds in the mid-1950s. Nationwide General, the country's first merit-rated auto insurance firm, was formed in 1956.

Nationwide established Neckura in Germany in 1965 to sell auto and fire insurance. Four years later the company bought GatesMcDonald, a provider of risk, tax, benefit, and health care management services. It organized its property/casualty operations into Nationwide Property & Casualty in 1979.

The company experienced solid growth throughout the 1980s by establishing or purchasing insurance firms, among them Colonial Insurance of California (1980), Financial Horizons Life (1981), Scottsdale (1982), and, the largest, Employers Insurance of Wausau (1985). Wausau wrote the country's first workers' compensation policy in 1911.

Earnings were up and down in the 1990s as the company invested in Wausau and in consolidating office operations. Nationwide set up an ethics office in 1995, a time of increased scrutiny of insurance industry sales practices, and made an effort to hire more women as agents. In 1996 the Florida Insurance Commission claimed the company discriminated against customers on the basis of age, gender, health, income, marital status, and location. Nationwide countered that the allegations originated from disgruntled agents.

In 1997 the company settled a lawsuit by agreeing to stop its redlining practices (it avoided selling homeowners' insurance to urban customers with homes valued at less than $50,000 or more than 30 years old, which allegedly discriminated against minorities). It also dropped a year-old sales quota system that was under investigation.

As the century came to a close, Nationwide began to narrow its focus on its core businesses. It spun off Nationwide Financial Services so the unit could have better access to capital, and it expanded both at home and abroad through such purchases as ALLIED Group (multiline insurance), CalFarm (agricultural insurance in California), and AXA subsidiary PanEuroLife (asset management in Europe). It jettisoned such operations as West Coast Life Insurance, its Wausau subsidiary, and its ALLIED Life operations. The company's discrimination woes came back to haunt it in 1999, and it created a $750,000 fund to help residents of poor Cincinnati neighborhoods buy homes.

At the end of 2000, Nationwide Health Plans asked regulators for permission to exit the profit-poor HMO business. The division plans to maintain its more popular PPO operations. The next year Nationwide's expansion in Europe continued with the purchase of UK fund manager Gartmore Investment Management.

Although Nationwide Financial and its Strategic Investments segment underperformed in 2002, the company swung to a net profit, helped in part by improved underwriting results by its insurance subsidiaries.

EXECUTIVES

Chairman: Arden L. Shisler, age 63
Vice Chairman: James F. Patterson, age 63
CEO and Director: William G. (Jerry) Jurgensen, age 53
President and COO, Nationwide Financial Services, Inc.: Mark R. Thresher, age 48
President and COO, Property and Casualty Insurance Operations: Stephen S. (Steve) Rasmussen, age 53
President, Nationwide Strategic Investments:
Donna A. James, age 47

EVP, General Counsel, and Secretary:
Patricia R. (Pat) Hatler, age 50
EVP and Chief Administrative Officer: Terri L. Hill, age 45
EVP, CFO, Finance, Investments, and Strategy:
Robert A. Rosholt, age 54
EVP and CIO: Michael C. Keller, age 45
EVP and Chief Marketing Officer:
Kathleen D. (Kathy) Ricord, age 54
President, Gartmore Group: Paul J. Hondros
President and COO, Scottsdale Insurance Company:
Michael D. (Mike) Miller
Auditors: KPMG LLP

LOCATIONS

HQ: Nationwide Mutual Insurance Company
1 Nationwide Plaza, Columbus, OH 43215
Phone: 614-249-7111   **Fax:** 614-249-7705
Web: www.nationwide.com

Nationwide operates in more than 35 countries around the world.

PRODUCTS/OPERATIONS

Selected Subsidiaries and Affiliates
Allied Property and Casualty Insurance Company
Colonial County Mutual Insurance Company
Depositors Insurance Company
Farmland Mutual Insurance Company
National Casualty Company
Nationwide Affinity Insurance Company of America
Nationwide Agribusiness Insurance Company
Nationwide Assurance Company
Nationwide Financial Services, Inc.
Nationwide General Insurance Company
Nationwide Insurance Company of America
Nationwide Lloyds
Nationwide Mutual Fire Insurance Company
Nationwide Property and Casualty Insurance Company
Nationwide Securities, Inc.
Scottsdale Indemnity Company

COMPETITORS

ACE Limited	Liberty Mutual
AIG	MassMutual
Allstate	MetLife
American Financial	New York Life
AXA	Northwestern Mutual
AXA Financial	Pacific Mutual
Blue Cross	Principal Financial
CIGNA	Prudential
Citigroup	St. Paul Travelers
CNA Financial	State Farm
Guardian Life	UnitedHealth Group
The Hartford	USAA
John Hancock	
Financial Services	

HISTORICAL FINANCIALS
Company Type: Mutual company

Income Statement

FYE: December 31

	ASSETS ($ mil.)	NET INCOME ($ mil.)	INCOME AS % OF ASSETS	EMPLOYEES
12/03	147,934	653	0.4%	30,000
12/02	117,930	252	0.2%	30,000
12/01	113,463	(295)	—	35,000
12/00	117,040	331	0.3%	35,000
12/99	115,760	526	0.5%	35,000
12/98	98,280	963	1.0%	32,815
12/97	83,214	1,031	1.2%	29,051
12/96	67,624	250	0.4%	33,184
12/95	57,420	183	0.3%	32,949
12/94	47,696	445	0.9%	32,600
Annual Growth	13.4%	4.4%	—	(0.9%)

2003 Year-End Financials

Equity as % of assets: 7.3%   Long-term debt ($ mil.): —
Return on assets: 0.5%   Sales ($ mil.): 16,803
Return on equity: 7.0%

Net Income History

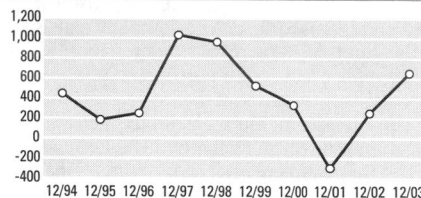

Navy Federal Credit Union

"Once a member, always a member," promises Navy Federal Credit Union (NFCU). This policy undoubtedly helped NFCU become one of the nation's largest credit unions, claiming more than 2.5 million members. Formed in 1933, NFCU provides US Navy and Marine Corps personnel and their families with checking and savings accounts, credit cards, insurance, investments, and a variety of loans, including mortgage, auto, and student loans. Members, who can retain their credit union privileges even after discharge from the armed services, get access to ATMs in Visa's PLUS Network and the CO-OP Network. NFCU has more than 100 locations in the US and overseas.

A wholly owned subsidiary, Navy Federal Financial Group, offers financial advice, brokerage services, and investments such as stocks, bonds, mutual funds, and annuities. NFCU added trust services in 2004.

EXECUTIVES

Chairman: John A. Lockard
First Vice Chairman: Mary Jane Miller
Second Vice Chairman: Bruce B. Engelhardt
President and CEO: Cutler Dawson
COO: William Earner
SEVP and Chief of Operations: John R. Peden
SEVP, Support Group: Brady M. Cole
EVP, Lending Department: Tom Steele
SVP, Marketing and Development: Patricia Schneck
VP, Regulatory Compliance and Public Policy:
Bill Briscoe
VP, Savings and Membership: Lynda McDaniel
Public Relations Manager: Susan Brooks
President and CEO, Navy Federal Financial Group:
Dennis J. Godfrey
Secretary and Director: Kenneth R. Burns
Treasurer and Director: Brian L. McDonnell
Auditors: PricewaterhouseCoopers LLP

LOCATIONS

HQ: Navy Federal Credit Union
820 Follin Ln., Vienna, VA 22180
Phone: 703-255-8000   **Fax:** 703-255-8741
Web: www.navyfcu.org

PRODUCTS/OPERATIONS

2004 Sales

	$ mil.	% of total
Interest		
Loans to members	931.9	69
Securities	126.3	9
Noninterest		
Overdrawn Sharechek fees	71.9	5
Sharechek card interchange	66.3	5
Credit card interchange	60.2	4
Mortgage servicing	36.4	3
ATM interchange	27.9	2
Other	39.4	3
Total	**1,360.3**	**100**

COMPETITORS

Bank of America	USAA
Citibank	Wachovia
JPMorgan Chase	Wells Fargo

HISTORICAL FINANCIALS
Company Type: Not-for-profit

Income Statement

FYE: December 31

	REVENUE ($ mil.)	NET INCOME ($ mil.)	NET PROFIT MARGIN	EMPLOYEES
12/04	1,360	274	20.1%	4,500
12/03	1,292	314	24.3%	4,000
12/02	1,201	181	15.1%	4,000
12/01	1,139	157	13.8%	4,000
12/00	1,016	185	18.2%	3,500
12/99	899	128	14.3%	3,100
12/98	848	113	13.3%	3,100
12/97	787	95	12.1%	3,597
12/96	709	—	—	3,423
12/95	664	—	—	3,304
Annual Growth	8.3%	16.3%	—	3.5%

Net Income History

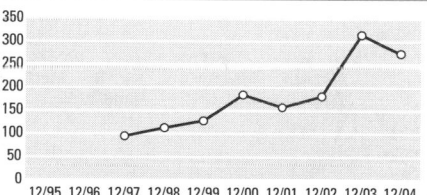

NBO Systems

This company can see its future in the cards — gift cards. NBO Systems creates gift card and gift certificate programs for shopping malls, individual retailers, and organizations seeking fund-raising opportunities. It covers the entire spectrum of services, from program development through order fulfillment. The company is transitioning from gift certificates to prepaid stored value cards for retailers. NBO Systems also offers fund-raising programs that use discounted gift certificates and cards sold at face value to raise money for school-based groups such as PTAs, boosters, sports organizations, and churches. Chairman and CEO Keith Guevara owns about 29% of the company. 13% of NBO's sales are attributed to "breakage," the term used when gift cards go unredeemed.

EXECUTIVES

Chairman, President, and CEO: Keith A. Guevara, age 55, $245,292 pay
CFO and Director: Christopher Foley, age 42, $139,508 pay
EVP: Robert H. Baker Jr., age 57, $78,419 pay
SVP: Chris Hutcherson
VP Technology and Information Systems and Acting COO and CTO: John J. Arego, age 46
Chief Accounting Officer, Secretary, and Treasurer: D. Kent Jasperson, age 56, $111,000 pay
Investor Relations: Diane S. Powers
SVP Business Development: Richard C. Pileggi
Auditors: Tanner + Co.

LOCATIONS

HQ: NBO Systems, Inc.
3676 W. California Ave., Bldg. D,
Salt Lake City, UT 84104
Phone: 801-887-7000   **Fax:** 801-973-4188
Web: www.nbo.com

PRODUCTS/OPERATIONS

2004 Sales

	$ mil.	% of total
Third-party gift certificates/cards	7.7	64
Gift certificate breakage	1.5	13
Merchant fees	1.2	10
Fees earned from customers	1.0	8
Other sales	0.6	5
Total	**12.0**	**100**

COMPETITORS

GiftCertificates.com
IncentOne
LoyaltyPoint
PrivaCash

HISTORICAL FINANCIALS

Company Type: Private

Income Statement

FYE: December 31

	REVENUE ($ mil.)	NET INCOME ($ mil.)	NET PROFIT MARGIN	EMPLOYEES
12/04	12	(4)	—	58
12/03*	9	(2)	—	65
3/03	6	(4)	—	—
Annual Growth	**46.4%**	—	—	**(10.8%)**

*Fiscal year change

Net Income History

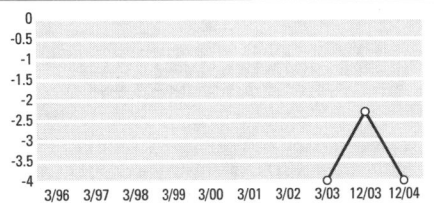

NCH

NCH Corporation has been cleaning up for years, and like everyone else, it's been using soaps and detergents to do so. The company makes and sells about 450 chemical, maintenance, repair, and supply products for customers in more than 60 countries throughout the world. NCH markets its products — including all kinds of cleaners — through a direct sales force to the agricultural, home-improvement, industrial, recreational, and utility industries. Other products include fasteners, welding supplies, plumbing parts, lubricants, and metal working fluids. Descendants of founder Milton Levy own the company.

NCH's cleaning products include hand cleaners, industrial cleaners, and housekeeping supplies. Specialty chemical products, including cleaning and water treatment chemicals, deodorizers, lubricants, paints and paint strippers, patching compounds, and flooring and carpet treatments, account for the majority of sales.

EXECUTIVES

Chairman and President: Irvin L. Levy
EVP: John I. Levy
EVP: Lester A. Levy Jr.
EVP: Robert M. Levy
EVP: Walter M. Levy
SVP, CFO, and Controller: Tom F. Hetzer, age 64
SVP: Earl Nicholson
VP and Treasurer: Glen Scivally
Director, Marketing: Mike Benton
Auditors: Grant Thornton LLP

LOCATIONS

HQ: NCH Corporation
2727 Chemsearch Blvd., Irving, TX 75062
Phone: 972-438-0226   **Fax:** 972-438-0707
Web: www.nch.com

NCH Corporation has roughly 20 manufacturing facilities in Asia, the Americas, and Europe, and office and warehouse facilities in Europe and the Americas.

PRODUCTS/OPERATIONS

Selected Operations and Products

Chemical Specialties
 Cleaning chemicals
 Deodorizers
 Floor and carpet care products
 HVAC products
 Lubricants
 Oil production facility chemicals
 Paint
 Paint removers
 Water-treatment chemicals
Landmark Direct
 First-aid supplies
 Workplace signage and productivity products
Partsmaster Group
 Cutting tools
 Electrical products
 Fasteners
 Welding alloys
Plumbing Products Group
 Plumbing products for new construction
 Plumbing repair and replacement parts

COMPETITORS

Acuity Specialty Products	Illinois Tool Works
Church & Dwight	JohnsonDiversey
Cintas	Lawson Products
Clariant International	Pioneer
Clorox	Quaker Chemical
Danaher	Safety-Kleen
Detrex	Smart & Final
Ecolab	Snap-on
H.B. Fuller	SYSCO
Hercules	WD-40
Hughes Supply	

HISTORICAL FINANCIALS

Company Type: Private

Income Statement

FYE: April 30

	REVENUE ($ mil.)	NET INCOME ($ mil.)	NET PROFIT MARGIN	EMPLOYEES
4/04	684	36	5.2%	6,500
4/03	650	—	—	6,500
4/02	658	—	—	6,500
4/01	680	—	—	8,404
4/00	728	—	—	9,330
4/99	787	—	—	10,093
4/98	784	—	—	10,373
4/97	767	—	—	10,458
4/96	773	—	—	10,543
4/95	735	—	—	10,569
Annual Growth	**(0.8%)**	—	—	**(5.3%)**

Revenue History

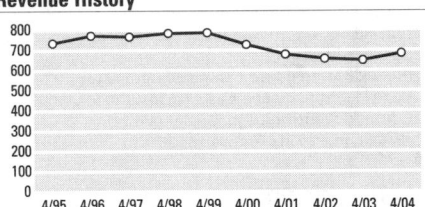

NCI

NCI takes great pride in information technology. The company provides a variety of information technology services to US government agencies. NCI's services include enterprise systems management, systems integration, consulting, legacy migration, implementation, maintenance, network design, application development, and network engineering. More than 70% of the company's sales come from defense and intelligence agencies, including the US Army, US Air Force, and the Defense Logistics Agency. Other clients include NASA and the Department of Energy. NCI was incorporated in 2005 to hold the stock of subsidiary NCI Information Systems, which was formed in 1989.

EXECUTIVES

Chairman and CEO: Charles K. Narang, age 63, $497,917 pay
President and Director: Michael W. (Mike) Solley, age 47, $363,613 pay
COO: Terry W. Glasgow, age 61, $276,645 pay
EVP: Linda J. Allan, age 57, $176,840 pay
SVP and CFO: Judith L. (Judy) Bjornaas, age 42, $276,834 pay
VP, Investor Relations: Maureen Crystal
Auditors: Ernst & Young LLP

LOCATIONS

HQ: NCI, Inc.
11730 Plaza America Dr., Reston, VA 20190
Phone: 703-707-6900　　**Fax:** 703-707-6901
Web: www.nciinc.com

PRODUCTS/OPERATIONS

2004 Sales

	% of total
Department of Defense & intelligence agencies	73
Federal civilian agencies & other	27
Total	**100**

COMPETITORS

Anteon	Northrop Grumman IT
CACI International	SAIC
Lockheed Martin Information & Technology	SRA International

HISTORICAL FINANCIALS

Company Type: Private

Income Statement   FYE: December 31

	REVENUE ($ mil.)	NET INCOME ($ mil.)	NET PROFIT MARGIN	EMPLOYEES
12/04	171	6	3.6%	1,450
12/03	136	6	4.5%	—
12/02	138	8	5.5%	—
Annual Growth	**11.3%**	**(10.4%)**	**—**	**—**

2004 Year-End Financials

Debt ratio: 56.2%　　　　Current ratio: 1.14
Return on equity: 43.2%　Long-term debt ($ mil.): 9
Cash ($ mil.): 0

Net Income History

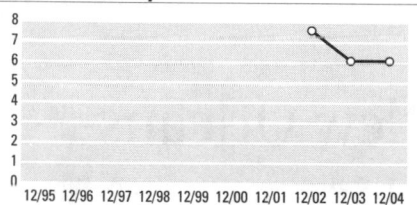

12/95 12/96 12/97 12/98 12/99 12/00 12/01 12/02 12/03 12/04

---

nCircle Network Security has attracted some $50 million in private equity funding from the likes of Alta Partners, BV Capital, Menlo Ventures, and Tall Oaks Capital.

EXECUTIVES

President and CEO: Abe Kleinfeld
CFO: Mark Elchinoff
SVP, Corporate Development: Karl Hutter
VP, Engineering: Rob Byrne
VP, Marketing: Elizabeth A. Ireland, age 43
VP, Product Management: Stefan Petry
VP, Worldwide Sales: Gus Malezis
CTO: Tim Keanini

LOCATIONS

HQ: nCircle Network Security, Inc.
101 Second St., Ste. 400, San Francisco, CA 94105
Phone: 415-625-5900　　**Fax:** 415-625-5982
Web: www.ncircle.com

COMPETITORS

Aventail
Forum Systems
Reactivity

HISTORICAL FINANCIALS

Company Type: Private

Income Statement   FYE: December 31

	ESTIMATED REVENUE ($ mil.)	NET INCOME ($ mil.)	NET PROFIT MARGIN	EMPLOYEES
12/04	10	—	—	100
12/03	6	—	—	60
Annual Growth	**66.7%**	**—**	**—**	**66.7%**

Revenue History

12/95 12/96 12/97 12/98 12/99 12/00 12/01 12/02 12/03 12/04

EXECUTIVES

Chairman and CEO: James S. (Jim) Davis, age 61
President and COO: Jim Tompkins
President Emeritus: John E. Larson
CFO: John Withee
EVP Administration: Anne Davis
EVP Global Marketing: Paul Heffernan
EVP Manufacturing and Procurement: Herb Spivak
VP Corporate Human Resources: Carol O'Donnell
VP International: Edward Haddad
VP International, Pacific/Asia: Joseph (Joe) Preston
VP Manufacturing: John Wilson
VP Sales, US and Canada: Fran Allen
Treasurer: Alan Rosen
Corporate Communications: Amy Vreeland

LOCATIONS

HQ: New Balance Athletic Shoe, Inc.
Brighton Landing, 20 Guest St., Boston, MA 02135
Phone: 617-783-4000　　**Fax:** 617-787-9355
Web: www.newbalance.com

COMPETITORS

adidas-Salomon
ASICS
Brooks Sports
Converse
Fila USA
K Swiss
Mizuno
NIKE
PUMA
Reebok
Roots
Saucony
Shoe Show

HISTORICAL FINANCIALS

Company Type: Private

Income Statement   FYE: December 31

	REVENUE ($ mil.)	NET INCOME ($ mil.)	NET PROFIT MARGIN	EMPLOYEES
12/03	1,200	—	—	2,600
12/02	1,200	—	—	2,400
12/01	1,160	—	—	2,400
12/00	1,100	—	—	2,400
12/99	890	—	—	2,000
12/98	630	—	—	1,600
12/97	560	—	—	1,500
12/96	483	—	—	1,300
12/95	380	—	—	1,200
Annual Growth	**15.5%**	**—**	**—**	**10.1%**

Revenue History

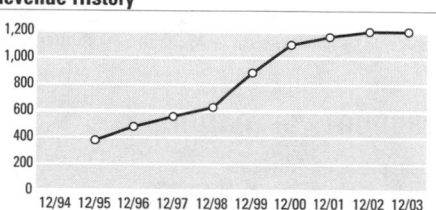

12/94 12/95 12/96 12/97 12/98 12/99 12/00 12/01 12/02 12/03

---

nCircle Network Security

Will the nCircle be unbroken? nCircle Network Security manufactures devices that assess and monitor enterprise network security, keeping hackers and other baddies out. It markets to corporations in the financial services sector, manufacturers, insurance companies, and other service organizations, as well as government agencies. Customers include the US Office of Naval Intelligence, Visa, Archer Daniels Midland, Aquila, Patelco, and USAID. nCircle was founded in 1998. The company has offices in Canada, Japan, the UK, and the US.

New Balance

New Balance Athletic Shoe's everyman appeal is what gives it a boost. Unlike its rivals, the company shuns celebrity endorsers; its lesser-known athletes show its emphasis on substance versus style. The approach attracts a clientele of aging boomer jocks who are less fickle than the teens chased by other shoe firms. Founded in 1906 to make arch supports, New Balance is known for its wide selection of shoe widths. Besides men's and women's shoes for running, cross-training, basketball, tennis, hiking, and golf, the company offers fitness apparel and kids' shoes and owns leather boot maker Dunham. Chairman and CEO Jim Davis bought New Balance on the day of the 1972 Boston Marathon.

New Jersey Devils

There was a time when it seemed as though this team didn't stand a snowball's chance in Hell of winning a Stanley Cup, but now the ranks of playoff-bound clubs is regularly possessed by the New Jersey Devils. The franchise, which entered the National Hockey League in 1974, won its first title in 1995 and scored two more championships in 2000 and 2003. Despite the team's recent successes, New Jersey suffers with one of the worst attendance rates in the pro ranks. The team was owned by uber-sports group YankeeNets (which also owned the New York Yankees and the New Jersey Nets), but former minority owner Jeffrey Vanderbeek and an investment group took it over in early 2005.

New Jersey's support from fans has been bedeviled by the team's strong defensive play (not exciting enough for some US patrons) and ongoing questions concerning the Devils' possible move away from Continental Airlines Arena at the Meadowlands. Vanderbeek has said he wants to move the team to a proposed $310 million arena in Newark. (Meanwhile, the Nets, also under new management after the dissolution of YankeeNets, have said they will exit the Garden State for a new arena in Brooklyn.)

EXECUTIVES

President, CEO, and General Manager:
Louis A. (Lou) Lamoriello, age 62
Head Coach: Larry Robinson, age 54
Goaltending Coach: Jacques Caron
Goaltending Coach, Albany: Chris Terreri, age 40
Head Coach, Albany: Robbie Ftorek, age 53
Assistant Coach: Jacques Laperriere
Assistant Coach: John MacLean
EVP: Peter S. McMullen
EVP: Chris Modrynski
VP and General Counsel: Joseph C. Benedetti
VP Finance: Scott Struble
VP Marketing and Community Development:
Jason Siegel
Director of Public Relations: Jeff Altstadter

LOCATIONS

HQ: New Jersey Devils
50 Rte. 120 North, East Rutherford, NJ 07073
Phone: 201-935-6050   **Fax:** 201-935-2127
Web: www.newjerseydevils.com

The New Jersey Devils play in the 19,040-seat capacity Continental Airlines Arena in East Rutherford, New Jersey.

PRODUCTS/OPERATIONS

Championship Trophies
Stanley Cup (1995, 2000, 2003)
Prince of Wales Trophy (1995, 2000-01, 2003)

COMPETITORS

New York Islanders
New York Rangers
Philadelphia Flyers
Pittsburgh Penguins

HISTORICAL FINANCIALS

Company Type: Private

Income Statement
FYE: June 30

	REVENUE ($ mil.)	NET INCOME ($ mil.)	NET PROFIT MARGIN	EMPLOYEES
6/04	61	—	—	—
6/03	73	—	—	—
6/02	61	—	—	—
6/01	70	—	—	—
6/00	63	—	—	—
6/99	52	—	—	—
6/98	54	—	—	150
6/97	44	—	—	—
6/96	30	—	—	—
6/95	27	—	—	110
Annual Growth	9.6%	—	—	10.9%

Revenue History

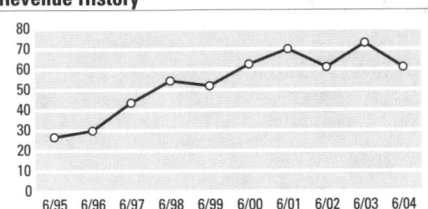

New Jersey Nets

It's nothing but the Nets in New Jersey. The New Jersey Nets posted just a few winning seasons in the past decade. Recent additions, such as guard Jason Kidd, have helped the team rebound into a contender; it made it to the NBA Finals in 2002-04, but lost all three outings. Arthur Brown started the Nets in 1967 as the New Jersey Americans. It moved across the Hudson the next year to become the New York Nets and won two ABA championships with Julius "Dr. J" Erving before joining the rival NBA in 1976. The Nets moved back to the Garden State that year. New York real estate developer Bruce Ratner bought the team from Lewis Katz and Ray Chambers in 2004 for $300 million. Ratner plans to move the team to Brooklyn.

EXECUTIVES

Owner: Bruce C. Ratner, age 60
President and CEO: Brett Yormark
CFO: Gordon Lavalette
President, Nets Basketball Operations and General Manager: Rod Thorn
Head Coach: Lawrence Frank
Assistant Coach: Gordon Chiesa
EVP, Marketing and Sales: Leo Ehrline
SVP: Lou Terminello
Executive Director, Corporate Sales: Joe Hocker
Director, Marketing: Matt Pazaras

LOCATIONS

HQ: Nets Sports & Entertainment, LLC
390 Murray Hill Pkwy., East Rutherford, NJ 07073
Phone: 201-935-8888   **Fax:** 201-939-7812
Web: www.nba.com/nets

PRODUCTS/OPERATIONS

Championship Titles
Eastern Conference Champions (2002-03)

COMPETITORS

Boston Celtics   Philadelphia 76ers
New York Knicks   Toronto Raptors

HISTORICAL FINANCIALS

Company Type: Private

Income Statement
FYE: June 30

	REVENUE ($ mil.)	NET INCOME ($ mil.)	NET PROFIT MARGIN	EMPLOYEES
6/04	93	—	—	—
6/03	94	—	—	—
6/02	91	—	—	—
6/01*	73	—	—	—
6/98	66	—	—	100
6/97	58	—	—	—
6/96	53	—	—	—
6/95	52	—	—	60
6/94	42	—	—	—
Annual Growth	10.5%	—	—	18.6%

*Irregular reporting interval

Revenue History

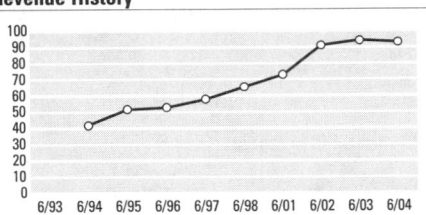

New Orleans Hornets

In North Carolina basketball didn't mean a thing and Charlotte no longer has that sting. The New Orleans Hornets, citing millions in losses and bad attendance, moved from Charlotte to New Orleans in 2002. The move proved successful with high attendance and great support from Crescent City fans. Then hurricane Katrina hit in 2005 and the team moved its game to Oklahoma City's Ford Center until its home city bounces back. The Hornets started play in the NBA in 1988. It has steadily reached the playoffs over its lifetime despite off court distractions like the move and rumors that owner George Shinn might sell or that the team might make the move to Oklahoma permanent.

EXECUTIVES

Majority Owner and Managing General Partner:
George Shinn
President: Paul Mott
General Manager: Allan Bristow
Head Coach: Byron Scott, age 44
Assistant Coach: Jim Cleamons
Assistant Coach: Kenny Gattison
Assistant Coach: Darrell Walker
EVP Business: Sam Russo
Director of Player Personnel: Jeff Bower
SVP Communications and Public Affairs: Steve Martin
SVP Corporate Development: Tim Hinchey
SVP Marketing and Business Development: John Lee
CTO: Tim Spero
VP Basketball Operations: Willis Reed, age 63
VP Community Relations: Suzanne Werdann
VP Finance: Barbara Booth
VP Public Relations: Harold Kaufman
Chief Marketing Officer: Tim McDougall
Human Resources: Donna Rochon

LOCATIONS

HQ: New Orleans Hornets
1501 Girod St., New Orleans, LA 70113
Phone: 504-301-4000 **Fax:** 504-301-4001
Web: www.nba.com/hornets

The New Orleans Hornets temporarily play at the 19,599-seat Oklahoma City Ford Center.

COMPETITORS

Dallas Mavericks
Houston Rockets
Memphis Grizzlies
San Antonio Spurs

HISTORICAL FINANCIALS

Company Type: Private

Income Statement

FYE: June 30

	REVENUE ($ mil.)	NET INCOME ($ mil.)	NET PROFIT MARGIN	EMPLOYEES
6/04	80	—	—	—
6/03	80	—	—	—
6/02	64	—	—	—
6/01	65	—	—	—
6/00	58	—	—	—
6/99	30	—	—	—
6/98	56	—	—	65
6/97	54	—	—	50
6/96	47	—	—	—
Annual Growth	**7.0%**	—	—	**30.0%**

Revenue History

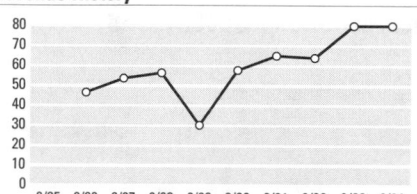

New United Motor Manufacturing

What do you get when a Japanese production process meets a California lifestyle? New United Motor Manufacturing, Inc. (NUMMI), a 50-50 joint venture between General Motors (GM) and Toyota. NUMMI makes Tacoma pickup trucks and Corolla sedans for Toyota. The Tacoma is made only at the NUMMI plant in Fremont, California. The company also makes GM's Pontiac division's Vibe sport wagon. NUMMI can produce 230,000 cars and 160,000 pickups a year. Together GM and Toyota are researching alternative-fuel vehicles. Since its formation in 1984 NUMMI has produced nearly 6 million vehicles.

NUMMI began as an experiment to see if Japanese management techniques emphasizing team decision-making would work in the US. The experiment has been a success story. Toyota's strategy to build more vehicles in the markets it serves (rather than transport them) helps the company reduce costs. NUMMI's production methods are considered to be among the world's most efficient.

HISTORY

Rivals General Motors (GM) and Toyota applied the old adage, "If you can't beat 'em, join 'em," in forming their 50-50 joint venture New United Motor Manufacturing, Inc. (NUMMI). During the early 1980s GM was sagging in the small-car market, and Japan's Toyota wanted to build cars in the US to ease trade tension. GM head Roger Smith and Toyota chairman Eiji Toyoda met in 1982 to discuss ways to achieve their goals.

After a year of negotiations, the two companies announced their partnership at GM's plant (which GM had closed in 1982) in Fremont, California. Toyota put up $100 million, and GM provided the plant (valued at $89 million) and $11 million cash. The companies also raised $350 million to build a stamping plant.

To gain FTC approval, the companies agreed to limit the venture to 12 years (extended later), make no more than 250,000 cars a year for GM, and refrain from sharing strategic information. In 1984 the FTC approved the deal and NUMMI was born.

The Fremont plant had a reputation for poor labor relations, and Toyota originally refused to rehire any of the workers from the plant; after prolonged negotiations with the United Auto Workers (UAW), it agreed to hire 50% plus one of the former workers. From the outset NUMMI was different, with fewer management layers and a blurred distinction between blue- and white-collar workers.

NUMMI's first car, a Chevy Nova, rolled off the assembly line in late 1984. The company began producing the Corolla FX, a two-door version of the four-door Nova, in 1986. NUMMI earned kudos for high worker morale and productivity and was selected that year as a case study on positive labor-management relations for the International Labor Organization Conference.

Despite its success on some fronts, NUMMI's sales slid during the late 1980s. It had earned a reputation for high-quality cars, but it struggled

with high overhead and weak Nova sales. In 1988 NUMMI halted Nova and Corolla FX production to build Geo Prizm and Corolla sedans.

By late 1989 NUMMI's production numbers had begun to rebound. In 1990 NUMMI began a major expansion as it geared up to build Toyota's half-ton pickup. Its first Toyota 4X2 pickup (the Toyota Hi-Lux) rolled off the assembly line in 1991, followed by the Toyota 4X4 pickup the next year.

In 1993 the FTC approved an indefinite extension of the original 12-year GM-Toyota agreement. Also that year NUMMI began building the Toyota Xtracab (an extended version of Toyota's pickup), and it began constructing a plastics plant to build bumper coverings for Prizms and Corollas. It also expanded the paint, body welding, and assembly plant facilities.

Although Toyota had produced half of its North America-bound pickups in Japan and half in the US for years, it shifted all compact truck production to the NUMMI plant with the 1995 launch of the Tacoma. NUMMI built its 3 millionth vehicle in 1997 and marked the event by donating three vehicles to charitable agencies in the Fremont area.

In 1998 Toyota introduced an updated Tacoma compact pickup, and GM changed the name of the Geo Prizm to the Chevrolet Prizm. The companies agreed in 1999 to a five-year partnership to develop and possibly produce alternative-fuel vehicles.

GM alluded to the possible discontinued production of the Prizm in 2000, and the last one left the NUMMI assembly line in 2001. The Prizm was replaced with the Pontiac Vibe the following year.

EXECUTIVES

Chairman, President, and CEO: Yuki Azuma
VP, Human Resources: Robert McCullough
VP, Manufacturing Operations:
Ernesto Gonzalez-Beltran
General Manager, Purchasing: Linda McColgan
General Manager, Truck Organization: Walt Odisho
Assistant Manager, Community Relations:
Rhonda Rigenhagen

LOCATIONS

HQ: New United Motor Manufacturing, Inc.
45500 Fremont Blvd., Fremont, CA 94538
Phone: 510-498-5500 **Fax:** 510-770-4116
Web: www.nummi.com

PRODUCTS/OPERATIONS

Selected Models

Pontiac Vibe (sport wagon)
Toyota Corolla (sedan)
Toyota Tacoma (pickup)

COMPETITORS

DaimlerChrysler	Mazda
Fiat	Nissan
Ford	Peugeot Motors
Fuji Heavy Industries	of America, Inc.
Honda	Saab Automobile
Isuzu	Suzuki Motor
Kia Motors	Volkswagen
Mack Trucks	

HISTORICAL FINANCIALS

Company Type: Joint venture

Income Statement

FYE: December 31

	ESTIMATED REVENUE ($ mil.)	NET INCOME ($ mil.)	NET PROFIT MARGIN	EMPLOYEES
12/98	4,699	—	—	4,800
12/97	4,600	—	—	4,800
12/96	4,700	—	—	4,700
12/95	4,500	—	—	4,800
12/94	3,700	—	—	4,500
12/93	2,700	—	—	4,300
12/92	2,200	—	—	3,969
Annual Growth	13.5%	—	—	3.2%

Revenue History

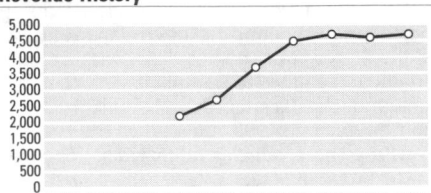

New York City Health and Hospitals

New York City Health and Hospitals Corporation (HHC) takes care of the Big Apple. HHC has facilities in all five boroughs of New York City. As one of the largest municipal health service systems in the US, HHC operates a health care network consisting of 11 acute care hospitals (including Bellevue, the nation's oldest public hospital), community clinics, diagnostic and treatment centers, long-term care facilities, and a home health care agency. HHC also provides medical services to New York City's correctional facilities and operates MetroPlus, a health maintenance organization.

In recent years HHC has lost paying patients to newer, better-equipped facilities and is left caring for a deluge of medically indigent and Medicaid patients, who tend to be sicker than the general population since they wait longer to seek care.

To streamline, HHC has slashed jobs, worked to reduce the average length of stay of patients, and shuttered unnecessary facilities.

HISTORY

The City of New York in 1929 created a department to manage its hospitals for the poor. During the Depression, more than half of the city's residents were eligible for subsidized care, and its public hospitals operated at full capacity.

Four new hospitals opened in the 1950s, but the city was already having trouble maintaining existing facilities and attracting staff (young doctors preferred private, insurance-supported hospitals catering to the middle class). Meanwhile, technological advances and increased demand for skilled nurses made hospitals more expensive

to operate. The advent of Medicaid in 1965 was a boon for the system because it brought in federal money.

In 1969 the city created the New York City Health and Hospitals Corporation (HHC) to manage its public health care system — and, it was hoped, to distance it from the political arena. But HHC was still dependent on the city for funds, arousing criticism from those who had hoped for more autonomy. A 1973 state report claimed "the people of New York City are not materially better served by the Health and Hospitals Corporation than by its predecessor agencies."

City budget shortfalls in the mid-1970s led to cutbacks at HHC, including nearly 20% of staff. Later in the decade several hospitals closed and some services were discontinued. Ed Koch became mayor in 1978 and gained more control over HHC's operations. Struggles between his administration and the system led three HHC presidents to resign by 1981. That year Koch crony Stanley Brezenoff assumed the post and helped transform HHC into a city pseudo-department.

The early 1980s brought greater prosperity to the system. Reimbursement rates and collections procedures improved, allowing HHC to upgrade its record-keeping and its ambulatory and psychiatric care programs. In the late 1980s sharp increases in AIDS and crack addiction cases strained the system and a sluggish economy decreased city funding. Criticism mounted in the early 1990s, with allegations of wrongful deaths, dangerous facilities, and lack of Medicaid payment controls. HHC lost patients to managed care providers, and revenues plummeted. In 1995 a city panel recommended radically revamping the system.

Faced with declining revenues and criticism from Mayor Rudolph Giuliani that HHC was "a jobs program," the company began cutting jobs and consolidating facilities in 1996. Under Giuliani's direction, HHC made plans to sell its Coney Island, Elmhurst, and Queens hospital centers. In 1997 the New York State Supreme Court struck down Giuliani's privatization efforts, saying the city council had a right to review and approve each sale. In 1998 Giuliani continued to seek to restructure HHC, and the agency itself contended it was making progress toward its restructuring goals, which were aimed at giving HHC more autonomy as well as more fiscal responsibility. In anticipation of a budget shortfall that year, the system laid off some 900 support staff employees. In 1999 the state court of appeals ruled HHC could not legally lease or sell its hospitals.

In 2000 HHC launched an effort to improve its physical infrastructure by beginning the rebuilding and renovation of facilities in Brooklyn, Manhattan, and Queens. The organization also began converting to an electronic (and thus more efficient) clinical information system. In 2001 HHC forged ahead with further restructuring initiatives. It introduced the Open Access plan, a cost-cutting measure designed to expedite the processes involved in outpatient visits.

EXECUTIVES

Chairperson: Charlynn Goins
Vice Chairman: Edwin Mendez-Santiago
Acting President and CEO; SVP, Queens Health Network: Alan D. Aviles
SVP and CFO: Marlene Zurack
SVP, Central Brooklyn Family Health Network; Executive Director, Kings County Hospital Center: Jean G. Leon
SVP, Corporate Planning, Community Health, and Intergovernmental Relations: LaRay Brown

SVP, Facilities Development: Phillip W. Robinson
SVP, Generations Plus Northern Manhattan Health Network; Executive Director, Lincoln Medical and Mental Health Center: Jose R. Sanchez
SVP, Medical and Professional Affairs: Van Dunn
SVP, North Bronx Healthcare Network; Executive Director, Jacobi Medical Center: William P. Walsh
SVP, Operations: Frank J. Cirillo
Corporate Director, Communications and Marketing: Kate McGrath
Acting General Counsel: Richard A. Levy
Auditors: KPMG LLP

LOCATIONS

HQ: New York City Health and Hospitals Corporation
125 Worth St., Ste. 514, New York, NY 10013
Phone: 212-788-3321   **Fax:** 212-788-0040
Web: www.ci.nyc.ny.us/html/hhc

HHC Networks

Central Brooklyn Family Health Network
   Dr. Susan Smith McKinney Nursing and Rehabilitation Center
   East New York Diagnostic & Treatment Center
   Kings County Hospital Center

Generations Plus Northern Manhattan Health Network
   Harlem Hospital Center
   Lincoln Medical and Mental Health Center
   Metropolitan Hospital Center
   Morrisania Diagnostic & Treatment Center
   Renaissance Health Care Network Diagnostic & Treatment Center
   Segundo Ruiz Belvis Diagnostic & Treatment Center

North Bronx Healthcare Network
   Jacobi Medical Center
   North Central Bronx Hospital

North Brooklyn Health Network
   Cumberland Diagnostic & Treatment Center
   Woodhull Medical and Mental Health Center

Queens Health Network
   Elmhurst Hospital Center
   Queens Hospital Center

South Brooklyn and Staten Island Health Network
   Coney Island Hospital
   Sea View Hospital Rehabilitation Center and Home

South Manhattan Healthcare Network
   Bellevue Hospital Center
   Coler-Goldwater Specialty Care and Nursing Facility
   Gouverneur Healthcare Services

COMPETITORS

Catholic Healthcare System	Mount Sinai NYU Health
Columbia University	North Shore-Long Island Jewish Health System
Cornell University	NYU
Memorial Sloan-Kettering	Saint Vincent Catholic
Montefiore Medical	Medical Centers

HISTORICAL FINANCIALS

Company Type: Government-owned

Income Statement

FYE: June 30

	REVENUE ($ mil.)	NET INCOME ($ mil.)	NET PROFIT MARGIN	EMPLOYEES
6/03	4,200	—	—	
6/02	4,300	—	—	31,544
6/01	4,300	—	—	32,385
6/00	4,100	—	—	33,500
6/99	4,131	—	—	33,403
6/98	3,835	—	—	31,600
6/97	4,069	—	—	33,000
6/96	4,461	—	—	35,000
6/95	4,134	—	—	41,711
6/94	3,949	—	—	45,000
Annual Growth	0.7%	—	—	(4.3%)

Revenue History

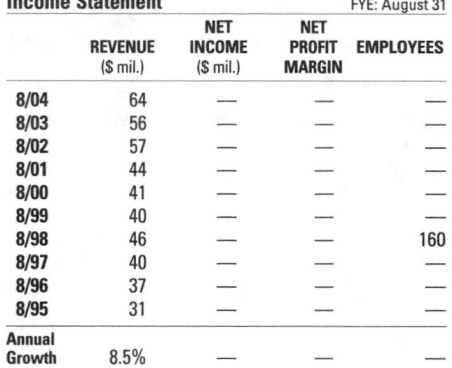

4,500
4,000
3,500
3,000
2,500
2,000
1,500
1,000
500
0

6/94 6/95 6/96 6/97 6/98 6/99 6/00 6/01 6/02 6/03

New York Islanders

These Islanders need to be surrounded by frozen water to be successful. Gotham's other hockey team, the New York Islanders entered the National Hockey League in 1972 and dominated the league in the early 1980s, winning four consecutive Stanley Cup titles until their streak was ended in 1984 by the Wayne Gretzky-led Edmonton Oilers. Since then, however, the Isles struggled for several years until the team was acquired by former Computer Associates chairman Charles Wang and CEO Sanjay Kumar in 2000. A return to postseason play has helped buoy home attendance at Nassau Veterans Memorial Coliseum.

Wang and Kumar bought the Islanders from Steven Gluckstern and Howard Milstein for about $190 million. They have made significant investments in talented players to improve the team's chances on the ice and are looking to replace the aging Nassau Coliseum.

EXECUTIVES

Co-Owner: Charles B. Wang, age 58
Co-Owner: Sanjay Kumar, age 41
General Manager: Mike Milbury, age 53
Head Coach: Steve Stirling
SVP and CFO: Arthur McCarthy
SVP Operations: Michael Picker
VP Corporate and Community Relations: Bill Kain
VP Marketing and Game Operations: Tim Beach
Director of Pro Scouting: Ken Morrow
Head Amateur Scout: Tony Feltrin, age 39
SVP Sales and Marketing: Paul Lancey
Media Relations Assistant: Corey Witt
Media Relations Coordinator: Jim Morlock

LOCATIONS

HQ: New York Islanders Hockey Club, L.P.
1535 Old Country Rd., Plainview, NY 11803
Phone: 516-501-6700   **Fax:** 516-542-9348
Web: www.newyorkislanders.com

The New York Islanders play at the 18,100-seat capacity Nassau Veterans Memorial Coliseum in Uniondale, New York.

PRODUCTS/OPERATIONS

Championship Trophies
Stanley Cup (1980-83)
Clarence S. Campbell Bowl (1978-79, 1981)

COMPETITORS

New Jersey Devils   Philadelphia Flyers
New York Rangers   Pittsburgh Penguins

HISTORICAL FINANCIALS

Company Type: Private

Income Statement

FYE: August 31

	REVENUE ($ mil.)	NET INCOME ($ mil.)	NET PROFIT MARGIN	EMPLOYEES
8/04	64	—	—	—
8/03	56	—	—	—
8/02	57	—	—	—
8/01	44	—	—	—
8/00	41	—	—	—
8/99	40	—	—	—
8/98	46	—	—	160
8/97	40	—	—	—
8/96	37	—	—	—
8/95	31	—	—	—
Annual Growth	**8.5%**	**—**	**—**	**—**

Revenue History

70
60
50
40
30
20
10
0

8/95 8/96 8/97 8/98 8/99 8/00 8/01 8/02 8/03 8/04

New York Life

New York Life Insurance has been in the Big Apple since it was just a tiny seed. The company (the top mutual life insurer in the US) is adding products but retaining its core business: life insurance and annuities. New York Life has added such products and services as mutual funds for individuals. It also offers its investment management services to institutional investors. Other lines of business include long-term care insurance and special group policies sold through AARP and other affinity groups or professional associations. The company, through New York Life International, is also reaching out geographically, targeting areas where the life insurance market is not yet mature.

After state legislators failed to approve its proposed company restructuring, New York Life announced it would not follow its rivals in demutualizing for fear of being gobbled up in a merger.

The insurer instead uses its considerable war chest to further expand its international operations (Asia is a major expansion target) and its investment management operations, which include New York Life Investment Management (mutual funds, group and individual retirement plans, college savings products), NYLIFE Securities (registered broker/dealer), and New York Life Trust Company, FSB (trust, investment management, custody, and administration services).

HISTORY

In 1841 actuary Pliny Freeman and 56 New York businessmen founded Nautilus Insurance Co., the third US policyholder-owned company. It began operating in 1845 and became New York Life in 1849.

By 1846 the company had the first life insurance agent west of the Mississippi River. Although the Civil War disrupted southern business, New York Life honored all its obligations and renewed lapsed policies when the war ended. By 1887 the company had developed its branch office system.

By the turn of the century, the company had established an agent compensation plan that featured a lifetime income after 20 years of service (discontinued 1991). New York Life moved into Europe in the late 1800s but withdrew after WWI.

In the early 1950s the company simplified insurance forms, slashed premiums, and updated mortality tables from the 1860s. In 1956 it became the first life insurer to use data-processing equipment on a large scale.

New York Life helped develop variable life insurance, which featured variable benefits and level premiums in the 1960s; it added variable annuities in 1968. Steady growth continued into the late 1970s, when high interest rates led to heavy policyholder borrowing. The outflow of money convinced New York Life to make its products more competitive as investments.

The company formed New York Life and Health Insurance Co. in 1982. It acquired MacKay-Shields Financial, which oversees its MainStay mutual funds, in 1984. The company's first pure investment product, a real estate limited partnership, debuted that year. (When limited partnerships proved riskier than most insurance customers bargained for, investors sued New York Life; in 1996 the company negotiated a plan to liquidate the partnerships and reimburse investors.)

Expansion continued in 1987 when New York Life bought a controlling interest in a third-party insurance plan administrator and group insurance programs. The company also acquired Sanus Corp. Health Systems.

New York Life formed an insurance joint venture in Indonesia in 1992; it also entered South Korea and Taiwan. The next year it bought Aetna UK's life insurance operations.

In 1994 New York Life grew its health care holdings, adding utilization review and physician practice management units. Allegations of churning (agents inducing customers to buy more expensive policies) led New York Life to overhaul its sales practices in 1994; it settled the resulting lawsuit for $300 million in 1995. Soon came claims that agents hadn't properly informed customers that some policies were vulnerable to interest-rate changes and that customers might be entitled to share in the settlement. Some agents lashed out, saying New York Life fired them so it wouldn't have to pay them retirement benefits.

As health care margins decreased and the insurance industry consolidated, New York Life in 1998 sold its health insurance operations and said it would demutualize — a plan ultimately foiled by the state legislature.

In 2000 the company bought two Mexican insurance firms, including the nation's #2 life insurer, Seguros Monterrey. It received Office of Thrift Supervision permission to open a bank, New York Life Trust Company. Also that year the company created a subsidiary to house its asset management businesses and entered the Indian market through its joint venture with Max India.

In 2002 New York Life entered into a joint life insurance venture with China's Haier Group.

EXECUTIVES

Chairman and CEO: Seymour (Sy) Sternberg, age 60
Vice Chairman; Chairman, New York Life International: Gary G. Benanav, age 59
President and Director: Frederick J. (Fred) Sievert
EVP and Co-Head, US Insurance Operations: Phillip J. (Phil) Hildebrand
EVP and Co-Head, US Insurance Operations: Theodore A. (Ted) Mathas
EVP and CFO: Michael E. Sproule
EVP; Chairman and CEO, New York Life Investment Management LLC: Gary E. Wendlandt
EVP, Law and Corporate Administration: Sheila K. Davidson
EVP; President and CEO, New York Life International, LLC: Joseph A. (Joe) Gilmour, age 49
SVP; President, New York Life Investment Management LLC: Brian A. Murdock
SVP and Treasurer: Jay S. Calhoun
SVP and CIO: Judith E. Campbell
SVP and General Counsel: Thomas P. English
SVP, Controller, and Chief Accounting Officer: John A. Cullen
SVP, Human Resources: Leonard J. Elmer
SVP and Chief Administrative Officer, US Insurance Operations: Frank M. Boccio
SVP and Chief Actuary: Joel M. Steinberg
SVP, Deputy General Counsel, and Secretary: Susan A. Thrope
SVP, General Auditor, and Chief Privacy Officer: Thomas J. Warga
SVP, Office of Governmental Affairs: Jessie M. Colgate
Auditors: PricewaterhouseCoopers LLP

LOCATIONS

HQ: New York Life Insurance Company
51 Madison Ave., New York, NY 10010
Phone: 212-576-7000   **Fax:** 212-576-8145
Web: www.newyorklife.com

New York Life Insurance Company operates in Argentina, China, Hong Kong, India, Mexico, the Philippines, South Korea, Taiwan, Thailand, the US, and Vietnam.

PRODUCTS/OPERATIONS

Selected Subsidiaries and Affiliates

MacKay Shields (institutional asset management)
Madison Square Advisors
MainStay Management (mutual funds)
Max New York Life Insurance Company, Ltd. (private life insurance joint venture with Max India, Ltd., India)
McMorgan & Company (institutional asset management)
Monitor Capital Advisors
New York Life Asset Management
New York Life Benefit Services (retirement benefits administration)
New York Life Insurance and Annuity Corporation (individual life insurance and annuities)
New York Life International (international sales)
NYLIFE Administration Corp. (long-term care and other specialty programs)

COMPETITORS

AEGON	Jefferson-Pilot
AIG	John Hancock Financial
AIG American General	Services
Allianz	Kemper Insurance
Allstate	MassMutual
American National	Merrill Lynch
Insurance	MetLife
AXA	Morgan Stanley
AXA Financial	Mutual of Omaha
Charles Schwab	Northwestern Mutual
CIGNA	Principal Financial
Citigroup	Prudential
CNA Financial	State Farm
Fortis SA/NV	T. Rowe Price
Guardian Life	TIAA-CREF
The Hartford	UBS Financial Services

HISTORICAL FINANCIALS

Company Type: Mutual company

Income Statement

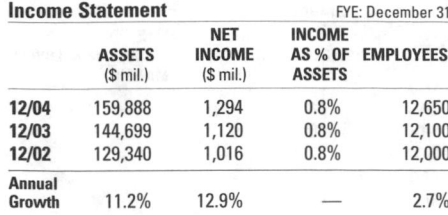

	ASSETS ($ mil.)	NET INCOME ($ mil.)	INCOME AS % OF ASSETS	EMPLOYEES
12/04	159,888	1,294	0.8%	12,650
12/03	144,699	1,120	0.8%	12,100
12/02	129,340	1,016	0.8%	12,000
Annual Growth	11.2%	12.9%	—	2.7%

FYE: December 31

2004 Year-End Financials

Equity as % of assets: 11.1%
Return on assets: 0.8%
Return on equity: 7.6%
Long-term debt ($ mil.): 2,455
Sales ($ mil.): 17,330

Net Income History

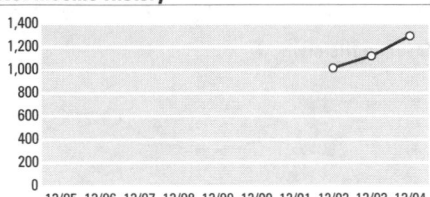

New York Power Authority

Question authority? Well, without question, authority for power lies in the Power Authority of the State of New York (commonly referred to as the New York Power Authority, or NYPA). The company generates and transmits more than 20% of New York's electricity, making it the largest state-owned public power provider in the US. It is also New York's only statewide electricity supplier. NYPA owns hydroelectric and fossil-fueled generating facilities that produce about 5,700 MW of electricity, and it operates more than 1,400 circuit-miles of transmission lines.

The authority sells power to government agencies, municipal systems, rural cooperatives, private companies, private utilities (for resale), and neighboring states. Its clients include some of the largest electricity users in the US, including the New York City government and the Metropolitan Transportation Authority. NYPA receives no state funds or tax credits. Instead, it finances new projects through bond sales.

Following its shift from a regulated monopoly to a competitor in an open power market, NYPA is aiming to grow by reducing the cost of the energy it provides and by developing electric transportation (such as electric cars) and other energy-efficiency projects, such as installing emergency power generators in metropolitan buildings. It is also working to improve the state's transmission grid and increase its generating capacity.

HISTORY

The Power Authority of the State of New York (aka New York Power Authority, or NYPA) was established in 1931 by Gov. Franklin Roosevelt to gain public control of New York's hydropower resources. The utility's major power plants came on line with the opening of the St. Lawrence-Franklin D. Roosevelt Power Project (1958) and the Niagara Power Project (1961). The Blenheim-Gilboa Pumped Storage Power Project opened in 1973.

In the mid-1970s NYPA shifted to nuclear power when it opened the James A. FitzPatrick Nuclear Power Plant (1975) and the Indian Point 3 Nuclear Power Plant (1976). The company then opened gas- and oil-powered plants: the Charles Poletti Power Project (1977) and the Richard M. Flynn Power Plant (1994).

In 1998 the authority allocated low-cost electricity to five companies that planned to invest $104 million in business expansions in western New York. The company suffered a loss in 1999 in part from reduced hydro generation and a drop in investment earnings. In 2000 NYPA sold its two nuclear plants (1,800 MW of capacity) to utility holding company Entergy for $967 million.

The company completed the installation of 11 gas-powered turbines at various locations in New York City and on Long Island in 2001; the program was initiated to prevent expected energy shortages that summer, but it also helped maintain power in areas of the city during the September 11 terrorist attacks.

EXECUTIVES

Chairman: Louis P. Ciminelli
Vice Chairman: Frank S. McCullough Jr.
President and CEO: Eugene W. Zeltmann
EVP, Secretary, and General Counsel: David E. Blabey
EVP Corporate Services and Administration: Vincent C. Vesce
EVP Power Generation: Robert A. Hiney
SVP and CFO: Joseph M. Del Sindaco
SVP Energy Services and Technology: Robert L. Tscherne
SVP Energy Services and Technology: Angelo S. Esposito
SVP Marketing, Economic Development, and Supply Planning: Louise M. Morman
SVP Public and Governmental Affairs: Brian Vattimo
SVP Transmission: Edward L. Hubert
VP and Controller: Arnold M. Bellis
VP Energy Risk Assessment and Control and Chief Risk Officer: Thomas H. Warmath
VP and Chief Engineer: Charles I. Lipsky
VP Ethics and Regulatory Compliance: Anne Wagner-Findeisen
VP Finance: Donald A. Russak
VP Major Accounts Marketing and Economic Development: James H. (Jim) Yates
Treasurer: Michael Brady
Regional Manager and Community Relations: Carol Simpson
Media Contact: Michael Saltzman
Auditors: PricewaterhouseCoopers LLP

LOCATIONS

HQ: Power Authority of the State of New York
123 Main St., White Plains, NY 10601
Phone: 914-681-6200   **Fax:** 914-681-6949
Web: www.nypa.gov

Selected Operations

Transmission Control Facility
  Frederick R. Clark Energy Center (Oneida County)
Fossil-Fueled Plants
  Charles Poletti Power Project (New York City)
  Richard M. Flynn Power Plant (Suffolk County)
  PowerNow! Turbines (11 units in New York City
    and Long Island)
Hydropower Plants
  Blenheim-Gilboa Pumped Storage Power Project
    (Schoharie County)
  Niagara Power Project (Niagara County)
  St. Lawrence-Franklin D. Roosevelt Power Project (St.
    Lawrence County)
Small Hydropower Plants
  Ashokan Project (Ulster County)
  Crescent Plant (Albany and Saratoga Counties)
  Gregory B. Jarvis Plant (Oneida County)
  Kensico Project (Westchester County)
  Vischer Ferry Plant (Saratoga and
    Schenectady counties)

PRODUCTS/OPERATIONS

2004 Sales

	$ mil.	% of total
Power sales	1,796	81
Wheeling charges	277	13
Transmission charges	142	6
Total	2,215	100

COMPETITORS

CH Energy	Entergy
Con Edison	KeySpan
Dynegy	Rochester Gas and Electric
Enbridge	TransCanada
Energy East	

HISTORICAL FINANCIALS

Company Type: Government-owned

Income Statement

FYE: December 31

	REVENUE ($ mil.)	NET INCOME ($ mil.)	NET PROFIT MARGIN	EMPLOYEES
12/04	2,215	82	3.7%	—
12/03	2,215	88	4.0%	—
12/02	2,060	84	4.1%	1,600
12/01	2,016	18	0.9%	1,600
12/00	2,034	170	8.3%	1,531
12/99	1,458	(233)	—	—
12/98	1,484	63	4.2%	—
12/97	1,481	106	7.1%	3,259
12/96	1,430	69	4.8%	3,200
12/95	1,413	—	—	3,300
Annual Growth	5.1%	2.2%	—	(9.8%)

2004 Year-End Financials

Debt ratio: 107.5%
Return on equity: 4.6%
Cash ($ mil.): 77

Current ratio: 1.66
Long-term debt ($ mil.): 1,976

Net Income History

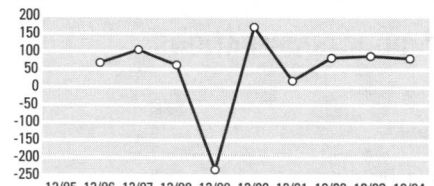

200									
150									
100									
50									
0									
-50									
-100									
-150									
-200									
-250									

12/95 12/96 12/97 12/98 12/99 12/00 12/01 12/02 12/03 12/04

New York State Lottery

Winning the New York State Lottery could make you king of the hill, top of the heap. The New York State Lottery is one of the largest and oldest state lotteries in the US (only New Hampshire's lottery is older). It offers players both instant-win games, as well as the multimillion-dollar jackpots of its lotto games. In addition, the New York lottery operates Quick Draw, a keno-style game in which numbers are picked every five minutes. The lottery sells tickets through more than 15,000 retailers and some 14,000 online terminals (maintained by GTECH Holdings).

The New York State Lottery has raised more than $20 billion for state educational programs (which get 33% of sales) since its inception. In addition to education, proceeds from the lottery have helped pay for the construction of New York City Hall, as well as bridges and roads for the state. The lottery returns more than half the money it takes in as prizes; 2% of sales are used to cover administrative costs, while retailers get 6%.

New York's legislature had resisted approving a multistate game, but finally caved late in 2001 and authorized a bill allowing New Yorkers to buy Powerball tickets. The New York State Lottery joined up with the nine-state Big Game Group in 2002 to launch the Mega Millions game. Mega Millions has since grown to 12 states, and New York has had nine winners in the game who have collectively earned more than $625 million.

HISTORY

In the mid-1960s the New York state legislature succeeded in sending a lottery amendment to voters, and 60% of New Yorkers voted in favor of the amendment in 1966. Lottery sales began in 1967 with a raffle-style drawing game. In its first year of operation, the lottery contributed more than $26 million to the state's education fund.

New York introduced its first instant game in 1976, with sales topping $18 million the first week. The state debuted its six-of-six lotto game two years later. Sales were slow until 1981, when Louie "the Light Bulb" Eisenberg — the state's first lottery celebrity — won $5 million, the largest single-winner prize at that time.

GTECH Holdings won the contract to operate New York's lottery terminal sales in 1987. The Quick Pick option — through which a terminal chooses a player's numbers — was introduced in 1989, as was a new lotto game and the state's first online computer terminal game. Autoworker Antonio Bueti set a record for the largest individual prize, winning $35 million in 1990. A jackpot of $90 million was split among nine players in 1991.

Through the mid-1990s, however, lackluster lottery sales were blamed on the Persian Gulf War, the recession, and poor publicity. During 1993 and 1994 lottery management revamped the state's lottery infrastructure and redesigned some games. The investment paid off in October 1994 when lotto fever pushed a jackpot to $72.5 million. During the height of the frenzy, sales reached $46,000 a minute.

Quick Draw, which lets players choose numbers every five minutes, was added in 1995. Sales of the game topped $1 million on the second

day, and soon it was grossing nearly $12 million a week. Real estate mogul Donald Trump unsuccessfully sued to stop Quick Draw, claiming that it was more addictive than (his) casinos and would encourage organized crime. That year the New York State Lottery became the first to reach $3 billion in sales in a single year.

In 1996 the state pulled its Quick Draw advertising after critics complained it encouraged compulsive gambling. Lottery officials replaced enticing ads with advertising stressing the lottery's benefits to state education. The lottery was the subject of a sting operation that year led by Governor George Pataki to crack down on lottery vendors selling tickets to minors. In 1997 the lottery spawned its own game show with the debut of *NY Wired*, a half-hour weekly program pitting vendor representatives against each other for cash prizes given to audience members and schools.

With sales slipping, the state left longtime ad partner DDB Needham Worldwide (now DDB Worldwide) in 1998 and signed a $28 million contract with Grey Advertising. Lottery director Jeff Perlee resigned the next year. He was replaced by Margaret DeFrancisco, who helped drum up sales with Millennium Millions, which paid out a record $100 million prize to Johnnie Ely, a cook from the South Bronx, on the eve of 2000. Two players shared a record $130 million jackpot later in the year.

After holding out for years, the New York legislature in late 2001 authorized a bill that would allow state residents to participate in the multistate Powerball lottery. In 2002 the New York Lottery joined with the nine-state Big Game Group to launch the Mega Millions game, which replaced the Big Game established in 1996. By 2005, Mega Millions had 12 participating states and New York had nine winners in the game.

EXECUTIVES

Director: Nancy Palumbo
Deputy Director: Susan E. Miller
Counsel: Robert J. McLaughlin
Director of Administration: Arthur DelSignore Jr.
Director of Communications: Carolyn M. Hapeman
Director of Data Processing: Debbie Doty
Director of Data Processing: Vincent Monitto
Director of Drawings: Brad Smi
Director of Human Resource Management:
  Lisa Fitzmaurice
Director of Internal Audit: John R. McNulty
Director of Operations: Joseph Seeley
Auditors: KPMG LLP

LOCATIONS

HQ: New York State Lottery
  1 Broadway Center, Schenectady, NY 12301
Phone: 518-388-3300   **Fax:** 518-388-3403
Web: www.nylottery.org

COMPETITORS

Connecticut Lottery
Massachusetts State Lottery
Multi-State Lottery
New Hampshire Lottery
New Jersey Lottery
Pennsylvania Lottery
Vermont Lottery

HISTORICAL FINANCIALS

Company Type: Government-owned

Income Statement

FYE: March 31

	REVENUE ($ mil.)	NET INCOME ($ mil.)	NET PROFIT MARGIN	EMPLOYEES
3/04	5,848	1,955	33.4%	—
3/03	5,396	1,787	33.1%	—
3/02	5,000	—	—	—
3/01	4,185	—	—	350
3/00	3,674	—	—	350
3/99	3,831	—	—	345
3/98	4,185	—	—	350
3/97	4,136	—	—	340
3/96	3,752	—	—	310
3/95	3,028	—	—	239
Annual Growth	7.6%	9.4%	—	6.6%

Net Income History

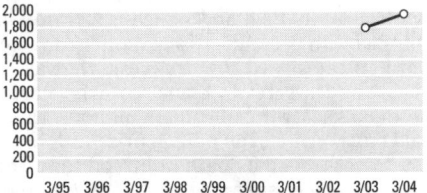

3/95 3/96 3/97 3/98 3/99 3/00 3/01 3/02 3/03 3/04

New York Stock Exchange

It's not called the Big Board for nothing: The New York Stock Exchange (NYSE) is one of the oldest and largest stock markets in the world. The member-owned, not-for-profit group lists nearly 2,800 companies, including most of the largest US corporations; it also recruits foreign companies seeking the liquidity available only in US markets. To better compete with electronic exchanges such as archrival Nasdaq, the NYSE broke from its long tradition of operating as an auction exchange (where stock prices are set largely by a throng of traders on the exchange floor) and adopted a hybrid system that permits automated trading. It is merging with Archipelago to fuel its transformation.

While the NYSE has always touted its people-driven exchange, stiff competition, not only from Nasdaq but also from foreign exchanges and electronic communications networks (ECNs), spurred the combination with Archipelago. The transaction will create a publicly traded for-profit company, NYSE Group, which will be about 70%-owned by NYSE stockholders; shareholders of Archipelago will control the other 30%.

In order to keep up with the Joneses, the NYSE has begun offering more and more new products, including ETFs (exchange-traded funds), such as the Qs. It also launched Open Book, a product that offers traders real-time access to specialist firms' buy and sell order information. Thanks to the Archipelago deal, the NYSE will add stock options and fixed income products to its trading menu, as well, after the merger closes.

The company owns two-thirds of Securities Industry Automation Corporation (SIAC), which provides communications, data processing, and clearing services primarily to the NYSE and to the American Stock Exchange, which owns the remainder of SIAC.

HISTORY

To prevent a monopoly on stock sales by securities auctioneers, 24 New York stockbrokers and businessmen agreed in 1792 to avoid "public auctions," to charge a commission on sales of stock, and to "give preference to each other" in their transactions. The Buttonwood Agreement, named after a tree on Wall Street under which they met, established the first organized stock market in New York. The Bank of New York was the first corporate stock traded under the Buttonwood tree.

Excluded traders continued dealing on the streets of New York until 1921 and later formed the American Stock Exchange.

In 1817 the brokers created the New York Stock & Exchange Board, a stock market with set meeting times. The NYS&EB began to require companies to qualify for trading (listing) by furnishing financial statements in 1853. Ten years later the board became the New York Stock Exchange.

Stock tickers began recording trades in 1867, and two years later the NYSE consolidated with competitors the Open Board of Brokers and the Government Bond Department. Despite repeated panics and recessions in the late 1800s, the stock market remained unregulated until well into the 20th century.

In the 1920s the NYSE installed a centralized stock quote service. Postwar euphoria brought a stock mania that fizzled in the crash of October 1929. The subsequent Depression brought investigation and federal regulation to the securities industry.

The NYSE registered as an exchange in 1934. In 1938 it reorganized, with a board of directors representing member firms, nonmember brokers, and the public; it also hired its first full-time president, member William McChesney Martin. As a self-regulating body, the NYSE policed the activities of its members.

The NYSE began electronic trading in the 1960s; in 1968 it broke 1929's one-day record for trading volume (16 million shares). It became a not-for-profit corporation in 1971.

Despite upgrades, technology was at least partly to blame for the crash of 1987: A cascade of large sales triggered by computer programs fueled the market's fall. NYSE's income suffered, leading to a $3 million loss in 1990.

In 1995 Richard Grasso became the first NYSE staff employee named chairman. The NYSE followed the other US stock markets in 1997 by switching trade increments from one-eighth point to one-sixteenth point (known as a "teenie" by arbitrageurs). New circuit-breaker rules halted trading on October 27 when the Dow Jones Industrial Average dropped 550 points in a day (the NYSE increased the trigger to 1,050 points in 1999).

The NYSE used a veiled threat to move to New Jersey to win itself the promise of some growing space. In 1999 the exchange named Karen Nelson Hackett as its first woman governor.

The Big Board in 2000 announced plans to go public, but the move stalled, then died altogether. It also extended its official pricing until 6:30 p.m. (Eastern). In the wake of the terrorism attacks that shook Wall Street and the nation, the NYSE and Nasdaq in 2001 began discussing a disaster plan that would see the two cooperating should a future incident cripple either market. Also that year the NYSE moved entirely to decimal pricing in accordance with SEC mandates.

Chairman Richard Grasso, who earned a reputation as something of a hero in the months following the 2001 terrorist attacks on New York City, resigned under fire two years later when his $187 million pay package was revealed. During the furor over Grasso's pay, the SEC launched an investigation, and many officials — including the heads of top pension funds — called for his resignation.

Former Citigroup chairman John Reed was named interim chairman and CEO following Grasso's departure; former Goldman Sachs president John Thain was subsequently tapped for the CEO role in 2004.

EXECUTIVES

Chairman: Marshall N. Carter, age 64
CEO: John A. Thain, age 50, $3,920,000 pay
President and Co-COO: Robert G. (Bob) Britz, age 54, $1,950,000 pay
President and Co-COO: Catherine R. Kinney, age 53, $1,950,000 pay
Chief Regulatory Officer: Richard G. (Rick) Ketchum, age 54, $1,084,615 pay
EVP, Market Operations: Anne E. Allen
EVP and General Counsel: Richard P. (Rich) Bernard, age 55, $1,150,000 pay
EVP, Technology and CTO: Roger Burkhardt, age 44
EVP and CFO: Amy S. Butte, age 37
EVP, Global Corporate Client Group: Noreen M. Culhane
EVP, Market Surveillance: Robert A. Marchman, age 46
EVP, Chief of Enforcement: Susan L. Merrill
EVP, Communications and Government Relations: Margaret Tutwiler, age 54
EVP, Member Firm Regulation: Grace B. Vogel
SVP, Corporate Communications: Richard C. (Rich) Adamonis, age 50
SVP and Chief Economist: Paul B. Bennett
SVP, Human Resources and Corporate Services: Dale B. Bernstein, age 50
SVP, Security: James C. Esposito, age 62
SVP, Market Data: Ronald Jordan, age 45
SVP, Institutional Client Group: Peter W. Jenkins, age 46
SVP, Member Firm Relations: Edward T. McMahon, age 50
SVP, Competitive Position: Robert J. McSweeney, age 53
SVP, International Relations: Alain Y. Morvan
SVP and Senior Advisor, Regulation: Regina C. Mysliwiec
SVP, Market Development and Hybrid Market Product Manager: Louis G. Pastina, age 48
SVP, Regulatory and Corporate Systems: Angela A. Posillico
SVP, Government Relations: Linda D. Rich, age 41
Auditors: PricewaterhouseCoopers LLP

LOCATIONS

HQ: New York Stock Exchange, Inc.
11 Wall St., New York, NY 10005
Phone: 212-656-3000   **Fax:** 212-656-2126
Web: www.nyse.com

PRODUCTS/OPERATIONS

2004 Sales

	$ mil.	% of total
Listing fees	320.9	30
Data processing fees	220.7	20
Market information fees	167.6	15
Trading fees	153.5	14
Regulatory fees	113.7	11
Facility & equipment fees	50.3	5
Membership fees	8.3	1
Investment and other income	40.9	4
Total	**1,075.9**	**100**

COMPETITORS

AMEX	Instinet
Archipelago	Investment Technology
CBOE	Knight Capital
Chicago Mercantile	London Stock Exchange
Exchange	Nasdaq Stock Market
Deutsche Börse	NYFIX
E*TRADE Financial	TRADEBOOK

HISTORICAL FINANCIALS

Company Type: Not-for-profit

Income Statement

FYE: December 31

	REVENUE ($ mil.)	NET INCOME ($ mil.)	NET PROFIT MARGIN	EMPLOYEES
12/04	1,076	25	2.3%	1,577
12/03	1,074	50	4.6%	1,522
12/02	1,066	28	2.6%	1,500
12/01	884	32	3.6%	1,500
12/00	815	73	8.9%	1,500
12/99	736	75	10.2%	1,500
12/98	729	101	13.9%	1,500
12/97	639	86	13.5%	1,475
12/96	562	74	13.3%	1,475
12/95	501	57	11.3%	1,450
Annual Growth	**8.9%**	**(8.9%)**	**—**	**0.9%**

2004 Year-End Financials

Debt ratio: 0.0%
Return on equity: 1.8%
Cash ($ mil.): —

Current ratio: —
Long-term debt ($ mil.): 0

Net Income History

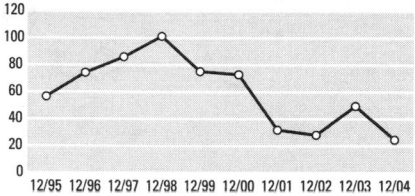

New York University

Higher education is at the core of this Big Apple institution. The setting and heritage of New York University (NYU) make it one of the nation's most popular educational institutions. With nearly 40,000 students attending its 14 schools and colleges, NYU is among the largest private schools in the US. It is well regarded for its arts and humanities studies, and its law school and Leonard N. Stern School of Business are among the best in the country. NYU occupies six major centers in Manhattan; its Washington Square campus is in the heart of Greenwich Village. The school was started in 1831. Alumni include Federal Reserve Chairman Alan Greenspan and film producer Ismail Merchant (*The Remains of the Day*).

With New York City experiencing a renaissance, NYU has become one of the more popular — and picky — schools, with more than 30,000 applicants for its 4,000 freshman seats. (Undergraduate tuition runs about $25,500 per year.) Its stature and location have also helped it attract the largest number of international students of any college in the US. To continue attracting students, NYU has also spent lavishly on facilities and top-notch faculty rather than increasing the size of its endowment (which now stands at about $1 billion).

EXECUTIVES

Chairman Board of Trustees: Martin Lipton
Vice Chairman Board of Trustees: Larry A. Silverstein, age 71
President: John E. Sexton, age 58
Provost: David W. McLaughlin
EVP: Jacob L. (Jack) Lew
SVP, General Counsel, and Secretary:
 S. Andrew Schaffer
SVP Development and Alumni Relations:
 Debra A. LaMorte
SVP Finance and Budget: Jeannemarie (Jeanne) Smith
SVP Health: Robert Berne
SVP University Relations and Public Affairs:
 Lynne P. Brown
SVP Operations and Administration: Cheryl Mills
VP Public Affairs: John Beckman
VP Public Resource Administration and Development:
 Richard N. Bing
Auditors: KPMG LLP

LOCATIONS

HQ: New York University
 70 Washington Sq. South, New York, NY 10012
Phone: 212-998-1212   **Fax:** 212-995-4040
Web: www.nyu.edu

PRODUCTS/OPERATIONS

Selected Schools and Colleges

College of Arts and Science (founded 1832)
College of Dentistry David B. Kriser
 Dental Center (1865)
Gallatin School of Individualized Study (1972)
Graduate School of Arts and Science (1886)
Leonard N. Stern School of Business (1900)
Robert F. Wagner Graduate School
 of Public Service (1938)
School of Continuing and Professional Studies (1934)
School of Law (1835)
School of Medicine (1841)
Shirley M. Ehrenkranz School of Social Work (1960)
Tisch School of the Arts (1965)

COMPETITORS

Columbia University
Juilliard School
New School
UC Berkeley
UCLA
University of Pennsylvania

HISTORICAL FINANCIALS

Company Type: School

Income Statement

FYE: August 31

	REVENUE ($ mil.)	NET INCOME ($ mil.)	NET PROFIT MARGIN	EMPLOYEES
8/03	2,005	—	—	15,010
8/02	1,866	—	—	10,136
8/01	1,692	—	—	13,000
8/00	1,546	—	—	13,000
8/99	1,410	—	—	13,000
8/98	1,296	—	—	12,790
8/97	1,771	—	—	12,937
8/96	1,669	—	—	15,000
8/95	1,524	—	—	15,400
8/94	1,409	—	—	15,300
Annual Growth	**4.0%**	**—**	**—**	**(0.2%)**

Revenue History

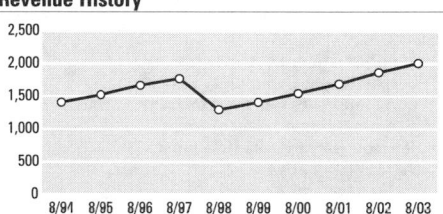

New York Yankees

Those damn Yankees are at it again. The New York Yankees have won a record 26 World Series titles and 39 American League pennants, making the team the most successful professional sports franchise in history. That success and the team's association with sports icons including Babe Ruth, Lou Gehrig, Joe DiMaggio, and Mickey Mantle help make the Yankees one of the most popular teams in the world as well. At home in the Bronx, the club draws some of the largest crowds in the league, while off the field the franchise generates huge sums from regional media deals. George Steinbrenner, who bought the team in 1973, also owns 60% of sports cable channel Yankee Entertainment & Sports.

Much to the dismay (or envy) of the rest of the league, the team is stocked full with such talented players as Derek Jeter, Hideki Matsui, and Alex Rodriguez, and (not surprisingly) has perennially had the highest payroll in baseball. The Texas Rangers traded Rodriguez to the Yankees in 2004 and the Yankees widened the gap between the haves and the have-nots further when they signed ace starting pitcher Randy Johnson to a $32 million, two-year deal in 2005, following a trade with the Arizona Diamondbacks. The addition of the "Big Unit" to the roster pushes the team's payroll to more than $200 million.

The downside to all this free spending on talent is that under Major League Baseball's collective bargaining agreement, the franchise has to give a percentage of its excess payroll back to the league to be distributed to smaller market teams. The Yankees are the only team to be hit with the luxury tax each year since the agreement was struck in 2002; its 2004 payment was about $25 million (more than the entire payroll of the Florida Marlins).

EXECUTIVES

Principal Owner: George M. Steinbrenner III, age 75
President: Randy Levine
COO: Lonn A. Trost
SVP and General Manager: Brian Cashman
SVP Baseball Operations: Mark Newman
SVP Marketing: Deborah A. (Debbie) Tymon
Manager: Joseph P. Torre, age 65
VP and CFO: Steven M. (Steve) Dauria
VP and Assistant General Manager: Jean Afterman, age 45
VP Administration: Sonny Hight
VP Corporate and Community Relations: Brian Smith
VP Corporate Sales and Sponsorships: Michael Tusiani
VP, Scouting: Damon Oppenheimer
Senior Director of Media Relations:
 Richard (Rick) Cerrone

LOCATIONS

HQ: New York Yankees Partnership
 Yankee Stadium, E. 161st Street and River Avenue,
 Bronx, NY 10451
Phone: 718-293-4300   **Fax:** 718-293-8431
Web: newyork.yankees.mlb.com

The New York Yankees play at 57,748-seat capacity Yankee Stadium in New York City.

PRODUCTS/OPERATIONS

Championship Titles
World Series (1923, 1927-28, 1932, 1936-39, 1941, 1943, 1947, 1949-53, 1956, 1958, 1961-62, 1977-78, 1996, 1998-2000)
American League Pennant (1921-23, 1926-28, 1932, 1936-39, 1941-43, 1947, 1949-53, 1955-58, 1960-64, 1976-78, 1981, 1996, 1998-2001, 2003)
American League East Division (1976-78, 1980-81, 1994, 1996, 1998-2005)

COMPETITORS

Baltimore Orioles	Tampa Bay Devil Rays
Boston Red Sox	Toronto Blue Jays

HISTORICAL FINANCIALS

Company Type: Private

Income Statement

	REVENUE ($ mil.)	NET INCOME ($ mil.)	NET PROFIT MARGIN	EMPLOYEES	FYE: December 31
12/04	315	—	—	—	
12/03	238	—	—	—	
12/02	223	—	—	—	
12/01	215	—	—	—	
12/00	200	—	—	—	
12/99	196	—	—	—	
12/98	176	—	—	175	
12/97	145	—	—	150	
12/96	133	—	—	120	
12/95	94	—	—	—	
Annual Growth	**14.4%**	**—**	**—**	**20.8%**	

Revenue History

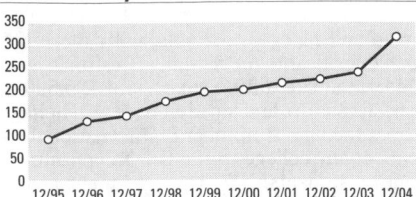

Newark Group

The Newark Group is proof that one man's trash is another man's treasure. Founded in 1912, the company is a major producer of paper products from recycled materials. Its recycled fibers division operates paper mills across the US and converts the 2.5 million tons of wastepaper it collects annually into several grades of paper and fiber products, including envelopes, corrugated cardboard, and newspaper. The paperboard division produces 1.3 million tons of paperboard per year from its 11 US mill sites. Recycled paperboard ends up in such products as books, puzzles, gameboards, and packaging. Brands include BreezeBoard (100% recycled paperboard), NewKote (boxboard), and Stress Relief (separator stock).

The Newark Group has five product lines: Recovered Paper; 100% Recycled Paperboard; Laminated Products and Graphicboard; Tube, Core and Allied Products; and Solidboard Packaging Products.

EXECUTIVES

Chairman: Fred G. von Zuben
Vice Chairman: Edward K. Mullen
President CEO and Director: Robert H. Mullen
VP and CFO: Joseph E. (Joe) Byrne
VP and Controller: Lynn M. Herro
VP and General Counsel: David Ascher
VP Human Resources: Carl R. Crook
Auditors: Deloitte & Touche LLP

LOCATIONS

HQ: The Newark Group, Inc.
 20 Jackson Dr., Cranford, NJ 07016
Phone: 908-276-4000   **Fax:** 908-276-2888
Web: www.newarkgroup.com

The Newark Group operates plants in Canada, France, Germany, the Netherlands, Spain, and the US. The group sells its products in these countries as well as the Pacific Rim region.

PRODUCTS/OPERATIONS

2004 Sales

	$ mil.	% of total
Paperboard	397.6	51
Converted products	246.9	31
International	143.1	18
Total	**787.6**	**100**

Selected Products

Recycled Fibers
 Corrugated products
 Envelopes
 Newspapers
 Printing grades
 Roll stock

Recycled Paperboard
 Boxboard
 Clay-coated folding board
 Separator stock
 Tube and core grades

COMPETITORS

Caraustar	Rock-Tenn
Georgia-Pacific Corporation	Smurfit-Stone Container
Green Bay Packaging	Sonoco Products
International Paper	Southern Container
Oji Paper	Stora Enso North America
Parsons & Whittemore	Unipapel
	Weyerhaeuser

HISTORICAL FINANCIALS

Company Type: Private

Income Statement

	REVENUE ($ mil.)	NET INCOME ($ mil.)	NET PROFIT MARGIN	EMPLOYEES	FYE: April 30
4/04	788	—	—	3,358	
4/03	798	—	—	3,500	
4/02	800	—	—	3,700	
4/01	883	—	—	4,150	
4/00	864	—	—	4,500	
4/99	800	—	—	3,900	
4/98	715	—	—	3,200	
4/97	690	—	—	3,000	
4/96	700	—	—	3,000	
4/95	700	—	—	2,700	
Annual Growth	**1.3%**	**—**	**—**	**2.5%**	

Revenue History

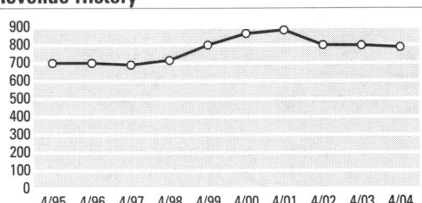

Newkirk Realty Trust

No, this company doesn't captain the Enterprise or consort with Vulcans, but it does intend to dabble in real estate. Newkirk Realty was formed to hold a controlling interest in The Newkirk Master Limited Partnership (Newkirk MLP), a real estate investment vehicle that primarily owns commercial triple-net leased properties. Newkirk MLP owns about 210 properties in more than 30 states. Its diverse portfolio includes office, retail, and industrial properties totaling approximately 18 million sq. ft. of space. Its largest tenants are Raytheon (17% of rent) and St. Paul Fire and Marine (10%). Newkirk Realty plans to operate as an externally managed umbrella partnership real estate investment trust (UPREIT).

Newkirk Realty's advisor, NKT Advisors, is also the manager of First Union. Newkirk Realty and First Union share a CEO in Michael Ashner; he also holds a controlling interest in NKT Advisors.

EXECUTIVES

Chairman and CEO: Michael L. Ashner, age 53
President and Director: Peter Braverman, age 53
CFO: Thomas C. Staples, age 49
EVP: Lara Sweeney Johnson, age 33
COO and Secretary: Carolyn Tiffany, age 38
Auditors: Deloitte & Touche LLP

LOCATIONS

HQ: Newkirk Realty Trust, Inc.
7 Bulfinch Place, Ste. 500, Boston, MA 02114
Phone: 617-570-4600   **Fax:** 617-742-4641

PRODUCTS/OPERATIONS

2004 Sales

	$ mil.	% of total
Rent	246.1	99
Interest	3.1	1
Management fees	0.3	—
Total	**249.5**	**100**

2004 Properties

	No.	% of total
Office	36	61
Retail	149	21
Industrial	12	10
Other	9	8
Total	**206**	**100**

COMPETITORS

Boston Properties
Brandywine Realty
Colonial Properties
Equity Office Properties
Inland Real Estate
Pennsylvania Real Estate
Prentiss Properties
Simon Property Group

HISTORICAL FINANCIALS

Company Type: Private

Income Statement

FYE: December 31

	REVENUE ($ mil.)	NET INCOME ($ mil.)	NET PROFIT MARGIN	EMPLOYEES
12/04	250	138	55.2%	75

NewYork-Presbyterian Healthcare

NewYork-Presbyterian Healthcare System serves New York City, as well as several counties in New York, Connecticut, and New Jersey. In fact, it serves nearly 25 percent of the patients located in the New York metropolitan area. The system, which maintains some 14,200 licensed beds, includes more than 30 hospitals. NewYork-Presbyterian Hospital is the system's flagship facility. All of its hospitals are affiliated with either Columbia University's College of Physicians and Surgeons or Cornell University's Weill Medical College. NewYork-Presbyterian Healthcare System also operates about 100 ambulatory sites, more than 15 nursing homes, and a few rehabilitation centers.

The NewYork-Presbyterian system has expanded its cardiac services by establishing cardiac-surgery programs at New York Hospital (Queens), St. Vincent's Hospital (Bridgeport, Connecticut), Valley Hospital (New Jersey), and New York Methodist Hospital (Brooklyn).

EXECUTIVES

President and CEO: Herbert Pardes
SVP and COO: Arthur A. Klein
SVP, CFO, and Treasurer: Phyllis R. F. Lantos
SVP and CIO: Aurelia G. Boyer
VP, Operations: David Alge
VP and Chief Administrative Officer: Laurence J. Berger
VP, Medical Affairs: Eliot J. Lazar
Senior Associate Dean, Clinical Affairs, Columbia University Medical Center: Joseph Tenenbaum
Associate Dean and Director, Office of Affiliations, Weill Cornell Medical College: Oliver T. Fein
Auditors: Ernst & Young LLP

LOCATIONS

HQ: NewYork-Presbyterian Healthcare System
525 E. 68th St., New York, NY 10021
Phone: 212-305-2500   **Fax:** 212-746-8235
Web: www.nypsystem.org

PRODUCTS/OPERATIONS

Facilities

Hospitals
  NewYork-Presbyterian Hospital
    The Allen Pavilion
    Children's Hospital of NewYork-Presbyterian
    NewYork-Presbyterian/Columbia
    NewYork-Presbyterian/Weill Cornell
    Westchester Division
  Bassett Healthcare
  The Brooklyn Hospital Center
  Holy Name Hospital
  Hospital for Special Surgery
  Lawrence Hospital Center
  New Milford Hospital
  New York Community Hospital
  New York Hospital Queens
  New York Methodist Hospital
  New York United Hospital Medical Center
  New York Westchester Square Medical Center
  Northern Westchester Hospital
  Nyack Hospital
  Orange Regional Medical Center
    Arden Hill Campus
    Horton Campus
  Palisades Medical Center
  The Rogosin Institute
  St. Barnabas Hospital — The Bronx
  St. Luke's Cornwall Hospital
  St. Vincent's Medical Center — Bridgeport
  South Nassau Communities Hospital
  Stamford Health System
  The Valley Hospital
  White Plains Hospital Center
  Winthrop-University Hospital
  Wyckoff Heights Medical Center
Long-Term Care Facilities
  Amsterdam Nursing Home
  Fort Tryon Center for Rehabilitation and Nursing
  Frankin Center for Rehabilitation and Nursing
  Friedwald Center for Rehabilitation and Nursing
  The Harborage at Palisades Medical Center
  Manhattanville Health Care Center
  Menorah Home and Hospital
  New York United Hospital Medical Center Skilled
    Nursing Pavilion
  St. Barnabas Nursing Home
  St. Mary's Hospital for Children — Queens
  Sea Crest Health Care Center
  Shore View Nursing Home
  The Silvercrest Center for Nursing and Rehabilitation
  Tandet Center for Continuing Care

Other Facilities
  The Burke Rehabilitation Hospital
  Community Healthcare Network
  Gracie Square Hospital
  Helen Hayes Hospital
  New York College of Podiatric Medicine &
    Foot Clinics of New York
  The Rogosin Institute

HISTORICAL FINANCIALS

Company Type: Not-for-profit

Income Statement

FYE: December 31

	REVENUE ($ mil.)	NET INCOME ($ mil.)	NET PROFIT MARGIN	EMPLOYEES
12/03	7,060	—	—	53,562
12/02	6,580	—	—	53,268
Annual Growth	**7.3%**	**—**	**—**	**0.6%**

Revenue History

NextiraOne

A next step toward convergence, NextiraOne provides voice and data systems integration, network infrastructure assessment and outsourcing, and call center applications. The company also offers consulting services focusing on technology, business protection, and education advisory services. NextiraOne operates a global network and teams up with such technology partners as Nortel Networks, Cisco Systems, and Alcatel to serve its more than 40,000 clients. The company is owned by Platinum Equity Holdings, which formed NextiraOne in 2001 by combining a group of companies that included the network services unit of Williams Communications Group (now WilTel) and assets from Alcatel.

EXECUTIVES

President and CEO: Dale A. Booth, age 44
EVP and CFO: Robert (Bob) Buhay
EVP, CTO and Chief Marketing Officer: Chuck Daniels
SVP, Sales and Marketing and General Manager, Central Region: Ernie Wallerstein
SVP, Service Operations: Charles Copeland Jr.
VP and CIO: Loren Tobey
VP, Eastern Region and General Manager: Ed Kelly
VP, National Markets and General Manager: Larry Underwood
VP, Western Region and General Manager: J.M. (Joe) Daly
Director, Human Resources: Randy Brown
Director, Marketing: Shannon DeYoung
VP, Marketing: David Stearns

LOCATIONS

HQ: NextiraOne, LLC
    2800 Post Oak Blvd., Ste 200, Houston, TX 77056
Phone: 713-307-4000   **Fax:** 713-307-4914
Web: www.nextiraone.com

NextiraOne has headquarters operations in
Houston and Paris.

PRODUCTS/OPERATIONS

Selected Services

Alarm monitoring and notification
Configuration management
Convergence readiness assessment
Data installation
Data network design
LifeCycle services (planning, design, implementation,
   management, and support)
Network discovery and documentation
Network performance baseline
PBX traffic and security assessment and analysis
Staging and configuration
Strategic consulting
Systems integration
Voice network design

COMPETITORS

Accenture
AT&T
Avaya
CIBER
Computer Sciences Corp.
Convergys
Deloitte Consulting
Deutsche Telekom
Dimension Data
EDS
Greenwich Technology Partners
HP Technology Solutions Group
IBM
Keane
Perot Systems
SBC Communications
Sprint Nextel
Verizon

HISTORICAL FINANCIALS

Company Type: Private

Income Statement
FYE: December 31

	REVENUE ($ mil.)	NET INCOME ($ mil.)	NET PROFIT MARGIN	EMPLOYEES
12/03	2,000	—	—	9,000
12/02	2,500	—	—	13,000
12/01	1,000	—	—	6,500
Annual Growth	41.4%	—	—	17.7%

Revenue History

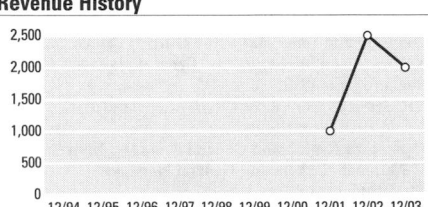

NextLinx

If some of the links in your supply chain involve
international trade, NextLinx can help with the
paperwork. NextLinx provides information management systems designed to automate the regulatory hurdles faced by international shipping
operations. It builds its applications around a
comprehensive database of international trade
regulations that helps determine the most efficient way of getting shipments from one country
to another. Its software also calculates tariffs and
automates licensing and compliance paperwork.
NextLinx's customers include Boeing, FedEx,
UPS, Fairchild Semiconductor, Rockwell Automation, Sotheby's, and VF Corporation. CEO Rajiv
Uppal founded the company as ExpoSoft in 1994.

NextLinx offers application suites targeted for
small businesses as well as international heavyweights. The company sells its software primarily through partnerships with enterprise
software vendors such as Oracle and SAP.

Shipping giant FedEx owns a stake in
the company.

EXECUTIVES

President and CEO: Rajiv Uppal
COO and Global Sales: Darren Maynard
SVP: Mona Babra
VP, Technology: Rajeev Jain
Director Finance: Robert Baker
Sales and Partnerships: Annika Olsen

LOCATIONS

HQ: NextLinx Corporation
    400B E. Gude Dr., Rockville, MD 20850
Phone: 301-315-4700   **Fax:** 301-315-0681
Web: www.nextlinx.com

NextLinx has offices in India, the UK, and the US.

COMPETITORS

Agile Software	JPMorgan Chase Vastera
Descartes Systems	Logility
EDS	Manugistics Group
G-Log	SAP
i2 Technologies	Supply Chain Consultants
IBM	TradeBeam
JDA Software	Transentric

HISTORICAL FINANCIALS

Company Type: Private

Income Statement
FYE: December 31

	ESTIMATED REVENUE ($ mil.)	NET INCOME ($ mil.)	NET PROFIT MARGIN	EMPLOYEES
12/04	10	—	—	180
12/03	10	—	—	180
12/02	10	—	—	200
12/01	19	—	—	500
Annual Growth	(20.4%)	—	—	(28.9%)

Revenue History

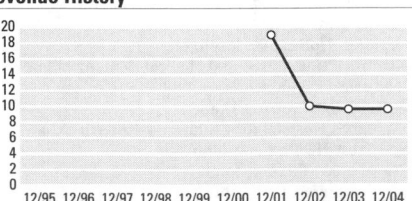

Noodles & Company

Forty lashes with a wet you-know-what if you
don't like what this company offers. Noodles &
Company operates about 100 Noodles & Company restaurants in ten states that feature entrees in a variety of American, Asian, and
Mediterranean flavors, from penne pasta to
chicken noodle soup. The chain's menu includes
noodle and vegetable bowls, soups, and green
salads with pasta. It also offers 'noodle-less'
dishes, such as mixed grill and shrimp sauté.
Chairman and CEO Aaron Kennedy, a former
brand manager at PepsiCo, founded Noodles &
Company in 1995. He and a group of private investors, including many friends and family members, own the company. The company opened its
first franchised location in 2004.

The fast-growing company has started a drive
to develop franchised units with the goal of expanding the chain to 300 locations in three years.
It has struck franchising deals with The Jan
Companies, which will develop 45 restaurants in
New England, and Casual Foods, a Midwestern
company that will open more than 10 shops in
Kansas and Missouri. In all, those franchisees
and four others will open more than 150 units
in the Midwest and New England.

EXECUTIVES

Chairman and CEO: Aaron Kennedy, age 42
President and COO: Kevin Reddy
CFO: Keith Kinsey
VP Finance: Tiffany Richards
VP Franchise Initiatives: Paul J. (P. J.) Evans, age 46
VP Human Resources: John R. Puterbaugh
VP Information Technology: John Lauderbach
VP Marketing: Dwayne G. Chambers
VP Restaurant, Culinary, and Supply Chain Services:
  David Berenson
Chief Development Officer: Dick Anderson
Director of Corporate Communications:
  Kelly Pascal Gould
Manager of Franchise Sales: Dana Rogers
General Counsel: Vikki Wulf
Executive Chef: Ross Kamens
Auditors: Deloitte & Touche; KPMG LLP

LOCATIONS

HQ: Noodles & Company
    2590 Pearl St., Boulder, CO 80302
Phone: 303-554-1963   **Fax:** 303-554-4404
Web: www.noodles.com

Noodles & Company operates restaurants in California,
Colorado, Illinois, Maryland, Michigan, Minnesota,
Texas, Utah, Virginia, and Wisconsin.

COMPETITORS

Atlanta Bread	Made In Japan Japanese
Benihana	Restaurants
Boston Market	New World Restaurants
Café de Coral	Panera Bread
Chevys	P.F. Chang's
Chipotle	Pickerman's Soup Cafe
Desert Island Restaurants	Qdoba
Fresh Enterprises	Todai
HuHot Mongolian Grill	Wild Noodles
Leeann Chin	Zoup!
	Zyng Asian Grill

HISTORICAL FINANCIALS

Company Type: Private

Income Statement

FYE: December 31

	REVENUE ($ mil.)	NET INCOME ($ mil.)	NET PROFIT MARGIN	EMPLOYEES
12/04	90	—	—	3,000
12/03	70	—	—	2,100
12/02	50	—	—	1,500
12/01	28	—	—	350
12/00	13	—	—	60
Annual Growth	61.0%	—	—	165.9%

Revenue History

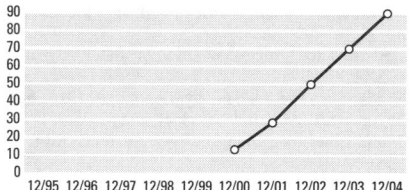

Nortek

Nortek Holdings, parent of Nortek, Inc., and other subsidiaries, makes and distributes building, remodeling, and indoor environmental control products for the residential and commercial construction, do-it-yourself, remodeling, and renovation markets. Products include range hoods and other spot ventilation products, heating and air-conditioning systems, indoor air quality systems, and specialty electronic products. It sells residential HVAC products under such brands as Frigidaire and Tappan. Nortek sold its Hoover Treated Wood Products and Ply Gem Industries (windows, doors, and siding) subsidiaries. Thomas H. Lee Partners, in partnership with company management, acquired Nortek Holdings in 2004.

Nortek, Inc., was reorganized as holding company Nortek Holdings in 2002 in order for it to be acquired. Kelso & Company and certain members of Nortek Holdings' management, including chairman and CEO Richard Bready, completed the acquisition in January 2003. Richard Bready's equity interest in the company was reduced from about 35% to 16%.

Nortek began the search for a buyer for its Ply Gem Industries, Inc. (windows, doors, and vinyl sidings) subsidiary by hiring UBS Securities LLC and Daroth Capital Advisors LLC as its scouts. In February 2004 the company sold the unit for about $560 million to investment vehicles associated with Caxton-Iseman Capital, Inc.

The company changed hands again in August 2004, when Thomas H. Lee Partners, in partnership with Nortek's management, acquired the company. In 2005 Nortek acquired speaker and audio/video signal distribution equipment maker Niles Audio.

EXECUTIVES

Chairman, President, and CEO: Richard L. Bready, age 58
VP and CFO: Almon C. Hall III
VP, General Counsel, and Secretary: Kevin W. Donnelly
VP and Treasurer: Edward J. Cooney
Director, Human Resources: Jane White
Auditors: Ernst & Young LLP

LOCATIONS

HQ: Nortek Holdings, Inc.
50 Kennedy Plaza, Providence, RI 02903
Phone: 401-751-1600   **Fax:** 401-751-4610
Web: www.nortek-inc.com

Nortek has manufacturing operations in Canada, China, France, Italy, and the US.

PRODUCTS/OPERATIONS

Selected Products and Brands

Exterior Residential Products
Air conditioners, heat pumps, gas/electric units (Nordyne — Frigidaire, Gibson, Kelvinator, Philco, Tappan)
Residential gate and door operating systems (OSCO — Operator Specialty Company)
Interior Residential Products
Cooking ranges (La Cornue, France)
Indoor-air quality systems (Venmar Ventilation, Canada)
Range hoods, bath fans, medicine cabinets, door chimes, central vacuum systems, and intercoms (Aubrey and Jensen divisions of the Broan-NuTone Group)
Wireless security and remote-control products (Linear)
Light Commercial Products
Access control (Linear)
Air conditioners, heat pumps, gas/electric units (Nordyne — Frigidaire, Gibson, Kelvinator, Philco, Tappan)
Exhaust fans, access doors, mailboxes, key keepers, collection boxes, and directories (Broan-NuTone)
Indoor air quality systems and heat and energy recovery systems (Venmar CES, Canada)
Residential gate and door operating systems (OSCO — Operator Specialty Company)
Self-contained V-Cube floor-by-floor units and water source heat pumps (Mammoth)
Commercial Products
Custom designed commercial HVAC systems and components (Eaton-Williams, UK)

COMPETITORS

AAON
American Standard
Andersen Corporation
Associated Materials
Black & Decker
Bocenor
Carrier
GE Security
Goodman Manufacturing
JELD-WEN
Lapeyre
Lennox
Masco
Masonite International
MasterBrand Cabinets
Mohawk Industries
NCI Building Systems
Owens Corning
Pella
Royal Group Technologies
Simpson Manufacturing
Stanley Works
ThermoView Industries
York International

HISTORICAL FINANCIALS

Company Type: Private

Income Statement

FYE: December 31

	REVENUE ($ mil.)	NET INCOME ($ mil.)	NET PROFIT MARGIN	EMPLOYEES
12/03	1,515	12	0.8%	4,139
12/02	1,888	63	3.3%	9,750
12/01	1,856	8	0.4%	9,900
12/00	2,195	42	1.9%	12,200
12/99	1,993	49	2.5%	12,100
12/98	1,738	35	2.0%	9,640
12/97	1,134	21	1.9%	9,262
12/96	970	22	2.3%	6,497
12/95	776	15	1.9%	6,423
12/94	737	18	2.4%	5,317
Annual Growth	8.3%	(4.1%)	—	(2.7%)

2003 Year-End Financials

Debt ratio: 661.6%	Current ratio: 2.65
Return on equity: 4.8%	Long-term debt ($ mil.): 1,325
Cash ($ mil.): 194	

Net Income History

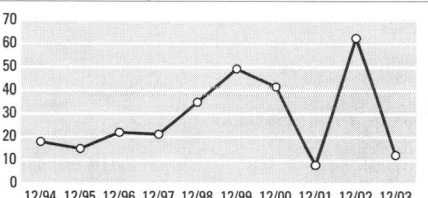

Northern Illinois University

Northern Illinois University is a public university in suburban Chicago. The school has more than 25,000 students enrolled at its flagship campus, located in DeKalb, and four satellite centers (Hoffman Estates, Naperville, Rockford, and Oregon). The university offers some 50 undergraduate programs and 70 graduate programs. Northern Illinois was founded in 1895.

EXECUTIVES

Chair: Barbara Giorgi Vella
Vice Chair: Cherilyn G. Murer
EVP Business and Finance, COO, and Treasurer: Eddie R. Williams
President: John G. Peters
EVP and Provost: J. Ivan Legg
Vice Provost: Earl J. (Gip) Seaver III
Vice Provost Academic Planning and Development: Virginia R. Cassidy
Vice Provost Resource Planning: Frederick Schwantes
Vice Provost Student Affairs: Gary Gresholdt
VP Research; Dean, Graduate School: Rathindra N. Bose
VP Student Affairs: Brian O. Hemphill
Associate VP Administration and Human Resource Services: Steven D. Cunningham
Associate VP and General Counsel: Kenneth L. Davidson
Associate VP Development and Chief Development Officer: Mallory M. Simpson
Assistant VP Public Affairs: Melanie Magara
Secretary and Trustee: Marc J. Strauss

HQ: Northern Illinois University
Northern Illinois University, DeKalb, IL 60115
Phone: 815-753-1000 **Fax:** 815-753-0430
Web: www.niu.edu

COMPETITORS

Illinois State
Southern Illinois University
University of Illinois

HISTORICAL FINANCIALS

Company Type: School

Income Statement

FYE: June 30

	REVENUE ($ mil.)	NET INCOME ($ mil.)	NET PROFIT MARGIN	EMPLOYEES
6/04	235	4	1.5%	3,841
6/03	218	29	13.4%	3,841
6/02	193	(5)	—	—
6/01	340	(9)	—	—
6/00	319	—	—	—
6/99	300	—	—	—
6/98	287	—	—	—
Annual Growth	**(3.3%)**	**—**	**—**	**0.0%**

2004 Year-End Financials

Debt ratio: 5.2%
Return on equity: —
Cash ($ mil.): —

Current ratio: —
Long-term debt ($ mil.): 10

Net Income History

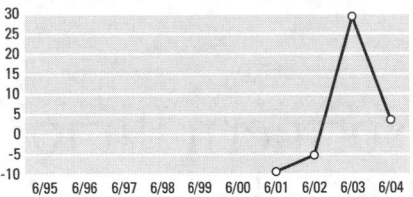

30									
25									
20									
15									
10									
5									
0									
-5									
-10									

6/95 6/96 6/97 6/98 6/99 6/00 6/01 6/02 6/03 6/04

Northwestern Mutual

Making sure it's not all quiet on the Northwestern front, Northwestern Mutual's 7,900 agents (meticulously recruited and trained) sell a lineup of life and health insurance and retirement products, including fixed and variable annuities and mutual funds to a clientele of small businesses and prosperous individuals. Other lines of business include institutional asset manager Frank Russell Company, known for the Russell 2000 stock index, and trust services subsidiary Northwestern Mutual Trust. The company in 2004 completed a series of transactions that returned ownership of midwestern investment bank Robert W. Baird & Co. to its employees.

Northwestern Mutual would "enter the 21st century as we left the 19th," according to its former chairman and CEO, John Ericson (who retired in mid-2001).

Well, not exactly. Although the company has resisted the industry trend of demutualizing and remains committed to ownership by its approximately 3 million policyholders, The Quiet Company has begun blowing its own horn — in a diffident, upper Midwest way. Reorganized to highlight its wealth management products, life insurance still accounts for the majority of the company's revenue. The company targets wealthy individuals over 55.

HISTORY

In 1854, at age 72, John Johnston, a successful New York insurance agent, moved to Wisconsin to become a farmer. Three years later Johnston returned to the insurance business when he and 36 others formed Mutual Life Insurance (changed to Northwestern Mutual Life Insurance in 1865). From the beginning, the company's goal was to become better, not just bigger.

The company continued to offer level-premium life insurance in the 1920s, while competitors offered new types of products. This failure to rise to new demands brought a decline in market share that lasted into the 1940s.

Northwestern Mutual automated in the late 1950s. In 1962 it introduced the Insurance Service Account, whereby all policies owned by a family or business could be consolidated into one monthly premium and paid with pre-authorized checks. In 1968 Northwestern Mutual inaugurated Extra Ordinary Life (EOL), which combined whole and term life insurance, using dividends to convert term to paid-up whole life each year. EOL soon became the company's most popular product.

Suffering from a low profile, in 1972 the insurer kicked off its "The Quiet Company" ad campaign during the summer Olympics. Public awareness of Northwestern Mutual jumped. But even in advertising, the company was staid; a revamped Quiet Company campaign made a return Olympic appearance 24 years later in another effort to raise the public's consciousness.

In the 1980s Northwestern Mutual began financing leveraged buyouts, gaining direct ownership of companies. Investments included two-thirds of flooring maker Congoleum (with other investors); it also bought majority interests in Milwaukee securities firm Robert W. Baird (1982) and mortgage guarantee insurer MGIC Investment (1985; later divested).

The firm stayed out of the 1980s mania for fast money and high-risk diversification. Instead, it devoted itself almost religiously to its core business, despite indications that it was a shrinking market.

In the early 1990s new life policy purchases slowed and the agency force declined — ominous signs, since insurers make their premium income on retained policies, and continued sales are crucial to growth. Northwestern Mutual reversed the trend, adding administrative support for its agents, using database marketing to target new customers, and increasing the cross-selling of products among existing customers. The result was a record-setting 1996.

With the financial services industry consolidating, Northwestern Mutual in 1997 moved into the mutual fund business by setting up its Mason Street Funds.

In the 1990s many large mutuals sought to demutualize, and in 1998 Northwestern Mutual, politically influential in Wisconsin, successfully lobbied for legislation to permit demutualization, citing the need to be able to move quickly in shifting markets.

The next year the company acquired Frank Russell Company, a pension management firm. The acquisition gave Northwestern Mutual a foothold in global investment management and analytical services (the Russell 2000 index).

The company followed up with an all-out reorganization, separating the office of president from the duties of chairman and CEO, and naming, for the first time, a marketing officer. In 2001 the firm opened Northwestern Mutual Trust, a wholly owned personal trust services subsidiary.

In 2004 the employees of Robert W. Baird completed a buyback of Northwestern Mutual's stake in the firm.

EXECUTIVES

President, CEO, and Director: Edward J. Zore, age 60
Director: James D. (Jim) Ericson, age 69
COO, Chief Compliance Officer, and Director: John M. Bremer, age 57
Chief Insurance Officer and Director: Peter W. Bruce, age 59
EVP, Planning and Technology: Deborah A. Beck, age 57
EVP, Agencies: William H. Beckley, age 57
EVP and Chief Investment Officer: Mason G. Ross, age 61
SVP and CIO: Barbara F. Piehler, age 54
SVP and CFO: Gary A. Poliner, age 51
SVP, Public Markets: Mark G. Doll, age 55
SVP, Life Product: Richard L. Hall, age 59
SVP and Chief Actuary: William C. Koenig, age 57
SVP, Insurance Operations: Gregory C. Oberland, age 47
SVP, Marketing: Marcia Rimai, age 49
SVP, Investment Products and Services: Charles D. Robinson, age 60
SVP, Investment Products and Services and Affiliates: John E. Schlifske, age 45
SVP, Investment Product Operations: Leonard F. Stecklein, age 58
SVP, Corporate and Government Relations: Frederic H. Sweet, age 61
VP, Secretary, and General Counsel: Robert J. Berdan, age 58
VP and Controller: John C. (Chris) Kelly, age 45
VP, Human Resources: Susan A. Lueger, age 51
VP, Communications: Brenda F. Skelton, age 49
VP, Communications: Ward White
Auditors: PricewaterhouseCoopers LLP

LOCATIONS

HQ: The Northwestern Mutual Life Insurance Company
720 E. Wisconsin Ave., Milwaukee, WI 53202
Phone: 414-271-1444
Web: www.northwesternmutual.com

PRODUCTS/OPERATIONS

2004 Sales

	$ mil.	% of total
Premiums	10,682	62
Net investment income	6,117	35
Other income	511	3
Total	**17,310**	**100**

COMPETITORS

AEGON USA	John Hancock Financial
AIG	Services
AIG American General	Liberty Mutual
Alliance Capital	MassMutual
Allianz	Merrill Lynch
AXA Financial	MetLife
CIGNA	Morgan Stanley
Citigroup	Mutual of Omaha
CNA Financial	Nationwide
Conseco	New York Life
FMR	Pacific Mutual
GenAmerica	Principal Financial
Genworth Financial	Prudential
Guardian Life	Sun Life
The Hartford	T. Rowe Price
ING	TIAA-CREF

HISTORICAL FINANCIALS

Company Type: Mutual company

Income Statement

FYE: December 31

	ASSETS ($ mil.)	NET INCOME ($ mil.)	INCOME AS % OF ASSETS	EMPLOYEES
12/04	123,957	817	0.7%	4,700
12/03	113,822	692	0.6%	4,500
12/02	102,935	158	0.2%	4,200
12/01	98,392	650	0.7%	4,100
12/00	92,125	1,829	2.0%	3,900
12/99	85,985	1,337	1.6%	3,700
12/98	77,995	809	1.0%	4,117
12/97	71,081	689	1.0%	3,818
12/96	62,680	620	1.0%	3,513
12/95	54,876	459	0.8%	3,344
Annual Growth	9.5%	6.6%	—	3.9%

2004 Year-End Financials

Equity as % of assets: 7.2%
Return on assets: 0.7%
Return on equity: 9.9%
Long-term debt ($ mil.): —
Sales ($ mil.): 17,310

Net Income History

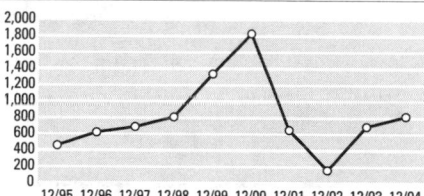

```
2,000
1,800
1,600
1,400
1,200
1,000
 800
 600
 400
 200
   0
     12/95 12/96 12/97 12/98 12/99 12/00 12/01 12/02 12/03 12/04
```

Northwestern University

Near the City of Big Shoulders is a place that shapes broad minds. With its main campus in the Chicago suburb of Evanston, Northwestern University serves its 17,000 students through 11 schools and colleges such as the McCormick School of Engineering and Applied Sciences and the Medill School of Journalism. Its Chicago campus houses the schools of law and medicine, as well as several hospitals of the McGaw Medical Center. Northwestern is home to several research centers, continuing education services, and community outreach programs. The university also supports 19 intercollegiate athletic programs. Founded in 1851, Northwestern is the only private institution in the Big 10 conference.

Among Northwestern's top-ranked programs are its law school, medical school, and its engineering program. Its J. L. Kellogg Graduate School of Management consistently ranks among the nation's top five business schools by *Business Week* and *U.S. News & World Report*. Its prestigious journalism and drama programs produced such alumni as Charlton Heston, Gary Marshall, and Julia Louis-Dreyfus. Current US Supreme Court Justice John Paul Stevens is also a former Wildcat.

The school's endowment and other trust funds have swelled to more than $4 billion, and it has exceeded its original Campaign Northwestern fund-raising goal of $1 billion by more than $15 million. The money is being used to increase endowment for student scholarships and fellowships, to help repair and build facilities, and to fund more faculty positions.

HISTORY

Northwestern University's Methodist founders met in 1850 to create an institution of higher learning serving the original Northwest Territory. The university was chartered in 1851, and two years later it acquired 379 acres of property north of Chicago on Lake Michigan. The town of Evanston was later named after John Evans, one of the school's founders.

Classes began in the fall of 1855 with two professors and 10 students. By 1869 Northwestern had more than 100 students and began to admit women. In 1870 Northwestern signed an affiliation agreement with the Chicago Medical College (founded 1859), and three years later it joined with the original University of Chicago (no relation to the current institution) to create the Union College of Law. When the University of Chicago closed in 1886 due to financial difficulties, Northwestern took control of the law school. The university reorganized in 1891, consolidating its affiliated professional schools (dentistry, law, medicine, and pharmacy) into the university.

By 1900 Northwestern had become the third-largest university in the US (after Harvard and Michigan), with an enrollment of 2,700. During the 1920s the university created the Medill School of Journalism, named after Joseph Medill, founder of the *Chicago Tribune*. In 1924 the school's athletic teams adopted the nickname Wildcats, and two years later the university completed the primary buildings that form its Chicago campus. Northwestern suffered a drop in enrollment during the Depression, but after WWII it saw student numbers swell as veterans took advantage of the GI Bill. Expansion continued throughout the 1960s and 1970s.

In 1985 the school and the City of Evanston began developing a research center to attract more high-tech industries to the area. The university's graduate school of business achieved national prominence in 1988 after it was ranked #1 in the US by *Business Week*. In 1995 Henry Bienen, a dean at Princeton, became the school's 15th president. That year Northwestern's football team, forever the doormat of the Big 10, achieved national fame when it won the conference championship.

In 1998 faculty member Professor John Pople won the Nobel Prize in Chemistry, the first Nobel Prize awarded to a faculty member while teaching at the university. To help pay for needed expansion, Bienen launched Campaign Northwestern that year with the goal of raising $1 billion. Northwestern won a significant legal battle in 1998 when a judge ruled that the university was not obligated to pay a faculty member simply because he had been granted tenure. Encouraged by its successful efforts, the college, in 2000, raised its fund-raising goal to $1.4 billion from $1 billion.

The university's dental school closed its doors in 2001, citing the difficulties posed for private schools in providing a competitive dental education.

EXECUTIVES

President: Henry S. Bienen, age 65
Provost: Lawrence B. Dumas
SVP Business and Finance: Eugene S. Sunshine
VP and General Counsel: Thomas G. Cline
VP Administration and Planning: Marilyn McCoy
VP Development: Sarah R. Pearson
VP Information Technology and CTO: Morteza A. Rahimi
VP Research: C. Bradley Moore
VP Student Affairs: William J. Banis
VP University Relations: Alan K. Cubbage
Associate VP Human Resources: Guy E. Miller
Director Media Relations: Charles R. Loebbaka
Auditors: Deloitte & Touche LLP

LOCATIONS

HQ: Northwestern University
633 Clark St., Evanston, IL 60208
Phone: 847-491-3741   **Fax:** 847-491-8406
Web: www.nwu.edu

Northwestern University has one campus in Chicago and one in Evanston, Illinois.

PRODUCTS/OPERATIONS

Selected Undergraduate Colleges and Schools

Medill School of Journalism
Robert McCormick School of Engineering and Applied Sciences
School of Communication
School of Education and Social Policy
School of Music
Weinberg College of Arts and Sciences

Graduate and Professional Schools

Feinberg School of Medicine
Interdisciplinary Biological and Life Sciences
J.L. Kellogg School of Management
McCormick School of Engineering and Applied Science
Medill School of Journalism
School of Communication (Speech)
School of Education and Social Policy
School of Law
School of Music

HISTORICAL FINANCIALS

Company Type: School

Income Statement

FYE: August 31

	REVENUE ($ mil.)	NET INCOME ($ mil.)	NET PROFIT MARGIN	EMPLOYEES
8/04	1,116	479	42.9%	7,100
8/03	1,055	325	30.8%	6,278
8/02	989	—	—	6,800
8/01	959	—	—	5,700
8/00	875	—	—	5,700
8/99	782	—	—	5,700
8/98	816	—	—	5,985
8/97	721	—	—	5,978
8/96	779	—	—	5,800
8/95	708	—	—	5,800
Annual Growth	5.2%	47.4%	—	2.3%

2004 Year-End Financials

Debt ratio: —
Return on equity: 10.7%
Cash ($ mil.): —
Current ratio: —
Long-term debt ($ mil.): —

Net Income History

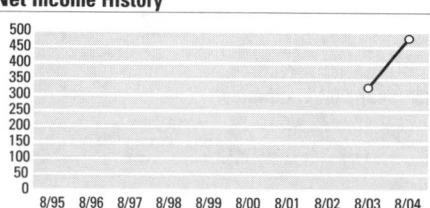

```
500
450
400
350
300
250
200
150
100
 50
  0
    8/95 8/96 8/97 8/98 8/99 8/00 8/01 8/02 8/03 8/04
```

NxStage Medical

NxStage Medical is giving a little life back to those suffering from kidney dysfunction. The medical device company's primary product, System One, is a portable dialysis machine, allowing users to treat themselves in the comfort of their homes. Dialysis is a necessary treatment for kidney failure as well as end-stage renal disease, from which more than 430,000 people in the US suffer. Typically, patients needing dialysis have to seek treatments at local clinics several times a week, with each session lasting several hours. System One received FDA approval for home use in mid-2005. The Sprout Group controls 37% of NxStage Medical.

EXECUTIVES

Chairman: Philippe O. Chambon, age 47
President, CEO, and Director: Jeffrey H. (Jeff) Burbank, age 43, $269,100 pay
SVP and COO: Philip R. (Phil) Licari, age 46, $52,284 pay (prior to promotion)
SVP and CFO: David N. Gill, age 50
SVP, Commercial Operations: Joseph E. (Joe) Turk Jr., age 37, $217,350 pay (prior to promotion)
SVP, General Counsel, and Secretary: Winifred L. (Winnie) Swan, age 41, $196,650 pay (prior to promotion)
VP, Disposables Engineering: James Brugger
VP, Manufacturing Operations: William (Bill) Weigel
VP, Research and Development: Dennis M. (Denny) Treu
VP, Quality Assurance and Regulatory Affairs: Michael J. (Mike) Webb
VP, Sales: Matt Pearman
Chief Medical Advisor: Alan R. Hull
Managing Director, EIR Medical: Martin Stillig
Auditors: Ernst & Young LLP

LOCATIONS

HQ: NxStage Medical, Inc.
439 S. Union St., 5th Fl., Lawrence, MA 01843
Phone: 978-687-4700   **Fax:** 978-687-4809
Web: www.nxstage.com

COMPETITORS

Aksys
Baxter
DaVita
Fresenius
Gambro
Renal Care

HISTORICAL FINANCIALS

Company Type: Private

Income Statement   FYE: December 31

	REVENUE ($ mil.)	NET INCOME ($ mil.)	NET PROFIT MARGIN	EMPLOYEES
12/04	2	(15)	—	127
12/03	0	(10)	—	—
12/02	0	(11)	—	—
Annual Growth	—	—	—	—

2004 Year-End Financials

Debt ratio: (5.2%)   Current ratio: 6.52
Return on equity: —   Long-term debt ($ mil.): 3
Cash ($ mil.): 6

Net Income History

Oakland Raiders

Who says you can't go home again? The Oakland Raiders set an NFL precedent when it returned to Oakland in 1995 after more than a decade in Los Angeles. The team is known for the "Just win, baby" slogan of majority owner Al Davis, who quickly discards coaches and routinely riles other owners. Founded in 1960, the Raiders won its first Super Bowl in 1977 under the leadership of quarterback Ken Stabler and legendary coach John Madden. The Raiders won two more Super Bowls in the early 1980s. As of late, the team has not only drawn back fans alienated by the move to LA, but also advanced to the Super Bowl in the 2002-03 season (it lost to the Tampa Bay Buccaneers). The E.J. McGah family owns 31% of the team.

EXECUTIVES

Majority Owner: Al Davis
CEO: Amy Trask
Head Coach: Norv Turner, age 51
Broadcasting: Chris Gargano
Business Affairs: Scott Fink
Business Affairs: Dawn Roberts
Finance: Marc Badain
Finance: Derek Person
Finance: Ed Villanueva
Finance/Technology: Tom Blanda
General Counsel: Jeff Birren
Public Relations Director: Mike Taylor

LOCATIONS

HQ: The Oakland Raiders
1220 Harbor Bay Pkwy., Alameda, CA 94502
Phone: 510-864-5000   **Fax:** 510-864-5160
Web: www.raiders.com

The Oakland Raiders play at McAfee Coliseum in Oakland, California.

PRODUCTS/OPERATIONS

Titles

Super Bowl Champions (1977, 1981, 1984)
AFC Champions (1976, 1980, 1983, 2003)
AFC Western Division Champions (1970, 1972-76, 1983, 1985, 1990, 2000-02)
AFL Champions (1967)
AFL Western Division Champions (1967-69)

COMPETITORS

Denver Broncos
Kansas City Chiefs
San Diego Chargers

HISTORICAL FINANCIALS

Company Type: Private

Income Statement   FYE: June 30

	REVENUE ($ mil.)	NET INCOME ($ mil.)	NET PROFIT MARGIN	EMPLOYEES
6/04	149	—	—	—
6/03	144	—	—	—
6/02	132	—	—	—
6/01	117	—	—	—
6/00	105	—	—	—
6/99	100	—	—	—
6/98	78	—	—	90
6/97	79	—	—	—
6/96	71	—	—	—
Annual Growth	9.7%	—	—	—

Revenue History

Ocean Spray

Ocean Spray Cranberries has transformed cranberries from turkey sidekick to the stuff of everyday beverages, cereal, and mixed drinks. Known for its blue-and-white wave logo, Ocean Spray controls more than half of the US cranberry drink market. A marketing cooperative owned by more than 900 cranberry and citrus growers in the US and Canada, Ocean Spray produces its line of juices by blending the cranberry with fruits ranging from apples to tangerines. It also makes other cranberry products (sauce, snacks), grapefruit juice, and Ocean Spray Premium 100% juice drinks for both retailers and food service providers.

To expand beyond the berry's traditional role, Ocean Spray has turned the fruit into a chewy snack (Craisins), and cranberries now show up in cobranded cookies and cereal. It has also introduced a "white juice" made from preripened cranberries that have a less tart taste. Promotional efforts have been aided by research showing that cranberry juice can reduce urinary tract infections and fight stomach ulcers.

The cooperative has expanded distribution internationally through partnerships with companies like Nestlé, Gerber, and even Sapporo in Japan. Closer ties to the alcoholic beverage industry will come as the company expands marketing with V&S Vin & Sprit's Absolut vodka.

Ocean Spray's Ingredient Technology Group processes fruit into juice ingredients.

HISTORY

Ocean Spray Cranberries traces its roots to Marcus Urann, president of the Cape Cod Cranberry Company. In 1912 Urann, who became known as the "Cranberry King," began marketing a cranberry sauce that was packaged in tins and could be served year-round. Inspired by the sea spray that drifted off the Atlantic and over his cranberry bogs, Urann dubbed his concoction Ocean Spray Cape Cod Cranberry Sauce.

It didn't take long for other cranberry growers to make their own sauces, and rather than compete, the Cranberry King consolidated. In 1930 Urann merged his company with A.D. Makepeace Company and with Cranberry Products, forming a national cooperative called Cranberry Canners. During the 1940s it added growers in Wisconsin, Oregon, and Washington and, to reflect its new scope, changed its name to National Cranberry Association.

Canadian growers were added to the fold in 1950. Urann retired in 1955, and two years later the co-op introduced its first frozen products. To take advantage of the popular Ocean Spray brand name, in 1959 the company changed its name to Ocean Spray Cranberries.

Two weeks before Thanksgiving that year, the US Department of Health mistakenly announced that aminotriazole, a herbicide used by some cranberry growers, was linked to cancer in laboratory rats. Sales of what consumers called "cancer berries" plummeted, and Ocean Spray nearly folded. However, the US government came to the rescue with subsidies in 1960, and the company stayed afloat.

The scare convinced Ocean Spray it needed to cut its dependence on seasonal demand, and it began to diversify more aggressively into the juice business, introducing a heavily promoted new line of juices blending cranberries with apples, grapes, and other fruits.

Ocean Spray allowed Florida's Indian River Ruby Red grapefruit growers to join the co-op in 1976. The company acquired Milne Food Products, a manufacturer of fruit concentrates and purees, in 1985, and three years later it signed a Japanese distribution deal.

To maintain its edge in a growing but increasingly competitive market, Ocean Spray automated plants and allied with food giants to create cranberry-flavored treats such as cookies (Nabisco, 1993) and cereal (Kraft Foods, 1996). In 1998 it unsuccessfully sued to block PepsiCo's purchase of juice maker Tropicana on grounds that it would interfere with PepsiCo's distribution of Ocean Spray's drinks. Ocean Spray also introduced a line of 100% juice blends to compete with rivals such as former co-op member Northland Cranberries.

Bumper harvests from 1997 through 1999 led to lower cranberry prices. As a result, in 1999 the company announced its third round of layoffs since 1997 (bringing the total to 500, or nearly one-fifth of its workforce). It also suspended its practice of buying back the stock of its growers, who must buy shares to join the co-op.

Amid criticism that it has been unable to compete effectively with for-profit rivals, Ocean Spray hired former Pillsbury executive Robert Hawthorne as CEO in 2000. Grower-owners voted not to explore a sale of the company at its 2001 annual meeting, a vote of confidence for the new management. The company supported a 32% crop reduction to help eliminate the crop surpluses that cause depressed prices. Ocean Spray also sold its interest in Nantucket Allserve (Nantucket Nectars) to Cadbury Schweppes, which folded Nantucket's brands into its Snapple unit.

In 2002 Hawthorne resigned. Barbara S. Thomas, a board member and former president of Warner Lambert's consumer health care division, was named interim CEO.

In February 2003 rival Northland Cranberries made a cash and stock bid to take over the juice business of Ocean Spray. The company rejected the offer the same month. Upset by their lack of input in the decision, cranberry growers voted in March to revamp the Ocean Spray board, reducing its size from 15 to 12 members and keeping just three of the board's previous members. Soon after, Ocean Spray laid off about 60 people, including several executives.

In 2004 the cooperative nearly revamped its board a second time in one year to again increase input from membership. As a compromise, the cooperative returned the size of its board to 15 members. Seven of the members were considered "compromise" candidates that would bring "additional viewpoints" to the Board. In June cooperative members rejected a proposed joint venture with PepsiCo. Also in 2004 Ocean Spray expanded its cranberry production line in Middleboro, Massachusetts.

Rounding out a busy year, in September 2004 Ocean Spray settled an antitrust lawsuit filed by Northland Cranberries and Clermont, Inc. As part of the settlement, Ocean Spray agreed to purchase Northland's production plant and pay more than $5 million to buy eight of Northland's cranberry marshes in Wisconsin. The agreement also stipulated that Ocean Spray would make cranberry concentrate for Northland.

EXECUTIVES

Chairman: Robert L. Rosbe Jr.
CEO: Randy Papadellis
SVP and COO: Kenneth G. (Ken) Romanzi, age 44
SVP and COO, Ocean Spray International: Stewart (Stu) Gallagher
SVP and CFO: Tim C. Chan
VP, Human Resources: Katie Morey
VP, Operations: Michael Stamatakos
VP, Research and Development: Geoffrey Woolford
Director of Beverage Marketing: Jared Konstanty
Director of Food: Keith Benoit
Group Marketing Manager, New Products: Kelly Reilly
National Account Business Manager: Michael Kuechle
National Sales Manager: John Gaither
Public Relations Manager: Cindy Taccini
PR Specialist: Sharon Newcomb
Team Leader, Food Service: Steve Harris
Auditors: Deloitte & Touche

LOCATIONS

HQ: Ocean Spray Cranberries, Inc.
1 Ocean Spray Dr., Lakeville-Middleboro, MA 02349
Phone: 508-946-1000   **Fax:** 508-946-7704
Web: www.oceanspray.com

Ocean Spray Cranberries operates four bottling facilities in Nevada, New Jersey, Texas, and Wisconsin and three fruit-processing sites in Florida, Washington, and Massachusetts.

PRODUCTS/OPERATIONS

Selected Products

Cranberry Juice Cocktails
  Cranberry Juice Cocktail
  Cranberry Juice Cocktail with Calcium
Cranberry Juice Drinks
  Cran Apple   Cran Raspberry
  Cran Cherry   Cran Strawberry
  Cran Grape   Cran Tangerine
  Cran Mango   Juice & Tea
Craisins Sweetened Dried Cranberries
  Cherry Flavor Sweetened Dried Cranberries
  Orange Flavor Sweetened Dried Cranberries
  Original Sweetened Dried Cranberries

Fresh Fruits and Sauces
  Citrus
  Cranberries
  Grapefruit
  Jellied Cranberry Sauce
  Whole Berry Cranberry Sauce
Light Cranberry Juice Drinks
  Light Cranberry Juice Cocktail
  Light Cran Grape
  Light Cran Raspberry
  Light White Cranberry
Premium 100% Cranberry Juices
  Cranberry Blend
  Cranberry and Concord Grape
  Cranberry and Georgia Peach
  Cranberry and Mixed Berry
  Cranberry and Pacific Raspberry
  Cranberry and Red Delicious Apple
  White Cranberry Blend
Premium 100% Grapefruit Juices
  Pink Grapefruit
  Ruby Red Grapefruit
  White Grapefruit
Ruby Grapefruit Juice Drinks
  Ruby Lemonade Grapefruit Juice Drink
  Ruby Mango Grapefruit Juice Drink
  Ruby Red Grapefruit Juice Drink
  Ruby Strawberry Grapefruit Juice Drink
  Ruby Tangerine Grapefruit Juice Drink
White Cranberry Juice Drinks
  White Cranberry
  White Cranberry and Apple
  White Cranberry and Peach
  White Cranberry and Strawberry

COMPETITORS

Altria	Mott's
Cadbury Schweppes	National Grape
Cadbury Schweppes	Cooperative
Americas	Northland Cranberries
Campbell Soup	Odwalla
Chiquita Brands	Old Orchard
Clement Pappas & Co.	Pepsi-Cola North America
Cliffstar	Smucker
Coca-Cola	Sunkist
Dole Food	Tropicana
Florida's Natural	Welch's
Hansen Natural	

HISTORICAL FINANCIALS

Company Type: Cooperative

Income Statement

FYE: August 31

	REVENUE ($ mil.)	NET INCOME ($ mil.)	NET PROFIT MARGIN	EMPLOYEES
8/04	1,400	—	—	2,000
8/03	1,000	—	—	2,000
8/02	1,068	—	—	2,000
8/01	1,104	—	—	2,200
8/00	1,400	—	—	2,000
8/99	1,360	—	—	2,000
8/98	1,480	—	—	2,350
8/97	1,438	—	—	2,300
8/96	1,433	—	—	2,300
8/95	1,361	—	—	2,300
Annual Growth	0.3%	—	—	(1.5%)

Revenue History

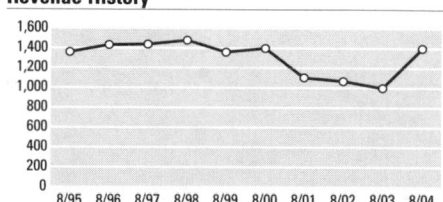

Oglethorpe Power

Much ogled, not-for-profit Oglethorpe Power Corporation is one of the largest electricity co-operatives in the US, with contracts to supply wholesale power to 38 member/owners (making up most of Georgia's electric distribution cooperatives) until 2025. Oglethorpe Power's member/owners, which also operate as not-for-profits, serve about 1.5 million residential, commercial, and industrial customers. The company, which was formed in 1974, has a generating capacity of more than 4,740 MW from fossil-fueled, nuclear, and hydroelectric power plants. In addition, Oglethorpe purchases power from other suppliers, and it markets power on the wholesale market.

Oglethorpe has stakes in 24 generating units. In 2004, Oglethorpe members Jackson EMC and Cobb EMC accounted for 12% and 10% of Oglethorpe's total revenues, respectively.

EXECUTIVES

Chairman: Benny W. Denham, age 74
Vice Chairman: J. Sam L. Rabun, age 73
President and CEO: Thomas A. (Tom) Smith, age 50, $481,373 pay
COO: Michael W. (Mike) Price, age 44, $278,854 pay
CFO: Elizabeth Bush (Betsy) Higgins, age 36, $260,126 pay (prior to title change)
SVP, Administration and Risk Management: W. Clayton (Clay) Robbins, age 58, $237,768 pay
SVP, Operations: Clarence D. Mitchell
VP and CIO: Barbara Hampton
VP and Controller: Mark Chesla
VP and Assistant to the COO: Billy Ussery
VP: George B. Taylor Jr.
VP, External Affairs: Robert D. Steele
VP, Finance: Anne F. Appleby
VP, Generation Projects: Dale R. Murphy
VP, Plant Operations: James A. (Jim) Messersmith
VP, Human Resources: Jami G. Reusch, age 42, $140,113 pay
Director, Public Relations: Greg Jones
Auditors: PricewaterhouseCoopers LLP

LOCATIONS

HQ: Oglethorpe Power Corporation
2100 E. Exchange Place, Tucker, GA 30084
Phone: 770-270-7600   **Fax:** 770-270-7827
Web: www.opc.com

PRODUCTS/OPERATIONS

2004 Sales

	$ mil.	% of total
Members	1,279.5	97
Non-members	33.3	3
Total	**1,312.8**	**100**

2004 Energy Mix

	% of total
Coal	32
Gas	30
Nuclear	25
Hydro	13
Total	**100**

COMPETITORS

AGL Resources
FPL Group
MEAG Power
Progress Energy
PS Energy
Southern Company
TVA

HISTORICAL FINANCIALS

Company Type: Cooperative

Income Statement

FYE: December 31

	REVENUE ($ mil.)	NET INCOME ($ mil.)	NET PROFIT MARGIN	EMPLOYEES
12/04	1,313	17	1.3%	168
12/03	1,204	17	1.4%	179
12/02	1,163	18	1.5%	173
12/01	1,139	18	1.6%	175
12/00	1,199	20	1.7%	160
12/99	1,176	20	1.7%	144
12/98	1,144	21	1.8%	125
12/97	1,048	22	2.1%	170
12/96	1,101	22	2.0%	—
12/95	1,150	22	1.9%	—
Annual Growth	**1.5%**	**(2.8%)**	**—**	**(0.2%)**

2004 Year-End Financials

Debt ratio: 766.9%
Return on equity: 4.3%
Cash ($ mil.): 134
Current ratio: 1.46
Long-term debt ($ mil.): 3,181

Net Income History

12/95 12/96 12/97 12/98 12/99 12/00 12/01 12/02 12/03 12/04

Ohio State University

The first student body of Ohio State University (OSU) had 24 students. Today the university has about 51,000 students at its flagship Columbus campus, edging out UT Austin and U of M (Twin Cities) for nation's largest campus in terms of enrollment. OSU also has four regional campuses and two agricultural institutes. The school's approximately 3,000 regular and research faculty members offer instruction in more than 170 undergraduate and 200 graduate programs. Its colleges and schools range from the Austin E. Knowlton School of Architecture to the College of Medicine and Public Health to the Fisher College of Business. OSU was established in 1870 as Ohio Agricultural and Mechanical College.

Noteworthy university alumni include astronaut Nancy Sherlock Currie, golfer Jack Nicklaus, author John Jakes, and Olympian Jesse Owens.

OSU is at the end of a five-year academic plan (unveiled in 2000) under which the university is spending $750 million to advance its national academic standing.

HISTORY

In 1870 the Ohio legislature, prompted by Governor Rutherford B. Hayes, agreed to establish the Ohio Agricultural and Mechanical College in Columbus on property provided by the Morrill Act of 1862 (the land-grant institution act, which gave land to states and territories for the establishment of colleges).

After a heated battle over whether the college should teach only agricultural and mechanical arts or foster a broad-based liberal arts curriculum, the college opened in 1873 offering agriculture, ancient languages, chemistry, geology, mathematics, modern languages, and physics courses. Two years later the school appointed its first female faculty member. The Ohio State University became the school's name in 1878; that year it graduated its first class. OSU graduated its first female student the next year.

OSU grew dramatically, adding schools of veterinary medicine (1885), pharmacy (1885), law (1891), and dairy sciences (1895). It awarded its first Masters of Arts degree in 1886.

The university continued to expand in the early 20th century, with enrollment surpassing 3,000 in 1908; by 1923 it had reached 10,000. New schools were added in education (1907), medicine and dentistry (1913), and commerce and journalism (1923). During WWI Ohio State designated part of its campus as training grounds and established the only college schools in the nation for airplane and balloon squadrons. Ohio Stadium was dedicated in 1922.

During the Great Depression Ohio State cut back salaries and course offerings. In the 1940s the school geared for war once again by establishing radiation and war research labs, as well as programs and services for students who were drafted. OSU captured its first national football championship in 1942.

The 1950s ushered in the era of legendary OSU football coach Woody Hayes. Hayes led his beloved Buckeyes to three national championships and nine Rose Bowl appearances before he was discharged for striking a Clemson player in 1978. The 1950s also saw the addition of four regional campuses at Lima, Mansfield, Marion, and Newark.

In the early 1960s the university was engaged in internal free-speech battles. By the end of that decade, enrollment had surpassed 50,000. OSU opened its School of Social Work in 1976.

In 1986 OSU and rival Michigan shared the Big 10 football conference title. Enrollment at OSU topped 54,000 in 1990 but then began declining. In response, the university tried to cut costs and beef up revenues. One way was through alliances: In 1992 it teamed with research group Battelle to develop a testing system for new drugs for the Food and Drug Administration. But when more savings were needed in 1995 and 1996, the university began streamlining operations, merging journalism and communications, and consolidating several veterinary departments. However, it also approved the creation of a new school of public health to provide education in environmental health, epidemiology, and health care management and financing.

But sports were not forgotten, and in 1996 OSU broke ground on the $84 million Schottenstein Center, a multipurpose facility for the university's basketball and ice hockey teams. In 1997 president Gordon Gee announced that he was leaving OSU for Brown University. The next year William Kirwan from the University of Maryland came on board as president.

In 2000 the university's "Affirm Thy Friendship" contribution campaign came to a close. The campaign increased OSU's endowment from $493 million in 1993 to $1.3 billion in 2000. In 2002 William Kirwan stepped down, and Karen Holbrook took over as president. Ohio State won the national football championship in early 2003.

EXECUTIVES

Chairman: Daniel M. Slane
Vice Chairman: Robert M. Duncan
President: Karen A. Holbrook, age 62
Chief of Staff and Special Assistant to the President: Pearl M. Bigfeather
EVP and Provost: Barbara R. Snyder
SVP Business and Finance: William J. (Bill) Shkurti
SVP External Relations: Curt Steiner
SVP Research: Robert T. McGrath
SVP; Executive Dean Health Sciences: Fred Sanfilippo
VP Agricultural Administration and University Outreach: Bobby D. Moser
VP Student Affairs: William H. Hall
VP University Development: James C. Schroeder
Associate VP Human Resources: Larry M. Lewellen
Vice Provost Minority Affairs: Mac A. Stewart
Secretary: David O. Frantz
General Counsel: Christopher Culley
Auditors: Deloitte & Touche LLP

LOCATIONS

HQ: The Ohio State University
Enarson Hall, 154 W. 12th Ave.,
Columbus, OH 43210
Phone: 614-292-3980   **Fax:** 614-292-0154
Web: www.osu.edu

The Ohio State University has campuses in Columbus, Lima, Mansfield, Marion, and Newark. It has two agricultural centers in Wooster, Ohio.

PRODUCTS/OPERATIONS

Selected Colleges and Schools
Austin E. Knowlton School of Architecture
College of Biological Sciences
College of Dentistry
College of Education
College of Engineering
College of Food, Agricultural, and Environmental Sciences
College of Human Ecology
College of Humanities
College of Law
College of Mathematical and Physical Sciences
College of Medicine and Public Health
College of Nursing
College of Optometry
College of Social and Behavioral Sciences
College of Social Work
College of the Arts
College of Veterinary Medicine
Graduate School
Max M. Fisher College of Business
School of Natural Resources
University College

HISTORICAL FINANCIALS

Company Type: School

Income Statement

FYE: June 30

	REVENUE ($ mil.)	NET INCOME ($ mil.)	NET PROFIT MARGIN	EMPLOYEES
6/04	3,060	—	—	34,000
6/03	2,721	—	—	33,772
6/02	2,000	—	—	33,000
6/01	1,661	—	—	32,000
6/00	1,554	—	—	31,302
6/99	1,923	—	—	29,502
6/98	1,749	—	—	31,268
6/97	1,630	—	—	29,000
6/96	1,531	—	—	29,266
6/95	1,575	—	—	29,500
Annual Growth	**7.7%**	**—**	**—**	**1.6%**

Revenue History

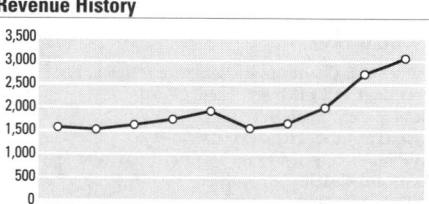

Old Dominion Electric

Ol' Virginny and neighboring states get power from Old Dominion Electric Cooperative, which generates and purchases electricity for its 12 member distribution cooperatives. These in turn serve nearly 500,000 customers in four northeastern states. The member-owned power utility has 2,000 MW of generating capacity from nuclear and fossil-fueled power plants and diesel generators; it purchases the remainder of its power from neighboring utilities and power marketers. Old Dominion transmits power to its members through the systems of utilities and transmission operators in the region. It also provides power to TEC Trading, a wholesale company also owned by the distribution cooperatives.

EXECUTIVES

President and CEO: Jackson E. (Jack) Reasor
SVP, Accounting and Finance and CFO: Daniel M. (Dan) Walker, $200,450 pay
SVP, Accounting and Finance and Secretary: Terri Young
SVP, Engineering and Operations: Gregory W. (Greg) White
VP and Controller: Robert L. (Bob) Kees
VP, Engineering and Operations: Ken Alexander
VP, Finance: Lynn Maloney
VP, Human Resources: Elissa Ecker
VP, Member and External Relations: John C. Lee Jr.
VP, Power Supply Planning: Rick Beam
Assistant VP, Rates and Regulations: Edward D. Tatum
Auditors: Ernst & Young LLP

LOCATIONS

HQ: Old Dominion Electric Cooperative
4201 Dominion Blvd., Glen Allen, VA 23060
Phone: 804-747-0592   **Fax:** 804-747-3742
Web: www.odec.com

Old Dominion Electric Cooperative operates in Delaware, Maryland, Virginia, and West Virginia.

2004 Sales

	$ mil.	% of total
Northern Virginia Electric Cooperative	159.8	27
Rappahannock Electric Cooperative	120.8	21
Delaware Electric Cooperative	61.0	10
Other cooperatives	246.9	42
Total	**588.5**	**100**

HISTORICAL FINANCIALS

Company Type: Cooperative

Income Statement

FYE: December 31

	REVENUE ($ mil.)	NET INCOME ($ mil.)	NET PROFIT MARGIN	EMPLOYEES
12/04	589	12	2.1%	84
12/03	536	12	2.3%	82
12/02	495	10	2.0%	—
Annual Growth	**9.1%**	**10.0%**	**—**	**2.4%**

Net Income History

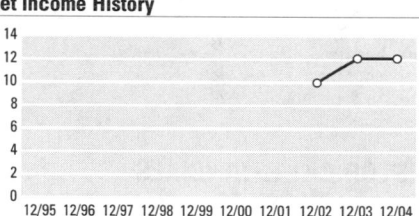

O'Melveny & Myers

O'Melveny & Myers is more than happy to play the role of legal guardian angel. Founded in 1885, O'Melveny & Myers is one of the oldest law firms in Los Angeles, and it has developed strong ties to the media and entertainment industry. Sony Pictures Entertainment, Walt Disney, and Time Warner Inc. are among the firm's clients. The firm has more than 900 lawyers located in 13 offices worldwide. O'Melveny & Myers' practice areas include labor and employment, litgation, and tax and transactions. The firm is expanding its services for high-tech companies, which include legal advice related to software licensing, intellectual property, and venture capital investments.

It also is known for political clout: Former US Secretary of State Warren Christopher is a senior partner.

EXECUTIVES

Chairman and CEO: Arthur B. Culvahouse Jr.
COO: Bruce Boulware
Director Finance: Joelle Nardone
Director Human Resources: Beth Naples

LOCATIONS

HQ: O'Melveny & Myers LLP
400 S. Hope St., Ste. 1500, Los Angeles, CA 90071
Phone: 213-430-6000   **Fax:** 213-430-6407
Web: www.omm.com

O'Melveny & Myers has 13 offices worldwide.

PRODUCTS/OPERATIONS

Selected Practice Areas

Asia Practice
Banking and financial institutions
Bankruptcy
Communications
Employee benefits
Entertainment and media
Environmental
Health care
Internet law
Labor and employment
Litigation
Real estate
White-collar crime

COMPETITORS

Akin Gump
Baker & McKenzie
Davis Polk
Gibson, Dunn & Crutcher
Greenberg Glusker
 Fields Claman
Latham & Watkins
Paul, Hastings
Skadden, Arps
Sullivan & Cromwell

HISTORICAL FINANCIALS

Company Type: Partnership

Income Statement

FYE: January 31

	REVENUE ($ mil.)	NET INCOME ($ mil.)	NET PROFIT MARGIN	EMPLOYEES
1/04	658	—	—	—
1/03	563	—	—	2,200
1/02	490	—	—	1,900
1/01	401	—	—	1,500
1/00	373	—	—	1,500
1/99	328	—	—	1,450
1/98	284	—	—	1,400
1/97	260	—	—	1,350
1/96	253	—	—	1,314
1/95	257	—	—	1,334
Annual Growth	11.0%	—	—	6.5%

Revenue History

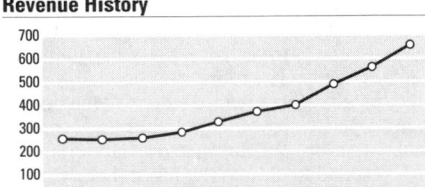

Orlando Magic

Perhaps there's destiny in a name. After dribbling onto the court in 1989, the Orlando Magic defied the odds against expansion teams, struggling for only a short time in its infancy. The team drafted Goliath-like center Shaquille O'Neal in 1992 and became a serious NBA competitor. The Magic, behind the talents of O'Neal, made the NBA Finals in 1995, but were swept by the Houston Rockets. The loss of O'Neal to the Los Angeles Lakers in 1996 hurt the team. The Magic hope to bring back the sparkle with high school sensation Dwight Howard. Rich DeVos, co-founder of Amway, has changed his mind about selling the team despite the fact that it loses about $10 million a year.

EXECUTIVES

Owner and Chairman: Richard (Rich) DeVos, age 79
President and CEO: Bob Vander Weide
Head Coach: Brian Hill
Assistant Coach: Randy Ayers
EVP Marketing and Franchise Relations: Alex Martins
Assistant Coach: Tom Sterner
SVP: Diana Basch
SVP: Julius W. (Dr. J) Erving II, age 55
SVP: Pat Williams, age 65
VP Corporate Sales and Broadcasting: Jack Swope
VP Business: Jim Fritz
VP Human Resources and Administration:
 Lorisse Garcia
VP Marketing: Chris D'Orso
Director of Communications: Joel Glass

LOCATIONS

HQ: Orlando Magic
 8701 Maitland Summit Blvd., Orlando, FL 32810
Phone: 407-916-2400   **Fax:** 407-916-2830
Web: www.nba.com/magic

The Orlando Magic play at the TD Waterhouse Centre in Orlando, Florida.

PRODUCTS/OPERATIONS

Titles

Eastern Conference Champions (1995)

COMPETITORS

Atlanta Hawks   Miami Heat
Charlotte Bobcats   Washington Wizards

HISTORICAL FINANCIALS

Company Type: Private

Income Statement

FYE: June 30

	REVENUE ($ mil.)	NET INCOME ($ mil.)	NET PROFIT MARGIN	EMPLOYEES
6/04	78	—	—	—
6/03	80	—	—	—
6/02	82	—	—	—
6/01	76	—	—	—
6/00	66	—	—	—
6/99	38	—	—	—
6/98	64	—	—	122
6/97	63	—	—	110
6/96	58	—	—	—
Annual Growth	3.8%	—	—	10.9%

Revenue History

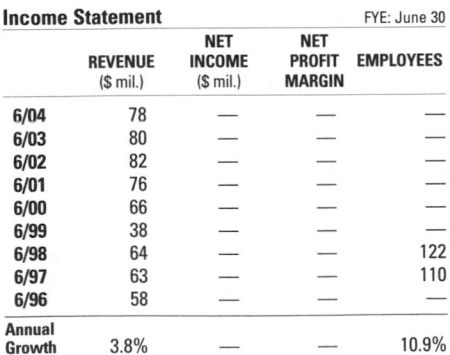

Outsourcing Solutions

Pay now or deal with Outsourcing Solutions (OSI) later. The accounts-receivable management firm and its subsidiaries perform consumer and commercial collections and other outsourced services such as billing and payment planning to its customers, which include credit card, financial, utility, retail, and health care companies, as well as educational and government entities. OSI also purchases new and delinquent accounts from creditors. The acquisitive company operates some 65 offices in about 25 states; it also offers its services in Canada, Mexico, and Puerto Rico. OSI, which is majority owned by Madison Dearborn Partners, filed for and emerged from Chapter 11 reorganization in 2003.

The Chapter 11 filing was primarily done to restructure debt, rather than necessitated by any loss in business volume. A major player in the company's rebound was Merrill Lynch, who provided OSI with a helping hand in the form of a $90 million credit facility to strengthen its debt-purchasing arm, OSI Portfolio Services.

EXECUTIVES

President and CEO: Kevin T. Keleghan
EVP and COO: Jeffrey S. (Jeff) Wahl
EVP and CFO: Gary L. Weller
EVP Business Development and Portfolio Acquisitions:
 Timothy J. Bauer
EVP, General Counsel, and Secretary: Eric R. Fencl
EVP and Chief Human Resources Officer:
 C. Bradford McLeod
EVP and President, Financial Services Business Group:
 Steve Richards
EVP: Michael B. Staed
SVP and CIO: J. Michael (Mike) Batton
SVP Operations: William (Bill) Cruz
Manager, Corporate Communications:
 Rita Holmes-Bobo
Auditors: Deloitte & Touche LLP

LOCATIONS

HQ: Outsourcing Solutions Inc.
 390 S. Woodsmill Rd., Ste. 350,
 Chesterfield, MO 63017
Phone: 314-576-0022   **Fax:** 314-576-1867
Web: www.osi.to

PRODUCTS/OPERATIONS

Selected Subsidiaries and Affiliates
Coast-to-Coast Consulting, LLC (health care staffing and consulting services)
Greystone Business Group, LLC (operations research and human performance improvement)
Jennifer Loomis & Associates, Inc. (out-of-state Medicaid billing services)
Medical Accounting Service (long-term health care payment planning)
North Shore Agency, Inc. (billing and recovery services)
OSI Collection Services, Inc. (third-party recovery services)
OSI Education Services, Inc. (third-party recovery services)
OSI Outsourcing Services, Inc. (first-party receivables management)
OSI Portfolio Services, Inc. (portfolio acquisitions and sales)
Qualink, Inc. (extended business office services to the health care industry)
RWC Consulting Group, LLC (financial operations services)
Transworld Systems Inc. (letter series profit recovery services)
University Accounting Services, LLC (student loan billing services)

COMPETITORS

Asta Funding
Equifax
GC Services
IntelliRisk Management
Nationwide Recovery
NCO Group
Portfolio Recovery

HISTORICAL FINANCIALS

Company Type: Private

Income Statement
FYE: December 31

	REVENUE ($ mil.)	NET INCOME ($ mil.)	NET PROFIT MARGIN	EMPLOYEES
12/04	475	—	—	6,100
12/03	488	—	—	6,200
12/02	592	—	—	7,200
12/01	612	—	—	9,000
12/00	543	—	—	7,600
12/99	504	—	—	7,000
12/98	479	—	—	7,000
12/97	272	—	—	5,000
12/96	106	—	—	—
12/95	30	—	—	—
Annual Growth	36.1%	—	—	2.9%

Revenue History

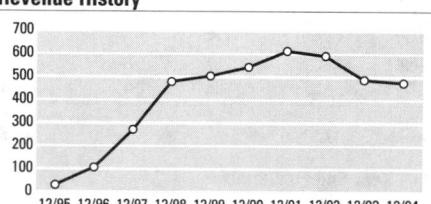

Pabst Brewing

The Pabst Brewing Company is a 19th century brewer retooled for the 21st century. Pabst, founded in 1844, today is a "virtual" brewer. It owns no brewery; instead, Pabst pays other brewers, such as Miller and Lion Brewery, to brew the beers, while it retains ownership of the brands (Pabst Blue Ribbon, Pearl, Lone Star, Old Milwaukee, Old Style, Schlitz, and Colt 45) and markets the products. Pabst is owned by the Kalmanovitz Charitable Trust.

Pabst's market share can't compare with those of the nation's top brewing giants, but its Pabst Blue Ribbon is enjoying a surge in popularity among rebel beer drinkers who resist the mass marketing of Pabst's rivals. The Kalmanovitz Charitable Trust is reportedly interested in selling Pabst.

EXECUTIVES

Chairman: Bernard Orsi
President and CEO: Kevin T. Kotecki, age 41
COO: James Walter
CFO: Kim James
VP and General Counsel: Yeoryios Apallas
VP National Sales: David Mahoney
VP Human Resources: Lee Wingert
Director, IT: Marc Smith
Director, Management Information Systems: Linda Ramos

LOCATIONS

HQ: Pabst Brewing Company
121 Interpark Blvd., Ste. 300,
San Antonio, TX 78216
Phone: 210-226-0231   **Fax:** 210-299-6807
Web: www.pabst.com

COMPETITORS

Anheuser-Busch	InBev USA
Constellation Brands	Miller Brewing
Gambrinus	Molson Coors
Heineken	Stone Brewing

HISTORICAL FINANCIALS

Company Type: Private

Income Statement
FYE: June 30

	ESTIMATED REVENUE ($ mil.)	NET INCOME ($ mil.)	NET PROFIT MARGIN	EMPLOYEES
6/03	600	—	—	700
6/02	575	—	—	700
6/01	750	—	—	300
6/00	1,000	—	—	750
6/99	1,200	—	—	700
6/98	500	—	—	1,500
6/97	550	—	—	1,600
6/96	550	—	—	1,604
6/95	600	—	—	1,300
6/94	595	—	—	2,400
Annual Growth	0.1%	—	—	(12.8%)

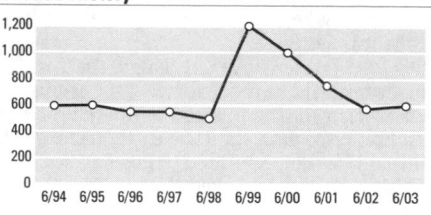

Pacific Mutual

Life insurance is alive and whale at Pacific Mutual Holding. The mutual holding company's primary operating subsidiary, Pacific Life Insurance, (whose logo is a breaching whale) is the largest California-based life insurer. Lines of business include a variety of life insurance products for individuals and small businesses; annuities and mutual funds (also geared to individuals and small businesses); institutional products (including funding agreements, annuities, and guaranteed investment contracts, or GICs) for pension plans and other institutional investors; and group insurance (medical, accident, and health insurance targeted to small and midsized employers).

Major operating subsidiaries of Pacific Mutual Holding include mutual fund and annuities distribution network Pacific Select Distributors; Pacific Asset Funding, which provides trade financing and related services; College Savings Bank, which offers a variety of college savings vehicles; and aircraft leasing operations Aviation Capital Group. Pacific Mutual, through Pacific Life, also owns a minority stake in Pacific Investment Management Company (PIMCO), a major investment management firm majority-owned by insurance giant Allianz, and held through Allianz Global Investors of America (formerly Allianz Dresdner Asset Management of America).

Pacific Life policyholders are members of Pacific Mutual Holding Company, which was created in 1997 following a conversion to the mutual holding company structure. Pacific LifeCorp is the intermediate stock holding company.

HISTORY

The Pacific Mutual Life Insurance began business in 1868 in Sacramento, California, as a stock company. Its board was dominated by California business and political leaders, including three of the "Big Four" who created the Central Pacific Railroad (Charles Crocker, Mark Hopkins, and Leland Stanford) and three former governors (Stanford, Newton Booth, and Henry Huntley Haight). Stanford (founder of Stanford University) was the company's first president and policyholder.

By 1870 Pacific Mutual Life was selling life insurance throughout most of the western US. Expansion continued in the early 1870s into Colorado, Kentucky, Nebraska, New York, Ohio, and Texas. The company ventured into Mexico in 1873 but sold few policies. It had more luck in China, accepting its first risk there in 1875, and in Hawaii, where it started business in 1877. In 1881 Pacific Mutual Life moved to San Francisco.

Leland Stanford died in 1893. The eponymous university and Stanford's widow, though rich in assets, found themselves struggling through a

US economic depression. The benefit from Stanford's policy kept the university open until the estate was settled.

In 1905 Conservative Life bought the firm. The Pacific Mutual Life name survived the acquisition just as its records survived the fire that ravaged San Francisco after the 1906 earthquake. Pacific Mutual Life then relocated to Los Angeles.

The company squeaked through the Depression after a flood of claims on its noncancellable disability income policies forced Pacific Mutual Life into a reorganization plan initiated by the California insurance commissioner (1936). After WWII, Pacific Mutual Life entered the group insurance and pension markets.

After 83 years as a stock company and an eight-year stock purchasing program, Pacific Mutual Life became a true mutual in 1959.

Pacific Mutual Life relocated to Newport Beach in 1972. During the 1980s it built up its financial services operations, including its Pacific Investment Management Co. (PIMCO, founded 1971). The company was in trouble even before the stock crash of 1987 because of health care costs and over-investment in real estate. That year it brought in CEO Thomas Sutton, who sold off real estate and emphasized HMOs and fee-based financial services.

In the 1990s the firm cut costs and increased its fee income. PIMCO Advisors, L.P. was formed in 1994 when PIMCO merged with Thomson Advisory Group. The merger gave Pacific Mutual Life a retail market for its fixed-income products, a stake in the resulting public company, and sales that offset interest-rate variations and changes in the health care system.

In 1997 the company assumed the corporate-owned life insurance business of failed Confederation Life Insurance; it also merged insolvent First Capital Life into Pacific Life as Pacific Corinthian Life. That year Pacific Mutual Life, which became Pacific Mutual Holding, became the first top-10 US mutual to convert to a mutual holding company, thus allowing it the option of issuing stock to fund acquisitions. Because the firm remained partially mutual, however, policyholders retained ownership but got no shares of Pacific LifeCorp, its new intermediate stock holding company.

To compete with such one-stop financial service behemoths as Citigroup, Pacific Mutual began selling annuities through a Compass Bank subsidiary in 1998. The next year it bought controlling interests in broker-dealer M.L. Stern and investment adviser Tower Asset Management. In 2000 the world's #2 insurer, Allianz, bought all of PIMCO Advisors (now Allianz Dresdner Asset Management of America) other than the interest retained by Pacific Mutual when it spun off the investment manager; Pacific Mutual gradually decreased its holdings in the firm through ongoing sales to Allianz.

Pacific Mutual Holding sharpened its focus on individuals and small businesses in 2001 with the sale of its reinsurance unit to what is now Scottish Re; Pacific Mutual holds a minority stake in the reinsurer. In 2004, Pacific Life agreed to sell its group health insurance business (which includes medical, dental, and life policies) to Pacificare.

EXECUTIVES

Chairman and CEO, Pacific Mutual Holding Company and Pacific Life Insurance Company:
Thomas C. Sutton, age 63
Chairman and CEO, Waterstone Financial Group, Inc.:
Thomas A. Hopkins

President and CEO, M.L. Stern & Co., LLC:
Milford L. (Mickey) Stern
EVP, Annuities and Mutual Funds Division, Pacific Life; Chairman and CEO, Pacific Select Distributors, Inc.: Gerald W. (Bill) Robinson
President and CEO, Associated Financial Group, Inc.:
G. John Hurley
CEO, College Savings Bank: Peter A. Roberts
Managing Director, Pacific Asset Funding:
Robert G. Denhert
Managing Director, Aviation Capital Group:
R. Stephen Hannahs
Chairman and CEO, Mutual Service Corporation; President, Pacific Select Distributors: John L. Dixon
Chairman and President, Associated Securities:
Neal E. Nakagiri, age 50
President and CEO, United Planners' Financial Services of America: Thomas H. Oliver
Auditors: Deloitte & Touche LLP

LOCATIONS

HQ: Pacific Mutual Holding Company
700 Newport Center Dr., Newport Beach, CA 92660
Phone: 949-219-3011   **Fax:** 949-219-7614

Pacific Mutual Holding has insurance operations throughout the US.

PRODUCTS/OPERATIONS

2004 Sales

	$ mil.	% of total
Net investment income	1,866	45
Policy fees	1,263	31
Commission revenue	270	6
Investment advisory fees	248	6
Net realized investment gain		
PIMCO	169	4
Other	4	—
Insurance premiums	104	3
Other income	191	5
Total	**4,115**	**100**

2004 Sales

	$ mil.	% of total
Life insurance	1,520	36
Institutional products	998	24
Broker-dealers	874	20
Annuities & mutual funds	850	20
Corporate & other adjustments	(127)	—
Total	**4,115**	**100**

2004 Assets

	$ mil.	% of total
Investments		
Securities available for sale, at estimated fair value		
Fixed maturity securities	26,605	34
Equity securities	389	1
Trading securities	226	—
Policy loans	5,629	7
Mortgage loans	3,286	4
Interest in PIMCO	606	1
Real estate	134	—
Other investments	1,249	2
Separate account assets	32,032	42
Deferred policy acquisition costs	3,278	4
Cash & cash equivalents	1,011	1
Accrued investment income	422	1
Other assets	2,270	3
Total	**77,137**	**100**

Selected Products and Services

Life Insurance Division
  Interest-sensitive whole life
  Joint and last-survivor life
  Term life
  Universal life insurance
  Variable universal life

Institutional Products Division
  Funding agreements
  Single premium group annuity contracts
  Stable value products
    Floating rate guaranteed interest contracts (GICs)
    Separate account GICs
    Synthetic GICs
    Traditional GICs
  Structured settlement annuities
Annuities and Mutual Fund Division
  529 College savings plans
  Fixed annuities
  Mutual funds
  Variable annuities
Group Insurance Division
  Dental and vision insurance
  Disability income insurance
  Life and accidental death and dismemberment insurance
  Medical and prescription drug insurance
  Stop loss contracts
Other
  Aircraft asset management for third-party financial institutions
  Aircraft joint venture investments
  Commercial jet aircraft for lease to airlines
  Commercial jet aircraft trading

COMPETITORS

Acordia	MetLife
Aetna	Mutual of Omaha
AXA Financial	Nationwide
Charles Schwab	Nationwide Financial
CIGNA	Network
GenAmerica	New York Life
Great-West Life Assurance	Northwestern Mutual
Guardian Life	PacifiCare
Hartford Life	Penn Mutual
Health Net	Principal Financial
John Hancock Financial	Prudential
Services	St. Paul Travelers
Liberty Mutual	StanCorp Financial Group
Life Investors Insurance	Transamerica Occidental
Lincoln Financial Group	Life
MassMutual	USAA

HISTORICAL FINANCIALS

Company Type: Mutual company

Income Statement

FYE: December 31

	ASSETS ($ mil.)	NET INCOME ($ mil.)	INCOME AS % OF ASSETS	EMPLOYEES
12/04	77,137	540	0.7%	—
12/03	67,422	418	0.6%	—
12/02	57,305	50	0.1%	3,700
12/01	56,055	247	0.4%	3,600
12/00	54,784	995	1.8%	3,600
12/99	50,123	371	0.7%	3,799
12/98	39,884	242	0.6%	2,700
12/97	34,009	176	0.5%	3,422
12/96	27,065	167	0.6%	2,750
12/95	17,589	85	0.5%	2,700
Annual Growth	17.9%	22.8%	—	4.6%

2004 Year-End Financials

Equity as % of assets: 7.1%   Long-term debt ($ mil.): 1,460
Return on assets: 0.7%   Sales ($ mil.): 4,115
Return on equity: 10.4%

Net Income History

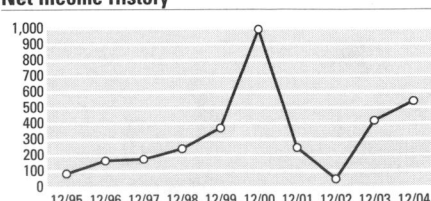

Packard Foundation

One of the wealthiest philanthropic organizations in the US, The David and Lucile Packard Foundation primarily provides grants to not-for-profit entities operating in three areas: conservation and science; children, families, and communities; and population. The foundation has approximately $5.2 billion in assets and awards about $200 million in national and international grants, with an extra focus on Northern California's Monterey, San Mateo, Santa Clara, and Santa Cruz counties. The late David Packard (co-founder of Hewlett-Packard) and his wife, the late Lucile Salter Packard, created the foundation in 1964. Their children now run the organization.

EXECUTIVES

Chairman: Susan Packard Orr
Vice Chairman: Nancy Packard Burnett
Vice Chairman: Julie E. Packard
President and CEO: Carol S. Larson, age 51
VP and CFO: George A. Vera, age 61
Secretary and General Counsel: Barbara P. Wright, age 56
Director Children, Families, and Communities Program: Lois Salisbury
Director Conservation and Science Program: James (Jim) Leape
Director Population Program: Sarah Clark
Auditors: Deloitte & Touche LLP

LOCATIONS

HQ: The David and Lucile Packard Foundation
300 2nd St., Los Altos, CA 94022
Phone: 650-948-7658   **Fax:** 650-948-5793
Web: www.packard.org

PRODUCTS/OPERATIONS

2004 Selected Grants

Conservation and Science
  Alaska Conservation Foundation ($250,000)
  Bridgespan Group ($30,000)
  California Institute of Technology ($625,000)
  Climate Policy Center ($200,000)
  Conservation Society of Pohnpei ($265,000; Federated States of Micronesia)
  Environmental Flying Services ($20,000)
  Harvard University ($625,000; $470,870; $250,000; $100,000)
  Iemanya Oceanica ($50,000)
  Kabang Kalikasan ng Pilipinas ($50,000)
  Massachusetts Institute of Technology ($625,000)
  Nature Conservancy ($500,000; $286,000; $100,000; $90,000; $50,000)
  Oregon State University ($43,200; $11,000)
  Pronatura Noroeste-Mar de Cortés ($200,000; Mexico)
  San Diego Society of Natural History Balboa Park ($20,000)
  Society for Conservation Biology ($110,000)
  Strategies for the Global Environment ($96,800)
  Trust for Conservation Innovation ($78,500)
  University of California, San Diego ($625,000)
  University of Papua New Guinea ($95,000)
  Wildlife Conservation Society ($500,000)

Population
  Action Health Incorporated ($550,000)
  Choice USA ($500,000)
  Feminist Majority Foundation ($450,000)
  Ipas ($2 million; $1.5 million; $900,000)
  Linangan ng Kababaihan ($380,000; Philippines)
  Planned Parenthood Federation of America ($1 million; $490,000)
  Population Reference Bureau ($250,000)
  University of California, Berkeley ($250,000)

Children, Families, and Communities
  Action Against Crime and Violence Education Fund ($375,200; $250,000)
  Asian Pacific American Legal Center of Southern California ($200,000)
  California Economic Development Lending Initiative ($150,000; $35,000)
  Center for Law and Social Policy ($100,000)
  Children Now ($650,000)
  Families USA Foundation ($500,000)
  Georgetown University ($330,000; $104,700)
  Labor Project for Working Families ($85,600; $50,000)
  Mexican American Legal Defense and Educational Fund ($155,000)
  National Women's Law Center ($100,000)
  Public Counsel Law Center ($125,000)
  San Francisco Foundation Community Initiative Funds ($1.4 million; $375,000; $34,100; $10,000)
  Sutton Group LLC ($25,000)
  Ventura County ($40,000)

Special Opportunities and Organizational Effectiveness Funds
  American Civil Liberties Union Foundation ($700,000)
  Cause Communications for Non-Profit Growth ($27,000)
  Central Coast YMCA ($12,900)
  Chartwell School ($500,000)
  Institute for Global Ethics ($500,000)
  Philanthropic Ventures Foundation ($130,000)
  Woodland Park Zoo ($118,900)

HISTORICAL FINANCIALS

Company Type: Foundation

Income Statement

FYE: December 31

	REVENUE ($ mil.)	NET INCOME ($ mil.)	NET PROFIT MARGIN	EMPLOYEES
12/03	1,501	—	—	83
12/02	92	—	—	90
12/01	121	—	—	100
12/00	146	—	—	—
12/99	5,570	—	—	—
12/98	1,017	—	—	—
12/97	663	—	—	100
12/96	462	—	—	100
12/95	907	—	—	—
12/94	289	—	—	—
Annual Growth	**20.1%**	**—**	**—**	**(2.6%)**

Revenue History

PAETEC

PAETEC gets its paychecks from institutional users of voice and data communication services. The integrated communications provider offers local and domestic and international long-distance voice services, as well as high-speed broadband data services, to midsized and large businesses such as colleges and universities, government organizations, and hospitals. PAETEC services are offered to end users and wholesale customers in 27 large markets from California to New Hampshire. Chairman and CEO Arunas Chesonis founded PAETEC in 1998.

EXECUTIVES

Chairman, President, and CEO, PAETEC and PAETEC Communications: Arunas A. Chesonis, age 42, $692,960 pay
EVP and CFO, PAETEC and PAETEC Communications: Keith M. Wilson, age 38, $460,361 pay
EVP and Director; Co-COO, PAETEC Communications: Bradford M. Bono, age 36, $398,125 pay
EVP; Co-COO, PAETEC Communications: Edward J. Butler Jr., age 44, $411,775 pay
EVP, PAETEC and PAETEC Communications: Richard J. Padulo, age 60
EVP and Treasurer, PAETEC and PAETEC Communications: Timothy J. Bancroft, age 56
EVP, Secretary, and General Counsel, PAETEC and PAETEC Communications: Daniel J. Venuti, age 45
EVP, Marketing and Training; Chief Marketing Officer, PAETEC Communications: John P. (Jack) Baron, age 44, $287,500 pay
EVP; President, South Region, and National Strategic Markets, PAETEC Communications: Joseph D. Ambersley, age 55
EVP; President, Strategic Channels and President, Alternate Channels, PAETEC Communications: Christopher Bantoft, age 58
EVP; EVP, Managed Services and Information Technology, PAETEC Communications: Jeffrey L. Burke, age 46
Communications Manager: David Mihalyov
Auditors: Deloitte & Touche LLP

LOCATIONS

HQ: PAETEC Corp.
1 PAETEC Plaza, 600 Willowbrook Office Park, Fairport, NY 14450
Phone: 585-340-2500   **Fax:** 585-340-2801
Web: www.paetec.com

PAETEC has operations in California, Connecticut, Florida, Illinois, Maryland, Massachusetts, New Hampshire, New Jersey, New York, Pennsylvania, Rhode Island, and Virginia.

PRODUCTS/OPERATIONS

2004 Sales

	$ mil.	% of total
Network services	316.7	77
Carrier services	70.7	17
Integrated solutions	26.2	6
Total	**413.6**	**100**

Selected Services

Data communications
Dedicated shared T1 access
Dedicated T1 access
Digital subscriber line (DSL) services
Managed data services
Virtual private networks
Web hosting

Voice Communications

Local exchange services
  Business lines
  Direct-dial trunks
Long-distance
  Dedicated 1+ and toll-free
  Domestic toll-free service
  International toll-free service
  Switched 1+ and toll-free
Wholesale
  Colocation
  IP/ISP services
  Local resale
  Network monitoring and reporting
  Off-net origination

COMPETITORS

ALLTEL
America Online
AT&T
BellSouth
Birch
Cavalier Telephone
Cingular Wireless
Comcast
Cox Communications
EarthLink
Level 3 Communications
MCI
Net2Phone
Primus Telecommunications
Qwest
SBC Communications
Sprint Nextel
Telephone & Data Systems
Time Warner
T-Mobile USA
Verio
Verizon
Verizon Wireless
Vonage

HISTORICAL FINANCIALS

Company Type: Private

Income Statement			FYE: December 31
	REVENUE ($ mil.)	NET INCOME ($ mil.)	NET PROFIT MARGIN	EMPLOYEES
12/04	414	79	19.1%	1,100
12/03	364	36	9.9%	—
12/02	289	(22)	—	975
Annual Growth	19.6%	—	—	6.2%

2004 Year-End Financials

Debt ratio: (253.7%)
Return on equity: —
Cash ($ mil.): 46

Current ratio: 1.59
Long-term debt ($ mil.): 124

Net Income History

80
60
40
20
0
-20
-40
12/95 12/96 12/97 12/98 12/99 12/00 12/01 12/02 12/03 12/04

Palmetto Bancshares

Palmetto Bancshares is the holding company for The Palmetto Bank, which operates about 30 branches concentrated in northwestern South Carolina. The bank's offerings include checking and savings accounts, money markets, IRAs, and CDs. Loans secured by commercial real estate account for the largest portion of its loan portfolio (almost 50%). Single-family residential mortgages are a distant second, at about 25% of the portfolio. Palmetto Bank also provides such investment services as financial planning, trust, and brokerage services, plus bond, mutual fund, and annuity sales. The Palmetto Bank was been serving South Carolina since 1906.

EXECUTIVES

Chairman and CEO: L. Leon Patterson, age 63, $476,580 pay
President, COO, and Director; Chairman and CEO, The Palmetto Bank: Paul W. Stringer, age 61, $431,460 pay
President and Chief Retail Officer, The Palmetto Bank: George A. (Andy) Douglas Jr., age 53, $246,750 pay
EVP, The Palmetto Bank: Teresa W. Knight, age 49, $178,365 pay
EVP and Chief Credit Officer, The Palmetto Bank: W. Michael Ellison, age 52
SVP and Regional Executive, Golden Strip, The Palmetto Bank: James C. (Jim) Peters Jr.
SVP and Regional Executive, Greenville, The Palmetto Bank: Robert A. (Rob) Hrubala
VP and Commercial Loan Officer, The Palmetto Bank: Peter J. Baldwin
VP, Chief Auditor, and Risk Manager, The Palmetto Bank: Valerie W. Stevenson
Treasurer; EVP, The Palmetto Bank: Ralph M. Burns III, age 54, $178,365 pay
Auditors: Elliott Davis LLC

LOCATIONS

HQ: Palmetto Bancshares, Inc.
  301 Hillcrest Dr., Laurens, SC 29360
Phone: 864-984-4551   **Fax:** 864-984-8415
Web: www.palmettobank.com

PRODUCTS/OPERATIONS

2004 Sales

	$ mil.	% of total
Interest		
Loans, including fees	46.2	70
Investment securities	4.7	7
Other	0.1	—
Noninterest		
Service charges on deposit accounts	8.6	13
Gains on sales of loans	0.6	1
Trust & brokerage services	0.6	1
Other	5.2	8
Total	**66.0**	**100**

COMPETITORS

Bank of America
BB&T
Community First Bancorp
First Citizens
  Bancorporation

First South Bancorp (SC)
GrandSouth
  Bancorporation
South Financial
Wachovia

HISTORICAL FINANCIALS

Company Type: Private

Income Statement			FYE: December 31
	ASSETS ($ mil.)	NET INCOME ($ mil.)	INCOME AS % OF ASSETS	EMPLOYEES
12/04	996	12	1.2%	374
12/03	898	11	1.2%	370
12/02	825	10	1.2%	368
Annual Growth	9.9%	12.3%	—	0.8%

2004 Year-End Financials

Equity as % of assets: 8.1%
Return on assets: 1.3%
Return on equity: 15.8%

Long-term debt ($ mil.): —
Sales ($ mil.): 66

Net Income History

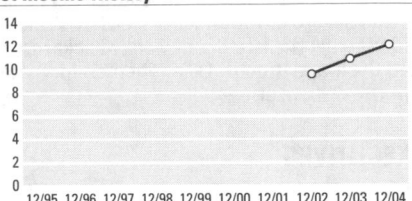

14
12
10
8
6
4
2
0
12/95 12/96 12/97 12/98 12/99 12/00 12/01 12/02 12/03 12/04

Parsons

Almost evangelically, Parsons carries its message — and its engineering, procurement, and construction management services — worldwide. The company provides design, planning, and construction management through four main operating groups: water & infrastructure, commercial technology, infrastructure & technology, and transportation. Among its many projects, Parsons has designed power plants; built dams, resorts, and shopping centers; and provided environmental services such as the cleanup of hazardous nuclear wastes. Parsons has also added improvements to airports and rail systems, bridges, and highways. Customers of the employee-owned company include government agencies and private industries.

Among Parsons' projects has been its participation since 1998 in the US Army's programs for alternative technologies for chemical weapons disposal. The company established the Parsons Fabrication Facility in Pasco, Washington, to test process systems for chemical weapon and bulk agent disposal. The events of September 11, 2001, prompted the US Army to accelerate the destruction of its chemical weapons, and Parsons' Newport, Indiana, chemical agent disposal facility has been developing a plan for speedy neutralization of the weapons. Parsons has also provided engineering management support for the construction of the Russian Chemical Weapons Destruction Complex.

Parsons has been developing its security services and has been selected to a team of companies that will be providing homeland security services at the Ports of New Jersey and New York to track containers.

Another project is the first major suspension bridge to be built in the US in more than 35 years. Parsons, which has been involved in the design and construction of more than 20 recent suspension bridges, is providing final design and engineering support during construction for the Carquinez Bridge near San Francisco.

Parsons is also designing and building military, police, and security sites in Iraq as well as more than 1,000 education and health facilities throughout the war-torn country. The group has had decades of experience internationally in infrastructure restoration, including work in Boznia-Herzegovina and Kosovo. The selection of Parsons and environmental engineering giant CH2M HILL by the Coalition Provisional Authority to manage four other contractors in Iraq has drawn criticism from some Democrats. The Democrats believe the contractors have conflicts of interest with the companies they are to manage because of existing partnerships in other projects.

HISTORY

Ralph Parsons, the son of a Long Island fisherman, was born in 1896. At age 13 he started his first business venture, a garage and machine shop, which he operated with his brother. After a stint in the US Navy, Parsons joined Bechtel as an aeronautical engineer. The company changed its name to Bechtel-McCone-Parsons Corporation in 1938. However, Parsons later sold his shares in that company and left in 1944 to start his own design and engineering firm, the Ralph M. Parsons Co., after splitting with partner John McCone (who later headed the CIA).

Parsons Co. expanded into the chemical and petroleum industries in the early 1950s. During that decade it oversaw the building of several natural gas and petroleum refineries overseas, including the world's largest, in Lacq, France.

In the early 1960s the company began working in Kuwait, which later proved to be one of its biggest markets. By 1969 Parsons had built oil refineries for all of the major oil companies, designed launch sites for US missiles, and constructed some of the largest mines in the world. In 1969 the company went public. With annual sales of about $300 million, it ranked second only to Bechtel in the design and engineering field. Ralph Parsons died in 1974.

The company built oil and gas treatment and production plants in Alaska in the 1970s and reorganized itself into The Parsons Corporation and RMP International in 1978. It went private in 1984 as The Parsons Corporation, taking advantage of a new tax law that favored corporations with employee stock ownership plans (ESOPs). Not all employees were happy, though. Several groups sued, maintaining that the plan disproportionately benefited executives, and that the buyout left the ESOP with all of the debt but no decision-making power. A Labor Department investigation later exonerated Parsons executives.

Parsons had just finished work on a power plant in Kuwait when Iraq invaded in 1990. Several employees were detained by the Iraqis but were released shortly before the Persian Gulf War. Two years later the company returned to Kuwait to rebuild some of the country's demolished infrastructure.

James McNulty, who had led the company's infrastructure and technology group, replaced Leonard Pieroni as CEO in 1996 after Pieroni died in the Bosnia plane crash that also claimed the life of US Secretary of Commerce Ronald Brown.

In 1999 Parsons was chosen to manage construction of a $5 billion refinery in Bahrain, a $1.4 billion gas plant in Saudi Arabia, and a $1 billion polyethylene project in Abu Dhabi.

Parsons partnered with TRW in 2000 to create TRW Parsons Management & Operations to bid

on the DOE's Yucca Mountain site in Nevada, a potential repository for the US's high-level radioactive waste and spent nuclear fuel. It also was awarded a three-year contract to help rebuild the war-torn Serbian province of Kosovo and the next year was awarded a similar contract for Bosnia-Herzegovina.

In 2001 the company won a US Federal Aviation Agency contract to upgrade air traffic control towers and other equipment and systems. Parsons also strengthened its 80-year-old bridge division by acquiring bridge engineering firm Finley McNary.

The next year Parsons won a contract from Dallas Area Rapid Transit (DART) to provide systems engineering and construction management services for the second phase of the buildout for the light-rail system, the largest expansion of its kind in North America. In 2003 it also won a contract for final design and construction management of the first light-rail system in Charlotte, North Carolina. In 2004 the Parsons' joint venture with Kellogg Brown & Root won a controversial defense contract for oil field and refinery engineering, construction, and maintenance in Iraq.

Parsons' Infrastructure & Technology Group subsidiary sold its Cultural Resources group to Versar, Inc. in 2005.

EXECUTIVES

Chairman and CEO: James F. (Jim) McNulty
President and COO: John A. (Jack) Scott
EVP and CFO: Curtis A. Bower
SVP and General Counsel: Gary L. Stone
VP Human Resources: David R. Goodrich
VP Safety: Andrew D. Peters
SVP Government Relations: James E. Thrash
VP Corporate Relations: Erin M. Kuhlman
President, Parsons Advanced Technologies: Clifford C. Eby
President, Parson Commercial Technology: Charles L. (Chuck) Harrington
President, Parsons Infrastructure & Technology Group: Thomas L. (Tom) Roell
President, Parsons Transportation: James R. (Jim) Shappell
President, Parsons Water and Infrastructure Inc. (PWI): David L. Backus
SVP and Manager, International Division, Infrastructure and Technology Group: Earnest O. Robbins II
VP and Director of Project Development, Rail & Transit Systems Division: Sallye Perrin
Principal Transportation Planner, Rail & Transit Systems: Peter Smoluchowski

LOCATIONS

HQ: Parsons Corporation
100 W. Walnut St., Pasadena, CA 91124
Phone: 626-440-2000   **Fax:** 626-440-2630
Web: www.parsons.com

Parsons Corporation operates in 46 states in the US and in 37 countries abroad.

PRODUCTS/OPERATIONS

Selected Markets and Services

Parsons Commercial Technology Group
Cable and component assembly
Equipment testing and system commissioning
Network planning and installation
Physical plants
Procurement, planning, and logistics
Project management
Remediation
Wireless and wireline network management systems

Parsons Infrastructure and Technology Group
Commercial and institutional facilities
Entertainment
Infrastructure
Mobile source air quality
Water resources
Parsons Transportation Group
Aviation
Bridges
Highways
Railroads
Systems engineering
Tunneling
Urban transport
Parsons Water and Infrastructure
Emergency response support
Master planning
Pump station design
Storm water management
Utility tunneling
Water/wastewater transmission

COMPETITORS

ABB	Jacobs Engineering
AECOM	Lend Lease
BE&K	Louis Berger
Bechtel	M. A. Mortenson
Black & Veatch	Michael Baker
Bouygues	Peter Kiewit Sons'
Day & Zimmermann	Stone & Webster
Fluor	TIC Holdings
Foster Wheeler	Turner Corporation
Gilbane	Tutor-Saliba
Granite Construction	URS
Halliburton	Vecellio & Grogan
Hyundai Engineering	Washington Group
and Construction	

HISTORICAL FINANCIALS

Company Type: Private

Income Statement

FYE: December 31

	REVENUE ($ mil.)	NET INCOME ($ mil.)	NET PROFIT MARGIN	EMPLOYEES
12/03	1,651	—	—	9,000
12/02	1,534	—	—	9,800
12/01	1,500	—	—	9,500
12/00	2,400	—	—	13,500
12/99	1,800	—	—	11,000
12/98	1,600	—	—	11,000
12/97	1,263	—	—	10,400
12/96	1,600	—	—	10,000
12/95	1,467	—	—	10,600
12/94	1,597	—	—	9,500
Annual Growth	0.4%	—	—	(0.6%)

Revenue History

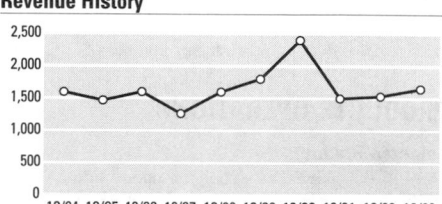

Passave

Passave develops semiconductors for broadband fiber access networks. The company designs system-on-a-chip devices for networking equipment that will bring "fiber to the home," providing broadband access to residences for voice, video, and high-speed Internet services. This market is often called the "first mile" in broadband fiber access, since it represents the initial step in building fiber-optic networks across the US and in other developed countries. All of Passave's customers are in Asia, with nearly all of them in Japan. UTStarcom accounts for about 70% of sales, while Mitsubishi Electric accounts for 14% and Sumitomo Electric Industries is good for 10%.

Passave's OEM customers are supplying Ethernet passive optical networking equipment to two main service providers in Japan, Nippon Telegraph and Telephone (NTT) and SOFTBANK Broadband.

The company is a fabless semiconductor supplier, meaning its chips are manufactured on a contract basis by other firms, known as silicon foundries. Passave's principal foundry contractors are Samsung Electronics, Semiconductor Manufacturing International Corp. (SMIC), and United Microelectronics Corp. (UMC).

Passave is an Israeli-American company, with most of its R&D conducted in Israel. The company established a Japanese subsidiary in 2004.

Entities affiliated with Walden Israel Ventures, Eurofund 2000 (Non-Israeli) entities, and BRM Capital Management each own nearly 19% of Passave. North Star Advisors/RSIS Business Trust holds about 12% of the company. Blue Orange Ventures and Pshoo each have an equity stake of around 8%. Intel owns about 7%.

EXECUTIVES

Chairman: Menashe Ezra, age 53
CEO and Director: Victor Vaisleib, age 39, $183,000 pay
President and Director: Ariel Maislos, age 32, $237,643 pay
COO: Ofer Bar-Or, age 39
CFO and Secretary: Yaron Garmazi, age 40
CTO: Onn Haran, age 34, $130,000 pay
VP, Business Development: Nadav Ben-Efraim

LOCATIONS

HQ: Passave, Inc.
2900 Lakeside Dr., Ste. 229, Santa Clara, CA 95054
Phone: 408-235-8790 **Fax:** 408-235-8791
Web: www.passave.com

Passave has offices in Israel, Japan, and the US.

PRODUCTS/OPERATIONS

Selected Products
PAS5001 (Gigabit Ethernet chip for optical line terminals or central office optical network units)
PAS6201 (Gigabit Ethernet passive optical network unit chip)

COMPETITORS

Agere Systems	Fujitsu Microelectronics
Applied Micro Circuits	Infineon Technologies
Broadcom	Mitsubishi Electric
Centillium	Sumitomo Electric
Communications	Teknovus
Conexant Systems	Texas Instruments
Freescale Semiconductor	

HISTORICAL FINANCIALS

Company Type: Private

Income Statement				FYE: December 31
	REVENUE ($ mil.)	NET INCOME ($ mil.)	NET PROFIT MARGIN	EMPLOYEES
12/04	21	8	38.4%	101
12/03	1	(2)	—	23
12/02	0	(2)	—	—
Annual Growth	927.1%	—	—	339.1%

2004 Year-End Financials
Debt ratio: 0.0%
Return on equity: 108.7%
Cash ($ mil.): 10
Current ratio: 4.68
Long-term debt ($ mil.): 0

Net Income History

Patriot Homes

Patriot Homes has remained loyal to the manufactured housing industry for more than 30 years. Founded in 1972 by owner and CEO Samuel Weidner Sr., the company builds single-, double-, and multiple-section manufactured homes. The company sells its modular homes through a network of about 600 national dealers, including about 100 that are exclusive to Patriot Homes or are company-owned retail sales centers. The enterprise also has a division to supply steel chassis. Patriot Homes operates 10 manufacturing facilities. It offers financing through Patriot Acceptance Corp. and insurance through Patriot Asset Protection.

EXECUTIVES

CEO: Samuel V. (Sam) Weidner Sr.
President: Dave Troyer
EVP, General Counsel, and Assistant Secretary: Steve Like
VP Administration and Marketing: Jacqueline (Jackie) Park
VP Finance, Treasurer, and Assistant Secretary: Tom Young
Secretary: Susan Richmond
President, Development: Samuel V. (Sam) Weidner Jr.
Assistant Secretary: Stacy Weidner

LOCATIONS

HQ: Patriot Homes, Inc.
307 South Main St., Ste. 200, Elkhart, IN 46516
Phone: 574-524-8600 **Fax:** 574-524-8638
Web: www.patriothomes.com

COMPETITORS

American Homestar	Fairmont Homes
Cavalier Homes	Fleetwood Enterprises
Champion Enterprises	Horton Industries
Clayton Homes	Palm Harbor
Dynamic Homes	Skyline

HISTORICAL FINANCIALS

Company Type: Private

Income Statement				FYE: September 30
	ESTIMATED REVENUE ($ mil.)	NET INCOME ($ mil.)	NET PROFIT MARGIN	EMPLOYEES
9/04	200	—	—	800
9/03	200	—	—	1,200
Annual Growth	0.0%	—	—	(33.3%)

Revenue History

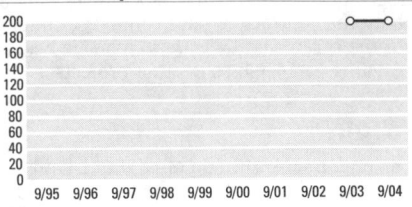

Paul, Hastings

Got a discrimination problem? Paul, Hastings, Janofsky & Walker may suit your needs. The law firm has built a solid reputation in employment law. Paul Grossman, a partner specializing in employment law, co-authored *Employment Discrimination Law* (the official treatise of the American Bar Association). Clients such as UPS and Hughes Aircraft have turned to Paul, Hastings for their expertise in the field. Real estate also is an area of strength for the firm. Other practice areas include business law, litigation, and tax. Founded in 1951, Paul, Hastings has nine offices in the US and eight in Europe and Asia.

EXECUTIVES

Chairman: Seth Zachary
Managing Partner: Greg M. Nitzkowski
CFO: Timothy (Tim) Wright
CIO: Stova Wong
Partner, Corporate: Tara Giunta, age 45
Chairman, San Diego office; Chairman, National Securities Litigation Practice Group: William Sullivan
Vice-Chairman, San Diego: Chris McGrath
Human Resources Officer: Jeanne Gervin

LOCATIONS

HQ: Paul, Hastings, Janofsky & Walker LLP
515 S. Flower St., 25th Fl., Los Angeles, CA 90071
Phone: 213-683-6000 **Fax:** 213-627-0705
Web: www.paulhastings.com

Paul, Hastings, Janofsky & Walker has offices in Atlanta; Costa Mesa, Los Angeles, Palo Alto, San Diego, and San Francisco, California; Stamford, Connecticut; New York City; and Washington, DC. It also has offices in Beijing, Brussels, Hong Kong, London, Milan, Paris, Shanghai, and Tokyo.

PRODUCTS/OPERATIONS

Selected Practice Areas
Business law
Employment law
Litigation
Real Estate
Tax

COMPETITORS

Gibson, Dunn & Crutcher	Perkins Coie
Latham & Watkins	Pillsbury Winthrop
Littler Mendelson	Shaw Pittman
Morrison & Foerster	Seyfarth Shaw
O'Melveny & Myers	Wilson Sonsini
Orrick	

HISTORICAL FINANCIALS

Company Type: Partnership

Income Statement

FYE: January 31

	REVENUE ($ mil.)	NET INCOME ($ mil.)	NET PROFIT MARGIN	EMPLOYEES
1/04	537	—	—	—
1/03	488	—	—	—
1/02	456	—	—	—
1/01	389	—	—	—
1/00	286	—	—	1,500
1/99	267	—	—	1,500
1/98	219	—	—	1,260
1/97	179	—	—	1,055
1/96	164	—	—	1,100
1/95	157	—	—	1,100
Annual Growth	14.7%	—	—	6.4%

Revenue History

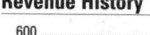
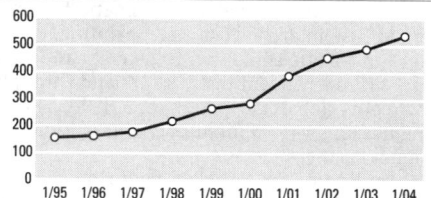

The PBSJ Corporation

The PBSJ Corporation provides planning, architectural, engineering, and construction management services through two main subsidiaries. It holds one of the largest US design firms, Post, Buckley, Schuh & Jernigan (PBS&J), which provides engineering, architectural, and planning services. The other unit, PBS&J Construction Services, provides construction management. The group targets the transportation and environmental markets, and nearly 80% of its sales are derived from public-sector projects. PBS&J is ranked among the top five pure design firms, the top 10 transportation designers, and the top 25 design firms worldwide. PBSJ is organized into four units: transportation, construction, civil, and environmental.

EXECUTIVES

Chairman and CEO: John B. Zumwalt III, age 53
EVP and Secretary; SEVP and COO, PBS&J:
  Robert J. Paulsen, age 52, $444,500 pay
CIO: Martin H. (Marty) Brown
EVP and CFO: W. Scott DeLoach
Corporate Controller: Kathryn J. Wilson
Corporate Internal Auditor: Melissa L. Eubanks
SVP; EVP, PBS&J: John S. Shearer, age 53,
  $366,250 pay

EVP and Director, Central Region:
  James W. (Jim) Bishop
EVP and National Service Director for Transportation:
  Max D. Crumit
SVP; EVP, PBS&J: Todd J. Kenner, age 43, $387,500 pay
Manager, Corporate Communications: Kathe R. Jackson
Auditors: Deloitte & Touche LLP

LOCATIONS

HQ: The PBSJ Corporation
  2001 NW 107th Ave., Miami, FL 33172
Phone: 305-592-7275   **Fax:** 305-599-3809
Web: www.pbsj.com

The PBSJ Corporation operates from 60 offices across the US.

PRODUCTS/OPERATIONS

2004 Sales

	% of total
Transportation	40
Environmental	25
Civil engineering	18
Construction management	17
Total	**100**

Selected Subsidiaries

HOH Associates, Inc.
PBS&J Construction Services, Inc.
Post, Buckley International, Inc.
Post, Buckley, Schuh & Jernigan, Inc.
Post Buckley de Mexico, S.A. de C.V.
Seminole Development Corporation

COMPETITORS

AECOM
Black & Veatch
Brown and Caldwell
CDM
CH2M HILL
HDR
HNTB
Jacobs Engineering
Louis Berger
MWH Global
Parsons
Parsons Brinckerhoff
STV
URS

HISTORICAL FINANCIALS

Company Type: Private

Income Statement

FYE: September 30

	REVENUE ($ mil.)	NET INCOME ($ mil.)	NET PROFIT MARGIN	EMPLOYEES
9/04	355	18	5.2%	3,800
9/03	307	17	5.6%	3,200
9/02	266	13	5.0%	2,800
Annual Growth	15.4%	16.9%	—	16.5%

2004 Year-End Financials

Debt ratio: 9.0%   Current ratio: 1.66
Return on equity: 23.4%   Long-term debt ($ mil.): 8
Cash ($ mil.): 3

Net Income History

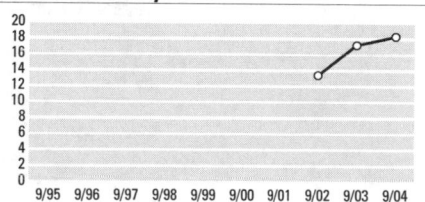

Pella

Window and door maker Pella got out of a jamb by offering its products through retailers. Originally Pella focused on upscale homeowners, builders, and designers, marketing its products through a network of distribution centers and high-end Pella Window & Door Stores retail outlets. The company now allows do-it-yourselfers to buy its ProLine windows and doors through building supply stores. Pella's products include sliding French and contemporary doors and awning, clad casement, and bay windows. The company holds more than 100 product and design patents. Pella was founded in 1925 as Rolscreen Company (after its first product, a roll-up window screen). The descendants of founder Pete Kuyper own the company.

Pella's plan for growth includes expanding its storm door, entry systems, and window product offerings. The company unveiled its Impervia window and door product line, manufactured from its exclusive Duracast five-layer fiberglass composite material, at the International Builders' Show in January 2003. The material is stated to be nine times stronger than vinyl and twice as strong as aluminum in tensile strength tests. The product line includes single-hung, sliding, and fixed window units.

Innovations in 2004 included its Architect Series double-hung wood windows, which meld traditional, old-world appearance with thermal efficiencies and modern performance features. For its fifth year in a row, Pella was distinguished in 2004 by *FORTUNE* magazine as one of the "100 Best Companies to Work For."

The next year Pella introduced its Designer Series windows and patio doors with changeable snap-in between-the-glass window fashions (light-filtering or room-darkening blinds, cellular shades, and unfinished wood grilles).

Pella provides environmental information about its products and services and is a member of the U.S. Green Building Council (USGBC).

EXECUTIVES

President and CEO: Mel Haught
SVP, CFO, and Secretary: A. Jacqueline (Jackie) Dout, age 50
SVP Finance: Herbert Liennenbrugger
SVP Sales and Marketing: Chris Simpson
VP Human Resources: Karin Peterson
VP Manufacturing: Denny Van Zanten
Corporate Public Relations: Kathy Krafka Harkema
President and COO, Entry Systems Division:
  Rich Allen
Director, Marketing, Entry Door Systems:
  Todd Friedman
Director, Sales and Marketing, Advanced Materials Division: Duane Putz

LOCATIONS

HQ: Pella Corporation
  102 Main St., Pella, IA 50219
Phone: 641-628-1000   **Fax:** 641-628-6070
Web: www.pella.com

Pella has manufacturing plants in Carroll, Pella, Shenandoah, Sioux City, and Story City, Iowa, and in Gettysburg, Pennsylvania.

PRODUCTS/OPERATIONS

Selected Products

Doors
  Entry door systems
  In-swing French
  Out-swing French
  Patio doors
  Sliding contemporary
  Sliding French
  Storm doors
Windows
  Awning
  Bow/bay
  Casement
  Circlehead
  Clad frame
  Cornerview
  Double-hung
  Replacement
  Single-hung

Selected Brands

Pease
Pella
ThermaStar by Pella
Viking

COMPETITORS

Andersen Corporation
Atrium
Bocenor
Designer Doors
HW Plastics
International Aluminum
JELD-WEN
Marshfield DoorSystems
Nortek
Pacesetter
Sierra Pacific Industries
Simonton Windows
Thermal Industries
Therma-Tru
ThermoView Industries
Tomkins

HISTORICAL FINANCIALS

Company Type: Private

Income Statement

FYE: November 30

	ESTIMATED REVENUE ($ mil.)	NET INCOME ($ mil.)	NET PROFIT MARGIN	EMPLOYEES
11/03	1,100	—	—	7,400
11/02	900	—	—	6,945
11/01	900	—	—	6,800
11/00	910	—	—	6,300
11/99	900	—	—	6,755
11/98	600	—	—	6,000
11/97	600	—	—	4,500
11/96	475	—	—	3,500
11/95	450	—	—	3,500
11/94	425	—	—	3,126
Annual Growth	**11.1%**	**—**	**—**	**10.0%**

Revenue History

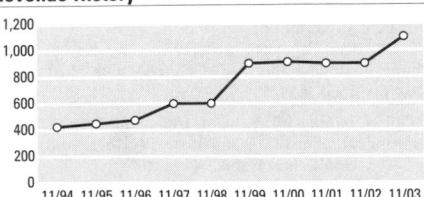

11/94	11/95	11/96	11/97	11/98	11/99	11/00	11/01	11/02	11/03	

Penhall International

Business can be both a grind and a groove for Penhall International, a leading provider of grinding services in the US, as well as highway and airport runway grooving. The company focuses on operated equipment rentals, supplying the skilled operators to go with the equipment if necessary. It also performs specialty contracting services such as asphalt cutting, concrete breaking, and demolition work. The group operates through nearly 40 locations in 17 states. Its rental fleet has some 700 units of equipment, including backhoes, excavators, compressors, saws, and drills..

Penhall International was founded in 1957 by Leroy Penhall. The company became a pioneer in the concrete and asphalt cutting industry. Environmental and oilfield services company Newpark Resources made an unsuccessful bid to acquire the company in 1995.

EXECUTIVES

Chairman, President, and CEO: John T. Sawyer, age 60, $283,103 pay
VP Finance and CFO: Jeffrey E. Platt, age 53, $223,789 pay
VP and Regional Manager, Southern California: C. George Bush, age 49, $196,760 pay
VP and Regional Manager, Southwest: Bruce F. Varney, age 52, $206,810 pay
VP and Regional Manager, Highway Services Division: Gary L. Aamold, age 54, $199,500 pay
Auditors: KPMG LLP

LOCATIONS

HQ: Penhall International Corp.
  1801 Penhall Way, Anaheim, CA 92803
Phone: 714-772-6450   **Fax:** 714-778-8437
Web: www.penhall.com

COMPETITORS

GE Equipment Services
H&E Equipment
Michigan Tractor
NationsRent Companies
Neff
NES Rentals
RSC Equipment Rental

HISTORICAL FINANCIALS

Company Type: Private

Income Statement

FYE: June 30

	REVENUE ($ mil.)	NET INCOME ($ mil.)	NET PROFIT MARGIN	EMPLOYEES
6/04	157	(6)	—	1,200
6/03	160	(6)	—	—
6/02	161	(2)	—	—
Annual Growth	**(1.3%)**	**—**	**—**	**—**

2004 Year-End Financials

Debt ratio: —
Return on equity: —
Cash ($ mil.): 1

Current ratio: 1.85
Long-term debt ($ mil.): 107

Net Income History

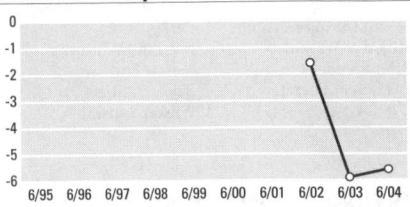

6/95	6/96	6/97	6/98	6/99	6/00	6/01	6/02	6/03	6/04

Penn Engineering

Penn Engineering's fasteners help sheet metal fabricators get a grip. The company's largest division, PEM Fastening, makes PEM-brand self-clinching, broaching, and insert fasteners for the computer, telecommunications, and electronics industries. It also sells installation equipment for its fasteners. Through its Pittman division, Penn Engineering produces magnetic DC motors for use in archival storage, printing, copying, and robotic equipment. The company sells through independent distributors and through its Arconix global distribution unit. In 2005 Penn Engineering was acquired by a unit of Tinicum Capital Partners.

Penn Engineering & Manufacturing adopted its identifying brand — PennEngineering — in 2000, in part to build worldwide recognition of its product lines under a unifying moniker.

The company actively seeks opportunities for growth through acquisitions of new technologies, product lines, smaller privately owned companies, and joint ventures the world over. In 2003 it acquired Maelux SA and its M.A.E. S.p.A operating company (stepper, brush, and brushless DC motors, Italy) for about $9.7 million.

EXECUTIVES

Chairman and CEO: Kenneth A. Swanstrom, age 65, $528,120 pay
President, COO, and Director: Martin Bidart, age 68, $568,560 pay
SVP Finance, CFO, Secretary, and Director: Mark W. Simon, age 66, $384,834 pay
President, PEM Fastening Systems: Francis P. Wilson, age 65, $335,291 pay
President, Arconix Group: Alan Kay, age 57, $214,580 pay
Corporate Controller and Assistant Secretary: William E. Sarnese, age 51
Treasurer and Assistant Secretary: Ronald J. Bean
Treasurer and Assistant Secretary: Richard F. Davies, age 55
Auditors: Ernst & Young LLP

LOCATIONS

HQ: Penn Engineering & Manufacturing Corp.
  5190 Old Easton Rd., Danboro, PA 18916
Phone: 215-766-8853   **Fax:** 215-766-7366
Web: www.penn-eng.com

Penn Engineering & Manufacturing has operations in China, Ireland, Italy, Mexico, Singapore, the UK, and the US (in California, North Carolina, Ohio, and Pennsylvania).

2004 Sales

	$ mil.	% of total
US	159.7	66
Europe		
UK	44.5	19
Italy	10.5	4
Ireland	2.2	1
Asia		
Singapore	19.3	8
China	4.7	2
Total	**240.9**	**100**

PRODUCTS/OPERATIONS

2004 Sales

	$ mil.	% of total
Fasteners	127.9	53
Distribution	62.4	26
Motors	50.6	21
Total	**240.9**	**100**

Selected Business Units

Arconix Group (distributes fastening and related products and offers logistical and inventory management services)

Atlas Engineering (manufactures metal tubular rivets)

PEM Fastening Systems (manufactures PEM-brand self-clinching and broaching fasteners, SI inserts for plastics, and STICKSCREW small screw insertion systems)

PennEngineering Motion Technologies (Europe) Srl (manufactures electronically-controlled, precision electric motors)

Pittman Motors (designs and produces brush-commutated and brushless DC servomotors and gearmotors)

COMPETITORS

Anixter Pentacon
Chicago Rivet
Fairchild
Fastenal
Federal Screw Works
Illinois Tool Works
Kinetek
MacLean-Fogg
MNP
Nidec
Park-Ohio Holdings
Textron
TriMas Corporation

HISTORICAL FINANCIALS

Company Type: Private

Income Statement

FYE: December 31

	REVENUE ($ mil.)	NET INCOME ($ mil.)	NET PROFIT MARGIN	EMPLOYEES
12/04	241	19	7.7%	1,361
12/03	191	5	2.6%	1,267
12/02	151	4	2.7%	1,166
12/01	188	9	4.9%	1,344
12/00	265	28	10.4%	1,657
12/99	198	17	8.6%	1,489
12/98	180	17	9.2%	1,423
12/97	168	15	8.6%	1,368
12/96	160	14	8.7%	1,330
12/95	141	14	9.8%	1,211
Annual Growth	**6.1%**	**3.3%**	**—**	**1.3%**

2004 Year-End Financials

Debt ratio: 1.3%
Return on equity: 9.1%
Cash ($ mil.): 33
Current ratio: 5.60
Long-term debt ($ mil.): 3

Net Income History

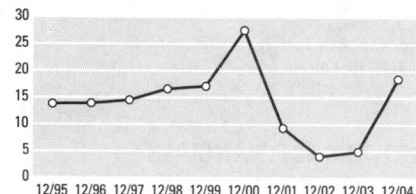

12/95 12/96 12/97 12/98 12/99 12/00 12/01 12/02 12/03 12/04

Penn Mutual Life Insurance

Founded in 1847, Penn Mutual Life Insurance offers life insurance, annuities, and investment products. The company's major subsidiaries include Penn Insurance and Annuity and brokerages Janney Montgomery Scott and Hornor, Townsend & Kent. Penn Mutual sells its products primarily to high-net-worth individuals, professionals, and business owners. Products include term, whole life, universal life, variable universal life, and disability income insurance policies, as well as a full range of deferred and immediate annuity products. The company also provides trust services and asset management to individuals and institutions.

EXECUTIVES

Chairman and CEO: Robert E. Chappell Jr., age 65
President and COO: Daniel J. Toran
EVP and CFO: Peter J. Vogt
EVP and Chief Human Resources Officer: Michael A. Biondolillo
EVP and Chief Investment Officer; Chairman, President, and CEO, Independence Capital Management: Peter M. Sherman
EVP and Chief Marketing Officer; President and CEO, Hornor, Townsend & Kent: Larry L. Mast
SVP Career Agency System: Ralph L. Crews
SVP Information, Management, and Technology: Terry Ramey
SVP Independence Financial Network: Steven O. Miller
SVP Market Conduct and General Auditor: Nina M. Mulrooney
VP Corporate Communications: Patricia Beauchamp

LOCATIONS

HQ: The Penn Mutual Life Insurance Company
600 Dresher Rd., Horsham, PA 19044
Phone: 215-956-8000   **Fax:** 215-956-8347
Web: www.pennmutual.com

Penn Mutual Life Insurance operates throughout the US.

PRODUCTS/OPERATIONS

2004 Assets

	$ mil.	% of total
Investments		
Debt securities	5,222.6	37
Equity securities	28.3	—
Real estate	16.0	—
Other	1,214.2	9
Other	4,653.3	32
Separate account assets	3,116.6	22
Total	**14,251.0**	**100**

2004 Sales

	$ mil.	% of total
Investment income	427.4	36
Premium & other product revenue	339.8	28
Other revenue	438.3	36
Total	**1,205.5**	**100**

Selected Subsidiaries and Affiliates

Hornor, Townsend & Kent, Inc. (NASD broker/dealer)
Independence Capital Management, Inc. (asset management)
Janney Montgomery Scott LLC (stock brokerage)
The Penn Insurance and Annuity Company (life insurance)
The Pennsylvania Trust Company (investment advisory & trust services)

COMPETITORS

Aetna
American National Insurance
AmerUs
AXA Financial
CIGNA
Erie Family Life Insurance
Fidelity & Guaranty Life
The Hartford
Jefferson-Pilot
John Hancock Financial Services
MassMutual
MetLife
Midland National Life
Minnesota Mutual
Nationwide Financial
Nationwide Financial Network
New York Life
Pacific Mutual
Primerica
Protective Life
Prudential
Security Benefit Group
Sentry Insurance
Union Central

HISTORICAL FINANCIALS

Company Type: Mutual company

Income Statement

FYE: December 31

	ASSETS ($ mil.)	NET INCOME ($ mil.)	INCOME AS % OF ASSETS	EMPLOYEES
12/04	14,251	137	1.0%	550
12/03	13,065	108	0.8%	1,100
12/02	11,335	73	0.6%	1,100
12/01	10,833	97	0.9%	1,100
12/00	10,708	139	1.3%	950
12/99	10,583	80	0.8%	850
12/98	10,086	58	0.6%	850
12/97	9,367	73	0.8%	848
12/96	8,757	49	0.6%	800
Annual Growth	**6.3%**	**13.8%**	**—**	**(4.6%)**

2004 Year-End Financials

Equity as % of assets: 12.4%
Return on assets: 1.0%
Return on equity: 8.0%
Long-term debt ($ mil.): 5,593
Sales ($ mil.): 1,206

Net Income History

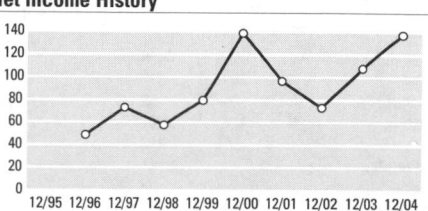

12/95 12/96 12/97 12/98 12/99 12/00 12/01 12/02 12/03 12/04

Pennsylvania Lottery

Even if they don't become millionaires, senior citizens in Pennsylvania can still benefit from the state lottery. Established in 1971, Pennsylvania Lottery proceeds are dedicated to programs geared toward seniors (property-tax relief, rent rebates, reduced-cost transportation, co-pay prescriptions). Proceeds also fund more than 50 Area Agencies on Aging across Pennsylvania. State law mandates that at least 40% of lottery proceeds must be awarded in prizes, and at least 30% must be used for benefit programs. Games range from the traditional Powerball to daily-wagering game Big 4. IGT Online Entertainment Systems operates the lottery's computer systems.

EXECUTIVES

Executive Director: Ed Mahlman
Executive Director, Administration and Finance: Tom Shaub
Executive Director, Marketing: Ed Trees
Director, Field Operations: Bob Siodlowski
Director, Product Delivery: Bill Powell
Director, Public Relations: Cris Stambaugh
Director, Research and Development: Drew Svitko
Director, Security: Jim Morgan
Manager, Instant Product: Kara Sparks
Division Chief, Computer Services: Byron Olenski
Press Secretary, Pennsylvania Lottery and Pennsylvania Department of Revenue: Steve Kniley

LOCATIONS

HQ: The Pennsylvania Lottery
    2850 Turnpike Industrial Dr., Middletown, PA 17057
Phone: 717-986-4699   **Fax:** 717-986-4767
Web: www.palottery.com

The Pennsylvania Lottery has offices throughout Pennsylvania in Clearfield, Erie, Harrisburg, Lehigh, Middletown, Philadelphia, Pittsburgh, and Wilkes-Barre.

PRODUCTS/OPERATIONS

Selected Games

Instant Games (scratch-off tickets)
    Doughman Dollars
    Lifetime Riches
    Lucky Day
    Money Farm
    Santa's List
    Sleigh Ride Riches
    Triple 777

Numbers Games
    Big 4 (daily)
    Cash 5 (daily)
    Daily Number (daily)
    Match 6
    Powerball
    Powerplay

2005 Game Sales

	$ mil.	% of total
Instant	1,302	49
Daily number	425	16
Big 4	272	10
Powerball	253	10
Cash Five	201	8
Match 6	113	4
Powerplay	41	2
Lucky lotto	28	1
Lucky instant	10	—
Total	**2,645**	**100**

COMPETITORS

Connecticut Lottery
Maryland State Lottery
Multi-State Lottery
New Jersey Lottery
New York State Lottery
Ohio Lottery
Virginia Lottery

HISTORICAL FINANCIALS

Company Type: Government-owned

Income Statement

FYE: June 30

	REVENUE ($ mil.)	NET INCOME ($ mil.)	NET PROFIT MARGIN	EMPLOYEES
6/05	2,645	—	—	—
6/04	2,352	—	—	—
6/03	2,143	—	—	—
6/02	1,947	—	—	—
6/01	1,803	—	—	—
6/00	1,707	—	—	—
6/99	1,669	—	—	169
6/98	1,682	—	—	152
6/97	1,719	—	—	178
6/96	1,674	—	—	181
Annual Growth	**5.2%**	**—**	**—**	**(2.3%)**

Revenue History

Penske

Penske, headed by race-car legend Roger Penske, seems to be on the right track as a diversified transportation firm. Penske is a partner with GE Equipment Management in Penske Truck Leasing, a commercial truck rental operation with about about 200,000 vehicles at about 1,000 locations. Penske owns more than 40% of publicly traded United Auto Group (UAG), which runs more than 250 franchised dealerships in some 20 states, Brazil, Puerto Rico, and the UK. Through Penske Automotive the company operates five car dealerships in California. Truck-Lite makes safety lights for boats, buses, cars, commercial trucks, construction equipment, and recreational vehicles. Roger Penske is the majority owner of the company.

Penske just can't seem to resist that new car smell. The company has sold its racetrack interests and upped its stake in the struggling UAG. Roger Penske personally visited most of UAG's dealerships to help return the chain to profitability. He now heads UAG. However, Penske plans to take joint control with DaimlerChrysler of a Detroit Diesel unit in Italy, VM Motori. Penske souped-up its Penske Truck Leasing unit with the purchase of Rollins Truck Leasing, which was the US's third-largest truck rental and leasing player.

Penske is also a lead investment partner in Transportation Resource Partners, which is part of a group that is acquiring Autocam.

HISTORY

As a teen Roger Penske earned money by repairing and reselling cars. At 21 he entered his first auto race; he was running second when his car overheated. His winning ways, however, were soon apparent, and in 1961 *Sports Illustrated* named him race car driver of the year.

Nonetheless, in 1965 Penske went looking for a day job. With a $150,000 loan from his father, he bought a Chevrolet dealership in Philadelphia and retired from racing to avoid loading his balance sheet with steep life-insurance premiums for the CEO. Penske teamed with driver Mark Donohue in 1966 to form the Penske Racing Team. Donohue died in a crash in 1975, but team Penske continued.

In 1969 Penske started a regional truck-leasing business, incorporated under the name Penske. The company established auto dealerships in Pennsylvania and Ohio in the early 1970s. In 1975 the company bought the Michigan International Speedway. Penske and fellow racing team owner Pat Patrick started the race-sponsoring organization Championship Auto Racing Teams (CART) in 1978.

In 1982 Penske's truck-leasing business formed a joint venture with rental company Hertz to form Hertz Penske Truck Leasing. Penske expanded its auto dealerships in the 1980s by acquiring dealerships in California, including Longo Toyota in 1985.

Racing legend Al Unser Sr. surprised Indy 500 watchers in 1987 by driving a car borrowed from an exhibition in a hotel lobby to a first-place finish for the Penske Racing Team.

In 1988 Penske bought 80% of GM's Detroit Diesel engine-making unit, which had a market share of only 3% and had lost some $600 million over the previous five years. Penske trimmed $70 million from the unit's budget by firing 440 salaried employees, streamlining manufacturing processes, and cutting administration expenses. Detroit Diesel's market share doubled in its first two years as a Penske unit. Also in 1988 Penske purchased Hertz's stake in Hertz Penske Truck Leasing, which it later combined with the truck-rental division of appliance maker General Electric to create Penske Truck Leasing.

By 1993 Detroit Diesel's market share had grown to more than 25%. That year the engine maker went public. Penske bought 860 Kmart auto centers for $112 million in 1995. The company's racing business, Penske Motorsports, went public in 1996, but Penske retained a 55% stake in the company. Also that year Penske bought Truck-Lite, Quaker State's automotive lighting unit.

Penske Truck Leasing formed Penske Logistics Europe in 1997 to offer information systems and other integrated logistics services on that continent. The next year it formed a logistics joint venture with Brazil-based Cotia Trading to serve US-based clients in the South American market, and Penske Logistics Europe opened a pan-European transport routing center in the Netherlands.

Penske sold its Penske Motorsports operations, which included racetracks in California, Michigan, North Carolina, and Pennsylvania, to International Speedway in 1999. The same year Penske invested about $83 million for a 38% stake in car retailer United Auto Group and Roger Penske became CEO of Penske. In 2000 the company sold its 48.6% stake in Detroit Diesel to DaimlerChrysler.

The following year Penske Corp. added three additional dealerships. Later in 2001 Penske Truck Leasing acquired Rollins Truck Leasing (then the US's third-largest player behind Ryder and Penske) for $754 million.

After Kmart filed Chapter 11 early in 2002, Penske expressed a "wait and see" strategy about the fate of its Penske Auto Centers business. Later that year Penske's Truck-Lite Industries bought Federal-Mogul's lighting business for $23 million.

Early in April 2002 Penske had waited long enough, and didn't like what it saw. It closed its 560-plus Penske Auto Centers at Kmart locations nationwide.

EXECUTIVES

Chairman and CEO: Roger S. Penske, age 68
President: Robert H. Kurnick Jr., age 43
EVP and CFO: J. Patrick Conroy
EVP: Walt Czarnecki
EVP, Administration: Paul F. Walters
VP: Tim Cindric
VP, Human Resources: Randall W. Johnson
Chairman, Truck-Lite, Inc.; Managing Partner, Transportation Resource Partners: Richard J. Peters, age 57

LOCATIONS

HQ: Penske Corporation
2550 Telegraph Rd., Bloomfield Hills, MI 48302
Phone: 248-648-2000   **Fax:** 248-648-2005
Web: www.penske.com

Penske operations include Penske Automotive, with five dealerships in California; Penske Truck Leasing, with about 1,000 rental locations in the US and Canada; and United Auto Group, with more than 250 franchise dealerships in some 20 states, Brazil, Puerto Rico, and the UK.

PRODUCTS/OPERATIONS

Selected Subsidiaries and Affiliates

Davco Technologies, LLC
(fuel filters and engine accessories)
Penske Automotive Group, Inc. (retail auto sales)
Penske Truck Leasing Co. LP (joint venture with GE Equipment Management, truck rental and leasing)
Truck-Lite Co., Inc. (automotive lighting)
United Auto Group, Inc.
(more than 40%, retail auto sales)

COMPETITORS

AMERCO
Asbury Automotive
AutoNation
DaimlerChrysler
Fiat
General Motors
Group 1 Automotive
Isuzu
Mack Trucks
Navistar
PACCAR
Prospect Motors
Ryder
Sonic Automotive
Tasha Inc.
Transport International Pool
Volvo

HISTORICAL FINANCIALS
Company Type: Private

Income Statement

FYE: December 31

	REVENUE ($ mil.)	NET INCOME ($ mil.)	NET PROFIT MARGIN	EMPLOYEES
12/03	14,000	—	—	36,000
12/02	12,000	—	—	36,000
12/01	11,000	—	—	36,000
12/00	10,000	—	—	34,000
12/99	6,400	—	—	34,000
12/98	6,000	—	—	28,000
12/97	5,800	—	—	28,000
12/96	5,200	—	—	25,000
12/95	3,900	—	—	16,700
12/94	3,287	—	—	16,000
Annual Growth	17.5%	—	—	9.4%

Revenue History

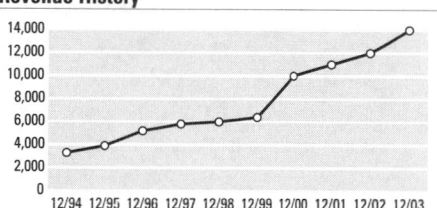

Penson Worldwide

Penson Worldwide works behind the scenes to help brokers do their jobs. The company offers a range of securities clearing services to brokers, investment advisors, and market makers, including integrated trade execution, clearing and custody services, customer account maintenance, and customized data processing. The firm's purchase of Worldwide Settlements (now Penson Financial Services, Ltd.) and ECE Electronic Clearing (renamed Penson Financial Services Canada) expanded its scope in the UK and Canada, respectively. Subsidiary Nexa Technologies (formerly Integrated Trading Solutions) offers online trading platforms for brokers and professional traders.

In early 2005 Penson acquired Tick Data, a Virginia-based firm that offers intraday securities trading data, including tick-by-tick trade and quote data on all US equities dating back to 1993. The company also is buying California-based Computer Clearing Services (CCS), a clearing firm specializing in the online trading market.

Penson was founded by EVP Phil Pendergraft as Service Asset Holdings in 1995.

EXECUTIVES

Chairman: Roger J. Engemoen Jr., age 52, $1,060,464 pay
CEO and Director; EVP, Pension Financial Services: Philip A. (Phil) Pendergraft, age 45, $1,680,000 pay
President and Director: Daniel P. (Dan) Son, age 67, $1,485,600 pay

SVP and CFO: Dave R. Henkel, age 53, $379,340 pay
SVP; COO, Penson Financial Services: Richard N. (Rich) Hart III
SVP and General Counsel: Andrew B. Koslow, age 44, $624,750 pay
Deputy Chief Executive, Penson Worldwide Settlements: Jay Proffitt
Director of Sales and Marketing, Penson Worldwide Settlements: Colin Thomas
Manager, Human Resources: Dawn Gardner
Auditors: BDO Seidman, LLP

LOCATIONS

HQ: Penson Worldwide, Inc.
1700 Pacific Ave., Ste. 1400, Dallas, TX 75201
Phone: 214-765-1100   **Fax:** 214-217-4978
Web: www.penson.com

Penson Worldwide has offices in Chicago, Dallas, London, Montreal, and Toronto.

PRODUCTS/OPERATIONS

2004 Sales

	$ mil.	% of total
Clearing	62.9	54
Interest	42.5	37
Technology	4.0	3
Other	6.7	6
Total	**116.1**	**100**

Selected Subsidiaries

Nexa Technologies, Inc.
Penson Financial Futures, Inc.
Penson Financial Services Canada, Inc.
Penson Financial Services, Inc.
Penson Financial Services, Ltd. (UK)

COMPETITORS

Banc of America Securities
Bank of New York
eSpeed
Goldman Sachs Execution & Clearing
Instinet
Knight Capital
Miller Johnson Steichen Kinnard
SWS Group

HISTORICAL FINANCIALS
Company Type: Private

Income Statement

FYE: December 31

	REVENUE ($ mil.)	NET INCOME ($ mil.)	NET PROFIT MARGIN	EMPLOYEES
12/04	116	8	6.7%	615
12/03	91	9	9.5%	—
12/02	80	(4)	—	—
Annual Growth	20.2%	—	—	—

2004 Year-End Financials

Debt ratio: 0.0%
Return on equity: 20.8%
Cash ($ mil.): —

Current ratio: —
Long-term debt ($ mil.): 0

Net Income History

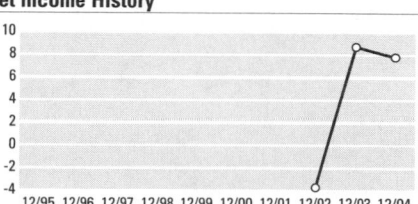

Peoples Bancorp, Inc.

Peoples Bancorp is the holding company for Peoples Bank of Kent County, a commercial bank with five branches in eastern Maryland's Kent County. The bank provides standard retail products services, including checking and savings accounts, NOW accounts, IRAs, and CDs. Commercial real estate loans make up the largest portion of the company's lending portfolio (40% of the total loan book), which also includes residential mortgages (30%), business loans, and a few construction and consumer loans. Peoples Bank of Kent County has offices in Chestertown (2), Galena, Millington, and Rock Hall, Maryland.

Company directors Elmer Horsey and Alexander Rasin own 8% and 7% of Peoples Bancorp, respectively.

The company is opening another branch location in Church Hill, Maryland, and may open another Chestertown location.

EXECUTIVES

President, CEO, and CFO, Peoples Bancorp and Peoples Bank: Thomas G. Stevenson, age 56, $129,518 pay
EVP and Loan Administrator, Peoples Bank: William G. Wheatley, age 51
EVP, Operations, Peoples Bank: H. Lawrence Lyons, age 51
EVP, Business Development, Peoples Bank: Thomas A. Tucker, age 45
Secretary: Robert A, Moore, age 70
Auditors: Rowles & Company, LLP

LOCATIONS

HQ: Peoples Bancorp, Inc.
100 Spring Ave., Chestertown, MD 21620
Phone: 410-778-3500   **Fax:** 410-778-2089
Web: www.pbkc.com

PRODUCTS/OPERATIONS

2004 Sales

	$ mil.	% of total
Interest		
Loans, including fees	9.6	83
US agency securities	0.9	8
Other	0.1	1
Noninterest		
Service charges on deposit accounts	0.7	6
Other	0.2	2
Total	**11.5**	**100**

COMPETITORS

Bank of America
BB&T
M&T Bank
Mercantile Bankshares
Shore Bancshares
SunTrust

Income Statement   FYE: December 31

	ASSETS ($ mil.)	NET INCOME ($ mil.)	INCOME AS % OF ASSETS	EMPLOYEES
12/04	203	3	1.4%	68
12/03	180	2	1.3%	63
12/02	169	2	1.4%	66
Annual Growth	9.5%	12.3%	—	1.5%

2004 Year-End Financials

Equity as % of assets: 10.5%   Long-term debt ($ mil.): —
Return on assets: 1.5%   Sales ($ mil.): 12
Return on equity: 14.1%

Net Income History

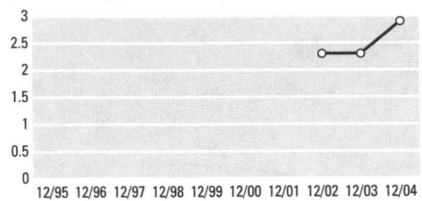

12/95 12/96 12/97 12/98 12/99 12/00 12/01 12/02 12/03 12/04

Percepta

This company helps make automakers perceptive to their customers' needs. Percepta provides outsourced customer contact services to automobile manufacturers, auto dealerships, and other companies in the automotive market. Its services include inbound and outbound call handling, customer support, telemarketing, and warranty administration. The company has seven call centers in the US, Canada, Europe, and Australia. Formed in 2000, Percepta is a joint venture between outsourcing firm TeleTech Holdings (which has a 55% stake in the company) and Ford Motor Company.

EXECUTIVES

CEO: Tom Loberto
CFO: Bruce Bell
CTO: Jeff Buckman
VP Solutions and Services: Dave Burns
VP Operations, North America: Donna Neale
General Manager, Europe and Asia: Trisha Roberts
Corporate Human Resources: Wanda Walkden

LOCATIONS

HQ: Percepta, LLC
3 Parklane Blvd., Ste. 430, Dearborn, MI 48126
Phone: 313-390-0135   **Fax:** 313-390-0168
Web: www.percepta-crm.com

Percepta has operations in Dearborn, Michigan; Melbourne, Florida; and Rockleigh, New Jersey. It also has operations in Glasgow, Scotland; Koln, Germany; Melbourne, Australia; and Toronto.

COMPETITORS

Accenture
Autobytel
Cobalt Group
Convergys
EDS
IBM Global Services
NCO Group
Reynolds and Reynolds
SITEL
SR.Teleperformance
Sykes Enterprises
West Corporation
Wipro Technologies

Income Statement   FYE: December 31

	REVENUE ($ mil.)	NET INCOME ($ mil.)	NET PROFIT MARGIN	EMPLOYEES
12/04	83	—	—	—
12/03	92	—	—	—
Annual Growth	(9.6%)	—	—	—

Revenue History

12/95 12/96 12/97 12/98 12/99 12/00 12/01 12/02 12/03 12/04

Perdue Farms

James Perdue makes Big Bird nervous. His family's company is one of the largest in the US poultry market, selling more than 48 million pounds of distinctly yellow chicken products and nearly 4 million pounds of turkey products each week. Vertically integrated, Perdue Farms sees its birds from the egg to the supermarket meat case. Perdue is expanding its value-added chicken parts and food service products and has established a plant in China through a joint venture. It also processes grain and makes vegetable oils and pet food ingredients. Founded by Arthur Perdue (James' grandfather) in 1920, the company sells its products in the East, Midwest, and South, and it exports to more than 40 countries.

While the company breeds and hatches the eggs, it ships the chicks off to supervised contract growers, who then send back fully grown birds. The company processes grain to make its own feeds and vegetable oils, and turns poultry by-products into pet food ingredients. In addition, in a joint venture with AgriRecycle, it makes fertilizer from used chicken litter.

James Perdue, who — like his famous father, Frank — had before him — appears in its advertisements. Perdue produces its own breed of chicken, the skin of which is a distinct yellow color, resulting from a diet that includes marigold petals.

HISTORY

If asked which came first, the chickens or the eggs, the Perdue family will tell you the eggs did. Arthur Perdue, a railroad express worker, bought 23 layer hens in 1920 and started supplying the New York City market with eggs from a henhouse in his family's backyard in Salisbury, Maryland. His son Frank joined the business in 1939.

The Perdues sold broiling chickens to major processors, such as Swift and Armour, in the 1940s and pioneered chicken crossbreeding to develop new breeds. The family started contracting with farmers in the Salisbury area in 1950 to grow broilers for them. Frank became president of the company in 1952. The next year it began mixing its own feed.

Frank persuaded his father to borrow money to build a soybean mill in 1961. (Arthur had not willingly gone into debt in his previous 40-plus years in the poultry industry.) The soybean mill was part of Frank's plan to vertically integrate the company — with grain storage facilities, feed milling operations, soybean processing plants, mulch plants, hatcheries, and 600 contract chicken farmers — to counter the threat of processors buying chickens directly from farmers rather than through middlemen like the Perdues. To differentiate their products, the Perdue name was applied to packages on retail meat counters in 1968.

Two years later the company began a breeding and genetic research program. During the following years Frank transformed himself from country chicken salesman to media poultry pitchman when the company decided to use him as spokesperson in its print, radio, and TV ads. Catchy slogans ("It takes a tough man to make a tender chicken") combined with Frank's whiny voice and sincere face helped sales. As Perdue Farms expanded geographically into new eastern markets such as Philadelphia, Boston, and Baltimore, it acquired the broiler facilities of other processors.

In 1983 James Perdue, Frank's only son, joined the company as a management trainee. In 1984 Perdue added processors in Virginia and Indiana and introduced turkey products. Two years later it acquired Intertrade, a feed broker, and FoodCraft, a food equipment maker. However, after enjoying a rising demand for poultry by a health-conscious society in the 1970s and early 1980s, the company found its sales leveling off in the late 1980s. When North Carolina fined Perdue for unsafe working conditions in 1989, the company increased its emphasis on safety.

James, who had become chairman of the board in 1991, replaced his folksy father in 1994 as the company's spokesman in TV ads. In the early 1990s Perdue's management determined future sales growth lay in food service and international sales; therefore, the poultry company quietly began laying the groundwork to support these new markets.

Perdue launched its Cafe Perdue entree meal kits in 1997. The following year it purchased food service poultry processor Gol-Pak and, through a joint venture, opened a poultry processing plant in Shanghai, China.

Settlements to chicken catchers and line workers in 2001 and 2002 cost the company over $12 million in back wages. Also in 2002 Perdue announced it would be shuttering a deboning plant purchased only three years earlier. During 2003 the company started work on a new research and development facility in Salisbury, Maryland. In January 2004 Perdue purchased a poultry processing facility from competitor Cagle's, Inc.

Frank Perdue died in April 2005. He was 84.

EXECUTIVES

Chairman, CEO, and CFO: James A. (Jim) Perdue
SVP, Retail, Sales, and Marketing: Steve Evans
VP, Business Development: Steven M. (Steve) Schwalb
VP, Corporate Research and Development: Dave Owens
VP, Foodservice Sales: Kerry Doughty
VP, Human Resources: Rob Heflin
VP, International Operations: Peggy Vining
VP, Supply Chain Management: Tom Kerber
President and General Manager, Grain and Oilseed Division: Dick Willey
President and General Manager, International Division: Robert (Bob) Turley
President and General Manager, Specialty Foods: Randy Day
CIO: Don Taylor
Director, Environmental Service: John Chlada
Director, Public Relations: Tita Cherrier
Manager, Western Division: Larry Nocerino
Manager, Foodservice, Eastern Division: Tom Engels

LOCATIONS

HQ: Perdue Farms Incorporated
31149 Old Ocean City Rd., Salisbury, MD 21804
Phone: 410-543-3000   **Fax:** 410-543-3292
Web: www.perdue.com

Perdue Farms has operations in Alabama, Connecticut, Delaware, Florida, Indiana, Kentucky, Maryland, New Jersey, North Carolina, Pennsylvania, South Carolina, Tennessee, Virginia, and West Virginia.

PRODUCTS/OPERATIONS

Selected Poultry Products and Brands

Fresh Poultry
  Chicken parts (Prime Parts)
  Cornish hens
  Ground chicken
  Roasters and turkeys (Oven Stuffer)
  Seasoned chicken
  Skinless, boneless poultry cuts (Fit 'N Easy)
  Turkey burgers
  Turkey sausage

Fully Cooked Poultry
  Cutlets
  Nuggets (Fun Shapes)
  Rotisserie-style chicken (TenderReady)
  Tenders

Other Products
  Pet food ingredients
  Vegetable oils

Other Brands

Chef's Choice
Cookin' Good
Gol-pak
Shenandoah
Short Cuts

COMPETITORS

AJC International
Allen Family Foods
Cagle's
Cargill
ConAgra
Cooper Farms
Gold Kist
Hormel
Keystone Foods
Murphy-Brown
Pilgrim's Pride
Sanderson Farms
Townsends
Tyson Foods

HISTORICAL FINANCIALS

Company Type: Private

Income Statement

FYE: March 31

	REVENUE ($ mil.)	NET INCOME ($ mil.)	NET PROFIT MARGIN	EMPLOYEES
3/04	2,800	—	—	18,000
3/03	2,700	—	—	20,000
3/02	2,700	—	—	20,000
3/01	2,700	—	—	19,500
3/00	2,501	—	—	19,500
3/99	2,515	—	—	20,500
3/98	2,200	—	—	18,000
3/97	2,200	—	—	18,000
3/96	2,100	—	—	19,000
3/95	1,700	—	—	18,600
Annual Growth	**5.7%**	—	—	**(0.4%)**

Revenue History

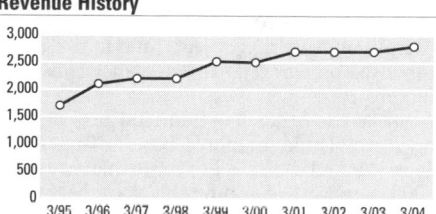

Peter Kiewit Sons'

Peter Kiewit Sons' has become a heavyweight in the heavy construction industry by building everything from tunnels to high-rises. The employee-owned general contractor was involved with projects in 28 US states and seven Canadian provinces in 2004. A transportation specialist (more than 60% of sales), typical undertakings include bridges, highways, railroads, airports, and mass transit systems. Other project areas include commercial buildings, mining infrastructure, petroleum, power, heating/cooling, and waste-disposal systems. The company, which also owns two coal mines, is owned by current and former employees and Kiewit family members.

Kiewit is a leader in the highway, bridge, water supply, and dam construction markets. Notable highway and bridge projects include the I-10 bridge repair in Florida, the Bay Bridge Skyway in Florida, the 91 Express Lanes in California, and the I-25 Southeast Corridor in Denver; water supply and dam projects include the Olivenhain and East dams in California, underground storage tanks for the Hollywood Hills Quality Improvement Project, and an intake valve at Lake Mead in Nevada. Public contracts accounted for 74% of sales in 2004.

Like most in its industry, Kiewit frequently undertakes projects through joint ventures to spread risk and share resources; about 27% of 2004's sales came through joint venture projects.

Kiewit Mining Acquisition Co., a subsidiary of the company, acquired the Buckskin mine in Wyoming from coal producer Arch Coal in 2004. The coal mine, in the Powder River Basin near Gillette, produced about 20 millions tons of coal in 2004, compared to 2 million tons at the company's Calvert mine in Texas. Kiewit also manages two other coal mines.

HISTORY

Born to Dutch immigrants, Peter Kiewit and brother Andrew founded Kiewit Brothers, a brickyard, in 1884 in Omaha, Nebraska. By 1912 two of his sons worked at the yard, which was named Peter Kiewit & Sons. When Peter Kiewit died in 1914, his son Ralph took over, and the firm took the name Peter Kiewit Sons'. Another son, Peter, joined Ralph at the helm in 1924 after dropping out of Dartmouth and later took over.

During the Depression, Kiewit managed huge federal public works projects, and in the 1940s it focused on war-related emergency construction projects.

One of the firm's most difficult projects was top-secret Thule Air Force Base in Greenland, above the Arctic Circle. For more than two years 5,000 men worked around the clock, beginning in 1951; the site was in development for 15 years. In 1952 the company won a contract to build a $1.2 billion gas diffusion plant in Portsmouth, Ohio. It also became a contractor for the US interstate highway system (begun in 1956).

Peter Kiewit died in 1979, after stipulating that the largely employee-owned company should remain under employee control and that no one employee could own more than 10%. His 40% stake, when returned to the company, transformed many employees into millionaires. Walter Scott Jr., whose father had been the first graduate engineer to work for Kiewit, took charge. Scott made his mark by parlaying money from construction into successful investments.

When the construction industry slumped, Kiewit began looking for other investment opportunities, and in 1984 it acquired packaging company Continental Can Co. (selling off noncore insurance, energy, and timber assets). Continental was saddled with a 1983 class action lawsuit alleging that it had plotted to close plants and lay off workers before they were qualified for pensions. In 1991 Kiewit agreed to pay $415 million to settle the lawsuit. In the face of a consolidating packaging industry, the company sold Continental in the early 1990s.

In 1986 Kiewit loaned money to a business group to build a fiber-optic loop in Chicago; by 1987 it had launched MFS Communications to build local fiber loops in downtown districts. In 1992 Kiewit split its business into two pieces: the construction group, which was strictly employee-owned; and a diversified group, to which it added a controlling stake in phone and cable TV company C-TEC in 1993. That year Kiewit took MFS public; by 1995 it had sold all its shares, and the next year MFS was bought by telecom giant WorldCom.

In 1996 Kiewit assisted CalEnergy (now MidAmerican Energy) in a hostile $1.3 billion takeover of the UK's Northern Electric. Kiewit got stock in CalEnergy and a 30% stake in the UK electric company, all of which it sold to CalEnergy in 1998.

That year Kiewit spun off its telecom and computer services holdings into Level 3 Communications. Scott, who had been hospitalized the year before for a blood clot in his lung, stepped down

as CEO, and Ken Stinson, CEO of Kiewit Construction Group, took over Peter Kiewit Sons'.

In 1999 Kiewit acquired a majority interest in Pacific Rock Products, a construction materials firm in Canada. Kiewit spun off its asphalt, concrete, and aggregates operations in 2000 as Kiewit Materials. Also that year the company created Kiewit Offshore Services to focus on construction for the offshore drilling industry. In 2001 the company acquired marine construction firm General Construction Company (GCC). The next year it expanded its offshore business further by buying a Canadian subsidiary from oil and gas equipment services company Friede Goldman Halter, which was trying to emerge from bankruptcy.

Kiewit made history in 2002 for the fastest completion of a project of its type when it completed the rebuilding of Webbers Falls I-40 Bridge in Oklahoma at the end of July. The bridge collapsed in May after being hit by a pair of barges, resulting in 14 fatalities. In August 2004 Kiewit greatly increased its coal sales and reserves with the acquisition of the Buckskin Mine in Wyoming from Arch Coal.

Kiewit underwent a changing of the guard at the end of 2004, when 22-year-veteran Bruce Grewcock took the reins as the company's fourth CEO since its founding. Ken Stinson stayed on as the company's chairman.

EXECUTIVES

Chairman Emeritus: Walter Scott Jr., age 73
Chairman: Kenneth E. (Ken) Stinson, age 62, $3,300,020 pay
President and CEO: Bruce E. Grewcock, age 51, $2,127,800 pay
EVP; EVP, Kiewit Corporation and Kiewit Pacific Co.: Richard W. Colf, age 61, $1,224,600 pay
EVP and Director: Douglas E. Patterson, age 54, $717,400 pay
SVP and CFO: Michael J. Piechoski, age 50
SVP, General Counsel, and Secretary: Tobin A. Schropp, age 42
SVP, Kiewit Corporation and Kiewit Construction; President, Gilbert Industrial Corp.: Scott L. Cassels, age 46
SVP, Kiewit Corporation, Kiewit Construction, and Kiewit Pacific Co.: Steven Hansen, age 59, $588,400 pay
SVP, Kiewit Corporation, Kiewit Construction, Kiewit Pacific Co., and Kiewit Western Co.; Director: R. Michael Phelps, age 52
SVP and Division Manager, Midwest Building: Bruce Tresslar
SVP, Building Division, Rocky Mountain Region: Robert J. (Bob) Mattuci
VP, Human Resources and Administration: John B. Chapman, age 59
VP and Treasurer: Ben E. Muraskin, age 41
VP; President, Kiewit Development Co.: Gerald S. (Jerry) Pfeffer, age 58
VP; SVP, Kiewit Corporation: Christopher J. Murphy, age 50
President, Kiewit Mining Group: Bruce McKay
Controller and Assistant Secretary; VP and Controller, Kiewit Corporation: Michael J. Whetstine, age 38
Auditors: KPMG LLP

LOCATIONS

HQ: Peter Kiewit Sons', Inc.
Kiewit Plaza, Omaha, NE 68131
Phone: 402-342-2052 **Fax:** 402-271-2939
Web: www.kiewit.com

Peter Kiewit Sons' has 20 principal operating offices in North America.

PRODUCTS/OPERATIONS

2004 Sales

	% of total
Transportation	61
Commercial building	10
Power, heat & cooling	8
Petroleum	7
Water supply/dams	7
Sewage & solid waste	1
Other operations	6
Total	**100**

2004 Sales

	$ mil.	% of total
Construction	3,265	97
Mining	87	3
Total	**3,352**	**100**

COMPETITORS

ABB	KBR
Balfour Beatty	Lane Construction
Construction	Parsons
Bechtel	Perini
Black & Veatch	Raytheon
Bovis Lend Lease	Skanska USA Civil
Fluor	Turner Corporation
Foster Wheeler	Tutor-Saliba
Granite Construction	Walsh Group
Halliburton	Washington Group
Hubbard Group	Whiting-Turner
ITOCHU	Williams Companies
Jacobs Engineering	

HISTORICAL FINANCIALS

Company Type: Private

Income Statement

FYE: Last Saturday in December

	REVENUE ($ mil.)	NET INCOME ($ mil.)	NET PROFIT MARGIN	EMPLOYEES
12/04	3,352	201	6.0%	14,000
12/03	3,375	157	4.7%	15,000
12/02	3,699	193	5.2%	15,000
12/01	3,871	175	4.5%	16,000
12/00	4,463	179	4.0%	11,146
12/99	4,013	165	4.1%	20,300
12/98	3,403	288	8.5%	16,200
12/97	2,764	155	5.6%	16,200
12/96	2,904	221	7.6%	14,000
12/95	2,902	244	8.4%	14,300
Annual Growth	**1.6%**	**(2.1%)**	**—**	**(0.2%)**

2004 Year-End Financials

Debt ratio: 2.7%
Return on equity: 16.5%
Cash ($ mil.): 677

Current ratio: 2.22
Long-term debt ($ mil.): 36

Net Income History

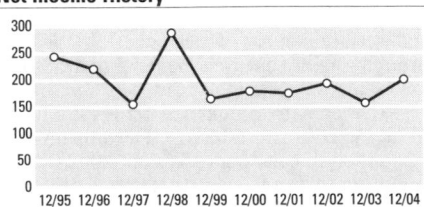

Petro Stopping Centers

Petro Stopping Centers is the center of attention for truckers who need a petro stop. The firm operates about 60 truck stops (more than a third of them franchised) in 31 states. Its truck stops sell Mobil-brand diesel fuel, gas, and travel merchandise such as food, toiletries, truck accessories, and electronics. (Fuel accounts for about 80% of sales.) The centers also provide Petro:Lube facilities (preventive maintenance services), showers, laundry services, game rooms, and Iron Skillet restaurants (home-style cooking). The company is run by chairman and CEO Jack Cardwell, who founded it in 1975, and his son, president and COO Jim Cardwell. Volvo Petro Holdings owns nearly 30% of Petro Stopping Centers.

EXECUTIVES

Chairman and CEO: James A. (Jack) Cardwell Sr., age 73, $846,154 pay
President, COO, and Director:
James A. (Jim) Cardwell Jr., age 44, $459,231 pay
CFO, Treasurer, and Secretary: Edward Escudero, age 34, $421,867 pay
VP, Petro:Lube: David (Dave) Latimer, age 46, $280,233 pay
Executive Director of Fuel/Store Operations: Keith Kirkpatrick, age 44, $290,715 pay
CIO: Richard Tisdale
Director, Engineering: Clark Rudy
Director, Franchise Business: Will Bowker
Director, Franchise Business: Michael Stuewe
Director, Human Resources: Rick Gonzalez
Director, Human Resources: Walter Kalinowski
Director, Marketing: David McClure
Auditors: KPMG LLP

LOCATIONS

HQ: Petro Stopping Centers, L.P.
6080 Surety Dr., El Paso, TX 79905
Phone: 915-779-4711   **Fax:** 915-774-7382
Web: www.petrotruckstops.com

PRODUCTS/OPERATIONS

2004 Sales

	$ mil.	% of total
Fuel	1,045.5	80
Non-fuel	261.0	20
Total	**1,306.5**	**100**

COMPETITORS

Bowlin Travel Centers
Chevron
Exxon Mobil
FFP Operating
Flying J
Love's Country Stores
Pilot
Rip Griffin Truck Service Center
TravelCenters of America
Valero Energy

Phibro Animal Health

Like many a pop star and pro wrestler (say, DJ Spooky or Andre the Giant), Phibro Animal Health has changed its name to better reflect its core business. Rather than spinning spooky discs or being large, the former Philipp Brothers Chemicals manufactures specialty chemicals for agricultural and industrial uses. Its largest segment by far, Animal Health and Nutrition, produces feed additives, including trace minerals, vitamins, and antibiotics. Its antibacterials protect against salmonellosis and fowl cholera. Phibro's Industrial Chemicals unit produces pigments, as well as minerals such as iron and manganese, which are used as colorants and in brick, masonry, and glass. Chairman Jack Bendheim owns the company.

Burdened by debt and losses, the company hired a few new executives (including CEO Gerald Carlson) in 2002, restructured some of its debt, and cut costs by closing some operations.

Phibro Animal Health sold subsidiary Agtrol (fungicides and plant growth regulators) following its acquisition of an animal feed additives business from Pfizer. In August 2003 Phibro sold its Mineral Resource Technologies subsidiary, which recycles coal combustion residue. Its Odda subsidiary in Norway also was discontinued, and Phibro sold Prince Manufacturing in December 2003.

HISTORICAL FINANCIALS

Income Statement

FYE: December 31

	REVENUE ($ mil.)	NET INCOME ($ mil.)	NET PROFIT MARGIN	EMPLOYEES
12/04	1,307	5	0.4%	4,226
12/03	1,063	9	0.8%	4,309
12/02	923	7	0.8%	4,202
12/01	914	(14)	—	4,108
12/00	981	(5)	—	4,186
12/99	720	2	0.3%	4,208
12/98	637	(9)	—	3,902
12/97	686	(13)	—	3,691
12/96	637	(9)	—	3,529
12/95	533	4	0.7%	—
Annual Growth	**10.5%**	**2.9%**	**—**	**2.3%**

2004 Year-End Financials

Debt ratio: —
Return on equity: 53.3%
Cash ($ mil.): 34
Current ratio: 1.18
Long-term debt ($ mil.): 246

Net Income History

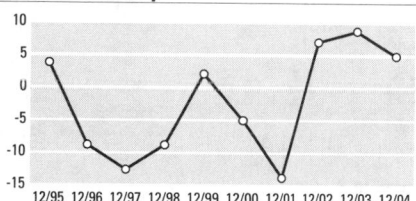

EXECUTIVES

Chairman and President: Jack C. Bendheim, age 58, $1,950,000 pay
Vice Chairman and President, Prince Agri: Marvin S. Sussman, age 58, $1,152,000 pay
CEO: Gerald K. Carlson, age 62, $1,044,000 pay
CFO: Richard G. Johnson, age 56, $411,917 pay
EVP; President, PhibroChem Group; and Director: James O. Herlands, age 63, $539,000 pay
SVP, Human Resources: Daniel A. (Dan) Welch, age 55
VP, General Counsel, and Secretary: Steven L. Cohen, age 61
CIO: Jeffrey (Jeff) Rose
President, Specialty Chemicals Group: Daniel M. Bendheim
President, PhibroChem: Mike Giambalvo
President, Phibro Tech: W. Dwight Glover
President, Animal Health Division: Keith R. Collins, age 50
Auditors: PricewaterhouseCoopers LLP

LOCATIONS

HQ: Phibro Animal Health Corporation
65 Challenger Rd., 3rd Fl.,
RidgeField Park, NJ 07660
Phone: 201-329-7300   **Fax:** 201-329-7399
Web: www.pahc.com

Phibro Animal Health has operations in Argentina, Australia, Belgium, Brazil, Canada, Chile, China, Costa Rica, France, Israel, Malaysia, Mexico, Norway, South Africa, Thailand, the UK, the US, and Venezuela.

2005 Sales

	$ mil.	% of total
US	251.5	69
Israel	40.1	11
Latin America	31.4	9
Asia/Pacific	24.2	7
Europe	17.1	4
Total	**364.3**	**100**

PRODUCTS/OPERATIONS

2005 Sales

	$ mil.	% of total
Animal Health & Nutrition	278.8	77
Industrial Chemicals	52.3	14
Distribution	33.2	9
Total	**364.3**	**100**

Principal Units and Products

Animal Health and Nutrition
  Agri-Tin
  Amprolium
  Animal feed ingredients
  Copper sulphate F.G.
  Nicarbazin
  Trace mineral premixes
  Trace minerals
  Ultra-flourish
Industrial Chemicals
  Alkaline etchant
  Calcium carbide
  Copper oxide
  Dicyandiamide
  Ferric chloride
  Fly ash
  Iron oxide
  Manganese dioxide
  Metal treatment
  Selenium disulfide
  Sodium flouride

COMPETITORS

Aceto
Akzo Nobel
Bayer Corp.
CFPI
Cognis
DuPont
LeaRonal, Inc.
MacDermid
Mitsui Chemicals
Sumitomo Chemical
Terra Industries
Trans-Resources

Income Statement

FYE: June 30

	REVENUE ($ mil.)	NET INCOME ($ mil.)	NET PROFIT MARGIN	EMPLOYEES
6/05	364	(20)	—	992
6/04	358	13	3.6%	1,051
6/03	355	(11)	—	1,126
6/02	389	(52)	—	1,423
6/01	364	(15)	—	1,550
6/00	318	10	3.2%	1,130
6/99	302	(1)	—	1,160
6/98	278	(9)	—	500
6/97	200	—	—	500
6/96	160	—	—	500
Annual Growth	**9.6%**	**—**	**—**	**7.9%**

Net Income History

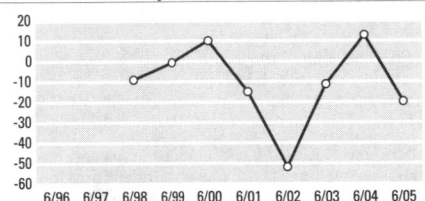

Philip Services

Philip Services Corporation (PSC) undertakes a wide range of industrial and environmental cleanup projects. Besides scrap metal recycling services, which have been the company's long-time focus, PSC provides on-site waste disposal and recycling, cleaning of industrial equipment, transportation of commercial and industrial waste, and emergency response to spills. In addition, PSC offers oil field services both onshore and offshore along the US Gulf Coast. Entities owned by investor Carl Icahn control PSC, which emerged from bankruptcy protection at the end of 2003.

EXECUTIVES

CEO: Vince Intrieri
SVP and CFO: Michael W. Ramirez
SVP and CEO Industrial Services Group:
Bruce E. Roberson
General Counsel: Debbie Huston
VP and Corporate Controller: Jim D. Graves
VP and Treasurer: David V. Andrews, age 45
VP Sales and Marketing, Industrial Services Group:
Brad Clark
Assistant Director of Tax and Assistant Treasurer:
Gerald Francis
Assistant Treasurer: Elisa Martinez
Auditors: KPMG LLP

LOCATIONS

HQ: Philip Services Corporation
5151 San Felipe Rd., Ste. 1600, Houston, TX 77056
Phone: 713-623-8777   **Fax:** 713-625-7185
Web: www.contactpsc.com

COMPETITORS

Clean Harbors
Commercial Metals
David J. Joseph
Halliburton Energy Services
Harsco
Metal Management
Onyx North America
Safety-Kleen
Schlumberger
Waste Management

HISTORICAL FINANCIALS

Company Type: Private

Income Statement

FYE: December 31

	REVENUE ($ mil.)	NET INCOME ($ mil.)	NET PROFIT MARGIN	EMPLOYEES
12/03	1,500	—	—	12,000
12/02	1,119	—	—	8,600
12/01	1,510	—	—	10,000
12/00	1,156	—	—	11,400
12/99	1,621	—	—	—
12/98	2,001	—	—	13,000
12/97	1,751	—	—	14,000
12/96	586	—	—	4,000
12/95	537	—	—	1,000
12/94	407	—	—	1,000
Annual Growth	**15.6%**	**—**	**—**	**31.8%**

Revenue History

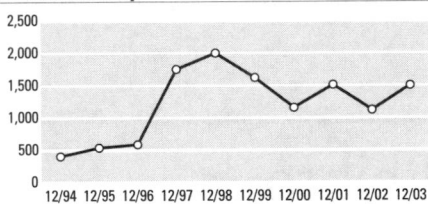

Phoenix Color

Phoenix Color Corp. does its work by the book. One of the largest book component printers in North America, the company's Book Components Division produces a variety of products such as book jackets, paperback covers, endpapers, and inserts for publishers. Its Rockaway Division teams up with printers in Asia to offer domestic and international illustrated and multicolor book printing options. In 2004 Phoenix Color closed down its own book manufacturing (one or two color books) division, called Book Technology Park, and sold its press and binding equipment to printing giant R.R. Donnelley. A group of 15 individuals, including chairman, president, and CEO Louis LaSorsa, founded the company in 1979. (LaSorsa owns a 10% stake in the company.)

Phoenix Color Corp.'s clients consist of such leading global publishing companies as HarperCollins, Pearson Publishing, Simon & Schuster, Random House, Holtzbrinck Publishers, and McGraw-Hill among others. Harper Collins accounts for 21% of sales; Pearson Publishing for 19% and the top 10 combined account for 85% of sales.

EXECUTIVES

Chairman, President, and CEO: Louis LaSorsa, age 58, $988,615 pay
EVP and COO, Book Components Division; Director: John Carbone, age 46, $540,461 pay
EVP, CFO, Secretary, and Director: Edward Lieberman, age 62, $646,381 pay
SVP Sales Northeast Region: John Sabella
VP Human Resources: Peggy Marfilius
VP Marketing: Kelly Hartman
VP Prepress Operations: John Hartman
VP Purchasing and Consumption: John Biancolli
VP Sales, East Central: Eric Henze
VP Sales, Midwest, South and Mountain States: Joseph Pezzuto
VP Sales, Mid-Atlantic: Andrew Ward
VP Sales, West Coast and Southwest: Sandy D`Amato
VP Sales, Western Region: Sandy D'Amato
Corporate Controller: Brian Keck
Auditors: PricewaterhouseCoopers LLP

LOCATIONS

HQ: Phoenix Color Corp.
540 Western Maryland Pkwy.,
Hagerstown, MD 21740
Phone: 301-733-0018   **Fax:** 301-791-9560
Web: www.phoenixcolor.com

Phoenix Color has operations in Maryland, New Jersey, and New York.

PRODUCTS/OPERATIONS

2004 Sales

	% of total
Book components	77
Illustrated multicolored books	23
Total	**100**

Selected Services

Finishing
  Binding
  Coating
  Die cutting
  Embossing
  Foil stamping
  Laminating
Prepress
  Assembly
  Color separations
  Digital file transfer
  Platemaking
  Proofing
  Retouching
Printing
  Book jackets
  Books
  Case covers
  Endpapers
  Illustrations
  Inserts
  Paperback books
  Paperback covers

COMPETITORS

Banta
Courier
Dai Nippon Printing
Quad/Graphics
Quebecor World
R.R. Donnelley
St Ives
Von Hoffmann Corporation
Worzalla

HISTORICAL FINANCIALS

Company Type: Private

Income Statement
FYE: December 31

	REVENUE ($ mil.)	NET INCOME ($ mil.)	NET PROFIT MARGIN	EMPLOYEES
12/04	99	(13)	—	690
12/03	137	(3)	—	769
12/02	138	(2)	—	818
12/01	129	(15)	—	862
12/00	148	(15)	—	899
12/99	141	(5)	—	780
12/98	108	1	0.9%	—
12/97	105	6	5.5%	506
12/96	95	2	1.9%	—
12/95	61	4	6.1%	—
Annual Growth	**5.5%**	**—**	**—**	**4.5%**

2004 Year-End Financials

Debt ratio: —
Return on equity: —
Cash ($ mil.): 0

Current ratio: 1.30
Long-term debt ($ mil.): 105

Net Income History

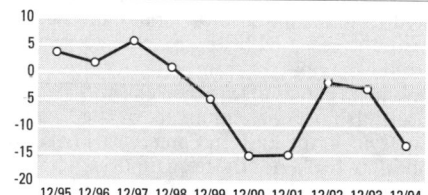

12/95	12/96	12/97	12/98	12/99	12/00	12/01	12/02	12/03	12/04

Phoenix Suns

After more than three decades, the Phoenix Suns still burn for an NBA Championship. The franchise was awarded to businessman Richard Bloch in 1968 and fronted by investors such as Tony Curtis and Henry Mancini. With players Ricky Sobers and Garfield Heard, the team made its first title bid in 1976 but lost to the Boston Celtics. The Suns' other runs at the championship ended against the Chicago Bulls in 1993 and the San Antonio Spurs in 2005. The team is coached by Mike D'Antoni. An investment group led by real estate executive Robert Sarver owns the team; former owner Jerry Colangelo, owner of the Arizona Diamondbacks, remains as the team's chairman and CEO.

EXECUTIVES

Chairman and CEO: Jerry J. Colangelo, age 65
President and COO: Rick Welts
President and General Manager: Bryan Colangelo, age 35
Assistant General Manager: Mark West, age 44
Head Coach: Mike D'Antoni
Assistant Coach: Dan D'Antoni
EVP Finance and Administration: Jim Pitman, age 40
SVP and General Counsel: Tom O'Malley
SVP Broadcasting: Al McCoy
SVP Business Development: John Walker
SVP Corporate Sales: Harvey Shank, age 59
SVP Marketing Communications: Ray Artigue
SVP Operations: Alvan Adams
SVP Player Personnel: Dick Van Arsdale, age 62
SVP Public Affairs: Thomas Ambrose, age 57
VP Finance: Jon Phillips
VP Human Resources: Peter Wong
VP Marketing: Jim Brewer, age 38

LOCATIONS

HQ: Phoenix Suns
201 E. Jefferson St., Phoenix, AZ 85004
Phone: 602-379-7900   **Fax:** 602-379-7990
Web: www.nba.com/suns

The Phoenix Suns play at America West Arena in Phoenix.

PRODUCTS/OPERATIONS

Titles
Western Conference Champions (1976, 1993)

COMPETITORS

Golden State Warriors
Los Angeles Clippers
Los Angeles Lakers
Sacramento Kings

HISTORICAL FINANCIALS

Company Type: Private

Income Statement
FYE: June 30

	REVENUE ($ mil.)	NET INCOME ($ mil.)	NET PROFIT MARGIN	EMPLOYEES
6/04	111	—	—	—
6/03	109	—	—	—
6/02	107	—	—	—
6/01	102	—	—	—
6/00	97	—	—	—
6/99	58	—	—	300
6/98	87	—	—	100
6/97	83	—	—	—
6/96	79	—	—	—
6/95	82	—	—	—
Annual Growth	**3.4%**	**—**	**—**	**200.0%**

Revenue History

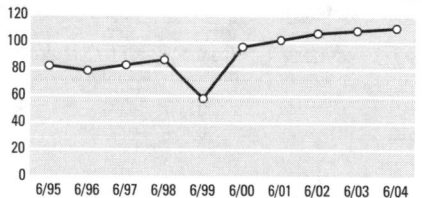

6/95	6/96	6/97	6/98	6/99	6/00	6/01	6/02	6/03	6/04

Pinnacle Foods

Pinnacle Foods Group (formerly Aurora Foods) has a mouthful of big-name brands. The firm produces grocery store staples such as Mrs. Butterworth's, Log Cabin, and Country Kitchen (syrup, pancake mix); Duncan Hines (baking mixes); Lender's (bagels); Van de Kamp's and Mrs. Paul's (frozen seafood); Chef's Choice (frozen skillet meals); and Celeste (frozen pizza). It has grown by buying well-known brands and then expanding those brand lines by adding new products. Upon Aurora's 2004 merger with Pinnacle Foods Holding Corporation, the company renamed itself Pinnacle Foods Group.

Pinnacle distributes its products nationwide to supermarket and other retail outlets. It also sells through club stores, as well as the private-label, military, and foodservice channels; it has a product development center in St. Louis. The merger of Aurora and Pinnacle added Swanson and Hungry-man frozen dinners, Lender's bagels, Open Pit Barbecue sauces, and Vlasic pickles to the company's product list.

EXECUTIVES

Chairman and CEO: C. Dean Metropoulos, age 58, $2,042,066 pay
EVP and Chief Administrative Officer: Michael J. Cramer, age 52
EVP and CFO: N. Michael Dion, age 47, $446,164 pay
EVP, Business Development and Acquisitions and Assistant Secretary: Louis Pellicano, age 58
EVP, Marketing: David Roe, age 40
EVP, Operations and Technical Services: Evan Metropoulos, age 51
EVP, Sales: William Toler, age 45
EVP, Sales and Marketing: Jon Roberts
EVP, Supply Chain: Bill Darkoch
SVP, Secretary, and General Counsel: M. Kelley Maggs, age 52
VP, Human Resources, Assistant General Counsel, and Assistant Secretary: John F. Kroeger, age 49
VP, Sales: Brian McCormick
Auditors: PricewaterhouseCoopers LLP

LOCATIONS

HQ: Pinnacle Foods Group Inc.
6 Executive Campus, Ste. 100,
Cherry Hill, NJ 08002
Phone: 856-969-7100   **Fax:** 856-969-7311
Web: www.pinnaclefoodscorp.com

Pinnacle operates seven manufacturing facilities located in Arkansas, Delaware, Illinois, Michigan, Nebraska, and Tennessee.

PRODUCTS/OPERATIONS

2004 Sales

	$ mil.	% of total
Frozen foods	271.2	53
Dry foods	240.0	47
Total	**511.2**	**100**

Selected Brand Names
All Day Breakfast
American Recipes
Aunt Jemima (frozen breakfast products only; licensed from The Quaker Oats Company)
Avalon Bay
Casa Brava
Casa Regina
Celeste
Country Kitchen
Duncan Hines
Fun Frosters
Great Starts
Grill Classics
Hearty Bowls
Hearty Hero
Hungry-Man
Lender's
Log Cabin
Milwaukee's
Mrs. Butterworth's
Mrs. Paul's
Open Pit
Snack'mms
Stackers
Steakhouse Mix
Swanson
Van de Kamp's
Vlasic

COMPETITORS

American Seafoods	Kraft Foods
Campbell Soup	Nestlé
Chelsea Milling	Nestlé USA
ConAgra	Nippon Suisan Kaisha
General Mills	Pacific Seafood
Gilster-Mary Lee	Red Chamber Co.
Goya	Rich Products
Heinz	StarKist
High Liner Foods	Thai Union
Interstate Bakeries	Trident Seafoods
Kellogg	Unilever

HISTORICAL FINANCIALS

Company Type: Private

Income Statement

FYE: Last Sunday in December

	REVENUE ($ mil.)	NET INCOME ($ mil.)	NET PROFIT MARGIN	EMPLOYEES
12/04*	511	(25)	—	2,600
7/04	756	(87)	—	—
7/03	575	8	1.5%	—
7/02	575	12	2.1%	—
Annual Growth	(3.8%)	—	—	—

*Fiscal year change

2004 Year-End Financials

Debt ratio: 238.3%   Current ratio: 1.31
Return on equity: —   Long-term debt ($ mil.): 938
Cash ($ mil.): 2

Net Income History

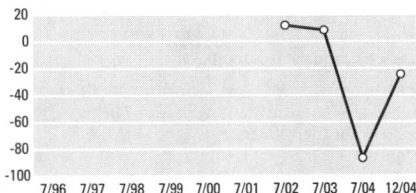

20	
0	
-20	
-40	
-60	
-80	
-100	7/96 7/97 7/98 7/99 7/00 7/01 7/02 7/03 7/04 12/04

Pismo Coast Village

Pismo Coast Village will prove that half the fun of owning an RV is parking it. The company runs a full-service recreational vehicle (RV) resort that accommodates up to 400 RVs. Vacationers have access to an onsite general store, heated swimming pool, laundry facilities, mini-golf course, recreation hall, video arcade, wireless Internet, and several playgrounds. Pismo Coast's recreation department aims to keep kids and families busy by renting out sports equipment and planning activities such as arts and crafts, mini-golf tournaments, pet costume contests, and scavenger hunts. The resort also offers an RV repair shop. Pismo Coast Village has been in operation since 1975.

EXECUTIVES

President: Jerald (Jerry) Pettibone, age 78
EVP: Glenn Hickman, age 71
VP and Secretary: Kurt Brittain, age 74
VP Finance and CFO: Jack Williams, age 54
VP Policy: Ronald Nunlist, age 66
COO, General Manager, and Assistant Corporate Secretary: Jay Jamison, age 51
Auditors: Brown Armstrong Paulden McCown Hill Starbuck & Keeter

LOCATIONS

HQ: Pismo Coast Village, Inc.
165 S. Dolliver St., Pismo Beach, CA 93449
Phone: 805-773-5649   **Fax:** 805-773-8079
Web: www.pismocoastvillage.com

PRODUCTS/OPERATIONS

2004 Sales

	$ mil.	% of total
Resort		
Site rental	2.5	76
Storage	0.6	18
Support	0.2	6
Retail		
General Store	0.6	67
RV Repair/Parts	0.3	33
Total	**4.2**	**100**

COMPETITORS

KOA
La Mesa RV
Outdoor Resorts
Thousand Trails

HISTORICAL FINANCIALS

Company Type: Private

Income Statement

FYE: September 30

	REVENUE ($ mil.)	NET INCOME ($ mil.)	NET PROFIT MARGIN	EMPLOYEES
9/04	4	0	4.8%	55
9/03	4	0	—	—
Annual Growth	7.7%	—	—	—

2004 Year-End Financials

Debt ratio: —   Current ratio: —
Return on equity: 2.9% Long-term debt ($ mil.): —
Cash ($ mil.): —

Net Income History

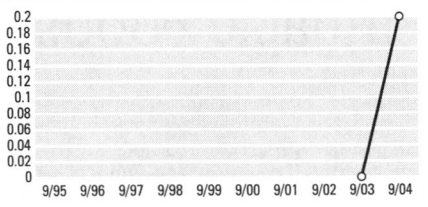

0.2	
0.18	
0.16	
0.14	
0.12	
0.1	
0.08	
0.06	
0.04	
0.02	
0	9/95 9/96 9/97 9/98 9/99 9/00 9/01 9/02 9/03 9/04

Pittsburgh Penguins

These penguins do their thing in downtown Pittsburgh, not the Antarctic. The Pittsburgh Penguins hockey franchise represents Steel City in the National Hockey League. Formed in 1967, the team brought home two Stanley Cup championships in 1991-92 but has fallen on hard times in recent seasons. Finishing at the bottom of its division for the past few years, the Pens draw some of the smallest crowds in the NHL. The Penguins play host in Pittsburgh's Mellon Arena (better known as "The Igloo"), the oldest facility in the league. Legendary forward Mario Lemieux controls the team through the Lemieux Group.

Financial woes under previous owner Howard Baldwin forced the Penguins to declare bankruptcy in 1998. Lemieux, who had led the Pens to its two championships before retiring in 1997, saved the club by rolling over nearly $30 million owed to him into an ownership bid. The next season he resigned his position as governor of the club to rejoin the team on the ice, scoring 35 goals in 43 games to take the Pens into the playoffs. (Pittsburgh was eliminated by the New Jersey Devils in the Eastern Conference finals.) He continues to play for the team (injuries not withstanding) and competed for Canada in the 2004 World Cup of Hockey. Lemieux also owns the minor league River City Lancers hockey team.

Baldwin helped form the New England Whalers of the World Hockey League (later to become the Carolina Hurricanes of the NHL) and later owned a stake in the Minnesota North Stars (now the Dallas Stars) before buying control of the Penguins in 1991 from Edward DeBartolo Sr.

EXECUTIVES

Chairman and CEO: Mario Lemieux, age 40
President and Governor: Ken Sawyer
EVP and General Manager: Craig Patrick
Assistant General Manager: Ed (E.J.) Johnston
Head Coach: Ed (Eddie) Olczyk, age 36
Assistant Coach: Randy Hillier
Assistant Coach: Joe Mullen
Head Scout: Greg Malone
VP Communications and Marketing: Tom McMillan
VP Sales and Marketing: David Soltesz
VP and General Counsel: Ted Black
VP and Controller: Kevin Hart
Director of Community Relations: Renee Petrichevich
Director of Marketing: Brian Magness
Director of Media Relations: Steve Bovino

LOCATIONS

HQ: Pittsburgh Penguins
1 Chatham Center, Ste. 400, Pittsburgh, PA 15219
Phone: 412-642-1300   **Fax:** 412-642-1859
Web: www.pittsburghpenguins.com

The Pittsburgh Penguins play in 17,000-seat capacity Mellon Arena in Pittsburgh.

PRODUCTS/OPERATIONS

Championship Trophies

Stanley Cup (1991-92)
Prince of Wales Trophy (1991-92)
Presidents' Trophy (1993)

HISTORICAL FINANCIALS

Company Type: Private

Income Statement

FYE: June 30

	REVENUE ($ mil.)	NET INCOME ($ mil.)	NET PROFIT MARGIN	EMPLOYEES
6/04	52	—	—	—
6/03	57	—	—	—
6/02	59	—	—	—
6/01	64	—	—	—
6/00	58	—	—	—
6/99	42	—	—	90
6/98	53	—	—	96
6/97	49	—	—	—
6/96	31	—	—	—
Annual Growth	**6.7%**	**—**	**—**	**(6.3%)**

Revenue History

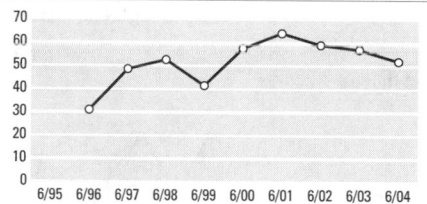

Plastipak Holdings

Plastipak likes to keep things bottled up. Doing business as Plastipak Packaging, the company manufactures plastic containers for four distinct industries: carbonated and noncarbonated beverages (soft drinks, bottled water, juice drinks, and beer); consumer cleaning (laundry detergent); food and processed juices (coffee creamers, relishes, and vegetable oils); and industrial, automotive, and agricultural (motor oil, antifreeze, windshield washer fluid). Plastipak Packaging makes high-density polyethylene (HDPE) resins and polyethylene terephthalate (PET) at its plants in the US and South America and is an exclusive packaging supplier to Procter & Gamble and Kraft Foods. The Young family owns and runs Plastipak.

The company's two largest business segments, which make containers for carbonated and noncarbonated beverages and the consumer cleaning industries, bring in 74% of its revenue.

Procter & Gamble is the company's largest customer, accounting for 27% of its sales. Plastipak is the exclusive supplier of plastic containers for Procter & Gamble's liquid laundry detergents (Tide, Cheer, Era, and Gain) and other

products like Bounce and Febreze; it is also the largest supplier of plastic containers for Kraft Foods salad dressing, barbecue sauces, and grated cheeses.

The company's Whiteline subsidiary serves 70% of Plastipak's transportation needs with a fleet of 300 tractors and 1,100 trailers. Its Clean Tech subsidiary, a plastics recycling firm, provides much of the company's raw material needs.

EXECUTIVES

Chairman, President, and CEO: William C. Young, age 63, $1,391,752 pay
VP, Finance; CFO, Treasurer, and Assistant Secretary: Michael J. Plotzke, age 46, $419,675 pay
VP, Controller and Strategic Operation Planning: Pradeep Modi, age 48
VP, International Sales and Marketing: Frank Pollock, age 48
VP, Operations and Manufacturing: William A. Slat, age 53, $390,475 pay
VP, Packaging Development: Richard Darr, age 54
VP, Product Supply: J. Ronald Overbeck, age 55
VP, Sales and Marketing: Gene W. Mueller, age 46, $377,871 pay
CIO: David Daugherty, age 48
President, Clean Tech: Thomas Busard, age 52, $400,892 pay
Corporate Legal Counsel and Secretary: Leann M. Underhill, age 58
Auditors: Grant Thornton LLP

LOCATIONS

HQ: Plastipak Holdings, Inc.
41605 Ann Arbor Rd., Plymouth, MI 48170
Phone: 734-455-3600   **Fax:** 734-354-7391
Web: www.plastipak.com

Plastipak has manufacturing facilities in Argentina, Brazil, the Czech Republic, the Slovak Republic, and the US.

PRODUCTS/OPERATIONS

2004 Sales

	$ mil.	% of total
Carbonated & non-carbonated beverage containers	442.2	44
Consumer cleaning containers	297.6	30
Food & processed juice containers	151.1	15
Industrial, agricultural & automotive containers	54.9	5
Other	58.2	6
Total	**1,004.0**	**100**

Selected Operations

Package development services
Plastic container manufacturing
High-density polyethylene (HDPE) resins
Polyethylene terephthalate (PET)
Technology licensing and equipment
EXI-PAK preform over-molding process technology (employs multi-layer, barrier, and post-consumer plastic technologies in PET bottles)
G.E.M. PAK container molding system

COMPETITORS

Amcor	Liqui-Box
Ball Corporation	Owens-Illinois
Consolidated Container	PVC Container
Constar International	Silgan
Crown	Silgan Plastics Corporation
Graham Packaging	
Husky Injection Molding Systems	

HISTORICAL FINANCIALS

Company Type: Private

Income Statement

FYE: Saturday nearest October 31

	REVENUE ($ mil.)	NET INCOME ($ mil.)	NET PROFIT MARGIN	EMPLOYEES
10/04	1,004	9	0.9%	3,865
10/03	898	4	0.5%	3,753
10/02	812	9	1.1%	3,700
10/01	810	—	—	3,300
10/00	566	—	—	3,000
Annual Growth	**15.4%**	**3.4%**	**—**	**6.5%**

2004 Year-End Financials

Debt ratio: 126.6%   Current ratio: 1.14
Return on equity: 20.5%   Long-term debt ($ mil.): 62
Cash ($ mil.): 12

Net Income History

Platinum Equity

Platinum Equity invests in information technology and other firms, often buying units of large corporations. These companies usually offer legacy products and services and have well-established customer bases and distribution operations. Platinum focuses on firms in such sectors as call center and help desk operations, data communications and networking, information systems, and software. It has operations on six continents. Platinum acquired Dallas-based CompuCom Systems and Frankfurt, Germany-based DyStar in 2004. Founder and CEO Tom Gores, who started Platinum in 1995, is the brother of Alec Gores, founder of another investment firm, Gores Technology Group.

EXECUTIVES

President and CEO: Tom T. Gores
EVP, Mergers and Acquisitions: Johnny O. Lopez
President, Portfolio Operations: Philip Norment
COO and Treasurer: Robert J. Joubran
CTO: David M. Anglin
EVP: John Diggins
EVP, General Counsel, and Secretary: Eva Kalawski
EVP: Gary Newton
EVP, Mergers and Acquisitions, Finance: Robert J. Wentworth
CFO: Jerome N. Gold
SVP, Mergers and Acquisitions and Operations: Rob Archambault
SVP, Corporate Relations: Mark Barnhill
SVP, Corporate Finance: Brian Duffy
VP, Human Resources: Barry D. Coleman
VP, Marketing Communications: Alanna Chaffin
VP, Corporate Communications: Bill Kobel
Director, Mergers and Acquisitions: Matt Young

LOCATIONS

HQ: Platinum Equity, LLC
    360 N. Crescent Dr., South Building,
    Beverly Hills, CA 90210
Phone: 310-712-1850   **Fax:** 310-712-1848
Web: www.platinumequity.com/site/action/home

Platinum Equity has offices in Beverly Hills, California;
New York; San Francisco; and Paris.

PRODUCTS/OPERATIONS

Selected Portfolio Companies
ACR Logistics (supply-chain management)
Altura Communication Solutions
    (voice and data communications)
Axcera (radio frequency transmission equipment)
Broadspire Services
    (insurance claims and risk management)
CompuCom Systems Inc. (IT services)
Data2Logistics (freight payment processing)
David Corporation (risk management software)
DCA Services (back office outsourcing for
    communications firms)
DyStar (textile dye manufacturing)
Excell Services (communications services)
Foresight Software (resource planning and customer
    relationship software)
GeoLogic Solutions (mobile communication equipment
    and wireless tracking service for transportation firms)
Gupta Technologies (Internet development and database
    tool applications)
iET Solutions (CRM and business planning software)
Matrix Telecom (telecommunications services for small
    and midsized firms)
NextiraOne (communications services)
Process Software (infrastructure software)
ProfitKey International (manufacturing software)
SourceOne Healthcare Technologies (medical imaging
    equipment and supplies)
Tesseract (human resources management software)
Vanguard Managed Solutions
    (Internet protocol access routers)

COMPETITORS

Apollo Advisors	KKR
CD&R	Texas Pacific Group
Hicks Muse	Thomas H. Lee Partners
Hummer Winblad	

HISTORICAL FINANCIALS

Company Type: Private

Income Statement

FYE: December 31

	REVENUE ($ mil.)	NET INCOME ($ mil.)	NET PROFIT MARGIN	EMPLOYEES
12/03	4,500	—	—	32,000
12/02	3,500	—	—	15,000
12/01	3,000	—	—	15,000
12/00	2,400	—	—	14,900
12/99	792	—	—	10,000
12/98	700	—	—	10,000
Annual Growth	**45.1%**	**—**	**—**	**26.2%**

Revenue History

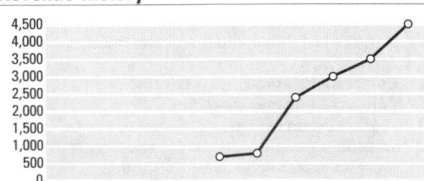

Pliant

Pliant is flexible when it comes to packaging. The company makes flexible packaging products and value-added films for a variety of uses. Pliant's specialty products include films used to make diapers, sterile films, and mulch films used for weed control. The company also produces industrial films such as stretch films (used to bundle palletized loads during shipping) and PVC films (used to wrap food products), along with engineered films, which are integrated into paper and foil packaging. Outside the US, Pliant makes and sells its products in Australia, Canada, Germany, and Mexico. Investment firm J.P. Morgan Partners owns 61% of the company; the family of former Pliant CEO Richard Durham owns 28%.

In 2004 the company sold its Pliant Solutions unit, which made films for decorative and surface covering applications, such as shelf paper. Pliant Solutions consisted primarily of businesses gained in Pliant's 2002 purchase of Decora Industries.

EXECUTIVES

Chairman: Edward A. Lapekas, age 61
President, CEO, Acting CFO, and Director:
    Harold C. Bevis, age 45, $1,537,307 pay
EVP and COO: R. David Corey, age 56, $558,213 pay
SVP and General Manager, Performance Films:
    Paul R. Franz, age 39, $296,167 pay
SVP, Technology and Innovation: Greg Gard, age 44,
    $305,333 pay
SVP, Sales: Glenn Harsh
SVP, Finance: Joseph J. Kwederis, age 58
SVP and General Manager, Industrial Films Division:
    Robert (Bob) Maltarich, age 53
SVP, Human Resources: Lori G. Roberts
SVP; President, Specialty Products:
    Kenneth J. Swanson, age 38, $369,500 pay
SVP and General Manager, Engineered Films:
    Coleman R. (Sonny) Wooldridge
Press Relations: Chris Sbertoli
Auditors: Ernst & Young LLP

LOCATIONS

HQ: Pliant Corporation
    1475 Woodfield Rd., Ste. 700,
    Schaumburg, IL 60173
Phone: 847-969-3300   **Fax:** 847-969-3338
Web: www.pliantcorp.com

Pliant Corporation has manufacturing facilities in Australia, Canada, Germany, Mexico, and the US.

2004 Sales

	$ mil.	% of total
US	780.0	81
Other countries	188.7	19
Total	**968.7**	**100**

PRODUCTS/OPERATIONS

2004 Sales

	$ mil.	% of total
Specialty products	390.7	40
Industrial films	254.1	26
Engineered films	219.0	23
Performance films	98.1	10
Other	6.8	1
Total	**968.7**	**100**

COMPETITORS

AEP Industries	Printpack
Bemis	Reynolds Food Packaging
Griffon	Sealed Air
Pactiv	Spartech
Polymer Group	

HISTORICAL FINANCIALS

Company Type: Private

Income Statement

FYE: December 31

	REVENUE ($ mil.)	NET INCOME ($ mil.)	NET PROFIT MARGIN	EMPLOYEES
12/04	969	(114)	—	3,025
12/03	929	(114)	—	3,250
12/02	879	(43)	—	3,250
12/01	840	(2)	—	3,500
12/00	844	(51)	—	3,150
12/99	814	18	2.2%	3,800
12/98	681	8	1.2%	3,000
Annual Growth	**6.0%**	**—**	**—**	**0.1%**

2004 Year-End Financials

Debt ratio: —
Return on equity: —
Cash ($ mil.): 6
Current ratio: 1.48
Long-term debt ($ mil.): 840

Net Income History

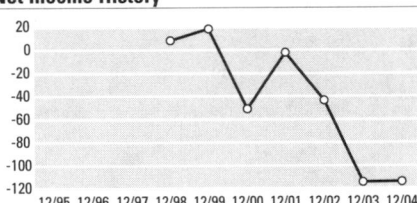

Plymouth Rubber

Despite its name, Plymouth Rubber doesn't bounce around — it sticks to the tape business. The company makes a range of vinyl and rubber electrical tapes, automotive harness tapes, industrial tapes and films, and highway striping tapes. It sells primarily to the auto and electrical supply and utility industries. Plymouth Rubber's Brite-Line Technologies subsidiary makes highway marking and safety products, and Spain-based Plymouth Rubber Europa makes vinyl and cloth-based insulating tapes. Delphi Corporation accounts for 32% of sales. The Hamilburg family owns nearly 60% of Plymouth Rubber. Failing to meet listing standards, the company was delisted from the American Stock Exchange (AMEX) in 2004.

Plymouth Rubber and Hebei Huaxia Group teamed up in 2005 to form a joint venture — Plymouth Yongle Tape (Shanghai) — to manufacture PVC adhesive tapes in China.

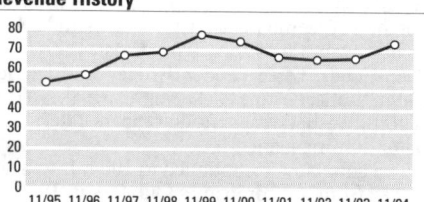
Port Authority of NY and NJ

The Port Authority of New York and New Jersey bridges the often-troubled waters between the two states — and helps with many of the region's other transportation needs. The bi-state agency operates and maintains airports, tunnels, bridges, a commuter rail system, shipping terminals, and other facilities within the Port District, an area surrounding the Statue of Liberty. A self-supporting public agency, the Port Authority receives no state or local tax money but relies on tolls, fees, and rents. The governors of the two states each appoint six of the 12 members of the agency's board and review the board's decisions.

The Port Authority's facilities include such international symbols of transportation and commerce as the George Washington Bridge, the Holland and Lincoln tunnels, and LaGuardia and John F. Kennedy airports. The Port Authority Trans-Hudson (PATH) rapid-transit system provides commuter rail service between New York and New Jersey.

The World Trade Center was among the agency's most visible assets before its twin towers and much of the rest of the complex were destroyed. The Port Authority is working with other agencies, government officials, and real estate interests on the rebuilding of the 16-acre site in Lower Manhattan. In 2003 it completed the reconstruction and reopening of the PATH rail station located at the World Trade Center site.

Future projects include upgrading the LaGuardia and Newark airports to accommodate anticipated increases in air traffic.

HISTORY

New York and New Jersey spent much of their early history fighting over their common waterways. In 1921 a treaty creating a single, bistate agency, the Port of New York Authority, was ratified by the New York and New Jersey state legislatures.

The agency struggled at first, although its early projects, such as the Goethals Bridge (1928, linking Staten Island to New Jersey), were far from timid. It merged with the Holland Tunnel Commission in 1930, which brought a steady source of revenue. In 1931 the George Washington Bridge (spanning the Hudson River from Manhattan to New Jersey) was completed. The Lincoln Tunnel (also linking Manhattan to New Jersey) opened in 1937.

After WWII the Port Authority broadened its focus to include commercial aviation. In 1947 the agency took over LaGuardia Airport, and the next year it dedicated the New York International Airport (renamed John F. Kennedy International Airport in 1963).

As trucking supplanted railroads in the late 1950s, The Port Authority experimented with more-efficient ways of transferring cargo. In 1962 it built the first containerport in the world. That year the agency acquired a commuter rail line connecting Newark to Manhattan, which became the Port Authority Trans-Hudson (PATH).

In the early 1970s the Port Authority completed the World Trade Center. The agency changed its name to The Port Authority of New York and New Jersey in 1972 to reflect its role in mass transit between the two states. Critics,

however, frequently assailed the agency for inefficiency and pork-barrel politics. In 1993 terrorists detonated a truck bomb in one of the World Trade Center towers, but within a year the building had largely recovered.

George Marlin became executive director in 1995. He cut operating expenses for the first time since 1943 and through budget cuts and layoffs, saved $100 million in 1996 and avoided hikes in tolls and fares. A privatization proponent, Marlin sold the World Trade Center's Vista Hotel to Host Marriott and arranged for the sale of other non-transportation businesses. He stepped down in 1997, and Robert Boyle took the post. That year the agency broke ground on the $1.2 billion Terminal 4 at JFK International Airport.

In 1998 the Port Authority authorized a $930 million design and construction contract for a light-rail line to JFK International Airport. New York City mayor Rudolph Giuliani proposed legislation in 1999 to place the Port Authority's LaGuardia and JFK airports under City Hall jurisdiction.

An 18-month standoff between the governors of New York and New Jersey regarding disputes over leases and agency spending was settled in 2000, which allowed the Port Authority to move forward with projects that had been blocked. Also in 2000 Boyle announced plans to resign. Neil Levin, New York's state insurance superintendent and a former Goldman Sachs vice president, replaced him the next year.

After the Port Authority and Vornado Realty Trust in 2001 failed to finalize an agreement for Vornado to lease the World Trade Center, the Port Authority that year signed a 99-year, $3.2 billion deal to lease portions of the World Trade Center's office space to a group led by Silverstein Properties while leasing the retail space to Westfield America.

Less than two months later, the World Trade Center's twin towers were destroyed when terrorists hijacked passenger jets and flew them into the buildings. Levin was killed, and 83 other Port Authority employees were listed as dead or missing.

The cleanup of the World Trade Center site, known as "Ground Zero," was completed in 2002, eight months after the attacks.

Director, Government and Community Affairs:
Arthur J. Cifelli
Director, Human Resources: Michael G. Massiah
Director, Office of Emergency Management:
John P. Paczkowski
Director, Public Affairs: Kayla Bergeron
Director, World Trade Center Redevelopment:
James T. Connors
Auditors: Deloitte & Touche LLP

LOCATIONS

HQ: The Port Authority of New York and New Jersey
225 Park Ave. South, New York, NY 10003
Phone: 212-435-7000   **Fax:** 212-435-6670
Web: www.panynj.gov

The Port Authority of New York and New Jersey operates primarily in the five boroughs of New York City, four suburban New York counties, and eight counties in northern New Jersey.

PRODUCTS/OPERATIONS

2003 Sales

	$ mil.	% of total
Air terminals	1,617	59
Interstate transportation	796	29
Port commerce	128	5
World Trade Center	126	4
Economic & waterfront development	97	3
Total	**2,764**	**100**

Selected Operations

Air Terminals
   Downtown Manhattan Heliport (New York)
   John F. Kennedy International Airport (New York)
   LaGuardia Airport (New York)
   Newark Liberty International Airport (New Jersey)
   Teterboro Airport (New Jersey)

Interstate Transportation
   Bayonne Bridge
      (Staten Island to Bayonne, New Jersey)
   George Washington Bridge
      (Manhattan to Ft. Lee, New Jersey)
   George Washington Bridge Bus Terminal
   Goethals Bridge
      (Staten Island to Elizabeth, New Jersey)
   Holland Tunnel (Manhattan to Jersey City, New Jersey)
   Lincoln Tunnel (Manhattan to Union City, New Jersey)
   Outerbridge Crossing
      (Staten Island to Perth Amboy, New Jersey)
   Port Authority Bus Terminal (Manhattan)
   The Port Authority Trans-Hudson System (PATH, rail
      transportation between New York and New Jersey)

Port Commerce
   Auto Marine Terminal (Bayonne, New Jersey)
   Brooklyn-Port Authority Marine Terminal (New York)
   Elizabeth Marine Terminal (New Jersey)
   Howland Hook Marine Terminal (New York)
   Port Newark (New Jersey)
   Red Hook Container Terminal (New York)

Economic and Waterfront Development
   Bathgate Industrial Park (Bronx, New York)
   Essex County Resource Recovery Center (municipal
      waste-to-energy electric generation plant;
      Newark, New York)
   Industrial Park at Elizabeth (Elizabeth, New Jersey)
   Newark Legal & Communications Center (office
      development; Newark, New Jersey)
   Queens West (mixed-use waterfront development;
      Queens, New York)
   Hoboken South (mixed-use waterfront development;
      Hoboken, New Jersey)
   The Teleport (communications center;
      Staten Island, New York)

COMPETITORS

Amtrak	MTA
Coach USA	Reckson Associates Realty
Covanta	Tishman
Helmsley Enterprises	Trump
Lefrak Organization	

HISTORICAL FINANCIALS

Company Type: Government agency

Income Statement

FYE: December 31

	REVENUE ($ mil.)	NET INCOME ($ mil.)	NET PROFIT MARGIN	EMPLOYEES
12/03	2,764	883	31.9%	7,000
12/02	2,671	740	27.7%	7,000
12/01	2,715	216	7.9%	7,000
12/00	2,648	372	14.1%	7,000
12/99	2,548	314	12.3%	7,200
12/98	2,361	299	12.7%	7,200
12/97	2,206	282	12.8%	7,500
12/96	2,154	199	9.2%	8,100
12/95	2,083	177	8.5%	9,250
12/94	1,980	153	7.7%	9,200
Annual Growth	**3.8%**	**21.5%**	**—**	**(3.0%)**

2003 Year-End Financials

Debt ratio: 109.8%
Return on equity: 13.9%
Cash ($ mil.): 29

Current ratio: 0.99
Long-term debt ($ mil.): 7,471

Net Income History

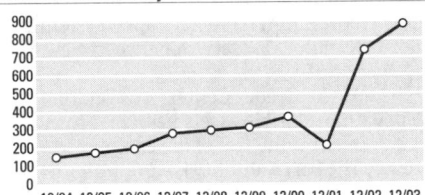

12/94 12/95 12/96 12/97 12/98 12/99 12/00 12/01 12/02 12/03

Portland Trail Blazers

The Portland Trail Blazers like to run over the competition. Founded in 1970 by Harry Glickman, the team won the NBA championship in 1977 with center Bill Walton. The Blazers have suffered only three losing seasons since but usually manage an early round exit from the playoffs except in 1992 when they lost to Michael Jordan's Chicago Bulls in the finals. Former Seattle SuperSonics coach Nate McMillan was named to the Blazer's top coaching post in 2005. Under the ownership of Microsoft co-founder Paul Allen, who also owns the Seattle Seahawks of the NFL, the Blazers frequently sell out the 21,000-seat Rose Garden.

EXECUTIVES

Chairman and Owner: Paul G. Allen, age 52
President: Steve Patterson
General Manager: John Nash
CFO: Gregg M. Olson
SVP Business Affairs: J. E. Isaac
VP and CIO: Chris Dill
VP and General Counsel: Michael Fennell
VP Blazers Broadcasting and Production:
   Dick Vardanega
VP Communications: Art Sasse
VP Marketing and Communications: Marta Monetti
Director of Community Relations: Traci Rose
Director of Human Resources: Traci Reandeau
Director of Marketing: Michele Daterman

LOCATIONS

HQ: Trail Blazers, Inc.
   1 Center Ct., Ste. 200, Portland, OR 97227
Phone: 503-234-9291   **Fax:** 503-736-2194
Web: www.nba.com/blazers

PRODUCTS/OPERATIONS

Championship Titles

NBA Finals (1977)

COMPETITORS

Denver Nuggets	Seattle SuperSonics
Minnesota Timberwolves	Utah Jazz

HISTORICAL FINANCIALS

Company Type: Private

Income Statement

FYE: June 30

	REVENUE ($ mil.)	NET INCOME ($ mil.)	NET PROFIT MARGIN	EMPLOYEES
6/04	88	—	—	—
6/03	97	—	—	—
6/02	96	—	—	—
6/01	101	—	—	—
6/00	97	—	—	—
6/99	57	—	—	—
6/98	94	—	—	1,425
6/97	90	—	—	1,420
6/96	86	—	—	—
6/95	47	—	—	—
Annual Growth	**7.1%**	**—**	**—**	**0.4%**

Revenue History

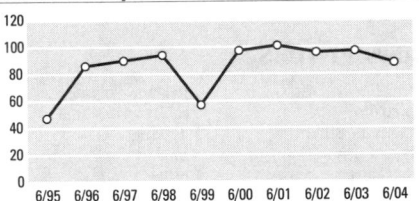

6/95 6/96 6/97 6/98 6/99 6/00 6/01 6/02 6/03 6/04

Portola Packaging

Portola Packaging brings closure to its customers' products. The company makes plastic bottles and closures and related equipment used for packaging applications in the noncarbonated beverage and institutional foods markets. It also manufactures and sell closures and containers for the cosmetics, fragrance, and toiletries market. Portola Packaging's brands include Snap Cap, Nepco, Portola, Tech Industries, Portola Tech International. The company's customers include Arla Foods, Avon, Coca-Cola, Dairy Crest, Dairyland, Dean Foods, Estée Lauder, Kroger, and Perrier Water/Nestle. Portola Packaging also makes a line of bottle washers, cappers, de-cappers, fillers, and water bottling plants.

The company was founded in 1964. It was acquired from the company's founders in 1986 by a group led by Jack Watts. Portola Packaging has grown through a series of acquisitions.

EXECUTIVES

Chairman: Jack L. Watts, age 55
President and CEO: Brian Bauerbach
VP, Finance and CFO: Dennis L. Berg, age 54
VP, Corporate Development: Laurie D. Bassin, age 54
VP, Engineering/R&D: Richard Lohrman, age 50
Auditors: PricewaterhouseCoopers LLP

LOCATIONS

HQ: Portola Packaging, Inc.
890 Faulstich Ct., San Jose, CA 95112
Phone: 408-573-2000   **Fax:** 408-453-8462
Web: www.portpack.com

Portola Packaging has 13 manufacturing facilities, including five in the US, four in Canada, and one each in China, the Czech Republic, Mexico, and the UK.

COMPETITORS

Amcor
IPEC Holdings
Owens-Illinois
Silgan Closures

HISTORICAL FINANCIALS

Company Type: Private

Income Statement

	REVENUE ($ mil.)	NET INCOME ($ mil.)	NET PROFIT MARGIN	EMPLOYEES
8/04	243	(21)	—	1,376
8/03	215	(2)	—	1,065
8/02	211	5	2.2%	—
Annual Growth	7.3%	—	—	29.2%

FYE: August 31

Net Income History

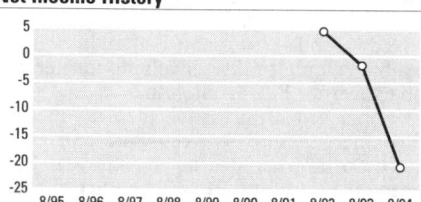

Precision Dynamics

The corporate name of this company doesn't give away much about its product focus. Precision Dynamics Corp. (PDC) doesn't suffer from identity problems, however. The company makes bar code and radio-frequency identification (RFID) wristbands for identifying hospital patients, ticket holders in entertainment venues, people in police custody, and the dead. Not the Grateful Dead, but deceased people in morgues. Precision Dynamics was established in 1956 by Walter Mosher Jr., the company's chairman and CTO. Mosher owns half of the company, while Robert Kraemer (corporate secretary and former EVP) owns the other half. PDC has facilities in Belgium, Mexico, and the US.

Precision Dynamics has long served the health care market with its different types of wristbands. The company introduced the Visa Band wristband for use in entertainment and recre-

ation programs in 1972, followed by the Clincher inmate ID wristband in 1976. The Smart Band RFID wristband was unveiled in 2000 and has been used by the South By Southwest festival in Austin, Texas, and the Triathlon Competition in Kona, Hawaii.

EXECUTIVES

Chairman and CTO: Walter W. Mosher Jr.
President, CEO, and Director: Gary Hutchinson
VP Advanced Marketing and Technology Group: Robin Barber
VP Engineering: Ed Hammerslag
VP Finance and CFO: Mark Segal
VP Intellectual Property: Ozzie Penuela
VP Operations: Hosmel Galan
VP Sales and Marketing: Nick Curtin
Secretary and Director: Robert B. Kraemer
Director Global Regulatory Affairs: Kalyna Snylyk
Media Relations Specialist: Paula Moggio

LOCATIONS

HQ: Precision Dynamics Corporation
13880 Del Sur St., San Fernando, CA 91340
Phone: 818-897-1111   **Fax:** 818-899-4045
Web: www.pdcorp.com

COMPETITORS

Digital Angel
Innovision
Intermec Technologies
National Ticket
Standard Register
Texas Instruments

HISTORICAL FINANCIALS

Company Type: Private

Income Statement

	REVENUE ($ mil.)	NET INCOME ($ mil.)	NET PROFIT MARGIN	EMPLOYEES
12/04	32	—	—	423

FYE: December 31

Predix Pharmaceuticals

Predix Pharmaceuticals, which merged with Physiome Sciences in 2003, is looking to streamline the drug discovery and development process by integrating 3D computational chemistry technologies with traditional medicinal chemistry. The company's drug discovery platform could accelerate the discovery of new drugs associated with ion channels and G-protein coupled receptors. Predix is developing its own drug candidates that could treat psychiatric and pulmonary diseases. Its drug PRX-03140 is being developed to treat Alzheimer's disease, and anxiety disorder drug PRX-0023 has completed Phase II clinical trials. It also is collaborating with large pharmaceutical companies to advance their drug discovery processes.

EXECUTIVES

Chairman: Frederick (Fred) Frank, age 72
President, CEO, and Director: Michael G. Kauffman, age 42, $382,500 pay
CFO: Kimberlee C. (Kim) Drapkin, age 37

SVP, Pipeline Management; General Manager, Israel: Silvia Noiman, age 49, $186,453 pay
VP, Clinical and Regulatory Affairs: Stephen R. (Steve) Donahue, age 41
VP, Drug Development Operations: Christine H. Wang, age 51, $192,186 pay
Chief Scientific Officer: Oren Becker, age 44
Chief Business Officer: Chen Schor, age 33, $266,666 pay
Senior Director and Product Leader, Alzheimer's Program: Sharon Shacham
Auditors: Ernst & Young LLP

LOCATIONS

HQ: Predix Pharmaceuticals, Inc.
4 Maguire Rd., Lexington, MA 02421
Phone: 781-372-3260   **Fax:** 781-372-3267
Web: www.predixpharm.com

COMPETITORS

Axonyx
Cephalon
Memory Pharmaceuticals
Panacea Pharmaceuticals
Samaritan Pharmaceuticals

HISTORICAL FINANCIALS

Company Type: Private

Income Statement

	REVENUE ($ mil.)	NET INCOME ($ mil.)	NET PROFIT MARGIN	EMPLOYEES
12/04	0	(19)	—	45
12/03	1	(25)	—	—
12/02	1	(11)	—	58
Annual Growth	—	—	—	(11.9%)

FYE: December 31

2004 Year-End Financials

Debt ratio: 9.6%
Return on equity: —
Cash ($ mil.): 14
Current ratio: 4.87
Long-term debt ($ mil.): 1

Net Income History

Prestwick Pharmaceuticals

Presto! Prestwick Pharmaceuticals hopes profits materialize from its work to develop drugs for chronic disorders of the central nervous system. The firm licenses drug candidates in late stages of development from other companies; it takes these candidates through their final paces of development and, hopefully, approval. Lead candidate tetrabenazine may treat chorea (irregular voluntary muscle movements) associated with Huntington's disease. Prestwick already markets tetrabenazine as Nitoman in Canada. Other drug candidates in the firm's pipeline are lisuride, a potential therapy for Parkinson's disease;

D-Serine, which Prestwick is developing to treat schizophrenia; and PPI-03306, a candidate for sleep apnea.

Prestwick Pharmaceuticals licensed US and Canadians rights to tetrabenazine from Cambridge Laboratories, which markets the drug as Xenazine in Europe. The drug candidate has orphan drug status in the US for Huntington's disease and another movement disorder, severe tardive dyskinesia.

In addition to bringing new drugs to market, the drugmaker aims to develop new formulations and find new indications for its candidates.

Investors in Prestwick include Atlas Venture, Vivo Ventures, and Sofinnova Ventures. Kathleen Clarence-Smith, founder and CEO, owns nearly 10% of the company.

EXECUTIVES

Chairman: Melvin D. Booth, age 59
CEO and Director: Kathleen E. Clarence-Smith, age 58
President and COO: David A. Cory, age 41, $279,639 pay
CFO and Assistant Secretary:
William H. (Bill) Washecka, age 57
Chief Medical Officer: Christopher F. (Chris) O'Brien, age 48, $320,000 pay
VP, Regulatory Affairs: Benjamin P. Lewis, age 62, $163,433 pay
Secretary and Director: Robert J. (Bob) Flanagan, age 49
Senior Director, Commercial Operations:
James P. Shaffer, age 38
Director, Legal Affairs: Richard P. Dulik, age 49

LOCATIONS

HQ: Prestwick Pharmaceuticals, Inc.
1825 K St. NW, Ste. 1475, Washington, DC 20006
Phone: 202-296-1400   **Fax:** 202-296-7450
Web: www.prestwickpharma.com

PRODUCTS/OPERATIONS

Drug Candidates

D-Serine (schizophrenia, autism, Alzheimer's disease)
Lisuride (Parkinson's disease, Restless Legs Syndrome)
PPI-03306 (sleep apnea)
Tetrabenazine (chorea associated with Huntington's disease, severe tardive dyskinesia)

COMPETITORS

Boehringer Ingelheim	Sandoz
Endo Pharmaceuticals	Schwarz Pharma
GlaxoSmithKline	UCB
Hi-Tech Pharmacal	XenoPort
Pfizer	

HISTORICAL FINANCIALS

Company Type: Private

Income Statement				FYE: December 31
	REVENUE ($ mil.)	NET INCOME ($ mil.)	NET PROFIT MARGIN	EMPLOYEES
12/04	1	(20)	—	29
12/03	0	(11)	—	—
12/02	0	(2)	—	—
Annual Growth	—	—	—	—

2004 Year-End Financials

Debt ratio: (0.1%)
Return on equity: —
Cash ($ mil.): 31
Current ratio: 13.54
Long-term debt ($ mil.): 0

Net Income History

Pricewaterhouse Coopers

Not merely the firm with the longest one-word name, PricewaterhouseCoopers (PwC) is also one of the world's largest accounting firms, formed when Price Waterhouse merged with Coopers & Lybrand in 1998, passing then-leader Andersen. The accountancy has offices around the world, providing clients with services in three lines of business: Assurance (including financial and regulatory reporting), Tax, and Advisory. The umbrella entity for the PwC worldwide organization (officially PricewaterhouseCoopers International) is one of accounting's Big Four, along with Deloitte Touche Tohmatsu, Ernst & Young, and KPMG. PwC serves some of the world's largest businesses, as well as smaller firms.

PwC puts its heft to good use: Non-North American clients make up nearly 65% of the firm's sales. Its bottom line, though, changed significantly in 2002, when PwC sold its consulting arm to IBM. A separation had been under consideration for years in light of SEC concerns about conflicts of interest when firms perform auditing and consulting for the same clients. The collapse of Enron and concomitant downfall of Enron's auditor and PwC's erstwhile peer Andersen undoubtedly hastened plans to spin off PwC's consultancy via an IPO, which was scrapped in favor of the IBM deal.

Like the other members of the (now) Big Four, PwC picked up business and talent as scandal-felled Andersen was winding down its operations in 2002. The former Andersen organization in China and Hong Kong joined PwC, accounting for about 70% of the approximately 3,500 Andersen alumni that came aboard.

In 2003 former client AMERCO (parent of U-Haul) sued PwC for $2.5 billion, claiming negligence and fraud in relation to a series of events that led to AMERCO restating its results.

HISTORY

In 1850 Samuel Price founded an accounting firm in London and in 1865 took on partner Edwin Waterhouse. The firm and the industry grew rapidly, thanks to the growth of stock exchanges that required uniform financial statements from listees. By the late 1800s Price Waterhouse (PW) had become the world's best-known accounting firm.

US offices were opened in the 1890s, and in 1902 United States Steel chose the firm as its auditor. PW benefited from tough audit requirements instituted after the 1929 stock market crash. In 1935 the firm was given the prestigious

---

job of handling Academy Awards balloting. It started a management consulting service in 1946. But PW's dominance slipped in the 1960s, as it gained a reputation as the most traditional and formal of the major firms.

Coopers & Lybrand, the product of a 1957 transatlantic merger, wrote the book on auditing. Lybrand, Ross Bros. & Montgomery was formed in 1898 by William Lybrand, Edward Ross, Adam Ross, and Robert Montgomery. In 1912 Montgomery wrote *Montgomery's Auditing*, which became the bible of accounting.

Cooper Brothers was founded in 1854 in London by William Cooper, eldest son of a Quaker banker. In 1957 Lybrand joined up to form Coopers & Lybrand. During the 1960s the firm expanded into employee benefits and internal control consulting, building its technology capabilities in the 1970s as it studied ways to automate the audit process.

Coopers & Lybrand lost market share as mergers reduced the Big Eight accounting firms to the Big Six. After the savings and loan debacle of the 1980s, investors and the government wanted accounting firms held liable not only for the form of audited financial statements but for their veracity. In 1992 the firm paid $95 million to settle claims of defrauded investors in MiniScribe, a failed disk-drive maker. Other hefty payments followed, including a $108 million settlement relating to the late Robert Maxwell's defunct media empire.

In 1998 Price Waterhouse and Coopers & Lybrand combined PW's strength in the media, entertainment, and utility industries, and Coopers & Lybrand's focus on telecommunications and mining. But the merger brought some expensive legal baggage involving Coopers & Lybrand's performance of audits related to a bid-rigging scheme involving former Arizona governor Fife Symington.

Further growth plans fell through in 1999 when merger talks between PwC and Grant Thornton International failed. The year 2000 began on a sour note: An SEC conflict-of-interest probe turned up more than 8,000 alleged violations, most involving PwC partners owning stock in their firm's audit clients.

As the SEC grew ever more shrill in its denunciation of the potential conflicts of interest arising from auditing companies that the firm hoped to recruit or retain as consulting clients, PwC saw the writing on the wall and in 2000 began making plans to split the two operations. As part of this move, the company downsized and reorganized many of its operations.

The following year PwC paid $55 million to shareholders of MicroStrategy Inc., who charged that the audit firm defrauded them by approving the client firm's inflated earnings and revenues figures.

The separation of PwC's auditing and consulting functions finally became a reality in 2002, when IBM bought the consulting business. (The acquisition took the place of a planned spinoff.)

EXECUTIVES

Global Chairman: Andrew Ratcliffe
Global CEO and Global Board Member:
Samuel A. DiPiazza Jr., age 45
Managing Partner, Global Markets: Willem L.J. Bröcker
Managing Partner, Global Operations:
Amyas C.E. Morse, age 55

Global General Counsel; Acting US General Counsel:
Lawrence Keeshan
Global Co-Leader, Human Capital: Richard L. Baird
Global Leader, Tax: Paul Boorman
**Global Leader, Assurance and Business Advisory
Services:** J. Frank Brown, age 45
Global Co-Leader, Human Capital: Marie-
Jeanne Chèvremont
Global Leader, Entertainment and Media Practice:
R. Wayne Jackson
Global Leader, Industries: Alec N. Jones
Global Leader, Regulatory: Richard Kilgust
Global Leader, Transaction Services: Colin McKay,
age 48
Global Strategy Leader: Edgargo Pappacena
Global Leader, Assurance: Gerald M. Ward
Territory/Regional Leader, Canada: Kevin J. Dancey
Territory/Regional Leader, South and Central America:
Luis E. Frisoni Jr.
Territory/Regional Leader, Australia:
Anthony P.D. Harrington
Territory/Regional Leader, UK: John K. Heywood
**Territory/Regional Leader, US; Chairman and Senior
Partner (US):** Dennis M. Nally
Territory/Regional Leader, UK: Kieran C. Poynter
Territory/Regional Leader, China and Southeast Asia:
Arshad Uda
Territory/Regional Leader, Continental Europe:
Wolfgang Wagner

LOCATIONS

HQ: PricewaterhouseCoopers International Limited
1177 Avenue of the Americas, New York, NY 10036
Phone: 646-471-4000   **Fax:** 646-471-3188
Web: www.pwcglobal.com

PricewaterhouseCoopers has offices in about
145 countries.

2004 Sales

	$ mil.	% of total
Europe	7,352	45
North America & Caribbean	6,028	37
Asia	1,497	9
Australasia & Pacific Islands	714	5
Middle East & Africa	358	2
South & Central America	305	2
Discontinued operations	29	—
Total	**16,283**	**100**

PRODUCTS/OPERATIONS

2004 Sales

	$ mil.	% of total
Assurance	8,713	54
Tax	4,464	27
Advisory	3,077	19
Discontinued operations	29	—
Total	**16,283**	**100**

2004 Sales By Industry

	% of total
Consumer & industrial products & services	
Services	19
Industrial products	15
Retail & consumer	10
Energy, utilities & mining	7
Automotive	3
Pharmaceuticals	3
Financial services	
Banking & capital markets & investment management	20
Insurance	5
Technology, infocomm & entertainment	
Technology	9
Entertainment & media	5
Infocomm	4
Total	**100**

Selected Products and Services

Audit and Assurance Services
  Actuarial services
    Audit support
    Financial modeling
    IFRS implementation
    Insolvencies and run-off solutions
    M&A and capital structuring
    Operational improvement
    Retirement, benefits, and actuarial
    Risk and capital management
  Assurance on capital market transactions
  Financial accounting
  IFRS readiness and conversions
  Independent controls and process assurance
  Internal audit
  Non-financial performance and reporting
  Regulatory compliance
  Sarbanes-Oxley readiness
  Statutory audit
  Web assurance solutions
Advisory Services
  Crisis management
    Business recovery services
    Dispute analysis and investigation
  Performance improvement
  Transaction services
    Corporate finance
    Valuation and strategy
Tax and Human Resource Services
  Customs and duties
  Finance and treasury
  Global compliance services
  Global VAT solutions
  Global visa solutions
  Human resource services
  International assignment solutions
  Mergers and acquisitions
  Transfer pricing

COMPETITORS

Bain & Company	H&R Block
Baker Tilly International	Hewitt Associates
BDO International	KPMG
Booz Allen	Marsh & McLennan
Boston Consulting	McKinsey & Company
Deloitte	Towers Perrin
Ernst & Young	Watson Wyatt
Grant Thornton	
International	

HISTORICAL FINANCIALS

Company Type: Partnership

Income Statement

FYE: June 30

	REVENUE ($ mil.)	NET INCOME ($ mil.)	NET PROFIT MARGIN	EMPLOYEES
6/04	16,283	—	—	122,471
6/03	14,683	—	—	122,820
6/02	13,800	—	—	124,563
6/01	24,000	—	—	160,000
6/00	21,500	—	—	150,000
6/99	15,300	—	—	155,000
6/98	15,000	—	—	140,000
6/97	5,630	—	—	60,000
6/96	5,020	—	—	56,000
6/95	4,460	—	—	53,000
Annual Growth	**15.5%**	**—**	**—**	**9.8%**

Revenue History

Primavera Systems

Primavera Systems serves up collaborative project, resource, and porfolio management software. Serving clients in the aerospace, construction and engineering, information technology, manufacturing, telecom, and utilities industries, Primavera offers applications for analyzing risk, assigning resources, tracking tasks, scheduling contractors, and keeping time and expense records for projects of all sizes. The company's software has been used to manage China's massive Three Gorges Dam project, the London Underground, and airports in Hong Kong, Philadelphia, and San Francisco. CEO Joel Koppelman and CTO Richard Faris co-founded Primavera in 1983; each owns about 40% of the company.

Boasting that its software is used to manage client projects worth more than $5 trillion altogether, Primavera counts Boeing, Motorola, FedEx, General Motors, and the US Navy among its 75,000 customers.

Primavera has expanded its product line over the years both through internal development efforts and through acquisitions of smaller companies. In 2003 Primavera grew its project portfolio management offerings when it bought the assets of Evolve Software (which had filed for Chapter 11 bankruptcy protection) for $13 million.

Primavera claims to have been profitable for more than 20 straight years. The company accepted outside investments for the first time in 2000, when it sold equity stakes to Intel Capital and i2 Technologies (which has since sold back its stake in Primavera) in order to fund development of its PrimeContract online construction project management offering.

EXECUTIVES

Chairman, President, and CEO: Joel M. Koppelman
EVP, Secretary, and CTO: Richard K. (Dick) Faris
VP, Business Development: Lawrence A. Spoerl
VP, Corporate Marketing: Nancy Allen
VP, Customer Support: Kristy C. Tan
VP, Evolve Development: Andrew Tahvildary
VP, Finance and CFO: Mitchell T. (Mitch) Codkind
VP, International Sales: David Oates
VP, Marketing: Michael E. (Mike) Shomberg
VP, Professional Services: Diane Nicolls
VP, Sales, Americas: Tom Dalle-Molle
General Manager, Primavera IT Operations:
Joanne McCool

LOCATIONS

HQ: Primavera Systems, Inc.
3 Bala Plaza West, Ste. 700, Bala Cynwyd, PA 19004
Phone: 610-667-8600   **Fax:** 610-667-7894
Web: www.primavera.com

Primavera Systems has offices in California, Illinois, Pennsylvania, and the UK.

PRODUCTS/OPERATIONS

Selected Software

Engineering and construction project management
  Expedition Professional
  Primavera Contractor
  Primavera Engineering and Construction
  Primavera Project Planner
  PrimeContract
  SureTrak Project Manager

Information technology project portfolio management
  Primavera IT Operations Management
  Primavera IT Project Office

Maintenance and turnaround project lifecycle
  Expedition Professional
  Primavera Maintenance and Turnaround

New product development project management
  Primavera New Product Development

Professional services resource management
  Primavera Professional Services

Services

Consulting
Online services
Training

COMPETITORS

Artemis International Solutions
Business Engine
Datastream Systems
Deltek
Indus International
Integrated Development
Lawson Software
Microsoft
MRO Software
Niku
Oracle
SAP
Timberline

HISTORICAL FINANCIALS

Company Type: Private

Income Statement

FYE: December 31

	REVENUE ($ mil.)	NET INCOME ($ mil.)	NET PROFIT MARGIN	EMPLOYEES
12/04	102	—	—	430
12/03	90	—	—	465
12/02	78	—	—	442
12/01	80	—	—	430
12/00	80	—	—	430
12/99	53	—	—	297
12/98	42	—	—	301
12/97	43	—	—	250
12/96	32	—	—	225
12/95	28	—	—	205
Annual Growth	15.5%	—	—	8.6%

Revenue History

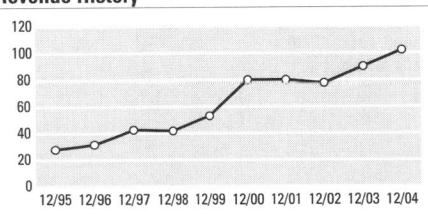

Princeton University

Princeton rules the Ivy League. The highly selective university accepts about 13% of those who apply. One of the US's richest universities (behind Harvard, Yale, and Texas), Princeton has an endowment of more than $8.7 billion. It offers degrees in 35 departments and has some 6,600 students (4,600 undergraduates and 2,000 graduate students). Tuition reaches $30,000 a year; more than 50% of students receive some financial aid. Nobel prize winners associated with Princeton include Woodrow Wilson (Princeton's president before becoming US president), writer Toni Morrison, and physicist Richard Feynman. The university also is loosely affiliated with the Institute for Advanced Study where Albert Einstein once taught.

Founded in 1746, Princeton is the fourth-oldest college in the nation. It was housed in Nassau Hall, which contained the entire college for nearly half a century. Nassau Hall served as the temporary capitol of the US in 1783.

EXECUTIVES

Chair: Stephen A. Oxman
Vice Chair: Anthony B. (Tony) Evnin, age 64
President and Trustee: Shirley M. Tilghman
Provost: Christopher L. Eisgruber
EVP: Mark Burstein
VP Campus Life: Janet Smith Dickerson
VP Development: Brian J. McDonald
VP Facilities: Michael E. McKay
VP Finance and Treasurer: Christopher McCrudden
VP Human Resources: Lianne Sullivan-Crowley
VP Information Technology and CIO: Betty Leydon
VP, Secretary, and Trustee: Robert K. Durkee
Dean of Admissions: Janet Lavin Rapelye
Dean of the College: Nancy Weiss Malkiel
General Counsel: Peter G. McDonough
Auditors: Deloitte & Touche LLP

LOCATIONS

HQ: Princeton University
  1 Nassau Hall, Princeton, NJ 08544
Phone: 609-258-3000   **Fax:** 609-258-1301
Web: www.princeton.edu

HISTORICAL FINANCIALS

Company Type: School

Income Statement

FYE: June 30

	REVENUE ($ mil.)	NET INCOME ($ mil.)	NET PROFIT MARGIN	EMPLOYEES
6/04	780	—	—	5,291
6/03	747	—	—	12,497
6/02	750	—	—	12,238
6/01	639	—	—	11,754
6/00	594	—	—	14,965
6/99	544	—	—	11,169
6/98	519	—	—	11,124
6/97	986	—	—	—
6/96	1,113	—	—	—
6/95	866	—	—	—
Annual Growth	(1.2%)	—	—	(11.6%)

Revenue History

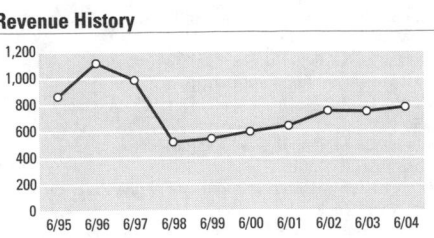

Printpack

And that's a wrap. Printpack wraps its flexible packaging around salty snacks, confections, baked goods, cookies, crackers, and cereal, as well as tissues and paper towels. The company's packaging includes plastic film, aluminum foil, metallized films and paper with specialized coatings, and cast and blown monolayer and co-extruded films. Customers include Frito-Lay, Georgia-Pacific, General Mills, and Quaker Oats. Printpack manufactures packaging materials at about 20 plants in the US, Mexico, and the UK. The Love family owns and manages the company; Dennis Love is Printpack president.

Printpack was founded by J. Erskine Love Jr., in 1956. By the early 1960s the company had established 50 to 60 accounts, including Frito-Lay and The Arkansas Rice Growers Co-op.

EXECUTIVES

Chairman: Gay M. Love, age 72
President, CEO, and Director: Dennis M. Love, age 49
VP, Finance and CFO: R. Michael Hembree, age 52
VP, Human Resources: Nicklas D. Stucky, age 55
VP, Engineering: August Franchini Jr., age 58
VP, Technology and Support: Terrence P. Harper, age 43
VP, General Manager, and Director: James E. Love III, age 44
VP and General Manager: Michael A. Fisher, age 54
VP and General Manager: James J. Greco, age 57
VP and General Manager: William E. Lewis, age 57
VP and General Manager: John N. Stigler, age 53
Director of Development, Technology, and Marketing: Thomas Dunn
Treasurer and Assistant Secretary: Dellmer B. Seitter III, age 36
Corporate Communications Manager: Susan Folds
Auditors: PricewaterhouseCoopers LLP

LOCATIONS

HQ: Printpack, Inc.
  4335 Wendell Dr., Atlanta, GA 30336
Phone: 404-691-5830   **Fax:** 404-699-7122
Web: www.printpack.com

Printpack operates 20 manufacturing plants in the US, Mexico, and the UK.

PRODUCTS/OPERATIONS

Selected Customers

Frito-Lay
General Mills
Georgia-Pacific
Hershey
Keebler
Kellogg
Mars
Nabisco
Nestlé
Quaker Oats

COMPETITORS

AEP Industries
Alcoa
Bemis
Madeco
Pliant
PMC Global
Reynolds Food Packaging
Sealed Air

HISTORICAL FINANCIALS

Company Type: Private

Income Statement

FYE: Saturday nearest June 30

	REVENUE ($ mil.)	NET INCOME ($ mil.)	NET PROFIT MARGIN	EMPLOYEES
6/04	1,091	—	—	3,872
6/03	1,053	—	—	3,906
6/02	1,100	—	—	4,300
6/01	1,027	—	—	3,800
6/00	907	—	—	3,800
6/99	846	—	—	3,600
6/98	832	—	—	3,500
6/97	782	—	—	3,500
6/96	443	—	—	2,330
6/95	455	—	—	2,663
Annual Growth	10.2%	—	—	4.2%

Revenue History

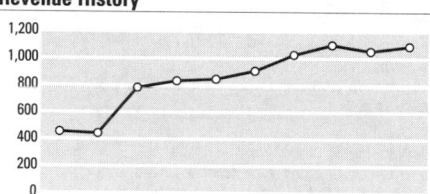

Director of Corporate Services: Cheryl Miller
Director of Sales and Business Operations:
 Fred Windhorst
Manager of Information Systems: Kirk Frickel
Auditors: Quick & McFarlin, P.C.

LOCATIONS

HQ: Professional Veterinary Products, Ltd.
 10077 S. 134th St., Omaha, NE 68138
Phone: 402-331-4440   **Fax:** 402-331-8655
Web: www.pvpl.com

HISTORICAL FINANCIALS

Company Type: Private

Income Statement

FYE: July 31

	REVENUE ($ mil.)	NET INCOME ($ mil.)	NET PROFIT MARGIN	EMPLOYEES
7/04	335	3	0.9%	307
7/03	299	3	1.1%	276
7/02	240	1	0.5%	244
7/01	196	1	0.3%	204
7/00	175	1	0.3%	—
7/99	119	0	0.1%	—
Annual Growth	23.1%	97.4%	—	14.6%

2004 Year-End Financials

Debt ratio: 46.6%   Current ratio: 1.13
Return on equity: 24.6%   Long-term debt ($ mil.): 6
Cash ($ mil.): 3

Net Income History

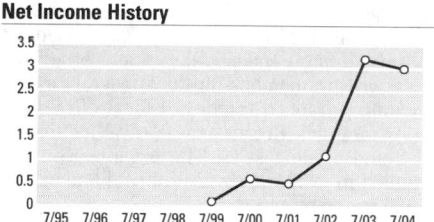

LOCATIONS

HQ: Promega Corporation
 2800 Woods Hollow Rd., Madison, WI 53711
Phone: 608-274-4330   **Fax:** 608-277-2516
Web: www.promega.com

Promega has facilities in Australia, Austria, China,
France, Germany, Italy, Japan, the Netherlands,
Singapore, Spain, Switzerland, the UK, and the US.

COMPETITORS

Applied Biosystems   Fisher Scientific
Bayer   Invitrogen
Beckman Coulter   Roche
Becton Dickinson   Sigma-Aldrich

HISTORICAL FINANCIALS

Company Type: Private

Income Statement

FYE: December 31

	REVENUE ($ mil.)	NET INCOME ($ mil.)	NET PROFIT MARGIN	EMPLOYEES
12/04	170	—	—	755
12/03	156	—	—	758
12/02	113	—	—	747
Annual Growth	22.6%	—	—	0.5%

Revenue History

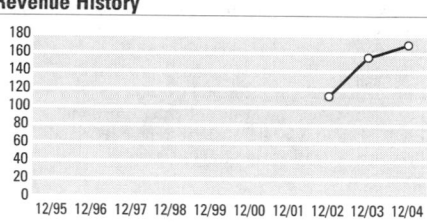

Professional Veterinary Products

Professional Veterinary Products distributes pharmaceuticals and supplies to licensed veterinarians. The company carries over 20,000 products ranging from diagnostic equipment to animal identification tags. PVPL has two subsidiaries: Exact Logistics (distributes to other animal health companies) and ProConn (supplies products directly to the consumer). The company was founded by a group of veterinarians in 1982.

EXECUTIVES

Chairman Emeritus: Raymond C. Ebert II
Chairman: Chester L. (Chet) Rawson
Vice Chairman: Steven E. Wright
President and CEO: Lionel L. Reilly
CFO: Neal B. Soderquist
Secretary: Michael B. Davis

Promega

Promega helps researchers plumb the depths of the life sciences. The company sells more than 1,200 products that allow scientists to conduct various experiments in gene, protein, and cellular research. Its reagents and other goods fall into about two dozen categories, including DNA and RNA purification; genotype analysis; protein expression and analysis; and DNA sequencing. Promega has customers in more than 90 countries around the world, although North America is its largest market. The firm sells its products directly and through distributors.

EXECUTIVES

Chairman, President, and CEO:
 William A. (Bill) Linton, age 57
VP and CTO: Randall Dimond
VP, Finance and CFO: Laura Francis
VP, Sales: Lisa Witte
Director, Information Systems: Jeff Christopher
Director, Marketing Communications: Roger Larrick
Manager, Corporate Communications: Penny Patterson
Auditors: Ernst & Young LLP

Providence Health System

Sisterhood is powerful in health care. The order of the Sisters of Providence runs not-for-profit Providence Health System in the Pacific Northwest (with outposts in Alaska and southern California). The system operates about 20 acute care hospitals, some of which offer specialized care centers for cancer and heart disease. Other services include long-term care and assisted-living facilities and primary care centers. All together, the health system has more than 3,700 acute care beds and nearly 1,750 long-term care beds. Providence Health System also offers health plans, low-income housing, and home health, hospice, and various community outreach services.

The Sisters of Providence were founded in 1843 in Montreal. Their work in the US began in 1856, when five members of the order established a mission in what was then Washington Territory.

EXECUTIVES

Chairman: Kay Stepp
President and CEO: John F. Koster, age 54
VP and CFO: Michael (Mike) Butler
VP and Chief Administrative Officer: Jan Jones
VP Clinical Excellence and Chief Medical Officer:
 Rocky Fredrickson
VP Government Affairs: Chuck Hawley
VP Human Resources: Sue Byington
VP Mission Leadership: Karin Dufault
VP Strategic Development: Claudia Haglund
VP Strategic Learning and Leadership Development:
 Adrienne McDunn
Interim CIO: Paul Anderson

LOCATIONS

HQ: Providence Health System
 506 2nd Ave., Ste. 1200, Seattle, WA 98104
Phone: 206-464-3355   **Fax:** 206-464-3038
Web: www.providence.org

Selected Facilities

Alaska
 Providence Alaska Medical Center (Anchorage)
 Providence Kodiak Island Medical Center (Kodiak)
 Providence Seward Medical Center (Seward)

California
 Providence Saint Joseph Medical Center (Burbank)
 Providence Holy Cross Medical Center (Mission Hills)
 Little Company of Mary Hospital (Torrance)

Oregon
 Providence Hood River Memorial Hospital
  (Hood River)
 Providence Medford Medical Center (Medford)
 Providence Milwaukie Hospital (Milwaukie)
 Providence Newburg Hospital (Newburg)
 Providence Portland Medical Center (Portland)
 Providence St. Vincent Medical Center (Porland)
 Providence Seaside Hospital (Seaside)

Washington
 Providence Centralia Hospital (Centralia)
 Providence Everett Medical Center (Everett)
 Providence St. Peter Hospital (Olympia)

COMPETITORS

Adventist Health	PacifiCare
Catholic Healthcare West	Sisters of Charity of
HCA	Leavenworth
Legacy Health System	Sutter Health
Los Angeles County	Tenet Healthcare
Health Department	Triad Hospitals
Memorial Health Services	UniHealth

HISTORICAL FINANCIALS

Company Type: Not-for-profit

Income Statement

FYE: December 31

	REVENUE ($ mil.)	NET INCOME ($ mil.)	NET PROFIT MARGIN	EMPLOYEES
12/03	3,780	177	4.7%	32,526
12/02	3,529	58	1.6%	33,920
12/01	3,274	95	2.9%	32,929
12/00	3,229	162	5.0%	32,238
12/99	3,000	—	—	27,000
12/98	2,709	—	—	23,000
12/97	2,346	—	—	21,800
12/96	2,137	—	—	20,368
12/95	1,579	—	—	17,956
12/94	1,503	—	—	17,362
Annual Growth	10.8%	2.9%	—	7.2%

2003 Year-End Financials

Debt ratio: 39.7%   Current ratio: —
Return on equity: 8.4% Long-term debt ($ mil.): 896
Cash ($ mil.): —

Net Income History

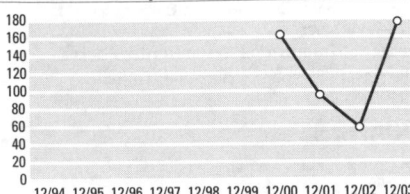

12/94 12/95 12/96 12/97 12/98 12/99 12/00 12/01 12/02 12/03

Public Broadcasting Service

More than just a showcase for a certain purple Teletubby, Public Broadcasting Service (PBS) serves up educational content to public TV stations across the country. A private, non-profit organization owned and operated by about 350 US public TV stations, PBS provides TV programming and related services such as distribution, fundraising support, and technology development. Programs include *NOVA*, *This Old House*, and *Masterpiece Theater*. Revenues come from underwriting, membership dues, federal funding (including grants from the not-for-profit Corporation for Public Broadcasting), royalties, license fees, and product sales. The organization was founded in 1969 to provide cultural and educational programming.

PBS has been on the receiving end of recent challenges from liberals and conservatives alike. When it planned to broadcast an animated children's show featuring a lesbian couple, PBS was denounced by religious groups and members of the Bush administration; CEO Pat Mitchell subsequently decided not to distribute the episode in question, and in turn faced criticism from left-leaning groups. In addition, conservatives have scorned PBS's liberal talk show *Now with Bill Moyers*. PBS has since added conservative commentators like Tucker Carlson and Paul Gigot to its line-up.

In the wake of such culture wars, Mitchell has announced that she will not renew her contract when it expires in June 2006.

EXECUTIVES

Chair: Mary G. Bitterman
Vice Chair: John E. Porter
Vice Chair: Jerrold F. Wareham
President, CEO, and Director: Patricia E. (Pat) Mitchell, age 62
EVP and COO: W. Wayne Godwin
SVP and CFO: Barbara L. Landes, age 49
SVP and Co-Chief Program Executive: John F. Wilson
SVP and Co-Chief Program Executive:
 Jacoba (Coby) Atlas
SVP and General Counsel: Katherine Lauderdale

**SVP Brand Management, Promotion, and Media
 Relations:** Lesli Rotenberg
SVP Interactive and Education:
 Cynthia (Cindy) Johanson
SVP Programming Services: Pat Hunter
SVP Technology and Operations: Edward P. Caleca
Controller and Assistant Treasurer: Chris DeCesaris
Ombudsman: Michael Getler
Auditors: PricewaterhouseCoopers LLP

LOCATIONS

HQ: Public Broadcasting Service
 1320 Braddock Place, Alexandria, VA 22314
Phone: 703-739-5000   **Fax:** 703-739-0775
Web: www.pbs.org

PRODUCTS/OPERATIONS

2004 Sales

	$ mil.	% of total
Underwriting	184.3	36
Member fees	155.5	30
Grants	80.2	15
Product sales	41.2	8
Royalties, license fees & other	56.1	11
Total	**517.3**	**100**

Selected Programming

Antiques Roadshow
Austin City Limits
Barney
Evening at Pops
Fawlty Towers
Frontier House
Frontline
Great Performances
HealthWeek
In The Mix
Jacques Pepin Celebrates!
Juila Child: Lessons with Master Chefs
Lawrence Welk Show
Live from Lincoln Center
Masterpiece Theater
McLaughlin Group
Mister Rogers' Neighborhood
MotorWeek
Mystery!
Nature
The NewsHour with Jim Lehrer
Newton's Apple
The New Yankee Workshop
NOVA
Now with Bill Moyers
P.O.V.
Sesame Street
Sit and Be Fit
Teletubbies
This Old House
Victory Garden
Washington Week
ZOOM

COMPETITORS

A&E Networks
BBC
Discovery Communications
National Geographic
NBC
NBC Universal TV Studio

HISTORICAL FINANCIALS

Company Type: Not-for-profit

Income Statement

FYE: June 30

	REVENUE ($ mil.)	NET INCOME ($ mil.)	NET PROFIT MARGIN	EMPLOYEES
6/04	517	—	—	507
6/03	498	—	—	—
6/02	534	—	—	500
6/01	542	—	—	—
Annual Growth	(1.5%)	—	—	0.7%

Revenue History

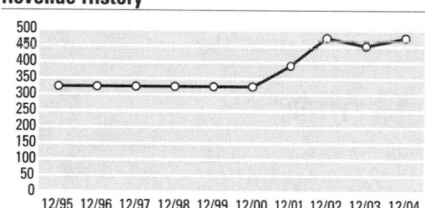

600
500
400
300
200
100
0

6/95 6/96 6/97 6/98 6/99 6/00 6/01 6/02 6/03 6/04

Publishers Clearing House

If your doorbell rings on Thanksgiving, it's probably just your Aunt Judy bringing more food. But it could be Publishers Clearing House (PCH) dropping by to let you know that you've won $1 million. PCH is one of the world's largest direct marketing organizations. Once known primarily for its magazines (and PCH giveaways), the company now makes most of its money from direct mail offerings for household items, personal care products, entertainment, collectibles, and food items in the US, the UK, and Canada. Close to half the company's profits go to charities. PCH was founded in 1953 by Harold and LuEster Mertz and is still owned largely by the Mertz family.

The company is highlighting the discount merchandise part of its business (which sells products such as DVDs, music, jewelry, and household items) from retailers including Sunbeam, Foster Grant, Vivitar, Coleman, and American Tourister.

EXECUTIVES

Chairman: Robin B. Smith, age 65
President and CEO: Andy Goldberg
EVP: Deborah Holland
CFO: Rick Busch
SVP, Marketing: John Princiotta
SVP: Todd Sloane
VP, Human Resources: Jordan Vargas
VP, pch.com: Eva Broker
Executive Director Advertising and Public Relations: Dave Sayer
Senior Director Consumer and Privacy Affairs: Christopher L. Irving

LOCATIONS

HQ: Publishers Clearing House
382 Channel Dr., Port Washington, NY 11050
Phone: 516-883-5432 **Fax:** 516-767-4567
Web: www.pch.com

COMPETITORS

Amazon.com	Reader's Digest
Amazon.co.uk	Synapse
EBSCO	Time

HISTORICAL FINANCIALS

Company Type: Private

Income Statement

FYE: December 31

	ESTIMATED REVENUE ($ mil.)	NET INCOME ($ mil.)	NET PROFIT MARGIN	EMPLOYEES
12/04	475	—	—	425
12/03	450	—	—	425
12/02	475	—	—	425
12/01	390	—	—	500
12/00	325	—	—	800
12/99	325	—	—	800
12/98	325	—	—	800
12/97	325	—	—	850
12/96	325	—	—	1,015
12/95	325	—	—	—
Annual Growth	4.3%	—	—	(10.3%)

Revenue History

500
450
400
350
300
250
200
150
100
50
0

12/95 12/96 12/97 12/98 12/99 12/00 12/01 12/02 12/03 12/04

Publix Super Markets

Publix Super Markets tops the list of privately owned supermarket operators in the US. By emphasizing service and a family-friendly image rather than price, Publix has grown faster and been more profitable than Winn-Dixie Stores and other rivals. Most of its 850 stores are in Florida, but it also operates in Alabama, Georgia, South Carolina, and Tennessee. Publix makes some of its own bakery, deli, and dairy goods, and many stores offer flowers, housewares, pharmacies, and banks. The company also operates five "Pix" convenience stores in the Sunshine State. Founder George Jenkins began offering stock to Publix employees in 1930. Employees own about 30% of Publix, which is still run by the Jenkins family.

Publix is expanding into the liquor market with the acquisition of two liquor stores adjacent to a pair of Kash n' Karry outlets in Florida that the company acquired from Delhaize America in 2004. Currently, Publix operates five liquor stores next to its supermarkets.

About 75% of the company's stores are in Florida. In 2005, Publix plans to open about 16 new supermarkets (12 in Florida).

To better serve its Latino customers, Publix has launched its own line of pre-packaged Hispanic foods, including frozen plantains and ready-to-eat black beans. It is also converting

two stores in Kissimmee and Hialeah, Florida, to its new Hispanic-themed format called Publix Sabòr. Soon after, the regional supermarket chain jumped onto the natural foods bandwagon with the introduction of a news store format called GreenWise, the name Publix has already given to its store-within-a-store natural/organic sections and private-label line of specialty foods. Two GreenWise stores are slated to open in 2006 in Miami and Boca Raton.

Publix is expanding its majority-owned restaurant chain Crispers with new menu items and plans to open 10 new locations in Florida this year, bringing the number of locations for the casual-dining restaurant chain to 40.

HISTORY

George Jenkins, age 22, resigned as manager of the Piggly Wiggly grocery in Winter Haven, Florida, in 1930. With money he had saved to buy a car, he opened his own grocery store, Publix, next door to his old employer. The small store (named after a chain of movie theaters) prospered despite the Depression, and in 1935 Jenkins opened another Publix in the same town.

Five years later, after the supermarket format had become popular, Jenkins closed his two smaller locations and opened a new, more modern Publix Market. With pastel colors and electric-eye doors, it was also the first US store to feature air conditioning.

Publix Super Markets bought the All-American chain of Lakeland, Florida (19 stores), in 1944 and moved its corporate headquarters to there. The company began offering S&H Green Stamps in 1953, and in 1956 it replaced its original supermarket with a mall featuring an enlarged Publix and a Green Stamp redemption center. Publix expanded into South Florida in the late 1950s and began selling stock to employees.

As Florida's population grew, Publix continued to expand, opening its 100th store in 1964. Publix was the first grocery chain in the state to use bar-code scanners — all its stores had the technology by 1981. The company beat Florida banks in providing ATMs and during the 1980s opened debit card stations.

Publix continued to grow in the 1980s, safe from takeover attempts because of its employee ownership. In 1988 it installed the first automated checkout systems in South Florida, giving patrons an always-open checkout lane.

The chain stopped offering Green Stamps in 1989, and most of the $19 million decrease in Publix advertising expenditures was attributed to the end of the 36-year promotion. That year, after almost six decades, "Mr. George" — as founder Jenkins was known — stepped down as chairman in favor of his son Howard. (George died in 1996.)

In 1991 Publix opened its first store outside Florida, in Georgia, as part of its plan to become a major player in the Southeast. Publix entered South Carolina in 1993 with one supermarket; it also tripled its presence in Georgia to 15 stores.

The United Food and Commercial Workers Union began a campaign in 1994 against alleged gender and racial discrimination in Publix's hiring, promotion, and compensation policies.

Publix opened its first store in Alabama in 1996. That year a federal judge allowed about 150,000 women to join a class-action suit filed in 1995 by 12 women who had sued Publix, charging that the company consistently channeled female employees into low-paying jobs with little chance for good promotions. The case, which at the time was said to be the biggest sex discrimination lawsuit ever, was set to go to trial, but in 1997 the company paid $82.5 million to settle and another $3.5 million to settle a complaint of discrimination against black applicants and employees.

Publix promised to change its promotion policies, but two more lawsuits alleging discrimination against women and blacks were filed in 1997 and 1998. The suit filed on behalf of the women was denied class-action status in 2000. Later that year the company settled the racial discrimination lawsuit for $10.5 million. Howard Jenkins stepped down as CEO in mid-2001; his cousin Charlie Jenkins took the helm.

In mid-2002 Publix made an equity investment in Florida-based Crispers, a chain of 13 quick-serve health-conscious diners targeting health-conscious diners. Also that year, Publix entered the Nashville, Tennessee, market with the purchase of seven Albertson's supermarkets, a convenience store, and a fuel center.

In mid-2003 Publix pulled the plug on its online store PublixDirect, which offered delivery service in parts of Florida, citing disappointing sales. However, it added 78 bricks-and-mortar stores in 2003.

In February 2004, Publix acquired three Florida stores from Kash n' Karry, a subsidiary of Belgium's Delhaize Group. Also in 2004 Publix became the majority owner of Crispers, the restaurant chain the company invested in initially in 2002.

EXECUTIVES

Chairman: Howard M. Jenkins, age 53
Vice Chairman: Hoyt R. (Barney) Barnett, age 61, $395,448 pay
CEO and Director: Charles H. (Charlie) Jenkins Jr., age 61, $713,931 pay
President and Director: William E. (Ed) Crenshaw, age 54, $588,357 pay
CFO and Treasurer: David P. Phillips, age 45, $467,498 pay
SVP and CIO: Daniel M. Risener, age 64
SVP, General Counsel, and Secretary:
John A. Attaway Jr., age 46
SVP, Manufacturing and Distribution:
R. Scott Charlton, age 46
SVP, Human Resources and Public Affairs:
John T. Hrabusa, age 49
SVP, Product Business Development: Todd Jones
VP, Internal Audit: Linda S. Hall, age 45
VP, Marketing: Mark R. Irby, age 49
VP, Public Affairs: M. Clayton Hollis Jr., age 48
Assistant Secretary and Executive Director, Publix Super Markets Charities: Sharon A. Miller, age 61
Director, Marketing and Research: Mark Lang
Director, Media and Community Relations:
Maria Rodamis Brous
Auditors: KPMG LLP

LOCATIONS

HQ: Publix Super Markets, Inc.
3300 Publix Corporate Pkwy., Lakeland, FL 33811
Phone: 863-688-1188   **Fax:** 863-284-5532
Web: www.publix.com

Publix Super Markets operates about 850 grocery stores in Alabama, Florida, Georgia, South Carolina, and Tennessee. The company also has three dairy processing plants (Deerfield Beach and Lakeland, Florida, and Lawrenceville, Georgia) and a deli plant and a bakery in Lakeland. Publix operates eight distribution centers in Florida (Boynton Beach, Deerfield Beach, Jacksonville, Lakeland, Miami, Orlando, and Sarasota) and Georgia (Lawrenceville).

2004 Stores

	No.
Florida	626
Georgia	159
South Carolina	37
Alabama	21
Tennessee	7
Total	**850**

PRODUCTS/OPERATIONS

Selected Supermarket Departments

Bakery
Banking
Dairy
Deli
Ethnic foods
Floral
Groceries
Health and beauty care
Housewares
Meat
Pharmacy
Photo processing
Produce
Seafood

Foods Processed

Baked goods
Dairy products
Deli items

COMPETITORS

Albertson's	Nash Finch
ALDI	The Pantry
BI-LO	Rite Aid
Bruno's Supermarkets	Royal Ahold
Costco Wholesale	Ruddick
CVS	Sedano's
Delhaize America	Smart & Final
IGA	Walgreen
Ingles Markets	Wal-Mart
Kerr Drug	Whole Foods
Kmart	Winn-Dixie
Kroger	

HISTORICAL FINANCIALS

Company Type: Private

Income Statement

FYE: Last Saturday in December

	REVENUE ($ mil.)	NET INCOME ($ mil.)	NET PROFIT MARGIN	EMPLOYEES
12/04	18,686	819	4.4%	128,000
12/03	16,946	661	3.9%	125,000
12/02	16,027	632	3.9%	123,000
12/01	15,370	530	3.5%	126,000
12/00	14,724	530	3.6%	126,000
12/99	13,069	462	3.5%	120,000
12/98	12,067	378	3.1%	117,000
12/97	11,224	355	3.2%	111,000
12/96	10,431	265	2.5%	103,000
12/95	9,393	242	2.6%	95,000
Annual Growth	**7.9%**	**14.5%**	**—**	**3.4%**

2004 Year-End Financials

Debt ratio: 0.0%
Return on equity: 24.3%
Cash ($ mil.): 472
Current ratio: 1.13
Long-term debt ($ mil.): 0

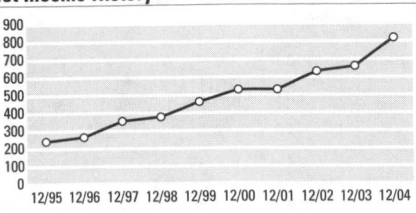

Net Income History

Purdue Pharma

Purdue Pharma makes drugs, not boilers. The company is best known for over-the-counter medicines like Betadine (an antiseptic) and Senokot (a laxative). Purdue concentrates its research and development on pain management and cancer. Prescription drugs include pain relievers MS Contin and OxyContin, as well as a generic version of OxyContin sold by partner IVAX Pharmaceuticals. It is also developing cardiac and respiratory therapies, as well as inhaled drug delivery systems. The firm markets products from other manufacturers in addition to its own products. Purdue is part of a network of affiliates with operations in Asia, North and South America, and Europe.

Founded in 1892, the company has been fighting pain for a long time. Purdue Pharma today sponsors the pain control organization Partners Against Pain.

The company's OxyContin has generated much controversy. The opiate-based drug has been criticized as too powerful and addictive and has a reputation of illegal use. The negative publicity has been amplified by such celebrities as singer and actress Courtney Love, who admitted overdosing on the drug, and talk radio host Rush Limbaugh, who spent time in rehab battling a reported OxyContin addiction. Purdue has taken steps to curb abuse of the painkiller, implementing a risk management program.

What Purdue could not curb was competition. After Teva Pharmaceutical won approval for its generic OxyContin, Purdue knew its sales of its billion-dollar best-selling drug would plummet. To reduce expenses, the company cut some 1,000 staffers and announced plans to close a research facility in New York.

A new pain medication may work to heal Purdue's wounds. It has acquired the rights to sell tramadol from Canadian drug maker Labopharm for $170 million. The drug is already being sold in the US to treat moderate pain, but requires several doses a day. Purdue will be the first to sell a once-a-day version of the drug.

EXECUTIVES

President and CEO: Michael Friedman
EVP and CFO: Edward B. Mahony
EVP and Chief Legal Officer: Howard R. Udell
EVP and Counsel to the Board of Directors:
Stuart D. Baker
EVP, Field Operations and Marketing: James Lang
SVP, Licensing and Business Development:
James Dolan

VP and CIO: Larry Pickett
VP, Human Resources: David Long
VP, Medical Affairs and Worldwide Drug Safety:
  Robert F. Reder
VP, Public Affairs: Robin Hogen
Senior Director, Corporate Communications:
  Merle Spiegel

LOCATIONS

HQ: Purdue Pharma L.P.
  1 Stamford Forum, 201 Tresser Blvd.,
  Stamford, CT 06901
Phone: 203-588-8000   **Fax:** 203-588-8850
Web: www.purduepharma.com

Purdue Pharma has facilities in Connecticut, New Jersey,
North Carolina, and Rhode Island.

PRODUCTS/OPERATIONS

Selected Products

Over-the-counter
  Betadine (antibiotic)
  Colace (laxative)
  Peri-Colace (stool softener)
  Gentlax (laxative)
  Senokot (laxative)
  Senokot-S (laxative)
  Slow-Mag (mineral supplement)
Prescription
  MS Contin (pain management)
  MSIR (pain management)
  OxyContin (pain management)
  OxyFast (pain management)
  OxyIR (pain management)
  Palladone (pain management)
  Spectracef (anti-infective)
  Uniphyl (asthma and other respiratory ailments)

COMPETITORS

Abbott GmbH	Merck
Bayer	Novartis
Bristol-Myers Squibb	Pfizer
Elan	Sanofi-Aventis
Endo Pharmaceuticals	Teva Pharmaceuticals
Johnson & Johnson	

HISTORICAL FINANCIALS

Company Type: Private

Income Statement

FYE: December 31

	REVENUE ($ mil.)	NET INCOME ($ mil.)	NET PROFIT MARGIN	EMPLOYEES
12/03	1,700	—	—	4,700
12/02	1,551	—	—	5,000
12/01	1,500	—	—	3,000
12/00	1,200	—	—	3,000
12/99	812	—	—	—
12/98	603	—	—	—
Annual Growth	23.0%			16.1%

Revenue History

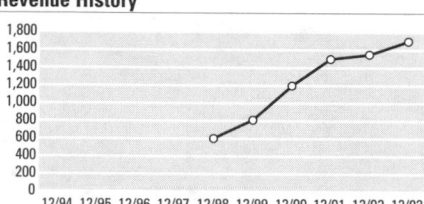

Purity Wholesale Grocers

Purity Wholesale Grocers (PWG) gets the goods to grocers. The company takes advantage of the discounts granted to large wholesalers and retailers (and of the promotional pricing offered in certain regions) by purchasing items and selling them to retailers not privy to those discounts. PWG moves groceries, health and beauty care items, pharmaceutical products, dairy foods, and dry goods to US grocery chains, drugstores, and convenience stores. PWG's marketing network is made up of about a dozen independently operated food distributors, marketers, and transportation firms in the US and Puerto Rico. The company is owned by Jeff Levitetz, who founded PWG in 1982.

EXECUTIVES

Chairman: Jeff Levitetz
President and CEO: Salvatore (Sal) Ricciardi
CFO: Alan Rutner
SVP, Operations: John Tarr
Director, Human Resources: Karen McGrath
Controller: Tom Jankus

LOCATIONS

HQ: Purity Wholesale Grocers, Inc.
  5400 Broken Sound Blvd. NW, Ste. 100,
  Boca Raton, FL 33487
Phone: 561-994-9360   **Fax:** 561-241-4628
Web: www.pwg-inc.com

COMPETITORS

Dot Foods	Spartan Stores
Eby-Brown	SUPERVALU
Nash Finch	SYSCO

HISTORICAL FINANCIALS

Company Type: Private

Income Statement

FYE: June 30

	REVENUE ($ mil.)	NET INCOME ($ mil.)	NET PROFIT MARGIN	EMPLOYEES
6/04	1,700	—	—	425
6/03	1,750	—	—	450
6/02	1,600	—	—	490
6/01	1,450	—	—	440
6/00	1,300	—	—	650
6/99	1,500	—	—	650
6/98	1,200	—	—	600
6/97	1,000	—	—	400
6/96	700	—	—	300
6/95	650	—	—	275
Annual Growth	11.3%	—	—	5.0%

Quad/Graphics

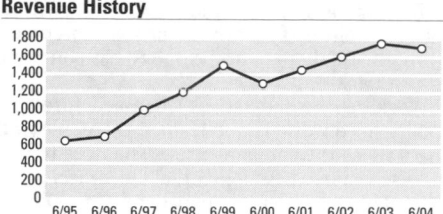

Revenue History

Your mailbox may be filled with Quad/Graphics' handiwork. One of the largest privately held printers in the US, the company prints catalogs, magazines, books, direct mail, and other items. It offers a full range of services, including design, photography, desktop production, printing, binding, wrapping, and distribution. At its printing facilities, five of which are in Wisconsin, the company prints catalogs for the likes of Bloomingdale's and Victoria's Secret, as well as periodicals such as *People, Newsweek,* and *Sports Illustrated.* Company employees and relatives of the founding Quadracci family own Quad/Graphics. The company sold its package delivery business Parcel Direct to FedEx in 2004 for $120 million.

Quad is one of the most employee- and community-oriented companies in the industry. The firm has been recognized for its fun work atmosphere, and it provides on-site day care centers, health clubs, and medical clinics. In addition, it sponsors sports leagues (softball, bowling), awards college scholarships to employees' children, and provides interest-free auto loans. Quad/Graphic's Windhover Fund manages the philanthropic distribution of 5% of the company's pretax profit for social, cultural, and educational projects.

HISTORY

Ink runs in Harry V. Quadracci's family. His father, Harry R., founded a printing business — Standard Printing — in Racine, Wisconsin, in 1930, when he was 16. Four years later Quadracci sold out to William A. Krueger. Though he worked to build Krueger into a major regional printer, the elder Quadracci had little equity in the company.

In the 1960s son Harry V. joined Krueger as a company lawyer. Within a few years he had worked his way up to plant manager. Krueger was a union shop, and in those days unions dictated the work rules and often salary levels. In 1970 there was a three-and-a-half-month strike. At odds with new management and reportedly dissatisfied with the way Krueger caved in to union demands and the adversarial relationship between company and union, the younger Quadracci left.

After 18 months of unemployment, in 1971 Quadracci formed a limited partnership with 12 others to get a loan to buy a press, which was installed in a building in Pewaukee, Wisconsin. The next year his father joined the company as chairman. Within two years the partners had recouped their initial investment, but the business' future remained in question until about

1976. One of its most innovative moves was to make its delivery fleet drivers into entrepreneurs by requiring them to find cargo to haul on their return trips.

Working on a shoestring, Quadracci hired inexperienced workers and trained them, moving them up as the company grew. The need to improvise fostered a flexibility that Quadracci institutionalized by keeping management layers flat and remaining accessible to his employees. Beginning in 1974, Quadracci rewarded his workers with equity in the company.

In the 1980s Quad/Graphics' commitment to technology enabled it to offer better service than many of its competitors. It was also immune to the merger-and-acquisition fever of the time. Free of acquisition debt, the company had excellent credit and was able to finance equipment upgrades with bank loans. Quad expanded by opening a plant in Saratoga Springs, New York (1985), and buying a plant in Thomaston, Georgia (1989).

But there were missteps, such as its 1985 attempt to break into the newspaper coupon insert business dominated by Treasure Chest Advertising. Quad/Graphics sold that operation three years later. The company could not avoid the national economic downturn that began about that time, which forced it to lay off employees in the late 1980s and early 1990s and prompted it to reduce weekend overtime pay (from double time to time-and-a-half). The firm was also hit when a major customer consolidated its printing outside the Midwest. In response, Quad/Graphics increased its capacity in other regions of the US during the 1990s.

In 1996 the company bought 40% of Argentine printer Anselmo L. Morvillo. Benefiting from the UPS strike and changes in the postal regulations, in 1997 Quad/Graphics expanded its shipping services with Parcel Direct, targeting parcels for large shippers such as catalog merchants, in cooperation with the US Postal Service. Also that year it created a joint venture color printing firm with Brazil's Folha Group.

In 1998 Quad/Graphics expanded its international reach, agreeing to a joint venture in Poland. The next year the company was awarded the pre-press business of Condé Nast magazines. In 2000 it launched a business-to-business portal called Smart Tools.

The company was shocked in 2002 when Quadracci died in an accidental drowning at age 66. Quadracci's brother, Tom, was then appointed president. In 2004, Tom Quadracci assumed the role of chairman and CEO, while Harry Quadracci's son, Joel, took over as president.

EXECUTIVES

Chairman and CEO: Thomas A. (Tom) Quadracci
President and COO: J. Joel Quadracci
SVP Finance and CFO: John C. Fowler
SVP Manufacturing: Thomas J. (Tom) Frankowski
SVP Sales and Administration: David Blais
VP and Controller: Linda Larson
VP Customer Service: Ron Nash
VP East Coast Sales: Bob Wachtendonk
VP Employee Services: Emmy M. LaBode
VP Information Systems: Steve Jaeger
VP Midwest Sales: Timothy Ohnmacht
VP West Coast Sales: Renee Lekan
President, QuadCreative Group and Publisher, Milwaukee Magazine: Betty Ewens Quadracci
Director Corporate Purchasing: Arthur W. (Art) Noe
Director Postal Affairs: Joe Schick

Manager Business Development: Chuck DuPont
Manager Credit: Pat Rydzik
Manager Corporate Purchasing: Mike Kaczmarek
Manager Marketing: Claire Ho
General Counsel: Andy Schiesl

LOCATIONS

HQ: Quad/Graphics, Inc.
N63 W23075 State Hwy. 74, Sussex, WI 53089
Phone: 414-566-6000   **Fax:** 414-566-4650
Web: www.qg.com

Quad/Graphics has production plants in Georgia, New York, West Virginia, and Wisconsin. It also operates joint ventures in Argentina, Brazil, and Poland.

PRODUCTS/OPERATIONS

Selected Services

Binding and finishing
Color correction
Design
Desktop production
Direct mailing
Imaging and photography
Ink jetting
Integrated circulation
Mailing and distribution
Mailing list management
Printing
Scanning

COMPETITORS

Arandell
Banta
Brown Printing
Consolidated Graphics
Dai Nippon Printing
Merrill
Perry Judd's
Quebecor World
R.R. Donnelley
Spencer Press
St Ives US Division
Toppan Printing

HISTORICAL FINANCIALS

Company Type: Private

Income Statement

	REVENUE ($ mil.)	NET INCOME ($ mil.)	NET PROFIT MARGIN	EMPLOYEES
12/03	2,000	—	—	12,000
12/02	1,800	—	—	11,000
12/01	1,700	—	—	10,500
12/00	1,800	—	—	14,000
12/99	1,500	—	—	13,000
12/98	1,400	—	—	11,000
12/97	1,200	—	—	11,000
12/96	1,042	—	—	9,500
12/95	1,002	—	—	8,444
12/94	801	—	—	7,500
Annual Growth	10.7%	—	—	5.4%

FYE: December 31

Revenue History

Qualitor

Qualitor keeps the big guys moving. The company makes automotive and heavy-duty truck parts, including brake components, wiper blades, and engine-control devices. Qualitor consists mainly of Anstro and International Brake Industries (brake manufacturers in the US), BLD (engine controls in the Netherlands), Sloan (truck and trailers components in the US), and Pylon (aftermarket wiper blades and replacement pieces in the US). The company's switches, sensors, brakes, repair kits, water pumps, and wipers are sold to OEM parts manufacturers, rebuilders, retailers, mass merchants, and auto dealers worldwide. Qualitor is majority-owned by Thayer Capital Partners.

EXECUTIVES

Chairman: Ralph E. Reins
President and CEO: Kevin Baird
CFO: Michael Borellis
President, BLD Products: Scott Bye
President, Hydraulic Brake Group: Robert Bosco
President, Pylon: Chuck Fesler

LOCATIONS

HQ: Qualitor, Inc.
24800 Denso Dr., Ste. 255, Southfield, MI 48034
Phone: 248-204-8600   **Fax:** 248-204-8619
Web: www.qualitorinc.com

HISTORICAL FINANCIALS

Company Type: Private

Income Statement

	ESTIMATED REVENUE ($ mil.)	NET INCOME ($ mil.)	NET PROFIT MARGIN	EMPLOYEES
12/04*	180	—	—	800
12/02	200	—	—	1,000
Annual Growth	(10.0%)	—	—	(20.0%)

FYE: December 31

*Irregular reporting interval

Revenue History

Quality Dining

Be it casual dining or fast food, you can find Quality Dining in seven states. A franchisee of both Burger King and Brinker International, the company operates more than 120 hamburger joints and nearly 40 Chili's Grill & Bar locations in a half dozen states. It also owns and operates about 10 restaurants under its own casual dining concepts: Grady's American Grill, Papa Vino's Italian Kitchen, Porterhouse Steaks & Seafood, and Spageddies Italian Kitchen. CEO Daniel Fitzpatrick owns more than 70% of the company after taking it private.

With its fast-food operations accounting for more than half the company's revenue, Quality Dining's top line has suffered from the price wars that have been waged between Burger King and McDonald's, as well as from the shift in consumer eater habits away from greasy burgers and fries and toward healthier alternatives. After acquiring more than 40 Burger King locations in 2001, the company has not added many new units to its portfolio.

Meanwhile, Quality Dining has been expanding its Chili's operations, opening three new locations per year. Its Grady's restaurants, however, have not fared as well, and the company has said it may not continue the concept.

Porterhouse is the newest concept featuring steak and seafood in an upscale atmosphere.

EXECUTIVES

Chairman, President, and CEO: Daniel B. Fitzpatrick, age 47, $470,570 pay
EVP, General Counsel, and Secretary: John C. Firth, age 47, $334,851 pay
SVP, Chief Development Officer, and Director: James K. Fitzpatrick, age 49, $266,476 pay
SVP, Full Service Dining: Lindley E. Burns, age 50
SVP, Burger King Division: Gerald O. Fitzpatrick, age 44, $252,282 pay
VP and CIO: Stephen G. Marquette
VP, Finance: Christopher L. Collier, age 43
VP, Marketing: Thomas D. Hanson
VP and Controller: Jeanne M. Yoder, age 38
VP, Burger King Division: William J. Lee
VP, Chili's Grill & Bar Division: Joseph E. Olin
Human Resources: Chad A. Hartzell
Auditors: PricewaterhouseCoopers LLP

LOCATIONS

HQ: Quality Dining, Inc.
4220 Edison Lakes Pkwy., Mishawaka, IN 46545
Phone: 574-271-4600   **Fax:** 574-271-4612
Web: www.qdi.com

2004 Locations

	No.
Michigan	98
Indiana	51
Pennsylvania	10
New Jersey	7
Ohio	6
Delaware	2
Georgia	1
Tennessee	1
Total	**176**

PRODUCTS/OPERATIONS

2004 Sales

	$ mil.	% of total
Burger King	122.2	53
Chili's Grill & Bar	87.7	38
Italian Dining Concepts	16.4	7
Grady's American Grill (includes Porterhouse)	5.8	2
Total	**232.1**	**100**

2004 Locations

	No.
Burger King	124
Chili's Grill & Bar	39
Italian Dining Division	9
Grady's American Grill	3
Porterhouse Steaks and Seafood	1
Total	**176**

COMPETITORS

AFC Enterprises
Applebee's
Avado Brands
B.T. Woodlipp
Carlson Restaurants
Cheesecake Factory
Chick-fil-A
CKE Restaurants
Dairy Queen
Darden
Frisch's
Houlihan's
J. Alexander's
Jack in the Box
Lone Star Steakhouse
McDonald's
Meritage Hospitality
Metromedia Restaurant Group
O'Charley's
Outback Steakhouse
RARE Hospitality
Ruby Tuesday
Subway
Triarc
Wendy's
YUM!

HISTORICAL FINANCIALS

Company Type: Private

Income Statement
FYE: Last Sunday in October

	REVENUE ($ mil.)	NET INCOME ($ mil.)	NET PROFIT MARGIN	EMPLOYEES
10/04	232	2	0.9%	7,176
10/03	227	1	0.4%	7,430
10/02	259	5	2.0%	8,300
10/01	227	(16)	—	10,000
10/00	228	(10)	—	7,000
10/99	231	(2)	—	9,000
10/98	232	0	0.0%	8,400
10/97	302	(197)	—	8,200
10/96	238	3	1.1%	10,000
10/95	105	6	5.6%	8,500
Annual Growth	**9.2%**	**(10.4%)**	**—**	**(1.9%)**

2004 Year-End Financials

Debt ratio: 295.8%
Return on equity: 8.5%
Cash ($ mil.): 2
Current ratio: 0.28
Long-term debt ($ mil.): 70

Net Income History

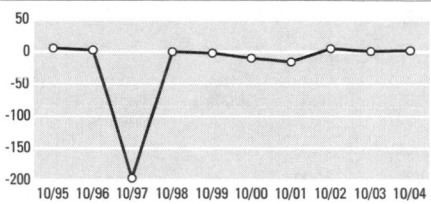

QuikTrip

QuikTrip provides a quick fix for people on the go. QuikTrip (QT) owns and operates more than 450 gasoline and convenience stores primarily in the Midwest. QT stores, which average 4,500 to 5,000 sq. ft., feature the company's own brand of gas, as well as brand-name beverages, candy, and tobacco, and QT's own Quik 'n Tasty and HOTZI lines of sandwiches. QuikTrip travel centers offer CAT scales, food, fuel, showers, and other services for truckers. The company's FleetMaster program offers commercial trucking companies detailed reports showing drivers' product purchases, amounts spent, and odometer readings. QuikTrip was co-founded in 1958 by chairman Chester Cadieux and partners. His son Chet runs the company.

QuikTrip is remodeling stores and expanding its hot and cold beverage selection. The icy "Koolee," introduced in 1963, has been phased out and replaced by a frozen carbonated beverage called a Freezoni, available in seven flavors.

The company is also testing a high-volume (capable of handling 120 cars per hour) car wash at a location in Tulsa.

EXECUTIVES

Chairman: Chester Cadieux
President and CEO: Chester (Chet) Cadieux III, age 38
SVP and CFO: Terry Carter
VP, Marketing: James (Jim) Denny
Treasurer: Paula Cotten
Director, Human Resources: Kimberly (Kim) Owen
Manager, Corporate Sales: Rodney Loyd
Manager, Public and Government Affairs: Mike Thornbrugh

LOCATIONS

HQ: QuikTrip Corporation
4705 S. 129th East Ave., Tulsa, OK 74134
Phone: 918-615-7700   **Fax:** 918-615-7377
Web: www.quiktrip.com

QuikTrip owns stores in Arizona, Georgia, Illinois, Iowa, Kansas, Missouri, Nebraska, Oklahoma, and Texas.

COMPETITORS

7-Eleven
Casey's General Stores
Chevron
CITGO
Exxon Mobil
E-Z Mart Stores
Krause Gentle
Motiva Enterprises
Racetrac Petroleum

HISTORICAL FINANCIALS

Company Type: Private

Income Statement				FYE: April 30
	REVENUE ($ mil.)	NET INCOME ($ mil.)	NET PROFIT MARGIN	EMPLOYEES
4/04	4,051	—	—	7,000
4/03	2,800	—	—	6,663
4/02	3,050	—	—	6,575
4/01	2,929	—	—	6,045
4/00	2,347	—	—	5,248
4/99	1,804	—	—	4,796
4/98	1,830	—	—	4,635
4/97	1,730	—	—	4,400
4/96	1,423	—	—	4,075
4/95	1,195	—	—	2,501
Annual Growth	14.5%	—	—	12.1%

Revenue History

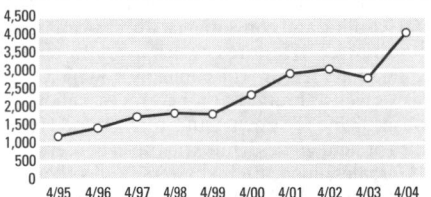

QuinStreet

QuinStreet connects companies with potential customers through the Internet. The online direct marketing company uses proprietary technologies to provide leads to companies. These clients, which have included DeVry and ADT, then use the leads as the targets of direct marketing campaigns. As a sign of its confidence in its quality, QuinStreet has adopted a pay for performance model of pricing where customers are charged based on lead performance.

EXECUTIVES

Chairman, President, and CEO: Doug Valenti
COO: Bronwyn Syiek
VP Client Strategy and Development: Scott Mackley
VP Direct Selling and Retail Network Services: Mihir Shah
VP Finance and Administration: Jeff Stephens
VP, General Counsel, and Manager, QuinStreet LLC: Michael McDonough
VP Media Strategy and Development: Tom Cheli
VP Product Management: Sherwin Faden
VP Product Development: Nina Bhanap
VP Products and Services: John Spottiswood
Editor-in-Chief, QuinStreet Publishing: Katrina Boydon

LOCATIONS

HQ: QuinStreet, Inc.
1051 E. Hillsdale Blvd., Foster City, CA 94404
Phone: 650-578-7700   **Fax:** 650-578-7604
Web: www.quinstreet.com

HISTORICAL FINANCIALS

Company Type: Private

Income Statement				FYE: June 30
	ESTIMATED REVENUE ($ mil.)	NET INCOME ($ mil.)	NET PROFIT MARGIN	EMPLOYEES
6/04	64	—	—	240

Quintiles Transnational

Quintiles Transnational has plenty to CRO about. One of the world's top contract research organizations (CROs), it provides services to help drug and medical device companies develop and sell their products. The firm's Product Development Services unit offers preclinical research and conducts clinical trials. Innovex, the CRO's commercialization unit offers regulatory consulting, as well as sales and marketing consulting, hiring, and training to get a product to buyers. Quintiles' PharmaBio Development unit teams with emerging health care firms to get new products approved and on the market by exchanging its R&D services for royalties. A group led by chairman Dennis Gillings took the firm private in 2003.

The CRO's Verispan joint venture with McKesson provides health care information products. Verispan, formed in 2002, brought McKesson's Kelly/Waldron unit together with Quintiles-owned Scott-Levin, a preeminent pharmaceutical industry market research company, and SMG Marketing Group. By bringing these marketing services firms under one umbrella, Quintiles can stay involved in a product's life span longer.

Quintiles Strategic Research Services, formed in late 2003, conducts research studies to gather drug data that isn't related to regulatory approval. Types of data generated by these studies can include cost effectiveness, population studies, and other such information. The results, for example, a drugmaker can use to persuade doctors and consumers its drug is safer and more effective than a close competitor's.

Quintiles, which operates in 50 countries, has suffered the double-whammy of pharmaceutical industry consolidation, which has trimmed its client list, and industry cost-cutting efforts. More drugmakers are bringing R&D work in-house to keep down expenses. Roche signed a three year clinical management services contract with the company in 2005.

Its PharmaBio Development and Verispan operations are among the company's attempts to continue to grow, even though they're in the risky business of pinning their hopes on drugs that may not make it onto the market. For instance, PharmaBio inked a deal with Eli Lilly to help market antidepressant Cymbalta, which it thinks could bring in a significant portion of the company's future revenues.

The company is selling off its preclinical technologies, pharmaceutical sciences, and packaging and logistics divisions to newly formed company Aptuit in a deal valued at $125 million. Collectively, these divisions' customers include almost all of the top 20 drug companies.

Quintiles ended its nearly 10-year stint as a public company in hopes that once it casts off the burden of meeting and beating Wall Street expectations, the CRO will have the freedom to grow its business as it chooses. The move brought founder Gillings back into the driver's seat; riding shotgun is financial backer BANK ONE's One Equity Partners. The returning CEO envisions Quintiles as an investor in the products it helps develop. However, the company loaded up on debt as part of its leap from NASDAQ.

HISTORY

Quintiles was founded by Dennis Gillings, a British biostatistician who had worked with Hoechst (now part of Sanofi-Aventis) on data analysis in the 1970s. Gillings set up Quintiles (Quantitative Information Technology In The Life and Economic Sciences) in 1982 at the University of North Carolina, where he was then teaching. The company grew as drug companies began outsourcing some of the more irksome tasks of drug development. Quintiles went public in 1994.

Quintiles used the proceeds of the IPO to expand its health economics segment with the purchases of Benefit International (1995) and Lewin Group (1996). These purchases introduced the company to such new clients as governments and HMOs. Quintiles' 1996 purchase of Innovex (unrelated to the computer hardware maker of the same name) made it the world's largest CRO. The buying spree continued in 1997 and 1998. Among the purchases were some intended to strengthen Quintiles' marketing services (Data Analysis Systems Inc., Q.E.D. International, and France-based Serval). The firm also formed new collaborations with such academic research organizations as Johns Hopkins Medicine.

In 1999 Quintiles expanded its marketing arm with the purchase of Pharmaceutical Marketing Services (parent of the leading pharmaceuticals industry research company, Scott-Levin) and jumped headlong into data mining with its purchase of ENVOY — which processed insurance claims. Quintiles found the core business uninspiring and sold it to Healtheon (now Emdeon, formerly WebMD) the next year. But it kept rights to ENVOY's stream of treatment, outcome, and insurance data, gleaned from health care providers, hospitals, payers, and pharmacies — a treasure house of information useful to salespeople and health providers.

The company continued in 2000 to add offices in Europe, Asia, and Latin America. The company also opened additional offices in the US and Europe to help Japanese pharmaceutical companies market their products in those regions. Late in the year, Quintiles bought the clinical development unit of Pharmacia.

In 2001 Quintiles became embroiled in a legal dispute with WebMD involving the availability of data associated with ENVOY; the company challenged WebMD's efforts to withhold such data. The two companies settled the squabble later that year and agreed to sever all ties. Also in 2001 Quintiles streamlined operations and cut about 5% of its workforce.

The future of the CRO came into question at the end of 2002. Gillings presented the company with a buyout offer; he planned to take the company private so he could pursue a new growth strategy Wall Street would surely find risky. The board rejected that offer in October 2002, but it opened up an auction. Some leading equity firms reportedly made offers, but Gillings — with backing from Blackstone Group and BANK ONE's One Equity Partners — placed another offer for Quintiles and won the prize in April 2003. Some five months later, Quintiles went private.

EXECUTIVES

Chairman and CEO: Dennis B. Gillings, age 60, $1,650,000 pay
EVP, Global Human Resources: Mike Mortimer, age 44
EVP and CFO: John Ratliff, age 45, $344,697 pay (partial-year salary)
EVP, General Counsel, and Chief Administrative Officer: John S. Russell, age 50, $550,000 pay
EVP, Corporate Development: Ronald J. (Ron) Wooten, age 44, $1,000,000 pay
EVP, Strategic Customer Relationships: Derek Winstanly
SVP and Head of Kansas City Facilities: Mike Baltezor
SVP, Strategic Planning and Investor Relations: Greg Connors
SVP, PharmaBio Development: Tom Perkins
SVP, Global Business Development: Tracy K. Tsuetaki, age 41
Global VP, e-Clinical Business: Graham Bunn
VP, Medical and Scientific Services: David Frakes
VP, Corporate Communications: Pat Grebe
VP, Biostatistical Services: Stephen C. Smeach
VP, Sales, Clinical Development Services, Americas: Paul Spreen
VP, Global Central Laboratory: Thomas Wollman
President, Clinical Development Services Americas: G. Stephen (Steve) DeCherney, age 52
President, Quintiles Europe: Hywel Evans
President and CEO, Quintiles Japan: Kiyotaka Fujii, age 48
President and CEO, AAA Region: Oppel Greeff, age 56, $550,000 pay (prior to promotion)
President, Innovex North America: Tony Yost
Chief Medical and Scientific Officer: Oren Cohen
Auditors: PricewaterhouseCoopers LLP

LOCATIONS

HQ: Quintiles Transnational Corp.
4709 Creekstone Dr., Ste. 200, Durham, NC 27703
Phone: 919-998-2000   **Fax:** 919-998-9113
Web: www.quintiles.com

Quintiles Transnational operates in 50 countries.

PRODUCTS/OPERATIONS

Selected Subsidiaries

Action International Marketing Services Limited (UK)
Benefit Holding, Inc.
Clin Data International (PTY) Limited (South Africa)
G.D.R.U. Limited (UK)
Innovex, L.P.
Laboratorie Novex Pharma Sarl (France)
The Lewin Group, Inc.
Medical Informatics KK (Japan)
Minerva Ireland Limited
PharmaBio Development, Inc.
Quintiles (Israel) Ltd.
Quintiles Hong Kong Limited
Quintiles Laboratories Limited
Source Informatics European Finance, Inc.
Spectral Laboratories Limited (India)
Transforce, S.A. de C.V. (Mexico)
Verispan, L.L.C.

COMPETITORS

Battelle Memorial	Nelson Communications
Covance	Ogilvy Healthworld
IMS Health	PAREXEL
Kendle	Pharmaceutical Product
Life Sciences Research	Development
NDCHealth	

HISTORICAL FINANCIALS

Company Type: Private

Income Statement
FYE: December 31

	REVENUE ($ mil.)	NET INCOME ($ mil.)	NET PROFIT MARGIN	EMPLOYEES
12/04	2,146	1	0.0%	16,986
12/03	2,046	30	1.5%	15,991
12/02	1,992	127	6.4%	15,548
12/01	1,620	(34)	—	17,224
12/00	1,660	419	25.2%	18,219
12/99	1,607	109	6.8%	20,453
12/98	1,188	84	7.0%	15,520
12/97	815	55	6.8%	10,900
12/96	538	4	0.8%	7,375
12/95	156	11	7.2%	2,000
Annual Growth	**33.8%**	**(23.6%)**	**—**	**26.8%**

2004 Year-End Financials

Debt ratio: 133.4%   Current ratio: 1.53
Return on equity: 0.2%   Long-term debt ($ mil.): 758
Cash ($ mil.): 536

Net Income History

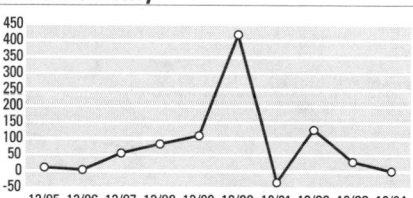

12/95	12/96	12/97	12/98	12/99	12/00	12/01	12/02	12/03	12/04

Quiznos

Quiznos is the toast of the sandwich world. The Quiznos Master operates the #2 sub sandwich chain (behind Subway), with about 3,500 quick-service Quiznos Sub restaurants that are popular for their made-to-order, oven-toasted subs. Patrons can choose from a variety of signature subs, such as the Honey Bourbon Chicken, BBQ Chipotle Carved Turkey, or Honey Bacon Club. Quiznos also serves salads, soups, and dessert items. The company operates in more than 20 countries, and nearly all of the company's restaurants are owned by franchisees. Quiznos started getting toasty in 1981 as a single Denver area restaurant. CEO Rick Schaden and his family control the company.

In 2004, a Denver judge approved the settlement of a multimillion class action lawsuit against Quiznos, in which the company was charged with breach of fiduciary responsibilities. The settlement called for the company to pay an additional amount per share on a tender offer from late 2000. (The per-share figure is about $7.35.) The court decision cost the sandwich chain about $5.25 million.

EXECUTIVES

Chairman, President, and CEO: Richard E. (Rick) Schaden
CFO, Treasurer, and Assistant Secretary: John L. Gallivan, age 55
EVP: Brooksy Smith
EVP Development: Dominick Voso
EVP Franchise Support: John Fitchett
EVP Operations: Steven B. Shaffer, age 51

SVP, International Development: Lee Vala
VP, Concept Development: Robert Forrester
VP, Public Relations: Stacie Lange
VP and General Counsel: Patrick E. Meyers
VP and Secretary: Richard F. (Dick) Schaden, age 64
Lead Co-Ordinator (HR): Christine Fisher
Auditors: Ehrhardt Keefe Steiner & Hottman PC

LOCATIONS

HQ: The Quiznos Master LLC
1475 Lawrence St., Ste. 400, Denver, CO 80202
Phone: 720-359-3300   **Fax:** 720-359-3399
Web: www.quiznos.com

Selected International Locations

Aruba	Japan
Australia	Jordan
Bahamas	Kuwait
Bahrain	Lebanon
Belize	Martinique
Bonaire	Mexico
Canada	Micronesia
Carpela	Nicaragua
Cayman Islands	Oman
Costa Rica	Panama
Curacao	Peru
Dominican Republic	Qatar
Egypt	Saudi Arabia
El Salvador	South Korea
Guadalupe	Syria
Guam	Turkey
Guatemala	UK
Honduras	United Arab Emerites
Iceland	Venezuela

COMPETITORS

Atlanta Bread
Blimpie
Burger King
Chick-fil-A
Chipotle
CKE Restaurants
Consolidated Restaurant Operations
Cousins Subs
Dairy Queen
Dunkin
Freebirds
Gosh Enterprises
Jack in the Box
Jersey Mike's
Jimmy John's
McDonald's
Mr. Goodcents
New World Restaurants
New York New York Franchising
Panera Bread
Penn Station
Port of Subs
Potbelly
Qdoba
Restaurant Developers
Roly Poly
Schlotzsky's
Sonic
Subway
Triarc
Wall Street Deli
Wendy's
YUM!

HISTORICAL FINANCIALS

Company Type: Private

Income Statement

FYE: September 30

	REVENUE ($ mil.)	NET INCOME ($ mil.)	NET PROFIT MARGIN	EMPLOYEES
9/04	130	—	—	450
9/03	100	—	—	400
9/02	75	—	—	400
9/01	50	—	—	400
9/00	41	—	—	421
9/99*	19	—	—	358
12/98	12	—	—	270
12/97	11	—	—	48
12/96	7	—	—	59
12/95	6	—	—	21
Annual Growth	40.2%	—	—	40.6%

*Fiscal year change

Revenue History

140	
120	
100	
80	
60	
40	
20	
0	
	12/95 12/96 12/97 12/98 9/99 9/00 9/01 9/02 9/03 9/04

RaceTrac Petroleum

RaceTrac Petroleum hopes it is a popular pit stop for gasoline and snacks in the Southeast. The company operates more than 525 company-owned and franchised gas stations and convenience stores in about a dozen states under the RaceTrac and RaceWay names. (RaceWay stores are franchised.) The chain plans to grow by adding between 35 and 45 new locations annually. Carl Bolch founded RaceTrac in Missouri in 1934. His son, chairman and CEO Carl Bolch Jr., moved the company into high-volume gas stations with long, self-service islands that can serve many vehicles at once. RaceTrac's convenience stores also sell fresh deli food, rent videos, and offer some fast-food fare. The Bolch family owns the company.

EXECUTIVES

Chairman and CEO: Carl E. Bolch Jr.
President: Max Lenker
CFO: Robert J. Dumbacher
SVP, Operations: Ben Tison
VP, Human Resources: Allison Moran

LOCATIONS

HQ: RaceTrac Petroleum, Inc.
300 Technology Ct., Smyrna, GA 30082
Phone: 770-431-7600   **Fax:** 770-431-7612
Web: www.racetrac.com

RaceTrac Petroleum operates in Alabama, Florida, Georgia, Kentucky, Louisiana, Mississippi, North Carolina, South Carolina, Tennessee, Texas, and Virginia.

COMPETITORS

7-Eleven	Gate Petroleum
Chevron	Motiva Enterprises
Cumberland Farms	The Pantry
Exxon Mobil	Pilot
E-Z Mart Stores	QuikTrip

HISTORICAL FINANCIALS

Company Type: Private

Income Statement

FYE: December 31

	REVENUE ($ mil.)	NET INCOME ($ mil.)	NET PROFIT MARGIN	EMPLOYEES
12/03	3,200	—	—	4,700
12/02	3,000	—	—	3,820
12/01	2,942	—	—	3,850
12/00	2,811	—	—	4,932
12/99	1,846	—	—	3,700
12/98	1,500	—	—	3,800
12/97	1,005	—	—	3,612
12/96	1,340	—	—	3,000
12/95	1,056	—	—	2,700
12/94	909	—	—	2,300
Annual Growth	15.0%	—	—	8.3%

Revenue History

3,500	
3,000	
2,500	
2,000	
1,500	
1,000	
500	
0	
	12/94 12/95 12/96 12/97 12/98 12/99 12/00 12/01 12/02 12/03

Radnor Holdings

The businesses of Radnor Holdings — food packaging and specialty chemicals — are related, although they don't exactly mix. A leading producer of foam cups and containers, Radnor's WinCup unit also makes polystyrene and polypropylene bowls, containers, cups, cutlery, plates, and stemware — the stuff in which fast food is carried and consumed. Radnor's StyroChem is a leading maker of cup-grade expandable polystyrenes (EPS) and related products, which are sold to companies in the food service, insulation, and protective packaging industries, including WinCup. President and CEO Michael Kennedy owns an 80% stake in Radnor Holdings.

EXECUTIVES

President, CEO, and Director: Michael T. Kennedy, age 50, $4,750,000 pay
EVP, Treasurer, and Director: R. Radcliffe Hastings, age 54, $571,154 pay
CFO: Paul D. Ridder, age 33

SVP, Human Resources and Administration: John P. McKelvey, age 64
SVP and Corporate Counsel: Caroline J. Williamson, age 37, $450,000 pay
SVP, Operations: Donald D. Walker, age 63, $337,500 pay
SVP, Sales and Marketing: Richard C. (Rich) Hunsinger, age 56, $337,500 pay
Head of Strategic Supply Chain Management: Michael V. Valenza, age 45, $337,500 pay (prior to promotion)
Controller: Michael P. Feehan
Auditors: KPMG LLP

LOCATIONS

HQ: Radnor Holdings Corporation
Radnor Financial Center, 150 Radnor Chester Rd., Ste. 300, Radnor, PA 19087
Phone: 610-995-2525   **Fax:** 610-995-2697
Web: www.radnorholdings.com

2004 Sales

	$ mil.	% of total
North America		
US	285.3	64
Canada	29.7	7
Europe	127.2	29
Total	442.2	100

PRODUCTS/OPERATIONS

2004 Sales

	$ mil.	% of total
Packaging	245.2	55
Specialty chemicals	197.0	45
Total	442.2	100

COMPETITORS

Alcoa	Huntsman Polymers
BASF Corporation	NOVA Chemicals
Berry Plastics	Pactiv
Dart Container	Solo Cup

HISTORICAL FINANCIALS

Company Type: Private

Income Statement

FYE: Last Friday of December

	REVENUE ($ mil.)	NET INCOME ($ mil.)	NET PROFIT MARGIN	EMPLOYEES
12/04	442	(12)	—	1,940
12/03	342	(10)	—	1,851
12/02	323	5	1.4%	1,692
12/01	332	2	0.5%	1,710
12/00	363	—	—	1,935
Annual Growth	5.1%	—	—	0.1%

2004 Year-End Financials

Debt ratio: —
Return on equity: —
Cash ($ mil.): 3
Current ratio: 1.35
Long-term debt ($ mil.): 299

Net Income History

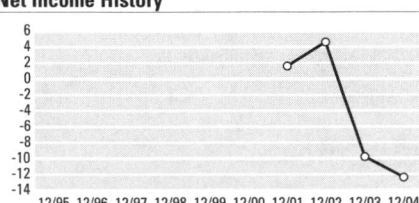

6	
4	
2	
0	
-2	
-4	
-6	
-8	
-10	
-12	
-14	
	12/95 12/96 12/97 12/98 12/99 12/00 12/01 12/02 12/03 12/04

Rand McNally

Rand McNally lets you know where you stand. The largest commercial mapmaker in the world, the company is famous for its flagship Rand McNally Road Atlas — the best-selling product in the history of mapmaking. In addition, the company produces travel-related software (TripMaker, StreetFinder) and educational products for classrooms (globes, atlases). It also operates a Web site and makes mileage and routing software for the transportation industry. Its Rand McNally Canada unit makes maps for the Canadian market. The company sells its products online and through some 50,000 retail outlets across the US, including a handful of Rand McNally stores. Rand McNally is majority-owned by Leonard Green & Partners.

Although it created a Web site in 1996, the company didn't really begin focusing on the Internet until 1999, years later than online rivals such as MapQuest.com. Rand McNally relaunched its Web site and increased its Web and software product offerings in hopes of catching up with its online competitors.

In early 2003 Rand McNally filed for Chapter 11 bankruptcy protection. The company exited bankruptcy within two months, with buyout firm Leonard Green & Partners as its new majority owner with a 60% stake. It has closed some retail stores as part of a new retail strategy.

HISTORY

Rand McNally was founded by William Rand and Andrew McNally in 1856. In 1864 the pair bought the job-printing department of the *Chicago Tribune,* and they expanded into the printing of railroad tickets and schedules. They published their first book, a Chicago business directory, in 1870.

In 1872 the company printed its first map for the *Railway Guide.* Rand McNally later expanded into publishing paperback novels (popular among train travelers), and by 1891 annual sales topped $1 million.

During the 1890s McNally bought Rand's share of the business, and the company branched into printing school textbooks. Rand McNally's first photo auto guide was issued in 1907, and the company introduced its first complete US road atlas in 1924.

When Hitler invaded Poland in 1939, Rand McNally's New York stock of European maps sold out in one day. WWII necessitated the revision of a number of maps — a challenge that the company continued to face throughout the 20th century.

Although the company had abandoned adult fiction and nonfiction in 1914, it reentered the field in 1948 when a company official persuaded explorer Thor Heyerdahl to write a book for the company about his adventures. First published in 1950, Heyerdahl's *Kon-Tiki* sold more than a million copies in its first six years.

Rand McNally produced its first four-color road atlas in 1960, and during the 1970s it began publishing travel guides for Mobil Oil. The next decade the company published several new road atlases to fill the void created when gas stations discontinued their practice of giving away free road maps. Rand McNally sold its textbook publishing business to Houghton Mifflin in 1980, and five years later it began computerizing its cartography operation.

In 1993 the company acquired Allmaps Canada Limited (now Rand McNally Canada). It introduced *TripMaker,* a CD-ROM vacation-planning program, the next year. Also in 1994 Rand McNally won a contract to create maps for a *Reader's Digest* atlas. The company debuted its StreetFinder street-level software in 1995 and created its Cartographic and Information Services division in 1996. It also established a Web site that year.

The next year, as part of a plan to focus on mapmaking and providing geographic information, Rand McNally sold a number of its subsidiaries (Book Services Group, DocuSystems Group). AEA Investors bought a controlling interest in the company later in 1997, bringing an end to more than 140 years of McNally family control (though it did retain a minority stake). While Rand McNally was still profitable, the sale to AEA underscored the challenges facing the company: Growth in earnings had slowed, and technological changes (Internet maps and software) had altered the mapmaking industry.

Rand McNally expanded in 1999 with acquisitions of mapmakers Thomas Bros. Maps and King of the Road Map Service. Later that year Henry Feinberg resigned as chairman and CEO. Richard Davis was appointed CEO, and John Macomber became chairman.

In 2000 the company relaunched its Web site with additional trip planning capabilities. Also that year it became the primary North American distributor of *National Geographic* maps and COO Norman Wells replaced Davis as CEO.

In 2001 Michael Hehir was named CEO, Wells replaced Macomber as chairman, and Macomber remained as a director on the board. In 2003 Hehir left the company and Allstate executive Robert Apatoff was named CEO. Wells was replaced by Peter Nolan, a managing partner at Leonard Green & Partners.

EXECUTIVES

President and CEO: Robert S. (Rob) Apatoff, age 46
SVP and CFO: Norman Smagley, age 42
SVP and CTO: Ken Levin
SVP and Chief Marketing Officer: Betsy Owens
SVP Geographic Information Services: Joel Minster
SVP Supply Chain Management: Tom Anderson
VP Consumer Sales and Distribution:
   Dennis FitzPatrick
VP Consumer Sales: Jeff Ventura
VP Local Travel Marketing: Gary Lancina
VP National Travel Marketing: Kendra Ensor
VP New Products and Strategy: Alan Yefsky
Director Educational Publishing: Pat Riley
Director Retail and Internet: David Rickabaugh
Editorial Director: Laurie Borman
Director Sales, Transportation Division:
   Bernie Hockswender
Media Relations: Paul Elsberg

LOCATIONS

HQ: Rand McNally & Company
   8255 N. Central Park Ave., Skokie, IL 60076
Phone: 847-329-8100   **Fax:** 847-329-6361
Web: www.randmcnally.com

Rand McNally operates in the US and Canada. It has retail stores in California, Massachusetts, and Texas.

PRODUCTS/OPERATIONS

Selected Products
Commercial Trucking Products
   IntelliRoute
   MileMaker
   Motor Carriers' Road Atlas
Consumer Products
   Children's Products
   Reference Maps and Books
   Road Atlases
      Motor Carriers' Road Atlases
      The Rand McNally Road Atlas Line
   Road and Street Maps
   Software
      StreetFinder
   Street Guides (street-level detail)
   Thomas Guides (spiral-bound format)
Educational Products
Online Business Locator
Wireless Products
   Mobile Travel Tools
   Rand McNally Traffic

COMPETITORS

American Automobile Association (AAA)
Analytical Surveys
Avalon Travel Publishing
DeLorme
ESRI
Expedia
Globe Pequot
Lonely Planet
MapInfo
MapQuest.com
Michelin
National Geographic
Piersen Graphics
R. L. Polk
TravRoute
Vindigo
Yahoo!

HISTORICAL FINANCIALS
Company Type: Private

Income Statement
FYE: December 31

	REVENUE ($ mil.)	NET INCOME ($ mil.)	NET PROFIT MARGIN	EMPLOYEES
12/00	200	—	—	1,000
12/99	179	—	—	920
12/98	175	—	—	1,000
12/97	175	—	—	1,000
12/96	163	—	—	1,000
12/95	469	—	—	4,650
12/94	438	—	—	4,200
12/93	395	—	—	4,000
12/92	342	—	—	4,000
12/91	307	—	—	4,000
Annual Growth	(4.6%)	—	—	(14.3%)

Revenue History

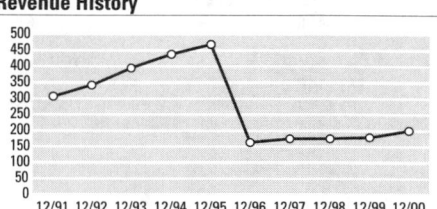

Real Mex Restaurants

This company is a real combinación grande. Real Mex Restaurants (formerly Acapulco Acquisition Corp.) operates about 200 Mexican restaurants in California and 12 other states nationwide. Its operations include restaurants under the El Torito and Acapulco names, as well as Casa Gallardo, GuadalaHarrys, Hola Amigos, Keystone Grill, Las Brisas, and Who-Song & Larry's. Backed by Bruckmann, Rosser, Sherrill & Co. and BancBoston Capital, the company acquired rights to the El Torito name from Prandium in 2000. Real Mex acquired the Chevys line of more than 110 Chevys and Fuzio restaurants in 2005, making Real Mex the largest Mexican restaurant operator in the US.

EXECUTIVES

President and CEO: Fred Wolfe
CFO: Steve Tanner
COO; President, Chevys Fresh Mex Restaurants and Fuzio Universal Pasta: Charles (Chuck) Rink
SVP Human Resources: Steve Wallace
SVP Research and Development and Executive Chef: Roberto (Pepe) Lopez
VP Facilities and Construction: Mark Turpin
VP Marketing: Julie Koenig-Browne
President, Real Mex Foods: Carlos Angulo
Banquet and Catering Specialist: Elaine Gies
Banquet and Catering Specialist: Brenda Perez

LOCATIONS

HQ: Real Mex Restaurants
5660 Katella Ave., Cypress, CA 90630
Phone: 800-735-3501   **Fax:** 562-346-1469
Web: www.eltorito.com

Real Mex Restaurants has restaurants in Arizona, California, Illinois, Indiana, Missouri, Oregon, and Washington.

COMPETITORS

Brinker	Metromedia
Chevys	Restaurant Group
Chipotle	Mexican Restaurants
CKE Restaurants	Outback Steakhouse
Consolidated Restaurant	Pancho's Mexican Buffet
Operations	Qdoba
Fresh Enterprises	Rubio's Restaurants
Luby's	Taco Bell
Margaritas	Taco Cabana

HISTORICAL FINANCIALS

Company Type: Private

Income Statement
FYE: August 31

	ESTIMATED REVENUE ($ mil.)	NET INCOME ($ mil.)	NET PROFIT MARGIN	EMPLOYEES
8/04	200	—	—	5,000

Recruitmax Software

If good help really is hard to find, Recruitmax has some detective skills to share. Founded in 1996, Recruitmax Software develops software for executive recruiters, temp agencies, and other types of staffing and human resources organizations. The company's Web-based software helps companies analyze their workforces and attract, hire, and retain employees more efficiently. Recruitmax offers its software in versions that target the needs of corporate human resources departments and staffing agencies, and it offers applications for monitoring skills and competency levels throughout an organization. The company also offers consulting, global deployment, and technology integration services related to its products.

With more than 500 customers, Recruitmax markets its products to clients in a wide variety of industries. The company offers versions of its recruiting software tailored to the needs of the financial services, health care, retail, technology, and staffing industries. Customers include EarthLink, the University of Washington, Affiliated Computer Services, and Janus Capital Group.

In 2004 Recruitmax acquired human resources management software and services company KnowledgePoint from its previous owner, Wolters Kluwer.

EXECUTIVES

CEO: Derek Mercer
President: Jim Philip
CFO: Mark S. Silverman
CTO: Angel Cabrera
SVP, Global Enterprise Solutions: Bertrand Dussert
SVP, Product Strategy and Development: Melissa Greene
VP, Business Development: Jamie Davis
VP, Customer Service: Alan Belser
VP, International Business: Andrew Geisel
VP, Sales and Marketing: Timothy (Tim) Beaumont
General Manager, Europe, Middle East, and Africa: Darren Jaffrey

LOCATIONS

HQ: Recruitmax Software, Inc
7660 Centurion Pkwy., Ste. 100,
Jacksonville, FL 32256
Phone: 904-394-5644   **Fax:** 904-493-9146
Web: www.recruitmax.com

Recruitmax Software has regional headquarters offices in Australia, the UK, and the US.

PRODUCTS/OPERATIONS

Selected Products

Aloha (new employee set-up automation software)
Beyond (enterprise software for managing relationships with staffing vendors)
Corporate Edition (recruitment and hiring software for corporate human resources departments)
Impact (workforce building and retaining software)
Resource Edition (labor planning and management software)
Staffing Edition (hiring software for staffing and recruiting agencies)

COMPETITORS

BrassRing	Unicru
iCIMS	VirtualEdge
Peopleclick	Webhire
ProAct Technologies	Workstream
Taleo	

HISTORICAL FINANCIALS

Company Type: Private

Income Statement
FYE: December 31

	ESTIMATED REVENUE ($ mil.)	NET INCOME ($ mil.)	NET PROFIT MARGIN	EMPLOYEES
12/04	25	—	—	320
12/03	10	—	—	100
12/02	5	—	—	66
12/01	4	—	—	—
Annual Growth	**87.4%**	**—**	**—**	**120.2%**

Revenue History

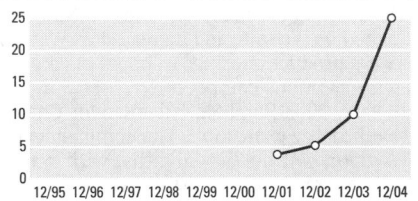

Red Apple Group

Red Apple Group sells more than just apples in the Big Apple. Subsidiary United Refining, which processes 65,000 barrels of oil a day, distributes fuel to its 372 Country Fair/Red Apple gas stations/convenience stores in New York, Pennsylvania, and Ohio. Red Apple controls Gristede's Foods, a leading New York City supermarket chain. It also has real estate, aircraft leasing, and newspaper operations. CEO John Catsimatidis owns the Red Apple Group, which lost out to Russian oil giant LUKOIL in a bid to acquire East Coast gasoline retailer Getty Petroleum Marketing.

EXECUTIVES

Chairman, President, and CEO, Red Apple Group and Gristede's Foods; Chairman and CEO, United Refining Company: John A. Catsimatidis, age 56
President and COO, United Refining: Myron L. Turfitt, age 52

LOCATIONS

HQ: Red Apple Group, Inc.
823 11th Ave., New York, NY 10019
Phone: 212-956-5803   **Fax:** 212-247-4509
Web: www.jacny.com

The Red Apple Group operates gasoline stations in New York, Ohio, and Pennsylvania. It owns commercial property in Florida, New Jersey, New York, and the Virgin Islands. The company also operates supermarkets in the New York City area.

COMPETITORS

7-Eleven
A&P
Ahold USA
Amerada Hess
D'Agostino Supermarkets
Getty Petroleum Marketing
King Kullen Grocery
Man-dell Food Stores
Motiva Enterprises
Pathmark
Sunoco
TOTAL
Wakefern Food

HISTORICAL FINANCIALS

Company Type: Private

Income Statement

FYE: February 28

	ESTIMATED REVENUE ($ mil.)	NET INCOME ($ mil.)	NET PROFIT MARGIN	EMPLOYEES
2/05	2,800	—	—	—
2/04	3,000	—	—	7,500
2/03	2,100	—	—	7,500
2/02	2,000	—	—	7,000
2/01	1,100	—	—	3,117
2/00	1,000	—	—	3,082
2/99	820	—	—	3,200
2/98	850	—	—	2,700
2/97	2,200	—	—	4,200
2/96	2,150	—	—	4,300
Annual Growth	3.0%	—	—	7.2%

Revenue History

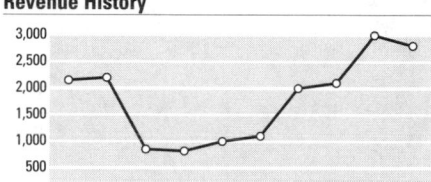

Refinery

Refinery pumps out Web sites. The company creates marketing Web sites, employee portals, and sales portals for such clients as Campbell Soup Company, Lenox, Merril Lynch, and Motorola. Its consulting and marketing services include custom application and e-commerce development. The company expanded its search engine marketing expertise with the 2005 acquisition of directMASS. Refinery was founded in 1994.

EXECUTIVES

CEO: Andrew Sullivan
SVP, Operations and CFO: Shaun Buss
SVP, Client Services: Joel Gehman
VP, Sales and Marketing: Sean Connelly
Director, Marketing: Heather L. Bonura
Director, Sales: Mike Derins
Director, Sales: Andrew Fegley

LOCATIONS

HQ: Refinery, Inc.
101 East County Line Rd., Hatboro, PA 19040
Phone: 215-706-5200 **Fax:** 215-706-5201
Web: www.refinery.com

COMPETITORS

AGENCY.COM
Akqa Inc.
Answerthink
aQuantive
Beyond Interactive
Dentsu
DiamondCluster International
Digitas
Grey Global
Havas
Idea Integration
Interpublic Group
LB Icon
Nurun
Organic
Publicis
Ripple Effects Interactive
Saltmine
Sapient
SiteLab International
U.S. Interactive
WPP Group

HISTORICAL FINANCIALS

Company Type: Private

Income Statement

FYE: December 31

	REVENUE ($ mil.)	NET INCOME ($ mil.)	NET PROFIT MARGIN	EMPLOYEES
12/04	15	—	—	121
12/03	11	—	—	78
12/02	10	—	—	71
12/01	6	—	—	55
Annual Growth	35.6%	—	—	30.1%

Revenue History

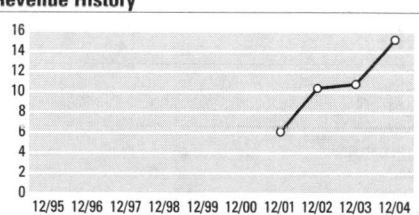

Regence Group

The Regence Group is the health care king of the Northwest, operating the largest group of Blue Cross Blue Shield companies in the northwestern US. Through its subsidiary companies, Regence BlueCross BlueShield of Oregon, Regence BlueShield, Regence BlueCross BlueShield of Utah, and Regence BlueShield of Idaho, the company provides health insurance products and

related services to nearly 3 million members. The company also provides life, disability, and short-term medical insurance through its Regence Life & Health Insurance subsidiary.

Although it faces stiff competition, The Regence Group has decided to remain not-for-profit. The company's strategy for remaining competitive consists of consolidating operations, upgrading the company's information technology infrastructure, and deploying new health insurance products.

EXECUTIVES

President and CEO: Mark B. Ganz
EVP; President, Regence BlueShield:
Mary O. McWilliams
EVP; President, Regence BlueCross BlueShield of Oregon: J. Bart McMullan Jr.
EVP and Chief Marketing Executive: Mohan Nair
EVP, Health Care Services: Jeffrey A. Robertson
SVP, Strategic Communications and Public Affairs:
Kerry Barnett
SVP, Human Resources: Tom Kennedy
VP and CFO: Steve Hooker
VP and Treasurer: Eric Tanaka
Chief Information Officer: Cheron Vail
President, Regence BlueShield of Idaho: John Stellmon
President, Regence BlueCross BlueShield of Utah:
D. Scott Ideson
President and CEO, Regence Life & Health Insurance:
Kathryn Kremin
SVP and Chief Medical Officer, Regence BlueShield:
Jeff Robertson
Auditors: Deloitte & Touche LLP

LOCATIONS

HQ: The Regence Group
200 SW Market St., Portland, OR 97201
Phone: 503-225-5221 **Fax:** 503-225-5274
Web: www.regence.com

The Regence Group's service area includes Idaho, Oregon, Utah, and Washington.

COMPETITORS

CIGNA
Kaiser Foundation Health Plan
PacifiCare

HISTORICAL FINANCIALS

Company Type: Private

Income Statement

FYE: December 31

	REVENUE ($ mil.)	NET INCOME ($ mil.)	NET PROFIT MARGIN	EMPLOYEES
12/03	6,700	—	—	6,000
12/02	6,250	—	—	6,600
Annual Growth	7.2%	—	—	(9.1%)

Revenue History

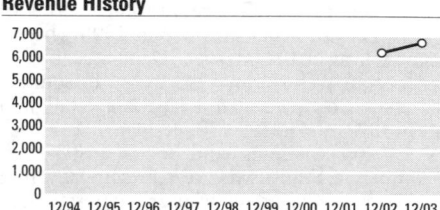

REI

Outdoor gear and clothing from Recreational Equipment, Inc. (REI) outfits everyone from mountain climbers to mall walkers. The company is one of the nation's largest consumer co-operatives, with over 2 million member-owners. Through nearly 80 outlets in about 25 states, REI sells high-end gear, clothing, and footwear (including private-label goods) for adventurous outdoor activities such as climbing, kayaking, and skiing, as well as for hiking, bicycling, and camping. The company also repairs gear, and it sells merchandise online and through occasional catalogs. Its adventure travel service, REI Adventures, offers trips such as cycling the Alps, sea kayaking Costa Rica, and hiking New Zealand.

REI's community and environmental involvement includes youth program support, community service, and designating a portion of its operating budget to environmental restoration projects. Through its partnership with US Bank (a subsidiary of U.S. Bancorp) the company offers members the REI Visa card.

REI stores feature product demonstrations, educational seminars, and gift registries. The company's MSR (Mountain Safety Research) subsidiary makes mountaineering equipment, outdoor clothing, and camping products. Customers can become co-op members by paying a one-time fee; its privileges include getting about 10% of their annual purchases refunded in the form of patronage dividends.

In March 2005 former president and CEO Dennis Madsen retired. He had joined the company as a stockroom clerk when he was 17 years old. Sally Jewell was named as his successor.

HISTORY

Lloyd Anderson founded REI in his Seattle garage in 1938 with his wife, Mary, and 23 other mountain climbers looking for high-quality mountaineering equipment at low prices. Uncomfortable about making money off of his friends, Anderson formed a co-op, returning a portion of the profits to its members. REI's first retail location (opened in 1944 in the back of a Seattle gas station) consisted of three shelves of Army surplus items. The company did not hire its first full-time employee until 1953.

Growth was slow yet steady. In 1971 the company operated one store; by 1983 REI had grown to seven stores with several additional product lines and a catalog business. That year Wally Smith became the company's CEO.

REI benefited from the growing interest in outdoor activities, expanding to 17 stores in 13 states in 1987. By 1991, when it built its first distribution center, REI had 27 stores in 16 states. The co-op reached for a new frontier in 1996 when it began selling on the Internet. It launched its REI-Outlet.com Web site in 1998 to sell discounted merchandise, and began a Japanese retail Web site in 1999. Also in 1999 REI decided to scale back its catalog mailings and focus instead on e-commerce. Smith, who grew the company from 9 to 54 stores during his 17-year reign, retired in early 2000 and was replaced by COO Dennis Madsen, a 34-year company veteran.

In 2000, the co-op rankled its rank and file when it moved its manufacturing operations to Mexico and closed its fleece-manufacturing subsidiary, Thaw. Also that year the company opened its first international location in Tokyo, but ended up closing the store and shutting down the Japanese Web site in 2001.

In January 2003, the company was named to *FORTUNE*'s "100 Best Companies" list for the sixth year in a row. It made the list again in January 2004, ranking 24th.

EXECUTIVES

Chairman: Bill Britt
Vice Chairman: Anne V. Farrell, age 69
President, CEO, and Director: Sally Jewell
Chief Administrative Officer, CFO, and Corporate Treasurer: Brad Johnson
SVP, Merchandising and Logistics: Matt Hyde
SVP, Sales, Service, and Store Development: Brian Unmacht
VP, General Counsel, and Corporate Secretary: Pam Myers
VP, Distribution: Clark Koch
VP, Human Resources: Michelle Clements
VP, Information Services: Brad Brown
VP, Logistics: David Presley
VP, Multi-Channel Programs: Joan Broughton
VP, Public Affairs: Michael Collins
VP, Real Estate: Jerry Chevassus
VP, Strategy, Marketing, and Communications: Atsuko Tamura
Director, Inventory and Logistics: John Strother
Director, Online Sales: Noel Nelson
Manager, Public Relations: Randy Hurlow

LOCATIONS

HQ: Recreational Equipment, Inc.
6750 S. 228th St., Kent, WA 98032
Phone: 253-395-3780   **Fax:** 253-395-4352
Web: www.rei.com

2004 Stores

	No.
California	18
Washington	8
Colorado	7
Texas	5
Massachusetts	4
Oregon	4
Georgia	3
Maryland	3
Arizona	2
Illinois	2
Michigan	2
Minnesota	2
Nevada	2
North Carolina	2
Utah	2
Virginia	2
Wisconsin	2
Alaska	1
Idaho	1
Missouri	1
Montana	1
New Jersey	1
New Mexico	1
Pennsylvania	1
Tennessee	1
Total	**78**

PRODUCTS/OPERATIONS

Selected Products and Services

Bicycles and accessories	Footwear
Books and maps	Gift registry
Camping gear	Racks (bike, boat, and ski mounts)
Canoes, kayaks, and related gear	REI repair service
Climbing gear	Sleeping bags
Clothing (children's, men's, and women's)	Snow sports gear
Fitness gear	Tents
	Travel accessories

COMPETITORS

Academy Sports & Outdoors	Hibbett Sporting Goods
Bass Pro Shops	Johnson Outdoors
Big 5	Lands' End
Cabela's	L.L. Bean
Dick's Sporting Goods	Patagonia
Eastern Mountain Sports	Sport Chalet
Eddie Bauer Holdings	Sports Authority
G.I. Joe's	Sportsman's Guide

HISTORICAL FINANCIALS

Company Type: Cooperative

Income Statement

FYE: December 31

	REVENUE ($ mil.)	NET INCOME ($ mil.)	NET PROFIT MARGIN	EMPLOYEES
12/04	888	25	2.8%	6,500
12/03	805	19	2.4%	—
12/02	735	16	2.2%	—
12/01	740	8	1.0%	6,000
12/00	698	(11)	—	7,000
12/99	621	10	1.7%	6,000
12/98	587	14	2.4%	6,000
12/97	536	15	2.8%	5,100
12/96	484	16	3.2%	4,800
12/95	448	13	2.8%	—
Annual Growth	**7.9%**	**8.1%**	**—**	**3.9%**

2004 Year-End Financials

Debt ratio: 12.6%   Current ratio: 1.30
Return on equity: 9.6%   Long-term debt ($ mil.): 35
Cash ($ mil.): 131

Net Income History

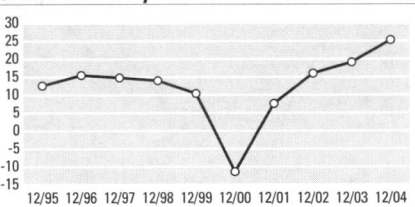

Reliant Pharmaceuticals

Reliant Pharmaceuticals gets to the heart of the matter. The company markets treatments for various cardiovascular ailments. Rather than go through the time and expense of developing drugs from start to finish in its own labs, the drugmaker instead buys rights to pharmaceuticals in late stages of development or drugs already approved by the FDA. Reliant's portfolio of drugs on the market includes high blood pressure meds DynaCirc and InnoPran XL and cholesterol fighters Lescol and Antara. Reliant and Novartis co-promote Lescol. PharmBay Investors owns 27% of the firm.

The company's bestsellers are the DynaCirc and Rythmol lines of products, accounting for nearly half of the company's 2004 revenues. Reliant's pipeline includes a potential therapy for herpes zoster (aka shingles).

The drugmaker in 2005 sold Axid, a stomach acid blocker, to Braintree Laboratories. Reliant had originally acquired rights to the drug from Eli Lilly.

Bay City Capital owns 20% of the company, and drug delivery technology developer Alkermes has a 12% stake.

EXECUTIVES

Chairman and CEO: Ernest Mario, age 66, $12,045 pay
Vice Chairman: Frederick B. (Fred) Craves, age 59
COO: Joseph S. Zakrzewski, age 41, $450,000 pay
CFO: Robert R. (Bob) Ferguson III, age 56, $325,000 pay
EVP, Business Development: Stefan Aigner, age 40, $450,000 pay
SVP, Research and Development: Steven B. Ketchum, age 40, $300,000 pay
SVP, Sales and Marketing: Martin (Marty) Driscoll, age 46, $391,458 pay
VP, Legal Affairs: Michael Lerner
VP, Sales: Vincent Angotti
VP, Scientific Affairs: George Bobotas
Director, Human Resources: Tim Soule
Auditors: Ernst & Young LLP

LOCATIONS

HQ: Reliant Pharmaceuticals, Inc.
110 Allen Rd., Liberty Corner, NJ 07938
Phone: 908-580-1200   **Fax:** 908-542-9405
Web: www.reliantrx.com

PRODUCTS/OPERATIONS

2004 Sales

	$ mil.	% of total
Product sales		
DynaCirc CR	34.0	15
Rythmol SR	26.1	12
Rythmol	22.7	10
DynaCirc	22.3	10
InnoPran XL	7.0	3
Axid	5.1	2
Promotion revenues		
Lescol & Lescol XL	105.1	48
Total	**222.3**	**100**

Selected Products

Approved
  Antara (high cholesterol)
  DynaCirc (hypertension)
  InnoPran XL (hypertension)
  Lescol (high cholesterol, with Novartis)
  Omacor (high cholesterol)
  Rythmol (arrhythmia)
In development
  Propranolol LA (hypertension, angina, migraines)
  RP-606 (herpes zoster)

COMPETITORS

Abbott Labs	King Pharmaceuticals
AstraZeneca	Kos Pharmaceuticals
Bristol-Myers Squibb	Pfizer
First Horizon Pharmaceutical	Purdue Pharma
Forest Labs	Shire Pharmaceuticals
	Wyeth

HISTORICAL FINANCIALS

Company Type: Private

Income Statement
FYE: December 31

	REVENUE ($ mil.)	NET INCOME ($ mil.)	NET PROFIT MARGIN	EMPLOYEES
12/04	222	(106)	—	1,152
12/03	172	(50)	—	—
12/02	177	(121)	—	—
Annual Growth	**11.9%**	—	—	—

2004 Year-End Financials

Debt ratio: —   Current ratio: 1.23
Return on equity: —   Long-term debt ($ mil.): 93
Cash ($ mil.): 58

Net Income History

0	
-20	
-40	
-60	
-80	
-100	
-120	
-140	

12/95 12/96 12/97 12/98 12/99 12/00 12/01 12/02 12/03 12/04

Remington Arms

They aim to arm at Remington Arms. The company makes shotguns and rifles, ammunition, and gear under the Remington brand. As the only US company to produce both guns and ammo, Remington is the top US seller of rifles and ammo and the #2 seller of shotguns behind Mossberg. Wal-Mart accounts for about 20% of the company's revenue. Other mass merchandisers, as well as sporting goods shops, sell Remington. The firm was founded in 1816 by Eliphalet Remington II, who took his first orders upon winning second place in a shooting contest with a gun he built. Equity firm Bruckmann, Rosser, Sherrill & Co. owns a majority stake in the company. Remington sold its Stren fishing line business to Pure Fishing in early 2004.

In 2004 Remington created a joint venture, Remington-Elsag, to serve the domestic security niche and distribute products using license plate technology. It developed a Remington LE Technologies Division to launch advanced-technology surveillance systems.

EXECUTIVES

Chairman: Leon J. (Bill) Hendrix Jr., age 63
President and CEO: Thomas L. (Tommy) Millner, age 51, $480,000 pay
EVP and COO: Ronald H. Bristol II, age 42, $260,000 pay
EVP, CFO, and Chief Administrative Officer: Mark A. Little, age 57, $245,000 pay
SVP, Manufacturing: Paul L. Cahan, age 63, $220,000 pay
VP, Accessories: Samuel G. (Sam) Grecco, age 51
VP, Finance, Treasurer, and Corporate Secretary: Stephen P. Jackson Jr., age 36
VP, Sales, Marketing, and Product Development, Ammunition and Clay Targets: John M. Dwyer Jr., age 46
VP, Sales, Marketing, and Product Development, Firearms: Jay M. Bunting Jr., age 47
Auditors: PricewaterhouseCoopers LLP

LOCATIONS

HQ: Remington Arms Company, Inc.
870 Remington Dr., Madison, NC 27025
Phone: 336-548-8700   **Fax:** 336-548-7801
Web: www.remington.com

Remington Arms makes black-powder metal parts, rifles, shotguns, and accessories in Ilion, New York; rimfire and centerfire rifles in Mayfield, Kentucky; ammunition and ammunition components in Lonoke, Arkansas; and clay targets in Ada, Oklahoma and Findlay, Ohio.

COMPETITORS

Alliant Techsystems	Mossberg
Beretta	Olin
Browning	Ruger
Colt Defense	Savage Arms
Colt's	U.S. Repeating Arms
Marlin Firearms	

HISTORICAL FINANCIALS

Company Type: Private

Income Statement
FYE: December 31

	REVENUE ($ mil.)	NET INCOME ($ mil.)	NET PROFIT MARGIN	EMPLOYEES
12/04	393	(4)	—	2,400
12/03	361	(3)	—	2,184
12/02	384	20	5.2%	2,334
12/01	383	14	3.6%	2,243
12/00	389	20	5.1%	2,229
12/99	403	23	5.7%	—
12/98	386	17	4.5%	—
Annual Growth	**0.3%**	—	—	**1.9%**

2004 Year-End Financials

Debt ratio: 1,914.2%   Current ratio: 2.58
Return on equity: —   Long-term debt ($ mil.): 203
Cash ($ mil.): 0

Net Income History

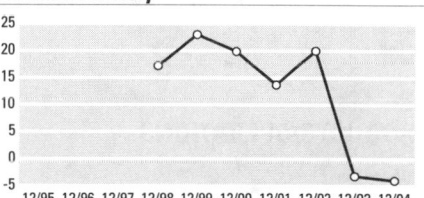

25	
20	
15	
10	
5	
0	
-5	

12/95 12/96 12/97 12/98 12/99 12/00 12/01 12/02 12/03 12/04

Remy

Carmakers get cranked up with the help of Remy International (formerly Delco Remy International), which manufactures and distributes starters and alternators for carmakers and light- and heavy-duty truck makers. The company, which is owned by Citicorp Venture Capital, also remanufactures engines, fuel systems, starters, and alternators for the automotive aftermarket. Remy's OEM customers include companies such as General Motors (28% of sales), Navistar (10%), Delphi, and Caterpillar; aftermarket customers include Pep Boys, Advance Auto Parts, and other automotive parts chains.

Remy also offers third-party core acquisition services that sell component cores to other remanufacturers. A core is a recycled, usually nonfunctioning auto part that is reclaimed at the time of its replacement so it can be remanufactured and used again.

Acquisitions boosted Remy's sales, but they failed to do much for the company's stock price, which consistently traded below its IPO price. The company was finally acquired by Citicorp Venture Capital in 2001. Berkshire Hathaway holds about a 20% stake.

EXECUTIVES

Chairman: Harold K. Sperlich, age 75
Vice Chairman: Erwin H. (Bill) Billig, age 78
President, CEO, and Director: Thomas J. Snyder, age 60, $786,300 pay
EVP and COO: Raj Shah, age 53, $581,400 pay (prior to promotion)
SVP and CFO: Jeffrey Potrzebowski, age 52
SVP, Human Resources and Communications: Roderick (Rod) English, age 53, $377,800 pay
SVP Operations and Supply Chain: David Abel
VP, Aftermarket Services: Al Rowley
VP and Corporate Controller: Amitabh Rai, age 44
VP; Managing Director, Europe: Patrick C. Mobouck, age 50, $477,900 pay
VP, Production Control and Logistics: Tania Wingfield
President, Remy Inc.: Richard L. Stanley, age 48, $433,600 pay
Auditors: Ernst & Young LLP

LOCATIONS

HQ: Remy International, Inc.
2902 Enterprise Dr., Anderson, IN 46013
Phone: 765-778-6499   **Fax:** 765-778-6404
Web: www.remyinc.com

Remy International has manufacturing facilities in Belgium, Brazil, Canada, China, Denmark, Germany, Hungary, India, Mexico, Poland, South Korea, Tunisia, the UK, and the US.

2004 Sales

	$ mil.	% of total
US	840	80
Europe	107	10
Mexico & Brazil	52	5
Asia/Pacific	51	5
Canada	1	—
Total	**1,051**	**100**

PRODUCTS/OPERATIONS

2004 Sales

	$ mil.	% of total
Electrical systems	913	87
Powertrain/drivetrain	79	7
Core services	59	6
Total	**1,051**	**100**

2004 Sales

	% of total
Electrical aftermarket	41
Automotive OEM	29
Heavy-duty OEM	17
Powertrain	7
Core services	6
Total	**100**

2004 Sales

	% of total
Aftermarket	54
Original equipment	46
Total	**100**

Selected Products

Alternators
Diesel and marine engines
Fuel systems
Gears
Power steering systems
Rack and pinions
Starters
Water pumps

COMPETITORS

Champion Parts
Dana
Federal-Mogul
General Parts
Genuine Parts
Hahn Automotive
Mitsubishi Motors
Motorcar Parts
Prestolite Electric
Robert Bosch
Valeo

HISTORICAL FINANCIALS

Company Type: Private

Income Statement

FYE: December 31

	REVENUE ($ mil.)	NET INCOME ($ mil.)	NET PROFIT MARGIN	EMPLOYEES
12/04	1,051	56	5.4%	6,800
12/03	1,053	(187)	—	6,159
12/02	1,069	(133)	—	6,338
12/01	1,054	(73)	—	7,422
12/00*	443	10	2.2%	7,424
7/00	1,091	12	1.1%	7,707
7/99	954	28	3.0%	6,845
7/98	815	(4)	—	4,833
7/97	690	(14)	—	4,949
7/96	637	(5)	—	3,000
Annual Growth	**5.7%**	**—**	**—**	**9.5%**

*Fiscal year change

2004 Year-End Financials

Debt ratio: —
Return on equity: —
Cash ($ mil.): 63
Current ratio: 1.56
Long-term debt ($ mil.): 610

Net Income History

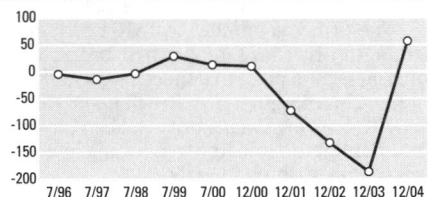

EXECUTIVES

Chairman, President, and CEO: Ira Leon Rennert, age 69
EVP and COO: Patrick G. Tatom, age 53
EVP: Marvin Koenig
VP Finance; VP Finance and CFO, Renco Steel: Roger L. Fay, age 57
VP Commercial: David A. Howard, age 43
Vice Chairman, President, and CEO, Doe Run: Jeffrey L. Zelms, age 57
President and CEO, WCI Steel: Ed Caine
VP Finance and CFO, Renco Steel: John P. Jacunski, age 39

LOCATIONS

HQ: Renco Group, Inc.
30 Rockefeller Plaza, New York, NY 10112
Phone: 212-541-6000   **Fax:** 212-541-6197

PRODUCTS/OPERATIONS

Selected Subsidiaries

AM General (manufactures the High Mobility Multipurpose Wheeled Vehicle known as the HUMVEE and the HUMMER, and diesel engines)
Consolidated Sewing Machine Corp. (manufactures industrial sewing machines, specialty machines, cutting machines, and motors)
Doe Run Company (lead smelter)
Renco Steel Holdings, Inc. (steel producer)
Rencoal, Inc. (coal miner)
WCI Steel, Inc. (steel producer)

COMPETITORS

AK Steel Holding Corporation
ASARCO
Nippon Steel
Nucor
Oshkosh Truck
Peugeot
RSR
Singer
United States Steel

HISTORICAL FINANCIALS

Company Type: Private

Income Statement

FYE: October 31

	REVENUE ($ mil.)	NET INCOME ($ mil.)	NET PROFIT MARGIN	EMPLOYEES
10/04	1,600	—	—	8,000
10/03	2,100	—	—	13,500
10/02	2,175	—	—	13,500
10/01	2,150	—	—	14,000
10/00	2,500	—	—	15,000
10/99	2,500	—	—	15,000
10/98	2,550	—	—	11,000
10/97	2,520	—	—	10,500
10/96	1,800	—	—	7,150
10/95	1,650	—	—	6,995
Annual Growth	**(0.3%)**	**—**	**—**	**1.5%**

Revenue History

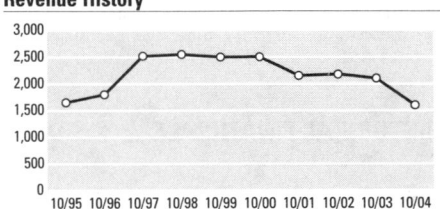

Renco

Renco Group is a holding company for a diverse bunch of businesses. Its AM General subsidiary (which Ronald Perelman's MacAndrews & Forbes Holding is acquiring) makes the HUMVEE, an extra-wide all-terrain vehicle used by the military, and the HUMMER, the HUMVEE's civilian counterpart. Renco Steel and WCI Steel manufacture, fabricate, and distribute steel. Renco was established in 1980 and is owned by industrialist Ira Rennert, a former business consultant whose Long Island, New York, home is double the size of the White House and is said to include 29 bedrooms, 42 bathrooms, a 100-car garage, and an English pub.

Other Renco Group companies include Doe Run, the world's #2 lead smelter; coal miner Rencoal; and Consolidated Sewing Machine, which makes industrial sewing machines.

Republic Bancshares of Texas

Republic Bancshares of Texas is the holding company for Republic National Bank, which has six branches in the metropolitan Houston area. Primarily serving consumers and small businesses, the bank offers checking and savings accounts, CDs, mortgages, business and personal loans, credit cards, and online banking. Consumer customer services also include individual retirement accounts and access to safety deposit boxes. Its small business customers include car washes, childcare facilities, gas stations, grocery stores, hotels, and restaurants. It was founded in 1998.

EXECUTIVES

Chairman, President, and CEO, Republic Bancshares and Republic National Bank: C. P. Bryan, age 54, $382,500 pay
CFO, Secretary, and Treasurer; EVP and CFO, Republic National Bank: R. John McWhorter, age 40, $190,000 pay
EVP and Chief Credit Officer, Republic National Bank: Leonard E. (Eddie) Parise
EVP, Republic National Bank: Steve Broadus
SVP, Accounting, Republic National Bank: Kim A. Doan
SVP, Loan Operations, Republic National Bank: Kristie L. Smith
SVP, Treasury Services and Operations, Republic National Bank: Ritana H. Layne
Assistant VP and Manager, Human Resources, Republic National Bank: Patricia Smith
Assistant VP, Bookkeeping, Republic National Bank: Linda Lambert
Assistant VP, Treasury Services, Republic National Bank: Monte C. Giebler
Technology Officer, Republic National Bank: Kevin Hajek
Auditors: KPMG LLP

LOCATIONS

HQ: Republic Bancshares of Texas, Inc.
4200 Westheimer, Ste. 101, Houston, TX 77027
Phone: 281-315-1100
Web: www.rnb-texas.com

PRODUCTS/OPERATIONS

2004 Sales

	$ mil.	% of total
Interest		
Loans, including fees	22.5	79
Investment securities	2.6	10
Federal funds sold & other	0.2	1
Noninterest		
Service charges on deposit accounts	1.9	6
Other	1.1	2
Total	**28.3**	**100**

COMPETITORS

Amegy Bancorporation	Hibernia Corporation
Bank of America	JPMorgan Chase
BOK Financial	MetroCorp Bancshares
Citibank	Regions Financial
Compass Bancshares	Sterling Bancshares
Cullen/Frost Bankers	Washington Mutual
Encore Bank	Wells Fargo
Franklin Bank	Whitney Holding
Golden West Financial	Woodforest Financial

HISTORICAL FINANCIALS
Company Type: Private

Income Statement
FYE: December 31

	ASSETS ($ mil.)	NET INCOME ($ mil.)	INCOME AS % OF ASSETS	EMPLOYEES
12/04	574	5	0.8%	133
12/03	435	4	0.9%	104
12/02	384	3	0.8%	105
Annual Growth	**22.2%**	**26.5%**	**—**	**12.5%**

2004 Year-End Financials

Equity as % of assets: 6.1%
Return on assets: 1.0%
Return on equity: 14.7%
Long-term debt ($ mil.): —
Sales ($ mil.): 28

Net Income History

12/95 12/96 12/97 12/98 12/99 12/00 12/01 12/02 12/03 12/04

Republic Property Trust

The future of the US republic lies in the American voter, but the future of Republic Property Trust lies in its American portfolio. A self-administered real estate investment trust (REIT), the company is engaged in the acquisition and development of commercial real estate, primarily in metropolitan Washington, DC. It will own 10 properties — some 21 Class A office buildings in all — upon the completion of its initial public offering. About half of the portfolio is leased to corporate tenants; a quarter is leased to the government. Republic Property Trust also provides third-party development and acquisition services; the company has built more than 5 million sq. ft. of office, industrial, and retail space.

Republic Property Trust is acquiring its portfolio from predecessor RKB Washington Property Fund, established in 2002 to invest in Washington, DC, real estate. In addition to its initial portfolio (some 2 million sq. ft. of space), the REIT holds options to acquire three Capital City office properties under various stages of development. Those properties are expected to eventually add another 1.1 million sq. ft. to the trust's holdings.

The company plans to partner with government entities to develop new or renovate older properties. It specializes in privately negotiated transactions; it secured nearly all of its initial portfolio in this manner.

Chairman Richard Kramer and president Steven Grigg are the founders and owners of Republic Properties Corporation, a real estate development and management firm with interests in the District of Columbia and the Southeast. Republic Properties Corporation will provide property management, leasing, and development services to Republic Property Trust.

EXECUTIVES

Chairman: Richard L. Kramer, age 56
Vice Chairman, President, and Chief Development Officer: Steven A. Grigg, age 57, $350,000 pay
CEO and Trustee: Mark R. Keller, age 54, $500,000 pay
SVP, Development: Peter J. Cole, age 43
SVP, Public Private Partnerships: Thomas G. Archer Jr., age 54, $300,000 pay
VP and Principal Financial Officer: Frank M. Pieruccini, age 43
VP, Acquisitions: Andrew G. Pulliam, age 34
VP, Leasing and Marketing: Michael C. Jones, age 40
Auditors: Ernst & Young LLP

LOCATIONS

HQ: Republic Property Trust
1280 Maryland Ave. SW, Ste. 280, Washington, DC 20024
Phone: 202-863-0300   **Fax:** 202-863-4049
Web: www.republicpropertytrust.com

PRODUCTS/OPERATIONS

2004 Sales

	$ mil.	% of total
Rent	24.0	91
Tenant reimbursements	2.2	8
Other	0.3	1
Total	**26.5**	**100**

Selected Properties

Campus at Dulles Technology Center (Herndon, VA)
Corporate Oaks (Herndon, VA)
Corporate Pointe IV (Chantilly, VA)
Presidents Park I and II (Herndon, VA)
The Republic Building (Washington, DC)
Willowwood III and IV (Fairfax, VA)

COMPETITORS

Boston Properties	Glenborough Realty Trust
Bresler & Reiner	Prentiss Properties
Columbia Equity Trust	Shorenstein
Douglas Development	Trizec Properties

HISTORICAL FINANCIALS
Company Type: Private

Income Statement
FYE: December 31

	REVENUE ($ mil.)	NET INCOME ($ mil.)	NET PROFIT MARGIN	EMPLOYEES
12/04	27	3	9.4%	65
12/03	13	2	14.4%	—
12/02	2	(0)	—	—
Annual Growth	**273.5%**	**—**	**—**	**—**

2004 Year-End Financials

Debt ratio: —
Return on equity: 6.0%
Cash ($ mil.): —
Current ratio: —
Long-term debt ($ mil.): —

Net Income History

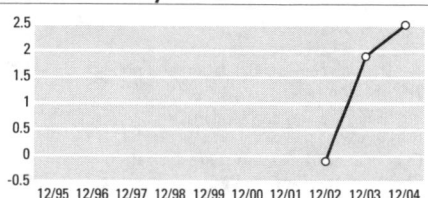

12/95 12/96 12/97 12/98 12/99 12/00 12/01 12/02 12/03 12/04

Research Triangle Institute

Pythagoras would find a happy home among the scientists at Research Triangle Institute (RTI). The not-for-profit enterprise conducts research in such areas as advanced technologies, education, environmental resources, health care, and medicine. It also provides such services as certification, training, and materials testing, as well as software used in laboratories and research projects. In addition, RTI offers analytical perspectives on public policy. The organization has more than 2,500 researchers working in about 30 countries. Duke University, North Carolina State University, and the University of North Carolina at Chapel Hill established RTI in 1958.

EXECUTIVES

Chairman: Earl Johnson Jr.
President and CEO: Victoria F. Haynes, age 57
Chief of Staff: Lon E. Maggart
SVP and CFO: James J. Gibson
SVP, International Development: Ronald W. Johnson
SVP, Science and Engineering: Satinder K. Sethi
SVP, Social and Statistical Survey: Richard A. Kulka
VP and CIO: John C. Crites
VP and Counsel for Legal and Regulatory Affairs: Lisa J. Gilliland
VP, Corporate Affairs: Sally S. Johnson
VP, Facility Strategic Services: Dennis F. Naugle
VP, Human Resources: Walter E. Goodlett Jr.
Corporate Secretary and Counsel to the President: J. Scott Merrell

LOCATIONS

HQ: Research Triangle Institute
3040 Cornwallis Rd.,
Research Triangle Park, NC 27709
Phone: 919-541-6000   **Fax:** 919-541-5985
Web: www.rti.org

Research Triangle Institute has operations in Alabama, the District of Columbia, Florida, Georgia, Illinois, Maryland, North Carolina, and Virginia, and in El Salvador, Indonesia, Poland, South Africa, United Arab Emirates, and the UK.

PRODUCTS/OPERATIONS

Selected Research Areas

Advanced technology
  Aerospace and defense
  Auditory prosthesis research
  Contamination control
  Energy technology
  Information technology
  Nanotechnology
  Semiconductors
  Technology assisted learning
  Technology commercialization and policy
  Thermoelectrics
Drug discovery and development
  Bioassays
  Chemical synthesis and characterization
  Chemoinformatics
  Clinical trials
  Drug design and synthesis
  Drug metabolism and pharmacokinetics
  General chemistry support
  Natural products chemistry
  Proteomics
  Therapeutic outcomes and safety
  Toxicology services

Economic and social development
  Crime and justice
  Economic development and technology
  Environment and natural resource management
  Public utilities and infrastructure
Education and training
  Adult education
  Disability policy and programs
  Elementary and secondary education
  Family and early childhood
  International education policy and systems
  Postsecondary education
  Technology assisted learning
Environment and natural resources
  Air, water, and land resources
  Energy and the environment
  Environmental and natural resource economics
  Environmental chemistry and toxicology
  Environmental information systems
  Management and engineering
  Measurement and monitoring
  Policies and regulations
  Risk management
Health
  Communication and education
  Health and the environment
  Health behaviors and interventions
  Health care access
  Health economics
  Genetics, proteomics, and bioinformatics
  Special populations
  Therapeutic outcomes and safety
International development
  Democratic governance
  Education
  Environmental management
  Financial systems
  Health
  Information and communication technology

COMPETITORS

Aerospace Corporation	Lockheed Martin
Alliant Techsystems	MITRE
Battelle Memorial	Northrop Grumman
Boeing	QSS Group
Booz Allen	RAND
CACI International	Raytheon
Cato Institute	SAIC
Charles Stark Draper	Southwest Research
Laboratory	Institute
Computer Sciences Corp.	SRI International
EDS	United Technologies
General Dynamics	Universities Research
Honeywell International	Association

HISTORICAL FINANCIALS

Company Type: Not-for-profit

Income Statement
FYE: September 30

	REVENUE ($ mil.)	NET INCOME ($ mil.)	NET PROFIT MARGIN	EMPLOYEES
9/04	510	17	3.4%	2,500
9/03	333	10	3.1%	2,301
9/02	286	5	1.9%	2,050
9/01	265	—	—	1,952
9/00	239	—	—	1,826
9/99	207	—	—	1,738
9/98	168	—	—	1,550
9/97	148	—	—	1,450
9/96	143	—	—	1,450
9/95	142	—	—	1,450
Annual Growth	**15.3%**	**78.5%**	**—**	**6.2%**

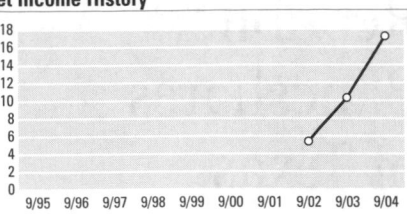

Net Income History

Resource Capital

Resource Capital is looking to pump some capital into real estate resources. The real estate investment trust (REIT) was launched in 2005 to invest in commercial and residential real estate-related securities, and to a lesser extent, commercial finance assets (syndicated bank loans, equipment leases). Residential mortgage-backed securities account for about 85% of the REIT's portfolio, although the company intends to diversify its holdings over time. Resource Capital raised almost $215 million through a private stock offering; it hopes to raise another $288 million through a planned IPO. The company's investments are managed by Resource Capital Manager, a subsidiary of Resource America.

Hedge fund Omega Advisors owns about 13% of the company.

EXECUTIVES

Chairman: Edward E. Cohen, age 66
President, CEO, and Director: Jonathan Z. Cohen, age 34
CFO, Treasurer, and Director: Steven J. Kessler, age 62
Chief Legal Officer and Secretary: Michael S. Yecies, age 37
SVP, Assets and Liabilities Management: Thomas C. Elliott, age 32
SVP, CDO Structuring: Jeffrey D. Blomstrom, age 36
SVP, Commercial Lending: Christopher D. Allen, age 35
SVP, Equipment Leasing: Crit S. DeMent, age 52
SVP, RMBS and CMBS: Andrew P. Shook, age 36
SVP, Real Estate Investments: David E. Bloom, age 40
SVP, Real Estate Investments: Alan F. Feldman, age 41
SVP, Syndicated Loans: Gretchen Bergstresser, age 42
Auditors: Grant Thornton LLP

LOCATIONS

HQ: Resource Capital Corp.
712 5th Ave., 10th Fl., New York, NY 10019
Phone: 212-974-1708

COMPETITORS

Anthracite Capital	Hanover Capital Mortgage
Bimini Mortgage	New York Mortgage Trust
Management	

HISTORICAL FINANCIALS

Company Type: Private

Income Statement
FYE: March 31

	REVENUE ($ mil.)	NET INCOME ($ mil.)	NET PROFIT MARGIN	EMPLOYEES
3/05	1	0	—	5

The Restaurant Company

Perkins is the restaurant chain for this company. The Restaurant Company operates and franchises about 400 Perkins family-style restaurants in 35 states and Canada. The full-service chain serves standard American fare for breakfast, lunch, and dinner. Locations doing business as Perkins Restaurant & Bakery also feature in-store bakeries serving fresh muffins, pies, cookies, and cakes. Some Perkins restaurants are open 24 hours. The company owns more than 150 of its units, while the rest are franchised. CEO Donald Smith, who is also chairman of Friendly Ice Cream, owns 70% of the company; a unit of Bank of America has a 21% stake. The Perkins chain was started in Cincinnati in 1958 by Matt and Ivan Perkins.

EXECUTIVES

Chairman and CEO: Donald N. Smith, $535,326 pay
President, COO, and Director: Joseph F. (Jay) Trungale, age 63
EVP, CFO, and Director: Michael P. Donahoe, age 53, $246,077 pay
EVP Foodservice Development: James F. Barrasso, age 53, $237,424 pay
Senior Director, Training and Development: Toni Kottom
Auditors: PricewaterhouseCoopers LLP

LOCATIONS

HQ: The Restaurant Company
6075 Poplar Ave., Ste. 800, Memphis, TN 38119
Phone: 901-766-6400   **Fax:** 901-766-6482
Web: www.perkinsrestaurants.com

2004 Locations

	No.
US	
Florida	50
Minnesota	50
Pennsylvania	50
Ohio	46
Wisconsin	42
Iowa	19
Tennessee	15
New Jersey	13
New York	13
Colorado	12
Nebraska	10
South Dakota	10
Michigan	9
Idaho	8
Missouri	8
Montana	8
North Dakota	8
Illinois	7
Indiana	7
Kansas	7
Washington	6
Arkansas	4
Kentucky	4
South Carolina	4
Wyoming	4
Other states	14
International	
Canada	1
Total	**429**

COMPETITORS

Applebee's	Frisch's
Big Boy Restaurants	Golden Corral
Bob Evans	IHOP
Brinker	Metromedia Restaurant
Buffets Holdings	Group
Carlson Restaurants	Outback Steakhouse
CBRL Group	Ruby Tuesday
Country Kitchen	Shoney's
Darden	Steak n Shake
Denny's	VICORP Restaurants

HISTORICAL FINANCIALS

Company Type: Private

Income Statement

FYE: Last Sunday in December

	REVENUE ($ mil.)	NET INCOME ($ mil.)	NET PROFIT MARGIN	EMPLOYEES
12/04	341	7	2.0%	8,400
12/03	333	4	1.1%	9,750
12/02	339	2	0.6%	10,700
12/01	331	(1)	—	9,700
12/00	336	4	1.2%	9,700
12/99	316	8	2.5%	9,800
12/98	299	1	0.4%	10,500
12/97	270	(0)	—	8,850
12/96	253	5	2.0%	9,000
12/95	875	—	—	40,000
Annual Growth	**(9.9%)**	**3.9%**	**—**	**(15.9%)**

2004 Year-End Financials

Debt ratio: 1,823.1%   Current ratio: 1.21
Return on equity: 118.9%   Long-term debt ($ mil.): 149
Cash ($ mil.): 18

Net Income History

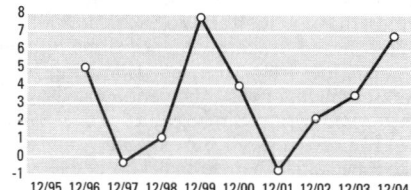

12/95 12/96 12/97 12/98 12/99 12/00 12/01 12/02 12/03 12/04

Reyes Holdings

Closely held Reyes Holdings has a grip on two things that are complementary — food and beer. Through its subsidiaries Reyes Holdings distributes products throughout North, Central, and South America. One of these, The Martin-Brower Company, supplies McDonald's restaurants in the US and Canada, as well as serving Brazil, Central America, and Puerto Rico. Reyes Holdings also counts Premium Distributors of Virginia, Chicago Beverage Systems, and California's Harbor Distributing among the wholesalers it owns. Reyes operates distribution centers in the US and six other countries. Co-chairmen Chris Reyes and Jude Reyes and VP David Reyes own the firm.

Reyes Holdings acquired Reinhart Food-Service, another family-owned firm, in 2004. Reyes hopes the acquisition, which added another 12 distribution centers to the company, will allow each firm to grow more quickly than either had anticipated alone.

EXECUTIVES

Co-Chairman: J. Christopher (Chris) Reyes, age 51
Co-Chairman: M. Jude Reyes
EVP, Business Development: Dean H. Janke
SVP: Richard F. (Dick) Strup
SVP and CFO: Daniel P. (Dan) Doheny
SVP, Human Resources: Phil Menzel
SVP, IT: Joe Crenshaw
SVP, Operations: Ray Guerin
VP: David K. Reyes
CEO, Reinhart FoodService Inc.: Mark Drazkowski

LOCATIONS

HQ: Reyes Holdings LLC
9500 West Bryn Mawr Ave., Ste. 700,
Rosemont, IL 60018
Phone: 847-227-6500   **Fax:** 847-227-6550

PRODUCTS/OPERATIONS

Selected Subsidiaries and Wholesalers

Chicago Beverage Systems LLC
Harbor Distributing LLC
The Martin-Brower Company LLC
Premium Distributors of Virginia LLC
Premium Distributors of Washington, D.C., LLC

COMPETITORS

Alex Lee
Anderson-DuBose
Ben E. Keith
Clark Products
Golden State Foods
Gordon Food Service
Keystone Foods
MBM
McLane Foodservice
Performance Food
Services Group
SYSCO
U.S. Foodservice

HISTORICAL FINANCIALS

Company Type: Private

Income Statement

FYE: December 31

	REVENUE ($ mil.)	NET INCOME ($ mil.)	NET PROFIT MARGIN	EMPLOYEES
12/03	4,630	—	—	4,100
12/02	4,180	—	—	3,994
12/01*	3,900	—	—	3,877
9/00	3,500	—	—	4,200
9/99	2,375	—	—	—
Annual Growth	**18.2%**	**—**	**—**	**(0.8%)**

*Fiscal year change

Revenue History

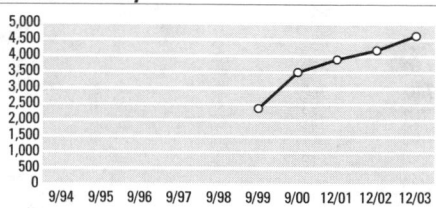

9/94 9/95 9/96 9/97 9/98 9/99 9/00 9/01 12/02 12/03

Riceland Foods

Riceland Foods is ingrained in the marketing and milling business. Started in 1921, the cooperative markets rice, soybeans, and wheat grown by its more than 9,000 member-owners in Arkansas, Louisiana, Mississippi, Missouri, and Texas. As one of the world's leading millers of rice, it sells long grain, brown, wild, and flavored rice (under the Riceland name as well as private labels) to grocery, food service, and food manufacturing customers. The co-op also sells oil and shortening products and processes soybeans, edible oils, and lecithin. Riceland markets its products throughout the US and over 75 countries internationally, mainly in the Caribbean, Mexico, the Middle East, South Africa, and Western Europe.

EXECUTIVES

Chairman: Thomas C. (Tommy) Hoskyn
President and CEO: K. Daniel (Danny) Kennedy, age 45
VP and CFO: Harry E. Loftis
VP, International Rice Marketing: Terry Harris
VP, Research: Don McCaskill
VP, Corporate Communications & Public Affairs:
 Bill J. Reed
VP, Soybeans and Grains: John B. Ruff
Director, Marketing, Food Ingredients: Dan Meins
Manager, Sales, Private Label: Randy Johnson
Manager, Sales, Rice Feed Ingredients: Sherry Brantley

LOCATIONS

HQ: Riceland Foods, Inc.
 2120 S. Park Ave., Stuttgart, AR 72160
Phone: 870-673-5500   **Fax:** 870-673-3366
Web: www.riceland.com

COMPETITORS

AarhusKarlshamn
American Rice
Cereal Byproducts
CHS
Connell Company
Ebro Puleva
Farmers' Rice Cooperative
Goya
Mars
Producers Rice Mill
Riviana Foods

HISTORICAL FINANCIALS

Company Type: Cooperative

Income Statement

FYE: July 31

	REVENUE ($ mil.)	NET INCOME ($ mil.)	NET PROFIT MARGIN	EMPLOYEES
7/04	951	—	—	1,900
7/03	873	—	—	1,900
7/02	750	—	—	—
7/01	683	—	—	—
7/00	694	—	—	—
7/99	813	—	—	1,850
7/98	804	—	—	1,850
7/97	868	—	—	1,850
7/96	734	—	—	1,850
7/95	737	—	—	1,850
Annual Growth	**2.9%**	**—**	**—**	**0.3%**

Revenue History

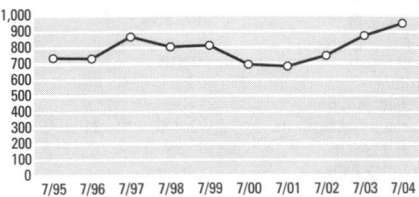

Rich Products

Starting in 1945 with "the miracle cream from the soya bean," Rich Products has grown from a niche maker of soy-based whipped toppings and frozen desserts to a major US frozen foods manufacturer. Since the 1960s the company has developed products, such as Coffee Rich (non-dairy coffee creamer), and expanded to include frozen bakery and pizza doughs and ingredients for the foodservice and in-store bakery markets, plus RICH-SEAPAK (seafood) and Byron's (barbecue). Rich Products markets more than 2,000 products in about 75 countries. The company, owned and operated by the founding Rich family, also owns the Buffalo Bisons, the Jamestown Jammers, and the Wichita Wranglers minor-league baseball teams.

In a move to grow its dessert offerings, Rich acquired Mother's Kitchen (gourmet cakes and cheesecakes) in 2003. Continuing to add to its offerings, that year Rich also acquired Morningstar Foods' brand frozen whipped topping and creamer lines from Dean Foods. Adding to its overall growth, in 2004 Rich announced a joint venture with Grupo Bimbo (called Fripan S.A. de C.V.) to make and sell frozen-dough and fresh-baked specialties to in-store bakery and foodservice companies.

Joining the industry trend toward more convenience foods, in 2005 Rich's introduced a line of "Thaw & Serve" cookies, which can be stored frozen for up to nine months and when thawed have a shelf life of five days. That year its European unit acquired UK bread and cookie maker David Powell Bakeries. The company also began test marketing smoothies and baked goods under the name Food Avenue Express at selected Target stores.

EXECUTIVES

Chairman: Robert E. (Bob) Rich Sr., age 91
President: Robert E. (Bob) Rich Jr.
COO: William G. (Bill) Gisel Jr.
CFO: Christopher Dunstan
EVP and Chief Administrative Officer, The People Network: Maureen O. Hurley
EVP, Innovation: Mindy Rich
SVP, Human Resources: Brian Townson
SVP, Information Systems and CIO: Paul Klein
SVP, Product Management and Innovation:
 Wendy Barth
VP and General Counsel: Jill Bond
President and COO, Rich Products Canada:
 Howard Rich
President, Food Service Division: Dennis Janesz
President, Europe: George Thomopoulos
President, Rich's US/Canada Group: Kevin R. Malchoff
Secretary: David E. Rich
Public Relations: Cindy Anderson

LOCATIONS

HQ: Rich Products Corporation
 1 Robert Rich Way, Buffalo, NY 14213
Phone: 716-878-8000   **Fax:** 716-878-8765
Web: www.richs.com

Rich's has US manufacturing facilities in California, Georgia, Illinois, New Jersey, New York, Ohio, Tennessee, Texas, and Virginia; its foreign operations are located in Argentina, Australia, Brazil, Canada, China, Colombia, India, Malaysia, Mexico, New Zealand, Puerto Rico, Singapore, South Africa, South Korea, Taiwan, Thailand, and the UK.

PRODUCTS/OPERATIONS

Selected Products

Bagels	Icings
Barbecue	Mini desserts
Brownies	Muffins
Cakes	Pies
Cheesecakes	Pizza
Donuts	Pretzels
Dough	Pudding
Bread	Sweet rolls
Cookie	Topping
Dry Mixes	On-top topping
Eclairs and puffs	Prewhipped topping
Fillings	Ready-to-whip topping

COMPETITORS

Campbell Soup	Kraft Foods
ConAgra	Michael Foods, Inc.
Dawn Food Products	Nestlé
Dean Foods	Pinnacle Foods
Del Monte Foods	Ralcorp
Dole Food	Sara Lee Bakery Group
Flowers Foods	Schwan's
Heinz	Unilever
Heinz U.S.	
Consumer Products	

HISTORICAL FINANCIALS

Company Type: Private

Income Statement

FYE: December 31

	REVENUE ($ mil.)	NET INCOME ($ mil.)	NET PROFIT MARGIN	EMPLOYEES
12/03	1,910	—	—	6,500
12/02	1,784	—	—	6,500
12/01	1,702	—	—	6,500
12/00	1,620	—	—	7,000
12/99	1,515	—	—	6,500
12/98	1,400	—	—	6,000
12/97	1,300	—	—	6,000
12/96	1,200	—	—	6,000
12/95	1,100	—	—	6,500
12/94	1,000	—	—	7,000
Annual Growth	**7.5%**	**—**	**—**	**(0.8%)**

Revenue History

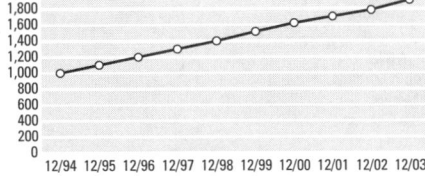

Ritz Camera

Ritz Camera Centers began as a one-man portrait studio and developed into the largest photographic chain in the US. More than 1,200 stores nationwide offer one-hour photofinishing, cameras, film, and related photographic and optical products and services. Stores operate under the Ritz, Camera Shop, Kits, Inkleys, and Wolf names; the company also sells online. Subsidiary Boater's World Marine Centers has more than 110 stores nationwide that offer gear and clothing for fishing and boating. CEO David Ritz owns Ritz Camera, which was founded in 1918. His cousin, Chuck Wolf, owned Wolf Camera (#2 photo chain in the US), which Ritz Camera bought in 2001. Still focused on growth, Ritz bought Camera World in 2002.

EXECUTIVES

Chairman, President, and CEO; Chairman, Ritz Interactive: David M. Ritz, age 56
Vice Chairman: Charles R. (Chuck) Wolf
CFO: Curtis Scheel
EVP: Richard Tranchida
President and CEO, Ritz Interactive: Fred H. Lerner, age 61
VP and Chief Marketing Officer, Ritz Interactive: Andre Brysha, age 58
VP and COO, Ritz Interactive: Peter Tahmin, age 47
VP and CFO, Ritz Interactive: Scott F. Neamand, age 42
Director of Human Resources: Alan MacDonald
Public Relations Manager: Brooke Ritz
Manager, Public Relations and Communications, Ritz Interactive: Mark Malkin

LOCATIONS

HQ: Ritz Camera Centers, Inc.
6711 Ritz Way, Beltsville, MD 20705
Phone: 301-419-0000 **Fax:** 301-419-2995
Web: www.ritzcamera.com

Ritz Camera Centers operates more than 1,200 stores throughout the US. The company also operates more than 110 Boater's World Marine Centers in more than 25 states.

PRODUCTS/OPERATIONS

Selected Merchandise and Services

Boater's World Marine Centers

Apparel
Foul weather gear
Gloves
Jackets
Shirts
Shoes
Shorts
Swimwear
T-shirts
Wetsuits
Electronics
Antennas
Audio-visual equipment
Autopilot equipment
Depth sounders
Fishfinders
GPS/chart plotters
Radar
VHF radios
Weather instruments

Fishing
Bait tanks
Bait well pumps
Downriggers
Nets and traps
Outriggers
Preserved bait and chum
Rods, reels, and combos
Tackle
Watersports
Kneeboards
Life jackets
Pool floats
Snorkeling and dive gear
Tubes
Wakeboards
Water skis

Ritz Camera Centers
Albums and frames
Batteries
Binoculars
Camera accessories
Camera attachments
Cameras
Cellular phones
Darkroom equipment and supplies
Digital imaging accessories
Digital imaging services
Film and processing
Lenses
Memory
One-hour photofinishing
Personalized photo products
Printers and scanners
Projectors and accessories
Studio lighting and accessories
Telescopes

COMPETITORS

Best Buy	PhotoWorks
Circuit City	Travis Boats & Motors
Costco Wholesale	Walgreen
CVS	Wal-Mart
MarineMax	West Marine
MOTO Franchise	

HISTORICAL FINANCIALS

Company Type: Private

Income Statement

FYE: December 31

	ESTIMATED REVENUE ($ mil.)	NET INCOME ($ mil.)	NET PROFIT MARGIN	EMPLOYEES
12/03	1,100	—	—	10,700
12/02	1,200	—	—	10,800
12/01	1,350	—	—	12,000
12/00	800	—	—	7,000
12/99	800	—	—	7,000
12/98	650	—	—	6,500
12/97	625	—	—	7,000
Annual Growth	**9.9%**	**—**	**—**	**7.3%**

Revenue History

Ritz Interactive

Ritz Interactive is all over the Web. The company, a network of e-commerce Web sites, sells digital cameras and photographic products, as well as marine, boating, and fishing gear, through e-retailers, including RitzCamera.com, WolfCamera.com, and BoatersWorld.com. The company also owns and operates a handful of content-based community portals, such as Photography.com and BoatingOnly.com. Its Ritz Interactive Big Print Gallery allows users to upload digital images, view images posted by other community members, and rate photos or post commentary. Ritz Interactive was founded by chairman David Ritz and president Fred Lerner in 1999. Ritz Interactive and Ritz Camera Centers are separate companies.

Each of Ritz Interactive's e-commerce Web sites (individually branded and marketed) employs outsourced distribution and shares a common technology infrastructure.

Ritz Interactive is an affiliate of Ritz Camera Centers (RCC). The two maintain a strategic relationship, whereby Ritz Interactive purchases almost all of its photographic, boating, marine, and fishing products (for resale) from RCC. David Ritz (also chairman and CEO of RCC) and his sister, Linda Dolphin, collectively own a little more than 30% of Ritz Interactive. Ritz Camera Centers owns an 11% stake in the company.

In 2002 Ritz Interactive acquired several of its biggest competitors, including CameraWorld.com and PhotoAlley.com.

EXECUTIVES

Chairman: David M. Ritz, age 56
President, CEO, and Director: Fred H. Lerner, age 61, $520,000 pay
EVP, CFO, and Secretary: Scott F. Neamand, age 42, $175,000 pay (partial-year salary)
VP, COO, and Assistant Secretary: Peter Tahmin, age 47, $215,832 pay
VP and Chief Marketing Officer: Andre Brysha, age 58, $277,782 pay
Auditors: Grant Thornton LLP

LOCATIONS

HQ: Ritz Interactive, Inc.
2010 Main St., Ste. 400, Irvine, CA 92614
Phone: 949-442-0202 **Fax:** 949-442-0210
Web: www.ritzinteractive.com

PRODUCTS/OPERATIONS

2004 Sales

	$ mil.	% of total
Service fees	20.4	98
Product sales	0.4	2
Total	**20.8**	**100**

Selected E-Commerce Web Sites

BoatersWorld.com
CameraWorld.com
eAngler.com
OuterBanksOutfitters.com
PhotoAlley.com
RitzCamera.com
RitzCards.com
ShopAtShark.com (official online retailer of Greg Norman's line of signature apparel and accessories)
WolfCamera.com

Selected Content-Based Web Sites

BoatingOnly.com
FishingOnly.com
Photography.com

COMPETITORS

Amazon.com	CompUSA
Bass Pro Shops	eBay
Best Buy	Overstock.com
Cabela's	Ritz Camera Centers
Circuit City	Wal-Mart

HISTORICAL FINANCIALS

Company Type: Private

Income Statement
FYE: December 31

	REVENUE ($ mil.)	NET INCOME ($ mil.)	NET PROFIT MARGIN	EMPLOYEES
12/04	21	3	13.5%	44
12/03	17	1	3.5%	—
12/02	15	0	2.0%	—
Annual Growth	18.2%	205.5%	—	—

2004 Year-End Financials

Debt ratio: —	Current ratio: 0.81
Return on equity: —	Long-term debt ($ mil.): 0
Cash ($ mil.): 17	

Net Income History

12/95 12/96 12/97 12/98 12/99 12/00 12/01 12/02 12/03 12/04

Rockefeller Foundation

The Rockefeller Foundation is one of the nation's oldest private charitable organizations. It supports grants, fellowships, and conferences for programs that try to identify and alleviate need and suffering around the world. These programs (or themes) include initiatives to foster fair implementation of health care, job opportunities for America's urban poor, creative expression through the humanities and arts, and agricultural policies that ensure food distribution to people in developing countries. The foundation's cross theme of global inclusion binds its programs to a global focus, ensuring that globalization gets doled out democratically and helps populations typically alienated from the global economy.

Former president Gordon Conway reorganized The Rockefeller Foundation's focus towards aiding the world's poor. The foundation's former divisions — such as Agricultural Sciences, Equal Opportunity, and Health Sciences — were placed under the themes of Food Security, Working Communities, and Health Equity. Its non-New York City offices (Bangkok; Mexico City; Nairobi, Kenya; Harare, Zimbabwe; and San Francisco) are taking on increasing responsibility in carrying out the group's global mission.

The foundation maintains no ties to the Rockefeller family or its other philanthropies. An independent board of trustees sets program guidelines and approves all expenditures.

HISTORY

Oil baron John D. Rockefeller, one of America's most criticized capitalists, was also one of its pioneer philanthropists. Before founding The Rockefeller Foundation in 1913, he funded the creation of The University of Chicago (with $36 million over a 25-year period) and formed organizations for medical research (1901), the education of southern African-Americans (1903), and hookworm eradication in the southern US.

Rockefeller turned the control of the foundation over to his son John D. Rockefeller Jr. in 1916. The younger Rockefeller separated the foundation from the family's interests and established an independent board. (The board later rejected a proposal from John Sr. to replace school textbooks that he claimed promoted Bolshevism.)

In the mid-1920s the foundation started conducting basic medical research. In 1928 it absorbed several other Rockefeller philanthropies, adding programs in the natural and social sciences and the arts and humanities. During the 1930s the foundation developed the first effective yellow fever vaccine (1935), continued its worldwide battles against disease, and supported pioneering research in the field of biology. Other grants supported the performing arts in the US and social science research. During WWII it supplied major funding for nuclear science research tools (spectroscopy, X-ray diffraction).

After the war, with an increasing number of large public ventures modeled after the foundation (e.g., the UN's World Health Organization) taking over its traditional physical and natural sciences territory, the organization dissolved its famed biology division in 1951. The following year emphasis swung to agricultural studies under chairman John D. Rockefeller III. The organization took wheat seeds developed at its Mexican food project to Colombia (1950), Chile (1955), and India (1956); a rice institute in the Philippines followed (1960). The Green Revolution sprouted 12 more developing-world institutes.

In the 1960s the foundation began dispatching experts to African and Latin American universities in an effort to raise the level of training at those institutions. The long bear market of the 1970s caused the foundation's assets to drop to a low of $732 million (1977).

The organization set up the Energy Foundation, a joint effort with the MacArthur Foundation and the Pew Charitable Trusts, in 1990 to explore alternate energy sources.

In the mid-1990s the Republican-led Congress launched three probes into the foundation and several other not-for-profits over allegations of political activities that could jeopardize their tax status.

In 1998 Gordon Conway, a British agricultural ecologist, became the foundation's 12th (and first foreign) president. He implemented a retooling of the organization's programs in 1999. He also led an effective campaign against bioengineering giant Monsanto's (now part of Pfizer) plan to market "sterile seeds" that do not regenerate. In 2000 James Orr III, a Rockefeller board member and CEO of Boston's United Asset Management Corporation, succeeded Alice Ilchman as chairman of the board of trustees.

The foundation pledged $5 million for disaster relief efforts in New York City following the September 11 terrorist attacks in 2001. The Rockefeller Foundation launched a multi-year initiative to promote fair intellectual property policies to the poor the following year.

Conway retired from the foundation at the end of 2004; former University of Pennsylvania president Judith Rodin was named as his successor.

EXECUTIVES

Chairman: James F. Orr III, age 61
SVP: Julia I. Lopez
President: Judith (Judy) Rodin, age 60
VP, Administration and Communication:
  Denise Gray-Felder
Director, Africa Region: John Lynam
Director, Creativity and Culture: Morris Vogel
Director, Food Security: Gary H. Toenniessen
Director, Health Equity: Timothy Evans
Associate Director, Health Equity: Joyce L. Moock
Programme Officer for Food Security: Pat Naidoo
Auditors: Ernst & Young LLP

LOCATIONS

HQ: The Rockefeller Foundation
  420 Fifth Ave., New York, NY 10018
Phone: 212-869-8500   **Fax:** 212-764-3468
Web: www.rockfound.org

The Rockefeller Foundation has field offices in Kenya, Thailand, and the US, and maintains the Bellagio Study and Conference Center in northern Italy.

PRODUCTS/OPERATIONS

Themes
Creativity & Culture
Food Security
Global Inclusion
Health Equity
Working Communities (employment, education, and representation for US urban poor)

HISTORICAL FINANCIALS

Company Type: Foundation

Income Statement
FYE: December 31

	REVENUE ($ mil.)	NET INCOME ($ mil.)	NET PROFIT MARGIN	EMPLOYEES
12/03	586	—	—	212
12/02	93	—	—	220
12/01	104	—	—	250
12/00	127	—	—	230
12/99	680	—	—	220
12/98	388	—	—	150
12/97	510	—	—	149
12/96	413	—	—	152
12/95	319	—	—	130
12/94	21	—	—	137
Annual Growth	44.8%	—	—	5.0%

Revenue History

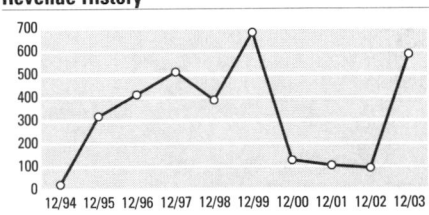

12/94 12/95 12/96 12/97 12/98 12/99 12/00 12/01 12/02 12/03

Rooms To Go

Need that sofa, recliner, table, and lamp in a hurry? Rooms To Go — with about 100 stores in Florida, Georgia, North Carolina, South Carolina, Tennessee, and Texas — has transformed itself into the top-selling furniture retailer in the US. The company markets its limited selection of furniture to brand-conscious, time-pressed customers. It packages low- to moderately priced furniture and accessories and offers discounts for those willing to buy a roomful. Rooms To Go also operates a Rooms to Go Kids chain with more than 20 stores in the Southeast, Texas, and Puerto Rico. President and owner Jeffrey Seaman and his father, Morty, founded the firm in 1990 after selling Seaman Furniture Company.

In August 2005 Rooms To Go won the bidding war for bankrupt Atlanta-based Rhodes Furniture. The company plans to convert an unspecified number of Rhodes' 50 stores in Florida, Alabama, and Georgia to the Rooms To Go format; it will sell the remaining stores to other furniture retailers.

EXECUTIVES

President and CEO: Jeffrey (Jeff) Seaman
COO: Steve Buckley
CFO: Lewis Lou Stein
VP Advertising: Richard Scobey
IT Director: Russ Rosen
Director Human Resources: Linda Garcia

LOCATIONS

HQ: Rooms To Go, Inc.
 11540 Hwy. 92 East, Seffner, FL 33584
Phone: 813-623-5400   **Fax:** 813-620-1717
Web: www.roomstogo.com

COMPETITORS

Bassett Furniture	J. C. Penney
Bombay Company	La-Z-Boy
Ethan Allen	Pier 1 Imports
Furniture.com	Rowe Companies
Havertys	Sears
IKEA	

HISTORICAL FINANCIALS

Company Type: Private

Income Statement

FYE: December 31

	REVENUE ($ mil.)	NET INCOME ($ mil.)	NET PROFIT MARGIN	EMPLOYEES
12/03	1,400	—	—	5,700
12/02	1,300	—	—	5,500
12/01	1,260	—	—	5,500
12/00	1,040	—	—	4,834
12/99	860	—	—	4,000
12/98	720	—	—	3,500
12/97	600	—	—	3,314
12/96	450	—	—	—
Annual Growth	17.6%	—	—	9.5%

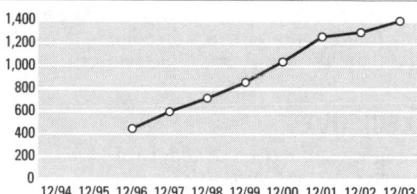

Revenue History

Chart showing revenue from 12/94 to 12/03, rising from about 450 to about 1,300.

Rooney Holdings

Film star Mickey isn't the only Rooney to have landed big contracts. Rooney Holdings (formerly Rooney Brothers), through Manhattan Construction and other subsidiaries, builds hospitals, government buildings (George Bush Presidential Library in Texas), offices, highways, and sports arenas (Reliant Stadium in Houston). It offers construction management, general contracting, and design/build services in the US, Mexico, Central America, and the Caribbean. It also assembles and distributes construction materials, operates an insurance agency, and manufactures electronics. The family-owned group was formed in 1984 to acquire Manhattan Construction Company, which was founded by patriarch L. H. Rooney in 1896.

EXECUTIVES

Chairman and CEO: L. Francis Rooney III
President and COO; CEO, Hope Lumber:
 James (Jim) Cavanaugh
CFO and Chief Administrative Officer: Kevin P. Moore
VP Information Technology: Duwayn Anderson
VP Administration: Jackie Proffitt
VP and Corporate Controller: Paul Vaughn
VP Human Resources: Bill Vogt
Auditors: Hogan & Slovacek

LOCATIONS

HQ: Rooney Holdings, Inc.
 1400 Gulf Shore Blvd., Ste. 184, Naples, FL 34102
Phone: 239-403-0375   **Fax:** 239-403-0316
Web: www.rooneybrothers.com

Rooney Holdings has offices in Naples, Florida and Tulsa, Oklahoma.

PRODUCTS/OPERATIONS

Selected Construction Areas

Airport and aviation
Corporate and commercial
Corrections
Entertainment
Government
Health care
Hospitality and leisure
Institutional and academic
Special projects
Sports and entertainment

COMPETITORS

84 Lumber	Home Depot
Austin Industries	Jacobs Engineering
Barton Malow	Lowe's
Bechtel	M. A. Mortenson
Beck Group	McCoy
Fluor	Siemens
Foster Wheeler	Skanska USA Building
Hensel Phelps	Turner Corporation
Construction	Washington Group

HISTORICAL FINANCIALS

Company Type: Private

Income Statement

FYE: September 30

	REVENUE ($ mil.)	NET INCOME ($ mil.)	NET PROFIT MARGIN	EMPLOYEES
9/04	1,457	—	—	2,625
9/03	1,262	—	—	2,400
9/02	1,201	—	—	2,500
9/01	1,053	—	—	2,400
9/00	1,002	—	—	2,400
9/99	925	—	—	2,400
9/98	769	—	—	2,000
9/97	611	—	—	1,800
9/96	500	—	—	1,800
9/95	230	—	—	750
Annual Growth	22.8%	—	—	14.9%

Revenue History

Chart showing revenue from 9/95 to 9/04, rising from about 230 to about 1,457.

Rotary

The rotary phone may be gone, but Rotary International is still going strong. The service organization addresses issues such as HIV/AIDS, hunger, and illiteracy, and includes about 31,000 clubs in more than 170 countries with a membership of nearly 1.2 million (predominantly men, although women are its fastest-growing segment). Its not-for-profit Rotary Foundation invests in international education and humanitarian programs (funds are raised through voluntary contributions). Rotary International also sponsors Interact clubs for secondary school students, as well as a network of about 8,000 Rotaract clubs for members ages 18-30. It is governed by a 19-member board and maintains offices globally.

Membership in Rotary clubs is by invitation only. Each club strives to include representatives from major businesses, professions, and institutions in its community. The organization's name arose from the early practice of rotating meetings among members' offices. Originally an all-male organization, women were first admitted in the US in 1986 and worldwide in 1989.

HISTORY

On Feb. 23, 1905, lawyer Paul Harris met with three friends in an office in Chicago's Unity Building. Inspired by the fellowship and tolerance of his boyhood home in Wallingford, Vermont, Harris proposed organizing a men's club to meet periodically for the purpose of camaraderie and making business contacts. The new endeavor was organized as the Rotary Club of Chicago and had 30 members by the end of the year.

As additional clubs followed, the organization assumed its role as a civic and service organization (the installation of public comfort stations in Chicago's City Hall was one of its first projects). At the first convention of the National Association of Rotary Clubs in 1910, Harris was elected president. International clubs soon followed, and by 1921 there were Rotary clubs on each continent.

In 1932, while struggling to revive a company with financial difficulties, Rotarian Herbert Taylor devised a statement of business ethics that later became the Rotarian mantra. Taylor's "4-Way Test" consisted of the following questions: "Is it the truth? Is it fair to all concerned? Will it build goodwill and better friendships? Will it be beneficial to all concerned?"

During WWII Rotary clubs promoted war relief and peace fund efforts. Following WWII the clubs assisted in efforts to aid refugees and prisoners of war. The extent of Rotarian involvement in international issues became clear when 49 members assisted in drafting the United Nations Charter in 1945.

The first significant contributions to The Rotary Foundation followed Harris' death in 1947. These funds formed the bedrock for the foundation's programs, and in 1965 the foundation created its Matching Grants and Group Study Exchange programs. Rotary International also welcomed younger members in the 1960s by creating its Interact and Rotaract clubs in 1962 and 1968, respectively.

The largest meeting of Rotarians occurred in 1978 when almost 40,000 members attended the organization's Tokyo convention. But controversy was fast approaching the male-only organization. In 1978 a California Rotary club defied the male-only requirement and admitted two women. Claiming that the club had violated the organization's constitution, Rotary International revoked the club's charter. A lengthy court battle ensued, and a series of appeals landed the issue on the docket of the US Supreme Court. In 1987 the court ruled that the all-male requirement was discriminatory. Two years later Rotary International officially did away with its all-male status.

In the 1990s membership in Rotary clubs grew, but at a slower pace than in the organization's past. Mary Wolfenberger was appointed the organization's first female CFO in 1993 (resigned 1997). In 1998 Rotary International joined with the United Nations to launch a series of humanitarian service projects in developing areas. In 1999 the organization spearheaded events to help flood victims in North Carolina and refugees in the Balkans. In 2000 the group created a program specializing in peace and conflict resolution. Rotary International established its first Internet-based Rotary club in early 2002. Also that year the group founded the Rotary Centers for International Studies which selects 70 scholars a year to participate in a master's-level peace studies program.

In addition to celebrating its 100th anniversary in 2005, the organization awarded grants in Sudan and Indonesia to stop polio and assisted victims of the Southeast Asian tsunami.

EXECUTIVES

President and Director: Carl-Wilhelm Stenhammar
President-elect and Director: William B. Boyd
VP and Director: Serge Gouteyron
General Secretary and Director: Edwin H. Futa
Treasurer and Director: Jocelyn I. Bolante
Controller: Mark A. Vieth
Director Human Resources: Carolyn Engblom
Communications Services General Manager: Kathy Kessenich
Membership Services General Manager: Theresa Nissen
Rotary Foundation General Manager: Duane Sterling
Corporate Services Manager: Andrew McDonald
Public Relations Manager: Susan Ross
Auditors: Deloitte & Touche LLP

LOCATIONS

HQ: Rotary International
1 Rotary Center, 1560 Sherman Ave.,
Evanston, IL 60201
Phone: 847-866-3000   **Fax:** 847-328-8281
Web: www.rotary.org

PRODUCTS/OPERATIONS

Selected Programs
Educational programs
  Ambassadorial Scholarships
  Grants for University Teachers
  Group Study Exchange (GSE)
  Rotary World Peace Scholarships
Humanitarian grants
  Discovery Grants
  Grants for Rotary Volunteers
  Matching Grants
  New Opportunities Grants
  Peace Program Grants
PolioPlus Program
  Polio Eradication Advocacy
  Polio Eradication Private Sector Campaign
  PolioPlus Partners

HISTORICAL FINANCIALS

Company Type: Not-for-profit

Income Statement

FYE: June 30

	REVENUE ($ mil.)	NET INCOME ($ mil.)	NET PROFIT MARGIN	EMPLOYEES
6/03	61	—	—	600
6/02	56	—	—	500
6/01	62	—	—	500
6/00	61	—	—	450
6/99	61	—	—	450
6/98	73	—	—	400
6/97	72	—	—	400
6/96	62	—	—	400
6/95	60	—	—	350
6/94	59	—	—	450
Annual Growth	0.3%	—	—	3.2%

Revenue History

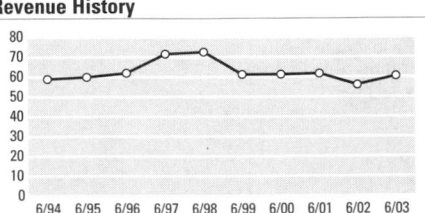

Roundy's

Roundy's rounds up name-brand and private-label goods and distributes them to warehouse and grocery stores throughout the Midwest. Roundy's services about 580 independent and licensee stores. The company also owns around 130 retail stores in Wisconsin, Minnesota, and other Midwest locations. Roundy's offers its members and customer stores support services, including accounting and inventory control, advertising, and store financing. Roundy's is a leading Wisconsin food retailer, with supermarket chains operating under the Pick 'N Save and Copps Food Centers banners. Roundy's was founded in 1872. It is owned by the private investment firm Willis Stein & Partners.

More than half of Roundy's sales come from its distribution business to independent Midwestern grocery stores. However, the company also aims to increase sales and profits in its retail division. To that end, Roundy's has been acquiring independent stores: in 2003 it bought 31 Rainbow Foods stores in the Minneapolis/St. Paul metro area from Fleming Companies and in 2004 Roundy's subsidiary Ultra Mart Foods purchased the seven Wisconsin retail Pick 'N Save grocery stores owned by McAdams Inc. The company has also been selling off its distribution centers.

Roundy's is the leading food retailer in Wisconsin, owning and operatating 89 stores in the state.

HISTORY

Migration from the eastern US and overseas was boosting Milwaukee's ranks when William Smith, Judson Roundy, and Sidney Hauxhurst formed grocery wholesaler Smith, Roundy & Co. in 1872. Smith left the firm in 1878 for his first of two terms as Wisconsin's governor, and William Peckham joined the enterprise, which was then renamed Roundy, Peckham & Co. Two years later Charles Dexter joined the company, by then operating in five Midwestern states and running a manufacturing business.

The wholesaler became Roundy, Peckham & Dexter Co. in 1902, following the death of Hauxhurst (Roundy died in 1907). The company introduced its first private-label product — salt — in 1922. In 1929 Dexter (then 84) came up with a plan to publicize the Roundy's name by handing out cookbooks that called for the company's goods.

Roy Johnson, who joined the company in 1912, was named president near the end of the Depression. In the 1940s the wholesaler acquired smaller companies in the region. The company became Roundy's in 1952 when Roundy, Peckham & Dexter was bought by a group comprising hundreds of Wisconsin grocery retailers. Johnson remained head of the new company until his death in 1962. James Aldrich led the company for the next 11 years.

In 1970 Roundy's started Insurance Planners, which offered insurance to retailers. Vincent Little became president of the company in 1973. Two years later Roundy's began a real estate subsidiary (Ronco Realty) and opened its first Pick 'n Save Warehouse Food store.

The company expanded in the mid-1980s through the purchase of distributors. But expansion hurt profits, and dividends were suspended in 1984 and 1985. In the late 1980s several Pick 'n Save stores opened throughout Wisconsin and other Midwestern states. Owners grew suspicious of Little's accounting practices and the special treatment given a Roundy's-owned store run by his son, and in 1986 they forced him out of his president and CEO positions. John Dickson replaced him.

By 1994 Pick 'n Save had vastly upgraded its image — one store sold $1,000 cognac and featured an $18,000 cappuccino machine. However, sales dropped off for the third straight year. COO Gerald Lestina was named CEO in 1995, replacing Dickson, who continued as chairman. Dickson died later that year.

Roundy's did not pay its members a dividend in 1995 as it made an effort to offset losses in Michigan and Ohio. To ease those losses, in 1997 the company closed 12 poorly performing stores in those states. A year later a fire destroyed its Evansville, Indiana, warehouse; the company rebuilt the facility in 1999. Also in 1999 Roundy's purchased three supermarkets in Indiana from Kroger and The John C. Groub Company.

The Mega Marts and Ultra Mart chains, which together operate 24 Pick 'n Save stores, primarily in Wisconsin, were acquired by Roundy's in 2000. In 2001 Roundy's launched an online grocery shopping service, called Pick 'n Save Online Shopping, in two test stores in Wisconsin (the plan was eventually scuttled). Also in 2001 the company purchased its competitor, The Copps Corporation, acquiring 21 stores in north and central Wisconsin and a wholesale business that distributes to retailers in Wisconsin and northern Michigan. Chicago-based Willis Stein & Partners bought Roundy's in 2002.

Dale Riley, who had been hired to revitalize Roundy's flagging Rainbow Food chain, resigned in 2004 after a year on the job. That year the company closed its distribution operations in Illinois.

Nash Finch bought Roundy's wholesale food distribution operations in Westville, Indiana, and Lima, Ohio, as well as two Ohio retail stores for about $225 million in 2005.

EXECUTIVES

Chairman, President, and CEO: Robert A. Mariano, age 55, $1,170,000 pay
EVP and CFO: Darren W. Karst, age 45, $855,000 pay
Group VP, Human Resources: Colleen J. Stenholt, age 54
Group VP, IT and Business Processes: John W. Boyle, age 47
Group VP, Legal, Risk, and Treasury; Corporate Secretyar: Edward G. Kitz, age 51
Group VP, Retail Operations and Customer Satisfaction: Gary L. Fryda, age 52, $498,297 pay
Group VP, Merchandising and Procurement: Robin S. Michel, age 50, $437,250 pay
Group VP, Sales and Marketing: Ronald Cooper, age 54
Group VP, Supply Chain: Donald S. Rosanova, age 55, $436,865 pay
Group VP, Wholesale Development & Real Estate: Michael J. Schmitt, age 56
VP, Procurement and Merchandising: DAvid Acchione
VP and General Manager, Minnesota Retail: Mark Beaty
Director, Communications: Lynn Guyer
Director, Floral: Kathy Hession
Auditors: Ernst & Young LLP

LOCATIONS

HQ: Roundy's, Inc.
875 E. Wisconsin Ave., Milwaukee, WI 53202
Phone: 414-231-5000   **Fax:** 414-231-7939
Web: www.roundys.com

Roundy's distributes its goods from five wholesale distribution centers located in Indiana, Ohio, and Wisconsin to approximately 580 licensee and independent retail operations throughout the Midwest. Its retail stores are located in Illinois, Michigan, Minnesota, Ohio, and Wisconsin.

2004 Company-Owned Retail Stores

	No.
Wisconsin	89
Minnesota	31
Michigan	2
Ohio	2
Illinois	1
Total	**125**

PRODUCTS/OPERATIONS

2004 Sales

	% of total
Wholesale	52
Retail	48
Total	**100**

2004 Retail Store Sales

	% of total
Company-owned stores	48
Independent retailers	38
Licensed Pick 'n Save stores	14
Total	**100**

Selected Private Labels
IGA
Old Time
Roundy's

Selected Product Lines
Bakery goods
Dairy products
Dry groceries
Fresh produce
Frozen foods
General merchandise
Meats

Selected Services
Centralized bakery purchasing
Business development
Financing
Group advertising
Insurance
Inventory control
Market analysis
Merchandising
Ordering assistance
Point-of-sale support
Pricing services
Purchasing reports
Retail accounting
Retail training

COMPETITORS

A&P	IGA
Albertson's	Kroger
ALDI	McLane
AWG	Meijer
Central Grocers Cooperative	Nash Finch
	S. Abraham & Sons
Certified Grocers Midwest	Spartan Stores
Costco Wholesale	SUPERVALU
Dominick's	SYSCO
GSC Enterprises	Wal-Mart
Hy-Vee	

HISTORICAL FINANCIALS
Company Type: Private

Income Statement

	REVENUE ($ mil.)	NET INCOME ($ mil.)	NET PROFIT MARGIN	EMPLOYEES
			FYE: Saturday nearest December 31	
12/04	4,777	61	1.3%	21,855
12/03	4,383	55	1.2%	19,999
12/02	3,638	31	0.9%	13,151
12/01	3,450	26	0.7%	13,451
12/00	2,984	21	0.7%	9,071
12/99	2,717	18	0.6%	5,617
12/98	2,579	12	0.5%	5,193
12/97	2,611	11	0.4%	5,071
12/96	2,579	10	0.4%	5,481
12/95	2,488	9	0.4%	4,839
Annual Growth	**7.5%**	**23.6%**	**—**	**18.2%**

2004 Year-End Financials

Debt ratio: 132.4%
Return on equity: 14.4%
Cash ($ mil.): 106
Current ratio: 1.07
Long-term debt ($ mil.): 596

Net Income History

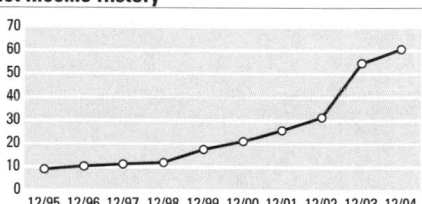

| 12/95 | 12/96 | 12/97 | 12/98 | 12/99 | 12/00 | 12/01 | 12/02 | 12/03 | 12/04 |

Royster-Clark

Royster-Clark has been spreading it on thick for more than 125 years. The company makes and distributes fertilizer and crop-protection products. It also processes seed for other companies and sells seed under its own label. Operations include some 30 fertilizer granulation and blending and seed-processing plants; 250 retail farm supply centers; and 75 distribution terminals and warehouses. The company operates primarily in the midwestern and southeastern US. A majority of Royster-Clark's sales come from the distribution of fertilizers bought from third parties. Members of the firm's management team collectively own 49% of the company. Investment firm 399 Venture Partners (a Citigroup affiliate) owns 38%.

EXECUTIVES

Chairman and CEO: Francis P. Jenkins Jr., age 62
President and COO: G. Kenneth (Ken) Moshenek, age 53, $485,000 pay
CFO: Paul M. Murphy, age 60, $310,000 pay
Senior Managing Director, International: Max Baer, age 72
Managing Director, Credit and Farm Financing: Michael J. Galvin, age 41
Managing Director, Crop Protection and Seed: Gary L. Floyd, age 50
Managing Director, Environmental, Health, and Safety: J. William (Billy) Pirkle, age 43
Managing Director, Human Resources: Kenneth W. (Ken) Carter, age 59
Managing Director and Controller: Joel F. Dunbar, age 56
Auditors: KPMG LLP

LOCATIONS

HQ: Royster-Clark, Inc.
1251 Avenue of the Americas, Ste. 900,
New York, NY 10020
Phone: 212-332-2965 **Fax:** 212-332-2999
Web: www.roysterclark.com

Royster-Clark has production facilities in Alabama, Florida, Georgia, Illinois, Kentucky, North Carolina, Ohio, South Carolina, Tennessee, Virginia, and Wisconsin.

PRODUCTS/OPERATIONS

2004 Sales

	$ mil.	% of total
Fertilizer	721.1	67
Crop Protection	178.8	17
Seed	81.3	8
Other	89.8	8
Total	**1,071.0**	**100**

Selected Products

Crop Nutrients
  Bagged and bulk dry fertilizers
  Custom-blended fertilizers
  Fertilizer materials
  Granulated fertilizers
  Lime and landplaster
  Liquid fertilizers
  Specialty fertilizers

Crop Protection
  Fungicides
  Herbicides
  Insecticides

Seeds
  Soybean
  Wheat

Selected Services

Agronomist services
Crop management
Crop protection application
Crop scouting
Custom blending
Custom spreading
Farm delivery
Soil sampling

COMPETITORS

Agriliance	GROWMARK
Agrium	Helena Chemical
Canpotex	Monsanto
Cargill	Southern States
ConAgra	Terra Industries
Dow Chemical	Tractor Supply
DuPont	UAP Holding
FMC	Wilbur-Ellis

HISTORICAL FINANCIALS

Company Type: Private

Income Statement

FYE: December 31

	REVENUE ($ mil.)	NET INCOME ($ mil.)	NET PROFIT MARGIN	EMPLOYEES
12/04	1,071	1	0.1%	2,820
12/03	960	(21)	—	3,120
12/02	898	(5)	—	3,130
12/01	954	(9)	—	3,130
12/00	913	(5)	—	3,130
12/99	715	7	0.9%	—
Annual Growth	**8.4%**	**(31.4%)**	**—**	**(2.6%)**

2004 Year-End Financials

Debt ratio: 588.7%   Current ratio: 2.19
Return on equity: 1.8%   Long-term debt ($ mil.): 325
Cash ($ mil.): 0

Net Income History

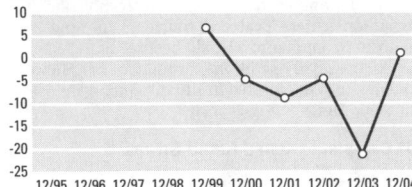

Rumpke

Rumpke Consolidated Companies provides waste collection, disposal, and recycling services for residential, commercial, and industrial customers in Kentucky, Indiana, and Ohio. The company operates nine landfills, seven transfer stations, and five recycling facilities. In addition, Rumpke rents portable toilets and repairs and distributes hydraulic components. The Rumpke family owns the company, which was founded in 1932.

EXECUTIVES

President and CEO: William J. (Bill) Rumpke Sr.
COO: William J. (Bill) Rumpke Jr.
CFO and Treasurer: Philip E. (Phil) Wehrman
Director, Engineering and Environmental Affairs: Jay Roberts
Director, Human Resources: Charla R. Cabe
Director, Marketing and Sales: Matthew J. (Matt) Bauer
Director, Safety: Lawrence R. (Larry) Stone
General Manager, Rumpke Recycling: Stephen J. (Steve) Sargent
General Counsel and Secretary: James E. (Jim) Thaxton
Senior Corporate Communication Executive: Amanda Pratt
Director, Hauling: Kevin Downey

LOCATIONS

HQ: Rumpke Consolidated Companies, Inc.
10795 Hughes Rd., Cincinnati, OH 45251
Phone: 513-851-0122 **Fax:** 513-851-2057
Web: www.rumpke.com

COMPETITORS

Allied Waste
Casella Waste Systems
Republic Services
Waste Management

HISTORICAL FINANCIALS

Company Type: Private

Income Statement

FYE: June 30

	REVENUE ($ mil.)	NET INCOME ($ mil.)	NET PROFIT MARGIN	EMPLOYEES
6/04	270	—	—	2,000
6/03	270	—	—	2,600
6/02	300	—	—	1,900
6/01	293	—	—	2,500
6/00	278	—	—	2,500
Annual Growth	**(0.7%)**	**—**	**—**	**(5.4%)**

Revenue History

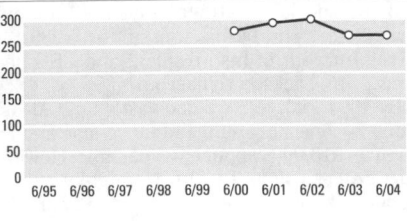

Sacramento Kings

The Sacramento Kings have been royally frustrated for most of their history. Les Harrison founded the team as the Royals in 1945 and coached it to an NBA title in 1951 by beating the New York Knicks in seven games. Afterward, the club became a bit of a vagabond and was known variously as the Cincinnati Royals, the Kansas City-Omaha Kings, and the Kansas City Kings. Then Gregg Lukenbill bought the team and moved it to Sacramento, California, in 1985. Brothers Joe and Gavin Maloof bought the team in 1998 through their Maloof Sports and Entertainment, which also owns the WNBA's Sacramento Monarchs and the teams' ARCO Arena, as well as the Palms Casino Hotel in Las Vegas.

EXECUTIVES

Co-Owner: Gavin Maloof
Co-Owner: Joe Maloof
President: John Thomas
President, Basketball Operations: Geoff Petrie
Head Coach: Rick Adelman, age 59
SVP, Business Operations: John Rienhart
VP, Arena Programming: Mike Duncan
VP, Basketball Operations: Wayne Cooper
VP, Human Resources: Donna Ruiz
VP, Marketing and Brand Development and Monarchs Business Operations: Danette Leighton
Senior Director, Public Relations and Community Service: Sonja Brown
Director, Finance: Ruth Hill

LOCATIONS

HQ: Sacramento Kings
ARCO Arena, 1 Sports Pkwy.,
Sacramento, CA 95834
Phone: 916-928-0000 **Fax:** 916-928-8109
Web: www.nba.com/kings

The Sacramento Kings play at the 17,317-seat ARCO Arena in Sacramento, California.

COMPETITORS

Golden State Warriors
Los Angeles Clippers
Los Angeles Lakers
Phoenix Suns
Portland Trail Blazers
Seattle SuperSonics

HISTORICAL FINANCIALS

Company Type: Private

Income Statement FYE: June 30

	REVENUE ($ mil.)	NET INCOME ($ mil.)	NET PROFIT MARGIN	EMPLOYEES
6/04	118	—	—	—
6/03	102	—	—	—
6/02	102	—	—	—
6/01	87	—	—	—
6/00	71	—	—	—
6/99	34	—	—	80
6/98	52	—	—	80
6/97	50	—	—	—
6/96	44	—	—	—
Annual Growth	**13.1%**	**—**	**—**	**0.0%**

Revenue History

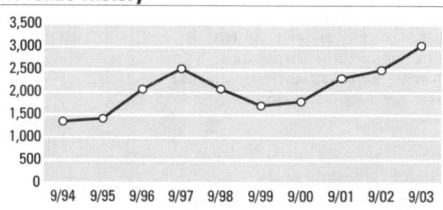

Salvation Army

The largest civil army in the land, the Salvation Army is about 2 million strong. Its faith-based programs assist alcoholics, drug addicts, the homeless, the handicapped, the elderly, prison inmates, people in crisis, and the unemployed through a range of services. These include day-care centers, programs for people with disabilities, substance abuse programs, and educational facilities for at-risk students. It also provides disaster relief in the US and abroad. The Salvation Army USA is a national unit of the Salvation Army, an international body based in London, which oversees Army activities in more than 100 countries.

The name Salvation Army may only ring a bell with you around Christmas, but Salvation Army USA is always working. Active as a church and a charity, the organization serves nearly 37 million people a year. It also provides disaster relief in the US and abroad. The Salvation Army usually tops the list of US not-for-profits in terms of donations received: In 2004 contributions reached about $1.5 billion.

Along with promoting charity, the Salvation Army seeks to save souls. As an evangelical church, it preaches the message of salvation through Jesus Christ. Before joining the organization and becoming a soldier (a lay member), one must sign an agreement known as the "Articles of War," a commitment to the avoidance of gambling, debt, and profanity and to abstention from alcohol, tobacco, and other recreational drugs. The US organization includes some 450,000 soldiers, more than 1 million volunteers, and nearly 5,400 officers, who are also ordained ministers.

Officers are expected to wear their uniforms at all times and to work full-time for the Salvation Army. They receive no salary; instead, they are provided with room and board and given a limited stipend.

The Salvation Army USA is only one of scores of national Salvation Army organizations around the world, which report to the group's global leader, Gen. John Larsson, at its international headquarters in the UK.

HISTORY

William Booth (1829-1912) started preaching the gospel as a Wesleyan Methodist in the UK, but the church expelled him because he insisted on preaching outside and to everyone, including the poor. In 1865 he moved to the slums of London's East End and attracted large crowds with his volatile sermons. Opposition to his message of universal salvation for drunks, thieves, prostitutes, and gamblers often caused riots. In fact, the first women in the organization wore bonnets designed with a dual purpose in mind — warmth and protection from flying objects.

At a meeting in 1878, a sign was used referring to the "Salvation Army." Booth adopted the reference as both the name and the style of his organization. Members became soldiers, evangelists were officers, and Booth was referred to as "General." Prayers became knee drills, and contributions were called cartridges.

The Salvation Army marched across the Atlantic to the US in 1880, led by seven women and one man. Women have always played an active role in the Salvation Army, both as officers and soldiers. Booth's wife, Catherine Mumford, was a leading suffragette, and Booth advocated equal rights for women.

In 1891 a crab pot was placed on a San Francisco street to collect donations, with a sign reading "Keep the Pot Boiling." The idea led to the Salvation Army's annual Christmas kettle program.

During WWI the organization became famous for the doughnuts that it served the doughboys fighting on the front lines. After some internal dissension, the Salvation Army took its only public political stance in 1928 with the endorsement of Herbert Hoover for his support of Prohibition during his presidential campaign. The charity opened its first home for alcoholics in 1939, in Detroit.

After WWII the Salvation Army began using such radio and TV programs as *Heartbeat Theater* and *Army of Stars* to spread its message.

Over the years the Salvation Army has provided assistance to victims of hurricanes, floods, and earthquakes. Volunteers rendered almost 70,000 service hours in the aftermath of the Oklahoma City bombing in 1995, counseling more than 1,600 victims and family members, helping with funeral arrangements, and providing food, clothing, and travel assistance. Indicative of the organization's readiness and extensive reach, its volunteers were helping victims in Guam within minutes of the 1997 Korean Air plane crash. The Salvation Army was quickly on the scene after a Jonesboro, Arkansas, shooting incident in 1998 when four students and one teacher were killed by fellow students. Late that year the organization received the largest donation in its history — $80 million from Joan Kroc, wife of McDonald's co-founder Ray Kroc.

In 2000 Gen. Paul Rader retired, and with incoming Gen. John Gowans the organization initiated its first reform in more than 100 years by allowing officers to marry outside the ranks. Following the September 11 attacks in 2001, the Salvation Army provided assistance to rescue workers and families affected by the tragedy through its Disaster Relief Fund.

In 2003 Joan B. Kroc left the Salvation Army a $1.5 billion donation. Receiving one of the largest individual charitable gifts ever was a boon for the Salvation Army's future, but the battles continue. The money is earmarked for community centers and cannot be used to support the Army's existing programs, so ask not for whom the bell tolls.

EXECUTIVES

Chairman National Advisory Board: Edsel B. Ford II, age 56
General (International Director): John Larsson
Commissioner (National Commander): W. Todd Bassett, age 64, $28,000 pay
Commissioner (Eastern Territory): Lawrence Moretz
Commissioner (Southern Territory): Philip Needham
Commissioner (Central Territory): Kenneth Baillie
Commissioner (Western Territory): Linda Bond
Commissioner (National President Women's Organizations): Carol Bassett
National Chief Secretary: Larry Bosh

LOCATIONS

HQ: The Salvation Army National Corporation
615 Slaters Ln., Alexandria, VA 22313
Phone: 703-684-5500   **Fax:** 703-684-3478
Web: www.salvationarmyusa.org

PRODUCTS/OPERATIONS

Selected Services

Alcohol and drug treatment centers	Military canteens and hostels
Clinics and hospitals	Nurseries and day care centers
Convalescent homes	
Counseling	Occupational centers
Crisis counseling	Prison ministry
Food distribution centers	Probation housing
Handicapped housing	Refugee centers
Homeless shelters	Science and trade schools
Institutes for the blind	Student housing
Leprosy clinics	Welfare aid

HISTORICAL FINANCIALS

Company Type: Not-for-profit

Income Statement FYE: September 30

	REVENUE ($ mil.)	NET INCOME ($ mil.)	NET PROFIT MARGIN	EMPLOYEES
9/03	3,040	—	—	42,530
9/02	2,497	—	—	40,000
9/01	2,313	—	—	45,000
9/00	1,803	—	—	45,096
9/99	1,707	—	—	43,318
9/98	2,078	—	—	39,883
9/97	2,525	—	—	40,770
9/96	2,070	—	—	44,626
9/95	1,421	—	—	38,999
9/94	1,355	—	—	39,591
Annual Growth	**9.4%**	**—**	**—**	**0.8%**

Revenue History

Sammons Enterprises

Sammons Enterprises summons its revenues from several sources. The diversified holding company's interests include insurance (Midland National Life Insurance and North American Company for Life and Health Insurance) and heavy equipment sales and rentals (Briggs Equipment). Sammons Enterprises also owns The Grove Park Inn Resort in Asheville, North Carolina. The late Charles Sammons, an orphan who became a self-made billionaire philanthropist (despite never attending college), founded the company in 1962 to consolidate his already varied holdings. His estate still owns the company, and his widow, Elaine Sammons, serves as chairman.

Sammons Enterprises continues to expand its horizons. Majority-owned private equity firm Sponsor Investments was launched in 2003; it has invested in North American Technologies Group's Tie Tek unit, which supplies railroad ties.

The company also is eyeing the Asia/Pacific region as a potential expansion area.

EXECUTIVES

Chairman: Elaine D. Sammons
President and CEO: Robert W. (Bob) Korba
COO: Robert W. (Bob) Black
SVP Finance and Treasurer: Joseph A. (Joe) Ethridge
VP Organization Development: Bob Kendall
VP Real Estate: Bill Daves
VP, Secretary, and General Counsel: Heather Kreager
VP: Joe Zimmerman
VP: Pamela Doeppe
Chairman and CEO, Sammons Financial Group:
  Michael M. (Mike) Masterson
President and CEO, Grove Park Inn Resort & Spa:
  J. Craig Madison
President and COO, Sammons Financial Group:
  John J. Craig II
Controller: Derek Claybrook
Director, Benefit Plans: Carol Cochran
Auditors: PricewaterhouseCoopers LLP

LOCATIONS

HQ: Sammons Enterprises, Inc.
  5949 Sherry Ln., Ste. 1900, Dallas, TX 75225
Phone: 214-210-5000   **Fax:** 214-210-5099
Web: www.sammonsenterprises.com

Sammons Enterprises and its subsidiaries have operations all across the US.

PRODUCTS/OPERATIONS

Selected Subsidiaries

Briggs Construction Equipment, Inc.
Briggs Industrial Equipment, Inc.
Midland National Life Insurance Company
North American Company for Life and
  Health Insurance Company
North American Company for Life and
  Health Insurance of New York
Sammons Annuity Group
Sammons Power Development, Inc.
Sammons Realty Corporation
Sammons Securities Company, LLC
The Grove Park Inn Resort & Spa

COMPETITORS

Caterpillar
CIGNA
CNH Global
Deere
MetLife
NationsRent Companies
NES Rentals
New York Life
Principal Financial
Prudential
United Rentals

HISTORICAL FINANCIALS

Company Type: Private

Income Statement

	REVENUE ($ mil.)	NET INCOME ($ mil.)	NET PROFIT MARGIN	EMPLOYEES
12/03	1,969	—	—	3,250
12/02	1,950	—	—	3,200
12/01	1,510	—	—	3,000
12/00	1,934	—	—	3,000
12/99	2,000	—	—	2,300
12/98	1,725	—	—	3,250
12/97	1,580	—	—	2,300
12/96	1,600	—	—	2,300
12/95	1,300	—	—	3,300
12/94	1,300	—	—	1,640
Annual Growth	**4.7%**	**—**	**—**	**7.9%**

FYE: December 31

Revenue History

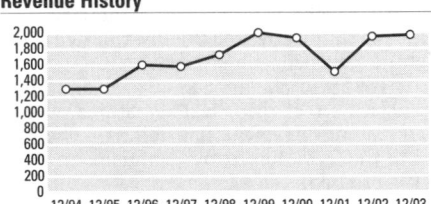

12/94 12/95 12/96 12/97 12/98 12/99 12/00 12/01 12/02 12/03

San Antonio Spurs

Spurred by Tim Duncan, the San Antonio Spurs roped their first NBA championship in 1999, and wrangled a second and third in 2003 and 2005. The club first hit the court as the Dallas Chaparrals in 1967 as part of the American Basketball Association. The Chaparrals became the San Antonio Spurs in 1973 and entered the NBA in 1976 when the leagues merged. Success came in the early 1980s behind George "The Iceman" Gervin, who led the Spurs to five division titles. A partnership led by chairman Peter Holt owns the team. The Spurs jingle in the $175 million SBC Center. The team owns a WNBA franchise, the San Antonio Silver Stars, which began play in the 2003 season.

The team's championship win in 2003 helped boost season ticket sales for the 2003-04 season by more than 30%.

Winning in 2005 was tough; it came in game seven against the defending champion Detroit Pistons.

EXECUTIVES

Chairman and CEO: Peter M. Holt
General Manager: R. C. Buford
EVP Basketball Operations and Head Coach:
  Gregg Popovich, age 56
EVP Business Operations: Russ Bookbinder
EVP Finance and Corporate Development: Rick A. Pych
SVP Broadcasting: Lawrence Payne
VP Community Relations; Executive Director, Spurs Foundation: Alison Fox
VP Finance: Lori Warren
VP Human Resources: Paula Winslow
VP Marketing: Bruce Guthrie
Controller: Jacee Hoggatt
Auditors: Ernst & Young

LOCATIONS

HQ: San Antonio Spurs LLC
  1 SBC Center, San Antonio, TX 78219
Phone: 210-444-5000   **Fax:** 210-444-5100
Web: www.nba.com/spurs

The San Antonio Spurs play at the 18,500-seat SBC Center in San Antonio.

PRODUCTS/OPERATIONS

Titles

NBA Champions (1999, 2003, 2005)
Midwest Division Champions (1981-83, 1990-91, 1995-96, 2001-02)

COMPETITORS

Dallas Mavericks
Houston Rockets
Memphis Grizzlies
New Orleans Hornets

HISTORICAL FINANCIALS

Company Type: Private

Income Statement

	REVENUE ($ mil.)	NET INCOME ($ mil.)	NET PROFIT MARGIN	EMPLOYEES
6/04	108	—	—	—
6/03	105	—	—	—
6/02	83	—	—	—
6/01	82	—	—	165
6/00	67	—	—	—
6/99	42	—	—	100
6/98	61	—	—	75
6/97	52	—	—	75
6/96	60	—	—	75
6/95	57	—	—	75
Annual Growth	**7.5%**	**—**	**—**	**14.0%**

FYE: June 30

Revenue History

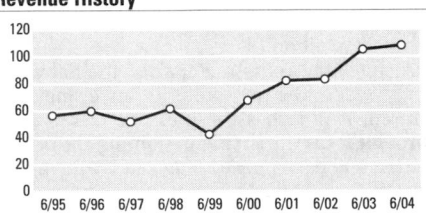

6/95 6/96 6/97 6/98 6/99 6/00 6/01 6/02 6/03 6/04

SAS Institute

Don't talk back to this company about business intelligence. SAS (pronounced "sass"), the world's largest privately held software company, leads the market in data warehousing and data mining software used to gather, manage, and analyze enormous amounts of corporate information. Clients such as Maytag, Air France, and the US Department of Defense use its software to find patterns in customer data, manage resources, and target new business. Founded in 1976, SAS also offers industry-specific integrated software and support packages. Chairman, president, and CEO James Goodnight owns about two-thirds of the company; co-founder and EVP John Sall owns the remainder.

SAS, which has reported 28 consecutive years of sales growth and profitability, continues to expand its product line with such offerings as financial management software and marketing automation and analysis applications. The company has also used acquisitions to shore up its position. In 2002 the company acquired ABC Technologies and event-triggering and behavioral tracking technology from Verbind. It purchased OpRisk Analytics and Risk Advisory, providers of risk measurement and management products the following year. These two acquisitions extended its offerings in corporate and consumer risk measurement and reporting.

Known for its tight-knit community, SAS offers its employees perks including on-site child-care centers, cafeterias, exercise facilities, walking trails, and a health care center.

HISTORY

SAS Institute was started in 1976 by North Carolina State University professors James Goodnight and John Sall. The two had developed a mainframe statistical analysis system (SAS) for the US Department of Agriculture to analyze data around the state. Its popularity grew at other southern campuses, enabling the two professors to go out on their own.

The company began rewriting SAS System software in 1984 to make it independent of hardware systems. While rewriting the package in C language, the company ran into a problem — none of the commercial C compilers supported the IBM 370 mainframe architecture. SAS Institute then began developing MultiVendor Architecture in C to enable the package to be hardware- and platform-independent.

SAS acquired Lattice Inc., a prominent maker of C language code translators, in 1986 to assist in the adaptation of SAS software to the PC environment. The next year the complete version of SAS System for the PC was released, and in 1988 the company unveiled systems for UNIX platforms.

In 1989 SAS released JMP software for the Apple Macintosh, developed a cooperative software program with IBM, and began offering consulting services. By 1990 the company had redesigned its SAS System software so it would be completely hardware-independent in the mainframe and minicomputer domains. SAS also introduced a new menu-driven, task-oriented interface to the SAS System that enabled access to those with limited computer experience.

The company released its first vertical market product for the pharmaceuticals and biotechnology industries in 1992, and the next year it introduced software for building customized executive information systems. In 1994 SAS released a version of its SAS/Access communications software, which tied its data analysis tools more closely to client/server applications. By that year almost all the top 100 companies in the *FORTUNE* 500 had site license agreements for SAS software.

In 1997 SAS acquired Abacus Concepts' StatView software, a statistical analysis program for the life sciences market. It also teamed up with Hewlett-Packard to create the Data Insight and Discovery Center, a data mining lab for financial services firms seeking information about their customers.

In 1998 SAS formed an alliance with business and information technology consulting firm American Management Systems to offer customized data warehousing and decision support systems to their clients. In 2000 the company spun off its first subsidiary, iBiomatics, to help life sciences professionals share information about drug compounds over the Internet. As part of a push to go public, the company hired Andre Boisvert, its first president and COO.

A year later, however, Boisvert abruptly resigned; Goodnight reassumed his duties, raising questions about SAS's plans to go public. Also in 2001 the company re-absorbed iBiomatics. The following year SAS acquired ABC Technologies, a provider of analytic management software, and Intrinsic, a campaign management software provider.

EXECUTIVES

Chairman, President, and CEO:
James H. (Jim) Goodnight
EVP: John P. Sall
EVP and Chief Administrative Officer:
W. Greyson Quarles Jr.
SVP and CFO: Kevin Thompson, age 40
SVP and Chief Marketing Officer: Jim Davis
SVP and CTO: Keith V. Collins
VP, General Counsel, and Secretary: John Boswell
VP, Human Resources: Jeff Chambers
Counsel to the CEO, Global Government Affairs:
Mary U. Musacchia
President, SAS International: Art Cooke
SVP, Strategy, SAS International: Allan Russell
CEO and Managing Director, SAS India: Sudipta Sen
Managing Director, Hong Kong: Peter Tsang
VP and Chief Accounting Officer: David Davis
Senior Director, Corporate Communications:
Mike Tindal
Manager, Community Relations: George Farthing
Manager, Corporate Public Relations: John Dornan

LOCATIONS

HQ: SAS Institute Inc.
100 SAS Campus Dr., Cary, NC 27513
Phone: 919-677-8000   **Fax:** 919-677-4444
Web: www.sas.com

2004 Sales

	% of total
Americas	46
Europe, Middle East & Africa	44
Asia/Pacific	10
Total	**100**

PRODUCTS/OPERATIONS

Selected Software

Customer relationship management
  Credit analysis
  Customer interaction management
  Customer retention
  Customer segmentation management
  Geographic reporting
  Marketing automation

Data analysis
Data mining
Data warehousing
E-commerce
Enterprise performance management
  Balanced score card reporting
Experimental design
Financial management
  Activity-based management
  Anti-money laundering
  Financial consolidation, reporting, and analysis
  Forecasting
  Planning and budgeting
Human resources management
Information technology systems management
  Cost management
  Resource optimization
  Security management
Management science
Patent discovery and analysis
Portfolio analysis
Process management
Project planning and management
Quality improvement
  Warranty analysis
Risk Management
Statistical analysis
Supplier relationship management
Supply chain analysis
Web traffic analysis

COMPETITORS

Actuate	Insightful
ANGOSS Software	Lawson Software
Ascential Software	Microsoft
Business Objects	MicroStrategy
Cognos	Oracle
Computer Associates	ProClarity
Epiphany	SAP
Fair Isaac	Siebel Systems
Hummingbird	SPSS
Hyperion	Sybase
IBM	Teradata
Information Builders	

HISTORICAL FINANCIALS

Company Type: Private

Income Statement

FYE: December 31

	REVENUE ($ mil.)	NET INCOME ($ mil.)	NET PROFIT MARGIN	EMPLOYEES
12/04	1,530	—	—	9,528
12/03	1,340	—	—	9,306
12/02	1,180	—	—	9,023
12/01	1,130	—	—	8,636
12/00	1,120	—	—	8,500
12/99	1,020	—	—	6,400
12/98	871	—	—	5,400
12/97	750	—	—	5,108
12/96	653	—	—	4,500
12/95	562	—	—	4,138
Annual Growth	**11.8%**	—	—	**9.7%**

Revenue History

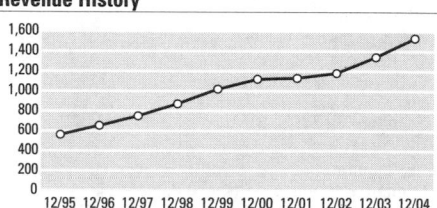

Sauder Woodworking

Sauder Woodworking takes the fear out of furniture and makes furniture for the God-fearing. The firm is the #1 US maker of ready-to-assemble (RTA) furniture (ahead of Bush Industries and O'Sullivan Industries) and, through Sauder Manufacturing, is also a top maker of church furniture and institutional seating. RTA products include computer workstations, desks, entertainment centers, and wardrobes. Subsidiary Archbold Container makes corrugated packaging and displays. Sauder's products are sold through retailers in more than 70 countries. In 2001 Sauder acquired Progressive Furniture, which makes fully assembled furniture. The company was founded in 1934 by Erie Sauder and is still family owned and operated.

EXECUTIVES

Chairman: Maynard Sauder
President and CEO: Kevin Sauder
EVP, Finance and CFO: Arnold Moshier
EVP, Marketing and Sales: John Yoder
EVP, Operations: Garrett Tinsman
VP, Engineering: Myrl Sauder
VP, Human Resources: Steve Webster
VP, Merchandising: Susan Dountas
VP, Sales: Brent Gingerich
VP, Supply Chain Management: David Yoder
SVP, Operations, Progressive Furniture: Paul Manley
President, Studio RTA: Bob Hughes

LOCATIONS

HQ: Sauder Woodworking Co.
   502 Middle St., Archbold, OH 43502
Phone: 419-446-2711   **Fax:** 419-446-3692
Web: www.sauder.com

PRODUCTS/OPERATIONS

Selected Products

Bedroom
   Armoires
   Chests
   Chifforobes
   Dressers
   Footboards
   Headboards
   Juvenile products
   Mirrors
   Night stands
   Wardrobes
Entertainment
   Audiovisual cabinets
   Corner units
   Entertainment centers and armoires
   TV/VCR carts and stands
Kitchen/Utility
   Buffet storage products
   Chair-side tables
   Cocktail tables
   End tables
   Telephone stands
   Utility carts
Office/Computer
   Computer armoires, carts, and desks
   File cabinets
   Workstations
Shelving/Storage
   Bookcases
   Storage cabinets

Selected Subsidiaries

Archbold Container Corporation (manufacturer of corrugated packaging, packaging materials, and point-of-purchase displays)
Historic Sauder Village (history museum focused on the founding settlers of northwest Ohio)
Progressive Furniture (manufacturer and importer of solid wood, veneered, and laminate furniture)
Sauder Manufacturing Company (manufacturer of institutional seating)
Studio RTA (importer and distributor of RTA furniture)

COMPETITORS

Bassett Furniture	Herman Miller
Bush Industries	HNI
Chromcraft Revington	IKEA
DMI Furniture	Jami
Dorel Industries	O'Sullivan Industries
Furniture Brands International	Stanley Furniture
Haworth	Steelcase

HISTORICAL FINANCIALS

Company Type: Private

Income Statement

FYE: December 31

	REVENUE ($ mil.)	NET INCOME ($ mil.)	NET PROFIT MARGIN	EMPLOYEES
12/04	750	—	—	4,000
12/03	700	—	—	3,500
12/02	700	—	—	3,500
12/01	700	—	—	3,500
12/00	700	—	—	3,950
12/99	565	—	—	3,900
12/98	545	—	—	3,200
12/97	500	—	—	3,300
12/96	500	—	—	3,200
12/95	467	—	—	3,200
Annual Growth	**5.4%**	**—**	**—**	**2.5%**

Revenue History

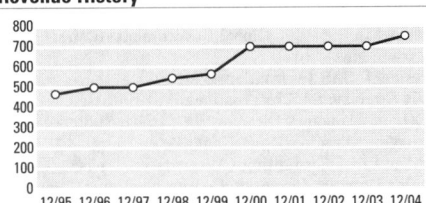

Save Mart

Save Mart Supermarkets is one of the big wheels in the California grocery business. A sponsor of the NASCAR Dodge/Save Mart 350, the company has about 120 grocery stores in Northern and Central California. Its supermarkets and warehouse stores operate under the S-Mart, Save Mart Foods, and FoodMaxx banners. The chain has been trying out different formats, including an upscale prototype with its own coffeehouse and expanded offerings of ethnic and organic foods and its popular private-label salad mix line, Fresh Favorites. Save Mart also owns distributor SMART Refrigerated Transport. CEO Robert Piccinini owns most of Save Mart, which was founded in 1952 by his father, Mike Piccinini, and uncle, Nick Tocco.

Save Mart grew its sales and store count in 2003 with the acquisition of 25 Food 4 Less stores from bankrupt grocery distributor Fleming Companies, which were quickly converted to the Food Maxx banner. The grocery chain has also been adding to its real estate holdings with the purchase of two shopping centers in Fresno and Visalia, California in mid-2004 and early 2005, and the purchase of four stores from rival Ralphs Grocery Co.

Save Mart president and COO Bob Spengler plans to retire at the end of 2005.

EXECUTIVES

Chairman and CEO: Robert M. (Bob) Piccinini, age 61
President and COO: Bob Spengler
VP, CFO, and CIO: Ronald (Ron) Riesenbeck
VP, Human Resources and Law: Mike Silveira
VP, FoodMaxx: Art Patch
VP, Operations: Steve Junqueiro
VP, Real Estate: Jim Watt

LOCATIONS

HQ: Save Mart Supermarkets
   1800 Standiford Ave., Modesto, CA 95350
Phone: 209-577-1600   **Fax:** 209-577-3857

PRODUCTS/OPERATIONS

2005 Stores

	No.
Save Mart	71
FoodMaxx	40
S-Mart Foods	8
Total	**119**

COMPETITORS

Albertson's	Rite Aid
Costco Wholesale	Safeway
Kroger	Smart & Final
Longs Drug	Trader Joe's
Raley's	Vons
Ralphs	Wal-Mart

HISTORICAL FINANCIALS

Company Type: Private

Income Statement

FYE: March 31

	REVENUE ($ mil.)	NET INCOME ($ mil.)	NET PROFIT MARGIN	EMPLOYEES
3/04	2,194	—	—	9,417
3/03	1,655	—	—	7,400
3/02	1,600	—	—	7,300
3/01	1,524	—	—	7,200
3/00	1,468	—	—	7,000
3/99	1,452	—	—	7,200
3/98	1,300	—	—	7,003
3/97	1,200	—	—	6,400
3/96	1,135	—	—	5,864
3/95	1,130	—	—	6,062
Annual Growth	**7.7%**	**—**	**—**	**5.0%**

Revenue History

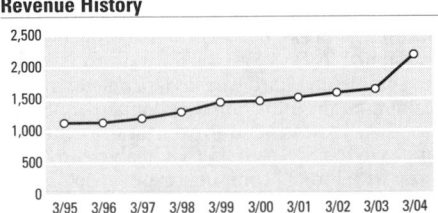

Sbarro

Sbarro lends an Italian flavor to that great American innovation, the shopping mall. The company operates and franchises nearly 1,000 cafeteria-style Italian-food stands across the US and about 30 other countries. Serving pizza, pasta, entrees, and salads, Sbarro's units are typically found in high-traffic locations, such as malls, downtown locations, and toll-road rest areas. It also has units in other food-court locations, such as airports, college campuses, and sports stadiums. In addition, Sbarro has stakes in about 30 other restaurants through joint ventures. Founded in 1954 by the late Gennaro Sbarro with his wife Carmela, the company was taken private by the Sbarro family in 1999.

Sbarro's newest restaurant brand is called Carmela's of Brooklyn. The first Carmela's opened in Orlando, Florida, and five more are scheduled to open in 2005.

EXECUTIVES

Chairman: Mario Sbarro
Vice Chairman and Treasurer: Anthony Sbarro
President and CEO: Peter J. Beaudrault, age 50
SEVP and Secretary: Joseph Sbarro
EVP and CFO: Anthony J. Puglisi, age 56
VP and CIO: Richar Guariglia
VP and Controller: Steven B. Graham
VP; President, Business Development: Anthony J. Missano
VP Administration: Carmela N. Merendino
President, Casual Dining: Jerry J. Sbarro
President, Franchise Development: John Brisco
President, Franchising and Licensing: Jerry A. Sbarro
Director Human Resources: Robert (Bob) Sabatino
Director Operations, UK: Eileen Phillips
Auditors: BDO Seidman, LLP

LOCATIONS

HQ: Sbarro, Inc.
   401 Broadhollow Rd., Melville, NY 11747
Phone: 631-715-4100   **Fax:** 631-715-4192
Web: www.sbarro.com

PRODUCTS/OPERATIONS

2004 Sales

	$ mil.	% of total
Restaurants	331.3	95
Franchises	12.1	4
Real estate & other	5.5	1
Total	**348.9**	**100**

2004 Sbarro Locations

	No.
Company-owned	511
Franchised	416
Other restaurant brands	22
Total	**949**

Other Restaurant Operations

Baja Grill (50%, quick-service Mexican, New York)
Boulder Creek Steaks & Saloon
   (40%, casual dining, New York)
Burton & Doyle (40%, fine dining, New York)
Carmela's of Brooklyn (casual dining)
Mama Sbarro (100%, quick-casual Italian, New York)
Rothmann's Steak House (40%, fine dining, New York)
Salute (70%, Italian & Mediterranean casual dining, New York)
Umberto of New Hyde Park (100%, quick-service Italian, mall locations, New York)
Vincent's Clam Bar (25%, New York)
Waves (50%, quick-service Mexican, New York)

COMPETITORS

AFC Enterprises	Mrs. Fields
Auntie Anne's	Nathan's Famous
Burger King	Noble Roman's
California Pizza Kitchen	Panda Restaurant Group
CiCi Enterprises	Pizza Hut
CKE Restaurants	Pizza Inn
Dairy Queen	Pizza Pro
Dunkin	Seed Restaurant
Famous Famiglia	Snappy Tomato Pizza
Freshëns	Triarc
Jerry's Subs	Wendy's
McDonald's	YUM!

HISTORICAL FINANCIALS

Company Type: Private

Income Statement				FYE: Sunday nearest December 31
	REVENUE ($ mil.)	NET INCOME ($ mil.)	NET PROFIT MARGIN	EMPLOYEES
12/04	349	(4)	—	6,500
12/03	332	(17)	—	5,600
12/02	360	5	1.3%	5,000
12/01	389	(15)	—	6,600
12/00	399	25	6.4%	6,800
12/99	380	30	7.8%	8,800
12/98	362	34	9.5%	7,500
12/97	338	36	10.7%	7,500
12/96	330	37	11.4%	7,770
12/95	319	21	6.7%	7,700
Annual Growth	**1.0%**	**—**	**—**	**(1.9%)**

2004 Year-End Financials

Debt ratio: 410.7%   Current ratio: 1.80
Return on equity: —   Long-term debt ($ mil.): 268
Cash ($ mil.): 63

Net Income History

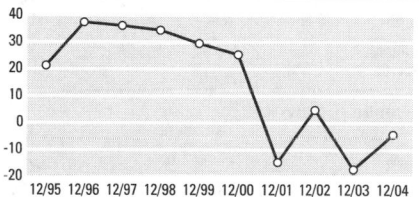

40	
30	
20	
10	
0	
-10	
-20	

12/95 12/96 12/97 12/98 12/99 12/00 12/01 12/02 12/03 12/04

S.C. Johnson

S.C. Johnson & Son helped consumers move from the flyswatter to the spray can. The company is one of the world's largest makers of consumer chemical products, including Drano, Glade, Johnson, OFF!, Pledge, Raid, Shout, Windex, and Ziploc. With operations on six continents, its international business accounts for about 60% of sales. The founder's great-grandson and once one of the richest men in the US, Samuel Johnson died in May 2004. His immediate family owns about 60% of S.C. Johnson; descendants of the founder's daughter own about 40%. President, CEO, and director Bill Perez left for Nike in late 2004 and chairman Dr. Fisk Johnson replaced him as CEO.

Many of S.C. Johnson's products have been and remain top sellers in their market categories. The company has operations in nearly 70 countries and its products are available in more than 100. In 2004 *Working Mother* magazine again recognized S.C. Johnson as one of the 100 best companies for working mothers.

The company's commercial products division (Johnson Wax Professional and Johnson Polymer) has been spun off as a private company owned by the Johnson family. The company also has sold most of its personal care line.

HISTORY

Samuel C. Johnson, a carpenter whose customers were as interested in his floor wax as in his parquet floors, founded S.C. Johnson in Racine, Wisconsin, in 1886. Forsaking carpentry, Johnson began to manufacture floor care products. The company, named S.C. Johnson & Son in 1906, began establishing subsidiaries worldwide in 1914. By the time Johnson's son and successor, Herbert Johnson, died in 1928, annual sales were $5 million. Herbert Jr. and his sister, Henrietta Lewis, received 60% and 40% of the firm, respectively. The original section of S.C. Johnson's headquarters, designed by Frank Lloyd Wright and called "the greatest piece of 20th-century architecture" in the US, was finished in 1939.

In 1954, with $45 million in annual sales, Herbert Jr.'s son Samuel Curtis Johnson joined the company as new products director. Two years later it introduced Raid, the first water-based insecticide, and soon thereafter, OFF! insect repellent. Each became a market leader. The company unsuccessfully attempted to diversify into paint, chemicals, and lawn care during the 1950s and 1960s. The home care products segment prospered, however, with the introduction of Pledge aerosol furniture polish and Glade aerosol air freshener.

After Herbert Jr. suffered a stroke in 1965, Samuel became president. In 1975 the firm banned the use of the chlorofluorocarbons (CFCs) in its products, three years before the US government banned CFCs. Samuel started a recreational products division that was bought by the Johnson family in 1986. That company went public in 1987 as Johnson Worldwide Associates, with the family retaining control.

The company launched Edge shaving gel and Agree hair products in the 1970s but had few products as successful in the 1980s. It moved into real estate with Johnson Wax Development (JWD) in the 1970s, but sold JWD's assets in the late 1980s.

S. Curtis Johnson, Samuel's son, joined the company in 1983. In 1986 S.C. Johnson bought Bugs Burger Bug Killers, moving into commercial pest control; in 1990 it entered into an agreement with Mycogen to develop biological pesticides for household use.

In 1993 it bought Drackett, bringing Drano and Windex to its product roster along with increased competition from heavyweights such as Procter & Gamble and Clorox. That year S.C. Johnson sold the Agree and Halsa lines to DEP. In 1996 it launched a line of water-soluble pouches for cleaning products that allow work to be done without touching hazardous chemicals. President William Perez became CEO the next year (and left in late 2004 to become president, CFO, and director of Nike, Inc.).

S.C. Johnson bought Dow Chemical's Dow-Brands unit, maker of bathroom cleaner (Dow), plastic bags (Ziploc), and plastic wrap (Saran Wrap), for $1.2 billion in 1998. It then sold off other Dow brands (cleaners Spray 'N Wash, Glass Plus, Yes, and Vivid) to the UK's Reckitt & Colman to settle antitrust issues.

A year later S.C. Johnson sold its skin care line, including Aveeno, to health care products maker Johnson & Johnson, and spun off its commercial products unit as a private firm owned by the Johnson family. Boosting its home cleaning line, in 1999 it introduced two new products: AllerCare (for dust mite control) and Pledge Grab-It (electrostatically charged cleaning sheets).

In 2000 S.C. Johnson pulled its AllerCare carpet powder and allergen spray from store shelves after some consumers had negative reactions to the fragrance additive in the products. That year Dr. Fisk Johnson succeeded his father (who became chairman emeritus) as chairman.

In 2001 the company was fined $950,000 for selling banned Raid Max Roach Bait traps in New York after agreeing to pull them from store shelves. Also that year S.C. Johnson's Japanese subsidiary agreed to buy that country's leading drain cleaner brand, Pipe Unish, from Unicharm.

In October 2002 the company acquired the household insecticides unit of German drug giant Bayer Group for $734 million. The following year S.C. Johnson invested in Karamchand Appliances Private Limited, which owns India's second-leading insect control brand *AllOut*.

Samuel C. Johnson died in May 2004 at the age of 76. Dr. Fisk Johnson became CEO of the company again in late 2004.

EXECUTIVES

Chairman and CEO: H. Fisk Johnson, age 44
President, Americas: Pedro Cieza
President, Asia: Steven P. Stanbrook, age 46
President, Europe/Africa and Near East Region (EurAFNE): Patrick O'Brien
President, North America: David L. May
President and General Manager, SC Johnson Canada: Brian Tuffin
SVP and CFO: W. Lee McCollum, age 55
SVP, General Counsel, and Secretary: David Hecker
SVP, Worldwide Research, Development, and Engineering: Richard S. Hutchings
SVP, Worldwide Corporate Affairs: Jane M. Hutterly
SVP, Worldwide Manufacturing and Procurement: Darcy D. Massey
VP and CIO: Daniel E. (Dan) Horton
VP, Global Environmental and Safety Actions: Scott Johnson
VP, New Products, North America: Gregory J. Barron
VP, North American Sales: Darwin Lewis
VP, Marketing Services: Patricia Penman
VP, Marketing Services — Worldwide: Ralph D. Perry
Director, Global Public Affairs and Communications: Kelly M. Semrau

LOCATIONS

HQ: S.C. Johnson & Son, Inc.
1525 Howe St., Racine, WI 53403
Phone: 262-260-2000   **Fax:** 262-260-6004
Web: www.scjohnson.com

S.C. Johnson & Son has operations in nearly 70 countries worldwide.

PRODUCTS/OPERATIONS

Selected Products and Brands
Air Care
Air freshener (Glade, Glade Duet)
Pillow and mattress covers (AllerCare)
Home Cleaning
Bathroom/drain (Drano, Scrubbing Bubbles, Vanish, Dow)
Cleaners (Fantastik, Windex, Windex Multi-Surface Cleaner with Vinegar)
Floor care (Pledge, Pledge Grab-It, Johnson)
Furniture care (Pledge, Pledge Wipes, Pledge Grab-it Dry Dusting Mitts)
Laundry/carpet care (Shout)

Home Storage
Plastic bags (Ziploc)
Plastic wrap (Handi-Wrap, Saran Wrap)
Insect Control
Insecticides (Raid, Raid Max)
Repellents (Deep Woods OFF!, OFF!, OFF! Mosquito Lamp, OFF! Skintastic)

COMPETITORS

3M
Alticor
Blyth
Church & Dwight
Clorox
Colgate-Palmolive
DuPont
Henkel
IWP International
Procter & Gamble
Reckitt Benckiser
Shaklee
Unilever
Yankee Candle

HISTORICAL FINANCIALS

Company Type: Private

Income Statement

FYE: Friday nearest June 30

	ESTIMATED REVENUE ($ mil.)	NET INCOME ($ mil.)	NET PROFIT MARGIN	EMPLOYEES
6/04	6,500	—	—	12,000
6/03	5,370	—	—	12,000
6/02	5,000	—	—	10,700
6/01	4,500	—	—	9,500
6/00	4,200	—	—	9,500
6/99	4,200	—	—	9,500
6/98	5,000	—	—	13,200
6/97	4,300	—	—	12,500
6/96	4,000	—	—	12,100
6/95	4,000	—	—	13,400
Annual Growth	5.5%	—	—	(1.2%)

Revenue History

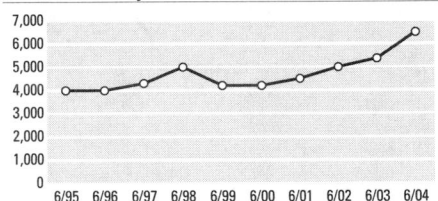

Scarborough Research

Scarborough Research provides marketing research studies for 75 local markets that delve into more than 1,700 consumer research topics such as lifestyle, home improvement, demographics, and travel. The company's more than 3,500 clients include the media, ad agencies, and sports teams. Its specialized services include His-

panic market research and custom analytics (helping clients better read customer data and make decisions based on that data). It is a joint venture owned by Arbitron (with a 49.5% stake) and VNU. The company was founded in 1975 and was originally developed as a newspaper measurement tool.

EXECUTIVES

President and CEO: Robert L. (Bob) Cohen
EVP Research: Gregg Linder
EVP and Director of Sales: Steve Seraita
SVP Advertiser, Agency, and Cable Services: Carol Hanley
SVP Information Systems: James H. (Jim) Collins
SVP Print and Internet Sales: Gary A. Meo
SVP Radio, Sports Marketing, and Outdoor Media: Howard Goldberg
VP Advertiser Marketer Services: Alisa Joseph
VP Cable: Carol Edwards
VP Finance: John Gilfillan
VP Human Resources: Debbie Morisie
VP Marketing and Communications: Deirdre McFarland
SVP Television: Cheryl Greenblatt

LOCATIONS

HQ: Scarborough Research
770 Broadway, New York, NY 10003
Phone: 646-654-8400   **Fax:** 646-654-8450
Web: www.scarborough.com

COMPETITORS

Edison Media Research
GfK NOP
International Demographics
Kantar Group
Mediamark
Opinion Research
Taylor Nelson
Zogby

HISTORICAL FINANCIALS

Company Type: Joint venture

Income Statement

FYE: December 31

	REVENUE ($ mil.)	NET INCOME ($ mil.)	NET PROFIT MARGIN	EMPLOYEES
12/04	55	—	—	—
12/03	50	—	—	—
12/02	44	—	—	—
12/01	40	—	—	—
12/00	36	—	—	—
12/99	31	—	—	—
12/98	28	—	—	—
Annual Growth	12.1%	—	—	—

Revenue History

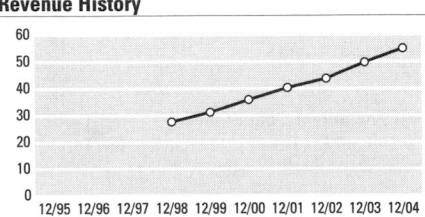

Schneider National

If you think that's the Great Pumpkin behind you, look again. With its signature bright-orange fleet of about 15,000 trucks and 47,000 trailers, Schneider National is one of the top truckload carriers in the US. The company's Schneider National Carriers unit provides truckload service throughout North America, including one-way van, expedited, dedicated, and intermodal offerings, as well as truck brokerage. Schneider Bulk Carriers transports liquid chemicals, and Schneider Specialized Carriers concentrates on the industrial glass industry. The company's Schneider Finance unit sells and leases commercial truck equipment. Schneider Logistics offers supply chain management services.

Not content to rely on its truckload business, Schneider National is expanding its intermodal offerings — freight transportation by a combination of road and rail — through a partnership with Burlington Northern Santa Fe. The company hopes to include other railroads in its intermodal business.

Schneider National is known for being an early adopter of new transportation technology — it was one of the first carriers to link all its trucks by two-way satellite. More recently, the company has invested in an in-cab e-mail system to help drivers stay in touch with their families. Schneider National plans to install global positioning units in its trailers in order to keep closer track of shipments.

Chairman and former CEO Don Schneider, son of the company's founder, is among its shareholders. He doesn't disclose how much of the company he owns.

HISTORY

A. J. "Al" Schneider bought a truck in 1935 with money earned from selling the family car. He drove the truck for three years, got another, and then leased them both to another firm. Becoming general manager of Bins Transfer & Storage in 1938, Schneider bought the company that year and changed the name to Schneider Transport & Storage. In 1944 Schneider stopped storing household goods and continued as an intrastate carrier in Wisconsin through the 1950s, transporting food and household goods. The Interstate Commerce Commission granted its first interstate license to Schneider in 1958.

Al's son Donald joined the company as general manager in 1961, and in 1962 the company dropped "Storage" from its name to become Schneider Transport. The 1960s also saw the first of many acquisitions. Donald became CEO in 1973, overseeing more acquisitions and the creation of Schneider National as a holding company for the organization. Donald also saw to the installation of computerized control systems, the first of many technical innovations Schneider would use in its trucks.

With the Motor Carrier Act's passage in 1980, restrictions eased and interstate shipping opened up. Schneider (and its competitors) saw the sky as the limit and founded Schneider Communications, a long-distance provider, in 1982. Eager to escape the Teamsters' thrall but choosing not to go head-to-head with the powerful union, Schneider formed Schneider National Carriers as a nonunion company out of three 1985 acquisitions, which signed on new recruits, while Schneider Transport remained unionized. Schneider focused on guaranteeing on-time delivery in the deregulated market: In 1988 Schneider became the first trucking company to install a satellite-tracking system in its trucks, setting the industry standard.

Schneider further expanded its services in the 1990s, starting with Schneider Specialized Services for carrying difficult items. It moved into Canada and Mexico in 1991. By 1993 some two-thirds of FORTUNE 500 companies used Schneider, and the company formed Schneider Logistics to help companies streamline their shipping operations. It sold Schneider Communications to Frontier Communications in 1995. The company moved into Europe in 1997.

It continued buying other US trucking firms, including Landstar Poole and Builder's Transport (both in 1998), mainly to acquire their drivers for its expanding fleet. In 1999 Schneider acquired the glass-transportation business of A. J. Metler & Rigging.

In 2000 Schneider acquired the freight payment services of Tranzact Systems and further boosted its e-commerce offerings through alliances with ContractorHub.com and Paperloop.com. The company also made plans to spin off Schneider Logistics and sell part of it to the public, but unfavorable market conditions put the IPO on hold. Schneider added expedited services to its portfolio in 2001 to provide time-definite delivery in Canada, Mexico, and the US.

Christopher Lofgren's promotion to president and CEO in 2002 made him the first person outside the founding family to lead Schneider National.

EXECUTIVES

Chairman: Donald J. (Don) Schneider, age 68
Vice Chairman and Secretary: Thomas A. (Tom) Gannon
President and CEO: Christopher B. (Chris) Lofgren
CFO: David Vander Ploeg
EVP and CIO: Judith A. (Judy) Lemke
SVP, Global Business Development: Brian Bowers
SVP, Sales: Dan Van Alstine
VP, Application Development: Bob Grawien
VP, Capacity Development and Safety: Don Osterberg
VP, Corporate Marketing; VP, Corporate Marketing, Schneider Logistics: Thomas (Tom) Nightingale
VP, Enterprise Recruiting: Rob Reich
VP, Human Resources: Tim Fliss
VP, Litigation: Frank Stackhouse
VP, Technology Services: Paul Mueller
President, Financial Services: Richard Palmieri
President, Schneider Logistics: Thomas I. (Tom) Escott
President, Transportation Services: Scott Arves
Chief Marketing Officer: Steve Matheys
VP and General Manager, Intermodal Services: Bill Matheson
VP and General Manager, Schneider Brokerage: Mark Rourke
VP, Schneider Logistics Payment Services: Philip Morse
VP, Sales, Transportation Services: Mark DePrey

LOCATIONS

HQ: Schneider National, Inc.
3101 S. Packerland Dr., Green Bay, WI 54306
Phone: 920-592-2000   **Fax:** 920-592-3063
Web: www.schneider.com

PRODUCTS/OPERATIONS

Selected Operating Units

Schneider Finance (commercial financing and leasing services)
Schneider Logistics, Inc. (supply chain management services)
Schneider Bulk Carriers (liquid chemical transport services)
Schneider National Carriers (full-truckload service, including intermodal, brokerage, expedited services, dedicated transport, and one-way van transport)
Schneider Specialized Carriers (open equipment transportation, specializing in industrial glass transport)

COMPETITORS

Burlington Northern Santa Fe
C.H. Robinson Worldwide
CNF
Crete Carrier
CSX
J. B. Hunt
Landstar System
Norfolk Southern
Ryder
Swift Transportation
Union Pacific
U.S. Xpress
Werner Enterprises

HISTORICAL FINANCIALS

Company Type: Private

Income Statement

	REVENUE ($ mil)	NET INCOME ($ mil)	NET PROFIT MARGIN	EMPLOYEES
12/03	2,900	—	—	20,733
12/02	2,627	—	—	20,756
12/01	2,388	—	—	19,349
12/00	3,089	—	—	18,775
12/99	3,000	—	—	19,000
12/98	2,711	—	—	17,000
12/97	2,510	—	—	16,500
12/96	2,156	—	—	17,550
12/95	1,700	—	—	15,500
12/94	1,325	—	—	15,300
Annual Growth	9.1%	—	—	3.4%

FYE: December 31

Revenue History

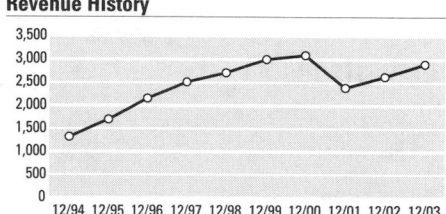

Schreiber Foods

If you order cheese on that burger, you might well get a taste of Schreiber Foods. The cheese processor is a major supplier of the cheese used on hamburgers by US fast-food restaurants. Schreiber primarily produces private-label processed and natural cheese for retailers, food-service distributors, and food manufacturers. Its few retail brands include American Heritage, Cache Valley, and Cooper. The company has bought up smaller cheese operations to expand it geographic reach and is now the leading private-label cream cheese maker. Founded in 1945, Schreiber opted in 1999 to transfer its ownership into an employee stock ownership plan.

The company has agreed to purchase the manufacturing assets of Galaxy Nutritional Foods, a maker of dairy-alternative products. Schreiber will manufacture and distribute Galaxy's products for at least five years.

EXECUTIVES

Chairman: John C. (Jack) Meng, age 60
President and CEO: Larry P. Ferguson
CFO: Brian Liddy
SVP, Information Services: Frederick Parker
VP, Industrial & Regulatory Affairs: Deborah Van Dyk

LOCATIONS

HQ: Schreiber Foods, Inc.
425 Pine St., Green Bay, WI 54301
Phone: 920-437-7601   **Fax:** 920-437-1617
Web: www.sficorp.com

Schreiber Foods has production facilities in Arizona, Georgia, Missouri, Pennsylvania, Texas, Utah, and Wisconsin, as well as in Brazil, Germany, and Mexico. It has joint ventures with companies in France, India, and Saudi Arabia.

PRODUCTS/OPERATIONS

Subsidiaries

Capri Packaging (packaging films)
Green Bay Machinery (cheese slicing and
  wrapping equipment)

Brands

American Heritage
Cache Valley
Clearfield
Cooper
Level Valley
Raskas
Schreiber

COMPETITORS

AMPI
Bongrain
Dairy Farmers of America
Darigold, Inc.
Foremost Farms
Fromageries Bel
Great Lakes Cheese
Kraft Foods
Land O'Lakes
Leprino Foods
Lucille Farms
Saputo
Sargento

HISTORICAL FINANCIALS

Company Type: Private

Income Statement

FYE: September 30

	ESTIMATED REVENUE ($ mil.)	NET INCOME ($ mil.)	NET PROFIT MARGIN	EMPLOYEES
9/04	2,200	—	—	4,500
9/03	2,000	—	—	4,200
9/02	1,450	—	—	4,400
9/01	1,350	—	—	3,100
9/00	1,300	—	—	3,000
9/99	1,160	—	—	2,600
9/98	1,100	—	—	2,600
9/97	1,400	—	—	2,600
9/96	1,375	—	—	2,300
9/95	1,320	—	—	2,400
Annual Growth	**5.8%**	**—**	**—**	**7.2%**

Revenue History

Schwan Food

Frozen pizza is the flashy part of The Schwan Food Company. With well-known pizza brands such as Tony's, Red Baron, and Freschetta, the company is one of the top frozen pizza makers in the US, along with Kraft Foods. Schwan is also a top supplier to the institutional frozen-pizza market and has operations in Europe. But pizza isn't the only slice of the company's revenue — its core business is a fleet of home-delivery trucks. Schwan delivers casseroles, ice cream, and frozen foods to homes in the continental US. The family of late founder Marvin Schwan owns the company.

With its unintentionally retro-hip freezer delivery trucks, The Schwan Food Company is definitely cool. The company maintains a home-delivery system that brings more than 300 frozen food products directly to customers in 48 of the US mainland states. Orders can include bagels or pancakes, and Schwan's ice cream has a devoted following.

The company's frozen pizza has almost 30% of the US market share (Kraft has almost 40%). Schwan's pizza is aboard Air Force One. In addition to its US pizza market, Schwan sells Chicago Town pizzas in Western Europe and supplies schools and other institutional cafeterias with frozen pizza and sandwiches. Due to falling sales of its Freschetta brand frozen pizza, in 2005 the company merged the pizzas into its Chicago Town line, renaming them Brick Oven and Oven Rise.

In conjunction with its Red Baron pizza brand, Schwan owns and operates the #1 civilian airshow act in the world, featuring the Red Baron Stearman Squadron, a formation aerobatics team that performs using vintage Stearman biplanes. Another Schwan unit produces food manufacturing equipment and systems to convert vehicles to using liquid propane.

The Schwan family is notoriously secretive (Marvin Schwan himself gave no interviews after 1982).

HISTORY

Paul Schwan bought out his partner in their dairy in 1948 and began manufacturing ice cream using his own recipes. His son, Marvin Schwan, made deliveries for the dairy for a few years. After attending a two-year college, Marvin came back in 1950 to work at the dairy full-time. Two years later he began using his delivery experience to take advantage of the increase in homes with freezers. He bought an old truck for $100 and began a rural route selling ice cream to farmers. He quickly developed a loyal customer base and expanded to two routes the following year.

In the 1960s the company diversified with two acquisitions: a prepared sandwich company and a condensed fruit juice company. A new holding company, Schwan's Sales Enterprises, was established in 1964. Schwan's began delivering pizza the next year. Paul died in 1969.

Deciding that frozen pizza was not a fad, Marvin bought Kansas-based Tony's Pizza in 1970 and quickly rose to the top of the new industry. In the late 1970s Schwan's entered the commercial leasing business, and it later added more leasing companies under the Lyon Financial Services umbrella (sold 2000).

The company entered the institutional-pizza market in the mid-1980s and bought out competitors Sabatasso Foods and Better Baked Pizza. Schools liked Schwan's use of their government surplus cheese to make pizzas, which the company then sold to the schools at a discount.

In 1992 the company bought two Minnesota-based food companies: Panzerotti, a stuffed pastry business, and Monthly Market, a specialty retailer that sells groceries to fund-raising groups. It also began selling its pizzas in the UK. The next year Schwan's bought Chicago Brothers Frozen Pizza, a San Diego-based company specializing in deep-dish pizza.

Marvin died of a heart attack in 1993 at age 64, with his worth estimated at over $1 billion. The previous year he had willed two-thirds of the company's stock to a charitable Lutheran trust, which was to be bought out by Schwan's after his death. In 1994 his brother, Alfred, and Marvin's friend Lawrence Burgdorf made arrangements to have the company repurchase the foundation's shares for a total of $1.8 billion. But Marvin's four children filed a lawsuit in 1995 against their uncle and Burgdorf over the action. They claimed the men did not have the financial health of the company at heart and were divided in their loyalty. The children, on the other hand, were called money-hungry and callous to their father's last wishes. (The case was settled in 1997, but no information was released.)

In 1994 more than 200,000 people in 28 states contracted salmonella food poisoning after eating E. coli-tainted Schwan's ice cream. The company's insurance company eventually paid out nearly $1 million to about 6,000 affected customers in exchange for their signing releases promising they would not sue Schwan's.

Lenny Pippin became the company's fourth CEO in 1999, replacing Alfred, who stayed on as chairman. Schwan's exited the Canadian market at the end of 1999 due to perennial losses. In 2000 Schwan's introduced irradiated frozen ground-beef patties.

In mid-2001 Schwan's expanded its offerings by acquiring frozen-dessert maker Edwards Fine Foods from private equity firm Ripplewood Holdings. In early 2002 the company sold off its Orion Food Systems fast-food subsidiary to Kohlberg Investors. That year Schwan joined the food industry trend toward handheld convenience foods by introducing a microwaveable, single-serve pizza slice designed to be eaten on the go.

The company began a reorganization of its business units and changed its name from Schwan's Sales Enterprises to The Schwan Food Company in early 2003.

In 2003 Schwan acquired the frozen-dessert business of Mrs. Smith's Bakeries from Flowers Foods for $240 million in cash. Flowers retained the frozen bread and roll dough segment of Mrs. Smith. The pies, cakes, cobblers, and pie crusts fit well with Schwan's other products. In 2004 the company launched Impromptu Gourmet, a catalog and Web site for ordering meals by mail.

The company was forced to recall more than 350,000 pounds of products in 2005 because they might have contained glass fragments. The recalled products, which were manufactured at Schwan's Minh plant in Pasadena, Texas, and were distributed to food stores nationwide and purchased by the federal school lunch program, included eggrolls, pizza twists, and tacos. Later that year, Schwan acquired Canadian frozen-pizza and bread-product maker T-and-N Foods.

EXECUTIVES

Chairman: Alfred Schwan
President and CEO: M. Lenny Pippin
SEVP and CFO: Tracy L. Burr
SEVP and COO, Sales and Manufacturing:
 John M. Beadle
SEVP, Strategic Development: David A. (Dave) Bunnell
EVP, Product and Market Strategy: Gregory D. Flack
EVP, Administration and General Counsel:
 David M. (Dave) Paskach
SVP, Consumer Brands: Ronald Frump
SVP, Foodservice: Steve Freeman
SVP, Human Resources: Bernadette M. Krunk
SVP and General Counsel: Brian R. Sattler
SVP and General Manager, Schwan's Bakery, Inc.:
 Bill Coban
VP, Corporate Relations: Howard Miller
VP, Human Resources: Sue Beary
VP, Marketing Consumer Brands North America:
 Brian Nau
VP, Marketing Foodservice Schwan's Bakery, Inc.:
 Andy Johnson
President, Global Consumer Brands:
 William O. McCormack
President, Global Food Service:
 Lawrence A. (Larry) Oberkfell
President, Global Home Service: Calvin C. Brink
President, Global Operations: Douglas J. (Doug) Olsem
President, Schwan Univeristy: Cheryl McConnaughey
Director, Government and Community Affairs:
 Gordon Crow
Manager, Corporate Communications: Mike Gunderson

LOCATIONS

HQ: The Schwan Food Company
 115 W. College Dr., Marshall, MN 56258
Phone: 507-532-3274　　**Fax:** 507-537-8226
Web: www.theschwanfoodcompany.com

The Schwan Food Company has manufacturing facilities in the US and in Europe; its products are sold in the 48 contiguous states and Western Europe.

PRODUCTS/OPERATIONS

Selected Consumer Brands

Asian Style Sensations (frozen Oriental foods)
Brick Oven (frozen pizza)
Chicago Town (frozen pizza, ready meals)
Edward's Fine Foods (desserts)
Impromptu Gourmet (mail-order meals)
Larry's (frozen potato side dishes)
Mrs. Smith (bakery)
Oven Rise (frozen pizza)
Red Baron (frozen pizza)
Tony's (frozen pizza)

COMPETITORS

Ben & Jerry's
Blue Bell
Celentano Brothers
Colorado Prime
ConAgra
Domino's
Dreyer's
Kraft Foods
Kraft Foods North America
Little Caesar's
Luigino's
Nation Pizza Products
Nestlé USA
Omaha Steaks
Papa John's
Pinnacle Foods
Southern Foods
SYSCO
YUM!

HISTORICAL FINANCIALS

Company Type: Private

Income Statement

FYE: December 31

	ESTIMATED REVENUE ($ mil.)	NET INCOME ($ mil.)	NET PROFIT MARGIN	EMPLOYEES
12/03	4,000	—	—	24,000
12/02	3,000	—	—	24,000
12/01	3,000	—	—	22,000
12/00	3,100	—	—	6,000
12/99	3,350	—	—	6,000
12/98	2,875	—	—	6,000
12/97	2,900	—	—	6,000
12/96	2,500	—	—	6,000
12/95	2,350	—	—	6,000
12/94	2,200	—	—	6,000
Annual Growth	6.9%	—	—	16.7%

Revenue History

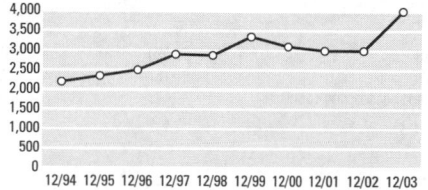

Schwarz Paper

Schwarz Paper Company is not just about paper — the diversified printing, packaging, paper, and distribution company makes a wide array of products, including bags, boxes, tissue paper, gift wrap, and other packaging materials used by retailers (such as The Gap and McDonald's) for promotional purposes. The commercial packaging group provides inventory management and distribution of corrugated packaging, tapes, strapping, tubes, cushioning, and cleaning supplies. The printing division prints tray liners, placemats, store fixtures, and point-of-purchase displays for customers including restaurants and airlines. Chairman Andrew McKenna Sr. (also chairman of McDonald's) owns the company.

EXECUTIVES

Chairman: Andrew J. McKenna Sr., age 75
CEO: Christopher J. Donnelly
President: Andrew J. (Andy) McKenna Jr., age 46
EVP and CFO: Warren J. Kelleher
VP and General Manager, Retail Sales:
 Courtney D. Wright
VP, Human Resources: Susan H. Bondy
VP, Procurement: Richard Rafdahl
VP, Technology: Thomas J. Lammers
Treasurer: Susan L. Donatello
Auditors: Deloitte & Touche

LOCATIONS

HQ: Schwarz Paper Company
 8338 Austin Ave., Morton Grove, IL 60053
Phone: 847-966-2550　　**Fax:** 847-966-1271
Web: www.schwarz.com

Schwarz's operations include facilities throughout the US and the UK.

PRODUCTS/OPERATIONS

Selected Products

Appliances
Furniture
Grocery paper products
Health and beauty products
HR forms, business forms, and ID products
Janitorial products
Leather and shoe care products
Lighting and electrical products
Maintenance equipment
Marking systems
Material handling products
Office supplies
Protective packaging products
Retail display products
Retail packaging products
Tape
Tools

COMPETITORS

Badger Paper Mills
Chesapeake Corporation
Field Container
Insignia Systems
MOD-PAC
OfficeMax
Rock-Tenn
Shorewood Packaging
Simon Worldwide
Smurfit-Stone Container
Stora Enso North America

HISTORICAL FINANCIALS

Company Type: Private

Income Statement

FYE: September 30

	REVENUE ($ mil.)	NET INCOME ($ mil.)	NET PROFIT MARGIN	EMPLOYEES
9/04*	400	—	—	350
9/02	450	—	—	350
9/01	454	—	—	850
9/00	435	—	—	820
9/99	363	—	—	765
9/98	322	—	—	715
9/97	302	—	—	650
9/96	271	—	—	610
9/95	240	—	—	565
9/94	209	—	—	520
Annual Growth	**7.5%**	—	—	**(4.3%)**

*Irregular reporting interval

Revenue History

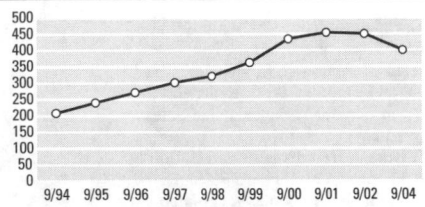

Science Applications International

This company puts science and technology to work for the government. SAIC (formerly Science Applications International Corporation) is a leading government services contractor offering a wide range of technical support and project management services. It provides networking, software development, and systems integration, as well as technical analysis and research for many federal and state agencies, and it offers maintenance and technical support to various branches of the military. The company also provides consulting and technology services for some commercial customers. Founded in 1969 by Dr. J. Robert Beyster, SAIC is the nation's largest employee-owned research and engineering company.

Ranking in the top 10 in several service segments, SAIC has seen revenue grow steadily in recent years thanks to robust federal spending in such areas as homeland security and new military programs. The company's respected expertise in these areas has helped it win many new contracts but having former government officials on payroll has also been a big help in its development: SAIC's alumni include such government insiders as former defense secretary William Perry and former CIA director John Deutch.

Big changes are afoot for SAIC under the leadership of CEO Ken Dahlberg, who took over when founder Beyster stepped down in 2004. The former General Dynamics executive has set the lofty goal of doubling the company's revenue before the end of the decade and has hinted that a major acquisition could be the springboard for such an expansion. Dahlberg has set the stage for growth by reorganizing the famously decentralized firm into a more traditional corporate structure and by shedding some non-core assets, including Telcordia Technologies. The former telecommunications services subsidiary was sold to investment firms Warburg Pincus and Providence Equity Partners for $1.3 billion in 2005.

The biggest shift for SAIC will come in 2006 when a planned IPO transforms the employee-owned company into a publicly traded enterprise. For years the company managed to grow while maintaining its private status (it last received $200,000 from outside investors in 1970), a feat executives have historically chalked up to the fact that employees have a direct stake in the success of the business. However, Dahlberg began hinting at a public stock offering as a means to raise capital for new acquisitions and to provide a more liquid market for employees looking to cash in their accumulated shares.

EXECUTIVES

Chairman, President, and CEO:
Kenneth C. (Ken) Dahlberg, age 60, $2,500,000 pay
EVP, COO, and Director: Duane P. Andrews, age 60, $1,428,842 pay (prior to promotion)
EVP and CFO: Thomas E. Darcy, age 55, $1,079,996 pay
EVP Strategic Investments: William A. Roper Jr., age 59, $1,276,586 pay
EVP, Chief Administrative Officer, and Director:
John H. Warner Jr., age 64, $1,025,980 pay
Chief Engineering and Technology Officer and Director: Donald H. (Don) Foley, age 61
EVP Business Development, Government Affairs, and Communications: Arnold L. Punaro, age 59
EVP Strategic Initiatives and Director:
Joseph P. (Joe) Walkush, age 53
Group President: Carl M. Albero, age 70
Group President: Mark V. Hughes III, age 60
President, Enterprise and Infrastructure Solutions Group: Larry J. Peck, age 58
President, Intelligence Group:
Lawrence B. (Larry) Prior III, age 49
Group President: George T. Singley III, age 60
President, Research, Development, Test and Evaluation Group: Theoren P. (Trey) Smith III, age 50
EVP: Randy I. Walker
SVP and Corporate Controller: John R. Hartley, age 39
SVP and Treasurer: Steven P. Fisher, age 45
SVP, General Counsel, and Secretary: Douglas E. Scott, age 48
VP Human Resources and Director of Corporate Diversity: Karen Penn
Auditors: Deloitte & Touche LLP

LOCATIONS

HQ: SAIC, Inc.
10260 Campus Point Dr., San Diego, CA 92121
Phone: 858-826-6000   **Fax:** 858-826-6800
Web: www.saic.com

SAIC has more than 400 offices in 43 states and additional operations in more than 20 other countries.

2005 Sales

	$ mil.	% of total
US	6,980	97
UK	161	2
Canada & other countries	46	1
Total	**7,187**	**100**

PRODUCTS/OPERATIONS

2005 Sales

	$ mil.	% of total
Government	6,738	93
Commercial	521	7
Corporate & other	(72)	—
Total	**7,187**	**100**

Selected Services and Operations

Government services
  Enterprise and infrastructure services
  Homeland security
  Naval engineering and technical services
  Research, development, test and evaluation, and intelligence
  Systems and networking services
  Transformation, training, and logistics
Commercial services
  Application development
  Enterprise systems management
  Networking
  Outsourcing
  Strategic consulting
  Systems integration
Other operations and services
  Bull, Inc. (broker-dealer)
  Campus Point Realty
  SAIC Venture Capital

COMPETITORS

Accenture	ITT Industries
Aerospace Corporation	L-3 Titan
Anteon	Lockheed Martin
Battelle Memorial	Lockheed Martin
BearingPoint	Information &
Boeing	Technology
Booz Allen	ManTech
CACI International	MITRE
Computer Sciences Corp.	Northrop Grumman
EDS	Raytheon
General Dynamics	SRA International
Halliburton	Thales
IBM Global Services	Unisys

HISTORICAL FINANCIALS

Company Type: Private

Income Statement

FYE: January 31

	REVENUE ($ mil.)	NET INCOME ($ mil.)	NET PROFIT MARGIN	EMPLOYEES
1/05	7,187	409	5.7%	42,400
1/04	6,720	351	5.2%	42,700
1/03	5,903	246	4.2%	38,700
1/02	6,095	19	0.3%	40,400
1/01	5,896	2,059	34.9%	41,500
1/00	5,530	620	11.2%	39,078
1/99	4,740	151	3.2%	35,200
1/98	3,089	85	2.7%	30,300
1/97	2,402	64	2.7%	22,600
1/96	2,156	57	2.7%	21,100
Annual Growth	**14.3%**	**24.4%**	—	**8.1%**

2005 Year-End Financials

Debt ratio: 51.7%   Current ratio: 2.17
Return on equity: 18.0%   Long-term debt ($ mil.): 1,215
Cash ($ mil.): 983

Net Income History

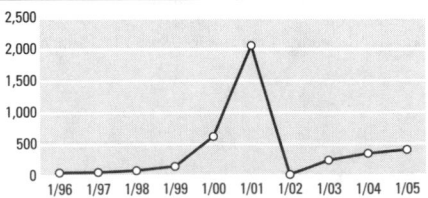

Scott Fetzer

The Scott Fetzer Company can help you cut through a soda can, vacuum up the mess, and then read about the vacuum that is outer space. The diversified manufacturer of commercial and industrial products owns a group of 20 companies, including Douglas/Quikut (makers of TV's Ginsu knives), The Kirby Company (home cleaning systems), and World Book (encyclopedias and other reference materials). The company's holdings also include Campbell Hausfeld (air compressors), Northland (electric motors), Stahl (commercial truck equipment), Scot Laboratories (cleaning products), and Western Plastics (plastic injection molding). Scott Fetzer is owned by Warren Buffett's Berkshire Hathaway.

Among Scott Fetzer's other holdings are recreational vehicle manufacturer Carefree of Colorado, France (which designs support mechanisms for neon signs), financial services firm UCFS, and a maker of patient-monitoring systems called ScottCare.

EXECUTIVES

President and CEO: Kenneth J. (Ken) Semelsberger
VP, CFO, and Treasurer: William W. T. Stephans
President and CEO, The Kirby Company: Robert (Rob) McBride
President, Campbell Hausfeld: Gary Heeman
Assistant Treasurer: John W. Gretta
Auditors: Deloitte & Touche LLP

LOCATIONS

HQ: The Scott Fetzer Company
28800 Clemens Rd., Westlake, OH 44145
Phone: 440-892-3000 **Fax:** 440-892-3060

PRODUCTS/OPERATIONS

Subsidiary Companies

Adalet
Altaquip (small equipment servicing)
Arbortech (forestry vehicle manufacturing)
Campbell Hausfeld (powered equipment manufacturer)
Carefree of Colorado (manufacturer of products for RVs, campers, etc.)
Douglas/Quikut (Ginsu, among others, knives)
France (designer and manufacturer of neon transformers and ballasts for the sign industry)
Halex (maker of fittings for the electrical industry)
Kingston
Kirby (vacuum cleaners and systems)
Meriam Process Technologies (measurement instrument)
Northland (electric motors)
Scot Laboratories (cleaning products)
ScottCare (patient monitoring systems)
Stahl
UCFS (financial services)
Wayne Combustion Systems (manufacturer of gas burners)
Wayne Water Systems (sump pump systems)
Western Plastics
World Book

COMPETITORS

Black & Decker
Electrolux
Encyclopaedia Britannica
Maytag

HISTORICAL FINANCIALS

Company Type: Private

Income Statement

FYE: December 31

	REVENUE ($ mil.)	NET INCOME ($ mil.)	NET PROFIT MARGIN	EMPLOYEES
12/04*	1,000	—	—	4,889
12/02	899	—	—	
12/01	914	—	—	
12/00	963	—	—	
Annual Growth	**1.3%**	**—**	**—**	**—**

*Irregular reporting interval

Revenue History

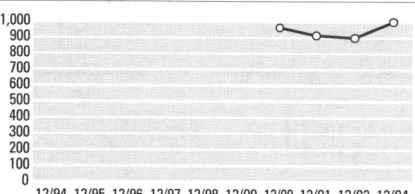

Scoular

The people who grow the wheat aren't usually the ones who grind it. The Scoular Company handles the process that goes on between the two groups. The company is best known for grain marketing, trading more than 400 million bushels of grain and more than 1 million tons of grain byproducts (used for animal feed) annually throughout North America. Other divisions offer fishmeal products for animal and aquaculture feeds, ingredients for food manufacturing, truck freight brokering, and livestock marketing. Founded in 1892 to run grain elevators, employee-owned Scoular operates elevators in Colorado, Nebraska, and South Dakota.

EXECUTIVES

Chairman: Marshall E. Faith
President and CEO: Randal L. (Randy) Linville
CFO: Roger L. Barber
SVP, Administration, Development, and Finance: John M. Heck
SVP, Corporate Development and Shareholder Relations: David M. Faith
SVP, Flourmill Markets: Charles (Chuck) Elsea
SVP, Industrial Markets: Eric H. Jackson
SVP, Processor Markets: Robert (Bob) Ludington
SVP, Producer Markets: George V. Schieber
SVP, Secretary, and General Counsel: Joan C. Maclin
VP and Chief Accounting and Control Officer: Randall Foster
Director, Human Resources: Yvonne Lutz
Managing Director, Emerging Markets: John H. Miller

LOCATIONS

HQ: The Scoular Company
9401 Indian Creek Pkwy., Bldg. 40, Ste. 850, Overland Park, KS 66210
Phone: 913-338-1474 **Fax:** 913-338-2999
Web: www.scoular.com

The company has locations in California, Colorado, Florida, Idaho, Iowa, Kansas, Minnesota, Missouri, Montana, Nebraska, New York, Ohio, Oregon, South Carolina, South Dakota, and Utah. Along with its facilities across the US, Scoular has subsidiaries operating in Canada and Mexico.

COMPETITORS

ADM	CHS
Ag Processing	ConAgra
Bartlett and Company	DeBruce Grain
Bunge Limited	GROWMARK
Cargill	Southern States

HISTORICAL FINANCIALS

Company Type: Private

Income Statement

FYE: May 31

	REVENUE ($ mil.)	NET INCOME ($ mil.)	NET PROFIT MARGIN	EMPLOYEES
5/04	2,000	—	—	340
5/03	1,900	—	—	330
5/02	2,100	—	—	330
5/01	2,098	—	—	400
5/00	2,015	—	—	379
5/99	1,729	—	—	400
5/98	1,606	—	—	267
5/97	1,900	—	—	278
5/96	1,955	—	—	285
5/95	1,130	—	—	225
Annual Growth	**6.5%**	**—**	**—**	**4.7%**

Revenue History

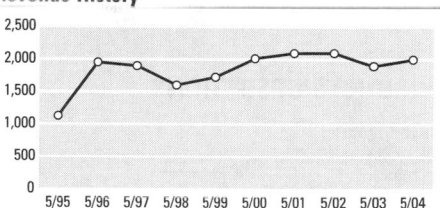

Sealy

Sealy is a slumbering giant. The company, North America's #1 maker of bedding products, manufactures mattresses and box springs and sells them in more than 7,000 stores. Its brands include Sealy, Bassett, and Stearns & Foster. Sealy's customers include sleep shops, furniture and department stores, warehouse clubs, and mass merchandisers, as well as the hospitality industry. Sealy also licenses its name to makers of other bedding products (pads, pillows) and home furnishings (sofas, futons). The company operates more than 30 factories worldwide. Sealy, formerly owned by Boston-based investment firm Bain Capital, was bought by Kohlberg Kravis Roberts (KKR) in 2004. It filed an IPO in 2005.

While the majority of Sealy's sales come from the US, the firm also has licensees and sales operations worldwide. Sealy is making acquisitions and building plants to expand its business in the Latin American region.

Sealy's merger agreement with affiliates of KKR, which closed in April 2004, was valued at about $1.5 billion. KKR and Sealy management acquired about 92% of Sealy in the transaction, while existing Sealy shareholders retained 8% of the company. The following year Sealy filed to go public.

EXECUTIVES

Chairman, President, and CEO:
David J. (Dave) McIlquham, age 50, $1,117,710 pay
EVP, CFO, and Director: James B. (Jim) Hirshorn, age 39, $548,620 pay
SVP, General Counsel, and Secretary:
Kenneth L. Walker, age 56
SVP Human Resources: Jeffrey C. Claypool, age 57, $381,782 pay
SVP National Accounts: Charles (Chuck) Dawson, age 48, $357,832 pay
SVP Operations: G. Michael Hofmann, age 46
SVP Marketing: Philip Dobbs, age 43
SVP Research and Development: Bruce G. Barman, age 59
SVP Sales: Alfred R. (Al) Boulden, age 58
President, International Bedding Group:
Lawrence J. (Larry) Rogers, age 56, $453,764 pay
Auditors: Deloitte & Touche LLP

LOCATIONS

HQ: Sealy Corporation
1 Office Pkwy. at Sealy Dr., Trinity, NC 27370
Phone: 336-861-3500   **Fax:** 336-861-3501
Web: www.sealy.com

Sealy has about 30 manufacturing facilities in Argentina, Brazil, Canada, France, Italy, Mexico, Puerto Rico, and 20 US states. It has licensees in Australia, Bahamas, the Dominican Republic, Israel, Jamaica, Japan, New Zealand, Saudi Arabia, South Africa, Thailand, and the UK.

PRODUCTS/OPERATIONS

Brand Names

Advanced Generation Sealy Posturepedic
Bassett
Bed Time
Carrington-Chase
Meyer
Sealy
Sealy Back Saver
Sealy Correct Comfort
Sealy Kids
Sealy Posture Premier
Sealy Posturematic
Sealy Posturepedic
Sealy Posturepedic Crown Jewel
Stearns & Foster

COMPETITORS

Mattress Giant   Simmons
Mattress Holding   Spring Air
Select Comfort   Tempur-Pedic
Serta   W. S. Badcock

HISTORICAL FINANCIALS

Company Type: Private

Income Statement			FYE: Sunday nearest November 30
	REVENUE ($ mil.)	NET INCOME ($ mil.)	NET PROFIT MARGIN	EMPLOYEES
11/04	1,314	(38)	—	6,399
11/03	1,190	18	1.5%	6,562
11/02	1,189	17	1.4%	6,480
11/01	1,197	(21)	—	6,410
11/00	1,102	30	2.7%	6,077
11/99	986	16	1.6%	5,460
11/98	891	(34)	—	5,193
11/97	805	7	0.9%	5,456
11/96	698	(1)	—	4,875
11/95	654	20	3.0%	4,520
Annual Growth	8.1%	—	—	3.9%

2004 Year-End Financials

Debt ratio: —   Current ratio: 1.17
Return on equity: —   Long-term debt ($ mil.): 966
Cash ($ mil.): 23

Net Income History

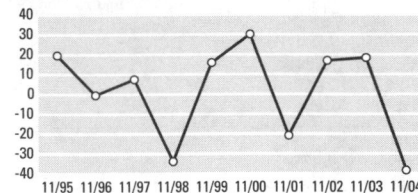

Seattle SuperSonics

Don't let the name confuse you: The Basketball Club of Seattle (TBCS) owns two teams — the Seattle SuperSonics of the NBA and the Seattle Storm of the WNBA. Sam Schulman founded the team in 1967 and sold it to Barry Ackerley who formed the Storm in 1999. A perennial playoff contender during most of the 1990s, the SuperSonics lost for years but has begun to pick up, going to the Western Conference Semifinals in 2005. The Storm won the WNBA championship in 2004 behind the play of stars Sue Bird and Lauren Jackson. Starbucks founder Howard Schultz, who owns 42% of TBCS (purchased in 2001) and leads the ownership group, cut ticket prices to boost Sonics attendance and rebuilt the team around all-star guard Ray Allen.

EXECUTIVES

Chairman: Howard D. Schultz, age 51
CEO: Wally Walker
CFO: Danny Barth
General Manager, Seattle SuperSonics: Rick Sund, age 54
Head Coach, Seattle SuperSonics: Nate McMillan, age 41
EVP Administration: Terry McLaughlin
EVP Sales and Marketing: Michael Humes
EVP: Billy McKinney
SVP Sales: Laura Kussick
VP Marketing: Rob Martin
Controller: Jean Webber
Director of Public Relations: Valerie O'Neal
Human Resources Manager: Karen Wheeler

LOCATIONS

HQ: The Basketball Club of Seattle, LLC
351 Elliot Ave. West, Ste. 500, Seattle, WA 98119
Phone: 206-281-5800   **Fax:** 206-281-5828
Web: www.nba.com/sonics

The Basketball Club of Seattle's two basketball teams play at 17,072-seat KeyArena in Seattle.

PRODUCTS/OPERATIONS

Seattle Storm Titles
WNBA Championship (2004)

Seattle SuperSonics Titles
NBA Championship (1979)
Western Conference Championship (1978-79, 1996)

COMPETITORS

Golden State Warriors
Los Angeles Clippers
Los Angeles Lakers
Phoenix Suns
Portland Trail Blazers
Sacramento Kings

HISTORICAL FINANCIALS

Company Type: Private

Income Statement				FYE: December 31
	REVENUE ($ mil.)	NET INCOME ($ mil.)	NET PROFIT MARGIN	EMPLOYEES
12/04	73	—	—	—
12/03	70	—	—	—
12/02	77	—	—	—
12/01	80	—	—	—
12/00	60	—	—	70
12/99	50	—	—	70
12/98	44	—	—	70
12/97	65	—	—	70
12/96	56	—	—	70
12/95	47	—	—	
Annual Growth	5.1%	—	—	0.0%

Revenue History

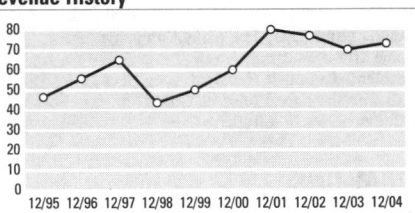

Security Benefit Group

The Security Benefit Group of Companies hopes to soar like a sunflower, not to be as flat as the Kansas plains. The group, which operates through Security Benefit Life Insurance Company and other subsidiaries, offers variable life insurance, annuities, mutual funds, and asset management services to individuals, investment advisors, and plan sponsors. After more than 100 years as a mutual company, the company made plans to convert to stock ownership but never followed through on those plans. Security Benefit's roots go back to the Knights and Ladies of Security, a benefit society begun in 1892 in Topeka, Kansas.

Security Benefit's assets under management were boosted when it took over some 25,000 variable annuity and life insurance accounts from Mutual of Omaha, which is exiting the variable annuity business, in 2004.

EXECUTIVES

Chairman: Howard R. Fricke, age 69
President and CEO: Kris A. Robbins
CFO: Tom Swank
SVP and Chief Marketing Officer: Kal Bakk
SVP and CIO: David (Dave) Keith
SVP and Chief Investment Officer:
  Michael G. (Mike) Odlum
SVP, Human Resources: Craig Anderson
VP, Corporate Communications and Brand Strategy:
  Michel' Philipp Cole
VP and Portfolio Manager: Mark Mitchell
VP, Marketing and Communications: Jenifer Purvis
VP and Head of Equity Asset Management:
  Cindy Shields
Auditors: Ernst & Young LLP

LOCATIONS

HQ: The Security Benefit Group of Companies
  1 Security Benefit Place, Topeka, KS 66636
Phone: 785-438-3000   **Fax:** 785-438-5177
Web: www.securitybenefit.com

PRODUCTS/OPERATIONS

Selected Subsidiaries

Security Benefit Life Insurance Company
Security Distributors, Inc.
Security Management Company, LLC

COMPETITORS

Aetna	Kansas City Life
American United Mutual	Mutual of Omaha
Americo	Principal Financial
CIGNA	Prudential
CNA Financial	Thrivent Financial
FMR	UnitedHealth Group
John Hancock	
Financial Services	

HISTORICAL FINANCIALS

Company Type: Private

Income Statement

FYE: December 31

	ASSETS ($ mil.)	NET INCOME ($ mil.)	INCOME AS % OF ASSETS	EMPLOYEES
12/03	9,905	37	0.4%	560
12/02	7,325	6	0.1%	700
12/01	7,463	31	0.4%	600
12/00	7,872	70	0.9%	—
12/99	8,310	69	0.8%	—
12/98	7,429	58	0.8%	—
12/97	6,403	52	0.8%	—
12/96	5,748	44	0.8%	—
12/95	4,914	37	0.8%	—
12/94	4,202	34	0.8%	—
Annual Growth	10.0%	0.9%	—	(3.4%)

2003 Year-End Financials

Equity as % of assets: —
Return on assets: 0.4%
Return on equity: —
Long-term debt ($ mil.): —
Sales ($ mil.): 2,969

Net Income History

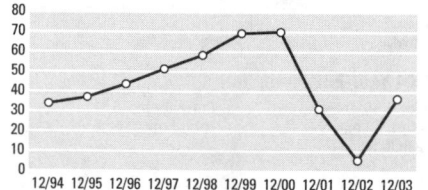

80
70
60
50
40
30
20
10
0
12/94 12/95 12/96 12/97 12/98 12/99 12/00 12/01 12/02 12/03

Sedgwick Claims Management

Unlike Kyra, this Sedgwick probably can't play the "Six Degrees of Kevin Bacon" game, but it does help employers save a little bacon playing today's insurance game. Sedgwick Claims Management Services offers major employers insurance claims administration services, focusing on workers' compensation; short- and long-term disability; and general, auto, and professional liability coverage. Through a partnership with insurance investigative firm MJM Investigations, it provides clients with fraud reporting, investigation, and resolution; its Sedgwick Managed Care division provides managed health care services. The company operates more than 80 offices throughout the US and Canada.

Sedgwick Claims Management Services specializes in serving clients in the entertainment, financial services, health care, public entity, manufacturing, and retail industries.

EXECUTIVES

President and CEO: David A. (Dave) North
CFO: Donald W. Burkett
EVP and COO: James B. (Jim) Wiertelak
EVP, National Operations: Donald Sloan
SVP and Corporate Medical Director: Pamela A. Hymel
SVP and Director of Integrated Services:
  Barry D. Bloom
SVP: Annette Sanchez, age 43
VP and Disability Practice Lead: Julie E. Norville
Director, Client Development: Glenn Fischer
Director, Corporate Communications: Frank J. Huffman
Director, National Sales and Marketing:
  Robert (Bob) Peterson
Corporate Staffing Specialist: Terry Peterson

LOCATIONS

HQ: Sedgwick Claims Management Services, Inc.
  1100 Ridgeway Loop Rd., Memphis, TN 38120
Phone: 901-415-7400   **Fax:** 901-415-7406
Web: www.sedgwickcms.com

PRODUCTS/OPERATIONS

Selected Services

Auto liability
Disability
General liability
Integrated disability management
Managed care
Special investigations
Workers' compensation

COMPETITORS

Brown & Brown	HealthSCOPE Benefits
Concentra	Meadowbrook Insurance
Crawford & Company	Selective Insurance

HISTORICAL FINANCIALS

Company Type: Private

Income Statement

FYE: December 31

	REVENUE ($ mil.)	NET INCOME ($ mil.)	NET PROFIT MARGIN	EMPLOYEES
12/04	325	—	—	3,500
12/03	271	—	—	3,500
Annual Growth	19.9%	—	—	0.0%

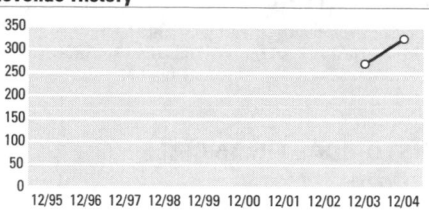

350
300
250
200
150
100
50
0
12/95 12/96 12/97 12/98 12/99 12/00 12/01 12/02 12/03 12/04

Sentara Healthcare

Health care's a beach for Sentara Healthcare. The not-for-profit organization provides medical services for about 2 million residents of southeastern Virginia and northeastern North Carolina. The system includes six hospitals, nine nursing and assisted-living centers, about 40 primary care offices, an integrated outpatient health care campus, and fitness centers. Sentara's Optima Health Plan provides HMO coverage to more than 312,000 members. The organization also provides home health services, ground and air medical transport, community health education programs, and mobile diagnostic vans.

EXECUTIVES

CEO: David L. Bernd
President and COO: Howard P. Kern
EVP; Administrator, Sentara Norfolk General Hospital:
  Rodney F. (Rod) Hochman
SVP and CFO: Robert A. (Rob) Broerman
SVP, Managed Care; President, Sentara Health Plans:
  Michael M. Dudley
SVP; President Sentara Peninsula Region:
  Kenneth M. (Ken) Krakaur
Corporate VP; President Sentara Life Care:
  Mary L. Blunt
VP; President, Sentara Enterprises: Donald V. Jellig
VP; Administrator, Sentara Virginia Beach General Hospital: Leslie A. (Les) Donahue
VP and CIO: Bertram S. (Bert) Reese
VP, Human Resources: Michael V. (Mike) Taylor
Chief Medical Officer: Gary R. Yates

LOCATIONS

HQ: Sentara Healthcare
  6015 Poplar Hall Dr., Norfolk, VA 23502
Phone: 757-455-7000   **Fax:** 757-455-7164
Web: www.sentara.com

Sentara operates in northeastern North Carolina and southeastern Virginia.

PRODUCTS/OPERATIONS

Selected Facilities

Sentara Bayside Hospital (Virginia Beach, VA)
Sentara CarePlex Hospital (Hampton, VA)
Sentara Leigh Hospital (Norfolk, VA)
Sentara Norfolk General Hospital (Norfolk, VA)
Sentara Virginia Beach General Hospital
  (Virginia Beach, VA)
Sentara Williamsburg Community Hospital
  (Williamsburg, VA)

COMPETITORS

Bon Secours Health
Carilion Health System
MAMSI
Novant Health
Wake Forest University
Baptist Medical Center

HISTORICAL FINANCIALS

Company Type: Not-for-profit

Income Statement

FYE: April 30

	REVENUE ($ mil.)	NET INCOME ($ mil.)	NET PROFIT MARGIN	EMPLOYEES
4/04	1,500	—	—	15,000
4/03	1,530	—	—	15,200
4/02	1,600	—	—	15,200
4/01	1,300	—	—	14,000
4/00	1,300	—	—	14,000
4/99	1,100	—	—	11,000
4/98	901	—	—	8,190
4/97	816	—	—	7,734
4/96	726	—	—	7,593
4/95	663	—	—	7,676
Annual Growth	**9.5%**	—	—	**7.7%**

Revenue History

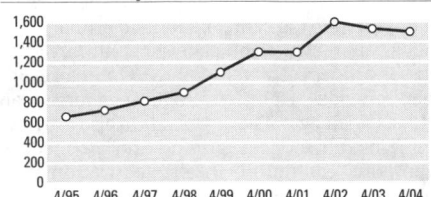

Sentry Insurance

Vigilant for its policyholders, Sentry Insurance (of the famous Minuteman statue logo) offers a variety of insurance coverage, including life, group health, auto, and property & casualty insurance. The mutual company (owned by its policyholders) offers coverage through several subsidiaries. Sentry Insurance also provides specialized insurance to small, midsized, and large businesses, including manufacturers and retailers. The company's Sentry Equity Services offers mutual fund services through its Sentry Fund. Formerly named Hardware Mutual, Sentry Insurance was founded in 1904 to provide insurance to members of the Wisconsin Retail Hardware Association.

In 2005 Sentry Insurance acquired ALF Insurance Agency, one of its brokerage partners. With about 15 Michigan locations, ALF continues to operates as an independent agency and sell other companies' products.

The Farm Equipment Manufacturer's Association gives Sentry Insurance an exclusive endorsement as a recommended insurance provider. The company works with a number of other member groups to create insurance programs, including Business Technology Association, Industrial Supply Association, and Power Transmission Distributors Association.

EXECUTIVES

Chairman, President, and CEO: Dale R. Schuh
VP and COO: Jim Clawson
VP, Finance: William J. Lohr
VP, Human Resources: Joe Fritzsche
VP, Investments: Jim Weishan
VP, Secretary, and General Counsel: William M. O'Reilly
Controller: Michael Zimmer
Auditors: PricewaterhouseCoopers

LOCATIONS

HQ: Sentry Insurance a Mutual Company
1800 N. Point Dr., Stevens Point, WI 54481
Phone: 715-346-6000 **Fax:** 715-346-7516
Web: www.sentry.com

Sentry Insurance has offices throughout the US.

PRODUCTS/OPERATIONS

Selected Subsidiaries

Dairyland County Mutual Insurance Company of Texas
Dairyland Insurance Company
Middlesex Insurance Company
Parker Services, L.L.C.
Patriot General Insurance Company
Sentry Casualty Company
Sentry Equity Services, Inc.
Sentry Life Insurance Company
Sentry Life Insurance Company of New York
Sentry Select Insurance Company

COMPETITORS

AIG
Allstate
CIGNA
CNA Financial
MetLife
Nationwide
New York Life
Prudential
Reliance Group
State Farm

HISTORICAL FINANCIALS

Company Type: Mutual company

Income Statement

FYE: December 31

	ASSETS ($ mil.)	NET INCOME ($ mil.)	INCOME AS % OF ASSETS	EMPLOYEES
12/04	8,570	218	2.5%	—
12/03	7,809	180	2.3%	4,400
12/02	6,945	46	0.7%	4,400
12/01	6,587	80	1.2%	4,300
12/00	6,499	217	3.3%	4,200
12/99	6,409	107	1.7%	4,200
12/98	5,782	134	2.3%	4,000
12/97	5,648	147	2.6%	4,479
12/96	5,363	115	2.1%	4,750
12/95	5,162	188	3.6%	3,909
Annual Growth	**5.8%**	**1.6%**	—	**1.5%**

2004 Year-End Financials

Equity as % of assets: 27.7%
Return on assets: 2.7%
Return on equity: 9.5%
Long-term debt ($ mil.): —
Sales ($ mil.): 2,213

Net Income History

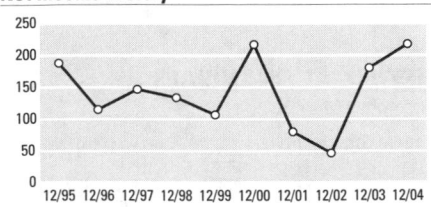

SGX Pharmaceuticals

SGX Pharmaceuticals is working FAST to develop new drugs. The development-stage company is using its proprietary technology, called Fragments of Active Structures (FAST), which identifies small molecule fragments that bind or inhibit drug discovery targets, to develop new drug candidates. Its lead product, Troxatyl, was created using FAST, and is designed as a third-line treatment of Chronic Myelogenous Leukemia. Third-line treatments are generally used when initial (first- and second-line) treatments have been unsuccessful. SGX is also exploring Troxatyl's usefulness in treating solid tumors. Major investors in SGX include BA Venture Partners and Atlas Venture.

EXECUTIVES

Chairman: Christopher S. Henney, age 64
President, CEO, and Director: Michael G. Grey, age 52, $370,500 pay (prior to title change)
CFO: James A. (Jim) Rotherham, age 40
SVP, Research and Chief Scientific Officer: Stephen K. Burley, age 47, $343,687 pay
VP, Human Resources: Julie Cooke, age 39
VP, Legal Affairs and Corporate Secretary: Annette North, age 39, $206,778 pay
VP, Drug Discovery: Peter L. Myers, age 61
Director, Business Development: Sean McCarthy, age 38
Auditors: Ernst & Young LLP

LOCATIONS

HQ: SGX Pharmaceuticals, Inc.
10505 Roselle St., San Diego, CA 92121
Phone: 858-558-4850 **Fax:** 858-558-4859
Web: www.stromix.com

COMPETITORS

ARIAD Pharmaceuticals
Avalon Pharmaceuticals
Genzyme
Johnson & Johnson
MGI PHARMA
Pharmion
Signal Pharmaceuticals
SuperGen
Vion Pharmaceuticals
Wyeth

HISTORICAL FINANCIALS

Company Type: Private

Income Statement

FYE: December 31

	REVENUE ($ mil.)	NET INCOME ($ mil.)	NET PROFIT MARGIN	EMPLOYEES
12/04	27	(19)	—	105
12/03	18	(19)	—	—
12/02	3	(33)	—	—
Annual Growth	**187.6%**	—	—	—

2004 Year-End Financials

Debt ratio: (1.8%)
Return on equity: —
Cash ($ mil.): 12
Current ratio: 0.61
Long-term debt ($ mil.): 1

Net Income History

Shamrock Foods

Milk does a business good too. And with Roxie as its "spokescow," Shamrock Foods has fortified itself from a mom-and-pop dairy into the fourth-largest independent foodservice distributor in the US serving supermarkets, convenience stores, restaurants, and institutional clients in 10 states in the West and Southwest, including California, Colorado, and Texas. The company's Shamrock Farms division processes dairy products, including milk, cottage cheese, and sour cream. Production of the company's ice cream is outsourced. Its products are sold under the Shamrock Farms and Sunland brands, as well as under private labels. Started in 1922, Shamrock Foods is owned and run by the founding McClelland family.

EXECUTIVES

Chairman and CEO: Norman McClelland
President and COO: Kent McClelland
SVP and CFO: F. Phillips (Phil) Giltner III, age 55
SVP and General Manager, Dairy Division: Michael Krueger
SVP and General Manager, Foods Division: Larry F. Yancy
VP, Human Resources: Robert (Bob) Beake
Secretary and Treasurer: Frances McClelland
Director of MIS: Charles Duncan

LOCATIONS

HQ: Shamrock Foods Company
2540 N. 29th Ave., Phoenix, AZ 85009
Phone: 602-233-6401   **Fax:** 602-233-2791
Web: www.shamrockfoods.com

Shamrock Foods does business in Arizona, California, Colorado, Kansas, Nebraska, Nevada, New Mexico, Texas, Utah, and Wyoming.

PRODUCTS/OPERATIONS

Selected Products

Beverages
Canned goods
Dairy products
Fresh produce
Fresh and frozen meat
Fresh and frozen poultry
Fresh and frozen seafood
Sanitation products
Tabletop and equipment

COMPETITORS

Dairy Farmers of America
Dean Foods
Land O'Lakes
McLane Foodservice
SYSCO
U.S. Foodservice

HISTORICAL FINANCIALS

Company Type: Private

Income Statement

FYE: September 30

	REVENUE ($ mil.)	NET INCOME ($ mil.)	NET PROFIT MARGIN	EMPLOYEES
9/04	1,354	—	—	2,250
9/03	1,186	—	—	2,258
9/02	1,093	—	—	2,143
9/01	1,100	—	—	2,196
9/00	1,177	—	—	2,426
9/99	1,081	—	—	2,337
9/98	995	—	—	2,284
9/97	892	—	—	2,168
9/96	818	—	—	2,064
9/95	703	—	—	1,783
Annual Growth	**7.6%**	**—**	**—**	**2.6%**

Revenue History

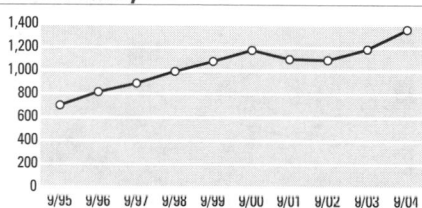

Sheetz

You might say Sheetz is to the convenience store business what Wal-Mart is to discount shopping. Noted for being exceptionally large (stores average 4,200 sq. ft., nearly twice the size of the average 7-Eleven, but new stores are planned to be 4,700 sq. ft.), Sheetz stores sell groceries, fountain drinks, baked goods, and made-to-order sandwiches and salads, self-service car washes, as well as discount gas and cigarettes. The company operates 300-plus combination convenience stores and gas stations, mostly in small and midsized towns in Pennsylvania, but also in five other states. Sheetz plans to open 25 new stores in 2005. Founded in 1952 by Bob Sheetz, the company is owned and run by the Sheetz family.

Increasing convenience is a priority at Sheetz stores. The company has begun installing gas machines that accept paper money at the pump, eliminating the walk inside for drivers on the go.

Sheetz is also going beyond traditional convenience store fare at locations in Altoona, Pennsylvania and Raleigh, North Carolina. The two new convenience restaurants are twice the size of a typical Sheetz store and have fried chicken, soups, and salads, in addition to sandwiches, on the menu. The stores seat 48 people. Sheetz hopes to sell beer at the Pennsylvania location.

EXECUTIVES

Chairman: Stephen G. Sheetz, age 57
President and CEO: Stanton R. (Stan) Sheetz, age 49
EVP, Marketing: Louie Sheetz
EVP, Operations: Dan McMahon

VP, Finance: Joseph S. Sheetz
VP and General Counsel: R. Michael (Mike) Cortez
VP, Distribution Services: Ray Ryan
VP, Human Resources: Phil Freeman
VP, Marketing: Bill Reilly
VP, Petroleum Supply: Mike Lorenz
VP, Real Estate: Joseph M. Sheetz
VP, Sales: Travis Sheetz
Director, Finance and Accounting: Tom Luciano

LOCATIONS

HQ: Sheetz, Inc.
5700 6th Ave., Altoona, PA 16602
Phone: 814-946-3611   **Fax:** 814-946-4375
Web: www.sheetz.com

Sheetz operates more than 300 stores in Maryland, North Carolina, Ohio, Pennsylvania, Virginia, and West Virginia.

PRODUCTS/OPERATIONS

Selected Products

Coffeez
Cupo'ccino
Dot'z Bakery items
MTO (Made to Order) sandwiches
Nachos
Salads
Schmuffin breakfast sandwiches

COMPETITORS

7-Eleven
BP
Convenience USA
Cumberland Farms
Exxon Mobil
Giant Eagle
Green Valley
Kroger
Motiva Enterprises
Sunoco
Wawa, Inc.

HISTORICAL FINANCIALS

Company Type: Private

Income Statement

FYE: September 30

	ESTIMATED REVENUE ($ mil.)	NET INCOME ($ mil.)	NET PROFIT MARGIN	EMPLOYEES
9/04	2,300	—	—	9,950
9/03	1,900	—	—	9,000
9/02	1,920	—	—	8,500
9/01	1,900	—	—	7,500
9/00	1,620	—	—	7,000
9/99	1,161	—	—	6,200
9/98	952	—	—	4,950
9/97	877	—	—	5,500
9/96	756	—	—	4,900
9/95	750	—	—	4,525
Annual Growth	**13.3%**	**—**	**—**	**9.1%**

Revenue History

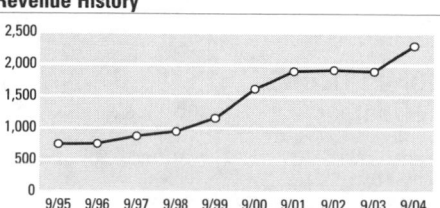

Sidley Austin Brown & Wood

Sidley Austin Brown & Wood aims to be a one-stop shop for corporate clients needing legal help. The law firm was created in 2001 by the merger of Chicago-based Sidley & Austin (founded by Norman Williams and John Thompson in 1866) and Wall Street-based Brown & Wood (established in 1914 in New York City). The firm employs more than 1,500 attorneys around the world, and its practices include financial transactions, antitrust, bankruptcy, intellectual property, and taxes. Clients have included AT&T and Citigroup. In 2005 federal attorneys charged Sidley Austin Brown & Wood with violating age-discrimination laws by forcing out or demoting older partners over the years.

EXECUTIVES

Chairman, Executive Committee: Thomas A. Cole
Chairman, Management Committee: Charles W. Douglas
Vice Chairman, Management Committee:
  Theodore N. Miller
Executive Director: Timothy Bergen
CIO: Nancy Karen
Head of EU Competition Practice: Stephen Kinsella
Director of Practice Development, Firmwide:
  Janet Zagorin
Director of Human Resources, Firmwide:
  Michael Prapuolenis
CFO: Christian Cooley

LOCATIONS

HQ: Sidley Austin Brown & Wood LLP
  Bank One Plaza, 10 S. Dearborn St.,
  Chicago, IL 60603
Phone: 312-853-7000   **Fax:** 312-853-7036
Web: www.sidley.com

Sidley & Austin has US offices in Chicago, Dallas, Los Angeles, New York City, San Francisco, and Washington, DC. It has international offices in Beijing, Brussels, Geneva, Hong Kong, London, Shanghai, Singapore, and Tokyo.

PRODUCTS/OPERATIONS

Selected Practice Areas
Antitrust and trade regulation
Banking and finance
Corporate
Cyberlaw
Employee benefits
Entertainment finance
Environmental
Intellectual property
Litigation
Real estate
Securities
Tax
Telecommunications

COMPETITORS

Baker & McKenzie
Hinshaw & Culbertson
Jenner & Block
Jones Day
Katten
Kirkland & Ellis
Latham & Watkins
Mayer, Brown, Rowe
  & Maw
McDermott, Will
Morgan, Lewis
Skadden, Arps
White & Case
Winston & Strawn

HISTORICAL FINANCIALS

Company Type: Partnership

Income Statement

FYE: December 31

	REVENUE ($ mil.)	NET INCOME ($ mil.)	NET PROFIT MARGIN	EMPLOYEES
12/03	926	—	—	—
12/02	831	—	—	2,913
12/01	715	—	—	3,000
12/00	670	—	—	3,000
12/99	446	—	—	2,000
12/98	421	—	—	2,000
12/97	360	—	—	1,952
12/96	303	—	—	1,848
12/95	277	—	—	1,623
12/94	255	—	—	1,606
Annual Growth	15.4%	—	—	7.7%

Revenue History

Sierra Club

Take a hike with the Sierra Club. The Sierra Club promotes outdoor activities and environmental activism on both the local and national level through political lobbies, education, outings, and publications. The club's approximately 750,000 members are organized into state and regional chapters throughout the US and Canada. Sierra Club publishes books, calendars, *SIERRA* magazine, and *The Planet,* an activist newsletter. Its current issues are clean water, stopping commercial logging in national forests, ending urban sprawl, and protecting wetlands. The group was founded in 1892 by naturalist John Muir.

EXECUTIVES

Executive Director: Carl Pope
President: Lisa Renstrom
VP: Chuck McGrady
Secretary: Ed Dobson
Director of Finance: Lou Barnes
Legislative, Political, Judicial Deputy Press Secretary:
  David Willett
National Press Secretary: Eric Antebi
National Media Director: Kerri Glover
Auditors: KPMG

LOCATIONS

HQ: Sierra Club
  85 Second St., 2nd Fl., San Francisco, CA 94105
Phone: 415-977-5500   **Fax:** 415-977-5799
Web: www.sierraclub.org

HISTORICAL FINANCIALS

Company Type: Not-for-profit

Income Statement

FYE: December 31

	REVENUE ($ mil.)	NET INCOME ($ mil.)	NET PROFIT MARGIN	EMPLOYEES
5/05*	82	—	—	330
2/05	84	—	—	330
Annual Growth	(2.1%)	—	—	0.0%

*Fiscal year change

Revenue History

Silicon Valley Sports & Entertainment

The San Jose Sharks are sinking their teeth into the competition. The team, controlled and operated by Silicon Valley Sports & Entertainment, entered the National Hockey League as an expansion club in 1991 and has quickly become a playoff caliber franchise. The team's success on the ice has translated into one of the higher attendance levels in the league. In addition to the Sharks, Silicon Valley Sports operates San Jose's HP Pavilion arena, the Cleveland Barons minor league hockey team, Logitech Ice (the Shark's practice rink), and the San Jose Stealth professional lacrosse team. Cleveland Cavaliers owner George Gund has a stake in the Sharks; president and CEO Greg Jamison owns most of Silicon Valley Sports.

The San Jose hockey franchise was originally awarded to brothers George and Gordon Gund after they sold the Minnesota North Stars (later the Dallas Stars) in 1990. In 2002 the Gunds sold control of the team to an investment group led by Jamison for about $80 million. A veteran sports executive, Jamison had previously worked for the Dallas Mavericks and Indiana Pacers before joining the Sharks organization in 1993, rising to become president of the team before leading the buyout of the franchise.

EXECUTIVES

President and CEO: Greg Jamison
EVP and CFO: Charles (Charlie) Faas, age 45
EVP and General Counsel: Don Gralnek
EVP and General Manager: Doug Wilson
EVP and General Manager, HP Pavilion at San Jose:
  Jim Goddard
EVP Business Operations: Malcolm Bordelon
Head Coach, San Jose Sharks: Ron Wilson, age 50
VP Sales and Marketing: Kent Russell
Senior Director of Media Relations and Publishing:
  Ken Arnold
Human Resources Manager: Cathy Chandler

LOCATIONS

HQ: Silicon Valley Sports & Entertainment LLP
525 W. Santa Clara St., San Jose, CA 95113
Phone: 408-287-7070   **Fax:** 408-999-5797
Web: www.sjsharks.com

Silicon Valley Sports & Entertainment operates the 17,483-seat capacity HP Pavilion in San Jose, California, home to the San Jose Sharks.

COMPETITORS

Dallas Stars   Mighty Ducks
Los Angeles Kings   Phoenix Coyotes

HISTORICAL FINANCIALS

Company Type: Private

Income Statement

FYE: July 31

	REVENUE ($ mil.)	NET INCOME ($ mil.)	NET PROFIT MARGIN	EMPLOYEES
7/04	74	—	—	—
7/03	65	—	—	—
7/02	71	—	—	—
7/01	63	—	—	—
7/00	61	—	—	—
7/99	51	—	—	90
7/98	49	—	—	130
7/97	42	—	—	—
7/96	31	—	—	—
Annual Growth	**11.5%**	**—**	**—**	**(30.8%)**

Revenue History

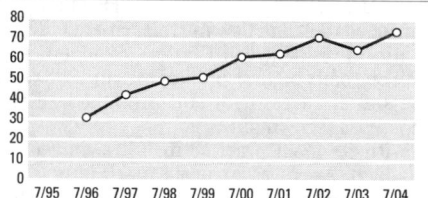

Sinclair Oil

Way out west, where fossils are found, brontosaur signs litter the ground. They belong to Sinclair Oil's more than 2,600 service stations and convenience stores in 22 western and midwestern US states. The company also operates three oil refineries, two pipelines (one jointly owned with ConocoPhillips), exploration operations, and a trucking fleet, all in the western US. It owns the Grand America Hotel, the Little America hotel chain, and two ski resorts (Sun Valley in Idaho and Snowbasin in Utah). Snowbasin was a venue of the 2002 Winter Olympics. The man behind all of this is Earl Holding, whose storied company, founded in 1916 by Harry Sinclair, was a central figure in the infamous Teapot Dome scandal.

EXECUTIVES

President and CEO: R. Earl Holding, age 77
VP Finance and Treasurer: Charles Barlow
VP Government Relations: Clint Ensign
VP: Kevin Brown
General Manager Retail: Larry Rogers
Auditors: PricewaterhouseCoopers LLP

LOCATIONS

HQ: Sinclair Oil Corporation
550 E. South Temple, Salt Lake City, UT 84102
Phone: 801-524-2700   **Fax:** 801-524-2880
Web: www.sinclairoil.com

Sinclair Oil's operations include marketing offices in Colorado, Kansas, Minnesota, Missouri, and Texas; refineries in Oklahoma and Wyoming; trucking terminals in Colorado, Idaho, Iowa, Kansas, Missouri, Nebraska, Oklahoma, and Wyoming; and Little America hotels and resorts in Arizona, California, Idaho, Utah, and Wyoming.

PRODUCTS/OPERATIONS

Selected Operations

Oil and Gas (marketing, pipelines, product terminals, refineries, trucking)
Little America Hotels & Resorts

COMPETITORS

BP
Cendant
ConocoPhillips
Exxon Mobil
Giant Industries
Hilton
Marriott
Royal Dutch/Shell Group
Vail Resorts
Valero Energy
Winter Sports

HISTORICAL FINANCIALS

Company Type: Private

Income Statement

FYE: December 31

	ESTIMATED REVENUE ($ mil.)	NET INCOME ($ mil.)	NET PROFIT MARGIN	EMPLOYEES
12/03	2,900	—	—	7,000
12/02	2,290	—	—	6,900
12/01	2,300	—	—	6,900
12/00	1,900	—	—	6,500
12/99	1,200	—	—	5,600
12/98	1,300	—	—	5,600
12/97	1,700	—	—	5,600
12/96	1,400	—	—	5,600
12/95	1,225	—	—	—
12/94	1,050	—	—	—
Annual Growth	**11.9%**	**—**	**—**	**3.2%**

Revenue History

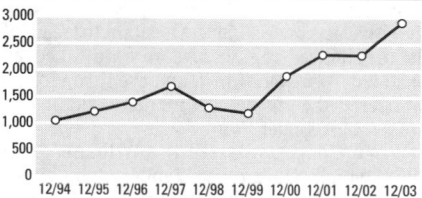

Sisters of Mercy Health System

Not to be confused with the goth rock band of the same name, Sisters of Mercy provides a range of health care and social services through its network of facilities in Arkansas, Kansas, Louisiana, Mississippi, Missouri, Oklahoma, and Texas. Through seven regional health systems units, the organization operates nearly 20 acute care hospitals and provides some 4,000 licensed beds. It also operates a psychiatric hospital, long-term care facilities, physician practices, and outpatient facilities. Sisters of Mercy Health System also runs several charitable foundations. For-profit subsidiary Mercy Health Plans offers managed care health plans, and third-party administrative services in Missouri, Illinois, and Texas.

Sisters of Mercy Health System was founded by the Sisters of Mercy of the St. Louis Regional Community in 1986. Catherine McAuley is the founder of the Sisters of Mercy religious communities now organized throughout the world.

EXECUTIVES

Chairman: Rev Joseph M. Sullivan
President and CEO: Ronald B. (Ron) Ashworth
EVP and COO: John Sullivan
SVP and CFO: James R. Jaacks
SVP and General Counsel: Bernard A. Duco Jr.
SVP: Robert E. (Bob) Schimmel
SVP, Resource Optimization: Lynn Britton
VP, Clinic Operations: George R. Flynn
VP, Enterprise Resource Planning: Steve Mattachione
VP, Healthcare Solutions: Shannon Sock
VP, Human Resources: Stephen Isenhower
VP, Medical Services: Jolene Goedken
Executive Director, Corporate Communications: Barbara W. (Barb) Meyer

LOCATIONS

HQ: Sisters of Mercy Health System
14528 S. Outer Forty Dr., Ste. 100,
Chesterfield, MO 63017
Phone: 314-579-6100   **Fax:** 314-628-3723
Web: www.smhs.com

PRODUCTS/OPERATIONS

Subsidiaries

St John's Mercy Health Care
  Mercy Medical Group
  St. John's Mercy Hospital (Washington, MO)
  St. John's Mercy Medical Center (Creve Coeur, MO)
  Unity Health Services
St. John's Health System
  St. John's Clinic
  St. John's Home Health
  St. John's Hospital (Springfield, MO)
  St. John's Hospital-Aurora (Aurora, MO)
  St. John's Hospital-Berryville (Berryville, AR)
  St. John's Hospital-Cassville (Cassville, MO)
  St. John's Hospital-Lebanon (Lebanon, MO)
  St. John's Mercy Villa
  St. John's St. Francis Hospital (Mountain View, MO)

Mercy Health System of Kansas
  Mercy Health Center (Fort Scott, KS)
  Mercy Hospital (Independence, KS)
  Mercy Physician Group
Mercy Health System of Oklahoma
  Mercy Health Center (Oklahoma City)
  Mercy Health Network
  Mercy Memorial Health Center (Ardmore, OK)
  Oklahoma Heart Hospital (Oklahoma City)
  Southern Oklahoma Physician Hospital Organization
    (Ardmore, OK)
Mercy Health System of Northwest Arkansas
  Mercy Health Center (Bentonville, AR)
  Mercy Medical Clinics
  St. Mary's Hospital (Rogers, AR)
St. Edward Mercy Health Network
  Health Point Physician Hospital Organization (Fort
    Smith, AR)
  Mercy Hospital of Scott County (Waldron, AR)
  Mercy Hospital/Turner Memorial (Ozark, AR)
  Mercy Medical Group
  Mercy Northside Clinic (Fort Smith, AR)
  North Logan Mercy Hospital (Paris, AR)
  St. Edward Mercy Medical Center (Fort Smith, AR)
St. Joseph's Mercy Health Center
  Mission Clinical Services
  St. Joseph's Mercy Health Center (Hot Springs, AR)
Mercy Ministries of Laredo

COMPETITORS

BJC HealthCare
CHRISTUS Health
HCA
Methodist Healthcare
Provena Health
Rush System for Health
Sisters of Charity of Leavenworth
SSM Health Care
Tenet Healthcare
Triad Hospitals

HISTORICAL FINANCIALS

Company Type: Not-for-profit

Income Statement

FYE: June 30

	REVENUE ($ mil.)	NET INCOME ($ mil.)	NET PROFIT MARGIN	EMPLOYEES
6/04	3,003	—	—	26,000
6/03	2,722	—	—	26,000
6/02	2,392	—	—	27,800
6/01	2,191	—	—	27,000
6/00	2,200	—	—	26,500
6/99	2,298	—	—	26,000
6/98	2,169	—	—	26,000
6/97	1,970	—	—	25,300
6/96	1,700	—	—	24,000
6/95	1,505	—	—	24,000
Annual Growth	8.0%	—	—	0.9%

Revenue History

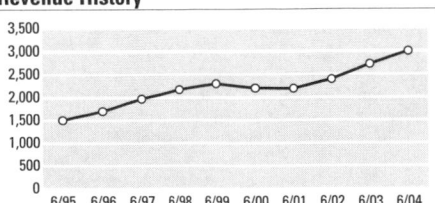

Skadden, Arps, Slate, Meagher & Flom

Have you heard about the law firm that sued the business information publisher for a profile that opened with a wickedly clever lawyer joke? Neither have we, and we would like to keep it that way. Skadden, Arps, Slate, Meagher & Flom, the largest US law firm and one of the largest in the world, has about 1,700 attorneys in 21 offices around the world. Founded in 1948, the firm offers counsel for corporate dealings, litigation, and international concerns. Skadden, Arps, Slate, Meagher & Flom has first-rate bankruptcy and securities practices and is a leader in mergers and acquisitions (M&A) work.

Long regarded for its M&A practice, Skadden, Arps is also a very big player in litigation work. In 2003 it defended Cendant Corporation against an investor class action lawsuit and it helped the National Football League in its conflict with Oakland Raiders owner Al Davis over revenue sharing. Embattled corporations WorldCom (now MCI) and HealthSouth are also among Skadden, Arps' litigation clients. Meanwhile, the firm's M&A practice kept up the pace in 2004, representing clients in more than 110 transactions that were worth more than $150 million.

One area of growth for the firm has been its corporate restructuring practice, which got a big boost from its work on Kmart's history-making bankruptcy and reorganization. The firm is looking to make the same kind of splash in the UK and throughout Europe.

HISTORY

Marshall Skadden, Leslie Arps, and John Slate hung out their shingle in New York City on April Fool's Day, 1948. Skadden and Arps came from a Wall Street law firm, and Slate had been counsel to Pan American World Airways. Without the reputation and connections of the established New York law firms, the firm found work one case at a time from referrals, handling mainly commercial, corporate, and litigations work. Marshall Skadden died in 1958.

Denied the luxury of steady clients, the firm was forced to be innovative and, at times, unorthodox. Joe Flom, who had joined as the firm's first associate, specialized in corporate law and proxy fights. During the 1960s, when tender offers and hostile takeovers increased, many of the more venerable firms referred clients engaged in the undignified corporate raids to Flom to preserve their gentlemanly reputations. With "white shoe" lawyers on Wall Street hesitant to tread into the uncivilized region of corporate takeovers, Skadden, Arps went for it, and the firm virtually pioneered the business of mergers and acquisitions (M&A) under Flom.

When Congress passed the Williams Act in 1968, which "legitimized" tender offers by providing regulation, other law firms started to get in on the act. Skadden, Arps was way ahead of the game, however, and as corporations and lawyers realized that aggressive legal tactics helped win corporate takeover battles, it also became apparent that Joe Flom was the expert. As takeover fights became more frequent in the early 1970s,

the firm earned more than just respect. Earnings came not just from some of the highest hourly rates in the industry, but from hefty retainers (now a common practice at many firms) on the theory that association with Flom would scare raiders off. The only other name that could strike such fear in people's hearts was Marty Lipton of rival takeover specialists Wachtell, Lipton, Rosen & Katz. From the late 1970s through the 1980s, Skadden, Arps was involved in almost every important M&A case in the US.

The firm used its success in mergers and acquisitions to build its practice in other areas. In the early 1980s it branched into bankruptcy, product liability, and real estate law. By then it had opened offices in Boston; Chicago; Los Angeles; Washington, DC; and Wilmington, Delaware. Les Arps died in 1987.

With the boom in mergers and acquisitions activity and bankruptcies in the late 1980s, the firm grew to almost 2,000 lawyers by 1989. Then came the recession, and M&A work virtually dried up. Skadden, Arps responded by shedding more than 500 lawyers between 1989 and 1990. It also scrambled to diversify and expand internationally. As takeover activity rebounded in the mid-1990s, the diversification strategy actually began to work against Skadden, Arps because profits didn't skyrocket like those of M&A specialist firms.

The firm opened an office in Singapore in 1995 to coordinate its Asian business, signaling that city's growing importance as a financial center. Two years later two-thirds of the firm's Beijing team defected to a rival firm. Headquarters shrugged it off and flew in replacements. Representing President Bill Clinton, Skadden, Arps won one of its highest-profile cases in 1998 when the sexual harassment suit brought by Paula Jones was thrown out.

With its M&A practice in full swing again, Skadden, Arps was involved in 70 announced M&A deals in 1999, including the $75 billion merger of oil companies Exxon and Mobil. It also became the first US law firm to reach $1 billion in revenue in 2000. The company announced an alliance with Italian law firm Studio Chiomenti the following year and took part in three of the top-10 M&A deals of 2002. Skadden, Arps helped struggling discount retailer Kmart emerge from its titanic bankruptcy the next year.

EXECUTIVES

Executive Partner: Robert C. Sheehan
Senior Partner: Joseph H. Flom
Senior Partner, Corporate Practice: Roger S. Aaron
Senior Partner, Litigation: William P. Frank
Finance Director: Carol A. Sawdye
Director of Associate Development: Jodie R. Garfinkel
Director of Human Resources: Laurel E. Henschel
Director of Legal Hiring: Carol Lee H. Sprague
Director of Marketing and Business Development:
  Sally J. Feldman
Director of Technology: Harris Z. Tilevitz

LOCATIONS

HQ: Skadden, Arps, Slate, Meagher & Flom LLP
  4 Times Square, New York, NY 10036
Phone: 212-735-3000   **Fax:** 212-735-2000
Web: www.skadden.com

Selected Office Locations

International	US
Beijing	Boston
Brussels	Chicago
Frankfurt	Houston
Hong Kong	Los Angeles
London	New York City
Moscow	Palo Alto, CA
Munich	San Francisco
Paris	Washington, DC
Singapore	Wilmington, DE
Sydney	
Tokyo	
Toronto	

PRODUCTS/OPERATIONS

Selected Practice Areas

Antitrust
Banking and institutional investing
Corporate finance
Government affairs
Health care
Insurance
Intellectual property
International trade
Internet and e-commerce
Labor and employment law
Litigation
Mass torts and insurance litigation
Mergers and acquisitions
Real estate
Tax
Trusts and estates
White-collar crime

COMPETITORS

Baker & McKenzie	O'Melveny & Myers
Clifford Chance	Shearman & Sterling
Davis Polk	Sidley Austin Brown
Gibson, Dunn & Crutcher	& Wood
Jones Day	Sullivan & Cromwell
Kirkland & Ellis	Wachtell, Lipton
Latham & Watkins	Weil, Gotshal
Mayer, Brown, Rowe	White & Case
& Maw	WilmerHale
McDermott, Will	

HISTORICAL FINANCIALS

Company Type: Partnership

Income Statement

FYE: December 31

	REVENUE ($ mil.)	NET INCOME ($ mil.)	NET PROFIT MARGIN	EMPLOYEES
12/03	1,330	—	—	4,200
12/02	1,310	—	—	4,490
12/01	1,225	—	—	4,350
12/00	1,154	—	—	4,235
12/99	1,025	—	—	3,600
12/98	890	—	—	3,200
12/97	826	—	—	3,000
12/96	710	—	—	3,150
12/95	635	—	—	3,000
12/94	582	—	—	3,100
Annual Growth	9.6%	—	—	3.4%

Revenue History

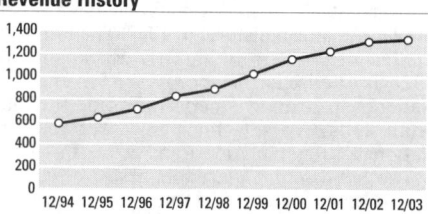

SkinMedica

SkinMedica hopes profit is skin deep. The firm develops prescription and over-the-counter skin care products. The FDA has approved two prescription products: VANIQA, which impedes the growth of unwanted facial hair on women, and EpiQuin Micro, a treatment for hyperpigmentation of skin. SkinMedica's pipeline includes NeoBenz Micro to treat acne and Hydrogel to treat atopic dermatitis. Its non-prescription products are primarily sold by dermatologists, plastic surgeons, and other medical professionals and include Tissue Nutrient Solution, a cosmeceutical to improve skin's appearance, and Ceratopic, a moisturizer. Other OTC products include a chemical facial peel, cleansers, moisturizers, and other care products.

Top customers are drug distributors Cardinal Health (which accounted for 41% of 2004 pharmaceutical product sales), McKesson (40%), and AmerisourceBergen (9%).

Perseus-Soros BioPharmaceutical Fund, led by famed investor George Soros, owns 21% of the company. Domain Associates controls 19% of SkinMedica. Other investors include Apax Partners (17%), HealthCare Ventures (12.5%), and The St. Paul Travelers Companies (10%).

EXECUTIVES

Chairman: David F. Hale, age 56
President, CEO, and Director: Rex Bright, age 65, $376,200 pay
SVP and CFO: Thomas H. Insley, age 54, $246,705 pay
SVP, Corporate Development: Diane S. Goostree, age 49, $302,130 pay
VP, Cosmeceutical Sales and Marketing: Theodore Schwarz, age 42
VP, Operations: Dennie W. Dyer, age 60, $206,425 pay
VP, Pharmaceutical Marketing: Dianne Denton, age 42
VP, Pharmaceutical Sales: Christopher J. (Chris) Foy, age 49
VP, Research and Development: Ronald Trancik, age 65
Auditors: Ernst & Young LLP

LOCATIONS

HQ: SkinMedica, Inc.
5909 Sea Lion Place, Ste. H, Carlsbad, CA 92008
Phone: 760-448-3600   **Fax:** 760-448-3601
Web: www.skinmedica.com

PRODUCTS/OPERATIONS

2004 Sales

	$ mil.	% of total
Cosmeceuticals	15.8	71
Prescription products	6.3	29
Total	**22.1**	**100**

Selected Products

In Development
  Desonate Hydrogel (atopic dermatitis)
  Mometasone Hydrogel (atopic dermatitis)
  NeoBenz Micro (acne)
Marketed
  Ceratopic (lotion)
  EpiQuin Micro (hyperpigmentation)
  Tissue Nutrient Solution Body Mist
  Tissue Nutrient Solution Illuminating Eye Cream
  Tissue Nutrient Solution Recovery Complex (skin appearance improvement)
  VANIQA (unwanted facial hair prevention)

COMPETITORS

Allergan	Obagi Medical
Bradley Pharmaceuticals	Ortho-Neutrogena
Connetics	PhotoMedex
Dermik Laboratories	Stiefel Laboratories
Inamed	Valeant
Medicis Pharmaceutical	

HISTORICAL FINANCIALS

Company Type: Private

Income Statement

FYE: December 31

	REVENUE ($ mil.)	NET INCOME ($ mil.)	NET PROFIT MARGIN	EMPLOYEES
12/04	22	(15)	—	110
12/03	13	(14)	—	—
12/02	7	0	—	—
Annual Growth	80.3%	—	—	—

2004 Year-End Financials

Debt ratio: (125.6%)
Return on equity: —
Cash ($ mil.): 14
Current ratio: 1.98
Long-term debt ($ mil.): 7

Net Income History

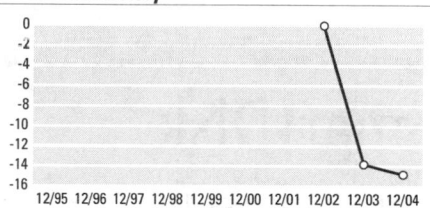

SL Corporation

SL Corp. provides software for real-time monitoring and control of data within an enterprise, using visualization technology. The company was established in 1983 as Sherrill-Lubinski Corp.; co-founder Peter Sherrill died in 1997. Co-founder and CEO Tom Lubinski is the majority owner. In 1998, SL established a Japanese subsidiary, of which it owns 74%. Customers include Harris, NASA, and Toshiba.

EXECUTIVES

President and CEO: Thomas C. (Tom) Lubinski, age 51
CFO: Nina Cartee
COO: Brian Z. King, age 42

LOCATIONS

HQ: SL Corporation
240 Tamal Vista Blvd., Ste. 110,
Corte Madera, CA 94925
Phone: 415-927-8400   **Fax:** 415-927-8401
Web: www.sl.com

COMPETITORS

AccuSoft
Advanced Visual Systems
CORDA Technologies
Dash Optimization
eNGENUITY
ILOG

HISTORICAL FINANCIALS

Company Type: Private

Income Statement

	REVENUE ($ mil.)	NET INCOME ($ mil.)	NET PROFIT MARGIN	EMPLOYEES
12/04	6	—	—	47
12/03*	4	—	—	38
12/97	8	—	—	—
12/96	9	—	—	—
12/95	9	—	—	—
Annual Growth	(7.1%)	—	—	23.7%

*Irregular reporting interval

Revenue History

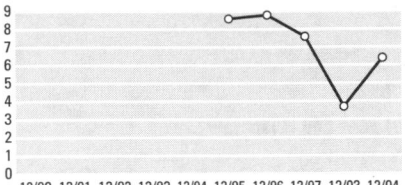

12/90 12/91 12/92 12/93 12/94 12/95 12/96 12/97 12/03 12/04

SmartDisk

SmartDisk eliminates digital device divides. The company develops products that enable data to be shared among electronic devices and PCs. SmartDisk's FlashPath, shaped like an ordinary 3.5-in. floppy, is used mainly to transfer digital camera images to PCs, but it also lets users perform digitized audio exchanges. SmartDisk also offers USB- and FireWire-based personal storage systems, including portable disk drives and expansion bay drives for desktop and notebook PCs. Its FlashTrax handheld device provides portable storage and a liquid crystal display for digital photos or other multimedia files. After operating for a number of years as a public company, SmartDisk opted to go private in 2003.

SmartDisk has acquired the business and certain assets of Zio Corp., a supplier of digital media readers, mobile telephone accessories, and video editing products.

The company offers its products through European and US portals on its corporate Web site. SmartDisk also sells through Amazon.com and Buy.com, and through such retailers as Best Buy, Dixons, Staples, and Wal-Mart.

EXECUTIVES

Chairman: Addison M. Fischer
President and CEO: Michael S. Battaglia
CFO: Andrew Warner, age 39
VP, Marketing and National Accounts: Charles Klinker
VP, Product Development: Stuart Cox
VP, Central Region Sales: Robert Pitzen
VP, Eastern Region Sales: Stephen McLaughlin
VP, Western Region Sales: Michael C. Battaglia
VP, Product Development: Steve Armfield
Auditors: Ernst & Young LLP

LOCATIONS

HQ: SmartDisk Corporation
12780 Westlinks Dr., Fort Myers, FL 33913
Phone: 239-425-4000 **Fax:** 239-425-4009
Web: www.smartdisk.com

SmartDisk has operations in Japan, the UK, and the US.

PRODUCTS/OPERATIONS

Selected Products

Card data and media manager (FoneMate)
Digital picture editing software (CameraMate ProPix)
Film scanners
Flash media readers
Flash memory adapter for floppy disk drives (FlashPath)
Handheld digital file storage and display (FlashTrax)
Personal storage systems
  CD-RW drives
  Flash drives (USB)
  Floppy drives
  Hard drives (expansion bay, FireWire, USB)
Universal reader/writer for digital camera, mobile phone media (Dazzle 990)

COMPETITORS

EZQuest
Fujitsu Computer Products
Hewlett-Packard
IBM
Imation
Iomega
Maxtor
Quantum
SanDisk
SCM Microsystems
Seagate Technology
SimpleTech
Sonic Solutions
Sony
TEAC
Toshiba
VisionTek
Western Digital
Yamaha

HISTORICAL FINANCIALS

Company Type: Private

Income Statement

	REVENUE ($ mil.)	NET INCOME ($ mil.)	NET PROFIT MARGIN	EMPLOYEES
12/04	39	(1)	—	—
12/03	29	(4)	—	—
12/02	41	(17)	—	45
12/01	70	(75)	—	90
12/00	97	(24)	—	125
12/99	40	1	2.5%	59
12/98	15	(6)	—	44
12/97	1	(4)	—	16
12/96	1	(10)	—	—
12/95	0	(2)	—	—
Annual Growth	71.9%	—	—	23.0%

2004 Year-End Financials

Debt ratio: 0.0%
Return on equity: —
Cash ($ mil.): 2
Current ratio: 1.69
Long-term debt ($ mil.): 0

Net Income History

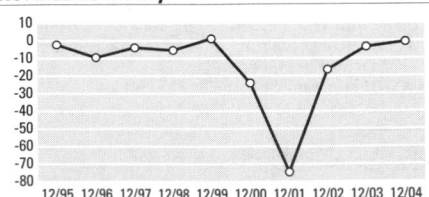

12/95 12/96 12/97 12/98 12/99 12/00 12/01 12/02 12/03 12/04

Smithsonian Institution

The Smithsonian Institution wears many hats, from the one worn by Harrison Ford in the Indiana Jones Trilogy to the one worn by Abraham Lincoln the night he was assassinated. The world's largest museum, the Smithsonian houses more than 140 million pieces in 18 museums and galleries. More than 35 million people every year come view its exhibits on art, music, TV and film, science, history, and other subjects. Admission to its museums, most of which are located on the National Mall in Washington, DC (two are in New York City), is usually free. The Smithsonian also operates the National Zoo and a handful of research facilities. The Smithsonian receives about 80% of its funding from the federal government.

The Smithsonian's exhibits display items such as the Declaration of Independence, the ruby slippers worn by Judy Garland in *The Wizard of Oz,* and the Wright Brothers' first airplane. A board of regents that includes Vice President Richard Cheney, six members of Congress, and nine private citizens leads the institution.

HISTORY

English chemist James Smithson wrote a proviso to his will in 1826 that would lead to the creation of the Smithsonian Institution. When he died in 1829, he left his estate to his nephew, Henry James Hungerford, with the stipulation that if Hungerford died without heirs, the estate would go to the US to create "an Establishment for the increase and diffusion of knowledge among men." Hungerford died in 1835 without any heirs, and the US government inherited more than $500,000 in gold.

Congress squandered the money after it was received in 1838, but perhaps feeling pangs of guilt, covered the loss. The Smithsonian was finally created in 1846, and Princeton physicist Joseph Henry was named as its first secretary. That year it established the Museum of Natural History, the Museum of History and Technology, and the National Gallery of Art. The Smithsonian's National Museum was developed around the collection of the US Patent Office in 1858. The Smithsonian continued to expand, adding the National Zoological Park in 1889 and the Smithsonian Astrophysical Observatory in 1890.

The Freer Gallery, a gift of industrialist Charles Freer, opened in 1923. The National Gallery was renamed the National Collection of Fine Arts in 1937, and a new National Gallery, created with Andrew Mellon's gift of his art collection and a building, opened in 1941. The Air and Space Museum was established in 1946.

More museums were added in the 1960s, including the National Portrait Gallery in 1962 and the Anacostia Museum (exhibits and materials on African-American history) in 1967. The Kennedy Center for the Performing Arts was opened in 1971. The Collection of Fine Arts was renamed the National Museum of American Art and the Museum of History and Technology was renamed the National Museum of American History in 1980.

The Smithsonian placed its first-ever contribution boxes in four of its museums in 1993.

A planned exhibit featuring the Enola Gay — the plane that dropped the atomic bomb on Hiroshima — created a firestorm in 1994 with critics charging that the exhibit downplayed Japanese aggression and US casualties in WWII. The original exhibit was canceled in 1995, the director of the Air and Space Museum resigned, and a scaled-down version of the exhibit premiered. In 2004 the exhibit attracted more protestors, prompting Smithsonian officials to evacuate and temporarily close the museum.

Large contributions from private donors continued in the 1990s; the Mashantucket Pequot tribe gave $10 million from its casino operations in 1994 for the Smithsonian's planned American Indian museum and prolific electronics inventor Jerome Lemelson donated $10.4 million in 1995. The museum celebrated its sesquicentennial in 1996 amid news that $500 million in repairs were needed over the next 10 years.

California real estate developer Kenneth Behring gave the largest cash donation ever to the museum in 1997 — $20 million for the National Museum of Natural History. Short of funds, the Smithsonian had to cut back on its 150th anniversary traveling exhibit that year. The Smithsonian announced a $26 million renovation for the National Museum of Natural History in 1998. Two years later Kenneth Behring quadrupled his record breaking 1997 donation of $20 million by giving $80 million to the National Museum of American History. Catherine Reynolds withdrew most of her $38 million gift in 2002 after the Smithsonian Institution refused to implement her ideas for an exhibit at the National Museum of American History.

The National Museum of the American Indian opened on the National Mall in 2004.

EXECUTIVES

Secretary: Lawrence M. Small, age 63
Director, External Affairs: Virginia B. Clark
General Counsel: John E. Huerta
Deputy Secretary and COO: Sheila P. Burke, age 52
Under Secretary for Science: David L. Evans, age 58
Under Secretary for Art; Director, Hirshhorn Museum and Sculpture Garden: Ned Rifkin
CFO: Alice Collier Maroni
CEO, Smithsonian Business Ventures: Gary Beer
CIO: Dennis R. Shaw
Treasurer: Sudeep Anand
Director, Communications and Public Affairs: Evelyn S. Lieberman
Acting Director, Human Resources: James Douglas

LOCATIONS

HQ: Smithsonian Institution
1000 Jefferson Dr. SW, Washington, DC 20560
Phone: 202-357-2700 **Fax:** 202-633-9835
Web: www.si.edu

The Smithsonian Institution has museums and galleries located in New York City and Washington, DC; its research centers are located in the US and Panama.

PRODUCTS/OPERATIONS

Museums and Research Centers

Anacostia Museum & Center for African American History and Culture
Archives of American Art
Arthur M. Sackler Gallery
Arts and Industries Building
Center for Folklife Programs and Cultural Heritage
Conservation and Research Center
Cooper-Hewitt, National Design Museum (New York City)
Freer Gallery of Art
Hirshhorn Museum and Sculpture Garden

National Air and Space Museum
National Museum of African Art
National Museum of American History
National Museum of Natural History
National Museum of the American Indian (New York City)
National Portrait Gallery
National Postal Museum
National Zoological Park
Smithsonian American Art Museum Renwick Gallery
Smithsonian Astrophysical Observatory
Smithsonian Center for Latino Initiatives
Smithsonian Center for Materials Research and Education
Smithsonian Environmental Research Center
Smithsonian Institution Building (The Castle)
Smithsonian Marine Station at Fort Pierce
Smithsonian Tropical Research Institute

HISTORICAL FINANCIALS

Company Type: Not-for-profit

Income Statement

FYE: September 30

	REVENUE ($ mil.)	NET INCOME ($ mil.)	NET PROFIT MARGIN	EMPLOYEES
9/03	691	—	—	—
9/02	691	—	—	—
9/01	665	—	—	—
9/00	604	—	—	6,500
9/99	563	—	—	6,400
9/98	775	—	—	—
9/97	729	—	—	6,469
9/96	703	—	—	6,487
9/95	750	—	—	6,600
9/94	605	—	—	6,671
Annual Growth	1.5%	—	—	(0.4%)

Revenue History

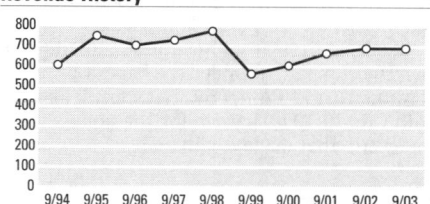

Software House

Software House International (SHI) wants to put software in houses across the globe. The company distributes more than 100,000 hardware and software products from suppliers such as Adobe, Corel, Microsoft, and IBM. SHI also offers professional services such as systems integration and application development through its Software House Enterprise Solutions division. The company counts Agilent, AT&T, Boeing, and Hewlett-Packard among its clients. Founded in 1982, SHI has grown from a company with less than $1 million in annual revenue in 1989, when entrepreneur Thai Lee assumed ownership, to a company with more than $1 billion in annual revenues.

EXECUTIVES

Chairman and Co-CEO: Leo Koguan, age 50
President and Co-CEO: Thai Lee, age 47
CFO: Paul Ng
Enterprise Solutions Program Champion: Caroline Change
Human Resources: Michael Haluska

LOCATIONS

HQ: Software House International, Inc.
2 Riverview Dr., Somerset, NJ 08873
Phone: 732-764-8888 **Fax:** 732-764-8889
Web: www.shi.com

Software House International has offices in Canada, France, Hong Kong, the UK, and the US.

PRODUCTS/OPERATIONS

Selected Products

Cameras	Printers
Copiers	Processors
Fax machines	Scanners
Hubs	Servers
Modems	Software
Motherboards	Storage products
Notebooks	Surge protection
PCs	equipment
Power supplies	Switchers and routers

Selected Services

Application development
Asset management
Contract staffing
Desktop installation
E-commerce
Network consulting
Security management
Systems integration
Technical support

COMPETITORS

Access Distribution	ICG
Agilysys	Ingram Micro
Arrow Electronics	Merisel
ASI Corp.	Pacific Magtron
Avnet	SARCOM
Bell Microproducts	Softmart
CDW	Supercom
CompuCom	Tech Data
Electrograph Technologies	

HISTORICAL FINANCIALS

Company Type: Private

Income Statement

FYE: December 31

	REVENUE ($ mil.)	NET INCOME ($ mil.)	NET PROFIT MARGIN	EMPLOYEES
12/03	1,652	43	2.6%	900
12/02	1,797	46	2.5%	1,000
12/01	1,730	43	2.5%	1,000
12/00	1,390	—	—	1,000
12/99	909	—	—	1,000
Annual Growth	16.1%	(0.6%)	—	(2.6%)

Net Income History

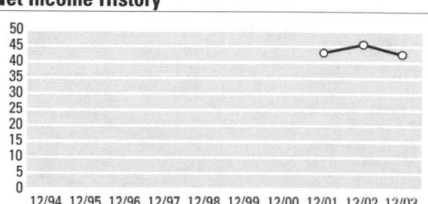

Softworld

Softworld provides recruiting and temporary staffing services in areas such as information technology, software engineering, life sciences, and business administration. Founded in 1993, Softworld serves clients through offices in Waltham, Massachusetts; Atlanta; Fort Lauderdale, Florida; and Washington, DC.

EXECUTIVES

Chairman: Michael Shuman
President and CEO: David S. (Dave) Teitelman
CFO: Warren Steinberg
VP Sales: Larry Agresto
Director of Sales and Alliances: Greg Flecke
Director of Staffing: Ray St. Martin
Director of IT Business Solutions and New Business Development: Jeff Schwartz
Director Human Resources: Stephanie Franklin

LOCATIONS

HQ: Softworld Inc.
281 Winter St., Ste. 301, Waltham, MA 02451
Phone: 781-466-8882   **Fax:** 781-466-8885
Web: www.softworldinc.com

COMPETITORS

Ablest
Adecco
Apex Systems
COMSYS IT Partners
Information Technology Professionals
Kelly Services
Kforce

HISTORICAL FINANCIALS

Company Type: Private

Income Statement

	REVENUE ($ mil.)	NET INCOME ($ mil.)	NET PROFIT MARGIN	EMPLOYEES
12/04*	14	—	—	—
12/01	9	—	—	90
Annual Growth	**53.4%**	—	—	—

FYE: December 31

*Irregular reporting interval

Revenue History

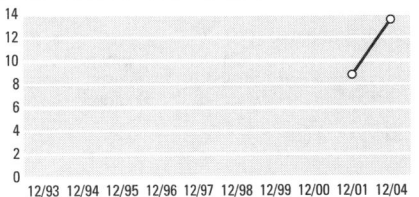

Solo Cup

Solo Cup married a Sweetheart, but kept its own name. In 2004, Solo Cup — which makes disposable cups, plates, containers, cutlery, and the like — bought and absorbed rival SF Holdings, parent company of disposable product maker Sweetheart Holdings (Sweetheart Cup). Solo Cup's plastic, paper, and foam items are sold through retailers and food-service distributors around the world, then used and thrown away by consumers. In addition to typical disposables, Solo also makes specialty party supplies, upscale disposable products, and plastic and paper packaging for snack food and dairy product manufacturers.

The company's Sweetheart of a deal was consummated in February 2004. The marriage of Solo and Sweetheart creates a company with more than 30 manufacturing facilities in North America (more than 20 from the Sweetheart side) and combined sales of $2 billion. Solo also operates factories in Japan, Panama, and the UK. The deal was helped along by a $220 million investment in Solo from equity firm Vestar Capital Partners in exchange for a minority stake in the new company. The acquisition of Sweetheart included Hoffmaster Tissues and Fonda Brands, two other paper product companies owned by Sweetheart parent SF Holdings Group.

Solo's consumer brands now include Solo (typical disposable tableware), SoloGrips (ergonomically designed cups and plates), Sensations and Hoffmaster (premium decorative tableware), and Creative Expressions (tableware and decorations for celebrations). Industrial brands include Flexstyle and Flex-E-Form frozen food packaging and Mtrene for refrigerated products.

Leo J. Hulseman, whose descendants still own the company, founded the Paper Container Manufacturing Company in 1936; it became Solo Cup in 1946, named for the cone-shaped paper cup that made it famous.

EXECUTIVES

Chairman and CEO: Robert L. Hulseman
President and COO: Ronald L. Whaley
EVP, CFO, and Assistant Secretary: Susan H. Marks
Group EVP: William Coad
SVP, Global Human Resources: Kathleen Wolf

LOCATIONS

HQ: Solo Cup Company
1700 Old Deerfield Rd., Highland Park, IL 60035
Phone: 847-831-4800   **Fax:** 847-831-5849
Web: www.solocup.com

Solo Cup sells its products in 50 countries around the world. It has distributors in Africa, Asia, the Caribbean, Europe, Latin America, the Middle East, the South Pacific, and the US.

PRODUCTS/OPERATIONS

Selected Products

Cold cups, lids, and straws
Cutlery
Dinnerware
Doilies
Fluted/Bakery products
Food containers
Hot cups, and lids
Napkins
Paper plates, bowls, and cups
Placemats
Plastic plates, bowls, cups, lids, deli, and food containers
Portion cups
Specialty tabletop disposables
Tablecovers

COMPETITORS

American Greetings
Amscan
Berry Plastics
Dart Container
EarthShell
Huhtamäki
Pactiv
Rexam
Reynolds Food Packaging

HISTORICAL FINANCIALS

Company Type: Private

Income Statement

	REVENUE ($ mil.)	NET INCOME ($ mil.)	NET PROFIT MARGIN	EMPLOYEES
12/04	2,116	(50)	—	11,500
12/03	880	(3)	—	—
12/02	837	17	2.0%	—
12/01	780	4	0.5%	—
12/00	707	8	1.1%	4,700
Annual Growth	**31.5%**	—	—	**25.1%**

FYE: December 31

2004 Year-End Financials

Debt ratio: 235.2%
Return on equity: —
Cash ($ mil.): 16
Current ratio: 2.21
Long-term debt ($ mil.): 1,005

Net Income History

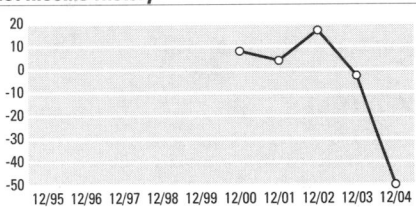

Sony BMG

There's nothing sweeter than when media conglomerates make beautiful music together. A 50-50 joint venture between Sony Corporation of America and Bertelsmann, Sony BMG Music Entertainment is the #2 record company in the world (behind Universal Music Group). It operates primarily through its stable of recording labels, such as Columbia, Epic, J Records, Jive, LaFace, and RCA, and boasts an artist roster that includes Aerosmith, Jennifer Lopez, Avril Lavigne, Alicia Keys, OutKast, Jessica Simpson, and Britney Spears. Sony BMG was formed through the 2004 merger of Sony Music Entertainment and BMG Entertainment.

While the mega-sized merger was able to catapult Sony and BMG (previously the third- and fifth-largest record companies, respectively) past EMI and into the #2 spot, the deal came as somewhat of a surprise given the industry's three-year long slide in album sales. But the gamble might yet pay off as the record industry begins to show some signs of recovery.

Contributing to increases in sales for Sony BMG is its involvement with the hit TV show *American Idol*, courtesy of music impresario and Arista Records founder Clive Davis. Winners Ruben Studdard and Fantasia Barrino have produced top selling albums for Davis' J Records while first-season winner Kelly Clarkson has shown some staying power recording for RCA.

Both Sony and Bertelsmann held onto the manufacturing and fulfillment arms as well as the music publishing operations that had been part of Sony Music and BMG.

EXECUTIVES

Chairman: Rolf Schmidt-Holtz, age 57
CEO and Director: Andrew R. (Andy) Lack, age 58
COO: Michael Smellie
EVP and CFO: Kevin Kelleher
EVP and Chief Business and Legal Affairs Officer:
Ron Wilcox
EVP and Chief Marketing Officer: Tim Prescott
EVP, Global General Counsel, and Secretary:
Daniel M. Mandil, age 48
EVP Sales: Tom Donnarumma
EVP Television: Jeremiah Bosgang
SVP and European Counsel: Jonathan Sternberg
SVP Communications: Cory Shields
SVP Feature Films: Sofia Sondervan
SVP Global Marketing: George Levendis
VP Global Marketing: Daniel Levy
VP Global Marketing: Ryan Wright
Chairman, BMG US; Chairman and CEO, J Records:
Clive Davis, age 72

LOCATIONS

HQ: Sony BMG Music Entertainment
550 Madison Ave., New York, NY 10022
Phone: 212-833-8000   **Fax:** 212-833-4818
Web: www.sonybmg.com

Sony BMG Music Entertainment has operations in more than 60 countries.

PRODUCTS/OPERATIONS

Selected Record Labels

Arista Records	RCA Records
BMG Heritage	RCA Victor Group
BMG International	Sony BMG Masterworks
Columbia Records	Sony Music International
Epic Records	Sony Music Nashville
J Records	Sony Wonder
Jive Records	Sony Urban Music
LaFace Records	So So Def Records
Legacy Recordings	Verity Records
Provident Music Group	

COMPETITORS

EMI Group
Universal Music Group
Warner Music

HISTORICAL FINANCIALS

Company Type: Joint venture

Income Statement				FYE: March 31
	ESTIMATED REVENUE ($ mil.)	NET INCOME ($ mil.)	NET PROFIT MARGIN	EMPLOYEES
3/05	5,000	—	—	10,000

Sound Surgical

Sound Surgical Technologies makes music your hips will really like. The company's ultrasonic medical devices use sound to break up and remove body fat. Sound Surgical's VASER System allows doctors to perform the increasingly common cosmetic surgery known as lipoplasty — which Sound Surgical has branded LipoSelection — without using suction cannulas and limiting post-surgical bruising and pain. The firm markets the VASER System to surgeons, surgery centers, and hospitals through a direct sales force in the US and through distribution agreements in Europe and South Korea. Sound Surgical hopes to open as many as four LipoSelection Centers of America, with the facilities making use of the VASER System.

Sound Surgical has installed more than 200 VASER Systems and makes the equipment available on a fee-per-procedure basis. Fee-per-procedure income accounted for nearly 20% of the company's 2004 sales.

Sales outside the US have been slow, contributing only 12% in 2004. These sales were primarily to buyers in Europe and South America.

Chairman and president William Cimino and CEO Donald Wingerter Jr. each owns 22% of the company. The company shelved its plans to go public in May 2005.

EXECUTIVES

Chairman and President: William W. Cimino
CEO and Director: Donald B. Wingerter Jr.
CFO, Secretary, and Treasurer: Douglas D. Foote
Chief Sales and Marketing Officer: Thomas J. Bogle
VP, Human Resources and Communication:
Stephen P. Kregstein
VP, International Sales and Business Development:
Carter E. Morgan
VP, Marketing: Sonya L. Courtney
VP, Operations: Peter D. Geary
VP, US Sales: Richard D. Harger
Auditors: Ehrhardt Keefe Steiner & Hottman PC

LOCATIONS

HQ: Sound Surgical Technologies LLC
357 S. McCaslin Blvd., Ste. 100,
Louisville, CO 80027
Phone: 303-926-8608   **Fax:** 303-384-9134
Web: www.soundsurgical.com

2004 Sales

	$ mil.	% of total
US	3.7	88
Other countries	0.5	12
Total	**4.2**	**100**

PRODUCTS/OPERATIONS

2004 Sales

	$ mil.	% of total
Product sales & services	3.2	76
Use fees	0.7	17
Gain on sale of sales-type leases	0.3	7
Total	**4.2**	**100**

COMPETITORS

Medtronic
Mentor Corporation
Palomar Medical

HISTORICAL FINANCIALS

Company Type: Private

Income Statement				FYE: December 31
	REVENUE ($ mil.)	NET INCOME ($ mil.)	NET PROFIT MARGIN	EMPLOYEES
12/04	4	(5)	—	58
12/03	2	(4)	—	49
12/02	0	(1)	—	—
Annual Growth	224.0%	—	—	18.4%

2004 Year-End Financials

Debt ratio: 0.0%   Current ratio: 2.03
Return on equity: —   Long-term debt ($ mil.): 0
Cash ($ mil.): 2

Net Income History

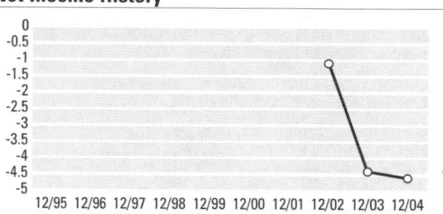

Southeastern Freight Lines

Less-than-truckload (LTL) carrier Southeastern Freight Lines hauls freight throughout the southeastern US. (LTL carriers consolidate freight from multiple shippers into single truckloads.) Through partnerships with other trucking companies, including A. Duie Pyle, Dayton Freight, and Oak Harbor Freight Lines, Southeastern Freight Lines provides service throughout the US and Canada. The company specializes in hauling carpet and carpet-related products. Its fleet includes about 2,000 tractors and 6,000 trailers. Southeastern Freight Lines is controlled by the Cassels family, which also owns truckload carrier G&P Trucking.

EXECUTIVES

Chairman: W. T. Cassels Jr.
President: W. T. (Tobin) Cassels III
SVP Corporate Planning and Development:
Braxton Vick
SVP Finance: Russ Burleson
SVP Operations: Rick Toburen
SVP Sales and Marketing: Mike Heaton
VP Management Information Systems: Dave Robinson
VP Quality and HR: David Scoggins

LOCATIONS

HQ: Southeastern Freight Lines, Inc.
420 Davega Rd., Lexington, SC 29073
Phone: 803-794-7300   **Fax:** 803-794-8131
Web: www.sefl.com

Southeastern Freight Lines operates service centers in Alabama, Florida, Georgia, Louisiana, Mississippi, North Carolina, South Carolina, Tennessee, Texas, Virginia, and in Puerto Rico.

COMPETITORS

AAA Cooper Transportation	FedEx Freight
Arkansas Best	Old Dominion Freight
Averitt Express	Overnite Transportation
Con-Way	Watkins Motor Lines
Estes Express	Yellow Roadway

HISTORICAL FINANCIALS

Company Type: Private

Income Statement

FYE: December 31

	ESTIMATED REVENUE ($ mil.)	NET INCOME ($ mil.)	NET PROFIT MARGIN	EMPLOYEES
12/04	546	—	—	6,000
12/03	484	—	—	—
12/02	446	—	—	—
12/01	435	—	—	—
12/00	449	—	—	—
12/99	410	—	—	—
12/98	377	—	—	—
12/97	347	—	—	—
12/96	304	—	—	—
12/95	264	—	—	—
Annual Growth	8.4%	—	—	—

Revenue History

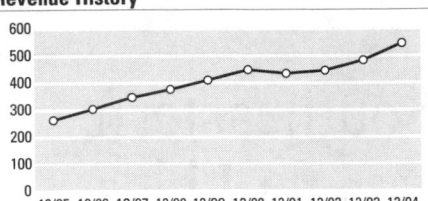

Southern Illinois University

Southern Illinois University enrolls more than 34,000 students at its two institutions — Southern Illinois University at Carbondale (which includes a School of Medicine) and Southern Illinois University at Edwardsville (which includes a School of Dental Medicine). The Carbondale campus oversees a university program in Niigata, Japan. The university was chartered as a teachers college in 1869.

EXECUTIVES

Chairman: Roger B. Tedrick, age 56
President: James E. Walker
Provost and Vice Chancellor: Sharon K. Hahs
Chancellor, Southern Illinois University Carbondale: Walter V. Wendler
Chancellor, Southern Illinois University Edwardsville: Vaughn Vandegrift
Provost and Dean, School of Medicine at Springfield: John Kevin Dorsey

Vice Chancellor for University Relations: G. Patrick Williams
VP Academic Affairs: John S. Haller
VP Financial and Administrative Affairs and Treasurer: Duane Stucky
Executive Director Internal Audit: Ronald E. (Ron) Cremeens
Executive Director University Development: Harold Melser
Executive Director University Marketing and Communications: Barbara O'Malley
Director Annual Fund: Lisa McKennedy
Director Human Resources, Carbondale: Kathleen M. Blackwell
Auditors: Kerber, Eck & Braeckel LLP

LOCATIONS

HQ: Southern Illinois University
425 Clocktower Dr., Carbondale, IL 62901
Phone: 618-536-3331   **Fax:** 618-536-3404
Web: www.siu.edu

HISTORICAL FINANCIALS

Company Type: School

Income Statement

FYE: June 30

	REVENUE ($ mil.)	NET INCOME ($ mil.)	NET PROFIT MARGIN	EMPLOYEES
6/04	341	—	—	—
6/03	331	—	—	—
6/02	314	—	—	7,250
Annual Growth	4.2%	—	—	—

Revenue History

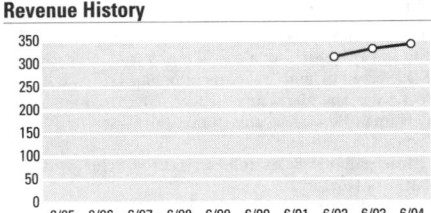

Southern States Cooperative

Founded to provide affordable, high-quality seed to Virginia farmers, Southern States Cooperative serves more than 300,000 members, mainly in midwestern and southern states. The co-op offers its farmer-owners feed and fertilizer manufacturing, seed processing, grain marketing, and petroleum and propane services, as well as wholesale farm supplies. Its Southern States and GardenSouth stores sell farm supplies, garden products, and fuel through some 1,200 retail outlets in more than 20 states. Other services include crop services, sales financing, and an aquaculture program. Southern States Cooperative, which was established in 1923, merged with Michigan Livestock Exchange in 1998.

With the bankruptcy and subsequent 2004 liquidation of Agway Inc., Southern States became the sole owner of Cooperative Milling Inc. It also obtained Agway's consumer wholesale dealer business, various Agway trademarks and its Internet domain name.

EXECUTIVES

President and CEO: Thomas R. Scribner
EVP and CFO: Leslie Newton
SVP, General Counsel, and Secretary: N. Hopper Ancarrow Jr.
EVP and COO: Wesley Wright
VP and CIO: Karen Lankford
VP and Controller: Philip Miller
VP, Agway: Dennis Marshall
VP, Crops Merchandising: Gregory Adlich
VP, Farm and Home Merchandising: Chuck Popik
VP, Feed Merchandising and Operations: Jim Moore
VP, Finance, and Treasurer: Fred Jezouit
VP, Human Resources: Jerry Walker
VP, Marketing and Independent Markets: Steve Patterson
Director, Corporate Communications, Member Relations, and Public Affairs: Jim Erickson
Auditors: PricewaterhouseCoopers LLP

LOCATIONS

HQ: Southern States Cooperative, Incorporated
6606 W. Broad St., Richmond, VA 23230
Phone: 804-281-1000   **Fax:** 804-281-1413
Web: www.southernstates.com

Southern States Cooperative operates retail locations in Alabama, Arkansas, Connecticut, Delaware, Florida, Georgia, Indiana, Kentucky, Louisiana, Maine, Maryland, Massachusetts, Michigan, Mississippi, New Hampshire, New Jersey, New York, North Carolina, Ohio, Pennsylvania, Rhode Island, South Carolina, Vermont, Virginia, and West Virginia.

COMPETITORS

ADM	Crop Production Services
Ag Processing	GROWMARK
Andersons	Rabo AgServices
Cargill	Scoular
CHS	Tennessee Farmers Co-op
ConAgra	Tractor Supply
Corn Products International	

HISTORICAL FINANCIALS

Company Type: Cooperative

Income Statement

FYE: June 30

	REVENUE ($ mil.)	NET INCOME ($ mil.)	NET PROFIT MARGIN	EMPLOYEES
6/04	1,294	68	5.2%	3,300
6/03	1,311	(55)	—	3,379
6/02	1,463	(68)	—	5,000
6/01	1,739	(15)	—	5,700
6/00	1,547	5	0.3%	5,425
6/99	1,366	(2)	—	6,000
6/98	1,120	11	1.0%	3,800
6/97	1,216	28	2.3%	3,800
6/96	1,123	28	2.5%	3,800
6/95	1,014	18	1.8%	3,800
Annual Growth	2.7%	15.8%	—	(1.6%)

2004 Year-End Financials

Debt ratio: 99.8%	Current ratio: 1.42
Return on equity: 98.1%	Long-term debt ($ mil.): 127
Cash ($ mil.): 12	

Net Income History

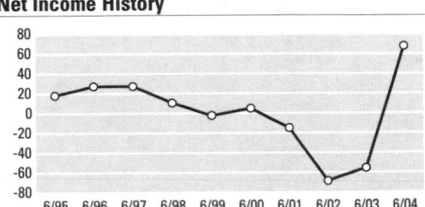

Southern Wine & Spirits

Fueled by alcohol and nicotine, Southern Wine & Spirits of America delivers market dominance. The firm is the #1 US distributor of wine and spirits, with operations in 19 states. In addition to importing and distributing wine and spirits, it sells imported brews, such as Grolsch and Steinlager; cigars, such as Don Diego and Montecristo; and nonalcoholic beverages, including Clamato and Rose's Lime Juice. The company also owns Premier Wine & Spirits of New York and large stakes in Pacific Wine & Spirits (part of Terlato Wine Group) and Romano Bros. Beverage, a spirits wholesaler in Illinois. Chairman and CEO Harvey Chaplin and his family own more than 50% of the company.

In 2005 Southern Wine became the majority owner in a newly formed joint venture with D.J. Koening & Associates, called Wine & Spirits of Mississippi. The joint venture marks Southern Wine's expansion into Mississippi.

EXECUTIVES

Chairman and CEO: Harvey R. Chaplin
President and COO: Wayne E. Chaplin
EVP; General Manager: Brad Vassar, age 47
EVP, Spirits: Rodolfo (Rudy) Ruiz, age 56
EVP, Wines, New York: James C. (Jim) Allen
VP, Finance and Administration: John R. Preston
VP; Secretary and Chief Administrative Officer: Lee F. Hager
VP and Director, Marketing: Lisa Barghahn
VP, Sales, National Accounts: Bill Edwards
Director, Human Resources Group and Shared Services: Rachel Seder

LOCATIONS

HQ: Southern Wine & Spirits of America, Inc.
1600 NW 163rd St., Miami, FL 33169
Phone: 305-625-4171   **Fax:** 305-625-4720
Web: www.southernwine.com

Southern Wine & Spirits of America distributes products from 15 warehouses in Arizona, California, Colorado, Florida, Hawaii, Illinois, Kentucky, Nevada, New Mexico, New York, Pennsylvania, and South Carolina. The company has exclusive rights to distribute Allied Domecq brands in California and Hawaii and a "first choice" agreement with Allied Domecq in South Carolina.

PRODUCTS/OPERATIONS

Selected Products
Beer
Cigars
Nonalcoholic beverages and mixes
Spirits
Wines

COMPETITORS

Altadis	National Wine & Spirits
Bacardi	Peerless Importers
Banfi Vintners	Rémy Cointreau
Ben E. Keith	Sunbelt Beverage
Constellation Brands	Synergy Brands
Geerlings & Wade	Topa Equities
Georgia Crown	UST
Glazer's Wholesale Drug	Wirtz
Johnson Brothers	Young's Market
National Distributing	

HISTORICAL FINANCIALS
Company Type: Private

Income Statement
FYE: December 31

	REVENUE ($ mil.)	NET INCOME ($ mil.)	NET PROFIT MARGIN	EMPLOYEES
12/03	5,400	—	—	8,000
12/02	4,400	—	—	7,100
12/01	3,750	—	—	5,680
12/00	3,500	—	—	5,600
12/99	3,100	—	—	5,400
12/98	2,600	—	—	4,500
12/97	2,450	—	—	4,500
12/96	2,200	—	—	4,000
12/95	2,125	—	—	4,000
12/94	1,985	—	—	3,925
Annual Growth	**11.8%**	**—**	**—**	**8.2%**

Revenue History

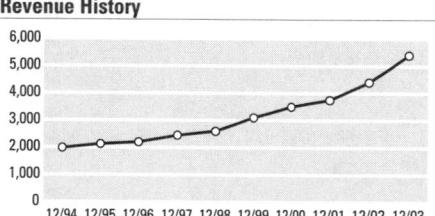

LOCATIONS

HQ: Southwire Company
One Southwire Dr., Carrollton, GA 30119
Phone: 770-832-4242   **Fax:** 770-832-4406
Web: www.mysouthwire.com

Southwire operates manufacturing plants in the US and sales offices in Hong Kong, Mexico City, and Paris.

PRODUCTS/OPERATIONS

Selected Products
Aluminum rod
Building wire
Communication cable
Copper rod
Electrical wire and cable
High voltage cable
Magnet wire
Specialty wire
Transit cable
Wire-making machinery

COMPETITORS

AFC Cable	Genesis Cable
Alcan	Hitachi Cable
Alcatel	International Wire
Alpine Group	IRCE
Anixter International	Nexans
Balfour Beatty	OFS BrightWave
Belden CDT	Phelps Dodge
Bridon	Pirelli & C.
Capro	Showa Electric Wire
Carlisle Companies	& Cable
Driver-Harris	Sumitomo Electric
Encore Wire	Superior Essex
General Cable	Volex

Southwire

Southwire hopes everyone's cable-ready. One of the world's largest cable and wire manufacturers, Southwire makes building wire and cable, utility cable products, industrial power cable, telecommunications cable, copper and aluminum rods, and cord products. The company also provides engineering and machining and fabrication services. Its Forte Power Systems subsidiary provides turnkey services for high-voltage systems using extruded-dielectric cable. Founded in 1950 by Roy Richards Sr. (the chairman's father), Southwire is owned by the Richards family.

Southwire will continue to build on its core operations, as evidenced by its purchase of General Cable Corporation's building wire assets, which made Southwire one of North America's largest producers of building wire. The company is also expanding its base of operations in Asia, such as the copper rod system deal with China's Jiangxi Copper Products Company that includes a furnace system complete with a loader, melter, holder and launder system, casting machine, and automatic metal pouring system.

EXECUTIVES

Chairman: Roy Richards Jr.
Vice Chairman and President, Business Development: Lee Richards
President and CEO: Stuart Thorn
VP, Finance: J. Guyton Cochran Jr.
VP, Information Technology Services: Lee Hunter
VP, Human Resources: Michael R. (Mike) Wiggins
VP, Legal: Stanley Tate
VP, Operations: Jeff Herrin
VP, Sales and Business Development, Energy Division: Norman Adkins
Manager, Communications: Gary Leftwich

HISTORICAL FINANCIALS
Company Type: Private

Income Statement
FYE: December 31

	ESTIMATED REVENUE ($ mil.)	NET INCOME ($ mil.)	NET PROFIT MARGIN	EMPLOYEES
12/03	1,500	—	—	3,100
12/02	1,400	—	—	3,300
12/01	1,500	—	—	3,300
12/00	1,500	—	—	3,000
12/99	1,300	—	—	4,000
12/98	1,400	—	—	4,500
12/97	1,700	—	—	4,900
12/96	1,700	—	—	5,000
12/95	1,900	—	—	5,200
12/94	1,600	—	—	5,000
Annual Growth	**(0.7%)**	**—**	**—**	**(5.2%)**

Revenue History

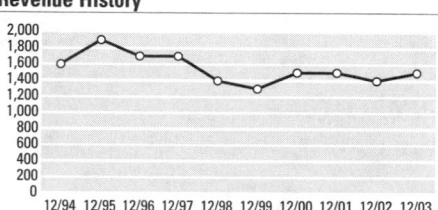

Spansion

Spansion favors flash expansion. Formerly called FASL, the joint venture between Advanced Micro Devices and Fujitsu makes and markets flash memory devices. The two chip heavyweights formed the company in 2003 as an outgrowth of their decade-long collaboration in non-volatile memory. Flash memory is used in a wide variety of electronic devices including wireless phones, networking equipment, and automotive subsystems. Spansion also provides hardware development tools and production manufacturing support. The company's products are marketed through Advanced Micro Devices and Fujitsu sales offices.

Spansion's blue-chip customers include Cisco Systems, Nortel Networks, and Volkswagen. Spansion is now the world's #2 maker of flash memory (behind Samsung).

EXECUTIVES

President and CEO: Bertrand Cambou, age 49, $602,570 pay
EVP and Chief Administrative Officer: Richard Previte, age 70
EVP and Chief Marketing Officer: Thomas T. (Tom) Eby, age 44, $395,199 pay
EVP and Chief Scientist: Masao Taguchi, age 54
EVP; President, Spansion Japan: Shinji Suzuki, age 58
EVP, Group Operations: Kazunori Imaoka, age 57
EVP, Worldwide Operations: James E. Doran, age 56, $434,393 pay
SVP; General Manager, Embedded Business Unit: Sylvia Summers, age 52, $399,311 pay
SVP; General Manager, Wireless Business Unit: Amir Mashkoori, age 43, $387,912 pay
VP, CFO, and Treasurer: Steven J. Geiser, age 36
VP, Corporate Development, General Counsel, and Secretary: Robert C. Melendres, age 40
VP, Worldwide Sales: Jeffrey W. (Jeff) Davis, age 45
Auditors: Ernst & Young LLP

LOCATIONS

HQ: Spansion Inc.
915 DeGuigne Dr., Sunnyvale, CA 94088
Phone: 408-962-2500
Web: www.spansion.com

Spansion has major operations in China, Japan, Malaysia, Thailand, and the US.

PRODUCTS/OPERATIONS

2004 Sales

	% of total
AMD	54
Fujitsu	46
Total	**100**

COMPETITORS

Atmel	SanDisk
Hynix	SANYO
Intel	Sharp
Macronix International	Silicon Storage
Micron Technology	STMicroelectronics
NEC	Toshiba
Renesas	Winbond Electronics
Samsung Electronics	

HISTORICAL FINANCIALS

Company Type: Joint venture

Income Statement

FYE: December 31

	REVENUE ($ mil.)	NET INCOME ($ mil.)	NET PROFIT MARGIN	EMPLOYEES
12/04	1,193	(129)	—	7,500
12/03	962	21	2.2%	6,900
Annual Growth	24.0%	—	—	8.7%

2004 Year-End Financials

Debt ratio: 27.5%
Return on equity: —
Cash ($ mil.): 138
Current ratio: 1.49
Long-term debt ($ mil.): 454

Net Income History

40									
20									
0									
-20									
-40									
-60									
-80									
-100									
-120									
-140									

12/95 12/96 12/97 12/98 12/99 12/00 12/01 12/02 12/03 12/04

SPARTA

This SPARTA relies on technology significantly more complex than that of its namesake city-state of ancient Greece to provide defense-related engineering, scientific, and technical services. As a prime contractor or a subcontractor, SPARTA contributes to the design and development of a variety of tactical and strategic weapons and defense systems, including ballistic missile defense systems. The company also fabricates prototype hardware and makes composite parts for aircraft and missile systems. The US Department of Defense and various intelligence agencies account for nearly all of SPARTA's sales. The company is owned by its employees.

EXECUTIVES

Chairman: Wayne R. Winton
CEO and Director: Robert C. (Bob) Sepucha
CFO: David E. Schreiman, age 42
CIO: Ray Gretlein
CTO: John Dyer
President, Hardware Systems Sector and Director: R. Stephen (Steve) McCarter
President, Mission Systems: Troy A. Crites, age 46
President, National Security Systems: Bill Sabean
President, Spiral Technology, Inc.: Archie L. Moore
President, Missile Defense Sector: Randy N. Morgan
Military Systems Operation, National Security Systems Sector: Bill Goodner
Director, Business Development and Director: Carl T. Case
Director, Human Resources: Jody Chiaro
Auditors: PricewaterhouseCoopers LLP

LOCATIONS

HQ: SPARTA, Inc.
25531 Commercentre Dr., Ste. 120, Lake Forest, CA 92630
Phone: 949-768-8161   **Fax:** 949-583-9113
Web: www.sparta.com

SPARTA has offices in Alabama, California, Colorado, Florida, Maryland, Massachusetts, Nebraska, Nevada, and Virginia.

COMPETITORS

BAE SYSTEMS
Boeing
General Dynamics
Lockheed Martin
Northrop Grumman
Raytheon
SAIC

HISTORICAL FINANCIALS

Company Type: Private

Income Statement

FYE: Sunday closest to December 31

	REVENUE ($ mil.)	NET INCOME ($ mil.)	NET PROFIT MARGIN	EMPLOYEES
12/04	252	16	6.4%	1,200
12/03	203	11	5.5%	1,000
12/02	162	9	5.5%	900
Annual Growth	24.5%	34.1%	—	15.5%

2004 Year-End Financials

Debt ratio: 14.6%
Return on equity: 35.6%
Cash ($ mil.): 29
Current ratio: 2.40
Long-term debt ($ mil.): 7

Net Income History

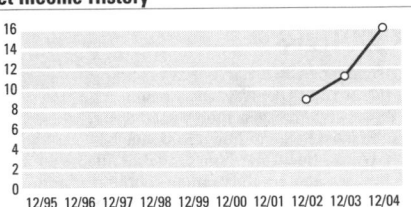

16									
14									
12									
10									
8									
6									
4									
2									
0									

12/95 12/96 12/97 12/98 12/99 12/00 12/01 12/02 12/03 12/04

Special Devices

Special Devices is blasting off as a leading US maker of initiators (pyrotechnic devices) used primarily in automotive airbag systems. The airbag initiators activate inflators that enable the airbag to be deployed. The company also makes micro gas generators that remove seatbelt slack in the event of a collision. Special Devices sells its products primarily to manufacturers of airbag initiators. Autoliv accounts for 26% of the company's sales; TRW Automotive and Inflation Systems account for 23% and 20%, respectively. Special Devices chairman John Lehman, through various investment entities, controls a 61% stake in the company.

One of just a few US manufacturers of airbag initiators, Special Devices is counting on increased demand for its products as carmakers install more so-called smart airbags.

To diversify, Special Devices is developing engineered pyrotechnic devices for use in the aerospace and mining industries. The company exited the aerospace market in 2001, but the expiration of noncompete agreements signed at that time allowed Special Devices to begin marketing products to aerospace customers in 2004.

EXECUTIVES

President, CEO, and Director: Thomas W. Cresante, age 57, $469,110 pay
VP, Advanced Product Development: Patrick J. Carroll, age 61, $168,690 pay
VP, Engineering: James L. Baglini, age 43, $191,129 pay
VP, Environmental, Health and Safety, and Regulatory Affairs: Thomas R. Cessario, age 50
VP, Finance and Assistant Secretary: James E. Reeder, age 47, $192,113 pay
VP, New Business Development and Strategy: Marty E. Sheber, age 45
VP, Operations: Nicholas J. Bruge, age 41, $235,533 pay
Assistant Secretary and Director: Louis N. Mintz, age 40
Secretary and Director: George A. Sawyer, age 73
Auditors: PricewaterhouseCoopers LLP

LOCATIONS

HQ: Special Devices, Incorporated
14370 White Sage Rd., Moorpark, CA 93021
Phone: 805-553-1200　　**Fax:** 805-553-1211
Web: www.specialdevices.com

Special Devices has manufacturing facilities in the US (Arizona and California) and in Thailand.

COMPETITORS

Autoliv
Goodrich
Hi-Shear Technology
Nippon Kayaku

HISTORICAL FINANCIALS

Company Type: Private

Income Statement

FYE: Sun. nearest the last day of Oct.

	REVENUE ($ mil.)	NET INCOME ($ mil.)	NET PROFIT MARGIN	EMPLOYEES
10/04	106	(2)	—	570
10/03	113	1	0.7%	621
10/02	120	(1)	—	784
10/01	123	12	9.4%	870
10/00	168	18	10.9%	720
10/99	141	11	7.6%	1,213
10/98	171	—	—	1,300
10/97	141	—	—	1,281
10/96	105	—	—	1,156
10/95	101	—	—	1,100
Annual Growth	0.5%	—	—	(7.0%)

2004 Year-End Financials

Debt ratio: —　　　　　Current ratio: 1.70
Return on equity: —　　Long-term debt ($ mil.): 75
Cash ($ mil.): 7

Net Income History

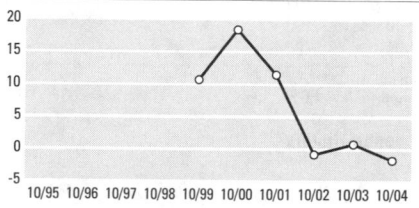

Specialty Restaurants

From Normandy to Nagasaki, Specialty Restaurants keeps its customers in plane view. The company operates about 35 upscale and casual-dining restaurants in more than a dozen states, including several themed locations that pay tribute to WWII aviation history. Carrying names such as 94th Aero Squadron, the flight-inspired restaurants feature replica military airplanes and an interior resembling a French farmhouse. Specialty Restaurants' other dining spots include Baby Doe's, Shanghai Red's, and Castaway. The company also offers catering and banquet services. Former WWII bomber pilot and aviation history buff David Tallichet founded the company in 1958 with George Millay, the founder of SeaWorld theme parks.

EXECUTIVES

Chairman and CEO: David C. Tallichet Jr.
President: Vincent E. (Vince) Kikugawa
CFO: John Kenny

LOCATIONS

HQ: Specialty Restaurants Corporation
8191 E. Kaiser Blvd., Anaheim, CA 92808
Phone: 714-279-6100　　**Fax:** 714-998-7574
Web: www.specialtyrestaurants.com

Specialty Restaurants operates about 35 restaurants in California, Colorado, Delaware, Florida, Georgia, Illinois, Maryland, Missouri, New Jersey, New York, Ohio, Tennessee, Texas, and Wisconsin.

PRODUCTS/OPERATIONS

Selected Restaurants

56th Fighter Group	HS Lordships
57th Fighter Group	Luminarias
94th Aero Squadron	Monterey Hill
100th Bomb Group	Odyssey
391st Bomb Group	Orange Hill
Air Transport Command	Pieces of Eight
Baby Doe's	Ports O' Call
Brady's Landing	Proud Bird
Brittany Hill	The Reef
Castaway	Rusty Pelican
Chili Pepper	Shanghai Red's
Confluence Park	Sunbird
Crawdaddy's	Whiskey Joe's

COMPETITORS

Ark Restaurants
Cohn Restaurants
Il Fornaio
Keg Restaurants
Kimpton
Lettuce Entertain You
Levy Restaurants
Morton's Restaurant Group
Outback Steakhouse
Restaurant Associates
Restaurants Unlimited
Ruth's Chris Steak House
Smith & Wollensky
Tavistock Restaurants

HISTORICAL FINANCIALS

Company Type: Private

Income Statement

FYE: June 30

	REVENUE ($ mil.)	NET INCOME ($ mil.)	NET PROFIT MARGIN	EMPLOYEES
6/04	109	—	—	2,000
6/03	105	—	—	2,000
6/02	100	—	—	—
6/01	102	—	—	—
Annual Growth	2.1%	—	—	0.0%

Revenue History

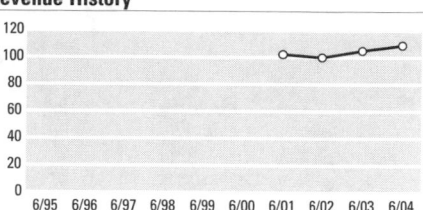

Spectrum Health

Spectrum Health is a regional health system serving western Michigan. The health network features seven hospitals, most of which operate under the Spectrum Health name. Residents and visitors to the area can also access Spectrum Health through its more than 140 service sites, which include urgent care centers, primary care physician offices, community clinics, rehabilitation and other outpatient facilities, and continuing care residences and services for the elderly. The health system also operates Priority Health, a health plan with about 450,000 members.

EXECUTIVES

President and CEO: Richard C. (Rick) Breon
EVP and CFO: Michael P. (Mike) Freed
SVP: John Mosley
SVP and CIO: Patrick O'Hare
SVP, Human Resources: Daniel Oglesby
SVP, System Quality: John Byrnes
VP, Clinical Operations: Jim Wilson, age 49
VP, Operations: Bill Ritscha
VP, Patient Care Services and Chief Nursing Officer: Shawn M. Ulreich
Auditors: Ernst & Young LLP

LOCATIONS

HQ: Spectrum Health
100 Michigan St. NE, Grand Rapids, MI 49503
Phone: 616-391-1774　　**Fax:** 616-391-2780
Web: www.spectrum-health.org

PRODUCTS/OPERATIONS

Hospitals

DeVos Children's Hospital (Grand Rapids)
Spectrum Health Blodgett Campus (Grand Rapids)
Spectrum Health Butterworth Campus (Grand Rapids)
Spectrum Health Kent Community Campus (Grand Rapids)
Spectrum Health United Campus (Greenville)
Spectrum Health Kelsey Campus (Lakeview)
Hackley Hospital (Muskegon)
Spectrum Health Reed City Campus (Reed City)
Hackley Lakeshore Hospital (Shelby)

HISTORICAL FINANCIALS

Company Type: Not-for-profit

Income Statement
FYE: June 30

	REVENUE ($ mil.)	NET INCOME ($ mil.)	NET PROFIT MARGIN	EMPLOYEES
6/04	1,868	—	—	14,000
6/03	1,538	—	—	14,000
6/02	1,373	—	—	—
Annual Growth	16.6%	—	—	0.0%

Revenue History

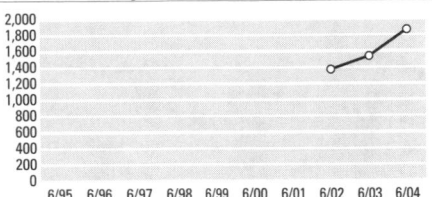

2,000 / 1,800 / 1,600 / 1,400 / 1,200 / 1,000 / 800 / 600 / 400 / 200 / 0
6/95 6/96 6/97 6/98 6/99 6/00 6/01 6/02 6/03 6/04

Spencer Stuart Management Consultants

When the board of directors ousts your CEO for running the company into the ground, it might look to Spencer Stuart Management Consultants for a replacement. Founded in 1956, the firm offers leadership consulting and executive search services, specializing in finding top-level executives and board directors. Clients hire Spencer Stuart to identify and recruit the best executives from its personal contacts and global database of business leaders. Citing the desire to protect client confidentiality, the firm's partners have declined to follow rivals into the public marketplace. Spencer Stuart is owned by its consultants.

EXECUTIVES

Chairman: Dayton Ogden
CEO: David S. Daniel
CFO and Chief Administrative Officer:
Richard M. (Rich) Kurkowski
SVP, Treasury: Robert Arnone
SVP, Training and Development: Mary Kay Jungbluth
VP, Systems: Rick Abel
Chief Marketing Officer: Ben Machtiger
Managing Director, Europe and South Africa:
Manuel Marquez
Managing Director, South America: Ignacio Marseillan
Regional Manager: Kevin M. Connelly
General Counsel: David J. Rasmussen

LOCATIONS

HQ: Spencer Stuart Management Consultants N.V.
401 N. Michigan Ave., Ste. 2600, Chicago, IL 60611
Phone: 312-822-0088   **Fax:** 312-822-0117
Web: www.spencerstuart.com

Spencer Stuart Management Consultants operates from more than 50 offices in 25 countries.

PRODUCTS/OPERATIONS

Selected Industries
Agribusiness
Aviation
Consumer goods and services
Financial services
Industrial
Life sciences
Not-for-profit
Technology

COMPETITORS

A.T. Kearney
Boyden
Christian & Timbers
Egon Zehnder
Heidrick & Struggles
J.C. Wilson Associates
Korn/Ferry
Michael Page
Monster Worldwide
Ray & Berndtson
Robert Half
Russell Reynolds
Solomon-Page Group

HISTORICAL FINANCIALS

Company Type: Private

Income Statement
FYE: September 30

	REVENUE ($ mil.)	NET INCOME ($ mil.)	NET PROFIT MARGIN	EMPLOYEES
9/04	362	5	1.3%	1,080
9/03	315	4	1.3%	1,055
9/02	272	4	1.3%	1,100
9/01	308	—	—	1,200
9/00	386	—	—	1,100
9/99	288	—	—	953
9/98	257	—	—	902
9/97	239	—	—	—
Annual Growth	6.1%	14.6%	—	3.0%

Net Income History

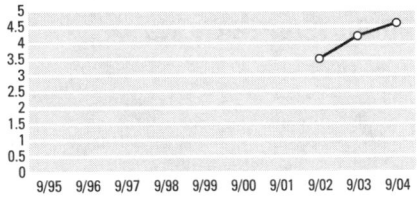

5 / 4.5 / 4 / 3.5 / 3 / 2.5 / 2 / 1.5 / 1 / 0.5 / 0
9/95 9/96 9/97 9/98 9/99 9/00 9/01 9/02 9/03 9/04

Spraylat

Stripping is OK at Spraylat. The company was founded in 1936 as a maker of strippable coatings (used to protect various products) and now has over 100 strippable coatings for use on a variety of surfaces. The company manufactures liquid and powder coatings, as well as coatings for signs, wheels, and electronics. Spraylat also makes mirror coatings through its Hilemn business segment. Customers include the aerospace, automotive, electronics, and general manufacturing industries. The US accounts for about 80% of the company's sales; European sales are handled through Spraylat's partner, UK-based Becker Industrial Coatings Corporation. The Borner family, including chairman James Borner, controls the company.

EXECUTIVES

Chairman: James Borner
CEO: Michael Borner
President: Ray Chlodney
EVP and General Counsel: William Borner
VP and CFO: John Ragazzini
VP, Operations: James Burrows
VP, Conductive Coatings: Roy Bjorlin
VP; Managing Director, Europe, Middle East, and Africa: Alain DeBlandre
VP and General Manager, Liquid Specialties:
Larry Nelson
VP and General Manager, Powder Coatings:
Robert (Bob) Schmuck
General Manager, Mirror Coatings: Dan Kovarik
Chairman, Spraylat Asia: John Million
Corporate Controller: Tom Klapatch
Director, Human Resources: Ken Breitman
Director, Strategic Planning and Marketing:
Gary Shawhan

LOCATIONS

HQ: Spraylat Corporation
143 Sparks Ave., Pelham, NY 10803
Phone: 914-738-1600   **Fax:** 914-712-2838
Web: www.spraylat.com

Spraylat Corporation has five manufacturing and two warehousing facilities in the US. It also has international offices in China, Germany, Japan, Korea, Mexico, Singapore, and Taiwan.

PRODUCTS/OPERATIONS

Selected Products
Conductive coatings
Liquid coatings
Powder coatings
Sign coatings
Tire coatings
Wheel coatings

COMPETITORS

Coatings Resource
DuPont Coatings
and Color Technologies
PPG
Schenectady International
Valspar

HISTORICAL FINANCIALS

Company Type: Private

Income Statement
FYE: December 31

	ESTIMATED REVENUE ($ mil.)	NET INCOME ($ mil.)	NET PROFIT MARGIN	EMPLOYEES
12/04	100	—	—	350
12/03	110	—	—	350
12/02	100	—	—	350
12/01	100	—	—	350
12/00	90	—	—	330
12/99	80	—	—	—
Annual Growth	4.6%	—	—	1.5%

Revenue History

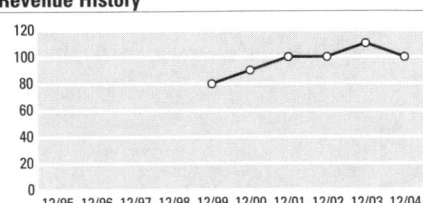

120 / 100 / 80 / 60 / 40 / 20 / 0
12/95 12/96 12/97 12/98 12/99 12/00 12/01 12/02 12/03 12/04

Springhill Lake Investors

Springhill Lake Investors not only has multiple owners and affiliates; it also has multiple tenants. The company was founded in 1984 to serve as the sole general partner of a series of limited partnerships that together own a single apartment community in Greenbelt, Maryland. The property has nearly 3,000 individual apartment units. AIMCO Properties and AIMCO IPLP, which are indirect subsidiaries of multifamily real estate giant AIMCO, own 80% of Springhill Lake Investors. Additionally, AIMCO/Springhill Lake Investors is the managing general partner of the company.

EXECUTIVES

VP Residential and Director, Three Winthrop: Martha J. Long, age 44
VP Residential and Chief Accounting Officer, Three Winthrop: Thomas M. Herzog, age 42
CEO Winthrop Financial Associates, Newkirk, First Union, Exeter Capital Corporation, and AP-Fairfield: Michael L. Ashner, age 53
Auditors: Ernst & Young LLP

LOCATIONS

HQ: Springhill Lake Investors Limited Partnership
55 Beattie Place, Greenville, SC 29602
Phone: 864-239-1000 **Fax:** 864-239-1031

PRODUCTS/OPERATIONS

2004 Sales

	$ mil.	% of total
Rent	31.1	95
Other	1.7	5
Total	**32.8**	**100**

COMPETITORS

BNP Residential Properties
Equity Residential
Lane Company

HISTORICAL FINANCIALS

Company Type: Partnership

Income Statement

FYE: December 31

	REVENUE ($ mil.)	NET INCOME ($ mil.)	NET PROFIT MARGIN	EMPLOYEES
12/04	33	2	6.4%	0
12/03	32	5	13.9%	0
12/02	32	3	9.9%	—
Annual Growth	0.8%	(19.0%)	—	—

Net Income History

Springs Industries

Springs Industries wants to cozy up in your bedroom. The company makes bath rugs, bedspreads, pillows, sheets, shower curtains, and towels under the Springmaid and Wamsutta brands. Springs also makes baby bedding, fabrics, hardware, infant apparel, and window blinds (Bali, Graber brands). The firm makes private-label items for Wal-Mart and Target, and licensed brands such as Harry Potter and NASCAR. Springs sells through catalogs, department stores, and mass retailers. The Close family, descendants of co-founder Leroy Springs, owns about 55% of Springs. Heartland Industrial Partners, with which the Close family took the firm private, owns the remaining 45%.

Wal-Mart represents about 25% of Springs' sales. The company also sells through about 60 of its own outlet stores. Historically an apparel textile maker, Springs has spent the last decade refocusing on home fashions through sales and acquisitions. In 2003 Springs acquired Charles D. Owen Manufacturing, the company's blanket supplier.

Springs Industries plans to operate its two business units, textiles home furnishings and window fashions, as separate companies beginning in 2006. The company has also announced a proposed merger with Brazilian company Cia. De Tecidos do Norte de Minas SA. The resultant company, named Springs Global and based in Brazil, is expected to be the world's largest sheet and towel manufacturer.

HISTORY

Springs Industries began in 1887 as Fort Mill Manufacturing Co., a cotton miller organized by Samuel Elliott White and a group of investors, including Leroy Springs, White's future son-in-law. Springs later founded his own cotton mill, Lancaster Cotton Mills, in 1895 and gained control of Fort Mill Manufacturing in 1914, three years after White died.

Leroy's only son, Elliott Springs, became president in 1931 when his father died. Left with massive debt and six aging cotton mills, Elliott rejuvenated the company by modernizing mill equipment and consolidating the plants into the Springs Cotton Mills (1933). During WWII the company's seven mills made fabric for military use.

In 1945 Springs started the Springmaid line of bedding and fabrics. Elliott's satiric, risqué, but effective ads (beginning in 1948) helped the company become a leading producer of sheets.

Elliott died in 1959 and his son-in-law, William Close, became president. With profits sharply declining, the company went public as Springs Mills in 1966.

The first non-family member to be president, Peter Scotese from Federated Department Stores, was hired in 1969. The next year Springs began working with designer Bill Blass. It diversified into synthetic fabrics in 1971 by buying a minority interest in a Japanese textile plant producing UltraSuede for apparel and cars.

Springs acquired Graber Industries (window-decorating products) in 1979 and three years later changed its name to Springs Industries. In 1985 it acquired M. Lowenstein, which made Wamsutta

home furnishings; the deal also gave it Clark-Schwebel Fiber Glass (industrial fabrics). Springs added Carey-McFall (Bali blinds) in 1989.

Declining economic conditions throughout the textile industry in the late 1980s and early 1990s forced Springs to close plants and trim its weakened finished-fabrics segment (the downsizing continued into 1993). A $70 million charge in 1990 led to a $7 million loss, its first in 25 years as a public company.

Historically a maker of apparel fabrics, Springs had grown vulnerable to imports and launched a long-term plan to focus on home furnishings through sales and acquisitions. In 1991 the company set up a bath group with the purchase of C. S. Brooks. Springs became a leading seller of home textiles in Canada the next year by buying the marketing and sales units of C. S. Brooks Canada and Springmaid distributor Griffiths-Kerr. A hostile takeover bid for rival Fieldcrest Cannon was rebuffed in 1993.

Expanding in 1995, Springs acquired Dundee Mills (baby and health care products, towels), Dawson Home Fashions (bath accessories, shower curtains), and Nanik Window Coverings (blinds, shutters). In 1996 the company sold its Clark-Schwebel subsidiary and the following year purchased half of American Fiber Industries (pillows, mattress pads, comforters).

Crandall Close Bowles became the eighth president of Springs in 1997. The next year she took over the chairman and CEO posts from Walter Elisha.

To further focus on its home furnishings business, in 1998 the company sold its UltraSuede business (but kept its UltraLeather business) and its industrial products division. In 1999 Springs finally exited the apparel fabrics business when it sold its Springfield division to a management group, then it purchased Regal Rugs (bath and accent rugs) and the remaining 50% of American Fiber Industries.

In April 2001 the Close family agreed to partner with private equity firm Heartland Industrial Partners to take Springs private. In September the deal was completed, increasing the family's stake to 55%, with Heartland owning the remaining 45%.

In March 2002 Springs acquired the rug division of Beaulieu Group, followed in April by its purchase of the sourced quilt division of Ultima Enterprises. In June Springs completed another acquisition, taking control of Burlington Industries' window treatments and bedding consumer products businesses.

In May 2003 Springs completed its acquisition of Charles D. Owen Manufacturing, one of the last remaining blanket makers in the US. The same year Springs acquired Oxford Bath.

EXECUTIVES

Chairman and CEO: Crandall Close Bowles, age 54, $637,504 pay
EVP and CFO: Kenneth E. Kutcher
EVP and CIO: Ray E. Greer
EVP, Operations: Dean Riggs
EVP; President, Marketing Group: Thomas P. (Tom) O'Connor, age 55, $396,672 pay
SVP and President, National Sales: Rick Canter
SVP and Chief Purchasing Officer: John R. Cowart
SVP, General Counsel, and Secretary: C. Powers Dorsett
SVP, Global Sourcing and International Marketing: Charles M. Metzler
SVP, Human Resources: Gracie P. Coleman

VP and Treasurer: Samuel J. Ilardo
VP, Brand Management: Leslie J. Gillock, age 48
VP, Corporate Communications and Public Affairs:
Ted Matthews
VP, Corporate Development: Jennifer Scott
VP, Creative Development: Gary Filippone
President, Decorative Flooring Division:
Kris Honeyman
President, Basic Bedding Strategic Business Unit:
Harvey Simon
Director of Juvenile Sales: Thomas McCaffrey
Business Manager, Freestanding Windows:
Gary Kitchens
Auditors: Deloitte & Touche LLP

LOCATIONS

HQ: Springs Industries, Inc.
205 N. White St., Fort Mill, SC 29715
Phone: 803-547-1500   **Fax:** 803-547-1636
Web: www.springs.com

Springs Industries operates about 30 manufacturing plants in 13 US states, Canada, and Mexico.

PRODUCTS/OPERATIONS

Selected Products and Brand Names

Home Furnishings (rugs, ceramic bath accessories, comforters, infant bedding, sheets, shower curtains, and towels)
Beaulieu
Dundee
Regal
Springmaid
Texmade (in Canada)
Wabasso (in Canada)
Wamsutta

Window Furnishings and Related Hardware
Bali
Graber
Nanik

COMPETITORS

Avondale Incorporated	Hollander Home Fashions
Burlington Industries	Hunter Douglas
Carter's	Keeco
Coats Holdings	Louisville Bedding
Croscill	Milliken
Crown Crafts	Mohawk Industries
Dan River	National Textiles
Galey & Lord Swift Denim	Newell Rubbermaid
Gerber Childrenswear	R. B. Pamplin
Guilford Mills	WestPoint Home

HISTORICAL FINANCIALS

Company Type: Private

Income Statement

FYE: Saturday nearest December 31

	REVENUE ($ mil.)	NET INCOME ($ mil.)	NET PROFIT MARGIN	EMPLOYEES
12/03	2,500	—	—	17,000
12/02	2,100	—	—	17,000
12/01	1,800	—	—	17,000
12/00	2,275	—	—	18,200
12/99	2,220	—	—	18,500
12/98	2,181	—	—	17,500
12/97	2,226	—	—	19,500
12/96	2,243	—	—	20,700
12/95	2,233	—	—	23,700
12/94	2,069	—	—	20,500
Annual Growth	**2.1%**	**—**	**—**	**(2.1%)**

Revenue History

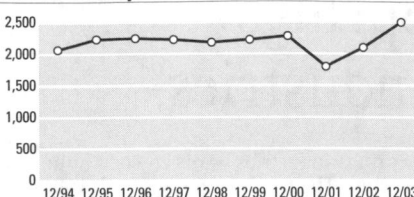

SRI International

Business Week magazine has called SRI International "Silicon Valley's soul." The not-for-profit think tank ponders advances in biotechnology, chemicals and energy, computer science, electronics, and public policy — and ways to commercialize those advances. SRI focuses on technology research and development, business strategies, and issues analysis. It has patents and patent applications in such areas as information sciences, software development, communications, robotics, and pharmaceuticals. Among SRI's clients are Visa, Samsung, NASA, and the US Department of Defense. Originally founded in 1946 as Stanford Research Institute, SRI became fully independent of Stanford University in 1970.

The organization has conceived such innovations as the computer mouse, magnetic encoding for checks, the videodisc, and high-definition television, not to mention some of the foundations of personal computing, the Internet, and stealth technology. Its 1,400 scientists and researchers work at research centers worldwide.

SRI's for-profit subsidiary the Sarnoff Corporation was formed in 1942 as RCA Laboratories. Formerly a unit of General Electric and gifted to SRI in 1987, Sarnoff specializes in creating and commercializing electronic, biomedical, and information technologies. SRI and Sarnoff together have spun off more than two dozen companies (*Business Week* has also called SRI "Spin-off City").

SRI Consulting (Chemical Business Services) was acquired from SRI International by Access Intelligence (formerly PBI Media) in 2004. The company's remaining consulting operations, SRI Consulting Business Intelligence (SRIC-BI), is an employee-owned spin-off of SRI International that focuses on such issues as organizational management, marketing technologies, and the commercialization of processes.

HISTORY

In the 1920s Stanford University professor Robert Swain envisioned a research center devoted to chemistry, physics, and biology. Swain received support from university president Ray Lyman and alumnus Herbert Hoover, but the Great Depression and WWII postponed the venture.

Finally, in 1946, the Stanford Research Institute was formed in conjunction with the university. That year the David Sarnoff Research Center

invented the color TV tube under the wing of RCA Laboratories.

During Stanford Research's early years, it worked on such projects as logistics for Disneyland, magnetic ink for character recognition, and strategies for combating air pollution. The think tank was the focus of student protests in the 1960s because of its defense work. In 1969 Stanford Research Institute was one of four nodes on the first computer network, the ARPANET. It became fully independent in 1970 as SRI International.

During the 1960s and 70s, SRI won large contracts from the US Department of Defense for research in such areas as radar, speech recognition, and noise cancellation technologies. It got a tremendous boost in 1987 when longtime client General Electric gave SRI the Sarnoff Research Center (as a tax write-off) plus $250 million in business, along with $65.2 million in cash.

In 1993 SRI founded Pangene to commercialize gene cloning and analysis technology. The next year it founded GeneTrace to develop genetics-related products for biomedical research and Nuance Communications to commercialize speech recognition products. Intuitive Surgical, which develops minimally invasive surgical technologies, was formed in 1995.

SRI developed two key components for use in an improved mail sorting program, which the US Postal Service announced in 1997 it would use to save millions in processing costs. The David Sarnoff Research Center changed its name to Sarnoff Corporation that year. SRI joined Motorola in 1997 to make semiconductors for digital TVs.

In 1998 SRI and the National Science Foundation teamed to develop innovative science and math teaching programs. The following year SRI began working with network equipment leader Cisco Systems and the US Army to develop a voice and multimedia communications system for the military. In 2001 SRI partnered with SPEEDCOM Wireless to co-develop wireless technology.

EXECUTIVES

Chairman: Samuel H. Armacost, age 66
President and CEO: Curtis R. Carlson, age 59
SVP and CFO: Thomas J. Furst
VP Biosciences Division: Walter H. Moos, age 50
VP Business Development and Marketing:
Leonard Polizzotto
VP Corporate and Marketing Communications:
Alice R. Resnick
VP Engineering and Systems Division: John W. Prausa
VP Human Resources: Jean E. (Jeanie) Tooker
VP Information and Computing Sciences Division:
William Mark
VP Legal and Business Affairs and General Counsel:
Richard Abramson
VP Physical Sciences Division: Lawrence H. Dubois
VP Policy Division: Dennis Beatrice
VP Ventures and Strategic Business Development:
Norman D. Winarsky
Acting VP Biosciences Division: Jon C. Mirsalis
Executive Director, SRI Japan: Osamu Karatsu
Senior Director Vaccine and Biotherapeutics Development: Rae Lyn Burke
Manager Corporate Marketing Communications:
Marty Mallonee
Auditors: PricewaterhouseCoopers LLP

LOCATIONS

HQ: SRI International
  333 Ravenswood Ave., Menlo Park, CA 94025
Phone: 650-859-2000   **Fax:** 650-326-5512
Web: www.sri.com

SRI International has offices and research centers in California, Maryland, Montana, New Jersey, Pennsylvania, and Washington, DC. It also has operations at four US Air Force bases (California, Florida, New Jersey, and Texas), and international locations in Greenland, Japan, and South Korea.

Air Force Base Locations

Eglin Air Force Base (Florida)
Fort Monmouth (New Jersey)
Lackland Air Force Base (Texas)
Vandenberg Air Force Base (California)

PRODUCTS/OPERATIONS

Selected Research Areas

Automation and robotics
Automotive and commercial equipment technologies
Chemistry, materials, and applied physics
Communications
Defense and intelligence
Homeland defense and national security
Information science and software development
Medical devices
Product engineering
Pharmaceutical services
Policy
Sensors and measurement systems

COMPETITORS

Aerospace Corporation	MIT
Battelle Memorial	MITRE
Bayer Corp.	PAREXEL
Booz Allen	Quintiles Transnational
CACI International	RAND
Charles Stark Draper	Research Triangle Institute
Laboratory	SAIC
DaVinci Institute	Southwest Research
DuPont	Institute
Educational Testing	Teknowledge
Service	University of California
Kendle	Wellcome Trust
LECG	Westat
McKinsey & Company	

HISTORICAL FINANCIALS

Company Type: Not-for-profit

Income Statement

FYE: December 31

	REVENUE ($ mil.)	NET INCOME ($ mil.)	NET PROFIT MARGIN	EMPLOYEES
12/03	320	—	—	2,800
12/02	318	—	—	2,800
12/01	315	—	—	2,750
12/00	307	—	—	2,700
12/99	330	—	—	2,700
12/98	350	—	—	2,700
12/97	363	—	—	2,783
12/96	326	—	—	2,700
12/95	320	—	—	1,900
12/94	312	—	—	1,973
Annual Growth	**0.3%**	—	—	**4.0%**

Revenue History

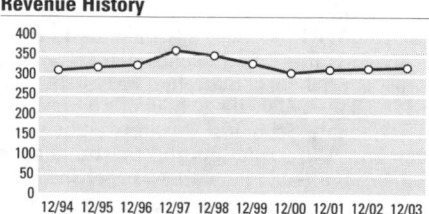

400
350
300
250
200
150
100
50
0
12/94 12/95 12/96 12/97 12/98 12/99 12/00 12/01 12/02 12/03

SSA Marine

On a ship, "port" means left, "starboard" means right, and "stevedoring" means heavy lifting, which means a call to SSA Marine, formerly Stevedoring Services of America. A leading marine terminal operator, SSA Marine loads and unloads ships at ports from Seattle to San Antonio, Chile. The company also maintains rail terminals and provides warehousing and distribution services at some of the ports where it operates. Overall, SSA Marine does business from about 150 locations worldwide. Founded in the 1880s, SSA Marine has been owned by the Smith and Hemingway families since 1949; president and CEO Jon Hemingway is the third generation of his family to head the company.

EXECUTIVES

President and CEO: Jon Hemingway
CFO, Carrix: Charles Sadowski
EVP Strategic Planning, Carrix: Daniel (Dan) Flynn
SVP Business Development and Marketing:
  Andrew McLauchlan
President, SSA Conventional: Claude Stritmatter
President, Tideworks Technology: Mike Schwank
President, SSA International: David Michou

LOCATIONS

HQ: SSA Marine
  1131 SW Klickitat Way, Seattle, WA 98134
Phone: 206-623-0304   **Fax:** 206-623-0179
Web: www.ssamarine.com

SSA Marine has operations in Africa, the Asia/Pacific region, North America, and South America.

COMPETITORS

Evergreen Marine
Grupo TMM
Hutchison Whampoa
Matson Navigation Company, Inc.
Mitsubishi Logistics
P&O

HISTORICAL FINANCIALS

Company Type: Private

Income Statement

FYE: January 31

	ESTIMATED REVENUE ($ mil.)	NET INCOME ($ mil.)	NET PROFIT MARGIN	EMPLOYEES
1/04	1,200	—	—	10,000
1/03	1,100	—	—	10,000
1/02	1,046	—	—	10,000
1/01	1,000	—	—	6,000
1/00	950	—	—	6,000
1/99	850	—	—	6,000
1/98	850	—	—	7,500
1/97	800	—	—	6,000
1/96	700	—	—	5,000
1/95	500	—	—	4,200
Annual Growth	**10.2%**	—	—	**10.1%**

Revenue History

1,200
1,000
800
600
400
200
0
1/95 1/96 1/97 1/98 1/99 1/00 1/01 1/02 1/03 1/04

SSM Health Care

The health care mission of SSM Health Care System began with five nuns who fled religious persecution in Germany in 1872 only to arrive in St. Louis in the midst of a smallpox epidemic. They formed their first hospital there in 1877 and later became pioneers in bringing health care to the rural frontier, founding the Oklahoma Territory's first hospital in 1898. Today the not-for-profit, sponsored by the Franciscan Sisters of Mary, owns and operates some 20 acute care hospitals with about 5,300 licensed beds. The company also operates nursing homes and rehabilitation clinics, and offers home health and hospice care. SSM's facilities are located in Illinois, Missouri, Oklahoma, and Wisconsin.

EXECUTIVES

President and CEO: Sister Mary Jean Ryan
EVP and COO: William C. Schoenhard
SVP Finance: Kris A. Zimmer
SVP Human Resources: Steven M. (Steve) Barney
SVP Mission and External Affairs: Dixie L. Platt
SVP Strategic Development: William P. Thompson
VP Ethics: Michael (Mike) Panicola, age 34
System VP; President and CIO, SSM Information Center: Thomas K. (Tom) Langston
President and CEO, SSM Health Care of Wisconsin:
  Mary Starmann-Harrison
Regional President and System VP, SSM Health Care St. Louis: Ronald J. Levy
Regional President and System VP, St. Mary's Good Samaritan: James M. Sanger
Corporate Communications Manager: Patty Klein
Corporate Communications Manager: Suzy Farren

LOCATIONS

HQ: SSM Health Care System Inc.
  477 N. Lindbergh Blvd., St. Louis, MO 63141
Phone: 314-994-7800   **Fax:** 314-994-7900
Web: www.ssmhc.com

SSM Health Care operates facilities in Illinois, Missouri, Oklahoma, and Wisconsin.

PRODUCTS/OPERATIONS

Selected Facilities

Illinois
  Good Samaritan Regional Health Center (Mt. Vernon)
  St. Francis Hospital & Health Center (Blue Island)
  St. Mary's Hospital (Centralia)
Missouri
  Pike County Memorial Hospital (Louisiana)
  St. Francis Hospital & Health Services (Maryville)
  St. Mary's Health Center (Jefferson City)
  SSM Cardinal Glennon Children's Hospital (St. Louis)
  SSM DePaul Health Center (Bridgeton)
  SSM St. Joseph Health Center (St. Charles)
  SSM St. Joseph Hospital of Kirkwood
  SSM St. Joseph Hospital West (Lake St. Louis)
  SSM St. Mary's Health Center (St. Louis)
  Villa Marie Skilled Nursing Facility (Jefferson City)
Oklahoma
  Bone & Joint Hospital (Oklahoma City)
  St. Anthony Hospital (Oklahoma City)
Wisconsin
  St. Clare Hospital and Health Services (Baraboo)
  St. Clare Meadows Care Center (Baraboo)
  St. Mary's Care Center (Madison)
  St. Mary's Hospital Medical Center (Madison)

COMPETITORS

Advocate Health Care
Allina Hospitals
BJC HealthCare
Greenville Hospital System
HCA
Mayo Foundation
Rush System for Health
Sisters of Mercy Health System
Tenet Healthcare

HISTORICAL FINANCIALS

Company Type: Not-for-profit

Income Statement

FYE: December 31

	REVENUE ($ mil.)	NET INCOME ($ mil.)	NET PROFIT MARGIN	EMPLOYEES
12/03	1,900	—	—	23,300
12/02	1,832	—	—	23,200
12/01	1,705	—	—	22,000
12/00	1,459	—	—	20,500
12/99	1,321	—	—	20,500
12/98	1,285	—	—	20,500
12/97	1,285	—	—	19,439
12/96	2,070	—	—	19,200
12/95	1,856	—	—	19,000
12/94	1,001	—	—	17,000
Annual Growth	7.4%	—	—	3.6%

Revenue History

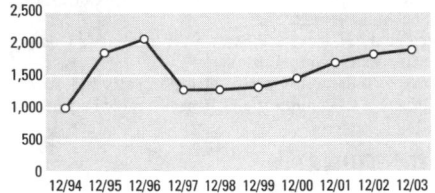

St. Louis Blues

With no championship title to call their own, St. Louis hockey fans have been singing the blues for a long time. The St. Louis Blues entered the National Hockey League in 1967 but has yet to capture a Stanley Cup championship despite making playoffs every year for more than two decades. (The Blues made its last finals appearance in 1970, losing to the Boston Bruins.) Still, the team enjoys one of the highest attendance levels in the league as loyal fans come out to support their team at St. Louis' Savvis Center. Bill Laurie and his wife Nancy (daughter of Wal-Mart founder James "Bud" Walton) bought the team and the arena in 1999. They are currently looking for a buyer after losing $60 million from 2003 to 2005.

EXECUTIVES

Chairman: William J. (Bill) Laurie
President and CEO: Mark Sauer, age 58
Head Coach: Mike Kitchen, age 48
Assistant Coach: Curt Fraser
Goaltending Coach: Keith Allain
SVP and General Manager: Larry Pleau, age 58
SVP Finance and Hockey Administration: Jerry Jasiek
SVP Marketing and Communications: Jim Woodcock
SVP and General Manager, Savvis Center:
  Dennis Petrullo
VP Building Operations: Fred Corsi
VP Human Resources: Dave Coverstone
VP Marketing: Jo Ann Miles
VP Sales: Bruce Affleck
Senior Director of Marketing and Public Relations:
  Cindy Underwood
Director of Human Resources: Lisa Schoeck
Community Relations Manager: Kim Mulherin

LOCATIONS

HQ: St. Louis Blues Hockey Club L.L.C.
  1401 Clark Ave., St. Louis, MO 63103
Phone: 314-622-2500   **Fax:** 314-622-2582
Web: www.stlouisblues.com

The St. Louis Blues play at the 19,022-seat capacity Savvis Center in St. Louis.

PRODUCTS/OPERATIONS

Championship Trophies

Clarence S. Campbell Bowl (1969-70)
Presidents' Trophy (2000)

COMPETITORS

Chicago Blackhawks
Columbus Blue Jackets
Detroit Red Wings
Nashville Predators

HISTORICAL FINANCIALS

Company Type: Private

Income Statement

FYE: June 30

	REVENUE ($ mil.)	NET INCOME ($ mil.)	NET PROFIT MARGIN	EMPLOYEES
6/04	66	—	—	—
6/03	67	—	—	—
6/02	70	—	—	—
6/01	64	—	—	—
6/00	57	—	—	—
6/99	62	—	—	—
6/98	70	—	—	150
6/97	62	—	—	—
6/96	55	—	—	—
6/95	29	—	—	—
Annual Growth	9.5%	—	—	—

Revenue History

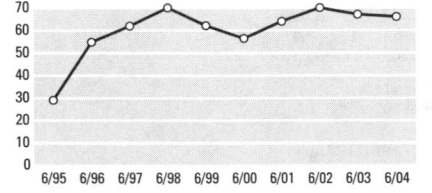

Stanford University

Prospectors panning for gold in higher education can strike it rich at Stanford University. The school is one of the premier educational institutions in the US, boasting respected programs in business, engineering, law, and medicine, among others. Its campus is home to more than 14,000 students as well as 1,775 faculty members. A private institution, Stanford supports its activities through a $10 billion endowment, one of the largest in the US. The university was founded in 1885 by Leland Stanford Sr. and his wife, Jane, in memory of their son, Leland Jr.

Stanford is also widely recognized as one of the top US research universities and sports a host of laboratories and research centers, including the Stanford Institute for Economic Policy Research and the Stanford Linear Accelerator Center. Its faculty members include 16 Nobel Prize winners and 21 National Medal of Science winners.

In 2000 the school welcomed its 10th president, former provost John Hennessy, who launched a campaign to raise $1 billion, the largest drive ever undertaken by a university. It quickly reached half that goal thanks to donations from such alumni as Jerry Yang (co-founder of Yahoo!), Charles Schwab, and Texas billionaire Robert Bass. However, its alumni ranks lost a prominent member in 2001 when William Hewlett (of Hewlett-Packard) died. The Hewlett Foundation's $400 million gift is the largest in university history.

HISTORY

In 1885 Leland Stanford Sr. and his wife, Jane, established Leland Stanford Junior University in memory of their son Leland Jr., who had died of typhoid at age 15. Stanford made his fortune selling provisions to California gold miners and as a major investor in the Central Pacific Railroad, one of the two companies that built the first transcontinental railway. It was Stanford who connected the tracks laid eastward by Central Pacific and westward by Union Pacific with a gold railway spike in 1869. He also served as California's governor and as a US senator.

The Stanfords donated more than 8,000 acres of land from their own estate to establish an unconventional university, one that was coeducational and nondenominational with a focus on preparing students for a profession. Stanford opened its doors in 1891 to a freshman class of 559 students. It awarded its first degrees four years later, and among the graduates was future US president Herbert Hoover.

Leland Stanford Sr. died in 1893, and in 1903 Jane Stanford turned the university over to the board of trustees. After weathering significant damage in 1906 from the Great San Francisco Earthquake, the university established a law school in 1908 and its medical school five years later.

During WWI the university mobilized half of its students into the Students' Army Training Corps. The School of Education was established in 1917, followed by the School of Engineering and Graduate School of Business eight years later. In 1933 a rule limiting the number of women admitted to Stanford was abolished.

Wallace Sterling, who became president of the university after WWII, initiated the transformation of Stanford into a world-class institution with a reputation for teaching and research. Under Sterling the university initiated development on the Stanford Research Park.

In 1958 Stanford opened its first overseas campus (near Stuttgart, Germany), and the Stanford Medical Center was completed the following year. The university created a computer science department in 1965 and two years later opened the Stanford Linear Accelerator Center dedicated to physics research.

Donald Kennedy became president in 1980. The next year students voted to abandon the university's official mascot, the "Indians," in response to concerns raised by Native American students. The nickname "Cardinal" was adopted in its place. The term refers to the school's color, cardinal red.

Also during Kennedy's tenure, it was revealed that Stanford had overcharged the Office of Naval Research for indirect costs associated with research. The scandal led to Kennedy's resignation in 1992, and in 1994 the Office of Naval Research and the university settled a related lawsuit for $1.2 million and a stipulation that Stanford had not committed any wrongdoing. Gerhard Casper succeeded Kennedy as president.

In 1997 Stanford and the University of California at San Francisco combined their teaching hospitals in a public/private merger. Two years later after the controversial experiment had harmed both hospitals' financial picture, the merger was terminated, and the two hospitals agreed to go their separate ways.

In 1999 Casper announced his intention to resign as president. The school tapped provost John Hennessy as his replacement. Soon after his appointment in 2000, Hennessey launched a campaign to raise $1 billion. Former Stanford professor and Netscape co-founder Jim Clark donated $150 million later that year to support Stanford's biomedical engineering and sciences program. The school also launched a new company, SKOLAR, which developed an online search engine for the medical industry.

EXECUTIVES

President: John L. Hennessy, age 52
Provost: John W. Etchemendy
VP and General Counsel: Deborah Zumwalt
VP, Business Affairs and CFO:
  Randall S. (Randy) Livingston, age 51
VP, Development: John B. Ford
VP, Public Affairs: David Demarest
CIO: Christopher Handley
Associate VP and Director, University Communications:
  Alan Acosta
Executive Director, Human Resources: Diane Peck
President, Stanford Alumni Association: Howard Wolf
University Manager, Public Relations: Gordon Earle

LOCATIONS

HQ: Stanford University
  655 Serra St., Stanford, CA 94305
Phone: 650-723-2300   **Fax:** 650-725-0247
Web: www.stanford.edu

PRODUCTS/OPERATIONS

Selected Schools
Undergraduate
  School of Earth Sciences
  School of Engineering
  School of Humanities and Sciences
Graduate
  School of Business
  School of Earth Sciences
  School of Engineering
  School of Education
  School of Humanities and Sciences
  School of Law
  School of Medicine

Selected Interdisciplinary Research Centers
Alliance for Innovative Manufacturing at Stanford
Center for Computer Research in Music and Acoustics
Center for Integrated Facility Engineering
Center for Integrated Systems

Selected Laboratories, Centers, and Institutes
Center for Research on Information Storage Materials
Center for the Study of Language and Information
Edward L. Ginzton Laboratory
Institute for International Studies
Institute for Research on Women and Gender
Stanford Center for Buddhist Studies
Stanford Humanities Center
Stanford Institute for Economic Policy Research
W.W. Hansen Experimental Physics Laboratory

Selected Medical Research Facilities
Center for Biomedical Ethics
Center for Research in Disease Prevention
Human Genome Center
Richard M. Lucas Center for Magnetic Resonance
  Spectroscopy & Imaging
Sleep Disorders Center

Other Selected Research Facilities
Hoover Institution on War, Revolution and Peace
Hopkins Marine Station
Martin Luther King, Jr. Papers Project
Stanford Linear Accelerator Center

HISTORICAL FINANCIALS
Company Type: School

Income Statement
FYE: August 31

	REVENUE ($ mil.)	NET INCOME ($ mil.)	NET PROFIT MARGIN	EMPLOYEES
8/03	2,300	—	—	—
8/02	2,600	—	—	—
8/01	2,940	—	—	—
8/00	1,957	—	—	—
8/99	1,749	—	—	—
8/98	1,558	—	—	9,535
8/97	1,474	—	—	8,677
8/96	1,416	—	—	8,702
Annual Growth	7.2%	—	—	4.7%

Revenue History

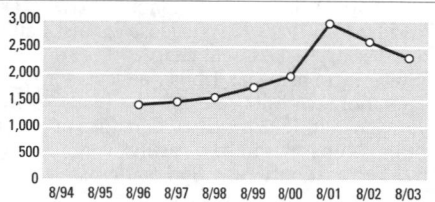

Staple Cotton Cooperative

Wear underwear? Chances are Staplcotn grew the cotton it's made of. Staple Cotton Cooperative Association (Staplcotn) serves approximately 12,000 member-owners in 10 southern states. Founded in 1921 by Mississippi cotton producer Oscar Bledsoe and 10 Delta growers, it sells almost 4 million bales of cotton annually. Most of the yield is sold to the US textile industry to make men's knit underwear, T-shirts, sheets, towels, and denim. Customers include Fruit of the Loom and Levi Strauss & Co. The co-op's Stapldiscount unit offers members low-interest loans for equipment, buildings, and land. Staple Cotton has 12 regional offices in six states and 15 warehouses in three states.

EXECUTIVES

Chairman; Chairman, Stapldiscount: Ben Lamensdorf
President and CEO; President and CEO, Stapldiscount:
  Woods E. Eastland, age 59
VP and Treasurer; VP and Treasurer, Stapldiscount:
  Mack L. Alford
VP and Treasurer: Charles Robertson
VP, Cotton Services: Sterling P. Jones
VP, Human Resources and Secretary; VP, Human Resources and Secretary, Stapldiscount:
  Eugene A. (Gene) Stansel Jr.
VP, Marketing: Meredith B. Allen
VP, Sales Operations: David C. Camp
VP, Systems and Controls; VP, Systems and Controls, Stapldiscount: L. A. (Larry) Gnemi
VP, Warehousing: Shane Stephens
General Counsel; General Counsel, Stapldiscount:
  Kenneth E. Downs
VP and COO, Stapldiscount: J. D. Hoover
Director, Communications and Public Relations:
  Vicki Wilkey

LOCATIONS

HQ: Staple Cotton Cooperative Association
  214 W. Market St., Greenwood, MS 38930
Phone: 662-453-6231   **Fax:** 662-453-6274
Web: www.staplcotn.com

COMPETITORS

Alabama Farmers Cooperative
Calcot
Cargill
Dunavant Enterprises
Plains Cotton
Southern States
Tennessee Farmers Co-op

Company Type: Cooperative

Income Statement
FYE: August 31

	REVENUE ($ mil.)	NET INCOME ($ mil.)	NET PROFIT MARGIN	EMPLOYEES
8/04	1,348	—	—	250
8/03	1,024	—	—	250
8/02	1,220	—	—	248
8/01	1,050	—	—	230
8/00	1,041	—	—	230
8/99	850	—	—	200
8/98	705	—	—	197
8/97	657	—	—	156
8/96	640	—	—	—
8/95	664	—	—	—
Annual Growth	8.2%	—	—	7.0%

Revenue History

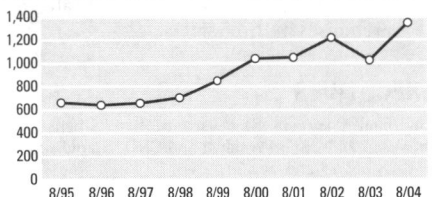

	8/95	8/96	8/97	8/98	8/99	8/00	8/01	8/02	8/03	8/04

State Farm

Like an enormous corporation, State Farm is everywhere. The leading US personal lines property/casualty company (by premiums), State Farm Mutual Automobile Insurance Company is the #1 provider of auto insurance. It also is the leading home insurer and offers nonmedical health and life insurance through its subsidiary companies. Its products are marketed via some 17,000 agents in the US and Canada. Competition has increased with the fall of barriers between the banking, securities, and insurance industries. State Farm's not-so-secret weapon is a federal savings bank charter (State Farm Bank) that offers consumer financial products through State Farm agents and by phone, mail, and the Internet.

The company is expanding its financial services, but insurance is still its main source of income. State Farm insures about 20% of the automobiles on US roads; auto insurance accounts for almost 70% of the company's property/casualty premiums. The insurer stopped writing new homeowners policies in some 15 states in an effort to improve profitability.

Although results have been improving and total revenue increasing since a low point in the early 2000s, State Farm is still experiencing lagging underwriting revenues in its flagship auto insurance segment.

Since its founding, the group's companies have been run by only two families, the Mecherles (1922-54) and the Rusts (1954-present).

HISTORY

Retired farmer George Mecherle formed State Farm Mutual Automobile Insurance in Bloomington, Illinois, in 1922. State Farm served only members of farm bureaus and farm mutual insurance companies, charging a one-time membership fee and a premium to protect an automobile against loss or damage.

Unlike most competitors, State Farm offered six-month premium payments. The insurer billed and collected renewal premiums from its home office, relieving the agent of the task. In addition, State Farm determined auto rates by a simple seven-class system, while competitors varied rates for each model.

State Farm in 1926 started City and Village Mutual Automobile Insurance to insure nonfarmers' autos; it became part of the company in 1927. Between 1927 and 1931 it introduced borrowed-car protection, wind coverage, and insurance for vehicles used to transport schoolchildren.

State Farm expanded to California in 1928 and formed State Farm Life Insurance the next year. In 1935 it established State Farm Fire Insurance. George Mecherle became chairman in 1937, and his son Ramond became president. In 1939 George challenged agents to write "A Million or More (auto policies) by '44." State Farm saw a 110% increase in policies.

During the 1940s State Farm focused on urban areas after most of the farm bureaus formed their own insurance companies. In the late 1940s and 1950s, it moved to a full-time agency force.

Homeowners coverage was added to the insurer's offerings under the leadership of Adlai Rust, who led State Farm from 1954 until 1958, when Edward Rust took over. He died in 1985 and his son, Edward Jr., currently holds the top spot.

Between 1974 and 1987 the insurer was hit by several gender-discrimination suits (a 1992 settlement awarded $157 million to 814 women). State Farm has since tried to hire more women and minorities.

In the early 1990s serial disasters, including Hurricane Andrew and the Los Angeles riots, proved costly. The 1994 Northridge earthquake alone generated more than $2.5 billion in claims and contributed to a 72% decline in earnings.

State Farm — the top US home insurer since the mid-1960s — canceled 62,500 residential policies in South Florida in 1996 to cut potential hurricane loss an estimated 11%. In response, Florida's insurance regulators rescinded a previously approved rate hike. That year the company agreed to open more urban neighborhood offices to settle a discrimination suit brought by the Department of Housing and Urban Development, which accused State Farm of discriminating against potential customers in minority-populated areas.

Legal trouble continued. In 1997 State Farm settled with a California couple who alleged the company forged policyholders' signatures on forms declining coverage and concealed evidence to avoid paying earthquake damage claims. That year a policyholder sued to keep State Farm from "wasting company assets" on President Clinton's legal defense against Paula Jones' sexual harassment charges (Clinton held a State Farm personal liability policy).

Relations with its sales force already rocky, State Farm in 1998 proposed to reduce up-front commissions and cut base pay in favor of incentives for customer retention and cross-selling. Reduced auto premiums and increased catastrophe claims from across the US eroded State Farm's bottom line that year. A federal thrift charter obtained in 1998 let the company launch banking operations the next year.

State Farm is appealing a 1999 Illinois state court judgment that it pay $1.2 billion to policyholders for using aftermarket parts in auto repairs. In 2000 the company was hit with a class-action lawsuit about its denial of personal-injury claims; previous suits had been individual cases.

In 2002, State Farm Indemnity, the company's auto-only New Jersey subsidiary, withdrew from the Garden State's auto insurance market but began phasing back into the market in 2005.

EXECUTIVES

Chairman and CEO: Edward B. (Ed) Rust Jr., age 54
Vice Chairman, President, and COO: Vincent J. Trosino, age 64
Vice Chairman and Chief Administrative Officer: James E. Rutrough
EVP, General Counsel, and Secretary: Kim M. Brunner
SEVP, Financial Services: Jack W. North
EVP; President, Indemnity: Brian V. Boyden
EVP: Barbara Cowden
EVP: William K. King
Vice Chairman, CFO, and Treasurer: Michael L. Tipsord
EVP; EVP, State Farm Life and Affiliates: Susan D. Waring
SVP, Investments: Paul N. Eckley
Vice Chairman and Chief Agency and Marketing Officer: Michael C. Davidson
EVP: Willie G. Brown
President and CEO, State Farm Bank: Stanley R. Ommen
SVP, Mid-America: Lee Baumann
SVP, Central: Mary Bitzer
SVP, Northeast: Brian Carlson
SVP, Canada: Bob Cooke
SVP, Great Lakes: Mary Crego
SVP, Texas: Ron Dodd
SVP, Great Western: Dave Gonzales
SVP, Pacific Northwest: Harold Gray
SVP, Heartland: James Thompson
SVP, California: Greg Jones
SVP, Florida: Joe Formusa
SVP, Mid-Atlantic: Doug Thompson
SVP, Southern: Robert (Bob) Trippel
VP, Marketing: Pam El
Auditors: PricewaterhouseCoopers LLP

LOCATIONS

HQ: State Farm Mutual Automobile Insurance Company
1 State Farm Plaza, Bloomington, IL 61710
Phone: 309-766-2311   **Fax:** 309-766-3621
Web: www.statefarm.com

PRODUCTS/OPERATIONS

2004 Assets

	$ mil.	% of total
Cash & invested assets		
Stocks (unaffiliated)	31,552	37
Bonds (long-term)	28,420	34
Investments in affiliates	15,253	18
Real estate	1,789	2
Cash & other invested assets	860	1
Premiums receivable	4,858	6
Other assets	1,673	2
Total	**84,405**	**100**

Selected Subsidiaries

State Farm Bank, FSB
State Farm County Mutual Insurance Company of Texas (high-risk auto insurance)
State Farm Federal Savings Bank
State Farm Fire and Casualty Company (homeowners, boat owners, and commercial insurance)
State Farm Florida Insurance Company (homeowners and renters insurance)
State Farm General Insurance Company (property insurance)
State Farm Indemnity Company (auto insurance in New Jersey)
State Farm Investment Management Corp
State Farm Life and Accident Assurance Company
State Farm Life Insurance Company
State Farm Lloyds
State Farm VP Management Corp

COMPETITORS

AIG	Liberty Mutual
Allstate	MetLife
American Family	Nationwide
Insurance	Progressive Corporation
CNA Financial	Prudential
COUNTRY Insurance	Safeco
GEICO	USAA
The Hartford	

HISTORICAL FINANCIALS

Company Type: Mutual company

Income Statement
FYE: December 31

	REVENUE ($ mil.)	NET INCOME ($ mil.)	NET PROFIT MARGIN	EMPLOYEES
12/04	58,800	5,300	9.0%	79,200
12/03	56,100	2,800	5.0%	79,000
12/02	49,700	(2,800)	—	79,400
12/01	46,700	(5,000)	—	79,400
12/00	47,863	408	0.9%	79,300
12/99	44,700	1,033	2.3%	79,300
12/98	38,678	996	2.6%	76,257
12/97	38,501	3,581	9.3%	—
Annual Growth	6.2%	5.8%	—	0.6%

Net Income History

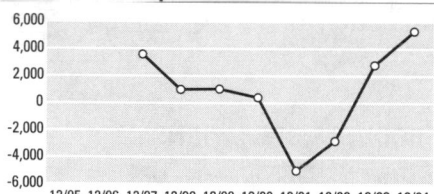

6,000	
4,000	
2,000	
0	
-2,000	
-4,000	
-6,000	

12/95 12/96 12/97 12/98 12/99 12/00 12/01 12/02 12/03 12/04

State University of New York

SUNY days are ahead for many New Yorkers seeking higher education. With more than 413,000 students, the State University of New York (SUNY) is running neck-and-neck with California State University for the title of largest university system in the US. The school maintains 64 campuses around New York State, including 13 university colleges and four university centers, 30 community colleges, five technical colleges, and three health centers. Its institutions' more than 6,000 programs of study include accounting, journalism, bioengineering, and computer science. The university system hands out some 70,000 diplomas each year, including nearly 9,000 post-graduate degrees.

Most students are residents of New York State (about 40% of all New York State high school graduates enroll at SUNY institutions) and pay about $4,400 a year in tuition. SUNY is also topnotch in research, boasting more than $700 million in federal, state, and local grants and contracts. Its laboratories have helped pioneer magnetic resonance imaging, implantable heart pacemakers, and supermarket bar code scanners.

HISTORY

The State University of New York was organized in 1948, but it traces its roots back to several institutions founded in the 19th century. In 1844 the New York state legislature authorized the creation of the Albany Normal School, which was charged with educating the state's secondary school teachers. Two years later, the University of Buffalo was chartered to provide academic, theological, legal, and medical studies. More normal schools later were founded between 1861 and 1889 in Brockport, Buffalo, Cortland, Fredonia, Geneseo, New Paltz, Oneonta, Oswego, Plattsburgh, and Potsdam.

In the early 1900s the state established several agricultural colleges, including schools in Canton (1907), Alfred (1908), Morrisville (1910), Farmingdale (1912), and Cobleskill (1916). New York also set up several schools as units of Cornell University, including colleges of veterinary medicine (1894), agriculture (1909), home economics (1925), and industrial and labor relations (1945).

After WWII, veterans began to fill US colleges and universities, taking advantage of the GI Bill to secure a college education. The legislature set up SUNY in 1948 to consolidate 29 institutions under a single board of trustees charged with meeting the growing demand. The board coordinated the state colleges into a single body and established four-year liberal arts colleges, professional and graduate schools, and research centers. During the 1950s and 1960s, new campuses were created at Binghamton, Stony Brook, Old Westbury, Purchase, and Utica/Rome, and enrollment began to take off, jumping from 30,000 in 1955 to 63,000 in 1959.

By the early 1970s SUNY had more than 320,000 students at 72 institutions. But budget constraints later that decade led to higher tuition, reduced enrollment goals, and employment cutbacks. In 1975 eight New York City community colleges were transferred to City University. SUNY's enrollment began growing again during the 1980s, reaching more than 400,000 by 1990. Early in the decade, the institution began implementing SUNY 2000, a plan that called for increasing access to education and diversifying undergraduate studies. Following his election in 1994, Governor George Pataki proposed more than $550 million in cuts to the SUNY system.

In 1997 John Ryan replaced Thomas Bartlett as chancellor. The following year SUNY became the exclusive sponsor of The College Channel, a guide to colleges and college life aimed at high school juniors and seniors and broadcast by PRIMEDIA's Channel One. In 1999 the governor's budget director, Robert King, was named chancellor to replace the retiring Bartlett. King challenged SUNY administrators and the state to increase levels of funding to help keep the university competitive against other top-flight institutions. In 2000 SUNY faced rising budget shortfalls at its teaching hospitals, in part because money was being siphoned off to other areas. That year King announced a set of initiatives to raise an additional $1.5 billion in federal research grants and $1 billion in private donations over five years.

King retired as the university's chancellor in June 2005.

EXECUTIVES

Acting Chancellor: John R. Ryan, age 59
Provost and Vice Chancellor Academic Affairs: Peter D. Salins
Vice Chancellor and CFO: David Richter
Vice Chancellor and Chief of Staff: Elizabeth D. (Betty) Capaldi
Vice Chancellor Business and Industry Relations: R. Wayne Diesel
University Counsel: D. Andrew Edwards Jr.
Vice Chancellor and Secretary; President, Research Foundation: John J. O'Connor
Assistant Provost: Peter Thomas
University Controller: Patrick J. Wiater
University Auditor: C. Kevin O'Donoghue
Assistant Vice Chancellor for Employee Relations: Joyce Villa
Director of Employee Relations: Raymond (Ray) Haines
Auditors: KPMG LLP

LOCATIONS

HQ: State University of New York
State University Plaza, Albany, NY 12246
Phone: 518-443-5555 **Fax:** 518-443-5322
Web: www.suny.edu

PRODUCTS/OPERATIONS

Selected Institutions

Colleges of Technology
  Alfred
  Canton
  Cobleskill
  Delhi
  Morrisville
  University Colleges of Technology

Health Science Centers
  Brooklyn
  Syracuse

Statutory Colleges
  College of Agriculture and Life Sciences at Cornell University
  College of Ceramics at Alfred University
  College of Human Ecology at Cornell University
  College of Veterinary Medicine at Cornell University
  School of Industrial and Labor Relations at Cornell University

University Centers
  Albany
  Binghamton
  Buffalo
  Stony Brook

University Colleges

Brockport	Old Westbury
Buffalo State	Oneonta
Cortland	Oswego
Empire State	Plattsburgh
Fredonia	Potsdam
Geneseo	Purchase
New Paltz	

HISTORICAL FINANCIALS

Company Type: School

Income Statement
FYE: June 30

	REVENUE ($ mil.)	NET INCOME ($ mil.)	NET PROFIT MARGIN	EMPLOYEES
6/04	6,176	279	4.5%	—
6/03	5,429	67	1.2%	—
6/02	5,386	292	5.4%	—
6/01	5,211	—	—	—
6/00	5,076	—	—	—
6/99	4,629	—	—	65,000
6/98	4,564	—	—	65,000
6/97	4,244	—	—	56,135
6/96	4,136	—	—	55,000
6/95	4,167	—	—	52,000
Annual Growth	4.5%	(2.2%)	—	5.7%

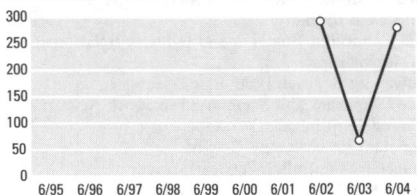
Stater Bros.

Stater Bros. Markets has no shortage of major league rivals, operating in the same Southern California markets as Ralphs, Albertson's, and Safeway-owned Vons. Stater Bros. Holdings has more than 160 full-service Stater Bros. Markets in some six counties, primarily in the Riverside and San Bernardino areas. The grocery chain also owns and operates milk and juice processor Santee Dairies, one of the state's largest milk processors. Founded in 1936 by twin brothers Leo and Cleo Stater, Stater Bros. is owned by La Cadena Investments, a general partnership consisting of Stater Bros. CEO Jack Brown and other company executives.

Competition from the grocery giants, and the purchase of stores from Albertson's, has put a strain on the company's profits. To distinguish itself from rivals, the chain refuses to offer promotional games and frequent shopper cards, boasting everyday low prices and chain-wide temporary price reductions (called Stater Savers) instead.

Stater Bros. is bracing itself for intense competition from Wal-Mart and Sam's Club stores, which are becoming more common in the area.

Stater Bros. Holdings is the largest privately held supermarket chain in Southern California. The company plans to open three to six new stores per year.

HISTORY

In 1936, at age 23, Cleo Stater and his twin brother, Leo, mortgaged a Chevrolet to make a down payment on a modest grocery store where Cleo had been working for five years in their hometown of Yucaipa, California. Later that year the brothers bought their second grocery in the nearby community of Redlands. Their younger brother, Lavoy, soon joined them to help build the company. In 1938 the brothers opened the first Stater Bros. market in Colton; by 1939 they had a chain of four stores.

The small, family-owned grocery chain continued to grow. In 1948 Stater Bros. opened its first supermarket (which was several times larger than its other stores and had its own parking lot) in Riverside. By 1950 the company had 12 stores.

Stater Bros. consolidated its offices and warehouse in Colton in the early 1960s and continued its expansion into nearby communities. By 1964 it operated 27 supermarkets in 18 cities in Los Angeles, Orange, Riverside, and San Bernardino counties. In 1968 the brothers sold the company's 35 stores to Long Beach, California-based petroleum services provider Petrolane for $33 million. Lavoy succeeded Cleo as president.

As a division of Petrolane, Stater Bros. kept growing. In the 1970s the company introduced a new store design that expanded sales area but required less land and a smaller building. The number of stores more than doubled (to over 80) between 1968 and 1979, when Lavoy retired.

Ron Burkle, VP of Administration for Petrolane, and his father, Joe, president of Stater Bros., attempted to buy the chain for $100 million in 1981. Infuriated by the low bid, Petrolane fired Ron and demoted his father, who left that year. Jack Brown was named president in his place. Petrolane sold the chain in 1983 to La Cadena Investments, a private company that included Brown and other top Stater Bros. executives.

Leo died in 1985. That year the company went public to reduce debt from the 1983 LBO and to provide funds for an extensive expansion plan. It also incorporated as Stater Bros. Inc. In 1986 a proxy fight for control of the company erupted between Brown's La Cadena group and chairman Bernard Garrett, who owned about 41% of Stater Bros. Brown had been suspended as president and CEO (Joe Burkle returned in his place), but Los Angeles-based investment firm Craig Corp. bought Garrett's stake and Brown returned; he was later elected chairman. That year Stater Bros. also became a co-owner in Santee Dairies with Hughes Markets (now part of Kroger).

The next year Craig and Stater Bros. executives took the grocery chain private again. Burkle bought a 9% stake in Craig in 1989 through Yucaipa Capital Partners. Also in 1987 Craig reduced its stake in Stater Bros., transferring some stock to La Cadena. Stater Bros. Holdings was created as a parent company for the grocery chain.

Stater Bros. expressed an interest in buying rival Alpha Beta stores when they were put up for sale, but Yucaipa Companies bought them in 1991. Craig considered selling its stake in Stater Bros. in 1992; it finally sold its half of the company to La Cadena in 1996.

In 1999 Stater Bros. acquired 33 Albertson's and 10 Lucky stores, as well as one store site. (The FTC required Albertson's to sell the stores in order to acquire American Stores, Lucky's parent.) The acquisition and the early retirement of debt resulted in its 1999 losses. In September 2001 company co-founder Cleo Stater died.

In early 2002 the company announced a partnership with Krispy Kreme Doughnuts to offer the treats at selected Stater Bros. supermarkets. In 2003, Stater Bros. introduced Topco private-label brand merchandise in its stores.

In February 2004 Santee Dairies became a wholly owned subsidiary of Stater Bros. when the grocery chain acquired Kroger's 50% stake in the operation.

Stater Bros. sales rose by about 5% during a four-and-a-half month long strike by employees of rivals Albertson's, Kroger, and Vons. The dispute, which diverted shoppers from those stores to Stater Bros. markets, ended in March 2004. In October Don Baker was promoted to president and COO of Stater Bros. Previously, Baker was EVP and COO of the company.

EXECUTIVES

Chairman and CEO: Jack H. Brown, age 64, $1,260,000 pay
Vice Chairman: Thomas W. Field Jr., age 69
President and COO: Donald I. (Don) Baker, age 62, $515,000 pay
SVP and CFO: Phillip J. (Phil) Smith, age 56, $215,000 pay
SVP, Retail Operations: Edward A. Stater, age 52, $182,000 pay
Group SVP of Marketing: Dennis L. McIntyre, age 43, $240,000 pay
Group SVP of Retail Operations: James W. (Jim) Lee, age 52, $232,000 pay
VP, Construction and Maintenance: Scott Limbacher
VP, Corporate Affairs: Susan Atkinson
VP, Human Resources: Kathy Finazzo
VP, Produce: Roger Schroeder
President and COO, Heartland Farms: Paul Bikowitz
Secretary and Director: Bruce D. Varner, age 67
Property Development Manager: Mike McCasland
Auditors: Ernst & Young LLP

LOCATIONS

HQ: Stater Bros. Holdings Inc.
21700 Barton Rd., Colton, CA 92324
Phone: 909-783-5000   **Fax:** 909-783-3930
Web: www.staterbros.com

Stater Bros. Holdings operates one distribution center and nearly 160 supermarkets in Southern California.

2004 Stores

	No.
San Bernardino County	47
Riverside County	42
Orange County	30
Los Angeles County	27
San Diego County	10
Kern County	2
Total	**158**

PRODUCTS/OPERATIONS

Selected Departments and Products

Bakery
Dairy products
Delicatessen
Floral
Fresh produce
Frozen foods
General merchandise
Health and beauty aids
Liquor
Meats
Seafood

COMPETITORS

Albertson's
Arden Group
Costco Wholesale
Longs Drug
Ralphs
SAM'S CLUB
Smart & Final
Trader Joe's
Vons
Walgreen
Wal-Mart
Whole Foods

HISTORICAL FINANCIALS

Company Type: Private

Income Statement			FYE: Last Sunday in September	
	REVENUE ($ mil.)	NET INCOME ($ mil.)	NET PROFIT MARGIN	EMPLOYEES
9/04	3,705	72	1.9%	15,700
9/03	2,754	10	0.4%	13,500
9/02	2,666	12	0.4%	13,400
9/01	2,574	8	0.3%	12,600
9/00	2,418	(6)	—	12,100
9/99	1,830	(9)	—	12,700
9/98	1,726	3	0.1%	8,700
9/97	1,718	14	0.8%	8,900
9/96	1,705	16	0.9%	8,900
9/95	1,580	7	0.4%	9,800
Annual Growth	**9.9%**	**30.2%**	**—**	**5.4%**

2004 Year-End Financials

Debt ratio: —
Return on equity: —
Cash ($ mil.): 302

Current ratio: 2.22
Long-term debt ($ mil.): 700

Net Income History

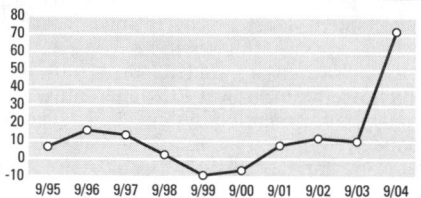

9/95 9/96 9/97 9/98 9/99 9/00 9/01 9/02 9/03 9/04

Sterling Sugars

Sterling Sugars grows and processes sugarcane to make raw sugar and blackstrap molasses for sale to sugar refiners and candy manufacturers. It also leases land for oil and natural gas exploration. The company is run by the Patout and Guarisco families, who own about 66% and 22% of Sterling Sugars, respectively. The two families and other shareholders took the company private in July 2005.

EXECUTIVES

Chairman and General Counsel:
Bernard E. Boudreaux Jr.
President and CEO: Craig P. Caillier
CFO: Randall Romero
VP and General Manager: Rivers M. Patout
Secretary: Tim Soileau
Auditors: Broussard, Poche, Lewis & Breaux, L.L.P.

LOCATIONS

HQ: Sterling Sugars, Inc.
611 Irish Bend Rd., Franklin, LA 70538
Phone: 337-828-0620 **Fax:** 337-828-1757

COMPETITORS

Amalgamated Sugar
American Crystal Sugar
C&H Sugar
Corn Products International
Cumberland Packing
Florida Crystals
Imperial Savannah
Imperial Sugar
Merisant Worldwide
Nippon Beet Sugar
NutraSweet
SMBSC
Sugar Cane Growers Cooperative of Florida
U.S. Sugar
Western Sugar Cooperative

HISTORICAL FINANCIALS

Company Type: Private

Income Statement

FYE: July 31

	REVENUE ($ mil.)	NET INCOME ($ mil.)	NET PROFIT MARGIN	EMPLOYEES
7/04	33	2	4.8%	188
7/03	40	(2)	—	197
7/02	43	1	2.4%	193
7/01	42	0	1.0%	175
7/00	48	1	1.9%	186
7/99	43	1	1.4%	192
7/98*	15	(1)	—	180
1/98	40	1	2.0%	207
1/97	39	2	5.2%	102
1/96	29	2	7.4%	86
Annual Growth	**1.7%**	**(3.0%)**	**—**	**9.1%**

*Fiscal year change

2004 Year-End Financials

Debt ratio: 24.0%
Return on equity: 9.3%
Cash ($ mil.): 2

Current ratio: 0.86
Long-term debt ($ mil.): 4

Net Income History

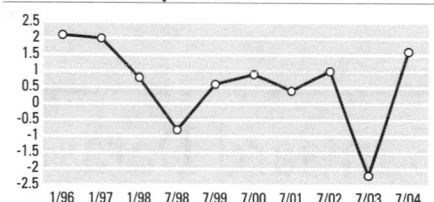

1/96 1/97 1/98 7/98 7/99 7/00 7/01 7/02 7/03 7/04

Stream

This company can handle a torrent of customer service calls. Stream (formerly Stream International) is a leading provider of outsourced customer and technical support services, with more than 20 call centers in more than a dozen countries. Its customer support staff can offer support services over the telephone, via e-mail, and through online chat sessions. In addition to customer service, Stream offers pre-sales and upsell services, as well as order processing. Stream was founded in the 1980s as part of R. R. Donnelley & Sons; today it is backed by investment firm H.I.G. Capital.

Stream has benefited from the growing interest in outsourcing as more companies look for ways to cut costs while still providing customer support. Its global presence offers its clients 24-hour coverage for their customers as well as localized services for an international customer base. In 2005 Stream added a contact center in the Dominican Republic, acquiring the operation from Supra Telecom.

Once an IPO candidate, Stream International was acquired by Bain Capital and later sold to contract manufacturing giant Solectron in 1999. H.I.G. acquired the firm in 2004 and merged it with two of its other portfolio companies, ECE Holdings and Infowavz. The combined enterprise took on the shortened moniker Stream.

EXECUTIVES

President and CEO: Toni J. Portmann
COO: Matt Kochan
CFO: Tom Andrus
VP Business Development: Todd Handy
VP Corporate Services: Larry Callahan
VP Human Resources: Laurie Brashear
VP Marketing and Business Strategy:
Katherin Dockerill
VP Sales: Jeff Evert
CIO: Jeff Jennings
Director of Communications: Curtis Niles Coats III
Marketing Manager: Missy Simone

LOCATIONS

HQ: Stream
2220 Campbell Creek Blvd., Ste. 100,
Richardson, TX 75082
Phone: 469-624-5000 **Fax:** 469-624-5902
Web: www.stream.com

Stream operates contact centers in Canada, the Dominican Republic, France, Germany, India, Ireland, Italy, the Netherlands, Spain, Sweden, Tunisia, the UK, and the US.

PRODUCTS/OPERATIONS

Selected Services

Post sales customer services
Pre-sales customer services
Professional and consulting services
Sales and marketing services
Technical support services

COMPETITORS

Accenture	SITEL
APAC Customer Services	SR.Teleperformance
BearingPoint	StarTek
ClientLogic	Sykes Enterprises
Convergys	TechTeam
EDS	TELESPECTRUM
IBM Global Services	TeleTech
Infosys	Unisys
Keane	West Corporation
NCO Group	Wipro Technologies
Perot Systems	

HISTORICAL FINANCIALS

Company Type: Private

Income Statement

FYE: December 31

	REVENUE ($ mil.)	NET INCOME ($ mil.)	NET PROFIT MARGIN	EMPLOYEES
12/04*	300	—	—	10,149
12/00	323	—	—	1,000
12/99	236	—	—	6,000
12/98	214	—	—	5,000
12/97	186	—	—	5,000
12/96	156	—	—	4,764
12/95	78	—	—	—
12/94	37	—	—	—
12/93	14	—	—	—
12/92	3	—	—	—
Annual Growth	**68.1%**	**—**	**—**	**16.3%**

*Irregular reporting interval

Revenue History

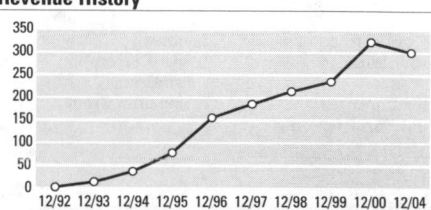

12/92 12/93 12/94 12/95 12/96 12/97 12/98 12/99 12/00 12/04

Structure Tone

Structured to set the right tone for its clients, The Structure Tone Organization develops corporate and commercial properties for major clients down the block and around the world. Through four main companies, the group provides general contracting, construction management, and project management services for building construction, interior fit-outs and renovations, and infrastructure upgrades. A top builder in the New York City area (it is a leader in telecommunications projects there as well), the company also works in Asia, Europe, and South America. Structure Tone was founded to focus on building interiors in 1971 by Lou Marino and Patrick Donaghy, whose family now owns the company.

EXECUTIVES

Chairman: James K. Donaghy
Vice Chairman: Brian M. Donaghy
President: Anthony M. Carvette
CEO: Robert W. Mullen
CFO: Ray Froimowitz
EVP and Secretary: John T. White
SVP Human Resources: Robert (Bob) Yardis
Director of IT: Steven Barber
VP Marketing: Robin Malacrea

LOCATIONS

HQ: The Structure Tone Organization
770 Broadway, 9th Fl., New York, NY 10003
Phone: 212-481-6100   **Fax:** 212-685-9267
Web: www.structuretone.com

The Structure Tone Organization has offices in Florida, Massachusetts, New Jersey, New York, Texas, and Virginia.

PRODUCTS/OPERATIONS

Companies
Constructors & Associates, Inc.
    Pavarini Construction
ST TECH Services, Inc.
Structure Tone International
Structure Tone, Inc.

Sectors
Commercial
Convention centers
Correctional facilities
Cultural centers
Educational
Entertainment
Health care
Hospitality
Interiors
Residential
Retail
Sports

COMPETITORS

AMEC, Construction	Opus
Management	PCL
Bovis Lend Lease	Perini
Clark Enterprises	Peter Kiewit Sons'
Devcon Construction	Skanska USA Building
DPR Construction	Tishman
Foster Wheeler	Turner Corporation
Gilbane	Walsh Group
HRH Construction	Washington Group
Hunt Construction	

HISTORICAL FINANCIALS

Company Type: Private

Income Statement

FYE: October 31

	ESTIMATED REVENUE ($ mil.)	NET INCOME ($ mil.)	NET PROFIT MARGIN	EMPLOYEES
10/04	1,950	—	—	1,200
10/03	1,700	—	—	1,500
10/02	2,100	—	—	1,600
10/01	2,100	—	—	1,600
10/00	2,000	—	—	1,300
10/99	1,600	—	—	1,000
Annual Growth	4.0%	—	—	3.7%

Revenue History

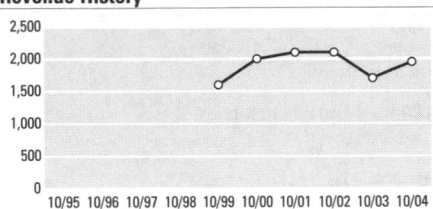

SunGard Data Systems

Just about every financial services company under the sun relies on SunGard Data Systems. About 70% of all Nasdaq trades pass through SunGard's investment support systems, which banks, stock exchanges, mutual funds, insurance companies, governments, and others use for transaction processing, asset management, securities and commodities trading, and investment accounting. SunGard's Availability Services division provides business continuity, managed information technology, and professional services for businesses that rely on information resources. SunGard, which also offers higher education and public sector administrative systems, serves more than 20,000 customers in 50 countries.

In 2005 a group of seven private investment firms — Silver Lake Partners (lead investor), Bain Capital, The Blackstone Group, GS Capital Partners, Kohlberg Kravis Roberts & Co., Providence Equity Partners, and Texas Pacific Group — acquired SunGard Data Systems for about $11.3 billion.

SunGard's aggressive acquisition strategy has helped the company expand its offerings and take a leading position in many of its markets. In 2003 the company completed nine acquisitions. Most notably, it spent $159 million to acquire Caminus, a provider of commodity trading software for the global energy industry, in order to grow its SunGard Trading and Risk Systems unit; it bought UK-based insurance and government software maker Sherwood International in order to expand SunGard Insurance Systems; and it spent $121 million to buy public sector software maker H.T.E., which became part of the SunGard Higher Education and Public Sector Systems segment. SunGard's acquisition spree continued into 2004: the company further expanded its Higher Education and Public Sector segment

with its $590 million purchase of Systems & Computer Technology (now SunGard SCT) and its purchase of Collegis, a provider of information technology services for higher education. Early in 2005 SunGard Availability Services closed its acquisition of Inflow, a provider of infrastructure management, disaster recovery, and information technology consulting services.

In 2004 SunGard sold its Brut subsidiary, which operates the Brut ECN alternative electronic trade-execution system, to Nasdaq for about $190 million in cash. Also that year, the company announced that it would spin off its Availability Services disaster recovery division (40% of sales) as a separate, publicly traded company, but it canceled those plans after it agreed to be taken private. The division has grown in recent years due to increased demand for disaster recovery services following the attacks on the US on September 11, 2001, and SunGard's purchase of Comdisco's Availability Solutions business.

SunGard counts most of the world's largest financial services institutions among its customers.

HISTORY

When Philadelphia-based Sun Company in 1983 shifted focus from its computer disaster recovery services business in favor of its oil-related operations, the subsidiary's founder and president, John Ryan, led a group of New York investment bankers in a leveraged buyout for $19 million. They changed the name to SunGard Data Systems, providing IBM mainframe users with disaster recovery services through four operating subsidiaries in California, Illinois, North Carolina, and Pennsylvania.

By 1985 half of sales came from financial processing and software development services. In 1986 SunGard went public and reached profitability on revenues of $70 million. That year former US Air Force pilot and IBM salesman James Mann, who joined SunGard after the buyout in 1983, was named chairman and CEO.

SunGard acquired four more companies in 1987, including Devon International, whose CEO, Cristóbal Conde, went on to launch SunGard's trading systems division in 1990 and became the company's president in 2000. The acquisition also marked SunGard's first expansion overseas.

SunGard grew rapidly in the early 1990s through acquisitions, mostly in the area of data recovery. By 1993, sales had eclipsed $380 million. Two years later SunGard entered the health care information systems market with the acquisitions of Intelus Corporation and MACESS (later renamed SunGard Workflow Solutions).

Propelled by 12 more acquisitions in 1997, including risk management software maker Infinity Financial Technology, SunGard reached $1 billion in sales in 1998. By the following year its focus had shifted toward providing software for asset management and trade execution to financial services companies. The strategy paid off; nearly 70% of all 1999 trades on the Nasdaq exchange were supported by SunGard software. Among its acquisitions that year was life insurance and pension software specialist FDP.

In 2000 SunGard realigned operations as part of a companywide move to better integrate and brand its 50 subsidiaries. The next year the company acquired Bridge Information Systems' PowerPartner financial information management software for $165 million.

In 2001 SunGard entered into a bidding war with Hewlett-Packard for Comdisco's computer services operations, eventually purchasing the business for about $850 million. The next year — during which SunGard completed nine more acquisitions — Mann turned over the CEO title to president and COO Conde, who had been slated to take over leadership of the company since he became an EVP in 1998; Mann remained as chairman. The company continued to buy up smaller companies in 2003 with nine acquisitions, including public sector software maker H.T.E., energy trading software maker Caminus, and insurance software provider Sherwood International.

EXECUTIVES

President, CEO, and Director: Cristóbal I. (Cris) Conde, age 45, $2,419,424 pay
EVP; Head of Investment Support Systems: Michael K. Muratore, age 58, $1,530,619 pay
SVP, Corporate Development: Richard C. Tarbox, age 52
SVP and Chief Marketing Officer: Brian Robins, age 46
SVP, Finance and CFO: Michael J. Ruane, age 51
SVP, Global Accounts Management: Bettina A. Slusar, age 41
SVP, Chief Administrative Officer, and Chief Legal Officer: Lawrence A. Gross, age 52
VP, Controller, and Assistant Secretary: Andrew P. Bronstein, age 46
SVP, Human Resources: Paul C. Jeffers, age 42
Group CEO, SunGard Asset Management Systems, SunGard Futures Systems, SunGard Securities Finance, SunGard Securities Processing, and SunGard Wealth Management Services: Donald W. (Don) Birdwell, age 52, $1,793,219 pay
Group CEO, SunGard Availability Services: James C. (Jim) Simmons, age 45
Group CEO, SunGard Data Management Solutions and SunGard Online Investment Systems: John Hyde
Group CEO, SunGard Employee Benefit Systems and SunGard Investor Accounting Systems: T. Ray Davis, age 56
Group CEO, SunGard Higher Education and Public Sector Systems: Robert F. (Bob) Clarke, age 60, $2,172,083 pay
Group CEO, SunGard Investment Management Systems: John E. (Jack) McArdle Jr., age 47
Group CEO, SunGard Trading and Risk Systems: James E. (Jim) Ashton III, age 46
Group CEO, SunGard Trading Systems: Ronald M. (Ron) Lang, age 53
Chairman and CEO, SunGard Higher Education and Public Sector Systems: Jeffrey P. (Jeff) Feather, age 61
Auditors: PricewaterhouseCoopers LLP

LOCATIONS

HQ: SunGard Data Systems Inc.
680 E. Swedesford Rd., Wayne, PA 19087
Phone: 484-582-2000   **Fax:** 610-225-1120
Web: www.sungard.com

SunGard Data Systems has offices in more than 30 countries.

2004 Sales

	$ mil.	% of total
US	2,638	74
Europe		
UK	382	11
Other countries	328	9
Canada	103	3
Asia/Pacific	57	2
Other regions	48	1
Total	**3,556**	**100**

PRODUCTS/OPERATIONS

2004 Sales

	$ mil.	% of total
Investment support systems		
Brokerage & trading	537	15
Benefit, insurance & investor accounting	385	11
Treasury & risk management	360	10
Wealth management	345	10
Investment management	212	6
Availability services	1,192	33
Higher education & public sector systems	525	15
Total	**3,556**	**100**

2004 Sales

	$ mil.	% of total
Services	3,180	89
License & resale fees	282	8
Reimbursed expenses	94	3
Total	**3,556**	**100**

Selected Products

BondMaster (interest and principal payments management systems)
Customer relationship management (BrokerWare, Cross-Seller, Contact Manager)
eTreasury (online cash management)
EXPEDITER (online mutual funds processing)
Investment support systems
   Asset management
   Banking and treasury
   Brokerage and execution
   Investor accounting
   Public sector
   Risk and derivatives
MINT (standardized messaging implementation)
Network Trade Model (XML-based data sharing between trading systems)
SunGard Direct (institutional trader, asset manager online processing)
SunGard Transaction Network (financial services firm trade processing exchange)
SunGard webRedirect (business continuity data collocation)

Selected Services

Application service processing
Business continuity (on-site and remote disaster recovery)
Collocation application hosting
Consulting
Data center outsourcing
Private network access
Training
Web hosting

COMPETITORS

ADP
Advent Software
Bloomberg
DST
EDS
First Data
Fiserv
IBM
Jack Henry
Merrill Lynch
Misys
Morgan Stanley
Reuters
Thomson Corporation

HISTORICAL FINANCIALS

Company Type: Private

Income Statement

FYE: December 31

	REVENUE ($ mil.)	NET INCOME ($ mil.)	NET PROFIT MARGIN	EMPLOYEES
12/04	3,556	454	12.8%	13,000
12/03	2,955	370	12.5%	10,000
12/02	2,593	326	12.6%	8,800
12/01	1,929	246	12.8%	8,700
12/00	1,661	213	12.8%	7,800
12/99	1,445	84	5.8%	6,900
12/98	1,160	119	10.3%	5,300
12/97	862	78	9.0%	4,500
12/96	670	35	5.2%	3,700
12/95	533	49	9.1%	2,900
Annual Growth	**23.5%**	**28.1%**	**—**	**18.1%**

2004 Year-End Financials

Debt ratio: 15.7%
Return on equity: 15.1%
Cash ($ mil.): 675
Current ratio: 1.30
Long-term debt ($ mil.): 509

Net Income History

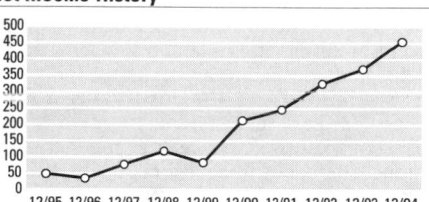

Sunkist Growers

Perhaps the US enterprise least susceptible to an outbreak of scurvy, Sunkist Growers is a cooperative owned by 6,500 citrus farmers in California and Arizona. Sunkist markets fresh oranges, lemons, grapefruit, and tangerines in the US and overseas. Fruit that doesn't meet fresh market standards is turned into juices, oils, and peels for use in food products. The Sunkist brand is one of the most recognized names in the US; through licensing agreements the name also appears worldwide on more than 600 beverages and other products, from vitamins to fruit rolls.

Sunkist is one of the largest marketing cooperatives in America and the largest cooperative in the world's fruit and vegetable industry. Sunkist's biggest export customers are Canada, Hong Kong, Japan, and South Korea. Sunkist has licensing agreements with companies in more than 50 countries.

HISTORY

Sunkist Growers was founded in the early 1890s as the Pachappa Orange Growers, a group of California citrus farmers determined to control the sale of their fruit. Success attracted new members, and in 1893 the Southern California Fruit Exchange was born. The name "Sunkissed" was coined by an ad copywriter in 1908, and it was soon reworked into "Sunkist" and registered as a trademark, becoming the first brand name for a fresh produce item. Eventually the co-op renamed itself after its popular brand: It became Sunkist Growers in 1952.

Sunkist began licensing its trademark to other companies in the early 1950s.

As early as 1916, efforts to increase citrus consumption included designing and marketing glass citrus juicers and encouraging homemakers to "Drink an Orange." The co-op also promoted the practice of putting lemon slices in tea or water and funded early research on the health benefits of vitamins (vitamin C in particular). In 1925 tissue wrappers gave way to stamping the Sunkist name directly on each piece of fruit.

Although Sunkist pioneered bottled orange juice in 1933, its juice marketing efforts were never as successful as those of its Florida competitors. Florida oranges are drippy and dowdy and thus better suited for juicing. Capitalizing on this aspect, Florida growers dominated the market for fresh and frozen juice.

In 1937 Congress created a system of citrus shipment quotas and limits (known as "marketing orders") that ultimately proved most beneficial to large citrus cooperatives. By the early 1990s the marketing order system was under political attack, and in 1992 the Justice Department filed civil prosecution against Sunkist, alleging that the co-op had reaped unfair extra profits by surpassing its lemon shipment limits. In 1994, after much legal wrangling, the quotas were abolished and the Justice Department dropped its case against Sunkist.

Inconveniently warm weather and increasing competition from imported citrus marked the harvests of 1996. That year the co-op had trouble maintaining discipline among its members; some undercut Sunkist price levels, while others flooded the market to sell their fruit at the higher early market prices, creating a supply surplus. Also that year the co-op relinquished the marketing of all Sunkist juices in North America to Florida-based Lykes Bros. in a licensing agreement.

The co-op agreed in 1998 to distribute grapefruit from Florida's Tuxedo Fruit, providing Sunkist with winter grapefruit supply and increasing its year-round consumer a-peel. Also in 1998 Russell Hanlin, Sunkist president and CEO since 1978, was succeeded by Vince Lupinacci. Lupinacci, who had held positions with Pepsi and Six Flags, became the first person from outside the citrus business to hold Sunkist's top post.

In 1998 the company sold 90 million cartons of fresh citrus — the greatest volume in its history — despite increased competition from imported Latin American, South African, and Spanish crops, a damaging California freeze, and the ill effects of El Nino. The next year production was almost halved because of adverse weather.

Lupinacci resigned in 2000, citing personal and family reasons. Chairman Emeritus James Mast then took the helm as acting president. Although the company grew its market through exports to China in 2000, its profits were squeezed that year by increasing foreign competition, a citrus glut, and lessened demand. In mid-2001 Jeff Gargiulo replaced Mast as Sunkist's president and CEO.

Sunkist formed a joint venture with strawberry shipper Coastal Berry Co. in 2003 to market strawberries under the Sunkist label year-round. Coastal Berry's president and CEO John Gargiulo and Sunkist's president and CEO Jeff Gargiulo are brothers. Also that year Sunkist began offering pre-cut bagged fruit to retail customers and restaurants in order to keep up with a changing market and consumer demand.

EXECUTIVES

Chairman: David W. Krause, age 43
President and CEO: Jeffrey D. (Jeff) Gargiulo
VP and COO: James A. (Jim) Padden
VP and Chief Administration Officer: Jeffrey E. (Jeff) Moxie
VP, Corporate Relations: Michael J. Wootton
VP, Finance and Treasurer: Richard G. French
VP, Domestic Sales: John B. McGuigan
VP, Global Licensing: Greg Combs
VP, International Sales and Sales Operations: Russell L. Hanlin II
VP, Licensing/International Development: Ashok D. Patel
VP, Law and General Counsel: Thomas M. Moore
VP, Marketing and Sales Promotion: Robert J. Verloop
VP, Processed Products, Research/Technical Services: Owen W. Belletto
VP: Mike Wootton
Director, Human Resources: John R. McGovern
Director, Sales Strawberry: John Corrigan III
Director, Trademark Licensing: Mario Kahn
Manager, Public Relations: Claire H. Smith
Leader, Citrus Juice and Oil Business: Frank Bragg
Corporate Secretary: Kristen J. Moyer
Auditors: KPMG LLP

LOCATIONS

HQ: Sunkist Growers, Inc.
14130 Riverside Dr., Sherman Oaks, CA 91423
Phone: 818-986-4800 **Fax:** 818-379-7405
Web: www.sunkist.com

COMPETITORS

Alico	Fresh Del Monte Produce
Chiquita Brands	Louis Dreyfus Citrus
Coca-Cola North America	Tropicana
Dole Food	UniMark Group
Florida's Natural	Vitality Foodservice

HISTORICAL FINANCIALS

Company Type: Cooperative

Income Statement

FYE: October 31

	REVENUE ($ mil.)	NET INCOME ($ mil.)	NET PROFIT MARGIN	EMPLOYEES
10/03	942	27	2.9%	—
10/02	964	(2)	—	—
10/01	993	4	0.4%	—
10/00	847	(4)	—	—
10/99	862	6	0.7%	—
10/98	1,069	6	0.6%	875
10/97	1,075	—	—	813
10/96	1,025	—	—	878
10/95	1,096	—	—	1,150
10/94	1,005	—	—	1,138
Annual Growth	(0.7%)	35.7%	—	(6.4%)

2003 Year-End Financials

Debt ratio: 34.0%
Return on equity: 42.5%
Cash ($ mil.): 6
Current ratio: 1.48
Long-term debt ($ mil.): 26

Net Income History

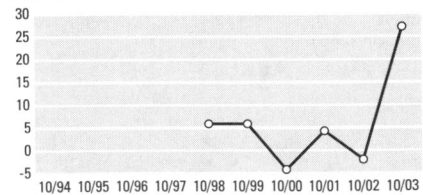

Sunsweet Growers

Being all dried up is a good thing at Sunsweet Growers. The 650-member, grower-owned cooperative processes and markets dried fruit. Sunsweet produces one-third of the world's prunes. Other Sunsweet fruit products include prune juice, as well as dried apples, apricots, dates, peaches, pears, pineapples, and more. It was founded in 1917 as the California Prune and Apricot Growers Association.

EXECUTIVES

Chairman: Gary S. Thiara
Vice Chairman: Tim D. Smith
CEO: Harold G. Schenker
VP, Finance, and CFO: Ana Spyres
President: Arthur Driscoll II
SVP, Human Resources: Sharon K. Braun
VP, Member Services, and President, Sunsweet Dryers: Mark Dalrymple
VP, Operations: Gene Dodson
VP, Global Sales and Marketing: Dane L. Lance
VP, Marketing, North America: Steve Ricardelli
VP, Sales, North America: Brad Schuller
Auditors: KPMG LLP

LOCATIONS

HQ: Sunsweet Growers Inc.
901 N. Walton Ave., Yuba City, CA 95993
Phone: 530-674-5010 **Fax:** 530-751-5395
Web: www.sunsweet.com

COMPETITORS

Birds Eye
Chiquita Brands
Del Monte Foods
Dole Food
Fresh Del Monte Produce
Global Berry Farms
Maui Land & Pineapple
Ocean Spray
Pro-Fac
Seneca Foods
Sun Growers
Sunkist

HISTORICAL FINANCIALS

Company Type: Cooperative

Income Statement

FYE: July 31

	REVENUE ($ mil.)	NET INCOME ($ mil.)	NET PROFIT MARGIN	EMPLOYEES
7/04	224	84	37.7%	—
7/03	214	74	34.4%	—
7/02	217	50	23.0%	—
Annual Growth	1.5%	30.1%	—	—

Net Income History

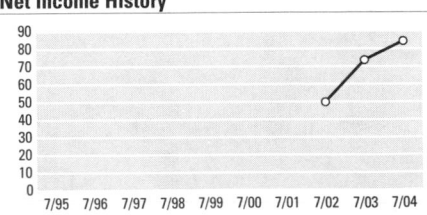

Sutter Health

Sutter Health is one of the nation's largest not-for-profit health care systems. It was organized in 1996 through the merger of Sutter Health and California Healthcare System. Today the company caters to residents of more than 100 Northern California communities. Its services are provided through the firm's approximately 3,600 affiliated doctors, from facilities of various types, including acute care hospitals, home health/hospice networks, medical groups, occupational health services centers, and skilled nursing facilities. Sutter Health's network also boasts several research institutes. Pat Fry became president and CEO in June 2005, when Van Johnson retired.

Nearly 40% of Sutter Health's patient services revenues comes from Medicare reimbursement; Medi-Cal, California's Medicaid program, accounts for about 15%.

The company's hospitals in Northern California felt a bit of a pinch after about a dozen of them were eliminated from the CalPERS HMO network. The two organizations fought bitterly over pricing and access, with CalPERS claiming Sutter Health charges 60% to 80% more than other hospitals.

To keep its San Francisco-based St. Luke's Hospital from shuttering its doors, Sutter Health plans to merge St. Luke's Hospital and its healthier California Pacific Medical Center in 2006. St. Luke's serves many of the city's uninsured and low-income population and has been logging losses of more than $20 million each year.

In an effort to reduce costs and errors, Sutter Health announced in 2004 plans to spend some $1.2 billion on IT systems over the next 10 years.

EXECUTIVES

Chairman: Ralph E. Andersen
SVP and CFO: Robert D. (Bob) Reed
President and CEO: Patrick E. (Pat) Fry
SVP and General Counsel: Gary F. Loveridge
SVP; President and CEO, Palo Alto Medical Foundation: David Druker
SVP, Chief Medical Officer, and Clinical Integration Officer: Gordon C. Hunt Jr.
SVP, Information Services and CIO: John Hummel
SVP, Strategy and Organization Development: James Farrell
SVP, Public Affairs: Cyndi Kettmann
VP, Communications and Marketing: Bill Gleeson
CIO and IT Strategist: Nelson Ramos
Auditors: Ernst & Young LLP

LOCATIONS

HQ: Sutter Health
   2200 River Plaza Dr., Sacramento, CA 95833
Phone: 916-733-8800   **Fax:** 916-286-6841
Web: www.sutterhealth.org

Hospitals

Sutter Delta Medical Center (Antioch, CA)
Sutter Auburn Faith Hospital (CA)
Alta Bates Medical Center (Berkeley, CA)
Mills-Peninsula Medical Center (Burlingame, CA)
Eden Medical Center (Castro Valley, CA)
Sutter Coast Hospital (Crescent City, CA)
Sutter Davis Hospital (CA)
Marin General Hospital (Greenbrae, CA)
Sutter Amador Hospital (Jackson, CA)
Sutter Lakeside Hospital (Lakeport, CA)
Memorial Hospital Los Banos (CA)
Memorial Medical Center (Modesto, CA)
Novato Community Hospital (CA)

Alta Bates Summit Medical Center (Oakland, CA)
Sutter Roseville Medical Center (CA)
Sutter Medical Center, Sacramento (CA)
   Sutter Center for Psychiatry
   Sutter General Hospital
   Sutter Memorial Hospital
California Pacific Medical Centers (San Francisco)
St. Luke's Hospital (San Francisco)
San Leandro Hospital (San Leandro, CA)
Sutter Maternity & Surgery Center of Santa Cruz (CA)
Sutter Medical Center of Santa Rosa (CA)
Sutter Warrack Hospital (Santa Rosa, CA)
Sutter Tracy Community Hospital (CA)
Sutter Solano Medical Center (Vallejo, CA)
Kahi Mohala, A Behavioral Healthcare System (Ewa Beach, HI)

COMPETITORS

Adventist Health	Providence Health System
Catholic Healthcare West	Stanford University
HCA	Medical
Memorial Health Services	Tenet Healthcare

HISTORICAL FINANCIALS

Company Type: Not-for-profit

Income Statement

FYE: December 31

	REVENUE ($ mil.)	NET INCOME ($ mil.)	NET PROFIT MARGIN	EMPLOYEES
12/03	5,672	—	—	41,000
12/02	4,931	—	—	39,678
12/01	4,216	—	—	36,000
12/00	3,500	—	—	35,000
12/99	2,919	—	—	35,000
12/98	2,881	—	—	35,000
12/97	2,663	—	—	35,000
12/96	2,453	—	—	35,000
12/95	2,226	—	—	—
12/94	1,940	—	—	—
Annual Growth	**12.7%**	**—**	**—**	**2.3%**

Revenue History

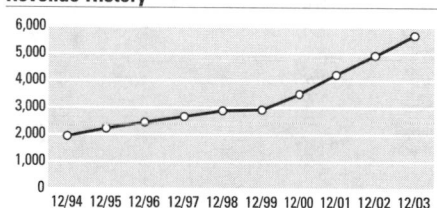

Swinerton

Swinerton is building up the West just as it helped rebuild San Francisco after the 1906 earthquake. The construction group, formerly Swinerton & Walberg, builds commercial, industrial, and government facilities, including resorts, subsidized housing, public schools, Hollywood soundstages, hospitals, and airport terminals. Through its subsidiaries, Swinerton offers general contracting and design/build services, as well as construction and program management. It also provides property management for conventional, subsidized, and assisted living residences. The employee-owned company, which has been expanding in the past decade in the Northwest and Southwest, traces its family tree to 1888.

Swinerton takes environmental stewardship to heart. As one of the top waste-reducing companies in California, Swinerton employs green building construction and design practices to conserve resources, reduce waste, and create healthier environments. The company's own headquarters building in San Francisco received Gold LEED-EB (Leadership in Energy & Environmental Design for Existing Buildings) certification from the U.S. Green Building Council.

EXECUTIVES

Chairman and CEO: James R. (Jim) Gillette
President and COO; President, Swinerton Builders: Gordon W. Marks
EVP and CFO: Michael Re
EVP Business Development: Jeffrey C. Hoopes
EVP; Northern California Regional Manager, Swinerton Builders: Charles P. (Charlie) Kuffner
SVP; Southern California Regional Manager, Swinerton Builders: Gary Rafferty
SVP and Colorado Regional Manager, Swinerton Builders: David White
SVP and Seattle Division Manager, Swinerton Builders: Keith M. Henrickson
Northwest Regional Manager and President, Swinerton Builders Northwest Inc.: Don Sundgren
SVP, Secretary, and General Counsel: Luke P. Argilla
VP and Controller: Linda G. Showalter
VP Operations Controller: Gregory A. (Greg) Elsea
Auditors: PricewaterhouseCoopers

LOCATIONS

HQ: Swinerton Incorporated
   260 Townsend St., San Francisco, CA 94107
Phone: 415-421-2980   **Fax:** 415-433-0943
Web: www.swinerton.com

Swinerton has offices in California, Colorado, Connecticut, Florida, Hawaii, Oregon, Texas, Utah, and Washington.

PRODUCTS/OPERATIONS

Selected Services

11-month follow-up
Budget studies/cost control
Building/site analysis
Constructability review
Construction management
Consulting
Design/build/assist
General contracting
Loan monitoring
On-line management — archival
Preconstruction
Procurement
Program scheduling
Property management
Quality control program
Regulatory approvals
Value management
Warranty administration

Selected Companies and Joint Ventures

Bud Bailey Construction (construction management, design/build, and general contracting)
Harbison-Mahony-Higgins Builders, Inc. (HMH, general contracting)
Lyda Swinerton Builders (general contracting)
Swinerton Builders (general contracting)
Swinerton Management & Consulting (property assessment)
Swinerton/Pacific (joint venture)
Swinerton Property Services (property management)
William P. Young Construction (engineering and civil construction)

COMPETITORS

Bechtel
Beck Group
Bovis Lend Lease
Charles Pankow Builders
Cordoba
Devcon Construction
DPR Construction
Gilbane
Hathaway Dinwiddie
 Construction
Hensel Phelps
 Construction

J.F. Shea
Kitchell
Rudolph & Sletten
S. J. Amoroso
 Construction
Skanska USA Building
Sundt
Turner Corporation
Tutor-Saliba
Webcor Builders
Whiting-Turner

HISTORICAL FINANCIALS

Company Type: Private

Income Statement

	REVENUE ($ mil.)	NET INCOME ($ mil.)	NET PROFIT MARGIN	EMPLOYEES
12/03	2,751	—	—	1,331
12/02	1,560	—	—	1,200
12/01	1,549	—	—	1,200
12/00	1,550	—	—	1,450
12/99	1,150	—	—	1,400
12/98	902	—	—	1,500
12/97	792	—	—	1,400
12/96	501	—	—	1,300
12/95	412	—	—	1,000
12/94	389	—	—	1,200
Annual Growth	24.3%	—	—	1.2%

FYE: December 31

Revenue History

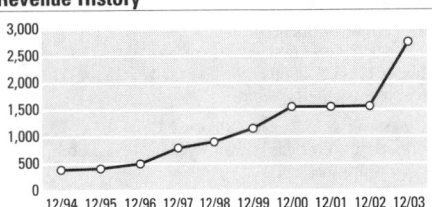

Sydran Services

This company has agreed to a Whopper of a deal. Sydran Services, the second-largest Burger King franchisee (behind Carrols), has agreed to sell its entire Burger King portfolio to Strategic Restaurants Acquisition as part of Sydran's Chapter 11 reorganization. The company runs more than 225 locations in eight states, primarily in California and Louisiana. CEO Matthew Schoenberg founded the company in 1992 when he acquired 14 Burger King locations in the San Francisco area. Sydran is backed by such institutional investors as New York Life, TCW, and Allied Capital.

EXECUTIVES

President and CEO: Matthew Schoenberg
SVP and General Counsel: Kenneth A. Freed
VP Finance: Steven (Steve) Grossman
VP Human Resources: Tammy Taylor
VP Information Systems: Mark Rhodes
VP Marketing: Myrna Schultz
Controller: Saundra Cleveland
Strategic Planning: Jacquie Bailey
Auditors: Deloitte & Touche LLP

LOCATIONS

HQ: Sydran Services, LLC
 Bishop Ranch 8, 3000 Executive Pkwy., Ste. 515,
 San Ramon, CA 94583
Phone: 925-328-3300   **Fax:** 925-328-3333
Web: www.sydran.com

Sydran Services operates more than 225 Burger King restaurants in Alabama, Arkansas, California, Florida, Kansas, Louisiana, Mississippi, and Missouri.

COMPETITORS

AFC Enterprises
Checkers Drive-In
Chick-fil-A
CKE Restaurants
Dairy Queen
Domino's
Jack in the Box
Little Caesar's
McDonald's
NPC International
Papa John's
PJ United
RPM Pizza
Sonic
Subway
Triarc
United States Beef
Wendy's
White Castle
YUM!

HISTORICAL FINANCIALS

Company Type: Private

Income Statement

	REVENUE ($ mil.)	NET INCOME ($ mil.)	NET PROFIT MARGIN	EMPLOYEES
6/04	207	—	—	6,000
6/03	215	—	—	7,000
6/02	278	—	—	12,000
6/01*	323	—	—	12,000
12/00	295	—	—	12,000
12/99	350	—	—	11,000
12/98	236	—	—	8,000
12/97	225	—	—	7,000
12/96	167	—	—	—
12/95	152	—	—	—
Annual Growth	3.5%	—	—	(2.2%)

FYE: June 30

*Fiscal year change

Revenue History

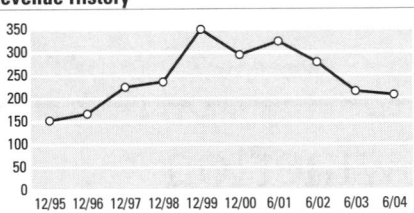

TAP Pharmaceutical

TAP Pharmaceutical Products taps into hot drug industry trends. The joint venture between Abbott Laboratories and Takeda Pharmaceutical Company develops and sells drugs in the US and Canada. The company's products target cancer, gastroenterology, gynecology, and urology. TAP's Lupron Depot was developed to treat advanced prostate cancer, but can also treat endometriosis in women and central precocious puberty in children. The company also markets Prevacid, which is used to treat acid reflux disease and ulcers, and is working on a second-generation formula of the proton pump inhibitor.

The company's pipeline includes drugs for hormone replacement therapy, obesity, and gout. Although erectile dysfunction treatment Uprima won European approval, TAP withdrew it from FDA consideration after questions arose over its efficacy and safety. It is continuing to improve the drug for resubmission. Febuxostat, TAP's gout treatment, is under consideration by the FDA and the company plans to submit asprisnil, a treatment for uterine fibroids, for approval in 2005.

Facing expiration of its patents on Prevacid, the company has developed two new formulations of the drug, a dissolving tablet and an intravenous version for hospital use.

TAP agreed to pay a record-setting $875 million to settle criminal and civil charges over its pricing and marketing of Lupron; a few executives and former executives have been indicted on allegations of criminal conspiracy.

EXECUTIVES

President: Alan MacKenzie, age 52
EVP: Glenn Warner, age 41
VP and General Manager, Prevacid and Gastrointestinal Marketing: Brian Luedtke
VP, Ethics and Compliance: L. Stephan Vincze
VP, Human Resources: Denise Kitchen
VP, Research and Development: Xavier Frapaise
Controller: Kevin Dolan
Public Relations: Kim Modory
Senior Scientific Director and Head of Urology Therapeutic Area: Stuart Atkinson
Director, Medical Affairs: Lawrence Stauback

LOCATIONS

HQ: TAP Pharmaceutical Products Inc.
 675 North Field Dr., Lake Forest, IL 60045
Phone: 847-582-2000   **Fax:** 800-830-6936
Web: www.tap.com

TAP Pharmaceutical Products has facilities in California, Georgia, Illinois, New Jersey, and Texas.

PRODUCTS/OPERATIONS

Products

Lupron/Lupron Depot (endometriosis, prostate cancer)
Prevacid (gastric acid inhibitor)

COMPETITORS

AstraZeneca
GlaxoSmithKline
ICOS
Pfizer
PRAECIS
Zonagen

HISTORICAL FINANCIALS

Company Type: Joint venture

Income Statement

FYE: December 31

	REVENUE ($ mil.)	NET INCOME ($ mil.)	NET PROFIT MARGIN	EMPLOYEES
12/04	3,362	750	22.3%	—
12/03	3,980	1,162	29.2%	3,300
12/02	4,037	1,334	33.0%	3,000
12/01	3,787	668	17.6%	3,000
12/00	3,539	963	27.2%	2,500
12/99	2,928	780	26.7%	2,300
12/98	2,063	533	25.8%	2,000
12/97	1,566	379	24.2%	1,500
12/96	1,129	259	23.0%	1,250
12/95	750	150	19.9%	1,000
Annual Growth	18.1%	19.6%	—	16.1%

Net Income History

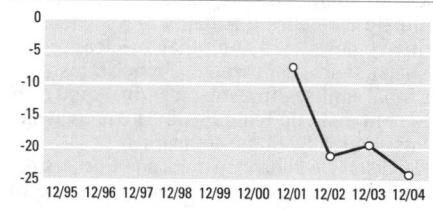

12/95 12/96 12/97 12/98 12/99 12/00 12/01 12/02 12/03 12/04

Targacept

For years we've heard about the dangers of nicotine. Targacept, however, hopes to put the nervous system's nicotinic receptors to good use. The biotechnology company is the result of nicotine research conducted by R.J. Reynolds Tobacco, which spun off the firm in 2000. Targacept's products treat conditions related to Alzheimer's disease (Ispronicline), depression (Mecamylamine), and hypertension (Inversine) by targeting nicotinic acetylcholine receptors (NNRs) in the nervous system using non-nicotine compounds. The firm hopes its drug candidates will reproduce the therapeutic effects of NNR interaction without the side effects of nicotine (but they may not offer that smooth, satisfying taste).

In addition to its product candidates in clinical trials, Targacept hopes to develop treatments for such conditions as inflammation, obesity, and schizophrenia. The company bought the rights to Inversine, which has FDA approval to treat moderately severe to severe hypertension, in 2002 from Layton BioScience.

Targacept's investors include CDIB BioScience, New Enterprise Associates, Nomura, and Oxford Bioscience Partners.

EXECUTIVES

Chairman: Mark B. Skaletsky, age 57
President, CEO, and Director: J. Donald deBethizy, age 54, $341,000 pay
VP, Preclinical Research: Merouane Bencherif, age 50, $199,640 pay
VP, Business and Commercial Development: Jeffrey P. (Jeff) Brennan, age 48, $88,500 pay (partial-year salary)
VP, Drug Discovery and Development: William S. Caldwell, age 51, $190,865 pay

VP, Clinical Development and Regulatory Affairs: Geoffrey C. Dunbar, age 58, $291,165 pay
VP, CFO, Treasurer, and Secretary: Alan A. Musso, age 43, $214,131 pay
Senior Director, Finance and Controller: Mauri K. Hodges
Senior Director and Corporate Counsel: Peter A. Zorn
Director, Human Resources: Karen A. Hicks
Community Affairs and Grants Specialist: Debra S. Perret
Auditors: Ernst & Young LLP

LOCATIONS

HQ: Targacept, Inc.
200 E. First St., Ste. 300, Winston-Salem, NC 27101
Phone: 336-480-2100   **Fax:** 336-480-2107
Web: www.targacept.com

PRODUCTS/OPERATIONS

Selected Disease and Disorder Targets

Alzheimer's disease
Depression
Hypertension
Obesity
Pain
Schizophrenia

COMPETITORS

Bristol-Myers Squibb
Eli Lilly
Forest Labs
GlaxoSmithKline
Johnson & Johnson
Merck
Novartis
Pfizer
Procter & Gamble
Shire Laboratories

HISTORICAL FINANCIALS

Company Type: Private

Income Statement

FYE: December 31

	REVENUE ($ mil.)	NET INCOME ($ mil.)	NET PROFIT MARGIN	EMPLOYEES
12/04	4	(24)	—	72
12/03	3	(19)	—	72
12/02	2	(21)	—	65
12/01	2	(7)	—	60
Annual Growth	29.6%	—	—	6.3%

2004 Year-End Financials

Debt ratio: (2.8%)
Return on equity: —
Cash ($ mil.): 53
Current ratio: 10.43
Long-term debt ($ mil.): 3

Net Income History

0
-5
-10
-15
-20
-25

12/95 12/96 12/97 12/98 12/99 12/00 12/01 12/02 12/03 12/04

Tastefully Simple

Taste buds get the Tupperware treatment at Tastefully Simple. The company promotes its line of gourmet soups, dips, desserts, and convenience foods through in-home parties where attendees can taste prior to buying. Its standard food items range in price from $4.99 for beer bread mix to $41.99 for a large gift pack. Most items cost $7 to $8. Many are ready-to-eat, while others require only one or two additional ingredients to prepare. Tastefully Simple has more than 20,000 sales representatives in all 50 US states, and it buys its products from specialty food vendors. Partners Jill Blashack and Joani Nielson founded the fast-growing company in 1995. Blashack owns about 70% of Tastefully Simple.

EXECUTIVES

President and CEO: Jill Blashack
CFO: Rick Miller
EVP and COO: Joani Nielson
VP Information Systems: Peter Bellavance
VP Operations: Jeff Rehovsky
VP Strategic Development: Nora I. Serrano
VP Team Relations: Edgar F. Timberlake
Director Information Systems: Jason Ebacher
Team Relations Senior Lead: Mary Atkinson Pergande
Communication Senior Lead: Lynn Grueneich

LOCATIONS

HQ: Tastefully Simple, Inc.
1920 Turning Leaf Ln. SW, Alexandria, MN 56308
Phone: 320-763-0695   **Fax:** 320-763-2458
Web: www.tastefullysimple.com

PRODUCTS/OPERATIONS

Selected Products

Beer bread
Cherry almond sauce
Chili mix
Corn and black bean salsa
Cranberry orange bread and muffin mix
Creamy wild rice soup
Dips
Dried tomato garlic pesto
Fudge brownies
Fudgy popcorn
Honey mustard
Marinara sauce
Party mixes
Potato cheddar soup
Pretzels
Raspberry salsa
Red pepper and onion preserves
Shortbread cookie mix
Spinach artichoke ball
Sweet pepper jalapeño jam

COMPETITORS

Fingerhut
Harry & David Holdings
Pampered Chef
Trader Joe's

HISTORICAL FINANCIALS

Company Type: Private

Income Statement

FYE: December 31

	REVENUE ($ mil.)	NET INCOME ($ mil.)	NET PROFIT MARGIN	EMPLOYEES
12/04	123	—	—	311
12/03	114	—	—	293
12/02	78	—	—	223
12/01	34	—	—	110
12/00	12	—	—	50
12/99	4	—	—	30
12/98	1	—	—	15
12/97	0	—	—	6
12/96	0	—	—	4
12/95	0	—	—	2
Annual Growth	120.5%	—	—	75.2%

Revenue History

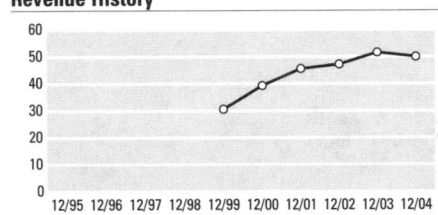

Taylor-Listug

You might say these guitars are Taylor-made to exacting specifications. Taylor-Listug, which does business as Taylor Guitars, is one of the premier acoustic guitar manufacturers in the US. It markets more than 130 models and styles of six- and 12-string guitars known for their quality workmanship. Played by such artists as Leo Kottke, Kenny Loggins, and Prince, the guitars range in price from under $1,000 to more than $11,700 (for a Brazilian rosewood 12-string model). Taylor also sells acoustic basses, guitar accessories, and apparel through about 850 dealers in the US and 25 other countries. The company is owned by president Bob Taylor and CEO Kurt Listug, who started the business in 1974.

EXECUTIVES

CEO: Kurt Listug
President: Bob Taylor
SVP Sales: Robert Sandell
VP Finance: Gary Correia
VP Human Resources: Shaun Paluczak
VP Public Relations: John D'Agostino
Media Relations Manager: Andy Robinson

LOCATIONS

HQ: Taylor-Listug, Inc.
1980 Gillespie Way, El Cajon, CA 92020
Phone: 619-258-1207   **Fax:** 619-258-1623
Web: www.taylorguitars.com

COMPETITORS

C. F. Martin & Co.
Carvin
Fender Musical Instruments
Gibson Guitar
Hoshino Gakki
Kaman Music
K.H.S. Musical Instrument
LaSiDo
Peavey Electronics
PRS
Rickenbacker
Samick
US Music
Yamaha

HISTORICAL FINANCIALS

Company Type: Private

Income Statement

FYE: December 31

	REVENUE ($ mil.)	NET INCOME ($ mil.)	NET PROFIT MARGIN	EMPLOYEES
12/04	50	—	—	376
12/03	52	—	—	375
12/02	47	—	—	357
12/01	46	—	—	375
12/00	39	—	—	350
12/99	31	—	—	322
Annual Growth	10.3%	—	—	3.1%

Revenue History

Team Health

Team Health hopes to score some points with its outsourced physician services. It has contracts with more than 470 hospitals in 44 states to provide medical staffing, management, administrative, and other support services. With about 4,700 health care providers in its network, the firm focuses on emergency medicine, but also specializes in radiology, pediatrics, anesthesia, and hospitalists (hospital physicians who coordinate care during patients' stays with their primary physicians and other medical professionals). It operates through physician-managed regional affiliates. Investment partners and management make up Team Health Holdings, which owns about 92% of the company.

Madison Dearborn Partners and Cornerstone Equity Investors each own 36% of Team Health; Beecken Petty O'Keefe and Company owns 8% of the company.

Team Health plans to grow by obtaining business with hospitals that currently do not outsource their hospital staffing functions, and by expanding its hospitalist, pediatrics, radiology, and anesthesiology service offerings. The company also intends to grow through acquisitions.

EXECUTIVES

CEO and Director: Lynn Massingale, age 52, $1,020,193 pay
President and COO: Greg Roth, age 48
CFO: David P. Jones, age 37, $359,650 pay
EVP and General Counsel: Robert C. (Bob) Joyner, age 57, $435,693 pay
EVP, Finance and Administration: Robert J. (Bob) Abramowski, age 54, $601,943 pay
EVP, Spectrum Healthcare Resources: George Tracy
SVP, Business Development and Marketing: Michael J. Shea
SVP, HCFS: Ron Matthews
SVP, New Business Ventures Team Health Anesthesia Management Services: Robert Stiefel
SVP, Operations and Technology Integration: Randall S. Aguiar
Corporate VP, Human Resources: Lisa Courtney
Chief Compliance Officer: Stephen Sherlin, age 59, $390,857 pay
Chief Information Officer: Harry Herman
Chief Medical Officer: Gar LaSalle
Auditors: Ernst & Young LLP

LOCATIONS

HQ: Team Health, Inc.
1900 Winston Rd., Ste. 300, Knoxville, TN 37919
Phone: 865-693-1000   **Fax:** 865-539-8003
Web: www.teamhealth.com

PRODUCTS/OPERATIONS

2004 Sales

	$ mil.	% of total
Fee-for-service	1,168.1	74
Contracts	373.9	24
Other	30.2	2
Total	1,572.2	100

COMPETITORS

EmCare	RehabCare
Emergency Medical Services	Sheridan Healthcare
Per-Se Technologies	Sterling Healthcare

HISTORICAL FINANCIALS

Company Type: Private

Income Statement

FYE: December 31

	REVENUE ($ mil.)	NET INCOME ($ mil.)	NET PROFIT MARGIN	EMPLOYEES
12/04	1,572	(49)	—	5,800
12/03	1,479	(3)	—	6,700
12/02	1,231	16	1.3%	6,800
12/01	965	—	—	3,500
12/00	919	—	—	1,804
12/99	852	—	—	1,500
12/98	548	—	—	1,388
Annual Growth	19.2%	—	—	26.9%

2004 Year-End Financials

Debt ratio: —
Return on equity: —
Cash ($ mil.): 18
Current ratio: 1.50
Long-term debt ($ mil.): 413

Net Income History

Teamsters

The International Brotherhood of Teamsters is the largest and arguably most (in)famous labor union in the US. With about 1.4 million members, the Teamsters represents nearly 20 trade groups, including truckers, UPS workers, warehouse employees, cab drivers, airline workers, construction crews, and railroad workers. The union negotiates with employers for contracts that guarantee members fair wages and raises, health coverage, job security, paid time off, promotions, and other benefits. The Teamsters union has about 570 local chapters in the US and Canada.

Elected in 1998, Teamsters chief James P. Hoffa (son of assumed-dead union leader Jimmy Hoffa) is working to shed the union's notorious image and has proposed ethics policies aimed at rooting out internal corruption and ties to organized crime. Hoffa wants the Teamsters to police themselves and put an end to the close governmental supervision under which the union has operated since 1989. He also is working to re-establish the union as a power in national politics, lobbying against plans to allow trucks from Mexico to traverse US highways.

The Teamsters have packed up and moved out from under the AFL-CIO umbrella and joined fellow unions UNITE HERE (textile, hotel, and restaurant workers), Service Employees International (SEIU), United Food and Commercial Workers, and others in the rival Change to Win Coalition. The group hopes to reverse the decline of labor jobs and union membership in the US by spending time and money on recruiting rather than contributing to political campaigns.

HISTORY

Two rival team-driver unions, the Drivers International Union and the Teamsters National Union, merged to form the International Brotherhood of Teamsters in 1903. Led by Cornelius Shea, the Teamsters established headquarters in Indianapolis. Daniel Tobin (president for 45 years, starting in 1907) demanded that union locals obtain executive approval before striking. Membership expanded from the team-driver base, prompting the union to add Chauffeurs, Stablemen, and Helpers to its name (1909).

Following the first transcontinental delivery by motor truck (1912), the Teamster deliverymen traded their horses for trucks. The union then recruited food processing, brewery, and farm workers, among others, to augment Teamster effectiveness during strikes. It joined the American Federation of Labor in 1920.

Until the Depression the Teamsters was still a small union of predominantly urban deliverymen. Then Farrell Dobbs, a Trotskyite Teamster from Minneapolis, organized the famous Minneapolis strikes in 1934 to protest local management's refusal to allow the workers to unionize. Workers clashed with police and National Guard units for 11 days before management acceded to the workers' demands. The strikes demonstrated the potential strength of unions, and Teamsters membership swelled. Although union power ebbed during WWII, the union continued to grow. It moved its headquarters to Washington, DC, in 1953.

The AFL-CIO expelled the Teamsters in 1957 when Teamster ties to the mob became public during a US Senate investigation. New Teamsters boss Jimmy Hoffa eluded indictment and

took advantage of America's growing dependence on trucking to negotiate the powerful National Master Freight Agreement (1964). Hoffa also organized industrial workers. He used a union pension fund to make mob-connected loans and was later convicted of jury tampering and sent to prison. In 1975, four years after his release, Hoffa vanished without a trace and is believed to have been the victim of a Mafia hit.

The Teamsters rejoined the AFL-CIO in 1987 and the following year settled a racketeering lawsuit filed by the US Justice Department by allowing government appointees to discipline corrupt union leaders, help run the union, and oversee its elections. The election of self-styled reformer Ronald Carey in 1991 (he received 49% of the vote) seemed to portend real changes for the union; each of his six predecessors had been accused of or imprisoned for criminal activities. However, membership dropped by 40,000 in both 1991 and 1992.

Carey won re-election as union president in 1996 over rival, and son of former boss Jimmy Hoffa, James P. Hoffa (whom Carey accused of having ties to organized crime). A 15-day strike by the Teamsters' UPS employees in 1997 led to the delivery company's agreement to combine part-time jobs into 10,000 new full-time positions. That year Carey's re-election was overturned amid a campaign finance investigation that netted guilty pleas from three Carey associates, and the Teamsters leader was disqualified from running for re-election in 1998. Carey was officially expelled from the Teamsters by the federal government, and Hoffa won the 1998 election over Tom Leedham (who was backed by the union's reform wing).

Promising to fight corruption, Hoffa hired former federal prosecutor Edwin Stier and several former FBI agents to help him operate Project RISE (respect, integrity, strength, and ethics), a new in-house anti-corruption program. In 2002 the union began lobbying against plans to allow Mexican trucking companies to transport goods across the US.

In 2005 the Teamsters joined four other unions representing more than 5 million workers to call for sweeping reform in the AFL-CIO. They released a proposal to revitalize the labor movement by focusing on growth and empowerment. When AFL-CIO president John Sweeney failed to heed their calls, the Teamsters joined the Service Employees International Union in boycotting the umbrella group's annual convention and joining the Change to Win Coalition.

EXECUTIVES

General President: James P. Hoffa, age 64
General Secretary-Treasurer: C. Thomas (Tom) Keegel
VP At-Large: Randy Cammack
VP At-Large: Fred Gegare
VP At-Large: Carl E. Haynes
VP At-Large: Thomas R. O'Donnell
VP At-Large: Ralph J. Taurone
VP, Canada; President, Teamsters Canada: Robert Bouvier
VP, Canada: Joseph McLean
VP, Canada: Garnet Zimmerman
VP, Central Region: Patrick Flynn
VP, Central Region: Walter Lytle
VP, Central Region: Dotty W. Malinsky
VP, Central Region: Lester A. Singer
VP, Central Region: Philip E. Young

VP, Eastern Region: Jack Cipriani
VP, Eastern Region: Richard K. Hall
VP, Eastern Region: John Murphy
VP, Eastern Region: Richard Volpe
VP, Southern Region: Tyson Johnson
VP, Southern Region: Ken Wood
VP, Western Region: Al Hobart
VP, Western Region: Chuck Mack
VP, Western Region: Jim Santangelo
Director Information Systems: Baker Killam

LOCATIONS

HQ: International Brotherhood of Teamsters
25 Louisiana Ave. NW, Washington, DC 20001
Phone: 202-624-6800   **Fax:** 202-624-6918
Web: www.teamster.org

2005 Membership

	% of total
United States	
Central	32
East	28
West	26
South	7
Canada	7
Total	**100**

PRODUCTS/OPERATIONS

Trade Divisions

Airline
Bakery and Laundry
Brewery and Soft Drink
Building Material and Construction
Carhaul
Dairy
Food Processing
Freight
Industrial Trades
Motion Picture and Theatrical Trade
Newspaper, Magazine, and Electronic Media
Parcel and Small Package
Port
Public Services
Rail
Tankhaul
Trade Show and Convention Centers
Warehouse

HISTORICAL FINANCIALS

Company Type: Labor union

Income Statement

FYE: December 31

	REVENUE ($ mil.)	NET INCOME ($ mil.)	NET PROFIT MARGIN	EMPLOYEES
12/04	155	10	6.4%	649
12/03	149	53	35.1%	649
12/02	118	4	3.4%	—
12/01	88	(15)	—	—
12/00	90	—	—	—
12/99	90	—	—	—
12/98	90	—	—	—
12/97	89	—	—	—
12/96	90	—	—	—
12/95	90	—	—	—
Annual Growth	**6.3%**	**—**	**—**	**0.0%**

Net Income History

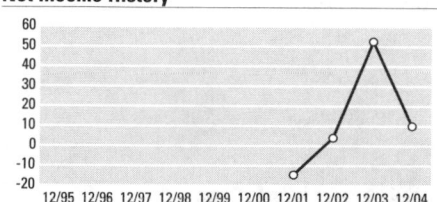

Technology Flavors & Fragrances

Technology Flavors & Fragrances (TFF) would like you to come to your senses by way of its products. Just as its name indicates, TFF makes flavors and fragrances used in a wide variety of beverages, cosmetics, foods, liquors, and pharmaceuticals. The company, founded in 1989, works with its clients to develop unique tastes and aromas for both consumer and institutional products; it has some 36,000 flavor and fragrance product formulations in its library. Formulations developed by TFF are used in more than 1,200 products sold worldwide. TFF has been acquired by industry rival FFG Industries, which is owned by investment firm Nautic Partners.

FFG completed its acquisition of 96% of TFF in June 2005 through a tender offer for TFF's common stock; it converted the remaining publicly held TFF shares into cash rights later that month, making TFF a wholly owned subsidiary. Together CEO and chairman Philip Rosner and his wife had previously owned more than 17% of the company. FFG intends to become a top provider of flavor and fragrance products.

EXECUTIVES

Chairman and CEO: Philip (Phil) Rosner, age 69, $306,973 pay
EVP and Director: A. Gary Frumberg, age 71, $264,074 pay
VP, CFO, Secretary, and Treasurer: Joseph A. Gemmo, age 59, $159,500 pay
SVP, Flavor Division: Harvey Farber, age 64, $183,600 pay
VP and Director, Fragrance Division: Virginia Bonofiglio
VP, Creative Perfumery: Richard Cerniglia
VP, Operations: Ronald J. Dintemann, age 61, $159,500 pay
Human Resources Coordinator: Dawn Fisher
Auditors: BDO Seidman, LLP

LOCATIONS

HQ: Technology Flavors & Fragrances, Inc.
10 Edison St. E., Amityville, NY 11701
Phone: 631-842-7600   **Fax:** 631-842-8332
Web: www.tffi.com

Technology Flavors & Fragrances maintains facilities in Canada, Chile, and the US.

PRODUCTS/OPERATIONS

Selected Subsidiaries
Technology Flavors and Fragrances, Inc. (Canada)
Technology Flavors and Fragrances S.A. (Chile)

COMPETITORS

BASF AG	M&F Worldwide
Bayer	McCormick
Imperial Chemical	Millennium Chemicals
Industries	Roche
International Flavors	Sensient
Kerry Group	

HISTORICAL FINANCIALS

Company Type: Private

Income Statement

FYE: December 31

	REVENUE ($ mil.)	NET INCOME ($ mil.)	NET PROFIT MARGIN	EMPLOYEES
12/04	16	(1)	—	67
12/03	16	(1)	—	63
12/02	17	1	4.2%	60
12/01	16	(1)	—	54
12/00	15	0	1.3%	61
12/99	15	1	4.7%	60
12/98	14	(2)	—	56
Annual Growth	**2.4%**	**—**	**—**	**3.0%**

2004 Year-End Financials
Debt ratio: 66.7%   Current ratio: 1.35
Return on equity: —   Long-term debt ($ mil.): 2
Cash ($ mil.): 0

Net Income History

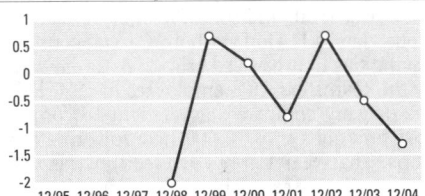

| | 12/95 | 12/96 | 12/97 | 12/98 | 12/99 | 12/00 | 12/01 | 12/02 | 12/03 | 12/04 |

Tekni-Plex

Combining packaging technology with a modicum of complexity, Tekni-Plex manufactures packaging, packaging products, and tubing products for the food, health care, and consumer industries. The company's packaging segment makes foam egg cartons, pharmaceutical blister films, poultry and meat processing trays, closure liners, foam plates, and aerosol and pump packaging components. Its tubing products division manufactures irrigation hoses, garden hoses, and pool and vacuum hoses. Tekni-Plex also makes vinyl resins and recycled PET used in a variety of industrial products. Over 85% of the company's sales are in the US. Dr. F. Patrick Smith (chairman and CEO) controls the company through Tekni-Plex Partners.

Originally the General Felt Products division of Standard Packaging Corp., the company was spun off as Tekni-Plex in 1967. The company's current management took control of Tekni-Plex in 1994.

EXECUTIVES

Chairman and CEO: F. Patrick Smith, age 56, $6,655,000 pay
President, COO, and Director: Kenneth W.R. Baker, age 60, $3,327,500 pay
VP and CFO: James E. Condon, $715,000 pay
VP, Human Resources: Joe Bruno
VP, International Sales and Marketing: Michael Franklin
Auditors: BDO Seidman, LLP

LOCATIONS

HQ: Tekni-Plex, Inc.
201 Industrial Pkwy., Somerville, NJ 08876
Phone: 908-722-4800   **Fax:** 908-722-4967
Web: www.tekni-plex.com

Tekni-Plex has manufacturing facilities in the US and in Argentina, Belgium, and Singapore.

2004 Sales

	$ mil.	% of total
US	545.6	86
Europe (primarily Belgium)	72.1	11
Canada	17.9	3
Total	**635.6**	**100**

PRODUCTS/OPERATIONS

2004 Sales

	$ mil.	% of total
Packaging	306.1	48
Tubing products	210.2	33
Other	119.3	19
Total	**635.6**	**100**

Selected Products
Consumer Packaging and Products
  Garden hose
  Irrigation hose
  Precision tubing and gaskets
Healthcare
  Blister packaging
  Cap liners and seals
  Coated film
  Co-extrusions
  Flexible film
  Laminations
  Medical tubing
  Rigid packaging film
  Semi-rigid film
  Vinyl compounds
Food Packaging
  Egg cartons
  Processor trays
Specialty Resins and Compounds
  Vinyl resins

COMPETITORS

Crown
Huntsman
Pactiv
RPC Group
Sealed Air
Smurfit-Stone Container
Sonoco Products
Teknor Apex

HISTORICAL FINANCIALS

Company Type: Private

Income Statement

FYE: Friday nearest June 30

	REVENUE ($ mil.)	NET INCOME ($ mil.)	NET PROFIT MARGIN	EMPLOYEES
6/04	636	(55)	—	3,200
6/03	611	3	0.6%	3,300
6/02	578	(7)	—	3,090
6/01	526	(19)	—	3,000
6/00	507	(21)	—	2,900
6/99	489	15	3.1%	2,950
6/98	310	9	2.8%	2,800
6/97	145	(12)	—	—
6/96	81	1	1.2%	—
6/95	45	0	0.4%	—
Annual Growth	**34.3%**	**—**	**—**	**2.3%**

2004 Year-End Financials

Debt ratio: —
Return on equity: —
Cash ($ mil.): 30

Current ratio: 3.34
Long-term debt ($ mil.): 732

Net Income History

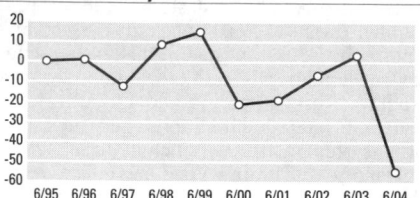

Teknor Apex

Teknor Apex is no retread. At least not any longer. Founded in 1924 as a tire distributor and retreader, Teknor Apex has sold off those assets to concentrate on chemical, plastic, and rubber. The company has eight divisions: chemicals (plasticizers and toll compounding), commercial products (floor mats and cutting boards), lawn and garden (garden hoses), rubber (custom mixing and molding of rubber compounds), specialty compounding (custom thermoplastic compound manufacturing and toll compounding of plastics compounds), Teknor Color Company (color concentrates for plastics), thermoplastic elastomers, and vinyl (custom PVC compounds). The founding Fain family owns a controlling interest.

The company is broadening its technology base as well as its graphic reach. Chem Polymer, its wholly owned subsidiary in the UK, was purchased in 2004. It makes specialty compounds for glass fiber, flame retardants, and other items. Teknor Apex is also exploring the uses of flexible PVC and alternate extrusion methods.

EXECUTIVES

President and CEO: Jonathan D. Fain
CFO: James E. Morrison
EVP and Secretary: Herbert Malin
SVP, Manufacturing: William (Bill) Murray
VP, Business Development: Robert S. Brookman
VP, Human Resources: Margaret North
VP and Business Manager, Thermoplastic Elastomer Division: Suresh Swaminathan
VP and Business Manager, Vynil Division: Lou Cappucci
VP and Business Manager, Hoses and Commercial Products: Jack McGrath
VP and Business Manager, Teknor Color Division: Jonathan C. Riley
Managing Director, Singapore Polymer Corporation: Cheah Sin Hua
Treasurer: Edward Massoud
Manager, Corporate Marketing Communications: Sandra L. (Sandy) Hopkins

LOCATIONS

HQ: Teknor Apex Company
505 Central Ave., Pawtucket, RI 02861
Phone: 401-725-8000   **Fax:** 401-725-8095
Web: www.teknorapex.com

Teknor Apex has operations in Singapore and the UK as well as in California, Florida, Kentucky, Massachusetts, Ohio, Rhode Island, South Carolina, Tennessee, Texas, and Vermont.

PRODUCTS/OPERATIONS

Selected Products and Services

Chemicals and Colorants
   Color concentrates
   Custom compounds
   Dry colors
   High-performance colors
   Plasticizers (trimellitates, adipates, phthalates, sebacates, and azelates)
   Pulverized colors
   PVC compounds
   Thermoplastic elastomers
Floor Mats and Cutting Boards
   Anti-fatigue floor matting
   Food cutting boards
   Industrial die-cutting pads
   Industrial hoses
   Spray nozzles
Garden Hose Products
   Cord, hose, and rope organizers
   Residential and commercial hoses
Rubber Products
   Custom rubber mixing
   Custom rubber molding

COMPETITORS

Advanced Elastomer
Atlantis Plastics
BASF AG
DuPont
GLS
Huntsman
PMC Global
PolyOne
R-B Rubber
Spartech
Tekni-Plex
Vulcan International
Yule Catto

HISTORICAL FINANCIALS

Company Type: Private

Income Statement

FYE: July 31

	REVENUE ($ mil.)	NET INCOME ($ mil.)	NET PROFIT MARGIN	EMPLOYEES
7/04	500	—	—	1,800
7/03	430	—	—	2,100
7/02	400	—	—	2,400
Annual Growth	**11.8%**	—	—	**(13.4%)**

Revenue History

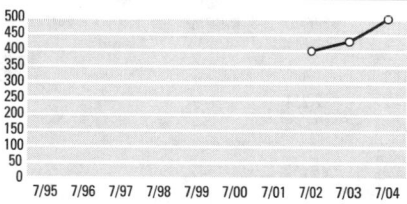

Telex Communications

Telex Communications makes sure its customers' voices are heard. The company makes audio and communications equipment for commercial, professional, and industrial customers — its sound systems can be heard in venues from the New York Metropolitan Opera to Wrigley Field. Telex derives more than 80% of its sales from professional audio products, which include speakers, microphones, and mixing consoles. The remaining revenue comes from audio and wireless products, such as military and aviation headsets. Telex was founded in 1936 as a hearing aid manufacturing company.

EXECUTIVES

Chairman: Brian P. Friedman, age 49
President, CEO, and Director: Raymond V. Malpocher, age 59, $349,316 pay
VP and CFO: Gregory W. Richter, age 43, $202,693 pay
VP and General Counsel: Kristine L. Bruer, age 54, $162,439 pay
VP, Finance: Leigh P. Hart, age 44
VP, Human Resources: Kathleen A. Curran, age 53, $151,384 pay
VP, Intercom Systems Group: Ralph K. Strader, age 51
VP, North American Operations: Terrence E. Martin, age 48
President, Audio and Wireless Technology: Thomas J. (Tom) Kulikowski, age 47
President, Worldwide Professional Audio: Mathias von Heydekampf, age 42, $278,668 pay
Auditors: Ernst & Young LLP

LOCATIONS

HQ: Telex Communications, Inc.
12000 Portland Ave. South, Burnsville, MN 55337
Phone: 952-884-4051   **Fax:** 952-884-0043
Web: www.telex.com

Telex Communications has operations in France, Germany, Hong Kong, Japan, Mexico, Singapore, the UK, and the US.

2004 Sales

	$ mil.	% of total
US	148.8	50
Europe	84.7	29
Asia	41.5	14
Other regions	21.8	7
Total	**296.8**	**100**

PRODUCTS/OPERATIONS

2004 Sales

	$ mil.	% of total
Professional audio	240.5	81
Audio & wireless technology	56.3	19
Total	**296.8**	**100**

Selected Products

Antennas	Intercoms
Assistive listening systems	Microphones
Audio duplication	Military aviation products
Auditory trainers	Paging systems
BTE receivers	Projectors
Computer audio	Vega signaling products
Conference phones	Signal Processing
Consoles	Sound field amplification
Digital conversion	Speakers
Electronics	Wireless LAN antennas
Headsets	

COMPETITORS

Bose	Shure
Eminence	Sony
Harman International	TEAC
Peavey Electronics	Yamaha

HISTORICAL FINANCIALS

Company Type: Private

Income Statement

FYE: December 31

	REVENUE ($ mil.)	NET INCOME ($ mil.)	NET PROFIT MARGIN	EMPLOYEES
12/04	297	(5)	—	1,838
12/03	269	(8)	—	1,900
12/02	267	(30)	—	1,983
12/01	285	61	21.4%	2,331
12/00	329	(18)	—	2,660
12/99	344	(22)	—	2,978
12/98	246	(5)	—	2,845
12/97	333	(51)	—	2,979
Annual Growth	(1.6%)	—	—	(6.7%)

2004 Year-End Financials

Debt ratio: —
Return on equity: —
Cash ($ mil.): 15
Current ratio: 2.86
Long-term debt ($ mil.): 197

Net Income History

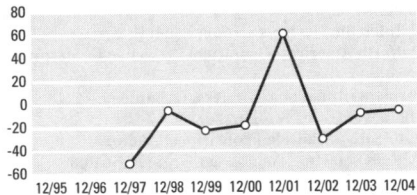

Tenaska

Tenaska is tenacious when it comes to producing and selling energy. The employee-owned company is a top natural gas marketer in the US; it also trades and markets electricity and develops, owns, operates, and maintains power plants, mostly in the Americas. Tenaska has interests in primarily gas-fired and hydroelectric generation facilities (some of which are under construction) that give it 7,600 MW of capacity. It also develops plants for third parties, providing engineering and construction, site development, financing, and management services. Other operations include fuel supply, power transmission, and gas transportation contracting. Tenaska was founded in 1987 by CEO Howard Hawks and EVP Thomas Hendricks.

EXECUTIVES

Chairman and CEO: Howard L. Hawks
CFO: Jerry K. Crouse
EVP: Thomas E. Hendricks
EVP and Chief Strategy and Legal Officer: Ronald N. Quinn
EVP Engineering, Construction, and Operations: Michael C. (Mike) Lebens
EVP and Treasurer: Michael F. (Mike) Lawler

VP and Managing Director, Tenaska-Oxy Power Services: Keith E. Emery
VP Asset Management: Todd Jonas
VP Development: David G. Fiorelli
VP Development: Ronald R. Tanner
VP Engineering and Construction: Nicholas N. Borman
Director Government and Public Affairs: Jana M. Martin

LOCATIONS

HQ: Tenaska, Inc.
1044 N. 115th St., Ste. 400, Omaha, NE 68154
Phone: 402-691-9500   **Fax:** 402-691-9575
Web: www.tenaska.com

Tenaska owns operating power projects in Alabama, Georgia, Oklahoma, Texas, Virginia, and Washington in the US, as well as in Bolivia and Pakistan.

PRODUCTS/OPERATIONS

Selected Subsidiaries

Tenaska Energy Holdings, LLC
Tenaska Energy, Inc.
Tenaska Marketing Canada (gas marketing)
Tenaska Marketing Ventures (gas marketing)
Tenaska Operations, Inc. (asset management)
Tenaska Power Fund (acquisitions)
Tenaska Power Services Co. (power marketing)

COMPETITORS

AES
BP
Calpine
Chevron
Cinergy
ConocoPhillips
Covanta
Edison Mission Energy
El Paso
Exxon Mobil
International Power
Mirant
National Energy & Gas Transmission
NRG Energy
Reliant Energy
Sempra Energy
Shell
Sithe Energies
Texas Genco

HISTORICAL FINANCIALS

Company Type: Private

Income Statement

FYE: December 31

	REVENUE ($ mil.)	NET INCOME ($ mil.)	NET PROFIT MARGIN	EMPLOYEES
12/03	5,600	—	—	475
12/02	2,231	—	—	460
12/01	2,665	—	—	450
Annual Growth	45.0%	—	—	2.7%

Revenue History

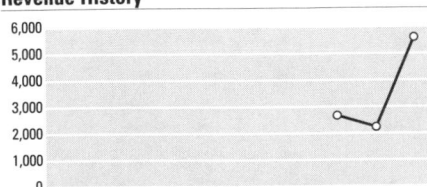

Texas A&M

Everything is bigger in Texas, even its universities. With about 100,000 students at nine institutions, The Texas A&M University System ranks among the largest in the US. Its flagship school at College Station is well-known not only for its programs in engineering and agriculture, but also for its long-held traditions and school spirit. Other system institutions include Tarleton State University and Prairie View A&M. The system also runs state extension agencies and a health sciences center. Texas A&M was founded in 1876 as the Agricultural and Mechanical College of Texas. The A&M system was formed in 1948; it is funded in part by a $7.7 billion state endowment (shared with the University of Texas).

Texas A&M in College Station is the largest campus in the university system, with an enrollment of about 44,000 students. Its campus is home to the George Bush Presidential Library Center, which opened in 1997.

At about 2,000 members, A&M's Corps of Cadets (commonly referred to as "the Corps") remains the largest uniformed body of students in the nation outside the US service academies.

In the wake of a bonfire collapse which took the lives of 12 students in 1999, Texas A&M has been charged by outsiders with trying to conceal its own involvement in the accident. Still others have called on Texas A&M to loosen some of its traditions. However, the school, students, and alumni have all stood fast against the tide of pressure. Texas A&M has embarked on a 20-year mission to renovate its facilities and secure status as a top public university.

HISTORY

The Texas Constitution of 1876 created an agricultural and mechanical college and stated that "separate schools shall be provided for the white and colored children, and impartial provisions shall be made for both." The white school, the Agricultural and Mechanical College of Texas (later Texas A&M), began instruction that year. Texas A&M was a men's school at first, and membership in its Corps of Cadets was mandatory. The Agricultural and Mechanical College of Texas for Colored Youth (later Prairie View A&M) opened in 1878.

To help fund the agricultural colleges and The University of Texas, the Legislature established the Permanent University Fund in 1876 to hold more than 1 million acres of land in West Texas as an endowment. An additional million acres was added in 1883. The Santa Rita well on the university land struck oil in 1923 and money flowed into the Permanent University Fund's coffers. Under the provisions of the constitution, The University of Texas got two-thirds of the income, and A&M got the rest.

In 1948 The Texas A&M College System was established to oversee Texas A&M, Prairie View A&M, Tarleton State, and Arlington State (which left the system in 1965 and is now The University of Texas at Arlington). By 1963 enrollment system-wide had reached 8,000. That year the system changed its name to The Texas A&M University System, the same year that Texas A&M went co-ed.

By the mid-1980s enrollment had surpassed 35,000 students. The system grew quickly in 1989 when it added Texas A&I University (now Texas A&M University-Kingsville), Corpus Christi State (now Texas A&M University-Corpus Christi), and Laredo State University (now Texas A&M International). West Texas State College in Canyon joined the system in 1990 and became West Texas A&M University in 1993.

The 91-year-old Baylor College of Dentistry (in Dallas) and East Texas State University, well known for training future teachers, joined the A&M system in 1996 (East Texas State was divided into Texas A&M University-Commerce and Texas A&M-Texarkana). In 1997 the system opened the first portion of the $82 million George Bush Presidential Library and Museum.

In early 1998 the system signed an alliance with the private South Texas College of Law in Houston, which was opposed by the Texas Higher Education Coordinating Board. (In 1999 a judge ruled that the two schools had to discontinue their affiliation.) That year Texas Instruments donated $5.1 million to the system (one of the largest donations in the institution's history) for the creation of an analog technology program. Chancellor Barry Thompson announced he would retire in 1999. The system appointed former Army general Howard Graves as the new chancellor (he died in September 2003).

Tragedy struck the College Station campus in 1999 when logs being stacked for the annual bonfire celebrating The University of Texas/Texas A&M football game collapsed and killed 12 people. Clinging to the 90-year tradition, many Aggies past and present insisted the bonfire go on in future years.

Texas A&M University has established "Vision 2020," an initiative to become a consensus top-10 public university by the year 2020.

EXECUTIVES

Chairman, Board of Regents: L. Lowry Mays, age 70
Vice Chairman, Board of Regents: Erle Nye, age 68
Chancellor: Robert D. (Bob) McTeer Jr., age 62
Deputy Chancellor: Jerry Gatson
General Counsel: Delmar Cain
Vice Chancellor of Governmental Relations: Stanton C. Calvert
Vice Chancellor of Administration: James A. Fletcher
Vice Chancellor of Business Services: Tom D. Kale
Vice Chancellor of Research and Federal Relations: Kenneth L. Peddicord
Vice Chancellor of Academic and Student Affairs: Leo Sayavedra
Chief Auditor: Catherine A. (Cathy) Smock
Director of Communications: Bob Wright
Associate Vice Chancellor and Treasurer: Gregory R. Anderson
Comptroller: Sandra K. Brown
Auditors: Texas State Auditor

LOCATIONS

HQ: The Texas A&M University System
A&M System Bldg., 200 Technology Way, Ste. 2043, College Station, TX 77845
Phone: 979-458-6000   **Fax:** 979-458-6044
Web: tamusystem.tamu.edu

PRODUCTS/OPERATIONS

Selected Texas A&M University System Components

Health Science Center
Baylor College of Dentistry
College of Medicine
Graduate School of Biomedical Sciences
Institute of Biosciences and Technology
School of Rural Public Health

State Agencies
Texas Agricultural Experiment Station
Texas Cooperative Extension
Texas Engineering Experiment Station
Texas Engineering Extension Service
Texas Forest Service
Texas Transportation Institute
Texas Veterinary Medical Diagnostic Laboratory
Universities
Prairie View A&M University
Tarleton State University
Texas A&M International University
Texas A&M University
Texas A&M University-Commerce
Texas A&M University-Corpus Christi
Texas A&M University-Kingsville
Texas A&M University-Texarkana
West Texas A&M University

COMPETITORS

Florida A&M University
University of Houston
University of Texas

HISTORICAL FINANCIALS

Company Type: School

Income Statement

	REVENUE ($ mil.)	NET INCOME ($ mil.)	NET PROFIT MARGIN	EMPLOYEES
8/04	1,323	(882)	—	24,500
8/03	1,257	—	—	38,500
8/02	2,254	—	—	25,000
8/01	1,928	—	—	24,000
8/00	2,620	—	—	23,000
8/99	1,792	—	—	23,000
8/98	1,695	—	—	23,300
8/97	1,550	—	—	22,800
8/96	1,425	—	—	22,600
8/95	1,299	—	—	20,000
Annual Growth	0.2%	—	—	2.3%

FYE: August 31

Revenue History

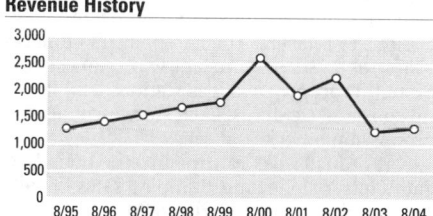

Former CenterPoint Energy subsidiary Reliant Resources had the option to purchase CenterPoint Energy's stake in Texas Genco in January 2004, but it decided not to exercise the option. After pursuing other options to divest its interest in Texas Genco, CenterPoint Energy has agreed to sell the unit to a consortium of investment firms for $3.65 billion; Texas Genco will first buy out its public shareholders.

The company will increase its stake in STP Nuclear to 44% by purchasing shares from AEP for $174 million.

EXECUTIVES

Chairman and CEO: Jack Fusco, age 43
CFO: Hamsa Shadaksharappa
EVP, Business Development and Strategic Planning: Thad Hill, age 37
EVP and Chief Legal Officer: Thad Miller, age 54
Investor Relations Contact: Neil Yekell
EVP, Human Resources: Margery M. (Margie) Harris, age 44
Investor Relations: Marianne Paulsen
Director, Corporate Communications: Joe Householder
Media Contact: Leticia Lowe
Auditors: Deloitte & Touche LLP

LOCATIONS

HQ: Texas Genco Inc.
12301 Kurland Dr., Houston, TX 77034
Phone: 713-795-6000
Web: txgenco.com

COMPETITORS

AEP
Duke Energy
Dynegy
El Paso Marketing
Mirant
National Energy
& Gas Transmission
Panda Energy
PSEG
Tenaska
TXU

HISTORICAL FINANCIALS

Company Type: Private

Income Statement

	REVENUE ($ mil.)	NET INCOME ($ mil.)	NET PROFIT MARGIN	EMPLOYEES
12/04	2,054	(99)	—	1,564
12/03	2,002	250	12.5%	1,511
12/02	1,541	(93)	—	1,639
12/01	3,411	128	3.8%	1,650
12/00	3,334	172	5.2%	—
12/99	2,816	(293)	—	—
Annual Growth	(6.1%)	—	—	(1.8%)

FYE: December 31

2004 Year-End Financials

Debt ratio: 0.0%   Current ratio: 1.04
Return on equity: —   Long-term debt ($ mil.): 0
Cash ($ mil.): 23

Net Income History

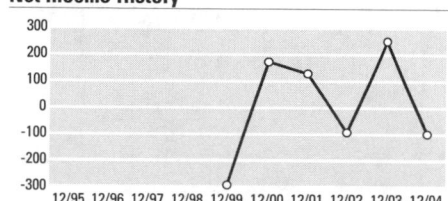

Texas Genco

From the get-go, Texas Genco aims to be a major producer of electricity in the Lone Star State. The company has interests in power plants across Texas that give it a generating capacity of more than 14,000 MW. Most of Texas Genco's plants are fossil-fueled; the firm also owns a 31% stake in the STP Nuclear facility. Texas Genco sells its power to wholesale customers in the state's newly deregulated market. The company has temporarily shut down about 3,000 MW of capacity due to low market demand. Parent CenterPoint Energy (formerly Reliant Energy) spun off 19% of Texas Genco to shareholders in 2003. Texas Genco filed an initial public offering in 2005.

Texas Health Resources

Texas Health Resources is takin' care of Texas with about 25 health care facilities in the Dallas/Fort Worth and North Texas region. Formed in 1997 by the merger of Harris Methodist Health System, Presbyterian Healthcare System, and Arlington Memorial Hospital Foundation, the not-for-profit system includes more than a dozen tertiary and acute-care hospitals, mental health centers, a retirement community, senior care centers, and home health services. Texas Health Resources' network includes more than 3,200 physicians and some 2,400 beds. The company's Texas Health Research Institute provides clinical studies management, medical device testing, and medical training services.

In order to keep up with the growing population of North Texas, Texas Health Resources is undergoing a $1.5 billion expansion of its facilities over a 10-year period.

EXECUTIVES

President and CEO: Douglas D. Hawthorne
EVP and CFO: Ron Bourland
EVP, Corporate Affairs: Margaret H. Jordan
EVP, Operations: Stephen C. (Steve) Hanson
EVP, People and Culture: Bonnie Bell
EVP; President, Arlington Memorial Hospital:
 Oscar L. Amparan
EVP, Strategy and System Development: Dave Ashworth
VP, Patient Care: Bob Lumpkins, age 54
CIO: David S. Muntz
Public Relations Manager: Kent Best

LOCATIONS

HQ: Texas Health Resources Inc.
 611 Ryan Plaza Dr., Ste. 900, Arlington, TX 76011
Phone: 817-462-7900   **Fax:** 817-462-6996
Web: www.texashealth.org

Selected Hospitals

Arlington Memorial Hospital (Arlington, TX)
Harris Methodist Erath County (Stephenville, TX)
Harris Methodist Fort Worth
Harris Methodist H-E-B (Bedford, TX)
Harris Methodist Northwest (Azle, TX)
Harris Methodist Southwest (Fort Worth, TX)
Harris Methodist Walls Regional Hospital (Cleburne, TX)
Presbyterian Hospital of Allen
Presbyterian Hospital of Dallas
Presbyterian Hospital of Kaufman
Presbyterian Hospital of Plano
Presbyterian Hospital of Winnsboro

COMPETITORS

Baylor Health
HCA
Triad Hospitals
VHA

HISTORICAL FINANCIALS

Company Type: Not-for-profit

Income Statement

FYE: December 31

	REVENUE ($ mil.)	NET INCOME ($ mil.)	NET PROFIT MARGIN	EMPLOYEES
12/03	1,900	—	—	16,800
12/02	1,700	—	—	16,500
12/01	1,500	—	—	16,000
12/00	1,340	—	—	16,000
12/99	1,291	—	—	15,000
12/98	1,286	—	—	15,000
12/97	1,250	—	—	15,000
Annual Growth	**7.2%**	**—**		**1.9%**

Revenue History

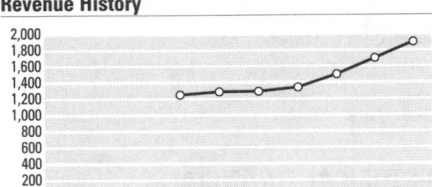

Texas Lottery

The Texas Lottery Commission hopes to have the eyes of Texans watching the lotto jackpot. The Texas Lottery Commission oversees one of the country's largest state lotteries, which has pumped more than $12 billion into state coffers since its inaugural in 1991. About 58% of lottery sales are paid out in prize money, while 30% goes to the state's Foundation School Fund; the remainder covers administration costs and commissions to retailers. The lottery offers numbers games and several instant-win games sold through grocery stores, gas stations, and liquor and convenience stores. Each store earns a small commission on tickets it sells.

A bit of luster has returned to the Lone Star State's lottery following slumping sales in 1998 and again in 2000. In 2004 and 2005 the lottery contributed more than $1 billion to the Foundation School Fund. However, lottery officials say certain lottery games will need continued tweaking to maintain consumer interest and that steady growth in sales cannot be guaranteed.

The Texas Lottery Commission offers numbers games (Lotto Texas, Pick 3, Cash 5, and Texas Two Step) in addition to Mega Millions, a multistate lottery game. Instant-win games are scratch-off cards sold under names like Super Lucky 7's, Blackjack Doubler, and Deuces Wild. The lottery commission also has a division that supervises charitable bingo games in the state of Texas.

HISTORY

A state lottery had been an issue in Texas for years before it was discussed in earnest in the mid-1980s. Falling oil and gas revenue had plunged the state into a recession, raising the specter of tax increases. In 1985 the state budget had a shortfall of $1 billion; that figure tripled by 1987. Adding fuel to the fire, the Texas Supreme Court ruled in 1989 that Texas had to change the way it funded public schools to avoid penalizing poor school districts. The ruling forced the state to seek new sources of revenue. In 1991 Gov. Ann Richards called a special session of the legislature to deal with the fiscal crisis, and House Bill 54 was passed, creating the state lottery. The measure was approved by 64% of voters.

In May 1992 Richards bought the symbolic first ticket at an Austin feed store (it was not a winner). Fourteen hours later Texans had spent nearly $23 million on tickets — breaking the California Lottery's first-day sales record — and had won $10 million in prizes. More than 102 million tickets were sold the first week. GTECH Holdings was awarded a five-year contract that year for lotto operations. Lotto Texas started in November with a winner taking nearly $22 million. By the end of the year, lotto sales in Texas had topped $1 billion. In its first 15 months, it contributed $812 million to the state's coffers.

In March 1994 five winners split a record $77 million jackpot. By that autumn sales from the lottery's beginning had surpassed $5 billion. In November a Mansfield, Texas, gas station owner picked up the largest single-winner jackpot, $54 million. By the end of 1994, Texas had the largest state lottery in the US. Cumulative sales topped $8 billion in mid-1995. In its first 37 months of operation, the Texas Lottery contributed $2.5 billion to the state's general fund. Cash 5 debuted that year, and instant ticket vending machines were installed at some sites.

In 1996 lottery director Nora Linares was dismissed following allegations that one of her friends received $30,000 from GTECH as a "hunting consultant." When a GTECH official was convicted in New Jersey of taking kickbacks from a lobbyist, questions were raised concerning payments to GTECH's Texas lobbyist, former Texas Lt. Gov. Ben Barnes. In 1997 Texas canceled its contract with GTECH to operate the lottery through 2002 and reopened bidding; GTECH filed suit to enforce the contract. Executive director Lawrence Littwin later was dismissed by the commission. Littwin sued GTECH, claiming the company had gotten him fired (the case was settled in 1999). Linda Cloud, his replacement, reinstated GTECH's contract. That year the Texas Legislature voted to increase the amount going to the state and to reduce prize payouts.

Lottery sales fell sharply in 1998, due in part to the reduced prize money. To combat suffering sales, the legislature reversed itself the next year and restored the level of prize payouts. The commission proposed lengthening the odds of winning to create larger jackpots, but public outcry scuttled the plan. In 2000 the commission agreed to change the wording on its scratch tickets after a San Antonio College professor and his students argued that breaking even is not winning.

The following year it introduced its first new lottery game in about three years, Texas Two Step, and discontinued Texas Million following slumping sales. It also changed its Lotto Texas game so that customers must match six numbers out of 54 numbers instead of 50. The extra four numbers changed the odds of winning from about one in 16 million to one in 26 million. The game was changed again in 2003 to a two-field game where players first select five numbers out of 44, and then select one number from a second field of 44. The new game has changed the odds of winning the jackpot to one in 48 million, while the odds of winning any prize have changed from one in 71 to one in 57.

HISTORICAL FINANCIALS

Company Type: Government-owned

Income Statement

FYE: August 31

	REVENUE ($ mil.)	NET INCOME ($ mil.)	NET PROFIT MARGIN	EMPLOYEES
8/02	2,966	64	2.2%	—
8/01	2,826	87	3.1%	—
8/00	2,658	(116)	—	335
8/99	3,156	(118)	—	300
8/98	3,106	1,213	39.0%	335
8/97	3,761	1,421	37.8%	304
8/96	3,449	1,101	31.9%	325
8/95	3,052	1,014	33.2%	325
8/94	2,772	932	33.6%	325
8/93	1,863	660	35.4%	325
Annual Growth	5.3%	(22.8%)	—	0.4%

Net Income History

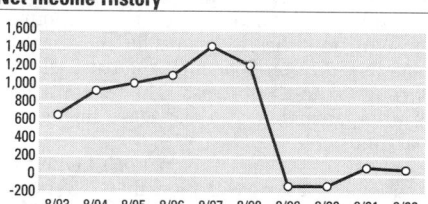

Texas Pacific Group

Yee-hah! Let's round us up some LBOs! Texas Pacific Group (TPG) has staked its claim on the buyout frontier with a reputation for roping in companies other investors wouldn't touch with a 10-foot pole. TPG, an active investor with over $20 billion under management, often takes control of the companies in which it invests. The firm is generally interested in resuscitating well-known consumer and *luxe* brands that have fallen on hard times. Investments have included stakes in technology (Seagate Technology, ON Semiconductor), consumer franchises/products (Burger King, Ducati), retailers (J. Crew, Petco), airlines (Continental, America West), and entertainment (Metro-Goldwyn-Mayer).

Despite its name, the company has invested extensively in Europe, where deals have included the turnaround of Punch Taverns. Recent European investments include UK retailer Debenhams (with CVC Capital Partners); restaurant, pub, and hotel chain Scottish & Newcastle (with CVC and Blackstone Group); Gate Gourmet (the world's second largest airline caterer); German bathroom fixtures manufacturer Grohe Water Technology; and luxury brand Bally Management. It has also agreed to buy (with Apax Partners) a controlling stake in Greek wireless operator TIM Hellas Telecommunications SA for about $1.4 billion.

It isn't always sunshine and flowers for TPG — the firm has encountered some recent setbacks: Magellan Heath Services' Chapter 11 agreement gave TPG a 2% share in the firm after reorganization (worth about $17 million); TPG had originally invested some $60 million in the firm. Bally, stunted by a slump in the luxury goods industry, is struggling to return TPG's investment as well.

Early in 2005, TPG and six other private investment companies (led by Silver Lake Partners) agreed to acquire SunGard Data Systems for $11.3 billion; the largest buyout since RJR Nabisco. TPG also bought a stake in computer maker Lenovo — which recently acquired IBM's PC business — and was part of a consortium that acquired Metro-Goldwyn-Mayer in a $4.9 billion deal. TPG's $2.35 billion bid for Enron subsidiary Portland General Electric was rejected by state regulators, however, and TPG abandoned its pursuit soon after. Around the same time, TPG's sweetened $1.3 billion bid for British Vita PLC, the UK's largest maker of foam rubber, was accepted. In May 2005 it was announced that TPG and Warburg Pincus had agreed to buy retailer Neiman Marcus for about $5.1 billion. Late in 2005 a consortium made up of Blackstone Group, Hellman & Friedman, Kohlberg Kravis Roberts, and Texas Pacific Group agreed to sell Texas Genco (which it acquired for $3.65 billion in 2004) to NRG Energy for $5.8 billion ($4 billion in cash and $1.8 billion in stock).

Co-founder and partner David "Bondo" Bonderman is known for turning around Continental Airlines. TPG usually holds onto a company for at least five years, although consistent moneymakers may be kept indefinitely.

HISTORY

The story of Texas Pacific Group is largely the story of David "Bondo" Bonderman. The magna cum laude Harvard law grad — an ardent Democrat and former law professor — built a reputation as an adviser who helped Texas billionaire Robert Bass rack up triple-digit returns.

After a decade with Bass, Bonderman struck out on his own in 1992. James Coulter, recruited to the Bass organization out of Stanford University's business school, went with him. William Price, a former Bain & Company consultant who advised Bonderman on some of his Bass deals, joined them, as did Richard Schifter (airlines background) and David Stanton (technology expertise).

Bonderman raised eyebrows in 1993 when TPG affiliate Air Partners recapitalized Continental Airlines, then in its second bankruptcy. At the time the airline industry was losing billions, and Bonderman was a little-known quantity. After an extensive restructuring and management shakeup, Bonderman turned Continental into the US's #5 airline, logging record profits for four consecutive quarters.

This type of deal would become Bonderman's modus operandi: jumping into troubled waters shunned by others, turning the company around, then (often) selling his interest for a profit. Of the head-rolling that frequently occurs after buyouts, Bonderman once said, "Generally speaking, you like to dance with the girl that brung you, and if you can't, sometimes you have to shoot her." In 1994 Bonderman worked his magic with America West Airlines. As with Continental, TPG sold shares in a second offering that made millions.

In 1997 TPG bought Paradyne and its GlobeSpan technology from Lucent (later taking it public in 1999). TPG also bought Del Monte Foods, the world's #1 maker of canned fruits and vegetables (later taking it public in 1999).

Bonderman and Air Partners in 1998 sold their interest in Continental to Northwest Airlines. Following its strategy of buying turnarounds, TPG threw lifelines to HMO Oxford Health Plans (1998) and Magellan Health Services (1999).

The group jumped into a European investment hotbed, taking a majority stake in Punch Taverns Group, which bought 3,600 pubs from Allied Domecq (TPG sold its Punch stake in 2003). In 1999 TPG bought the Bally fashion house and a stake in Italian scooter maker Piaggio. In 2000 TPG bought a 22% stake in French smart-card maker Gemplus and netted more than $1 billion by selling a large portion of its GlobeSpan stake (TPG's original investment was about $5 million).

In 2002 TPG took off and picked up Gate Gourmet, an airline catering company, from the bankrupt Switzerland-based Swissair Group. It also smelled a good deal and bought Burger King Corporation. TPG raked in a hefty profit in 2003 when Hotwire, in which it held a 30% stake, was acquired by InterActiveCorp.

TPG did a lot of liquidating in 2004, unloading its remaining stakes in Del Monte, Petco, Paradyne, Denbury, and Belden and Blake.

In brighter 2005 news, a consortium consisting of TPG, Comcast, Sony, Providence Equity Partners, and DLJ Merchant Banking Partners completed a $4.9 billion acquisition of MGM.

EXECUTIVES

Managing Partner: David Bonderman, age 63
Managing Partner: Jim Coulter, age 45
Managing Partner: Bill Price, age 49
CFO: John Viola
Partner, Investor Relations: Jamie Gates
Partner, European Portfolio Companies:
  Vincenzo Morelli
Partner, Operations: Dick Boyce
Partner: Vivek Paul, age 46
Managing Director, UK: Philippe Costeletos
Managing Director, UK: Andrew Dechet
Managing Director, UK: Stephen Peel
**General Partner, TPG Ventures for European
  Investment:** Badri Nathan
General Counsel: David Spuria

LOCATIONS

HQ: Texas Pacific Group
  301 Commerce St., Ste. 3300,
  Fort Worth, TX 76102
Phone: 817-871-4000   **Fax:** 817-871-4001

Texas Pacific Group has offices in Fort Worth, Texas;
San Francisco; and London.

PRODUCTS/OPERATIONS

Selected Holdings

Bally Management
Burger King Corporation
Debenhams
Ducati Motor SpA
Eutelsat
Gate Gourmet
GlobeSpan
Grohe Water Technology AG
IASIS Healthcare Corporation
Isola GmbH
J. Crew Group Inc.
KRATON Polymers Corp.
MEMC
Metro-Goldwyn-Mayer
ON Semiconductor
Piaggio
Quintiles Transnational
Scottish & Newcastle plc
Seagate

COMPETITORS

AEA Investors
Apollo Advisors
Berkshire Hathaway
Blackstone Group
Carlyle Group
CD&R
Goldman Sachs
Haas Wheat
Heico
Hicks Muse
Jordan Company
Kelso & Company
Keystone
KKR
Oaktree Capital
Sevin Rosen
Silver Lake Partners
Thomas H. Lee Partners
Wingate Partners

HISTORICAL FINANCIALS

Company Type: Partnership

Income Statement

FYE: December 31

	REVENUE ($ mil.)	NET INCOME ($ mil.)	NET PROFIT MARGIN	EMPLOYEES
12/04	125	—	—	9,900

Thrivent Financial

The Spirit moved Aid Association for Lutherans (AAL) to merge with Lutheran Brotherhood and form a new entity, christened Thrivent Financial for Lutherans. The fraternal benefit society now includes nearly 3 million members, and brings under one steepled roof some $65 billion in assets under management in mutual funds, bank and trust services (AAL Bank and Trust and LB Community Bank & Trust merged into Thrivent Financial Bank), and other financial services. Thrivent Financial, which operates all over the US, also has more than $155 billion in life insurance in force. The company also funds the Thrivent Financial for Lutherans Foundation, which contributed more than $6 million in 2004 to charitable causes.

EXECUTIVES

Chairman, President, and CEO: Bruce J. Nicholson, age 58
EVP and Chief Administrative Officer:
  Jon M. Stellmacher
EVP Marketing and Products: Pamela J. (Pam) Moret
SVP: David Francis
SVP and CIO: Larry Robbins
SVP and Chief Investment Officer:
  Russell W. (Russ) Swansen
SVP Finance and Treasurer:
  Randall L. (Randy) Boushek
SVP Business Development: Nikki Sorum
SVP Communications: Marie A. Uhrich
SVP Field Distribution: James A. (Jim) Thomsen
SVP Financial Services Operations:
  David (Dave) Anderson
SVP Fraternal Industry Relations: Frederick A. Ohlde
SVP Fraternal Operations: Bradford L. (Brad) Hewitt
SVP Human Resources: Jennifer H. Martin, age 57
Auditors: Ernst & Young LLP

LOCATIONS

HQ: Thrivent Financial for Lutherans
  625 4th Ave. South, Minneapolis, MN 55415
Phone: 800-847-4836
Web: www.thrivent.com

PRODUCTS/OPERATIONS

2004 Sales

	$ mil.	% of total
Net investment income	2,194	49
Insurance revenue	1,786	40
Net realized investment gains	269	6
Other	220	5
Total	**4,469**	**100**

COMPETITORS

American Express
Citigroup
FMR
MetLife
Modern Woodmen
New York Life
Security Benefit Group
State Farm
TIAA-CREF

HISTORICAL FINANCIALS

Company Type: Not-for-profit

Income Statement

FYE: December 31

	ASSETS ($ mil.)	NET INCOME ($ mil.)	INCOME AS % OF ASSETS	EMPLOYEES
12/04	56,750	488	0.9%	2,676
12/03	52,667	252	0.5%	2,979
12/02	47,892	(292)	—	3,420
12/01	23,478	139	0.6%	3,733
12/00	22,112	228	1.0%	2,086
12/99	21,158	226	1.1%	3,914
12/98	19,418	134	0.7%	1,751
12/97	17,975	210	1.2%	1,596
12/96	16,671	130	0.8%	1,559
Annual Growth	**16.5%**	**18.0%**	**—**	**7.0%**

2004 Year-End Financials

Equity as % of assets: 11.7%   Long-term debt ($ mil.): —
Return on assets: 0.9%   Sales ($ mil.): 4,469
Return on equity: 7.6%

Net Income History

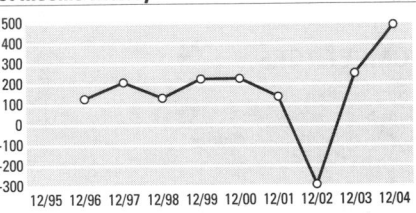

TIAA-CREF

It's punishment enough to write the name once on a blackboard. Teachers Insurance and Annuity Association — College Retirement Equities Fund (TIAA-CREF) is one of the largest, if not longest-named, private retirement systems in the US, providing for more than 3 million members of the academic community and for investors outside academia's ivied confines. It also serves some 15,000 institutional investors. TIAA-CREF's core offerings include financial advice, investment information, retirement accounts, pensions, annuities, individual life and disability insurance, tuition financing, and trust services (through TIAA-CREF Trust). The system, a non-profit organization, also manages a line of mutual funds.

TIAA-CREF — one of the nation's heftiest institutional investors, with more than $350 billion in assets under management — has not been afraid to throw its weight around corporate boardrooms. The organization is known for active and choosy investing and is a vocal critic of extravagant executive compensation packages. With an increasing share of its investment assets overseas, TIAA-CREF is also leading the crusade for global corporate governance standards. (TIAA-CREF faced its own corporate governance issue in 2004, when two directors stepped down after it was revealed they had a business relationship with the company's auditor, Ernst & Young.)

HISTORY

With $15 million, the Carnegie Foundation for the Advancement of Teaching in 1905 founded the Teachers Insurance and Annuity Association (TIAA) in New York City to provide retirement benefits and other forms of financial security to educators. When Carnegie's original endowment was found to be insufficient, another $1 million reorganized the fund into a defined-contribution plan in 1918. TIAA was the first portable pension plan, letting participants change employers without losing benefits and offering a fixed annuity. The fund required infusions of Carnegie cash until 1947.

In 1952 TIAA CEO William Greenough pioneered the variable annuity, based on common stock investments, and created the College Retirement Equities Fund (CREF) to offer it. Designed to supplement TIAA's fixed annuity, CREF invested participants' premiums in stocks. CREF and TIAA were subject to New York insurance (but not SEC) regulation.

During the 1950s, TIAA led the fight for Social Security benefits for university employees and began offering group total disability coverage (1957) and group life insurance (1958).

In 1971 TIAA-CREF began helping colleges boost investment returns from endowments, then moved into endowment management. It helped found a research center to provide objective investment information in 1972.

For 70 years retirement was the only way members could exit TIAA-CREF. Their only investment choices were stocks through CREF or a one-way transfer into TIAA's annuity accounts based on long-term bond, real estate, and mortgage investments. In the 1980s CREF indexed its funds to the S&P average.

By 1987's stock crash, TIAA-CREF had a million members, many of whom wanted more protection from stock market fluctuations. After the crash, Clifton Wharton (the first African-American to head a major US financial organization) became CEO; the next year CREF added a money market fund, for which the SEC required complete transferability, even outside TIAA-CREF. Now open to competition, TIAA-CREF became more flexible, adding investment options and long-term-care plans.

John Biggs became CEO in 1993. After the 1994 bond crash, TIAA-CREF began educating members on the ABCs of retirement investing, hoping to persuade them not to switch to flashy short-term investments and not to panic during such cyclical events as the crash.

In 1996 it went international, buying interests in UK commercial and mixed-use property. TIAA-CREF filed for SEC approval of more mutual funds in 1997. Although Federal tax legislation took away TIAA-CREF's tax-exempt status in 1997, the change was made without decreasing annuity incomes for the year.

The status change let TIAA-CREF offer no-load mutual funds to the public in 1998. A trust company and financial planning services were added; all new products were sold at cost, with TIAA-CREF waiving fees. TIAA-CREF in 1998 became the first pension fund to force out an entire board of directors (that of sputtering cafeteria firm Furr's/Bishop's). Also that year TIAA-CREF's crusade to curb "dead hand" poison pills (an anti-takeover defense measure) found favor with the shareholders of Bergen Brunswig (now AmerisourceBergen), Lubrizol, and Mylan Labo-

ratories. Late in 1999 the organization sold half of its stake in the Mall of America to Simon Property Group, keeping 27%. The next year it made a grab for more market share when it launched five new mutual funds.

Biggs retired in 2002 and was succeeded by Herbert Allison.

EXECUTIVES

Chairman, President, and CEO:
Herbert M. (Herb) Allison
EVP and CTO: Susan S. Kozik
EVP and Chief Investment Officer: Scott C. Evans
EVP and General Counsel: George W. Madison, age 49
EVP, Marketing: Jamie DePeau
EVP, Public Affairs: I. Steven (Steve) Goldstein
EVP, Risk Management: Erwin W. Martens
EVP, Client Services: Frances Nolan
EVP, Human Resources: Dermot J. O'Brien
EVP, Product Management: Bertram L. Scott, age 52
EVP and Head of Fixed Income and Real Estate:
John A. Somers
SVP and Head of Corporate Governance: John C. Wilcox
VP and Corporate Secretary: E. Laverne Jones
VP, Internal Audit and Acting CFO: Russell Noles
Director, Corporate Governance and Senior Counsel:
Hye-Won Choi
Director, Social Investing: Amy Muska O'Brien
Director, Corporate Governance: Linda E. Scott
Head of Equity Investments: Susan E. Ulick
Head of Global Equity Research: Thomas M. Franks
Director, Corporate Media Relations:
Stephanie Cohen Glass

LOCATIONS

HQ: Teachers Insurance and Annuity Association —
College Retirement Equities Fund
730 3rd Ave., New York, NY 10017
Phone: 212-490-9000 **Fax:** 212-916-4840
Web: www.tiaa-cref.org

Teachers Insurance and Annuity Association — College Retirement Equities Fund (TIAA-CREF) has major offices in Charlotte, North Carolina; Denver; and New York City. It also has dozens of smaller offices throughout the US.

PRODUCTS/OPERATIONS

Selected Subsidiaries and Units
Teachers Personal Investors Services, Inc.
  (mutual fund management)
TIAA-CREF Individual & Institutional Services, Inc.
  (broker-dealer)
TIAA-CREF Institute (think tank)
TIAA-CREF Institutional Mutual Funds
  (investment company)
TIAA-CREF Life Insurance Company
  (insurance and annuities)
TIAA-CREF Mutual Funds (investment company)
TIAA-CREF Trust Company, FSB (trust services)
TIAA-CREF Tuition Financing, Inc. (state tuition savings
  program management)

Selected Mutual Funds
Bond Plus
Equity Index
Growth & Income
Growth Equity
High-Yield Bond
Inflation-Linked Bond
International Equity
Large-Cap Value
Managed Allocation
Mid-Cap Growth
Mid-Cap Value
Money Market
Real Estate Securities
Short-Term Bond
Small-Cap Equity
Social Choice Equity
Tax-Exempt Bond

COMPETITORS

Aetna	MassMutual
AIG	Merrill Lynch
AXA Financial	MetLife
Bank of New York	New York Life
Berkshire Hathaway	Northwestern Mutual
CalPERS	Principal Financial
Charles Schwab	Prudential
CIGNA	T. Rowe Price
Citigroup	U.S. Global Investors
FMR	USAA
John Hancock	VALIC
Financial Services	Vanguard Group
JPMorgan Chase	

HISTORICAL FINANCIALS

Company Type: Private

Income Statement

FYE: December 31

	ASSETS ($ mil.)	NET INCOME ($ mil.)	INCOME AS % OF ASSETS	EMPLOYEES
12/03	300,000	—	—	6,000
12/02	261,252	—	—	6,500
12/01	274,390	—	—	6,700
12/00	281,383	—	—	5,000
12/99	289,248	—	—	5,000
12/98	249,715	—	—	5,000
12/97	214,296	—	—	4,920
12/96	182,612	—	—	4,490
Annual Growth	7.3%	—	—	4.2%

Asset History

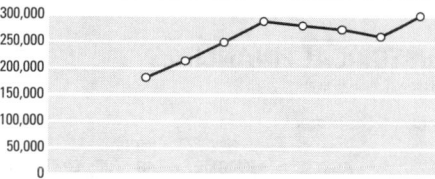

300,000	
250,000	
200,000	
150,000	
100,000	
50,000	
0	

12/94 12/95 12/96 12/97 12/98 12/99 12/00 12/01 12/02 12/03

Tidelands Bancshares

Tidelands Bancshares is the holding company for Tidelands Bank, which opened in October 2003 with an office in Mount Pleasant, South Carolina. The bank offers such retail services and products as checking and savings accounts, money market accounts, and commercial and consumer loans. Real estate loans make up the majority of its loan portfolio, with mortgages accounting for about 55% and construction loans accounting for some 30% of all loans. Tidelands Bank also operates two loan production offices in Summerville and Myrtle Beach, South Carolina. The company plans to expand with new stores in the tri-state area.

Company executives and directors collectively own nearly one-quarter of Tidelands Bancshares.

EXECUTIVES

Chairman: Barry I. Kalinsky, age 44
President, CEO, and Director, Tidelands Bancshares and Tidelands Bank: Robert E. (Chip) Coffee Jr., age 57, $123,750 pay
EVP and CFO, Tidelands Bancshares and Tidelands Bank: Alan W. Jackson, age 43, $111,875 pay
EVP and Senior Credit Officer, Tidelands Bank: Robert H. (Bobby) Mathewes Jr., age 38, $111,875 pay
SVP and Senior Commercial Banker, Tidelands Bank: Ken Pickens
SVP, Commercial Lending, Tidelands Bank: James A. Kimbell III
VP and Commercial Lender, Tidelands Bank: David Tomlinson
VP and Head of Operations, Tidelands Bank: Debbie Roumillat
VP and Mortgage Manager, Tidelands Bank: Steve Humphreys
Human Resources Manager, Tidelands Bank: Barbara P. McKenzie
Auditors: Elliott Davis LLC

LOCATIONS

HQ: Tidelands Bancshares, Inc.
875 Lowcountry Blvd., Mt. Pleasant, SC 29464
Phone: 843-388-8433   **Fax:** 843-388-8081
Web: www.tidelandsbank.com

COMPETITORS

First Financial Holdings
Regions Financial
Southcoast Financial
Synovus

HISTORICAL FINANCIALS

Company Type: Private

Income Statement

FYE: December 31

	ASSETS ($ mil.)	NET INCOME ($ mil.)	INCOME AS % OF ASSETS	EMPLOYEES
12/04	76	(1)	—	23
12/03	29	(1)	—	17
12/02	0	(1)	—	1
Annual Growth	1,487.5%	—	—	379.6%

2004 Year-End Financials

Equity as % of assets: 11.0%   Long-term debt ($ mil.): 7
Return on assets: —   Sales ($ mil.): 3
Return on equity: —

Net Income History

Timex

Branching out from its original "takes a licking" designs, Timex is strapping on new faces in order to tap new markets worldwide. The US's largest watch producer has expanded its lines from simple, low-cost watches to include high-tech tickers capable of paging or downloading computer data. Its sports watches have gone upscale and gadgety with lines such as Reef Gear and Ironman. (The brightness of its Indiglo watch helped a man lead a group of people down 34 flights of dark stairs after the first World Trade Center bombing in 1993.) Timex also makes watches for Guess?, Nautica, and Versace, under license. Founded in 1854 as Waterbury Clock, Timex is owned by Fred Olsen, whose father bought the company in 1942.

About 15 women who painted glow-in-the-dark dials on watchfaces for the Waterbury Clock Co., dubbed "radium girls," died from radium poisoning during the 1920s and 1930s; dozens of others suffered from crumbling jaws from a technique that required the women to dip their paintbrushes into the glowing paint and then sharpen the brushpoints with their lips.

In 2001 Timex closed its last US-based factory. The following year, the company signed a licensing agreement with MEDport, LLC to manufacture and sell medical devices for the home (such as digital thermometers) under the Timex brand name.

The company dropped its famed "It takes a licking and keeps on ticking" in favor of the more updated "Timex. Life is ticking." in 2003. In 2004 Timex purchased Versace's Swiss watch subsidiary; the renamed Vertime SA will continue producing watches, jewelry, and writing tools for the Italian fashion house.

In the summer of 2005 Timex purchased Versace's precious goods division, including its watch and jewelry collections. The division was renamed Versace Precious Items.

EXECUTIVES

Chairman: Annette Olsen
President and CEO: Jose Santana
CFO: Theresa Yerkes
SVP Americas: Ken Lewis
General Counsel, Secretary, and SVP Human Resources: Frank Sherer
VP Marketing: Mario Sabatini
VP Licensing: Helen Prial
Director of Advanced Products: Wilson Keithline
Communications Director: Jim Katz
Director of Information Technology: Steve Beaudry
Systems Manager: James Jackson

LOCATIONS

HQ: Timex Corporation
555 Christian Rd., Middlebury, CT 06762
Phone: 203-346-5000   **Fax:** 203-346-5139
Web: www.timex.com

Timex Corporation sells its products worldwide. It has operations in Brazil, China, France, Germany, India, Israel, the Philippines, and the US.

COMPETITORS

Benetton	Measurement Specialties
Bulova	Movado Group
CASIO COMPUTER	NIKE
Citizen Watch	SDI Technologies
E. Gluck	Seiko
Emerson Radio	Swatch
Fossil	Swiss Army Brands
GE	

HISTORICAL FINANCIALS

Company Type: Private

Income Statement

FYE: December 31

	ESTIMATED REVENUE ($ mil.)	NET INCOME ($ mil.)	NET PROFIT MARGIN	EMPLOYEES
12/03	800	—	—	7,500
12/02	600	—	—	5,500
12/01	600	—	—	—
12/00	600	—	—	7,500
12/99	600	—	—	8,000
12/98	600	—	—	8,000
12/97	600	—	—	7,500
12/96	650	—	—	7,500
12/95	650	—	—	—
12/94	650	—	—	—
Annual Growth	2.3%	—	—	0.0%

Revenue History

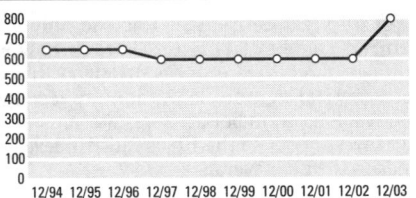

Tin Star Restaurants

Tin Star gets a gold star for rethinking the traditional Tex-Mex menu. The Dallas-based company owns and franchises Tin Star restaurants in the Lone Star State, Arizona, California, Colorado, Florida, Georgia, Nebraska, Nevada, and Oklahoma. The fast-casual restaurant offers salads, burgers, ribs, and fajitas. It is known for its copyrighted Cheeseburger Tacos, but customers can also create their own tacos, choosing gourmet toppings like steak, whitefish, or tempura shrimp. President Rich Hicks (formerly of Brinker) started Tin Star in 1999. He intends to develop as many as 50 more Tin Star franchises throughout the southwestern US by 2009.

EXECUTIVES

President: Richard (Rich) Hicks
VP Franchising: Michael Mabry
Administrative Director: Paula Holt
Public Relations: Kellie McCrory

HQ: Tin Star Restaurants
1800 Preston Park Blvd., Ste. 104, Plano, TX 75093
Phone: 972-665-4000   **Fax:** 972-665-4001
Web: www.tinstar.us

COMPETITORS

Brinker	Mission Burritos
Chipotle	Panda Restaurant Group
Del Taco	Qdoba
El Pollo Loco	Taco Bell
El Taco Tote	Taco Bueno
Extreme Pizza	Taco Cabana
Kahala	Taco Time
McDonald's	Wendy's

HISTORICAL FINANCIALS

Company Type: Private

Income Statement

FYE: December 31

	REVENUE ($ mil.)	NET INCOME ($ mil.)	NET PROFIT MARGIN	EMPLOYEES
12/04	6	—	—	130
12/03	5	—	—	130
Annual Growth	10.0%	—	—	0.0%

Revenue History

6	
5	
4	
3	
2	
1	
0	

12/95 12/96 12/97 12/98 12/99 12/00 12/01 12/02 12/03 12/04

Tishman Realty & Construction

Tishman Realty & Construction is an immigrant success story writ large. The company builds office, hospitality, recreational, industrial, and other property for itself and for others. It offers third-party developers a full menu of real estate design, construction, management, and financing services. High-profile projects handled by the company (or its publicly-owned predecessor) include Disney World's EPCOT Center, Madison Square Garden, the ill-fated World Trade Center (as well as its rebuilding), and Chicago's John Hancock Center. The Tishman family — scions of immigrant founder Julius Tishman, who began building tenements in 1898 — own Tishman Realty & Construction.

Affiliates of Tishman Realty & Construction include Tishman Construction, which provides development and construction services; Tishman Technologies, which equips buildings with data and communications infrastructure; Tishman Real Estate Services, which provides leasing, landlord and tenant representation, and other commercial services; Tishman Hotels, which provides management services to about 160 properties; and Tishman Realty, which finances the firm's activities.

Tishman Realty & Construction's E Walk entertainment and retail development in New York's Times Square district includes the Westin New York hotel (which opened in 2002), specialty retail shops, restaurants, and entertainment venues. The company also manages four boutique hotels in Manhattan owned by Credit Suisse First Boston's Principal Transactions Group.

CEO John Tishman has expanded the company beyond its Big Apple origins, most notably through a partnership with the Walt Disney Company to build hotels and theme parks in Florida. Among the company's completed non-New York projects are the Dolphin and Swan hotels at Disney's EPCOT Center, the Sheraton Chicago Hotel & Towers, and the Westin Rio Mar Beach Resort & Casino in Puerto Rico.

HISTORY

Julius Tishman escaped the Russian pogroms of the late 19th century by emigrating to the US in 1885. Five years later he opened a store in Newburgh, New York. In 1898, as eastern European immigrants inundated New York City, Tishman began building tenements on the Lower East Side. He named his business Julius Tishman & Sons. By the 1920s, the firm had moved uptown and upscale, building luxury apartment buildings. The firm went public in 1928 as Tishman Realty & Construction, with the family retaining an ownership stake. Julius was chairman; son David was CEO.

The pitfalls of going public were soon obvious. The offering raised less than $2 million, not enough to finance projects, and because the stock market favored profit generation over asset appreciation, the company was undervalued. When the Depression hit, David's involvement as a director of the Bank of the United States and the family's participation in bad loans made by the bank forced the firm to sell assets. Tishman's lenders, including insurer Metropolitan Life, took over some of its buildings, leaving the firm to manage them. In the 1930s and 1940s, the company focused mainly on managing its properties. It continued its construction operations on a contract basis for the Federal Housing Authority.

After WWII, Tishman moved away from residential development and into office construction. Meanwhile, David's younger brothers Paul and Norman began jockeying for position to replace him as CEO; in 1948 David chose Norman to succeed him (Paul resigned to form his own construction company). A nephew, John, became head of the firm's construction arm.

By the early 1950s, Tishman had moved into management and leasing services and expanded nationally, opening offices in Chicago and Los Angeles. In 1962 David relinquished his chairmanship to Norman, who was in turn replaced as CEO by his brother Bob. Under Bob's leadership, Tishman divested residential properties to focus on office space, mostly company-owned.

In 1972 the company completed the World Trade Center complex, including twin 110-story towers which were then the tallest buildings in the world. The iconic structures stood more than 1,300 feet above Manhattan until they collapsed as a result of a terrorist attack in 2001.

Tishman was hit hard by recession in the 1970s. In 1976 Bob took the company private again, selling off the firm's New York assets, and split the company into Tishman Speyer Properties (headed by Bob and son-in-law Jerry Speyer); Tishman Management and Leasing (now part of Grubb & Ellis); and Tishman Realty & Construction (headed by John and promptly bought by the Rockefeller Center Corporation).

John Tishman bought back Tishman Realty & Construction in 1980 and steered it into high-profile partnerships with the likes of the Walt Disney Company. He also added project management and real estate financial services to his company's repertoire and continued to take part in highly visible construction projects.

Since the late 1990s, Tishman's major projects have centered around the revitalization efforts of Times Square and 42nd street in New York City — including the construction of 4 Times Square (the Conde Nast building), 3 Times Square (Reuters America headquarters), and E Walk, a mixed-use entertainment and retail center.

EXECUTIVES

Chairman and CEO: John L. Tishman
President and CEO: Daniel R. Tishman
CFO and Treasurer: Larry Schwarzwalder
SVP Public Relations: Richard M. Kielar
SVP and General Counsel: Linda Christensen
Chairman and CEO, Tishman Hotel Corp. and Tishman Realty Corp.: John A. Vickers
President and CEO, Tishman Real Estate Services: Joseph J. Simone
President and COO, Tishman Urban Development: John T. Livingston
President, Tishman Realty Corp.: William J. Sales
COO, Tishman Construction Eastern Region: Jay Badame
EVP, Tishman Real Estate Services: Ronald Bowman
SVP, Tishman Real Estate Services: Paul Diamond
SVP, Tishman Real Estate Services: Charles A. Wojcik
EVP, Tishman Technologies: Joseph B. Ryan Jr.

LOCATIONS

HQ: Tishman Realty & Construction Co. Inc.
666 5th Ave., New York, NY 10103
Phone: 212-399-3600   **Fax:** 212-397-1316
Web: www.tishman.com

PRODUCTS/OPERATIONS

Selected Subsidiaries

Tishman Construction Corp. (construction operations)
Tishman Hotel Corp. (hotel development and management)
Tishman Interiors Corp. (interior build-out and renovation)
Tishman Real Estate Management Co. (property management for third-party clients)
Tishman Real Estate Services Co. (real estate consulting and management)
Tishman Research Corp. (building materials research and consulting)
Tishman Technologies Corp. (communication and data systems development)

COMPETITORS

CB Richard Ellis
Cushman & Wakefield
Forest City Ratner
Gilbane
Grubb & Ellis
JMB Realty
Jones Lang LaSalle
Lefrak Organization
Lincoln Property
Reckson Associates Realty
Starrett Corporation
Trammell Crow Company
Trump
Witkoff Group

HISTORICAL FINANCIALS

Company Type: Private

Income Statement

FYE: June 30

	ESTIMATED REVENUE ($ mil.)	NET INCOME ($ mil.)	NET PROFIT MARGIN	EMPLOYEES
6/04	2,000	—	—	900
6/03	2,000	—	—	900
6/02	2,100	—	—	920
6/01	1,640	—	—	920
6/00	1,109	—	—	890
6/99	1,005	—	—	800
6/98	937	—	—	650
6/97	650	—	—	620
6/96	580	—	—	600
6/95	572	—	—	575
Annual Growth	**14.9%**	**—**	**—**	**5.1%**

Revenue History

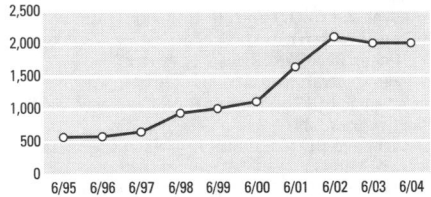

Topco Associates

Topco Associates is principally into private-label procurement. Topco uses the combined purchasing clout of more than 50 member companies (mostly supermarket operators) to wring discounts from suppliers. Serving grocery wholesalers, retailers, and food service firms, Topco markets more than 5,000 private-label items, including fresh meat, dairy and bakery goods, and health and beauty aids. Its brands include Food Club, Shurfine, and a line of "Top" labels such as Top Crest. In 2001 Topco Associates, Inc. merged operations with Shurfine International to form Topco Associates LLC. The new entity is 86%-owned by Topco Holdings, Inc. (formerly Topco Associates).

Holding company Shurfine International owns 14% of the merged entity, which also has members in Israel and Japan. But most of Topco's member companies are in the consolidating US market, where many stores have been bought by giant chains.

In addition to the Shurfine, Food Club, and Top Crest brands, Topco distributes Ultimate Choice and Shurfresh products. Topco also helps members market their own brands. Topco's cost-saving scheme goes beyond product offerings; its buying power cuts costs for its members' stores. Its warehouse equipment purchase and a financial services program also create savings for members.

HISTORY

Food Cooperatives was founded in Wisconsin in 1944 to procure dairy bags and paper products during wartime shortages. A few years later it merged with Top Frost Foods, with which it had some common members. In 1948 the name Topco Associates was adopted (created by com-

bining the word "Top" from Top Frost with the "Co" in Cooperatives). The member companies involved in the merger included Alpha Beta, Big Bear Stores, Brockton Public Market, Fred Meyer, Furr's, Hinky Dinky, Penn Fruit Company, and Star Markets.

Topco initially sold basic commodities to private-label retailers. It added fresh produce in 1958 and expanded its product line further in 1960, moving into general merchandise, health and beauty care items, and store equipment. In 1961, when the company moved its headquarters to Skokie, Illinois, revenues topped the $100 million mark. In the 1960s other leading supermarkets, including Giant Eagle, King Soopers, McCarty-Holman, and Tom Thumb, joined Topco.

Also that decade it came under attack from the Justice Department when it was accused of antitrust activity in granting its members exclusive distribution rights for Topco-branded products. In 1972 the Supreme Court ruled against Topco. It then agreed to sell products under the private labels of its members.

In the late 1970s the company introduced Valu Time, the first nationally marketed line of branded generic products. This concept was then adopted by many US supermarkets. By 1979 Topco surpassed $1 billion in annual revenues.

By the end of the 1980s, Topco's membership had expanded to include Randall's, Riser Foods, Pueblo International, Schnuck Markets, and Smith's Food & Drug Centers. In 1988 it introduced World Classics, a premium line of high-volume, high-margin products promoted as national brands.

During the early 1990s Topco ran through a number of CEOs. In 1990 Robert Seelert replaced 10-year CEO Marcel Lussier. In 1992 John Beggs took over, and the next year Steven Rubow was handed the reins.

The early 1990s also saw rapid growth, with 20 new members bringing the company's total to 46 by 1995 (its membership later declined in number through acquisition and consolidation). Topco also expanded internationally, with the membership of Oshawa Group in Canada and the associate membership of SEIYU in Japan in 1995. Also that year the company lured upscale Kings Super Markets away from distributor White Rose.

Topco began offering members utility accounting and natural gas services through Illinova Energy Partners in 1998. The company expanded its Top Care line of personal care products in 1999, using a variety of packaging designed to resemble several name brands within a single category. Rubow retired late that year and was replaced by Steve Lauer. Topco took aim at consumers who prefer natural foods in 2000, launching the Full Circle line of organically grown items.

In November 2001 Topco combined operations with co-op operator Shurfine International and re-formed as a limited liability company. Topco Associates, Inc., and Shurfine International became holding companies with stakes in Topco Associates LLC. Lauer, the CEO of Topco Associates, Inc., was named president and CEO of the new company. In 2004 IGA became a member of Topco.

EXECUTIVES

Chairman: Joseph V. Fisher
Vice Chairman: Steven C. (Steve) Smith
President, CEO, and Director: Steven K. (Steve) Lauer
SVP, CFO, and Treasurer: Randall (Randy) Skoda
SVP Cost Containment Programs/Support Services: Ian Grossman
SVP Member Development: Kenneth H. Guy
SVP Center Store: Daniel F. Mazur
SVP and Chief Procurement Officer: Jeffrey Posner
SVP and President, Wholesale Channel: John Stanhaus
SVP Perishables: Russel Wolfe
SVP World Brands: Michael Ricciardi
VP Purchasing: Dennis Dangerfield
VP Non-Foods: Curt Maki
VP Best Practices, Cost Containment, and Purchasing: David McMurray
VP Sales and Marketing, Wholesale Channel: Mike Nugent
VP Dairy: Laird Snelgrove
VP Produce and Floral: Rob O'Rourke
VP Brand and Product Innovation: Maryruth Wilson
Manager, Human Resources: Dennis Pieper
Director, Media Relations: Annette McMillan
Auditors: KPMG LLP

LOCATIONS

HQ: Topco Associates LLC
7711 Gross Point Rd., Skokie, IL 60077
Phone: 847-676-3030 **Fax:** 847-676-4949
Web: www.topco.com

Topco Associates purchases products on behalf of its members in the US, Israel, Japan, and Puerto Rico.

PRODUCTS/OPERATIONS

Selected Private-Label Brands

Food Club
Full Circle
Pet Club
Price Saver
Savers Choice
Shurfine
Shurfresh
Shurtech
Top Care
Top Crest
Ultimate Choice

Selected Member Companies

Ace Hardware
Acme
Ahold USA
Alex Lee
Associated Grocers, Inc.
Big Y Foods
Blue Square-Israel
Eagle Food Centers
F.A.B. Inc.
Food City
Fred W. Albrecht Grocery Co.
Fresh Brands (Piggly Wiggly)
Furr's Supermarkets
Giant Eagle
Haggen
Harris Teeter
Hy-Vee
IGA, Inc.
Kings Super Markets
K-VA-T Food Stores
Meijer
Penn Traffic Company
Piggly Wiggly Carolina
Pueblo International
Raley's Supermarkets
Schnuck Markets
THE SEIYU
Ukrop's Super Markets
Unipro Food Service
Wegmans
Weis Markets

COMPETITORS

Ahold USA	SYSCO
C&S Wholesale	Wakefern Food
Kroger	Wal-Mart
SUPERVALU	

HISTORICAL FINANCIALS

Company Type: Cooperative

Income Statement

FYE: December 31

	REVENUE ($ mil.)	NET INCOME ($ mil.)	NET PROFIT MARGIN	EMPLOYEES
12/03	4,600	—	—	400
12/02	4,000	—	—	300
12/01*	3,300	—	—	300
3/00	3,400	—	—	275
3/99	4,000	—	—	359
3/98	3,900	—	—	365
3/97	3,700	—	—	400
3/96	3,900	—	—	390
3/95	3,700	—	—	375
3/94	3,500	—	—	400
Annual Growth	**3.1%**	**—**	**—**	**0.0%**

*Fiscal year change

Revenue History

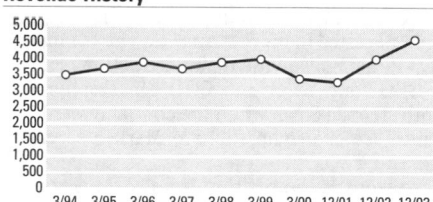

Toresco Enterprises

Auto malls — what a concept! Donald Toresco, owner of Toresco Enterprises, helped pioneer the idea. The company's Autoland of New Jersey sells new and used Chrysler, Dodge, Jeep, and Toyota cars, trucks, and SUVs. The dealership also offers service, financing, and fleet sales. Visitors to the company's Web site can search inventory, build and price a car, apply for financing, schedule service, and order parts. Chairman Toresco founded his company in 1965 as a used-car dealership and created the auto mall in 1985. Toresco also has interests in the real estate and insurance industries.

After taking space from Ford to expand the Toyota part of the dealership, Ford gave Toresco an ultimatum: restore the space or give up the franchise. Toresco shocked the American auto maker by resigning the franchise and happily giving the Ford space to Toyota product.

EXECUTIVES

Chairman: Donald Toresco
EVP: Andrea Karsian

LOCATIONS

HQ: Toresco Enterprises, Inc.
170 Rte. 22 East, Springfield, NJ 07081
Phone: 973-467-2900   **Fax:** 973-467-1824
Web: www.1800autoland.com

COMPETITORS

AutoNation	Planet Automotive Group
Holman Enterprises	Sansone Auto Network
Hometown Auto	

HISTORICAL FINANCIALS

Company Type: Private

Income Statement

FYE: December 31

	REVENUE ($ mil.)	NET INCOME ($ mil.)	NET PROFIT MARGIN	EMPLOYEES
12/04	507	—	—	548
12/03	490	—	—	700
12/02	498	—	—	692
12/01	530	—	—	682
12/00	550	—	—	682
12/99	495	—	—	700
12/98	500	—	—	750
12/97	463	—	—	598
12/96	437	—	—	650
12/95	430	—	—	782
Annual Growth	**1.8%**	**—**	**—**	**(3.9%)**

Revenue History

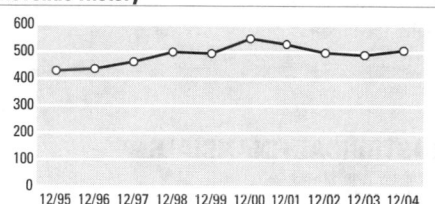

Towers Perrin

Refusing to live in an ivory tower, this company aims to offer practical advice. One of the leading management consulting firms in the world, Towers Perrin serves an extensive list of corporate clients, including more than 700 of the *FORTUNE* 1000 companies. The firm's core focus is on human resources consulting. Its Tillinghast-Towers Perrin unit focuses on risk management and actuarial services to financial companies, and its Towers Perrin Reinsurance serves clients primarily as a reinsurance intermediary. In addition to consulting, the company produces several publications and surveys investigating business trends and challenges.

After guiding its clients through the downsizing and consolidating 1990s, Towers Perrin has been working to streamline its own operations. The company has pared down its client roster, keeping mainly its biggest customers. At the same time it has been creating new business by expanding into new practice areas, such as public relations and corporate communications.

The company joined with EDS to form a new firm called ExcellerateHRO, which is focused on human resources outsourcing. Towers Perrin owns 15% of the new company; EDS, 85%.

Towers Perrin was founded by four partners in 1934 and is now owned by more than 630 partners.

EXECUTIVES

Chairman and CEO: Mark Mactas
CFO: Mark L. Wilson
CIO: Tony Candito
Managing Director: Donald L. (Don) Lowman
Managing Director and Chief Administration Officer: Garrett L. Dietz
Managing Director, Global Marketing: Sharon Clark
Managing Director, Global Markets: Michael (Mike) Ponicall
Managing Director, Global Retirement Services, Health & Welfare, and Administration Services: Robert G. Hogan
Managing Director, Human Resources: Anne Donovan Bodnar
Managing Director, Tillinghast and Towers Perrin Reinsurance: Patricia L. (Tricia) Guinn
General Counsel and Secretary: Kevin Young
Head of Global Consulting Group, UK: Nigel Bateman
Reinsurance Practice, Europe: Amar Shah

LOCATIONS

HQ: Towers Perrin
1 Stamford Plaza, 263 Tresser Blvd., Stamford, CT 06901
Phone: 203-326-5400   **Fax:** 203-326-5499
Web: www.towers.com

Towers Perrin has about 80 offices in 24 countries worldwide.

PRODUCTS/OPERATIONS

Selected Operations

Tillinghast-Towers Perrin
Financial Reporting
Mergers, Acquisitions, and Restructuring
Products, Markets, and Distribution
   Distribution strategy, economics, and operating solutions
   Market entry, analysis, and positioning
   Product development and management
   Group life and health insurance
Risk Management
   Corporate risk management and self-insured management
   Insurance and financial services
   Health care professional liability
Value-Based Management

Towers Perrin

Administration Solutions
Change Management
Communication
Executive Compensation
Global Databases and Surveys
Health and Welfare
HR Delivery Solutions
Mergers, Acquisitions, and Restructuring
Retirement Services
Rewards and Performance Management
Sales Compensation
Superannuation in Australia

COMPETITORS

Accenture	Gallup
Aon	Hewitt Associates
A.T. Kearney	KPMG
Bain & Company	Marsh
Benecon Group	Marsh & McLennan
Booz Allen	McKinsey & Company
Boston Consulting	Mercer
Deloitte	PricewaterhouseCoopers
Drake Beam Morin	Right Management
Ernst & Young	Watson Wyatt

HISTORICAL FINANCIALS

Company Type: Private

Income Statement

FYE: December 31

	REVENUE ($ mil.)	NET INCOME ($ mil.)	NET PROFIT MARGIN	EMPLOYEES
12/03	1,500	—	—	8,384
12/02	1,441	—	—	9,000
12/01	1,469	—	—	9,009
12/00	1,448	—	—	8,919
12/99	1,338	—	—	8,600
12/98	1,125	—	—	6,314
12/97	1,000	—	—	6,350
12/96	855	—	—	6,361
12/95	822	—	—	5,050
12/94	767	—	—	5,000
Annual Growth	7.7%	—	—	5.9%

Revenue History

[Revenue History line chart, 12/94 to 12/03, values from 0 to 1,600]

Town Sports International Holdings

Town Sports International wants to be the apple a day that keeps the doctor away in NYC. The company owns and operates about 140 full-service health clubs, two-thirds of which are in the New York City area under the New York Sports Club banner. The company claims nearly 400,000 members. Memberships are sold in three classes varying in price. The least expensive gives access to clubs during off-peak hours; premium membership allows use of all Town Sports' facilities at any time. Town Sports also has three clubs in Switzerland. Directors Bruce Bruckmann and J. Rice Edmonds together own about 38% of the company through Bruckmann, Rosser, Sherrill & Co. Town Sports was founded in 1973.

Town Sports clubs in other cities go by the names Washington Sports Clubs (DC), Boston Sports Clubs, and Philadelphia Sports Clubs.

The company will use the funds from its IPO to pay down debt.

EXECUTIVES

Chairman: Mark N. Smith, age 46, $872,286 pay
CEO: Robert J. Giardina, age 47, $770,133 pay
COO: Randall C. Stephen, age 48, $345,913 pay
CFO: Richard G. Pyle, age 46, $524,869 pay
SVP Strategic Planning and Special Projects: Frank J. Napolitano
VP Finance: Daniel Gallagher
VP Human Resources: Maureen A. McGovern
VP and Controller: Margaret (Peggy) Houren
VP Sales: Margaret Stevens

VP and General Counsel: Robert (Bob) Herbst
VP Marketing: Merrill Richmond
CIO: Jennifer Prue
Chief Development Officer: Alexander A. Alimanestianu, age 46, $524,869 pay
Auditors: PricewaterhouseCoopers LLP

LOCATIONS

HQ: Town Sports International Holdings, Inc.
888 7th Ave., New York, NY 10106
Phone: 212-246-6700   **Fax:** 212-246-8422
Web: www.mysportsclubs.com

2004 Locations

	No.
New York metro	94
Boston metro	19
Washington, DC metro	18
Philadelphia metro	6
Switzerland	3
Total	**140**

PRODUCTS/OPERATIONS

2004 Sales

	$ mil.	% of total
Membership	295.2	84
Personal training & other ancillary club	53.0	15
Fees & other	4.8	1
Total	**353.0**	**100**

COMPETITORS

Bally Total Fitness	YMCA
Gold's Gym	YWCA
The Sports Club	

HISTORICAL FINANCIALS

Company Type: Private

Income Statement

FYE: December 31

	REVENUE ($ mil.)	NET INCOME ($ mil.)	NET PROFIT MARGIN	EMPLOYEES
12/04	353	(4)	—	7,440
12/03	343	7	2.2%	7,200
12/02	319	11	3.3%	7,700
12/01	283	7	2.5%	7,150
12/00	225	5	2.1%	6,400
12/99	160	0	—	4,400
12/98	82	0	0.4%	2,600
12/97	57	(1)	—	—
12/96	44	1	1.1%	—
12/95	33	(1)	—	—
Annual Growth	30.0%	—	—	19.2%

2004 Year-End Financials

Debt ratio: —	Current ratio: 1.11
Return on equity: —	Long-term debt ($ mil.): 395
Cash ($ mil.): 58	

Net Income History

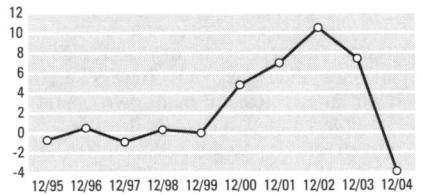

[Net Income History chart, 12/95 to 12/04, values from -4 to 12]

Toys "R" Us

The only Monopoly that Toys "R" Us holds these days is on its shelves. The company is still one of the world's largest toy retailers, but it has lost its #1 US position to Wal-Mart. Toys "R" Us sells its wares through about 1,500 stores in the US and abroad, and Web sites (run by Amazon.com). In addition to about 680 US namesake stores selling toys, games, and other items for kids, Toys "R" Us sells infant and toddler apparel, furniture, and feeding supplies at some 215 Babies "R" Us stores. The company closed its Kids "R" Us children's clothing stores in 2004. Tough times in toyland led to the acquisition of Toys "R" Us by two private equity firms and a real estate company for about $6.6 billion in mid-2005.

Toys "R" Us had been expected to split its ailing toys and fast-growing baby businesses through a sale of the toy business or a spin-off of Babies "R" Us. Instead, Kohlberg Kravis Roberts & Co and Bain Capital Partners (owner of KB Toys), together with real estate firm Vornado Realty Trust, beat out competing bidders in a deal that took the entire company private. The inclusion of Vornado suggests that the acquirers are interested in more than toys. The company's real estate may be the major attraction.

CEO John Eyler and COO Christopher Kay both stepped down when the company went private. Vice chairman Richard Markee serves as interim CEO.

To fend off competition from consumer electronics makers for the "tween" market (kids ages 8 to 12), Toys "R" Us and other toymakers are stocking up on youth electronics for the holidays. This is the first holiday season that Toys "R" Us will carry products such as MP3 players and digital cameras for kids. The company has also been adding apparel to many Toys "R" Us stores in the US.

To improve its lagging position in the toy retail game, Toys "R" Us is emphasizing top-selling and proprietary items (like special Barbie dolls available only at its stores) and making a concerted effort to improve customer service. It is also opening Toys "R" Us Toybox sections in selected supermarkets, which includes an exclusive toy provider agreement with Albertson's. There are currently some 900 toy sections now in place at Albertson's.

In order to increase store traffic during the non-holiday season, Toys "R" Us opened four Geoffrey stores that combine products from Toys "R" Us and Babies "R" Us, as well as apparel, and include activity centers, play areas, party rooms, photo studios, and hair salons.

The company's Toysrus.com subsidiary is suing Amazon.com for violating its 10-year exclusivity agreement that began in 2000. The agreement gives Toysrus.com exclusive selling rights in the game, toy, and baby products categories on the Amazon.com e-commerce platform; however, Toys "R" Us has found there are currently over 4,000 items from competitors being sold within these categories on the same platform. Amazon.com is counter-suing, stating Toys "R" Us broke the agreement.

HISTORY

Charles Lazarus entered retailing in 1948, adding his $2,000 savings to a $2,000 bank loan to convert his father's Washington, DC, bicycle repair shop into a kids' furniture store. Customers persuaded him to add toys, and he renamed the store Children's Supermart.

By 1966 sales had reached $12 million. He sold his company to discounter Interstate Stores for $7.5 million, with the condition that he would retain control of the toy operation. By 1974 Lazarus' division had expanded to 47 stores and $130 million in annual sales, but the parent had filed for bankruptcy.

In 1978, Lazarus raised Interstate from the dead, or at least pulled them out of bankruptcy and into his control. The company adopted the name Toys "R" Us. With 72 toy stores (and 10 Interstate stores) and a 5% toy market share, it posted $349 million in sales that year.

From 1978 to 1983 earnings grew 40% annually, market share climbed to 12.5%, and the number of toy stores reached 169. The company opened two Kids "R" Us clothing stores in 1983, copying the toy stores' discount formula. Toys "R" Us entered the Japanese market in 1991.

Toys "R" Us pushed rivals Child World and Lionel into bankruptcy in 1992. In 1993 Toys "R" Us continued its international expansion before Lazarus stepped aside as CEO in 1994. The company opened its first franchise (in Dubai, United Arab Emirates) in 1995. The toy seller paid $376 million for Baby Superstore in 1997 to strengthen its fledgling Babies "R" Us; by 1998 Babies "R" Us had become the largest US baby store chain.

Trouble came in 1997 when a federal judge decided Toys "R" Us violated trade laws by conspiring with manufacturers to keep toys priced artificially high and out of warehouse clubs like Costco. Toys "R" Us appealed, then settled with the FTC for $40.5 million, including $27 million in donated toys.

In 1998 president and COO Bob Nakasone became CEO, and the company began selling online and launched its first mail-order catalog.

Toys "R" Us was passed in US toy sales in 1999 by Wal-Mart. Later that year, as Toys "R" Us struggled to win back lost market share and after seven straight quarters of earnings decline, CEO Nakasone left the company.

In early 2000 the company hired John Eyler away from FAO Schwarz as president and CEO. That year Toys "R" Us sold 32% of its Japanese subsidiary, Toys — Japan, to the public, retaining a 48% stake. toysrus.com, haunted by its failure to deliver toys in time for Christmas 1999, launched a co-branded Internet store (toys, video games) with Amazon.com later in 2000.

In 2001 the company said it would close 37 Kids "R" Us stores and 27 of the non-remodeled stores, in many cases converting nearby stores to the combo format; it also said it would cut 1,900 jobs. Weak holiday sales and continued competition from mass retailers prompted the company to lay off 700 of its management and supervisory employees in late January 2002.

Citing continued sales declines in some of its freestanding operations, the company closed the majority of its 146 Kids "R" Us clothing stores and all 36 Imaginarium stores in early 2004. The company sold 124 of the Kids "R" Us stores to Office Depot, and converted 14 of the remaining stores to the Babies "R" Us format.

In 2004 Toys "R" Us launched its Toysrus.ca and Babiesrus.ca e-commerce Web sites in Canada. The next year, two private investment firms (KKR and Bain Capital) and a real estate company (Vornado Realty Trust) bought Toys "R" Us for $6.6 billion.

EXECUTIVES

Interim CEO; Vice Chairman; President, Babies "R" Us: Richard L. (Rick) Markee, age 51, $2,151,287 pay
EVP and CFO: Raymond L. (Ray) Arthur, age 46
EVP; President, Toys "R" Us United States: John Barbour, age 45, $1,668,040 pay
EVP, Human Resources: Deborah M. (Deb) Derby, age 41
EVP; President, Merchandising, Toys "R" Us United States: James E. (Jim) Feldt, age 50, $1,240,320 pay
EVP and CIO: John Holohan, age 47
EVP, Strategic Planning and Business Development: Francesca L. Brockett, age 44
EVP, Supply Chain: Karen Duvall
SVP and General Counsel: David J. Schwartz
SVP, Treasurer, and Assistant Secretary: Jon W. Kimmins
SVP, Human Resources: John Butler
SVP, Logistics: Michael C. Jacobs
SVP, Marketing: Amy J. Parker
SVP, Operations, Toys "R" Us United States: Steven J. Krajewski
SVP, Taxes: Peter W. Weiss
SVP; General Merchandise Manager, Toys "R" Us International: Joan W. Donovan
VP, Asia Pacific Operations: Adam Szopinski
VP, Investor Relations: Ursula H. Moran
Auditors: Deloitte & Touche LLP

LOCATIONS

HQ: Toys "R" Us, Inc.
1 Geoffrey Way, Wayne, NJ 07470
Phone: 973-617-3500   **Fax:** 973-617-4006
Web: www7.toysrus.com

Toys "R" Us operates or has franchised stores in the US and some 30 other countries. The company's four Geoffrey stores are located in Mississippi, North Carolina, Texas, and Wisconsin.

2005 Sales

	% of total
US	75
Other countries	25
Total	**100**

2005 Toys "R" Us US Stores

	No.
California	82
Texas	50
Florida	46
New York	45
Pennsylvania	33
Illinois	32
Ohio	32
New Jersey	26
Michigan	25
Virginia	22
Georgia	20
Maryland	18
Massachusetts	18
North Carolina	15
Washington	15
Tennessee	14
Indiana	13
Missouri	13
Arizona	11
Wisconsin	11
Connecticut	10
Minnesota	10
Louisiana	9
South Carolina	9
Colorado	8
Iowa	8
Kentucky	8
Other states	64
Puerto Rico	4
Total	**681**

2005 Non-US Stores

	No.
Japan	153
UK	67
Canada	63
Germany	48
Spain	34
France	33
Australia	32
Turkey	26
Israel	21
Netherlands	15
South Africa	13
Denmark	12
Sweden	11
Austria	10
Taiwan	10
Portugal	8
Hong Kong	7
Malaysia	6
Norway	6
Saudi Arabia	6
Singapore	4
Switzerland	4
Indonesia	3
United Arab Emirates	3
Other countries	6
Total	**601**

PRODUCTS/OPERATIONS

2005 Sales

	$ mil.	% of total
Toys "R" Us (US)	6,104	55
Toys "R" Us (non-US)	2,739	25
Babies "R" Us	1,863	17
Toysrus.com	366	3
Kids R Us	28	—
Total	**11,100**	**100**

Store Chains

Toys "R" Us (toys, games, books, sporting goods, electronics, furniture)
Babies "R" Us (infant care products, car seats and strollers, furniture, toys)
Geoffrey (combination store format)

Toys "R" Us Departments

Apparel (clothing for children from newborn to age 10)
Core toy (boys and girls toys)
Geoffrey's Box Office (DVD and VHS movies)
Imaginarium (educational and developmental products, accessories, games, puzzles)
Juvenile (baby products and apparel for newborn to age 4)
Pre-school (activities, learning, toys)
R Zone (video game software and hardware, electronics, computer software, related products)
Seasonal (Christmas, Halloween, summer, bikes, sports, playsets)

COMPETITORS

Best Buy
The Children's Place
Circuit City
Costco Wholesale
Dillard's
Discovery Toys
Disney
Electronics Boutique
Excellige Learning
Federated
GameStop
Gap
Gymboree
KB Toys
KidsStuff.com
Kmart
May
Mothercare
OshKosh B'Gosh
Sears
Target
Wal-Mart

HISTORICAL FINANCIALS

Company Type: Private

Income Statement

FYE: Saturday nearest January 31

	REVENUE ($ mil.)	NET INCOME ($ mil.)	NET PROFIT MARGIN	EMPLOYEES
1/05	11,100	252	2.3%	157,000
1/04	11,566	88	0.8%	113,000
1/03	11,305	229	2.0%	114,000
1/02	11,019	67	0.6%	113,000
1/01	11,332	404	3.6%	121,000
1/00	11,862	279	2.4%	119,000
1/99	11,170	(132)	—	114,000
1/98	11,038	490	4.4%	116,000
1/97	9,932	427	4.3%	107,000
1/96	9,427	148	1.6%	111,000
Annual Growth	**1.8%**	**6.1%**	**—**	**3.9%**

2005 Year-End Financials

Debt ratio: 43.0%
Return on equity: 5.9%
Cash ($ mil.): 1,250
Current ratio: 1.69
Long-term debt ($ mil.): 1,860

Net Income History

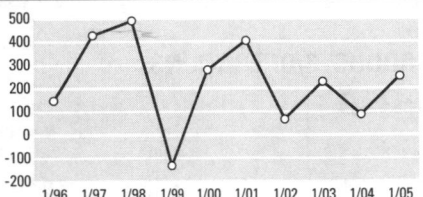

| | 1/96 | 1/97 | 1/98 | 1/99 | 1/00 | 1/01 | 1/02 | 1/03 | 1/04 | 1/05 |

Traffic.com

No, Traffic.com does not provide information about Steve Winwood. Instead, the leading commercial supplier of digitally gathered traffic data offers real-time data about specific speeds, travel times, and delay times generated by roadside sensors placed on monitored routes. The company covers 24 of the country's largest cities (home to some 55 million commuters), including Houston and New York. Traffic.com also offers an advanced service that delivers updated, custom traffic information by text to cell phones and other wireless devices. In addition, the company provides data for dashboard navigational systems in cars, as well as for XM Satellite Radio, The Weather Channel, and Comcast Cable Communications.

Traffic.com earns most of its money through providing traffic information to radio and TV stations in exchange for selling advertising time that is generally adjacent to the stations' traffic, news, and weather reports.

EXECUTIVES

Chairman: Mark J. DeNino, age 52
CEO and Director: Robert N. Verratti, age 62, $300,000 pay
President and Director: David L. Jannetta, age 53, $201,200 pay
COO: Christopher M. (Chris) Rothey, age 35, $181,666 pay
CFO: Andrew Maunder, age 48

SVP Business Development: Michael Nappi, age 51
SVP Media Affiliation: Peter Doyle, age 56
SVP Operations and Systems Architecture: Peter Menninger, age 44
SVP Sales: William Powers, age 38
SVP Software Development: Brian Smyth, age 37
VP ITS and Telematics and Corporate Counsel: John J. Collins
VP Marketing: Joan Silver
CIO: Joseph A. Reed, age 40, $185,000 pay
Director Programming: Margaret Cronan
Auditors: Ernst & Young LLP

LOCATIONS

HQ: Traffic.com, Inc.
851 Duportail Rd., Ste. 220, Wayne, PA 19087
Phone: 610-725-9700   **Fax:** 610-725-0530
Web: www.traffic.com

PRODUCTS/OPERATIONS

2004 Sales

	$ mil.	% of total
Advertising	39.4	89
Traffic data	4.7	11
Total	**44.1**	**100**

Selected Offerings

Electronic feeds to third parties
   (The Weather Channel, Comcast)
In-vehicle traffic data services (Acura RL, Cadillac CTS)
Traffic.com
   City Pages (US city traffic information)
   Jam Factor (traffic measurement system)
   myTraffic.com (personalized traffic information)
TrafficInform (consumer wireless subscription service)
Traffic Pulse Broadcaster (radio product)
Traffic Pulse NeXgen (television product)

COMPETITORS

Clear Channel
MetroCommute
Westwood One

HISTORICAL FINANCIALS

Company Type: Private

Income Statement

FYE: December 31

	REVENUE ($ mil.)	NET INCOME ($ mil.)	NET PROFIT MARGIN	EMPLOYEES
12/04	44	(15)	—	527
12/03	39	(21)	—	—
12/02	29	(27)	—	—
Annual Growth	**24.4%**	**—**	**—**	**—**

2004 Year-End Financials

Debt ratio: —
Return on equity: —
Cash ($ mil.): 5
Current ratio: 1.50
Long-term debt ($ mil.): 0

Net Income History

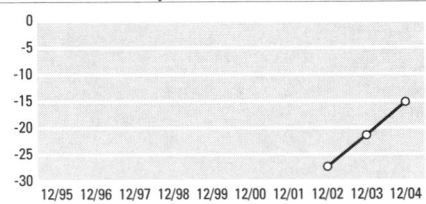

| | 12/95 | 12/96 | 12/97 | 12/98 | 12/99 | 12/00 | 12/01 | 12/02 | 12/03 | 12/04 |

Trammell Crow Residential

Trammell Crow Residential builds and maintains quite the nest. A developer and manager of upscale apartment complexes, the company operates regionally through national and divisional partners. These partners work with the company to handle the purchase, development, and building of multifamily rental properties. Subsidiary Trammell Crow Residential Services manages nearly 200 in about 20 states, with the heaviest concentrations of properties located in Texas, the Southeast, and the West. The company split off from mammoth real estate management firm Trammell Crow in 1977 but is still associated with the Crow family empire.

Trammell Crow Residential is selling Trammell Crow Residential Services to members of the subsidiary's executive team. After the sale, the name of the management firm is expected to change. Although the spun-off company will completely separate from Trammell Crow Residential, it will continue to manage Trammell Crow's properties.

EXECUTIVES

Chairman and CEO: J. Ronald Terwilliger
EVP and Chief Accounting Officer: Rachel Purcell
EVP, Human Resources and Information Systems: Tim Swango
EVP, Risk Management and Legal Services: Thomas J. (Tom) Patterson
Executive Managing Director, Capital Markets: Michael G. Melaugh
Senior Managing Director, Affordable Housing: Chris Bergmann
Managing Director, Acquisitions: Susan D. Vickery

LOCATIONS

HQ: Trammell Crow Residential
2859 Paces Ferry Rd., Ste. 1100, Atlanta, GA 30339
Phone: 770-801-1600   **Fax:** 770-801-5395
Web: www.tcresidential.com

2004 Properties under Management

	No.
Texas	50
North Carolina	27
Florida	25
Colorado	24
Oregon	10
Georgia	8
Washington	7
California	6
Louisiana	6
South Carolina	6
Maryland	4
New York	4
Virginia	4
Arizona	3
Connecticut	2
New Jersey	2
Washington, DC	2
Massachusetts	1
Total	**191**

COMPETITORS

AIMCO
Berkshire Realty
Cousins Properties
Gables Residential Trust
Great Atlantic Management
Hines Interests
Inland Group
JPI
Lincoln Property
LNR Property
Roberts Realty Investors
Stratus Properties
The Vandenburg Organization

HISTORICAL FINANCIALS

Company Type: Private

Income Statement

FYE: December 31

	REVENUE ($ mil.)	NET INCOME ($ mil.)	NET PROFIT MARGIN	EMPLOYEES
12/03	1,592	—	—	2,300
12/02	2,000	—	—	2,300
12/01	2,000	—	—	2,000
12/00	2,000	—	—	4,000
12/99	1,800	—	—	4,000
12/98	1,617	—	—	3,500
12/97	1,322	—	—	3,000
12/96	920	—	—	2,500
12/95	510	—	—	900
Annual Growth	15.3%	—	—	12.4%

Revenue History

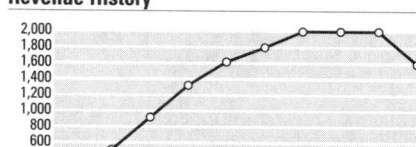

Transammonia

Fertilizers, liquefied petroleum gas (LPG), and petrochemicals form the lifeblood of international trader Transammonia. The company trades, distributes, and transports these commodities around the world. Transammonia's fertilizer business includes ammonia, phosphates, and urea. Transammonia's Sea-3 subsidiary imports and distributes propane to residential, commercial, and industrial customers in the northeastern US and in Florida. The company's Trammochem unit trades in petrochemicals, specializing in aromatics, methanol, methyltertiary butyl ether (MTBE), and olefins. Trammo Petroleum trades oil products including gasoline, heating oil, jet fuel, and naphtha from its office in Houston.

EXECUTIVES

Chairman and CEO: Ronald P. Stanton
SVP and CFO: Edward G. Weiner
CIO: Benjamin Tan
Director Human Resources: Marguerite Harrington

LOCATIONS

HQ: Transammonia, Inc.
320 Park Ave., 10th Fl., New York, NY 10022
Phone: 212-223-3200 **Fax:** 212-759-1410
Web: www.transammonia.com

Transammonia operates offices in 18 countries, with major trading centers in Darien, Connecticut; Tampa, Florida; and Houston in the US and in Amman, Jordan; Beijing; Hong Kong; Lachen, Switzerland; London; and Paris.

PRODUCTS/OPERATIONS

Major Subsidiaries

Sea-3 (liquefied propane)
Trammochem (petrochemicals)
Trammo Gas (LPGs)
Trammo Petroleum (crude oil and oil products)
Transammonia (fertilizers)

COMPETITORS

Cargill
CF Industries
ConAgra
Dynegy
HELM
Magellan Midstream
Norsk Hydro
Terra Industries

HISTORICAL FINANCIALS

Company Type: Private

Income Statement

FYE: December 31

	REVENUE ($ mil.)	NET INCOME ($ mil.)	NET PROFIT MARGIN	EMPLOYEES
12/03	4,000	—	—	300
12/02	2,309	—	—	269
12/01	2,434	—	—	237
12/00	2,447	—	—	218
12/99	1,480	—	—	205
12/98	1,380	—	—	249
12/97	2,100	—	—	262
12/96	2,480	—	—	235
12/95	2,469	—	—	200
12/94	1,330	—	—	207
Annual Growth	13.0%	—	—	4.2%

Revenue History

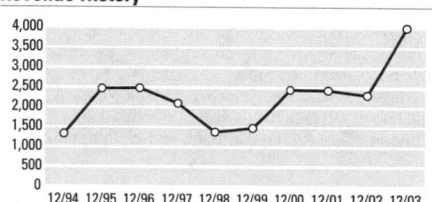

TransDigm Holding

TransDigm operates through subsidiaries that manufacture and distribute aircraft components. Subsidiary companies include AeroControlex (pumps, valves, controls), AdelWiggins (fuel line connectors, hoses, connectors), Marathon Power Technologies (batteries, chargers, inverters), Adams Rite Aerospace (hardware, water systems, oxygen systems, control consoles), and Champion Aerospace (spark plugs, oil filters, igniters). TransDigm acquired Avionics Instruments, a maker of conversion devices, in 2004, and Skurka Engineering Company, a maker of electric motors and components, in 2005. Investment firm Warburg Pincus owns TransDigm.

EXECUTIVES

Chairman and CEO: W. Nicholas Howley, age 52, $625,500 pay (prior to title change)
EVP and CFO: Gregory Rufus, age 48, $275,000 pay (prior to promotion)
President, Adams Rite Aerospace, Inc.: John F. Leary, age 57, $247,125 pay
EVP and President, AdelWiggins Group: Robert S. Henderson, age 48, $249,500 pay (prior to promotion)
President and COO: Raymond Laubenthal, age 43, $249,500 pay (prior to promotion)
President, Champion Aerospace Inc.: W. Todd Littleton, age 41
Auditors: Ernst & Young LLP

LOCATIONS

HQ: TransDigm Holding Company
1301 E. 9th St., Ste. 3710, Cleveland, OH 44114
Phone: 216-289-4939
Web: www.transdigm.com

COMPETITORS

Goodrich
Honeywell International
United Technologies

HISTORICAL FINANCIALS

Company Type: Private

Income Statement

FYE: September 30

	REVENUE ($ mil.)	NET INCOME ($ mil.)	NET PROFIT MARGIN	EMPLOYEES
9/04	301	30	9.8%	1,100
9/03	293	(73)	—	—
Annual Growth	2.5%	—	—	—

2004 Year-End Financials

Debt ratio: —
Return on equity: 5.6%
Cash ($ mil.): —

Current ratio: —
Long-term debt ($ mil.): —

Net Income History

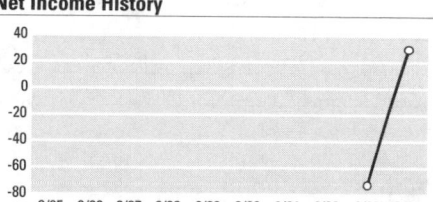

TransPerfect Translations

TransPerfect Translations can get your message through no matter what language it's in. In addition to translation and interpretation services, the company offers subtitling and voice-over work as well as multi-cultural marketing (including multilingual graphics and Web design services). The company's network of more than 4,000 linguists cross cultural barriers and communicate in more than 100 languages. TransPerfect serves corporate clients from a variety of industries including legal, financial, life sciences, technology, and advertising and marketing. Phil Shawe and CEO Elizabeth Elting founded TransPerfect in 1992. Royal Caribbean Cruises, Exxon Mobil, and Bechtel have all relied on TransPerfect's services.

EXECUTIVES

President and CEO: Elizabeth (Liz) Elting, age 39
SVP, Global Sales: Brooke Christian
VP, International Sales: Angela O'Sullivan
VP, US Sales: Kevin Obarski
VP, Global Production: Mark Peeler
President, Document Management: Steven R. Kaplan
Co-Founder: Phil Shawe

LOCATIONS

HQ: TransPerfect Translations, Inc.
3 Park Ave., 39th Fl., New York, NY 10016
Phone: 212-689-5555   **Fax:** 212-689-1059
Web: www.transperfect.com

TransPerfect Translations has 30 offices on three continents. The company's US headquarters are in New York and its European headquarters are in London.

PRODUCTS/OPERATIONS

Selected Services
Document management
Interpreting
Multicultural marketing
Translation
Typesetting and graphics
Voice-overs and subtitling

COMPETITORS

Albors & Associates
ALT Services
BabelFish
Bowne Global Solutions
JLS Language Corporation

HISTORICAL FINANCIALS

Company Type: Private

Income Statement

	REVENUE ($ mil.)	NET INCOME ($ mil.)	NET PROFIT MARGIN	EMPLOYEES
12/04*	50	—	—	250
12/02	25	—	—	150
Annual Growth	100.0%	—	—	66.7%

*Irregular reporting interval

FYE: December 31

Revenue History

TransWestern Publishing

TransWestern Publishing's probably got your number. The company is one of the country's largest independent telephone directory publishers, with more than 330 directories spanning 25 states. TransWestern Publishing has more than 230,000 advertising accounts, primarily consisting of small to midsized businesses. The company also offers its directories via the Internet through its WorldPages.com subsidiary. TransWestern Publishing has been on a buying spree; it has acquired about 110 directories since 2000. Its 2001 acquisition of WorldPages.com was one of TransWestern's largest. Investment firm Thomas H. Lee owns a stake in the company.

EXECUTIVES

Chairman: Laurence H. Bloch
President and CEO: Ricardo Puente
CFO: Joan M. Fiorito
EVP Sales: Steve Boucher
EVP Sales: Jim Durance
EVP Sales: David Raymond
EVP Sales: Dennis Reimert
EVP Sales: Ita Shea-Oglesby
VP Human Resources: Cynthia M. Hardesty
EVP Sales: Steve Sparks
VP Internet Business Development: Richard Larkin
CTO: Beth Brennan
Manager Marketing: Kimberley (Kim) Beales
Auditors: Ernst & Young LLP

LOCATIONS

HQ: TransWestern Publishing Company LLC
8344 Clairemont Mesa Blvd., San Diego, CA 92111
Phone: 858-467-2800   **Fax:** 858-292-4125
Web: www.worldpages.com

TransWestern Publishing has directories in Alabama, Arizona, California, Connecticut, Florida, Georgia, Indiana, Kansas, Kentucky, Louisiana, Massachusetts, Michigan, New Jersey, Nevada, New York, Ohio, Oklahoma, Oregon, Pennsylvania, Rhode Island, Tennessee, Texas, Utah, Vermont, and Washington.

COMPETITORS

DAG Media	R.H. Donnelley
Dex Media	Switchboard
Google	USADATA
Hearst	Yellow Book USA
InfoSpace	Yellow Pages Group
infoUSA	YP
Monster Worldwide	YPM

HISTORICAL FINANCIALS

Company Type: Private

Income Statement

FYE: December 31

	REVENUE ($ mil.)	NET INCOME ($ mil.)	NET PROFIT MARGIN	EMPLOYEES
12/04	371	—	—	2,511
12/03	324	—	—	2,346
12/02	335	—	—	1,941
12/01	242	—	—	1,843
12/00	177	—	—	1,247
12/99	146	—	—	978
12/98	61	—	—	819
12/97	100	—	—	680
12/96	91	—	—	—
12/95	78	—	—	—
Annual Growth	19.0%	—	—	20.5%

Revenue History

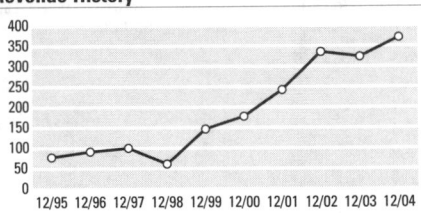

Traq-wireless

While you're searching for areas to cut business costs, Traq-wireless wants you to consider how your employees are using their cell phones and other wireless devices, and whether they're using the devices at all. For firms that don't have the funds or room to hire in-house analysts to monitor their cell phone and wireless device usage, Traq-wireless finds the appropriate plan for each wireless device based on how it's used. Because not all plans are for all employees, the company pairs wireless users with cost-savings plans by regularly mining some 40,000 rate plans. Clients include Burlington Northern Santa Fe, FedEx Freight, Cadbury Schweppes, Nova Chemicals, and Target.

Traq-wireless has developed mobile communications management software, which regularly crunches data for cell phones, PDAs, laptops, pagers, remote access services, and other untethered devices.

EXECUTIVES

President, CEO, and Director: Richard S. (Rick) Pontin, age 47
CFO: Mike Fitzpatrick
VP, Development and Operations: Scott Snyder
VP, Marketing: Jeff Fugitt
VP, Business Development: Steven (Steve) Anderson
Chief Product Officer: Bill Marsh
Director of Professional Services: Randy De Lorenzo

LOCATIONS

HQ: Traq-wireless, Inc.
8300 N. Mopac Expwy., Ste. 310, Austin, TX 78759
Phone: 512-344-0100   **Fax:** 512-345-0945
Web: www.traq.com

COMPETITORS

mindWireless

HISTORICAL FINANCIALS

Company Type: Private

Income Statement

FYE: December 31

	REVENUE ($ mil.)	NET INCOME ($ mil.)	NET PROFIT MARGIN	EMPLOYEES
12/04	14	—	—	50
12/03	5	—	—	70
12/02	1	—	—	75
Annual Growth	318.3%	—	—	(18.4%)

Revenue History

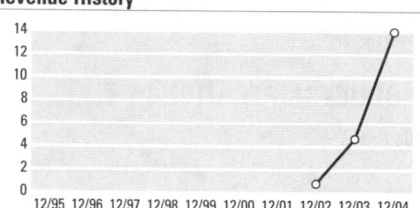

TravelCenters of America

TravelCenters of America is in the food, fuel, and relaxation business for the long haul. The company's network of 160 interstate highway travel centers in 41 US states and Ontario, Canada is the nation's largest. Company-owned, leased, and franchised truck stops provide fuel, fast-food and sit-down restaurants (Country Pride, Buckhorn Family), convenience stores, and lodging. With professional truck drivers as TravelCenters' main customers, some outlets also offer "trucker-only" services such as laundry and shower facilities, telephone and TV rooms, and truck repair. The company was formed in 1992 and is owned by a group of investors led by Oak Hill Capital Partners, Freightliner, and company officers.

TravelCenters of America acquired the Rip Griffin chain of 11 truck stops in Arizona, Arkansas, California, Colorado, New Mexico, Texas, and Wyoming for a purchase price of $120 million in December 2004. The Rip Griffin locations are all full-service travel centers that include full-service and quick-service restaurants, truck maintenance and repair shops, convenience and travel stores, and other driver amenities.

EXECUTIVES

Chairman and CEO: Edwin P. (Ed) Kuhn, age 62, $901,250 pay
President and COO: Timothy L. Doane, age 47, $595,000 pay
EVP, CFO, and Secretary: James W. (Jim) George, age 53, $567,875 pay
SVP, Development and Franchising: Peter Greene
SVP, Marketing: Joseph A. Szima, age 53, $336,000 pay
SVP, Sales: Michael H. (Mike) Hinderliter, age 55, $516,250 pay

---

VP and General Counsel: Steven C. Lee, age 41
VP, Human Resources: Bruce Sebera
VP, Shop Marketing: Randy Graham
Director, Advertising and Public Relations: Tom Liutkus
Director, Restaurant Marketing: Fred Dobson
Auditors: PricewaterhouseCoopers LLP

LOCATIONS

HQ: TravelCenters of America, Inc.
24601 Center Ridge Rd., Ste. 200,
Westlake, OH 44145
Phone: 440-808-9100   **Fax:** 440-808-3306
Web: www.tatravelcenters.com

PRODUCTS/OPERATIONS

2004 Sales

	$ mil.	% of total
Fuel	1,959.2	73
Non-fuel	708.0	27
Other	10.7	—
Total	**2,677.9**	**100**

2004 Stores

	No.
Company-operated	138
Leased	12
Franchisee-owned	10
Total	**160**

COMPETITORS

Bowlin Travel Centers	Marathon Petroleum
Chevron	Petro Stopping Centers
Exxon Mobil	Pilot
Flying J	Royal Dutch/Shell Group
Love's Country Stores	Stuckey's

HISTORICAL FINANCIALS

Company Type: Private

Income Statement

FYE: December 31

	REVENUE ($ mil.)	NET INCOME ($ mil.)	NET PROFIT MARGIN	EMPLOYEES
12/04	2,678	15	0.6%	11,510
12/03	2,176	9	0.4%	10,500
12/02	1,870	1	0.1%	10,000
12/01	1,935	(10)	—	10,255
12/00	2,060	(38)	—	10,635
12/99	1,455	(25)	—	11,000
12/98	924	(15)	—	9,800
12/97	1,039	(6)	—	8,000
12/96	696	6	0.8%	—
12/95	456	10	2.2%	—
Annual Growth	21.7%	4.6%	—	5.3%

2004 Year-End Financials

Debt ratio: 1,804.1%
Return on equity: 47.4%
Cash ($ mil.): 46
Current ratio: 1.32
Long-term debt ($ mil.): 683

Net Income History

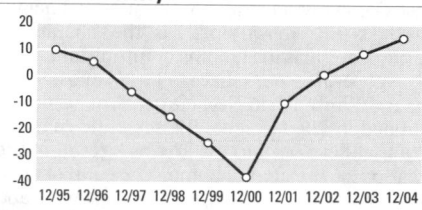

Trek Resources

The long trek that Trek Resources is on has it exploring for and producing oil and natural gas primarily in Texas, but also in Oklahoma. The company has proved reserves of 10 billion cu. ft. of gas and 1.4 million barrels of oil. Trek Resources has interests in 370 wells and operates 298. The company's business strategy is to refurbish and improve the production potential of existing oil and gas producing properties and to develop non-producing and undeveloped reserves on other properties that it owns. Trek Resources was taken private in a reverse stock split in May 2005; chairman and CEO Michael Montgomery owns a controlling stake in the company.

EXECUTIVES

Chairman, President, CEO, and CFO:
Michael E. Montgomery, age 51, $123,600 pay
Secretary: Kenneth R. Smith, age 52
Auditors: Hein + Associates LLP

LOCATIONS

HQ: Trek Resources, Inc.
4925 Greenville Ave., Ste. 955, Dallas, TX 75206
Phone: 214-373-0318   **Fax:** 214-373-8035
Web: www.trekresources.com

PRODUCTS/OPERATIONS

2004 Sales

	$ mil.	% of total
Oil	5.0	56
Gas	3.9	44
Total	**8.9**	**100**

COMPETITORS

Brigham Exploration
Exploration Company of Delaware
Parallel Petroleum

HISTORICAL FINANCIALS

Company Type: Private

Income Statement

FYE: September 30

	REVENUE ($ mil.)	NET INCOME ($ mil.)	NET PROFIT MARGIN	EMPLOYEES
9/04	9	2	23.6%	7
9/03	8	1	16.0%	5
9/02	6	(1)	—	6
9/01	7	1	10.0%	8
Annual Growth	8.3%	44.2%	—	(4.4%)

2004 Year-End Financials

Debt ratio: 144.1%
Return on equity: —
Cash ($ mil.): —
Current ratio: —
Long-term debt ($ mil.): 8

Net Income History

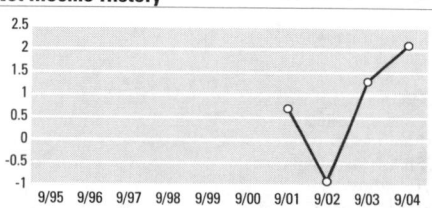

TriMas
Corporation

Whether you're hitching your wagon or seeking closure, TriMas' business mix is always fastenating. The company's Cequent Group unit makes trailers, hitches, and roof racks for SUVs and trucks. TriMas' Rieke Packaging Systems unit makes containers, closures, dispensers, and other packaging items for consumer products. The Industrial Specialties unit manufactures a range of products, including precision tools, gaskets, and tapes. TriMas' Fastening Systems division makes large-diameter bolts used to assemble construction and agricultural equipment. Heartland Industrial Partners controls TriMas; part of Heartland's stake is held by former TriMas parent Metaldyne, which also is controlled by Heartland.

Heartland might have been able to cash out at least part of its stake in Trimas, but a proposed IPO filed by Trimas in March 2004 was withdrawn in May 2005.

EXECUTIVES

Chairman: Samuel Valenti III, age 59
President, CEO, and Director: Grant Beard, age 44, $1,018,900 pay
CFO: E. R. (Skip) Autry Jr., age 50
EVP Corporate Development: Benson K. Woo, age 49
VP Human Resources: Dwayne Newcom, age 44
VP Finance and Treasurer: Robert J. Zalupski, age 46
President, Rieke Packaging Systems: Lynn Brooks, age 51, $616,000 pay
President, Cequent Transportation Accessories: Scott Hazlett, age 49, $546,757 pay
President, Industrial Specialties and Fastening Systems: Edward L. Schwartz, age 43, $586,500 pay
General Counsel and Secretary: Joshua A. Sherbin, age 41
Auditors: KPMG LLP

LOCATIONS

HQ: TriMas Corporation
39400 Woodward Ave., Ste. 130, Bloomfield Hills, MI 48304
Phone: 248-631-5450   **Fax:** 248-631-5455
Web: www.trimascorp.com

TriMas has operations in Australia, Canada, China, Germany, Italy, Mexico, the UK, and the US.

PRODUCTS/OPERATIONS

2004 Sales

	$ mil.	% of total
Cequent Transportation Accessories	511.3	49
Industrial Specialties	248.7	24
Fastening Systems	156.0	15
Rieke Packaging Systems	129.2	12
Total	**1,045.2**	**100**

Selected Products

Cequent Transportation Accessories
Ballmounts
Cargo liners
Couplers
Floor mats
Hitch accessories
Portable toilets
Roof racks
Splash guards
Tie downs
Trailer brakes
Trailer lighting products
Travel carriers
Winches

Industrial Specialties
Cylinders for acetylene
Fasteners
Fiberglass facings
Flame retardant facings
Heat jacks
Industrial gaskets
Precision cutting tools
Fastening Systems
Blind bolt fasteners
Large diameter bolts
Rieke Packaging Systems
Bottle closures and dispensers
Drum closures and dispensers
Pail closures and dispensers
Plastic industrial closures and dispensers
Specialty pumps
Specialty sprayers

COMPETITORS

AptarGroup
Atwood Mobile Products
Dutton-Lainson

Harsco
Johns Manville
Saint-Gobain Calmar

HISTORICAL FINANCIALS

Company Type: Private

Income Statement   FYE: December 31

	REVENUE ($ mil.)	NET INCOME ($ mil.)	NET PROFIT MARGIN	EMPLOYEES
12/04	1,045	(2)	—	5,200
12/03	905	(31)	—	4,736
12/02	750	(35)	—	3,770
12/01	748	(11)	—	—
Annual Growth	**11.8%**	**—**	**—**	**17.4%**

2004 Year-End Financials

Debt ratio: 182.5%
Return on equity: —
Cash ($ mil.): 3
Current ratio: 1.45
Long-term debt ($ mil.): 739

Net Income History

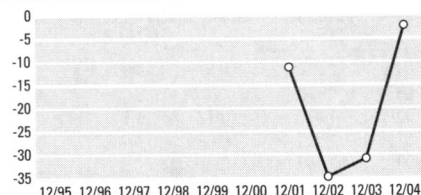

Trinity Capital

The three parts of this Trinity are Los Alamos National Bank (LANB), Title Guaranty & Insurance Company, and the communities that neighbor the facility known simply as "the Laboratory." Trinity Capital is the holding company for LANB, which operates four offices in Los Alamos, Santa Fe, and White Rock, New Mexico. The bank was founded in 1963 to serve the scientific community that developed in the area as a result of the creation of the atomic bomb. The bank offers a range of deposit, lending, asset management, and trust services. Trinity acquired its title insurance company subsidiary in 2000.

EXECUTIVES

Chairman, Trinity Capital and Los Alamos National Bank: Jerry Kindsfather, age 54
Vice Chairman, Trinity Capital and Los Alamos National Bank: Jeffrey F. Howell, age 51
President and CEO; Chairman and CEO, Los Alamos National Bank and Trinity Guaranty & Insurance Company: William C. Enloe, age 55, $355,819 pay
Secretary; President and Chief Administrative Officer, Los Alamos National Bank: Steve W. Wells, age 48, $255,078 pay
CFO; VP and CFO, Los Alamos National Bank: Daniel Bartholomew, age 38
Auditors: Neff & Ricci LLP

LOCATIONS

HQ: Trinity Capital Corporation
1200 Trinity Dr., Los Alamos, NM 87544
Phone: 505-662-5171   **Fax:** 505-662-0329
Web: www.lanb.com

PRODUCTS/OPERATIONS

2004 Sales

	$ mil.	% of total
Interest		
Loans, including fees	50.3	78
Investment securities	3.8	6
Other	0.2	—
Noninterest		
Gain on sale of loans	3.1	5
Mortgage loan servicing fees	2.4	4
Loan & other fees	2.4	4
Service charges on deposits	1.4	2
Other	1.1	1
Total	**64.7**	**100**

COMPETITORS

BOK Financial
First State Bancorporation
Wells Fargo

HISTORICAL FINANCIALS

Company Type: Private

Income Statement   FYE: December 31

	ASSETS ($ mil.)	NET INCOME ($ mil.)	INCOME AS % OF ASSETS	EMPLOYEES
12/04	1,080	10	1.0%	271
12/03	1,007	13	1.3%	282
12/02	912	10	1.1%	258
12/01	810	8	1.0%	—
Annual Growth	**10.1%**	**9.6%**	**—**	**2.5%**

2004 Year-End Financials

Equity as % of assets: 5.1%
Return on assets: 1.0%
Return on equity: 20.3%
Long-term debt ($ mil.): 60
Sales ($ mil.): 65

Net Income History

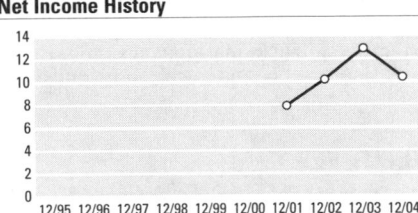

Trinity Health

One needn't believe in the holy trinity to come to Trinity Health. The Catholic health care system runs nearly 50 hospitals and has some 400 outpatient facilities, as well as long-term care facilities, home health agencies, and hospice programs in seven states. Combined, Trinity Health has some 6,500 acute care and non-acute care beds. Its subsidiary, Trinity Health Plans, operates the Care Choices HMO in southeastern Michigan. Another subsidiary, Trinity Design, offers health care facility architectural and interior design services. Catholic Health Ministries sponsors the organization.

Trinity Health is really more of a duo than a trio: The not-for-profit company is the result of a coupling between Mercy Health Services and Holy Cross Health System.

EXECUTIVES

Chairman: William Kreykes
President and CEO: Joseph R. Swedish
COO: Edgar T. (Ed) Carlson
Chief Development Officer:
James (Jim) Peppiatt Combes, age 67
EVP, Western Division: Marsha Casey
EVP, Clinical and Physician Services: M. Narendra Kini
SVP and CFO: Edward Chadwick, age 46
SVP and CIO: James (Jim) Elert
SVP and General Counsel: Daniel G. (Dan) Hale
SVP, Human Resources: William (Bill) Anderson
SVP, Mission Integration: Sister M. Gretchen Elliott
SVP, Strategic Planning and Support: Bruce Goldstrom
VP, Clinical Quality and Patient Safety: Paul Conlon
VP, Corporate Communications and Public Relations:
Stephen M. Shivinsky
Auditors: Deloitte & Touche LLP

LOCATIONS

HQ: Trinity Health
27870 Cabot Dr., Novi, MI 48377
Phone: 248 489 5004   **Fax:** 248 489 6039
Web: www.trinity-health.org

Selected Operations

California
Saint Agnes Medical Center (Fresno)
Idaho
Saint Alphonsus Regional Medical Center (Boise)
Indiana
Saint Joseph's Regional Medical Center (South Bend)
Iowa
Mercy Medical Centers (Clinton, Dubuque, Mason City, New Hampton, Sioux City)
Maryland
Holy Cross Hospital (Silver Spring)
Michigan
Saint Joseph Mercy Health System (Ann Arbor)
Mercy Hospital (Cadillac)
Trinity Design (Farmington Hills)
Trinity Health International (Farmington Hills)
Trinity Health Plans (Farmington Hills)
Saint Mary's Mercy Medical Center (Grand Rapids)
Mercy Hospital (Grayling)
St. Mary Mercy Hospital (Livonia)
Mercy General Health Partners (Muskegon)
St. Joseph Mercy Oakland (Pontiac)
Mercy Hospital (Port Huron)
Ohio
Mount Carmel Health System (Columbus)
Ambulatory Management Services (Westerville)

COMPETITORS

Ascension Health	Henry Ford Health System
Beverly Enterprises	Mayo Foundation
Blue Cross (MI)	Triad Hospitals
Detroit Medical Center	William Beaumont
HCA	Hospital

HISTORICAL FINANCIALS

Company Type: Not-for-profit

Income Statement

FYE: June 30

	REVENUE ($ mil.)	NET INCOME ($ mil.)	NET PROFIT MARGIN	EMPLOYEES
6/04	5,287	553	10.5%	44,100
6/03	4,957	(236)	—	43,900
6/02	4,697	5	0.1%	44,500
6/01	4,500	—	—	45,700
6/00	4,100	—	—	45,700
6/99	3,300	—	—	36,000
6/98	2,534	—	—	26,436
6/97	2,399	—	—	27,510
6/96	2,303	—	—	30,000
6/95	2,201	—	—	26,584
Annual Growth	**10.2%**	**911.8%**	**—**	**5.8%**

2004 Year-End Financials

Debt ratio: 56.8%   Current ratio: 2.10
Return on equity: 19.3%   Long-term debt ($ mil.): 1,790
Cash ($ mil.): 862

Net Income History

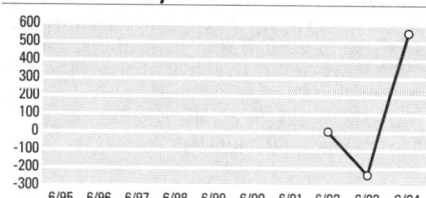

Tronox

Tronox (formerly New-Co Chemical) comes into the chemical world with a lofty status. The company, a subsidiary of Kerr-McGee that filed to go public in June 2005, will take over its parent's status as the third-largest global titanium dioxide (TiO2) producer. (DuPont and Millennium Chemicals are the top players in the market.) Its products are sold under the TRONOX brand and are used as a whitening pigment in coatings, plastics, and paper. TiO2 sales account for the majority of the unit's revenues; it also produces other chemicals, including electrolytic, boron-based, and specialty products. Tronox will combine the chemical operations of several Kerr-McGee subsidiaries, including Kerr-McGee Chemical.

EXECUTIVES

Chairman: Robert M. Wohleber, age 54
President, CEO, and Director: Thomas W. (Tom) Adams, age 44, $455,113 pay
VP and CFO: Mary Mikkelson, age 44, $217,240 pay (partial-year salary)
COO and Director: Marty J. Rowland, age 48, $263,264 pay
VP, General Counsel, and Secretary: Roger G. Addison, age 53, $335,693 pay
Auditors: Ernst & Young LLP

LOCATIONS

HQ: Tronox Incorporated
123 Robert S. Kerr Ave., Oklahoma City, OK 73102
Phone: 405-270-1313   **Fax:** 405-270-3609

Tronox has manufacturing, sales, and service operations in the Asia/Pacific region, Europe, and North America and serves customers in more than 100 countries.

PRODUCTS/OPERATIONS

2004 Sales

	$ mil.	% of total
Pigment	1,209	93
Electrolytic & other chemical products	93	7
Total	**1,302**	**100**

COMPETITORS

Altair Nanotechnologies	Kronos
DuPont	Millennium Chemicals
Huntsman Corp	Rockwood Holdings
Kemira	TOR Minerals

HISTORICAL FINANCIALS

Company Type: Private

Income Statement

FYE: December 31

	REVENUE ($ mil.)	NET INCOME ($ mil.)	NET PROFIT MARGIN	EMPLOYEES
12/04	1,302	(128)	—	2,150
12/03	1,158	(84)	—	—
12/02	1,064	(97)	—	—
Annual Growth	**10.6%**	**—**	**—**	**—**

2004 Year-End Financials

Debt ratio: 0.0%   Current ratio: 1.66
Return on equity: —   Long-term debt ($ mil.): 0
Cash ($ mil.): 24

Net Income History

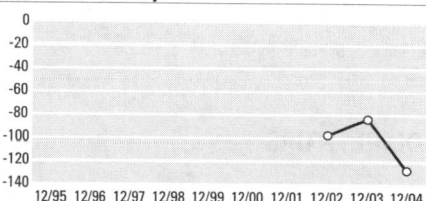

True Temper Sports

True Temper's golf shafts have probably withstood many golf course temper tantrums. The company primarily makes golf shafts and bicycle tubing, forks, and seat posts. Its steel manufacturing facility in Amory, Mississippi makes steel products for the bicycle, automobile, and golfing industries and its composite production facilities in El Cajon, California and Guangzhou, China make graphite golf shafts and lacrosse and hockey sticks. True Temper's golf shafts are used by club makers such as Callaway, Golfsmith, TaylorMade, and Mizuno. Members of management, along with Gilbert Global Equity Partners, purchased the company from Cornerstone Equity Investors in mid-2004.

EXECUTIVES

Co-Chairman: Steven J. Gilbert, age 57
Co-Chairman: Steven Kotler, age 58
President and CEO: Scott C. Hennessy, age 46, $400,000 pay
SVP, CFO, and Treasurer: Fred H. Geyer, age 44, $200,000 pay
SVP, Global Distribution and Sales: Adrian H. McCall, age 47, $175,000 pay
VP, Engineering, Research, and Development: Graeme Horwood, age 60, $130,000 pay
VP, Finance: Jason A. Jenne, age 35
VP, Human Resources: Stephen M. Brown, age 39
VP, Manufacturing: L. Gene Pierce, age 38, $154,000 pay
Director, Marketing and Tour Operations: Chad Hall
Manager, Sales and Marketing: Corey Bush
Assistant Manager, Marketing Communications: Cara Polinski
Tour Manager: Bob Montgomery
Auditors: KPMG LLP

LOCATIONS

HQ: True Temper Sports, Inc.
8275 Tournament Dr., Ste. 200, Memphis, TN 38125
Phone: 901-746-2000   **Fax:** 901-746-2160
Web: www.truetemper.com

2004 Sales

	% of total
US	63
Other countries	37
Total	**100**

PRODUCTS/OPERATIONS

2004 Sales

	% of total
Golf shafts	94
Performance Sports	6
Total	**100**

COMPETITORS

Aldila	Graphite Design
Cannondale	Royal Precision

HISTORICAL FINANCIALS

Company Type: Private

Income Statement

FYE: December 31

	REVENUE ($ mil.)	NET INCOME ($ mil.)	NET PROFIT MARGIN	EMPLOYEES
12/04	98	(20)	—	649
12/03	116	11	9.4%	—
12/02	107	9	8.7%	—
Annual Growth	(4.3%)	—	—	—

Net Income History

True Value

To survive against home improvement giants such as The Home Depot and Lowe's, True Value (formerly TruServ) is relying on the true value of service. Formed by the merger of Cotter & Company (which was the supplier to the True Value chain) and ServiStar Coast to Coast, the cooperative serves some 6,025 retail outlets (down from nearly 7,200 in 2001), including its flagship True Value hardware stores. The company sells home improvement and garden supplies, as well as appliances, housewares, sporting goods, and toys. Members use the Taylor Rental, Grand Rental Station, Home & Garden Showplace, Induserve Supply, and other banners. True Value also manufactures its own brand of paints and applicators.

The merger of Cotter & Company and ServiStar Coast to Coast (operator of Coast to Coast and ServiStar hardware stores, most of which converted to the True Value banner) gave members — many of them mom-and-pop outlets — more buying clout to compete against the do-it-yourself mega-retailers, plus retail advice and advertising support. True Value has been growing its business in the rental and maintenance, repair, and operation (MRO) arenas, and it plans to begin supplying lumber and building materials once again. (The company had sold its lumber and building materials business in 2000.) At the store level, True Value has been developing "lite" or smaller versions of its signature programs, such as Platinum Paint Shop, for the co-op's stores (more than half) that are less than 6,000 sq. ft.

Outside the US the company serves about 700 stores in nearly 60 countries.

HISTORY

Noting that hardware retailers had begun to form wholesale cooperatives to lower costs, John Cotter, a traveling hardware salesman, and associate Ed Lanctot started pitching the wholesale co-op idea in 1947 to small-town and suburban hardware retailers, and by early 1948 they had enrolled 25 merchants for $1,500 each. Cotter became chairman of the new firm, Cotter & Company.

The co-op created the Value & Service (V&S) store trademark in 1951 to emphasize the advantages of an independent hardware store. Acquisitions included the 1963 purchase of Chicago-based wholesaler Hibbard, Spencer, Bartlett, giving Cotter 400 new members and the well-known True Value trademark, which soon replaced V&S signs. Four years later Cotter broadened its focus by buying the General Paint & Chemical Company (Tru-Test paint). The V&S name was revived in 1972 for a five-and-dime store co-op, V&S Variety Stores.

In 1989 Cotter died and Lanctot retired. (Lanctot died in October 2003.) By 1989 there were almost 7,000 True Value Stores. Cotter moved into Canada in 1992 by acquiring hardware distributor and store operator Macleod-Stedman (275 outlets).

Juggling variety-store and hardware merchandise and delivering very small amounts of merchandise to a lukewarm co-op membership did not allow for economies of scale, so in 1995 the company quit its manufacturing operations and its US variety stores (though it still serves variety stores in Canada, operating as C&S Choices),

tightened membership requirements, and introduced new services.

Two years later Cotter formed TruServ by merging with hardware wholesaler Servistar Coast to Coast. ServiStar had its origins in the nation's first hardware co-op, American Hardware Supply, which was founded in Pittsburgh in 1910 by M. R. Porter, John Howe, and E. S. Corlett. By 1988, the year it changed its name to ServiStar, the co-op topped $1 billion in sales.

ServiStar expanded in the upper Midwest and on the West Coast in 1990 when it acquired the assets of the Coast to Coast chain (founded in 1928 as a franchise hardware store in Minneapolis); ServiStar brought Coast to Coast out of bankruptcy two years later, making it a co-op. Merging its 1992 acquisition of Taylor Rental Center with its Grand Rental Station stores in 1993 made ServiStar the #1 general rental chain. In 1996 it consolidated Coast to Coast's operations into its own and changed its name to ServiStar Coast to Coast.

President Don Hoye became CEO of the company in 1999. That year TruServ slashed 1,000 jobs and declared it would convert all its hardware store chains to the True Value banner. But TruServ lost $131 million in 1999 over bookkeeping gaffs, and co-op members received no dividends. Of 2,800 ServiStar dealers, only 1,900 raised the True Value flag. Others either declined to switch or were never offered the change because other True Value stores already shared their market area. In addition, stores began deserting the co-op because of inventory and other problems. In late 2000 the company sold its lumber and building materials business.

As competition continued to increase in 2001, the company was facing falling sales, lawsuits from shareholders, and accusations by retailers of unfair practices intended to pressure them into adopting the cooperative's flagship True Value banner. TruServ also had to confront a $200 million loan default. It made cuts in its corporate staff and divested its Canadian interests. In July 2001 Hoye resigned. The company's CFO and COO, Pamela Forbes Lieberman, was named the new CEO that November.

In April 2002 the company reported a net loss of $50.7 million during 2001, which it attributed to restructuring charges, inventory writedowns, and finance fees. Also that month the company announced that it had received $200 million in long-term financing. TruServ, under SEC investigation for alleged inventory, accounting, and other internal-control problems, was one of several companies that failed in August 2002 to meet a government requirement to swear by their past financial results.

In January 2003 TruServ received about $125 million in financing from investment firm W. P. Carey & Co. in a sale-leaseback deal on seven of TruServ's distribution centers. In March 2003 TruServ settled the SEC's allegations, without admitting or denying them, and agreed to follow measures intended to ensure compliance with securities laws.

Lieberman resigned in November 2004. Director Thomas Hanemann was named interim CEO. TruServ changed its name to True Value in Janaury 2005. In June 2005 Hanemann turned over the reins to Sears veteran Lyle G. Heidemann who joined True Value as its new president and CEO.

EXECUTIVES

Chairman: Bryan R. Ableidinger, age 56
President, CEO, and Director: Lyle G. Heidemann, age 60
SVP and CFO: David A. (Dave) Shadduck, age 44, $443,019 pay
SVP and CIO: Leslie A. Weber, age 48, $353,851 pay
SVP and Chief Merchandising Officer:
Steven L. Mahurin, age 45
SVP, General Counsel, and Secretary:
Cathy C. Anderson, age 55, $386,805 pay
SVP, Human Resources and Communications:
Amy W. Mysel, age 52
SVP, Logistics and Manufacturing:
Michael (Mike) Haining, age 49, $361,246 pay
(prior to promotion)
VP, Corporate Controller: Donald J. Deegan
VP and Corporate Treasurer: Barbara L. Wagner
VP, Marketing: Carol Wentworth, age 47
VP, Retail Development: Brian Kiernan, age 46
VP, Retail Finance: Jon Johnson
VP, Retail and Specialty Businesses Development:
Fred Kirst, age 53
Director, E-Business: Eric Lane
General Manager, Rental: Tony Sabo
Auditors: PricewaterhouseCoopers LLP

LOCATIONS

HQ: True Value Company
8600 W. Bryn Mawr Ave., Chicago, IL 60631
Phone: 773-695-5000 **Fax:** 773-695-6516
Web: www.truevaluecompany.com

True Value is a hardware store cooperative serving some 6,025 stores in the US.

PRODUCTS/OPERATIONS

2004 Sales

	$ mil.	% of total
Hardware goods	495.0	25
Farm & garden	430.8	21
Electrical & plumbing	350.7	17
Painting & cleaning	320.3	16
Appliances & housewares	218.5	11
Sporting goods & toys	102.8	5
Other	105.7	5
Total	**2,023.8**	**100**

Selected Operations

Grand Rental Station (General rental)
Home & Garden Showplace (Nursery and giftware)
Induserve Supply (Commercial and industrial)
Party Central (Parties and corporate events)
Taylor Rental (General rental)
True Value (Hardware)

COMPETITORS

84 Lumber
Ace Hardware
Akzo Nobel
Benjamin Moore
Do it Best
Fastenal
Hertz
Home Depot
Kmart
Lanoga
Lowe's
McCoy
Menard
Northern Tool
Orgill
Réno-Dépôt
Sears
Sherwin-Williams
Stock Building Supply
Sutherland Lumber
United Rentals
Valspar
Wal-Mart
Wolohan Lumber

HISTORICAL FINANCIALS

Company Type: Cooperative

Income Statement

				FYE: December 31
	REVENUE ($ mil.)	NET INCOME ($ mil.)	NET PROFIT MARGIN	EMPLOYEES
12/04	2,024	43	2.1%	2,800
12/03	2,024	21	1.0%	3,000
12/02	2,176	21	1.0%	3,200
12/01	2,619	(51)	—	4,000
12/00	3,994	34	0.9%	4,300
12/99	4,502	(131)	—	5,500
12/98	4,328	21	0.5%	6,500
12/97	3,332	43	1.3%	5,800
12/96	2,442	52	2.1%	3,825
12/95	2,437	59	2.4%	4,186
Annual Growth	**(2.0%)**	**(3.4%)**	**—**	**(4.4%)**

2004 Year-End Financials

Debt ratio: 493.7%
Return on equity: 269.3%
Cash ($ mil.): 7
Current ratio: 1.22
Long-term debt ($ mil.): 139

Net Income History

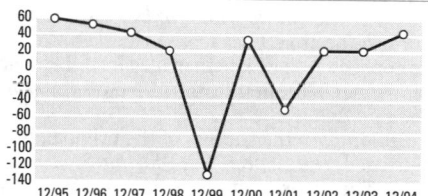

12/95 12/96 12/97 12/98 12/99 12/00 12/01 12/02 12/03 12/04

TruFoods

No matter your craving — whether by land or by sea — TruFoods has you covered. The company operates and franchises more than 300 restaurant locations across the US, including more than 100 Arthur Treacher's Fish & Chips restaurants, located primarly along the East Coast. It also runs Pudgie's Famous Chicken, the Wall Street Deli, and Burritoville chains.

EXECUTIVES

President and CEO; CEO, Wall Street Deli:
Jeffrey Bernstein
EVP and COO; COO, Wall Street Deli: Ritu Dewan
VP: Larry Feierstein
VP and Treasurer; CFO, Wall Street Deli:
Barry Knepper, age 54
Secretary and General Counsel, Wall Street Deli:
Scott Y. Stuart
Controller: Ken Manne
Director of Marketing: Jacque Vandekieft
Executive Chef: David LaPointe
Human Resources: Susie Szalai
Auditors: Amper, Politziner & Mattia, P.C.

LOCATIONS

HQ: TruFoods Systems, Inc.
5 Dakota Dr., Ste. 302, Lake Success, NY 11042
Phone: 516-358-0600 **Fax:** 516-358-5076
Web: www.trufoods.com

COMPETITORS

AFC Enterprises
Blimpie
Burger King
Captain D's
Chick-fil-A
CKE Restaurants
Dunkin
Galardi Group
Jack in the Box
Jerry's Famous Deli
Jerry's Subs
Jersey Mike's
Long John Silver's
McDonald's
Nathan's Famous
Panera Bread
Quiznos
Schlotzsky's
Subway
Triarc
Ultimate Franchise Systems
Wendy's
YUM!

HISTORICAL FINANCIALS

Company Type: Private

Income Statement

				FYE: June 30
	REVENUE ($ mil.)	NET INCOME ($ mil.)	NET PROFIT MARGIN	EMPLOYEES
6/04	15	—	—	150
6/03	15	—	—	150
6/02*	15	—	—	150
6/00	14	—	—	300
6/99	22	—	—	350
6/98	23	—	—	700
6/97	18	—	—	700
6/96	8	—	—	—
Annual Growth	**9.6%**	**—**	**—**	**(22.6%)**

*Irregular reporting interval

Revenue History

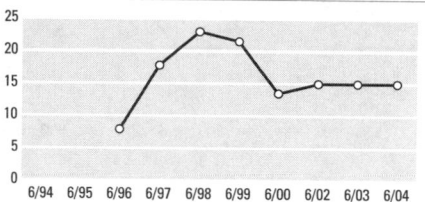

6/94 6/95 6/96 6/97 6/98 6/99 6/00 6/02 6/03 6/04

Truman Arnold

This jobber gets the job done by distributing wholesale petroleum across the US. Truman Arnold Companies (TAC) markets and distributes more than 100 million gallons of petroleum products a month to customers located in 48 states in the US through its TAC Energy subsidiary. Through its TAC Air unit, the company offers fixed-base operations (FBO), including aircraft fueling, hanger, and ground transportation services, through 11 general aviation facilities in the US. The company also operates convenience stores and provides trucking, real estate, and construction services.

The family-owned and -operated company was founded in 1964 by Texarkana businessman Truman Arnold. The company expanded its FBO business through the acquisition of Cherokee Aviation in 2005.

EXECUTIVES

Chairman and CEO: Truman Arnold
President and COO: Gregory A. (Greg) Arnold
VP, CFO, and Treasurer: Steve McMillen
VP Administration: James Day
Director Information Technology: Michael Davis
Director Marketing: Cheryl May

LOCATIONS

HQ: Truman Arnold Companies
701 S. Robison Rd., Texarkana, TX 75501
Phone: 888-370-8273 **Fax:** 903-831-4056
Web: www.tacenergy.com

Truman Arnold Companies operates in 48 states in the US, as well as in five Canadian provinces.

COMPETITORS

Getty Petroleum Marketing
Gulf Oil
Streicher Mobile Fueling
Sun Coast Resources
Warren Equities

HISTORICAL FINANCIALS

Company Type: Private

Income Statement

FYE: September 30

	REVENUE ($ mil.)	NET INCOME ($ mil.)	NET PROFIT MARGIN	EMPLOYEES
9/04	1,205	—	—	500
9/03	1,200	—	—	500
9/02	1,150	—	—	400
9/01	1,120	—	—	400
9/00	650	—	—	400
Annual Growth	**16.7%**	**—**	**—**	**5.7%**

Revenue History

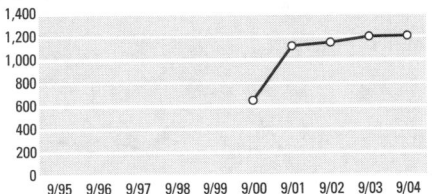

Trump Organization

When it comes to betting on big business, The Donald always pulls out a Trump card. Through The Trump Organization, Donald Trump can claim several pieces of glitzy real estate in the Big Apple, including Trump International Hotel & Tower, Trump Tower (26 floors of it, anyway), and 40 Wall Street. Trump also owns 29% of Trump Entertainment Resorts (formerly Trump Hotels & Casino Resorts), owner and operator of Atlantic City, New Jersey, casinos Trump Taj Mahal, Trump Plaza, and Trump Marina. Other holdings include a Florida resort and 50% of the Miss USA, Miss Teen USA, and Miss Universe beauty pageants (CBS owns the rest). Trump Entertainment Resorts has emerged from Chapter 11 bankruptcy.

The reorganization of Trump Entertainment Resorts allows The Donald to remain chairman, but passed on a provision that would give him a base salary of $1.5 million per year and a possible annual bonus of equal value.

Never one to quit in the face of adversity, The Donald continues to excel on the strength of his deal-making prowess. The flamboyant tycoon is renowned for setting up real estate partnerships in which other firms put up most of the cash while he retains most of the control. In the Trump World Tower, for example, he invested $6.5 million, while Korean firm Daewoo pumped in more than $58 million.

Trump also has profited from his famous moniker — which he has trademarked — and his public image: Developers can pay to co-brand their properties using the Trump name, as long as they meet Trump's super-luxury standard.

Trump dumped his stake in the now-tallest building in New York City. His interest in the Empire State Building leasehold brought in only a paltry $2 million per year. He was also ordered by the courts — after a lengthy legal battle — to sell his 50% stake in the General Motors Building to co-owner Conseco; the two parties agreed to sell the building.

Trump renovated New York City's landmark Delmonico Hotel into luxury condos — rechristened Trump Park Avenue — in 2004. It also plans to provide Canada with its tallest building — Toronto's Trump International Hotel & Tower.

Trump is developing the Trump International Hotel & Tower Chicago at the site formerly leased by the *Chicago Sun-Times*. Slated to open in 2007, the project has scored a marketing coup: Its construction will be managed by Bill Rancic, the winner of the first season of Trump's hit show *The Apprentice*.

Building on the success of the original, NBC launched *The Apprentice: Martha Stewart* in 2005. The new show follows the same format as the original, but revolves around Stewart's penchant for entertaining, design, and style. She was released from federal prison March 4, 2005. Trump and *The Apprentice* creator Mark Burnett serve as the new show's executive producers.

HISTORY

The third of four children, Donald Trump was the son of a successful builder in Queens and Brooklyn. After graduating from the Wharton School of Finance in 1968, his first job was to turn around a 1,200-unit foreclosed apartment complex in Cincinnati that his father had bought for $6 million with no money down. Managing the Cincinnati job gave Trump a distaste for the nonaffluent; he wanted to get to Manhattan to meet all the right people.

Operating as The Trump Organization, he took options on two Hudson River sites in 1975 for no money down and began lobbying the city to finance his construction of a convention center. The center was built, but not by Trump, who nevertheless got about $800,000 and priceless publicity. He and hotelier Jay Pritzker turned the Commodore Hotel near Grand Central Station into the Grand Hyatt Hotel in 1975.

In 1981 he built the posh Trump Tower on Fifth Avenue and proceeded to wheel and deal himself into 1980s folklore. In 1983 he joined with Holiday Inn to build the Trump Casino Hotel (now Trump Plaza) in Atlantic City using public-issue bonds (he bought out Holiday Inn's interest in 1986), and he bought the Trump Castle from Hilton in 1985. In 1987 he ended up with the unfinished Taj Mahal in Atlantic City, then the world's largest casino, after a battle with Merv Griffin for Resorts International (Griffin won). He bought the Plaza Hotel in Manhattan in 1988, and the Eastern air shuttle (renamed the Trump Shuttle) the next year.

As the 1990s dawned, though, Trump's balance sheet was loaded with about $3 billion in debt. At the same time, his marriage to Ivana broke up in a splash of publicity. Trump's 70 creditor banks consolidated and restructured his debt in 1990.

In 1995 Trump formed Trump Hotels & Casino Resorts and took it public. He also paid a token $10 for 40 Wall St. (now home to American Express). The next year he sold his half-interest in the Grand Hyatt Hotel to the Pritzker family and unloaded more than $1.1 billion in debt by selling the Taj Mahal and Trump's Castle to Trump Hotels.

In 1997 he published *The Art of the Comeback*, a follow-up to *The Art of the Deal* (1987), and started work on Trump Place, a residential development on New York's Upper West Side. In 1999 he began building the Trump World Tower — a 90-story residential building near the United Nations complex. Residents of nearby high rises brought lawsuits in 2000, claiming that the new building would block their view and lower their property value. The court sided with Trump.

The following year Trump and publisher Hollinger International announced plans to transform the former riverfront headquarters of the *Chicago Sun-Times* into a residential and commercial development. Originally planned to be the world's tallest skyscraper, Trump decided to scale back the project in the wake of terrorist attacks on the World Trade Center; Hollinger sold its stake in the venture to Trump in 2004.

In 2004 Trump ventured into reality television as the star and executive producer of *The Apprentice*. A hit with viewers and critics (it garnered four Emmy Award nominations), the show featured candidates competing for a position as a divisional president within The Trump Organization. Riding the wave of fascination with all things Donald, Trump published two more best-selling books (*How to Get Rich* and *Think Like A Billionaire*) that year.

In mid 2005 the Trump Organization and a group of investors sold a parcel of land and three buildings on the Manhattan waterfront to Extell Development Corp. and The Carlyle Group for about $1.8 billion. Later that year The Donald inked a deal with Nakheel, a developer in the United Arab Emirates, to develop resort destinations in the Middle East.

EXECUTIVES

Chairman, President, and CEO: Donald J. Trump, age 59
EVP and COO: Mathew F. Calamari
EVP and CFO: Allen Weisselberg
EVP: Carolyn Kepcher
EVP and General Counsel: Bernard Diamond
EVP and Assistant General Counsel: Jason Greenblatt
EVP Golf Course Development: Vincent Stellio
EVP Construction: Andrew Weiss
VP and Controller: Jeffrey McConney
VP Development: Jill Cremer
VP Development: Donald J. Trump Jr.
VP Media Relations and Human Resources: Norma Foerderer
VP Operations and Residential Buildings: Thomas Pienkos
VP Leasing and Insurance: Nathan Nelson

LOCATIONS

HQ: The Trump Organization
725 5th Ave., New York, NY 10022
Phone: 212-832-2000 **Fax:** 212-935-0141
Web: www.trumponline.com

PRODUCTS/OPERATIONS

Trump Hotels & Casino Resorts, Inc.
Indiana Riverboat at Buffington Harbor
Trump 29 Casino (management only)
Trump Marina Hotel Casino
Trump Plaza Hotel and Casino
Trump Taj Mahal Casino Resort

Other Holdings
40 Wall Street
General Motors Building at Trump International Plaza
Mar-A-Lago (private club; Palm Beach, FL)
Miss Teen USA pageant
Miss Universe pageant
Miss USA pageant
Trump Grande Ocean Resort (Sunny Isles Beach, FL)
Trump National Golf Club
Trump International Hotel and Tower
Trump Palace
Trump Parc
Trump Place
Trump Tower
Trump World (Seoul)
Trump World Tower

COMPETITORS

Alexander's
American Real Estate Partners
Aztar
Boston Properties
Harrah's Entertainment
Helmsley Enterprises
Hyatt
Lefrak Organization
Marriott
Mashantucket
 Pequot Gaming
MGM MIRAGE
Port Authority of NY & NJ
Ritz-Carlton
Tishman
Vornado Realty Trust

HISTORICAL FINANCIALS
Company Type: Private

Income Statement
FYE: December 31

	ESTIMATED REVENUE ($ mil.)	NET INCOME ($ mil.)	NET PROFIT MARGIN	EMPLOYEES
12/03	8,500	—	—	15,000
12/02	8,500	—	—	22,000
12/01	8,500	—	—	22,000
12/00	8,000	—	—	22,000
12/99	7,000	—	—	22,000
12/98	6,800	—	—	22,000
12/97	6,500	—	—	22,000
12/96	6,000	—	—	19,000
12/95	4,000	—	—	19,000
12/94	2,750	—	—	15,000
Annual Growth	13.4%	—	—	0.0%

Revenue History

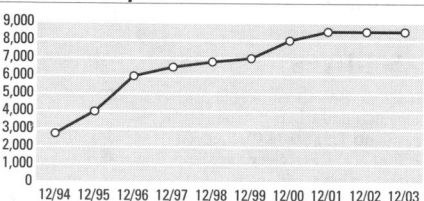

TTI

TTI has a passion for passives. Each year the company distributes more than 1.7 million electronic components, including passive components such as resistors and capacitors, and interconnects such as cables, sockets, and filter connectors. Suppliers of its 160,000 line items include AVX, Tyco Electronics, Molex, KEMET, and Vishay Intertechnology. TTI also offers services such as connector assembly, packaging, testing, and supply chain management. TTI, which majority owner and CEO Paul Andrews founded in 1971 as a supplier to the military, serves manufacturers of aerospace and defense systems, computers, telecom equipment, medical devices, and industrial products.

TTI's Mouser Electronics subsidiary specializes in catalog sales of passive components in North America. TTI acquired Mouser in 2000.

Customers in commercial markets account for about three-quarters of sales. The company is expanding its presence in Europe and Asia.

EXECUTIVES

Chairman and CEO: Paul E. Andrews Jr.
SVP Finance and CFO: Nick M. Kypreos
SVP and Chief Marketing and Strategic Planning Officer: Craig Conrad
SVP North American Sales; President, TTI Europe: Gene Conahan
SVP Corporate Materials and Logistics Management: Mike Morton
President and CEO, Mouser Electronics: Glenn Smith
President, TTI Asia: John V. Davidson
VP Corporate Product Marketing: Michael Knight
VP Corporate Operations and Logistics: Allen Clem
VP Supplier Marketing: Lew LaFornara
Director Human Resources: Myran Dill
Director Marketing: Tim Scott
Corporate Communications Coordinator: Cathy Walensky

LOCATIONS

HQ: TTI, Inc.
 2441 Northeast Pkwy., Fort Worth, TX 76106
Phone: 817-740-9000   **Fax:** 817-740-9898
Web: www.ttiinc.com

TTI has offices in Austria, Canada, China, Denmark, France, Germany, Hong Kong, Italy, Mexico, the Netherlands, Singapore, Sweden, Switzerland, Taiwan, the UK, and the US.

PRODUCTS/OPERATIONS

Selected Products
Capacitors
Circuit protectors
Connectors
Crystals
EMI filters
Magnetics/inductors
Passive integrators
Potentiometers
Relays
Resistors
Resonators
Sensors
Sound components
Switches
Wire and tools

Services
Connector assembly
Connector hot solder dipping
Documentation
Inspecting
Labeling
Lead forming, cutting, and trimming
Marking
Packaging
Parts remarking
Solder testing of passive components
Supply chain management
Taping and reeling
Testing

COMPETITORS

Advanced MP Technology
All American
 Semiconductor
Arrow Electronics
Avnet
ce CONSUMER
 ELECTRONIC
Digi-Key
Electrocomponents
Future Electronics
Jaco Electronics
Memec
N.F. Smith
Nu Horizons Electronics
Premier Farnell
ROHM
Sager Electrical

HISTORICAL FINANCIALS
Company Type: Private

Income Statement
FYE: December 31

	REVENUE ($ mil.)	NET INCOME ($ mil.)	NET PROFIT MARGIN	EMPLOYEES
12/04	877	—	—	1,750
12/03	525	—	—	1,500
12/02	630	—	—	1,500
12/01	750	—	—	1,550
12/00	955	—	—	1,050
12/99	555	—	—	1,055
12/98	461	—	—	985
12/97	450	—	—	933
12/96	411	—	—	819
Annual Growth	10.0%	—	—	10.0%

Revenue History

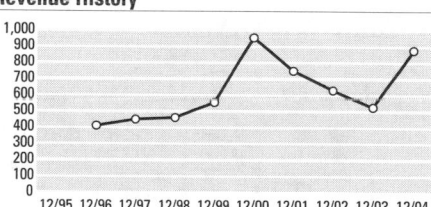

Tubby's Sub Shops

With a name like Tubby's, the sandwiches had better be big. Tubby's Sub Shops franchises about 100 Tubby's submarine sandwich restaurants located primarily in Michigan. Each Tubby's serves a variety of made-to-order submarine and pita sandwiches, along with soups, salads, curly fries, and desserts. Many of its restaurants are free-standing units while others are in shopping malls. Tubby's also has some co-branded locations. The company was co-founded in 1968 by Rick Paganes and his brothers Robert

(CEO) and Peter (VP). The Paganes family continues to own the Tubby's chain.

The company began franchising its units in 1978 and went public in 1986, but struggled financially. The Paganes took Tubby's private in 2000 after a failed merger attempt with Popeyes franchiser Interfoods of America.

EXECUTIVES

President and CEO: Robert M. (Bob) Paganes
VP: Peter T. Paganes
VP Human Resources: Shanon Oddo
Controller: Larry Hein
Director of Marketing: Michelle DeLand
Media Relations: Shanon Rupkus
Auditors: BDO Seidman, LLP

LOCATIONS

HQ: Tubby's Sub Shops, Inc.
 35807 Moravian Rd., Clinton Township, MI 48035
Phone: 586-792-2369 **Fax:** 586-792-4250
Web: www.tubby.com

COMPETITORS

Blimpie
Burger King
Chick-fil-A
Cousins Subs
Hot Brands
Jack in the Box
Jersey Mike's
Jimmy John's
McDonald's
Miami Subs
Penn Station
Potbelly
Quiznos
Restaurant Developers
Schlotzsky's
Subway
Triarc
Wendy's
YUM!

HISTORICAL FINANCIALS

Company Type: Private

Income Statement				FYE: November 30
	REVENUE ($ mil.)	NET INCOME ($ mil.)	NET PROFIT MARGIN	EMPLOYEES
11/04	10	—	—	15
11/03	10	—	—	15
11/02	9	—	—	15
11/01	10	—	—	—
11/00	10	—	—	—
11/99	10	—	—	68
11/98	7	—	—	45
11/97	4	—	—	86
11/96	3	—	—	81
11/95	4	—	—	52
Annual Growth	12.0%	—	—	(12.9%)

Revenue History

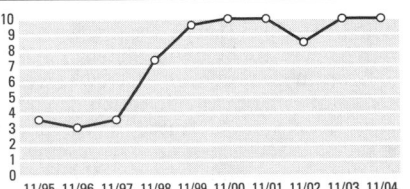

11/95 11/96 11/97 11/98 11/99 11/00 11/01 11/02 11/03 11/04

Tufts Associated Health Plans

Managed health care headaches in the New England states have made times tough for Tufts Associated Health Plans. The for-profit company provides administrative, management, advertising, and marketing services for its subsidiaries, including not-for-profit Tufts Associated Health Maintenance Organization (TAHMO), and Tufts Insurance Company (life insurance). The company's provider network serves about 750,000 members. Tufts Associated Health Plans offers HMO, PPO, point-of-service, and other health care plans to its customers. The company also provides third-party administrative services through its Tufts Benefit Administrators subsidiary.

EXECUTIVES

President and CEO: James Roosevelt Jr.
CFO: J. Andy Hilbert
SVP and CIO: Tricia Trebino
SVP Human Resources: Carol Corcoran
SVP Planning and Development: Jon M. Kingsdale
SVP Sales, Marketing, and Member Services:
 Kevin J. Counihan
VP and Secretary: Deborah E. Benjamin
Chief Medical Officer: Allen Hinkle
VP Secure Horizons: Patricia Blake
Auditors: Ernst & Young LLP

LOCATIONS

HQ: Tufts Associated Health Plans, Inc.
 333 Wyman St., Waltham, MA 02454
Phone: 781-466-9400 **Fax:** 781-466-8583
Web: www.tufts-healthplan.com

PRODUCTS/OPERATIONS

Health Plans
Advantage PPO
Choice CoPay (copay options)
Common Wealth PPO (state employee plan)
EPO (exclusive provider option)
HMO
Liberty Plan (consumer driven plans)
POS (point-of-service)
PPO (preferred provider organization)
Secure Horizons Tufts Health Plan
 for Seniors (Medicare)

COMPETITORS

Aetna
Blue Cross (MA)
CIGNA
ConnectiCare
Harvard Pilgrim
Prudential
UnitedHealth Group

HISTORICAL FINANCIALS

Company Type: Private

Income Statement				FYE: December 31
	REVENUE ($ mil.)	NET INCOME ($ mil.)	NET PROFIT MARGIN	EMPLOYEES
12/03	2,300	57	2.5%	2,500
12/02	2,329	—	—	2,500
12/01	2,000	—	—	2,500
12/00	2,000	—	—	3,000
12/99	2,000	—	—	3,000
12/98	1,600	—	—	2,500
12/97	1,210	—	—	2,341
12/96	865	—	—	1,200
12/95	670	—	—	1,128
12/94	542	—	—	—
Annual Growth	17.4%	—	—	10.5%

Revenue History

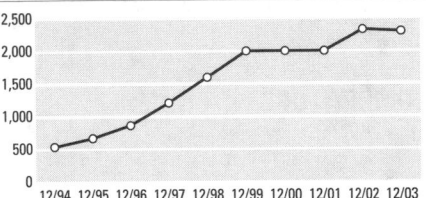

12/94 12/95 12/96 12/97 12/98 12/99 12/00 12/01 12/02 12/03

Turner Industries

Turner Industries Group turns out industrial services. The company is a top US player in industrial construction, contract maintenance, and outsourcing. Its customers include oil refiners, petrochemical companies, power generators, and pulp and paper mills. Through its divisions, the Group provides such services as scaffolding equipment rental, environmental remediation, heavy hauling and rigging, pipe fabrication, and tank cleaning. Turner Industries also offers materials management and training workshops and staffing services. Chairman emeritus Bert Turner, the company's principal shareholder, founded the company in Baton Rouge, Louisiana in 1961.

Turner Industries Group is the largest privately owned enterprise for industrial construction and maintenance in Louisiana. It consistently ranks as a leading firm in *Engineering News-Record's* lists of "The Top 400 Contractors" in the US (based on revenue); it ranked 45th in 2005.

EXECUTIVES

Chairman Emeritus: Bert S. Turner, age 83
Chairman and CEO: Roland M. Toups
President: Thomas H. Turner
VP Finance, CFO, Secretary, and Treasurer:
 Lester J. (Les) Griffon Jr.
President, Harmony: Donald L. McCollister
President, International Maintenance, National Maintenance, Turner Company, and Turner Industrial Services: Joseph W. Guitreau
President, International Piping Systems:
 Robert L. Pearson
President, Nichols Construction and Scafco:
 Davis J. Lauve

LOCATIONS

HQ: Turner Industries Group, L.L.C.
8687 United Plaza Blvd., 5th Fl.,
Baton Rouge, LA 70809
Phone: 225-922-5050   **Fax:** 225-922-5055
Web: www.turner-industries.com

Turner Industries Group operates from offices in
Alabama, Florida, Louisiana, and Texas.

PRODUCTS/OPERATIONS

Selected Services

Construction
Contract maintenance
Environmental remediation
Equipment rental
Heat exchanger bundle extraction and cleaning
Heavy hauling
Hydroblasting and lancing
Painting and blasting
Petrochemical wastewater treatment construction
    and project management
Pipe fabrication and bending
Preventive maintenance
Project management
Procurement
Rigging
Scaffolding
Specialty welding
System integration
Tank cleaning
Turnarounds and shutdowns

COMPETITORS

ABB	Halliburton
Aker Kværner	HydroChem
APi Group	Jacobs Engineering
Austin Industries	McDermott
Bechtel	Parsons
Black & Veatch	Peter Kiewit Sons'
Centerline Piping	Philip Services
CH2M HILL	Shaw Group
Chicago Bridge & Iron	TIC Holdings
Fluor	Zachry
Foster Wheeler	

HISTORICAL FINANCIALS

Company Type: Private

Income Statement
FYE: October 31

	REVENUE ($ mil.)	NET INCOME ($ mil.)	NET PROFIT MARGIN	EMPLOYEES
10/04	800	—	—	12,000
10/03	800	—	—	12,000
10/02	800	—	—	12,000
10/01	790	—	—	11,000
10/00	741	—	—	12,000
10/99	673	—	—	10,000
10/98	600	—	—	9,800
10/97	553	—	—	10,500
10/96	500	—	—	10,000
10/95	486	—	—	8,100
Annual Growth	**5.7%**	**—**	**—**	**4.5%**

Revenue History

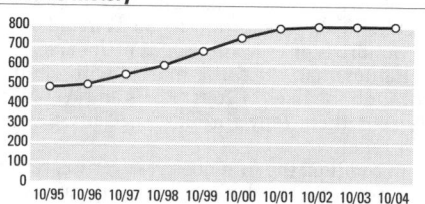

Turtle & Hughes

Founded in 1923 as an electrical supply
house, Turtle & Hughes has plodded and plotted to become an industrial maintenance, repair,
and operations supply center of hare-raising
proportions. Turtle & Hughes supplies its customers with products including wiring, saws,
janitorial supplies, alarms, and pneumatics. The
company uses customized databases to track its
clients' operations and needs. Industrial plants,
industrial construction companies, and contractors make up the core of Turtles & Hughes'
client base. Chairman and CEO Suzanne Turtle
Millard is a third-generation leader of the
family-controlled business, 33% of which is
owned by employees. Turtles & Hughes has operations in the northeastern US and Texas.

EXECUTIVES

Chairman, President, and CEO: Suzanne Turtle Millard
EVP: Frank Millard
SVP: Jack Sniagra
VP and Controller: Trevor Barnett
Director, Human Resources: Maria Penland
President, Industrial Division: Jay Drummond
President, Schlecter Industrial Division: Alan Schlecter
Operations Manager, Bridgewater: Andrea Strong
Auditors: Amper, Politziner & Mattia, P.C.

LOCATIONS

HQ: Turtle & Hughes, Inc.
1900 Lower Rd., Linden, NJ 07036
Phone: 732-574-3600   **Fax:** 732-574-3723
Web: www.turtle.com

Turtle & Hughes operates eight distribution centers in
Connecticut, New Jersey (6), and Texas.

PRODUCTS/OPERATIONS

Selected Products
Adhesives and tapes
Alarms, annunciators, and signals
Anchors and plugs
Ballasts and transformers
Batteries and flashlights
Breakers, panels, and switchgears
Brushes and brooms
Cable trays and struts
Carbide tools
Conduit fittings
Cord connectors
Cutting tools
Dimming controls
Fans
Fuses holders and terminal blocks
Hand tools
Heat shrink
Janitorial paper supplies
Ladders
Lamps
Lighting
Locks
Lubricants
Lugs and terminals
Pneumatic tools
Power tools accessories
Precision tools
Programmable controls
Relays
Saw blades
Shim and shim stock
Solenoid valves
Time clocks
Wiring devices

COMPETITORS

C. R. Laurence	Kennametal
Consolidated Electrical	Lab Safety Supply
CPAC	MSC Industrial Direct
Dillon Supply	Prime Advantage
Foster Wheeler	Rexel, Inc.
Graybar Electric	Sonepar USA
Hughes Supply	Steiner Electric
Indoff	WESCO International
Interline Brands	W.W. Grainger

HISTORICAL FINANCIALS

Company Type: Private

Income Statement
FYE: September 30

	REVENUE ($ mil.)	NET INCOME ($ mil.)	NET PROFIT MARGIN	EMPLOYEES
9/04*	217	—	—	450
9/02	195	—	—	350
9/01	146	—	—	324
9/00	150	—	—	300
9/99	175	—	—	430
9/98	170	—	—	320
9/97	150	—	—	310
9/96	150	—	—	300
9/95	135	—	—	300
9/94	125	—	—	300
Annual Growth	**6.3%**	**—**	**—**	**4.6%**

*Irregular reporting interval

Revenue History

TVA

Although the Tennessee Valley Authority (TVA)
may not be an expert on Tennessee attractions
like Dollywood and the Grand Ole Opry, it is an
authority on power generation. TVA is the largest
government-owned power producer in the US,
with nearly 32,000 MW of generating capacity. Its
power facilities include 11 fossil-powered plants,
29 hydroelectric dams, three nuclear plants, and
six combustion turbine plants. The federal corporation transmits electricity to 158 local distribution utilities, which in turn serve 8.5 million
consumers. It also provides power for industrial
facilities and government agencies, and it manages the Tennessee River system for power production and flood control.

TVA is the sole power wholesaler, by law, in an
80,000-sq.-mi. territory that includes most of
Tennessee and portions of six neighboring states
(Alabama, Georgia, Kentucky, Mississippi, North
Carolina, and Virginia). Generating and transmitting power to local distribution utilities accounts for 86% of TVA's sales.

Most of TVA's power comes from traditional
generation sources, but the company is also exploring alternative energy technologies. It has
developed solar, wind, and methane gas facilities,

and it is offering green choice options through its distribution affiliates.

TVA has also agreed to produce tritium, a radioactive gas that boosts the power of nuclear weapons, for the US Department of Energy (a first for a civilian nuclear power generator). The company is making modifications at its Watts Bar and Savannah River plants to produce and extract the gas; it plans to begin producing tritium by 2007.

TVA's rates are among the nation's lowest, which would-be competitors attribute to its exemption from federal and state income and property taxes. To prepare for deregulation, the authority is trying to reduce its $25 billion debt.

HISTORY

In 1924 the Army Corps of Engineers finished building the Wilson Dam on the Tennessee River in Alabama to provide power for two WWI-era nitrate plants. With the war over, the question of what to do with the plants became a political football.

An act of Congress created the Tennessee Valley Authority (TVA) in 1933 to manage the plants and Tennessee Valley waterways. New Dealers saw TVA as a way to revitalize the local economy through improved navigation and power generation. Power companies claimed the agency was unconstitutional, but by 1939, when a federal court ruled against them, TVA had five operating hydroelectric plants and five under construction.

During the 1940s TVA supplied power for the war effort, including the Manhattan Project in Tennessee. During the postwar boom between 1945 and 1950, power usage in the Tennessee Valley nearly doubled. Despite adding dams, TVA couldn't keep up with demand, so in 1949 it began building a coal-fired unit. Because coal-fired plants weren't part of TVA's original mission, in 1955 a Congressional panel recommended the authority be dissolved.

Though TVA survived, its funding was cut. In 1959 it was allowed to sell bonds, but it no longer received direct government appropriations for power operations. In addition, it had to pay back the government for past appropriations.

TVA began to build the first unit of an ambitious 17-plant nuclear power program in Alabama in 1967. However, skyrocketing costs forced it to raise rates and cut maintenance on its coal-fired plants, which led to breakdowns. In 1985 five reactors had to be shut down because of safety concerns.

In 1988 former auto industry executive Marvin Runyon was appointed chairman of the agency. "Carvin' Marvin" cut management, sold three airplanes, and got rid of peripheral businesses, saving $400 million a year. In 1992 Runyon left to go to the postal service and was replaced by Craven Crowell, who began preparing TVA for competition in the retail power market.

TVA ended its nuclear construction program in 1996 after bringing two nuclear units on line within three months, a first for a US utility. The next year it raised rates for the first time in 10 years, planning to reduce its debt. In response to a lawsuit filed by neighboring utilities, it agreed to stop "laundering" power by using third parties to sell outside the agency's legally authorized area.

In 1999 the authority finished installing almost $2 billion in scrubbers and other equipment at its coal-fired plants so that it could buy Kentucky coal along with cleaner Wyoming coal. That year, however, the EPA charged TVA with vi-

olating the Clean Air Act by making major overhauls on some of its older coal-fired plants without getting permits or installing updated pollution-control equipment. It ordered TVA to bring most of its coal-fired plants into compliance with more current pollution standards. The next year TVA contested the order in court, stating compliance would jack up electricity rates.

TVA was fined by the US Nuclear Regulatory Commission in 2000 for laying off a nuclear plant whistleblower. Crowell resigned in 2001, and Glenn McCullough Jr. was named chairman.

EXECUTIVES

Chairman: Glenn L. McCullough Jr.
President and COO: Tom D. Kilgore, age 56
EVP and General Counsel: Maureen H. Dunn
EVP, Financial Services and CFO:
 Michael E. (Mike) Rescoe
EVP, Administration: D. LeAnne Stribley
EVP, Communications and Government Relations:
 Ellen Robinson
EVP, Customer Service and Marketing:
 Kenneth R. Breeden
EVP, Fossil Power: Joseph R. Bynum
EVP, River System Operations and Environment:
 Kathryn J. (Kate) Jackson
EVP, Human Resources: John E. Long Jr.
EVP, Transmission and Power Supply: Terry Boston
SVP, Economic Development: John J. Bradley
SVP, Investor Relations and Treasurer: John M. Hoskins
SVP, Power Resources and Operations Planning:
 Jack A. Bailey
SVP, Strategic Planning and Analysis: Theresa A. Flaim
VP, Bulk Power Trading: Amy T. Burns
VP, Corporate Communications: Tracy Williams
VP, Performance Initiatives: Anda A. Ray
Chief Nuclear Officer; EVP, TVA Nuclear:
 Karl W. Singer
**General Manager, Business and Community
 Development:** Amy Bunton
**General Manager, Marketing Development and Field
 Operations:** Heidi T. Smith
Manager, Community Development: Phil Scharre
Auditors: PricewaterhouseCoopers LLP

LOCATIONS

HQ: Tennessee Valley Authority
 400 W. Summit Hill Dr., Knoxville, TN 37902
Phone: 865-632-2101 **Fax:** 865-632-4760
Web: www.tva.gov

The Tennessee Valley Authority's service area covers most of Tennessee and parts of Alabama, Georgia, Kentucky, Mississippi, North Carolina, and Virginia.

PRODUCTS/OPERATIONS

2004 Sales

	$ mil.	% of total
Electric		
Municipalities & cooperatives	6,457	86
Industries directly served	842	11
Federal agencies & other	140	2
Other	94	1
Total	**7,533**	**100**

2004 Energy Mix by Net Capacity

	% of total
Fossil	50
Nuclear	19
Hydro	16
Combustion turbine & diesel generators	15
Total	**100**

HISTORICAL FINANCIALS
Company Type: Government-owned

Income Statement
FYE: September 30

	REVENUE ($ mil.)	NET INCOME ($ mil.)	NET PROFIT MARGIN	EMPLOYEES
9/04	7,533	386	5.1%	12,742
9/03	6,952	456	6.6%	13,000
9/02	6,835	73	1.1%	13,000
9/01	6,999	(3,311)	—	13,000
9/00	6,762	24	0.4%	13,400
9/99	6,595	119	1.8%	13,322
9/98	6,729	233	3.5%	13,818
9/97	5,552	8	0.1%	14,500
9/96	5,693	61	1.1%	16,021
9/95	5,375	10	0.2%	16,559
Annual Growth	**3.8%**	**50.1%**	**—**	**(2.9%)**

2004 Year-End Financials

Debt ratio: 854.1% Current ratio: 0.43
Return on equity: 22.4% Long-term debt ($ mil.): 19,337
Cash ($ mil.): 519

Net Income History

Ty

Take some fabric, shape it like an animal, fill it with plastic pellets, and you, too, could own luxury hotels. That's the lesson taught by Ty Warner, sole owner of Ty Inc., the firm behind Beanie Babies and their worldwide cult following — popular with kids and adults alike. Since 1993 Ty has produced more than 365 different Beanie Babies with colorful names such as California Poppy (current) and Cheeks the baboon (retired). Other products include Beanie Buddies (bigger versions of traditional Beanies), Ty Classics (stuffed animals), Beanie Boppers (preteen dolls), and Punkies (squeezable beanbag pals). Beanie bucks enabled Warner to buy three luxury hotels (in New York and California) in recent years.

Ty's marketing smarts have kept Beanies popular for years rather than for a single holiday season, a la Furby or Tickle Me Elmo. The company limits production so that supply never outstrips demand, keeping only 40 or 50 Beanie Babies in circulation at any one time. Ty's "retirement" of a Beanie can cause its price among collectors to skyrocket from its $5-$7 retail debut to hundreds or even thousands of dollars.

Rather than flood the market with Beanies through the likes of Toys "R" Us and Wal-Mart, Ty sells them only through specialty toy and gift retailers.

In addition, the firm doesn't advertise, relying instead on the word of mouth that is rampant in Beanie culture. Books, magazines, newsletters, and Web sites stoke collectors' enthusiasm. This collectors' market — which Ty frowns upon (officially, anyway) — shows signs of fading, however.

The company's first ever character licensing agreement was with Paws, Inc., the licensing studio for comic strip cat *Garfield*. The deal consisted of a line of Beanies specifically created for the 2004 summer release of *Garfield: The Movie* and included Garfield, Nermal, Odie, and Arlene.

HISTORY

Ty Warner, the son of a plush-toy salesman, started his toy career selling stuffed animals to specialty shops for stuffed-bear manufacturer Dakin. Warner left Dakin in 1980, moved to Europe for a few years, and in the mid-1980s returned to the US and founded Ty Inc. The company first designed a line of $20, understuffed Himalayan cats.

Beanie Babies first debuted at a 1993 trade show. In January 1994 the first nine Beanies went on sale — at prices low enough for kids to afford — in Chicago specialty stores. As Warner had learned at Dakin, selling stuffed animals through specialty retailers rather than through mass merchandisers meant bigger profits for suppliers and longer-term popularity. By 1995 there were about 30 different Beanies, and Ty's estimated sales were $25 million.

The popularity of Beanies exploded in 1996, first in the Midwest, then along the East Coast, and then across the US. By midyear, Beanies — along with the public's mania for getting them before they sold out — were receiving widespread media coverage. Ty heightened the frenzy among collectors when it started announcing Beanie retirements on its Web site in 1997.

That same year, McDonald's got on the bandwagon: The fast-food giant issued some 100 million "teenie" Beanie Babies in a Happy Meal promotion. McDonald's ran out of the toys and had to end the promotion early, causing a public relations mess. McDonald's doubled its toy order in 1998 and teamed up with Ty again in 1999 and 2000.

In 1998 Warner paid $10 million for a 7% stake in marketing company Cyrk. In return, Cyrk developed the Beanie Babies Official Club, which turned stores that sell Beanies into "official headquarters" offering club membership kits. Ty introduced its Attic Treasures and Beanie Buddies lines that year.

By spring 1998 Beanies had become a customs issue at the Canadian border, where Ty's limit of one imported Beanie per person into the US resulted in tears and fisticuffs. (The company later raised the personal limit to 30.) That summer the crowds at Major League Baseball games featuring Beanie giveaways were 26% bigger than average.

Warner bought the Four Seasons hotel in New York City in 1999. He also provided auditing documents and correspondence to *The New York Post* indicating that Ty had 1998 profits of more than $700 million — more than Hasbro and Mattel combined.

After an August 1999 announcement that it would retire the Beanies at the end of the year, the company held a New Year's vote to determine their fate. In the most shocking outcome since *Rocky IV*, the public voted overwhelmingly in favor of continuing the Beanies. Ty introduced its humanoid Beanie Kids line in early 2000. Later that year Warner bought the Four Seasons Biltmore Hotel and the San Ysidro Ranch — the hostelry where JFK and Jackie honeymooned; both are near Santa Barbara, California.

In 2001 Ty debuted its pre-teen Beanie Boppers (boy and girl dolls designed for kids from 8 to 12 years of age). To round out his Four Seasons Hotels and Coral Casino properties in California, in 2003 Warner purchased nearby Sandpiper Golf Course. Also that year, the Beanie Baby celebrated its 10th anniversary, and Ty marked the event with the introduction of the Decade Beanie Baby.

EXECUTIVES

Chairman and CEO: H. Ty Warner
EVP and CFO: Michael W. Kanzler
VP: Tania Lundeen

LOCATIONS

HQ: Ty Inc.
　280 Chestnut Ave., Westmont, IL 60559
Phone: 630-920-1515　　　**Fax:** 630-920-1980
Web: www.ty.com

PRODUCTS/OPERATIONS

Selected Products

Attic Treasures
Baby Ty
Beanie Babies
Beanie Boppers
Beanie Buddies
Beanie Kids
Pluffies
Punkies
Teenie Beanie Boppers
Ty Classics

COMPETITORS

Boyds Collection	Mattel
Build-A-Bear	North American Bear
Dakin	Russ Berrie
Enesco Group	Sanrio
Gund	Vermont Teddy Bear
Hasbro	

HISTORICAL FINANCIALS

Company Type: Private

Income Statement

FYE: December 31

	ESTIMATED REVENUE ($ mil.)	NET INCOME ($ mil.)	NET PROFIT MARGIN	EMPLOYEES
12/03	485	—	—	500
12/02	750	—	—	600
12/01	750	—	—	650
12/00	850	—	—	1,000
12/99	1,250	—	—	1,000
12/98	1,000	—	—	1,000
12/97	400	—	—	500
12/96	250	—	—	200
12/95	25	—	—	50
Annual Growth	44.9%	—	—	33.4%

Revenue History

1,400	
1,200	
1,000	
800	
600	
400	
200	
0	
12/94 12/95 12/96 12/97 12/98 12/99 12/00 12/01 12/02 12/03	

Typhoon

Customers at Typhoon! restaurants swear the phad see ewe, chaphlu leaves, and ka-thong tong are as delicious as they are tongue-twisting. The company operates six upscale Thai and pan-Asian restaurants in the Portland, Oregon, and Seattle areas that offer both traditional and retro Thai food, including hor mok (shrimp in red curry) and miang kum (a leafy crepe appetizer). The restaurants also feature an extensive tea menu. President and executive chef Bo Lohasawat Kline, a native of Bangkok, and her husband, secretary and treasurer Stephen Kline, own the company they founded in Portland in 1995.

EXECUTIVES

President and Executive Chef: Bo Lohasawat Kline
Secretary and Treasurer: Stephen Kline, age 59

LOCATIONS

HQ: Typhoon, Inc.
　720 SW Washington, Ste. 305, Portland, OR 97205
Phone: 503-222-7991　　　**Fax:** 503-222-7993
Web: www.typhoonrestaurants.com

COMPETITORS

Benihana
Café de Coral
Consolidated Restaurants
Made In Japan Japanese Restaurants
McCormick & Schmick's
P.F. Chang's
Restaurants Unlimited
Schwartz Brothers Restaurants
Todai

HISTORICAL FINANCIALS

Company Type: Private

Income Statement

FYE: November 30

	ESTIMATED REVENUE ($ mil.)	NET INCOME ($ mil.)	NET PROFIT MARGIN	EMPLOYEES
11/04	20	—	—	300
11/03	25	—	—	300
Annual Growth	(20.0%)	—	—	0.0%

Revenue History

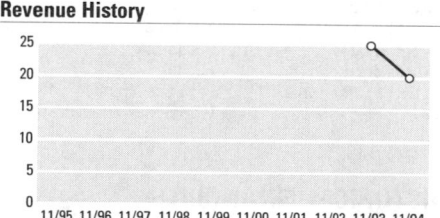

25	
20	
15	
10	
5	
0	
11/95 11/96 11/97 11/98 11/99 11/00 11/01 11/02 11/03 11/04	

Under Armour

Under Armour has yet to show a chink. Since its 1995 foray into the sporting goods market, the maker of performance athletic undies and apparel has risen to the top of the industry pack, boasting more than 90% of the compression garment market. Under Armour is the official supplier of MLB and the NHL. Specializing in sport-specific garments, the company dresses its consumers from head (Cold Weather Hood) to toe (Team Sock). Most products are made from its moisture-wicking and heat-dispersing fabrics, able to keep athletes dry during workouts. Under Armour, owned by founder Kevin Plank and two other officers, sells its apparel via the Internet, catalogs, and 3,000 US sporting goods stores.

Thus far, the company's primary consumer segment has been men, but it is actively working to expand its apparel offerings for women and children. Under Armour sells its product lines to almost 400 women's sports teams at NCAA Division I-A colleges.

EXECUTIVES

Chairman, President, and CEO: Kevin A. Plank, age 33, $1,907,597 pay
SVP and CFO: Wayne A. Marino, age 44, $409,697 pay
CIO: Joseph D. Giles, age 42
Chief Administrative Officer: J. Scott Plank, age 39, $333,591 pay
SVP, Merchandising: Scott R. Gilbertson, age 36
SVP, Sales: Ryan S. Wood, age 33, $386,329 pay
VP, International Sales: Mark R. MacKay, age 44
VP, Marketing: Stephen J. (Steve) Battista, age 31
VP, Product Creation and Merchandising:
Raphael J. Peck, age 35
VP, Sports Marketing, Team Sales, and Licensing:
William J. Kraus, age 41, $340,870 pay
VP, US Sales: Matthew C. Mirchin, age 45
Auditors: PricewaterhouseCoopers LLP

LOCATIONS

HQ: Under Armour, Inc.
1020 Hull St., 3rd Fl., Baltimore, MD 21230
Phone: 410-454-6428 **Fax:** 410-468-2516
Web: www.underarmour.com

COMPETITORS

adidas-Salomon	L.L. Bean
Calvin Klein	NIKE
Columbia Sportswear	North Face
Cotton Inc.	Patagonia
Fruit of the Loom	Reebok
Jockey International	Sara Lee Branded
K2	Warnaco Swimwear

HISTORICAL FINANCIALS

Company Type: Private

Income Statement

FYE: December 31

	REVENUE ($ mil.)	NET INCOME ($ mil.)	NET PROFIT MARGIN	EMPLOYEES
12/04	205	16	7.9%	546
12/03	115	6	4.9%	—
12/02	50	3	5.7%	175
Annual Growth	103.6%	141.3%	—	76.6%

2004 Year-End Financials

Debt ratio: 13.1%
Return on equity: 98.5%
Cash ($ mil.): 1
Current ratio: 1.21
Long-term debt ($ mil.): 3

Net Income History

UNICCO Service

UNICCO Service Company isn't afraid to get its hands dirty. The company provides an array of janitorial and other facilities management services to some 1,000 industrial, commercial, education, government, and retail clients in the US and Canada. UNICCO's long list of services includes HVAC maintenance, landscaping, lighting design and maintenance, engineering services, administrative support, and plant operation. UNICCO's staff has even been known to plow snow and serve as switchboard operators. Herb Kletjian founded the company in 1949. The Kletjian family (including chairman and CEO Steven Kletjian and vice chairmen Richard and Robert Kletjian) continues to own and operate UNICCO.

The company sold its Boston-based window washing division to PureView LLC in September 2005. The sale will allow UNICCO to focus on its core businesses.

EXECUTIVES

Chairman and CEO: Steven C. Kletjian
Vice Chairman: Richard J. Kletjian
Vice Chairman and EVP: Louis J. Lanzillo Jr.
Vice Chairman and VP: Robert P. Kletjian
President and COO: George A. Keches
SVP and General Manager: Bruce L. Charboneau
VP and CFO: James E. (Jim) Lawlor
VP and General Counsel: Walter W. Crow
VP Business Development: Michael F. Dunn
VP Human Resources: Arthur Mushkin
VP Information Technology: Jeffery P. Peterson, age 44
VP Marketing: George R. Lohnes
Auditors: PricewaterhouseCoopers LLP

LOCATIONS

HQ: UNICCO Service Company
275 Grove St., Newton, MA 02466
Phone: 617-527-5222 **Fax:** 617-969-2210
Web: www.unicco.com

UNICCO Service Company has offices in Connecticut, Florida, Hawaii, Illinois, Maine, Massachusetts, New Jersey, Texas, and Virginia, in the US and Alberta, British Columbia, Ontario, and Quebec, in Canada.

PRODUCTS/OPERATIONS

Selected Services

Administration
Audiovisual services
Mail distribution
Minority contract management
Reprographics and copy center services
Secretaries and clerical services
Service call desk
Switchboard and receptionist services

Cleaning
Acoustical tile
Carpet
Clean room
Housekeeping
Steam cleaning
Engineering
CAD Services
Central energy plant operation
Environmental and energy services
Mechanical engineering
Planning and scheduling
Plant engineering
Space planning
Maintenance
Chemical distribution
Construction project management
Elevator and escalator maintenance
Facility maintenance and repair
Fleet maintenance
Inventory control
Landscaping and grounds maintenance
Pest control
Recycling
Roof repair
Snow plowing
Operations
Air quality management
Lighting
Matron and porter services
Pipefitting
Wells and pump stations
Route maintenance
Building and grounds
Carpentry
Carpet care
Electrical troubleshooting
Painting
Transportation

COMPETITORS

ABM Industries	Johnson Controls
ARAMARK	Onesource Facility
Chemed	Services
Colin Service	Rentokil Initial
Davey Tree	Rollins
Dwyer Group	ServiceMaster
Ecolab	Sodexho
Fluor	Swisher Hygiene
Healthcare Services	

HISTORICAL FINANCIALS

Company Type: Private

Income Statement

FYE: June 30

	REVENUE ($ mil.)	NET INCOME ($ mil.)	NET PROFIT MARGIN	EMPLOYEES
6/04	690	—	—	20,500
6/03	650	—	—	20,500
6/02	600	—	—	20,500
6/01	590	—	—	20,500
6/00	555	—	—	20,000
6/99	522	—	—	19,000
6/98	491	—	—	19,000
6/97	472	—	—	22,000
6/96	98	—	—	—
6/95	88	—	—	—
Annual Growth	25.7%	—	—	(1.0%)

Revenue History

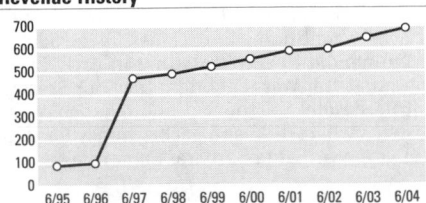

Unified Western Grocers

Unified Western Grocers guarantees that food and general merchandise reach mostly independent grocery stores in nine western states and several countries in the South Pacific. The food wholesaler and cooperative supplies a full line of groceries, as well as its own bakery and dairy goods. In addition to name-brand items, its offerings include private labels Cottage Hearth, Golden Creme, and Western Family. The co-op also provides member support services such as store remodeling, financing, and insurance. The company was formed in 1999 when Certified Grocers of California merged with United Grocers of Oregon.

Consolidation and the trend toward self-distribution among food retailers has hurt wholesale grocery distributors. Certified Grocers and United Grocers merged to match the buying power afforded to large supermarket chains and wholesalers. Unified helps independent grocers capture an increasing share of the Hispanic market in places like Los Angeles by supplying ethnic foods and targeted marketing campaigns to its member stores.

HISTORY

Certified Grocers of California evolved from a group of 15 independent Southern California grocers that formed a purchasing cooperative in 1922 to compete against large grocery chains. Certified Grocers of California incorporated in 1925 and issued stock to 50 members.

The co-op merged with a small retailer-owned wholesale company called Co-operative Grocers in 1928. It acquired Walker Brothers Grocery in 1929 and nearly tripled the previous year's sales. By 1938 the co-op had grown to 310 members and 380 stores, and sales passed $10 million.

Certified launched a line of private-label products under the Springfield name in 1947. In the early 1950s it added nonfood items and began processing its own private-label coffee and bean products. The co-op added delicatessen items in 1956. During the 1960s and 1970s, Certified added a meat center, a frozen food and deli warehouse, a produce distribution center, a creamery, a central bakery, and a specialty foods warehouse.

In 1989 the co-op opened several membership warehouse stores called Convenience Clubs. The Save Mart and Boys Markets chains left the fold in 1991. The co-op lost about 30% of its business during the next two years, including the Bel Air and Williams Bros. chains. After disappointing returns, in 1992 Certified sold its warehouse stores, cut staff, and consolidated warehouses.

CFO (and former Atlantic Richfield executive) Al Plamann was appointed CEO in 1994, succeeding Everett Dingwell. In 1996 the co-op began to convert its customers' older retail stores to Apple Markets in Southern California. Revenues began to dip in 1997 as the result of reduced purchases from some supermarkets and the sale the previous year of one of its subsidiaries, Hawaiian Grocery Stores.

Member chain Stumps converted to the Apple Markets banner in 1998. Faced with a declining customer base, in 1999 Certified merged with United Grocers of Oregon to form Unified Western Grocers.

Dr. R. Norton, F. L. Freeburg, and A. C. Brinckerhoff founded United Grocers of Oregon in 1915 as a way for grocers in Portland to cooperate in purchasing merchandise. By the next year the co-op had 35 members. In the 1950s United formed a trucking department and established a general merchandise division. It also grew rapidly in the 1950s through acquisitions, buying Northwest Grocery Company and the Fridegar Grocery Company. In 1963 United formed its frozen food department when it purchased Raven Creamery.

By 1975 the company's Northwest Grocery Company subsidiary had 14 Cash and Carry warehouses that sold goods to small grocers and restaurants. In 1995 United bought California food distributor Market Wholesale. Three years later the company sold its Cash and Carry warehouse-style stores to Smart & Final.

Upon completion of the merger in 1999, Certified's president and CEO, Plamann, was named to head the new organization. Soon after, Unified consolidated warehouse operations, eliminated duplicate personnel, and combined its private labels. Also in 1999 the company acquired California-based Gourmet Specialties.

The next year it bought the specialty foods business of J. Sosnick and Son, another California company, and Central Sales of Washington State. The company attributed net losses during 2001 to delays in moving the source for northern California specialty merchandise from southern to northern California and to the costs of entering the Washington marketplace, among other factors.

In 2002 Unified closed seven retail stores in Northern California and Oregon (under the Apple Markets and SavMax Foods banners) that accounted for sales of about $140 million as part of its plan to reduce debt and focus on wholesaling. In 2003 the co-op sold or closed all 12 of its company-owned SavMax Foods stores as part of its plan to exit its unprofitable retail business and focus on its wholesale division (99% of total sales).

EXECUTIVES

President and CEO: Alfred A. (Al) Plamann, age 62, $995,250 pay
EVP, Finance and Administration and CFO: Richard J. Martin, age 59, $463,846 pay
EVP, General Counsel, and Secretary: Robert M. Ling Jr., age 47, $528,577 pay
EVP and Chief Marketing and Procurement Officer: Philip S. Smith, age 54, $414,269 pay
SVP, Distribution: Rodney L. VanBebber, age 49
SVP, Retail Support Services; President, SavMax Foods: Daniel J. Murphy, age 58, $309,596 pay
VP, Human Resources: Don Gilpin
VP, Insurance: Joseph A. Ney, age 56
VP, Procurement: Robert Lutz
VP and CIO: Gary S. Herman
VP and Controller: William O. Coté, age 47
VP and Treasurer: Christine Neal, age 51
President, Pacific Northwest: Dirk T. Davis
President, Northern California: Joe Falvey
President, Southern California: Luis de la Mata
Auditors: Deloitte & Touche LLP

LOCATIONS

HQ: Unified Western Grocers, Inc.
5200 Sheila St., Commerce, CA 90040
Phone: 323-264-5200   **Fax:** 323-265-4006
Web: www.uwgrocers.com

PRODUCTS/OPERATIONS

2004 Sales

	% of total
Wholesale distribution	99
Insurance	1
Total	**100**

Selected Co-op Members

Alamo Market
Berberian Enterprises, Inc.
Bristol Farms
Evergreen Markets, Inc.
Gelson's Markets
Goodwin & Sons, Inc.
Joe Notrica, Inc.
Mar-Val Food Stores, Inc.
Mollie Stone's Markets
Pioneer Super Save, Inc.
Pokerville Select Market
Pro & Son's, Inc.
Sentry Market
Stump's Market, Inc.
Super A Foods, Inc.
Super Center Concepts, Inc.
Sweet Home Thriftway
Tresierras Bros. Corp.
Wright's Foodliner

Selected Support Services

Financing
Information technology
Insurance
Private labels
Real estate development
Store design
Transportation

COMPETITORS

Associated Food	Shurfine International
Associated Grocers	SUPERVALU
C&S Wholesale	Wal-Mart
Nash Finch	WinCo Foods

HISTORICAL FINANCIALS

Company Type: Cooperative

Income Statement

FYE: Saturday nearest September 30

	REVENUE ($ mil.)	NET INCOME ($ mil.)	NET PROFIT MARGIN	EMPLOYEES
9/04	3,040	7	0.2%	2,900
9/03	2,819	5	0.2%	3,000
9/02	2,793	(45)	—	3,600
9/01	2,930	(14)	—	4,200
9/00	3,067	(11)	—	4,000
9/99	1,894	3	0.1%	3,945
9/98	1,832	3	0.2%	2,200
9/97	1,927	2	0.1%	2,400
9/96	1,949	2	0.1%	2,400
9/95	1,823	1	0.0%	2,470
Annual Growth	5.8%	28.0%	—	1.8%

2004 Year-End Financials

Debt ratio: 160.8%
Return on equity: 6.7%
Cash ($ mil.): 24
Current ratio: 1.36
Long-term debt ($ mil.): 192

Net Income History

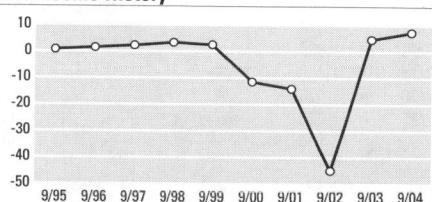

UniGroup

Moving household goods has made many of UniGroup's companies household names. The moving services company transports household goods and other items in more than 100 countries through subsidiaries United Van Lines, Mayflower Transit, and UniGroup Worldwide UTS. UniGroup's Total Transportation Services unit sells and leases trucks and trailers and provides moving supplies, and its Vanliner Group offers insurance to movers. Subsidiary Allegiant Move Management offers relocation management and assistance, and Insite Logistics provides third-party logistics services. Founded in 1987, UniGroup is owned by a 250-person group that includes agents of United Van Lines and Mayflower Transit and company managers.

EXECUTIVES

Chairman and CEO; Chairman, United Van Lines: Gerald P. (Gerry) Stadler
President and COO; COO, United Van Lines: Richard H. (Rich) McClure
CFO: James G. (Jim) Powers
EVP Sales and Marketing: John Lograsso
VP Organization Development and Quality Management and Assistant to the President: George Mitsch
CIO: Randall C. (Randy) Poppell
President and CEO, Transportation Services Group and United Van Lines: Patrick (Pat) Larch
President, Total Transportation Services: Patrick G. Baehler
President, UniGroup Worldwide: Michael Kranisky
EVP and COO, Vanliner Group: Gale Preston
VP, InSite Logistics: Frank Fischer
Director Human Resources: Sherry Fagin
General Counsel: Jan R. Alonzo
Manager Public Relations and Communications: Jennifer Bonham

LOCATIONS

HQ: UniGroup, Inc.
1 Premier Dr., Fenton, MO 63026
Phone: 636-326-3100   **Fax:** 636-326-1106
Web: www.unigroupinc.com

COMPETITORS

AMERCO	Nelson Westerberg
Atlas World Group	Penske Truck Leasing
Bekins	SIRVA
Budget	Starving Students
Graebel	

HISTORICAL FINANCIALS

Company Type: Private

Income Statement

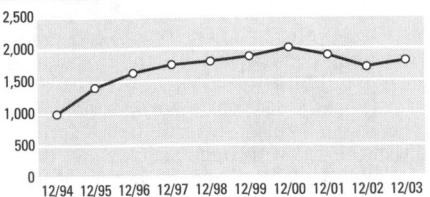

Revenue History

FYE: December 31

	REVENUE ($ mil.)	NET INCOME ($ mil.)	NET PROFIT MARGIN	EMPLOYEES
12/03	1,809	—	—	1,836
12/02	1,708	—	—	1,335
12/01	1,896	—	—	1,400
12/00	2,009	—	—	1,871
12/99	1,878	—	—	1,800
12/98	1,800	—	—	1,600
12/97	1,749	—	—	1,650
12/96	1,626	—	—	1,600
12/95	1,406	—	—	1,000
12/94	995	—	—	950
Annual Growth	6.9%	—	—	7.6%

Union Drilling

A leading independent US drilling contractor, Union Drilling unifies hydrocarbons and pipelines via the drill bit. Operating 65 drilling rigs, the company provides contract land drilling services, primarily in the Appalachian Basin, where the majority of its rigs operate. It also has rigs operating in the Arkoma and Fort Worth basins, the Uinta Basin and the Piceance Basin in eastern Utah and western Colorado. Union Drilling's primary customers include Columbia Natural Resources, Equitable Resources, and Great Lakes Energy. Union Drilling is owned by a unit of Morgan Stanley.

Union Drilling was formed in 1997 to acquire the drilling equipment assets of Equitable Resources Energy. In 2005 the company acquired drilling contractors Thornton Drilling Company and SPA Drilling, LP.

EXECUTIVES

Chairman: Thomas H. O'Neill Jr., age 63
Vice Chairman: William H. (Henry) Harmon, age 50
Vice Chairman: William R. Ziegler, age 63
President and CEO: Christopher D. (Chris) Strong, age 46, $358,871 pay
EVP Operations: J. Michael Poole, age 45, $215,886 pay
VP, CFO, Treasurer, and Secretary: Dan E. Steigerwald, age 64, $151,150 pay
Northern Division Manager: William H. (Bill) Ei
Central Division Manager: Byron L. (Doc) Musselman
Southern Division Manager: Charlie S. Hull
Human Resources Director: Lee Spangler
Environment, Health, and Safety Director: Rick Waltemire
Controller: Gary Impellicerri
Auditors: Ernst & Young LLP

LOCATIONS

HQ: Union Drilling, Inc.
South Pittsburgh Technology Park, 3117 Washington Pike, Bridgeville, PA 15017
Phone: 412-257-9390   **Fax:** 412-257-9392
Web: www.uniondrilling.com

Union Drilling has offices and operating facilities in Buckhannon, West Virginia; Norton, Virginia; Pittsburgh and Punxsutawney, Pennsylvania; and Vernal, Utah.

COMPETITORS

Grey Wolf	Petroleum Development
Helmerich & Payne	Pride International
Nabors Industries	Resource America
Patterson-UTI Energy	Unit Corporation

HISTORICAL FINANCIALS

Company Type: Private

Income Statement

FYE: December 31

	REVENUE ($ mil.)	NET INCOME ($ mil.)	NET PROFIT MARGIN	EMPLOYEES
12/04	68	4	5.2%	1,060
12/03	58	(3)	—	—
12/02	47	(3)	—	—
12/01	78	—	—	800
12/00	51	—	—	573
12/99	39	—	—	—
12/98	44	—	—	—
Annual Growth	7.6%	—	—	16.6%

2004 Year-End Financials

Debt ratio: 9.5%	Current ratio: 1.62
Return on equity: 8.3%	Long-term debt ($ mil.): 4
Cash ($ mil.): 4	

Net Income History

Unisource

This company has a singular mission to distribute paper to North America. Unisource Worldwide is a leading distributor of paper products and other supplies, providing commercial printing and business imaging paper and specialty paper products though more than 80 distribution centers. Its offerings include ink jet and laser paper, Xerox paper, and toner cartridges, in addition to coated and uncoated commercial printing paper. Unisource also distributes packaging supplies (corrugated papers, foam and bubble sheeting), packaging systems (pallet systems, shrink packaging systems), and cleaning supplies and equipment. The company is 60%-owned by Bain Capital; paper manufacturer Georgia-Pacific owns about 40%.

In addition to its traditional distribution business, Unisource offers paper supply services to publishers and other commercial operators through its Websource paper brokerage. Its Rollsource unit specializes in business forms and products for customers in the direct mail industry. The company also sells retail paper products online and operates about 50 retail stores under the Paper Plus banner.

HISTORY

Tinkham Veale II, a mechanical engineer from Cleveland, got help from his father-in-law, A. C. Ernst of Ernst & Ernst accounting firm, to buy a stake in a prosperous engineered goods manufacturer in 1941. Veale retired at age 37 to breed and race horses. He invested his earnings, became a millionaire by 1951, and joined the board of Alco Oil and Chemical. In 1960 he and his associates formed a holding company, V & V Associates, and bought a large minority share in Alco.

Renamed Alco Chemical two years later, the company bought four fertilizer companies, and in 1965 (by then renamed Alco Standard) it merged with V & V Associates, which had stakes in machinery producers. At the helm, Veale implemented the partnership strategy that would serve Alco for 25 years: He bought small, privately owned companies, usually in exchange for cash and Alco stock, and let the owners continue to run them.

The company took advantage of several Supreme Court antitrust decisions in the 1960s that forced papermakers to divest marketing companies acquired in the 1950s. Alco acquired Garrett-Buchanan of Philadelphia and Monarch Paper in 1968 as the basis for its national paper distribution network. After acquiring other paper distributors, the company formed a paper distributor unit called Unisource. Veale brought in former Kimberly-Clark executive Ray Mundt in 1970 to guide the growing division. Unisource's profitability prompted Alco to enter other distribution businesses, including pharmaceuticals, hospital supplies, steel products, food service equipment, and liquor.

Alco also acquired several manufacturers (plastics, machinery, rubber, and chemicals), but they were not as prosperous. By 1981, with large warehouses and computerized ordering and delivery systems, Unisource was the most efficient, cost-effective distributor in the US. It continued to buy distributors, such as Saxon Industries (1984), an international paper seller valued at $378 million.

Mundt succeeded Veale as chairman two years later and switched Alco's focus to office products and paper distribution, eliminating seven divisions. In the 1990s Mundt oversaw a restructuring that included installing a state-of-the-art distribution software system across the network and consolidating the company's service center operations (Mundt cut Unisource's locations by half). He also expanded the supply products offered to include disposable paper and plastic supplies, packaging systems, and sanitary maintenance equipment in order to offset cyclical downturns in the paper market.

Unisource continued to grow, acquiring more than 40 companies (including 15 in Mexico) in fiscal 1996, and eventually accounting for 70% of Alco's revenues. In late 1996 Alco (which soon after became IKON Office Solutions) spun off Unisource Worldwide with Mundt as its chairman and CEO. The next year Unisource bought National Sanitary Supply (the #1 specialized distributor of sanitary maintenance supplies in the US) and 13 other companies (mostly supply systems). It also sold its $300 million grocery systems operation to Bunzl in 1997.

In 1998 the company announced a restructuring plan that included reducing its US workforce by 15% and cutting its number of distribution facilities almost in half (it took a $370 million charge for the year). Also that year Unisource divested its businesses in Mexico, where the economy was too uncertain.

In early 1999 Unisource agreed to be acquired by UGI Corporation, majority shareholder of AmeriGas Partners, the largest US propane distributor. However, UGI shares fell shortly after the offer, reducing the value of the deal. Georgia-Pacific made an unsolicited bid that Unisource couldn't refuse and the $1.2 billion deal was completed later that year. Unisource became the sole authorized distributor of Ecolab's Professional Products-branded janitorial supplies in 2001.

The next year Georgia-Pacific sold a 60% stake in the company to Bain Capital. It also sold 38 of Unisource's warehouses to Cardinal Capital Partners, which leased them back to the company. Unisource acquired paper broker Graphic Communications in 2003 and merged it with Websource, its existing paper brokerage division.

EXECUTIVES

CEO: Allan (Al) Dragone, age 49
SVP and CFO: Gordon Glover
SVP Human Resources: James M. (Jim) Lynde
VP, General Counsel, and Secretary: Zygmunt Jablonski
VP Corporate Diversity: Don Roberts
President, Packaging and Facility Supplies: Thomas (Tom) Pitera
President, Paper: Newell E. Holt, age 57
President, Supply Chain: Thomas H. (Tom) Shortt
President, Unisource Canada: Yves Montmarquette
VP and General Manager, PaperPlus: Glenn Shiroff
VP, Unisource West: Kenneth Vuylsteke
VP, Marketing, Coated Paper: Mark Potter
VP, Marketing, Packaging and Facility Supplies: Timothy M. (Tim) O'Connor
Director of Corporate Communications: Michelle Wagner
Director of Marketing, Great Lakes Region: John M. Pavloff
Director of Organizational Development and Training: Linda Brenner
Director of Talent Acquisition: Amy Ivers
Auditors: Ernst & Young LLP

LOCATIONS

HQ: Unisource Worldwide, Inc.
6600 Governors Lake Pkwy., Norcross, GA 30071
Phone: 770-447-9000   **Fax:** 770-734-2000
Web: www.unisourcelink.com

Unisource operates about 50 Paper Plus retail stores and more than 80 distribution centers in the US and Canada.

PRODUCTS/OPERATIONS

Selected Products

Envelopes, computer paper, and specialty paper
  Computer paper (blank and proprietary grades)
  Envelopes (mailing, shipping, commercial)
  Specialty products (engineering rolls, labels)
Facility supplies and equipment
  Production supplies (degreasers, work wear)
  Sanitary supplies and equipment
    (can liners, matting systems)
Packaging
  Case erecting, packaging, and sealing systems (case packers, gummed tapes)
  Case and pallet coding systems
    (ink jet printers, label materials)
  Packaging Supplies (foam and bubble sheeting)
  Pallet unitization systems (conveyers, stretch films)
  Shrink packaging, bundling, bagging, and overwrapping systems
Printing papers
  Coated and uncoated sheet-fed papers
  Premium text, cover, and writing papers
  Uncoated and coated web papers
Specialty businesses
  Paper Plus (smaller orders of paper, packaging, and supplies)
  Rollsource (paper conversion to forms, direct mail)
  Websource (large web paper orders)

COMPETITORS

Bradner Central	Midland Paper
Central National-Gottesman	Office Depot
	OfficeMax
Domtar	Ris Paper
Ecolab	S.P. Richards
Gould Paper	Staples
International Paper	United Stationers
Katy Industries	Weyerhaeuser
Menasha	

HISTORICAL FINANCIALS

Company Type: Private

Income Statement				FYE: Saturday nearest December 31
	REVENUE ($ mil.)	NET INCOME ($ mil.)	NET PROFIT MARGIN	EMPLOYEES
12/03	5,900	—	—	7,100
12/02	5,900	—	—	8,000
12/01	6,200	—	—	—
12/00	6,900	—	—	—
12/99*	7,000	—	—	—
9/98	7,417	—	—	13,400
9/97	7,108	—	—	14,200
9/96	7,023	—	—	11,800
9/95	6,987	—	—	11,800
9/94	5,757	—	—	11,200
Annual Growth	0.3%	—	—	(4.9%)

*Fiscal year change

Revenue History

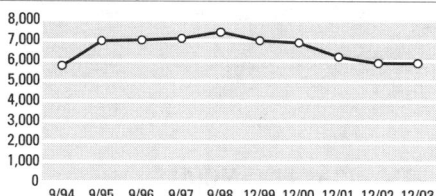

United Supermarkets

From Muleshoe up to Dalhart and on over to Pampa, United Supermarkets keeps the Texas Panhandle well fed. The grocer has nearly 50 supermarkets, mostly in rural towns. Its stores feature deli, floral, and bakery shops, as well as groceries, pharmacies, and gas at some locales. The company's larger format, Market Street, stocks more specialty foods. United Supermarkets runs its own distribution facility. H. D. Snell founded the firm in Sayre, Oklahoma, in 1916 as United Cash Store. He bucked the norms of the day — when grocers sold on credit — by selling for cash at lower prices. United Supermarkets is owned and run by the Snell family. (Co-presidents Gantt and Matt Bumstead are the great-great-grandsons of the founder.)

EXECUTIVES

Co-President: R. Gantt Bumstead
Co-President and EVP, Customer and Community Service: Matt Bumstead
CEO and EVP: Dan Sanders
SVP and COO: Sidney Hopper
SVP, Sales and Merchandising: Wes Jackson
SVP, Sales and Operational Support: Gerald Critz
SVP, Technology and Logistics: Kyle Gayler
VP and CFO: Suz Ann Kirby
VP, Facilities Design and Development: Michael Molina
VP, Human Resources: Phil Pirkle
VP, Marketing: Renée Underwood
CIO: Peter Wellman
Controller: Amanda Tomlin

LOCATIONS

HQ: United Supermarkets, Ltd.
  7830 Orlando Ave., Lubbock, TX 79423
Phone: 806-791-0220   **Fax:** 806-791-7491
Web: www.unitedtexas.com

PRODUCTS/OPERATIONS

Retail Operations
Market Street
United Supermarkets
United Supermercado

COMPETITORS

Albertson's
H-E-B
Homeland Stores
IGA
Kroger
Minyard Group
Randall's
Wal-Mart

HISTORICAL FINANCIALS

Company Type: Private

Income Statement

FYE: January 31

	ESTIMATED REVENUE ($ mil.)	NET INCOME ($ mil.)	NET PROFIT MARGIN	EMPLOYEES
1/04	900	—	—	7,000
1/03	700	—	—	7,000
1/02	600	—	—	5,000
1/01	575	—	—	5,000
1/00	570	—	—	4,500
1/99	560	—	—	4,000
1/98	520	—	—	4,000
1/97	450	—	—	4,000
1/96	400	—	—	3,300
1/95	350	—	—	3,000
Annual Growth	11.1%	—	—	9.9%

Revenue History

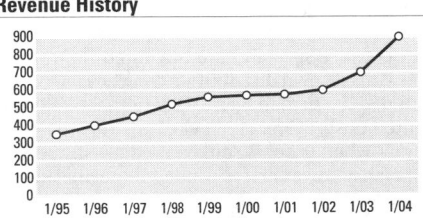

United Systems Technology

United Systems Technology, Inc. (USTI) is big on big government. The company's software helps county and local governments throughout North America keep track of bills, records, and licenses. USTI offers financial software for budgets, accounts payable, and payroll; public works software for utility billing and collections; general administration software for managing building permits and animal licenses; and public safety software for managing jails, courthouses, and law enforcement records. The company, which sells its software under the Legacy, asyst, AutoAdmin, and Quest names, also sells third-party computers and offers installation, training, and support services.

Software maintenance services bring in about 60% of the company's sales. About a quarter of USTI's sales come from customers in Minnesota and Texas.

CEO Thomas Gibbs owns 12% of the company.

EXECUTIVES

Chairman, President, and CEO: Thomas E. Gibbs, age 56, $230,925 pay
VP, CFO, Secretary, Treasurer, and Director: Randall L. (Randy) McGee, age 48
Sales Manager: Lisa Bush
Account Representative: Barbara Barnes
Account Representative: Patrick McGarrity Jr.
Account Representative: Bridget Starr
Bill Cards, Checks, and Hardware: Nancy Murphy
Training and Professional Services: Debbie Jones
Auditors: Hein + Associates LLP

LOCATIONS

HQ: United Systems Technology, Inc.
  1850 Crown Rd., Ste. 1109, Dallas, TX 75234
Phone: 972-402-8600   **Fax:** 972-402-9922
Web: www.unitedsystech.com

United Systems Technology has offices and sales representatives in Kentucky, Louisiana, Minnesota, North Carolina, Tennessee, and Texas, and in Canada.

2004 Sales

	$ mil.	% of total
US	2.3	64
Canada	1.3	36
Total	**3.6**	**100**

PRODUCTS/OPERATIONS

2004 Sales

	$ mil.	% of total
Maintenance	2.2	61
Software packages	0.6	17
Installation, training & customer support	0.4	11
Equipment & other	0.4	11
Total	**3.6**	**100**

Selected Software Products

Financial Systems
  Accounts payable and receivable
  Budget preparation
  Centralized cash receipts
  General ledger and budgetary accounting
  Payroll
  Purchase orders
  Reports
  Tax billing
General Administration
  Animal licenses
  Building permits
  Business licenses
  Code enforcement
Public Safety
  Computer-aided dispatch
  Court administration
  Jail management
  Law enforcement records management
Public Works
  Bank drafts
  Handheld meter reading
  Utility billing and collections

Selected Brand Names

asyst
AutoAdmin
Legacy
Quest

COMPETITORS

ABM
Affiliated Computer Services
CACI International
EDS
IBM
Indus International
Manatron
SunGard HTE
Telos
Tyler

HISTORICAL FINANCIALS

Company Type: Private

Income Statement

FYE: December 31

	REVENUE ($ mil.)	NET INCOME ($ mil.)	NET PROFIT MARGIN	EMPLOYEES
12/04	4	0	8.3%	34
12/03	4	0	11.4%	37
12/02	4	1	16.7%	36
12/01	3	1	16.7%	29
12/00	2	0	15.0%	26
12/99	2	0	19.0%	16
12/98	2	0	15.8%	16
12/97	2	(0)	—	19
12/96	2	(1)	—	23
12/95	2	(1)	—	27
Annual Growth	8.0%	—	—	2.6%

2004 Year-End Financials

Debt ratio: 0.0%
Return on equity: 12.3%
Cash ($ mil.): 2
Current ratio: 1.41
Long-term debt ($ mil.): 0

Net Income History

United Way

United Way of America (UWA) has been described as a mutual fund for charitable causes, and with thousands of agencies receiving financial support from UWA's 1,350 local organizations, the epithet seems fitting. The not-for-profit organization focuses on health and human services causes. Its local organizations help to fund a multitude of endeavors, including the American Cancer Society, Big Brothers/Big Sisters, Catholic Charities, Girl Scouts and Boy Scouts, and The Salvation Army. In 2004-2005, UWA raised more than $3.8 billion (mostly through its annual campaign and about 22% from corporations). UWA's administrative expenses average about 13% of funds raised.

Each of the local organizations is an independent entity governed by local volunteers, and UWA acts as a national services and training center, supporting the local organizations with services such as national advertising and research. To advance the understanding of its role, UWA has launched an initiative to raise awareness of how it serves local communities.

In the aftermath of Hurricane Katrina, UWA has teamed up with the Red Cross and Salvation Army to form a Coordinated Assistance Network to address the needs of evacuees by providing emergency and recovery services.

HISTORY

The first modern Community Chest was created in 1913, laying the foundation for the practice of allocating funds among multiple causes. Five years later, representatives from 12 fundraising organizations met in Chicago and established the American Association for Community Organizations, the predecessor of the present-day United Way. By 1929 more than 350 Community Chests had been established.

Payroll deductions for charitable contributions debuted in 1943. In 1946 the United Way's predecessor organization initiated a cooperative relationship with the American Federation of Labor and the Congress of Industrial Organizations (which merged to become the AFL-CIO in 1955); the two groups agreed to provide services to members of organized labor. (The relationship continues today, with the organizations collaborating on projects such as recruiting members of organized labor to lead health and human services organizations.)

The Uniform Federal Fund-Raising Program was created by order of President Dwight Eisenhower in 1957, enabling federal employees to contribute to charities of their choice. (The program later evolved into the Combined Federal Campaign.) Six years later Los Angeles became the first city to adopt the United Way name when more than 30 local Community Chests and United Fund organizations merged. The national organization, which had been operating under the United Community Funds and Councils (UCFCA) name, adopted the United Way of America (UWA) name in 1970. It established its headquarters in Alexandria, Virginia, the next year.

Congress made its first grant for emergency food and shelter to the private sector in 1983, and UWA was selected as its fiscal agent. UWA created its Emergency Food and Shelter National Board Program the same year. In 1984 UWA created the Alexis de Tocqueville Society to solicit larger donations from individuals (it attracted such members as Bill Gates and Walter Annenberg).

In 1992 William Aramony, UWA's president for more than two decades, resigned after coming under fire for his lavish expenditures. Former Peace Corps head Elaine Chao was tapped to replace him, and in 1995 Aramony was sentenced to seven years in prison for defrauding the organization of about $600,000. Former UWA CFO Thomas Merlo and Stephen Paulachak (former president of a UWA spinoff) were convicted on related charges. After four years spent burnishing UWA's tarnished image, Chao resigned in 1996 and was succeeded the next year by Betty Beene, who had served as CEO of the Tri-State United Way.

In an effort to stress the manner in which its local organizations benefit their communities, UWA launched a brand-initiative campaign in 1998. The following year UWA's local organization in Santa Clara, California, found itself in serious financial straits when donations began slipping despite its location in the wealthy Silicon Valley. Infoseek (now Walt Disney Internet Group's GO.com) founder Steve Kirsch and Microsoft founder Gates chipped in $1 million and $5 million, respectively, to help keep the organization afloat.

Beene, who drew the ire of some chapters for suggesting a national pledge-processing center and national standards, stepped down in January 2001. That same year UWA began funneling more funds into smaller community projects instead of national charities. In 2002 Brian Gallagher took over as president and CEO.

EXECUTIVES

Chairman, Board of Trustees: Johnnetta B. Cole
President and CEO: Brian A. Gallagher
COO: Joseph V. Haggerty
CFO: Usha Chaudhary
Enterprise Services: Michael Schreiber
Controller: Cynthia Smith
Legal Counsel: Patti Turner
Human Resources: Evelyn Amador
Director, Media and Public Relations: Sheila Consaul
Auditors: Ernst & Young LLP

LOCATIONS

HQ: United Way of America
701 N. Fairfax St., Alexandria, VA 22314
Phone: 703-836-7100   **Fax:** 703-683-7840
Web: national.unitedway.org

United Way of America has 1,350 local organizations across the US.

PRODUCTS/OPERATIONS

Selected Recipients of United Way Funds

American Cancer Society
American Red Cross
Big Brothers/Big Sisters of America
Boy Scouts of America
Catholic Charities USA
Girl Scouts of the United States of America
The Salvation Army
The Urban League

HISTORICAL FINANCIALS

Company Type: Not-for-profit

Income Statement

FYE: December 31

	REVENUE ($ mil.)	NET INCOME ($ mil.)	NET PROFIT MARGIN	EMPLOYEES
12/04	45	—	—	—
12/03	35	—	—	—
12/02	42	—	—	15,166
12/01	52	—	—	8,500
12/00	41	—	—	—
12/99	92	—	—	—
Annual Growth	(13.5%)	—	—	78.4%

Revenue History

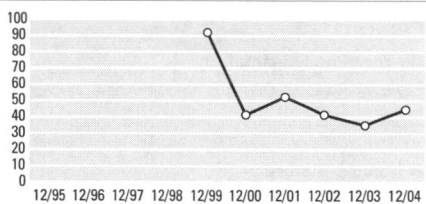

Unity Holdings

Northwestern Georgians say "amen" to Unity Holdings, the holding company for Unity National Bank. Through branches in Adairsville, Calhoun, Cartersville, and Rome, Unity National Bank offers such standard banking products as personal, business, money market, and individual retirement accounts, as well as personal and home equity loans.

EXECUTIVES

President, CEO, and Director: Michael L. McPherson, age 56, $187,793 pay
EVP and Senior Lender: W. Stewart Griggs, $136,333 pay
SVP and CFO: Eli D. Mullis, $100,003 pay
Mortgage Specialist: Dianne Gilbert
Mortgage Specialist: Ellis Tucker
Mortgage Specialist: Karen Turco
Auditors: Mauldin & Jenkins, LLC

LOCATIONS

HQ: Unity Holdings, Inc.
950 Joe Frank Harris Pkwy., SE,
Cartersville, GA 30121
Phone: 770-606-0555   **Fax:** 770-606-1855
Web: www.unitynationalbank.com

PRODUCTS/OPERATIONS

2004 Sales

	$ mil.	% of total
Interest		
Loans, including fees	10.3	86
Securities & other	0.6	5
Noninterest		
Deposit service charges	0.7	6
Mortgage loan fees	0.3	2
Other	0.1	1
Total	**12.0**	**100**

COMPETITORS

AmSouth
Regions Financial
SunTrust

HISTORICAL FINANCIALS

Company Type: Private

Income Statement

FYE: December 31

	ASSETS ($ mil.)	NET INCOME ($ mil.)	INCOME AS % OF ASSETS	EMPLOYEES
12/04	200	2	0.8%	48
12/03	160	1	0.9%	49
12/02	131	1	0.6%	49
Annual Growth	23.5%	41.4%	—	(1.0%)

2004 Year-End Financials

Equity as % of assets: 7.5%
Return on assets: 0.9%
Return on equity: 11.4%
Long-term debt ($ mil.): —
Sales ($ mil.): 12

Net Income History

Universal Hospital Services

The yearning for medical equipment is universal, as Universal Hospital Services well knows. The company leases movable medical equipment to more than 6,250 hospitals and care providers across the US. It has a pool of some 150,000 pieces of equipment in four main categories: critical care, monitoring, respiratory therapy, and newborn care. Universal Hospital's programs include Pay-Per-Use pricing, which charges customers on a daily basis, and Asset Management Partnership, which supplies, maintains, manages, and tracks equipment for customers. The company also sells new and used equipment and disposable supplies. J.W. Childs owns about three-quarters of the firm.

EXECUTIVES

Chairman: David E. Dovenberg, age 60
President, CEO, and Director: Gary D. Blackford, age 47, $514,686 pay
SVP and CFO: Rex T. Clevenger, age 47
SVP, Human Resources: Walter T. Chesley, age 50, $236,761 pay
SVP, Medical Equipment Services: Timothy R. Travis, age 46
SVP, Sales: Joseph P. Schiesl, age 50, $333,427 pay
SVP, Asset Optimization: Jeffrey L. Singer, age 43, $232,443 pay

SVP, Technology, Marketing, and Facilities: David G. Lawson, age 48, $239,642 pay
VP, Customer Service: Timothy W. Kuck, age 47
Controller and Chief Accounting Officer: Andrew P. Weaver
Auditors: PricewaterhouseCoopers LLP

LOCATIONS

HQ: Universal Hospital Services, Inc.
7700 France Ave. South, Ste. 275, Edina, MN 55435
Phone: 952-893-3200 **Fax:** 952-893-0704
Web: www.uhs.com

Universal Hospital Services operates 75 district offices and 62 regional service centers in all 50 US states and the District of Columbia.

PRODUCTS/OPERATIONS

2004 Sales

	$ mil.	% of total
Medical equipment outsourcing	156.5	78
Technical & professional services	25.5	13
Medical equipment sales & remarketing	17.6	9
Total	**199.6**	**100**

COMPETITORS

MEDIQ
Medline Industries
Owens & Minor
PSS World Medical

HISTORICAL FINANCIALS

Company Type: Private

Income Statement

FYE: December 31

	REVENUE ($ mil.)	NET INCOME ($ mil.)	NET PROFIT MARGIN	EMPLOYEES
12/04	200	(4)	—	1,188
12/03	171	(20)	—	971
12/02	154	(0)	—	827
12/01	126	(4)	—	765
12/00	106	(5)	—	648
12/99	92	(5)	—	553
12/98	69	(8)	—	462
12/97	60	3	4.5%	384
12/96	56	1	1.6%	384
12/95	52	3	5.3%	309
Annual Growth	16.0%	—	—	16.1%

2004 Year-End Financials

Debt ratio: —
Return on equity: —
Cash ($ mil.): 0
Current ratio: 1.48
Long-term debt ($ mil.): 297

Net Income History

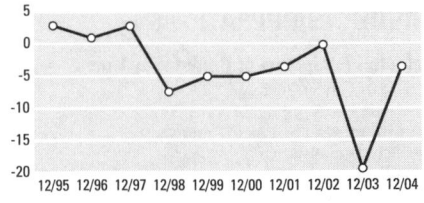

University of Alabama

Students in the Heart of Dixie can choose from among three campuses overseen by The University of Alabama system. The flagship Tuscaloosa campus offers about 215 degree programs to its more than 20,000 students. The University of Alabama at Birmingham offers about 140 degree programs and has an enrollment of about 17,000 students; it is also home to the university's school of medicine and a 900-bed hospital. The system's Huntsville campus has about 7,000 students enrolled in its five colleges and graduate school. Each campus offers bachelor's, master's, and Ph.D. degree programs. The University of Alabama was founded in Tuscaloosa in 1831 as the state's first public university.

EXECUTIVES

Chancellor: Malcolm Portera, age 59
President: Robert E. Witt
Vice Chancellor Academic Affairs: Charles Nash
Vice Chancellor Financial Affairs: Lynda Gilbert
Vice Chancellor Information Technology; Vice Provost Information Technology, University of Alabama: Priscilla Hancock
Vice Chancellor System Relations: Kellee Reinhart
VP Academic Affairs and Provost: Judith L. (Judy) Bronner
VP Student Affairs: Margaret Ingram King
Interim VP University Advancement: Pat Whetstone
Assistant VP University Relations: Janet L. Griffith
Associate VP Human Resources: Charlotte Harris
President, University of Alabama at Birmingham: Carol Z. Garrison
President, University of Alabama in Huntsville: Frank A. Franz
Secretary and Executive Assistant to the Chancellor: Michael A. Bownes
Director Financial Operations: Sandra Horne
Interim General Auditor; Director Internal Audit, University of Alabama: Newt Hamner
Auditors: KPMG LLP

LOCATIONS

HQ: The University of Alabama System
401 Queen City Ave., Tuscaloosa, AL 35401
Phone: 205-348-6010 **Fax:** 205-348-9788
Web: www.ua.edu

The University of Alabama System oversees campuses in Tuscaloosa, Birmingham, and Huntsville.

PRODUCTS/OPERATIONS

Selected Colleges and Schools

The University of Alabama (Tuscaloosa)
Capstone College of Nursing
College of Arts and Sciences
College of Communication
College of Community Health Sciences
College of Continuing Studies
College of Education
College of Engineering
College of Human Environmental Sciences
Culverhouse College of Commerce and Business Administration
Graduate School
School of Law
School of Social Work

The University of Alabama at Birmingham
School of Arts and Humanities
School of Business
School of Dentistry
School of Education
School of Engineering
School of Health Related Professions
School of Medicine
School of Natural Sciences and Mathematics
School of Nursing
School of Optometry
School of Public Health
School of Social and Behavioral Sciences
The University of Alabama in Huntsville
College of Administrative Science
College of Engineering
College of Liberal Arts
College of Nursing
College of Science
School of Graduate Studies

HISTORICAL FINANCIALS

Company Type: School

Income Statement

	REVENUE ($ mil.)	NET INCOME ($ mil.)	NET PROFIT MARGIN	EMPLOYEES
9/04	462	—	—	—
9/03	459	—	—	—
9/02	360	—	—	—
9/01	384	—	—	20,000
9/00	365	—	—	20,000
9/99	340	—	—	19,775
Annual Growth	6.3%	—	—	0.6%

FYE: September 30

Revenue History

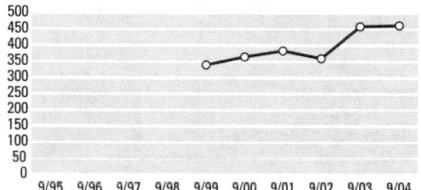

| | 9/95 | 9/96 | 9/97 | 9/98 | 9/99 | 9/00 | 9/01 | 9/02 | 9/03 | 9/04 |

University of California

The University of California (UC) system has approximately 208,000 students at its 10 campuses (which include three law schools and five medical schools) located in Berkeley, Davis, Irvine, Los Angeles (UCLA), Merced (which opened in the fall of 2005 with an enrollment of 875 students), Riverside, San Diego, San Francisco, Santa Barbara, and Santa Cruz. The schools, with more than 120,000 faculty and staff, offer areas of study in more than 150 disciplines ranging from the arts to bioengineering. UC also operates three US Department of Energy research labs in California and New Mexico.

In the wake of the 1996 approval of California's Proposition 209, which eliminated state affirmative-action programs, enrollment of minorities and the hiring of female faculty both dropped in the UC system. To help restore minority admissions to pre-Prop 209 levels, UC guarantees admission to the top 4% of students at each California high school and operates outreach programs aimed at low-income students.

More than 14% of California high school students were meeting UC's minimum eligibility requirements, a rate higher than the state guideline requiring the school to draw from only the top 12.5%. In 2004 the school agreed to raise the grade point level for students beginning in 2007 in order to shrink its applicants to meet the state guideline. Opponents to the plan argued that the higher standards would unfairly reduce the enrollment of minority and disadvantaged students.

HISTORY

The founders of California's government provided for a state university via a clause in the state's constitution in 1849. The origins of the College of California, opened in Oakland in 1869, date back to the Contra Costa Academy, a small school established by Yale alumnus Henry Durant in 1853. Durant ran Contra Costa, and then the college, until 1872. Women were allowed to enter the school in 1870. The college moved to Berkeley and graduated its first class (12 men) in 1873.

As California's economy and population grew, so did its university system. Renamed University of California (UC) in 1879, it had 1,000 students by 1895. Agriculture, mining, geology, and engineering were among its first fields. A second campus was established at Davis in 1905, followed by campuses in San Diego (1912) and Los Angeles (1919).

The Depression brought cutbacks in funding for UC, but the system rebounded in the 1940s. It opened its fifth campus (Santa Barbara) in 1944, and during WWII it also began gaining recognition for research. Between 1945 and 1965 enrollment quadrupled, spurred by GI Bill-sponsored veterans and a population shift to the West. The state legislature formulated the Master Plan for Higher Education in 1960, which reorganized university administration and established admission requirements. Campuses were established at Irvine and Santa Cruz in 1965.

The first of several important demonstrations in the 1960s at UC Berkeley came in 1964 over the university's attempts to ban political activity on a strip of UC-owned land. The People's Park riot of 1969, touched off when UC tried to close a parcel of land in Berkeley that students had turned into a kind of playground for the counterculture, left one dead and more than 50 wounded.

Aware of the changing demographics of its student body, especially its growing Asian enrollment (28% in 1990), UC Berkeley gave the chancellor's job to Chang-Lin Tien in 1990 — the first person of Asian descent to hold that position at a major US university (Tien served as chancellor until 1997). A California recession in the early 1990s resulted in budget cuts for UC. Strapped for cash, the university launched a for-profit entity in 1992 to tap its extensive library of patents.

UC San Diego chancellor Richard Atkinson succeeded Jack Peltason as UC president in 1995, the same year the UC Board of Regents approved a new campus — the university's 10th — in the San Joaquin Valley. That year it voted to phase out race- and sex-based affirmative action. The board, in an effort to be competitive with other top universities in recruiting faculty, voted to offer health benefits to the partners of gay employees in 1997. Also that year UC created the California Digital Library and began putting its library collection online.

Entrepreneur Alfred Mann donated $100 million to UCLA in 1998 for biomedical research. Also that year admissions of non-Asian-American minorities to the fall freshman classes of UCLA and UC Berkeley fell sharply. The following year the UC system began guaranteeing admission to the top 4% of students in each of the state's high schools. UC took some heat in 1999 and 2000 for two separate instances of security breaches at the Los Alamos National Laboratory.

Robert Dynes, previously chancellor of UC San Diego, became president of the UC system in October 2003.

EXECUTIVES

President: Robert C. Dynes
SVP, Academic Affairs and Provost: M.R.C. (Marci) Greenwood, age 62
SVP, Business and Finance: Joseph P. Mullinix
SVP, University Affairs: Bruce B. Darling
VP, Clinical Services: William H. Gurtner
VP, Agriculture and Natural Resources: W. R. (Reg) Gomes
VP, Budget: Lawrence C. (Larry) Hershman
VP, Financial Management: Anne C. Broome
VP, Health Affairs: Wyatt R. Hume
VP, Student Affairs: Winston C. Doby
VP Laboratory Management: S. Robert Foley
Associate VP, Human Resources and Benefits: Judith Boyette
Director, International Strategy Development: Gretchen Kalonji
Interim Treasurer and Interim VP, Investments: Marie N. Berggren
Auditors: PricewaterhouseCoopers LLP

LOCATIONS

HQ: University of California
1111 Franklin St., Oakland, CA 94607
Phone: 510-987-0700   **Fax:** 510-987-0894
Web: www.universityofcalifornia.edu

Campuses
UC Berkeley
UC Davis
UC Irvine
UC Los Angeles (UCLA)
UC Merced
UC Riverside
UC San Diego
UC San Francisco
UC Santa Barbara
UC Santa Cruz

PRODUCTS/OPERATIONS

Department of Energy Laboratories
Ernest Orlando Lawrence Berkeley National Laboratory (Berkeley, CA)
Lawrence Livermore National Laboratory (Livermore, CA)
Los Alamos National Laboratory (New Mexico)

HISTORICAL FINANCIALS

Company Type: School

Income Statement

FYE: June 30

	REVENUE ($ mil.)	NET INCOME ($ mil.)	NET PROFIT MARGIN	EMPLOYEES
6/04	15,122	—	—	120,786
6/03	14,166	—	—	118,533
6/02	15,980	—	—	114,282
6/01	15,887	—	—	108,827
6/00	14,048	—	—	103,767
6/99	13,074	—	—	99,890
6/98	9,375	—	—	130,000
6/97	9,022	—	—	130,000
6/96	8,363	—	—	137,874
6/95	7,958	—	—	131,660
Annual Growth	7.4%	—	—	(1.0%)

Revenue History

University of Chicago

The University of Chicago ranks as one of the world's youngest and most-esteemed major universities. Its undergraduate branch, The College, offers a core curriculum based on the "Great Books." The school is associated with 78 Nobel Prize recipients including Enrico Fermi, Milton Friedman, and Saul Bellow. Undergraduates can major in more than 50 areas. Among the U of C's graduate programs are the University of Chicago Law School and Graduate School of Business, both of which consistently rank in the top 10 by *U.S. News & World Report*. Founded in 1890 by John D. Rockefeller, the university has an endowment of about $3.5 billion. The U of C has more than 13,000 students and some 2,100 faculty.

The University of Chicago has steadfastly stood its ground against trendiness in education curricula. All students take courses that expose them to the social, biological, and physical sciences, as well as humanities, mathematics, and language. While the university's list of those who graduated is impressive, the list of those who did not is equally prominent, including Oracle's Larry Ellison and author Kurt Vonnegut.

Students attending the U of C study primarily at its 200-acre main campus on the South Side of Chicago, but the university's Graduate School of Business also maintains campuses in downtown Chicago, London, and Singapore. Among the many institutions affiliated with the U of C are the University of Chicago Hospitals and Health System, the Argonne National Laboratory, and the Yerkes Observatory. The University of Chicago Press, founded in 1892, is the largest university press in the US.

HISTORY

The University of Chicago took its name from the first U of C, a small Baptist school that operated from 1858-1886. The school, incorporated in 1890, was born when William Rainey Harper, the man who was to become the University's first president, convinced Standard Oil's John D. Rockefeller to provide a founding gift of $600,000. Members of the American Baptist Education Society chipped in another $400,000, and department store owner Marshall Field donated the land for the campus.

The university opened in 1892 with a faculty of 103 and 594 students. As it grew, the university took over property that had been used in the Columbian Exposition of 1892-93, eventually surrounding the fair's former midway. (The school's football team later earned the nickname "Monsters of the Midway" while being coached by the legendary Amos Alonzo Stagg; this was before withdrawing from intercollegiate play in 1939. Legend has it that the university retains the right to rejoin the Big Ten.)

Only four years after its founding, the university's enrollment of 1,815 exceeded Harvard's. By 1907, 43% of its 5,000 students were women. Robert Maynard Hutchins, president from 1929 to 1951, revolutionized the university and American higher education by insisting on the study of original sources (the Great Books) and competency testing through comprehensive exams. He organized the college and graduate divisions into their present structure, reaffirming the role of the university as a place for intellectual exploration rather than vocational training. In 1942 the U of C ushered in the nuclear age when Enrico Fermi created the first controlled nuclear chain reaction in the school's abandoned football stadium.

From the 1950s through the 1970s, the university purchased and restored Frank Lloyd Wright's famed Robie House and built the Joseph Regenstein Library (1970). In 1978 Hanna Holborn Gray became the first woman to be named president of a major university. Gray abolished the decade-old Lascivious Costume Ball, a major social event (some would say the only social event) at the university. Hugo Sonnenschein succeeded Gray in 1993. The beginning of his tenure coincided with a period of financial difficulty for the school as increases in costs outpaced revenue growth. In 1996 Sonnenschein announced plans to boost enrollment by as much as 30% in order to invigorate the school's finances.

U of C graduate and former professor Myron Scholes shared the Nobel Prize in economics in 1997. The next year the school announced plans for a $35 million athletics center to be named after Gerald Ratner, a former student who donated $15 million toward construction of the facility. The university later signed an agreement to supply content to Internet distance-learning startup UNext.com (now Cardean Learning Group), founded by trustee Andrew Rosenfield. (This agreement was controversial within the university community.) Cardean University, UNext.com's online university, began operating in 2000.

Sonnenschein resigned in 2000 and was replaced by Don Randel, former provost of Cornell University. That year the University of Chicago Graduate School of Business opened a campus in Singapore, and U of C economist James Heckman was awarded the Nobel Prize for his work in microeconomics.

EXECUTIVES

Chairman: James S. Crown, age 51
President: Don M. Randel, age 64
Provost: Richard P. Saller
VP Administration and CFO: Donald J. Reaves, age 55
VP and CIO: Gregory A. (Greg) Jackson
VP and Chief Investment Officer: Peter Stein
VP and General Counsel: Beth A. Harris
VP Community and Government Affairs: Henry S. Webber
VP; Dean, Students in the University: Stephen P. Klass
VP Development and Alumni Relations: Randy L. Holgate
VP Medical Affairs; Dean, BSD/Pritzker School of Medicine: James L. Madara
VP Research and Argonne National Laboratory: Thomas A. Rosenbaum
VP University Relations; Dean, College Enrollment: Michael C. Behnke
Dean, The College: John W. Boyer
Secretary: Kineret S. Jaffe
Comptroller: William J. Hogan Jr.
Director Library: Judith Nadler
Auditors: KPMG LLP

LOCATIONS

HQ: The University of Chicago
5801 S. Ellis Ave., Chicago, IL 60637
Phone: 773-702-1234 **Fax:** 773-702-4155
Web: www.uchicago.edu

The University of Chicago has campuses in the Hyde Park area of Chicago; downtown Chicago; London; and Singapore.

PRODUCTS/OPERATIONS

Selected Majors at The College (Undergraduate)

African and African American Studies
Ancient Studies
Art History
Biological Chemistry
Cinema and Media Studies
Classical Studies
Early Christian Literature
East Asian Languages and Civilization
English Language and Literature
Geography
Geophysical Sciences
Germanic Studies
History
History, Philosophy, and Social Sciences
International Studies
Jewish Studies
Latin American Studies
Medieval Studies
Music
Near Eastern Languages and Civilizations
Physics
Political Science
Psychology
Public Policy Studies
Religion and the Humanities
Romance Languages and Literatures
Russian Civilization
Sociology
South Asian Languages and Civilizations
South Asian Studies
Tutorial Studies
Visual Arts

Selected Affiliated Institutions

Argonne National Laboratory
Chapin Hall Center for Children
Consortium on Chicago School Research
Institute for Mind & Biology
University of Chicago Hospitals and Health System
Yerkes Observatory

Selected Graduate Schools and Programs

Divinity School
Graduate School of Business
Irving B. Harris Graduate School of
  Public Policy Studies
Law School
Pritzker School of Medicine
School of Social Service Administration

HISTORICAL FINANCIALS

Company Type: School

Income Statement

	REVENUE ($ mil.)	NET INCOME ($ mil.)	NET PROFIT MARGIN	EMPLOYEES
6/03	1,699	—	—	12,623
6/02	1,650	—	—	12,460
6/01	1,617	—	—	12,000
6/00	1,639	—	—	11,900
6/99	848	—	—	11,900
6/98	892	—	—	12,869
6/97	1,377	—	—	12,000
6/96	1,395	—	—	12,000
6/95	1,313	—	—	10,954
6/94	1,217	—	—	11,400
Annual Growth	3.8%	—	—	1.1%

FYE: June 30

Revenue History

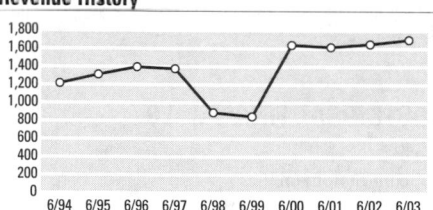

University of Illinois

The log cabins that used to dot the landscape in the Land of Lincoln have given way to the three campuses of the University of Illinois. Established as a land grant institution in 1867, the university has grown to include campuses in Chicago, Springfield, and Urbana-Champaign. Its nearly 70,000 students (more than half of whom study at the Urbana-Champaign campus) can choose from academic fields such as business, fine arts, and medicine. The Urbana-Champaign campus is the site of the National Center for Supercomputing Applications (which developed Mosaic, the basis for popular Internet browsers such as Netscape Navigator); the university's Springfield campus houses the Institute for Public Affairs.

EXECUTIVES

President: B. Joseph White, age 57
VP Administration and Comptroller:
  Stephen K. (Steve) Rugg
VP Academic Affairs: Chester S. Gardner
VP Technology and Economic Development:
  David L. Chicoine
President, Alumni Association: Loren R. Taylor
President, University of Illinois Foundation:
  Sidney S. Micek

Secretary: Michele M. Thompson
**Executive Director Governmental Relations and
  Director Federal Relations:** Richard M. Schoell
Executive Director University Relations: Thomas Hardy
University Counsel: Thomas R. Bearrows
Chancellor, UI Chicago: Sylvia Manning
Chancellor, UI Springfield: Richard D. Ringeisen
Chancellor, UI Urbana-Champaign: Richard Herman
Auditors: BKD, LLP

LOCATIONS

HQ: University of Illinois
  Henry Administration Bldg., 506 S. Wright St.,
  Urbana, IL 61801
Phone: 217-333-1000   **Fax:** 217-244-2282
Web: www.uillinois.edu

The University of Illinois has campuses in Chicago, Springfield, and Urbana-Champaign, as well as health professions sites and continuing education centers throughout the state.

PRODUCTS/OPERATIONS

Selected Colleges and Instructional Units

College of Agricultural, Consumer and Environmental
  Sciences
College of Applied Life Studies
College of Commerce and Business Administration
College of Communications
College of Education
College of Engineering
College of Fine and Applied Arts
College of Law
College of Liberal Arts and Sciences
College of Medicine at Urbana-Champaign
College of Veterinary Medicine
Graduate College
Graduate School of Library and Information Science
Institute of Aviation
Institute of Labor and Industrial Relations
School of Social Work

HISTORICAL FINANCIALS

Company Type: School

Income Statement

	REVENUE ($ mil.)	NET INCOME ($ mil.)	NET PROFIT MARGIN	EMPLOYEES
6/04	2,900	—	—	23,483
6/03	2,850	—	—	24,000
6/02	2,800	—	—	25,000
6/01	2,750	—	—	25,500
6/00	2,722	—	—	26,500
6/99	2,566	—	—	26,667
6/98	2,446	—	—	26,148
6/97	2,285	—	—	26,150
6/96	1,959	—	—	25,105
6/95	1,944	—	—	20,000
Annual Growth	4.5%	—	—	1.8%

FYE: June 30

Revenue History

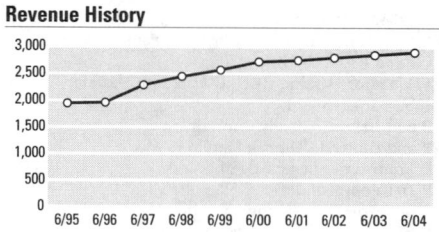

University of Iowa Hospitals and Clinics

University of Iowa Hospitals and Clinics partners with the University of Iowa Roy J. and Lucille A. Carver College of Medicine to make up the University of Iowa Health Care network. The organization provides residents of the Hawkeye State with an acute care hospital serving a variety of inpatient and outpatient needs. The facility also houses the Children's Hospital of Iowa and the Holden Comprehensive Cancer Center. The health care system has some 800 beds.

EXECUTIVES

Director and CEO: Donna M. Katen-Bahensky
Senior Associate Director: John H. Staley
**Senior Assistant Director and Assistant Dean of
  Clinical Affairs, UI Carver College of Medicine:**
  Daniel S. Fick
**Senior Assistant Director and Assistant Dean of
  Clinical Affairs, UI Carver College of Medicine:**
  Barbara A. Muller
Associate Director and COO: Ann Madden Rice
Associate Director and CFO: Anthony DeFurio
**Associate Director, Director of Nursing Sevices, and
  Patient Care/Chief Nursing Officer:** Linda Q. Everett
**Associate Director, External Relations and Legal
  Services:** William W. Hesson
Chief of Staff: Charles M. Helms

LOCATIONS

HQ: University of Iowa Hospitals and Clinics
  200 Hawkins Dr., Iowa City, IA 52242
Phone: 319-356-1616   **Fax:** 319-384-7099
Web: www.uihealthcare.com/uihospitalsandclinics

PRODUCTS/OPERATIONS

Selected Specialties

Acute and chronic pain medicine
AIDS consultation
Dermatology
Emergency medicine
Family medicine
Gynecology
Head surgery
Hospital dentistry
Internal medicine
Neurology
Neurosurgery
Obstetrics
Ophthalmology
Orthopaedics
Neck surgery
Pathology
Pediatrics
Psychiatry
Radiation oncology
Radiology
Surgery
Urology

Selected Centers
Children's Hospital of Iowa
Holden Comprehensive Cancer Center
James A. Clifton Center for Digestive Diseases

HISTORICAL FINANCIALS
Company Type: Not-for-profit

Income Statement   FYE: June 30

	REVENUE ($ mil.)	NET INCOME ($ mil.)	NET PROFIT MARGIN	EMPLOYEES
6/04	701	—	—	7,229
6/03	594	—	—	7,013
6/02	592	—	—	—
Annual Growth	8.8%	—	—	3.1%

Revenue History

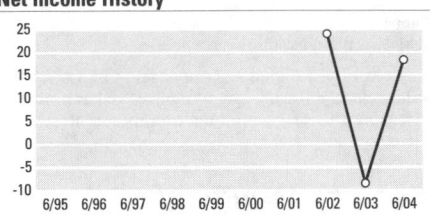

University of Louisville

The origins of the University of Louisville date back to 1798 with a meeting to establish Jefferson Seminary, which didn't open its doors until 1813 and closed 16 years later. Subsequent incarnations eventually led to the creation of the University of Louisville in 1846. A major focus then and now has been health care, and the University of Louisville Hospital is a part of the school's medical programs. The university now has more than 21,000 students enrolled in 12 colleges and schools on three campuses.

EXECUTIVES
President: James R. Ramsey, age 56
EVP and Acting Provost: Shirley C. Willihnganz
Interim EVP, Health Affairs: Larry Cook
VP, Business Affairs: Larry L. Owsley
VP, Finance: Michael J. Curtin
VP, Information Technology: Ronald L. (Ron) Moore
Associate VP, Administration: Mitchell Payne
Associate VP, Communications and Marketing: Rae Goldsmith
Associate VP, Human Resources: Julien C. Carter
Head Coach, Men's Basketball: Rick Pitino, age 53
Chairman, Department of Surgery, U of L School of Medicine: Kelly M. McMasters, age 44
Auditors: Deloitte & Touche LLP

LOCATIONS
HQ: University of Louisville
2301 S. 3rd St., Louisville, KY 40292
Phone: 502-852-5555   **Fax:** 502-852-7658
Web: www.louisville.edu

HISTORICAL FINANCIALS
Company Type: School

Income Statement   FYE: June 30

	REVENUE ($ mil.)	NET INCOME ($ mil.)	NET PROFIT MARGIN	EMPLOYEES
6/04	384	18	4.8%	5,521
6/03	328	(9)	—	5,100
6/02	327	24	7.3%	4,700
Annual Growth	8.3%	(12.7%)	—	8.4%

Net Income History

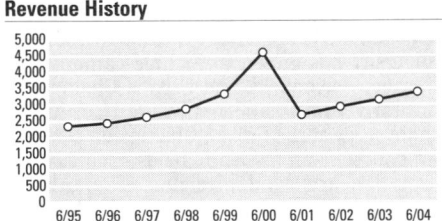

University of Michigan

Michigan — it's shaped like a mitten, and higher education fits the state like a glove. The University of Michigan has been a leader in the state's education effort since its founding in 1817. With more than 51,000 students and about 5,600 faculty members scattered across three campuses in Ann Arbor, Dearborn, and Flint, the university's diverse academic units span such areas of study as architecture, education, law, medicine, music, and social work. Notable alumni include former President Gerald Ford (the university is home to the Gerald R. Ford Library and the Ford School of Public Policy) and playwright Arthur Miller. In addition to state funding, the university is supported by a $4.3 billion endowment.

The university was founded in Detroit but moved to Ann Arbor in 1837. There are seven museums on campus — including the Museum of Art, the Exhibit Museum of Natural History (with a planetarium), and the Kelsey Museum of Archaeology — as well as the Nichols Arboretum and the Mattaei Botanical Gardens.

EXECUTIVES
President: Mary Sue Wilson Coleman, age 61
EVP Academic Affairs and Provost: Paul N. Courant
EVP and CFO: Timothy P. Slottow
EVP Medical Affairs; CEO, U-M Health System: Robert P. (Bob) Kelch
VP and Secretary: Sally Churchill
VP and General Counsel: Marvin Krislov
VP Communications: Lisa M. Rudgers
VP Development: Jerry A. May
VP Government Relations: Cynthia H. Wilbanks
VP Student Affairs: E. Royster Harper
Associate VP and Chief Human Resource Officer: Laurita E. Thomas

Associate VP Development: Chacona Johnson
Chancellor, UM-Dearborn: Daniel Little
Chancellor, UM-Flint: Juan E. Mestas
Auditors: PricewaterhouseCoopers LLP

LOCATIONS
HQ: The University of Michigan
3074 Fleming Administration Bldg.,
Ann Arbor, MI 48109
Phone: 734-764-1817   **Fax:** 734-764-4546
Web: www.umich.edu

PRODUCTS/OPERATIONS

Selected Academic Units
Architecture and urban planning
Art and design
Business administration
Dentistry
Education
Engineering
Kinesiology
Law
Literature, science, and the arts
Medicine
Music
Natural resources and environment
Nursing
Pharmacy
Public health
Public policy
Social work

HISTORICAL FINANCIALS
Company Type: School

Income Statement   FYE: June 30

	REVENUE ($ mil.)	NET INCOME ($ mil.)	NET PROFIT MARGIN	EMPLOYEES
6/04	3,384	770	22.7%	—
6/03	3,157	—	—	—
6/02	2,944	—	—	—
6/01	2,696	—	—	—
6/00	4,609	—	—	—
6/99	3,334	—	—	—
6/98	2,881	—	—	23,000
6/97	2,630	—	—	23,000
6/96	2,444	—	—	22,596
6/95	2,348	—	—	—
Annual Growth	4.1%	—	—	0.9%

Revenue History

University of Minnesota

More than 64,000 students come seeking higher education in the Land of 10,000 Lakes. A major land grant university system, the University of Minnesota (U of M) offers undergraduate and graduate degrees in some 370 academic fields. Its Twin Cities campus, with about 50,000 students, ranks among the largest in the country in terms of enrollment (along with the main campuses of Ohio State and The University of Texas). U of M serves additional students through campuses in Crookston, Duluth, and Morris, and a collaborative center in Rochester. It is also a top research institution with numerous research centers. U of M was founded as a prep school in 1851 and became a land grant institution in 1867.

EXECUTIVES

President: Robert H. (Bob) Bruininks
SVP Academic Affairs and Provost:
 E. Thomas (Tom) Sullivan
SVP Health Sciences: Frank B. Cerra
SVP System Administration: Robert J. Jones
VP, CFO, and Treasurer: Richard H. Pfutzenreuter
VP and Chief of Staff: Kathryn F. Brown
VP Human Resources: Carol Carrier
VP University Services: Kathleen O'Brien
Associate VP and Controller: Michael D. Volna
**Associate VP Community Partnerships and
 Development:** Sheila Ards
General Counsel: Mark B. Rotenberg
University Librarian: Wendy Pradt Lougee
Auditors: Deloitte & Touche LLP

LOCATIONS

HQ: University of Minnesota
 234 Morrill Hall, 100 Church St., Southeast,
 Minneapolis, MN 55455
Phone: 612-625-5000   **Fax:** 612-626-1693
Web: www.umn.edu

The University of Minnesota has campuses in Crookston, Duluth, Minneapolis-St. Paul, and Morris. It also operates facilities in Rochester through a partnership with Minnesota State University.

PRODUCTS/OPERATIONS

Selected Colleges and Schools

Carlson School of Management
College of Agricultural, Food, and Environmental
 Sciences
College of Architecture and Landscape Architecture
College of Biological Sciences
College of Continuing Education
College of Education and Human Development
College of Human Ecology
College of Liberal Arts
College of Natural Resources
College of Pharmacy
College of Veterinary Medicine
General College
Graduate School
Hubert H. Humphrey Institute of Public Affairs
Institute of Technology
Law School
Medical School
School of Dentistry
School of Nursing
School of Public Health

HISTORICAL FINANCIALS

Company Type: School

Income Statement

FYE: June 30

	REVENUE ($ mil.)	NET INCOME ($ mil.)	NET PROFIT MARGIN	EMPLOYEES
6/04	1,381	—	—	17,918
6/03	1,237	—	—	18,287
6/02	1,131	—	—	17,881
6/01	2,301	—	—	17,416
6/00	3,224	—	—	16,602
6/99	2,204	—	—	16,062
6/98	2,051	—	—	15,290
6/97	1,872	—	—	15,249
6/96	1,880	—	—	17,570
6/95	2,079	—	—	16,936
Annual Growth	(4.4%)	—	—	0.2%

Revenue History

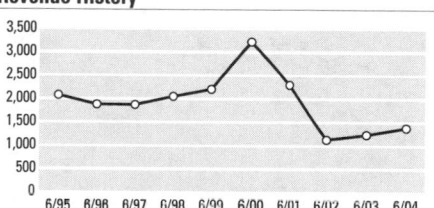

University of Missouri

Education isn't just for show in the "Show Me" state. The University of Missouri, founded in 1839, educates more than 60,000 students at four campuses and through a statewide extension program; some 25% of the students are in graduate or professional programs. Nicknamed "Mizzou," the university's cadre of campuses includes flagship UM-Columbia (home to some 27,000 students, 20 schools and colleges, and the University of Missouri Health Sciences Center), UM-Kansas City, UM-Rolla, and UM-St. Louis. Offering fields of study ranging from journalism to law to fine arts, the university has about 7,100 faculty and members.

EXECUTIVES

President: Elson S. Floyd, age 47
EVP and Director Cooperative Extension:
 Ronald J. Turner
Chancellor, UM-Kansas City: Martha W. Gilliland
Chancellor, UM-Rolla: Gary Thomas
Chancellor, UM-St. Louis: Thomas F. (Tom) George
VP Academic Affairs: Stephen W. Lehmkuhle
VP Finance and Administration:
 Natalie R. (Nikki) Krawitz
VP Human Resources: R. Kenneth Hutchinson
VP Government Relations: Stephen Knorr
Secretary to the Board: Kathleen M. Miller
Treasurer: Shirley S. DeJarnette
Director University Relations: David R. Russell
Director Planning and Budget: Cuba Plain
General Counsel: Marvin E. (Bunky) Wright
Auditors: Deloitte & Touche LLP

LOCATIONS

HQ: University of Missouri System
 321 University Hall, Columbia, MO 65211
Phone: 573-882-2121   **Fax:** 573-882-2721
Web: www.umsystem.edu

The University of Missouri has campuses in Columbia, Kansas City, Rolla, and St. Louis.

PRODUCTS/OPERATIONS

Selected Colleges and Schools

Accountancy
Agriculture
Art
Arts and Science
Business
Education
Engineering
Food Science
Graduate School
Health Professions
Honors College
Human Environmental Sciences
Information Science and Learning Technologies
Journalism
Law
Medicine
Natural Resources
Nursing
Social Work
Veterinary Medicine

Campuses

University of Missouri-Columbia (about 27,000 students)
University of Missouri-Kansas City
 (about 14,000 students)
University of Missouri-Rolla (about 5,000 students)
University of Missouri-St. Louis (about 15,000 students)

HISTORICAL FINANCIALS

Company Type: School

Income Statement

FYE: June 30

	REVENUE ($ mil.)	NET INCOME ($ mil.)	NET PROFIT MARGIN	EMPLOYEES
6/04	1,344	272	20.2%	23,513
6/03	1,252	—	—	26,246
6/02	1,253	—	—	26,316
6/01	1,446	—	—	27,914
6/00	1,356	—	—	32,870
6/99	1,487	—	—	20,000
6/98	1,396	—	—	15,818
6/97	1,336	—	—	15,283
6/96	1,226	—	—	17,400
6/95	1,164	—	—	18,997
Annual Growth	1.6%	—	—	2.4%

Revenue History

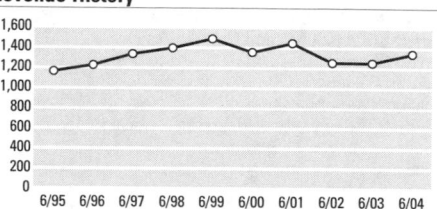

University of Nebraska

The University of Nebraska has sprouted four campuses out in the fields of the Cornhusker State. Founded in 1869, the state university system offers bachelor's, master's, and doctoral degrees in such programs as agriculture, business, education, and engineering at its campuses in Kearney, Lincoln, and Omaha. The university's Medical Center in Omaha trains doctors, performs research, and is affiliated with a 700-bed teaching hospital. The University of Nebraska also operates research and extension services across the state. Nearly 47,000 students attend classes in the university system, which is recovering from a severe 1997 enrollment drop caused by tighter admissions standards.

EXECUTIVES

President: James B. (J. B.) Milliken
EVP and Provost: Jay Noren
VP Business and Finance: David E. Lechner
VP University Affairs: Peter G. (Pete) Kotsiopulos
VP; Vice Chancellor, Agriculture and Natural Resources: John C. Owens
VP and General Counsel: Richard R. Wood
Associate EVP, Provost, and Corporation Secretary: Donal Burns
Assistant EVP and Provost: Royce Ballinger
Assistant VP Administration: Deb Thomas
Assistant VP and Director Facilities Planning Management: Rebecca Koller
Assistant VP and Director Finance: Michael Justus
Assistant VP and Director Human Resources: Ed Wimes
Assistant VP Communications and Marketing: Sharon Stephan
Auditors: Deloitte & Touche

LOCATIONS

HQ: The University of Nebraska
3835 Holdrege St., Lincoln, NE 68583
Phone: 402-472-2111   **Fax:** 402-472-1237
Web: www.nebraska.edu

PRODUCTS/OPERATIONS

University Campuses

The University of Nebraska at Kearney
The University of Nebraska-Lincoln
The University of Nebraska Medical Center
The University of Nebraska at Omaha

Selected Colleges and Programs

Agricultural Science and Natural Resources
Architecture
Arts and Sciences
Business Administration
Dentistry (University of Nebraska Medical Center)
Engineering and Technology
Fine and Performing Arts
Graduate Studies
Human Resources and Family Science
Law
Medicine (University of Nebraska Medical Center)
Nursing (University of Nebraska Medical Center)
Pharmacy (University of Nebraska Medical Center)
Teachers College

HISTORICAL FINANCIALS

Company Type: School

Income Statement

FYE: June 30

	REVENUE ($ mil.)	NET INCOME ($ mil.)	NET PROFIT MARGIN	EMPLOYEES
6/04	1,336	93	6.9%	21,624
6/03	1,253	—	—	21,432
6/02	1,133	—	—	—
6/01	1,157	—	—	—
6/00	1,071	—	—	—
6/99	1,016	—	—	—
6/98	1,249	—	—	—
6/97	1,270	—	—	16,000
6/96	1,100	—	—	15,000
6/95	1,081	—	—	15,000
Annual Growth	2.4%	—	—	4.1%

Revenue History

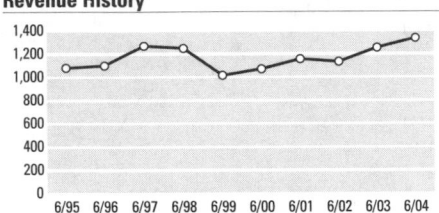

University of Pennsylvania

The University of Pennsylvania was established by Benjamin Franklin when he had a little down time between establishing a country and experimenting with lightning. Since opening its doors to students in 1751, the Ivy League university has accumulated a notable list of accomplishments, including the creation of the first medical school in the US and the invention of the ENIAC computer. The university's more than 23,000 students pursue their studies in four undergraduate schools and a dozen graduate and professional schools, including the renowned Wharton School and the Annenburg School for Communications. Former president Judith Rodin was the first female to head an Ivy League university.

EXECUTIVES

President: Amy Gutmann
Provost: Ronald J. Daniels
EVP: Craig Carnaroli
EVP University of Pennsylvania Health System and Dean School of Medicine: Arthur H. Rubenstein, age 66
SVP and General Counsel: Wendy White
SVP Facilities and Real Estate Services: Omar H. Blaik

VP and Chief of Staff: Joann Mitchell
VP Budget and Management Analysis and Executive Director Administrative Affairs: Bonnie Gibson
VP Development and Alumni Relations: John H. Zeller
VP Division of Public Safety: Maureen Rush
VP Finance and Treasurer: Scott R. Douglass
VP Human Resources: John J. Heuer
VP Information Systems and Computing: Robin H. Beck
VP University Communications: Lori Doyle
Secretary: Leslie Laird Kruhly
Comptroller: John F. Horn
Auditors: PricewaterhouseCoopers LLP

LOCATIONS

HQ: The University of Pennsylvania
3451 Walnut St., Philadelphia, PA 19104
Phone: 215-898-5000   **Fax:** 215-898-9659
Web: www.upenn.edu

Located in Philadelphia, The University of Pennsylvania also offers study abroad programs in 36 countries.

PRODUCTS/OPERATIONS

Selected Schools

Annenberg School for Communication
The College at Penn (School of Arts and Sciences)
Graduate School of Education
Graduate School of Fine Arts
Law School
School of Arts and Sciences
School of Dental Medicine
School of Engineering and Applied Science
School of Medicine
School of Nursing
School of Social Work
School of Veterinary Medicine
The Wharton School

HISTORICAL FINANCIALS

Company Type: School

Income Statement

FYE: June 30

	REVENUE ($ mil.)	NET INCOME ($ mil.)	NET PROFIT MARGIN	EMPLOYEES
6/03	3,786	—	—	11,949
6/02	3,563	—	—	—
6/01	3,191	—	—	12,290
6/00	3,007	—	—	—
6/99	2,823	—	—	18,331
6/98	2,602	—	—	20,619
6/97	2,197	—	—	22,934
6/96	1,994	—	—	21,803
6/95	1,778	—	—	20,500
6/94	1,714	—	—	20,000
Annual Growth	9.2%	—	—	(5.6%)

Revenue History

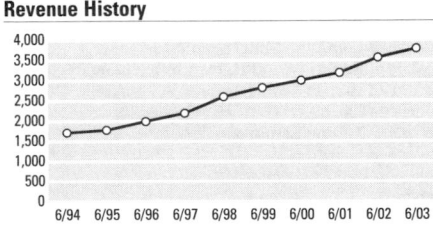

University of Rochester

The buzz about the University of Rochester is music to some ears. The private, upstate New York institution is nationally recognized for its programs in medicine, engineering, and business, and its Eastman School of Music (founded by Eastman Kodak creator George Eastman) is one of the top music schools in the US. The university, which has an endowment of more than $1.1 billion, offers some 175 bachelor's, master's, and doctoral degrees to about 8,500 full- and part-time students. Founded as a Baptist-sponsored institution in 1850, the university is nonsectarian today.

EXECUTIVES

President: Thomas H. Jackson
Provost: Charles E. Phelps
SVP Administration and Finance, CFO, and Treasurer: Ronald J. Paprocki
SVP Institutional Resources: Douglas W. Phillips
VP and General Secretary: Paul J. Burgett
Auditors: KPMG LLP

LOCATIONS

HQ: University of Rochester
   Administration Bldg., Rochester, NY 14627
Phone: 585-275-2121   **Fax:** 585-275-0359
Web: www.rochester.edu

PRODUCTS/OPERATIONS

Selected Schools

Eastman School Campus
   Eastman School of Music
Medical Center
   Eastman Dental Center
   School of Medicine and Dentistry
   School of Nursing
   Strong Memorial Hospital
River Campus
   Margaret Warner Graduate School of Education and
      Human Development
   William E. Simon Graduate School
      of Business Administration

Other Operations

C. E. K. Mees Observatory (Bristol Hills, NY)
Center for Optoelectronics and Imaging
Laboratory for Laser Energetics
Memorial Art Gallery
Mt. Hope Campus

HISTORICAL FINANCIALS

Company Type: School

Income Statement

FYE: June 30

	REVENUE ($ mil.)	NET INCOME ($ mil.)	NET PROFIT MARGIN	EMPLOYEES
6/04	1,809	—	—	16,554
6/03	1,653	—	—	16,040
6/02	1,427	—	—	11,200
6/01	1,419	—	—	12,242
6/00	1,340	—	—	13,656
6/99	1,160	—	—	12,968
6/98	1,061	—	—	12,568
6/97	865	—	—	11,859
6/96	822	—	—	11,801
6/95	846	—	—	11,956
Annual Growth	8.8%	—	—	3.7%

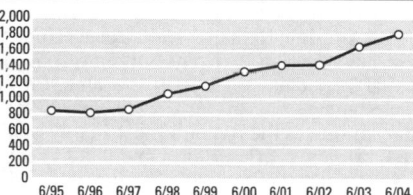

Revenue History

University of Southern California

This Trojan horse, filled with more than 31,000 students, is more than welcome at the University of Southern California (USC). Founded in 1880, the private university (home of the Trojans) grew up with the city of Los Angeles. It offers 77 undergraduate majors and 139 postgraduate degrees. Recognized for distinguished programs in business, engineering, film, law, medicine, public administration, and science, USC boasts two Los Angeles campuses and a string of research centers and health care facilities. The university also supports medical staffs at five Los Angeles hospitals. USC is the largest private employer in Los Angeles.

The university's focus on fund raising under current president Steven Sample has resulted in four individual donations of $100 million or more for his efforts to improve USC's undergraduate programs and medical school, as well as attract top-flight teachers.

Notable USC alumni include Marion Morrison (also known as John Wayne), who played tackle on the school's football team, as well as the first man on the moon, Neil Armstrong. Directors Ron Howard and Robert Zemeckis are both USC film school graduates.

EXECUTIVES

Chairman: Stanley P. Gold
Vice Chairman: Kathleen L. McCarthy
President and Trustee: Steven B. Sample, age 64
SVP Academic Affairs and Provost: C. L. Max Nikias
SVP Administration: Dennis F. Dougherty
SVP University Advancement: Alan Kreditor
SVP University Relations: Martha Harris
SVP and General Counsel: Todd R. Dickey
Associate SVP Budget and Planning: Robert A. Cooper
Associate SVP Financial and Business Services: Robert V. Johnson
Senior Associate VP Administration: Michelle McCarthy
Associate VP University Public Relations: Susan Heitman
Treasurer: Ruth Wernig
University Controller: Erik Brink
Auditors: PricewaterhouseCoopers LLP

LOCATIONS

HQ: The University of Southern California
   University Park Campus, Los Angeles, CA 90089
Phone: 213-740-2311   **Fax:** 213-740-5229
Web: www.usc.edu

PRODUCTS/OPERATIONS

Schools and Programs

Annenberg School for Communication
College of Letters, Arts and Sciences
Graduate School
Independent Health Professions
Keck School of Medicine
The Law School
Leonard Davis School of Gerontology
Marshall School of Business
Rossier School of Education
School of Architecture
School of Cinema-Television
School of Dentistry
School of Engineering
School of Fine Arts
School of Pharmacy
School of Policy, Planning, and Development
School of Social Work
School of Theatre
Thornton School of Music

Campuses

Health Sciences Campus
University Park Campus

Health Facilities

Childrens Hospital Los Angeles
Doheny Eye Institute
Los Angeles County+USC Medical Center
USC University Hospital
USC/Norris Comprehensive Cancer Center

HISTORICAL FINANCIALS

Company Type: School

Income Statement

FYE: June 30

	REVENUE ($ mil.)	NET INCOME ($ mil.)	NET PROFIT MARGIN	EMPLOYEES
6/04	1,500	—	—	14,000
6/03	1,568	—	—	17,000
6/02	1,480	—	—	17,000
6/01	1,399	—	—	17,000
6/00	1,186	—	—	17,000
6/99	1,142	—	—	17,000
6/98	1,307	—	—	17,000
6/97	1,239	—	—	17,000
6/96	1,233	—	—	17,100
6/95	1,152	—	—	17,000
Annual Growth	3.0%	—	—	(2.1%)

Revenue History

University of Texas

These students are hooked on higher education. The University of Texas System runs nine universities throughout the Lone Star State with a total enrollment of about 183,000 students, making it one of the largest university systems in the US. Its flagship Austin campus, with some 50,000 students, ranks as one of the nation's largest student populations (neck-and-neck with the main campuses at Ohio State and the University of Minnesota). UT also runs six health institutions, including four medical schools, and receives some $1.5 billion a year for research. Its $10 billion endowment fund (managed by the University of Texas Investment Management Co.) is the country's third largest (after Harvard and Yale).

Established in 1876, UT Austin opened in 1883. The UT System was formally organized in 1950.

With the bulging ranks of Generation Y looming on the horizon, the UT System expects its enrollment to swell to 250,000 by the end of the decade. To accommodate the increase, the system has laid out plans to spend an estimated $5 billion on construction projects over the next six years. It also hopes the improvements will put it on par with research institutions such as California State University.

HISTORY

The Texas Declaration of Independence (1836) admonished Mexico for having failed to establish a public education system in the territory, but attempts to start a state-sponsored university were stymied until after Texas achieved US statehood and fought in the Civil War. A new constitution in 1876 provided for the establishment of "a university of the first class," and in 1883 The University of Texas (UT) opened in Austin. Eight professors taught 218 students in two curricula: academics and law.

The school's first building opened in 1884, and in 1891 the university's medical school opened in Galveston. By 1894 UT-Austin had 534 students and a football team. UT opened a Graduate School in 1910 and various other colleges over the years. The university added its first academic branch campus when the Texas State School of Mines and Metallurgy (opened in 1914 in El Paso) became part of the system in 1919.

UT's financial future was secured in 1923 when oil was found on West Texas land that had been set aside by the legislature as an education endowment. The income from oil production, as well as the proceeds of surface-use leases, became the Permanent University Fund (PUF), from which only interest and earnings on the revenues can be used: two-thirds by UT and one-third by Texas A&M University. UT continued to grow, thanks to the PUF, which topped $100 million by 1940.

UT sported the black eye of racial prejudice (as did many other institutions at the time) when it refused to admit Heman Sweatt, a black student, to its law school in 1946. The Supreme Court ordered UT to admit him in 1950, the same year the UT System was officially organized. Sixteen years later, in one of the nation's most highly publicized crimes, Charles Whitman killed 14 people and wounded 31 others with a high-powered rifle fired from atop the UT-Austin administration tower. The observation deck wasn't closed until 1975, however, after a series of suicides. (It was later reopened in 1999.)

In the meantime, UT added a medical center in Dallas and several graduate schools in Austin. The 1960s through the 1980s were a time of geographic expansion for the system as it absorbed other institutions, started several new campuses, and expanded its network of medical centers. In 1996 the UT System became the first public university to establish a private investment management company (University of Texas Investment Management Co.) to invest PUF money (by that time over $9 billion) and other funds.

The race issue reared its head again in 1996 when a federal court ruled in the Hopwood decision (named for the plaintiff) that the UT System could no longer use race to determine scholarships and admissions. Minority enrollments declined the following year, prompting the Texas Legislature to enact a law granting admission to the top 10% of graduates from any Texas high school to the state university of their choice.

Chancellor William Cunningham announced plans in 2000 to expand the UT System by 100,000 students over the decade. After he resigned that year, R. D. Burck took over as his successor. In 2001 UT received a $50 million donation, the largest gift in its history, from Texas businessman and Minnesota Vikings owner Red McCombs. The following year Burck stepped down and was replaced by Mark Yudof, former president of the University of Minnesota.

EXECUTIVES

Chairman, Board of Regents: James R. Huffines
Vice Chairman, Board of Regents: Rita C. Clements
Vice Chairman, Board of Regents: Woody L. Hunt
Vice Chairman, Board of Regents: Cindy T. Krier
Counsel and Executive Secretary, Board of Regents: Francie A. Frederick
Chancellor: Mark G. Yudof, age 61
Executive Vice Chancellor Academic Affairs: Teresa A. Sullivan
Executive Vice Chancellor Business Affairs: Scott C. Kelley
Vice Chancellor and General Counsel: Cullen M. Godfrey
Vice Chancellor Administration: Tonya M. Brown
Vice Chancellor Community Relations: John De La Garza Jr.
Vice Chancellor External Affairs: Randa S. Safady
Vice Chancellor Federal Relations: William H. Shute
Vice Chancellor for Governmental Relations and Policy: E. Ashley Smith, age 59
Vice Chancellor for Health Affairs: Kenneth I. Shine
Associate Vice Chancellor and Chief Information Officer: Clair Goldsmith
Asscoiate Vice Chancellor for Finance: Philip R. Aldridge
Executive Director of Employee Group Benefits: Dan Stewart
Auditors: Texas State Auditor

LOCATIONS

HQ: The University of Texas System
601 Colorado St., Austin, TX 78701
Phone: 512-499-4200 **Fax:** 512-499-4215
Web: www.utsystem.edu

PRODUCTS/OPERATIONS

University of Texas System Component Institutions

Academic Institutions
The University of Texas at Arlington (established 1895; fall 2004 enrollment 25,297)
The University of Texas at Austin (1883; 50,377)
The University of Texas at Brownsville (1991; 11,546)
The University of Texas at Dallas (1961; 14,092)
The University of Texas at El Paso (1914; 18,918)
The University of Texas-Pan American (Edinburg; 1927; 17,030)
The University of Texas of the Permian Basin (Odessa; 1969; 3,291)
The University of Texas at San Antonio (1969; 26,175)
The University of Texas at Tyler (1971; 5,326)

Health Institutions
The University of Texas Health Science Center at Houston (established 1972; fall 2004 enrollment 3,399)
The University of Texas Health Science Center at San Antonio (1959; 2,837)
The University of Texas Health Center at Tyler (1947; 5,326)
The University of Texas M.D. Anderson Cancer Center (Houston, 1941; 70)
The University of Texas Medical Branch at Galveston (1891; 2,121)
The University of Texas Southwestern Medical Center at Dallas (1943; 2,273)

HISTORICAL FINANCIALS

Company Type: School

Income Statement

FYE: August 31

	REVENUE ($ mil.)	NET INCOME ($ mil.)	NET PROFIT MARGIN	EMPLOYEES
8/03	5,235	—	—	66,845
8/02	4,806	—	—	65,689
8/01	6,461	—	—	63,054
8/00	5,943	—	—	79,430
8/99	4,131	—	—	78,000
8/98	5,244	—	—	77,112
8/97	4,803	—	—	75,517
8/96	4,624	—	—	74,364
8/95	4,300	—	—	72,395
8/94	4,030	—	—	70,000
Annual Growth	2.9%	—	—	(0.5%)

Revenue History

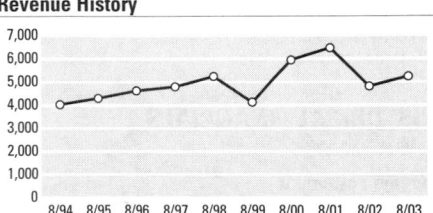

University of Washington

The University of Washington (UW) is Husky indeed, with more than 39,000 students enrolled at its main Seattle campus. Founded in 1861 as the Territorial University of Washington, UW (pronounced "U-dub" by those on campus) also has smaller branches in Tacoma and Bothell. The university maintains 17 schools and colleges for both undergraduate and graduate students (more than 70% of students on the main campus are undergrads). It also operates a health sciences center and an academic medical center, which includes the University of Washington Medical Center and Harborview Medical Center.

EXECUTIVES

President: Mark A. Emmert
EVP: Weldon E. Ihrig
VP Academic Affairs and Provost: Phyllis Wise, age 60
VP Computing and Communications:
  Ronald A. Johnson
VP Diversity: Nancy Barceló
VP Development and Alumni Relations: Connie Kravas
VP Financial Management: V'Ella Warren
VP Human Resources: Joanne I. Suffis
VP Student Affairs: Ernest R. Morris
VP Medical Affairs; Dean, School of Medicine:
  Paul G. Ramsey
Auditors: KPMG LLP

LOCATIONS

HQ: University of Washington
  University of Washington, Seattle, WA 98195
Phone: 206-543-2100
Web: www.washington.edu

The University of Washington has campuses in Bothell, Seattle, and Tacoma, Washington.

PRODUCTS/OPERATIONS

Schools and Colleges

The College of Architecture and Urban Planning
The College of Arts and Sciences
The College of Education
The College of Engineering
The College of Forest Resources
The College of Ocean and Fishery Sciences
The Graduate School
The Graduate School of Public Affairs
Information School
The School of Business Administration
The School of Dentistry
The School of Law
The School of Medicine
The School of Nursing
The School of Pharmacy
The School of Public Health and Community Medicine
The School of Social Work

Health and Medical Centers

Academic Medical Center
  Alcohol and Drug Abuse Institute
  Center on Human Development and Disability
  Harborview Medical Center
  Institute on Aging
  Regional Primate Research Center
  Research Center in Oral Biology
  University of Washington Medical Center
Warren G. Magnuson Health Sciences Center
  Department of Environmental Health and Safety
  Hall Health Primary Care Center

HISTORICAL FINANCIALS

Company Type: School

Income Statement

FYE: June 30

	REVENUE ($ mil.)	NET INCOME ($ mil.)	NET PROFIT MARGIN	EMPLOYEES
6/04	2,263	—	—	26,750
6/03	2,050	—	—	29,077
6/02	1,814	—	—	23,680
6/01	2,647	—	—	23,462
6/00	2,696	—	—	25,917
6/99	2,456	—	—	25,281
6/98	1,748	—	—	34,757
6/97	1,615	—	—	32,080
6/96	1,990	—	—	30,000
6/95	1,785	—	—	22,655
Annual Growth	**2.7%**	**—**	**—**	**1.9%**

Revenue History

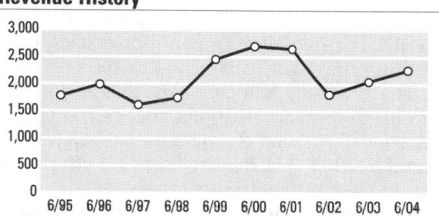

University of Wisconsin

There is no School of Cheese in the University of Wisconsin System, but there are 13 four-year universities, 13 two-year campuses, and a statewide extension program. The University of Wisconsin System is one of the largest public university systems in the US, with more than 160,600 students. Its top school is the University of Wisconsin at Madison, which offers undergraduate, graduate, and doctoral degrees and regularly ranks as one of the top public schools in the US. It has some 40,000 students and a nationally recognized graduate program in sociology. The system's other major campus is the University of Wisconsin at Milwaukee, with about 26,000 students.

Nearly one-third of the UW System's annual budget comes from state funds. Student fees, federal grants, fund raising, and other sources account for the remainder.

HISTORY

When Wisconsin became a state in 1848, its constitution called for the establishment of a state university. A board of regents was named, and it first established a preparatory school because regents felt Wisconsin's secondary schools were not advanced enough to prepare students for university studies. The school began classes in 1849 with 20 students in the Madison Female Academy Building. The University of Wisconsin's first official freshman class began studies in the fall of 1850. A campus was established a mile west of the state capitol in Madison. By 1854, when it held its first commencement (with two graduates), the school had 41 students.

Enrollment dipped during the Civil War (all but one of the school's senior class joined the army) but soon rebounded, and by 1870 the university had almost 500 students. Meanwhile, it established a school of agriculture (1866) and a school of law (1868). The state established normal schools (teachers colleges) in Platteville (1866), Whitewater (1868), Oshkosh (1871), and River Falls (1874).

There was also a teachers' course for women at the university in Madison. However, when John Bascom became president in 1874, he transformed the university into a truly coeducational institution, putting women "in all respects on precisely the same footing" with the men.

While the university at Madison remained Wisconsin's primary seat of learning, the state continued to establish normal schools. It opened institutions in Milwaukee (1885), Superior (1893), Stevens Point (1894), La Crosse (1909), and Eau Claire (1916). The nine normal schools eventually became a system of state colleges called Wisconsin State Universities.

The university at Madison also continued to grow, and by the late 1920s it had almost 9,000 students. WWII brought a drop in enrollment, but afterward it took off, jumping from about 7,000 in 1945 to over 22,000 by the late 1950s. The University of Wisconsin-Milwaukee branch was founded in 1956. Other branch campuses were established in Green Bay (1965) and Kenosha (1968).

The Madison campus became a focal point for student protests during the Vietnam War. Events came to a head in 1970 when President Fred Harrington resigned during a four-day standoff between students and the National Guard. War protesters also placed a bomb outside Sterling Hall, which housed the Army Math Research Center; the explosion killed one student and injured three others.

The state legislature merged the University of Wisconsin and the Wisconsin State Universities in 1971 to create The University of Wisconsin System. By the early 1980s it had an enrollment of nearly 160,000. Later that decade, however, it tightened admission standards, and enrollment began to fall.

A property-tax reform bill passed by the legislature in 1994 cut into The University of Wisconsin System's funding the next year. The system announced it would cut 500 jobs in 1997, use more part-time instructors, and increase class sizes to deal with the $43 million it lost in the budget cuts.

UW-Madison broke ground on the $22 million Fluno Center for Executive Education in 1998, a 100-room dorm, classroom building, and dining hall rolled into one. The next year enrollment at The University of Wisconsin System's two-year colleges broke 10,000 for the first time in five years. The licensing of technologies invented at the UW-Madison campus was expanded to include all four-year universities in the UW System in 2000. The System's mandatory student-fee policy was ruled unconstitutional later that year. The demand for enrollment for The University of Wisconsin System increased from 2001 to 2002, with the number of applications for undergraduate admissions growing 10%. The UW System raised the price of tuition to help offset cuts in state funding in 2003 and 2004.

EXECUTIVES

Chairman: Toby E. Marcovich
Vice Chairman: David G. Walsh
President: Kevin P. Reilly
Executive SVP: Donald J. Mash
SVP Academic Affairs: Cora B. Marrett
SVP Administration: David W. Olien
VP Finance: Deborah A. Durcan
VP University Relations: Linda L. Weimer
Associate VP Academic Affairs: Ronald M. Singer
Associate VP Budget and Planning: Freda J. Harris
Associate VP Financial Administration: Doug Hendrix
Associate VP Human Resources: George H. Brooks
Associate VP Learning and Information Technology:
  Edward Meachen
Associate VP University Relations: Margaret Lewis
**Assistant VP Academic Affairs and Senior Advisor to
  the President for Academic Diversity:** Andrea-
  Teresa (Tess) Arenas
Assistant VP Administrative Services: Ruth Anderson
Assistant VP Budget and Planning: Lynn Paulson
Assistant VP Capital Planning and Budget: David Miller
Assistant VP Human Resources: Alan Crist
Assistant VP University Relations: Kris Andrews
Secretary: Judith A. Temby
General Counsel: Patricia A. Brady
Auditors: State of Wisconsin Legislative Audit Bureau

LOCATIONS

HQ: The University of Wisconsin System
  Van Hise Hall, 1220 Linden Dr., Madison, WI 53706
Phone: 608-262-2321   **Fax:** 608-262-3985
Web: www.uwsa.edu

HISTORICAL FINANCIALS

Company Type: School

Income Statement			FYE: June 30	
	REVENUE ($ mil.)	NET INCOME ($ mil.)	NET PROFIT MARGIN	EMPLOYEES
6/03	3,273	—	—	28,030
6/02	3,059	—	—	26,650
6/01	3,160	—	—	24,000
6/00	2,922	—	—	23,981
6/99	2,558	—	—	25,889
6/98	2,543	—	—	25,500
6/97	2,399	—	—	25,399
6/96	2,612	—	—	28,626
6/95	2,556	—	—	30,410
6/94	2,442	—	—	30,341
Annual Growth	3.3%	—	—	(0.9%)

Revenue History

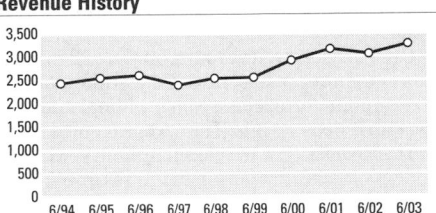

Uno Restaurant Holdings

One is the loneliest number . . . unless it's Uno Restaurant Holdings. The company operates and franchises about 200 Uno Chicago Grill restaurants known for their deep-dish, Chicago-style pizza. The casual-dining spots also serve pasta, steak, seafood, and sandwiches. The company's restaurants are located in about 30 states, primarily in the Northeast. About 120 of its locations are company-owned, and the rest are franchised. Through subsidiary Uno Foods, the company sells its pizza products to airlines, food courts, hotels, supermarkets, and theaters. Ike Sewell opened the first Pizzeria Uno in Chicago in 1943. Private equity firm Centre Partners Management purchased a controlling share in the company in 2005.

The company is looking to expand both its company-owned operations and its franchised locations, doubling the number of total restaurants by 2008. It also sees a lot of growth potential in the consumer products segment.

Uno Restaurants also owns one Mexican restaurant, Su Casa, in Chicago.

EXECUTIVES

Chairman: Aaron D. Spencer, age 73
CEO: Frank W. Guidara
EVP Finance, CFO, and Treasurer: Robert M. Vincent,
  age 52
EVP; President, Uno Foods: Alan M. Fox, age 57
SVP and General Counsel: George W. Herz II, age 49
SVP Franchising: Randy M. Clifton
SVP Human Resources and Training: Roger C. Ahlfeld
SVP Marketing: M. Heyward Whetsell Jr., age 57
SVP Operations: William J. (Bill) Golden
VP Design and Construction: James M. Carey Jr.
VP Food and Beverage and Executive Chef:
  Christopher S. (Chris) Gatto
VP Marketing: Daniel J. Wheeler
Auditors: Ernst & Young LLP

LOCATIONS

HQ: Uno Restaurant Holdings Corp.
  100 Charles Park Rd., Boston, MA 02132
Phone: 617-323-9200   **Fax:** 617-218-5376
Web: www.unos.com

Uno's domestic restaurants are located in 34 states and Washington, DC. The company is internationally located in Puerto Rico, South Korea, and the United Arab Emirates.

COMPETITORS

Applebee's	Darden
Back Bay Restaurant	Johnny Carino's
Bertucci's	Metromedia
BJ's Restaurants	Restaurant Group
Brinker	Outback Steakhouse
BUCA	The Pasta House
California Pizza Kitchen	Paul Revere's Pizza
Carlson Restaurants	Pizza Inn
Cheesecake Factory	Rock Bottom Restaurants
Consolidated	Ruby Tuesday
Restaurant Operations	Snappy Tomato Pizza

HISTORICAL FINANCIALS

Company Type: Private

Income Statement			FYE: Sunday nearest September 30	
	REVENUE ($ mil.)	NET INCOME ($ mil.)	NET PROFIT MARGIN	EMPLOYEES
9/04	500	—	—	8,200
9/03	260	—	—	8,100
9/02	255	—	—	8,000
9/01	242	—	—	7,800
9/00	231	—	—	7,644
9/99	214	—	—	6,435
9/98	191	—	—	5,590
9/97	178	—	—	6,389
9/96	172	—	—	6,227
9/95	159	—	—	5,815
Annual Growth	13.6%	—	—	3.9%

Revenue History

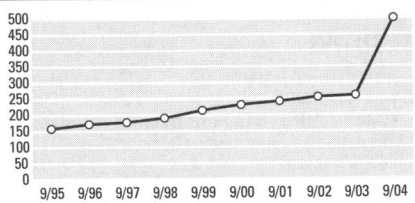

U.S. Can

If any company can make aerosol cans, U.S. Can can. The company makes a variety of steel and plastic containers that hold products ranging from shaving cream to paint — but not beverages. U.S. Can's steel aerosol cans, which account for the largest portion of the company's sales, are used to package automotive, household, paint, and personal care products. The company also makes nonaerosol paint cans, steel containers for products such as turpentine, and plastic pails for products such as paint, pool chemicals, and spackle. In addition, U.S. Can offers custom and specialty products such as decorative tins. Investment firm Berkshire Partners owns 77% of U.S. Can.

U.S. Can's approximately 5,600 customers have included Gillette and Sherwin-Williams. The company is a leading seller of aerosol cans in both the US and Europe.

The company operates in South America through a 37% stake in Argentina-based Formametal, an aerosol can manufacturer.

EXECUTIVES

Co-Chairman: George V. Bayly, age 62
Co-Chairman: Carl Ferenbach
CEO and Director: Philip R. Mengel, age 60
**EVP and General Manager, Business Units of the
  Americas:** Thomas A. Scrimo, age 56, $353,738 pay
SVP and CFO: Sandra K. Vollman, age 46, $244,777 pay
SVP, Metal Manufacturing and Lithography Operations:
  Larry S. Morrison, age 51, $257,600 pay
SVP, Sales and Marketing: Sarah T. Macdonald, age 40,
  $285,162 pay

VP and CTO: Emil P. Obradovich, age 58
VP and Controller: Robert Burkhardt, age 45
VP, Corporate Marketing and CIO: Sheleen Quish, age 56
VP, Human Resources: Thomas J. Olander, age 56
VP, Production Engineering: Frank Azzarello
Assistant General Counsel: Patricia Cosgrove
EVP, International: Anthony P. MacLaurin, $247,263 pay
Auditors: Deloitte & Touche LLP

LOCATIONS

HQ: U.S. Can Corporation
700 E. Butterfield Rd., Ste. 250, Lombard, IL 60148
Phone: 630-678-8000   **Fax:** 630-678-8131
Web: www.uscanco.com

U.S. Can has manufacturing facilities in Denmark, France, Germany, Italy, Spain, the UK, and the US.

2004 Sales

	$ mil.	% of total
US	546.7	65
Europe	298.1	35
Total	**844.8**	**100**

PRODUCTS/OPERATIONS

2004 Sales

	$ mil.	% of total
Aerosol	371.6	44
International	298.1	35
Paint, plastic & general line	134.1	16
Custom & specialty	41.0	5
Total	**844.8**	**100**

Selected Products

Aerosol containers
  Steel aerosol cans
International
  Steel aerosol cans
  Steel food cans
Paint, plastic, and general line containers
  Oblong steel cans
  Plastic pails and other containers for industrial
    and consumer products
  Steel paint and coating containers
Custom and specialty containers
  Collectible items (such as decorative metal signs
    and canister sets)
  Functional and decorative containers and tins
  Stampings

COMPETITORS

Ball Corporation	Owens-Illinois
BWAY	Silgan
CCL Industries	Silgan Containers
Crown	Sonoco Products

HISTORICAL FINANCIALS

Company Type: Private

Income Statement

FYE: December 31

	REVENUE ($ mil.)	NET INCOME ($ mil.)	NET PROFIT MARGIN	EMPLOYEES
12/04	845	(30)	—	2,200
12/03	823	(14)	—	2,300
12/02	797	(72)	—	2,400
12/01	772	(40)	—	2,600
12/00	810	(12)	—	2,700
12/99	714	21	3.0%	3,000
12/98	710	(16)	—	3,195
12/97	739	(32)	—	4,478
12/96	761	12	1.5%	4,065
12/95	627	4	0.6%	3,678
Annual Growth	**3.4%**	**—**	**—**	**(5.6%)**

US Oncology

US Oncology wants to get on the frontlines in the war against cancer, having restructured to focus on services more directly related to treating cancer. These services include oncology pharmaceutical management (such as the purchase and distribution of drugs), research and development assistance (such as the supervision of clinical trials), and outpatient cancer center operations. US Oncology serves more than 900 cancer physicians and cancer centers across the US. The company was formed from the 1999 merger of American Oncology Resources and Physician Reliance Network. Investment firm Welsh, Carson, Anderson & Stowe purchased the company in 2004.

US Oncology's network offers health care services from 460 sites, including about 85 cancer centers. The company plans to grow by providing a wide range of care management support services to medical oncologists.

EXECUTIVES

Chairman and CEO: R. Dale Ross, age 57
Vice Chairman: Lloyd K. Everson, age 60
EVP and COO: George D. Morgan, age 51
EVP, Pharmaceutical Services and CFO:
  Bruce D. Broussard, age 41
EVP and Chief Administrative Officer: Leo E. Sands, age 56
SVP, Marketing and Development: Richard J. Hall
President, Cancer Information Research Group:
  Atul Dhir, age 41
General Counsel: Phillip H. Watts, age 38
Director, Corporate and Marketing Communications:
  Kimberly Rutherford
Manager, Public Relations and Marketing:
  LeeAnn Donnelly
Auditors: PricewaterhouseCoopers LLP

LOCATIONS

HQ: US Oncology, Inc.
16825 Northchase Dr., Ste. 1300,
Houston, TX 77060
Phone: 832-601-8766   **Fax:** 832-601-6282
Web: www.usoncology.com

US Oncology operates in 32 states.

COMPETITORS

Aptium Oncology	Memorial Sloan-Kettering
Cancer Treatment Holdings, Inc.	Orion HealthCorp
	Sheridan Healthcare
Caremark	Sterling Healthcare
Medco Health Solutions	

HISTORICAL FINANCIALS

Company Type: Private

Income Statement

FYE: December 31

	REVENUE ($ mil.)	NET INCOME ($ mil.)	NET PROFIT MARGIN	EMPLOYEES
12/03	1,966	71	3.6%	8,096
12/02	1,651	(46)	—	8,957
12/01	1,505	46	3.1%	8,254
12/00	1,324	(73)	—	7,716
12/99	1,093	48	4.4%	7,182
12/98	456	30	6.6%	1,293
12/97	322	23	7.1%	1,162
12/96	206	18	8.6%	937
12/95	99	12	11.7%	737
12/94	20	1	5.9%	613
Annual Growth	**66.1%**	**57.3%**	**—**	**33.2%**

2003 Year-End Financials

Debt ratio: 32.6%   Current ratio: 1.37
Return on equity: 12.2%   Long-term debt ($ mil.): 188
Cash ($ mil.): 125

Net Income History

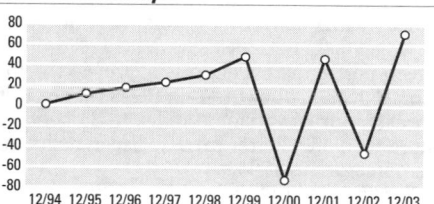

12/94 12/95 12/96 12/97 12/98 12/99 12/00 12/01 12/02 12/03

U.S. Postal Service

The United States Postal Service (USPS) handles cards, letters, and packages sent from sea to shining sea. The USPS delivers billions of pieces of mail a year to more than 142 million addresses. The independent government agency relies on postage and fees to fund operations. Though it has a monopoly on delivering nonurgent letters, the USPS faces competition for services such as package delivery. The US president appoints nine of the 11 members of the board that oversee the USPS. The presidential appointees select the postmaster general, who, along with the deputy postmaster general, is a board member. Delivery of standard mail (letters) and periodicals has been suspended in areas hit by Hurricane Katrina.

A challenge for the agency is the growing use of the Internet, which the USPS expects will cause the volume of "snail mail" to decline. To keep pace, the USPS is launching e-commerce initiatives such as computerized postage. The agency has also tapped into online shopping with its priority mail, merchandise return, and delivery confirmation services. It has formed limited alliances with express delivery companies, including a deal in which FedEx provides air transportation for EXPRESS MAIL, PRIORITY MAIL, and FIRST-CLASS MAIL shipments (but doesn't deliver the mail).

With an eye on its bottom line, the USPS has scaled down its construction program and accel-

---

2004 Year-End Financials

Debt ratio: —   Current ratio: 1.34
Return on equity: —   Long-term debt ($ mil.): 551
Cash ($ mil.): 7

Net Income History

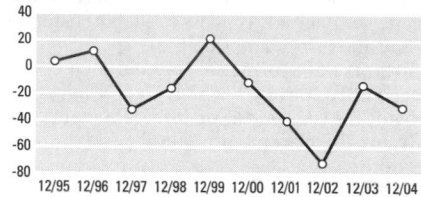

12/95 12/96 12/97 12/98 12/99 12/00 12/01 12/02 12/03 12/04

erated the pace of its rate increases, although officials don't expect the next increase to take effect until 2006. In addition, the agency is reducing its workforce through attrition and cutting hours of operation at some post offices.

A commission appointed by President Bush has recommended that the USPS adopt some private-sector management practices in order to ensure the agency's long-term financial health and to preserve universal mail service. The Bush administration expects the commission's recommendations to lead to the most significant revamp of postal operations since the early 1970s. Congress has yet to approve postal reform legislation, however.

HISTORY

The second-oldest agency of the US government (after Indian Affairs), the Post Office was created by the Continental Congress in 1775 with Benjamin Franklin as postmaster general. The postal system came to play a vital role in the development of transportation in the US.

At that time, postal workers were riders on muddy paths delivering letters without stamps or envelopes. Letters were delivered only between post offices. Congress approved the first official postal policy in 1792: Rates ranged from six cents for less than 30 miles to 25 cents for more than 450. Letter carriers began delivering mail in cities in 1794.

First based in Philadelphia, in 1800 the Post Office moved to Washington, DC. In 1829 Andrew Jackson elevated the position of postmaster general to cabinet rank — it became a means of rewarding political cronies. Mail contracts subsidized the early development of US railroads. The first adhesive postage stamp appeared in the US in 1847.

Uniform postal rates (not varying with distance) were instituted in 1863, the year free city delivery began. The start of free rural delivery in 1896 spurred road construction in isolated US areas. Parcel post was launched in 1913, and new mail-order houses such as Montgomery Ward and Sears, Roebuck flourished.

The famous pledge beginning "Neither snow nor rain . . . " — not an official motto — was first inscribed at the main New York City post office in 1914. Scheduled airmail service between Washington, DC, and New York City began in 1918, stimulating the development of commercial air service. The ZIP code was introduced in 1963.

As mail volume grew, postal workers became increasingly militant under work stress. (Franklin's pigeonhole sorting method had barely changed.) A work stoppage in the New York City post office in 1970 spread within nine days to 670 post offices, and the US Army was deployed to handle the mail. Later that year the Postal Reorganization Act was passed. The new law established a board of governors to handle postal affairs and choose the postmaster general, who became CEO of an independent agency, the US Postal Service (USPS). The next year USPS negotiated the first US government collective-bargaining labor contract. Express mail service began in 1977, and USPS stepped up automation efforts.

In 1995 USPS launched Global Package Link, a program to expedite major customers' shipments to Canada, Japan, and the UK. The next year it overhauled rates, cutting prices for larger mailers who prepared their mail for automation and raising prices for small mailers who didn't.

Postmaster General Marvin Runyon — whose six-year tenure took the agency from the red into the black — retired in 1998 and was succeeded by USPS veteran William Henderson. The next year a 1-cent hike in the price of first-class postage took effect. (Another 1-cent increase took effect in 2001, and the rate rose once again the following year.) In a nod to the Internet, USPS in 1999 contracted with outside vendors to enable customers to buy and print stamps online.

In 2001 USPS formed a strategic alliance with rival FedEx through which FedEx agreed to provide air transportation for USPS mail, in return for the placement of FedEx drop boxes in post offices.

Henderson stepped down at the end of May 2001, and EVP Jack Potter was named to replace him. That year several postal workers in a Washington, DC, branch office were exposed to anthrax-tainted letters.

Potter launched a series of cost-cutting programs, which together with rate increases enabled the USPS to post back-to-back profitable years in 2003 and 2004 — the agency's first years in the black since 1999.

EXECUTIVES

Chairman: James C. Miller III, age 62
Vice Chairman: John F. Walsh
Postmaster General and CEO: John E. (Jack) Potter
Deputy Postmaster, EVP, and COO: Patrick R. Donahoe
EVP and CFO: Richard J. Strasser Jr.
EVP and Chief Human Resources Officer:
 Anthony Vegliante
SVP and Chief Marketing Officer: Anita J. Bizzotto
SVP Government Relations: Ralph Moden
SVP Government Relations: Thomas G. (Tom) Day
SVP Intelligent Mail and Address Quality:
 Charles E. (Charlie) Bravo
SVP Operations: William P. Galligan
SVP Operations: John A. Rapp
VP and CTO: Robert L. (Bob) Otto
VP Finance and Controller: Lynn Malcolm
VP and General Counsel: Mary Anne Gibbons
VP Sales: Jerry Whalen
VP and Treasurer: Robert J. Pedersen
VP Public Affairs and Communications:
 Azeezaly S. Jaffer
Chief Postal Inspector: Lee R. Heath
Auditors: Ernst & Young LLP

LOCATIONS

HQ: United States Postal Service
 475 L'Enfant Plaza SW, Washington, DC 20260
Phone: 202-268-2500 **Fax:** 202-268-4860
Web: www.usps.com

PRODUCTS/OPERATIONS

2004 Sales

	$ mil.	% of total
FIRST-CLASS MAIL	36,377	53
Standard mail	18,123	26
PRIORITY MAIL	4,421	7
Package services	2,207	3
Periodicals	2,191	3
International airmail	1,551	2
EXPRESS MAIL	853	1
Certified	630	1
Other services	2,643	4
Total	**68,996**	**100**

COMPETITORS

BAX Global	Postal Connections
DHL	UPS
FedEx	Western Union

HISTORICAL FINANCIALS

Company Type: Government agency

Income Statement

FYE: September 30

	REVENUE ($ mil.)	NET INCOME ($ mil.)	NET PROFIT MARGIN	EMPLOYEES
9/04	68,996	3,065	4.4%	707,485
9/03	68,529	3,868	5.6%	826,955
9/02	66,463	(676)	—	854,376
9/01	65,834	(1,680)	—	797,795
9/00	64,540	(199)	—	787,538
9/99	62,726	363	0.6%	800,000
9/98	60,072	550	0.9%	792,041
9/97	58,216	1,264	2.2%	765,174
9/96	56,402	1,567	2.8%	760,966
9/95	54,294	1,770	3.3%	753,384
Annual Growth	**2.7%**	**6.3%**	**—**	**(0.7%)**

2004 Year-End Financials

Debt ratio: 0.0%
Return on equity: 127.8%
Cash ($ mil.): 877
Current ratio: 0.19
Long-term debt ($ mil.): 0

Net Income History

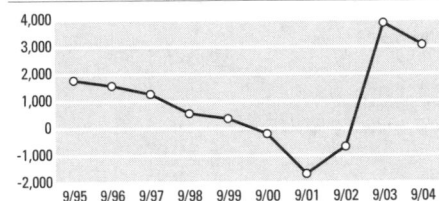

4,000	
3,000	
2,000	
1,000	
0	
-1,000	
-2,000	
	9/95 9/96 9/97 9/98 9/99 9/00 9/01 9/02 9/03 9/04

USAA

USAA has a decidedly military bearing. The mutual insurance company serves more than 5 million customers, primarily military personnel, military retirees, and their families. Its products and services include property/casualty (sold only to military personnel) and life insurance, banking, discount brokerage, and investment management. USAA relies largely on technology and direct marketing to sell its products, reaching clients via the telephone and Internet. The company also has a large mail-order catalog business (computers, furniture, jewelry, and home and auto safety items), and it offers long-distance telephone service, travel services, and Internet access to its members.

The company is expecting its membership to continue growing, projecting it to nearly double by 2010. In an attempt to increase revenue, the company has entered new markets by making efforts to target people less affluent than military officers.

Facing rising claims and a decline in value of its investments, USAA has streamlined operations by reducing staff and closing down divisions (including mailing, printing, and information technology offices).

HISTORY

In 1922 a group of 26 US Army officers gathered in a San Antonio hotel and formed their own automobile insurance association. The reason? As military officers who often moved, they had a hard time getting insurance because they were considered transient. So the officers decided to insure each other. Led by Major William Garrison, who became the company's first president, they formed the United States Army Automobile Insurance Association.

In 1924, when US Navy and Marine Corps officers were allowed to join, the company changed its name to United Services Automobile Association. By the mid-1950s the company had some 200,000 members. During the 1960s the company formed USAA Life Insurance Company (1963) and USAA Casualty Insurance Company (1968).

Robert McDermott, a retired US Air Force brigadier general, became president in 1969. He cut employment through attrition, established education and training seminars for employees, and invested in computers and telecommunications (drastically cutting claims-processing time). McDermott added new products and services, such as mutual funds, real estate investments, and banking. Under McDermott, USAA's membership grew from 653,000 in 1969 to more than 3 million in 1993.

During the 1970s, in an effort to go paperless, USAA became one of the insurance industry's first companies to switch from mail to toll-free (800) numbers. In the early 1980s the company introduced its discount purchasing program, USAA Buying Services. In 1985 it opened the USAA Federal Savings Bank. USAA began installing an optical storage system in the late 1980s to automate some customer service operations.

McDermott retired in 1993 and was succeeded by Robert Herres. The following year USAA Federal Savings Bank began developing a home banking system, offering members information and services over advanced screen telephones provided by IBM.

In the early 1990s USAA's real estate activities increased dramatically. In 1995 USAA restructured its interest in the Fiesta Texas theme park in San Antonio in order to focus on previously developed properties in geographically diverse areas. That year Six Flags Theme Parks (now Six Flags, Inc.) assumed operation and management of Fiesta Texas (which purchased it from USAA in 1998).

In 1997 USAA began including enlisted military personnel as members. It also started to experiment with a "plain English" mutual fund prospectus. In 1998 USAA also began offering Choice Ride in Orlando, Florida. For about $1,100 per quarter and a promise not to drive except in emergencies, the pilot program provided 36 round trips and a 90% discount on car insurance, in hopes of keeping older drivers from unnecessarily getting behind the wheel.

Also in 1998, as part of its new Financial Planning Network, USAA began offering retirement and estate planning assistance aimed at 25- to 55-year-olds for a yearly $250 fee. In 1999 claims doubled largely due to the impact of Hurricane Floyd and spring hail storms hitting military communities in North Carolina and Virginia.

USAA also moved in 1999 to consolidate its customers' separate accounts (such as mutual fund holdings, stocks and bonds, and life insurance products) into one main account to strengthen customer relationships and reduce operational costs. The next year, after completing a number of technology projects, it laid off workers for the first time in its history.

In 2002, Robert Herres resigned as chairman and was succeeded by CEO Robert Davis. The next year the company saw increased sales and an improved net income thanks to the rebounding stock market and membership growth.

EXECUTIVES

Chairman and CEO: Robert G. (Bob) Davis
EVP, Enterprise Business Operations, and COO: Robert T. Handren
EVP, CFO, and Corporate Treasurer: Josue (Joe) Robles Jr., age 59
EVP, Corporate Services: David H. Garrison
EVP, Marketing: Karen B. Presley
EVP, General Counsel, and Corporate Secretary: Steven A. Bennett
EVP, Human Resources: Elizabeth D. Conklyn
EVP, Corporate Communications: Wendi E. Strong
President and CEO, USAA Alliance Services Company: Dawn M. Johnson
President and CEO, USAA Federal Savings Bank: Mark H. Wright
President and CEO, USAA Investment Management Company: Christopher W. Claus
President and CEO, USAA Real Estate: Edward B. Kelley
President and CEO, USAA Financial Planning Services: Stuart Parker
President, USAA Life Insurance Company: Kristi A. Matus
President, USAA Property and Casualty Insurance Group: Henry Viccellio Jr.
Auditors: Ernst & Young LLP

LOCATIONS

HQ: USAA
9800 Fredericksburg Rd., San Antonio, TX 78288
Phone: 210-498-2211   **Fax:** 210-498-9940
Web: www.usaa.com

USAA has major regional offices in Colorado Springs, Colorado; Las Vegas; Norfolk, Virginia; Phoenix; Sacramento, California; and Tampa, Florida. It operates international offices in London and Frankfurt, Germany.

PRODUCTS/OPERATIONS

2004 Assets

	$ mil.	% of total
Investments	18,866	41
Bank loans, net	15,520	33
Real estate investments, net	1,267	3
Cash & cash equivalents	1,972	4
Premiums due from policyholders	1,494	3
Property & equipment, net	1,336	3
Securities lending collateral	1,481	3
Other assets	4,546	10
Total	**46,482**	**100**

2004 Sales

	$ mil.	% of total
Insurance premiums	8,408	75
Fees, sales, & loan income, net	1,347	12
Investment income, net	934	8
Real estate investment income	294	3
Other revenues	290	2
Total	**11,273**	**100**

Selected Operations

USAA Alliance Services Company (merchandising and member services)
USAA Federal Savings Bank
USAA Financial Planning Services
USAA Investment Management Company (mutual funds, investment and brokerage services)
USAA Life Insurance Company
USAA Property and Casualty Insurance Group (including automobile, home, boat, and flood insurance)
USAA Real Estate Company

COMPETITORS

21st Century	Kemper Insurance
AIG	Liberty Mutual
AIG American General	MassMutual
Allstate	MetLife
American Express	Morgan Stanley
American Financial	Mutual of Omaha
AXA Financial	Nationwide
Berkshire Hathaway	New York Life
Charles Schwab	Northwestern Mutual
Chubb	Pacific Mutual
CIGNA	Prudential
Citigroup	St. Paul Travelers
CNA Financial	State Farm
FMR	T. Rowe Price
Guardian Life	UBS Financial Services
The Hartford	
John Hancock Financial Services	

HISTORICAL FINANCIALS

Company Type: Mutual company

Income Statement

	REVENUE ($ mil.)	NET INCOME ($ mil.)	NET PROFIT MARGIN	EMPLOYEES
12/04	11,273	1,597	14.2%	21,000
12/03	10,593	1,501	14.2%	21,000
12/02	9,222	500	5.4%	22,000
12/01	8,970	604	6.7%	22,000
12/00	8,551	669	7.8%	22,000
12/99	8,319	765	9.2%	21,795
12/98	7,687	980	12.7%	20,120
12/97	7,454	1,189	16.0%	17,967
12/96	6,890	855	12.4%	16,571
12/95	6,611	730	11.0%	15,677
Annual Growth	**6.1%**	**9.1%**	**—**	**3.3%**

Net Income History

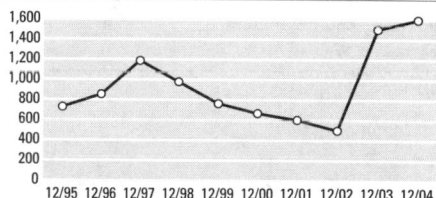

Valera Pharmaceuticals

Valera Pharmaceuticals makes it easy for patients to take their medicine. Focusing on treatments for urological and endocrine diseases, the company uses its Hydron Technology to develop implants that continuously deliver drugs directly to the bloodstream for up to a year. Its FDA-approved Vantas administers histrelin to patients with prostate cancer. In addition, Valera is developing several drug candidates to treat interstitial cystitis, addictive disorders, and other conditions. The company sells its products primarily to urologists in the US. Chairman James Gale controls about 49% of the company.

EXECUTIVES

Chairman: James C. Gale, age 55
President, CEO, and Director: David S. Tierney, age 42, $375,000 pay
CFO: Andrew T. Drechsler
VP, Marketing and Commercial Development:
Matthew L. Rue III, age 54, $193,000 pay
VP, Research and Development: Petr F. Kuzma, age 61, $155,000 pay
VP, Sales: Pete J. Perron, age 38, $149,109 pay (partial-year salary)
Director, Finance and Administration: Daniel J. Hayes
Senior Director, Regulatory Affairs: William B. Gray
Auditors: Ernst & Young LLP

LOCATIONS

HQ: Valera Pharmaceuticals, Inc.
8 Clarke Dr., Cranbury, NJ 08512
Phone: 609-409-9010   **Fax:** 609-409-1650
Web: www.hydromed.com

COMPETITORS

AstraZeneca
Novartis Pharmaceuticals
Pfizer
Sanofi-Aventis
TAP Pharmaceutical Products

HISTORICAL FINANCIALS

Company Type: Private

Income Statement

FYE: December 31

	REVENUE ($ mil.)	NET INCOME ($ mil.)	NET PROFIT MARGIN	EMPLOYEES
12/04	6	(12)	—	79
12/03	0	(8)	—	—
12/02	0	(6)	—	—
Annual Growth	—	—	—	—

2004 Year-End Financials

Debt ratio: (0.1%)   Current ratio: 3.54
Return on equity: —   Long-term debt ($ mil.): 0
Cash ($ mil.): 5

Net Income History

0									
-2									
-4									
-6									
-8									
-10									
-12									

12/95 12/96 12/97 12/98 12/99 12/00 12/01 12/02 12/03 12/04

ValleyCrest

ValleyCrest Companies hit pay dirt with plant care. The company uses its green thumb to provide landscape construction and maintenance, irrigation, golf course construction, lawn care, nurseries, and site engineering. ValleyCrest grows more than 2 million trees (for relocation), maintains indoor and outdoor gardens, and restores wetlands. It also franchises landscape maintenance services. Co-founder and CEO Burton Sperber and his family control the company, which began operations in 1949 as a small neighborhood landscape retail nursery in North Hollywood, California.

ValleyCrest purchased the landscape construction operations of TruGreen LandCare in 2001 to expand operations in Maryland, Massachusetts, Illinois, Minnesota, and Texas. In 2004 the company acquired the landscaping division of Omni Facility Services, which will be integrated into ValleyCrest's landscape maintenance division. The acquisition expands ValleyCrest's operations in the eastern US.

EXECUTIVES

Chairman and CEO: Burton S. (Burt) Sperber
Vice Chairman and CEO, Valley Crest Tree:
Stuart J. Sperber
President and COO: Richard A. Sperber
EVP and CFO: Andrew J. (Andy) Mandell
VP and CIO: John D. Johnston
SVP Asset and Risk Management:
Michael L. (Mike) Dingman
VP Risk Management: Katie Bouvier
VP and Corporate Counsel: William N. (Bill) Cohen
VP and Corporate Controller: Anthony (Tony) Garruto
VP and Assistant COO: Renu Nallicheri
VP Customer Satisfaction: Pamela S. (Pam) Stark
Director Human Resources: Raúl Díaz de León
Director Public Relations: Cheryl Steelberg
Corporate Secretary: Anita Legg

LOCATIONS

HQ: ValleyCrest Companies
24151 Ventura Blvd., Calabasas, CA 91302
Phone: 818-223-8500   **Fax:** 818-223-8142
Web: www.valleycrest.com

ValleyCrest Companies has operations in Arizona, California, Colorado, Florida, Georgia, Illinois, Indiana, Kentucky, Maryland, Massachusetts, Michigan, Minnesota, Missouri, Nevada, North Carolina, Pennsylvania, Tennessee, Texas, and Virginia.

PRODUCTS/OPERATIONS

Selected Subsidiaries and Operating Divisions
U.S. Lawns
ValleyCrest Landscape Development
ValleyCrest Landscape Maintenance
ValleyCrest Golf Course Maintenance
Valley Crest Tree Company

COMPETITORS

Davey Tree
FirstService
GreenSmart
Griffin Land & Nurseries
Hines Horticulture
OneSource Landscape and Golf Services
Skinner Nurseries
TruGreen Landcare

HISTORICAL FINANCIALS

Company Type: Private

Income Statement

FYE: April 30

	ESTIMATED REVENUE ($ mil.)	NET INCOME ($ mil.)	NET PROFIT MARGIN	EMPLOYEES
4/04	700	—	—	8,000
4/03	620	—	—	8,000
4/02	605	—	—	—
4/01	500	—	—	5,500
4/00	450	—	—	5,000
4/99	400	—	—	4,000
4/98	350	—	—	4,000
4/97	340	—	—	4,100
4/96	300	—	—	4,689
4/95	265	—	—	—
Annual Growth	11.4%	—	—	6.9%

Revenue History

700	
600	
500	
400	
300	
200	
100	
0	

4/95 4/96 4/97 4/98 4/99 4/00 4/01 4/02 4/03 4/04

Vanderbilt University

The house that Cornelius built, Vanderbilt University was founded in 1873 with a $1 million grant from industrialist Cornelius Vanderbilt. The university's endowment has grown to about $2 billion, and the school today is a haven for more than 11,000 students and more than 2,200 full-time faculty. Vanderbilt has 10 schools and colleges; its Owen Graduate School of Management and its medical school rank near the top of national surveys. A major research university, Vanderbilt receives millions of dollars annually in sponsored awards to fund its facilities. Vanderbilt offers undergraduate and graduate programs in areas such as education and human development, engineering, and the arts and sciences.

For its first 40 years of existence, Vanderbilt was under the auspices of the Methodist Episcopal Church, South. The Vanderbilt Board of Trust severed its ties with the church in 1914 after a dispute with the bishops over who would appoint University trustees.

EXECUTIVES

Chairman: Martha R. Ingram, age 69
Vice Chairman: Darryl D. Berger
Vice Chairman: Dennis C. Bottorff
Chancellor: E. Gordon Gee, age 61
Vice Chancellor Academic Affairs and Provost:
Nicholas S. Zeppos
Vice Chancellor Administration and CFO:
Lauren J. Brisky, age 54
Vice Chancellor Health Affairs: Harry R. Jacobson, age 57
Vice Chancellor Public Affairs: Michael J. Schoenfeld
Vice Chancellor Investments and Treasurer:
William T. Spitz
Vice Chancellor Student Life and University Affairs, General Counsel, and Secretary: David Williams II
Associate Vice Chancellor Finance and Controller:
Betty Price
Assistant Vice Chancellor Research Finance: Jerry Fife
Assistant Vice Chancellor Management Information Systems: Timothy R. (Tim) Getsay
Secretary of the Board: William W. Bain Jr.
Auditors: KPMG LLP

LOCATIONS

HQ: Vanderbilt University
2201 West End Ave., Nashville, TN 37235
Phone: 615-322-7311
Web: www.vanderbilt.edu

PRODUCTS/OPERATIONS

2004 Sales

	$ mil.	% of total
Health care services	1,188.0	60
Government grants & contracts	238.6	12
Tuition, fees, room & board	204.8	10
Endowment distributions	101.9	5
Facilities & administrative costs recovery	87.6	4
Gifts, private grants & contributions	59.5	3
Auxiliary services	45.0	3
Other	45.5	3
Total	**1,970.9**	**100**

Selected Schools and Colleges

Blair School of Music
College of Arts and Science
Divinity School
Graduate School
Law School
Owen Graduate School of Management
Peabody College of Education and Human Development
School of Engineering
School of Medicine
School of Nursing

HISTORICAL FINANCIALS

Company Type: School

Income Statement

FYE: June 30

	REVENUE ($ mil.)	NET INCOME ($ mil.)	NET PROFIT MARGIN	EMPLOYEES
6/04	1,971	—	—	18,551
6/03	1,799	—	—	17,700
6/02	1,590	—	—	16,679
6/01	1,419	—	—	15,427
6/00	1,280	—	—	16,532
6/99	1,181	—	—	16,161
6/98	1,246	—	—	13,993
6/97	1,125	—	—	13,739
6/96	1,121	—	—	12,937
6/95	1,021	—	—	12,040
Annual Growth	**7.6%**	**—**	**—**	**4.9%**

Revenue History

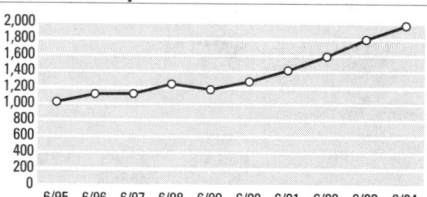

Vanguard Group

If you buy low and sell high, invest for the long term, don't panic, and generally disapprove of those whippersnappers at Fidelity, then you may end up in the Vanguard of the financial market. The Vanguard Group offers individual and institutional investors a line of highly sought-after mutual funds and brokerage services; it is the #2 fund manager after FMR (aka Fidelity), but is closing the gap, claiming some $750 billion of assets under management. Vanguard's fund options include more than 150 stock, bond, mixed, and international offerings, as well as variable annuity portfolios; its Vanguard 500 Index Fund is one of the largest in the US.

The company is known as much for its puritanical thriftiness and conservative investing as for its line of index funds, which track the performance of such groups of stock as the S&P 500. Retired company founder John Bogle is sometimes derisively called "St. Jack" for his zealous criticism of industry practices, but the company's reputation for being squeaky clean appears to have paid off: Vanguard so far remains untainted by the mutual fund industry scandals that began unfolding in late 2003.

Unlike other funds, Vanguard is set up like a mutual insurance company. The funds (and by extension, their more than 18 million investors) own the company, so fees are low to nonexistent; funds are operated on a tight budget so as not to eat into results. The company spends next to nothing on advertising, relying instead on strong returns and word-of-mouth.

And despite its no-broker, no-load background, Vanguard has developed cheap ways to dole out advice, especially through the use of toll-free numbers and the Internet and by quietly touting its online brokerage service.

HISTORY

A distant cousin of Daniel Boone, Walter Morgan knew a few things about pioneering. He was the first to offer a fund with a balance of stocks and bonds, serendipitously introduced early in 1929, months before the stock market collapsed. Morgan's balanced Wellington fund (named after Napoleon's vanquisher) emerged effectively unscathed.

John Bogle's senior thesis on mutual funds impressed fellow Princeton alum Morgan, who hired Bogle in 1951. Morgan retired in 1967 and picked Bogle to replace him. That year Bogle engineered a merger with old-school investment firm Thorndike, Doran, Paine and Lewis. After culture clashes and four years of shrinking assets, the Thorndike-dominated board fired Bogle, who appealed to the mutual funds and their separate board of directors. The fund directors decided to split up the funds and the advisory business.

Bogle named the fund company The Vanguard Group, after the flagship of Lord Nelson, another Napoleon foe. Vanguard worked like a cooperative; mutual fund shareholders owned the company, so all services were provided at cost. The Wellington Management Company remained Vanguard's distributor until 1977, when Bogle convinced Vanguard's board to drop the affiliation. Without Wellington as the intermediary, Vanguard sold its funds directly to consumers as no-load funds (without service charges). In 1976 the company launched the Vanguard Index 500, the first index fund. These measures attracted new investors in droves.

Vanguard rode the 1980s boom. Its Windsor fund grew so large the company closed it, launching Windsor II in 1985. Vanguard weathered the 1987 crash and began the 1990s as the US's #4 mutual fund company. The actively managed funds of FMR (better known as Fidelity), most notably its Magellan fund, led the market then. The retirement of legendary Magellan manager Peter Lynch and the fund's consequential underperformance spurred a rush to index funds. Vanguard moved up to #2.

Vanguard played against type in 1995 when it introduced the Vanguard Horizon Capital Growth stock fund, an aggressively managed fund designed to vie directly with Fidelity's funds.

In 1997 Vanguard added brokerage services and began selling its own and other companies' funds on the Internet to allow clients to consolidate their financial activities. In 1998 Bogle passed the chairmanship to CEO John Brennan, a soft-spoken technology wonk. Morgan died that year at age 100.

Investors were ruffled when 70-year-old Bogle announced that corporate age limits would force him to leave the board of directors at the end of 1999. (Bogle retains an office at Vanguard headquarters, and remains popular on the speaker circuit.)

Despite Vanguard's stated commitment to the little guy, by late 2002 the company was forced to mitigate realities of the economy and started courting investors with bigger bankrolls; it also raised fees for some customers with smaller accounts.

EXECUTIVES

Chairman and CEO: John J. Brennan
Chief Investment Officer: George U. (Gus) Sauter
Managing Director, Legal Department, and General Counsel; Secretary, Vanguard Fiduciary Trust Company: R. Gregory Barton
Managing Director, Investment Programs and Services: James H. Gately
Managing Director, Human Resources: Kathleen C. Gubanich
Managing Director, Client Relationship Group: F. William McNabb III
Managing Director, Planning and Development Group: Michael S. Miller
Managing Director, Finance Group: Ralph K. Packard
Managing Director, Information Technology: Mortimer J. (Tim) Buckley

LOCATIONS

HQ: The Vanguard Group, Inc.
100 Vanguard Blvd., Malvern, PA 19355
Phone: 610-648-6000   **Fax:** 610-669-6605
Web: www.vanguard.com

The Vanguard Group has offices in Malvern, Pennsylvania; Charlotte, North Carolina; and Scottsdale, Arizona; as well as in Brussels, Melbourne, Singapore, and Tokyo.

PRODUCTS/OPERATIONS

Selected Funds

500 Index Fund
Admiral Treasury Money Market Fund
Asset Allocation Fund
Balanced Index Fund
California Long-Term Tax-Exempt Fund
California Tax-Exempt Money Market Fund
Calvert Social Index Fund
Capital Opportunity Fund
Capital Value Fund
Convertible Securities Fund

Developed Markets Index Fund
Dividend Growth Fund
Emerging Markets Stock Index Fund
Energy Fund
Equity Income Fund
European Stock Index Fund
Explorer Fund
Extended Market Index Fund
Federal Money Market Fund
Florida Long-Term Tax-Exempt Fund
Global Equity Fund
GNMA Fund
Growth and Income Fund
Growth Equity Fund
Growth Index Fund
Health Care Fund
High-Yield Corporate Fund
High-Yield Tax-Exempt Fund
Inflation-Protected Securities Fund
Insured Long-Term Tax-Exempt Fund
Intermediate-Term Bond Index Fund
Intermediate-Term Tax-Exempt Fund
International Explorer Fund
International Growth Fund
International Value Fund
Large-Cap Index Fund
LifeStrategy Conservative Growth Fund
LifeStrategy Growth Fund
LifeStrategy Income Fund
LifeStrategy Moderate Growth Fund
Limited-Term Tax-Exempt Fund
Long-Term Investment-Grade Fund
Long-Term Tax-Exempt Fund
Massachusetts Tax-Exempt Fund
Mid-Cap Growth Fund
Mid-Cap Index Fund
Morgan Growth Fund
New Jersey Long-Term Tax-Exempt Fund
New York Tax-Exempt Money Market Fund
Ohio Long-Term Tax-Exempt Fund
Ohio Tax-Exempt Money Market Fund
Pacific Stock Index Fund
Pennsylvania Long-Term Tax-Exempt Fund
Pennsylvania Tax-Exempt Money Market Fund
Precious Metals and Mining Fund
Prime Money Market Fund
PRIMECAP Fund
PRIMECAP Core Fund
REIT Index Fund
Selected Value Fund
Short-Term Bond Index Fund
Short-Term Federal Fund
Short-Term Tax-Exempt Fund
Small-Cap Growth Index Fund
Small-Cap Index Fund
Small-Cap Value Index Fund
STAR Fund
Strategic Equity Fund
Target Retirement 2005 Fund
Target Retirement 2015 Fund
Target Retirement 2025 Fund
Target Retirement 2035 Fund
Target Retirement 2045 Fund
Target Retirement Income Fund
Tax-Managed Capital Appreciation Fund
Tax-Managed Growth and Income Fund
Tax-Managed International Fund
Tax-Managed Small-Cap Fund
Total Bond Market Index Fund
Total International Stock Index Fund
Total Stock Market Index Fund
Treasury Money Market Fund
U.S. Growth Fund
U.S. Value Fund
Value Index Fund
Wellesley Income Fund
Wellington Fund
Windsor Fund

COMPETITORS

AIG	Legg Mason
AIM Funds	Mellon Financial
Alliance Capital	Mellon Investor Services
Management	Merrill Lynch
American Century	MFS
AMVESCAP	Principal Financial
AXA Financial	Putnam
Charles Schwab	T. Rowe Price
FMR	TIAA-CREF
Franklin Resources	USAA
Janus Capital	

HISTORICAL FINANCIALS

Company Type: Private

Income Statement

FYE: December 31

	ASSETS ($ mil.)	NET INCOME ($ mil.)	INCOME AS % OF ASSETS	EMPLOYEES
12/03	730,000	—	—	10,000
12/02	560,000	—	—	10,000
12/01	590,000	—	—	11,000
Annual Growth	11.2%	—	—	(4.7%)

Asset History

800,000	
700,000	
600,000	
500,000	
400,000	
300,000	
200,000	
100,000	
0	

12/94 12/95 12/96 12/97 12/98 12/99 12/00 12/01 12/02 12/03

Vanguard Health Systems

Hospitals shouldn't let their guard down with Vanguard Health Systems hanging around the block. The company buys up acute care hospitals and other health care facilities primarily in urban areas. Vanguard seeks to partner with, develop, or convert non-profit hospital systems to investor-owned entities as independent hospitals seek to capitalize on the benefits of becoming part of a larger hospital company. Vanguard also operates a prepaid Medicaid managed health plan called Phoenix Health Plan, serving nearly 70,000 members in Arizona. Blackstone Group owns the company.

EXECUTIVES

Chairman and CEO: Charles N. (Charlie) Martin Jr., age 62, $3,160,228 pay
Vice Chairman: Keith B. Pitts, age 48, $3,689,558 pay
President and COO: Kent H. Wallace, age 50, $1,147,564 pay
EVP, CFO, and Treasurer: Joseph D. (Joe) Moore, age 58, $1,331,450 pay
EVP, Secretary, and General Counsel: Ronald P. (Ron) Soltman, age 59

SVP and CIO: Alan N. Cranford, age 47
SVP and Chief Medical Officer: James Bonnette, age 54
SVP, Assistant General Counsel, and Assistant Secretary: James H. (Jim) Spalding, age 46
SVP, Compliance and Ethics: Bruce F. Chafin, age 49
SVP, Controller, and Chief Accounting Officer: Phillip W. Roe, age 44
SVP, Development: Robert E. Galloway, age 60
SVP, Human Resources: James Johnston, age 61
SVP, Managed Care and Physician Integration: Thomas M. Ways, age 55
SVP, Market Strategy and Government Affairs: Reginald M. Ballantyne III, age 61
Auditors: Ernst & Young LLP

LOCATIONS

HQ: Vanguard Health Systems, Inc.
20 Burton Hills Blvd., Ste. 100, Nashville, TN 37215
Phone: 615-665-6000   **Fax:** 615-665-6099
Web: www.vanguardhealth.com

Vanguard operates some 20 hospitals in the Chicago, Phoenix, and San Antonio markets, as well as in Framingham, Natick, and Worcester in Massachusetts and in Orange County in California.

PRODUCTS/OPERATIONS

Selected Facilities

Arrowhead Hospital (Phoenix)
Baptist Medical Center (San Antonio)
Huntington Beach Hospital (Orange County)
La Palma Intercommunity Hospital (Orange County)
Louis A. Weiss Memorial Hospital (Chicago)
MacNeal Hospital (Chicago)
Maryvale Hospital (Phoenix)
MetroWest Medical Center-Framingham Union Hospital (Framingham, MA)
MetroWest Medical Center-Leonard Morse Hospital (Natick, MA)
North Central Baptist Hospital (San Antonio)
Northeast Baptist Hospital (San Antonio)
Paradise Valley Hospital (Phoenix)
Phoenix Baptist Hospital (Phoenix)
Phoenix Memorial Hospital (Phoenix)
Southeast Baptist Hospital (San Antonio)
St. Luke's Baptist Hospital (San Antonio)
Saint Vincent Hospital at Worcester Medical Center (Worcester, MA)
West Anaheim Medical Center (Orange County)
West Valley Hospital (Phoenix)

COMPETITORS

HCA	Tenet Healthcare
Rush System for Health	Triad Hospitals

HISTORICAL FINANCIALS

Company Type: Private

Income Statement

FYE: June 30

	REVENUE ($ mil.)	NET INCOME ($ mil.)	NET PROFIT MARGIN	EMPLOYEES
6/04	1,783	40	2.2%	14,300
6/03	1,341	17	1.3%	13,500
6/02	911	7	0.7%	8,000
6/01	668	10	1.5%	7,300
6/00	305	(1)	—	—
6/99	92	(5)	—	—
Annual Growth	81.1%	—	—	25.1%

2004 Year-End Financials

Debt ratio: 149.8%
Return on equity: 10.2%
Cash ($ mil.): 108

Current ratio: 1.68
Long-term debt ($ mil.): 617

Net Income History

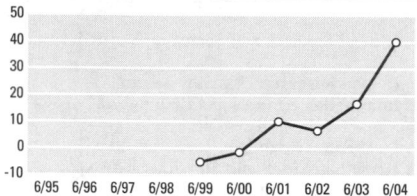

Vertis

Vertis is ready to bring its marketing cross hairs to bear for grocery stores, retail chains, newspapers, and ad agencies. The company provides targeted marketing services from conception through design, production, and distribution for more than 3,000 clients. Vertis' services include market research, media planning, advertising production, digital production, and fulfillment services. Vertis produces newspaper inserts such as color comics, TV magazines, and supplements and provides direct mail, package design, interactive marketing, and media planning services to clients in the US and the UK. An investor group led by Thomas H. Lee Company and Evercore Partners owns Vertis.

In addition to its advertising services Vertis also provides digital services, online marketing, and strategic consulting, as well as direct mailing, response management, Internet integration, and database management. Vertis' customers include grocery stores, retailers, newspapers, consumer good manufacturers, advertising agencies, and any other organization seeking to reach a large number of consumers within certain demographic range.

Vertis has undergone significant restructuring in recent years. It began relying less and less on its traditional commercial printing business in the late 1990s as it expanded into areas of marketing and advertising. Later it consolidated its three primary divisions (all the better to create cross-selling opportunities), took itself private, moved its headquarters from New York City to Baltimore (headquarters of its TC Advertising division), and changed its name from Big Flower Holdings to Vertis. In 2002 the company consolidated all its operations (LTC Group, TC Advertising, and Webcraft) under the Vertis name. The consolidation continued in 2003 and into 2004 as the company realigned operations based on geography rather than marketing discipline and downsized its European and North American operations.

Vertis' changes were motivated by a desire to streamline operations, cut costs, and ultimately grow revenue. Saddled with debt and with zero to little growth in the advertising sector Vertis' future relies on an economic recovery happening sooner rather than later.

EXECUTIVES

Chairman and CEO: Donald E. (Don) Roland, age 62, $650,000 pay
COO: Dean D. Durbin, age 52, $400,000 pay (prior to promotion)
CFO: Stephen E. Tremblay
Chief Legal Officer and Secretary: John V. Howard Jr., age 43, $273,000 pay (prior to title change)
Chief Strategy Officer: Ann Raider
SVP and General Manager, Advertising Insert Platform: David Laverty
SVP Human Resources: Catherine S. Leggett, age 54
SVP National Sales and Marketing: Janice Mayo
SVP Sales, North America: Joe Scott, age 62
VP Marketing Research: Thérèse Mulvey
CIO: Gary L. Sutula, age 60
Managing Director, Vertis Europe: Adriaan Roosen, age 53, $302,575 pay
Group President, Vertis North America East: Dave Colatriano, age 42
Group President, Vertis North America West: Thomas R. Zimmer, age 56, $366,401 pay
Human Resources: Gary Dupree
Communications: Grace Platon
Auditors: Deloitte & Touche LLP

LOCATIONS

HQ: Vertis, Inc.
250 W. Pratt St., 18th Fl., Baltimore, MD 21201
Phone: 410-528-9800   **Fax:** 410-528-9287
Web: www.vertisinc.com

Vertis operates through more than 120 locations in the US and Europe.

2004 Sales

	$ mil.	% of total
North America	1,506.3	92
Europe	138.7	8
Total	**1,645.0**	**100**

PRODUCTS/OPERATIONS

Selected Products and Services

Retail and Newspaper Services
    Ad insert programs for retailer and manufacturers
    Newspaper products including TV magazines, comics, and supplements
    Consumer research
    Creative services for ad insert page layout and design
    Digital advertising design and transmission
    Freight and logistics management
Direct Marketing Services
    Customized one-to-one marketing programs
    Automated digital fulfillment services
    Direct mail production
    Data design, collection, management
    Mailing management services
    Effectiveness measurement
Ad Technology Services
    Digital content management
    Graphic design and animation
    Digital photography, compositing, and retouching
    In-store displays and billboards
    Consulting services
    Newpaper advertisment development
    Media planning and placement software
    Response management, warehousing, and fulfillment services
    Call center and telemarketing services

COMPETITORS

ACG Holdings
Acxiom
ADVO
communisis
Harte-Hanks
News America Marketing

Polestar
Quebecor World
R.R. Donnelley
Schawk
Valassis

HISTORICAL FINANCIALS

Company Type: Private

Income Statement

FYE: December 31

	REVENUE ($ mil.)	NET INCOME ($ mil.)	NET PROFIT MARGIN	EMPLOYEES
12/04	1,645	(11)	—	8,000
12/03	1,586	(96)	—	8,000
12/02	1,675	(120)	—	8,700
12/01	1,851	(55)	—	9,000
12/00	1,986	(25)	—	10,000
12/99	1,800	—	—	10,000
12/98	1,740	—	—	10,000
12/97	1,377	—	—	8,500
12/96	1,202	—	—	6,410
12/95	532	—	—	4,000
Annual Growth	**13.4%**	**—**		**8.0%**

2004 Year-End Financials

Debt ratio: —
Return on equity: —
Cash ($ mil.): 3

Current ratio: 0.78
Long-term debt ($ mil.): 1,031

Net Income History

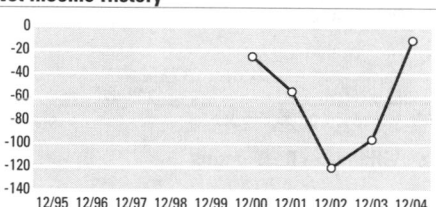

VICORP Restaurants

VICORP Restaurants keeps its eyes on the pies. VICORP operates or franchises about 375 family-style, medium-priced restaurants in the US — mainly in Arizona, California, Florida, the Rocky Mountain region, and the upper Midwest. Its restaurant chains are Village Inn (more than 220 locations), known primarily for its breakfast menu and pies, and Bakers Square (about 150 locations), serving lunch and dinner and emphasizing fresh-baked pies. The company makes all its own pies through VICOM, its bakery production division, which operates three baking plants. VICORP is owned by Chicago-based investment firm Wind Point Partners.

With intense competition for the family dining dollar, VICORP has struggled to compete against larger casual dining chains. The once public company was taken private in 2001 by BancBoston Capital and Goldner Hawn Johnson & Morrison. Retreating from Wall Street did little to help its market position, however, and two years later Wind Point Partners ponied up $225 million to buy the restaurant business. The new ownership brought in former McDonald's executive Debra Koenig to try and turn the company around. As revenues inched up, Koenig announced plans in late 2004 to revamp the Bakers Square menu and image in an effort to be more than a pie place.

Current management under Koenig and owner Wind Point Partners have sued former and current company executives as well as former owners, including BancBoston. The dispute is over claims that Wind Point was not properly notified prior to its purchase of VICORP of nine lawsuits brought against the company concerning the Americans with Disabilities Act.

EXECUTIVES

Chairman: Walter Van Benthuysen, age 65
CEO: Debra Koenig, age 52
COO: Robert E. Kaltenbach, age 59
CFO: Anthony J. (Tony) Carroll, age 53
SVP Purchasing, Production, and Distribution:
Timothy R. (Tim) Kanaly
VP and Treasurer: Michael R. Kinnen
VP Human Resources and Training: Jill Bagley
VP Purchasing: Mark Hampton
Regional VP, Bakers Square: Tom Rink
Regional VP, Village Inn: Jeff Guido
Director of Research and Development: Ellen Hayes
General Counsel: Gary Burke
General Counsel: David Sidran
Public Relations: Karen Slye
Auditors: Grant Thornton LLP

LOCATIONS

HQ: VICORP Restaurants, Inc.
400 W. 48th Ave., Denver, CO 80216
Phone: 303-296-2121   **Fax:** 303-672-2668
Web: www.vicorpinc.com

2004 Village Inn Restaurants

	Company Operated	Franchised	Total
Colorado	33	16	49
Florida	11	16	27
Arizona	25	—	25
Iowa	16	4	20
Nebraska	16	3	19
New Mexico	9	5	14
Utah	11	2	13
Kansas	—	10	10
Wyoming	—	9	9
Texas	—	8	8
Oklahoma	—	6	6
Arkansas	—	4	4
Missouri	—	4	4
Oregon	1	3	4
Alaska	—	3	3
Illinois	2	1	3
Minnesota	—	3	3
Washington	—	3	3
North Dakota	—	2	2
Virginia	—	1	1
Total	**124**	**103**	**227**

2004 Bakers Square Restaurants

	Company Operated
California	50
Illinois	44
Minnesota	25
Michigan	8
Ohio	8
Wisconsin	8
Indiana	4
Iowa	3
Total	**150**

COMPETITORS

Applebee's
Big Boy Restaurants
Bob Evans
Brinker
Buffets Holdings
Carlson Restaurants
Catalina Restaurant Group
CBRL Group
Cheesecake Factory
Country Kitchen
Denny's
Fresh Choice
Huddle House
IHOP
Marie Callender
Metromedia Restaurant
 Group
Perkins
Shari's Restaurants
Shoney's
Waffle House

HISTORICAL FINANCIALS

Company Type: Private

Income Statement

FYE: October 31

	REVENUE ($ mil.)	NET INCOME ($ mil.)	NET PROFIT MARGIN	EMPLOYEES
10/04	400	1	0.2%	11,382
10/03	387	(2)	—	13,000
10/02	383	11	2.7%	13,000
10/01	350	—	—	13,000
10/00	372	—	—	13,071
10/99	359	—	—	11,800
10/98	346	—	—	11,800
10/97	326	—	—	12,400
10/96	343	—	—	12,400
10/95	374	—	—	13,500
Annual Growth	**0.7%**	**(74.2%)**	**—**	**(1.9%)**

2004 Year-End Financials

Debt ratio: —
Return on equity: 1.0%
Cash ($ mil.): —
Current ratio: —
Long-term debt ($ mil.): —

Net Income History

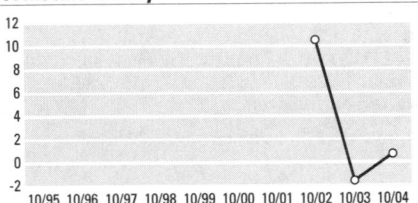

ViewSonic

ViewSonic has a display for every occasion. The company makes CRT and LCD computer displays, including the Professional Series for high-end computer-aided design, desktop publishing, and graphic design; the Graphics and E2 lines for homes and small offices; and the A Series for replacing monitors included in bundled systems. ViewSonic also offers LCD and plasma TVs, wireless networking equipment, LCD projectors, handheld computers, and tablet PCs. CEO James Chu, who founded ViewSonic in 1987, is the company's majority owner. ViewSonic has also received financing from the venture capital arm of chip giant Intel, which partnered with the company to develop inexpensive chipsets for high-definition TV.

A leading provider of displays, ViewSonic has managed to hold its own in an industry where Asian giants such as NEC-Mitsubishi, Samsung, and Sony vie for market share. ViewSonic sells directly and through resellers and distributors to consumer, corporate, government, and education customers. The company gets more than half of its sales from the Americas.

ViewSonic entered the home networking market in 2004, releasing a line of wireless equipment that includes media gateways and adapters.

EXECUTIVES

Chairman and CEO: James Chu, age 46
CFO: James A. Morlan, age 56
President, Global Products Group; President, ViewSonic International: H. C. Ho
SVP, Business Development and Strategy:
Matthew (Matt) Milne
VP, General Counsel, and Secretary: Robert J. Ranucci, age 39
VP, Human Resources: Timothy Ashcroft
VP, Information Services and CIO: Robert Lee Moon, age 54
VP, Field Sales: Brian Igoe
VP, Marketing, ViewSonic Americas: Jeff Volpe
VP, Operations: Lorraine Meng
VP, Visual Solutions Group: Michael Holstein
VP, Sales, ViewSonic Americas: Steve Woo
President, Viewsonic Europe: Jan Jensen
Director, Public Relations: Duane Brozek
Auditors: Deloitte & Touche LLP

LOCATIONS

HQ: ViewSonic Corporation
381 Brea Canyon Rd., Walnut, CA 91789
Phone: 909-444-8888   **Fax:** 909-468-1202
Web: www.viewsonic.com

2003 Sales

	$ mil.	% of total
Americas	668	62
Asia/Pacific	227	21
Europe	180	17
Total	**1,075**	**100**

PRODUCTS/OPERATIONS

2003 Display Sales

	% of total
CRT	49
LCD	42
Other	9
Total	**100**

Selected Products

LCD projectors
Monitors (CRT, LCD)
Personal digital assistants
Tablet PCs
Televisions (high-definition, plasma)
Wireless networking equipment
 (routers, adapters, access points)

COMPETITORS

Acer
Apple Computer
BenQ
Daewoo International
Dell
Fujitsu
Gateway
Hewlett-Packard
InFocus
LG Electronics
LG.Philips LCD
Matsushita
Mitsubishi Corporation
NEC
NEC Display Solutions of America
Palm
Philips Electronics
Philips North America
Planar Systems
Princeton Digital
Samsung Electronics
Sharp
Sony

HISTORICAL FINANCIALS

Company Type: Private

Income Statement

FYE: December 31

	REVENUE ($ mil.)	NET INCOME ($ mil.)	NET PROFIT MARGIN	EMPLOYEES
12/03	1,075	5	0.4%	743
12/02	884	19	2.2%	600
12/01	962	(18)	—	600
12/00	1,371	—	—	800
12/99	1,040	—	—	700
12/98	941	—	—	700
12/97	826	—	—	675
12/96	510	—	—	600
12/95	350	—	—	550
12/94	200	—	—	120
Annual Growth	20.5%	—	—	22.5%

2003 Year-End Financials

Debt ratio: 85.1%
Return on equity: 7.7%
Cash ($ mil.): 92
Current ratio: 1.28
Long-term debt ($ mil.): 55

Net Income History

20									
15									
10									
5									
0									
-5									
-10									
-15									
-20									

12/94 12/95 12/96 12/97 12/98 12/99 12/00 12/01 12/02 12/03

Visa

Paper or plastic? Visa International hopes you choose the latter. Visa operates the world's largest consumer payment system (ahead of MasterCard and American Express) with more than 1 billion credit and other payment cards in circulation. The company is owned by nearly 21,000 financial institutions, each of which issues and markets its own Visa products. They all participate in the VisaNet payment system, which provides authorization, transaction processing, and settlement services for purchases from 20 million merchants worldwide. In addition to credit cards, Visa also provides its customers with debit cards, Internet payment systems, value-storing smart cards, and traveler's checks.

Visa International oversees Visa's worldwide interests as well as regional organizations Visa Asia Pacific; Visa Central and Eastern Europe, Middle East and Africa (CEMEA); and Visa Latin America and the Caribbean (LAC). The company also runs the Interlink and PLUS automated teller machine (ATM) networks.

Visa is accelerating its push to introduce chip cards over magnetic stripe technology, and it is maneuvering its Open Platform technology into position against the MasterCard-supported Mondex platform and Microsoft's Smart Card for Windows. The company also has some 2,000 pre-paid card programs in 30 countries and has begun offering government- issued cards for social benefits.

Both Visa U.S.A. and main rival MasterCard International were recently in some 4 million retailers' sights. Led by retail giant Wal-Mart, the merchants claimed Visa and MasterCard violated antitrust laws and attempted to monopolize a legally defined market for debit cards. The plaintiffs sought up to $200 billion in damages in their class-action suit. Just as the 1996 lawsuit was to go to trial in early 2003, Visa settled, agreeing to pay $2 billion (twice that of co-defendant MasterCard) over the next decade. Both agreed to pay $25 million immediately, as well as reduce the fee merchants pay for signature-based debit cards. At the time of settlement, some 129 million consumers carried the Visa debit card.

HISTORY

Although the first charge card was issued by Western Union in 1914, it wasn't until 1958 that Bank of America (BofA) issued its BankAmericard, which combined the convenience of a charge account with credit privileges. When BofA extended its customer base outside California, the interchange system controlling payments began to falter because of design problems and fraud.

In 1968 Dee Hock, manager of the BankAmericard operations of the National Bank of Commerce in Seattle, convinced member banks that a more reliable system was needed. Two years later National BankAmericard Inc. (NBI) was created as an independent corporation (owned by 243 banks) to buy the BankAmericard system from BofA.

With its initial ad slogan, "Think of it as Money," the Hock-led NBI developed BankAmericard into a widely used form of payment in the US. A multinational corporation, IBANCO, was formed in 1974 to carry the operations into other countries. People outside the US resisted BankAmericard's nominal association with BofA, and in 1977 Hock changed the card's name to Visa. NBI became Visa USA, and IBANCO became Visa International.

By 1980 Visa had debuted debit cards, begun issuing traveler's checks, and created an electromagnetic point-of-sale authorization system. Visa developed a global network of ATMs in 1983; it was expanded in 1987 by the purchase of a 33% stake in the Plus System of ATMs, then the US's second-largest system. Hock retired in 1984 with the company well on its way to realizing his vision of a universal payment system.

The company built the Visa brand image with aggressive advertising, such as sponsorship of the 1988 and 1992 Olympics, and by co-branding (issuing cards through other organizations with strong brand names, such as Blockbuster and Ford).

In 1994 Visa teamed up with Microsoft and others to develop home banking services and software. Visa Cash was introduced during the 1996 Olympics. Visa pushed its debit cards in 1996 and 1997 with humorous ads featuring presidential also-ran Bob Dole and showbiz success story Daffy Duck.

Visa expanded its smart card infrastructure in 1997. It published, with MasterCard, encryption and security software for online transactions. The gloves came off the next year as the companies vied to convince the world to rally around their respective e-purse technology standards.

During the 1990s, Visa fought American Express' attempts to introduce a bank credit card of its own by forbidding Visa members in the US from issuing the product; the Justice Department responded with an antitrust suit against Visa and MasterCard. The case went to trial in 2000 with the government claiming that Visa and MasterCard stifle competition and enjoy an exclusive cross-ownership structure.

Also that year, the company made a deal with Gemplus, the French smart card company, to enable payments over wireless networks; Visa also inked a billing deal with wireless technology company Aether Systems, as well as e-commerce agreements with telecommunications companies Nokia and Ericsson.

The company continued its technology push in 2000 with a deal with Financial Services Technology Consortium to test biometrics — the use of fingerprints, irises, and voice recognition to identify cardholders. The company also launched a pre-paid card, Visa Buxx, targeted at teenagers.

That year the European Union launched an investigation into the firm's transaction fees, alleging that the fees could restrict competition. The following year Visa International agreed to drop its fee to 0.7% of the transaction value over five years.

EXECUTIVES

Chairman: William P. Boardman, age 64
President and CEO: Christopher J. Rodrigues
EVP and CFO: Kenneth F. (Ken) Sommer
EVP, Global Brand and Marketing: John Elkins
EVP, Global Marketing Partnerships and Sponsorship: Tom Shepard
EVP, Human Resources: Elizabeth Rounds
SVP, Risk Management: Brian Buckley
SVP, Commercial Solutions: Aliza Knox
SVP, Global Acceptance and Operations: Roger Swales
CTO: Terence V. (Terry) Milholland
Chief Commercial Officer: Matthew Piasecki
President and CEO, Inovant: John Partridge
President and CEO, Visa U.S.A.: John Philip Coghlan, age 54
President, Visa Central and Eastern Europe, Middle East, and Africa: Anne L. Cobb
President, Visa Latin America and the Caribbean: Eduardo Eraña
President, Visa Canada: Derek A. Fry
President, Visa Asia Pacific: Rupert G. Keeley
President, Visa Europe: Johannes I. (Hans) van der Velde
Auditors: KPMG LLP

LOCATIONS

HQ: Visa International
900 Metro Center Blvd., Foster City, CA 94404
Phone: 650-432-3200   **Fax:** 650-432-7436
Web: www.visa.com

Visa cards are accepted at 20 million merchant locations in 150 countries around the world.

PRODUCTS/OPERATIONS

Selected Products and Services

Electron (debit card outside of US)
smartVisa card (computer-chip-embedded card that is accepted worldwide)
Visa Business card (for small businesses and professionals)
Visa Cash (smart cards)
Visa Classic card (credit/debit card issued by Visa's 21,000 member banks)
Visa Corporate card (for travel and entertainment expenses)
Visa Debit card (accesses bank account for immediate settlement of payments)
Visa Gold card (higher spending limits)
VisaNet (electronic transaction processing network)
Visa Purchasing card (for corporate purchases)
Visa Travelers Cheques
Visa TravelMoney (prepaid card in any currency)

COMPETITORS

American Express
Citigroup
MasterCard
Morgan Stanley

HISTORICAL FINANCIALS

Company Type: Private

Income Statement

FYE: September 30

	ESTIMATED REVENUE ($ mil.)	NET INCOME ($ mil.)	NET PROFIT MARGIN	EMPLOYEES
9/04	6,000	—	—	6,000
9/03	5,400	—	—	6,000
9/02	4,800	—	—	6,000
9/01	3,600	—	—	6,000
9/00	3,000	—	—	5,000
9/99	2,800	—	—	5,000
9/98	2,550	—	—	5,000
9/97	2,050	—	—	5,000
9/96	1,650	—	—	4,800
9/95	1,330	—	—	4,000
Annual Growth	**18.2%**	—	—	**4.6%**

Revenue History

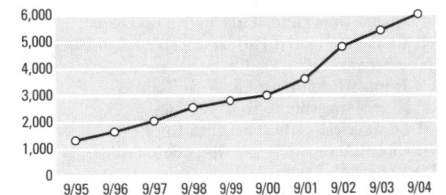

Vision Service Plan

Thanks to Vision Service Plan (VSP), you can see clearly now. One of the top eye care benefits providers in the US (with more than 38 million members, about one in eight people in the US use the company's services), VSP offers vision coverage ranging from general plans to laser vision correction procedures. VSP has more than 20,800 clients. The company's Sight for Students program provides uninsured children with vision exams and glasses. The VSP network includes thousands of doctors who provide both eye exams and eyewear nationwide. The company was founded in 1955.

VSP's strategy for growth consists of forming alliances with managed care companies, eyeglass makers, and others in order to sell its services. The company expects to do well as aging baby boomers are expected to increase demand for the company's services.

EXECUTIVES

President and CEO: Roger J. Valine, age 56
SVP, Marketing and Corporate Development: Don Yee
SVP, Operations: Gary Brooks
VP and CFO: Patricia Cochran
VP, Marketing: Kate Renwick-Espinosa
VP and Legal Counsel: Barclay Westerfeld
VP, Client Services: Mary Ann Cavanagh
VP, Customer Service: Laura Costa
VP, Health Care Services: Cheryl Johnson

VP, Human Resources: Walter Grubbs
VP, Information Systems: Steve Scott
VP, Provider Relations: Don Price
VP, Sales: Ric Steere
Brand Specialist: Matthew Mason

LOCATIONS

HQ: Vision Service Plan
3333 Quality Dr., Rancho Cordova, CA 95670
Phone: 916-851-5000 **Fax:** 916-851-4858
Web: www.vsp.com

PRODUCTS/OPERATIONS

Selected Vision Plans
Computer VisionCare
Laser VisionCare
Primary EyeCare
Safety EyeCare
VSP WellVision Plan

COMPETITORS

EyeMed Vision Care
Guardian Life
Kaiser Foundation
 Health Plan
Oxford Health
PacifiCare
Spectera
UnitedHealth Group

HISTORICAL FINANCIALS

Company Type: Private

Income Statement

FYE: December 31

	REVENUE ($ mil.)	NET INCOME ($ mil.)	NET PROFIT MARGIN	EMPLOYEES
12/03	1,970	—	—	2,000
12/02	1,860	—	—	2,300
12/01	1,770	—	—	2,300
12/00	1,500	—	—	2,300
Annual Growth	**9.5%**	—	—	**(4.6%)**

Revenue History

Vistar

Vistar Corporation is a growing distributor of specialty food products and related supplies to vending and food service operations nationwide through its more than 35 warehouses. Vistar was formed in 1997 through the merger of Multifoods Distribution — specializing in Italian markets — and VSA, which provided vending and office coffee products. In 2004 Vistar acquired Atlanta's pizza, deli, and Italian restaurant supplier Original Brand Foods. In early 2005 Vistar brought in the assets of Italian food supplier Roma Food Enterprises and acquired the assets of Luna Vend Distributing. Vistar is owned by Wellspring Capital Management LLC.

EXECUTIVES

President and CEO: George Holm
SVP and CFO: Tom McGonagle
VP, Merchandising, Specialty Markets: Pat Hagerty
SVP and General Counsel: Kent Berke
EVP, Sales and Marketing, Roma Food Enterprises:
 Stephen J. Piancone
President and CEO, Roma Food Enterprises:
 Louis G. Piancone
AVP, Finance: Kathy McBride

LOCATIONS

HQ: Vistar Corporation
12650 E. Arapahoe Rd., Centennial, CO 80112
Phone: 303-662-7100 **Fax:** 303-662-7565
Web: www.vistarvsa.com

COMPETITORS

ARAMARK
Compass Group USA, Inc.
Performance Food
Pierre Foods
SYSCO

HISTORICAL FINANCIALS

Company Type: Private

Income Statement

FYE: February 28

	REVENUE ($ mil.)	NET INCOME ($ mil.)	NET PROFIT MARGIN	EMPLOYEES
2/04	2,500	—	—	2,500
2/03	2,400	—	—	2,500
Annual Growth	**4.2%**	—	—	**0.0%**

Revenue History

Vivid Entertainment

Vivid Entertainment Group, one of the world's top adult film producers, leaves little to the imagination. Fans of the form know the company best for its Vivid Girls, a gaggle of porn starlets such as Sunrise Adams, Jenna Jameson, Briana Banks, and Savanna Samson, who are signed to exclusive contracts much like in the bygone days of the Hollywood studio system. Vivid sells its titles to the retail and rental markets and directly to consumers through its online mail-order site. Vivid also distributes the films to cable and satellite channels and offers its Internet subscribers pay-per-view access. Co-CEOs Steven Hirsch, David James, and Bill Asher own the company that Hirsch and James founded in 1984.

Leading the pack in the adult film industry, the company has been credited with bringing porn into the mainstream through its marketing efforts and by placing its actresses in mainstream films, television shows, and music videos. The company has inked promotional deals with footwear maker Pony and snowboard manufacturer Sims Sports.

Vivid is also expanding its Internet operations by gradually making all of its film titles available for pay-per-view streaming access on its Web site. Its book publishing acheivements include 2004's *How to Have a XXX Sex Life: The Ultimate Vivid Guide* written by the Vivid Girls and produced by HarperCollins. The company opened its first nightclub in the Venetian hotel and casino in Las Vegas in 2005.

EXECUTIVES

Co-chairman and Co-CEO: William (Bill) Asher
Co-chairman and Co-CEO: Steven Hirsch, age 41
Co-chairman and Co-CEO: David James
Head of Production: Marci Hirsch
VP Licensing: David Schlesinger
National Sales Manager, Vivid Video: Howard Levine
General Manager, Vivid Cash: Leslie Sharp
Media Contact: Ellie Reeve

LOCATIONS

HQ: Vivid Entertainment Group
3599 Cahuenga Blvd. West, Los Angeles, CA 90068
Phone: 323-436-2001   **Fax:** 323-436-2006
Web: www.vivid.com

PRODUCTS/OPERATIONS

Selected Film Titles
Bad Girls
Bad Wives
Boiling Point
Briana Loves Jenna
Center Stage
Fade To Black
Filthy Rich
Gettin' Lucky
I Dream of Jenna
Secrets and Lies
Sex at Six
Where the Boys Aren't

COMPETITORS

Beate Uhse
Digital Playground
LFP
New Frontier Media
Penthouse Media Group
Playboy
Private Media Group
Sin City
Wicked Pictures

HISTORICAL FINANCIALS

Company Type: Private

Income Statement

FYE: December 31

	ESTIMATED REVENUE ($ mil.)	NET INCOME ($ mil.)	NET PROFIT MARGIN	EMPLOYEES
12/04	100	—	—	—
12/03	100	—	—	—
12/02	95	—	—	—
12/01	90	—	—	—
12/00	80	—	—	—
12/99	50	—	—	150
12/98	40	—	—	150
Annual Growth	**16.5%**	**—**	**—**	**0.0%**

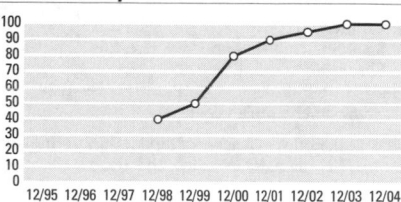

Revenue History

Vocus

Vocus' focus is simplifying public and government relations processes. Vocus produces software that helps automate some public relations duties; it organizes media contacts, manages news collection, and analyzes public relations effectiveness. Its government relations software offers a state and federal legislative contact list and project management tracking and lobbying analysis tools. Users vary from not-for-profits and the government to corporations and public relations professionals. The company acquired privately held Gnossos Software in 2004, boosting its government relations software business.

The company's roster of strategic partners includes companies such as Dow Jones, eWatch, CyberAlert, Thomson, Xpedite, and the Australian Associated Press.

EXECUTIVES

Chairman, President, and CEO:
Richard (Rick) Rudman, age 44, $383,950 pay
CFO and Treasurer: Stephen (Steve) Vintz, age 36, $238,580 pay
VP Account Sales: Norman Weissberg, age 44, $304,136 pay
VP Client Services: Darren Stewart, age 37
VP Corporate Development: Matthew (Matt) Siegal, age 41
VP Marketing: Gary McNeil, age 41
VP Sales: William (Bill) Donnelly, age 49, $356,319 pay
CTO and Director: Robert (Bob) Lentz, age 44, $266,975 pay
Managing Director, Vocus International: Andrew Muir, age 49
Public Relations: Erin Lindsay
Public Relations: Erin Sweeney
Auditors: Ernst & Young LLP

LOCATIONS

HQ: Vocus, Inc.
4296 Forbes Blvd., Lanham, MD 20706
Phone: 301-459-2590   **Fax:** 301-459-2827
Web: www.vocus.com

COMPETITORS

Biz360
Medialink
PR Newswire
Siebel Systems

HISTORICAL FINANCIALS

Company Type: Private

Income Statement

FYE: December 31

	REVENUE ($ mil.)	NET INCOME ($ mil.)	NET PROFIT MARGIN	EMPLOYEES
12/04	20	(2)	—	170
12/03	15	(3)	—	112
12/02	12	(3)	—	115
Annual Growth	**32.9%**	**—**	**—**	**21.6%**

2004 Year-End Financials

Debt ratio: —
Return on equity: —
Cash ($ mil.): 8

Current ratio: 0.71
Long-term debt ($ mil.): 3

Net Income History

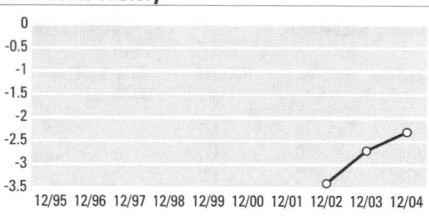

Voyager Pharmaceutical

Voyager Pharmaceutical is tackling some of the age-old problems of getting older. The company is developing a variety of treatments for age-related diseases such as Alzheimer's Disease, Parkinson's, atherosclerosis, osteoarthritis, and osteoporosis, as well as colon and brain cancer. One of Voyager's potential Alzheimer treatments (which incorporates Leuprolide acetate) has completed Phase II clinical trials. Chairman Richard Bowen owns about 24% of the company, with Patrick Smith (president and CEO) holding a 23% stake. The company was originally incorporated as Angel Care, Inc. in 2001, merging with Voyager Pharmaceutical Corporation in November 2001.

EXECUTIVES

Chairman and Chief Scientific Officer:
Richard L. Bowen, age 47, $307,500 pay
President, CEO, and Director: Patrick S. Smith, age 53, $358,749 pay
EVP, CFO, and Director: David J. Corcoran, age 57, $280,000 pay
SVP Corporate Development: Sheldon Goldberg, age 57
VP Business Operations: Michael J. (Mike) Giannini, age 47, $231,250 pay
VP Finance and Chief Accounting Officer:
Timothy J. (Tim) Creech, age 44
VP Manufacturing and Technical Operations:
Maynard E. Lichty, age 55
VP Sales and Marketing: Steven J. (Steve) Fiander, age 52
VP Sales and Marketing: Laurence C. (Larry) Tusick, age 49
Senior Director Clinical Operations: Barbra LaPlante
Director Research: Christopher W. (Chris) Gregory
Auditors: PricewaterhouseCoopers LLP

LOCATIONS

HQ: Voyager Pharmaceutical Corporation
8540 Colonnade Center Dr., Ste. 501,
Raleigh, NC 27615
Phone: 919-846-4880   **Fax:** 919-846-4881
Web: www.voyagerpharma.com

COMPETITORS

First Horizon Pharmaceutical
Forest Pharmaceuticals
Novartis
Pfizer
Shire Pharmaceuticals

HISTORICAL FINANCIALS

Company Type: Private

Income Statement

FYE: December 31

	REVENUE ($ mil.)	NET INCOME ($ mil.)	NET PROFIT MARGIN	EMPLOYEES
12/04	0	(12)	—	29
12/03	0	(7)	—	—
12/02	0	(3)	—	—
Annual Growth	—	—	—	—

2004 Year-End Financials

Debt ratio: 89.5%
Return on equity: —
Cash ($ mil.): 4

Current ratio: 1.83
Long-term debt ($ mil.): 3

Net Income History

LOCATIONS

HQ: VT, Inc.
8500 Shawnee Mission Pkwy., Ste. 200,
Shawnee Mission, KS 66202
Phone: 913-895-0200   **Fax:** 913-789-1039
Web: www.vanenterprises.com

VT has dealerships in Arizona, Florida, Illinois, Indiana, Missouri, Nebraska, New Mexico, and Texas.

COMPETITORS

Asbury Automotive
AutoNation
CarMax

Hendrick Automotive
Jordan Automotive
United Auto Group

HISTORICAL FINANCIALS

Company Type: Private

Income Statement

FYE: December 31

	REVENUE ($ mil.)	NET INCOME ($ mil.)	NET PROFIT MARGIN	EMPLOYEES
12/03	5,229	—	—	—
12/02	5,250	—	—	—
12/01	5,299	—	—	7,000
12/00	4,300	—	—	6,000
12/99	3,600	—	—	5,805
12/98	2,587	—	—	5,000
12/97	2,423	—	—	5,000
12/96	2,075	—	—	4,300
12/95	1,755	—	—	3,950
12/94	1,681	—	—	3,874
Annual Growth	13.4%	—	—	8.8%

Revenue History

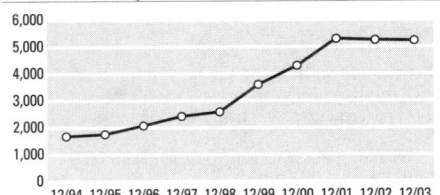

VT

VT is in pursuit of the pole-position as one of the top three US car dealers. The company operates more than 30 dealerships in some 10 states, primarily Texas and Missouri. It offers about 20 brands of new and used cars (and RVs) made by General Motors, Ford, Honda, Isuzu, and Nissan, among others. VT also engages in fleet sales and receives a portion of its revenue from back-shop operations such as parts and service and body shop sales. Founder and co-CEO Cecil Van Tuyl began his automotive empire in 1955. He owns the company with son and co-CEO Larry Van Tuyl.

EXECUTIVES

President and Co-CEO: Cecil Van Tuyl
Co-CEO: Larry Van Tuyl
Secretary and Treasurer: Robert J. Holcomb
Head, Finance and Insurance School: Chris Depperman
National VP Sales: Doug Scallorn

Vulcan

Even with all his Vulcan logic, could Spock invest like *this?* Brainy billionaire Paul Allen organizes his business and charitable ventures under Vulcan (formerly Vulcan Northwest). Vulcan includes Allen's slim stake in the industry-defining juggernaut Microsoft, as well as holdings in dozens of companies providing computer, technology, multimedia, and communications products and services; some recent portfolio additions include biotechnology ventures, energy (Plains Resources), and real estate assets. Allen also owns professional sports teams like the NBA's Portland Trail Blazers and the NFL's Seattle Seahawks, as well as stakes in six charitable organizations.

Vulcan's charities support the arts, medical research, land conservation, and other causes. Allen, who co-founded Microsoft with Bill Gates, promotes a "wired world" vision, in which everyone is united through interconnecting communications, entertainment, and information systems. CEO Jody Patton, Allen's sister, oversees both his business and charitable ventures.

Many of Allen's investments in the "wired world" took a beating with the stock market downturn. He even saw his own personal wealth take a dip by a third. The most recent casualty, communications company RCN Corporation, has filed for bankruptcy, rendering Allen's 15% stake essentially worthless.

Allen is finally dumping the last of his unprofitable stakes in tech-boom companies, and has cleaned house in other ways — long-time right-hand man William Savoy has left the firm. Meanwhile, Vulcan Ventures, the VC arm of Allen's empire, has started investing in cutting-edge biotechnology firms. In more prosaic investments, Vulcan acquired energy firm Plains Resources in 2004. Lastly, Allen has bought a good deal of Seattle real estate and is intent on redeveloping it.

HISTORY

Paul Allen and Bill Gates first worked together on computer projects as schoolmates in Seattle. They developed a program to determine traffic patterns and launched Traf-O-Data, an operation that failed because the state provided the information for free. When Allen saw an article on the MITS Altair 8800 minicomputer in 1975, the two realized it needed a simplified programming language to make it useful. They offered MITS a modified version of BASIC they had written for Traf-O-Data. The company set them up in an office in Albuquerque, New Mexico. They then began their biggest collaboration of all: Microsoft. While Gates concentrated on business, Allen focused on technical issues.

They moved to Bellevue, a Seattle suburb, in 1979. The next year IBM asked them to create a programming language for a PC project. Allen bought Q-DOS (quick and dirty operating system) from Seattle Computer; the pair tweaked it and renamed it MS-DOS. Allen and Gates made a key decision to structure their contract with IBM to allow clones. They also helped design many aspects of the original IBM PC.

Allen developed Hodgkin's disease in 1982. Facing his own mortality, he ended his daily involvement in Microsoft (keeping a chunk of the company and a board seat) and began to play more (traveling and playing the electric guitar). With his cancer in remission in 1985, Allen founded multimedia software company Asymetrix. The next year he set up Vulcan to hold his diversified interests and Vulcan Ventures. He also began helping startups, indulging his interests (buying the NBA's Portland Trail Blazers in 1988 and donating some $60 million to build a museum honoring his musical idol, Jimi Hendrix, and other Pacific Northwest artists). He has also funded Seattle-area civic improvements.

In 1990 Allen hired William Savoy to help organize his finances; Savoy later became president of Vulcan Ventures. Seeing a need for more R&D in the US, Allen in 1992 started Interval Research. He also invested in America Online (sold 1994). In 1993 Allen bought 80% of Ticketmaster (sold 1997), and in 1995 he invested in DreamWorks SKG, the multimedia company of Steven Spielberg, Jeffrey Katzenberg, and David Geffen.

Allen made a rare buy outside the entertainment and high-tech worlds through a 1996 investment in power turbine maker Capstone Turbine. To prevent the Seattle Seahawks from moving to California, Allen bought the team in 1997 and made plans for a new stadium. He consolidated his management operations under Vulcan and dissolved Paul Allen Group (founded 1994), keeping Vulcan Ventures.

Allen moved into cable in 1998 and 1999; his Charter Communications eventually became the #4 US cable firm. In 1999 several Allen investments (Charter Communications, Vulcan Ventures, RCN, High Speed Access, and Go2Net) joined to form wired-world venture Broadband Partners.

In 2000 it was nearly impossible to ignore Allen's influence on Seattle as several major projects took shape or were completed, including the new Seahawks' arena, the Experience Music Project, and the renovation of a 90-year-old train station as part of a complex that will include Vulcan's new headquarters. That year he provided a $100 million infusion to struggling Oxygen Media. In 2001 Vulcan Ventures bought sports games Web site operator Small World Media to boost its sports holdings, which was later folded into the online fantasy sports operations of another Allen holding, *The Sporting News*.

Tech-boom losses accounted for only about 5% of Allen's portfolio, but things looked very bleak indeed in 2002 when the US attorney's office began investigating Charter Communications — for accounting irregularities. Four former executives were later indicted for fraud in 2003.

In late 2003, Allen began to restructure his holdings, dumping remaining unprofitable holdings (including RCN), and laying off many employees, including William Savoy. TechTV was sold to Comcast in 2004; the network was merged in to Comcast's existing gaming and technology network, G4 TV. It is now called G4techTV.

Notable investments in 2004 include the acquisition of Plains Resources, which marked the company's first foray into the energy sector. Plains Resources owns 44% of Plains All American Pipeline, which provides oil and gas transportation services.

EXECUTIVES

Chairman: Paul G. Allen, age 52
President and CEO: Jo Allen (Jody) Patton, age 47
EVP Investment Management: Lance Conn
VP Tax, Risk, and Asset Management: Joseph Franzi
VP Corporate Communications: Steven C. Crosby
VP Corporate Development and Operations: Denise Wolf
VP Finance and CFO: Nathaniel T. (Buster) Brown
VP Technology: Chris Purcell
VP Investment Management; Managing Director, Vulcan Captial: Nathan Troutman
VP Media Development: Richard E. Hutton
VP Real Estate Development: Ada M. Healey
Managing Director, Private Equity, Vulcan Ventures: Hoon Cho

LOCATIONS

HQ: Vulcan Inc.
505 5th Ave. South, Ste. 900, Seattle, WA 98104
Phone: 206-342-2000   **Fax:** 206-342-3000
Web: www.vulcan.com

PRODUCTS/OPERATIONS

Selected Holdings
Audience
Charter Communications (57%, TV system)
Click2learn, Inc. (27%, multimedia development software)
Cytokinetics, Inc. (small molecule drugs)
Dick's Clothing & Sporting Goods (9%, sporting goods retailer)
Digeo, Inc. (interactive television)
DreamWorks SKG (entertainment company)
Microsoft Corporation
Oxygen Media (Internet and television content provider)

Perlegen Sciences, Inc. (genetics research)
Plains Resources (oil and gas pipeline, transportation, and storage)
Portland Trail Blazers (professional basketball team)
PTC Therapeutics, Inc. (small molecule drugs)
Seattle Seahawks (professional football team)
The Sporting News (print and online sports magazine)
Xcyte Therapies, Inc. (cell-based therapies)

COMPETITORS

Accel Partners	Matrix Partners
Austin Ventures	Mayfield Fund
Benchmark Capital	Menlo Ventures
Boston Ventures	Microsoft
Draper Fisher Jurvetson	SOFTBANK
Harris & Harris	Sutter Hill Ventures
Hummer Winblad	Trinity Ventures
Institutional Venture Partners	US Venture Partners
Kleiner Perkins	Venrock
	Veronis Suhler Stevenson

VyStar Credit Union

The largest credit union in its region, VyStar provides a galaxy of financial services from about 20 locations in northeastern Florida. The credit union offers traditional banking services including deposit accounts, credit cards, and loans; its VyStar Financial Group subsidiary specializes in financial management and insurance services to members and non-members. Credit union membership is available for any who live or work in one of 15 area counties and their families. Founded in 1952 (as Jax Navy Federal Credit Union) to serve the Naval Air Station in Jacksonville, VyStar now boasts more than 330,000 members nationwide.

VyStar's loan portfolio is comprised largely of consumer mortgages (40%) and automobile loans (35%); the credit union also services loans for others.

Residents and workers in Alachua, Baker, Bradford, Clay, Columbia, Duval, Flagler, Gilchrist, Levy, Marion, Nassau, Putnam, St. Johns, Union, and Volusia Counties are eligible to join VyStar.

EXECUTIVES

Chairman: Ralph R. Story
Vice Chairman: George R. Berry
President and CEO: Terry R. West
EVP and CFO: John H. Turpish
EVP, Call Center and COO: Richard G. Alfirevic
SVP, Branch Services: Randy Swift
SVP, Human Resources: Willie R. Williams
SVP, Lending: Kathryn Bonaventura
SVP, Marketing: Judith T. Walz
VP, Accounting: Joan M. Hill
CIO: Terry L. Mayne
Secretary: Esther T. Schultz
Treasurer: Lawrence R. Jacobs
Auditors: Nearman, Maynard, Vallez, CPAs and Consultants, P.A.

LOCATIONS

HQ: VyStar Credit Union
4949 Blanding Blvd., Jacksonville, FL 32210
Phone: 904-777-6000   **Fax:** 904-908-2488
Web: www.vystarcu.org

PRODUCTS/OPERATIONS

2004 Sales

	$ mil.	% of total
Interest		
Loans	93.3	57
Investment	30.8	19
Trading gains	0.2	—
Noninterest		
Fees & charges	34.5	21
Security gains	0.9	1
Other	3.3	2
Total	**163.0**	**100**

COMPETITORS

AmSouth	Compass Bancshares
Bank of America	SunTrust
BB&T	Wachovia

HISTORICAL FINANCIALS

Company Type: Not-for-profit

Income Statement

FYE: December 31

	ASSETS ($ mil.)	NET INCOME ($ mil.)	INCOME AS % OF ASSETS	EMPLOYEES
12/04	2,852	17	0.6%	900
12/03	2,688	23	0.9%	—
12/02	2,464	22	0.9%	—
Annual Growth	7.6%	(10.8%)	—	—

2004 Year-End Financials

Equity as % of assets: 95.5%   Long-term debt ($ mil.): 111
Return on assets: 0.6%   Sales ($ mil.): 163
Return on equity: 0.7%

Net Income History

W. B. Doner & Company

This company brings marketing skills to the party. W. B. Doner & Company (which does business as Doner) is the largest independent advertising agency in the US, boasting a client roster that includes Circuit City, Sirius Satellite Radio, and Mazda. It provides creative ad development and campaign management services, along with media planning and buying. Founded by Wilfred Broderick Doner in 1937, the firm has created classic campaigns for such customers as Timex ("Takes a licking and keeps on ticking") and Klondike Bar ("What would you do for a Klondike Bar?"). It is controlled by a management group that includes chairman and CEO Alan Kalter and vice chairmen John DeCerchio and Barry Levine.

Doner has picked up several top brands in the past year, including Circuit City, Hotels.com, and Lexmark. It also struck a chord with its Mr. Six campaign for theme park operator Six Flags.

In addition to offices in Cleveland, Detroit, Los Angeles, and Tampa, Florida, Doner has offices in Canada and an outpost in London operating under the banner Doner Cardwell Hawkins.

EXECUTIVES

Chairman and CEO: Alan Kalter
Vice Chairman and CFO: H. Barry Levine
Vice Chairman and Chief Creative Officer:
 John DeCerchio
EVP and Chief Marketing Officer: Bryan Yolles
EVP and Chief Media Officer: Shane Ankeney
EVP and General Manager, Cleveland: David DeMuth
EVP and Director of Operations: Sue Guise
EVP and Account Management Director:
 Kevin Weinman
EVP: Barbara Yolles
SVP and Creative Director: George Levy
Director of Marketing: Mary Scott
Director of Human Resources: Carol Cothern

LOCATIONS

HQ: W. B. Doner & Company
 25900 Northwestern Hwy., Southfield, MI 48075
Phone: 248-354-9700 **Fax:** 248-827-0880

COMPETITORS

Arnold Worldwide	Hill, Holliday
BBDO Detroit	JWT
Campbell Mithun	Leo Burnett
Campbell-Ewald	Martin Agency
C-K	Publicis USA
Deutsch	Saatchi & Saatchi
Euro RSCG	TBWA Worldwide
Fallon Worldwide	Team One
Foote, Cone & Belding	Wieden and Kennedy
GSD&M	Young & Rubicam

HISTORICAL FINANCIALS

Company Type: Private

Income Statement

FYE: February 28

	REVENUE ($ mil.)	NET INCOME ($ mil.)	NET PROFIT MARGIN	EMPLOYEES
2/05	156	—	—	1,200
2/04	137	—	—	1,000
2/03	122	—	—	930
2/02	114	—	—	982
2/01	110	—	—	908
2/00	86	—	—	832
2/99	70	—	—	1,000
2/98	57	—	—	1,000
2/97	63	—	—	—
2/96	61	—	—	600
Annual Growth	11.1%	—	—	8.0%

Revenue History

W. L. Gore & Associates

W. L. Gore & Associates would like your clothing to take a deep breath. The company makes a variety of fluoropolymer products; best known is its breathable, waterproof, and windproof GORE-TEX fabric. Product uses range from clothing and shoes to guitar strings, dental floss, space suits, and sutures. In addition to its apparel (popular among hikers and hunters), W. L. Gore makes insulated wire and cables, filtration products, and sealants. Fabrics are offered under such brands as GORE-TEX and WINDSTOPPER. The Gore family owns about 75% of the company; Gore associates own the rest.

W. L. Gore is known for its unusual style of management — the lattice system. There is no fixed authority, as the company has "sponsors," not bosses, and all employees are considered associates. Company goals and tasks are determined by consensus.

HISTORY

In 1941 Bill Gore, a DuPont scientist, started researching and developing plastics, polymers, and resins. One project at DuPont that Gore worked on was the development of a synthetic substance commonly known as teflon.

Seeing an untapped market for teflon-type products, Gore quit DuPont and in 1958 started his own business. He worked with his wife and his son Bob, a chemical engineering student. Bob helped him develop the company's first major product line — teflon-insulated electronic wires and cables.

With the success of its cables, the company was able to move out of the family basement and into a facility in Newark, Delaware. By 1965 Gore employed 200 people and soon implemented the lattice structure of management, eschewing demands for personal commitments and emphasizing cooperation and teamwork as paramount tenets of the business. A second plant was opened in Flagstaff, Arizona, in 1967.

Bob Gore, who had earned a doctorate in chemistry, hit the synthetic plastic motherlode in 1969. While experimenting with teflon, he discovered a way to stretch the material at microscopic levels, creating a fabric with holes large enough for body heat and moisture to escape, but small enough to deflect raindrops. Gore applied for a patent on its GORE-TEX fabric in 1970 and received it six years later. The company experienced an explosive period of growth as GORE-TEX found its way into space suits, sporting apparel, filters, and artificial arteries. Bob Gore became the company's president during this time.

By the 1980s GORE-TEX-related products generated the majority of sales. Globally, Gore operated about 30 plants, locating most in smaller cities since the Gores believed that small towns offered a better quality of life. Bill Gore died in 1986. The business continued and developed new uses for GORE-TEX. Various patent lawsuits emerged at the time, and when the company lost a case in 1990, Gore's exclusive patent on GORE-TEX ended, although it retained patents on certain products and processes.

The door was open for competition by 1993, but Gore still had the advantages of experience and a perception of higher quality and durability. It continued to introduce new uses for GORE-TEX, spooling out dental floss in 1993. The company also moved into the computer market that year by acquiring Supercomputer Systems.

Gore expanded its US medical product line in 1996 by marketing a membrane made from GORE-TEX-related material for use as a replacement for dura mater (the membrane that protects the brain and spinal cord) and in 1997 with the purchase of Prograft Medical.

In 1999 Gore introduced its REMEDIA catalytic filter system, which destroys carcinogenic dioxins and furans produced during industrial combustion by converting them into water and harmless chemicals.

The company exited the circuit packaging business in 2000 when it sold its Eau Claire, Wisconsin, plants to 3M. The following year Gore entered into a strategic agreement with Singapore-based photonic component manufacturer Flextronics Photonics to manufacture optical transmitter and receiver modules. In 2002 Gore sold its fiber optic operations to focus on electrical interconnects and materials. Pall Corporation and Gore entered into a business alliance, which allowed Pall rights to the GORE-TEX filter technology to be used in bachwashable filtration systems in 2003.

EXECUTIVES

CEO: Terri Kelly, age 42
Associate Chief Information Officer: Justin Kershaw
Medical Marketing Director: Thom O'Hara
Human Relations Chief: Donna Frey

LOCATIONS

HQ: W. L. Gore & Associates, Inc.
 555 Papermill Rd., Newark, DE 19711
Phone: 410-506-7787 **Fax:** 410-996-8585
Web: www.gore.com

W. L. Gore & Associates operates manufacturing facilities in China, Germany, Japan, the UK, and the US, with sales and customer service offices in those countries as well as in Argentina, Australia, Austria, Brazil, Finland, France, Greece, Hong Kong, India, Italy, Malaysia, the Netherlands, New Zealand, Poland, Russia, Singapore, South Korea, Spain, Sweden, and Taiwan.

PRODUCTS/OPERATIONS

Selected Divisions, Products, and Brands

Consumer Products
 CleanStream vacuum cleaner filters
 ELIXER guitar strings
 GLIDE dental floss
 GORE WINDSTOPPER fabrics
 ReviveX water and stain repellent
Electronics and Electrochemical Materials
 Cable and assembly products
 Flat cables
 High data rate cables
 Hook-up wire
 Microwave products
 Round cables
 Electronic packaging and materials
 Conductive adhesives
 EMI/RFI shielding — GORE-SHIELD
 PWB materials
 Thermal interfaces
Fabrics and Fibers
 AIRVANTAGE
 CROSSTECH fabrics
 DRYLOFT fabrics
 GORE-TEX BEST DEFENSE outerwear
 GORE-TEX fabrics
 GORE-TEX IMMERSION TECHNOLOGY products
 GORE-TEX OCEAN TECHNOLOGY outerwear

Filtration
  Cleanroom garments
  CleanStream vacuum cleaner filters
  Disk drive filters
Filter Bags and Cartridges
  GORE-SORBER exploration survey
  GORE-SORBER screening survey
  Liquid filtration tubular filter socks
  Microfiltration filter media
  Particulate and fluid filters for nonimpact printing
    components
  PRIMEA power assemblies
  PRISTYNE UX filter media
  RASTEX sewing thread and weaving fiber
Medical and Health Care
  GLIDE floss
  GORE cast liner
  Implantable medical devices
  GORE RESOLUT XT regenerative material
  GORE subcutaneous augmentation material
  GORE-TEX DualMesh biomaterial
  GORE-TEX DualMesh PLUS biomaterial
  GORE-TEX MycroMesh biomaterial
  GORE-TEX MycroMesh PLUS biomaterial
  GORE-TEX regenerative material
  GORE-TEX stretch vascular graft
  GORE-TEX suture
  GORE-TEX vascular grafts
  PRECLUDE dura substitute
  PRECLUDE peritoneal membrane
  SEAMGUARD staple line-reinforcement material
Sealants
  GFO fiber packing
  GFO marine service packing
  GORE-TEX gasket tape
  GORE-TEX GR sheet gasketing
  GORE-TEX joint sealant
  GORE-TEX valve stem packing
  ONE-UP pump diaphragms
  RASTEX fiber
  SEQUEL fiber packing
  STA-PURE peristaltic pump tubes

COMPETITORS

Belden CDT	Malden Mills
Burlington Industries	Milliken
CardioTech	Superior Essex
Donaldson	Thoratec Corp
Kellwood	Timberland

HISTORICAL FINANCIALS

Company Type: Private

Income Statement   FYE: March 31

	REVENUE ($ mil.)	NET INCOME ($ mil.)	NET PROFIT MARGIN	EMPLOYEES
3/04	1,579	—	—	6,900
3/03	1,330	—	—	6,600
3/02	1,230	—	—	6,000
3/01	1,400	—	—	6,600
3/00	1,350	—	—	5,888
3/99	1,280	—	—	7,000
3/98	1,150	—	—	6,600
3/97	1,064	—	—	6,100
3/96	958	—	—	5,860
3/95	825	—	—	5,700
Annual Growth	7.5%	—	—	2.1%

Revenue History

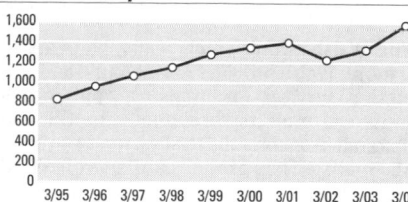

Wakefern Food

Started by seven men who each invested $1,000, Wakefern Food has grown into the largest retailer-owned supermarket cooperative in the US. The co-op is now owned by 38 independent grocers who operate more than 200 ShopRite supermarkets in seven eastern states, including New Jersey (where it is a leading chain). More than half of ShopRite stores offer pharmacies. In addition to name-brand and private-label products (ShopRite, Chef's Express, Reddington Farms), Wakefern supports its members with advertising, merchandising, insurance, and other services. Wakefern's ShopRite Supermarkets subsidiary acquired the assets of Florida-based Big V Supermarkets, which filed for bankruptcy in 2000.

The cooperative provides members and other customers with more than 20,000 name-brand items, including groceries, dairy and meat products, produce, frozen foods, and general merchandise. It also sells more than 3,000 items under the ShopRite label. All members are given one vote in the co-op, regardless of size.

Wakefern is moving its distribution operations from its facility in Wallkill, New York to Allentown, Pennsylvania after failing to reach an agreement with labor there on a new contract.

HISTORY

Wakefern Food was founded in 1946 by seven New York- and New Jersey-based grocers: Louis Weiss, Sam and Al Aidekman, Abe Kesselman, Dave Fern, Sam Garb, and Albert Goldberg (the company's name is made up of the letters of the first five of those founders). Like many cooperatives, the association sought to lower costs by increasing its buying power as a group.

They each put in $1,000 and began operating a 5,000-sq.-ft. warehouse, often putting in double time to keep both their stores and the warehouse running. The shopkeepers' collective buying power proved valuable, enabling the grocers to stock many items at the same prices as their larger competitors.

In 1951 Wakefern members began pooling their resources to buy advertising space. A common store name — ShopRite — was chosen, and each week co-op members met to decide which items would be sale priced. Within a year, membership had grown to over 50. Expansion became a priority, and in the mid-1950s co-op members united in small groups to take over failed supermarkets. One such group, called the Supermarkets Operating Co. (SOC), was formed in 1956. Within 10 years it had acquired a num-

ber of failed stores, remodeled them, and given them the ShopRite name.

During the late 1950s sales at ShopRite stores slumped after Wakefern decided to buck the supermarket trend of offering trading stamps (which could then be exchanged for gifts), figuring that offering the stamps would ultimately lead to higher food prices. The move initially drove away customers, but Wakefern cut grocery prices across the board and sales returned. The company also embraced another supermarket trend: stocking stores with nonfood items.

The co-op was severely shaken in 1966 when SOC merged with General Supermarkets, a similar small group within Wakefern, becoming Supermarkets General Corp. (SGC). SGC was a powerful entity, with 71 supermarkets, 10 drugstores, six gas stations, a wholesale bakery, and a discount department store. Many Wakefern members opposed the merger and attempted to block the action with a court order. By 1968 SGC had beefed up its operations to include department store chains as well as its grocery stores. In a move that threatened to break Wakefern, SGC broke away from the co-op, and its stores were renamed Pathmark.

Wakefern not only weathered the storm, it grew under the direction of chairman and CEO Thomas Infusino, elected shortly after the split. The co-op focused on asserting its position as a seller of low-priced products. Wakefern developed private-label brands, including the ShopRite brand. In the 1980s members began operating larger stores and adding more nonfood items to the ShopRite product mix. With its number of superstores on the rise and facing increased competition from club stores in 1992, Wakefern opened a centralized, nonfood distribution center in New Jersey.

In 1995, 30-year Wakefern veteran Dean Janeway was elected president of the co-op. The company debuted its ShopRite MasterCard, co-branded with New Jersey's Valley National Bank, in 1996. The following year the co-op purchased two of its customers' stores in Pennsylvania, then threatened to close them when contract talks with the local union deteriorated. In 1998 Wakefern settled the dispute, then sold the stores.

The company partnered with Internet bidding site priceline.com in 1999, offering customers an opportunity to bid on groceries and then pick them up at ShopRite stores. Big V, Wakefern's biggest customer, filed for Chapter 11 bankruptcy protection in 2000 and said it was ending its distribution agreement with the co-op. In July 2002, however, Wakefern's ShopRite Supermarkets subsidiary acquired all of Big V's assets for approximately $185 million in cash and assumed liabilities.

Infusino retired in May 2005 after 35 years with Wakefern Food. He was succeeded by former vice chairman Joseph Colalillo.

EXECUTIVES

Chairman and CEO: Jospeh Colalillo
President and COO: Dean Janeway
CFO: Ken Jasinkiewicz
EVP, Marketing: Joseph Sheridan
SVP and CIO: Natan Tabak
VP, Corporate and Consumer Affairs: Mary Ellen Gowin
VP, Human Resources: Ernie Bell
VP, Corporate Merchandising and Advertising:
  Bill Crombie
VP, Information Services Division: Alan Aront
VP, Logistics: Pete Rolandelli
President and COO, ShopRite Supermarkets:
  Kevin Mannix

Director, Advertising: Karen McAuvic
Manager, Consumer Affairs: Cheryl Macik
**Manager, Corporate Communications and Media
Relations:** Karen Meleta

LOCATIONS

HQ: Wakefern Food Corporation
600 York St., Elizabeth, NJ 07207
Phone: 908-527-3300   **Fax:** 908-527-3397
Web: www.shoprite.com

Wakefern Food's 38 members operate more than 200 ShopRite supermarkets in Connecticut, Delaware, Massachusetts, New Jersey, New York, Rhode Island, and Pennsylvania.

PRODUCTS/OPERATIONS

Major Members
Foodarama Supermarkets
Inserra Supermarkets
Village Super Market

Selected Private Labels
Black Bear (deli items)
Chef's Express
Reddington Farms (poultry)
ShopRite

COMPETITORS

A&P	Pathmark
C&S Wholesale	Royal Ahold
Di Giorgio	Shurfine International
IGA	Stop & Shop
King Kullen Grocery	SUPERVALU
Kings Super Markets	Wal-Mart
Krasdale Foods	White Rose Food

HISTORICAL FINANCIALS

Company Type: Cooperative

Income Statement

FYE: September 30

	REVENUE ($ mil.)	NET INCOME ($ mil.)	NET PROFIT MARGIN	EMPLOYEES
9/03	6,578	—	—	50,000
9/02	6,208	—	—	50,000
9/01	5,900	—	—	—
9/00	5,800	—	—	—
9/99	5,500	—	—	—
9/98	5,000	—	—	—
9/97	4,613	—	—	—
9/96	4,304	—	—	—
9/95	3,700	—	—	—
9/94	3,740	—	—	—
Annual Growth	6.5%	—	—	0.0%

Revenue History

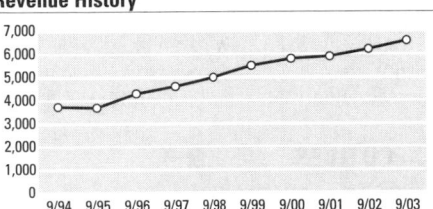

Walsh Group

The Walsh Group erects walls, halls, malls, and more. Walsh provides design/build and construction services for industrial, public, and commercial projects throughout the US. Projects range from prisons to skyscrapers to shopping malls. The group consists of Walsh Construction and Archer Western Contractors. Walsh provides complete project management services, from planning and demolition to general contracting and finance. It is a major player in bridge and highway construction, as well as in water treatment facilities, and also renovates and restores buildings. Among its projects is work on Chicago's Millenium Park. The Walsh family still owns the firm, founded in 1898.

EXECUTIVES

Chairman; CEO, Walsh Construction:
Matthew M. Walsh
President; President, Walsh Construction:
Daniel J. Walsh
CFO, Secretary, and Treasurer: Larry J. Kibbon
VP Business Development: Patrick M. Donley
Human Resources Manager: Rhonda Hardwick
Auditors: Wolf & Company, P.C.

LOCATIONS

HQ: The Walsh Group
929 W. Adams St., Chicago, IL 60607
Phone: 312-563-5400   **Fax:** 312-563-5466
Web: www.walshgroup.com

The Walsh Group's Archer Western Contractors has offices in Arlington, Texas; Atlanta; Jacksonville, Florida; Phoenix; Raleigh, North Carolina; Richmond, Virginia; and San Diego. Its Walsh Construction Company has offices in Boston; Chicago; Detroit; LaPorte, Indiana; and Pittsburgh.

PRODUCTS/OPERATIONS

Projects
Apartment complexes
Correctional facilities
Data centers
Education facilities
Health-care facilities
Highways and bridges
Hotels
Industrial parks
Interiors
Laboratories
Parking garages
Renovations
Retail centers
Senior housing
Skyscrapers
Treatment plants

Selected Services
Construction management
Design/build
General contracting
Preconstruction
Project financing
Project and tenant analysis

COMPETITORS

APAC	Jacobs Engineering
Bechtel	Lane Construction
Black & Veatch	McCarthy Building
Bovis Lend Lease	Modern Continental
Brasfield & Gorrie	Companies
CH2M HILL	MWH Global
Flatiron Construction	Peter Kiewit Sons'
Fluor	Skanska
Granite Construction	TIC Holdings
Hunt Building	Turner Corporation
Hunt Construction	Vecellio & Grogan

HISTORICAL FINANCIALS

Company Type: Private

Income Statement

FYE: December 31

	REVENUE ($ mil.)	NET INCOME ($ mil.)	NET PROFIT MARGIN	EMPLOYEES
12/03	1,725	—	—	3,750
12/02	1,754	—	—	3,691
12/01	1,450	—	—	3,000
12/00	1,304	—	—	2,600
12/99	1,080	—	—	1,000
12/98	1,170	—	—	3,500
12/97	992	—	—	2,000
12/96	740	—	—	1,500
12/95	604	—	—	1,000
12/94	450	—	—	4,000
Annual Growth	16.1%	—	—	(0.7%)

Revenue History

Warren Equities

Warren Equities fills car tanks and stomachs in the US Northeast. The holding company sells fuel and groceries from over 400 Xtra Mart brand service stations and convenience stores from Maine to Virginia. Warren's distribution companies supply those stores, as well as independent outlets, with gasoline, grocery, and tobacco products. Other Warren companies trade and store petroleum, provide environmental testing services, and make promotional signs and clothing. Chairman and owner Warren Alpert's foundation gives annual grants to medical researchers; he has donated more than $20 million to Harvard Medical School.

Warren Alpert founded the company in 1950 after Standard Oil awarded him a distributorship. Over time, Alpert built Warren Equities into the holding company for six separate businesses.

EXECUTIVES

Chairman: Warren Alpert, age 84
Vice Chairman: Edward M. Cosgrove
President and CEO: Herbert (Herb) Kaplan
CFO and Treasurer: John Dziedzic
EVP: Francis K. (Fran) La Forge
Controller and Assistant Treasurer: Richard J. Sawicki
Director Human Resources: Thomas (Tom) Palumbo
Media Contact: Diana Paulik

LOCATIONS

HQ: Warren Equities, Inc.
27 Warren Way, Providence, RI 02905
Phone: 401-781-9900   **Fax:** 401-461-7160
Web: www.warreneq.com

Warren Equities operates in Connecticut, Maine, Maryland, Massachusetts, New Hampshire, New York, Pennsylvania, Rhode Island, and Virginia.

PRODUCTS/OPERATIONS

Subsidiaries

Auburn Merchandise Distributors, Inc.
  (wholesale marketing)
Convenient Graphics (promotional products)
Drake Petroleum Company, Inc. (wholesale gasoline)
Warex Terminals Corporation (wholesale marketing)
Xcel Environmental, Inc. (environmental services)
Xtra Mart Convenience Stores (convenience stores)

COMPETITORS

7-Eleven	Global Partners
BP	Motiva Enterprises
Casey's General Stores	Sunoco
Crown Central Petroleum	SUPERVALU
Cumberland Farms	Wawa, Inc.
Getty Petroleum	
Marketing	

HISTORICAL FINANCIALS

Company Type: Private

Income Statement

	REVENUE ($ mil.)	NET INCOME ($ mil.)	NET PROFIT MARGIN	EMPLOYEES
				FYE: May 31
5/04	1,000	—	—	2,200
5/03	1,000	—	—	2,200
5/02	1,000	—	—	2,200
5/01	984	—	—	2,200
5/00	797	—	—	2,100
5/99	587	—	—	2,100
5/98	620	—	—	2,100
5/97	700	—	—	2,300
5/96	900	—	—	2,100
5/95	786	—	—	1,600
Annual Growth	2.7%	—	—	3.6%

Revenue History

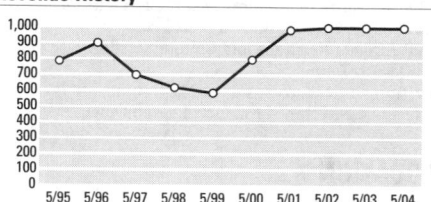

Washington Capitals

The Washington Capitals are far from being the seat of power in the National Hockey League. Operated by Lincoln Hockey, the team has reached the Stanley Cup finals just once in 1998 (losing to the Detroit Red Wings) and has since been on the decline. The lack of playoff success has hurt the team in ticket sales with attendance at home games dwindling to among the lowest levels in the league. Washington Wizards owner Abe Pollin formed the Capitals in 1974. Ted Leonsis, a mover and shaker at America Online, today controls the team through Lincoln Holdings, an investment group that includes team president Dick Patrick and Capital One Financial chairman Richard Fairbank.

Lincoln Holdings bought the Capitals from Pollin in 1999 for about $85 million. The deal also included a 44% stake in the Wizards and Washington's MCI Center, the home arena for both teams.

Leonsis had boasted a five-year plan to turn the Capitals into a championship winner when he bought the team and signed former NHL scoring champion Jaromir Jagr to a seven-year, $77 million contract in 2001. The team failed to make the playoffs that season and were ejected in the first round the next. In 2004 Leonsis began dismantling the money-loosing team, trading away Jagr and several other highly paid veterans such as Peter Bondra, Sergei Gonchar, and Robert Lang.

EXECUTIVES

Chairman: Ted Leonsis
President: Richard M. (Dick) Patrick
Alternate Governor, VP, and General Manager:
  George McPhee
Assistant General Manager: Frank Provenzano
Head Coach: Glen Hanlon
VP Marketing: John Vidalin
Chief Marketing Officer: Kevin Morgan
Controller: Keith Burrows
Senior Director of Communications: Kurt Kehl
Director of Operations: George Parr
Manager Community Relations: Elizabeth Wodatch

LOCATIONS

HQ: Lincoln Hockey LLC
  401 9th St. NW, Ste. 750, Washington, DC 20004
Phone: 202-266-2200   **Fax:** 202-266-2360
Web: www.washingtoncaps.com

The Washington Capitals play in the 20,000-seat capacity MCI Center in Washington, DC.

PRODUCTS/OPERATIONS

Championship Trophies

Prince of Wales Trophy (1998)

COMPETITORS

Atlanta Thrashers	Florida Panthers
Carolina Hurricanes	Tampa Bay Lightning

HISTORICAL FINANCIALS

Company Type: Private

Income Statement

	REVENUE ($ mil.)	NET INCOME ($ mil.)	NET PROFIT MARGIN	EMPLOYEES
				FYE: July 31
7/04	61	—	—	—
7/03	62	—	—	—
7/02	61	—	—	—
7/01	50	—	—	—
7/00	49	—	—	—
Annual Growth	5.6%	—	—	—

Revenue History

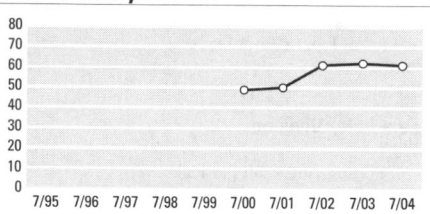

Wawa

It's not baby talk — when folks say they need to go to the Wawa, they need groceries. Wawa runs about 550 Wawa Food Markets in Delaware, Maryland, New Jersey, Pennsylvania, and Virginia. Wawa stores are noted for their coffee and their salad and deli offerings, including hoagie sandwiches; more than 150 stores sell gas. Unlike many convenience store chains, Wawa has its own dairy, supplying Wawa stores and about 1,000 hospitals, schools, and other institutions. The company opened its first store in 1964, but its roots go back to an iron foundry begun in 1803 by the Wood family; food operations began in 1902 when George Wood started a dairy in Wawa, Pennsylvania. The Wood family owns 52% of the company.

Howard Stoeckel succeeded Richard Wood as CEO of the company in January 2005. Stoeckel is the first non-family member to lead Wawa, Inc. There DuPont, who was was named president of Wawa when Stoeckel became CEO, is Wood's nephew.

EXECUTIVES

Chairman: Richard D. (Dick) Wood Jr., age 66
CEO: Howard B. Stoeckel, age 59
President and CFO: There du Pont, age 38
SVP and Chief Marketing Officer: Rob Price
SVP, Operations: Harry McHugh
VP, Human Resources: Carol Jensen
VP, Procurement and Logistics: Jim Bluebello
CIO: Neil McCarthy
Director, Food Service: Michael Sherlock
Director, IT Architecture: Marty Maglio
Director, Store Operations Technology:
  John Cunningham
Manager, Network and Telecommunications:
  Julius Colina
Manager, Public Relations: Lori Bruce
Product Manager: Jane Coleman
Manager, Real Estate Technology: Michael McCabe

LOCATIONS

HQ: Wawa, Inc.
260 W. Baltimore Pike, Wawa, PA 19063
Phone: 610-358-8000 **Fax:** 610-358-8878
Web: www.wawa.com

PRODUCTS/OPERATIONS

Selected Products and Private-Label Brands

Bakery (Wawa)
Cold beverages (Wawa)
Hoagies (Built-to-Order, Shorti)
Hot breakfast
Coffee (Freshly Brewed Coffee)
Hash browns
Hot breakfast sandwiches (Sizzli)
Party platters
Ready-to-eat foods (Wawa Express)
Sides
Soups

Wawa Dairy Division

Products
100% orange juice (All Florida)
Butter
Cappuccino
Fruit juices and drinks
Ice cream mixes
Milk (including lactose-free, chocolate,
and strawberry)
Non-dairy coffee blend
Spring water (Deer Park)
Tea
Yogurt (Dannon)

COMPETITORS

7-Eleven	Green Valley
A&P	Kroger
Albertson's	Motiva Enterprises
Amerada Hess	Rutter's Dairy
Chevron	Sheetz
Cumberland Farms	Subway
Exxon Mobil	Village Super Market
Foodarama Supermarkets	Warren Equities
Genuardi's Family Markets	Wegmans
Getty Realty	

HISTORICAL FINANCIALS

Company Type: Private

Income Statement			FYE: December 31
	REVENUE ($ mil.)	NET INCOME ($ mil.)	NET PROFIT MARGIN	EMPLOYEES
12/03	2,819	51	1.8%	15,000
12/02	2,272	35	1.5%	13,400
12/01	2,010	36	1.8%	13,000
12/00	1,500	—	—	13,000
12/99	1,398	—	—	12,000
12/98	1,000	—	—	12,000
12/97	1,010	—	—	12,500
12/96	959	—	—	12,000
12/95	901	—	—	10,000
12/94	838	—	—	—
Annual Growth	14.4%	19.2%	—	5.2%

Net Income History

12/94 12/95 12/96 12/97 12/98 12/99 12/00 12/01 12/02 12/03

Wayport

Whether away from home or office, travelers can access the Internet with Wayport's help. The company provides high-speed fixed-line and Wi-Fi (802.11) wireless Internet access in hotel rooms, airports, and meeting rooms, allowing users with laptops equipped with Ethernet network cards to access the Web, company networks, and e-mail for a fee. Major customers include Austin-Bergstrom International Airport and Dallas/Fort Worth International Airport. Want fries with your Internet access? The company has also announced it will be providing wireless Internet access at 8,000 McDonald's locations in the US. Major investors include Sevin Rosen Fund and New Enterprise Associates.

While the company originally sold Internet access directly to users, it has switched to selling services wholesale, as in the McDonald's deal. Car rental agency Hertz has also decided to offer Wayport's wireless access service in its facilities at more than 50 airports in the US. Wayport also has agreements with companies such as SBC Communications, Sprint, and MCI to cooperate on services and roaming.

EXECUTIVES

CEO: Dave Vucina
COO: Greg Williams
CFO: Kenneth C. (Ken) Kieley, age 54
VP Corporate Development: David Hampton
VP Engineering Development: Jim Keeler
VP Business Development and Marketing:
Daniel (Dan) Lowden
VP Network Engineering: Timothy G. Smith
VP McDonald's Partnership and Human Resources:
Phillip (Phil) Waters
VP Sales: Jack Alton
VP Strategic Business Development: Steven E. Fulford
VP and General Counsel: Robert (Bob) Kroll
Human Resources: Debbie Primera
Auditors: PricewaterhouseCoopers

LOCATIONS

HQ: Wayport, Inc.
4509 Freidrich Lane, Southpark Commerce Center
2, Bldg. 3, Ste. 300, Austin, TX 78744
Phone: 512-519-6000 **Fax:** 512-519-6450
Web: www.wayport.com

Wayport has operations in Canada, the Czech Republic, France, Germany, Ireland, Portugal, the UK, and the US.

COMPETITORS

Boingo	On Command
Cardinal Communications	Speedus
The Cloud	STSN
GoAmerica	T-Mobile HotSpot
ICOA	US Wireless Online

HISTORICAL FINANCIALS

Company Type: Private

Income Statement			FYE: June 30
	ESTIMATED REVENUE ($ mil.)	NET INCOME ($ mil.)	NET PROFIT MARGIN	EMPLOYEES
6/04	38	—	—	230
6/03	19	—	—	—
Annual Growth	105.4%	—	—	—

Revenue History

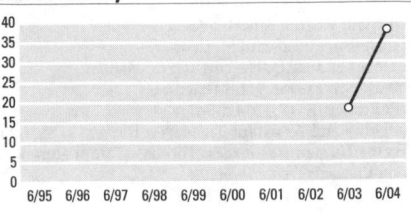
6/95 6/96 6/97 6/98 6/99 6/00 6/01 6/02 6/03 6/04

WB Television Network

The WB Television Network is looking to grow up and get over the teen angst. After primarily catering to Generation Y with hits like *Charmed* and *Smallville,* the upstart network that took to the airwaves in 1995 is trying to combat low ratings by attracting an older audience to newer shows such as *Everwood.* The WB broadcasts primetime programming six nights a week, and under the guise of Kids' WB!, the network also provides Saturday morning children's programming, including *The Batman* and *Teen Titans.* In addition, The WB is producing original movies for the first time to boost non-serialized programming. Warner Bros. Television Group owns 78% of The WB, Tribune Company owns the rest.

In 2005 the network dropped weekday afternoon Kids' WB! programming in favor of sitcom reruns. The move came as The WB realized that its initial strategy of courting young viewers in the afternoon with the hope that their parents would stick with the network during primetime was unfeasible in the world of almost unlimited cable television programming. Instead, the afternoon rerun block will court older teenagers and the 18-34 demographic.

EXECUTIVES

Chairman: Garth Ancier
COO: John Maatta
President, Entertainment: David Janollari
Co-President, Marketing: Bob Bibb
Co-President, Marketing: Lew Goldstein
Co-EVP Comedy Development: Michael Clements
Co-EVP Comedy Development: Tracey Pakosta
EVP Current Programming: Michael Roberts
EVP Drama Development: Carolyn Bernstein
EVP Finance and Operations: Mitch Nedick
EVP Media Sales: Bill Morningstar
EVP Network Communications: Brad Turell
EVP Talent/Casting: Kathleen Letterie
SVP Affiliate Relations and Communications:
Elizabeth Tumulty
VP Human Resources: Valerie Masterson
Executive Director of Finance: Lauren Odle

LOCATIONS

HQ: The WB Television Network
4000 Warner Blvd., Bldg. 34R, Burbank, CA 91522
Phone: 818-977-5000 **Fax:** 818-977-6771
Web: www.thewb.com

PRODUCTS/OPERATIONS

Selected Programs

7th Heaven	*One Tree Hill*
Beauty and the Geek	*Reba*
Blue Collar TV	*Related*
Charmed	*Smallville*
Everwood	*Supernatural*
Gilmore Girls	*Twins*
Living with Fran	*What I Like About You*

COMPETITORS

ABC	NBC
CBS	UPN
FOX Broadcasting	

HISTORICAL FINANCIALS

Company Type: Joint venture

Income Statement
FYE: December 31

	REVENUE ($ mil.)	NET INCOME ($ mil.)	NET PROFIT MARGIN	EMPLOYEES
12/04	700	—	—	—
12/03	660	—	—	—
12/02	589	—	—	400
12/01	450	—	—	340
12/00	453	—	—	—
12/99	384	—	—	—
12/98	260	—	—	—
12/97	136	—	—	—
12/96	87	—	—	—
Annual Growth	29.8%	—	—	17.6%

Revenue History

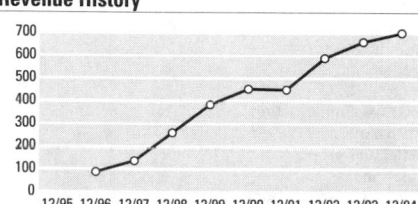

webloyalty.com

Webloyalty.com offers services such as consumer membership programs for companies that are looking to garner better relationships with its customers. The company serves e-commerce, travel, and other fee-based Web sites by providing travel discounts and promotional offers on entertainment, retail merchandise, and home computer protection software seamlessly (Webloyalty sends the offers out but they are branded with the clients' Web sites), building customer loyalty. Private equity firm General Atlantic LLC acquired a majority stake in the company in 2005.

EXECUTIVES

CEO: Richard J. Fernandes, age 43
President: Vincent R. D'Agostino
CTO: Gary Cacace
SVP Operations and Administration: Jeffrey Kendall
SVP Business Development: Shane Spitzer
SVP Marketing: Martin Isaac

LOCATIONS

HQ: webloyalty.com
101 Merritt 7, 7th Fl., Norwalk, CT 06851
Phone: 203-846-3300   **Fax:** 203-846-4100
Web: webloyalty.com

COMPETITORS

Advantex Marketing	Loyaltyworks
LoyaltyPoint	Maritz Loyalty Marketing

HISTORICAL FINANCIALS

Company Type: Private

Income Statement
FYE: December 31

	REVENUE ($ mil.)	NET INCOME ($ mil.)	NET PROFIT MARGIN	EMPLOYEES
12/04	86	—	—	175
12/03	55	—	—	
Annual Growth	55.6%	—	—	

Revenue History

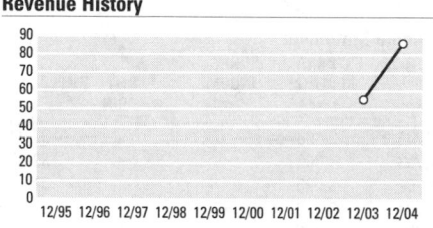

Website Pros

Website Pros has everything a growing business needs to get on the Internet. The company provides Web site building software, custom design consulting, and Web hosting. Its eWorks! XL program also helps companies improve their visibility online through search engine optimization and Internet advertising. Website Pros sells to more than 40,000 small and medium-sized businesses in the US, mostly on a subscription basis. In 2005 the company acquired E.B.O.Z. and Leads.com, expanding its lead generation and Internet marketing offerings. Principal investors in Website Pros include Insight Venture Partners and Norwest Venture Partners.

EXECUTIVES

President, CEO, and Director: David Brown, age 51, $281,385 pay
EVP: Edward Hechter, age 41, $185,000 pay
SVP Business Development and Corporate Development: Darin Brannan, age 37, $151,850 pay
SVP Marketing: Roseann Duran, age 53, $126,231 pay
VP Finance and CFO: Kevin Carney, age 41, $163,877 pay
VP Acquisition Services: Lisa Anteau, age 33
VP Operations: Joel Williamson, age 57
Auditors: Ernst & Young LLP

LOCATIONS

HQ: Website Pros, Inc.
12735 Gran Bay Pkwy. West, Bldg. 200, Jacksonville, FL 32258
Phone: 904-680-6600   **Fax:** 904-880-0350
Web: www.websitepros.com

Website Pros has offices in California, Florida, Virginia, and Washington.

PRODUCTS/OPERATIONS

2004 Sales

	$ mil.	% of total
Subscription	19.4	83
License	3.4	15
Professional services	0.6	2
Total	23.4	100

COMPETITORS

Adobe	Microsoft
Macromedia	Business Solutions

HISTORICAL FINANCIALS

Company Type: Private

Income Statement
FYE: December 31

	REVENUE ($ mil.)	NET INCOME ($ mil.)	NET PROFIT MARGIN	EMPLOYEES
12/04	23	1	4.3%	337
12/03	17	(2)	—	—
12/02	14	(6)	—	—
Annual Growth	30.7%	—	—	—

2004 Year-End Financials

Debt ratio: 0.0%
Return on equity: —
Cash ($ mil.): 7
Current ratio: 1.98
Long-term debt ($ mil.): 0

Net Income History

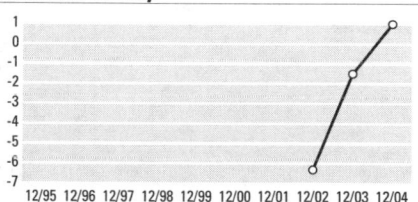

Wegmans

One name strikes fear in the hearts of supermarket owners in New York, Pennsylvania, New Jersey, and now, Virginia: Wegmans Food Markets. The grocery chain owns nearly 70 stores, but they are hardly typical. Much larger than most supermarkets (up to 130,000 sq. ft.), they offer specialty shops such as huge in-store cafes, cheese shops with some 400 different varieties, and French-style pastry shops. The company is known for its gourmet cooking classes and an extensive employee-training program. Wegmans also runs about 15 Chase-Pitkin Home and Garden home-improvement stores and a restaurant. Founded in 1916, the company is owned by the family of founder John Wegman. His nephew, Robert Wegman, is chairman.

Robert Wegman stepped down as CEO of the company in January 2005 and was succeeded by his son Danny Wegman. Concurrently, Colleen Wegman, Danny Wegman's daughter, was named president of the grocery chain.

Wegmans won the #1 spot on *FORTUNE* Magazine's 2005 list of the "100 Best Companies to Work For." While Wegmans has appeared on the FORTUNE list since its inception, 2005 marks the first time the grocery chain captured the top spot.

Wegmans opened its first store in Virginia in 2004, followed by a second store there in early 2005. Its first supermarket in Maryland opened in October 2005.

Citing competition from national home improvement chains Home Depot and Lowe's, Wegmans has decided to close its 14 Chase-Pitkin Home and Garden Centers in 2006. (Chase-Pitkin employs 507 full-time and 1,660 part-time workers.)

EXECUTIVES

Chairman: Robert B. Wegman, age 86
CEO: Daniel R. (Danny) Wegman, age 57
President: Colleen Wegman, age 33
EVP, Operations: Jack DePeters
SVP and CFO: James (Jim) Leo
SVP, Consumer Affairs: Mary Ellen Burris
SVP, Distribution: Mike Bargmann
SVP, Information Technology: Donald (Don) Reeve
SVP, Real Estate: Ralph Uttaro
VP, People: Karen Shadders
VP, Produce: Dave Corsi
Secretary and General Counsel: Paul S. Speranza Jr.
Director, Human Resources: Gerald Pierce

LOCATIONS

HQ: Wegmans Food Markets, Inc.
1500 Brooks Ave., Rochester, NY 14624
Phone: 585-328-2550   **Fax:** 585-464-4664
Web: www.wegmans.com

2004 Stores

	No.
New York	51
Pennsylvania	10
New Jersey	5
Virginia	1
Total	**67**

PRODUCTS/OPERATIONS

Products/Operations

Asian foods
Bath and body
Bulk foods
Cheeses
Coffee/cappuccino Bar
Cooking classes
Deli
Dry cleaning
European bread bakery
Floral department
Gift and fruit baskets
Kosher deli
Market café
Meat service
Nature's Marketplace (organic health and food items)
Organic produce
Pasta Station
Pharmacy
Photo processing and photo enlarging
Pizza Primo

Ready-to-cook meat and seafood
Rotisserie
Seafood
Sub sandwiches
Sushi bar
UPS parcel service
Video player and game system rentals
Videos and DVDs
WKids Fun Center
Wokery

COMPETITORS

A&P	IGA
Albertson's	Pathmark
Foodarama Supermarkets	Penn Traffic
Foodtown	Safeway
Genuardi's Family Markets	SUPERVALU
Giant Eagle	Tops Markets
Giant Food Stores	Wal-Mart
Golub	Wawa, Inc.
Home Depot	Weis Markets

HISTORICAL FINANCIALS

Company Type: Private

Income Statement

FYE: December 31

	ESTIMATED REVENUE ($ mil.)	NET INCOME ($ mil.)	NET PROFIT MARGIN	EMPLOYEES
12/04	3,600	—	—	32,000
12/03	3,300	—	—	32,000
12/02	3,020	—	—	31,300
12/01	2,920	—	—	29,072
12/00	2,800	—	—	29,826
12/99	2,670	—	—	28,766
12/98	2,450	—	—	25,000
12/97	2,340	—	—	25,000
12/96	2,250	—	—	25,000
12/95	2,130	—	—	—
Annual Growth	**6.0%**	**—**	**—**	**3.1%**

Revenue History

Weil, Gotshal & Manges

The seeds of Weil, Gotshal & Manges (WGM) may have been planted in New York City, but its branches have grown globally. Founded in 1931, the law firm has 20 offices worldwide. WGM strives to integrate the expertise of its more than 1,200 lawyers across all practice areas for the benefit of clients such as General Electric, Hicks, Muse, Tate & Furst, and CBS. Its office in Washington, DC, for example, lends legislative support and its Silicon Valley office offers technology know-how. WGM is well-known for its business finance and restructuring practice; other practice areas include energy, real estate, tax law, and trusts and estates.

EXECUTIVES

Chairman and Executive Partner:
Stephen J. Dannhauser
Executive Director: John W. Neary
CFO: Norman W. LaCroix
CIO: Jim McGinnis
Chief Marketing Officer: Katherine D'Urso
Associate Executive Director: Rob Singer
Associate Relations Director: Brad Scott
Auxiliary Legal Services Director: Kevin Curtin
Director Global Diversity: Lisa Cuevas
Human Resources Director: Pat Bowers
Management Information Systems Director:
Randy Buckart
Professional Development Director: Victoria Alzapiedi
Library Services Manager: Deborah Cinque
Associate Relations Manager, Diversity: Larry Perkins

LOCATIONS

HQ: Weil, Gotshal & Manges LLP
767 5th Ave., New York, NY 10153
Phone: 212-310-8000   **Fax:** 212-310-8007
Web: www.weil.com

Weil, Gotshal & Manges has US offices in Austin, Dallas, and Houston; Texas; Boston; Miami; New York City; Providence, Rhode Island; Redwood Shores, California; Washington, DC; and Wilmington, Delaware. It has international offices in Brussels; Budapest, Hungary; Frankfurt and Munich, Germany; London; Paris; Prague, Czech Republic; Shanghai; Singapore; and Warsaw, Poland.

PRODUCTS/OPERATIONS

Selected Practice Areas

Advertising
Aviation finance
Bankruptcy
Business finance and restructuring
Capital markets
Corporate
Energy
Executive compensation
Health care
Intellectual property
Litigation
Mergers and acquisitions
Real estate
Securities
Sports
Tax
Technology
Trade practices and regulatory law
Trusts and estates

COMPETITORS

Cleary Gottlieb
Clifford Chance
Cravath, Swaine
Paul, Weiss, Rifkind
Proskauer Rose
Shearman & Sterling
Sidley Austin Brown & Wood
Simpson Thacher
Skadden, Arps
Sullivan & Cromwell
Wachtell, Lipton
White & Case

HISTORICAL FINANCIALS

Company Type: Partnership

Income Statement
FYE: December 31

	REVENUE ($ mil.)	NET INCOME ($ mil.)	NET PROFIT MARGIN	EMPLOYEES
12/03	801	—	—	—
12/02	688	—	—	—
12/01	581	—	—	—
12/00	506	—	—	—
12/99	440	—	—	1,800
12/98	400	—	—	1,700
12/97	354	—	—	1,600
12/96	322	—	—	—
12/95	306	—	—	—
12/94	311	—	—	—
Annual Growth	**11.1%**	**—**	**—**	**6.1%**

Revenue History

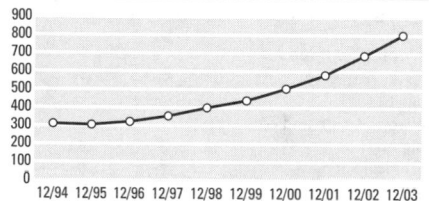

Werner

If a man's reach exceeds his grasp, perhaps he should buy a Werner — the company is the world's #1 producer of ladders. For the do-it-yourselfer, Werner makes extension, step, attic, and platform ladders made of wood, fiberglass, or aluminum; professional products include work platforms and ladder jacks. In addition to traditional ladders, Werner manufactures a full line of professional grade planks, scaffolding, specialty ladders, stages, and ladder accessories. The company also makes extruded products and fabricated parts for the architectural, automotive, construction, and electronics industries. Investment group Investcorp controls Werner.

Werner Co. was founded in 1922 by Richard Werner, as R. D.Werner Co. The company pioneered the industry's first aluminum ladders in 1951, and the first fiberglass ladders in 1963. Investcorp helped recapitalize Werner in 1997 and subsequently took control of the company.

EXECUTIVES

Chairman: Donald M. Werner, age 71
Interim President and CEO: Dana R. Snyder, age 58
President and CEO Holding (PA) and Holding (DE), and Director: Steven P. Richman
SVP, Operations: Peter R. O'Coin, age 57, $285,577 pay
SVP, Product Marketing and Development: John M. Remmers
SVP, Product Development: John J. Fiumefreddo, age 50
SVP, Sales: Edward W. Gericke, age 47, $228,462 pay
VP, CFO, and Treasurer: Larry V. Friend, age 58, $228,462 pay
VP, Secretary, and General Counsel: Eric J. Werner, age 42, $392,385 pay
VP, Manufacturing: Steven R. Bentson, age 55, $259,615 pay
Director, Human Resources: John Guyton
Auditors: PricewaterhouseCoopers LLP

LOCATIONS

HQ: Werner Co.
93 Werner Rd., Greenville, PA 16125
Phone: 724-588-8600 **Fax:** 724-588-0315
Web: www.wernerladder.com

Werner Co. has manufacturing locations in Alabama, California, Illinois, Kentucky, and Pennsylvania.

PRODUCTS/OPERATIONS

2004 Sales

	$ mil.	% of total
Climbing products	373.5	84
Extruded products	72.7	16
Total	**446.2**	**100**

COMPETITORS

Aarque
Columbus McKinnon
Danaher
JLG Industries
Nippon Light Metal
Terex

HISTORICAL FINANCIALS

Company Type: Private

Income Statement
FYE: December 31

	REVENUE ($ mil.)	NET INCOME ($ mil.)	NET PROFIT MARGIN	EMPLOYEES
12/04	446	(12)	—	1,800
12/03	501	16	3.2%	2,500
12/02	520	27	5.3%	2,800
12/01	536	16	2.9%	3,000
12/00	545	12	2.3%	3,100
12/99	485	11	2.3%	3,400
12/98	436	0	0.0%	—
12/97	416	(91)	—	—
12/96	367	19	5.3%	—
12/95	329	6	1.9%	—
Annual Growth	**3.5%**	**—**	**—**	**(11.9%)**

2004 Year-End Financials

Debt ratio: —
Return on equity: —
Cash ($ mil.): 37
Current ratio: 1.82
Long-term debt ($ mil.): 311

Net Income History

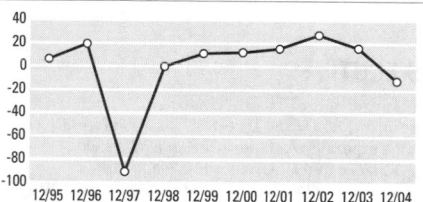

West Suburban Bancorp

West Suburban Bancorp can loan you money to buy that new Suburban. It's the holding company for West Suburban Bank, a community-oriented institution with more than 30 branches serving Chicago's western suburbs. It offers personal and business deposit products such as checking, savings, and money market accounts, and certificates of deposit, as well as loan products including commercial, consumer, and home mortgage loans. Rounding out its offerings are Visa debit, credit, and gift cards, electronic banking, and investment and trust services offered through West Suburban Financial Services.

West Suburban Bancorp also runs an insurance agency, West Suburban Insurance Services, which offers auto, home, life, and major medical insurance, and a travel agency, Travel With West Suburban.

EXECUTIVES

Chairman, CEO, and VP; SVP, Marketing, West Suburban Bank: Kevin J. Acker, age 55, $300,245 pay
President, CFO, and Director; SVP, Trust Officer, and Comptroller, West Suburban Bank: Duane G. Debs, age 48, $230,347 pay
COO; President, Trust Officer, and Director, West Suburban Bank: Keith W. Acker, age 55, $329,294 pay
VP; SVP, Commercial Lending and Community Reinvestment Act Officer, West Suburban Bank: Michael P. Brosnahan, age 54, $247,702 pay
Chief Compliance Officer, West Suburban Bancorp and West Suburban Bank: David J. Mulkerin
Director, Internal Audit; VP and Director, Internal Audit, West Suburban Bank: Michael J. Lynch
Secretary and Treasurer; VP, Assistant Comptroller, and Investment Officer, West Suburban Bank: George E. Ranstead
Chairman, West Suburban Bank: Robert W. Schulz
SVP, Business Development and Prepaid Solutions, West Suburban Bank: Daniel P. Grotto, $212,204 pay
SVP, Consumer Lending, West Suburban Bank: James T. Chippas

LOCATIONS

HQ: West Suburban Bancorp, Inc.
711 S. Meyers Rd., Lombard, IL 60148
Phone: 630-629-4200 **Fax:** 630-629-0278
Web: www.westsuburbanbank.com

PRODUCTS/OPERATIONS

2004 Sales

	$ mil.	% of total
Interest		
Loans, including fees	59.2	61
Securities	19.7	20
Federal funds sold	0.4	—
Noninterest		
Service fees on deposit accounts	7.8	8
Stored value cards	5.7	6
Debit card fees	1.8	2
Other	2.9	3
Total	**97.5**	**100**

HISTORICAL FINANCIALS

Company Type: Private

Income Statement

FYE: December 31

	ASSETS ($ mil.)	NET INCOME ($ mil.)	INCOME AS % OF ASSETS	EMPLOYEES
12/04	1,748	24	1.4%	613
12/03	1,711	26	1.5%	629
12/02	1,586	18	1.1%	598
Annual Growth	5.0%	15.1%	—	1.2%

2004 Year-End Financials

Equity as % of assets: 5.5%
Return on assets: 1.4%
Return on equity: 24.3%
Long-term debt ($ mil.): —
Sales ($ mil.): 98

Net Income History

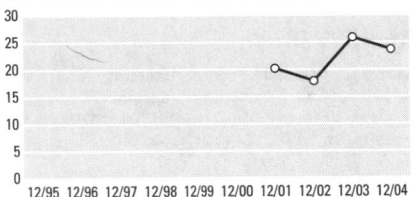

12/95 12/96 12/97 12/98 12/99 12/00 12/01 12/02 12/03 12/04

Westbrook Technologies

Westbrook Technologies is a supplier of document management software and custom software development services. The company's products are resold by a number of vendors, including IKON Office Solutions. Fortis — Westbrook's flagship software product — enables document management both within individual offices and departments and across entire enterprises. Other products include tools for Web imaging, enterprise resource management, and workflow management. Fortis and related packages are used in accounting, education, government, health care, manufacturing, publishing, telecommunications, and utilities, among other industries.

Westbrook Technologies was started in 1990 by Intelligent Optics Corporation, which later became known as IOC Westbrook; Westbrook is now owned by outside investors.

EXECUTIVES

President and CEO: Paul Lord
CFO: Paul Remington
VP, North American Sales and Regional Sales Manager, Northeast: Paul Maxwell
CTO: Marshall Pimenta
Director, Marketing: Mitchell Hallock
Director, Professional Services: Brent Wesler
Corporate Communications Manager: Tara Lallo
Marketing Research Manager: Margie Sleboda
Inside Sales: Michael Frattini

LOCATIONS

HQ: Westbrook Technologies, Inc.
22 Summit Place, Branford, CT 06405
Phone: 203-483-6666   **Fax:** 203-483-3350
Web: www.westbrooktech.com

COMPETITORS

Compulink Management Center
FileNet
Hummingbird
Hyland Software
Stellent

HISTORICAL FINANCIALS

Company Type: Private

Income Statement

FYE: December 31

	REVENUE ($ mil.)	NET INCOME ($ mil.)	NET PROFIT MARGIN	EMPLOYEES
12/04	15	—	—	60

Westcon

The Westcon Group sees more pros than cons in networking equipment. The company's three divisions — Comstor, Westcon, and Voda One — resell networking and communications equipment made by Avaya, Cisco Systems, Nortel Networks, and other top manufacturers. Networking servers, switches, and routers; network security systems; and virtual private network systems top Westcon's product list. The company also provides a variety of support services, including training, network design, and logistical support. South Africa-based networking company Datatec Ltd. owns a controlling stake in Westcon.

The company filed to raise $115 million in an IPO in March 2004, but the filing was withdrawn in March 2005. Previously, Westcon had filed to go public in January 2001; that filing was withdrawn in January 2004.

Philip Raffiani and company president and CEO Thomas Dolan founded Westcon in 1985.

EXECUTIVES

Chairman: John McCartney, age 52
President, CEO, and Director: Thomas (Tom) Dolan
SVP Corporate Operations: Brian E. Weisfeld
VP Finance and CFO: John P. O'Malley III
VP Worldwide Business Operations and Chief Risk Officer: Russ Fein, age 40
VP Marketing and Investor Relations: Jenny Pappas
VP Worldwide Marketing: Duncan Potter
VP Technology Solutions Group: Paul Cunningham
CIO: Jason Molfetas
SVP and General Manager, the Americas, Westcon Group North America: Anthony Daley, age 39, $377,456 pay
VP and General Manager, U.S., Westcon Group North America: Carol Rivetti, age 42, $333,692 pay
Managing Director, Comstor Europe: Simon J. England, age 39, $312,601 pay
Communications: Jeff Touzeau
Auditors: Deloitte & Touche LLP

LOCATIONS

HQ: Westcon Group, Inc.
520 White Plains Rd., Ste. 100,
Tarrytown, NY 10591
Phone: 914-829-7000   **Fax:** 914-829-7137
Web: www.westcongroup.com

Westcon Group has operations in Australia, Austria, Belgium, Brazil, Canada, Denmark, France, Germany, Ireland, the Netherlands, Norway, Singapore, South Africa, Spain, Sweden, the UK, and the US.

PRODUCTS/OPERATIONS

Selected Products

Data caching servers
Integrated communication systems
Internet servers
Network security systems
Network switches and routers
Videoconferencing systems
Virtual private network systems
Wireless network access systems

Selected Services

Inventory management
Logistics
Network design and consulting
Support
Technical services
Training

COMPETITORS

Avaya
CDW
Cisco Systems
CompuCom
En Pointe
Ingram Micro
Nortel Networks
Pomeroy IT
Resilien
ScanSource
Tech Data

HISTORICAL FINANCIALS

Company Type: Private

Income Statement

FYE: Last day in February

	REVENUE ($ mil.)	NET INCOME ($ mil.)	NET PROFIT MARGIN	EMPLOYEES
2/04	1,885	6	0.3%	1,000
2/03	1,649	(92)	—	1,000
2/02	1,687	16	0.9%	1,000
2/01	2,066	59	2.8%	1,059
2/00*	1,168	21	1.8%	1,057
3/99	587	22	3.7%	—
3/98	334	7	1.9%	—
Annual Growth	33.4%	(1.9%)	—	(1.4%)

*Fiscal year change

2004 Year-End Financials

Debt ratio: 13.2%
Return on equity: 2.1%
Cash ($ mil.): 114
Current ratio: 1.66
Long-term debt ($ mil.): 37

Net Income History

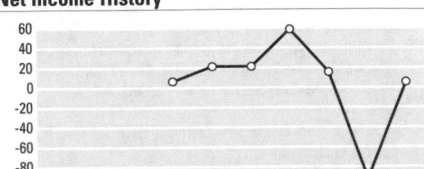

3/95 3/96 3/97 3/98 3/99 2/00 2/01 2/02 2/03 2/04

Western Family Foods

From mayo to mops, Western Family Foods supplies private-label products to more than 3,500 independent grocery retailers in 23 US states, including Alaska and Hawaii. It also sells in Mexico, Russia, Japan, China, Hong Kong, and other Pacific Rim countries. Its main brands are Better Buy, Market Choice Shur Saving, Shurfine (no relation to competitor Shurfine International), and Western Family. Western Family coordinates with manufacturers and wholesalers to produce more than 6,000 products, including dry grocery, frozen, deli, household, and heath and beauty care items.

Founded in 1934, Western Family Foods is part of a consortium that buys general merchandise and sells it to independent retailers. Wholesalers Affiliated Foods, Associated Food Stores, Associated Grocers, and Unified Western Grocers own Western Family.

EXECUTIVES

President and CEO: Ronald S. King
SVP and CFO: Russ Jones
SVP, Procurement: Robert Cutler
SVP Sales and Marketing: David (Dave) Hayden
VP, Information Systems: Gregg Floren
VP, International: Charlie Rotta
VP, Quality Assurance: Roy Besand
Manager, Human Resources: Martina Nilles

LOCATIONS

HQ: Western Family Foods, Inc.
6700 SW Sandburg St., Tigard, OR 97223
Phone: 503-639-6300   **Fax:** 503-684-3469
Web: www.westernfamily.com

In addition to distributing its products in 23 states, Western Family Foods exports to Chile, China, Fiji, Hong Kong, Indonesia, Japan, Malaysia, Mexico, Micronesia, Panama, Guam, the Philippines, Russia, Singapore, South Korea, Taiwan, Thailand, and Vietnam.

PRODUCTS/OPERATIONS

Selected Private Labels

Better Buy
Market Choice
Shur Saving
Shurfine
Western Family

COMPETITORS

AWG
Colgate-Palmolive
Kraft Foods
Kraft Foods North America
McLane
Nash Finch
Procter & Gamble
Ralcorp
Rich Products
Sara Lee
SUPERVALU
SYSCO
Unilever
Unilever NV
Unilever PLC

HISTORICAL FINANCIALS

Company Type: Private

Income Statement   FYE: April 30

	ESTIMATED REVENUE ($ mil.)	NET INCOME ($ mil.)	NET PROFIT MARGIN	EMPLOYEES
4/05	630	—	—	75
4/04	612	—	—	75
4/03	590	—	—	75
4/02	560	—	—	75
4/01	500	—	—	74
4/00	500	—	—	74
4/99	500	—	—	74
4/98	500	—	—	70
Annual Growth	3.4%	—	—	1.0%

Revenue History

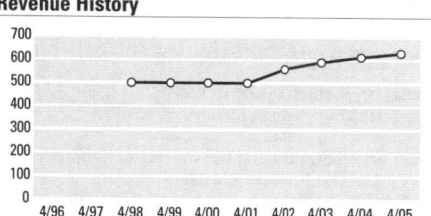

Western Refining

It's not its refined air but its refined products that make Western Refining a major player in the West. The independent oil refiner and marketer operates primarily in Arizona, New Mexico, and West Texas. Western Refining's refinery has a crude oil refining capacity of 108,000 barrels per day. More than 90% of its refined products are made up of light transportation fuels, including diesel, gasoline, and jet fuel. In addition, the refinery has a storage capacity of 4.3 million barrels and a 43,000 barrels-per-day product marketing terminal. Western Refining's refinery complex has access to both crude oil and refined product pipelines, courtesy of Kinder Morgan Energy Partners and Chevron.

The company's refined products sell at a premium on the Gulf Coast due to increasing demand and limited local refining capacity. In Phoenix, Western Refining also benefits from tighter EPA fuel specifications that require the use of cleaner burning gasoline. As a consequence, Phoenix CBG fuel is the company's highest-margin product.

EXECUTIVES

President, CEO, and Director: Paul L. Foster, age 47, $1,036,808 pay
COO: Ralph A. Schmidt, age 59, $785,769 pay (prior to promotion)
CFO and Treasurer: Gary R. Dalke, age 53, $326,000 pay (prior to promotion)
EVP and Director: Jeff A. Stevens, age 41, $891,962 pay
VP Services: Emmett Reagan
Chief Administrative Officer, Secretary, and Director: Scott D. Weaver, age 47, $630,904 pay (prior to title change)
Manager Safety: Larry Whipple
Auditors: Ernst & Young LLP

LOCATIONS

HQ: Western Refining, Inc.
6500 Trowbridge Dr., El Paso, TX 79905
Phone: 915-775-3300   **Fax:** 915-881-0002
Web: www.westernrefining.com

COMPETITORS

Alon USA Energy
ConocoPhillips
Giant Industries
Holly
Valero Energy

HISTORICAL FINANCIALS

Company Type: Private

Income Statement   FYE: December 31

	REVENUE ($ mil.)	NET INCOME ($ mil.)	NET PROFIT MARGIN	EMPLOYEES
12/04	2,215	68	3.0%	350
12/03	925	41	4.4%	—
12/02	446	26	5.8%	—
Annual Growth	122.8%	60.8%	—	—

2004 Year-End Financials

Debt ratio: 41.8%
Return on equity: 76.6%
Cash ($ mil.): 45

Current ratio: 1.45
Long-term debt ($ mil.): 45

Net Income History

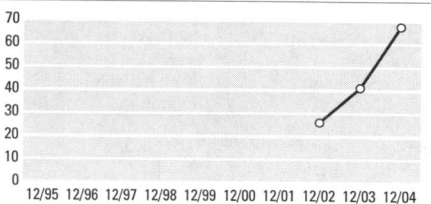

Whataburger

When you see that familiar orange and white roof, you know you're in for a Whataburger. With more than 600 owned and franchised outlets, the company operates a popular fast-food chain in Texas, Oklahoma, and eight other southern states. Whataburger restaurants are typically open 24 hours a day and serve burgers and fries along with breakfast items (taquitos, pancakes), fajitas, chicken, and salads. Less than half of the company's restaurants are franchised. Loyal Whataburger fans can don the company's line of apparel sporting the chain's logo. The late Harmon Dobson founded Whataburger in Corpus Christi, Texas, in 1950. His family (including Dobson's son, chairman and CEO Thomas Dobson) owns the company.

Despite the fact that Whataburger has a much smaller presence than its national competitors, the chain continues to be a powerful player in its native Texas because of the intense loyalty of its customers.

The company is expanding through new franchising agreements and repurchased franchise outlets. It bought some 100 franchised locations in Texas, New Mexico, Oklahoma, and Louisiana and in Mexico from its largest franchisee, Whataco, in April 2004.

EXECUTIVES

Chairman, President, and CEO:
Thomas E. (Tom) Dobson
EVP and COO: Preston L. Atkinson
CFO: Wendy A. Beck
EVP: John M. McLellan
Chief Restaurant Operations Officer: Robert R. Moore
VP Benefits Services: Jim Langenkamp
VP Franchise Development: James G. Turcotte
VP Supply Management: Dino Del Nano
VP Regional Operations: Jeffery Bankston
VP Brand Management: Todd A. Coerver
Controller: Ed Nelson
Human Resources: Marianne Dowdy
Human Resources: Debbie Nunez
Corporate Communications Coordinator: Lori Smith
Auditors: KPMG LLP

LOCATIONS

HQ: Whataburger, Inc.
1 Whataburger Way, Corpus Christi, TX 78411
Phone: 361-878-0650   **Fax:** 361-878-0473
Web: www.whataburger.com

Whataburger has about 600 fast-food restaurants in Alabama, Arizona, Arkansas, Florida, Georgia, Louisiana, Mississippi, New Mexico, Oklahoma, and Texas, as well as a small number in Mexico.

COMPETITORS

AFC Enterprises	Krystal
Braum's	McDonald's
Burger King	Quiznos
Checkers Drive-In	Schlotzsky's
Chick-fil-A	Sonic
CKE Restaurants	Steak n Shake
Dairy Queen	Subway
Fatburger	Taco Bueno
Hardee's	Taco Cabana
In-N-Out Burgers	Triarc
Jack in the Box	Wendy's
Jason's Deli	YUM!

HISTORICAL FINANCIALS

Company Type: Private

Income Statement

	REVENUE ($ mil.)	NET INCOME ($ mil.)	NET PROFIT MARGIN	EMPLOYEES
9/04	500	—	—	13,000
9/03	460	—	—	12,000
9/02	448	—	—	11,000
9/01	395	—	—	9,500
9/00	352	—	—	8,800
9/99	309	—	—	8,400
9/98	291	—	—	8,800
9/97	265	—	—	8,000
9/96	248	—	—	7,500
9/95	240	—	—	7,200
Annual Growth	**8.5%**	**—**	**—**	**6.8%**

FYE: September 30

Revenue History

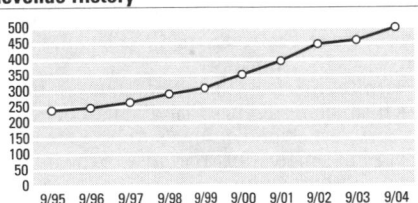

White & Case

What do you call a law firm with some 1,700 lawyers? Well, the safe answer would be White & Case. One of the world's largest law firms, White & Case has buoyed its global reputation by establishing some 35 international offices in locations such as Bangkok, Thailand; Budapest, Hungary; Istanbul, Turkey; London; Paris; Riyadh, Saudi Arabia; and Warsaw, Poland (the firm also maintains six US offices, including its New York City headquarters). Among White & Case's practice areas are bankruptcy, corporate, intellectual property, litigation, project finance, and tax. The firm's client list has included Deutsche Bank and Royal Ahold. White & Case was founded in 1901.

EXECUTIVES

Managing Partner: Duane D. Wall
Administrative Partner: David N. Koschik
CFO: James Latchford
Chief Knowledge Officer: Eugene Stein
Chief Marketing Officer: Liz Pava
Director Media Relations: Roger J. Cohen
Director Administration: Richard M. McKenna
Director Finance: Gregory J. Dolan
Director Human Resources: Jill Connors
Director Marketing, Americas: Helene R. Freymann
EU Law & Policy Advisor, Brussels: Vincent Artis
Associate, Frankfurt: Christian Bartels

LOCATIONS

HQ: White & Case LLP
1155 Avenue of the Americas, New York, NY 10036
Phone: 212-819-8200   **Fax:** 212-354-8113
Web: www.whitecase.com

White & Case has offices in Africa, the Americas, Asia, Europe, and the Middle East.

PRODUCTS/OPERATIONS

Selected Practice Areas

Antitrust
Arbitration and alternative dispute resolution
Bankruptcy and reorganization
Corporate
Employee benefits
Insurance
Intellectual property
Litigation
Mergers and acquisitions
Project finance
Public Finance
Tax
Telecommunications

COMPETITORS

Akin Gump	Marks & Clerk
Baker & McKenzie	Mayer, Brown,
Bryan Cave	Rowe & Maw
Clifford Chance	Milbank, Tweed
Cravath, Swaine	Morgan, Lewis
Debevoise & Plimpton	Pillsbury Winthrop
Dewey Ballantine	Shaw Pittman
Freshfields	Proskauer Rose
Holland & Knight	Schulte Roth & Zabel
Jones Day	Sidley Austin Brown
Kaye Scholer	& Wood
Latham & Watkins	Skadden, Arps
LeBoeuf, Lamb	Weil, Gotshal

HISTORICAL FINANCIALS

Company Type: Partnership

Income Statement

FYE: December 31

	REVENUE ($ mil.)	NET INCOME ($ mil.)	NET PROFIT MARGIN	EMPLOYEES
12/03	811	—	—	—
12/02	675	—	—	—
12/01	603	—	—	—
12/00	491	—	—	—
12/99	405	—	—	2,500
12/98	352	—	—	2,300
12/97	318	—	—	2,200
12/96	282	—	—	—
12/95	247	—	—	—
12/94	233	—	—	—
Annual Growth	**14.9%**	**—**	**—**	**6.6%**

Revenue History

White Castle

The treasure room of this fast food fortress contains Slyders. White Castle System owns and operates more than 390 hamburger joints known for their little square burgers called Slyders. The meat patty is steamed over a bed of onions rather than grilled and served on a steamed bun with a single slice of pickle. Patrons typically consume a sack of Slyders at a time. White Castle restaurants can be found in about a dozen states, primarily in the Midwest. The company also sells frozen Slyders through supermarket chains. The first fast food chain in the US, White Castle was founded by Walter Anderson and real estate broker E. W. "Billy" Ingram in 1921. The Ingram family continues to control the company.

Little has changed at White Castle over the years, from its Slyders to its castle-shaped buildings. That has helped the chain establish strong loyalty among both customers and employees. However, its reluctance to franchise and its lack of television advertising have caused the venerable chain to fall far behind fast food giants such as McDonald's and Burger King. Yet in 2004 the company lent its name and product to the movie *Harold and Kumar Go to White Castle* — a rare high-visibility moment for the chain. White Castle does sell branded items (caps, mugs, and shirts) to keep its loyal fans happy and engaged.

In addition to its hamburger business, White Castle System owns PSB Company, a subsidiary that makes metal products and equipment, including fixtures and cooking tools used at the company's restaurants. PSB also makes lawn spreaders under the PrizeLAWN brand.

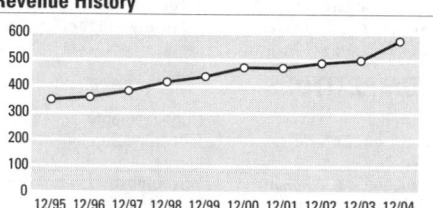
Whiting-Turner Contracting

Whiting-Turner Contracting is a big fish in an ocean of builders. The employee-owned firm provides construction management, general contracting, and design/build services, primarily for large commercial, institutional, and infrastructure projects in the US. It subcontracts roughly 85% of its volume, but also offers in-house mechanical and electrical review, concrete forming, foundation, and structural steel services. A key player in retail construction, the company also undertakes such projects as biotech cleanrooms, educational facilities, stadiums, and corporate headquarters for such clients as AT&T and General Motors. G. W. C. Whiting and LeBaron Turner founded the company in 1909 to build sewer lines.

Whiting-Turner Contracting's recent projects include the Joseph B. Whitehead Building at Emory University, Vanderbill Hall at Yale University, and a vaccine facility at Chesapeake Biological Laboratories, Inc. Projects for the firm's hometown of Baltimore have included the city's convention center and Harborplace.

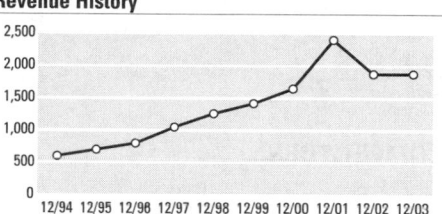
WinCo Foods

WinCo Foods isn't just big on self-service — it's giant. Inside the immense stores (average size is 90,000 sq. ft.) of this mostly employee-owned supermarket chain, customers shop for food in bulk and bag their own groceries. The company's 40-plus stores also feature pizza shops, bakeries, health and beauty products, and organic foods. WinCo Foods, formerly known as Waremart Foods, was renamed as a shortened version of "winning company." The name is also an acronym for its states of operation, which include Washington, Idaho, Nevada, California, and Oregon. Founded in 1968, WinCo Foods formerly operated stores under the Cub Foods and Waremart names. Employees, past and present, own about 80% of the company.

SUPERVALU, the nation's leading grocery wholesaler, sold its minority stake in Winco back to the company in April 2003.

EXECUTIVES

Chairman and CEO: William D. (Bill) Long
President COO, and Director: Scott Preece
VP, Finance and Director: Gary R. Piva
EVP, Retail Operations: Steve Goddard
VP, Advertising: Sharon Kadell
VP, Engineering: Dick VanderLinden
VP, Information Technology: Glen Reynolds
VP, Labor and Human Resources: Roger Cochell
VP, Marketing and Promotions: Dave Strausborger
VP, Public and Legal Affairs: Michael (Mike) Read
Controller: Del Ririe

LOCATIONS

HQ: WinCo Foods, Inc.
650 N. Armstrong Place, Boise, ID 83704
Phone: 208-377-0110　　**Fax:** 208-377-0474
Web: www.wincofoods.com

2005 Stores

	No.
Oregon	16
California	14
Idaho	8
Washington	7
Nevada	2
Total	**47**

PRODUCTS/OPERATIONS

Selected Store Departments

Bakery
Bulk foods
Delicatessen
Fresh meat
Health and beauty aids
Organic products
Pizza shop
Produce
Seafood

COMPETITORS

Albertson's	Raley's
Associated Food	Safeway
AWG	Stater Bros.
Costco Wholesale	Unified Western Grocers
Fred Meyer Stores	Wal-Mart
Haggen	

HISTORICAL FINANCIALS

Company Type: Private

Income Statement

FYE: March 31

	REVENUE ($ mil.)	NET INCOME ($ mil.)	NET PROFIT MARGIN	EMPLOYEES
3/04	2,000	—	—	7,500
3/03	1,700	—	—	7,100
3/02	1,540	—	—	6,500
3/01	1,300	—	—	5,300
3/00	1,160	—	—	5,000
3/99	940	—	—	4,900
Annual Growth	**16.3%**	**—**	**—**	**8.9%**

Revenue History

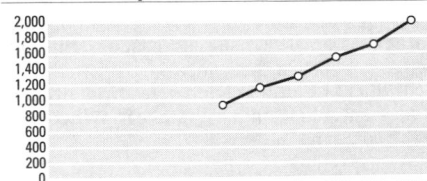

---

wine.com

Maybe you heard it through the grapevine — wine.com (formerly eVineyard) is the largest online wine retailer in the US. wine.com sells more than 14,000 domestic and imported wines in 36 states and sells wine accessories in all 50 states. The company also does business in Japan via a Japanese version of its Web site and a local distributor, SanSonoma. eVineyard bought top competitor wine.com in 2001 and adopted the wine.com name in 2002. Launched in 1999, wine.com is owned by private investors, including Angel Investors and Bear Creek Corp.

Wine.com now sells wine through the help of Amazon.com. The online retailer has partnered with wine.com because the company has leaped many hurdles to shipping wine to multiple US states. Wine.com does business with wholesalers in states that require a three-step process to wine sales (manufacturer-distributor-retailer), does not ship wine to counties that prohibit the sale of alcohol, and requires wine shipments to be signed and verified online.

EXECUTIVES

Chairman: Chris Kitze
President and CEO: George R. Garrick
CFO: John Belchers
SVP, Business Development: Russell (Russ) Fradin
SVP, Gift Services: Lisa Consani
SVP, Operations: David Standridge
SVP, Internet Marketing: Lincoln Silver
CIO/CTO: Francis Juliano
General Manager, Gift Services: Jay Shaffer
General Manager, Wines: Michael J. (Mike) Osborn
Manager, Human Resources: Tina Estrada
Auditors: PricewaterhouseCoopers

LOCATIONS

HQ: wine.com, Inc.
114 Sansome St., 6th Fl., San Francisco, CA 94104
Phone: 415-291-9500　　**Fax:** 415-291-9599
Web: www.wine.com

COMPETITORS

1-800-FLOWERS.COM
Geerlings & Wade
M. Shanken Communications
Sam's Wines & Spirits

HISTORICAL FINANCIALS

Company Type: Private

Income Statement

FYE: December 31

	REVENUE ($ mil.)	NET INCOME ($ mil.)	NET PROFIT MARGIN	EMPLOYEES
12/04	32	—	—	—
12/03	22	—	—	60
12/02	14	—	—	34
12/01	25	—	—	58
12/00	10	—	—	50
Annual Growth	**33.7%**	**—**	**—**	**6.3%**

Revenue History

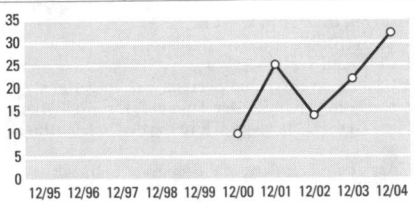

WinWholesale

You Win some, you Win some more. So it goes for WinWholesale (formerly Primus). The company is invested in more than 430 small-to-medium wholesale distributors in about 40 states that sell plumbing, heating, air-conditioning, electrical, and other supplies to contractors and other professional customers. The companies are easily recognizable by their Win-prefixed names, such as Columbia Winnelson, Salt Lake Windustrial, and Dayton Winfastener. WinWholesale supports these companies with bulk purchasing, warehousing, accounting, and data processing. After operating as Primus for more than 40 years, the company (owned by heirs of the investors who founded it in 1956) changed its name to WinWholesale in 2004.

EXECUTIVES

President: Richard W. Schwartz
CIO/CTO: Jeffrey Dana
VP, National Sales, WinWholesale: Gary Benaszeski
Treasurer/Comptroller: Jack W. Johnston
Director, Corporate Communications and Secretary: Bruce Anderson
Director, Finance: Ward Allen
Director, Human Resources: Thomas Snow

LOCATIONS

HQ: WinWholesale Inc.
3110 Kettering Blvd., Dayton, OH 45439
Phone: 937-294-6878　　**Fax:** 937-293-9591
Web: www.winholesale.com

PRODUCTS/OPERATIONS

Selected Businesses

Winair (heating, ventilation, air conditioning, and refrigeration)
Windustrial (industrial pipes and valves)
Winfastener (specialty fasteners)
Winlectric (electrical supplies and products)
Winnelson (plumbing)
Winpump (pumps and accessories)
Wintronic (electronic parts and equipment)
Winwaterworks (waterworks and utility supplies)

COMPETITORS

Fastenal	Hughes Supply
Ferguson Enterprises	Johnstone Supply
Gensco	Lowe's
Groeniger & Company	MSC Industrial Direct
Hajoca Corporation	Noland
Home Depot	W.W. Grainger

HISTORICAL FINANCIALS

Company Type: Private

Income Statement — FYE: January 31

	REVENUE ($ mil.)	NET INCOME ($ mil.)	NET PROFIT MARGIN	EMPLOYEES
1/04	1,200	—	—	3,000
1/03	1,100	—	—	3,195
1/02	1,001	—	—	3,195
1/01	1,040	—	—	3,093
1/00	931	—	—	3,037
1/99	780	—	—	2,175
Annual Growth	9.0%	—	—	6.6%

Revenue History

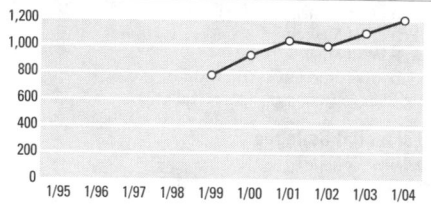

Wirtz

Wirtz does best on ice. Led by CEO William Wirtz, it owns the Chicago Blackhawks hockey team and is partnered with Jerry Reinsdorf, of the Chicago Bulls basketball team, for ownership of the United Center, where both teams play. Wirtz owns liquor distributorships, including Judge & Dolph, the largest in Illinois, and Edison Liquor Co. The firm owns property in Wisconsin, Mississippi, Texas, Nevada, and Florida. Arthur Wirtz (father of William Wirtz) founded the family-controlled empire in 1922.

Wirtz's Judge & Dolph is the exclusive distributor of Allied Domecq brands in Illinois and also has rights to distribute some key Diageo brands such as Crown Royal, Johnny Walker, J&B, and Tanqueray.

The Wirtz family gave thousands of dollars to state lawmakers in 1999 to pass a law protecting liquor distributors by making it difficult for liquor producers to switch distributors. (The law later was declared unconstitutional.)

EXECUTIVES

CEO: William W. Wirtz, age 76
CFO: Max Mohler
VP: W. R. (Rocky) Wirtz
VP Human Resources: Cindy Kirch
VP, Judge & Dolph Ltd.: Julian Burzynski
Controller: Linda Bescalli

LOCATIONS

HQ: Wirtz Corporation
680 N. Lakeshore Dr., 19th Fl., Chicago, IL 60611
Phone: 312-943-7000   **Fax:** 312-943-9017

Wirtz operates liquor distributorships in Illinois, Iowa, Minnesota, Nevada, Texas, and Wisconsin.

PRODUCTS/OPERATIONS

Selected Distribution Companies
DeLuca Liquor and Wine (Las Vegas)
  Nevada Wine Agents
  Silver State Distributors (Reno)
Edison Liquor Corp. (Brookfield, Wisconsin)
Griggs, Cooper & Co. (St. Paul, Minnesota)
Judge & Dolph, Ltd. (Wood Dale, Illinois)
Mediterranean Imports Wine Company
  (Elk Grove, Illinois)

COMPETITORS

Columbus Blue Jackets	National Distributing
Detroit Red Wings	National Wine & Spirits
Glazer's Wholesale Drug	Southern Wine & Spirits
Johnson Brothers	St. Louis Blues
Nashville Predators	Young's Market

HISTORICAL FINANCIALS

Company Type: Private

Income Statement — FYE: June 30

	ESTIMATED REVENUE ($ mil.)	NET INCOME ($ mil.)	NET PROFIT MARGIN	EMPLOYEES
6/04	1,000	—	—	2,200
6/03	1,000	—	—	2,200
6/02	865	—	—	2,100
6/01	850	—	—	2,000
6/00	880	—	—	2,100
6/99	830	—	—	2,100
6/98	700	—	—	2,100
6/97	675	—	—	2,100
6/96	600	—	—	2,100
6/95	600	—	—	1,800
Annual Growth	5.8%	—	—	2.3%

Revenue History

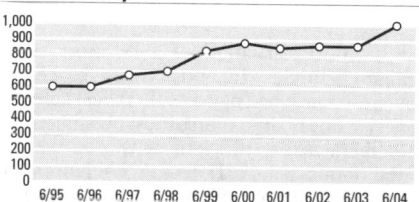

WL Homes

WL Homes, doing business as John Laing Homes, is one of the largest homebuilders in Southern California; it also builds in Colorado. John Laing Homes builds homes and communities for first-time to luxury homebuyers. Its John Laing Urban division develops communities in Southern California. The company sells more than 2,045 homes a year. It offers financing through JLH Mortgage. WL Homes was created from the 1998 merger of John Laing Homes (UK) and Watt Homes in the US. In 2001 John Laing Homes (UK) sold more than half of its stake in the company (retaining 22%) to an investor group led by chairman Ray Watt and CEO Larry Webb. *Professional Builder* magazine named John Laing Homes its 2004 Builder of the Year.

EXECUTIVES

Chairman: Ray Watt
CEO: H. Lawrence (Larry) Webb
CFO: Wayne J. Stelmar
EVP Sales and Marketing: William B. (Bill) Probert
VP People: Alejandro Macia
Treasurer: Shahram Gheysari
Region President, Colorado; Division President, Denver: Richard (Rich) Staky
Region President, Northern California: Jack Davidson
Region President, Southern California; Division President, South Coast (Orange County/San Diego, CA): Steve Kabel
Division President, Colorado Springs: Ron Covington
Division President, Inland Empire, CA: Terry Neale
Division President, Los Angeles/Ventura: Bill Rattazzi
Division President, Sacramento: Kevin Carson
Division President, Laing Luxury (Southern California): Tom Redwitz

LOCATIONS

HQ: WL Homes LLC
895 Dove St., Ste. 200, Newport Beach, CA 92660
Phone: 949-265-2400   **Fax:** 949-265-2500
Web: www.johnlainghomes.com

WL Homes operates divisions in California: Inland Empire, Los Angeles/Ventura, Orange County/South Coast, Sacramento, San Diego, John Laing Urban (Culver City), and Laing Luxury (Southern California). It also has divisions in Colorado in Colorado Springs and Denver.

COMPETITORS

Brookfield Homes	NVR
Centex	Pulte Homes
D.R. Horton	Ryland
Fannie Mae	Standard Pacific
Freddie Mac	Taylor Woodrow, Inc.
Hovnanian Enterprises	Toll Brothers
Larwin Company	Wells Fargo
Lennar	Home Mortgage
M.D.C. Holdings	

HISTORICAL FINANCIALS

Company Type: Private

Income Statement — FYE: December 31

	REVENUE ($ mil.)	NET INCOME ($ mil.)	NET PROFIT MARGIN	EMPLOYEES
12/04	1,480	—	—	—
12/03	744	—	—	—
12/02	701	—	—	—
12/01	600	—	—	—
12/00	603	—	—	—
Annual Growth	25.2%	—	—	—

Revenue History

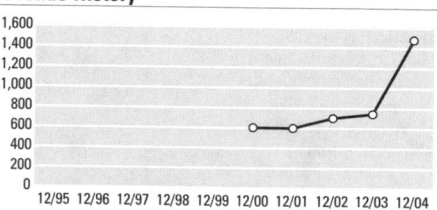

Wyle Laboratories

Wyle Laboratories provides engineering, testing, and other technical support services to clients in such industries as aerospace, life sciences, telecommunications, and transportation. In addition to serving commercial and industrial customers, the company is also a large government contractor providing services to the various branches of the US military, as well as NASA. Wyle Laboratories was founded in 1949 and operates more than a dozen research and testing facilities around the country. In 2005 it acquired the aeronautics services business of General Dynamics.

EXECUTIVES

Chairman: Constantinos D. (Gus) Yiakas
President and CEO: George R. Melton
EVP and CFO: L. Craig Smith
SVP: Joe Kerwin
SVP and General Manager, Life Sciences Systems and Services: Bob Ellis
SVP and General Manager, Technical Support Services: Drexel Smith
VP Contracts: Bob Houser
Controller: Doug Van Kirk
Director of Acoustics Research and Consulting: Ben Sharp
Director of Engineering: Gordon Bakken
Director of Human Resources: Tom Stinson
Director of Information Services: Bach Tran
Corporate Communications Manager: Dan Reeder

LOCATIONS

HQ: Wyle Laboratories, Inc.
128 Maryland St., El Segundo, CA 90245
Phone: 310-322-1763   **Fax:** 310-322-3603
Web: www.wylelabs.com

PRODUCTS/OPERATIONS

Selected Operations

Life Sciences Systems and Services
  Aircrew performance
  Biotechnology
  Environmental research
  Medical operations and research
  Space flight hardware
Technical Support Services
  Calibration and repair services
  Computer system support
  Digital systems repair and maintenance
  Engineering services
  Laboratory operations outsourcing
  Laboratory services
  Logistics management
  Metrology management
Test and Engineering
  Aerospace and defense testing
  Acoustic research
  Commercial testing
  Special test systems
  Utility services

COMPETITORS

Bureau Veritas
Exponent
Intertek
National Technical Systems
Orbital Research
SGS
SRI International

HISTORICAL FINANCIALS

Company Type: Private

Income Statement

FYE: December 31

	REVENUE ($ mil.)	NET INCOME ($ mil.)	NET PROFIT MARGIN	EMPLOYEES
12/04	450	—	—	3,000
12/03	200	—	—	1,500
12/02	150	—	—	1,500
Annual Growth	73.2%	—	—	41.4%

Revenue History

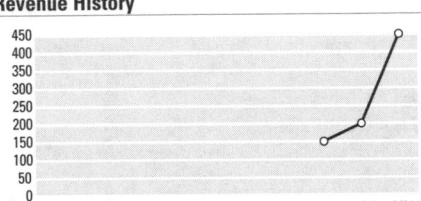

Yale University

What do President George W. Bush, writer William F. Buckley Jr., and actress Meryl Streep have in common? They are all Yalies. Yale University is one of the nation's most prestigious private liberal arts institutions, as well as one of its oldest (founded in 1701). Its $12.7 billion endowment ranks second only to Harvard's in the US. Yale comprises an undergraduate college, a graduate school, and 10 professional schools. Programs of study include architecture, law, medicine, and drama. Its 12 residential colleges (a system borrowed from Oxford) serve as dormitory, dining hall, and social center. The school has more than 11,200 students and some 3,200 faculty members.

EXECUTIVES

President: Richard C. Levin
Provost: Andrew D. Hamilton
VP and Secretary: Linda Koch Lorimer, age 52
VP and General Counsel: Dorothy K. Robinson
VP Development: Ingeborg T. (Inge) Reichenbach
VP Finance and Administration: John E. Pepper Jr., age 66
VP; Director, New Haven and State Affairs: Bruce D. Alexander
Associate VP Human Resources and Chief Human Resources Officer: Robert Schwartz
Associate VP Administration: Janet E. Lindner
Assistant VP and Controller: Cary B. Scapillato
Executive Director Alumni Association: Jeffrey Brenzel
Auditors: PricewaterhouseCoopers LLP

LOCATIONS

HQ: Yale University
246 Church St., New Haven, CT 06520
Phone: 203-432-2331   **Fax:** 203-432-2334
Web: www.yale.edu

PRODUCTS/OPERATIONS

Colleges and Schools

Graduate School of Arts and Sciences
Professional schools
  School of Architecture
  School of Art
  School of Divinity
  School of Drama
  School of Forestry & Environmental Studies
  School of Law
  School of Management
  School of Medicine
  School of Music
  School of Nursing
Yale College (undergraduate studies)

Residential Colleges

Berkeley College
Branford College
Calhoun College
Davenport College
Ezra Stiles College
Jonathan Edwards College
Morse College
Pierson College
Saybrook College
Silliman College
Timothy Dwight College
Trumbull College

COMPETITORS

Brown University
Columbia University
Cornell University
Dartmouth
Harvard University
Princeton University
University of Pennsylvania

HISTORICAL FINANCIALS

Company Type: School

Income Statement

FYE: June 30

	REVENUE ($ mil.)	NET INCOME ($ mil.)	NET PROFIT MARGIN	EMPLOYEES
6/03	2,565	—	—	8,071
6/02	1,467	—	—	7,577
6/01	1,353	—	—	7,398
6/00	1,264	—	—	10,800
6/99	1,150	—	—	10,318
6/98	1,083	—	—	9,685
6/97	992	—	—	10,000
6/96	931	—	—	9,200
6/95	948	—	—	10,000
6/94	902	—	—	9,600
Annual Growth	12.3%	—	—	(1.9%)

Revenue History

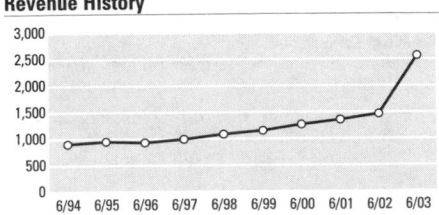

YMCA

If the Village People can be believed, it's fun to stay at the YMCA. One of the nation's largest not-for-profit community service organizations, YMCA of the USA assists the more than 2,500 individual YMCAs across the country and represents them on both national and international levels. YMCAs serve almost 19 million people across the US. One of the largest child-care providers in the US, YMCAs also offer programs in areas such as aquatics, arts and humanities, health and fitness, and teen leadership. The first YMCA in the US was established in 1851 as an outgrowth of the YMCA movement launched by George Williams in the UK in 1844.

Dedicated to continuing education, YMCA of the USA has created YMCA University through a partnership with Cornell University and its online program eCornell. The program provides professional development classes to the staff and volunteers at YMCAs across the country. John R. Mott, who won a Nobel Peace prize in 1946 for his leadership of the YMCA, graduated from Cornell.

EXECUTIVES

Chairman: Daniel A. Casey
National Executive Director: Kenneth L. Gladish
CFO: Kate Spencer
CIO: Jeff Bundy
General Counsel and Secretary: Jan Koran
Chief Marketing Officer: JoAnna Taylor
National Director for Arts and Humanities:
Jason Shinder
Director of Movement Advancement: Sam Evans
Director of Association Financial Development:
Stephen Burns
Director of Corporate Relations: Monique Hanson
Director of Development: Tom Colligan
Director of Human Resources: Sharon Rakowski
Director of International Group: Jerry Prado Shaw
Director of Leadership Development: Daniel Nussbaum
Director of Membership and Program Development Group: Carmelita Gallo
Director of National Philanthropic Initiatives:
Mark C. Johnson
Director of Operations and Chief Solution Officer:
Marie Lynch
Director of Philanthropy and Financial Development:
Bruce L. Berglund
Director of Public Relations & Communication:
Kevin Shermach

LOCATIONS

HQ: YMCA of the USA
101 N. Wacker Dr., Chicago, IL 60606
Phone: 312-977-0031   **Fax:** 312-977-9063
Web: www.ymca.net

YMCAs are located in all 50 states in the US and more than 120 countries worldwide.

PRODUCTS/OPERATIONS

Selected YMCA Programs
Aquatics
Arts and humanities
Camping
Child-care
Community development
Family
Health and fitness
International
Older adults
SCUBA
Sports
Teen leadership

HISTORICAL FINANCIALS
Company Type: Not-for-profit

Income Statement
FYE: June 30

	REVENUE ($ mil.)	NET INCOME ($ mil.)	NET PROFIT MARGIN	EMPLOYEES
6/03	77	1	1.2%	340
6/02	72	(1)	—	303
6/01*	44	3	6.4%	240
12/00	80	12	14.9%	—
12/99	60	(1)	—	—
Annual Growth	6.5%	—	—	19.0%

*Fiscal year change

Net Income History

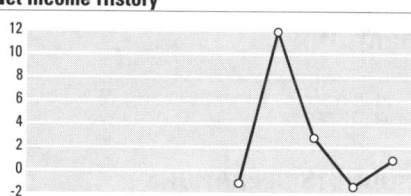

Young's Market

Although no longer young, Young's Market Company is in high spirits. Young's Market is one of the largest distributors of beer, wine, and distilled spirits in the US. The company is a major supplier along the Pacific coast. It also operates in Hawaii through its Better Brands subsidiary. Young's Market distributes products for Bacardi, Brown-Forman, and other distillers and winemakers. In California it distributes wines of the Chalone Wine Group and Brown-Forman's Sonoma-Cutrer Vineyards. John Young founded the company in 1888, which at one time included grocery retailing and specialty food distribution. The Underwood family, relatives of the Youngs, bought Young's Market in 1990.

EXECUTIVES

Chairman and CEO: Vernon O. Underwood
President: Jeffrey Underwood
EVP and CFO: Dennis J. Hamann
EVP, Operations: John Klein
VP, Human Resources: Craig Matsuda

LOCATIONS

HQ: Young's Market Company, LLC
2164 N. Batavia St., Orange, CA 92865
Phone: 714-283-4933   **Fax:** 714-283-6175

Young's Market Company primarily distributes to Alaska, California, Hawaii, Oregon, and Washington.

COMPETITORS

Beauchamp Distributing
Glazer's Wholesale Drug
National Distributing
National Wine & Spirits
Southern Wine & Spirits
Topa Equities
WinterBrook Beverage

HISTORICAL FINANCIALS
Company Type: Private

Income Statement
FYE: February 28

	REVENUE ($ mil.)	NET INCOME ($ mil.)	NET PROFIT MARGIN	EMPLOYEES
2/04	1,400	—	—	1,800
2/03	1,200	—	—	1,800
2/02	1,300	—	—	1,700
2/01	1,300	—	—	1,700
2/00	1,100	—	—	1,700
2/99	1,090	—	—	1,600
2/98	1,000	—	—	1,500
2/97	960	—	—	1,400
2/96	1,000	—	—	1,600
2/95	910	—	—	1,650
Annual Growth	4.9%	—	—	1.0%

Revenue History

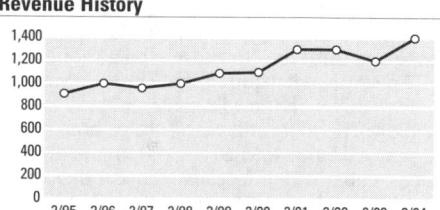

Yucaipa

Yucaipa has a hungry eye for picking out ripe bargains in different industries, but made its name with grocery stores. The investment company forged its reputation as the ultimate grocery shopper, executing a series of grocery chain mergers and acquisitions that put the company on the supermarket map. The Yucaipa Companies owns Jurgensen's, Falley's, and Alpha Beta, among other chains. The company's chairman, billionaire Ron Burkle, is a prominent Democratic activist and fundraiser; former president Bill Clinton and the Rev. Jesse Jackson serve on the company's board.

Yucaipa maintains a link to the food industry through a miniscule stake in Kroger (less than 2%), as well as a minority stake in Simon Worldwide (formerly Cyrk), a promotional marketing company whose largest customer is McDonald's. Yucaipa's portfolio also includes Alliance Entertainment (a distributor of music, videos, and games), TDS Logistics (automotive logistics services), and Piccadilly Restaurants. The firm has provided $100 million in financial backing to rapper/mogul Sean "Diddy" Combs' clothing line, Sean John.

Yucaipa sold its 50% stake in McDonald's supplier Golden State Foods to that firm's management and Wetterau Associates in early 2004.

Some of its investments have run into bumps in the road: Kmart filed for bankruptcy in 2002, and Simon Worldwide faced numerous lawsuits stemming from a scandal after an employee allegedly rigged its client McDonald's Monopoly games and stole the cash.

HISTORY

Ronald Burkle launched his career in the grocery industry as a box boy at his dad's Stater Bros. grocery store. By age 28 Burkle had moved up to SVP of administration, but he was fired after botching a buyout of the company in 1981.

Burkle and former Stater Bros. colleagues Mark Resnik and Douglas McKenzie founded Yucaipa (named after Burkle's hometown of Yucaipa, California) in 1986 when they bought Los Angeles gourmet-grocery chain Jurgensen's. The next year Yucaipa bought Kansas-based Falley's, which had 20 Food 4 Less stores in California.

In 1989 Yucaipa merged with Breco Holding, operator of 70 grocery stores, and bought Northern California's Bell Markets. It acquired ABC Markets in Southern California in 1990. The next year the company bought the 142-store chain Alpha Beta. Thirty-six Yucaipa stores were damaged in the 1992 Los Angeles riots, but Yucaipa rebuilt, working with unions to keep workers employed until the stores were operational.

The company acquired the 28-store Smitty's Super Valu chain (now Fred Meyer Marketplace) in 1994. The following year Yucaipa bought the 70-year-old family-owned chain Dominick's Finer Foods. Later in 1995 Yucaipa's Food 4 Less chain merged with Los Angeles competitor Ralphs Grocery (founded in 1873 by George Ralphs), making Yucaipa #1 in Southern California.

Yucaipa sold Smitty's to Utah-based Smith's in 1996, acquiring a minority stake in Smith's (Burkle became Smith's CEO). Dominick's went public in 1996, and Yucaipa retained a minority stake. The next year Fred Meyer bought Smith's for $1.9 billion. Burkle became the acquired company's chairman, and Yucaipa gained a 9% interest in Fred Meyer.

In 1998 Fred Meyer bought Ralphs and 155-store Quality Food Centers (QFC). Yucaipa and Wetterau Associates, a management firm, bought Golden State Foods, giving Yucaipa a 70% stake in the McDonald's food supplier. Yucaipa sold Dominick's to Safeway.

After Kroger bought Fred Meyer in 1999, Yucaipa turned away from the consolidating grocery industry and moved into cyberspace. That year Burkle and former Walt Disney president Michael Ovitz launched CheckOut Entertainment Network, which operated CheckOut.com, an entertainment Web site at which Web surfers could buy books, music, and videogames. Yucaipa hired Richard Wolpert, former president of Disney Online, to oversee its Internet and technology activities.

Yucaipa added to its portfolio in 1999 by taking stakes in GameSpy (online games), Talk City (later LiveWorld, online chat service), OneNetNow (online communities), ClubMom (Web site for mothers), and Cyrk (now Simon Worldwide, promotional marketing). Yucaipa also bought music, video, and games distributor Alliance Entertainment. The company also holds a minority stake in Simon Worldwide.

Music and video retailer Wherehouse Entertainment became a 50%-owner of CheckOut.com after it merged its online retailing operations with CheckOut.com in 1999. (As the Internet economy faltered, Yucaipa sold CheckOut.com in 2001.)

In 2000 the company digressed from its focus on the Web to invest in Kole Imports, an importer of merchandise sold in discount stores.

Yucaipa sold its stakes in grocery distributor Fleming and discount retailer Kmart in 2001 before both companies crashed and burned into bankruptcy.

YWCA

Although it has yet to be immortalized in a song like its male counterpart, YWCA of the U.S.A. promotes the empowerment of women and girls through thousands of locations across the US. The not-for-profit organization provides 2.5 million women with services such as sports and physical fitness programs, shelters, child care, employment training and job placement, and youth development programs. It also sponsors racial justice, antiviolence, and human rights advocacy programs. YWCA of the U.S.A. is a founding member of World YWCA, which represents more than 25 million women in about 100 countries. The first YWCA in the US was founded in New York City in 1858. The national organization was created in 1907.

HISTORICAL FINANCIALS

Company Type: Not-for-profit

Income Statement   FYE: August 31

	REVENUE ($ mil.)	NET INCOME ($ mil.)	NET PROFIT MARGIN	EMPLOYEES
8/99	18	5	27.8%	—
8/98	15	(0)	—	90
8/97	26	8	32.2%	125
8/96	20	1	3.5%	100
8/95	12	—	—	75
8/94	10	—	—	65
Annual Growth	12.3%	92.6%	—	8.5%

Net Income History

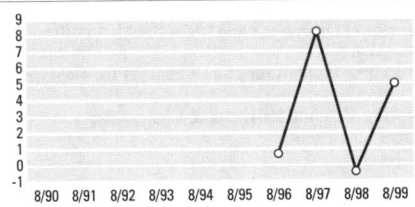

Zachry Construction

H. B. Zachry began building roads and bridges in 1924, and now his son and grandsons are running the show. Zachry Construction builds and maintains power and chemical plants, steel and paper mills, refineries, roadways, dams, airfields, and pipelines. Operating mostly in Texas and the southeastern US, Zachry has built facilities for companies such as Alcoa, DuPont, Honeywell, and Southern Company. It also operates internationally and has worked on several US embassy projects. In addition, Zachry owns interests in ranches and in oil exploration, cement, hospitality, and realty companies, as well as a stake in the San Antonio Spurs basketball team. The Zachry family owns the firm.

The company has agreed to acquire Denver-based energy engineering firm Utility Engineering, including its Precision Resource, Proto-Power, and Universal Utility Services subsidiaries, from Xcel Energy.

EXECUTIVES

Chairman: H. Bartell Zachry Jr.
CEO and Director: John B. Zachry
President, COO, and Director: David S. Zachry
SVP: Edward R. Bardgett
SVP, Controller, and Director: Joe J. Lozano
SVP Corporate Business Development:
Keith D. Manning
SVP and Manager, Power: Robert J. (Bob) Kalt
SVP Corporate Development: Kenneth A. (Ken) Oleson
SVP Finance and Director: D. Kirk McDonald
VP Administration, Accounting, and Director:
Charles Ebrom
VP, General Counsel, Secretary, and Director:
Murray L. Johnston Jr.
VP Employee Relations: Stephen L. (Steve) Hoech
Director Public Affairs: Victoria Waddy
Auditors: Ernst & Young

LOCATIONS

HQ: Zachry Construction Corporation
527 Logwood Ave., San Antonio, TX 78221
Phone: 210-475-8000   **Fax:** 210-475-8060
Web: www.zachry.com

Zachry Construction has offices in Arizona, Florida, Louisiana, Texas, and North Carolina. It also has an international office in Saudi Arabia.

COMPETITORS

Aker Kværner
Alberici
APAC
Austin Industries
Barton Malow
Bechtel
Black & Veatch
Dick Corporation
Fluor
Foster Wheeler
Gilbane
Granite Construction
Hensel Phelps
  Construction
Hoffman Corporation
Holloman
Jacobs Engineering
KBR
M. A. Mortenson
McCarthy Building
MWH Global
Parsons
Peter Kiewit Sons'
Polysius
Shaw Group
Sumitomo Mitsui
  Construction
TIC Holdings
Turner Industries
Washington Group
Williams Brothers
  Construction

HISTORICAL FINANCIALS

Company Type: Private

Income Statement

FYE: December 31

	REVENUE ($ mil.)	NET INCOME ($ mil.)	NET PROFIT MARGIN	EMPLOYEES
12/04	966	—	—	9,096
12/03	1,007	—	—	12,000
12/02	1,700	—	—	14,000
12/01	1,940	—	—	14,000
12/00	1,400	—	—	14,000
12/99	1,195	—	—	11,000
12/98	670	—	—	7,500
12/97	660	—	—	7,500
12/96	775	—	—	7,625
12/95	780	—	—	10,100
Annual Growth	2.4%	—	—	(1.2%)

Revenue History

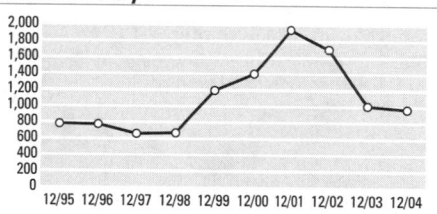

Zephyr Software

Zephyr Software, formerly Zephyr Development, was founded in 1985 as a custom software development and information technology consulting firm. The company now specializes in terminal emulation software packages for older IBM computers and other "legacy" systems. Customers include Banner Health, Charles Schwab, the Cook County (Illinois) government, Eastern Illinois University, Scott & White Memorial Hospital, and Willis Group Holdings. President Greg Ledford and EVP David Muck started Zephyr.

EXECUTIVES

President and CTO: Vernon G. (Greg) Ledford, age 49
EVP: David L. Muck, age 46

LOCATIONS

HQ: Zephyr Software Ltd.
8 E. Greenway Plaza, Ste. 1414, Houston, TX 77046
Phone: 713-623-0089   **Fax:** 713-623-0091
Web: www.zephyrcorp.com

COMPETITORS

Blueprint Technologies
Liant Software
Micro Focus

HISTORICAL FINANCIALS

Company Type: Private

Income Statement

FYE: December 31

	REVENUE ($ mil.)	NET INCOME ($ mil.)	NET PROFIT MARGIN	EMPLOYEES
12/04	3	—	—	8

Hoover's Handbook of

Private Companies

The Indexes

Index by Industry

Midwest Research Institute 341
Research Triangle Institute 428
SRI International 466
Wyle Laboratories 554

CHARITABLE ORGANIZATIONS

American Cancer Society 41
American Red Cross 46
Feed The Children 197
Goodwill 217
Heifer Project International 239
Salvation Army 437
United Way 515

CHEMICALS

Agricultural Chemicals
Phibro Animal Health 399

Basic & Intermediate Chemical & Petrochemical Manufacturing
Astaris 64
Badger State Ethanol 69
Chevron Phillips Chemical 125
J.M. Huber 275
Technology Flavors & Fragrances 482
Tronox 501

Chemical Distribution
Royster-Clark 435

Paints, Coatings & Other Finishing Product Manufacturing
Daubert Industries 157
Spraylat 464

Plastic & Fiber Manufacturing
Dow Corning 175
Teknor Apex 483

Specialty Chemical Manufacturing
Flint Ink 200
Hexion Specialty Chemicals 244
Koppers (KI Holdings Inc.) 293
NCH 364

COMPUTER HARDWARE

Computer Networking Equipment
AESP 29
nCircle Network Security 365

Computer Peripherals
SmartDisk 456
ViewSonic 534

COMPUTER SERVICES

Computer Generated Solutions 138

Computer Products Distribution & Support
ASI Corp. 60
D&H Distributing 152
Derive Technologies 165
Electrograph Technologies 186
Software House 457
Westcon 548

Information Technology Services
Alion Science and Technology 33
Caritor 112
DecisionOne 161
Forsythe Technology 206
InfoReliance 260
NCI 364

Science Applications International 446

COMPUTER SOFTWARE

Asset Management Software
Primavera Systems 409

Business Intelligence Software
SAS Institute 439

Collaborative Software
IntraLinks 266

Content & Document Management Software
eCopy 185
Westbrook Technologies 548

Customer Relationship Management, Marketing & Sales Software
Blue Martini Software 89
Vocus 537

Development Tools, Operating Systems & Utilities Software
California Software 105
Green Hills Software 223
SL Corporation 455

E-commerce Software
Model N 346

Education & Training Software
Datatel 156

Engineering, Scientific & CAD/CAM Software
Engineous Software 189

Enterprise Resource Planning Software
Activant Solutions 23

Financial Services, Legal & Government Software
BancTec 72
DealerTrack 160
SunGard Data Systems 474
United Systems Technology 514

Health Care Management Software
IMPAC Medical Systems 258
Medical Information Technology 327

Human Resources & Workforce Management Software
Recruitmax Software 422

Multimedia, Graphics & Publishing Software
ArcSoft 55

Networking & Connectivity Software
Zephyr Software 557

Security Software
eAcceleration 182

Supply Chain Management & Logistics Software
NextLinx 376

CONSTRUCTION

Construction & Design Services
Adams Homes 23
AECOM Technology 28
A. G. Spanos 17

American Homestar 44
Barton Malow 73
BE&K 76
Bechtel 77
Black & Veatch 85
Brand Intermediate 97
CH2M HILL 124
Choice Homes 127
Day & Zimmermann 158
Drees Co. 178
Dunn Industries 180
Gilbane 213
Hensel Phelps Construction 242
J.F. Shea 273
John Wieland Homes 276
Kimball Hill 287
Kitchell 289
Louis Berger Group 307
McCarthy Building 323
Parsons 388
Patriot Homes 390
The PBSJ Corporation 391
Peter Kiewit Sons' 397
Rooney Holdings 433
Structure Tone 474
Swinerton 477
Turner Industries 506
Walsh Group 542
Whiting-Turner Contracting 551
WL Homes 553
Zachry Construction 557

Construction Materials
Andersen 53
Associated Materials 61
G-I Holdings 211
Hampton Affiliates 232
JELD-WEN 272
Kohler 292
McFarland Cascade 324
Nortek 377
Pella 391

CONSUMER PRODUCTS MANUFACTURERS

Apparel
Broder Bros. 98
Crocs 149
Levi Strauss 300
New Balance 365

Appliances
Alliance Laundry 35
BISSELL Homecare 84
Conair 139
iRobot 267
Minuteman International 345

Cleaning Products
JohnsonDiversey 277
S.C. Johnson 441

Consumer Electronics
Bose 94
Telex Communications 483

Hand Tools, Power Tools, Lawn & Garden Equipment
MTD Products 349

Home Furniture
Ashley Furniture 60
Berkline/BenchCraft 80
Sauder Woodworking 440

Housewares
American Achievement 39
Amscan 50
Home Products International 249
Jostens 280

Jewelry & Watch Manufacturing
Timex 490

Linens
Springs Industries 465

Mattress & Bed Manufacturers
Sealy 447

Musical Equipment
Taylor-Listug 480

Office & Business Furniture, Fixtures & Equipment
Haworth 235

Personal Care Products
Alticor 37
Forever Living 206
John Paul Mitchell 275
MacAndrews & Forbes 310
Mary Kay 317

Pet Products
Doane Pet Care 171
Professional Veterinary Products 411

Sporting Goods & Equipment
Colt Defense 135
Colt's Manufacturing 136
Golfsmith 216
ICON Health 256
Remington Arms 425
True Temper Sports 501

Toys & Games
Ty 508

CONSUMER SERVICES

Automotive Service & Collision Repair
American Tire 48

Car & Truck Rental
Enterprise Rent-A-Car 189
Frank Consolidated Enterprises 207

Travel Agencies & Services
Carlson Wagonlit 113

CULTURAL INSTITUTIONS

National Geographic 357
Smithsonian Institution 456

EDUCATION

Child Care Services & Elementary & Secondary Schools
LPA Holding 309

Colleges & Universities
California State University 106
City University of New York 130
Columbia University 136
Cornell University 145
Harvard University 234
Indiana University 259
Michigan State University 338
New York University 373
Northern Illinois University 377
Northwestern University 379
Ohio State University 382
Princeton University 410
Southern Illinois University 460
Stanford University 468
State University of New York 471
Texas A&M 484
University of Alabama 516

Index by Headquarters

ALABAMA

Birmingham
BE&K 76
EBSCO 184
Jack's Family Restaurants 270
McWane 326

Tuscaloosa
University of Alabama 516

ALASKA

Anchorage
Chugach Electric 128

ARIZONA

Chandler
Bashas' 73

Phoenix
Best Western 81
Desert Schools Federal Credit
 Union 166
Kitchell 289
Leslie's Poolmart 299
Phoenix Suns 401
Shamrock Foods 451

Scottsdale
Cold Stone Creamery 134
Coyotes Hockey 148
Desert Island Restaurants 166
Discount Tire 169
Forever Living 206

ARKANSAS

Little Rock
Heifer Project International 239

Stuttgart
Riceland Foods 430

CALIFORNIA

Alameda
Oakland Raiders 380

Aliso Viejo
Buy.com 103

Anaheim
The Mighty Ducks of Anaheim 341
Penhall International 392
Specialty Restaurants 463

Artesia
California Dairies 105

Beverly Hills
Academy of Motion Picture Arts and
 Sciences 21
John Paul Mitchell 275
Platinum Equity 403

Burbank
WB Television Network 544

Calabasas
ValleyCrest 530

Carlsbad
Jazzercise 272
SkinMedica 455

Colton
Stater Bros. 472

Commerce
Unified Western Grocers 511

Concord
JCM Partners 272

Corte Madera
SL Corporation 455

Costa Mesa
Anna's Linen 54

Cypress
Real Mex Restaurants 422

El Cajon
Taylor-Listug 480

El Segundo
Los Angeles Lakers 306
Wyle Laboratories 554

Fontana
California Steel 107

Foster City
QuinStreet 418
Visa 535

Fountain Valley
Kingston Technology 288

Fremont
ArcSoft 55
ASI Corp. 60
New United Motor Manufacturing 367

Glendale
DreamWorks 176

Hayward
Mervyn's 333

Inglewood
Herbalife 242

Irvine
El Pollo Loco 186
Golden State Foods 215
Ritz Interactive 431

Lake Forest
InSight Health Corp. 262
SPARTA 462

Livingston
Foster Poultry Farms 207

Long Beach
California State University 106
Holthouse Carlin & Van Trigt 248
It's A Grind Coffee Franchise 269

Los Altos
Harman Management 233
Packard Foundation 387

Los Angeles
AECOM Technology 28
Cook Inlet Energy Supply 144
DMX MUSIC 170
Forever 21 205
Latham & Watkins 298
Los Angeles Clippers 306
Los Angeles Kings 306
Metro-Goldwyn-Mayer 334
O'Melveny & Myers 383
Paul, Hastings 390
University of Southern California 523
Vivid Entertainment 536
Yucaipa 555

Menlo Park
SRI International 466

Modesto
E. & J. Gallo 181
Save Mart 440

Moorpark
Special Devices 462

Mountain View
IMPAC Medical Systems 258

Newport Beach
Irvine Company 268
Pacific Mutual 385
WL Homes 553

Nicasio
Lucasfilm 309

North Hollywood
Academy of Television Arts &
 Sciences 21

Oakland
Crowley Maritime 149
Golden State Warriors 216
Kaiser Foundation Health Plan 282
Kaiser Permanente 283
University of California 517

Ontario
Kaiser Ventures 283

Orange
Young's Market 555

Pasadena
Parsons 388

Pismo Beach
Pismo Coast Village 402

Rancho Cordova
Vision Service Plan 536

Redwood City
Genomic Health 210

Roseville
Adventist Health 26

Sacramento
CalPERS (California Public
 Employees' Retirement System) 108
Sacramento Kings 436
Sutter Health 477

San Clemente
California Software 105

San Diego
It's Just Lunch 269
Memec 330
Science Applications
 International 446
SGX Pharmaceuticals 450
TransWestern Publishing 498

San Fernando
Precision Dynamics 407

San Francisco
Bechtel 77
Blue Shield of California 89
Catholic Healthcare West 119
Delta Dental of California 164
Jamba Juice 271
Levi Strauss 300
nCircle Network Security 365
Sierra Club 452
Swinerton 477
wine.com 552

San Jose
Fry's Electronics 208
Portola Packaging 406
Silicon Valley Sports &
 Entertainment 452

San Mateo
Blue Martini Software 89

San Ramon
24 Hour Fitness 16
Caritor 112
Sydran Services 478

Santa Ana
GeoLogistics 210

Santa Barbara
Green Hills Software 223

Morton Grove
Schwarz Paper 445

Mt. Sterling
Dot Foods 173

Mundelein
Medline Industries 328

Naperville
Eby-Brown 184

Northbrook
Culligan 150

Oak Brook
Ace Hardware 22
Advocate Health Care 27
Inland Retail Real Estate Trust 262

River Grove
Follett 203

Rolling Meadows
Kimball Hill 287

Rosemont
Reyes Holdings 429

Schaumburg
Pliant 404

Skokie
Forsythe Technology 206
Rand McNally 421
Topco Associates 492

Springfield
Illinois Lottery 258

Urbana
University of Illinois 519

Westmont
Ty 508

INDIANA

Anderson
Remy 425

Bloomington
Indiana University 259

Elkhart
Patriot Homes 390

Evansville
BPC Holding 96

Indianapolis
Aearo 28
Indiana Pacers 259
National Wine & Spirits 361

Mishawaka
Quality Dining 417

IOWA

Breda
Breda Telephone 98

Des Moines
MidAmerican Energy 339

Hills
Hills Bancorporation 247

Iowa City
University of Iowa Hospitals and
Clinics 519

Pella
Pella 391

West Des Moines
Hy-Vee 255

KANSAS

Kansas City
Associated Wholesale Grocers 63
Interconnect Devices 263

Leawood
Houlihan's Restaurants 251

Overland Park
Black & Veatch 85
Scoular 447

Shawnee Mission
VT 538

Topeka
Security Benefit Group 448

Wichita
Airxcel 32
Koch Industries 290

KENTUCKY

Ashland
International Coal Group 265

Bowling Green
Houchens 250

Fort Mitchell
Drees Co. 178

Louisville
Kentucky Lottery 285
University of Louisville 520

LOUISIANA

Baton Rouge
Turner Industries 506

DeRidder
AMERISAFE 49

Franklin
Sterling Sugars 473

New Orleans
New Orleans Hornets 366

MAINE

Freeport
L.L. Bean 304

MARYLAND

Baltimore
The Chimes 127
Maryland State Lottery 318
NAACP 352
Under Armour 510
Vertis 533
Whiting-Turner Contracting 551

Beltsville
Ritz Camera 431

Bethesda
Clark Enterprises 131
FLAVORx 200

Chestertown
Peoples Bancorp, Inc. 396

Germantown
Avalon Pharmaceuticals 67

Hagerstown
Phoenix Color 400

Hanover
Allegis Group 34

Lanham
Vocus 537

Rockville
Goodwill 217
NextLinx 376

Salisbury
Perdue Farms 396

Silver Spring
Discovery Communications 169

MASSACHUSETTS

Boston
ABP 20
Boston Red Sox 95
CombinatoRx 138
Eastern Bank 183
FMR 202
Houghton Mifflin 250
International Data Group 265
Liberty Mutual 302
New Balance 365
Newkirk Realty Trust 374
Uno Restaurant Holdings 526

Burlington
iRobot 267

Cambridge
Harvard University 234

Canton
Cumberland Farms 150
Plymouth Rubber 404

Chelsea
Gulf Oil 228
HP Hood 252

Framingham
Bose 94

Lakeville-Middleboro
Ocean Spray 380

Lawrence
NxStage Medical 380

Lexington
Predix Pharmaceuticals 407

Littleton
Dover Saddlery 174

Needham
Fresh Concepts 207

Newton
UNICCO Service 510

Northborough
Bertucci's 81

Pittsfield
KB Toys 284

Springfield
Big Y Foods 82
Massachusetts Mutual Life
Insurance 320

Tewksbury
Demoulas Super Markets 165

Waltham
Softworld 458
Tufts Associated Health Plans 506

Westford
Cynosure 151

Westwood
Medical Information Technology 327

MICHIGAN

Ada
Alticor 37

Ann Arbor
Flint Ink 200
University of Michigan 520

Auburn Hills
Guardian Industries 226

Battle Creek
Kellogg Foundation 284

Bloomfield Hills
Penske 394
TriMas Corporation 500

Clinton Township
Tubby's Sub Shops 505

Dearborn
Percepta 396

Detroit
Blue Cross Blue Shield of
Michigan 88
Detroit Medical Center 167
Henry Ford Health System 241

East Lansing
Michigan State University 338

Grand Rapids
BISSELL Homecare 84
Meijer 329
Spectrum Health 463

Holland
Haworth 235

Kentwood
Autocam 66

Lansing
Auto-Owners Insurance 67

Livonia
Market Strategies 315

Madison Heights
Hungry Howie's Pizza & Subs 253

Mason
Dart Container 155

Midland
Dow Corning 175
Midland Cogeneration Venture 340

Novi
Trinity Health 501

Plymouth
Metaldyne 334
Plastipak Holdings 403

Southfield
Barton Malow 73
Qualitor 416
W. B. Doner & Company 539

Southgate
ASC 58

Sterling Heights
Key Safety Systems 286

Warren
Cold Heading Company 134

MINNESOTA

Alexandria
Tastefully Simple 479

Arden Hills
Land O'Lakes 296

Index of Executives

A

Aamold, Gary L. 392
Aaron, Roger S. 454
Abel, David 426
Abel, Gregory E. 339
Abel, Rick 464
Abeles, Jon C. 119
Abell, G. Hughes 308
Abernethy, David S. 237
Abfalter, Dan 16
Abington, Bill 328
Ableidinger, Bryan R. 503
Abney, Donald R. 97
Abold, Phillip 33
Abraham, Jay 353
Abrahamson, James R. 255
Abramowski, Robert J. 480
Abrams, Jim 328
Abrams, Sarah K. 203
Abramson, Richard 466
Abutaleb, Mona 170
Acacio, R. Bruce 106
Acchione, David 435
Accordino, Daniel T. 116
Achermann, Hubert 294
Achtenberg, Roberta 106
Acker, Keith W. 547
Acker, Kevin J. 547
Ackerman, Greg 301
Acone, Adam 360
Acosta, Alan 469
Acosta, Belen J. 158
Adair, Janna 333
Adamonis, Richard C. 372
Adams, Alvan 401
Adams, Andy 166
Adams, Ben C. Jr. 71
Adams, Carolyn 258
Adams, Daniel (Midland Financial) 340
Adams, Daniel L. (The Fund) 66
Adams, Donna 109
Adams, Edward 190
Adams, J. Phillip 201
Adams, James 209
Adams, Melvin L. 32
Adams, Mike 214
Adams, Ralph G. 164
Adams, Richard C. 76
Adams, Staci 169
Adams, Stan 26
Adams, Stephen 30
Adams, Thomas W. 501
Adams, Wayne 23
Adamson, Terrence B. 358
Adante, David E. 157
Addison, Roger G. 501
Adelman, Rick 436
Adkins, Norman 461
Adler, Peter G. 225
Adlich, Gregory 460
Admire, Dan 251
Afable, Mark V. 43
Affleck, Bruce 468

Afterman, Jean 374
Agarwal, Shisir 301
Agre, Ross D. 92
Agres, Robert E. 71
Agresto, Larry 458
Aguiar, Randall S. 480
Ahearn, Joseph A. 124
Ahern, Joe 349
Ahlfeld, Roger C. 526
Ahlquist, David A. 322
Ahmad, Asif 179
Ahrens, E. Edward 182
Ahrold, Robbin 90
Aiello, Greg 357
Aigner, Stefan 425
Akin, Steven P. 203
Alayeto, George 141
Albarian, Mark 37
Albero, Carl M. 446
Alberts, Charles 284
Albright, Carl 260
Album, Jeff 164
Aldape, Porfirio 100
Alderman, Ken 213
Aldridge, Philip R. 524
Alexa Strauss, Julie 198
Alexander, Bruce D. 554
Alexander, Jimmy 22
Alexander, John 58
Alexander, Ken 383
Alexander, Leslie L. 252
Alexander, S. Tyrone 246
Alfirevic, Richard G. 539
Alfonsi, Thomas J. 284
Alford, Mack L. 469
Alge, David 375
Alic, James M. 25
Alifano, John 152
Alimanestianu, Alexander A. 494
Allain, Keith 468
Allan, Linda J. 364
Allbritton, Barbara B. 34
Allbritton, Robert L. 34
Alldian, David P. 90
Allen, Anne E. 372
Allen, Ashley 342
Allen, Christopher D. 428
Allen, Dale 124
Allen, David W. 227
Allen, Eric 245
Allen, Floyd 167
Allen, Fran 365
Allen, James C. (Southern Wine & Spirits) 461
Allen, James R. (NASD) 354
Allen, Jeff 289
Allen, Katherine 196
Allen, Keith 103
Allen, Kenneth 230
Allen, Matthew N. 256
Allen, Meredith B. 469
Allen, Nancy 409
Allen, Paul G. 406, 539
Allen, Rich 391
Allen, Robert C. 124

Allen, Ward 552
Allen, William 328
Allison, Herbert M. 489
Allison, Linda 100
Alm, Nancy 162
Almassy, Stephen E. 192
Almond, Stephen 164
Alonzo, Jan R. 512
Alpert, Richard H. 359
Alpert, Warren 542
Alspaugh, Robert W. 294
Altendorf, Michael J. 22
Alterman, Simon 194
Altherr, Jack R. Jr. 68
Altieri, Michael 306
Altman, Lawrence B. 250
Altman, Steven J. 147
Alton, Jack 544
Altstadter, Jeff 366
Alvarez, Michael 23
Alvarez, Scott G. 197
Alzapiedi, Victoria 546
Amador, Evelyn 515
Amaral, José 235
Amato, Thomas 334
Ambersley, Joseph D. 387
Ambrose, Jill 213
Ambrose, Lou 251
Ambrose, Thomas 401
Amburn, Linda 236
Amendola, Michael 254
Amenita, Chris 58
Amidon, Paige 143
Ammon, Donald R. 26
Amos, Christopher 33
Amparan, Oscar L. 486
Amsigner, Gary 323
Anand, Sudeep 457
Ancarrow, N. Hopper Jr. 460
Ancier, Garth 544
Andelin, Roger 103
Andereck, Mike 180
Andersen, Ralph E. 477
Anderson, Brian (Allina Hospitals) 36
Anderson, Brian (ContiGroup) 144
Anderson, Bruce 552
Anderson, Cathy C. 503
Anderson, Cindy 430
Anderson, Craig 449
Anderson, David (Thrivent Financial) 488
Anderson, David R. (American Family Insurance) 43
Anderson, Dick (Noodles & Company) 376
Anderson, Douglas L. 339
Anderson, Duwayn 433
Anderson, Gary E. 175
Anderson, Gregory R. 485
Anderson, J. William 99
Anderson, James G. 322
Anderson, John (Fatburger) 195
Anderson, John F. (Catholic Health Initiatives) 118
Anderson, Ken 355

Anderson, Mark (DeCrane) 162
Anderson, Mark R. (AMERISAFE) 49
Anderson, Milton C. 193
Anderson, Mitch 341
Anderson, Paul (Providence Health System) 412
Anderson, Paul W. (Minnesota Mutual) 344
Anderson, R. John 301
Anderson, Richard (Encyclopædia Britannica) 188
Anderson, Ron 109
Anderson, Ruth (KPMG) 294
Anderson, Ruth (University of Wisconsin) 526
Anderson, Steven 498
Anderson, Tom 421
Anderson, Walter 24
Anderson, William 501
Andow, David 134
Andreassen, Inge 47
Andree, Timothy P. 356
Andrejccyk, Donald R. 405
Andreola, Albert V. 248
Andrews, David V. 400
Andrews, Duane P. 446
Andrews, Gloria Moore 108
Andrews, Kris 526
Andrews, Michael 213
Andrews, Paul (Denver Nuggets) 165
Andrews, Paul (Grant Thornton International) 220
Andrews, Paul E. Jr. (TTI Inc.) 505
Andrews, R. Michael Jr. 100
Andrews, Theron 110
Andrulonis, David L. 219
Andrus, Tom 473
Anger, Michael 487
Angle, Colin 268
Anglin, David M. 403
Angotti, Vincent 425
Angulo, Carlos 422
Ankeney, Shane 540
Annetta, John 168
Anschuetz, Christopher 327
Anschutz, Philip F. 306
Anson, Mark J.P. 108
Anstey, Judd 57
Anteau, Lisa 545
Antebi, Eric 452
Anthony, J. Rodger 146
Antonvich, Mark S. 244
Apallas, Yeoryios 385
Apatoff, Robert S. 421
Appell, Lawrence 309
Apperson, Kevin 34
Appleby, Anne F. 382
Appleby, C.G. 93
Archambault, Rob 403
Archer, Thomas G. Jr. 427
Archey, Paul 312
Archibald, Ed 332
Ards, Sheila 521
Arego, John J. 364
Arena, Michael 131

Morgan, Jim 394
Morgan, Kevin 543
Morgan, Randy (Louis Berger) 307
Morgan, Randy N. (SPARTA) 462
Morgensen, Jerry L. 242
Morgenstern, Jay 58
Moriarty, Dan 235
Moriarty, Ed 95
Moriarty, Laura B. 93
Morisie, Debbie 442
Morlan, James A. 534
Morlock, Jim 369
Morlok, Jane A. 98
Morman, Louise M. 370
Morningstar, Bill 544
Moroney, Patrick E. 236
Morra, Marion E 42
Morrice, Robert R. 121
Morris, Diana 487
Morris, Ernest R. 525
Morris, John L. 74
Morris, Kenneth C. 179
Morris, R. Steven 25
Morrison, Andrew J. 315
Morrison, Craig O. 244
Morrison, Gregory B. 147
Morrison, James E. 483
Morrison, Joe 150
Morrison, John M. 36
Morrison, Larry S. 526
Morrison, Scott D. 158
Morrow, Ken 369
Morrow, Robert H. 117
Morse, Amyas C.E. 408
Morse, John 188
Morse, Philip (Schneider National) 443
Morse, Phillip H. (Boston Red Sox) 96
Mortensen, Steve 556
Mortimer, Mike 419
Morton, C. Hugh 244
Morton, Mike (H.T. Hackney) 253
Morton, Mike (TTI Inc.) 505
Morton, Peter A. 232
Morvan, Alain Y. 372
Morway, David 259
Moser, Bobby D. 383
Moser, Sara 27
Mosey, Ed 92
Moshenek, G. Kenneth 435
Moshier, Walter W. Jr. 407
Moshier, Arnold 440
Moskow, Michael H. 197
Mosley, John 463
Moss, Douglas 148
Mossler, Jeffrey A. 49
Mostert, Thomas J. Jr. 26
Mosticchio, Dennis P. 227
Mostrom, Michael 50
Mott, Daniel C. 42
Mott, Paul 367
Moxie, Jeffrey E. 476
Moyer, Christine K. (Center Oil) 123
Moyer, Kristen J. (Sunkist) 476
Moylan, Kienan 274
Moylanhas, Kiernan P. 274
Muchnick, Ed 122
Muck, David L. 557
Mudd, John O. 59
Mueller, Gene W. 403
Mueller, Guy 176
Mueller, Paul 443
Muellner, Paul E. 65
Muir, Andrew 537
Mulders, Abbe 175
Muleski, Robert T. 302
Mulherin, Kim 468
Mulkerin, David J. 547
Mullen, Edward K. 374
Mullen, Joe 402
Mullen, Robert H. (Newark) 374
Mullen, Robert W. (Structure Tone) 474
Muller, Barbara A. 519
Mulligan, Donald 165

Mullin, Bernard J. 65
Mullin, Chris 216
Mullin, Kathy A. 248
Mullinix, Joseph P. 517
Mullis, Eli D. 515
Mulrooney, Nina M. 393
Multari, Alfred M. 234
Mulvey, Thérèse 533
Munick, Paul S. 347
Munneke, Jeff 345
Muntz, David S. 486
Muraskin, Ben E. 398
Muratore, Michael K. 475
Murchison, Bradley D. 71
Murdock, Brian A. 370
Murdock, David H. 173
Murdock, Kent H. 264
Murer, Cherilyn G. 377
Murphy, Christopher J. 398
Murphy, Dale R. 382
Murphy, Daniel J. 511
Murphy, E. Ray 325
Murphy, Elizabeth A. 156
Murphy, Jeremiah T. 17
Murphy, John (Teamsters) 481
Murphy, John V. (MassMutual) 320
Murphy, Mark 111
Murphy, Michele 333
Murphy, Nancy 514
Murphy, Paul M. 435
Murphy, Reg 358
Murphy, Susan H. 145
Murray, Andy 306
Murray, Cathy 303
Murray, Gerald P. 284
Murray, John M. 156
Murray, Kathy 19
Murray, Patrick M. 178
Murray, Peter 357
Murray, Stephen P. 309
Murray, Wayne P. 185
Musacchia, Mary U. 439
Musacchio, Robert A. 45
Muse, John R. 245
Mushkin, Arthur 510
Musick, Larry R. 80
Musselman, Byron L. 512
Musso, Alan A. 479
Myatt, Bob 47
Myer, David F. 22
Myers, Pam 424
Myers, Peter L. 450
Myers, William 156
Mynsberge, Steven C. 323
Myrick, Bill J. 17
Mysel, Amy W. 503
Mysliwiec, Regina C. 372

N

Nachtigal, Jules 139
Naddaff, Alfred 208
Nadeau, Richard J. (Colt Defense) 135
Nadeau, Rick (Colt's) 136
Nadelmman, Michele 170
Nadler, Judith 518
Nadosy, Peter A. 235
Naegele, Robert O. Jr. 344
Nagaraja, Mysore L. 337
Nagel, David C. 56
Nagle, Thomas 287
Naidoo, Pat 432
Nair, Mohan 423
Nairn, Richard 148
Nakagiri, Neal E. 386
Nakis, Dominic J. 27
Nallicheri, Renu 530
Nally, Dennis M. 409
Napier, Bill 60
Naples, Beth 383
Napolitano, Frank J. 494
Nappi, Martin V. 223

Nappi, Michael 496
Narang, Charles K. 364
Nardi, Robert J. 307
Nardone, Joelle 383
Nash, Charles 516
Nash, John 406
Nash, Ron 416
Nathan, Badri 488
Nattier, James A. 178
Nau, Brian 445
Naugel, Scott A. 248
Naugle, Dennis F. 428
Nauman, Joan 184
Navarro, Benito 487
Nazarian, Robert H. 333
Neal, Christine 511
Neal, Elise 20
Neal, James G. 137
Neal, Robin 132
Neal, T. Webber 215
Neale, Donna 396
Neale, Terry 553
Nealy, Mike 344
Neamand, Scott F. 431
Neary, Daniel P. 351
Neary, John W. 546
Neaves, William B. 341
Nedick, Mitch 544
Needham, Philip 437
Neff, Richard B. 168
Neibauer, Rob 89
Neill, George 145
Neiss, Woodie 200
Nelms, Charlie 259
Nelson, Curtis C. 113
Nelson, Donnie 155
Nelson, Ed 550
Nelson, Gary 353
Nelson, Gordon L. Jr. 279
Nelson, Gregory V. 71
Nelson, Jim 225
Nelson, John (Follett) 204
Nelson, John C. (AMA) 45
Nelson, Jon (AMPI) 62
Nelson, Linda 84
Nelson, Nathan 504
Nelson, Noel 424
Nelson, Richard 297
Nelson, Scott (Hobby Lobby) 247
Nelson, Scott W. (Advantis) 26
Nelson, Shanna Missett 272
Nelson, Thomas C. 18
Nelson, Vern L. 124
Nelson, William E. (Captain D's) 109
Nelson, William H. (Intermountain Health Care) 264
Neroni, Mike 158
Nesbitt, Steven S. 184
Netchvolodoff, Alexander V. 147
Neugebauer, Toby R. 304
Neuman, Eric C. 245
Neumann, Paul G. 118
New, Kim 303
Newby, Larry 285
Newcom, Dwayne 500
Newcomb, Sharon 381
Newell, Janice 225
Newhouse, Donald E. 24
Newhouse, Samuel I. Jr. 24
Newman, Eric 145
Newman, Mark 374
Newman, Paul R. 179
Newman, Richard G. 29
Newsome, Mark 325
Newstead, Laura 39
Newton, Gary 403
Newton, Leslie 460
Ney, Joseph A. 511
Ng, Paul 457
Nguyen, Linda 556
Nguyen, Thuan 251
Nichlos, Kenneth L. 22
Nichols, John D. 316
Nicholson, Bruce J. 488

Nicholson, Earl 364
Nicholson, Pamela M. 190
Nicholson, Roger L. 265
Nicolls, Diane 409
Niehus, Dean A. 333
Niekamp, Randy W. 150
Nielson, Joani 479
Niemi, John R. 123
Nightingale, Paul C. 252
Nightingale, Thomas 443
Nigro, Paul N. 99
Nikias, C. L. Max 523
Nikol, Eleonora 70
Nilles, Martina 549
Nishan, Mark A. 197
Nishikawa, Morio 277
Nissen, Theresa 434
Nitzkowski, Greg M. 390
Nix, Jack 180
Nixon, Lynn Marie 99
Nobers, Jeff 17
Noble, Emmalee 90
Noble, Rex A. 133
Nocerino, Larry 397
Nodland, Jeffrey M. 244
Noe, Arthur W. 416
Noe, Stephen P. 158
Noel, Christy 170
Noiman, Silvia 407
Nolan, Frances 489
Nolan, Mike 161
Nolan, Robert 284
Nolan, Thomas J. 345
Noland, Rick 274
Noles, Russell 489
Nollman, Mitch 95
Noonan, Trey 79
Nordin, Elizabeth A. 109
Norelli, Mark 252
Noren, Jay 522
Norman, Chris 330
Norman, Paul E. 92
Norment, Philip 403
Norris, William 266
North, Annette 450
North, David A. 449
North, Jack W. 470
North, Margaret 483
Norville, Julie F. 449
Noto, Robert A. 338
Novak, Steve 289
Novelli, Bob 89
Novelli, William D. 18
Novik, Steven 278
Nowak, Joseph 334
Nowak, Tom 217
Nowlin, Charles F. 326
Nudd, Kevin 70
Nugent, Mike 492
Nunemaker, Richard A. 51
Nunez, Debbie 550
Nunlist, Ronald 402
Nurkin, Matthew 133
Nussbaum, Daniel 555
Nussdorf, Lawrence C. 131
Nutzinger, Karl 210
Nye, Erle 485
Nygaard, Loyd 81
Nyquist, John S. 343

O

Oates, David 409
Obarski, Kevin 498
Ober, Gordon L. 157
Oberkfell, Lawrence A. 445
Oberland, Gregory C. 378
Obert, Steve 341
Obradovich, Emil P. 527
O'Brien, Amy Muska 489
O'Brien, Christopher F. 408
O'Brien, David M. 246

Pyne, George 353

Q

Quadflieg, Frank 54
Quadracci, Betty Ewens 416
Quadracci, J. Joel 416
Quadracci, Thomas A. 416
Qualley, Michael J. 206
Quandt, Fred 216
Quarles, W. Greyson Jr. 439
Queally, Paul B. 140
Quellhorst, Timothy S. 150
Quenneville, Joel 135
Quigley, Bryan 88
Quigley, Michael 170
Quinn, Jon 155
Quinn, Ronald N. 484
Quinn, Thomas H. 279
Quiring, James 328
Quirk, James S. 331
Quish, Sheleen 527
Qureshi, Pervez 23

R

Raba, Todd M. 339
Rabb, Anthony A. 97
Rabin, Edward W. Jr. 255
Rabun, J. Sam L. 382
Radine, Gary D. 164
Radtke, Karen A. 334
Raether, Paul E. 291
Rafdahl, Richard 445
Rafferty, Gary 477
Raffo, Charlie 17
Ragazzini, John 464
Ragozzino, Kathy 99
Ragsdale, Dorothy 45
Ragsdale, Perry A. 126
Rahimi, Morteza A. 379
Rahn, William M. 242
Rahr, Stewart 288
Rai, Amitabh 426
Raible, Robert 333
Raichlen, Rob 306
Raider, Ann 533
Rainey, Brian M. 174
Raisbeck, David W. 111
Rajewski, James M. 340
Rake, Michael 294
Rakow, Jay 335
Rakowski, Sharon 555
Raksis, Joseph W 200
Rambach, Ralph 88
Rambis, Kurt 307
Ramey, Terry 393
Ramey, Thomas C. 302
Ramirez, Julio 102
Ramirez, Michael W. 400
Ramleth, Geir 78
Ramos, Linda 385
Ramos, Nelson 477
Ramsdale, Doug 249
Ramsey, Boyd J. 229
Ramsey, Craig R. 38
Ramsey, J. Douglas 193
Ramsey, James R. 520
Ramsey, Mike 344
Ramsey, Paul G. 525
Rancourt, Wayne M. 91
Rand, Mike 63
Randel, Don M. 518
Rankin, Mark D. 74
Ranstead, George E. 547
Ranton, James D. 227
Ranucci, Robert J. 534
Rao, Srikanth 112
Rapaport, Michael 288
Rapelye, Janet Lavin 410
Rapier, Donella 235

Rapp, John A. 528
Raquet, Bonnie E. 111
Rasikas, Kreigh 145
Rasmusen, Vicki 113
Rasmussen, David J. 464
Rasmussen, Earl R. 332
Rasmussen, Patti 166
Rasmussen, Stephen S. 362
Ratcliffe, Andrew 408
Ratliff, John 419
Ratner, Bruce C. 366
Rattazzi, Bill 553
Rau, Gregory J. 345
Rau, Michael A. 345
Raufast, Jean-Charles 192
Rausch, Elizabeth M. 109
Rautio, Trudy 113
Raven, Peter 358
Rawal, Rajesh 102
Rawlings, Hunter R. III 145
Rawson, Chester L. 411
Ray, Anda A. 508
Ray, Doug 276
Ray, Gene W. 214
Ray, Jerry M. 179
Ray, Robert 122
Ray, Wendell 329
Rayburn, Greg 352
Raymond, David 498
Raymond, Kathy 319
Re, Michael (Swinerton) 477
Re, Michaeline (John Paul
    Mitchell) 275
Read, Mark 174
Read, Michael 552
Reagan, Emmett 549
Reagan, Martin P. 31
Reamey, Gary D. 278
Reandeau, Traci 406
Reardon, Valerie A. 237
Reasor, Jackson E. 383
Reaves, Benjamin F. 27
Reaves, Donald J. 518
Rebok, Douglas E. 26
Rebula, Enzo 202
Reck, Una Mae 260
Records, George J. Jr. (Midland
    Financial) 340
Records, George J. Sr. (Midland
    Financial) 340
Redding, Thomas L. 241
Reddy, Kevin 376
Reder, Robert F. 415
Redlick, Mike 331
Redman, Chuck 78
Redmon, Dwayne 216
Redmon, John W. 76
Redmond, David L. 49
Redwitz, Tom 553
Reed, Bill J. (Riceland Foods) 430
Reed, Bruce 99
Reed, Charles B. 106
Reed, Gary 48
Reed, John D. III 261
Reed, Joseph A. 496
Reed, Randal R. 243
Reed, Robert D. 477
Reed, Willis (New Orleans
    Hornets) 367
Reeder, Dan 554
Reeder, James E. 463
Reedy, John D. 337
Reedy, Scott 103
Rees, Brandon 30
Rees, Norma S. 107
Reese, Bertram S. 449
Reese, Stuart H. 320
Reeve, Donald 546
Reeve, Ellie 537
Reeves, Mike 344
Reeves, Sam 80
Rego, Anthony C. 212
Rehl, John 174
Rehovsky, Jeff 479

Reich, Rob 443
Reich, Ronald E. 108
Reichard, Joseph F. 246
Reichenbach, Ingeborg T. 554
Reid, John 62
Reiff, Melissa 143
Reilly, Bill 451
Reilly, James G. 35
Reilly, Kelly 381
Reilly, Kevin P. 526
Reilly, Lionel L. 411
Reimer, Richard 58
Reimert, Dennis 498
Rein, Brian S. 272
Reinders, Mark 339
Reinhart, Kellee 516
Reins, Ralph E. 416
Reinsdorf, Jerry 126
Reinstein, Bruce 208
Reinstein, Larry 208
Reis, Glenn 189
Reissig, Michael P. (Colt Defense) 135
Reissig, Mike (Colt's) 136
Reister, Jane 264
Reitz, Phillip 201
Rekers, John 342
Rekowski, Jerry G. 43
Remboldt, Darwin 26
Remington, Paul 548
Remmel, Lee 223
Remmers, John M. 547
Rendulic, Donald 209
Rennert, Ira Leon 426
Renstrom, Lisa 452
Renwick, Ed 556
Renwick-Espinosa, Kate 536
Rescoe, Michael E. 508
Resnick, Alice R. 466
Ressler, Rickie 36
Restaino, Michael N. 79
Reum, W. Robert 51
Reusch, Jami G. 382
Reuter, Lawrence G. 337
Revels, Claude 274
Rew, Richard II 23
Rexach, Frank 235
Reyes, David K. 429
Reyes, J. Christopher 429
Reyes, M. Jude 429
Reynolds, Craig A. 44
Reynolds, Glen 552
Reynolds, J. Scott 48
Reynolds, John T. 243
Reynolds, Robert A. Jr. (Graybar
    Electric) 221
Reynolds, Robert L. (FMR) 203
Reynolds, Thomas A. 156
Rhinehart, June Acie 276
Rhodes, Mark 478
Rhodes, Rhonda 45
Ricardelli, Steve 476
Ricciardi, Michael 492
Ricciardi, Salvatore 415
Rice, Alan J. 26
Rice, Ann Madden 519
Rice, Douglas C. 140
Rich, David E. 430
Rich, Howard 430
Rich, Linda D. 372
Rich, Mindy 430
Rich, Nancy 100
Rich, Robert E. Jr. (Rich Products) 430
Rich, Robert E. Sr. (Rich Products) 430
Richards, Lee 461
Richards, Margaret E. 128
Richards, Mark R. 55
Richards, Michael S. 159
Richards, Roy Jr. 461
Richards, Stephen (Houghton
    Mifflin) 251
Richards, Steve (OSI) 384
Richards, Tiffany 376
Richardson, Barbara J. 52

Richardson, Jamie 551
Richardson, Jane 47
Richardson, William C. 285
Richer, Clare S. 203
Richey, Frank 93
Richman, Steven P. 547
Richmond, Merrill 494
Richmond, Rollin C. 107
Richmond, Susan 390
Richter, David 471
Richter, Gregory W. 483
Richter, Wolfgang 164
Rickabaugh, David 421
Rico, Tony 218
Ricord, Kathleen D. 363
Riddell, Mark 198
Ridder, Paul D. 420
Ridder, Raymond 216
Rienhart, John 436
Rieny, Robert 241
Rienzi, Michael J. 52
Riesenbeck, Ronald 440
Rifkin, Ned 457
Rigenhagen, Rhonda 367
Riggio, Leonard S. 73
Riggs, Dean 465
Rijos, John P. 99
Riley, Jonathan C. 483
Riley, Pat (Miami Heat) 239
Riley, Pat (Rand McNally) 421
Riley, Sean P. 321
Rimai, Marcia 378
Rinaldi, Catherine A. 337
Rinat, Zack 346
Rinehart, Kathleen 210
Riney, Robert 241
Ringeisen, Richard D. 519
Ringler, Kenneth J. Jr. 405
Rink, Charles 422
Rink, Tom 534
Rinne, Kristin S. 129
Rinner, Richard D. 40
Rios, Sandra 319
Ririe, Del 552
Risberg, Elizabeth 164
Risebrough, Doug 344
Risener, Daniel M. 414
Rissman, Paul C. 35
Rist, Larry 316
Ritch, Charles H. 183
Ritcher, Peter A. 129
Ritscha, Bill 463
Rittenberg, Gerald C. 50
Ritter, Keith 360
Ritz, Brooke 431
Ritz, David M. 431
Rivera, Marcy 206
Rivers, Nelson B. III 352
Rivetti, Carol 548
Rizzo, James M. 179
Rizzotti, Al 143
Roach, Mike 80
Roach, Randy A. 92
Roach, Tim 182
Roadarmel, Rick 209
Roark, Stephen R. 271
Robbins, Clifton S. 331
Robbins, Earnest O. II 389
Robbins, Kris A. 449
Robbins, Larry 488
Robbins, Ray 278
Robbins, Roger 274
Robbins, W. Clayton 382
Roberson, Bruce E. 400
Roberts, Bill 79
Roberts, Dawn 380
Roberts, Don 513
Roberts, George R. 291
Roberts, Harry (Boscov's) 94
Roberts, Harvey (Kentucky
    Lottery) 285
Roberts, Jay 436
Roberts, Jesse M. 324
Roberts, Jon 401